THE NEW INTERPRETER'S BIBLE
COMMENTARY

In Ten Volumes

Volume I
Introduction to the Pentateuch; Genesis; Exodus; Leviticus; Numbers; Deuteronomy

Volume II
Introduction to Narrative Literature; Joshua; Judges; Ruth; 1 & 2 Samuel; 1 & 2 Kings; 1 & 2 Chronicles

Volume III
Introduction to Hebrew Poetry; Job; Psalms; Introduction to Wisdom Literature; Proverbs; Ecclesiastes; Song of Songs

Volume IV
Ezra; Nehemiah; Introduction to Prophetic Literature; Isaiah; Jeremiah; Baruch; Letter of Jeremiah; Lamentations

Volume V
Ezekiel; Hosea; Joel; Amos; Obadiah; Jonah; Micah; Nahum; Habakkuk; Zephaniah; Haggai; Zechariah; Malachi

Volume VI
Esther; Additions to Esther; Tobit; Judith; 1 & 2 Maccabees; Book of Wisdom; Sirach; Introduction to Apocalyptic Literature; Daniel; Additions to Daniel

Volume VII
The Gospels and Narrative Literature; Jesus and the Gospels; Matthew; Mark

Volume VIII
Luke; John

Volume IX
Acts; Introduction to Epistolary Literature; Romans; 1 & 2 Corinthians; Galatians

Volume X
Ephesians; Philippians; Colossians; 1 & 2 Thessalonians; 1 & 2 Timothy; Titus; Philemon; Hebrews; James; 1 & 2 Peter; 1, 2 & 3 John; Jude; Revelation

EDITORIAL BOARD

THE NEW INTERPRETER'S™ BIBLE
COMMENTARY

VOLUME THREE

Introduction to Hebrew Poetry
Job
Psalms
Introduction to Wisdom Literature
Proverbs
Ecclesiastes
Song of Songs

ABINGDON PRESS
Nashville

THE NEW INTERPRETER'S BIBLE COMMMENTARY
VOLUME III

Copyright © 2015 by Abingdon Press

This volume is a compilation of the following previously published material:
The New Interpreter's® Bible in Twelve Volumes, Volume IV (Introduction to Hebrew Poetry, Job, Psalms), Copyright © 1996 by Abingdon Press.
The New Interpreter's® Bible in Twelve Volumes, Volume V (Introduction to Wisdom Literature, Proverbs, Ecclesiastes, Song of Songs), Copyright © 1997 by Abingdon Press.

This book is printed on acid-free paper.

ISBN 978-1-4267-3580-6

17 18 19 20 21 22 23 24—10 9 8 7 6 5 4 3

MANUFACTURED IN THE UNITED STATES OF AMERICA

CONTRIBUTORS

ADELE BERLIN
    Robert H. Smith Professor of Hebrew Bible
    Associate Provost for Faculty Affairs
    University of Maryland
    College Park, Maryland
      Introduction to Hebrew Poetry

CAROL A. NEWSOM
    Professor of Old Testament
    Candler School of Theology
    Emory University
    Atlanta, Georgia
    (The Episcopal Church)
      Job

J. CLINTON McCANN, JR.
    Evangelical Professor of Biblical Interpretation
    Eden Theological Seminary
    St. Louis, Missouri
    (Presbyterian Church [U.S.A])
      Psalms

RICHARD J. CLIFFORD, S.J.
    Professor of Old Testament
    Weston Jesuit School of Theology
    Cambridge, Massachusetts
    (The Roman Catholic Church)
      Introduction to Wisdom Literature

RAYMOND C. VAN LEEUWEN
    Professor of Religion and Theology
    Eastern College
    Saint Davids, Pennsylvania
    (Christian Reformed Church in North America)
      Proverbs

W. SIBLEY TOWNER
    The Reverend Archibald McFayden Professor
      of Biblical Interpretation
    Union Theological Seminary in Virginia
    Richmond, Virginia
    (Presbyterian Church [U.S.A])
      Ecclesiastes

RENITA J. WEEMS
    Associate Professor of Hebrew Bible
    The Divinity School
    Vanderbilt University
    Nashville, Tennessee
    (African Methodist Episcopal Church)
      Song of Songs

* The credentials listed here reflect the positions held at the time of the original publication.

CONTENTS

VOLUME III

Introduction to Hebrew Poetry
Adele Berlin _____ 1

Job
Carol A. Newsom _____ 17

Psalms
J. Clinton McCann, Jr. _____ 271

Introduction to Wisdom Literature
Richard J. Clifford, S.J. _____ 731

Proverbs
Raymond C. Van Leeuwen _____ 749

Ecclesiastes
W. Sibley Towner _____ 947

Song of Songs
Renita J. Weems _____ 1021

Abbreviations _____ 1081

Introduction to Hebrew Poetry

Adele Berlin

t has been recognized since ancient times that the Hebrew Bible contains poetry, but the definition of what constitutes biblical poetry, the description of poetic features, and the identification of poetic passages have varied greatly over the centuries. This article will present a summary of the poetic features considered most relevant by contemporary biblical scholars, and will show how an understanding of them may lead to better interpretations of biblical poetry.

INTERNAL EVIDENCE FOR THE DEFINITION OF POETRY

A good starting place would seem to be the Bible's own terminology. Certain terms occur in superscriptions or within passages that may indicate poetic genres. The broadest of these is *šîr* (שיר) or *šîrâ* (שירה), meaning "song" or "poem." *Šîr* may stand alone, as in Judg 5:12 and Ps 65:1, or it may be qualified, as in *šîr hamma'ălôt* (שיר המעלות, "pilgrimage song"; Psalms 120–134), *šîr ṣiyyôn* (שיר ציון, "Zion song"; Ps 137:3), *šîr ḥādāš* (שיר חדש, "new song"; Pss 96:1; 98:1; 149:1). For other types of *šîr,* see Pss 30:1; 45:1; 137:4. The "feminine" form, *šîrâ,* is found, e.g., in Exod 15:1; Deut 31:30; Num 21:17. Another frequent term is *mizmôr* (מזמור, "song," "psalm"), which appears in numerous psalms, sometimes in combination with *šîr* (e.g., Pss 67:1; 68:1). A third term, *qînâ* (קינה, "lament"), is known from 2 Sam 1:17; Amos 8:10. While these terms provide a useful entrée into ancient notions of literary, or perhaps musical, genres, they do not encompass every passage that a modern reader would consider poetry.

Likewise, the ancient scribal tradition, practiced from rabbinic times, of writing certain sections of the Hebrew Bible stichographically (i.e., with space left between lines of a poem; see, e.g., Exodus 15; Deuteronomy 32; Judges 5) is suggestive of what may have been perceived as poems. Yet it is not a sufficient criterion by today's standards because, like the term *šîr,* stichographic writing was not used for all poetic passages and is occasionally used for non-poetic lists (Josh 12:9-24; Esth 9:7-9).

The internal features of the biblical text neither adequately define nor identify poetry. Moreover, no ancient Israelite or ancient Near Eastern treatises on poetry or poetics have been found. Hence, scholars in each time and place, beginning with the Greco-Roman period, have applied to the biblical text definitions of poetry from their own literary tradition. Early Christian scholars discussed biblical poetry in terms of classical metrical systems, medieval Jewish scholars searched the Bible for the types of rhyme and metrical patterns found in medieval Hebrew poetry, and English Renaissance scholars sought the attributes of their style of poetry in the Bible. We do the same today, applying all we know of systems of versification, poetic syntax and vocabulary, symbolic and metaphoric representation—in short, all the ways in which language may be distinguished as poetic (as opposed to non-poetic)—to the study of biblical poetry. The result is an increasingly complex and sophisticated view of the Hebrew Bible's poetry and, by extension, all biblical language, as well as an ever-deepening aesthetic appreciation for it.

VERSE OR POETRY?

When we speak of verse we mean a type of discourse with formal properties, generally quantifiable, such as meter or rhyme, that distinguish it from other types of discourse. The search for such properties in biblical poetry has a long and largely unsuccessful history. For most of this history, attempts were made to uncover the Bible's metrical system. Biblical verse has been, at various times and places, described as quantitative, syllabic, or accentual. But despite much effort, no one has been able to demonstrate convincingly the existence of a consistently occurring metrical system. (See the section "Meter and Rhythm," below.)

M. O'Connor has suggested that instead of looking for formal arrangements built on the recurrence of phonological units (which is what most metrical systems are), we will find the formal properties of biblical verse in the arrangement of syntactic units. O'Connor proposed a system of syntactic constraints to define a line of verse.[1] The terms that he employs are *clause,* a verbal clause or a verbless clause; *constituent,* each verb and nominal phrase and the particles dependent on it; and *unit,* the independent verb or

noun along with the particles dependent on it (generally equivalent to a word). According to this system, a line of biblical verse may contain no more than three clauses; it may contain between one and four constituents; and it may contain between two and five units. The dominant line form, according to O'Connor's description, contains one clause and either two or three constituents of two or three units. For example, Exod 15:7 may be analyzed as

7a.	וברב גאונך תהרס קמיך	*ûběrōb gě'ôněkā*
		tahărōs qāmêkā
7b.	תשלח חרנך	*těšallaḥ ḥărōněkā*
7c.	יאכלמו כקש	*yō'kělēmô kaqqaš*

In your great majesty, you smash your foes,
You send forth your anger,
It consumes them like stubble.[2]

Line 7a contains one clause of three constituents, 7b contains one clause of two constituents, and 7c contains one clause of two constituents. While O'Connor's work is frequently cited, and is generally recognized as an innovative description grounded on a sound linguistic basis, it has rarely been applied to analyses of biblical poetry. Perhaps his description has not replaced the older types of search for meter because it is technical and complex, or because it is difficult to imagine that a native poet would have thought in these syntactic categories.

Other scholars, including myself, feel that the quest for a formal system of versification should be abandoned because it does not exist. It is preferable, therefore, to speak of "poetry" rather than "verse." By "poetry" I mean a type of discourse that employs a high degree of the tropes and figures that are described below. Poetry can be distinguished from non-poetic discourse (historical narrative, legal discourse) by the comparatively high density of these tropes and by the structuring of some of them into recurring patterns. Poetry also employs sound and joins it to meaning in interesting ways. In stating this, I espouse a Jakobsonian view, which sees poetry as focusing on the message for its own sake. A poem conveys thought, and, moreover, it conveys

1. M. O'Connor, *Hebrew Verse Structure* (Winona Lake, Ind.: Eisenbrauns, 1980).

2. Unless otherwise specified, translations of the biblical text are the author's.

that thought in a self-conscious manner, through a special structuring of language that calls attention to the "how" of the message as well as to the "what." At the same time, the "how" and the "what" become indistinguishable. Robert Alter, taking his approach from New Criticism, puts it slightly differently: "Poetry . . . is not just a set of techniques for saying impressively what could be said otherwise. Rather, it is a particular way of imagining the world."[3]

GENRES OF BIBLICAL POETRY

There does not seem to have been a formal or structural distinction between different kinds of poems. Hebrew poetry has no fixed number of lines or type of patterning that is characteristic of a particular genre. If the ancient Israelites did make genre distinctions, those genres are largely lost to us. (They are presumably similar to the genres of other ancient Near Eastern literatures.)[4]

As one might have expected, form-critical studies have discovered genres or subtypes of poetry, especially as they can be related to a specific *Sitz im Leben,* such as victory songs or communal laments. Hermann Gunkel's work remains the classic source on form-critical types of psalms.[5] Following Gunkel, most scholars find the following genres in the book of Psalms: individual and communal laments, hymns of praise, thanksgiving songs, royal psalms, songs of Zion, and wisdom psalms.

Modern scholars tend to impose their own notions of genre, based for the most part on analogy with the tone and contents of genres in other literatures, when they divide up the poetic territory in the Bible. This division corresponds to a large degree with the biblical books in which the poems are found; thus Proverbs and Job are wisdom literature; Psalms contains praise (or lyric) or perhaps liturgy; Lamentations has laments; Song of Songs is love poetry (or perhaps wedding songs). In other books, one may find

victory songs (Exodus 15; Judges 5; Num 21:28) or elegies (2 Sam 1:19-27; 3:33-34). Prophetic writing makes an interesting test case, as Robert Alter has observed, for some prophetic speeches are written as poetry and others as prose. Alter has suggested that the vocative (addressing the reader in the second person) and monitory (admonishing) nature of prophetic poetry distinguishes it from other poetic genres.

Actually, most studies of biblical poetry are not concerned with genre per se, but concentrate on the common features of all biblical poetry. These are presented in the following sections.

TERSENESS

Scholars of comparative literature who have searched for a universal definition of poetry have noticed that poetic lines tend to be shorter and terser than lines of prose. This feature seems to occur whether or not there are metrical constraints on the length of lines. Whatever the reason, poetry has a tendency to be more terse, more concise, than non-poetic discourse, both within a single line and, in the case of biblical poetry, over the discourse as a whole. Biblical poems are relatively short, usually thirty verses or less; there are no epic poems in the Bible. Lines are short, and the relationships or transitions between lines are often unexpressed. This gives the impression that in poetry each word or phrase is more loaded with meaning, since fewer words must bear the burden of the message. In biblical poetry, terseness within lines is achieved largely by the omission of the definite article (ה *ha*), the accusative marker (את *'ēt*), and the relative pronoun (אשר *'ăšer*). The decreased usage of these particles has been documented in computerized counts.[6] The relationship between lines is frequently not made explicit, but is implied by the parallelism that compels the reader to construe some type of relationship.

We can see some of the terseness and the effect of parallelism in a comparison of

3. Robert Alter, *The Art of Biblical Poetry* (New York: Basic Books, 1985) 151.

4. For biblical terms that may possibly indicate different genres, see above, "Internal Evidence for the Definition of Poetry."

5. Hermann Gunkel, *Einleitung in die Psalmen. Die Gattingen der religiösen Lyrik Israels* (Göttingen, 1933).

6. See F. I. Andersen and A. D. Forbes, " 'Prose Particle' Counts of the Hebrew Bible," in *The Word of the Lord Shall Go Forth,* ed. C. Meyers and M. O'Connor (Winona Lake: Eisenbrauns, 1983) 165-83.

Judg 4:19 and 5:25, a poetic and a prose version of the same incident:

> Then he said to her, "Please give me a little water to drink; for I am thirsty." So she opened a skin of milk and gave him a drink and covered him.
> (Judg 4:19 NRSV)

> He asked water and she gave him milk,
> she brought him curds in a lordly bowl.
> (Judg 5:25 NRSV)

The poetic version is both more concise and more redundant. The parallelism in 5:25 sets up an exact equivalence, a reciprocity, which brings into focus the contrast between what was requested and what was served. The addition of "she brought him curds in a lordly bowl" does not add to the sequence of actions but doubles back upon the milk, stressing once more its "dairiness" (as opposed to water) and the noble flourish with which it was offered. The prose version carries the reader step-by-step along the narrative sequence, giving more information but not highlighting any part of it as the poetic version does.

PARALLELISM

Since the work of Robert Lowth, parallelism has come to be viewed as one of the two identifying markers of poetry.[7] And since the other marker, meter, is notoriously resistant to analysis, parallelism, which is relatively easy to perceive (at least since Lowth called attention to it), has emerged as the predominant feature of biblical poetry. We should note at the outset, however, that parallelism is also present in non-poetic discourse, albeit to a more limited extent. So the mere existence of parallelism is not a sufficient indication of poetry, although a high frequency of parallelism in adjacent lines or verses has a high correlation with what we consider poetic discourse.

Parallelism may be defined as the repetition of similar or related semantic content or grammatical structure in adjacent lines or verses. The repetition is rarely identical, and it is the precise nature of the relationship between the two lines that has been the focus of most discussion. Indeed, the flexibility of this relationship, its capacity for variation, makes parallelism rhetorically interesting.

The Semantic Relationship. There have been two schools of thought on how to describe the semantic relationship between parallel lines. The first, introduced by Lowth and followed until recently, emphasizes the sameness of the relationship and the types and degree of correspondence between the lines. Lowth's classic definition is

> The correspondence of one Verse, or Line, with another I call Parallelism. When a proposition is delivered, and a second subjoined to it, or drawn under it, equivalent, or contrasted with it, in Sense; or similar to it in the form of Grammatical Construction; these I call Parallel Lines; and the words or phrases answering one to another in corresponding Lines Parallel Terms.[8]

Lowth advanced his description by proposing discrete categories into which parallelisms could fit, depending on the nature of the correspondence of the lines. His categories are synonymous, antithetic, and synthetic. In synonymous parallelism, the same thought is expressed in different words, as in Ps 117:1:

> Praise the LORD, all you nations!
> Extol him, all you peoples! (NRSV)

In antithetic parallelism, the second line contradicts, or is opposed to, the first line, as in Prov 10:1:

> A wise child makes a glad father,
> but a foolish child is a mother's grief. (NRSV)

Synthetic parallelism, a much looser designation, accounts for parallelisms that lack exact correspondence between their parts but show a more diffuse correspondence between the lines as a whole. An example is Cant 2:4:

7. Robert Lowth, *De sacra poesi Hebraeorum* (*Lectures on the Sacred Poetry of the Hebrews*), 1753; *Isaiah: A New Translation with a Preliminary Dissertation and Notes Critical, Philological, and Explanatory,* 1778.

8. Lowth, *Isaiah,* 10-11.

He brought me to the banqueting house,
and his intention toward me was love.
(NRSV)

This tripartite system of categorization of types of parallelisms gained wide popularity, for it accounted for large numbers of parallel lines.

As scholars continued to study parallelism, they refined Lowth's original categories, furthering his typological approach by adding subcategories, such as staircase parallelism, in which the second line repeats part of the first but moves beyond it, as in Jer 31:21:

Return, O virgin Israel,
return to these your cities. (NRSV)

and janus parallelism, hinging on the use of a single word with two different meanings, one relating to what precedes it and one to what follows, as in Cant 2:12:

The flowers appear on the earth;
the time of singing [הזמיר *hazzāmîr*,
  or "pruning"] has come
and the voice of the turtledove/ is heard in
  our land.

In such an approach, the weak link was synthetic parallelism, because at best it appeared to be nothing more than a catchall of undefined categories or, at worst, a grouping of lines containing no parallelism. But the weakness of synthetic parallelism began to spread, as it was observed that no set of parallel lines is exactly synonymous or antithetic.

A major turning point came in the 1980s with the work of Robert Alter and James Kugel. Whereas Lowth's approach emphasized the similarity between parallel lines, Alter and Kugel emphasized their differences. Kugel rejected the notion of the synonymity of parallel lines and substituted the notion of continuity, phrasing his definition of parallelism as "A, what's more, B." Alter, moving independently in the same direction, spoke of the "consequentiality" of parallel lines. He saw the relationship between the lines as one of progression or intensification.

Indeed, both approaches contain elements of truth, for parallelism contains relationships of both similarity and difference. Take, for example, Ps 18:9 (Eng. 18:8 = 2 Sam 22:9):

Smoke went up from his nostrils,
  and devouring fire from his mouth;
  glowing coals flamed forth from him.
(NRSV)

There is a grammatical and semantic similarity among the three lines: *smoke/fire/coals* coming forth from his *nostrils/mouth*. But at the same time, within the general sameness there is an intensification, an escalation of the sense of burning. A clearer example is Lam 5:11:

They raped women in Zion,
Virgins in the Judean towns.

At first glance, these lines are synonymous, but on further reflection one sees intensification as one moves from *women* to *virgins* and progresses from *Zion* to *the Judean towns*.

Parallel Word Pairs. Lowth's definition had called attention to "parallel terms"— that is, "words or phrases answering one to another in corresponding lines"—but it was only with the discovery of Ugaritic poetry and the widespread acceptance of the theory of oral composition that efforts to analyze parallelism focused on parallel word pairs, or, as they came to be called, "fixed word pairs." Scholars noticed that certain sets of terms regularly recurred in parallel lines, such as *day/night* (e.g., Ps 121:6: "The sun shall not strike you by day,/ nor the moon by night" [NRSV]) and *heaven/earth* (e.g., Isa 1:2: "Hear, O heavens, and listen, O earth" [NRSV]). Such pairs were taken to have been the functional equivalents of the formulas in Greek and Yugoslavian poetry that enabled the poet to compose orally. The pairs were thought to have been fixed—i.e., they were stock pairs of words learned by poets who would then use them as the building blocks around which a parallelism could be constructed. Much research concentrated on discovering and listing these pairs (which were often the same in Hebrew and Ugaritic) and charting their frequency, the order in which the members of a set occurred, their grammatical form, and the semantic relationship between them. This last element led to categories not unlike those elicited by Lowth: synonyms and antonyms. But new categories were also noted, such as a whole and a part, abstract and concrete, common term and archaic term, and the breakup of stereotyped phrases. Examples of recurring word pairs abound: *Jerusalem/Judah* (Isa 3:8; Jer 9:10); *father/mother* (Ezek 16:3; Prov 1:8); *right/left* (Gen 13:9; Ezek 16:46; Cant 2:6).

Research on word pairs advanced the scholarly understanding of the components of parallel lines and the lexical and poetic similarities between Hebrew and Ugaritic. But because the study was largely based on an unproven hypothesis about the oral composition of Greek poetry and a tenuous analogy between Greek formulas and Hebrew word pairs, it misconstrued the nature of word pairs. They are not "fixed," and they do not drive the composition of parallel lines. Rather, the process of composing parallel lines calls forth word pairs, which are nothing more than commonly associated terms that can be elicited by any speaker of the language (as word association games have shown). In fact, many of the same pairs occur together in non-parallel discourse (e.g., right/left, Num 20:17; 22:26).

Linguistic Models. In the 1970s and 1980s the focus of research on parallelism began to move away from word pairs and back to the lines as a whole. By then, however, there were new theories and models from the field of linguistics that offered new and better possibilities for understanding parallelism. Among the scholars employing linguistic models were A. Berlin, T. Collins, S. Geller, E. Greenstein, D. Pardee, and W. G. E. Watson. They drew on structural linguistics and transformational grammar for a grammatical analysis of parallelism. The major influence came from the work of Roman Jakobson, whose most famous dictum on parallelism was:

> Pervasive parallelism inevitably activates all the levels of language—the distinctive features, inherent and prosodic, the morphological and syntactic categories and forms, the lexical units and their semantic classes in both their convergences and divergences acquire an autonomous poetic value.[9]

This statement suggests that not only lexical units (word pairs) or semantic relationships, but all linguistic features as well come into play in parallelism.

Parallelism can be viewed as a phenomenon involving linguistic equivalences or contrasts that may occur on the level of the word, the line, or across larger expanses of text. (However, the analysis of parallelism generally operates at the level of the line.) Linguistic equivalence not only means identity, but also refers to a term or construction that belongs to the same category or paradigm, or to the same sequence or syntagm. This kind of equivalence can easily be seen in word pairs. Pairs like day and night or father and mother belong to the same grammatical paradigm (nouns) and might be said to belong to the same semantic paradigm ("time" and "family members").

Similarly, entire lines can be grammatically equivalent—that is, contain the same grammatical deep structure (and perhaps surface structure). I call this the *grammatical aspect*. In fact, Lowth had called attention to lines with similar grammatical construction in his definition of parallelism, but this feature had never been carefully analyzed before. With the advent of transformational grammar, it began to receive major attention.

For example, Ps 103:10:

> Not according to our sins did he deal
> with us,
> And not according to our transgressions
> did he requite us.

These lines have the same surface structure as well as the same deep structure. More often, though, the surface structure varies in some way, while the deep structure remains the same. For instance, in Mic 6:2*b* a nominal clause is paired with a verbal clause:

> For the Lord has a quarrel with his people,
> And with Israel will he dispute.

In Prov 6:20, a positive clause is paired with a negative clause:

> Guard, my son, the commandments of
> your father,

9. Roman Jakobson, "Grammatical Parallelism and Its Russian Facet," *Language* 42 (1966) 423.

And do not forsake the teaching of
  your mother.

The subject of one clause may become the object in the parallel clause, as in Gen 27:29:

Be lord over your brothers,
  and may the sons of your mother bow
  down to you. (NIV)

Parallelism may pair lines of different grammatical mood, as in Ps 6:6 (Eng. 6:5) where a negative indicative clause parallels an interrogative one:

For in death there is no mention of you,
In Sheol, who can acclaim you?

All parallelism involves the pairing of terms, the *lexical aspect*; as already suggested, the process whereby specific terms are paired is similar to the process that generates associations in psycholinguistic word association games. Linguists have discovered rules that account for the kinds of associations made, much as biblical scholars had tried to discover the principles at work in "fixed word pairs." They have noted that in word association games a word may elicit itself; so, too, in parallelism a word may parallel itself or another word from the same root—e.g., 2 Sam 22:7: *I called//I called*; Job 6:15: *stream//bed of streams.* Linguists have also noted that a word may have a number of different associates and that some are likely to be generated more often than are others, thereby giving rise to the perception that some associations are "fixed."

The rules for word association are categorized by linguists as paradigmatic and syntagmatic (like the rules for the grammatical, and other, aspects of parallelism). Paradigmatic pairing involves the selection of a word from the same class as a previous word. The most common type of paradigmatic pairing is one with minimal contrast, which produces an "opposite," such as *good/bad* or *man/woman.* Other linguistic rules explain other paradigmatic choices.

Syntagmatic responses involve the choice of an associate from the same sequence rather than from the same class. This is often realized in the completion of idiomatic phrases or conventional coordinates, like *horses/chariots* or *loyalty/truth.* (This phenomenon is similar to what had been called the breakup of stereotyped phrases.) Another type of syntagmatic pairing involves the splitting of the components of personal or geographic names; e.g., *Balak//king of Moab* (Num 23:7) and *Ephrathah//Bethlehem* (Ruth 4:11).

While this lexical aspect of parallelism generally accompanies the grammatical aspect (the pairing of lines with equivalent syntax), it may occur in the absence of grammatical parallelism (strictly speaking, lines with paradigmatic grammatical equivalence). An example is Ps 111:6:

The power of his deeds he told to his
  people,
In giving to them the inheritance of
  nations.

The grammatical relationship of the lines is not paradigmatically equivalent. Moreover, *people* and *nations* do not refer to the same entity in this verse (*people* refers to Israel, and *nations* refers to non-Israelite nations). But the pair *people/nation* is a known association that occurs frequently, usually referring to the same entity. The manner in which this pair is used is somewhat novel, but the use of a common pair helps to draw the two lines together, making them appear more parallel.

Even in the presence of grammatical equivalence, word pairs may run counter to this equivalence instead of reinforcing it, as is more usual. An example is Job 5:14:

By day they encounter darkness,
And as at night they grope at noon.

Both lines express a similar thought (semantic content); during the daytime it will seem like nighttime. The semantic and syntactic equivalent terms here are *day/noon* and *darkness/night.* But the poet has employed a common word association, *day/night,* and has placed these terms in the same position in each line. In this case, the lexical pairing is at odds with the semantic and syntactic pairing, creating a tension between the two, which in turn sets up a competing relationship between the lines, thereby binding them even more closely together.

This illustration reminds us that the sense of the entire verse comes into play in the selection of word pairs, for words are chosen to express or emphasize a particular message. Just as the selection of parallel words is not totally random, so also it is not totally fixed. Through linguistics, we have come to understand better the process of word selection, and so to understand better the workings of parallelism and the effect of a particular word choice. Another illustration will demonstrate the subtle difference that the choice of a word pair can make. Compare, for example, Ps 102:13 (Eng. 102:12) with Lam 5:19:

> But you, O Lord, are enthroned forever;
> your *name* endures to all generations.
> (NRSV, italics added)

> But you, O Lord, reign forever;
> your *throne* endures to all generations.
> (NRSV, italics added)

The difference in the choice of one word underscores the difference in the messages of these two passages. Psalm 102 contrasts the weakness and fleetingness of a human being with the permanence of God. God's name—that is, God's existence—lasts forever. The author of Lamentations, on the other hand, laments the destruction of the Temple, the locus of God's throne. Despite its physical destruction, he maintains that God's throne—the metaphoric seat of God's rulership—will remain intact.

I have made reference to the *semantic aspect* of parallelism, which pertains to the relationship between the meaning of the parallel lines. Lowth characterized this relationship as synonymous, antithetic, or synthetic; and Kugel called it "A, what's more, B." From a linguistic perspective, the semantic relationship between lines (like the lexical and grammatical relationships) can be described as either paradigmatic or syntagmatic. It is not always easy, however, to decide specific cases, for often one reader sees similarity where another sees sequential development (see above the discussion on Lowth vs. Alter and Kugel). Part of the confusion arises because both paradigmatic and syntagmatic elements may be present.

> Ascend a high hill, Herald (to) Zion,
> Lift your voice aloud, herald (to) Jerusalem.
> (Isa 40:9)

The actions of the herald are sequential (syntagmatic), but the vocatives, "herald (to) Zion/ Jerusalem," are paradigmatic. It seems to be the nature of parallelism to combine syntagmatic and paradigmatic relationships on different levels or in different aspects. The effect is to advance the thought, while at the same time creating a close relationship between the parallelism's constituent parts.

Another linguistic aspect that may come into play in parallelism is phonology. Equivalences in sound may be activated in parallelism just as equivalences in grammar are. This is the *phonological aspect,* which often takes the form of pairing words with similar consonants. These pairs may also be semantic or lexical pairs, such as שלום (*šālôm*)// שלוה (*šalvâ*), "peace" // "tranquility" (Ps 122:7); or they may be unrelated, as in Ps 104:19:

> He made the moon for time-markers
> [מועדים *mô'ădîm*],
> The sun knows its setting
> [ידע מבואו *yāda' měbô'ô*].

Sound pairs reinforce the bond between lines created by grammatical and lexical pairings, providing an additional type of linguistic equivalence in the parallelism. The more linguistic equivalences there are, the stronger is the sense of correspondence between one line and the next. Such similarity, in turn, promotes the sense of semantic unity.

There are infinite ways to activate linguistic equivalences, and hence there are infinite ways to construct a parallelism. No one type is "better" or "worse" than another. Each is designed for its own context and purpose.

METER AND RHYTHM

Although I earlier rejected meter as a demonstrably formal requirement of biblical verse, it is appropriate to summarize some of the modern analyses of meter because they are so pervasive in discussions of biblical poetry, and because they raise important questions about the nature of that poetry. Moreover, it is practically impossible for someone raised in a modern North American or European tradition to imagine poetry without meter.

Strictly speaking, meter requires the recurrence of an element or group of elements with mathematical regularity. The element to be measured may be the syllable (or a certain type or length of syllable), the accent or stress, or the word. (M. O'Connor's system of syntactic constraints is a substitute for meter, or a metrical system of a different order.) There have been various metrical theories of biblical poetry involving one or more of these elements. The theory of word meter assumes that there is a fixed number of word units in each line of verse. Related to word meter is the theory of thought meter, in which the thought unit (usually one or two words receiving one major stress) constitutes the basic unit of measurement. A third theory counts the number of syllables (without respect to whether they are open or closed, or stressed or unstressed). While technically not a metrical theory, syllable counting is related to discussions of syllabic meter. The most popular theory of biblical meter is accentual, which counts the number of accents or stresses per line. This approach is sometimes combined with the counting of the number of words or syllables.

All of these metrical theories suffer from several deficits. First, none has gained sufficient acceptance among scholars to place it clearly above its competitors. Second, all have had problems defining precisely the unit to be counted. For instance, what constitutes a "word"? Does it include affixed prepositions? Is a construct noun (a noun linked grammatically to an adjacent noun, as in "mountain top") a separate word? Finally, when the counting is done, the pattern of recurrence of the unit does not appear with sufficient regularity, even within a few lines, not to mention throughout an entire poem. While there are certain parameters for the number of words or syllables that may occur in a line, these parameters do not appear to result in a metrical system. They are, rather, a factor of the biblical Hebrew language, the terseness of poetic lines, and parallelistic construction. It seems best, therefore, to abandon the quest for meter in the poetry of the Bible.

The absence of a real metrical system notwithstanding, sounds do seem to recur with some regularity in biblical poetry, and this recurrence can be differentiated from non-poetic discourse. I prefer to use the term *rhythm* rather than *meter* for this type of recurrence because *rhythm* conveys the notion of the recurrence of sound, or the patterning of sound, without the requirement of measured regularity.

The rhythm of biblical poetry results from terse parallel lines. The number of thoughts and, therefore, of words and of stresses in each line of a parallelism tends to be about the same—not necessarily precisely the same, but about the same. Benjamin Hrushovski has described this as "semantic-syntactic-accentual free parallelism,"[10] which, as far as the recurrence of sound is concerned, produces "free accentual meter." In this system, most lines have between two and four stresses. More important, the lines within a parallelism tend to have the same number of stresses. Thus parallel lines are rhythmically balanced. Lines throughout a poem may vary in number of stresses (within linguistic constraints), but sets of parallel lines tend to be of the same "length." An exception is the so-called *qinah* meter, the rhythm found in laments, which has an unbalanced 3-2 stress pattern. Many lines in the Songs of Ascent collection (Psalms 120–134) have similarly unbalanced lines, but the pattern is not consistent. On the whole, though, a rhythmic balance within a parallelism, and sometimes over larger textual expanses, seems to be present, no matter what elements are counted. This rhythm, a by-product of parallelism, may be viewed as the "metrical" aspect of biblical poetry.

REPETITION AND PATTERNING

All discourse entails repetition, but we have come to expect more of it in poetry because we expect poetry to be more formally organized around certain structures and patterns. Patterning depends on repetition. We have already seen that parallelism, the most dominant characteristic of biblical poetry,

10. Benjamin Hrushovski, "Note on the Systems of Hebrew Versification," in *The Penguin Book of Hebrew Verse*, ed. T. Carmi (New York: Penguin, 1981) 58.

involves many types of linguistic repetition or equivalences—grammatical structures, semantic terms, words, and sounds. While much of the repetition described in this section occurs in parallelism, and some is a direct result of parallel structuring, other forms of repetition occur independently of parallelism. Whether or not they are found in discourse formally designated as poetic, they add to the poetic nature of the discourse because they encourage the reader to focus on the message for its own sake; in Jakobsonian terms, they contribute to the poetic function.

The repetition described below involves repeating the same word or triliteral Hebrew root, or the same or closely related basic sounds. The repetition may occur in various combinations or patterns. Sometimes it seems designed to emphasize the message or to focus attention on only a part of that message. At other times, the effect is less discernible, but nevertheless creates an agreeable impression.

Key Words. The same word or root may occur numerous times throughout a passage. For example, the root שמר (*šāmar*, "guard") occurs six times in the eight verses of Psalm 121. In Psalm 137 (nine verses) the root זכר (*zākar*, "remember") occurs three times, and the root שיר (*šîr*, "sing/song") occurs five times. In both cases, the key words point to the essence of the psalm's message. Psalm 121 assures us that God is the guardian who never sleeps, and Psalm 137 struggles with the conflict between remembering Zion and singing Zion-songs—that is, between the need to remember the Temple and the impossibility of performing the temple worship.

Anaphora. Several consecutive lines may begin with the same word or phrase. An excellent example is Psalm 150, in which every line begins with "praise him." Compare also Eccl 3:2-8: "a time to . . . and a time to . . ." More often, the repetition occurs within just a few lines, as in Ps 13:2-3: "How long" (four times).

Cataphora (Epiphora). Consecutive lines end with the same word or phrase. This is rare in the Hebrew Bible and may be considered incidental. An example is Isa 40:13-14; both of these verses end with "instructed him."

Anadiplosis. In this type of repetition, the last word or phrase of a line is repeated at the beginning of the next line. Examples are Ps 96:13:

> before the LORD; for he is coming,
>> for he is coming to judge the earth.
> He will judge the world with righteousness.
> (NRSV)

and Ps 98:4b-5:

> break forth into joyous song and sing praises.
> Sing praises to the LORD with the lyre,
>> with the lyre and the sound of melody.
> (NRSV)

Side-by-Side Repetition. This is the immediate repetition of the same word (a device used also in prose); for example, "Comfort, O comfort my people" (Isa 40:1 NRSV); "Awake, awake,/ put on your strength" (Isa 52:1 NRSV). Isaiah 28:10 (NRSV) makes extensive use of this form:

> For it is precept upon precept,
>> precept upon precept,
> line upon line, line upon line,
> here a little, there a little.

Refrain. A refrain is a phrase that is repeated after every verse or at major subdivisions of the poem. The refrain may have been chanted by a chorus in liturgical poems, such as Psalm 136, in which every verse contains the refrain "for his steadfast love endures forever" (cf. Ps 107:1, 8, 15, 21, 31). An example of a refrain in a non-liturgical poem occurs in David's lament over the death of Saul and Jonathan: "How the mighty have fallen!" (2 Sam 1:19, 25, 27 NRSV).

Inclusio (Envelope Figure, Frame). In this figure, the passage or poem begins and ends with the same word or phrase. The inclusio in Psalm 8 is "O LORD, our Sovereign,/ how majestic is your name in all the earth!" (NRSV). In Psalm 103 it is "Bless the LORD, O my soul" (NRSV). The framing of a poem gives a sense of closure and completeness.

Chiasm (ABBA Word Patterning). There are many types of chiasm, or reverse patterning, ranging from within one verse to entire books. The figure has been widely documented. I cite here only two examples of the ABBA patterning of words in one verse or two:

> Ah, you who call evil good and good evil,
> who put darkness for light
>   and light for darkness,
> who put bitter for sweet
>   and sweet for bitter! (Isa 5:20 NRSV)

> Even youths will *faint* and be *weary,*
>   and the young will fall exhausted;
> but those who wait for the LORD
>   shall renew their strength,
>   they shall mount up with wings
>   like eagles,
> they shall run and not be *weary,*
>   they shall walk and not *faint.*
> (Isa 40:30-31 NRSV, italics added; this is part of a larger patterning of these words)

ABAB Word Patterning. Isaiah 54:7-8:

> For a brief *moment* I abandoned you,
> But with great *compassion* I will gather you.
> In overflowing wrath for a *moment* I hid my face from you,
> But with everlasting love I will have *compassion* on you.

Notice that the patterned words in Isa 54:7-8 are not semantically related, as they are in Isa 51:6:

> Lift up your eyes to the *heavens,*
> And look at the *earth* beneath.
> For the *heavens* will vanish like smoke,
> And the *earth* will wear out like a garment.

Sound Patterning. Various types of sound patterning are possible in poetry. I have already mentioned the use of sound pairs, terms in parallel lines that share the same or similar phonemes (see the section "Parallelism," above). The most common type of sound patterning that one might expect is rhyme, but such rhyme as can be found in the Bible is incidental. There are many examples of alliteration, the repetition of the same sound or sounds (or more precisely, consonance, the repetition of consonant sounds).

For example, Isa 1:2 contains what may be viewed as consonance in an AABB pattern: שמעו שמים והאזיני ארץ (*šim'û šāmayim wĕhaʾazînî ʾereṣ*; cf. also Ps 46:10; Job 5:8).

Closely related to consonance and to parallel sound pairs is paronomasia, or word play—the use of words with different meanings but similar sounds. This is a favorite technique in the Hebrew Bible, and it occurs in prose as well as in poetry. A classic example is in Isa 5:7:

ויקו למשפט והנה משפח	*wayĕqav lĕmišpāṭ wĕhinnēh miśpāḥ*
לצדקה והנה צעקה	*liṣdāqâ wĕhinnēh ṣĕʿāqâ*

This play on words is rendered in the Tanakh translation as:

> And He hoped for justice,
> But behold, injustice;
> For equity,
> But behold, iniquity!
> (See also Isa 61:3; Zeph 2:4.)

The discussion thus far has focused on repetition and patterning within small passages of text, usually a line or two. Many more possibilities may occur in an entire poem. Of course, the most obvious structuring device is the alphabetic acrostic (Psalms 9–10; 25; 34; 37; 111; 112; 119; 145; Prov 31:10-31; Lamentations 1–4). Daniel Grossberg has analyzed centripetal and centrifugal structures. An adequate appreciation of the ways in which poems may be structured requires a separate study. I cite here only an example of the manner in which the various types of repetition presented above may intertwine and interact in one poem, Psalm 122.[11]

The key words of the psalm are *Jerusalem* (3 times) and *peace* (3 times), and they are good pointers to the message. The phonemes of *Jerusalem* echo in the word *peace* (שלום *šālôm*) and in several other words throughout the poem, so the entire poem reverberates with the sound of the city's name. *House*

---

11. See also Grossberg's analysis of this poem in Daniel Grossberg, *Centripetal and Centrifugal Structures in Biblical Poetry* (Atlanta: Scholars Press, 1989).

of the Lord (Temple) forms an inclusio, and at the midpoint, in verse 5, is *House of David.* Anadiplosis occurs in vv. 2-3 in the repetition of *Jerusalem,* and in two lines in v. 4: "To it the tribes go up,/ the tribes of the LORD" (NRSV). There is anaphora in the repetition of *there* in vv. 4-5 and *for the sake of* in vv. 8-9. The words שלום (*šālôm,* "peace") and שלוה/שלה (*šālâ/ šálvâ,* "have peace"/ "ease") alternate in an ABAB pattern in vv. 6-7; v. 6 has a high degree of consonance. Moving away from the repetition of words and sounds, we might note that the poem employs five verbs of speaking (*say, praise, ask, speak, request*) and four verbs of motion (*walk/go, stand, ascend, sit*). All of these forms of repetition help to bind the poem into a tight unity of sound and meaning.

IMAGERY

Metaphor and simile are hallmarks of poetry in all languages, to the extent that some theorists would define poetry in terms of the presence or dominance of metaphor rather than in terms of formal linguistic structures, like meter or parallelism. While biblical scholars generally do not view metaphor as the *sine qua non* of poetry, there is widespread acknowledgment that metaphor abounds in the Bible's poetic discourse. At the same time, there is widespread ignorance of how metaphor operates in biblical poetry, both from a theoretical point of view and on the practical level of how it affects the message of the poem.[12] An introductory article such as this one does not permit a full treatment of the theory of metaphor, or of the wealth of biblical examples, but a few observations on the use and effect of metaphor may be offered.

Imagery involves more than a simple comparison of one object to another. By placing the two objects in juxtaposition, a relationship between them is established such that their qualities become interchanged. This can be seen in Ps 42:2-3 (Eng. 42:1-2):

As a deer longs for flowing streams,
[אפיק *'āpîq*]
so my soul longs for you, O God.
My soul thirsts for God. (NRSV)

Water, the life-sustaining element, is equated with God; and the psalmist's thirst for God is like the deer's thirst for water. It is a natural, intuitive thirst for a basic substance. Thus the qualities of the deer image are transposed to the psalmist. But "longing" is not an emotion usually associated with a deer. It is a human emotion, transposed from the psalmist's longing for God onto the deer. The verb that one would expect in v. 1 in connection with the deer, "to thirst," is used for the psalmist in v. 2. There is a crossover effect: The deer longs (like a human) for water, and the human thirsts (like a deer) for God. (The psalm continues in v. 4 with "My tears have been my food day and night" [NIV]—continuing the parallelism between "water" and "food/bread" and doing so through another metaphor, equating "tears" [water, non-food, a symbol of despair] with "food.")

Even stock images like water can be used creatively. Let us see how the same term found in Ps 42:2, "stream" (*'āpîq*), is used in two other passages:

My brothers are treacherous like a wadi,
Like a wadi-stream [*'āpîq*] that runs dry.
(Job 6:15)

Restore our fortunes, O LORD,
like streams [*'āpîq*] in the Negev.
(Ps 126:4 NIV)

The image in both verses is taken from nature: the wadis that flow with water in the winter and dry up in the summer. The primary transfer of qualities in Job 6:15 is from the water to the friends. They are treacherously inconsistent like the wadis; they are unreliable, changing with the seasons. The choice of water imagery may also suggest that, like water, the friends should be life-giving and that, therefore, their betrayal is all the more disappointing. But there is also a transfer in the other direction. One does not normally think of wadis as traitors; yet that is what is suggested here in a hint of personification of the wadis. (The root "to betray,

12. One of the few volumes devoted to this topic, G. B. Caird, *The Language and Imagery of the Bible* (London: 1980), is not helpful except as a catalog of common images. The interpretations of Harold Fisch and Meir Weiss on specific passages are much more successful in explaining the workings of metaphor. See Harold Fisch, *Poetry with a Purpose* (Bloomington: Indiana University Press, 1988); Meir Weiss, *The Bible from Within* (Jerusalem: Magnes, 1984).

be treacherous" [בגד *bāgad*] is never used of inanimate objects.)

The same natural reference serves a more optimistic purpose in Ps 126:4, where the return of the streams in the rainy season forms the basis of the image. Is the restoration of fortunes, like the streams in their cyclical return, a certainty? Or is it unpredictable (as in the Job verse), and therefore an act of grace?

Sometimes multiple metaphors are linked to one subject, generally to clarify or to reinforce the thought. The metaphors derive from different images and are linked only in that they convey a shared idea.

> [two different images for speed]:
> They go by like skiffs of reed,
>   like an eagle swooping on the prey.
> (Job 9:26 NRSV)

> And it [the sun] is like a bridegroom
>   coming out from his wedding canopy,
> It rejoices like a strong man in running
>   his/its course. (Ps 19:6 [Eng. 19:5])

In the example from Psalm 19, which I have translated literally, it is not clear whether both images have the same sense—eagerness—or whether the first represents happiness/brightness and the second eagerness/strength. Again there is a crossover, this time between the two images, for "rejoices" (שוש *śûś*) is a verb more aptly used for a bridegroom than for a runner. The NRSV has neatly bound the two images together:

> which comes out like a bridegroom from
>   his wedding canopy,
> and like a strong man runs its course
>   with joy.[13]

There may also be a series of metaphors deriving from a central image—a conceit—as in Eccl 12:1-7; or a series of different metaphors for different parts of the subject, like the *wasfs* in Song of Songs 4–7.

When the Bible talks about God, it must speak, by necessity, metaphorically. God is *sui generis* and abstract, having no form, shape, color, or size. The deity is not like anything else, hence the only way to picture God is to compare God to other things. The most commonly used metaphor is that of a human, which results in anthropomorphisms, but aspects of God may also be compared to natural phenomena (Deut 32:11; Ps 36:5-7) or to the works God created (Ps 48:13-15).

On occasion, the same image may recur in close proximity with a new twist that gives a jarring effect, thereby reinforcing the power of the image, as in Isa 1:9-10:

> If the LORD of hosts
>   had not left us a few survivors,
> we would have been *like Sodom,*
>   and become *like Gomorrah.*
> Hear the word of the LORD,
>   you rulers of *Sodom!*
> Listen to the teaching of our God,
>   you people of *Gomorrah.*
> (NRSV, italics added)

Because the Sodom-and-Gomorrah image has two different connotations, Isaiah is able to use it for two different effects. He first invokes the association of Sodom and Gomorrah with total destruction, suggesting that the destruction that he describes might have been, but for the grace of God, just as catastrophic. But then, in an arresting reversal, he calls upon the association of Sodom and Gomorrah with total corruption, equating his present audience with the wickedness of Sodom and Gomorrah, which must inevitably lead them to a similarly catastrophic end:

> Raise your eyes to the heavens,
> And look upon the earth beneath.
> Though the heavens should evaporate
>   like smoke,
> And the earth wear out *like a garment,*
> And its inhabitants in like manner die out,
> My salvation shall stand forever.
> My deliverance shall not cease.
> Listen to me, you who know the right,
> You people with my teaching in its heart.
> Fear not human insults,
> And be not dismayed at their jeers.
> For the moth shall eat them up *like*
>   *a garment,*
> The caterpillar shall eat them like wool.

---

13. But the NRSV may have gone astray here. The word occurs in Job 39:21 in connection with strength or eagerness. It may well be that the image in Psalm 19 is not one of joy, but of virility. See my article "On Reading Biblical Poetry: The Role of Metaphor," forthcoming in *VT*.

But my deliverance shall endure forever,
My salvation through the ages. (Isa 51:6-8)

The image of the earth's wearing out like a garment makes the earth, which does not wear out nearly so quickly, seem ephemeral compared to the permanence of God's victory. Then, in v. 8, the jeering enemy will be eaten as a garment eaten by a moth, making the enemy not only ephemeral but also powerless before the attack of a small insect that will come to punish it. While the single use of "Sodom and Gomorrah" and "being eaten like a garment" would be effective, the reuse of these images strengthens the rhetoric by forcing the audience to give deeper thought to the image and its range of associations.

Finally, when reading the Bible, especially Hebrew poetry, it is not always easy to know when to read the text figuratively and when literally. What are we to make of Ps 114:3-4?

The sea looked and fled;
 Jordan turned back.
The mountains skipped like rams,
 the hills like lambs. (NRSV)

It seems clear that the personification of the sea and the Jordan refers to a "literal" event, the crossing of the Reed Sea and the crossing of the Jordan, which form a frame around the wandering in the wilderness at the time of the exodus. But what of the animation of the mountains and hills? Was this earth imagery made up to match the water imagery, to provide a kind of figurative background? Or does it, perhaps, also refer to a "literal" event, the theophany at Sinai?

Psalm 133:1 presents a different case:

How very good and pleasant it is
 when kindred live together in unity!
(NRSV)

Most modern scholars interpret this verse literally as a reference to family harmony. They perceive the entire psalm as a practical teaching on correct conduct. But, as I have shown elsewhere, this verse is both more concrete and more metaphoric than is generally understood. The phrase "live together in unity" is a technical legal term for joint tenancy (cf. Gen 13:6; 36:7; Deut 25:5), but the psalm uses the phrase metaphorically. The joint tenancy refers to the united monarchy. The psalm is expressing an idealistic hope for the reunification of Judah and Israel, with Zion as the capital and focal point.

FIGURES OF SPEECH

The notion of "figures of speech" is a Greek invention, as is much of the terminology used to describe poetic diction, but many of the phenomena that the Greeks identified in their own poetry and rhetoric may be found in other literatures as well. There is no clear consensus among modern scholars as to the figures of speech used in biblical poetry.[14] Among the figures of speech usually cited are allusion, apostrophe, hendiadys, hyperbole and litotes, irony, merismus, oxymoron, personification, and rhetorical questions. It should be noted that these figures also appear in the non-poetic sections of the Hebrew Bible, with the same rhetorical force. They are rhetorical figures, not poetic figures per se. These figures are not critical to the structuring of the poetry, nor do they dominate the poetic landscape like repetition or parallelism. They are merely decorative, enhancing the rhetorical effect of the message.

For example, in Ps 107:26 sailors tossed about in a storm are described through hyperbole (extravagant exaggeration) and merismus (the expression of a totality through mention of its representative components) as: ". . . mounted up to the heavens and went down to the depths" (NIV). Often hyperbole is conveyed through metaphor or simile, as in Obadiah 4: "If she [Edom] soars aloft like an eagle; if she places her nest among the stars."

Personification of death can be seen in Isa 28:15 and Ps 49:15; and wisdom is personified as a woman in Prov 1:20-33 and Proverbs 8.

Rhetorical questions may occur in series (Job 38; Amos 3) or singly. The effect can be as varied as the message in which the question is contained: anguish in Lam 5:21;

---

14. The standard reference is W. Bühlmann and K. Scherer, *Stilfiguren der Bibel* (Fribourg: 1973), but compare, for example, the list of "Figures of Speech" in L. Alonso Schökel, *A Manual of Hebrew Poetics* (Rome: Pontificio Istituto Biblico, 1988); and the list of "Poetic Devices" in W. G. E. Watson, *Classical Hebrew Poetry* (Sheffield: JSOT, 1986).

sarcasm in Job 8:12 and Zeph 2:15; instruction in Prov 31:10; amazement in Ps 8:5. A rhetorical question is a good way to draw the listener into the argument, and it is effectively employed by the prophets, as in Isa 5:4 and Jer 5:7, 9.

MOTIFS AND THEMES

A number of motifs or themes recur throughout or are specific to certain types of biblical poetry. These devices, no less than parallelism and repetition, are part of the forms of poetic expression. The recognition of motifs and themes allows the reader to understand them as overarching cultural references or metaphors and to compare their use in different contexts. They may be taken from the natural world, from human relationships, or from historical or mythical references.

Some themes are well-known, but even these have rarely been studied systematically. Among these are the prophetic use of familial relationships—i.e., husband-wife, father-child—to represent the relationship between God and Israel. Familial imagery is found throughout prophetic writing and reaches its height in the book of Hosea. Brief examples are:

I accounted to your favor
The devotion of your youth,
Your love as a bride. (Jer 2:2)

For I am ever a father to Israel,
Ephraim is my firstborn. (Jer 31:9)

Another pervasive theme is creation, which may be used to demonstrate God's infinite power over the enemy (Isaiah 40); God's benevolence to the natural world (Psalm 104); the awe and mystery of God's deeds (Job 38); the appreciation of the place of humans in the cosmos (Psalm 8); or the venerability of wisdom (Proverbs 8). Each iteration of the creation theme is different—in the wording used, in the items enumerated, in the aspects omitted or emphasized—so that the effect in each instance is tailored to the specific tone and message of the poem in which it is located.[15]

15. See A. Berlin, "Motif and Creativity in Biblical Poetry," *Prooftexts* 3 (1983) 231-41.

Other common motifs include God as a shepherd (Ps 23:1; Isa 40:11) and water as a metaphor for the life-sustaining nature of God (Ps 1:3; Jer 2:13). Less commonly recognized as a motif, but used frequently in the psalms, is the enemy or foe. This may be taken literally, but it is just as likely that it is intended to be an image for a more generalized type of danger or distress, physical or psychological.

O LORD, how many are my foes!
  Many are rising against me.
(Ps 3:1 NRSV)

O LORD my God, I take refuge in you;
  save and deliver me from all who
    pursue me. (Ps 7:1 NIV)

Lest my enemy say, "I have overcome
    him,"
My foes exult when I totter. (Ps 13:5)

An individual poet or prophet may have his own motifs or refrains, as Jeremiah does with "to uproot and tear down, to destroy and overthrow, to build and to plant" (Jer 1:10 NIV; 18:7-9 and passim) and Ezekiel does with "O, human being" (12:2, 9 and passim).

READING A POEM

Most scholarly analysis of biblical poetry has concentrated on its measurable features, such as formal structuring devices, repetition, parallelism, meter, and the like. Commentaries generally offer line-by-line interpretations focusing on difficult words and constructions or unusual references. Occasionally provided by the exegete, but often left to the reader, has been the actual reading of the poem—the making of sense and beauty from its sounds, words, and structures, the perception that it is a unified entity with a distinctive message. This, after all, is the raison d'etre for all the analysis, but because it requires more art than science, there has been some reluctance to engage in it. But there are ways to approach the reading of poetry and some guidelines to direct the reading process. One might look for the movement within the poem, the repeated words or phrases, unexpected expressions or images, and the general tone and the effect that it produces. It is also useful to compare similar passages, with an eye to their differences. (Meir Weiss does this with great skill and insight.) An introductory article does not permit a full-blown discussion of these points, but a few examples may be offered.

Movement in Psalm 13. The psalm begins at the depths of despair: "How long, O LORD? Will you forget me forever?" (v. 1 NRSV). It slowly moves toward the possibility of hope: "Look at me, answer me, O Lord, my God" (v. 3). Then it reaches its climax in hope and exultation: "But I trust in your faithfulness . . . I will sing to the Lord for he has been good to me." The reader of this psalm, if identifying with the speaker, traverses the same emotional path from despair to hope.

Repetition in Job 38. Job 38 contains numerous rhetorical questions that involve first- and second-person pronouns: "Where were you when I laid the earth's foundation?" (v. 4 NIV); "Do you know who fixed its dimensions?" (v. 5); "Who closed the sea behind doors . . . when I clothed it in clouds?" (vv. 8-9); "Have you ever commanded the day to break?" (v. 12); "Have you penetrated the vaults of snow . . . which I have put aside for a time of adversity?" (v. 22). The effect of these pronouns is to create an opposition between the "you" and the "I"—Job and God—and the answers to the rhetorical questions prove that Job lacks even a fraction of God's knowledge and power. The combined effect is to show that Job is no match for God.

BIBLIOGRAPHY

The bibliography on biblical poetry is extensive, and much of it is extremely technical. It includes monographs and articles on specific features of poetry as well as explanations of poetic verses and sections in the Hebrew Bible. I have listed here only the most broad-based studies. References to more narrowly focused studies were made in the body of the discussion when appropriate.

For additional bibliography, see Berlin, *The Dynamics of Biblical Parallelism*; O'Connor, *Hebrew Verse Structure*; and Watson, *Classical Hebrew Poetry* (all cited below).

Alonso Schökel, L. *A Manual of Hebrew Poetics.* Rome: Pontificio Istituto Biblico, 1988.

Alter, R. *The Art of Biblical Poetry.* New York: Basic Books, 1985.

Berlin, A. *Biblical Poetry Through Medieval Jewish Eyes.* Bloomington: Indiana University Press, 1991.

———. *The Dynamics of Biblical Parallelism.* Bloomington: Indiana University Press, 1985.

———. "Parallelism." *Anchor Bible Dictionary.* New York: Doubleday, 1992. 5:155-62.

Fisch, H. *Poetry with a Purpose.* Bloomington: Indiana University Press, 1988.

Freedman, D. N. "Pottery." In *Poetry and Prophecy: Collected Essays on Hebrew Poetry.* Winona Lake, Ind.: Eisenbrauns, 1980.

Garr, W. "The Qinah: A Study of Poetic Meter, Syntax and Style," *ZAW* 95 (1983) 54-75.

Grossberg, D. *Centripetal and Centrifugal Structures in Biblical Poetry.* Atlanta: Scholars Press, 1989.

Hrushovski, B. "Prosody, Hebrew." In *EncJud.* 13:1195-1203.

Kugel, J. *The Idea of Biblical Poetry: Parallelism and Its History.* New Haven: Yale University Press, 1981.

Kuntz, J. K. "Recent Perspectives on Biblical Poetry," *RelSRev* 19, 4 (1993) 321-27.

O'Connor, M. *Hebrew Verse Structure.* Winona Lake, Ind.: Eisenbrauns, 1980.

Petersen, D., and K. Richards. *Interpreting Hebrew Poetry.* Minneapolis: Fortress, 1992.

Watson, W. G. E. *Classical Hebrew Poetry.* Sheffield: JSOT, 1986.

Weiss, M. *The Bible from Within.* Jerusalem: Magnes, 1984.

THE BOOK OF JOB

INTRODUCTION, COMMENTARY, AND REFLECTIONS
BY
CAROL A. NEWSOM

THE BOOK OF
JOB

INTRODUCTION

here was once a man in the land of Uz whose name was Job." With these words, the Bible introduces one of its most memorable characters. In the popular imagination Job is an icon, emblematic of the sufferer who endures the unendurable without complaint. Yet what many generations have tended to remember about Job is only one aspect of his story. The "patience of Job" has become a cliché that obscures the much more complex figure who appears in the biblical book. Although the book of Job begins with just such a depiction of Job the pious, patiently enduring calamity, that initial image serves as a foil for the contrasting representation of Job that follows: Job the rebel, who debunks the piety of his friends and boldly accuses God of injustice. In contrast to the majority of Jewish and Christian interpreters over the centuries, who have often seemed somewhat embarrassed by Job's unrestrained blasphemies, many twentieth-century readers, reeling from a century of unparalleled horror, have been drawn to Job's anger as a voice of moral outrage against a God who could permit such atrocities. The attempt to claim Job as the patron saint of religious rebellion, however, also encounters embarrassment, for at the end of the book, after God's speech from the whirlwind, Job withdraws his words against God. Neither the character nor the book of Job yields to an easy appropriation. To the reader who is willing to forgo simplistic answers, however, the book offers a challenging exploration of religious issues of fundamental importance: the motivation for piety, the meaning of suffering, the nature of God, the place of justice in the world, and the relationship of order and chaos in God's design of creation.

READING THE BOOK OF JOB: ISSUES OF STRUCTURE AND UNITY

Job is a challenging book to read, not only because of the theological issues it treats but also because of the form in which it is written. It begins with a simple prose story (1:1–2:13) describing Job's piety, the conversation between God and the *satan,* which leads to a decision to test Job, and the disasters that befall Job as the test of his piety. Abruptly, the style of the book changes in chap. 3, as Job and the friends who have gathered to comfort him begin to debate the meaning of what has befallen him and the proper posture Job should assume toward God. In contrast to the simple prose of the first two chapters, this dialogue is composed in elegant, sophisticated poetry, full of rare words and striking images. The climax of this section is the long speech of God from the whirlwind and Job's brief reply (38:1–42:6). At that point, just as abruptly, the style again shifts back to simple prose for the conclusion, as Job's well-being is restored and the remainder of his long life is briefly described (42:7-17). The changes between the beginning, middle, and end of the book are not merely stylistic, but also correspond to changes in the representation of characters and in the nature of the religious issues under consideration.

Although the relationship between the prose and the poetic sections poses the most intriguing questions about how one is to read the book of Job, the form of the central poetic dialogue also presents issues that affect one's understanding of the book. The dialogue takes shape initially as an exchange between Job and the three friends who have come to comfort him. Following Job's initial speech (chap. 3), this exchange exhibits a regular and symmetrical pattern throughout two cycles, but appears to break down in the third (see Fig. 1, "Dialogue Between Job and the Three Friends," below). In this third cycle, Bildad's speech is only six verses long (25:1-6), and Zophar has no speech at all. Even more perplexing, what Job says in parts of chaps. 24, 26, and 27 seems to contradict his own previous words and to assert views like those of the friends.

Figure 1: Dialogue Between Job and the Three Friends

		Eliphaz	Job	Bildad	Job	Zophar	Job
First cycle:	chaps.	4–5	6–7	8	9–10	11	12–14
Second cycle:	chaps.	15	16–17	18	19	20	21
Third cycle:	chaps.	22	23–24	25	26	——	27

Between the end of the third cycle and Job's long speech in chaps. 29–31 comes a poem on the elusiveness of wisdom (chap. 28). No heading introduces the chapter, yet its style and content are so different from the surrounding speeches that it is difficult to imagine its being spoken by any of the characters. Job's long closing speech in chaps. 29–31 is no longer addressed to the friends as part of the dialogue but contains a challenge to God (31:35-37). Yet instead of God's reply, the following chapters introduce a new character, Elihu, whose speech is uninterrupted for six chapters (chaps. 32–37). Only then does the divine speech occur, bringing an end to the poetic section of the book.

In scholarly discussions of the past century, these various elements have usually been interpreted as evidence that the book of Job grew by stages, the various parts attributable to different authors working at different times. Although there are many different versions of this hypothesis,[1] it usually includes at least the following claims.

Stage 1. The oldest form of the book would have been the prose tale, an ancient story, originally told orally, about Job the pious. This stage is represented by chaps. 1–2 and 42:7-17. The middle part of this form of the story is no longer extant, but would have included some sort of brief dialogue between Job and his friends in which they spoke disparagingly of God, while Job steadfastly refused to curse God.

Stage 2. An Israelite author who considered the old story inadequate and in need of critique decided to use it as the framework for a much more ambitious, sophisticated retelling of the story in which the figure of Job does not remain the patiently enduring character of the traditional tale, but challenges God's treatment of him. According to this hypothesis, the author substituted a new poetic dialogue between Job and his friends (3:1–31:37) in place of the discussion in which they engaged in the older story and added a long speech by God as the climax (38:1–42:6). The author used the conclusion of the old story (42:7-17) as the conclusion of

1. See the discussions in H. H. Rowley, "The Book of Job and Its Meaning," in *From Moses to Qumran* (London: Lutterworth, 1963) 151-61; M. Pope, *Job*, 3rd ed., AB 15 (Garden City, N.Y.: Doubleday, 1979) xxiii-xxx; J. E. Hartley, *The Book of Job*, NICOT (Grand Rapids: Eerdmans, 1988) 20-33.

his thoroughly transformed new version of the book. The poem on wisdom in chap. 28 may be a composition by this author, who used it as a transition between Job's dialogue with his friends and Job's dialogue with God, or it may be an addition by a later hand.

Stage 3. Another author, writing sometime later, considered the new version of the book of Job unsatisfactory, because he perceived that Job had gotten the better of his three friends in their argument, and because he did not find the divine speeches to be an entirely adequate answer to Job. Consequently, he created a new character, Elihu, and inserted his long speech into the book in order to provide what seemed to him a decisive refutation of Job's arguments.

Stage 4. Sometime during the transmission of the book, copyists who were shocked by Job's blasphemous words attempted to soften their impact by rearranging the third cycle of speeches, putting some of Bildad's and Zophar's speeches into Job's mouth.

Perhaps the least persuasive part of the hypothesis is the supposed rearrangement of the third cycle of speeches. Although some disruption may have occurred, the final result suggests incoherence more than a depiction of Job in the process of rethinking his views. Much more persuasive is the claim that the Elihu speeches are a secondary intrusion. The removal of his speeches would create no disruption in the rest of the book, for Elihu is not mentioned outside of chaps. 32–37, either in the frame story or in the dialogues. The absence of Elihu from the conclusion of the story is difficult to explain if he were an original part of the composition of either the prose frame story or the poetic dialogue. Also pointing to the secondary nature of the Elihu material is the fact that Elihu's speeches stand apart as a long monologue, unlike the speeches of Job's three friends, which are interspersed more or less regularly with Job's replies in the body of the dialogue. Elihu's discourse is also written differently, as he is the only character who explicitly cites other characters' words, a feature that suggests that the author of this section had the book of Job before him as he composed Elihu's speech. Since Elihu is the only character who bears a Hebrew name, it is possible, although quite speculative, that Elihu is actually the name of the writer who added these chapters—i.e., that he is a disgruntled reader who quite literally wrote himself into the book.

The hypothesis of growth by stages also provides a plausible account of the relationship between the prose tale and the poetic dialogue, and it offers an explanation for the incongruity that exists between the end of the poetic section and the final prose conclusion. In 42:7-9, God rebukes the friends for not having spoken correctly about God, as Job has done. This comment is difficult to reconcile with the book as we know it, but it seems to point back to a different form of the story, the "missing middle" that was displaced to make room for the poetic dialogues. No direct evidence for the independent existence of the old prose tale exists, but there is indirect testimony. Bishop Theodore of Mopsuestia (c. 350–428 CE) was familiar with an oral version of the story of the pious Job that did not contain the angry speeches of the canonical book and that was popular among both Jews and others. Indeed, Bishop Theodore considered the oral story to be the true story of Job, considering the biblical version as a literary production composed to show off the learning and poetic skill of its author.[2]

Critics who argue that the book of Job developed in this way rarely address the question of how one is supposed to read the book as it now exists. Indeed, one of the unfortunate consequences of this hypothesis about the composition of Job is that it has often led to interpretations of the book that fail to take its final or canonical form seriously. In recent years there has been a reaction against this tendency to treat the book as an assortment of parts rather than a single whole. Increasingly, even commentators who consider that the book may well have undergone some form of growth and redaction have nevertheless argued that one should read the book "as if" it were the product of a single author.[3] Occasionally, the claim is made that the book possesses a literary, thematic, and even stylistic unity best accounted for as the work of a single author.[4]

---

2. See the report of Isho'dad of Merv, the ninth-century CE author who summarizes Bishop Theodore's views, cited in D. Zaharopoulos, *Theodore of Mopsuestia on the Bible: A Study of His Old Testament Exegesis* (New York: Paulist, 1989) 45-48. B. Zuckerman has suggested that the epistle of James alludes to the familiar oral tale rather than to the canonical book of Job when it says, "You have *heard* of the patience of Job" (James 5:11) rather than "you have *read* [in the Bible] of the patience of Job" (Zuckerman, *Job the Silent: A Study in Historical Counterpoint* [New York: Oxford University Press, 1991] 13-14).

3. E.g., F. Andersen, *Job: An Introduction and Commentary*, Tyndale Old Testament Commentaries (Downers Grove, Ill.: Inter-Varsity, 1976) 55; J. G. Janzen, *Job*, Interpretation (Atlanta: John Knox, 1985).

4. N. Habel, *The Book of Job*, OTL (Philadelphia: Westminster, 1985) 35-40. Cf. Hartley, *The Book of Job*, 20.

Supporting the argument in favor of a single author is the contention that the prose tale in chapters 1–2 and 42 cannot be understood as more or less a transcription of an oral folktale but is a highly sophisticated piece of narrative art written in a deliberately "pseudo-naive" style.[5] To make that claim is not to reject the evidence for the existence of oral tales and traditions about Job, but only to recognize that the form of the story as we have it in Job 1–2; 42 is the product of a skilled author who has written an artistic imitation of such a popular story as the framework for his retelling of the story of Job.

Apart from the Elihu speeches, which seem quite clearly to be a later addition to the book, I confess to being an agnostic on the question of whether the book of Job grew by stages or was written by a single author, although I incline to the latter view. Interpretively, the important issue is not how the book attained its present form but how the shape of the book contributes to its meaning. In this regard, the presence of Elihu, the incoherence of the third cycle, and the role of the poem on wisdom raise interesting but relatively minor interpretive issues. The vital question is how one understands the significance of the abrupt juxtaposition of the two very different ways of telling the story of Job one finds in the prose and poetic parts of the book. The position taken in this commentary is that the incongruities produced by the transition to the prose conclusion in 42:7-9 are intentionally designed to call attention to these differences and to frustrate attempts to read the book as a single coherent narrative.[6] Whether this structure was produced by an editor who chose to let the discrepancies stand when the prose tale was adopted as a framing device, or whether it was produced by a single author who composed both prose and poetry, cleverly planning the incongruities, the effect is of a book "at odds with itself."[7]

Far from being an embarrassment, recognition that the book is at odds with itself is key to understanding its meaning and purpose. Dialogue is at the heart of the book of Job. The clash of divergent perspectives is represented in the three cycles of disputation between Job and his friends (chaps. 3–27). Job's final speech of self-justification (chaps. 29–31) stands over against God's answer from the whirlwind (chaps. 38–41) in dialogical relationship. By means of the cleverness of editor or author, the book as a whole is also structured as a dialogue of two very different prose and poetic voices, two very different ways of telling the same story that cannot be harmonized into a single perspective.

Representing two different ways of telling the same story within a single composition presents an artistic challenge. One could, of course, tell one version of the story in its entirety and then tell the other. The dialogic relationship is enhanced, however, by having one way of telling the story interrupt the other, as happens in the book of Job. This structure of two intersecting ways of telling the story may be visualized as follows:

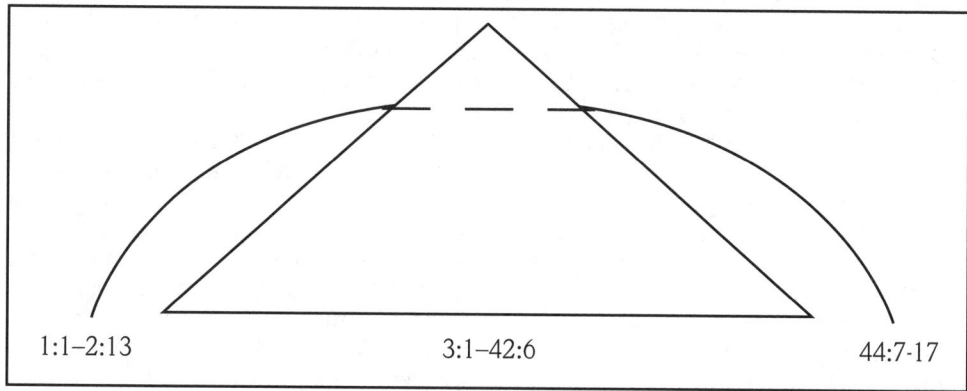

1:1–2:13   3:1–42:6   44:7-17

Figure 2: The Narrative Structure of Job

5. D. Clines, "False Naivete in the Prologue to Job," HAR 9 (1985) 127-36. The extensive and symmetrical repetition, highly stylized characters, and studied aura of remote antiquity imitate but exaggerate features of folktale style. Alongside these features are subtle word plays and verbal ambiguities that suggest an ironic distance from the aesthetic of simple naivete.

6. See C. Newsom, "Cultural Politics in the Book of Job," *Biblical Interpretation* 1 (1993) 119-34. In contrast, cf. the interpretive position taken by Habel, *The Book of Job*, 25-35.

7. Zuckerman, *Job the Silent*, 14.

This design works artistically because the frame story, whether considered as a naive popular tale or a "pseudo-naive" tale, invokes certain narrative conventions belonging to traditional storytelling that give such stories a high degree of predictability. As surely as a story that begins "Once upon a time . . . " must end with " . . . and they all lived happily ever after," readers know almost immediately what kind of story is being told in Job 1–2, how it will develop, and how it must end. One can plot the trajectory of the story line on the basis of these conventions. After God and the narrator have vouched for Job's character against the detractions of the *satan,* there can be no doubt about how Job will conduct himself. Since significant features often cluster in sequences of three in traditional storytelling, one expects three trials of Job's piety, before the obligatory happy ending. Thus, when the author of Job interrupts the frame story with the very different material in 3:1–42:6, a dialogical relationship is set up between what one knows is "supposed" to happen in this sort of a tale and what is actually happening in the story.

The tension set up by this structure is not only an aesthetic one. Social, moral, and religious values and assumptions are always embedded in particular modes of telling a story. By disrupting the prose tale, the poetic section of Job also challenges its assumptions about the nature of piety, the grounds of the relationship between humans and God, the proper stance toward suffering, etc.

If the book of Job had ended with a smooth transition from the poetic section to the concluding prose, then perhaps a synthesis of perspectives might have been fashioned. In the book as we have it, however, the transition to the prose tale is both abrupt and incongruous. The prose conclusion takes no account of the poetic dialogue but gestures back to the missing middle of the traditional tale, to what was "supposed" to happen according to its conventions. Moreover, as the Commentary on 42:7-17 will discuss, the presence of the prose conclusion following the dialogue and divine speeches actually creates both dissonance and irony, which threaten to unravel the sense of closure created by God's speech and Job's reply at the end of the poetic section. The book of Job thus presents the reader with unresolved perspectives. The theological implications of this structure are considered below.

DATE AND PROVENANCE

When, by whom, and for whom a book is written are important in understanding its meaning and significance. As the preceding discussion already suggests, those are difficult questions to answer with respect to Job, since different parts of the book may have been composed at different times for different audiences. Estimates for the date of the book as a whole (excepting the Elihu speeches), have ranged from the tenth century to the second century BCE, with most scholars opting for dates between the seventh and fifth centuries BCE.[8] Part of the difficulty in establishing a date for the book is that it contains no references to historical events or persons. Attempts to date the book according to its themes or place within the history of the religion of Israel are precarious, since it is difficult to demonstrate that the issues and religious values of the book of Job would be at home in only one era. More persuasive is the argument that certain motifs, such as the representation of the *satan* in chaps. 1–2, have their closest parallels in literature from the early post-exilic period (cf. 1 Chr 21:1; Zech 3:1-2).

Linguistic evidence has also been used to date the book; yet even here one encounters ambiguity. The poetic dialogues contain linguistic forms that one would expect to find in archaic Hebrew, from approximately the tenth century BCE.[9] Since these speeches appear to be written in a deliberately archaizing style and lack other poetic features one associates with very ancient Hebrew poetry, the argument for such an early date has not been generally accepted. The prose tale also contains narrative and stylistic details that suggest great antiquity.[10] Yet here, too, one must distinguish between what is genuinely archaic from an artistic imitation of archaic style. The most careful linguistic study has argued that the prose tale in its present form is no older

---

8. See J. Roberts, "Job and the Israelite Religious Tradition," *ZAW* 89 (1977) 107-14.
9. D. Robertson, *Linguistic Evidence in Dating Early Hebrew Poetry,* SBLDS 3 (Missoula, Mont.: SBL, 1972) 153-56.
10. N. Sarna, "Epic Substratum in the Prose of Job," *JBL* 76 (1957) 13-25.

than the sixth century BCE.[11] If that is the case, the book of Job as a whole is best taken as a composition of the early post-exilic period (sixth–fifth centuries BCE), whether one considers the book to have been composed by a single author, writing in two different styles, or by an author who appropriated an existing prose tale as the framework for a new composition.[12]

The Elihu speeches are difficult to date for many of the same reasons. The latest date for their composition is determined by their presence in the Aramaic translation of Job found in the Dead Sea Scrolls. Although that manuscript dates from the first century CE, the translation may have taken place as early as the second century BCE.[13] The only other basis upon which to date the Elihu speeches is the similarity of their ideas and expressions to other literature. While such evidence is not decisive, recent scholarship on the Elihu speeches has tended to place them in the third century BCE.[14]

Arguably more important than date is the question of by whom and for whom the book was written. Since no independent evidence exists, this question has to be posed in terms of the assumptions and values embodied in the book. Although much remains elusive, there are certain clues to its intellectual context and social class perspectives.

The book of Job is an immensely learned and cosmopolitan work. One recognizes this quality in the texture of the language itself, which is full of rare vocabulary and archaic verbal forms. The complex and beautiful poetry contains numerous mythological allusions, some of which appear to be based on Egyptian and Mesopotamian traditions. Furthermore, the poetic dialogue presents Job in terms of a sophisticated reworking of the Mesopotamian tradition of "the righteous sufferer" (see "The Book of Job and Ancient Near Eastern Tradition"). This same command of cultural and literary forms is evident in the author's treatment of genres and stylistic features drawn from Israelite tradition. The speeches of Job and his friends are largely shaped as disputations and make use of a rich variety of rhetorical devices one finds in wisdom, prophetic, and legal argumentation (e.g., rhetorical questions, wisdom sayings, appeals to ancient tradition). The author also displays a similar command of the genres of Israelite piety, in particular the hymn, the psalm of praise, and the complaint psalm. Not only are these forms cited in their traditional modes, but in the speeches of Job they are also rendered as exquisite parodies. Legal vocabulary, categories, and practices are similarly drawn upon for the development of a forensic metaphor through which to explore Job's relationship with God. The overall impression is of an author who has a remarkable command of the religious literature and traditions of Israel and its neighbors.

Although the author of Job orchestrates motifs, genres, and themes from a variety of different discourses in a way that is not characteristic of the books of Proverbs and Ecclesiastes, one should identify the book of Job primarily with the wisdom tradition. The very subject matter of the book suggests as much. Wisdom literature is centrally concerned with the nature of the proper moral and religious conduct of an individual and with the relation of such conduct to personal and communal well-being. Moreover, wisdom tends to pursue such questions in ways that do not make use of distinctively national religious traditions so much as they employ the conventions, styles, and language of an international discourse of wisdom. This orientation characterizes the book of Job, in which traditions about the non-Israelite Job are used to develop a critical reflection on the assumption that good conduct and well-being are related. More specifically, the theme of "fearing God," which is programmatic for the book of Proverbs (Prov 1:7; 9:10), also occurs in significant places in the framing of the book of Job, not only in the prose tale but also in the poem that concludes the dialogue between Job and his friends (1:1, 8; 2:3; 28:28). The friends' speeches, too, contain the sort of advice and admonition that has been described as "sapiential counselling."[15] The theme of wisdom is most explicit in the poem in

---

11. A. Hurvitz, "The Date of the Prose Tale of Job Linguistically Reconsidered," *HTR* 67 (1974) 17-34.

12. Zuckerman, *Job the Silent*, 26, however, argues that the linguistic evidence as a whole indicates that the dialogues are chronologically older than the prose tale.

13. Here, too, the basis for that date is linguistic. See J. P. M. van der Ploeg and A. S. van der Woude, *Le Targum de Job de la Grotte XI de Qumran* (Leiden: Brill, 1972) 4.

14. H.-M. Wahl, *Der Gerechte Schoepfer*, BZAW 207 (Berlin and New York: Walter de Gruyter, 1993) 182-87. Cf. T. Mende, *Durch Leiden zur Vollendung*, Trierer Theologische Studien 49 (Trier: Paulinus-Verlag, 1990) 419-27.

15. Habel, *The Book of Job*, 118.

chap. 28, in the refrain, " 'But where shall wisdom be found?' " (28:12, 20 NRSV). The prominence of creation motifs, both in chap. 28 and especially in the divine speeches, is also characteristic of wisdom, which often sets the question of the moral order of the world in terms of the structures of creation (e.g., Proverbs 3; 8; Ecclesiastes 1; Sirach 24). Finally, the wisdom tradition as a whole is typified both by conventional voices, which one largely hears in Proverbs, and skeptical, subversive voices, such as Ecclesiastes. In Job these two voices are joined in dialogue, not only in the dialogue between Job and his friends but also in the very form of the book, as discussed above. Thus the book of Job, although unique in many respects, is best understood as a part of the intellectual and cultural world of wisdom.

There is little consensus about the social identity of Israel's sages.[16] Although the sources of wisdom thought may lie in the social structures of families and tribes, wisdom *books* like Job are likely to emerge from a different institutional setting. Analogies with Egyptian wisdom literature suggest that such works were the product of a scribal class, the members of which served as administrators in the court or temple. Alternatively, it has been suggested that schools for the education of upper-class youths provided the social context for the composition of wisdom books. But the existence of such institutions is speculative. Although it is clear that Job is the product of an intellectual milieu, the exact nature of the social context in which it was produced and read cannot be known.

The issue of social class perspectives in the book of Job is complicated by the fictional setting of the book. Simply because the characters are depicted as wealthy aristocrats, one cannot necessarily assume that the author and audience are of that class. The more appropriate question to ask is what ethos is reflected in the book; when the issue is framed in those terms it is easy to agree that, whatever the actual social class of the author, the book addresses issues through the perspective of aristocratic sensibilities and values. In particular, Job's final speech (chaps. 29–31) provides an extended statement of the moral values of an aristocratic and patriarchal culture.[17] Attempts have been made to locate the social context of Job more specifically within the socioeconomic changes of the Persian period, when disruptions in traditional economic and social relations threatened to displace many old aristocratic families and brought increased suffering to the very poor, while the *nouveau riche,* who lacked traditional aristocratic religious and social values, exploited the new possibilities for their own benefit (cf. Nehemiah 5).[18] Although it is plausible to consider the author of the Joban dialogues as representing the perspectives of the old aristocratic culture in the context of the economic upheavals of the Persian period, it would be difficult to claim that the social conflicts presupposed by Job and his friends were unique to that period.

THE BOOK OF JOB AND ANCIENT NEAR EASTERN TRADITION

Scholars agree that neither the character Job nor the story about his misfortunes originated in Israel. The name "Job" is not a typically Israelite name, although forms of the name are attested in Syria-Palestine in the second millennium BCE.[19] Moreover, the story itself associates Job with the land of Uz, a place that is to be located either in Edomite or Aramean territory. Job's three friends—Eliphaz the Temanite, Bildad the Shuhite, and Zophar the Naamathite—also come from non-Israelite locales. (See Commentary on Job 1:1; 2:11.) The story as we have it in the Bible has been adapted for an Israelite religious context, however, so that Yahweh is assumed to be the God whom Job serves.

16. See, e.g., R. N. Whybray, "The Social World of the Wisdom Writers," in R. E. Clements, *The World of Ancient Israel* (Cambridge: Cambridge University Press, 1989) 227-50; M. B. Dick, "Job 31, the Oath of Innocence, and the Sage," *ZAW* 95 (1983) 31-53.

17. C. Newsom, "Job," in *The Women's Bible Commentary,* ed. C. Newsom and S. Ringe (Philadelphia: Westminster/John Knox Press; London: SPCK, 1992) 133-35; Dick, "Job 31, the Oath of Innocence, and the Sage," 31-53.

18. See F. Cruesemann, "Hiob und Kohelet: Ein Beitrag zum Verstaendnis des Hiobbuches," *Werden und Wirken des Alten Testaments* (Westermann Festschrift), ed. R. Albertz et al. (Goettingen and Neukirchen: Vandenhoeck & Ruprecht and Neukirchener Verlag, 1980) 373-93; R. Albertz, "Der sozialgeschichtliche Hintergrund des Hiobbuches und der 'Babylonischen Theodizee,' " *Die Botschaft und die Boten* (Wolff Festschrift), ed. J. Jeremias and L. Perlitt (Neukirchen: Neukirchen Verlag, 1981) 349-72.

19. Pope, *Job,* 5-6.

Although no trace of a pre-Israelite Job story exists in sources yet discovered from the ancient Near East, there is one biblical text that associates Job with two other non-Israelite characters whose stories had been incorporated into Israelite tradition. The prophet Ezekiel refers to Job in the context of an oracle from God concerning judgment against Jerusalem:

> "Mortal, when a land sins against me by acting faithlessly, and I stretch out my hand against it, and break its staff of bread and send famine upon it, and cut off from it human beings and animals, even if Noah, Daniel, and Job, these three, were in it, they would save only their own lives by their righteousness, says the Lord [Yahweh] . . . as I live, says the Lord [Yahweh], they would save neither son nor daughter; they would save only their own lives by their righteousness." (14:13, 20 NRSV)

Noah, the hero of the flood story, is a non-Israelite (or pre-Israelite) character whose story is told in Genesis 6–9. Although the name "Noah" is known only from biblical tradition, the character and his story originate in Mesopotamia, where he is variously known as Utnapishtim and Atrahasis.[20] Dan'el is not the Judean exile, hero of the book of Daniel, but a legendary Canaanite king. Although he is otherwise mentioned in the Bible only in Ezek 28:3, his story is told in the Ugaritic epic of Aqhat, the text of which was found in the second millennium BCE tablets excavated at Ras Shamra.[21]

Ezekiel's brief allusion takes for granted that his audience knows the stories of all these ancient paragons of righteousness. Yet it is difficult to say in detail exactly what stories about these figures Ezekiel and his audience know, whether they are the same ones preserved in the written accounts or from different oral traditions. The reference in Ezek 14:20 appears to suggest that all three somehow save their children from danger by means of their own righteousness. In Genesis 6–9, Noah's righteousness saves not only his own life but also those of his children when he takes them aboard the ark. Dan'el's story from the Ugaritic tablets is unfortunately broken off at a critical place, but it does involve the death of his son at the hand of the goddess Anat, the recovery of his body, and Dan'el's seven years of mourning for Aqhat. Whether the story told of Aqhat's restoration to life because of Dan'el's righteousness, as Ezekiel's allusion might suggest, is not known. With respect to Job, Ezekiel's allusion may refer to Job's attempting to protect his children by sacrificing on their behalf, in case "my children have sinned, and cursed God in their hearts" (Job 1:5 NRSV). In the canonical story of Job, the children are eventually killed as a part of the test of Job's righteousness. Ezekiel, however, may have known versions of the stories different from the ones preserved in written sources. Like Noah and Dan'el, Job appears to have been an ancient non-Israelite or pre-Israelite whose story, originally developed in other parts of the ancient Near East, had been incorporated into Israelite religious culture by the sixth century BCE.

In contrast to the prose tale, for which there are only tantalizing hints but no clear ancient Near Eastern parallels, the poetic dialogue in the book of Job has been compared to a variety of ancient Near Eastern texts from Egypt, Mesopotamia, and Ugarit.[22] For the most part, however, the similarities are much too general to be significant and do little to illumine the specific literary tradition to which the poetic dialogue of Job belongs. Only two categories of texts warrant discussion. The first is the tradition of Mesopotamian liturgical texts from the second millennium BCE in which a sufferer praises his god for deliverance from suffering. Among these are the Sumerian composition known as "Man and His God: A Sumerian Variation on the 'Job' Motif"[23] and the Babylonian text "I Will Praise the Lord of Wisdom," often called the "Babylonian Job."[24] Although these texts offer some parallels to the description of suffering one finds in Job, their importance for understanding the literary tradition to which Job belongs has been overrated.

---

20. For the Mesopotamian versions of the flood story, see James B. Pritchard, ed., *Ancient Near Eastern Texts Relating to the Old Testament (ANET)*, 3rd ed. with supplement (Princeton: Princeton University Press, 1969) 93-95, 104-6.

21. *ANET*, 149-55.

22. See, e.g., J. Gray, "The Book of Job in the Context of Near Eastern Literature," *ZAW* 82 (1970) 251-69; J. Leveque, *Job et son Dieu* (Paris: J. Gabalda, 1970) 13-90; Pope, *Job*, lvi-lxxi.

23. *ANET*, 589-91.

24. *ANET*, 596-600.

They are much closer in form and function to biblical psalms of thanksgiving than to the book of Job.[25] At most they provide background for the general ancient Near Eastern conventions for describing physical suffering and social ostracism.[26]

Much more significant is the striking similarity of form and content between Job and the text known as the Babylonian Theodicy. In contrast to the liturgical poems discussed above, the Babylonian Theodicy is a wisdom text.[27] Written c. 1000 BCE, the text was apparently quite popular even in the Hellenistic period, when a commentary on it was written by a Mesopotamian scribe from Sippar.[28] The Babylonian Theodicy consists of a dialogue between a sufferer and his friend and is composed as an acrostic poem of twenty-seven stanzas of eleven lines each, with a strict alternation of stanzas between the two characters. This formal design is quite similar to the dialogue in Job, although in Job the role of the friend is divided among three characters: Eliphaz, Bildad, and Zophar. Equally striking is the similarity in the way the individual speeches begin. In the Babylonian Theodicy, most of the stanzas begin with a compliment to the general intelligence of the other party. When the friend speaks, this general compliment is followed by a criticism that in this particular case the sufferer has said something irrational, erroneous, or blasphemous. For example:

> "Respected friend, what you say is gloomy.
> You let your mind dwell on evil, my dear fellow.
> You make your fine discretion like an imbecile's." (ll. 12-14)
> "My reliable fellow, holder of knowledge, your thoughts are perverse.
> You have forsaken right and blaspheme against your god's designs." (ll. 78-79)[29]

Similarly, when the sufferer speaks, his opening compliment is followed by a request that his friend truly listen to what he has to say:

> "My friend, your mind is a river whose spring never fails,
> The accumulated mass of the sea, which knows no decrease.
> I will ask you a question; listen to what I say.
> Pay attention for a moment; hear my words." (ll. 23-26)

In Job many of the speeches begin with a similar characterization of the previous speaker's words and wisdom, although the tone is generally sarcastic rather than the polite-but-frank tone that typifies the Babylonian Theodicy. As Job says:

> "Doubtless you are the people,
>   and wisdom will die with you!
> But I have a mind as well as you;
>   I am not inferior to you.
>   Who does not know all these things?" (12:2-3 NIV)

Similarly, Eliphaz replies:

> "Would a wise man answer with empty notions
>   or fill his belly with the hot east wind?
>
> .   .   .   .   .
>
> But you even undermine piety
>   and hinder devotion to God." (15:2, 4 NIV)

---

25. M. Weinfeld, "Job and Its Mesopotamian Parallels—A Typological Analysis," in W. Claassen, ed., *Text and Context: Old Testament and Semitic Studies for F. C. Fensham* (Sheffield: Sheffield Academic Press, 1988) 217-26; Gray, "The Book of Job in the Context of Near Eastern Literature," 256.

26. But see Zuckerman, *Job the Silent,* 93-103, who suggests a larger role for this genre in the development of the book of Job.

27. Gray, "The Book of Job in the Context of Near Eastern Literature," 267-68; S. Denning-Bolle, *Wisdom in Akkadian Literature* (Leiden: Ex Oriente Lux, 1992) 136-58.

28. W. G. Lambert, *Babylonian Wisdom Literature* (Oxford: Oxford University Press, 1960) 63.

29. Translation according to Lambert, *Babylonian Wisdom Literature,* 71-89.

Like the sufferer of the Babylonian Theodicy, Job asks that his words be heard, yet Job spoke without the confidence that his friends are capable of true understanding: " 'Listen carefully to my words,/ and let this be your consolation./ Bear with me, and I will speak;/ then after I have spoken, mock on' " (21:2-3 NRSV).

The content of the "Babylonian Theodicy" and of the Joban dialogues contains close parallels. In each of his speeches, the Babylonian sufferer complains about either personal misfortune or his perception that the world itself is morally disordered, with the unworthy and the criminal prospering while the deserving and the pious languish in misery.

> "My body is a wreck, emaciation darkens [me,]
> My success has vanished, my stability has gone.
> My strength is enfeebled, my prosperity has ended,
> Moaning and grief have blackened my features."

Compare Job:

> "My skin grows black and peels;
>   my body burns with fever.
> My harp is tuned to mourning,
>   and my flute to the sound of wailing." (30:30-31 NRSV)

The Babylonian sufferer complains that the impious flourish:

> "[. . .]the nouveau riche who has multiplied his wealth,
> Did he weigh out precious gold for the goddess Mami?" (ll. 52-53)
> "Those who neglect the god go the way of prosperity,
> While those who pray to the goddess are impoverished and dispossessed." (ll. 70-71)

Similarly, Job:

> "Why do the wicked live on,
>   reach old age, and grow mighty in power?
>
> .   .   .   .   .
>
> They say to God, 'Leave us alone!
> We do not desire to know your ways.' " (21:7, 14 NRSV)

Like Job's friends, the friend in the Babylonian Theodicy argues that retribution will come eventually to the wicked, whereas the pious one who bears temporary distress patiently will have his prosperity returned to him:

> "The godless cheat who has wealth,
> A death-dealing weapon pursues him.
> Unless you seek the will of the god, what luck have you?
> He that bears his god's yoke never lacks food, though it be sparse.
> Seek the kindly wind of the god,
> What you have lost over a year you will make up in a moment." (ll. 237-42)

Compare Eliphaz's words:

> "Consider now: Who, being innocent, has ever perished?
>   Where were the upright ever destroyed?

As I have observed, those who plow evil
and those who sow trouble reap it." (4:7-8 NIV; cf. 5:17-26)

Similarly, just as the Babylonian friend argues that "the divine mind, like the centre of the heavens, is remote; Knowledge of it is difficult; the masses do not know it" (ll. 256-57), so also Zophar asks Job:

"Can you fathom the mysteries of God?
Can you probe the limits of the Almighty?
They are higher than the
heavens—what can you do?
They are deeper than the depths of
the grave—what can you know?
Their measure is longer than the earth
and wider than the sea." (11:7-8 NIV)

Despite the striking similarities between particular arguments, the dialogues end quite differently. In the Babylonian Theodicy, when the sufferer complains that people praise the wicked and abuse the honest person, his friend not only agrees with him but also attributes this sad state of affairs to the gods, who "gave perverse speech to the human race. With lies, and not truth, they endowed them for ever" (ll. 279-80). Apparently satisfied that he has been heard, the sufferer thanks his friend, repeats his claim that he has suffered even though he has behaved properly, and concludes with an appeal to the mercy of the gods:

"May the god who has thrown me off give help,
May the goddess who has [abandoned me] show mercy,
For the shepherd Shamash guides the peoples like a god." (295-97)

By contrast, there is no rapprochement between Job and his friends. Following Job's lengthy concluding defense of his conduct, he does not appeal for God's mercy but wishes for a legal confrontation with his divine adversary (31:35-37). The Babylonian Theodicy contains nothing like the speech from the whirlwind, which forms the climax of the book of Job.

Although it is possible that the author of Job knew and drew upon the Babylonian Theodicy itself, it is more likely that the relationship is indirect and that there was a larger tradition of wisdom dialogues about the problem of the righteous sufferer and the general issue of moral disorder in a world supposedly governed by divine justice.[30] If that is so, then the similarities between Job and the Babylonian Theodicy, coming from different times and different national and religious contexts, allow one at least to identify the contours of that genre: the formal structuring of the dialogue, the rhetorical acknowledgment by speakers of each other, the characteristic arguments for and against the just ordering of the world. The lack of a narrative framework, as in the Babylonian Theodicy, is probably also a characteristic of the genre. Even if one assumes that the dialogue in Job was written explicitly with the frame tale in mind, it is striking that, except for the names of the characters, the dialogue makes no reference whatsoever to the particulars of the frame story. The dialogue appears to have been left intentionally unintegrated. As compared to the Babylonian Theodicy, the Joban dialogue is a much more sophisticated literary work. Without other examples, however, one cannot say whether the more ambitious scope and daring tone of the Joban dialogues mark a radical departure from the tradition or build on examples more fully developed than the Babylonian Theodicy.

Having traced what can be known of the ancient Near Eastern background to the prose and poetic parts of the book of Job, it is possible to venture a suggestion about the composition of the biblical book. All suggestions are necessarily speculative. They amount to claims that the shape

---

30. Lambert, *Babylonian Wisdom Literature*, 90-91, suggests that another very fragmentary text may be a second example of such a dialogue.

of the book and its component parts make the most sense if one assumes that it arose in such and such a fashion. They are in that sense suggestions about how one should read the book. With that caution in mind, I suggest that one read the book "as if" it came into existence in the following fashion. One might assume that an Israelite sage from the sixth or fifth century knew various oral traditions about the legendary Job and also knew the literary wisdom tradition of the dialogue of a righteous sufferer and his friend. Since Job was such an archetypal righteous sufferer, it is possible that the name "Job" had already been attached to versions of such dialogues. The religious perspectives of the two traditions, however, would have been sharply different, the tale of Job stressing a model of righteousness that takes the form of legendary endurance of extraordinary misfortune without protest, and the dialogue tradition casting Job in the role of skeptical protester against unwarranted personal misfortune and general moral disorder. How might one bring these traditions together so that they may both assert their claims and be challenged by the other's vision of reality? The solution devised by this clever Israelite sage was the artistic device of inter-cutting, beginning the book with a version of the traditional story, then sharply interrupting the telling of the tale with a version of the skeptical dialogue of the righteous sufferer, abruptly followed by the resumption of the traditional tale. Although it is possible that the speech from the whirlwind has antecedents in some other literary tradition, one might be inclined to think that the divine speech is the author's innovation, a reinterpretation of wisdom traditions about creation that serves to set the entire conversation about the experience of suffering in a quite different context than that envisioned either by the old tale or by the conventions of the dialogue of the righteous sufferer.

THEOLOGICAL ISSUES

However the book of Job achieved its present form, it presents a series of thought-provoking theological issues. The initial theological question of the book is framed in the prose tale by the *satan,* who asks about the motives of piety (1:9-11). Why does Job, and by extension any person, reverence God? Is it an implicit bargain for security and well-being, or is the relationship independent of circumstances? Traditional religion often talks about the blessings that come from piety and obedience to God, and the *satan*'s probing question asks whether such expectations subtly corrupt the relationship between human beings and God. The prose story, taken by itself, describes Job's piety as unshaken by extreme and inexplicable misfortune, and so affirms the possibility of wholly unconditional love of God. As important as such a question is, the way in which it is treated in the prose tale leaves a great deal unexplored. *Should* one serve God unconditionally and without question? What *is* the nature of the relationship between God and human beings? What is the character of God, and how does one have knowledge of that character? The dialogue and the divine speeches serve as a vehicle for considering these further questions, as well as other religious issues as they emerge from the experience of suffering.

Perhaps the most prominent issue in the dialogues is that of the proper conduct of a person in suffering. For the friends, suffering is an occasion for moral and religious self-examination and reflection. Although there is no single "meaning" for suffering, it is to be understood in some way as a communication from God. For the wicked, it is judgment (15:20-35); for the ethically unsteady, it is a warning (33:14-30); for the morally immature, it is a form of educational discipline (5:17-19); and for the righteous, it is simply something to be borne with the confidence that God will eventually restore well-being (4:4-7; 8:20-21). In every case the proper response is to turn to God in humility, trust, and prayer (5:8; 8:5; 11:13-19; 22:21-30). Implicit in the friends' view is the assumption that God is always right and that it is the human being who must make use of the experience to learn what God is trying to communicate. Although Job does not engage the friends' arguments explicitly, his own stance toward God implies a very different understanding of the divine-human relationship. Rather than turning inward in self-examination, Job demands an explanation from God (7:20; 10:2; 13:23; 23:5; 31:35). For Job, God has no right to cause suffering to come upon a person unless that person deserves punishment. The proper response where suffering appears to be undeserved is not humble prayer but confrontation of God. Thus Job rejects the notion of unconditional piety, at least insofar as it would mean submission to a God who acts without regard to what is just.

The differences between Job and the friends on the matter of proper conduct in suffering also bring into focus the issue of the character of God and God's governance of the world. In contrast to the conventional views of the friends, which take God's goodness and justice to be axiomatic (8:3; 34:12), Job often depicts God as a violator of justice (27:2) who acts out of obsessive and malicious curiosity (7:17-20; 10:8-14) or in a spirit of sadistic rage (16:9-14). The world over which God exercises supposed "moral" governance is characterized by anarchic destruction (12:14-25), the prosperity of the wicked (21:30-33), and the pervasive abuse of the poor (24:1-12). If Job is correct when he depicts God in these ways, then the very possibility of reverence for God is at an end, for God is a monster of cruelty. Job's speeches set up the theological issue in a more complex fashion, however, for Job's view of God's character is contradictory. He cannot give up the idea that, despite the evidence of his experience and his observations, God will ultimately be revealed as a God of justice (13:15-22; 23:3-7). The theological and emotional power of the book is due in large measure to the apparently insoluble nature of this contradictory experience. Job is not unique in raising the problem of a just God and the existence of injustice in the world (cf. Psalm 73). What is unusual about Job is the way in which he attempts to pursue and ultimately resolve this excruciating dilemma.

Some of the most intriguing theological issues in the book are never raised to the level of explicit debate between Job and his friends but can be teased out by attentive readers. One of these is the way claims to knowledge are authorized. Job and his friends not only hold different positions about the nature of God, the moral order of the world, and the meaning of what has befallen Job, but they also authorize their claims on very different grounds. The friends appeal to common sense, what "everybody" knows (4:7). Consequently, they assume that Job, too, will share their perceptions (5:27). Sometimes they argue deductively from what they consider to be universally agreed principles (34:10-12). At other times they cite anecdotal evidence (4:8; 5:3) or even the transcendent authority of private revelation (4:13-16). Most important of all, however, is their reliance on the authority of tradition. Not only do they appeal explicitly to ancestral tradition (8:8-10), but by filling their speeches with the forms of traditional religious language (e.g., sayings, didactic examples, doxologies), they also embody that authority. Job opposes this arsenal of common sense, rational argument, revelation, and tradition because he knows that what the friends claim is inconsistent with his own experience. Job often expresses the vivid immediacy of this experience and the claims to knowledge that it warrants in terms of the body's organs of perception (tongue, eyes, ears; 6:30; 13:1). Thus the book stages a conflict between different ways of grounding and authorizing knowledge.

Related to the conflict over the grounds for knowledge of truth is the book's exploration of the adequacy and limits of various kinds of religious language. Job's parodies of traditional psalmic and hymnic forms (7:17-19; 12:13-25) expose what appears to him to be their pervasive hypocrisy about the real nature of the divine-human relationship. Such forms of religious speech allow one to speak only of the goodness of God's transforming power, care for human beings, etc., but exclude from view the terrible experiences that give rise to the crisis of religious doubt about the nature of God. Traditional prayer also, which the friends keep urging upon him, is inadequate for the kind of conversation Job seeks to have with God, because it has no means of imposing accountability on God. Rejecting the conventional alternatives, Job's speeches gradually explore the possibilities of a new religious language based on a radically different underlying metaphor of the divine-human relationship. Job reimagines the relationship in legal categories, most concretely in terms of the possibility of a trial with God. This idea occurs first as parody (9:2-4) but eventually develops into a serious model for engaging God (23:3-7; 31:35-37). It serves Job's purposes well, for the model envisions a relationship of mutual accountability, undistorted by discrepancies of power, in which both parties acknowledge common standards of justice as binding. Such a way of talking about God and with God would have radical implications for the nature of religion. The book never fully develops these implications but leaves them as a provocative possibility.

Throughout the long dialogues between Job and his friends, theological issues and options are set up as alternatives between the traditional positions championed by the friends and the radical challenges posed by Job. The friends argue for the goodness of God, the moral order of the world, the purposiveness of suffering, and the importance of humble submission to God. Job questions the justice of God, describes the world as a moral chaos, depicts suffering in terms of victimization, and stakes his life on the possibility of legal confrontation with God. What goes largely unnoticed is the extent to which both positions depend on the same paradigm of understanding. They both take as unquestionable the assumption that justice, specifically retributive justice, should be the central principle of reality. They disagree only as to whether such justice is operative in the world or whether God should be called to account for failing to enforce such justice. The speeches of God from the whirlwind, however, challenge the paradigm that both Job and the friends have taken for granted. When God speaks of the "design" of the cosmos, which Job has obscured (38:2), the categories that underlie God's descriptions are not categories of justice/injustice but order/chaos.

The divine speeches do not explicitly engage the particular arguments Job had made but implicitly call into question their fundamental assumptions. As the juxtaposition of Job's final speech (chaps. 29–31) and the divine speeches (chaps. 38–41) shows, Job's theological categories had been derived from the social and moral assumptions that structured community life and social roles in his own experience. From these assumptions Job had extrapolated his expectations concerning God and the world. God's speeches, by beginning with the great structures of creation and speaking scarcely at all of the place of human beings in the cosmos, expose the limits of Job's anthropocentric categories. Similarly, Job's legal model for understanding divine-human relationships is also implicitly challenged. In Job's understanding, the fundamental categories are "right and wrong." No place exists in such a schema for the chaotic. Yet in God's speeches, the play between fundamental order and the restricted but still powerful forces of the chaotic is crucial for understanding the nature of reality. Through images of the sea (38:8-11), the criminal (38:12-15), the anarchic wild animals (38:39–39:30), and finally the legendary beasts Behemoth and Leviathan (40:15–41:34[41:26]), God confronts Job with things that his legal categories cannot possibly comprehend. The evocative but elusive language of the divine speeches provides resources for the reconstruction of theological language of a very different sort than that employed by Job and his friends, but the divine speeches do not do that work themselves. Theological construction properly remains a human task.

The provocative challenge of the divine speeches, which incorporate an image of God and the world quite different from that embodied in either the prose tale or the dialogues, brings one back to the original theological issue of the book: Why does one reverence God? What had been a question about the nature of human piety in the prose tale was transformed in the dialogues into a question about the character of God. Job's reply suggests that the divine speeches have provided him with a transformed vision of God and thus a very different basis for reverence (42:5); but his brief and enigmatic words (42:1-6) do not make clear exactly how his understanding has changed. If the author had made Job's interpretation of the divine speeches more explicit, then the reader would have been left with little to do beyond approving or disapproving of Job's response. By making Job's response so elusive, however, the author forces the reader to grapple more directly with the meaning of the divine speeches and so enter into the work of theological reconstruction that they invite.

One final theological issue remains to be considered, an issue that arises from the overall structure of the book, as discussed above. This issue might be stated in language taken from the book of Job itself: "Where can wisdom be found?" (28:12 NIV)—i.e., to which of the many voices in the book should one listen for the word of truth? One might reasonably assume that the divine speeches contain the essential truth of the book of Job. Not only does the voice of God carry transcendent authority, but the structure of the book up to that point seems to encourage such a judgment as well. The book appears to have been directing the reader from less to more adequate perspectives. The naive prose tale presents a moral perspective that is made to appear inadequate by the more literarily and theologically sophisticated dialogues. Within the dialogues, the friends' moral perspectives are shown to be inadequate by the compelling power of Job's words. The inadequacy of Job's perspective, however, is disclosed by the extraordinary speeches of God from the whirlwind. Surely one is supposed to adopt and endorse the perspective articulated by none other than God. Yet the book gives the last word to the prose tale. Moreover, the transition to the prose conclusion creates ironies that undermine the conviction that the book as a whole endorses the perspective of the divine speeches as the one true point of view. By having God declare that *Job* has spoken rightly (42:7), and by having events turn out just as the *friends* had predicted, the book wryly affirms perspectives that had appeared to be superseded and rejected.

What gets challenged in this process is the very notion that discerning truth is a matter of choosing one perspective and rejecting all others, that the truth about a complex question can be contained in a single perspective. Each perspective in the book of Job, taken by itself, contains valid insights. Yet each one, by virtue of its distinctive angle of vision, is of necessity oblivious to other dimensions of the question. When one looks back at the various views articulated by the different voices in the text, one finds that they are not so much contradictory as incommensurable.

It may be that the truth about a complex question can only be spoken by a plurality of voices that can never be merged into one, because they speak from different experiences and different perspectives. This is not to suggest that every position has equal validity or that with enough conversation consensus will be reached. As the book of Job illustrates, serious theological conversation places different voices in relationship precisely so that their limitations as well as their insights may be clearly identified. The dialogic truth that emerges from such a conversation is not to be found either in the triumph of one voice over the others or in an emerging consensus. It is to be found in the intersection of the various voices in their mutual interrogation. Such a perspective does not mean that one never gets beyond talk to decision. On the contrary, every person must choose how to live. In terms of the issues posed by the book of Job, choosing how to live involves deciding about the character of God, the structure of creation, the place of suffering in the world, and the significance of the moral and pious life. What the structure of the book challenges, however, is the assumption that such a decision, once made, accounts for everything and resolves every question. Instead, the significance of a choice can be appreciated only when it is questioned from other perspectives and by persons who have made different choices. The book of Job models a kind of theological inquiry in which multiple perspectives are not merely helpful but essential. By closing in a manner that frustrates closure, the book signals that the conversation it has begun about the nature of divine-human relations is not finished but requires to be continued by new communities of voices.

BIBLIOGRAPHY

1. Commentaries

Andersen, F. I. *Job: An Introduction and Commentary.* Tyndale Old Testament Commentaries. Downers Grove, Ill.: Inter-Varsity, 1976. An exceptionally good short commentary, written from an evangelical perspective.

Clines, David J. A. *Job 1–20.* WBC 17. Dallas: Word, 1989. A superb exegetical commentary with many original insights into Job.

Good, Edwin M. *In Turns of Tempest: A Reading of Job with a Translation.* Stanford, Calif.: Stanford University Press, 1990. A somewhat idiosyncratic but often provocative commentary, informed by contemporary literary approaches to the Bible. The translation is noteworthy for its attempt to render the Masoretic Text without emendation.

Habel, Norman C. C. *The Book of Job.* OTL. Philadelphia: Westminster, 1985. One of the best commentaries on Job, especially valuable for its sensitivity to literary dimensions of the book.

Hartley, John E. *The Book of Job*. NICOT. Grand Rapids, Mich.: Eerdmans, 1988. A thorough, helpful, and well-balanced commentary.

Janzen, J. Gerald. *Job*. Interpretation. Atlanta: John Knox, 1985. An accessible and thoughtful commentary that makes the existential questions raised by Job central to the theological interpretation of the book.

Pope, Marvin H. *Job*. 3rd ed. AB 15. Garden City, N.Y.: Doubleday, 1979. A classic commentary with excellent linguistic notes and comparisons with other ancient literature. The introduction is particularly valuable.

2. The following books and collections of essays by biblical scholars and theologians are particularly recommended.

Duquoc, Christian, and Casiano Floristan, eds. *Job and the Silence of God.* New York: Seabury, 1983.

Gordis, R. *The Book of God and Man: A Study of Job.* Chicago: The University of Chicago Press, 1965.

Gutiérrez, Gustavo. *On Job: God-Talk and the Suffering of the Innocent.* Translated by M. J. O'Connell. Maryknoll, N.Y.: Orbis, 1987.

Perdue, Leo G. *Wisdom in Revolt: Metaphorical Theology in the Book of Job.* JSOTSup 112. Sheffield: JSOT Press, 1991.

Perdue, Leo G., and W. Clark Gilpin, eds. *The Voice from the Whirlwind: Interpreting the Book of Job.* Nashville: Abingdon, 1992.

Zuckerman, Bruce. *Job the Silent: A Study in Historical Counterpoint.* New York: Oxford University Press, 1991.

3. Job's status as literary classic as well as sacred Scripture for both Judaism and Christianity has encouraged many who are neither biblical scholars nor theologians to write about the book. The following are particularly engaging recent examples of such work.

Bloom, Harold, ed. *The Book of Job.* New York: Chelsea House, 1988. Essays by philosophers and literary critics.

Girard, Rene. *Job: The Victim of His People.* Translated by Yvonne Freccero. Stanford, Calif.: Stanford University Press, 1987. An interpretation that considers Job in the light of the author's understanding of sacred violence and the phenomenon of the scapegoat.

Mitchell, Stephen. *The Book of Job.* San Francisco: North Point, 1987. A translation of Job by a poet who takes a poet's liberties with the text. The result is one of the most powerful artistic renderings of Job available.

Wiesel, Elie. *The Trial of God: A Play in Three Acts.* Translated by M. Wiesel. New York: Schocken, 1979. Set in the anti-Jewish pogroms of seventeenth-century Russia, the play engages issues raised by the book of Job by means of characters who correspond to Job, his friends, and the *satan.*

Wilcox, J. T. *The Bitterness of Job: A Philosophical Reading.* Ann Arbor: University of Michigan Press, 1989. An exploration of the necessity of affirmation in a world that cannot be adequately comprehended in moral categories.

OUTLINE OF JOB

I. Job 1:2–2:13, The Prose Narrative: Introduction

    A. 1:1-22, The First Test

1:1-5, Scene 1: Introduction to Job
1:6-12, Scene 2: A Dialogue About Job
1:13-22, Scene 3: The Test–Destruction of "All That He Has"
B. 2:1-10, The Second Test
2:1-6, Scene 4: A Second Dialogue About Job
2:7-10, Scene 5: The Test–Disease
C. 2:11-13, Scene 6: The Three Friends

II. Job 3:1–31:40, The Poetic Dialogue Between Job and His Friends

A. 3:1–14:22, The First Cycle
3:1-26, Job Curses the Day of His Birth
4:1–5:27, Traditional Understandings of Misfortune
6:1–7:21, Job Defends the Vehemence of His Words
6:1-30, Anguish Made Worse by the Failure of Friendship
7:1-21, Job Confronts God
8:1-22, A Metaphor of Two Plants
9:1–10:22, Job Imagines a Trial with God
11:1-20, Zophar Defends God's Wisdom
12:1–14:22, Job Burlesques the Wisdom of God and Struggles with Mortality
12:1–13:2, Job Parodies Traditional Praise of God
13:3-19, Job Criticizes Deceitful Speech
13:20–14:22, Job Experiences the Destruction of Hope
B. 15:1–21:34, The Second Cycle
15:1-35, Eliphaz Describes the Fate of the Wicked
16:1–17:16, Job Complains of God's Criminal Violence
18:1-21, Bildad Describes the Fate of the Wicked
19:1-29, Job Denounces God's Injustice
20:1-29, Zophar Describes the Fate of the Wicked
21:1-34, The Fate of the Wicked Is Prosperity and Honor
C. 22:1–27:23, The Third Cycle
22:1-30, Eliphaz Urges Job to Repent
23:1–24:25, Divine Justice Is Elusive
25:1–26:14, Bildad and Job Argue About the Power of God
27:1-23, Job Defends His Integrity
D. 28:1-28, Interlude: Where Can Wisdom Be Found?
E. 29:1–31:40, Job's Concluding Speech
29:1-25, Job Recalls an Idyllic Past
30:1-31, Job Laments His Present Humiliation
31:1-40, Job's Oath of Innocence

III. Job 32:1–37:24, The Speeches of Elihu

A. 32:1–33:33, Elihu Attempts to Answer Job
32:1-22, Elihu's Compulsion to Speak
33:1-33, God Uses Suffering to Warn and Redeem
B. 34:1-37, God, the Absolute Sovereign, Always Acts Justly
C. 35:1-16, God Does Not Answer the Prideful
D. 36:1–37:24, Elihu Describes the Character of God
36:1–21, God Redeems by Affliction
36:22-37:24, God Manifest in the Thunderstorm

IV. Job 38:1–42:6, God's Speeches from the Whirlwind and Job's Replies

    A. 38:1–40:5, Understanding the Divine Plan in the World
        38:1-38, The Cosmic Structures
        38:39–39:30, The World of Wild Animals
        40:1-5, Job's Response
    B. 40:6–42:6, Understanding the Nature of Divine Governance
        40:6-14, The Challenge
        40:15-24, Behemoth
        41:1-34, Leviathan
        42:1-6, Job's Response

V. Job 42:7-17, The Prose Narrative: Conclusion

JOB 1:2–2:13

THE PROSE NARRATIVE:
INTRODUCTION

OVERVIEW

The story of Job has often been called a folktale, and there are certain elements of the folktale in Job 1–2. The main character is a traditional figure, one whose story was apparently told not only in Israel but also among other peoples (see Introduction). The style of chaps. 1–2 has many of the marks of traditional folklore: repetition, economy of plot, characters who are types rather than complex figures.[31] Moreover, the central plot device, the testing of a character who does not know that he or she is being tested, recurs not only in the Old Testament (the testing of Abraham in Genesis 22) but also in many other cultures.

Although the term *folktale* is somewhat helpful in describing what kind of a story Job 1–2 is, it is not specific enough to account for the more distinctive features of the story and the way it is told. Compared with other biblical narratives containing elements of traditional or folk style (e.g., the wife-sister stories of Genesis 12; 20; and 26 or the wise courtier stories of Joseph in Genesis 41 and Daniel in Daniel 2), the story of Job is told in an exaggeratedly schematized style. The design of the story is symmetrically structured, organized around pairs of complementary scenes. Also notable is the extensive repetition of key words, phrases, sentences, and even whole passages. Schematic and symbolic numbers abound, both explicitly and in the structuring of scenes. Characters and events are described in exaggerated and hyperbolic terms, and the characters exemplify traits rather than undergo development. Also distinctive is the syntax of the opening line, literally, "a man there was . . . " rather than

the more common "there was a man." The narrator is explicitly evaluative, both at the beginning of the story and at crucial points within it. Although some of these features can be found in traditional folk narratives, taken together they point to a different genre.

In terms of both its style and its function, the story of Job is best understood as a didactic story, very much like the story that Nathan tells to David about a rich man and a poor man (2 Sam 12:1-4). There, too, the story opens with the same unusual subject-verb word order ("two men there were"). The setting of the story is similarly vague ("in a certain city"). Most important, the narrative style is characterized by highly schematic, parallel, and exaggerated descriptions of characters and events, as well as by extensive verbal repetition. The plot of the story is simple in the extreme, serving, as in Job, to disclose the character of the rich man. The comparison of Job with Nathan's story also suggests something of the function of this type of storytelling. Corresponding to the narrative schematization of the story is a moral schematization. In Nathan's story there are no shades of gray; right and wrong are unmistakable. It is a didactic story used to orient its audience (in this case David) to clear moral values. David responds to the story appropriately by voicing his outrage at the rich man's behavior. That judgment is just what the story is designed to provoke, although David does not foresee that he will be identified with the rich man.

Like Nathan's story, the tale of Job uses its schematic style to orient its audience to certain judgments about the existence and nature of true piety. Very frequently, such didactic stories serve to explore and resolve apparent contradictions in the values or

31. S. Niditch, *Folklore and the Hebrew Bible* (Minneapolis: Fortress, 1993) 6.

beliefs of a community. That is clearly how the story of Job 1–2 is structured. The *satan* is given the role of casting doubt. The plot of the story shows such doubt to have been wrong, and in so doing reaffirms the belief of the community in the possibility of disinterested piety. The simplicity of that story and its moral views will be challenged in the poetic dialogue that begins in chap. 3. In order for that challenge to have its full effect, however, one must first appreciate the didactic tale on its own terms.

The story of Job 1–2 is composed of a series of six distinct scenes (1:1-5; 1:6-12; 1:13-21; 2:1-7*a*; 2:7*b*-10; 2:11-13), the first five of which alternate between earth and heaven. Scenes 2 and 3 and scenes 4 and 5 form symmetrical pairs, each consisting of a dialogue in heaven about Job and a test of Job on earth. With the arrival of the friends after the conclusion of the second test, the symmetry of alternation between earth and heaven is broken, and the story prepares for the beginning of the dialogue between Job and his friends. The anticipated seventh scene, in which Job is restored, occurs in 42:7-17.

JOB 1:1-22, THE FIRST TEST

Job 1:1-5, Scene 1: Introduction to Job

COMMENTARY

1:1. The character of Job is the pivot upon which the entire book turns. In the first verse the reader is told three things about Job: his homeland, his name, and the qualities of his character. The location of the land of Uz is not entirely certain; probably it refers to an area south of Israel in Edomite territory (Jer 25:20; Lam 4:21; cf. Gen 36:28), although some traditions associate the name with the Arameans, who lived northeast of Israel (Gen 10:23; 22:21). In any event it is not an Israelite location. Similarly, the name "Job" would have had a foreign and archaic ring to it. It was not a name used in Israel, but similar names are known from ancient Near Eastern texts of the second millennium BCE.[32] Although later Jewish and Christian interpreters were concerned with whether Job was an Israelite or a Gentile,[33] his ethnicity plays no role in the story itself. Whatever the origins of the figure of Job, his story has been naturalized into Israelite religious culture, so that Job is presented unself-consciously as a worshiper of Yahweh (1:21). Job's archaic name and foreign homeland help to establish a sense of narrative distance, which facilitates the presentation of Job as a paradigmatic figure.

The crucial information about Job is the description of his character: "blameless and upright, one who feared God and turned away from evil." These are all very general moral and religious terms, particularly frequent in the wisdom literature and the book of Psalms (see, e.g., Pss 25:21; 37:37; Prov 3:7; 14:16; 16:6, 17). Although their content is important, the form of their presentation is also meaningful: two pairs of parallel terms. There is something hyperbolic in this piling up of adjectives. Even Noah, that other legendary righteous man (see Ezek 14:14), is described with only two (Gen 6:9).[34] More significant, the use of the numerical schema of four qualities, neatly paired, suggests completeness and perfection (cf. below on the fourfold destruction of "all that he has"). The leading term of the sequence, "blameless" (תם *tām*), carries connotations of wholeness and is often translated "integrity." This term becomes central to the story, as both God and Job's wife characterize him as one who "persists in his integrity" (תמה *tûmmâ*, 2:3, 9). The first term of the second pair, "one who fears God," is also echoed in a thematically crucial verse (1:9). "Fearing God" is a traditional Hebrew term for respectful and unsentimental piety.

32. Pope, *Job*, 5-6.
33. J. Baskin, *Pharaoh's Counsellors*, BJS 47 (Chico, Calif.: Scholars Press, 1983) 8-26.
34. A. Brenner, "Job the Pious? The Characterization of Job in the Narrative Framework of the Book," *JSOT* 43 (1989) 41.

1:2-3. The description of Job continues with an account of his children, his property, his household, and his status. Although it is not often reflected in the translations, the first word of v. 2 is "And" (וְ *wĕ*). It is grammatically possible to translate it simply as "and," a word that coordinates two independent observations, or it could be translated "and so," indicating a causal relationship. Does Job just happen to be rich and have a large family, or does he have these things because he is a man of exemplary piety? Although the narrator does not say explicitly, the very description of Job's family and wealth suggests a connection. All the numbers used are symbolic, suggesting completeness and perfection: seven sons and three daughters, for a total of ten children; sheep and camels in the same ratio of seven thousand and three thousand; and agricultural animals in a balanced distribution of five hundred plus five hundred. Just as Job's piety is complete and perfect, so also his family and property are complete and perfect. The reader is encouraged to see these as two things that fit naturally together. What binds them is the religious notion of blessing. Although the word "blessing" is not yet used, the picture the narrator draws of Job is easily recognized as the image of the righteous person blessed by God (cf. Pss 112:1-3; 128:1-4; Prov 3:33; 10:22). As with Isaac (Gen 26:12-14) Job's greatness (v. 3), i.e., his wealth and the status that accompanies it, can also be seen as a mark of divine blessing.

1:4-5. These verses illustrate the untroubled happiness of Job's family and the extraordinary piety of Job himself. Directing the reader's attention to the children foreshadows their crucial place in the destruction that follows (vv. 13, 18-19). Job's sons live like a king's sons, each in his own home (cf. 2 Sam 13:7; 14:31). Some interpreters see the series of banquets that the sons host "each on his day" as nonstop partying every day of the week,[35] but that interpretation seems unlikely. Since the brothers formally invite their sisters to each banquet and Job conducts sacrifices on their behalf "when the feast days had run their course," it is more likely that what is referred to here is a cycle of banquets

lasting several days, hosted by each son on the occasion of his birthday (cf. 3:1, where "his day" refers to Job's birthday). In contrast to the frequent OT narrative theme of conflict between brothers (e.g., Cain and Abel in Genesis 4; Absalom and Amnon in 2 Samuel 13), Job's sons live harmoniously and honor their sisters with particular attention. Nothing seems amiss in this picture.

Job's action, however, is the focal point of the passage. "To send and sanctify" suggests that Job summons his children to a solemn occasion at the conclusion of each banquet in order to offer sacrifice on their behalf (cf. Exod 19:10, 14; Lev 25:10; Joel 1:14; 2:15).[36] The sin that Job fears, cursing God, is a serious one, punishable by death (Exod 22:28 [27]; Lev 24:14-16; 1 Kgs 21:10). Job, however, does not even imagine that his children have cursed God aloud, but only "in their hearts." Moreover, the children may not be guilty of any misdeed at all. Job offers the sacrifice just in case his children have sinned. As with almost every other detail in this story, there is something a little exaggerated in the description of his careful intercession. The image of Job, protectively sacrificing on behalf of his children, recalls Ezekiel's allusion to Job (Ezek 14:14-20) as a legendary figure whose own righteousness sufficed to save the lives of sons and daughters. The irony of this scene is that it is precisely Job's righteousness that will set in motion events leading to the deaths of his children.

The English reader often misses a peculiarity of the text that is present in the Hebrew. Where the translations render "cursed God" in v. 5, the Hebrew text actually reads, "perhaps my children have sinned and *blessed* God in their hearts." The translators correctly recognize that "blessed" (ברך *bārak*) is used euphemistically here in place of "curse" (קלל *qll*), as in 1 Kgs 21:13. This euphemism is probably not a later substitution of the scribes who transmitted the biblical text; if it were, one would expect the euphemism to be standard throughout the Bible. There are, however, passages in which the literal words "curse God" (יקלל אלהיו *yĕqallēl 'ĕlōhāw*) appear (Lev 24:15; see Exod 22:28 [27]). Instead, this rather prim euphemism is a matter of the stylistic preference of the author.

---

35. E. Dhorme, *A Commentary on the Book of Job,* trans. H. Knight (London: Nelson, 1967) 4; G. Fohrer, *Das Buch Hiob,* KAT xvi (Guetersloh: Gerd Mohn, 1963) 77; H. Rowley, *The Book of Job,* rev. ed., NCB (Grand Rapids, Mich.: Eerdmans, 1976; original ed., 1970) 29.

36. Dhorme, *A Commentary on the Book of Job,* 4.

It may even be a part of the artistry of the story. Each of the seven times the word occurs in the prose tale (1:5, 10, 11, 21; 2:5, 9; 42:12), the reader must negotiate its meaning. Does it mean "bless" or "curse"? Even though most of the instances are easily enough resolved, the antithetical use of the word "bless" draws attention to itself. The word is thematically crucial. Just as "blessing" is used in a self-contradictory way, the story will explore a contradiction deeply hidden in the dynamic of blessing itself. (See Reflections at 2:11-13.)

Job 1:6-12, Scene 2: A Dialogue About Job

COMMENTARY

1:6. The first scene closed with the observation that "this is what Job *always* did," literally, "all the days." Scene 2 opens with the contrasting punctual phrase, "One day. . . . " The divine council is the setting of scene 2. Like its neighbors in the ancient Near East, Israel often imagined God as a king holding court, taking counsel, and rendering judgments about various matters (see 1 Kgs 22:19-23; Psalm 82; Isa 6:1-8; Dan 7:9-14).[37] The divine court consists of heavenly beings who are generally presented as an anonymous group, rarely distinguished by title or function. In Hebrew they are called the "sons of God." The term does not refer to a family relationship but is a Hebrew idiom for specifying the group to which an individual belongs. Thus "sons of cattle" means "cattle," "sons of Israel" means "Israelites," and "sons of God" means "divine beings" (see Gen 6:2, 4). Here

the divine beings "present themselves before Yahweh," a formal gesture (see Deut 31:14; Judg 20:2). The image is one of divine beings reporting to God, receiving commissions to execute, and reporting back from their missions. The most suggestive parallel to Job 1:6 is Zech 6:5, where the chariots of the four winds/spirits of heaven are described as setting out to patrol the earth after having "presented themselves before Yahweh."

It is unfortunate that so many translations, including the NRSV and the NIV, render the Hebrew השטן (*haśśāṭān*) in Job 1–2 as "Satan," which is linguistically inaccurate and highly misleading. The word *satan* is a common noun, meaning "accuser," "adversary," and is related to a verb meaning "to accuse," "to oppose." Here, where the noun is accompanied by the definite article, it cannot be understood as a personal name but simply as "the accuser." To read back into Job 1–2 the much later notions of Satan-the-devil is seriously to misunderstand the story of Job.

37. E. T. Mullen, "Divine Assembly," in *The Anchor Bible Dictionary,* ed. D. N. Freedman (New York: Doubleday, 1992) 2:214-17.

EXCURSUS: THE ROLE OF SATAN IN THE OLD TESTAMENT

Elsewhere in the OT the word *satan* is used to describe both human (1 Sam 29:4; 1 Kgs 5:4 [18]; Ps 109:6) and heavenly beings (Num 22:22; Zech 3:1), who act as adversaries or accusers. The context may be personal, legal, or political, but in each case the noun simply defines a function. It is likely that by the early post-exilic period, when the book of Job was probably written, the expression "the satan" had come to designate a particular divine being in the heavenly court, one whose specialized function was to seek out and accuse persons disloyal to God. The chief evidence for this is Zech 3:1, which describes the heavenly trial of the high priest Joshua, who is "standing before the angel of Yahweh, with the accuser [*ha-satan*] standing at his right hand to accuse [*satan*] him" (author's trans.). Some scholars have speculated that the figure of the accuser in Zechariah and Job may be modeled on officials in the Persian court who served as informers ("the eyes and ears of the king" [cf. Zech 4:2, 10*b*]) and even as *agents provocateurs*,[38] although this is less certain.

There is an ambivalence in the relation between Yahweh and the accusing angel that is important for understanding the development of this figure. The accusing angel is a subordinate of God, a member of the divine court who defends God's honor by exposing those who pose a threat to it. In that sense he is not *God's* adversary but the adversary of sinful or corrupt human beings. Yet in Zech 3:2, Yahweh rejects the accuser's indictment of the high priest and rebukes the accuser instead. In Job 1–2, Yahweh and the accuser take opposing views of the character of Job. As one who embodies and perfects the function of opposition, the *satan* is depicted in these texts as one who accuses precisely those whom God is inclined to favor. In this way the ostensible defender of God subtly becomes God's adversary.

Many scholars have seen in the development of the *satan* a process whereby ambivalent characteristics of God are externalized as a subordinate divine character. The *satan*'s actions are therefore not directly attributable to God and may even be rejected. The story of David's census of Israel is often cited as evidence of this process. In 2 Sam 24:1, the narrative says that "the anger of Yahweh was kindled against Israel" (author's trans.) and that Yahweh incited David to sinful behavior in conducting the census. In the later, parallel story in 1 Chr 21:1, however, the verse says, "Satan stood up against Israel, and incited David to count the people of Israel" (NRSV). In 1 Chronicles 21 the term *satan* is apparently used as a proper name for the first time,[39] and Satan represents an externalization, or hypostasis, of divine anger. In Zech 3:1, the accusing angel is the externalizing of the divine function of strict judgment in contrast to divine graciousness, which is then exercised by God (Zech 3:2).[40] In Job 1–2, the accuser is the externalizing of divine doubt about the human heart, which allows God to voice confident approval of Job's character.

In later centuries the figure of Satan develops into the dualistic opponent of God.[41] This hostile image of Satan is presumed by the New Testament (see, e.g., Mark 3:22-30; Luke 22:31; John 13:27; Rev 20:1-10). In the story of Job, however, that later development has not yet taken place. The accuser is simply the wily spirit who embodies his given function to perfection. In Goethe's famous phrase, he is *der Geist der stets verneint*, "the spirit who always negates."

38. N. H. Tur-Sinai, *The Book of Job: A New Commentary* (Jerusalem: Kiryath Sepher, 1957) 41; Pope, *Job*, 9-11.
39. But cf. P. Day, *An Adversary in Heaven: Satan in the Hebrew Bible*, HSM 43 (Atlanta: Scholars Press, 1988) 141-42.
40. Day, *An Adversary in Heaven*, 117.
41. V. P. Hamilton, "Satan," *ABD*, 5:985-89.

❖   ❖   ❖   ❖

1:7. There is a formal, almost ritual quality to the initial exchange between Yahweh and the *satan*. As a sovereign receiving a subordinate returned from his mission, Yahweh inquires whence he has come, and the *satan* replies (v. 7). His answer is neither evasive nor disrespectful.[42] The verbs

42. Contra R. Gordis, *The Book of Job: Commentary, New Translation, and Special Studies* (New York: Jewish Theological Seminary, 5738/1978) 15; Andersen, *Job*, 83.

are the same ones used in Zechariah of the "eyes of Yahweh who range [שׁוט *šûṭ*] through the earth" (Zech 4:10) and of the "divine horsemen and chariots who patrol [הלך *hālak*] it" (Zech 1:11; 6:5). At the same time, the *satan*'s reply presents him as a figure of wit and intelligence. His words are cast in poetic parallelism (AB//A´ B´) and contain a visual pun on his own title. The first verb, "to rove," "to go to and fro," is spelled *šûṭ*, and *satan* is *śāṭān*.

1:8. From his title one can assume that the *satan* has been patrolling the earth looking for disloyalty or sinful behavior to indict before Yahweh. Before the *satan* can give his report, however, Yahweh challenges him with a pre-emptive question. This is not a request for information. Narratively, Yahweh's challenging question suggests an ongoing rivalry with the *satan.* The grounds for such an edgy relationship are implicit in the *satan*'s function. One who defends a king's honor by zealously ferreting out hidden disloyalty simultaneously exposes the king to dishonor by showing that he is disrespected. Here, Yahweh pre-empts such activity and in effect defends his own honor by directing attention to "my servant Job" (cf. Gen 26:24; Exod 14:31; 2 Sam 7:5), the one person whose perfect loyalty and regard for God cannot be doubted. Yahweh's words in v. 8 *b* are precisely those by which the narrator introduced Job in v. 1 *b,* but God's praise is even more hyperbolic than the narrator's. Job is not merely the "greatest of all the people of the east" (v. 3); in God's judgment, "there is none like him on the earth."[43]

1:9-10. One of the conventions of Hebrew narrative is that the narrator can be trusted. When God confirms what the narrator says, the structures of narrative authority are doubly reinforced. Job's perfect character would seem to leave no crack for the accuser's doubt to penetrate. But as an accuser the *satan* must be true to type. The *satan*'s strategy is to shift the grounds of the debate. He meets God's rhetorical question with a rhetorical question of his own. "Is it for nothing [חנם *ḥinnām*] that Job fears God?" (v. 9, author's trans.). The *satan* shifts the focus to the question of what motivates Job's behavior. This is not necessarily, as it first appears, merely a questioning of Job's sincerity. The following rhetorical question is directed at God's activity in protecting and blessing Job. It is blessing itself that casts doubt on the very possibility of disinterested piety, even in such a paragon as Job. The *satan*'s insinuation suggests the symbolic image used by Henry James in *The Golden Bowl,* a vessel gleaming and perfect

on the surface, but flawed by a hidden crack within. The crack in the golden bowl that the accuser claims to see is the subtly corrupting influence of blessing on piety, which then becomes a tool of manipulation.

The *satan*'s language in v. 10 is vivid. As an image of God's protection, the hedge is an agricultural metaphor. The well-tended vineyard protected by a thorn hedge is safe from the destructive trampling of wild animals and theft by passers by (Ps 80:8-13 [9-14]; Isa 5:1-7). What is thus protected for Job is described in a three-part sequence that proceeds from the most intimate to the most distant: himself, his house (i.e., family), his possessions. While protection is described with a metaphor of containment (the hedge [שׂוך *śûk*]), Job's blessing is depicted as a "bursting forth" of flocks and herds (פרץ *pāraṣ*; see Gen 30:30).

1:11-12. The words that the *satan* utters in v. 11 are no wager but a challenge to a test. Job and God are mutually self-deceived in thinking that piety can ever be freely offered when it is routinely met with blessing. Breaking the nexus will prove the accuser right. If God breaches the protective hedge and destroys what Job has, Job will openly repudiate God. The language of the challenge requires comment. Literally translated, the sentence reads, "but stretch out your hand and touch all that he has—if he doesn't 'bless' you to your face." The euphemistic substitution of "bless" for "curse" is recognizable here, as in v. 5. The clause beginning with "if" is a form of self-curse. The full form contains both a protasis (an "if" statement) and an apodosis (a "then" statement), as in Ps 7:4-5 [5-6] ("If I have repaid my ally with harm/ or plundered my foe without cause,/ then let the enemy pursue and overtake me,/ trample my life to the ground,/ and lay my soul in the dust" [NRSV]). Commonly, a shortened form of the self-curse, without the apodosis, functions as an exclamation (Gen 14:23; 1 Sam 3:14; 14:45). Although occasionally an interpreter will argue that the accuser's exclamation is a seriously intended self-curse,[44] most recognize the conventional nature of the expression. Both the form and the nuance of the *satan*'s statement can be

43. For a somewhat different understanding of the dynamics of the exchange, see Janzen, *Job,* 39; D. Clines, *Job 1–20,* WBC 17 (Dallas: Word, 1989) 23-25.

44. E. Good, *In Turns of Tempest: A Reading of Job with a Translation* (Stanford, Calif.: Stanford University Press, 1990) 194-95.

colloquially but aptly rendered as "stretch forth your hand and strike all that he has, and I'll be damned if he doesn't curse you to your face!" The *satan's* challenge makes Job's *speech* about God the decisive factor in the drama. As Gutiérrez astutely observes, how to talk about God becomes the central issue in the whole book.[45]

The concluding words of v. 11 echo and contrast with v. 5. Where Job sacrificed on behalf of his children because he feared they might have cursed God in their hearts, the accuser challenges God to sacrifice Job's well-being to see if he will curse God to God's face.

45. G. Gutiérrez, *On Job: God-Talk and the Suffering of the Innocent,* trans. M. O'Connell (Maryknoll, N.Y.: Orbis, 1987) 3.

God consents and sets the terms. For the third time in as many verses, the phrase "all that he has" is repeated. The protective hedge is removed; God reserves for protection only the person of Job. Note that the threefold distinction of v. 10 has now become a twofold distinction. Job's family is incorporated into the category of "all that he has."

Yahweh will not personally "stretch forth his hand" against Job, as the *satan* suggested, but the difference is not significant. Yahweh and the *satan* have, metaphorically, joined hands to destroy Job. The scene ends dramatically: The accuser, having received a new commission, goes out from Yahweh's presence (v. 12; cf. 1 Kgs 22:22; Zech 6:5). (See Reflections at 2:11-13.)

Job 1:13-22, Scene 3: The Test—Destruction of "All That He Has"

COMMENTARY

1:13. This scene opens with two verbal echoes that set an ominous tone. Its first words, "one day . . . , " are the same as those that opened the preceding scene of the heavenly council at which the destruction was decreed. The description of the sons and daughters "eating and drinking wine" echoes v. 4. Although ostensibly the verse serves only to set the scene, it foreshadows the transformation of celebration into destruction and grief. There is also an ironic echo of the divine council. Just as emissaries come to Yahweh to report, so also messengers come to Job with reports. But Job is not sovereign over the events that befall him.

1:14-19. The account of the four messengers in vv. 14-19 is an astonishing piece of verbal art, using symmetrical structures and closely patterned repetition and variation. In vv. 2-3 Job's blessings were enumerated in the sequence of (1) sons and daughters, (2) herds of sheep and camels, (3) agricultural animals (oxen and asses), and (4) servants. In the reports of the messengers, the sequence is presented in almost the reverse order. The destruction of the servants, however, is distributed throughout the four reports. To keep the numerical total of four, the accounts of

the destruction of the camels and sheep are separate events. Thus the disasters are reported in the order: (1) oxen and asses, (2) sheep, (3) camels, (4) children. Other symmetries are present as well. The first and the fourth reports (vv. 14-15, 18-19) are longer and begin with a description of the peaceful scene before the destruction. The second and the third reports begin with an immediate identification of the agent of destruction (vv. 16-17). The agents of destruction alternate between human predators (Sabeans, Chaldeans) in the first and third reports and natural forces (lightning and a storm wind) in the second and fourth.

It becomes clear in the fourth messenger's report why the author has chosen to distribute the death of the servants throughout the account. A different term is used for the servants in vv. 14-19, not *'abûdâ* (עבדה) as in v. 3, but *nĕ'ārîm* (נערים). Although *nĕ'ārîm* is often used to mean "servants," its primary meaning is "boys," "young people." This strategic shift on the author's part allows a momentary ambiguity when the fourth messenger, reporting on the destruction of the eldest brother's house, says that it "fell on the *nĕ'ārîm* and they are dead." But Job and the reader know that this time the term includes both the servants and the children. For the reader, too, another echo is recognizable. In the fourth messenger's description of the situation before the disaster, he repeats word for word the narrator's scene-setting description in v. 13. The ominous anticipation has been fulfilled; the destruction is complete.

What is one to make of the narrative art of this description? At one level it is simply part of a schematic and hyperbolic style. But form always has meaning, although it may be elusive. Clearest is the use of the number four to suggest totality.[46] The interlinking of the four distinct reports in the various ways described underscores the fact that they are aspects of a single event. At a more comprehensive level of analysis, the totality is part of the story's structure. The completeness of Job's piety (v. 1) and the completeness of his blessing (vv. 2-3) are answered by the completeness of his destruction (vv. 14-19).

The interlocking of the four messenger reports, the formulaic repetition of the way the narrator introduces each ("while this one was speaking, another came and said," vv. 16-18), and the way each messenger ends his speech ("and I alone have escaped to tell you," vv. 15-17, 19) contribute not only to the scene's unity but also to its emotional impact. No time has been allowed for Job to respond to each individual destruction. The terms of the test were that "all that he has" be destroyed. Only now is it time for Job's response.

In contrast to the nonstop, overlapping words of the messengers, Job's response is initially nonverbal. He expresses himself in the ancient gestures of mourning, which the narrator enumerates in a series of brief clauses (v. 20). Tearing the robe in grief (see Gen 37:34; Josh 7:6; 2 Sam 1:11; 3:31; 13:31; Ezra 9:3, 5; Esth 4:1) and shaving the head (see Ezra 9:3; Isa 22:12; Jer 7:29; Ezek 7:18; Mic 1:16) are customary responses to catastrophe. Falling to the ground may also be (see Josh 7:6; cf. 2 Sam 13:31). The last verb in the sequence (lit., "to prostrate oneself" [השתחוה *hištaḥăwâ*]) is not otherwise used in a context of grieving. It is distinctly a gesture

of worship (1 Sam 1:3; Ps 95:6; Ezek 46:9). This is the decisive moment of Job's response. Why Job understands it to be an appropriate sequel to his gestures of grief is disclosed in his words.

1:20-21. Contrary to what one might expect, Job does not use the language of the funeral song or the lament. Those genres guide the grieving to experience and to express loss by contrasting what was with what is ("How the mighty have fallen" [2 Sam 1:25*a* NRSV]; "She that was a princess . . . has become a vassal" [Lam 1:1*c* NRSV]). Job also reaches for traditional words to orient himself in the face of shattering loss, but the words he chooses are proverbial ones from the wisdom tradition (v. 21). Variants of the saying about the mother's womb occur in Eccl 5:15 and Sir 40:1. Differences in form and context suggest that those later authors are not borrowing directly from Job. More likely the saying in Job 1:21*a* was traditional. Unlike the contrastive structure of the lament, the wisdom saying Job repeats is shaped according to a structure of equivalence. The governing image is that of the naked body, glimpsed as just-birthed infant and as corpse. The image is even more apt if one recalls that in the ancient Near East bodies were often arranged in the fetal position for burial. Thus the womb of the mother becomes the metaphor for the grave, and indeed for the earth, from which one comes and to which one returns (cf. Gen 3:19*b*; Ps 139:13-15). If the privileged image is that of the naked body at birth and death, then all else—not only possessions but also human relationships—is implicitly likened to the clothes one wears. However much clothes may feel like a second skin, they are put on and eventually must be put off. By means of the proverbial saying, Job is orienting himself to the hard but necessary reality of relinquishing what cannot be held on to.

The proverbial saying in v. 21*a* is followed by a specifically religious one in which the orientation is no longer to the experience of the human individual but to the activity of Yahweh. Fohrer is probably correct that the saying presumes an ancient idea that possessions are a loan from God, who may require them back at any time (cf. the notion of the present moment as a gift in Ecclesiastes).[47]

---

46. Fohrer, *Das Buch Hiob*, 88-89. Fohrer notes the use of fourfold destruction in Ezek 14:12-23; Zech 2:3; and in ancient Near Eastern literature in the story of Gilgamesh, 11:177-85.

47. Fohrer, *Das Buch Hiob*, 93.

But how would such a notion and such a statement lead to the final benediction, "blessed be the name of Yahweh"? First one must notice that the word order of the saying places the emphasis not on the verbs but on the subject. "It is *Yahweh* who has given and *Yahweh* who has taken away." The parallelism between the first saying and the second one is also important. In the first saying, the terror of birth and death, the vulnerability of nakedness, is contained through the image of the mother. It is she who sends and she who receives back again. In the second saying, Yahweh occupies the same place as the mother and is to be understood in the light of that image. The fragility of the gift and the desolation of the loss are endurable only if it is Yahweh who gives and Yahweh who takes (cf. Ps 104:27-30). Human words of blessing addressed to God are an act of worship that reaffirms relationship with God. It is not in spite of his loss but precisely because of its overwhelming dimensions that Job moves from the ritual of grief to words of blessing, which echo the liturgical formula in Ps 113:2.

1:22. in the Hebrew text the crucial word "blessed" (מברך *měbôrāk*) comes last in Job's speech. Its occurrence reminds the reader of what is at stake in Job's response. What Job has said contradicts the accuser's prediction that Job would curse God openly. Rather, in the light of the euphemism in 1:11, Job ironically says precisely what the *satan* predicted: He blesses God. The narrator sums up Job's response in v. 22. The word תפלה (*tiplâ*), which the NRSV and the NIV translate as "wrongdoing," is obscure. It is related to a word that means "insipid," "without taste" (Job 6:6; Lam 2:14), but the precise nuance of *tiplâ* remains uncertain. According to Clines, the context suggests that attributing *tiplâ* to God must be the most modest form of cursing God.[48] Job does not do even this. Thus Job's words are judged to have been absolutely blameless. The narrator's comment serves as a guide to what issues are central and how the reader is supposed to respond. Job's words demonstrate that piety can be disinterested, that it is not necessarily corrupted by divine blessing or destroyed by loss. There is no hidden crack in the golden bowl after all. The narrator's summing up also has a restrictive function. Other issues and questions that the reader might wish to raise about the characters, their actions, and their values are subtly discouraged as beside the point. Perhaps the author of Job has emphasized this stylistic trait of narrative control in order to make Job's outburst in chapter 3 all the more powerful. (See Reflections at 2:11-13.)

48. Clines, *Job 1–20*, 40.

JOB 2:1-10, THE SECOND TEST

Job 2:1-6, Scene 4: A Second Dialogue About Job

COMMENTARY

2:1-3. The fourth scene begins in a way virtually identical to the second (1:6-12). The addition of the phrase "to present [himself] before Yahweh" at the end of v. 1 points to the *satan*'s report as the one that matters for this story.[49] God initiates the dialogue as before, and the *satan* replies in the same way. Such repetition has several functions. It reinforces the stylized quality of the narrative. Repetition also increases the reader's

49. Contra Gordis, *The Book of Job*, 19.

sense of participation, as well as the sense of familiarity. Moreover, repetition increases anticipation. Whatever words break the repetition become the focus of attention. These crucial words occur in v. 3*b*. In the first part of that statement God echoes the narrator's positive judgment about Job, using the key term "integrity" (תמה *tûmmâ*). The following part of God's statement requires more reflection, however: "although you incited me against him, to destroy him for no reason." The wording shifts the focus momentarily from Job's character to the actions of God and the *satan*. Consider the difference if the storyteller had written, "He still holds fast to his integrity, even when the hedge around him is removed." The momentary loss of focus on Job runs counter to the highly controlled style of the didactic tale. It serves the design of the book as a whole, however. In the poetic dialogues God's character will become one of the main issues.

The author signals the thematic importance of this brief line more directly. The last word of Yahweh's statement ("without cause" [חנם *ḥinnām*]) is in Hebrew the same as the first word of the *satan*'s crucial question in 1:9 ("for nothing"). The Hebrew term *ḥinnām* has a range of meanings: "without compensation," "in vain," "without cause," or "undeservedly." It is possible to translate the line *"in vain* you incited me to destroy him," the point being that the test did not work as the *satan* predicted.[50] The word order, however, makes it more likely that the phrase is to be translated "to destroy him for no reason"—i.e., undeservedly. Something of the play on words can be suggested in English by the related words *gratis* and *gratuitously*. The use of the same word with different nuances in 1:9 and 2:3 suggests that the issues of the story are more complex than first envisioned. The didactic tale has been guiding the reader to affirm that disinterested piety, a fully unconditional love of God, is both possible and commendable. Yahweh's echo of the term *ḥinnām* in the context of "gratuitous destruction," however, suggests

the dark possibilities inherent in a relationship that is radically unconditional.

2:4-6. The *satan* is a formidable adversary. Unwilling to concede defeat, he shifts ground again. The proverbial saying that the *satan* cites is obscure.[51] It probably derives from a marketplace setting and has to do with comparative values. As Good argues, it should not be translated "skin for skin," which would be expressed in Hebrew with a different preposition. Rather, it is better translated "skin up to skin."[52] A person trying to trade for a skin would be willing to offer anything of value, up to an equivalent skin. But if the cost of a skin is another skin, then the deal is off, because there is no advantage in it. So the *satan* argues in the following line, which uses the same preposition, "All that a man has he will give, *up to* [בעד *běʿad*] his life."

The *satan*'s rhetoric is persuasive because it builds on Job's own images. Job used the image of the naked body as the essential self. So the *satan* turns to the image of skin, the reality of bone and flesh. The expression "bone and flesh" is an idiom elsewhere used to describe the identity of kinship, as in Laban's greeting of Jacob in Gen 29:14. Following the same wording as in the previous challenge (1:11), the *satan* now predicts that if God strikes Job's body, Job will openly curse God. As before, God places Job under the power of the accuser, this time preserving only his life (v. 6). Parallel to 1:12, the *satan* departs from the presence of God (1:7*a*). (See Reflections at 2:11-13.)

50. Andersen, *Job*, 90.

51. See Clines, *Job 1–20*, 43-46, for a survey of various interpretations.
52. Good, *In Turns of Tempest*, 52, 198.

Job 2:7-10, Scene 5: The Test—Disease

COMMENTARY

2:7. Since the second test is an attack on Job's body, there is no place for a scene such as 1:14-19. Instead, the destruction is briefly described in a narrative summary (2:7*b*). Here, too, however, there is a symbolic representation of the totality of Job's affliction, as he is struck with skin sores "from the soles of his feet to the top of his head." The identity of Job's disease has long intrigued

interpreters; attempts at diagnosis are beside the point, however. It is significant that it is a disease of the skin. Perhaps because so much of a person's identity is invested in the skin and because at least hands and face are involved in the public presentation of the self, diseases of the skin often evoke social revulsion. In the ancient Near East, where disease in general was often seen as a sign of divine displeasure, serious and intractable skin disease was particularly likely to be so interpreted.[53] There is, for instance, a strong echo between the description of Job's disease and the disease threatened as one of the curses for disobedience to the covenant in Deut 28:35. Similarly, in the Prayer of Nabonidus, a fragmentary Aramaic narrative from Qumran, a Babylonian king is stricken with "painful sores" (the same phrase as in Job 2:7). He recovers only when a "Jewish exorcist" pardons his sins and teaches him to worship the Most High God. Thus the disease with which the *satan* afflicts Job is one that would easily lend itself to interpretation as a mark of divine displeasure.

2:8. Job's response to this new disaster is described in quite different terms from the parallel scene. Job engages in no new acts of mourning. The NIV translation, "as he sat among the ashes," reflects well the syntax of the Hebrew. The clause identifies existing circumstances, not new action. As Clines observes, the implication is that Job has been sitting in the ashes as part of his mourning for his previous losses (cf. Jer 6:26; Ezek 27:30).[54] Now Job's only response to this new, terrible suffering is a purely physical one: He picks up a piece of a broken pot and scratches himself with it. The gesture communicates nothing explicit about Job's inner state, although its very noncommunicativeness has a somewhat ominous quality.

2:9. The silence is broken by Job's wife. For a character with only one line to speak, she has made an indelible impression on interpreters of the book of Job. The ancient tradition, reflected in Augustine, Chrysostom, Calvin, and many others, that she is an aide to the *satan* underestimates the complexity of her role. Verbally, her speech echoes both God's evaluation of Job (2:3) and the *satan*'s prediction of what Job will eventually say (1:11; 2:5; she, too, employs the euphemistic "blessed" [ברך *brk*]). Her words contain an ambiguity seldom recognized, one having to do with the thematically important word "integrity" (*tûmmâ*).[55] That word and its cognates denote a person whose conduct is completely in accord with moral

and religious norms and whose character is one of utter honesty, without guile. (In Psalm 101, for instance, integrity of heart and conduct is contrasted with images of a twisted heart, secret slander, deceit, and lies.) Ordinarily, it would be unthinkable that a conflict would exist between the social and personal dimensions of the word. Just such a tension, however, is implicit in the words of Job's wife. One could hear her question as a frustrated, alienated cry of bitterness stemming from immeasurable loss and pity, the equivalent of "Give up your integrity! Curse God, and in so doing, put yourself out of your misery!" More hauntingly, one could hear her words as recognition of a conflict between integrity as guileless honesty and integrity as conformity to religious norms. If Job holds on to integrity in the sense of conformity to religious norm and blesses God as he did before, she senses that he will be committing an act of deceit. If he holds on to integrity in the sense of honesty, then he must curse God and violate social integrity, which forbids such cursing.

2:10. However Job hears the words of his wife, he rejects them with strong language of his own, characterizing her as talking like one of the נבלות (*něbālōt*). Often translated "foolish women," this term has both moral and social connotations.[56] In English, one could capture something of the nuance by saying that she "talks like trash." Job's reply may also contain an element of social disdain for the outspoken woman (cf. Prov 21:9, 19; 25:24; 27:15-16). Although Job's criticism of his wife has largely set the tone for her evaluation by interpreters, there are more sympathetic interpretations of her character. The Septuagint gives her a longer speech, allowing her to talk about Job's sufferings and her own. In the *Testament of Job,* a Jewish retelling of the story of Job from the first century BCE, she is a character of pathos, whose suffering as she tries to care for her husband is vividly described. In both of these accounts, however, Job is the morally superior character who corrects her understanding. The sympathetic interpretation, as much as the hostile interpretation, obscures the role of Job's wife in articulating the moral and theological dilemma of his situation. Significantly, Job's rebuke of his wife is the last thing that he says

53. See K. van der Toorn, *Sin and Sanction in Israel and Mesopotamia,* SSN 22 (Assen and Maastricht: Van Gorcum, 1985) 72-75.

54. Clines, *Job 1–20,* 5, 49.

55. See Janzen, *Job,* 50, for a similar interpretation.

56. van der Toorn, *Sin and Sanction in Israel and Mesopotamia,* 107.

for some time. When he speaks again in chap. 3, his words bear traces of hers. Although he does not curse God, he curses the day of his birth. Although he does not die, he talks longingly of death. In subsequent chapters, his persistence in his integrity—both in the sense of his moral conduct and in the sense of his absolute honesty—motivates his own angry speech. His wife's troubling question will have become his own.[57]

Those developments lie in the future, however. In the present scene Job responds to his wife's question with another rhetorical question. Although it is not otherwise attested in wisdom literature, the rhythmic balance of the saying suggests that here, too, Job turns to tradition for words to orient himself and his wife to a proper response. The notion that both "weal and woe" come from God is a conventional way of acknowledging God's sovereignty (Isa 45:7; cf. Deut 32:39).

The artistic use of parallel scenes in the story directs the reader back to the equivalent scene and words in 1:20-21. There are contrasts: Job's words here are much less personal; there is no concluding blessing. At the same time, nothing in Job's words can be construed as cursing God. The comparison of the narrator's concluding evaluation is even more striking. The first words are the same: "In all this Job did not sin." But whereas the narrator in 1:22 went on to add "or charge God with wrongdoing" (NRSV), the narrator now adds only the phrase "with his lips." That phrase could with equal legitimacy be construed in two contradictory ways. It could be taken to mean that Job, like the ideal righteous person, was in control of himself from the inside out (cf. Ps 39:2; Prov 13:3; 18:4; 21:23).[58] Alternatively, it could suggest, as the Talmud says, that "Job did not sin with his lips; but in his heart he did."[59] That, after all, was what Job imagined his children might do, simply in the careless spirits of a feast (1:5). Of course, even if one conceded what the Talmud suggests, the terms of the test were about cursing God to God's face. Nevertheless, a merely technical victory is not a very satisfying outcome. This entire scene has suggested increasing strain on Job, and the ambiguous concluding verse raises the level of narrative tension. That tension must be resolved in a third and decisive scene.

It is almost disingenuous to talk about narrative tension, however, in this sort of story. The reader has been told by the authoritative narrator and by God that Job is "blameless and upright," etc. The situation is similar to that in a melodrama, where the audience knows that the hero will triumph over the villain and so can enjoy the pseudo-anxiety of the conflict. So here, the reader of the tale can enjoy the pseudo-anxiety that the hero will fall from perfection, knowing that in the third and decisive test the hero will triumphantly dispel all doubt about his character. Or so one could expect if the whole book of Job were told as a traditional tale. (See Reflections at 2:11-13.)

57. Newsom, "Job," *The Women's Bible Commentary*, 131-32.

58. So Gordis, *The Book of Job*, 22; Fohrer, *Das Buch Hiob*, 103; Andersen, *Job*, 94.

59. *b. B. Bat.* 16a. See M. Weiss, *The Story of Job's Beginning* (Jerusalem: Magnes, 1983) 71-74.

JOB 2:11-13, SCENE 6: THE THREE FRIENDS

COMMENTARY

The alternation of scenes between earth and heaven breaks off as the perspective shifts to another location on earth. The reader first sees the three friends of Job come together with the intention of visiting him in his grief (v. 11), and then sees Job through the eyes of the friends as they approach (v. 12).

Like Job in 1:1, the three friends are identified by name and place. The significance of the names and locations is no longer entirely clear, although the likelihood is that the three are presented as Edomites and, therefore, countrymen of Job.[60]

60. So Dhorme, *A Commentary on the Book of Job*, xxvi-xxvii; Gordis, *The Book of Job*, 23; Clines, *Job 1–20*, 57. For a different opinion, see Fohrer, *Das Buch Hiob*, 105-6.

The friends' action, going to Job "to console and comfort" him, is a traditional expression of solidarity in grief. To be deprived of this gesture of friendship made suffering even more difficult to endure (cf. Ps 69:20[21]; Isa 51:19; Nah 3:7, where the same pair of words occurs). Although the text says that the friends did not recognize Job, they clearly do, for it is the sight of him, changed *almost* beyond recognition, that provokes their gestures and cries of grief (cf. Isa 52:14). Weeping and tearing one's robe are both conventional expressions of mourning and distress, as is the use of dust. The precise nature and significance of "sprinkling dust in the air upon their heads" is obscure. The particular verb (זרק *zāraq*) and direction (lit., "heavenward" [השמימה *haššāmāymâ*]) recall how Moses flung soot into the air (Exod 9:10) to bring on the plague of "boils" (שחין *šĕḥîn*, the same word as in Job 2:7). The meaning and purpose of the actions, however, seem quite different.[61] Perhaps the word "heavenward" was not originally part of the text (cf. LXX) but was added as a gloss by a scribe who noted other similarities with Exod 9:10. Others suggest that the word may be an error for

a similarly written word, "appalled" (השמם *haŝamēm,* ; cf. Ezek 3:15; Ezra 9:3).[62]

Symbols of completeness and "perfection" are present in this scene, as in every other: the numerical symbols of three friends and seven days; the complementary images of seven days and seven nights. (Elsewhere periods of grief or silent distress may be described as seven days [Gen 50:10; 1 Sam 31:13; Ezek 3:15] but never as seven days and seven nights.)[63] The final words in 2:13 about the greatness of Job's suffering ironically echo the introduction of Job in 1:3 as the greatest among the peoples of the east. He has now exceeded all in suffering as he had in good fortune.

The picture of Job's friends sitting in silence on the ground is a conventional image of grieving, recalling Lam 2:10. The narrator focuses the scene through their eyes ("for they saw that his suffering was very great"). The friends' silence is respectful, even awed. In their silence they present a contrast to Job's wife, who, whatever her motives and meaning, sought to bring an end to Job's suffering by urging him to curse God. Ironically, the space created by the friends' silent presence is what finally provokes Job to a curse, moving the story out of the safe confines of the simple tale.

61. But see Gordis, *The Book of Job,* 24; Weiss, *The Story of Job's Beginning,* 76; Habel, *The Book of Job,* 97, who all argue that it is some form of magical gesture, though they disagree as to whether the intent is to express empathy or to ward off a similar fate.

62. So Tur-Sinai, *The Book of Job,* 30; Janzen, *Job,* 58.
63. Clines, *Job 1–20,* 63.

REFLECTIONS

This seemingly simple story presents any number of issues for reflection. Three of them will be examined: (1) the relation of blessing and self-interested religion; (2) attachment, loss, and grief; (3) the disturbing image of God in Job 1–2 and the cultural context it assumes.

In the OT blessing is primarily an expression of a close relationship or bond between God and an individual or a people. Divine blessing makes people flourish, and that flourishing is often talked about in very concrete terms: a large family, material prosperity, social power and status (e.g., Psalms 112; 128). Moreover, often one finds the promise of blessing offered as motivation for good conduct (Gen 17:1-2; Deuteronomy 28). That is the problem addressed by the *satan*'s cynical question: Hasn't the way people understand divine blessing slipped into essentially a barter religion? "If you will do this for me, I will do that for you." "If you will guarantee me this, then I will agree to do that." It does not take long, listening to religious talk shows or browsing through religious book stores, to feel the force of the *satan*'s question. Explicitly or implicitly, much of religion seems preoccupied with striking a bargain with God.

It is easy enough to deplore crude expressions of self-interested religion. The *satan*'s challenge goes deeper, however, suggesting that the distortion in the religious relationship is so deeply ingrained that people are not even aware of its presence until something happens to upset their assumptions. One finds out what people really believe when they face a crisis. The baby lies gravely ill, and the father rejects God in rage. The question that Job 1–2 poses to such a situation is not about the proper pastoral response or even about whether it is emotionally and religiously healthy to express the anger one feels. The story's question is about the theology implied by that rage, a theology that contains the unspoken assumption of a contract with God: God is bound to protect me from tragedy because I have been good or simply because I belong to God. Such a brittle faith will not sustain a person in crisis; yet it is often taught subliminally in the way religious communities talk about God. (There is, of course, much more to be said about the relation between anger and faith; later parts of the book will provide opportunity to reflect on different dimensions of that issue.)

It can be difficult to make the distinction between the appropriate human desire to protect what is precious and the inappropriate belief that one can strike a bargain with God. The story in Job 1–2 explores this subtle distinction by showing the reader a character who is fully aware of the human fears that drive so many to try to bargain with God but who does not understand his own piety and religious acts as a guarantee of security. The story engages readers by drawing them into emotions that readers have themselves experienced, as well as drawing them into situations and feelings that seem foreign or strange. Job's gathering his children and offering sacrifice for them "just in case" is the representative of every parent who has sat looking at his or her children around the dinner table, knowing that there is so much danger in the world and longing to protect them from it. The very exuberance and high spirits that make young people so dear is one of the things that produces anxiety in a parent's heart. Job knows this, like any parent, and evidently worries that his children would not think through the consequences of their actions, would get caught up in the partying and do something foolish, or in the process of trying to impress one another would make a bad judgment with possibly fatal consequences. It is a rare parent who has not, like Job, offered up a prayer to God on behalf of her or his children.

Such prayers are not necessarily attempts to strike a bargain with God, although the temptation is always there. Praying on behalf of another is an act of caring. When that prayer concerns a sin that the other person is unable or unwilling to bring before God, then it can be an act of reconciliation. Only when such prayer is assumed to have struck a deal is the proper function of prayer abused. Job's response to the sudden loss of children, property, and health shows that his piety was not the sort corrupted by the assumption of an implicit bargain. To understand the religious perspective that grounds piety like that of Job, it is necessary to look at the issues of attachment, loss, and grief, and at the way in which they are illustrated by Job.

The agony of love is that it cannot ensure the safety of the one we love so deeply. All the prayers, all the good advice, all the superstitious rituals ("if I imagine all the bad things that could happen, then they won't happen") cannot guarantee it. Loving is risky business; there is no way to bargain with God about that. Vulnerability is a condition of our being finite and mortal creatures. The greater evil would be to fear loss too much to risk loving at all.[64]

Job's blessings, especially as they are manifested in his children, but also in his prosperity and in his health, may appear to the *satan* as a hedge of security, but they can be seen equally well as a measure of Job's vulnerability. Health, financial security, family—these things matter. There is nothing venal or sinful or wrong in caring about them very much. It is because they are so important that the story insists that it is also important to think about the experience of losing them, and about the related but distinct experience of letting them go. Losing something one cares about deeply

---

64. Mary Oliver says this well in the poem "In Blackwater Woods," in *American Primitive*, 83.

---

is a devastating experience. Numbness, disorientation, anger, an overwhelming sense of helplessness—all of these emotions and more wash over a person in waves. This is the first part of grieving, but the work of grief requires something more. Finally, one has to let go of what has been lost. This does not mean forgetting or no longer feeling the aching absence. Letting it go does mean recognizing the reality of loss and accepting its finality. Both aspects of this process are reflected in Job's response, the first in the silent gestures of grief, the second in the words that he utters.

There are many ways to accept the finality of loss, because people bring different understandings of the world and of God to that process. For Job, letting go is made possible precisely because all things—both good and bad—ultimately come from God. To many readers, this is a baffling, if not an outrageous, position. There is a wisdom in Job's words, however, that is deep and powerful. Job's words are not about causality in the narrow sense. They do not deny the reality of tornadoes or bandits. Especially in the case of human violence it is right to be angry, to seek justice, to prevent such violence from occurring again. Energies directed in those directions are important, but they do not finish the work of grieving. One also has to come to grips with the terrible fragility of human life itself, the vulnerability that attends all of existence. It is God the creator who has made us as we are, capable of love and attachment, but also susceptible to disease, accidents, violence. In this sense, it is God who gives and takes away, from whom we receive both what we yearn for and what we dread. There is a tendency to want to associate God with only what is good. If one does that, however, then when trouble comes it is easy to feel that one has fallen into a godforsaken place. At the time, when one most needs the presence of God, there is only the experience of absence. The wisdom of Job's stance is that it allows him to recognize the presence of God even in the most desolate of experiences. Job blesses God in response to that presence.

This kind of reflection, which focuses on the religious values of Job and views God only through Job's statements about God, does not get at all of the difficult issues raised by this story. After all, the reader knows what Job does not—namely, what has gone on in heaven. No reflection on this story can be complete that has not wrestled with the difficult question of what to do with the image of God presented by the narrative itself. Some readers are so outraged by God's treatment of Job that they can hardly focus on any other aspect of the story. Others do not see this as an important issue at all. After all, they would say, this is not "really" God but a fictional story in which God is represented as a character. The whole business of testing Job is necessary to the plot, and without it there would be no story. Both of these responses have merit. It is important to be attuned to the genre and style of the story—to its playfulness and freedom of the imagination. Like some parables, it adopts a frankly outrageous premise to enable its readers to see something important. On the other hand, it would be a mistake to set Job 1–2 aside as "just a story," as though other speech about God could be literally descriptive. That is not so. *All* speech about God is the making of an image of God. All verbal or visual images of God are attempts to make a claim about who God is and what God is like. These images are suggestive, of course, rather than literal. Taking the genre of Job 1–2 fully into account, it remains necessary to reflect on the story's claim about who God is.

The representation of God as king of the universe in Job 1–2 is quite familiar from other biblical imagery and serves as a graphic way of attributing authority and sovereignty to God. The way the story represents God's motives in the actions that constitute the plot, however, puzzles many modern readers. What is God doing in bringing up Job's name, almost as a provocation, and then responding to the *satan*'s counter-provocation? To many readers, the exchange seems childish and quite unworthy as a representation of God.[65] Why the characters act as they do can be understood only

65. Cf. Robert Frost's humorous lines in "A Masque of Reason," when God confesses to Job: "I was just showing off to the Devil, Job,/ As is set forth in Chapters One and Two" (*The Poetry of Robert Frost*, ed. Edward Connery Latham [New York: Holt, Rinehart and Winston, 1969] 484-85, ll. 327-28).

when one recognizes that they represent the values of a culture of honor. When the *satan* casts doubt on Job's motives, he also besmirches God's honor by suggesting that even the best humans do not love God for God's own sake, but simply for what they can get out of it. Since God has just praised Job, God appears as a dupe. In cultures in which honor is a paramount value and losing face is a matter of shame, such a challenge cannot be ignored. Not only God's dignity but also God's authority would be compromised if the issue remained unaddressed. Readers who share those assumptions are not likely to consider God's response as "just showing off" but as something much more serious.

The narrative of Job 1–2 makes a radical case for the religious values accompanying a culture of honor. In doing so, it also exposes the limits of those religious values. Most readers of this commentary probably belong to communities in which honor, although important, is not such a central moral value as it appears in the narrative of Job 1–2. It takes a stretch of the imagination to enter into its worldview and theological values. Only after one has made the effort to appreciate those values, however, is criticism of their limitations legitimate.

God's honor and Job's freely given piety are two sides of the same religious values. Giving such devotion to God not only honors God but also provides the source of Job's own identity and self-worth. He is not a mercantile, self-oriented person, but one whose values are emphatically non-materialistic. That is what the story honors in Job and holds up as an ideal value. It is because of the integrity of his own devotion that Job can experience God's blessing as free grace. He places absolutely no conditions on his loyalty to God, and so does not feel forsaken by God even in the midst of his loss. Søren Kierkegaard praised Abraham as a "knight of faith." Yet Job excels Abraham.

The analogy with Abraham, however, raises questions about the intent of the Job narrative. In a sense, it radicalizes the story of Abraham. God tested Abraham, apparently uncertain of whether Abraham would sacrifice Isaac. When Abraham made it clear that he would, God spared Isaac—and Abraham. God has no doubts about Job. Yet neither Job's children nor Job is spared. It is as though the narrative asks the reader to look at values believed to be true—God's honor and Job's unconditional piety—and then forces the reader to evaluate those values under the most extreme circumstances. Can either value stand when weighed against the death of ten children and the torment of a loyal servant? The narrative appears to ask the reader to say yes by presenting Job's response as a sublime example of selfless piety. But is Job's response an example of sublime faith or of religious masochism? If the honor of God is absolutized, then nothing is too precious to be sacrificed to it—not the lives of children, not the body of a devoted worshiper. Job's own self-worth has been invested in his integrity as one who "fears God for nothing." But has his integrity itself become such a fetish that he cannot recognize the perversity of blessing the one who destroys him for no reason?

The literary genius of the prose tale is that one genuinely cannot say whether it intends to be a straightforward didactic tale that represents the sublime expression of a true knight of faith who loves God unconditionally, or whether it is a subversive didactic tale that exaggerates the traditional style just sufficiently to reveal the obscenity lurking behind the values of God's honor and the integrity of disinterested piety.

JOB 3:1–31:40

THE POETIC DIALOGUE BETWEEN JOB AND HIS FRIENDS

OVERVIEW

The narrative of chaps. 1–2 has created the expectation that Job will speak one final time, the conflict will be resolved, and the story will move on to its happy ending. Job speaks in chap. 3, but in a way that confounds narrative expectations and makes immediate resolution impossible. His long, highly developed poetic speech in chap. 3 belongs to a very different literary style from that of the prose tale. Biblical critics have generally assumed that this sharp contrast preserves the literary seam where a sophisticated poetic dialogue was inserted into a pre-existing traditional tale. Perhaps this is so, but it is also possible to understand the sharp change in literary styles as an intentional strategy on the part of a single author (see the Introduction).

Job's bitter outburst, so different in style and tone from his previous remarks, provides the occasion for the friends who have come to comfort him to speak. The dialogue through which this takes place, however, has a highly formal, stylized structure. Each friend speaks to Job in a set order, and Job replies to each, giving the sequence Eliphaz-Job; Bildad-Job; Zophar-Job. This sequence is followed for two complete cycles (first cycle, chaps. 4–14; second cycle, chaps. 15–21). In the third cycle (chaps. 22–27) the sequence breaks down, and it is not clear whether this disruption is due to mistakes made in the long history of the text's transmission or whether it is a literary representation of the breakdown of the dialogue itself.

The word *dialogue* may be misleading if the reader thinks of speakers who reply directly to each other's specific arguments. Although there are occasional instances in which one speaker appears to allude intentionally to what another has said, for the most part this is not so. Moreover, virtually none of the concrete details of Job's situation, as developed in the prose tale, are referred to in the dialogue, while many topics not seemingly germane to Job's particular case are discussed at length. To a great extent, the dialogue is best thought of as a disputation concerning traditional religious ideology and its ability to make sense of misfortune. Job, the archetypal righteous sufferer, provides the occasion for the debate, but the scope of the disputation is not limited to his case.

It is not evident why there should be three friends instead of one, as in the Babylonian Theodicy, or why the dialogue should be structured in three cycles. Presumably the three friends are a traditional feature of the Job legend and not a detail that the author of the book of Job was free to alter. A more perplexing question is whether any significant differentiation exists in the characterization or in the content of the three friends' arguments.[66] Interpreters frequently attempt to distinguish the three as having different styles. Eliphaz is often described as a character of great dignity and urbanity, primarily on the basis of his first speech, which is carefully solicitous of Job.[67] Bildad and Zophar are by contrast dogmatic

---

66. The most developed argument for a clear differentiation in the character and argument of the three friends is that of D. Clines, "The Arguments of Job's Three Friends," in *Art and Meaning: Rhetoric in Biblical Literature*, ed. D. Clines, D. Gunn, A. Hauser, JSOTSup 19 (Sheffield: JSOT, 1982) 199-214.

67. E.g., R. Gordis, *The Book of God and Man: A Study of Job* (Chicago: University of Chicago Press, 1965) 77-78. Some, however, consider Eliphaz to be sarcastic, e.g., J. C. Holbert, "The Function and Significance of the 'Klage' in the Book of 'Job,' with Special Reference to the Incidence of Formal and Verbal Irony" (Ph.D. diss., Southern Methodist University, 1975) 123. A much more subtle reading is that of K. Fullerton, who suggests that Eliphaz "is simply a rather stupid good person, blundering into words that would cut Job to the quick because he did not have a sufficiently sympathetic imagination to realize what impression he was likely to make by them." See Fullerton, "Double Entendre in the First Speech of Eliphaz," *JBL* 49 (1930) 340.

and mean-spirited. Differences between the styles of Bildad and Zophar, however, are much more difficult to establish. The whole question of character differences may well be the wrong one to ask. If it were a stylistic feature of the book, one would expect Bildad and Zophar to be more clearly distinguished. Moreover, the distinctions that one can make in the first cycle appear to evaporate in the second cycle, where the three friends all say essentially the same thing in essentially the same way. Throughout the dialogue the crucial contrast is between the three friends on the one hand and Job on the other. In this regard, they function as a collective character, similar to the way Shadrach, Meshach, and Abed-nego in Daniel 3 serve collectively as a contrast to Nebuchadnezzar. If Job's three friends have slightly different roles in the first cycle, it may be more a function of the sequence in which they speak rather than a character type that they represent.

The issue of the differentiation (or lack thereof) among the friends cannot be separated from the issue of the relation between the different cycles of speeches and between the friends' speeches and those of Job. In his first speech in chaps. 4–5, Eliphaz actually presents the whole repertoire of arguments that the friends will employ in all three cycles. There is, however, a clear progression in the perception of Job in the friends' first three speeches, from Eliphaz's assertion of Job's blamelessness (4:6), through Bildad's conditional language about Job's purity and uprightness (8:6), to Zophar's assumption that Job is guilty of something (11:6). Also characteristic of the first cycle is the friends' use of a number of different arguments and illustrations. In the second cycle there is only one issue: the retribution that befalls the wicked. This narrowing of focus implies that defense of this belief is central to the defense of the whole religious tradition represented by the friends. The relation between Job's situation and the fate of the wicked is left ambiguous. In the second cycle none of the friends identifies Job with the wicked person they describe. Only in the first speech of the third cycle does Eliphaz explicitly accuse Job of great wickedness and identify his evildoing as the cause of his suffering. Unfortunately, the disarray of the third cycle makes it impossible to know

if there was a particular focus to the friends' speeches beyond the indictment made by Eliphaz.

Taken as a set, Job's speeches do not show a simple developmental pattern. Themes are repeated throughout, and Job's mood vacillates from beginning to end. Various features, however, give his speeches a certain dynamic movement. One such feature is the theme of death. In chaps. 3 and 6–7, death is depicted as a refuge from God, a desirable alternative to the suffering of life. In chap. 10, even though life is something Job would rather not have experienced, death is no longer presented as a desirable state. Chapter 14 presents death as a terrible fate that destroys hope. By chaps. 16 and 19, death is an obstacle threatening what Job seeks from God, so that Job attempts to imagine a way around that obstacle.

To understand the changing role that death plays in Job's imagination, one has to note the emergence of another theme in Job's speeches, the lawsuit with God. In the early speeches (chaps. 3; 6–7), Job has rejected traditional approaches to suffering offered by religious convention. He has no reason to live. In chaps. 9–10, however, Job begins to toy with the notion, absurd on the face of it, of meeting God in a court trial (9:2-4, 14-24, 28-35; 10:1-2). As that model of engaging God begins to take shape in Job's mind, he gradually loses his desire to die. Even if it is a chimerical hope, the notion of a trial organizes his energy. The lawsuit metaphor appears in only a limited number of verses, yet it occupies an increasingly important place in Job's imagination (13:3, 17-19; 16:18-21; 19:23-29), until it becomes the mode by which Job attempts to force a confrontation with God (chap. 31).

A connection also exists between the development of Job's thought and the change in the way his friends respond to him. In the first cycle the vehement and even sarcastic tone of Job's replies in chaps. 6–7 and 9–10 is directly related to the hardening of the friends' responses to him. Job's final speech in the first cycle, however, shifts the focus of his attack (chaps. 12–14). He speaks less about his own distress and turns his attack more generally to the inadequate and deceptive modes of speaking about God and the world that characterize the friends' traditional religion. Apparently, this general attack on religious ideology provokes Eliphaz's direct accusation that Job's speech is sinful (15:2-16) and calls forth the friends' defensive demonstration of the reality of retributive justice in the speeches concerning the fate of the wicked. In the second cycle of speeches, when the friends reiterate their defense of retributive justice (chaps. 15; 18; 20), Job does not reply directly to their words in his first two speeches. In chap. 21, however, he refutes their depiction by a counterspeech concerning the good fortune of the wicked. Immediately following Job's direct repudiation of this most cherished notion of the friends, Eliphaz explicitly accuses Job of wickedness (chap. 22).

Unfortunately, the structure of the third cycle is too uncertain to make it clear how it relates to the preceding speeches. The disarray of the third cycle is followed, however, by the interlude of the poem on wisdom in chap. 28. This poem provides important connections to the major parts of the book. Its claim that wisdom cannot be found by mortals, but only by God, serves as a critique of the preceding dialogue and an anticipation of the voice from the whirlwind. The echo of the prose tale in 28:28 (cf. 1:1) reminds the reader of the alternative moral vision of the traditional story with its veneration of unconditional piety. As an interlude, however, the poem does not serve to resolve the book's conflicts so much as it provides an opportunity for the reader to detach from the intensity of the dialogue.

The final part of the dialogue is Job's concluding speech (chaps. 29–31), which corresponds structurally to his opening speech in chap. 3. This speech is quite different from what has preceded and serves as an important indication of how Job understands that his conflict with God can be resolved. Somewhat nostalgically, he describes his place in society before disaster overtook him (chap. 29). In so doing, he articulates a moral vision of the good society as he understands it. Job contrasts that vision with a detailed description of the social misery of his current plight (chap. 30). Finally, he challenges God with a great oath to present the charges against him (chap. 31). Implicitly, Job's assurance and his challenge are grounded in his assumption that God's relation to him is analogous to Job's relation to those in society dependent upon him, that God's values are analogous to Job's values. With Job's bold challenge to God, the dialogue ends.

JOB 3:1–14:22, THE FIRST CYCLE

Job 3:1-26, Job Curses the Day of His Birth

COMMENTARY

3:1-2. Chapter 3 begins with two introductory sentences, one in the style of the prose tale (v. 1), the other in the style of the dialogue that follows (v. 2). The opening phrase ("after this") establishes continuity with the seven days and seven nights of silence during which Job's friends have sat with him. This period of silence occupies the narrative place of a third test of Job. Just as the other two tests hinged on whether Job would "curse God," so also here Job's speech is critical, solemnly introduced by the statement "he opened his mouth." According to the conventions of traditional storytelling, which often use patterns of three, the third repetition should provide both heightened tension and definitive resolution. Just at the critical moment, the narrator says he "opened his mouth and cursed." The word is not the euphemistic "blessed" (ברך *bērēk*, as in 1:5, 11; 2:5, 9), but the word it has masked in chaps. 1–2, "cursed" (קלל *qillēl*). Only with the last word of the sentence does the narrator apparently resolve the tension: "he opened his mouth and cursed *his day*" (i.e., the day of his birth; see v. 3).

What does it signify to curse the day of one's birth? In antiquity curses and blessings were understood to be acts that had real effect under the proper conditions. Although some interpreters assume that Job is attempting an effective curse,[68] other references in the Bible to cursing the day of one's birth suggest that it is a rhetorical gesture. Most obviously, it is a highly charged way of expressing the wish that one had never been born (Sir 23:14[19]). The curse takes the energy of self-directed aggression and transfers it to an external object, the day of one's birth. Apart from Job 3 there is only one other preserved example of such a curse, Jer 20:14-18. Like Job 3, it contains four elements: a curse on the day of birth itself (Jer 20:14; Job 3:3a, 4-5), a curse on the messenger who brought the news (Jer 20:15-16; Job 3:3b, 6-9), the reason for the curse (Jer 20:17; Job 3:10), and a lament for having been born (Jer 20:18; Job 3:11-16). In the case of Jeremiah, even though the words are framed as a curse, one can argue that Jeremiah intends them as an implicit appeal to God, what Zuckerman calls "a lament-of-final-resort," the function of which was "to portray a sufferer's distress in the most nihilistic terms possible for the purpose of attracting God's attention and thus leading to the rescue of the sufferer from affliction."[69] As an implicit appeal, it is an act of faith.

Understood in this context, the announcement in Job 3:1 is perfectly in keeping with the dynamics of the prose story and with the image of Job created there. Even in extremis he will curse the day of his birth rather than God, his words of despair a tacit plea for deliverance. If that is what the friends and the reader expect, however, the actual words Job uses overturn those expectations and decisively break open the closed world of the prose tale. Job subverts the conventions of the birthday curse through his radical use of (anti-) creation imagery, his inversion of divine speech, and his bitterly ironic description of life as oppression and death as a valuable treasure. Whatever this is, it is not a tacit appeal for deliverance.

3:3-10. Job's speech divides into two major sections: the curse proper (vv. 3-10) and the lament over having been born (vv. 11-26). The former begins in v. 3 with a curse on the day of birth and on the night of conception. First, day is cursed with a deprivation of light (vv. 4-5). Then night is cursed with a deprivation of fellowship and frustration of desire (vv. 6-9). Finally, the reason for the curse is given: the failure of that day to prevent Job's birth (v. 10).

The object of the curse, identified generally as "his day" in v. 1, is divided into two distinct times, the day of birth and the night of conception (v. 3). In Jeremiah, not only is the day cursed but also the messenger who brought the news to the father (Jer 20:15-16). Job's curse personifies the night as announcing the news of the conception. Since ordinarily birth is announced rather than conception, some interpreters rationalize the image by translating the Hebrew word as "born" instead of "conceived" (on the basis of 1 Chr 4:17; see the NIV) or by assuming a textual error and reading "behold!"[70] In so doing they underestimate the extravagant quality of Job's language.

"Day of birth" and "night of conception" are complementary terms in that conception and birth mark the beginning and end of gestation. "Night" and "day" are also complementary terms that designate the corresponding parts of a single day (cf. "evening and morning" in Genesis 1). The double resonance of these terms creates a poetically condensed image of Job's coming into being. It also allows Job to exploit the ambiguities of the term "day."

The day of one's birth might be understood to refer either to a unique historical day or to a calendar day that occurs once each year. Although the limited amount of evidence concerning such curses makes it difficult to know what was customary, the references in Sirach and in Jeremiah focus on the unique historical day. Jeremiah, for instance, draws attention to the events and persons attending his birth. Clines declares such curses to be rhetorical rather than magical acts, because a day that is already passed cannot be affected.[71] In sharp contrast to Jeremiah, however, Job develops his curse through images that minimize the sense of the historical particularity of the day and instead focus

68. M. Fishbane, "Jeremiah iv 23-26 and Job iii 3-13: A Recovered Use of the Creation Pattern," *VT* 21 (1971) 153-55.
69. Zuckerman, *Job the Silent,* 125-26.
70. So de Wilde, following the LXX. See A. de Wilde, *Das Buch Hiob, OTS* xxii (Leiden: Brill, 1981) 97.
71. Clines, *Job 1–20,* 79.

on the calendrical and cosmic aspects of day/ night. Job may well be breaking with traditional expectations here and exceeding the bounds of what was "appropriate" in such a rhetorical gesture. Certainly the images give his curse a disturbing quality.

Unlike Jeremiah, who begins his curse with a technical formula ("cursed be the day . . . ," Jer 20:14), Job begins with a specific word of destruction ("let the day . . . the night perish," v. 3; cf. Ps 109:6-19). But how does one imagine the perishing of a day or a night? What is a suitable fate to wish upon them? The dominant motif in his curse on "that day" is the reversal of light into darkness. To deprive day of light is to deprive it of its essential characteristic, but it is also a punishment that fits the crime. Because that day allowed Job to "see light" (cf. v. 16), Job deprives that day of light. Six different expressions for darkness appear in vv. 4-5, but its most powerful formulation is the opening phrase "that day— let it be darkness!" (יהי חשך *yĕhî ḥōšek*). As is often noted, this phrase is an allusion to and reversal of God's words of creation in Gen 1:3, "let there be light" (יהי אור *yĕhî ʾôr*). A secondary motif, having to do with abandonment/possession, is introduced in the following phrase, "Let Eloah above not seek it." Perhaps this is a mythic allusion that we can no longer recognize, but "seeking" is elsewhere used of God's protective relation (Deut 11:12; Isa 62:12); not to be sought is to be an outcast (Jer 30:17). The third image ("let light not shine upon it") assumes that light is not an intrinsic quality of day but something that must be given to it. Taken together, the two sentences suggest that Job would thwart a divine creation of day.

Verse 5 complements the image of God's abandonment of day with the image of hostile possession by others. The word translated "claim" is the same word elsewhere rendered "redeem" (גאל *gāʾal*). It is from the language of family law relating to the responsibility of the next-of-kin to buy back the family's mortgaged property or family members sold into slavery (Lev 25:25-55). Here gloom and deep darkness (lit., "the shadow of death") are cast as the next of kin who "buy back" that day, a shrewd image, since in cosmogonic terms day is the offspring of night.[72] This is no true

redemptive moment, as the following images indicate. There is something claustrophobic in the image of the cloud bank settling on the day. Even more ominous is the hostility expressed in the image of the "blackness of the day" (כמרירי יום *kimrîrê yôm*), presumably an eclipse, terrifying that day. This expression is actually vocalized to read "like the biternesses of the day." Most interpreters, however, assume that a rare word meaning "blackness" is the original reading.[73] Gordis and Habel translate "demons of the day," following a medieval Jewish interpretation.[74]

The curse on "that night" is pronounced in vv. 6-9. Continuity with vv. 2-5 is provided through the opening image of ominous "thick darkness," but the dominant motif of these curses is the denial of joy in relationships. Here, too, the curse corresponds to the offense. Because the night presided over the sexual union of Job's parents and announced his conception, night will be punished by exclusion from joy and fellowship and by a frustration of desire.

Where day was grotesquely "redeemed," night is "seized," "taken away" (v. 6). Like a captive, it can no longer enjoy the company of its fellows. The difference between the NIV and the NRSV in the translation of v. 6*b* points to a play on words. Literally, the text reads "let it not rejoice" (אל-יחד *ʾal-yiḥad*). But the parallelism with "come into," "enter" in the next line suggests that one read instead the similar sounding "not be included" (אל-יחד *ʾal-yēḥad*; cf. also Gen 49:6, where the parallelism is "enter"//"be included"). Poetic speech often exploits echoes between two similar sounding words with different meanings. Since both deprivation of joy and exclusion from fellowship are thematic, one should read "let it not rejoice" and hear the echo of "let it not be included."

That Job should curse the night of his conception with "barrenness" (גלמוד *galmûd*, a rare word otherwise used only in Isa 49:21) is not surprising, but he intensifies the punishment by excluding also the cry of joy. In context, this would refer to the exclamations of sexual pleasure. What Job envisions is that on this night of the year, sexual union will

72. Clines, *Job 1–20*, 84.

73. See Pope, *Job*, 29.
74. Gordis, *The Book of Job*, 33; Habel, *The Book of Job*, 100.

mysteriously produce neither pleasure nor conception.

In v. 8 the imagery shifts toward the cosmic plane. As in v. 6, an unexpected word, "day" (יוֹם *yôm*), occurs where the parallelism with Leviathan leads one to expect "Sea" (יָם *yām*; cf. NIV, NRSV). Leviathan is the name of the primordial dragon-like creature associated with the mythic Sea (Ps 74:14; Isa 27:1; cf. Isa 51:9; Hab 3:8; it is to be equated with Lotan in Ugaritic mythology). As symbols of chaos, Leviathan and Sea are often depicted as opponents whom God overcomes in the cosmogonic battle.[75] Some interpreters assume that a mistake has been made in the text and that v. 8 originally read "Sea."[76] Supporting that suggestion is the fact that there is no evidence of persons in ancient Israel who were expert in "cursing day," but there are later Jewish magical texts that invoke Sea and Leviathan as a parallel pair: "I enchant you with the adjuration of Sea, and the spell of Leviathan the serpent."[77] Nevertheless, the substitution of "sea" for "day" in v. 8, although initially appealing, will not work. In contrast to the Jewish magical text, Job is not appealing to a spell that binds Leviathan but to a spell that rouses Leviathan. Similarly, he does not wish to curse Sea, i.e., the forces of chaos.[78] As vv. 4-5 indicate, Job seeks to let loose the chaotic forces of darkness (see Gen 1:2) to attack his "day." The shock effect of v. 8 is precisely in its calculated misuse of the formulae of "white magic."

In v. 9, Job curses night precisely by breaking the bond that joins night to day: the time of dawn, when dark mingles with first light. Night is personified in ways that suggest a lover, one who waits expectantly, desiring to look upon the eyes of its partner, dawn. Job's curse would deny that union. The cosmic horror lurking in Job's curse is that it would break the dependable alternation of opposites upon which creation is established. God's promise to humankind after the flood was that "As long as the earth endures,/ seedtime and harvest, cold and heat,/ summer and winter, day and night,/ shall not cease" (Gen 8:22 NRSV).

The reason for Job's curse finally appears in v. 10: "because it did not shut the doors of my mother's womb,/ and hide trouble from my eyes." The expression "opening/closing the womb" is an idiom for the ability to conceive (Gen 29:31; 1 Sam 1:5). Thus v. 10 appears to be tied most closely to the curse on night and only secondarily to the curse on the day of birth. In Israelite thought, of course, it is not night but God who opens or closes the womb. Job's poetic displacement of this function may indicate that the object of his anger is God, although he does not acknowledge this, perhaps even to himself. His feelings are revealed, however, by his choice of images. The second part of Job's reason in v. 10 is also closely related to v. 9*b*. Because night did not prevent Job from seeing what he did not wish to see, Job's curse will prevent night from seeing what it most desires.

3:11-26. This section is often called a lament. That label can be misleading if one thinks in terms of the psalms of lament, where the individual addresses God directly and seeks relief. Here, even though some terms and images from the lament tradition are used, Job does not address his words to anyone in particular.[79] What Job says is not a lament in the classic sense but the rhetorical wish that one had never been born, which formally belongs to the curse on the day of one's birth (Jer 20:18; Sir 23:14*b* [19*b*]). This wish never to have been born is not the same as the wish to die, which a number of characters in the Bible express (Rebekah, Gen 27:46; Elijah, 1 Kgs 19:4; Jonah, Jonah 4:3; Tobit and Sarah, Tob 3:6, 10, 13, 15; Mattathias, 1 Macc 2:6, 13). Except for 1 Macc 2:6, these are requests that the person should no longer continue to live, rather than the specific desire that one had never lived or had died at birth.

Job transforms what is a briefly expressed wish in Jeremiah into a baroque fantasy of death. The death wish is expressed in vv. 11-12 as the desire to have died as a newborn and in v. 16 as the desire to have been stillborn. In vv. 13-15 and 17-10, Job describes

75. J. Day, *God's Conflict with the Dragon and the Sea,* University of Cambridge Oriental Publications 35 (Cambridge: Cambridge University Press, 1985).

76. So Pope, *Job,* 30, following H. Gunkel, *Schoepfung und Chaos in Urzeit und Endzeit* (Göttingen: Vandenhoeck und Ruprecht, 1895) 59n. 1; L. Perdue, *Wisdom in Revolt: Metaphorical Theology in the Book of Job,* Bible and Literature Series 29 (Sheffield: JSOT, 1991) 92.

77. C. D. Isbell, *Corpus of the Aramaic Incantation Bowls,* SBLDS 17 (Missoula, Mont.: Scholars Press, 1975) 19.

78. Gordis, *The Book of Job,* 34.

79. C. Westermann, *The Structure of the Book of Job,* trans. C. A. Muenchow (Philadelphia: Fortress, 1981) 37-38.

the advantages of such death without life. He expands the wish for death with a reflection on the irony that life is given to those who crave death (vv. 20-24). Finally, Job concludes by stating the reason for his vehement curse (vv. 25-26).

Job begins this section with rhetorical questions expressing the desire to have died during birth (v. 11) or, if not, then to have been refused the life-sustaining nurture an infant requires. Why? If he had not been held and suckled, Job says, now he would be lying down, quiet and asleep (v. 13). With bitter irony Job takes the image of the child who sleeps after feeding and applies it to himself as a child fortunately dead from lack of nurture.

The images that follow are more perplexing, for it is not immediately clear why Job would speak of the company of rulers and wealthy princes as a particular feature of death (vv. 14-15). As "the greatest of all the people of the east" (1:3), Job certainly enjoyed their company in life. The meaning of the image is to be sought in the contrasts and similarities that the passage sets up between the lives and deaths of infants and magnates. Unlike the infant, the rulers engaged in intensive activity. This contrast is expressed most ironically in v. 14*b*, where the text says literally that they "built ruins for themselves." The phrase captures the ambiguity of such activity. Ancient Near Eastern kings took great pride in rebuilding ancient ruins of cities and temples (Ezra 6:1-5; Isa 44:26-28);[80] yet whatever was built eventually would fall into ruin again. Similarly, the silver and gold that princes amassed (v. 15) remained in their houses at death. What the infant and the magnates share in death is rest, the one desirable thing in Job's view. The infant who died at birth, however, received this good without either "toil" or "trouble" (v. 10; עמל [*ʿāmāl*] has both meanings).

Verse 16 resumes the rhetorical question of v. 11. Job's desire for death is expressed in an image even more extreme. Here he envisions not the brief life of the infant but the stillborn child who "never saw the light." Parallel to the account of kings and princes now at rest, vv. 17-19 also describe the quietness that comes in death to various social groups who had been bound together in oppressive relationships, characterized by agitation and exhaustion. "Wicked" (רשעים *rěšāʿîm*) in v. 17 is a term that, as Clines has shown, has not only moral but also specifically antisocial overtones.[81] Thus those "exhausted by power" (v. 17*b*) are victims of the wicked, just as the captive corresponds to the taskmaster and the slave to the master.[82] Common to all of these relations is a disproportion of power and an inability of the weaker member to resist the will and violent energy ("turmoil, troubling") of the stronger.

These are not idly chosen images; yet they seem initially incongruous for Job. He has said nothing about his particular suffering, the loss of possessions, servants, children, and health, even though that is what motivates his words. Somehow those specific losses have been transmuted during seven days of silence (2:13) into these defining images of death and life. Perhaps these images indicate that Job's fundamental perception of the world has changed. A person can survive devastating losses if the sense of the world as a fundamentally trustworthy place is still intact, as Job's words in 1:21 were meant to suggest. Now his images suggest that he perceives the world as crushing and inescapable bondage, from which death is the only release. It is tempting to interpret Job's use of the images of social oppression as an indication that his sufferings have caused him to identify with the oppressed of the earth.[83] As later chapters will show, however, Job's social perceptions, even as they are shaped by his suffering, are complex (cf. Job 24 and 30).

A second rhetorical question, which begins in v. 20 and is resumed in v. 23, explores the irony of unwelcome life. Literally, the sentence begins "why does he give light to one in misery . . . ?" Hebrew often uses such a construction as the equivalent of a passive (i.e., "Why is light given . . . ?"), but the words could also be understood as a reference to God as the one who gives, echoing 1:21 and more faintly 2:10.[84] Job often responds to the bitter ironies he perceives by exposing them through parody. He develops the image

80. Cf. the reports of rebuilding by Cyrus and Antiochus Soter in *ANET,* 315, 317.

81. Clines, *Job 1–20,* 96; F. Horst, *Hiob,* Biblischer Kommentar xvi (Neukirchen-Vlun: Neukirchener Verlag, 1960) 53.
82. Good, *In Turns of Tempest,* 56.
83. Clines, *Job 1–20,* 93.
84. Janzen, *Job,* 65.

of the embittered sufferer, first as one whose expectant waiting for death is disappointed (v. 21a). Then the passivity changes to activity as Job employs the image of the treasure hunter, with death as the prize (v. 21b). That is an ideal image for Job's purposes, since as Clines observes, most buried treasure in the ancient world consisted of valuables placed with the dead in tombs.[85] Thus Job invokes the familiar picture of the graverobber. The graverobbers' eagerness and exultant delight at the discovery of a rich grave grotesquely becomes the image of the one for whom the grave itself is the treasure (v. 22).

The resumption of the rhetorical question in v. 23 provides insight into the way Job experiences his situation. His images are those of restricted movement: one whose way is hidden, whom Eloah has hedged in. "Way" (דרך *derek*) is a frequent and important image in Israelite moral discourse. Based on the concrete image of the path along which one walks, it refers to a course of conduct, the knowledge of how to proceed (1 Kgs 2:4; 2 Chr 13:22; Ps 1:6).[86] The image of the hedge was used by the *satan* as a metaphor of God's protection of Job in 1:10 (a slightly different verb). Here, however, it has an obstructive, hostile sense, as in Hos 2:6 (2:8). Job is trapped in a perverse, unintelligible world. Under such circumstances life is, quite literally, meaningless; hence his ironic rhetorical question about the pointlessness of light and life.

85. Clines, *Job 1–20,* 100.
86. See N. Habel, "The Symbolism of Wisdom in Proverbs 1–9," *Int.* 26 (1972) 131-57.

Verse 24 provides a transition. Using images familiar from traditional psalms of lament (cf. Ps 102:4-5, 9[5-6, 10]), Job again speaks in the first person. The following words of v. 25 are elliptical: "What I feared has come upon me;/ what I dreaded has happened to me." To what does Job refer? The character of Job in the prose tale had seemed a rather transparent figure, and the only anxiety he expressed was concern about the careless thoughts of his children (1:5). With these words, however, the author has created a character of depth and complexity who is not immediately accessible to the reader. What has Job feared? A clue appears in v. 26. The poetic construction of the line is powerful. Even readers who do not know Hebrew can appreciate the effect:

לא שלותי ולא שקטתי   *lōʾšālawtî wĕlōʾ šāqaṭṭî*
ולא־נחתי ויבא רגז   *wĕlōʾ-nāḥĕtî wayyābōʾ rōgez*

("I have no ease, no quiet, no rest—what comes is turmoil"). Here, a threefold repetition of the same grammatical construction produces a repetition of sounds, almost like the tolling of a bell. Each phrase is also synonymous. The fourth element contrasts grammatically, as well as in meaning. The verb that introduces the last word is "come" (בוא *bôʾ*), the same verb used in v. 25 ("what I dreaded has come to me"). The parallel points to רגז (*rōgez,* "turmoil") as the word that Job chooses to identify his dread. The reliability of his world, the quality of existence that had allowed Job to experience the quietness of trust, has been shattered.

REFLECTIONS

The nihilism of Job's words is frightening. Like Samson, pulling down the pillars of the temple of Dagon, Job seems intent on pulling down the pillars of the cosmos itself. The pain that produces such words is like a black hole, the enormous gravitational force of which draws everything into itself. As unsettling as Job's words are, there is one thing that would be even more disturbing. Imagine how vastly different the book of Job would be if the seven days and seven nights of silence were never broken. The withdrawal into permanent silence would have been a withdrawal into despair and apathy. The fact that Job *can* speak of a despair so profound that it threatens to consume the cosmos is vital.

Theologian Dorothee Soelle has examined what she describes as necessary phases of suffering.[87] First of all comes mute suffering. It is a time of numbness and

87. D. Soelle, *Suffering,* trans. E. Kalin (Philadelphia: Fortress, 1975) 68-74.

disorientation, in which the person experiences an acute sense of helplessness. Extreme suffering turns a person inward, making communication almost impossible and intensifying a sense of isolation. In this phase nothing can be done. Suffering has to find a voice before it can be worked on. That process is not an easy one, nor does it take place in the same way for every person. The first two chapters of Job show him attempting to make use of inherited words of proverbial wisdom to find a resolution for his grief. Perhaps because Job tries to resolve his suffering before he has adequately given voice to its enormity, his attempts fail, and he sinks into a prolonged period of mute suffering.

In some way the friends' presence facilitates Job's speaking in chap. 3. Even though he does not address them, the fact that they sit before him and with him is instrumental in bringing forth his cry. Certainly what Job says is not what they would have anticipated, yet it moves Job into the second phase of suffering in which he finds a language of pain and lament.

One of the things that makes this stage of suffering so difficult to enter into or even to witness is that it initially intensifies suffering. The anesthesia of numbness is gone, as is any attempt to deny the reality and severity of what has happened. To speak, however, is to begin to emerge from passivity and utter helplessness. The one who speaks names what is wrong or broken and so begins to organize the experience. Perhaps most important, speaking begins to break down the isolation that is so much a part of the devastation of acute suffering. Although a sympathetic listener may be the most helpful in enabling a sufferer to speak, it is also possible for some of this process to take place through writing down one's words when there is no one to whom they can be spoken. The page itself can become the image of the one who would know how to listen.

One should not think that the words a suffering person first finds will necessarily be "constructive" words. Certainly Job's are not. Gustavo Gutiérrez gives insight into the nature of the first language of suffering when he compares Job's words in chap. 3 with a poem by César Vallejo.[88] Vallejo's poem is an unrelenting cry of pain. Paradoxically, as Gutiérrez observes, the poem is entitled "I Am Going to Talk about Hope." Vallejo does not explain the title, nor is there anything in the content of the poem that looks remotely like what one ordinarily thinks of as hope. The title can refer only to the act of speaking itself. That startling dissonance between title and content provokes one into a new way of listening to words of pain, words of anger, and even words of nihilistic despair. Job cannot remain forever in his nihilism any more than the speaker in Vallejo's poem can remain forever in a cry of pain. In both cases, however, nothing can be done until suffering has been given a voice. In that sense even a cry of pain or an angry curse on the day of one's birth is also a token of hope.

A sufferer's friends and community often find it difficult to accept anger such as Job utters as a legitimate way of finding a voice for suffering. Anger is a very common element in the experience of suffering and grief, yet the expression of anger is one of the most frequently discouraged actions in many religious communities. The reason why is not difficult to understand. Anger claims not only that the situation is painful but also that something is fundamentally not right about the situation, that what has happened *should not* have happened. Anger is frightening because it often exposes contradictions in the community or points to a scandal in the belief system. It claims to disclose a disturbing reality that others are covering over with self-deceiving illusions. Anger directed at other members of the community is difficult because it requires facing up to responsibility and admitting and assessing guilt. Anger directed at God or, as in Job's words, at life itself is disturbing because it questions fundamental beliefs of the culture. If a religious community is supple and resilient, it is easier for it to allow and even encourage the expression of anger in connection with suffering. If a community and its beliefs are fragile or brittle, however, the reaction to anger is more likely to be

88. Gutiérrez, *On Job,* 9-10, 111-12n. 8.

defensive and repressive. One cannot minimize what is at stake. As the book of Job shows, once the contradictions are pursued, an entire belief system may be shattered. Yet that may be the only way forward to a more mature and adequate faith.

Israelite religion is often admired for making a place for anger within religious language. The psalms of lament are particularly noted for allowing the speaker to articulate anger. Although this is true, it is often overlooked that even there expressions of anger are strictly circumscribed by the form of the lament, which begins and ends with expressions of trust. If the response of the friends to Job can be taken as indicative, exceeding the appropriate bounds for the expression of anger created anxiety and the need to contain such expressions in ancient Israel as it does in many other cultures. One should remember, however, that even though God criticizes Job's words, it is Job who is commended for "speaking rightly" of God (42:7). The book of Job validates the legitimacy of anger arising out of the experience of suffering, even when that anger makes others uncomfortable, and even when that anger is directed at God. Anger that settles into bitterness is not the final resting place, but often the anger of suffering has to be expressed and explored in all its dimensions before it can be transmuted into something else.

As discussed above, Job's curse on the day of his birth is a token of hope because it marks his ability to enter into the phase of suffering in which muteness is replaced by speaking. There is also a third phase of suffering, one that is enabled in part by the process of finding a voice. Soelle calls this phase "changing" and characterizes it as a phase in which active behavior is possible, objectives can be identified, and solidarity with other persons forms new community. Although she is thinking largely in terms of the suffering produced by social oppression, what Soelle says about this phase of suffering also applies to other forms of grief and loss. The young woman paralyzed from a car accident who has found the language in which to express her anger and to grieve her loss is better able to organize her energies for learning a new way of living. Sometimes, as in Job's case, this phase of changing is first of all a matter of changing one's own perspectives, no longer being willing to accept what everyone else says is so. In such circumstances, solidarity may not be so easy to find, as Job discovers; yet the energy that comes from engaging in this change is an important part of overcoming the power of suffering.

Job 4:1–5:27, Traditional Understandings of Misfortune

COMMENTARY

Eliphaz's speech is composed of several distinct parts. After the narrator's introduction (4:1), Eliphaz acknowledges Job's vulnerability and explains his own need to speak (4:2). He reminds Job of how he had previously sustained others who were distraught and encourages him to find confidence in the very fact of his piety and uprightness (4:3-6). Eliphaz supports his claim by reminding Job of the beliefs they have shared concerning the moral structure of the world (4:7-11). In the following passage, Eliphaz tells Job of a visionary experience that bears on the moral implications of human frailty (4:12-21). What Eliphaz says next is difficult to interpret, but has to do with the consequences of foolish behavior (5:1-5) and the source of evil and trouble (5:6-7). Encouraging Job to turn to God, Eliphaz grounds his advice by reciting a hymn in praise of God's power to transform (5:8-16). Finally, Eliphaz interprets suffering as a form of correction. If embraced, this hard pedagogy results in security and blessedness (5:17-26). A final call for Job to hear and acknowledge the truth of Eliphaz's words concludes his speech (5:27).

4:1-6. The solicitude in Eliphaz's opening words indicates his concern for Job. The nuance of the first part of v. 2 is difficult to render in English, but the Tanakh captures it better than either the NRSV or the NIV: "If one ventures a word with you, will it be too much?" (v. 2 TNK). A sage does not rush to speak prematurely (Prov 15:14), and one shows respect by listening in silence (Job 29:9). Only Job's evident distress as manifested in his terrible curse overcomes Eliphaz's reluctance to speak (v. 2*b*).

Eliphaz's admonition is designed to show Job how he has lost perspective, unable to appropriate for his own situation the very instruction he had given to others (vv. 3-5). In Eliphaz's view, Job has lost sight of who he is and consequently of the stability that comes from such knowledge. The metaphors that describe the person overcome with affliction are those of weakness in the limbs and joints, an apt metaphor for the emotional and psychic prostration that accompanies traumatic experiences and profound fear (2 Sam 4:1; Ps 109:24; Isa 13:7; Ezek 7:17). Correspondingly, the sage's words are intended to provide the stiffening to put someone "back on his feet," as we might say. The term translated "instruct" (יסר *yissar*, v. 3) identifies the type of assistance Eliphaz is attempting to render. The word is capable of a variety of nuances, ranging from instruction to warning to discipline to punishment. At the heart of its meaning is the idea of correction.[89] This activity is different from the support rendered simply by a sympathetic presence. Instruction refers to the support, both sympathetic and confrontational, that has as its goal keeping a person oriented to the life-giving beliefs, values, and behaviors of the community.

The reorientation Eliphaz attempts to effect is succinctly stated in the rhetorical question of v. 6: "Is not your piety (the grounds of) your confidence, your hope the integrity of your conduct?" Unknowingly, the qualities that Eliphaz attributes to Job, piety (lit., fear [of God]) and integrity of way, are the same words used by the narrator and God to characterize Job (1:1, 8; 2:3). This echo serves first of all to make clear that Eliphaz does not assume Job is sinful. It also reminds the reader that questions raised in the prose tale about the relationship between well-being and moral character are also going to play an important but different role in the dialogue.

The surface simplicity of v. 6 conceals a complex set of assumptions about God, the world, and how one chooses to talk about suffering. Note how Eliphaz's question frames the issues. His words do not address what has happened to Job or his present distress but are oriented wholly to the future. Job should concentrate on hope, which Habel eloquently describes as "the hidden source of new life and purpose in the face of death and disaster."[90] That is no small thing. Eliphaz's words are based on an assumption, axiomatic for much of Israel's piety, that a person's moral character and ultimate well-being are inherently linked (Pss 18:20[21]; 112:1-10; Prov 11:8; 23:18; 24:14). Thus because Job knows that he is a person of piety and integrity, he can have confidence in his future. If the assumption is correct, then the conclusion must follow. The book of Job is going to subject that assumption to a rigorous scrutiny, however.

4:7-11. These verses serve as a more detailed argument in support of the assumption that moral character and ultimate fate are organically related. The rhetorical features of these verses are just as important as the content. Eliphaz begins with an imperative, "recall, now," followed by a rhetorical question. Asking Job to remember shifts the claim from something for which Eliphaz can vouch to something Job himself can authenticate on the authority of his own knowledge. Similarly, a rhetorical question presumes that the answer is so self-evident that everyone must agree. Eliphaz's claim, however, is problematic on its very face: "who that was innocent ever perished?/ Or where were the upright cut off?" (cf. Ps 37:25[24]). Yet Ps 10:8; Jer 22:17; and 2 Kgs 21:16 all refer to the murder of the innocent. Eliphaz, of course, does not mean that such things never happen. His words are a rhetorical exaggeration. Eliphaz would not be swayed by a counterexample, however, because he is not interested in "isolated cases" but in the fundamental regularities of the world that he perceives and that he is certain Job also perceives. Eliphaz's call

89. Dhorme, *A Commentary on the Book of Job*, 43.

90. Habel, *The Book of Job*, 125.

for Job to "remember" suggests something important about the way perception and memory and meaning are related. Human perceptions of the world are necessarily based on selective memory. Myriad facts and events exist, but not all are treated as interpretively significant. Ordinarily, those events that confirm the worldview one already holds have greater significance; those that contradict it appear as mere anomalies. Hence Eliphaz's confidence in v. 7. The same process underlies Eliphaz's claim that *as I have seen,* those who plough mischief and sow trouble reap it" (v. 7). He sees clearly only what the screen of his worldview allows him to see. His belief in the intrinsic relation of act and consequence, a fundamental tenet of wisdom thinking, is evident also in his choice of the agricultural metaphor of sowing and reaping (cf. Prov 14:22; 22:8; also Hos 10:13). The book of Job can be understood as a crisis in moral perception, which emerges when the organizing schemata are challenged as radically distorting (see Reflections).

Eliphaz pairs his statement about the organic relationship of evil and its consequences with a claim about divine punishment, phrased in the image of the breath of God and wind of God's anger (v. 9). These are simply alternative ways of expressing the same reality as v. 8. The catchword "perish" serves as a link with the concluding saying (vv. 10-11), a verbally sophisticated proverb that uses five different terms for "lion." Here, as often, the lion is a symbol for the wicked (Ps 17:12; Prov 28:15; Nah 2:11-12[12-13]).

It is evident why Eliphaz would speak about the fate of the innocent and upright person, but why does he devote most of this section to the issue of the fate of the wicked? Eliphaz is not subtly insinuating that Job is one of the wicked, as v. 6 makes clear. Since the appropriate fates of the upright and the wicked are complementary aspects of the same moral order, these comments can serve to reassure Job. Nevertheless, as will become evident, Eliphaz and his friends do talk much more extensively about the fate of the wicked than about the hope of the righteous (15:20-35; 18:5-21; 20:4-29; 22:5-20; see the Commentary and Reflections on chap. 18.).

Although Eliphaz does not intend to imply that Job is among the wicked, his actual words come disconcertingly close to describing the fate that has actually befallen Job. The punishing wind that Eliphaz alludes to in v. 9 recalls the "great wind" (1:19) that crushed Job's children. The "irony and innuendo" of these words is not, as Fullerton properly observes, "the irony and innuendo of Eliphaz at the expense of Job but the irony and innuendo of the author at the expense of Eliphaz and of the orthodox reader whose position he represents."[91] That the classic description of the fate of the wicked should match the situation of one who is righteous undermines the cogency of Eliphaz's moral language, even if he is not aware of it.

4:12-21. While dreams and visions are not usually associated with the wisdom tradition as represented by Proverbs, Ecclesiastes, and Sirach, another tradition, sometimes called mantic wisdom, does include revelatory dreams and visions among the sources of the sage's wisdom. In the biblical tradition, Daniel is an example of this type of sage (Dan 1:17; 2:19-23). More generally, dreams and night visions are associated with a variety of biblical characters, including patriarchs, kings, prophets, and ordinary individuals (e.g., Gen 15:12-17; 28:10-15; 37:5-11; 40:8-19; 41:1-7; 1 Sam 3:1-14; 2 Sam 7:17; 1 Kgs 3:5; Zech 1:8). Although dreams and visions could be deceptive (Zech 13:4), they are accepted as legitimate channels of divine revelation.

Eliphaz spends almost half of his account describing the experience, turning to its content only in v. 17. That description is not unrelated to the content but prepares for it. A person who experiences a revelatory dream or vision enters into a liminal state, "betwixt and between" ordinary states of being, where the divine and human meet. It is a space of numinous power, hence the seer's ability to receive a revelation, but it is also a space of intense vulnerability and danger. Isaiah implicitly likens the danger to that of an unclean person entering the zone of holiness in the Temple (Isa 6:5). Daniel experiences weakness and helplessness, including prostration, during the vision (Dan 10:8), exhaustion, and illness afterward (Dan 8:27). Since the two themes of human uncleanness/unrighteousness and physical human frailty are the subject of the

91. Fullerton, "Double Entendre in the First Speech of Eliphaz," 340.

revelation Eliphaz receives, the experience of the vision underscores the message and may account for the lengthy description.

4:12-14. The elusiveness of the experience is well expressed in Eliphaz's opening description of the word approaching him with stealth (NIV: "secretly"; NRSV more literally, "stealing"). The word translated "whisper" (שמץ *šēmeṣ,*) is obscure but more likely means "a small piece," "fragment" (Sir 10:10; 18:32).[92] Thus "my ear seized only a fragment of it." From the first Eliphaz is in the presence of something that eludes his grasp. Verse 13 does not describe the vision itself but the temporal and psychological context. Although the term "deep sleep" (תרדמה *tardēmâ*) can refer to a trance-like state, such as Abraham experiences (Gen 15:12; cf. 1 Sam 26:12), it can also describe ordinary deep sleep (Prov 19:15; cf. Jonah 1:5).[93] Eliphaz uses the term to describe what we know as that part of the sleep cycle associated with dreaming. Moreover, Eliphaz is already experiencing anxiety from vaguely identified "disquieting dreams" when a more intense terror seizes him (v. 14). This scene setting is not only evocative but also significant for the content. The middle of the night is the time when persons are most isolated from their fellows, when they feel most vulnerable, most aware of their own fragility.

4:15. Eliphaz's words in v. 15 are more ambiguous than the NIV and the NRSV indicate. Although רוח (*rûaḥ*) is once used in the Bible to mean a heavenly being (1 Kgs 22:21//2 Chr 18:20) and becomes a common term for angels in post-biblical literature, it most frequently means "wind." (Cf. Hab 1:11, where the same noun and verb are used: "they sweep past like the wind" [NIV].) The most natural understanding of Eliphaz's words is that he is describing a physical phenomenon, an eerie movement of air across his face, which increases his terror. A number of commentators, including Gordis, Habel, and Clines, render the parallel line as "a whirlwind made my flesh shiver"[94] rather than "the hair of my flesh bristled." The words for

"hair" (שערה *śa'ărâ*) and "whirlwind" (שערה *śě'ārâ*) are very similar. Bristling hair is a common reaction to the uncanny in ancient Near Eastern literature, however, and there is no need to emend the text.[95]

4:16. Verse 16 begins abruptly with a verb that has only an indefinite subject ("it stood still"). Eliphaz underscores the eerie sense of amorphous presence by saying that he could not recognize what it was. Similarly, the ancient Mesopotamian king Gudea said of a mysterious being who appeared to him in a dream, "I could not recognize him."[96] Eliphaz's choice of terms in the last part of the verse thus intimates but never explicitly claims that the apparition is a manifestation of God. "Form" (תמונה *těmûnâ*) is elsewhere used of God (Num 12:8; Deut 4:12, 17; Ps 17:15). The words "silence" (דממה *děmāmâ*) and "voice" (קול *qôl*) echo the terms describing the theophany to Elijah (1 Kgs 19:12).

4:17. The KJV and many older translations render v. 17 as a question of whether mortals can be "more righteous" and "more pure" than God. Although that translation is grammatically possible, the context makes it unlikely. Most modern translations render righteous or pure "before" God (cf. Num 32:22). Even that does not quite get the nuance right. The entrance liturgies in the psalms indicate that moral purity and righteousness are expected of one who comes before God in the sanctuary (Psalms 15; 24), yet the rhetorical question of v. 17 points to something obviously impossible. What is at stake is a comparison between the very being of God and mortals, and so one should translate "in relation to" or "as against" God (so the NAB).[97]

4:18-21. The comparative nature of the claim is evident in the following verses (vv. 18-19), which argue from the greater to the lesser, from the angelic to the human. There appears to be a shift in categories, however, from morality to mortality as the focus turns to human beings. The physicality of human existence (the metaphor of the body as a house of clay; see Wis Sol 9:15; cf. Gen 3:19)

---

92. So Gordis, *The Book of Job,* 48; Clines, *Job 1–20,* 111; contra de Wilde, *Das Buch Hiob,* 107.
93. D. Clines, "Job 4,13: A Byronic Suggestion," *ZAW* 92 (1980) 289-91.
94. Gordis, *The Book of Job,* 42; Habel, *The Book of Job,* 113; Clines, *Job 1–20,* 107.

95. S. Paul, "Job 4,15—A Hair Raising Encounter," *ZAW* 95 (1983) 119-21.
96. Cited by Dhorme, *A Commentary on the Book of Job,* 51.
97. See B. Waltke and M. O'Connor, *An Introduction to Biblical Hebrew Syntax* (Winona Lake, Ind.: Eisenbrauns, 1990) 11.2.11e[3] and 14.4e.

and the susceptibility to sudden death are introduced to substantiate the claim of v. 17. The apparent illogicality of the connection irritates some,[98] but the connection is a symbolic, not a logical, one. The same process is reflected in the development of our word *corrupt*. Although now used primarily as a moral term, it derives from a Latin word meaning "broken in pieces." This link between mortality and moral culpability is unusual in the Hebrew Bible, although it occurs twice more in Job (15:14-16; 25:4-6). Some Mesopotamian texts have a similarly negative view of human moral capacity,[99] but the closest ancient parallel comes from the texts of the Dead Sea Scrolls. Although written much later, these passages do not appear to be based on Job but reflect an independent development of the same idea. For example, "and I am a creature of clay and a thing kneaded with water, a foundation of shame and a well of impurity, a furnace of iniquity and an edifice of sin, a spirit of error, perverted, without understanding, and terrified by righteous judgments."[100]

There are several obscure words and phrases in vv. 19-21, although they do not greatly affect the overall meaning. Since "moths" (עָשׁ ʿāš) are otherwise used as images of destructiveness rather than of vulnerability (Isa 50:9; 51:8), some read the quite similar word "birdnest" (so the NEB).[101] In v. 20 it is not clear whether the sentence intends to say that people may die without anyone else noticing or that people are taken by death unawares.[102] In either case, the end is the same: People die without wisdom (v. 21). The relevance of Eliphaz's message to Job's situation and its relation to theodicy in general are discussed below in the Reflections.

5:1-7. This passage is the most difficult part of Eliphaz's speech to understand. First, the text is garbled in v. 5; second, it is not clear how the verses fit together; third, vv. 6-7 can be interpreted in contradictory ways. Any interpretation must therefore be tentative.

5:1-2. The sense of the inevitability of the human condition, with which the previous section concluded, is echoed in the opening rhetorical question in 5:1, which insists on the futility of appealing to angelic beings for help. The proverb that follows (v. 2) appears to be logically disconnected, although it should probably be viewed as Eliphaz's rebuke of Job's violent outburst in chap. 3.[103] The Hebrew terms are difficult to render in English, because they are capable of a variety of nuances. "Vexation" and "jealousy" are not appropriate for this context. "Resentment" and "anger" are closer. The wisdom ethos Eliphaz represents considered extreme anger and its unregulated expression as not just unwise (Prov 12:16) but dangerous, since uncontrolled anger has the power to consume a person's very essence (Prov 14:30). Since human beings are inescapably subject to sudden death, railing against the inevitability of the human condition is just such a dangerously foolish obsession in Eliphaz's view.

5:3-5. Eliphaz's proverb used the term "fool" (אֱוִיל ʾĕwîl) for the person who gives in to angry resentment. To illustrate the fatal danger Eliphaz employs a little set piece about the fool. It does not have to do specifically with anger and so is not entirely germane to the point Eliphaz is making. But that is the nature of Eliphaz's way of thinking and speaking; he joins together pieces of received wisdom as though that would do his thinking for him. Just how problematic this can be is evident in the ghastly inappropriateness of this set piece to Job's situation. The text appears garbled in several places, but its basic meaning is clear. The contrast expressed in v. 3 is between the fool seeming to be secure ("taking root") and "suddenly" encountering disaster. The Hebrew text of v. 3*b* literally says "and suddenly I cursed their dwelling." Many interpreters plausibly emend the text to a passive, "and suddenly his house was cursed," since it is not evident why Eliphaz would be doing the cursing. Moreover, the fundamental contrast of the fool's security/sudden disaster is weakened if attention shifts to the onlooker and his act of cursing. Verse 4 refers to the helplessness of the fool's children against those who would oppress them in business and legal dealings. "The gate" is the place of such activities, where the poor

98. See Clines, *Job 1–20*, 133.
99. de Wilde, *Das Buch Hiob*, 108; Perdue, *Wisdom in Revolt*, 118.
100. 1QH 1.21-23.
101. Gordis, *The Book of Job*, 50.
102. Gordis, *The Book of Job*, 51.
103. Fohrer, *Das Buch Hiob*, 146.

were often subject to abuse if they lacked a more powerful advocate (29:7; 31:21; Prov 22:22; Amos 5:12). Although the text of v. 5 is obscure, the basic image is of the greedy (lit., "hungry" and "thirsty") consuming all of the fool's possessions. If this is indeed meant to serve as a warning to Job of the dangers of persisting in the folly of anger, it could scarcely be more grotesque, for Job has already lost his children and his possessions. As one with literally nothing left to lose (since he does not even wish to keep his life), why should Job not persist in the "folly" of his rage? But Eliphaz apparently does not notice the irony of his own words.

5:6-7. Following the digression of vv. 3-5, the main line of thought is completed with the explanation of why Job's anger is misplaced, and he cannot reasonably expect assistance from the holy ones. The clearest part of the statement is v. 7*a* with its statement that mortals "are born to trouble." The second part of the verse supplies an analogy ("as sparks fly upward"), which underscores the fatalism. Verse 6 is open to two possible interpretations. Both the NIV and the NRSV render it as a contrasting statement—i.e., misery and trouble do not come from nature but from human nature.[104] In Hebrew, however, questions are sometimes not expressly marked as such, so that it would also be possible to translate the verse as a claim that trouble is inherent in nature, and hence in human nature: "Does not misery come from the dust and trouble spring from the soil?"[105] Many commentators resolve the tension between vv. 6 and 7 in a different way, emending the text of v. 7 to read "human beings *give birth to* trouble."[106] This emendation is prompted by a desire to make Eliphaz's statement consistent with his argument in 4:7-11 that people create their own trouble. The more immediate context, however, is Eliphaz's reflections on the intrinsic moral and physical frailty of human nature as such (4:12-21). A fatalistic reading of 5:6-7 ("Does not misery come from the dust and trouble spring from the soil?") seems the most appropriate.

Whether or not there is an intentional allusion to Gen 3:17-19 in vv. 6-7, it is striking that four of the same terms are used in discussing a similar theme, the genesis of the hardship that is the heritage of all human existence. Both passages contain a play on words between "human beings" (אדם 'ādām) and "soil" (אדמה 'ădāmâ), as well as references to things that "sprout" (צמח ṣāmaḥ; thorns and thistles in Gen 3:18; misery in Job 5:6). In Gen 3:19, humans come from and return to the "dust" (עפר 'āpār), while in Job 5:6 it is a question of whether trouble comes from that source.

5:8-16. Eliphaz shifts the focus from human nature to divine nature and from the inappropriate stance of uncontrolled anger to what he urges as the proper stance: committing the situation to God. The introductory verse is poetically striking. Of the nine words in the verse, all but the last begin with the same letter, א ('aleph). Form embodies content also in that the phrases that occupy the center of the verse, concluding the first half-line and beginning the second, are "to El, to Elohim" (see the NRSV). Eliphaz urges Job to orient himself to God.

Eliphaz supports this advice by reciting a doxology in praise of God as one who transforms situations (vv. 9-16). Here traditional language, images, and forms function in their most sympathetic role in Eliphaz's speech. Although Eliphaz may be composing the doxology for the occasion, it is constructed almost wholly out of phrases and images that are a familiar part of the repertoire of worship and wisdom. The power of such familiar words and forms at a time of chaos resides in their ability to reconnect a disoriented person with a reality once experienced as reliable and trustworthy, and that has not ceased to exist despite the present collapse of the individual's world. Such, at least, is Eliphaz's belief.

The doxology begins with a summary acknowledgment of the "great" and "wonderful things" that God does (cf., e.g., Pss 26:7; 40:5[6]; 105:5; 106:21-22). The first substantiation of this general praise is the giving of rain (v. 10). As Clines notes, in the Near Eastern desert climate the rain that marks the change of seasons transforms the appearance of the land with great suddenness from dry and brown to green and colorful

---

104. Similarly, Fohrer, *Das Buch Hiob,* 128.
105. See Pope, *Job,* 42; Habel, *The Book of Job,* 117; and Perdue, *Wisdom in Revolt,* 120, for a similar interpretation on different grammatical grounds.
106. So Clines, *Job 1–20,* 116; Gordis, *The Book of Job,* 55; Rowley, *The Book of Job,* 53.

with flowers.[107] The doxology's most important image, God's transforming the situation of the lowly and grieving (v. 11), is a central motif in Israelite religious language (cf. 1 Sam 2:7-8; Pss 113:7-8; 147:6). The passage will return to a closely related image in its concluding verses (vv. 15-16). Linking these two crucial parts, vv. 12-14 present a complementary image, God's transforming into harmlessness the power of those who scheme. The vocabulary of vv. 12-13 is more characteristic of wisdom than of psalms, but the general idea often appears both in Proverbs and in Psalms (e.g., Pss 7:15-16; 9:16; 35:8; 57:6[7]; Prov 26:27; 28:10). Whereas vv. 11 and 12-14 dealt with the lowly and the powerful separately, v. 15 brings the two together in an image of deliverance. Incidentally, v. 13 is the only verse from Job cited in the New Testament (1 Cor 3:19).

Note that Eliphaz does not deny the existence of drought, oppression, grief, scheming villains, or poverty. But by making the image of transformation central to his language, he strategically shifts the focus from situation to process. Implicitly, Eliphaz claims that the crucial aspect of reality is that it is always open. The final verse of the doxology contains the word that is thematically central for Eliphaz: "hope" (תקוה *tiqwâ*; see also 4:6). This word is important because hope contains an ineradicable element of the future (cf. Jer 29:11). Job's preoccupation with death in chap. 3 had closed off both hope and the possibility of a future. In his recourse to the traditional language of God as transformer of situations, Eliphaz attempts to restore that possibility to Job.

5:17-27. The concluding part of Eliphaz's long speech begins with what is known as a macarism, a statement in the form "happy is X." Such sayings are frequent in Proverbs and Psalms, but what is striking in Eliphaz's macarism is his use of the form in connection with something painful. The general notion that misfortune could be "correction" or "discipline" from God is very much a part of the moral thinking of the ancient Near East. In Psalms 6 and 38 the psalmists, using the same terminology, acknowledge their sufferings as divine discipline, but pray that God not discipline them in anger. The particular

understanding that lies behind Eliphaz's bold macarism is that expressed in Prov 3:11-12, where divine discipline is understood as being motivated by love, such as a father has for a son. The general statement is illustrated in v. 18 with the imagery of wounding and healing, striking and binding up. As shocking as such images may be to modern readers, the use of beatings in education was considered appropriate and compatible with a loving relationship (cf. Prov 20:30; 22:15; 23:13-14).

Although introduced by the macarism about discipline, vv. 19-26 actually shift the focus to the sustaining protection of God in occasions of distress that are more collective than personal in nature. Verse 19 also uses a traditional sayings pattern, the ascending numerical form ("six . . . seven"; cf., e.g., Ps 62:11-12[12-13]; Prov 6:16; 30:15-16; Amos 1:3-15). That the following list exceeds seven is not atypical of the form.[108] But what is Eliphaz's point? The rhetorical exaggeration in Eliphaz's words in vv. 19-22 makes them easy to dismiss. The imagery moves from mere survival in v. 20 (not dying from famine, not being killed in war) to secure protection in v. 21 (being hidden from slander and its destructive power) to active confidence in v. 22 (the ability to laugh fearlessly at the disasters of famine and predatory animals). Read literally, Eliphaz's speech seems to be promising the magical protection of a lucky charm. Read more sympathetically, and with more appreciation of the nature of poetic language, Eliphaz's imagery evokes something of the life-giving power of God, which sustains a person even in calamity, the inextinguishable source of strength that prevents a person who is gravely suffering from shattering entirely and even enables that person to flourish again.

Eliphaz's final set of images describes just such flourishing after great suffering. Here, too, the images are extravagant but evocative. The notion of a covenant with the stones of the field is not otherwise attested, but clearly suggests the reversal of the ancient conflict between human cultivation and the earth's resistance, described in somewhat different images in Gen 3:17*b*-18. Moreover, peace

---

107. Clines, *Job 1–20*, 144-45.

108. Cf. W. M. W. Roth, *Numerical Sayings in the Old Testament: A Form-Critical Study*, VTSup 13 (Leiden: Brill, 1965) 68n. 2.

with the wild animals is an image associated with eschatological blessedness (cf. Isa 11:6-9). The general images in vv. 24-25 of security in the house and field, coupled with abundant descendants, are evocative of the types of blessings enumerated in more concrete detail in the covenant blessings of Lev 26:3-13 and Deut 28:1-14. The concluding verse describes death under the figure of the harvest of a sheaf of grain. In contrast to the debility that can make old age fearful (Eccl 12:1-7), Eliphaz describes death in the fullness of one's powers, a death like that granted to Moses (Deut 34:7).[109]

109. Clines, *Job 1–20*, 153.

The reader who finds Eliphaz's words in vv. 19-26 trite should compare them with Psalm 23. If Eliphaz's words are to be dismissed, so too is much that religious people are accustomed to affirming. At the same time, how can one hear Eliphaz's words about a safe home and a fold with nothing missing and not think of Job's flocks decimated and his children crushed? The book of Job forces one to listen to traditional religious language in a much more complex way than one is accustomed to, experiencing its truth and its falsity in uncomfortable ways. This unease is not part of Eliphaz's experience, however. In v. 27, he again asks Job to acknowledge for himself the traditional insights that the community has examined and found true.

REFLECTIONS

Even if one takes account of cultural differences and listens to Eliphaz as one who speaks from a somewhat different moral world than one's own, and even if one gives Eliphaz full credit for consciously good intentions, his speech remains deeply disturbing. Although Eliphaz speaks out of genuine concern for Job, at the heart of his speech lies fear. He is afraid because of what has happened to Job, but he is also afraid of Job. In part, what makes Eliphaz's speech troubling is the ambiguity about whose needs he is tending. Eliphaz's situation is not an unusual one. Anyone who has confronted another whose suffering is great and irremediable knows the fear and the temptation. The cry of despair is so terrible, opening onto a seeming abyss, that one desires to make it stop, to muffle it, to silence it. At such moments it is very easy to confuse the needs of the sufferer with the impulses of one's own anxiety. The silence that comes when a suffering voice is repressed, however, is not the quiet of true consolation.

One way of reflecting on what Eliphaz does is to consider whether he aids Job in finding a voice or whether he acts to silence Job. Eliphaz, one can be certain, would understand himself as restoring Job's true voice to him. After all, he is reminding Job of how Job used to talk to others (4:3-4). That, however, is an evasion and a self-deception. Eliphaz attempts to speak *in place of* Job, saying what he thinks Job should have said, and that is the antithesis of helping Job find his voice. However kindly the intention, the person who says to a grieving widow, "It was God's will," or who says to a father whose child has died, "God needed your baby in heaven," or who says to a terminal cancer patient, "God works miracles," is signaling to that person what the acceptable limits of speech are. Perhaps those words coincide with the suffering person's own speech, but if they do not, they serve as a means of silencing a grief that needs to find its own expression.

It would be a mistake to understand Eliphaz's response to Job as a purely individual shortcoming. Although suffering is a radically individual experience, it is also a culturally shaped experience. The inbreaking of great suffering, like a flood or an earthquake, threatens to overwhelm the structures that give life order and direction. At such a time, both sufferers and comforters tend to reach for the traditional rituals and formulas their culture has developed to shape the experience and guide the persons through it. Particular cultures and subcultures vary enormously in what they encourage and discourage. Some cultures disapprove of any but the most minimal display of emotion.

Others encourage extravagant gestures of grief. Whatever the prevailing expectations within a particular culture, however, very little deviation from the norm is usually tolerated. The person who behaves "inappropriately" or who rejects the traditional formulas is seen as a threat to the community's worldview, even if no one would be comfortable in admitting it. As discussed in the Reflections on chap. 3, Job transgresses the cultural assumptions about the ways in which anger arising from suffering may be expressed. This is what makes Eliphaz afraid of Job, and his fear gives an edge of aggressiveness to the words he intends kindly.

The tension between Job and Eliphaz cannot be resolved simply by declaring that Job is right and Eliphaz is wrong. It would be inappropriate to suggest that anger is the only appropriate response to suffering or that there is something misguided in the attempt to try to place an experience of suffering in a context of meaning. On the contrary, in some way, integrating the disrupting and disorienting experiences of suffering into a larger understanding of life and world is essential. That effort to find meaning may be as simple as a belief that the power of a person's life transcends death through the impact that person had on the lives of others. Or meaning may be found in a community's resolve to remedy an unjust situation so that a victim's suffering "will not have been in vain." Meaning may be a matter of recognizing that God's love is powerful even in the midst of suffering. Other more rationalistic approaches will attempt to give reasons for the occurrence of suffering. What is common to all these efforts is the impulse to deny the last word to suffering, to refuse to let it be the ultimate reality. There is a fine line to be walked, however, between denying ultimacy to suffering and simply engaging in denial.

What makes chaps. 4–5 so deeply offensive is not that they attempt to integrate suffering into a context of meaning but that they are the attempt of someone who is not suffering to silence the "unacceptable" words of one who is. Chapters 4–5 would have a very different resonance if they were Job's own words. Readers might argue about whether the individual passages represented good or bad ways of grappling with the disorientation of radical suffering, but they could be seen as authentic attempts to use traditional beliefs to incorporate the suffering into a structure of meaning capable of sustaining a future.

Since statements of the type present in chaps. 4–5 are often made by sufferers struggling to come to terms with their own situations, it is important to reflect on the nature of these arguments and the reasons why people are drawn to them. There are two distinct impulses in the material in chaps. 4–5. One, which is not very strongly developed in these chapters, is to attempt to justify suffering by endowing it with an intrinsic logic and purpose. The other, much more pronounced impulse is to bypass questions of cause and to focus instead on the grounds for hope beyond suffering.

The approach that attempts to justify suffering is represented by Eliphaz's statements about suffering as divine discipline (5:17-19) and hinted at in his observations about the wicked, who reap what they sow (4:8-9). The idea of suffering as disciplinary has been a persistent notion in Judaism and Christianity from antiquity to the present. As problematic as such an idea is, it has a strong appeal because it brings terrifying and chaotic events into a structure of meaning and purpose. Suffering understood that way can be incorporated into the context of a personal relationship with a deity in whom love predominates over anger. Although there is never any explicit criticism of this view in the book of Job (Job himself never answers it directly), the book exposes the lurking obscenity in this perspective simply by the disproportionate way it is applied. The suffering that Eliphaz identifies as divine "correction" includes the deaths of ten children.

Eliphaz makes one other extended attempt to justify suffering: his contrast between the nature of divine and human being (4:17-21). Many readers find this argument bizarre, and yet it is a type of argument that recurs in various forms in biblically based religion. Eliphaz places Job's catastrophe in the context of all human vulnerability to sudden death. In so doing, he attempts to take away the terror of a unique and incomprehensible suffering. That is not the main point, however. By stressing the enormous gulf between human and divine nature, Eliphaz makes human perishing seem not simply inevitable but intrinsic to the affirmation that all values, meaning, and being itself are located in God. God and humanity are posited as opposites. By this logic, the more one affirms the presence of certain values in God, the more one must negate them in human beings. In his study of how religious meaning is developed and sustained, Peter Berger refers to this type of thinking as a "masochistic theodicy."[110] God is absolute being; the human over against God is absolute nothingness. Out of this dynamic arises a kind of ecstasy. It is not comfort in the traditional sense but ecstatic transcendence through self-negation that the sufferer receives.

The psychological cost of this type of theodicy is evident. Its theological problems are just as grave, however. The goodness of creation, a fundamental tenet of biblical religion, has to be ignored. Moreover, the richly nuanced biblical understanding of divine holiness as not only dangerous but also life-giving is reduced to an image of all-consuming sterility.

For the most part, however, chaps. 4–5 are not concerned with arguments that attempt to justify suffering in general or Job's situation in particular. Rather, they are concerned with establishing hope. Over and over again, the ultimacy of suffering is denied. "Lions" are real, but their power to destroy is checked (4:10). Human beings are "born to trouble" (5:7), but God can transform situations (5:8-16). Disasters abound, but the power of God sustains even in the face of destruction (5:19-26). These types of statements are more frequently in the mouths of sufferers than are rationalizations and justifications; they have a legitimacy that rationalizations do not. What is characteristic of this way of talking is its narrative quality. Suffering becomes an episode in a larger story. As important as that way of understanding can be for someone attempting to live through a crisis, it also has its dangers. Not all stories have happy endings. A way of talking about suffering that can describe meaning only in terms of happy endings is defective. Although the way Eliphaz talks about suffering is not without value, his speech is ultimately flawed by denial. Even if these were Job's own words, they would not suffice.

110. P. Berger, *The Sacred Canopy* (Garden City, N.Y.: Doubleday, 1967) 73-76.

Job 6:1–7:21, Job Defends the Vehemence of His Words

OVERVIEW

Job is not silenced by Eliphaz's words. In chaps. 6–7, Job replies with a spirited defense of his own speech, a sharp indictment of the friends' failure, and a bold accusation against God. Although the two chapters are linked by the themes of rash speech and human frailty, they have different emphases and serve different purposes in Job's reply. Chapter 6 is primarily concerned with a justification of Job's way of speaking and his insistence on what is necessary for a true dialogue with his friends. The chapter begins (vv. 2-3) and ends (vv. 28-30) with Job's defense of both the vehemence and the truth of his words. The long section in which Job criticizes his friends (vv. 14-27) focuses specifically on the failure of the friends to take Job's words seriously and to respond to him with the same degree of integrity that he exhibits. A second topic, developed in vv. 4-13, concerns Job's rejection of life. It continues the death-wish theme of chap. 3, using language and images from the lament tradition.

Although briefly treated, the theme of unrestrained speaking plays a crucial role in chap. 7, occurring in the central verse of the chapter (v. 11). In the verses leading up to this declaration, Job justifies his need to speak without restraint through a reflection on the misery of the human condition in general (vv. 1-2) and of his own condition in particular (vv. 3-6). Directly addressing God (v. 7), he meditates on the ephemeral quality of human life (vv. 7-10). Impelled by misery and mortality to speak without restraint (v. 11), Job addresses God in words utterly without parallel in the Bible. The content of his accusation (vv. 12-21) is that God has a misplaced and inappropriate obsession with inspecting and punishing human behavior. What makes Job's words both powerful and shocking, however, is his use of sarcasm and parody. Unlike the expression of simple anger, sarcasm and parody do not have a recognized place in the language of Israel's religious traditions. When Job introduces them into his speech, he defies all the conventions of piety.

Job 6:1-30, Anguish Made Worse by the Failure of Friendship

COMMENTARY

6:1-2. Throughout his speech, Job echoes a number of words previously used by Eliphaz.[111] Such repetition of words used by the previous speaker is a fairly frequent device in the dialogue. Whether or not the characters are to be understood as replying explicitly to each other's arguments, the struggle over the meaning of certain words is an important part of the conflict. In 5:2, Eliphaz chided Job for his outburst with a proverb concerning anger. Here, Job picks up that same word (כעש *ka'aś*), now used with the nuance of "anguish," and incorporates it into an image of weight and measure, part of his defense of the way he is speaking (v. 2). Heaviness is a common metaphor in many cultures for the oppressiveness of suffering. In Job's extravagant image the weight of anguish bearing down on him is imaginarily objectified and displaced from his own body to a set of giant scales. Scales belong to the cultural sphere of the public market, where they serve to establish agreement between parties who are by the nature of things inclined to mistrust each other's valuations. Job's use of the image implies that Eliphaz has underestimated the weight of his suffering.

6:3. The specific comparison establishes the magnitude of Job's anguish as something that wholly transcends human scale, since the sand of the sea was itself proverbial for its weight (Prov 27:3; Sir 22:15) and for its numberless grains (Gen 22:17; cf. Isa 48:19; Jer 15:8). Thus the image serves as a justification for Job's speaking rashly. Although rash speech was understood in the wisdom tradition as something that one later regretted (Prov 20:25), the rest of the chapter makes clear that Job is by no means apologizing for what he has said.

6:4. Job identifies the source of his calamity through images of divine violence, specifically, images of God as warrior (cf. Deut 32:23-24; Lam 2:4; Hab 3:3-12). This is conventional language, and Job simply states the obvious. According to his worldview, so much devastation was almost certainly the result of divine anger (cf. Pss 38:1-3[1-4]; 90:7-8; Lam 3:1, 12-13). In the biblical tradition, God's dangerousness can express itself in sudden violence, as in the stories about the incineration of Nadab and Abihu (Lev 10:1-7), Miriam's leprosy (Numbers 12), and the striking down of Uzzah (2 Sam 6:6-11). In every case it was assumed that God's anger was not arbitrary but was provoked by something that the individual had done. Divine compassion, however, was understood to be more profound than anger, so that an afflicted person could turn in yearning to God, who was always inclined to respond by turning anger into compassion. Psalm 38 is an

111. Habel, *The Book of Job*, 141.

excellent example of just the sort of response that a person in Job's situation might be expected to make. Job, however, resolutely rejects that expected response. Just how "rash" Job's words are can be better appreciated if one first reads Psalm 38 and then reads the rest of chap. 6.

6:5-7. Job continues with two proverbial sayings in the form of rhetorical questions (vv. 5-6). Following after vv. 3-4, v. 5 initially serves as a further defense of Job's outcry, using the images of animals who do not bray or bellow when they have food. The second saying does not continue the focus on noisy complaint, however, but shifts to the food itself. The last phrase in v. 6 is quite obscure, as the divergent translations of the NRSV and the NIV suggest.[112] The general image is clear, however: Food that has no taste does not appeal. Verse 7, also obscure at the end, strengthens the image, with its suggestion of revulsion at such food. The embedded metaphor is that of life as food, and the will to live as the appetite. Job's situation differs from that of the wild ass or ox in an essential way. Their food is appropriate and appealing.[113] Job's food (= life) is so disgusting that he has no attachment to it and certainly will not cry out for more of it, as Job makes clear in what follows.[114]

6:8-9. In the following verses, Job does not actually pray.[115] As will become increasingly evident, the fundamental trust governing the relationship between the person and God in Israelite prayer traditions has been shattered for Job. He is left with only the fragments of a language of prayer, which he employs in parodistic fashion. Traditionally, those who prayed psalms of lament begged God for life because they were in danger of being swallowed up by death (Pss 22:12-21[13-22]; 143:7-12). Job's wish for death (v. 9) turns the language of prayer upside down. It is not just death but specifically death by divine violence that Job desires, parodying other psalmists who pray for God's hand to be lifted from them (Pss 32:4; 39:10[11]), who pray not to be cut off (Ps 88:5; Isa 38:12), and who pray for relief from being crushed by God (Ps 38:2, 8[3, 9]).

Job's identification of this as his "hope" (v. 8) mocks Eliphaz's use of the word (4:6; 5:16). In Eliphaz's moral world, hope is the openness of life to a future; Job's only "hope" is to close off the future through a quick death.

6:10. Disagreement over the translation of v. 10 leads to sharply differing interpretations. It is quite unclear whether Job refers to "exulting" in unrelenting pain (so NRSV and NIV) or whether he speaks of "recoiling" in unrelenting pain (so TNK). The evidence does not allow a certain decision. More important is the translation of the last phrase. Most translations render something like "for I have not denied the words of the Holy One." The interpretation lying behind this translation is exemplified by Clines, who likens Job to a prisoner under torture, longing for death to come before he breaks down and curses God.[116] In this way, Job still "holds fast to his integrity." Although this interpretation offers a fascinating psychological portrait of Job, it runs into trouble on the grounds that the verb כחד (*kāḥad*) does not really mean "deny." The literal meaning is much closer to "hide," "conceal" and always has to do with the control of information.[117] This is clear from other instances in which the verb occurs, as when Eli tells Samuel not to conceal anything that God has told Samuel (1 Sam 3:17-18; cf. 2 Sam 14:18; Jer 38:14, 25). "Hide" or "conceal" is also the meaning of the verb elsewhere in Job (15:18; 27:11). The phrase "words of the Holy One" need not refer only to the teachings of God in general but can also refer to divine decisions,[118] in this case God's decision to attack Job (v. 4). Thus Job would find ironic "comfort," even in the midst of unrelenting pain, in that he had not hidden the fact that it is God who has decreed his affliction.[119] Although it is uncertain whether Psalm 119 was extant when Job was written, an ironic echo exists between Job 6:10 and Ps 119:50, which reads: "This is my comfort in affliction: that your word gives me life." Life, as he has just made clear, is the last thing Job wants.

112. See Clines, *Job 1–20*, 158.
113. Cf. Fohrer, *Das Buch Hiob*, 169.
114. For a different understanding of these verses, see Habel, *The Book of Job*, 145-46.
115. Contra Andersen, *Job*, 128.
116. Clines, *Job 1–20*, 174.
117. See Dhorme, *A Commentary on the Book of Job*, 82; Habel, *The Book of Job*, 140.
118. Dhorme, *A Commentary on the Book of Job*, 82; Perdue, *Wisdom in Revolt*, 42-46.
119. Similarly, Habel, *The Book of Job*, 147.

6:11-13. Waiting with hope and expectation is the traditional stance of the psalmists (e.g., Pss 33:18, 22; 71:14; 147:11). In vv. 11-13, Job explains why he cannot take up the stance of hopeful waiting. That reason is his body. The contrast with stones and bronze underscores the limits set by the fragility of flesh. The psalmists, too, often invoke the body's weakness as part of their rhetoric, urging God to come quickly because they are in distress (Pss 22:12-21[13-22]); 38:3-8, 22[4-9, 23]; 69:1-3, 16-18[2-4, 17-19]). The psalms of lament frame a moment when the situation is urgent but open to transformation. They never look at the eventuality in which help comes too late. Job exposes the blindness of traditional piety to the real limits of human endurance. To wait for God's help (e.g., Ps 33:20), Job would have to have help and resources within himself; yet that has been driven out of him (v. 13). Neither can he find the strength he needs in the support of his friends, as the next section makes clear.

6:14-21. Another fragment from the language of psalms of lament is the motif of being abandoned by one's friends (Pss 31:11[12]; 38:11[12]; 88:8[9], 18[19]). Echoing that tradition, Job transforms it into an accusation and the basis for a direct appeal to the friends, rather than using the motif as part of a plea to God. The text of v. 14 is difficult and possibly corrupt. The divergent translations of the NRSV and the NIV reflect the two main options.[120] "Loyalty" (a better translation in this context for חסד [*hesed*] than "kindness" or "devotion") was prized in ancient Israel as the primary quality of friendship (1 Sam 18:1; 20:14-15; Prov 17:17; 18:24). According to the NIV, Job radicalizes the claims of such loyalty so that they must be honored even toward a person who has rejected God.[121] Yet when Job makes explicit what he asks of his friends (vv. 24-30), it is nothing so heroic. More likely, v. 14 should be construed as in the NRSV, equating failure to meet the claims of friendship with a failure of piety.

Job characterizes the failure of the friends in a strikingly developed metaphor, comparing them with the "treachery" of a Near Eastern wadi, a stream bed that alternates between

120. Cf. Clines, *Job 1–20,* 176-78.
121. See N. Habel, " 'Only the Jackal Is My Friend': On Friends and Redeemers in Job," *Int.* 31 (1977) 230.

torrential flow and dryness (vv. 14-17; cf. Jer 15:18). Although translation difficulties occur, they do not obscure the basic image of a stream that has abundant water when it is least needed but dries up during the heat of summer. In an expansion of the metaphor (vv. 18-20), Job implicitly likens himself to desperate caravaneers who futilely relied upon the presence of water in the streams. How seriously Job takes the failure of the friends is suggested by the comparison; it is a matter of life and death (v. 18). The intermingling of the metaphorical imagery with the psychological and social reality it describes is evident in the verbs of vv. 19-20. The expectant looking of v. 19 is appropriate to the image of the caravaneers, but the verbs of v. 20 ("be ashamed," "be confounded" [בוש *bôš*]) come from the language of social relations. They connote the shame experienced by those who have lost status or the respect with which they were formerly treated (Isa 24:23; Jer 15:9; Mic 3:7). In Job's world, the failure of his friends' loyalty itself undercuts his standing and leaves him publicly shamed, a theme to which he will return in chaps. 19 and 30.

Another textual problem obscures the first half of v. 21, but the main point is clear. Job uses a play on words between "you see" (תראו *tir'û*) and "you are afraid" (תיראו *tîrā'û*) to explain the metaphorical drying up of his friends' loyalty. *That* Job believes his friends have failed him and *why* he thinks they have are explicitly stated. But Job has not yet said *how* his friends have fallen short or what he expects of them.

6:22-24. Through a series of rhetorical questions, Job lists several substantial claims that one friend might make on another, all of which involve money or an element of danger (vv. 22-23); yet Job has asked nothing like this from his friends. What he does want is described in vv. 24-26. The reader should be careful not to assume that Job wants what the reader might want in a friend. Job expresses himself in the categories of sapiential friendship. He needs his friends to help him understand the truth about his situation. The "error" to which he refers (v. 24*b*) could be either some fault that has led to the divine anger, or an error of understanding that has led him to misconstrue the significance of his experience. In either case, Job's plea, "Teach me, and I will be silent," echoes the beginning of the chapter, where Job acknowledged the rashness of his own words. Only understanding will bring Job genuine quietness. His words underscore a major theme of the rest of the book. The subsequent failure of the friends to meet Job's need for understanding will serve to expose the inadequacies of the traditional discourse of wisdom and piety. Job will become silent after the divine speeches (chaps. 38–41), and the reader will have to decide whether the divine speeches have finally given Job the understanding that he craves or whether he has merely been silenced by divine might.

6:25. One can imagine Eliphaz's surprise at Job's words. Has he not tried to show Job where he has erred? Why is Job unsatisfied with his efforts? Just where Job faults Eliphaz is evident in v. 25, as he refers to the painfulness of straight talk. Translations that emend the expression to "how pleasant" (cf. NAB)[122] or that soften the expression to "how forceful" (NRSV) miss the point. Job knows that only painful words could do justice to his deeply painful situation. Eliphaz's words were full of hope for a bright future. He deftly avoided laying blame for the situation with either Job or God, except in broad generalizations about the universal human condition. Eliphaz's words lack the relentless honesty that Job demands of himself and of his friends, an honesty that will not conceal (v. 10). In an alliterative phrase that mocks the surface prettiness of Eliphaz's words, Job dismisses Eliphaz's arguments as meaningless (v. 25*b*).

6:26-27. Job carries the issue further in v. 26. To reprove or correct "words" is a fundamental task of the sage. But Job resents that his words are treated as so much "wind"— i.e., trivialized—precisely because he is desperate. Job would not think kindly of the statement made concerning him in the Talmud: "a person is not held responsible for what he says while in distress."[123] Although Job had earlier characterized his own words as rash (v. 3), he insisted that they were motivated by his circumstances. Now he makes a much bolder defense of his own ability to discern the truth, not in spite of but because

of the fact that he has been driven to the margins of life itself. In v. 27, Job boldly asserts that refusing to take seriously the words of a sufferer is the moral equivalent of casting lots for an orphan or selling out a friend. These words, too, strike some commentators as rash overstatement,[124] but Job's comparison requires that one consider what unites these cases. In each instance one who is vulnerable is devalued and treated as less than a person.

6:28. In vv. 28-30, Job attempts to set the conditions for a true dialogue about his situation. The image dominating v. 28 is that of the face. The phrase translated "look at me" is literally "face me" (פְּנוּ־בִי *pĕnû-bî*). In the following half-line Job uses a solemn oath formula to declare to his friends that he will not lie "to your face" (עַל־פְּנֵיכֶם *'al-pĕnêkem*). The image of the face is a profound symbol of human identity. Faces are what an infant first learns to recognize visually as it establishes a sense of social relationship. A face always makes a moral claim on another face.

6:29. The imperatives with which Job addresses his friends can be translated conceptually, as in the NIV's "relent . . . reconsider." After the vividness of "face me," however, the underlying physical nuance of these verbs is better expressed by "turn" or "turn back." The two terms that Job contrasts in v. 29 (עַוְלָה *'awlâ*; צֶדֶק *sedeq*) have a range of meanings. They could be translated as "injustice" and "vindication" respectively, anticipating the legal language that will occupy so much of Job's thinking.[125] As Habel observes, however, *'awlâ* is often associated in the book of Job with speech, so that it takes on the nuance of "deceit,"[126] contrasting with the "rightness" (*sedeq*) or integrity that Job claims is at stake for him.

6:30. In the final verse, Job brings together images of the body (tongue, palate) with the metaphor of taste as discernment, recalling the similar images of vv. 4-7. What does Job claim to be able to discern? The two words used have double meanings, both of which should be heard. As noted above, *'awlâ* means both "injustice" and "deceit." Similarly, the very last word of the line can mean "calamity," as it does in v. 2, yet it can also

122. Pope, *Job*, 55.
123. *b. B. Bat.* 16b.

124. Andersen, *Job*, 133.
125. See Good, *In Turns of Tempest*, 214-15.
126. Habel, *The Book of Job*, 150.

carry the meaning of "deceit," "falsehood" (Ps 5:9[10]; Mic 7:3).[127] Thus Job is making two claims, which, significantly, he does not distinguish. Through these words he asserts that he is not lying to his friends, since his own tongue can detect deceit and falsehood.

127. Gordis, *The Book of Job*, 78.

At the same time he claims that he is able to tell the objective truth about his situation, since his own tongue is able to discern injustice and calamity when he tastes it. These are, in fact, claims of a quite different nature. Whether Job is aware of the difference is difficult to say but of great importance.

REFLECTIONS

Job's speeches are highly imagistic, inviting the reader to search for meaning among the images as well as in the explicit claims he makes. The reader who expects to find a transparent, consistently worked out system of metaphors and symbols is often frustrated, however, discovering instead a hodgepodge of apparently "ill-connected images."[128] Yet what is ill-connected on one level may prove quite coherent on another. It is always worth investigating when a person shows a preference for certain types of images or for words from a particular semantic field, even if these images and words are used in superficially disparate contexts. The individual may not be aware of it, but in such imagistic play the symbolic processes of speech itself are at work, exploring and attempting to resolve some fundamental dilemma that hovers on the edges of conscious discourse. So it is with Job's speech.

The body in all its physicality serves as a point of reference for Job. He thinks by means of the body in several ways. First, Job makes use of the image of the body as limit (see Commentary on Job 7). Even the relationship with God must take account of the finitude of the human body. It is surprisingly easy for moral and religious language to become abstract, to fail to take the body into account or to represent the body in unrealistic ways. Job uses a variety of images that insist on the vulnerability of the body. He graphically portrays his affliction in terms of arrows that have penetrated his body (v. 4), twice uses words for pain (vv. 10, 25), and explicitly contrasts the limited strength of flesh with that of the unfeeling, invulnerable strength of stones and bronze (v. 12). In this way Job's speech sharply contrasts with Eliphaz's sanitized references to binding up wounds and healing bruises (5:18) and to the swords and famines that in Eliphaz's miraculous world leave no scars or ravages (5:19-22). A religious language that cannot be realistic about the body is suspect, and Job calls into question the traditional language of prayer, because it does not acknowledge the limits of the body as one waits for God's deliverance (see Commentary above).

Second, the image of the body as the organ of perception dominates chap. 6. Almost all of Job's language about perception, judgment, and discrimination is developed in terms of body imagery, most important the bodily function of eating and drinking. He perceives his affliction in terms of his spirit's "drinking" poison (v. 4). He compares his outburst to animals who bray or bellow when deprived of food (v. 5). He describes his life in terms of insipid, tasteless food (v. 6). Even the image of nauseated revulsion is a bodily image (v. 7; the word for "appetite" [נפשׁ *nepeš*] concretely means "throat," "gullet"). Job images loyalty in terms of water and himself as one who dies of thirst when he fails to find it in his friends (v. 18). At the end of the chapter, Job refers to the tongue and palate, which are both the organs of speech and of taste, as he makes a claim about his ability to judge and discriminate (v. 30).

Third, for Job the question of how one knows something has to be referred to the body's experience. The body's knowledge is immediate and direct. What is significant

128. Good, *In Turns of Tempest,* 214.

about such images is that they depict a kind of knowledge that is at the same time indisputable and radically subjective. No one else can tell me whether I am hungry or thirsty or nauseated. Only I can know. Moreover, these are not things about which I am likely to be confused or in doubt. I know such things with the immediacy and certainty of the body's knowledge. By using such imagery, Job makes a very powerful claim for the authority of what he knows. There is, however, something troubling and problematic about that imagery when it is used to authenticate knowledge about the world. Nothing is more subjective than taste. We use the phrase "a matter of taste" when we want to say that there are no objective standards to which one can appeal. Yet Job represents the tongue and the palate as the privileged organs of discrimination and judgment. The problem that lurks in the appeal and the limit of these images is the problem of how to make a subjective claim valid intersubjectively. How can I make what seems as clear to me as the taste of salt equally clear to you?

Job struggles with this problem through his use of images. His opening image of transferring his inner anguish onto a set of scales is just such an attempt. He recognizes the need for a way of perceiving that can be shared between persons who do not have the same immediacy of experience. The problem, of course, is that this is a fantasy image. Anguish cannot be made as tangible as the weight of sand. At the end of the chapter Job tries again for an image that will be faithful to his primary commitment to the body as the privileged organ of perception and yet adequate to the reality of intersubjective distance. He finds what he is seeking in the image of the face (v. 28). Such an image is faithful to Job's concern for the body, because there is no other part of one's physical self in which identity is invested more than in the face. The face is also that part of the body that is the primary means of establishing connection with another person, through the expression of the eyes and the mouth. The mutual scrutiny of face meeting face creates an environment that discourages a lie (v. 28b). Yet for all his concern to acknowledge the claims of intersubjective distance, Job returns in the end to claim for himself the final authority in adjudicating the truth of his own speech and the judgment on his own situation (v. 30).

The issue lying behind Job's images of the body as the organ of perception remains quite lively in contemporary theological discussion—namely, the issue of the role of experience in establishing knowledge about the world and about God. Increasingly, persons whose experience has not traditionally been taken into account insist that they be heard. Often this experience is understood quite specifically in terms of the body—the body that is female rather than male, the body whose skin is not white, the disabled body, the body crushed by poverty. As with Job, there is an immediacy and authenticity in such experience that commands respect. As with Job, there is also the difficulty of translating what is a wholly convincing subjective experience into a mode of communication that is genuinely dialogical. The danger is that the gap will not be bridged and that competing subjectivities will find no common ground.

Job 7:1-21, Job Confronts God

COMMENTARY

7:1-10. Having made the solemn claim that he would speak the truth, Job begins to describe the human condition. Although he ostensibly continues to address his friends in vv. 1-6, Job is primarily concerned to speak to God. Job first addresses God directly in v. 7 and continues to do so for the rest of the chapter. The unifying topic of the chapter is the nature of human existence, which Job invokes both to justify his own behavior and to bring God's into question.

7:1-2. As in chap. 6, Job's argument is developed through a grim play with several clusters of interrelated images. In the opening verses these include metaphors of work, payment, rest, and time. The three governing images for life in vv. 1-2—forced labor, day-labor, and slavery—are all characterized by subjection to someone else's power and will. Job's focus is more precise, however. As indicated by the clause "like the *days* of a day-laborer are his *days*," Job draws attention specifically to the way such conditions affect the experience of time. For such workers, the horizon of expectation is severely limited. The slave's sense of time is governed by the coming of evening shade (v. 2*a*), when the slave might cease work for the day. The day-laborer's expectation is also focused on the end of the day, when the worker was supposed to be paid (Deut 24:15), an arrangement often abused (Jer 22:13; Mal 3:5). Implicitly, the only satisfaction was in cessation of work and in meager reward, not in the work itself. As metaphors, these images create a relentlessly negative depiction of human existence.

7:3-5. In v. 3, Job applies the image to his own condition, which fails even to offer the meager rewards of the day-laborer. The theme of time is emphasized, as Job describes himself as being paid in the coin of time—months and nights. It is a defective payment, however, as the qualifying words "emptiness" (שוא *šāw*) and "trouble" (עמל *'āmāl*) make clear. The phrase "nights of trouble" provides the transition to Job's examination of the other image, the slave who seeks rest in the shadows of evening. For Job there is no rest. What is striking about v. 4 is its rendering of the reality of time as experienced by one who cannot rest. Expected values are reversed. The night that should be desirable is treated with impatience. Time that should seem all too short is experienced as frustratingly prolonged. Verse 5 interrupts the sequence of images having to do with work and time. In one of the most graphically physical descriptions in the book, it describes Job's ravaged skin. Following v. 4, the description serves to explain why Job can get no rest. The reference to worms, which are part of the traditional

imagery of death and decay (17:14; 21:26; 24:20; Isa 14:11), suggests how close to the border between death and life Job is.

7:6. The sense of contradictoriness in the experience of time, which was developed in v. 4, is renewed in v. 6 by the image of days moving quickly. The image of life as a cloth woven of a person's days is a common one in many cultures. Hezekiah speaks of his death in a similar image: "like a weaver I have rolled up my life;/ he cuts me off from the loom" (Isa 38:12 NRSV). The medieval Jewish writer Ibn Ezra invokes the image when he says "man in the world weaves like a weaver, and certainly his days are the thread."[129] Job's use of the image is characteristically subversive. He does not take the product of weaving—the cloth—as the image of life, as do Hezekiah and Ibn Ezra. Rather, the metaphor is the shuttle itself, specifically its repetitive back-and-forth movement. Job makes the same point with this image as he did with the image of the slave and the day-laborer. There is no accomplishment in Job's image of the shuttle. What makes the metaphor so devastating, however, is the play on words Job makes between the words "thread" and "hope" (both תקוה *tiqwâ*). The shuttle's incessant, repetitive movement simply stops abruptly "when the thread [*tiqwâ*] runs out," just as life abruptly stops "without hope [*tiqwâ*]."

7:7a. The sense of the tenuousness of life, developed in vv. 5-6, motivates Job's direct appeal to God in v. 7. Calling upon God to remember is a traditional motif of prayer. God may be asked to remember many things: the individual who prays (Judg 16:28), particular deeds or sufferings of the individual (2 Kgs 20:3; Ps 89:50[51]), or God's own mercy (Ps 25:6). When the psalmists say that God remembers that humans are mortal beings, creatures of dust (Ps 103:14) like a passing wind (Ps 78:39), the context has to do with God's compassionate restraint. Job, too, will ask for God's restraint, but in a way quite different from the psalmists.

7:7b-10. In v. 7*b*, Job introduces an image that will become increasingly important in the book, the image of the eye that gazes and the object of its gaze. In keeping with his theme of the transitoriness of human

129. Cited in Dhorme, *A Commentary on the Book of Job*, 101.

existence, in vv. 7-10 Job primarily uses the image to talk about what the eye cannot hold and fix. His own eye will not again "see happiness." More important is Job's association of the image of the gazing eye with God (vv. 8, 19). The association of God with sight is frequently made in the OT. Hagar calls God *El-roi,* "God of seeing" (Gen 16:13), and the psalmists often refer to God's attentive vision (Pss 11:4; 33:18; 34:15[16]; 139:16). Job's use of the motif, however, stresses the limits of that seeing, in particular the powerlessness of even God's gaze to hold its object in the face of the dissolution of death (v. 8*b*). Death is depicted as a kind of vanishing, compared with the way a cloud simply vanishes (v. 9*a*). Although Job invokes the traditional motif of death as a journey without return (v. 9*b*-10*a*),[130] he ties this motif to the imagery of vision in the last line of this series. The term rendered "know" is more properly a perceptual verb, "recognize" (נכר *nākar*), often associated with seeing (Gen 42:7; Ruth 3:14).[131] Although the connection is not made explicitly, this section is also about time. The limit of mortality on human time must always be considered. Moreover, the transition between life and death is a matter of an instant; it happens "in the blink of an eye," as we say.

7:11. The misery of human life (vv. 1-6), which deprives experienced time of satisfaction, and the limits and suddenness of mortality (vv. 7-10) combine to create an urgent need to speak (v. 11). Cultural inhibitions against unrestrained speech were considerable. The wisdom tradition valued control of speech highly (Prov 10:19; 17:27). Job's situation, however, might better be compared with the psalmists'. They, too, recommended restraint of rash speech and trust in God (Ps 4:4[5]). Psalm 39 offers the closest comparison with Job 7, since in that psalm a sufferer struggles to keep silent but finally must speak out. There are even a number of motifs shared by the psalm and Job's words (cf. Ps 39:5[6] with Job 7:16*b* ; Ps 39:11[12] with Job 7:18, 20; Ps 39:13[14] with Job 7:19); yet the difference in tone could not be more marked. The psalmist manages to shape the

words forced out by burning anguish into the forms and sentiments sanctioned by tradition (Ps 39:2-3[3-4]). Job, however, will deliberately savage traditional forms (vv. 17-18). Job describes his speech as being characterized by "anguish of spirit" and "bitterness of soul" (v. 11). Although these can be conventional terms for someone deeply grieved (Ps 4:1[2]; Isa 38:15; Ezek 27:31), "bitterness of soul" can also describe those who are so alienated that they defy social conventions and can even be dangerous (Judg 18:25; 1 Sam 22:2). Such alienation distinguishes Job's ironic and parodying speech from that of the psalmist.

7:12. Job begins his complaint with an ironic rhetorical question based on a mythological allusion (v. 12). Throughout the ancient Near East there were stories about the conflict between the deities who create and govern and the forces of chaos represented by the sea or sea monsters. In Mesopotamia, conflict between the god Marduk and the primordial sea Tiamat forms the central plot of the creation epic, the *Enuma Elish.*[132] In Ugarit, Baal's kingship is secured by his victory over Yam, the sea. The goddess Anat also fights Yam and muzzles the dragon Tannin.[133] Israel, too, recounted Yahweh's victory over Yam the sea and Tannin the dragon as part of the creation and governance of the world (Ps 74:13; cf. Isa 27:1; 51:9).[134]

The ironic contrast in v. 12 between Job, a person of fleeting days, and the great cosmic opponents of God serves as an accusation that God is treating Job with an intensity wholly disproportionate to his significance, a point that Job will make more explicitly in vv. 17-19 and v. 20. What is less transparent is the way in which Job characterizes this divine treatment. Unlike 6:4, where he used the image of an attack, Job here speaks of God's putting a "guard" or a "watch" on him. Although it has been suggested that Job is making an allusion to a specific mythic motif, such as Marduk's posting a guard to keep the waters of the sky in place, the analogy is not that close.[135] Job's image of a "guard" appears not to be drawn specifically from a myth but

---

130. N. Tromp, *Primitive Conceptions of Death and the Nether World in the Old Testament,* BibOr 21 (Rome: Pontifical Biblical Institute, 1969) 189-90.

131. Dhorme, *A Commentary on the Book of Job,* 103, translates "see again."

132. *ANET,* 60-72.

133. *ANET,* 129-42.

134. See D. A. Diewert, "Job 7:12: Yam, Tannin and the Surveillance of Job," *JBL* 106 (1987) 203-15, for a thorough review of the ancient Near Eastern and biblical parallels.

135. Diewert, "Job 7:12," 204.

represents his interpretation of his own situation. Although the Hebrew term involved (שמר *šāmar*) is not semantically related to words for seeing, as the English word *watch* is, the aspect of surveillance is very much a part of the concept of "setting a guard against" someone (see Neh 4:22-23[4:16-17]). Job will develop this notion of surveillance in the following verses.

7:13-16. In v. 13, Job turns to a traditional psalmic motif: the sufferer in the privacy of the sickbed. In the psalms, the bed is the place of quiet introspection (Ps 4:4[5]), or the place of weeping, to which God hears and responds (Ps 6:6[7]), healing the sick (Ps 41:3[4]). Job, however, undercuts that traditional motif by charging that instead of finding comfort and relief in his bed, he is subjected by God to terrifying dreams and visions (v. 14). The image is an aggressive, invasive one, a psychic counterpart to the physical image of piercing arrows in 6:4. Dreams and visions are a type of forced seeing and serve here as a counterpart to God's surveillance of Job; God watches Job, but Job's vision is filled with horrors. The notion of dreams as a means of divine aggression is unusual, although it may be what Eliphaz and Bildad refer to as the nameless terrors that pursue the wicked (15:21; 18:11; cf. Sir 40:6).

In Job's case, such divine aggression reinforces his desire to die (v. 15). As in chap. 6, Job's language for himself is graphically physical, much more so than the translations usually suggest. The word translated simply as "I" is נפש (*nepeš*), which literally designates the air passage in the throat. The word rendered "body" is literally "bones" (עצם *'eṣem*). Thus "my throat would choose strangling, [and I would choose] death rather than my own bones." Job concludes this section with the image of his life's being as transient as a puff of air (v. 16*b*), echoing his appeal to God in v. 7.

7:17-21. The last section of the chapter opens with Job's bitter parody of Psalm 8:4[5]. In the psalm, humankind's confessed insignificance vis-à-vis the moon and the stars serves as a foil for grateful acknowledgment that God has given humans an exalted place of dominion over creation (cf. Ps 144:3). Job draws the image into the themes of divine surveillance and of God's absurd exaggeration

of danger, already introduced in v. 12. Thus the first verb, "make great," "magnify" (גדל *gādal*), echoes the descriptions of exaltation in Ps 8:5-6[6-7]; here, however, the sarcastic intent is unmistakable, as Job questions God's sense of proportion. Where the psalmist marveled at God's mindfulness of human beings and care for them, Job reinterprets this divine attentiveness as unwelcome scrutiny (v. 17*b*). Hebrew allows a particularly clever word play, since the same verb that the psalmist uses to mean "care for" (פקד *pāqad*) can also mean "inspect" or even "call to account" (v. 18*a*).

The paradoxes of time, which were explored at the beginning of the chapter, return in v. 16 and in vv. 17-19. As a human being, Job's days are as transient as a breath of air (v. 16*a*). Yet he would not choose to live forever (v. 16*b*), because of God's unrelenting presence, which is expressed in successively smaller units of time—every morning, every moment (v. 18). When Job speaks of a period of relief, he does so characteristically in terms of time as measured by the body, long enough to "swallow my spit" (v. 19*b*). This image, like those of v. 14-15, also suggests the invasive quality of divine scrutiny, which interferes with even the most intimate of bodily functions.

Job's alienation from the traditional language of prayer is underscored when one compares vv. 19-21 with Psalm 39. As in Job 7:19, the psalmist also makes the unusual plea that God turn away God's gaze (Ps 39:13[14]). The accompanying reflection on sin, however, is quite different. The psalmist pleads with God to "deliver me from all my [transgressions]" (Ps 39:8[9] NRSV), acknowledging the legitimacy of divine anger but pleading for relief because human existence is "mere breath" (Ps 39:11[12]; cf. Job 7:16) and the psalmist will soon "be no more" (Ps 39:13[14]; cf. Job 7:21). Whether one takes Job's opening words in v. 20 to be hypothetical, as most do, or confessional,[136] what Job says is no prayer. Pursuing the logic of his meditation on human transiency and insignificance, Job insists that he cannot have harmed God, a calculation that would be utterly alien to the psalmist. This assertion motivates his question of why God does not simply pardon

---

136. So Andersen, *Job*, 132.

whatever offenses Job has committed. Neither sin nor the forgiveness of sin would be of much consequence to God. This is not the thinking of traditional piety, in which the seriousness of sin and the generosity of God's compassion are taken with utmost seriousness (e.g., Psalm 32).

That Job's mode is parody rather than prayer is evident also from the epithet "watcher of humans" (v. 20). The related verb (נצר *nāṣar*) is often used in the psalms to describe God as protector (e.g., Pss 12:7[8]; 32:7; 40:11[12]; 140:1, 4[2, 5]). Job's development of the theme of divine surveillance, however, gives this epithet a wholly different and more threatening character.

It is more difficult to determine Job's tone in the last half-verse of the chapter (v. 21 *b*). At issue is how one takes the introductory words. They can be translated "for now"/"for soon," as in the NRSV and the NIV, indicating that God must act quickly, since Job will soon be dead. If God then seeks Job out in order to restore him, it will be too late. In this interpretation, Job ends his speech on a pleading note, not unlike the ending of Psalm 39. Given what has preceded, it seems likely that Job is imitating the words of a plea but subverting the meaning. One can also take the first two words as introducing a consequence, "for then" (i.e., "If you forgive me, then thus and so will happen").[137] In this reading, Job says in essence that the consequence of divine forgiveness will be that he is allowed to die.[138] And when God searches for him in renewed surveillance, Job will be safely beyond God's power, for he "will be no more" (cf. v. 8).[139] Such a sentiment would provide a fitting conclusion for Job's anti-psalm.

137. Cf. Fohrer, *Das Buch Hiob*, 164.
138. Gordis, *The Book of Job*, 68, 83.
139. Habel, *The Book of Job*, 167.

REFLECTIONS

The bitterness Job expresses through his savage parody of the language of psalms arises from his sense of contradiction between the image of God as it has been traditionally rendered in psalms and the image of God that seems necessary to account for Job's recent experiences. Job takes over unchallenged from his culture the assumption that extraordinary suffering is to be understood as the action of God, specifically a response to sin (vv. 20-21). The lack of proportion between whatever sin he might have committed and the extent of his devastation is incomprehensible to him, however, and in order to make it comprehensible, he must imagine the type of God capable of acting in such a fashion. The disparity of his experience leads him to conclude that only a God madly obsessed with scrutinizing and punishing human behavior could act this way.

The assumptions of Job and his friends about suffering as punishment for sin is not entirely a relic of the past. It crops up from time to time in religious polemics, almost always in a mean-spirited way. It also emerges, sometimes to the surprise of the individual in question, in the instinctive response to misfortune: "What have I done to deserve this?" One of the distinctive features of contemporary religious thinking, however, is a tendency to reject the notion that God intentionally inflicts suffering on people as punishment. One might think, therefore, that people who do not share the assumptions of Job concerning sin and punishment would read chap. 7 with a sense of detachment. Yet often, even people who do not in any way share that perspective are nevertheless deeply drawn into Job's anger. What makes Job's outcry so compelling even to persons who do not share his theological assumptions? It may be because Job speaks so powerfully about the fragility of human life and its propensity to misery. For many human beings there is no escape from harassing powers and oppressive structures. As in Job's description, their lives are deprived of even the most limited autonomy as they struggle from day to day, all dignity denied by incessant oppression. For those who suffer unrelentingly, there is no luxury of unlimited time. As Job observes, human life is bounded inexorably by death. This is the reservoir of outrage that Job's words open.

Modern reflection on human suffering often focuses on the role of the immediate causes of misery: political oppression, economic exploitation, the destruction of family and social structures, the deadly combination of ethnic prejudice and power. For the religious, however, Job's question about the nature of the God who presides over a world in which such things happen is finally inescapable. In his speech, Job models a kind of theological reflection that insists on beginning with the concrete realities of life. What image of God makes sense in the context of undeniable, incessant, unending misery? Job's answer is that it is a God who gazes, like a child poking an anthill, entranced by the spectacle of brokenness and confusion. The temptation, when one is confronted with such a radical claim, is to reject and dismiss it as the raving of someone whose misfortunes have caused him to lose perspective (6:26). It may be the case, however, that those who are pushed to the limits of endurance are precisely the ones who no longer deceive themselves with the platitudes that blind the comfortable with an easy self-deception.

How does someone who is that angry and that alienated speak about God or to God? Anyone who has experienced such intense alienation knows how infuriating much conventional religious language can be. The cheerful hymns of assurance and the bland responsive readings appear intentionally blind to all the pain in the world. The benign image of God they project seems disconcertingly like the packaged images of politicians running for office and deflects serious questioning in much the same way. At such times, it is not surprising that one wants to tear apart conventional religious language that seems intent on denying the spiritual agony of religious persons struggling with the hard realities of life. Taking the words of easy assurance and placing them in a context in which their shallowness is exposed, as Job does in chap. 7, is not only satisfying but also an important step toward making a more honest and adequate religious language possible.

Although exposing the inadequacy of much conventional religious language is part of what is involved in the "anti-psalms" Job utters, there is another dimension that should not be overlooked. The poignancy of these words arises from the sense of betrayal that echoes through them. Savaging the words of a traditional prayer or hymn can often be a way of expressing the painful sense that God has betrayed the relationship. The old familiar words expressed who one had understood God to be; they were the promises of God's love and presence. Now it is God who seems to make a mockery of everything upon which one had relied. Like a betrayed lover, one feels a fool for having been taken in. Flinging the shreds of that language of prayer and praise back at God is a way of protesting such treatment. The Bible does not shy away from this way of talking to God. Although Job's speeches are the most sustained words of protest, Jeremiah also voiced the sense of having been betrayed by God, when he said:

> O LORD, you deceived me, and I was deceived;
>   you overpowered me and prevailed.
> I am ridiculed all day long;
>   everyone mocks me. (Jer 20:7 NIV)

The Commentary argued that Job's words are not prayer. This is certainly true in the sense that Job does not use conventional forms of prayer or compose his emotions into those traditionally shaped by psalmic prayers. But in the more profound sense, is it prayer? One should not answer that question too quickly. Not all angry language addressed to God is prayer. It may make a pastor or a spiritual adviser more comfortable to think so, but one should probably make distinctions. Such discrimination requires careful listening. There are some angry words that are a prelude to the indifference that comes from the death of a relationship. Yet other angry words, no matter how laced with the protective rhetoric of sarcasm, do not have the mark of finality about them. In subtle ways they seek a response. So it is with Job's speech, above all in the ambiguity with which he uses the expression "you will search for me" in his concluding words (v. 21). Job's words are the prayer of a person who cannot "pray," but whose conversation with God is far from over.

Job 8:1-22, A Metaphor of Two Plants

COMMENTARY

In chap. 6, Job complained about the failure of his friends to respond to him as they should (see 6:24, 26, 30). Bildad attempts to address Job's challenge, at least according to his own understanding of it. Job's invitation to "teach me" is certainly congenial to Bildad, whose speech has a distinctly didactic flavor. How one understands the structure of Bildad's speech depends on the resolution of difficult interpretive problems in vv. 16-19 (see below). The speech is best understood as organized throughout according to a set of contrasts. After a verse referring to the nature of Job's words (v. 2), Bildad begins the first part of his speech with the general principle that governs his whole understanding (v. 3). Following from this general principle, Bildad contrasts the fate of Job's children (v. 4) with Job's own prospects (vv. 5-7). The second part of the speech is introduced by an appeal to the authority of ancient tradition (vv. 8-10). Two contrasting metaphorical descriptions compare the fate of the godless (vv. 11-15) with that of the blameless person (vv. 16-19). The point of this metaphorical comparison is made explicit in v. 20, which contrasts God's relation to the blameless and the evildoer. The speech comes to an end with a prediction of the very different futures in store for Job (v. 21) and his enemies (v. 22).

8:1-2. Bildad begins, as will most of the speakers, with a criticism of the previous speaker's words (cf. 11:2-3; 12:2-3; 15:2-6; 16:2-3; 18:2-3; 19:2-3; 20:2-3; 21:2-3; 26:2-4). This technique is a familiar part of a disputation, not only in Israel but also in Mesopotamian wisdom literature. In the Babylonian Theodicy, for instance, one of the characters says to the other, "My reliable fellow, holder of knowledge, your thoughts are perverse, you have forsaken right and blaspheme against your God's designs."[140] The frequency

of such remarks in Job is unusual, however. It draws attention to the crisis of human words and human wisdom that is thematic in the book of Job.

The way Bildad formulates his criticism echoes Job's complaint in 6:26 that the friends treat his words as so much "wind." Most commonly, "wind" (רוח *rûaḥ*) connotes something insubstantial and empty (cf. Job 15:2; 16:3; Isa 41:29; Jer 5:13; Mic 2:11). Bildad, however, changes the traditional image by referring to Job's words as a "mighty wind" (רוח כביר *rûaḥ kabbîr*). Something that is *kabbîr* is the very opposite of insubstantial; it must be reckoned with, like the "mighty waters" of Isa 28:2 (cf. Job 15:10; 34:17, 24; Isa 17:12). Calling Job's words a "mighty wind" draws attention not only to their emptiness but also and almost paradoxically to the destructiveness inherent in their emptiness (cf. the "great wind" that destroyed the house of Job's eldest son, 1:19).[141]

8:3-7. To refute Job's unsatisfactory words, Bildad produces an axiom in the form of a rhetorical question. The word order puts the emphasis on "El" (אל *ʾēl*) and "Shaddai" (שדי *šadday*), the terms for God. Thus Bildad makes God's character the issue. The values Bildad specifies, "justice" (משפט *mišpāṭ*) and "the right" (צדק *ṣedeq*), are frequently used in combination to describe the just order of the world established and commanded by God.[142] According to tradition, nothing could be more intrinsic to God's nature than *mišpāṭ* and *ṣedeq*. They are the foundation of God's throne (Ps 97:2), what God loves (Ps 33:5), God's gift to the king (Ps 72:1-2), what God expects of Israel (Isa 5:7), and what God will give to Zion (Isa 33:5). *Mišpāṭ* and *ṣedeq* are the basis of the covenant in Hosea (2:19 [21])

---

140. Lambert, *Babylonian Wisdom Literature*, 77. This and other examples are cited in Habel, *The Book of Job*, 173.

141. Clines, *Job 1–20*, 202; contra Fohrer, *Das Buch Hiob*, 188.
142. J. J. Scullion, "Righteousness (OT)," *ABD* 5:727, 731.

and God's demand in Amos (5:24). The notion that God would pervert them is, according to tradition, simply unthinkable. Bildad's faith in the axioms of tradition may be unshakable, but for Job the question Bildad poses in v. 3 is not rhetorical but painfully real.[143]

For Bildad, the axiom about God serves as the fixed point from which Job's situation can be properly understood. In Hebrew, vv. 4, 5, and 6 all begin with the same word, "if" (אם *'im*). As the NIV recognizes, however, v. 4, concerning the sin of Job's children, is not hypothetical for Bildad, but a deduction from the fact of their violent and unexpected deaths and the axiom that God does not pervert the right.[144] Unbeknownst to Bildad, Job, too, had entertained concerns about the possible sins of his children, but had assumed that his actions on their behalf would protect them (1:5; cf. Ezek 14:20). Bildad's words seem grossly insensitive, and it may well be that he is presented as the type of the rigid, doctrinaire moralist who loses his humanity in his desire to perceive the world according to a set of rules. His certitude is implicitly ridiculed by the author, who has let the reader know that the deaths of Job's children have nothing to do with any sin at all. It will not do simply to dismiss Bildad as a caricature, however, for he articulates one side of a complex moral problematic in ancient Israel concerning sin and its consequences. The larger context of Bildad's position is discussed in the Reflections below.

Bildad does not explicitly say whether he thinks Job has sinned. Given Bildad's views, he must assume so, else how could he account for Job's other catastrophic losses and his ominous skin disease? The critical difference is that God has not taken Job's life, perhaps indicating that Job's sin was not as serious as that of his children.[145] In any event, that is not Bildad's main concern. Like Eliphaz, he is primarily concerned to reassure Job about the prospects for his future restoration. Bildad's advice in v. 5 echoes that of Eliphaz in 5:8. In contrast to Eliphaz's advice, however, Bildad's words in vv. 5-6 are true

conditionals. Job must do two things. First, he must approach God in the spirit of true piety, seeking God (cf. Ps 63:1[2]; Isa 26:9; Hos 5:15) and imploring God's favor (cf. Pss 30:8[9]; 142:1[2]). Second, Job must be morally "pure and upright." The image of restoration at the end of v. 6 may be understood in more than one way. Some translate "restore your righteous abode"[146] or "safeguard your righteous dwelling."[147] The interpretation reflected in the NRSV and the NIV, however, better reflects Bildad's understanding of how God acts. The verb translated "restore" (שלם *šillam*) is often used in legal contexts for restitution, or in contexts of payment of debt or other settling of accounts. Frequently, it serves an image of divine judgment, in which God "pays back" a person for deeds committed, both negatively (e.g., Deut 32:41; 2 Sam 3:39; Jer 51:56) and positively (e.g., Ruth 2:12; 1 Sam 24:19[20]). Similarly, the translation "rightful place" captures Bildad's belief that a person's outward circumstances should correspond to that person's character, and he believes in Job's fundamentally good character (vv. 20-21).

Bildad concludes his description of Job's restoration with a rhetorical flourish, contrasting past and future (v. 7). Like Eliphaz in 5:17-26, Bildad avoids talking about Job's present sufferings, preferring to focus on the future. Bildad's schematic terms for time contrast sharply with Job's perception of time as constricted by suffering (7:1-3) and measured by the body's experience (7:4-6).

Throughout this section the reader's knowledge of the real cause of Job's misfortunes creates irony at Bildad's expense. His pompous certainty is exposed as false and his ideas discredited. The chapter lays the groundwork for a more difficult irony, however. What Bildad predicts in v. 7 is close to what actually happens. There is even a verbal echo when it is said in 42:12 that "Yahweh blessed the *latter* days of Job more than his *former* days," describing how Job's possessions were restored to him twofold (42:10).

8:8-10. Bildad invokes the authority of ancestral tradition to introduce his comparison of the fate of the wicked and the fate of the righteous (vv. 11-19). The appeal to

143. Janzen, *Job*, 87-88.

144. So Gordis, *The Book of Job*, 88; Pope, *Job*, 64; Habel, *The Book of Job*, 169; Clines, *Job 1–20*, 198; contra Dhorme, *A Commentary on the Book of Job*, 113; Good, *In Turns of Tempest*, 68.

145. Fohrer, *Das Buch Hiob*, 189-90; Clines, "The Arguments of Job's Three Friends," 206.

146. Habel, *The Book of Job*, 167; Clines, *Job 1–20*, 197.

147. Gordis, *The Book of Job*, 86.

ancient tradition is a familiar motif in biblical rhetoric (cf. Deut 4:32-35; 32:7-9; Isa 40:21-24; 46:8-11).[148] Here, Bildad creates a sense of the chain of tradition by referring first to a former generation and then to the ancestors who preceded them (cf. Sir 8:9). Although some argue that Bildad is referring to "the previous generations in the more recent past,"[149] similar appeals stress the primordial nature of tradition (cf. Deut 4:32; Isa 40:21).[150] Both in Mesopotamia and in Israel there was a belief that the antediluvian generations possessed special knowledge. One of the oldest existing wisdom texts, The Instructions of Shuruppak, is presented as the instructions of the survivor of the flood to his son.[151] In post-exilic Israel, too, traditions developed about the wisdom of the long-lived, antediluvian patriarchs, especially Enoch.[152] Wisdom itself is personified as a primordial figure (Prov 8:22-31).

The crucial role that antiquity plays in authenticating and discrediting claims to wisdom is embodied in the contrast between the vista of generations receding into antiquity in v. 8 and the abrupt metaphor in v. 9a ("we are but of yesterday, and we know nothing"). In v. 9b, Bildad echoes ideas and words Job had used in his speech ("shadow," 7:2; "days," 7:1, 6, 16; "upon the earth," 7:1). The notion of the ephemerality of human life is a common motif, especially in the psalms (e.g., Pss 90:5-6; 102:11[12]; 103:14-16; 109:23). There, however, it is used, as Job employs it, to establish a contrast between the nature of divine and human existence, not as Bildad uses it, to discredit knowledge based on an individual's experience.

Job had asked his friends to teach him and show him where he had been wrong (6:24). Bildad both demurs and accepts this invitation. *He* cannot teach Job, for Bildad includes himself in the category of those who "know nothing" (v. 9). It is the ancestors who must teach Job (v. 10). Although he does not say so explicitly, Bildad presents himself as a conduit through which tradition passes, pure and undistorted.

8:11-15. Bildad's teaching is traditional. First, he cites a proverb (v. 11), which might be used in any of a number of contexts to make various points. Next, he develops the proverb in a mini-narrative. Staying within the metaphorical world of the proverb, he unfolds the features of the saying that are relevant to the situation he addresses (v. 12). Finally, he makes explicit application to human experience (v. 13). A second comparison with an image from nature underscores the moral (vv. 14-15).

The saying in v. 11 is a nature proverb concerning the relation of cause and effect. Such proverbs are to be found in every culture. Compare the Mesopotamian proverb, "The mother brew is bitter. How is the beer sweet?"[153] Or the Israelite proverb, "For lack of wood the fire goes out" (Prov 26:20a NRSV). Bildad develops the relevant aspects of the proverb by describing how an apparently flourishing and green plant withers before its time (v. 12). The cause: no water; the effect: premature death. Proverbs work by establishing analogies. Thus in the application in v. 13 God is implicitly compared to the water essential for life, whereas "those who forget God" and "the godless" correspond to the plants. The analogy with Job's children is unmistakable (v. 4).

In v. 13a, the NRSV follows the MT, "the *paths* of all who forget God" (ארחות *'orḥôt*), while the NIV follows the LXX, "the *destiny*" (τὰ ἔσχατα *ta eschata* = אחרית *'aḥărît*). The parallelism with the future-oriented word "hope" (תקוה *tiqwâ*) in v. 13b might favor reading "destiny," but perhaps the author is playing with the similar sounds and appearance in Hebrew of the two words "paths"/"destiny" to suggest the close connection between chronic behavior and ultimate consequences (cf. Prov 1:19).

The smooth translations of v. 14a in the NRSV and the NIV mask difficult textual problems.[154] The basic meaning is clear, however, from the parallel in v. 14b, where what the godless person relies upon is compared with a spider's web, literally, a spider's "house," which cannot support the weight of one who leans upon it (v. 15).

148. The classic study is that of N. Habel, "Appeal to Ancient Tradition as a Literary Form," *ZAW* 88 (1976) 253-72.

149. Dhorme, *A Commentary on the Book of Job,* 116; similarly Gordis, *The Book of Job,* 89.

150. Habel, "Appeal to Ancient Tradition as a Literary Form," 255.

151. *ANET,* 594-96.

152. J. Collins, "The Sage in Apocalyptic and Pseudepigraphic Literature," in *The Sage in Israel and the Ancient Near East,* ed. J. Gammie and L. Perdue (Winona Lake, Ind.: Eisenbrauns, 1990) 344-47.

153. Lambert, *Babylonian Wisdom Literature,* 271.

154. See Pope, *Job,* 66-67; and Clines, *Job 1–20,* 199-200.

8:16-19. These verses pose the most difficult exegetical problem of chap. 8. Do they provide a second comparison of the godless to a plant that first thrives and then dies?[155] Or do they provide a contrasting comparison of the blameless person who endures despite harsh conditions and thrives after apparent disaster?[156] The latter interpretation, already suggested by the medieval Jewish commentator Saadiah,[157] appears the more likely. It fits well with Bildad's preference for contrasting fates in vv. 4-7 and 20-22. Moreover, the comparison of the righteous and the wicked under the image of two plants is a rhetorical device that also occurs in Jer 17:5-8 and Psalm 1. Although no transitional phrase in v. 16 signals a change in topic, the contrast is established by the first word in the verse. Whereas vv. 11-12 were concerned with the plant that lacked water, the first word of v. 16 is "the well-watered (plant)." (The NRSV, misleadingly, supplies the phrase "the wicked" and translates the adjective "well-watered" as a verb.)

8:17. Like the tree planted by water in Jer 17:8, which stays green even during the hottest times, the well-watered plant in v. 16 grows healthily even under the hot sun. The growth of the shoots in v. 16*b* finds its counterpart in the growth of the plant's roots in v. 17*a*. The notion of a plant "looking for" or "gazing at" a house of stones (v. 17*b*; יחזה *yehĕzeh*) strikes some interpreters as so odd that they prefer to emend the text to "live" (יחיה *yihyeh*, following the LXX; so the NRSV) or to "grasp" (יאחזו *y'ōhĕzû*).[158] Whatever the verb, the image of the house of stones, with its suggestion of strength, contrasts with the insubstantial spider's house of v. 14. A plant that winds its roots around rocks is solidly grounded.

8:18. Surprisingly, however, v. 18 describes the plant being torn from its place. The contrast between two symbolic plants does not ordinarily contain such a detail (cf. Jer 17:5-8; Psalm 1). Bildad, however, is applying the traditional motif to Job's situation. Just as his earlier proverb corresponded

to the premature deaths of Job's children (v. 12), so also the traditional motif of the well-watered plant is adapted to correspond to the situation of Job, a basically good person who has experienced an unexpected disaster. There is even an echo of Job's own rhetoric in the personification of the place that does not recognize (7:10) or denies having seen (8:18) its former occupant.

8:19. Unfortunately, v. 19 is difficult to interpret. The first part of the verse reads, "See, such is the joy of his way" (cf. NRSV). Those who understand the passage as applying to the wicked must either take the phrase ironically or emend the text, as the NIV does (reading "withers" [מסוס *mĕsôs*] instead of "joy" [משוש *māsôs*]). More naturally, the phrase seems to introduce the good news of the plant's revival. The last part of the verse can be translated in ways that complement either interpretation. The ambiguity is that one word (אחר *'ahēr*) may be read as a noun ("another"), as an adjective ("other soil"), or as an adverb ("later," perhaps emending to *'ahar*). In keeping with their interpretation of the plant as a symbol of the wicked, the NRSV and the NIV adopt the first alternative. Those who understand the passage as referring to the righteous translate either "such is the joy of its way, that from other soil it sprouts forth"[159] or "such is the joy of its way, that from the soil later it sprouts forth."[160] The latter translation seems better. The "later" (*'ahēr/'ahar*) return of the plant echoes the restoration in the "latter days" (*'aharît*) that Bildad foresees for Job in v. 7.[161]

8:20-22. Verse 20, with its contrast between the blameless and the evildoers, serves as a summary of the preceding teaching, as well as a reaffirmation of Bildad's initial axiom about God's justice (v. 3). The term "blameless" (תם *tām*) was used to describe Job by the narrator (1:1) and by God (1:8). In the last two verses, Bildad again addresses Job in the second person. The image of a mouth filled with laughter and exuberant shouts is elsewhere associated with restoration from calamity (Job 33:26; Ps 126:2; cf. Ps 27:6). In making reference to God's shaming Job's

155. So Horst, *Hiob*, 133-34; Fohrer, *Das Buch Hiob*, 193; Clines, *Job 1–20*, 209-10; Good, *In Turns of Tempest*, 219-20.

156. So Gordis, *The Book of Job*, 521, followed by Habel, *The Book of Job*, 177-78; Hartley, *The Book of Job*, 161-63; Janzen, *Job*, 85-86.

157. Saadiah ben Joseph al-Fayyumi, *The Book of Theodicy*, trans. by L. E. Goodman (New Haven: Yale University Press, 1988) 217, 220.

158. E.g., Pope, *Job*, 67.

159. Similarly, Gordis, *The Book of Job*, 93; cf. Habel, *The Book of Job*, 168.

160. Similarly, Janzen, *Job*, 86.

161. Janzen, *Job*, 86.

enemies (v. 22), Bildad simply draws on the traditional language of the psalmists. Ironically, in Psalms these enemies are sometimes described as persons who turn against the one who suffers, because they take such suffering as proof of sin (cf. Ps 35:11-15; 109:29).[162] By the end of the dialogue, Job's friends will have become just such enemies.

162. Fohrer, *Das Buch Hiob,* 194.

REFLECTIONS

It is all too easy to dismiss Bildad as boorish and insensitive to Job's suffering. To judge him simply according to the standards of pastoral care, ancient or modern, is to overlook the fact that the book of Job is a drama of ideas as much as it is a drama of human suffering. The moral position Bildad represents was an important part of a long and never fully resolved deliberation in ancient Israel concerning the moral consequences of deeds and the relation between the individual and the community. It is not possible to do justice to the complexity of the issue in this brief reflection. At its most basic level, however, the issue concerns whether the responsibility and consequences for sin were understood to be corporate (whether within a family or settlement, or extending between generations, or between ruler and people) or limited to the individual. Intergenerational inheritance of the consequences of sin is reflected in the popular proverb cited by both Jeremiah and Ezekiel, "The fathers have eaten sour grapes,/ and the children's teeth are set on edge" (Jer 31:29 NIV; Ezek 18:2; cf. also Joshua 7; 2 Sam 13:13-14; 21:1-9). Both Jeremiah and Ezekiel, however, repudiate the popular proverb (Jer 31:27-30; Ezekiel 18; cf. Deut 24:16; 2 Kgs 14:5-6). Ezekiel's long treatment of individual responsibility is particularly important for understanding Bildad's moral stance. Although Ezekiel was addressing the problem that the generation of the Babylonian exile had with accepting responsibility for its own situation, he formulates his teaching in terms of case examples concerning a father, a son, and a grandson. Ezekiel's conclusion in every case is that each one bears the responsibility for and the consequences of his own actions: "The person who sins shall die" (Ezek 18:20*a* NRSV). Even in the course of an individual life, the sinner who repents will live and not die (Ezek 18:21-23). This is precisely the stance that Bildad embodies in his reply to Job (vv. 3-7). Job's children were their own moral agents, not extensions of Job's moral identity. Job's fate remains in his own hands. It is critical to recognize the context that shapes Bildad's thinking and hence the way in which a longstanding moral controversy is introduced into the book of Job.

It is difficult for a modern person to take Bildad seriously because he does not question two crucial assumptions. First, Bildad does not question the assumption that he can deduce the cause (sin) from the effect (death); second, neither he nor Job questions the theological assumption that God uses illness, destruction, and death as punishment for individual sins. If, however, one takes the issue of individual vs. corporate moral responsibility out of the limits of Bildad's frame of reference and places it in a more general framework, then one suddenly discovers that far from being an obvious question that was settled long ago, the question of who bears the moral responsibility for sin is a very lively question in our own time. The consequences of one person's sin often do fall upon another. Justice may demand that one generation make right the wrongs of a previous generation, even at great cost to itself. And yet there is something compelling in the insistence that morally no person can be treated as simply an extension of another. These are the complex issues that the post–World War II generation in Germany has struggled with. Although these persons were not responsible for the Holocaust, they have largely acknowledged that they have a moral duty to make reparations, to uncover the truth, to warn others. Americans have been much more conflicted about acknowledging intergenerational responsibility for the consequences of the sin of slavery. The complex question of individual vs. corporate responsibility is also present in smaller contexts in the events of everyday life. Especially in fairly small, closed communities, it is easy for the sins of the parents to be unfairly visited on the children, at least in terms of reputation and public opinion.

There are times, however, when it is appropriate for an individual to take responsibility for the misdeeds of others. It is disappointing to see a person who has taken on a position of leadership and oversight in a business, church, or civic group respond to the exposure of wrongdoing in the organization by hurrying to say, "It's not *my* fault," instead of acknowledging the corporate responsibility that comes with leadership. These diverse examples are simply intended to indicate that, even though one may find Bildad's remarks about Job's children not worth taking seriously, the larger context out of which he speaks remains an area of moral and pastoral concern.

The other significant issue raised by Bildad concerns the sources of trustworthy moral knowledge. By and large, Israelite wisdom understood tradition and individual experience to be complementary sources of knowledge. Job and Bildad, however, polarize the issue. Job's championing of subjective experience was discussed in the Reflections on chap. 6. But what is implied by Bildad's insistence that only ancestral tradition is valid? He clearly believes that insight into the moral structures of the world can be obtained through observing the regular patterns that emerge only over long periods of time. That, in and of itself, is a valid insight.

What is troubling about Bildad's position is not his championing of tradition, but his understanding of tradition as a closed body of knowledge. He does not see tradition as being continually modified by the incorporation of new observations and experiences. If he did, he could not speak of the present generation as one that "knows nothing" (v. 9). For Bildad, the ancestors discovered truths that were valid for all time. Individual experience that contradicts those truths has to be wrong. Anyone who has ever lived through a time of change knows that it is not that simple.

A community's social relations are strongly shaped by inherited traditions, "the way we do things around here." Individual experience that does not fit those traditional ways poses a challenge. The proper roles of women and men, the nature and structure of families, acceptable modes of sexuality—many of the currently contested social issues involve a tension between the claims of tradition and the claims of experience. The same is true of many volatile issues in the church concerning how to understand and talk about God. The way forward is not found by polarizing the claims of tradition and experience and arguing about which has the superior claim, but by realizing that experience and tradition are part of a continuum. Tradition, after all, is the deposit of experience in the past; present experience may be tradition in the making. Once that is recognized, then it is possible to ask about the presuppositions, assumptions, and values that shape both tradition and present experience in order to see what is valuable and should be retained, and what should be modified in the light of new perspectives and changed circumstances.

An important part of the reflection on tradition always needs to be an examination of *whose* experience has contributed to the formation of tradition. One of the misunderstandings about the nature of tradition that Bildad makes is overestimating the objectivity of this process. Bildad does not appreciate the way in which the perspectives of observers shape what they see. The conclusion that people get what they deserve and deserve what they get is more likely to be reached by the comfortable than by the miserable. A tradition that does not incorporate the perspectives of persons from various parts of the social order confuses the self-interest of a few with truth itself. Many of the most vehemently contested issues of the present involve the complaint that people whose experience should have been incorporated had no part in shaping the traditions that they are now expected to uphold. In Bildad, one sees not the failure of tradition as such, but the ease with which tradition can be distorted both by the temptation to make it a closed body of knowledge and by the temptation to absolutize its insights.

Job 9:1–10:22, Job Imagines a Trial with God

COMMENTARY

Job's speech begins with an ironic rhetorical question about the possibility of being "in the right" with God (9:2). The question leads Job to the image that will dominate not only this speech but also his whole understanding of his situation: the notion of a lawsuit with God (9:2-4). Such a lawsuit is transparently impossible to Job because of the enormous disparity between God's power and his own (9:5-13); yet Job cannot leave off his exploration of the idea. Convinced that God's overwhelming power would prevent a just outcome (9:14-21), Job's conclusions about God become increasingly negative (9:22-24). Lamenting the brevity of his life (9:25-26), Job tries three times to imagine a resolution to his situation (9:27-28, 29-32, 33-35). The extent to which the image of a lawsuit has taken hold of his imagination is evident from the fact that the impossibility of a resolution is expressed each time in legal language (9:28b, 32-33).

Job imagines the kind of speech he would make if he could engage God in a trial (10:1-7). His imaginary speech slips gradually into speculation about God's intentions toward him, a reflection that combines pathos and bitter accusation (10:8-17). Job concludes bleakly, with an appeal for a moment's respite before the unrelenting darkness of death (10:18-22).

9:1-4. As v. 2 is translated in the NRSV and the NIV, Job appears to agree with what Bildad has just said. If so, Job is being ironic. More likely, the "truth" to which Job assents is contained in the rhetorical question in v. 2b: "Truly, I know that this is so: how can . . . " (see REB, TNK).[163] That rhetorical question contains a crucial play on different nuances of the Hebrew verb צדק (*ṣādaq*), which an English translation cannot capture. The verb can have a general moral meaning, "to be righteous," but it can also have a distinctly forensic connotation, "to be [legally] in the right" (see Exod 23:7; Deut 25:1).

Initially, Job appears simply to be agreeing with Eliphaz's words in 4:17a ("Can mortals be righteous before God?"). The next verse, however, changes the context. The words "contend"/"dispute" and "answer" are often used specifically for legal disputes (Exod 23:2-3; Deut 19:16-19; Prov 18:17). In that context it becomes apparent that underlying Job's ostensible agreement with Eliphaz is a very different question: "How could a mortal be legally vindicated against God?"

The ambiguity of the Hebrew pronouns in v. 3 makes it grammatically possible to understand Job's words in three different ways: (1) "if [God] wished to dispute with one, one could not answer him one in a thousand"; (2) "if [one] wished to dispute with [God], one could not answer him" (cf. NRSV); (3) "if [one] wished to dispute with him, [God] would not answer" (cf. 33:13).[164] For the most part, Job's use of the legal metaphor in chaps. 9–10 casts God as the one bringing charges and Job as the one accused (e.g., 9:15, 20; 10:2). Consequently, I am inclined to translate v. 3 according to the first alternative.

A more important issue than ambiguous syntax, however, is the question of the image's background. Legal metaphors occur in Israelite religion, most frequently in the context of the relation of God and the people as a whole (entering into litigation with the people, as in Isa 3:13-14; Mic 6:1-2, or arguing the case of the people, as in Isa 49:25b; Jer 50:34). Although less common, there are some instances of legal imagery in personal piety. God is said to "enter into judgment with" a person in Ps 143:2 and Eccl 11:9, and in Ps 119:154a God is asked to "argue the case" of the psalmist. In none of these instances, however, is a person represented as a plaintiff against God. Only in the prophetic rhetoric of Jeremiah does one find such a boldly imagined use of the metaphor: "You will win, O LORD, if I make claim against You,/ Yet I shall present charges against You" (Jer 12:1 TNK). For Jeremiah, the metaphor is

163. A. B. Davidson, *The Book of Job*, Cambridge Bible for Schools and Colleges 15 (Cambridge: Cambridge University Press, 1891) 66; Clines, *Job 1–20*, 227.

164. Habel, *The Book of Job*, 189.

merely a rhetorical flourish. For Job, however, the metaphor gradually moves from being a bold piece of rhetoric to becoming the organizing model for his relationship with God.[165]

Job explores the contradictoriness of the notion of a trial with God. The qualities that make someone successful in arguing a case, cleverness and forcefulness, belong overwhelmingly to God (v. 4; cf. Isa 40:26). Job could not answer God in a lawsuit (v. 14). Before he states that conclusion, however, Job takes time to substantiate his statement about God's power and cleverness by reciting fragments of language traditionally used to praise God.

9:5-13. Job links together two doxologies (vv. 5-7, 8-10), followed by two conditional statements (vv. 11-12) and a simple concluding sentence (v. 13). Traditional doxological style is formally indicated in Hebrew by the use of introductory participles (with the article in vv. 5-7, without it in vv. 8-10). The NRSV suggests this style through its use of clauses introduced by "who."

9:5-7. Although many commentators claim that Job is parodying traditional doxologies by presenting God's power as violent and destructive (vv. 5-7),[166] the content of Job's words has parallels elsewhere in biblical praise of God. The appearance of God, the divine warrior, is often described in terms of the quaking of the earth, the disruption of the mountains, and the general disturbance of nature (Pss 18:7-15 [8-16]; 97:1-5; 114:1-8; Nah 1:1-6; Hab 3:3-13). The darkening of the light of the sun and the stars is part of the divine warrior's struggle against the dragon Egypt in Ezek 32:7-8. This is not violence directed at nature per se. When God appears to fight against God's enemies, however, the effects of the struggle are felt by the entire cosmos. This representation of God is traditionally a positive one, since divine violence is associated with God as mythic victor over chaos (Psalm 29), as champion of Israel against its oppressors (Nah 1:1-6;

Hab 3:3-13), and as deliverer from distress (Psalm 18). Even where the anger is directed against Israel, it is set in the context of God's righteous judgment (Isa 5:25; Jer 4:23-26). Job, however, has contextualized the images of divine violence differently. What is reassuring when imagined as the champion who rescues one from danger (e.g., Psalm 18) becomes terrifying when imagined as one's opponent in court.

9:8-11. The second doxology in vv. 8-10 substantiates God's power and wisdom by describing God's creative acts. Stretching out the heavens (v. 8*a*) is a common motif (Ps 104:2; Zech 12:1), occurring most frequently in Second Isaiah (40:22; 42:5; 44:24; 45:12). In Jer 10:12, it is associated explicitly with divine wisdom. The NRSV and the NIV translations of v. 8*b* obscure the mythological allusion to God's trampling the "back of Sea" (NRSV mg), a reference to the cosmogonic battle by which God secures the order of creation against the forces of chaos.[167] The ordering of the heavens and the subduing of Sea are complemented by the creation of constellations. It is no longer possible to identify with certainty which constellations are intended,[168] but the making of constellations and control over the stars are motifs used in other doxologies to praise God's effective power (Isa 40:26; Amos 5:9). Moreover, God will refer to the motif in the speeches from the whirlwind (38:31-33). Even more clearly than in vv. 5-7, the second doxology contains only traditional words of praise of God. There is no overt parody, yet Job will set the traditional words in a context in which they become troubling rather than comforting.

The key to this reversal is the summary verse of the doxology (v. 10), which is virtually identical to the line Eliphaz used to introduce his praise of God in 5:9. For Eliphaz, the key words in the line are "great things" and "wonders," by which he means God's actions in transforming situations. For Job, the key words are the modifiers, "beyond understanding," "without number." What troubles Job is the way God eludes human understanding. Job's own words immediately following the doxology have to do with his

165. Cf. J. J. M. Roberts, "Job's Summons to Yahweh: The Exploitation of a Legal Metaphor," *ResQ* 16 (1973) 161-62. Because the legal metaphor plays such a prominent role in Job's thought, it is unfortunate that we know so little about trial procedure. The only narrative account of a trial in the OT concerns the blasphemy charges brought against Jeremiah (Jer 26:7-19).

166. E.g., Gordis, *The Book of Job*, 522; Westermann, *The Structure of the Book of Job*, 73-74; Janzen, *Job*, 90-91; K. Dell, *The Book of Job as Sceptical Literature*, BZAW 197 (Berlin and New York: de Gruyter, 1991) 148.

167. F. M. Cross and D. N. Freedman, "The Blessing of Moses," *JBL* 67 (1948) 196, 210.

168. See de Wilde, *Das Buch Hiob*, 142-47; G. Schiaparelli, *Astronomy in the Old Testament* (Oxford: Clarendon, 1905).

incapacity to "see" or to "perceive" God. The NIV suggests the close relation between these verses through its fourfold repetition of the word "cannot" (לֹא . . . לֹא . . . אֵין . . . אֵין *ʾên . . . ʾên . . . lōʾ . . . lōʾ*). In v. 11, the verbs "pass by" (עָבַר *ʿābar*) and "move on" (חָלַף *ḥālap*) recall God's elusive manifestation to Moses (Exod 33:18-23) and to Elijah (1 Kgs 19:11-12). Those episodes, however, were occasions of revelation, even as they preserved the awful transcendence of God. For Job, there is no such revelatory disclosure, only the sense of divine hiddenness.

9:12-13. Similarly, in v. 12 Job invokes traditional expressions for the autonomy of God's power (cf. Job 11:10; Isa 43:13; 45:9; Dan 4:35[32]). Although God's willingness to revoke anger is often affirmed in tradition (Deut 13:17; Ps 78:38), in v. 13*a* Job draws attention to the countertheme of the relentlessness of divine anger (cf. 2 Kgs 23:26; Isa 9:12[11], 17[16], 21[20]; 10:4). Job's final image (v. 13*b*) is drawn from the mythic tradition. Rahab is the name of a chaos monster, similar to Leviathan. Like the Mesopotamian chaos monster Tiamat, Rahab is depicted as having allies.[169] In Ps 89:10-14[11-15] the violent defeat of Rahab is connected with the creation of the world and of a just order. That is not, however, the way Job's following words contextualize the allusion.

9:14-16. Job creates a sense of estrangement from traditional words of praise of God's power and wisdom by juxtaposing them to legal imagery (vv. 14-16). The direct consequence of God's superiority in strength and cleverness is that Job would be unable to answer charges brought against him (v. 14). Verse 15 provides a succinct example of how Job's legal metaphor transforms the significance of a traditional word of piety. Bildad had urged Job to "make supplication" (חָנַן *ḥānan*) to God (8:5), a stance frequently taken by psalmists, regardless of whether they have sinned against God (Pss 45:5; 51:3) or not (Pss 6:2[3]; 26:11; 119:132; *ḥānan* trans. as "be gracious"). Having to "plead for mercy" (*ḥānan*) with an adversary when one is in the right is an intolerable perversion of what should be (Deut 16:18-20). Similarly, Job cannot imagine God respecting the solemn injunction that a full hearing be given to every party without partiality (Deut 1:17) in his case (v. 16).

9:17-18. These verses may be either Job's imagination of the violence that would disrupt his lawsuit (so NIV)[170] or a reference to his experience, which makes him doubt God's capacity for restraint (so NRSV).[171] Although v. 17 reads "crush me with a *tempest*" (שְׂעָרָה *śěʿārâ*), many commentators emend to "crush me for a *hair*" (שַׂעֲרָה *saʿărâ*), i.e., a trifle.[172] The emendation improves the parallelism with "for no reason" in 17*b*. Yet as the rabbis recognized (*b. B. Bat.* 16*a*), there may be an ironic foreshadowing here, since God will speak to Job "from a tempest" in 38:1. Similarly, Job's complaint that God increases his wounds "for no reason" (חִנָּם *ḥinnām*) repeats the thematically significant word from 1:9 and 2:3.

9:19-21. In v. 19, Job contrasts two forms of resolution: a trial of strength and a trial at law. Both are impossible for Job because of God's superior power. The devastating effects of this power are explored in vv. 20-21. In his earlier words to his friends, Job had expressed great confidence in his own ability to speak the truth in a face-to-face encounter (6:28). His tongue would be free of deceit, and his palate would discern falsehood (6:30). Now, as he contemplates a trial with God, Job envisions his own mouth speaking a lie. Horrifyingly, it is a lie against his own innocence (v. 20; the NRSV's "though" is to be preferred to the NIV's "even if"). What Job envisions as the effect of a trial with God is not the recovery of truth but the loss of the integrity that has characterized his very essence. Significantly, the thematically crucial word "blameless" (תָּם *tām*; cf. 1:1, 8; 2:3, 9) occurs twice, as the self-affirmation that Job knows his own mouth will repudiate (vv. 20*b*, 21*a*). The statement that follows, "I do not know myself" (NRSV), is sometimes taken as an idiom (NIV),[173] but its literal meaning is preferable here. To be forced to confess a lie about oneself is to risk a dissolution of the self. When that occurs, the will to live also disintegrates (v. 21*b*).

169. *ANET*, 67.

170. Habel, *The Book of Job,* 193.
171. Clines, *Job 1–20,* 235.
172. E.g., Dhorme, *A Commentary on the Book of Job,* 136; Pope, *Job,* 72; Clines, *Job 1–20,* 214.
173. S. M. Paul, "An Unrecognized Medical Idiom in Canticles 6,12 and Job 9,21," *Bib* 59 (1978) 545-47; Clines, *Job 1–20,* 237.

9:22. The collapse of the essential moral distinction between innocence and guilt in his own case leads Job to generalize about God's governance of the world (v. 22-24). Although one can find a number of statements acknowledging that God is the source of both good and bad fortune (as Job himself says in 2:10), weal and woe (Isa 45:7), life and death (Deut 32:39), stating that God destroys the blameless and the wicked alike (v. 22) makes a claim of a different sort. The fundamental distinction between the righteous and the wicked was the foundation of moral thought in the ancient Near East, including Israel (see Pss 1:6; 7:8-9[9-10]; 9:4-5[5-6]). The role of the gods as ultimate authority for and upholders of the moral order was axiomatic (Ps 89:14[15]).[174] Job's assertion that God makes no such distinction is a radical denial of the basis of the moral order.[175]

9:23-24. Job inverts the traditional moral thought represented by Bildad in two ways. First, in 8:21-22 Bildad claims that God would fill Job's mouth with laughter, the laughter of the triumph of good and the end of evil. The laughter that Job describes, however, is quite different. The book of Proverbs warns that "those who mock the poor insult their Maker;/ those who are glad at calamity will not go unpunished" (Prov 17:5 NRSV). Yet in the topsy-turvy moral world of Job's perception, God's derisive laughter mocks the death of the innocent in their catastrophe (v. 23). Second, God's justice and righteousness (8:3) were understood to be the source of the justice exercised by human rulers (e.g., Ps 72:1-2). So, Job argues, a God whose own ways are corrupt must be the source of abuse and judicial corruption on earth (v. 24).

9:25-28. Job abruptly shifts from his parody of divine morality to a lament about the brevity of his own life (vv. 25-26). The images—drawn from land, water, and air—depict movements of increasing swiftness.[176] As in 7:16, Job's sense of limited life adds urgency to the need for resolution and

relief. Yet each movement of his imagination encounters the limits that render such hope futile. First, Job imagines a change in his own expression and response (v. 27). Such a gesture would be a claim of personal autonomy, the ability to exercise a measure of control over his situation. The dread that prevents such a course is not fear of physical pain but fear of what that pain means (v. 28). God, not Job, controls the situation, refusing to declare Job innocent. Note that Job addresses God directly here for the first time in this speech.

9:29-31. Job's second attempt to imagine resolution is introduced by a statement of futility, also phrased in legal language (v. 29). Although echoes of a legal ritual may be present in the washing of hands (v. 30; cf. Deut 21:1-9), Job's vividly imagined scene reaches back to the symbolic power of cleanness and filth. The metaphorical connection between dirt and guilt, cleanness and innocence, is deeply embedded in the human psyche (Deut 21:6-7; Pss 26:6; 51:2[4]; 73:13; Isa 1:18).[177] Job's image, however, is not a static contrast between clean and dirty, but between the actions of making clean and making filthy. Job's inability to control his own body lies at the heart of the image. He powerfully expresses his dehumanization at the hands of God in the final image, "my clothes will abhor me." This image reverses a person's actual revulsion at wet and dirty clothes.[178] Personifying the clothes makes Job himself into the object of disgust (cf. 30:19).

9:32-35. In v. 32, Job again negates his final image of resolution in advance, by stating the condition that renders it impossible. God is not a human being. What would be an obvious and wholly unproblematic theological statement in many other contexts here becomes the essence of the problem. The legal metaphor upon which Job builds assumes a rough equality of power between the parties, if justice is to be done. As Job has argued (vv. 2-14), this condition does not obtain between himself and God. Therefore, he can have no justice. Grammatically, it is not clear whether Job continues in the indicative ("There is no umpire" [v. 33 NRSV]) or states a condition contrary to fact ("If only there were someone

---

174. Zuckerman, *Job the Silent,* 109; van der Toorn, *Sin and Sanction in Israel and Mesopotamia,* 45.

175. There is one known parallel to Job's words. In the Babylonian poem the Erra Epic, the pestilence god Erra confesses that "the righteous and the wicked, I did not distinguish, I felled." Quoted in P. Dion, "Formulaic Language in the Book of Job," *SR* 16 (1987) 189. The Erra Epic, however, is precisely a story about the collapse of the moral order and its restoration.

176. Fohrer, *Das Buch Hiob,* 210; Gordis, *The Book of Job,* 109.

177. P. Ricoeur, *The Symbolism of Evil,* trans. E. Buchanan (Boston: Beacon, 1967) 25-46.

178. Habel, *The Book of Job,* 196.

to arbitrate" [v. 33 NIV]). The meaning is much the same. What is significant, however, is the extent to which Job's imagination draws him into the details of this impossible desire, so that it momentarily takes on the concreteness of reality.

The figure Job refers to as an "umpire" or "arbitrator" (מוכיח *môkîaḥ*) is a recognized part of Israelite legal procedure, although the precise nature and extent of the *môkîaḥ's* role is not well understood (hence the variety of translations).[179] The basic function of the *môkîaḥ* seems to have been that of deciding between two parties (Gen 31:37) or alternatives (1 Chr 12:17[18]). Two texts locate the *môkîaḥ* "in the gate," the setting of civil lawsuits, and underscore the necessity for the independence and impartiality of the *môkîaḥ* if justice was to be done (Isa 29:21; Amos 5:10). Job's words stress the mediating, restraining role of the *môkîaḥ* (v. 33). Most likely, the *môkîaḥ* should be taken as the subject of the first verb in v. 34 (so NIV), as the one who restrains God's rod. The absurd contradictoriness of Job's fantasy is transparent. Traditionally, the image of *môkîaḥ* was applied to God, as one who judged persons and nations (1 Chr 12:17[18]; Isa 2:4; Mic 4:3). To imagine a *môkîaḥ* who decides between God and Job is to envision a legal authority superior to the very God who was traditionally understood as the ultimate source of law and authority.[180]

The final half verse of chap. 9 is grammatically obscure (lit., "for not thus am I with myself"). Probably, it represents Job's recognition that the conditions necessary for speaking to God in a trial do not exist (so NIV).[181] The NRSV follows an interpretive tradition stemming from the medieval Jewish commentator Ibn Ezra, taking the line to refer to Job's defense of what he knows about himself against God's misapprehension of him.

10:1-2. As in chap. 7, Job's sense of the brevity of his life and the futility of his situation, which he has explored in 9:25-35, leads him to speak boldly (v. 1). Even though Job had denied that the conditions exist that would allow him to speak without fear before God (9:32-35), nevertheless he can imagine what he would say if he could confront God (v. 2). The metaphor of affliction as legal action by God against a person is not original with Job. It is probably already present in Ps 143:2 and is explicit in a Mesopotamian prayer to the God Shamash: "In the (legal) cause of the illness which has seized me, I am lying on my knees for judgment. Judge my cause, give a decision for me."[182] In contrast to the psalm and the Mesopotamian prayer, however, Job asks neither for a judgment nor to be spared a judgment. He asks for a statement of the charges, which he is prepared to refute. By treating a conventional metaphor as a creative one, Job turns it to his advantage.

10:3-17. Job continues to imagine how he would press God concerning the irrationality of God's actions toward him. The argument Job makes can be understood on its own terms but is better grasped against the background of a prayer like Psalm 139. That psalm begins and ends with images of God "searching" the psalmist, examining the speaker's moral condition. There is even an element of aggression in the way this is described (Ps 139:5), and yet the overall impression is one of complete solidarity between the speaker and God. In particular, the themes of God's knowledge of the psalmist and of God's intimate creation of him in the womb are closely connected. The psalmist describes himself as completely united with God in sharing the same enemies and prays that God will destroy the wicked. Likely Job is parodying not Psalm 139 itself but the complex of religious themes to which Psalm 139 gives expression.

10:3. The phrase "work of your hands" (יגיע כפיך *yĕgîaʿ kappekā*) employs a word that connotes actual toil rather than the more common, bland words for making or forming (עשה *ʿāśâ*, כון *kûn*; e.g., Ps 119:73). In vv. 8-12, the image is developed in quite specific terms. Comparison with Psalm 139 helps to illumine the otherwise odd contrast in v. 3 between "the work of your hands" and "the wicked." As in the psalm, divine toil in creating the individual should serve as a symbol of the special bond between the individual and God. Thus the wicked would be the mutual enemies of God and the speaker. For Job, however, this relationship has been reversed.

179. M. B. Dick, "The Legal Metaphor in Job 31," *CBQ* 41 (1979) 46.
180. Zuckerman, *Job the Silent*, 111.
181. But cf. Clines, *Job 1–20*, 244.

182. Cited in Dick, "The Legal Metaphor in Job 31," 39-40.

10:4-7. In these verses, Job parodies the theme of God's complete and effortless knowledge of the individual (cf. Ps 139:2-6). The difference between divine and human sight was proverbial (1 Sam 16:7; see also Ps 139:12, 16), yet Job complains that God is acting like a human who cannot readily see what is in the heart of another (v. 4). Similarly, the urgency of mortality that motivates Job's words could hardly be a consideration for God (v. 5), whose transcendence of the ages is often noted (Ps 90:4; Isa 48:12). The contradiction for Job is that God seems to be searching obsessively for something that God already knows does not exist (vv. 6-7*a*).[183] The unit concludes with an expression ordinarily used in praise of God's power ("there is no one to deliver out of your hand"; cf. Deut 32:39; Isa 43:13), but here ironically indicating Job's entrapment (cf. Ps 139:5).

10:8-12. Job now returns to the theme of himself as the work of God's hands. In v. 8, the general contrast is between making and destroying, the latter word being the same one used in 2:3. Verses 9-12 develop the image of Job as the work of God's hands in concrete, sensuous terms. As anyone who has made a craft object knows, a piece has value not only for its intrinsic usefulness but also because the intimacy of its crafting creates a bond between creator and creation. Hence the pathos of v. 9, which envisages the creator as destroyer. The image of God as potter is familiar (Gen 2:7; Isa 64:8[7]; Jer 18:5). Less common is the image of God the creator as cheesemaker. The metaphor of gestation as a "curdling" of the father's semen and the mother's blood in Wis 7:2 suggests that the comparison of cheesemaking to the formation of the embryo may be implicit in v. 10.[184] The development of the fetus as a divine crafting is more explicit in v. 11, where weaving and sewing are images for the development of the skeletal structure, soft tissues, and skin. Job extends the imagery beyond physical creation to the gift of life and nurture (v. 12). The parallel between vv. 9-12 and Ps 139:13-18 is particularly close. But whereas the motif in

Psalm 139 connects the intimate knowledge God has of the psalmist with God's providential care (Ps 139:16), in Job's case the divine intention is more sinister.

10:13-14. With most commentators, I take v. 13 as introducing v. 14 (so NIV).[185] What appeared to be loving creation was only a cover for God's true intention of inspecting for sin. Nor would this searching out and testing lead to a reformed life, such as the psalmist prays for (Ps 139:23-24), but rather a judgmental inspection with neither justice nor mercy (vv. 14-15). Job returns in these verses to judicial language ("acquit," "guilty," "innocent").

10:15-17. A series of images of Job's affliction and God's implacable aggression complete this section. Several textual and grammatical problems stand behind the different translations in the NIV and the NRSV. In v. 15*c*, the word translated "look upon" (ראה *rā'â*) is probably only a variant spelling of the word for "drenched" (רוה *rāwâ*),[186] which is preferable on the basis of parallelism. The subject of the first word in v. 16 is uncertain, and one must assume either that "my head" (v. 15) is the subject ("if my head is high"; cf. NIV) or that the text should be changed to "if I raise up" (ואגאה *wĕ'eg'eh* in place of ויגאה *wĕyig'eh*). The NRSV's adverb "boldly" is the product of a similar emendation (to וגאה *wĕgĕ'eh*). The more interesting question is whether God or Job is portrayed as a lion. Grammatically, either is possible. The tradition of royal lion hunts in the ancient Near East as manifestations of the king's prowess suggests that God is here depicted as the hunter of Job, the lion.[187] The last verse appears to mix judicial and military imagery ("witnesses . . . troops"), although it is possible that the word translated "witnesses" (עדיך *'ēdeykā*) is a rare word meaning "military forces."[188] Throughout his speeches, Job will alternate between judicial imagery and imagery of divine violence. Both are ways of

---

183. See A. C. M. Blommerde, *Northwest Semitic Grammar and Job*, BibOr 22 (Rome: Pontifical Biblical Institute, 1969) 59-60; Pope, *Job*, 80; Clines, *Job 1–20*, 246-47, for a different understanding of the grammar of v. 7.

184. Dhorme, *A Commentary on the Book of Job*, 149-50, lists parallels from later literature.

185. Gordis, *The Book of Job*, 114; and Andersen, *Job*, 154, assume that v. 13 points back to the images of intimate creation in vv. 9-12. Thus God's intentions were originally benevolent but have somehow become mysteriously hidden away in God's mind. As Andersen notes, however, this interpretation makes the transition to v. 14 quite abrupt.

186. Clines, *Job 1–20*, 222.

187. Cf. James B. Pritchard, ed., *The Ancient Near East in Pictures Related to the Old Testament* (*ANEP*) (Princeton: Princeton University Press, 1954) 56-57, pls. 182-84.

188. W. G. E. Watson, "The Metaphor in Job 10,17," *Bib* 63 (1982) 255-57.

depicting God's aggression. The image of a trial at least permits a way of imagining the containment of such aggression through legal procedures, even though at this point Job can only imagine such constraints being overrun by uncontrollable divine power and anger. The images of the hunt and of the battle, on the other hand, are figures in which uncontrolled violence is of the essence. From these images, Job turns to a concluding lament and complaint in vv. 18-22.

10:18-22. The final verses of the chapter echo motifs from Job's earlier speeches in chaps. 3 and 7, although there are subtle but significant differences. Job's wish to have died at birth (v. 18) is similar to 3:11. In chap. 3, however, Job simply lamented the conditions of his birth. Now, following chapters in which he has begun to reflect on God's actions toward him, Job decries his birth in terms of God's active role. Whereas earlier Job spoke of the advantage of never having seen the light (3:16*b*), here he speaks of the advantage of not having been seen by any eye (cf. 7:8, 12). Although Job still considers nonexistence preferable to life (v. 19; cf. 3:16*a*), and failing that seeks respite from God's oppressive presence (v. 20; cf. 7:16*b*, 19), his attitude toward death seems to have changed. In 3:17-18, 21-22, Job described death in highly desirable terms, something to be actively sought. Even in chap. 7, Job spoke of death as a form of protection from the relentlessness of God (7:21). Now, however, Job's description of death is decidedly negative. The irreversibility of death confronts Job (v. 21*a*), and his dread is communicated through the piling up of images of darkness (vv. 21*b*-22). Although these are traditional ways of describing Sheol (cf. Ps 88:7, 13; Isa 45:18-19),[189] Job intensifies them. He invokes images that suggest the chaos prevailing before creation, particularly through the phrase "darkness without order" and the paradoxical statement that the land of death "shines like darkness."[190] In Gen 1:2, darkness is the primordial characteristic of chaos. Even after the creation of light, light and darkness are mingled and must be separated and given structure for day and night to appear (Gen 1:3-4). In contrast to chap. 3, where Job seemed to relish the idea of invoking chaos, now he dreads it.

189. See Tromp, *Primitive Conceptions of Death and the Nether World in the Old Testament,* 95-98.
190. So Pope, *Job,* 79. Pope aptly cites Milton's description from *Paradise Lost* I.63: "No light, but rather darkness visible."

REFLECTIONS

What has changed Job, causing him to move from asking for death (6:8-9) to at least a subjective resistance of death (10:18-22)? Nothing has changed in his circumstances; no acceptable response has come from his friends; nor has he received any word from God. The change has to be sought in Job's own words. Although his words in chaps. 3 and 6–7 were remarkable for their expressiveness and imaginative power, they were primarily reactive, without an organizing center. In chaps. 9–10, however, Job finds such a center in the metaphor of a trial with God. Even though Job happens upon the metaphor almost by accident in the course of a satire of Eliphaz (9:2-4), and even though Job repeatedly denies that the metaphor can correspond with reality, the very act of engaging in such an imaginative exploration of his situation vis-à-vis God gives Job a desire to live, however tenuous at this point. Metaphor is a creative act, a reorganizing of perception. Ricoeur calls it a redescription of reality.[191] As such, it gives to the one using it a measure of power in relation to a situation. For this reason, writing, and poetry in particular, has always been a strategy of resistance and a source of strength for political prisoners, for the chronically ill, and for others who must endure situations in which much of their power is taken away.

One can think about metaphor's ability to empower in relation to Soelle's three phases of suffering (see Reflections on Job 3). Soelle identified these phases as mute

191. P. Ricoeur, *The Rule of Metaphor,* trans. R. Czerny, University of Toronto Romance Series 37 (Toronto: University of Toronto Press, 1977) 229-39.

suffering, lamenting, and changing. In lamenting, a person begins to describe what the oppressive situation is like. Many of the initial metaphors and similes that a person uses may simply serve to confirm the awfulness of the situation, expressing self-pity and even despair. The man who is blinded in an accident may lament that he is like a child lost in the woods at night, vulnerable and terrified, afraid to move. Playing with such images in order to give suffering a voice may be grim play, but it is play nonetheless, and play is an intrinsically creative activity. Different images begin to overlap and compete with the initial ones. One can imagine others besides lost children who may find themselves alone in the woods, such as explorers in a strange land. Explorers are wary and cautious, knowing that danger can come unexpectedly; but they are also courageous, knowing how to acknowledge their fear without being paralyzed by it. With the shift in metaphor, the nature of the situation is changed, at least in the realm of the imagination. That "redescription of reality" makes it significantly easier to change one's way of acting and so make some significant changes in the situation itself. As the man who is blind discovers the undeveloped capacities of his senses of hearing, touch, and smell to orient him in the world, the metaphor of the explorer may be transformed into the metaphor of the forest dweller. To such a person the forest itself speaks in many ways that are unrecognizable to those who do not live there or know its language.

The use of metaphor to open up new ways of perceiving is one of the important ways that a person moves from the phase of lamenting to the phase of changing. Job first uses the legal metaphor to depict himself as one who could not possibly hope for justice in a trial with an opponent as powerful as God. In his grim play with the image, however, the metaphor allows Job to see himself as a person with rights, no matter how badly abused those rights are. The ability to imagine a trial, even if it seems a practical impossibility, is enough to make Job no longer desire death.

The role of metaphor in the process of suffering is related to the role of metaphor in theology. It is not too bold to say that metaphor is at the heart of theology. One cannot speak literally of God, because God is transcendent and human language is finite. Consequently, all of our affirmations of God partake of metaphor. Calling God Father or Mother, saying that God is love, or speaking of God as judge uses categories from human experience to speak of what transcends. All theological metaphors organize experience of God into images that can be grasped. But not all metaphors have the same scope and interpretive capacity. To speak of God as "the rock that shelters me" is an evocative image of security, but one with little capacity for organizing other aspects of experience. The more significant metaphors for God tend to be drawn from the realms of human social organization: the family, political community, etc. Speaking of God as parent leads naturally to a richly developed theological vocabulary based on that governing metaphor. Speaking of God as ruler leads to an equally rich, but quite different, theological vocabulary. Both the power and the limit of metaphors are found in their selectivity. Metaphors bring certain aspects of experience into clear focus by obscuring others. In order to be adequate to the complexity of experience, religious language uses a variety of overlapping metaphors. Even so, experiences often occur for which there is no adequate language, or even more critically, experiences occur that are contradicted by traditional religious language.

Job's response to his experience reveals much about the way in which theological language changes. He does not set to work systematically but responds to an acute, specific problem: his need to articulate his inchoate sense of being treated wrongly. Legal language seems most adequate for this purpose. Once the legal metaphor is introduced into Job's speech, however, it takes on a life of its own. Indeed, part of metaphor's power is its ability to do its work beneath the surface of consciousness. Once one accepts the power of a metaphor to disclose the truth about one aspect of a situation, it is easy to accept the application of other aspects of the metaphor to other dimensions of reality. The legal metaphor will thus come to dominate Job's thinking about God, the world, and himself. Although there is little explicit critique of Job's legal metaphor (the friends, except Elihu, simply ignore it), the book itself reveals the problems with Job's metaphor by showing how its logic finally leads to a set of untenable alternatives (see Reflections on Job 31). It can be hard to give up a religious metaphor that has shaped one's understanding in important ways. In Job's case, one could even say that the legal metaphor saved his life. Eventually, however, the legal metaphor comes to be more of an obstacle than a help in understanding the nature of God, the world, and Job's relationship to both. Wisely, Job will let it go.

Job makes it easier to see why and how metaphors matter, how powerfully they can remake theological understanding, and how they sometimes need to be given up when they have served their purpose or when they have been shown to be less useful than they first appeared. There is, however, no simple "lesson" from Job to apply to contemporary debates about the adequacy of traditional theological language and the viability of new metaphors. One who reads Job attentively, however, begins to listen differently to the metaphors in religious discourse and to understand their powers and their limitations.

Job 11:1-20, Zophar Defends God's Wisdom

COMMENTARY

Zophar is the last of Job's friends to reply. Although his speech is the shortest of the three, it crystallizes the terms on which the conflict between Job and his friends will be carried out. Unlike Eliphaz, who stressed Job's blamelessness as the grounds for his hope, and unlike Bildad, who used the presumed sinfulness of Job's children to urge Job to seek God in purity and uprightness, Zophar bluntly accuses Job himself of sin (v. 6). Beginning with a sharp rebuke of Job's glib and hostile rhetoric (vv. 2-3), Zophar contrasts Job's false self-assessment with the profound knowledge God could reveal (vv. 4-6). Zophar uses a traditional figure of speech to reinforce his argument that God's wisdom far exceeds human abilities to understand (vv. 7-9). His specific point, however, is that God's superior knowledge reliably detects evil (vv. 10-11). Despite his exasperation at Job's empty-headedness, expressed in a clever proverb (v. 12), Zophar reassures Job that if he will reorient himself to God and reform his conduct (vv. 13-14), then the troubles he has endured will pass away, and he will experience a secure and blessed future (vv. 15-19). The wicked, however, will have neither security nor hope (v. 20).

11:1-3. The wisdom tradition had a deep suspicion of one who was too facile with words (Prov 10:8, 14). Job's dazzling but parodic way of speaking is itself an indication

of falsehood to someone like Zophar, steeped in the sober and conservative values of the sages. Indeed, the first two words of Zophar's speech echo Prov 10:19, "In a multitude of words, sin is not lacking." Zophar attempts to rebut Job's whole way of understanding; in his first sentence, he uses the word Job made central to his last speech: "to be righteous," "in the right" (צדק ṣādaq). Following Job's use of the word in a forensic sense, one immediately hears a legal nuance, hence the translation "vindicated" in the NRSV and the NIV. Zophar, however, has no intention of accepting Job's way of setting the terms for debate. As his speech will make clear, Zophar is primarily interested in the sapiential and religious sense of ṣdq, the sense of the right order of the world established by God's wisdom and maintained by God's oversight of the world. Zophar will advise Job to internalize this right order. A "man of lips," the literal meaning of the phrase in v. 2b, is one who talks superficially (cf. the primordial elders who speak from the "heart," the center of the body, in 8:10). Job's wild and iconoclastic words mark him out as someone who is not "in right order."

Although Zophar pejoratively declares Job's words to be "babbling," he is concerned that they not go unrefuted (v. 3a). More specifically, Zophar characterizes Job's words as mockery, a form of verbal aggression (v. 3*b*). To mock is to treat with sarcastic disrespect something that others take quite seriously. This is precisely what Job's bitter parodies do. His words are his only weapons against a religious ideology that now seems monstrous to him. Zophar attempts to respond with a weapon from the same arsenal, "shaming" Job—i.e., depriving him of social respect in an effort to restore him to a sense of proper values. But Job is already far too alienated from his former world of values for Zophar's shaming to have the desired effect.

11:4-6. Zophar ostensibly cites Job's words. They are not literally Job's words, however, but a representation of what Zophar has heard Job say, filtered through his own understanding of what is at stake. This subtle distortion is most evident in the first half of the verse, lit., "you say, 'My teaching is pure.'" The phrase "my teaching" (לקחי *liqḥî*) seems so inapt that the NRSV emends it to "my conduct" (לכתי *lēktî*). But "teaching," a sapiential term, reflects well the way Zophar would have understood Job. Zophar is not prepared to hear in Job's words the agony of a person whose world has collapsed. All he can hear is the theology, and Zophar is prepared to argue theology. It is true, as suggested in the Reflections on chaps. 9–10, that there are implicit theological claims in Job's words. But what distinguishes Job and Zophar is that for Job theology emerges out of the concrete experience of his life, whereas Zophar thinks that theology is primarily a matter of doctrine. And doctrine is what Zophar hears in Job's words.

Job had insisted that he was "blameless" (9:21) and that God knew he was "not guilty" (10:7), so Zophar's second quotation in v. 4*b* is less interpretive than his first, although the terms "pure" and "clean" are not terms Job himself used. It is notable, however, that Zophar avoids the specifically forensic terminology Job made central to his speech. Zophar does not want to argue with Job on those terms.

The contrast between Job and Zophar is also evident in vv. 5-6. Job had wanted God to tell him something quite specific: "what charges you have against me" (10:2). Zophar wishes that God would talk to Job at a much higher level of abstraction (v. 6). The sapiential

orientation of Zophar is disclosed in two key words: "wisdom" (חכמה *ḥokmâ*) and "efficacy" (תושיה *tûšiyyâ*; translated "true wisdom" in the NIV). "Efficacy" is awkward, but the Hebrew word refers to the practical knowledge that allows one to solve problems and act effectively.[192] In short, Zophar says that what Job needs to know is the hidden workings of God in ordering the world. Only from this overarching perspective can Job's particular situation be understood.

In the last part of v. 6, Zophar moves to his conclusion about Job's sin, which refutes the self-evaluation of Job quoted in v. 4. In 10:7, Job had claimed that God *knew* he was not guilty. Echoing that word, Zophar says, *"Know* this. . . . " The difference in the translations of the NRSV and the NIV in v. 6*b* reflects uncertainty about which of two similarly spelled Hebrew words is used here. The NIV is more likely.[193] Fohrer suggests that Zophar is alluding to Job's request in 7:21 that God forgive his sins rather than continue punishing him.[194] Zophar's retort is that God's justice has already been tempered with mercy in Job's case. There is a certain exasperated, rhetorical exaggeration in Zophar's words. Yet the question is irrepressible: How does he know? Zophar does not claim that he has access to the "secrets of wisdom," yet he is certain about Job's guilt. This is not an inconsistency on Zophar's part. He believes in God's wise and effective governance of the world; consequently, to borrow the words of Alexander Pope, Zophar believes that "whatever is, is right."[195] Because God governs wisely and with skill, Job's acute suffering can only be interpreted as punishment for his guilt. Therefore, Job must be guilty. Insofar as both mercy and justice are characteristic of God, God will have applied both qualities to Job's situation.[196]

11:7. Zophar reiterates his argument in the following verses, using a traditional

192. M. Fox, "Words for Wisdom," *ZAH* 6 (1993) 163-65. The word translated "two sides" or "many-sided" (כפלים *kiplayim*) is peculiar in this context. It is often suggested that a similarly spelled word meaning "like wonders" (כפלאים *kiplāʾîm*) should be read here, parallel to "secrets" in the first half of the verse. See Fox, "Words for Wisdom," 164n. 44; similarly, Gordis, *The Book of Job*, 121.
193. See Clines, *Job 1–20*, 254-55; but cf. Habel, *The Book of Job*, 203.
194. Fohrer, *Das Buch Hiob*, 226.
195. See Alexander Pope *An Essay on Man*.
196. As Fohrer, *Das Buch Hiob*, 226, observes, the emphasis on divine mercy is more characteristic of prophetic rather than wisdom traditions. Similarly, see Clines, *Job 1–20*, 261-62.

figure of speech. The metaphorical image underlying Zophar's beliefs is a spatial one: the smallness of the human being in a vast world, which itself only gestures toward the transcendent vastness of divine wisdom. The spatial quality of v. 7 is somewhat obscured in translation. The noun חקר (ḥēqer; lit., "the process or object of searching") can have the sense of uttermost limit, as in 38:16 ("the recesses of the deep"). The parallel word תכלית (taklît, "boundary," "limit") adds to the sense of physical distance, as does the verb מצא (māṣāʾ), which means not only "find out" in an intellectual sense but also "reach," "arrive." Thus one might translate, "Have you reached the uttermost limits of God, or have you arrived at the boundary of Shaddai?" There is an evocation here of the ancient Near Eastern motif of the heroic journey, as it appears in the story of Gilgamesh. In that narrative, the hero's journey to the uttermost limits ends in a confrontation with his human finiteness.[197]

11:8-9. Zophar contrasts transcendent divine wisdom and corresponding human incapacity by placing each in relation to his symbolic map of the cosmos (vv. 8-9). Based on the number four, a symbol of totality, Zophar's map identifies the four dimensions of height, depth, length, and breadth with the four regions of the cosmos: heaven, Sheol, land, and sea (cf. Pss 135:6; 139:8-9; Hag 2:6). A Mesopotamian text uses a similar motif to express human limitedness: "Who is tall enough to ascend to heaven? Who is broad enough to embrace the earth?"[198] The Mesopotamian saying expresses despair that human beings cannot attain the perspective that makes choosing the right course of action possible. In Zophar's speech, too, rhetorical questions that must be answered in the negative (vv. 7-8) reinforce the sense of human incapacity. For Zophar, however, the conclusion is not one of despair but one of confidence in the wisdom of God, which is greater than the reaches of the cosmos.

11:10-11. The specific purpose of Zophar's comparison is expressed in these verses, in which he echoes and contests Job's complaint about God (9:10-12). There Job had objected that the "unsearchable" God (אין חקר

'ên ḥēqer) is one whom he cannot "see" (ראה rāʾâ) or "perceive" (בין bîn), who "passes by" (חלף ḥālap) and seizes, "unhindered" (מי ישיבנו mî yĕšîbennû). Having made the point that Job cannot search out God (v. 7), Zophar turns Job's words inside out. Using the same expressions Job had used, Zophar describes God's passing through (חלף ḥālap) to inspect the earth (v. 10a). Where Job had referred to God's seizing or "snatching," a word with criminal implications, Zophar reverses the image, referring to God's imprisoning and convening a court, terms drawn from legal procedure (v. 10; cf. Lev 24:12; Num 15:34; Ezek 16:40; Neh 5:7). That no one can "hinder" God (v. 10b) is in Zophar's opinion not only true but proper as well. The issue is not, as Job had complained, whether Job can see and perceive God, but what God sees and considers (v. 11b). Although Zophar makes no explicit reference to Job in v. 11, there is no doubt that he considers God to have seen deceit and evil in Job (cf. v. 6c).

11:12. Here the author's irony at the expense of Zophar is palpable. Zophar's rhetorically and philosophically sophisticated arguments, which are genuinely powerful on their own terms, have led him to absolutely wrong conclusions. As the reader knows, what God has seen is that Job is a person unlike anyone else on earth, blameless and upright, one who fears God and turns from evil (1:8). Zophar's elegant a priori reasoning is false. Thus, when Zophar in exasperation applies the proverb about the unlikeliness of an empty-headed person getting understanding (v. 12), the reflective reader knows that the saying applies more readily to Zophar than to Job.

The proverb itself is clever. The first half of the line has a striking use of assonance (איש נבוב ילבב ʾîš nābûb yillābēb). Unfortunately, a syntactical problem in the second half makes the translation uncertain. There are two words for "ass" in the line, the first meaning "domesticated ass" (עיר ʿayir; not "colt," as in the NIV), the second meaning "wild ass" (פרא pereʾ). Probably these are variants and one of the terms should be deleted (so the NRSV).[199]

11:13-20. Having rebuked Job as a donkey-brain for not seeing what is so evident to

197. See *ANET*, 72-99.
198. *ANET*, 438.

199. Pope, *Job*, 86, discusses the grammatical basis for the reading given in the NIV.

himself, Zophar appeals to Job to take the steps that will restore hope and security to him (cf. 5:17-27; 8:5-7, 20-22). Zophar had described an orderly cosmos, in its fourfold divisions and dimensions. The proper human stance within that cosmos is not a Promethean attempt to rival and challenge God's wisdom. For Zophar, destruction comes into people's lives precisely because they are "out of order" with the rightness of God's wisdom. The proper response to such a situation is to reorder one's life in harmony with the rightness (צדקה *ṣĕdāqâ*) of God's world. The reordering is first of all a matter of the body: heart, palms, hands, face (vv. 13-15). As Clines notes, "directing the heart" is an idiom used by the rabbis for the mindfulness that prepares one for prayer.[200] Here, too, it precedes the advice to spread out the palms in prayer. Throughout the ancient Near East, the posture of prayer was to stand with the palms raised, facing outward (Exod 9:29, 33; 1 Kgs 8:22, 38).[201] The sense of reordering of life is reinforced by the following images of separation from evil. To have wrongdoing in one's hand is a common idiom for guilt (cf. 1 Sam 24:12; 1 Chr 12:17[18]; Ps 7:3[4]). Putting iniquity away from one's hand implies that moral reordering is a matter of the will, since "hand" is a metaphor for power and control.[202] Like the hand, the tent is an image of what is closely associated with a person (18:6; 29:4), and Job is urged to distance deceit from the hospitality of his dwelling.

The result of this reordering is described first in terms of the body, the lifting up of the face, which Job said God denied to him (v. 15a; cf. 10:15). For Zophar, however, it is not a matter of the vindication of Job but of the healing of Job, as the accompanying phrase "without blemish" suggests. Although used in a moral sense, "blemish" (מום *mûm*) is primarily a term for physical disfiguration, which makes an animal unfit as an offering to God or a priest unfit to approach the altar (Lev 21:17; Deut 15:21). Thus, graphically, Zophar describes Job as lifting up a face no longer disfigured by sin.

Other striking images elaborate the transformation that comes from this reordering of the self. In v. 15b, a Job who is "firm" (מצק *muṣāq*; lit., "cast" like metal) is contrasted with troubles that flow away like water (v. 16a). Clines notes the striking synonymous use of "forget" and "remember" to describe the psychological reality of being able to recall a past trauma without its having power over one any longer.[203] In v. 17, Zophar also reverses Job's images of the fearful darkness of approaching death (10:21-22). In contrast to Job's image of light that is "like darkness" (10:22), Zophar says of Job's life that "its darkness will be like the morning" (v. 17b; cf. Isa 58:10b). Whereas Job lamented the brevity of his days (10:20), Zophar describes a "lifespan" (חלד *ḥeled*) that will rise higher than the sun at noon (v. 17a).

The concluding images in vv. 18-19 develop the theme of security and hope. Here Zophar is true to the moral imagination of the wisdom tradition, which understands such security as coming from conducting oneself in harmony with the wisdom and right order of God (cf. Prov 3:21-26). The two images of v. 19 are coordinate descriptions of the social dimensions of security: having no enemies but only those who seek one's favor. The image in v. 19a is concretely that of a flock, safe from predators (see Zeph 3:13, where it is also associated with moral wholeness). The final image of having one's favor courted (lit., "soften the face") may strike a jarring note with modern readers, but in highly communal, paternalistic cultures, it is a strong image of being embedded securely in the social networks that sustain the community.

Zophar's final word, which speaks of the loss of security and hope for the wicked, initially resembles Bildad's contrast between the blessed fate that awaits Job and the destruction of his enemies (8:21-22). But Zophar does not identify the wicked of v. 20 with Job's enemies. He switches from the "you" of direct address to Job (v. 19) to a third-person plural comment about the wicked in general (v. 20). Thus Zophar sets before Job a word of warning like that of Prov 10:28, for at this point Zophar considers Job to be at risk of experiencing the fate of the wicked.

200. Clines, *Job 1–20*, 267.

201. O. Keel, *The Symbolism of the Biblical World: Ancient Near Eastern Iconography and the Book of Psalms* (New York: Seabury, 1978) pls. 415, 416, 422.

202. Clines observes that Zophar's approach to sin is characteristic of wisdom thinking: "How does Zophar propose Job can get rid of his sin? Not by sacrifice or atonement, not even by repentance, but by . . . a distancing of himself from it, putting himself far from it . . . (cf. Ps 1:1; Prov 1:10-15; 4:14, 24; 5:8; 30:8)" (*Job 1–20*, 268).

203. Clines, *Job 1–20*, 269.

REFLECTIONS

Job's speech in chaps. 9–10 and Zophar's in chap. 11 present the reader with a clash of certainties. Job is certain that he is innocent; Zophar is certain that he is guilty. Job is certain that he knows the truth about himself; Zophar is certain that only God can know such a thing. The clash between the two extends also to their favored images of truth. For Zophar, truth resides in the "hidden things" of knowledge, the mysteries of God's ways, which no human can grasp. It is not necessary for humans to know the details, only to trust in the wisdom of God. For Job, truth can—indeed, must—be open to scrutiny, as in a trial. A human being can know the truth about himself or herself, and, if not overpowered, can defend that truth before God. Resolution comes not from human submission to a mystery of divine knowledge, as for Zophar, but from mutual acknowledgment of the truth.

The fascinating thing about such contradictory positions is that they often point to a common assumption that neither party is capable of recognizing. Both Job and Zophar assume a world of complete rationality and tight causality, a world with no randomness in it, at least so far as acute human suffering is concerned. Zophar and Job are willing to pay a terrible price to avoid considering Job's suffering simply as part of the contingency of living. Zophar is willing to declare Job guilty; Job is willing to consider the criminality of God. Neither seems capable of seeing, let alone questioning, the assumption they share. It is so obvious to them both that it is invisible.

It is not just Job and his friends who are determined to find a unifying explanation for disturbing events. That impulse remains intensely strong in many people. The words that echo in the mind of a person to whom a catastrophe has occurred are frequently, "Why? Why did this happen?" Even those who do not want to claim that "sin" is always the cause of suffering nevertheless may be heard to say, "Everything happens for a reason."

Why is the impulse to deny the contingent quality of life so strong? Most likely, the answer lies in our fragility as human beings, our intense vulnerability. Part of the passion for discerning a reason behind distressing events has to do with a desire to have as much control as possible. If one can understand why something happens, then one can sometimes influence what will happen. The intense need for a reason, however, most often emerges after a catastrophe has taken place, when there is no chance of changing events. In those instances, the terrible experience to which the question "Why?" gives voice is the collapse of the world into chaos, where anything can happen and nothing is secure. Asking "Why?" is an attempt to gain some control over that horrifying sense that everything is falling into an abyss. Distinguishing between the ostensible question ("Why did *this* happen?") and the underlying request ("Please reassure me that the chaos I feel is not all there is") is critical. What is needed is not an explanation of the causes of an accident or an illness but words that communicate the sustaining structures of God's creation, which contain chaos, and the reliable presence of God's love even in the experiences of deep darkness. Israel recognized the connection between the disorienting experience of disaster and the power of creation traditions to provide a measure of reassurance. One often finds images of God's containment of chaos and establishment of orders of creation incorporated into psalms of lament (e.g., Psalms 74; 77).

The common human sense of vulnerability is not the only factor involved in the attempt to find a reason for catastrophes. Much traditional religious language about God contributes to the assumption that Job and Zophar take for granted that God is directly responsible for what happens to people. The biblical image of God as a ruler who governs the world, an image with which the book of Job itself begins, is often implicit in such thinking. If God is the one who runs things, then God must be responsible. As Job puts it, "If it is not he, who then is it"? (9:24).

In fact, biblical reflection on such matters is remarkably diverse. Especially in the narrative traditions, the unpredictability of the consequences of other people's choices and the simple contingency of existence are presented as part of the texture of human life. Hagar and Ishmael's suffering happened for no particular divine reason, but was the consequence of some poorly conceived decisions made by Sarah and Abraham and the social pressures that made Hagar and Sarah into rivals. Neither the famine that drove Naomi's family from Judah nor the premature death of her two sons is represented by the narrator as anything other than simple misfortune. And even though he is not happy about it, the author of Ecclesiastes acknowledges that "time and chance happen to them all" (Eccl 9:11 NRSV). The Bible simply does not speak with a single voice on the question of the causes of human suffering.

Zophar and Job are both so eloquent, however, that it is difficult not to get drawn into their vision of things and to assume that one must choose between the two positions they articulate, even though these are not the only ways of looking at what happens to people. That is not to suggest, however, that some obvious third alternative waits just offstage. What one can say is that both of their responses evade acknowledging the way radical suffering refuses to be confined and contained by rational explanations. Neither Zophar nor Job is willing to contemplate the tragic dimension of human life. Neither is willing to imagine suffering that cannot be reduced to fault, whether human or divine. To risk thinking along those lines will necessitate a very different image of God than that which exists in the mind of either Zophar or Job. There will be an opportunity to return to these questions in the Reflections on chaps. 38–41.

Job 12:1–14:22, Job Burlesques the Wisdom of God and Struggles with Mortality

OVERVIEW

Job's final speech in the first cycle is the longest and most complex. The traditional division into three chapters identifies important differences in tone and mode of speech, as well as in content. What is obscured by that structure, however, is the division of the speech into two parts, according to whom Job addresses. In 12:1–13:19, Job addresses his friends; in 13:20–14:22, he addresses God. Although Job's words are directed to all his friends in 12:1–13:9, he is most directly engaged with Zophar's claims about his asinine intelligence, the superiority of hidden wisdom, and God's careful supervision and right ordering of the world. Savage parody is Job's chosen weapon in this part of his speech, introduced by his mocking compliment to the friends' wisdom (vv. 2-3). A brief aside in which Job bitterly comments on the contradictoriness of his own fate as

a righteous person and that of the wicked suggests Job's true feelings (vv. 4-6). When he resumes, however, Job gives a parodic imitation of a wisdom discourse, burlesquing Zophar's claims about the inaccessibility of wisdom (vv. 7-10) and "granting" the traditional belief that wisdom resides with the aged (vv. 11-12), only to turn that premise into the basis of a sarcastic doxology that parodies God's wisdom and counsel (vv. 13-25).

Chapter 13 is linked to chap. 12 by repetition of the claim that Job's knowledge is equal to that of the friends (12:2-3//13:1-3). This repetition marks a turning point in the speech, however, as Job abandons parody and sarcasm. The rest of his words consist of an earnest and passionate speech that is thoroughly shaped by the legal metaphor Job began to explore in chaps. 9–10. Job criticizes the friends as lying witnesses for God (vv. 4-12) and reflects on the urgency of bringing his case before God (vv. 13-19).

In 13:20, Job begins to address God directly, as though a trial were in fact beginning (vv. 20-28). The intensity of Job's imagination, as he is gripped by the vision of a lawsuit with God, leads him to a sense of confident strength and expectation unparalleled in his other speeches (vv. 16-19). Almost as soon as he has begun to speak to God, however, his confidence falters as he again confronts the reality of the overwhelming inequality of power (vv. 25-28).

Consequently, in chap. 14 Job abandons the language of legal disputation and instead takes up a meditative reflection on the ephemerality of human life (vv. 1-6). For the rest of the chapter, Job struggles with the tension between mortality and hope. A series of vivid images from nature in vv. 7-12 and 18-19 articulates the problem and frames Job's bold attempt to imagine a place for hope (vv. 13-17). In the end, however, death has the last word (vv. 20-22).

Job 12:1–13:2, Job Parodies Traditional Praise of God

COMMENTARY

12:1-3. By this point in the dialogue, the reader expects each speech to begin with a sharp criticism of the previous speaker and/ or a defense of the present speaker's words. Here, as Job concludes the first round of speeches, he offers a tongue-in-cheek compliment to his friends. The syntax of v. 2 is difficult, and it is not clear what Job means by referring to his friends as the "people." Suggestions that the phrase means something like "the gentry" lack supporting evidence.[204] It is better to translate "truly, you are the people with whom wisdom will die."[205] The exaggeration is Job's caricature of the way his friends have been presenting themselves as the ultimate representatives of wisdom. (The verse is also susceptible to the satirical reading that the friends are killing wisdom.)[206] Corresponding to the rhetorical exaggeration of v. 2 is the rhetorical modesty in what Job claims for himself (v. 3). He does not claim anything special, but only such things as everyone knows (v. 3c). In part, this may be a reply to Zophar's appeal for a revelation of hidden mysteries (11:5-6). That is not necessary, Job implies; all that it is necessary to know is common knowledge. These introductory verses set up the primary work of the chapter, which is to subject such "common knowledge" to a critical scrutiny.

12:4-6. Although they seem to interrupt the logical flow of thought between v. 3 and v. 7, vv. 4-6 perform a very important role in the rhetoric of Job's speech. As in a play, they are an "aside," which discloses the speaker's mood and inner thoughts, giving a context within which to hear the speaker's following words.

In v. 4, the NRSV and the NIV insert the first-person pronoun in places where the Hebrew text has the third person. One can make sense of the literal words, however, if one reads them as Job's echoing of the way people have talked about him in the past and in his present distress. One needs to hear traces of quotation marks around these stock phrases. Thus "a 'laughingstock-to-his-friends' I have become. 'One-who-calls-on-God-and-he-answers-him,' 'a righteous-and-perfect person,' (I have become) a laughingstock." The phrase "righteous and perfect" (צדיק תמים *ṣaddîq tāmîm*) evokes the hyperbolic language of the narrator's description of Job in 1:1 (cf. Gen 6:9). To be known as "one who calls upon God and he answers him" is to be known as one in God's favor (see Ps 99:6). By contrast, a community tends to make a laughingstock out of someone who is deemed out of favor with God and thus a safe target. (For the special misery of being mocked by friends, see Ps 55:12-15[13-16].)

In v. 5, Job reflects briefly on the social dynamics at work. It is a disturbing but well-recognized phenomenon that the precipitous

204. Pope, *Job*, 89; but cf. Clines, *Job 1–20*, 278.
205. J. A. Davies, "A Note on Job XII 2," *VT* 25 (1975) 670-71.
206. Good, *In Turns of Tempest*, 234.

misfortune of someone previously respected and successful sometimes evokes contempt rather than sympathy. Perhaps this is the reflex of a need to rationalize inexplicable misfortune, a need for those "at ease" to believe that it could not happen to them. The contradiction that Job experienced between his own "righteous and perfect" conduct and the way he has been treated as a laughingstock finds its counterpart in another contradiction described in v. 6, the peace and security of those who have been actively evil. Zophar had described such security as the blessing for those whose lives reflected the right order of God's world (11:13-19). What Job observes, however, is a world in which something is fundamentally not right. The issue of the fate of the wicked, introduced only briefly here, will become the primary topic of the friends' speeches in the second cycle (chaps. 15; 18; 20) and will dominate Job's final speech in that cycle (chap. 21).

The last clause in v. 6 is obscure. The words could be translated either "the one who brings God in his hand" or "the one(s) whom God brings into his hand." The sentence is generally taken, according to the first reading, to refer to the arrogance of the wicked, who trust in their own power. A somewhat similar idiom appears in Gen 31:29; Deut 28:32; Neh 5:5; Mic 2:1,[207] although the wording is not the same. Moreover, it is odd that the verb in v. 6c is singular, whereas the rest of v. 6 is cast in the plural. Clines, following the second alternative, translates "those whom God has in his own power."[208] Although it, too, has problems, that translation is probably to be preferred. It anticipates the reference in the last verse of the next unit, vv. 7-10, to what God has "in his hand."

12:7-10. Verse 7 resumes the line of thought in v. 3. Job will demonstrate that he is not less intelligent than his friends by giving a wisdom discourse in just their style. That this speech has something of the quality of a performance is suggested by Job's use of second-person singular verbs and pronouns in vv. 7-10, instead of the plural forms Job used at the beginning of his speech (v. 2-3), a distinction that cannot be represented in

English. Moreover, there is not a word from vv. 7-13 that could not have been said by the friends. Job is not *quoting* his friends,[209] however, but imitating the type of speech they use. Job's relationship to this manner of talking is complex. The dominant tone is one of parody. Job will show the bankruptcy of this platitudinous, cliché-ridden way of speaking. Yet there are genuinely "Joban" elements in what he says, especially in vv. 7-10. Perhaps these verses can be understood best as Job's forcing even a language of hypocrisy to bear witness to the truth. This double-voicing of Job's words is facilitated by vv. 4-6 immediately preceding, which indicate Job's passionate sense that the world is not rightly ordered.

12:7-8. Job opens his wisdom discourse with an appeal to authority that acknowledges and challenges the similar appeals made by his friends. The words "but ask . . . and they will teach you" echo Bildad's appeal to ancient generations in 8:8-10. Job also engages Zophar's reflections on knowledge in 11:5-9. Zophar attempted to persuade Job that he could not attain the boundary of God's knowledge, which transcends the four dimensions of the cosmos. Here Job shifts the issue away from what is not accessible to what is readily accessible to all the creatures who inhabit the land, the air, and the sea. One could make Job's figure parallel Zophar's more exactly by translating "earth" (ארץ *'ereṣ*) as "underworld."[210] The underworld, however, was seldom treated as a source of knowledge in Hebrew wisdom,[211] so that "earth" is more likely. The NRSV and the NIV differ in translating v. 8, depending on whether the Hebrew word שׂיח (*śîaḥ*) is read as a verb ("speak") or as a noun ("plant"). The parallelism is better if one translates "plant" or "shrub," since then each line contains a reference to a creature.

Although Hebrew literature sometimes contrasts human intelligence with that of animals (Job 18:3; Dan 4:16[13]), nature is generally a positive source of knowledge in the wisdom tradition (Prov 6:6; 30:24-28; see also 1 Kgs 4:33[5:13]). Job's point, however,

207. Dhorme, *A Commentary on the Book of Job,* 171; Pope, *Job,* 90; Habel, *The Book of Job,* 213.

208. Clines, *Job 1–20,* 275.

209. Cf. R. Gordis, "Quotations as a Literary Usage in Biblical, Oriental and Rabbinic Literature," *HUCA* 22 (1949) 157-219; Gordis, *The Book of Job,* 523-24; Clines, *Job 1–20,* 292.

210. M. Dahood, *Proverbs and Northwest Semitic Philology* (Rome: Pontifical Biblical Institute, 1963) 58; followed by Pope, *Job,* 91.

211. Perdue, *Wisdom in Revolt,* 152n. 1.

is not a comparative one but a direct challenge to Zophar's wish that God would reveal to Job the "hidden things of wisdom" (11:6). To the contrary, Job says, all that it is necessary to know is readily available, anywhere in the cosmos.

12:9-10. What is the crucial knowledge that every creature understands? In keeping with his rhetorical strategy, Job states it in the form of a well-known saying: "that the hand of the LORD has done this" (v. 9). The exact words are also found in Isa 41:20b, and it is likely that both authors are simply using a familiar formula. In fact, the cliché quality of this statement is indicated by the presence of the divine name "Yahweh." Throughout the poetic section of Job, the divine name is otherwise never used by the author. Whether the poet used it intentionally to signal Job's citation of a common saying, or whether a scribe accidentally substituted the more familiar form of the saying, the "slip" is a telling one. This phrase is on everyone's lips.

The ambiguity of the word "this" in v. 9 is calculated. Does it point forward to the platitudinous statement in v. 10? Or does it point backward to what Job said in vv. 4-6 about the contradictions between what should be and what is? By allowing the ambiguity to remain unresolved, Job forces his audience to recognize that the clichés they thought protected their complacent view of the world can be turned against them. Even the platitude in v. 10 serves Job's purposes. None of the friends would contradict such a statement, and yet the phrase "in his hand" or "in his power" echoes Job's description of the rampant injustice he described in v. 6. All that one needs to know, Job suggests, is that God is ultimately responsible.

12:11. Job is not finished with his parodic performance of a wisdom discourse. He introduces the second part in v. 11 with a traditional saying used to invite agreement with the speaker. Elihu will use the same saying in 34:3 at the beginning of his second discourse. The saying is based on the image of the discriminating palate as a metaphor of critical judgment. Here, too, Job chooses his platitude carefully. As Clines notes, the saying has a disingenuous quality to it. Although it ostensibly honors the hearer's judgment, it is used as an assertion that the speaker is right and

that the audience members naturally all share the same tastes.[212] Job's own testing of words, as the following verses will make abundantly clear, is a genuinely critical exercise. He takes seriously the individual, experiential basis of knowledge implicit in the words of the saying but largely ignores the way it is customarily employed (cf. 13:1-2).

12:12-13. The words that Job asks his audience to test belong to another clichéd sentiment—that wisdom and understanding are characteristic of age (v. 12). The issue that engages many commentators, whether Job could possibly believe such a claim himself,[213] is not entirely to the point. Job is playing a sophisticated game with his friends, and he first offers them a saying that they could certainly test and find sound. Following the traditional style of logic that argues from the lesser to the greater, Job goes on to assert that God (who, after all, is the ancient of days) possesses not only wisdom and understanding, but also power and counsel, qualities having to do with the ability to effect what one plans (v. 13). Again, the friends would certainly find this statement to their taste. As often noted, the four qualities attributed to God in v. 13 are also the God-given qualities of the ideal ruler (Isa 11:2). It is precisely these words—*wisdom, understanding, counsel, strength*—that Job wishes to test in order to determine their real meaning in relation to God's governance of the world, not the debased meaning they have in the platitudes of common speech.

Verse 13 is not just the second part of a lesser-to-greater argument. It also introduces the satirical doxology that occupies the rest of the chapter. Verses 13, 16, and 22 provide the general statements illustrated by the concrete examples in the following verses. Ostensibly serving to substantiate the divine qualities listed in v. 13, the examples actually destabilize their meaning.

12:14-25. Job's rhetorical strategy begins to change in vv. 14-25. Whereas previously he had used the very platitudes that characterized the friends' speech, now he uses traditional hymnic style but gives the content a

212. Clines, *Job 1–20*, 295.
213. E.g., Pope, *Job*, 92; Rowley, *The Book of Job*, 94; Clines, *Job 1–20*, 295.

decidedly negative cast. Even here, however, Job uses much of the phraseology and themes from familiar hymnic praise of God. Psalm 107 is particularly close and may even be specifically quoted by Job (Ps 107:40 = Job 12:21*a*, 24*b*). Isaiah 44:24-28 and Dan 2:20-23 also have striking similarities to this passage. The important issue is not whether Job alludes specifically to any of these passages. It is, rather, the way in which the common idioms of praise, which in Job's opinion have served as a kind of verbal fog, obscuring real knowledge of God, are now used by him in a subversive way to disclose the truth about God's governance of the world.

12:14-15. The subtlety of Job's inflections of traditional speech can be seen in vv. 14-15, which offer substantiations for v. 13. The pairs of verbs in v. 14 ("tears down . . . rebuild"; "shut in . . . open up") are conventional ones, elsewhere used in positive contexts to define power and authority (cf. Isa 22:22; Jer 1:10). In those contexts, however, the actions are complementary. In Jeremiah, reconstruction follows destruction; in Isaiah, opening and closing suggest proper regulation. By contrast, Job highlights only the destructive, restrictive element of each pair. More distantly, Job's words parody Eliphaz's hymn of God's transforming power (5:8-16). Here, however, constructive activity is precisely what is prevented.

In contrast to v. 14, where only one type of action was featured, v. 15 describes God's engaging in two complementary actions— but with similarly devastating results. The unmotivated, destructive manipulation of water in v. 15 contrasts with Ps 107:33-37, where water is dried up and released specifically as punishment and blessing.

12:16-21. These verses constitute the second part of the satirical doxology. The first line of v. 16 is closely parallel to v. 13, merely adding "strength" and "effectiveness" to the list of divine qualities. But the second line is startling. Job employs a merismus, a figure of speech that indicates totality by naming opposite categories, such as "bond and free" (Deut 32:36; 1 Kgs 14:10) or "great and small" (Esth 1:5). The categories Job chooses are not social ones, however, but "deceived and deceiver." For Job the heart of human experience is error and the cynical manipulation of

truth, and it is God to whom this situation must be attributed. By placing these words at the end of the sequence of divine qualities in vv. 13 and 16, Job creates an utterance that is at the literal level contradictory. The God of wisdom and understanding is the God of error and manipulation.

The implicit contradiction is explored further in the substantiating examples in vv. 17-21. Here, as Habel notes, Job satirizes the claim made by passages such as Prov 8:14-16 that divine wisdom is the source of just and effective human government.[214] In Proverbs, personified wisdom claims: "to me belong *counsel* and *effectiveness*; I am *understanding*; to me belongs *strength.* By me *kings* govern and leaders decree what is right; by me rulers rule, and *nobles,* all who *judge* rightly" (words in common with Job 12:13-21 are italicized). In vv. 17-21, Job lists nine categories of persons who provide leadership for a community in its political, religious, and social life. In contrast to the claims of Proverbs 8, however, Job's doxology describes the activities of God that destroy just governance. One way is by insidiously depriving leaders of reason, so that they do not have the "counsel and understanding" of wisdom (vv. 17*b*, 20). God also causes leaders to be defeated and humiliated, that is, deprived of "strength and effectiveness" (vv. 17*a*, 18-19, 21). Several images refer to the practice of stripping, a symbolic act represented in ancient Near Eastern art.[215] Since the garments of leaders are often badges of office, the humiliation is not merely personal but also an act of violence against the community.

A discordant echo occurs in v. 21*a*, where Job incorporates the exact words of Ps 107:40*a*. In the psalm, God is praised for the action of "pouring contempt upon nobles," represented as God's intervention to save the poor from their oppressors and restore right order (Ps 107:39-42). Job, however, takes the same "snapshot" of divine intervention and sets it in a different context, giving it a wholly different and deeply disturbing meaning.

12:22-25. Verse 22 introduces the final strophe of the doxology. Although the verse shares some vocabulary with Ps 107:10, 14, its celebration of God's knowledge of things

214. Habel, *The Book of Job,* 216.
215. *ANEP,* 98-99, 111; pls. 305, 332.

"deep and dark" is closer to the language of the doxology in Dan 2:20-23, in which Daniel celebrates God as a revealer of mysteries. Job 12:22 *a* is almost identical to Dan 2:22 *a*. Job's deviation from standard, orthodox language in v. 22 is very slight but highly significant. The only word that is out of place is צלמות (*ṣalmāwet*), literally, "shadow of death" (NRSV, "deep darkness"; NIV, "deep shadows"). This word is not part of the semantics of mystery, as simple "darkness" is (חשך *ḥōšek*; as in Dan 2:22), but always connotes danger and evil. When Job uses both words together, he intends them to signify something sinister (3:5; 10:21). Now the allusion to Ps 107:10, 14 can be properly understood. The psalmist describes prisoners who sit in "darkness and the shadow of death," prisoners whom God "brings forth." Job, however, metaphorically treats this menacing shadow of death as itself the prisoner whom God brings forth and sets free.

The fruits of this divine activity are described in the examples of vv. 23-25. These verses are also best understood against the background of Psalm 107. The image with which Psalm 107 begins and ends is that of a scattered and directionless people being brought together and settled in an orderly and prosperous land (Ps 107:2-9, 33-41).

Their oppressors were the ones whom God caused to wander, lost in the wilderness (Ps 107:40 *b*). But here God's action has a disturbing quality of purposelessness. Nations are apparently made great only to be destroyed (v. 23). Citing Ps 107:40 *b*, Job depicts God's power to disorient as directed not at oppressors but at those whose responsibility it is to lead (v. 24). The final verse (v. 25) departs from the participial style of the doxology (represented in the NRSV and the NIV by the initial "he" in vv. 17-24). The focus shifts from inexplicable divine activity to the pathos of disoriented leaders, groping and staggering like drunks.

13:1-2. Although the chapter division segments Job's speech here, these verses correspond in form and content to the words with which Job opened his speech in 12:3, reasserting his claim to be equal to his friends in knowledge. Job's knowledge is grounded differently than that of the friends, however. Zophar had argued in an *a priori* fashion from the premise of the superior wisdom of God. Bildad had insisted upon the authority of ancestral tradition. Eliphaz had grounded his teachings on a revelatory encounter. But Job insists on the authority of experience: what his own eye has seen, what his own ear has heard (13:2).

REFLECTIONS

There is a great deal to think about in this part of Job's speech, but one issue seems particularly important: Job's devastating critique of a theological language constructed of clichés and platitudes. Job's parody of such language hits close to home. Although the problem is not unique to religious discourse, one cannot help remembering the sermons, Sunday school lessons, funeral homilies, and words of appreciation for volunteers that seemingly consist of nothing but a string of platitudes. More alarmingly, one hears one's own voice mouthing those tired phrases and trite words.

What is wrong with platitudes? If the issue were simply one of style or a lack of sophistication, then very little would be at stake. Job, however, is talking about something much more serious. The issue is how language serves or fails to serve truth. In Job's view, a language riddled with platitudes is a diseased language that can no longer serve this essential function. Platitudes are ready-made, standard-issue speech, and they suffer from the problem that besets other one-size-fits-all products: They seldom fit. The richness, complexity, and ambiguity of situations are lost when a speaker attempts to force them into the simplistic patterns of perception provided by a language of clichés.

Even in the most innocuous cases, one senses what is wrong with such language. Think of a typically trite appreciation speech. Even if the words are truly applied and the person being honored is in fact "generous to a fault," "a pillar of the community," "always ready to lend a helping hand," "the backbone of the church," "beloved by his/her children," etc., saying such words drains the person of individuality. It reduces the person to a monochromatic blandness, and so ends up being false.

The emptiness of such speech makes it easy to use in a more perniciously false way, by misapplying the platitudes. When words have been debased, one does not treat them with value and care. They become pretend words that describe the way one wants a situation to be, even if it is actually the opposite. So one introduces the new chair of the board as a "devoted family man," even if it is known that he is abusive to his children. One refers to the mayor who lined her pockets while in office as a "dedicated public servant." Such a language of collective self-deception is the verbal equivalent of the emperor's new clothes. It is not just the language of personal evaluation that is corrupted by cliché and platitude. Social and moral problems also are reduced to formulas by such speech. It becomes impossible to see what the problems actually are because the platitude substitutes for discriminating judgment. Once the label is applied, no further thought is needed.

People succumb to the temptations of clichéd speech for many reasons, including simple laziness. Social insecurity, too, leads people to say words they have heard before, words that they hope will make them fit in. More disturbingly, people are drawn to platitudinous language when they are uneasy in the presence of something they do not understand and fear to examine. Religious leaders in particular often assume that they are supposed to have answers for every human dilemma. How much easier it is to speak in an authoritative voice of "the wisdom of God which we cannot comprehend" or "the plan of God for your life" than to admit that there is no simple answer for the pain, confusion, and devastation that erupt unexpectedly in people's lives. How much easier it is to mouth the conventional words of comfort than to find words for the unspeakable contradiction between a God of love and a world of cruelty and broken bodies.

Job will not stand for this. He knows that his friends are frightened by the anomaly he represents and that they use language to defend themselves against having to look into the truth of his devastation. In their response to him, they reveal how debased their religious language has become. It provides them with only so many pigeonholes, and they are determined to make Job's situation fit one of them: "Think now, who that was innocent ever perished?" (4:7 NRSV). "Happy is the one whom God reproves" (5:17 NRSV). "Does God pervert justice?" (8:3 NRSV). "If you will seek God . . . [God will] restore to you your rightful place" (8:5-6 NRSV). "Know then that God exacts of you less than your guilt deserves" (11:6 NRSV).

Even worse, in Job's view, they misapply words until such words literally have no meaning. His friends are ready to speak of God's "wisdom and understanding." But the reality Job experiences cannot be appropriately described as the result of God's wisdom and understanding. When words no longer refer to some reality, then they are simply nonsense syllables that can be used in any way at all. Perhaps the worst result of the friends' corrupt language is that they have allowed it to become a substitute for seeing and hearing. Their platitudes persuade them that they already know, without needing to look or listen, what the world is like and why things happen as they do.

A language so debased and corrupted as the one the friends speak is almost impervious to criticism. How does one break in and interrupt its self-satisfied noise? One effective strategy is parody—mimicking the tone and favored vocabulary of debased speech, exaggerating its characteristic features, and bringing into full view the ugly things such speech tries so hard to hide. That, of course, is precisely what Job does in chap. 12. He mimics the way the friends talk, exaggerating the use of wisdom figures, proverbs, traditional sayings, and hymnic forms. In doing so, he draws attention to the problems inherent in using language worn too smooth by too many mouths. The most important part of Job's parody, however, is the way he creates a thoroughly incoherent speech to show just how the friends' words have lost their meaning. Job aggressively juxtaposes the words *wisdom* and *understanding* with concrete examples that cannot possibly be included in anybody's definition of them. Job forces the contradiction between words and reality, which the friends have ignored, into his own parodic speech, where the contradiction between one word and another cannot be missed.

After one has heard an effective parody, after it has disrupted the smoothness of familiar forms of speech, it becomes hard to hear the traditional speech without also hearing an echo of the parody. The mocking voice, the dissenting opinion, is always there like a whisper. Parody of the sort Job uses disrupts the universalizing claims made by "straight" speech by posing an undeniable counterexample. After Job has spoken, one cannot hear Psalm 107 and its confident claims about God's leading a people to a settled and orderly life without also hearing the echo of Job's counterexample of a whole leadership class destroyed and the senseless destruction of a nation. One hears religious leaders claiming to recognize God's power in the movements toward democracy in the modern world; the Joban parodist would mimic their speech, saying that one has only to look at the increasing number of genocidal conflicts in the world to see evidence of God's power.

As much as such language needs to be questioned, there are limits to what parody can accomplish. Parody is a critical, but not constructive, tool. It can expose the inadequacies of someone's speech, but it cannot by itself provide an alternative way to talk about reality. Moreover, parody has its own dangerous seductions. There is great energy in its negative power. Without equal commitment to a constructive alternative, the negativity of parody can become a cynical nihilism. Job seems to recognize this danger. In chap. 13, he will turn from his scathing critique of the way the friends talk about God to explore an alternative way of talking about God and with God that he finds more adequate to the rigorous demands of speaking the truth.

Job 13:3-19, Job Criticizes Deceitful Speech

COMMENTARY

13:3-12. Despite his expressed intention to speak with God (v. 3), Job has not finished his critique of the friends' speech. Although the expression "smear with lies" (v. 4) is a traditional phrase for slander (Ps 119:69; Sir 51:5), the context suggests that Job uses it in a different way. As the following verses indicate, what bothers Job is not lies about himself but misrepresentations of the nature of God (v. 7). Verse 4 makes most sense if one assumes that both lines are part of a medical image.[216] The friends are "worthless physicians" because the salves or plasters with which they have tried to heal Job are but lies they have spoken about God.

Job's sarcastic comment that the friends could best show their wisdom by remaining silent (cf. Prov 17:28) is perhaps an ironic

216. So the LXX; cf. Fohrer, *Das Buch Hiob,* 247; and Clines, *Job 1–20,* 306.

allusion to Zophar's claim that Job's babblings have silenced others (11:2). If only it were so! The call to be silent and listen (vv. 5-6) here introduces Job's criticism of the friends (vv. 7-12), but is repeated in vv. 13 and 17, as Job introduces his address to God. In both places Job uses legal terminology to characterize his words, in v. 6 as "pleadings" (רבות *ribôt;* cf. Deut 17:8) and in v. 18 as a "case" (משפט *mišpāṭ).*

Having framed his remarks in legal terminology, Job's accusation that the friends have spoken "falsely" and "deceitfully" for God (v. 7) amounts to a charge that they have borne "false witness." Job reinforces the legal metaphor by describing the friends as "showing partiality" to God in arguing God's case (v. 8). The friends, of course, have not thought of themselves as participating in a trial. They are simply counseling a friend about the proper religious understanding of his situation. By insisting on viewing their words through the lens of legal categories, however, Job is demanding that theological language be held to the same strict standards of truth required of participants in a trial. The severe penalties prescribed for those who give false witness (Deut 19:16-19; cf. Exod 20:16; Deut 5:20) and the stringent prohibition of partiality (Exod 23:2-3, 6-8) indicate how seriously such matters were taken.

There is an irony in Job's imagining God examining and rebuking the friends (vv. 9-10). Although Job will be examined in God's searching speeches at the end of the book, the friends will be rebuked because they "have not spoken of me what is right" (42:7 NRSV). In v. 10, Job speaks of the friends "showing partiality in secret." From their own perspective, the accusation is wrong on both counts. Their defense of God is not partiality, and they have been quite open in their views. Job's words are psychologically acute, however. The friends' motives and the character of their words are hidden, even from themselves. Their lack of perception is evident in the glibness with which they speak deceit, without a sense of the awfulness of an angry God (v. 11). Job knows of what he speaks, for he has experienced the terror of the divine presence, even though he is blameless (6:4; 7:14; 9:34-35).

Job's passionate depiction of a God enraged by false witness and partiality contrasts sharply with his earlier depiction of a God whose power overrides justice (9:14-20; 10:15) and who even corrupts judges (9:24). Both images appear true to Job, and yet they are contradictory.

The terms Job uses in v. 12 to summarize his dismissal of the friends' speech as worthless are quite comprehensive. "Maxims" (זכרון zikkārôn, lit. "something remembered") alludes to tradition.[217] "Proverbs" (משל māšāl,) are the commonplaces of speech by which people order their thinking. The final term is actually a play on words, for it means both "replies" and "defenses" (גב gab),[218] suggesting the friends' rhetorical argumentation. In the wisdom tradition,

wise and appropriate words are compared to precious and desirable objects (choice silver, honeycomb, apples of gold in a setting of silver; see Prov 10:20; 16:24; 25:11) because they have the capacity to save and to give life (Prov 10:11; 11:14; 12:6; 15:4). By contrast, all of the resources of language at the friends' disposal are "clay" and "ashes," images of what crumbles into nothingness (Job 4:4-19; Ezek 28:18; Mal 4:3[3:21]).

13:13-16. Since the friends' speech is worthless, they should be silent (v. 13a). In contrast to the friends, who seem to be oblivious to the danger of speaking falsely about God, Job assesses the risk he takes in speaking honestly before God (vv. 13b-16). Formally, this passage is like the statements in 7:11 and 10:1 with which Job introduced his earlier address to God. There Job referred to the "bitterness of spirit" forcing him to speak. Here the urgency is expressed somewhat differently.

As often happens, ambiguities in the text allow for more than one translation and somewhat different depictions of Job's state of mind. The NRSV and the NIV make quite different interpretive choices, and the issues deserve careful attention. In v. 14, the phrase meaning "why" (על-מה 'al-mâ) is probably an accidental recopying of the last letters in v. 13 ("upon me what may" [עלי מה 'ālay mâ]). The NIV retains the phrase and takes v. 14 as a rhetorical question answered in vv. 15-16. The NRSV, following the LXX, omits the phrase and takes v. 14 as a statement of determination, further developed in v. 15 and qualified in v. 16. Although the image of taking one's life into one's hands is attested elsewhere (Judg 12:3; 1 Sam 19:5; 28:21), the parallel image of taking one's flesh into one's teeth is not.

The most famous textual problem in the book of Job occurs in v. 15. There are several ambiguities. The first word (הן hēn) may be translated either as "behold," "see" (so NRSV) or as the word that means "if," "even if" (so NIV). The second verb (יחל yiḥēl) means "to wait" and, since it can suggest expectant waiting, is sometimes translated "to hope." The crux of the textual problem is reflected in the difference between the NRSV ("I have no hope") and the NIV ("yet will I hope in him"). The Hebrew Bible preserves

---

217. Cf. Gordis, *The Book of Job,* 143, who associates the term with Bildad's appeal to ancient authority.
218. L. Koehler and W. Baumgartner, *Hebräisches und Aramäisches Lexicon,* 3rd ed. (Leiden: Brill, 1967) 170.

both traditions in the marginal notation known as *Ketib/Qere,* which means "what is written"/"what is read." While the body of the text clearly contains the negative (לֹא *lō';* hence, "I cannot wait" or "I have no hope"), the marginal note records an ancient alternative reading "to/for him" (לוֹ *lô;* hence, "I will wait for him" or "I will hope in him"). Both traditions were known to the rabbis, as *Mishnah Sota* 5.5 indicates in its discussion of Job: "The matter is undecided—do I hope in him [*lô*] or not hope [*lō*]?"[219]

How one resolves these ambiguities is as much a matter of context as text. The NIV presents Job as still entangled in the paradox of a God whose irrational violence is real but whose commitment to truth is just as real. There is genuine danger that if Job presses his case, God will kill him (cf. 9:17-18). The "hope" (v. 15) and the "deliverance" (v. 16) of which Job speaks are not that he will escape death but that he will be vindicated, since his integrity will be attested by the very fact of his daring to come before God (v. 16*b*). Such an interpretation is both textually and contextually defensible. Only when v. 15 is taken out of context and made into a slogan of masochistic piety is the authenticity of this reading abused.

The NRSV interpretation, equally defensible, presents Job in a more defiant mode. Job does not pose a rhetorical question about why he is willing to risk death, but makes a statement (v. 14), intensified into a certainty (v. 15), that God will kill him. Such a dramatic claim sets off Job's determination to speak in defiance of all the power of God. One could also stress the note of urgency rather than defiance with a slightly different translation: "See, he may kill me; I cannot wait, but I must argue my ways to his face."[220] Such a translation would parallel the reference to the urgency of impending death with which Job introduces his address to God in 7:7-11. The textual ambiguities in 13:14-16 are not

mere annoyances but occasions for pondering the image of Job: Is he a figure pressed by the urgency of death, a Promethean rebel, or a person wracked by the paradoxes of God? Meditating on alternative interpretations is more valuable than choosing one too quickly.

13:17-19. Although Job is primarily concerned to address God, he cares that his friends hear and understand what he says (v. 17). As his language in vv. 18-19 makes clear, Job continues to think of his encounter with God in terms of a court case. An interpretive choice must be made here, too. If one translates v. 18*b* as "I know I shall be vindicated," then Job appears to be expressing a confidence in God's justice that contradicts his earlier feelings (9:15, 29). Such an interpretation gives Job a certain psychological complexity, although Habel prefers to translate Job's words as conditional: "I should be vindicated."[221] The line, however, need not refer to what God will do at all, but to Job's own certainty about himself: "I know that I am innocent."[222] (Cf. 9:20-21, where Job's self-knowledge threatened to disintegrate under the pressure of God's overwhelming power.) This interpretation fits well with the following line (v. 19*a*), in which Job asks rhetorically who could bring charges against him (cf. Isa 50:8, where the same expression is used in a similar expression of confidence). There is no real doubt in Job's mind about his own innocence when he says, "For then I would be silent and die" (v. 19). What the line reveals is how closely linked speech and life are for Job. In chap. 3, Job did not want to live. Even in chaps. 6–7 death was as much desired as feared. Beginning in chap. 9, however, the image of a trial with God has given Job a conceptually powerful way to articulate his sense of grievance. Now, the desire to state his case has given Job the will to live. If, to his surprise, a case were proven against him, then his ability both to speak and to live would evaporate together.

219. Gordis, *The Book of Job,* 144. Zuckerman, *Job the Silent,* 170, discusses the evidence for the antiquity of the variant reading.
220. Similarly Good, *In Turns of Tempest,* 85.

221. Habel, *The Book of Job,* 224, 231. Cf. Gordis, *The Book of Job,* 130.
222. So Clines, *Job 1–20,* 277; and Good, *In Turns of Tempest,* 85.

REFLECTIONS

Job is the representative of those whose resistance to suffering takes the form of a determination to bring truth to light. From the perpetrators of genocide who attempt to destroy all witnesses to their crime to the incest survivor who is threatened so that she or he will never tell anyone, silence continues the violence against the abused. Bearing witness is both a means of survival and an act of defiance. The passion to speak is the power to live.

Speaking out can be especially difficult where society's uneasiness about a problem takes the form of blaming the victim, as has often been the case with survivors of sexual crimes, such as rape and incest. Undeserved shame serves as a strong deterrent to their publicly disclosing what happened to them. Even close friends and family members who are otherwise supportive may become uneasy and even embarrassed if a survivor insists on speaking out. Job's situation is strikingly similar, which makes his struggle particularly instructive. As discussed in the Commentary to chaps. 1–2, overwhelming catastrophes in general and skin diseases in particular carried with them the suggestion that the victim had perhaps done something wrong and was being punished for it. Such suffering was associated with a taint of shamefulness, as the description of the suffering servant suggests: "He was despised and rejected by others;/ a man of suffering and acquainted with infirmity;/ and as one from whom others hide their faces,/ he was despised, and we held him of no account" (Isa 53:3 NRSV). For Job to demand a trial in which he could be vindicated and God's wrongful action exposed is to reject the implication that he should feel shame for what has happened to him. One wishes that such courage always brought forth support from others. Often it does not, and speaking out can be lonely. As the example of Job shows, however, the very act of speaking can become a source of energy, confidence, and the will to live.

Bearing witness is also an act of faith. It testifies to the belief that if people only knew the truth, they would do something to change the situation, because they desire justice. The Chinese dissident who smuggles out an account of forced labor camps, the Central American widow who publishes the names of the army officers who tortured and murdered her husband, the small-town newspaper reporter who writes about the conditions of migrant workers—such people bear witness not only to the existence of evil but also to the possibility of good. Sometimes their faith is rewarded; other times, it is disappointed, when their testimony is met with chilling indifference. That such people continue to call upon others to hear is an act of faith that the community has more goodness and power than it has yet acknowledged. This dynamic sheds light on the apparent contradictoriness of Job's appeal for justice to a God he has accused of corrupting justice. Unlike the friends, Job does not flinch from the realities that appear to show God's indifference, if not cruelty. Nevertheless, Job's act of faith is that God is fundamentally a God of justice who will yet respond, if only God will listen.

In one important respect, Job's situation is different from that of persons bearing witness against human abuse and oppression. In those instances, the criminal nature of the acts themselves is clear. Job's life, however, has been devastated by a series of catastrophes, the origin and significance of which are not at all clear. He knows that the traditional explanations provided by the friends are unsatisfactory, but he is groping to find a way of talking about what has happened that will be more adequate to his experience. His characterization of what has happened and what it implies about God and his relation to God has an exploratory quality. Only after Job has taken up the legal metaphor does the notion of bearing witness become essential. One is still left with the question, however, of whether the metaphor of a trial is the appropriate one for Job's situation. In the end, it may not be, a possibility that will raise its own issues for reflection. At this point, however, it is the most compelling model available to Job for understanding his situation, and he is prepared to follow what it requires of him, courageously bearing witness to the truth, even if it means risking his life in a confrontation with God.

Job 13:20–14:22, Job Experiences the Destruction of Hope

COMMENTARY

Since the friends lack the wisdom necessary to help him (cf. 6:24), Job desires to speak directly to God (v. 3), which he now does. The pattern of Job's direct speech to God is perplexing. In the speech with which he broke his silence (chap. 3), Job did not address God at all. Each of his three speeches in the first cycle concludes with an extended address to God (7:7-21; 10:2-22; 13:20–14:22). After the first cycle, however, Job does not address God again in any extended fashion. Two verses in 17:3-4, perhaps two in 16:7-8, and a brief passage in 30:20-23 are the only words Job addresses directly to God before he replies to God's own speech in 40:3-5 and 42:1-6. What role this use and avoidance of direct address to God plays in the dramatic structure of the book and in the development of Job's character is not immediately self-evident. It can best be understood by recalling that the traditional language for direct address to God is the language of prayer, and Job does not wish to pray. In his three addresses to God, he attempts to find an alternative language. In chap. 7, Job burlesques the language of lament and praise, the traditional language of prayer. In chap. 10, he attempts to cast his words not as prayer but as a legal speech, and a hypothetical one at that. The motifs and language of prayer seep into his speech, however, especially in evocations of the creator/creature relationship in 10:8-12, although Job bitterly repudiates the possibility that such language could provide the basis for an appeal to God, and reasserts the categories of legal language (10:13-17). In chaps. 13–14, too, Job introduces his words as legal speech (13:17-22). In the latter part of this speech, however, Job starts to be drawn into the language of prayer (14:13-17). Nowhere else is his yearning for God expressed in such a direct way. At the last moment, however, Job turns away from prayer's traditional words of appeal (14:18-22). The language of prayer is still too powerful and too seductive for Job to trust himself to speak in its accents. After this, he will talk about God, but not to God, and the legal metaphor will increasingly direct his speech.

13:20-28. As in chaps. 9–10, Job recognizes that the imbalance of power between himself and God is a barrier to a fair trial. In contrast to 9:32-35, however, Job addresses God directly (v. 20). A lawsuit with God is not impossible—*if* God voluntarily removes the fearsomeness and the oppressive peremptory punishment that leave Job scarcely able to breathe (v. 21; cf. 7:13-16). Job imagines the encounter as a structured dialogue with either party taking the initiative. The wrong impression may be created by commentators who interpret v. 22 as offering God the position of either plaintiff or defendant.[223] The roles of parties in legal disputes in the ancient Near East were not differentiated in quite the same way as in modern systems and could be quite fluid.[224] Moreover, in Job the metaphor of a trial as the way in which speech with God can be envisioned remains a suggestive metaphor rather than a literal event.

Job's rhetorical demand to know the number and nature of his iniquities, sins, and offenses is modeled after similar expressions often used in legal disputes to assert innocence. (Cf. Gen 31:36, where Jacob says to Laban, "What is my offense? What is my sin?" [NRSV], as he calls upon those present to act as judges in the dispute.)[225] A number

223. So Pope, *Job,* 101; Habel, *The Book of Job,* 231.
224. H. J. Boecker, *Law and the Administration of Justice in the Old Testament and Ancient East,* trans. J. Moiser (Minneapolis: Augsburg, 1980) 23; Dick, "The Legal Metaphor in Job 31," 38.
225. Dick, "The Legal Metaphor in Job 31," 38n. 10, cites a similar example from a Babylonian letter of a man accused by his superior. He defends his innocence by saying, "What offense have I committed against my lord?"

of commentators are at pains to argue that Job does not claim never to have sinned, as though he were in danger of saying something "religiously incorrect."[226] That is not the issue, for Job's complete innocence is the narrative premise on which the story is built.[227] What is important here is the way in which the introduction of legal language changes the way Job talks about sin before God. No parallel exists for this kind of challenging question in the traditional language of Israelite prayer or in the cultic laws that govern relations between individuals and God. By transferring the patterns and idioms of language used to talk about the legal resolution of disputes between persons, Job begins to remap the territory of divine-human relations.

Although the image of God's hiding God's face (v. 24) is a familiar motif in psalms (Pss 27:9; 30:7[8]; 104:29), the rhetoric of vv. 24-25 is quite similar to that used by David in his dispute with Saul (1 Samuel 24). There, too, the issue is why Saul unjustly considered David an enemy (v. 24b; cf. 1 Sam 24:9, 19). Just as David asks rhetorically why Saul pursues "a dead dog? A single flea?" (1 Sam 24:14), so also Job chides God for pursuing "a windblown leaf . . . dry chaff" (v. 25). Job's accusations continue in v. 26. Exactly what it means to "write bitter things against" a person is not clear. The verb can refer to the writing out of an indictment (cf. 31:35), but since Job complains that he has not been told what he is charged with, the phrase is better taken as the writing of a decree allotting bitter things to Job (cf. Isa 10:1).[228] The harsh nature of God's treatment is suggested also by the reference to "the sins of my youth" in v. 26b. Children were assumed to have a less fully formed moral understanding than adults (Deut 1:39; cf. Jonah 4:11). Even though a child was culpable for sins committed, God's mercy could be invoked to overlook the sins of youth (Ps 25:7). For such to be charged against Job implies a merciless harshness on God's part. The theme of obsessive divine scrutiny, raised by Job in 7:17-20 and 10:14-17, is repeated in v. 27. Although the verse is grammatically difficult, the images all have to do with circumscribed movement. The NIV interprets the last image according to a fanciful hypothesis about an ancient custom of inscribing an owner's name on the soles of the feet of slaves.[229] The NRSV more plausibly understands the verb to refer to inscribing a boundary to restrict movement.[230]

Verse 28 interrupts syntactically (lit., "and he . . . ") and is thematically more closely related to what follows than to the preceding lines. Many commentators suggest moving the verse to follow 14:2.[231] Although the image of decay and disintegration would not be inappropriate as a transition between chaps. 13 and 14, translations such as those of the NIV and the NRSV, which attempt this reading, have to paraphrase in order to minimize the syntactical problem.

14:1-6. The vocabulary and tone of legal challenge are abandoned in chap. 14, as Job turns instead to contemplate the ephemerality of human existence. The first six verses of chap. 14 divide into three groups, with the main point expressed in the middle pair. An initial comment on the transient quality of human life (vv. 1-2) leads to the central objection that God's bringing Job into judgment is cruelly absurd (vv. 3-4). The power that God has over the human lifespan becomes an argument for a brief respite (vv. 5-6).

14:1-2. Job's reflections, although prompted by his own experience, are expressed in universal terms. Commentators who see in the phrase "born of woman" (v. 1) an allusion to female weakness or impurity disclose their own misogyny, not that of the text.[232] The phrase simply means "every person," since there is no one who is not born of a woman (cf. 15:14; 25:4; Sir 10:18; 1QS 13.14; 1QH 18.12-13). The phrase may also contain the suggestion of inescapable mortality.[233] In the narratives of Genesis 3–4, birth takes place only outside the garden, when death has been sealed as humanity's fate. Birth is inextricably linked with death.

226. Dick, "The Legal Metaphor in Job 31," 167-68; Gordis, *The Book of Job*, 146; Hartley, *The Book of Job*, 226-27.

227. Clines, *Job 1–20*, 318.

228. Andersen, *Job*, 168.

229. Tur-Sinai, *The Book of Job*, 230; Gordis, *The Book of Job*, 146; cf. the critique of Clines, *Job 1–20*, 322.

230. Davidson, *The Book of Job*, 101; A. S. Peake, *Job*, NCB (London: T.C. & E.C. Jack, 1904) 145; so Tanakh.

231. Dhorme, *A Commentary on the Book of Job*, 193; Pope, *Job*, 106; Horst, *Hiob*, 206.

232. Peake, *Job*, 145; Dhorme, *A Commentary on the Book of Job*, 194; Rowley, *The Book of Job*, 103.

233. de Wilde, *Das Buch Hiob*, 172.

Job laments not only mortality but also the fleeting quality of life. The images of v. 2 are traditional (Job 8:6; Pss 37:2; 90:5-6; 103:15; 144:4; Eccl 6:12; Isa 40:6-8). The similes work by making phenomena that even human beings experience as ephemeral—flowers and shadows—into the symbols of human life itself. Job's bitterness is evident in the way his phrase "few of days and full of trouble" (v. 1 *b*) reverses the traditional phrase "old and full of days" (Gen 25:8; 35:29; 1 Chr 29:28).

14:3-4. God's seemingly absurd determination to treat Job as a powerful adversary is a theme Job has broached before (7:12, 17-18). Here he casts it in terms of God's legal aggression against him (v. 3; whether one follows the MT in reading a first-person reference to Job [so NRSV] or the ancient versions in seeing a general reference to humanity [so NIV] makes little difference). Commentators are often perplexed by v. 4 because they fail to recognize it as a figure of speech expressing an impossible transformation. It has the same general structure as the saying that one cannot "make a silk purse out of a sow's ear" or that one cannot "spin straw into gold." The comparison is even sharper, however, because "clean and unclean," categories drawn from the sphere of cultic practice, are logical opposites. The saying as a whole, not the individual terms, is to be applied to the situation at hand. God and Job cannot be appropriate adversaries at law because God and human beings are logical opposites, like clean and unclean, whereas parties at law must share a common legal status. Job is facing the same dilemma that he articulated in 9:32: "For he is not a mortal, as I am . . . that we should come to trial together."

14:5-6. The notion of a rivalry between humans and God and God's decision to limit the human lifespan or otherwise restrict human power are common mythic motifs throughout the ancient Near East. In the Bible, they are featured in the expulsion from the garden. After the humans eat the fruit that makes them "like God," they must be excluded from the tree of life, which would allow them to live forever (Gen 3:22). A similar divine restriction on human life follows the intermarriage of divine beings and human women in Gen 6:3. Job alludes to these

traditions in v. 5. God has nothing to fear from human beings, since God has already set limits to human life. Consequently, God might drop the obsessive scrutiny (v. 6*a*). The NRSV and the NIV differ in their translations of v. 6*b* depending on which of two Hebrew homonyms (רצה *rāṣâ*) each translates; the NIV ("put in his time") is preferable (cf. Lev 26:34).[234]

14:7-12. The consequences of "the bounds that [humans] cannot pass" are worked out in a series of striking comparisons and contrasts with natural phenomena. Descriptive images in Hebrew poetry are generally brief and undeveloped. Job's vivid and extensively developed image of the tree (vv. 7-9) draws part of its power from its contrast with ordinary style. More important, however, is the complex pattern of cross-identification that the image creates. The expression "there is hope for a tree" has become so familiar that one seldom notices the figure of personification. Hope is an emotion, a characteristic of human beings. One does not ordinarily attribute hope to trees. Such personification, however, establishes a point of contact between the nature of the tree and of human experience. What "hope" means will be defined metaphorically by what the poet says about the tree. The images of vulnerability, too, invite metaphorical appropriation. The felling of a tree in its prime (v. 7) and the aging and death of roots in dry ground (v. 8) are evocative of human susceptibility to violence and to loss of vitality in old age. Hope is concretely imaged in the growth of new shoots from a cut-off trunk (v. 7) and in the green response of dry roots to water (v. 9). Hope is the power of regeneration.

There is bitter irony in the complex figure. Although the poet "inappropriately" transfers the human emotion of hope to the tree at the beginning, the pursuit of the metaphor discloses that it is only the tree, and not human beings, who can truly lay claim to hope, for only the tree has the power of regeneration (v. 10).

The use of the tree for this metaphorical exploration needs to be understood in the context of the ambivalence of tree symbolism in the ancient Near East. Very commonly

---

234. Dhorme, *A Commentary on the Book of Job,* 198; Perdue, *Wisdom in Revolt,* 157.

the tree is a symbol of life, longevity, and the power of renewal available to the righteous (Pss 1:3; 92:12-14[13-15]). The life-giving power of wisdom (Prov 3:18; Sir 24:13-17), of the king (Dan 4:10-12[7-9]), and of God (Hos 14:5-8[6-9]) are all expressed by the symbolism of the tree.[235] Over against all of the images that stress identification with the tree and its life-giving powers, however, must be set the image of the cherubim with the flaming sword who forever bar the way to the tree of life (Gen 3:24). Although expressed in poetic and not mythic terms, the tree in Job 14 represents that capacity for regenerative life from which humans are definitively excluded.

The second image from nature that Job chooses to represent the human situation, the vanishing of water from lakes and rivers, is unexpected but perceptive (v. 11). There are plenty of examples in the Near East of seasonal wadis and other bodies of water that might give rise to an image of regeneration, but seasonal dryness is not what Job is talking about. His image is that of the irreversible loss of water that occurs, for instance, when an earthquake cuts off the spring that feeds a stream or a lake. In ancient cosmology, this process was envisioned as the sealing up of a fountain of the great underground freshwater sea that was thought to lie beneath the earth (cf. Gen 2:6; 8:2). One expects lakes and rivers to be permanent features, and human beings, despite knowing that they will die, persist in an irrational but deeply held conviction of their own permanence; yet the death of each is irreversible.

Job subtly attacks another human evasion in his play with the image of death as sleep (v. 12). That image, common in many cultures, attempts to obscure death's finality, since sleep and waking are logically coordinate terms. Job insists, however, that there is no rising from this lying down, no rousing from this sleep. The phrase "until the heavens are no more" is an idiom meaning "forever."

14:13-17. Trapped between the anger of God and the inexorability of death, Job's imagination attempts to secure a place for hope. Even though Job speaks of Sheol in v. 13, he does not see death as a refuge

from God, as he did in 3:13-19 and 7:8-10, 21. Death has become part of the problem, because Job's desire has changed. He wishes to have the mutuality of his relation with God restored. This longing is expressed poignantly in v. 15. The words "you would call, and I would answer you" echo those of 13:22 and by so doing underscore how torn Job is. In 13:22, the words are part of the adversarial vocabulary of legal challenge and reply; in 14:15, they are part of a vocabulary of piety expressed in the most personal terms. Job's imagining God "longing for the work of your hands" also contradicts his earlier sense of God's despising the "work of [God's] hands" (10:3). The very verb Job uses ("to long for" [כסף *kāsap*]) has connotations of the most instinctive, elemental urges: the hunger of a lion for prey (Ps 17:12), the desire of a bird to nest (Ps 84:2[3]), the homesickness of a person in a faraway land (Gen 31:30). Such is the bond that connects God and the creature God has made. Death threatens the restoration of this bond, since death in ancient Israelite thought is a realm cut off from God's presence. As the psalmist laments, "I am set apart with the dead,/ like the slain who lie in the grave,/ whom you remember no more,/ who are cut off from your care" (Ps 88:5[6] NIV).

This very idea, however, becomes the seed of Job's imaginary solution. If Sheol could become his temporary refuge, he could be protected from God's anger until it had passed (v. 13), in much the same way that Israel traditionally spoke of God hiding people from their enemies (Ps 27:5; 31:20[21]; Isa 49:2; cf., however, Amos 9:2-4). But as a living human being, Job cannot enter Sheol on his own; that act would have to be God's. The contradictions in Job's image of God are here projected into God's very will; God would hide Job from God's own anger, which seeks to destroy Job.

That Job is not talking about death and resurrection is made clear by the rhetorical question of v. 14.[236] He imagines the time in Sheol as a kind of "pressed service" (צבא *ṣābā'*), as in a labor gang or an army, with a set time and an occasion for release. The same image is used in Isa 40:2 for the exile in Babylon. Here, too, Job inverts his previous

---

235. Perdue, *Wisdom in Revolt*, 158-60; Keel, *The Symbolism of the Biblical World*, figs. 46, 47, 48, 479, 480.

236. Fohrer, *Das Buch Hiob*, 257-58.

words. Whereas in 13:15 he declared "I have no hope," now he says that "all the days of my service I would wait[/hope]."

Job also has to imagine how his relationship with God could be resumed without a renewal of God's obsession to find fault, which has led to his suffering (vv. 16-17). As earlier, Job must project a contradiction into God's behavior, a simultaneous seeing and not seeing. God would count Job's steps but not observe his sin. As Fohrer notes, counting the steps is never an image of providential care, but scrutiny of conduct (cf. 31:4; 34:21; Lam 4:18).[237] How could God scrutinize yet not see? This could happen only by a kind of divine self-interference analogous to what Job imagined in v. 13, God's sealing up offenses in a bag or painting over iniquities, so that God does not see them. When Job thought in legal terms, he demanded disclosure of his alleged sins, offenses, and iniquities, so that he could refute them (13:23). When he thinks in the relational terms of personal religion, images of concealment provide the resolution (14:16-17). Two rival ways of thinking about his relationship with God compete in Job's imagination, each with its own set of images and metaphors that organize his thinking about how to speak with God (13:22//14:15), whether or not hope is possible (13:15// 14:14), and how to deal with sin (13:23//14:16-17).

14:18-22. Abruptly, the imaginary vision is displaced by another scene. In Hebrew the change is marked by an introductory disjunctive word, "but" (ואולם *wĕʾûlām*). With exceptional artistry, the poet delays explicit interpretation of the figure (v. 19*b*), but form and meaning are closely interrelated. As erosion is the governing metaphor, so the images move sequentially from mountain to crag to stones to dust (vv. 18-19*a*). Grammatically, the first two scenes are described in the passive voice, with no agent mentioned. In the second two, however, the eroding agents, water and torrents, are the subjects of active verbs. In the final line, which identifies God as the agent, the verb is causative (lit., "cause to perish" ([האבדת *heʾĕbadtā*]).

Most extraordinary is Job's choice of the mountain as an image of human hope. In contrast to fragile, transient flowers and shadows, which Job used to describe the fleetingness of life (v. 2), hope is as strong and resistant as a mountain. It can be destroyed only by relentless and inexorable abrasion of almost unimaginable duration; but it can be destroyed. As opposites, water and stone are natural enemies, joined in a struggle in which water will always eventually triumph. To employ this metaphor for the relationship between God and human beings is to suggest that their opposite natures make them inevitable opponents, with the slow destruction of what is human a foregone conclusion.

The fundamental opposition underlying Job's metaphor is that of life, which belongs to God, and death, which is the lot of human beings. This sense of the fundamental chasm between the divine and human haunted ancient Near Eastern reflections. It permeates the book of Ecclesiastes and lies also at the heart of the ancient Babylonian poem of Gilgamesh ("Gilgamesh, whither rovest thou? The life thou pursuest thou shalt not find. When the gods created mankind, death for mankind they set aside, life in their own hands retaining").[238] For Job, this difference is experienced not simply as a difference of nature but as active antagonism. Like water against stone, God "prevails against" (v. 20) human beings.

Job's concluding images of death are governed by the figure of separation. The notion, alluded to earlier, that death is the realm where one is cut off from God, is echoed in Job's use of verbs of movement: "he is gone"; "you send him away" (v. 20). Job also notes that death is a separation from the bonds of kinship. In a culture that had no belief in immortality, descendants formed a link between the dead and the living community. The childless Absalom poignantly set up a memorial stone, "for he said, 'I have no son to keep my name in remembrance' " (2 Sam 18:18 NRSV). Job, however, reverses the ordinary perspective. He considers not what the living remember of the dead but what the dead can know about the living—which is nothing, neither their good fortune nor their bad (v. 21; cf. Eccl 9:5-6, 10). The final verse does not describe a postmortem pain, but moves back to the process of dying.[239] As so

---

238. *ANET*, 90.
239. So Clines, *Job 1–20*, 336; Fohrer, *Das Buch Hiob*, 261; contra Pope, *Job*, 111; Rowley, *The Book of Job*, 107.

237. Fohrer, *Das Buch Hiob*, 259.

often, Job's perception is acute. There comes a stage when the dying person becomes wholly concentrated on the business of dying. This turning inward, which separates the dying from their community even before the last breath is taken, becomes for Job the symbol of death as utter isolation.

REFLECTIONS

Hope is one of the most fundamental experiences of human life; yet it is not easy to describe. Anyone who has ever looked at a beloved child or started a new business or sat beside a hospital bed listening to quiet breathing knows what hope feels like, including the way in which hope and fear shadow each other. Most people know, too, what loss of hope feels like—the sensation that accompanies the rejection letter, the foreclosure notice, or the results of the medical test confirming the worst. Recovering hope can be difficult, and for those who have repeatedly had their hopes crushed, despair may seem more attractive. Despair at least does not tantalize, then disappoint. The problem of hope and despair is one to which Job and his friends repeatedly return in the course of their dialogue. Their different perspectives illumine some of the complexities of hope and suggest what is needed in order to resist the suicide of the spirit that is despair.

Eliphaz understands hope as the horizon of a future open to change, the prospect that things may yet be other than they are (5:8-16). The transforming power of God to open such a future is grounds for "the poor [to] have hope" (5:16 NRSV). Unquestionably, Eliphaz is correct in linking the sustaining power of hope with a sense of an open future. Perhaps that connection sheds light on one of the perplexing aspects of hope and despair among young people. Teenagers often lack a realistic sense of the future: Everything is possible; nothing can change. This tendency to see the future in such radically different and equally unrealistic ways is not a defect but an ordinary part of the process of maturation. The ability to dream a bright future gives some young people the resiliency to endure hardships and deprivations that would crush a more "realistic" adult. The other side of this phenomenon, however, is despair that comes from believing that nothing can ever change. Consequently, problems that do not seem so severe to an adult—the breakup of a relationship, being teased or ridiculed by others at school—can seem overwhelming to a young person who cannot imagine that someone else will love him or that she could ever be admired.

Eliphaz's extravagant language of a future completely turned around raises other questions. When does hope become false hope? Can such language be not only insensitive but even dangerous? Assurances that everything will turn out for the best are especially offensive when they are offered as a rote response. Even in the mouth of the sufferer, extravagant hope may be simply a form of denial that interferes with the person's ability to address the realities of a situation. Yet one should be cautious in assessing the meaning and function of the language of hope, especially in communities whose culture is different from one's own. Communities in which hard living and recurrent tragedy are all too familiar often have a more vivid language of hope than do communities in which tragedy is an infrequent visitor. Where people are not accustomed to *needing* hope, such language can be looked at with suspicion, dismissed as mere "pie in the sky" talk. Distinguishing between language that sustains and language that deceives is in part a matter of knowing the individual and the traditions of the community.

In any cultural context, cultivating a language of hope that does justice to the reality of loss as well as to the possibility of renewal requires appropriate images. The contrast between Zophar's image of hope and Job's is instructive. For Zophar, the fulfillment of hope means that "you will forget your misery;/ you will remember it as waters that have passed away" (11:16 NRSV). Perhaps that is true for some situations, but Job has lost his children as well as his possessions and his health. Any way of talking about hope for someone like Job has to acknowledge the emptiness that will always remain. Even though Job invokes the tree as a symbol of hope, only to reject it (14:7-9), it is worth looking more closely at that image. As a figure of the power of regeneration, the tree that is cut down but sprouts again incorporates a sense of the future as essential to the meaning of hope. The regenerative new growth of the tree, however, does not abolish the cut stump. In Job's way of envisioning hope, its fulfillment does not negate pain and loss but incorporates it into new being. Even in the tree's renewed life, the stump gestures to the now invisible outlines of the tree that once was but is no more.

The most difficult issue still remains. Throughout the book, Job repeatedly raises the objection that death puts an end to hope and so renders talk about hope empty. This association is present in the word play and metaphor of 7:6, in which life is likened to the rapid movement of a shuttle that ceases abruptly, without "thread," or "hope" (תקוה *tiqwâ*). The drained sea and dried-up river of 14:11, the eroded mountain of 14:18-19, and the uprooted tree of 19:10 are all images of the destruction of hope by death. In 17:15-16, Job asks rhetorically whether his hope will accompany him into Sheol. In this way, he exposes the evasion contained in the speech of the friends. In the friends' representation there is always time, always a limitless future to which hope can attach itself; but there is not. To talk of hope without facing the limit of death is dishonest.

In part, the issue is a matter of what one hopes for. The person with an incurable disease needs to give up unrealistic hopes, but that is not the same as giving up hope. Rather, hope is allowed to find its appropriate objects. Such a person's hope may be for the chance to put affairs in order, to seek reconciliation with an estranged loved one, to revisit a place that was important, or simply to find peace. Pursuing those hopes gives meaning to a life that is drawing to a close.

This discussion, however, does not quite get to the issue that Job is raising. Death as a temporal limit is not the whole point, and perhaps not even the main problem for him. Even if Job could be assured of limitless years, that would not necessarily provide him with the power of regeneration. Death is a threat not merely because it cuts off the future, but also because it would make permanent Job's condition of isolation, evocatively described in 14:20-22. At the heart of Job's struggle with despair is the sense of utter isolation. Like the psalmist in Psalm 88, he is as one already dead.

Hope as the power for regeneration, even from moment to moment, is nurtured by the sense of another's presence, communion, and fellowship. That presence is the water that stirs response in dry roots. No one can sustain hope in utter isolation. To that extent, hope is as much a gift of grace as it is an act of courage. The presence of the other sustains and makes possible the energy and even pain involved in regeneration. Despite the implications of Eliphaz's initial comment (4:6), hope is not a facile confidence in full recovery. The content of hope varies and often takes surprising forms, but it is always a green presence. Where there is hope, there is life.

Job's sense that death is the enemy of hope has often led Christian interpreters to see the problem of Job as being solved by resurrection. One must be very careful in thinking about these issues, however, for the notion of resurrection is one that is easily abused. The book of Job itself addresses the problem of Job's hopelessness without recourse to any notion of resurrection, which was not a part of Israel's religious thinking before the Hellenistic period. Thus to see the book as presenting a problem that can only be addressed by resurrection is simply false. Moreover, Job's challenge to the justice of God certainly cannot be addressed by any idea of resurrection and reward. Doing so would be to treat resurrection as religious hush money, used to cover over a moral scandal at the heart of faith.

Christian thinking about resurrection nevertheless does have a place in the dialogue initiated by Job. Resurrection, rooted in the religious imagination of Jewish apocalyptic, represents the inbreaking of the kingdom of God even into the realm of death. No more can death be thought of as a place cut off from the power and presence of God, a place of isolation. As Paul says, "Who will separate us from the love of Christ? Will hardship, or distress, or persecution, or famine, or nakedness, or peril, or sword? . . . I am convinced that neither death, nor life, nor angels, nor rulers, nor things present, nor things to come, nor powers, nor height, nor depth, nor anything else in all creation, will be able to separate us from the love of God in Christ Jesus our Lord" (Rom 8:35, 38 NRSV). In that assurance of ineradicable presence is the ground of hope.

JOB 15:1–21:34, THE SECOND CYCLE

OVERVIEW

With chap. 15, the second cycle of speeches begins. In each cycle, Eliphaz's initial speech plays a key role in setting the theme and tone. The sympathetic concern and didactic content of his speech in chaps. 4–5 established the model of sapiential counseling prominent in the first cycle. In the second cycle, Eliphaz shifts emphasis. The key to this difference lies in Eliphaz's accusation that Job's words are undermining religion (15:4). For the friends the issue becomes defending religious ideology against a blasphemer. What must be defended at all costs is the doctrine of retribution. The importance of this belief can be gauged by the fact that it is the only topic addressed by the friends in the second cycle. Moreover, they each use the same form to do so: a vivid poetic description of the fate of the wicked (15:17-35; 18:5-21; 20:4-29). More than anywhere else in the book, the friends speak here with one voice.

Commentators usually assume that the friends are using the topos of the fate of the wicked to accuse Job of wickedness, even though none of the friends specifically relates his description to Job's case. Although the similarity between Job's own situation and what the friends say about the wicked raises an important question, the structure of the second cycle suggests that at this point the issue is more a struggle over religious ideology than an accusation against Job. During his first two speeches in this cycle (chaps. 16–17 and 19), Job does not directly engage the fate of the wicked, preferring instead to focus on the issue of divine violence. In his third and final speech, however, Job explicitly addresses the matter, directly contradicting all that the friends have said (chap. 21) and prompting the accusations of heinous sin with which Eliphaz will begin the third cycle of speeches.

Job 15:1-35, Eliphaz Describes the Fate of the Wicked

COMMENTARY

Chapter 15 divides into two distinct parts. The first (vv. 2-16) corresponds formally to the introductory remarks by which a speaker justifies his own words or denigrates those of the previous speaker. What has been a brief rhetorical introduction in previous instances (4:2; 6:2-3; 8:2; 9:2a; 11:2-3; 12:2-3), however, occupies fully half of Eliphaz's entire

speech, suggesting that it has a thematic as well as a rhetorical function. The issue Eliphaz engages is religious epistemology—the sources, nature, methods, and limits of knowledge about God and the moral order of the world. Eliphaz begins by discrediting Job's claims to speak as a sage (vv. 2-6), contrasting them with the reliable authority on which the friends' speech is based (vv. 7-10). Eliphaz shames Job for his rash words (vv. 11-13), reminding him of the basic truth about human nature, its inherent corruptness in the eyes of God (vv. 14-16).

In contrast to Job's defective knowledge, Eliphaz sets out reliable knowledge (vv. 17-19). His words are not a rebuttal to a specific argument made by Job but an attempt to refute Job's basic claim: that God's world is morally incoherent. As evidence for the moral order of the world, Eliphaz chooses the traditional topos of the fate of the wicked, who becomes a prey to terrifying anxiety (vv. 20-24) because of his moral hubris (vv. 25-26). Despite initial appearances, the wicked person's fate is dispossession and futility (vv. 27-30), described further in images of profitless commerce, unfruitful vegetation, and barrenness (vv. 31-34). The underlying moral order of the world is evident. It is the wicked who give birth to wickedness (v. 35)—not, as Job has implied, an amoral and irrational God.

15:1-6. Eliphaz's initial rebuke of Job's words in vv. 2-6 has a chiastic structure. Verses 2-3 claim that Job does not speak as a wise person speaks; vv. 5-6 make the contrasting claim that iniquity directs his mouth. At the center of the passage (v. 4) is the scandal itself: What Job is saying destroys religion. Although some commentators suggest that Eliphaz is concerned about Job's destroying his own faith,[240] v. 4 does not support such a limited application of Eliphaz's words. If Job is correct, then God is not worthy of worship.

The term that Eliphaz uses, "fear" (יראה yir'â) is an abbreviation of the phrase "fear of God" (יראת אלהים yir'at 'ĕlōhîm; cf. 1:1, 8). Especially in the wisdom literature, it is the comprehensive term for that orientation to God that organizes a person's understanding and conduct (Ps 111:10; Prov 9:10). "Meditation before God," as Pope observes, has the nuance of the English word *devotion,* in the sense of a religious exercise (see Ps 119:23, 27, 48, 78, 97, 99).[241] From Eliphaz's conventional perspective the trusting, submissive relationship necessary for such piety is destroyed by the way Job speaks. It would be completely alien to Eliphaz's understanding that Job's words could be a terrible but faithful meditation before God.

Eliphaz's values are also implicit in the way he says that a wise person should speak. Such words should be "useful" and "profitable" (v. 3), or as one might say today, constructive rather than negative. Characterizing Job's words as "wind" (v. 2) marks them as empty (cf. Isa 41:29; Eccl 1:14, 17) and perhaps also as destructive (cf. 1:19; Hos 12:1[2]). Eliphaz's defensiveness is such that he cannot entertain the question of whether critical speech directed toward God (or toward traditional beliefs about God) is true or false. By its very nature, it must be false; therefore, it serves to indict the one who speaks it (v. 6). Moreover, one can deduce from such speech the motives giving rise to it, motives that cannot be noble but must be of the same nature as the speech itself (v. 5). To one not sharing his perspective, Eliphaz's logic is hopelessly circular. From his own perspective, however, his certainty is a legitimate deduction from the unquestionable truth that God is just.

There is no doubt that Eliphaz here accuses Job of sin, specifically the sin of speaking blasphemously and destructively. Possibly, Eliphaz's words in vv. 5-6 also mean that he now believes Job to be a "hardened sinner and rebel against God."[242] More likely, Eliphaz is himself caught in a contradiction of perception that he does not know how to resolve. He believes that Job is fundamentally a person of integrity who fears God, as he said in 4:6. Yet now Job is destroying "fear of God" by speaking in the rash and angry way Eliphaz warned against in 5:2. Not until chap. 22 will Eliphaz resolve the contradiction by concluding that Job is, and has long been, an evil person. Even then Eliphaz will hold out the possibility of redemption to Job. The way he resolves the cognitive dissonance, however, reveals much about Eliphaz. Faced with a contradiction between his personal knowledge of the goodness of his friend and that friend's rejection of the religious ideology by which they both had lived, Eliphaz chooses faithfulness to ideology over faithfulness to his friend.

240. See Andersen, *Job,* 175; Hartley, *The Book of Job,* 245; Clines, *Job 1–20,* 348.

241. Pope, *Job,* 114.

242. Pope, *Job,* 114. Clines, *Job 1–20,* 346-54, overstates the case for Eliphaz as a sympathetic voice in chap. 15, but his remarks are a good counter to the prevailing opinion.

15:7-10. In vv. 2-6, Eliphaz attacked Job's words on the basis of their destructive effect. In vv. 7-10, he takes on the issue of authority. Job had claimed authority on the basis of what "my eye has seen . . . my ear has heard" (13:1 NRSV). In vv. 7-8, Eliphaz attacks the individualism implicit in Job's assertion. The only *individual* who could claim authentic knowledge superior to the communal knowledge of the elders would be the "firstborn of the human race" (v. 7). Here Eliphaz invokes an old creation tradition, different from the canonical story of Genesis 2–3, but one that has left its traces in Ezekiel 28. Later Jewish tradition combined this myth with the Genesis account to produce a portrait of primordial Adam, perfect in wisdom and beauty.[243] Not only in Israel, but also in Mesopotamia, the earliest inhabitants of the earth, especially those from "before the flood," were believed to possess exceptional knowledge, because the lines separating the divine and human realms were not so sharply drawn. Eliphaz's words describe the firstborn human as birthed "before the hills" and as one who listens in the "council of God," the assembly of divine beings who consult with God (cf. 1 Kgs 22:19-22; Ps 82; Jer 23:18). In the wisdom tradition, these characteristics of the firstborn human were applied to personified wisdom itself (Prov 8:22-31; Sir 24:1-12). Thus Eliphaz mocks what appears to him as Job's arrogance and pretense to superior knowledge, citing Job's own words (13:1) in v. 9.

How does one establish a claim to superior knowledge? In Eliphaz's opinion, two criteria authenticate wisdom: age and consensus. Both of these criteria are invoked in v. 10, where Eliphaz refers to the "gray-haired and the aged," who are in agreement with what the friends have been saying. Job had dismissed both age and consensus in his parody of the wisdom of the aged in chap. 12 and in his championing of individual judgment (13:2). In Eliphaz's opinion, since no ordinary person can claim the superior knowledge of the firstborn human (vv. 7-8), the surest source of reliable wisdom is that preserved in the communal tradition of the elders, passed down from generation to generation (cf. Ps 78:1-4).

15:11-13. There is poignancy in Eliphaz's words about the "consolations of God" and the "word that deals gently" (v. 11), by which he refers to his own attempt to counsel Job according to ancestral traditions (chaps. 4–5). Eliphaz knows that every person and every society must face painful and perplexing aspects of life and attempt to integrate them into some structure of meaning.[244] Although Eliphaz might not agree, there is always an element of denial, a compromise with reality, in such attempts. Nevertheless, some such peacemaking with the pain of existence is necessary if one is to continue to live. What Eliphaz sees clearly is the price one pays for rejecting such "consolations": alienation from God expressed in just such angry words as Job has used (v. 13). What Eliphaz cannot fathom is the turn of mind (v. 12; in Hebrew, the heart [לבּ *lēb*] is the organ of reason) that leads Job to choose alienation over consolation.

15:14-16. The teaching that Eliphaz chooses to restate from his previous speech (cf. 4:17-19) is not randomly chosen, but shows that Eliphaz has heard Job clearly. Job's resistance to traditional wisdom is grounded in his insistence that he is innocent (9:15, 21; 10:23-24). Eliphaz argues that such a claim is literally nonsensical, since no human being is innocent before God (v. 14). He even uses the comprehensive "born of woman," which Job himself had employed (14:1). As in chap. 4, Eliphaz invokes the comparison with heavenly beings to argue from the greater to the lesser (v. 15). The terms Eliphaz uses to characterize human nature, "abhorrent" (נתעב *nitā'b*) and "corrupt" (נאלח *ne'ĕlāḥ*) are strongly emotive words, suggesting the almost visceral revulsion he imagines God to feel. The image of human beings "drinking iniquity like water" is a vivid and economical representation of the idea that sin is both intentional (since drinking, unlike breathing, is a conscious act) and unavoidable (since one must drink water to live). In this way of thinking, Job's claim to innocence is meaningless.

By themselves, Eliphaz's words do not look much like consolation to modern readers. One must place them in the context of ancient Near Eastern religious assumptions and practices. In Israel, as in Mesopotamia, it was assumed that God related to human

---

243. See R. Gordis, "The Significance of the Paradise Myth," *AJSL* 52 (1936) 86-94.

244. Cf. Berger, *The Sacred Canopy*, 53-80.

beings in a number of different ways. From the perspective of justice, God distinguished between the righteous and the wicked. From the perspective of loving creator, God's mercy was like that of a parent for a child. From the perspective of transcendent purity, however, divine revulsion at human iniquity could cause God to turn away God's protecting presence from an individual, or even to unleash divine wrath. Eliphaz seems to suspect that, for unknown reasons, Job has somehow become the object of such divine revulsion at corrupt human nature. If Job leaves this possibility out of consideration, he cannot make sense of his situation. By attending to Eliphaz's counsel, Job can not only understand his situation, but also act to change it. Ancient traditions of prayer recognize the great gulf between divine being and human being and God's wrath at corrupt human nature (e.g., Ps 90:1-12), but they also appeal to God to set aside this way of perceiving human existence and to draw instead on divine mercy (e.g., Ps 90:13-17; cf. also Psalm 25). Ultimately, God's love proves more profound than God's revulsion at inherent human sinfulness. Prayer is answered, and the relationship is restored. These are the consolations of God, traditional religion's way of coping with the inexplicable sorrows of life.[245]

15:17-19. Eliphaz introduces the second part of his speech with an instruction formula (v. 17). Like Job, he refers to "what he has seen," but Eliphaz does not privilege individual experience as such. For him there can be no contradiction between individual experience and the teaching of the sages, which goes back to ancestral tradition (v. 18). As Clines puts it, Eliphaz "has sold his soul to tradition, and has so ensured that he will never have any experience that runs counter to it."[246] Eliphaz's statement that this tradition comes from a time when there was no alien in the land is not well understood but appears to suggest the unadulterated origin of the tradition to which he is heir.

15:20-24. Eliphaz wants Job to accept the fact, articulated in vv. 14-16, that all human beings are vile before God, so that Job can understand how he, a basically righteous

person, has nevertheless been subject to such suffering. Although that insight is necessary for accounting for certain apparent anomalies, it is not the central fact about the world. Eliphaz and his friends believe deeply that the moral order of the world nurtures good and rejects evil. This is the conviction that Eliphaz expressed at the beginning of his first speech (4:7-8) and of which Job appears to be losing sight (cf. 12:4-6).

One common way of dealing with the apparent contradiction that the wicked prosper is to argue that their retribution is only delayed (e.g., Psalms 37; 73). Eliphaz, however, makes the more sophisticated argument that the wicked are already in torment ("all the days" of the wicked, "all the years" in store for the ruthless, v. 20). He takes the traditional belief that the wicked have no security (cf. 8:13; 11:20; Ps 73:18; Prov 12:3) and reflects on the psychological implications of knowing that destruction is certain to occur (vv. 22*b*, 23*b*), but at an unknown time (v. 21*b*). The anticipation of disaster creates present terror. Verse 21 is best understood as depicting the subjective state of the wicked person, in which every sound is interpreted as a harbinger of destruction that could erupt even in the midst of apparent peace. Such insecurity leads to loss of confidence (v. 22*a*). The same Hebrew letters in v. 23*a* can be read one way to state that the wicked person wanders about searching for food (so NRSV, following MT) or in another way to say that the wicked wanders about as food for vultures (so NIV, following LXX). The clustering of images of violence and destruction ("sword" in v. 22*b* and "day of darkness" in v. 23*b*; cf. Amos 5:18-20) makes the image of the wicked as carrion quite apt. Being eaten by birds and animals is the fate of those defeated in battle (cf. Ezek 32:4-6; 39:5); the wicked, however, experience themselves as carrion even though they are not yet slain. The psychic insecurity that terrifies the wicked finally takes shape as the image of an attacking king (v. 24).

15:25-26. The wisdom tradition was quite taken by the notion that actions rebound on their perpetrators with a kind of poetic justice (e.g., Prov 26:27). So here, there is an ironic appropriateness that the wicked person's terrors take the shape of a warrior, since his own

---

245. See further T. Jacobsen, "Personal Religion," in *Treasures of Darkness* (New Haven: Yale University Press, 1976) 147-64.

246. Clines, *Job 1–20*, 355.

sin was to "play the hero" against God (vv. 25-26). Note that the NRSV breaks the passage differently, reading vv. 25-27 as reasons for the consequences described in vv. 28-30. In the NIV, vv. 25-26 give the cause for the psychological terror of vv. 20-24. Verse 27 introduces a separate section that is organized around another motif: the inability of the wicked person to retain the good fortune that is briefly and tantalizingly his.

15:27-30. Commentators are quite divided about the moral significance of the wicked person's fat (v. 27),[247] in part because the OT itself reflects an ambivalent attitude toward fatness. On one occasion, obesity figures as a crucial detail in a satirical story (Judges 3), but obesity is generally not what the biblical text has in mind when it refers to fatness. In an agricultural economy in which famine and scarcity are recurrent problems (see, e.g., Gen 12:10; 26:1; 41:25-32; Ruth 1:1), fatness is positively associated with adequate food, good health, strength, and security (2 Sam 1:22; Neh 9:25). Negative associations arise when security becomes complacency and satiety becomes self-satisfaction (Deut 32:15; Ps 119:70; Jer 5:28). If one takes v. 27 as introducing the following verses (so NIV), then fatness represents the material good fortune that fails to provide security for the wicked.

To dwell in uninhabited ruins (v. 28) is to be dispossessed from human society. Such places were deeply dreaded as the haunt of hostile animals and demons (Isa 13:19-22; 34:8-15; Jer 50:39-40; 51:37-44).[248] In the poetic tradition they are often described as godforsaken, compared with Sodom and Gomorrah. Such lands are the opposite of the rich, settled agricultural land such as Israel was promised, where "you shall eat your fill and bless the LORD your God for the good land" (Deut 8:10 NRSV; see Deut 8:7-10).

The motif of the instability of the wicked person's good fortune continues in v. 29. As Gordis argues, the point is not whether the wicked person can become rich, but that he or she cannot remain rich (cf. Prov 13:11).[249]

Although the last part of the verse is obscure (the meaning of מִנְלָם [minlām] is not certain), the general point is clear.

Verse 30 summarizes the fate of the wicked. The first line echoes v. 22*a*, with the emphasis now on external event rather than internal fear. As in Bildad's allegory of the withering plant (8:11-13), Eliphaz uses the image of a sun-blasted sprout to suggest the insubstantiality of the wicked person's flourishing. Once again the end of the line is obscure. A slight emendation produces a continuation of the plant metaphor (so NRSV).[250] Others read the MT's "the breath of his mouth" as a reference to God's action (so NIV) or to that of personified death.[251]

15:31-35. The admonition in v. 31 gives the principle that explains the fate of the wicked: Relying on nothingness provides nothing on which to rely. The examples that illustrate the results of such behavior are somewhat akin to futility curses in which a person's actions fail to produce normal consequences (see Deut 28:30, 38-41). Some commentators object to the introduction of a commercial metaphor in vv. 31*b*-32, emending the text to produce a consistent plant metaphor.[252] Quickly changing metaphors are not alien to Hebrew poetry, however, and the notion of being paid back emptiness in full, even before the due date, is a striking image of an ironically futile commercial transaction. The images of the vine that casts its grapes prematurely and of olive fruit that fails to set are related to traditional images of divine curse and punishment (cf. Deut 28:40; Isa 18:5). Here they are simply the outward manifestation of the emptiness on which the wicked person is established. Similarly, barrenness and the loss of one's tent, conventional images of the family (29:4-5), reinforce the motif of the inability of the wicked to be established (v. 34).

Although the last verse is related to v. 34 through its use of birth imagery, its point is quite different. Verse 35 focuses not on the self-depleting and self-destroying nature of the wicked but on the way the wicked bring trouble and deceit into being. On its own

247. For negative views, see Pope, *Job*, 118; Habel, *The Book of Job*, 259; Dhorme, *A Commentary on the Book of Job*, 221; Andersen, *Job*, 178. For positive views, see Fohrer, *Das Buch Hiob*, 275; Clines, *Job 1–20*, 360.

248. O. Keel, *Jahwes Entgegnung an Ijob*, FRLANT 121 (Goettingen: Vandenhoeck & Ruprecht, 1978) 64-65.

249. Gordis, *The Book of Job*, 165.

250. Dhorme, *A Commentary on the Book of Job*, 223; Clines, *Job 1–20*, 344.

251. Habel, *The Book of Job*, 248.

252. Tur-Sinai, *The Book of Job*, 259; Habel, *The Book of Job*, 248; Clines, *Job 1–20*, 344; Hartley, *The Book of Job*, 250; Pope, *Job*, 119.

terms it is an example of the traditional wisdom claim that like begets like. In the context of the dialogues, however, it responds to Job's claim that God produces social futility and destruction (12:14-25). On the contrary, Eliphaz argues that the world is morally coherent. The wicked generate trouble, but because they derive their being from nothingness, that nothingness ultimately claims them.

REFLECTIONS

The intensity of Eliphaz's attack on Job's claims and his defensiveness about his own words indicate the presence of a crisis in religious knowledge. The particular issue of whether Eliphaz or Job is right is in many respects less significant than the broader questions. What makes a claim about the world trustworthy and reliable? What is the authority for believing anything? What makes such claims and beliefs persuasive—to oneself as well as to others?

The crisis in knowledge in the book of Job does not concern simple facts: whether it was Sabeans or Edomites who made off with Job's cattle, or whether Job's disease is leprosy or something else. The question that triggers the crisis is, What does it all mean? How is one to make sense of what has happened? What can one know about how the world works, so that one knows its moral foundation—or whether there *is* a moral foundation to the world? How does one know where to place one's trust, what to value, how to choose what to do or what stance to take? These are the perennial questions of religion, of philosophy, of ethics, and of politics. Although they may become quite abstract, such questions most often arise out of dilemmas posed by very concrete situations, as in Job.

The book of Job is not a treatise on religious epistemology. It does, however, offer an opportunity to experience characters attempting to state their beliefs persuasively and to defend them authoritatively. How they go about this business is actually quite similar to the way people today talk about the bases for their beliefs. Although the friends make many different arguments and appeals in the course of their speeches, these can be roughly grouped into three types, depending on the nature of the authority the friends invoke. First is the appeal to external (i.e., non-human) authority. Second is the appeal to consensus within the human community. Third is the appeal to individual experience. Although some of these appeals are explicit and self-conscious, in many instances the friends may not be aware that they are making such claims. Rather, authenticating words and phrases are woven into speech as a natural part of talking. Once one begins to listen for such attempts to underwrite the truth, one discovers that they are a constant presence, in both the friends' speech and one's own.

The appeal to external authority in the friends' speeches takes two forms. One is the claim of direct divine revelation (e.g., 4:17-19; cf. 11:5-6). This kind of an appeal to authority is fairly rare in modern religious language, but it does occur. The televangelist may say that God has revealed to him God's plans for a mighty, new ministry, for which he is now soliciting funds. In a more subtle form, one also hears people speak of God's guidance in a difficult decision or God's showing them the truth about themselves, which they had not wanted to see. Whatever one thinks about the content of the claim, the appeal to authority is similar. The insight is claimed to be reliable because it comes from God.

The other appeal to external authority is the appeal to nature. Analogies with nature are virtually universal in the moral language of human cultures[253] and are very common in the friends' speeches (e.g., 4:10-11, 19; 5:6-7; 8:10-19). Their persuasive force seems to reside in the assumption that the same structure underlies all of creation.

---

253. M. Douglas, *How Institutions Think* (Syracuse, N.Y.: Syracuse University Press, 1986) 45-53.

Significant patterns that are more easily identified in the plant or animal world can be transferred to illumine the truth about human experience. For example, talking about the "seasons" of a person's life authenticates the claim that certain tasks or experiences are characteristic of different ages by invoking the analogy of the very different activities that occur in nature in spring, summer, autumn, and winter.

The second category, the appeal to the authority of consensus, is perhaps the most pervasive. When everyone else believes something to be so, it is extremely difficult to believe otherwise. People seldom explicitly say that they believe something just because everybody else does, but the appeal to the authority of consensus is reflected in the way people use certain catch-words and slogans that are on everyone's lips. These words seem true because others use them, and no one challenges them. The rhetoric of biblical inerrancy sounds self-evidently true in a fundamentalist church; the rhetoric of historical criticism sounds self-evidently true in a modernist church. Similarly, in Job, the friends' astonishment that Job does not agree with what seems so obvious to them is manifested in every speech they make. Consensus among the contemporary community is a weighty claim, but it is made even stronger when it is connected with the authority of tradition, which is a consensus that spans generations.

In the third category, claims to truth are grounded in an appeal to individual experience. The claim "this happened to me" or "I saw this myself" (5:3) is powerful. More generally, anecdotes of various kinds are persuasive not only because they "actually happened," but also because they cast complex issues in personal terms. The personal dimension makes them seem more immediate and emotionally involving. In contemporary political rhetoric, the anecdote is one of the most frequently used persuasive devices, as anecdotes about the abuse of a government program serve to arouse public sentiment against the program, or anecdotes about the violation of human rights in a foreign country garner support for sanctions against that country.

The problem with all of these appeals to authority, of course, is that they prove nothing. The ancient world, no less than the modern, was aware of the difficulty of distinguishing true from false revelation. Analogies from nature can be used to support contradictory propositions, and Job is as adept at invoking nature as are his friends. Consensus is vulnerable to the weakness of collective opinion. As an ancient Egyptian proverb puts it, "one who raves with the crowd is not counted a fool." Nor is tradition a guarantee. There are old lies, as well as old truths. Even experience is no guarantee of truth. For every anecdote there is one that points in the opposite direction. Not every event has genuine explanatory power. Some things may be true in the sense that they actually happened but may be quite false if taken as indicative of underlying reality.

But where does this leave us? Cynicism is no resting place. Every human society must have a broadly shared commitment to certain basic beliefs and values if it is to be a moral community. As much as people would like to have a simple and definitive way of establishing those truths, however, there is no shortcut. The work of establishing moral values requires a great deal of listening to many voices—voices of tradition, voices of dissent. The moral understandings of a community must always be under negotiation, as aspects of that community's beliefs are reexamined, challenged, overturned, or reaffirmed. The reader is given access to one such negotiation in the book of Job. This process can be painful, and it is easy to understand the appeal of simplistic alternatives, such as one finds in the bumper-sticker assertion: "God said it. I believe it. That settles it." Such a comment is both deceptive and evasive, however. It is deceptive because it pretends that one does not have to be an active listener to the word of God, which must be taken into ever-changing situations. It is evasive because it seeks to avoid moral responsibility for interpreting what it means to be faithful to God in the face of unanticipated circumstances.

There is no escape from the hard work of moral dialogue, no escape from trying to give an account of one's values and commitments and the bases for them, no escape from listening to a person whose experience runs counter to one's own. Such a process does not mean embracing a lazy relativism or an abandonment of judgment. On the contrary, when one realizes that there is no simple appeal to the answer book, the act of moral judgment takes on a weighty seriousness. Nor does it mean disregarding the authority of divine disclosure, the teachings of nature, tradition, the prevailing consensus of the community, or personal experience. Each of these is a resource for the work of moral reflection, but none of them alone suffices. God has made humans as moral beings and entrusted us with the work of creating communities of value in an ever-changing world. Fidelity to God lies in the honesty and openness with which we take up the task, as it also lies in the concrete commitments we make.

Job 16:1–17:16, Job Complains of God's Criminal Violence

COMMENTARY

In the opening speech of the second cycle, Eliphaz had bitterly criticized Job for undermining piety (15:4), amazed at Job's disdain for the traditional consolations of religion (15:11). Job's reply ridicules the inadequacy of conventional responses (16:1-6). Job's alienation from traditional religious language becomes evident as he takes up one form of traditional lament language that would seem adequate to his situation: the depiction of God as adversary (16:7-17; cf. Lam 3:1-20). Just at the point at which the traditional form would lead to acceptance and prayerful turning to God (cf. Lam 3:21), Job disrupts the form, calling out in legal language for the avenging of his blood and an advocate who will vindicate his name (16:18-21).

The impending death, which lends urgency to his words (16:22), also undermines his hope. Job is exhausted by the mockery to which God has exposed him (17:1-7). Ironically, Job has become an object lesson that reinforces the complacent certainties of the "upright" (17:8-10). Even the reassurances of his friends (17:11-12) are fatuous because they fail to deal seriously with the power of death to destroy hope (17:13-16).

16:1-6. As usual, Job's speech begins with criticism of the friends' words. The structure of the passage is obscured by the inability of English translations to distinguish between "you" (plural) and "you" (singular). In vv. 2 and 4-5, Job uses the plural. In v. 3, he uses the singular. Since Job does not ordinarily address the friends individually, it is more

likely that v. 3 represents Job's quotation of what the friends have said to him (cf. 15:2).[254]

Job's characterization of the friends in v. 2b exploits an ambiguity in Hebrew syntax. The phrase is literally "comforters of misery," and that is undoubtedly how the friends see themselves. In Hebrew, however, the prepositional phrase "of misery" can also be the equivalent of an adjective, hence "miserable comforters." The quotation in v. 3 illustrates how the friends increase rather than comfort Job's misery. Job represents them as asking what ails him to make him keep arguing (v. 3b). They should not need to ask. What ails Job physically is apparent to the eye. What ails him emotionally is what he has been trying to say. The friends refuse to see or to hear him as he really is, and this is what makes them miserable comforters.

Job criticizes the conventional, ready-made quality of traditional consolation. Already in v. 2a he devalues it by saying that he has heard "many things like these." As in chap. 12, where Job gave an imitation of a wisdom speech, so here, Job says that he, too, knows how to console (vv. 4-5). The nuance of these verses can be taken in various ways. Many understand Job to be saying that he would know how to be unsympathetic but would choose instead to be a genuine comforter (NIV).[255] More plausibly, Job may be saying

---

254. Clines, *Job 1–20*, 378-79. Other commentators understand Job to be addressing Eliphaz in v. 3. E.g., Hartley, *The Book of Job*, 257; Fohrer, *Das Buch Hiob*, 284; Habel, *The Book of Job*, 271.

255. E.g., Clines, *Job 1–20*, 379-80; Habel, *The Book of Job*, 271; Hartley, *The Book of Job*, 257.

that he, too, is master of all the various strategies of conventional consolation. He knows how to be critical (v. 4a) or to nod in sympathy (v. 4b; to "shake the head" can be a positive as well as a negative gesture). He knows how to speak strengthening words (v. 5a) or how to be silent (v. 5b; the line can be translated "sympathy would restrain my lips").[256] He is as well-trained a sapiential counselor as any of them (cf. 4:3-4) and could perform as well, if the roles were reversed. Job's suffering has taught him the hollowness of the wisdom he had shared with the friends. It has not, however, given him words that will assuage such affliction. Nothing, neither speech nor silence, lessens the pain (v. 6).

16:7-17. Job does not speak in order to ease his pain; he speaks in order to discover the truth about his situation. In vv. 7-17, Job speaks vividly of God as his adversary. Many readers are shocked by the descriptions of divine violence. In order to understand this passage, however, one must recognize that Job speaks in thoroughly traditional terms. The biblical lament tradition includes a way of speaking about affliction that understands some suffering as direct divine violence. Elements of this language occur in the psalms (e.g., Pss 32:4; 38:2[3]; 39:10b[11b]), but it is most clearly represented in Lamentations 3. Even though the book of Lamentations responds to the national catastrophe of Zion's destruction, chap. 3 takes the form of an individual lament. Lamentations 3 and Job 16:7-17 share so many similarities, both general and particular, that it is possible Job alludes specifically to that lament. If not, he certainly engages this type of lament.

16:7-8. These verses introduce the lament. Oddly, the verbs switch from third person in v. 7a to second person in vv. 7b and 8a, and back to third person in vv. 9-14. Although some scholars defend the alternation as consistent with Hebrew poetic style,[257] it is more likely that the passage, as description, should be in the third person throughout.[258] Themes of personal exhaustion and isolation from a community of support, introduced in v. 7, will be developed in chap. 17 (vv. 1-2, 7-9, 11-14). Verse 8 is more closely related to the imagery of the rest of chap. 16, specifically that of the body (prominent in vv. 9-17) and forensic imagery (developed in vv. 18-21). At one level, Job's comment simply alludes to the common assumption that emaciation resulting from illness is a sign of divine punishment for sin.[259] By invoking the image of his own body as a hostile witness, however, Job indicates the way this religious belief results in an inescapable self-alienation (cf. 9:20, where Job imagines his own mouth betraying him).

16:9-14. Divine violence is more directly depicted through a series of increasingly intense images. The sequence begins in v. 9 with a personification of God's anger (lit., "his anger tore me and hated me"). Through the verb "to tear" (טרף ṭārap), God is implicitly visualized as an animal attacking prey. Such a comparison is quite rare, but significantly occurs in Lam 3:10-11 (see also Hos 5:14; 6:1). The image is concretely developed through reference to the parts of the face that convey focused rage: gnashing teeth and "sharpened" eyes. Even the word for "anger" is an old facial metaphor, literally, "nose" (אף ʾap). For Job, this savage malice is the face of God.

In strictly logical terms, one might expect v. 11, which describes how God has given Job over into the power of the wicked, to precede v. 10, which describes their assault on Job. The transition, however, is more cinematic than logical. The visual focus on the threatening face of God in v. 9 bleeds into the image of the gaping mouths of the crowd. The devouring God is merged with the jeering crowd. Such overlap is not incidental. In laments, the aggression of a human mob is often taken as a sign that God has forsaken or is punishing the speaker (e.g., Pss 22:12-13[13-14]; Lam 3:30).

Military images dominate the second part of the description (vv. 12-14). In Job's words, the violence is presented as personal physical assault(seizing by the neck; cf. Gen 49:8). Its annihilating character is suggested by the choice of verbs, which not only denote a shattering into pieces but also are employed elsewhere to describe God as a divine warrior "breaking open" (פרר pārar; see Ps 74:13)

256. Gordis, *The Book of Job,* 175.
257. Gordis, *The Book of Job,* 175.
258. Clines, *Job 1–20,* 381 (so NRSV). The NIV makes all verbs in vv. 7-8 second person, adding "O God" to the text for clarity.

259. For "shrivel" (NRSV) instead of "bound" (NIV) see S. R. Driver and G. B. Gray, *A Critical and Exegetical Commentary on the Book of Job,* ICC (Edinburgh: T. & T. Clark, 1921) Part II, 105; Gordis, *The Book of Job,* 176.

the chaotic sea and "shattering" (פצץ *pāṣaṣ*; see Hab 3:6) the mountains. What the English reader misses, however, is the powerful effect generated by the repetition of sounds in v. 12, which suggests the relentlessly repeated assaults of God (ויפצפצני . . . ויפדפרני *wayparpĕrēnî . . . waypaṣpĕṣēnî*). A similar device is used in v. 14, where the breaking of Job is expressed in Hebrew as יפרצני פרץ על־פני־פרץ (*yiprĕṣēnî pereṣ 'al-pĕnê-pāreṣ*; lit., "he breaches me breach upon breach").

In vv. 12c-13, the assault is reimaged as an arrow attack against Job as the target. As in vv. 9-11, the agency of the attack is fluid, alternately God and the archers whom God directs. The image of being helpless, surrounded, and attacked appears frequently in the lament tradition (Pss 22:12-13[13-14]; 31:21b[22b]; 35:15). Here, however, the image culminates in the fatal penetration of Job's body by God's arrows (cf. 6:4; Ps 38:2[3]; and esp. Lam 3:12-13). To the modern reader, the kidneys are simply internal organs particularly susceptible to pain and essential to life. To the ancient reader, however, the kidneys were not only a part of the physical body but also a central part of the emotional being. We often speak in symbolic terms about a person's heart as the emotional center, and the Hebrew word for "kidneys" (כליה *kilyâ*) is often translated as "heart" to capture that nuance. In describing the intimacy of divine creation, the psalmist says "you formed my kidneys" (Ps 139:13). Here that symbol of intimacy becomes the site of violent assault. Job's pairing of the image of the assaulted kidneys with that of gall spilled upon the ground is evocative. Similar to the way the English word *gall* has an emotional as well as a physical nuance, the Hebrew for "gall" (מררה *mĕrērâ*) is related to the word meaning "bitter" (מרר *mārōr*). As Clines remarks, "If the affections and sympathies are assaulted, it is bitterness that spills out."[260]

In the final image of violence, Job represents himself as a besieged city (v. 14; cf. Lam 3:5-9, where the speaker is besieged and imprisoned by God). Job does not develop the image as one of constriction, as Lamentations does. Instead, Job exploits the image of the breaching of the city wall. Like the preceding

figure of an arrow that tears the kidneys, the breaching is an image of forced penetration, not just once but "breach upon breach." Attributing this violence to God the warrior sets up various echoes. In contrast to Eliphaz, who represented the wicked as one who charges against God like a warrior (15:25-27), Job claims that it is God who attacks him. More disturbingly, the image of God as warrior was traditionally a positive image of the one who fights for Israel (Exod 15:3-4; Ps 24:8; Isa 42:13) and for the suffering psalmist (Pss 7:12[13]; 64:7[8]).[261] Here, as in Lamentations 3, God the warrior's violence is turned against the one who laments.

16:15-16. Throughout this section, the image of violence against the body has become increasingly savage and invasive, from the insult of having one's cheek slapped (v. 10), to being seized by the neck (v. 12), to having one's kidneys pierced (v. 13), to having one's body broken open like a breached city invaded by hostile warriors (v. 14). In vv. 15-16, Job describes the effects of such violence. Although sackcloth is a familiar image of mourning (Gen 37:34; 2 Kgs 6:30; Ps 35:13), there is no other reference to sewing it upon oneself. Perhaps Job suggests that his grief is so profound that he will never be able to leave off mourning, and so the symbolic garments may be permanently sewn in place as a second skin (cf. Ps 30:11[12]). The paired image, literally, "I have thrust my horn in the dust," connotes abject humiliation, a reversal of the uplifted bull's horn, commonly used as a metaphor of strength (1 Sam 2:1; Pss 75:4-5[5-6]; 92:10[11]). Dust itself is symbolic both of the humiliation of one defeated and of the abjection of one who grieves (cf. Lam 3:16, 29). Finally, the furious face of God, who savages Job (v. 9), which introduced this description of violence, contrasts with the closing image of Job's face (v. 16), reddened by weeping (cf. Lam 2:11) and marked not just with darkness but with the dark "shadow of death" (צלמות *ṣalmāwet*).

16:17. At this point, the comparison with Lamentations 3 is crucial for understanding Job 16. In Lamentations 3, the transition between the recital of divine violence and the

260. Clines, *Job 1–20*, 385.

261. For a discussion of the motif of God as divine warrior, see F. M. Cross, *Canaanite Myth and Hebrew Epic* (Cambridge, Mass.: Harvard University Press, 1973) 91-111; P. D. Miller, *The Divine Warrior in Early Israel*, HSM 5 (Cambridge, Mass.: Harvard University Press, 1973).

rest of the poem begins with the comment, "But this I call to mind,/ and therefore I have hope:/ the mercies of God do not end" (Lam 3:20). In the following verses, the speaker reflects on God's goodness (Lam 3:21-24) and the appropriateness of accepting affliction quietly (Lam 3:25-30), because it comes reluctantly from God, as punishment for sin (Lam 3:31-39). Consequently, one should confess and turn to God (Lam 3:40-42), portraying to God vividly the suffering God has inflicted (Lam 3:43-48). The pattern of plea to God and description of suffering recurs throughout the rest of the chapter (Lam 3:49-66).

Job has imitated the pattern of the lament in vv. 7-16 in order to portray God's violence against him. At the point where the traditional form would direct Job to accept his suffering and confess his guilt, however, he ruptures the form by asserting his innocence. Some have suggested that Job is here echoing another cultic form of speech, the declaration of righteousness (cf. Pss 17:1; 24:4).[262] Habel argues that the terminology has a legal resonance.[263] In either case, Job breaks the cultural form and the way it seeks to direct and control the experience of affliction. One cannot go on with the lament after v. 17.

16:18-22. Unlike Job's use of parody to disrupt traditional forms of speech in 7:17-18 and 12:13-25, here Job uses the technique of juxtaposing the discourse of the lament with discourse of a very different type: legal speech. Whether or not Habel is correct about v. 17, the legal language in vv. 18-21 is explicit. Job invokes the ancient principle that shed blood must be avenged (Gen 9:5-6; cf. Num 35:16-21). If blood was covered over and not perceived, then the crime might not be avenged (Isa 26:21; Ezek 24:7-8). Calling upon the earth not to cover his blood (v. 18a), Job invokes the image of the murdered Abel (Gen 4:10). The parallel line in v. 18b is part of the same image, since Abel's blood, too, is personified as "crying out from the earth." By invoking this tradition, Job names God's violence against him as murder, not justified punishment, as the lament tradition would interpret it.

Even before his death, Job seeks legal vindication for the injustice done to him. Corresponding to the help he pleads for from the earth, Job also looks for help from heaven in the form of a witness who will advocate for him (v. 19). Widespread attempts to interpret the heavenly witness as none other than God[264] are not grounded in the text but result from an anachronistic imposition of monotheistic categories.[265] As v. 21 makes clear, Job speaks of someone who will argue his case *with God.* The type of figure Job envisions is one like the angel of Yahweh in Zechariah 3, who defends the high priest against the accusations of the *satan.* Such a figure is mentioned by other characters in the book of Job itself, both by Eliphaz, who doubts the willingness of the "holy ones" to answer Job's call (5:1), and by Elihu, who is confident that an angel will intercede with God on behalf of an essentially upright person who has fallen into sin and is punished by God (33:23-26).[266] Although Job had earlier rejected as impossible the notion of a mediator who could adjudicate between himself and God (9:33), here he speaks not of a judge but of an advocate, similar to the redeemer/avenger to whom he will refer in 19:25.

Unfortunately, the text of v. 20 is obscure and ambiguous. Pope outlines the alternative readings of v. 20a succinctly: "My interpreter[s]/scorner[s] [is/are] my friend[s]/ thought[s]/shepherd[s]."[267] These alternatives are not all equally plausible, however. The NIV's translation of v. 20a is more likely than that of the NRSV, since the Hebrew word מליץ (*mēlîṣ*) elsewhere refers to an intermediary of some sort, a translator (Gen 43:23), advocate (Job 33:23), envoy (2 Chr 32:31), spokesperson (Isa 43:27), or minister of a ruler (Sir 10:2), but does not otherwise mean "scorner," which is expressed by the Hebrew word ליץ (*lēṣ*). Since the word translated "friend" (רע *rēaʿ*) is spelled the same as that meaning "thoughts," it is possible to translate "interpreter of my thoughts."[268] Yet Job does

262. Hartley, *The Book of Job,* 262; similarly, Fohrer, *Das Buch Hiob,* 290, citing Isa 53:9 and 1 Chr 12:18.

263. Habel, *The Book of Job,* 265, following S. Scholnick, "Lawsuit Drama in the Book of Job" (Ph.D. diss., Brandeis University, 1975) 27n. 37.

264. Dhorme, *A Commentary on the Book of Job,* 239; Rowley, *The Book of Job,* 121; Fohrer, *Das Buch Hiob,* 292; Andersen, *Job,* 183.

265. Contra Gordis, *The Book of Job,* 527.

266. Clines (*Job 1–20,* 390) interprets the witness as a personification of Job's own outcry (v. 18). Zuckerman, *Job the Silent,* 115, understands the figure as an imaginary divine figure, a countergod conjured out of the traditional imagery of God as champion of the oppressed.

267. Pope, *Job,* 125.

268. So Pope, *Job,* 125-26.

not need someone to explain his thoughts to God, a task he handles quite well on his own. What he needs is a member of the heavenly council who can intervene on his behalf with God.[269] How Job would conduct himself while his advocate speaks for him is obscured by a difficult word (v. 20). Hebrew דלף (*dālap*) may mean "drip" (hence, "my eyes pour out tears"), or it may mean "be sleepless" (hence, "my eyes look sleeplessly to God").[270] What is most important, however, is not Job's weeping or sleeplessness, but the way Job imagines the heavenly figure advocating his case, as a person does for a friend (v. 21; cf. Judah's interceeding for Benjamin in Gen 44:18-34). The idea of a heavenly advocate also appears in Mesopotamian religion.[271]

The last verse of the chapter (v. 22) expresses Job's urgency for vindication in the face of impending death and provides a transition to the lament over his loneliness and hopelessness in chap. 17. Job's reference to death as "the way of no return" expresses both the separation and the finality that death imposes (cf. 2 Sam 12:23).[272]

17:1-5. Unlike some of Job's other speeches, chap. 17 does not have a clear structure. What unifies it is the theme of isolation. The hostility of mockers, the inability of his friends to understand and support him, and the complicity of God in his humiliation leave Job with no companion but death. His allusion to the grave in v. 1 anticipates his bitterly ironic description of Sheol, which concludes the chapter in vv. 13-16.

The role of mockery and social ostracism in Job's suffering (v. 2) is a topic that he first broached in chap. 16, but which becomes increasingly important, not only in this chapter (vv. 6, 8) but also in later speeches (19:13-19; 30:1-15). Honor and shame, incorporation and exclusion from human fellowship are powerful modes of social control. Although such behavior may serve to establish the moral boundaries of a community, it may just as easily express jealousy, rivalry, and resentment. In the book of Psalms and other literature related to the lament, as in

the book of Job, one hears the voice of persons who experience social humiliation (Pss 22:6-8[7-9]; 31:11-13[12-14]; Isa 50:6). No matter how confident one may be of one's own uprightness, rejection by one's community is devastating. As the psalmists' words make evident, an assurance of God's solidarity with the rejected person is absolutely crucial (Pss 22:9-11[10-12]; 31:14-18[15-19]; Isa 50:7).

Given this cultural pattern of seeking support from God in the face of social ostracism, it is not surprising that Job addresses God directly in vv. 3-4. Job's sense of God's enmity, however, precludes his confident reliance on God's solidarity. Unfortunately, as so often, obscurity in the text prevents certainty about what Job says. The motif Job uses is that of "surety," a pledge given to ensure the performance of some act or to support a claim. Property, or even a life, might be pledged (Gen 43:9; 44:32; Prov 11:15). One person might pledge on behalf of another, or one might pledge for oneself (Jer 30:21). Some interpreters understand Job to be asking God to "go surety for him" as an act of solidarity (so NRSV, NIV). Such an expression does occur in other laments and psalms (Ps 119:122; Isa 38:14). In such a reading, Job speaks much like the psalmists, contrasting God's support with his inability to find support anywhere among his own community. What Job says is slightly different, however, from what one finds in Isaiah 38 or Psalm 119. In Job 17:3, God *receives* the pledge.

Job's statement is best understood as a claim that he is willing to place his own life in pledge in order to come before God and clear his name: "Put my pledge by you" (i.e., "accept my pledge"; cf. Jer 30:21).[273] Such an interpretation is similar to Job's earlier statement in 13:14-16. Thus, unlike the psalmists who turn from human mockers to seek support from God, Job believes that God is actually behind the mockers (v. 6) and that God's actions have caused the failure of his friends to support him (vv. 3b-4a). Job must be his own surety.

Grammatical obscurity also plagues 17:4. The verb in v. 4b does not make sense as written, and every translation requires some modest emendation. The NRSV and the NIV

269. Perdue, *Wisdom in Revolt*, 172.

270. Fohrer, *Das Buch Hiob*, 281; Clines, *Job 1–20*, 372; Good, *In Turns of Tempest*, 95.

271. Jacobsen, "Personal Religion," 159-60.

272. Fohrer, *Das Buch Hiob*, 294, notes similar expressions in Babylonian literature. See *ANET*, 106.

273. Habel, *The Book of Job*, 266; Clines, *Job 1–20*, 393-4.

add an object for the verb ("them"), but the resulting sentence is very strange, even on the assumption that God is of two minds about Job. The reading of the verb as a passive is much more plausible: "Since you have closed their minds to understanding, therefore you will not be exalted."

Verse 5 is even more problematic. It is apparently a traditional saying, but the words are susceptible of quite different translations. The interpretation represented by the NRSV and the NIV understands it as a saying that rebukes the friends for betraying the obligations of friendship.[274] Alternatively, one can translate the proverb as "a person invites his friends to share his bounty, while the eyes of his own children grow faint (with hunger)."[275] So translated, the proverb might be an ironic criticism of the friends for inviting Job to share the "bounty" of their wisdom, when in fact it is too meager even to feed their own children. Fohrer, however, suggests that the saying applies to the relation between God and Job, by comparing God with one who favors outsiders while his own child (i.e., Job) is starved.[276] That interpretation fits well with the complaint against God in v. 6 and with Job's use of the image of failing eyes to describe himself in v. 7.

17:6-9. Verses 6-7 mirror vv. 1-2 as they repeat the themes of mockery (cf. Deut 25:9; Pss 44:14[15]; 69:11-12[13-14]) and physical exhaustion (cf. Pss 6:7[8]; 31:9-10[10-11]). The following verses are best taken ironically, representing the self-understanding of those who mock and spit at Job (cf. TNK). They perceive themselves as upright persons, shocked at the ungodliness of Job now revealed through his punishment (v. 8). As a consequence of this object lesson, the "righteous" hold more firmly than ever to their way of life (v. 9; the first word of the Hebrew text may be read either as "and" or "but").[277] Like the cathartic effect of a Greek tragedy,

the spectacle of Job's fate purges and purifies those who witness it.[278] All of this from Job's mouth, of course, is a parody of self-righteous judgment.

17:10-16. it seems improbable that Job is inviting his friends to change their minds and take a more sympathetic approach to him.[279] More likely, he is mockingly inviting them to try once more to present their positions. Job exposes the fatuous quality of what they say by contrasting the reality of his situation (v. 11) with the false comfort that the friends give (v. 12).[280] Especially in the first cycle of speeches, each of the friends suggested to Job the prospects of a reversal of fortune (5:19-26; 8:21; 11:15-19), even using the image of darkness that "will be like the morning" (11:17). Job seeks to contest the friends' insistence on the power of hope. As discussed in the Reflections on chap. 14, hope cannot endure without the presence of fellowship. For Job, death renders such fellowship impossible. His community, destroyed by the suffering God has imposed on him (16:7), can only be reconstituted as a community of nothingness in Sheol. Job's sardonic wit in describing Sheol as the only "house" he can hope to occupy (v. 13) perhaps alludes to the practice in the ancient Near East of making ossuaries in the shape of houses. Similarly, the bier on which a corpse was laid (2 Chr 16:14) is imagined as a bed in Sheol (Isa 14:11; Ezek 32:25). Job elaborates on the reconstitution of this nihilistic household, using the recognition formulas ("my mother," "my sister"; v. 14) that acknowledge close relationships (cf. Pss 2:7; 89:26[27]; Prov 7:4; Jer 2:27). The rhetorical questions of vv. 15-16 assume a negative answer (cf. Ps 49:17[18]).[281] As in his previous speeches, the reflection on death brings his words to an end (7:21; 10:21-22; 14:18-22). Job 16–17 are, however, the last of the speeches to conclude in this fashion.

274. Similarly, Habel, *The Book of Job*, 277; Hartley, *The Book of Job*, 269; Andersen, *Job*, 184.

275. Peake, *Job*, 173; Gordis, *The Book of Job*, 181-82; Clines, *Job 1–20*, 395.

276. Fohrer, *Das Buch Hiob*, 294; Clines, *Job 1–20*, 395.

277. See Janzen, *Job*, 126, for an interpretation along the lines of the NRSV and the NIV translations.

278. Rene Girard, *Job: The Victim of His People*, trans. Y. Freccero (Stanford: Stanford University Press, 1987) 71.

279. Hartley, *The Book of Job*, 270; cf. Habel, *The Book of Job*, 278.

280. For a very different interpretation, reading vv. 11-12 as a statement of pathos on the loss of the heart's desires, see Gordis, *The Book of Job*, 184; Habel, *The Book of Job*, 278; Clines, *Job 1–20*, 398.

281. So Fohrer, *Das Buch Hiob*, 295-96; Clines, *Job 1–20*, 400; contra Habel, *The Book of Job*, 279.

Reflections

The book of Job presents no more difficult issue for reflection than that of divine violence. Although readers rightly associate Job with the theme, it is actually Eliphaz who introduces it: God "wounds, but he binds up;/ he strikes, but his hands heal" (5:18). The very casualness with which Eliphaz describes God's violence should be more disturbing than Job's painfully graphic description. Eliphaz's remark is an index of the extent to which the violence of God is so much woven into the language of piety as to have become almost invisible: "Day and night your hand was heavy upon me;/ my strength was dried up as by the heat of summer" (Ps 32:4 NRSV); "Your arrows have sunk into me,/ and your hand has come down on me" (Ps 38:2[3] NRSV); "I am worn down by the blows of your hand" (Ps 39:10*b* [11 *b*] NRSV); "let the bones that you have crushed rejoice" (Ps 51:8*b* [10*b*] NRSV); "You have put me in the depths of the Pit,/ in the regions dark and deep" (Ps 88:6[7] NRSV); "you have lifted me up and thrown me aside" (Ps 102:10*b* [11 *b*] NRSV); "The Lord has punished me severely,/ but he did not give me over to death" (Ps 118:18 NRSV); "He has made my teeth grind on gravel,/ and made me cower in ashes" (Lam 3:16 NRSV).

Christians cannot escape from a confrontation with the issue of the violence of God by disingenuously asserting that such violence is a characteristic of the OT but not the NT. Divine violence is present in the NT (one has only to think of Heb 12:5-11 or the book of Revelation). Moreover, Christian prayer and piety have also been traditionally influenced by images of divine violence. The poet John Donne wrote:

Batter my heart, three-personed God, for you
As yet but knock, breathe, shine, and seek to mend;
That I may rise and stand, o'erthrow me; and bend
Your force to breake, blow, burn, and make me new.
("Holy Sonnets," 10.1-4)

The issue of divine violence cannot be understood in isolation from other related language about God. In the psalms from which the statements above are excerpted, it is evident that the words about the anger, rejection, and violence of God are part of a broader and more complex way of talking about God, in which God is experienced as personal and emotive. The angry emotions, however, are only a part of the picture. The relation between God and person is intimate and mutual, founded on a deep and primary bond of love. The individual offers love and obedience to God. Utterly dependent on God for all, the individual expects compassion and active protection from enemies, but also expects correction and punishment in cases of disobedience. The relationship is a deeply personal one, and the sense of closeness and trust is one of the most profound needs and satisfactions expressed in the psalms. The origins of this language of piety in the older religious literature of Mesopotamia have been traced. The root metaphor that generates this way of talking about God is that of parent and child.[282] In Israelite psalms, even though other social relationships (e.g., king and people) influence the religious language, the relation between parent and child is the hidden "deep structure," shaping the way in which God is experienced and talked about.

The relationship between parent and child, the most primary of human relationships, provides a religious metaphor of immense power, resonance, and richness, one capable of nurturing a complex and nuanced religious life. Like all root metaphors, however, the analogies it makes available for understanding experience may create as well as resolve problems. Nowhere is this clearer than in the problem of understanding acute suffering. The image of God as an all-powerful parent virtually requires the

---

282. Jacobsen, "Personal Religion," 157-60.

---

understanding that God must be responsible for an individual's suffering, either by directly causing it or by neglecting to protect that person. Although the psalms primarily address suffering in terms of urging God to save and protect the psalmist from the aggression of enemies, they also speak of God as the source of violence, as in the citations above. In such instances, when the logic of the metaphor is fully developed, what emerges is the image of God as abusive parent. Because the underlying parental metaphor is so deeply a part of religious language, however, the image of God as abusive is difficult to resist or critique. Instead, the one who prays may be drawn into the pathological thought patterns of the cycle of abuse.

One can see this happening in Lamentations 3, the text that so engages Job. The violence inflicted on the speaker is represented as being for his own good. Indeed, the one who is subjected to violence has to internalize this message ("It is good for a person to bear a yoke when he is young, to sit alone in silence when [God] has imposed it, to put his mouth in the dust [Lam 3:27-29a]). There is no question of proportionality. Whatever the punishment (Lam 3:1-20), it must be accepted as such ("Why should any person who lives complain when punished for his sin?" [Lam 3:39]). There can be no question of resistance (It is appropriate "to give one's cheek to the smiter, and be filled with insults" [Lam 3:30]). The relationship is not simply one of absolute dependency on a God experienced as all powerful (Lam 3:27) and as the source of good as well as of pain (Lam 3:38). There is also the memory of a relation that includes tenderness and affection ("The LORD is good to one who waits on him, to the soul that seeks him" [Lam 3:25]; "you came near when I called on you; you said, 'Do not be afraid' " [Lam 3:57]). Consequently, the one who is hurt attempts not only to justify the abuse but also to excuse the abuser ("Although [God] causes grief, he will have compassion . . . for he does not willingly afflict or grieve anyone" [Lam 3:32a-33 NRSV]). The one who is abused thus takes responsibility for the abuse ("Let us test and examine our ways,/ and return to the LORD. . . . We have transgressed and rebelled" [Lam 3:40, 42 NRSV]).

There are, to be sure, differences between Lamentations 3 and the thought processes of an abused child, which would require a much longer reflection to explore. An ancient Israelite lament cannot be read as the transcript of a modern counseling session. Nevertheless, the similarities in the modes of thinking and perceiving are striking enough to be deeply disturbing. There is something grotesquely wrong with a religious language that deals with suffering as justified abuse, whether the individual is guilty or innocent of wrongdoing. Job's speech in chap. 16 recognizes, exposes, and challenges the pathology embedded in the lament tradition. Job's description of God's violence against him differs in no essential way from the description in Lam 3:1-20. At the point at which tradition calls upon him to justify the punishment and to speak words of confidence in God's compassion, however, Job refuses. When Job says, "O earth, do not cover my blood," he renames this violence as abuse, as murder. With these words, Job delegitimizes the language of divine violence that the lament tradition had represented as natural. He takes the language of violence out of the context of prayer and insists that one consider it in the context of criminality.

What is one to do with Job's exposure of the scandal that lies in this traditional language of lament? One alternative has been to understand Job's words as a fatal critique of the religious imagination that bases itself on the metaphor of a personal God and to seek a radically different language about God based on a different root metaphor. It is possible to read the divine speeches in chaps. 38–41 as an attempt to do just that, depicting a God whose image is to be found not so much in human parents as in the rhythms of nature, the balance of light and darkness, life and death.[283] A religious language constructed upon such an image would deal with the issue of suffering quite differently than do the psalms. Suffering would not be seen as implying either the

---

283. Cf. N. Habel, "In Defense of God the Sage," in *The Voice from the Whirlwind*, ed. L. G. Perdue and W. Clark Gilpin (Nashville: Abingdon, 1992), 35.

violence of God or divine neglect, for the image of God would not be that of a passionate, acting, and reacting being, but an image of the creator and sustainer of a world in which the destructive energies of chaos are contained but not eliminated. Whether or not this is the intent of the divine speeches will be considered later, but in either case, this position is a possible response to the crisis exposed by Job's recognition that traditional language about God can lead to the sanctification of a model of abuse.

Another alternative, perhaps even more radical, is championed by those who wish to claim that the personal, parental root metaphor provides the most adequate model for experiencing God, and who are also persuaded that Job's dilemma is not merely a problem of language.[284] This alternative requires the recognition that God *is* abusive. It is not just a matter of how God is portrayed but a matter of how God acts. Like human parents who physically abuse their children, however, God is not always abusive but may also be loving, nurturing, and responsive. As moral agents who answer to God for their own behavior, humans have the right to call God to answer for what God does or fails to do, when it results in abusive violence. As outrageous, even blasphemous, as such a position may sound, it has a biblical pedigree. Abraham confronts God with the immoral implications of God's intentions in Gen 18:23-25. In Psalm 44, the nation accuses God of a neglect that amounts to abuse. Job's critique is the most direct and sustained confrontation of God for abuse of the innocent, but it is not an isolated one. Jewish writers have long maintained the tradition of moral argument with God,[285] but it is the attempt to think about God in the wake of the Holocaust that has produced the most systematic exploration of divine violence and human response. For some, confrontation of God, like that in Job 16, is psychologically, morally, and religiously necessary. It is God and not Job who should repent. It is God who must confess to having remained a bystander while God's chosen people were slaughtered.[286]

For many people wrestling with the issue of suffering and the traditional language of divine violence, which Job has so powerfully exposed in chaps. 16–17, these two alternatives may seem to polarize the issues in an unacceptable way. Only if one takes the language about God as parent or ruler in a naively literal fashion, describing a being who regularly intervenes directly in the affairs of the world, does it seem necessary to take up the stance of confronting God as abusive parent. Giving up personal language about God entirely, however, would impoverish the richness of traditional imagery for God, changing Judeo-Christian religion beyond recognition. The middle ground is not easy to stake out. The contradiction between a God of love and a world in which pain is so much a presence defies resolution. Perhaps the only way of addressing such a paradox is the one that the Bible follows. Instead of attempting to define a single true image that resolves all contradictions, the Bible works instead with the complexities of human experience. In some circumstances, God's presence *feels* violently oppressive. At other times, God's presence *feels* like the love of a mother. In still other contexts, God may be experienced as the foundation that restrains chaos but does not protect individuals from the risks that are intrinsic to creation. Religious language can speak only in fragments. That limitation may frustrate human desire for a clearer understanding of issues that have a burning urgency, but what it is possible to say within the contradictory but honest language of religious experience can produce a tradition capable of addressing the complexity of emotions faced by those who bring their suffering before God.

284. See D. R. Blumenthal, *Facing the Abusing God: A Theology of Protest* (Louisville: Westminster/John Knox Press, 1993).

285. See A. Laytner, *Arguing with God: A Jewish Tradition* (Northvale, N.J.: Jason Aronson, 1990).

286. See, e.g., the character of Michael in Elie Wiesel's *The Town Beyond the Wall* (New York: Holt, Reinhart and Winston, 1964) 52-53.

Job 18:1-21, Bildad Describes the Fate of the Wicked

COMMENTARY

Bildad's reply begins with the typical objection to the previous speaker's words and attitudes (vv. 2-3), although, curiously, he uses second-person plural forms. In v. 4, he identifies the scandal he hears in Job's words, which motivates his own reply. The rest of his speech is devoted to a descriptive account of the fate of the wicked (vv. 5-21), developed through images of extinguished light (vv. 5-6), loss of vigorous movement (v. 7), entrapment like a hunted animal (vv. 8-10), predation by the forces of destruction (vv. 11-13), seizure and arraignment by death's servants (v. 14), and the annihilation of all traces of existence, including place, progeny, and memorial (vv. 15-19). The description concludes with a universal reaction of horror (v. 20) and Bildad's summary appraisal (v. 21). What makes the passage difficult to interpret is that Bildad never explicitly indicates the purpose of his speech or how he intends his words to be taken.

18:2-4. Although the problem is not evident in an English translation, Bildad's words in vv. 2-3 are couched in the second-person plural. Occasional attempts have been made to understand these verses as being addressed to Eliphaz and Zophar rather than to Job,[287] but this suggestion is not persuasive. It is easier to assume a textual error and to read these verses as being directed at Job. Whether Bildad is irritated by Job's "hunting for words" or impatient for him to "end these speeches" depends on the interpretation of a rare Hebrew word (קנץ *qēneṣ*). The Aramaic targum of Job from Qumran supports the NIV.

As so often, the first issue in the speech deals with what is preventing genuine dialogue. In Bildad's view, such conversation can take place only within a framework of essential, shared presuppositions and in an atmosphere of respect. For Bildad, dialogue is not simply a matter of exchanging words. Indeed, Job's words are making serious discussion impossible. Bildad wants Job to stop talking and "recognize" certain essential

things (בין *bîn*; NRSV, "consider"; NIV, "be sensible"; the Hebrew word has connotations of both perception and understanding). Only then can useful dialogue take place (v. 2*b*). Bildad's concern for the foundations of moral discourse is also reflected in the images of v. 4, where "the earth" and "the rock" are symbols of the encompassing structures and secure bases on which all else rests. He rightly perceives that Job's words in such passages as 12:13-25 are a challenge to the very foundations of the world.

Bildad's objection that Job considers the friends to be "like cattle" (v. 3) is acute. Even though Job has not used such a term, he has ridiculed the herd mentality embedded in the clichéd and platitudinous language of the friends (see Reflections on Job 13). Bildad's request for respect seems innocuous enough. Sometimes, however, insistence on civility can be a means of control by those who do not want a discussion to disturb the foundations of things in which their security and their very identities are invested. A comparable rhetorical strategy is evident in Bildad's characterization of Job as one who "tears" himself "in his anger" (v. 4*a*). Bildad recasts Job's serious attack on the foundations as mere self-destructive behavior. His words have subtle overtones of animality ("tear" [טרף *ṭārap*] is used of animals attacking prey) and of madness, since only if he were insane would Job mutilate himself in his anger. By these means, he belittles Job's words and patronizes him.

18:5-21. At this point Bildad introduces his description of the fate of the wicked. The context of the preceding verses gives some clue as to the description's function. This vision is what Bildad wants Job to perceive, a precondition for further dialogue. Bildad presents this description as the rock that cannot be moved from its place without endangering the whole superstructure of piety and morality (cf. 15:4). That the wicked come to a bad end is a commonplace in the wisdom literature (cf. the numerous sayings in Proverbs 11–13). In these proverbs the fate

287. Dhorme, *A Commentary on the Book of Job,* 257, noting Elihu's rebuke of the friends in 32:3.

of the wicked is usually presented in a binary saying, in which the complementary half of the verse describes the good fortune of the righteous. What is at stake in such proverbs is the claim that the world is founded on a just moral order. A developed description of the fate of the wicked also occurs in a number of psalms. In Ps 7:14-16[15-17], it is part of the prayer of an innocent person who is reassured about the moral order of the world by envisioning the recoil of evil upon the wicked (cf. also Ps 49:13-20[14-21], where the issue is the power of wealth). In Psalm 64, the description serves to resolve the psalmist's complaint about the predations of the wicked. In Ps 73:17-28, it explicitly answers the psalmist's question of theodicy.

The apparent good fortune of the wicked seems to have been a much more problematic issue than the misfortune of the righteous. Perhaps this is because there were so many possible explanations for the temporary distress of the righteous, many of them catalogued in Eliphaz's speech in chaps. 4–5. Moreover, religious practice always provided something for the righteous sufferer to do about the situation: pray to an ever compassionate God. But if, as Van der Toorn has suggested, the fundamental conviction throughout the ancient Near East was that "nothing happens on earth unless it is decreed in heaven,"[288] then the good fortune of the wicked was a theological scandal, a contradiction of the moral order of the world. Moreover, there was no religious practice comparable to a prayer of lament by which one could reverse the good fortune of the wicked and so restore coherency to the world. It remained a scandal. The vividness of the descriptions of Eliphaz, Bildad, and Zophar are in part attempts to create a virtual reality in which the ultimate downfall of the wicked can be experienced. One might object that the friends are answering a question Job has not asked. As elsewhere, they are responding with prefabricated replies. Nevertheless, they are right to recognize in Job's words an attack on the plausibility of the belief that the world has a moral structure. Their replies reiterate that moral structure at the place where they feel it to be most vulnerable.

Those who interpret Bildad's words as an identification of Job as one of the wicked and an announcement of his fate are not entirely wrong,[289] but they collapse a more complex process that takes place over several chapters. Bildad is not yet ready to declare Job wicked. The moral order Bildad reaffirms, however, has no place for an anomaly such as Job represents. Almost inevitably, the resolution of that intolerable contradiction will be made by declaring Job to be one of the wicked, which Eliphaz will say in chap. 22. Since the reader knows what none of the characters do, that all this disaster has in fact happened to a person who is "blameless and upright, one who feared God and turned away from evil" (1:1 NRSV), the reader's confidence in the religious ideology that results in such a false accusation is seriously undermined.

18:5-6. The images Bildad invokes throughout his description are primarily those of disintegration.[290] The first of these is the image of a light going out (vv. 5-6). In Hebrew, none of the verbs used denotes an active agent. Rather, the light simply "goes out" (דעך *dāʿak*) and "grows dark" (חשך *ḥāšak*); the flame "does not shine" (לא־יגה *lōʾ-yiggah*), and the lamp "goes out" (*dāʿak*). As in Bildad's previous image of a plant that withers for lack of life-giving water (8:11-13), the life and power of the wicked are self-limited because they are cut off from the source of all life. The symbolic association of light/darkness with life/death is common in the OT and particularly frequent in Job (e.g., 3:20; 10:21-22; 15:22; 17:13). The lamp in the tent is more specifically an image of security and protection, as in Job's evocative use in 29:3.

The saying "the lamp of the wicked goes out" is a traditional one (Prov 13:9; 24:20; cf. Prov 20:20). Throughout the description, Bildad shows a particular fondness for familiar images and phrases. In his earlier speech, he had insisted on the reliability of ancestral words as bearers of truth. By populating his speech with traditional figures, Bildad makes his own words a conduit of that authoritative, ancestral voice.

289. E.g., Andersen, *Job*, 190; Pope, *Job*, 137; Habel, *The Book of Job*, 282; Janzen, *Job*, 128. Contrast Clines, *Job 1–20*, 409.
290. Good, *In Turns of Tempest*, 253.

288. van der Toorn, *Sin and Sanction in Israel and Mesopotamia*, 56.

18:7-10. In this section, Bildad's images have to do with arrested movement. Shortening steps (v. 7) are an evocative image of diminishing vitality, a contrasting image to the broad strides that the books of Psalms and Proverbs use as an image of the vigor that comes from divine support (Ps 18:36[37]; Prov 4:12). In those passages, the parallel image of walking without stumbling also contrasts with Bildad's description of the wicked being cast down by their own schemes. The notion that the evil planned by the wicked eventually causes their own ruin is a very common motif in wisdom thought (e.g., Prov 11:3*b*, 5*b*, 6*b*; 26:27). Behind this notion lies the belief that the world is structured to respond supportively to good and to resist evil. Thus the plans of the wicked, no matter how clever, are doomed to failure because they are contradictory to the fundamental moral order of the world.

Bildad's description of traps in vv. 8-10 is a tour de force of imagery. Unfortunately, it is not possible to identify the particular types of traps, snares, nets, and other devices referred to by the six different words he uses. What they all have in common is that they work because the victim cannot perceive them and so blunders into destruction. For Bildad, what is morally significant is not that wicked people exist but that their existence is tenuous, because the world for them is a field baited with snares that they cannot see and so cannot escape. Imagery of the snare and trap appears in many contexts to express anxiety about a hostile and uncontrollable situation (Pss 9:16; 124:7; 140:5[6]; 142:3*b*[4*b*]; Jer 18:22*b*; 48:44).

18:11-14. The imagery now shifts from hidden menace to the aggression of death's forces, represented as a pack of hunting predators. Verse 11 describes the chase, v. 12 the cornering of the prey, and v. 13 the devouring. The agents are variously described but are all traditional designations for the servants of death. The word "terrors" (בלהות *ballāhôt*), for instance, does not primarily refer to subjective psychological reactions but to the servants of personified Death who cause terror (v. 11).[291] Similarly, "calamity" (און *'ōn*) and "disaster" (איד *'ēd*) are agents

of death (v. 12). The graphic image of death's firstborn consuming the skin and limbs brings the image of predation to its logical conclusion, but it also alludes to the specific effects of deadly diseases that eat away flesh (v. 13). This is probably an allusion to plague as the personified firstborn of Death, as in Mesopotamian mythology the plague god Namtar is the vizier and apparently the firstborn of Erishkigal, queen of the underworld.[292]

Textual problems and grammatical ambiguities in vv. 12-13 permit an alternative interpretation in which death itself is described, personified as the "Hungry One" (v. 12), and named with the honorific title "First-Born Death" (v. 13),[293] as in Habel's translation: "The Hungry One will be his strength,/ Calamity ready as his escort./ He consumes his skin with both hands;/ First-born Death consumes with both hands."[294] The god Mot (Death) is an important figure in Ugaritic mythology, and death is often represented in mythic terms in the OT. Death is also associated with an insatiable hunger (Isa 5:14; Hab 2:5). In Ugaritic myth, Mot is described as having "one lip to earth and one to heaven, [he stretches his to]ngue to the stars. Baal enters his mouth, descends into him like an olive-cake."[295] As that image suggests, however, personified Death is not characteristically represented as roaming the earth in search of victims but as the king of the underworld to whom all come. Thus it seems less likely that vv. 12-13 refer to personified Death. Dramatically, Death appears only at the climax of Bildad's description. In v. 14, the imagery of the "hounds of Hell" modulates into that of sudden arrest by unnamed agents who march the victim off to the presence of Death, the "king of terrors."

18:15-19. A series of images of annihilation follows. Textual problems obscure the first line. The initial words can be translated "nothing of his dwells in his tent" (see NRSV), although it is very awkwardly expressed in Hebrew. It is also possible to emend the text slightly and read "fire" as a parallel to

---

291. Tromp, *Primitive Conceptions of Death and the Nether World in the Old Testament*, 74; Pope, *Job*, 134; Clines, *Job 1–20*, 416.

292. Dhorme, *A Commentary on the Book of Job*, 265; J. B. Burns, "The Identity of Death's First-Born (Job xviii 13)," *VT* 37 (1987) 363; cf. N. Sarna, "The Mythological Background of Job 18," *JBL* 82 (1963) 315-17.

293. Pope, *Job*, 135; Habel, *The Book of Job*, 287.

294. Habel, *The Book of Job*, 280.

295. *ANET*, 138.

"sulfur" (NIV).[296] Fire and sulfur, traditionally "fire and brimstone," are associated as agents of destruction (Gen 19:24; Ps 11:6; Ezek 38:22). The sprinkling of land with sulfur, as with salt (Judg 9:45), renders it unfruitful and unfit for habitation (Deut 29:23[22]). In Greek tradition, sprinkling sulfur served as a disinfectant for corpse contamination.[297] Either connotation would fit the context.

In the following verses, Bildad uses merismus, the rhetorical device of expressing totality by naming paired opposites: root and branch in v. 16, farmlands and grazing lands in v. 17,[298] one's own kin and place of sojourn in v. 19, and westerners and easterners in v. 20. Note also the use of polar terms in the phrase "from light to darkness" (v. 18) and the synonymous terms "offspring or descendants" (v. 19). Although Bildad's speech is not, properly speaking, magical, he empowers his words by imitating the reality he wishes to evoke in the texture of his language, the totality of the annihilation of the wicked.

In v. 16, the withering of "root and branch" (Mal 4:1[3:19]; Sir 23:25), like that of "root and fruit" (Ezek 17:9; Hos 9:16; Amos 2:9),[299] expresses the failure of possessions and progeny, those things that the individual has "put forth" like a tree.[300] Verse 17 makes the same point more directly by referring to the cessation of the mention of the deceased person's name, which is connected less with reputation than with the children who carry the name into succeeding generations (cf. 2 Sam 14:7; 18:18; Ps 109:13). In v. 19, the extinction of the entire line is explicitly stated, not even excepting a survivor dwelling in a foreign land. In a culture that did not believe in immortality or continued existence after death except through one's progeny, the protection of that continuity was a matter of anxiety and considerable creativity. The problem of childlessness is a recurrent one in ancient Israelite and Canaanite literature (cf. the stories of Abraham in Genesis 16–22 and of Keret and Dan'el in Ugaritic literature),[301] and the variety of social practices designed to ensure offspring (polygamy, concubinage, adoption, Levirate marriage) attests to the importance of progeny.[302] The horror of such an end is captured in Bildad's image that such a person is "driven out of the world" (v. 18).

18:20-21. The description concludes by evoking the horrified reaction of the whole world to the spectacle of the annihilation of the wicked and his line (v. 20). Picking up the references to habitation (v. 15) and tent (vv. 6, 14-15), Bildad uses the terms "dwelling" (משכן *miškan*) and "place" (מקום *māqôm*) as metaphors for the existence of the "one who knows not God" (v. 21). The term "place" also echoes v. 4, where Bildad asked rhetorically if the rock should be moved from its place. Bildad's summary appraisal in v. 21 thus frames the vivid immediacy of the poem and succinctly states his didactic theme.

296. M. Dahood, "Some Northwest-Semitic Words in Job," *Biblica* 38 (1957), 312-14, followed by Pope, *Job*, 136; Habel, *The Book of Job*, 282; Clines, *Job 1–20*, 407.

297. See Homer *Odyssey* 22.480-81.

298. Translation following Clines, *Job 1–20*, 404; cf. Dhorme, *A Commentary on the Book of Job*, 267.

299. See Eshumunazar Inscription in *ANET*, 662.

300. Clines, *Job 1–20*, 420.

301. *ANET*, 142-55.

302. Pope, *Job*, 136-37. Perpetuation of the "name" is the issue associated with male childlessness. In narratives about childless women, social status is the problem.

REFLECTIONS

As dramatic poetry, the three speeches on the fate of the wicked (chaps. 15; 18; 20) are among the most compelling in the book of Job. They also model a provocative way of imagining evil and the people who embody it. Many readers may feel that the moral imagination evoked by these poems is strange and alien to modern sensibilities. As one explores them more closely, however, one may recognize some familiar and disturbing modes of thinking.

To understand this way of thinking about evil, it is necessary to look briefly at the way good and evil were envisioned in Israel's wisdom tradition. Ancient Israelite wisdom tended to think of good and evil as active forces in a world composed of active forces.[303] Good and evil are not merely matters of the disposition of the human heart, but forces that have the power to create or destroy things of value: contentment, reputation, possessions, a life, a family, a community. As active qualities, good produces good and evil produces evil, for self and for others. The created order, however, has a bias toward life and thus toward the good. The world responds favorably to good but resists and rejects evil. Evil can be described as participation in the realm of death. An evil person spreads death among the community, but in the end is claimed by the same power of death. This understanding is illustrated in Prov 1:10-19, where violent persons use the imagery of death to describe their own activity (Prov 1:12a), yet in the end destroy themselves (Prov 1:18). By identifying their violence with death, they give death a claim over them. So, too, in Bildad's speech, the forces of life reject the wicked person (vv. 5-7), who is claimed by death (vv. 11-14).

Similar ideas inform the understanding of the curse that falls on a people because they have done evil or repudiated the covenant. The curse also often takes the form of unleashing the enmity of the powers of life itself against the ones who are cursed. In Deuteronomy 28, for instance, one section of the covenant curse describes the refusal of sky and earth to open themselves to the accursed. Vividly stated, the sky becomes bronze and the earth iron; the rain that falls turns into dust, until all perish (Deut 28:23-24). Similarly, the fundamental trustworthiness of the world, which allows one to act and accomplish the basic functions of life, does not hold for the one accursed. In the so-called futility curses, actions no longer produce dependable results, whether in the production of food, in the establishment of a family, or in social and community relations (Deut 28:30-32, 38-44). These curses create the image of someone's being rejected by the powers of life, subjected to terror and confusion because that person no longer has a place in the domain of life. As in Bildad's account (18:20), the cursed person becomes an object of horror (Deut 28:37). This reaction is not simple moral disapproval but a much more visceral reaction against someone whom life itself seems to have rejected.

Just as the natural world expelled evil that was identified as accursed by God, so also the human community's reaction might take a similar shape, as in the story of Achan in Joshua 7. After an unexpected defeat, oracular inquiry reveals that the defeat was caused by a person's having violated the principles of holy war. When the guilty party is identified, the entire community participates in the destruction of Achan, together with "his sons and daughters, with his oxen, donkeys, and sheep, and his tent and all that he had. . . . And all Israel stoned him to death; they burned them with fire, cast stones on them, and raised over him a great heap of stones that remains to this day" (Josh 7:24b-25a, 26a NRSV). Like the wicked person described by Bildad, Achan is "driven out of the world," annihilated "root and branch" as his possessions and his progeny are destroyed along with his own life (cf. Job 18:15-19).

The understanding of good and evil as active forces bearing life and bearing death is a powerful model that envisions the world as a holistic environment in which what is good is nurtured and what is evil is isolated and expelled. Nevertheless, this way of imagining evil and the world's response to it is deeply disturbing. Most obviously, it becomes very easy to identify suffering itself as a sign of rejection by the life-giving forces of the world, and thus as a sign that the person who suffers is in some way evil. That elements of this perception are present in modern culture is evident from the common reactions of fear, disgust, and even hatred that people sometimes experience when confronted by a person whose body is deformed or disfigured by illness and suffering. These reactions are residual elements of a subconscious, subrational chain of association: a horribly suffering body, which death is so visibly claiming, is seen as a body rejected by life and all the goodness associated with life. It is seen as a body cursed and, therefore, a presence of evil. Healthy persons, anxious to associate

303. This analysis is based on G. von Rad, *Wisdom in Israel,* trans. J. D. Martin (Nashville: Abingdon, 1972) 77-81.

themselves with the powers of life and dissociate themselves from death, react by driving the suffering one away, either literally or figuratively.

A number of diseases have particularly evoked such a response. There is a trace of it in one of the synonyms for *cancer*: *malignancy,* a malign or evil thing. Not too many years ago, cancer was spoken of in whispers; a vague sense of shame was attached to it, and people often attempted to conceal the nature of their disease. More dramatic has been the response to leprosy. Even though the disease is not highly contagious, it evoked such horror that sufferers were expelled from the community and forced to live as outcasts. Most recently, AIDS sufferers have encountered similar reactions. Despite the fact that the mechanisms of the disease's transmission are well understood and controllable, the announcement of plans for an AIDS hospice is likely to produce a nearly hysterical reaction from neighbors. In each of these diseases, the powers of life and health, which normally protect the body, fail spectacularly, leaving the body open to the ravages of disease and death, which attack with virulence. For people who are influenced by the type of thinking reflected in Bildad's speech, the rejection of the body by the forces that normally protect it appears as a rejection of the person by God. This symbolic association, which may take place on a subconscious level, encourages the communal response of expulsion and annihilation, all in a spirit of great self-righteousness. The cruel injustice of this reaction, a form of blaming the victim, is obvious once it is exposed. Because such associations tend to be rooted deep in the psyche, however, they are often difficult to bring to surface where they may be examined and corrected.

To be fair to Bildad, one could say that the confusion of the physical with the moral is a *mis*application of his understanding of how the world expels evil from its midst. What he is trying to talk about is moral evil, not physical suffering. Yet there are reasons to be uneasy about Bildad's vision of things even when it is applied to the case of a person who is truly and deeply evil. Janzen expresses the concern well in his recollection of the crowds that savaged the lifeless body of Mussolini, "dragging it through the streets, hanging it heels-up against the wall, then pelting it with stones and spitting at it. In viewing the scene, one was drawn into the moral energy of the action; yet more deeply, one felt a pathos of horror that any human being, no matter in what moral state, could be so driven out of the world."[304] Bildad's vision dehumanizes the wicked. The wicked become objectified, something wholly other than "good people"; they become monsters against whom any violence is legitimate. Such dichotomizing between the wicked and the righteous leads to a deceptively dangerous misapprehension of the nature of evil. In fact, no one is completely free of the taint of evil. The crowds who attacked the body of Mussolini were not themselves wholly innocent of complicity in evil. Indeed, the knowledge of that complicity may have been the source of some of their fury. The understanding of evil articulated by Bildad and his friends and enacted by avenging mobs encourages the hypocrisy of pretending that evil is something we can expel from ourselves (individually or communally) by exterminating one whom we have judged to be radically evil.

304. Janzen, *Job,* 130.

Job 19:1-29, Job Denounces God's Injustice

COMMENTARY

Although Job echoes Bildad's opening words (cf. 18:2 and 19:2), his speech is not so much a reply to Bildad as a further investigation of the themes and issues of his previous speech in chap. 16. Following a reproach to the friends for their aggressive and misplaced attacks on him (vv. 2-6), Job uses traditional lament motifs to describe his suffering at God's hand. Job describes both God's violent aggression against him (vv. 7-12) and his alienation from friends and family (vv. 13-19), concluding with a description of his own body's deterioration (v. 20). Whereas the tradition of psalmic laments would direct Job to plead to God for mercy, Job makes an ironic appeal to the friends instead (vv. 21-22). Rather than prayer, he thinks in terms of legal confrontation with God, expressing the wish that his words could be permanently preserved (vv. 23-24). Although Job expresses certainty that a defender will arise to take up his case after he is dead (vv. 25-26a), what he most wants is to confront God before his death (vv. 26b-27). For the first time in the dialogue, Job does not close his speech with a meditation on death but closes with a final rebuke and warning addressed to the friends who persecute him.

19:1-6. In his previous opening comments, Job parodied the words of the friends (9:2-3), made fun of their pretense to knowledge (12:2), and criticized them as "miserable comforters" whose talk is both empty and destructive (16:2-3). Here, however, Job's reproach is more severe, as he accuses them of acts of verbal violence (v. 2). In vv. 21-22 and 28-29 as well, Job will explicitly accuse the friends of a kind of obsessive aggression manifested in their slanders. Job does not distinguish among his friends or between their first and second speeches but lumps all that they have said together ("ten times," v. 3, is a round number; cf. Gen 31:7; Num 14:22). Whatever the friends' intentions, Job has heard their words as impugning his integrity. He casts the issue in terms of honor and shame. By attempting to expose him to shame, they have actually exposed their own shameful conduct (v. 3; "cast reproach" does not capture the nuance of the Hebrew [כלם *kālam*]; "insult" or "humiliate" is closer to the meaning). Job's sense of the social dimension of well-being and suffering is acute, as vv. 13-19 illustrate. He will return to the theme in chaps. 29–30.

The same theme of agonistic social relations appears in v. 5, as Job depicts the

friends' "making themselves big" by using Job's humiliation against him. Their attitude would be improper under any circumstance (cf. 31:29), but it is particularly abhorrent because it is not Job who has done wrong but God who has wronged Job (v. 6). The word Job uses in v. 6a is the same one Bildad employed in 8:3 in his rhetorical question "does God *pervert* (עות *'ivvēt*) justice?" Note also Job's echo of the word "justice" (משפט *mišpāṭ*) in v. 7b.

The enigmatic v. 4 is best understood in the context of vv. 5-6. The NRSV gives a fairly literal translation of the verse, although the verb translated "remains" is, more concretely, "lodges" (לין *lîn*). The conduct referred to is inadvertent sin, i.e., sin committed in ignorance or without intent.[305] Although real sin with real consequences, it was not considered to be as serious as intentional, willful sin. In this verse, Job is not admitting that he has committed this less serious type of sin, but is stating a conditional proposition: "If it were true that I had inadvertently sinned. . . . " But what does Job mean by saying that "my inadvertent sin would lodge with me"? The NIV understands Job to say that such sin is his business alone. Sin was not so clearly a purely private matter in ancient Israel, however. In the wisdom tradition in particular, public reproach for behavior that "departs from the way" was necessary and expected (e.g., Prov 12:1; 13:1; 15:5). More plausibly, Job acknowledges that if he had sinned, even inadvertently, then that sin and its consequences would indeed lodge with him. In such a case, the friends would have grounds to reproach him (v. 5). But the true state of affairs is that the wrongdoing is God's, not Job's (v. 6).

19:7-12. In another context there would be little in these verses, or in vv. 13-20, that would strike one as untraditional. Job uses conventional lament vocabulary, imagery, and motifs. Following Job's statement in v. 6 that God has wronged him (lit., "twisted"), however, these verses take on the connotation of an accusation rather than a proper lament. This rhetorical strategy is similar to what Job uses in 9:2-14 and 16:9-21, where he recontextualizes a doxology and a lament, respectively. As in chap. 16, there are many

---

305. J. Milgrom, "The Cultic Segaga and Its Influence in Psalms and Job," *JQR* 58 (1967) 73-79.

similarities between vv. 7-12 and Lamentations (esp. Lam 3:5-9).

Although Job uses a variety of images in vv. 7-12, most have overtones of violent aggression and evoke a sense of powerlessness. It has been suggested that the cry "Violence!" (v. 7) is the equivalent of the English plea "Help!"—a cry of alarm that should bring aid.[306] In Lam 3:8 and Hab 1:2, such cries are addressed to God, who, however, refuses to hear or delays action. Following v. 6b, which describes God as casting a net (or possibly a siegework)[307] against Job, he vainly cries out against God's violence. What Job seeks is not rescue, but justice; yet that is precisely what is absent (v. 7b; cf. Hab 1:2-4).

As in Lam 3:8-9, the image of futile outcry is followed by that of a blocked way. Blocking a road or obscuring a path (v. 8) controls a person's movement and options, depriving him or her of self-determination (cf. Hos 2:6[8]). The emotional overtone of being in someone else's power is also present in the image of being stripped of dignity and crown (v. 9; cf. Lam 5:16). The social background for such an image is the humiliation of a captive, as in 12:17-19, where Job described the stripping of leaders by God. Verse 10 intensifies the sense of powerlessness. In 14:7-9, Job had evocatively described hope as the power of regeneration, likening it to the ability of a hewn tree's roots to put forth new growth. Here, however, Job describes his hope as being torn up by the roots, so that the capacity for self-regeneration is utterly destroyed.

The concluding set of images reinforces the theme of powerlessness. Job attributes his destruction to God's having intentionally increased his anger against Job, treating him as an enemy (cf. Lam 2:5). The outcome of such hostility is expressed in the image of a military operation: the gathering of troops, the building of a siege ramp, and the final besieging of Job's tent (cf. Lam 3:5, 7). As often noted, a disproportion exists between the description of preparations, which would suffice for an attack on a city, and the object of the operation, which is merely a tent.[308]

Here perhaps is a trace of Job's ironic, subtly mocking voice, as in 7:17-18.

19:13-20. There is no irony in the following section, however. In these verses, Job also employs a traditional lament motif, the alienation of the speaker from family and friends (cf. Pss 31:11-13[12-14]; 38:11[12]; 41:9[10]; 55:12-14[13-15]; 69:8[9], 18[19]. In contrast to the psalms, Job's account is much longer and more detailed. Verses 13-19 contain some twelve different terms for social and kinship categories. Unfortunately, the precise meaning of many of them is unknown or disputed. Even without such knowledge, however, one has the impression that Job is giving a detailed map of the relational world from which he is now excluded. The account begins (vv. 13-14) and ends (vv. 18-19) with the broader social contexts, placing the intimate domestic sphere at the center (vv. 15-17). The verbs used trace a different pattern, a crescendo of repudiation. The sequence begins with passively expressed alienation (distancing, estrangement, forgetting; see vv. 13-14), then records the changed attitudes of others, which result in the refusal of customary relations (vv. 15-16). A description of visceral repulsion follows (v. 17), concluding with active rejection and antagonism (vv. 18-19). The very first verb in the series stands out for another reason as well. While the passage is primarily descriptive, the first clause speaks of causation: God is responsible for the terrible isolation Job experiences (v. 13a).

In vv. 13-14, paired terms identify the extended family and friends in general. The NIV's "brothers" (אחים ʾaḥîm) in v. 13, although literal, obscures that word's broader nuance, "kin." The parallel term in v. 14 (קרוב qārôb) refers to the closer family circle (cf. Lev 21:2-3; Num 27:11). Probably, the two terms for friends (ידע yōdēaʿ and מידע měyūdāʿ) also designate "friends" and "familiar friends," respectively,[309] although the evidence is less clear (cf. 2 Kgs 10:11; Ps 55:13[14]).

The NRSV and the NIV divide the lines differently in vv. 14 and 15, with the NRSV following the opinion of most commentators. The precise meaning of the phrase translated "guests in my house" (גרי ביתי gārê bêtî) is

---

306. H. Haag, "chamas," G. Johannes Botterweck and Helmer Ringgren, eds., *Theological Dictionary of the Old Testament* (*TDOT*), 5 vols. (Grand Rapids: Eerdmans, 1974–86) 4:484.
307. Gordis, *The Book of Job*, 201; Habel, *The Book of Job*, 291; Clines, *Job 1–20*, 428.
308. Hartley, *The Book of Job*, 286; Habel, *The Book of Job*, 301.

309. Driver and Gray, *A Critical and Exegetical Commentary on the Book of Job*, Part I, 167.

uncertain. Since גר (*gēr*) refers to resident aliens, the phrase means something like "retainers," persons not related by blood to the community but who are protected by the patronage of a householder (cf. Exod 3:22, where the phrase means "tenant").[310] Such a person would ordinarily be bound by the strongest motives of loyalty to the one who had given the outsider a place in the social order.

Verses 15-16 describe a social world turned upside down. Maidservants were not only low-ranking members of a household but were also often ethnic foreigners, captured in war or sold into slavery (Lev 25:44-46; 2 Kgs 5:2). For the maidservants to treat the master of the house as the "stranger" and the "foreigner" reverses the relationship. Similarly, the manservant was expected to attend to the needs of the master, taking his cue from the master's gestures as well as words (cf. Ps 123:2). For Job not only to have to verbalize his request ("with my mouth" is emphatic in v. 16*b*) but even to beg, and still to get no response (NIV) is to experience the collapse of a social relationship previously taken for granted.

The dissolution of the most intimate relationships is described in v. 17. Word play in the initial phrase (רוחי זרה *rûḥî zārâ*) allows it to be read both "my spirit is alien" and "my breath is repulsive" to my wife. Whether or not the pun is intentional, it captures the way in which revulsion at a previously insignificant physical characteristic often serves as the focus for and symbol of the alienation between two persons. Another pun occurs in the second half of the verse. In context the verb must mean "be loathsome"; yet it is spelled the same as the verb "to seek favor" (חנתי *ḥannōtî*). Opinion is divided as to whether those who find Job repellent (בני בטני *bĕnê bitnî*, lit., "sons of my belly") are his own children (i.e., those whom his loins have engendered) or his uterine brothers (i.e., sons of the same womb from which he came). The objection to the first alternative is that Job's children are dead (1:19). In this passage, however, Job is using a conventional form of lament, which might well be employed as a traditional topos, whether or not the details fit the narrative framework.

Parallelism favors "wife and children" here. Whichever interpretation is elected, the painful sense of intimacy turned to repulsion is clear.

In vv. 18-19, the description turns again to the larger social world but also to more marked expressions of rejection. The collapse of two very different kinds of social relations is depicted. In the first it is the respect of children for elders, which was taken with great seriousness in the ancient world (cf. 2 Kgs 2:23-24). In the second, it is the solidarity of persons who belong to a circle of friends bound by mutuality. The intensity of such relationships and the particular pain when they turned to enmity is expressed also in the poignancy of Ps 55:12-14[13-15].

A single verse describes Job's physical disintegration (v. 20). Such descriptions are not uncommon in laments, but the precise meaning of this verse is unusually obscure. Clines's suggestion for v. 20 is the best.[311] Flesh and skin are ordinarily supported by the structure of the bones. When the bones "cling to" or are supported by soft tissues, then the normal relationships of the healthy body are reversed. Although there is a close parallel to v. 20*a* in Ps 102:5[6], v. 20*b* is unique. The KJV's literal translation, "and I am escaped with the skin of my teeth," has provided the English language a memorable proverb, but Job is not talking about a narrow escape here, as the adage has come to mean. Teeth, of course, have no skin, so that the expression is a paradoxical way of saying "nothing." Thus "and I have escaped with [or am left with] nothing."

19:21-22. In the preceding verses Job has used a conventional topos from the lament tradition to describe his radical isolation. As in chap. 16, however, he rejects the stance of humble appeal to God to which the lament form would direct him. His subversion of the form is ironic. The imperative "have pity on me" is ordinarily addressed by the sufferer to God (occurring some eighteen times in Psalms; e.g., 4:1[2]; 6:2[3]; 41:10[11]; 57:1[2]). In Ps 41:9-10[10-11], for instance, the psalmist recounts the betrayal by his trusted friend as a reason for God to take pity on him. But Job has no intention of appealing to God for mercy. Rather, he parodies this convention of traditional piety. Inverting the

---

310. Clines, *Job 1–20*, 446-47.

311. Clines, *Job 1–20*, 450-52.

relationships, he calls on the *friends* to have pity because *God* has struck him. A second level of irony in Job's appeal can be gauged by the fact that he has already criticized his cautious friends' readiness to take God's side, even if it means acting as false witnesses (13:7-8). They are certainly not going to take pity on one whom God has struck.[312] The subversion of traditional religious categories is also present in v. 22. Even though ostensibly addressed to the friends as a criticism of their persecution and insatiable appetite for Job's flesh, the sting in v. 22 is the phrase "like God" (כמו־אל *kĕmô-'ēl*). In contrast to the conventions of psalmic piety in which God is deliverer, Job identifies God's role as like that of the wicked who pursue the psalmist (e.g., Ps 7:1[2]; 31:15[16]; 71:11).

19:23-27. In addition to the serious textual problems in this section, the most difficult exegetical challenge of these verses may be their excessive familiarity. Only the rare individual can read v. 25*a* without hearing the strains of Handel's *Messiah* in the background. The very term "redeemer" (גאל *gō'ēl*) has been so Christianized that the use of that word in translations tends to distort the contextual meaning of the underlying Hebrew. Unfortunately, both the NRSV and the NIV improperly capitalize the word "redeemer," as though it were a title rather than a simple noun. In addition to christological interpretation of v. 25*a*, early Christian tradition also found in vv. 25-27 a proof text for bodily resurrection. Although that position is rarely advanced in scholarship today, the issue still draws a disproportionate amount of attention to these verses. To understand this passage in terms of its original context and significance, one must set aside the later history of its appropriation in Christianity.

Since Job has parodied and rejected the language of prayer (vv. 21-22) and realized that his outcry brings no response or justice (v. 7), there appears to be no way for him to bring his words before God. Already in 16:18-22, Job struggled to find a way to keep his cry for justice alive after his own death. Now, in 19:23-26*a*, he returns to that problem. Initially his imagination turns to the distant future, as the words "forever" (לעד *lā'ad*, v. 24) and "at the last" (אחרון *'aḥărôn*, v. 25) indicate. The

first part of his reflection is distinctly marked as an impossible wish ("Oh that . . . " [מי־יתן *mî yittēn*]), as Job fantasizes the preservation of his words as a future testimony (vv. 23-24). Although there is some uncertainty about the interpretation of the imagery, it appears that Job describes three materials on which his words might be recorded—scroll, lead tablet, engraved rock—each more enduring than the last (so NIV).[313] Alternatively, it is possible to interpret all three lines as describing the inscription of words on stone, as in Habel's translation: "Oh, if only it were inscribed on a stela/ With iron stylus and lead,/ Carved on rock forever!"[314]

Just as in 16:18-19, where the cry of Job's blood was paired with his assurance that a witness on high would take his part, so also here Job's words of testimony are paired with his certainty that he has a kinsman-defender (*gō'ēl*, v. 25). The term *gō'ēl* comes from the field of family law. It designates the nearest male relative, who was responsible for protecting a person's interests when that individual was unable to do so. The *gō'ēl* would buy back family property sold in distress (Lev 25:25; Ruth 4:4-6; Jer 32:6-7), recover what had been stolen (Num 5:8), redeem a kinsman sold into slavery (Lev 25:28), or avenge a murdered kinsman's blood (Deut 19:6-12; 2 Sam 14:11). The *gō'ēl* is the embodiment of family solidarity. There is perhaps a note of defiance in Job's confidence that his "*gō'ēl* lives," following his account of how God has alienated all his friends and relatives. In Israelite tradition, God is sometimes referred to as the *gō'ēl* of the orphan and the widow (Prov 23:11; Jer 50:34) and of others who experienced helplessness (Ps 119:154; Lam 3:58), yet Job is clearly seeking a *gō'ēl* to defend his interests against God.[315] Indeed, there may be reproach in his very choice of that term.

To whom does Job refer? The close similarity between 16:18-21 and 19:23-26 suggests that the *gō'ēl*, like the witness, is a heavenly figure, similar to the intercessory angel to whom Elihu refers in 33:23-24.[316]

312. See Hartley, *The Book of Job,* 290, for a contrasting interpretation.

313. Driver and Gray, *A Critical and Exegetical Commentary on the Book of Job,* 171.

314. Habel, *The Book of Job,* 290, 292.

315. Habel, *The Book of Job,* 305-6, and S. Terrien, "Job" *The Interpreter's Bible,* ed. G. Buttrick (Nashville: Abingdon, 1954) 3:1052, provide detailed refutations of the arguments of those who have suggested that the redeemer is God.

316. S. Mowinckel, "Hiob's go'el und Zeuge im Himmel," BZAW 41 (1925), 207-12; Pope, *Job,* 146; Terrien, "Job," 1052.

Or it has been argued that the *gō'ēl* is simply the personified figure of Job's own cry for justice.[317] The issue of the identity of the *gō'ēl*, however, is less important than the function this figure plays in Job's thought. For Job, the notion of the *gō'ēl* supplies the certainty that there is someone with the power and the presence to take up his case with God (the verb "arise" [קום *qûm*] can have a forensic connotation, as in Deut 19:16). It is also clear that Job envisions this as taking place sometime in the future. That this is understood to be after Job's death is likely from the general context, even if the phrase "upon the dust" more likely means "upon the earth" (cf. 41:33[25]) than referring to Job's grave.[318] Unfortunately, v. 26*a* is linguistically obscure but is generally taken also as referring to a time after Job's death. Although the verb is unusual in this context, it is possible to achieve a plausible meaning with only a modest emendation ("thus" [כזאת *kĕzō't*], instead of "this" [זאת *zō't*]), so that the text reads "and after my skin has been stripped off thus."

Additional confusion has been introduced into the interpretation of this passage by the assumption that vv. 26*b*-27 refer to the same scene that Job envisions in vv. 25-26*a*. If read all together, then Job sees his vindication by God after his death. This is a most unlikely notion to ancient Israelites, who did not believe in a bodily resurrection and assumed that the dead know nothing, as Eccl 9:5 succinctly puts it (cf. Job 14:12, 21). Commentators who attempt to read all of these verses together are consequently forced into assuming that a religious leap toward the notion of resurrection is being squeezed out of Job's agony,[319] or that Job as a disembodied shade will be granted a special vision of his vindication by God (NRSV).[320] Neither approach is persuasive.

A much simpler solution has been suggested by Clines, anticipated to a degree by Habel.[321] The key to this interpretation is the recognition that vv. 25-26*a* and 26*b*-27 do not refer to the same scene. In vv. 25-26*a*, Job describes his certainty that a redeemer

will arise and vindicate him after his death. As important as that certainty is to Job, it is not what he most desires. What he desires is expressed in vv. 26*b*-27, not a post-mortem vindication but a vindication that he can experience before he dies, in his flesh and with his own eyes. This interpretation requires no emendation, only a recognition that the conjunction in v. 26*b* can be read as "but," and that the following verbs are not to be translated as simple futures but as modal imperfects expressing a wish. Thus "I know that my defender lives, and that at the last he will arise upon the earth—after my skin has been stripped off! But I would see God from my flesh, whom I would see for myself; my eyes would see, and not a stranger." Although it is linguistically possible to translate v. 27*a* "whom I shall see *on my side,*" as the NRSV does, the interpretation proposed here makes it more likely that Job is emphasizing his desire to see for himself (so NIV).

This understanding of vv. 25-27 fits well with the development of Job's thought. As Job has explored the legal metaphor as a model for his confrontation with God, he has imagined various heavenly figures who might assist him: an arbitrator (9:33), a witness (16:18), and a defender (19:25). The necessity of these figures has been forced on him by the increasing certainty of his impending death. Yet just as Job's confidence in the presence of such a figure reaches its climax, he realizes that such a solution would not truly satisfy him. He desires what he described in 13:13-22, a direct presentation of his case to God and God's reply. After 19:25, Job says no more about heavenly intermediaries; rather, in chaps. 23 and 31 he pursues his determination to carry his case to God's presence. Whether Job experiences yearning or fear (v. 27*c*), there is no doubt about the enormity of what he desires.

19:28-29. At least for the present Job is certain about finding vindication, as his final words to his friends indicate. In v. 22, Job had spoken of the friends persecuting him like God; now he threatens them with judgment. Although Job does not mention God explicitly, his belief in his own vindication is closely connected with his sense that the moral order of the world will be reaffirmed and that the friends will receive judgment

317. Clines, *Job 1–20*, 459.
318. Dhorme, *A Commentary on the Book of Job*, 283.
319. Janzen, *Job*, 144.
320. G. Hoelscher, "Hiob 19, 25-27 und Jubil 23, 30-31," *ZAW* 53 (1935) 277-83.
321. Clines, *Job 1–20*, 457-8, 461-62; Habel, *The Book of Job*, 290-91, 308-9.

for their behavior toward Job (vv. 28-29) and toward God (13:7-11). Just where one expects a despairing meditation on death, Job instead speaks boldly of judgment against his accusers. After chap. 19, Job does not again speak of death, either in longing or in despair.

REFLECTIONS

No one could have anticipated, when this story began as a simple narrative about the nature of true piety, that it would come to this. Even Job was uncertain for a long time about the nature and meaning of his story. His first reaction was to understand it as a story of immense, boundless, and irresistible suffering, the only response to which was bitterness and a desire to die (chaps. 3; 6–7). Gradually, however, Job has recast the nature of his story. By the time one reaches chap. 19, it is no longer the story of a suffering man but that of a man unjustly accused.

The story of the unjustly accused is a paradigmatic one in our own culture, a story that we tell over and over, with different characters, exploring different dimensions of its significance. It is the story told in the novels *The Ox-Bow Incident* and *To Kill a Mockingbird,* in the film *In the Name of the Father,* in the documentary *The Thin Blue Line,* and in countless other works. Whenever a community tells the same story over and over, it signals that the problem presented goes to the foundations of that community. These repeated stories tell of an anxiety that will not go away, even as they re-affirm a truth that is necessary for existence. The story of the unjustly accused emerges as a paradigmatic story only in cultures that organize themselves upon the basis of law and justice. In ancient Israel, justice was such a foundational value. "Righteous-ness and justice are the foundation of your throne," says the psalmist (Ps 89:14*a* [15*a* NRSV), and "O God, give your justice to the king and your righteousness to the king's son; may he judge your people with righteousness, and your poor with justice" (Ps 72:1-2). In ways that combine both religious and secular traditions, American culture is also deeply committed to the "self-evident truths" that make justice the essential foundation of society.

Justice does not always prevail, even in societies in which justice is a basic value. The people who exercise responsibility for justice are fallible and sometimes corrupt. Systems designed to serve justice do not always do so. Anxieties and fears having noth-ing to do with justice cloud vision. Only a blind dogmatist could insist that nothing ever goes wrong. Telling the story of the miscarriage of justice is a way of exploring the moral significance of such failures, reflecting on the qualities of character necessary to maintain a society based on justice, and ultimately determining whether the underlying structure can still be trusted and affirmed. Where God's character and governance of the world are understood in large part through the category of justice, telling such a story also becomes an important exercise in the testing and reformation of religious beliefs.

There are many ways to organize a story of the unjustly accused. One can place the focus on the community and its complicity in a desire not to know the truth. Or the focus can fall on the tireless defender who brings truth to light. The most compelling stories, however, are those that focus on the person of the unjustly accused, as in Job. It is remarkable how many of the dramatic elements that one would find in a contempo-rary narrative of the unjustly accused occur in Job 19: the unheeded cry for justice (v. 7); the sense of powerlessness (vv. 8-12); the gradual withdrawal of social support and the resultant isolation (vv. 13-19); the sense of having been left with absolutely nothing (v. 20). What is perhaps most unendurable is having to hear one's story unrecogniz-ably and falsely told by others who are certain that they recognize the pattern of the criminal or the terrorist or the sinner in one's own case—"broken in pieces by words" is how Job puts it (vv. 2-3). Society is made uncomfortable by an accused person who will not confess, for that raises anxiety about the reliability of the system of justice. It is not "satisfied with the flesh" of the unjustly accused (v. 22) but seeks the victim's own complicity.

In the paradigmatic story, a moment arrives when the unjustly accused must make a fundamental decision: whether to give in to overwhelming pressures and sink into passivity and disintegration or to find the will to fight. Job exemplifies this transition. As angry as his words were in chap. 3, they were essentially the words of a defeated person seeking nothing more than oblivion. His sharp wit and capacity for parody gave him some energy (chaps 7; 9; 12), but they could not keep him from sinking into despair, as the recurrent concluding reflections on death indicate (10:18-22; 14:18-22; 17:13-16). Even though the strength of character of the unjustly accused person is a crucial element, that person cannot succeed alone. The ability to resist is catalyzed by the presence of someone who will stand in solidarity and publicly defend the innocence of the accused. For Job, that crucial assurance comes in 16:18 and in 19:25 with his certainty that a witness and a defender will stand up for him. Even as Job determines to pursue his case himself, he is strengthened by the vision of his witness and his defender.

The unjustly accused persons who seek justice accomplish more than simply personal vindication. They also redeem a compromised system. Their determination to right the wrong done to them is a commitment to the belief that the system of justice is not wholly corrupt, but that through the exposure of its own failures it can be called back to its true nature. That is why Job has become such a compelling figure by chap. 19, and why the narrative of the unjustly accused is such a crucial story in our own culture. It is possible for such stories to be misleading, if they convey the impression that *all* miscarriages of justice are eventually corrected. At their best, however, such stories provide a nuanced and complex way of exploring the elements that lead to a failure of justice. They allow for an honest confrontation of the corruption that besets even the best systems of law. Such stories also serve as models of the moral character and kind of social commitment that is essential for the hard work of maintaining justice. By doing so, they provide an alternative to the complacency of those who refuse to see evil and the cynicism of those who refuse to believe that anything can be done about it.

Job 20:1-29, Zophar Describes the Fate of the Wicked

COMMENTARY

Like Eliphaz and Bildad before him, Zophar's speech in the second cycle consists almost wholly of a conventional poem on the fate of the wicked. After the typical introduction to the disputation, in which he characterizes Job's words as offensive and explains his own need to reply (vv. 2-3), Zophar appeals to ancient authority (v. 4) for the truth of the proposition he wishes to illustrate: that the joy of the wicked is short-lived (v. 5). Zophar first describes the insubstantial nature of the wicked person and his complete destruction (vv. 6-11). The second part of the poem explores the self-destructive nature of evil through a striking series of metaphors pertaining to eating (vv. 12-23). In the third part, Zophar describes the inescapable destruction of the wicked by all the elements of the earth and the heavens (vv. 24-28). A concluding summary underscores that this destruction is God's decree (v. 29).

What Job has said about his own innocence and the wrong done him by God threatens Zophar at a basic level. As Clines puts it, "If Job is right everything Zophar stands for is wrong."[322] Zophar's speech should not be interpreted as an intentional but indirect accusation that Job is one of the wicked who perish so miserably. Like Eliphaz and Bildad, Zophar reasserts the foundations of his moral world in the face of the implications of Job's claims. That foundation is his conviction that evil does not have the same grounding in reality that good has, and that, consequently, its flourishing is ephemeral. This is the fate God has apportioned and decreed for the wicked. That Job hears Zophar's speech (and, indeed, those of Eliphaz and Bildad) as a general claim about the moral order of the world rather than as a personal attack is indicated by the nature of Job's reply in chap. 21, where he refutes the general proposition that the wicked come to an early, miserable end. Only after Job explicitly refutes the moral foundation of their world will Eliphaz resolve the intolerable contradiction by declaring Job guilty of great wickedness and thus an example of precisely the dynamics the friends have been describing as a general proposition (chap. 22).

20:1-3. Most of the opening statements have been directed at the content of the previous speaker's words (8:2-3; 9:2*a*; 11:2-3; 12:2-3; 15:2-3; 18:2-4), although Job has also referred to the social dynamics of the exchange, describing the friends as "comforters" who increase misery (16:2-3), and charging them with using words as weapons to crush him (19:2-3). Zophar opens with words that show that he, too, is upset by the dynamics of the disputation. His agitation and emotional disturbance (v. 2) are caused by the fact that Job has insulted the friends. In a culture strongly oriented to the values of honor and shame, insults are taken seriously. From the friends' perspective, they are warranted in giving Job the kind of tough-minded counsel that characterized wisdom instruction, even if it involves confronting Job with prima facie evidence of his sin (11:6*b*) or with evidence of a sinful disposition expressed in his very words (15:4-6). For Job to characterize their intentions and actions as vicious aggression and as shameful conduct (19:2-3), deserving "punishment by the sword" (19:29), is in Zophar's view an intolerable smear on their

character. Job, of course, sees things very differently. Knowing himself to be innocent of any wrongdoing, he hears all of the friends' direct rebukes and their teachings about the fate of the wicked as an intolerable insult to his own character (19:3). Given the different assumptions that each side brings to the dialogue, this impasse was inevitable. Now that Job and Zophar have cast the dispute in terms of personal insult, the dialogue is doomed.

20:4-5. The foundational nature of what Zophar will say is already implicit in his appeal to ancient authority (v. 4). The moral order was established with the placing of human beings upon the earth (cf. Deut 4:32). Zophar articulates that moral order in terms of the fleeting nature of the joy of the wicked, an idea expressed in similar terms in Ps 37:2, 10. To modern minds, that notion may seem like a peculiar choice for a fundamental insight into the structure of the world. In the moral imagination of ancient wisdom, however, the contrast between the enduring and the ephemeral was of greatest importance. This is not simply a contrast of chronological duration; the difference has ontological significance—that is, it has to do with the nature of reality. A teaching from the Egyptian wisdom text "The Instruction of Ptahhotep" makes this point in describing *maat*, a concept that has connotations of order, justice, and integrity, somewhat similar to the Hebrew word for "righteousness" (צדק *ṣedeq*). The text says, "Great is justice [*maat*], lasting in effect,/ Unchallenged since the time of [the god] Osiris. . . . Baseness may seize riches,/ Yet crime never lands its wares;/ In the end it is justice [*maat*] that lasts."[323] Both evil and good, criminality and justice exist in the world. No one would deny that. The saying insists, however, that, by the nature of things, justice is grounded in the foundations of reality in a way that criminality is not, so that justice eventually reasserts itself, and evil loses its hold. In Hebrew thought, too, God is עולם (*ʿôlām*), the lasting one. Divine wisdom, the foundation of justice, is likewise "from eternity" (see Prov 8:23). Those persons and actions that are grounded in wisdom and partake of God's nature participate in that reality

---

322. Clines, *Job 1–20*, 482.

323. Translation adapted from M. Lichtheim, *Ancient Egyptian Literature: A Book of Readings*, vol. 1 (Berkeley: University of California Press, 1973) 64.

and stability in a way that evil does not. The imagery of Psalm 1 is illustrative. The righteous are like durable live trees with deep roots fed by streams of water; by contrast, the wicked are ephemeral dry chaff, material no longer rooted or living but subject to being blown off by the wind (Ps 1:3-4). Although Israelite thought is expressed in concrete rather than abstract terms, these images make a fundamental philosophical claim about the nature of reality and the difference between good and evil.

20:6-11. Zophar substantiates his claim about the fleeting nature of the joy of the wicked with a series of images. Although varied, all illustrate the inability of the wicked to secure a hold either on the objects of their ambition or, indeed, on existence itself. The image of reaching to the clouds and the heavens (v. 6) echoes mythic stories about human ambition, such as the tower of Babel (Gen 11:4). In that story, the purpose of building the tower was to secure the builders' reputation and to protect against being scattered and dispersed. Just as the activity of the builders of the tower brought about the very thing they most feared, so also the wicked person's ambition to transcend earthly limits results in a most earthy fate: perishing like his or her own excrement (v. 7a). Although it is possible that the image here is of animal dung destroyed by being burned for fuel (cf. 1 Kgs 14:10), the suffixed expression *"his* excrement" more likely refers to the practice of discarding human excrement like dirt (cf. Zeph 1:17). In either case, the wicked person is no longer to be seen (v. 7b; cf. Ps 37:10, 20).

Verses 8-9 continue the imagery of seeing, begun in v. 7b. Dreams seem quite vivid while they occur, but they have no reality in the external world (cf. Isa 29:8), and so they "fly off" or are "chased away" by the act of waking. In Zophar's view, this is also the nature of the wicked (v. 8). Lacking reality, the wicked are subject to the same sudden dispersal into nothingness. Verse 9 shifts the perspective to that of an observer who looks at an object that is suddenly no longer there. Job had used similar imagery to speak of the vanishing of a person in death (7:8-10), but for Zophar the disappearance of the wicked has a significance different from that of general human transiency (e.g., Ps 103:15-16).

The final two verses in this section seem quite different, and some commentators move v. 10 to another place,[324] or simply delete it (so NAB),[325] because of its reference to the children of the wicked person. The verses are, however, consistent with the underlying theme that the wicked, because they lack "reality," are unable to secure their hold on what is desirable. Neither the NRSV nor the NIV gives an adequate translation. Better is the TNK, "His sons ingratiate themselves with the poor;/ His own hands must give back his wealth." The possession of secure wealth, which could be left to one's children as a heritage, was an important value in ancient society (cf. Ruth 4:6; Prov 19:14). Because the wicked cannot secure anything (cf. Prov 11:18; 20:21; 28:8, 22), they have nothing to pass on to their children, who are then so destitute that they must beg even from those who are poor.[326] The last verse describes the inability of the wicked to hold on to life itself. As Clines notes, the first clause is concessive, "though his bones are full of vigor."[327] (For the premature death of the wicked, see Ps 55:23[24].)

20:12-23. In this central section of the speech, Zophar explores the self-destructive nature of the wicked person's obsession with evil through a brilliant succession of metaphors, all related to eating. This life-giving and sustaining activity, which is ordinarily the source of pleasure as well as nourishment, becomes an occasion of pain and death for the wicked.

20:12-15. The first image developed is that of evil as a delicious morsel of food, held in the mouth and savored for all its sweetness. The wicked person's sensuous pleasure in evil is suggested by the threefold description of hiding under the tongue, reluctance to let go of the pleasure, and holding on to the food (vv. 12b-13). Evil is by nature deceptive, however, attractive on the surface but deadly in its essence. Zophar's image captures this quality by the contrast of "sweet"/"bitter poison" and "in the mouth"/"in the belly." The same dynamic is expressed in Proverbs not only through images of food (Prov 9:17; 20:17; 26:22) but also through images of evil

324. Dhorme, *A Commentary on the Book of Job*, 299.
325. Clines, *Job 1–20*, 472, 487, marks it as "unsuitable."
326. Similarly, Fohrer, *Das Buch Hiob*, 329; Andersen, *Job*, 196.
327. Clines, *Job 1–20*, 488.

as illicit sexual pleasure, seductive but ultimately deadly (Prov 7:6-27). Zophar relentlessly follows the logic of his metaphor. Just as poison often induces vomiting, so also the wicked person vomits up what he or she has swallowed (v. 15). In this verse, however, Zophar breaks out of metaphorical speech to identify the evil of v. 12 specifically as economic crime, for what the wicked swallows is property ("riches"). That the wicked cannot keep food down, as we would say, is a representation of the same inability to secure possession that was addressed in vv. 6-11.

20:16. This verse takes up a term from v. 14 and restates the preceding description in terms of the image of snake venom. The term for "bitter poison" in v. 14 is literally "the gall of asps." It was believed in antiquity that the venom of snakes was actually their bitter gall, released through the tongue.[328] In v. 16, the wicked persons' activity is redescribed, not through their own self-deception that evil is sweet, but in the light of its actual nature. When they thought they were savoring delicious food, they were actually sucking on snake venom, which will kill them.

20:17-19. Whereas vv. 14-16 describe the effect of the wicked person's ingesting fatal poison, vv. 17-19 describe the inability of the wicked to ingest truly desirable food. Honey and milk curds (v. 17) are traditional images of plenty, often associated with the land of Canaan (Exod 3:8, 17). In 29:6, Job refers to milk and streams of oil as symbols of his blessedness (cf. the similar description in the Ugaritic Baal epic, "the heavens rain oil, the wadis flow with honey").[329] The wicked are excluded not only from these manifestations of divine blessing, but even from the enjoyment of the fruit of their own toil and trade as well (v. 18). This verse underscores once again the motif that the wicked cannot secure their hold on anything.

Finally, Zophar identifies the crimes of the wicked, which are the reason for the futility of their efforts. As in v. 15, they are economic and social offenses, neglect and oppression of the poor, and the seizure of houses built by others. To a certain extent, these are stereotypical images of evil. Treatment of the poor

is a measure of righteousness and wickedness in the book of Job (22:5-9; 29:12-17; 31:13-23), as in Proverbs (Prov 14:31; 19:17; 22:23; 29:7), and in the prophetic tradition (Isa 10:1-4; 58:6-10; Jer 22:13-17; Amos 5:11-12; 8:4-8). It is also possible, however, that something more specific lies behind the prominence of economic and social themes in the book of Job. If the book of Job was composed in the fifth century, then it may be that the social and economic issues addressed in Nehemiah 5 lie behind the repeated references to economic crimes and the plight of the poor in the book of Job.[330]

20:20-23. The final image in this series is the uncontrollable appetite of the wicked, which leads to punishment by God. These verses are somewhat difficult to translate, but the development of the theme is clearer in the NRSV translation than in the NIV. Zophar's imagery is graphic, as he describes the incessant, restless craving of the belly, which leads the wicked to consume everything. There is perhaps a trace of grotesque personification in v. 21, where the term "nothing left" ordinarily designates a human survivor (שָׂרִיד śārîd). The wicked person's appetite is like a destroying army that lets none escape. There is a certain fascinating energy in phenomena that do not know the regulating limits of satiety, as in the saying of Prov 30:15b-16: "Three things are never satisfied;/ four never say, 'Enough':/ Sheol, the barren womb,/ the earth ever thirsty for water,/ and the fire that never says, 'Enough' " (NRSV). As the proverb suggests, however, the paradox of such insatiability is that such forces consume incessantly, yet have nothing to show for all that effort. This, too, is the paradox of the wicked. For all their greed, they cannot establish lasting prosperity (v. 21b).

The punishment that Zophar describes for the wicked is ironically fitting. The moment of greatest fullness is at the same time the moment when distress (lit., "narrowness" [צַר ṣar]) comes upon him (v. 22a). The mode of his punishment, which corresponds to the insatiable appetite of the wicked, echoes the description of God raining manna upon the hungry Israelites in the wilderness

328. D. Pardee, "mĕrorat-pĕtanim 'Venom' in Job 20.14," *ZAW* 91 (1979) 401-16.

329. *ANET*, 140.

330. The most sustained attempt to provide such a social context for the book of Job is the work of Ranier Albertz, "Der sozialgeschichtliche Hintergrund des Hiob-buches und der 'Babylonischen Theodizee'," 349-72.

(Exod 16:4). Here, however, God's anger rains upon the wicked as food, which he must unwillingly now consume (v. 23).

20:24-29. The final section recounts the rejection and utter extermination of the wicked by all the forces of the world (cf. 18:5-21). Verses 24-25 use the imagery of deadly wounds in a context of battle, whereas vv. 26-28 describe the enmity of darkness, fire, heaven, earth, and flood. The motif of escaping one peril only to fall victim to another (vv. 24-25) is conventional (cf. Isa 24:18; Amos 5:19). Here, poetically, the wicked person flees from personified weapons, rather than from the warriors who wield them. In many cultures weapons are symbolically represented as having personal qualities or even wills of their own. In Ugaritic myth, Baal's two clubs are named Chaser and Driver and are directly exhorted to chase and drive away Baal's enemy Yam.[331] Elsewhere in the OT swords are personified as thirsting for and drinking blood (e.g., Isa 34:5-6). Verse 24 mentions two weapons, one of iron, the other of bronze (lit., a "bronze bow," although often translated as "bronze arrow"). Perhaps the metals iron and bronze are specifically mentioned to form a link with the other natural phenomena listed in vv. 26-28 (darkness, fire, heaven, earth, flood) as seeking out the wicked person for destruction.

331. *ANET,* 131.

Verse 26*a* contains a more clever image than comes across in English translation. The word for "treasures" is literally "things hidden away" (צפונים *ṣĕpûnîm*) so that Zophar describes darkness as concealing itself in order to seize what the wicked person has concealed. An "unfanned fire" (v. 26*b*) is not necessarily a divine fire.[332] In the context of the poetic imagination in this section, it is simply one of the active forces of nature intent on destroying the wicked person.

Analogously, heaven and earth take on the role of witnesses and accusers against the wicked (v. 27; cf. Deut 32:1; Isa 1:2; Mic 6:1-2; and cf. Job 16:18). Textual and grammatical problems obscure v. 28. The difficult word יבול (*yĕbûl*) is best taken as "flood" rather than "produce" (so NIV), in keeping with the parallel term נגרות (*niggārôt*) in v. 28*b*, which means "torrents."[333] Thus, after the heavens and the earth have borne witness against the wicked, the floods carry out the sentence. Although the elements act directly, they all act as agents of divine anger (v. 28*b*).

Zophar concludes his speech with a summary evaluation emphasizing the role of God. Ironically, in view of the futile efforts of the wicked to lay secure hold of any of the objects of their desire, his utter destruction is the one thing that can be called their "portion" and their "inheritance" (v. 29).

332. Contra Gordis, *The Book of Job,* 221; Pope, *Job,* 153; Fohrer, *Das Buch Hiob,* 333.
333. So Dhorme, *A Commentary on the Book of Job,* 306; Gordis, *The Book of Job,* 221; Pope, *Job,* 153.

REFLECTIONS

Is Zophar right? The modern reader's strong identification with Job often means that what the friends say is dismissed simply because they say it. Yet Zophar's underlying claim, that good and evil have a different relation to fundamental reality, deserves more thoughtful consideration. Part of the difficulty in giving Zophar a hearing lies with the way he develops the argument in terms of the fate of individual persons. Job will make short work of that form of the argument in chap. 22. Nevertheless, there is something provocative about the notion that good and evil are different in nature—that there is a resilient, lasting quality to good that derives from its participation in the fundamental structures of God's creation, and that evil, no matter how large it looms, is nevertheless fragile and subject to sudden collapse precisely because it is not part of that creation but a distortion of it.

The claim made by Zophar and by ancient wisdom in general cannot be confirmed or refuted simply by citing examples and counterexamples. It is not so much a conviction deduced from observation as it is a claim of faith, which in turn shapes perception.

Even those who are initially skeptical about its validity, however, may be more willing to consider its merits when the question is phrased in terms of what gives persons the strength to oppose massive evil. A long struggle can be sustained only if a deeply held conviction exists that evil is inherently unstable and must eventually break apart. The opponents of official racial segregation in the United States and of apartheid in South Africa were sustained by the conviction that such injustice simply could not preserve itself in the face of the claims of simple human justice. The dissidents in the Soviet Union and Eastern Europe resisted in the knowledge that the massive structures of oppression would eventually show themselves to be hollow. The democracy movement in China is supported by the certainty that such repressive power will one day crumble. At its most profound, Zophar's perception offers not a denial of evil, but a bulwark against despair.

Criticisms can be brought against the position Zophar articulates, however. It does not seem able to account for the insidious persistence of evil. A cruel system of repression may vanish like a dream or die suddenly, poisoned by its own appetite for evil. In the aftermath, however, new evil often seems to sprout as vigorously as good. The claims of Zophar and the wisdom tradition in general about the lasting nature of good and the ephemeral nature of evil have little explanatory power in those situations.

Rather than simply deciding for or against the understanding of good and evil represented by Zophar, one might do better to reflect on the variety of ways in which the Bible talks about good and evil and how they differ from Zophar's perspective. Although there is not space here to explore them in detail, three models in particular suggest something of the range of thinking found in the OT. Drawing on ancient Near Eastern mythic traditions, biblical accounts of the struggle between Yahweh and the primordial chaos monster represent evil as something that is contained and restrained by God but never fully eliminated from the world (Job 38:8-11; Psalms 74; 114). Although the great victory that occurred in connection with the establishment of the created world was decisive, elements of the chaotic continue to break forth. In quelling them, God reenacts the great cosmogonic victory (Isa 51:9-11). This is a very insightful way of thinking about evil, one that deserves greater presence in contemporary theological reflections. In its own mythic language, this perspective acknowledges that disruptive and painful elements are and always have been part of the world. In contrast to Zophar's view of evil as ephemeral, such an understanding has no difficulty in accounting for the persistence of evil, for the very nature of the chaotic is to break out suddenly and unexpectedly. The psalmists often used the image of the surging waters of chaos to evoke the personal sense of being overwhelmed by illness, danger, and death. It is equally evocative of the disasters that overtake whole communities and threaten their existence.

For Zophar, hope is mostly a matter of waiting. One need do nothing if evil will self-destruct. The mythic tradition of God's battle with chaos suggests a different stance. Hope is assured because the decisive victory is already won, and the power of the creating God is now present in every struggle, sustaining and restoring the community of life. Such a perspective leads to a less passive stance than Zophar's, for it is in one's own struggles against the inbreaking of chaos that one experiences the power of God the creator. Finally, one possible misapprehension should be addressed. The mythic account is not a dualistic model, and it is perhaps somewhat misleading to talk about it primarily in terms of good and evil. It is a more comprehensive vision of the tensions that exist within creation between order and disorder, chaos and cosmos, death and regeneration, as well as good and evil.

The apocalyptic tradition, by contrast, does develop a model of good and evil that becomes increasingly dualistic. The struggle between good and evil on earth mirrors a struggle between good and evil heavenly forces (Daniel 7; 10-12). Although the OT does not speak of a chief of heavenly forces of evil, other non-canonical Jewish literature and certain books of the NT do present a malign angelic being—variously called Mastema, Satan, Belial, or Beelzebub—who is the source of evil and God's opponent. In sharp contrast to Zophar's view, apocalyptic stresses the reality of evil. Evil does not self-destruct, but has to be violently overcome. The apocalyptic perspective accounts for the persistence of evil, as cycles of evil and its defeat recur in the history of the world until eventually God triumphs decisively over all evil (e.g., *1 Enoch* 85–90).

One of the most serious problems with apocalyptic approaches to evil, however, is that they tend to overschematize the problem. Simple human stupidity, venality, insecurity, and alienation are responsible for a great deal of the woe in the world, and it is implausible to see much of this as part of a great cosmic drama. In this respect, Zophar's images of individual ambition, greed, and self-absorption are much more apt. Apocalyptic can also be a very dangerous model of evil, because its black-and-white scenario allows for no shades of gray. It becomes all too easy to demonize one's opponents and to fail to see the evil that may lodge in one's own self and community. This tendency to divide the world into two categories is not limited to apocalyptic. Zophar, too, thinks in terms of righteous and wicked *people* rather than in terms of people who are variously capable of doing righteous and wicked deeds.

In this respect, the understanding of good and evil presented in Genesis 2–3 is a refreshing alternative. One must be careful not to import into this story later Christian reinterpretation, which tends to read it through the lens of apocalyptic. On its own terms, Genesis 2–3 is the one account that chooses not to locate good and evil in relation to cosmic structures but in relation to the complexities of being human. This subtle story locates the issue in the human desire to imitate God's ability to choose for oneself between what is desirable and undesirable, good and bad. The problem is that such choices are always made with respect to a center of value. When that center of value becomes the human self, then the way is open both to great creativity and to great destructiveness. The consequences of this divine prerogative, now lodged in human beings with limited wisdom, are evident in the stories that follow Genesis 2–3: fratricidal murder (4:8) but also the founding of civic culture (4:17); the development of the arts of civilization, including animal husbandry, music, and metalworking (4:20-22), but also the impulse to revenge (4:23-24). Good and evil are inextricably mixed in the restless human heart, which is always engaged in exercising power for which it lacks adequate wisdom. Such a vision of good and evil is much more radically open than the others described; there is no guarantee that goodness will triumph. Indeed, the opposite is most likely, as the human descent into almost universal corruption suggests (Gen 6:1-4). From this perspective, the grace of God, not the fundamental structures of reality, ensures the continuation of life and goodness (Gen 8:21-22).

The challenge presented by Job's account of his situation and his radical reinterpretation of the nature of the world has forced Zophar to articulate his fundamental understanding of the world's moral structure. Readers who take these issues seriously are similarly forced to consider how they understand the nature of the world, the structure of good and evil, and God's role. What is evil like? Is it mostly an illusion, something that lacks the grounding in reality that good possesses? Or is it very much a part of the structure of the world, always threatening, but ultimately limited in its power to destroy? Is it a malign will that seeks out and tries to annihilate every good thing? Or is it largely the side effect of human self-centeredness and lack of understanding? It is not easy to decide what one thinks about these questions, and perhaps no one of these perspectives is adequate by itself. How one understands the nature of evil, however, plays a very important role in the way a person responds to the crises of life and community.

Job 21:1-34, The Fate of the Wicked Is Prosperity and Honor

COMMENTARY

Throughout the second cycle of speeches, the friends have focused on one theme only: the fate of the wicked (chaps. 15; 18; 20). In his first two speeches, Job did not reply directly to their claims but pursued the theme of God's violence against him, using legal imagery to explore a way of securing his vindication (chaps. 16–17; 19). Now, however, in his final speech in this cycle, Job addresses the cumulative arguments of the friends concerning the fate of the wicked. Job's speech is a simple one. He introduces his words by asking for a hearing, sarcastically granting the friends permission to mock him when he is finished (vv. 2-3). Job recognizes the radical nature of what he is about to say. Not only will it shock his friends, but the thought of it is also enough to terrify Job himself (vv. 4-6). Modern readers may miss the horror implicit in Job's words. In the ancient wisdom tradition, however, the notion of the punishment of the wicked was the fulcrum of the entire moral order. By denying that the wicked are regularly punished, Job in effect denies the moral order of the world. He develops his claim in four parts. First, he describes the actual fate of the wicked in terms that orthodox thought would use to describe those blessed by God (vv. 7-16). In the second section, Job argues that disaster seldom overtakes the wicked and that a punishment visited upon the wicked person's descendants is no punishment at all (vv. 17-21). Next, Job points out the apparent randomness of fate and the common end awaiting all persons (vv. 22-26). Finally, Job engages the anecdotal claims of the friends concerning the destruction of the wicked by appealing to an equally familiar scene: the wicked person who escapes judgment in life and is honored in death with a splendid funeral and memorial (vv. 27-33). Job concludes by judging the friends' words to be not only empty but also a betrayal of the truth (v. 34).

21:1-6. The ironic use of the motif of consolation opens and closes Job's speech (vv. 2, 34). In the first speech of this cycle, Eliphaz used the phrase "the consolations of God" to refer to the teachings through which a person could be reassured about the nature of God and the world. Job has had more than enough of such teachings, however. The only consolation the friends could give him is to listen to what he has to say. This is not unlike the appeal Job made in 6:24-30. Then, however, Job still considered it possible for a genuine exchange of truth to take place. Now, after having heard what the friends have to say, Job no longer expects them to listen with understanding, but only asks them to hold their mockery until the end of his speech (v. 3).

As Job indicates through a rhetorical question, the issue at stake is not a mere dispute with another human being, but something much more fundamental (v. 4*a*). The term translated "impatient" (קצר *qāṣar*), however, does not quite capture the nuance of his words, which literally mean "my spirit is short" (v. 4*b*). Elsewhere, this and similar phrases designate the psychological state of a person immediately before some decisive word is spoken or action is taken (Num 21:4; Judg 10:16; 16:16; Zech 11:8). The pent-up tension can no longer be held in; what is said or done will change the course of events.

It is not his appalling physical condition to which Job directs the attention of his friends (v. 5); they have seen that before. Rather, it is what he is about to say. The expression "look at me" is the same one Job used in 6:28 when he asked the friends to attend to the truthfulness of his words. The gesture of placing the hand to the mouth indicates silence (Judg 18:19), although it may be silence induced by respect (29:9), shame (Prov 30:32; Mic 7:16; cf. 40:4), or shock, as here. Despite the boldness of Job's words, he, too, is aware that what he is about to say will destroy the foundations of the moral world in which he, as well as his friends, have lived. It is not the audacity of his saying it that makes him tremble, however, but the terrifying nature of what confronts him as simple truth (v. 6).

21:7-16. Job announces the topic of his complaint in v. 7. Contrary to what should be, the wicked actually live long and prosperous lives. In the following verses, he gives a detailed description of their experience. If encountered out of context, vv. 8-13 would appear to be a description of God's blessings upon the righteous. Job recounts the security of descendants (v. 8; cf. Pss 112:2; 128:3, 6; 144:12), a peaceful household, free from fear or divine punishment (v. 9; cf. Ps 112:7-8; Prov 1:33), multiplication of herds (v. 10; cf. Gen 30:29-30; Ps 144:13; also note Deut 28:4, 18), the carefree frolicking of children and general festivity (vv. 11-12; cf. Ps 21:6[7]; Prov 10:28; Jer 31:4; Zech 8:5), and a life of unbroken prosperity concluding in a peaceful death (v. 13; cf. Gen 25:8). The description is quite similar to Eliphaz's account of the fate of the righteous (5:23-26), which includes peace, security, prosperity, descendants, and a long life ending in a good death. Job's account completely contradicts the traditional claims, repeated by the friends, about the fate of the wicked, that their offspring are cut off (18:19; 20:10; Ps 37:28b, 38b), that their households are destroyed (18:14-15; 20:28; Prov 14:11; 21:12), that their wealth dissipates (15:29; 20:10, 15; Prov 11:18; 13:22; 28:22), that they are subject to terrors (15:21), and that they experience violent and premature death (15:30; 18:13-14; 20:23-25; Pss 37:20; 55:23[24]; Prov 11:19, 23; 14:32; 21:7).

Those who have experienced the goodness that Job describes are not the righteous, however, but those who have repudiated God. Job dramatizes their attitude by quoting the words that they might have said, a device often used in depicting the wicked (see Pss 10:4, 6, 11; 12:4[5]; 14:1; 53:1[2]; 94:7). In this case, the wicked are portrayed as not desiring to know the ways of God (v. 14), the very opposite stance from the righteous, who ask for such knowledge (e.g., Ps 25:4-5). The wicked calculate the possible benefits and decide that righteousness is not worthwhile (v. 15). Job is perhaps slyly mocking the tendency of traditional religious discourse to stress the material benefits of righteousness as a motive for obedience to God (Deut 28:1-2; Psalm 128; Prov 13:21-22, 25). As Fohrer

notes, the entire plot of Job begins with the question of whether the benefits of piety corrupt its purity.[334]

The translation and interpretation of the final verse of this section (v. 16) is disputed.[335] The NRSV takes 16a as an implicit rhetorical question, to the effect that the wicked are indeed responsible for their own prosperity. This interpretation fits well with vv. 14-15, but it leaves unexplained why Job would rather primly distance himself from "the plans of the wicked" (v. 16b). The NIV takes v. 16a as a simple statement that the prosperity of the wicked is *not* in their own control. This judgment, contradicting vv. 14-15, does not seem consistent with Job's other statements in this chapter. The problem of interpretation disappears if one understands this verse as Job's mimicking of a typical pious platitude. This statement, as the NIV translates it, is just the sort of thing that the friends would say; indeed, it is the theme of Zophar's last speech. Thus conventional wisdom responds to the claims of the wicked (vv. 14-15) by saying that they are not really in control of their fleeting prosperity; God is (v. 16a). Consequently, the pious distance themselves from the way the wicked think (v. 16b). But Job will refute such conventional wisdom by pointing out that God seldom seems to do anything about the prosperity of the wicked (vv. 17-21).

Job is not the first person to have noticed and been troubled by the apparent contradiction between the claims of religious ideology and the evidence of experience. This problem was addressed in a number of writings in the ancient Near East, particularly in Mesopotamia and in Israel. The Mesopotamian text most closely resembling Job, the Babylonian Theodicy, is also framed as a dialogue between a sufferer, who is innocent of wrongdoing, and his friend. In his complaints, the sufferer observes that the moral order seems to be the reverse of what it should be. "Those who do not seek the god go the way of prosperity, While those who pray to the goddess become destitute and impoverished" (ll. 70-71).[336] In Israelite tradition, Psalms 10; 37; and 73 are sustained examinations of this

334. Fohrer, *Das Buch Hiob*, 343.
335. Gordis, *The Book of Job*, 230, and Habel, *The Book of Job*, 322, emend the text. Pope, *Job*, 159, suggests that the verse is misplaced or is a pious gloss.
336. *ANET*, 602.

problem and the threat it posed to faith. In Psalm 73, the psalmist's description of the good fortune of the wicked (Ps 73:4-11) is as long and as vivid as Job's. The difference, however, is that in all of these instances the problem is expressed in a context that contains and finally defeats the threat to orthodox faith. In the Babylonian Theodicy, the friend's replies are appreciatively accepted and finally seem to overcome the sufferer's alienation, for he ends with a humble plea for mercy (ll. 295-97).[337] The tone of Psalm 37 is consistently one of assurance that the wicked will be quickly cut off. Even Psalm 73 represents its anxiety about the good fortune of the wicked as a danger to faith that troubled the psalmist in the past but was later overcome through the psalmist's experience of God's presence. These texts operate as safety valves, allowing the pressure of perceived contradictions to be expressed in a controlled manner, without doing harm to the basic structure of belief. Job, by contrast, can no longer be satisfied with such measures. He is determined to expose the radical nature of the contradiction between what orthodoxy claims and what experience knows to be the case.

21:17-21. Job refutes two arguments in this section. The first is the claim that the wicked have a tenuous existence and are quickly destroyed (cf. v. 16*a* NIV). In vv. 17-18, Job alludes to several popular images by which this idea was expressed, that the lamp of the wicked is extinguished (cf. 18:5; Prov 13:9; 24:20), that the wicked are like chaff blown off by the wind (cf. Pss 1:4; 35:5), that God's anger apportions destruction to the wicked (cf. 20:28-29), and that calamity overtakes them (cf. 18:12; Prov 6:15). To all of this Job simply asks, "How often?" To claim that a pattern of events is part of a true moral order, one must be able to show that the events occur in a regular and predictable way. It is not enough to say that sometimes the wicked are cut off, but sometimes they are not.

In v. 19*a*, Job cites a possible objection, that even if a wicked person is not punished, it is because God has stored up the punishment for the wicked person's children. (The phrase "you say" or "it is said" is not explicit in the text but added for clarity in the translations.)

The notion that God might punish a later generation for the sin of a former generation was common in ancient Israel (Exod 20:5; Deut 5:9; 2 Sam 12:13-14; Lam 5:7), but was also contested (Jer 31:29-30; Ezek 18:1-4). Curiously, however, it is not used elsewhere in the context of theodicy, as Job uses it here. When the friends speak of the fate of the children of the wicked, it is as an extension of their punishment, not as a substitute for it (5:4; 18:19; 20:10).[338] Perhaps the idea was more common than the surviving literature suggests, or perhaps Job, like a confident debater, is adding an argument to the friends' repertoire, only to dismantle it. In either case, Job's reply to this hypothetical objection is of a piece with his previous reflection on the limit imposed by death (14:21-22). In death all knowledge and all concern for one's descendants are cut off (v. 21). Thus only direct recompense during the individual's life suffices. Job's imagery is highly sensory: seeing and drinking (v. 20). This kind of immediacy is necessary for one to *know* a moral order, to understand a correlation between evil and punishment (v. 19*b*). Although he does not draw the conclusion, what Job has been doing in this section is to establish the conditions necessary for a principle to be recognized as part of a moral order. Such a principle must be direct enough to be perceived as a response to one's actions (vv. 19-21), and it must be regular enough to be perceived as a structure rather than as an accident of existence (vv. 17-18). The claim about the punishment of the wicked meets neither criterion.

21:22-26. In contrast to the implicit conditions for a moral order Job has just articulated, he now demonstrates that existence is actually characterized by a lack of rational discrimination between one person's fate and another's. Job introduces his argument with a citation of a common cliché: No one can teach God understanding, since God is the judge of the highest (v. 22; cf. Isa 40:13-14). The ability to make discriminating judgments is, after all, the distinguishing characteristic of divinity (Gen 3:5). Yet Job follows this cliché with the claim that two persons, otherwise indistinguishable ("one . . . another . . . " [זה . . . זה *zeh . . . zeh*], NRSV), suffer diametrically opposite fates (vv. 23-25). To look at the

337. *ANET*, 604.

338. Fohrer, *Das Buch Hiob*, 344.

situation from another perspective, no matter how deserving of different fates they were, in death they experience the same end (v. 26). Whichever way one looks at it, the world is characterized more by randomness than by discriminating moral judgment exercised by a powerful God. Job's critique is also developed in Ecclesiastes, where the inability to discern a moral order leads to the judgment that existence itself is absurd (Eccl 2:14-15; 9:1-3).

21:27-34. Most commentators think that v. 27 is Job's barbed reply to the friends' attempt to identify him indirectly as one of the wicked (i.e., the wicked are destroyed; Job has been destroyed; therefore, Job is one of the wicked).[339] Certainly the phrasing "the schemes by which you would wrong me" fits this interpretation. The problem, however, is that what follows this statement has nothing to do with Job personally but is his reply to another typical argument of theodicy. The entire attempt to interpret the friends' arguments in the second cycle as veiled accusations against Job stresses the personal dimension too much and ignores the more general argument about the moral structure of the world, which is what Job actually engages. The terminology of v. 27 is probably to be understood in relation to the disputation ("I know the devices by which you plan to attack me," i.e., my arguments) rather than as Job's reply to subtle personal accusations.

The sudden disappearance of the establishments of the wicked (v. 28) is one of the most pervasive moral themes in biblical piety. It is a claim made by each of the three friends (8:14-15; 15:34; 18:15-21; 20:26-28), and it is prominent in Proverbs (Prov 6:15; 10:30; 14:11) and Psalms (Pss 37:10, 20, 35-36;

52:7[9]; 73:18-20; 112:10). Such a claim is essentially anecdotal. Job, in reply, appeals to those who have access to a wide range of anecdotal information, those who travel the roads (v. 29), whether as vagabonds, itinerant laborers, or traders (cf. Pss 80:13; 89:42; Prov 9:15; Lam 1:12; 2:15). Such people, Job claims, will be able to give accounts that directly contradict prevailing orthodoxies, accounts of how the evil person was spared in the day of calamity (v. 30; cf. 20:28; Prov 11:4; Zeph 1:18).

Even more strongly, Job insists that such persons are never confronted with their conduct or paid back for what they have done in life (v. 31; cf. Prov 11:31). The dishonoring of the corpse was the final way in which such a wicked person might be repaid (e.g., Jer 22:18-19). Job, however, recounts the irony of the wicked person's being given a distinguished burial. Far from having memory of that person perish (Prov 10:7), a watch will be kept over the tomb (v. 32*b*), and a great funeral procession will accompany the interment (v. 33; cf. Eccl 8:10).

In the final verse of his speech, Job returns to the motif of consolation. What the friends have offered him is "emptiness" (הבל *hebel*), the same word that serves as the theme of Ecclesiastes. Even more strongly, Job identifies their consolation as fraudulent (מעל *ma'al*). As Gordis observes, in priestly contexts the term designates the violation of something sacred, an act of faithlessness or treachery.[340] In using this word, Job implies that the friends' attempt to answer him with empty platitudes is a violation of truth, which is itself sacred (cf. Prov 16:10).

---

339. Andersen, *Job*, 201; Habel, *The Book of Job*, 329.

340. Gordis, *The Book of Job*, 236.

REFLECTIONS

Does the world possess a fundamental moral order, or are events and fates merely random? We are accustomed to assume that such radical questions, which go to the heart of traditional religious belief, only emerged in the modern period. Not so. These honest questions are embedded within the Bible itself. In the psalms there may be a certain nervousness about raising such questions and a too hasty attempt to put the lid back on. But in Job and in Ecclesiastes questions about whether a moral order exists in the world are asked with all the freedom and passion imaginable. In these books, the doubts that are raised are not introduced in order to be triumphantly refuted. In

Ecclesiastes, Qoheleth works out the nature of a faith that remains deeply skeptical about the accessibility of a clear moral order. In Job, even though God will reject Job's arguments as "words without knowledge" (38:2), God's own words about the nature of the world are as much a challenge to the orthodoxies of the friends as are Job's questions. Far from closing off the discussion, the book as a whole invites it to continue.

Too often religious people repress hard questions and expressions of doubt, embarrassed that they cannot simply accept what others seem to believe so easily. In many Sunday school classes, Bible studies, and discussion groups anyone attempting to voice such doubts might be criticized and made to feel "unchristian" for having said so. Many leave, concluding that their questions have no place within the church. One should remember, however, that at the end of the book, Job—not the friends—is commended for "speaking rightly." Those who are hostile to doubt fail to understand that doubt is not merely compatible with faith but also essential to it. Mature and resilient faith is nurtured by the honest exploration of all the questions arising from experience. Fearful, unexamined faith is brittle and unsustaining, as the contrast between Job and his friends shows. By placing the radical questions of Job and Ecclesiastes squarely within its bounds, the Bible models the confidence of a mature community of faith for whom these questions are a natural part of religious life.

It is one thing to celebrate the freedom to ask hard questions; it is quite another to grapple with the content of Job's challenge. Does the world have a moral order or not? Job's insistence on looking at what actually happens in the world leads to skepticism if not outright rejection of the notion that people regularly get what they deserve and deserve what they get. Although people sometimes do bring trouble upon themselves, just as often it seems to be a random fate or victimization by others. Taken on his own terms, Job is right; there is no discernible moral order in the world. But Job and his friends have all been assuming that a moral order somehow operates (or should operate) automatically, like a cosmic "happy-ending machine," producing the proper pattern of outcomes for everyone. Perhaps that is not the appropriate way to think about the moral order of the world.

A moral order is something that has to be created, or more properly, co-created. It comes into being and continues to exist through the actions of individual moral agents. This notion is easier to grasp if one thinks in terms of moral order in relation to an actual community, such as the community formed by people who work together in a business. Everyone knows the content of a moral order in such a community. It means fairness in dealing with others, respectful treatment, honesty, diligent work, etc. Under such conditions, everyone flourishes. That moral order does not happen automatically, but comes into existence through the actions of the people who make up the community. Those who violate the moral order can cause great damage, both to individuals and to the community. An employee who spreads malicious gossip or a supervisor who abuses power threatens the moral order that has been created. Restoring the health of the organization requires the hard work of those who understand the importance of the moral order and are willing to take risks in order to support it. In the world at large, the moral order is more complex but not fundamentally different in nature.

What is the role of God in the moral order? It is clear to Job and to anyone who observes the gross injustices occurring every day that God is not a heavenly "enforcer" who guarantees that everyone acts properly, meting out rewards and punishments to make certain that they do. Some might say that God commands persons to live morally but leaves humans free to obey or disobey. That perspective is partially correct but overlooks an important way in which God is also related to the moral order through creation. Every moral order must be grounded on a notion of value. God brings the moral order into being through God's judgment that each created being is "good" (Gen 1:10, 12, 18, 21, 26, 31). Thus each being is a center of value that must be treated with respect. In addition to value, a moral order requires relationships of "rightness."

These relationships are in part a matter of mutual limits that secure a place for each being. They are also a matter of cooperative behavior that ensures mutual flourishing. Such an order of harmony and flourishing is described in Genesis 1, where each aspect of creation must respect the limits proper to it to make room for its opposite, and where cooperative interaction between these different creatures makes possible the flourishing of all. These orders of rightness, experienced in the rhythms and structures of nature, are the pattern for the moral order. As creatures endowed with freedom, human beings have to choose to perceive and embody such an order of rightness and respect in community. To covet, to steal, to commit adultery, to bear false witness, to kill—all such actions violate the integrity of a fellow human. To honor one's parents and to respect God enhance the cooperative bonds that form community. To keep the sabbath, the sign of God's creation, is to recognize the close relationship between the order of rightness embodied in creation and the order of rightness embodied in the moral law.

Israel's wisdom tradition offers ways of thinking about the moral order that are congenial to this understanding. According to the wisdom tradition, animals are wise by nature (Prov 30:24-28), living "rightly" in harmony with the order of creation. But for human beings, living rightly is not so simple. It requires above all the cultivation of insight, the perception of the wisdom that lies at the heart of creation (Prov 3:19-20), the righteousness and justice that are the foundations of God's throne (Ps 89:14[15]). Such insight is not easy to achieve, since it is always tempting to confuse one's personal interest with transcendent values. Yet it is possible to know what is right. Understanding is the first act, but it is also necessary not just to know what is right but, as the biblical idiom puts it, to "do righteousness" as well. Doing righteousness is a cosmos-creating activity, an activity that brings into being the very values that direct it. The moral order is a co-creative activity of God and human beings as moral agents.

Thinking of the moral order in these dynamic terms also requires that one acknowledge the possibility of cosmos-destroying activities. The wisdom tradition names this folly. It is primarily a failure of understanding (Prov 28:5). Without insight into the moral order, persons do destructive things with devastating consequences. By asserting that wisdom is part of the fabric of creation itself, however, the wisdom tradition does not leave the moral order as a merely contingent phenomenon dependent on the weak minds and wills of individual human beings. No matter how destructive the folly and malice of those who lack insight, the grounding of the moral order in creation provides it with a resiliency and vitality that cannot be ultimately destroyed.[341]

341. For a philosophical development of the idea of the relation between the moral order and the order of nature, see Erazim Kohak, *The Embers and the Stars: A Philosophical Inquiry into the Moral Sense of Nature* (Chicago: The University of Chicago Press, 1984).

JOB 22:1–27:23, THE THIRD CYCLE

OVERVIEW

In the first two cycles of speeches the sequence of speakers has been regular and symetrical: Eliphaz-Job; Bildad-Job; Zophar-Job. Although the third cycle begins in a similar manner with speeches by Eliphaz and Job, the expected sequence soon begins to break down. Bildad's speech in chap. 25 is only 6 verses long. Although Job replies to Bildad in chap. 26, chap. 27 begins with the unusual heading "And Job again took up his discourse and said . . . " (27:1), as though Job's speech had been interrupted. In the third cycle there is no speech attributed to Zophar. The content of the speeches presents difficulties. Each of the speeches attributed to Job contains material that sounds more like the opinions and style of the friends, especially in 24:18-25; 26:5-14; 27:13-23. Since the poem on wisdom in chap. 28 contains no separate heading, it is occasionally taken as a continuation of Job's speech,[342] but most recognize it as a separate composition placed after the dialogue, which concludes with chap. 27. Its independence from both what precedes and what follows is suggested by the fact that 29:1 begins with the heading "and Job again took up his discourse and said . . . " (cf. 27:1).

The majority of modern scholars have made the assumption that the third cycle originally contained the same sequence of speakers as the first two cycles. The present state of disarray is presumed to be the result either of unintentional scribal error or a deliberate attempt by a concerned copyist to put some traditionally pious words into the mouth of Job, borrowing them from the speeches of Bildad and Zophar. Although it is quite possible that some such disturbance of the text occurred, there is no independent evidence of it. The earliest translations, the targum of Job from Qumran and the Septuagint, exhibit the same distribution of speeches that one finds in the MT. Those who assume that the third cycle has been disturbed have made a bewildering variety of proposals for reconstructing the original cycle.[343] Gordis serves as a good example of the most modest rearrangement. In his view the third cycle had the following original structure: Eliphaz, 22:1-30; Job 23:1–24:25; Bildad, 25:1-6 + 26:5-14; Job 26:1-4 + 27:1-12; Zophar, 27:13-23.[344] Others typically add all or part of 24:18-25 to Zophar's or, more rarely, to Bildad's speech.[345] The problem with this approach is that such rearrangement creates a text that may never have existed except in the scholarly reconstruction.

There are good reasons for being cautious about resorting to textual surgery. The assumption that the third cycle must be structured like the first two overlooks the fact that the dialogue has broken down. It is entirely possible that the disarray of the third cycle is an artistic representation of the impasse that Job and his friends have reached in their attempt to persuade each other. Giving Bildad a short speech and having Zophar fail to speak at all are apt ways of suggesting that the friends have nothing more to say or see no point in saying it again.[346] The apparent contradictoriness in what Job says in chaps. 24, 26, and 27 is a more difficult matter. Nevertheless, it is quite possible to read and interpret those speeches as belonging entirely to Job, if, for instance, one assumes that Job is citing the friends in order to refute them (24:18-25) or sarcastically mimicking their predictable ways of speaking (26:5-14; 27:13-23). This approach is not without its own difficulties, however, for it depends on recognizing literary techniques that are somewhat different from those used in earlier parts of the dialogue.

Neither approach to the third cycle solves all the interpretive problems. In the commentary to the third cycle, I attempt to read the text without rearrangement, although I think that a case can be made for taking 26:5-14 as part of Bildad's speech (see Commentary on Job 25–26).

The beginning of the third cycle is closely related to the end of the second cycle of speeches. In chap. 21 Job attacked the central element of the friends' moral imagination, their belief in divine retribution as reflected in the miserable fate of the wicked. At the beginning of the third cycle in chap. 22 Eliphaz responds by accusing Job of being one of the wicked, even as he holds out the continuing possibility of repentance and restoration. Job, alienated from the entire tradition of religiosity represented by Eliphaz, seeks a vindication of his integrity not through prayer but through a legal hearing (chap. 23). The questions that trouble him, however, do not just concern the chances for his vindication by God but also the failure of God to ensure a moral order in the world (chap. 24). Bildad's reply to Job (25:1-6; 26:5-14), sarcastically interrupted by Job (26:1-4), attempts to shift the focus of the conversation away from Job's personal situation and even from the fate of the wicked. He wishes to speak of the wholly otherness of the cosmic creator and the comparative nothingness of all human existence. But Job

342. E.g., Janzen, *Job*, 187-201.

343. Leveque, *Job et son dieu*, 217n. 1, contains a long list.

344. Gordis, *The Book of Job*, 534-35. Gordis thinks that some original material is now missing, however.

345. See, e.g., Dhorme, *A Commentary on the Book of Job*, 386; Pope, *Job*, 188-89.

346. Davidson, *The Book of Job*, 180, 186; Andersen, *Job*, 214; Janzen, *Job*, 171-86.

refuses to be swayed from his determination to confront the God "who has taken away my right" (27:2), and in chap. 27 swears an oath defending his integrity. His mocking imitation of the friends' platitudes in the second half of the chapter pre-empts Zophar's reply and brings the dialogue to an end.

Job 22:1-30, Eliphaz Urges Job to Repent

COMMENTARY

Throughout their responses to Job, the three friends have never yet identified Job with the wicked. In the first cycle, Eliphaz spoke of him as a pious person who only needs to wait for restoration (4:6), whose misfortunes are a form of divine discipline leading to a secure future (5:17-26), and who is part of sinful humanity and so shares in its fate (4:17-21; cf. 15:14-16). Bildad argued that Job's children were the sinners (8:4). Zophar assumed that Job must have sinned in some fashion, but perhaps in a way that Job himself was not conscious of, since he lacks divine wisdom (11:4-6). Such inadvertent sin, although punishable, did not carry with it the stigma of much more serious willful and blatant sin. In the opening speech of the second cycle, Eliphaz warned that the destructive words Job now speaks are prompted by a sinful disposition (15:5-6), but he made no judgment on Job's previous life. In the course of the second cycle, the friends reaffirmed the foundation of their moral world: the order of retribution as it is evident in the horrifying fate of the wicked (chaps. 15; 18; 20). Even here, none claims that Job is one of the wicked. Job's last speech in the second cycle, however, in which he flatly denies the principle of retribution, pushed Eliphaz to the inevitable conclusion that the friends have resisted until this moment: Job must be a blatant, willful sinner.

Eliphaz begins without the customary introductory complaint about windy words, lack of wisdom, or insulting speech. Instead, he launches directly into his argument that since God derives no benefit from human righteousness, Job's punishment must recompense for his wickedness (vv. 2-5). In support of this insight, Eliphaz details the sins Job must have committed, concluding that he has been punished for just this conduct (vv. 6-11). In a second argument, Eliphaz accuses Job of denying God's knowledge and judgment, conduct that since ancient times leads to certain ruin (vv. 12-20). Despite his conviction that Job's behavior is characterized by great evil, Eliphaz does not conclude his speech with judgment, but with an appeal. If Job returns to God and reforms his conduct under God's instruction, then not only will he be restored, but also his favor with God will be so great that he can even intercede on behalf of others (vv. 21-30). For Eliphaz, the resources of traditional religion are always sufficient. All that he asks of Job is that he acknowledge his sin. What Eliphaz asks, however, is the one thing that Job's integrity will not allow him to do.

22:1-3. In 21:15, Job had represented the wicked as dismissing piety because there was no benefit in it. Eliphaz begins his reply with a series of rhetorical questions denying that God receives any benefit from human righteousness (vv. 2-3). At the end of his speech, he will return to this theme, arguing that humans benefit from piety, for turning to God brings complete well-being (vv. 21-30).

22:4-5. Eliphaz's words assert the impartiality of God (cf. 35:6-8). Consequently, Job's claim of complete innocence (9:21; 16:17) is implausible to Eliphaz. Since he believes with Bildad that God does not pervert justice, Eliphaz's rhetorical questions in v. 4 have a tone of exasperated incredulity about them. Ironically, it is precisely Job's piety (lit., "fear [יראה *yir'â*] of God") that has resulted in his devastation, even though that devastation is neither rebuke nor judgment, as Eliphaz assumes. Eliphaz's moral imagination encompasses only certain possibilities. Having interpreted Job's suffering as divine judgment, and knowing that God does not punish piety, he inevitably concludes that Job must be a wicked person (v. 5).

22:6. Eliphaz supports his claim with a detailed accusation. The form of this section is evocative of prophetic judgment speeches, with the accusations introduced by "because" (כי *kî*, v. 6; NRSV, "for"), and the judgment introduced by "therefore" (על־כן *'al-kēn*; v. 10).[347] As in the poems on the fate of the wicked, the crimes are specifically abuses of social and economic power. The seizing of pledges for repayment of debt (v. 6) was strictly regulated in Israel, precisely because the poor, who had little with which to secure a debt, were so vulnerable. If the tools by which they made their living or the cloak in which they slept were taken, then their very lives were at risk (Exod 22:25-26; Deut 24:6, 17). If v. 6*b* is intended to specify the nature of the pledge taken, then Eliphaz clearly refers to someone who possesses nothing of value except the clothes they wear. To seize a pledge "for no reason" suggests a particular hardness; extracting it from one's family, toward whom one had a special obligation, is heinous.

22:7-9. Callous disregard for elemental human solidarity is reflected in the accusation that Job refused water to the thirsty or bread to the hungry (v. 7). Response to or rejection of these basic needs was the touchstone of human decency and faithfulness to the creator of all (Isa 58:7; Ezek 18:7, 16; Matt 25:34-45). Similarly, protection of the widow and the orphan (v. 9) was one of the most fundamental obligations of those possessing power and position within ancient society. This theme occurs in the Code of Hammurapi[348] and in the Ugaritic epics of Keret and Aqhat,[349] as well as in the Bible (Exod 22:22[21]; Deut 10:18; 24:17; Isa 1:17; Jer 22:3; Zech 7:10). The widow and the orphan were especially under God's protection (Exod 22:22-23[21-22]; Pss 10:14; 68:5[6]; 146:9). To show cruelty toward the widow and the orphan was to show contempt for the moral foundation of the social order. It is difficult to imagine a more serious accusation.

In the midst of these accusations, v. 8 stands out. Some interpret this verse as an accusation that Job has favored the powerful,[350] or as a reference to Job himself as a land-grabber who dispossessed neighbors.[351] The Aramaic translation of the book of Job found at Qumran introduces this verse with the phrase "and you say," as though the words were Job's self-satisfied justification for selfishness.[352] Verse 8, however, contains no moral condemnation in itself. It is rather like certain proverbs that simply make observations about the world. The powerful and influential in a very real sense do "possess the land." For Eliphaz and the social ethic he advocates, such power entails corresponding responsibilities. Job, as just such a powerful person, has betrayed the social contract by the crimes against the poor detailed in vv. 6-7, 9 (so NIV).[353] There is no disagreement between Eliphaz and Job on the nature of the social ethic, only about whether Job has violated it. Job will defend himself as a righteous person precisely by referring to these values (chaps. 29; 31).

22:10-11. Having laid out the accusation, Eliphaz delivers the judgment in vv. 10-11. The imagery of snares and terror (v. 10) evokes Bildad's description of the fate of the wicked (18:8-11). Darkness and flood are also part of the repertoire of those accounts (18:5-6; 20:28).

22:12-20. In 21:22, Job used a pious cliché about God's knowledge and judgment in a sarcastic manner to introduce his claim that experience shows no rational discrimination between the fates of people. Here Eliphaz attempts to reclaim the truth of that traditional belief in the face of Job's cynical denial and to warn Job against the consequences of the beliefs he seems to be embracing.

22:12-14. For Eliphaz, the loftiness ascribed to God is an index of God's ability to see and know all things (v. 12; cf. Ps 33:13-14; Isa 40:22, 26-27). The contrasting position, which he attributes to Job (vv. 13-14), is traditionally associated with sinners, a claim that God's transcendence is such that God cannot see or is not interested in what people do on earth (e.g., Pss 10:11; 73:11; Isa 29:15; Jer 23:23-24; Ezek 8:12). The impious, as

---

347. Good, *In Turns of Tempest,* 273. See C. Westermann, *Basic Forms of Prophetic Speech,* trans. H. C. White (Lousiville: Westminster/John Knox, 1991) 137-68.
348. *ANET,* 178.
349. *ANET,* 149, 151.

350. Dhorme, *A Commentary on the Book of Job,* 329.
351. Pope, *Job,* 165.
352. Similarly, Gordis, *The Book of Job,* 246.
353. See Gordis, *The Book of Job,* 245, for the justification of such a translation.

Eliphaz represents them, cleverly employ the very images used to praise God: the shielding dark cloud associated with theophanies (ערפל *'arāpel;* cf. Exod 20:21; 1 Kgs 8:12; Ps 18:11[12]), the clouds signifying the presence of the divine warrior (cf. Judg 5:4; Ps 18:12[13]), and the heavenly dome formed by God (cf. Prov 8:27; Isa 40:22). Yet the impious exploit different nuances of these images: connotations of obscurity and distance. That has not been the burden of Job's accusations against God. When Job has used the imagery of sight, it has been in the context of a complaint of incessant divine scrutiny (e.g., 7:17-20; 10:4-6). Eliphaz, however, is not concerned to answer Job's particular claims. Having concluded that Job is a sinner, Eliphaz can only see him in the stereotyped image of the sinner that tradition describes.

22:15-20. Here Eliphaz begins the first of two appeals to Job. Verses 15-20 consist of negative examples of the destruction of the wicked; in vv. 21-30, the motivation for repentance is developed through images of a close relationship with God. The metaphor of a path, representing habitual conduct (v. 15), is an important part of wisdom imagery.[354] It implies that moral conduct is not simply a series of particular choices but a commitment to a pattern of behavior leading in a particular direction. Jeremiah develops the image vividly, describing his audience as standing at a crossroad, faced concretely with the dilemma of discerning and choosing "the good way" (Jer 6:16). The expression "ancient paths" (נתבות עולם *nĕtibôt 'ôlām;* cf. Jer 6:16; 18:15) even suggests that alternative patterns of conduct were established in antiquity, so that in choosing between them one participates in a community of moral conduct rooted in ancient times. In early Jewish moral instruction, examples of the "two ways" drawn from remote antiquity were particularly popular.[355]

Eliphaz contrasts the actual destruction that befalls the wicked (v. 16) with their own self-deceiving perception (v. 17), dramatizing the supposed words of the wicked (cf. Ps 10:4, 6, 11; 94:7). These lines are quite close to Job's representation of the wicked in

21:14-16. Both Eliphaz and Job agree that the wicked contemptuously dismiss God. Job represents them as denying that God can do anything *for* them, and Eliphaz represents them as denying that God can do anything *to* them. But Eliphaz directly engages Job's sarcastic citation of the pious cliché " 'their prosperity is not in their own hands,/ so I stand aloof from the counsel of the wicked'" (21:16 NIV). To Job's mind, the cliché, which supposedly denied the autonomy of the wicked, actually served as evidence that God favors the wicked. Eliphaz surprisingly agrees with Job that the prosperity of the wicked does come from God (v. 18*a*); yet in the context of Eliphaz's speech that claim serves to show up the ingratitude of the wicked, who accept the gracious bounty but reject the one who gives it. Thus when Eliphaz restates the line "the counsel of the wicked is far from me," he restores it to its non-ironic, non-sarcastic meaning. Eliphaz concludes this section with a motif familiar from the psalms: the rejoicing of the righteous over the destruction of the wicked (vv. 19-20; see Pss 52:6-7[8-9]; 58:10-11[11-12]; 107:42).

22:21-22. A second and much more developed appeal concludes Eliphaz's speech. In vv. 21-22, he uses imperative sentences to establish what Job must do. A word play in v. 21 cannot be represented in English. The same verb meaning "benefit" in v. 2 (סכן *sākan*) has a related form that means "accustom oneself to," "submit to" in v. 21*a* (הסכן *hasken*). The relationship between God and humanity is not symmetrical. Although a person cannot benefit (*sākan*) God through any conduct, submitting (*hasken*) to God is the source of all that is good for a person. A textual problem obscures v. 21*b* and leads to disagreement about the tenor of Eliphaz's claim. A garbled word (תבואתך *tĕbô'ātĕkā*) might be corrected either to a noun ("your yield" [תבואתך *tĕbû'ātkā*]) or a verb ("will come to you" [תבואך *tĕbô'ākā*]). The first alternative ("by this means your yield will be good") would give Eliphaz's advice a rather materialistic overtone.[356] Eliphaz, however, defines the benefits of being at peace with God in the following verses, and they are decidedly not materialistic.[357] In this context the NIV's

---

354. See N. Habel, "The Symbolism of Wisdom in Proverbs 1–9," *Int.* 26 (1972) 131-57.

355. E.g., T. Asher; *Damascus Document* 2:14–3:12.

356. So Dhorme, *A Commentary on the Book of Job,* 336; Pope, *Job,* 167; Hartley, *The Book of Job,* 331.

357. Contra Dhorme, *A Commentary on the Book of Job,* 336.

"prosperity" is too narrow for the sense of holistic well-being that the Hebrew word טוב (*tôb*) signifies. The wisdom background for Eliphaz's advice is evident in his choice of words in v. 22, not only "instruction" (תורה *tôrâ*; cf. Prov 4:2; 13:14) and "word" (Prov 4:5; 5:7; 7:24), but also the imagery of mouth and heart (e.g., Ps 119:11; Prov 10:11).

22:23-25. The motivation for Eliphaz's appeal to Job is developed in a series of conditional sentences (see Isa 58:13-14 for a very similar appeal). It is possible to divide the sentences differently (cf. v. 25 NRSV and NIV), although the NRSV probably reflects the grammatical structure of the Hebrew text better. Eliphaz begins in v. 23*a* with a simple statement that summarizes all that he will say: "if you return to Shaddai, you will be restored." Eliphaz's vision is of a gracious God, always ready to receive the repentant. In v. 23*b*, he begins to specify the nature of repentance (cf. 11:14). Reordering the self according to God's teaching (v. 22) leads to reordering commitments (what is "in one's tent," v. 23) and values (vv. 24-25). The contrast between those who put their trust in material things and those who put their trust in God is a staple of psalmic and wisdom piety (31:24-25; Ps 119:36; Prov 11:4; Sir 5:7-8). Eliphaz vividly develops the theme by depicting Job as actually returning gold to the places from which it was dug (the NIV's "assign," not the NRSV's "treat") and taking God as his gold and silver instead (v. 25; in Proverbs, wisdom is often compared favorably to gold and silver; e.g., Prov 3:14-15; 8:10-11, 19). Returning gold to the far away and legendary land of Ophir (28:16; 1 Kgs 9:28; Ps 45:9[10]; Isa 13:12) would be a gesture of extravagant proportions. Yet Job would receive something more valuable than what he parted with, which would more than repay his efforts.

22:26-28. The first result of Job's reformation of self, commitments, and values is the transformation of his desire. Now God becomes the source of his pleasure (v. 26*a*; cf. Ps 37:4). Moreover, Job's relationship with God is transformed from alienation to intimacy and trust. The imagery of lifting up the face (v. 26*b*) can describe the trust required

for individuals to look at each other directly (cf. Gen 4:6; 2 Sam 2:22). Just as sin makes a person ashamed to lift the face to God in prayer (Ezra 9:6), so also repentance restores that intimacy. The context of prayer is explicit in v. 27, as Eliphaz assures Job that God will hear his prayers. Vows (v. 27*b*) were often made in the course of petitionary prayer, so that the fulfillment of a vow is another indication that prayer has been answered (cf. 1 Sam 1:10-11; Pss 22:25[26]; 61:5-8[6-9]; 65:1-2[2-3]; Jonah 2). The ability to determine a course of action and to see where one is going (v. 28) connotes someone whose will is in harmony with God's (e.g., Deut 28:29; Prov 4:18-19), the opposite of the condition described in futility curses (e.g., Deut 28:38-44).

22:29-30. Eliphaz's culminating image of well-being, the ability to intervene on behalf of sinners, is obscured in the NRSV. The difficulty comes from confusion about how to translate the Hebrew word גוה (*gēwâ*, v. 29*a*). It is one of a family of words that connote height, and so often have come to represent pride or arrogance. Here, however, the contrast with "brought low" suggests that it is used as an exhortation—"be lifted up."[358] That word of encouragement is grounded on Job's ability to draw from his own uprightness to save the guilty (v. 30).[359] In this way, Job would be like Abraham interceding for Sodom (Gen 18:21-33) or Moses for the people of Israel (Exod 32:9-14). The prophet Ezekiel remembered Job, together with Noah and the Canaanite king Dan'el, as persons whose righteousness was popularly thought to be sufficient to save others (Ezek 14:14, 20). The irony in Eliphaz's depiction of Job's restoration as an intercessor is that it truly comes to pass, when Job intercedes with God to spare Eliphaz and his two friends from God's anger (42:8).

---

358. Similarly, Gordis, *The Book of Job*, 252; Habel, *The Book of Job*, 333.

359. See R. Gordis, "Corporate Personality in the Book of Job," *JNES* 4 (1945), 54-55, for a brief survey of the theme of intercession in biblical and rabbinic thought, what Gordis calls "horizontal corporate responsibility."

REFLECTIONS

Eliphaz's speech is a masterpiece of prophetic and pastoral counseling. Now, at last, he thinks he understands Job's situation and knows the right words to speak. Eliphaz's speech is a powerful evocation of the fundamental religious theme of sin and redemption. The parallels between Eliphaz's depiction and the story of Daniel and King Nebuchadnezzar in Daniel 4 are striking. Both Eliphaz and Daniel perceive themselves to be faced with a person who is a great sinner, a person whose true humanity has been distorted by arrogance, but who can be redeemed by repentance and by turning in humility toward God (cf. Dan 4:27[24], 33-34[30-31]).

The story of the redeemed sinner is a popular one that has great power in Judeo-Christian tradition. Second Chronicles 33 turns the story of the reign of the evil King Manasseh into an edifying narrative about his suffering, repentance, and reformation (2 Chr 33:10-17; cf. 2 Kings 21). The canon of the Orthodox Church even includes the text of his prayer of repentance (Prayer of Manasseh). In the NT book of Acts, the story of Paul, the persecutor who becomes an apostle (Acts 8–9), draws its narrative power in part from this paradigm of the transformed sinner. Popular moral literature also makes use of this theme. The figure of Ebenezer Scrooge in Charles Dickens' *A Christmas Carol* has become an icon of the hard and selfish miser transformed into a person of true humanity and generosity. These stories and the religious paradigm they embody provide an alternative to the harsh "fate of the wicked" vision of judgment. They appeal to us because they allow us to envision good overcoming evil in a redemptive rather than a judgmental manner.

Eliphaz thinks that the paradigm of the repentant sinner can resolve the problem of Job. He had initially been faced with an apparent contradiction: why a good person would experience the fate normally associated with divine punishment. That contradiction is resolved as soon as Eliphaz concludes that Job must be a great sinner. Yet Eliphaz does not mean to abandon his friend. Instead, he holds out to Job the promise of redemption, the transformation of Job the oppressor of the widow and the orphan into Job the intercessor. Job need only accept this portrait of himself and act according to the paradigm. The problem, of course, is that Eliphaz's depiction of Job has nothing to do with the reality of Job's situation or the truth about Job's character.

This sobering observation leads one back to the most scandalous aspect of this chapter: Eliphaz's denunciation of Job in vv. 6-11. There is no doubting Eliphaz's sincerity at this point. But how could he do this? How could he throw such accusations against someone he has known so well? It is tempting to be smug and dismissive of Eliphaz, but the phenomenon he represents is more common than it is comfortable to admit. The bizarre allegations of anti-Semitic propaganda from the Middle Ages to the present have often found a large audience willing to believe them. Christians who defended their Jewish neighbors against such egregious slanders were all too rare. In seventeenth-century Salem, accusations of witchcraft against well-known and respected persons were widely credited as true. Few who experienced the "red scare" of the 1950s and 1960s can forget how easily the claim that someone was a communist agent could be believed, even when the accused was wholly innocent. Another manifestation of this phenomenon takes the form of allegations of systematic child abuse, often linked with satanic cult practices. In all of these cases there is an element of hysteria that obliterates a community's ability to distinguish between actual problems (communist agents did exist; child abuse does occur) and wild accusations that are only the concrete manifestations of a community's anxiety about many things over which it has no control. Although it is disturbing enough to observe how such allegations can be believed about strangers, it is truly frightening that people can be willing to believe the most heinous accusations about neighbors and friends whom they have known well for many years.

What is common to all of these situations is an unacknowledged sense of the fragility of the social order. Life together requires a fundamental trust in other people. That trust is sometimes broken, even in shocking ways. In a healthy society, those betrayals can be acknowledged and confronted while still leaving intact the grounding faith in the trustworthiness of the members of the community. Faith is not easy, however, and the fear that such faith may be misplaced is always present. All too quickly a community can give in to the anxiety that the bland surface of normality is only a thin cover over something horribly and dangerously wrong, an unseen threat that will seize from below. A breakdown of fundamental social trust is replaced with a belief that deception may be the rule, not the exception. If that is so, then it is entirely possible to believe that one's next-door neighbor, who has always seemed a friendly and kind person, is actually a monster of evil. Sometimes even the victims of false accusations are so swept up in the hysteria that they, too, believe the whole scenario and, no longer trusting their own sense of themselves, confess to crimes they never committed.

This type of social paranoia is most common where religious or political beliefs are highly dualistic, conceived of as a battle between good and evil. In such a context, it takes enormous courage to say no to collective hysteria. It also requires a deep faith in the goodness of God's creation and in the persons whom God has created in God's image. It requires a belief that truth is more fundamental than deception and, therefore, that it is possible to distinguish the evil that actually exists from the fantasies created by anxiety.

Job 23:1–24:25, Divine Justice Is Elusive

COMMENTARY

Job's first speech in the third cycle presents some of the most difficult exegetical problems in the entire book. Not only are there many grammatical problems and obscurities in the individual verses, but also the ending of the speech (24:18-24) sounds in some ways more like the words of one of Job's friends than Job's own words. The interpretation taken here, however, is that the entire speech belongs to Job and that the difficult last part of the speech is to be understood as Job's provocative demand that God act to bring judgment against the wicked and so resolve the intolerable contradiction between a God of justice and a world of unpunished criminality.

Job's speech begins on a note of bitter defiance (23:2). After Eliphaz's last speech, one might have imagined that the model of the repentant sinner would have been an appealing one for Job to adopt, for it would have put a shattered world together again. For Job, however, integrity is everything. He has not betrayed his community or his God, and he will not betray himself. Although he does not reply directly to Eliphaz's accusations

that he is wicked, Job repeats his assertions of innocence and integrity. Whereas Eliphaz had advised Job to seek God through prayer, repentance, and submission (22:21-30), Job seeks the resolution of a trial, in which he is certain God will give him a hearing, and he will be vindicated (23:3-7). Job's confidence is checked by his inability to find God (23:8-9), but it returns as he considers that God knows his integrity (23:10). In striking contrast to his earlier imaginings (e.g., 9:20, 28), Job is persuaded that God's judgment of him and his own testimony to his uprightness will be the same (23:10b-12). At the peak of his confidence, Job's dread returns, grounded in the overwhelming power of a God who completes what has been decreed (23:13-16). At the very end, however, the grim determination with which he began reappears, as Job refuses to be silenced (23:17).

The second part of the speech in chap. 24 returns to the problem that Job addressed in chap. 21: the absence of moral order in the world. He begins with a question that governs the rest of the chapter: Why does God not set times of judgment that are discernible to the faithful (24:1)? Job describes the world as he knows it, a world in which the most heinous types of oppression regularly occur (24:2-4) and the destitute suffer unspeakably (24:5-12*b*). In the absence of divine judgment, however, Job concludes that apparently God sees nothing amiss (24:12*c*). Job resumes with an account of the criminal violence that is a nightly occurrence (24:13-17). Challenging God's failure, Job invokes judgment on these wicked persons in almost curse-like language (24:18-20). Again, Job describes God's indulgence of the mighty who prey on the most defenseless in society (24:21-23) and demands that the retribution they deserve finally come upon them (24:24). He concludes his speech with a challenge to anyone to refute him (24:25).

23:1-7. Job's opening words echo 21:4, where he also spoke of his "complaint" against God and the urgency that gripped him. Neither Eliphaz's accusations against him nor his plea for Job to submit to God has changed anything. Now Job characterizes his complaint as "defiant" (מרי *měrî*). The LXX, followed by the NRSV and the NIV, reads instead the similar Hebrew word "bitter" (מר *mar*). It is likely that there is a play on words and that the word "bitter" brings the echo of the similar-sounding "defiant" in its wake. Job has earlier spoken of the bitterness of his soul (7:11; 10:1). Job correlates his own bitter defiance with the unrelenting pressure of God's hand.[360]

Job's defiance consists precisely of his insistence on seeking resolution for his complaint through a legal hearing rather than through the traditional religious practices of prayer and lament. As in his previous speeches, the notion of a trial with God remains in the realm of the imagination, for Job does not know how to find his way into God's presence (23:3). This time his words are altogether more confident than before. In chaps. 9–10, when the notion of a trial first occurred to him, he treated it as a subject for satire,

although he could not help imagining what he would say if there were a way to restrain the overwhelming power of God. When he considered the idea again in chap. 13, Job fluctuated between confidence that he could defend himself before God and be vindicated, and fear that God's power would annihilate him. Nevertheless, he rehearsed the arguments that he would bring before God. In chap. 16, Job seemed to have given up the notion of defending himself, but envisioned an advocate who would argue his case even after his death. His thoughts began much the same way in chap. 19, envisioning a heavenly defender (גאל *gō'ēl*) who would advocate for him (19:25-26*a*). In the end, however, Job reasserted his ardent desire to see God for himself (19:26*b*-27).

Now he returns to imagining this direct encounter with God. In contrast to the earlier chapters in which Job rehearsed particular arguments (e.g., 10:2-7; 13:23-28), here he focuses on the respectful attention of the parties, as Job imagines first stating his case and supporting arguments (23:4) and then considering what God would say in reply (23:5; cf. 13:22*b*). Previously, the issue of God's overwhelming power blocked Job from envisioning a trial (9:32-35; 13:20-21), but now he can imagine God's restraint (23:6). The elliptical syntax of the Hebrew in 23:6*b* (lit., "he would fix upon me") gives rise to both the NRSV's "give heed to" and the NIV's "press charges." What makes it possible for Job to imagine a fair trial before God is Job's affirmation (23:7) that in such a setting one could reason with God and depend upon God for a just verdict. Despite the injustice of his own situation, Job cannot let go of the fundamental belief, rooted in everything that has shaped him, that God is a god of justice.

23:8-12. Job's desire for a trial, however, is blocked by the elusiveness of God. In 23:8-9, Job names the four directions of bodily orientation (NRSV), which are the same in Hebrew as the four compass directions (NIV; cf. Gen 14:15; 1 Sam 23:19; Isa 9:12[11]). Like Zophar's listing of the four components of the cosmos (heaven, Sheol, earth, sea; 11:8-9), it is an image of totality. In 23:9, the presence of possible homonyms (עשה *'āśâ*, "to act" or "to hide"; עטף *'āṭap*, "to turn" or "to cover oneself") and certain differences in

---

360. Accepting a slight emendation of the text and reading "his hand" (ידו *yādô*) instead of "my hand" (ידי *yādî*), with the LXX. Dhorme and Good retain the MT, interpreting the line as describing suppression of grief (Dhorme, *A Commentary on the Book of Job,* 343) or the discouragement that comes from grief (Good, *In Turns of Tempest,* 112). Cf. the similar expression in the Babylonian poem of the righteous sufferer, *Ludlul bel nemeqi:* "His hand was heavy [upon me]. I could not bear it" (Lambert, *Babylonian Wisdom Literature,* 49).

the versions lead to a variety of translations. Each half line of these two verses, however, ends by reiterating the crucial point: "he is not there"; "I cannot perceive him"; "I cannot see him"; "I cannot glimpse him" (cf. 9:11). Job's frustrated search is an ironic contrast to the psalmist's imaginary flight from God in Ps 139:7-12.

Job's unwillingness to let go of the vision of vindication glimpsed in 23:4-7 leads him to attempt to overcome the problematic realization that he cannot search out the elusive God. He does this by returning to a theme that he had introduced in earlier speeches: God's scrutiny of his way (23:10; cf. 7:17-19; 10:4-7). Even if he cannot see God, God can perceive Job (cf. Ps 139:1-4). In the earlier passages, God's scrutiny and testing were experienced as hostile and unwelcome. Now, however, Job invokes the notion with the assurance that God's knowledge of him will ensure his vindication. He will be like an unknown metal that is tested and proves to be gold (v. 10b; cf. Ps 17:3). Ironically, Job has unwittingly described the scenario of the prose tale in which God's knowledge of Job's way is coupled with God's assurance that Job will prove as good as gold when tested. As Prov 17:3 notes, gold is tested in a crucible. Job, however, does not pursue the possible connection between suffering and testing.

In 23:11-12, Job comes closest to speaking in the accents of traditional prayer and wisdom. His "way" (23:10) is defined metaphorically as walking in the steps of God, without turning aside (23:11; cf. Pss 17:5; 44:18[19]; 119:3, 59; Prov 4:27). Job describes his piety in terms of the sapiential orientation to "the precepts of his lips" and "the words of his mouth" (23:12; cf. Ps 119:13, 72, 88; Prov 2:1). Although the NIV attempts to render the MT in 23:12b ("more than my daily bread" [מחקי *mēḥuqqî*]),[361] most translations follow the LXX in reading "in my bosom" (בחקי *bĕḥēqî*). The heart or bosom is often used to suggest the integral and intimate relationship between the pious and God's word (22:22; cf. Deut 6:6; 30:14; Ps 119:11; Jer 31:33). For one brief moment, Job is once again at home with his inherited religious

language and can use it to express his unity with God. That moment is fleeting, however, as Job recalls an aspect of God's character that fills him with dread.

23:13-17. Although the expression Job uses at the beginning of v. 13 is somewhat peculiar (lit., "but he is as one"), it is probably either an idiom for "unchangeable"[362] or an expression of divine sovereignty.[363] Its meaning is best judged by the rest of the verse, which describes an unopposable God who does what he pleases (cf. 9:12; 11:10). There are strong similarities between this verse and the language of Second Isaiah (e.g., Isa 43:13). What would be words of praise in Second Isaiah have a very different meaning in Job's mouth, however. The decree that God will complete concerning Job (23:14a) is God's inexplicable determination to destroy him.

The outcome of Job's meditation is a return of the terror and dread that has plagued him every time he has attempted to consider what confrontation with God really means (23:15; cf. 3:25-26; 9:34-35; 13:21). The difficult exegetical issue is how to translate 23:17 and understand its relationship to 23:16. That terror has made his heart faint (23:16) is clear, but does Job succumb to his discouragement with a return of the death wish that concluded his earlier speeches (23:17 NRSV; cf. 3:11-24; 7:21; 10:18-22)? Or does Job resist the terror and recover the note of defiant complaint with which he began (23:17 NIV)? Unfortunately, the crucial verb (צמת *ṣāmat*) is not well attested in Hebrew. Etymologically, it could mean either "be destroyed" or "be silenced." In fact, it is possible that both meanings were current in Hebrew.[364] The second half of the verse can be translated grammatically either with the NRSV or the NIV. Those who favor the NRSV reading, however, must change the initial negative word "not" (לא *lō*) to the similar-sounding word "if only" (לו *lû*). The context also favors a reading like that of the NIV. Job's following words in chap. 24 are more consistent with a recovered determination to resist than with a desire for oblivion. The better reading is "Yet

---

361. Since the word means "prescription" or "rule," as well as "portion," Habel, *The Book of Job*, 344, translates the same term as "beyond that required of me."

362. Gordis, *The Book of Job*, 262.
363. Andersen, *Job*, 210.
364. See the discussion in Koehler and Baumgartner, *Hebräishes und Aramäisches Lexikon*, fasicle III, 970.

I am not silenced by the darkness, or by the thick darkness that covers my face."[365]

24:1-4. Job's complaint in chap. 24 is that, in opposition to all that traditional religion has claimed, oppression and criminality flourish on the earth without any discernible sign of God's judgment. It is, nonetheless, grammatically questionable to translate the first line with either the NRSV or the NIV.[366] Gordis provides a more grammatically defensible translation: "Why, since times of judgment are not hidden from Shaddai, do His Friends not see His day (of judgment)?"[367] Following Gordis's translation, Job first cites a theological commonplace: God knows the days of judgment. Then he pointedly asks why that day never seems to arrive. After all, psalms such as Ps 37:34 promise that the pious will "inherit the land" and "look on the destruction of the wicked." Yet the friends of God see a world in which basic moral constraints are violated with impunity.

Land for agriculture and herds for pasturing were the bases of ancient Israelite economy. Moreover, land was a family heritage, so that the theft of land by moving boundary markers was an assault on the social stability of the community (24:2a). The seriousness of this crime is suggested by the frequency with which it is mentioned in laws (Deut 19:14), covenant curses (Deut 27:17), prophetic denunciations (Hos 5:10), and wisdom teachings (Prov 22:28; 23:10). Laws concerning animals underscore the social solidarity of the community. Not only was animal theft prohibited, but a person was also required to go after and return a neighbor's straying animal, even if that meant caring for it until it could be returned (Deut 22:1-3). Theft of entire flocks (24:2b) implied the utter absence of social bonds, as between warring nations (Jer 51:23) or bandits and their victims (Job 1:14, 17).

In the moral world of ancient Israel, treatment of the orphan and the widow (24:3) was the most fundamental measure of a society's moral status. As vulnerable members of the community, they were under the special protection of God and the king (Deut 10:18; Ps 72:12-14; Prov 23:11; Isa 1:23). Laws specifically restricted what could be taken in pledge from such persons (Deut 24:17). To take an ox or ass, essential for subsistence farming, was reprehensible (1 Sam 12:3). The vivid image of the powerful forcing the needy off the road and into hiding (24:4) concludes the listing of abuses and introduces Job's more detailed description of the wretchedness of the destitute in the following verses.

24:5-12. Job's metaphor of the destitute as wild asses that are not fed, as domestic animals are, but must forage in the dry land (24:5), captures the social and economic exclusion of the poor. The term "fodder" (בליל *bĕlîl*) in 24:6 strikes some as odd. The NRSV redivides the word and translates "not their own" (בלי לו *bĕlî lô*); others emend slightly and translate "at night" (בליל *bĕlayil*)[368] or "in the field of the villain [בליעל *bĕliyyaʿal*]."[369] The use of the word "fodder," however, provides a link with the animal imagery of 24:5 and suggests that the two verses be interpreted in the light of each other. The fields and vineyards where the poor scavenge are like the sparse vegetation of the wasteland. Israelite law specifically forbade the owner to go back over fields, orchards, and vineyards a second time to collect the overlooked crops; those were to be left for the poor (Lev 19:10; Deut 24:19-22). A generous owner, like Boaz in the story of Ruth, made certain that plenty was left (Ruth 2:15-16). By contrast, the owner here is described as "evil." Moreover, the word translated "glean" (לקש *liqqēš*) is not the usual one but may refer to picking fruit that ripens only after the main harvest.[370] If so, then the food available is extremely scanty.[371]

The destitution of these wretched of the earth is absolute (24:7-8). They are without adequate clothes against the cold, without shelter from the driving rain. Homeless, they huddle against a rock for protection. The "rock" is a traditional image of God as

---

365. Similarly, Dhorme, *A Commentary on the Book of Job*, 352; contra Pope, *Job*, 173; cf. Gordis, *The Book of Job*, 263; Habel, *The Book of Job*, 346.

366. The expression נצפנו מן (*nispĕnû min*) means "hidden from" or possibly "stored up by," but scarcely "kept by" or "set." Moreover, judging from the context, Job does not seem to be asking why God does not *delay* retribution, as the translation "why are times (of judgment) not stored up by Shaddai" would suggest (cf. 21:19-20, where Job rejects delayed retribution as morally worthless).

367. Gordis, *The Book of Job*, 264.

368. Dhorme, *A Commentary on the Book of Job*, 358.

369. Pope, *Job*, 176.

370. Driver and Gray, *A Critical and Exegetical Commentary on the Book of Job*, Part II, 166-67.

371. See Dhorme, *A Commentary on the Book of Job*, 356-58, for a different interpretation of these verses.

protector (Pss 18:2[3]; 62:2[3], 6-7[7-8]; 71:3; 94:22). Use of that word here gives Job's words an added sting. Job's language also echoes the imagery of passages like Isa 25:4, which says of God: "you have been a stronghold for the poor, a stronghold for the needy in their distress; a shelter from the driving rain, shade from the heat" (author's trans.).

The indigent are also vulnerable to the cruelty of their creditors (24:9). Second Kings 4:1-7 tells the story of a widow whose children had been taken as slaves because she could not pay her debt. In that story, the prophet of God works a miracle of abundance that redeems the children and provides for their future security; Job draws attention to the vast majority for whom there is no wonder-working prophet.

Without resources of their own, the poor must work as day laborers in the fields of those who have much (24:10-11). The scandal of the hungry carrying grain and the thirsty treading the wine grapes is enhanced by the echo of Deut 25:4, which prohibits a farmer from muzzling an ox as it treads out the grain. The exploited laborer lacks even the consideration afforded the ox.

This grim panorama of wretchedness ends, appropriately, with a scene of the wounded and dying who groan and cry out vainly for help (24:12ab). The shock comes as Job suddenly shifts perspective from human misery to divine perception (24:12c). In the face of misery and oppression that contradicts all that covenant law tries to establish, Job observes that "God charges no one with wrongdoing." The NRSV's translation, "yet God pays no attention to their prayer," depends on a slight emendation of the Hebrew text (from תפלה [tiplâ, "wrongdoing"] to תפלה [tĕpillâ, "prayer"]). Although there is no sufficient reason to change the Hebrew text, poetic language often exploits the relationship between the word actually written and the echo of similar words with different meanings. Both translations are required for one to hear the text in all the fullness of its meaning, the NIV representing the primary tone, the NRSV a poetic overtone. God's responses of judgment and salvation alike depend on God's hearing the cry of the oppressed and taking note of the crimes of the oppressor (cf. Exod 2:21-25).

In 24:12, Job's initial question about why the friends of God do not see God's day of judgment (24:1) finds an ironic answer: God does not perceive anything wrong with the world. The word "wrongdoing" (tiplâ) has another significant echo. It is the same word used in 1:22, where after the loss of his wealth, servants, and children, "Job did not sin by charging God with wrongdoing" (NIV).

24:13-17. In these verses, Job evokes the moral chaos of criminality. The term *chaos* is particularly apt, since Job uses the image of the reversal of the values of light and darkness, the primordial structures of creation (Gen 1:3-5), to suggest the destructiveness that results when fundamental prohibitions are violated. The three types of criminals whom Job names—the murderer, the adulterer, and the house-breaker (cf. Hos 4:2; Jer 7:9)—respectively threaten the life of the individual, the integrity of the marital bond, and the security of the household. These are the elements upon which the social life of the entire community depends. Thus it is appropriate that Job calls the criminals "rebels against the light" (24:13). In contrast to his own close adherence to the "steps" and "way" of God (23:11), the threatening, chaotic nature of criminals is suggested by their alienation from the established ways and paths of light (24:13).

In successive verses, Job describes the inverted worlds of the three types of criminals. Reversing the normal order, the murderer rises at dusk to do his work in the night (24:14). Job's critique of criminality is related to his social critique in 24:2-12, for he observes that the victims tend to be precisely the vulnerable "poor and needy." The adulterer is described through a poetic play with the image of the "eye," a part of the body closely associated with illicit desire (cf. 31:1; Prov 6:25). The adulterer's eye watches for dusk (cf. Prov 7:8), when there is insufficient light for another eye to discern him (24:15). Similarly, the house-breaker digs at night (24:16; cf. Exod 22:2) when others do not work, and seals himself up during the day when others go out to work (Ps 104:23). Job concludes his account of this counterworld of the criminal in 24:17 with an ironic comment. Traditionally, morning is the time of security and returning hope, and deep darkness (lit., "shadow of death") the time of fearfulness; but for these perverted beings the values are reversed.

24:18-25. If these verses are taken as simple declarative sentences, as in most translations, then the whole section is completely incongruous in Job's mouth, for it would be a statement about the certainty of God's judgment against the wicked. This incongruity leads many commentators to assume that these verses are part of the missing speech of Zophar or Bildad, somehow erroneously attached to Job's speech (see Overview above). The early versions—the LXX, the Vulgate, and the Peshitta—point to a better understanding of these verses, however. They translate them as optatives—that is, as Job's wish for what should happen. This interpretation is not without its own grammatical problems.[372] Nevertheless, this approach offers an interpretation that does justice to the tensions with which Job is struggling in chaps. 23–24 and is consistent with rhetorical techniques he has already used in chap. 21. Of the current translations, the Tanakh, which translates these verses as Job's curse upon the criminal, comes closest to the interpretation proposed here.[373]

Job believes passionately and fervently in justice. Moreover, he cannot abandon the belief that God is a god of justice. That is why the legal metaphor is so important to Job's thinking and why he begins his speech in chap. 23 with a vivid evocation of a trial in which God appears as the just and reasonable judge. When Job says in 24:1, "why, since times of judgment are not hidden from God, do his friends not see his days?" it is partly a rhetorical question, but partly a genuine one. Verses 2-17 express Job's angry conviction that there are in fact no days of judgment. Verses 18-25 express Job's anguished demand that his belief in God's justice not turn out to be a lie. The rhetorical form in which this urgent plea is expressed is not unlike 21:17-21, where Job's struggle with the absence of evident judgment leads him to a demand: Let it be done.

24:18-20. This section begins with a peculiar statement: "קל [*qal*] is he upon the face of the water" (24:18). Job is presumably speaking of the criminal, whose perverted values he has just finished describing. The Hebrew word *qal* can mean "swift" (NRSV) or "light," "insignificant," hence the NIV's "foam." Since there is a close similarity with the word "cursed" (קלל *qillēl*), which appears in the second half of the verse, one suspects that *qal* is pejorative. Although it is not certain, the REB may have the right nuance, "Such men are scum [*qal*] on the surface of the water." Job's evaluative description provides the transition from his account of the criminals to his wish/curse/demand for their punishment: "let their portion of the land be cursed [תקלל *tĕqullal*], so that no one goes to the vineyards."

In an earlier speech, Job used the image of a wadi that dries up in the heat as a symbol of something disastrously changed from what one expects (6:15-17). Here Job invokes the image as a metaphor for the power of Sheol over the sinner: "let dryness and heat consume snow waters, Sheol those who have sinned" (24:19; cf. Ps 49:14[15]). The imagery of life and death, initiated in 24:19, is developed in 24:20 with the contrasting reactions of the womb, a symbol of life, and the worm, a symbol of death. Since a person who died continued to be part of the community through the memory of others, the motif of forgetting contributes to the picture of the sinner's utter annihilation: "let the womb forget him, the worm find him sweet, until he is no longer remembered." The final image, "and let iniquity be broken like a stick," recalls the type of symbolic images of destruction often included in treaty curses.[374] In Ezek 37:15-23, the joining of two sticks is a symbol of reunification.

24:21-25. Grammatical ambiguities and words with a wide range of possible meanings permit a bewildering variety of translations for these verses (e.g., NRSV, NIV, TNK). None of these translations is without difficulties, but neither is any so arbitrary as to be impossible. I am inclined to follow the NRSV's translation of 24:21-23 as both defensible in its grammatical interpretations and consistent with the overall content of the chapter. The cruelty of the wicked toward the defenseless is the central feature of Job's description

---

372. Driver and Gray, *A Critical and Exegetical Commentary on the Book of Job*, 211; but see Hartley, *The Book of Job*, 350-51.

373. See also Hartley, *The Book of Job*, 350-54.

374. *ANET*, 539.

of the world, and no one represents such defenselessness more than the widow without children (24:21). The contradiction tormenting Job is that God, who is supposed to defend just such persons (Deut 10:18; cf. Isa 54:1), instead appears to favor the powerful oppressor of the weak (24:22-23). As Job said earlier in a similar context, "If it is not he, who then is it?" (9:24 NRSV). The burden of this chapter is Job's urgent need to resolve the contradiction and to see clearly the days of judgment supposedly known to God. Thus in 24:24 he returns to his demand that what tradition has claimed should be done. One may translate: "Exalted for a little while, let them be no more. Let them be brought low and shriveled up like grass; and like the heads of grain let them be cut off."

Job ends in a defiant mood. At the conclusion of his previous speech, he had rejected the friends' arguments as worthless and false. Correspondingly, he now defends the truth and significance of his own words with an angry challenge (24:25).

REFLECTIONS

There is no stronger indictment of God in the book of Job than the depiction in chap. 24 of divine indifference in the face of the pervasive misery, abuse, and injustice endured by the most vulnerable of people. We tend to think of the twentieth century as unique in its experience of evil so enormous that it makes the very idea of God a scandal. It is not just because of the Holocaust, although that event remains the most numbing of horrors. There is also the experience of wars of unparalleled destruction, oppression on a previously unimaginable scale, and crushing poverty created by the very forces that brought unprecedented wealth to a minority of the world's population. The book of Job reminds us that others have also struggled with the theological scandal presented by a world where injustice is rampant.

For those nurtured in the religious traditions of the Bible, belief in God and belief in God as a champion of justice and a protector of the vulnerable are inseparable ideas. The central event in the faith of Israel is the exodus, portrayed as God's response to the suffering of God's people: " 'I have observed the misery of my people who are in Egypt; I have heard their cry on account of their taskmasters. Indeed, I know their sufferings, and I have come down to deliver them from the Egyptians' " (Exod 3:7-8*a* NRSV). This is the God who says, "You shall not wrong or oppress a resident alien. . . . You shall not abuse any widow or orphan. If you do abuse them, when they cry out to me, I will surely heed their cry" (Exod 22:21-23 NRSV). This is the God whom the psalmist calls "lover of justice" who establishes equity (Ps 99:4). This is the God whom Amos represents as "roaring" in anger at the war crimes, social abuses, and lawlessness of many nations (Amos 1–2). Taking the Bible seriously requires that one take seriously its claims about God's active role in establishing and preserving justice. But how can one say those words over the body of an abandoned child who starved to death or speak those words to a peasant woman raped and tortured by soldiers? How can one say those words in the shadow of Auschwitz?

It is hard to stay with this contradiction between what the Bible affirms about God and the atrocities that speak of God's absence. One is tempted to speak instead about human evil and the need for human resistance to evil, or to change the focus and talk about God's sustaining presence with the victim, or to reinterpret God's power in terms of non-coercive love. These are not irrelevant matters—they have their place— but they must not be engaged too quickly or used as a means of evading the painful contradiction itself. Martin Buber aptly calls this contradiction "the rent in the heart of the world."[375]

375. M. Buber, *The Prophetic Faith* (New York: Harper and Bros., 1949) 191.

In a paradoxical way, one often comes to know the meaning of a thing through its absence rather than its presence. An illustration, which originally derives from the philosopher Heidegger, makes this point. It speaks of a carpenter who goes into his well-furnished workshop, with its stacks of wood, containers of nails, and racks of tools. Intent on the activity of the project, the carpenter pays little attention to the individual items. The wood, the nails, the hammer are simply taken for granted as part of the whole of the carpenter's activity. But suddenly, the hammer breaks, the shaft snapping off at the head. For the first time the carpenter becomes genuinely aware of the hammer. It has never been so vivid in its wholeness as it has become in its brokenness. The image of the hammer, what it does, how essential it is to the task of carpentry, are all inescapably present to the carpenter precisely because of its absence. So it is with Job. One can imagine Job before his catastrophe speaking fluently about God, justice, and the moral order of the world. In a certain sense, he would have understood what he was talking about, but only in a way comparable to the carpenter who, as he walked into the workshop, could have described the wood, the nails, and the hammer. Only now that Job has experienced the brokenness of justice and the absence of the God of justice does he possess the urgent, existential knowledge of justice and of God.

This illustration also suggests why Job and so many others who have experienced the unendurable do not simply dismiss God as an illusion. It would seem so much easier to do so, yet for these persons God's love and passion for justice are no more an illusion than the hammer is for the carpenter. They have known it and experienced it and can doubt its existence no more than their own reality. What is unbearable is the equally undeniable experience of its brokenness and its absence, just where it should be most present. This is the unresolved contradiction in Job's speech (chaps. 23–24), which contains his passionate belief in a God of justice and his devastating expose of a God indifferent to a world of injustice.

What kind of faith is possible for a person who refuses to let go of either reality? Martin Buber says of Job that in spite of all that he experienced, "Job's faith in justice is not broken down. But he is no longer able to have a *single faith* in God and in justice. . . . He believes now in justice in spite of believing in God, and he believes in God in spite of believing in justice. But he cannot forego his claim that they will again be united somewhere, sometime, although he has no idea in his mind how this will be achieved."[376]

The faith of Job, as expressed in chaps. 23–24, is the prototype of the defiant post-Holocaust faith of many of the characters in the books and plays of Elie Wiesel. In *The Trial,* a play with many similarities to the book of Job, the character Berish is just such a Job-like figure. A survivor of a pogrom in which virtually the entire Jewish community of the village of Shamgorod was destroyed, Berish engages a troupe of Purim actors to stage a "trial" of God, with Berish acting as the prosecutor. He speaks as witness for all the slaughtered: "Let their premature, unjust deaths turn into an outcry so forceful that it will make the universe tremble with fear and remorse!"[377] The trial is interrupted by the news that a second pogrom is about to occur. Berish refuses to save himself by accepting a priest's offer to baptize him, saying, "My sons and my fathers perished without betraying their faith; I can do no less."[378] He denies, however, that this decision suggests a reconciliation with God. "I lived as a Jew, and it is as a Jew that I shall die—and it is as a Jew that, with my last breath, I shall shout my protest to God! And because the end is near, I shall shout louder! Because the end is near, I'll tell Him that He's more guilty than ever!"[379] Berish's decision is to live and die in faithful defiance/defiant faithfulness. As difficult as that may be, for many it is the only authentic response to the biblical God.

376. Buber, *The Prophetic Faith,* 192.
377. E. Wiesel, *The Trial* (New York: Schocken Books, 1979), 130.
378. Wiesel, *The Trial,* 154.
379. Wiesel, *The Trial,* 156.

Job 25:1–26:14, Bildad and Job Argue About the Power of God

COMMENTARY

Chapters 25–26 pose difficult interpretive questions. As the text stands, Bildad's speech in chap. 25 is only six verses long. Job begins his speech in chap. 26 with sarcastic remarks of the sort that have opened several of his other speeches. The body of the speech in 26:5-15, however, a description of God's creative power, lacks the ironic touches that characterize Job's previous use of that theme (e.g., 9:2-10; 12:13-25) and is not what one expects to hear from Job. No speech by Zophar follows chap. 26. Instead, chap. 27 begins with the unusual notice "Job again took up his discourse and said . . . " (27:1). That same notice is used to introduce Job's speech in chaps. 29–31, following the poem on wisdom in chap. 28.

Although the third cycle of speeches may have been damaged and garbled in the copying of the text, one should be cautious in attempting to reconstruct what may never have existed. The text itself gives certain clues as to how the speeches are to be sorted out, although these clues are not unambiguous. The starting place is the unique introductory formula that occurs in 27:1 and 29:1. To say that Job "again" took up his discourse suggests that it has been interrupted. Most scholars regard chap. 28 as an independent poem separating Job's final speech in the dialogue (chap. 27) from his summation and challenge to God (chaps. 29–31). Thus, even though chap. 28 is not marked at the beginning as an independent poem, the notice in 29:1 is an *ex post facto* acknowledgment that it should be read as such. The relationship of chaps. 28 and 29 provides an analogy for understanding the significance of 27:1. There, too, the notice that Job "again" took up his discourse suggests that it had been interrupted by the immediately preceding material. As with chap. 28, the beginning of that interruption is not marked in the text, but the change in style and content suggests that the interruption consists of 26:5-14.[380]

If this is the case, then whose words are 26:5-14? Although it is possible to understand them as an independent poem, like chap. 28,[381] most scholars regard them as the second part of Bildad's speech.[382] What happens in these chapters represents the deterioration of the dialogue. Bildad begins to speak in 25:1-6, but is interrupted by Job, who sarcastically mocks what Bildad has said (26:1-4). Undeterred, Bildad completes his speech (26:5-14), at which point Job resumes his discourse. Such a structure may be the author's attempt to represent the interruptive and even overlapping speech of the parties to a conversation that has irretrievably broken down.

25:1-6. Like Eliphaz in 22:2, Bildad begins abruptly, without the introductory remarks that have characterized his previous speeches (8:2-4; 18:2-4). His theme is announced in the first words he speaks: the dominion and awesomeness of God (25:2a). Throughout his speech, this theme will be developed by reference to the mythic acts of God as creator and governor of the cosmos. Although many details of his description are distinctive, it has been suggested that his account employs a sequence of themes similar to the creation poem in Psalm 104.[383]

Bildad's statement that God "makes peace" ("establishes order" [NIV]) in the heights of heaven alludes to traditions about conflict among the gods or a rebellion in heaven. The OT itself contains only a few allusions to these myths (e.g., Isa 14:12-15). The narratives lying behind these allusions, however, seem to have influenced later apocalyptic traditions of a revolt of the angels and war in heaven (cf. Daniel 10; *1 Enoch* 6–11; 1QM). The troops

---

380. Alternatively, Davidson, *The Book of Job*, 186; and Good, *In Turns of Tempest*, 286, suggest that the notice in 27:1 does not reflect an interruption but Job's pause, as he waits in vain for Zophar to speak. See also Hartley, *The Book of Job*, 368.

381. So Fohrer, *Das Buch Hiob*, 381-85.

382. E.g., Gordis, *The Book of Job*, 534-35; Pope, *Job*, 180-86; Habel, *The Book of Job*, 366-68. Janzen assumes that Job is the speaker, but that in these verses Job "finishes Bildad's speech for him . . . with an angry sureness of eloquence and tone" (Janzen, *Job*, 173). Janzen's suggestion is a very appealing one, although it does not entirely account for the unique form of the introduction in 27:1.

383. R. J. Clifford, *Creation Accounts in the Ancient Near East and in the Bible*. CBQMS 26 (Washington: Catholic Biblical Association, 1994) 190.

of God the divine warrior, to which Bildad refers in 25:3a, are a frequent motif in epic poetry (Deut 33:2-3; Judg 5:20), in psalms (Ps 68:17[18]), and in prophetic poetry (Isa 40:26; Hab 3:5). Similarly, the shining of God's light in 25:3b is also associated with the appearance of the divine warrior, much as Deut 33:2-3 speaks of God "dawning" from Seir and "shining forth" from Mount Paran, as God approaches with the heavenly army.

In terms of poetic imagery, the continuation of Bildad's description appears in 26:5, where the trembling of the "shades" is described. Bildad, however, inserts a parenthetical observation into his description of the divine warrior's might, indicating the significance of his words for the issue at hand (25:4-6). Taking up the theme introduced by Eliphaz twice before (4:17-19; 15:14-16), Bildad asks rhetorically whether a mere human being can be righteous or pure before God (25:4). The first line of Bildad's question is also a literal citation of Job's words in 9:2b. Whereas Job framed the question in legal terms, Bildad develops the line in a way that makes it clear he understands the issue to pertain to human existence itself.

Like Eliphaz, Bildad refers to the human as one "born of woman" (25:4b), a phrase that connotes mortality. That which is born also must die. In 25:6, Bildad makes this point in a striking figure of speech. Calling a human being "worm" and "maggot" draws attention to the brutal fact that bodies decay; where flesh was, worms will be. Throughout Job's speeches the worm is a symbol of death and Sheol (7:5; 17:14; 21:26; 24:20). Bildad juxtaposes this earthy image to that of the moon and the stars, heavenly entities characterized by light rather than mortal flesh (Gen 1:14-16; Isa 60:20; Jer 31:35). These are creatures of God that stand high in the hierarchy of the cosmos (Pss 8:3[4]; 148:3), entrusted with responsibility (Ps 136:9), symbols of what is not mortal (Ps 72:7). The moon is even designated a "faithful witness" (Ps 89:37[38]). Bildad uses a pun to make his point. The word that means "morally pure" (זכה zākâ, 25:4b) is related to a word that means both "morally pure" and "bright" (זכך zākak, 25:5). If even the heavenly luminaries are not "bright"/"pure" before God, how could what is characterized by dark, wormy decay be so?

The implicit logic in Bildad's comparison is that physical corruption and moral corruption are two aspects of the same reality.

26:1-4. Job interrupts Bildad at this point (26:1). In contrast to most of Job's opening words, these are not addressed to the friends as a group, but to Bildad alone (cf. 21:3b). Since Bildad has characterized human existence in terms of its physical and moral inferiority, Job makes this the starting point of his remarks. He sardonically refers to himself, the recipient of Bildad's help, rescue, and counsel, as one "without power . . . without strength . . . without wisdom" (26:2-3a). There is a subtle linguistic play, however. The words that at first glance appear to describe Job could also be taken as phrases describing Bildad's advice. "How you have helped, without strength! How you have rescued, with a powerless arm! How you have counseled, without wisdom! And you have given your advice so abundantly!"[384] Job's rhetorical question in 26:4 concerning the source of Bildad's remarkable words hovers between personal insult and blasphemy. It suggests on the one hand that Bildad needed assistance even to mouth such banalities. On the other hand, if Bildad is understood to speak divine truths, then Job's contempt for those words extends to their divine source as well.

26:5-14. As suggested above, Bildad's and Job's speeches are interwoven. Ignoring Job's interruption, Bildad continues with his invocation of God's majesty. Job will resume his own interrupted words in 27:1.

26:5-6. In 25:2-3, Bildad described God the divine warrior. Now in vv. 5-6 he describes the terror with which the underworld responds to God's appearance. The "shades" (רפאים rĕpā'îm) are the dead who persist in shadowy form in Sheol (see Ps 88:10[11]; Prov 2:18; 9:18; 21:16). In Isaiah 14:9, there is a trace of the old mythological tradition that the rĕpā'îm are the spirits of dead heroes and kings. As in several other places in the OT, the presumption is that the underworld is situated at the bottom of the sea (26:5b; cf. 2 Sam 22:5-6; Pss 18:4-5[5-6]; 88:6-7[7-8]; Jonah 2:2-6). The motif of the exposure of the channels of the sea by the divine warrior's gusty breath (cf. Ps 18:15[16]) and the

---

384. Translated similarly by the NEB, the TNK, and Habel, *The Book of Job*, 375.

motif of the visibility of Sheol and Abaddon to God's eye (Prov 15:11) may be merged in Bildad's image (26:6). Bildad, however, adds a vivid note of personification in his use of the terms "naked" (ערום *ʿārôm*) and "without covering" (אין כסות *ʾên kĕsût*; cf. 24:7). The term "Abaddon" is a synonym for "Sheol," derived from the Hebrew verb "to perish" (אבד *ʾābad*).

26:7-9. Bildad changes both the focus of his description and the literary form. Here his gaze moves from the underworld to the cosmic mountain of God, and his style becomes hymnic (in Hebrew vv. 7-9 all begin with participles; cf. the style of 5:9-13). Instead of the expected poetic image of stretching out the heavens (cf. 9:8; Ps 104:2; Isa 40:22), Bildad refers to God stretching out "the north" (26:7). The north (צפון *ṣāpôn*) is the designation of the mythic mountain that is the site of the divine assembly, Mount Zaphon (see Isa 14:13; Mount Zaphon has the same function in Ugaritic mythology). In this way, Bildad's image of the establishment of the cosmos incorporates an image of divine governance. The striking imagery of 26:7 uses "chaos" (תהו *tōhû*; cf. Gen 1:2, "formless and empty" [תהו ובהו *tōhû wābōhû*]) and "nothing" (בלי־מה *bĕlî-mâ*, lit., "without-what") as contrasting parallels to the heavenly mount of assembly and the earth. The figure of the void provides a vivid contrast for the creative power of God in stretching out the celestial north and suspending the earth from it. Because of the poetic nature of the language, it is difficult to say whether Bildad's description represents a significant departure from traditional Israelite cosmology,[385] or whether it is simply an alternative way of speaking of the tripartite structure of heavens, earth, and chaotic waters.[386]

Control over rain is a divine power (5:10; 36:27-29; Deut 28:12; 1 Kgs 18:1; Ps 65:9-10[10-11]; Prov 30:4), and rain is often represented as being held in celestial storehouses (Jer 10:13; Sir 43:14). Here the clouds are depicted as the storage containers (cf. 38:37). The use of the verb "split" (בקע *bāqaʿ*) in 26:8b suggests the concrete image of the clouds as waterskins. The concluding image of this section of Bildad's poem in 26:9 is

connected to the preceding by the focus on clouds. Because of an ambiguous word, it is not clear whether Bildad refers to God covering "the full moon" (כסה *keseh*)[387] with a screen of clouds or covering his "throne" (כסא *kissē*; cf. 22:14; Ps 97:2).[388] Given the immediate context, "full moon" seems more appropriate.

26:10. The horizon has always held a strong fascination for the human imagination, because it is such a visible marker of the structure of the cosmos. As in Prov 8:27, Bildad understands it to be a circle inscribed on the cosmic waters, a boundary marker dividing the light from the darkness (26:10; cf. Isa 40:22). In the Mesopotamian story of Gilgamesh, the Mashu mountains are a similar cosmic boundary marker, the very place where the sun moves from the upper world to the nether world.[389]

26:11-14. The concluding verses of Bildad's description return to the dynamic myth of the creation of the cosmos in the divine warrior's battle with the watery chaos monster. As in other accounts, the appearance of the divine warrior with his thunderous battle cry causes shaking and fear among the mountains, here described as the "pillars of the sky" (26:11; cf. Pss 18:7[8]; 29:3-9; 114:3-7). Verse 12 describes the cosmic battle with the Sea/Rahab. Yahweh's battle with the sea is of the same type and has the same significance as Baal's battle with Yam in Ugaritic mythology[390] and Marduk's battle with Tiamat in Mesopotamian religion.[391] The name "Rahab," which is frequently used in biblical texts for the sea monster, means something like "the boisterous" or "stormy one" (see 9:13; Pss 89:10[11]; Isa 51:9). Only with the subjugation of chaotic forces, so aptly represented in the shapeless but powerful waters of the sea, can the structures necessary to support life be established.

Bildad names both "power" and "wisdom" as the means by which God's victory is achieved (see also Jer 10:12). As Pope observes, cleverness or the assistance of a

385. So Habel, *The Book of Job*, 371.
386. So Hartley, *The Book of Job*, 366.

387. See Fohrer, *Das Buch Hiob*, 382; Pope, *Job*, 184. The suggestion goes back to the medieval Jewish scholar Ibn Ezra.
388. So Gordis, *The Book of Job*, 279; Habel, *The Book of Job*, 365.
389. *ANET*, 88.
390. *ANET*, 130-31.
391. *ANET*, 66-67. For a broad overview, see Clifford, *Creation Accounts in the Ancient Near East and in the Bible*; Day, *God's Conflict with the Dragon and the Sea*.

clever helper is a characteristic in Mesopotamian and Ugaritic myths as well.[392] Curiously, the verb in 26:12*a* (רגע *rāga'*) can mean either "stir up" (NIV, "churned up") or "still" (NRSV). Since the Sea rather than the divine warrior is typically depicted as the aggressor in the cosmogonic battle, "stilled" is preferable here, signifying the subjugation of the chaotic forces. Although wind or breath is a characteristic weapon of the divine warrior against the sea (26:13*a* ; e.g., Exod 15:8; Ps 18:15[16]), a reference to the sky's becoming fair is not otherwise associated with such accounts. Attempts to emend the text have produced some intriguing suggestions, but none is entirely persuasive.[393] Piercing the fleeing serpent, however, is a familiar image, both from Ugaritic mythology[394] and from Israelite accounts (see Isa 27:1; 51:9).

Bildad concludes his account of God's dominion and awesomeness in a rhetorically effective manner (26:14). Having given a remarkably vivid account of the cosmogonic battle and the structures of the cosmos, he minimizes what he has said, declaring that all of this is only the "outskirts," a "whisper." The full force of the powerful thunder of God's majesty is beyond human comprehension.

392. Pope, *Job*, 185.

393. Pope, *Job*, 181, suggests "By his wind he bagged the Sea," an image that evokes the strategy used by Marduk to subdue Tiamat.

394. *ANET*, 137.

REFLECTIONS

The clash in perspective between Job's speech in chaps. 23–24 and Bildad's in chaps. 25–26 could not be more profound. Job's religious imagination is deeply grounded in the ethical and the personal (see Commentary on Job 23; 24). By contrast, Bildad's religious imagination is grounded in a profound sense of the holy and of the "wholly otherness" of God. He is drawn to the experience of the transcendent, as his imagery reflects. In Bildad's speech, one encounters absolute heights and depths, immense voids, distant horizons, mythic conflicts. Both Job's perspective and that of Bildad have deep roots in Israelite religion. Yet juxtaposed as they are here, one is aware of their radical differences and not surprised that these two individuals cannot communicate with each other.

One can deduce what Bildad finds unacceptable in Job's speech. From his perspective, Job has let the "personal" quality of God become an intimacy that destroys the necessary and proper sense of awe that should be present in religious experience. Job has made God accountable to Job himself and talks as though they were two neighbors with a quarrel. Anyone who has listened closely to Job knows, of course, that his language about God is more complex than that. Nevertheless, the general point is worth thinking about. The Judeo-Christian tradition uses personal and intimate language about God with a striking boldness, especially in traditions of prayer and psalmody. To speak of God, the creator of the universe, in parental images or to pour out one's innermost pains in the confidence that God will listen is an extraordinary claim to make. If the necessary tension between the augustness of God and intimacy with God is lost, however, personal language becomes a shallow sentimentality. One sees this in certain traditional hymns, as well as in much contemporary Christian music. Or it may find expression in the general domestication of the image of God, so that God becomes an amiable caregiver, rather like the congregation's image of the ideal pastor. Bildad may be shocked at Job's language about God; he would be absolutely appalled if he listened to the language about God that flows freely at Sunday morning services in many contemporary churches.

Bildad champions a very different kind of experience of God and language about God. It is very close to what historian of religion Rudolf Otto wrote about in his classic study *The Idea of the Holy.* Otto stressed what he called a quality of "wholly otherness," which cannot be evoked by personal imagery. Its characteristics are an awefulness that produces a profound dread, an overpowering sense of majesty, a forceful energy, and yet an element of fascination. The great theophanic images of Yahweh in the Bible use imagery that attempts to communicate such an experience: the imagery of whirlwind, of fire, of the numinous cloud that glows from within and yet shields the divine presence from view. Bildad's language, although it is more graphically mythic, has many of these same qualities of the *mysterium tremendum et fascinans* that Otto describes.

In another respect, too, Bildad draws out an implication similar to what Otto discusses. An encounter with the holy, Otto noted, produces an experience of "creature-consciousness," which he describes as "the emotion of a creature, submerged and overwhelmed by its own nothingness in contrast to that which is supreme above all creatures."[395] It is an experience of the "annihilation of the self" that comes with contemplation of that which is absolute being. This is the experience to which Bildad refers in 25:4-6, when he contrasts the exalted being of God, before whom even the moon and stars are not bright, with the nothingness of mortal decay, which is human existence. Such an experience is far from a negative one, for it is accompanied by a sense of participating in that transcendent reality.[396] In mystical encounter, the structures of the individual ego are broken down and one's identity is taken up into the holy itself. Otto cites the experience recounted by William James: "The perfect stillness of the night was thrilled by a more solemn silence. The darkness held a presence that was all the more felt because it was not seen. I could not any more have doubted that *He* was there than that I was. Indeed, I felt myself to be, if possible, the less real of the two."[397] Although Bildad is not so explicit, he renders this experience poetically by drawing the reader so much into the transcendent description of God's majesty that it comes almost as a shock when he shifts the perspective back to that of the finite mortal in 26:14, declaring that all this majesty is but a whisper of the ineffable thunder of the divine reality.

Although Bildad may simply be reacting to what he considers the blasphemous familiarity and lack of respect in Job's way of talking about God, one needs to ask how the language of "the holy" would address the experience of suffering and whether it possesses resources for consolation. In at least one important respect it does. One of the characteristics of acute suffering is its tendency to obliterate all other experience. It can become almost impossible to see, hear, or feel anything beyond one's own suffering, as though that suffering were all that existed in the world. In such a situation, images of God that stress the intimate, personal quality of God, likening God to one who suffers with the grieving, may not be what is needed. What one craves is reassurance that one's own suffering is *not* the whole of reality. The religious experience of the holiness of God, of God as wholly otherness, is capable of providing such reassurance. As Bildad's speech suggests, religious language that speaks of the transcendence of God often does so in terms of creation. God's power in overcoming chaos and establishing the reliable structures of the cosmos can be an important support for one whose own experience is a wilderness of pain and anxiety. Thus one should not assume that only the religious traditions that speak of God in personal and intimate terms are of importance to one who suffers. There is also solace to be found in the language of God's majesty and transcendence.

395. R. Otto, *The Idea of the Holy*, 2nd ed., trans. J. W. Harvey (London: Oxford University Press, 1958; 1st ed. 1923) 10.
396. Otto, *The Idea of the Holy*, 21-22.
397. Otto, *The Idea of the Holy*, 22-23.

Job 27:1-23, Job Defends His Integrity

COMMENTARY

Chapter 27, the final chapter in the third cycle of speeches, poses many of the same interpretive difficulties as chaps. 23–24 and

25–26. The perspectives that were clearly separated into coherent, contrasting points of view in the earlier parts of the dialogue, seem jumbled together in a bewildering manner in these speeches. As in the case of chaps. 23–24 and 25–26, scholars have tended to resolve the problem by dividing up the material, assigning part of chap. 27 to Job (usually vv. 1-12) and part to Zophar (usually vv. 13-23).[398] Such a solution does not solve all the problems, however. One is left with two fragments instead of two complete speeches, and even that surgical separation does not remove all of the seeming inconsistencies from Job's speech. It is more appropriate to struggle with the text as it stands. The third cycle's difficulties, incoherencies, and tensions are an apt representation of a disintegrating dialogue. Although begun in classical symmetry, it ends incomplete and without clarity. These are persons who finally have no more to say to one another and no desire to hear one another any longer.

It is possible to read chap. 27 without reassigning the verses. By this point in the book, Job has emerged as a very complex character who has an extremely complicated relationship to the traditional moral language that had once seemed so uncomplicated to him. There is more than one legitimate way a reader might understand how the words of chap. 27 are used by Job and what they mean coming from his mouth.[399] The interpretation offered here is only one of those possibilities.

After the heading (v. 1), Job begins with a series of oaths in which he defends the honesty of his speech, his integrity, and his determination not to declare his friends right (vv. 2-6). Following these oaths, Job utters a curse on any enemy who would rise up against him (vv. 8-10). In vv. 11-12, Job declares his intention to instruct the friends in the true nature of God's power and criticizes them for merely "blowing wind." In vv. 13-23, Job satirically and dismissively imitates just such drivel as the friends have been speaking. By doing so, Job in effect preempts Zophar, who never speaks in the third cycle. Job's promise to disclose the nature of God's power is fulfilled in his final oration in chaps. 29–31, where he recalls the God who once protected but now

persecutes him and challenges the God who has "taken away my right" (27:2).

27:1-6. As noted in the Overview to chaps. 25–26, the unusual heading in 27:1 and 29:1 ("Job again took up his discourse") implies that his discourse has been interrupted. Thus 26:5-14 may be taken as the conclusion of Bildad's speech, begun in 25:1-4.

In 26:2-4, Job had already dismissed the sort of speech Bildad was making. Now he moves directly to his own statement. Job begins by swearing on the life of God (cf., e.g., Judg 8:19; 1 Sam 14:45; 2 Sam 2:27). Frequently, such an oath formula is expanded with an epithet for God, as when Saul says, "As Yahweh lives, who saves Israel . . ." (1 Sam 14:39; cf. 1 Kgs 2:24; Jer 16:14; 23:7). The use of God's name in an oath was intended to invoke God as a witness and guarantor of the oath, and the epithet served to remind the oath taker and the ones before whom the oath was taken of the power and effectiveness of the God in whose name the oath is made.[400] Job's formula, however, is paradoxical to the point of contradiction, for he swears by the life of the God who has "taken away my right" and "embittered my soul" (v. 2). This contradiction is the unavoidable consequence of the legal metaphor Job has invoked. His integrity has been called into question not only by what his friends have said, but also by God's actions. In this manner, "his right" to be treated as an innocent person has been violated. In the context of the legal metaphor, the resolution of his situation is understood in terms of vindication. Job's vindication requires two things: that his own word about himself be acknowledged as true and that he receive divine affirmation of his innocence. By means of his oath in 27:2-4, Job attempts to establish the veracity of his word. The great oath in chap. 31 will constitute his demand for vindication from God. In both cases, Job is staking everything on his belief that, despite all that he has experienced, God is ultimately a God of justice and will vindicate him.

The expressions Job uses in v. 3 to set the duration of the oath also point to the irony of his situation and to the ground of his paradoxical hope. The commonplace expression,

398. E.g., Dhorme, *A Commentary on the Book of Job,* xlvii-l; Habel, *The Book of Job,* 37; Rowley, *The Book of Job,* 174-78.

399. Contrast, e.g., the interpretations of Andersen, *Job,* 219-22; Janzen, *Job,* 172-74; and Good, *In Turns of Tempest,* 286-90, all of whom attribute chap. 27 in its entirety to Job.

400. M. Pope, "Oaths," IDBSup, 577; H. Ringgren, "chayah," *TDOT* IV, 339-40.

"while my breath is still in me," generally warrants no particular notice. It simply means "while I am still alive" (cf. 2 Sam 1:9). Job, however, scrutinizes the term "breath" (נשׁמה *nĕšāmâ*) and turns the cliché into a provocative claim. "Breath" is not some autonomous possession of human existence. It is a gift of God (Gen 2:7; Ps 104:29-30; Isa 42:5). Indeed, God's own breath or spirit enlivens a person (v. 3*b*). Just as Job speaks with God's own breath, he makes his claim against God with God's own passion for justice.

In v. 4, Job states the content of his oath; he will speak neither falsehood nor deceit. (The NIV's "wickedness" is too general. When עולה [*'awlâ*] is used with verbs of speaking, it refers specifically to lies; cf. Isa 59:3; Zeph 3:13.) Job made a similar claim in his first reply to Eliphaz (6:30), bitterly condemning his friends for speaking "falsehood" and "deceit" about God (13:7). At this point, speaking the truth means that Job can never declare the friends to be right, for that would be a betrayal of his own integrity (v. 5). Consequently, the resolution they had hoped to achieve by dialogue with Job is absolutely impossible. The dialogue is at an end.

In v. 6, Job describes the determination that has been the central feature of his character throughout the dialogues: to hold fast to his righteousness and to know that his own conscience (lit., "heart") will never have anything for which to reproach him. Here, too, there are echoes of the prose tale in the terms "integrity" (תמה *tummâ*) in v. 5 and "hold fast" or "persist" (החזיק *heḥĕzîq*) in v. 6. After the first test, when Job spoke words of acceptance, God said to the *satan,* "He still persists in his integrity" (2:3*a* NRSV). Later in that same chapter, Job's wife urged him to a different course of action, saying, " 'Do you still persist in your integrity? Curse God and die!' " (2:9 NRSV).

27:7-10. Job completes the section of his speech containing his oath by invoking a curse against his "enemy" (v. 7). In this context, the enemy is not God, as some have suggested.[401] The content of the curse makes no sense on that supposition. Although it is possible that Job refers specifically to his friends, it seems more likely that the curse is generic. Dhorme is probably correct in suggesting that it is a rhetorical form of speech. "Instead of saying: 'May I not suffer the fate of the wicked!' he says: 'May my enemy suffer the fate of the wicked.' "[402] The central enigma for Job has been that he, a righteous person, has experienced what tradition said is the fate of the wicked. It is his opposite, the one who rises up against him with malice, who deserves such a fate.

The tension between what should be and what Job has experienced lends an ironic element to his description of the wicked person's situation. Job phrases the question in terms of "hope," a word that resonates with Job's previous words about the destruction of his own hope (cf. 14:7, 19; 17:15; 19:10). Here, he specifically identifies hope with God's willingness to hear a person in distress (v. 9*a*). Verse 10 is better taken, not as a second set of questions following v. 9*a* (as in NIV and NRSV), but as further development of the situation in v. 9*b*, as in the TNK's translation: "Will God hear his cry/ When trouble comes upon him,/ When he seeks the favor of Shaddai,/ Calls upon God at all times?" The wicked person has no such hope, but can Job hope for God to hear him, a righteous person? That remains the unresolved question that Job will put to the test in the great oath that constitutes his challenge to God (chap. 31).

27:11-12. With v. 11, the style changes, as Job addresses the friends directly, adopting a didactic manner of speaking. He is perhaps mocking them, as in chap. 12, when he imitated a typical wisdom discourse. In v. 11, Job offers to teach them concerning God's power, but in v. 12 he alters his focus, drawing attention to the inanity of what the friends have said. For Job, the direct evidence of eyes and ears is the basis for speaking truth (see 13:1). Since the friends can see (v. 12*a*), it is incomprehensible that they speak nonsense (v. 12*b*). More literally, Job says that they "blow wind," using the noun הבל (*hebel*), a word that concretely means "puff of wind," and the related verb (*hābal*; cf. 21:34).

27:13-23. These verses are best understood as Job's imitation of just such empty words as he has been hearing from his friends.

---

401. So Habel, *The Book of Job,* 381-82, and Good, *In Turns of Tempest,* 287-88.

402. Dhorme, *A Commentary on the Book of Job,* 382. In Dan 4:19*b* (16*b*), Daniel uses a similar expression when he is reluctant to interpret Nebuchadnezzar's dream: " 'My lord, may the dream be for those who hate you, and its interpretation for your enemies' " (NRSV).

As an example of prefabricated tradition, they will contrast with the testimony of his own experience in chaps. 29–31. That these are not Job's own words but an imitation of the friends' speech is indicated by the way the introductory verse 13 mimics the last verse of Zophar's speech from the second cycle (20:29). As Janzen suggests, Job is in essence giving Zophar's speech for him.[403]

Traditional elements abound in Job's version of the fate of the wicked. In describing the destruction of the wicked person's offspring in vv. 14-15 (cf. 18:19), Job invokes a version of the traditional threefold disaster: war, famine, and pestilence (cf. Ezek 6:11-12). Here, as in Jeremiah, the term "death" serves as an epithet for plague (Jer 15:2; 43:11; cf. Job 18:13, where "death's firstborn" is a plague-like disease). Verse 14 evokes the so-called futility curses, in which what appears to be good fortune only prepares for disaster (cf. Deut 28:41). To be "buried by death" (v. 15) implies having no proper burial at all, a fate greatly dreaded in the ancient world (see Isa 14:18-20; Jer 22:18-19). For widows not to lament suggests a destruction so overwhelming that the most elemental obligations to the dead are no longer honored (see Ps 78:64).

Verses 16-19 describe the ephemeral nature of the wealth of the wicked. In the first example, vv. 16-17, Job pairs "silver" with "clothing" rather than the more common "silver and gold" (cf. Zech 9:3, which also uses the comparison with dust/dirt). The impending loss is already implied in the very terms used to describe the wicked person's abundance. Dust functions as a symbol both of abundance (Gen 13:16; 28:14) and of decay (17:16).[404] That the righteous enjoy the wealth that the wicked have gathered is a cliché of wisdom literature (Prov 13:22b; 28:8; cf. Eccl 2:26). The second example, the insubstantiality of the wicked person's house, is a theme already canvassed by Eliphaz

(5:3-5) and Bildad (18:15). The imagery of v. 18a is obscured by uncertainty about the meaning of the word עָשׁ (ʿāš). In addition to "moth" and "bird's nest," it has been suggested that the word means "guard."[405] If so, then the two parts of the verse are more nearly parallel, and the point is that the house of the wicked is like the flimsy shelters put up by guards and sentinels (cf. Isa 1:8; 24:20). The third example, of wealth that vanishes between sleeping and waking (v. 19; cf. Prov 23:4-5), completes the series.[406]

The culmination of the destruction of the wicked is depicted in ways that suggest expulsion from the world. The "terrors" of v. 20a are not subjective fears, but as in Bildad's speech (18:11, 14), objective forces of death unleashed into the world. These terrors are compared to the mighty flood waters that figure frequently as a symbol of death and destruction (Pss 18:16[17]; 32:6; Isa 28:17). Similarly, the storm (v. 20b) and east wind (v. 21a) that carry off the wicked are traditional symbols of disaster and punishment (Prov 1:27; 10:25; Jer 18:17; Hos 13:15). The clapping and whistling in v. 23 are gestures of contempt and scorn (Jer 49:17; Lam 2:15; Zeph 2:15), ways of punishing by shame. Since the subject of a verb need not be separately expressed in Hebrew, it is not clear who or what is the subject of the verbs in vv. 22-23. Perhaps the ambiguity is deliberate. Certainly, it adds to the eerie quality of the description that one cannot quite be certain whether it is the personified east wind that hurls itself against the wicked, clapping and whistling, or the generic "people" who do this,[407] or perhaps God (NRSV mg). Reality dissolves, as divine judgment and human contempt are made present in the incessant whistling and snapping of the wind that pursues the wicked.

403. Janzen, *Job*, 174.
404. Habel, *The Book of Job*, 386.
405. Pope, *Job*, 193.
406. Habel, *The Book of Job*, 387, suggests that the verse refers to the wicked person's life rather than to wealth.
407. Dhorme, *A Commentary on the Book of Job*, 397.

REFLECTIONS

Job's words in 27:2-6 offer an opportunity to reflect on some of the painful ironies that may confront a person who is determined to speak without falsehood or deceit about an experience of betrayal. Telling the truth about his situation as he understands it has required Job to say things he previously could not have imagined himself saying. Job's words against God have been so bitter that one can seriously ask whether Job has cursed God.[408] Although Job has not used a technical curse formula, there is no doubt that he has spoken blasphemy—i.e., reviling words against God. Alleging that God has given the earth into the hands of the wicked and even corrupted judges (9:24) is blasphemy. So is Job's depiction of God as one who acts destructively in apparent random fashion against whole peoples (12:13-25). One could add many such statements. One rather cynical comment in the rabbinic discussion of Job in *b. Bat.* 15*b* says, "There was a certain pious man among the heathen named Job, but he [thought that he had] come into the world only to receive [here] his reward, and when the Holy One, blessed be He, brought chastisements upon him, he began to curse and blaspheme, so the Holy One, blessed be He, doubled his reward in this world so as to expel him from the world to come."[409]

That judgment is too hard on Job and misconstrues the nature of his words. An important distinction needs to be made between Job's blasphemy and what the *satan* had in mind when he said that Job would "curse God." The *satan* assumed that Job would repudiate God. It is certainly true that one may speak bitterly and disparagingly of a person one has repudiated, with whom there can be no further relationship; but not all bitter and abusive words are acts of repudiation. Sometimes they are acts of a harrowing intimacy. Job's blasphemous words are not a farewell to God but a searing truth-telling to the God he will not leave. In a paradoxical way that completely escapes the friends, Job's "holding fast to his integrity," even though it means speaking blasphemy, is the only way he can hold fast to God. It is doubtful that Job could sustain indefinitely the moral energy required to support this position, but at this point Job has not cursed God.

One of the ironic truths of life is that in certain circumstances loyalty and fidelity can only be expressed in opposition. Perhaps the most familiar instance of this paradoxical loyalty through opposition is to be found in the figure of the political dissident. For the dissident, love of country does not mean blind endorsement of whatever policies are developed by its leaders. Love of country means deep and abiding commitment to the values that make it worthy of love. When those values are betrayed, then love expresses itself in opposition and in an attempt to recall the country to its true identity. In ancient Israel, the role of the dissident was often borne by the prophet. Jeremiah is the most poignant example, as one sees how painful it was for Jeremiah to confront Judah with its fatal inability to be faithful, how excruciating it was to be hated by former friends and by relatives for speaking the truth given to him by God. Jeremiah also reflects the desire often expressed by dissidents who would keep silent if only they could, and yet who know that the word of protest is a fire shut up in their bones (see Jer 20:9). In the contemporary church, this role of reluctant dissident has come to many women whose denominations refuse to acknowledge the legitimacy of the ministries to which they have been called. To outsiders it appears a simple matter for such women to leave and take their gifts where they would be welcomed. But the true dissident has a deep identity with the object of her protest and is bound by love for the institution she seeks to call to repentance. This sense of identity is what Job alludes to when he refers to speaking against God by means of the breath of God and when he swears in the name of the very God who has deprived him of his right (vv. 2-3).

Confronting a person or an institution with the contradiction between what is and what should be is painful beyond all reckoning. To attack what one loves in the name of that love forces one into a bewildering confusion of emotions. It is morally dangerous,

408. J. T. Wilcox, *The Bitterness of Job: A Philosophical Reading* (Ann Arbor: University of Michigan Press, 1989) 51-70.

409. I. Epstein, ed., *The Babylonian Talmud: Seder Nezikin: Baba Bathra,* vol. 1, trans. M. Simon (New Work: Rebecca Bennet Publications, 1959) 75.

too, for it is but a small step into self-righteousness. Being the object of such anger and accusation is equally wrenching. As individuals and as members of institutions, there is always the temptation to resort to defensiveness, seeing the accuser as merely destructive, motivated by resentment rather than love. It is a difficult encounter to negotiate to the end, unpredictable in its outcome, but it is often the only alternative to ending things with a curse.

JOB 28:1-28, INTERLUDE: WHERE CAN WISDOM BE FOUND?

COMMENTARY

The poem on wisdom in chap. 28 is one of the most exquisite poetic compositions of the entire Bible. Precious jewels serve as an important image within the poem and might also serve as an image for the poem itself. Like a gemstone, this poem is beautifully crafted, clear and luminous, yet full of mysterious depths. Its unique literary form and meditative tone have led many commentators to conclude that it must be a late addition to the book, rather than an integral part of its composition; but that view betrays a rather wooden notion of the book's composition. Moreover, it overlooks the fact that the diction, grammar, and style of chap. 28 are quite similar to other passages in the dialogues and the divine speeches. The similarities between chaps. 28 and 38 are especially close.[410] The important issue is not whether chap. 28 belongs where it is placed, but what role it plays.

The first issue to be resolved is the speaker's identity. Since no heading separates chap. 28 from chap. 27, it would initially appear that it is a continuation of Job's speech. The abrupt change of tone, topic, and imagery, however, makes a distinct break from the preceding material. Similarly, the heading introducing chap. 29, which indicates that Job is "resuming" his discourse, implies that chap. 28 is not Job's speech. Moreover, the contrast between the content and the perspective of chaps. 28 and 29-31 is so striking that it is virtually impossible to imagine chap. 28 as Job's

words at this point in the story.[411] It is equally unlikely that chap. 28 contains the "missing" speech of Zophar for the third cycle. Even though the theme of the poem bears some resemblance to Zophar's comments in 11:7-12, the style and mood of chap. 28 are completely different from any of the speeches in the dialogue. Both those who consider the speech to be original and those who consider it to be a later addition agree that it serves as a sort of meditative interlude, reflecting on the dialogue that precedes it, and preparing for the final section of the book, which will reach its climax in the divine speeches in chaps. 38–41.[412]

The structure of the poem is clearly marked. The first section of the poem (vv. 1-11) describes the place of precious metals in the world and the heroic human search to find and obtain them. These verses serve as a foil to the second section of the poem (vv. 12-27), which describes the inability of humans, in contrast to God, to find or obtain wisdom. This second section is divided into two parts both by the repetition of the thematic rhetorical question concerning the source and place of wisdom (vv. 12, 20) and by the repetition of the statement that neither living beings nor the personified cosmic realms of Sea and Death are able to locate and so gain access to wisdom (vv. 13-14, 21-22). Thus the structure of the poem draws attention to the contrast between the inability

---

410. See the list compiled by S. A. Geller, " 'Where Is Wisdom?' A Literary Study of Job 28 in Its Settings," in *Judaic Perspectives on Ancient Israel,* eds. J. Neusner, B. Levine, and E. S. Frerichs (Philadelphia: Fortress, 1987) 177n. 1. See also Habel, *The Book of Job,* 392.

411. Janzen, *Job,* 187-201, is the only recent commentator to defend the speech as Job's. Good, *In Turns of Tempest,* 290-93, concludes that it was not originally composed as a speech of Job, but that its insertion within the book has made it appear to be Job's, and so he attempts to interpret it as such.

412. E.g., Andersen, *Job,* 222-24; Hartley, *The Book of Job,* 26-27; Habel, *The Book of Job,* 391-94.

of humankind to obtain wisdom, even in exchange for all the riches procured by mining (vv. 15-19), and God's knowledge of the way and place of wisdom in the cosmos, expressed most fully in God's encounter with wisdom in the act of creation (vv. 23-27).

The final verse of the poem (v. 28) stands apart from the comprehensive structure and provides an unexpected conclusion to the poem. In contrast to the contention that humans cannot obtain wisdom, v. 28 presents God as saying that, for humans, piety ("fear of the LORD") is the equivalent of wisdom, and morality ("turning from evil") the equivalent of understanding. Stylistically, the verse echoes the prose narrative with which the book began, as well as presenting its point of view. Interpreters who judge every deviation in style or perspective to be a sign of later editorial tampering with the text tend to treat v. 28 as an intrusion. One should remember, however, that the entire book of Job is structured dialogically, setting one perspective over against another. Not only is this true of the dialogue between Job and his friends or between Job and God, but it is also true of the way that the prose narratives at the beginning and end of the book are set over against the poetic material in the middle. Verse 28 should be taken as an integral part of the chapter. It imitates in miniature the structure of the end of the book in which the long poetic speeches about creation are followed by a return to the voice of the prose narrative. The interpretive problem of understanding v. 28 in relation to the preceding poem anticipates the similar interpretive problem of understanding the narrative conclusion of the book in relation to the divine speeches.

28:1-11. The first part of the poem, concerning the godlike power of human beings to search out and mine precious minerals, is divided into a series of small strophes. In the first (vv. 1-2), the topic is announced. Verses 3-4 recount the search for minerals in a distant and inaccessible land. Verses 5-6 describe the land and its subterranean riches. The extraordinary human achievement in locating the source of such riches is underscored by contrasting the animals' ignorance concerning its location (vv. 7-8). The climax comes in the account of the mining operation

itself and the successful bringing to light of hidden treasures (vv. 9-11).

Verse 1 has a double function in the chapter. In its immediate context, it is paired with v. 2 and introduces the list of precious minerals (silver, gold, iron, copper), together with the places in which they are found and the material from which they are derived. But v. 1 is also the first part of a parallel that is not completed until v. 12. The verbal similarities between the two verses are obscured in English translation, but the two key words in v. 1 are "mine" (מוצא *môṣāʾ*; lit., "place of coming forth") and "place" (מקום *māqôm*). In v. 12*b*, *māqôm* is also used; and in v. 12*a* the verb "be found" (מצא *māṣāʾ*), although from a different Hebrew root than *môṣāʾ*, has a similar sound. Thus the contrast is established. There is a site where silver can be *found* and a *place* for gold, but where can wisdom be *found,* or where is the *place* of understanding?

Verses 3-4 are quite difficult to translate and to interpret. Although individual words are problematic, the main question is whether the verses refer to prospecting or to mining. (The NRSV's "miners" is interpretive; the Hebrew text simply has "he" or "one.") Although these verses have generally been interpreted to refer to the act of mining, a good case can be made that the mining and extraction procedures are not described until vv. 9-11.[413] Verse 3 summarizes the entire process and its goal. Specifically, the allusion to "putting an end to darkness" anticipates the result that is not made explicit until v. 11*b*, in which the "hidden things" of the earth are "brought to light." One should not miss the overtones of godlike activity in this phrase (cf. Gen 1:2-3); themes of power and creation are used in complex ways in this chapter. That prospecting is in view seems especially clear from the phrase "searching to the farthest limit." In 26:10 the same word (תכלית *taklît*) was used to identify the horizon as the boundary between darkness and light. Zophar used the phrase "the limit of Shaddai" to talk about divine wisdom in 11:7*b*, employing the four cosmic dimensions as comparison. In v. 3 the sense of the direction of this search to the limits of the cosmos is suggested by the description of the ore that is sought as the

---

413. Cf. Geller, " 'Where Is Wisdom?' A Literary Study of Job 28 in Its Settings," 158-59.

"stone of gloom and the shadow of death." These phrases are used elsewhere to describe the darkness of Sheol (10:21-22). The enterprise of prospecting and mining leads to the far reaches of the world and from thence into the depths of the earth, where the boundary between the land of life and the land of death is easily crossed. Such a quest is fraught with both power and danger.

As Andersen says, "Everyone is reduced to despair by v. 4, and, comparing several versions . . . it is hard to believe that they all had the same Hebrew text in front of them."[414] There are two problems with the translations of the NRSV and the NIV. First, the term translated "shafts" (נחל *naḥal*) is nowhere else attested with that meaning, but is the ordinary word for "wadi," the dry river bed that crosses the desert landscape. Second, the expression "dangles and sways" or "sway suspended" is based on a very problematic interpretation of the Hebrew verb דלל (*dālal*). With minimal emendation, Geller tentatively proposes a much more likely translation, which I would adapt as follows: "They spread out through wadis far from habitation, they wandered through (wadis) forgotten by travelers, poor in population."[415] However one translates v. 4, its contribution to the imagery is captured in its threefold repetition of the expression "far from," followed by some expression that suggests human presence. Whether the text refers to prospecting or mining, the one who seeks out precious minerals journeys deep into utter isolation.

Verses 5-6 describe this remote region where precious minerals are found (cf. Deut 8:9). The contrast in v. 5 is between the surface and the depths.[416] Volcanic activity was recognized as an indication of fire under the earth. It is possible that the expression "stones of fire," used as a term for gemstones in Ezek 28:14, suggests a belief that precious stones were formed in such environments.[417] In any event the fiery depths of this region are associated with lapis lazuli and with gold.[418]

The references to not knowing the path, not seeing, and not traversing the area all indicate that vv. 7-8 refer to the hidden and inaccessible location of the land that is so rich in minerals. Birds of prey are used as an example because of their extraordinary eyesight and ability to look over large territories from great heights (cf. 39:29). The significance of lions and the other wild animals referred to in Hebrew as "children of pride" is less clear. An ingenious case has been made that the word translated "lion" (שחל *šaḥal*) should be rendered "snake," which would give a fitting parallelism between creatures of the air and creatures of the dust. The "children of pride" are elsewhere mentioned only in Job 41:34[26], in connection with the reptilian Leviathan, and so might designate lizards, which, as Prov 30:29 notes, find their way into unlikely places.[419] The problem with this otherwise appealing suggestion is that *šaḥal* is clearly used with the meaning "lion" in Eliphaz's list of five different terms for lions (4:10-11).

Verses 9-11 form the climax of this section of the poem, describing the technical power by which human beings delve into the earth. Here, as in the search for mineral lands, there are overtones of godlike ability. "Overturning the roots of the mountains" evokes the similar image of God's power in 9:5 (cf. Hab 3:6). Not only mountains but also waters are controlled, as vv. 10*a* and 11*a* contrast "forcing open" (בקע *biqqēa'*) channels and binding the sources of rivers. There is no reason to emend the text of v. 11*a* to "search," as the NRSV and the NIV do. It destroys the parallelism and does not improve the sense. Although one can imagine the sort of mining techniques that would involve the control of water, the godlike qualities of the acts are equally important for the symbolism of the poem. Habakkuk 3:9 refers to God "splitting" (*bāqa'*) the earth with rivers. Similarly, in a description of creation, Ps 74:15 contrasts God's "forcing open" springs and channels with God's drying up of rivers. The cosmic overtones of the scene in Job 28 are underscored by the term used for "sources of the

414. Andersen, *Job,* 225.
415. Geller, " 'Where Is Wisdom?' A Literary Study of Job 28 in Its Settings," 178n. 9.
416. An alternative interpretation, which takes this verse to refer to mining operations, suggests that a technique of heating rocks to make them crack is what is described here. See Pope, *Job,* 201.
417. Habel, *The Book of Job,* 396.
418. The translation "sapphire," instead of "lapis lazuli" is anachronistic. That gem was not known until Roman times, as Rowley notes, *The Book of Job,* 181.
419. See S. Mowinckel, *"shahal",* in *Hebrew and Semitic Studies Presented to Godfrey Rolles Driver,* ed. D. Winton Thomas and W. D. McHardy (Oxford: Clarendon, 1963) 95-103. His suggestion is adopted by Geller, " 'Where Is Wisdom?' A Literary Study of Job 28 in Its Settings," 179-80.

rivers" (מבכי נהרות *mibkî nĕhārôt*, v. 11), for it is the same term used in Ugaritic mythology to describe the abode of the god El, "at the sources of the two rivers, in the midst of the channels of the two seas."[420] Human activity extends to the very doorstep of the gods. The success of the enterprise in seeing the precious things (v. 10*b*) and bringing "the hidden things to light" (v. 11*b*) also echoes the divine ability to bring the things of darkness to light (12:22; cf. Dan 2:22).

One should note that these divine overtones are not used in a critical fashion to condemn human technological power. To the contrary, they celebrate it as the means by which human beings approximate the extraordinary powers of God. In the overall strategy of the poem, however, the pinnacle of power and achievement that mining represents is used as a foil for the utter inability of human striving to find and secure something much more precious: wisdom.

28:12-19. Only now, approximately 40 percent of the way through the poem, is its true theme announced. Although one usually speaks of "wisdom" as the subject of the poem, actually two words are used, "wisdom" (חכמה *ḥokmâ*) and "understanding" (בינה *bînâ*; cf. Prov 1:2; 4:5, 7; 9:10; 16:16). *Hokmâ* is a very general term, the precise meaning of which depends on the context in which it is used. *Bînâ*, by contrast, has a somewhat more restricted meaning, referring to intellectual discernment, both as a capacity that an individual might possess and as the knowledge produced by such discernment.[421] By pairing these terms and setting them in the context of imagery that has already established the whole cosmos as its frame of reference, the poet is apparently asking about the kind of understanding that would provide insight into the nature and meaning of the entire cosmos. There are several examples within wisdom literature of this type of poem, which reflect on wisdom as the organizing principle of the cosmos (Prov 8:22-31; Wis 7:15-30; Sir 1:1-10; 24:1-29; Bar 3:9–4:4). In contrast to Proverbs 8 and Sirach 24, however, wisdom is not personified in Job 28.[422]

420. *ANET*, 133.
421. Fox, "Words for Wisdom," 154.
422. Contra Habel, *The Book of Job*, 394.

As noted above, v. 12 complements v. 1. The use of similar terminology of place establishes a metaphorical relationship between precious minerals and wisdom. But the "place" of wisdom is precisely what is problematic about it. Verse 13 bluntly states that human beings do not know the way to the place of wisdom (NRSV, following LXX; the NIV's "value," following MT, is apparently influenced by the topic of comparative value introduced in vv. 15-19). Verse 13*b* denies that wisdom can be found in the entire "land of the living," a term used in contrast to the pit and the watery depths that are the realm of death (Ezek 26:19-20; cf. Isa 38:10-11). But wisdom is not to be found in those watery depths either, as the personified cosmic deep testifies in v. 14 (cf. vv. 21-22, which similarly pair the realms of the living and the dead).

The next section, vv. 15-19, transforms certain commonplaces of wisdom teaching. In the book of Proverbs one frequently encounters the admonition to "acquire" wisdom (e.g., Prov 4:5, 7), an expression whose commercial overtones are playfully exploited (Prov 23:23). The value of wisdom is also compared with that of silver, gold, and jewels (Prov 3:13-15), and the two themes are combined in the advice that one "buy" wisdom rather than gold (Prov 16:16). Here, however, the poet reverses the traditional imagery. One cannot buy wisdom for all the precious metals and jewels in the world.

The entire passage has a list-like quality, as the same point is made in subtly varying sentences. One notes this in the long list of precious gems and metals named. In addition to silver, there are five different expressions for "gold," impossible to render in English, but suggesting a connoisseur's familiarity with rarities among rarities. Seven different gemstones are named. Although it is not always possible to be certain which particular gems are intended, the very enumeration has a sensuous quality that suggests all the fabled riches coming from widely differing places in the world. As the products of mining, they represent not only wealth but also evidence of the technological power of mining celebrated in vv. 1-11. There is also a list-like quality in the synonymous verbs for exchange or value: "given," "weighed out" (v. 15); "be paid for" (v. 16); "valued" (v. 17).

The sequence is interrupted in v. 18 with the humorous phrase "don't even mention . . ." and completed in v. 19 with a repetition of the verbs "valued" and "be paid for." The governing repetition, however, which is not varied but tolls like a bell, is the negative particle "not" (לֹא *lō*). It begins each verse, except the next to last (v. 18), where it is the third word.

28:20-27. The final section of the poem opens with a repetition of the rhetorical question of v. 12, differing only in the use of the verb "come" (בוא *bō*) rather than "be found" (מצא *māṣā*). Verses 21-22 parallel vv. 13-14, excluding the notion that wisdom can be found either among the living or in the realm of the dead. In terms of scope, the phrase "all living" includes not only humans (v. 13) but also animals (cf. Gen 6:19; 8:21) and is complemented by mention of the "birds of the heavens." Verse 21 teases the reader with the notion that wisdom has a place, albeit elusively hidden. Analogously, the words of personified Abaddon and Death in v. 22 have a teasing quality when compared with v. 14. In contrast to the simple negative of the Deep and Sea, these regions report having heard a rumor of the place of wisdom. At the same time, such statements underscore how far removed from human reach such a place must be.

These tantalizing words prepare for the climactic statement in v. 23: "God understands the way to it." Both the word "God" (אלהים *ĕlōhîm*) and the pronoun "he" (הוא *hû*) are in emphatic positions in the sentences, marking the contrast between God and humanity. Verse 24 continues to tease the reader with the notion of wisdom's place, as it seems to connect God's knowledge of wisdom's place with God's ability to see to the ends of the earth and everything under heaven.

It is thus somewhat surprising that the text shifts from spatial language to temporal language with v. 25. Grammatically, both v. 25 and v. 26 are subordinate clauses that introduce the main clause in v. 27. Thus, literally and somewhat woodenly, one might translate "at (the time of) the setting of weight for the wind . . . in the setting of a limit for the rain . . . then he saw it." Or, more fluidly, "when . . . when . . . then." This grammatical structure is important because

it is typical of the way in which many stories and poems about creation are told. The Babylonian creation myth, the Enuma Elish, begins: "When on high the heaven had not been named. . . . When no gods whatever had been brought into being. . . . Then it was that the gods were formed within [the waters of Apsu and Tiamat]."[423] There is a similar grammatical structure in the Israelite creation story in Gen 2:4b-7: "In the day that the LORD God made the earth and the heavens, when no plant of the field was yet in the earth . . . then the LORD God formed man from the dust of the ground" (NRSV). In the wisdom poem of Prov 8:22-31 the same grammatical structure appears: "When there were no depths I was brought forth. . . . Before the mountains had been shaped. . . . When he assigned to the sea its limit . . . when he marked out the foundations of the earth, then I was beside him" (NRSV). In each case the main clause, the one introduced by "then," contains the crucial element.

There is a subtle difference between the creation accounts just mentioned and the creation language of vv. 25-27. In the Enuma Elish and Genesis 2, the "when" clauses establish conditions that exist before the crucial event. Proverbs 8 plays with this tradition by reversing it. Wisdom exists prior to all the things named in the "when" clauses. Job 28:25-27 does something slightly different. Instead of setting up a before and after relationship, the "when" clauses establish a relationship of simultaneity. It was "in the act of" (לעשות *laʿăśôt*, בעשתו *baʿăśōtô*, vv. 25a, 26a) creating the world that God perceived wisdom. Now the poet's teasing references about wisdom's "place" appear in a new light. Wisdom's place is not a location; wisdom is found in an act of creativity.[424] The particular acts that vv. 25-26 recount all have to do with bringing order to things that have a certain formlessness about them: wind, water, rain, thunderstorms (cf. 36:27-33; 38:4-38; Isa 40:12). Weight and measure (v. 25) are purely physical terms, but the corresponding terms in v. 26, "limit" (חק *hōq*; lit., "groove," by extension "decree" or "rule")[425] and "way" or "path" (דרך *derek*) have both

423. *ANET*, 61.
424. Similarly, Janzen, *Job*, 197.
425. Pope, *Job*, 205.

physical and moral connotations, depending on context. In the activity of making order, of giving substance to creatures and of simultaneously setting limits for them, God perceives wisdom.

The specific verbs used in v. 27 are difficult to translate appropriately, as a comparison of various translations shows. The first verb phrase, "he saw it," is simple enough (cf. v. 24). But what is one to make of the other verbs? The NIV translation attempts to bring out nuances of the verbs that would support the metaphor of wisdom as a jewel, tested and confirmed as without flaws.[426] Although an appealing interpretation, it is not clear that the Hebrew words have those precise connotations. Certainly the point could have been made more explicitly. Gordis suggests a more likely explanation in noting that the Hebrew words "innumerable" (אין מספר 'ên mispār) and "unsearchable" (אין חקר 'ên ḥēqer), elsewhere used of divine wisdom (Ps 147:5; Isa 40:28), are related to the verbs used here, "declared" or "appraised" (ספר sippēr) and "searched" (חקר ḥāqar).[427] These verbs suggest the complete and thorough knowledge of wisdom that God obtains. Although some would emend the verb "confirmed" or "established" (כון kûn) to "discerned" (בון bîn) in order to make it parallel to "saw,"[428] the meaning of the verse does not require it.

What has the poem asserted about wisdom and its place in the world? Wisdom cannot be found by mining, because it is not a thing deposited somewhere in the world and waiting to be dug up. Searching for it as though it were is an act of futility doomed to failure. Similarly, wisdom is not a commodity that can be possessed. Even God's relation to wisdom is described in ways that challenge notions of wisdom as some objectified thing. Wisdom is perceived and known fully only in the act of creation itself. What the poet describes is rather like what an artisan experiences. The wisdom that makes the crafting possible is known only in the exercise of that skill. It is a faculty of the maker, and yet that wisdom is also worked into every aspect of the thing that is made. If that is what the poem says,

then wisdom is in the world, worked into its very fabric (cf. Prov 3:19-20), yet not in a way that allows it to be extracted. The poem has not yet said, however, whether and how human beings can experience wisdom, once its true nature is recognized.

28:28. One expects some sort of summary or conclusion after v. 27, but not the one that actually appears. The introductory words of v. 28, "and he said to humankind," have the syntax of prose, not poetry, and consequently draw attention to themselves as interruptive. The allusion to 1:1 in the phrases "fear of the Lord" (יראת אדני yir' at 'ădōnāy; cf. "fears God" [וירא אלהים wîrē' 'ĕlōhîm] in 1:1) and "turning from evil" (סור מרע sûr mērā') give this interrupting voice the tone of the narrator of the prose tale.[429] The use of the word "Lord" ('ădōnāy), otherwise unattested in the book of Job, leads some commentators to regard v. 28 as a later addition to the text. Whether secondary or original, however, v. 28 does provide an interpretive conclusion to the poem by means of a voice that distinguishes itself from the voice of the poem and so sets up a dialogue with it.

There is something shocking and outrageous about coming to the end of such a profound poem and being met by a cliché. These are the shopworn phrases of conventional instruction found in Prov 1:7; 3:7; 9:10; and in Ps 111:10. Moreover, hearing these phrases in the accents of the prose narrator gives them an unbearable smugness, as though chaps. 3–27 have meant nothing. But perhaps the affront is part of the artistic design and pedagogical strategy. Readers are accustomed to finding the meaning of a work at the end. The process is not unlike mining, where the precious thing one wishes to extract lies at the bottom of the pit or the far end of the tunnel. So here, even though the poem has been at pains to tell us that wisdom is not a thing to be located and extracted, we have still been expecting to find the extractable nugget at the end. To be met with dross instead of gold is disconcerting.

Disorientation can be a useful pedagogical tool, however, for it often makes one look at the familiar in new ways. Only if the proverbial saying is taken in isolation is it something

---

426. Similarly, Habel, *The Book of Job*, 400.
427. Gordis, *The Book of Job*, 311.
428. See Dhorme, *A Commentary on the Book of Job*; Pope, *Job*, 206; Geller, " 'Where Is Wisdom?' A Literary Study of Job 28 in Its Settings." A few manuscripts actually read "discerned it."

429. So Dhorme, *A Commentary on the Book of Job*, 414; Pope, *Job*, 206; Fohrer, *Das Buch Hiob*, 392.

that the reader already knows. Here it is set in a context that permits it to disclose something previously unperceived. The interpretive v. 28 sets up a parallel with vv. 25-27. "Fear of the Lord" and "turning from evil" play the same role in relation to humans that "giving weight to the wind" and "setting a limit for the rain" play in relation to God. God's acts are cosmos-creating acts, and God perceives and establishes wisdom in the midst of that activity. The human actions of true piety—fearing God and turning from evil—those too are acts of creation. They are cosmos-creating acts, not as acts of physical creation but as acts of moral creation. Humankind cannot find wisdom by searching for it as though it could be mined or purchased. One cannot possess wisdom; one can only embody it.

REFLECTIONS

Chapter 28 speaks of a paradox, of something that cannot be found because it is everywhere, of a quest whose end is the same as its beginning. To understand this paradox, one needs to think more about the nature of wisdom. Habel calls wisdom that which integrates the phenomena of the cosmos.[430] One might rephrase that definition by saying that wisdom is the point of coherence of the universe, the point from which the integrity of creation can be perceived, the point from which the interrelatedness of things can be understood. Wisdom of that sort brings both profound peace and profound security. There is no one who does not yearn for that, and yet it seems so elusive.

Job and his friends have been seeking wisdom in terms of an explanatory principle that will make sense of everything. Their efforts have failed and are doomed to fail, although they are not yet ready to acknowledge this. Wisdom is not a principle of explanation. Chapter 28 talks of it instead as a means of participation in the world. In identifying that mode of participation, v. 28 uses the two phrases "fear of the Lord" and "turning from evil."

The notion of "fear of the Lord," a general term for piety, is not so different from what is sometimes called mindfulness. It is an orientation to God developed and nurtured by the disciplines of piety: prayer, meditation, and other religious observances that serve to remind one of God's continual presence. The forms that such disciplines of piety take vary from one religious tradition to another and from one individual to another. In the monastic tradition, for instance, it is the daily observance of the divine liturgy. For others it may be silent meditation. In the tradition of Psalm 119, it is reflection on the beauty of Torah. Whatever form it takes, the function of such practices is to integrate the individual into the same realities that are expressed by the reference to God's "setting a weight for the wind and establishing the waters by measure, establishing a limit for the rain, and a way for the thunderstorm" (vv. 25-26, author's trans.).

"Turning from evil" is a condensed expression for the moral capacity of human beings. That, too, is a form of participation in divine creativity. Love does not exist without someone who will love. Justice does not come into being without someone to do justice. This notion is embedded in the Hebrew phrase to *"do* righteousness," a phrase used of humans as well as of God (see, e.g., Ps 106:3; Prov 21:3; Isa 56:1; 58:2; Jer 9:23; Ezek 18:21). To do righteousness and to turn from evil are acts of moral creation. The philosopher Erazim Kohak puts it this way: "There is an order, a rightness as well as a rhythm of time. The generations of the porcupines, the phases of the forest, even the death of the chipmunk, all attest to a rightness of time. The glory of being human is the ability to recognize the pattern of rightness and to honor it as a moral law. The horror of being human is the ability to violate that rightness, living out of season—doing violence to the other, perverting the most sacred human relationships,

---

430. Habel, *The Book of Job,* 397.

devastating the world in greed, overriding its rhythm, not in the name of necessity and charity, but in the compulsion of coveting."[431]

In the disciplines of piety and of moral order, human beings may also perceive and participate in wisdom, experiencing in mindfulness and in moral action the integrity of creation. Through this participation in wisdom comes a peace and security that are not a denial of the tragic dimension of life, but an ability to be sustained in tragedy by experiencing the creating, sustaining presence of God. This is what is portrayed by the Job of the prose tale.

The story has shown, however, that Job did not, after all, "fear God for naught." Like his friends, Job had tacitly assumed that by embodying wisdom he somehow secured himself and his household from tragedy. If not, he would not be so furious at his "unjust" treatment. By the end of chap. 28, however, the reader knows that the world is not as Job wishes it were. Job has shown, not only from his own story but also from the experiences of others, that suffering comes even to those who fear God and turn from evil. If one believes Job, and if one also believes the poet of chap. 28, then one has to believe that it is possible through a life of true piety to experience something of the coherency of the universe, to experience something of the wisdom embodied in divine creative activity through one's own participation in that creation. In such participation there is real presence and strength. But one also has to recognize that such participation will not make one secure from suffering. In that sense, there is no choice about it; one *must* "fear God for naught," for God does not offer insurance against all harm.

As Job discovers, giving up such a claim upon God is harder than one would expect, even for those who think that they have made no such claims. That is not to say that one must give up anger at the fact of a life cut short by death or outrage at the callous violation of life by those who engage in the cosmos-destroying activity of violence. The absence of those emotions in Job's initial responses to loss (1:21; 2:10) suggests that there was something incomplete and truncated in his reaction. But now that Job has explored the depths of his anger, there is a danger that he will remain mired in what Wilcox calls "moral bitterness."[432] If he is to avoid this, Job must find his way back to what was true about his original stance. Yet there is no simple going back into naiveté. The quest may end where it began, but the hero will have been transformed.

The provocative echo of the first verse of the book in the last verse of chap. 28 suggests that the resolution of Job's anguish must somehow be made in terms of where he began. Just how that might happen is not spelled out. This process is not restricted to the particulars of Job's story, of course. It is a familiar part of human experience, in the lives of individuals and institutions. The structures of meaning that once seemed so necessary and that later come to seem so hollow and even oppressive may yet be encountered in a way that renews and transforms them. The following lines from T. S. Eliot's "Little Gidding" might well serve as a gloss on Job 28:

We shall not cease from exploration
And the end of all our exploring
Will be to arrive where we started
And know the place for the first time.[433]

---

431. Kohak, *The Embers and the Stars*, 84.
432. Wilcox, *The Bitterness of Job*, 100-17.
433. T. S. Eliot, *Collected Poems 1909–1962* (New York: Harcourt, Brace & World, 1963) 208.

JOB 29:1–31:40, JOB'S CONCLUDING SPEECH

Job 29:1-25, Job Recalls an Idyllic Past

COMMENTARY

Job begins his final speech in chap. 29 with a retrospective reflection on the conditions that gave his life meaning and value before disaster shook him to the foundations. By speaking in this way, Job gives the reader insight into his moral world. Only in the light of this description can one understand the full nature of Job's suffering and loss. Since Job's image of God is shaped so strongly by his understanding of his own place in this moral world, one also learns a great deal about the sources and nature of Job's theology. Job's description of "the good life," in the sense of moral goodness as well as of deep satisfaction, is noteworthy first of all for its deeply social orientation. As Job describes the various categories of persons with whom he interacts, he virtually draws a map of his social world. There is, indeed, a spatial quality to his account, which moves from the household to the city gate. This sense of a social map will continue in the following chapter, as Job describes the boundary of his social world and his own sense of having been cast out from it.

The ethical sense that pervades Job's moral world is a paternalistic one, in which the most important ethical actions are those involving the protection of the powerless against exploitation. The deepest satisfactions for a person like Job in this society are the gratitude of those he has aided and the respect of his peers. Both gratitude and respect are important measures of honor, the preeminent value in a moral world such as Job inhabited. Job begins his account with the image of God's protective presence, expressed in terms of personal relationship, and with the image of the household and its well-being, expressed in terms of progeny and abundance (vv. 2-6). Next the horizon moves outward to encompass Job's interaction with his peers in social rituals of honor at the city gate (vv. 7-10). The longest part of the description is given over to Job's paternal care for marginalized members

of society (vv. 11-17). The mutually life-giving nature of Job's relation with his community is evoked first in images of Job's anticipated long life, nurtured by resources that would sustain and renew him (vv. 18-20). Job's description of his expectations for himself are matched by his final word concerning the way in which his leadership gave life, direction, and comfort to his community (vv. 21-25).

29:1. As in 27:1, Job's speech opens with the observation that he "again" took up his discourse, implying that it has been interrupted. In this case, the poem on wisdom separates Job's reply to Bildad in chap. 27 from this, his final speech.

29:2-6. In describing the wholeness and meaningfulness of the life he has lost, Job first recounts his sense of God's protective presence (vv. 2-4). His language is personal, relational, and richly emotive. For God to "watch over" (v. 2b) someone connotes a deep sense of security (cf. Psalm 121, where the sixfold repetition of the same verb creates a sense of protection). In keeping with the general spatial organization of the speech, Job begins with the most intimate horizon, depicting God as light in relation to his own body and movement (v. 3). The imagery is traditional (cf. Pss 18:28[29]; 36:9[10]; Mic 7:8; cf. Job 18:5-6). The imagery of light connotes security, as suggested by the reference to walking through darkness. Darkness represents unseen dangers that cannot be eliminated from the world. But the one who is illumined by God's light may see and avoid them, in contrast to the one whose light is extinguished and so blunders helplessly into danger (18:7-10).

In the next verses, the horizon moves slightly outward to the "tent" or household under the protection of God's friendship (v. 4b; cf. Ps 25:14). This relationship is visualized in terms of the patriarch's relation to his children gathered round about him. The fundamental relationship in this social and moral world, and the one with the strongest emotional meaning, is the relationship between parents and children (cf. Gen 15:2; Ps 127:3). The patriarch also provides for his household. Job had spoken of the horror of the destitute who are not able to provide for their children (24:5, 9). The contrasting blessing is overflowing abundance (v. 6). The word translated "cream" or "milk" (חמה *ḥēmâ*) denotes a yogurt-like food, often associated with gestures of hospitality (Gen 18:8; Judg 5:25). Olive oil, too, is an evocative symbol, not only of the goodness of food, but also of the pleasures of the body. Deuteronomy 32:13 describes Asher's blessing in terms of bathing his feet in oil, and Psalm 133 likens the joy of brotherly unity to the pleasure of oil poured on the head and dripping into the beard. For such richness to come from the very rocks is a traditional image of abundance (Deut 32:12; cf. Ps 81:16).

29:7-10. In the next section the horizon moves outward to the city gate and the plaza, where prominent men of the community met to take counsel, resolve disputes, and conduct business (cf. Deut 21:19; Ruth 4:1; 2 Chr 32:6). God's presence with Job finds expression in the respect and honor accorded to him by his peers. Spatial imagery is important here, too. Much as his children were depicted as gathered round about him in v. 5, so here, when Job goes out to the plaza to take his seat (v. 7), he becomes the center around which others station themselves. Young men "hide themselves," withdrawing to the margins (v. 8*a*), but even the elders, who had previously been seated as centers of attention, now arise and stand, acknowledging Job's place (v. 8*b*; cf. Lev 19:32; Isa 49:7). The same social rearrangement that took place in terms of physical position also occurs with respect to speech. Even princes and nobles, who would normally give counsel, fall silent when Job appears, waiting respectfully for him to speak (vv. 9-10). Job's understanding of what brings satisfaction finds its symbolic form in images of center and periphery. To be the dynamic center that reorganizes social space is an expression of what is highly valued.

29:11-17. It would be a mistake to understand Job's pleasure in the honor paid to him simply in terms of ego satisfaction. As this section of the speech makes clear, Job receives

honor because he embodies the values of the community. In vv. 9-10, Job spoke of the respectful silence with which his presence was greeted. That does not mean that his peers did not evaluate him, however. What Job said and did was continuously judged by the ear and eye of the community (v. 11). There are few experiences so gratifying as to receive the approbation of one's peers for having embodied the shared values of the group.

What those values are can be judged from the following verses (vv. 12-17). Here the focus shifts from the inner circle of Job's peers to persons occupying a more marginal place in the social map: the poor, the orphan, the wretched, the widow, the blind, the lame, the needy, the stranger. The responsibility of the leaders of a community for its weakest members is one of the foundations of the ancient Near Eastern moral world (see Ps 72:1-4, 12-14).[434] It is easy to see how these persons depend upon Job, but one should not overlook the fact that Job also depends on them in certain significant ways. The powerful one gives protection and intervention; in return, he receives gratitude, described in v. 13 as the blessing of the wretched and the widow's song. This recognition by the powerless is as important in establishing the patriarch's social identity as is the respect and approbation of his peers. Job identifies his intervention on behalf of the powerless as "righteousness" and "justice." How essential these aspects are to his sense of identity is indicated through his use of clothing imagery in v. 14, for clothes are one's "public skin."

Job's language of aid is personal and intimate. In v. 16, he uses paternal imagery, and in v. 15 he even identifies his assistance in terms corresponding to the damaged bodies of the needy. Job's championing of the poor is not merely a matter of largess, however, but a protective rage against their victimization. His metaphor in v. 17 is implicitly that of the shepherd, someone like David, who would risk his own life to rescue a sheep carried off by a predator (cf. 1 Sam 17:34-35). The poor are Job's flock, and his sense of responsibility for them in large measure defines his identity.

The values and identity that Job articulates for himself are very similar to those Israel

434. See also the Epilogue to Hammurapi's Law, *ANET*, 178; the inscription of Kilamuwa, *ANET*, 654-55.

attributed to God. God, too, is a champion of the oppressed (Deut 24:17-22; Prov 23:10-11), a father to the orphan and a protector of widows (Ps 68:5[6]), closely identified with righteousness and justice (Ps 89:14[15]), a shepherd (Ps 23:1) who delivers victims from the jaws of the wicked (Ps 3:7[8]).

29:18-20. As in Eliphaz's description of the righteous person in 5:17-26, Job describes a good death as the culmination of a meaningful life (v. 18). The verse is susceptible of two quite different translations, reflected in the NRSV and the NIV. At issue is the translation of the word חול (*ḥôl*) in v. 18*b*. Ordinarily, the word means "sand" (NIV),[435] and the image of sand traditionally represents a vast number (Gen 32:12; 41:49; Ps 139:18; Isa 48:19). The image in the first line of the verse, however, "Then I thought, 'I shall die in my nest'" (NRSV; NIV paraphrases), suggests translating *ḥôl* as "phoenix," the mythical bird that lived for a vast number of years and then renewed its life by rising from the ashes of its burned nest.[436] This interpretation is already attested in the Talmud,[437] and is supported by certain evidence from Ugaritic texts.[438] Ironically, this *will* be Job's fate. He will experience renewed life that arises out of the ashes of his previous existence and will die in the midst of his family at a very advanced age, "old and full of days" (42:12-17).

Additional images of sustaining strength and renewal occur in vv. 19-20. Job implicitly compares himself to a tree (v. 19), whose roots are fed by underground water (cf. Ps 1:3; Jer 17:8; Ezek 31:7) and whose leaves are refreshed by dew (Deut 33:28; Ps 133:3; Zech 8:12). Renewal of "glory" in v. 20*a* may be a more physical image than first appears, since the same word can occasionally mean "liver" (cf. Ps 7:5[6]; 16:9).[439] Analogously, the "bow" in 20*b* is a familiar symbol for masculine prowess (Gen 49:24; 1 Sam 2:4; Ps 37:15[16]).

29:21-25. The final section of the chapter turns from the sustaining strength Job received to the way he sustained his community. Job's leadership was expressed first of all through his role as counselor (vv. 21-23). The great respect with which a wise counselor was held is suggested by the reputation of Ahitophel, of whom it was said that it was "as if one consulted the oracle of God" (2 Sam 16:23 NRSV). Similarly, Job's advice was literally the last word to his fellows. The metaphor of life-giving rain in v. 23 echoes the water imagery of v. 19. Just as Job was sustained by transcendent sources of strength represented as water, so also he became a transcendent source of strength for his community (cf. Deut 11:14; Jer 5:24; Hos 6:3). Although v. 24 can be legitimately translated in more than one way (cf. NRSV and NIV), the basic sense is clear. The expressions of goodwill communicated by Job's face were themselves enough to sustain those who depended on him.

The final cluster of images in v. 25 surprises some readers. The first three all have to do with leadership in terms of royal authority and the ability to make decisions on behalf of the entire community. The final image, however, is that of "one who comforts mourners." A few commentators, seeking consistency, emend the last words to read "where I led them, they were willing to go."[440] Leadership in ancient Israel, however, was understood to be personal and nurturing, as well as a matter of decisive action. The image of the king as shepherd, and of God as shepherd, reflects well the combination of these qualities (e.g., Isa 40:10-11; Ezekiel 34). That Job should make the role of comforting mourners the final word of his description of leadership is significant. This is the task the friends undertook and failed to perform for Job. One senses from chap. 29 why Job would have been a better comforter. Comfort is not a matter of supplying reasons but of providing a sense of supportive community in a time when chaos threatens to overwhelm.

It is striking how many of Job's images for himself in chap. 29 are elsewhere applied to kings and even to God. Proverbs 16:15 refers to the life-giving quality of the "light of

435. Driver and Gray, *A Critical and Exegetical Commentary on the Book of Job*, Part I, 249; Part II, 201-4; Pope, *Job*, 208, 213-16; Hartley, *The Book of Job*, 392.

436. See R. van den Broek, *The Myth of the Phoenix According to Classical and Early Christian Traditions*, EPRO 24 (Leiden: Brill, 1972).

437. See *b. Sanh.* 108*b*.

438. M. Dahood, "*Ḥôl* 'Phoenix' in Job 29:18 and in Ugaritic," *CBQ* 36 (1974) 85-8; L. Grabbe, *Comparative Philology and the Text of Job: A Study in Methodology*, SBLDS 34 (Missoula, Mont.: Scholars Press, 1977) 98-101; Gordis, *The Book of Job*, 321-22; but see Pope, *Job*, 213-16.

439. Habel, *The Book of Job*, 411.

440. Dhorme, *A Commentary on the Book of Job*, 422; similarly, Pope, *Job*, 212.

a king's face" and even compares the king's favor to the clouds bringing spring rain. Similarly, the king is compared to rain in Ps 72:6. Wise counsel is a quality of the ideal ruler in Isa 9:6. The protection of the powerless, a function Job claims in vv. 11-17, is also that of the king in Ps 72:12-14, and the association of the king with righteousness and justice is a commonplace (e.g., Isa 9:7). Perhaps more striking is the parallel between Job's self-description and traditional images of God. God brings life-giving rains (Deut 11:14; Jer 5:4; Hos 6:3). Most strikingly, "the light of your face" is a phrase most often associated with God's presence (Num 6:25; Pss 4:6[7]; 44:3[4]; 89:15[16]). Readers who take these

similarities as evidence of Job's arrogance misunderstand their function.[441] Job uses these images because they characterize the ideals of leadership in his community, whether that is the leadership of the patriarch, of the king, or of God. Indeed, to a very large extent the image of God is shaped according to the ideal model of a patriarch or king. The expressions that echo traditional language about God are also the poet's way of reminding the reader that Job's expectations of God are similar to what he expects of himself (see Commentary on Job 31).

441. Habel suggests that "Job virtually usurps the functions of God" (*The Book of Job*, 406), and Perdue says that "the language of this chapter borders on self-idolatry" (*Wisdom in Revolt*, 192).

REFLECTIONS

Job's long speech about his past and present experience is both appealing and disturbing. Readers often wonder, however, whether it is appropriate to make judgments about the moral values presented by figures from another culture and another time. There is certainly a danger that one will either romanticize the past or dismiss it simply because it is different from one's own set of values. It is both appropriate and necessary, however, to take seriously the claims about the nature of the moral life as they are made in a text like Job 29. Because modern readers stand largely outside that cultural world, it is easier to see some of the limitations and problems with its vision of character and culture than it would have been for contemporaries. The judgment does not proceed in one direction only, however. Reflecting on the moral vision that informs Job's sense of himself can also lead to a clearer vision of the limitations and problems in one's own moral world.

Perhaps the most striking feature of Job's moral sense is its deeply relational character. In his world, persons are not autonomous individuals so much as they are persons in relation. Job locates himself in relation to God, to his children, to his peers, to those who need his protection, to those who need his leadership. These sets of relationships are what feed and refresh him, root and branch. His is a world in which community has an organic quality. Both the best and the most troubling aspects of Job's moral world concern his relationship with the marginal and vulnerable members of his community. That his own worth should be so connected with his role as their defender and helper is admirable, but what Job cannot see is the limitations of an essentially paternalistic relationship. Such a relationship is necessarily tied to the logic of inequality. The binary relationship of dominant/subordinate or donor/recipient undergirds the sense of moral obligation. The limitation of such a structure is that it can embrace amelioration of suffering on an individual basis, but it cannot comprehend the transformation of the very structures that generate the inequalities that produce suffering. The social rewards that such a system offers to its leading members are based on the gratitude of the poor and the respect of one's peers—in short, the reward of honor. Such a social system requires a measure of inequality and even a vulnerable, marginal class in order to function.

Using Job's speech as a model, it is worth thinking how a modern citizen of the United States might look over his or her life and talk about what elements gave it meaning and value. The modern culture is much more complex than the world of ancient Israel, of course, and so there would undoubtedly be many different accounts. Nevertheless, a number of the elements would be fairly common to our stories of what matters in life. Undoubtedly, relationships would have a prominent place, but they would be quite different in nature and scope from Job's account. Most citizens of the U.S. would speak of the importance of family, much as Job did. On closer investigation, however, the scope of "family" would be quite different. For modern Americans, the nuclear family is what is primarily meant, not the extended kinship group that had so much greater importance in traditional societies like that of ancient Israel. A modern person would also be very likely to mention a romantic relationship as central to well-being, something completely absent from Job's account. Perhaps the most striking difference would be the modern individual's references to personal autonomy. The word *choice* shows up frequently in people's accounts of their lives: choosing a mate, choosing a career, choosing a church, choosing a life-style, choosing values for oneself. Such a language and its implications for the nature of the individual would be absolutely incomprehensible to someone like Job. Although it is often difficult to get enough distance to reflect on it, the immense value placed on personal autonomy points to some of the limitations of our own moral world. It can easily become a kind of moral consumerism, in which there is no common good, only personal preference.

The other striking difference between Job's moral world and that of the modern world concerns the public or civic sphere. Modern persons also seek the respect of their peers. Most often, however, the context for this social validation is the workplace. That is where, at least in good situations, persons experience the satisfaction of teamwork and the commendation of a job well done. In our society, self-worth is deeply tied up with having a job in the first place and in being respected for the work one does. It is not so closely tied to one's efforts on behalf of the poor. Whereas for Job such care for the socially vulnerable was at the very core of his identity, in modern society such matters are generally considered admirable, but optional. Civic work, charity, and social justice involvements are things that one does as a volunteer, an indication of their marginal status. This is not to say that such work might not be of central importance for a particular individual, but that the culture in general does not consider it to be an essential measure of a person's worth.

Finally, the place of religion would be a great variable. For some it would be the starting point, as it is in Job's narration. For others, including some readers of this commentary, it would be an element that has a place in the story of what is meaningful, but not the obvious starting place. And for many, it would not appear at all. The fact of such variability is itself an indication of the great distance between Job's cultural world and our own.

Such reflections do not lead to simple conclusions. The point is not to judge one vision of moral community better or worse than another so much as it is to underscore the importance of learning how to articulate one's understanding of what constitutes the life worth living and to develop the critical distance necessary for perceiving both its limitations and its strengths. In a recent study of American moral self-understanding, the authors of *Habits of the Heart* noted the great difficulty many persons had in being able to explain the foundation for the values they held and the vision of moral worth and community implied by them. The language in which most persons attempted to articulate their moral sense was a language of radical individualism. Quite apart from the limitations such a moral vision might entail in itself, the authors also noted that such language simply failed to describe adequately the much richer lives that most of the persons interviewed actually lived.[442] The church is the bearer of a long tradition of moral discourse that can provide alternatives and correctives to the prevailing language of individualism. It is, of course, neither possible nor desirable simply to take up a biblical model, such as the one Job gives voice to. Our world is not his world and never can be; nor is it clear that one would want to return to such a world even if it were possible. What engagement with a text like Job can do is to challenge some of our assumptions and lead us into a much richer sense of how we might rethink the meaning of moral community.

442. R. Bellah et al., *Habits of the Heart: Individualism and Commitment in American Life* (Berkeley: University of California Press, 1985), esp. 81-83.

Job 30:1-31, Job Laments His Present Humiliation

COMMENTARY

Idyllic recollections of a world that was satisfying and meaningful are shattered as Job turns his attention to his present situation. Three times Job punctuates his account with the introductory phrase "but now . . . " as he describes a world turned upside down. The particular quality of Job's suffering is closely linked to the features that made his previous life so fulfilling. Just as he derived his sense of identity from being a person of honor, honored by others, so also he experiences his devastation most acutely in terms of being an object of contempt, even to the contemptible. As he describes his anger and sense of betrayal at what has happened to him, Job reveals certain disturbing features of his moral world that were only barely visible in chap. 29. Job's baffled disappointment in what he took to be the moral structures of his world, however, lends a note of poignancy to his speech.

The chapter divides into four major sections, the first three marked by the repeated phrase "but now" (עתה 'atâ, vv. 1, 9, 16), and the last introduced by the word "surely" (אך 'ak, v. 24). In vv. 1-8, Job begins to describe the mockery to which he is subjected (v. 1), but interrupts himself to utter his own contemptuous description of those who treat him with such disrespect (vv. 2-8). Resuming his account of the scorn with which he is regarded, Job shows how such contempt can quickly become savage maltreatment by those whose resentment is unleashed (vv. 9-15). The third section (vv. 16-23) turns from an account of the social dimensions of Job's suffering to an account of physical and psychic suffering. As Job talks about God's enmity, he addresses God directly (vv. 20-23). In the final section of the chapter (vv. 24-31), Job expresses his outraged sense of having received evil in the place of good and concludes with striking images of his alienation from a world that has no place for him.

30:1-8. The phrase "but now" introduces the contrast with the ideal lost world of "months of old" (29:2). Where Job had been the object of respect even by those older than

he (29:8*b*), now he is the object of mockery by those who are younger (v. 1). Although public mockery is painful in any society, there are certain cultures in which it is particularly devastating. Where group ties are especially strong and identity is fixed by one's place in the group, rather than by achievements as an autonomous individual, the shame of public ridicule is one of the most excruciating experiences imaginable. Only in this context can one understand the social dimensions of Job's suffering. Cultures in which the values of honor and shame are central are also often organized by a strong sense of social hierarchy.[443] Job's first words here reflect the values of a hierarchy of age, in which youth respects age. Thus an insult that would be hard enough to bear from a contemporary is even more painful when it comes from someone who is younger.

Youth and age are not the only aspects of the social hierarchy of Job's moral world. Social stigma may be passed from generation to generation, and so Job expresses his own contempt for his mockers by insulting their fathers (v. 1*b*). Job is a master of the insult. The ostensible point of his comment is that he would not even have hired these men to be his shepherds; but that is not the way Job phrases it. He says instead that he would not have "put them with the dogs of [his] flock," thus insinuating that these men were not worthy even to be associated with his dogs. Since the term "dog" (כלב *keleb*) was itself a serious insult if applied to others and a term of deep self-abasement if used of oneself (cf. 1 Sam 24:14; 2 Sam 9:8; 2 Kgs 8:13), Job could scarcely have said anything more contemptuous.

Opinion is divided as to whether vv. 2-8 describe the young men who insult Job (so NRSV) or their fathers (so NIV; "their sons" in v. 9 is not in the Hebrew text but is added by the translators). Although either

443. See, e.g., J. Pitt-Rivers, *The Fate of Shechem*, Cambridge Studies in Social Anthropology 19 (Cambridge: Cambridge University Press, 1977); B. Malina, *The New Testament World: Insights from Cultural Anthropology*, rev. ed. (Louisville: Westminster/John Knox, 1983).

interpretation is possible, the continuity of imagery is clearer if one understands Job to be talking primarily about the young men. In truth, there is little distinction between them, since they share each other's characteristics. What makes these people so contemptible is their abject poverty. In v. 2, Job comments on their lack of strength. In vv. 3-4, it becomes obvious why they have lost their vigor: They have nothing to eat. Job represents them as scavengers who live off the meager foods that can be gathered in wastelands not fit for cultivation. The location that Job assigns them is symbolically significant. Traditionally, the unsown land beyond the cities and their surrounding fields was associated with dangerous and hostile forces. Beyond the boundaries of ordered and civilized society, wild animals and even demonic beings lurked.[444] The destitute may roam the wastelands out of necessity, but their association with that eerie place makes it easy to treat them as dangerous and alien, and so to exclude them from a place in the social order. This is precisely what is reflected in v. 5. Note that Job does not say that they *are* thieves, but that people drive them out from society, shouting at them *as if* they were thieves. Simply by being who they are, these people evoke the fear and rejection appropriate to criminals.

Verses 6-8 largely recapitulate the previous description in vv. 3-5. Here, however, the contrast between these alien outsiders and the people of the town is not made in terms of food, as in vv. 3-4, but in terms of their dwellings. They are homeless. They do not live in houses like everyone else, but in makeshift dwellings: caves, rock shelters, and gullies (cf. 1 Sam 14:11). The fact that they live in the scrubland, outside the normal place for human beings, makes it easy to compare them with the wild animals whose land they share, as Job implicitly does by referring to their "braying" among the bushes (v. 7), a term elsewhere used of the wild ass (6:5). In such subtle symbolic ways these marginal figures are dehumanized. Corresponding to v. 5, Job again underscores the judgment that these people have no place in human society (v. 8), but are "whipped out of the land."

It is difficult to render Job's terms for them in colloquial English. He calls them "sons of a fool" and "sons of a 'no-name.' " Although the term "fool" (נבל *nābāl*) can have a general sense, it originates as a social term, designating the poverty, but even more, the lack of proper values to be found in the lower classes.[445] Thus when Job told his wife that she spoke as "one of the foolish women" (2:10a), one might get the gist by saying that she "talks like trash." The social dimensions of the insult are explicit in Job's designation of his tormentors as "sons of a 'no-name.' " In Job's world, an important part of a person's dignity and honor comes from having a distinguished lineage. These persons are by birth destined for low status and are despised for it.

One of the interpretive problems posed by this section is its striking contrast with Job's sympathetic description of the destitute in 24:3-8. It will not do to attempt to evade the contradiction by supposing that Job is talking about two different groups, the deserving poor vs. the rabble.[446] Both accounts use the same imagery: exclusion from the public sphere, scavenging for food, lack of shelter, and even comparison with the wild asses. What is different is Job's point of view. The collapse of Job's world, and with it the collapse of his complacency, had given him a certain ability to look at his world through the eyes of those who have nothing and who are rejected by others. This he expresses clearly in 24:3-8. There are barriers to any true solidarity between Job and the wretched of the earth, however. For all the insight that his recent experience has brought him, Job was not born destitute; rather, he was born to privilege. The social resentment that lurks in strongly hierarchical societies often finds intense expression when a high-ranking member of society falls from his or her position.[447] Consequently, Job is not welcomed by the outcasts as someone who has become one of them, but becomes the object for their pent up rage. Not surprising, Job reacts to this hostility by taking refuge in his own social class perceptions and values, lashing out with words that reinscribe the distinctions between "those people" and Job

444. See A. Haldar, *The Notion of the Desert in Sumero-Accadian and West-Semitic Religions* (Uppsala: A.-B. Lundequistska Bokhandeln, 1950).

445. van der Toorn, *Sin and Sanction in Israel and Mesopotamia*, 107; Gordis, *The Book of Job*, 332. The social dimensions of the term can be seen in Prov 30:21-23.

446. Contra Habel, *The Book of Job*, 419.

447. See Girard, *Job*, 51-52.

himself. In these two passages, the author of Job has given a dismal but acutely observed depiction of an all too familiar social drama.

30:9-15. Repeating the phrase "and/but now," Job returns to his main topic, a description of his mockery and ill-treatment by this rabble. There is a crescendo pattern in Job's account, beginning with verbal aggression in v. 9, proceeding to insulting gestures in v. 10, and culminating in images of physical violence in vv. 12-14. In a society in which dignity and reputation are highly valued, having satirical songs made up about one and one's name used as a byword is devastating (v. 9; cf. Lam 3:14). Although in modern cultures persons are expected to develop a measure of indifference to such talk, most readers can sense the dynamics by remembering the terrible power of taunts and jokes in the different social world of the playground and the school. Gestures of shunning and spitting have a more aggressive edge to them, since they are enacted in the despised person's presence. (For spitting, see 17:6 and Isa 50:6b.)

In v. 11, Job reflects on how it is that these "nobodies" have gained the nerve to attack one who was once so powerful and high ranking. Both Job and the rabble understand the catastrophe that has overtaken him as God's own aggression against and humiliation of Job. As such, it gives permission for anyone else to treat Job similarly. The image of the loosening of the bowstring is a telling one, for it suggests that God has deprived Job of the ability to defend himself. By contrast, Ps 18:34[35] describes divine protection as bringing with it the ability to bend a bow of bronze.

A number of obscurities in the Hebrew text lead to slightly different translations of vv. 12-14 in the NRSV and the NIV. The overall imagery of military aggression is somewhat clearer in the NIV. The roadworks (or seige ramps) of the aggressors are built up, while those of Job are torn down (vv. 12-13; cf. 19:12). As in 16:14, Job describes his destruction in terms of soldiers breaching the walls of a beseiged city (v. 14).

Despite the very physical imagery, Job makes it clear that what these people have succeeded in destroying is his dignity (v. 15). The word that Job uses is נדיבה (*nĕdîbâ*), an abstract term related to the noun meaning

"a noble" (נדיב *nādîb*). The parallel term is translated in the NRSV as "prosperity" and in the NIV as "safety," but the TNK is probably correct in understanding the word to be related to שׁוע (*šôaʿ*), "noble." It is Job's honor (ישעתי *yĕšûʿātî*) that has been assaulted.

30:16-23. In this section, Job turns from the social dimensions of his degradation to its physical and psychic counterpart. Here again, the phrase "and/but now" serves to contrast his description of the "days of affliction" (v. 16) with the "days when God watched over me" (29:2). Job begins with an account of physical pain that is especially acute at night, similar to 7:4-5. As in his previous references to physical distress, Job experiences it as direct divine violence (cf. 7:13-16; 10:16-17; 16:9, 12-14). Unfortunately, the Hebrew text of v. 18 is so difficult that it is simply not possible to be certain what image Job uses to describe God's action against him. In v. 19, however, Job echoes an image he had used earlier, of God's forcing him into filth (cf. 9:30-31). Such a gesture is intended to be symbolic, and Job acknowledges its effect on his identity; he is made to feel like dirt (lit., "dust and ashes"). Given Job's symbolic universe, it is very difficult for acute and prolonged suffering not to feel like degradation. It is experienced as God's rejection of and contempt for a person (v. 11), echoed in the social contempt expressed by others (vv. 9-10).

For the first time since chap. 16, Job addresses God directly in vv. 20-23. His words recall earlier accusations about God's silence and Job's unanswered cry (v. 20a; cf. 19:7), the obsessive but uncommunicative scrutiny to which God subjects him (v. 20b; cf. 7:17-19), and God's enmity toward him (v. 21; cf. 16:9, where the same verb is used). Although the NIV takes v. 22 simply as a negative image of God's buffeting Job like a storm wind (cf. 27:20-21), it is possible to take the first part of the verse in a positive sense. God is often represented as "riding the wind" (see Ps 18:10[11]); 104:3), and this verse may assert that God has first lifted Job up to an almost divine status, only to bring him down.[448] Such a contrast would echo the

448. Similarly, Habel, *The Book of Job,* 421. Textual problems allow for additional ways of interpreting this verse. Compare Gordis, *The Book of Job,* 336, and Habel, *The Book of Job,* 416.

larger structure of chaps. 29–30. Although the notion has been implicit in much that Job has said, here he states explicitly that that God is seeking his death (v. 23; cf. 10:8-9).

30:24-31. Unfortunately, the verse that introduces the final section of the chapter is extremely obscure. Literally, it reads, "surely one does not stretch out a hand against a ruin, if in his calamity therefore a cry." Modest emendations produce a variety of plausible translations, although none of them is certain. Given the context of what follows, it appears that Job states a general moral principle that one does not answer a person in distress with violence. This has been the rule of his own conduct (cf. 29:12a, which is similar in wording, if one emends "ruin" [עִי 'î] to "poor" [עָנִי 'ānî] in 30:24). Inexplicably, God has behaved in just the opposite way to Job.

Verses 25-26 express Job's bafflement at the incoherence of the moral world he now experiences. Wisdom traditions insisted that good produced good and evil produced evil, both for others and for oneself (11:17, 24-25, 31; 13:2; 14:14; 15:27; 26:27). Yet Job's compassion for others has not resulted in compassion for himself. Rather, his expectations have been met by their opposites (for this figure of speech, see Isa 5:7b; Jer 8:15). These verses stand in considerable tension with Job's words in 2:10b, "Shall we receive the good at the hand of God, and not receive the bad?" (NRSV). At least in some sense the *satan* appears to have been right; Job did not "fear God for nothing" (1:9). Job assumed, much as his friends did, that the principle of moral retribution was an essential part of the relationship between God and human beings. Upon this basis, he formed his expectations (cf. 29:18-20), and he is now outraged at God's injustice.

Job's description of his present situation is an inversion of his past. Whereas he previously experienced physical vigor and the renewal of inner strength (29:19-20), now he experiences inner turmoil (v. 27a; cf. Lam 1:20; 2:11). The respectful reception by his peers (29:10) is parodied in the greeting he receives from personified "days of affliction" (v. 27b). The darkness to which Job refers in v. 28a is probably not the discoloration of his skin by disease (so NIV) but Job's sense that he now walks in gloom (so NRSV), in contrast to the light of God, which previously illumined his way (29:3). Whereas Job used to preside in the assemblies at the gate (29:7), now his role is that of suppliant (v. 28b), like the poor who once cried out to him (29:12). The kin and friendship relations who provided his social identity (29:5) now take the grotesque form of a kinship with the animals of the wasteland, the jackal and the ostrich (v. 29; the NIV's "owl" is less likely). Like the wild ass, the jackal and the ostrich are associated with desolate land (cf. Ps 44:19[20]; Jer 9:10-11),[449] the place of exclusion where Job located the despised "sons of a 'no-name.'" Job recognizes that his calamity has turned him into a figure who instills fear and rejection by those belonging to the protecting world of the town. In vv. 30-31, Job concludes with references to his physical and psychic suffering, much as he had described them in vv. 16-17. His concluding reference in v. 31 to his own songs of mourning recalls the mocking songs others sing about him (v. 9). More poignantly, Job's isolation in his mourning contrasts with the culminating line of Job's own self-description in 29:25 as "one who comforts mourners."

449. Keel, *Jahwes Entgegnung an Ijob,* 83-84.

REFLECTIONS

Despite the poignancy of Job's words, one cannot help being shocked by the way he expresses his contempt for the outcasts who now mock him. This is not to criticize Job as a person but to recognize that, given his moral world, such language and views are inevitable. Job's world is a highly stratified one that makes sharp distinctions. It distinguishes "vertically" between the nobles and the lowly who depend on them (29:11-17), and it distinguishes "horizontally" between the grateful poor and the mocking rabble (30:1-10). This social stratification is also related to the moral and social values of honor and shame. Although the sense of what is honorable and what is shameful is intended to apply to conduct, it often gets drawn into distinctions of social class and wealth. Society is predisposed to assume that a person of high birth and wealth is a good person, and that a person who is poor and a "nobody" is also likely to have bad morals. From there it is only a short step to associating poverty itself with what is contemptible.

Even though the ancient Near East, including ancient Israel, was a culture deeply invested in the values of honor and shame, Israelite religion often provided a critical judgment against the tendency to associate these values with differences in wealth and status. Israel reminded itself often of its own lowly origins, that its ancestors had been slaves (Exod 20:2; Deut 5:15). The Israelites' obligation not to reject or oppress the alien does not arise out of a sense of *noblesse oblige* (as it may for Job), but is mandated because Israelites, too, knew what it meant to be alien (Exod 22:21). The prophets criticize the arrogance of "all that is lifted up and high" (Isa 2:12 NRSV), recognizing that wealth and status could lead to greediness and cruelty as easily as to social responsibility. Eventually, terms such as "poor" and "lowly" came to be associated not with moral laxity but with righteousness and piety (e.g., Zeph 3:12-13; Luke 1:46-55). In the NT, too, Jesus showed acceptance of "shameful" people, of prostitutes (Luke 7:36-50), of tax collectors (Matt 9:9-12), of beggars (Luke 18:35-42), even of despised Samaritans (John 4:4-42).

We would like to think that our culture, and in particular our churches, has learned these lessons and that we do not treat the marginal, the destitute, and the outsider with contempt. Unfortunately, those attitudes are very deeply ingrained. It is the rare middle-class parent who lets her child play with a friend who lives in the trailer park. It is the rare storeowner who does not watch the migrant worker with a careful eye, because everyone "knows" that "those people steal." Even in churches with night shelters, it is rare that homeless persons feel welcome at worship. To a disturbing extent, we still make unconscious judgments about moral character on the basis of social and economic class, and those judgments communicate themselves not only through words but also through gestures and glances. The poor know when they are regarded with fear and contempt. It is not necessary to "shout" (v. 5).

In Job's world, the two categories of the poor show very clearly where the boundaries of community lie. Even though the "deserving poor" may occupy the fringes of society, their claim on the attention of the nobles marks their place within the protecting boundaries of the social structure. By contrast, the outer boundary of community is marked by the exclusion of the rabble, whose place is literally outside the city walls in the wilderness. That social boundary marking function of an excluded group is a disturbingly recognizable feature. In our own society, that excluded group may be sociocultural, such as the distinction between "poor white trash" and the deserving poor. Much more often, however, those boundaries have been marked along racial and ethnic lines. It is an all too familiar story how the exclusion and dehumanization of blacks has been used to form a secure boundary, a sense of community identity, for a white society.

This tendency to define a community by who is excluded from it is quite pervasive. In some instances it may be innocuous, but more often it is used as an instrument of social power. Women may be kept out of particular occupations or organizations in order to reassure men of their superiority. Recent immigrants may be kept out of certain jobs or housing in order to reassure the grandchildren and great-grandchildren of earlier immigrants that they are truly Americans. Anxiety about identity, however, cannot be assuaged by excluding others. Yet expecially when an individual or a community feels vulnerable, as Job so clearly does in chapter 30, it is easy to translate that sense of vulnerability into social polarization.

Job 31:1-40, Job's Oath of Innocence

COMMENTARY

The final chapter in Job's last speech begins abruptly. It is immediately clear, however, that the tone is different from the words of lament with which chap. 30 ended. In a manner similar to the rhetorical strategy of chaps. 16 and 19, lament language is interrupted by legal language. Job's words in chap. 31 are cast in the form of an elaborate oath, by means of which he attempts to establish his innocence of any wrongdoing (cf. 1 Sam 24:10-16; 1 Kgs 8:31-32). His speech has been compared to the process by which an accused person whose opponent refuses to produce evidence compels his accuser to come to court.[450] This is a suggestive analogy, although Job's reference to a hearing in vv. 35-37 appears as something of an afterthought and an impossible desire. Moreover, it should be remembered that Job uses the oath in an adapted, rhetorical manner, not as an actual legal proceeding. The rhetorical adaptation is apparent in that the behaviors of which Job claims to be innocent are largely matters that the law does not cover. Rather, they are elements of what Gordis calls Job's "code of honor,"[451] the revered moral values of his culture by which he has defined himself.[452]

The chapter has several functions. For Job, it serves to support his claim that he is indeed a person of honor, much as he described himself in chap. 29, not deserving of the contempt and humiliation to which he has been subjected by others and even by God. For the reader, Job's words reaffirm and give specific content to the narrator's original description of Job as a person of integrity and uprightness, who fears God and turns from evil. Not only Job's values are in evidence here, however. At several points, Job refers to God's passion for these values as the basis for his own moral seriousness. In this way the reader again sees the extent to which Job assumes a continuity between his own moral being and that of

God. This assumption provides the basis for a possible resolution of the conflict between Job and God and a resolution of the issues of the book. That approach to a resolution is not one that God chooses, however; hence the book challenges many of Job's assumptions about God and the relationship between God and the world.

The structure of the chapter can be perceived if one examines the oath forms that are used and attends to the way they are grouped by topic. Two forms of the oath appear here. The complete oath has the form, "If I have done X, may Y happen to me" (vv. 7-10, 21-22, 38-40). An abbreviated oath has the form, "If I have done X . . . " with the consequences left unspecified. In effect, it serves as an assertion of innocence: "I have not done X." There are some ten examples of the abbreviated oath in chap. 31 (vv. 5, 13, 16, 19, 24, 25, 26, 29, 31, 33). Only the first claim of innocence is expressed in a non-oath form (v. 1). The topical structure of the chapter has largely escaped notice, and yet it seems quite straightforward. There are five groups of oaths, interrupted by Job's wish for a hearing in vv. 35-37. The general issues covered are (1) sexual and general morality (vv. 1-12), (2) justice and social obligation (vv. 13-23), (3) proper allegiance (vv. 24-28), (4) social relations (vv. 29-34), and (5) land ethics (vv. 38-40). Within several groups the structure is chiastic (i.e., having an ABBA or an ABA pattern; see below). The inclination of many commentators to see Job's desire for a hearing as the climax of the passage (to the extent that some even rearrange the text)[453] imposes the commentators' own sense of how the speech "should" have been composed. The oath of clearance is itself the point of the speech. The NIV correctly places all of vv. 35-37 in parentheses to indicate that these words are an aside by Job, not the goal of his speech.

450. Dick, "The Legal Metaphor in Job 31," 42.

451. Gordis, *The Book of Job*, 339.

452. G. Fohrer, "The Righteous Man in Job 31," in *Studien zum Buch Hiob*, 2nd ed., BZAW 159 (Berlin: Walter de Gruyter, 1983) 78-93; and Dick, "Job 31, the Oath of Innocence, and the Sage," 31-53, discuss various genres to which Job 31 bears a resemblance.

453. E.g. Dhorme, *A Commentary on the Book of Job*, liii; Gordis, *The Book of Job*, 545; Pope, *Job*, 230; Hartley, *The Book of Job*, 422; but see Habel, *The Book of Job*, 427-31; and Good, *In Turns of Tempest*, 312, who retain the order of the biblical text.

31:1-12. The first group of four oaths begins and ends with sexual ethics, specifically, conduct toward a virgin (vv. 1-4) and toward the wife of another man (vv. 9-12). The two oaths in the middle address ethical conduct in general (vv. 5-8).[454] There is greater unity to the section than might first appear. Imagery in v. 4 concerning ways and steps anticipates the imagery of walking that introduces the second oath in v. 5, and reference to the heart toward the end of the third oath in v. 8 is echoed by the use of the same word at the beginning of the fourth oath in v. 9. Moreover, advice about sexual ethics in the wisdom tradition often had more than a literal application. It was the favorite image for proper conduct in general and was often used to introduce ethical admonitions of various sorts.[455] In a strongly patriarchal society, sexual restrictions are important in both social and symbolic ways as a means of articulating the order of the social world.[456] Thus the combination of topics is quite in keeping with literary conventions in wisdom literature and an appropriate starting point for a comprehensive oath of innocence. These verses also employ a rhetorical device familiar from Proverbs, the use of particular parts of the body as images of the moral will (e.g., feet, heart, eyes, hands; see Prov 4:20-27).

31:1-4. The seduction or rape of an unmarried woman was a serious offense primarily because it threatened the rights of the father and thus undermined the social organization of the community (Exod 22:16-17[15-16]; Deut 22:23-29). Job, however, asserts that he has controlled not just his behavior but even his desire (v. 1). The eye often symbolizes desire (Ps 119:37; Isa 33:15), especially in sexual matters (Sir 9:5, 8). Job's image of making a covenant with his eyes is an unusual one, and the syntax of v. 1 *a* is that of the imposition of a covenant by a superior on an inferior party.[457] Job claims to be master of his passions.

Verses 2-4 give the reasons why Job takes this commitment so seriously. His moral language is quite close to that of the friends, as he talks of the "portion" and "heritage" God allots to persons according to their conduct (v. 2; cf. Zophar in 20:20), the disaster that overtakes the evildoer (v. 3; cf. Bildad in 18:12), and God's scrutiny of an individual's behavior (v. 4; cf. Zophar in 11:11). Like that of the friends, Job's entire moral world and the motives for his own conduct have been shaped by the conviction that God directly rewards and punishes moral and immoral behavior. Precisely because what has happened to him threatens the meaningfulness of this fundamental belief, Job is determined to put this structure of meaning back together again. His words here indicate that he can conceive of no alternative to the beliefs by which he has lived.

31:5-8. The second oath in this series (vv. 5-6) uses the common wisdom metaphor of "walking" for behavior (cf. Ps 1:1; Prov 2:13), as well as the general moral terminology of falsehood and deceit, contrasted with integrity (cf. Ps 24:4). The image of God as one who "weighs" the hearts of persons is traditional (Prov 16:2; 24:12), but Job's use of the phrase "honest scales" also echoes legal and moral traditions in which God commands that honest scales be used among persons engaged in trade (Lev 19:35-36; Prov 20:10, 23; Ezek 45:10). Job assumes that the same morality governing relations between persons, according to God's command, will also govern his relation with God.

The first complete oath formula appears in vv. 7-8. The various parts of the body named (feet [lit. "steps"], eyes, heart, hands) suggest the totality of an individual's will and action (cf. Prov 4:25-27). There is no particular relation between the conduct described and the content of the curse in v. 8.[458] For someone to eat what another has sown, however, is a frequent image of divine punishment (Lev 26:16; Mic 6:15; cf. Isa 65:22).

31:9-12. Job rounds off the first series of oaths with the fundamental principle of Israelite ethics, sexual avoidance of a neighbor's wife (Exod 20:17; Deut 5:21; Prov 6:24-35; 7:6-27; Sir 23:18-27). "Door" is a double entendre, suggesting both the doorway of the

454. Gordis's suggestion, *The Book of Job*, 345, that these verses concern specifically business ethics is not persuasive.
455. Dick, "Job 31, the Oath of Innocence, and the Sage," 46. The attempt by Pope, *Job*, 229, to understand "virgin" as a reference to the Canaanite goddess Anat overlooks this traditional function of sexual topics in ethical discourse.
456. C. Newsom, "Woman and the Discourse of Patriarchal Wisdom: A Study of Proverbs 1-9," in P. Day, ed., *Gender and Difference in Ancient Israel* (Philadelphia: Fortress, 1989) 142-60.
457. Pope, *Job*, 228.
458. Contra Andersen, *Job*, 241.

neighbor's house and the sexual "doors of the womb" (3:10; cf. Cant 4:12). Although legal tradition treats adultery as a crime against the community and against God,[459] the sense that the husband is the injured party also appears in biblical literature (e.g., Prov 6:34-35). This perception underlies Job's oath that if he has violated the wife of another man, his own wife should be violated in return (cf. Deut 28:30; 2 Sam 12:11). The imagery in v. 10 ("grind," "kneel") has sexual connotations, as traditional Jewish interpretation recognized.[460] The vulnerability of servant women to sexual exploitation is perhaps alluded to in the play of literal and figurative meanings of the expression "may my wife grind for another" in v. 10*a*. The seriousness with which Job considers adultery is explicit in vv. 11-12. Fire is also used as a metaphor of the destructiveness of adultery in Prov 6:27-29, although here its terrible effect is virtually cosmic.

31:13-23. The second group of four oaths is concerned with the topics of justice and social obligation. As in the preceding series, there is a chiastic structure. In the first and fourth oaths Job denies depriving the weak of justice (vv. 13-15, 21-23), and in the second and third he denies ever having refused food and clothing to the needy (vv. 16-20). All of these oaths concern the ethics of power in a relationship of inequality.

31:13-15. First, Job asserts that he has never denied justice to his male or female slaves when they have had a grievance (ריב *rîb*) against him (v. 13). Although various laws governed the limited rights of slaves (e.g., Exod 21:1-11, 20-21; Lev 25:39-55; Deut 5:14; 15:12-18; 23:15-16; cf. Jer 34:8-22), Job's language suggests a more general concern for fairness, the basis for which is given in v. 15: God is the maker of both master and servant (cf. Prov 14:31; 22:2). Job clearly assumes that he will be answerable to God for anything less than justice toward his slaves (v. 14). Although this section does not receive particular emphasis within the chapter, it contains the implicit analogy that grounds Job's conviction that his complaint (*rîb*) against God can be resolved fairly. Just as

God demands justice *of* him, so also God will show justice *to* him, despite the difference in power, if Job can gain a hearing (cf. 23:2-7).

31:16-20. The central two oaths of this series concern the essential ancient Near Eastern moral value of generosity to the poor. When Eliphaz attempted to depict Job as wicked, abuse of the orphan, the widow, and the poor was precisely the example he chose (22:7-9). Here, as in 29:12-17, Job refutes those accusations. The sharing of food and clothes, basic necessities of existence, is often mentioned in admonitions (Prov 22:9; Isa 58:7; Tob 4:6-11, 16-17; cf. Ezek 18:7). Job's familial imagery in v. 18 reflects the analogy that undergirded the sense of moral obligation to vulnerable members of society. The ancient Syrian king Kilamuwa recounts his care for the poor in these terms: "to some I was a father. To some I was a mother. To some I was a brother."[461]

31:21-23. The final oath in the series contains the complete formula. Job recognizes the truth of the proverb that "the poor are shunned even by their neighbors,/ but the rich have many friends" (Prov 14:20 NIV). Here he asserts that he never abused his influence to exploit the powerless in legal affairs. The hand (v. 21) is a symbol of power and perhaps more specifically of condemnation and judgment (cf. Isa 19:16; Zech 2:9).[462] In this instance, Job envisions a form of poetic justice for the abuse of such power: the breaking of his arm. Similarly, he knows that he would have to answer to one wielding even greater power (v. 22). Once again, the relation between Job and a more vulnerable member of the community is mirrored by Job's relation to God.

31:24-28. The third series of oaths concerns ultimate allegiance, the first two oaths involving wealth and the third other deities. Wealth brings with it a measure of security and confidence (Sir 40:26); for that very reason, it is morally ambiguous. "Trust," "confidence," and "joy" (vv. 24-25) define attitudes properly directed to God, not to wealth (cf. Pss 40:4[5]; 49:6[7]; 52:7[9]; 62:10[11]; 71:5; Prov 11:28; Jer 17:7; Sir 5:1-3; 31:5-11). Like shining gold, the luminous sun and moon have a seductive appeal (v. 26-27*a*).

459. T. Frymer-Kensky, "Deuteronomy," in C. Newsom and S. Ringe, *The Women's Bible Commentary* (Louisville: Westminster/John Knox, 1992) 58.

460. Gordis, *The Book of Job*, 346.

461. *ANET*, 654.

462. Habel, *The Book of Job*, 436.

The Deuteronomic tradition is particularly concerned to warn against worship of the sun and the moon (see Deut 4:19; 17:2-3; 2 Kgs 21:3-5; 23:5; Jer 8:1-2). Although the gesture described in v. 27b is not entirely clear, it is probably similar to what we describe as "blowing a kiss."[463] Job is clear about the moral significance of such compromised allegiance. It is a betrayal of God and so deserving of punishment (cf. Josh 24:27; Deut 17:2-7).

31:29-34. The three oaths making up the fourth series appear to be the most diverse, although they all have to do with situations in which the bonds of social solidarity are threatened.

31:31-32. The central oath of this series treats the exercise of hospitality to strangers. As outsiders not covered by the moral obligations that members of a clan or village have to each other, traveling strangers were particularly vulnerable to abuse, often expressed as sexual violence. The episodes at Sodom (Genesis 19) and Gibeah (Judges 19) are illustrative. In such cases, hospitality was more than a gracious gesture. It offered protection and a social bond where none existed before. Although there are difficulties with the translation of v. 31, the clear reference of v. 32 to the plight of the stranger makes the NRSV's v. 31 preferable. In that verse, Job denies that any members of his household ever expressed the desire to abuse the stranger sexually; on the contrary, Job's house was a place of refuge (v. 32).[464] The NIV takes v. 31 to refer to Job's generosity with food as part of his hospitality.[465]

31:29-30, 33-34. The first and third oaths of this series (vv. 29-30, 33-34) correspond. In societies in which the dynamics of honor and shame are strong, social relations are often highly competitive. Concern for who is higher and lower in public esteem, for flaunting good fortune and hiding what would bring one into disrepute are very strong pressures. The book of Psalms, with its frequent references to enemies who taunt and boast, and with its heartfelt curses against such enemies, gives a sense of the dynamics of such a society (see, e.g., Psalms 52; 59; 64; 69; 109).

Jeremiah, who in so many other instances is similar to Job, called down God's wrath upon his enemies in traditional terms (Jer 11:20; 12:3). When Job swears that he has neither rejoiced in the ruin of his enemies nor sought to curse them, he lays claim to the most difficult ideals of moral behavior (cf. Prov 17:5b; 24:17-18). In vv. 33-34, Job refers to the corresponding moral issue, the proper conduct of a person who has done wrong, or who at least has done something of which the community would disapprove. For certain categories of infractions, the legal literature assumes that a person who has incurred guilt must make it right in a fairly public way, through an offering and restitution (e.g., Lev 4:1-6:7). Although the way in which psalms were used is not known, it is possible that psalms of confession were also used in public confessions (e.g., Psalm 51). Whatever the expectations, in a society in which shame was a primary sanction, the temptation to conceal sins would have been intense. Job indicates as much in his vivid depiction of the contempt to which such a person would be exposed (v. 34). Although the phrase at the end of v. 33a can be translated "as others do," it may also be rendered "as Adam did," invoking the primordial story of the one whose reluctance to have his failure exposed led to concealment and thus a breaking of the social bond (Gen 3:8-13). Significantly, Job does not claim that he has never done anything wrong. His honor consists in having always been willing to take responsibility for his actions, even when it would have been possible to conceal them.

31:35-37. It is not accidental that Job interrupts the oath of clearance at this juncture with his ardent desire that someone give him a legal hearing. He knows that in this instance he has done nothing wrong and has nothing to hide; the moral outrage is that he is being treated as guilty without having been charged with any wrongdoing. Although Job's oath by itself need not have legal significance, his words have a distinct legal nuance and so give the entire chapter a more forensic connotation. (An oath of clearance was often part of a demand for a trial.)[466]

The Hebrew word for "mark" (תו *tāw*, v. 35b) designates the last letter of the Hebrew alphabet and was formed like an *x*. In

---

463. See Pope, *Job,* 235, for an extended discussion. A possible illustration of this religious gesture is found in *ANEP,* pls. 204, 622.
464. See Pope, *Job,* 236-37, for a defense of the interpretation of v. 31 as pertaining to sexual abuse.
465. Similarly, Hartley, *The Book of Job,* 420.

466. Dick, "The Legal Metaphor in Job 31," 42.

Ezek 9:4, 6 it is used to identify those who are to be spared God's judgment. Here it apparently indicates Job's signature. The legal response that Job expects in return is an "indictment in writing," indicated in the Hebrew by the term "document" (ספר *sēper*). That term is used to designate a variety of legal documents, including divorce decrees (Deut 24:1; Isa 50:1) and deeds (Jer 32:11-12). In the context of the expression "adversary at law" (איש ריב *'îš rîb*) the meaning "charge" or "indictment" is likely, although it is also possible that the document might be a decree of release or acquittal.[467] The reference in v. 37 to approaching the adversary to give an account of conduct makes the interpretation of a written indictment the most probable.

The image in v. 36 is somewhat obscure, for there are no clear parallels for someone wearing a legal document; perhaps the image was more apparent to its original audience. Persons did wear stamp and cylinder seals, which were used to authenticate transactions. Isaiah 22:22 refers to the official Eliakim ben Hilkiah wearing a key on his shoulder as a sign of his authority. The instruction in Deut 6:8; 11:18 to bind the commands of God upon the wrist and forehead gave rise to the practice in Judaism of wearing phylacteries (cf. Exod 13:16). Whatever the precise meaning, it is clear that far from facing shame, Job regards the occasion as an opportunity for displaying his dignity and honor (v. 37).

31:38-40. Job's words in vv. 35-37 constitute an aside, although an important one for understanding the intent of his oath. With vv. 38-40, he returns to complete his oath of clearance with a final double oath concerning land ethics. In v. 38, the land is personified as crying out and its furrows weeping. Although Job does not specify the reasons for which land might protest, a number of laws in Israelite tradition served to protect the land.[468] It was to remain fallow during sabbath and jubilee years (Exod 23:10-11; Lev 25:1-22), and regulations forbade the mixing of different types of seeds (Lev 19:19; Deut 22:9), as well as eating the produce of newly bearing trees for three years (Lev 19:23-25). More broadly, certain kinds of sin were considered to pollute the land (Deut 24:3). The book of Chronicles interprets the exile as a time of rest for the land to compensate for the sabbaths that were not observed (2 Chr 36:21; cf. Lev 26:34-35, 43).

The corresponding oath in v. 39 concerns ethical obligations to those who own and/or work the land. The judicial murder of Naboth and the seizure of his land by Ahab and Jezebel (1 Kings 21) are the most notorious examples of what was a recurrent issue of social justice (Isa 5:8; Neh 5:1-13; cf. Lev 25:23-38). Workers on the land were often at the mercy of owners for payment of the meager wages to which they were entitled (24:10-11; Lev 19:13; Deut 24:14-15; Mal 3:5). The curse Job invokes for such behavior is a fitting one, the growth of weeds instead of grain (cf. Gen 3:17-18; Jer 12:13).

The chapter concludes with the narrator's comment that "the words of Job are ended" (cf. Ps 72:20; Jer 51:64), signaling the end of the dialogue.

---

467. See Habel, *The Book of Job*, 439. For an example from the Jewish colony of Elephantine in Egypt, see *ANET*, 491.

468. Perdue, *Wisdom in Revolt*, 187-88.

REFLECTIONS

Throughout his final speech in chaps. 29–31, Job presents himself as a man of honor and gives a fairly full account of the values entailed by that identity. Particularly in the long oath of clearance in chap. 31, Job often invokes God as the source and guarantor of the values constituting his sense of self. Clearly, Job assumes that the values that give content to his own character also define the character of God. The values that structure his relations with others are the values he assumes should structure God's relation with him. Job's image of God is developed out of the highest and best values of his society, values that Job has always tried to embody.

This implicit analogy provides Job with the possibility of a resolution of the inexplicable events that have cast doubt on his integrity. Among the affirmations Job makes of himself in chap. 31 is the claim that he never rejected the grievance of his own slaves when they brought a just complaint against him. That is how a man of honor behaves. One can think of the patriarch Judah, who was ready to have his daughter-in-law Tamar killed for adultery. Yet when she showed him evidence that he was the father of her child, Judah recognized his own failure to sustain the rights of his daughter-in-law and confessed, "She is more in the right than I." King Saul groundlessly believed that David was his enemy and tried on numerous occasions to kill him. When David finally managed to confront Saul with the unmistakable evidence that David was not his enemy, however, Saul acknowledged it with the statement, "You are more in the right than I." The words that Job wants to hear from God are the same words: "You are more in the right than I." By configuring his claim in terms of the code of honor, Job provides for a resolution that would confer dignity on both parties. Like a person of honor, God will hear Job's complaint and judge justly, vindicating Job's innocence. Far from demeaning God, such an action will show God's honor, just as Job claimed that hearing the complaints of his own slaves was a demonstration of his honor.

The book could find its resolution on the terms Job has laid out. Many wish that it did. The task for reflection, however, is to think carefully about both the theological method implicit in the workings of Job's imagination and the content of the image of God he generates. These questions are scarcely separable. The workings of Job's theological imagination are very much in keeping with the larger Judeo-Christian tradition, which encourages thinking about God by means of metaphors drawn largely from the realm of human relations. The Bible speaks of God's emotions (e.g., love, anger, regret, forgiveness), as well as of God's intentions and actions. This language is so ubiquitous in the traditional way of thinking about God that one tends to forget that it is metaphorical, a way of talking about God in terms drawn from the model of human nature and expression. More easily recognized as metaphors are representations of God in terms of human relations (e.g., God as parent, king, kin-redeemer). The conviction that such metaphors provide knowledge of God is based on the belief that one can in some way know the creator through the creation. Even though metaphors based on human existence are not the only ones used of God, they are particularly important in the light of the Bible's claim that humans are made in the image and likeness of God. In some significant, but not fully articulated way, a continuity exists between human nature and divine nature. Job has good warrant for trying to know God by knowing what is best about himself.

One danger of theological metaphors is that one forgets that they are metaphors and treats them as literal statements. Unconsciously, one comes to think of God as a sort of ideal person who feels, thinks, and behaves (or ought to) according to the highest human standards. What gets lost in such a literalizing of language is the sense of God as "wholly other," to use Rudolph Otto's phrase.[469] Certain religious experiences disclose where metaphors drawn from human experience meet their limits and, indeed, are revealed as simply incapable of rendering God's nature. To a great extent, Job has become so caught up by the power of his generative metaphor for God that he has lost sight of its limits and inadequacies.

The temptation to literalize metaphor is not the only problem. A related problem concerning the metaphorical language that informs Job's thinking, and indeed much of Judeo-Christian theology, involves the scope of the dominant metaphors. To put it concretely, Job has attempted to understand the nature of the cosmos on the basis of his understanding of the social world of village patriarchy. Metaphors drawn from primary human relationships such as Job describes (e.g., parent-child, patron-dependent, leader-community) are powerful because they are so richly endowed with meaning for human beings and are so accessible. Meaning is readily given when one starts from one's embeddedness in a particular social context. But metaphors based on such local

469. See Otto, *The Idea of the Holy.*

relationships may not be comprehensive enough for understanding the fundamental nature of reality. The most serious problem is the ease with which certain parochial social arrangements can become "sacralized" when used as religious metaphors. Despite the genuine power of Job's use of his own social reality to gain insight into God's nature, modern readers are likely to have some reservations about the analogy Job seems to imply between his own social values and God's just order. Job's assumption that a fitting punishment if he committed adultery would be the sexual abuse of his own wife strikes most people today as utterly abhorrent. Nor would one like to see the paternalism and contempt for outcasts that are such an unself-conscious part of Job's moral vocabulary inform understandings of God's righteousness.

Many of these problems with the use of human metaphors to understand God can be addressed by critical reflection and self-consciousness about the nature of religious language. But a more intractable dilemma lurks in the analogy Job establishes between his values and God's, one that remains a deeply troubling problem for all people of faith. As Job's words in chaps. 29–31 make clear, he believes that his own passion for justice and rage against victimization of the weak by the strong are grounded in a similar passion of God. The whole of the Judeo-Christian tradition affirms with Job that this is so. Moreover, only metaphors drawn from human experience are capable of expressing this aspect of the divine nature, for only human beings possess the distinctive traits that make us "like God," the reflective knowledge of good and evil and the will to choose. The painful contradiction embedded in Job's anger against God is the recognition that no human parent filled with love for a child, no redeemer bound by ties of kinship, no king committed to the protection of the vulnerable would stand by in the face of abuse, murder, and genocide. Yet these things happen in God's world. One cannot evade the contradiction by talking about human responsibility for human deeds. Nature, too, is constructed with violence as an essential part of its order, a food chain that requires the painful death of some creatures as the price of life for others. Language about God that is based solely on metaphors of human beings and human relationships is simply not adequate to comprehend the presence of so much pain, violence, and oppression in God's world. To a certain extent, the divine speeches will address this issue, representing God and creation by means of images quite different from those that have informed Job's own theological imagination. Although the divine speeches will provide new resources for thinking about the presence of pain and disorder in a world created by a good God, the book as a whole will not attempt to resolve the matter in any simple way. It is an issue with which Judaism and Christianity must always struggle.

JOB 32:1–37:24

THE SPEECHES OF ELIHU

OVERVIEW

Whatever one expects to follow Job's oath of clearance, it is not Elihu. The appearance of this new character, with his long, uninterrupted discourse, poses two distinct but related questions. First, are the Elihu speeches part of the original composition of the book, or a later addition to it? Second, what is their purpose in the book as it now stands?

There are very strong reasons for recognizing the Elihu speeches as a later addition. Elihu is not mentioned in the prose tale that begins the book, where all other characters are introduced, and he does not appear in the epilogue. When God rebukes Job's friends by name in 42:7-9, Elihu is not mentioned. This omission is inexplicable if Elihu were one of the original characters but makes more sense if his speeches were added by a later writer who valued the ideas put into Elihu's mouth and did not want him included in the divine rebuke of the friends. Many compositional and stylistic features also suggest a different author. Elihu is the only character bearing an Israelite name. The prose by which he is introduced in 32:1-5 differs in tone and style from the spare, pseudo-naive style of the prologue and epilogue. In the speeches themselves, certain linguistic traits give Elihu a distinctive profile—e.g., preference for the divine name El and for the short form of the first-person pronoun (אני *ʾănî* rather than אנכי *ʾānōkî*), use of a word for "knowledge" (דע *dēaʿ*) not found elsewhere in the book, the presence of more Aramaisms than in the other speeches.[470]

Much more significant, however, is the distinctive way in which Elihu calls Job by name (32:12; 33:1, 31; 34:5, 7, 35, 36;

35:16; 37:14) and quotes fragments of Job's speeches (see 33:8-13; 34:5-6; 35:2-3). Since this trait is not characteristic of the original dialogue, it strongly suggests the work of an author who knows the written text and is intent on refuting specific statements. More generally, Elihu appears to engage in "correcting" the entire book. Not only does he refute Job explicitly, but also he criticizes the arguments of the friends as inadequate, indicating his intention to use arguments different from theirs (32:10-14). Although he does not criticize God explicitly, Elihu's speech in 36:22–37:24 anticipates elements of the divine speeches, while at the same time altering their nature so as to engage issues raised by Job more explicitly. The overall impression is that chaps. 32–37 derive from a later writer, dissatisfied with the failure of a powerful book and confident of his ability to supply the voice it lacks.

In recent years, perhaps in reaction to the excesses of historical-critical disassembly of the book of Job, some commentators have argued that the Elihu speeches are an integral part of the original composition of the book.[471] Their arguments, however, are more ingenious than persuasive. It is certainly true that the original author *could* have given Elihu a different style and diction in an effort to distinguish him from the other characters; yet such an explanation begs the question of why the three friends are not so clearly distinguished from one another in their speech and style. Those who argue for the orginality of Elihu sometimes explain his absence from

---

470. This is difficult evidence to evaluate. See the discussions in Driver and Gray, *A Critical and Exegetical Commentary on the Book of Job,* xlii-xlviii; Dhorme, *A Commentary on the Book of Job,* civ-cv; Gordis, *The Book of Job,* 547-48.

471. Cf. esp. Habel, "The Role of Elihu in the Design of the Book of Job," in *In the Shelter of Elyon: Essays on Palestinian Life and Literature in Honor of G. W. Ahlstrom,* JSOTSup 31, ed. W. B. Barrick and J. S. Spencer (Sheffield: JSOT, 1984) 81-88; Habel, *The Book of Job,* 36-37, 443-47; Janzen, *Job,* 217-18, 221-25. See also Andersen, *Job,* 49-52. Gordis, *The Book of God and Man,* 104-16, argues that the Elihu speeches are a later addition, but written by the author of the rest of the book of Job. Cf. D. N. Freedman, "The Elihu Speeches in the Book of Job," *HTR* 61 (1968) 51-59.

the prologue by making him a bystander who takes up the role of adjudicator. If so, it is odd that the prose tale gives the impression that Job and his three friends are the only actors on the scene, with no bystanders around. The assumption that an author with a controlling design wrote the Elihu speeches as part of an original composition virtually requires the conclusion that Elihu be understood as a self-destructing character, a self-parody undermined by his own words and by the rest of the book. Perhaps this interpretation derives much of its appeal from the fact that Elihu's style and argumentation are so little to the taste of modern readers. That modern readers have difficulty taking Elihu seriously, however, does not necessarily mean that his speech was intentionally composed to be unpersuasive. In short, arguments for the Elihu speeches as original to the book do not account for features of the speeches and their relation to the rest of the book as persuasively as does the hypothesis that they are the work of a somewhat later author who was dissatisfied with the book as it existed.

Assuming that the Elihu speeches were later additions to the book of Job, it is not clear when they were composed. They are present in the first century CE targum of Job from the Dead Sea Scrolls, but more precise evidence is elusive. Certain ideas in the Elihu speeches bear an intriguing resemblance to notions current in Jewish literature from the Hellenistic period, leading some to suggest a third century BCE date for their composition.[472] Although far from certain, the date is plausible. Modes of thinking about moral and religious issues underwent considerable development during the Hellenistic period, so that an intellectual of that age might well judge the book of Job unsatisfactory in not setting the religious issues in terms that had recently become influential and persuasive. Zuckerman suggests that this "generation gap" between the original book and the author of Elihu is symbolized in the representation of Elihu as a younger character.[473] Thus the conflict of the author's desire to correct the book, coupled with a reluctance to tamper with it, are given expression in the long self-justification with which Elihu begins his speech.

The Elihu speeches are best understood as disputations, as the narrative introduction and Elihu's own self-introduction make clear. While the speeches of the friends are at least somewhat embedded in the dramatic setting of the book and reflect the pastoral dimensions of sapiential friendship, Elihu's speeches are more exclusively engaged in a battle of ideas.[474] Elihu's primary idiom is that of wisdom, although he does engage Job's legal language more than the other friends have. His speeches, however, should not be understood as an attempt to make a legal case against Job in the strict sense.[475]

After a prose paragraph introducing Elihu (32:1-5), narrative headings divide Elihu's words into four speeches: 32:6–33:33; 34:1-37; 35:1-16; 36:1–37:24. The first speech begins with a long self-justification for speaking (32:7-22). In the main body of the speech, Elihu addresses Job, explaining ways in which, contrary to Job's assertion, God does "speak" to persons through dreams and through illness, in order to lead them to moral insight and so preserve them from destruction (33:1-33). Elihu concludes that speech with an offer to teach Job wisdom, an offer that is fulfilled in the following discourse. In 34:1-37, Elihu's style imitates a general wisdom discourse, addressed to an audience of "sages" and "men of reason" who are invited to judge Job's words. Contrary to Job's accusations, Elihu argues for the righteousness of God's character, exhibited in just governance and in judgment executed against abusive rulers. In the following speech (35:1-16), Elihu again directly challenges Job concerning the validity of his words about himself and about God. Elihu explains the implications of divine transcendence and the reasons why certain protests against oppression, including Job's, do not seem to receive divine response. Elihu's long final discourse divides into two parts. In 36:1-21, Elihu recapitulates many of the themes previously addressed. With 36:22–37:24, he begins to anticipate the divine speeches, describing the wonders of God as Lord of the weather and reminding

---

472. Wahl, *Der Gerechte Schoepfer,* 182-87. Cf. Mende, *Durch Leiden zur Vollendung,* 419-27.
473. Zuckerman, *Job the Silent,* 148, 153.

474. Westermann, *The Structure of the Book of Job,* 146.
475. Contra Habel, *The Book of Job,* 445-47, 452; and, rather differently, Zuckerman, *Job the Silent,* 151-53.

Job of his comparative powerlessness and ignorance. In Elihu's account, the wonders of God testify to God's righteous providence, before which the only possible response is awe and praise. A concluding description of a theophany leads directly to the speeches of God from the stormwind, which follow in chap. 38.

JOB 32:1–33:33, ELIHU ATTEMPTS TO ANSWER JOB

Job 32:1-22, Elihu's Compulsion to Speak

COMMENTARY

Chapter 32 introduces Elihu, first through narrative (vv. 1-5) and then through self-presentation (vv. 6-22). Both introductions are concerned primarily with establishing the motivation for Elihu's intervention. The *leitmotif* of the narrative introduction is Elihu's anger, which is mentioned four times. In the self-presentation Elihu establishes three things: that he will speak (vv. 6-10), that he can speak (vv. 11-14), and that he must speak (vv. 15-22).[476]

32:1-5. Although good reasons exist for regarding chaps. 32–37 as the work of a later author, nonetheless the chapters have been artfully crafted to fit into the book. By explaining why the three friends cease to answer Job, the author of the Elihu speeches provides closure for the friends' role in the dialogue. As in 2:11-13, a shocking perception leads to silence. In 2:12, the friends "lift up their eyes" to see Job, transformed by illness almost beyond recognition. As a consequence they sit before him for seven days and nights in silence (2:13). Now the friends, here called "these three men," are again silenced by the perception of a Job who is morally transformed almost beyond recognition. They now see Job as he sees himself, "righteous in his own eyes" (v. 1). In one sense, that is simply the literal truth; Job does consider himself innocent, in the right (cf. 27:1-6). But the idiom ("X in his own eyes") is a pejorative one that in wisdom discourse describes a fatuous and complacent person, a fool or worse (cf. Prov 12:15; 26:5, 12, 16;

28:11; 30:12). The friends have no more to say to such a person.

Elihu is introduced in v. 2. The narrator gives his name (Elihu), his father's name (Barakel), the city or territory from whence he comes (Buz), and his clan affiliation (Ram). The name "Elihu," which belongs to several minor biblical characters (1 Sam 1:1; 1 Chr 12:20[21]; 26:7; 27:18), means "He is my God," a variant of the name "Elijah," "Yahweh is my God." Although the name "Barakel" ("God has blessed") is not known from biblical sources, it was borne by certain diaspora Jews from Nippur.[477] The territory of Buz is mentioned in Jer 25:23, along with Dedan and Tema, cities located in northwest Arabia. The name "Ram" is not otherwise known as a clan designation, although it occurs as the name of one of David's ancestors (Ruth 4:19; 1 Chr 2:9-10, 25, 27).

Two things are puzzling about Elihu's designation: why his identification is so much longer than those of the other characters, and why he alone bears an Israelite name. Some have suggested that the names are semantically significant,[478] but the meanings do not seem especially crafted to describe his role. Moreover, whereas Ram would have positive significance ("lofty" [רם *rām*]), the name "Buz" (בוז *bûz*) puns on a negative word ("shame" [בוש *bôš*]). One can only speculate, but Elihu may simply be the name of the author of chapters 32–37, an angry reader who literally wrote himself into the book. If it

---

476. G. Fohrer, "Die Weisheit des Elihu (Hi 32-37)," *Studien zum Buche Hiob (1956–1979),* 2nd ed. (Berlin: Walter de Gruyter, 1983) 95.

477. See M. Coogan, *West Semitic Personal Names in the Murashu Documents* (Cambridge, Mass.: Harvard Semitic Museum, 1975) 16-17.

478. E.g., Gordis, *The Book of God and Man,* 115; Hartley, *The Book of Job,* 429; and rather differently, Good, *In Turns of Tempest,* 320.

is the case that the Elihu speeches come from the third or early second century BCE, then a precedent exists for a wisdom writer's using his own name in his composition. In the epilogue of Sirach, the author writes, "Instruction in understanding and knowledge/ I have written in this book,/ Jesus son of Eleazar son of Sirach of Jerusalem,/ whose mind poured forth wisdom" (Sir 50:27 NRSV).

Whether or not Elihu is the name of an actual person who has fictionalized himself as a character in the book of Job, the representation of Elihu in vv. 2-5 is an artful psychological portrait. First his anger is described in absolute terms (v. 2*a*). Next his anger against Job and the reason for it (v. 2*b*), and his anger against the friends and the reason for it (v. 3), are recounted in parallel clauses. Elihu is angry at Job for much the same reason that the friends cease to speak: because of Job's opinion that he, and not God, is in the right (the same Hebrew root [צדק *ṣādaq*], appears in vv. 1 and 2*b*). His anger at the three friends is more intriguing; Elihu thinks they have failed in their responsibility to overcome Job's disturbing claims. Thus his anger is evidence that ancient readers, not just modern ones, consider Job to have gotten the better of the friends in the dialogue.

Ancient Masoretic tradition identifies the end of v. 3 as one of the "corrections of the scribes" (*tiqqune sopherim*), a correction of the text made in the interests of piety.[479] Accordingly, the original text would have read "and so put God in the wrong," a perception that would fit well with Elihu's anger against the friends.

The syntax of v. 4 is awkward. Although it probably means that Elihu had been waiting during the entire dialogue (cf. v. 11), Gordis suggests that it be read "Elihu waited with Job for them to speak,"[480] drawing attention to the silence that signals the friends' refusal to argue further with Job (v. 5; cf. v. 13). In either case, Elihu's reticence is motivated by the strong cultural value of respect for elders (cf. 15:10; 30:1; Sir 32:7-9). Their inability to answer Job sets up a conflict of values for Elihu: respect for elders vs. the need to defend God, a conflict that expresses itself emotionally as anger (v. 5).

32:6-10. Although Elihu is often faulted for being long-winded and overly self-conscious,[481] he must overcome the strong prohibition against putting himself forward in the presence of elders. Elihu's reference to his own youth as a reason for holding back (v. 6) is a traditional self-deprecating remark, part of the rhetoric of politeness. Such a statement often occurs, however, in stories of remarkable leaders singled out by God for special service, such as Gideon (Judg 6:15), Saul (1 Sam 9:21), and Jeremiah (Jer 1:6). Elihu may wish for his politeness to intimate similar moral leadership.

An inclusio marks the limits of the first argument, as Elihu transforms the statement "I was afraid to tell you what I know" (v. 6*b*, author's trans.) into the assertion "I myself will tell you what I know" (v. 10*b*, author's trans.). Elihu presents the transformation as one taking place within himself, although his goal is to make it plausible to his audience, so that they will be willing to listen to him despite his youth. He presents as his own initial belief the traditional axiom that age should speak, because age possesses wisdom (v. 7; cf. 8:8-10; 15:10). Next he confronts it with a different axiom, but one that was also traditional and widely shared: the Spirit of God gives understanding (v. 8; cf. Exod 31:3; Num 11:26-30; 27:18). Implicitly assuming that the second axiom takes precedence over the first, Elihu concludes that age (alone) does not provide insight (v. 9). Thus he can move from his initial assumption ("I said, 'Let age speak' " [v. 7*a*, author's trans.]) to his new conclusion ("Therefore I say, 'Listen to me' " [v. 10*a*]).

Whether Elihu refers in v. 8 to a special inspiration[482] or to a general knowledge available to all is disputed.[483] The terms "spirit"/"breath" (רוח *rûaḥ* / נשמה *nĕšāmâ*) can refer to that which gives life to all (cf. 27:3; 33:4; Gen 2:7), or to that which gives wisdom to a select few (Gen 41:38; Judg 6:34; Isa 11:2). Only the context can determine the appropriate meaning; in this case, Elihu clearly is talking about an unusual quality that overrides the presumptive association

479. Gordis, *The Book of Job*, 366.
480. Gordis, *The Book of Job*, 367.

481. E.g., Habel, *The Book of Job*, 444; Rowley, *The Book of Job*, 207; Good, *In Turns of Tempest*, 321.
482. So Janzen, *Job*, 218; de Wilde, *Das Buch Hiob*, 311; J. W. McKay, "Elihu—A Proto-Charismatic?" *ExpTim* 90 (1979) 168.
483. Habel, *The Book of Job*, 451; Perdue, *Wisdom in Revolt*, 248.

of wisdom with age. He is attempting to present himself according to the model of the young man whose God-given wisdom allows him to surpass those older and more experienced than he (cf. Joseph in Genesis 41 or Daniel and his three friends in Dan 1:17-20). In the LXX version of Susanna, the contrast between youth and age is drawn very sharply, with the clever youth Daniel foiling the plot of the wicked elders. The LXX draws the moral of that story as follows: "Wherefore the youths are the beloved of Jacob because of their integrity. . . . For if the youths live reverently, a spirit of understanding and insight will be in them for ever."[484] A similar, rather pointed claim appears in Ps 119:99-100 that meditation on and obedience to Torah gives the speaker "more insight than all my teachers . . . more understanding than the elders." These various passages from the literature of the late Persian and Hellenistic periods suggest that the challenge to the dominance of elders was part of a broader intellectual and social phenomenon.

32:11-14. In this second section of his self-introduction, Elihu establishes his ability to contribute to the dialogue. He underscores his attentiveness to the friends' words, thus rhetorically establishing both his own proper behavior and his authority as one who knows and thus can judge what they have said (v. 11). The failure with which Elihu charges the friends is the same one that vv. 1-5 indicated as the source of Elihu's anger: their failure to refute Job (v. 12). In v. 12, Elihu echoes a term Job had used earlier, "confuted" (מוכיח *môkîaḥ*, NRSV). Whereas Job used the term to refer to one who would arbitrate between oneself and God (9:33), Elihu uses it in its more general sense of "one who corrects, rebukes" (NIV, "proved Job wrong"; NRSV, "confuted Job").[485] Elihu interprets the friends' silence as their conclusion that no one but God can successfully answer Job (v. 13), perhaps a sly acknowledgment that the author of the Elihu speeches knows the structure of the whole book. For Elihu to make a place for himself, he has to claim that his arguments will be different from those of the friends (v. 14). A number of commentators

scoff at his claims, insisting that he brings little new to the conversation,[486] but Elihu's arguments differ significantly from those of the friends, as the discussion of succeeding chapters will show.

32:15-22. Elihu ends with a vivid representation of his urgent need to speak. Like an actor addressing an aside to the audience, Elihu describes the defeated silence of the friends (v. 15) and rhetorically asks if he need wait any longer to speak, when they clearly have no more to say (v. 16). Answering his own rhetorical question with a bold announcement that he will speak (v. 17), Elihu repeats the concluding words of v. 10b. The phrase "I also," which Elihu uses three times in vv. 10 and 17, is artful, for the Hebrew words "also" and "anger" are homonyms (אף *'ap*). Even as Elihu presents his words within the discipline of sapiential politeness and careful argumentation, his anger is underscored, as his self-asserting words "I also" echo the claim "I am angry."

It is almost impossible for a modern reader to listen with a straight face as Elihu describes himself as having a belly full of words like a wineskin full of fermenting wine (v. 19). Those who view Elihu as a parody created by the author of the rest of the book of Job make much of this passage.[487] What is humorous in one culture, however, is no reliable guide to what is humorous in another. Within the context of ancient values and metaphors, Elihu says nothing absurd. Because discipline in speech was so highly valued, words that might sound excessive required justification. For example, Eliphaz acknowledged the boldness of his own first reply to Job with the rhetorical question, "but who can keep from speaking?" (4:2b NRSV). Job also justified his "speaking rashly" by making a reference to the immensity of his anguish (6:2-3), and Zophar spoke of the "agitation" impelling him to speak (20:2). More graphically, the prophet Jeremiah likened God's word within him to "fire shut up in my bones" (Jer 20:9 NRSV). The wineskin bursting from the pressure of fermentation would have been a vivid and appropriate image (cf. Matt 9:17).

484. R. Doran, "The Additions to Daniel," *HBC*, ed. J. L. Mays et al. (San Francisco: Harper & Row, 1988) 865.

485. Contra Habel, *The Book of Job*, 452, who assumes that Elihu also uses the term in a forensic context.

486. E.g., Driver and Gray, *A Critical and Exegetical Commentary on the Book of Job*, xli; Pope, *Job*, xxvii-xxviii.

487. E.g., Habel, "The Role of Elihu in the Design of the Book of Job," 91.

Elihu concludes by insisting that he will not abuse the authority of speech by showing partiality or using flattery (vv. 21-22). Since he has made it clear that he intends to be critical both of Job and of the friends, partiality is not likely to be a problem. Ironically, Elihu notes that God would carry him away if he did flatter or show partiality. It does not occur to Elihu that his judgments are uncritically partial to God. This is precisely the blindness of piety that Job has attempted to expose but that Elihu cannot begin to accept as a legitimate issue for discussion. Thus Elihu cannot engage Job in a significant way, because their presuppositions about the way one must talk about God are so radically different.

REFLECTIONS

Why do people loathe Elihu? The strong identification of modern readers with Job tends to generate criticism of all his opponents, but no one comes in for such vituperative comments as Elihu: "a pompous, insensitive bore,"[488] "a fanatic and a bigot,"[489] and "ridiculous"[490] are typical judgments. Perhaps one reason for the intense reactions Elihu generates is hinted at in the title Gordis gives him, "Elihu the Intruder."[491] Elihu intrudes into an intense moment, not just among the characters in the book, but also between the reader and the book. He breaks the dramatic spell and spoils the integrity of an aesthetic, emotional, and religious encounter at the climax of the book. The author of the Elihu speeches chooses a strategic location in which to insert his words. His location allows him a privileged position from which to interpret the dialogues. They are now completed, so that his voice is not simply one among others, but one that looks back over the whole and declares what the critical issues are. As much as a reader may recognize the distortions Elihu introduces, it is difficult to prevent them from having their effect. By the end of chap. 37, Elihu has distanced the reader from the immediacy of Job's passion and has changed the nature of the reader's experience of the book, so that ideas dominate over passions. Elihu also changes the experience of the divine speeches that follow. In everyday life one can recognize the need to control that is manifested when a friend insists on giving a strongly evaluative description of a person whom one is soon to meet. Similarly, Elihu's need to control—to control the reader's perception of God and perhaps even to control God—is amply on display when he speaks. This dynamic, coupled with Elihu's unconcealed conviction that he alone understands what is said and can point out and remedy its defects is what earns Elihu the undying resentment of generations of readers.

One can reflect on Elihu, or perhaps one should say on the author of the Elihu speeches, as a cautionary example of the temptations that beset all interpreters. Whether one is preaching a sermon, teaching a Bible study, or writing a commentary, there is often a temptation to use one's authoritative role in an improperly controlling fashion. By selecting some issues and passing over others in silence, by subtle distortions of what the text says, or by caricaturing and ridiculing other interpretations, one can make it appear that there is no other way to understand the text and the issues it presents. This temptation is particularly acute when texts bear on controversial issues. In our own day biblical texts concerning matters of sexuality or the role of women are often subjected to such tendentious interpretations by people on both sides of the issue. It can be very difficult to allow a text to speak in its own voice, especially when one thinks that the text is wrong. Like Elihu, we experience the impulse to argue the text into silence or to put a "spin" on it so that it will be read in a way that we approve.

488. Good, *In Turns of Tempest,* 321.
489. J. B. Curtis, "Why Were the Elihu Speeches Added to the Book of Job?" *Proceedings of the Eastern Great Lakes and Midwest Biblical Societies* 8 (1988) 93.
490. Rowley, *The Book of Job,* 209.
491. Gordis, *The Book of God and Man,* 104-16.

This is not to say that an interpreter can be utterly objective or should be wholly dispassionate. All interpretation is interpretation from a particular, and limited, perspective. Many factors, including the interpreter's age, gender, ethnicity, social class, denomination, and particular life experience, will shape what a person is able to see in a text. The author of the Elihu speeches, for instance, is able to see omissions in the discussion of suffering (see chap. 33) because he comes from a later age that reflected on such issues differently. Nor is anger at a text necessarily a bad thing. A text that offends can be a stimulus to think about issues in a way that one otherwise would not have to. It is not Elihu's anger that sets a bad example, but what he does with it.

Part of what is troubling about the role of the Elihu speeches in the book of Job is the way in which they change the nature of the discourse. The preceding speeches, and indeed the book as a whole, are structured as a dialogue between very different points of view. The Elihu speeches, however, do not integrate themselves into this dialogical structure but privilege themselves as a long monologue. They do not allow another voice to answer back. In certain settings of interpretation, for instance in Bible studies, it is comparatively easy to set interpretation in the context of a dialogue of voices. Other interpretive genres, such as sermons and commentaries, have the form of a monologue. Even in such forms of speech, however, it is often possible to acknowledge and sometimes even incorporate other voices with their differing interpretive possibilities. It is always possible to speak and write in a way that recognizes that one's interpretation is only *an* interpretation, not *the* interpretation. Such a stance should not be a wishy-washy claim that one interpretation is as good as another but rather a recognition of the inexhaustible richness of texts that require many different voices to engage in the work of interpretation.

Job 33:1-33, God Uses Suffering to Warn and Redeem

COMMENTARY

With chap. 33 Elihu begins the task of answering Job. He introduces his discourse in vv. 1-7 with a call to hear (v. 1) and a self-recommendation of what he has to say (vv. 2-3), along with a claim that, as a fellow human, he speaks to Job as an equal (vv. 4-7). He summarizes Job's complaint (vv. 8-11) by drawing primarily on Job's speeches in chaps. 9 and 13. The gist of Job's complaint, as Elihu interprets it, is that even though Job is innocent, God has treated him as an enemy and punished him. Elihu sets up his refutation of Job by citing one of the specific complaints Job had made: that God refuses to reply to a person's words (vv. 12-13).

The main body of Elihu's speech is set off by the inclusio in vv. 14 and 29-30 ("once, twice . . . two times, thrice" [author's trans.]), referring to God's attempts to communicate with a person and to turn the person back from death. Although Elihu draws in various ways on what the friends have said, the distinctive quality of his argument is the account of God's comprehensive concern to warn and correct humans and so to save them from destruction. Elihu describes a three-stage process, involving dreams (vv. 15-18), illness (vv. 19-22), and the intervention of an angelic mediator (vv. 23-28), who finally effects the recognition of wrongdoing, restoration, and reconciliation. A concluding call to Job to hear and reply (vv. 31-33), if he has anything to say, brings this part of Elihu's speech to a conclusion and provides for the transition to chap. 34.

Elihu's preoccupation with the process of moral regeneration is distinct from the arguments of the friends. Although the date of composition of the Elihu speeches is not certain (see Overview of Job 32:1–37:24), there was a growing interest in Jewish moral literature of the Persian and Hellenistic periods in issues of character, and particularly in the acknowledgment of sin and repentance. The chronicler provides an account of the repentance of King Manasseh, for instance (2 Chr 30:10-20), and later tradition even supplied the text of his penitential prayer (Prayer of Manasseh). The stories of King Nebuchadnezzar in Daniel 2–4 show how a proud king is warned by dreams (Daniel 2; 4) and by suffering (Daniel 4) to humble himself and confess the Most High God. Similarities between these narratives and the account Elihu gives of the process of moral regeneration suggest that the author of the Elihu speeches comes from a generation in which this topic was central to any understanding of the meaning of suffering.

33:1-7. The first three verses of Elihu's introduction are a fairly typical piece of didactic rhetoric, consisting of a call to hear addressed explicitly to Job (v. 1; cf. Deut 5:1; Prov 1:8; Isa 1:10) and a self-recommendation of what he has to say (vv. 2-3; cf. Prov 8:6-8). Verses 4-7, however, specifically engage the concerns Job had expressed in chap. 13, that the unrestrained power of God makes dialogue impossible. Here Elihu presents himself as one who, as a mere human like Job, can engage him in dialogue without intimidation. The argument is organized in an ABAB pattern, v. 4 corresponding to v. 6 and v. 5 to v. 7. In vv. 4 and 6, human nature is described in terms of the breath of God (v. 4) and clay (v. 6), as in Gen 2:7. The motif of being snipped off from clay was also known in Mesopotamian[492] and Egyptian[493] literature. Elihu invites Job to "answer" and "prepare" his words in terms evocative of Job's own challenge to God (13:18a, 22b). The phrase "if you are able" (v. 5) has a double nuance. When Job considered confronting God, Job's ability to answer was put in question by the inequality of power. But here, as Elihu's words suggest, Job's ability to reply depends on the intrinsic strength of his arguments, which, Elihu subtly suggests, are inadequate. Elihu closes his argument with a pointed allusion to Job's words in 13:21b, where Job asked God not to allow God's fearfulness to terrify him when they spoke together (cf. also 9:34). If one follows the NIV in taking the word אכפי (ʾakpî) as a variant form of כפי (kapî, "my hand"),[494] then Elihu also echoes 13:21a.

33:8-18. Elihu summarizes what he considers to be the essence of Job's complaint, making use of explicit citations as well as more general summaries. As Habel notes, these verses pair four claims to innocence (v. 9) with four complaints against God (vv. 10-11).[495] Although v. 9 does not use Job's exact words, Job had claimed to be innocent of serious wrongdoing (9:20-21; 27:4-6; 31:1-40). Verses 10-11 contain a nearly verbatim quotation of Job's words in 13:24b and 27a.

Having set forth a summary of Job's arguments, Elihu announces his judgment and his intent to refute (v. 12a), stating the principle that grounds all the arguments he will make: God is greater than humankind.[496] In Elihu's opinion, Job's entire understanding of God is wrong, but he introduces his own interpretation of God's motives and methods by means of another specific complaint Job has made about God: that one could not "contend" with God (13a; cf. 9:3a) because God would not "answer" (13b; cf. 9:3b). In fact, the pronouns in 9:3b are ambiguous, and it is not clear whether Job is saying that a person *could not* answer God or that God *would not* answer a person (see Commentary on Job 9:2-4). Elihu has taken it in the latter sense, and it is certainly the case that Job complains about the elusive, non-responsiveness of God (23:8-9).

In singling out 9:2-4 and 13:18-27, Elihu draws attention to the legal metaphor that has been important in shaping Job's complaint, but that the other three friends have not acknowledged in their replies. Some commentators think that Elihu's engagement of the legal metaphor constitutes his distinctive contribution to the book,[497] but that does not seem to be borne out by the way Elihu engages Job's legal language. Elihu does not point Job toward a solution by using legal categories but by showing how they have confused and misled Job. Job had complained that God would not answer his words in the context of a legal case; Elihu points out that God often speaks, but in ways that go unnoticed by people like Job (v. 14).

495. Habel, *The Book of Job*, 465.
496. Gordis, *The Book of Job*, 374; and Habel, *The Book of Job*, 467, take v. 12b as part of Elihu's citation of Job's arguments. As Habel translates: "Well, in this you are not in the right. I will answer you./ If 'Eloah is greater than humans,'/ Then why do you bring a suit against him,/ Since (as you claim), 'He answers none of my charges' " (Habel, *The Book of Job*, 455).
497. Habel, *The Book of Job*, 56, 445; Zuckerman, *Job the Silent*, 150-53.

492. E.g., the *Gilgamesh Epic* (*ANET*, 74).
493. E.g., in the Instructions of Anememopet, (*ANET*, 424).
494. M. Dahood, "Hebrew-Ugaritic Lexicography I," *Biblica* 44 (1963), 293.

God's mode of communication is not a trial but dreams and night visions that carry warnings (vv. 15-16). Job had complained that God terrified him with dreams and visions (7:14), implying an obsessive and sadistic character for God. Elihu reinterprets these phenomena as attempts by God to turn a person away from wrongful deeds or pridefulness (v. 17). Far from being acts of hostility, they are attempts by God to save a person's life. (Parallelism makes the NRSV's "traversing the River [of death]," more likely than the NIV's "perishing by the sword," although both are linguistically possible.) In general, dreams and visions are recognized in the Bible as means of divine revelation (see Gen 15:1; 28:10-17; 31:10-13, 24; 40:8-18; 41:1-32). Similar to Elihu's description, God sends Abimelech a dream, warning him against unintentionally committing the serious sin of sexual intercourse with Sarah, wife of Abraham (Gen 20:3-7).

Elihu identifies two objects of divine warning: an "act" that might be committed and a disposition, "pride," the character flaw that leads to wrongful deeds (cf. the dream of Nebuchadnezzar in Dan 4:10-11[7-8], where the lofty tree whose top "touched the heavens" symbolizes pride). The choice of this characteristic is significant, since, as Gordis notes, hubris is the flaw to which good people are particularly susceptible,[498] and Job's insistence on his own rightness over against God would seem to Elihu evidence of just such arrogance.

33:19-22. A second and more emphatic form of divine communication is illness, which Elihu characterizes as a kind of reproof or chastening (v. 19). Eliphaz had briefly mentioned such divine correction in 5:17, using the same term. He focused on the objective outcome of such divine correction, however, whereas Elihu is more concerned with the process itself and the moral regeneration of the individual. The psalms, too, sometimes interpret illness in terms of divine reproof (cf. Pss 6:1[2]; 38:1[2]). Yet they associate divine reproof with anger, whereas Elihu assumes that the divine intent is not punitive but salvific (v. 30). Although Elihu's words engage those of Eliphaz and the psalmists, they are most specifically directed at Job's interpretation of

his illness as a sign of God's enmity and desire to humiliate him (19:20; 30:16-19, 30-31). This section reaches its climax at the point where the sufferer approaches death itself (v. 22). In the psalms the approach to death is often the moment of appeal to God and of God's deliverance (Pss 18:4-6[5-7]; 30:1-3[2-4]; cf. Isa 38:9-20; Jonah 2:2-9).

33:23-28. Although Elihu generally follows the scenarios of the lament and thanksgiving psalms in vv. 19-22, his imagination differs from those scenarios in that the psalms simply depict the person in trouble calling out to God and being delivered. They seldom if ever attempt to explore what makes that appeal to God possible. For Elihu that process, which the psalms pass over in silence, is of utmost importance. How is it that repentance, restoration, and reconciliation become possible for a person who is blind and deaf to God's warnings (cf. Isa 42:18-25)? The impasse, Elihu claims, is broken by an angelic mediator (מליץ *mēlîṣ*). The term refers primarily to an interpreter (e.g., Gen 42:23), but also comes to have a broader meaning of "intermediary," "advocate." Job used the term in 16:20 in the sense of a legal advocate who would argue his case with God. In later Judaism, the notion of an angelic defense attorney became part of traditions concerning the high holy days, when each person would be judged by the heavenly court.[499] Intercessory angels are already attested in *1 Enoch* 9:3; 15:2 and in the *Testaments of the Twelve Patriarchs.*[500]

What Elihu says must be interpreted on its own terms and in its own context, however, and does not necessarily imply later ideas about angels and their functions. It is not clear, for instance, whether the phrase "one of a thousand" (v. 23) is intended to suggest the rarity of such an angelic mediator or its ready availability. Equally ambiguous is the following phrase, which could be translated either "to declare a person upright" (see NRSV),[501] or "to tell a person what is right for him," i.e., his duty (see NIV).[502] Although the later tradition of the intercessory angel would support the translation "to declare a

498. Gordis, *The Book of Job,* 375.

499. See Gordis, *The Book of Job,* 377.
500. *T. Levi* 3:5-6; *T. Dan* 6:2-6.
501. See Gordis, *The Book of Job,* 377; Habel, *The Book of Job,* 470.
502. J. F. Ross, "Job 33:14-30: The Phenomenology of Lament," *JBL* 94 (1975) 40.

person upright," the case that Elihu has been building about the inability of a person to perceive the divine message would support the translation "to tell a person what is right for him." The angelic interpreter translates the "language" of suffering into words that a person can understand. Perhaps the ambiguity is intentional. Elihu is both appropriating and correcting the idea that Job advanced in chap. 16. The angelic mediator's speech expresses belief in the sufferer's essential uprightness; yet the sufferer's life is endangered by a moral flaw to which he remains oblivious. In that sense, Elihu claims that the angel speaks both *for* and *to* the sufferer.

The results of this activity are seen in the words of the angel to God (vv. 24-25) and in the transformed understanding and words of the sufferer (vv. 27-28). Although it has been objected that God should be understood as the subject of the verbs in v. 24, because an angel does not possess the authority to redeem (cf. v. 24 TNK),[503] the words "deliver him from the Pit" are not a command but an urgent plea to God. The nature of the "ransom" (כפר *kōper*) is ambiguous. In the legal literature, *kōper* designates the compensation paid by an injuring party to the injured party (e.g., Exod 21:30; Num 35:31-32). Correspondingly, here the ransom would be the repentance of the sinner.[504] A ransom may be paid by another (cf. Isa 43:3), however, and so this may be the angel's pledge to stand surety for the person.[505]

Verse 26 is a highly condensed account of the cultic process of prayer and reconciliation that forms the setting for psalms of lament and thanksgiving. In contrast to the person's failure to perceive and respond to God's "speaking" (v. 14) through dreams and illness, God accepts the person's prayerful entreaty (v. 26). The joy of God's life-giving presence (cf. Num 6:24-26; Pss 4:7; 17:15; 31:16[17]) contrasts with the previous pain, depression, and emaciation (vv. 19-21). God's concluding and most significant act is ambiguously phrased, as the contrasting translations of v. 26b in the NRSV and the NIV suggest. As in v. 23b, the ambiguity may be strategic. Corresponding to the person's essential righteousness, "God repays him for his righteousness" (NRSV), but through the difficult process of turning the person from wrongful deeds and suppressing pride, he has been "restored by God to his righteous state" (NIV).

Until this point the individual has been talked about, but the individual's own understanding of events has not been described. Elihu brings together the theme of the transformation of moral self-understanding with the theme of cultic reconciliation as he dramatizes the individual's own words in the performance of the vow of praise. (The vow of praise is a frequent feature in psalms of lament; cf. Ps 22:22-31[23-32]). In v. 27, the individual confesses sin and perversion of "what is right" (ישר *yāšār*; cf. ישר *yōšer* in v. 23b), presumably the pride that distorted the person's understanding of God's message, but also acknowledges God's essential graciousness ("it was not paid back to me"). Elihu shifts the focus away from suffering as retributive, seeing it rather as redemptive, a notion expressed in images of redemption from the Pit and restoration to the light in v. 28.

33:29-30. Elihu summarizes in vv. 29-30, using inclusio to indicate the completion of the argument. The numerical figure of speech in v. 14 ("once, twice") is echoed in v. 29 ("two times, thrice"), and images used in the thanksgiving in v. 28 are echoed in v. 30. It is no accident that the grammatical construction in v. 30 is a purpose clause, for Elihu's point throughout has been to stress the redemptive purposefulness of what appears to Job to be God's arbitrary or hostile action.

33:31-33. The final three verses renew the call to hear with which Elihu began his speech (v. 1//v. 33) and the invitation for Job to speak (v. 5//v. 32a). One should look at these words not so much in terms of Elihu's rhetoric but in terms of the strategic role of these words in the work of the *author* of the Elihu speeches. That author has no intention of letting Job reply and so turn Elihu's monologue into a dialogue. Rhetorically, having Elihu invite Job to speak and yet having Job remain silent make it appear that Elihu's speeches are more persuasive to Job than those of the friends had been. Verse 33, which presumes Job's silence, provides the transition to Elihu's further words in the following chapters.

---

503. Gordis, *The Book of Job*, 377.
504. Fohrer, "Die Weisheit des Elihu (Hi 32-37)," 97; Wahl, *Der Gerechte Schoepfer*, 67.
505. Habel, *The Book of Job*, 470, thinks that it is a combination of the person's past behavior and surety by the angel.

REFLECTIONS

Elihu is a formidable thinker—and a dangerous one. In this chapter he articulates a powerful idea: God intentionally sends suffering to people in order to make them better—indeed, to save them. There is so much that is repugnant in this idea that it can be difficult to understand why it has had such a persistent grip on the moral imagination of countless generations of Jews and Christians. Yet it has been extremely influential, both in popular piety and in learned reflection.[506] In an almost uncanny echo of Elihu, the Christian scholar and novelist C. S. Lewis wrote the following in his book *The Problem of Pain:*

> Now God, who has made us, knows what we are and that our happiness lies in Him. Yet we will not seek it in Him as long as He leaves us any other resort where it can even plausibly be looked for. While what we call "our own life" remains agreeable we will not surrender it to Him. What then can God do in our interests but make "our own life" less agreeable to us, and take away the plausible sources of false happiness? . . . We are perplexed to see misfortune falling upon decent, inoffensive, worthy people—on capable, hard-working mothers of families or diligent, thrifty, little trades-people, on those who have worked so hard, and so honestly, for their modest stock of happiness and now seem to be entering on the enjoyment of it with the fullest right. . . . Let me implore the reader to try to believe, if only for the moment, that God, who made these deserving people, may really be right when He thinks that their modest prosperity and the happiness of their children are not enough to make them blessed: that all this must fall from them in the end, and that if they have not learned to know Him they will be wretched. And therefore He troubles them, warning them in advance of an insufficiency that one day they will have to discover.[507]

Lewis captures not only the essence of Elihu's argument but also the smugness of tone and the abstract quality of his reasoning. One might think that these are the arguments of someone who has never suffered, but that is not the case. Lewis's mother died when he was a child. It appears, however, that through ideas such as these he attempted to deal with his grief through a rationalization that seemed to give meaning and purpose even to such a terrible event.

That is apparently why the idea of suffering as divine pedagogy has such a strong appeal. Like the notion of suffering as punishment for sin, it organizes the disorienting chaos of suffering into a meaningful pattern. Fearing meaninglessness almost above all else, people are willing to pay a great deal to restore a meaningful structure to experiences over which they have no control. Moreover, the explanation of suffering as a warning is superior to the idea of suffering as punishment in that it provides not only reason but also purpose. What was evil from one perspective can be seen as positively good from another, and people are extremely reluctant to admit the reality of things that are simply and truly evil. The belief that God has a purpose in bringing suffering enlists the energies of the one who suffers to discern that purpose and to work toward fulfilling it. Suffering as redemptive discipline may also seem more appealing than retribution in its image of God. Instead of an angry God, it offers the image of a caring God who desires a person to live and be whole and uses pain only as a last resort.

When one begins to examine these ideas, however, their grotesque nature becomes apparent. A parent who would break a child's arm or kill a child's dog to draw the child's attention to some moral lesson or to remind the child of its absolute dependence

---

506. See J. A. Sanders, *Suffering as Divine Discipline in the Old Testament and Post-Biblical Judaism* (Rochester, N.Y.: Colgate Rochester Divinity School, 1955).

507. C. S. Lewis, *The Problem of Pain* (New York: Macmillan, 1940) 84-85.

is no loving parent but a sadist who takes a perverted pleasure in cruelty. No ultimate good for the child, even if it were the parent's sincere purpose, could make those actions anything other than evil. This is too high a price to pay for meaning. Yet this is essentially the image of God offered by Elihu and by Lewis in *The Problem of Pain.*

It should not be surprising that a belief in suffering as divine pedagogy often leaves the one who believes it terribly vulnerable when tragedy occurs. The brittleness of the explanation is swept away by the reality of grief. We do not know what might have happened to the character Elihu in later life, but C. S. Lewis was overtaken by a second terrible loss when his wife died of cancer. In his response to that grief, he leaves behind all his Elihu-like complacent rationalizations. Instead, his voice echoes the pain, rage, and sense of betrayal that one hears in Job:

> Meanwhile, where is God? . . . When you are happy, so happy that you have no sense of needing Him, so happy that you are tempted to feel His claims upon you as an interruption, if you remember yourself and turn to Him with gratitude and praise, you will be—or so it feels—welcomed with open arms. But go to Him when your need is desperate, when all other help is vain, and what do you find? A door slammed in your face. . . . After that, silence. . . . Not that I am (I think) in much danger of ceasing to believe in God. The real danger is of coming to believe such dreadful things about Him. The conclusion I dread is not "So there's no God after all," but "So this is what God's really like. Deceive yourself no longer."[508]

Lewis's honest grappling with his pain and bewilderment is, like Job's, the voice of a deep faith. Like Job, he does not find a simple answer.

Part of the problem with attempts to grapple with the meaning of suffering is that suffering does not a have a single cause or a single shape, and so it cannot have a single meaning. It may arise out of human cruelty, out of self-inflicted folly, out of the inescapable reality of finitude, or any number of things. The notion that God wills particular suffering in order to teach something, however, can lead only to the conclusion that God is a monster of cruelty. It is a false belief that should be rejected.

The connection between suffering and learning is an important one, however, once it is detached from the notion that learning is the *purpose* of suffering. Suffering is not meaningful or purposeful in and of itself. Some kinds of suffering can never be anything but meaningless, but that is not always the case. One of the dehumanizing aspects of suffering is that it tends to make persons experience themselves as powerless and passive. Suffering takes away so much. The determination to learn from suffering, to wrest something back from it, can be a powerful means of resisting its soul-destroying force. One sees this in the struggles of the abused and the oppressed who are able to learn how to transmute suffering into solidarity. But one also sees this in the bereaved, whose suffering arises from the natural event of death, when they take back from the experience of immeasurable loss the capacity for a new compassion. Suffering is not sent, nor does it *have* meaning and purpose. Rather, the ability to take its emptiness and to put it to the service of meaning and purpose is the power to resist the evil in suffering. In that experience, one discovers the power and presence of God in suffering.

508. C. S. Lewis, *A Grief Observed* (San Francisco: Harper, 1989) 17-19.

JOB 34:1-37, GOD, THE ABSOLUTE SOVEREIGN, ALWAYS ACTS JUSTLY

COMMENTARY

Chapter 34 is a very different kind of speech from chap. 33. Whereas chap. 33 is addressed specifically to Job and concerned with the very personal process of moral regeneration, chap. 34 is addressed to a general audience of the wise and presents an almost philosophical reflection on God's nature and governance of the world. As in chap. 33, however, Elihu is concerned to refute a specific claim made by Job that God has "taken away Job's right." Although there is only one explicit citation of Job's words (v. 5b, citing 27:2a), Elihu refutes the attacks Job has made on God's governance in the world in chaps. 12; 21; and 24.

The speech has a fairly clear structure. Following the introductory heading (v. 1), Elihu begins with a developed rhetorical appeal to his audience to listen and judge with him the words of Job (vv. 2-9). A similar, briefer appeal and judgment closes the speech (vv. 34-37). The body of the speech is developed in a series of related arguments. Elihu defends the just governance of God by appealing to God's absolute sovereignty (vv. 10-15) and character as a disinterested lover of justice (vv. 16-20). In response to Job's complaint that times for judgment are not evident, Elihu describes the sudden and surprising ways in which God overturns the wicked (vv. 21-30). Satirizing Job's insistence on being restored on his own terms while refusing to admit guilt (vv. 31-33), Elihu renews his call for the judgment of all right-thinking people against Job's rebellious and ignorant words (vv. 34-37).

34:1-9. Three times in the course of his speech Elihu addresses his audience as "wise men," "people of learning," and "men of reason" (vv. 2, 10, 34). According to the narrative context, the only people present are Job and his three friends, none of whom Elihu considers wise. Elihu is rhetorically addressing an imaginary audience, the truly wise, for whom Elihu is the spokesperson. This device serves as an appeal to readers who

may assume the title of wise by agreeing with Elihu's judgment.

The introductory appeal is tightly structured. Following the call to hear (v. 2; cf. Deut 5:1; Prov 1:8; Isa 1:10), Elihu cites a proverb (v. 3), which authorizes his appeal for the audience to exercise discriminating judgment (v. 4). Next, he cites the words of Job, which are to be judged (vv. 5-6), makes his own judgment about Job's character as reflected in his words (vv. 7-8), and reinforces his conclusion by adding another citation of Job's obviously impious words (v. 9).

The proverb Elihu cites in v. 3 is the same one Job used in 12:11 to introduce his satirical doxology of God's governance in 12:13-25, and the echo suggests something of Elihu's attempt to turn Job's words to his own purposes. The theme of the chapter is introduced in Elihu's invitation to determine "what is right" (משפט *mišpāṭ*). The term *mišpāṭ* occurs six times in the course of the speech, although with varying nuances. Here, as in v. 6a, it means the determination of what is correct in a particular case, as the parallel line in v. 4b confirms. To "know what is good" is to be able to make discriminating judgments between good and bad, sound and unsound (cf. Gen 3:22; 2 Sam 14:20). Elsewhere in the chapter, *mišpāṭ* designates a legal right or judgment (vv. 5, 12, 23), on the one hand, and the broader principle of just governance (v. 17) on the other. For Elihu, as for Job, these various dimensions of meaning are related. Job has argued inductively from the sense of injustice done to him to a critique of divine governance in general. Elihu will argue deductively from a conviction of God's righteous governance to the conclusion that God could not have acted unjustly in Job's case. Both assume that only one view can be judged correct.

The words of Job that Elihu cites are a pastiche of 27:2a ("As God lives, who has taken away my right" [NRSV]), 9:20 ("Though I am innocent, my own mouth would condemn me" [NRSV]), and 6:4 ("the arrows of the Almighty" [NRSV]). Elihu's composite citation is a fair representation of Job's views. For the moment Elihu does not seek to refute them so much as to disqualify them by characterizing them as "scorn," the sort of mockery associated with the impious (cf. Ps 1:1; Prov 1:22). By using the idiom "to drink X like water" (cf. 15:16), Elihu implies that such derisive speech is habitual with Job. With his rhetoric, Elihu shifts the focus away from the content of Job's words in order to make Job's character the issue. Similarly, without explicitly saying that Job is a bad person, Elihu accuses him of being a "fellow traveler" of the wicked (v. 8), because Job says the same sort of things they say (v. 9). In reality, Job had attributed words like those in v. 9 to the wicked, from whom he certainly distinguished himself (21:15). Elihu, however, implies that Job's complaints (e.g., that God destroys both blameless and wicked persons [9:22], that the wicked prosper [21:7-17], and that, despite his own upright behavior, he has received evil instead of good [30:26]), all amount to much the same thing as the wicked say.

34:10-15. Repeating his summons to "men of reason" (v. 10*a*), Elihu introduces the first of his arguments in support of God's righteous governance. His initial statements are not so much arguments as assertions (vv. 10*b*-12). The oath formula in v. 10*b* ("far be it from . . . ") and the emphatic exclamation in v. 11*a* ("of a truth") establish a rhetorical stance that the NIV captures well in its rendering of v. 11. Elihu presents it as literally unthinkable that God could do evil or pervert justice. It is a logical contradiction. The grounds for Elihu's claims are articulated in vv. 13-15; yet their obliqueness requires the reader to work out the connection. When Elihu asks rhetorically who appointed God over the earth (v. 13), he draws attention to God's absolute sovereignty. God has no superiors, only creatures who depend on God for every breath they draw (vv. 14-15). Here Elihu echoes Job's similar assertion in 12:10 that in God's "hand is the life of every living thing/ and the breath of every human being" (NRSV). Whereas Job used this observation to introduce his complaint about God's mismanagement of the world, Elihu's words point to the question of motive. Why would one who

is absolutely sovereign do evil or pervert the right? Those are rather the actions of individuals who are insecure and have something to gain by doing evil.

34:16-20. What was only obliquely indicated in vv. 10-15 becomes explicit in the following argument. Elihu's call to hear is expressed in the singular in v. 16. Although he addresses Job directly in v. 33, here it is more likely that Elihu is addressing each member of the audience who "has understanding." Modern readers, skeptical and suspicious of official power, may be inclined to answer in the affirmative Elihu's rhetorical question, "Can one who hates justice govern?" Tyranny provides ample evidence. But that misses Eliphaz's subtle, philosophical point about the relationship between the character and action of God. Elihu has already established that God's authority over the world is freely chosen, neither derivative nor imposed. The two nuances of *mišpāṭ*, "governance" and "justice," assist Elihu in making his point. If God chooses to govern, it must be because it is in the nature of God to love justice. It would be self-contradictory for God to choose to do what God hates. Elihu makes the same point even more sharply in v. 17*b*. "Righteousness" (צדקה *ṣĕdāqâ*) and "wickedness" (רשע *rāšāʿ*) are logically contradictory terms. Given that God is not only the "righteous one" (צדיק *ṣadîq*) but also the "(all-)powerful one" (כביר *kabbîr*), it is logically contradictory that God would do evil.

Elihu substantiates his claims with illustrations of God's behavior toward human rulers, whom God judges according to the standards of righteousness and good governance (v. 18; the NRSV and the NIV follow the LXX; cf. the TNK). Divine judgment against unjust rulers is commonplace in prophetic literature (e.g., Isa 10:1-4; Jer 22; Amos 7:10-17) and in the historical books (e.g., 1 Kgs 15:1-5; 2 Kgs 16:1-4; 21:1-26). God's impartiality toward nobles and the poor (v. 19; cf. Deut 10:17) is also required by God of human judges (Deut 16:18-20).

The mysterious suddenness with which the powerful die and are swept away (v. 20) is taken by Elihu as evidence of God's judgment. Here, as elsewhere (see Overview of Job 33), similarities exist between Elihu's words and the stories in Daniel 1–6. The story of

Belshazzar (Daniel 5) illustrates sudden and mysterious divine judgment against a prideful king at the very height of his glory, one who is killed "in the very night" that judgment is decreed (Dan 5:30). Like the powerful one removed "without human hand" in Job 34:20, the statue symbolizing imperial rule in Dan 2:34 is shattered by a rock cut "without human hand" (cf. Dan 8:25).

34:21-30. Elihu's third argument addresses several charges raised by Job in 24:1-17. In 24:13-17, Job had described the way in which criminals take advantage of the dark to carry out their crimes, because "no eye will see me." Furthermore, Job had complained that the times of judgment are not seen by God's friends (24:1; see comm.). In his description of the misery of the destitute, Job had also observed that while the murdered cry out, God seems to notice nothing wrong (24:12). Elihu attempts to address each of these issues.

Using several of the same words that Job used in 24:13-17, Elihu insists that God's eyes *do* see human deeds and that even deep darkness provides no cover for evildoers (vv. 21-22). In v. 23, he responds to Job's complaint about times of judgment. There are various ways of understanding the grammar and text of v. 23. The translations of both the NRSV and the NIV can be defended, although the NIV requires a fairly tortuous understanding of the syntax, and the meaning of the NRSV is not entirely clear. The simplest reading is that suggested by Gordis, "It is not for man to set the times to go to God for judgment."[509] Elihu is also implicitly challenging Job's obsession with a legal hearing, although the focus here remains on the judgment of the wicked. Elihu's argument is that since God knows all that the wicked do, no investigation and no set time for judgment are needed. God simply acts suddenly and decisively to overthrow the mighty and put others in their place (vv. 24-27; cf. Dan 2:21). This overthrow of the wicked also serves as Elihu's evidence that the cry of the oppressed comes before God and is acted upon (vv. 28, 30). The NRSV cleverly interprets v. 30 as the completion of the sentence, with v. 29 as an

interjection, but the grammatical construction of the Hebrew makes this interpretation unlikely. Although not without its own problems, the NIV is to be preferred.

The conclusion that Elihu draws from his reflection on God's preferred way of dealing with oppressive rulers is twofold. First, God's silence cannot be judged (v. 29*a*; cf. v. 24), nor can God's seeming absence from human history be made transparent to human inquiry (v. 29*b*). At the same time, God's sovereignty is the warrant that the godless will not triumph (v. 30). The issues with which Elihu struggles are similar to those found in apocalyptic literature, although his solution is somewhat different. As in apocalyptic, Elihu tends to set the issue of theodicy in terms of kings and nations. God's sovereignty is a similarly important theme (cf. Dan 2:44; 4:34-35[31-32]). Both Elihu and apocalyptic texts conceive of God's power as sudden and mysterious, expressed in the dramatic overturning of established rulers (Dan 2:21; 8:8, 25). But whereas Elihu accepted the inability of humans to know the times of judgment, apocalyptic writers, appealing to mysterious divine revelation, came to believe that it was possible to know the plan of God (Dan 7:15-28) and even the times of judgment (Dan 9:24-27; 12:7-12) and so endure the dissonance produced by the presence of evil in a world where God is sovereign.

34:31-37. These verses are extremely difficult to interpret. By means of a modest emendation of v. 31, they can be read as Elihu's advice to Job, "But say instead to God, 'I have borne my punishment, I will offend no more.' "[510] Others suggest, with somewhat different emendations, that Elihu is sarcastically describing the kind of divine apology Job expects from God, "Should God say to you, 'I have erred, I will offend no more'?"[511] The NIV, however, proposes a translation that involves minimal emendation, yet makes good sense of the lines. In its interpretation, Elihu contrasts a properly repentant and teachable person (cf. 33:26-28) with the obdurate Job, who appears to Elihu to expect restoration even though he refuses to repent. (The verb translated "refuse" or "reject" [מאס *māʾas*] in

509. Gordis, *The Book of Job,* 390; cf. also Habel, *The Book of Job,* 474, 484; Guillaume, *Studies in the Book of Job* (Leiden: E. J. Brill, 1968) 120.

510. Gordis, *The Book of Job,* 393; similarly Habel, *The Book of Job,* 476.

511. Fohrer, *Das Buch Hiob,* 465; Wahl, *Der Gerechte Schoepfer,* 89-91.

v. 33 has no expressed object in the Hebrew text; the NIV supplies "to repent" according to its understanding of the passage.) The NIV translation of vv. 31-33 also allows for a smooth transition to the final verses in the chapter, which again call upon the "men of reason" to judge Job's words as ignorant and obtuse (vv. 34-35). This judgment anticipates Elihu's words at the conclusion of his next speech (35:16).

In v. 35, the author of the Elihu speeches appropriates the similar criticism of Job's words by God in 38:2. Whether God's objection is actually the same as Elihu's is a different question, but by creating an anticipatory echo of the divine words, the author of these chapters sets up what appears to be an endorsement of his insight. There is a similarly opportunistic quality to Elihu's wish that Job be "tested to the limit" (v. 36). That, after all, has been agreed to in the prologue (1:12; 2:6), although none of the original parties to the dialogue know it. Elihu's call for such testing, however, does not concern Job's character before disaster struck him, but the quality of his words in response to that calamity (v. 37).

REFLECTIONS

Elihu's speech provides an opportunity to reflect on the way in which rigidly dogmatic religion attempts to use rationalistic argument to avoid the discomforting claims of individual experience. Job, as Elihu represents him, speaks out of the immediacy of his experience. He knows himself to be innocent, yet experiences violence from God, and so concludes that God is acting unjustly toward him (vv. 4-6). From Elihu's point of view, Job's experience cannot be trusted as a reliable source of knowledge about God for the simple reason that it contradicts propositions about the nature of God that are part of accepted tradition ("it is unthinkable . . . that the Almighty would pervert justice," v. 12; cf. vv. 10, 17). In effect, Elihu argues deductively. Since God could not act inconsistently with God's nature, it is impossible that God could act unjustly. Therefore, Job must not know what he is talking about.

What is disturbing about the type of argument in which Elihu engages is not the use of rational argument itself, or even of deductive reasoning. The ability to reflect clearly and systematically about the nature of religious experience and the primary metaphors that speak of God is essential to theology. But Elihu attempts to use deductive arguments to exclude the very possibility that an individual's experience might put in question his or her propositions about God. In Elihu's hands, rational argument serves to defend a closed dogmatism.

One often encounters a kind of pseudo-rationalistic theology in fundamentalist churches, although it can appear in other religious traditions as well. Propositions are lined up and conclusions drawn to "prove" the various claims that the preacher or evangelist wishes to make. It does not matter that the logic of the arguments would generally not stand up to scrutiny. What is being offered in this type of religious ethos is the appearance of certainty. Even those who are not drawn to such religious cultures can recognize their appeal. It is difficult to live in a world that often seems to make no sense at all, and the desire for certainty is an understandable response to a disturbingly confusing world. The offer of absolute clarity and certainty is a strong part of the appeal of fundamentalism and other dogmatic approaches to faith. One can memorize the arguments and so have a ready answer for every doubting thought, whether it comes from others or from one's own heart.

The problem, of course, is that the alluring simplicity and certainty offered by dogmatic religion is often too rigid to stand up to the complexities of real life. People faced with tragedies may find themselves led to question the goodness of God. Or they may be caught in moral dilemmas, torn between the claims of conflicting values. A theology that rejects the legitimacy of such questioning leaves people without the resources to sustain faith, for they must either deny their own experience or risk rejection by their religious community. Not everyone has the courage of Job and is willing to endure the criticism that outspokenness in a dogmatic community entails. Some people hide their doubts, blaming themselves for a failure of faith, and so bear the double burden of the doubt itself and of the guilt for having been prey to doubt.

A mature and resiliant faith requires a willingness to let go of the need for absolute certainty. It requires the ability to trust, even when one does not know where questions may lead. Much as a human relationship develops in richness as persons become increasingly free to be honest with each other, the relationship that is faith in God draws strength from the ability to bring all experiences and all questions before God.

JOB 35:1-16, GOD DOES NOT ANSWER THE PRIDEFUL

COMMENTARY

In this address Elihu takes up two of Job's complaints and attempts to set them in a larger religious context: the complaint that no benefit accrues from refraining from sin (v. 3) and the complaint that God takes no notice of his case (v. 14). The body of the speech is enclosed by a rhetorical question at the beginning, which asks whether Job's evaluation of himself is correct (v. 2), and by a statement of judgment at the end, which declares Job's words to be empty and ignorant (v. 16). Elihu introduces the first issue with an alleged quotation of Job's words (v. 3) and an announcement of his intent to reply to them (v. 4). The substance of his argument appears in vv. 5-8. The second issue is structured in reverse fashion. Elihu begins to explain in general why the cries of some oppressed people go unanswered (vv. 9-12) and then relates the general theme to Job's particular case (v. 13), concluding with a quotation of Job's words (vv. 14-15). The summary judgment in v. 16 brings the speech to an end.

35:1-8. At the beginning of his last speech Elihu invited the "wise" to judge for themselves what was "right" (משפט *mišpāṭ*, 34:4), following that invitation with a citation of Job's words, "For Job says, 'I am in the right [צדקתי *ṣādaqtî*].'" Eliphaz now poses the same challenge to Job (v. 2), and the words of Job that he quotes are a variation of those in 34:4. The word צדק (*ṣādēq*) has both a general moral sense and a legal one (cf. 4:17; 9:2), so one might translate either

"I am more righteous than God" (cf. NIV mg) or "I am more in the right than God." Both nuances are relevant to Elihu's speech. Curiously, both the NRSV and the NIV soften the statement by eliminating the comparative force of the preposition מן (*min*), which can mean "more than." The stronger claim seems more in keeping with Elihu's representation of Job.

In v. 3, Elihu cites another alleged statement of Job, that there is neither advantage nor profit in refraining from sin. This statement is similar to the citation of Job's supposed words in 34:9. As noted there, Job has not said anything quite like this, although Elihu is confident that this is the implication of Job's general position. Although no verbal similarity exists, the theme is related to the question posed by the prologue, whether Job is pious only because there is an advantage in being so. Why Elihu should address his refutation not only to Job but also to "your friends with you" is not clear, since Eliphaz has already made an argument similar to the one Elihu will propose (22:2-3).

The heavens and the high clouds (v. 5), which in a pre-industrial age seemed untouchable by human activity, serve Elihu as a metaphor for the relationship between God and humans. Elihu organizes his argument systematically, considering first the effect of human sin (v. 6) and then the effect of human righteousness (v. 7) on God, concluding that human good and evil affect only other humans (v. 8). Job had used a similar argument ironically (7:20) to suggest that since his sins did not affect God, God should not act so obsessively and violently toward him. But Elihu is not much given to irony when talking about God.

The content of Elihu's refutation does not exactly match the alleged quotation from Job. Job had supposedly asked how it profited *him* to refrain from sin, and Elihu replies that Job can neither harm nor benefit *God* by his sin or by his righteousness. The difference between their two arguments, as Elihu would presumably see it, is that Job's thinking is self-centered, whereas his own is God-centered.

35:9-16. A new argument begins with v. 9. Elihu describes a situation like that Job described in 24:12, in which people in distress cry out and yet do not seem to be heard by God. Elihu explains this apparent anomaly. The people may "cry out," but they do not cry out *in prayer.* The words "where is God my creator" are not words of alienation but the traditionally sanctioned words of faithful appeal to God for deliverance. The same argument appears in Jer 2:5-6, where God rebukes the people for abandoning God and failing to say, "Where is Yahweh who brought us up out of Egypt?" Analogous to the way God is addressed in terms of saving deeds in Jer 2:6, Elihu represents the proper prayer as addressing God as the one "who gives strength in the night" (v. 10; cf. Exod 15:2). The word translated "strength" (זמרות *zĕmirôt*) has a homonym that means "songs." Either meaning is plausible here. It seems odd, however, that persons suffering from oppression would congratulate themselves that God has made them wiser than animals and birds (v. 11). A more plausible translation is "who teaches us *by means of* the animals and makes us wise *by means of* the birds of the air" (cf. NIV mg). Elihu is echoing Job's satiric invitation to "ask the animals, and they will teach you, or the birds of the air, and they will tell you . . . that the hand of Yahweh has done this" (12:7, author's trans.). Here, as in vv. 5-8, Elihu attempts to reclaim a traditional saying from

Job's ironic subversion. Elihu does believe that the hand of God is at work even when oppression seems to go unchecked (cf. 34:24-28). That is the wisdom that the pious learn from the animals.

In vv. 9-16, however, Elihu is concerned with those who do not address their cries to God in prayer. People who merely cry aloud receive no answer (v. 12*a*). Opinion is divided as to whether the phrase "because of the pride of evildoers" modifies "cry out" (so NIV) or "does not answer" (so NRSV). The word order of the Hebrew favors the NRSV. Although it might seem odd that Elihu would describe oppressed persons as themselves "evil," pride is the particular flaw to which he draws attention in his account of the person brought to the brink of death (33:17). A prideful person who does not turn to God in suffering is evil in Elihu's eyes.[512] He concludes his general description by characterizing the outcry not addressed to God as "empty" (v. 13).[513] That Job is the object of his description is fairly obvious, for Job has continually rejected the friends' advice to turn to God in prayer (5:8; 8:5; 11:13; 22:17) and has cast his own cries in terms of legal accusations (19:7). In v. 14, Elihu makes this point explicitly, casting his words in the form of an indirect quotation of Job, echoing the sentiments of Job expressed in 23:8-9. The NIV is probably correct in taking v. 15 as a continuation of Elihu's quotation, with "you say" in v. 14 governing both verses. Here, too, although the exact words are not Job's, they reflect his complaints in chaps. 21 and 24.

In the concluding v. 16, Elihu himself answers the question he posed to Job in v. 2 and declares Job's words to be empty and ignorant. The phrase "words without knowledge" is the same one God will use in 38:2, creating the impression that God is endorsing Elihu's judgment. It apparently does not occur to Elihu that he is afflicted by the sin of pride.

512. Rowley, *The Book of Job,* 226.
513. For an alternative translation and interpretation of this verse, see Gordis, *The Book of Job,* 402.

REFLECTIONS

There is no doubt that Job's speeches have produced considerable anxiety in the author of the Elihu speeches. One of the consequences of the anxiety that can arise in the course of religious debate is the tendency of those who feel threatened to become narrow and rigid, taking refuge in carefully controlled behaviors and words. Anything that does not fit one's model of proper religious values can be judged illegitimate and forced out. This tendency is evident in Elihu's response to Job. Job has refused to make use of the traditionally validated language of prayer, because his experience has made it impossible for him to use that language with integrity. That the only language he can now use in order to voice his outcry is structured largely by legal imagery does not mean that he is not faithful, as Elihu seems to suppose (vv. 14-16). Job's cries of outrage are a dark and anguished form of prayer, but one that Elihu cannot recognize (see Reflections on Job 7). Job's words, provoked by extreme suffering, are not without their own problems. Nevertheless, it is essential for Job to explore the alternative language that he creates, searching out its potential to deal more adequately with his experience. But because Job's radical departure from the language of tradition frightens Elihu, he hurries to declare it illegitimate and to suggest that God only hears cries when they are addressed in the traditionally approved form (vv. 12-13).

Elihu is on shakier ground than he might wish to acknowledge. The Bible as a whole does not make the distinction that Elihu tries to make. Although it assumes that people who cry out generally address their cries in prayer to God, it recognizes other types of expression as well. In the exodus story, for instance, it is said that "the Israelites groaned in their slavery and cried out, and their cry for help because of their slavery went up to God. God heard their groaning and he remembered his covenant with Abraham, with Isaac and with Jacob. So God looked on the Israelites and was concerned about them" (Exod 2:23*b*-35 NIV). The text leaves it quite uncertain whether the Israelites "pray" in the sense that Elihu would recognize or simply "groan" and "cry out." Even the words "for help" are not in the Hebrew text, so there is no indication that the Israelites' cry is specifically addressed to anyone at all. It may simply be a cry of anguish that cannot be contained. But the cry itself "goes up" to God and evokes a response, not because it is addressed in the proper form, but because the covenant people are in need.

The positions represented by Job and Elihu have echoes in many contemporary churches, where arguments about the "idolatry" of traditional religious language and the "heresy" of alternative religious language threaten to tear communities apart. Perhaps both sides of this often acrimonious debate might reflect on the confrontation of Job and Elihu. Job witnesses to the fact that experience may make it necessary to challenge traditional ways of speaking about God and to God. He also witnesses to the fact that searching for an alternative way of speaking is a groping, exploratory process, as new metaphors are tested for their possibilities. Driven by its own pressing need, such a search may produce new and valid religious insight, but it also has its own blindness. As the character of Job illustrates, it can be arrogant. Job is no role model for civil debate. However justified by the extremity of his own pain, his sarcasm and contemptuous dismissal of the friends' traditional language ignores much that remains powerful and valid in that tradition. Protest movements are inherently susceptible to the sin of smug superiority, because they are filled with the conviction of having perceived something to which others are blind. The protestors often do not realize that singleminded focus on one aspect of an issue may also make them blind to other important values embedded in the tradition they would so easily dismiss. Such an attitude undermines the possibility of community and of transformative dialogue.

Although a challenge like Job's may be disturbing and disruptive, a vibrant and healthy religious community is invigorated by the presence of a Joban voice, faithful in its protest, even if irritating in its manner of speaking. Elihu is potentially the more dangerous to faith, because he secures his own voice by silencing others. Although sincerely believing himself to serve God, Elihu arrogantly attempts to usurp God's role, declaring what language God finds acceptable. The danger that religious people like Elihu pose is that they will succeed in preserving the form but lose the substance of faith, standing guard over an empty shrine. If Elihu's were the last voice to answer Job, no doubt Job would turn away in utter alienation. Certainly many in the church would be relieved if all those who were unhappy with traditional language and practices would just go away. But complex problems of faith, practice, and belief are never resolved by recourse to a simplistic "love it or leave it" stance.

The book of Job recognizes that arguments sometimes reach an impasse. The voice from the whirlwind surprises us by undercutting the assumptions and arguments of all the parties, enabling a new vision that neither side could accomplish while stuck in the polarization of endless debate. Although the mechanism may not be quite so dramatic as in the book of Job, divine disclosure that has the power to transform understanding and reconcile opponents occurs more often than many people realize.

JOB 36:1–37:24, ELIHU DESCRIBES THE CHARACTER OF GOD

OVERVIEW

Elihu's final speech faces in two directions. In the first part (36:1-21), he remains concerned with correcting the views Job and his friends have advanced in the dialogues. The second part of the speech (36:22–37:24), however, anticipates the divine speeches. That chaps. 36–37 function as a conclusion is indicated by the fact that Elihu no longer explicitly quotes and refutes Job. Instead, in introducing the speech Elihu again commends his own words (36:1-4), as he did in his first address (32:6-22). In the first part of the body of the speech (36:5-15), Elihu reprises several of his themes: God's superiority, divine justice, God's redemptive concern for those who err, expressed through the disciplines of affliction. An admonition and warning to Job concludes the first part of the speech (36:16-21). A very different kind of discourse begins in 36:22. In this part of the speech, the author of the Elihu speeches attempts to shape the reader's understanding of the speeches from the whirlwind by drafting a poem that uses several of the motifs of chap. 38 but incorporates them into Elihu's own understanding of

God. Thus Elihu is positioned to stage manage the introduction of God. In 36:22-33, Elihu both introduces and summarizes the rest of his speech. The structure of this section is indicated by the threefold repetition of the introductory exclamation "behold" or "see" (הן hēn) in vv. 22, 26, and 30 (not clearly reflected in the NRSV and the NIV). The first part (36:22-25) praises the irreproachable greatness of God and exhorts Job to join in praise; the second (36:26-29) praises God as Lord of the rain, and the third (36:30-33) describes God's control of lightning. Elihu's personal exclamation in 37:1 marks a new section in which he first expounds the theme of lightning as the voice of God (37:1-5), followed by a celebration of the power of God manifested in winter storms (37:6-13). A series of rhetorical questions that imitate the style of the divine speeches serve as an admonition to Job (37:14-20), while a brief description of a theophany (37:21-24) provides the segue to God's appearance in the stormwind in the next chapter.

Job 36:1-21, God Redeems by Affliction

COMMENTARY

36:1-4. The beginning of Elihu's final speech differs from earlier ones in that no words of Job are cited (cf. 33:8-11; 34:5-6; 35:3). Instead, Elihu turns attention to his own speech, rhetorically appealing for patience for the rest of what he has to say about God (v. 2) and commending the soundness of his knowledge (vv. 3*a,* 4). Elihu also gives a succinct summary of the purpose of his speech: to ascribe righteousness to God (v. 3*b*; cf. 35:2*b*). The expression "perfect in knowledge" leads many to comment about Elihu's arrogance,[514] but in fairness to him the Hebrew word (תמים *tāmîm*), the same word used of Job's integrity, is merely a claim to "sound," "whole-some" knowledge.

36:5-15. Verse 5 introduces Elihu's first major argument concerning the character and acts of God. In this brief statement Elihu makes three claims, which echo what he has said in his previous speeches and anticipate what he will say in the remainder of this speech. First, Elihu stresses God's sovereign power through his twofold repetition of the word "mighty" (כביר *kabbîr*; cf. 34:17). Next he alludes to God's receptiveness (lit, "he does not despise"; the verb is without an object, which the NRSV and the NIV supply according to sense; cf. 33:26). Finally, he appeals to God's powerful mind (cf. 36:22).

Elihu sets up his argument more specifically by means of an axiom asserting God's just retribution to the wicked and the afflicted alike (v. 6). The common term of contrast for "the wicked" (רשע *rāšā'*) in wisdom writings is not "the afflicted" (עניים *ăniyyîm*) but "the righteous" (צדיק *ṣaddîq*), an expression Elihu uses in v. 7, apparently as a further designation of the afflicted (cf. Ps 14:6). In the psalms, however, and particularly in psalms of lament, the "wicked" and the "afflicted" are often used as contrasting types, the wicked preying on the poor (cf. Psalm 10).[515] Elihu appears to be influenced by the lament tradition, which he combines in his distinctive way with a concern for moral pedagogy.

In vv. 7-12, Elihu develops the theme of the afflicted and in vv. 13-14 that of the wicked. God's exaltation of the righteous (v. 7) is a familiar motif, present in Eliphaz's hymn in 5:11 and in thanksgiving psalms such as 1 Sam 2:8 and Ps 113:7-8. But Elihu's understanding of God's care for the afflicted righteous is more complex than that of the traditional thanksgiving psalm, since it also involves redemption by means of affliction. Complementing his description of illness as a means of moral redemption (33:19-22), Elihu mentions the social misery of imprisonment in fetters and ropes (v. 8). Although this language may be figurative, it is grounded in an all too familiar social reality (cf. 2 Kgs 25:7; 2 Chr 33:11; Nah 3:10). As in chap. 33, Elihu interprets such a time of affliction as an occasion for God to disclose to persons their sins and to provide an opportunity for repentance (vv. 9-10; cf. 2 Chr 33:10-17). Characteristically for Elihu, arrogance is the distinguishing feature of the sinner's wrongdoing (cf. 33:17). In an artful conclusion, Elihu contrasts the consequences of the person's fateful choice: "if he listens . . . if he does not listen . . . " (vv. 11-12). A word play not visible in translation but present in the Hebrew text enhances the contrast, as "serve" (עבד *'ābad*) is echoed by "perish" (עבר *'ābar*). The representation of the moral life as a decisive choice between two antithetical modes of being is common in Israelite thought, as in early Jewish and Christian writings (cf. Deut 30:15-20; Jer 21:8-9; Sir 15:14-17; *T. Asher* 1:3-9; Matt 7:12-14; *Didache* 1).

The reference to the one who chooses not to listen provides the transition to the case of the utterly godless (vv. 13-14; cf. v. 6*b*). Elihu's characterization of their anger and refusal to cry for help suggests the kind of pridefulness he finds so offensive. It may well be an indirect characterization of Job. Like those who refused to listen to God's word in affliction (v. 12), the fate of the godless is death, and an early death at that. Elihu parallels the term "youth" (נער *nō'ar*) with the word קדשים (*qĕdēšîm*), usually rendered

---

514. E.g., Good, *In Turns of Tempest,* 331.
515. D. Pleins, "Poor, Poverty," *ABD* 5:409-10.

"male temple prostitutes." Although little is known about this phenomenon, apparently both men and women were at times employed as temple prostitutes, their wages going to the temple treasury. The Deuteronomic tradition was violently opposed to this practice (Deut 23:17-18[18-19]; 2 Kgs 23:7).[516] Elihu concludes by restating his primary point concerning the redemptive use God makes of affliction (v. 15).

36:16-21. This text is extremely difficult and obscure, leading to significantly different translations. There are a few clues to its structure and meaning, however. Clearly, Elihu attempts to apply to Job's specific situation the general message he has articulated in vv. 5-15. This much is indicated by the introductory words "and also" in v. 16 and by the similar summary references to purposive affliction in vv. 15 and 21. The repetition of the two key words סות (*sût*, "woo," "allure," "entice") and צר (*ṣar*, "narrow straits," "distress") in v. 16 and vv. 18-19 suggest that Elihu structures his argument by contrasting what God has done for Job with the destructive dangers posed by anger (NRSV) or wealth (NIV). The images of spaciousness and abundance in v. 16 are typical images of salvation (cf. Pss 18:19[20]; 23:5; 31:8[9]). The NRSV and the NIV differ as to whether v. 17 describes objective conditions of judgment that have befallen Job (NIV)[517] or Job's own obsession with a legal resolution of his case and of all such instances of injustice (NRSV).[518] Although certainty is not

possible, the interpretation of the NRSV fits with Elihu's contrast between the proper language of prayer and the improper pursuit of a legal case in 35:14.

About all that is clear in vv. 18-19 is that Elihu describes the enticement of a dangerous alternative that will lead to distress rather than away from it. Although the majority of commentators follow the line of interpretation presupposed by the NIV,[519] it is not clear why Elihu would warn Job about the dangers of wealth. To be sure, the prologue had explored whether wealth as a divine "hedge" corrupted piety, but that has not been a concern of Elihu. Although not without its own grammatical difficulties, the translation of the NRSV is consistent with Elihu's themes.[520] The warning against "wrath" recalls the "anger" of the godless in v. 13. Similarly, the noun translated "scoffing" (ספק *sepeq*) is related to the verb Elihu uses to characterize Job in 34:37 ("He claps his hands [in mockery]"). The "great ransom" that might turn Job aside is the necessary acceptance of affliction and humble repentance that allows the mediating angel to say "I have found a ransom" (33:24). Verse 19 also refers to one of Elihu's themes, the destruction of sinners that takes place suddenly in the night (34:20-22).

The translation of v. 21*b* in the NRSV requires a very modest emendation (revocalizing the verb from active to passive) and is more in keeping with Elihu's themes than that of the NIV. Although the referent of "this" is rather vague, Elihu is the only character who points to the actual reason for Job's affliction: God's decision to allow Job's piety to be tested.

516. K. van der Toorn, "Prostitution (Cultic)," *ABD* 5:511-12.
517. Hartley, *The Book of Job*, 472.
518. Habel, *The Book of Job*, 495. Pope, *Job*, 270; and Gordis, *The Book of Job*, 416, following Tur-Sinai, *The Book of Job*, 499, redivide the consonants of the text to produce a different reading: "But you did not plead the cause of the poor, nor the suit of the orphan" (Gordis, *The Book of Job*, 416).

519. See Habel, *The Book of Job*, 498-99; Pope, *Job*, 271; and Wahl, *Der Gerechte Schoepfer*, 111, for the grammatical issues involved.
520. See also Fohrer, *Das Buch Hiob*, 477; de Wilde, *Das Buch Hiob*, 337-38.

Job 36:22–37:24, God Manifest in the Thunderstorm

COMMENTARY

36:22-25. In praising God as powerful and an incomparable teacher, Elihu brings together two traditional themes. The closest parallel to Elihu's words in vv. 22-23 is Isa 40:12-14. There, using the same type of

rhetorical questions, Second Isaiah praises God as the incomparable creator who needed no counselor (cf. Isa 40:14, "Whom did the LORD consult to enlighten him,/ and who taught him the right way?" [NIV]). Although

Elihu's point is similar in v. 23, he reaccents this motif by describing God not only as one who is not taught, but also as the supreme teacher (v. 22*b*). The theme of God as moral teacher is an important one for Elihu (33:14-22; 34:32; 35:11). In chaps. 33–35 he develops this theme in ways similar to the psalms (cf. Pss 25:8-14; 94:12). Although Elihu's description of storms and lightning mostly exalt God's power, he interprets God's presence in the storms as having a moral purpose (36:31-32; 37:13, 23-24), thus uniting the themes of God as Lord of creation and as moral teacher. Whether consciously or not, the author of the Elihu speeches appears to be remedying what must have seemed to him a defect in the divine speeches of chaps. 38–41: the lack of any apparent connection between God as creator and the moral dimensions of creation.

The form of Elihu's rhetorical questions in vv. 22*b*-23 presumes not only a negative answer but also the very absurdity of anything but a negative answer. Yet Job *has* in essence said to God, "You have done wrong" (v. 23*b* ; cf. 19:7; 24:12; 27:2). By characterizing such a charge as absurd and urging Job instead to speak the words of praise that all people sing (v. 24), Elihu attempts to silence Job's alienated voice and reintegrate him into the collective voice of universal praise. Elihu describes this communal praise as a response to *seeing* (v. 25), and in what follows Elihu attempts to provide such an experience of seeing through the highly visual quality of the poetic imagery. It may be that Elihu is attempting to anticipate (and take a measure of credit for) Job's confession of the decisive significance of "seeing" God (42:5).

36:26-29. Elihu introduces his celebration of the wonders of God with a statement of praise (v. 26) similar in form to v. 22. Here, however, the emphasis is not on God's greatness per se but on the inability of human understanding to grasp it (cf. 5:9; Eccl 8:17; Sir 43:27-33). Thus, like Bildad, he characterizes his own description as no more than a "whisper" of divine thunder (26:14).

The cycle of rain is the topic of vv. 27-29. As Wahl observes, Elihu's description uses less of the mythic language that characterizes the motif of rain in the divine speeches (cf.

38:22-30).[521] The precise mechanism Elihu describes is not entirely clear, however. Most translations assume that Elihu refers to the evaporation cycle in vv. 27-28. The NRSV retains the translation "mist" for אד ('ēd), even though it is now generally agreed that the word refers to the primordial underground reservoir from which rivers emerge (cf. Gen 2:5-6).[522] The image of the spreading clouds with their attendant thunder (v. 29) provides the transition to the next topic, God's control of lightning (vv. 30-33; note the repetition of "spread out," "scatter" [פרש *pāraś*] in vv. 29-30).

36:30-33. The imagery of v. 30*b* is somewhat obscure. The NRSV renders the Hebrew literally as "and covers the roots of the sea." Some translate it as *"un*cover the roots of the sea," either by emending the verb or by arguing that it means both "covers" and "uncovers," or that to cover something with light is to uncover it.[523] A modest emendation produces the reading "the roots of the sea are his throne."[524] Such imagery would be similar to that of Psalm 29, which celebrates the thundering of God's voice and speaks of God's being "enthroned over the flood" (Ps 29:10 NRSV). It is also possible that the verse simply presents a contrast between the illumination of God's pavilion in the heavens and the covered depths of the sea below.

For Elihu, appreciation of God's majesty reflected in the grandeur of storms is not the whole point. Storms also have purposes related to God's governance of the world. Although some argue that poetic parallelism requires the verb "nourish" in v. 31*a*,[525] there is no reason to reject the ordinary meaning "judges" (or "governs"). The thunder, lightning, clouds, and rain of storms are frequently associated with the activities of God the divine warrior (cf. Pss 18:7-15[8-16]; 97:1-9). Whereas v. 31*a* points forward to God's use of lightning as a weapon in judgment (v. 32), v. 31*b*, with its reference to food, points back to the rain of vv. 27-28 and the nurture of God (cf. the relation between water, God's providence, and food in Ps 104:10-16).

521. Wahl, *Der Gerechte Schoepfer,* 120.
522. Pope, *Job,* 273.
523. Gordis, *The Book of Job,* 422; Habel, *The Book of Job,* 499; Hartley, *The Book of Job,* 476.
524. Pope, *Job,* 267.
525. Pope, *Job,* 274.

Obscurity plagues the final verse of the chapter. The first half can be fairly literally translated "his roar announces him," referring to the approaching thunder. The second half of the verse reads "the cattle also [announce] the one who comes up." Although it is not impossible that the text refers to a presentiment of storms by cattle, the words can be revocalized to render a more likely meaning. Gordis suggests that originally the word for "storm" (עלעולה *ʿilʿôlâ*) was misread as "concerning the one who comes up" (על־עולה *ʿal-ʿôleh*) and that "[his] indignant wrath" (מקנה אף [from מקנא *miqnēh ʾap*) was misread as "the cattle also" (מקנה אף *miqneh ʾap*). Thus without changing the consonantal text one can read with Gordis: "His thunderclap proclaims His presence; His mighty wrath, the storm."[526] The emendation underlying the NRSV is similar in its interpretation of *miqneh ʾap*. It differs from Gordis in reading "concerning iniquity" (על־עולה *ʿal-ʿawlâ*).

37:1-5. Elihu develops the themes of lightning in these verses. A new section is marked first by his reference to his own emotional reaction to the dramatic scene he has just described (v. 1) and by his call to others to listen (v. 2). Here, even more explicitly, thunder is described as the voice of God in a manner reminiscent of Psalm 29. The function of this passage is sensuous, inviting the reader to "listen, listen" (v. 2). In v. 5*b*, Elihu returns to the theme he announced in 36:26, the inability of humans to comprehend God and God's works (cf. 5:9).

37:6-13. In this section, Elihu describes the particular qualities of winter storms (cf. Sir 43:13-20). Snow occurs occasionally in Israel, especially in the northern areas, but cold rain is the distinctive feature of winter weather (v. 6).[527] As so often, v. 7 is obscure. The key to understanding, however, is in its parallel with v. 8. Just as animals go into their dens to avoid the winter storms, so also people stay indoors. With two small emendations (reading the preposition בעד [*bĕʿad*] in place of the phrase ביד [*bĕyad*], "on the hand" and adding one letter (אנשים *ʾănāšîm* ["people"] instead of אנשי *ʾanšê* ["people of"] one can translate "he shuts in every person, so that

all people may know his work" (author's trans.).[528]

The image of humans and animals shut up tight in their dwellings is complemented by that of the cold stormwind emerging from its chamber (v. 9; cf. 38:22-24; Ps 135:7; Jer 10:13; 51:16; Sir 43:14). Elihu juxtaposes two different poetic images for the wind. One is of wind stored away and called out at God's command (v. 9); the other is of wind as the breath of God (v. 10 cf. Exod 14:21; 15:8, 10; Ps 18:15[16]; the closest parallel to Elihu's image is Ps 147:16-18). Returning to the two images that have governed his poem, Elihu speaks again of rain and lightning (v. 11). In vv. 12-13, he brings this section of the poem to a close with an observation about the moral purposes of such natural phenomena. The language of command and guidance (v. 12) is similar to that of the divine speeches (e.g., 38:10-12), although in Elihu's speech it is given a climactic prominence that quite alters its significance. Nowhere in the divine speeches is the moral intent of God's control of nature as pronounced as in Elihu's summary that God uses weather "for punishment or for acceptance or for love" (37:13, author's trans.; cf. *1 Enoch* 59:1). The interpretation of the phrase here translated "for acceptance" is contested. The Hebrew text reads "for his land" (cf. NRSV), but a geographical expression fits awkwardly between "punishment" and "love." The NIV attempts to join the phrases with the following words, but the translation eases over very difficult syntactical problems. It is possible that the middle phrase does not have to do with the word for "land" (ארץ *ʾereṣ*) but with the word for "pleasure" or "acceptance" (רצה *rāṣâ*). Thus the three terms could describe a range of divine purposes: punishment, acceptance, love.[529]

37:14-20. Elihu's direct summons to Job to "hear this" (v. 14) marks the final part of his speech (cf. 33:1, 31). The theme of general human inability to comprehend the ways of God is applied specifically to Job's case as a way of mocking his pretensions. Here, more explicitly than before, Elihu mimics the style of the divine speeches, with their series of rhetorical questions designed to contrast God's

526. Gordis, *The Book of Job*, 424.
527. Wahl, *Der Gerechte Schoepfer*, 122.

528. For similar translations, see Pope, *Job*, 281; Fohrer, *Das Buch Hiob*, 481.
529. Cf. Andersen, *Job*, 266.

power and wisdom with Job's ignorance and lack of control. By imitating the style Elihu also attempts to appropriate the authority of the divine speeches, as though he and God think and speak alike. The examples Elihu uses are largely those already addressed in his celebration of God as lord of the weather, although the reference to the cosmogonic act of stretching out the sky introduces a new element (v. 18; cf. Isa 40:22; Sir 43:12; for mirrors of bronze, see Exod 38:8). In contrast to God's control of all the earth's weather, Job is powerless to keep himself cool when the hot south wind casts a pall upon all activity (v. 17).

Elihu's sarcastic appeal to Job to "teach us what we should say to him" contrasts with both his designation of God as teacher (36:22) and his own attempts to instruct Job and the three friends. The "darkness" (v. 19*b*) that characterizes human ignorance contrasts with the brightness of God's appearance, which Elihu will describe in vv. 21-22. Elihu apparently mocks Job's eagerness to speak with God (9:35; 13:22; 23:4-5; 31:35-37) by rejecting with horror the notion that God should be informed that Elihu wished to speak with God, for that would be tantamount to a death wish (v. 20).

37:21-24. The final verses serve both to sum up Elihu's main points and to prepare the way for the theophany. The impossibility of looking upon the sun (אור *'ôr,* lit., "light") in a clear sky is implicitly compared with the impossibility of confronting God (v. 21; cf. Sir 43:1-5). In almost cinematic fashion Elihu invites the reader to imagine the brilliance of the sun, only to overlay that image with one of surpassing brilliance, the theophany of God appearing in golden splendor. Although much less elaborate, Elihu's description shares several features with the divine vision Ezekiel describes. In both instances the divine appearance comes "from the north," the

mythic home of the deity (Ezek 1:4; cf. Ps 48:2[3]; Isa 14:13). The appearance is characterized by movement ("coming"; cf. Ezek 1:4). Although "gold" is not ordinarily associated with theophanies, Ezekiel describes the radiance of the divine vision as like חשמל (*ḥašmal*), an enigmatic term often translated "electrum" (NIV, "glowing metal"). The "fearful majesty" surrounding God (v. 22*b*) is a frequent description of the numinous splendor of the divine presence (Ps 104:1-2; Hab 3:3-4). One feature of Ezekiel's description that is absent from Elihu's is that of the stormy wind (סערה *sĕʿārâ*), but that is precisely the element that will be mentioned in the narrative heading to the divine speeches in 38:1.

Elihu cannot conclude without an explicitly moral comment. As he has been at pains to argue throughout his speech, God's power is coordinate with justice and righteousness (v. 23). As is too often the case, the last verse is textually obscure. The first line is clear enough, and it draws a conclusion concerning human response: "therefore people revere him" (lit., "fear"). The parallel line should not be translated as the NRSV does, however, since "wise of heart" is a positive and not a pejorative designation.[530] Following the LXX, some take "all the wise of heart" as the subject and render "indeed, all the wise of heart see him."[531] But Andersen makes a more intriguing suggestion. The verb that means "regard" (ראה *rāʾâ*) is quite similar to that meaning "to fear" (ירא *yārēʾ*), and Andersen suggests that one repoint the verb and read "surely all wise of heart fear him." The use of the same verb in both lines of a verse is common in the poetry of Job. With such a reading, as Andersen observes, "we have come full circle to Job 28:28."[532]

530. Gordis, *The Book of Job,* 434.
531. E.g., Hartley, *The Book of Job,* 483.
532. Andersen, *Job,* 268.

REFLECTIONS

In the second part of his speech, Elihu uses a description of nature, specifically of the processes of weather, for two purposes: to instill a sense of wonder and to show how God's presence in the order of nature has a moral purposiveness that points to the moral character of God. In this way, Job's challenge to God's righteousness can be answered. Elihu's attempt to relate the realm of nature to the realm of moral order warrants a closer look. It is a persistent but quite perplexing issue that has preoccupied religious thinkers from ancient times until the present.

Elihu has a distinctive way of talking about the function of weather. The manipulation of rain and lightning, he says, is the way that God "judges the nations" (36:31 a). More specifically, he refers to the provision of food (36:32 b) and to God's commanding the lightning to strike its target (36:32). Later, Elihu says that God uses the clouds, loaded with moisture and filled with lightning, in order to punish or to show God's love (37:13). The thunder, as the voice of God, expresses God's anger (36:33 b). In Elihu's perception, nature is filled with specific divine intentionality. Weather is understood in instrumental terms, as the means by which God expresses emotions and judgments.

Elihu's perspective reflects a quite traditional notion. Exodus 14:21-22; 15:8-10 speak of God's intentional use of wind and water to achieve the rescue of the Israelites and the destruction of Pharaoh's army. In Judg 5:20-21 the stars and the rivers engage in battle with the Canaanite armies. Heat, drought, blight, and even mildew are instruments of God's punishment for covenant disobedience, according to Deut 28:22-24. A three-year long drought is announced by Elijah and ended dramatically as part of his struggle against Ahab and his support of the worship of Baal (1 Kings 17–18). The control of rain as warning and punishment, along with the use of crop blight and devouring locusts, is described vividly by Amos (Amos 4:7-9). Although the counter observation that the rain falls upon the just and the unjust also appears (Matt 5:45), the image of weather as a direct instrument of God's judgment is the prevalent one.

This way of representing the forces of nature is, of course, part of a pre-scientific understanding of the natural world. One occasionally still hears these views. When earthquakes or extraordinary floods devastate an area or prolonged drought causes famine, there are always those who will identify them as divine judgments, even though it is difficult to see why the residents of Missouri or of Bangladesh are more culpable than the rest of the human race. These arguments are less and less common, however, in part because of increasing knowledge about how natural processes work and in part because of changing notions about God's relationship with the world. One can, of course, continue to use the old language in an extended sense, talking about the judgment of earthquakes on the folly of humans who persist in building rigid buildings on known fault lines, or about devastating floods as judgment against deforestation. As valid as these observations may be on their own terms, this is not what Elihu has in mind when he talks about divine judgment exercised through rain, storm, and lightning.

It is tempting simply to declare Elihu's language out of date and no longer useful. As post-Enlightenment people, moderns tend to draw a sharp distinction between the natural order and the moral order. In certain circles any comment about the moral sense of nature suffices to bring on the criticism that one is talking nonsense. But even if one cannot (and would not want to) speak like Elihu, with his image of God hurling lightning bolts at unsuspecting sinners, the larger question of whether one can speak of a relationship between the order of nature and the moral order is an extremely important one. The ancient religious perception that a relationship exists should not be facilely dismissed.

Part of the problem with Elihu's way of talking is that he has a very restricted, even impoverished sense of the moral. For him, the justice of God visible in the natural order can only be understood in terms of intentional acts of reward and punishment. The role of nature in disclosing the character of God as moral "teacher" (36:22) is to communicate these specific judgments. This narrow view must be abandoned as false. Lightning may be attracted to metal, but it is not attracted to evil.

There are other ways of thinking about the relationship between the natural order and the moral order, however. As was suggested in the Reflections on Job 21, the place to start is not with the question of retribution but with the question of value. What gives value to a being, and so makes it a proper object of moral concern, is the status of that being as God's creation. The goodness of a thing—the earth, the seas, the plants, the animals, and human beings—is established, not by means of a utilitarian calculation of worth, but absolutely by virtue of being a creature of God (cf. Genesis 1). When a being has intrinsic value, it must be treated with respect. Thus the moral obligation to do justice is indeed part of the structure of creation.

Elihu touches on another aspect of the moral sense of nature when he draws attention to seasonality in the way animals and humans alike withdraw to their shelters during cold and rainy winter. Contemplation of nature leads inevitably to the perception of the order it embodies: the alternation of night and day, of seasons, of activity and rest, of birth and death. These are not random or discordant orders but coordinate ones that nurture life. There is a rightness in them, what in Hebrew could be called *ṣĕdāqâ*, a rightness that is disturbed only at a terrible price. Human beings are part of this order of rightness. Our bodies are attuned to the rhythms of the physical order of being. But humans are not simply like other creatures who are attuned to the natural order of rightness by instinct. For humans, the understanding and the will are involved in responding to the order of rightness in creation and extending it to the order of rightness in social community. As the wisdom poem cited in Ecclesiastes puts it, "For everything there is a season, and a time for every matter under heaven" (Eccl 3:1 NRSV). Taking that insight further, a modern philosopher has said, "the glory of being human is the ability to recognize the pattern of rightness and to honor it as a moral law. The horror of being human is the ability to violate that rightness, living out of season—doing violence to the other, perverting the most sacred human relationships, devastating the world in greed, overriding its rhythm, not in the name of necessity and charity, but in the compulsion of coveting."[533]

Elihu wants to believe that the horror of being human is closely circumscribed by a God who pours out grain for proper behavior and delivers electric shocks for improper behavior (36:31-32). He wants to believe that the world operates as a giant "Skinner box," such as those used to induce learning in laboratory rats. The world is not like that, of course. Human beings do, by and large, "love righteousness," as the wisdom tradition would put it. A sense of peace and joy comes from experiencing life in harmony. One who has known it yearns for it and seeks to embody it. But if that is the case, why do human individuals and communities so often act in disorder and in violation of the order of rightness? Israel's wisdom tradition sometimes spoke of an unruly will or of undisciplined appetites as destructive forces, but for the most part the wisdom tradition regards the problem as a failure of understanding. "The evil do not understand justice,/ but those who seek the LORD understand it completely" (Prov 28:5 NRSV). "A ruler who lacks understanding is a cruel oppressor" (Prov 28:16a NRSV). "The righteous know the rights of the poor;/ the wicked have no such understanding" (Prov 29:7 NRSV). For the wisdom tradition, to *know* the good was to do the good. One who had truly understood the order of creation would embody its order of rightness in the moral will. Thus the contemplation of nature is no irrelevancy or merely the source of casual illustrations but the essential place in which moral understanding is grounded.

Elihu is right in intuiting that God's speaking to Job in terms of creation and the orders of nature had something to do with answering Job's questions about the moral order of the world. But Elihu seriously misunderstands the import of God's speech from the storm.

533. Kohak, *The Embers and the Stars*, 84.

JOB 38:1–42:6

GOD'S SPEECHES FROM THE WHIRLWIND AND JOB'S REPLIES

OVERVIEW

There is no more dramatic moment in the book of Job than that signaled by the words "then [Yahweh] answered Job out of the whirlwind" (38:1). Job has both sought and dreaded a confrontation with God (9:14-20, 32-35; 13:3, 15-24; 23:3-7, 15-17; 31:35-37). For the reader, too, this is a moment of high anticipation. Job's words have exposed the inadequacies of the traditional "consolations of religion" articulated by the friends. His characterization of God as unjust, capricious, and savagely violent has cast doubt on the very basis for religious trust. Job has refused, however, to abandon completely his belief that God will ultimately turn out to be a God of justice who acknowledges Job's claim of right. He has initiated a way of speaking about his relationship with God based on a legal metaphor and developed by means of reflection on his own moral identity as a person of honor. The presence of the Elihu speeches, which attempt to reinterpret Job's situation along other lines, merely adds to a sense of frustration. Job has so dominated the dialogue that no other way of talking seems credible. Consequently, expectations for what God will say are shaped by the deep investment that both Job and the reader have in the assumptions and moral claims embedded in Job's way of perceiving the issues.

God's answer comes as a complete overturning of these expectations and a frustration of the desire for an explicit reply to Job's own words. That Job is rebuked and confronted with his limits is clear (38:2; 40:2, 8-14). But the bulk of what God has to say seems to concern cosmology, meteorology, and zoology, rather than the specific issues of justice Job had raised. Not surprisingly, readers' reactions vary considerably. Some may be angry and disappointed; others, intrigued. It is generally recognized that God's frustration of expectations is strategic. The very obliqueness of the speeches is part of the way they function as an answer. Having recognized that, most commentators develop interpretations that incorporate the disorienting quality of the divine speeches into an interpretation of the way by which the speeches serve to reorient Job. Yet interpreters come to strikingly different conclusions about the meaning of the divine speeches and thus the nature of that reorientation.[534]

These differences are not necessarily the product of good vs. bad exegesis. Instead, they point to the way in which certain irreducible ambiguities embedded in the divine speeches legitimately permit more than one interpretation of their meaning and significance. The most important ambiguity is the oblique relationship of the divine speeches to Job's complaints, since neither God nor the narrator ever says explicitly how the divine speeches pertain to Job's quite different questions. But there are others. The tone of the speeches, for example, could be interpreted as one of dominating power, playful mockery, or slightly exasperated instruction. The richly visual quality of the speeches also contributes to the surplus of meaning, since visual imagery tends to be more polyvalent than conceptual language, more evocative and saturated with subtle emotional dimensions that resist reduction to simple propositions. Most important, in the course of the speeches God draws upon language and imagery from many different discourses: wisdom discourse,

---

534. See, for example, the side-by-side interpretations of "God the sage" (N. Habel) and "God the victor" (T. Mettinger) in *The Voice from the Whirlwind*, ed. L. G. Perdue and W. Clark Gilpin (Nashville: Abingdon, 1992) 21-49.

mythic discourses of creation and of the divine warrior, legal discourse, the discourse of honor and shame, royal discourse, etc. As each type of language is invoked, the values, meanings, and images of God connected with it are evoked. Yet the various ways of talking do not all fit together smoothly; indeed, they may not be entirely compatible. Many of the different interpretations arise as readers make one of these discourses the interpretive key to the divine speeches as a whole, muting or repressing the significance of the other discourses.

This teasing ability of the divine speeches to evade a single definitive interpretation is not mere evasion. Like the juxtaposition of different styles, genres, and perspectives in the structure of the book as a whole, the elusiveness of the divine speeches requires the reader to assume a more active role in making meaning than does a text in which the "message" is simple and transparent. Since no single interpretation can adequately incorporate all elements of the text, every interpretation remains to a degree unsatisfactory and unstable, as what it has left out demands to be taken into account. The interpretation of the divine speeches given here is only one possibility. It should serve primarily as a stimulus to the reader's own wrestling with the evocative but elusive divine disclosure.

Not all is puzzlement. The outline of the divine speeches is quite clear.[535] Each of the two speeches (38:1–39:30; 40:1–41:34[26]) begins with an identical narrative introduction (38:1; 40:6). Challenges to Job follow (38:2-3; 40:7-14), each of which contains the identical demand for Job to gird up his loins and to answer God's questions (38:3; 40:7). These challenges articulate important themes that the body of the speeches are designed to address. In the first speech, the theme is divine "counsel" or "plan" (עצה 'ēṣâ; 38:2); in the second it is משפט (mišpāṭ, 40:7), a word that may have legal connotations ("judgment," "justice," "right") or administrative ones ("governance" or "sovereignty").[536] The body of the speech follows (38:4–39:30; 40:15–41:34[26]). Each speech divides into two main parts, according to its content. In the first speech, God talks first about cosmological and meteorological phenomena (38:4-38), then about five pairs of animals (38:39–39:30). The second speech concerns a single pair of animals, Behemoth (40:15-24) and Leviathan (41:1-34[40:25–41:26]). After each speech Job responds. Following the first speech, God specifically asks for a response (40:1-2), and Job replies by declining to speak (40:3-5). Following the second speech, Job replies without a specific divine request (42:1-6).

In terms of both form and function the divine speeches are best understood as disputations. Like many of the speeches of Job and his friends, they begin with challenges and satirical characterizations of the inadequacies of the opponent's speech and ability. The rhetorical questions and imperatives, along with the descriptive passages, are typical devices of disputations. Although the divine speeches do not address the issues Job raised in the terms in which Job and the friends argued, they are designed to change Job's mind and to cause him to withdraw his charges, which in fact happens. With respect to form and function the closest parallel to the divine speeches is found in the disputation speech of Isa 40:12-31. As Isa 40:27-31 shows, that disputation is intended to refute the complaint of the people that " 'My way is hidden from [Yahweh];/ and my right is disregarded by my God' " (Isa 40:27 NRSV). In order to do this, the prophet uses many of the same rhetorical devices one finds in Job 38–41: rhetorical questions, imperatives, and descriptive passages that challenge the inadequate perception of the people and assert God's sovereignty, primarily through images of God as creator.[537]

Disputations often incorporate and make allusion to other genres as a means of shaping their own arguments. The genre upon which the disputation in Job 38–41 primarily draws is the hymn of God the creator, especially as it is represented in Psalm 104. Both the similarities and the differences in the way motifs are presented in that psalm are important for understanding the divine speeches. The sequence of topics is generally similar between the two compositions, with

535. Cf. V. Kubina, *Die Gottesreden im Buche Hiob*, FThSt (Freiburg: Herder, 1979) 121.

536. S. Scholnick, "The Meaning of Mishpat in the Book of Job," *JBL* 101 (1982) 521-29.

537. Cf. Kubina, *Die Gottesreden im Buche Hiob*, 131-42; H. Rowold, "Yahweh's Challenge to Rival: The Form and Function of the Yahweh-Speech in Job 38–39," *CBQ* 47 (1985) 207-9.

the description of the foundation of cosmic structures (Ps 104:1-9; cf. Job 38:4-38) preceding the account of care for the animals (Ps 104:10-23; cf. Job 38:39–39:30). The final descriptive passage of the psalm, marked as a separate section by the introductory word of praise, concerns the sea creatures, Leviathan in particular (Ps 104:24-26; cf. Job 41:1-35[40:25–41:26]). There are also several points of similarity in details. The long list of particular animals in the psalm (wild ass, stork, mountain goat, rock badger, lion, Leviathan) is unusual in a hymn, and four of the six also occur in the divine speeches in Job. The motif of lions seeking food from God is unique to Psalm 104 and Job 38. Moreover, the function of the sun in setting a limit to the predation of the lions is analogous to the function of dawn setting a limit to the activity of the wicked in Job 38:12-15. There are, of course, many differences between the two compositions, but two particular ones suggest the way in which the Job poet is intentionally transgressing the motifs of the psalm. First, the harmonious alternation between descriptions of animals and humans in Psalm 104 contrasts with the utter absence of reference to humans in the divine speeches. Second, the peaceful image of Leviathan playing in the sea where ships sail contrasts with the prolonged description of Leviathan as a creature of terror in Job 41. The use the divine speeches make of this tradition of creation hymns is a complex but essential part of the way they construct their meaning.

As helpful as similarities with other texts and genres are, the most important clue to the way the divine speeches attempt to change Job's perception is found in the sequence of themes and images in the speeches themselves. The first part of the first speech (38:4-38), which concerns the structures of creation, makes use of images of boundary, path, way, and place to create the sense of a secure and well-ordered cosmos. The second part of that speech, with its focus on the five pairs of animals (38:39–39:30), invokes themes of providential care, especially through its images of food, birth, and freedom. But the animals chosen as examples almost all belong to the hostile and alien realm of the wild, lying outside the boundaries of cultivated land. Thus the animals evoke emotions of ambivalence, if not threat. When Job's answer to the first divine speech proves equivocal and unsatisfactory, God uses an extended description of a single pair of animals as the sole subject of the second speech. What was subtly present in the previous descriptions comes to the fore here. Behemoth and Leviathan are not ordinary animals but legendary creatures with mythic overtones. Leviathan in particular is a creature of utter terror whose associations with primeval chaos make it the ultimate symbol of the alien and threatening other. Leviathan is at the heart of God's answer to Job, and Job gives his definitive reply immediately following the account of Leviathan.

As this brief summary suggests, the divine speeches move Job, imaginatively, from places of secure boundaries to places where boundaries are threatened. In narrative sequence, they run counter to the traditional mythic schema in which the creator god's defeat of the chaos monster precedes the creation of the structures of the cosmos (as in the Enuma Elish; cf. Ps 74:12-17; Isa 51:9-11).[538] An element of "uncreation" takes place in the experience provided by means of the divine speeches, as Job is led to a sustained and intimate encounter with the symbol of the chaotic.

538. *ANET*, 66-68.

JOB 38:1–40:5, UNDERSTANDING THE DIVINE PLAN IN THE WORLD

OVERVIEW

One does not envy the Job poet the task of writing the speech from the whirlwind. The literary and dramatic problems are nearly as daunting as the theological ones. In a book already flooded with words, how does one make space for God's words? How is it possible to imagine God's speech so that the divine words engage what has gone before without sounding merely like one of the previous characters? In no other speech are rhetorical issues so closely related to the meaning and function of the speech itself.

Several features give the first divine speech its distinctive quality. First is the unrelenting use of rhetorical questions: "Who?" "Where?" "How?" "What . . . can you . . . have you . . . do you know . . . ?" These questions focus attention in three directions: Job, God, and creation itself. Second is the intensely visual quality of the divine speech. Other speakers have used striking images, but only incidentally. Here pictorial imagery is primary. Third is the highly structured form of the divine speech, which sets it apart from the speeches of the other characters. Following the narrative introduction (38:1) and the

challenge to Job (38:2-3), the first part of the divine speech concerns itself with cosmology and meteorology: the structuring of the earth (38:4-7); the control of the sea (38:8-11); the functions of the dawn (38:12-15); the place of the abysses of sea and death (38:16-18); the dwellings of light and darkness (38:19-21); the storehouses of snow, hail, lightning, and wind (38:22-24); the course of rain for the desert (38:25-27); the origin of rain, dew, ice, and frost (38:28-30); the movement of constellations (38:31-33); the control of clouds and rain (38:34-38). After cosmology and meteorology come the five pairs of animals: (1) the lions and ravens (38:39-41); (2) the mountain goats and deer (39:1-4); (3) the onager and wild ox (39:5-12); (4) the ostrich and the war horse (39:13-25); (5) the hawk and the vulture (39:26-30). What unifies form and content is the theme announced in the challenge to Job: the "design" of God (עצה *'ēṣâ*).

Job 38:1-38, The Cosmic Structures

COMMENTARY

38:1. A storm often accompanies a divine appearance in biblical tradition (Pss 18:7-15[8-16]; 50:3; 68:8[9]; Ezek 1:4; Nah 1:3; Zech 9:14). The particular term used here, סערה (*sĕ'ārâ*), can refer specifically to a whirlwind (2 Kgs 2:11), although in other instances it seems to refer more generally to a violent storm (e.g., Ps 107:29; Ezek 13:11, 13). The same term is used to describe the theophany in Ezek 1:4.

More difficult to determine is the significance of the use of the divine name Yahweh in this verse. Although the name "Yahweh" is associated with theophanies elsewhere in the Bible,[539] the distribution of divine names within the book of Job itself is more directly pertinent. The name "Yahweh" otherwise occurs only in the prose narration (1:1–2:13; 42:7-17).[540] In the dialogues only the names "El," "Eloah," "Elohim," and "Shaddai" appear. The use of the name "Yahweh" in

the headings to the divine speeches thus reasserts the voice of the narrator as the one who frames the entire book.

The reappearance of this name from the narrative world of the prose tale provides an occasion for thinking about the issue that occasioned the events of the story. The *satan* had alleged that Job's respect for God was based only on the "hedge" of blessing and that, if everything were lost, Job would curse God to God's face. Now there is to be a face to face encounter, and the decisive word has yet to be spoken. But the dialogues have changed the nature of what is at stake. No longer is the question simply whether unconditional piety exists; one needs to know how such a stance could be meaningful. From the perspective of Job, who makes justice the central value, the notion of radically unconditional piety is at best meaningless and at worst monstrous, for it would appear to sanction divine arbitrariness and cruelty. The task God faces is to articulate a theological vision that will make such a stance not only meaningful but also profound. It is a high-stakes gamble.

---

539. Hartley, *The Book of Job*, 491.
540. The occurrence of "Yahweh" in 12:9 is either a scribal error or occurs because the verse contains the quotation of a popular proverb.

38:2-3. The very first words of God's speech ("Who is this . . . ?") set both tone and theme. The question raises the issue of Job's standing to challenge God's counsel. It is not Job's humanity per se that disqualifies his challenge, but that he speaks "words without knowledge." One might object that God is being evasive in not replying to Job's explicit demand that God "tell me what charges you have against me" (10:2*b*, author's trans.), and declare "how many wrongs and sins have I committed? Show me my offense and my sin" (13:23, author's trans.). The problem, however, is that those demands make sense only within the context of a certain paradigm of understanding, a paradigm that God is contesting. God makes an ironic allusion to Job's demands and the legal context in which he had placed them by echoing Job's words from 13:22, "Then call, and I will answer;/ or let me speak, and you reply" (NRSV). That Job's challenge to God is accepted, although not in the way Job anticipated, is reflected in God's command that Job gird his loins, a preparation for action (Jer 1:17) that may refer to tucking the ends of one's robe into a belt, so that movement will be unimpeded (Exod 12:11; 1 Kgs 18:46). In this case, Job will need unimpeded intellectual agility.

The use of the vocabulary of "counsel" and "knowledge" in v. 2 sets the divine speeches within the context of wisdom traditions.[541] The theological assumptions and presuppositions of wisdom tradition are particularly evident in the importance the divine speeches place on insight into the primordial structures of creation as a means of understanding God and the world (cf. Job 28; Proverb 8; Sirach 24).

The translation of עצה (*'ēṣâ*) as "counsel" is less than clear. The word refers to careful thinking and planning and to the capacity to do such planning.[542] "Plan" or "design" is better, so long as those words are understood in the active sense. In chap. 12, Job had mocked the "wisdom and power . . . counsel and understanding" of God, as Job described an irrational world of destructive forces,

confusion, and the contemptuous undermining of human attempts to construct wise social order (12:13-25). What God's design "brought to light," Job contended, was deep darkness, "the shadow of death" (12:22). It is appropriate that God chooses this ground on which to engage Job, for all of Job's specific accusations are ultimately rooted in his challenge to God's design.

38:4-7. The rhetorical questions of the divine speech manage to do several things at once. While they confront Job with the limits of his knowledge and capacity, and contrast it with the wisdom and resourcefulness of God, they also create vivid pictorial images of the cosmos. In 38:4-7, the earth is imaged as a great building that God, as architect and builder, constructs. The general notion is quite traditional (cf. Pss 24:2; 89:11[12]; 102:25[26]; 104:5; Prov 3:19; Isa 48:13; 51:13; Zech 12:1), although nowhere else is it developed with so many concrete details. The combination of planning activities (making measurements, stretching out the line) and the accomplishment of structurally crucial physical activities (sinking footings, laying foundations) makes the image a particularly apt illustration of divine *'ēṣâ* as planning and design.[543] The concluding image of the morning stars and heavenly beings singing and shouting for joy is not simply a festive grace note but serves to interpret the creation of the earth as the building of God's temple (cf. Isa 66:1-2*a*). The laying of a temple's foundations and the placing of the capstone were liturgical occasions when musicians and singers praised God, and the people joined in shouts of blessing and praise (Ezra 3:10-11; Zech 4:7; cf. 2 Chr 5:11-14).[544] The motif may be more distantly echoed in personified wisdom's joyful response to God's creation of the cosmos (Prov 8:30-31).

38:8-11. The sea, the traditional symbol of primordial chaos, is a frequent image in creation accounts. In mythic tradition, the sea is often represented as a hostile force, subdued in battle by the creator god (e.g.,

---

541. Cf. Habel, "In Defense of God the Sage," 21-38.

542. Fox, "Words for Wisdom," 160. The term *'ēṣâ* does not necessarily have connotations of God's action *in history*, as Lévêque, *Job et son Dieu*, 511, has argued. Attempts to load this term with connotations of historical providence (e.g., Kubina, *Die Gottesreden im Buche Hiob*, 122-23; Gutiérrez, *On Job*, 69) run counter to the content of the divine speeches.

543. Various passages in other contexts refer to details of building, including the use of measuring and plumb lines (2 Kgs 21:13; Isa 34:11; Jer 31:39; Zech 1:16), foundation or capstones (Ps 118:22; Isa 28:16; Jer 51:26), and footings for pillars (Exod 26:19; Cant 5:15).

544. Cf. also the celebration that accompanies the building of Babylon as the gods' sanctuary in Enuma Elish (*ANET*, 68-72) and the building of Baal's house/temple in the Baal cycle (*ANET*, 134).

Ps 74:13-14; 89:9-13[10-14]; Isa 51:9-10).[545] A somewhat different tradition speaks of the establishment of boundaries for the sea in the process of creation (Ps 104:5-9; Prov 8:29; Jer 5:22). The waves of the sea, which restlessly lap at the shore and which, during storms, reach aggressively across the boundary separating land from sea, suggest a force that would break out if it were not contained. For these reasons the sea became a potent image by which to describe personal or national distress that threatened to overwhelm and from which only God could rescue (Pss 18:4-10[5-20]; 77:16-20[17-21]; 144:7; Isa 17:12-14).

The divine speeches both adapt and transform these traditions. The language of boundaries, bars, and doors as well as of verbal command (38:10-11) is all in keeping with the tradition of restricting the aggressive sea to its appointed place. Here that aggressiveness is depicted in the image of "proud waves," anticipating the theme of pride, which is of such importance in the second divine speech. In striking contrast to the motif of battle between God and the sea, however, God here appears as the midwife who births the sea and wraps it in the swaddling bands of cloud and darkness. Whether this image is a creation of the Job poet or the appropriation of an otherwise unknown tradition cannot be determined. The metaphorical connections between this image of birthing and the more traditional language can be traced, however. Birth is an event in which an irrepressible force breaks through containment and transgresses boundaries. Specifically, the breaking through of water from the womb signals the onset of the process. Swaddling bands in which babies were wrapped were restraints to prevent the baby's arms and legs from moving about and were believed to calm the child. Thus both the aggressive force of the sea and the restraints placed upon it are taken up into this new image. The image of the baby in turn transforms the emotional resonance of the image of the sea. Far from being a hostile, alien power it is associated with the vigor of new life, and the restraints placed upon it are associated with nurture and protection. In Job 38:8-11, this new imagery does not displace the more traditional language; rather, it stands side by side with it. The chaotic waters

have a place in God's design of the cosmos, yet one that is clearly circumscribed. They are the object not only of divine restriction but also of divine care.

38:12-15. Ironic echoes of Job's opening speech occur in God's words. God asks rhetorically if Job has ever commanded the morning and shown dawn its place (38:12). Job had in fact attempted to command dawn through a curse (3:9). In God's design the coming of the light of dawn has a different task. The imagery suggests that the darkness of the earth at night is like the cloak with which sleepers cover themselves. The term "skirts" (כנפות *kĕnāpôt*) is a standard figure of speech for the edges of the earth (37:3; Isa 11:12 ; 24:16; cf. its literal use in Ruth 3:9). For dawn to take the "skirts" of the earth and shake the wicked out of them (38:13) implicitly likens the wicked to vermin, which are attracted to the warmth and darkness of such a cover.[546]

It is easy for modern readers to be amused at the image of shaking out the cosmic bedbugs and to miss the more profound dimensions of this section. In the ancient Near East, each morning was considered a recapitulation of creation, or perhaps better, each morning was part of the continuing work of creation.[547] In a pair of striking images, the poet describes the power of dawn's light to "create" the earth by bringing it from undifferentiated formlessness into the order that is creation (cf. Genesis 1). Just as precise images are stamped onto clay by a seal, so also light brings forth the distinct shapes of the earth's features. Similarly, colors, which merge into indistinguishable gray in darkness, are brought back into being by light.[548]

The final verse returns to the topic of the wicked. To say that the coming of dawn deprives the wicked of their "light" is to draw on the same motif that Job used in 24:13-17, that for criminals day and night are inverted, and "deep darkness is morning to all of

---

545. See also Enuma Elish IV (*ANET,* 66-67).

546. See, e.g., the Egyptian Hymn to the Aton (*ANET,* 370). In Ps 104:19-23, night is the time when lions prowl, seeking prey, and humans sleep. When dawn comes, the lions sleep, and humans go out to work. Symbolically, lions represent danger and are sometimes used as symbols of the wicked (cf. 4:10-11).
547. B. Janowski, *Rettungsgewissheit und Epiphanie des Heils,* WMANT 59, Bd. I, 1989, 183-84.
548. Since the expression "they stand forth like a garment" makes little sense, most emend the Hebrew verb יצב (*yāṣab*) to the similar verb צבע (*ṣābāʿ,* "to dye"; so NRSV). See Dhorme, *A Commentary on the Book of Job,* 581; Pope, *Job,* 295.

them" (24:17*a* NRSV). In Job's mouth, the words were a criticism of God's order. Here, however, containment of the violence of the wicked is set in the context of the work of creation, which is renewed each day. Like the hedging in of the sea with bars and doors, the light of day contains and limits but does not eliminate the wicked from the world.

38:16-21. In these sections, God questions Job about his experience of the four dimensions of the world: the great deep (38:16), the underworld (38:17), the expanse of the earth (38:18), and the heavens (38:19-21; cf. 11:7-9; 28:14, 22). The vocabulary evokes a journey: enter, walk, see, gaze upon; recesses, gates, way, place, territory, paths. One could compare the epic journey of the Mesopotamian hero Gilgamesh, who sought to evade the inevitability of death. In his journey he roamed the steppe, came to the mountains that are the gates of sunrise and sunset, ventured through the dark underworld passage where the sun travels at night, and even crossed the waters of death.[549] For this he was called "he who saw everything to the ends of the land, who all things experienced, considered all."[550] As God's rhetorical question makes clear, Job cannot claim such a heroic journey, although in a certain way the divine speeches with their vivid descriptive imagery evoke the sense of a virtual journey to these hidden places. The outcome for Job will be like that for Gilgamesh: a recognition of the necessity to renounce a deeply held but ultimately impossible desire (42:6). Yet that renunciation makes reintegration into community and return to the activities of life possible.

The cosmic geography in vv. 16-17 is thematically more closely related to the preceding sections than might first appear. The springs of the sea and the great deep refer to the primordial waters, which were divided and contained by God at creation (Gen 1:6; cf. Ps 33:6-7). Although they are the sources of oceans and of fresh waters that well up from the earth, their sudden release can return the world to its chaotic, pre-creation state. In the Priestly account of the deluge, the opening of the springs of the great deep and of the floodgates of the heavens destroys the earth and

its inhabitants (Gen 7:11). Similarly, the gates of death designate the boundary between the realms of life and death (Pss 9:13[14]; 107:18; Isa 38:10; Jonah 2:6[7]). The Mesopotamian myth of the Descent of Ishtar to the netherworld contains a graphic description of the progress of the goddess through seven gates, as she is progressively stripped of all the attributes of life.[551] In Israel, the image of the gates of death primarily figures as a symbol of the fact that one who goes down to Sheol cannot return (Jonah 2:6[7] speaks of the bars of the underworld). Gates also mark the limit of death's domain. Although the servants of death may carry off persons to the King of Terrors (18:14), the realm of death may no more burst through its gates to devour all life than the sea may break through its restraining doors.

Verses 18-19 refer to the most primordial of all the acts of creation (cf. the sarcastic comment in v. 21 that Job must know, since he was born then, as though he were as primordial as wisdom itself; cf. 15:7-8; Prov 8:22-31). In Gen 1:3, the creation of light and the separation of light from darkness is the first of God's acts, a separation that makes possible the alternation of day and night. In Gen 8:22, the assurance that "as long as the earth endures,/ seedtime and harvest, cold and heat,/ summer and winter, day and night,/ shall not cease" (NRSV) is the divine promise that the fundamental structures of creation, which make life possible, will not be destroyed. The Bible does not otherwise speak of the dwelling places of light and darkness (38:20; cf. Ps 19:4-6[5-7]); the Greek poet Hesiod refers to a house at the edge of the world, where Atlas lifts up the heavens. There night and day dwell alternately, each entering when the other leaves.[552]

38:22-24. With v. 22 the poem turns from the great cosmogonic structures of creation to meteorological phenomena (vv. 22-38), things that are closer and more accessible to humans than the primordial structures of creation. Yet in each sphere Job's ignorance and inability to control are complete.

The image of storehouses for the various phenomena of weather is common (37:9;

549. *ANET*, 88-91.
550. *ANET*, 73.

551. *ANET*, 107.
552. Hesiod *Theogony* 745-57. See also G. Fuchs, *Mythos and Hiobdichtung* (Stuttgart: Kohlhammer, 1993) 207.

Deut 28:12; Jer 10:13; Sir 39:29; 43:14). Because knowledge of such matters was regarded as utterly beyond the reach of human ability, it later becomes part of the esoteric mysteries revealed to the apocalyptic seer. Enoch's heavenly journey, for instance, includes a detailed examination of the cosmic storehouses (*1 Enoch* 41:4; 60:11-21). Hail frequently appears as a weapon of God (Exod 9:22-26; Josh 10:11; Isa 28:17; 30:30; Ezek 13:11, 13; Hag 2:17; Sir 39:29), along with other things that may fall from the sky. Since it would seem odd for "light" (38:24*a*) to be included in this sequence, the word should be understood as a synonym for "lightning" (so NIV), as in 37:11. The east wind is, with perhaps one exception (Ps 78:26), always associated with destruction (e.g., Gen 41:6; Exod 10:13; Jer 18:17; Ezek 27:26; Jonah 4:8). Thus three of the four elements mentioned do damage on earth. They are associated here, however, with words of regulation and control: storehouses, proper times, way, place, reserve, distribute, disperse.

38:25-27. In contrast to the east wind, which destroys vegetation in cultivated lands (Gen 41:6; Ezek 19:12; Jonah 4:8), the rains bring forth grass in the desolate wasteland. The imagery is provocative. Constructing water channels was one of the defining acts of human civilization in the ancient Near East. Although more characteristic of Mesopotamia and Egypt, artificial canals were also known in Israel. God uses the language paradoxically, to talk of the channeling of rain onto desert lands, which are, it is twice emphasized, "empty of human life." Some commentators interpret this section as a repudiation of the idea of God's use of rain as reward or punishment (e.g., 37:13; Jer 3:3; Hos 6:3),[553] but that does not seem to be quite the point. The contrast challenged in these verses is between the sown and the unsown, between cultivated land, which is associated with order and creation, and desolate land, which is associated with chaos.[554] Although the term "desert" (מדבר *midbār*) may have many connotations, the characterization of this land as "waste and desolate" (שאה ומשאה *šō'â ûměšō'â*) gives it strongly

negative associations. This is a term often associated with the desolation that accompanies destruction (Ps 35:8; Isa 10:3; 47:11; Ezek 38:9). Job himself made use of the negative connotations of the phrase *šō'â ûměšō'â* when he described the outcast and despised "persons of no name" as grubbing out their meager existence in the "waste and desolate" land (30:3). In Job's view, such a place is both dehumanized and godforsaken. Yet this is precisely the place that God "satisfies" with rain and causes to bring forth grass, an image associated with creation (Gen 1:11; 2:5-6). This is not to say that the dry land is permanently transformed into a paradise, as may be the implication of certain eschatological passages (e.g., Isaiah 35). Rather, in the same way that each morning partakes in the work of creation, when the occasional heavy rains come, the land that is ordinarily desolate and hostile becomes for a while a place of lushness and beauty.

38:28-30. The theme of water continues in these verses. Since the questions are rhetorical and not requests for information, it is unlikely that one should search for mythological identities for a father of rain or a mother of ice. The questions identify wondrous and mysterious phenomena, like the listing of "three things [that] are too wonderful for me;/ four I do not understand" in Prov 30:18-19 (NRSV). Imagery of begetting and birth directs attention to the mysterious way in which various forms of water come into being or are transformed from one to another. What makes some clouds produce rain and not others? Dew seemingly appears from nowhere. Ice and frost are absent one cold day but present the next. The reference to ice, in particular, points to the odd transformation of which water is capable. Job 38:30*a* literally reads, "water hides itself like a rock." Ice is water in hiding.

38:31-33. The section concerning the constellations is the only one in the second half of the chapter that does not deal with water. Perhaps it has been misplaced from an earlier part of the chapter, although there is no evidence in the texts and translations. It may be, however, that the changing visibility and times of rising and setting of the constellations were signs associated with seasonal changes in rainfall, so that their mention here

553. M. Tsevat, "The Meaning of the Book of Job," *HUCA* 37 (1966) 99-100.
554. Keel, *Jahwehs Entgegnung an Ijob*, 58.

would seem thematically appropriate to an audience familiar with those traditions.[555] If so, then the references to binding and loosing would refer to the ability to control not only the movement of the stars but also the rainy and dry seasons associated with them. Some connection between what happens in the heavens and what happens on earth is presupposed in the question to Job about knowing the ordinances of the heavens and establishing their rule on earth (38:33). As in several other sections of this chapter, the vocabulary of order is prominent.

Where possible, English translations use familiar names derived from Greek to specify the constellations. In Hebrew, the Pleiades were called "the herd" (כימה *kîmâ*) and Orion "the fool" (כסיל *kĕsîl*). Mazzaroth (מזרות) cannot be identified with certainty; possibly it is a form of the word that means constellations in general (see NIV; cf. 2 Kgs 23:5). A. de Wilde argues that it refers to Sirius, the dog star, whose appearance was associated with the rising of the Nile.[556] The bear and its children are commonly taken as Ursa Major, although de Wilde argues for Aldebaran and the Hyades. As he notes, Orion,

Sirius, and Aldebaran appear together at the time when the Pleiades would be "bound," i.e., not visible.[557]

38:34-38. Anyone who has endured long days of drought knows the longing to command the clouds to pour out rain or to summon the lightning of the thunderstorm (38:34-35). Such power does not belong to humankind, nor does the wisdom to know when rain will fall. It was popularly believed, however, that certain birds had such knowledge. In 38:36 the translation of the Hebrew words טחות (*ṭūḥôt*) and שׂכוי (*śekwî*) is probably not "mind" and "heart," but rather "the ibis" and "the cock."[558] The ibis was believed to announce the rising of the Nile, and the cock the coming of rain.[559] The concluding image (38:37-38) is one of stewardship. Here the clouds are metaphorically represented as waterskins or jars (cf. Sir 43:8). Since water is a precious commodity, it requires the wisdom of a careful steward to know the number of containers and determine how many may be poured out upon the dry ground. (See Reflections on 40:1-5.)

---

555. See de Wilde, *Das Buch Hiob*, 142-47, 366-67.
556. de Wilde, *Das Buch Hiob*, 367.

557. de Wilde, *Das Buch Hiob*, 144.
558. Dhorme, *A Commentary on the Book of Job*, 593; Gordis, *The Book of Job*, 452-53; Fohrer, *Das Buch Hiob*, 508-9; but see Pope, *Job*, 302.
559. Jussen, "Le Coq et la pluie," *RB* (1924) 574-82. In classical sources, see Virgil *Georgics* I.374ff.

Job 38:39–39:30, The World of Wild Animals

COMMENTARY

The transition to the second part of the divine speech is marked simply by an abrupt change of topic, from the phenomena of weather to the lives of animals. Animals are powerful symbols in all human cultures, although their emotive and symbolic significance varies greatly from one culture to the next. Consequently, one must be careful not to assume that the values a modern reader would automatically associate with the animals named are the same as those in an ancient text like Job. In the religious and cultural contexts of the ancient world, the sphere of the wild is the Other against which human society defines itself. Consequently, attitudes toward it are ambivalent but largely negative. The desert waste in particular is

contrasted with inhabited land as a hostile and dangerous place (Deut 32:10; Ps 107:4-7). Since the desert is a symbol of chaos, divine punishment often takes the form of making a city into just such an uninhabited wilderness (Ps 107:33-38; Isa 34:8-15; Hos 2:3*b*[5*b*], 12[14]). The punished city, which had been structured and ordered like creation itself, now partakes of the disorder and confusion of chaos (cf. Isa 34:11-12, echoing Gen 1:2). Wild animals are also part of this pattern of opposition and enmity. Those that lived in the desolate places and ruined cities took on the aura of those places (Isa 13:19-21; 34:8-15; Jer 50:39-40; Zeph 2:13-15; animals mentioned in those contexts include several described in the divine speech: the lion, the raven, the wild ass, and the ostrich). Divine punishment was often depicted as letting wild animals savage a land, predators attacking persons and livestock (Lev 26:22; Ezek 5:17; Isa 56:9), and other animals trampling and eating crops (Ps 80:13[14]; Isa 5:5-6; Hos 2:12[14]). This deep divide between humans and animals goes back to the re-creation of the world after the deluge, when God declared to Noah that all living creatures would be in "fear and dread of you" (Gen 9:2 NIV). The ideal of a "covenant" with the animals of the earth (Job 5:23; Hos 2:18[20]) and of an eschatological transformation in which wild animals "will neither harm nor destroy" (see Isa 11:6-9) only underscores the enmity that was understood to define the relationship between wild animals and humans in the present.

Two motifs in ancient Near Eastern art illustrate this perception of animals. One is the motif of the royal hunt. Both Egyptian and Mesopotamian kings are depicted as hunting a variety of animals, including lions, mountain goats, deer, wild asses, wild oxen, ostriches, and birds of prey of all kinds—virtually all of the animals listed in Job 39. The king's hunt was not simply a recreational activity, but a symbolic act. Just as the king protected the integrity of the land against hostile human enemies by going out to war, so also he enacted his role as protector of the land against the hostile forces represented by animals by engaging in the hunt.[560] The other motif is that of the "Lord of the animals." Mesopotamian art has numerous representations of a divine figure flanked by wild animals, which he holds in each hand. The gesture is clearly one of control. Again, although there are variations according to region and date, most of the animals represented in the king's hunt and in Job 39 are also represented in the "Lord of the animals" motif.[561] It is always difficult to interpret pictorial symbolism without an accompanying text, but it appears that control of the animals by a divine figure is analogous to the mythic motif of the restriction of the chaotic sea. A wild force that is part of the world is limited by a divine power as part of an orderly creation. Although no exact counterpart to these representations appears in biblical literature, a similar idea is expressed in Jer 27:5-7, where God grants sovereignty to Nebuchadnezzar, including the promise that even the beasts of the field will serve him.

These are not the only ways in which animals were represented. The wisdom tradition regarded particular animals as examples of wise behavior (Prov 6:6-8; 30:24-28; cf. 1 Kgs 4:32-33) and of wondrous ways that eluded human comprehension (Prov 30:18-19). Certain psalms that praise God as creator include references to wild animals and the provision God has made for them in creation, alongside human beings (Pss 104:10-30; 147:8-9, 12-14; cf. Ps 148:7-12; as noted above in the overview to the divine speeches, Psalm 104 is particularly important as a background for God's words). These psalms may be compared with the motif of the "world tree" in Mesopotamian art. There a stylized tree or a divine figure with tree motifs is represented as providing food for animals.[562] In the Bible the motif is also used as a royal symbol. Daniel 4:12[9] describes the tree that represents Nebuchadnezzar: "Its foliage was beautiful,/ its fruit abundant,/ and it provided food for all./ The animals of the field found shade under it,/ the birds of the air nested in its branches,/ and from it all living beings were fed" (NRSV; cf. Ezek 31:1-9). In Mesopotamian art, the motif of the "Lord of the animals" is sometimes combined with that of the "world tree," so that the animals turn their heads to eat from the tree while also being restrained by the divine figure. In this way the themes of abundance and control of the wild are brought together.

All of these traditions provide important background, but the meaning of the divine speech depends on the particular way in which traditions are put to use. First, as in 38:4-38, all but one of the individual sections in 38:39–39:30 are introduced by the familiar rhetorical questions that serve to point out the limits of Job's knowledge and ability, while underscoring God's power and wisdom. Second, each section also includes a closely observed description of the animal in a characteristic activity. Elsewhere in the Bible references to animals are brief and incidental. Only here is sustained attention given to the

---

560. Keel, *Jahwehs Entgegnung an Ijob*, 71.
561. Keel, *Jahwehs Entgegnung an Ijob*, 87.
562. *ANEP*, pl. 464.

simple description of animals. The animals are presented, not as they were traditionally perceived in human perspective, but in ways that challenge human perspective. Thus, in interpreting the significance of the passage one must attend to the background of the various traditions, the rhetorical setting, and the unprecedented focus on animal activity.

38:39-41. It is no accident that the sequence should begin with the image of the lion, which was *the* wild animal in the imagination of ancient Israel. The detail that most engaged attention was the lion's prowess as a predator, a feature that occurs in the vast majority of references to the lion in the Bible (e.g., Gen 49:9; Num 23:29; Ps 17:2; Isa 5:29; Amos 3:4; Nah 2:12). As noted above, this passage has particularly close connections with Ps 104:21. There the lion's roar is interpreted as its request to God for food. Here the imagery is even bolder. The rhetorical questions posed to Job point out something he cannot do, but that God can do. Asking Job if he can "hunt" on behalf of the lions depicts him, and by extension God, as a lioness who brings down prey to satisfy the hunger of members of the pride. The implications of this image of God are important. Although lions hunt many different kinds of prey, the Bible often refers to the lions' attack on flocks of sheep and the consequent enmity between lions and shepherds (1 Sam 17:34-37; Isa 31:4; Jer 25:38; Mic 5:8). Like the image of God's treating the sea with protective care, hunting on behalf of the lions is an image of nurture toward an element of creation perceived as hostile by humans.

Why the raven is grouped with the lion is not certain.[563] As with the lion, the feeding of the raven figures in a creation psalm (Ps 147:9). The Job poet appears to have combined two traditional motifs in such hymnody. The image in Ps 147:9 is quite similar to that of 38:41, as both refer to the raven's offspring and to the sound of their crying out for food. The symbolic significance of the raven is more elusive, however. It is one of the unclean birds (Lev 11:15; Deut 14:14), a scavenger (Prov 30:17) associated with desolate places (Isa 34:11). Yet ravens fed Elijah when the prophet hid in a wadi east of the Jordan (1 Kgs 17:4-6).

There is perhaps an oblique parody of Job in these verses. Job had represented himself as a provider, one who heard the cries of the poor (29:12; the same verb as in 38:41), and before whom others opened their mouths as if to receive rain (29:23). But Job's vision of society has no place for literal or metaphorical lions and ravens. His world is sharply delineated between the village and the wasteland, the latter symbolic of all that was feared and rejected. Lions appear in Job's speech only as an image of the wicked (29:17), to be dealt with violently.

39:1-4. Although the mountain goat and the deer are objects of the king's hunt in Mesopotamian and Egyptian art and are frequently represented as animals controlled by the "Lord of the animals,"[564] they do not bear connotations of threat in Israelite literature. Instead, they are noted for their agility (2 Sam 22:34; Isa 35:6) and beauty (Gen 49:21; Prov 5:19), and even appear in love poetry (Cant 2:7, 9, 17; 3:5); one song was entitled "The Doe of the Dawn" (Ps 22:1). Deer also appear in Israelite poetry as images of suffering, since they are vulnerable to hunger and thirst during times of drought (Ps 42:1[2]; Jer 14:5; Lam 1:6).

Mountain goats and deer, as browsing animals, are similar to domestic sheep and goats. The questions God poses to Job imply just such a comparison, as a means of underscoring how different are the relations of domestic and wild animals to human beings. Knowledge of the seasons of birth and of the precise gestation periods of domestic sheep and goats was essential if the flocks were to increase. Although the Bible does not provide much detail about actual practices, the story of Jacob's clever breeding suggests a strong preoccupation with all aspects of the reproduction of the flocks (Gen 30:31-43). Yet Job knows nothing of the reproduction of these wild creatures. Similarly, lambing season is a time of intense activity for the shepherd, who must not only protect the safety of vulnerable ewes and lambs but also assist with difficult births. Translations often miss the proper nuance of the verb rendered "watch" and "observe" (שׁמר *šāmar*) in 39:1*b*. It should be translated by its meaning of "watch over," "guard." What the passage implies is that

---

563. Hartley, *The Book of Job*, 505n. 4, notes the word play between "ambush" (ארב *'ārab*) and "raven" (ערב *'ōrēb*), in vv. 40-41.

564. Keel, *Jahwehs Entgegnung an Ijob*, 72-75, 87-94.

these animals are alien to the protective relation between shepherd and sheep, which was important not only to the economic but also to the symbolic life of ancient Israel. These animals need no shepherd, nor are they considered to form a flock. Instead, they are represented as reaching maturity and leaving, not to return (39:4). Job's symbolic world, which has been structured primarily in terms of dependence and protection, cannot comprehend such beings within its categories.

39:5-12. The resistance of the sphere of the wild to incorporation within Job's organizing categories, implicit in the description of the mountain goat and deer, becomes explicit in the representation of the wild ass and the wild ox. These animals have exact counterparts within the domestic world, and the contrast with those domestic animals forms the focus of these sections. The wild ox, perhaps the now extinct aurochs, is mentioned elsewhere in the Bible primarily in connection with its remarkable strength (Num 23:22; 34:8; Deut 33:17; Pss 22:22; 92:11). Here, however, emphasis falls on the absolute impossibility of domesticating this wild creature. The hallmark of domestication is the exchange of food in return for service (Isa 1:3), yet that is what 39:9 treats as an absurdity. Domestication involves domination (39:10), but also a relationship of trust (39:11-12). These categories, so evocative of Job's hierarchical and paternalistic moral world, break down when confronted with the wild ox. The aurochs's utter alienness confounds Job's customary ways of thinking.

The wild ass, or onager, is an even more evocative subject, for it holds a more developed position in Israel's symbolic world, and in Job's. Throughout the Bible the wild ass stands for everything opposed to the world of human order and culture. Ishmael is called "a wild ass of a man" precisely because "his hand will be against everyone and everyone's hand against him, and he will live in hostility toward all his brothers" (see Gen 16:12). The wild ass is associated with ruined and deserted cities destroyed by the judgment of God (Isa 32:14). Thus they are evocative of the resurgence of the chaotic into what had once been the sphere of creation. Job twice draws on the connection between the wild ass and the barren wasteland it inhabits

(24:5; 30:7; cf. Jer 14:6). He uses the wild ass as a symbol for a certain social category, the destitute and outcast. Given the symbolic function of the wild ass as defining what is opposed to the sphere of the human, there can be few more powerful symbols of rejection and dehumanization.

The divine description draws on traditional depictions in associating the wild ass with the barren salt flats (39:6) and with rugged areas where vegetation is scarce (39:8). From the human perspective such places are the opposite of fruitful, habitable land. They are, rather, a place of punishment (Ps 107:34; Jer 17:6). Yet for the wild ass they are home. As in Ps 104:11, the wild ass is an object of divine care. The divine speeches exploit the traditional contrast between the human and the wild ass, but in a way that reverses the values. The city, the emblem of human culture, is represented as a place of noise and oppression (39:7), a place of bondage from which God has set the wild ass free (39:5). When Job had looked on the wasteland and its inhabitants, whether in sympathy or in contempt, all that he could see was a place of rejection. God's presence in such a place had utterly eluded him.

13:13-18. The ostrich and the war horse (39:19-25) are both uncanny animals, associated here because of their speed, their exuberance, and their disdain for fear. The passage concerning the ostrich does not begin with the characteristic rhetorical questions and refers to God in the third person (39:17). Possibly, it is a set piece incorporated from another context. Be that as it may, its imagery and themes fit well into divine speech.

Identifying symbolic associations with the ostrich is unfortunately complicated by a disagreement concerning names. In 39:13 the unique term "screechers" (רננים *rěnānîm*) is used, instead of the ordinary term for "ostrich" (יען *yā'ēn*; see Lam 4:3, which also mentions its alleged cruelty to its offspring). The dispute is whether the related term יענה (*ya'ănâ*), which occurs frequently in the Bible, should be understood as referring to ostriches (so NRSV) or to owls (so NIV). What makes this rather technical issue important is that the *ya'ănâ* bird is frequently associated with uninhabited places, especially ruins of cities destroyed by God. There it keeps company with other eerie and ominous animals, including jackals, hyenas, buzzards, owls, the demon Lilith, and other creatures often associated with the demonic, including wild cats and feral goats (Isa 13:21; 34:13; 43:20; Jer 50:30). Most important, in describing his own sense of ruin and exclusion, Job had called himself "a brother of jackals,/ and a companion of ostriches [ya'ănâ]" (30:29 NRSV). The argument in favor of owls is that they do have a fondness for living in ruins. As Keel has argued, however, one should not confuse naturalistic observation with symbolic language. Destruction transfers a city from the sphere of the inhabited to the sphere of the wasteland, and the ostrich is one of the characteristic animals of uninhabited wasteland.[565] The clear pairing of the jackal and the ostrich (yā'ēn) in Lam 4:3 suggests that the fixed pair of the jackal and the ya'ănâ bird in Isa 34:13; 43:20; Mic 1:8; and in Job 30:29 also refers to the jackal and the ostrich. These observations, together with the evidence of the versions and cognate languages, suggest that the NRSV is correct in translating ya'ănâ as "ostrich."

This detour into bird names allows one to consider the symbolic evocations of the ostrich and the way in which this passage both alludes to and overturns them. In 39:13-18, Job is confronted with an animal with which he had claimed companionship (30:29) in order to evoke a sense of isolation from human society and perhaps also the mourning with which the ostrich's sound was associated (30:31; cf. Mic 1:8). Here in radical contrast the ostrich appears as an image of pure heedless joy. Its shrill sound becomes the basis for its name, rĕnānîm, but that word means "cry of joy," not mourning. Moreover, the verb translated "flap wildly" literally means "to be glad," "rejoice" (עלס 'ālas). The second half of 39:13 is corrupt, although it clearly has something to do with the feathers of the bird's wings. More likely than either the NRSV or the NIV is the suggestion of Gordis, "is her wing that of the stork or the falcon?"[566] The ostrich's joyous wings are not

for flight, as are those of other birds; yet the ostrich is not put at a disadvantage. As the concluding v. 18 notes, the ostrich, spreading its plumes, laughs at the pursuit of horse and rider. This image is particularly important in relation to the symbolic significance of the hunt, which, as discussed above, represents the opposition between culture and nature and the defense of order against the chaotic.[567] The laughter of the ostrich echoes that of the wild ass (39:7), which similarly evades human control.

The central part of the description (39:14-17) concerns the strange lack of parental concern displayed by ostriches. That ostriches do not in fact abandon their eggs is beside the point. Such was the belief not only in ancient Israel, but also in Egypt.[568] That supposed behavior was so alien to the nurture of the young characteristic of animals and humans alike that Lam 4:3 uses it as a symbol of the collapse of elemental social bonds in a destroyed community. What is most remarkable in this passage, however, is that God explicitly takes credit for the arrangement, having deprived the ostrich of the wisdom and understanding by which other animals care for their young. Whatever the "design" of God signifies (38:3), it is not something that one could comprehend simply from the imagery of lamplight and the family circle (29:3-5). The harshness and joy of the ostrich's character are also part of that design.

39:19-25. The reference to horse and rider in v. 18 provides a transition to the section on the horse. The horse is an apparent anomaly in the series, since it is the only domesticated animal, but that is precisely the point of departure for the passage. In domesticating a horse one can make it tractable, but one cannot give it the wild lust for battle described here. That character comes from another source. In participating in battle, the horse is no more a "servant" of humans than is the wild ass.

Translators attempt to "domesticate" the text by rendering רעמה (ra'mâ) in 39:19 as "mane."[569] Yet the word means "thunder," and the striking image should not be obscured. As Habel observes, the horse is

565. Keel, Jahwehs Entgegnung an Ijob, 67-68n. 232.
566. Gordis, The Book of Job, 459; similarly, Fohrer, Das Buch Hiob, 514. Alternatively, Dhorme, A Commentary on the Book of Job, 603, suggests "she possesses a gracious plumage and pinions." See also Habel, The Book of Job, 525.

567. For a depiction of Pharaoh Tutankhamen hunting ostriches, see Keel, Jahwehs Entgegnung an Ijob, 72.
568. Pope, Job, 309.
569. E.g., Pope, Job, 311.

presented with the same terminology used of a warrior god.[570] "Might" (12:13), "thunder," (40:9), "majesty" (37:22), and "terror" (9:34; 13:21) are all characteristic terms for the appearance of God in glory. The comparison of the horse to the leaping locust is part of the same complex of imagery by which the prophet Joel compares the sight of a locust plague to an approaching army of horses, the army of God on the day of Yahweh (Joel 2:1-11).

The war horse is like the ostrich in its lack of concern for consequences. As the ostrich feels no "anxiety" (פחד *paḥad*) for eggs that might be crushed and "laughs" (שׂחק *śāḥaq*) at the pursuit of the hunt, so the horse laughs at fear (ישׂחק לפחד *yiśḥaq lĕpaḥad*) as it charges into the midst of flailing weapons. The image is not exactly one of courage, however, but of something more radical, as the image of unrestrained eagerness at the smell of battle and the sound of the trumpet suggests (39:25). Animals ordinarily are drawn by the smell of water when thirsty or by the hormonal smells and characteristic cries that signal the time for breeding (Jer 2:24; 14:6). For the war horse, however, the desire for battle is as compelling as the drive for water or sex.

39:26-30. The final vignette will conclude with one of the most disturbing images in the entire series, yet it is introduced with an allusion to one of the wisdom tradition's more beautiful themes, the mystery of the flight of birds (cf. Prov 30:18-19). What is "too wonderful" for the sage and beyond Job's insight and power of command is nevertheless part of God's design. The flight of the hawk to the south (39:26) perhaps alludes to the annual

migration of hundreds of thousands of raptors from eastern Europe to their wintering territory in Africa.[571] The horizontal imagery of great distance in v. 26 is paired with vertical imagery of great heights in vv. 27-28. A natural association leads from the theme of secure nests to the provision of food for the nestlings and occasions the observation about the extraordinary vision of raptors (39:29). Only in the final verse does the grim object of the bird's sight come into view for the reader: the corpses of those slain in battle. Here is the blood that the brood will drink. This detail makes it clear that most translations err in rendering "eagle" instead of "vulture." Although נשׁר (*nešer*) can refer to either bird, it is evident that this bird is a carrion eater, not a predator (cf. Ezek 32:4; 39:4-5; Matt 24:28; Luke 17:37). Nor can one think of the vulture's food as simply another dead animal. The term "slain" (חלל *ḥālāl*) is used almost exclusively of humans in biblical Hebrew.[572] Literally, it means "pierced" and is the common term used for those killed in battle, pierced by the sword (see, e.g., Judg 9:40; 1 Sam 17:52; Jer 14:18; Ezek 31:17).

In the most disconcerting way, the divine speech asks Job and the reader to look at battle not from the human perspective of victory or punishment, liberation or oppression, but through the eyes of the horse, who finds it exhilarating, and through the eyes of the vulture, who finds it nourishing. The end of the series is marked by an inclusio. The feeding of the vulture's brood (39:29-30) corresponds to the provision of prey for the raven and its hungry fledglings (38:41). (See Reflections at 40:1-5.)

---

570. Habel, *The Book of Job*, 547.

571. E. Firmage, "Zoology (Animal Profiles)," *ABD* 4:1144.
572. Dhorme, *A Commentary on the Book of Job*, 613.

Job 40:1-5, Job's Response

COMMENTARY

God's first words to Job had announced God's intention to question Job and receive an answer (38:2-3). Now following the questions of the first divine speech, God demands that answer. Although the NRSV and the NIV disagree as to which word should be

the subject and which the verb in 40:2*a*, it is clear that God casts the relationship with Job in terms of a disputation. Job has reproached God publicly; God has responded. Now Job must answer. One might assume at this point that there will be a resumption of the type of disputation Job engaged in with the friends. Those disputation speeches often began with words characterizing and criticizing the opponent's speech (e.g., 8:2; 11:2-3; 12:2-3; 15:2-3; 16:2-3; 18:2-3; 19:2-3; 21:2-3; 38:2-3). Job's first words, however, characterize himself and signal his withdrawal from the disputation (40:4-5). The language and images he uses belong to the discourse of honor.[573] The NIV paraphrases the Hebrew, but what Job says literally is, "I am small" or "light" (קלל *qālal*). "Small" is the opposite of the word "honor" (כבד *kābēd*; lit., "heavy"), as is clear from the way both terms are used in 2 Sam 6:22, where Michal and David argue about his conduct. It is difficult to determine the precise nuance in 40:3. Although the word "small" can be used to signify shame and contempt (Gen 16:4-5; 2 Sam 6:22), that nuance comes to the fore when the issue is how one appears in the eyes of others. But "small"

and "heavy" are also words of status and hierarchy. By applying the term to himself, Job acknowledges the difference in status between God and himself. The accompanying gesture, placing the hand over the mouth (40:4*b*), is the same gesture of deference and respect that Job's own presence evoked among even high-ranking members of his own community when he appeared among them (29:9). They refrained from speaking in his presence (29:9-10) in much the same way that Job indicates that he will no longer speak before God (40:5). The significance of what Job says and does, however, has to be seen in terms of what he had previously said about his honor and status. In 31:35-37, in the context of his long oath of clearance, Job had challenged God to answer him, declaring that he would approach God "like a prince." From that perspective, Job here does engage in an act of self-humiliation, as he implicitly acknowledges the gross impropriety of having ventured to rebuke God.

573. See C. Muenchow, "Dust and Dirt in Job 42:6," *JBL* 108 (1989) 608.

REFLECTIONS

Why does the enounter with God not end here? Why is this not enough? By word and gesture Job has indicated his intention to discontinue his argument and his acknowledgment of God's superiority in power, status, and honor. The issue of divine honor is an important one for the book of Job, but it is not the only issue. God has addressed Job concerning the way Job's words have obscured the design of God (38:2). Nothing in Job's reply indicates that he has yet perceived and understood the nature of that design and its significance for his own situation. Until he does, the encounter with God cannot find closure.

Everything that God has to say to Job is contained in this first speech. Like many people who have experienced catastrophe, Job's world had been shattered, and along with it his ability to trust. Job would draw into the abyss of his own pain the very creation that had brought him into being only to expose him to such suffering (chap. 3). For such a person, recovery of trust in the fundamental structures of existence is essential. The situation is like that of a clergy couple who undertook to foster three children whose lives had been devastated by tragedy, witnessing their mother kill their father and then be arrested. On the first night the children were in the clergy couple's care, the family gathered and read together the creation account in Genesis 1. As the husband later explained, the children had experienced the sudden and violent loss of so much that they needed to know there was something upon which they could still rely. To hear the measured and ordered words of God's creation of a good world in the presence of adults who would stand by them was a first step to restoring a sense of trust to these children. God's words of creation have something of this function for Job, although Job does not seem capable of hearing and responding to them.

God's task in responding to Job is rather more complicated than that of the foster parents caring for the devastated children, since God not only has to persuade Job of the fundamental reliability of the structures of creation but also simultaneously has to persuade him to recognize the presence of the chaotic as a part of the design of creation. As noted in the Commentary, God incorporates this theme in various ways throughout the first divine speech, in the representation of the sea (38:8-11), in the remarks about the persistence of the wicked (38:12-15), and above all in the long description of animals who are associated with the anarchic and chaotic forces in the world (38:39–39:30). Yet Job seems equally incapable of hearing and responding to this part of the divine speech.

Fundamental changes of perception do not happen easily, whether in the realm of therapeutic understanding, political commitment, or spiritual transformation. For the longest time one may hear the arguments that are supposed to persuade one or lead one to insight and yet be completely baffled by them. One may even, like Job, shrug in resignation, willing to concede without ever having understood. What blocks understanding is not an intellectual inability to comprehend. One must be ready to understand. Sometimes, too, people protect themselves, consciously or unconsciously, from having to examine the one thing they fear confronting, because that is precisely where their carefully built edifices of belief are vulnerable. By announcing one's intention to say no more, one can continue to protect from scrutiny whatever it is that one fears to examine. It takes a shrewd partner in dialogue to recognize what that protected area is and to know how to require a person to confront a reality that he or she must face if life is to be transformed. In the book of Job, God recognizes Job's inability to confront the existence of the chaotic as the source of his entrapment in a system of beliefs that can lead only to isolation and moral bitterness. Thus God's second speech to Job is one that makes confrontation with the chaotic inescapable.

JOB 40:6–42:6, UNDERSTANDING THE NATURE OF DIVINE GOVERNANCE

OVERVIEW

Compared with the long series of brief but vivid descriptions of the cosmos and its creatures that give the first divine speech its panoramic character, the focus of the second speech is tight and intense. If the rhetorical strategy of the first speech was enumeration and repetition, here it is close encounter, mediated by vivid poetry. After a brief thematic introduction (40:6-14), Job is directed to "look at Behemoth," the description of whom continues for some ten verses (40:15-24). Without transition, the focus shifts to Leviathan, who is described in a poem of thirty-four verses (41:1-34[40:25–41:26]). In the course of this poem, Job is brought, figuratively speaking, face to face with Leviathan. Immediately after the description of Leviathan, Job utters his second response, reflecting the changed understanding that leads to

his withdrawing the challenge (42:1-6). Both conceptual language and poetic language play an important role in constructing the meaning of this speech. If conceptual language alone were sufficient, the speech could be much briefer; the introductory section would suffice. But the meaning of the speech is also constructed and communicated as experience. For that, the primary images and their power to evoke emotional response and recognition are also essential.

The old dispute about whether Behemoth and Leviathan are animals (e.g., the hippopotamus and the crocodile) or mythical monsters engages in a false dichotomy. They are animals in the sense that they are creatures of God. That much is said explicitly about Behemoth (40:15), and Leviathan also is best understood, as in Ps 104:26, as a creature made by

God (41:33[25]; cf. Gen 1:21). Although the description of these creatures may well draw details from the hippopotamus and the crocodile, they are not "mere" animals. There is a suggestion of the primordial about Behemoth (40:15), and Leviathan is described in terms that clearly evoke the mythic traditions associated with its name (41:18-21[10-13]). These are liminal creatures, betwixt and between the categories of ordinary animal and mythic being. As with medieval maps in which the outer oceans bear the inscription "Here be dragons," Behemoth and Leviathan are creatures that mark the limits of the symbolic map of the world. Even more than the wild animals of chaps. 38–39, they represent the frightening and alien "other," bearing the terror of the chaotic in their very being. The subtler articulation of this theme in both parts of the first divine speech evoked no response from Job. Now it is amplified in a way that permits no evasion.

Job 40:6-14, The Challenge

COMMENTARY

40:6-8. The beginning of the second divine speech in v. 6 is marked by the same narrative introduction as in 38:1, and the challenge statement of 38:3 is repeated in 40:7. The thematic question corresponding to 38:2 is announced in v. 8 and elaborated in vv. 9-14. In v. 8, God uses three words that have been of key importance for Job. In Job's mouth they have had legal connotations: "a claim of right" (משפט *mišpāṭ*; 9:15; 27:2), "declare guilty" (רשע *rāšaʿ*; 9:20; 10:2), "declare innocent" (צדק *ṣādēq*; 9:15, 20). But *mišpāṭ* has other connotations as well. It belongs to the language of governance, as well as to the language of judging.[574] In the question of v. 8, the double resonance of *mišpāṭ* points to unexamined problems inherent in Job's paradigm of understanding. Job's legal paradigm is a system of simple oppositions: For one party to be right, the other must be wrong; for one to be innocent, the other must be guilty. If *mišpāṭ* is simply about judicial decisions, then the choice is between God's taking away Job's right (27:2), and Job's discrediting God's justice (40:8). But the *mišpāṭ* that is God's governance of the world cannot be reduced to legal categories. In attempting to do so, Job has fundamentally misconstrued the nature of the world and God's role. Thus the thematic question about governance in 40:8 is analogous to the question about the design of creation in 38:2.

40:9-14. These verses introduce a shift in language and imagery. Here the topics are power and pride, anticipating the imagery associated with Behemoth and Leviathan in the body of the speech. Reduced to its barest outlines, this section rhetorically asks Job if he has power comparable to God's and the ability to bring down the proud. If so, then God will recognize Job's ability to win his own victory. Behemoth and Leviathan thus serve as examples of creatures of power and pride whom Job could not possibly overcome. That much is clear. The more difficult question is what this speech says about the nature of the world and divine governance. As in the first speech, one must carefully note not only how traditional speech and images are invoked but also how they may be used differently than in other settings, in order to determine what they mean in this particular context.

The challenge to Job in vv. 9-14 is constructed out of traditional, almost clichéd language about God. The arm (Exod 15:16; Pss 77:15[16]; 89:13[14]; Isa 63:5) and thundering voice (37:4; Pss 18:13[14]; 77:18[19]; 104:7) are typical attributes of the divine warrior. Similarly, the abstract terms of v. 10—"majesty," "dignity," "glory," and "splendor"—all connote the awe-inspiring quality of divinity (Exod 15:7; Pss 96:6; 104:1; 138:5; Isa 2:10, 19, 21; 24:14).

This description of God introduces the vocabulary of pride that is thematically important throughout the second speech. Terms for "pride" in Hebrew are frequently derived from words referring to height. For instance, the waves of the sea in 38:11 are described literally as "high" (גאון *gāʾôn*), metaphorically

---

574. Scholnick, "The Meaning of Mishpat in the Book of Job," 522.

as "proud." Similarly, here in v. 10 the words translated "majesty" and "dignity" ("glory" and "splendor") literally have to do with height (*gāʾôn* and גבה *gōbah*). A related word (גאה *gēʾeh*) is the negative term for "pride" in vv. 11*b* and 12*a*. As these examples already suggest, "height" is a complex category in biblical imagery. In its associations with God it is wholly positive. But precisely because it is godlike, it provokes ambivalence as a human characteristic. As "majesty," it is tolerated and in certain contexts even encouraged, unless it becomes excessive "pride." Then what has grown too high is "brought low" and "abased" (40:11*b*, 12*a*).[575] In the allegories of Ezekiel 31 and Daniel 4 the goodness of the trees that nurture all the creatures of the world is in part a virtue of their height; yet height as arrogance is the fatal flaw that finally requires that they be cut down (Ezek 31:10-12; Dan 4:30[27]). One cannot say of *gāʾôn* that it is either good or bad, right or wrong. The issue is one of appropriate limits. Thus the symbolic system associated with *gāʾôn* and related words is one of regulation and containment. Such a way of imagining the world and its governance belongs to an entirely different paradigm from Job's legal categories.

575. In apocalyptic literature, this symbolic system is turned into a veritable philosophy of history. See Daniel 8; 10–12.

The only power capable of this kind of regulation, the reversal of high into low, arrogance into abasement, is God. Thus the transcendent height of God in 40:10 parallels images of depth in 40:13 (dust and the hidden place—i.e., the underworld). Echoing the image of the "arm of God" with which the passage began, God says that if Job can abase the proud, then God will acknowledge that Job's "own right hand" can give him victory (40:14), for he will be like God.

The ambivalence surrounding the category of pride is in large part what makes the interpretation of the figures of Behemoth and Leviathan so difficult. Following vv. 9-14, they are clearly examples of the proud, whom Job is challenged to "bring low." Leviathan, in particular, is traditionally associated with the chaos monster, whom God defeats in battle. Yet in chaps. 40–41 they are not presented as enemies of God. Although God's capacity to overcome them is acknowledged, hostility between God and these creatures plays no role in the description. Rather, they appear as magnificent creatures whose pride is appropriate to their place in creation. One should not attempt to resolve the ambiguity in their representation. It is an irreducible part of the role they play in the divine speeches. (See Reflections at 41:1-34.)

Job 40:15-24, Behemoth

COMMENTARY

The name "Behemoth" is simply the "plural of majesty" of the ordinary word for "animal" or "cattle."[576] Thus it is the animal *par excellence*. Unlike Leviathan, a name attested in several other places in biblical and non-biblical sources, there are no earlier instances of the name "Behemoth." Possibly, it is a creation of the Job poet, who needed a land animal to pair with the sea creature Leviathan, or it may be the poet's rendering of an older tradition otherwise unattested.

576. The earlier attempt to relate Behemoth to a supposed Egyptian term for "hippopotamus" is now recognized as erroneous. See Dhorme, *A Commentary on the Book of Job,* 618.

What sort of animal is the model for Behemoth? Its habitat is described as a marshy place where reeds, wadi poplars, and the thorny lotus grow (40:21-22). It is closely associated with rivers, in particular the Jordan, although its food is said to come from the mountains (40:20, 23). Its fondness for water suggests to many that Behemoth is modeled after the hippopotamus, although the mention of mountains is something of an embarrassment for this interpretation. That there were no hippopotamuses in the Jordan in antiquity is no fatal objection, since a legendary creature may live where a poet wishes to place it. In Egyptian mythology, the hippopotamus was an ominous creature, associated with the god Seth, the opponent of Horus. The temple of Edfu, for example, contains illustrations of the god Horus hunting Seth in the form of a hippopotamus.[577] Such a background would provide Behemoth with an aura comparable to that of Leviathan. It is also possible, however, that the primary animal imagery from which Behemoth is shaped is that of the water buffalo, which also enjoys submerging itself in rivers and marshy areas and inhabited the Lake Huleh region in northern Palestine in antiquity. Behemoth is said to "eat grass like an ox," and numerous bull-like monsters appear in Ugaritic and Mesopotamian mythology.[578] The terrifying "Bull of Heaven" let loose by the goddess Ishtar and killed by Gilgamesh and Enkidu is the best-known example.[579] Later apocalyptic literature speculated on the nature of Behemoth and Leviathan. According to 2 Esdras 6:49-52, they were formed on the fifth day of creation. Because the sea was not large enough to hold both of them, Behemoth was given a part of the dry land where a thousand mountains stood, and Leviathan was left in the sea (cf. Apoc. Bar. 29:4; *1 Enoch* 60:7-9).

The passage about Behemoth divides into two parts, vv. 15-19 and vv. 20-24. The first section begins and ends with references to Behemoth's creation (40:15, 19) and contains a description of its extraordinary strength.

40:15-19. Earlier in the chapter God had rhetorically asked if Job could compare with God in power (v. 9). Here Job's attention is directed to Behemoth, a creature that, God says, "I made along with you." Yet even this fellow creature's power greatly exceeds Job's. The focus on the loins and belly in v. 16 and the thighs in v. 17*b* makes it quite likely that the word "tail" (זנב *zānāb*) in v. 17 is a euphemism for "penis," as is often suggested.[580] Although it is not at all clear why a literal tail would be a symbol of strength or be compared to a cedar tree, the masculine association of a large erection with power fits the context well. Bulls often symbolize sexual potency, another reason for thinking of Behemoth as a bovine creature rather than as one modeled after the hippopotamus. Corresponding to the impressive sinews in v. 17, the bones are described in v. 18 as being made of bronze and iron. In summarizing, God praises the powerful Behemoth as "the first" or "the best" of God's works (v. 19*a*; the word ראשית [*rē'šît*] can have either or both senses). What exactly is meant by this claim? The same phrase is used to describe primordial wisdom in Prov 8:22, where it clearly has a temporal meaning. Behemoth is possibly being depicted as the most ancient of all creatures,[581] but the focus on Behemoth's extraordinary power suggests that its superiority is praised (so NIV). Such a claim parallels the presentation of Leviathan, too, as a creature "without equal," a king over all the proud (41:33-34[25-26]).

Often, an obscure line can become the basis for an interpretation of the whole passage. The sentence "only its Maker can approach it with the sword" (v. 19*b*) is just such a case. The text and grammar of v. 19*b* are much more ambiguous than the NRSV and the NIV suggest. There are no words in the Hebrew for "only" or "yet" or "with." The verse literally reads: "He is the first of the ways of God; his maker brings near his sword." As the NRSV and the NIV render the line, the verse implies that God does, or at least could do, battle with Behemoth. Basing their ideas on such a translation, some commentators attempt to understand the divine speeches as an allusion to the old *Chaoskampf* myth, the ancient battle between the creator god and the chaos monster.[582] A translation of v. 19*b* that implies a confrontation between God and Behemoth is not impossible in the larger context of the chapter, especially in the light of the reference to "bringing low the proud" as a godlike act (40:9), but it does not fit the immediate context well. The force of the descriptions of both Behemoth and Leviathan is not containment of their power but the vivid representation of the immensity of their prowess.

Alternatively, some have argued that the sword in question is Behemoth's[583] and that

577. Keel, *Jahwehs Entgegnung an Ijob*, 138-39; Kubina, *Die Gottesreden im Buche Hiob*, 71.

578. Pope, *Job*, 321-22.

579. *ANET*, 83-85.

580. E.g., Pope, *Job*, 324; Habel, *The Book of Job*, 553.

581. Fuchs, *Mythos und Hiobdichtung*, 238.

582. E.g., T. Mettinger, "God the Victor," in *The Voice from the Whirlwind*, ed. L. Perdue and C. Gilpin (Nashville: Abingdon, 1992) 45-46; J. C. L. Gibson, "On Evil in the Book of Job," *Biblical and Other Studies in Memory of P. C. Craigie*, JSOTSup 67 (Sheffield: JSOT Press, 1988) 399-419.

583. Rowley, *The Book of Job*, 257.

Yahweh brings the sword to Behemoth as a token of his lordship over other animals (40:20). The word translated "his maker" (העשׁו *hāʿōśô*) is grammatically anomalous, however, and the Hebrew consonants suggest that it is actually the word "made" (*heʿāśû*), the same word that occurs in the description of Leviathan as "made without fear" (41:33[25]). Without changing the consonantal text of v. 19 *b*, the line could be revocalized to read: "He is the first of the ways of God, made to dominate his companions."[584] Such a translation fits smoothly into the context. But the point is not so much to recommend this

emendation as to caution against reading into this passage a version of the *Chaoskampf* on a shaky textual basis. Violence is not what the passage associates with Behemoth.

40:20-24. The second part of the description concerns Behemoth's idyllic life. The mountains provide food (v. 20 *a*; cf. Ezek 36:8) in a setting of peace where animals frolic (v. 20 *b*), while the marshlands provide a shady resting place (vv. 21-22). Far from being an aggressive creature, Behemoth is associated with security. The very Jordan at flood (Josh 3:15) does not cause him to flee (v. 23). Even less need Behemoth fear capture by humans (v. 24). (See Reflections at 41:1-34.)

584. See the discussion in Rowley, *The Book of Job*, 256. Similarly, Dhorme, *A Commentary on the Book of Job*, 621; Fohrer, *Das Buch Hiob*, 522.

Job 41:1-34, Leviathan

COMMENTARY

Whereas Behemoth's extraordinary power finds its artistic representation in images of repose and security, Leviathan is rendered in images of violence, fire, and turmoil. The segue between the two poems is hunting imagery, which closes the poem on Behemoth (40:24) and opens the one on Leviathan (41:1[40:25]). As a motif, hunting is much more extensively developed in the Leviathan section, since it provides a way to talk about Leviathan's dangerous violence.

Unlike "Behemoth," the name "Leviathan" brings with it a well-developed set of symbolic associations. Both in Ugaritic mythology and in the Bible, "Leviathan" (or "Lotan") is the name of a sea monster with which Yahweh, Baal, and Anat do battle. In the Baal epic, the god Mot refers to a victory of Baal, "when you killed Lotan, the Fleeing Serpent, finished off the Twisting Serpent, the seven-headed monster." Elsewhere, the goddess Anat says, "Didn't I demolish El's Darling, Sea? didn't I finish off the divine river, Rabbim? didn't I snare the Dragon? I enveloped him, I demolished the Twisting Serpent, the seven-headed monster."[585] In the Bible, the psalmist praises Yahweh, saying, "It was

you who split open the sea by your power;/ you broke the heads of the monster in the waters./ It was you who crushed the heads of Leviathan/ and gave him as food to the creatures of the desert" (Ps 74:13-14 NIV). Establishment of the orders of creation follows this victory. Isaiah 27:1 describes the eschatological future as involving the same act: "In that day Yahweh will punish with his sword, his fierce, great and powerful sword, Leviathan the gliding serpent, Leviathan the coiling serpent; he will slay the monster of the sea" (author's trans.). Similar associations are in Job's mind when he refers to those prepared to "rouse up Leviathan" in a curse (3:8). As the Ugaritic quotations suggest, Leviathan is one of a group of closely related figures, all of whom are associated with the sea in its symbolic value as chaotic power, represented in the Bible by Rahab the dragon (9:13; 26:12; Ps 89:10[11]; Isa 51:9) and the sea monster תנין (*tannîn*; 7:12; Ps 74:13; Isa 27:1; Ezek 29:3; 32:2).

The fluid boundary between the mythical and the nonmythical, as well as the ambivalent status of the chaotic in relation to creation, is suggested by texts in which *tannîn* and Leviathan are creatures formed by God and not at all hostile. In Gen 1:21, the *tannînim* are sea animals created as part of

585. M. Coogan, *Stories from Ancient Canaan* (Philadelphia: Westminster, 1978) 92, 106.

the work of the fifth day of creation, concerning which God said that "it was good." In Ps 148:7, the *tannînim* are called upon to praise God as part of universal praise. Similarly, Leviathan in Ps 104:26 is an animal that God has formed to play in the sea. The representation of Leviathan in chap. 41 [chaps. 40–41] draws associations from both the mythic tradition and the tradition represented in Genesis and the book of Psalms.

The passage on Leviathan can be divided into three parts: (1) 41:1-12[40:25–41:4], which consists of rhetorical questions about hunting Leviathan and God's comments upon such an enterprise; (2) 41:13-24[5-16], the physical description of Leviathan; and (3) 41:25-32[17-24], Leviathan's defiance of attack and movement out to sea. A concluding description of Leviathan as king over all the proud concludes the poem (41:33-34[25-26]).

41:1-8. The barrage of rhetorical questions in 41:1-7 [40:25-31] is predicated upon absurdity. Images of capture begin and end the series. So little is known about the technologies of ancient hunting and fishing that it is not entirely clear whether an ancient audience would have recognized the use of hook and cord, harpoon and spear as specific to a particular kind of hunting.[586] In any case, these would be ludicrously inadequate for Leviathan. The practice of controlling captives with a rope passed through a hole in the nose or cheek is well attested (2 Kgs 19:28; Isa 37:29; Ezek 29:4; 38:4),[587] but creates an absurd image when applied to Leviathan. In Egyptian myth, Isis warns Horus not to listen to the crocodile if it speaks sweetly to him.[588] The image in vv. 3-4 (40:29-30) is of Leviathan begging not to be killed and offering perpetual servitude as an alternative. The height of domestication is the image of Leviathan as a child's pet (41:5[40:30]). In 41:6[40:31], the rhetorical question imagines the dead Leviathan cut up and sold as meat (41:6[40:31]), so huge that it has to be divided among many traders. That image provides a transition back to the topic of hunting,

which brings the series of rhetorical questions to a close (41:7[40:31]), rounded off by the comment that the memory of one encounter would be enough to prevent one's ever attempting another (41:8[40:32]).

41:9-12. The following four verses provide a transition between the rhetorical questions and the description of Leviathan's appearance and behavior. Escalating the imagery from that of 41:8[40:32], which spoke of laying hands on Leviathan, 41:9[1] insists that the mere sight of it is enough to cast one down. The syntax of the line is awkward, and some translators follow the Greek text of Symmachus and the Syriac in reading "the gods were cast down at the sight of him" (so NRSV), which would require only a modest emendation of the Hebrew. The fear of the gods is a frequent motif in both Ugaritic and Mesopotamian myth. The threatening message that Yam (Sea) sends Baal causes the assembled gods to drop their heads onto their knees in fear.[589] In the Enuma Elish, after the first unsuccessful confrontation with the chaos monster Tiamat, the gods are of the opinion, "No god can go [to battle and], facing Tiamat, escape [with his life]."[590] Following the NRSV, the text alludes to the mythic character of Leviathan.

Textual problems and ambiguous references make the next three verses susceptible to more than one interpretation, leading to radically different interpretations of the meaning of the entire speech. Since so much hangs on the issue, it is necessary to explain the alternatives. The first half of 41:10[2] is clear, echoing 3:8. In the second half of the verse, however, the Hebrew manuscripts are divided between "who is able to stand against him" (so NRSV) and "who is able to stand against me" (so NIV). One cannot decide between the two alternatives until the problems of the following verse are resolved.

The text of 41:11[3] is clearly first-person speech. Some interpreters consider this first-person reference out of place and change it to third-person speech, so that the passage is understood as God's describing the inability of anyone to confront the powerful Leviathan.[591]

---

586. These are considered not to be the weapons of crocodile hunting in any case. E. Ruprecht, "Das Nilpferd im Hiobbuch. Beobachtungen zu der sogennanten zweiten Gottesrede," *VT* 21 (1971) 221-22; Kubina, *Die Gottesreden im Buche Hiob*, 91.

587. See also *ANEP*, pls. 296, 447.

588. Kubina, *Die Gottesreden im Buche Hiob*, 74.

589. *ANET*, 130.

590. *ANET*, 64.

591. E.g., Dhorme, *A Commentary on the Book of Job*, 631; Rowley, *The Book of Job*, 261; Fohrer, *Das Buch Hiob*, 527; Gordis, *The Book of Job*, 483; de Wilde, *Das Buch Hiob*, 387-99.

Those interpreters also read 41:10[2] as third-person. The advantage of this interpretation is that it preserves the consistency of the references. Accordingly, a new section begins in 41:12[4] with God declaring the intention to describe Leviathan's appearance.

Other interpreters keep the first-person references in 41:11[3] and interpret them as referring to God (so NIV).[592] They generally also choose the first-person pronoun in 41:10[2]. In this way, Leviathan serves as a point of comparison for God. If Job (or anyone else) cannot confront Leviathan, how much less could Job confront God? This is not an impossible interpretation, since God has mockingly challenged Job to gird his loins (40:7) and has rhetorically asked if he has an arm and a voice like God's (40:9). Nevertheless, the appearance of this topic in the midst of the description of Leviathan seems abrupt. Those who take 41:10b-11[2b-3] as referring to God are divided on their interpretation of 41:12[4]. Some take it as beginning a new section in which God will describe Leviathan's appearance (so NIV). Others, however, translate 41:12[4] very differently: "Did I not silence his boasting, his mighty word and his persuasive case?"[593] The difficult question is whether this translation fits the context. In 40:12, God had challenged Job to humble the proud. Accordingly, 41:12[4] would be an example of God's humbling Leviathan's proud boasting. The problem is that confrontation between God and Leviathan does not seem to be the point of the speech. What follows does not describe God's victory over the chaos monster but a celebration of the awesome and terrifying power of Leviathan, culminating in the declaration that he is unequalled on earth, king over all the children of pride (41:33-34[25-26]). Moreover, the interpretation of 41:12[4] as God's silencing Leviathan's boasting does not fit well with the problem Job presents. Job has not questioned God's power, but he has been unable to recognize the presence of the chaotic within God's design and governance of the world.

Consequently, the translations and interpretations of 41:10-12[2-4] that take these verses as referring simply to the power and dangerousness of Leviathan are to be preferred (e.g. NRSV). The linguistic arguments of Habel, Rowold, and Mettinger, however, suggest an even more provocative possibility. One might take 40:10[2] as God's speech to the effect that no one can stand against Leviathan, 40:11[3] as a quotation of Leviathan's boast, and 40:12[4] as God's statement that God will *not* silence Leviathan's boast.[594] Thus:

God:	Who is so fierce as to rouse him up? Who is there who could stand against him?
Leviathan:	Whoever confronts me, I will repay. Under all the heavens, he is mine!
God:	I will not silence his boasting, his mighty word, and his persuasive case.

Leviathan's claim to repay any who confront it simply repeats what God has already said (41:8[40:32]) and will shortly describe in more detail (41:25-29[17-21]). Significantly, Leviathan describes the sphere of its dominion as "under all the heavens." Leviathan does not challenge heaven itself. Its boasting is confined to the domain appropriate to its status. Moreover, God seems to endorse just this claim, since God will end the poem by declaring, "on earth it has no equal" or, as the words might also be translated, "on earth there is no one who can dominate it" (41:33[25]). Because it says only what it is entitled to say, God shocks Job by refusing to silence Leviathan's boasting. The description of Leviathan that follows in 41:13-32[5-24] is thus designed not only to make the validity of Leviathan's claim indisputable but also to provide an experience of this chaotic force whose place in the world cannot be ignored.

41:13-17. As Perdue notes, beauty as well as power characterizes Leviathan in Yahweh's description of this extraordinary creature.[595] Armored like a warrior, its head is wreathed about with fire and smoke, impervious to any form of weapon,

---

592. E.g., Habel, *The Book of Job,* 555; Hartley, *The Book of Job,* 531-32; Perdue, *Wisdom in Revolt,* 227.

593. Mettinger, "God the Victor," 235n. 34. Similarly, Habel, *The Book of Job,* 551; H. Rowold, "Mi hu? Li hu!" *JBL* 105 (1986) 104-9. The verse is not marked as a question in the text but is taken as an implicit question by these scholars.

594. Although talking animals are not common in the Bible (see only the snake in Genesis 2–3 and Balaam's ass in Numbers 22), the motif of Leviathan's speech has already been introduced in the poem in 41:3[40:27]. In contrast to those imagined "soft words," Leviathan's boast is proud and defiant.

595. Perdue, *Wisdom in Revolt,* 230n. 7.

---

its thrashing is capable of transforming the appearance of the sea itself. The description of Leviathan begins by visualizing its skin as a coat of impenetrable mail (41:13[5] NRSV, reading with the LXX; cf. the description of Goliath's armor in 1 Sam 17:5). Leviathan's terrifying face is the next focus of attention. Its jaws, poetically described as "the doors of its face," are the setting for its fearsome teeth, similar perhaps to the "sharp-toothed" dragons created by Tiamat for her battle with the gods in the Enuma Elish.[596]

The common practice of emending "pride" to "back" in 41:15[7] and interpreting vv. 16-17[8-9] as referring to Leviathan's scales is questionable. Words for "pride" are of such thematic importance in this speech (40:10, 12; 41:34[26]) that one should hesitate to emend. It is perfectly meaningful to translate "his rows of shields are his pride" (cf. TNK). Moreover, the emendation also obscures the focus on the description of the face. The rows of shields are Leviathan's teeth, set so close that there is no space between them.[597]

41:18-21. The description next moves to the fiery phenomena that stream from Leviathan's mouth, eyes, and nose. Fieriness is a characteristic of divine beings, both gods and monsters. In Ugaritic myth, when the messengers of Sea deliver their words to the gods, "fire, burning fire doth flash; a whetted sword [are their e]yes."[598] When the god Marduk speaks, he blazes forth fire.[599] Yahweh's face, too, is a source of fire, as Ps 18:8[9] indicates: "Smoke went up from his nostrils,/ and devouring fire from his mouth;/ glowing coals flamed forth from [it]" (NRSV; cf. Ps 29:7). In the context of so much terror the image of "eyes like the rays of the dawn" disorients by its beauty. As the NIV's translation suggests, the word does not refer to a physical part of the eye (NRSV, "eyelids") but to the glance coming from the eye, imaged as a beam of light. Dawn's light has a reddish glow to it, as the German word *morgenrot* (lit., "the red of morning") and the Homeric formula "rosy-fingered dawn" reflect. Here the inner fire that burns in Leviathan is projected out

through its glance, as dawn sends out its reddish rays.[600]

41:22-24. moving on from the face, the poet traces Leviathan's neck, the folds of flesh below the neck, and the chest. The artistry in the sequence of this description is subtle, for one would see those features only if Leviathan raised itself up, which is precisely what is described in the following verse (41:25[17]). It is as though the visual description itself introduces motion into the picture. The images of 41:22-24[14-16] are mostly of hardness and impenetrability, culminating in the description of Leviathan's chest (lit., "heart") as like a lower millstone.

41:25-32. The raising up of Leviathan (41:25[17]) should present an adversary with the opportunity to strike it. Yet even the gods are terrified of Leviathan because it is invulnerable to any weapon. The catalogue of weaponry in 41:26-29[18-21]—sword, spear, dart, javelin, iron, bronze, arrow, slingstone, club, lance—freezes the moment when Leviathan lifts itself up and allows the eye to contemplate its invincibility. In the final line of the sequence the motif of the wild animal's laughter is again introduced. Just as the wild ass laughs at the noisy town (39:7), the ostrich laughs at the pursuing horse and rider (39:18), the war horse laughs at fear (39:22), and the animals of the field frolic (lit., "laugh") in the company of Behemoth (40:20), so also Leviathan laughs at the rattling lance (41:29[21]). These creatures and the anarchistic, chaotic element of creation that they represent are utterly beyond the control of the human will.

The physical description of Leviathan, interrupted by the catalogue of weapons, resumes in 41:30[22], with a comparison of its rough and scaly belly to jagged potsherds. But the focus is on the transformation of shore and sea as Leviathan moves over them. Habel is probably right that "mire" (טיט *ṭîṭ*; cf. Isa 57:20), "the depths" (מצולה *mĕṣûlâ*; cf. Jonah 2:4), and "the deep" (תהום *tĕhôm*; cf. 28:14; 38:16) are evocative of the chaotic, as is the image of churning water.[601] Yet the three images used are progressively less violent and increasingly beautiful. The image of

596. *ANET*, 62.
597. So Tur-Sinai, *The Book of Job*, 569; Kubina, *Die Gottesreden im Buche Hiob*, 99.
598. *ANET*, 130.
599. *ANET*, 62.

600. Hartley, *The Book of Job*, 532n. 42, notes that in ancient Egyptian hieroglyphs the eyes of the crocodile stand for the red morning light.
601. Habel, *The Book of Job*, 573.

the threshing sledge is elsewhere associated with violence (e.g., Amos 3:1; Isa 41:15). A pot of boiling ointment is also an image of agitation, yet is one not associated with danger. The small size of such a pot subtly introduces an element of visual distance into the picture, as though one were watching the sea from far away. The sense of distance is further enhanced in the last verse of the series, as one looks not at Leviathan, but at its wake as it swims away. The image with which the wake is visualized is no longer one of agitation, but a calm image of the deep as white-haired.

41:33-34. As God declared Behemoth's status as "first in rank among the works of God," so Leviathan's place is proclaimed.

Leviathan is no threat to God, but upon earth it is supreme. As noted above, the word for "without equal" is spelled the same way as the phrase "none can dominate him" (אין משלו *'ên mošlô*; 41:33[40:25]); both meanings are probably intended here. The preceding poem is ample testimony to that claim and to the statement that he is "made without fear." As in chap. 39, the conclusion of the poem is marked by an inclusio, as 41:34[26] echoes 40:11*b*. There Job was challenged to "look on every proud one and bring him low." Here it is said that Leviathan "looks on all that are haughty." Far from being brought low, Leviathan is their king.

REFLECTIONS

At the end of the dialogue, as Job prepared to make his decisive challenge to God, he gave a lengthy account of his moral world and the basis upon which he was confronting God and seeking vindication. Job's moral thinking, both its admirable qualities and its disturbing elements, have been considered in the Reflections to Job 29–31. Here one may simply note that it was a fairly rigid moral perspective, quite without resources for dealing with the ineradicable presence of the chaotic as a part of the natural or the social world. What Job has been confronted with in the divine speeches will have rendered his old moral categories no longer adequate to his new perception. Indeed, anyone who approaches the divine speeches with a dogmatic, legally oriented moral system is likely to feel a similar disorientation. How is one to rebuild a coherent moral perspective after the experience of the voice from the whirlwind?

The divine speeches do not contain an explicit moral teaching that can be simply summarized. Indeed, they do not seem to employ much explicitly "moral" language at all. God does not remake Job's moral world for him; that remains properly a human task. But God does provide Job and the reader with the resources for that undertaking. The divine speeches contain the lumber from which a new house of meaning can be built. The resources God offers to Job and to each reader include provocative questions about identity, new ways of perceiving the world, patterns and structures of thought different from accustomed ones, and, above all, images that can become generative metaphors for a renewed moral imagination.

As Janzen has noted, the rhetorical questions God addresses to Job (Who is this? Where were you? Are you able?) are not merely rhetorical questions, but in an ironic sense real, existential questions about identity and vocation.[602] Questions of identity and vocation are fundamentally moral questions. The way a person answers such questions is in large part a matter of the horizon of meaning within which a person thinks. The contrast between the horizon within which Job presents himself in chaps. 29–31 and the horizon within which God asks Job to locate himself could not be sharper. Job's primary horizon of meaning was the village and the family. God challenges the parochialism of Job's moral imagination by making the starting point nothing less than the whole of creation. We, too, often tend to think of the moral world as having to do simply with the relation of humans to other humans. Yet human abuse of creation in

602. Janzen, *Job,* 225-28.

the wanton destruction of the environment should make modern readers particularly alert to the significance of God's insistence that the questions of human identity and vocation must first be answered in the context of the whole of creation. Not only does such a horizon of meaning alter one's relation to non-human creation, but it also causes one to understand human relations differently. By the choice of their starting place, the divine speeches suggest that one understand human identity and human community in the light of creation, rather than attempting to understand God and the cosmos on the basis of particular human social arrangements.

Not only the scope of the horizon but also the disciplines of attention that God requires of Job and the reader contribute to the remaking of the moral sense. Readers may be impatient for explicit moral discourse, but the divine speeches require a prolonged and disciplined act of contemplation as the first task. There are probably not many ethics courses in colleges or seminaries that spend the first three days in silence—one day in the forest, one day at the shore of the sea, one night in a field gazing at the stars. Yet something like that is what God requires of Job as the starting point for a new moral understanding. As was discussed in the Reflections to Job 36–37, the "moral sense of nature" is above all an affirmation that the natural world has intrinsic value. The morning stars' cry of joy (38:7) is the recognition of the intrinsic value that God speaks of as "goodness" in Genesis 1. The starting point for the development of the moral sense in the divine speeches is a contemplation of the goodness of the natural world: earth and rain and raven.

The account of creation in the divine speeches contains metaphors that are strongly suggestive of the formation of a moral order. The imagery of place, limit, and nonencroachment recurs frequently. Most explicitly, it occurs in the account of the sea, which is told that it may come so far and not farther (38:11). Such imagery is also present in the pervasive language of gates, paths, ways, storage chambers, channels. The language of place, limit, and nonencroachment is a language of balance, what we would speak of today as an ecological language. What kind of an ethic might emerge from meditation on these formative images? If one realizes that each thing, each person has place, purpose, and limit, then there are places where I must not tread, places where the energy and vitality, indeed, the violence of my being must meet its limit. Correspondingly, I do have a place, which none must violate.[603]

Where the language of limit challenges much customary moral thinking is in its application to the case of the wicked. God's description of the coming of dawn as setting a limit to the activity of the wicked (38:12-15) is quite different from Job's description of breaking the jaws of the wrongdoer and wresting the prey from his teeth (29:17). Neither image can be taken out of context and used, for example, as a proof text in an argument over the proper response to the problem of violent crime in modern society. Each image, however, can be a starting place for reflection on the very different visions of moral thinking and social order it implies. The heroism and decisiveness of Job's image are immensely appealing. Yet it is an image of meeting violence with violence that in no way transcends the cycle of violence. Job's figure of speech contains an implicit analogy that compares the criminal with the lion that raids the flock. The implication is that the criminal is not a member of the community who has done evil but one who is wholly an enemy, to be driven out and if necessary annihilated. The dehumanization of the criminal is inscribed in the image. Such an understanding of the criminal is very much a part of moral thinking that draws sharp lines between insiders and outsiders. God's image of setting limits to criminal activity emerges out of a different vision of social relations. It implicitly acknowledges that the antisocial impulse is always present in human communities and that, while it may be restrained, it will certainly return. The divine speeches do not develop the image, but

603. C Newsom, "The Moral Sense of Nature: Ethics in the Light of God's Speech to Job," *The Princeton Seminary Bulletin* 15 New Series (1994) 9-27.

certain implications might be traced out. Once a community has recognized that it cannot deal with the criminal by expulsion or annihilation, then it has also acknowledged the criminal as a part of the community, however disruptive a presence. Only on the basis of that recognition is redemption possible.

It is important to remember that the divine speeches do not primarily serve to lay out a moral teaching about the world. They serve, rather, as a revelatory experience. Such moments of revelation always have an elusive, enigmatic quality that escapes reduction to a "message." This is true not only of the stories of revelatory disclosure in the Bible but also in the epiphanies that occur in every person's life. Yet a person is repeatedly drawn to remember those moments out of a recognition that they contain the generative seed of a wholly new way of understanding God, the world, and oneself. Teasing out the possibilities of such a moment may require a lifetime, but in that process one engages the existential questions of identity and vocation that God poses to each person.

Job 42:1-6, Job's Response

COMMENTARY

Immediately following God's speech concerning Behemoth and Leviathan, Job replies. As the decisive word that Job speaks in God's presence, this reply provides the dramatic climax anticipated since the *satan*'s prediction that, once deprived of his family, possessions, and health, Job would curse God to God's face (1:11; 2:5). Job's words are not a curse, but the significance of what he says is not easily discerned. His words are elusive and enigmatic. That Job will no longer attempt to argue with God is clear, but his state of mind and the reasons for his withdrawal can be understood in more than one way. The ambiguity is perhaps strategic. By making Job's reply enigmatic, the poet requires readers to assume a more active role in construing the meaning and significance of the divine speeches and how they might resolve the conflict between Job and God.

The outline of Job's brief response is clear. He begins with a confession of God's effective power (42:2). Two quotations from God's speech (42:3a, 4; the NIV supplies "You asked . . . you said") introduce Job's two conclusions, each marked with a form of the word "therefore" (לכן *lākēn*, 42:3b, 5-6). The meaning of his reply is more difficult to judge. Although he uses somewhat different terminology from that employed by God, Job's confession (42:2) acknowledges God's power (cf. 40:9) and ability to implement plans

(cf. 38:2; 40:8). In 42:3a, Job echoes God's words from 38:2 in a slightly altered form. By incorporating God's words into his own speech, Job suggests that he now views himself from God's perspective. More explicitly, with his following words (42:3b) Job accepts God's judgment that he has spoken without knowledge and understanding (38:2). Those words do not make clear, however, how Job has understood the substantive meaning of the divine speeches.

In 42:4, Job again echoes God's words, as 42:4b ("I will question you,/ and you shall answer me") cites 38:3b and 40:7b. The beginning of the verse ("Hear, and I will speak") is not a direct quotation of God's words, but a poetic expansion of 42:4b. It allows Job to introduce the word "hear" (שמע *šāma*ʿ), which is significant for his own reply in v. 5. Most interpreters assume that in v. 5 Job is contrasting past hearing with present seeing.[604] The "hearing of the ear" can be used of rumors or secondhand reports (cf. 28:22b; Ps 18:44[45]). The theologies of Job and his friends would be just such secondhand constructions of God. By contrast, the immediacy of the divine revelation could be characterized as "seeing." Although this interpretation is entirely plausible, it overlooks the relationship between v. 4 and

604. See Dhorme, *A Commentary on the Book of Job,* 646; Gordis, *The Book of Job,* 492; Pope, *Job,* 347.

v. 5. Job characterizes God's command to him as a command to listen while God speaks. It would be odd if Job's next words were a denigration of "hearing." Instead, one should take 42:5*a* as Job's confirmation that he has indeed listened, as God has commanded him; the consequence of that hearing is that Job now "sees" God (i.e., "I have listened to you with my ears, and now my eye sees you" [author's trans.]).[605] The language of "seeing" God has a special place in Israelite religious tradition. Seeing God is rarely permitted and often associated with a momentous occasion in the life of an individual or a people (Gen 16:13; Exod 24:9-11; 33:20-23; Isa 6:1). Job had earlier expressed the fervent desire to see God with his own eyes (19:26-27). The context in which that desire has been fulfilled, however, is quite different from what Job had anticipated. His words in 42:5 say nothing about the way in which his understanding of God has been changed by this new "seeing."

One expects the final verse of Job's reply in v. 6 to clarify matters. Instead, it is not only as terse and enigmatic as the preceding verses but also grammatically ambiguous.[606] Almost every word in v. 6 is susceptible of more than one interpretation, as a brief survey of the grammatical problems, followed by a sampling of alternative translations, will illustrate. The word translated "despise" or "reject" (מאס *mā'as*) ordinarily requires an object, yet none is present in 42:6, and so it must be supplied by context. Hence, "I despise myself" or "I reject my words"—i.e., "I retract" or "I recant."[607] One could argue, however, that the object is present in the words "dust and ashes" (עפר ואפר *'āpār wā'ēper*).[608] Alternatively, it may be that the verb is a variant of another Hebrew verb meaning "to melt" (מסס *māsas*), and might be translated here as "I submit."[609]

Similar ambiguities affect the translation of the phrase ונחמתי על (*wěniḥamtî 'al*). It may be translated "I repent upon/on account of . . ." or "I am consoled concerning . . ." or "I have changed my mind concerning . . ."

or "I forswear. . . . "[610] The translation of the phrase "dust and ashes" is straightforward enough, but the expression has two related yet different metaphorical meanings. It can refer to human mortality, especially the human condition as contrasted with divine being (cf. Gen 18:27; Sir 10:9). The phrase can also be used to describe particular humiliation or degradation (Job 30:19; Sir 40:3).[611] Other suggestions that the phrase refers to the ash heap upon which Job sits (2:8)[612] or to dust as a symbol of mourning (2:12)[613] are less likely, since they involve only one term of what is clearly a set phrase; but they are not impossible.

Taking account of these various possibilities, one could legitimately translate v. 6 in any of the following ways:

(1) "Therefore I despise myself and repent upon dust and ashes" (i.e., in humiliation; cf. NRSV; NIV);

(2) "Therefore I retract my words and repent of dust and ashes" (i.e., the symbols of mourning);[614]

(3) "Therefore I reject and forswear dust and ashes" (i.e., the symbols of mourning);[615]

(4) "Therefore I retract my words and have changed my mind concerning dust and ashes" (i.e., the human condition);[616]

(5) "Therefore I retract my words, and I am comforted concerning dust and ashes" (i.e., the human condition).[617]

With a slightly different understanding of the grammar, the TNK translates, "Therefore, I recant and relent,/ Being but dust and ashes." These examples do not exhaust the various nuances that might be heard in the ambiguity of the Hebrew of 42:6, but they suggest something of the possible range of meaning.

Asking which possibility is correct misses the interpretive significance of the ambiguity of Job's reply, which corresponds to

605. See Good, *In Turns of Tempest,* 373-75.

606. See W. Morrow, "Consolation, Rejection, and Repentance in Job 42:6," *JBL* 105 (1986) 211-25, for a thorough discussion of the grammatical issues.

607. L. Kuyper, "The Repentance of Job," *VT* 9 (1959) 91-94; Fohrer, *Das Buch Hiob,* 536; Habel, *The Book of Job,* 582.

608. D. Patrick, "The Translation of Job 42.6," *VT* 26 (1976) 369-71.

609. Dhorme, *A Commentary on the Book of Job,* 646-47.

610. Morrow, "Consolation, Rejection, and Repentance in Job 42:6," 215-17.

611. Morrow, "Consolation, Rejection, and Repentance in Job 42:6," 216-17.

612. E.g., Dhorme, *A Commentary on the Book of Job,* 646-47; Pope, *Job,* 349.

613. Cf. Habel, *The Book of Job,* 583.

614. Cf. Habel, *The Book of Job,* 575.

615. Cf. Patrick, "The Translation of Job 42.6," 369-70.

616. Cf. Janzen, *Job,* 6-57.

617. Cf. Perdue, *Wisdom in Revolt,* 232.

the ambiguity that is also part of the divine speeches. A reader who has interpreted the divine speeches as a defense of God's honor and a rebuke to the audacity of a mere human in challenging God will tend to hear Job's words more or less according to the first alternative suggested above, or as the TNK renders the line. A reader who understands the book largely in terms of the legal metaphor and takes God's speeches as a rebuttal of Job's lawsuit might be inclined to hear Job's words in terms of the second alternative. One who emphasizes the celebratory tone of the divine speeches might hear Job's words according to the third alternative. In the interpretation of the divine speeches proposed here, which understands them as challenging Job's legal paradigm and placing the question of human existence in terms of a world in which the chaotic must be acknowledged, either the fourth or the fifth alternative appears fitting. The ambiguities inherent in the divine speeches and Job's reply resist every attempt to reduce them to a single, definitive interpretation. That ambiguity does not mean that a reader should refrain from arguing for a particular interpretation of the divine speeches and Job's reply, but only that a reader must recognize that more than one legitimate interpretation is possible. Here, it is appropriate to consider how one should understand Job's reply in the light of the interpetation of the divine speeches developed in this commentary.

In v. 3, Job repudiated his previous words as having been spoken without understanding. He had attempted to speak of "wonderful things" (נפלאות *niplā'ôt*), i.e., God's design (38:2), without realizing that such knowledge was beyond his scope. Thus it is appropriate to assume that in v. 6 Job rejects or retracts his previous words. He also refers to what he has heard about God (v. 5*a*), a hearing that has led to a new way of perceiving God (v. 5*b*). Job had earlier been caught in a dilemma. He could attribute the wretchedness of the human condition to only the arbitrariness and perhaps the hostility of God. Now, given what has been disclosed to him in the divine speeches, Job is able to perceive a world in which the vulnerability of human existence can be understood, not in terms of divine enmity, but in terms of a creation within which the chaotic is restrained but never fully eliminated. Thus it is fitting that Job should speak of a change of mind and perhaps of a consolation concerning the human condition. His final words signal his appropriation of the vision of reality and the nature of God disclosed in the divine speeches.

REFLECTIONS

1. Job's observation that he now "sees" (42:5*b*) is the key to the significance of his reply to God. However one chooses to translate 42:6, Job confesses that he now perceives God in a way that transforms his understanding of himself and his situation. As Job's reply suggests, "seeing" is a complex business, involving much more than simply having one's eyes physically open. An old proverb makes the point nicely: "Ninety percent of what a person sees lies behind the eyes." Even at the literal level, this proverb is true, for the brain structures visual stimuli into meaningful patterns. By means of these patterns, some features are made to appear prominent and others are virtually screened out, so that the visual stimulus may be recognized as a meaningful thing— e.g., an apple, a knife, a face. Without the templates that organize raw perception, a person could not see in any real sense. The proverb is even more true at the level of moral perception. What a person is able to see in a situation depends a great deal on the organizing and interpretive frameworks that person brings to it. Some aspects of an experience will be made to appear significant and others will be relegated to the periphery or not perceived at all, so that the experience may be interpreted—e.g., as a situation of injustice, an act of caring, a show of indifference. Most of the time we are not aware of these frameworks, because they lie "behind the eyes," at the level of subconscious presuppositions, but they very directly influence what we are capable of seeing. So it was with Job. He could see only injustice in his situation, because his interpretive paradigm, based on a legal metaphor, organized his experience in terms of rights and wrongs.

As Job discovered, events do occur that challenge and sometimes overturn the paradigms that have shaped one's perceptions. Yet people do not readily let go of the frameworks that have shaped their vision of reality. Often, it is when we have already begun to suspect that something is wrong with our paradigms that we become most resistant to allowing them to be challenged. It is not just that we *cannot* see something, but that we are *afraid* of looking squarely at what we can glimpse just at the periphery of our vision. Like the characters in the book of Job, many people are reluctant to confront the reality that human beings cannot secure their lives and their families against harm. We do not want to see that bad things happen to good people. Yet horrible things can happen, without apparent rhyme or reason. Premature death, accidents, violence, and illness can happen to anyone at any time. We all know that to be true, and yet we resist it with all our being. Drunk drivers exist, but why must one kill *my* child? Cancer is a reality, but why must it strike *my* spouse? The seeming randomness of such events is terrifying, and so we cling to interpretive paradigms of experience that will mask the reality, organize it in a way that makes it appear to be something else. Job's friends employed a number of such frameworks, which allowed disaster to be seen as moral discipline, punishment, etc. Job rejected those frameworks but embraced an alternative, legal paradigm that allowed him to declare the disasters morally wrong and to have someone to blame. All of these paradigms allowed them not to see what they were afraid to see—that the chaotic is an irreducible aspect of creation that must be taken into account in any adequate understanding of experience. To that extent, their moral paradigms served them as a means of denial.

The reality that Job has to confront in the divine speeches is the ineradicable presence of the chaotic in existence. God's speeches do not invite speculation as to *why* the chaotic is a part of creation. They are not a theodicy in the sense that a theodicy attempts to explain or to justify the presence in God's creation of those things that render human existence fragile and vulnerable. Theodicies, too, are explanatory frameworks that often serve to mask or obscure something that is difficult to acknowledge. When, in their attempts to justify death, pain, or suffering, theodicies speak of such things as only "appearing" to be evils but "really" being for some greater good, then they are forms of denial. Job's friends had attempted just such justifications (see Reflections on Job 4; 5), as they suggested that suffering was divine discipline, but the divine speeches make no such claims. They insist that the presence of the chaotic be acknowledged as part of the design of creation, but they never attempt to justify it. The pain caused by the eruption of the chaotic into human life must be recognized as such.

Sometimes a dramatic confrontation is required to overcome the resistance people often experience in acknowledging the reality of something they have tried hard not to see. Leviathan plays that role in God's speech to Job. Job had concluded his first speech in chap. 3, which was filled with the imagery of chaos, with the words, "the dread which I dreaded has come upon me" (3:25*b*, author's trans.). Like many people, Job intuited but was not yet willing to face what he most feared. Job's quarrel with God has been a long attempt to keep that dread at bay by trying to engage God in a very different kind of argument. God's wisdom, however, is to know that Job can neither make his decision about God (1:1; 2:5) nor continue with his life until he has acknowledged the reality of what he fears. Finally, in the divine speeches Job encounters the very image of his dread in the face of Leviathan. When that happens, it is as though a spell is broken. Job is released from his obsession with justice and can begin the process of living beyond tragedy. Putting one's life together again is not easy. For most people, the "happy ending" does not come in the quick and apparently simple resolution that the book of Job describes in 42:7-17. But the book of Job is wise in its recognition that false or distorting frameworks to which people cling in an attempt to defend themselves against what they dread may prevent them from seeing what they need to acknowledge, if they are to get on with their lives.

2. Confronting the reality of the presence of the chaotic in the design of the world is essential, but if the divine speeches had nothing to say to Job except that pain is part of life, then they would hardly be worth reading. One has to ask how they comfort and strengthen. It is essential to remember that Leviathan is not the only topic in the divine speeches. Before God speaks of that emblem of the chaotic, God has already described a world in which the chaotic, although present, is contained within the secure boundaries of a created order that is also rich with goodness. The power of these speeches to comfort was powerfully articulated by a mother whose teenage son had been killed in an automobile accident. She described how, on the morning of his funeral, she rose early and reached for her Bible, reading to herself the speeches of God from the whirlwind. When asked why she chose those chapters, she said, "I needed to know that my pain was not all there was in the world." Her anguish was like that of Job's in chap. 3, an inward spiral of pain that threatened to swallow all of creation. What she needed was the reassurance of a God whose power of creation and re-creation is stronger than the power of the chaotic. Job had been ready in his pain to give in to the overwhelming sense of despair, to use a curse to destroy the structures of creation that had led to his unbearable existence (3:3-10). God cannot now take away the defenses that Job has erected in the succeeding chapters without addressing that original cry of despair. The first divine speech in chaps. 38–39 acknowledges Job's sense of a fall into the abyss. With its orderly pattern of visually powerful images, this divine speech is a verbal re-creation of the world. Hearing the words of the establishment of the earth on secure foundations, the reliable return of the dawn each day, the regulation of life-giving water, and the nurture of the animals is a reassurance that in spite of the reality of pain and loss, God's creation supports and sustains.

The divine speeches offer comfort in another way, too. A person who has suffered a great loss or who has finally faced up to a painful reality long denied often experiences an overwhelming sense of isolation, alienation, and godforsakenness. There is a need to share the burden, and yet such sharing may be difficult. Cultures often make sharing more difficult than it need be, for instance, by placing too much value on stoic endurance or, as in Job's culture, by treating suffering as somehow a sign of divine rejection. The result is to increase the burden of isolation. The divine speeches address this issue by means of the creation imagery they employ. Speaking of the relation of the created world to issues of pain and grief, Kohak talks explicitly about the book of Job:

> A human alone, surrounded by the gleaming surfaces of his artifacts, cannot bear the pain. He can do that only when the grief can disperse, radiate out and be absorbed. [Even] fellow humans and their works, bearing the same burden, cannot absorb it. . . . To reconcile, that is what the forest does, silent and accepting, as if God were present therein, taking the grief unto Himself. When humans no longer think themselves alone, masters of all they survey, when they discern the humility of their place in the vastness of God's creation, then that creation and its God can share the pain. . . . That is the age-old wisdom of the book of Job. . . . When God speaks . . . [God] speaks not of pain but of the vastness of the creation, of the gazelle in her mountain fastness and the mighty creatures of the deep sea. God is not avoiding the issue. [God] is teaching Job the wisdom of bearing the pain that can neither be avoided nor abolished but can be shared when there is a whole living creation to absorb it. . . . When the human, in the solitude of dusk, surrenders his pride of place and learns to bear the shared pain, he can begin to understand the pain that cannot be avoided as a gift which teaches compassion and opens understanding. . . . It opens him to receive, in empathy, the gift of the other, not in censure but in gratitude and love.[618]

618. Kohak, *The Embers and the Stars,* 45-46.

Kohak's words explain why the divine speeches enable Job to take up his life again. The acknowledgment of the reality of "pain that can neither be avoided nor abolished" may have broken the spell of denial, but living beyond tragedy requires the ability to receive and to give within community.

3. The divine speeches also challenge Job's understanding of where the presence of God may be found. Like many who suffer, Job experienced himself as godforsaken. In his way of thinking, God's presence was to be found in the peace and fulfillment of the family circle and the satisfaction of doing good within the community (chap. 29). To a certain extent, Job was not wrong, for God is to be found there. Job found it impossible, however, to experience the presence of God in desolation (chap. 30). As a symbol of his outcast condition, Job described himself as "a brother of jackals,/ a companion of ostriches" (30:29 NRSV), identifying in his misery with the creatures who inhabit desolate places. God's view of such creatures and their world is quite different from Job's. The vivid image of God's "satisfying the desolate wasteland" with rain, symbol of divine blessing, strongly suggests that Job is wrong in thinking that there is any place or any condition beyond the sustaining power of God's presence.

God's nurture of and pleasure in the animals of the wasteland is a provocative image. As noted in the Commentary, these animals were symbolic of the hostile and alien "other." In Job's imagination, they provided an image for describing the rejected and despised human "beasts" cast out of society (30:5-8). It is worth pursuing that connection. In our own society, many groups of people cluster at the margins of society; the mentally ill and the homeless are those we think of first. But one should also think of the biker culture, petty criminals, and others who live on the fringes of the law. The lives of such people often seem to be desolate wastelands, and the emotions they provoke in others are often a mixture of pity and fear. They seem so alien, so far outside the bounds of the ordinary social life that most people take as normative. But that is to view them from Job's perspective. From God's perspective, there is no alien outsider; there are only children of God. It can be difficult for "good Christian people" to imagine, but the destitute may know more of the grace of God than do the comfortable, and the petty criminal's life may be touched by the love of God in ways that the "respectable" person can scarcely imagine. God's revivifying rain continues to satisfy the desolate places. Indeed, those places are the ones most likely to respond with exuberant flowering, even though that beauty may go unseen by most of the world.

JOB 42:7-17

THE PROSE NARRATIVE: CONCLUSION

COMMENTARY

Immediately following Job's reply to God, the voice of the prose narrator takes up the story and brings it to a conclusion. This shift is more than a change in style, for the prose conclusion seems to presume a significantly different story line from the one that has just been enacted in the dialogues and divine speeches. First, Yahweh's rebuke of the friends, that they "have not spoken of me what is right, as my servant Job has" (vv. 7-8), is difficult to square with the iconoclasm of Job's words in the dialogue and God's rebuke of Job as having spoken "words without knowledge" (38:2*b*). Second, the resolution of the story by means of the restoration of Job's wealth and the birth of a new family, which fits with the narrative and moral world of the didactic story in chaps. 1–2 (see Commentary on Job 1; 2), clashes with the moral complexity of the dialogue and the divine speeches.

As discussed in the Introduction, some commentators have attributed the discrepancy between the frame story and the poetic material to an editor who combined the beginning and end of an old traditional tale with a long poetic dialogue from a different author, not bothering to smooth out the inconsistencies created by joining the two. Yet it is also possible that a single author wrote the entire book, artfully using contrasting styles and sharply disjunctive transitions between the frame story and the dialogue to create the illusion of two different compositions joined together. Whichever way the book of Job achieved its present shape, that shape gives 42:7-17 two different functions. It serves as the conclusion to the simple, didactic prose story, and it serves as the conclusion to the book of Job as a whole. When considered as the conclusion to the didactic tale, the happy ending provides a smooth and satisfying conclusion. When considered as the conclusion to the book as a whole, the ending creates dissonance and disruption. Commentators who attempt to read the entire book as a unity often soften these discrepancies. Thus attempts are made to interpret Job's "speaking rightly" in terms of sincerity, i.e., his avoidance of "dissembling and flattery."[619] The happy ending is read as an act of the free grace of God[620] or as a narrative symbol of Job's putting aside moral bitterness and experiencing reconciliation with God and community.[621] Such interpretive moves evade rather than engage the dissonance of the ending of the book of Job. The position taken in this commentary is that the dissonance is part of the narrative strategy of the book (see Introduction). By leaving the tension between the two parts unresolved, the book as a whole allows the frame story and the dialogue to explore different dimensions of the complex question of the moral basis for divine-human relations. That dissonance both recognizes and refuses the reader's desire for closure to the story and a definitive resolution of the issues it has raised.

The prose conclusion divides into two parts: vv. 7-9 concern God's rebuke of Job's three friends and Job's role as intercessor for them; vv. 10-17 describe the restoration of Job's wealth, family, and well-being, concluding with an account of his long life.

42:7-9. The impossibility of harmonizing v. 7 with the preceding material in chaps. 3:1–42:6 is clearly indicated in the connotation of the word "right" (נכונה *nĕkônâ*). As

619. Habel, *The Book of Job*, 583.
620. Habel, *The Book of Job*, 584; Janzen, *Job*, 267; Hartley, *The Book of Job*, 540.
621. Wilcox, *The Bitterness of Job*, 209.

Pope argues, it does not have the nuance of "sincerity." Instead, its basic meaning is "correct" (cf. 1 Sam 23:23).[622] Job cannot be both praised for speaking "correctly" (42:7) and rebuked for speaking "words without knowledge" that obscure the design of God (38:2). Verse 7 thus gestures back to the story line begun by the didactic prose tale in chaps. 1–2, in which Job is the model of piety and his friends warrant rebuke.

In the didactic story itself, without 3:1–42:6, Job is the hero of unconditional piety who never wavers in his commitment, despite extraordinary and inexplicable adversity (1:21-22; 2:10). The test of fidelity having been completed, restoration of the hero's fortunes is the ending that this sort of narrative requires. Generously, the story even includes the rebuked friends in its happy ending. The sacrifice of vv. 8-9, commanded by Yahweh, reaffirms Job's role as intercessor (cf. 1:5) and serves as the mechanism for the reconciliation of God and the friends. The extravagant offering of seven bulls and rams is in keeping with the exaggerated style and use of symbolic numbers characteristic of the prose tale (see Commentary on Job 1; cf. also the folkloristic Balaam story, in which seven bulls and seven rams are sacrificed on seven altars [Num 23:1, 4, 14, 29-30]).

42:10-17. Following the reconciliation between God and Job's three friends, the story describes the restoration of Job's fortunes. That Job should receive twice as much as before (v. 10) is an appropriate feature in this type of story (cf. the restoration of good fortune that comes to the pious and long-suffering Tobit and Sarah in the book of Tobit). Rather than taking the visit of Job's family and friends as subsequent to the restoration of his fortunes,[623] one should interpret v. 11-12 as describing the *way* in which God restored the fortunes of Job. That is, even before Job's fortunes are restored, his family and friends come to share a meal and offer gestures of comfort. The solidarity of Job's family in sorrow echoes the family solidarity of the joyful birthday celebrations shared by the brothers and sisters in 1:4. Job's family and friends all give him gifts, a piece of money (קשיטה

qĕśîtâ) and a gold ring. The value of a *qesita* is not known, but it was apparently a modest but not insignificant gift (see Gen 33:19; Josh 24:32). From these shared gifts, God's blessing would create the enormous fortune Job enjoyed in the latter part of his life (v. 12; cf. Gen 30:30).

A new family is also born as part of Job's restoration, seven sons and three daughters (v. 13). An unusual form of the word for "seven" is used here (שבענה šib'ānâ), leading some to interpret it as a dual form, indicating that Job's second family included fourteen sons (cf. 1 Chr 25:5, where a family of fourteen sons and three daughters are given to Heman the seer "through the promises of God to exalt him").[624] If that is the correct interpretation, then the extraordinary number of Job's sons would be matched by the extraordinary beauty of Job's daughters (v. 15a). The narrator lingers on the daughters, giving their names. The first is named Jemimah, which means "dove"; the second is named Keziah, which means fragrant "cinnamon" (cf. Ps 45:8); the third is named Keren-Happuch, which means "cosmetics box" (lit., "Horn of Eyeshadow"; cf. 2 Kgs 9:30; Jer 4:30). The image of a joyful and harmonious society is underscored by the note that Job gave his daughters an inheritance along with their brothers (v. 15b). That this detail should receive special mention apparently indicates that it was not the normal state of affairs (cf. Num 27:3-4).

It may seem shocking that the story seems to overlook that beloved children cannot be replaced by new ones, as wealth may be replaced. Without knowing more about the conventions of storytelling in ancient Israel, it is difficult to say whether such "outrageous" features are supposed to be accepted simply as part of the way one tells a story like this, or whether the author is subtly using this detail to make readers uncomfortable with a story that they would otherwise accept without question. The narrator makes no evaluative comment but continues with the account of Job's restoration.

The final indication of Job's blessedness lies in the length of life granted to him (v. 16a).

---

622. Pope, *Job*, 350.
623. So, e.g., Dhorme, *A Commentary on the Book of Job*, 651; Pope, *Job*, 351.

624. So the Targum to Job. See Dhorme, *A Commentary on the Book of Job*, 651-52; Gordis, *The Book of Job*, 498. See also Sarna, "Epic Substratum in the Prose of Job," 18.

As his fortunes and the number of his sons were doubled, so the years of his life after his calamity (140 years) are the equivalent of two normal lifetimes (cf. Ps 19:10). An ordinarily blessed life includes seeing one's children's children, two generations (Ps 128:6); thus Job's doubly blessed life allows him to see four generations of his descendants (v. 16*b*). Echoing the language used of Israel's patriarchs, the final verse of the story describes Job's death as occurring when he was "old and full of days" (v. 17; cf. Gen 25:8; 35:29; 1 Chr 29:28).

When vv. 7-17 are read as the conclusion to the didactic tale, every detail contributes to the coherency of the story. In the book as we have it, however, the conclusion follows the dialogue and divine speeches, not the didactic tale. In this actual context, the conclusion produces ironic dissonance rather than coherency. The effect is to reawaken questions that had ostensibly been resolved. This ironic affirmation that Job has spoken "correctly" of God directs the reader's attention back to what Job has in fact said: that God has treated him with cruel injustice and has abdicated proper governance of the world. A reader who has too quickly put aside Job's passionate argument with God in the face of the divine speeches' alternative paradigm is given a chance to reconsider. Can God be the ultimate source of the moral order without behaving as a moral being toward Job or acting responsibly toward the world? Is not Job's challenge to God concerning the misery of the destitute still valid, and still awaiting an answer? The narrative compounds the irony through its depiction of the twofold restoration of Job's fortunes. A reader who knows Israelite legal tradition may recall that a thief or a negligent trustee of another's property was required to pay double to the injured party (Exod 22:4,

7, 9[3, 6, 8]). Thus in the light of Job's accusations against God in the dialogue, the restoration in vv. 10-12 seems to be a piece of narrative irony at God's expense, as God performs the act of restitution expected of a criminal. Yet a person persuaded by the justice of Job's accusations is not likely to be satisfied that the fundamental issues are resolved by such restitution.

Just as the affirmation of Job's words in vv. 7-8 produces ironic dissonance, so too does the rebuke of the friends' words. The friends repeatedly urged Job to endorse the wisdom of traditional piety, turning to God in prayer and humble self-examination, trusting that God would restore him to peace and security (e.g., 11:13-19). In fact, when Job does confess humbly before God, his arrogance in speaking rashly about "what I did not understand" (v. 3), events turn out just as the friends said they would. The statement that God "blessed the latter days" (אחרית *'aḥărît*) of Job more than his beginning (ראשית *rē'šît*, v. 12) is a verbal echo of what Bildad had said in 8:7: "Though your beginning [*rē'šît*] was small,/ your latter days [*'aḥărît*] will be very great" NRSV). Moreover, Eliphaz's description of God as one who "wounds, but binds up" is an apt account of Job's experience of God. Just as Eliphaz had anticipated, God does preserve Job from absolute destruction even in the midst of calamity, and then restores him to a blessed old age (cf. 5:19-26), culminating in a peaceful death (v. 17) in which Job might be said to "come to [his] grave in ripe old age,/ as a shock of grain comes up to the threshing floor in its season" (5:26 NRSV). Despite God's rebuke of the friends, the ironic structure of the narrative as a whole seems to ratify this dimension of the friends' understanding of the divine-human relationship.

REFLECTIONS

The prose conclusion in 42:7-17, which ostensibly serves to give closure to the book of Job, in fact does just the opposite. Throughout the course of the book, four different perspectives have been presented: that of the didactic prose tale, that of the friends, that of Job, and that of the divine speeches. Although initially the structure of the book appeared to be leading to a progressive rejection of the first three perspectives, the device of giving the last word to the prose tale undercuts this seeming momentum toward closure. Through its ironic dissonance with what has gone before, the prose conclusion makes it less clear which voice, if any, holds the key to the troubling issues raised by the book of Job. Just where one expects resolution, the book offers frustration instead. One could easily be angry at the book for having asked its readers to work hard at difficult moral and religious questions and then ended with a tease instead of an answer.

This sense of betrayal can be especially acute since the book of Job is part of Scripture. People want answers to difficult questions, and many people assume that the Bible is the place to find them. The teasing quality of the book of Job is actually more characteristic of biblical teaching than one might think. For example, Jesus' parables have a similar frustrating elusiveness for those who look to them for simple moral directions. Rather than merely being irritated at the ending of Job, one might reflect on what the book is trying to teach us by refusing to give the clear answers we crave.

Especially in our modern culture, there is a tendency to assume that every issue has a single answer; every problem has a single solution. If one works hard at it, then the answer will appear, the problem will be resolved, and one can move on. In religious terms, this assumption expresses itself in the expectation that study, prayer, and instruction will result in knowing the answers to the questions of life. The structure of the book of Job draws our attention to the fallacy in this assumption. Not all the things that trouble us are issues that can be resolved; instead, some of them are dilemmas with which we must continue to live. As the book of Job demonstrates, the anguish that wells up in the question, "Why?" is one such dilemma. There is no single answer that can put an end to that question once and for all.

To deny that there is a single definitive answer is not to say that one cannot gain insight into the problem of suffering in a world created by a loving God. What the book of Job models is a community of voices struggling to articulate a range of perspectives, each one of which contains valid insights as well as blindness to other dimensions of the problem. At different times and in different circumstances, one or another of the voices may seem more powerful, may be the word we need to hear in order to work our way through a particular experience. By refusing to give the book a neat resolution and declare one of the perspectives to be *the* solution, the book of Job draws us toward a recognition that our craving for an answer is an attempt to evade what we know to be true. Especially in times of religious crisis, richness of meaning and even a sense of peace are not to be found in a pre-packaged answer but emerge from the experience of wrestling with God.

Nevertheless, one must reflect on the author's choice to conclude the book of Job not merely with a "happy ending" but with one that takes the reader back to the beginning of the book. The presence of the happy ending is provocative. As much as it may remind readers of unfinished questions, it also poses a new issue that must be reckoned with. Readers must decide whether such an ending "fits." Is the image of reconciliation and flourishing new life an appropriate ending, or is it a betrayal of what has gone before? When people compare their opinions about the fittingness of 42:7-17 as a conclusion for the book of Job, differences of opinion about the book's ending often turn out to be related to differences of opinion about the nature of life itself, whether existence has a fundamentally tragic structure or a comedic structure.

Finally, one needs to consider the significance of a return at the end of the book to the same narrative style with which the book began. As in chap. 28, which also echoed the prose of 1:1 in its concluding verse, one is invited to consider Job's experience as a journey that ends where it began; and yet neither Job nor those who have accompanied him vicariously as readers can experience that place in the same way. It is possible, I think, to imagine Job again uttering the words of 1:21 ("Yahweh has given and Yahweh has taken away; may the name of Yahweh be blessed") and 2:10 ("Shall we accept good from God, and not trouble?" [NIV]). What those words mean, or are capable of meaning, is quite different after one has encountered the voice from the whirlwind from what they meant when one first read them.

THE BOOK OF PSALMS

INTRODUCTION, COMMENTARY, AND REFLECTIONS
BY
J. CLINTON McCANN, JR.

THE BOOK OF

PSALMS

INTRODUCTION

O ne of the most outstanding and highly respected international leaders of the twentieth century was Sweden's Dag Hammarskjöld. As Secretary-General of the United Nations, he devoted the final years of his life to pursuing the principles espoused in the United Nations Charter—international cooperation and reconciliation toward a peaceful world. As Dorothy V. Jones points out, Hammarskjöld viewed his work not simply as a political role but as a religious calling. Jones reports:

> On his travels around the world Hammarskjöld always took three items with him. These items were found in his briefcase that was recovered after the plane crash that took his life in September 1961: a copy of the New Testament, a copy of the Psalms and a copy of the United Nations Charter.[1]"

Hammarskjöld apparently understood—quite correctly—that the book of Psalms presents nothing short of God's claim upon the whole world and that it articulates God's will for justice, righteousness, and peace among all peoples and all nations. It is the purpose of this commentary to elucidate that claim and to enable the reader to hear the Word of God as it comes to us in the psalms. I write as a Christian biblical scholar and theologian, and, like Hammarskjöld, I consciously and constantly hold side by side the psalms and the New Testament. A careful reading of each reveals that the psalms anticipate Jesus' bold presentation of God's claim upon the whole world ("the kingdom of God has come near" [Mark 1:15 NRSV]) and that Jesus embodied the psalter's articulation of God's will for justice, righteousness, and peace among all peoples and all nations. In other words, the approach to the psalms in this commentary is explicitly *theological,* and it takes seriously the canonical shape of the book of Psalms itself as well as the psalter's place in the larger canon of Scripture.

To be sure, this approach differs from the predominant scholarly approach to the psalms in the twentieth century. For the most part, Psalms scholarship has been explicitly *historical.*

---

1. Dorothy V. Jones, "The Example of Dag Hammarskjöld: Style and Effectiveness at the UN," *The Christian Century* 111, 32 (Nov. 9, 1994) 1050.

Undoubtedly, the historical-critical method has produced exciting, enduring, and important results. For instance, when scholars asked historical questions that were informed by sociological analysis (see below on form criticism), they arrived at the understanding that the psalms are not just the products of pious individuals in ancient Israel and Judah but that they are the liturgical materials used in ancient Israelite and Judean worship. In short, the psalter represents the hymnbook or the prayer book of the Second (and perhaps the First) Temple. This conclusion is not incorrect, but it is only partially correct. When scholars began to ask historical questions that were informed by literary sensitivity (see below on rhetorical criticism), they arrived at a new appreciation of the psalmists as highly skilled and sophisticated poets and of each psalm as a unique poetic creation. This conclusion is not incorrect either, but it too is only partially correct.

As important as it is to view the psalms as the sacred poetry that was used in ancient Israelite and Judean worship, this conclusion fails to do justice to another crucial dimension of the psalms: It fails to deal with the fact that the psalms were appropriated, preserved, and transmitted not only as records of human response to God but also as God's word to humanity. As Brevard Childs puts it:

> I would argue that the need for taking seriously the canonical form of the Psalter would greatly aid in making use of the Psalms in the life of the Christian Church. Such a move would not disregard the historical dimensions of the Psalter, but would attempt to profit from the shaping which the final redactors gave the older material in order to transform traditional poetry into Sacred Scripture for the later generations of the faithful.[2]

In short, the book of Psalms has been preserved and transmitted as Scripture, a dimension that is more evident when the final shape of the book of Psalms is taken seriously and when the psalms are heard in conversation with the whole canon of Scripture.

It is my intent in the following commentary to interpret the psalms both as humanity's words to God and as God's word to humanity. Underlying this intent is a very *incarnational* view of Scripture, but the origin and transmission of the psalms in this regard is really no different from other parts of the canon. *All* Scripture originated as the record of humanity's encounter with and response to God, a record that generations of God's people judged to be authentic and true; thus it was preserved and transmitted as the Word of God. To be sure, such an incarnational view of Scripture is scandalously particularistic, but no more so than the fundamental Jewish and Christian convictions that God chose Israel or that God is fully known finally in one Jesus of Nazareth, who was "fully human"—"the Word became flesh and lived among us" (John 1:14 NRSV).

To interpret the psalms both as human words to God and as God's word to humans means that a multiplicity of methods is necessary. To appreciate the psalms as humanity's response to God—as sacred poetry as well as songs and prayers used in worship—it is necessary to employ form criticism and rhetorical criticism. To be sure, these methods may yield insights that lead to fruitful theological reflection; however, as Childs suggests, to appreciate the psalms more fully as God's word to humanity—as Scripture—it is helpful to consider the canonical shape of the psalter itself. Thus the following commentary consciously employs a multiplicity of methods in an attempt to interpret the psalms both historically and theologically. To illustrate what this means in practice, it is helpful to consider the history of the critical study of the psalms in the twentieth century.

CRITICAL STUDY OF THE BOOK OF PSALMS

For centuries, interpreters of the psalms assumed that they were written by the persons whose names appear in the superscriptions. Since David's name appears in the superscriptions of seventy-three psalms, interpreters often have assumed by generalization that David must

---

2. Brevard Childs, "Reflections on the Modern Study of the Psalms," in *Magnalia Dei, the Mighty Acts of God: Essays in Memory of G. Ernest Wright,* eds. F. M. Cross, W. E. Lemke, P. D. Miller, Jr. (Garden City, N.Y.: Doubleday, 1976) 385.

have written most of the untitled psalms as well. With the emergence of critical scholarship in the nineteenth century, these assumptions began to be questioned. Even so, at the beginning of the twentieth century, the psalms were still understood primarily as the work of pious individuals (although not necessarily the persons whose names appear in the superscriptions) who composed prayers and songs either for their private devotional use or in response to particular historical events. Thus scholars were intent upon determining and attempting to describe the authors of the psalms, to discern the historical circumstances of their composition, and to date each psalm as specifically as possible. The tendency was to date most of the psalms very late (third to second century BCE) and to view them as evidence of an individualized spirituality that was superior to the corporate worship of earlier centuries of Israelite and Judean history.

This approach has been characterized by W. H. Bellinger, Jr., as "the personal/historical method."[3] It is still being practiced in some circles, not only by interpreters who tend to read the Bible literally, but also by critical scholars. Michael Goulder, for instance, has recently proposed that Psalms 51–72, a collection attributed to David, actually date from David's time, that they were probably written by one of David's sons, and that they are in chronological order, with Psalm 51 deriving from the events of the David/Bathsheba episode in 2 Samuel 11–12 and subsequent psalms reflecting the succeeding events narrated in the rest of 2 Samuel through 1 Kings 1. Thus 1 Kings 1, which narrates Solomon's accession to the throne, corresponds to Psalm 72, which is attributed to Solomon.[4] A major weakness in Goulder's proposal is that the historical superscriptions of Psalms 52; 54; 56; 57; 59; 60; and 63 do not fit the scheme, since they allude to events much earlier in David's life. Thus most scholars remain unconvinced by Goulder's proposal, which, although ingenious and skillfully argued, contains a high degree of speculation. Nevertheless, Goulder's work illustrates well the variety of possible approaches to the psalms; and the personal/historical method at least reminds us that the psalms grew out of concrete historical situations in which real people sought to live their lives under God. While this reminder is valuable, most scholars agree that dating the psalms with any degree of precision or certainty is virtually impossible. To be sure, there are a few exceptions (see Psalm 137), and it often makes sense to relate certain psalms or groups of psalms to broad historical eras (see below on the shaping of the psalter in response to the exile). By and large, however, scholars have abandoned the personal/historical method in favor of a method that has dominated the study of Psalms in the twentieth century: form criticism.

Form Criticism. Early in the twentieth century, German scholar Hermann Gunkel became convinced of the inadequacy of the personal/historical method. He noted the many references in the psalter to liturgical activities (singing, dancing, shouting, sacrifice, prayer, etc.) and places (the Temple, the house of the Lord, gates, courts, etc.); he concluded that the psalms were as much or more related to the corporate worship of ancient Israel and Judah than to the meditation of pious persons. Gunkel pioneered a method known as form criticism. He classified the psalms as various forms or types or genres, and then sought to determine where each type would have fit into the worship of ancient Israel or Judah—its "setting in life."[5] Although Gunkel's work has been modified, extended, and refined (see below), it remains the foundation of a method that dominated psalms scholarship for much of the century and that still remains a viable and vital approach. Gunkel's types are described in the following sections, which also include observations concerning how subsequent scholars have responded to Gunkel's work and how the following commentary generally deals with the issues.

Lament of an Individual. The lament of an individual, which some scholars prefer to call the complaint or prayer for help, is the most frequent type in the psalter. Characteristic elements include:

❖ Opening address, often including a vocative, such as, "O LORD"
❖ Description of the trouble or distress (the lament or complaint proper)

3. W. H. Bellinger, Jr., *Psalms: Reading and Studying the Book of Praises* (Peabody, Mass.: Hendrickson, 1990) 15.
4. Michael Goulder, *The Prayers of David (Psalms 51–72): Studies in the Psalter II*, JSOTSup 102 (Sheffield: JSOT, 1990) 24-30.
5. See Hermann Gunkel, *The Psalms: A Form-Critical Introduction*, trans. T. M. Horner, FBBS 19 (Philadelphia: Fortress, 1967).

❖ Plea or petition for God's response (the prayer for help), often accompanied by reasons for God to hear and act

❖ Profession of trust or confidence in God (Gunkel's "certainty of being heard")

❖ Promise or vow to praise God or to offer a sacrifice

Not all of the typical elements appear in every prayer. Furthermore, the order of the elements varies from psalm to psalm, and the elements vary considerably in length and intensity among the prayers. This means that each lament has some degree of uniqueness, an observation that is especially important to rhetorical critics (see below).

When it came to the question of the setting in life for the laments of an individual, Gunkel did not break completely with the older personal/historical approach. He still maintained that the prayers were late spiritual compositions by individuals, but he claimed that the authors based their creations upon prototypes that had originated in the worship of an earlier period. In Gunkel's view, the cultic prototypes arose out of a situation in which a sick person came to the Temple to pray for God's help. Recurring features of the prayers were explained in relation to this basic situation. For instance, the dramatic turn from complaint and petition to trust and praise is explained as the psalmist's response to a priestly salvation oracle, which is not preserved in the text. The wicked or enemies are those who slandered or sought to take advantage of the psalmist's distress. Some prayers include the psalmist's plea for revenge against the enemies (Gunkel's Imprecatory Psalms). In some prayers, as a way of asserting that the distress is undeserved, the psalmist explicitly defends his or her behavior (Gunkel's Protestations of Innocence). In other prayers, the psalmist admits her or his guilt and is content to leave the situation with God (Gunkel's Penitential Psalms).

Needless to say, subsequent scholarship has not been entirely content with Gunkel's conclusions. In particular, the question of the setting in life of the laments has been and still is much debated. While it is true that the language and imagery of several of the laments of an individual clearly suggest an original situation of sickness (see Psalms 6; 38; 41; 88), such is not the case with many others. Rather than sickness, the primary distress in some cases seems to be persecution by ruthless opponents. Consequently, several scholars have suggested that some of the prayers have arisen out of a situation in which the psalmist was falsely accused of some offense (see Psalms 5; 7; 11; 17; 26; 59; 109). According to this view, the psalmist has come to the Temple—perhaps has even taken up residence there—to seek asylum and to request redress from God (see 1 Kgs 1:50-53). This situation explains the protestations of innocence and the need to request revenge against the enemies, or in short, to ask that justice be done. The existence of praise following the complaint and petition is explained as a portion of the psalm that was added later, when the psalmist had been exonerated.

Still other laments of an individual seem to have arisen from circumstances involving neither sickness nor false accusation. The imagery is primarily military (see Psalms 3; 35; 56–57). This has led some scholars to identify the speaker in these psalms as the king, the military leader of the people. In the absence of any explicit indications in this regard, however, it is more likely that the military imagery is metaphorical. Indeed, the imagery of sickness and accusation may also be metaphorical. If this is the case, then the attempt to specify precisely the original circumstances of these prayers is finally futile and unnecessary. The work of Erhard Gerstenberger points to this conclusion. Maintaining that scholars "know little about the exact use of individual complaint psalms," Gerstenberger concludes that they "belonged to the realm of special offices for suffering people who, probably assisted by their kinfolk, participated in a service of supplication and curing under the guidance of a ritual expert."[6] While Gerstenberger's work is clearly historical and form critical, it is to be noted that his conclusions are fairly modest in comparison to earlier attempts and that his focus is on primary social groups, like the family, rather than on the Temple and its rituals.

---

6. Erhard S. Gerstenberger, *Psalms: Part 1, with an Introduction to Cultic Poetry,* Forms of the OT Literature 14 (Grand Rapids: Eerdmans, 1988) 13-14.

In the following commentary, scholarly proposals concerning the possible origins of the laments will be regularly noted. The emphasis, however, will lie elsewhere, for this reason: Regardless of the circumstances out of which the prayers arose, the language and imagery were eventually heard and appropriated metaphorically (and perhaps were even *intended* to function metaphorically from the beginning). This means that the language and imagery are symbolic and stereotypical enough to be applicable to a variety of situations. While this may be a frustration to scholars who are attempting to pin down precisely the historical circumstances of a psalm's origin, it is a distinct advantage to faithful communities and people who actually pray the prayers and look to them for a word about God and their own lives under God. As Patrick D. Miller, Jr., suggests:

> The search for a readily identifiable situation as the context for understanding the laments may, however, be illusory or unnecessary. The language of these psalms with its stereotypical, generalizing, and figurative style is so open-ended that later readers, on the one hand are stopped from peering behind them to one or more clearly definable sets of circumstances or settings in life, and on the other hand, are intentionally set free to adapt them to varying circumstances and settings.[7]

In other words, the really pertinent questions in approaching the laments are *not,* What was wrong with the psalmist? Who were her or his enemies? Rather, the crucial interpretive questions are these: What is wrong *with us?* Who or what are *our* enemies? This approach opens the way for an explicitly *theological,* as well as historical, understanding of the laments of an individual. For instance, rather than approaching the transition from complaint/petition to trust/praise chronologically or liturgically, the interpreter can take the simultaneity of complaint and praise as an expression of the perennial reality of the life of faith. Such an approach has profound implications for understanding human suffering and the suffering of God (see below on "The Theology of the Psalms" as well as Commentary and Reflections on Psalms 3; 13; 22; 31; 51; 69; 88; 109; 130).

Thanksgiving Song of an Individual. The thanksgiving song of an individual can be thought of as the offering of the praise that is regularly promised in the concluding sections of the laments (see above). It may have originally accompanied a sacrifice offered in the Temple, including perhaps a sacrificial meal. Typical elements include:

- ❖ expressions of praise and gratitude to God
- ❖ description of the trouble or distress from which the psalmist has been delivered
- ❖ testimony to others concerning God's saving deeds
- ❖ exhortation to others to join in praising God and acknowledging God's ways

Because the thanksgiving songs seem to look back on the kinds of distressing situations described in the laments, the same basic interpretive issues come into play (see above). In fact, because of the difficulty of translating Hebrew verb tenses, scholars sometimes disagree on whether a psalm should be classified as a lament or a thanksgiving song (see Psalms 28; 56; 57). From a theological perspective, the difference is not crucial, since the larger context of the book of Psalms suggests that deliverance is finally experienced not beyond but in the midst of suffering. In the following commentary, historical matters will not be ignored, but the emphasis will fall on the consideration of what it means to make gratitude one's fundamental posture toward God (see Commentary and Reflections on Psalms 30; 34; 92; 107; 116).

Lament of the Community. The characteristic elements of the lament of the community are essentially the same as those of the lament of the individual (see above), but the prayer is offered in the first-person plural. In addition, the communal prayers frequently include a reminder to God of the history of God's relationship with the people and of God's mighty deeds on behalf of

---

7. Patrick D. Miller, Jr., *Interpreting the Psalms* (Philadelphia: Fortress, 1986) 8; see also 48-52.

the people. The communal prayers are less likely to include the turn from complaint and petition to trust and praise. Like the laments of an individual, however, each communal prayer is unique.

The communal prayers obviously originated amid situations of communal distress, and scholars offer a range of proposals for each psalm. The most dramatic communal setback in the biblical period was the destruction of Jerusalem in 587 BCE and the subsequent exile. While it is not clear that all of the communal laments arose in response to this crisis, it is likely that several of them did; it is even more likely that all of them were eventually read and heard in view of this crisis. In the following commentary, the possible historical origins of the communal prayers will be noted. More attention will be given, however, to the apparently intentional attempt to place strategically the communal laments in the final form of the psalter. The second psalms in Books II and III are communal laments (Psalms 44; 74), and several more communal prayers appear in Book III (Psalms 79; 80; 83; and perhaps 77; 85; and 89; see "The Shape and Shaping of the Psalter"). The placement of these prayers encourages a theological as well as a historical approach to them, and it gives them a significance greater than their relative paucity might indicate. In particular, the communal laments encourage reflection on what it means to continue to profess faith in God's sovereignty in situations of severe extremity (see "The Theology of the Book of Psalms" as well as the Commentary and Reflections on Psalms 44; 74; 79; 80).

Hymn or Song of Praise. Whereas there are elements of praise in the above-mentioned types, the hymn or song of praise is oriented exclusively in this direction. The basic form is very simple:

- ❖ Opening invitation to praise
- ❖ Reasons for praise, often introduced by the Hebrew particle translated "for" (כִּי *kî*)
- ❖ Recapitulation of invitation to praise

As with the other types, these elements may vary in length and arrangement, thus giving each song of praise a certain individuality. For instance, in some hymns, the invitation is greatly extended and occupies most or all of the psalm (see Psalms 100; 148; 150). Then, too, the reasons for praise cite a variety of events, themes, and characteristics of God, and they employ a variety of vocabulary and imagery.

The songs of praise ordinarily refer to God in the third person rather than addressing God directly, as in the prayers, but there are exceptions (see Psalm 8). While it is clear that the communal laments are the corporate correlate of the laments of individuals, it seems to be that the hymns or songs of praise serve as the corporate correlate of the thanksgiving songs of individuals. In several cases where God is addressed directly in praise, however, some scholars prefer to categorize the psalm as a thanksgiving song of the community (see Psalms 65–67). In the final analysis, though, precision of categorization is not crucial. Claus Westermann, for instance, has chosen not to use "song of thanksgiving" at all in categorizing the psalms. Rather, he prefers to distinguish between descriptive praise, which celebrates God's general character and activity, and declarative praise, which celebrates God's deliverance in a specific situation of distress.[8]

Usually treated as sub-categories of the songs of praise are two more groupings customarily known as the enthronement psalms and the songs of Zion. The enthronement psalms are those that explicitly proclaim the reign of God (see Psalms 29; 47; 93; 95–99), and the songs of Zion are poems that focus praise on the city of Jerusalem (see Psalms 46; 48; 76; 84; 87; 122). While Gunkel was inclined to treat these psalms as "Eschatological Hymns" directed toward a vision of the end of time, his form-critical successors sought a liturgical setting for these psalms. For instance, Sigmund Mowinckel began by criticizing Gunkel's view that cultic prototypes had been spiritualized. Mowinckel characterized his own approach as the cult-functional method, and he made the enthronement psalms the foundation for an overarching proposal for a liturgical setting in life of many psalms. In particular, Mowinckel suggested that the enthronement psalms can be taken as evidence that Israel, like certain other ancient Near Eastern peoples, celebrated annually the enthronement or re-enthronement of their deity, Yahweh, as king of the universe.[9]

---

8. Claus Westermann, *Praise and Lament in the Psalms,* trans. K. R. Crim and R. N. Soulen (Atlanta: John Knox, 1981) 30-35.
9. Sigmund Mowinckel, *The Psalms in Israel's Worship,* 2 vols., trans. D. R. Ap-Thomas (Nashville: Abingdon, 1962) 1:106-92.

According to Mowinckel, this New Year Festival formed the setting in life of not just the enthronement psalms but many others as well. In a similar move, but one that went in a different direction, Hans-Joachim Kraus focused on the songs of Zion and the royal psalms (see below) in his proposal that many of the psalms were used liturgically in an annual Royal Zion Festival, which celebrated God's choice of Jerusalem and the Davidic dynasty. The basic problem with these two proposals, as well as with Artur Weiser's attempt to relate many psalms to a Covenant Renewal Festival, is that there is simply no solid biblical evidence for such festivals.[10]

Because of the lack of biblical evidence, subsequent scholarship has generally abandoned the proposals of Mowinckel, Kraus, and Weiser. Even so, they were not totally misguided. They had the value of emphasizing the liturgical origins and use of the psalms, and they served to highlight crucial themes in the psalter, especially the reign of God and the centrality of Zion. While the proposals of Mowinckel and Kraus may have gone beyond the confines of the evidence, it can hardly be doubted that the kingship of God and God's choice of Zion were celebrated cultically in some manner in ancient Israel or Judah. Neither can it be doubted that the songs of praise played a major role in such celebrations and more generally in worship at the major pilgrimage festivals (see the festal calendars in Exod 23:14-17; Lev 23:3-44; Deut 16:1-17).

In the following commentary, possible liturgical origins and uses of the songs of praise will be noted; however, in keeping with the shape of the psalter itself (see below, "The Shape and Shaping of the Psalter"), the emphasis will fall on hearing the hymns as proclamations of the reign of God. Not only do the enthronement psalms proclaim God's reign (see Psalms 29; 47; 96), but so also do the other songs of praise (see Psalms 8; 33; 100; 103; 104; 113), including the songs of Zion (see Psalms 46; 48; 122).

Royal Psalms. The royal psalms are actually not a form-critical category but rather a grouping based on a particular *content*. In this category, Gunkel included all the psalms that deal primarily with the Israelite or Judean king or the monarchy. For instance, Psalm 2 seems to be a portion of a coronation ritual; Psalm 45 celebrates a royal wedding; Psalm 72 is a prayer for the king, perhaps originally upon his coronation day (see also Psalms 18; 20; 21; 89; 101; 110; 132; 144).

Form-critical appropriation of the royal psalms involves the attempt to determine a precise setting for each psalm; such attempts will be noted in the following commentary. More emphasis will be given, however, to the function of the royal psalms in the final form of the psalter. Gerald Wilson has noted that royal psalms occur at the "seams" of Books I–III.[11] It may also be important, as Childs suggests, that the royal psalms are generally scattered throughout the psalter (see below "The Shape and Shaping of the Psalter").[12] The effect is to give these psalms themselves and the psalter as a whole a messianic orientation; that is to say, the royal psalms are not only poetic relics from the days of the Davidic dynasty but are also expressions of the ongoing hope that God will continue to manifest God's sovereignty in concrete ways in the life of God's people and in the life of the world. Such an appropriation of the royal psalms takes seriously the historical fact that they were preserved and were found meaningful long after the disappearance of the monarchy (see below on "The Theology of the Book of Psalms" and the Commentary and Reflections on Psalms 2; 18; 89; 101; 110; 132; 144).

Wisdom/Torah Psalms. Gunkel suggested that certain psalms should be identified as wisdom poetry (see Psalms 1; 37; 73; 128). Like the royal psalms, wisdom poetry is not strictly a form-critical category. Rather, for Gunkel, wisdom psalms "consist entirely of pious reflections."[13] Mowinckel also distinguished certain psalms as wisdom poetry, and he suggested that these poems were the only non-cultic material in the psalter.[14] Subsequent scholars have debated

10. See H.-J. Kraus, *Psalms 1–59: A Commentary*, trans. H. C. Oswald (Minneapolis: Augsburg, 1988) 56-58; Artur Weiser, *The Psalms*, OTL, trans. H. Hartwell (Philadelphia: Westminster, 1962) 23-52.
11. Gerald H. Wilson, *The Editing of the Hebrew Psalter*, SBLDS 76 (Chico, Calif.: Scholars Press, 1985) 207-8.
12. Brevard Childs, *Introduction to the Old Testament as Scripture* (Philadelphia: Fortress, 1979) 515-16.
13. Gunkel, *The Psalms*, 38.
14. Mowinckel, *The Psalms in Israel's Worship*, II:104-25.

these conclusions, sometimes trying to identify various characteristics or themes as constitutive of wisdom psalmody and sometimes seeking a cultic setting for the wisdom psalms.[15]

In the following commentary, it will be noted when a psalm shares characteristics and themes with the wisdom literature. More important, however, is the fact that one of the wisdom psalms opens the psalter and serves as a kind of preface. Psalm 1, along with Psalms 19 and 119, is often identified as a torah psalm (NIV and NRSV "law" in Ps 1:2 translates the Hebrew word תורה [tôrâ]; see also Ps 19:7; 119). As James L. Mays points out, these three psalms, along with numerous other expressions throughout the psalter of a didactic intent (see Psalms 18; 25; 33; 78; 89; 93; 94; 99; 103; 105; 111; 112; 147; 148), serve to give the whole psalter an instructional orientation. The effect, according to Mays, is this: "Form-critical and cult-functional questions are subordinated and questions of *content and theology* become more important."[16] In short, the existence of the wisdom/torah psalms is finally a stimulus to interpret the psalms theologically as well as historically (see below on "The Shape and Shaping of the Psalter").

Entrance Liturgies. Although a relatively minor category, since it contains only Psalms 15 and 24, the psalms that Gunkel called entrance liturgies have commanded a good deal of scholarly attention. The similarity between the two psalms is evident:

❖ The question apparently asked by those approaching the Temple or sanctuary
❖ The answer, perhaps delivered by a priestly voice, involving standards of admission
❖ Concluding blessing or affirmation

While the liturgical origin and use of Psalms 15 and 24 are perhaps more evident than with any other genre, the following commentary will move beyond an investigation of historical matters. In particular, the entrance liturgies invite theological reflection on what it means to enter God's reign and to submit to God's sovereign claim upon the life of God's people and the world.

Prophetic Exhortation. Gunkel noticed prophetic sayings or oracles in several psalms, an insight developed by Mowinckel and subsequent scholars to the point that Psalms 50, 81, and 95 are often called prophetic exhortations. More recently, Gerstenberger has suggested that these psalms may represent what he calls a "liturgical sermon."[17] In any case, as with the wisdom/torah psalms, the instructional intent is evident. These psalms challenge the reader to make a decision regarding God's sovereign claim, and thus they will be treated in the following commentary as a further indication of a theological appropriation of the psalms.

Psalms of Confidence/Trust. According to Gunkel, the psalms of confidence are to be explained as derivatives of the lament of an individual; that is, when the "certainty of being heard" (see above) became detached from the elements of complaint and petition, the result was psalms like Psalms 16, 23, and 91. It is not at all clear that this explanation is correct; however, it has been largely adopted by subsequent scholars, and it does make sense to categorize certain psalms under the rubric of confidence or trust. In the following commentary, a consideration of the historical or liturgical origin of these psalms is subordinated to the theologically significant fact that these psalms offer eloquent professions of faith in God's protective presence and power amid threatening circumstances. In short, these psalms assert God's sovereignty, despite appearances to the contrary.

Mixed Types and the Move Beyond Form Criticism. Even though his methodological emphasis would seem to belie it, Gunkel was well aware of the individuality of each psalm. When psalms were especially unique, and thus resistant to easy categorization, Gunkel resorted to a category that he called "mixed types."[18] In retrospect, it is clear that the very existence of this category would eventually undermine the basic goals of the form-critical and cult-functional approaches. Gunkel, Mowinckel, and their successors sought first of all to discern what was

---

15. See Roland E. Murphy, "A Consideration of the Classification 'Wisdom Psalms'," VTSup 9 (1962) 156-67; J. K. Kuntz, "The Canonical Wisdom Psalms of Ancient Israel—Their Rhetorical, Thematic, and Formal Dimensions," in *Rhetorical Criticism: Essays in Honor of J. Muilenburg*, eds. J. J. Jackson and M. Kessler (Pittsburgh: Pickwick, 1994) 186-22; L. Perdue, *Wisdom and Cult: A Critical Analysis of the View of Cult in the Wisdom Literature of Israel and the Ancient Near East*, SBLDS 30 (Missoula, Mont.: Scholars Press, 1977).

16. James L. Mays, "The Place of the Torah-Psalms in the Psalter," *JBL* 106 (1987) 12; italics added.

17. Gerstenberger, *Psalms: Part 1*, 210.

18. Gunkel, *The Psalms*, 36-39.

typical about particular psalms. Thus practitioners of the form-critical and cult-functional methods tended to overlook the *individuality* of each psalm. This neglect opened the way for James Muilenburg and others to issue the call for scholars to supplement form criticism with rhetorical criticism in an attempt to appreciate the unique literary features of each psalm. It is to rhetorical criticism, the immediate successor of form criticism, that we now turn. But first, it should be noted that Gunkel's explanation of the existence of mixed types also anticipates a further scholarly move beyond form criticism. In Gunkel's words: "Mixtures or inner transformations occur with great frequency when the literature we are discussing becomes old, especially when the original setting of the literary types has been forgotten or is no longer clear."[19]

In short, Gunkel recognizes that discernment of the types and liturgical origins of the psalms is not sufficient for understanding them in their final form and literary setting. It is precisely this recognition that eventually invited the movement beyond a method that aims at appreciating the *typical* and the *original* to methods that aim at appreciating the *individual* and the *final*. In other words, the limited aims of form criticism invited the movement first toward rhetorical criticism and then toward a consideration of the importance of the shape and the shaping of the book of Psalms as a literary context for interpreting the individual psalms.

Rhetorical Criticism. In 1968, James Muilenburg issued his widely heeded call for biblical scholarship "to venture beyond the confines of form criticism into an inquiry into other literary features which are all too often ignored today."[20] Muilenburg did not advocate the abandonment of form criticism, but rather suggested that it be supplemented by what he called rhetorical criticism. As applied to the book of Psalms, rhetorical criticism has meant an attention to literary features that leads to an appreciation of each psalm as a unique poetic creation.

Just as the following commentary will attend to the possible liturgical origins and uses of the psalms, so it will also attend to the literary features that make the psalms good poetry. The more prominent of these features are described below, including an indication of how these features will be treated in the commentary.

Parallelism. Perhaps the most persistent poetic feature of the psalms is parallelism. While several of the psalms' poetic features cannot readily be captured in translation, parallelism can be, and even a casual reader is likely to notice that the second half of a typical poetic line is often related somehow to the first half of the line. Earlier generations of scholars categorized parallelism as either synonymous (the second part of the line echoes the first), antithetical (the second part of the line states opposition to the first), or synthetic (which is a catch-all category and often really meant that no parallelism could be detected). In these terms, the most frequent type of parallelism is synonymous; however, recent scholars have pointed out that the echoing involved is only rarely precisely synonymous. Rather, the second part of the poetic line usually has the effect of intensifying or specifying or concretizing the thought expressed in the first part of the line.[21] While there are far too many instances of parallelism for it to be noted regularly, the commentary will point out particularly striking instances of parallelism (see Commentary on Psalms 1; 3; 13; 90; see also the article entitled "Introduction to Hebrew Poetry").

Repetition. Another very common, and probably the most important, poetic feature of the psalms is repetition. While it is often considered bad writing style to use the same word repeatedly, such apparently was not the case in Hebrew. Consequently, repetition occurs frequently in a variety of patterns and for a variety of purposes. For instance, the same word will occur several times in a psalm in order to draw the reader's attention to a key word or concept, such as salvation/deliverance (Psalm 3), righteousness (Psalms 71; 85), justice/judgment (Psalm 82), or steadfast love (Psalms 103; 109; 136). Unfortunately, both the NIV and the NRSV sometimes obscure the Hebrew repetition by choosing different English words to translate the same Hebrew word. In the commentary, such instances will be identified, and such instances will often serve as a primary clue to the theological significance of the psalm.

19. Gunkel, *The Psalms*, 36.
20. James Muilenburg, "Form Criticism and Beyond," *JBL* 88 (1969) 4.
21. See James L. Kugel, *The Idea of Biblical Poetry* (New Haven: Yale University Press, 1981); Robert Alter, *The Art of Biblical Poetry* (New York: Basic Books, 1985). For a more technical discussion that proposes a broader understanding of parallelism, see Adele Berlin, *The Dynamics of Biblical Parallelism* (Bloomington: Indiana University Press, 1985).

When a word, phrase, or poetic line occurs in both the opening and the closing line of a psalm or section of a psalm, the repetition is called an *inclusio,* or envelope structure. This framing technique again often identifies a crucial theological theme or concept (see Psalms 8; 21; 67; 73; 103; 107; 118). The same effect is frequently achieved by the use of a refrain, a poetic line that occurs in exactly or essentially the same form two or more times in the psalm (see Psalms 8; 42–43; 46; 49; 56; 57; 59; 62; 80; 99; 107; 116; 136). Still another form of repetition is known as step-like or stair-like repetition, since it involves repeating a word either in both parts of the same line or in juxtaposed lines. Not coincidentally, it occurs most frequently in the Songs of Ascents or Songs of the Steps (Psalms 120–134; see Commentary on Psalms 120–122 and others in the collection). While it is not necessary to categorize every instance of repetition, and while some instances are clearly more noticeable and significant than others, this commentary will regularly call attention to cases of repetition and will take them as a primary stylistic clue to discern the theological message and significance of the psalms.

Chiasm. A special form of repetition is known as a chiasm. *Chiasm* is a word derived from the Greek letter *chi* (X), and it denotes the arrangement of elements in an ABBA or ABCBA pattern. The number of elements in a chiasm may vary, but the effect is to provide a sort of multiple envelope structure that focuses attention on the center of the chiasm. Chiasm occurs frequently, and on various scales, in the psalms. It may involve the arrangement of words in a single poetic line (see Pss 3:7; 6:10; 25:9; 83:1; 100:3; 142:2); it may involve the arrangement of corresponding words or phrases in several poetic lines (see Pss 1:5-6; 3:1-2; 36:6-7, 10-11; 56:3-4; 72:1-2; 87:3-7; 90:1-2, 5-6; 97:6-7; 101:3-7; 137:5-6); or it may involve the arrangement of the poetic lines or sections of a psalm with the effect of focusing attention on a central panel or pivotal verse (see Psalms 1; 5; 11; 12; 17; 26; 67; 86; 92). In the commentary, chiasm will be treated not only as an important literary device but also as a clue to appropriate directions for theological reflection and appropriation.

Structure. Whereas form critics are interested in the structure of a psalm in order to discern characteristic elements and their typical arrangement, rhetorical critics are more interested in what is unique about the way a psalm is structured. In this commentary, an attempt is made to treat the structure of a psalm not only as a literary issue but also as a clue to theological significance and appropriation. To be sure, some psalms are more amenable to such analysis than others (e.g., Psalms 8; 73; 122). In many cases, it seems fairly clear that a poem falls into distinct sections, sometimes even into formal stanzas or strophes (although I have avoided these terms because such formal regularity is rare). In several cases, however, the structure of a psalm can justifiably be perceived in several ways, depending upon which structural clues one chooses to focus. In this case, it is not necessary to declare one structural proposal correct to the exclusion of others. Rather, it is proper to conclude that the structure or movement of the psalm occurs at more than one level (see Psalms 62; 77; 87; 94; 101; 113; 122; 128; 129; 136; 140; 142; 145; 146).

Other Figurative Uses of Language. The literary features described above can be captured in English translation, at least to a certain extent. Nevertheless, other figurative uses of language in the psalms are virtually impossible to render recognizably into English. For instance, although there is disagreement over how to define it and even over whether it exists, most scholars are willing to speak of the meter of Hebrew poetry. There is no really satisfactory way to capture the rhythmical quality of psalms, except perhaps to render the psalms in poetic lines rather than as continuous prose; and both the NIV and the NRSV do this. Also difficult to capture in English are instances in which Hebrew syntax or word order is unique or striking; however, in the commentary, the more prominent of such cases will be mentioned and described (see Pss 3:1-2, 6-7; 5:1; 22:9-10; 31:15; 36:5-6; 38:15; 62:7; 90:4; 93:2; 114:7; 123:3). So will other figures of speech that cannot be readily rendered into English, such as alliteration (see Pss 54:3-4; 63:1, 11; 122:6-8), onomatopoeia (see Pss 29:3-7; 140:3), and plays on words (see Pss 28:5; 39:4-5; 48:4; 146:3-4).

Another literary feature of the psalms that cannot be captured in English is the apparently intentional ambiguity of some Hebrew words, phrases, and grammatical constructions. Although an English translation cannot preserve the ambiguity, it will be pointed out in the commentary (see Pss 1:3; 25:12; 40:9; 51:14; 71:7; 87:4-5; 96:13; 100:3; 122:3; 127:3; 135:3; 147:1).

Aside from specific instances of intentional ambiguity, however, there is a sense in which all poetry is inevitably ambiguous. That is, poetry aims not so much at describing things objectively as it does at evoking the reader's imagination. As Thomas G. Long puts it, "Psalms operate at the level of the imagination, often swiveling the universe on the hinges of a single image."[22] This means that the psalms put the reader in touch with a source of mystery that cannot be precisely defined, objectively described, or even fully comprehended. As S. E. Gillingham says of biblical poetry, including the book of Psalms:

> Its diction is full of ambiguity of meaning. As with all poetry, but perhaps especially in this case, the concealing/revealing aspect of biblical verse means that any interpretation involves as much the power of imaginative insight as any so-called "objective" analysis. . . .
> . . . The language of theology needs the poetic medium for much of its expression, for poetry, with its power of allusion, reminds us of the more hidden and mysterious truths which theology seeks to express. Poetry is a form which illustrates our need for a sense of balance in our study of theology. On the one hand, good poetry still testifies to the need to be properly analytical in our pursuit of knowledge, but on the other, it illustrates the importance of being open to the possibility of mystery and ambiguity in our pursuit of meaning.[23]

In keeping with the direction Gillingham suggests, the following commentary will attend analytically to the literary and stylistic devices that make the psalms good poetry, but it will always do so with an eye toward theology—that is, to the way the psalms encounter the reader with the majesty of God and with the mystery of God's involvement with the world.

The Shape and Shaping of the Psalter. As already suggested, Hermann Gunkel's own conclusions about the psalms left the way open for the emergence of rhetorical criticism and for the scholarly consideration of individual psalms in the context of their final *literary* setting within the book of Psalms. It is in the latter direction that Psalms scholarship has moved in the past fifteen years. Although they did not make much of them, scholars have long been aware of various features that pointed to a process involving the gradual collection of individual psalms and groups of psalms into what we now have as the book of Psalms. Such features are described below, including an indication of their significance for the following commentary.

Superscriptions. Of the 150 psalms, 117 have a superscription, ranging from a single phrase (see Psalms 25–28) to several lines (see Psalms 18; 60; 88). The superscriptions contain three kinds of information:

(1) *Personal Names.* The superscriptions of seventy-three psalms mention David; others mention Jeduthun (Psalms 39; 62; 77; see 1 Chr 16:41-42; 25:1-8), Heman (Psalm 88; see 1 Kgs 4:31; 1 Chr 2:6; 6:17; 16:41-42; 25:1-8), Ethan (Psalm 89; see 1 Kgs 4:31; 1 Chr 2:6), Solomon (Psalms 72; 127), Moses (Psalm 90), the Korahites (Psalms 42; 44–49; 84–85; 87–88), and the Asaphites (Psalms 50; 73–83). While it is possible in some cases that these names indicate authorship (see above on the personal/historical method), it is more likely that they originated in the process of collection. David, for instance, was remembered as the initiator of psalmody in worship (see 1 Chr 16:7-43). To be sure, the chronicler wrote hundreds of years after the actual time of David, but the memory may be an ancient one. In any case, it is more likely that many psalms were attributed to David as a result of this memory rather than as a result of Davidic authorship. Similarly, the process of collection accounts for the association of thirteen psalms with specific moments in David's life (see Psalms 3; 7; 18; 34; 51; 52; 54; 56; 57; 59; 60; 63; 142). These references should not be construed as historically accurate, but neither should they be dismissed as irrelevant. Rather, they provide an illustrative narrative context for hearing and interpreting particular psalms as well as a clue to the appropriateness of imagining narrative contexts for other psalms that do not contain superscriptions.

22. Thomas G. Long, *Preaching and the Literary Forms of the Bible* (Philadelphia: Fortress, 1989) 47.
23. S. E. Gillingham, *The Poems and Psalms of the Hebrew Bible,* Oxford Bible Series (Oxford: Oxford University Press, 1994) 277-78.

Not surprisingly, several of the other names found in the superscriptions are also associated with David's establishment of worship—Jeduthun, Heman, Korah (see 1 Chr 6:22, 37; 9:19), and Asaph (1 Chr 6:39; 9:15; 16:5, 7; 37; 25:1-8). The significant Korahite and Asaphite collections probably point to a process of both authorship and collection of psalms within Levitical guilds. It is not clear how well these collections reflect the actual work of these guilds, and this issue remains the subject of scholarly debate.[24] Of more relevance for the consideration of the shape and shaping of the psalter is the appearance of those collections at the beginning of Books II and III. Interestingly, too, the name Solomon occurs at the end of Book II and the name Moses at the beginning of Book IV. This pattern seems more than coincidental, and I shall return to these observations later.

(2) *Liturgical Instructions.* Fifty-five superscriptions contain the phrase "to the leader" (למנצח *lamnaṣṣēaḥ*; see NRSV). As the NIV suggests with its translation, "for the director of music," this phrase is probably some sort of liturgical instruction (see NIV "directing" and NRSV "lead" in 1 Chr 15:21, where the Hebrew word occurs as a verb). Its precise significance is unknown, as is that of other words and phrases that probably indicate moods, modes, or even melodies accompanying the original singing of certain psalms (see *sheminith* [השמינית *haššĕmînît*] in Psalms 6; 12; and 1 Chr 15:21; *gittith* [הגתית *haggittît*] in Psalms 8; 81; 84; NRSV, *Muth-labben* [עלמות לבן *ʿalmût labbēn*]; NIV, "the tune of 'The Death of the Son'" in Psalm 9; NRSV, "The Deer of the Dawn"; NIV, "the tune of 'The Doe of the Morning' " in Psalm 22 [אילת השחר *ʾayyelet haššaḥar*]; "Lilies" [ששנים *šōšannîm*] in Psalms 45 and 69; "Lily of the Covenant" [שושן עדות *šûšan ʿēdût*] in Psalm 60; NRSV, "Lilies, a Covenant"; NIV, "the tune of 'The Lilies of the Covenant' " in Psalm 80 [*šōšannîm ʿēdût*]; *alamoth* [עלמות *ʿălāmôt*] in Psalm 46 and 1 Chr 15:20; *mahalath* [מחלת *māḥălat*] in Psalm 53; *mahalath leannoth* [מחלת לענות *māḥălat lĕʿānôt*] in Psalm 88; NRSV, "Dove on Far-off Terebinths"; NIV, "to the tune of 'A Dove on Distant Oaks' " in Psalm 56 [יונת אלם רחקים *yônat ʾēlem rĕḥōqîm*]; and "Do Not Destroy" in Psalms 57–59; 75 [אל-תשחת *ʾal-tašḥēt*]). According to some scholars, however, these mysterious terms may designate musical instruments or the original liturgical settings of certain psalms, as is more clearly the case with other words and phrases. For instance, musical instruments are mentioned in the superscriptions of Psalms 4; 5; 6; 54; 55; 61; 67; 76, and several superscriptions indicate a particular setting or use for their psalms. Psalms 30 and 92 are the most specific in this regard, but the superscriptions of Psalms 38; 45; 70; and 100 may also point to cultic occasions. The liturgical instructions in the superscriptions clearly suggest that many of the psalms were meant to be sung, but we know very little about actual performance. Consequently, little attention will be devoted to the liturgical instructions in the following commentary. The same applies to the term *selah,* which occurs in the body of several psalms. While it almost certainly represents a liturgical instruction of some kind—perhaps a signal to the musical director or levitical choir—its precise meaning and significance are not known.

(3) *Genre Designations.* The term "Genre designation" may be misleading, since it is clear that the ancient authors and performers of the psalms were not form critics in the contemporary sense (see above). For instance, while the most important contemporary rubrics are "prayer" and "praise," these terms occur infrequently in the superscriptions—"praise" only in Psalm 145 and "prayer" only in Psalms 17; 86; 90; and 102 (and only in Psalm 102 does the superscription further identify the prayer as a "lament"; see the NIV). Even so, the ancient collectors did apparently distinguish among types of poems. The most frequent designation in the superscriptions is the Hebrew word מזמור (*mizmôr,* 57 times), which is traditionally rendered "psalm," an English transliteration of the Greek translation (ψαλμός *psalmos*) of *mizmôr* and the term that has provided the Greek and English names for the entire collection (the Hebrew title of the book is תהלים [*tĕhillîm,* "Praises"]). The Hebrew root occurs frequently in the Psalms as a verb, and it describes both singing and the musical accompaniment to singing. Aside from "psalm," the most frequent designation in the superscriptions is "song" (שיר *šîr*), and it too points to the musical performance of the poems. What difference the ancient authors and collectors perceived

24. See M. D. Goulder, *The Psalms of the Sons of Korah,* JSOTSup 20 (Sheffield: JSOT, 1982); H. D. Nasuti, *Tradition History and the Psalms of Asaph,* SBLDS 88 (Atlanta: Scholars Press, 1988).

between a "psalm" and a "song" is not clear, especially in view of the fact that thirteen psalms are identified as both and that both labels are applied to psalms that contemporary form critics categorize in a variety of ways. Psalm 88 is even triply identified as a "song," a "psalm," and a "maskil" (משׂכיל *maśkîl*). This term, which occurs in the superscriptions of thirteen psalms as well as in Ps 47:7 (see NIV and NRSV notes), appears to derive from a root that means "be attentive, prudent, wise." Thus it may mean something like "contemplative poem" or "didactic poem." Certainty of meaning is impossible, however, and the term is best left untranslated. The same conclusion applies to the terms מכתם (*miktām*, Psalms 16; 56–60) and שׁגיון (*šiggāyôn*, Psalm 7; see the similar term in Hab 3:1), which are even more obscure. Since the origin, meaning, and significance of the ancient genre designations are so elusive, little further is said of them in the commentary.

Collections. The existence of collections within the Psalter has long been obvious, but the exact process behind the compilation of these collections to form the book of Psalms remains unknown. While the superscriptions of many psalms may not be original, they do offer a clue as to which psalms were perceived as somehow belonging together. For instance, psalms with the same ancient genre designation often occur in sequence (see Psalms 42–45; 52–55; 56–60), but more important, the personal names mentioned in the superscriptions indicate the existence of a collection. With the exception of Psalms 1–2; 10; and 33, the superscription of every psalm in Book I mentions David. Another Davidic collection is formed by Psalms 51–72. While Psalms 66–67 and 71–72 do not mention David, the notice in 72:20 suggests the ancient editors' awareness of a collection. Interestingly, most of the psalms in the two Davidic collections are laments of an individual, although the ancient genre designations vary. Between the two Davidic collections that form the bulk of Books I–II are a Korahite collection (Psalms 42–49) and a single Asaph psalm (Psalm 50) that anticipates the Asaphite collection (Psalms 73–83), which forms the bulk of Book III.

A mysterious feature of Books II–III is the existence of another kind of collection, the so-called Elohistic psalter (Psalms 42–83), a grouping in which the divine name *Elohim* occurs far more frequently than it does in Psalms 1–41 or 84–150 (*Elohim* occurs 244 times in Psalms 42–83 as opposed to only 49 times in Psalms 1–41 and 70 times in Psalms 84–150). For years, scholars have usually concluded that the Elohistic psalter is the result of the work of a redactor who changed many of the occurrences of *Yahweh* to *Elohim*; however, this conclusion is questionable. For instance, it does not satisfactorily explain why 44 occurrences of *Yahweh* remain in Psalms 42–83 or why the redactor would have stopped with Psalm 83 rather than continuing through Psalm 89, the end of Book III. Thus it appears likely that the occurrences of *Elohim* are original to the composition of Psalms 42–83 and that these psalms originated and existed independently. Only later, it seems, were they joined to Psalms 3–41 (or 1–41) and only later were Psalms 84–89 attached as a sort of appendix to form Books I–III.[25]

It appears that Books I–III were in place prior to Books IV–V. Indications to this effect include the facts that 28 of the 33 untitled psalms occur in Books IV–V and that the psalters found at Qumran show a great deal more variation from the MT in Books IV–V than they do in Books I–III.[26] In short, it is likely that a different and later process of collection was operative for Books IV–V. For instance, the name of David is not nearly so prominent (see only Psalms 101; 103; 108–110; 122; 124; 131; and the Davidic collection, Psalms 138–145). At the same time, the laments of an individual are far less prominent and songs of praise become predominant (see below). Collections are marked more by the theme of praise, as with Psalms 93–99 (the reign of God) and Psalms 113–118 (or 111–118). More formally, Psalms 146–150 all begin and end with the imperative "Praise the LORD!" Book V contains what is clearly a discrete collection, the Songs of Ascents (Psalms 120–134; see Commentary on Psalm 120).

While scholars have long noticed the existence of various collections, only recently have they begun to try to discern the significance of the shape of the whole book of Psalms. While much

---

25. Beth L. Tanner, " 'Where Is Your God?' The Shape of the Elohistic Psalter," unpublished paper delivered at the Annual Meeting of the SBL, Nov. 20, 1994, Chicago, Illinois.

26. Gerald H. Wilson, "Shaping the Psalter: A Consideration of Editorial Linkage in the Book of Psalms" in *The Shape and Shaping of the Psalter*, ed. J. C. McCann, Jr., JSOTSup 159 (Sheffield: JSOT, 1993) 73-74.

about the process of collection remains and will undoubtedly always remain unknown, certain directions can be detected and will be discussed under the heading "The Editorial Purpose of the Psalter."

The Five-Book Arrangement. As both the NIV and the NRSV suggest, the doxologies in Pss 41:13; 72:19; 89:52; and 106:48 have the effect of dividing the psalter into five books:

Book I	Psalms 1–41
Book II	Psalms 42–72
Book III	Psalms 73–89
Book IV	Psalms 90–106
Book V	Psalms 107–150

This is not a new observation. Indeed, the *Midrash Tehillim* states, "As Moses gave five books of laws to Israel, so David gave five books of Psalms to Israel."[27] Despite this ancient tradition, some scholars conclude that the five-book arrangement is coincidental rather than intentional; that is, the doxologies are simply original parts of Psalms 41; 72; 89; and 106 and were never meant to serve any editorial function. This conclusion has recently been definitively refuted by Gerald H. Wilson, who points out that the movements from Psalms 41 to 42, 72 to 73, and 89 to 90 are marked not only by doxologies but also by shifts in the ancient genre designation and in the personal names mentioned in the superscriptions.[28] Thus, while a five-book arrangement may not have been the original goal of the earliest editors or collectors, it did become a goal of those who put the psalter in its final form. Wilson's work has been a major stimulus in moving Psalms scholarship in the direction of attempting to discern the editorial purpose of the psalter, and it is to this issue that we now turn.

The Editorial Purpose of the Psalter. The detection and description of an editorial purpose for the psalter does not involve the attempt to explain how each individual psalm reached its current literary placement. The following commentary will point out relationships between adjacent psalms and among several psalms that seem to form a coherent sequence or pattern, and it will take these literary relationships seriously as a context for theological interpretation. At the same time, however, the commentary reflects the attempt not to force relationships or to read too much into patterns that may simply be coincidental. It by no means assumes that every psalm can be tied to an overarching editorial purpose, but rather that the psalter in its final form often reflects the earlier shape of the smaller collections of which it is composed. Following Wilson's lead, the commentary's governing assumption is that editorial activity most likely took place at the "seams" of the psalter—that is, at the beginning or conclusion of the whole or of the various books.[29] Proceeding on this assumption, the interpreter of the whole psalter notices several patterns that seem too striking to be coincidental.

Books I–III (Psalms 1–89). The most striking observation about Books I–III is that royal psalms occur near the beginning of Book I (Psalm 2) and at the conclusion of Books II (Psalm 72) and III (Psalm 89). To be sure, the pattern would be even more striking if Psalm 41 were a royal psalm; but even so, it is impressive enough as Psalm 2 forms with Psalm 72 an envelope structure for Books I–II and with Psalm 89 an envelope structure for Books I–III. As Wilson points out, the progression from Psalms 2 to 72 to 89 is revealing. Psalm 2 establishes the intimate relationship between God and the Davidic king; Psalm 72 reinforces this relationship; and while Psalm 89 begins as a comprehensive rehearsal of all the features of this relationship (vv. 1-37), it concludes with a wrenching description of God's rejection of the covenant with David (vv. 38-45) and with the pained, poignant prayer of the spurned anointed one (vv. 45-51). As Wilson concludes concerning the effect of this progression, "The Davidic covenant introduced in Psalm 2 has come to nothing and the combination of these books concludes with the

---

27. William G. Braude, *The Midrash on Psalms* (New Haven: Yale University Press, 1954) 1:5.
28. Wilson, *The Editing of the Hebrew Psalter,* 139-97.
29. See Wilson, *The Editing of the Hebrew Psalter,* 207-8; see also G. H. Wilson, "The Use of Royal Psalms at the 'Seams' of the Hebrew Psalter," *JSOT* 35 (1986) 85-94. For a survey, see David M. Howard, Jr., "Editorial Activity in the Psalter: A State-of-the-Field Survey," in *The Shape and Shaping of the Psalter,* 52-70.

anguished cry of the Davidic descendants."[30] In other words, Books I–III document the failure of the Davidic covenant—at least as traditionally understood—that was made evident by the destruction of Jerusalem in 587 BCE and the subsequent exile. Thus Books I–III call out for a response, and, according to Wilson, this response is offered by the proclamation of God's reign, which is prominent in Books IV–V.

Before considering Books IV–V in detail, however, it should be noted that the opening psalms of Books II–III already begin both to anticipate the crisis of exile that is fully articulated in Psalm 89 and to point toward a constructive response. Again, a strikingly similar pattern exists between Books II and III. Not only does each of these books conclude with royal psalms, but also each begins with psalms in which an individual voice expresses deep alienation from God and God's place (Psalms 42–43; 73). In each case, these opening psalms are followed by communal laments that are strongly reminiscent of the destruction of Jerusalem and the exile (Psalms 44; 74). Furthermore, impressive verbal links exist between Psalms 42–43 and 44 and between Psalms 73 and 74 (see the Commentary there). The effect is to provide a corporate orientation and context for hearing Psalms 42–43; 73 as well as other individual expressions of opposition and defeat in Books II–III. Such expressions predominate in Book II (see Psalms 51–71). They occur also in Book III (see Psalms 86; 88), although Book III is actually pervaded by communal laments (Psalms 74; 79; 80; 83; 89:38-51), which suggests that the whole book may have been decisively shaped by the experience of exile. In any case, the opening psalms of Books II–III effectively instruct the community to face exile (Psalms 44; 74) with "Hope in God" (Pss 42:5, 11; 43:5) and with the assurance that "God is the strength of my heart and my portion forever" (Ps 73:26 NRSV).[31]

Although not exactly the same as the opening of Books II and III, a similar pattern creates the same effect at the beginning of Book I. Psalm 1 states the problem of the wicked and the righteous in individual terms, and then Psalm 2 states the same problem in corporate terms. Like Psalms 42–44 and 73–74, Psalms 1 and 2 are connected by significant verbal links (see Commentary on Psalms 1 and 2). Although, unlike Psalms 44 and 74, Psalm 2 is a royal psalm, it does feature a problem that was preeminent in the exilic and postexilic eras: the reality and continuing threat of the domination of Israel by the nations. By portraying God as judge of the wicked (Ps 1:4-6) and ruler of the nations (Psalm 2), Psalms 1–2 affirm the possibility of hope amid the hard realities of the exilic and postexilic eras. By standing at the head of Book I (and the whole psalter; see further below), Psalms 1 and 2 provide a literary context for hearing Psalms 3–41. As in the case of Book II, the shape of Book I suggests that the laments of an individual, which heavily dominate Book I, may be heard also as expressions of communal plight. In short, the final form serves to instruct the community to face crises in the same manner as the "I" of the laments, who always accompanies the articulation of distress with expressions of trust and praise (see above on the laments of an individual).

Because the laments of an individual are so numerous in Book I, psalms of other types are quite noticeable (see Psalms 8; 15; 19; 24; 29; 33; 37). It may be that these other psalms have been placed intentionally between small collections of laments.[32] In any case, however, the juxtaposition of complaint and praise both within a single psalm and between psalms is theologically significant, and it will serve as a basis for theological reflection in the commentary.

In view of the foregoing discussion of Books I–III and in anticipation of the consideration of Books IV–V, it is necessary to define further what is meant here and throughout the following commentary by reference to the exile. To be sure, the exile was a historical event that began with the deportation of Judeans to Babylon in 597 BCE, continued with the destruction of Jerusalem in 587 by the Babylonians, and lasted until 539 when Cyrus permitted the Judean exiles in Babylon to return to Palestine. But in a broader sense, the exile was a theological problem, and it represented an ongoing theological crisis well beyond 539. The destruction of Jerusalem and the deportation to Babylon meant that the people of God lost their three most fundamental

30. Wilson, *The Editing of the Hebrew Psalter*, 213.

31. See J. C. McCann, Jr., "Books I–III and the Editorial Purpose of the Hebrew Psalter" in *The Shape and Shaping of the Psalter*, 93-107.

32. See Lawrence Boadt and William J. Urbrock, "Book I of the Psalter: Unity, Direction, and Development," unpublished paper delivered at the Annual Meeting of the SBL, Nov. 20, 1994, Chicago, Illinois.

and cherished religious institutions: the Temple, the land, and the monarchy. To say that this loss precipitated a crisis is an understatement. Although some of the exiles returned to Palestine after 539, and although the Temple was rebuilt by 515, things were never really the same as before. National autonomy was never achieved again except briefly in the second century BCE. Furthermore, the Davidic monarchy was never reestablished. The Davidic king had been viewed as nothing less than God's own adopted son (see Ps 2:7), and the monarchy represented theologically the concrete embodiment of God's purposes on earth (see Psalm 72). The loss of the monarchy was thus an ongoing theological crisis that made it necessary for the people of God to come to a new understanding of God and of their existence under God. When the commentary refers to the exile, it means primarily not the historical event but the ongoing theological crisis.[33] Because this theological crisis persisted for centuries, the fact that we cannot precisely date the final formation of the psalter is not of crucial significance. The Hebrew psalter may have taken final form in the fourth to third centuries BCE, as many scholars suggest; however, the manuscript evidence from Qumran complicates this conclusion, since it suggests the fluidity of Books IV–V into the second century BCE or beyond.[34] But even if the psalter did not take final form until the first century CE, its shape can still be understood as a response to the exile in the sense of an ongoing theological crisis. This crisis called for new understandings of God and of human faithfulness to God. The shape of the psalter indicates that its editors intended the psalms to participate in the theological dialogue that resulted in new perspectives on both divine and human sovereignty and suffering (see further below on "The Theology of the Psalms").

Books IV–V (Psalms 90–150). The anguished questions of the Davidic descendants (Ps 89:46; 49) cry out for a response, and a fitting answer is provided by Psalm 90 and the subsequent psalms in Book IV—namely, Israel's true home is, always has been, and always will be God alone (Ps 90:1-2). There is, of course, no better voice to deliver this assurance than that of Moses, whose intimate experience of God and leadership of the people occurred before there ever was a temple or a monarchy and before entry into the land! Not coincidentally, the superscription of Psalm 90 is the only one to bear the name of Moses, and seven of the eight references to Moses in Psalms occur in Book IV.[35]

Furthermore, Book IV affirms that Israel's true monarch is not the Davidic king but Yahweh—again, the way it was in Moses' time (see Exod 15:18) and before the monarchy (see 1 Samuel 8). This affirmation is found explicitly in Book IV in the so-called enthronement psalms (Psalms 93; 95–99), a collection that dominates Book IV and that Wilson properly called "the theological 'heart' " of the psalter.[36] While it appears at first sight that Psalm 94 is an intrusion into this collection, it has significant thematic parallels with the enthronement psalms. This fact, plus the verbal links between Psalms 92 and 94, suggest that the placement of Psalm 94 may be intended to bind the enthronement collection more closely to Psalms 90–92, which also share significant verbal links (see Commentary on Psalms 90–92; 94).[37] It may also be more than coincidental that Psalms 95 and 100 are similar (cf. 95:7 and 100:3) and that they form a frame around Psalms 96–99. Furthermore, Psalm 100 recalls Psalm 2, since 2:11 and 100:2 are the only two occurrences in the psalter of the imperative, "Serve the LORD" (NIV and NRSV "Worship" in 100:2). That the theological heart of the psalter recalls its beginning may be a coincidence, but if so, it is an auspicious one that reinforces the psalter's pervasive proclamation of God's sovereignty (see further on "The Theology of the Psalms").

The intent of Book IV to address the crisis of exile helps to explain the placement of Psalms 101–102, which have proven extremely enigmatic in the light of earlier approaches. If Psalm 89 has documented the failure of the Davidic monarchy, for instance, why is a royal psalm like Psalm 101 in Book IV at all? While absolute certainty is elusive, it is crucial to note that

---

33. See Ralph W. Klein, *Israel in Exile: A Theological Interpretation* (Philadelphia: Fortress, 1979) 1-8.

34. G. H. Wilson, "A First Century CE Date for the Closing of the Hebrew Psalter?" in *Haim M. I. Geraryahu Memorial Volume* (Jerusalem: World Jewish Bible Center, 1990) 136-43.

35. See Marvin E. Tate, *Psalms 51–100*, WBC 20 (Dallas: Word, 1990) xxvi. Tate characterizes Book IV as a "Moses-book."

36. Wilson, "The Use of Royal Psalms at the 'Seams' of the Hebrew Psalter," 92. See also James L. Mays, *The Lord Reigns: A Theological Handbook to the Psalms* (Louisville: Westminster John Knox, 1994) 12-22.

37. Wilson, "Shaping the Psalter," 75-76. See also David M. Howard, "A Contextual Reading of Psalms 90–94," in *The Shape and Shaping of the Psalter,* 114-22.

when 101:2 is not emended (cf. the NIV with the NRSV), Psalm 101 can be reasonably read as a royal lament. In view of the concluding verses of Psalm 89 (see above), the placement of this royal complaint makes perfect sense. As a lament out of the experience of exile, Psalm 101 also anticipates Psalm 102, vv. 12-17 of which have baffled commentators, since these verses represent a corporate profession out of exile following an apparently individual prayer in vv. 1-11. But together, Psalms 101–102 rehearse the three crucial elements of the crisis of exile: loss of monarchy, Zion/Temple, and land. Fittingly, and congruent with the move from Psalms 89 to 90, Psalm 103 returns the reader to a Mosaic perspective, even though it is labeled "Of David." Not surprisingly, Book IV ends with a historical review, which concludes with the exile (Ps 106:40-46) and the people's plea to be gathered "from among the nations" (Ps 106:47).

In view of the sevenfold occurrence of the Hebrew word for "steadfast love" (חסד *ḥesed*, NRSV) in Psalm 89, culminating in the question of v. 49 ("Lord, where is your steadfast love of old . . . ?" [NRSV]), it is significant that Ps 90:14 prays for God's steadfast love and that Psalm 106 features this word as well (see vv. 1, 7, 45). Furthermore, Psalm 103, which follows immediately the two psalms in Book IV that most clearly articulate the pain of exile (see above on Psalms 101–102), contains four occurrences of the word (vv. 4, 8, 11, 17; see also Pss 92:2; 94:18; 98:3; 100:5). What is more, the six occurrences of the word in Psalm 107, the opening psalm of Book V, suggest that Book V picks up where Book IV left off—that is, it continues the response to the crisis of exile (cf. also Pss 106:47 and 107:2-3). Indeed, Psalm 107 can properly be considered a sermon on God's steadfast love that sounds as if it could have been written in response to Ps 89:49 (see Commentary on Psalm 107). Psalms 108 (v. 3) and 109 (vv. 21, 26) continue the focus on God's steadfast love, and the opening verse of Psalm 107 reappears as the first and last verses of Psalm 118. While Psalms 113–118 are a traditional liturgical unit within Judaism, the literary connections between Psalms 107 and 118 (107:1; 118:1, 29) suggest that Psalms 107–118 may form a redactional unit within Book V. Psalms 107 and 118 both recall the exodus, but the language is also appropriate for describing the return from exile. Significant in this regard, however, Psalm 118 moves toward a petition for continuing help (see v. 25). In short, even after the historical return from exile (see Pss 107:2-3; 118:21-24), the crisis persisted, and the shape of Book V continues the psalter's response.

The imposing Psalm 119, for instance, whenever it may have originated, admirably articulates the experience of the post-exilic generations. While the psalmist is faithful to God and God's instruction, he or she nonetheless is scorned and persecuted and so must live in waiting as a suffering servant—just like the post-exilic generations. This perspective is what the following commentary regularly calls "eschatological," since it involves the proclamation of God's reign amid circumstances that seem to deny and belie it—that is, it leaves the people simultaneously celebrating and awaiting God's reign (see below on "The Theology of the Psalms").

This same eschatological perspective characterizes the movement of the Songs of Ascents (Psalms 120–134) and is particularly evident in Psalm 126. Not surprisingly, the final three psalms (135–137), which form a sort of appendix to the Songs of Ascents, are the most explicit statement in the psalter of the pain of exile (see Commentary on Psalm 137). Psalms 135–137 are the prelude to a final Davidic collection, the first and last psalms of which return to the theme of God's steadfast love, which is prominent at key points in Books IV–V (see Pss 138:2, 8; 145:8; see above on Psalms 89; 90; 106; 107; 118). The core of this collection consists of psalms of lament, culminating in Psalm 144, which is a royal lament. Thus, near the end of both Books IV and V, there are royal laments (see above on Psalm 101) that effectively call to mind the ongoing theological crisis of exile. Significantly, Psalm 145 responds to Psalm 144 by affirming God's steadfast love, just as Psalm 103 had responded to Psalms 101–102 (see Pss 103:8; 145:8). Of further significance, Psalm 145 begins by addressing God as "King," thus also recalling Psalms 93; 95–99, the dominant collection of Book IV and the theological heart of the psalter.

Actually, Psalm 145 proves to be transitional. Not only does it conclude the Davidic collection, forming with Psalm 138 an envelope of praise around a core of laments, but it also anticipates Psalms 146–150. Each psalm in this concluding collection is bounded by "Praise the Lord

[הללו־יה *hallelu-yah*]!" The psalter's final invitation to praise (150:6) has been anticipated by 145:21. Furthermore, the explicit proclamation of God's sovereignty, reintroduced in Ps 145:1, recurs in Pss 146:10 and 149:2, thus recalling the theological heart of the psalter and its beginning as well. More particularly, Ps 149:6-9 features the same cast of characters present in Psalm 2: the rebellious "nations" and "peoples" and "kings." In contrast to Psalm 2, however, Psalm 149 assigns to the "faithful" (see vv. 1, 5, 9)—*not* to the Davidic king as in Psalm 2—the task of concretely implementing God's reign in the world. Thus Psalm 149 completes a direction that was initiated earlier in Books IV–V and that is another piece of the psalter's response to the crisis of exile—namely, the transfer to the whole people of claims and promises formerly attached to the Davidic monarchy (see the Commentary on Psalms 105; 110; 132; 144; 149). The literary and conceptual links and contrasts between Psalms 2 and 149 are another reminder of the crucial significance of Psalms 1–2, and further consideration of their role is necessary.

Psalms 1–2 as an Introduction to the Psalter. As already suggested, Psalms 1–2 are a fitting introduction to Books I and to Books I–III as a unit. As the psalter progresses, however, it becomes increasingly clear that Psalms 1–2 have set the interpretive agenda and provided an orientation for reading the whole book of Psalms. Scholars have traditionally concluded that Psalm 1 represents an intentional preface or introduction to the psalter, but the introductory function clearly belongs to Psalms 1 and 2 together. Neither psalm has a superscription, and they are bound by several literary links, including the crucial word translated "happy" (אשרי *'ašrê*), which forms an envelope structure (Pss 1:1; 2:12).

Psalm 1 portrays happiness as constant openness to God's "instruction" (v. 2; NIV and NRSV "law"), the fundamental orientation of life to God. The repetition of "instruction" (תורה *tôrâ*) is emphatic and suggests that the book of Psalms itself will serve as a source of divine instruction. While Psalm 1 counsels the reader to be open to God's instruction, including the subsequent psalms, Psalm 2 introduces the basic content of that instruction—namely, that God rules the world. Although the role of the Davidic monarch as an agent of God's rule will change as the psalter proceeds (see above), nothing will alter the pervasive proclamation of God's reign, which is first articulated in Ps 2:11-12. Thus happiness essentially belongs to those who "take refuge in" *God* (Ps 2:12), *not* in the Davidic monarch! In short, happiness is essentially trusting God, living in dependence upon God, an affirmation to which the conclusion of the psalter will return (see Ps 146:5). As Psalms 1 and 2 already make clear, and as subsequent psalms will clarify even further, the rule of God is persistently opposed. Thus the perspective of the psalter from the beginning is eschatological—that is, God's reign is proclaimed as a present reality, but it is always experienced by the faithful amid opposition. In this sense, the faithful live both with fulfillment and in waiting (see below, "The Theology of the Psalms").

Beyond Psalms 1 and 2, the rest of the psalter will portray the shape of the faithful life—including what it looks like and feels like and leads people to say and do—and it will reveal how the faithful life constitutes happiness. The portrayal of the faithful life is congruent with the portrayal of the character of God in Psalms, and both portrayals constitute a profoundly important revelation about the nature of divine sovereignty. In other words, while the book of Psalms originated as liturgical responses to God, it has been preserved and transmitted as God's word to humanity. As such, it not only represents a theological resource for dealing with the crisis of exile, but is also a theological resource for the people of God in every generation.

Methodological Conclusion. As suggested at the beginning of this Introduction, the approach to the psalms in the commentary that follows is explicitly theological. To be sure, it is theologically significant that Israel sang songs of praise to God, addressed honest and heartfelt prayers to God, and composed sacred poetry either addressed to or devoted to God. Thus the methods of form criticism and rhetorical criticism will be employed regularly. As traditionally practiced, however, form criticism and rhetorical criticism have not yielded theological conclusions. It is sustained attention to the shaping and final form of the psalter that pushes the interpreter toward theological interpretation. Klaus Seybold summarizes well the purpose of the psalter in its final form:

With the new preface ([Psalm] 1) and the weight of the reflexive proverbial poem ([Psalm] 119), which in terms of its range is effectively a small collection in itself, the existing Psalter now takes on the character of a documentation of divine revelation, to be used in a way analogous to the *Torah,* the first part of the canon, and becomes an instruction manual for the theological study of the divine order of salvation, and for meditation.[38]

As a theological instruction manual that aims at nothing less than the "documentation of divine revelation," the psalter in its final form demands to be interpreted theologically. Thus, while form criticism and rhetorical criticism will regularly be employed to arrive at historical, sociological, and literary conclusions, the ultimate purpose in the commentary is "to compose a commentary based on the book itself as the interpretive context of the psalms."[39] In short, I shall attempt to discern how the psalter was for Israel and is for us "an instruction manual for the theological study of the divine order of salvation"—in other words, what the psalter reveals about the life of God and the life God intends for humankind and for the world.

THE THEOLOGY OF THE PSALMS

Given the importance of the final form of the psalter, it is necessary to begin a consideration of the theology of the psalms with Psalms 1–2; even more specifically, with the very first word of the psalter: "Happy" (NRSV). In a real sense, the rest of the psalter will portray the shape of human happiness, and it is clear from the beginning and throughout Psalms that the definition of human happiness is thoroughly God-centered. The "happy" are those who constantly delight in God's "instruction" (תורה *tôrâ*, Ps 1:2; NIV and NRSV, "law"). In short, happiness derives from the complete orientation of life to God, including perpetual openness to God's instruction. Not only does Ps 1:2 have the effect of orienting the reader to approach the rest of the psalter as Scripture, as "an instruction manual for the theological study of the divine order of salvation" (see Seybold quotation above), but it also introduces a key concept—happiness—and begins to give it a thoroughly theocentric definition. Not surprisingly, the word for "happy" (אשרי *'ašrê*) will occur throughout Book I and the rest of the psalter, including as soon as the conclusion of Psalm 2 (see also Pss 32:1-2; 33:12; 34:8; 40:4; 41:4; 65:4; 84:4-5, 12; 89:15; 94:12; 106:3; 112:1; 119:1-2; 127:5; 128:1; 137:8-9; 144:15; 146:5).

Psalm 2:12 begins to fill out the portrait of the happy person, and it does so by introducing another key word that will also occur throughout Book I and the rest of the psalter: "refuge" (חסה *ḥāsâ*; see Pss 5:11; 7:1; 11:1; 14:6; 16:1; 18:30; 25:20; 31:1, 19; 34:8, 22; 36:7; 37:40; 46:1; 57:1; 61:3-4; 62:7-8; 64:10; 71:1, 17; 73:28; 91:2, 4, 9; 94:22; 118:8-9; 141:8; 142:5; 144:2). The happy are those who "take refuge in" God. In short, happiness derives from living in complete dependence upon God rather than upon the self. The word *ḥāsâ* has several synonyms that also occur frequently throughout the psalms (variously translated as "refuge," "fortress," "stronghold"), the most important of which is "trust"(see Pss 4:5; 9:10; 13:5; 21:7; 22:4-6; 25:2; 26:1; 28:7; 31:6, 14; 32:10; 37:3, 5; 40:3; 52:8; 55:23; 56:3-4, 11; 62:8; 84:12; 86:2; 91:2; 115:9-11; 125:1; 143:8). To be happy is to entrust one's whole self, existence, and future to God. As one would expect, there are several instances in which the words for "refuge" and "trust" occur in the same context (see Pss 31:1, 4, 6, 14, 19; 52:7-8; 62:7-8; 71:1, 3, 5; 91:2, 4, 9; 143:8-9); in addition to 2:12, the word "happy" is associated with either "refuge" or "trust" in Pss 34:8; 84:12; and 146:3, 5. Not surprisingly too, several of the occurrences of *ḥāsâ* or related words occur at key places in the psalter (see Pss 2:12; 91:2, 4, 9; 146:3, 5). Indeed, Jerome F. D. Creach argues that the editors of the psalter intended by the placement of certain psalms to call particular attention to the word *ḥāsâ* and related words.[40] In any case, whether intentional or not, the sheer repetition of "refuge," "trust," and several other synonyms

---

38. Klaus Seybold, *Introducing the Psalms*, trans. R. G. Dunphy (Edinburgh: T. & T. Clark, 1990) 24. See also Harvey H. Guthrie, Jr., *Israel's Sacred Songs: A Study of Dominant Themes* (New York: Seabury, 1966) 188-93; J. Clinton McCann, Jr., "The Psalms as Instruction," *Int.* 46 (1992) 117-28.

39. James L. Mays, *Psalms*, Interpretation (Louisville: John Knox, 1994) 19.

40. See Jerome F. D. Creach, *The Choice of YHWH as Refuge and the Editing of the Hebrew Psalter* (Sheffield: Sheffield Academic Press, 1996).

effectively portrays the happy, faithful life as one characterized by complete dependence upon God (see Commentary and Reflections on Psalms 1; 2).

This fundamental dependence upon God for life and future defines another key word in Psalms, at least insofar as it applies to human beings: "righteousness" (צדק *ṣĕdeq*) or "the righteous" (צדיק *ṣaddîq*). "Righteousness" is not primarily a moral category but a relational term. To be sure, behavior follows from one's commitments, but the righteous in the psalms should not be seen as morally superior persons whose good behavior lays an obligation on God to reward them. Rather, the righteous are persons who acknowledge their fundamental dependence upon God for life and future. Their happiness derives ultimately from God's forgiveness (see Ps 32:1-2) and the gift of God's faithful love (see Ps 32:10-11). In short, the happy, the righteous, are those who live by grace. As is evident from Psalm 1 onward, the righteous live constantly in the presence of the wicked, who are also called "scoffers," "sinners," "enemies," "foes," "adversaries," etc. As follows from the above definition of the righteous, the wicked are not outrageously or even obviously bad people, but are persons who live in fundamental dependence upon the self rather than upon God. In short, the wicked are persons who consider themselves to be autonomous, which means literally "a law unto oneself." Self-centered, self-directed, and self-ruled, the wicked see no need for dependence upon God or for consideration of others. The really frightening thing about this conclusion is that the essence of wickedness in the psalms—autonomy—is often what North American culture promotes as the highest virtue (see Commentary and Reflections on Psalm 1).

The definitions of "happiness" and "righteousness" in terms of refuge, the fundamental dependence upon God for life and future, makes sense only in the light of the affirmation that lies at what has been identified as the theological heart of the psalter: the Lord reigns (Psalms 93–99)! Indeed, this affirmation pervades the psalter. God is frequently addressed as "King" (see Pss 5:2; 10:16; 24:7-10; 29:10; 44:4; 47:2, 7; 48:2; 68:24; 74:12; 84:3; 95:3; 98:6; 145:1; 149:2), but even when the language of kingship and reigning is not explicitly present, God's rule is articulated by means of other words and concepts. For instance, God's role as universal judge is a function of God's cosmic sovereignty (see Pss 7:7-11; 9:7-8), as is God's role as the divine warrior who enacts the divine will for the world (see Pss 24:8; 68:1-3; 89:5-18).

Furthermore, the royal psalms, which are scattered throughout the psalter, located in strategic places (see above, "Royal Psalms"), serve to articulate God's sovereignty. To be sure, these psalms focus directly on the earthly kings of Israel and Judah, but the earthly kings are presented as agents of God's rule. Psalm 2, for instance, culminates not in an invitation to serve the earthly king but to "Serve the Lord" (v. 11 NRSV). God's reign involves the enactment of justice and righteousness among all people (see Pss 96:10-13; 97:1-2; 98:4-9), and it is precisely the mission of the earthly king as God's agent to embody justice and righteousness on a cosmic scale (see Psalm 72). In this way, too, the royal psalms articulate God's sovereign claim on the whole world.

Even the songs of Zion, although they focus on a very particular place, are finally affirmations of God's universal reign. Psalms 46 and 48, for instance, surround Psalm 47, which explicitly celebrates God's kingship. Not surprisingly, both Psalms 46 and 48 portray God in the role of a warrior who wages peace (see also Ps 76:4-9), and Psalm 48 addresses God as "King" and describes the effect of God's worldwide involvement as "righteousness" (v. 10 NIV) and justice (v. 11; cf. "judgments" in NIV and NRSV; see Ps 122:5). In short, a particular place, Jerusalem, has become a concrete symbol of the extension of God's rule in all places and times. God claims the whole world and all its peoples (see Psalm 87).

At the same time that they affirm God's cosmic reign, however, the royal psalms and songs of Zion also make it clear that God's rule is constantly and pervasively opposed. As the psalter begins, the nations and peoples are aligned against God and God's chosen king (Ps 2:1-3). Jerusalem is regularly the target of attack (see Pss 46:6; 48:5; 76:3-6). This apparent anomaly—constant and powerful opposition to the cosmic rule of God—calls attention to a crucial characteristic of the psalter that I frequently refer to in the commentary as its *eschatological* perspective. Because this word may be subject to misunderstanding, it needs to be carefully defined. By *eschatological,* I mean the proclamation of God's universal reign amid circumstances that seem to deny it and belie it. The word *eschatological* literally means "a word about last things," and it is popularly perceived as having to do primarily with the future. But in the commentary, the word focuses attention on the *present.* That is, the psalms regularly affirm God's reign as a *present* reality. To be sure, the reality of opposition implies the future consummation of God's reign, but the emphasis in the psalms is clearly on the presence of God's reign as the only true source of refuge, happiness, and, indeed, life.

While the eschatological perspective of the psalter is clear enough from Psalm 2, the movement from Psalm 2 to Psalm 3 makes it clear that not only are God's chosen king and God's chosen place constantly opposed, but so also are God's people. In other words, happiness (Pss 1:1; 2:12), prosperity (Ps 1:3), and refuge (Ps 2:12) exist not beyond but rather in the midst of opposition and suffering. Consequently, in addition to "the righteous" and synonyms such as "the upright," the most frequent designations the psalmists use for themselves include "the poor," "the afflicted," "the meek," "the humble," "the needy," "the helpless," and "the oppressed" (see Psalms 9–10). Not surprisingly, therefore, the dominant voice in the psalter is that of prayer. Indeed, prayer is a way of life for those who entrust themselves fully to God's care. Prayer is the offering of the whole self to God, including pain, grief, fear, loneliness, and sinfulness as well as expressions of innocence and desire for vengeance (which in the final form of the psalter are to be understood as pleas for justice; see Psalms 58; 109; 137).

Although prayer and praise are usually treated as separate voices involving distinct categories of psalms (that is, laments/complaints and songs of praise; see above on form criticism), it is of crucial theological significance to notice that prayer and praise are finally inseparable. Almost without exception, each prayer for help moves toward expressions of trust and praise. Furthermore, Books I–III, the portions of the psalter dominated by laments, include songs of praise at regular intervals, that are often linked verbally to the preceding prayer (see below Commentary on Psalms 7; 8; 32; 33) as if to remind the reader of the inseparability of prayer and praise. Thus, while laments and songs of praise may have represented in ancient Israel separate liturgical movements or moments, their regular juxtaposition within the same psalm and in the final arrangement of the psalter suggests theological connections. The juxtaposition prevents the conclusion that the songs of praise represent merely the ideology of the rich and powerful that is used to celebrate the status quo.[41] To state it positively, the juxtaposition means that for the faithful, suffering and glory are inseparable. In explicitly Christian terms, the people of God are inevitably and always identified by *both* the cross and the resurrection (see Reflections on Psalms 13; 22; 31; 69).

When construed as ultimately inseparable voices, both prayer and praise are means of expressing complete dependence upon God. While prayer is the offering of the whole self to God by way of direct address to God involving bitter complaint, brutally honest confession of sin or innocence, and poignant petition and intercession, praise is the offering of the whole self to God by way of joyful affirmation of God's sovereignty, enthusiastic celebration of God's character and activity, and direct address to others to invite them to join in the song. Praise affirms a simple but profound good news—namely, that the whole cosmos and all its peoples, creatures, and things belong to God. This good news has extraordinary political, socioeconomic, and ecological implications.

Because our lives belong to God, we are not our own. Thus the autonomy that much of North American culture promotes is a dead end; it will lead only to a society of isolated selves rather than to the community of justice and righteousness that God wills among all people (see Commentary on Psalms 1; 100).

Because our lives belong to God, and because God wills life for all people, "justice for all" becomes far more than a phrase out of a pledge or a matter of democratic fairness. Rather, "justice for all" means that God wills political and economic systems that exclude *no one* from access to provision for life and future; God will be content with nothing less than peace on earth (see Commentary on Psalms 29; 46; 68; 72; 82). Because God wills life for the whole creation as

---

41. See Walter Brueggemann, *Israel's Praise: Doxology Against Idolatry and Ideology* (Philadelphia: Fortress, 1988).

well as for all people, ecological awareness becomes not simply a matter of preserving limited natural resources in order to maintain for ourselves and our children the standard of living to which we have grown accustomed. Rather, ecology and theology are inseparable. To live under God's rule is to live in partnership with all other species of creature and in partnership with the earth itself (see Commentary on Psalms 8; 19; 29; 104; 147; 148).

The psalter's eschatological character has profound significance for understanding the fundamental identity of both humanity and God. As for humanity, the psalms teach us that human happiness—indeed, authentic human life—exists only when people acknowledge God's reign and respond by taking refuge in God. Because God's reign is constantly opposed by humans, however, happiness and life inevitably involve suffering. Therefore, the faithful, righteous life consists of suffering servanthood.

As for God, the reality of constant opposition to God's reign calls for an understanding of divine sovereignty that differs from the usual view of sovereignty. Sovereignty is ordinarily thought of as the power to enforce one's will. But God simply does not do this. Rather, God invites, encourages, and empowers people to do God's will. But from the very beginning of the biblical story, people have chosen *not* to do God's will (see Genesis 3). God's only choice is either to enforce the divine will, which will mean the destruction of humanity, or to suffer the consequences of human disobedience (see Genesis 6–9). God chooses the latter, and it is a monumentally important choice, for it means that God willingly becomes vulnerable for the sake of relating genuinely to humankind. Terence Fretheim calls God's choice "a divine *kenosis,* a self-emptying, an act of self-sacrifice," and he concludes, "The very act of creation thus might be called the beginning of the passion of God."[42] In other words, God suffers, too, and it is necessary to conclude that divine sovereignty consists not of sheer force but of sheer love. The eschatological perspective of the psalter—the proclamation of God's reign amid persistent opposition—reinforces the conclusion that God's power is essentially that of pure, unbounded love. God's life, too, consists of suffering servanthood!

This being the case, it is not an exaggeration to say that the most important theological concept in the book of Psalms is represented by the Hebrew word חסד (*hesed*), which the NIV often translates as "unfailing love" and the NRSV regularly translates as "steadfast love." It occurs as early as Ps 5:7 and frequently thereafter in all five books of the psalter, often in crucially placed psalms (see Psalms 42; 89; 90; 106; 107; 118; 138; 145). Its range is not restricted to a particular type. Rather, Israel appeals to God's *hesed* in prayer (see Commentary on Psalms 6; 13; 31; 44; 51; 63), and Israel celebrates God's *hesed* in songs of praise (see Psalms 33; 100; 103; 136; 145; 147). Indeed, the opening line of several psalms constitutes a brief hymn in itself as it celebrates God's *hesed* (see Pss 107:1; 118:1; 136:1; cf. 100:5; 113:2), and this formulation appears to have functioned as a sort of "favorite hymn," which also has the character of a basic profession of faith (see 2 Chr 5:13; 7:3; 20:21; Ezra 3:11).

Given that the final form of the psalter has the character of "instruction" (*tôrâ*; see above), it is not surprising that the importance of *hesed* in the psalms matches its importance in the Pentateuch, the Torah. At a crucial turning point when the future of Israel hangs in the balance, God reveals Godself to be "merciful and gracious, slow to anger, and abounding in steadfast love and faithfulness" (Exod 34:6 NRSV). In fact, this or a very similar formulation occurs several more times in the Pentateuch and beyond; it seems to constitute a basic profession of Israel's faith (see Num 14:18; Neh 9:17; Joel 2:13; Jonah 4:2). Not unexpectedly, it also occurs in the psalms (see Pss 86:15; 103:8; 145:8). The other terms in the formulation of Exod 34:6 are also important in the psalms. The NRSV's "merciful" (רחום *rahûm*) is from the same root as a noun that means "womb" (רחם *rhm*); thus it conveys God's motherly compassion (see also Pss 25:6; 40:11; 51:1; 69:16; 79:8; 106:45; 111:4). The word "gracious" (חנון *hanûn*) is regularly paired with "merciful" (*rahûm*), and another form of the root indicates that God's grace is the basis for appeals to God for help (e.g., see "Be gracious" in Pss 4:1; 6:2). The words "faithfulness" (אמת *'ĕmet*) and "steadfast love" (*hesed*) are paired frequently in the psalms as in Exod 34:6 (see Pss 25:10; 36:5; 40:10-11; 57:3; 61:7; 85:10; 89:14; 117:2). The word "faithfulness" occurs

42. Terence Fretheim, *The Suffering of God: An Old Testament Perspective* (Philadelphia: Fortress, 1984) 58.

alone as well (see Pss 54:5; 71:22; 91:4; 143:1), but the word *hesed* appears more frequently and serves virtually as a one-word summary of Israel's understanding of the character of God.

That God is fundamentally compassionate, gracious, faithful, and loving does not mean that anything goes with God. From the beginning, the psalter recognizes the wrath of God (see Ps 2:5, 12). The psalmists appeal to God's wrath against their enemies (Pss 56:7; 59:13), and they are aware of experiencing God's wrath (Pss 6:1; 38:1; 78:59, 62; 88:7, 16; 89:38, 46; 90:7, 9, 11). Again, this picture is consistent with Exodus 34, where God's self-revelation as *hesed* (v. 6) is followed closely by the statement that God "does not leave the guilty unpunished" (v. 7 NIV). But how can God be both loving and wrathful, gracious and just, forgiving and punishing? The question is not easily answered for us—or for God! Indeed, this very dilemma is the inevitable result of God's choice to love a sinful humanity, and it bespeaks God's willingness to be vulnerable and to suffer for love's sake. What we can say is that retribution is clearly not operative as a mechanistic scheme. Rather, reward is the experience of authentic life in dependence upon God, and punishment is the inevitable outcome of the choice not to be related to God. The book of Psalms affirms that evil will not endure (see Psalm 1). But given Israel's awareness of its own sinfulness (see Psalms 32; 51; 78; 106; 130) and the sinfulness of all humanity (see Psalms 1–2; 14; 143), one must finally conclude that God's justice is ultimately manifest as love. For Christian readers, the psalter's presentation of the mystery of sovereignty made perfect in steadfast love comes into sharpest focus on the cross of Jesus Christ.

THE PSALMS AND THE NEW TESTAMENT

The early church's use of the psalms was in keeping with both major directions suggested by recent scholarly study of the book of Psalms—that is, the church used the psalms both as liturgical materials in early Christian worship and as a theological resource. Evidence for the first use is found in Paul's advice to the Colossians to "sing psalms, hymns, and spiritual songs to God" (3:16 NRSV; see also Eph 5:19). Although it is not clear precisely what each of these three terms designates, it is almost certain that "psalms" (and perhaps "hymns") refers to material from the book of Psalms. After all, the earliest followers of Jesus were Jews, so it only makes sense that they would continue to use in worship some of the same materials they had always used. To be sure, new materials were used in Christian worship as well, and it is likely that "spiritual songs" refers explicitly to Christian material that may have been created with inspiration from the psalms. For instance, Mary's Song (Luke 1:46-55) contains echoes of Psalms 98 and 113, and the Song of Simeon (Luke 2:28-32) echoes Ps 119:123.

While it is likely that the early Christians prayed and sang the psalms, it is absolutely clear that they used the psalms as a theological resource. The book of Psalms is quoted and alluded to in the NT more than any other OT book. This is not at all surprising in view of the fact that the theology of the psalms is congruent with the core of Jesus' preaching and teaching. What was identified earlier as the theological heart of the psalter—God reigns—is precisely the fundamental good news that Jesus announced from the beginning of his public ministry (see Mark 1:14-15). Jesus proclaimed the reign of God as a present reality, and he invited people to enter it and experience it immediately. Thus Jesus' preaching was eschatological in the sense in which this term was defined—that is, he proclaimed the reign of God amid constant opposition. This persistent opposition meant that Jesus' own life, as well as the lives of his followers and of those to whom his ministry was most often directed, may be characterized in the same terms that regularly describe the psalmists: *afflicted, oppressed, poor, needy, weak, meek,* and *persecuted.* But as in the psalms, it is precisely the afflicted whom Jesus pronounces "Happy" or "Blessed" (see Matt 5:1-11; Luke 6:20-23).

In short, like the psalms, Jesus' ministry of suffering servanthood pushes toward a radical redefinition of the usual understanding of sovereignty. Sovereignty is not the demonstration of sheer power but the embodiment of sheer love, which ultimately is revealed to be the most powerful reality of all. The gracious, incarnational involvement of God with humanity, already evident in the psalms (and elsewhere in the OT), is, from the Christian perspective, completed in Jesus' ministry of suffering servanthood. Thus, in reflecting on Jesus' identity, the early Christians concluded that Jesus was nothing less than God incarnate, "the Word became flesh and lived among us" (John 1:14 NRSV). Because Jesus had fully revealed what God is like, thus fulfilling the role of the ancient kings of Judah and Israel to enact God's justice and righteousness, the early church saw in Jesus the culmination of the monarchical ideal. Thus they accorded Jesus the royal titles "anointed" (מָשִׁיחַ *māšîaḥ*; Χριστός *Christos*; see Ps 2:4; Mark 1:1) and Son of God (see Mark 1:1; Ps 2:7). The cross, far from being a sign of defeat, was the clearest demonstration of God's character and sovereignty. The resurrection did not remove the scandal of the cross but instead validated its revelation that the power of sheer love is the only authentic source of life. Thus Jesus' invitation to discipleship is essentially an invitation for people to share his ministry of suffering servanthood: "let them deny themselves and take up their cross and follow me" (Mark 8:34 NRSV). The lives of Jesus' followers, like Jesus' own life, will replicate the lives of the psalmists, who are pronounced "happy" not beyond but in the midst of their constant affliction.

Given the congruence between the portrayal of God and the faithful life in the psalms and by Jesus, it is not surprising that the Gospel writers cannot tell the story of Jesus without frequently referring or alluding to a psalm. For instance, the words of the heavenly beings in Luke's account of Jesus' birth recall the content and movement of Psalm 29, thus suggesting that Jesus' birth signals the presence of God's reign (see Luke 2:13-14 and Commentary on Psalm 29). The heavenly voice at Jesus' baptism quotes a portion of Ps 2:7, thus introducing Jesus as the one who would ultimately embody God's will and finally fulfill the purpose of the monarchy (see Matt 3:17; Mark 1:11; Luke 3:22). Psalm 2:7 is cited again at Jesus' transfiguration, immediately after the first prediction of his passion in the synoptic Gospels (see Matt 17:5; Mark 9:7; Luke 9:35). The effect is to reinforce the message that Jesus will embody God's character and will do so precisely by way of his suffering servanthood.

This message is, of course, regularly reinforced as well by Jesus' ministry of compassion and his teaching (see Commentary on Psalms 24; 37; and 73, which are specifically recalled by Jesus' Beatitudes; see also Psalms 41; 126). But it is seen most clearly in Jesus' passion, and in telling this part of Jesus' story, the Gospel writers rely most heavily on the psalms. Jesus' entry into Jerusalem is narrated with reference to Psalm 118, thus suggesting that Jesus' upcoming passion is to be viewed in sequence with the exodus and return from exile, God's saving deeds of old (see Matt 21:9; Mark 11:9-10; Luke 19:38; John 12:12). The account of the crucifixion in all four Gospels has been shaped by Psalm 22, and in Matt 27:46 and Mark 15:34, the words Jesus speaks from the cross are a quotation of Ps 22:1. These words are not present in Luke and John, but Jesus' final words in Luke are a quotation of Ps 31:5 (Luke 23:46), and Jesus' final words in John seem also to allude to Ps 31:5 and perhaps to Ps 22:31 (John 19:30). The passion accounts have also been influenced by Psalm 69 (cf. Matt 27:48; Mark 15:36; John 19:28-29 with Ps 69:21; and Ps 69:4 with John 15:25). In short, the Gospel writers drew upon the three longest and most impressive of the laments of an individual in order to relate the story of Jesus' suffering (see also Psalms 38; 41). In other words, Jesus is presented as the ultimate paradigm of the faithful sufferer. What is more, it is precisely Jesus' faithful suffering on behalf of others that reveals what God is like. Thus, as suggested already, the cross is for Christians the ultimate revelation of the mystery the Psalms present—that is, divine sovereignty manifested as perfect love.

The paradox of strength made perfect in weakness (see 2 Cor 12:9), although "a stumbling block to Jews and foolishness to Gentiles" (1 Cor 1:23 NRSV), should not be misunderstood. God's strength—the power of sheer love—is *real* strength. As William Placher, citing Jürgen Moltmann's *The Crucified God,* puts it: "It would be a weak, poor God . . . who could not love or suffer. Such a God would be caught in a prison of impassability."[43] It is precisely the God revealed in Psalms and in Jesus Christ that is strong enough to be vulnerable. This apparent weakness turns out to be the greatest strength of all, as the resurrection of Jesus demonstrated. For us to understand properly the paradox of divine sovereignty, the cross and the resurrection must be inseparable, and the NT always presents them this way.[44] Indeed, the inseparability of

---

43. William C. Placher, *Narratives of a Vulnerable God: Christ, Theology, and Scripture* (Louisville: Westminster John Knox, 1994) 19.
44. See Charles B. Cousar, *A Theology of the Cross: The Death of Jesus in the Pauline Letters* (Philadelphia: Fortress, 1990) 103-8.

cross and resurrection is analogous to the way in which lament and praise are finally inseparable in the psalms (see above). Given this analogy, it is appropriate that the resurrection as well as the crucifixion is proclaimed in the NT by way of the psalms. The first recorded Christian sermon—Peter's sermon on the Day of Pentecost—is based primarily on Pss 16:8-11; 110:1; and 132:11 (see Acts 8:25-34); Psalm 110 is often quoted or alluded to in articulating the glory of the crucified one (see 1 Cor 15:25; Eph 1:20; Col 3:1; Heb 1:3; 8:1; 10:12-13; 12:2).

The radical implications of Jesus' embodiment of God's sovereignty in suffering love were not lost on the apostle Paul. As Elsa Tamez points out, Jesus' proclamation of the reign of God becomes, in Pauline terms, justification by grace—or better yet, "the revelation of the justice of God."[45] As Jesus revealed and as Paul clearly understood, God's justice is ultimately manifested as grace. The traditional exposition of justification by faith as the forgiveness of sins is not incorrect, but it is not broad enough. The revelation of God's justice involves fundamentally the good news that God's gracious love extends to *all* people. God's justice means the affirmation of life for all people, not based on any system of human merit but as a result of God's loving gift. The message is again congruent with that of the psalms, and Paul appeals to the psalms to support his case. No human being can deserve God's gift of life (see Rom 3:9-20, where Paul cites several psalms, including 14:1-3; 143:2). The gift of divine forgiveness (see Rom 4:7-8, which cites Ps 32:1-2) means the leveling of all distinctions and human systems that exclude. This theology of divine justice revealed as gracious love—which Paul found in the psalms and which Jesus had embodied—led Paul to the radical step of casting aside sacred but exclusivistic symbols, such as circumcision and dietary regulations, in order to open the church to all people. It is appropriate that Paul found warrant for this step in the psalms (see Rom 15:9-11, which quotes Pss 89:49; 117:1).

It is appropriate that a final word about the psalms and the NT come from the Revelation to John. While direct quotation of the psalms is rare (see only Rev 2:26-27, which cites Ps 2:8-9), the Revelation is full of singing and songs that could well have been inspired by the psalter. The Revelation shares the psalter's fundamental conviction that God rules the world (see Rev 11:15; 12:10; 15:3), and the mention of "a new song" (Rev 5:9; 14:3) explicitly recalls Psalms 96; 98; and 149, all of which assert God's reign. It is particularly interesting that the Revelation, like Psalm 149, envisions God's people reigning with God in a redeemed world that includes "the healing of the nations" (Rev 22:1-5 NRSV; see also 2:26-27; 5:10; and cf. Ps 149:5-9). While the Revelation is usually classified as apocalyptic literature, it should not be construed as a timetable for the chronological end of the world. Rather, it portrays the future that God wills, which is possible because God rules the world, and which, indeed, becomes a present reality for those who acknowledge God's claim and enter God's realm of life. Insofar as it depicts the "end" or destiny of the world, it portrays the faithful gathered to God and singing a song that recalls Pss 86:9-10 and 145:17 (see Rev 15:3-4). As a vision of the "end," it might be beneficial for contemporary folk to hold this scenario alongside secular apocalyptic scenarios like nuclear winter, nuclear holocaust, or an earth laid waste by the radiation that enters through an atmosphere depleted of ozone. To be sure, such warnings should not be dismissed, although it is unlikely that we shall be frightened into reform. What will go further than anything else to prevent such catastrophes will be living toward a different vision, the biblical vision of faithful folk from all times and places, gathered, like the psalmists of old, to acknowledge God's reign by singing a new song.

45. Elsa Tamez, *The Amnesty of Grace: Justification by Faith from a Latin American Perspective,* trans. Sharon H. Ringe (Nashville: Abingdon, 1993) 157.

BIBLIOGRAPHY

Commentaries:

Allen, Leslie C. *Psalms 101–150.* WBC 21. Waco: Word, 1983. Contains the author's translation, a survey of scholarly treatment, and theological reflection. Especially rich in structural and stylistic analysis.

Bratcher, Robert G., and William D. Reyburn. *A Translator's Handbook on the Book of Psalms*. New York: United Bible Societies, 1991. Provides analysis of many recent translations with a focus on the RSV and the GNB. Also provides many helpful structural and stylistic insights.

Brueggemann, Walter. *The Message of the Psalms: A Theological Commentary*. Minneapolis: Augsburg, 1984. Organized according to a contemporary typology (orientation, disorientation, new orientation), this treatment of fifty-eight psalms is rich in literary insights and theological appropriation.

Craigie, Peter. *Psalms 1–50*. WBC 19. Waco: Word, 1983. Contains the author's translation, a survey of scholarly treatment, and theological reflection. Heavily oriented to form criticism with attention to ancient Near Eastern backgrounds.

Gerstenberger, Erhard S. *Psalms: Part 1, with an Introduction to Cultic Poetry*. Forms of the OT Literature 14. Grand Rapids: Eerdmans, 1988. Although thoroughly form critical, this volume proposes that psalms should be understood as rituals originally set in small primary groups, such as the family or the local synagogue. Contains commentary on Psalms 1–60.

Kraus, Hans-Joachim. *Psalms 1–59* and *Psalms 60–150*. Translated by H. C. Oswald. Minneapolis: Augsburg, 1988 and 1989. Although still primarily form critical, Kraus has modified his earlier stance. His work is full of sensitive theological insights and references to classical sources, especially Luther and Calvin.

Mays, James L. *Psalms*. Interpretation. Louisville: John Knox, 1994. Excellent commentary for preachers and teachers. Reflects the best of all recent methods with results that are theologically profound, relevant to pastors, and shaped with an eye toward the church's liturgical calendar.

Stulmueller, Carroll. *Psalms 1* and *Psalms 2*. OT Message 21 and 22. Wilmington, Del.: Michael Glazier, 1983. Employs a variety of approaches to interpret the psalms in their original contexts but always with an eye toward NT use and contemporary appropriation.

Tate, Marvin E. *Psalms 51–100*. WBC 20. Dallas: Word, 1990. Contains the author's translation, a survey of scholarly treatment, and very helpful theological reflection. Reflects judicious use of all methods, including attention to the shape and shaping of the psalter.

Weiser, Artur. *The Psalms*. Translated by H. Hartwell. OTL. Philadelphia: Westminster, 1962. The theory of a Covenant Renewal Festival is pervasively evident, but this volume contains many keen theological insights and illustrates them with frequent references to classical Lutheran sources and hymnody.

Westermann, Claus. *The Living Psalms*. Translated by J. R. Porter. Grand Rapids: Eerdmans, 1989. Organized according to form-critical categories, this volume contains commentary on forty-six psalms by a sensitive exegete and theologian.

Other Studies:

Bellinger, W. H., Jr. *Psalms: Reading and Studying the Book of Praises*. Peabody, Mass.: Hendrickson, 1990. A brief introduction that aims at preparing persons to engage in their own informed study of Psalms.

Brueggemann, Walter. *Praying the Psalms*. Winona, Minn.: St. Mary's, 1982. A sensitive treatment of the theological issues involved in reading and praying the psalms.

Gillingham, S. E. *The Poems and Psalms of the Hebrew Bible*. Oxford Bible Series. Oxford: Oxford University Press, 1994. Accessible, helpful introduction to Hebrew poetry and to what it means to read the psalms as poems.

Gunkel, Hermann. *The Psalms: A Form-Critical Introduction*. Translated by T. M. Horner. FBBS 19. Philadelphia: Fortress, 1967. Makes available in English the basis of Gunkel's classical work on Psalms.

Guthrie, Harvey H. *Israel's Sacred Songs: A Study of Dominant Themes.* New York: Seabury, 1966. Departs from form-critical insights but is constantly concerned with how and why the psalms continue to be spoken and to speak to contemporary persons.

Holladay, William L. *The Psalms Through Three Thousand Years: Prayerbook of a Cloud of Witnesses.* Minneapolis: Fortress, 1993. Illustrates how the psalms have functioned throughout history and also addresses contemporary theological issues in interpreting and using the psalms. Good companion to Prothero's work (see below).

Kraus, Hans-Joachim. *Theology of the Psalms.* Translated by Keith Crim. Minneapolis: Augsburg, 1986. Illumines basic topics in their ancient setting—God, people, Zion, the king, the enemies, the individual—and concludes with a consideration of the use of the psalms in the NT.

Levine, Herbert J. *Sing Unto God a New Song: A Contemporary Reading of the Psalms.* Bloomington: Indiana University Press, 1995. A sensitive discussion of the psalms and their use in view of the conflict between faith and experience and the consequent issue of theodicy, concluding with a chapter on Jewish interpretation of the psalms after the Holocaust.

Limburg, James. *Psalms for Sojourners.* Minneapolis: Augsburg, 1986. Brief essays on psalms of various types with constant concern to address their meaning for today. Very useful for preachers and teachers.

McCann, J. Clinton, Jr. *A Theological Introduction to the Book of Psalms: The Psalms as Torah.* Nashville: Abingdon, 1993. Focuses on hearing the psalms in the contemporary context as Scripture—as instruction about God, humanity, and the faithful life.

Mays, James L. *The Lord Reigns: A Theological Handbook to the Psalms.* Louisville: Westminster John Knox, 1994. A series of essays on the theological issues involved in the ongoing use of the psalms as both Scripture and liturgy. Excellent companion to Mays's Psalms commentary (see above).

Miller, Patrick D., Jr. *Interpreting the Psalms.* Philadelphia: Fortress, 1986. Introductory essays on contemporary issues in Psalms interpretation are followed by excellent expository essays on ten psalms.

Mowinckel, Sigmund. *The Psalms in Israel's Worship.* Translated by D. R. Ap-Thomas. Nashville: Abingdon, 1962. Presents Mowinckel's influential cult-functional approach and his conclusions concerning the use and setting of the various types, several of which are involved in his theoretical Enthronement Festival of Yahweh.

Nowell, Irene. *Sing a New Song: The Psalms in the Sunday Lectionary.* Collegeville, Minn.: Liturgical Press, 1993. Organized by form-critical type, this volume relates the psalms lection to the other readings in the Roman Catholic lectionary and makes a plea for the use of the psalms in the Sunday service.

Peterson, Eugene H. *Answering God: The Psalms as Tools for Prayer.* San Francisco: Harper & Row, 1989. An accessible rationale for and guide to the use of the psalms in contemporary prayer.

Pleins, J. David. *The Psalms: Songs of Tragedy, Hope, and Justice.* Maryknoll, N.Y.: Orbis, 1993. Takes seriously the contemporary realities of socioeconomic oppression as a point of departure for hearing the psalms as "poetry of justice" and for considering their theological implications for worship and work.

Prothero, Rowland E. *The Psalms in Human Life and Experience.* New York: E. P. Dutton, 1903. Illustrates the use of Psalms in Christian history through the nineteenth century. A good companion to Holladay's work (see above).

Sarna, Nahum M. *Songs of the Heart: An Introduction to the Book of Psalms.* New York: Schocken, 1993. Introduces Psalms primarily by way of nine essays on individual psalms of various types. Especially useful for treating the psalms in their ancient Near Eastern context and for relating them to rabbinic sources as well as to medieval and contemporary Jewish commentators.

Smith, Mark S. *Psalms: The Divine Journey.* New York: Paulist, 1987. Drawing on ancient Near Eastern solar imagery, this volume treats Psalms primarily from the perspective of the psalmists' experience of God in the Temple.

Wilson, Gerald H. *The Editing of the Hebrew Psalter.* SBLDS 76. Chico, Calif.: Scholars Press, 1985. Ground-breaking study of the shape and shaping of the psalter that is responsible for much of the impetus to interpret the book of Psalms in its final literary context.

Zenger, Erich. *A God of Vengeance? Understanding the Psalms of Enmity.* Translated by Linda M. Maloney. Louisville: Westminster John Knox, 1995. A comprehensive rationale and plea for the use of the psalms of enmity in Christian worship so as to be liturgically sound, theologically faithful, and not Marcionite or anti-Jewish.

OUTLINE OF PSALMS

I. Psalms 1–41, Book I

    A. 1:1-6, Delight in God's Teaching
    B. 2:1-12, The Reign of God
    C. 3:1-8, God Helps Those Who Cannot Help Themselves
    D. 4:1-8, You Alone, O Lord
    E. 5:1-12, Lead Me, O Lord
    F. 6:1-10, O Lord—How Long?
    G. 7:1-17, O Righteous God!
    H. 8:1-9, The Majesty of God and the Glory of Humanity
    I. 9:1–10:18, The Needy Shall Not Always Be Forgotten
    J. 11:1-7, The Upright Shall Behold God's Face
    K. 12:1-8, I Will Now Arise
    L. 13:1-6, But I Trust in Your Steadfast Love
    M. 14:1-7, No One Does Good
    N. 15:1-5, They Shall Not Be Moved
    O. 16:1-11, I Keep the Lord Always Before Me
    P. 17:1-15, Beholding Your Likeness
    Q. 18:1-50, Steadfast Love to the Anointed
    R. 19:1-14, God's Instruction Is All-Encompassing
    S. 20:1-9, We Trust in the Name of the Lord Our God
    T. 21:1-13, The King Trusts in the Lord
    U. 22:1-31, My God, My God, Why Have You Forsaken Me?
    V. 23:1-6, Like a Child at Home
    W. 24:1-10, The Earth Is the Lord's
    X. 25:1-22, To You, O Lord, I Offer My Life
    Y. 26:1-12, Establish Justice for Me, O Lord
    Z. 27:1-14, Your Face, Lord, Do I Seek
    AA. 28:1-9, The Lord Is My Strength
    BB. 29:1-11, Glory to God!
    CC. 30:1-12, So That My Soul May Praise You
    DD. 31:1-24, My Life and Future Are in Your Hand
    EE. 32:1-11, You Forgave the Guilt of My Sin
    FF. 33:1-22, The Earth Is Full of God's Unfailing Love
    GG. 34:1-22, I Will Teach You the Fear of the Lord
    HH. 35:1-28, O Lord, Who Is Like You?
    II. 36:1-12, In Your Light

JJ. 37:1-40, The Meek Shall Inherit the Land
KK. 38:1-22, There Is No Soundness in My Flesh
LL. 39:1-13, My Hope Is in You
MM. 40:1-17, I Delight to Do Your Will
NN. 41:1-13, Happy Are Those Who Consider the Poor

II. Psalms 42–72, Book II

A. 42:1–43:5, Hope in God
B. 44:1-26, Like Sheep for Slaughter
C. 45:1-17, For the Cause of Truth, Humility, and Righteousness
D. 46:1-11, Our Refuge and Strength
E. 47:1-9, King of All the Earth
F. 48:1-14, Great Is the Lord
G. 49:1-20, God Will Redeem My Life
H. 50:1-23, Offer to God a Sacrifice of Thanksgiving
I. 51:1-19, According to Your Steadfast Love
J. 52:1-9, I Trust in God's Unfailing Love
K. 53:1-6, No One Does Good
L. 54:1-7, Surely, God Is My Helper
M. 55:1-23, Cast Your Burdens on the Lord
N. 56:1-13, In God I Trust
O. 57:1-11, Be Exalted, O God, Above the Heavens
P. 58:1-11, There Is a God Who Establishes Justice
Q. 59:1-17, The God Who Shows Me Steadfast Love
R. 60:1-12, Human Help Is Worthless
S. 61:1-8, The Rock Higher Than I
T. 62:1-12, Trust in God at All Times
U. 63:1-11, Your Love Is Better Than Life
V. 64:1-10, What God Has Done
W. 65:1-13, You Crown the Year with Your Bounty
X. 66:1-20, God Has Kept Us Among the Living
Y. 67:1-7, That God's Ways May Be Known on Earth
Z. 68:1-35, My God, My King!
AA. 69:1-36, For Your Sake I Have Borne Reproach
BB. 70:1-5, O Lord, Do Not Delay!
CC. 71:1-24, I Will Hope Continually
DD. 72:1-20, May Righteousness Flourish and Peace Abound

III. Psalms 73–89, Book III

A. 73:1-28, It Is Good to Be Near God
B. 74:1-23, Do Not Forget Your Afflicted People
C. 75:1-10, God Says to the Arrogant, "Do Not Boast"
D. 76:1-12, God Indeed Is Awesome
E. 77:1-20, God's Footprints Were Unseen
F. 78:1-72, Trusting in God
G. 79:1-13, The Nations Say, "Where Is Their God?"
H. 80:1-19, Restore Us, O God
I. 81:1-16, If My People Would Only Listen to Me!
J. 82:1-8, Show Justice to the Weak
K. 83:1-18, Let Your Enemies Know

L. 84:1-12, Happy Are Those Whose Strength Is in You
M. 85:1-13, Surely God's Salvation Is Near
N. 86:1-17, You Alone Are God
O. 87:1-7, This One Was Born in Zion
P. 88:1-18, The Darkness Is My Closest Friend
Q. 89:1-52, Lord, Where Is Your Steadfast Love of Old?

IV. Psalms 90–106, Book IV

A. 90:1-17, Have Compassion on Your Servants
B. 91:1-16, The Shelter of the Most High
C. 92:1-15, But You, O Lord, Are Exalted Forever!
D. 93:1-5, God Has Established the World
E. 94:1-23, Justice Will Return
F. 95:1-11, Listen to God's Voice
G. 96:1-13, God Is Coming to Establish Justice
H. 97:1-12, Rejoice That the Lord Reigns
I. 98:1-9, Joy to the World
J. 99:1-9, The Lord Our God Is Holy
K. 100:1-5, Know That the Lord Is God
L. 101:1-8, I Will Sing of Your Love and Justice
M. 102:1-28, God Hears the Prayer of the Destitute
N. 103:1-22, Bless the Lord, O My Soul
O. 104:1-35, God as Creator and Provider
P. 105:1-45, All God's Wonderful Works
Q. 106:1-48, Out of Great Love, God Relented

V. Psalms 107–150, Book V

A. 107:1-43, Consider the Steadfast Love of God
B. 108:1-13, With God We Shall Do Valiantly
C. 109:1-31, God Saves Those Who Are Needy
D. 110:1-7, Sit at My Right Hand
E. 111:1-10, Great Are the Works of the Lord
F. 112:1-10, Happy Are Those Who Fear the Lord
G. 113:1-9, Who Is Like the Lord Our God?
H. 114:1-8, Tremble, O Earth, at the Presence of the Lord
I. 115:1-18, Trust in the Lord
J. 116:1-19, I Will Lift Up the Cup of Salvation
K. 117:1-2, Praise the Lord, All You Nations
L. 118:1-29, This Is the Day on Which the Lord Has Acted
M. 119:1-176, How I Love Your Instruction
N. 120–134, Songs of Ascents
    120:1-7, I Am for Peace
    121:1-8, God's Protective Care
    122:1-9, The Peace of Jerusalem
    123:1-4, Our Eyes Look to the Lord
    124:1-8, If the Lord Were Not for Us . . .
    125:1-5, Those Who Trust in the Lord
    126:1-6, Restore Our Fortunes, O Lord
    127:1-5, Unless the Lord Builds the House
    128:1-6, You Shall Be Happy

129:1-8, God Has Cut the Cords of the Wicked
130:1-8, Out of the Depths
131:1-3, Like the Weaned Child That Is with Me
132:1-18, For the Lord Has Chosen Zion
133:1-3, In Praise of Unity Among God's People
134:1-3, May the Lord Bless You from Zion
O. 135:1-21, Your Name, O Lord, Endures Forever
P. 136:1-26, God's Steadfast Love Endures Forever
Q. 137:1-9, By the Rivers of Babylon
R. 138:1-8, Thanksgiving and Praise for God's Deliverance
S. 139:1-24, Search Me, O God, and Know My Heart
T. 140:1-13, A Cry for Protection from Violence
U. 141:1-10, Deliver Me from Wickedness
V. 142:1-7, No One Cares for Me
W. 143:1-12, No One Living Is Righteous Before You
X. 144:1-15, Happy Are the People Whose God Is the Lord
Y. 145:1-21, God Is Great and Good
Z. 146:1-10, Justice for the Oppressed
AA. 147:1-20, God Sends Out God's Word
BB. 148:1-14, Let Them Praise the Name of the Lord
CC. 149:1-9, The Justice That Is Written
DD. 150:1-6, Praise the Lord!

PSALMS 1–41

BOOK I

PSALM 1:1-6, DELIGHT IN GOD'S TEACHING

COMMENTARY

1:1. The book of Psalms begins with a beatitude, a form usually associated with wisdom literature but that occurs most frequently in Psalms (see e.g., Pss 2:12; 32:1-2; 33:12; 34:8; 40:4; 41:1; 106:3; 112:1; 119:1-2; "blessed" or "happy" [אשרי *ʾašrê*] occurs 25 times in the Psalms and 8 times in Proverbs). Because the opening phrase stands outside the parallel structure of the remainder of the verse, and because Psalm 1 is a preface or introduction to the psalter (see the Introduction), the effect is to offer the exclamation, "Happy are those . . . " as an interpretative clue both to this particular psalm and to the whole psalter. In some sense, *all* of the psalms will involve a portrayal of what it means to be "happy" or "blessed."

The remainder of v. 1 describes the happy person over against the "wicked" (רשעים *rĕšāʿîm*), "sinners" (חטאים *ḥaṭṭāʾîm*), and "scoffers" (לצים *lēṣîm*). The effect of defining the happy person initially in negative terms is to sharpen the contrast between what will in v. 6 be called "the way of the righteous" and the "way of the wicked." The two occurrences of "way" (דרך *derek*) in v. 6, along with the occurrence in v. 1 in the phrase "way of sinners" (דרך חטאים *derek ḥaṭṭāʾîm*; NRSV "path"), suggest that this psalm and the entire psalter will offer a choice between two fundamentally different ways of life or life-styles. The outcomes of one's choice of ways are described by the first and last words of the psalm. That choice will either make one "happy" or will lead one to "perish." In short, the way one chooses is a matter of life and death. The comprehensiveness of this choice is probably reinforced poetically by the fact that "happy" (*ʾašrê*) begins with the first

letter of the Hebrew alphabet, and "perish" (תאבד *tōʾbēd*) begins with the last letter—that is, Psalm 1 is an all-embracing presentation of what it means to be "happy."

As the only three-part line in the psalm, v. 1 effectively emphasizes that the way of the wicked is to be studiously avoided. The vocabulary of this verse also begins to suggest what Psalm 1 and the psalter mean by wickedness and righteousness. As is often the case, the parallelism in v. 1 is not precisely synonymous. The general term "wicked" is followed by a more specific term, "sinners," suggesting those who miss the mark or choose the wrong way. The most specific term is "scoffers," which elsewhere connotes persons who are arrogantly unwilling to accept instruction (see Prov 1:22; 9:7-8; 13:1; 14:6; 15:12). This specific term prepares for the positive presentation of the happy person as one whose "delight is in the *instruction* [תורה *tôrâ*] of the LORD" (see v. 2).

The three verbs in v. 1 are important: "walk" (הלך *hālak*; NRSV "follow"), "stand" (עמד *ʿāmad*; NRSV, "take"), "sit" (ישב *yāšab*). The variety of postures covered by these verbs not only reinforces the importance of how one positions oneself, but also has the effect of associating motion and thus instability with the wicked. Insofar as the wicked do achieve stability—the verb for "to sit" also means "to dwell"—it is in the wrong place. Like the nouns in v. 1, the verbs prepare for the positive presentation of the happy person, whose fruitfulness is made possible by a stable rootedness in a favorable location (v. 3).

1:2. The negative characterization of v. 1 is followed by a strong adversative particle ("but" [כי אם *kî ʾim*]) at the beginning of v.

2, which introduces the positive portrayal of happy persons. While the NRSV and the NIV regularly translate the Hebrew word *tôrâ* as "law," this translation is misleading. Many interpreters have understood "the law" in v. 2 to mean the Deuteronomistic code, and they have taken Psalm 1 as recommending a rigid legalism that is accompanied by a mechanistic system of reward and punishment for obedience or disobedience. Consequently, Psalm 1 has often been dismissed as simplistic and naive. Such a conclusion is not necessary. The word *tôrâ* fundamentally means "instruction." In contrast to scoffers who arrogantly refuse all instruction, happy persons delight in God's instruction, having it always before them. What is commended, therefore, is not a close-minded legalism, but a posture of constant openness to God's instruction. That this openness to God's instruction was not a burden but a source of delight is indicated by Psalms 19 and 119, which along with Psalm 1 are often categorized by scholars as torah psalms (see Introduction).

Verse 2*b* is reminiscent of Josh 1:8. As Joshua succeeds Moses, he is told by God that "this book of the law" is something he is to "meditate on . . . day and night" in order to "make your way prosperous" (NRSV; cf. "prospers" in Ps 1:3). The king of Israel also is to have "a copy of this law" and is to "read . . . it all the days of his life" (Deut 17:18-19 NRSV). It is likely that "law" in these two texts does, indeed, designate the Deuteronomistic code; however, such need not be the case in Ps 1:2. There is no mention of a book or a copy of the law. "Instruction" here refers not to a particular corpus of stipulations, but more broadly to the whole sacred tradition of God's revelation. It is helpful to recall that the Torah for Judaism—the Pentateuch—contains both stipulations and identity-forming stories of God's dealings with the world and God's people. But even the Pentateuch is too narrow a referent for the "instruction" of v. 2. The two occurrences of *torah* here, especially in conjunction with the division of the psalter into five books, suggests that the psalms are to be received in a manner analogous to the Pentateuch—that is, as an identity-forming, life-shaping source of God's instruction. What Psalm 1 commends, therefore, is a devotion that looks to tradition, to Scripture, and to

contemporary words and events as sources of God's revelation (see Commentary on Psalm 119). What the righteous, "happy" life involves is constant openness to God's teaching.

1:3-4. These verses lie at the center of the psalm, and each contains a simile. Persons who are open to God's instruction are like trees transplanted beside a source of water; they are never without a resource to sustain their lives—namely, God's life-giving instruction (see Ps 19:7). What the tree imagery highlights is not primarily the aspect of fruitfulness but the importance of a stable rootedness. The root is in precisely the proper place—beside water, which represents God's life-giving instruction (see the importance of water in Job 14:7-9). The identical image appears also in Jer 17:8, which specifically mentions the tree's roots. It is deep rootedness in the proper ground that allows the tree to withstand drought and to always bear fruit. As Jer 17:7 suggests, when read along with Ps 1:1-3, to be open to God's teaching is to trust God and to entrust one's life to God. Those who do so always have a resource to sustain their lives. This understanding of the simile illumines the meaning of the final line of v. 3, which has often been interpreted to mean that obedience is materially rewarded. Instead, to "prosper" in "all that they do" should be understood as an affirmation that persons who trust God have a resource for sustaining their lives under any circumstance. As James L. Mays puts it, the way of the righteous is "not so much a reward as a result of life's connection with the source of life."[46]

Verse 4 is introduced by an emphatic form of the negative particle, which has already occurred three times in v. 1 and once in v. 3 and will occur again in v. 5. This sixfold repetition sharpens the contrast between the righteous and the wicked. The second simile (v. 4*b*) is preceded by the same adversative particle ("but") that introduced v. 2 and that reinforces the contrast. The similarity of the Hebrew words for "tree" (עץ *'ēṣ*) and "chaff" (מץ *mōṣ*)—both are two-letter nouns ending in the same letter—also serves to highlight the contrasting sense of the two similes. While the righteous are like a well-placed tree whose stability allows it to live and bear fruit,

46. Mays, *Psalms*, 43-44.

the wicked are like chaff, which is the insubstantial waste product that "the wind blows away" while the heavier fruit of the grain falls back to the threshing floor. The wicked have no stability, no rootedness, no place to stand. As suggested already by v. 1, the wicked are always in motion. The instability or "lightness" of the wicked is represented by the relatively brief amount of space accorded to the second simile. The simile of the tree occupies three poetic lines, while the simile of the chaff occupies only one.

1:5. The instability and uselessness of the chaff prepare for the description of the wicked in v. 5. The wicked "will not stand in the judgment." The Hebrew word used here for "stand" (קום *qûm*) is different from the one translated "stand" in v. 1 (עמד *ʿāmad*), but the effect of each is to communicate that the wicked have no foundation, no connection with the source of life. The meaning of v. 5 is disputed. It may mean that the wicked will not endure when the judgment of God occurs. Dahood, for instance, finds here a description of "the final judgment," and concludes that Psalm 1 offers "a rather advanced concept of resurrection and immortality."[47] Most scholars disagree. Craigie, for instance, understands v. 5 to assert that "the wicked hold no weight or influence in the important areas of human society."[48] When persons meet to determine matters of "judgment" (or "justice" [משפט *mišpāṭ*], as the word may be translated), the wicked will have no influence, no place in "the assembly of the righteous." Insofar as vv. 5 and 6b do suggest a kind of judgment, it need not be understood mechanistically as punishment (see below on v. 6).

What is clearer about v. 5 is its literary correspondence with v. 1. The same characters are involved—the "wicked" and "sinners"—and the similarity of the Hebrew words for "counsel" (עצה *ʿēṣâ*) and "assembly" (עדה *ʿēdâ*) also suggests a correspondence. Petersen and Richards take this correspondence as one piece of a larger chiastic structure (see Introduction) of vv. 1-5, which they outline as follows:

A Description of the righteous (vv. 1b-2)
  B Simile (v. 3a-b)
    C Objectifying conclusion (v. 3c)
    C´ Objectifying introduction (v. 4a)
  B´ Simile (v. 4b)
A´ Description of the wicked (v. 5)

This analysis identifies "a hinge" (C/C´) consisting of the following two lines (vv. 3c-4a):

> And (in) everything which he(it) does, he(it) prospers.
> Not so the wicked!

Verse 3c may be understood as the continuation of the tree simile if the subject of the verbs is taken as "it," or the verse may be understood as an "objectifying conclusion" to the simile if the subject is taken as "he" (i.e., the person open to God's instruction). The Hebrew permits either construal, and the ambiguity is probably intentional. Since v. 4a precedes the simile, it can more clearly be taken as an "objectifying introduction." The effect is to create a "hinge" that demonstrates again that the whole psalm turns on the crucial contrast between the wicked and the righteous.[49]

1:6. The concluding verse of Psalm 1 stands outside the chiastic structure outlined above, thus effectively emphasizing again the contrast between "the way of the righteous" and "the way of the wicked." The conjunctive particle at the beginning of v. 6 suggests, however, that it should not be totally isolated from v. 5. Furthermore, the repetition of "righteous" and "wicked" links v. 6 to v. 5; not surprisingly, the pattern of the repetition is chiastic: "wicked . . . righteous . . . righteous . . . wicked." The effect is to present the righteous as central and preeminent, both literarily and theologically. In vv. 5-6, the wicked perish on the periphery (note "judgment" in v. 5a and "perish" in v. 6b), while the righteous are at the center of God's attention. Indeed, for the first time in the psalm, the Lord is the subject of a verb. The Lord "knows" (ידע *yāda*, RSV; NIV and NRSV, "watches over"), which in other contexts suggests a relation as intimate as sexual intercourse. The happy or righteous persons

47. Mitchell Dahood, *Psalms I (1–50)*, AB 16 (Garden City, N.Y.: Doubleday, 1966) 4.

48. Peter C. Craigie, *Psalms 1–50*, WBC 19 (Waco: Word, 1983) 61.

49. D. L. Petersen and K. H. Richards, *Interpreting Hebrew Poetry* (Minneapolis: Fortress, 1992) 95-96.

are those who are constantly open to God's teaching, thus always connected to God, who is the source of life.

The wicked, on the other hand, are those who refuse to attend to God's teaching, thus cutting themselves off from the source of life. That they "perish" is not so much a punishment, but the inevitable outcome of their own choice not to be related to God. In short, wickedness in Psalms is fundamentally to be self-centered rather than God-centered. It is autonomy, which literally means to be a "law unto oneself," or in terms of my translation of *torah,* to be wicked is to be self-instructed rather than open to God's instruction.

By offering the sharpest possible contrast between "the way of the righteous" and "the way of the wicked," Psalm 1 prepares the reader to hear the rest of the psalter. These two "ways" and their results will be in view again and again, and the reader will be challenged to choose the way of openness to God's instruction, the way that leads to happiness and life.

REFLECTIONS

Psalm 1 offers an understanding of happiness, life, prosperity, and righteousness/ wickedness that differs profoundly from the way these things are ordinarily understood. The understanding of reality in Psalm 1 is thoroughly God-centered; the perception of reality among contemporary persons is almost inevitably self-centered. This means that happiness tends to be understood essentially as enjoying oneself; one's life goal is understood in terms of self-actualization or self-fulfillment; prosperity becomes a matter of attaining what one wants; and righteousness and wickedness become moral categories that are measured among some by the ability or inability of persons to obey a set of rules and among others by the ability or inability to enact particular programs and policies. In either case, righteousness is measured in terms of a capacity of the self; it is essentially self-righteousness.

For Psalm 1 (and the rest of the psalter), happiness involves not enjoying oneself but delight in the teaching of God. The goal of life is to be found not in self-fulfillment but in praising God (see the Introduction concerning the songs of praise). Prosperity does not involve getting what one wants; rather, it comes from being connected to the source of life—God. The righteous are not primarily persons who make the proper choices or implement the proper policies (although some psalms include the psalmist's affirmation of innocence), but those who know that their lives belong to God and that their futures are secured by God (see Ps 2:12). In the book of Psalms, the righteous are constantly assailed, persecuted, and threatened (Pss 3:1; 34:19), while the wicked visibly prosper (Pss 37:7; 73:3). The prosperity of the righteous is real but hidden. It is an openness to and connectedness with God that sustains life amid all threats. It is real, but not "as the world gives" (John 14:27 NRSV).

What is so unsettling about all of this is that what Psalm 1 and the rest of the psalter call "wickedness" is perhaps what North American culture promotes as the highest virtue—autonomy. What generally marks maturity among contemporary North Americans is self-sufficiency. Wanting or needing help, whether from others or from God, is taken as a sign of weakness or instability. The effect is to produce a society of isolated selves. The irony is tragic—the pursuit of self-fulfillment yields self-alienation (see Mark 8:35).

In her story "A Good Man Is Hard to Find," Flannery O'Connor strikingly portrays "the way of the wicked." When a character called the Misfit is asked why he does not pray, he replies: " 'I don't want no hep,' he said, 'I'm doing all right by myself.' "

The Misfit represents what Psalm 1 and the rest of the psalter call wickedness—the conviction that we are doing all right by ourselves, that we need no help. It is not surprising that the Misfit's words conclude the story: " 'It's no real pleasure in life.' "[50]

50. Flannery O'Connor, *The Complete Stories* (New York: Farrar, Straus, and Giroux, 1971) 130, 133.

He is telling the truth. Failing to trust God and to make connection with God as the source of life, persons cannot be "happy." It is not surprising that contemporary societies of isolated selves consistently fail to produce people who are "happy," even though these societies are among the wealthiest, healthiest, and most educated in human history. In biblical terms, to be autonomous, to be alienated from God and other people, is to "perish."

The choice presented by Psalm 1 is always contemporary. We may choose to be self-instructed and self-directed, or we may choose to open ourselves to God's teaching and to God's direction. In a real sense, what Psalm 1 commends is what John Calvin described as "a teachable frame."[51] This "teachable frame" means a reverence for Scripture, God's written "instruction" (see Luke 11:28), as well as an openness to new ways in which God continues to act and be revealed in the lives of persons and the life of the world. Or, as Calvin insisted, the written Word must be read under the inspiration of the Holy Spirit.

What is commended, therefore, is not a self-righteous legalism but a commitment of the whole self to God. The call to decision presented by Psalm 1 is not unlike Jesus' call to repent and to enter the reign of God (Mark 1:14-15)—that is, to give up self-sovereignty to live under the sovereignty of God (see Mark 8:34). Like Psalm 1, Jesus also promised that his followers would be "blessed" or "happy" (Matt 5:3-11). As in the psalms, this happiness is not incompatible with persecution and suffering (Matt 5:10-11); as in the book of Psalms, the way Jesus commends constitutes a righteousness that fulfills the law (Matt 5:17-20) without being a self-justifying legalism (see Matt 5:21, which initiates a series of new teachings introduced by, "But I say to you . . . "). As an introduction, Psalm 1 not only orients us to read and hear the psalms as Scripture or "instruction," but it also prepares us to hear the affirmation of God's sovereignty, which is explicit in Psalm 2 and which pervades the psalter.

51. John Calvin, *Commentary on the Book of Psalms*, Calvin Translation Society, 5 vols. (Calvin's Commentaries, vols. IV-VI; Grand Rapids, Mich.: Baker, rep. 1981) IV:1:xl.

PSALM 2:1-12, THE REIGN OF GOD

COMMENTARY

Psalm 2 joins Psalm 1 as a paired introduction to the book of Psalms. It makes even more explicit what Psalm 1 has already clearly suggested by its sharply drawn contrast between the righteous and the wicked— namely, "happy" persons are those who know that their lives depend on God (2:12). While Psalm 1 orients the reader to receive the whole collection as instruction, Psalm 2 makes explicit the essential content of that instruction—the Lord reigns! The entire psalter will be about the "happy"/"blessed" life, and it will affirm throughout that this life derives fundamentally from the conviction that God rules the world.

That Psalms 1 and 2 are meant to be read together is indicated by the literary links between them. Most significant is the repetition of "happy"/"blessed" at the beginning of Psalm 1 and the end of Psalm 2, forming an envelope structure that holds the two together. To delight in and to be constantly open to God's instruction (1:2) means that one will "take refuge in" God (2:12). Both psalms commend a dependence upon God that is the antithesis of autonomy.

2:1-3. Another impressive literary link between Psalms 1 and 2 is the Hebrew repetition represented by "plot" (הגה *hāgâ*) in 2:1 and "meditate" (*hāgâ*) in 1:2. The repetition creates a contrast between persons who meditate on God's instruction and those whose thinking is vain, empty, purposeless. The effect is to identify "the nations," "the peoples," "the kings," and "the rulers" of 2:1-2 with the wicked of Psalm 1. Therefore, it is not surprising that their destiny, if they persist in opposing God, is described the same way as in Psalm 1: "you will *perish* in the *way*" (2:12, italics added; see "perish" [אבד *'ābad*] and "way" [דרך *derek*] in 1:6). In effect, Psalm 2 portrays in corporate terms what Psalm 1 depicts in individual terms: the contrast between the righteous, who are open to God's teaching and God's rule, and the wicked, who assert themselves and make their own plans in opposition to the reign of God.

Twentieth-century scholarship has focused attention more on the theology of the Davidic monarchy than on the reign of God. Psalm 2 is ordinarily classified as a royal psalm that was used either upon the coronation of a new king or at a yearly celebration of God's choosing Jerusalem and the Davidic house. Indeed, it is not difficult to imagine Psalm 2 as a coronation liturgy. Verses 1-3 focus on the desire of the nations to rebel, a desire that would have been heightened by the relative instability during a change of administrations. "Bonds" and "cords" (v. 3) elsewhere indicate servanthood (Jer 2:20; 30:8) as well as knowledge of and obedience to the "way of the LORD" (Jer 5:5). But the kings and rulers have no intention of recognizing God's sovereignty, which v. 2 suggests is exercised through God's "anointed," or messiah—the king.

2:4-6. God's response to the rebellious kings and rulers is given in these verses. The NIV's "enthroned" is better than the NRSV's "sits." Because God is the real ruler, God can laugh at the opponents (see Pss 37:13; 59:9; cf. 52:6 where the righteous "laugh" at the defeat of "the evildoer"). In another key text, the Song of Moses (Exod 15:1-18), God's "fury" (Exod 15:7) and ability to "terrify" (Exod 15:15) God's opponents are associated with God's everlasting reign (Exod 15:18). As in vv. 1-3, v. 6 suggests that God's sovereignty is exercised through a chosen agent—"my king," as opposed to the other "kings of the earth" (v. 2; see v. 10). The pronoun "I" in v. 6 is emphatic; God is the primary actor. It is God's king who occupies God's chosen place—"my holy hill" (see Pss 3:4; 15:1; 43:3; 48:2)—elsewhere a designation of Mount Zion. Verse 6 may have been spoken by a priest or prophet at the climactic moment in a coronation ceremony.

2:7-9. If v. 6 was used during a coronation, then the speaker changes in v. 7. The first "I" of v. 7 is the king, and the king's speech in vv. 7-9 describes the relationship God has established with him and rehearses the accompanying promises. The declaration of the king's sonship in v. 7 recalls Nathan's oracle to David (esp. 2 Sam 7:14; see also 1 Chr 28:6; Ps 89:26-27). Other ancient Near Eastern cultures also viewed their kings as sons of the divinity. Several Egyptian texts suggest a physical relationship between the king and the god, whereas the Mesopotamian conception involved adoption of the king. The Israelite conception is closer to the Mesopotamian. By "decree" (see Ps 105:10 where "decree" is virtually synonymous with "covenant"), God gives birth to a new agent of God's rule. The "today" of v. 7 thus refers to the day of enthronement.[52] The second "I" in v. 7, like the "I" of v. 6, is emphatic; God's initiative and activity are crucial. The promises in vv. 8-9 are also part of the ancient Near Eastern ideology of kingship. The king has the prerogative to request the benefit of God's power (see Pss 20:2; 21:4). The rebellious nations (see v. 1) will be subject to God, and the king will share God's universal sovereignty (see Ps 72:8). The difference between the NRSV's "break" and the NIV's "rule" in v. 9a may reflect an original play on words. The Hebrew verbs for "to break" (רעע *rā'a'*) and "to shepherd, rule" (רעה *rā'â*) are very similar. The Hebrew text supports the NRSV, while the LXX supports the NIV. Either meaning is appropriate, and the noun in v. 9a can designate a shepherd's implement (Ps 23:4; Ezek 20:37), a ruler's scepter (Gen 49:10; Ps 45:6), or an implement for inflicting blows (2 Sam 7:14; Ps 89:32; Mic 5:1). Throughout the ancient Near East, kings were perceived as shepherds of the people (see Ezek 34:1-10). While the parallelism of v. 9a with v. 9b suggests that the NRSV meaning is primary; the ambiguity is appropriate.

2:10-12. The psalm concludes with a warning to the rebellious leaders who had spoken in v. 3. Being "wise" is defined elsewhere for Israel as meditating day and night

---

52. For details, including citing of Egyptian and Mesopotamian texts, see Kraus, *Psalms 1–59*, 129-32.

on God's instruction (see "successful" in Josh 1:8 [NRSV]; cf. Ps 1:2), and being "warned" or "disciplined" elsewhere consists of being taught God's instruction (Ps 94:12). In other words, the kings and rulers are invited to be like the "happy"/"righteous" persons of Psalm 1—open to God's instruction, God-directed rather than self-assertive. Verse 11*a* puts it even more explicitly: To "serve the LORD" means to live under the rule of God, to depend on God for life. The only other invitation in the psalms to "serve the LORD" occurs in 100:2 (NIV and NRSV "worship"), a psalm that immediately follows a group of psalms that proclaim the Lord's reign (Psalms 93; 95–99). It is significant that the introduction to the psalter and the theological heart of the psalter (see Introduction) make the same proclamation: The Lord reigns! This is the essential claim underlying and pervading the book of Psalms. The final line of v. 12 both reinforces this claim and suggests the proper response to God's rule. To "take refuge" (חסה *ḥāsâ*) in God means to depend on God, to trust God, to entrust one's life and future to God. Like the proclamation of God's rule, the theme of refuge is pervasive (see, e.g., 5:11; 7:1; 11:1; 16:1; 25:20; and Introduction).

The end of v. 11 and the beginning of v. 12 are probably also meant to exhort the leaders of the earth to acknowledge God's rule (see "trembling" in Exod 15:15; Ps 48:6; both contexts affirm God's kingship); however, the meaning is uncertain, as shown by a comparison of the NIV with the NRSV. The NIV attempts to follow the Hebrew word order more closely; however, "Kiss the Son" is doubly problematic. First, the Hebrew underlying "Son" is actually the Aramaic word for "son" (בר *bar*; the Hebrew word for "son" [בן *bēn*] occurs in v. 7), so the text seems to be corrupt. Second, the NIV has capitalized the word "son" (see v. 7 as well), thus strongly implying a christological meaning that is foreign to the original. On the assumption that

the text is corrupt, the NRSV has followed a widely adopted scholarly emendation. The safest route is to admit that the meaning of vv. 11*b*-12*a* "is difficult if not impossible to understand."[53]

The disparity between the affirmations of vv. 8-9 and historical accuracy is very evident. At no time did an Israelite or Judean king possess "the ends of the earth" (v. 8); neither was any king able to dominate opponents the way v. 9 promises. To be sure, Psalm 2 can be treated simply as an example of ancient Near Eastern royal ideology with its characteristic tendency toward hyperbole. But Psalm 2 was preserved by the community of faith as something more than a historical artifact of the Davidic dynasty. In periods of monarchical weakness and even after the disappearance of the monarchy, Psalm 2 was preserved and treasured as Israel's poetic answer to the fundamental question, Who rules the world? And the answer is clear: The Lord reigns! When it appeared otherwise, as it always does, Psalm 2 thus served as a powerful affirmation of faith and hope. In short, this psalm functioned eschatologically (see Introduction).[54] It enabled its readers and hearers to perceive amid contrary indications the reality of God's reign and to hope for the consummation of God's rule. That hope took different forms. Some in the post-exilic era may have hoped for a literal restoration of the Davidic dynasty and the political independence of bygone days.[55] Others saw their hope fulfilled in Jesus of Nazareth, who proclaimed and embodied the fundamental affirmation of Psalm 2 and the psalter: God rules the world (see Mark 1:14-15).

53. R. G. Bratcher and W. D. Reyburn, *A Translator's Handbook on the Book of Psalms* (New York: United Bible Societies, 1991) 32.

54. See J. W. Watts, "Psalm 2 in the Context of Biblical Theology," *HBT* 12 (1990) 79-80.

55. See Gerstenberger, *Psalms: Part 1*, 48. Gerstenberger suggests that Psalm 2 originated in the exilic or post-exilic eras as an expression of the hope for a Davidic savior who would liberate the people "by overthrowing the world powers that held Israel captive."

REFLECTIONS

1. The crucial questions Psalm 2 addresses are always contemporary: Who rules the world? Who is in control? Verses 1-2 are as timely as today's headlines—nations conspiring, peoples plotting, world leaders posturing to be as powerful as possible. Conditions in our cities—not to mention our schools and homes and churches—seem out of control. Just as it must have seemed to ancient Israelites and Judeans during a variety of monarchical crises, and just as it must have seemed to a restored but embattled post-exilic community, so also it seems to us: It does *not* appear that God rules the world.

But it is precisely the disparity between the proclamations and promises of Psalm 2 and historical actualities that presents us with the crucial interpretative issue. This disparity reveals the strange way that God exercises sovereignty. The power of God is not the absolute power of a dictator but the power of committed love. In worldly terms, might makes right. But on God's terms, right makes might. The righteous—those who live under God's sovereignty—will be vulnerable to the powers of the world (Ps 3:1-2), but they will never be without help (3:8). The striking claim of Psalm 2 is that true happiness is found by those "who take refuge in" God (2:12).

Thus, like Psalm 1, Psalm 2 calls for a decision: Who rules the world? Whom shall we trust? Will we trust the apparent power of the kings and rulers of the earth—the wicked? Or will we trust God? The "happy," the righteous, are those who, amid competing claims and powers, put their trust in God. In the eyes of the world, this decision makes no sense.

2. Given the choice presented by the disparity in Psalm 2, it is not surprising that the church would later identify God's "anointed" (v. 2), God's "son" (v. 7), with the suffering Jesus. At Jesus' baptism, the heavenly voice declares, "You are my son" (Mark 1:11 NRSV; cf. Ps 2:7; Matt 3:17; Luke 3:22). The declaration continues with an apparent allusion to Isa 42:1, one of the suffering servant songs in Isaiah 40–55. Jesus is thus portrayed from the beginning as God's suffering messiah. At the transfiguration, the heavenly voice again alludes to Ps 2:7 and adds "listen to him" (Mark 9:7 NRSV; cf. Matt 17:5; Luke 9:35). What Jesus had been saying, and would say again, is that he must suffer and die (Mark 8:31-33; 9:30-32; 10:32-34). The opposition to Jesus can be seen as analogous to the opposition of the nations, peoples, kings, and rulers to God's reign (see Ps 2:1-2, which is quoted in Acts 4:25-26). To the world, Jesus' proclamation of the reign of God, and his embodiment of it in suffering, made no sense (see 1 Cor 1:23).

The relationship between Psalm 2 and Jesus is highlighted by Flannery O'Connor in a story entitled "Why Do the Heathen Rage?" (Ps 2:1 KJV). In this story, a dominating mother laments the fact that her grown son will not take over the responsibilities of running the family farm after her husband has had an incapacitating stroke. Instead of attending to practical matters, the son "read books that had nothing to do with anything that mattered now." One day the mother picked up one of the books and was struck by a passage her son had underlined. It was from a letter of St. Jerome to Heliodorus, who had abandoned his avowed calling:

> "Listen! The battle trumpet blares from heaven and see how our General marches fully armed, coming amid the clouds to conquer the whole world. Out of the mouth of our King emerges a double-edged sword that cuts down everything in the way. Arising finally from your nap, do you come to the battlefield! Abandon the shade and seek the sun."

The final lines of the story record the mother's reaction: "This was the kind of thing he read—something that made no sense for now. Then it came to her, with an unpleasant little jolt, that the General with the sword in his mouth, marching to do violence, was Jesus."[56]

As O'Connor suggests, King Jesus—although he conquers by the power of love, and although his crown is a cross—is content with nothing less than claiming the whole world for God. Psalm 2, like Jesus, calls us to affirm the jolting good news that God rules the world, and it calls us to live under God's reign. To the world, that decision

---

56. O'Connor, *The Complete Stories*, 486-87.

will make no sense for now. But to the psalmist and to Jesus, that decision is the source of happiness beyond all the world can give and the promise of a future of incomparable glory (see the citing of Ps 2:8-9 in Rev 2:26-27; see also Rev 11:15; 22:5).

PSALM 3:1-8, GOD HELPS THOSE WHO CANNOT HELP THEMSELVES

COMMENTARY

The plight of the psalmist (vv. 1-2) and the faith he or she displays in the midst of threat (vv. 3, 5-6, 8) illustrate the truth of Ps 2:12: The psalmist finds a "refuge" in God. The movement from Psalms 1–2 to Psalm 3 also effectively demonstrates that to "prosper" (1:3) or to be "happy" (1:1; 2:12) does not mean to live without struggle or opposition. As the first actual prayer for help in the psalter (although the prayer is accompanied by professions of faith in vv. 4-6, 8), Psalm 3 dramatically introduces the situation and the faith that is evident in all the prayers: "Many are the afflictions of the righteous,/ but the LORD rescues them from them all" (Ps 34:19 NRSV).

3:1-2. The most evident stylistic feature of the psalm is the threefold repetition of "many" (רב *rab*) in these verses. Each occurrence intensifies the threat. While the foes are simply present in v. 1*a*, they actively oppose the psalmist in v. 1*b* (see the verb "rise" [קום *qûm*] in 54:3; 86:14), and they directly address the psalmist in v. 2*a* with a statement that flatly contradicts 2:12*b*. Their words reveal them to be opponents not only of the psalmist but also of God. Like the peoples and leaders in 2:1-2 and the wicked in Psalm 1, the foes embody autonomy. They trust no one but themselves and recognize no rule other than their own.

The plight of the psalmist is highlighted by the syntax of v. 1. The first word is "LORD" and the last is "me"; thus the word order represents what the foes are attempting to do—to stand between the psalmist and God.[57] Their words also reveal this intent: "Don't look to God for help." Interestingly, the foes introduce the concept to which the

psalmist will return in his or her own plea (v. 7) and profession (v. 8): "help" (ישע *yš'*; NIV, "deliver"; the NIV helpfully uses the same English word in vv. 2, 7, 8 to capture the effect of the Hebrew repetition). While the syntax of v. 1 underscores the psalmist's dilemma, the syntax of vv. 1-2 together offers a clue to the psalmist's hope. The last word in v. 2 is "God" (אלהים *'ĕlōhîm*). Thus the two references to Lord/God open and close this section. God has the enemies surrounded.

3:3-4. God also surrounds the psalmist. In the battle against the foes, the Lord is the psalmist's shield (see Pss 7:10; 18:2; 28:7; 33:20; 59:11; 84:9, 11; 115:9-11; 119:114; see esp. 18:30; 144:2, where "shield" is associated with taking "refuge" in God, as in 2:12). The phrase "my glory" (כבודי *kĕbôdî*) may refer to the Lord, but the NIV probably has captured the proper sense. In Ps 4:2, "my glory" is threatened by others; whereas in 62:7; 84:11, "my glory" (NIV and NRSV, "my honor") depends on God as in Psalm 3. The vocabulary of Psalm 3 is also present in both contexts—"deliverance" in 62:7 and "shield" in 84:11. The lifting up of the head also signifies deliverance or preeminence (see Pss 27:6; 110:7; 140:9). Verse 4 seems to suggest that the deliverance still lies in the future (see v. 7), but the psalmist is confident that God will respond (see v. 8).

3:5-6. Thus in vv. 5-6, the psalmist can rest assured. The pronoun "I," which begins v. 5, is emphatic, recalling the pronoun "you," which began v. 3, and providing a link between the two sections. Because the "you" is "a shield around [בעדי *ba'ădî*] me" (v. 3), the "I" can sleep and awake normally (v. 5), unafraid of "ten thousands . . . all around" (סביב *sābîb*, v. 6; the prepositions differ in Hebrew, but convey the same idea).

57. See John S. Kselman, "Psalm 3: A Structural and Literary Study," *CBQ* 49 (1987) 574-75.

The word translated "ten thousands" (רבבה *rĕbābâ*) is related to the word "many" in vv. 1-2. The opposition is real, but the governing reality of the psalmist's life is his or her relatedness to God. While the foes presume to stand between the psalmist and God (vv. 1-2), the psalmist knows better. As if to signify the inseparability of the psalmist and God, the syntax has changed in vv. 3-4 and vv. 5-6. Noting phrases such as the Lord "answers me" (v. 4) and "the LORD sustains me" (v. 5), John Kselman suggests, "Yahweh and the psalmist are in constant interaction."[58] The psalmist trusts that no amount of opposition will separate her or him from God (see Rom 8:38-39).

The above discussion has assumed the NIV and NRSV division of the psalm into vv. 1-2, 3-4, 5-6, 7-8; but several scholars propose a division as follows: vv. 1-3 (the foes and God's response), vv. 4-6 (the psalmist and God), vv. 7-8 (petition and profession).[59] The effect of this alternate proposal is to focus attention on v. 5 as the center of the psalm. In fact, the tradition apparently has focused on v. 5 in designating Psalm 3 for use as a morning prayer. A focus on v. 5 also suggests a conceptual parallel between the psalmist and the "happy" person, who is open to God's instruction "day and night" (Ps 1:1-2). Constant dependence on God rather than on self has the very practical effect of making rest and refreshment a daily possibility (see 4:8). Given the psalmist's circumstances (vv. 1-3), this is not an inconsiderable achievement. The daily equilibrium of life is possible, because God "sustains" (סמך *sāmak*; see "upholds"/"upholder" in Pss 37:17, 24; 54:4; 145:14).

3:7-8. The final section contains petition (vv. 7*a*, 8*b*) and profession (vv. 7*b*-8*a*). The opening imperatives clearly recall vv. 1-2. While the foes are "rising against me" (v. 1), the psalmist appeals in faith for God to "Rise up" (see Pss 7:6; 9:19; 10:12; 17:13; 44:26; 74:22). Then the psalmist appeals to God to do precisely what the foes had said God could not do: "Deliver me" (cf. v. 2). The autonomous foes trust only themselves. The psalmist trusts the one to whom he or she is inseparably related: "my God!" The verbs in v. 7*b* are not grammatical imperatives, despite the

58. Kselman, "Psalm 3," 573-80.
59. Kselman, "Psalm 3," 573-80.

NIV's rendering. Verse 7*b* probably should be understood as the beginning of the psalmist's profession of faith, as the NRSV suggests. The NRSV does not preserve the chiastic structure (see Introduction), however. The verbs "strike" (נכה *nkh*) and "break" (שבר *šābar*) begin and end the poetic line. Again, the enemies are surrounded (see Commentary on vv. 1-2). Fittingly, God's activity strikes at the organs of speech, which uttered the presumptuous words of v. 2 (see Ps 58:6).

In v. 8*a*, the psalmist directly contradicts the words of the foes (v. 2): God does help those who cannot help themselves! The affirmation of God's "deliverance"/"help"/"salvation" pervades the psalter (see "deliverance" in 14:7 and "salvation" in 35:3; 62:1; 69:29; 70:4; 91:16; 96:2; 118:14, 21; see also Exod 15:2 and Introduction). Verse 8*b* introduces the concept of "blessing" (see Pss 5:12; 28:9; 29:11; 67:1, 6, 7; 115:12-13; 133:3; 134:3; 147:13). Biblical theologians often distinguish between God's saving—deliverance from particular crises—and God's blessing—the sustenance of life on an ongoing, daily basis. The psalmist had experienced both—the actual or assured anticipation of rescue from foes (vv. 3-4), which led to the ongoing possibility of normal life on a daily basis (v. 5). The psalmist concludes with a prayer that all God's people would share this experience.

The superscription assigns the psalm to David and specifies a setting (see 2 Samuel 15–18). This should not be taken as a historically accurate remembrance, but some scholars do conclude from the superscription that the person praying was a king and that Psalm 3 is a royal psalm. The juxtaposition with Psalm 2 and the shared phrase "holy hill" (2:6; 3:4) may provide support for this conclusion; however, it is by no means necessary, nor is it the majority view. It is more likely that the superscription is intended to encourage the reader to imagine a situation like that of David's during Absalom's revolt. In this episode, David appeared as anything but kingly. His family—indeed, his life—was a wreck. Absalom had killed his brother Amnon for raping his sister Tamar (2 Samuel 13). David forgave Absalom (2 Samuel 14), but Absalom rebelled against his father and drove him from Jerusalem (2 Samuel 15). The whole sorry situation is illustrative of the messy situations we regularly experience—violence, turmoil, rebellion, threats to job and even to life itself. Following Psalms 1–2, Psalm 3 proclaims that "happiness"/"blessedness" consists of the good news that God's help (v. 8) is forthcoming precisely in the midst of such threats in order to make life possible (vv. 3-4) and to offer us a peace (v. 5) that the world says is not possible (v. 2).

REFLECTIONS

1. The good news the psalmist affirms—that God helps those who cannot help themselves—is not the prevailing profession of contemporary society. In fact, it is the *foes* who express what functions as a credo for a secular world: "There is no help for you in God" (v. 2). To put it in the form we usually hear it: "God helps those who help *themselves.*" Interestingly and tellingly, many people assume that this cultural creed is in the Bible! As suggested above (see Commentary on Psalm 1), autonomy, or *self*-sufficiency, is often promoted as the highest virtue.

It is ironic that even our best intentions are frequently motivated by, and thus promote, the persuasive notion that God helps those who help themselves. Speaking of the church's ministry and mission, Stanley Hauerwas and William H. Willimon observe:

> Most of our social activism is formed on the presumption that God is superfluous to the formation of a world of peace with justice. Fortunately, we are powerful people who, because we live in a democracy, are free to use our power. *It is all up to us.*
> The moment that life is formed on the presumption that we are not participants in *God's* continuing history of creation and redemption, we are acting on unbelief rather than faith."[60]

In directly contradicting the foes' assertion, the psalmist affirms that human identity and destiny are shaped ultimately by the reality of God. The psalmist thus proclaims the paradoxical good news that full human selfhood is experienced in the yielding of oneself to God (see Mark 8:35).

2. The psalmist's thoroughly theological comprehension of reality is a challenge to us who live in a world where the human self is preeminent, a world that promotes self-fulfillment, self-reliance, self-help. As did Psalms 1 and 2, Psalm 3 calls for a decision. Concerning the foes' assertion in 3:2, Mays comments:

> One can either believe it or believe in God. The psalm is composed to encourage faith and to give it language. . . . It recites the doctrine that "salvation belongs to the LORD" to remind the distressed that no trouble is beyond help and no human hostility can limit God's help. In all these ways the psalm encourages and supports faith and invites the distressed to pray, the ultimate act of faith in the face of the assault on the soul.[61]

In other words, prayer is for those who know they are *not* self-sufficient; it is for those who know they need help. It is both word and act, language and life-style. As Eugene Peterson puts it, "Prayer is the language of people who are in trouble and know it, and who believe or hope that God can get them out." Peterson goes on to quote Isaac Bashevis Singer, "I only pray when I'm in trouble, but I'm in trouble all the time."[62] Prayer is both the language and the life-style of persons who know that their

60. Stanley Hauerwas and William H. Willimon, *Resident Aliens: Life in the Christian Colony* (Nashville: Abingdon, 1989) 36-37, italics added.
61. Mays, *Psalms,* 53.
62. Eugene A. Peterson, *Answering God: The Psalms as Tools for Prayer* (San Francisco: Harper & Row, 1989) 36.

lives, their futures, and the destiny of the world depend on God (3:8; see 1:1-2; 2:12). To pray subverts the prevailing worldly wisdom that God helps those who help themselves. Therefore, to pray in our kind of world is a revolutionary act, but it is one that may yield indirectly the same practical consequence for us as it did for the psalmist—a good night's sleep (vv. 4-5).

PSALM 4:1-8, YOU ALONE, O LORD

COMMENTARY

The similarities between Psalms 3 and 4 have led a few scholars to suggest their original unity, and even more propose that the confident conclusion in 3:8 is the point of departure for Psalm 4 (see "answer" [ענה *'ānâ* in 3:4; 4:1; "glory" [כבוד *kābôd*] in 3:3; 4:2 [NRSV, "honor"]; "cry aloud" [קרא *qārā'*] in 3:4 = "call" in 4:1, 3; "lie down and sleep" [שכב *šākab* and ישן *yāšēn*] in 3:5; 4:8). In any case, both psalms clearly identify God as the source of "deliverance" (3:8) and its results, "peace" and "safety" (4:8; note too the confident conclusions in 1:6; 2:12). Like Psalm 3, Psalm 4 is basically a prayer for help, but one in which the psalmist also addresses other people with questions and exhortations that function as professions of faith (4:2-5; cf. 3:4-6, 8).

After an initial plea and acknowledgment of past help, the psalmist addresses others in vv. 2-5. The opponents seem clearly in view in vv. 2-3, but vv. 4-5 could be addressed to the faithful congregation as well. Thus the NRSV and the NIV propose a break between vv. 3 and 4. In v. 6*a* the psalmist quotes what others say, and then gives a response in vv. 6*b*-7. Verse 8 may be understood as a continuation of v. 7 (NIV) or as a sort of independent concluding prayer (NRSV). A division into vv. 1, 2-3, 4-5, 6-7, 8 focuses attention on vv. 4-5 as a central panel surrounded by a pair of contrasts in vv. 2-3 and 6-7. Verses 2-3 contrast those who pursue vanity or "false gods" with the faithful, who belong to the Lord. Verses 6-7 contrast those who always want more with the psalmist, who is content with God's provision.[63]

4:1. "Answer me" is a frequent petition (see Pss 13:3; 55:2; 69:13, 16, 17; 86:1;

108:6; 143:7; see esp. 27:7; 143:1). It is addressed to "O God of my right." "Righteousness" is both an attribute of God and a characteristic of God's reign (see, e.g., 9:8; 96:13; 97:2, 6). God's ability to set things right is the foundation of the psalmist's advice to "trust in the LORD" (v. 5). The petition is followed by an example of God's past righteousness (following the NRSV). The verb (רחב *rāḥab*) in "gave me room" literally means "wide," and the noun translated "distress" (צר *ṣār*) means "narrow." In a contemporary idiom, the psalmist says, "You gave me some space when I was in a tight spot." But now the psalmist is needy again, and the petition continues with two characteristic pleas (see "be gracious" in Pss 6:2; 9:13; 25:16; 26:11; 27:7; 30:10; 31:9; and "hear my prayer" in 39:12; 54:2; 84:8; 102:1; 143:1). Like the appeal to God's righteousness, the prayer that God "be gracious" is an appeal to God's character (see Exod 34:6, God's self-revelation to Moses as "gracious").

4:2-3. In v. 2, the question "How long?" (often addressed to God; see Ps 13:1-2) is addressed to the psalmist's opponents. They are apparently responsible for injuring the psalmist's reputation (see "shame" in Ps 69:7) with their "vain words." The word "vain" (ריק *rîq*) recalls Ps 2:1 and thus suggests that the psalmist's opponents are opponents of God as well. This lends plausibility to the NIV's translation, "seek false gods" (see Ps 40:4; Amos 2:4 NIV); however, the Hebrew word elsewhere designates the false and damaging speech of the wicked, as the NRSV suggests (Pss 5:6; 58:3; 62:4). In contrast to the opponents, the psalmist belongs to God (v. 3; see Exod 33:16, where "be distinct" [פלה *pālâ*] is the same as "set apart" here). The designation "faithful" (חסיד *ḥāsîd*) is a form of the noun that the NRSV ordinarily translates as

63. See Peterson, *Answering God*, 63.

"steadfast love" and that, like righteousness and grace (v. 1), is a fundamental attribute of God (see Exod 34:6-7; see "faithful" in Pss 12:2; 30:5; 31:24; 32:6; 37:28; 85:9; 86:2; 97:10, and see the Introduction). Persons who belong to God are those whose identity has been formed by God's character. Their opponents may slander them and question their reputation, but the "glory" or "honor" of the faithful is secure because it derives from God (see Pss 3:3; 62:6). Thus "the faithful" can be confident that God "hears" when they "call" (see both verbs in v. 1).

Verses 2-3 may offer a clue to the original setting of Psalm 4. It is possible that the falsely accused psalmist has been vindicated in a ritual court proceeding held in the Temple.[64] If so, then the advice in vv. 4-5 may be offered not only to the opponents but also to anyone who was present to hear it, including the contemporary reader.

4:4-5. Verse 4 is usually understood as the psalmist's command to the opponents to refrain from their harmful speech; however, it can be heard also as advice to the faithful. In 1 Sam 7:10, being "disturbed" is a state caused by enemies. Thus v. 4 may exhort the faithful to stand firm in their identity and not be led into temptation by their opponents. In this case, "be silent" (דמם *dāmam*) would better be translated "be quieted" and would advise composure and peace of mind (see v. 8, which has to do with nighttime activity). The NIV's "anger" derives from the LXX and perhaps was chosen because v. 4 is quoted in this form in Eph 4:26—where, by the way, it is advice to the faithful.

The exhortation in v. 5 would be appropriate for either the foes or the faithful. In Ps 51:19, "right sacrifices" are apparently a

possibility for those who have first been reconciled to God and have offered their whole selves to God (see vv. 16-17). To "trust in the LORD" also involves yielding the whole self to God. It is essentially synonymous with taking refuge in God (Ps 2:12); like the theme of refuge, the theme of trust is pervasive in Psalms (see, e.g., 9:10; 21:7; 22:4-5; 25:2; 26:1; 28:7; 32:10; 37:3; 40:4; 55:23; 56:3, 11; 84:12; 115:9-11; 125:1; 143:8; see esp. 62:8; 91:2, where "refuge" occurs with "trust" in the same verse; see also the Introduction).

4:6-7. In v. 6, the psalmist quotes what others say, although the NIV and the NRSV disagree on the extent of the quotation; the NIV seems preferable. When vv. 6-7 are read as a unit, it appears that the "many" were praying for material prosperity, whereas the psalmist desires a different kind of fulfillment—the light of God's face (see Num 6:25; Pss 31:16; 67:1; 80:3, 7, 19). In contrast to the "many" and their "restless dissatisfaction with what they have," the psalmist "has been given more joy by the sign of God's acceptance [see v. 3] than would be gained from an abundance of meat and drink. The gift of trusting God transcends the value of any material good."[65] Again, the psalmist's identity is secured by her or his relationship to God.

4:8. This relationship to God, this gift of trusting God, dispels anxiety (see Ps 3:5) and makes for genuine "peace" (*shalom*) and "safety" (בטח *beṭaḥ*; the Hebrew word is related to "trust" in v. 5). Neither the "vain words" nor the material prosperity of others can direct the psalmist's attention from what is truly essential for life—namely, "You alone, O LORD" (v. 8).

---

64. See Kraus, *Psalms 1–59*, 146-47.

65. Mays, *Psalms*, 56.

REFLECTIONS

The psalmist apparently was tempted by two things that still have a way of keeping us from appreciating what life is truly all about: (1) concern over reputation—what other people think and say about us (vv. 2-3)—and (2) concern over material possessions, particularly the fact that others may have more than we do (vv. 6-7). To be sure, these may be legitimate concerns, especially when persons are impugned unjustifiably, as the psalmist apparently was. The point, however, is that not even this kind of pressure could shake the psalmist's conviction that his or her life was of inestimable value because it belonged to God. Belonging to God changes everything—values, priorities, life-style. The "faithful"—those whose identity is shaped by experience of God's "steadfast love"—are different, "set apart" (v. 3). So the psalmist can advise others, to paraphrase vv. 4-5: "When things work against you, don't let it throw you off [the root sense of "sin" is "to miss the mark"]. Don't lose any sleep over it. Keep your composure. Offer your entire self to God. Entrust your life to God." Mays suggests: "The psalmist has a basis of identity that transcends the judgments of others—the relation to God."[66] As the apostle Paul put it, "If God is for us, who is against us?" (Rom 8:31 NRSV; see also Isa 50:7-9). In the topsy-turvy world where God reigns and everything is different, it is even possible to say, as Jesus did, "Blessed are you when people revile you and persecute you and utter all kinds of evil against you falsely on my account" (Matt 5:11 NRSV).

Those who belong to God know, too, that material possessions can be of only relative importance. Jesus said, "One does not live by bread alone, but by every word that comes from the mouth of God" (Matt 4:4 NRSV; cf. Deut 8:3), and "One's life does not consist in the abundance of possessions" (Luke 12:15 NRSV). The psalmist knew this good news, and so he or she could sleep without anxiety (v. 8; see Matt 6:25-33) in the enjoyment of that "peace of God, which surpasses all understanding" (Phil 4:7 NRSV). In our media culture, which leads us daily to believe that life does consist in the abundance of possessions, and in which presenting the proper self-image is paramount, the psalmist has a powerful lesson to teach us and a timely challenge to offer us. God alone is the guarantor of ultimate security (v. 8), so "put your trust in the LORD" (v. 5).

66. Mays, *Psalms*, 55.

PSALM 5:1-12, LEAD ME, O LORD

COMMENTARY

Like Psalms 3 and 4, this prayer for help illustrates that righteousness does not go unopposed (see v. 8). The psalmist is apparently threatened by violent schemes and is already the victim of deceit and lies (vv. 6, 9-10). The psalm may have originally been prayed in the Temple by a person who had been slandered or falsely accused, perhaps of idolatry (vv. 1-3, 7; see Psalms 7; 17; the Introduction). The psalmist's final appeal rests with God, perhaps in a ritual involving a priestly oracle or sign. Be that as it may, the psalm was and is appropriate for wider use. For instance, it is an appropriate prayer for persecuted individuals, like Jeremiah or Jesus or contemporary political prisoners, or for persecuted communities like postexilic Israel or the early church or Christian communities today who live under repressive regimes.[67]

67. Mays, *Psalms*, 58.

The structural divisions in the NIV and the NRSV are helpful: vv. 1-3, 4-6, 7-8, 9-10, 11-12. The psalm consists of sections that alternate between a focus on the psalmist's appeal and approach to God (vv. 1-3, 7-8) and on the wicked and God's dealing with them (vv. 4-6, 9-10; note that both vv. 4 and 9 begin with "For" in the NRSV). A final section (vv. 11-12) also involves appeal and approach to God, but now all the righteous are involved. The alternation focuses attention on vv. 7-8 as a structural and theological center.

5:1-3. The Hebrew word order in v. 1 is significant; "my words" is the first and "my sighing" the last element of the line, and the middle word is "LORD." In effect, the psalmist surrounds God with petitions (see "give ear" in Pss 17:1; 39:12; 54:2; 55:1; 80:1; 84:8; 86:6; 140:6; 141:1; 143:1). The plea continues in v. 2 (see "listen" or "attend" in Pss 17:1; 55:2; 61:1; 86:6) where the NIV's "cry for help" is a more accurate translation (see Pss 18:6, 41; 22:24; 28:2; 30:2; 31:22; 88:13, and a different form of the word in Exod 2:23). The address of God as "my King" represents the first occurrence in the psalter of the Hebrew root מלך (*mālak*, "to reign," "to be king"), and it serves to connect Psalm 5 and similar prayers for help to the affirmation that pervades and forms the theological heart of the psalter: The Lord reigns (see Psalm 2 and the Introduction). Here, as in Psalm 2 and throughout Psalms, the affirmation of God's kingship is made in the presence of the competing claims of evildoers and enemies (vv. 5-6, 8). In short, it is eschatological. It articulates the psalmist's conviction that God rules, but it also anticipates a future consummation of that reign. Trust in the present reality of God's rule explains why the psalmist continues to pray and appeal his or her case to God (see Job 23:4) with confidence that God hears (v. 3; morning seems to have been a set time for prayer and praise, as in Pss 55:17; 59:16; 88:13; 92:2). That God's reign is yet to be fully manifested explains why the psalmist continues to "wait in expectation" (see Mic 7:7; Hab 2:1).

5:4-6. As one of "the righteous" (v. 12), the psalmist appeals to a king whose righteous royal policy (see v. 8) is to oppose "wickedness" (v. 4; note that the two contrasting ways of Ps 1:6 are present here). To "sojourn" or "dwell" with God (Ps 15:1) involved being a "doer of righteousness" and a "speaker of truth" (15:2); it meant controlling the tongue, avoiding evil and opposing the wicked, and protecting the neighbor and the innocent (15:3-5). Thus "evil" and "the wicked" cannot "sojourn" or "dwell" with God (v. 4). The wicked are "doers of iniquity" (v. 5), who "speak lies" (v. 6; see 4:2; cf. v. 9); they are "deceitful" (see Pss 10:7; 24:4; 52:4; 35:20; 34:13; 36:3; 43:1) and prey on others (see "bloodthirsty" in Pss 20:9; 55:23; 59:2; 139:19; Prov 29:10). There are seven words for "evil" in vv. 4-6, perhaps suggesting the completeness of God's opposition, which is stated in the strongest possible terms— "hate" (שנא *śānēʾ*; See Ps 11:5) and "abhors" (תעב *tāʿab*; see Ps 106:40; the noun form of this word is usually translated "abomination" [תועבה *tôʿēbâ*] and covers a variety of evils; see, e.g., Jer 6:15; 8:12). The word for "destroy" (אבד *ʾābad*) in v. 6 means literally

"cause to perish," recalling Pss 1:6 and 2:12. Those who oppose God's sovereignty will ultimately perish, because they cut themselves off from the giver of life.

5:7-8. In contrast to the "boastful" or "arrogant" (see Pss 73:3; 75:4), who will not stand before God, the psalmist will enter God's house. The psalmist humbly attributes this, not to personal worthiness but to God's merciful love (v. 7). This is the first occurrence in Psalms of the word חסד *ḥesed*, which the NRSV ordinarily translates as "steadfast love" and the NIV as "unfailing love." If any one Hebrew word serves to describe the character of God, it probably is this one (see Exod 34:6-7). It is difficult to translate because it rolls into one the concepts of God's grace, mercy, compassion, patience, faithfulness, loyalty, and love. It is frequently celebrated in Israel's songs of praise and is appealed to in the prayers for help (see, e.g., Pss 23:6; 31:7, 16, 21; 32:10; 33:5, 18, 22; 100:5; 103:4, 8, 11, 17; 130:7; and the Introduction). The psalmist makes the proper response to such grace. "Bow down" (שחה *šḥh*) indicates what subjects do in the presence of a monarch (see 1 Sam 24:8; 2 Sam 14:4). Thus the psalmist takes the position of a loyal servant before "my King" (see "bow down" or "worship" in Pss 29:2; 95:6; 96:9; 99:9, all in the context of God's kingship; see also Exod 34:8, and note that "awe" or "fear" is also associated with the recognition of God's sovereignty in Ps 2:11). Psalm 5 represents the strange notion of sovereignty that is present throughout the Bible. God's sovereignty is exercised not as absolute power but as committed love. A royal policy of committed love is true "righteousness" (see Commentary on Ps 4:1 and the Introduction), and the psalmist humbly requests to be led in this way (see "lead" in Pss 23:2; 26:11; 31:3; 61:2; 72:21; 139:10, 24; 143:10). This petition at the center of the psalm indicates a relinquishing of self-reliance in dependence upon God and anticipates the celebration of refuge and protection in vv. 11-12. The mention of "my enemies" (שוררי *šôrĕray*) links the central section with vv. 4-6 and 9-10. The particular word used here means more literally "those watching for me" (see Pss 27:11; 54:5; 56:2; 59:10; 92:11).

5:9-10. Verse 9 is dominated by anatomy, as if to say that the wicked are evil through and through. Actually, three of the four parts mentioned are organs of speech, which is appropriate in view of vv. 5-6. Similar descriptions of the wicked are found elsewhere. Their character or speech amounts to "destruction" (cf. Pss 38:12; 52:2; 91:3; 94:20). Their flattering tongues are deadly (see Pss 12:3-4; 52:2; 57:4; 64:2-3; 140:3). In v. 10 the psalmist prays that the deadly threats of the wicked may fall back upon them (see vv. 4-6). The word "transgressions" connotes willful rebellion against God, and the final line of v. 10 completes the portrait of the wicked as those who reject the Lord's sovereignty. "Counsels" is the same word as "advice" in Ps 1:1. As suggested there and reinforced here, the righteous (see v. 12) are those open to God's instruction (1:2), whereas the wicked live only for themselves.

5:11-12. One of the responsibilities of a king was to provide for and protect his people, and the psalmist appeals in vv. 11-12 for the fulfillment of that role. These are the things for which the psalmist waits "in expectation" (v. 3)—joy (see 4:7), blessing (see 3:8), favor. The verbs could be translated as future indicatives—"will rejoice" and so on. The psalmist is certain that the future holds security and joy for those whose refuge is in God (see Ps 2:12). As in Pss 1:1-2; 2:12; 3:5; 4:8, this conviction enables the psalmist, amid persistent opposition (vv. 4-6, 9-10), to live with reverent purpose (v. 7), unshakable hope (v. 3), and enduring joy (v. 11).

REFLECTIONS

1. Because it affirms the sovereignty of God (v. 2) amid continuing opposition from the wicked and evil (vv. 4-6, 8-10), Psalm 5 is an eloquent profession of the faith that underlies all the prayers for help. Indeed, bold affirmation of God's reign while simultaneously waiting patiently (vv. 2-3) is the perennially appropriate posture for the people of God. Jesus invited persons to enter and live under the rule of God, but he made it clear that the life of disciples involves bearing a cross. Thus Jesus taught his disciples to pray, "Thine is the kingdom," and simultaneously, "Thy kingdom come."

2. The apostle Paul quoted Ps 5:9 in Rom 3:13 as part of his argument that all people "are under the power of sin" (Rom 3:9 NRSV). Paul seems unconcerned by the fact that v. 9 functions within the psalm as an indictment of particular enemies (see v. 8) rather than a characterization of all humanity. Even so, Paul's use of Psalm 5 and the psalmist's life of humble reliance upon God challenge the contemporary reader to make a decision. Are we among the boastful, who rely essentially on their own resources and live for themselves at the expense of others? Or do we take refuge in God? Do we seek first our own wills and our own way? Or do we pray with the psalmist, "Lead me, O LORD, in your righteousness" (5:8 NRSV), or in effect, "Thy will be done"? As Craigie suggests, Psalm 5 can be for us "a prayer of self-examination and a request for forgiveness and deliverance."[68]

3. Psalm 5 can also serve to remind us of the power of human speech and of its importance in standing with or against God. Walter Brueggemann suggests that human beings are "the speech creature *par excellence.*"[69] It matters what we say. Words can give life, and, as the psalmist testifies, words can kill (vv. 6, 9). As the Letter of James recognizes, "no one can tame the tongue—a restless evil, full of deadly poison. With it we bless the Lord and Father, and with it we curse those who are made in the likeness of God" (James 3:8-9 NRSV; see vv. 5-12). The psalmist was the victim of such a curse, and his or her plight instructs us that destructive speech does violence to other people and fails to conform to God's will. The righteous rule of God requires the truth to be

---

68. Craigie, *Psalms 1–50*, 89.
69. Walter Brueggemann, *The Book of Genesis*, Interpretation (Atlanta: John Knox, 1982) 31.

---

told for God's sake and the sake of others. Thus Psalm 5 reinforces the importance of the ninth commandment, "You shall not bear false witness against your neighbor" (Exod 20:16 NRSV). Mays concludes: "So this psalm asks us whether we take the opposition between truth and lie seriously enough as a matter of faith, whether we are ready to stand with those damaged by falsehood and propaganda, and whether we are alert to the lies to us and about us told by the powers and opinions of our culture."[70] The conventional wisdom is that "talk is cheap," but, as the psalmist reveals, the effects of human speech can be terribly costly.

70. Mays, *Psalms*, 58.

PSALM 6:1-10, O LORD—HOW LONG?

COMMENTARY

Like Psalms 3–5, Psalm 6 is a prayer for help. As in the preceding psalms, foes are present (vv. 7-8, 10); however, these foes are not the psalmist's main problem. Rather, the real problem is God! The language and imagery suggest that Psalm 6 was originally composed by a sick person as a prayer for healing (cf. Psalms 38; 41; see also the Introduction), and the psalmist begins by attributing the sickness to the wrath of God (v. 1). But if God is the problem, God is also the solution. So the psalmist appeals immediately for God's mercy and God's healing action (v. 2). This thoroughly theocentric understanding of reality presents both interpretive problems and possibilities (see Reflections).

While Psalm 6 seems to describe a physical illness that threatens the psalmist with death, it is also possible that the language functions metaphorically. In short, the psalm need not be heard exclusively as a prayer for healing from physical illness. The expressions of terror (vv. 2-3) and grief (vv. 6-7) may arise from a variety of circumstances. For instance, several scholars have suggested that Psalm 6 reflects threatening circumstances in the life of Jeremiah; Patrick D. Miller has suggested the appropriateness of reading Psalm 6 against the narrative background of Hannah's plight in 1 Samuel 1.[71] That the language and imagery of Psalm 6 are capable of being heard on several levels is indicated by the fact that Psalm 6 became by the fifth century one of the church's seven penitential psalms (see

71. Miller, *Interpreting the Psalms*, 56-57.

also Psalms 32; 38; 51; 102; 130; 143), even though it has no explicit confession of sin and only the mildest implication of sinfulness in vv. 1-2. Nevertheless, the psalm's articulation of disease, mortality, and grief serves as a reminder of human finitude and fallibility, which impel persons to confront their essential neediness and to depend ultimately for life on the grace of God. This humble dependence on God for life is the essence of penitence.

As the NIV and the NRSV suggest, the psalm is best understood in four sections: vv. 1-3, 4-5, 6-7, 8-10. Verses 1-3 and 4-5 consist of petition and supporting reasons. Verses 6-7 focus on the psalmist's sorrowful present, while vv. 8-10 focus on the psalmist's hopeful future. Verse 6 is the only three-part line in the psalm. The way the editors of a recent Hebrew Bible have arranged the poetry serves to isolate v. 6*a* as a kind of hinge that functions as the culmination of vv. 1-5 and the introduction of vv. 6*b*-10.

6:1-3. The key to understanding v. 1 is the use of the words "anger" (אף *'ap*) and "wrath" (חמה *ḥēmâ*). The Lord's "rebuke" and "discipline" are seen elsewhere as signs of God's loving guidance (see Prov 3:11-12), but the psalmist can see nothing educational about the present experience—be it sickness or otherwise—because it threatens his or her very life (see Ps 38:1). The psalmist knows God to be a God of grace (see Exod 34:6; Ps 4:1) and of healing (see Exod 15:26; Pss 30:2; 41:4; 103:3; 147:3; Isa 57:18-19; Jer 3:22; 33:6; Hos 7:1; 14:4), and so can interpret the present experience only as an indication of God's wrath. Psalm 6 may testify to the ancient belief that sin caused sickness (see Ps 41:4; Mark 2:1-12); however, because it lacks an explicit confession of sin, the psalm testifies even more strongly to the psalmist's conviction that every experience of life is somehow an experience of God (see Deut 32:39). "Terror" (or "dismay" [בהל *bhl*], vv. 2-3) is associated elsewhere with the experience of God's presence as judgment or wrath (Pss 2:5; 48:5 [NIV]; 83:15; 90:7 [NIV]; see also Exod 15:15) or with the experience of God's absence (Pss 30:7; 104:29). It is often the wicked whom God terrifies. In effect, the psalmist concludes that he or she is being treated by God as an *enemy,* and this conclusion shakes the psalmist's whole being (see Pss 31:9-10; 35:9-10, where "bones" and "soul" appear in the same context to describe the pervasive effect of grief or joy). But firm in the conviction that God is the only hope, the psalmist can only ask, "How long?" (v. 3; see Pss 13:1-2; 35:17; 74:10; 79:5; 80:4; 89:46; 90:13; 94:3; 119:84).

6:4-5. As in Ps 90:13-14, here the question "How long?" is juxtaposed with the plea that God "turn" or "repent" and with an appeal to God's "steadfast love." The request is also reminiscent of Exod 32:12-14, where Moses intercedes for the people with the plea, "Turn from your fierce wrath" (32:12 NRSV; cf. Ps 6:2). The problem in Exod 32:1-14 was the people's sinfulness, and it is possible that this fundamental story from the Pentateuch influenced the appropriation of Psalm 6 as a penitential psalm. The outcome of the episode in Exod 32:1-14 is the revelation of God as a God of "steadfast love" (Exod 34:6-7)—precisely the basis of the appeal in Ps 6:4 (see Ps 5:7 and the Introduction). At issue in Exodus 32–34 was the very life of the people, and the very life of the psalmist also hangs on the plea in 6:4. The psalmist appeals to the grace and love that God had historically shown to the chosen people. The pronoun "me" is a translation of the same Hebrew word rendered "my soul" in v. 3 (נפש *nepeš*). The psalmist's whole being, terrified at experiencing God as an enemy, depends ultimately on God's steadfast love (on "deliver," see Ps 3:2, 7-8).

Verse 5 and similar expressions throughout Psalms are often viewed as attempts to appeal to God's self-interest (see 30:9; 88:10-12); that is, since the dead went to Sheol, and since Sheol was ordinarily understood to be beyond even God's reach, God would have one less worshiper if the psalmist died. While this approach is plausible, it is also possible to hear v. 5 as the psalmist's affirmation of God's good gift of life. Consider the words of Jürgen Moltmann: "In this world, with its modern 'sickness unto death,' true spirituality will be the restoration of the love of life—that is to say, *vitality.* The full and unreserved 'yes' to life, and the full and unreserved love for the living, are the first experiences of God's spirit."[72] If this be the case, then v. 5 can be heard as the psalmist's " 'yes' to life" and an affirmation of "love for the living." To make such an affirmation is, in essence, to praise God. Thus the question in v. 5*b* is itself an act of praise, and, as is regularly the case in the psalms, praise is offered amid difficult circumstances (see the Introduction).

6:6-7. Although perhaps surprising to contemporary folk, it is not unusual in Psalms that the psalmist's praise—the love of life and desire to live—occurs in the midst of an experience summarized by a poetic line that stands at the very center of the psalm (v. 6*a*): weariness (see Ps 69:3). This weariness is manifested and compounded by incessant weeping (vv. 6*bc*-7; cf. Ps 31:9). The foes (v. 7) apparently are not the direct cause of the psalmist's plight but are persons who fail to support the psalmist and thereby exacerbate the suffering. Verse 6*a* is duplicated exactly in Baruch's lament in Jer 45:3, to which God responds with the promise, "I will give you your life . . . in every place to which you may go" (Jer 45:5 NRSV). While no such divine promise is recorded here, a similar conviction on the psalmist's part seems to underlie the expression of confidence in vv. 8-10.

6:8-10. In any case, vv. 8-10 are remarkably different in tone from vv. 1-7. The psalmist trusts that he or she has been "heard" (vv. 8-9). The repetition of vocabulary from vv. 1-4 marks the reversal. "Be merciful" was the plea in v. 2, and now the psalmist is sure that the "cry for mercy" (v. 9; "supplication" [NRSV]) has been heard. Whereas "terror" had pervaded the psalmist's being (vv. 2-3),

---

72. Jürgen Moltmann, *The Spirit of Life: A Universal Affirmation* (Minneapolis: Fortress, 1992) 97.

now the enemies will be "struck with terror" (v. 10). The psalmist trusts that God will heed the plea to "turn" (v. 4), and the result is that enemies shall "turn back" (v. 10). The chiastic structure (see Introduction) of v. 10 is significant. The verb "be ashamed" (בּוֹשׁ *bôš*) is the first and the penultimate word in the line, suggesting that the enemies (see vv. 7-8) will be surrounded by shame.

Scholars continue to debate the cause and significance of the transition from vv. 1-7 to vv. 8-10 (see Introduction). Perhaps the psalmist is responding to a priestly oracle or a promise that the text no longer records. Perhaps the psalmist has recovered from illness. But there is no solid evidence for either of these proposals. As the psalm now stands, the psalmist's physical condition and circumstances remain unchanged. Thus vv. 8-10 represent a profession of the trust that God makes life and hope possible even amid the stark daily realities of terror, disease, weariness, and grief. Praise and complaint remain inseparable realities (see Psalms 13; 22; Introduction).

REFLECTIONS

The thoroughly theocentric understanding of reality that characterizes the book of Psalms is thrown into particularly sharp relief by Psalm 6. God is both the problem and the solution. On the one hand, God is responsible for the psalmist's plight; on the other hand, God is the psalmist's only hope. If physical illness lies behind the origin of the prayer, as seems likely, then we are presented with troubling interpretive issues. In our world, we have other explanations for sickness and suffering—germs, viruses, chemical pollutants, improper diet, abuse of our own bodies. To suggest that God's wrath causes sickness and suffering seems to be dangerous reinforcement for a cruel doctrine of retribution that enables us to conclude that the prosperous must deserve God's favor and the afflicted must deserve God's wrath. Indeed, this is precisely what Job's friends unjustifiably concluded about Job (see, e.g., Job 11:2-6; 22:4-11).

Nevertheless, the psalmist's insistence that his or her plight be understood in relation to God may be instructive for contemporary readers. If all we can talk about in regard to sickness and suffering is viruses or germs, then we are in danger of removing God from the whole realm of the human experience of sickness, suffering, and death. Psalm 6 resists such a move. On the basis of Psalm 6, we need not make the mistake Job's friends made by adopting a doctrine of retribution that would interpret all sickness and suffering as God's direct action to punish particular sins. Rather, Psalm 6 encourages us to understand sickness, suffering, and death as the conditions of creatureliness that should make it obvious to us that the ability to secure our lives lies ultimately beyond our control. This relinquishment of self-control in dependence upon the grace and love of God has the liberating effect of allowing us to accept sickness, suffering, and death as inevitable realities of being mortal, finite, fallible. Like the psalmist, we live daily with the stark realities of terror, disease, weariness, grief, and the awareness of our mortality. The good news the psalmist offers is that none of these realities is sufficiently powerful to separate us from the love of God (see Rom 8:31-39). Amid them all, it is possible to live with integrity, purpose, and hope—by the grace of God. Without minimizing the difficulties of life, Psalm 6 offers a resounding " 'yes' to life," grounded not in self-confidence but in the steadfast love of God (v. 4). Thus, while this first penitential psalm does not even mention sin, it articulates the essence of penitence: humble reliance on the grace of God.

PSALM 7:1-17, O RIGHTEOUS GOD!

COMMENTARY

Psalm 7 is a prayer for help from a person whose enemies are bearing down. It is likely that the psalmist had been falsely accused by opponents and appealed to God for help, perhaps in a judicial proceeding in the Temple (see Psalms 5; 17; Introduction). The psalm is sometimes labeled a protestation of innocence, since the psalmist makes the appeal on the basis of "my righteousness" (v. 8; cf. vv. 3-5 and Psalms 17; 26). The historical note in the superscription is enigmatic, since no Cush appears in the Davidic narratives.

A comparison of the NIV with the NRSV reveals different ways of understanding the structure and movement of the psalm; the NIV translation is preferable. An opening affirmation and a petition (vv. 1-2) are followed by an oath of innocence (vv. 3-5). Petition is resumed in vv. 6-9, and it is followed by sections of affirmation. Verses 10-13 affirm God's protection and righteous judgment, while vv. 14-16 affirm that the evil of the wicked will eventually fall back upon them. Verse 17 is a concluding promise to praise God.

7:1-2. The opening affirmation in v. 1 recalls Pss 2:12 and 5:11. Both psalms proclaim God's sovereignty, which the psalmist here recognizes. Thus he or she entrusts life, including the present crisis, to God. As in Psalm 3, the psalmist recognizes that "deliverance belongs to the LORD" (3:8). The plea, "Save me," translates the same Hebrew word as "deliver"/"deliverance" (ישע *yš'*) in 3:2, 7-8. The opposition is real and strong (v. 2; see "pursue"/"persecute" in Pss 31:15; 35:3; 69:26; 109:26; 142:6; 143:3; see similar animal imagery in Pss 10:9; 17:12; 22:13, 21), but not as strong as God.

7:3-5. Here the psalmist proclaims innocence with an oath formula—in effect, "Let me be cursed if I'm in the wrong." The "wrong" (v. 3) or "harm" (v. 4) that the psalmist is apparently accused of is not specified. The word "soul" in v. 5 is more literally "glory" (כבוד *kābôd*; see Pss 3:3; 4:2). The psalmist would be willing to be dishonored and humiliated if such was deserved, but it is not. The closest biblical parallel to vv. 3-5 is

Job 31, where Job uses the same formula to affirm his innocence as he rests his case with God. Indeed, Psalm 7 as a whole is reminiscent of Job, whose friends end up finally pursuing him (Job 19:22, 25) with false accusations (see Job 11:2-6; 22:4-11; 42:7). Verses 3-5 anticipate the petition of v. 8.

7:6-9. In v. 6, God is summoned to action against the enemies (see "rise up" in Ps 3:7; "awake"/"rouse" in Pss 44:23; 59:4). The divine "anger" that the psalmist hoped to avoid in Ps 6:1 is appropriate for the enemies, because they are in the wrong. The psalmist is certain that God has "appointed a judgment," or more literally, "ordained justice." Verse 7 affirms the worldwide sovereignty over "the peoples" (see Ps 2:1) that gives God the prerogative to judge. Both the NIV and the NRSV understand the disputed verb (שובה *šûbâ*) in v. 7*b* to be the same verb translated as "enthroned" in 2:4, and God's position "on high" is associated with God's kingship in Ps 93:1, 4. Using a different verb, the psalmist again affirms God's role as judge (v. 8*a*; see Ps 96:10, which also affirms God's kingship); the psalmist does not hesitate to request that the cosmic judge of the world "judge me" (the same root [שפט *šāpaṭ*] as "judgment" in v. 6). The basis for the appeal is "my righteousness" and "integrity" (see Pss 25:21; 26:1; 41:12). Verse 8 is again reminiscent of Job, who declares his own righteousness (see Job 29:14) and integrity (31:6; and see the NRSV's "blameless" in Job 1:1, 8; 2:3; 8:20; 9:20-22). Verse 9 can be translated in a jussive (NRSV), an imperative (NIV), or an indicative sense. In any case, it articulates the policy of the cosmic judge—to oppose the wicked and establish the righteous (see Ps 1:6). As cosmic judge, God operates with the most personal information (see "test"/"try" [בחן *bāḥan*] in Pss 11:5; 17:3; 26:2; 139:23; Jer 11:20; 17:10; 20:12).

7:10-13. Because God's knowledge and sphere of influence are both cosmic and personal, the psalmist in v. 10*a* can claim "God Most High" as "my shield" (cf. Ps 3:3). In v. 10*b*, the psalmist, who is among "the upright in heart" (cf. Pss 11:2; 32:11; 36:10; 64:10; 94:15; 97:11), affirms what he or she had prayed for in v. 1: God saves. The protection God offers grows out of God's role as "righteous judge" (v. 11). The word "righteous" (צדק *ṣedeq*; צדיק *ṣaddîq*) occurs five times in this psalm (vv. 8, 9 [twice], 11, 17), and the word "judge" (*šāpaṭ*; משפט *mišpāṭ*) occurs three times (vv. 6, 8, 11). These key words emphasize that it is God's will to enact justice and righteousness on a daily basis and a cosmic scale.

In vv. 12-13, the subject of the verbs is not specified. The NRSV suggests that the wicked should be understood as the subject of the first verb and that God be understood as subject of the remaining verbs, whereas the NIV suggests that God is the subject of all the verbs. Some interpreters suggest that the wicked be understood as subject of all the verbs, in which case, anticipating vv. 15-16, the military preparations of v. 12 must be understood as backfiring in v. 13 so that the wicked themselves are destroyed. Certainty

is elusive, but the immediate antecedent of the pronouns in vv. 12-13 is "God," so the NIV translation seems preferable. Elsewhere, God is portrayed as executing judgment as a warrior (see Deut 32:41-42; Pss 38:3; 64:7; Lam 2:4; 3:12).

7:14-17. The subject of the verbs in these verses remains unspecified, but is clearly the wicked. The procreation imagery in v. 14 is striking; the whole process is perverse (see Job 15:35; Isa 59:4). The words "evil" (און *ʾāwen*) and "mischief" (עמל *ʿāmāl*) are also paired elsewhere (cf. Ps 55:10: "iniquity and trouble"; Job 4:8; 15:35). These verses affirm the faith that the wicked will ultimately destroy themselves (see Pss 9:16; 35:7-8; 57:6; 141:10; Prov 26:27). "Violence" (חמס *ḥāmās*) characterizes the wicked (see Pss 27:12; 25:19; 58:2; 73:6), and God opposes it (Pss 11:5; 18:48; 55:9; 140:1, 4, 11). The juxtaposition of vv. 16 and 17 suggests that the destruction of the wicked is ultimately the working out of God's "righteousness" (see vv. 9, 11), for which God is to be praised.

REFLECTIONS

Like the preceding psalms, Psalm 7 affirms that the sovereign God will ultimately secure the lives of the righteous and the downfall of the wicked (see Pss 1:6; 2:12; 3:7-8; 5:4-6, 11-12; 6:8-10; see also Reflections on Psalm 6). The affirmation is eschatological, reflecting hope in God's future victory, for wickedness persists in the present; however, God's work is *already* effective, and the psalmists already experience God as a "shield" (3:3; 5:12; 7:10) and a "refuge" (2:12; 5:11; 7:1).

The problematic aspect of Psalm 7 is that the prayer for help in this case appears to be based on the psalmist's own righteousness and integrity (v. 8). This problem, however, is more apparent than real. The psalm is not a profession of general perfection or sinlessness but of the psalmist's innocence or rightness in a *particular* case that the enemies are pressing (vv. 1-2). This psalm's similarities with the book of Job are instructive at this point. Job also defended his own righteousness and integrity (see 29:14; 31:6) against his friends' accusations, and God declared that Job spoke "what is right" (42:7). Neither the book of Job nor Psalm 7 is about *self*-righteousness. Rather, both are fundamentally about the righteousness of God. Like Job, the psalmist rests the case with God, trusting God to be a "righteous judge" (v. 11; see also v. 9) and celebrating finally God's "righteousness" (v. 17), not the psalmist's own. If anyone is self-righteous in Psalm 7, it is the enemies who presumptuously usurp the prerogative of God by condemning the psalmist.

What the enemies need to hear is "Do not judge, so that you may not be judged" (Matt 7:1 NRSV). As for the psalmist, to defend righteousness and integrity against the enemies is, in effect, to profess trust in God and loyalty to God's ways (see Ps 26:1-3). In his interpretation of Psalm 7, Luther cites Paul's submission to the judgment of God (1 Cor 4:1-6) and issues a call for Christians to stand for justice and truth:

Thus we see that it is not enough that if someone suffers for a just cause or for the truth, he commits the matter to God and is ready to yield and to be turned to dust together with his glory, but he should diligently pray that God judge and justify the cause of the truth, not for the petitioner's own advantage, but for the service of God and the salvation of the people. . . . We must pray that the truth may triumph.[73]

In Psalm 7, the psalmist prayed for the triumph of truth. In doing so, like Jesus, the psalmist "entrusted himself to the one who judges justly" (1 Pet 2:23 NRSV).

73. Quoted in Kraus, *Psalms 1–59*, 176.

PSALM 8:1-9, THE MAJESTY OF GOD AND THE GLORY OF HUMANITY

COMMENTARY

Psalm 8 has several distinctions. It is the first hymn or song of praise in the psalter. Unlike other hymns that consist of an invitation to and reasons for praise, Psalm 8 is unique in addressing God throughout in the second person. In a different sphere, Psalm 8 had the distinction of being the first biblical text to reach the moon, when the Apollo 11 mission left a silicon disc containing messages from seventy-three nations, including the Vatican, which contributed the text of this psalm.[74] Psalm 8 was clearly an appropriate choice for this cosmic journey, for it is both an eloquent proclamation of the cosmic sovereignty of God and a remarkable affirmation of the exalted status and vocation of the human creature.

8:1a, 9. The most obvious stylistic feature of Psalm 8 is the refrain in vv. 1*a*, 9. As if to fulfill the promise in Ps 7:17 that "I will . . . sing praise to the *name* of the LORD," vv. 1*a*, 9 enthusiastically proclaim the majesty of God's *"name* in all the earth!" The word "name" (שׁם *šēm*) connotes character and essence; everything in the world gives evidence of God's sovereign activity. The title "our Lord" or "our Sovereign" is used elsewhere to address a king (see 1 Kgs 1:11, 43, 47), and the adjective "majestic" (אדיר *'addîr*) is used of kings in Ps 136:18 (NIV, "mighty"; NRSV, "famous") and of God in Ps 93:4 in the context of the proclamation that "the LORD is

74. See James Limburg, "Who Cares for the Earth? Psalm 8 and the Environment," *Word and World Supplement Series* 1 (1992) 43. Limburg's source is NASA News Release No. 69-83F (July 1969).

king" (Ps 93:1). In short, the proclamation of God's reign frames the psalm. The subsequent affirmation of humanity's royal status and dominion must be understood within the context of God's reign.

8:1b-2. Before the focus shifts to humanity, however, vv. 1*b*-2 explicitly extend the reach of God's sovereignty beyond "all the earth" to "above the heavens." The word "glory" (הוד *hôd*) is also used of earthly kings (Ps 45:3; see also "splendor," Ps 21:5) and of God to support the proclamation of God's reign (see also Pss 96:6 [NIV, "splendor"; NRSV, "honor"]; 145:5, "majesty"). The text of v. 1*b* is difficult, and there are numerous proposals for translating it and relating it to the beginning of v. 2. The NIV and the NRSV agree in construing the Hebrew as literally as possible and in taking v. 1*b* as a self-contained thought; however, many translations render v. 1*b* differently and take v. 2*a* as a continuation of v. 1*b*: "Thou whose glory above the heavens is chanted/ by the mouth of babes and infants" (RSV). In this reading, the idea is that even babies recognize God's cosmic sovereignty. The NIV's rendering of v. 2, following the LXX, would support this idea. The NRSV's translation of v. 2, however, seems to assert that God can use even the speech of vulnerable, helpless infants as a power to oppose God's foes. The "foes"/"enemy"/"avenger" are probably the chaotic forces that God conquered and ordered in the sovereign act of creation. Understood this way, v. 2 anticipates the assertion of vv. 3-8 that God uses the weak and seemingly insignificant human creature as a partner in caring for a creation that is constantly threatened by its enemy, chaos (see Gen 1:1–2:4, to which Ps 8:6-8 is obviously related; see also Job 38:8-11; Pss 29:10; 74:12-17; 89:9-11; 104:5-9).

8:3-4. In v. 3, the focus shifts to humanity, but even in vv. 3-8, the primary actor is God. The only time a human is the subject of a verb is in v. 3, and the action of looking is very passive. When looking into the night sky, the psalmist is struck by the vastness of God's "work" (see Ps 102:25). How does the God who is responsible for the creation and care of such an immense universe have time to attend to the tiny human creature? This question lies at the structural and thematic center of the psalm (v. 4). Whereas the boundaries of the psalm deal with the issue of God's "name" or identity, the heart of the psalm raises the issue of the identity of humanity. The two issues are inseparable. Indeed, vv. 1*a*, 9 and 4 are verbally linked by the Hebrew particle מה (*mâ*), translated "how" in vv. 1*a*, 9 and "what" in v. 4. In short, the character of God's sovereignty cannot be understood apart from the knowledge that God *does* choose to be "mindful" and to "care for" humanity; the identity of humanity cannot be understood apart from this relationship with God.

8:5-8. The identity of both God and humans is addressed even more explicitly in these verses. That God rules the world has already been proclaimed (vv. 1-2), but now it is affirmed that humanity has royal status, too—indeed, "a little lower than God" (v. 5; the Hebrew word translated "God" [אלהים *'ĕlōhîm*] may also be translated "heavenly beings" as in the NIV and as the NRSV note suggests). The attributes with which humans are "crowned" (see 2 Sam 12:30; Ps 21:3; Jer 13:18; Ezek 21:26) are royal ones. Both human kings and God as king possess "glory" (see Pss 21:5; 24:7-10; 29:1-3, 9; cf. 145:5,

12, "glorious"; the Hebrew word differs here from the one translated "glory" in v. 1) and "honor" (cf. Pss 21:5, "majesty"; 145:5-12, "splendor"). The sovereign God has bestowed sovereignty upon the human creature. This remarkable affirmation is described in different terms in vv. 6-8. The human exercises the kingly function of "dominion" (see NRSV "rule"/"ruler"/"sovereign" in Gen 45:8, 26; Judg 8:22-23; 9:2; 2 Sam 23:3; 1 Kgs 4:21) over "all things" (v. 6). Although the Hebrew words translated "dominion" differ in v. 6 (משל *māšal*) and Gen 1:26-28 (רדה *rādâ*), Psalm 8 clearly recalls Genesis 1. The phrase "image of God" does not occur in Psalm 8, but the language and movement of Psalm 8 suggest that humans represent God in the world. This, of course, has profound implications for understanding both God and humanity. God and humans are partners in the care of creation, because God has made the risky choice to share God's power!

8:9. This conclusion is reinforced by the second occurrence of the refrain. Verse 9 is an exact verbal repetition of v. 1*a*, but the second occurrence has a fuller sense that is achieved primarily by repetition of the word "all" (כל *kōl*, vv. 1*a*, 6-7, 9). When the refrain occurs the second time, it is clear that the majesty of God's name, which is known "in all the earth," includes the dominion of humanity, for God has given them dominion over God's "works" (v. 6; cf. v. 4) by putting "all things under their feet" (v. 6; see v. 7).[75] God's "name" or reputation is bound up with the human performance of dominion, and human dominion is a responsibility that is to be bounded by God's ultimate sovereignty (see Reflections). The identity and destiny of God, of humanity, and of the creation are inextricably intertwined. Theology, anthropology, and ecology are inseparable.

75. See Alter, *The Art of Biblical Poetry*, 119.

REFLECTIONS

For Psalm 8, structural and canonical observations are starting points for theological reflection.

1. As suggested above, the psalm is framed by proclamation of God's sovereignty, and at the center of the psalm (v. 4) is the question that leads to the proclamation of

God-given human sovereignty (vv. 5-8). Walter Brueggemann suggests that the crucial interpretative move is to hold the boundaries and the center together.[76] To fail to take seriously the central importance of humanity in God's plan for the creation is to abdicate the God-given responsibility to be partners with God in caring for the earth (see Ps 115:16). At the same time, it is necessary to recognize that the proclamation of human sovereignty is bounded, both structurally and theologically, by the proclamation of God's sovereignty. In other words, human sovereignty is derivative. Apart from the limits of God's sovereign will, the exercise of dominion is in danger of becoming simply human autonomy, or self-rule. As suggested above (see Commentary on Psalms 1; 2), the attempt to live beyond the claim of God is the essence of wickedness. In other words, dominion without the recognition of God's claim on us and on the earth becomes domination. To leave God out of the partnership invites disaster; indeed, frightening signs of ecological disaster are all around us, from eroding soil to polluted streams to the possible depletion of the ozone layer. Psalm 8 is thus a reminder "that the God-praising and the earth-caring community are one."[77]

2. The canonical placement of Psalm 8 also invites theological reflection. The juxtaposition of Psalms 3–7 and Psalm 8 suggests another crucial interpretative question: What should we conclude about the human creature who both suffers miserably (Psalms 3–7) and is "little lower than God" and "crowned . . . with glory and honor" (v. 5)? The movement from Psalms 3–7 to Psalm 8 suggests at least that the royal status and vocation of humanity are not diminished by suffering. In fact, as regards the human, we may conclude that to be created in the "image of God" inevitably means that we will suffer. As regards God, we may conclude that divine partnership with humanity inevitably involves God in suffering. These same conclusions are articulated in the book of Job. Given that Psalm 7 recalled the book of Job at several points (see above), it is not surprising that Psalm 8 figures prominently in Job. In the beginning, Job's suffering leads him to deny the royal status and vocation of humanity that is voiced by Ps 8:4-5 (cf. Job 7:17 with Ps 8:4; Job 19:9 with Ps 8:5). Job eventually moves toward reclaiming the vision of Psalm 8 (see the royal imagery in Job 31:36-37), and God's challenge at the end of the book (40:10) leads Job to change his mind. Job finally concludes: "I . . . change my mind about dust and ashes [vulnerable humanity]" (Job 42:6; see Gen 18:27; Job 30:19).[78] What Job has learned is that the royal status and vocation of humanity involves suffering as well as glory. The clear implication of Job's conclusion is that God suffers too and that human suffering should be understood ultimately as part of the experience of sharing in partnership with God a burden of responsibility in caring for the earth.

The juxtaposition of Psalms 3–7 and Psalm 8, along with the use of Psalm 8 in the book of Job, anticipate the NT understanding of the identity of God and humanity. Hebrews 2:6-8 quotes Ps 8:4-5, 6b, and Heb 2:9 applies Ps 8:5 to Jesus (see also 1 Cor 15:27; Eph 1:22). It appears on the surface that the author of Hebrews has simply understood the phrase "son of man" in Ps 8:5 as a christological title. This may be the case; however, it is also the case that Hebrews 2 as a whole points in the same direction as Psalm 8—namely, the inseparability of suffering and glory for both God and humanity. It is Jesus—"the reflection of God's glory" (Heb 1:3) and the complete embodiment of authentic humanity (see Heb 2:14, 17; 4:15)—who conclusively reveals that God's glory is not incompatible with suffering and thus that the suffering of human beings does not preclude their sharing in the glory of God (Heb 2:10-18; see esp. "glory" in 1:3 and 2:10). Finally, then, the use of Psalm 8 in Hebrews 2 is faithful to the

---

76. Walter Brueggemann, *The Message of the Psalms* (Minneapolis: Augsburg, 1984) 37-38.

77. Limburg, "Who Cares for the Earth?" 51.

78. For an explanation, see J. Gerald Janzen, *Job,* Interpretation (Atlanta: John Knox, 1985) 254-59. This translation differs significantly from the NIV and the NRSV.

message of the original. Psalm 8, Hebrews 2, and the NT as a whole call human beings to live under God's rule and to exercise "dominion over . . . all things" in the same way that God exercises dominion: as a suffering servant (see Mark 10:41-45; Phil 2:5-11).[79]

79. Portions of the treatment of this and several other psalms in this commentary are similar to the author's comments in C. B. Cousar, B. R. Gaventa, J. C. McCann, Jr., J. D. Newsome, *Texts for Preaching: A Lectionary Commentary Based on the NRSV—Year C* (Louisville: Westminster John Knox, 1994).

PSALMS 9:1–10:18, THE NEEDY SHALL NOT ALWAYS BE FORGOTTEN

COMMENTARY

As the NIV note indicates, it is likely that Psalms 9 and 10 were originally a single acrostic poem with every other line beginning with a successive letter of the alphabet. The pattern remains largely intact, and there are further indications of unity, including the fact that the LXX treats Psalms 9–10 as a single psalm and that Psalm 10 is one of only four psalms in Book I without a superscription (see Psalms 1; 2; 33). In addition, a shared vocabulary links the two psalms, especially the designations of the major human characters—the wicked (9:5, 16-17; 10:2-4, 13, 15) and the "afflicted"/"poor"/"oppressed"/ "meek" (9:12, 18; 10:2, 9, 12, 17; additional links are noted below).

Psalms 9 and 10 seem to have no discernible structural regularity, perhaps due to the acrostic pattern. This does not mean, however, that the progression of thought is simply random. Psalm 9 begins like a psalm of thanksgiving and retains this basic character throughout. After an initial announcement of thanks (vv. 1-2) and account of deliverance (vv. 3-4), the psalmist generalizes from his or her experience to God's treatment of "the nations" and "the wicked" (v. 5). The nations remain particularly in view in Psalm 9 (see vv. 15, 17, 19-20), while the wicked will be especially prominent in Psalm 10 (see above). Verses 5-8 contrast the disappearance of the wicked (vv. 5-6) with the permanent enthronement of God (vv. 7-8). This leads to an affirmation of God's protection (vv. 9-10), invitation to praise (vv. 11-12), petition (vv. 13-14), assessment of the contrasting fates of the wicked and the poor (vv. 15-18), and renewed petition (vv. 19-20). The two sections of petition in Psalm 9 anticipate the character of Psalm 10, which in contrast to

Psalm 9 is primarily a prayer for help. This is evident from the complaint in vv. 1-2, which is followed by an extended description of the wicked (vv. 3-11) and by alternating petitions (vv. 12-13, 15) and affirmations of trust (vv. 14, 16-18).

The original setting of Psalms 9–10 is unclear (see the Introduction), but there are indications that these psalms would have been especially appropriate for post-exilic worship. The post-exilic community was subject to domination by the nations, yet in the midst of such oppression, the community affirmed the rule of God (see 9:4, 7, 11; 10:16; Introduction). The post-exilic situation evoked both complaint and confidence, which may explain the juxtaposition of thanksgiving (Psalm 9) and prayer for help (Psalm 10) as well as the alternating expressions of petition and confidence within both psalms.

9:1-8. Perhaps not coincidentally, vv. 1-2 recall Ps 7:17. The "righteousness" mentioned there, and thematic in Psalm 7, will also be thematic in Psalms 9–10 (cf. 9:4 with 7:11). The thanksgiving the psalmist intends to offer seems to consist not simply of sacrifice but of proclamation (see v. 15; Ps 26:7). God's "wonderful deeds" could include historic events like the exodus (see Exod 3:20; 15:11; see also Pss 77:11, 14; 78:12) or personal experiences of deliverance (see Ps 88:10, 12). In fact, the psalmist cites a personal episode in vv. 3-4. The enemies have "perished," an outcome that recalls the destiny of the wicked (and the nations) in Pss 1:6 and 2:12, and that signals a thematic word in Psalms 9–10 (see 9:5, "destroyed"; 9:6, 18; 10:16). Verse 4 also introduces key themes of Psalms 9–10—God rules (see 9:7, 11, where "enthroned" and "dwells" translate the same word rendered in v. 4 as "sat" [ישב *yāšab*]; see also "king" in 10:16), and God's royal policy is to enact justice (see "just"/"judgment"/ "judge"/"justice" here and in 9:7-8, 16, 19; 10:5, 18; see also 89:14; 97:2).

The psalmist apparently sees his or her experience as paradigmatic. What happened to the psalmist's enemies has happened to "the nations" and "the wicked" as well— God has "destroyed" (v. 5; lit., "caused to perish"). Indeed, even their "memory . . . has perished" (v. 6; see also Ps 34:16). The destruction of the nations and the wicked is also testimony to God's reign and to the goal of God's royal policy—justice, righteousness, and equity (vv. 7-8; see v. 4; Pss 96:10, 13; 98:9; 99:4).

Figure 1: The Hebrew Alphabet

א	*'āleph*	ט	*ṭêt*	פ	*pē'*
ב	*bêt*	י	*yôd*	צ	*ṣādê*
ג	*gîmel*	כ	*kaph*	ק	*qôph*
ד	*dālet*	ל	*lāmed*	ר	*rêš*
ה	*hē'*	מ	*mēm*	שׂ	*śîn*
ו	*wāw*	נ	*nûn*	שׁ	*šîn*
ז	*zayin*	ס	*sāmek*	ת	*tāw*
ח	*ḥêt*	ע	*'ayin*		

(In alphabetic acrostics, the letters *śîn* and *šîn* are treated as a single letter.)

9:9-12. Because of God's commitment to justice and righteousness, there is hope for the "oppressed" (see 10:18). God is their "stronghold" (see "refuge"/"fortress"/"sure defense" in Pss 18:2; 46:7, 11; 48:4; 59:9, 16-17; 62:2, 6; 94:22; 144:2). Those who "know" God's character and reputation know that God stands for justice (see 9:16), and their response is well-founded trust (see Ps 4:5; Introduction). Thus the psalmist invites others to do what he or she will do: "sing praises" (v. 11; see also v. 2) and proclaim God's deeds (v. 11; see also v. 1). Verse 12, like v. 10, emphasizes the reliability of God. One "who avenges blood" means one who values human life (see Gen 9:5; Ezek 33:6). Because God values life, God "remembers" those who entrust themselves to God and who cry for help. This dynamic was operative in the historic deliverance of the people (see "cry" in Exod 3:7, 9; 14:10; Deut 26:7; Josh 24:7) and in a variety of other crises, both corporate and personal (Pss 34:17; 77:1; 88:1; 107:6, 28). Verse 12 contains the first occurrence of a Hebrew root (ענה *'ānâ*) that appears in two similar forms in Psalms 9–10 and is translated by the NRSV as "afflicted" (9:12), "poor" (9:18; 10:2, 9), "oppressed" (10:12), and "meek" (10:17). This sevenfold repetition is part of a cluster of words that designate those who belong to God—the "oppressed" (9:9; 10:18), the "needy" (9:18), the "innocent" (10:8), and the "helpless" (10:8, 10, 14). The "afflicted" are those who know they are not self-sufficient. They know they need help (see Psalm 3), and so entrust their lives and future to God. Elsewhere, these people are called "the righteous" (see Pss 1:5-6; 5:12).

9:13-18. While the psalm began by celebrating deliverance, it seems that not all is settled. Verse 13 consists of petition (v. 13*a*; see Ps 4:2) and complaint (v. 13*b*), but there is also confidence (v. 13*c*; see Job 38:17; Ps 107:18), which enables the psalmist to envision again declaring (the NRSV's "recount" is the same Hebrew word [ספר *sāpar*] as "tell" in v. 1) God's "praise" (see Pss 22:4; 34:2; 51:15; 71:6; 100:4; 102:21; 106:2, 12). Those who cannot help themselves will rejoice in God's help (NRSV, "deliverance"; NIV, "salvation"; see also Ps 3:2, 7-8). The expression of confidence continues in vv. 15-18. As the working out of God's justice is revealed, the nations and the wicked will be victims of their own designs (see Ps 7:15-16), and death is their destiny (see "Sheol" in Ps

6:5 and the description of the results of forgetting God in Deut 8:17-20). Verse 18 reinforces v. 12: God will not forget the helpless. In contrast to the enemies who perish (9:3, 5-6), the "hope of the poor" (see Pss 62:5; 71:5) will not perish.

9:19-20. The focus on the nations continues in these verses and the petition is another link with Psalm 10 (see 10:12; see also 3:7; 7:6). The Hebrew word for "mortals"/"human" (אנוש *'ĕnôš*) seems to have the connotation of weakness. The strength of the nations is no match for God's sovereignty. The parallelism of "judge" (v. 19*b*) and "know" (v. 20*b*) recalls v. 16. Unlike the power of mortals, God's power is always exercised for justice. The word translated as "mortals"/"human" (*'ĕnôš*) in vv. 19-20 occurs also in the final verse of Psalm 10 in the NRSV's phrase "those from earth." There, too, their defeat means "justice" for those who need help (10:18).

10:1-11. The petitions in vv. 13, 19-20 have anticipated the change of tone marked by the complaint of 10:1-2 (see Ps 22:1). That things remain unsettled for the psalmist is indicated by the fact that 10:1 contradicts 9:9, and 10:2*b* prays for what 9:15-16 has already celebrated. Clearly, the poor are still being persecuted by the arrogant wicked (see Ps 30:11), who become the focus of Psalm 10 (see vv. 2-4, 13, 15). In fact, an extended description of the wicked follows in vv. 3-11 (see Ps 73:3-12). The wicked "boast" (v. 3; see Pss 5:5; 73:3, "arrogant"; 75:4) of their selfishness. Unlike the afflicted, the wicked see themselves as self-sufficient, so they "renounce" God (v. 3; see v. 13) and see themselves accountable to no one (v. 4; see Psalm 14). Even so, the wicked seem to prosper with impunity (v. 5); with apparent justification, they consider themselves untouchable. To not be "moved" or "shaken" (v. 6) is elsewhere supposed to be the result of righteousness (see Pss 15:5; 16:8; 62:2, 6). Here, however, the wicked perceive themselves

to be secure, despite their deceitful, violent treatment of the helpless, the poor, and the innocent (vv. 7-10; see 5:6, 9; 7:2, 14; 17:10-12; 22:13; 55:10-11; 140:1-5). In v. 11, the wicked arrogantly contradict the faith of the psalmist: God "has forgotten" (cf. 9:12, 18). The wicked cruelly attempt to deepen the doubt expressed in 10:1: God "has hidden." According to the wicked, there will be no help from God (see Ps 3:2).

10:12-14. The petition in v. 12 responds directly to v. 11 as it asks God not to forget, and v. 13 quotes the wicked again so as to remind God directly of their arrogant assertions. The expression of confidence in v. 14 also responds directly to v. 11. The wicked say that God does not "see," but the helpless know better: "You do see!" The "you" here and in the final line of v. 14 is an emphatic use of the Hebrew pronoun (אתה *'attâ*). The word "trouble" (עמל *'āmāl*) here is the same as "mischief" in v. 7. God sees both the "mischief" of the wicked and the "trouble" and "grief" (see Ps 6:7) it causes the helpless, and God responds as "helper" (see Pss 33:20; 70:5; 115:9-11; 146:5) of the "orphan" (see v. 18; Exod 22:22-23; Deut 24:17-20; Pss 68:5; 94:6; 146:9).

10:15-18. This expression of trust is followed by further petition, which includes the request that God do precisely what the wicked said God could not do: "call . . . to account" (v. 15; see v. 13 NIV). The psalm ends in trusting affirmation. Verse 16 recalls the affirmation of God's reign that followed the descriptions of the enemies' demise in 9:3-4, 5-8. The psalmist's confidence is ultimately founded on the conviction that God rules the world and that God will enact the royal policy of justice (v. 18). While the wicked boast of the "desires of their heart" (10:3), God hears the "desire of the meek," and it is "their heart" that God "will strengthen" (v. 17). Because God rules the world, the meek will ultimately inherit the earth (see Ps 37:11; Matt 5:5).

REFLECTIONS

In a sense, Psalms 9–10 are a mirror image of Psalms 1–2. Psalm 1 framed the problem of rebellion against God in terms of the wicked (vv. 1, 5-6), whereas Psalm 2 put the problem in terms of peoples and nations (vv. 1, 8). Conversely, Psalm 9 focuses attention primarily on the rebellion of the nations, while Psalm 10 speaks mainly in terms of wicked persons. Both Psalms 1–2 and 9–10 affirm that, appearances to the contrary, God rules the world.

A crucial clue to recognizing the eschatological orientation of Psalms 9–10 is the apparent contradiction between 9:9 and 10:1, as well as the juxtaposition of thanksgiving (Psalm 9) and complaint (Psalm 10). Kraus writes:

> Godforsakenness and triumph are juxtaposed in one and the same psalm, and that quite abruptly. Jubilation and lament permeate the song. Two experiences lie adjacent to each other, just as they are met with under the world reign of God on Zion: wondrous rescue and incomprehensible delay.[80]

In other words, Psalms 9–10 leave the faithful where Jesus' proclamation of the reign of God leaves them. We are invited both to enter the reign of God as a present reality (Mark 1:14-15; Luke 17:20-21) and to await its consummation (Mark 13:23, 28-31; Luke 21:29-36).

As we wait, we pray as the psalmist prayed in Psalms 9–10—as one of the "poor" and the "helpless." Mays suggests that the prayer is for all the poor: "It is, so to say, a class action appeal. 'Blessed are you poor, for yours is the kingdom of God' (Luke 6:20); it is the lowly who by dependence and anticipation already live in the rule of God."[81] To be sure, we live in the rule of God amid competing rules and claims from wicked persons and nations, among whom we must certainly at times count ourselves and our nation. North American culture trains people to be self-centered, and it encourages us to be accountable to no one but ourselves. Whatever nation we live in, we can be sure it pursues above all its own national security with little or no consideration of the impact on others and even less for something as elusive as the will of God. Yet, despite the wickedness in ourselves, in others, and in society, we dare to trust with the psalmist that the "LORD is king forever and ever" (10:16) and that justice will prevail. This conviction and hope impels us into the struggle to join God at God's work in the world.

80. Kraus, *Psalms 1–59*, 199.
81. Mays, *Psalms*, 73.

PSALM 11:1-7, THE UPRIGHT SHALL BEHOLD GOD'S FACE

COMMENTARY

Because of its uniqueness, Psalm 11 is difficult to categorize. It is usually classified as a song of trust, but if the verbs in vv. 6-7 are understood as jussives ("let [God] rain coals . . ."), then vv. 6-7 can be construed as petition, and the psalm may be heard as an individual complaint or prayer for help. Gerstenberger suggests that Psalm 11 is a unique sort of complaint that he calls a Psalm of Contest, and he suggests that an accused person is given a chance in the context of a worship service to confront his or her opponents and offer a defense.[82] Other scholars suggest that the psalmist has found asylum in the Temple and is awaiting a ritual judicial proceeding that will result in vindication (see Psalms 5; 7; 17; Introduction). While the advisers recommend flight (v. 1), apparently due to the degree of opposition and the hopelessness of the case (vv. 2-3), the psalmist expresses confidence in God's sovereign righteousness and entrusts his or her destiny to God (vv. 4-7).

82. Gerstenberger, *Psalms: Part 1*, 77, 79; he cites Psalms 4; 52; 62; Jer 11:18-23; 18:18-23; 20:7-13 as similar texts.

The above proposals support the NIV and the NRSV divisions of the psalm into two major sections: vv. 1-3, 4-7. It often makes sense to view the structure or movement of a psalm on more than one level, and an alternative perspective in this case involves a chiastic arrangement (see the Introduction), as follows:

A v. 1 the security of the psalmist (the righteous)
 B vv. 2-3 the threat of the wicked
  C v. 4 the sovereignty of God
 B´ vv. 5-6 the destiny (punishment) of the wicked
A´ v. 7 the destiny (security) of the righteous

This proposal highlights v. 4, which, like several of the preceding psalms, affirms that God rules the world and enacts a royal policy of setting things right (see Psalms 1–2; 5; 7:7-11; 9:7-8; 10:15-18; Introduction).

11:1-3. Regardless of the accuracy of the proposals for a cultic setting, it is clear that Psalm 11 poses two alternatives for the faithful when confronted by the wicked and their threats—the faithful can either flee or stand firm in their profession of trust in the righteous rule of God. The psalm begins by stating the alternative that the psalmist has chosen: to trust God (see "refuge" in Pss 2:12; 5:11; 7:1; see also Isa 28:16; Introduction). Thus the psalmist categorically rejects the advice of those who say to "flee" like a bird to a mountain hideaway (see Pss 102:7; 124:7, where the psalmist is portrayed as a bird). Instead, the psalmist will find a home with God, as do the birds in Ps 84:3. It is not clear how far to extend the quote of the advisers. Some commentators conclude it with v. 1 or v. 2, but the NIV and the NRSV seem justified in carrying the quote through v. 3. In any case, whether the words of the advisers or the psalmist's own assessment, vv. 2-3 describe the desperate situation the psalmist faces. The wicked are a deadly threat (v. 2; see similar imagery in Pss 7:12-13; 37:14; 57:4; 64:2-4; 91:5). The situation appears hopeless (v. 3). The Hebrew word translated "foundations" (שֵׁת *šāt*) is rare, but it seems to

refer to the basic structures of society. Thus v. 3 asks, in effect, "What can be done when things are falling apart?" The question opens the way for the psalmist to elaborate upon the chosen alternative; vv. 4-7 tell what it means to "take refuge" in God.

11:4-7. To trust God means fundamentally to affirm, despite appearances (vv. 2-3), that God is in control. God is properly positioned on earth—in the "holy temple" (v. 4; see Ps 5:7)—and "in heaven," where God's "throne" is located (see Ps 9:4, 7). God sees what is going on, and God is involved. As the NIV suggests, the same Hebrew word (בחן *bāḥan*, "examines") occurs in v. 4*b* and v. 5*a*. This same activity is associated in Ps 7:9 (NRSV, "test"; NIV, "search") with God's judgment of the wicked and establishment of the righteous. The same parties are involved in Ps 11:5. As in Psalm 7, God's royal policy stands in opposition to the "violence" of the wicked (see 7:16); the wicked will be judged. Verse 6 recalls Gen 19:24, the judgment upon Sodom and Gomorrah, and the image of a "cup" of judgment occurs in Ps 75:9; Isa 51:17; Jer 25:15. The judgment occurs because God "is righteous" (v. 7*a*). God's righteousness is both the assurance of the downfall of the wicked and the hope of the righteous. Whereas the wicked are "lover[s] of violence" (v. 5), God "loves righteous deeds" (v. 7*b*). This phrase contains the fourth occurrence in this psalm of the Hebrew root meaning "righteous" (צדק *ṣdq*, vv. 3, 5, 7*a*, 7*b*). Righteous persons derive their identity and hope from God. Because the "eyes" of the righteous judge "behold" what is going on among the wicked and the righteous (vv. 4-5), the righteous shall "behold" God's "face" (v. 7). God's vision of humanity leads ultimately to humanity's vision of God. To "behold" God's face may suggest an original setting in the Temple (see Ps 24:3-6, esp. v. 6); however, more generally, to behold God's face means that the "upright" (v. 7; see v. 2) take their stand with God in the assurance that God stands with them. When things seem to be falling apart, this is what the righteous can do (v. 3).

Reflections

The message of Psalm 11 can be effectively summarized in the words of a familiar hymn: "Though the wrong seems oft so strong, God is the ruler yet." Faced by hostile powers that made the situation seem utterly hopeless (vv. 2-3), the psalmist professes faith in God's rule (v. 4) and lives out of the hope that God's rule will be fully manifested (vv. 5-7). In short, Psalm 11 is eschatological; when it least appears that God rules, the psalmist proclaims God's reign. Faced with a choice, the psalmist chooses not flight but faith. The choice, in effect, is the relinquishing of self-sufficiency in dependence upon God (see Commentary on Psalms 1–3). As Kraus puts it, "This trust is a confession to God's ability to protect and a rejection of all self-help."[83]

Like the psalmist, we live in a world whose "foundations" seem to be "destroyed" (v. 3). Things seem to be falling apart around us. Basic social structures and institutions are threatened—family, school, neighborhood, city, church. We often find ourselves asking essentially the same question raised by the psalmist's advisers (or perhaps by the psalmist) in v. 3: What can we do? The overwhelming temptation is to do what the psalmist was advised to do—give up. We may not literally be tempted to flee, but we are tempted to seek refuge in sheltered enclaves—perhaps in the latest home-security system or in the comfort of insulated congregations that convince us that things are not really as bad as they seem. Seldom does it occur to us even to consider what it might mean to reject self-help and to take refuge in God.

For us to take refuge in God may mean, as for the psalmist, for us to reject flight in order to fight—that is, to stand firm in contesting the forces of hostility and violence, which God hates. The final verse of Psalm 11 suggests that to take refuge in God, in the face of seemingly overwhelming opposition, means to be motivated by hope to do the "righteous deeds" that God loves. A contemporary confession of faith says it well:

We know that we cannot bring in God's kingdom.
But hope plunges us into the struggle
    for victories over evil that are possible now in
    the world, in the church, and our individual
    lives.

Hope gives us courage and energy
to contend against all opposition,
however invincible it may seem,
for the new world and the new humanity
that are surely coming.[84]

Psalm 11 is, indeed, a Psalm of Contest, a psalm that calls for the confrontation of God's enemies. It impels us into the contest for righteousness, upheld by a righteous God whose face we behold precisely in the midst of the struggle.

83. Kraus, *Psalms 1–59*, 203.
84. "A Declaration of Faith" (10.5) in *The Proposed Book of Confessions of the Presbyterian Church in the U.S.* (Atlanta: Materials Distribution Service, 1976) 172.

PSALM 12:1-8, I WILL NOW ARISE

COMMENTARY

Psalm 12 is a prayer that would be particularly appropriate in the circumstances described in Psalm 11—that is, when "the foundations are destroyed" (Ps 11:3). As in Psalms 9–11, the problem is the wicked (v. 8; see 11:2, 6; 9:5, 16-17; 10:2-4, 13, 15). The Lord's response to the wicked in 12:5 recalls especially Pss 9:18-19 and 10:12-13, for God promises to "rise up" on behalf of the "poor" and "needy," as requested in Psalms 9–10.

Psalm 12 may be the prayer of an individual or that of the community.[85] Because of the word from the Lord in v. 5, many commentators suggest that this psalm was originally spoken by a cultic prophet. The lament over the prevalence of wickedness may also suggest a prophetic character (see Isa 57:1-13; 59:1-21; Jer 5:1-3; Hos 4:1-3; Mic 7:1-7).

Both the NIV and the NRSV divide the psalm into four two-verse sections. The repetition of "lips" (vv. 2-4) and the focus on speech suggest that vv. 1-4 belong together as a larger unit of plea and complaint. Verses 5-8 then offer God's response and express confidence in divine protection by contrasting the reliability of God's speech with the empty, deceitful speech of the wicked. Just as with Psalm 11, so also it is possible to detect a chiastic structuring (see the Introduction) of Psalm 12. This alternative proposal serves especially well to emphasize the contrast:

A   v. 1 plea amid human corruption
   B   v. 2 empty, deceptive speech of the wicked
      C   vv. 3-4 plea for the LORD to cut off boasters
      C´   v. 5 the LORD's response
   B´   v. 6 the reliable speech of the LORD
A´   vv. 7-8 the LORD's protection amid human corruption[86]

12:1-4. The psalm begins with perhaps the most basic human prayer: "Help!" (see "deliver" in Pss 3:7; 6:4 and "save" in 7:1).

The "godly" are identified in Ps 4:3 (see NIV) as persons who belong to God, but they, not the wicked, have come to an end (see Ps 7:9). The faithful individual or community seems to be alone in the world (see 1 Kgs 19:10), surrounded by those whose speech is characterized by deception and hypocrisy (v. 2; see similar descriptions of speech in Pss 5:9; 41:6; 144:8, 11; Isa 59:4; Ezek 13:8). Verses 3-4 suggest that the speech of the wicked is indicative of their character. They boast in their own strength. Verse 4*b* is literally "our lips are with us," perhaps a play on what would be the proper profession, "God is with us." But the wicked do not recognize God's sovereignty. In their minds, they are accountable to no one but themselves (see Pss 10:4, 6; 73:8-9). Such autonomy is the essence of wickedness (see Psalms 1–2; Introduction).

12:5-8. The wicked apparently intend their question in v. 4*b* to be rhetorical. They expect no response, least of all from God. This makes the divine speech in v. 5 all the more effective. The true word exposes the wicked and their illusions of grandeur. Because God is sovereign, God has not only seen the behavior of the wicked (see Ps 11:4) and heard their boasting, but also has seen the despoiling of "the poor" (v. 5*a*; the Hebrew word translated "despoiled" [שֹׁד *šōd*] occurs elsewhere almost exclusively in prophetic books; see, e.g., "violence" in Jer 6:7; 20:8; Ezek 45:9; Hos 12:1; Amos 3:10; Hab 1:3; "desolation" in Isa 59:7; "devastation" in Isa 60:18) and heard their groaning (see Pss 79:11; 102:20). Just as the speech of the wicked reveals their character, so also God's speech reveals the divine character. God acts (see "rise up" in 3:7; 9:19; 10:12) to help the poor and needy (see Exod 22:21-24; 1 Sam 2:8-9; Pss 3:8; 10:17-18). The NRSV's "safety" is from the same Hebrew root as the opening plea for help. The prayer will be answered; God helps those who cannot help themselves (cf. Psalm 3). This good news lies at the heart of Psalm 12. The chiastic structure emphasizes its centrality, and even commentators with differing structural proposals

85. See Gerstenberger, *Psalms: Part 1*, 80. He categorizes Psalm 12 as both a "Complaint of the Individual" and a "Congregational Lament."
86. See Bratcher and Reyburn, *A Translator's Handbook on the Book of Psalms*, 115.

recognize v. 5 as the "focal point."[87] The final phrase in v. 5 is difficult, but the basic sense of the verse is clear.

The "words" or "promises" in v. 5 can be relied on (v. 6), in contrast to the deceptive words of the wicked (v. 2). This reliability grounds the expression of confidence in v. 7. Both the NRSV and the NIV follow the LXX in rendering the objects of both verbs as "us" rather than "them" and "him," as in the Hebrew. The initial "You" is emphatic. God

87. Kraus, *Psalms 1–59*, 209.

will assure the future of God's people. This assurance derives ultimately from God's word in v. 5. Verse 8 recalls v. 1, and the effect is a reminder that the promises of God are always surrounded by the apparent triumph of the wicked. In short, Psalm 12, like the preceding psalms, is eschatological (see Commentary on Psalms 2; 5; 7; 9–11; Introduction). Trust in God's word and character is indeed a blessed assurance in the present, but it also leaves the faithful awaiting the fuller experience of this foretaste of glory divine (see Ps 31:23-24).

REFLECTIONS

While the assessment in vv. 1, 8 of the pervasiveness of the wicked among humankind may be hyperbolic, it is not too much of an exaggeration to say that the church exists now, as it always has, as a beleaguered minority. In a thoroughly secularized society, it is almost impossible not to buy in to the credo of the wicked in v. 4—that is, we are masters of our own destiny, and we are accountable to no one but ourselves. Nevertheless, as the people of God, we profess that we live not by these selfish, sinful words but by the Word of God. We profess that our security lies in God's activity, not our own. We profess that God is our master, which positions us as servants whose lives are not our own. This radical departure from the secular norm means nothing less than that, in effect, we live as "resident aliens," as a distinctive colony in a prevailing culture dedicated to self-sufficiency and self-fulfillment.[88] In Jesus' words, we have been sent "into the world," but we "do not belong to the world" (John 17:16, 18). In the final analysis, Psalm 12 can be heard as a challenge to the church to claim its distinctiveness. Charles B. Cousar suggests, "The issue that confronts the church, then, is one of identity, of understanding and articulating who it is, of claiming its distinctiveness."[89] It is revealing that in John 17, Jesus prayed for precisely the same thing the psalmist prays for and celebrates in this psalm: God's protection (vv. 1, 7; cf. John 17:11, 15).

88. See Hauerwas and Willimon, *Resident Aliens*, 92.
89. See Cousar, *A Theology of the Cross*, 176.

PSALM 13:1-6, BUT I TRUST IN YOUR STEADFAST LOVE

COMMENTARY

Because it is the shortest and simplest of the prayers for help, Psalm 13 is often cited by commentators as the textbook example of an individual lament or complaint. The complaint appears in vv. 1-2, petition in vv. 3-4, and expression of trust and praise in vv. 5-6.

13:1-2. Both the impatience and the desperation of the psalmist are emphasized

by the fourfold occurrence of "How long . . . ?" in vv. 1-2. Robert Alter points out that each occurrence introduces a question that "reflects an ascent on a scale of intensity, the note of desperate urgency pitched slightly higher with each repetition."[90] It seems at

90. Alter, *The Art of Biblical Poetry*, 65.

first that God may simply have forgotten (see Pss 9:12, 10:12). But no, it is worse than that. God has intentionally turned away, an action often indicative of God's wrath (see Deut 31:17; 32:20; Pss 22:24; 27:8-9; 30:7; 69:17; 88:14; 102:2; 143:7; Isa 8:17; 54:8; Jer 33:5; Mic 3:4). God's apparent apathy or anger is a source of anxiety for the psalmist. The NIV translation of v. 2*a* is preferable; it suggests the psalmist's inner agitation and turmoil. The NRSV note indicates that the translators have followed the Syriac, although some scholars claim that the Hebrew word in question (עצה *'ēṣâ*) can mean "pain" as well as "counsels" or "thoughts." The word "sorrow" (יגון *yāgôn*) in v. 2*b* indicates the urgency of the situation; it is used elsewhere in the context of the death of individuals (Gen 42:38; 44:31) or of the nation (Jer 8:18). Thus v. 2 implies what vv. 3-4 will make explicit: The crisis at hand is a matter of life and death. Verse 2 is a three-part poetic line; it serves to isolate and emphasize the climactic element, v. 2*c*. In the psalms, it is supposed to be God who is "exalted" (see 18:46; 21:13; 46:11; 57:5, 11; 108:5). In short, it seems to the psalmist that God has been displaced. The place to which one looks for help is occupied by the enemy. This is the worst possible news.

It has traditionally been suggested on the basis of vv. 1-2 that the psalmist was seriously ill and facing imminent death. A related notion is that the enemy in v. 2*c* should be understood as death. These proposals make some sense, but the precise nature of the problem and the identity of the enemy are by no means certain. It is more likely that the language and imagery are intended to be stereotypical and open-ended (see Introduction). What is more clear is that vv. 1-2 portray the interrelation of the three major "characters" in Psalms: the psalmist, the enemy, and God. The psalms consistently hold together the three corresponding realms of experience that we contemporary people are inclined to separate—the psychological, the sociological, and the theological. For the psalmist, every experience of the self or the other is also an experience of God. While this view of reality may be problematic—leading, for instance, to the conclusion that God causes sickness and suffering—it does at least affirm God's intimate involvement in the world. The value of the psalmist's view of reality is that it can remind us of the marvelous complexity and ambiguity of human life, amid which God is somehow present. Thus, even while the psalmist complains of God's absence (v. 1), the psalmist addresses the complaint and the subsequent petition precisely to "my God" (v. 3; see Ps 22:1).

13:3-4. In these verses a threefold petition is supported by three reasons why God should act. The NIV's "Look" is more accurate than the NRSV's "Consider"; the request calls for God to reverse the action of hiding God's face (v. 1; see Ps 10:14: NRSV, "note"; NIV, "consider"). The request that God "answer" is also particularly appropriate, since the complaint in vv. 1-2 was framed as a series of questions (on the plea "answer," see Ps 4:1). The final petition may also recall v. 1, since God's face is often described as a source of light (see Num 6:25; Pss 4:6; 31:16; 67:1; 80:3, 7, 19; 119:135). In any case, the request is for strength (see 1 Sam 14:27, 29; Pss 6:6; 38:10; Lam 5:17). Without renewed strength, the psalmist will die (see Dan 12:2). As in v. 2, the "enemy" in v. 4*a* could be death, but the plural "foes" in v. 4*b* suggest human enemies who will rejoice over the psalmist's defeat or demise (see "shake"/"shaken" in Pss 10:6; 15:5; 16:8; 21:7; 30:6; 62:2, 6; 112:6 NIV).

13:5-6. The movement from complaint to petition seems logical, but the transition from vv. 1-4 to vv. 5-6 is more of a surprise. To be sure, the prayers for help regularly become expressions of trust and praise, but the transition here seems unusually abrupt. The NIV's translation of the verb (בטח *bāṭaḥ*) in v. 5*a* in the present tense is preferable. The psalmist's trust is ongoing (see "trust" in Pss 4:5; 9:10; see also the Introduction); trust is properly directed to the fundamental attribute of God's character: "steadfast love" (see Pss 5:7; 21:7; Introduction). Trust is accompanied by rejoicing in God's "salvation" (see Commentary on Ps 3:2, 7-8). The transition is brought into even sharper focus by the repetition of several words from vv. 1-4. The "sorrow in my heart" (v. 2) has been replaced by a "heart" that "shall rejoice" (v. 5). Only a verse earlier, the enemies were the ones who would "rejoice" (v. 4). The last words of the psalm, "with me"

(עָלַי *'ālāy*), are a repetition of the last words of v. 2, "over me." Whereas the enemy had been "exalted over me," now God has "dealt bounty over me." The psalmist seems now to be unshakable.

Scholars disagree concerning both the nature and the explanation of the remarkable transition between vv. 1-4 and vv. 5-6 (see Introduction). Some scholars suggest that vv. 5-6 reflect a materially changed situation; that is, the psalmist has been cured, the enemies have been defeated, or some other problem has been solved. In this case, vv. 5-6 must have been written after vv. 1-4 and added to the complaint and petition. A more frequent conclusion is that the change reflected in vv. 5-6 involves not the psalmist's situation or condition but the psalmist. In this view,

vv. 5-6 constitute an affirmation of faith that anticipates future deliverance, perhaps made in response to a promise of salvation delivered by a priest or some other religious functionary in the context of a temple or synagogue ritual or house prayer service.

To be sure, it is possible that the psalmist either looks back in gratitude or forward in trust, but the text remains ambiguous. This very ambiguity, however, is a theological gain, for it invites the interpreter to view complaint and praise as simultaneous rather than separate moments. Thus the ambiguity and complexity of the psalm accurately represent the ambiguity and complexity of the life of faith. As people of faith, we will always find it necessary to pray, "How long, O LORD?" even as we simultaneously profess that the Lord "has been good to me."

REFLECTIONS

1. The juxtaposition of complaint and praise in Psalm 13 bears reflection. According to Mays:

> Luther in his exposition of the Psalm calls the mood of the prayer the "state in which hope despairs, and yet despair hopes at the same time. . . . "
> There is a coherence which holds the apparently separate moments together. . . . This is the deep radical knowledge of faith which cannot separate God from any experience of life and perseveres in construing all, even life's worst, in terms of relation to God. . . .
> . . . The Psalm is not given to us to use on the rare occasions when some trouble seems to make it appropriate. It is forever appropriate as long as life shall last. We do not begin at one end and come out at the other. The agony and the ecstasy belong together as the secret of our identity.[91]

In other words, by holding together complaint and praise, we are taught about both God and ourselves. God is involved in all of life—even life at its worst. Such a conviction opens the way to see God's involvement even in such an apparently God-forsaken event as the crucifixion (see Commentary on Psalm 22).

As for us, we are simultaneously confronted with our own perpetual neediness and comforted by the proclamation of God's unfailing love. The agony and the ecstasy belong together. In Christian terms, we are simultaneously people of the cross and people of the resurrection. Thus Psalm 13 anticipates the message of the Gospels and the letters of Paul. In effect, Psalm 13 reminds us both that there is no following Jesus without bearing a cross (Mark 8:34) and that those who lose their life for Jesus' "sake, and for the sake of the gospel, will save it" (Mark 8:35 NRSV). In his discussion of Phil 3:2-11 and the way Paul's theology of the cross and resurrection affects the Christian life, Charles B. Cousar writes: "Instead of discovering that sufferings may be endured for a time because the sufferers will ultimately be vindicated, we find in the text that

91. J. L. Mays, "Psalm 13," *Int.* 37 (1983) 281-82.

the resurrection-power comes to expression in the very midst of the tribulations."[92] Here, too, as in Psalm 13, "the agony and the ecstasy belong together as the secret of our identity."

2. Because it is such a succinct example, Psalm 13 also serves to teach us about prayer. It involves not only the nice, positive expressions of vv. 5-6, but also the bold, brutally honest complaints and accusations of vv. 1-2 and the urgent petitions of vv. 3-4. This kind of prayer challenges us to locate and articulate both our pain and the suffering of others in a way that we often hesitate to do out of fear of offending God, shocking others, or embarrassing ourselves. Psalm 13 gives voice to things we often do not talk about—forsakeness, abandonment, anxiety and inner turmoil, defeat, the fear of death. As Walter Brueggemann suggests of these kinds of prayers, "How wondrous that these Psalms make it clear that precisely such dimensions of our life are the stuff of prayer."[93]

92. Cousar, *A Theology of the Cross,* 161.
93. Walter Brueggemann, *Praying the Psalms* (Winona, Minn.: St. Mary's Press, 1988) 31.

PSALM 14:1-7, NO ONE DOES GOOD

COMMENTARY

Like Psalm 12, Psalm 14 has a prophetic character. The psalmist's observations in vv. 1-3 serve as an indictment that apparently targets all humanity (see Ps 12:1, 8). Verses 1-3 are perhaps hyperbolic, for v. 4 narrows the indictment to "all the evildoers" (see below on the tension between vv. 1-3 and vv. 4-6). These persons victimize God's people (v. 4). Verses 5-6 function as an announcement of judgment upon the evildoers and as an oracle of salvation for the righteous. Verse 7 expresses the conviction that God will help the victimized people, and it celebrates the anticipated deliverance. Psalm 14 appears in a slightly different version as Psalm 53 (see Commentary on Psalm 53).

Because of its prophetic character, and because it is neither prayer nor praise, Psalm 14 is often categorized as a prophetic exhortation. Pointing to the mention of "fools" in v. 1 as well as the words "wise" (v. 2) and "knowledge" (v. 4), some scholars also detect an affinity with wisdom literature. In any case, Psalm 14 does have an instructional intent.

14:1. The NIV note suggests that the term "fool" (נבל *nābāl*) is more a moral assessment than an intellectual one. As the second half of v. 1 suggests, foolishness is not a lack of knowledge in general but the

failure to acknowledge God in trustful obedience (see v. 4; see also Deut 32:6; 2 Sam 13:13; Ps 74:18, 22; Jer 17:11). The failure to acknowledge God will inevitably mean misplaced priorities and misguided behavior. What the fools say to themselves in v. 1*a* should not be understood as a statement of philosophical atheism. Rather, the issue is a much more subtle and widespread practical atheism—that is, acting as if there is no God to whom one is accountable in any way. Thus foolishness turns out to be synonymous with wickedness—that is, autonomy, being a "law unto oneself" (see Commentary on Psalm 1). Indeed, the wicked in Ps 10:4 say precisely what the fools say in Ps 14:1 (see also Pss 10:5-6, 13; 73:11).

14:2. This verse asserts precisely what the wicked and the foolish ignore—namely, God's sovereignty. God is positioned *over* humankind. In Psalm 102:18-22, God's looking down from heaven occurs in the same context with peoples and kingdoms gathering to serve the Lord. The Hebrew word translated "serve" means essentially "to be subject," "to live under the sovereignty of another." In Ps 14:2, God is looking for those who are "wise," which Psalm 2 earlier defined precisely in terms of serving when it exhorted the kings of the earth to "be wise" (2:10) and to "Serve the LORD" (2:11). To seek God also suggests recognizing God's rule. Seeking God means trusting God (9:10), worshiping God (22:6-7), taking refuge in God (34:8-10; see 14:6).

14:3. This verse is clearly similar to v. 1. The verbs that describe human behavior in vv. 1 and 3 recall two key events in the Pentateuch: the flood story (see "corrupt"/"corrupted" in v. 1 and Gen 6:12) and Israel's worship of the golden calf (see Exod 32:7, where the verb here translated "corrupt" in v. 1 appears as "acted perversely" in the NRSV; and Exod 32:8, where "gone astray" in v. 3 appears as "turn aside"). Both of these episodes prove to be paradigmatic. The history of both Israel and humankind reveals that the repeated assessment in vv. 1 and 3 is not much of an exaggeration: "there is no one who does good." The added "no, not one" in v. 3 emphasizes the point. This phrase represents the fourth occurrence of a Hebrew negative particle (אֵין 'ên), and the effect is to reinforce the negative assessment of humankind. This message of universal human perversity is used by the apostle Paul in Rom 3:10-18, where he quotes portions of Ps 14:1, 3 as well as several additional verses of a longer version of Psalm 14 that is found in the Greek Old Testament (see below).

14:4-6. These verses seem to contradict vv. 1-3, since vv. 4-6 distinguish between "the evildoers" and those identified as "my people" (v. 4), "the righteous" (v. 5), and "the poor" (v. 6). These verses may reflect a divided society in which a strong upper class oppressed the majority of the people. Such a situation is suggested, for instance, in Mic 3:1-4, which also uses the image of some people's being fed upon by others (Ps 14:4; Mic 3:3). As in Pss 9:17-18; 10:17-18; and 12:5-7, God will act on behalf of the poor. The oppressors will be terrified (see Exod 15:16), for God is on the side of the righteous; and the poor will find their refuge in God (see Pss 2:12; 5:11; 7:1; 11:1; Introduction). The word "there" (שָׁם šām) in v. 5 is difficult, but it may suggest that the evildoers will be terrified somehow precisely in the midst of their attempts to oppress others.

14:7. Many scholars consider v. 7 to be a post-exilic addition to the psalm in order to make it especially applicable to a situation in which Israel was dominated by other nations. This is certainly possible and may find support in the appearance of the phrase "restore the fortunes," which often specifically indicates return from exile and always suggests restoration from a major setback, such as the exile and its aftermath (see Deut 30:3; Jer 29:14; 30:3, 18; 31:23; 32:44; 33:7, 11; Pss 85:2; 126:1). Verse 7a is actually stated in the form of a question, "Who will give from Zion help for Israel?" The answer is God. Despite what the foolish or the wicked may say (Pss 3:2; 10:4; 14:1), God is the help of God's people, individual persons or the body as a whole (Pss 3:8; 10:14; 14:5-7).

REFLECTIONS

Reflection on Psalm 14 must begin with the apparent contradiction between vv. 1-3 and vv. 4-6. It is possible in the light of vv. 4-6 to conclude that the seemingly universal indictment of humanity in vv. 1-3 is hyperbole; however, as Mays suggests, "theologically we would do well to let the tensions stand unresolved."[94] When we allow vv. 1-3 to speak apart from vv. 4-6, they assert that all humans are sinful, a lesson that should not be ignored (see Luke 18:9-14). Indeed, this is precisely the message that Paul derived from Ps 14:1, 3 and used to argue that all people "are under the power of sin" (Rom 3:9 NRSV). As Kraus puts it, we "must come to realize how shocking the assertions of Psalm 14 actually are."[95] He is right. What is truly shocking is that what Psalm 14 calls foolishness, and what other psalms call wickedness, is essentially what our culture teaches people to be—autonomous, self-directed, self-sufficient. Of course, such cultural wisdom makes some sense psychologically, but we often unconsciously

94. Mays, *Psalms,* 83.
95. Kraus, *Psalms 1–59,* 223-24.

translate the message into theological conclusions: We don't need other people, and we don't need God! While philosophical atheism is relatively rare, this kind of practical atheism is rampant. For us, in effect, "there is no God." Lest we think that our advanced, sophisticated era has left corruption and perversity behind, all we need do is remind ourselves of the persistent, daily realities of our world—poverty, hunger, homelessness, political corruption, violence in our homes and cities as well as throughout the world. Although our rugged individualism (that is, our autonomy) may lead us to deny it, not one of us is uninvolved in or unaffected by these realities—"no, not one."

While vv. 1-3 remind us of the pervasive sinfulness of humanity, vv. 4-6 proclaim that sin does not have the final word. The good news is that God is able to gather sinners into "the company of the righteous"—Israel, the church. Paul knew this too. After arguing on the basis of Ps 14:1, 3 that all "are under the power of sin" (Rom 3:9 NRSV), he goes on to proclaim the good news that all people "are now justified by his grace as a gift, through the redemption that is in Christ Jesus" (Rom 3:23-24). As Paul makes clear, this justification or righteousness is not a human achievement but a gift. We remain sinners and victims of sin; however, we know that our inability to do good is not the final word. This is true "knowledge" (v. 4), the wisdom for which God is looking (v. 2), for it amounts to dependence upon God rather than upon self. In short, the Lord is our refuge (v. 6).

Of course, this kind of wisdom—dependence upon God rather than self—may appear foolish to the world. But Paul also proclaims, "God chose what is foolish in the world to shame the wise" (1 Cor 1:27 NRSV). According to Paul, the wisdom for which God is looking ultimately takes the shape of a cross (1 Cor 1:24-25). Indeed, the cross reveals clearly the two realities with which Psalm 14 confronts us: the reality of human sin (vv. 1-3) and the reality of God's grace (vv. 5-6). To live among "the company of the righteous" is to trust that the reality of God's grace is the ultimate reality, the final word about our sinful human existence. Thus we are to live not by what we see so pervasively around us (vv. 1, 3) but by what we believe and what we hope for (see v. 7).

PSALM 15:1-5, THEY SHALL NOT BE MOVED

COMMENTARY

Along with Psalm 24, Psalm 15 is ordinarily classified as an entrance liturgy (see also Isa 33:13-16; Mic 6:6-8), a question-and-answer ritual enacted as persons prepared to enter the temple gates. There is evidence from Israel and other ancient Near Eastern sources that there were requirements for entering a holy place (see Deut 23:1-8; 2 Chr 23:19); however, Psalm 15 concludes not with a judgment about admission but with an observation that has the character of a promise. While perhaps modeled on an entrance liturgy, Psalm 15 in its present form has more the tone of liturgical instruction. In its present literary context, it serves to portray the shape of the lives of those who have been mentioned frequently in preceding psalms—those who take refuge in God (Pss 2:12; 5:11; 7:1; 11:1; 14:6), the poor/oppressed/afflicted/meek (Pss 9:9, 12, 18; 10:2, 9, 12, 17-18; 12:5; 14:6), the righteous or "company of the righteous" (Pss 1:5-6; 5:12; 7:9; 11:3, 5; 14:5). In fact, there is a revealing progression from Psalm 13 to Psalm 15. The movement is from the threat of being "shaken" (13:6) to the affirmation that "God is with the company of the righteous" (14:5) to the portrayal of the righteous dwelling with God, the result being that they "shall never be moved" (15:5c; "moved" here is the same Hebrew word [מוט môṭ] as "shaken" in 13:4 NRSV).

The questions in v. 1 are followed by a series of answers in vv. 2-5*ab*, the origin and organization of which are variously understood. Many scholars suggest that the answers have been shaped by the influence of the Ten Commandments, but it is not clear that there are actually ten items. The organization of the items is also debated. Bratcher and Reyburn detect twelve items, arranged in an alternating pattern of three positive statements (vv. 2, 4*abc*) and three negative statements (vv. 3, 4*d*-5*b*; the last line of v. 4 actually contains a positive and a negative that are obscured by the NRSV and the NIV—lit., "he swears to his hurt and he will *not* change"). In their view, "the contrast of plusses and minuses ... serves the purpose of focusing attention upon the exemplary conduct of those who would enter the Temple for worship."[96] A different (or perhaps complementary) proposal construes v. 2 as an answer to v. 1 in general terms, while vv. 3-5*ab* offer specific illustrations in the realms of dealing with neighbors (v. 3), with the religious community (v. 4*ab*), and with people and practices in society at large (vv. 4*c*-5*b*).[97] Support for this view may be derived from the fact that each item in v. 2 is introduced by an active participle, whereas the other items use finite verb forms (with the exception of v. 4*a*, where the NRSV's "the wicked" is the subject and is accompanied by a passive participle). Complicating this proposal is the observation that each item in v. 2 is paralleled in v. 3—that is, vv. 2*a* and 3*a* have to do with walking (the word "slander" [רגל *rāgal*] in v. 3*a* is more literally "tread" or "foot it"); vv. 2*b* and 3*b* have to do with acting (see "do" in both cases, although the Hebrew differs [פעל *pāʿal* in v. 2*b* and עשה *ʿāśâ* in v. 3*b*]); and vv. 2*c* and 3*c* have to do with speech. It is possible that several structural patterns are operating simultaneously.

15:1. The word "tent" (see Exod 33:7-11; Num 12:5, 10; Pss 27:5-6; 61:5) and the phrase "holy hill" (Pss 2:6; 3:4; 43:3) may certainly refer to the Temple on Mount Zion, God's chosen dwelling place on earth (see Pss 24:3; 46:4-5; 48:1-3; 132:13-14; 1 Kgs 8:1-11). The Temple symbolized God's presence. Thus, in effect, v. 1 inquires about the identity

or life-position of those who belong to God (see Ps 1:1, 5). The first verb in v. 1 (גור *gûr*) means literally "sojourn, be a resident alien." It suggests that no one can *deserve* to reside in God's presence. Rather, persons dwell with God only because of God's gracious permission (see Ps 5:7).

15:2-5b. God's gracious acceptance of persons into the divine presence has an important implication for understanding the answers in vv. 2-5*ab*. These answers should not be understood as requirements; rather, they portray the character of persons whose lives have been shaped in conformity with God's character. Mays suggests of vv. 2-5*ab*, "It is a picture, not prescription."[98] Not surprisingly, the words that describe the deeds and speech of those who belong to God are used elsewhere to describe God's own character, work, or word. For instance, God is "blameless" or "perfect" in God's way (Ps 18:30), work (Deut 32:4), and instruction (Ps 19:7). Those who belong to God mirror God's character. This is not to say that they are absolutely sinless (see Commentary on Ps 14:1-3) but that their lives are completely oriented to and dependent upon God (the Hebrew root of "blameless[ly]" [תמים *tāmîm*] means essentially "to be complete"; see Deut 18:13 NRSV, where this word is translated as "completely loyal"). Persons identified elsewhere as blameless include Noah (Gen 6:9), Abraham (Gen 17:1), David (1 Kgs 9:4; NRSV, "integrity"), Job (Job 1:1, 8; 2:3), and the psalmist (Pss 18:23; 26:1, 11; NRSV, "integrity"; see also Ps 119:1). Psalm 101 is particularly reminiscent of Psalm 15, for here the psalmist, probably the king, studies "the way that is blameless" (101:2), walks "with blameless heart" (101:2), and admits into his presence those "whose walk is blameless" (101:6; cf. Ps 101:4-5 with 15:3 and 101:7 with 15:2).

Those who belong to God also mirror God's character as they "do what is right," for God is righteous (see Pss 5:8; 7:9, 11; 9:4, 8; see esp. 11:7). God is also characterized by "faithfulness" (see Exod 34:6), and those who speak faithfulness or truth mirror God's character and embody God's will (see Jer 9:5; Zech 8:16; cf. Ps 5:6; Amos 5:10). As God's character is manifested in concrete actions,

96. Bratcher and Reyburn, *A Translator's Handbook on the Book of Psalms*, 133.
97. Mays, *Psalms*, 84.
98. Mays, *Psalms*, 84.

341

the character of those who belong to God will be manifested as well. Their tongues will not be instruments of deceit or oppression (v. 3; see Pss 5:9; 12:4). They will bring no harm upon their neighbor by speech or action (v. 3; see Exod 20:16-17; Lev 19:18; Ps 28:3; 101:5). They will oppose those who oppose God, and honor those who honor God (v. 4*ab*; see Ps 1:1). They will keep their word even when they suffer for it (see Ps 24:4; Matt 5:33-37). Just as God acts on behalf of the poor and oppressed (see Pss 9:18, 10:17-18; 12:5), so also the business practices of those who belong to God will benefit the poor (v. 5*a*; see Exod 22:25; Lev 25:36-37, where the refusal to exact interest is to protect the poor; see also Deut 23:20; Ezek 18:8, 13, 17). As God avoids bribery to enact justice (Deut 10:17-18; Ps 9:4), those who belong to God will do the same (v. 5*b*; see Exod 23:7-8; Deut 16:19-20; 1 Kgs 8:3; cf. Ps 10:8).

15:5c. This verse concludes the psalm with a statement that is both an affirmation and a promise. Just as God has established the earth (Pss 93:1; 96:10; 104:5) and Zion (Pss 46:5; 125:1) so that they cannot be "moved" or "shaken" by chaotic forces, so also God secures the lives of those who belong to God. In view of the rest of the book of Psalms, this clearly does not mean that the righteous will live unopposed (see Pss 3:1-2; 5:7-8; 7:6; 9:13-14; 10:1-2; 12:1-4; 13:1-4; 14:4; 34:19). Rather, in even the worst of circumstances, the righteous will have in God's presence and power a resource to sustain their lives. That promise is equivalent to the promise of happiness to those who take refuge in God (Ps 2:12) and of prosperity for the righteous in all they do (Ps 1:3). That is to say, those who trust God will always have a solid foundation for facing the world; they will not be moved (see Pss 10:6; 13:4; 16:8; 17:5; 21:7; 30:6; 62:2, 6; 112:6).

REFLECTIONS

The refrain of a well-known African American spiritual consists of references to both Ps 1:3 and Ps 15:5*c* : "Like a tree that's planted by the water, we shall not be moved."[99] The juxtaposition reveals a profound understanding of both psalms. While Psalm 15 may be modeled on an entrance liturgy, its present form and context suggest that its primary purpose is to portray what it means to be constantly open to God's instruction (Ps 1:2), to take refuge in God (Pss 2:12; 5:11; 7:1; 11:1; 14:6; 16:1; 17:7), to live under God's rule (Pss 2:11; 5:2; 7:7-8; 8:1, 9; 9:7-8; 10:16; 11:4; 14:2).

The answers to the questions in v. 1, therefore, are not requirements or prescriptions. Rather, like the content of the Sermon on the Mount in Matthew 5–7, vv. 2-5*b* portray what life is like when it is lived under God's reign instead of in reliance upon oneself (see Commentary on Psalm 24). While the answers in vv. 2-5*b* and the teachings in the Sermon on the Mount are not requirements, both do suggest that the lives of those who are loyal and faithful to God will look different from the lives of the wicked and foolish, who autonomously deny God's claim (see Pss 10:3-4; 14:1; see also Matt 7:21-23). The character and behavior of the righteous will inevitably mirror God's character and God's values. Recipients of grace (see Commentary on v. 1) will inevitably be gracious.

Consideration of Psalm 15 in terms of entry into the Temple, or simply in terms of preparation for or participation in worship, raises the question, What does God desire from the worshiper? A traditional answer was that God desires sacrificial offerings; however, the prophets proclaimed that sacrifice was not sufficient. God desires justice, righteousness, knowledge, goodness, and love (see Isa 1:12-17; Hos 6:6; Amos 5:21-24; Mic 6:6-8). Psalm 15 is consistent with these prophetic texts. In short, God desires the loyalty of the whole self—lifestyle (see "walk" in v. 2), action (see "do" in v. 2), and speech (see "speak" in v. 2). The proper gift to bring into God's presence is the

99. See, e.g., *The United Methodist Hymnal* (Nashville: United Methodist Publishing House, 1989) 738.

gift of one's life (see Pss 25:1; 50:12-15, 23; 51:15-17; 86:4; 143:8). Psalm 15 calls for "a living sacrifice, holy and acceptable to God, which is your spiritual worship" (Rom 12:1 NRSV). As Paul recognized, such a gift involves being transformed rather than "conformed to this world" (Rom 12:2 NRSV). In other words, those who live under God's rule rather than the rule of self will be different (see Reflections on Psalm 12). Such faithfulness will invite opposition, as the life of Jesus reveals, but God's promise to the faithful is a peace greater than the world can give (see John 14:27). Indeed, persons who entrust themselves to God "shall never be moved" (v. 5c).

PSALM 16:1-11, I KEEP THE LORD ALWAYS BEFORE ME

COMMENTARY

After a brief opening petition, the rest of v. 1 "strikes the main theme of the prayer"—refuge or trust.[100] Accordingly, Psalm 16 is usually classified as a psalm of confidence/trust. There is a meaningful progression from Psalm 13 to Psalm 15 (see Commentary on Psalm 15), and Psalm 16 fits well with this sequence. Psalm 15 portrayed the identity of those who enter God's presence and dwell with God; the focus there was on deeds. Psalm 16 also portrays the identity of those who abide in God's presence (see esp. vv. 8, 11; cf. v. 8 with Pss 13:6; 15:5c), but the focus here is on the psalmist's joyful attitude (vv. 8-9, 11; cf. v. 9 with Ps 14:7) and speech (v. 2). Indeed, Gerstenberger aptly labels Psalm 16 a "Confession of Faith" as well as a "Song of Confidence," and he concludes, "The psalm can be compared in its function with the Apostles' Creed in Christian worship."[101]

16:1. The opening petition of Psalm 16 occurs also in Pss 17:8; 25:20; 86:2; 140:5; 141:9 (NRSV, "guard," "keep," or "preserve"; see also Psalm 121 and the sixfold repetition of "keep[s]"/ "keeper"). It is followed immediately by a supporting rationale that ties the psalm to a pervasive theme in the psalter, especially in Psalms 1–72: refuge (see 2:12; 5:11; 7:1; 11:1; 14:6; 17:7; Introduction). Some scholars give a geographical interpretation to the act of taking refuge; that is, the psalmist flees to the Temple to gain asylum from persecutors or visits the Temple to seek healing or social restoration. More broadly, however, to take refuge in God means to trust God, to recognize God's sovereignty, to live in dependence upon God rather than on self.

16:2. As in Psalm 2, the concepts of sovereignty and refuge are explicitly linked. In v. 2a, the psalmist addresses God as "master" or "Lord," thus accepting the role of God's servant. The Hebrew of v. 2b is uncertain. Most translators agree essentially with the NIV and the NRSV translations, which suggest the psalmist's dependence on God. Dahood seeks to make sense of the Hebrew, suggesting a translation that highlights God's sovereignty: " 'You are my Lord, my Good,/ there is none above you.' "[102]

16:3-4. These verses are even more uncertain than v. 2b. Both the NIV and the NRSV construe the "saints"/"holy ones" and the "glorious ones"/"noble" to be other members of God's people. Thus an affirmation of loyalty to the people of God (v. 3) accompanies a profession of loyalty to God alone in keeping with the first commandment (v. 4). Many scholars suggest, however, that the terms in v. 3 refer to other gods, and many translations of v. 3 differ significantly from the NIV and the NRSV (see the NIV note). The New American Bible, for instance, reads: "Worthless are all the false gods of the land./ Accursed are all who delight in them." In any case, vv. 3-4 are almost certainly the psalmist's assertion that he or she will have no other gods. There will be no participation in idolatrous sacrifices or worship.

---

100. Gerstenberger, *Psalms: Part 1*, 90.
101. Gerstenberger, *Psalms: Part 1*, 92.
102. Dahood, *Psalms I (1–50)*, 86.

16:5-6. As if to emphasize as sharply as possible the contrast between loyalty to other gods and loyalty to the true God, v. 5 begins with the most personal of the divine names: "LORD." Doubly emphatic is the appearance of the Hebrew pronoun "you" (אתה *'attâ*) in v. 5*b*. Indeed, it recalls the appearance of the pronoun in v. 2 in the phrase, "You are my Lord." In short, there is no doubt that the psalmist belongs to God. And in a sense, God belongs to the psalmist as well—not in the sense of ownership but in the sense of relatedness. The word "portion" (חלק *ḥēleq*) is used in the book of Joshua to designate every Israelite's share in the land (see Josh 19:9). Thus it represented the possibility of sustenance, life, future. For the psalmist, God is the source of all these good things (see v. 2). To call God "my cup" suggests the same idea (see Pss 23:6; 116:13). The word "lot" (גורל *gôrāl*) recalls both the method and the results of apportioning the land in the book of Joshua (18:6, 8, 10; 19:51); the lot was also a method for determining duty or function (see 1 Chr 24:5, 7). The final line of v. 5 thus affirms again that the psalmist's life and future lie with God and that the psalmist is willing to be used by God for God's purposes. Since the priests and the Levites had no portion in the land and were specifically told that God was their portion (see Num 18:20; Deut 10:9; 12:12), some scholars conclude that the psalmist was a priest or Levite serving in the Temple. While this is possible, it is more likely that the language and conceptuality of the book of Joshua are being used symbolically and poetically (see Pss 73:26; 119:57; 142:6; Lam 3:24). More language from Joshua occurs in v. 6: "boundary lines" (see 17:5; NIV, "share," NRSV, "portions") and "inheritance"/"heritage" (see 14:3; 17:6). The images effectively communicate the psalmist's affirmation that entrusting one's life to God has favorable consequences. God has provided (see v. 2).

16:7-8. This verse develops further an idea found in v. 5: the psalmist's willingness to be used by and for God. The word "bless" (ברך *bārak*) in its root sense means "to kneel," as in paying homage to a superior (see Pss 26:12; 34:1; 63:4; 103:20-22; 104:1, 35). As suggested earlier by the word "refuge" (v. 1), the psalmist recognizes God's

sovereignty. And as one who subjects oneself to God, the psalmist is open to God's instruction or "counsel" (v. 7*a*; see Commentary on Psalm 1, esp. v. 2; see also Ps 32:8). Verse 7*b* implies that the psalmist may be involved in self-instruction, but that is not necessarily so, since the heart (lit., "kidneys") was especially accessible to God's examination and influence (see Pss 7:9; 26:2; Jer 11:20; 20:12). The verb "instructs" (יסר *yāsar*) recalls Ps 2:10, where it is rendered "be warned" and parallels the command to "Serve the LORD" (2:11). Thus, even v. 7*b* represents the psalmist's intention to be subject to God in every way. Verse 8 conveys the same idea; for the psalmist, God is "always before me," the constant center of attention. Somehow—whether it be the psalmist's entry into the Temple or a keen awareness of God's pervasive presence (see Ps 139:1-12)—the psalmist finds that God is always accessible and available (see "right hand" in Pss 73:23; 109:31). In apparent contrast to Psalm 13, in which the psalmist's perception of God's absence led to the fear of being "shaken" (see 13:4), here the psalmist's perception of God's presence provides an unshakable foundation (see Commentary on Pss 13:4; 15:5*c*; see also Psalm 1).

16:9-11. The trust expressed in v. 8 is a source of joy. In v. 9, the psalmist is and does precisely what Ps 14:7 says Israel will be and do when it experiences God's help. The psalmist's whole being is involved—"heart," "soul" (lit., "glory"; see Pss 3:3; 4:2; 7:5: NRSV, "soul"; NIV, "me"), and "body." The word "secure" (בטח *beṭaḥ*) is from a Hebrew root that means "trust." Security for the psalmist is not an achievement but a result of a life entrusted to God (see Pss 4:5; 9:10; Introduction). As vv. 10-11 suggest, God is the guarantor of life and life's constant guide. What vv. 10-11 affirm precisely remains unclear. Perhaps it is the psalmist's profession of faith that death—Sheol or the Pit—will be averted when the prayer for healing is answered in the Temple. Dahood even suggests that vv. 10-11 articulate the psalmist's belief "that he will be granted the same privilege accorded Enoch and Elijah; he is convinced that God will assume him to himself, without suffering the pains of death."[103] While this may be

103. Dahood, *Psalms I (1–50)*, 91.

possible (see also Pss 49:15; 73:24), it is unlikely. Mays suggests a more likely approach for understanding the conclusion of Psalm 16:

> It can be read as the general prayer of the faithful who, without any doctrine of resurrection or eternal life to explain just how, nonetheless trust the LORD to keep them with such total confidence that they cannot imagine a future apart from life in God's presence. The language of the psalm presses toward an unbroken relation between LORD and life.[104]

In the vision of poetic outreach, the psalmist is convinced "that neither death, nor life . . . will be able to separate us from the love of God" (Rom 8:38-39 NRSV; see also Commentary on Psalm 22, esp. v. 27). The psalmist's "pleasant" lot in the present (v. 6) becomes a promise of a presence that yields "pleasures forevermore" (v. 11). The present joy (v. 9) will be complete (v. 11).

104. Mays, *Psalms*, 88.

REFLECTIONS

1. One can detect a sort of progression from Psalm 13 to Psalm 16. Actually, the apparent movement from complaint (Psalm 13) to trust (Psalm 16) is already present within Psalm 13 in the movement from vv. 1-4 to vv. 5-6. In a sense, Psalm 16 is a kind of elaboration upon 13:5-6, articulating more fully the trust and joy and experience of bounty mentioned there. Psalm 16 should not be understood as a better profession of faith than Psalm 13. Rather, just as vv. 1-4 and vv. 5-6 of Psalm 13 should be understood as simultaneous moments (see Commentary on Psalm 13), so also should Psalms 13 and 16 be understood as equally legitimate and simultaneous professions. Indeed, only one who is facing the full force of death's assaults (13:1-4) need pray, "Protect me" (16:1), and is in a position to utter the assurance of v. 10. Thus Psalm 16 articulates the experience of life and joy, not apart from suffering, but in the midst of it. For those who entrust their lives and futures completely to God, suffering and glory are inseparable. To be sure, this was Jesus' experience, but it is also the experience of his followers—from bold first-century martyrs, like Peter and Paul, to courageous twentieth-century martyrs, like Martin Luther King, Jr.

2. While the psalmist probably did not possess a doctrine of resurrection, it is theologically appropriate that 16:8-11 is one of the texts Peter used on the Day of Pentecost to proclaim the resurrection of Jesus (Acts 2:25-28; see also 13:35). Faced with the full force of death's assault, Jesus both complained (Mark 15:34; see Ps 22:1) and petitioned for the removal of the cup of suffering (Mark 14:36); yet, at the same time he completely entrusted his life and future to God (Mark 14:36). Jesus' life, death, and resurrection are testimony to the truth that Psalm 16 already articulates: Suffering and glory are inseparable. Indeed, the author of Hebrews can even speak of Jesus' enduring the cross "for the sake of the joy that was set before him" (Heb 12:2 NRSV).

3. Those who entrust their lives to God experience a depth of stability (v. 8) and joy (v. 9*a*) and security (v. 9*b*) that not even death can undermine. In the contemporary world, where the fear of death often motivates frantic attempts to achieve our own security and joy, frequently through material abundance, Psalm 16 points us in an entirely different direction. Abundant life will not be something we achieve but something we receive. We begin to experience this gift when we say with the psalmist, "You are my Lord" (v. 2). This act of humility promises exaltation. Psalm 16 is thus both a challenge to keep the Lord always before us and a promise that the experience of God's presence is its own reward: abundant life and fullness of joy (see John 10:1-11; 16:16-24; see also Commentary on Psalm 73).

PSALM 17:1-15, BEHOLDING YOUR LIKENESS

COMMENTARY

Psalm 17 is a prayer for help that contains near its beginning a protestation of innocence (vv. 3-5; see Pss 7:3-5; 26:1-7; Introduction) and concludes with a striking expression of trust (v. 15). Structural division of the psalm varies. A focus on form and content units yields the following: opening petition (vv. 1-2), protestation of innocence (vv. 3-5), petition (vv. 6-9), complaint (vv. 10-12), petition (vv. 13-14), affirmation of trust/confidence (v. 15). An eye to poetic symmetry, however, suggests an alternative: opening petition (God and the psalmist) and trust (vv. 1-3), description of the psalmist (vv. 4-6), central petition (vv. 7-9), description of the wicked (vv. 10-12), concluding petition (God and the wicked) and trust (vv. 13-15). Verses 4-6 and 10-12 also display a chiastic arrangement (see Introduction):

A   v. 4 the psalmist's non-violence
  B   v. 5 the psalmist's stability
    C   v. 6 the psalmist's humble speech
      D   vv. 7-9 central petition
    C´   v. 10 the wicked's arrogant speech
  B´   v. 11 the wicked's attempt to destabilize
A´   v. 12 the wicked's violence

The chiasm effectively focuses attention on the central petition (vv. 7-9), including the exact structural center of the psalm (v. 8). Not surprisingly, in terms of poetic symmetry, v. 8 is linked conceptually to the beginning and end of the psalm. The request to be "the apple [lit., "pupil"] of the eye" highlights the function of seeing and calls to mind God's face. The request thus recalls v. 2, which reads literally, "From your *face* let my justification come; let your *eye see* the right." The request also anticipates v. 15, in which the psalmist "will *see* your *face*." Because God sees (vv. 2, 8), the psalmist too will see (v. 15). God and the psalmist stand face to face.

It may be more than coincidental that the conclusion of Psalm 17 locates the psalmist in the very same place that the end of Psalm 16 does. Psalm 16:11*a* reads literally, "Fullness of joy [is] with your *face.*" As in Psalm 16, the sight of God's face in 17:15 yields the experience of fullness: "I shall be satisfied" ("satisfied" [שׂבע *śābaʿ*] is the same Hebrew root as "fullness" in 16:11). Like Psalm 16, Psalm 17 may have originally been set in the Temple, where perhaps the psalmist sought refuge (v. 7; see Ps 16:1) and vindication (v. 2) from enemies who had made false accusations (see Psalms 5; 7; 26; Introduction). The mention of night in 16:7 and 17:3 (see also "awake" in 17:15) suggests the possibility that the original use of these psalms involved the psalmist's spending the night in the Temple. Further links between the two psalms include the mention of God's "right hand" (16:11; 17:7), the identical plea to "keep" (16:1; 17:8), and the affirmation of not being "moved" (16:8; 17:5).

17:1-3. The opening plea already suggests that the psalmist is on the defensive; it reads literally, "Hear a righteousness" (see v. 15; cf. Ps 7:8). The word "cry" (רנה *rinnâ*) usually indicates a joyful exclamation, but here it indicates petition (see Pss 61:2; 88:2; 142:6). The psalmist's description of her or his lips as "free of deceit" suggests both that the psalmist has been falsely accused and that she or he is prepared to face God (see Ps 24:4*c*; see also Pss 10:7; 34:13; 35:20; 36:3). Indeed, it is "from your face" (v. 2) that justice will come for the psalmist. God will see that the psalmist is in the "right," because God judges with "right" (or "equity"; see Pss 9:8; 96:10; 98:9; 99:4). The psalmist is sure that she or he can stand God's most careful examination (v. 3; see Pss 7:9; 11:4-5; 26:2; 66:10). The last line of v. 3 recalls the final line of v. 1.

17:4-6, 10-12. Verse 4 is difficult, and Bratcher and Reyburn point out, "There are almost as many different renditions of these lines as there are commentaries and translations."[105] The Hebrew appears to read literally, "As for the deeds of others, by the word of your lips I have kept the paths of the violent." The NIV supplies the preposition "from" to give the verse the opposite sense, and the NRSV seems to have achieved the same effect with a paraphrase. It is possible to construe the verb in the sense of "observe" rather than "keep," thus mitigating the problem (cf. NIV). Perhaps the best alternative is offered by *Biblica Hebraica Stuttgartensia,* which suggests reading the last portion of v. 3 with v. 4, and the last portion of v. 4 with v. 5. The result is:

> My mouth has not crossed over into the
>   deeds of others,
> The word of your lips, I have kept.
> (On) the violent way, my steps hold fast.
> On your paths, my feet are not moved.
> (vv. 3c-5, author's trans.)

In any case, the intent seems to be to contrast the psalmist and the wicked (see Pss 7:9-11; 11:4-5; 12:1-2, 7-8). The chiastic arrangement of vv. 4-6, 10-12 reinforces the contrast, as do the two first-person pronouns in vv. 4, 6, which emphasize that the psalmist's action and speech are directed to God. While the psalmist lives by God's word (v. 4), the wicked prey on others (v. 12; see Pss 7:2; 10:9; 22:13, 21; 58:6). The wicked seek to bring down the psalmist (v. 11), but the psalmist is not moved (v. 5; see Pss 13:4; 15:5; 16:8). The psalmist directs her or his words to God (v. 6), while the wicked "speak arrogantly" (v. 10). Verse 6*b* returns to the imperative, and the plea "hear" is repeated, recalling v. 1. The psalmist wants God to hear the "words" (v. 6), since they issue from "lips free of deceit" (v. 1) and a "mouth [that] does not transgress" (v. 3).

17:7-9. While vv. 1-6 have dealt almost exclusively with the psalmist, vv. 7-9 specifically introduce the "adversaries"/"foes" (v. 7) and "the wicked" (v. 9), who are the primary subject of vv. 10-14. In the midst of arrogant and violent opponents, the psalmist humbly requests God's "steadfast love" (v. 7; see Pss 5:7; 13:5; Introduction). Aware of personal need, the psalmist looks to God as "savior" (see "deliver"/"deliverance" in Ps 3:2, 7, 8 NIV). Life is entrusted to God's care (see "refuge" in Pss 2:12; 5:11; 7:1; 11:1; 14:6; 16:1; Introduction). The "right hand" of God symbolizes both presence and power. The psalmist stakes her or his life on both (see vv. 13, 15). Craigie points out that v. 7 is reminiscent of Exod 15:11-13, where the words "wonders" (v. 11), "right hand" (v. 12), and "steadfast love" (v. 13) also occur. The psalmist's recollection of the exodus is a source of strength, and he or she envisions a sort of "personal 'exodus.' "[106]

Verse 8 is also reminiscent of God's care for all Israel (see Deut 32:10-11). To be hidden in the shadow of God's wings may originally have had a geographical referent; that is, the wings may be those of the seraphs that were associated with the ark in the Temple. The phrase is associated with "refuge" in Pss 36:7 and 57:1. In Pss 36:7 and 63:7, God's house or sanctuary is the apparent setting for this experience of protection. It is also possible that the imagery of God's wings derives from the observation of a mother bird protecting her young (see Matt 23:37); such feminine imagery for God occurs elsewhere in Psalms (see Psalm 131) and the OT (see Isa 66:13). In any case, the imagery was eventually understood metaphorically.

17:13-15. The word "adversaries"/"foes" in v. 7 is literally "risers"; in v. 13, the psalmist requests God to "rise" (see Pss 3:7; 9:19; 10:12) against the wicked and, literally, "meet their face." The psalmist desires to see God face to face and wants the same experience for the wicked, for the psalmist is confident that God's "eyes see the right" (v. 2). Verse 14 is difficult. The first part may be construed as a continuation of v. 13 that further defines the wicked. In contrast to those whose portion is God (Ps 16:5), the wicked are those who look for security in worldly things and accomplishments. The remainder of v. 14, according to the NRSV, says, in effect, "If that's what they want, let them have it." The tone should be understood as sarcastic (see Num 11:19-20 and Matt 6:2, 16 concerning "reward"). In

---

105. Bratcher and Reyburn, *A Translator's Handbook on the Book of Psalms,* 152.

106. Craigie, *Psalms 1–50,* 163.

contrast to those who can "be filled" (מלא *mālā'*) by stuffing "their bellies," the psalmist will "be satisfied" (*śāba'*, the same word as "have more than enough" in v. 14) only by the higher good of seeing God's face (v. 15; see Pss 11:7; 24:6) and "likeness." In short, the psalmist will be privileged to see God face to face, as Moses did (see Num 12:8, where "form" is the same word as "likeness" [תמונה *tĕmûnâ*] here). This interpretation of v. 14*b* and its relationship to v. 15, however, is by no means certain. The NIV, for instance, construes v. 14*b* in a good sense as an articulation of God's provision for the psalmist and others who seek refuge in God.

REFLECTIONS

The psalmist's certainty of the rightness of his or her cause (vv. 1-2) and the protestation of innocence (vv. 3-5) seem problematic; they may suggest that the psalmist is proud or self-righteous. But as suggested in the Reflections on Psalm 7, the psalmist asserts not sinlessness in general but rightness in a particular case involving false accusation by opponents. In this sense, Psalm 17, like Psalm 7, is reminiscent of the book of Job. If anyone is arrogant in Psalm 17, it is the psalmist's opponents, who have apparently condemned the psalmist and do not hesitate to exact punishment. The psalmist actually displays humble trust in God's steadfast love and willingness to save (v. 7). The protestation of innocence is essentially an expression of the psalmist's willingness to be completely open and honest to God. In sharp contrast to the adversaries, the psalmist professes to live by God's word (v. 4).

We are not told the outcome of the psalmist's appeal for righteousness and justice (vv. 1-2); however, in view of v. 15, this issue becomes irrelevant. The assurance that the psalmist will somehow see God's face and likeness puts the opposition of enemies in a new perspective. The psalmist now knows that nothing will be able to separate her or him from God's protecting love (see v. 8; see also Ps 16:8-11; Rom 8:38-39). We are not told how the psalmist will see God. Israel was prohibited from making any likeness of God (Exod 20:4); yet, there is testimony that people "saw the God of Israel" (Exod 24:10; see Num 12:8; Isa 6:1-8; Pss 11:7; 24:6; 42:2; 63:2). Perhaps this experience involved worshiping in the Temple (see Isa 6:1-8; Psalms 24; 42; 63). Christians profess to see God in worship, and that experience is celebrated in prayer and song (e.g., the communion hymn "Here, O My Lord, I See Thee Face to Face"). There may be other ways that Israel and we see God—in momentous historical events, like the exodus or the dismantling of apartheid in South Africa, or in daily rituals that sustain and nourish, or in the faces of friends and loved ones, or in the faces of strangers, who may be among the least of our sisters and brothers. In any case, the psalmist is convinced of and apparently transformed by the possibility of experiencing unbroken communion with God. The psalmist anticipates the experience that Jesus proclaimed: "Blessed are the pure in heart, for they will see God" (Matt 5:8 NRSV). Christian tradition has interpreted v. 15 as a reference to the resurrection. While the psalmist probably had no doctrine of resurrection, her or his language pushes toward the notion of a communion with God that nothing—not even death—can interrupt (see Commentary on Pss 16:10-11; 22:27; see also Rom 8:38-39). It is thus appropriate that Christians hear in v. 15 an added dimension.

The final two verses of Psalm 17 leave modern believers with the challenge of considering what it is that truly satisfies. Shall we be content with a "portion in life" that consists only of what the world can cram into our greedy stomachs and minds? One of the real dangers of a culture of affluence is the boredom that results from satiation. We have our reward, but it does not truly satisfy. Luxuriance does not constitute life (see Luke 12:15). We hunger for a higher good. Psalm 17 promises a satisfaction that does not fade, for it involves nothing less than seeing God's likeness—unbroken communion with God, whose "eyes see the right" (v. 2). Again, the psalmist antici-pates the experience Jesus proclaimed: "Blessed are those who hunger and thirst for righteousness, for they will be filled" (Matt 5:6 NRSV; see also John 4:13-14; 6:27, 35).

PSALM 18:1-50, STEADFAST LOVE TO THE ANOINTED

COMMENTARY

Psalm 18 is one of the longest and most literarily complex in the psalter. Since David is mentioned in v. 50, and since David recites in 2 Samuel 22 a song that is virtually iden-tical to Psalm 18, scholars have traditionally categorized Psalm 18 as a royal psalm. It rehearses and celebrates God's deliverance of the king from some dire threat; thus, more specifically, it seems to be a royal song of thanksgiving.

Partly because of the link to 2 Samuel 22, and partly because of the nature of its lan-guage and syntax, Psalm 18 is traditionally understood as having originated in David's time and used by him and his descendants, perhaps upon occasions of victorious military battles. While this view may not be ruled out, it is by no means certain. Gerstenberger, for instance, concludes that Psalm 18 originated in the post-exilic era. Using older theophanic (see vv. 7-15) and monarchical traditions, the early Jewish community created "a messianic thanksgiving song" for use in synagogal wor-ship. According to Gerstenberger, the intent of Psalm 18 is: "The psalmist sought to keep hope alive in hard-pressed Jewish communi-ties. As Yahweh had always intervened for Israel—in mighty theophanies, in individual acts of redemption, in special aid to the kings of old—he would thus always take the side of his struggling faithful and lead them toward a bright future."[107]

The disparity between the traditional dat-ing of Psalm 18 and Gerstenberger's date is approximately 500 years! While historical certainty is impossible, Gerstenberger's pro-posed date does greater justice to the message of Psalm 18 in its placement within the psal-ter. The psalter in its final form has an escha-tological orientation; that is, it proclaims the reign of God amid circumstances that sug-gest God does *not* reign (see the Introduc-tion). Even if Psalm 18 originated very early, it would have taken its place in the collected psalter at a time when the monarchy had dis-appeared (see the Introduction; see also Com-mentary on Psalm 144, which appears to be a post-exilic re-reading of Psalm 18). Thus its function, as Gerstenberger suggests, was to keep hope alive by proclaiming God's sover-eignty over the nations. In this regard, Psalm 18 is like Psalm 2; Mays even suggests that "Psalm 18 is a sequel to Psalm 2."[108]

The structure of Psalm 18 is complicated enough that some scholars contend that it should be viewed as two separate psalms, (1) vv. 1-30 and (2) vv. 31-50; however, there is a unifying plot. Out of his distress, the king calls upon God (vv. 1-6), and God comes down to rescue him (vv. 16-19), an action that is introduced as a dramatic theophany (vv. 7-15). The praise that is expected follow-ing the account of deliverance is postponed until vv. 31-50, being preceded by descrip-tions of the king's righteousness (vv. 20-24) and God's faithfulness (vv. 25-30). Thus, in terms of its basic structure and movement, Psalm 18 does have the form of a royal song of thanksgiving for God's deliverance from distress. The fact that it functions eschato-logically is suggested by the observation that each part of the psalm contains universalis-tic, cosmic language and imagery. The king's plight involves "torrents" (v. 4) and "mighty waters" (v. 16), which are reminiscent of the watery chaos that God commands to become an orderly cosmos. God's arrival has cosmic effects—the earth shakes, the heavens part, and there is participation by mountains, clouds, wind, lightning, and hail (vv. 7-15).

107. Gerstenberger, *Psalms: Part 1*, 100.

108. Mays, *Psalms*, 90.

The rescue also has universal proportions; the king becomes "head of the nations" (v. 43) and praises God "among the nations" (v. 49). This hyperbolic description is congruent with those in other royal psalms. In Psalm 2, God is sovereign over peoples and nations (vv. 4, 10-12), and in Psalm 72, the king's righteous rule is to be recognized and reinforced by hills and mountains (v. 3) as well as by kings and "all nations" (vv. 11, 17). These hyperbolic descriptions obviously exceed the reality that any Israelite or Judean king actually experienced. In short, the descriptions affirm Israel's faith in God's rule amid circumstances that seem to deny it. Psalm 18, as the other royal psalms, functions eschatologically.

Even the superscription reinforces the eschatological dimension. There never was really a day when David was delivered from *all* of his enemies. Even 2 Samuel 22, where David sings this song near the end of his career, is followed by further threats to David and to the kingdom. And if the use of David's name in the superscription is meant to allude to the Davidic house (see v. 50), it reinforces even more strongly the eschatological dimension.

18:1-6, Invocation and Distress. The opening "I love you" is unusual, and it is not in 2 Sam 22:2. The text can be emended slightly to read "I exalt you," which seems more fitting here. There follows an impressive series of metaphors in v. 2 indicating effectively that God is the source of the king's life and "strength" (v. 1; see vv. 32, 39, where the Hebrew word [חיל *ḥāyil*] differs from the one here [חזק *ḥēzeq*]). Metaphors for God occur throughout the psalter—"rock" (סלע *selaʿ*, Pss 31:3; 42:9; 71:3), "fortress" (מצודה *mĕṣûdâ*, Pss 31:2-3; 71:3; 91:2; 144:2); "rock" (צור *ṣûr*, see vv. 31, 46; Pss 19:14; 28:1; 31:2; 62:2, 6-7; 73:26 NIV and NRSV, "strength"; 78:35; 89:26; 92:15; 95:1; 144:1; see also Deut 32:4, 18); "refuge" (חסה *ḥāsâ*, Ps 2:12; see the Introduction); "shield" (מגן *māgēn*, Ps 3:4); "stronghold" (משגב *miśgāb*, Ps 9:10). The words "salvation" (v. 2) and "saved" (v. 3) are from the same Hebrew root (ישע *yšʿ*), which is a key word throughout the psalm (see vv. 27, 35, 41, 46). It emphasizes that the king owes his life to God. The repetition of the root underlying "deliver" (פלט *pālaṭ*) has the same effect (see vv. 43, 48).

Whoever or whatever the enemies (v. 3) may be, the threat is urgent. Indeed, the king is already in the clutches of death (vv. 4-5) and Sheol (see Ps 6:5; see also Jonah 2:1-9 for similar language and imagery). Verse 6 repeats the verb "call" from v. 3, and there are also two occurrences of the root that means "cry for help" (v. 6b, 6d; see also Pss 5:3; 22:24; 28:2; 30:2; 31:22; 34:15; 39:12; 72:12; 88:13; 145:19; Exod 2:23; Jonah 2:2). The repetition emphasizes the urgency of the situation, but God has heard. God's "temple" probably indicates God's heavenly abode, but the Jerusalem Temple symbolized the point where heaven touched earth, so it too may be implied here (see Ps 28:1-2).

18:7-19, God's Response. Preceding the actual account of deliverance (vv. 16-19) is an extended account of a theophany (vv. 7-15). God "was angry" (v. 7), because God's chosen agent was being threatened, and so God "came down" (v. 9). The language of theophany is generally expressive of God's presence and power (see Pss 50:2-3; 68:7-8). It occurs elsewhere in contexts that specifically assert God's sovereignty (see Pss 29:3-9; 97:1-5; 99:1; see also Psalm 144, which is reminiscent of Psalm 18 and where the plea for a theophany in vv. 5-8 accompanies in vv. 9-11 an appeal for deliverance and a celebration of the God who "rescues his servant David"). It occurs also in passages that celebrate God's historic deliverance of the people—exodus and entry into the land (cf. Ps 18:7, 15 with Exod 15:8, 10, 14-16 and Judg 5:4-5). The cosmic effects of God's coming down are emphasized by the repetition of "foundations" in vv. 7, 15. The cosmic dimension is also evident in the description of the threat—"mighty waters" (v. 16) and the phrase "confronted me" (v. 18), which recalls v. 5 and the deadly power of Sheol. The cosmic language is a reminder that the one threatened is the king, the earthly representative and sign of God's universal claim. To oppose God's anointed is to oppose God. At issue ultimately is God's sovereignty, and the deliverance of the king asserts God's rule. The deliverance is described in spatial terms (v. 19; see NRSV's "broad place" in Pss 31:8 and 118:5; the verb is used as a figure for deliverance in v. 36 and Ps 4:1; see also Exod 3:8, where an adjectival form of the root describes the promised land as "broad"). The rationale for the deliverance provides a transition to vv. 20-30 (see 1 Kgs 10:9; Pss 22:8; 41:11).

18:20-30, Character of the King and God. Just as the presence of the cosmic dimension in vv. 7-19 is attributable to the psalm's royal subject matter, so also is its presence in vv. 20-30. Verses 20-24 sound like the self-righteous boasting of the king, but the chiastic structure (see Introduction) of vv. 20-24 focuses attention on v. 22. That is, God's "ordinances" (more literally, "justices") and "statutes" are the source of the king's "righteousness" and "cleanness" (vv. 20, 24; see Pss 24:4; 73:1). In short, the king is simply saying that he has been what God has intended and enabled him to be (see Deut 17:18-10; Ps 72:1-7). In fact, v. 22 is reminiscent of Ps 1:1-2; the king is constantly open to God's instruction.

The king's dependence on God is reiterated in vv. 25-30, which are linked to vv. 20-24 by repetition of the words "blameless" (תמים *tāmîm*, vv. 23, 25; "perfect" in v. 30 is also the same Hebrew word) and "cleanness"/"pure" (vv. 20, 24, 26). This section ends by affirming God as "refuge," recalling not only v. 2 but also Ps 2:12. David was known as the "lamp of Israel" (2 Sam 21:17), and here the king says to God, "You light my lamp" (v. 28). The initial pronoun "you" in vv. 27-28 is emphatic, reinforcing God's initiative and the conclusion that the king's righteousness is but a reflection of God's own character. Verses 25-26 suggest even more strongly that the "loyal," "blameless," and "pure" are mirroring God's own character. Blamelessness means essentially completeness or reliability (see Ps 15:2). God's complete reliability (vv. 25, 30) enables the king to be "blameless" (v. 23)—to depend utterly on God (see also Ps 19:13, which clearly suggests that "blamelessness" does not mean sinlessness). Loyalty to or trust in God is well placed, for God is trustworthy and loyal (v. 25*a*). Not coincidentally, these crucial affirmations about God lie "at the psalm's midpoint" and perform the "pivotal function" of proclaiming why God delivers the king—namely, because God is steadfast in love.[109] The verb in "show yourself loyal" (חסד *ḥsd*, v. 25*a*) is the same root as the noun "steadfast love" (*ḥesed*, see v. 50), which more than any other word serves to describe what God is like (see Exod 34:6-7; Pss 5:7; 6:4; 13:5; Introduction). The word "shield" in v. 30, along with the word "refuge," recalls v. 2 and the series of metaphors for God.

18:31-50, The King's Response of Praise. The genre of vv. 31-50 may be a victory hymn, but the function is to articulate the king's praise for deliverance. There are clear lines of continuity with vv. 1-30. As in v. 1, God is the source of the psalmist's strength (vv. 32, 39). This affirmation is reinforced by repetition of the rock metaphor (vv. 2, 31, 46) as well as by the assertion that God "makes my way perfect" (v. 32), which corresponds to v. 30. In short, God protects the life and future of the king. God equips and prepares the king (vv. 33-36), enabling him to defeat his enemies (vv. 37-48). While the king shares in the action (vv. 37-38, 42), his victory is God's victory (vv. 40-41, 43-48, 50). It is evidence of God's sovereignty over peoples (v. 47) and nations (vv. 43, 49; see also Psalm 2), and it is testimony to God's steadfast love (v. 50; see also v. 25; 2 Sam 7:15).

109. J. Kenneth Kuntz, "Psalm 18: A Rhetorical-Critical Analysis," *JSOT* 26 (1983) 19; see also 18.

REFLECTIONS

If Psalm 18 is viewed simply as a royal psalm of thanksgiving used by David or one of his descendants upon the occasion of a military victory, then it must be viewed essentially as a literary artifact—an interesting museum piece, but not something for contemporary handling and use. Taking a clue from Gerstenberger, however, the interpreter may move in a different direction. Gerstenberger's proposal that Psalm 18 was intended "to keep hope alive in hard-pressed Jewish communities" is all the more likely when we consider that, in some post-exilic circles, the promises originally attached to the Davidic monarchy were applied to the whole community (see, e.g., Isa 55:3-5, in which v. 5 even seems to echo Ps 18:43; see also Pss 105:15; 144; Introduction). In essence, then, Psalm 18 was and is a profession of faith in God's will and ability to reverse the fortunes of the humble and the oppressed (see v. 27). The focus is on God, as suggested from the beginning of the psalm with its impressive series of metaphors for God (v. 2). Donald K. Berry says of v. 2, "The effect is to focus acute attention upon Yahweh himself, a feature which flavors the reading of the entire poem."[110] In other words, Psalm 18 is more about God than about David; insofar as it is about David and his descendants, they represent persons who were chosen as agents of *God's* rule. Psalm 18, therefore, is a powerful affirmation of the cosmic, universal reign of God, and it is upon this foundation of faith that hope is built.

In the post-exilic era—indeed, always—the assertion of God's sovereignty is made amid circumstances and powers that deny it (see vv. 4-5). Psalm 18, therefore, like Psalm 2, is eschatological (see Commentary on Psalm 2; Introduction). It is no more evident in our day than it was in the post-exilic era that God rules the world. Yet that is exactly what Jesus preached (Mark 1:14-15) and what the church continues to proclaim as the basis of its hope.

This apparent disparity between what we proclaim and what is reality—evil, sin, violence, destruction—is precisely what calls us to a decision. It is the same decision with which Jesus confronted his hearers. Shall we enter the hidden reign of God, where strength is made perfect in weakness? Shall we trust that "this God" shows us the "way" that "is perfect," and thus is indeed a reliable "refuge" (v. 30)? If we decide to trust the righteous and steadfastly loving God rather than the forces of hatred and greed that are so evidently at work in the world, then we will find that we are in for a fight—like the king in Psalm 18 (vv. 33-42) and like King Jesus. Our fight, however, involves not waging war but waging peace. It will be no less a struggle, and, like the king in Psalm 18, we will need God's strength—indeed, the "whole armor of God" (Eph 6:11, 13; cf. Eph 6:10-17 with Ps 18:33-42; in Eph 6:10-17 as in Psalm 18, the battle has cosmic dimensions). At issue is nothing less than the ultimate question of who rules the world.

The circumstances and faith of the psalmist, as well as the intent of Psalm 18 to keep hope alive, are captured in Jesus' parting words to his disciples: "Peace I leave with you; my peace I give to you. I do not give to you as the world gives. Do not let your hearts be troubled, and do not let them be afraid. . . . I have said this to you, so that in me you may have peace. In the world you face persecution. But take courage; I have conquered the world!" (John 14:27; 16:33 NRSV). Our hope is built on nothing less than the conviction that pervades Psalm 18: God will ultimately fulfill God's steadfastly loving purposes for the world and for all its peoples (Ps 18:43-50; see John 3:16-17).

110. Donald K. Berry, *The Psalms and Their Readers: Interpretive Strategies for Psalm 18*, JSOTSup 153 (Sheffield: JSOT, 1993) 115.

PSALM 19:1-14, GOD'S INSTRUCTION IS ALL-ENCOMPASSING

COMMENTARY

Like Psalms 1 and 119, Psalm 19 highlights the importance of God's *torah,* "instruction" (v. 7, "law"). Despite the fact that Psalm 19 can be understood as an artistic unity, scholars have often divided it into two separate poems: Psalm 19A (vv. 1-6), which deals with creation, and Psalm 19B (vv. 7-14), which deals with *torah*. This approach, however, failed to detect that there are actually three separate sections to the psalm: (1) vv. 1-6, (2) vv. 7-10, (3) vv. 11-14. While vv. 1-6 do focus on creation and vv. 7-10 on *torah,* vv. 11-14 focus on the psalmist, "your servant" (vv. 11, 13), and the words and thoughts the psalmist offers to God (v. 14).

The traditional approach also failed to detect unifying features of the psalm. For instance, "speech" (vv. 2-3) and "words" (v. 14) are the same Hebrew word (אמר *'ōmer),* thus linking vv. 11-14 to vv. 1-6. And "perfect" (v. 7) is the same Hebrew word as "blameless" (v. 13), linking vv. 11-14 to vv. 7-10. On a conceptual level, the theme of the rising and setting of the "sun" unifies the three parts. The sun is explicitly mentioned in v. 4, and language that describes the effects of the sun is applied to *torah* in vv. 7-10 and 11-14—"giving light" (v. 8) and "illuminated" (v. 11; the NIV and the NRSV prefer another sense of the word with their translation "warned"). Nahum M. Sarna even suggests that each of the attributes and actions of *torah* in vv. 7-10 is applied to the sun god in various ancient Near Eastern texts. He proposes that Psalm 19 was composed as "a tacit polemic" in the time of Josiah to oppose the Assyrian-influenced worship of astral deities, including the sun.[111] In any case, to hear Psalm 19 as a unity is to appreciate its bold and sweeping claims about God's *torah,* "instruction." In short, Psalm 19 intends to teach. Its instructional intent may be emphasized by its placement within a series of royal psalms (Psalms 18, 20–21); that is, Psalm 19, especially vv. 7-14, describes the orientation to life that faithful kings were supposed to embody and model for the people (see Pss 18:20-30; 21:7; note especially the repetition of "blameless" in 18:23, 25 and 19:13).[112]

19:1-6. As traditional commentary has recognized, vv. 1-6 focus on creation. The sun was an object of worship in the ancient Near East, and it is likely that an original hymn to the sun lies behind vv. 1-6. But here the sun is not a god. Rather, along with the heavens, the firmament, and day and night

(see Genesis 1), the sun is a created object that testifies to the sovereignty of its creator. The testimony is characterized first as "glory," a word that often appears in contexts that explicitly affirm that God reigns (see Pss 24:7-10; 29:1-3, 9; 145:5, 12). Without actually speaking, the universe itself instructs humanity (see "knowledge," v. 2) about God's rule. No corner of the cosmos is unreached. The "words" of day and night reach "to the end of the world" (the word for "world" here often occurs in contexts that celebrate God's reign; see Pss 93:1; 96:10; 97:4; 98:7, 9), and the course of the sun reaches to "the end of the heavens" (v. 6). The heat of the sun, from which nothing is hidden, suggests the sun's pervasive, energizing, life-giving power.

19:7-10. As suggested above, the movement from vv. 1-6 to v. 7 has caused problems for many commentators, but the transition is really not so abrupt. In vv. 1-6, the created order has proclaimed God's sovereignty, and it is the privilege and responsibility of a sovereign to provide life-sustaining guidance and instruction for the servants (see vv. 11, 13; see also Ps 93:1, 5, where the assertion of God's reign culminates in an assessment of God's decrees that is similar to Ps 19:7*b*). This *torah,* "instruction," is the focus of vv. 7-10. Verse 7*a* would be translated better as: "The instruction of the LORD is all-encompassing, restoring life." As vv. 4*b*-6 describe the all-encompassing circuit of the sun, so v. 7*a* asserts that God's *torah* is all-encompassing. Because "nothing is hidden from its heat" (v. 6*b*), the sun constantly energizes the earth and makes life possible. So it is, the psalmist claims, with God's *torah*; it makes life possible. In short, when vv. 7-10 are heard following vv. 1-6, they present *torah* on a cosmic scale. God's instruction is built into the very structure of the universe, and life depends on *torah* as much as it depends on the daily rising of the sun.

Following the mention of *torah* in v. 7*a* are five more words that describe God's revelation, each of which is accompanied by a phrase that either indicates the effect of God's word on humanity (vv. 7*b*-8) or further elaborates the nature of God's word (v. 9). God's *torah* accomplishes what God intends for human life: wisdom (see Deut 4:6; Ps 2:10), joy (see Ps 4:8), enlightenment (see Ps

111. Nahum M. Sarna, *Songs of the Heart* (New York: Schocken, 1993) 74.

112. See Leslie C. Allen, "David as Exemplar of Spirituality: The Redactional Function of Psalm 19," *Biblica* 67 (1986) 544-46.

36:9). The "fear of the LORD" in v. 9a actually describes not God's revelation but the human response of conformity to God's word. Living by God's word makes one pure. The word for "pure" (טהורה *ṭĕhôrâ*) elsewhere indicates ritual cleanness, which could be conditional and temporary (see Lev 7:19; 13:13, 17, 37; 15:8). Living by *torah,* however, constitutes a cleanness that endures. The word "ordinances" (משפטים *mišpāṭîm*) in v. 9b is literally "judgments"/"justices"; the Hebrew root is often paired with the word "righteous," as here (see also Amos 5:24). In short, living by *torah* constitutes righteousness—life as God intends it. Neither wealth nor the richest food can make life possible the way that God's instruction does (v. 10), because God's *torah* makes accessible to humanity the "speech" and "knowledge" of the cosmos. It is revealing that the personal name for God, Yahweh ("LORD"), occurs six times in vv. 7-9, whereas it does not occur at all in vv. 1-6. What makes life possible is relatedness to God, and this personal relatedness is mediated by *torah.* The creation speaks (vv. 1-6), but more important, God has spoken a personal word to humanity that enables the human creature to live in harmony with God and with the whole creation (vv. 7-10).

Indeed, this is the "great reward" of v. 11. The phrase would be better translated "great consequence" in order to avoid the implication that God's *torah* represents a mechanistic system of reward and punishment for obedience and disobedience. God's *torah* does not consist of a static body of revelation but a dynamic, living relationship. The great consequence of keeping God's *torah* is fundamentally the same thing that Ps 1:3 means when it says that those who meditate constantly on God's *torah* "prosper." The prosperity or reward consists of connection to the true source of life: God (see Commentary on Psalm 1).

19:11-14. That the psalmist means by *torah* something other than a static system of reward/punishment is further indicated by vv. 12-14. In the final analysis, even God's personal instruction to humanity is not sufficient to ensure that human behavior will be in harmony with God and God's ordering of the world. Verse 12 indicates that inevitably there will be "errors" and "hidden faults." Verses 12b-13b are essentially a petition for forgiveness, and v. 13c suggests that the psalmist will be "blameless" (see "perfect" in v. 7a; see also Pss 15:2; 18:23, 25, 30, 32) and "innocent" (the word is from the same root [נקה *nqh*] as "forgive" in v. 12b) as a result of God's grace. To be "blameless" is not to be sinless but to live in dependence upon God (see Commentary on Psalms 15; 18). This dependence upon God for forgiveness and for life itself is what makes one's words and thoughts "acceptable" to God (v. 14). By the grace of God, the psalmist's words are in harmony with the "speech" (vv. 2-3) of the cosmos. In other contexts, "acceptable" designates a worthy sacrifice (see Exod 28:38; Lev 22:19-20). Thus Ps 19:14 suggests that the kind of sacrifice God ultimately desires consists of human lives that are lived in humble dependence upon God (see Pss 50:22-23; 51:15-17; Rom 12:1-2).

The psalmist's address of God as "my rock" reinforces this conclusion; the psalmist's strength is from God (see Ps 18:2, 31, 46). The address of God as "my redeemer" suggests that this strength is experienced very personally. The term derives from the realm of family relationships, where it was the responsibility of family members to buy back, or "redeem," relatives who had fallen into slavery (see Lev 25:47-49). Thus "redeemer" connotes intimacy; the NRSV sometimes translates גאל (*gōʾēl*) as "next of kin" (see Ruth 4:1, 3). Considering the way Psalm 19 begins, the implications of this address are astounding: The God who set the sun on its course is the same God the psalmist has experienced personally as "my next of kin"!

REFLECTIONS

C. S. Lewis considered Psalm 19 to be "the greatest poem in the Psalter and one of the greatest lyrics in the world."[113] As remarkable as the lyrical quality of Psalm 19,

113. C. S. Lewis, *Reflections on the Psalms* (New York: Harcourt, Brace, and Company, 1986) 63.

however, is its extraordinary theological claim. In essence, Psalm 19 affirms that love *is* the basic reality. According to the psalmist, the God whose sovereignty is proclaimed by cosmic voices is the God who has addressed a personal word to humankind—God's *torah.* Furthermore, this God is experienced ultimately by humankind not as a cosmic enforcer but as a forgiving next of kin! God is love, and love is the force that drives the cosmos. This is, indeed, an extraordinary thought!

This extraordinary thought has radical implications for a scientifically oriented, secular culture. Psalm 19 is not anti-science, but it does offer a view of the universe as something more than an object to be studied and controlled. To be sure, nature is not divine, but it is incomprehensible apart from God. In some sense, nature "knows" God (v. 2), and thus it can proclaim God's sovereignty. In short, like the human who addresses God as "next of kin" (see v. 14), the creation is related to God. On some level, we are *all* part of the same family. The Hebrew language itself recognizes the family resemblance—the word for "humanity" is אדם (*'ādām*), and the word for "earth"/"ground" is אדמה (*'ădāmâ*). The ecological implications of this view of the world are astounding. In God's ordering of the cosmos, the future of the creature is linked inextricably to the future of the creation.

None of this implies that Psalm 19 offers simply a natural theology. The creation does offer knowledge (v. 2), but God has also addressed a personal word to humanity: God's *torah,* which makes human life possible (v. 7*a*) and orders it rightly (v. 9*b*). Again, the implications are radical. Human life can be adequately understood only in relationship to God. This is the antithesis of secularity and its creed of autonomy (see Commentary on Psalm 1). According to the psalmist, humans live not by our ability to earn, achieve, or possess (see v. 10, which suggests the insufficiency of money and the finest food), but by "every word that comes from the mouth of God" (Matt 4:4 NRSV; see Deut 8:3).

The juxtaposition of creation and *torah,* then, is theologically significant. Not surprisingly, the same juxtaposition characterizes the Pentateuch, where the story of creation (the book of Genesis) precedes the story of redemption from bondage and revelation at Sinai (the book of Exodus). What this movement suggests is that creation is not secondary. God's instruction to humanity works toward the fulfillment of God's creational purposes (see Commentary on Psalms 33; 65–66). The love that motivated God to create humankind and bear the burden of human disobedience (Genesis 1–11) is the same love manifested in the story of Israel (see esp. Exodus 32–34), in the life of the psalmist (vv. 11-14), and, as Christians profess, in the life, death, and resurrection of Jesus. Love is the basic reality of the universe.

PSALM 20:1-9, WE TRUST IN THE NAME OF THE LORD OUR GOD

COMMENTARY

Psalm 20 is almost unanimously classified as a royal psalm, due to the mention of the "anointed" (v. 6) and "the king" (v. 9). The uniqueness of the psalm lies in the fact that only v. 9 is an actual prayer. This peculiarity raises the question of its origin and setting. Several features point to a liturgical ceremony in the Temple: the mention of "sanctuary" and Zion in v. 2 and sacrifices in v. 3, as well as the public character of the psalm and the king's need to pray for help (vv. 1, 4-5). The traditional conclusion is that Psalm 20 was performed originally in the Temple as a king prepared to go into battle. The king was there to pray for help (see 1 Sam 7:7-11; 13:9-12; 1 Kgs 8:44-45), and the people wished him well in the name of God (vv. 1-5), professed their faith in God's help for king and nation (vv. 6-8), and prayed directly for the king and themselves (v. 9).

This proposal may well account for the original use of Psalm 20; however, it may also be insufficient for understanding how the psalm was finally heard and how it functions in the psalter as a literary collection. As suggested about Psalm 18, another royal psalm that has to do with the king in battle (see esp. vv. 31-50), the psalm is really more about God than it is about the king. The same is true about Psalm 20. While the king is not unimportant, the primary actor in the psalm is God. The post-exilic and subsequent generations of God's people would have preserved and transmitted the psalm not so much as a historical recollection of a long-lost monarchy but as testimony to God's continuing ability to save the people. This is especially likely when one considers that the promises attached to the monarchy seem to have been applied to the people as a whole (see Psalms 18; 144; 149; Isa 55:3-5; Introduction).

The three key words in Psalm 20 emphasize the role of God. The word "answer" (עֲנָה *ʿānâ*) occurs three times, including the first and last verses (vv. 1, 6, 9). God must answer if there is going to be "help"/"victory"/"victories" (יֵשַׁע *yšʿ*). This word occurs four times (vv. 5, 6, 9; see NIV, "save," "saving power"). Psalm 20 illustrates the affirmation of the concluding verse of Psalm 3: "From the LORD comes deliverance" (Ps 3:8; the Hebrew root is again *yšʿ*). The threefold occurrence of "name" (vv. 1, 5, 7) also emphasizes God's primacy. The "name" of God not only is synonymous with God's presence and power, but also suggests the importance of identity and character. It is to God's character that the people appeal, and God's character will assure the future of king and people.

20:1-5. The wishes expressed in vv. 1-5 are for the protection and welfare of the king, but the subject of each verb is God (with the exception of v. 5*a*). In the light of the mention of the "God of Jacob" in v. 1*b*, it is perhaps not surprising that v. 1*a* recalls Jacob's words in Gen 35:3 (see "answer" also in Pss 3:4; 4:1). As here, God's protection is associated with God's name in Ps 91:14. Verses 1-2 are reminiscent of Ps 18:6, where help for the king also comes from God's dwelling in a time of distress. As suggested above, vv. 3-5 seem to indicate an original liturgical setting. Sacrifices regularly accompanied prayers for help, and help is precisely what the king needs (vv. 4, 5*b*). As reflected in vv. 4, 5*b*, it was the prerogative of the king to make requests of God (see Commentary on Ps 2:8-9; see also 1 Kgs 3:5-14; Ps 21:4). Verse 5*a* indicates that the welfare and future of the people are bound up with that of the king.

20:6-8. The same reality is evident in these verses. Help from God for the "anointed" (v. 6; see Pss 2:2; 18:50; 28:8; 89:38, 51; 132:10, 17) accompanies the deliverance of the people. In contrast to those who "trust" in the instruments of warfare, the people of God trust God (v. 7; see Ps 33:16-17). The verb that the NIV translates as "trust" (זכר *zākar*) more literally means "to cause to remember." Thus persons who cause God's name to be remembered will live (v. 8). Memory leads to hope.

20:9. Verse 9 can be construed in several ways, as the NRSV note suggests. Both the NRSV and the NIV have chosen to follow the LXX, which seems to make more sense than the Hebrew. As these translations construe v. 9, it is a prayer for both king and people. This is particularly appropriate in the light of vv. 6-8, and it also made and makes the psalm more appropriate for the generations of God's people that came after the disappearance of the monarchy.

REFLECTIONS

1. On one level, it is possible to hear Psalm 20 as nothing more than a piece of ancient Judean political propaganda—that is, God is on our side, and God will give us the victory. It seems to be an ancient example of the kind of thinking that is so dangerous and frightening in our day, thinking that leads people to conclude that God sanctions whatever our nation does and to label our opponents as evil empires.

On the other hand, it is possible to hear Psalm 20 quite differently, building upon the insight that the primary actor in the psalm is God, not the king or the people. Keeping this in mind, we can hear in Psalm 20 the lesson that the people of any nation in some sense depend on their leaders, as well as the admonition that both the people and their leaders are to depend on God. Mays concludes:

> As Scripture the psalm teaches the church to pray for those who hold the power of office, because they, like us, are dependent on the Lord. It warns against ever letting our dependence on their service turn into the trust we owe to God alone. It warns against allowing their fascination with military strength to make us support policies based on trust in military might.[114]

In other words, Psalm 20 is actually anti-militaristic. It exhorts us to submit our will to God's will rather than pretend that our will is God's will. It is another invitation to live under God's reign (see Introduction): "Thy kingdom come, thy will be done."

2. The Christian tradition has often read Psalm 20 christologically, especially on the basis of v. 6. If this approach is followed, one should not hear v. 6 as a prediction of Jesus' coming. Rather, Christians may see in Jesus the "anointed one" (*messiah*) who really did submit himself fully to God's will (see Mark 14:36), who did not resort to violence on account of his complete trust in God, and who gathered around himself a community of people who also professed to find life as "we trust in the name of the LORD our God" (v. 7).

114. Mays, *Psalms,* 103.

PSALM 21:1-13, THE KING TRUSTS IN THE LORD

COMMENTARY

Like Psalm 20, to which it is closely linked, Psalm 21 is a royal psalm. Verses 1-6 are a thankful celebration of the fulfillment of the wishes expressed for the king in Ps 20:1-5 (cf. 20:4 and 21:2) and of the arrival of the anticipated "victory"/"help" from God in Ps 20:5-9 (see the Hebrew root for "help"/"victories" [יֵשַׁע *yš*] in 20:5, 6, 9; 21:1, 5).

Verse 7 is the structural center of the psalm and also its theological heart. This verse makes it clear that Psalm 21, like other royal psalms (see 2; 18; 20; Introduction), is really more about God than about the king. The king lives in dependence upon God and God's loving purposes, as vv. 1-6 have already described. As the midpoint of the psalm, v. 7 is transitional. Whereas vv. 1-6 addressed God directly, vv. 8-12 address the king (although there is some ambiguity here), anticipating

future victories. Verse 13 again focuses attention directly on God and on God's "strength," recalling the mention of God's "strength" in v. 1 and forming an envelope structure. In other words, everything that can be said about the king begins and ends with God's strength.

Like Psalm 20, Psalm 21 may have been used originally in a military context, either upon the king's departure for or return from battle. Several scholars suggest that it may have been used as a coronation ritual (see v. 3; Psalm 2) or as a liturgy for the anniversary of a king's coronation. In any case, it is clear that the psalm must have functioned differently in the post-exilic era and that it functions differently in its current literary setting. Gerstenberger concludes: "As a possible synagogal prayer—which it became in any case, earlier or later—it would have implored the protection and help of Yahweh for the local congregation, which still existed in the traditions of the past."[115] Because the real subject of Psalm 21 is God's sovereignty, the psalm can continue to serve for every generation of God's people as an affirmation of trust in God and in God's commitment to the people and their future (see esp. v. 7).

21:1-6. The focus on God's sovereignty is evident in v. 1. God's strength is elsewhere explicitly associated with God's reign (Pss 29:1; 93:1; 96:6-7; 99:4; see also Exod 15:13, 18). God's "strength" and "help" are determinative, not the king's. As suggested above, vv. 1-2 recall Psalm 20. Verse 1 repeats the key word "help" (ישועה *yĕšûʿâ*; see Ps 20:5, 6, 9), and v. 2 asserts that the wish of 20:4 has been answered. In fact, every good thing the king enjoys has come from God—the king's office (v. 3*b*; see Ps 2:6-7) and the eminence associated with royalty (v. 5), abundant daily provision (see "blessings" in vv. 3, 7; see also Pss 45:2; 72:15), indeed, life itself (v. 4; see 1 Kgs 3:11). The gift of life and the attendant blessings are to endure "forever" (vv. 4, 6; see Ps 72:17). Such language should probably be understood as poetic hyperbole rather than an indication of the king's divinity, although some ancient Near Eastern cultures did view the king as divine. Although different Hebrew words are used, the concept of joy (vv. 1, 6) envelopes the first section. Again, the source is God's character and activity—indeed, God's very "presence" (v. 6; lit., "your face").

21:7. Considering the list of benefits the king has experienced from God (vv. 1-6), it appears that the king's trust in God is well-founded. In any case, it is significant that the king is to relate to God just as any faithful Israelite should: by trusting God (see Pss 4:5; 9:10; 22:4-5; 31:6; 32:10; see also

2 Kgs 18:5) and by depending on God's steadfast love (see Pss 5:7; 31:7, 16, 21; 32:10; Introduction; note that "trust" and "steadfast love" are associated in Pss 31:6-7; 32:10; see also 2 Sam 7:15; 1 Kgs 3:6). Like other psalmists, the king "shall not be moved" (see Pss 15:5; 16:8; 62:2, 6; note the occurrence of "trust" in 62:8 and "steadfast love" in 62:12). The reason why is God.

21:8-12. Most commentators understand vv. 8-12 as being addressed to the king. Several commentators, however, construe the addressee as God. The ambiguity is theologically appropriate. The king's victories, described in vv. 8-12, are God's doing, as v. 9*b* makes explicit. In any case, whereas God's blessing (that is, daily provision) of the king is elaborated in vv. 1-6, God's saving help (vv. 1, 5) is described in detail in vv. 8-12. Verse 10 seems particularly brutal, but such rhetoric was standard ancient Near Eastern fare for communicating victory (see 2 Kgs 8:12; Ps 137:8-9; Isa 13:16; Hos 10:14; 13:16; Nah 3:10). Other descriptions in the royal psalms of the king's relationship to the nations are more uplifting (see, e.g., Ps 72:17*b*).

21:13. This verse clearly addresses God directly. The imperative "Be exalted" may have been intended as an ascription of praise, as v. 13*b* seems to suggest (see Pss 46:11; 99:2). Given the military context of vv. 8-12, it could be understood as a request for God to arise—namely, in preparation for battle, as in the holy war traditions. Strength is exerted elsewhere by God against enemies (see Exod 15:13; Pss 66:3; 68:28; 77:15), and "power" occurs often in military contexts (see Ps 20:6). In either case, by referring again to God's strength (see v. 1), v. 13 reinforces the conclusion that both the king and the people depend for their lives and futures on the presence and power of God, which is experienced as steadfast love.

115. Gerstenberger, *Psalms: Part 1*, 108.

REFLECTIONS

As was the case with Psalm 20, it is possible to see in Psalm 21 a literary artifact of the monarchical period; however, it can be more. Like Psalms 2; 18; 20 and other royal psalms, Psalm 21 is ultimately testimony to God's sovereignty, not the king's sovereignty. Corresponding to Psalm 20, in which the people profess, "We trust in the name of the LORD our God" (v. 7), is the assertion in Psalm 21 that "the king trusts in the LORD" (the Hebrew words translated "trust" differ; see Commentary on Ps 20:7).

In essence, the king is portrayed in Psalm 21 as the model of faith, one who lives not in dependence upon self but in dependence upon God. The king thus demonstrates what Psalm 1 means by happiness and prosperity (see vv. 1, 3) and what Psalm 2 means by taking refuge in God (see v. 12). The king may be surrounded by foes (21:8-12), but he knows that there is "help . . . in God" (Ps 3:2; see "deliver"/"deliverance" in 3:7-8; cf. 21:1, 5).

While the king is presented here as the model of faith (see Deut 17:14-20), and while a few kings actually embodied this model (see 2 Kgs 18:5-7), the monarchy for the most part modeled self-assertion and self-reliance. Even Solomon, who asked God for understanding and discernment (1 Kgs 3:3-14) rather than for more material things (cf. 1 Kgs 3:11 with Ps 21:2-6), could not manage finally to control his desire for riches, power, and fame (see 1 Kgs 5:13-14; 6:38–7:1; 11:1-13). King Ahaz, invited by the prophet Isaiah to trust God's ability to deliver, appealed instead to Assyrian military might for security (Isa 7:1-17). Even Hezekiah, who is commended for his trust in 2 Kgs 18:5, lapsed in his later years (Isaiah 39). In actuality, the king often did not trust God; neither did the people, and neither do we.

It would fall to Jesus to model authentic kingship and authentic humanity. The ancient kings were known as sons of God (see Ps 2:7) and were viewed in some sense as sharing God's sovereignty and even God's attributes (see Ps 21:5). Christians profess Jesus Messiah as Son of God, sharing God's sovereignty and attributes to the point of being fully divine as well as fully human. King Jesus "did not regard equality with God as something to be exploited, but emptied himself, taking the form of a slave" (Phil 2:6-7 NRSV). Jesus "humbled himself" (Phil 2:8) in the way that kings, living in dependence upon God, were supposed to do (Ps 21:7). He served as kings were supposed to do (see Psalm 72), and he called his followers to do the same (Mark 8:34-35). The basics of faithfulness are present in Psalms 20–21: trusting God and living in dependence on God's steadfast love (20:7; 21:7)—even if leaders and people, then and now, fail to measure up.

PSALM 22:1-31, MY GOD, MY GOD, WHY HAVE YOU FORSAKEN ME?

COMMENTARY

The haunting words that open Psalm 22 anticipate the alternation of complaint and trust/praise that characterizes the psalm. The psalmist complains of being forsaken, yet still addresses God as "my God." To be sure, the presence of both complaint and trust/praise is typical of the prayers for help, as is the element of petition. In a sense, then, Psalm 22 is a typical prayer for help; however, commentators have long suggested that Psalm 22 is unique. Of course, one may suspect that Psalm 22 is singled out because v. 1a is quoted by Jesus from the cross (Matt 27:46; Mark 15:34) and because Psalm 22 figures prominently in the passion story (see the use of v. 7 in Matt 27:34 and Mark 15:29; v. 8 in Matt 27:43; v. 15 in John 19:28; v. 18 in Matt 27:35; Mark 15:24; Luke 23:34; John 15:24).

But there is more to this psalm's uniqueness than that. There is an intensity and inclusiveness that sets Psalm 22 apart. While recognizing that it is composed of the typical elements, Mays suggests that this psalm represents "a development of the type that raises it to its very limits and begins to transcend them."[116] For instance, the complaint is extended, consisting of two major parts

116. James L. Mays, "Prayer and Christology: Psalm 22 as a Perspective on the Passion," *TToday* 42 (1985) 322.

(vv. 1-11, 12-21), which in turn consist of two parts (vv. 1-5, 6-11 and vv. 12-15, 16-21). The praise section of the psalm (vv. 22-31) is also extended. It consists of two parts (vv. 22-26, 27-31), the second of which draws everyone—living and dead alike—into the sphere of God's reign. This elaborate construction and elevated conceptuality led Ellen F. Davis to speak of the "balanced extravagances of the lament and the vow or call to praise." Davis noted that it is the "poet's extravagance of expression" and the "exuberance of the poetic vision that explodes the limits" both of the typical form and of "Israel's traditional understandings" of God, of the world, of life, and of death.[117] In short, the expansiveness—indeed, explosiveness—of Psalm 22 makes it unique and made it particularly suitable for use in recounting the revolutionary story of Jesus' suffering and death. Psalm 22 is not unique because it is used in the NT; rather, it is used in the NT because it is unique.

22:1-11. These verses consist of two complaints (vv. 1-2, 6-8), each of which is followed by an expression of trust that looks back to a better time, either in the life of the whole people (vv. 3-5) or in the psalmist's own life (vv. 9-10). A petition closes the unit (v. 11). The poignant alternation of complaint and trust serves only to make the psalmist's current distress seem all the more bitter. Actually, the effect is already achieved in the opening line. The particular form of the address, "my God," is rare and seems to represent an especially intimate form of address based on close personal attachment (see also v. 10; Exod 15:2; Pss 63:1; 68:14; 89:26; 102:24; 118:28; 140:6; Isa 44:17). If this is indeed the case, the subsequent question is all the more urgent: Why? Why has God "forsaken" God's own? The verb means more literally "to leave" (עזב *'āzab*). God, who had been experienced personally and closely, is now "far" (v. 2). The word "far" (רחוק *rāḥôq*) recurs in the two petitions as the psalmist asks for a reversal (vv. 11, 19).

The memorable v. 3 is difficult to translate; the NIV and the NRSV give two major options. In either case, v. 3 asserts God's sovereignty (see vv. 27-31) and suggests that in the past God had given Israel reason to

117. Ellen F. Davis, "Exploding the Limits: Form and Function in Psalm 22," *JSOT* 53 (1992) 97, 103.

praise: the deliverance and salvation mentioned in vv. 4-5. The verb "trusted" (בטה *bāṭaḥ*) occurs three times in vv. 4-5 (see Pss 4:5; 9:10; 21:7; Introduction). The ancestors trusted and were delivered when "they cried," which is supposed to be the case (see Ps 9:10). The psalmist has also cried to God (v. 2; the Hebrew words differ in vv. 2, 5), and vv. 1-2 imply that the psalmist has also trusted God (see v. 10 NIV), but finds no help. Thus the affirmation of trust in vv. 3-5 actually communicates the psalmist's despair. It may be coincidental, but three key words from Psalms 20–21 recur in vv. 1-5: "helping" (עשׁי *yš'*, v. 1; see Pss 20:5-6, 9; 21:1, 5), "answer" (ענה *'ānâ*, v. 2; see Ps 20:1, 6, 9), and "trust" (*bāṭaḥ*, vv. 4-5; see Ps 21:7). In Psalms 20–21, there is the certainty that the sovereign God will answer and help the king, who lives by his trust in God. Thus the canonical sequence emphasizes the sharp contrast; there is no help and no answer for the psalmist.

Complaint resumes in vv. 6-8. While the deliverance experienced by earlier generations led them to enthrone God on their praises (v. 3), the psalmist's experience is utterly dehumanizing (see "worm" in Job 25:6; Isa 41:14). Apparent rejection by God leads to the psalmist's being "scorned by others" as well (see Pss 31:11; 69:7; 69:19-20; Psalms 31 and 69 also figure prominently in the story of Jesus' passion). Their words are biting and cruel. The word "deliver" in v. 8 recalls "delivered" in v. 4, thus reminding the psalmist of past glories that contrast with current pain. The words of the mockers imply that the psalmist must have been mistaken about the closeness of his or her relationship with God (cf. v. 8 with Ps 18:20).

The mocking words move the psalmist to recall not just the past of the whole people but his or her own past with God (vv. 9-10). The "you" in v. 9*a* is emphatic—"it was *you.*" The same Hebrew pronoun concludes v. 10, thus reinforcing literarily the closeness to God that the psalmist claimed with the address "my God," which is repeated in v. 10—namely, his or her life from the beginning was surrounded by "you," God. The psalmist was not mistaken; he or she and God go way back together. The NIV translation of v. 9*b* is more literal: "you made me trust." Thus v. 9 recalls

vv. 4-5. Like the ancestors, the psalmist has trusted God, but apparently to no avail. God is now "far" (see v. 1); only "trouble is near."

22:12-21. The imagery shifts in vv. 12-21 to provide a terrifying description of the trouble. Like vv. 1-11, this section is composed of two complaints (vv. 12-15, 16-18), each with two elements, followed by a petition (vv. 19-21). The first element in each case employs animal imagery (vv. 12-13, 16*ab*). In both cases, the psalmist is surrounded (vv. 12, 16; see NIV), by either bulls (see Deut 32:14; Amos 4:1) or dogs. The animal imagery is apparently used to represent powerful and rapacious people (see Pss 7:2; 10:9; 27:2; 68:30; Isa 10:13; Jer 4:7; 5:6). In some ancient Near Eastern texts, however, animals are used to represent demonic forces; this dimension of the metaphor should be considered here as well. In other words, the powers of evil are unleashed against the psalmist so as to make it appear that the only possible consequence is death.

This leads to the second element of each complaint: descriptions employing anatomical terms to indicate the nearness of death (vv. 14-15, 16*c*-18). The first bodily part mentioned in vv. 14-15 and the last in vv. 16*c*-18 is "bones," but also involved are the heart, breast, mouth, tongue, jaws, hands, and feet. The text is unclear at v. 16*c* (the NIV retains the more familiar reading; see the NIV's note); more generally, the precise nature of the affliction remains unclear. What the imagery does clearly communicate is that the psalmist is as good as dead. Indeed, he or she says to God that "you lay me in the dust of death" (v. 15), while the enemies also assume that death is imminent and so begin to appropriate the psalmist's possessions (v. 18).

Like the first larger complaint (vv. 1-11), the second ends with petition (vv. 19-21), which features animal characters from the previous complaints and is linked to the previous petition by the repetition of "far" and "help" (v. 19; see v. 11). The recurrence of the animal imagery indicates that the psalmist's plight continues, but something is changing. Whereas the psalmist had concluded that there was no one to help (v. 11), here the psalmist addresses God as "my help" or "my strength" (v. 19). This is the first clue that vv. 19-21 are transitional. Further

evidence is provided by the three verbs in vv. 20-21: "deliver," "save" (NIV, "rescue") and "answer" (NRSV, "rescued"; NIV, "save"). Each of these verbs occurs in vv. 1-11 with a negative sense. The taunts of the enemy imply that God cannot deliver (v. 8; NRSV, "rescue" [נצל *nṣl*]). The psalmist complains that God is "so far from saving me" (v. 1; or "helping") and that God does "not answer" (v. 2). But the addressing of God as "my help," as well as the continuing plea for God to deliver and to save, indicates a remarkable depth of faith in an apparently hopeless, deathful situation.

The final line of vv. 19-21 is particularly important, and it completes the transition as it moves beyond petition to affirmation. A comparison of the NIV with the NRSV reveals that v. 21*b* can be translated variously (see the RSV and the NAB for another frequent reading that is based on the LXX, Syriac, and the work of Jerome). The Hebrew text, however, is readable and should be translated literally here: "from the horns of the wild oxen you have answered me." In short, the opening complaint has been reversed (see "answer" in v. 2). God has answered! The answer comes, not beyond the suffering, however, but precisely in the midst of and even from the suffering! God is somehow present in the depths and even amid death (v. 15; see vv. 17-18).

22:22-31. As suggested above, the extravagant affirmation of v. 21*b* prepares for the praise section of Psalm 22; the NRSV even includes v. 21*b* with vv. 22-26. It is characteristic of the prayers for help that they end with either praise or expressions of trust (see Commentary on Psalm 13, esp. vv. 5-6; Introduction). Even so, the exuberance and extent of the praise here are surprising. Earlier in the psalm, the memory of the whole community had only increased the psalmist's despair (vv. 3-5), but here the psalmist becomes a witness to the congregation (v. 22). The psalmist's invitation for others to "glorify" God (v. 23) indicates renewed recognition of God's sovereignty (see Isa 24:15 and 25:3, where glorifying God occurs in the context of the affirmation of God's reign in 24:23; see also Isa 43:20; 23 in the context of 43:15).

The congregation is also invited to join the psalmist in praising God (vv. 22-23). Indeed, the Hebrew root for "praise" occurs in every verse of vv. 22-26 except the middle verse (v.

24), which gives the reason for praise: God "did not despise or abhor the affliction of the afflicted." This reason sounds quite unbelievable in view of vv. 1-21, but something has changed! The affliction is still very real, but the affliction itself has somehow become an answer (v. 21 b). What the psalmist now affirms is that God is present with the afflicted (see also Pss 9:12; 34:6; 35:10; 40:17; 140:12, where God is with or for the afflicted; the Hebrew word here translated "afflicted" [עָנִי ʿānî] occurs elsewhere in the NRSV as "weak," "poor [soul]," "needy"). The praise the psalmist offers (v. 22) and invites the congregation to offer (v. 23) comes out of the depths in the midst of suffering. The four occurrences of hll in vv. 22-26 recall v. 3, "enthroned on the praises of Israel" and removes the bitterness of that phrase. Now the psalmist also enthrones God on praise, but for God still to be enthroned on Israel's praises in vv. 22-26 must mean that God is "enthroned" or "dwells" (the Hebrew word [יָשַׁב yāšab] can mean either one) in the depths. In short, God is positioned among the afflicted. God is not hiding God's face, and God can hear the psalmist's cry (v. 24; see v. 2), because God is present. God does not despise the suffering of the afflicted. God shares it! The forsakenness of the psalmist (v. 1) is the forsakenness of God. If God is the source of the psalmist's death (v. 15), God is also the source of the psalmist's praise (v. 25a). To praise God is to live, and so v. 26b forms an appropriate conclusion to the first unit of the praise section: "May your hearts live forever!" In the face of the traditional Israelite understanding that death constantly encroaches upon life, the psalmist affirms that life encroaches upon death! Traditional boundaries are transcended.

The payment of vows is a typical element of the prayers for help and songs of thanksgiving (v. 25; see Pss 56:12; 61:8; 65:1; 66:13; 116:14, 18), and such payment apparently involved a thank offering and the sharing of a sacrificial meal. The participants, those who "fear" God (vv. 23, 25), are the "poor" (v. 26), a word that derives from the same root as "afflicted" in v. 24. They "shall eat and be satisfied" (v. 26). In short, the afflicted psalmist, having been assured of God's presence in his or her affliction, becomes a source of life for other sufferers. Life defies death.

Traditional boundaries and borders are obliterated even more completely in vv. 27-31. The testimony and praise offered by and on behalf of the afflicted in vv. 22-26 have universal effects. "All the ends of the earth" and "all the families of the nations" will recognize God's reign (vv. 27-28; the word translated here as "dominion" [מְלוּכָה mĕlûkâ] occurs in Pss 103:19; 145:11-13 ["kingdom"]; it derives from the Hebrew root for "to reign" [מלך mālak]). Ethnic and national boundaries are superseded; God's people include the whole world (see Gen 12:1-3). God's rule is extended not only in space but also in time. There will be an unbroken communion of God's servants, because "future generations will be told" (v. 30), and they in turn will proclaim God's "righteousness to a people yet unborn" (v. 31). Even more remarkably, the dying and even those already dead will worship God (v. 29). To be sure, this affirmation is not the traditional Israelite view of life and death, and v. 29 is difficult to translate. The middle portion of v. 29, however, is clear and is translated literally by both the NIV and the NRSV. The phrase "go down to the dust" indicates that death is almost a certainty in view of v. 15, which mentions "the dust of death." Davis offers a cogent analysis of the psalmist's remarkable affirmation:

> Emerging suddenly out of a deathlike loss of meaning, the psalmist's joyful confidence that God is responsive to his plea demands that the dead above all may not be excluded from celebration and worship. It is the exuberance of the poetic vision that explodes the limits of Israel's traditional understandings. The shift in thought occurs first within the linguistic sphere, when a poet's productive imagination glimpses a possibility that only later (perhaps even centuries later) will receive doctrinal formulation as the resurrection of the dead.[118]

Thus Psalm 22 anticipates Paul's affirmation that "whether we live or whether we die, we are the Lord's" (Rom 14:8 NRSV), as well as the Christian doctrine of the communion of saints.

118. Davis, "Exploding the Limits," 102-3.

REFLECTIONS

The communal dimension of Psalm 22 is particularly worthy of note. It is present from almost the beginning of the psalm (vv. 3-5), even when it seems to be a meager source of comfort and hope. But immediately upon being answered by God (v. 21*b*), the psalmist turns to the congregation, praising God and inviting their participation (vv. 22-23). Then the psalmist gathers a table-sharing community consisting of "the afflicted" (v. 24) and "the poor" (v. 26), who will "be satisfied" and join the chorus of praise—indeed, who will experience life in all its fullness (v. 26). Even more remarkable, this community of afflicted ones will be the stimulus for the formation of a community that knows no bounds, consisting of people from all nations—living, dead, and yet unborn! God's reign will be universally acclaimed.

We might cynically conclude that the poet's exuberance has gotten out of control or that the poetic imagination has gone wild. This community of the faithful from all times and places sounds like neither Israel nor the church, both of which could and can be terribly parochial and exclusivistic. But if the psalmist was not merely misguided or mistaken, what do we make of this remarkable psalm? To state it positively, we must conclude that Psalm 22, like the psalter as a whole, has an eschatological character (see Introduction). It portrays what God intends for the world. It affirms God's reign over all peoples and nations in all times and places, despite appearances to the contrary. The poet's exuberant vision is not a mistake but a challenge, a call to enter the reign of God.

Mays points out that throughout the OT God deals with the nations through the agency of the whole people, Israel, or of a unique individual, the Davidic king (the messiah, "anointed one"; see Psalms 20–21, which may be juxtaposed intentionally with Psalm 22, and see above concerning the linguistic links between Psalms 20–21 and 22:1-5). Thus Mays concludes concerning Psalm 22 and its speaker:

> Psalm 22 cannot be the prayer of just any afflicted Israelite. Though we cannot know for certain for whom it was written and through what revisions it may have passed in the history of its use, in its present form the figure in the psalm shares in the corporate vocation of Israel and the messianic role of David.[119]

For the Gospel writers, who saw in Jesus the fulfillment of Israel's history and the arrival of the Messiah, Psalm 22 thus represented an ideal resource. The effect of their use of Psalm 22 is in keeping with the central thrust of Jesus' proclamation, for as a commentary on Jesus' death and resurrection, Psalm 22 "interprets Jesus' passion and resurrection as a summons to the world (in the most inclusive sense of that term) to believe in the reign of the Lord."[120]

The inclusiveness of Psalm 22 touches on another aspect that made it an ideal resource for articulating the story of Jesus—namely, its poetic explosion of limits, which resulted in a new and expanded vision of God, of human life and vocation, and of death. By telling the story of Jesus using Psalm 22, the Gospel writers affirm that in Jesus' faithful suffering, as in the psalmist's faithful suffering, God was present. God's presence with the afflicted and dying opens up new possibilities for understanding and living human life, as well as for understanding and accepting death. Because of these new possibilities, the Gospel writers saw in Psalm 22 a source for articulating the meaning of both the cross and the resurrection. Thus Jesus' cry from the cross (Matt 27:46; Mark 15:34; cf. Ps 22:1) is not simply a cry of dereliction; it is an affirmation of

119. Mays, "Prayer and Christology," 329.
120. Mays, "Prayer and Christology," 330.

faith in a God who, as the psalmist comes to understand and articulate, shares human affliction and enables even the dead to praise God.

Entrusting one's life to this kind of God, as the psalmist did and as Jesus did, changes everything. For instance, life can be understood not as a frantic search for self-satisfaction and self-security, but as a matter of dependence upon God (see Matt 6:25-33). Suffering can be understood not as something to be avoided at all costs, but as something to be accepted—even embraced on behalf of others—with the knowledge that God shares the suffering of the afflicted (see Heb 2:14-18). Death can be understood not as the ultimate insult to human sovereignty, but as something to be entrusted to God with the assurance that nothing in all creation can separate us from God (see Rom 8:31-39).

It is not surprising that Jesus embodied these transformed perspectives. He lived in humble dependence on God. He did not welcome suffering, but embraced it on behalf of others. He faced death with the conviction that God's power is greater than death's power. All of this may be summarized in Jesus' words, "Not what I want, but what you want" (Mark 14:36 NRSV). In short, Jesus lived, like the psalmist, as one of the afflicted, but in the knowledge that God does not despise the afflicted (Ps 22:24). Rather, God loves the afflicted, and God shares their suffering. So Jesus, like the psalmist, gathered around himself a community of the afflicted, the poor, the outcast. He sat at table with them, and he still invites to his table those who profess to live in humble dependence upon God rather than self.

In essence, the Gospel writers recognized that Psalm 22 affirms what the life, death, and resurrection of Jesus affirm. Suffering and glory are inseparable, both for the people of God and for God's own self![121]

---

121. Portions of the treatment of this and several other psalms in this commentary are similiar to the author's comments in J. Clinton McCann, Jr., *A Theological Introduction to the Book of Psalms: The Psalms as Torah* (Nashville: Abingdon, 1993).

PSALM 23:1-6, LIKE A CHILD AT HOME

COMMENTARY

Certainly the most familiar psalm, and perhaps the most familiar passage in the whole Bible, Psalm 23 is a challenge for the interpreter. On the one hand, its familiarity and obvious power seem to make commentary superfluous. On the other hand, its very familiarity invites the attempt to hear it in a fresh way. The challenge in this regard is the fact that Psalm 23 has become what William L. Holladay calls "an American Secular Icon,"[122] and it is almost exclusively associated with a particular contemporary setting: the funeral service. To be sure, it is appropriate that Psalm 23 be read and heard in the midst of death and dying. It may be more important, however, that this psalm be read and heard as a psalm about living, for it puts daily activities, such as eating, drinking, and

seeking security, in a radically God-centered perspective that challenges our usual way of thinking. Furthermore, it calls us not simply to claim individual assurance but also to take our place with others in the household of God.

23:1-3. The psalm begins with a simple profession. In the ancient world, kings were known as shepherds of their people. Thus to profess "The Lord is my shepherd" is to declare one's loyalty to God and intention to live under God's reign. It was the responsibility of kings to provide for and protect the people, but they frequently failed to do so (see Jer 23:1-4; Ezek 34:1-10). In contrast to the failure of earthly kings, God does what a shepherd is supposed to do: provide life and security for the people (see Ezek 34:11-16). Thus the psalmist affirms, "I shall lack nothing," as v. 1*b* is better translated (see Deut 2:7; Neh 9:21). The rest of the psalm explains

122. William L. Holladay, *The Psalms Through Three Thousand Years: Prayerbook of a Cloud of Witnesses* (Minneapolis: Fortress, 1993) 359; see also 359-71.

how God fulfills the role of a good shepherd (see also Gen 49:24; Pss 28:9; 74:1; 79:13; 80:1; 95:7; 100:3; Isa 40:11; Jer 31:10; Mic 7:14).

Contrary to the usual understanding, the imagery in vv. 2-3 is not aimed primarily at communicating a sense of peace and tranquility. It does this, to be sure, but its primary intent is to say that God keeps the psalmist alive. For a sheep, to be able to "lie down in green pastures" means to have food; to be led "beside still waters" means to have something to drink; to be led "in right paths" means that danger is avoided and proper shelter is attained (see Pss 5:8; 27:11). In short, God "restores my soul," or, better translated, God "keeps me alive." The sheep lack nothing, because the shepherd provides the basic necessities of life—food, drink, shelter. Thus the psalmist professes that his or her life depends solely on God and that God keeps the psalmist alive "for his name's sake" (v. 3*b*)—that is, in keeping with God's fundamental character.

By alluding to God's character, v. 3*b* anticipates the mention of "goodness and mercy," two fundamental attributes of God (see below on v. 6). Not surprisingly, the vocabulary of vv. 2-3 occurs elsewhere in relation to key events that reveal God's character. For instance, the two Hebrew verbs translated "leads" in vv. 2-3 occur together in Exod 15:13 in the song that celebrates the exodus. The verb in v. 2 also occurs in Isa 40:11, where God is also portrayed as a shepherd who leads the people home from exile (see also Isa 49:10-11). Although the psalmist's personal address to God as "my shepherd" is unique, the way the psalmist experiences God is entirely in keeping with God's character and historic deeds.

23:4. This is the structural and theological center of Psalm 23. Even in the most life-threatening situation, God's provision is sufficient. The word that the NIV translates "the shadow of death" elsewhere seems to mean simply "darkness" or "deep darkness" (see Job 3:5; 10:22; 12:22; 16:16; Pss 44:19; 107:10; Amos 5:8). The word, however, is unusual. It appears to be a compounding of words meaning "shadow" and "death," and in Job 10:22 it describes the realm of the dead. Thus the traditional translation seems appropriate (see v. 4 NIV). The similarity

between the Hebrew words for "evil" (רע *ra'*) and "my shepherd" (רעי *rō'î*) is striking, and the effect is to pit dramatically the shepherd against the threatening evil. The threat is real, but it is not to be feared, for the shepherd's provision is sufficient. The expression "fear no evil" is reminiscent of the central feature of the prophetic salvation oracle, which is particularly prominent in Isaiah 40–55 (see Isa 41:11-13, 14-16; 43:1-7; 44:6-8; 54:4-8). The word "comfort" (נחם *nḥm*) is also thematic in Isaiah 40–55 (see Isa 40:1-2; 49:13; 51:3, 12, 19; 52:9). The historical setting of Isaiah 40–55 is that of exile, Israel's "darkest valley." The message of the prophet is that even in exile, God will provide. Indeed, the introductory oracle concludes that God "will feed his flock like a shepherd" (Isa 40:11 NRSV).

The central affirmation, "you are with me," is made even more emphatic by the shift from third to second person in referring to God and by the presence of the Hebrew pronoun for "you." The direct address heightens the expression of the intimacy of God's presence. As Brueggemann points out, the only two occurrences of the personal name for God, Yahweh (LORD), occur in vv. 1 and 6, as if to indicate that Yahweh's presence is all-surrounding.[123]

The "rod" in v. 4 makes sense as a shepherd's implement; however, the word even more frequently signifies royal authority and rule (see "scepter" in Gen 49:10; Ps 45:6; Isa 14:5). What is ultimately comforting is the assurance that God is sovereign and that God's powerful presence provides for our lives.

23:5-6. While some interpreters discern the sheep/shepherd imagery in these verses, it is more likely that God is here portrayed as a gracious host. In any case, whether the metaphor shifts is not crucial. The gracious host does for the guest exactly what the shepherd did for the sheep—provides food ("You prepare a table"), drink ("my cup overflows"), and shelter/protection (v. 6).

Like vv. 1-4, vv. 5-6 suggest that it is God's very character to provide for God's people. The clue in vv. 1-4 is the phrase "for his name's sake." The primary indication in vv. 5-6 is the Hebrew word חסד (*ḥesed*), which

---

123. Brueggemann, *The Message of the Psalms,* 154-55.

the NRSV translates as "mercy" and the NIV as "love." God's *ḥesed* lies at the very heart of God's character, as suggested by the fact that the word occurs twice in God's self-revelation to Moses in Exod 34:6-7 (see the Introduction). The word "goodness" (טוב *ṭôb*) is also reminiscent of God's self-revelation to Moses, for God's "goodness" passes before Moses in Exod 33:19 (see Pss 100:5; 106:1; 107:1; 118:1, where "goodness" and *ḥesed* are paired as reasons for praising God).

Most translations suggest that God's goodness and *ḥesed* will "follow" the psalmist, but the Hebrew verb (רדף *rādap*) has the more active sense of "pursue." God is in active pursuit of the psalmist! This affirmation is particularly noteworthy in view of "the presence of my enemies." Ordinarily in the psalms, it is precisely the enemies who "pursue" the psalmist (see 7:5; 71:11; 109:16). Here the enemies are present but have been rendered harmless, while God is in active pursuit.

The mention of "the house of the LORD" in v. 6 may indicate the Temple and, along with the mention of "a table" in v. 5, may be a clue to the psalm's original cultic setting. It is possible that the psalm was used at a meal sponsored by a worshiper as part of his or her thanksgiving offering (see Commentary on Ps 22:22-26), perhaps in gratitude for deliverance from enemies (v. 5). Other scholars take v. 6b very literally and conclude that the psalmist was one of the temple personnel or that she or he spent the night in the Temple during a distressing time to await a reassuring oracle. It is more likely, however, that the "stay in the sanctuary is probably metaphorical for keeping close contact with the personal God."[124]

In any case, the mention of "the house of the LORD" is significant. To be in "the house of the LORD," literally or metaphorically, provides a communal dimension to this psalm that is usually heard exclusively individualistically. This communal dimension is reinforced when Psalm 23 is heard in conjunction with Psalm 22, as the editors of the psalter may have intended. Not only can the depth of trust expressed in Psalm 23 be appreciated more fully after reading Psalm 22, but also the conclusion of Psalm 22 (vv. 22-31) seems to anticipate the ending of Psalm 23 (vv. 5-6). Psalm 22 ends with the psalmist in the "congregation" (vv. 22, 25), which would have been found in the house of the Lord (23:6). Thus the personal assurance articulated by the psalmist is finally experienced in the community of God's people.

124. Gerstenberger, *Psalms: Part 1*, 115.

REFLECTIONS

1. In a consumer-oriented society, it is extremely difficult to hear the simple but radical message of Psalm 23: God is the only necessity of life! While v. 1 is best translated "I shall lack nothing," the traditional translation preserved by the NIV and the NRSV is particularly appropriate in a culture that teaches people to want everything. Driven by greed rather than need, we can hardly imagine having only the necessities of life—food, drink, shelter/protection. Clever advertisers have succeeded in convincing us that what former generations considered incredible luxuries are now basic necessities. To say in our prosperous context that God is the only necessity of life sounds hopelessly quaint and naive. Then again, the words of Jesus also strike us as naive:

> "Therefore I tell you, do not worry about your life, what you will eat or what you will drink, or about your body, what you will wear. . . . But strive first for the kingdom of God and his righteousness, and all these things will be given to you as well." (Matt 6:25, 33 NRSV)

In effect, to make Psalm 23 our words is to affirm that we do not need to worry about our lives (or our deaths). God will provide, and God's provision is grounded in the reality of God's reign. The proper response to the simple good news of Psalm 23 and Jesus

Christ is to trust God. But this is precisely the rub. In a secular society, we are encouraged to trust first ourselves and to work first to secure our own lives and futures. Psalm 23 thus challenges us to affirm with the psalmist: "The LORD is my shepherd, I shall not want." To say that means to live humbly and gratefully as a child of God.

The third stanza of Isaac Watts's beautiful metrical version of Psalm 23 expresses eloquently the simple trust that Psalm 23 communicates and commends to us:

> The sure provisions of my God
> Attend me all my days;
> O may Your House be my abode,
> And all my work be praise.
> There would I find a settled rest,
> While others go and come;
> No more a stranger or a guest,
> But like a child at home.[125]

Not only does Watts's paraphrase capture the childlike trust articulated by Psalm 23, recalling Jesus' words about entering the reign of God "like a little child" (Mark 10:15 NIV), but also it calls to our attention the communal dimension of Psalm 23.

To be a child at home means inevitably to be part of a family, to share community around a table (see v. 5). Thus we are led to reflect on what it means to be a part of God's household (see v. 6). The implications are profound and radical: We are not our own! We belong to God and to one another! In his book *God the Economist,* M. Douglas Meeks recognizes the radical implications of Psalm 23. He quotes Aubrey R. Johnson's rendering of Psalm 23:6:

> Yea, I shall be pursued in unfailing kindness every day of my life,
> finding a home in the Household of Yahweh for many a long year.

Meeks understands Psalm 23 to be an articulation of the same message ultimately embodied in the Lord's Supper, which also has to do with God's gracious provision of food, drink, and security within God's household. Meeks puts it as follows:

> The celebration of the Lord's Supper is under orders from God the Economist and is a concrete instance of God's providential *oikonomia* [the Greek word from which our word *economy* is derived; it means literally "law of the household"] with implications for all eating and drinking everywhere. For this reason, the disciples of Jesus should pray boldly for daily bread (Luke 11:3). They should keep the command to eat and drink, recognizing that it includes the command that they should share daily bread with all of God's people.
>   . . . Psalm 23 depicts the work of God's economy overcoming scarcity in God's household.[126]

Because, as Psalm 23 affirms, God is the source of all food and drink and security, because we belong first and forever to God's household, our lives are transformed. Daily realities are not to be taken for granted and certainly not to be treated as rewards we have earned. Psalm 23, like the Lord's Supper, becomes finally an invitation to live under God's rule and in solidarity with all God's children. Thus to make Psalm 23 our own is a profoundly radical affirmation of faith that transforms our lives and our world. To be sure, Psalm 23 is to be heard in the midst of death and dying, but it is also to be

---

125. Isaac Watts, 1719, altered 1972, in *Hymns, Psalms, and Spiritual Songs* (Louisville: Westminster/John Knox, 1990) no. 172.
126. M. Douglas Meeks, *God the Economist: The Doctrine of God and Political Economy* (Minneapolis: Fortress, 1989) 180.

heard amid the ordinary daily activities of living. And it gives these daily activities an extraordinary significance, for it invites us to share daily bread with all of God's people.

2. It is inevitable that Christians hear in Psalm 23 testimony to Jesus Christ. Jesus became the gracious host who prepares a table that reconciles enemies and offers life (see Mark 14:22-25; interestingly, Mark 14:27 alludes to Zech 13:7, a passage about sheep and shepherds). In a story with obvious eucharistic overtones (Mark 6:30-44, esp. vv. 41-42), Jesus feeds people. The crowd is to "sit down . . . on the green grass" (Mark 6:39 NRSV), a detail that recalls Ps 23:2. That the allusion is not coincidental is suggested by Mark's description of Jesus' motivation for having compassion on the crowd: "they were like sheep without a shepherd" (Mark 6:34 NRSV). Jesus serves as both host and shepherd, acting out the two metaphors of Psalm 23.

Jesus is cast even more clearly in the role of shepherd in John 10:1-17. As in Psalm 23, the shepherd leads the sheep (John 10:3), providing food (John 10:9) and protection (John 10:12-13) for the purpose of sustaining life itself (John 10:10). And Jesus says specifically, "I am the good shepherd" (John 10:11, 14 NRSV). Interesting too in John 10 is the enigmatic mention of "other sheep that do not belong to this fold" (v. 16 NRSV). Does this refer to Christians beyond the Johannine community? Does this refer more broadly to adherents of other world religions? The solution is unclear, but in the light of the communal conclusion to Psalm 23 (especially in view of the conclusion of Psalm 22, where "all the ends of the earth" and "all the families of the nations" are to "turn to the LORD" and "worship before him" [22:27]); it is worthy of note that John 10 envisions God's household in very open terms, with room perhaps for "enemies" (Ps 23:5) and even for "all the families of the nations" (Ps 22:27).

This thrust toward universality is present too in the relationship between Jesus and Ps 23:4, "you are with me." According to Matthew, Jesus is to be named "Emmanuel . . . 'God is with us' " (Matt 1:23 NRSV). This affirmation provides a frame for the Gospel, the final words of which are "I am with you always, to the end of the age" (Matt 28:20 NRSV). This final affirmation of Emmanuel is in the context of Jesus' commission to "make disciples of all nations" (Matt 28:19 NRSV). God intends for God's household to include "the ends of the earth" (Ps 22:27).

In short, in NT terms, Jesus is shepherd, host, Emmanuel. When Psalm 23 is heard in the context of Psalm 22 and of Jesus Christ, its profoundly radical implications are even clearer: God is with us, but God is not ours to own; the God who shepherds us to life also gives life to the world; the table at which we are hosted is one to which the whole world is invited.

PSALM 24:1-10, THE EARTH IS THE LORD'S

COMMENTARY

Perhaps more than any other psalm, Psalm 24 allows the interpreter to imagine a liturgical ceremony in which it may have been used. Like Psalm 15, it is usually classified as an entrance liturgy (see also Isa 33:13-16; Mic 6:6-8). Verses 1-2 consist of an opening profession of faith by the worshipers; vv. 3-6 offer an exchange between worshipers (v. 3) and priests (vv. 4-6) concerning entrance into the sanctuary; and vv. 7-10 consist of a responsorial liturgy that takes place as the processional prepares to enter the temple gates. It is very possible that the procession accompanied the bringing of the ark into the sanctuary (see 2 Samuel 6; Ps 132:8-10). Earlier generations of scholars associated Psalm 24 with an annual enthronement of the Lord or celebration of Zion and the Davidic dynasty; however, Gerstenberger has suggested more modestly that "Psalm 24 has to do with some ritual celebrated at the Second Temple (see Ezekiel 43–44), the coming of Yahweh into his sanctuary, and his passing through heavily guarded temple gates," or perhaps an "even more symbolic enactment of such a coming in a templeless, synagogal environment."[127]

While the identification of Psalm 24 as an entrance liturgy is reasonable and the attempts to describe its liturgical setting are plausible, they do not necessarily do justice to the psalm as a literary product in its final form. Whatever may have been its original setting and use, Psalm 24 in its current form is a powerful affirmation of the sovereignty of God, the identity of humankind, and the relationship between humanity and God.

24:1-2. While the reign of God is not explicitly proclaimed in vv. 1-2, and neither is God called "King" as in vv. 7-10, the sovereignty of God is clear enough. The whole world belongs to God, including all its people! The reason is simple: God created it. The "seas" and "rivers" are symbolic of the chaos that God has ordered into a cosmos, a world. God has "founded" it (see Pss 78:69; 89:11; 102:25; 104:5; Isa 48:13; 51:13, 16). The words translated here as "world" (תבל *tēbēl*) and "established" (יסד *yāsad*) also occur together in Pss 93:1 and 96:10, both of which explicitly affirm, "The LORD reigns." Thus vv. 1-2 anticipate vv. 7-10, where God is addressed five times as "the King of glory."

24:7-10. In addition to the word "king," other elements of the vocabulary of vv. 7-10 also focus attention on God's reign. The adjective "strong" (עזוז *'izzûz*, v. 8) occurs elsewhere only in Isa 43:17, almost immediately following an affirmation of God's kingship in Isa 43:15. A related noun, "strength" (עז *'ōz*), is prominent in the psalms that explicitly proclaim God's reign (see 29:1; 93:1; 96:6-7; 99:4). The same can be said of the noun "glory" (כבוד *kābôd*, vv. 7-10). Although the phrase "King of glory" is unique to Psalm 24, the concept of "glory" is frequently associated with God's reign (see Pss 29:1, 3, 9; 96:3, 7-8; 97:6; 145:11-12). The phrase "mighty in battle" (v. 8) recalls the description of the Lord as a "man of war" near the beginning of the Song of the Sea (Exod 15:3), a song that concludes with the affirmation "The LORD will reign forever and ever" (Exod 15:18 NRSV).

The portrayal of God as a warrior provides another link between vv. 1-2 and 7-10, for creation was often viewed in the ancient Near East as a battle. God has won the battle against chaos, thus demonstrating sovereignty. The title "LORD of hosts" may also be a military term, since the word "host" (צבא *ṣābā*) can designate an army. This title also occurs in Pss 46:7, 11 and 48:8, psalms that celebrate God's protection of Zion in apparent military confrontations with hostile kings and nations. The word "hosts" may also refer to the assembly of heavenly beings that form God's heavenly court (see Pss 29:1-2; 82:1; 89:6-8). In any case, the phrase "LORD of hosts" appears immediately following the title "King" in Isa 6:5, as if it were God's throne name. It points to God's sovereignty and is also associated with the ark, God's earthly throne (see 1 Sam 4:3-4). If vv. 7-10 were a liturgy of entrance for the ark, the ritual would have been a visible enactment of God's sovereignty. "The entrance liturgy of verses 7-10 is the dramatic version of the confession of verses 1-2."[128]

24:3-6. Verse 3 recalls Ps 15:1 and refers to the Temple on Mount Zion, symbolic of God's earthly dwelling place (see Isa 2:3; 30:29; Mic 4:2 for occurrences of the phrase "mountain of the LORD," which the NIV and the NRSV translate here as "hill of the LORD"). God's place is "holy" (see Pss 2:6; 3:4; 15:1; 43:3; 48:1), and those entering God's presence should be holy as well. It should be recalled that the two affirmations of God's sovereignty frame vv. 3-6. Thus, when the questions of v. 3 and responses of vv. 4-6 are heard in the context of vv. 1-2, 7-10, the issue becomes larger than entrance into the Temple. Rather, the questions in v. 3 ask, in effect, Who will live under God's sovereignty? Who will enter the reign of God?

This concern is addressed in v. 4. That v. 4a should not be interpreted simply as requirements for entering the Temple is indicated by the lack of specificity in the response to the questions of v. 3. "Clean hands" and "pure hearts" may be intended to indicate outward behavior and inward motivation respectively; however, these phrases do not designate ritual holiness or preparation that could easily be measured. Rather, they

---

127. Gerstenberger, *Psalms: Part 1,* 119.

128. Mays, *Psalms,* 123.

seem to indicate proper relatedness to God and neighbor in every aspect. The phrase "pure of heart" occurs elsewhere only in Ps 73:1, where the parallel is "Israel." Perhaps not coincidentally, the psalmist also says in Ps 73:13, "I have . . . washed my hands in innocence" (NRSV); and the word "innocence" (נקי *nāqî*) is from the same Hebrew root as "clean" in Ps 24:3. While Psalm 73 offers no more indication than Psalm 24 of the specific behavior involved, the psalmist does suggest that if she or he did not wash the "hands in innocence," the psalmist would be forsaking the "generation of your [God's] children" (Ps 73:15 NRSV). Psalm 24:6 also concludes that "those who have clean hands and pure hearts" constitute "the generation of those who seek" God. Thus v. 4*a* serves more as an invitation than an examination. Those who will stand in God's presence are persons whom God has claimed as God's own and whose lives reflect the intention to live together under God's rule.

Verse 4*bc* reinforces this conclusion. Verse 4*b* recalls the third commandment of the Decalogue (Exod 20:7), which could be translated literally: "You shall not *lift up* the name of the LORD your God to *nothingness* [the same Hebrew word (שוא *šāwě*) as "what is false," NRSV], for the LORD will not *hold clean* [the same Hebrew root (*nāqî*) as "clean" in v. 4*a*] the one who *lifts up* his name to *nothingness.*"

As the NIV suggests, the noun "nothingness" can have the sense of "idol" (see Ps 31:7; Jer 18:5). Thus both Exod 20:7 and Ps 24:4 affirm that cleanness results from nothing less than trusting God completely and unreservedly. It is significant that the idiom "to lift up the soul" occurs again in Ps 25:1. In this case, and the two other cases where the psalmist lifts her or his soul to God, the word "trust" occurs in the immediate context (see Pss 25:1-2; 86:2, 4; 143:8). While v. 4*b* describes proper relation to God, v. 4*c* communicates solidarity with neighbor. Although the vocabulary differs, v. 4*c* recalls the ninth commandment: "You shall not bear false witness against your neighbor" (Exod 20:16 NRSV). In short, persons who will enter God's reign are those whose lives are shaped by complete loyalty to God and love of neighbor. It is not a matter of earning entrance by displaying this behavior but of being shaped by the claim of the sovereign God upon the world and all its people (vv. 1-2).

Those who entrust their lives to God receive blessing (v. 5); that is, their daily needs are provided for. Thus, like Psalm 23, Psalm 24 affirms that the sovereign God provides for God's people (see esp. 23:1). They also receive "righteousness" (or "vindication"). "Righteousness" (צדקה *ṣĕdāqâ*) is a term that can describe an attribute of the sovereign God (see Pss 36:7; 71:19), proper relatedness among human beings (in which case, it is often parallel to "justice" [משפט *mišpāṭ*]; see Amos 5:24), and even proper relatedness between humanity and the created order (in which case, it is often parallel to "salvation" [ישע *yēša*]; see Isa 45:8). In other words, those who enter God's reign—those who know that "the earth is the LORD's" (v. 1)—will discover what it means to live in harmony with God, with other people, and with the whole creation. This is the ultimate blessing for those "who seek the face of the God of Jacob" (v. 6; see Ps 11:7).

REFLECTIONS

The Commentary suggests that Ps 24:4 recalls the Ten Commandments, the first in a series of commandments given at Sinai. The Ten Commandments are not rules for earning God's favor; rather, they are given only *after* God has already shown favor and after God's reign has been proclaimed (Exod 15:18). In short, they are instruction for those who are committed to live under God's sovereignty. Given the points of contact between Psalm 24 and the Ten Commandments, the OT instruction *par excellence,* it is not surprising that there are also points of contact between Psalm 24 and the NT instruction *par excellence,* the Sermon on the Mount (Matthew 5–7). The same proclamation found in Ps 24:1-2, 7-10 lies at the heart of the Sermon on the Mount: God reigns. In Matthew's terms, "the kingdom of heaven has come near" (Matt 4:17

NRSV), the announcement that inaugurates Jesus' public ministry and the concept that pervades the Sermon on the Mount. For instance, the first and last of what appear to be the original eight Beatitudes (Matt 5:3, 10; vv. 11-12 seem to be an expansion of v. 10) mention the kingdom of heaven, thus providing an envelope for the series. That is to say, the proclamation of God's reign surrounds the Beatitudes, both structurally and theologically (see also Matt 5:19-20; 6:33; 7:21).

Furthermore, just as Psalm 24 features the concepts of blessing and righteousness (v. 5), so also does the Sermon on the Mount. Each of the Beatitudes begins with "Blessed," and the concept of righteousness is central to the Beatitudes and to the entire sermon (see Matt 5:6, 10, 20; 6:33; see also Matt 3:15). Just as in Psalm 24, so also it is clear that righteousness is not simply a matter of meeting a list of requirements (see Matt 5:21-22, 27-28, 33-34, 38-39, 43-44) but of yielding one's whole life to God's claim. It is interesting, too, that one of the Beatitudes speaks in terms of seeing God: "Blessed are the pure in heart, for they will see God" (Matt 5:8 NRSV). The similarity to Ps 24:4-6 is clear; persons with "pure hearts" (v. 4) constitute "the company of those . . . who seek the face of the God of Jacob" (v. 6). In Exod 33:17-23, seeing God's face is prohibited; even Moses can see only God's back. Thus it is rather extraordinary for Ps 24:6 to speak of seeking God's face and for Matt 5:8 to speak of those who will see God (see Pss 11:7; 17:15). What a monumental experience is in view—indeed, nothing short of the creation of a new world that turns the current world upside down (see Acts 17:6). Such is the import of Psalm 24 and the Sermon on the Mount as they invite persons to enter the extraordinary new world of God's reign.

As for Matthew, the determining factor for Psalm 24 is the reality of God's universal claim (see esp. vv. 1-2, 7-10). Like Matthew 5–7, Psalm 24 is eschatological; it proclaims God's reign amid the reality of sin and amid the reality of opposition, which God must fight (see Psalm 2; Introduction). When read and heard in its final literary form and setting, it calls for a decision: Who is sovereign? Who rules the world? Who will enter the reign of God (v. 3)?

The Sermon on the Mount is often considered under the rubric of ethics. So is Psalm 24, especially vv. 4-6. Verses 4-6 do not reduce ethical activity to following a specific set of rules and regulations. This same position is argued forcefully by Stanley Hauerwas and William H. Willimon: "So the primary ethical question is not, What ought I now to do? but rather, How does the world really look? . . . Our ethics derive from what we have seen of God."[129]

This is precisely the theological point of Psalm 24. Indeed, v. 1 gives a very clear and specific answer to "the primary ethical question": "The earth is the LORD's." For those who see the world first and foremost as the sphere of God's reign, every human activity and ethical decision—personal, political, ecological, and otherwise—will be grounded in and result from unreserved trust in God and the desire to embody God's loving, life-giving purposes for "the world, and all who live in it" (v. 1).

129. Hauerwas and Willimon, *Resident Aliens*, 88, 90.

PSALM 25:1-22, TO YOU, O LORD, I OFFER MY LIFE

COMMENTARY

As the NIV note indicates, Psalm 25 is an acrostic poem. This form, in which each verse begins with a successive letter of the Hebrew alphabet, may account for the frequent scholarly perception that Psalm 25 lacks a clear structure and organization; however, some scholars do detect a degree of regularity. Bratcher and Reyburn, for instance, identify a series of five petitions (vv. 2b-3, 4-7, 11, 16-18, 19-22) following an opening address (vv. 1-2a). The middle petition (v. 11) is set off from the others by a section of praise (vv. 8-10) and assurance (vv. 12-15).[130]

There are other indications that the psalmist intended to focus attention on the center of the psalm. For instance, the words "shame" (vv. 2-3) and "wait" (vv. 3, 5, 21) occur only near the beginning and end of the psalm, thus directing attention to the center. The same effect is achieved by the change in person. Verses 1-7 are in the first person (except v. 3), as are vv. 15-21. In contrast, vv. 8-14 are in the third person, with the exception of v. 11. Again, attention is focused on v. 11, which is also the middle line in the psalm. Furthermore, if the first letters of vv. 1, 11, and 22 (which actually lies outside the acrostic structure) are taken in order, they spell out the word אלף (*'ālep*), the first letter of the alphabet.

To be sure, all of the above may be simply coincidental; yet, the evidence does suggest that there are structural and stylistic regularities in Psalm 25 that focus attention on v. 11. At the same time, there is a compelling reason not to draw too sharp a distinction between v. 10 and v. 11—namely, a cluster of vocabulary in these two verses that clearly recalls Exod 34:6-10: "steadfast love" (v. 10; cf. Exod 34:6); "faithfulness" (v. 10; cf. Exod 34:6); "covenant" (v. 10; cf. Exod 34:10); "pardon" (v. 11; cf. Exod 34:9); "guilt"/"iniquity" (v. 11; cf. Exod 34:7, 9). Thus it seems that vv. 10-11 function as a kind of theological center for Psalm 25, the effect of which is to focus attention on the character of God and to offer a narrative background (Exodus 32–34) for hearing and understanding major words and concepts throughout the psalm.

In form, Psalm 25 is a prayer for help—for deliverance from enemies (vv. 2-3, 19-21), for relief from distress (vv. 16-18, 22), for forgiveness (vv. 6-7, 11, 18b), for guidance and instruction (vv. 4-5). It is voiced mainly in the first-person singular, but it seems appropriate

130. See Bratcher and Reyburn, *A Translator's Handbook on the Book of Psalms*, 244.

also for corporate use, especially in the light of v. 22. On account of the acrostic form and didactic interests (see esp. vv. 4-5, 8-9, 12), some scholars conclude that Psalm 25 would not have been used in congregational worship, but this conclusion is not compelling. On the other hand, it is clear that the psalm is a prayer that serves the purpose of instruction or catechesis; that is, it teaches about the character of God, the identity of humankind, and the relationship between God and people. There is no reason why such a purpose would have disqualified Psalm 25 from liturgical use.

Using the same idiom found in Ps 24:4 (see Commentary on Psalm 24), the opening line of Psalm 25 anticipates the central affirmation and plea of vv. 10-11. Because God is loving and faithful, the psalmist entrusts her or his life to God. The verse could also be translated, "To you, O LORD, I offer my life" (see Ps 96:8; Ezek 20:32, where the verb translated "lift up" also means "to bring an offering"). To offer one's life to God means to trust God amid threatening circumstances (v. 2; see Pss 4:5; 9:10; 21:7; 22:5-6; 26:1; Introduction). As is always the case, faith and hope are inseparable (see Heb 11:1). Thus to offer one's life to God means also to wait for God, to live with hope (v. 3; see vv. 5, 21; see also Pss 27:14; 37:34; 39:7; 40:2; 130:5). In God is the psalmist's only hope of not being defeated or destroyed by enemies or circumstances (that is, "put to shame," v. 2; see vv. 3, 20 and Pss 35:4; 26; 40:14; 69:6; 71:24).

In two other psalms, the psalmist also says, "I lift up my soul" to God (86:4; 143:8). In both of these contexts, as in Psalm 25, the psalmist affirms trust in God (86:2; 143:8) and appeals to God's steadfast love as the basis for trust (86:5, 13, 15; 143:8, 12). As in Ps 25:4-5, the offering of the self to God is accompanied by the request that God teach the psalmist God's way (86:11; 143:8, 10). Verse 5a could also be translated, "Lead me by your faithfulness" (see v. 10). Thus faith and hope in God are characterized by openness to God's instruction and God's faithful leading. The word "way[s]" (דרך *derek*) occurs four times (vv. 4, 8, 9, 12), and the same Hebrew root underlies the translation "lead[s]" (or "guide[s]") in vv. 5, 9. The word connotes "way of life" or "life-style," and in this regard, v. 9 is particularly interesting. Its chiastic structure ("leads . . . humble . . . humble . . . way") has the visual effect of surrounding the humble with God's way or leading. The life-style of those who trust God will be characterized by humility—openness to God's teaching and reliance not on the self but on God (see Commentary on Psalms 1; 2). The result will be "justice" (or "what is right"). In short, by way of God's instruction, God justifies sinners.

The psalmist is confident that God does teach and lead (vv. 8-9, 12), but is also very much aware of failing to follow God (vv. 7, 11, 18). Thus the basis of the offering of self to God (v. 1) is not one's own worthiness, but the need for forgiveness. In vv. 6-7, the psalmist appeals to God's "mercy" (better translated, "motherly compassion" [רחמים raḥămîm]; the word is related to the Hebrew word that means "womb"; see Exod 33:19; 34:6) and steadfast love (see Introduction). The word "remember" (זכר zākar) occurs three times in vv. 6-7 (see NIV). What the psalmist requests is that God remember God's own character—the way that God has revealed God's own self to be "from of old" (v. 6).

The mention of "mercy," "steadfast love," "sins," and "transgressions" in vv. 6-7 anticipates the theological center in vv. 10-11. The vocabulary of these four verses is strongly reminiscent of Exod 34:6-10; the revelation "from of old" of God's self to Moses and Moses' response at the conclusion of the golden calf episode, which begins in Exod 32:1 (see above on vv. 10-11 and Exod 34:6-10; note that the adjectival form of "mercy" occurs in Exod 34:6 and that "sins" and "transgressions" occur in Exod 34:7). Especially when heard against the narrative background of Exodus 32–34, Psalm 25 is eloquent testimony to the character of God, whose commitment to sinful people requires that God's fundamental attributes, all of which occur in Psalm 25, be those rehearsed in Exod 34:6-7—"steadfast love" (vv. 6-7, 10), "faithfulness" (v. 10; the word also occurs in v. 5 as "truth"), "mercy" (v. 6), and "grace" (see "gracious" in v. 16). These attributes take concrete form in God's willingness to "pardon" (v. 11; see Exod 34:9) and to "forgive" (v. 18; see Exod 34:7), which is

the good news that enables the psalmist to offer her or his life to God (v. 1).

As for vv. 10-11, there is the same inevitable tension that is present in Exod 34:6-9, where God forgives iniquity but without "clearing the guilty" (34:7 NRSV). Psalm 25 implies that the steadfast love and faithfulness of God are reserved for those who obey God, but the psalmist has *not* obeyed, as v. 11 makes clear. The psalmist's ultimate appeal is to God's character, God's "name's sake" (v. 11), which the psalmist trusts will ultimately manifest itself in forgiveness (see Commentary on Psalms 99; 103).

Verse 12 returns to the theme of instruction, which pervades Psalm 25. The psalmist has already asked God to teach her or him (vv. 4-5) and has affirmed that God does teach and guide (vv. 8-9). Three different verbs meaning "teach" are used in vv. 4-5, 8-9, 12. The one that the NIV translates as "instruct(s)" in vv. 8, 12 represents the same root as the noun *torah*, "instruction," which is fundamental in approaching the psalter (see Ps 1:2; Introduction). In short, v. 12 functions as the psalmist's exhortation to others to posture themselves as the psalmist has, trusting God and being open to God's instruction (see Psalms 1–2). Verse 12b is grammatically ambiguous. In contrast to the NRSV and the NIV, it could be translated: "He [God] will teach them the way that he [God] chooses." This translation would make v. 12 more congruent with vv. 8-9.

Verses 13-15 describe the lives of persons who offer themselves to God. The translation of טוב (tôb) as "prosperity" in v. 13a is probably misleading, because contemporary persons tend to hear it exclusively in material terms. The Hebrew word is the same one translated as "good" in v. 8 ("goodness" in v. 7 is a very similar word from the same Hebrew root). In other words, those open to God's instruction will share in the "goodness" that characterizes God. As was the case with Ps 1:3 (where the word "prosper" is a different Hebrew word), the reward is that one's life is connected with the source of life: God. It was God who had given the land to Israel as a source of livelihood, so v. 13b suggests too that those who entrust themselves to God will experience life in all its fullness (see Ps 37:11; Matt 5:5). Verse 14 reinforces the conclusion that the real issue is relatedness to God. "Covenant" is obviously a relational word, and God is the initiator (see "Make me . . . know" in v. 4 NRSV). The NIV and the NRSV differ in translating v. 14*a*, but each translation suggests intimacy with God. The Hebrew word סוד (*sôd*) elsewhere describes the place or process whereby prophets receive revelation from God (see "council" in Jer 23:18, 22; see also Amos 3:7). As an example to others, the psalmist affirms that her or his life is safe from the traps of opponents (see "net" in Pss 9:15; 10:9; 31:4; 35:7; 140:5).

The final two petitions occur in vv. 16-18 and 19-21. Verse 16 may be a standard petition (see Pss 86:16; 119:132), but it appeals to God's character (see "gracious" in Exod 34:6) and activity "from of old" on behalf of the afflicted (see "affliction" also in v. 18; see also Deut 26:7, where the word also occurs; the word "toil" in Deut 26:7 is also the same as "trouble" in Ps 25:18). Verses 19-21 recall the opening address and first petition with its mention of foes, as well as the repetition of "soul" (cf. "life" in v. 1), "shame" (see vv. 2-3), and "wait" (see vv. 3, 5). To take refuge

in God is synonymous with trusting, hoping, offering one's life to God (see Pss 2:12; 5:11; Introduction). This utter dependence on God constitutes "integrity" or wholeness (see Pss 7:8; 26:1, 11; 41:12).

Verse 22 stands outside the acrostic structure and may have been appended to an original version of Psalm 25 to give it a more specifically corporate application; however, it is a thoroughly appropriate theological conclusion. Although the psalm appears to articulate primarily the prayer of an individual, the identity and speech of this individual are incomprehensible apart from Israel's basic understanding of the character and historic activity of God in dealing with God's people (see above on Exodus 32–34). To pray "deliver me" (v. 20) and "Redeem Israel" (v. 22) is finally, in the psalmist's view, to pray the same thing. The psalmist's faith and hope derive from and represent the faith and hope of Israel in a God who teaches the people the way that God chooses (vv. 8-9, 12) and yet who persistently forgives them for failing to follow (vv. 11, 18).

REFLECTIONS

1. Psalm 25 offers a model of prayer and a model of living that are increasingly difficult to appreciate or even to comprehend in the midst of a secular culture that promotes self-actualization, self-sufficiency, and instant gratification. Instead of living for self, the psalmist prays, and that prayer is an offering of his or her life to God (v. 1; see Rom 12:1-2). Instead of depending on self and personal resources, the psalmist depends on God in trust, finding security or refuge in God (vv. 2, 20). Instead of seeking instant gratification, the psalmist is content to wait for God (vv. 3, 5, 20) in the confidence that being related to God is the essence of fullness of life (vv. 5, 12-15, 21). For the psalmist, prayer is not a way to pursue what one wants. Rather, it is a means to seek God's ways (vv. 4-5, 8-9, 12): "Thy will be done."

Although apparently persecuted (vv. 2, 19), "lonely and afflicted" (v. 16), troubled and distressed (vv. 17-18), the psalmist nonetheless models what Psalms 1–2 call "happiness"—openness to God's instruction (1:1-2) and dependence upon God (2:12). The psalmist's awareness of personal shortcomings (vv. 7, 11), accompanied by humbly seeking God's direction (vv. 4-5, 8-9, 12), offers an example to every generation of God's people. This example may be especially timely as the church faces new and controversial issues that call for discernment of the will of God for our place and time. For many of the issues we confront, there are no clear, unambiguous biblical answers. Thus these questions generate strong differences of opinion. In such circumstances, humility is called for, as is the conviction that God really does continue to teach us God's ways. In essence, the psalmist's openness to God's instruction seems to be an example of what the Reformers called for when they insisted that the Bible must be read under the direction of the Spirit. As Mays concludes, Psalm 25 "teaches the church to pray for the Spirit to bring into our lives not only the power and mercy of God but as well a being-taught the way we are to live through the knowledge of God's ways with us."[131]

2. Worthy of reflection, too, is the psalmist's awareness of the faith stories of Israel. As Mays suggests, the psalmist seeks new insight into God's ways, but out of awareness of God's character and activity "from of old" (v. 6). This is why the psalmist's petitions and affirmations clearly recall Exodus 32–34, for instance, and why the psalm is both a prayer and an eloquent testimony to the essential character of God. There are lessons here for us. Tradition is crucial and needs to be taken seriously, but not simply for tradition's sake. Rather, awareness of the tradition becomes the foundation for openness to further instruction from God. This ongoing revelation will be consistent with God's character and the motivation for God's historic activity—"merciful and gracious, slow to anger, and abounding in steadfast love and faithfulness" (Exod 34:6 NRSV; cf. Ps 25:6-7, 10, 16)—but it will also be genuinely new and will call for openness on our part.

3. Psalm 25 is traditionally used during both Advent and Lent. The psalmist's posture of humble penitence is clearly appropriate for the season of Lent. The trust that yields both present assurance and hope is obviously appropriate for Advent, a season that both celebrates God's coming in Jesus Christ and anticipates the consummation of God's rule. Indeed, the psalmist's dependence on God is appropriate for all seasons.

131. Mays, *Psalms*, 127.

PSALM 26:1-12, ESTABLISH JUSTICE FOR ME, O LORD

COMMENTARY

Psalm 26 has affinities with several psalms that precede it in the psalter. It is most often classified with Psalms 7 and 17. In all three psalms, the psalmist requests that justice be done (7:8; 17:1-2; 26:1*a*) and accompanies this plea with the invitation for God to test him or her (7:9; 17:3; 26:2) and with a so-called protestation of innocence (7:3-5; 17:4-5; 26:1*b*, 3-5, 11*a*; see Introduction). It is usually assumed that Psalms 7; 17; and 26 reflect a setting in which the psalmist has been falsely accused by enemies and visits the Temple to appeal to God for justice (see Psalm 5; Introduction; see also Exod 22:7-8; Deut 17:8-9; 1 Kgs 8:31-32).

Psalm 26 is also occasionally classified with Psalms 15 and 24 as an entrance liturgy, since vv. 1-5 seem to anticipate and perhaps prepare for activities that would be carried out in the Temple (vv. 6-8, 12). Furthermore, the words "blameless" in v. 1 and "truth" in v. 3 recall Ps 15:2, and the phrase "in innocence"

in v. 6 corresponds in Hebrew to "clean" in Ps 24:4. It is used of hands in both instances and may reflect ritual preparation for entering the Temple.

The protestation of innocence in Ps 26:4-5 also recalls Ps 1:1. In both cases, the psalmist defines herself or himself over against "the wicked." Thus the implication is that the psalmist in Psalm 26 is among the happy or the righteous who live in dependence upon God and in openness to God's instruction (see Commentary on Psalm 1). In this regard, Psalm 26 is akin also to Psalm 25; it is not surprising that several key words link the two psalms. For instance, Ps 25:9 affirmed that "God leads the humble into justice" (author's trans.), and Ps 26:1 opens with the plea, "Establish justice for me" (author's trans.). The basis for this plea involves the psalmist's "integrity" (v. 1; see 25:21) as well as the fact that the psalmist has trusted God (26:1; see 25:2) and has been guided by God's steadfast love and faithfulness (26:3; see 25:10). Both psalms include near their end the petition that God "be gracious" (25:16; 26:11) and "redeem" (25:22; 26:11). Thus, in both psalms, the psalmist recognizes that life and future ultimately depend on the grace of God.

While the affinities between Psalm 26 and Psalms 1; 7; 15; 17; 24; and 25 are interesting, they are not conclusive, and the issue of genre and setting remains elusive. Paul Mosca has criticized the standard proposals and has sought to determine a setting based not on the usual categories but on the content of the psalm itself. Pointing out the likelihood that only priests could "go around your altar" (v. 6b) and that priests were required to wash their hands and feet before approaching the altar lest they die (see Exod 30:17-21), Mosca concludes that Psalm 26 originated as the private prayer of a priest for approval to serve at the temple altar.[132] While Mosca may be correct about the origin of Psalm 26, his proposal does not account for its continued use. In short, we must consider the possibility that v. 6 was meant to be understood figuratively rather than literally or that it came to be understood figuratively so as to make the psalm suitable for broader use. In its current literary form and setting, there is no explicit indication of exclusively priestly use. Thus Psalm 26 functions as both a prayer for justice and a profession of loyalty to God, to God's ways, and to God's people.

There is a variety of ways to understand the structure and movement of Psalm 26. The NRSV's divisions are convincing, except that v. 8 belongs with vv. 6-7 rather than with vv. 9-10. The psalm is organized chiastically (see Introduction). Verses 1-3 and 11-12 focus on the psalmist and God, and they are linked by repetition of the verb "walk" and the noun "integrity." Verses 4-5 and 9-10 focus on the psalmist and the wicked, sharply contrasting them and their ways. The central section, vv. 6-8, again focuses on God and the psalmist; but it is distinctive in that no petition is present and in that it gives prominence to a particular place: the Temple.[133]

26:1-3. Verses 1 and 2-3 show a similar structure: an imperative (v. 1) or imperatives

(v. 2) followed by a profession of loyalty or trust. The opening imperative would be translated better as "Judge me" or "Establish justice for me" (see Pss 7:8; 9:4; 10:18; 43:1; 96:13; 98:9). It is the prerogative and responsibility of a sovereign to judge or establish justice. Thus the psalmist recognizes God's sovereignty and appropriately expresses loyalty to God. The word translated "my integrity"/"blameless life" (תמ *tōm*) does not indicate personal achievement or sinlessness. The Hebrew root has the sense of completeness or wholeness, and its use here indicates complete devotion or total orientation of one's life to God (see Gen 17:1; 1 Kgs 9:4; Job 1:1, 8; 2:3; Pss 7:8; 15:2; 18:23; 25:21; 41:12; see also Commentary on Psalms 15; 18). As vv. 2-3 suggest, integrity in this sense derives from trusting God (see Pss 4:5; 9:10; 21:7; 22:5-6; Introduction) and from being led by God's steadfast love (see Pss 5:7; 21:7; 25:10; Introduction) and faithfulness (see Ps 25:5a, which could be translated, "Lead me by your faithfulness"). As a means of expressing complete devotion to God, the psalmist invites God's examination (see similar requests or statements, including use of the same vocabulary in Pss 7:9; 11:4-5; 17:3; 66:10; 139:23). The repetition of "walk" (הלך *hālak*) in vv. 1, 3 binds this section together. The verb "walk" connotes "walk of life" or "life-style." Again, the psalmist's whole life is oriented to God. As a poetic means of expressing this reality, "heart and mind" are mentioned in v. 2, to be followed by "eyes" (v. 3), "hands" (v. 6), and "foot" (v. 12). In short, from the core of the being to the tips of the bodily extremities, the psalmist's whole self belongs to God (see "my soul" in v. 9 NIV).

26:4-5. Continuing the protestation of innocence, but now in the negative, vv. 4-5 shift the focus to the psalmist and "the wicked." Occurrences of the verb for "to sit" (ישׁב *yāšab*) at the beginning of v. 4 and the end of v. 5 recall the occurrences of this root in Ps 1:1, as does the mention of the wicked (see Ps 1:1, 4-6) and the three accompanying synonyms. The NRSV's "worthless men" is more literally "men of emptiness" (see "false" in Job 11:11; Pss 24:4; 31:6 NRSV; as Ps 31:6 and the NIV of 24:4 suggest, the word is sometimes associated with idolatry), and

---

132. Paul Mosca, "Psalm 26: Poetic Structure and the Form-Critical Task," *CBQ* 47 (1985) 212-37.
133. Mosca, "Psalm 26," 220-29.

the word "hypocrites" (נעלמים *naʿălāmîm*) is more literally "those who conceal themselves." As the NIV suggests, the word "assembly" (מקהלים *maqhēlîm*) is repeated in v. 12 (see v. 5 NIV) to designate God's worshiping community, to which the psalmist belongs. The effect is to contrast sharply the psalmist and the wicked, as in Psalm 1. The assertion "I hate" (v. 5) emphasizes the contrast as well. It should be understood not as an emotional reaction but as an expression of resolute opposition. God opposes evil (see Ps 5:5), and so does the psalmist.

26:6-8. The central section, vv. 6-8, returns the focus to God and the psalmist with an added spatial dimension: the Temple. As suggested above, it is possible to interpret literally the activities in v. 6; however, this is by no means necessary. Verse 6*a* is identical in Hebrew to Ps 73:13*b,* and the phrase "clean hands" in Ps 24:4 is essentially the same. Neither Psalm 24 nor Psalm 73 seems to deal exclusively with priests. If the imagery originated in priestly experience, it came to be understood more broadly. In effect, the psalmist continues to profess loyalty to God. His or her faithful life-style (vv. 1-5) is accompanied by faithful worship in the Temple, including joyful expression of gratitude (perhaps accompanied by the bringing of a thank offering) and witness to God's activity (v. 7; see Pss 9:1; 73:28). While hating evil, the psalmist loves the Temple (v. 8*a*), because there God's presence is experienced (v. 8*b;*

see "glory" in Exod 16:7, 10; Pss 24:7-10; 63:3; Isa 60:1-2; Ezek 43:4-5).

26:9-10. Although the terms for the wicked differ, vv. 9-10 correspond in the chiastic structure to vv. 4-5 and seem to sharpen the contrast between the psalmist and the wicked. Unlike the "bloodthirsty" (see Pss 5:6; 55:23; 59:2; 139:19), whose hands are polluted by destructive plans (which elsewhere include murder, sexual misconduct, idolatry) and dishonest gain (see "bribe" in Exod 23:8; 1 Sam 8:3; Isa 1:23; Mic 3:11), the psalmist's hands are clean (see v. 6). The petition in v. 9 is essentially the equivalent of v. 1*a.*

26:11-12. Verse 11*a* forms with v. 1 an envelope structure. That the psalmist's "integrity" does not mean absolute sinlessness is indicated by the petitions in v. 11*b.* The essence of wickedness is dependence on self (see Psalm 1); the psalmist lives in dependence on the grace of God. The psalmist does not "stand in the way of sinners" (Ps 1:1) but on "level ground," a phrase that could be understood in view of v. 12*b* to mean the safety of the Temple floor or to designate the life-style of the psalmist. In a final act of submission to God, the psalmist takes his or her place in the congregation, blessing God, kneeling in homage to the one upon whom life depends (see Pss 16:7; 34:1; 63:4; 103:20-22; 104:1, 35; 135:19-20; esp. 145:2, following the address of God as "King" in 145:1).

REFLECTIONS

Two aspects of Psalm 26 may prove bothersome. First, it may seem that the psalmist bases this appeal for justice on self-righteousness—"my integrity" (vv. 1, 11). Second, the psalmist seems rather elitist in separating from the wicked to the point of even hating them. Christians may wonder about all this. The psalmist may sound like the Pharisee whom Jesus criticizes for exalting himself, thanking God that he was "not like other people" (Luke 18:11 NRSV). And did not Jesus regularly mingle with sinners and tax collectors, loving and forgiving rather than hating and condemning?

These problems, however, are more apparent than real. As was the case with Psalms 7 and 17, it is likely that the psalmist defends his or her innocence in a specific case in which the psalmist has been falsely accused by the wicked. At any rate, the psalmist's integrity or wholeness derives not from self-achievement but from entrusting life to God and attempting to follow God's direction in matters of life-style (vv. 1-5), worship (vv. 6-7), and witness (vv. 7, 12*b*). The final petition is "be gracious" (v. 11).

As for the apparent separatism, the psalmist's positioning of self over against the wicked is actually an act of humility rather than one of arrogance. In the psalter, wickedness is fundamentally self-rule (see Commentary on Psalm 1), so the stand against the wicked is equivalent to yielding oneself to God's rule. It is helpful at this point to remind ourselves that while Jesus did love and forgive sinners and tax collectors, he also had some pointed and condemning words for persons who failed to yield to God's sovereignty: "Hypocrites!" (Matt 23:13-36; see Ps 26:4).

Psalm 26 reminds us, then, that there is a legitimate form of separatism. Not anything goes! God opposes evil. Those who submit their lives to God's sovereignty will be different from those who follow only the direction of the self. There is a particular shape to the faithful life. It involves daily "walk" (vv. 1, 3). It involves participation in worship, where unlike "those who conceal themselves" (v. 4), the faithful publicly proclaim their gratitude to God and testify to the source of their wholeness and life (vv. 6-8). It involves taking one's place in the proper assembly (vv. 5, 12)—the worshiping community of persons who deny themselves in recognition of God's sovereign claim upon their lives. W. H. Bellinger concludes, "Participation in the worshiping community brings renewal for the significant life of trust and integrity."[134]

In short, Psalm 26 offers a challenge: "Choose this day whom you will serve" (Josh 24:15 NRSV), the challenge to recognize the truth of Jesus' claim, "No one can serve two masters. . . . You cannot serve God and mammon" (Matt 6:24 RSV).

134. W. H. Bellinger, Jr., "Psalm XXVI: A Test of Method," *VT* 43 (1993) 458.

PSALM 27:1-14, YOUR FACE, LORD, DO I SEEK

COMMENTARY

The first six verses of Psalm 27 are a remarkable profession of faith in God. The shift to direct address of God in v. 7 marks the beginning of a prayer for help that extends through v. 12. Verse 13 returns to profession, and v. 14 is an exhortation to the congregation or readers. Because of the shift between vv. 6 and 7, Psalm 27 has often been treated as two separate psalms. The verbal links between vv. 1-6 and 7-14, however, support the unity of the psalm (see "my salvation" in vv. 1, 9; "adversaries" in vv. 2, 12; "heart" in vv. 3, 8, 14; "rise up"/"risen against" in vv. 3, 12; "seek" in vv. 4, 8; "life"/"living" in vv. 1, 4, 13). There is a conceptual unity, too. The profession of faith serves as the basis for the prayer (vv. 7-12) as well as the concluding testimony and exhortation (vv. 13-14). The sequence conveys an important point. Faith in God does not spare God's servants from difficulties. But it equips them (v. 9) to live with courage and hope despite difficulties (vv. 13-14).

27:1-6. The opening line of the psalm summarizes its entire message. The Hebrew words translated "light" (אור *'ôr*) and "fear" (ירא *yārē'*) are similar, and the word play highlights the available alternatives—fear or faith (see Mark 5:36). Elsewhere, the blessing or saving presence and activity of God are associated with light (see Isa 9:2; 51:4; John 1:4-5; 8:12; 12:46; see also Isa 42:6; 49:6). The addressing of God as "my light" also anticipates vv. 8-9, since God's "face" appears as light or "shines" upon people (see Num 6:25; Pss 4:6; 31:16; 44:3; 67:1; 80:3, 7, 19; 89:15; 119:135). Thus, in both profession and prayer, the psalmist affirms the desire and intention to live in God's presence. The address of God as "my salvation" (see Exod 15:2; Pss 18:3; 24:5; 25:5; 95:1) and "my stronghold" (see "refuge" in Pss 28:8; 31:2, 4; 37:39; 43:2) reinforces the psalmist's conviction that God is the source and sustainer of life.

This faith casts out fear, even amid the dire threats to life described in vv. 2-3 (cf. v. 2 to

Ps 14:4). The same alternatives are evident again in v. 3. The psalmist "shall not fear" (see v. 1) but "will be confident," which represents the Hebrew root that the NRSV and the NIV usually translate as "trust" (בטח *bāṭaḥ*; see Pss 4:5; 9:10; Introduction). While the military language need not be taken literally, vv. 2-3, along with v. 12, may indicate the psalmist's problem: persecution by enemies. Likewise, vv. 4-6 may indicate that the psalmist sought asylum in the Temple. But again, the language may well have been intended metaphorically; it certainly came to function that way eventually. In short, what the psalmist singlemindedly seeks is the experience of God's presence (v. 4; see "seek" in v. 8; see also Ps 23:6). It is not clear what specific activities are described in v. 4c. To "behold the beauty of" may mean something like to "experience the favor of" (see Ps 90:17, where the word here translated "beauty" [נעם *nōʿam*] appears as "favor"). If "inquire" or "seek" originally indicated a specific ritual, it is not clear what—perhaps awaiting an answer to prayer (see Ps 5:3).

The psalmist is convinced that God will be his or her protection and deliverance (vv. 5-6a). As in v. 4, it is possible to read literally and interpret the Temple as the place of shelter (v. 5a; see Pss 31:20; 76:2 [NRSV, "abode"]; Lam 2:6 [NRSV, "booth"]). Recalling Israel's early history, the psalmists sometimes refer to the Temple as God's "tent" (v. 5b; see Pss 15:1; 61:4; see also 2 Sam 7:2). The Temple mount was a "rock" (see Isa 30:29), and perhaps by extension, God too is often the psalmist's "rock" (Pss 31:3; 61:2; 62:7; 71:3). The NRSV's "set me high" (v. 5) and "lifted up" (v. 6a; see Pss 3:3; 110:7) are the same Hebrew word (רום *rûm*). The humbled one will be exalted and will respond with gratitude, joy, and praise (v. 6bc; see Exod 15:1; Pss 9:11; 89:15-16; 107:22).

27:7-12. The prayer for help that begins with the petitions in v. 7 is clearly linked to vv. 1-6 by the occurrences of "my heart" (v. 8; see v. 3) and "seek" (v. 8; see v. 4). As vv. 1-6 have already suggested, the psalmist seeks God's presence, which is symbolized by the three occurrences of "face" in vv. 8-9. The psalmists are convinced elsewhere of the benefits of seeing God's face (see Pss 11:7; 17:15; 24:6; 42:2; 102:2; the word "presence" [פנים

pānîm] in Pss 16:11; 21:6; 140:13 is literally "face"). This is striking, given the tradition that one could not see God's face and live (see Exod 33:20), but it powerfully articulates the intimacy of communion with God that the psalmist seeks.

Verse 9 begins a series of seven imperatives that ask God to be present and involved in the psalmist's life. Expressions of assurance accompany the petitions, recalling vv. 1-6: God is "my help" (v. 9; see Pss 22:19; 40:17; 46:1; 63:7; 115:9-11) and "my salvation" (v. 9; see v. 1). The assurance in v. 10 picks up the verb "forsake" (עזב *ʿāzab*) in v. 9 (see Pss 22:1; 38:21). Even when forsaken by family, a serious threat to life in ancient cultures, the psalmist can depend on God to "take me up" (see Isa 40:11 [NRSV, "gather"]). The request in v. 11 is reminiscent of the claim in Psalm 1 (see also Pss 25:8, 12; 86:11) that those who are continually open to God's instruction (1:2 [NRSV, "law"]; the noun in 1:2 and the verb "teach" in 27:11 are from the same Hebrew root) are truly happy. Such happiness is not freedom from trouble and threat (see vv. 2-3, 12), but a solid grounding of faith that enables one to endure trouble and threat. The word "level" (מישור *mîšôr*) in v. 11 is the same as "level ground" in 26:12, where the context suggests a location in the Temple—that is, in God's presence (see also Ps 5:7-8). God's presence sustains the solid foundation on which the psalmist stands.

27:13-14. These verses conclude the psalm with another expression of the psalmist's faith (v. 13, "I believe"), and its inseparable companion, hope (v. 14; see Ps 37:34; Rom 8:24-25; Heb 11:1). Verse 13 recalls Ps 25:13, where God's "goodness" is also mentioned in the context of a plea for instruction (see 25:4-5, 12). It also recalls Exod 33:19-20, where Moses is prohibited from seeing God's face but is shown God's "goodness." Thus the psalmist trusts that he or she will be privileged to share the same experience as Moses. God will reveal God's own self to the psalmist. As an exhortation to others, v. 14 has the character of a public witness. The psalmist had earlier declared in v. 3 that "my heart shall not fear" and had been exhorted by his or her own heart (v. 8). Now the psalmist exhorts others to "let your heart take courage" (see Ps 31:24; Deut 31:7-8).

This exhortation is surrounded by "Wait for the LORD," suggesting that strength and courage begin and end with hope. Thus vv. 13-14 invite others, including contemporary readers, to join the psalmist in a community of faith, hope, and courage.

REFLECTIONS

1. When Jesus overheard people tell Jairus that his daughter was dead, Jesus exhorted Jairus: "Do not fear, only believe" (Mark 5:36 NRSV). Jesus' words effectively summarize the message of Psalm 27. In the presence of dire threat to life (vv. 2-3, 12), the psalmist dares to believe: "even then will I be confident" (v. 3*d*, which could also be translated, "through this I am trusting") and "I believe" (v. 13). Twice the psalmist uses "my salvation" to refer to God (vv. 1, 9). In biblical terms, salvation means life, especially life made possible when death is threatening (see Exod 15:2). Threatened by deadly forces, the psalmist lives by faith.

As both Mark 5:36 and Psalm 27 suggest, the opposite of faith is not so much doubt as it is fear. For the psalmist to say, "My heart shall not fear" (v. 3*b*; see v. 1), is to say, "I believe" (v. 13; see v. 3*d*). Psalm 27:3 recalls Ps 23:4. There, too, the psalmist is threatened by deadly forces but is able to say, "I fear no evil." The determining factor is trust in God's presence—"you are with me"—and it is precisely God's presence that the psalmist both affirms and continues to seek in Psalm 27 (see vv. 1, 4-5, 8-11; cf. v. 4 with Ps 23:6).

Our era has been called the Age of Anxiety, which makes the psalmist's example of faith all the more important. Kraus suggests that the psalmist is an example of one who "has anchored his life entirely in Yahweh."[135] How difficult this is in our secular world! The real measure of the difficulty is not outright doubt—still relatively few people profess to be atheists or agnostics—but the pervasive anxiety that characterizes contemporary existence. This anxiety is often interpreted as a failure of nerve, but Psalm 27 suggests that it is a failure to trust. Left to depend on ourselves instead of on God, we fail to experience joy (v. 6) and life in all its fullness (v. 13).

2. Verse 14 is a call to anchor our lives entirely in God. As the psalmist's address to others, v. 14 envisions a community of people who will "wait for the LORD"—an eschatological community. We wait for the Lord, but, like the psalmist, our waiting contains already (see "Now" in v. 6) the possibility of joy, strength, and courage. It should be noted that waiting for God is active rather than passive. The psalmist, for instance, resolutely seeks God through active involvement in worship, in the Temple or elsewhere (vv. 4-6). Mays states that "trust is nurtured and strengthened by the exercise and discipline of religion. . . . Trust needs the stimulus and renewal that come from confronting and contemplating religion's representation of the revelation of God in liturgy, architecture, and proclamation."[136]

3. In several ways, Psalm 27 is reminiscent of the final chapter of the book of Micah. Violence and oppression surround the prophet. He cannot trust even the closest of kin (Mic 7:1-6; cf. Ps 27:10). His response is to "wait for the God of my salvation" (Mic 7:7 NRSV; cf. Ps 27:9, 14), who is "a light to me" (Mic 7:8 NRSV; cf. Ps 27:1). Amid the anxiety, inhumanity, brutality, and greed of our world, Micah 7 joins Psalm 27 and Jesus in inviting us to trust rather than fear—to seek light, life, strength, courage, and direction in God. When the church located the presence of God in the Word that became flesh, the accompanying good news was the same as Psalm 27: "The light shines in the darkness, and the darkness did not overcome it" (John 1:5 NRSV). Such is the faith and hope that give us life and peace (see John 8:12; 14:27).

135. Kraus, *Psalms 1–59*, 337.
136. Mays, *Psalms*, 133.

PSALM 28:1-9, THE LORD IS MY STRENGTH

COMMENTARY

Psalm 28 begins as a prayer for help, including the psalmist's plea to be heard (vv. 1-2) and the petition that the wicked get what they deserve (vv. 3-4). Verse 5 is transitional. It expresses the confidence that God will deal with the wicked; thus it prepares for the praise, profession of faith, and thanksgiving of vv. 6-7. Verse 8 broadens the profession to include the whole people and the king, and v. 9 closes the psalm with renewed petition.

Because of its variety of component parts, Psalm 28 is difficult to categorize. Most scholars conclude that vv. 6-7 indicate that the petitions of vv. 1-4 have been answered, in which case it makes sense to label Psalm 28 a song of thanksgiving. Gerstenberger, however, concludes that vv. 6-7 anticipate deliverance, suggesting that v. 7cd is a vow that could be translated, " 'If helped, I will rejoice and give thanks.' "[137] He classifies the psalm as an individual complaint. Because of the mention of the "anointed" in v. 8, others view Psalm 28 as a royal psalm; however, there is nothing that would have prevented an individual from praying for the king, especially in the context of praying for the whole people, as here.

28:1-2. The psalm opens with the prepositional phrase "To you," suggesting immediately the urgency of the call that the rest of the verse reinforces. If God is "silent" (see Pss 35:22; 39:12; 83:1; 109:1; Isa 64:11; 65:6), the psalmist will be as good as dead. The "pit" is synonymous with Sheol, the realm of the dead (see Pss 6:5; 30:3; 88:4; 143:7; Isa 14:19). At the same time, the address of God as "my rock" implies confidence in God's ability to help (see Pss 18:2, 31, 46; 19:14; 31:22; 62:2, 6-7; 73:26). The plea continues in v. 2. The NIV's "cry for mercy" better captures the sense of the Hebrew root (חנן ḥānan; see Pss 31:23; 86:6; 130:2; 140:6; 143:1). It and the word translated "cry . . . for help" (שוע šwʿ; see Pss 18:6, 41; 30:2; 31:22) effectively communicate the psalmist's need without specifically identifying what it

is. The psalmist's words are accompanied by the proper posture of prayer: hands lifted (see Pss 63:4; 134:2; 141:2), perhaps toward the holy of holies where God was symbolically enthroned (see 1 Kgs 6:5; 8:6, 8).

28:3-5. The substance of the psalmist's prayer is contained in these verses. Although the vocabulary differs, the essence of the request in v. 3 is the same as in Ps 26:9-10. If the behavior of the wicked is an indication of what the psalmist has personally experienced (v. 3bc; see Pss 5:9; 7:14), then the psalmist may have been slandered or falsely accused. At any rate, the prayer is an implicit protestation of innocence (see Psalms 7; 17; 26; Introduction). Jeremiah 9:8-9 promises retribution for those who speak peacefully but act violently, and it is this sort of promise to which the psalmist appeals. The prayer that the wicked get what they deserve is not a matter of personal revenge but a matter of divine justice (see Ps 94:2). A comparison of vv. 4 and 5 makes this clear. The same Hebrew root (פעל pʿl) occurs in v. 4 in the phrase "their work" and in v. 5 in the phrase "works of the LORD." Similarly, a different but synonymous Hebrew word (מעשה maʿǎśeh) occurs in v. 4 in the phrase "work of their hands" and in v. 5 in the phrase "work of his [God's] hands." The effect of the repetition is to say that the wicked are completely self-absorbed. Their deeds show no comprehension of or participation in the goodness and order that God wills for creation and humanity. In effect, the behavior of the wicked sows the seeds of its own destruction. They leave God nothing with which to work. As a just and righteous God, God has no choice but to "break them down and build them up no more" (see Pss 10:3-4; 54:5; 73:18-20). This conclusion is reinforced by a play on words in v. 5. Because the wicked do not "regard" (יבינו yābînû), God will not "build them" (יבנם yibnēm).

28:6-7. These verses apparently assume that the petitions of vv. 1-4 have been answered and that the promise of v. 5 has been effected (see esp. v. 6b, which the NIV

137. Gerstenberger, *Psalms: Part 1,* 129.

correctly suggests is a direct response to v. 2a). God has proven to be the psalmist's strength (see Exod 15:2; Pss 46:1; 59:1). "Strength" is elsewhere associated with God's sovereignty (see Pss 29:1, 10-11; 93:1; 96:7), and the word occurs again in v. 8 in relation to the whole people (see Ps 29:11). The psalmist and the whole people live as a result of God's claim on them and on their world. The word "shield" (מגן māgēn) also communicates empowerment as well as protection (see Pss 3:4; 7:10). Recognizing God's sovereignty, the "heart" of the psalmist "trusts" (see Pss 4:5; Introduction) and rejoices (v. 7), whereas the "hearts" of the wicked were filled with "mischief" (רעה rā'â, v. 3). This word is often translated elsewhere as "evil," as in Ps 15:3, which suggests that those who recognize God's claim on their lives "do no evil to their friends." As suggested throughout the Psalms (see Commentary on Psalm 1), wickedness is essentially dependence on self. In contrast, the psalmist entrusts life to God—God is "my strength"—and responds to God's help (see Pss 10:14; 22:19; 37:40; 46:1) with gratitude (see Pss 7:17; 9:1).

28:8-9. The psalm concludes with a communal affirmation (v. 8) and a prayer for the community (v. 9). What God is for individuals, God is also for the entire people and the king, who embodies the life of the community:

"strength" (עז 'ōz, vv. 7-8) and "refuge" (מעוז mā'ōz, v. 8; the Hebrew word used here is the same as "stronghold" in Ps 27:1). The words "strength" and "salvation" (ישועה yĕšû'â, see v. 8 NIV) also occur together in Exod 15:2 at the beginning of the Song of the Sea, which concludes with an affirmation of God's reign (Exod 15:18). Again, God's claim upon the world and its people is the source of empowerment and protection. While "salvation" is claimed in v. 8, it is nonetheless prayed for in v. 9. "Save" (see "deliver"/"deliverance" in Pss 3:7-8; 6:4; 7:1) and "bless" (see Gen 12:1-3; Pss 3:8; 5:12; 29:11) suggest respectively rescue from distress and daily provision for needs. The plea "be their shepherd" could more literally be translated, "feed them," which is what shepherds did for their flocks (see Ps 23:1-3). The term "shepherd" again calls to mind the reality of God's sovereignty, since kings were often designated as shepherds in the ancient Near East (see Ezek 34:1-16). Whereas the language of v. 8 alluded to the exodus (Exod 15:2), the language of v. 9 alludes to return from exile (see Isa 40:11). These two great saving events are recalled as the psalmist prays for the people. Communal conclusions to predominantly individual psalms are also found in Pss 3:8; 5:11-12; 14:7; 25:22; 31:23-24; 51:18-19; and 130:7-8.

REFLECTIONS

1. The communal conclusion of Psalm 28 is instructive. While the psalms speak frequently of individuals' being saved or helped (see 28:7), Ps 28:8-9 reminds us that ultimately there is no such thing as individual salvation. To live under God's claim, to live as God intends, is to live as part of God's people. To belong to God means also to belong to others. Artur Weiser concludes that the psalmist lives "*in* the fellowship of faith and *from* that fellowship."[138]

2. It is instructive, too, that the psalm claims both strength and salvation for the people (v. 8) and yet still prays for saving and blessing (v. 9). In short, the perspective is eschatological. The psalmist and the people already experience the benefits of God's reign—"strength" (vv. 7-8), "help" (v. 7), "salvation" (v. 8)—yet not completely. As is always the case, the reign of God is proclaimed amid circumstances and powers that seem to deny it (see Psalm 2; Introduction).

In effect, the psalmist's perspective in prayer is the one articulated by Jesus when he taught his disciples to pray both "thine is the kingdom" and "thy kingdom come." The particular petitions in Psalm 28 also bring to mind the Lord's prayer. The prayer for justice in vv. 3-4 could well be paraphrased, "Thy will be done . . . deliver us from

138. Weiser, *The Psalms*, 258.

evil." And the petition "be their shepherd," or literally, "feed them," could well be paraphrased, "Give us this day our daily bread." Psalm 28, like the Lord's prayer, affirms that God's people live in dependence upon God rather than upon self. Indeed, the poignant words of v. 1 suggest that the psalmist will live ultimately "by every word that comes from the mouth of God" (Matt 4:4 NRSV; see Deut 8:3).

3. The lives of those who recognize God's claim will have a particular character that begins with trust (v. 8). Psalm 2:12 claims that happiness belongs to "all who take refuge in" God, and Psalm 28 also represents this claim. The trusting heart is the joyful, singing heart (v. 7). Those who attempt to make their way by "the work of their hands" (v. 4)—who live in dependence upon self—will be characterized by pride that is ultimately destructive of community (see v. 3). Those who attend to the work of God's hands (v. 5)—who receive life as a gift to be lived in dependence upon God—will be characterized by gratitude (v. 7) that impels them into the community of God's people (vv. 8-9).

PSALM 29:1-11, GLORY TO GOD!

COMMENTARY

Psalm 29 is often considered to be the oldest of the psalms, due in part to what seems to be an archaic pattern of repetition (see vv. 1-2), but due primarily to the observation that it seems to be an Israelite adaptation of an ancient Canaanite hymn to Baal, a god of weather and fertility. Following the opening invitation to praise (vv. 1-2), vv. 3-9 consist of a poetic description of a thunderstorm, responsibility for which the Canaanites attributed to Baal. Psalm 29 is fundamentally polemical, for it clearly attributes all power to Yahweh (LORD), who is enthroned in v. 9 with the exclamation, "Glory!" That enthronement is indeed the effect of v. 9 is indicated by the affirmation of Yahweh's kingship in v. 10, followed by the appeal for Yahweh to fulfill the royal role of blessing the people.

While Psalm 29 is traditionally categorized as an enthronement psalm (see also Psalms 47; 93; 95–99; Introduction) and shares several typical features of such psalms, much about it is unique. For instance, in vv. 1-2, the invitation to praise is addressed not to any earthly congregation but to "heavenly beings" (cf. Ps. 96:7-8, where the same invitation is addressed to "families of the peoples"). Although these beings could be understood as angels, more likely they should be viewed as the deposed gods of the Canaanite pantheon—another indication of the psalm's polemical thrust.

In any case, Psalm 29 preserves the ancient conception of a divine council (see Gen 1:26; 1 Kgs 22:19; Pss 58:1; 82:1; 89:7; 103:19-21; 148:1-2), whose members are invited to acknowledge (which is the sense of "ascribe to") Yahweh's glory and strength, in other words Yahweh's absolute sovereignty. Both of these attributes are associated frequently with God's reign (see "glory" in Pss 24:7-10; 96:3, 7-8; 145:5, 11-12; Isa 6:3; and "strength" in Exod 15:2, 13; Pss 93:1; 96:6-7; 99:4 [NRSV, "Mighty"]). "Glory" (כבוד *kābôd*) recurs in v. 2, not surprisingly in an invitation involving God's "name." The personal name "Yahweh" occurs eighteen times in Psalm 29 so as to emphasize the exclusiveness of Yahweh's claim. God's "glory," which becomes the key word in the psalm (see vv. 1-3, 9), consists of the strength mentioned in v. 1, described in detail in vv. 3-9 and exercised on behalf of God's people in v. 11. The imperative "worship" (השתחוו *hištaḥăwû*) also bespeaks God's sovereignty; it means literally "to bow down" before a monarch (see 1 Sam 24:8; 1 Kgs 1:31 of earthly kings; and Pss 95:6; 96:9; 99:5, 9 in the context of God's kingship). It is not clear exactly what "holy splendor" (הדרת-קדש *hadrat-qōdeš*) indicates. It may refer to the appropriate attitude or even the proper attire of those called upon to glorify

Yahweh (see 1 Chr 16:29; 2 Chr 20:21; Ps 96:9).

The polemical thrust of Psalm 29 is also clear in vv. 3-9. In these verses, the phrase "the voice of the LORD" occurs seven times, with the number 7 symbolizing fullness or completion. Yahweh's strength, which is represented by the sevenfold mention of the voice, is all-powerful. Yahweh's sovereignty—not Baal's—is absolute. As the verb in v. 3b suggests, the "voice of the LORD" is thunder (see 1 Sam 2:10; Job 37:4-5; Ps 18:13). The noun here translated "voice" (קול $q\hat{o}l$) is sometimes translated "thunder" by the NRSV (see Exod 19:19). The repetition may be intended to be onomatopoeic. The "waters" in v. 3 could be a reference to the Mediterranean Sea, over which the thunderstorm gathers force before crashing into the coast of Palestine. It is likely, too, that we should hear an allusion to the cosmic waters above and below the earth (see v. 10; Gen 6:17; 7:6, 7, 10; see also Psalm 93). In other words, the effects of the storm are to be understood as testimony to Yahweh's sovereignty over all creation. The two adjectives that describe the voice in v. 4 also connote sovereignty, occurring elsewhere in contexts that affirm earthly or divine kingship (see "power" in Exod 15:6; 1 Chr 22:12; 2 Chr 20:6; "majesty" in Ps 21:5; "splendor" in Ps 145:5).

Verses 5-9 offer a poetic description of the effect of a violent thunderstorm. Trees are uprooted and ripped apart (vv. 5, 9ab; see Exod 9:25); lightning flashes (see Exod 9:24; Pss 83:14; 97:3-4; Rev 4:5); the earth itself seems to shake (vv. 6, 8; see Pss 97:5; 114:4,

6). The described effects are similar to those generally found in theophanies, portrayals of appearances of God (see Pss 18:7-15; 68:4, 8, 33; 77:16-18; 97:1-5; 104:3-4). In the ancient Near East, thunder would have been the loudest sound known. Not surprisingly, thunderstorms were associated with divine appearances, especially manifestations of the Canaanite god Baal, whose voice was supposed to be the thunder. But here the heavenly beings interpret this powerful display as testimony to Yahweh's sovereignty over all, which they affirm in v. 9c (see vv. 1-3). The temple in v. 9c seems to designate God's heavenly abode, where the divine council would have gathered (see Pss 11:4; 18:6; Isa 63:15); however, the reference is ambiguous. In all likelihood, human worshipers who would have gathered in the Jerusalem Temple are also invited to join in acknowledging Yahweh's reign.

This likelihood is supported by the first explicit mention of human beings, which comes in the conclusion of the psalm (vv. 10-11). As the eternal ruler of all creation (the word "flood" [מבול $mabb\hat{u}l$] occurs only here and in Genesis 6–11; see Gen 6:17; 7:6-7; 9:11, 15), God is in a position to provide strength (see v. 1; see also Exod 15:2; Pss 28:7-8; 46:1; 68:35; 84:5; 86:16; 138:3) and the blessing (see Ps 28:9) of *shalom* (see Num 6:26). Just as it was the role of the earthly king to provide peace for his people (see Ps 72:1-7, esp. vv. 3, 7; *shalom* is translated "prosperity" in v. 3), so also it is the duty of Yahweh, the heavenly king, to provide peace for all creation.

REFLECTIONS

1. Psalm 29 is a marvelous profession of the message that lies at the heart of the psalter and the gospel: The Lord reigns! It speaks eloquently what Christians affirm regularly in the conclusion to the Lord's prayer: "for thine is the kingdom, and the power, and the glory forever." This message had a polemical thrust in the ancient Near Eastern context as well as in the time of Jesus—and it does still today. To be sure, contemporary persons are not tempted to worship Baal as such, but what the Baalistic cult represented is a major temptation to us. H. D. Beeby states, "This religion was for the Canaanites (and for most of the Israelites) what scientific humanism and technology are for people of the 20th century: essential to the means of production and for ensuring regular increase of the Gross National Product."[139] In short, the religion of Baal

139. H. D. Beeby, *Grace Abounding: A Commentary on the Book of Hosea,* International Theological Commentary (Grand Rapids: Eerdmans, 1989) 2.

asserted what humans are all too inclined to believe in any era, that ultimately *we* are in control and that *our* efforts can ensure security. While Psalm 29 is not necessarily anti-science or anti-technology, it does suggest definite limits to both. The universe is the sphere of God's reign. It derived from and belongs to God and thus is not simply an object for our study, much less for our manipulation and control. Similarly, our strength (v. 11)—including our scientific knowledge and technological capabilities—are gifts from God, not simply results of human inquiry and ingenuity. Thus *shalom*—peace, well-being, security—does not begin with our efforts but with our openness to God's claim upon us and the ways God has gifted us.

2. Needless to say, to view the world as the sphere of God's sovereignty rather than the arena of human progress would have profound ecological and economic implications. Creation does not exist simply for the sake of humanity. When we act as if it does, the results are disastrous—dirty water, polluted air, soil erosion, and perhaps even depletion of the ozone layer. Inequitable distribution of land and resources threatens life in our cities and destabilizes delicate international relations. Ironically, the more we seek to secure our own future, the less secure we become. Psalm 29 becomes a call to yield control to the sovereignty of God. Enduring strength and *shalom* will derive from joining the heavenly beings in their cry, "Glory!" (v. 9*c*). To paraphrase the first answer in the Westminster Shorter Catechism, the chief end of humankind is to glorify God and enjoy God forever. Obviously, this assertion is a monumental challenge in the midst of a culture that teaches us that our chief end is to enjoy ourselves—another indication of the polemical thrust of Psalm 29.

3. The use of Psalm 29 on the First Sunday After the Epiphany is particularly appropriate. Epiphany follows Christmas; Psalm 29 spans the two seasons. The movement of Psalm 29 from proclaiming God's glory (v. 9*c*) to peace on earth (v. 11) recalls the account of Jesus' birth in Luke (Luke 2:14). The birth of Jesus is the event by which God's universal reign became manifest. In addition, the cosmic proclamation of God's reign in Psalm 29 is appropriate for the season of Epiphany (which means "manifestation"), because Jesus' baptism is celebrated on the First Sunday After the Epiphany (Luke 3:15-22). Immediately following his baptism, a heavenly voice proclaims Jesus "my Son" (Luke 3:22), publicly manifesting Jesus as the one who would soon proclaim and enact "the good news of the kingdom of God" (Luke 4:43-44 NRSV). Mays's conclusion about the pairing of Psalm 29 and the baptism of Jesus applies as well to the similarity between Psalm 29 and Luke 2: "The Christology is not adequate unless its setting in cosmology is maintained. The Old Testament doxology is necessary to the gospel."[140] For the NT, Jesus becomes the ultimate embodiment of God's kingdom, power, and glory (see John 1:14; 1 Cor 2:8; 2 Cor 4:6).

140. Mays, *Psalms*, 138.

PSALM 30:1-12, SO THAT MY SOUL MAY PRAISE YOU

COMMENTARY

The superscription makes Psalm 30 one of the few psalms associated with a specific occasion. Rabbinic sources identify Psalm 30 with the Feast of Dedication (Hanukkah), which originated as a celebration of the restoration of proper worship under the Maccabees in

165 BCE after the desecration of the Temple by Antiochus IV Epiphanes (see 2 Maccabees 10). Most scholars conclude that the association of Psalm 30 with Hanukkah is secondary, since the psalm is likely to be much older than the second century BCE, since it appears to have no specific relevance for a dedication, and since the prayer is offered in the first-person singular. For the latter reason as well, Psalm 30 is usually categorized as an individual song of thanksgiving.

Even so, it would not be entirely exceptional to articulate in the first-person singular the experience of a communal deliverance. Psalm 118, for instance, which is also regularly categorized as an individual thanksgiving, clearly recalls the exodus and was (and is) traditionally used at Passover. Thus the expression of thanksgiving and joy in Psalm 30 would have made it quite appropriate for use in celebrating Hanukkah (see 2 Macc 10:7: "they offered hymns of thanksgiving" [RSV]), or perhaps even the return from exile, which led to the construction and dedication of the Second Temple in 515 BCE. Of course, Psalm 30 is appropriate for individual use as well, and most scholars identify it as the celebratory prayer of a person who has recovered from sickness (see v. 2). In short, regardless of how it originated, Psalm 30 may well have functioned in a variety of settings. Of enduring theological significance is the fact that while the psalm is predominantly a prayer, the substance of the prayer is praise.

30:1-3. The psalmist's praise in prayer is voiced in the opening words using the verb "extol" (רום *rûm*). God is extolled elsewhere simply because God is king (see Pss 99:5, 9; 145:1) or because God has demonstrated sovereignty by delivering the people from their enemies (cf. Exod 15:2; Ps 118:28) or other distress (cf. Pss 34:3; 107:32). The word "extol" more literally means "to lift up"; it is an appropriate choice here, since God has "lifted . . . out" the psalmist (v. 1*b*; see Exod 2:16, 19, where the verb is used of drawing water from a well). The imagery anticipates v. 3, where God has "brought up" those who have "gone down." Sheol (see Ps 6:5) and the Pit (see Ps 28:1) are designations for the realm of the dead (see Ps 88:3-4 and Isa 38:18, where the terms occur together). In other words, the distress, which the foes (v.

1) have either caused or seek to take advantage of, is life-threatening. The different imagery in v. 2 suggests a sickness from which the psalmist had been "healed" when he or she "called . . . for help" (see Pss 5:2; 18:41). It is possible that Psalm 30 originated as a prayer to celebrate deliverance from a serious illness (see Psalm 6 and Isa 38:9-20, each of which shares vocabulary and conceptuality with Psalm 30). The verb "to heal" (רפא *rāpā*), however, can be used metaphorically (see Ps 147:3; Hos 6:1; 11:3; 14:4; Jer 3:22; 33:6); as Kraus suggests of vv. 2-3, "In this formulary, room could be found for many of the misfortunes of life."[141]

30:4-5. These verses interrupt the prayer as the psalmist invites the congregation (see Ps 4:3) to join in the praise and thanksgiving. The two verbs in v. 4 recur in v. 12, where the psalmist makes a lifetime commitment to these activities. The word "name" (זכר *zēker*) in v. 4 is more literally "remembrance" (see Ps 97:12). As Ps 6:5 suggests, there is no "remembrance" or praise of God in Sheol (see below on v. 9). Praise and thanksgiving are the vocation of the living (Isa 38:19). Indeed, as Kraus concludes, what the psalmist has learned from the whole experience is that "the purpose of his existence is to praise God."[142] This new understanding of life motivates the psalmist to be a witness to others concerning the character of God (v. 5*a*; see "favor" in v. 7 and Pss 5:12; 89:17; 106:4). It also prompts a reevaluation of suffering (v. 5*b*). God's commitment to life (v. 3) and lifetime commitment of favor mean that the ultimate end of human suffering is not "weeping" but "rejoicing" (see Ps 6:8; Isa 65:19; Jer 31:16). Thus v. 5 anticipates v. 11, just as v. 4 anticipates v. 12.

30:6-12. The reevaluation continues in v. 6 as the prayer resumes. Verses 6-12 seem to be a sort of flashback in which the psalmist reviews the former distress (vv. 6-10) and deliverance (vv. 11-12), even quoting a portion of the prayer for help mentioned in v. 2 (vv. 9-10). The psalmist's former approach to life apparently involved a false sense of security (v. 6). Even though there is something compelling about attributing prosperity to God's favor and misfortune or "dismay" to

141. Kraus, *Psalms 1–59*, 355.
142. Kraus, *Psalms 1–59*, 356.

God's absence, as the psalmist does in v. 7 (see Ps 104:29; see also Ps 6:2-3, where the same root is rendered by the NRSV as "shaking with terror" and "struck with terror"), this theology is ultimately not profound enough. Although the psalmist says in v. 6, "I shall not be shaken forever" (author's trans.; see Pss 10:6; 15:5; 16:8), the psalmist *was* shaken by the experience of misfortune. This experience leads the psalmist, however, to plead for the mercy of God (see vv. 8, 10). The two pleas for mercy frame the questions of v. 9, which are often interpreted as the psalmist's attempt to appeal to God's self-interest (see the similar question or assertions in Pss 6:5; 88:10-12; Isa 38:18), but which may more positively be heard as the psalmist's affirmation of the desire to live, despite suffering. Indeed, the psalmist's question about praise is a question about life, since for the psalmists to live is to praise God and to praise God is to live (see Reflections).

By v. 12, the psalmist is committed to being thankful "forever," in contrast to the false confidence that was presumed to be "forever" in v. 6. To be sure, it seems that the psalmist's situation has improved (v. 11), but one is left with the impression that when the next round of distress arrives, as it inevitably does, the psalmist will remain "forever" thankful even as she or he offers a new prayer for help. In short, the psalmist has arrived at a new awareness of God's presence, even amid suffering, when God appears to be absent (see Commentary on Psalm 22). And the psalmist will not be silent; that is, the psalmist will be a faithful witness to this new and deeper understanding of the availability of God's gracious presence and help. Now, in distress as well as in prosperity, the psalmist will live to praise God "forever."

REFLECTIONS

1. Mays speaks of the psalmist's experience as risky, since it is possible to hear Psalm 30 in a very simplistic way—that is, pray long enough and God will make everything all right.[143] But it is also possible to hear Psalm 30 differently. Kraus suggests that the psalmist's new orientation to life means a reevaluation of suffering and joy: "Suffering is fitted into the course of life in a comprehensive way . . . the new reality of the nearness of God and the help of God fills life and determines the understanding of existence."[144] In short, suffering need not be an indication of the absence of God for those who take refuge in God (Ps 2:12). The existence of suffering does not negate the good news that life is a gift from God.

But if this is the case, then joy is possible in the depths. And praise is not reserved for seasons of prosperity; rather, it becomes a constant way of life. As Mays concludes:

> The psalmist had made the loss of praise the very basis of his supplication and thereby dared to make one of the most important statements in the Bible about the theological value of praise. . . . Praise is the way the faithfulness of the LORD becomes word and is heard in the LORD's world (v. 9). For people, it is the language of joy and gladness that goes with life and is life in contrast to the silence of death (vv. 11-12). And salvation is here understood as reaching its goal, not just in the restoration of the needy, but finally in the praise of God.[145]

The psalmist prays to live and lives to praise.

2. Psalm 30 is traditionally used during the season of Easter. It is appropriate for Easter, because it is an affirmation of both God's life-giving power and life as God's good gift. In a real sense, the psalmist's deliverance is not so much from physical sickness

---

143. Mays, *Psalms*, 142.
144. Kraus, *Psalms 1–59*, 356-57.
145. Mays, *Psalms*, 141.

to physical health as it is from a deadly misunderstanding of human security (vv. 6-7) to a lively awareness of God's presence in all of life (vv. 11-12). This awareness engenders thanks, praise, and dancing (vv. 4, 11-12; see Reflections on Psalm 6). In this light, as suggested above, v. 9 need not be understood as an appeal to God's self-interest, but may be heard as the psalmist's embrace of life as a God-given gift. Clothed with joy (v. 11) and giving thanks to God forever, the psalmist's whole life becomes praise (v. 12).

PSALM 31:1-24, MY LIFE AND FUTURE ARE IN YOUR HAND

COMMENTARY

This prayer for help is traditionally classified as an individual complaint, but Gerstenberger points out that it shows "neither logical nor literary order."[146] Perhaps its irregularity is an appropriate representation of the psalmist's chaotic life (see vv. 9-13). In any case, it is clear that expressions of trust alternate with petitions accompanied by reasons that indicate the severity of the psalmist's plight. The effect is a psalm that begins (v. 1a), ends (vv. 19-24), and is pervaded by expressions of trust in God (vv. 3a, 4b-8, 14-15a). While it is possible to divide the psalm into two (vv. 1-8, 9-24) or three parts (vv. 1-8, 9-18, 19-24), its most prominent feature is the frequent alternation between petition and trust.

31:1-2. The opening line, which the NIV translates better than the NRSV does, effectively summarizes the message of the whole psalm and much of the psalter. In entrusting his or her life to God, the psalmist arrives at what the introduction to the psalter calls "happy" (Ps 2:12; see "refuge" also in Pss 5:11; 7:1; 11:1; 14:6; 16:1; 31:19; and esp. 71:1-3, which is almost identical to 31:1-3; see Introduction). The initial expression of trust is followed by a series of petitions in vv. 1b-2 that make it clear that the psalmist depends on God. The psalmist's integrity depends on God (v. 1b; see "shame" in v. 17 and Pss 25:2-3, 20; Ps 25:20 specifically associates not being ashamed with taking refuge in God). Indeed, the psalmist's life depends on God as the three nearly synonymous verbs suggest: "deliver" (פלט *pālaṭ*; see Ps 22:5, 9), "rescue" (נצל *nṣl*; see Ps 7:2), and "save"

(ישע *yš'*; see Pss 3:2 [NIV, "deliver"; NRSV, "help"]; 6:4; 7:1). The variety of nouns also emphasizes the psalmist's dependence upon God—"rock" (see Pss 18:2, 31, 46; 19:14; 28:1), "refuge" (a different Hebrew word than in v. 1; cf. "stronghold" in Ps 27:1), "fortress" (see Pss 18:2). By appealing to God's righteousness, vv. 1b-2 anticipate vv. 3-8. The psalmist affirms that it is God's character to set things right. Subsequent verses will also highlight two of God's fundamental characteristics: faithfulness (v. 5) and steadfast love (vv. 7, 16, 21).

31:3. The psalmist returns briefly to another expression of trust in v. 3a, repeating "fortress" from v. 2 and using a different Hebrew word for "rock" (see Pss 18:2; 42:9). The piling up of synonyms for the original "refuge" in v. 1 makes the point emphatically: the psalmist's life depends on God. The syntax of v. 3a reinforces the point. The line contains no verb, thus necessitating the use of the personal pronoun "You," which emphasizes God's role in the psalmist's life. The return to petition in v. 3b is marked by the phrase "for your name's sake," which again directs attention to God's character. The two verbs in v. 3b also occur together in Ps 23:2-3 (see NIV). There, too, the provision God makes for the psalmist's need is "for his [God's] name's sake" (see also Ps 25:11). The two verbs also occur in Exod 15:13, where Moses and the Israelites celebrate the exodus and guidance effected by God's steadfast love. In Psalm 31 as well, the psalmist will rejoice and appeal to God's steadfast love (vv. 7, 16, 21).

146. Gerstenberger, *Psalms: Part 1*, 137.

31:4-5. The prayer for God to "take me out" (v. 4a) is also reminiscent of the exodus, which is often described with the same verb (see Exod 13:9, 14, 16; 18:1; 20:2). The psalmist requests a sort of personal exodus, based on his or her awareness that God's past activity has revealed God to be one who sees affliction (Ps 31:7; see Exod 3:7, 17) and liberates captives. It is not clear exactly what type of affliction is indicated in v. 4a (see "net" in Pss 10:9; 25:15; 35:7; 57:6; 140:6). The imagery in vv. 4, 9-13 is sufficiently graphic to suggest real affliction, but it is open-ended enough to apply to a variety of circumstances. Obviously, the psalmist is being persecuted somehow; he or she is suffering precisely on account of faith in God.

Verse 4b contains another emphatic personal pronoun—*"you* are my refuge" (the same word as in v. 2)—and introduces another expression of trust that extends through v. 8. The most direct affirmation of the psalmist's dependence on God is v. 5a, which is quoted by Jesus from the cross in Luke 23:46. In Jesus' case, this affirmation comes at the moment of death, which is certainly appropriate; but for the psalmist, this affirmation is as much for living as for dying. The word "spirit" (רוח *rûaḥ*) can also mean "breath," and it is virtually synonymous with "life" (see Job 34:14-15; Ps 104:29-30). The psalmist says, in effect, "I put my life in your hand," or "I turn my life over to you." The psalmist's confidence is obviously not *self*-confidence; it is grounded in God's activity ("you have redeemed"; see Pss 25:22; 26:11) and God's character ("faithful God"; see Exod 34:6, where God's self-revelation includes faithfulness).

31:6-8. As the NIV suggests, v. 6 should begin with "I hate." Thus the psalmist expresses loyalty to God by affirming opposition to those who oppose God (see Pss 5:5; 26:5). It is another way of saying what the psalmist has affirmed all along and says explicitly in v. 6b : "I trust in the LORD" (see Pss 4:5; 9:10; Introduction). The "I" is emphatic, effectively contrasting the psalmist and those who are loyal to "worthless idols" (see Jonah 2:8; for the word here translated "worthless," see "false" in Ps 24:4; see also Jer 18:15). The progression in vv. 5-6 from "into your hand" to "I trust" anticipates vv. 14-15a, the next expression of trust, where

the sequence is reversed. The psalmist's trust in God allows the psalmist to "exult and rejoice" (v. 7). Again, the goal for rejoicing is God-centered rather than self-centered—"in your steadfast love" (see vv. 16, 21). Like the word "faithful" in v. 5, the word "steadfast love" occurs in Exod 34:6-7 in God's self-revelation (see Pss 5:7; 6:4; Introduction). The psalmist depends on God to do what God had done in the book of Exodus—namely, to see affliction (v. 7; Exod 3:7, 17) and to break the power of the enemy for the sake of the life of God's people. "Broad place" in v. 8 connotes safety and security or, in a more contemporary idiom, "You have given me some space." Given the recollections of the exodus noted above, it is perhaps not coincidental that the same Hebrew root (רחב *rḥb*) is used in Exod 3:8 to designate the land of promise as a "broad" land (see also Pss 4:1; 18:19; 118:5).

31:9-13. Whereas vv. 7-8 make one think that deliverance has already occurred (see also vv. 19-22), vv. 9-13 return to a petition ("Be merciful" [חנן *ḥānan*]; see Pss 4:1; 6:2) followed by an extended description of the psalmist's "distress" (צר *ṣar,* see the same Hebrew root in v. 7 [NRSV, "adversities"; NIV, "anguish"]). The language is open-ended; it seems to suggest simultaneously grief, sickness, depression, and persecution. Not surprisingly, several of the formulations are echoed in other complaints. For instance, v. 9b recalls Ps 6:7a (the verb "waste[s] away" [עשש *'āšēš*] occurs only in Pss 6:7 and 31:9-10); and the vocabulary of v. 10 appears elsewhere—"sorrow" (v. 10a; see Pss 13:2b; Jer 20:18); "groaning"/"sighing" (v. 10b; see Pss 6:6; 38:9; 102:5); "strength" (v. 10c; see Pss 38:10; 71:9; 102:23); "bones" (v. 10d; see Pss 6:2; 22:14, 17; 102:3). Elsewhere, too, the psalmist is an object of "scorn" or "contempt" (v. 11; see Pss 22:6; 39:8; 69:7, 9-10 [NRSV, "reproach" and "insult(s)"]; see also Jer 20:8 [NRSV, "reproach"]). The image of a "broken vessel" in v. 12 is particularly graphic and poignant (see Jer 22:28). The phrase is more literally "perishing vessel," thus suggesting that despite, or perhaps because of, his or her trust in God, the psalmist is experiencing what is supposed to be reserved for the wicked (see "perish" in Pss 1:6; 2:12). Support for the latter option is found in the similarity between Psalm 31 and the book of Jeremiah, which is particularly evident in v. 13 (see Jeremiah 20; see esp. "terror all around" in Ps 31:13 and Jer 20:3, 10; note also "sorrow" in Ps 31:10 and Jer 20:18; "scorn"/"reproach" in Ps 31:11 and Jer 20:8; and "shame" in Ps 31:1, 17 and Jer 17:18; 20:18). Jeremiah suffers *because of* his trust and his faithfulness in proclaiming the word of God (see Jer 20:8). Like the psalmist, Jeremiah's very life was threatened by his persecutors (see Jer 38:4-6).

31:14-24. Like the psalmist, too, Jeremiah alternates between petition/complaint and trust, ultimately turning his case over to God (Jer 20:10-12). The psalmist returns emphatically to trust in vv. 14-15*a*, which, as suggested above, reverses the sequence of affirmations in vv. 5-6. Here *"I trust"* (v. 14; as in v. 6, the "I" is emphatic) leads to "My times are in your hand" (v. 15), or better translated, "in your hand is my *future."* In vv. 5-6, 14-15, the psalmist entrusts life and future to God. The word "hand" (יד *yād*) connotes "grasp" or "power." Thus the psalmist affirms that the operative power in his or her life is ultimately God and not the enemy (see "hand" in association with enemies in vv. 8, 15). The syntax of v. 15 is revealing; the first word is the emphatic pronoun "I," and the last word is the pronoun "you." The effect is to highlight the intimacy of relation on which the psalmist stakes his or her life and future.

Verses 15*b*-18 renew the petition, repeating earlier pleas ("deliver" in v. 15*b* is the same as "rescue" in v. 2; see "save" in vv. 2, 16*b* and "shame" in vv. 1, 17) and adding a new one in v. 16*a*: "Let your face shine" (see Num 6:25; Pss 4:6; 67:1; 80:3, 7, 19; see "face" in Pss 11:7; 17:15; 27:8-9). God's "face" symbolizes God's presence, and as is often the case, the request seems to correlate good fortune with God's presence and suffering with God's absence. This correlation is understandable and even helpful to the extent that it attempts to relate all of life to God; however, it also represents a limited understanding of God, and the psalmists regularly push beyond it. Psalm 31:20 moves in this direction; that is, "the shelter of God's face" (author's trans.) is available to the persecuted. And v. 22 goes further, as the psalmist suggests that he or she was mistaken in the earlier conclusion that suffering had completely separated him or her from God. This is certainly the faith that Luke

articulates as Jesus quotes Ps 31:5*a* from the cross (Luke 23:46; see Introduction and Commentary on Psalms 13; 22; 30).

In addition to recalling the petition with which the psalm began (see v. 1), vv. 17-18 juxtapose the contrasting alternatives that are present in Psalm 1 and throughout the psalter: "the wicked" (v. 17) and "the righteous" (v. 18). As vv. 19-20 make clear, Psalm 31 affirms, as do Psalms 1 and 2, that there is much to be gained—"abundant . . . goodness"—from being open to God's instruction (Ps 1:1-3) and taking refuge in God (v. 19; see Ps 2:12). This "reward" is clearly not material prosperity or an easy life (see vv. 4, 9-13, 15*b*-18) but the conviction that one's life and future really are in God's hand. This conviction issues in praise that celebrates God's fundamental character—steadfast love (v. 21). For the psalmist, to praise God is to live abundantly, regardless of outward circumstances. Interestingly, the psalmist envisions the future of the wicked as lying "silent" (v. 17), whereas Ps 30:12 had concluded with the affirmation that the psalmist would "not be silent" as a result of God's life-giving power. The psalmist's "unsilence" consists of unending praise—the offering of the self to God—which constitutes life as God intends.

Meanwhile, of course, all is not as God intends. The psalmist is opposed (vv. 7, 11, 13, 15, 18), and so is God. Thus Psalm 31, like Psalms 1 and 2 and the psalter as a whole, is eschatological (see Introduction). God's goodness is simultaneously something to be experienced in the present and something to be awaited, hoped for (v. 24; see Ps 27:14). Thus the psalmist both celebrates deliverance as already having occurred (vv. 5*b*, 7-8, 21-22) and continues to pray for it (vv. 1*b*-2, 3*b*-4*a*, 9-13, 15*b*-18). This tension is the persistent reality of the life of faith. As we wait, there is the possibility of strength and courage, because we wait as God's "saints . . . the faithful" (v. 23). These two words are related to the two fundamental attributes of God celebrated in Psalm 31: steadfast love (vv. 7, 16, 21; "saints" חסידים *ḥāsîdîm*] could be translated "steadfastly loving ones" or "steadfastly loved ones") and faithfulness (v. 5). In short, the people of God derive their identity from God's identity, and therein lies genuine hope (v. 24) and the possibility of love (v. 23).

REFLECTIONS

Scholars regularly observe that the frequent expressions of trust in Psalm 31 give it a creedal character or even a didactic thrust. What John Calvin said about v. 5 applies to the whole psalm, "This is one of the principle places of Scripture which are most suitable for correcting distrust."[147] In short, Psalm 31 is a prayer that teaches us about trusting God, both in dying and in living.

As suggested above, Psalm 31 became a resource for the gospel writers in understanding and relating the passion and death of Jesus (see also Psalms 22; 41; 69; Introduction). Jesus' quotation of v. 5a makes the final act of his earthly life an affirmation of trust in God that anticipates the resurrection. God's power to redeem will not be thwarted even by death (see also Rom 14:8). Following the example of Jesus, several great saints of the church—Jerome, Martin Luther, John Knox—died with the words of Ps 31:5 on their lips (see also Acts 7:59).[148] Psalm 31 can teach us how to die.

But just as important, Psalm 31 teaches us how to live. Jesus' words from the cross are not simply an interpretation of how Jesus died but also an interpretation of how Jesus lived his whole life—trusting God, proclaiming and embodying the reign of God in word and deed. The affirmations in vv. 5, 15 are for living, but this is precisely the difficulty we have with Psalm 31. What does it mean for us to turn our lives and futures over to God? What does it mean to live as a "servant" (v. 16) under God's sovereignty? The difficulty of answering these questions is indicated by the way contemporary people are inclined to hear vv. 4, 9-13, 15b. People tend to think the psalmist is paranoid. How can anybody be that threatened or persecuted? To be sure, it is a legitimate question for those of us who manage fairly well to order our lives satisfactorily most of the time. But that's also the real rub; we manage to order our lives. And that makes it very difficult to appreciate what Psalm 31 is fundamentally about: "the act of self-surrender to Yahweh."[149] Perhaps the most important thing Psalm 31 can teach us is that persons who trust God unreservedly should expect opposition from those who choose to trust themselves or any of the "worthless idols" (v. 6) that abound in our culture and in our churches.

In this regard, it is significant that much of the language of Psalm 31 is similar to the book of Jeremiah, especially those portions in which Jeremiah complains that his very faithfulness in proclaiming God's word has disrupted his life. Like Jeremiah, Jesus' very faithfulness to the reign of God engendered opposition, culminating in the cross, from which Jesus spoke the words of Ps 31:5. Those of us whom Jesus calls to "deny themselves and take up their cross and follow me" (Mark 8:34 NRSV) can also expect opposition. To surrender self in order to follow God is no more popular today than it was in the time of Jeremiah or Jesus. What Reinhold Niebuhr wrote in the 1920s is just as true today, and it is particularly pertinent to preachers:

> The real meaning of the gospel is in conflict with most of the customs and attitudes of our day at so many places that there is an adventure in the Christian message, even if you only play around with its ideas in a conventional world. . . .
>
> An astute pedagogy and a desire to speak the truth in love may greatly decrease opposition to a minister's message and persuade a difficult minority to entertain at least, and perhaps to profit by, his message; but if a gospel is preached without opposition it is simply not the gospel which resulted in the cross. It is not, in short, the gospel of love.[150]

The faithful psalmist knew in her or his life the kind of opposition that resulted in the cross. The psalmist also knew the paradoxical secret of what Scripture calls "happy":

147. Calvin, *Commentary on the Book of Psalms,* IV:1:503.
148. See Rowland E. Prothero, *The Psalms in Human Life and Experience* (New York: E. P. Dutton, 1903) 93, 199.
149. Kraus, *Psalms 1–59,* 367.
150. Reinhold Niebuhr, *Leaves from the Notebook of a Tamed Cynic* (San Francisco: Harper & Row, 1980) 27, 140.

that to surrender one's life to God is truly to claim one's life (see Mark 8:35). Psalm 31 can teach us how to live.

To entrust our lives and futures to God, to belong to God in living and dying means ultimately that we derive our identity not from the worthless idols of our culture but from the character of God, to whom we entrust ourselves. The two fundamental characteristics of God that are emphasized in Psalm 31 are God's faithfulness (v. 5) and God's steadfast love (vv. 7, 16, 21), and the psalmist's closing admonition addresses the people of God as God's steadfastly loved (or loving) ones and "the faithful" (v. 23). God's faithfulness and love enable and empower the existence of a people who in turn can be faithful and loving to God and to each other. In our world—full of isolated selves and with "terror all around" (v. 13)—that good news invites a commitment to God and to the church that makes it possible to "be strong . . . take courage . . . wait for the LORD" (v. 24).[151]

151. Portions of the above treatment of Psalm 31 appeared originally in substantially the same form in J. C. McCann, Jr., "Psalm 31:1-8: Psalm for the Fifth Sunday of Easter," *No Other Foundation* 13/2 (Winter 1992–93) 30-35.

PSALM 32:1-11, YOU FORGAVE THE GUILT OF MY SIN

COMMENTARY

On account of its description of deliverance from sin and its harmful effects (vv. 3-5), as well as the elements of testimony (vv. 6-7) and invitation (v. 11), Psalm 32 is often classified as a psalm of thanksgiving. Several scholars, however, categorize it as a wisdom psalm, because of the opening beatitudes (vv. 1-2) and the explicitly instructional intent (vv. 8-9). Drawing on both sets of observations, Gerstenberger suggests that Psalm 32 "comes very close to being a homily on penitence."[152] For this reason, church tradition has named Psalm 32 the second of the penitential psalms (see also Psalms 6; 38; 51; 102; 130; 143). While there is no actual confession of sin in the psalm, it does report the psalmist's experience of confessing sin and receiving forgiveness (vv. 3-5). Psalm 32 is thus instructive testimony as to the nature and benefits of confession, as well as to God's character as a gracious, forgiving God. The psalm may originally have been used in ceremonies of confession or cleansing in the Temple, although most scholars suggest a later date, associating its origin and use with the post-exilic synagogue (see Ezra 9; Nehemiah 9; Daniel 9). In any case, it continues to function as instruction for readers in any generation, and it

continues to invite the people of God to confession of sin, to trust, and to joy (vv. 6-11).

Psalm 32 begins with two beatitudes that recall the beginning of the psalter (see 1:1; 2:12). Several other items of the vocabulary of Psalm 32 also recall Psalms 1–2: "sin" (vv. 1, 5; see "sinners" in 1:1, 5), "day and night" (v. 4; see 1:2), "teach" (v. 8; the root is the same as "law" or "instruction" in 1:2), "way" (v. 8; see 1:1, 6; 2:12), "wicked" (v. 10; see 1:1, 4-6), and "righteous" (v. 11; see 1:6). By defining happiness in terms of forgiveness, Psalm 32 functions as an important check against any tendency to misunderstand Psalm 1. That is, to be righteous is not a matter of being sinless but a matter of being forgiven, of being open to God's instruction (Ps 1:2; see 32:8-9), and of trusting God rather than self (v. 10; see Ps 2:12). In fact, as Psalm 32 suggests, sin and its effects are pervasive in the life of the righteous. Verse 2*c* apparently anticipates v. 5 and the confession of sin described there; that is, confession of sin must be made honestly and humbly. The pervasiveness of sin is not an excuse for further sinning but an opportunity to seek forgiveness sincerely.

The pervasiveness of sin is represented literarily by the fact that three words for sin in vv. 1-2, 5 envelope the psalmist's self-description in vv. 3-4: "transgression(s)" (vv. 1, 5), "sin(s)"

152. Gerstenberger, *Psalms: Part 1,* 143.

(vv. 1, 5), "iniquity"/"guilt" (עון *'āwōn*, vv. 2, 5). While there are other words for "sin," these words represent Israel's basic vocabulary (see Ps 51:1-5). The word "sin" (פשע *peša'*) is the most general, meaning fundamentally "to miss the mark." "Transgression" connotes willful rebellion, and "iniquity"/"guilt" (חטאה *ḥăṭā'â*) suggests the enduring, destructive effects of disobedience. The psalmist's life is characterized by all three (v. 5), and the results are very real, even physical, causing the psalmist's "bones" (see Pss 22:14; 31:10; 38:3) to waste away (cf. Job 13:28) through "groaning" (cf. Job 3:24; Pss 22:1; 38:8). While the imagery of v. 4 suggests God's judgment (see 1 Sam 5:11; Ps 38:4), the impression left by vv. 3-4 is that the real problem is not God's wrath but the psalmist's silence. As v. 5c indicates, God is fully willing to forgive. But first the psalmist's silence must be broken, for "the silence is the rejection of grace."[153]

That the reality of divine forgiveness is even more encompassing than the reality of sin is also represented by the literary structure of the psalm. Whereas sin encompassed the description of the psalmist's life, God's forgiveness encompasses sin (see "forgiven"/"forgave" in vv. 1a, 5c). Those who do "not *cover up* . . . iniquity" (v. 5) will be the "happy" ones whose "sins are *covered*" (v. 1). Verse 5c, which marks the turning point of the psalm, is crucial. Its pronoun "you" is emphatic; it is nearly, perhaps exactly, the central poetic line. After the announcement of forgiveness in v. 5c, none of the words for "sin" occur again. The situation changes for persons who acknowledge their sin in reliance on God's grace.

While the psalmist focuses on himself or herself in vv. 3-5, the reality of forgiveness directs the psalmist outward. Attention is now focused on "the faithful" (v. 6), the Hebrew word for which (חסיד *ḥāsîd*) anticipates the occurrence of the related steadfast love in v. 10. The faithful derive their identity not from their own accomplishments but from *God's* faithfulness in forgiving and renewing them (see Ps 31:23). Prayer becomes a way of life for those who know that their own accomplishments, capabilities, and intentions are always inadequate. That is, it is a way of life for those "who trust in the LORD" (v. 10).

Attention is also focused on God. Prayer, of course, is directed "to you"—to God (v. 6), and the three affirmations in v. 7 focus directly on God as well. The first word in v. 7 is the emphatic pronoun "You," which recalls the emphatic "you" that began v. 5c. In each of the three affirmations in v. 7, God is the subject and the psalmist is the object of God's action. God's character and activity are determinative; God is a faithful protector (the word for "hiding place" [סתר *sēter*] also occurs as "cover" or "shelter" in Pss 27:5; 31:20; 61:4; 91:1). Robert Jenson points out that "the psalmist's own stance is that of *witness*, to his experience and to the grace of God."[154] The substance of the psalmist's witness in v. 7c anticipates vv. 10-11, which also underscore God's character and activity. The word "surround(s)" recurs in v. 10 in connection with God's steadfast love, a fundamental divine attribute (see Exod 34:6-7, where the issue is also forgiveness; see also Introduction). The Hebrew root translated "songs of deliverance" (רנה *rinnâ*) in v. 7c underlies "sing" in v. 11. The psalmist can invite others to sing, because God has already surrounded the psalmist with "songs of deliverance." Verses 6-7 and 10-11 are also linked structurally in a chiastic pattern (see Introduction): "invitation" (v. 6), profession of faith (v. 7), profession of faith (v. 10), invitation (v. 11).

The chiastic pattern of these verses serves to emphasize vv. 8-9, which are probably another instance of the psalmist's witness. Several scholars understand the "I" of v. 8 to be God, and thus view vv. 8-9 to be a divine word delivered by a priest or prophet; however, in view of the psalmist's witness in vv. 6-7, 10-11, it is more likely that the psalmist is speaking in vv. 8-9 to offer instruction to others. As in Psalm 51, which is another penitential psalm, the forgiven sinner teaches God's ways to others (see 51:13). This educational ministry is not presumptuous, for the psalmist witnesses not to his or her own righteousness but to divine grace—God's willingness and God's ability to set things and persons right. Thus "the way you should go" (v. 8) points to the psalmist's example of breaking silence to confess sin (vv. 3, 5) and to his or her conviction of God's willingness to forgive and restore (vv. 7, 10). The psalmist's witness

153. Mays, *Psalms,* 147.

154. Robert W. Jenson, "Psalm 32," *Int.* 33 (1979) 175.

in vv. 6-11 is in essence an invitation to others, including the readers of Psalm 32, to confess their own sinfulness and to live in dependence upon the grace of God (see "trust" in Pss 4:5; 9:10; Introduction). The invitation is explicit in v. 11, which is a final reminder that the "righteous" (see Ps 1:5-6) and the "upright in heart" (see Pss 7:10; 11:2; 36:10; 64:10; 94:15; 97:11; 125:4) are not the sinless but the forgiven. Joy and happiness (vv.

1-2) derive not from human achievement but from God's gracious activity on behalf of sinners. Perhaps not coincidentally, Psalm 33 begins with essentially the same invitation that concludes Psalm 32; it is an extended celebration of the divine steadfast love (vv. 5, 18, 22; see 32:10), which surrounds the penitent (32:10) and, indeed, fills the earth (33:5; see Commentary on Psalms 19; 33).

REFLECTIONS

As the Commentary shows, Psalm 32 recalls Psalm 1 and reinforces the understanding of righteousness articulated on the basis of Psalm 1. That is to say, to be righteous is not to manage somehow to obey all the rules, to be sinless. Rather, as Psalm 32 suggests, the lives of the righteous are pervaded by sin and its consequences (vv. 3-5). To be righteous is to be forgiven (v. 5). To be righteous is to be a witness to God's grace (vv. 6-11).

Not surprisingly, one of the greatest witnesses to God's grace, the apostle Paul, knew Psalm 32 and cited vv. 1-2a in his own teaching in Rom 4:6-8. Paul did not invent the notion of justification by grace. He found it in the story of Abraham (see esp. Gen 15:6) and in psalms like Psalm 32 (see also Psalm 51). Another of the great witnesses to God's grace, Augustine, is said to have had the words of Psalm 32 inscribed above his bed so that they would be the first thing he saw upon awakening.[155]

The experience of being happy (vv. 1-2), of being forgiven (v. 5), of being in the right (v. 11), is an important dimension of human life in any era. Indeed, "facing up to one's errors and being pardoned are important modes of interaction even today, which go far beyond all the existing penitential rites of religious and ideological groups."[156] While Gerstenberger is undoubtedly correct, it is also true that we contemporary folk do not readily think of ourselves as being sinners; neither are we inclined to think in terms of sin as an explanation for our corporate ills. Karl Menninger pointed this out several years ago in a book entitled *Whatever Became of Sin?* After documenting the disappearance of sin, Menninger makes a simple proposal:

> My proposal is for the revival or reassertion of personal responsibility in all human acts, good and bad. Not total responsibility, but not zero either. I believe that all the evildoing in which we become involved to any degree tends to evoke guilt feelings and depression. These may or may not be clearly perceived, but they affect us. They may be reacted to and covered up by all kinds of escapism, rationalization, and reaction or symptom formation. To revive the half-submerged idea of personal responsibility and to seek appropriate measures of reparation might turn the tide of our aggressions and of the moral struggle in which most of the world population is engaged.[157]

Menninger recognizes what Ps 32:3-4 also recognizes: the devastating physical, emotional, and spiritual effects of failing to acknowledge our sinfulness. Like the psalmist, he calls on us to break our silence (v. 3). Menninger calls on everyone to contribute to the revival of the term *sin,* but he suggests that the clergy have a special responsibility: "It is their special prerogative to study sin—or whatever they call it—to identify it, to define it, to warn us about it, and to spur measures for combating and rectifying it."[158]

---

155. See Prothero, *The Psalms in Human Life and Experience*, 29.
156. Gerstenberger, *Psalms: Part 1*, 141.
157. Karl Menninger, *Whatever Became of Sin?* (New York: Hawthorn Books, 1973) 178.
158. Menninger, *Whatever Became of Sin?* 192.

For clergy and laity alike, Psalm 32 is an impetus and a resource to study sin. It also suggests how to begin to combat it and rectify it: by forthright confession of sin, acceptance of the grace of God, and humble dependence on God's steadfast love rather than on human initiative and ingenuity.

PSALM 33:1-22, THE EARTH IS FULL OF GOD'S UNFAILING LOVE

COMMENTARY

One of the few songs of praise in Books I–II of the psalter, Psalm 33 seems to be a direct response to the invitation of Ps 32:11 (note the absence of a superscription for Psalm 33). Verse 1 addresses an invitation to the same parties addressed in 32:11—the "righteous" and the "upright"—and the NRSV's "shout for joy" (32:11) and "rejoice" (33:1) translate the same Hebrew verb. Furthermore, the culminating affirmation of Ps 32:11 highlighted the concepts of steadfast love and trust, both of which are also prominent in Psalm 33. The word "trust" (בטח *bāṭaḥ*) is featured in the culminating affirmation of Psalm 33 (v. 21), and v. 5*b* boldly proclaims that the steadfast love, which surrounds those who trust God (32:11), also fills the earth! This is the crucial verse in the psalm; everything that follows is essentially an explanation of it.[159] What is affirmed as the psalm unfolds is that God is sovereign over all (note the word "all" in vv. 6, 8, 13, 14, 15)—creation (vv. 6-9), the nations and peoples (vv. 10-12), humanity in general (vv. 13-15), human teachers and symbols of power (vv. 16-17), as well as those who explicitly acknowledge their hope in God's steadfast love (vv. 18-19).

The intent of Psalm 33 to acknowledge God's comprehensive sovereignty is reinforced by the fact that it consists of 22 lines—the same number of lines as the letters in the Hebrew alphabet. The psalm is not an acrostic, but its structure does bespeak completeness. When Psalms 32 and 33 are read in sequence, the striking claim is that the grace God shows in forgiving sinners (Psalm 32) is the force that accounts for the origin of the world (vv. 6-9), the unfolding of history (vv. 10-12), the care of individual persons

(vv. 13-15), the real power behind human illusions of power (vv. 16-17), and the hope of God's own people (vv. 18-19). Appropriately, the psalm concludes with a joyful affirmation of faith in God's beneficence and power (vv. 20-21) and a prayer for what constitutes the fundamental reality of the universe: God's steadfast love (v. 22).

33:1-3. The invitation in v. 1 extends into vv. 2-3. Praise is appropriate to those who acknowledge their dependence on God (see Ps 147:1), for praise is essentially the offering of the self to God, including one's musical gifts. Verse 2 represents the first reference to musical instruments in the psalms (see Pss 43:4; 57:8; 71:22; 81:2; 92:3; 98:5; 108:2; 137:2; 144:9; 147:7; 149:3; 150:3; see also 1 Sam 16:16; 2 Sam 6:5; 1 Chr 13:8. Verses 1-2 together suggest that what is important about praise is more the motive and the goal than the means. Instrumentation is appropriate, as is the human voice, singing or shouting (v. 3). The Hebrew root of "loud shouts" (תרועה *těrû'â*) occurs in verbal form in Pss 47:1; 95:1-2; 98:4 (see also Ps 100:2), all of which specifically celebrate God's reign. The motive for praise is the recognition of God's reign, and the goal is to offer oneself and one's best gifts to the source of one's existence. The singing of a "new song" is also associated elsewhere with the celebration of God's reign (see Pss 96:1; 98:1; 149:1; see also Pss 40:3; 144:9; Isa 42:10).

33:4-5. As is typical in the songs of praise, the invitation is followed by reasons for praise. God's "word" and "work" are manifestations of God's own self (v. 4); God is elsewhere described as "upright" (see Pss 25:8; 92:15; see also Pss 32:11; 33:1, which suggest that God's people derive their identity

159. See Mays, *Psalms,* 149.

from God) and possessing "faithfulness" (see Pss 36:5; 88:12; 89:1-2, 5, 8, 33, 49; 92:2; 98:3; 100:5). Verse 5 describes the goal of God's speaking and acting in terms associated elsewhere with God's character and rule: "righteousness and justice" (see Pss 97:2; 99:4), manifested in steadfast love (Pss 98:3; 145:8; see also Exod 34:6-7; Pss 5:7; 119:64; Introduction). As suggested above, the rest of the psalm is an elaboration upon v. 5*b*, illustrating the full extent of the reach of God's loving purposes.

33:6-9. Verse 6*a* repeats the key terms from v. 4: "word" (דבר *dābār*) and the root "to do," "to make" (עשה *'āśâ*; "work" in v. 4 and "made" in v. 6). The focus is on God's Word, as suggested by the mention of "the breath" of God's "mouth" (v. 6*b*) and by the verbs in v. 9. God's Word effects God's work. Verse 6 and 9 especially recall the creation account in Genesis 1, and vv. 7-8 allude to the exodus, which, as Terence Fretheim persuasively argues, represents the fulfillment of God's creational purposes.[160] Verse 7 clearly recalls Exod 15:8 (see "deeps" in both verses, as well as the word the NRSV renders as "heap"/"bottle"; see the NIV's note); and v. 8 describes precisely the response of the Israelites when they saw what God "did" (the same root as "work" in v. 4) against the Egyptians—they "feared the LORD" (Exod 14:31 NRSV).[161] The two occurrences of "he" in v. 9 represent the emphatic use of the pronoun—*God* is behind it all!

33:10-12. The focus shifts from God's word to God's will and from the sphere of creation to the sphere of history (insofar as the two can be separated). As the NIV suggests, the two key terms from v. 10 are repeated in v. 11, effectively contrasting God's enduring will with the transient human will (see Neh 4:15; Prov 19:21, 30-31; Isa 14:26-27; 25:1; 46:10-11). Contrary to a frequent appropriation of v. 12, it is *God* who chooses a nation and a people, not vice-versa. The unremitting focus in Psalm 33 is on God's sovereignty.

---

160. Terence Fretheim, *Exodus,* Interpretation (Louisville: Westminster/John Knox, 1991) 12-14.
161. See Craigie, *Psalms 1–50,* 273.

33:13-15. God's sovereignty is clearly in view in v. 14 (see "sits" or "enthroned" or both in Pss 2:4; 9:8; 29:10; 99:1). Because God rules over all, God sees everyone and everything (vv. 13-15; see Pss 11:4; 14:2; 102:19). The universality of vv. 13-14 recalls v. 8, but there is a particularity here as well. As creator or fashioner of every heart (see "formed" in Gen 2:7), God knows each person.

33:16-19. The greatest of human personages and their trappings of power are negated in vv. 16-17. Kings, of course, represent human sovereignty, and armies and horses are their means for enforcing their own will to power. Such apparent greatness (see "great" three times in vv. 16-17) is an illusion (see Prov 21:30-31). Salvation ("saved" in v. 16 and "victory" in v. 17 represent the same Hebrew root [ישע *yš'*]), or life, is God's gift, not a human achievement. Those who "fear" God (v. 18; cf. v. 8) know that God delivers them from death and keeps them alive (v. 19; see Ps 107:4-9, where sustenance and life result from God's steadfast love).

33:20-22. Thus, they "wait in hope" (v. 20). חכה (*ḥākâ*) is not a commonly used word for "hope" in the psalter (elsewhere only Ps 106:13), but it is essentially synonymous with the more frequently used words that occur here and elsewhere (see "hope" in vv. 18, 22; see also Pss 27:14; 31:24; 130:7; 131:3). Faith, hope, and joy characterize the lives of those who recognize God as a "help" (see Pss 22:19; 27:9; 40:17; 70:5; see esp. Ps 115:9-11, where the admonition to trust accompanies the same affirmation as here) and a "shield" (see Pss 3:3; 7:10; 28:7; 115:9-11). The psalm concludes with a prayer for what it earlier had affirmed fills the earth: God's steadfast love (v. 22; see also vv. 5*b*, 18). Like the psalter as a whole, Psalm 33 is eschatological. It proclaims God's reign amid persons and circumstances that deny it. Thus God's rule is something both to be celebrated with joyful praise (vv. 1-3; see v. 21) and to be awaited in fervent hope (vv. 20-22).

REFLECTIONS

As Peter Craigie suggests, Psalm 33 is a "timely reminder of the essence of biblical theology."[162] That is to say, Psalm 33 proclaims what lies at the heart of the good news of all of Scripture, including the psalter as a whole and the preaching of Jesus: God rules the world (see Psalm 2; Mark 1:14-15; Introduction). The reminder is timely, because the message is so difficult to believe in the context of contemporary, secularized culture. Seldom does it occur to us that life and the resources that sustain life (see vv. 18-19) are the provision of a gracious, steadfastly loving God! Instead, we view life simply as a biological fact, or perhaps as a "human right," and the resources that sustain life are seen as the product of our sophisticated educational and economic system, the benefits of which we attain personally by our own hard work. We earn it!

Likewise, seldom do we understand the world (vv. 6-9) in anything other than scientific terms; so creation becomes not a sacred trust but a realm to be explored and then exploited. Seldom, if ever, do we think of international politics in terms of God's will; we have made even human relatedness a "political science," the subject of which is exclusively "the counsel of the nations" and the "plans of the peoples" (v. 10). In fact, we do believe that nations are saved by their great armies and that security is found in the implements of war (vv. 16-17), and this faith has been and still is the cornerstone of the foreign policy of the United States and every other nation in the world. The great irony, as Reinhold Niebuhr pointed out years ago, is that the very efforts to secure our own destiny and future have rendered us even more insecure and vulnerable. To be sure, neither Niebuhr nor Psalm 33 calls us to passivity but to properly motivated activity. Niebuhr characterized the biblical view of human history: "The evil in human history is regarded as the consequence of man's wrong use of his unique capacities. The wrong use is always due to some failure to recognize the limits of his capacities of power, wisdom, and virtue. Man is an ironic creature because he forgets that he is not simply a creator but also a creature."[163]

We forget that God rules the world and we do not. Instead of praising God, our first inclination is to congratulate ourselves (see Commentary on Psalm 65). Psalm 33 is finally, then, a call to humility and to trust in God rather than in human power, wisdom, or virtue. To heed this call means nothing less than a revolutionary transmutation of values. The things and people that seem so obviously powerful—politicians, armies, weapons—are exposed in the light of God's sovereignty to be illusions. The real power behind the universe, human history, and personal existence is the steadfast love of God, which fills the earth (Ps 33:5b) and is revealed ultimately not by God's absolute enforcement of God's will but by God's forgiveness of sin (Psalm 32). The astounding good news is that the ultimate reality and power in the universe is love (see Commentary on Psalm 19). This power, to be sure, is made perfect in weakness (see 2 Cor 12:9). Indeed, Christians profess to see it revealed most clearly in the cross of Jesus Christ.

162. Craigie, *Psalms 1–50*, 275.
163. Reinhold Niebuhr, *The Irony of American History* (New York: Charles Scribner's Sons, 1952) 156.

PSALM 34:1-22, I WILL TEACH YOU THE FEAR OF THE LORD

COMMENTARY

Psalm 34 is an acrostic poem (see NIV note) that is similar in several ways to Psalm 25 (see above). For instance, as in Psalm 25, v. 22 lies outside the acrostic structure, and if the first letters of vv. 1, 11 (the central poetic line), and 22 are taken in order, they spell the word אלף (*ʾālep*), the first letter of the alphabet. This apparently intentional literary cleverness is often associated with wisdom literature (see the acrostic poem in Prov 31:10-31), and Psalm 34 shares other characteristics with the wisdom literature as well. It explicitly intends to teach, as is clear in v. 11, which addresses "children" as in the book of Proverbs (see Prov 1:8; 3:1; 4:1). Furthermore, the topic of the teaching—"the fear of the LORD"—is a major theme in Proverbs (see Prov 1:7, 29; 2:5; 9:10; 15:33). And the goal of the teaching—to impart "life"—also is in keeping with Proverbs (see Prov 3:2, 16, 18; 4:22-23; 5:6; 10:17). So is the behavior involved in fearing God—proper speech (Prov 4:24, 27; 6:17, 19; 10:18), departure from evil and doing good (Prov 2:20; 3:7; 4:14), the pursuit of peace (Prov 3:17).

Psalm 34 is usually classified as a song of thanksgiving, due to the psalmist's expressed intent to praise God (vv. 1-3), as well as to the account of deliverance in v. 4, which is echoed in vv. 6, 15, 17-18. It is also possible that v. 8 alludes poetically to the sacrificial meal that accompanied a thank offering, but the language may be metaphorical (see below). In any case, it is not necessary to conclude, as most scholars have done, that Psalm 34 was a private composition intended for personal use. To be sure, it can be used for personal meditation, but Gerstenberger suggests that Psalm 34 was probably used originally in synagogue services where "the individual's anxieties and hopes, suffering and salvation were dealt with in meditation, adoration, and instruction."[164]

The superscription is enigmatic. It is most closely related to 1 Sam 21:13, but the king

in that story is named Achish, so what the editor may have intended is not clear. Within the overarching acrostic structure, it is possible to identify several divisions. The opening section expresses the psalmist's intent to praise God (vv. 1-2) and invites others to participate (v. 3). The next section is marked by the repetition of "sought"/"seek" (vv. 4-10). The psalmist narrates his or her own experience of deliverance (vv. 4, 6). This experience, as well as the generalizations the psalmist makes from this experience (vv. 7, 9b-10), serve as the basis for inviting others to turn to God (vv. 5, 8). Hence, even before v. 11, Psalm 34 is instructional; however, vv. 11-14 are more explicitly so. The instruction continues in vv. 15-22 by way of a series of affirmations that are united by their concern with how God relates to the righteous and the wicked.

34:1-3. The psalmist's opening statements make it clear that she or he lives in dependence upon God. To "bless" means essentially to kneel before a sovereign (see Pss 16:7; 26:12). The words "praise" and "boast" are derived from the same Hebrew root (הלל *hll*); praise involves the offering of the self to God (see Pss 22:22-23, 25-26; 33:1; Introduction). Interestingly, while the praise is directed to God, it is also intended to be overheard by the "humble" (cf. NRSV: Pss 9:12, "afflicted"; 10:12, "oppressed"; 22:26, "poor"; 25:9; 69:32, "oppressed"), who are immediately invited to join the psalmist in magnifying (see Ps 69:30) and exalting God (Exod 15:2; see "extol" in Pss 30:1; 99:5, 9; 145:1; note the connections with proclamations of God's reign). As in Ps 69:30-33, the psalmist here offers his or her own life and praise as an example to others who are oppressed, not in an arrogant way but as testimony to God's character (see Ps 20:7; 1 Cor 1:31; 2 Cor 1:12; 10:12-18; 12:1-10).

34:4-10. The psalmist's intent to be an example is clear in these verses. Following the recountings of his or her own experience

164. Gerstenberger, *Psalms: Part 1*, 149.

(vv. 4, 6), the psalmist says to others, in effect, "Experience it for yourselves" (vv. 5, 8-9)! What has been experienced is deliverance (v. 4), salvation (v. 6)—in short, life (see v. 12). It is not something the psalmist has to offer, for he or she is one of the "poor" (v. 6; "poor" [עָנִי *'ăni*] is the same Hebrew root as "humble"/"afflicted" in v. 2). Rather, life is something that *God* offers. The psalmist's advice is not, "Look to me," but, "Look to God" (v. 5)—or, as v. 8 puts it, "Taste and see." In other words, "Get a taste of it yourself, and you'll see" (see Prov 31:18, where the verb translated "taste" is used figuratively as "perceive" [NRSV]; see also Job 12:11; 34:3, where tasting suggests trying something out). What others will "see" is that God is "good"; that is, they will be put in touch with one of Israel's fundamental professions (see Pss 73:1; 86:5; 100:5; 106:1; 107:1; 118:1, 29; 136:1; see also Exod 33:19). Entrusting their lives to God, they will be "radiant" (see Isa 60:5), "happy" (v. 8; see Pss 1:1; 2:12; Introduction), and will be fully provided for (vv. 8-9; see Deut 2:7; 15:18; Ps 23:1).

The key word in vv. 4-10 is "fear" (ירא *yārē'*, vv. 7, 9; see Pss 22:25; 25:12, 14; 31:19; 33:8). While a few OT references to fearing God suggest actual fright (see 1 Sam 12:18; 2 Sam 6:9), fearing God usually connotes reverence for, trust in, and dependence upon God. In effect, it is synonymous with taking refuge in God (v. 8; see Pss 2:12; 5:11; 7:1; 11:1; Introduction) or seeking God (v. 10).

34:11-14. The three occurrences of "fear" in vv. 7, 9 anticipate v. 11, where "fear of the LORD" is the subject of the psalmist's instruction. The fear of God leads to life (v. 12), and, as vv. 13-14 suggest, obedience is involved as well. In the book of Deuteronomy, fearing

God appears to be virtually synonymous with obeying God's commandments (see Deut 6:2, 24; 10:12-13). Evil (vv. 13-14; see also vv. 16, 21) and deceit (see Pss 10:7; 17:1; 24:4; 36:3) are to be avoided; good and peace are to be pursued (cf. Amos 5:14-15).

34:15-22. The movement from vv. 11-14 to vv. 15-16 seems to suggest that the righteous earn life (v. 12) by their good behavior while God punishes evildoers; however, the situation is more complex. The righteous have plenty of troubles about which to cry to God (vv. 15, 17; see also v. 6; the Hebrew words translated "cry"/"cried" differ in each case). Indeed, "Many are the afflictions of the righteous" (v. 19). Faithfulness to God will mean anything but a carefree life! As v. 18 suggests, the good news is that God is with "the brokenhearted" (see Ps 51:17; Isa 61:1) and the "crushed in spirit" (see Ps 51:17; Isa 57:15). In other words, "life" will be experienced in the midst of suffering, not beyond it. Indeed, God will be experienced in the midst of suffering (see Commentary on Psalms 13; 22; 31). Fear of God is rewarded not in a material, mechanistic sense but with the nearness of God (see Commentary on Psalm 1, where it is suggested that the prosperity of the righteous consists in their being connected to the source of life; see also Commentary on Psalm 73). To take refuge in God, to belong to God, is to live (v. 22). To separate oneself from God, which is the essence of wickedness (see Commentary on Psalm 1, esp. 1:6), is to die. To be a servant of God (v. 22) means to recognize God's sovereign claim on one's life. Thus to be a servant of God is to live in dependence on God, which is the essence of righteousness (see Commentary on Psalms 1; 2).

REFLECTIONS

Psalm 34 employs four different Hebrew roots to describe God's activity on behalf of persons who cry out to God in their affliction or trouble. Each word points to God's life-giving activity and serves to focus attention on the question that lies at the heart of Psalm 34 and that is as current as this morning's newspaper: "Which of you desires life?" (v. 12).

Of course, we all desire life. There are further questions, however, such as What is life? And how do we attain it? Psalm 34 offers some answers, but they are not ones we can easily comprehend, because they contradict what culture often teaches us about life. For instance, the culture of the United States would lead one to believe that life consists of driving the classiest car, being surrounded with the most beautiful people, carrying the proper credit card, drinking the right beverages, and generally enjoying oneself to the fullest every moment of the day and night. Millions of advertising dollars are spent every day to try to convince us that life *does* consist in the abundance of possessions (see Luke 12:15), and most of us believe it most of the time. We are good consumers.

In striking contrast to what our culture may teach us, Psalm 34 teaches us that life begins with fearing God—life is a gift from God for which God makes gracious provision (vv. 8-9). What culture teaches us fosters greed, whereas what Psalm 34 teaches us fosters gratitude (vv. 1-3). If life is defined the way our culture defines it, there is no allowance for suffering or for comprehension of the dilemma of the human condition—in short, no possibility for happiness or joy except in the most shallow of senses. Again, Psalm 34 offers a sharp contrast, as Peter Craigie points out:

> The fear of the Lord establishes joy and fulfillment in all of life's experiences. It may mend the broken heart, but it does not prevent the heart from being broken; it may restore the spiritually crushed, but it does not crush the forces that may create oppression. The psalm, if fully grasped, dispels the naiveté of that faith which does not contain within it the strength to stand against the onslaught of evil.[165]

The psalmist experiences life amid suffering, not beyond it. His or her faith is thus the kind that Jesus embodied and to which Jesus calls his disciples—faith that knows the paradoxical good news that to lose one's life for God's sake is truly to find it (see Mark 8:35). Thus it is easy to imagine the psalmist, like the apostle Paul, enumerating her or his "many afflictions" (Rom 8:31) and then concluding that nothing "will be able to separate us from the love of God" (Rom 8:38 NRSV; see also 2 Cor 4:7-12). Like Paul, too, the psalmist says to others, in effect, "be imitators of me" (1 Cor 4:16; 11:1; see also Phil 3:17). This is not arrogance but testimony to God's grace at work in one's life. The boast is in the Lord (v. 2; see 1 Cor 1:31).

Psalm 34 is traditionally associated with the Lord's supper, primarily because of the word "taste" in v. 8. In a sense, this connection is superficial; however, as a whole, Psalm 34 is appropriately associated with the Lord's Supper. The Lord's Supper celebrates God's gracious provision for life, which is the good news proclaimed by Psalm 34. The proper response is gratitude (vv. 1-3)—eucharist!

165. Craigie, *Psalms 1–50*, 282.

PSALM 35:1-28, O LORD, WHO IS LIKE YOU?

COMMENTARY

Psalm 35 is a prayer for help that is traditionally classified as an individual lament or complaint. The usual elements are present, but the psalm moves back and forth among them in a way that makes it difficult to identify neat structural divisions. There is petition for deliverance (vv. 1-3, 17, 22-25), petition for judgment upon enemies (vv. 4-6, 8, 19, 26), complaint (vv. 7, 11-12, 15-16, 20-21), vow to praise (vv. 9-10, 18, 28), an apparent expression of innocence (vv. 13-14), and even a brief petition for the supporters of the psalmist (v. 27). Some scholars suggest a division of the psalm into three major sections: (1) vv. 1-10, (2) vv. 11-18, (3) vv. 21-28—each of which concludes with a vow to praise. Perhaps it is best not to attempt to discern too much literary order in the psalm, but to interpret the apparent literary disarray as an appropriate indication of the chaotic conditions that prevailed in the life of the psalmist.

The attempt to identity precisely the nature of these conditions has led to strikingly divergent understandings of the origin and setting of Psalm 35. It is often viewed as the prayer of a falsely accused person (see Psalms 5; 7; 17; 26; Introduction), perhaps one who is sick (v. 13) and whose opponents interpret this sickness as a sign of wrongdoing that justifies persecution. This approach relies heavily on the legal imagery in the psalm (vv. 1a, 11, 23-24). Other scholars focus more on the military imagery (vv. 1b-3). Craigie, for instance, labels Psalm 35 as "A Royal Prayer for International Crisis," suggesting that it is similar to Psalm 20 in being the prayer of a king for God's help in dealing with national enemies.[166] Both of these approaches construe the legal and military language literally, but Gerstenberger is probably correct in proposing that the language is metaphorical. He concludes that the original setting of Psalm 35 was a "private cultic" ritual and that the psalm would have been used by a suffering individual "as a central part of the recitations that were obligatory for the sufferer who underwent such rehabilitating ritual in the circle of friends and family."[167]

The very existence of such different proposals is sufficient indication that the language and imagery of Psalm 35 are open-ended enough to be applicable to a variety of circumstances. Thus Psalm 35 has remained a resource for sufferers throughout the generations, serving both as a prayer for help and as a testimony to God's character. In fact, this latter function is highlighted by a unique feature of this psalm: the psalmist's quoting of God (v. 3), of his or her own bones (v. 10), of enemies (vv. 21, 25), and of supporters (v. 27). Verses 3, 10, and 27 in particular offer instruction about God's character as one who helps, delivers, and provides for the weak, the needy, and the vulnerable.

35:1-3. The plea for God to "contend" (v. 1a) has a legal background, but it is usually

166. Craigie, *Psalms 1–50*, 282-86.
167. Gerstenberger, *Psalms: Part 1*, 150, 153.

used figuratively of God's calling oppressors to accountability (see v. 23, "my cause"; see also Ps 43:1; Isa 3:13; 49:25; Lam 3:58). Military imagery dominates the rest of vv. 1-3. The verb "fight" (לחם *lāham*) usually refers to battle, but it is used elsewhere of general opposition by enemies (see Pss 56:2; 109:3, where "attack" is accompanied by "without cause" as in 35:7, 19; Jer 1:19; 15:20). Elsewhere, God is addressed as "shield" (Pss 3:3; 7:10), and God's protection is described as covering with a buckler (a large shield; see Pss 5:12; 91:4). Likewise, the subsequent plea is frequent in Psalms: "rise" (Pss 3:7; 9:19; 10:12), and God is often seen as the psalmist's "help" (Pss 22:19; 30:10; 33:20; 54:4; 115:9-11). The "spear" is a weapon, of course, but it also symbolizes the presence and authority of a king (see 1 Sam 26:7-8, 11). In effect, the psalmist asks God to take charge of the situation, which means in this case to deal with the "pursuers" (cf. Pss 7:1; 31:15). Entrusting his or her life to God, the psalmist desires to hear God say precisely what the foes in Ps 3:2 deny—that is, that God is a source of "help"/"salvation" (ישועה *yēšûʿâ*; the Hebrew word is the same in 3:2; 35:3).

35:4-8. Verses 4-6 elaborate upon what it will mean when God rises against the enemies. For the psalmist to escape from those seeking his or her life (see Pss 38:12; 40:14; 54:3; 63:9; 70:2; 86:14; see also 1 Sam 23:15; 1 Kgs 19:10; Jer 38:16), the enemies must be stopped—"put to shame" (see v. 26; see also, e.g., Pss 6:10; 69:6) and "dishonored" (see Pss 40:14; 69:6; 70:2) and "confounded" (see "confusion" in v. 26; see also Pss 71:24 [NRSV, "disgraced"]; 40:15 and 70:2 [NRSV, "confusion"]; 83:17 [NRSV, "dismayed"]). The psalmist's plea in v. 5a recalls Ps 1:4, implying the wickedness of the enemies. The root of the word "slippery" (חלקלקות *hălaqlaqqôt*, v. 6) is also used elsewhere to describe the destiny of the wicked (Ps 73:18). Verse 6 asks that the "pursuers" (v. 3) become the pursued (see "angel," or messenger, in Pss 34:7; 91:11). The effect of vv. 7-8 is the same: "ruin" (see Ps 63:10: "those who seek my life will come to ruin" [NAB]; 73:18)—that is, let them experience what they are attempting to perpetrate (see "net" in Pss 9:15; 10:9; "pit" in Pss 7:15;

9:15). The two occurrences of the phrase "without cause" in v. 7 (see v. 19) anticipate the psalmist's self-defense in vv. 13-14.

35:9-18. Verse 9 articulates the promise of joy when God effects "deliverance" (*yěšû'â*; the word is the same as "salvation" in v. 3). The psalmist anticipates too the role of witness. Quoting his or her "bones"—that is, whole being (see Ps 6:2)—the psalmist first asks a question focused on God's character, and then answers it. God acts on behalf of the "weak"/"afflicted"/"poor"/ "oppressed," as the NRSV variously translates the word עָנִי ('*ānî*; see Pss 9:12; 10:2, 9; 12:5; 14:6; 25:16; 37:14; 40:17; 70:5; 74:21; 82:3; 86:1; 109:16, 22). This affirmation lies at the heart of Israel's faith (see "misery" in Exod 3:7; 4:31; see also Deut 26:7). Suffering is not an indication of God's disfavor but an opportunity for God's presence and activity (see Commentary on Psalms 9–10; 13; 22; 31).

The psalmist's enemies clearly do not interpret the suffering this way. Just as Job's "friends" interpreted his suffering as evidence of his sinfulness, so apparently do the psalmist's associates as well. Thus, they think, the psalmist can justifiably be persecuted. The complaint in v. 11 returns to legal imagery; more literally, "witnesses of violence" oppose the psalmist (see Ps 27:12, where the same vocabulary is present). The opposition leaves the psalmist "forlorn" (שְׁכוֹל *šěkôl*); this word is often associated with the bereavement of childlessness or barrenness (see Isa 47:8). Thus it is a particularly poignant choice of words in view of the way the psalmist responded to the suffering of others—that is, as a family member. When others were afflicted, the psalmist joined them in their affliction (v. 13*c*; the root of "afflicted" is the same as "weak" in v. 10). Thus the psalmist's response contrasts sharply with that of the enemies, who "exalt themselves against me" (v. 26). This insensitive, self-centered manner is evident in vv. 15-16. Wild beasts, not other people, ordinarily tear at people (v. 15; see Hos 13:8), an action perhaps related to the image of gnashing teeth (v. 16; see Job 16:9; Pss 37:12; 112:10; Lam 2:16; Job 16:9). And the enemies are explicitly called "lions" in v. 7 (see Ps 58:6). Having been utterly dehumanized, the psalmist perceives that his or

her life is in danger, and the psalmist again returns to petition (v. 17*b*), followed by the anticipation of deliverance in v. 18 (see vv. 9-10, 28; Pss 22:22-25; 26:12).

35:19-27. The petition in v. 19 employs another legal term; "treacherous" often describes false testimony in court (see "false" in Ps 27:12). The word also occurs in Ps 69:4, where the psalmist is again hated without cause (cf. John 15:25). By not speaking *shalom* (v. 20), the enemies reveal themselves to be opponents also of God, who does will *shalom* (cf. "welfare," v. 27) for God's servants. The opponents' self-centered arrogance is also revealed in their exclamation in v. 22*a* (see v. 25; Ps 40:15). What the opponents do not realize is that they are not the only ones who have "seen"; God has seen too (v. 22), and so the psalmist can confidently address a series of petitions to God in vv. 22-26. The enemies have spoken, and now the psalmist wants God to speak (v. 22*a*; see also Pss 83:1; 109:1). The enemies have been present, and now the psalmist wants God to be present (v. 22*b*; see also Pss 22:11, 19; 38:21; 71:12), even if it takes a wake-up call (v. 23*a*; see Ps 59:5). Legal terminology again dominates vv. 23-24. The phrase "my defense" (v. 23*a*) could be translated "my justice"; the same root in verbal form opens v. 24, where it could be translated, "Establish justice for me." As the rest of the verse makes clear, the appeal is to God's character as sovereign judge—that is, to God's righteousness (see Pss 7:17; 9:8; 96:13; 97:2), to which the psalmist promises to be a witness (v. 28; see above on v. 10). The psalmist also invites others—specifically, those who desire his or her "vindication" (צֶדֶק *ṣedeq*; the root is the same as "righteousness" in vv. 24, 28)—to join in the affirmation of what God is like. In contrast to the enemies, who "make themselves great" (or "exalt themselves," v. 26), the psalmist's supporters will proclaim God's greatness (v. 27; see also Ps 40:16), a greatness that consists of God's identification with and setting things right for the suffering and the vulnerable (vv. 1-3, 10, 23-24, 27).

REFLECTIONS

As Gerstenberger suggests, Psalm 35 is a particularly "aggressive and defensive" prayer for help.[168] For this reason, perhaps, contemporary readers may find various aspects of this psalm troubling—the military imagery (vv. 1-3), the psalmist's prayer for the punishment of enemies (vv. 4-6, 8, 26), the psalmist's self-commendation (vv. 13-14). However, the psalmist prays, in effect, exactly what Jesus taught his disciples to pray: "Deliver us from evil." The psalmist's self-commendation should not be a problem; it is simply a way of affirming loyalty to God and faithfulness to others. The psalmist's prayer against the enemies is not a selfish, vengeful prayer. Rather, it should be understood as a prayer for justice for the oppressed—"thy will be done on earth as it is in heaven." For justice to be done on earth, however, requires that evil oppressors be opposed. It is for God's opposition to oppressors that the psalmist prays. She or he recognizes, quite realistically, that oppressors do not give up without a fight. Thus God's opposition to oppression (v. 10), God's work of setting things right in the world (vv. 23-24, 27), will necessarily mean that God has to "fight" (v. 1b). In this sense, the military imagery is understandable and appropriate (see Eph 6:10-17).

To put it in different terms, the psalmist prays for the enactment of what Jesus expressed in his saying, "all who exalt themselves will be humbled, but all who humble themselves will be exalted" (Luke 18:14 NRSV). While the enemies "exalt themselves" (v. 26), the psalmist and his supporters humble themselves and exalt God (vv. 13, 27). The petitions for deliverance and the petitions against the enemies represent requests that God reveal God's character, for God is for the weak and the needy (v. 10). The petitions imply, of course, that persons who exalt themselves have not yet been humbled. Thus Psalm 35, like the psalter as a whole, is eschatological; it asserts God's sovereignty amid the existence of competing claims and powers (see Psalm 2; Introduction). The psalmist trusts God's sovereign will and ability to help (vv. 1-3, 10, 22-24, 27), and yet still prays for and awaits God's help.

While Psalm 35 is testimony to God's character and activity, it also teaches about suffering and the life of faith. It is easy to imagine Psalm 35 as the prayer of Elijah or Jeremiah or Job or Jesus (see John 15:25), all of whom were hated without cause, all of whom were pursued by their enemies, all of whom suffered on account of their righteousness and faithfulness to God. Clearly, suffering in these cases cannot be understood as punishment. If anything, suffering must be understood as the inevitable cost of discipleship. In this regard, then, Psalm 35 offers us a model of discipleship and invites our decision. Are we willing, like the psalmist and like Jesus, to humble ourselves in identification with the affliction of others (v. 13)? Are we willing, like the psalmist and like Jesus, to entrust our lives to God, praying all the while, "Thy will be done . . . deliver us from evil"?

168. Gerstenberger, *Psalms: Part 1*, 153.

PSALM 36:1-12, IN YOUR LIGHT

COMMENTARY

Although scholars generally agree in classifying Psalm 36 as an individual lament/complaint or prayer for help, only vv. 10-11 are petition. Verses 5-9, while addressed to God, have more the character of a profession of faith, and vv. 1-4, 12 consist of a description of the behavior and destiny of the wicked. The apparent discontinuity between vv. 1-4,

12 and vv. 5-11 has led numerous scholars to treat Psalm 36 as two separate psalms; however, it is preferable to treat the psalm as a unity (note the occurrence of "wicked" in vv. 1, 11 (רשע *rāšā'* in v. 1; רשעים *rĕšā'îm* in v. 11), linking the two supposedly separate sections). When the psalm is read as a unity, vv. 1-4, 12 provide a framework for hearing the words addressed to God in vv. 5-11. This framework suggests that the psalmist's praise (vv. 5-9) and prayer (vv. 10-11) arise not from untroubled circumstances, but from the midst of opposition and threat.

36:1-2. A comparison of the NIV and the NRSV discloses that the translation of v. 1*a* is a problem. The Hebrew reads literally, "utterance of rebellion to the wicked in the midst of my heart." The NIV's translation may be an attempt to paraphrase this literal reading, but it misses the point that the oracle is *to* the wicked. Some Hebrew manuscripts and the Syriac version read "his heart," a reading on which the NRSV depends—and it is preferable. The intent seems to be sarcastic. The word "utterance" (נאם *nĕ'um*; or "speaks," "oracle") elsewhere is almost always followed by the divine name, and the resultant phrase—usually translated "says the LORD"—occurs almost exclusively in the prophetic books to indicate an oracle from God. Thus the psalmist says, in effect, that all the wicked hear is "says rebellion." In short, "rebellion" or "transgression" is their god. They perceive no reason whatsoever to be accountable to the true God, as v. 1*b* suggests. Together, v. 1*a* and v. 1*b* cover hearing and seeing. Verse 2 develops the latter; it repeats the word "eyes" (עינים *'ênayim*) from v. 1, linking the wicked's failure to honor God and their self-assertion. In other words, idolatry and selfishness are inseparable. The NIV and the NRSV construe v. 2*b* differently, but either reading suggests the arrogant autonomy of the wicked (see Commentary on Psalms 1; 2). Given the way the psalm begins, the unique superscription takes on even fuller significance. As opposed to the wicked, who serve only themselves, David is identified as "the servant of the LORD."

36:3-4. The arrogance of the wicked manifests itself in speech (v. 3*a*), in action (v. 3*b*), and in thought (v. 4*a*). As the NRSV suggests, the word "mischief" (און *'āwen*) occurs in vv.

3-4, although "mischief" probably does not communicate the seriousness of the behavior (cf. the NIV's "wicked" and "evil"; see also v. 12, where the term "evildoers" also contains the same Hebrew word). The word designates the destructive effects of evil, and, not surprisingly, it is elsewhere associated with idolatry (see "iniquity" in Hos 12:11 NRSV). The word "deceit(ful)" often characterizes the speech and thinking of the wicked (see Pss 5:6; 34:13; 35:20; 38:12 [NRSV, "treachery"]; 52:4; 109:2). Elsewhere, "to be wise" (v. 3*b*) is associated with serving God (Ps 2:10-11)—that is, acknowledging God's sovereignty. It is precisely this, of course, that the wicked do not do. Rather, their hearing, seeing, speaking, acting, and thinking (cf. v. 4*a* with Mic 2:1) are focused on themselves. Rejecting "good" (vv. 3-4), they embody "evil" (v. 4; see Ps 34:13-14).

36:5-6. While clearly aware of the reality of the wicked and their threatening thoughts and deeds, the psalmist perceives a more profound reality. His or her profession, praise, and prayer center on God's "steadfast love" (vv. 5, 7, 10); and there is no other word in the OT that serves so well to describe the character of God (see Exod 34:6-7; Pss 5:7; 6:4; 13:5; 33:5, 18, 22; Introduction). In vv. 5-6, it is joined by three other central aspects of God's character (see also Ps 89:14, where essentially the same four attributes are present). God's love is unbounded (v. 5*a*; see Pss 33:5; 57:10; 71:19). God is ultimately dependable (v. 5*b*, "faithfulness"; see Pss 89:24; 92:2; 98:3, where "steadfast love" and "faithfulness" are paired). In ancient Near Eastern cosmology, the mountains anchor the dry land, holding up the firmament and holding back the waters of the deep. Just as the life and future of the earth thus depend on the mountains, so also the world depends on God's "righteousness"—God's will and ability to set things right (v. 6*a*). As the "great deep" represents inexhaustible power, so it is with God's "justice" (v. 6*b*; see Pss 89:14; 97:2; 99:4). To be noted is that each attribute of God in vv. 5-6 is described in cosmic terms that are arranged in descending order according to the ancient view—"heavens" above all, "clouds" above the earth, "mighty mountains" as the highest earthly point, and "the great deep" below the earth. In short,

God's character is built into the very structure of the universe. Everything and every creature—"humans and animals alike" (v. 6c)—depends on God for its existence and future. This affirmation is reinforced by the syntax of vv. 5-6. The first word in v. 5 and the last word in v. 6 is "Yahweh" ("LORD"). God surrounds it all!

36:7-8. The exclamation of v. 7a is founded on the conviction that the life of the whole world depends on God's love. To take refuge in God (see the same image in Pss 17:8; 57:1; 63:7) means simply to acknowledge dependence on God. This is the precise opposite of the wicked, who assert their self-sufficiency (vv. 1-2) and who pursue their own selfish ways (vv. 3-4). Psalm 36 ends by professing the faith that the way of the wicked will ultimately prove futile (v. 12), thus recalling the beginning of the psalter, which affirms that "the way of the wicked will perish" (1:6) and "happy are those who take refuge in [God]" (2:12 NRSV; see also 5:11; 7:1; 11:1; 16:1; Introduction).

Verse 8 portrays God's provision of life for people. They are fed and given drink. God's "house," as well as the "shadow of your wings" in v. 7c (see Commentary on Ps 17:8), may designate the Temple and indicate an original liturgical setting for the psalm, but the meaning need not be literal (after all, there is no river in the Temple). As Mays suggests, the language is symbolic and intends to express poetically the conviction that life is a gift received from and nurtured by God: "It is this receiving from God that occurs in complex and related ways—through common life, liturgy, and the inner world of the spirit—that the psalm seeks to describe."[169] The affirmation is similar to that of Ps 23:5-6 (see Isa 55:1-3).

36:9-12. The psalmist's profession culminates with the memorable v. 9, which sums up vv. 6c-8: God is the source of life (see Ps 68:27; Prov 14:27; Jer 2:13; 17:13). As elsewhere, God's presence itself is described poetically as "light" (אור 'ôr, Pss 4:6; 44:3; 69:15; see "shine," the verbal form of the Hebrew root, in Num 6:25; Pss 4:6; 31:16; 67:1; 80:3, 7, 19). Likewise, the experience of God's presence is described as light (see Pss 27:1; 97:11; 118:27; Isa 9:2; 10:17; Mic 7:8). Again, the language is richly symbolic. The same imagery is used by the Gospel of John, which locates God's presence in Jesus Christ, in whom "was life, and the life was the light of all people" (John 1:4 NRSV). The prologue of John goes on to acknowledge the presence of darkness but affirms that God's presence in Christ affords a light that cannot be overcome (John 1:5). In effect, Psalm 36 ends the same way; the psalmist prays in v. 10 for the continuation of God's steadfast love (see Jer 31:3) and "righteousness" (see v. 6) for the "upright in heart" (see Pss 7:10; 11:2; 32:11). The psalmist acknowledges the presence of evil (v. 11) but affirms that God's presence (see "there"—that is, wherever God is present—in v. 12; see also Ps 14:5) affords a power that the wicked cannot overcome.

169. Mays, *Psalms*, 157.

REFLECTIONS

A consumer-oriented culture teaches people to view life as a reward to be earned; Psalm 36, however, is a radical profession of faith. It teaches us that life is not a reward to be earned but a gift to be received! God gives life (vv. 6c, 9), and God will provide for the life of the world and its people (vv. 7-8). This remarkable affirmation of faith lies at the heart of the book of Psalms and the entire Bible (see Psalms 23; 34, esp. v. 12; 73, esp. vv. 25-26).

It is not surprising that the NT employs the same imagery to affirm God's gracious gift of and provision for life. The Gospel of John, for instance, affirms that Jesus is the "living water" (John 4:10; cf. Ps 36:8b-9a), "the bread of life" (John 6:35; cf. Ps 36:8a), and "the light of the world" (John 8:12, see also 1:4; cf. Ps 36:9). Jesus says, "I come that they may have life, and have it abundantly" (John 10:10 NRSV), and the Gospel of John professes that those who believe in Jesus will have "eternal life" (3:16). Life in Christ is effective now, and the joy and peace are real (16:24, 33). But life is experienced amid persistent opposition from "the world," and so Jesus must pray for the ongoing protection of his followers (17:14-19). In the same way, Psalm 36 is eschatological; God's sovereignty is asserted amid persistent opposition (see Psalm 2; Introduction). Those who belong to God (see v. 10a, "those who know you") already experience refuge and abundant provision (vv. 5-9), but this gift of life (v. 9) is experienced amid persistent opposition from the wicked (vv. 1-4, 11-12), and so the psalmist must pray for the continuation of God's love and God's work of setting things right (v. 10).

The psalmist can be confident in praying for God's steadfast love and righteousness, because the psalmist trusts that God's love is the fundamental reality in the universe (v. 5; see Commentary on Psalms 19; 33) and that God's righteousness holds the world together (v. 6). Again, Psalm 36 is a radical profession of faith, since hatred and violence seem so prevalent among us, and, indeed, it often seems that the world is falling apart. Here again, Psalm 36 anticipates the NT affirmation that God is love (1 John 4:8, 16) and that God's love relates to, as Col 1:20 puts it, "all things, whether on earth or in heaven" (cf. Ps 36:5-6). Indeed, Col 1:17 attributes to Jesus what Psalm 36 attributes to God's righteousness: "in him all things hold together" (NRSV).

Obviously, this remarkable affirmation of faith has profound implications for the way we view the world and our place in it. This affirmation is simultaneously good news and a warning. Consider, for instance, the ecological implications. The good news is that there is hope for the world despite the fact that in caring for the earth we have acted the part of the wicked; we "have ceased to act wisely and do good" (v. 3b). The affirmation that God saves "humans and animals alike" (v. 6c) is good news as well, but it also functions as a warning that calls for a reverence for all creatures and their habitats that is seldom evidenced in our relentless desire for development and "progress." Our plans for the future (ecological and otherwise) often reveal a self-flattery that our "iniquity cannot be found out" (v. 2)—that is, that we are not accountable (see Commentary on Psalms 1; 2). God so loves the world, and God calls us to do the same.

PSALM 37:1-40, THE MEEK SHALL INHERIT THE LAND

COMMENTARY

Psalm 37, as Gerstenberger suggests, "can perhaps be called a homily."[170] It addresses a theological issue that is a perennial pastoral concern: the apparent prosperity of the wicked. Like any good sermon, Psalm 37 proclaims the faith, instructs the faithful, and calls for a decision. Because of its clearly instructional intent, Psalm 37 is generally classified as a wisdom psalm. This classification is adequate, as long as Psalm 37 is not understood simply as a private meditation. The central issue of Psalm 37 was a characteristic concern of the wisdom tradition (e.g., the book of Job). The psalm also contains between the righteous and the wicked is

also characteristic of wisdom literature. To be sure, the contrast between the righteous and the wicked is also characteristic of the book of Psalms, beginning with Psalm 1. By sheer repetition, Psalm 37 raises the intensity of the contrast. The "righteous" (צדיק ṣaddîq) are mentioned nine times in Hebrew (vv. 12, 16, 17, 21, 25, 28, 29, 32, 39), and the "wicked" (רשע rāšāʿ) even more (vv. 10, 12, 14, 16, 17, 20, 21, 28, 32, 34, 35, 38, 40, plus vv. 1, 9, where a different Hebrew word [מרעים mĕrēʿîm] is used). As in Psalm 1, the righteous are those who are attentive to God's instruction (v. 31; cf. 1:2) and are known by God (v. 18; cf. 1:6 NIV). Thus they will "inherit the land" (see vv. 9, 11, 22, 29, 34; cf. v. 3). Although it is possible to understand this

170. Gerstenberger, *Psalms: Part 1*, 158.

affirmation literally, it is better to approach it symbolically. Since possession of the land afforded access to the resources necessary to sustain life, the righteous "live," whereas the wicked "perish" (v. 20; see 1:6) and "shall be cut off" (vv. 9, 22, 28, 34, 38; cf. "destruction" in v. 34 NRSV).

This conclusion is based on the psalmist's conviction that God rules the world, a conviction that underlies everything in Psalm 37 and that is most explicit in the assertion that "the LORD laughs at the wicked" (v. 13). This assertion recalls Psalm 2 (see v. 4), which is fundamentally an affirmation of God's sovereignty over the nations and rulers of the earth (see 2:10-12). As in Psalm 2, so it is in Psalm 37 that the affirmation of God's rule is made in circumstances that seem to deny it. In short, Psalm 37 is eschatological. For *now,* the wicked *do* "prosper in their way" (v. 7; cf. 1:3). Thus the future tense of the two refrains is significant—"*shall* inherit" and "*shall be* cut off."

37:1-11. The contrast between what is (present) and what shall be (future) provides the context for understanding the imperative exhortations in vv. 1, 3-5, 7-8, as well as the attached promises in vv. 2, 6, 9-11. The righteous live their lives not on the basis of present appearances, but based on what they know is assured in the future. Thus, in the midst of the present prosperity of the wicked, the psalmist can say, "Do not fret" (vv. 1*a*, 7-8) and "do not be envious" (v. 1*b*; see also Ps 73:3), or, to state the same exhortation positively, "Trust in the LORD" (v. 3; see also v. 5; Pss 4:5; 9:10; Introduction). The verb "delight" (v. 4*a*; see v. 11) is associated elsewhere with God's provision of resources for life (see Isa 55:2; 58:14; 66:11). In other words, God's providence can be trusted, as v. 4*b* also suggests. The righteous will live by faith and by what is always inseparable from faith: hope (v. 7*a*; see vv. 9, 34, where a different Hebrew word from the one used in v. 7*a* is translated "wait" by the NRSV).

But to live eschatologically means not only to live *for* the future but also to live *by* the future. Living by faith and hope has a profound impact on the present, in terms of emotion and behavior. The verb in the phrase "do not fret" (חרה *ḥārâ*) and the noun "wrath" (חמה *ḥēmâ*, v. 8) have similar root meanings:

"to be kindled" or "to be hot." Thus the psalmist's advice in vv. 1, 7-8, in modern parlance, is "Be cool." Trusting God enables one to live in the present with a certain serenity (see "be still" in v. 7; see also Ps 62:1, 5) and peace of heart and mind (vv. 1, 7-8). Trusting God also enables one to live constructively in the present, to continue to "do good" (vv. 3, 27) even when it appears that evil pays quite well.

The promises attached to the exhortations declare the transience of the wicked (v. 2; see also Ps 129:6) and their ultimate demise (vv. 9*a*, 10; the verb translated "cut off" [כרת *kārat*] refers in Gen 9:11 to the destruction of all humanity in the flood and elsewhere is used in association with the death penalty; see also Prov 2:22). On the other hand, things will be set right for those who trust God (v. 6*a*); "justice" will prevail (v. 6*b*; see also vv. 28, 30). Life belongs ultimately to those who "wait for" God (v. 9)—the "meek" (v. 11; see also Pss 10:17; 22:26; 25:9; 34:2; see also the closely related term usually translated "poor"/"afflicted"/"weak"/"oppressed" [עני *ʿānî*] in Pss 9:12; 10:2, 9; 14:5; 35:10; see also Matt 5:5). It is they who enjoy *shalom* (v. 10; see v. 37), even if it is not "as the world gives" (John 14:27 NRSV).

37:12-20. The imperatives that predominate in vv. 1-11 are much less frequent in vv. 12-40 (only in vv. 27, 34), which consist primarily of observations about the righteous, the wicked, and their respective destinies. Verses 12-15 focus on the wicked. While they "plot" (see Ps 31:13) and "gnash their teeth" (see Pss 35:16; 112:10), God laughs. While they seek to live at the expense of others ("poor" [*ʿānî*] in v. 14 is the same Hebrew root as "meek" in v. 11), they will not succeed. In effect, vv. 14-15 assert that those who live by the sword will die by the sword (see vv. 2, 10).

Verse 17 makes essentially the same observation (see "broken" in vv. 15, 17). It is paired with the proverbial saying in v. 16; because the wicked will disappear, their abundance is illusory. Contrary to worldly calculations, less can be better (see Prov 15:16; 16:8; 28:6). Verse 18 tells why. The "blameless" may have only a little, but it "will endure forever" (cf. Prov 28:10). As suggested above (see Psalms 15; 18; 19), blamelessness connotes not sinlessness but dependence on God. This mode of life is a form of wealth that retains its value in all seasons (v. 19; see also Matt 5:6). Recalling "perish" in Ps 1:6, v. 20 again affirms that the wicked will disappear.

37:21-26. Verses 21 and 26 are linked verbally by the words "borrow"/"lend" (the two English words translate the same Hebrew root) and "generous(ly)"; and vv. 21-26 illustrate what was affirmed in vv. 3-4. Those who trust in God are motivated and enabled to "do good" (v. 3). Even though they already have more, the wicked greedily seek more, while the righteous share their resources (see Ps 12:5; Prov 14:31; 19:17; 28:8, 17). The Hebrew word translated "generous(ly)" (חונן ḥônēn) is more literally "gracious," and it is one of God's essential characteristics (see Exod 34:6; Introduction). In short, the righteous are persons whose character has been shaped by God's character; having known grace, they can be gracious. Because they trust God to protect and provide (vv. 23-25; note the repetition of "upholds" in vv. 17, 24; see 54:4; 119:116; 145:14; see also "sustains" in Ps 3:5), the righteous are able to know the happiness of giving (see Acts 20:35). Having been blessed (v. 22), they become a blessing (v. 26; see also Gen 12:1-3).

37:27-29. Whereas vv. 21-26 recall vv. 3-4, v. 27 explicitly repeats the exhortation of v. 3, "do good." Not surprisingly, the motivation is explicitly linked to the way God is. The word "justice" (משפט mišpāṭ) in v. 28a recalls v. 6 and anticipates v. 30, where again the righteous reflect God's character by their own behavior. The designation "faithful ones" also moves in this direction; it could also be translated "steadfastly loved [or loving] ones," thus linking it as well to a primary characteristic of God (see Exod 34:6-7; Introduction).

37:30-40. The vocabulary of vv. 30-31 recalls Ps 1:2. The word translated "utter" (הגה hāgâ) here appears as "meditate" in 1:2, which also twice mentions God's "law" or "instruction" (see Commentary on Psalm 1). Here the righteous meditate on or utter "wisdom" (see Ps 49:3; Prov 31:26), but wisdom begins with fearing God (see Job 28:28; Ps 111:10; Prov 1:7; 9:10; 15:33). Thus, as in Psalm 1, the righteous are those who do not pursue their own ways but are open to God's instruction because they recognize God's sovereignty. God's instruction is the solid foundation on which their lives are built.

The word "abandon" (עזב ʿāzab, v. 33) represents the third occurrence of this Hebrew root in the psalm (see "forsaken"/"forsake" in vv. 25, 28). In the confidence that God will not forsake the righteous, the psalmist offers a final exhortation in v. 34, "Wait" (קוה qāwâ; see also v. 9, and a different Hebrew word translated "wait" in v. 7 [חול ḥûl]). The humble (see "meek" in v. 11 and "poor" in v. 14) *will be* exalted. Verses 35-36 articulate again the theme of the transience of the wicked (see vv. 2, 10, 13-15, 17, 20), as does v. 38. The word "posterity" (אחרית ʾaḥărît) in vv. 37-38 is better translated "future." In contrast to the wicked, the "blameless" (v. 37; see also v. 18) have a future! It is not due to their own efforts, of course, as the wicked would conclude; rather, it is "from the LORD" (v. 39). In biblical terms, salvation (v. 39; see "saves" in v. 40) means life in the fullest sense of the word. It is a gift from God. It does not mean a trouble-free existence (v. 39; see also vv. 19, 24) or the absence of opposition (v. 40; see also vv. 7, 12, 14, 32, 35), but it does mean God's availability as a source of help (see Pss 22:19; 30:10; 54:4) and a reliable "stronghold" (v. 39; see also Ps 27:1) and "refuge" (see Ps 2:12; Introduction).

REFLECTIONS

Psalm 37—along with Psalms 49; 73; and the book of Job—is often labeled a theodicy, because it implies the question, How can God be just while there is so much evil in the world? "Theodicy" means literally, "justice of God"; while this label may be too restrictive, there is some rationale for considering Psalm 37 to be a homiletical exploration of the issue of God's justice. The word "justice" (משפט mišpāṭ) occurs in vv. 6, 28, 30 (the phrase "when brought to trial" in v. 33 NIV also represents the same

Hebrew root). If God "loves justice" (v. 28) and will bring justice to light (v. 6), then why are the wicked able to "prosper in their way" (v. 7)? To put the question from the human side: Why do the righteous suffer?

To be sure, Psalm 37 does not satisfactorily answer these questions, but it does as much as any sermon can do. As Thomas G. Long says in an article entitled "Preaching About Suffering": "We can only go so far down the path of theodicy. . . . We must admit that we have been placed in the middle of life and that, from our vantage point, suffering is an unsolvable mystery. We must affirm that the meaningful question is not 'Is theism unintelligible because I am suffering?' but 'Is God a God of salvation—is God one who can help?' "[171]

If this is the meaningful question, then Psalm 37 does offer an answer. Yes, salvation "is from the LORD. . . . The LORD helps them . . . and saves them" (vv. 39-40). And so Psalm 37 invites trust (vv. 3, 5) and hope (vv. 7, 9, 34) in God's will and ability to set things right.

Long goes on to say that for Christians, the response to the question above is finally "a story, *the* story of the love of God and the passion of Jesus Christ."[172] Of course, Psalm 37 does not tell the story of Jesus Christ, but it does proclaim God's love and thus anticipates the story of Jesus. For instance, Psalm 37 proclaims the sovereignty of God as the basis for trust and for doing good (vv. 3, 13, 27), and the same message forms the core of Jesus' preaching: "the kingdom of God has come near; repent, and believe in the good news" (Mark 1:15 NRSV). For Jesus, the reality of God's rule turned worldly values upside down. Because God rules the world, "the meek . . . will inherit the earth" (Matt 5:5 NRSV; see also Ps 37:11*a*). Because God rules the world, "those who hunger and thirst for righteousness . . . will be filled" (Matt 5:6 NRSV; see also Ps 37:19). Because God rules the world, there is a source of joy and an experience of peace greater than the world can give (see John 14:27; 16:24, 33; see also Ps 37:11*b*). Because God rules the world, "life does not consist in the abundance of possessions" (Luke 12:15 NRSV; see also Ps 37:16). Because God rules the world," 'It is more blessed to give than to receive' " (Acts 20:35 NRSV; see also Ps 37:21, 26). Because God rules the world, there is no need to "worry about your life" (Matt 6:25 NRSV; see also Ps 37:4).

As Jesus' life showed, trusting God and doing good engender opposition, and the opposition to the righteous is very clear in Psalm 37 (see esp. vv. 14, 32). But as Jesus' life and death and resurrection demonstrated, and as Psalm 37 also proclaims, God "rescues them from the wicked" (v. 40) and creates a future "for the peaceable" (v. 37). Psalm 37 thus promises what Jesus promised too: "all who exalt themselves will be humbled, but all who humble themselves will be exalted" (Luke 18:14 NRSV; see also Ps 37:34; Commentary on Psalm 35).

To be sure, all of these affirmations and promises are eschatological. There is no proving them to the wicked, except insofar as we embody them in our lives. The only proof we can offer that God rules the world is the tangible existence of a community that is shaped by the character of God and God's claim. We prove that God rules the world when we trust in God (vv. 3, 5), "do good" (vv. 3, 27), commit our way to God (v. 5), "give generously" (v. 21), "speak justice" (v. 30), open ourselves to God's instruction (v. 31), and "take refuge in" God (v. 40). Such humble dependence on God is, in effect, to "inherit the land"—it is life as God intends it, abundant and eternal.

171. Thomas G. Long, "Preaching About Suffering," *Journal for Preachers* 15/2 (Lent 1992) 13.
172. Long, "Preaching About Suffering," 13.

PSALM 38:1-22, THERE IS NO SOUNDNESS IN MY FLESH

COMMENTARY

Psalm 38 is, according to Gerstenberger, among "the most impressive individual laments."[173] Although not as familiar or widely used as the others, Psalm 38 is one of the church's seven penitential psalms (see also Psalms 6; 32; 51; 102; 130; 143). Like Psalm 6, the language and imagery of Psalm 38 suggest that it may have originally been used by sick persons as a prayer for help (see vv. 1, 21-22). Like Psalm 6, too, Psalm 38 begins with a petition that seems to indicate that the sickness is the result of God's wrath (vv. 1-2). More explicitly than Psalm 6, Psalm 38 suggests that God's wrath has been provoked by the psalmist's sinfulness (vv. 3-4; see also "foolishness" or "sinful folly" in v. 5; cf. v. 18).

Thus Psalm 38 is evidence of the ancient belief that sin causes sickness (see Pss 32:3-5; 39:10-11; 41:4; 88:7, 16; 107:17-18; Mark 2:1-12). This belief, which is also a contemporary one in some circles, is very problematic; but the association of sin and sickness holds interpretive possibilities, especially if the link is not viewed mechanistically or individualistically (see Reflections). Actually, the nature of the imagery and its extent discourage an individualistic or biographical interpretation of Psalm 38. Although several commentators conclude that the psalmist must have had leprosy (see Leviticus 13–14), the description of the disease is too stereotypical and hyperbolic to make such a specific diagnosis. As Craigie points out, if the description is taken clinically, it would appear that the psalmist "has almost every disease in the book."[174] But the description is poetic, and so the psalm could be and has been perceived to be applicable to a variety of persons and situations throughout the centuries.

After the initial petition and accompanying rationale (vv. 1-2), the psalmist describes his or her condition in vv. 3-10. The social effects of the disease and the psalmist's response are

described in vv. 11-14, followed by an expression of trust in God in vv. 15-16. Verses 17-20 are a sort of review of the whole situation in preparation for the concluding petition in vv. 21-22.

A comparison of the NIV and the NRSV reveals that the meaning of the final phrase of the superscription is unclear (see the same phrase in Psalm 70). Translated literally, it means "to cause to remember." Whether this should be understood as a reference to "the memorial offering" (cf. Lev 2:2, 9, 16 NIV) is not clear. It is just as likely, as the NIV suggests, that the phrase refers to the purpose of the prayer—that is, to cause God to remember the psalmist's need or perhaps to remember God's own gracious character and promises (see Exod 2:24; 32:12).

38:1-4. Verse 1 is identical to Ps 6:1, except that different Hebrew words underlie the translation "anger" (קצף *qeṣep*, 38:1; אף *'ap*, 6:1) in each verse. While "rebuke" (יכח *ykḥ*) and "discipline" (יסר *yāsar*) are elsewhere indications of God's guidance (see Prov 3:11-12), this is not the case when they are done in "anger" and "wrath." Instead of being experienced as guidance, they are experienced as punishment (v. 2), as "arrows" (see Pss 7:13; 64:7) and the blow of God's hand (see Pss 32:4; 39:10). The identical syntax of the two parts of v. 3 emphasizes the point: God's "indignation" (see Pss 69:24; 102:10) and the psalmist's "sin" are parallel. The result is "no soundness in my flesh" (cf. Isa 1:6). The phrase is repeated in v. 7*b*; between the two occurrences lies a chilling description of physical disease. While "flesh" suggests the bodily exterior, the interior body is indicated by "bones" (v. 3*b*; see also Job 30:17, 30; Pss 22:14; 31:10; 102:3). The NRSV's "health" in v. 3*b* translates the Hebrew *shalom*; the psalmist knows no "peace." The mention of "sin" (חטאת *ḥaṭṭā't*) in v. 3*b* is followed in v. 4*a* by the occurrence of "iniquities" (or "guilt" [עון *'āwôn*]; see also Pss 32:1-2, 5; 51:2, 5). The two words also occur together

173. Gerstenberger, *Psalms: Part 1*, 160.
174. Craigie, *Psalms 1–50*, 303.

in v. 18. The iniquities rise like flood waters (v. 4a), while at the same time they pull the psalmist down like a heavy weight (v. 4b). It appears that the psalmist will drown in his or her own guilt.

38:5-8. The seriousness of the situation is also clear in vv. 5-8. The verb translated "grow foul" (באש *bāʾaš*) is more literally rendered "stink." Both it and the verb "fester" or "rot" (מקק *mqq*) are used elsewhere of corpses (see "stench" in Isa 34:3 and "rot away" in Isa 34:4). Again, it appears that the psalmist is as good as dead. The cause was iniquities in v. 4; in v. 5, it is "foolishness" (אולת *ʾiwwelet*), a word that, as the NIV suggests, has more to do with morality than intelligence (see Ps 107:17 [see the NIV and NRSV notes]; Prov 1:7; 14:9; Jer 4:22). The words "prostrate" and "mourning" occur together in Ps 35:14 to indicate the psalmist's sympathy for those who are suffering. Here it is the psalmist who seems to be irreversibly "crushed" (see Ps 51:8).

38:9-10. But v. 9 interjects a glimmer of hope, anticipating vv. 15-16, 21-22. The psalmist's "longing(s)" (or "desire"; see Ps 10:17) are before God, as well as his or her "sighing" (cf. "moaning"/"groaning" in Job 3:24; Pss 6:6; 31:10; 102:5). Verse 10, however, returns to complaint, repeating "heart" from v. 8. Verse 10 may indicate failing sight as the psalmist loses strength, but "light" may also be symbolic of life (see Job 33:30; Pss 13:3; 56:13).

38:11-14. These verses continue the complaint but with a shift of focus from the psalmist's condition to the social effects of the situation. The psalmist is abandoned by those who would be expected to provide support (see Job 19:13-19; Ps 88:8, 18). Verse 11b reads literally, "and my near ones stand far off." Thus it anticipates the petition in v. 21b, where the psalmist asks God to "not be far." The psalmist's friends have become enemies, seeking the psalmist's life (see Pss 35:4; 40:14). Their opposition is demonstrated by their actions (v. 12a), by their speech (v. 12b), and by their thoughts (v. 12c). As ones who meditate treachery or "deceit" (see Pss 10:7; 34:13; 36:3), the psalmist's opponents reveal themselves to be opponents of God as well. Those loyal to God are called to meditate on or utter something different—namely, God's

instruction (Ps 1:2) or wisdom (Ps 37:30). Verses 13-14 seem to describe the psalmist's reaction to the opposition of former friends; the psalmist pretends not to hear and makes no response. In view of such treachery, there is nothing left to say (see Matt 26:63; 27:11-14).

38:15-16. Given the human response to his or her suffering, the psalmist's only possible appeal is to God. So the psalmist will "wait" for or hope in God (see Pss 31:24; 33:18, 22; 69:3; 71:14; 130:7; 131:3). The syntax of v. 15 emphasizes God's role. The poetic line starts with the prepositional phrase "for you" (כי־לך *kî-lĕkā*), and the appearance of the personal pronoun "you" in v. 15b adds emphasis. *God* is the psalmist's only hope; God "will answer" (see Pss 3:4; 4:1; 22:21 NRSV note). God does not rejoice in the psalmist's suffering, and God is the only one who can prevent others from doing so (v. 16; see Pss 13:4; 35:24).

38:17-22. Verses 17-20 review the major aspects of the situation. Verse 17 summarizes the complaint and its urgency (see vv. 2-10). Using the two words from vv. 3b-4a, v. 18 rehearses the psalmist's confession. The verb in v. 18b means more literally "troubled"; however, the fact that the psalmist is troubled seems to indicate a penitent stance, as the NRSV suggests. Verse 19a, which the NIV translates more accurately, recalls vv. 11-12. Verses 13-14 have implied that the opposition to the psalmist is wrong, but v. 19b states this explicitly, and v. 20 reinforces this statement. Verse 20b seems to contradict what the psalmist had said earlier; that is, the psalmist had asserted his or her sinfulness (vv. 3-5, 18), but now says "I follow after good." But this need not be a contradiction; rather, it likely suggests that the psalmist, having been "troubled by" his or her sin (v. 18b) and having experienced the destructive effects of sinfulness (vv. 2-10), has repented.

Thus, even if the indignation of God may once have been deserved, such is the case no longer. In any case, the response of others to the psalmist's suffering is not justified. As Ps 35:13-14 suggested, the proper response to the suffering of others is sympathy and even participation in the suffering, not further accusation (see Ps 69:26). There has thus been some movement between vv. 1-10 and vv. 17-20. According to the psalmist, sin has produced pain (v. 17), but it is precisely pain that God sees (v. 9) and responds to compassionately (v. 15; see Exod 3:7, where the word "sufferings" [מכאוב *mak'ôb*] is the same as "pain" in Ps 38:17). The repentant, suffering psalmist thus has a solid foundation for the complaint against the opponents (v. 20) and for the final appeal in vv. 21-22. These verses are especially reminiscent of Psalm 22. The petition in v. 21*a* recalls Ps 22:1, and the pleas in vv. 21*b*-22 recall Ps 22:11, 19 (see also Ps 35:22*b*). While Psalm 38 does not make the dramatic turn to praise that is found in Psalm 22, the final petitions do indicate the psalmist's trust that neither one's own sinfulness, nor suffering (whatever the cause), nor the opposition of others will be able to separate one from the one properly addressed as "my salvation" (v. 22; see "salvation"/"deliverance" in Pss 3:8; 88:1; 118:14, 21; Exod 15:2).

REFLECTIONS

As suggested above, the ancient belief that sickness or suffering could be directly explained as the punishment of God is very problematic. Indeed, there is ample protest within Scripture against such a mechanistic doctrine of retribution that would lead one to conclude that the prosperous must have earned God's favor and suffering persons must be experiencing God's wrath. The book of Job, for instance, clearly demonstrates that Job's suffering is not punishment from God, and it severely criticizes Job's friends for accusing Job of deserving his plight (cf. Job 11:2-6 and 22:4-11 with 42:7).

At the same time, it may be proper to retain some association of sin and suffering, even of sin and sickness. Sin—the failure to honor God and the way God has ordered human life and the world—has destructive consequences, including physical consequences. For instance, abuse of one's body, including overwork and stress, can literally make one sick. This does not mean, however, that all sickness and suffering can be interpreted as God's punishment of particular sins on a one-to-one basis. This would be to make the mistake of Job's friends. Rather, like the book of Job, Psalm 38 invites us to view sickness, suffering, and death as inevitable realities of being mortal, finite, and fallible. To be sure, sin causes suffering, but the suffering we experience is not necessarily the result of our own particular sins. As a penitential psalm, Psalm 38 may serve as an invitation to personal confession and repentance, but it also serves as an invitation to live constantly in humble reliance upon God in a world where our sufferings may have much more to do with the sinfulness of others than with our personal misdeeds (see Reflections on Psalm 6).

While Psalm 38 has implications for understanding our own suffering, it is especially instructive in terms of how we are called to respond to the suffering of others. The "friends," "companions," and "neighbors" of v. 11 are clearly a negative example, as suggested by vv. 12 and 20 and by the literary context of Psalm 38 (see Ps 35:12-14). In short, it is not proper to treat those who are suffering as if they deserve their suffering (even if they might deserve it, as the psalmist suggests of himself or herself!). Rather, we are called to be forgiving and compassionate, as God is forgiving and compassionate. This lesson is easily forgotten. The inclination of many individual Christians and congregations is to *blame* those who suffer. We often conclude that if people are poor or homeless or carriers of HIV, they must have done something to deserve it. It is a convenient excuse for allowing ourselves to "stay far away" (v. 11) rather than to love those whom God loves. It is also a cruel and proudly self-deceptive response, since it involves our condemnation of others and our congratulation of ourselves.

Unlike several other of the more impressive individual laments (see Psalms 22; 31; 69), Psalm 38 does not figure prominently in the narrative of Jesus' suffering and death. The reason why almost certainly is that the psalmist attributes the suffering to sinfulness. Nevertheless, v. 11 anticipates Jesus' experience (see Matt 26:56; 27:55), and vv. 13-14 anticipate Jesus' response to the treachery committed against him (see Matt 26:63; 27:11-14). Jesus, though sinless, suffered, and other people were perfectly willing to interpret his suffering as God's punishment (see Matt 26:65-68; 27:20-23, 38-44). Thus the cross of Jesus constitutes the ultimate sign of the rejection of a doctrine of retribution that would interpret all suffering as the punishment of God. The cross too proclaims the good news that Psalm 38 affirms: God is a source, not of condemnation, but of hope (v. 15), and sinners may address God as "my God" (v. 21) and "my salvation" (v. 22).

PSALM 39:1-13, MY HOPE IS IN YOU

COMMENTARY

In some ways, Psalm 39 is like other prayers for help. Like Psalm 38, for instance, it could have originated from a person who was ill (see v. 10), and it implies a connection between sickness and sin (vv. 8, 10-11; the NRSV's "chastise" and "punishment" in v. 11 are from the same roots as the words "rebuke" and "discipline" in Ps 38:1 NRSV). Even the psalmist's opening resolve to be silent (vv. 1-2) has a possible parallel in Ps 38:13-14, and in both the psalmist places hope in God ("wait" in 38:15 and "hope" in 39:7 translate the same Hebrew root [יחל *yḥl*]). Despite these similarities, Psalm 39 is unique. Major commentators describe it using words like *enigma, unusual,* and *strange.* The extended opening meditation (vv. 1-3) is not typical, nor is the final petition that seems to ask for God's inattention (v. 13). Perhaps the most unique feature of Psalm 39, however, is the content of the complaint (vv. 4-6), which articulates not specific problems but the general condition of human transience.

The uniqueness of Psalm 39 has given rise to widely divergent understandings. Kraus, for instance, concludes that "the psalm breaks off in despair; it is plunged into darkness without parallel."[175] Craigie, on the other hand, suggests that Psalm 39 is the product of mature spiritual reflection; the psalmist "has regained his perspective on the transitory nature of human life and can face death with calmness."[176] These contradictory viewpoints suggest another possibility. As Robert Alter puts it, "the speaker flounders in a world of radical ambiguities."[177] In other words, Psalm 39 articulates despair and hope *simultaneously.* In so doing, it portrays the way life really is: terrifyingly short, yet awesomely wonderful. And it represents the tension inevitably involved in our response to life—that is, both hopeful awe and nearly unspeakable despair that finally cannot be silenced.

As both the NIV and the NRSV suggest, Psalm 39 falls into four sections. As important as these structural divisions, however, is Alter's observation that the movement of Psalm 39 involves the presentation and interweaving of three themes: silence (vv. 1-3, 9, 12*c*), human transience (vv. 4-6, 11*c*-12), and sin/suffering (vv. 8, 10-11*b*). The first two, which are more prominent, come together in the climactic v. 13, and v. 7, the exact middle line of the poem, functions as a turning point.[178] The existence of these themes and their complex interrelatedness contribute to the sense of ambiguity and tension mentioned above.

39:1-3. The psalm begins with the unusual, "I said." What is then stated is the psalmist's intention not to speak. Apparently, the psalmist wants to avoid the sin of accusing God of wrong-doing (see Job 1:22; 2:10); furthermore, the psalmist does not want to provide the wicked with ammunition for their attacks. So the psalmist "was silent" (see Isa 53:7) and "still" (see "silence" in Ps 62:1, 5, where it seems to connote patience). Although v. 2*b* may be variously construed (cf. the NIV with the NRSV), the verb means "to keep silence" (חשה *ḥāšâ*; see Eccl 3:7).

175. Kraus, *Psalms 1–59,* 420.
176. Craigie, *Psalms 1–50,* 310.
177. Alter, *The Art of Biblical Poetry,* 69.
178. Alter, *The Art of Biblical Poetry,* 68-73.

But silence does not work. The worsening "distress" (v. 2; cf. Job 2:6) has internal effects—heartburn, as it were (v. 3a; see Deut 19:6, where a similar phrase is translated "hot anger"), indicating an overwhelming compulsion (see Jer 20:9). The phrase "I spoke" in v. 3 recalls v. 1a, and the repetition of "tongue" recalls v. 1b. Like Job, the psalmist moves from pious, resigned silence to speech (cf. Job 1–2 with Job 3).

39:4-6. The content of the speech that begins in v. 4, however, is surprising—no cursing the day of his or her birth (see Job 3:1), no accusing God or asking "how long?" (see Ps 13:1-2). Indeed, there seems nothing particularly sinful about what the psalmist says in vv. 4-6. Verse 4 is framed as a request for information about "my end" (see Job 6:11), although v. 4c suggests that the psalmist already knows about the transience of life. The Hebrew word translated "fleeting" (חדל ḥādēl) anticipates v. 5 by way of a play on words with the Hebrew word translated by the NRSV as "lifetime" (חלד ḥeled), and v. 5 confirms the knowledge that v. 4c implied. In v. 5ab, the psalmist focuses on his or her own life, concluding it is "as nothing" (כאין kĕʾayin; cf. Ps 103:16, "it is gone"). This word occurs again as the final word of the psalm ("no more," v. 13), and it is also the foundation for the following three generalizations about all human life (vv. 5c-6b), each of which is introduced by the particle "surely" (אך ʾak).

Two Hebrew words are used in vv. 5c-6 to describe the human situation (v. 5c), human vocation (v. 6a), and human aspiration (v. 6b). The word translated "shadow" or "phantom" (צלם ṣelem) more literally denotes a likeness or "image" (see Gen 1:26-27). Here it clearly implies an image devoid of actual reality; so the psalmist suggests that human life is really an illusion (see Ps 73:20, where the word is translated "phantoms" or "fantasies" and is used of the wicked). The words "breath" (v. 5c) and "for nothing" (v. 6b) translate the same Hebrew word (הבל hebel), which is related by alliteration to the nouns in vv. 4c, 5b. It indicates a vapor, a puff of wind, a breath—something insubstantial and fleeting (see Job 7:16; Pss 62:9; 94:11; 144:4; Isa 57:13). It is especially prominent in Ecclesiastes, where it occurs over thirty times (e.g.,

Eccl 1:2, 14; 2:1, 15; 12:8). By describing a situation that Ecclesiastes identifies as "vanity," v. 6c also recalls Eccl 2:18-21).

39:7-8. Just as the emphatic expression of the intent to be silent unexpectedly issued in speech (vv. 1-3), so also the psalmist's emphatic expression of human transience (vv. 4-6) unexpectedly issues in hope in v. 7. This verse uses both of the primary Hebrew roots for "hope" (for the word here translated "wait for" [qāwâ], see Pss 25:5, 21; 27:14; 37:34; for the word here translated "hope" [תוחלת tôḥelet], see Pss 31:24; 33:18, 22; 38:15). The exact center of the psalm, v. 7 represents a turning point. It is followed immediately by the introduction of the third theme: sin/suffering. There is still no accusation or railing at God. Rather, the psalmist, implicitly confessing sin, makes a humble request for forgiveness. As in v. 1, the psalmist is again concerned about the response of the wicked or, as they are called here, fools (see Ps 14:1). Both petitions are much more typical of other prayers for help (see "scorn" in Ps 31:10) than were the opening meditation (vv. 1-3) and complaint (vv. 4-6).

39:9-11. Verse 9 returns to the theme of silence and makes better sense in the past tense, as in the NIV. The personal pronoun "you" in v. 9b is emphatic. In vv. 9b-11b, the psalmist seems to affirm the traditional connection between sin and sickness as God's punishment (see Commentary on Psalm 38; the Hebrew word translated "stroke" [נגע negaʿ] in 39:10a also underlies the NRSV's "affliction" in 38:11). Verse 11 again represents a generalization from the psalmist's own experience to all humanity (see vv. 5-6), and v. 11c links the themes of sin/suffering and transience by means of the repetition of "breath" from vv. 5-6. This linkage is reminiscent of Psalm 90.

39:12. The three petitions in v. 12 are the most traditional-sounding part of Psalm 39 (see also Ps 4:1). The third petition returns to the theme of silence with a twist, requesting that God *not* be silent at the psalmist's "tears" (see Pss 6:6; 56:8). The accompanying rationale involves the theme of transience again. The two terms elsewhere designate non-Israelite residents of the land, but Lev 25:23 suggests that in view of God's ownership of the land, all Israelites "are but aliens and tenants" (NRSV). David's final praise of God in 1 Chronicles cites this tradition, recognizing that it seems to imply hopelessness but that it actually serves to emphasize God's gracious provision (see 1 Chr 29:15). Thus v. 12*de* offers an appropriate basis for the petitions in v. 12*abc* by reminding God of how God has historically provided for the people.

39:13. This allusion to God's gracious provision makes v. 13 all the more surprising, even in a poem that is full of surprises. One might expect at this point something like, "Let the light of your face shine on us" (Ps 4:6*b*); however, v. 13*a* requests just the opposite! Like Job, the psalmist asks for God to "look away" (the verb also occurs in Job 7:19; cf. Job 7:17-21; 10:20-22; 14:1-6; the word

the NRSV translates as "smile" [בלג *blg*] in Ps 39:13 also appears in Job 10:20 as "comfort"). The apparent contradiction between v. 13 and v. 12 may be softened by assuming that the psalmist associates God's gaze with punishment, as Job seems to do in Job 7:20-21. However, this approach does not remove the tension between the psalmist's experience of God as "my hope" to whom appeal is made (v. 12) and the experience of God as an oppressive presence who is responsible for human transience (v. 11). The themes of silence and transience come together in the final word of the psalm: "no more," which anticipates the psalmist's death—the ultimate silence. The ambiguity is not resolved. Hope and despair stand side by side.

REFLECTIONS

The ambiguity or tension that characterizes Psalm 39 invites theological reflection. The place to begin is with the similar movement in vv. 1-3 and vv. 4-7. In vv. 1-3, the psalmist moves from silence to speech. In vv. 4-7, the articulation of despair moves toward hope. The movements are related; that is, the psalmist *speaks* his or her way to hope. In other words, the very existence of the psalmist as a speech-partner with God belies the apparent insignificance of humanity. Walter Brueggemann says, "The Psalm evidences courage and ego strength before Yahweh which permits an act of hope, expectant imperatives, and an insistence that things be changed before it is too late."[179] In effect, the psalm suggests a paraphrase of Descartes: "I speak; therefore, I am."

A further clue in this direction is the repetition of "as nothing"/"no more" in vv. 5, 13. In the light of v. 13, in which the psalmist speaks about death, v. 5 implies that "my lifetime" is really no better than death. But again, the very act of speech subverts this implication. Any being that has the courage to tell God, "Look away" (v. 13), cannot be entirely insignificant, even if life is fleeting. In this sense, the fact that the psalmist speaks is of more importance than the content of the speech.

On the other hand, the content of the psalmist's speech is important as well. Particularly noteworthy is the ambiguity or tension already pointed out. In language reminiscent of Ecclesiastes and Job, the psalmist articulates the fleeting quality and apparent futility of life (vv. 4-6), even suggesting that God's presence is a hindrance (v. 13). At the same time, however, the psalmist expresses hope in God (v. 7), articulates in very traditional language a relationship between sin and suffering (vv. 10-11), and invokes God's forgiveness and help (vv. 8, 12). This juxtaposition may indicate, as Alter suggests, "a psychological dialectic in the speaker,"[180] but it has theological significance as well. It suggests that Psalm 39, like Job and Ecclesiastes, deals with the issue of theodicy, that it is an exploration of the issue of God's justice in view of sin and human suffering (see Reflections on Psalm 37). The simultaneous use of and subversion of traditional formulations is revealing. The psalmist does not give up on God or relinquish the conviction of God's governance of the world; rather, like Job and Ecclesiastes, the psalmist articulates hope in God on a new basis. The inability to keep silent and

179. Walter Brueggemann, "The Costly Loss of Lament," *JSOT* 36 (1980) 66.
180. Alter, *The Art of Biblical Poetry*, 70.

the honest articulation of the transience and futility of human life suggest that God's governance of the world cannot be reduced to a simple moral calculus, a mechanistic system of reward and punishment. In this sense, the psalmist's speech is fundamentally a protest, as was Job's speech, not so much against God as against a too simple understanding of God. As both Psalm 39 and the book of Job suggest, God is not a score-keeper of human rights and wrongs but a partner with humanity in the complex matter of life. That humanity speaks and God listens is crucial. Not only is God made accessible to humanity, and hence vulnerable to human shortcoming, but also humanity is given the exalted status of partnership with God. Paradoxically, the psalmist's articulation of fleetingness and futility is eloquent testimony to the importance of humanity. To be sure, human transience is a reality, and life is uncertain and difficult. But the good news is that hope and joy are possible, because human beings live as partners of God.

Finally, then, Psalm 39 is not an affirmation of futility but a profession of faith. As the NT recognizes as well, to live as a "passing guest" is to entrust one's life and future to God amid all the uncertainties and ambiguities of the world (see Heb 11:13; 1 Pet 2:11). Like the psalmist, we must live with hope in an apparently hopeless world. In the face of discouragement and despair, we must dare to speak to God and thus claim our partnership with God. While it may be coincidental, it is interesting that the word "shadow" or "image" in v. 6 is used in Gen 1:26-27 to describe humankind's creation in the "image of God." It is a bold affirmation that our finite, creaturely status does not mean insignificance. It does not detract from the royal vocation of "dominion" (Gen 1:28)—in effect, the calling to participate with God as a partner in ruling the world! Just as God spoke humanity into being, so also humanity is called to continue the conversation, as the psalmist does so honestly and eloquently in Psalm 39.

PSALM 40:1-17, I DELIGHT TO DO YOUR WILL

COMMENTARY

Because of the marked difference between vv. 1-10 and vv. 12-17, Psalm 40 is often treated as two separate psalms that have been placed together by an editor, who perhaps provided v. 11 as a transition. Recalling and celebrating a past deliverance, vv. 1-10 have the character of a song of thanksgiving. Verse 11 shifts to petition, however, and vv. 12-17 constitute a typical lament or complaint. Further impetus to treat the two sections as separate psalms is provided by the fact that vv. 13-17 are virtually identical to Psalm 70.

Even so, there are compelling reasons to treat Psalm 40 as a unity, regardless of its compositional history. For instance, several repeated words or roots bind the two sections ("see" in vv. 3, 12; "thought[s]" in vv. 5, 17; "more" in vv. 5, 12; "counted"/"number" in vv. 5, 12; "desire"/ "delight" in vv. 6, 8, 14; "will"/"be pleased" in vv. 8, 13; "salvation"

in vv. 10, 16; plus the emphatic pronoun "you" in reference to God in vv. 5, 9, 11, 17, although the NIV and the NRSV obscure its appearance in v. 11). Furthermore, there is a coherence to Psalm 40 in its final form. This coherence may well be a "liturgical integrity," as Gerstenberger suggests.[181] In any case, it makes sense that a past deliverance would be recalled (vv. 1-10) as the basis for a prayer for help in a new situation of distress (vv. 11-17). While this sequence may not be typical, neither is it without parallel in the psalter (see Psalms 9–10; 27; 44; 89).

40:1-3. In v. 1, the psalmist affirms emphatically that she or he has done what several psalms exhort and encourage: waited for God (see Pss 25:3, 5, 21; 27:14; 37:34; 39:7). And the waiting was not in vain.

---

181. Gerstenberger, *Psalms: Part 1*, 169.

God's hearing the "cry" (שׁועה *šawʿâ*; see Pss 18:6; the word "cry" also occurs in Ps 39:12, which makes an interesting juxtaposition to Ps 40:1, especially in light of 39:13; see Commentary on Psalm 39) is accompanied by God's active response (v. 2). The poetic language of v. 2*ab* does not permit an exact determination of the distress but does indicate its life-threatening nature. The word "pit" (בור *bôr*) in v. 2*a* often occurs in parallel with "Sheol," the realm of the dead (see Pss 30:3; 88:3-4, 7; see "pit" alone in Pss 28:1; 143:7). In Ps 7:15, the enemies endanger the psalmist by digging a pit. Similarly, the same word designates the pit where Joseph's brothers threw him to be eaten by animals (Gen 37:20, 22, 24, 28) and the cistern where Jeremiah's enemies left him to die of hunger (see Jer 38:6). The parallel to "pit" in v. 2*b* would be more literally translated "mud of the mire" (טיט היון *ṭîṭ hayāwen*), again recalling Jer 38:6, where "mud" (*ṭîṭ*) appears twice (the same word also occurs in Pss 18:42; 69:14, where it is translated "mire" by the NRSV). Thus the Joseph and Jeremiah narratives illustrate literally what the psalmist here describes poetically, although the parallels suggest that enemies may have been involved in the former and current threat to the psalmist's life (see v. 14).

In any case, whatever brought the psalmist down, God brought the psalmist up, establishing a solid foundation for life (see "rocks" in Isa 33:17 and God as "rock" in Pss 18:2; 31:3). Elsewhere, God's "word" or "law" secures the psalmist's "steps" (v. 2; see also Pss 17:4-5; 37:31), suggesting that God is the real source of life; this conclusion is reinforced by v. 3. Even the response to deliverance—the "new song"—is something for which God is responsible. The new song elsewhere is explicitly associated with God's sovereignty (see Pss 96:1; 98:1; 149:1; see also 33:3; 144:9), the proper response to which is trust (see Pss 4:5; 9:10; Introduction). Thus, when others see the deliverance God has effected for the psalmist, they too will be led to fear, which is synonymous with trust ("see and fear" represent a play on two similar Hebrew words [ראה *rāʾâ* and ירא *yārā*] see also Ps 52:6; for "fear" and "trust" used in the same context, see Ps 33:18, 21).

40:4-5. Repeating the word "trust" (מבטח *mibṭāḥ*), v. 4 recalls the beginning of the psalter, which suggests that happy persons are those who are open to God's instruction (1:2) and "who take refuge in" God (Ps 2:12). In short, happiness is derived from dependence on God, not from powerful humans or from other gods. To support the affirmation of v. 4, the psalmist in v. 5 breaks into praise addressed to God. Perhaps v. 5 is even the new song mentioned in v. 3*a*. In any case, the pronoun "you" in v. 5 emphasizes God's initiative in terms of God's activity (see Pss 9:1; 26:7) and God's will (see v. 7; Ps 92:5; Isa 55:8, 9). The effect of v. 5 is to place the psalmist's deliverance (vv. 2-3) in continuity with God's historic activity on behalf of the whole people (see "wonders" in Exod 3:20; 34:10 NIV). God's deeds are incomparable (see Isa 40:18) and incalculable. Verse 5 anticipates vv. 9-10, where the psalmist will serve as witness to God's activity and character, as well as v. 12, where the psalmist's troubles are described as incalculable.

40:6-8. These verses address the issue of response to God's activity (see Ps 116:12)—that is, what God may desire (v. 6) and thus what the psalmist will desire (v. 8). Ordinarily, response to God's activity would have included some form of sacrifice as well as a song of thanksgiving (see Pss 56:12; 107:22; 116:17), but, in words reminiscent of several prophetic texts, the psalmist concludes that God does not really—or at least primarily—want sacrifice (see 1 Sam 15:22; Isa 1:12-17; Hos 6:6; Amos 5:21-24). The four terms for various sacrifices surround a statement that reads literally, "ears you have dug for me" (v. 6*b*). This statement seems to suggest that what the psalmist can hear is more important than what he or she may do. And what the psalmist can hear and be open to is God's will (v. 8*a*; see Pss 103:21; 143:10) and God's instruction (v. 8*b*). Like v. 4, v. 8 recalls the beginning of the psalter; it contains two words from Ps 1:2 ("delight" and "law"). In short, what the psalmist presents to God is her or his own self (see v. 7*a*), open to God's instruction and committed to living in dependence upon God alone (see v. 4).

The nature and significance of the "scroll" (מגלה *mĕgillâ*) in v. 7 is unclear; this verse may be a way of supporting the "Here I am" of

v. 7a. To be written about in God's book is to belong to God and to be fully known by God (see Pss 56:8; 69:28; 139:16), so perhaps the psalmist affirms that she or he offers God the whole self. Another plausible explanation is that the scroll contained written testimony to the psalmist's deliverance (all or part of vv. 1-5) and perhaps to the psalmist's resolve to do God's will (v. 8). If so, it may have been brought as an offering in place of a sacrifice. Thus it would have provided a material representation and witness to the psalmist's offering of her or his transformed, committed self to God. The scroll would have provided the visible evidence of the psalmist's profession that God's instruction is internalized "within my heart" (v. 8b; cf. Jer 31:31-34).

40:9-10. If the scroll was a witness of sorts, it was not the only witness. In vv. 9-10, the psalmist describes the public witness (see vv. 9b, 10c) that he or she has made, or perhaps continues to make (cf. the tenses in NRSV and NIV). The Hebrew verb "told the glad news" (בשׂר *bśr*) in v. 9a underlies the Greek word κήρυγμα (*kērygma*). The psalmist preaches the good news. The word *kērygma* occurs most frequently in Isaiah 40–55 to describe the prophetic proclamation of the good news of forgiveness, which led to the end of the exile (see Isa 40:9; 41:27; 52:7; also Isa 60:6; 61:1). It also occurs in Ps 96:2, where to tell of God's salvation is accompanied by "a new song" (Ps 96:1; cf. 40:3) and leads ultimately to the proclamation of God's reign (96:10; cf. Isa 52:7). In short, the psalmist proclaims God's rule, which here and elsewhere is characterized by "righteousness" (צדק *ṣedeq*, v. 9a), God's setting things right (see Pss 96:13; 97:2; 99:4). It happened at the exodus; it happened with the return from exile; it happened in the psalmist's life—God sets things right. The word "righteousness" (in a slightly different Hebrew form) occurs again in v. 10a. While the psalmist had internalized God's will (v. 8), it does not remain "in my heart" (v. 10a; the Hebrew words translated "heart" differ in vv. 8b [מעה *mē'eh*] and 10a [לב *lēb*]). Supporting the proclamation of God's righteousness is the psalmist's reference to key words that describe the essence of God's character—"faithfulness" (vv. 10b, 10c; the Hebrew forms differ but are from the same root [אמן *'mn*]) and "steadfast love"

(חסד *hesed*, v. 10b; see Exod 34:6-7; Pss 5:7; 6:4; Introduction)—and God's purpose for humanity: salvation (see v. 16).

40:11-12. Verse 11 can be read as either a petition, as the NIV and the NRSV suggest, or a statement. The verb "withhold" (כלא *kālā'*) is the same Hebrew word as "restrained" in v. 9. The psalmist has not withheld testimony to God and now either asks that God not withhold or affirms that God will not withhold mercy. Perhaps the ambiguity is intentional. In any case, the effect of v. 11 is to express confidence for the future on the basis of God's character, the description of which employs the vocabulary of v. 10 and adds "mercy" or "motherly compassion." (See "merciful" in Exod 34:6, which also contains "steadfast love" and "faithfulness"; see also Ps 25:6; Introduction.) Trust in God's character and recollection of past manifestations of it (vv. 5, 9-11) form the foundation for the complaint in v. 12 and the petition in vv. 13-15.

The complaint in v. 12 reveals the current distress but without real specificity. Several repetitions from earlier verses make the description all the more poignant. As God's wonderful deeds had been described as incalculable (v. 5), so now are the present troubles. While previously others could see the psalmist's example and be led to trust (v. 3), now the psalmist "cannot see." Although the psalmist's heart has been filled with knowledge of God's instruction and righteousness (vv. 8, 10), now the heart "fails." So the psalmist prays for help.

40:13-17. The opening petition (v. 13) is from the same Hebrew root as "will" in v. 8. In other words, "make my deliverance part of your will." Verse 13 indicates the urgency of the situation (see essentially the same plea in Pss 22:19b; 35:26). Verse 14 indicates that, as is often the case in the prayers for help, enemies are at least one aspect of the crisis. On the content of the petitions in vv. 14-15, see Pss 35:4, 21, 26; 71:13, 24. Verse 14b contains the third occurrence of "desire" (see vv. 6, 8). While the psalmist's desire is focused on God's will, the desire of the enemies involves the injury of others.

Similarly, the enemies and the faithful are contrasted by what they seek (vv. 14, 16) and by what they say (vv. 15-16). Again, the enemies seek the psalmist's life, and their speech is mocking. The faithful seek God and declare God's greatness; they recognize God's rule (see Pss 35:27; 47:2; 95:3; 96:4; 99:2-3, where God's greatness is recognized in the context of the proclamation of God's reign). The psalmist, too, concludes by aligning with God; the sight of the poor and the needy motivates God to action (see Pss 12:6; 86:1; 109:22, 31; see Commentary on Psalms 9–10). Verse 17cd indicates trust in God (see "help" in v. 13; Pss 22:19; 38:22), but the final petition also indicates the urgency of the current situation; it is especially noticeable in the light of the psalm's opening words. Patient waiting may not always be possible!

REFLECTIONS

The somewhat unusual movement of Psalm 40 from thanksgiving to complaint and urgent petition is significant and instructive. It suggests that, whether individually or corporately, we always pray out of need, at least in the sense that no deliverance is final in this mortal life. To be sure, we can testify to experiences of deliverance, to God's life-giving power at work in our lives and in our churches. But with each new deliverance comes a new threat, imposed perhaps by our own shortcomings (see v. 12) or by external sources. The story of Israel demonstrates this reality. The deliverance from Egypt led immediately to a new threat, precipitated by the people's own "iniquities"—their worship of the golden calf (Exodus 32–34). Delivered from themselves and from external enemies in the wilderness, the people entered the land, where new threats awaited them (the book of Judges narrates several cycles of deliverance/new threat). The monarchy was instituted as a means of deliverance from the Philistine threat, but it in turn threatened the life of the people from within, resulting in exile and eventual restoration. The story of the Christian church or of our individual lives is no different; we are perpetually needy. Mays concludes, "The psalm teaches that the *torah* in the heart does not prevent sin, nor does the experience of salvation spare us from the need of God's help."[182] Patient waiting for the Lord is a way of life for the people of God—we live eschatologically.

But to live eschatologically is to live in the paradox of being perpetually needy and experiencing new life simultaneously. Quite appropriately, then, Psalm 40 not only instructs us about our neediness but also offers in vv. 4-10 what Brueggemann calls "a comprehensive proposal for what the new life should look like."[183] The new life involves trust in God alone (v. 4), the offering of the whole self to God in openness to God's instruction (vv. 6-8), and the sharing with others of the good news of God's will and ability to set things right (vv. 5, 9-10). In effect, the psalmist fulfills Paul's injunction in Rom 12:1-2, offering the self as a living sacrifice (v. 7), committed to discerning the will of God (v. 8). The exhortation in Rom 12:1-2 is made to those who live in the midst of "the sufferings of this present time" (Rom 8:18 NRSV; cf. Ps 40:12) and those who live "in hope" (Rom 8:24) and who wait "with patience" (Rom 8:25 NRSV; cf. Ps 40:1, 13-17) for what they "do not see" (Rom 8:25 NRSV; cf. "see" in Ps 40:3, 12). As much in adversity as in security, the psalmist proves to be a faithful witness. In commenting on v. 11, which he suggests be read as a statement of trust rather than as a petition, Mays concludes: "The psalmist trusts himself to the gospel he has proclaimed in the situation in which he now is. He does what is usually so difficult to do—live by the gospel you preach."[184]

Psalm 40:6-8, in a form that differs from both the Hebrew text and the LXX, is quoted by the author of Hebrews in 10:5-7. The words of the psalm are attributed to Jesus and are interpreted by the author to support the abolition of the OT sacrificial

---

182. Mays, *Psalms,* 169.
183. Brueggemann, *The Message of the Psalms,* 130.
184. Mays, *Psalms,* 168-69.

system in view of Jesus' "once for all" offering of himself (Heb 10:10). While the attribution should not be taken literally, it is significant that the author of Hebrews viewed the psalmist as a type of Christ. As in Psalm 40, the proper sacrifice is the offering of the obedient self. Because Jesus invited his followers to pick up their crosses and follow him (Mark 8:34), the psalmist also becomes a type for all disciples. Psalm 40 and the gospel call us, in recognition of God's sovereign claim upon us (vv. 3-5, 16), to offer God our whole selves, our lives—open to God's instruction and delighting to do God's will (v. 8).

PSALM 41:1-13, HAPPY ARE THOSE WHO CONSIDER THE POOR

COMMENTARY

At the heart of Psalm 41 (vv. 4-10) lies a prayer for help, which is framed by identical petitions in vv. 4 and 10 and contains in vv. 5-9 a fairly typical complaint against the enemies. What is unclear, however, is whether the complaint describes the psalmist's current situation or whether the psalmist is rehearsing what he or she had said during a past situation of distress. The introduction to v. 4 suggests the latter, as does the affirmation in vv. 11-12, which seems to indicate that the psalmist has already been delivered from the threats described in vv. 5-9 (note the repetition of "enemies"/"enemy" in vv. 5, 11). Thus most scholars suggest that Psalm 41 is an individual song of thanksgiving, and this seems to be the soundest conclusion. It is possible, though, to construe the verb tenses in vv. 11-12 as future and to conclude that the psalmist still awaits deliverance. In this case, priority is given to vv. 4-10, and Psalm 41 is understood as an individual lament or complaint.[185]

41:1-3. In any case, the psalm begins in a unique way—with a beatitude. Two other psalms in Book I begin with beatitudes (see Pss 1:1; 32:1-2), and there are four more beatitudes in Book I (see Pss 2:12; 33:12; 34:8; 40:4); but in each of these, happiness has to do with the psalmist in relationship to God. In Psalm 41, however, happiness belongs to "those who consider the poor" (v. 1*a*; cf. Prov 14:21), but this beatitude should not be understood as contradictory to the others. Rather, it follows from the others

and from the character of God as it has been portrayed in the preceding psalms in Book I. Because Psalm 41 is the last psalm in Book I, the opening "happy" especially recalls Ps 1:1-2, where happiness involves openness to God's instruction, including the subsequent psalms themselves as sources of instruction (see Commentary on Psalm 1). If Psalms 2–40 have made anything clear, it is that God considers the oppressed (see Pss 9:9, 18; 10:17-18; 12:5; 14:6; 22:24; 34:19; 37:11; 40:17). Thus those who are open to God's instruction and God's leading, those who live under God's rule, will also "consider the poor." (The word translated "poor" [דל *dal*] occurs here for the first time in the psalter, but it is synonymous with other terms that have occurred frequently in Book I; the word occurs later as "weak" in Pss 72:13; 82:3-4; in 113:7, it is parallel to several of the more frequently used terms.) In other words, the way one treats the poor follows from the way one relates to God.

We may reasonably conclude that the psalmist is among "those who consider the poor," since vv. 1*b*-3 anticipate what apparently actually happens to the psalmist. That is, as vv. 11-12 suggest, the psalmist is delivered, kept alive, and not subdued by the enemies, all of which seems to involve recovery from sickness (see vv. 3-4). But even if one assumes that the psalmist still awaits healing, the affirmation of v. 1*a* is still effective. Happiness is not simply material good fortune. Rather, it involves the connectedness of one's life to the source of life; it means fundamentally

185. See Gerstenberger, *Psalms: Part I*, 174-77.

dependence upon God (see Commentary on Psalms 1; 2). As v. 2*a* suggests, *God* "keeps them alive"; and v. 2*b* reinforces this conclusion. To be "in the land" need not be taken literally, since the land represented access to the God-given resources necessary to sustain life (see above on Ps 37:3, 9, 11, 22, 29, 34). Regardless of whether he or she has actually been healed or still awaits healing, the psalmist's opening affirmation (v. 1-3), prayer for help (vv. 4-10), and concluding assurance (vv. 11-12), indicate that the psalmist lives in dependence upon God.

41:4-9. The petition in v. 4*a* is used frequently (see Ps 4:1). Especially in the light of v. 3, v. 4*b* (see Ps 6:2) makes a connection between sickness and sin. As suggested above, however, the connection is a complex one (see Commentary on Psalms 6; 38). The sickness is an occasion for the psalmist to confess sin, but it does not justify the enemies' inconsiderate response, which is described in vv. 5-9. The enemies clearly do not show any awareness of the beatitude in v. 1*a*; they either do not know or do not care that God acts on behalf of the weak and the needy. Instead, they interpret the psalmist's need as punishment for sin and as license to inflict further punishment. Thus they attempt to capitalize on the psalmist's misfortune. Their speech is malicious (v. 5*a*), "empty" (v. 6*a*; see the NRSV "lies" in Pss 12:3; 144:8, 11), and slanderous (vv. 6*c*-7*a*). Their thoughts and intentions are characterized by "mischief" (אָוֶן *'āwen*; v. 6*b*; see Ps 36:3-4) and "the worst" (lit., "evil" [רָעָה *rā'â*], 7*b*; the word is from the same root [רעע *r'*] as "malice" in v. 5 and "trouble" in v. 1). The phrase in v. 8*a* that the NRSV translates as "deadly thing" means more literally, "thing of worthlessness." As the NIV suggests, it may refer to the psalmist's sickness. The phrase also occurs in Deut 15:9 to describe the "wicked thought" of those who would greedily take advantage of their needy neighbor. Thus, while the referent of the phrase differs in Deut 15:9 and Ps

41:8, the concern of Deut 15:9 is to prevent the kind of greed and exploitation that the enemies demonstrate in Psalm 41. Indeed, even the psalmist's "close friend" (v. 9*a*; lit., "person of my peace," suggesting those who had formerly worked for the psalmist's well-being) has become an opponent (see Pss 38:11; 88:8, 18; see also Job 29–30; John 13:18).

41:10-13. As already suggested, the setting of the petition and complaint (vv. 4-10) between the opening affirmation (vv. 1-3) and concluding assurance (vv. 11-12) suggests that the enemies' behavior is not justified (see Commentary on Psalm 38). The final petition in v. 10 reinforces this conclusion. While the enemies think that the psalmist "will not rise again" (v. 8*b*), the psalmist's petition indicates that she or he trusts God can "raise me up." The psalmist's expressed intent to repay them is not simply an expression of personal revenge. Rather, it may be interpreted as a matter of justice (see Ps 31:23). Liberation for the oppressed means judgment upon oppressors. As v. 11 demonstrates, the failure of the enemies is not just the psalmist's will but God's will as well. The psalmist is "upheld" in his or her "integrity" (v. 12*a*; see Ps 63:8; Isa 42:1, where the mission of the servant in 42:6-8 clearly involves consideration of the poor, in keeping with Ps 41:1*a*). Integrity is not a matter of the psalmist's merit (as the NRSV seems to suggest) but indicates the psalmist's dependence upon God for life and future (see the discussion of "blameless"/"integrity" above in Pss 7:8; 15:2; 18:25; 19:13; 25:21; 26:1, 11). The phrase "in your presence" (לְפָנֶיךָ *lĕpānêkā*; lit., "to your face") may indicate a liturgical setting in the Temple (see "face" in Pss 11:7; 17:15; 24:6; 27:8-9), but it more generally articulates symbolically the psalmist's assurance that God is with him or her. Verse 13 is a doxology that marks the end of Book I (see Pss 71:19; 89:52; 106:48; Introduction).

REFLECTIONS

As the conclusion of Book I, Psalm 41 forms with Psalm 1 an appropriate frame for the whole. Both psalms begin with a beatitude. While Psalm 1 commends openness to God's instruction, Psalm 41 commends openness to the needs of others. The two beatitudes are not contradictory but complementary. In effect, then, the framework of Book I portrays happy persons as those who love God and love neighbor.

A verbal link between Pss 1:2 and 41:11 offers another connection. The root (חפץ *ḥāpēṣ*) translated "delight" in 1:2 is translated "pleased with" in 41:11. Book I opens with a portrayal of those who delight in God, and it concludes with an affirmation of God's delighting in the psalmist. The effect is to articulate the mutuality of the relationship between God and humanity. From the human side, the essence of the relationship is trusting or taking refuge in God, which is the subject of the beatitudes in Pss 2:12; 34:8; 40:4 (see Introduction). From the divine side, the relationship is grounded in the way God is: fundamentally gracious (see vv. 4, 10) and steadfastly loving (see Pss 5:7; 40:10-11; Introduction). In particular, God is committed to those persons variously described in Book I as weak, poor, needy, afflicted, humble, meek, and oppressed. In short, God helps those who cannot help themselves (see Psalm 3). This conviction underlies both the appeal and the opening beatitude in Psalm 41. In essence, happiness belongs to those who are like God—those who consider the poor. As Jesus would say it, "Blessed are the merciful, for they will receive mercy" (Matt 5:7 NRSV).

This basic conviction that God helps the afflicted undercuts any mechanistic doctrine of retribution. The psalmist may be motivated by sickness to confess sins (v. 4), but there is no justification for us to conclude that the psalmist deserves the sickness as punishment for sin, and there is clearly no justification for us to reject the sufferer or take advantage of the suffering (see Commentary on Psalms 6; 38).

In John 13:18, Judas's betrayal of Jesus is interpreted as a fulfillment of Ps 41:9*b*. Thus, like other psalms (see esp. 22; 31; 69), Psalm 41 illuminated for the Gospel writers the suffering of Jesus. Judas's betrayal was motivated, in part at least, by greed, so that he became a representation of the enemies who throughout the psalms seek to take advantage of the humble and the afflicted. As Judas's destiny suggests, this way—the way of self-aggrandizement—is the way of death. The way Jesus walked— the way of suffering that led to a cross—is the way of life. Jesus becomes the ultimate paradigm of the faithful sufferer, who entrusts life and future to God and who likewise considers the poor. The good news of Psalm 41 is that the seemingly rejected one is the one who can finally say to God, "You . . . set me in your presence forever" (Ps 41:12 NRSV). This movement anticipates the NT. The humble are exalted. The crucified one is raised. Suffering and glory belong together as the secret of our identity and God's identity as well (see Commentary on Psalms 13; 22).

PSALMS 42–72

Book II

PSALMS 42:1–43:5, HOPE IN GOD

Commentary

Because of their shared vocabulary, themes, and refrain, Psalms 42–43 are a unit. They open a collection attributed to the Korahites (Psalms 42–49; see also Psalms 84–85; 87–88; Introduction), which in turn opens Book II. While Psalms 42–43 appear to be the prayer of an individual, the rest of the collection has a communal character. This fact, plus the linguistic links between Psalms 42–43 and 44 (see "taunt"/"taunters" in 42:10 and 44:13, 16; "oppress"/"oppression" in 42:9; 43:2; 44:24; "cast off"/"rejected" in 43:2; 44:10; "forgotten"/"forget" in 42:9; 44:24; "face" in 42:2; 44:24; "light" in 43:3; 44:3; "steadfast love" in 42:8; 44:26), suggests that the "I" of Psalms 42–43 speaks for the people (see Reflections below). Not coincidentally, perhaps, the speaker in Psalms 42–43 seems to be exiled from the Temple, and Psalm 44 is a communal lament that recalls the Babylonian exile and dispersion (see esp. 44:9-12). Interestingly, Book III begins in a similar way, with an "I" psalm (Psalm 73) followed by a communal lament (Psalm 74) as the first two psalms in the Asaph collection, which like the Korah collection has a communal orientation. The pattern with which both books begin provides a context for reading subsequent psalms throughout the books—for instance, the Davidic collection of Psalms 51–72—with a communal orientation. This would have particularly suited both books for addressing the exilic and post-exilic eras (see Introduction).

Several scholars conclude that Psalms 42–43 in particular are suited for addressing concerns of the post-exilic era. Gerstenberger, for instance, places these psalms in "the synagogal worship of the Persian times," but he also recognizes that Psalms 42–43 speak "in

very general terms of danger, threats, anxiety, trust, and hope."[186] This fact has made Psalms 42–43 adaptable to a variety of situations. Indeed, they express the fundamental biblical conviction that human life depends on relatedness to God.

The poem may be divided into three sections, each concluding with the refrain: (1) 42:1-5; (2) 42:6-11; (3) 43:1-5. The first two sections are primarily complaint. The final section is primarily petition, giving the whole the character of a prayer for help. Psalms 42–43 also share the spirit of the songs of Zion, in that the psalmist longs to return to Jerusalem and to enter the Temple again (see 43:3-4).

42:1-5. The opening verses articulate the psalmist's need for God with the image of thirst. The opening simile (see Joel 1:20) is followed by a direct statement of the psalmist's need. The two occurrences of "soul" (vv. 1b, 2a) anticipate the refrain. The psalmist's soul "thirsts for God" (v. 2a; see Pss 63:1; 143:6). Thirst is not just a desire, for the human body cannot live without water. For the psalmist, God is a necessity of life. Verse 2b begins to suggest that the psalmist is exiled or at least is prevented from making a pilgrimage to the Temple to "behold the face of God." More symbolically, the psalmist desires a communion with God that is not currently available. The mention of "the face of God" (v. 2) and "bread" (v. 3) reinforces the conclusion that the desire for communion with God is expressed as the wish to visit the Temple, which contained the "bread of the face" (or "bread of the Presence"; see Exod 25:30; 1 Sam 21:6; 1 Kgs 7:48). The psalmist is unable to visit the Temple, so his or her "bread" has

---

186. Gerstenberger, *Psalms: Part I*, 182.

been tears (see Ps 80:5). The grief of absence has been made worse by the question of others, "Where is your God?" (v. 3; see also v. 10; Pss 79:10; 115:2; Joel 2:17; Mic 7:10).

Unable to visit the Temple, all the psalmist can do is remember (v. 4; see also Ps 137:1, 6; Lam 1:7), so she or he recalls the joy of past visits. The poignancy of the scene is expressed by the expression "pour out my soul," for it continues the thirst imagery of vv. 1-2. God's absence means that there is no water to be poured to alleviate the psalmist's thirst; therefore, the psalmist must "pour out" her or his soul by praying (see 1 Sam 1:15; see Pss 62:8; 102:1; 142:2; Lam 2:19). The happy memories that accompany the prayer, however, exacerbate the present sense of despair, which is expressed in the refrain by the verbs "cast down" (שחח šḥḥ, which translates the same verb as "bowed down" in Ps 35:14 and "prostrate" in Ps 38:6) and "disquieted" (המה hāmâ, which translates the same verb as "moan" in Pss 55:17; 77:4). The refrain also articulates the possibility of hope (see Pss 31:24; 33:18, 22; 38:15) and help (more literally, with a slight emendation that makes the refrain here virtually identical to 42:11 and 43:5, "the salvation of my face"; see Exod 15:2; Pss 3:2; 22:1). Although the refrain remains the same, these hopeful notes will be heard more clearly by the conclusion of the poem, which provides the refrain with a different context.

42:6-11. The beginning of the second section echoes the first line of the refrain, thus emphasizing the note of despair. Again, the psalmist's response is to "remember you" (v. 6; see v. 4). The geographical terms in v. 6 are sometimes understood literally and are thus cited by those who want to locate the psalmist outside the land. The names seem to indicate the region where the Jordan River begins, and it is more likely that the psalmist refers to this region as a poetic way of introducing the water imagery of v. 7. Whereas scarcity of water had been the poetic image used to describe the psalmist's need in vv. 1-2, there is too much water in v. 7. The "deep" (תהום těhôm) represents the chaotic forces that plague (cf. Jonah 2:5) and threaten to overwhelm the psalmist (see Pss 69:1-2; 124:4-5; Jonah 2:3).

Verse 8 is unexpectedly hopeful, and commentators often treat it as the psalmist's recollection of a happier time (see 42:4). The reference to "day" and "night" recalls v. 3, and v. 8 even seems to answer the question raised in v. 3, affirming the presence of God's steadfast love (see Pss 5:7; 23:6; 31:7, 16, 21; 32:10; 33:5, 18, 22; Introduction). The refrain has already hinted at hope and help, and the psalm is moving in the direction of assurance (see 43:3-4), so perhaps the expression of confidence here should not be so surprising. After all, despair and hope may exist simultaneously (see Commentary on Psalm 13), and, again, the refrain clearly demonstrates this. In fact, v. 9 also points to the simultaneity of hope and despair. While addressing God as "my rock" (see Pss 18:2; 31:3), the psalmist also wonders why God has "forgotten me" (see Ps 13:1) and why mourning must continue (see Pss 35:14; 38:6) as "the enemies oppress me" (cf. Exod 3:9; Deut 26:7; Pss 56:1; 106:42). The enemies' haunting and taunting question is repeated from v. 3 (see "taunt"/"scorn" in Pss 22:6; 31:11; 55:12; 79:12 NRSV), leading to the second occurrence of the refrain.

43:1-5. The final section moves from complaint to petition. "Vindicate me" (שפטני šōpṭēnî) could also be translated "Establish justice for me" (v. 1; see also Pss 10:18; 26:1). The second petition in v. 1 is framed in legal terms (see Ps 119:154; Lam 3:58; cf. Ps 74:22). The enemies in the psalms are often described as "deceitful" (see Pss 5:6; 10:7; 36:3) and "unjust" (cf. Pss 37:1; 58:2). Verse 2 demonstrates again the simultaneity of hope and despair. While the psalmist still has questions (see 42:9), she or he is clearly moving toward a more hopeful conclusion as the visit to the Temple is envisioned. The psalmist anticipates being led (see Ps 31:3) to the "holy hill" (Pss 2:6; 3:4; 15:1; 48:2) by God's "light" (see Ps 27:1) and "faithfulness" (NIV and NRSV "truth"). Usually, "steadfast love" and "faithfulness" are paired in the psalms (see 57:3; 85:10; 89:14), and Ps 5:7 even affirms that God's steadfast love leads the psalmist to the Temple. Perhaps the normal pairing is altered to include "light" here, since light is often associated with God's "face," which the psalmist longs to see (see Ps 42:2; see also Ps 4:6). Psalm 43:4 articulates the joy of arriving at the Temple, where the psalmist will respond with praises on the harp (see Ps 33:2). The word "praise" (ידה *yādâ*) in v. 4 serves this time to emphasize the hopeful aspect of the refrain: "I shall again praise."

REFLECTIONS

1. The spirit of Psalms 42–43 pervades the opening paragraph of Augustine's *Confessions:* "The thought of [God] stirs [the human being] so deeply that he cannot be content unless he praises you, because you made us for yourself and our hearts find no peace until they rest in you."[187] The imagery of Psalms 42–43 was used by early Christians as symbols for baptism: "The hart [or "deer"; 42:1] . . . was the emblem of those thirsting souls who, in the cooling streams of the baptismal font, drank deeply of the fountain of eternal life."[188] This psalm was sung when Augustine was baptized on Easter Sunday 387 CE. Such use of this symbolism is appropriate, for Psalms 42–43 affirm what Christians profess in baptism: Each human life derives from and belongs to God, and life can be lived authentically only in relationship to God. In short, human life depends on God.

2. As memorable as the opening line of Psalm 42 is the threefold refrain. Although the refrain seems to be intensely personal, it may actually be more liturgical than autobiographical, as Mays suggests:

> "In it the ego who speaks to the downcast soul is the liturgical and confessional ego speaking to the consciousness shaped by a society and circumstances that do not support faith. . . .
> . . . For Christians who live in a world that constantly raises the question, "Where is your God?" these psalms are indispensable liturgy and Scripture. They disclose the real nature of our souls' disquiet as thirst for God. They turn us toward the worship of praise, sacraments, and preaching in and through which our Lord wills to be present for the congregation."[189]

In other words, the refrain and Psalms 42–43 as a whole profess the faith of the people of God, the church. That they did so in a hostile environment makes them all the more timely. As Hauerwas and Willimon put it, the church is in a sort of permanent exile, at least in North America. Christians live as "resident aliens" in a culture that clearly does not support faith or affirm that human life derives from and depends on God. Instead, our culture teaches us that we are self-grounded and self-directed; "It is all up to us."[190] In this cultural context, the most important thing we can do is to hope in God and to claim God as our help (Pss 42:5, 11; 43:5).

3. To hope in God means that we live eschatologically, that we know and articulate hope and despair simultaneously (see Commentary on Psalm 2; Introduction). That we cannot escape this inevitable reality is demonstrated by Jesus, who echoes the refrain of Psalms 42–43 in his prayer in the Garden of Gethsemane (Matt 26:38; John 12:27). Even Jesus, who fully embodied dependence upon God, could not escape disquietude of soul. Neither shall we. The good news, however, is that neither shall we be able to escape the steadfast love and faithfulness of God, which are manifested in God's desire to lead us back to God's own self (see 42:8; 43:3). This is the source of our hope and, indeed, the hope of the world.

187. Augustine, *Confessions*, I.1, trans. R. S. Pine-Coffin (New York: Penguin Books, 1961) 21.
188. Prothero, *The Psalms in Human Life and Experience*, 9-10.
189. Mays, *Psalms*, 175-76.
190. Hauerwas and Willimon, *Resident Aliens*, 36; see also Commentary on Psalm 3.

PSALM 44:1-26, LIKE SHEEP FOR SLAUGHTER

COMMENTARY

Psalm 44 is the first communal lament or complaint in the psalter. Two major issues have dominated the scholarly discussion of the psalm: (1) the circumstances in which it arose, and (2) the identity of the speaker(s). As for the first issue, a wide variety of proposals has been offered. The origin of the psalm is sometimes placed during the monarchy (see 2 Chr 20:1-12) and is often associated with Sennacherib's campaign of 701 BCE (see 2 Kgs 18:13–19:37; Isa 36:1–37:37). Then, too, Psalm 44 is clearly reminiscent of the exile, which involved the scattering of the people (see v. 11). Since vv. 17-22 seem inconsistent with the dominant OT view that the exile was a deserved punishment (see 2 Kgs 17:19-20; 24:4-5), other dates have also been proposed, including the second-century BCE Maccabean period, when the Temple was desecrated by Antioches IV Epiphanes. The very fact that these proposals cover a range of over 500 years suggests the difficulty of dating the psalm. As John Calvin suggested long ago, almost any date after the exile would fit, "for after the return of the Jews from the captivity of Babylon, they were scarcely ever free from severe afflictions."[191]

The second issue is related to the first. Noting that vv. 4, 6, 15-16 depart from the predominant first-person plural, several scholars suggest that this speaker must be the king, who speaks as a representative of the nation during the crisis. Obviously, this view necessitates a pre-exilic dating of the psalm. Craigie, for instance, argues that Psalm 44 originated during some unknown pre-exilic crisis and was used during subsequent crises throughout the history of the nation.[192] But as Gerstenberger points out, the alternating of plural and singular speakers can be attributed to the liturgical use of the psalm, and he suggests that the origin and use of Psalm 44 are to be associated with "Jewish worship in Persian times," the purpose of which in part was to

encourage and strengthen congregations in a threatening environment.[193]

Perhaps more accessible than the question of the origin of Psalm 44 is the issue of its final placement. There are striking linguistic links between Psalms 42–43 and 44 (see Commentary on Psalms 42–43), which open Book II. While Psalms 42–43 seem to be the prayer of an exiled individual, Psalm 44 is the prayer of a scattered people. Together, they set the tone for hearing the rest of the psalms in Book II, and thus they reinforce the ability of the collection to address the perpetually threatened people of God (see Introduction). This recognition allows Psalm 44 to be heard not simply as a historical artifact but as an ongoing theological resource for the people of God as they confront their vocation and the suffering that it inevitably involves (see Reflections below).

Psalm 44 can be divided into four major sections. Verses 1-8 have the character of a profession of faith that is motivated by historical recollection. In view of v. 8b, the section of bitter complaint in vv. 9-16 is unexpected, thus increasing its rhetorical impact. The vehemence of the complaint is perhaps more understandable in the light of vv. 17-22, the people's protestation of innocence. The psalm culminates in the petition of vv. 23-26.

44:1-8. The book of Deuteronomy directs that children be told of God's deliverance of the people from Egypt and of God's gift of the land (Deut 6:20-25), and Psalm 44 begins by affirming that this has happened (see Judg 6:13; Ps 78:3-4). The "you" that begins v. 2 is emphatic. God's power—symbolized by God's "hand" (v. 2), "right hand" (v. 3; see Exod 15:6, 13), and "arm" (v. 3; see Exod 15:16; Ps 77:15)—has been operative in the people's history. The latter is specifically contrasted in v. 3 with "their own arm." As in the exodus and holy war traditions (see Exodus 15; Joshua 8–12), God is portrayed as a warrior. The result is "victory" (ישועה *yĕšûʿâ*,

191. Calvin, *Commentary on the Book of Psalms,* V:2:148.
192. Craigie, *Psalms 1–50,* 331-33.
193. Gerstenberger, *Psalms: Part I,* 186.

v. 3; lit., "salvation"; see vv. 4, 6, 7; and Exod 15:2 NIV); the nations have been driven out (see Deut 7:17) and the people "planted" (see Exod 15:17; Jer 24:6; 32:41). Whereas in Ps 42:2, the psalmist could not see "the face of God," Ps 44:3 attributes victory to "the light of your face" (see also Ps 4:6). The section concludes with the observation that Israel's past has been evidence of God's love (see Deut 7:7-11, where the same observation is made with different vocabulary; see also Ps 149:4, where the NRSV's "takes pleasure" translates the same verb here translated "delighted" [רצה *rāṣâ*] and where it also accounts for the people's "victory").

The emphatic pronoun "you" opens v. 4 as it did v. 2, focusing attention on God. God's control of the destiny of nations and peoples—God's victory—is evidence of God's sovereignty; so God is addressed as "my King" (see Pss 5:2; 68:24; 74:12; 84:3; see also Exod 15:1-18; Pss 98:1-3; 149:1-7, where God's "victory"/"salvation," God's control of the nations, and God's reign are explicitly associated; see also Psalm 2; Introduction). In addition to the repetition of "victory," vv. 4-8 are linked to vv. 1-3 by the repetition of "sword" (vv. 3, 6). While the participation of the people is somewhat more evident in v. 5 than in vv. 2-3, the victory still belongs to God (the word translated "tread down" [בוס *bûs*] is used elsewhere of God as warrior; see Pss 60:12; 108:13; Isa 14:21; 63:6). The people's trust (v. 6; see Pss 4:5; 9:10; Introduction), boasting (v. 8; see Ps 34:2; cf. Pss 52:1; 97:7), and gratitude (see Pss 75:1; 79:13) are properly directed to God.

44:9-16. Nothing in vv. 1-8 has prepared for the complaint in vv. 9-16. Suddenly, delight has become rejection (v. 9; see v. 23 NIV; see also Pss 43:2; 60:1, 10; 74:1; 77:7; 88:14; 89:38; 108:11); victory has become retreat and defeat (v. 10). God is no longer the good shepherd of the "sheep" (see Pss 74:1; 79:13; 95:7; 100:3). Rather, the sheep are either being killed (v. 11*a*; see v. 22; Jer 12:3) or scattered (see Ezek 5:12; 12:14; 20:23). The word "sold" (מכר *mākar*, v. 12) recalls former times that were not so auspicious (see Judg 2:14; 3:8; 4:2). The language

of vv. 13-16 is similar to that of other individual and communal complaints. The people are taunted (v. 16; see Ps 22:6), derided (see Ps 22:7), and scorned (see Ps 79:4, where all three words occur). The word "byword" (see Ps 69:11) occurs in Deut 28:37 as part of the curses for violating the covenant, thus preparing for the people's defense in vv. 17-22.

44:17-22. In vv. 20-21, the people suggest that they could accept their misfortune if they had worshiped a "strange god" (see Ps 81:9; Isa 43:12). But they have neither forgotten God (vv. 17, 20) nor violated the covenant (see Deut 4:23; 2 Kgs 17:15). They have not "turned back" (see Ps 78:57), yet they suffer (v. 19; on v. 19*a*, cf. Isa 34:13; Jer 9:11; 10:22; on v. 19*b*, cf. Pss 23:4; 107:10). Thus all they can conclude is that their suffering is "Because of you" (v. 22). Verse 22 recalls v. 11*a*, although the Hebrew words translated "slaughter" differ in the two verses (מאכל *ma'ăkāl*, v. 11*a*; טבחה *ṭibḥâ*, v. 22). The one in v. 22 occurs also in Isa 53:7 (see Ps 69:7), which is part of the climactic Suffering Servant song, another text that pushes toward new and deeper understandings of suffering (see Reflections below).

44:23-26. Given the people's conclusion in v. 22, all that they can do is desperately plead for God to wake up (see Pss 7:6; 35:23; 59:4-5) as they bombard God with questions. God is not supposed to sleep (see Ps 121:4); God is not supposed to hide God's face (see Pss 13:1; 22:24; 27:9); God is not supposed to forget affliction (see Pss 9:12, 18; 10:12; 42:9). A final complaint (v. 25; the NRSV's "sinks down" translates a verb [שחה *šāḥâ*] that is very similar to "cast down" in Pss 42:5, 11; 43:5) precedes the threefold petition of the concluding verse: "Rise up" (see Pss 3:7; 74:22), "help" (see Pss 22:19; 38:22; 40:13), "redeem" (see Pss 25:22; 34:22). The appeal is to God's fundamental character: steadfast love (see Exod 34:6-7; Pss 5:7; 6:4; Introduction). While God is the problem, God is also the solution. As Mays suggests, "the last hope of a faithful people is the faithfulness of God."[194]

194. Mays, *Psalms*, 178.

REFLECTIONS

The unexpected movement from vv. 1-8 to vv. 9-16 reveals the pathos of Psalm 44; God's faithful people suffer, even when they do not deserve it (vv. 17-22). Thus they are left to appeal for help (vv. 23-26) to the one who is apparently the source of the problem (vv. 11, 22). This is the paradox of the individual complaints and of the book of Job as well. For the psalmists and for Job, every experience of life is somehow an experience of God. Like Psalm 44, for instance, Psalm 13 moves from bitter complaint (cf. Ps 13:1 to 44:24) to petition and to the psalmist's taking a stand on God's steadfast love (cf. 13:5 to 44:26). The paradox of the complaints pushes toward a profound understanding of suffering (see Commentary on Psalms 13; 22).

Crucial in this regard in Psalm 44 are vv. 11 and 22. In commenting on v. 22, Mays concludes:

> "For your sake" meant they could see no other meaning and purpose in their confession and trust [see vv. 1-8] than that they were accounted as sheep for slaughter. But that minimal and doleful interpretation of their suffering opens on the prospect of an understanding of suffering as a service to the kingdom of God. The prospect leads to the suffering servant of Isaiah 53, to Jewish martyrs, and to the cross of Calvary.[195]

For Israel, the experience of exile and the ongoing afflictions of the post-exilic era necessitated a reconsideration of suffering. While it is not clear that the origin of Psalm 44 can be related to the exile, it is certain that Psalm 44 and other complaints assisted Israel to reach in the post-exilic era a new and profound understanding of its suffering and its vocation. In this regard, the similarity to Isaiah 53 is not surprising (cf. Ps 44:11, 22 to Isa 53:7). Israel came to understand its mission to the world in terms of a suffering that is somehow redemptive.

This understanding of suffering, election, and vocation makes comprehensible the life and death of Jesus Christ. Jesus could even pronounce his followers blessed when they experienced the kind of rejection and derision described in Ps 44:13-16 (see Matt 5:10-11). In his consideration of "the sufferings of this present time" (Rom 8:18 NRSV) that are experienced by "God's elect" (Rom 8:33 NRSV), the apostle Paul quoted Ps 44:22 (see Rom 8:36) to illustrate the nature of the Christian life. Suffering is not a sign of separation from God or from God's love; rather, it marks those who have been chosen to follow Jesus Christ (see Mark 8:34-35).

195. Mays, *Psalms,* 179.

PSALM 45:1-17, FOR THE CAUSE OF TRUTH, HUMILITY, AND RIGHTEOUSNESS

COMMENTARY

Unique in the book of Psalms and the entire OT, Psalm 45 is essentially a song of praise addressed to a human being: the king (see esp. vv. 1, 16-17). As the superscription suggests, it is a love song, or more specifically, a wedding song. Almost certainly this royal psalm was composed for use at the wedding of some Israelite or Judean king to a princess from another country. Scholars frequently suggest the wedding of Ahab to Jezebel, since v. 12 mentions the "Daughter of Tyre." But it is not clear that this title designates the new queen, nor is any certainty possible regarding the time and place of the origin of Psalm 45. All that can safely be said is that it originated during the existence of the monarchy and was probably used at several royal weddings.

A crucial question is, Why was this seemingly secular psalm included in the book of Psalms? After the disappearance of the monarchy, Psalm 45 came to be understood messianically by Jews as well as by Christians (see Heb 1:8-9, which quotes Ps 45:6-7), and this fact may account for its inclusion in the psalter. It is misleading, however, to view Psalm 45 simply as a secular psalm. The king was not just a secular ruler; rather, he represented God's own sovereignty, to the point that he was known as God's own son (see Commentary on Psalm 2). Verse 6 even seems to address the king with a term ordinarily reserved for divinity. Regardless of how v. 6 is interpreted, however, it is clear that God is intimately involved with the life and future of the king (see vv. 2, 7), and that the king is entrusted with the implementation of God's royal policy—that is, God's will (vv. 4, 6-7). An important event in the life of the king—such as a royal wedding—is thus an important event in the life of God's kingdom. Thus, even apart from a messianic interpretation, Psalm 45 would with reason have been preserved as part of the book of Psalms. And apart from a messianic interpretation, it still has an important message for contemporary readers (see Reflections below).

45:1. Unlike any other psalm, this one begins with the author's description of his or her task. The phrase "goodly theme" is more literally "good word." It is possible, as some have suggested, that the author was a cultic prophet; however, the matter is unclear. The psalmist may have been a court poet or "scribe" (see Ezra 7:6), although the latter is used in a simile and does not necessarily designate the author's position. As suggested above, the addressing of praise to a human being is also unique.

45:2-5. The judgment of v. 2a may be understood as part of the ancient Near Eastern ideology of kingship (see 1 Sam 16:12, where the narrator cannot help noting that David is handsome, even though God has already announced through Samuel in 1 Sam 16:7 that outward appearance is unimportant;

see also 1 Sam 9:2). While v. 2b is primarily intended to describe the king's speaking ability, it may be significant that "grace" (חֵן ḥēn) is an element of God's character and something God bestows (see Exod 34:6; Pss 4:1; 6:2). Thus v. 2b may anticipate v. 2c, where it is explicitly stated that "God has blessed you forever" (see 2 Sam 7:29; Pss 21:3, 6; 72:15). In other words, the king enjoys a special relationship with God that is elaborated on in the following verses.

The prerogatives of this relationship include military strength (v. 3a) and, more generally, the splendor of the royal office (v. 3b; the word the NIV translates "splendor" [הוד hôd] is also associated with the earthly king in Ps 21:6 and 1 Chr 29:25 and with God's kingship in Pss 96:6; 145:5; for the word the NIV and the NRSV translate "majesty" [הדר hādār] see Pss 21:6; 96:6; 145:5). But this power and majesty (vv. 3-4) are not intended for the king's personal benefit. Rather, they are to be directed toward the enactment of God's royal policy, beginning with "faithfulness." That is, as the sovereign God demonstrates faithfulness to God's people (see Exod 34:6; Pss 25:10; 54:5; 57:3; 71:22), so also should the king, the earthly agent of God's reign. As a comparison of the NIV with the NRSV indicates, the next phrase in v. 4 may be understood differently. It seems to mean, literally, "the oppression of righteousness." The word "righteousness" elsewhere appears in association with God's reign to designate God's will for the world (see Pss 9:8; 96:13; 97:2; 98:9). The phrase in question may indicate the suppression of God's policy, which the king is to address with the power and majesty that God has bestowed upon him (see "righteousness" also in v. 7 and Ps 72:1, 7; see the similar notion in Ps 101:1). The word "oppression" in this form, however, is unusual. The root of the word is the same as the word that occurs frequently in Psalms to designate persons whom God especially responds to—the afflicted/humble/poor/oppressed (see Pss 9:12; 10:2, 9; 14:6). As the NIV suggests, the phrase may suggest more specifically that the king is to join God as an advocate of the oppressed. The "awesome deeds" that the king is to learn are elsewhere what God performs (see Exod 34:10; Ps 66:3, 5), again suggesting that the king's power is to be directed to the fulfill-ment of God's will. The king's enemies in v. 5 are enemies of God as well (see Pss 2:1-3; 21:8-12; 72:8-11).

45:6-7. These verses reinforce the direc-tion of vv. 4-5. The king, the one whom God has "anointed" (v. 7*b*; see also Ps 2:2), embodies God's values. The word "righteous-ness" recurs in v. 7 (see v. 4), and the contrast of "righteousness" and "wickedness" recalls Psalm 1. In contrast to the wicked, who pur-sue their own ends, the king pursues God's purposes. The king's "scepter," symbolic of his power and authority (see Ps 2:9), pro-motes equity, another of God's values, often parallel to righteousness (see Pss 9:8; 67:4; 96:10; 98:9; 99:4). In fact, the poet so iden-tifies the king with God's purposes that the psalmist even addresses the king in v. 6*a* as "elohim" (אלהים *'ĕlōhîm*). This name is most frequently used for God, as the NIV and the NRSV suggest; however, it occasionally des-ignates human beings who exercise God-given authority over others (see Exod 4:16, where Moses is "God" for Aaron, and Exod 7:1, where Moses is "God" to Pharaoh; the same kind of usage may be intended in Exod 21:6; 22:8-9, as the NIV and NRSV notes suggest; see also Zech 12:8). This seems to be the case here. While other ancient Near Eastern cultures viewed the king as divine, and while Israel certainly accorded the king special relatedness to God (see Ps 2:7), it is not likely that Israelite or Judean kings were viewed as divine (see Isa 9:6, where the simi-lar term "el" [אל *'ēl*] is used at the birth of a royal child, but this term, too, can occasion-ally designate powerful human beings as well

as gods and God). Verse 7*b* clearly traces the king's authority to God.

45:8-9. These verses more clearly suggest the setting of a royal wedding. The king's gar-ments exude sensuality. The setting is elegant (see "ivory" in Amos 3:15); the music con-tributes to the joyous mood; the prestigious attendants are in place and so is the queen (see Neh 2:6; the wedding setting prompts the NIV's "royal bride") in elegant attire (see 1 Chr 29:4; Job 28:16; Isa 13:12). The men-tion of the queen in v. 9 prepares for the next section of the poem.

45:10-17. Verses 10-15 focus on the queen, who is addressed in vv. 11-12 and described in vv. 13-15, especially as regards her participation in the wedding ceremony. The queen is encouraged to embrace the new relationship (v. 10), which will involve sub-mission to the king (v. 11), but which will also bring recognition and honor to her (v. 12). Verses 16-17 seem to be addressed again to the king (see the NRSV note), anticipating the continuation of the dynasty (see 2 Sam 7:12-17, 29). The "I" in v. 17 may be the poet, whose poem will "perpetuate the king's memory." Or the "I" may be God, whose promise of sons will perpetuate the king's memory (see 2 Sam 18:18). The latter under-standing would provide a more logical pro-gression between vv. 16 and 17. The words "therefore" and "forever" in v. 17*b* recall the beginning of the poem (v. 2). God's blessing of the king will be matched by human rec-ognition. Ordinarily, praise is reserved for God, but, as suggested above, to recognize the king's sovereignty is also to recognize the sovereignty of God.

REFLECTIONS

1. It would be possible to dismiss Psalm 45 as a relic of the ancient Near Eastern ideology of kingship or as a piece of Israelite or Judean political propaganda. Indeed, if its portrayal of women is taken as a criterion, Psalm 45 should be dismissed (see vv. 10-15). But it seems that the psalm was preserved as Scripture, because it has the potential to facilitate theological reflection about the nature of legitimate political authority. Such reflection is crucial, especially in the light of the apostle Paul's assertion that "those authorities that exist have been instituted by God" (Rom 13:1 NRSV), as well as in the light of the persistent human tendency to be fascinated with powerful people, be they royalty or politicians or even self-appointed dictators.

In fact, Psalm 45 may serve as testimony to the seemingly inevitable human ten-dency to glorify political leaders. Perhaps there is even a certain necessity in this tendency, for it helps to maintain the structure and stability of a society. However, Psalm 45 also warns us about this tendency. While the king could be lavishly honored and addressed, and while the events of his life could be opulently celebrated, it is clear that his power is finally derivative. Thus, while the poet praises the king and contributes material for the celebration, he or she also reminds the king of his responsibility to embody not his own will but the will of God—faithfulness, righteousness, equity (vv. 4-7). By implication, at least, the failure to enact God's will removes one's God-given authority, as indeed the prophets frequently reminded the kings.

2. As for the contemporary scene, perhaps Psalm 45 suggests that we can allow a degree of pageantry and splendor in our state houses and governors' mansions; however, it also reminds us that among the criteria for discerning which authorities are indeed "instituted by God" must be the question of whether our leaders get around to acting "in behalf of truth, humility and righteousness" (v. 4 NIV). If they do not, our fascination with them and loyalty to them are misdirected.

As suggested in the commentary, Psalm 45 came to be read messianically within Judaism; that is, given the failure of the monarchy, people longed for the arrival of one who would indeed rule as God intended. The early church identified this one—this Son of God (see Ps 2:7)—as Jesus of Nazareth, "the reflection of God's glory and the exact imprint of God's very being" (Heb 1:3 NRSV; see Heb 1:8-9). In short, as a king was supposed to do, Jesus embodied God's faithfulness, ministered to the humbled and afflicted, and enacted God's will for rightly ordering the world. In view of Jesus' person and work, as Mays points out, "Christians have traditionally understood the psalm as a song of the love between Christ and his church." This kind of allegorical interpretation is legitimate, at least insofar as it serves as "a safeguard against attributing the divine right of rule to any other save Christ, in whose hands it is utterly safe."[196] In short, Psalm 45 reminds us of what Jesus also proclaimed: that our ultimate political loyalty is to God's reign.

196. Mays, *Psalms*, 182.

PSALM 46:1-11, OUR REFUGE AND STRENGTH

COMMENTARY

"God is our refuge and strength." Whether in this traditional translation or in Martin Luther's paraphrase, "A mighty fortress is our God," the opening line of Psalm 46 is one of the most memorable and powerful in all the book of Psalms. After the opening affirmation of faith (vv. 1-3), vv. 4-6 shift the focus to the city of God and to God's activity on behalf of it. Following the first occurrence of the refrain (v. 7), the final section begins with an invitation to consider God's "works" (v. 8*a*), which are then described in vv. 8*b*-9. Another invitation is issued in v. 10, but this time it is in the divine first person. It effectively summarizes the message of the entire

psalm in preparation for the final refrain (v. 11). Because of the focus on the city of God in vv. 4-6, Psalm 46 is usually classified as a song of Zion (see Psalms 48; 76; 84; 87; 122; Introduction); however, its significance is much broader than the focus on Zion. It is fundamentally an affirmation of faith—not in Zion, but in God. Thus it is often classified as a song of confidence or trust.

46:1. The psalm begins with a threefold description of God: "refuge," "strength," and "help." The word "refuge" (מחסה *maḥseh*) is one of the most important in the book of Psalms, especially in Books I–II (Psalms 1–72). It occurs for the first time in Psalm

2, which, along with Psalm 1, serves as an introduction to the book of Psalms: "Happy are all who take refuge in" God (2:12 NRSV). This beatitude sets the tone for what follows, and in Books I–II the word "refuge" becomes a sort of one-word refrain, occurring twenty-three more times (see Pss 5:11; 7:1; 11:1; 14:6; 16:1; 57:1; 61:3; 62:7-8; 71:7; Introduction). To "take refuge in" God means to trust God, and not surprisingly, trust is also a key theme in the psalms, especially in Books I–II (see Pss 4:5; 9:10; 22:4-5; 25:2; 26:1; 31:6, 14; 55:23; 56:3-4, 11; 62:8; Introduction). Thus Psalm 46 begins with the affirmation that God is a reliable refuge; God is worthy of trust.

Underlying this affirmation is the conviction that God rules the world; God's strength or power lies behind the origin and continuing life of the universe. In short, God is in control—*not* the wicked or the enemies or the nations that regularly threaten the life of the psalmist or the existence of God's people (see Pss 2:1-3, 11; 7:1; 11:1-2; 25:19-20; 31:19-20). The word "strength" (עֹז *'ōz*) points to this conviction of God's sovereignty. It occurs frequently in the psalms that explicitly announce God's reign (see 29:1; 93:1; 96:7; 99:4). God can be trusted, because God rules the world. Perhaps not coincidentally, the very next psalm explicitly refers to God as "a great king over all the earth" (47:2 NRSV).

Psalm 46 affirms that the strength behind the universe is not simply a neutral power. Rather, it is "for us" (v. 1 *a* in Hebrew reads literally, "God is *for us* a refuge and strength"). Or, as v. 1 *b* suggests, this power is inclined toward our "help" (see God as "help" or "helper" in Pss 10:14; 22:19; 28:7; 30:10; 33:20; 37:40; 40:17).

46:2-3. To illustrate how powerful a help God can be in trouble, these verses present the ultimate worst-case scenario. The "change" in the earth described in vv. 2-3 seems like a simultaneous 10.0 earthquake and class-five hurricane, but actually it is even worse! According to the ancient Near Eastern view of the universe, the mountains were both the foundations that anchored the dry land in the midst of a watery chaos and the pillars that held up the sky. Thus the worst thing that could happen would be for the mountains to shake (v. 2) or tremble (v.

3), for the earth would be threatened from below by water and from above by the sky's falling. Verses 2-3, then, may be thought of as an ancient version of the contemporary doomsday scenarios that are more familiar to us—nuclear winter or the depletion of the ozone layer and the rapid rise of the earth's temperature. To use the words of Luther's hymn, vv. 2-3 depict circumstances that "threaten to undo us." Even in this degree of trouble—when the very structures of the universe as we know it cannot be depended upon, when our world is falling apart—God is still a reliable refuge. God can be trusted. Therefore, the astounding affirmation in the face of the ultimate worst-case scenario is simply, "We will not fear" (v. 2; see Ps 23:4).

46:4-7, 11. The trouble, which is portrayed in cosmic terms in vv. 2-3, is described in human terms in vv. 4-6. The "nations are in an uproar" (v. 6; "uproar" translates the same Hebrew word as "roar" [המה *hāmâ*] in v. 3). The "kingdoms totter" (v. 6; "totter" translates the same Hebrew word as "shake" [מוט *môṭ*] in v. 2). As in vv. 2-3, and even using the same vocabulary, v. 6 suggests that everything is in motion. In the midst of the mayhem, there is one point of stability: "the city of God" (v. 4), in whose midst is God (v. 5), and "it shall not be moved" (v. 5). The verb translated "moved" is the same one translated "shake" in v. 2 and "totter" in v. 6 (the NIV translates the verb "fall" in each case). The pattern of repetition emphasizes the assurance; God's presence can be solidly depended upon.

The "city of God" is Jerusalem, in which is located the Temple, "the holy habitation of the Most High" (v. 4). Without intending to confine God to Zion or the Temple, the prevailing theology did view Zion as God's special place. In this and other Zion songs, "the city of God" is thus symbolic of God's presence. The refrain (vv. 7, 11) summarizes the assurance: God is "with us," "our refuge." The Hebrew word translated "refuge" in vv. 7, 11 differs from the one used in v. 1, but it is virtually synonymous (see the NRSV's "stronghold" in Pss 9:9; 18:2; 94:22; 144:2; "sure defense" in 48:3; and "fortress" in 59:9, 16-17; 62:2, 6). In the midst of international, and even cosmic, chaos, God can be trusted.

The title "LORD of hosts" is particularly appropriate following vv. 4-6. Verse 4 has referred to God's "habitation," and the title "LORD of hosts" is elsewhere associated with the ark, God's symbolic throne (see 1 Sam 4:3-4). The title also seems to have a military background, since "hosts" (צבאות *ṣĕbā'ôt*) can mean "armies" (see 1 Sam 17:45; see also Commentary on Psalm 24). The uproar in v. 6 apparently is meant to suggest an attack on Jerusalem. In this confrontation, the Lord of the armies is on Jerusalem's side—"with us." The word "refuge" also functions elsewhere as a military term (in addition to the occurrences and translations cited above, see Isa 25:12 where it is part of the phrase that the NRSV translates as "high fortifications"). Thus the vocabulary of the refrain anticipates vv. 8-10, where God is a warrior, but is one who wages peace.

The significance of the "river" in v. 4 is metaphorical rather than geographical. The threatening, chaotic waters of vv. 2-3 have become a life-giving stream. That there is actually no river flowing through Jerusalem is no problem. This river is symbolic, like the river in Ezek 47:1-12, which flows from the Temple, and like the river in Rev 22:1-12, which flows from the throne of God, which has replaced the Temple in the New Jerusalem. Both of these rivers yield sustenance for life (Ezek 47:9-12; Rev 22:2). In other words, the river in Ps 46:4 is another way of symbolizing the assurance of God's power and provision, even amid the worst imaginable trouble (v. 2). As v. 5 suggests, repeating a key word from v. 1, the presence of God means help when the world should threaten to undo us.

Verse 6*b* is another indication of God's sovereignty. God's voice is powerful. When the psalmist says, "the earth melts," it sounds as if God has taken over the role of destroyer; however, the word "melts" serves elsewhere to describe poetically the effects of God's appearing (see Amos 9:5; Nah 1:5), including God's melting human opposition in order to enact the divine will (see Exod 15:15; Josh 2:9, 24; Jer 49:23). This seems to be the meaning here, as the refrain suggests; God's

presence ("with us") means protection for God's people.

46:8-10. Verses 8 and 10 begin with imperatives, between which lies a description of God's "works" (vv. 8*b*-9). The invitation to "Come and see" (v. 8) calls to mind Philip's similar invitation to Nathanael in John 1:46. When Nathanael saw Jesus' works, he hailed him as "the king of Israel" (John 1:49). The same movement is intended in Psalm 46, which moves toward the explicit acknowledgment of God's sovereignty in v. 10*b*. The verb translated "exalted" (רום *rûm*) in v. 10*b* is used elsewhere in the context of kingship, both of earthly kings (Num 24:7; Ps 89:19) and of God as king (see Pss 99:5, 9; 145:1). Thus, in the climactic divine speech in v. 10, God proclaims sovereignty over the nations (see v. 6) and the earth (see vv. 2, 6). God rules the world!

In the ancient Near East, it was the particular responsibility of rulers to establish peace for their people. This is precisely what God's works involve, according to v. 9 (see Isa 2:4; Mic 4:3-4); v. 10*a* should be understood in close relationship to v. 9. The imperatives in v. 10*a* are explicitly instructional (see "know" in Ps 100:3). Although the NIV and the NRSV retain it because of its familiarity, "Be still" (רפה *rāpâ*) is not a good translation. Contemporary readers almost inevitably hear it as a call to meditation or relaxation, when it should be heard in the light of v. 9 as something like "Stop!" or "Throw down your weapons!" In other words, "Depend on God instead of yourselves."

In the light of the description of God's activity in v. 9, it seems that v. 8*b* may be sarcastic. The "desolations" that God brings, in contrast to human efforts, involve the cessation of war and the destruction of all human implements of destruction. In the light of v. 9, the military imagery of the refrain is given a new orientation. Whereas Israel often sought security in military might, v. 9 affirms that God the warrior fights for peace. The final occurrence of the refrain thus reinforces what v. 9 and the whole psalm have affirmed: Ultimate security derives from God alone.

REFLECTIONS

Although Christians do not view Jerusalem as the symbolic locus of God's presence and power as Psalm 46 does, that concrete and particularistic way of thinking is not entirely foreign to Christianity. For the early Christians, Jesus Christ became what the Temple had once represented. Indeed, Jesus became the new locus of God's presence and power to such a degree that the Gospel of John can say that "the Word became flesh" (1:14 NIV, NRSV). Jesus was God incarnate; Jesus was also known as Emmanuel, "God is with us" (Matt 1:23 NRSV; see "with us" in Ps 46:7, 11).

It should not be surprising, then, that the fundamental message Jesus proclaimed and embodied is essentially the same as that of Psalm 46: God rules the world (see Mark 1:14-15). Like Jesus, too, Psalm 46 calls people to decision (vv. 8, 10); that is, it invites its hearers to enter the reign of God, to live in dependence upon God, to find ultimate security in God rather than in self or in any human systems or possessions. Because it eloquently affirms that the ruling power in the universe is for us (v. 1) and inclines toward our help (vv. 1, 5), Psalm 46 has been a source of strength, consolation, and hope to believers throughout the centuries in a variety of situations—in ancient Judah, in the Protestant Reformation, in the lives of countless Jews and Christians who humbly look to God for help in trouble (v. 1). Indeed, Psalm 46 suggests a spiritual exercise that might be thought of as the opposite of positive thinking. Perhaps we should regularly imagine, as the psalmist did (vv. 2-3, 6), the *worst* possible thing that could happen to us, as a way of preparing ourselves to say in the midst of the crises that will inevitably come, "We will not fear" (v. 2).

The affirmation in Psalm 46 of God's sovereignty and God's will for peace among nations and in the cosmos is eschatological, as was Jesus' proclamation of the reign of God, for it does not appear that God reigns or that peace prevails. But it is precisely this eschatological orientation that calls us to decision: Shall we see the world as the sphere of God's rule? In our day, as much as in the days of the psalmist and Jesus, the decision to recognize God's sovereignty is crucial. We are tempted more than ever to conclude that our security finally depends on ourselves or our possessions or our technology or our weapons. The governments of the world attempt to justify terribly repressive and destructive activities in the name of national security. And, of course, our implements of destruction are no longer just arrows and spears and shields. We have tanks and submarines and nuclear missiles, and more readily than any generation in history, we are able to picture a "worst-case scenario" resulting from our own actions. Faced with the temptation to self-assertion, yet aware of its frightening results, we hear in Psalm 46 the good news that our ultimate security lies not in our own strength or our own efforts or our own implements, but in the presence and power of God.[197]

197. Portions of the above treatment of Psalm 46 appear in substantially the same form in J. Clinton McCann, "Psalm 46: Psalm for the Third Sunday After Pentecost," *No Other Foundation* 14/2 (Winter 1993–94) 32-36.

PSALM 47:1-9, KING OF ALL THE EARTH

COMMENTARY

Along with Psalm 24, Psalm 47 offers perhaps the clearest view of a liturgical procession to celebrate the kingship of God. As if in response to the concluding imperatives of Psalm 46 (see vv. 8, 10), Psalm 47 begins by inviting everyone to acknowledge God's sovereignty (v. 1). The invitation to praise is renewed in v. 6. The fundamental reason for praise in each case is God's kingship over "all the earth" (vv. 2, 7). Evidence for and results of God's kingship are given in vv. 3-4 and vv. 8-9. In between these two hymnic forms stands v. 5, and this central verse seems to depict the liturgical enthronement of God. As Mowinckel suggested, v. 5 describes the "royal entry of Yahweh, at which he himself is present, symbolized by his holy 'ark.' " For Mowinckel, v. 5 portrayed "the preeminent visible center of the experiences connected with the enthronement festival."[198]

Mowinckel's theory of an annual celebration of God's enthronement at the New Year festival (as part of the Feast of Booths) is questionable; however, it cannot be doubted that the theological heart of the psalter—God reigns! (see Psalms 29; 93; 95–99; Introduction)—was celebrated liturgically upon some occasion, perhaps in a procession involving the ark (see 2 Samuel 6; Pss 24:7-10; 132:8). It is simply impossible to know whether such a liturgical enactment took place as part of a New Year festival, as part of one of the three pilgrimage feasts, or as Gerstenberger has suggested, as a regular part "of early Jewish worship liturgy that jubilantly recalls the history of Israel's election by Yahweh (vv. 4-5) and glorifies his supreme, as yet unrealized, power over all the earth (vv. 3, 8, etc.)."[199] Given this uncertainty, one must conclude that more important than the original setting of Psalm 47 is the actual content of the psalm: God rules the earth!

47:1-2. Because God rules over all the earth, "all you peoples" are included in the invitation in v. 1. Hand clapping was apparently a gesture of celebration or triumph, as it still can be today (see Nah 3:19). Shouting sometimes served as a battle cry, but here it bespeaks joyful praise. The verb for "shout" (רוע *rûa'*) occurs in several other songs of praise as well, often in the context of the proclamation of God's reign (see Pss 66:1; 81:2; 95:1-2; 98:4, 6; 100:1; see also 1 Sam 10:24; Zech 9:9, where earthly kings are also greeted with a shout). The characterization of God as "awesome" in v. 2*a* recalls historic manifestations of the sovereignty that is explicitly affirmed in v. 2*b* (see "awesome" in Exod 15:11, the Song of the Sea, which culminates in Exod 15:18

with the proclamation of God's reign; cf. Ps 68:35 with 68:24, and 145:6 with 145:1). In addition to the enthronement psalms that explicitly affirm God's reign, several psalms scattered throughout the psalter describe or address God as "king" (see 5:2; 10:16; 44:4; 48:2; 68:24; 74:12; 84:3; 145:1; 149:2), and the adjective "great" is frequently associated with God's rule (see 95:3; 96:4; 99:2).

47:3-4. These verses offer a specific illustration of God's rule: the conquest and possession of the land. It is all God's doing. What preceding psalms have said that God did for the king, vv. 3-4 affirm that God the King has done for the whole people: God "subdued peoples" (see Ps 18:47) and provided a "heritage" (see Ps 2:8; see also Josh 11:23). The "pride of Jacob" seems to mean the land and its wealth and defenses (see Amos 6:8; 8:7). All of this God provided out of love (see Deut 7:8; Ps 78:68; Isa 43:4; Hos 11:1).

47:5. The *selah* after v. 4 serves to set vv. 1-4 apart from v. 5. It is possible to construe v. 5 as the beginning of a new section that extends through v. 6 (NIV) or v. 7 (NRSV) or perhaps to the end of the psalm; however, since v. 6, like v. 1, is an invitation to praise, it is also possible to construe v. 5 as a central panel surrounded by two hymnic sections (vv. 1-4, 6-9). The vocabulary of v. 5 reinforces this conclusion. On the one hand, v. 5 recalls v. 1, repeating "shout" and the Hebrew word the NIV translates as "cries" in v. 1 and "sounding" in v. 5 (קול *qôl*). On the other hand, v. 5 anticipates v. 9 by way of repetition of the key root "gone up"/"ascended" (עלה *'ālâ*), which appears in v. 9 as "exalted." Thus both the pattern of repetition and the structure of the psalm serve to highlight the liturgical enactment of God's enthronement. To borrow Mowinckel's words, v. 5 itself is a "preeminent visible center." In contrast to Mowinckel, however, we may conclude that what is celebrated—God's reign—lay at the heart of *all* Israelite worship, just as the proclamation of God's reign lies at the theological heart of the psalter (see Introduction). Just as a trumpet blast accompanied the coronation of earthly kings (see 1 Kgs 1:34, 39), so also here it accompanies the celebration of God's enthronement (see Ps 98:6).

47:6-9. In v. 6, four of the six Hebrew words are the verb "sing praises" (זמר

---

198. Mowinckel, *The Psalms in Israel's Worship*, 1:171.
199. Gerstenberger, *Psalms: Part 1*, 198.

zimmēr, cf. Pss 9:11; 68:32). Thus each half of the verse literally surrounds either God or "our King" with praise. The effect is appropriate, for "the king of all the earth" (v. 7; cf. v. 2) deserves no less. The word "king" occurs again in v. 8 (although in a verbal form in Hebrew), thus emphasizing God's sovereignty. References elsewhere to God's "throne" occur in the context of God's cosmic rule (see Pss 89:15; 93:2; 97:2; 103:19). Thus v. 8*a* proclaims God's rule over all persons, and v. 8*b* proclaims God's rule over all things. What was celebrated liturgically (v. 5) both derives from and shapes the Israelite view of the world; it and all of its people are subject to God (v. 8; cf. Ps 24:1-2, 7-10). Thus the congregation of God's people—"the people of the God of Abraham" (v. 9)—can include nothing less than the gathering of all the peoples (see v. 1) and their leaders. The word "shields" (מגן *māgēn*) probably is figurative for leaders (see the NIV; cf. Ps 89:18); they and their people belong to God. Verse 9 recalls Gen 12:1-3, where the promise of blessing to Abraham and his descendants is somehow to involve "all peoples on earth" (Gen 12:3 NIV; see also Isa 19:23-25).

By the end of Psalm 47, the word "earth" (ארץ *ereṣ*) has occurred three times (vv. 2, 7, 9), recalling Psalm 46, where it occurred five times (vv. 2, 6, 8, 9, 10). Both psalms proclaim God's sovereignty over all the earth, concluding in each case with a proclamation that God is exalted (46:10; 47:9; the Hebrew words differ, however). When read together, they also offer a compelling rationale for God's opposition to all warfare (46:9)—namely, in any war, God is always the loser, because it is always God's people who are killed.

REFLECTIONS

It was a persistent temptation for the people of Israel, and it has been and is a persistent temptation for the church to make our God too small. We are quick to recall that God "chose our heritage for us" and loves us (v. 4), but we are quick to forget that God loves the world and that all the world's rulers and people "belong to God" (v. 9). The Christian practice of speaking about Jesus as a personal Savior may be symptomatic of our forgetfulness, for often we seem to mean that we own God rather than that God owns us. To worship the God of Abraham and the God revealed in Jesus Christ is to worship a universal sovereign, and it means claiming every other person in the world as a sister or brother. To acknowledge God's universal sovereignty might even mean that we give our assent and support to the simple proposal that we Christians take a first step toward world peace by refusing to kill each other!

By virtue of its structure as well as its content, Psalm 47 highlights the nature and importance of liturgy. In worship, we say and act out our conviction of who God is and of what the world is really like. In accordance with Psalm 47 and in accordance with the proclamation of Jesus (see Mark 1:14-15), we say that God rules over all and thus that the world is the sphere of God's sovereignty. Our profession is eschatological, because it does not appear that God rules, and the world is full of opposition to God's sovereignty (see Commentary on Psalm 2; Introduction). But our profession is thereby no less real. In liturgy, we say and act out the reality that our lives and our world have been shaped by God's loving rule. At the same time, our speaking and acting contribute to the further shaping of ourselves and of our world in conformity to God's claim. For us, the "real world" exists insofar as God's sovereignty is acknowledged in word and in deed. In short, liturgy is indispensable for both experiencing God's rule and expressing the reality of that experience.

Psalm 47 is traditionally used by the church on Ascension Day. The church thereby claims that the life, death, and resurrection of Jesus represent the essential claim of Psalm 47: that God rules the world and lovingly claims all the world's peoples.

PSALM 48:1-14, GREAT IS THE LORD

COMMENTARY

The opening verse of Psalm 48 is a superbly appropriate response to Psalm 47, which has depicted God's enthronement (v. 5) and proclaimed God's universal sovereignty (vv. 2, 7-9). Without abandoning the universal perspective, Psalm 48 focuses on God's particular place, Mount Zion (v. 2). Like Psalm 46, this psalm is a song of Zion (see also Psalms 76; 84; 87; 122; Introduction). In fact, because of the similarities among Psalms 46; 47; and 48, these psalms can be viewed as a "trilogy . . . honoring Jerusalem."[200] More accurately, however, they could be called a trilogy *honoring God.* As Psalm 48 suggests, Jerusalem is important because it is God's place; thus it can serve as a witness to God's character. What Psalm 48 really celebrates is God's greatness (v. 1); God's protection (v. 3); God's steadfast love, righteousness, and justice (vv. 9-11); and God's enduring presence (vv. 13-14). Because the focus is really more on God than on Zion, Psalm 48 has continued to be used throughout the centuries to express the faith of the people of God.

Psalm 48 may have served originally as a song to be used by pilgrims as they approached and entered Jerusalem. Verses 1-3 give the impression of viewing Zion from afar, a position that allows the visitor to imagine how Jerusalem may have appeared to invading kings (vv. 4-7). Verses 8-11 locate the pilgrim in the city, including the Temple (v. 9), which serves as testimony to God's character and activity throughout the world (vv. 10-11). Verses 12-14 suggest that every architectural feature of the city can serve a similar purpose. The city itself proclaims God's greatness.

48:1-3. The psalm begins with an affirmation of God's greatness, an attribute that is explicitly associated elsewhere with God's sovereignty (cf. Pss 95:3; 96:4; 99:2). The praise due the sovereign God is to take place "in the city of our God"; however, what follows in v. 2 appears to be not praise of God

but praise of the city itself. The seven designations for Jerusalem in vv. 1*b*-2 clearly emphasize the importance of the city; however, even these designations suggest that the city derives its importance from God, and the dramatic element of the series even makes God's sovereignty explicit with the title "great King" (the Hebrew word translated "great" [רב *rab*] here differs from the one used in v. 1; in fact, the phrase occurs only here in the OT, although an analogous phrase occurs in other ancient Near Eastern literature to designate human or divine monarchs).

Several of the designations for Jerusalem occur elsewhere—for instance, "city of our God" (see Ps 46:4), "holy mountain" (see Pss 2:6; 3:4; 15:1), Mount Zion. Other terms are more distinctive. The phrase "in the far north" is puzzling. As the NIV suggests, the word translated "north" (צפון *ṣāpôn*) should probably be understood as "Zaphon," the name of the mountain that the Canaanites believed was the residence of the gods. Thus this designation seems to be a way of affirming that Yahweh has displaced the Canaanite deities; Yahweh is the true sovereign of the universe, the genuine "great King" (see Ps 82:1). In short, the designations in v. 2 are more symbolic than geopolitical. Jerusalem does occupy a mountain, but to affirm that it is "beautiful in elevation" is to say more about its significance to the eye of faith than about its actual altitude. Similarly, to say that Jerusalem is the "joy of all the earth" (cf. Isa 60:15; 65:18; Lam 2:15) is to make the confessional claim that Jerusalem is the indisputable capital of the world! In other words, God reigns, and Jerusalem is God's city, within which God has proven to be "a sure defense" (v. 3; the Hebrew word is the same one translated "refuge" in Ps 46:7, 11 NRSV). Verse 3 is apparent testimony to the belief in Zion's indestructibility, a conviction upon which Isaiah's advice to King Ahaz seems to be based (see Isa 7:1-16) and that Jeremiah later opposes (see Jer 7:1-15).

48:4-7. Of course, the claim of Jerusalem's centrality was regularly disputed, as these

---

200. Carroll Stuhlmueller, "Psalm 46 and the Prophecy of Isaiah Evolving into a Prophetic, Messianic Role," in *The Psalms and Other Studies on the Old Testament,* ed. J. C. Knight and L. A. Sinclair (Nashotah, Wis.: Nashotah House Seminary, 1990) 21.

verses make clear. That is to say, God's sovereignty was disputed. In opposition to "the great King," other "kings joined forces." The Hebrew for "joined forces" (נועדו *nôʿădû*) recalls the claim of v. 3*b*, which could literally be translated, "God has made Godself known [נודע *nôdaʿ*] as a fortress." The play on words emphasizes the contrast. The kings' *joining of forces* will be futile in the face of God's *revelation*. Indeed, as soon as the kings *saw* Jerusalem, they were as good as defeated. The description of their reaction recalls Exodus 15, the Song of the Sea following the deliverance from the Egyptian king and his forces. In Psalm 48, the kings "were in panic" (v. 5; see "dismayed" in Exod 15:15 NRSV; Ps 2:5); "trembling took hold of them" (v. 6; see "trembling seized" in Exod 15:15 NRSV) as did "pains" (v. 6; see "pangs" in Exod 15:14 NRSV). Furthermore, the "east wind" in v. 7 recalls the "east wind" of Exod 14:21, which drove back the sea for the Israelites' passage. The song in Exod 15:1-18 concludes with a reference to "the mountain," which is God's "own possession" (15:17 NRSV). This place is the one God has established (15:17) and presumably the place from which God "will reign forever and ever" (15:18 NRSV). This is precisely what Psalm 48 is about—the "great King" (v. 2) ruling from the city that God "establishes forever" (v. 8). The numerous allusions in Psalm 48 to the Song of the Sea also explain perhaps the curious circumstance that Jerusalem is depicted as the site of a sea battle (v. 7). The battle is more metaphorical than geographical.

48:8-11. The very sight of Jerusalem is overwhelming, not only to the invading kings but also to approaching pilgrims. What they have seen (v. 8; see v. 5) in Jerusalem has a profound effect on their perception of space and time. The sight of Jerusalem connects their current experience with the past deliverance from Egypt and with God's universal dominion "to the ends of the earth" (v. 10; see v. 2)—the spatial extension of God's reign. The present sight of Jerusalem takes the worshiper back in time to the exodus and forward in time to "forever" (v. 8; see vv. 13-14)—the temporal extension of God's reign. Robert Alter aptly sums up the perspective of Psalm 48: "Thus, the towering

ramparts of the fortress-city become a nexus for all imagined time and space."[201]

One further link between Psalm 48 and Exodus 15 is the occurrence of the word translated "steadfast love" (חסד *ḥesed*, v. 9; Exod 15:13). In Exodus 15, God's guidance in "steadfast love" brings people to God's place (see Ps 5:7); and in Psalm 48, it is precisely "steadfast love" that the people think about in the Temple. The word *ḥesed* describes God's fundamental character (see Exod 34:6-7; Pss 13:5; 17:7; Introduction). As the exodus revealed God's fundamental character, so the present experience in Jerusalem puts the pilgrim in touch with God's historical (past) and enduring (future) essence. Not surprisingly, v. 10 mentions God's "name," a word expressive of reputation or character, as well as God's "righteousness," a word expressive of God's character in action (see Pss 7:17; 9:8; 96:13; 97:6). As is often the case, God's righteousness is mentioned in conjunction with God's "judgments" (v. 11; see Pss 9:4; 97:2). That is to say, God's implementation of justice is in keeping with God's character.

48:12-14. Just as the city of Jerusalem proclaims God's greatness (vv. 1-3), so also it proclaims God's character (vv. 8-11). This is the rationale for the invitation in vv. 12-14 to consider Jerusalem in all its concrete detail—towers, ramparts, citadels (see v. 4). The five imperatives in vv. 12-13 are thus not simply an invitation to take an architectural tour of the city. Much more is at stake, as is emphasized by the repetition of the Hebrew root ספר (*sāpar*), translated "count" in v. 12 and "tell" in v. 13. In the third and central of the five imperatives, worshipers are invited to "count" Jerusalem's towers so that they may "tell" future generations about God. Alter's translation captures the pun: *"count* its towers. . . . So that you may *recount* to the last generation:/ That this is God, our God,/ forever."[202] In short, observation of spatial detail leads to proclamation about God. God is "our God forever and ever" (v. 14)—the temporal extension of God's reign. God "will be our guide forever" (v. 14)—the spatial extension of God's reign as Israel is led from place to place. The movement in vv. 12-14,

201. Alter, *The Art of Biblical Poetry*, 124; I am indebted to several of Alter's insights found on pp. 121-29.
202. Alter, *The Art of Biblical Poetry*, 122, italics added.

emphasized by the repetition of *sāpar*, is remarkable testimony to the power of sacred space. The seemingly simple matter of seeing a particular place—Jerusalem—leads to the powerful proclamation of God's reign in all times and places.

REFLECTIONS

To contemporary readers, the claims made about Jerusalem are likely to seem highly exaggerated or perhaps even extremely parochial and dangerously wrong. To assert that Jerusalem is the indisputable and indestructible capital of the world was probably as inflammatory in ancient times as it would be today. Besides, we know that Jerusalem was not indestructible; hostile kings and their forces were not put to flight by the very sight of Jerusalem. Indeed, the city was destroyed in 587 BCE by the Babylonians and again in 70 CE by the Romans. Was the psalmist simply mistaken? Was his or her perception blurred by an overly zealous nationalism? Was the psalmist a political propagandist? So one might cynically conclude. But before dismissing the psalmist as a naive optimist or a misguided patriot or a clever politician, we must remember that the details of Psalm 48 are as much metaphorical as geopolitical. What Psalm 48 embodies is "poetic form used to reshape the world in the light of belief."[203] In this case, Jerusalem, a seemingly ordinary place, has become to the eye of faith "the city of the great King" (v. 2), a powerful symbol of God's reign in all places (vv. 2, 10) and in all times (vv. 8, 14). In effect, the psalmist has created in poetic form an alternative worldview, a new reality that for the faithful becomes the deepest and most profound reality of all: God rules the world, now and forever! Psalm 48 articulates the faith that no power on earth or the passing of any amount of time can ultimately thwart the just and righteous purposes of a steadfastly loving God (see vv. 9-11).

The spirit of Psalm 48 is captured eloquently in a novel by Elie Wiesel:

JERUSALEM: the face visible yet hidden, the sap and blood of all that makes us live or renounce life. The spark flashing in the darkness, the murmur rustling through shouts of happiness and joy. A name, a secret. For the exiled, a prayer. For all others, a promise. Jerusalem: seventeen times destroyed yet never erased. The symbol of survival. Jerusalem: the city which miraculously transforms man into pilgrim; no one can enter it and go away unchanged.[204]

The psalmist knew precisely this about Jerusalem: "no one can enter it and go away unchanged"—not because Jerusalem is indestructible or universally acclaimed. Rather, for believers, Jerusalem becomes a spatial, temporal symbol for the reality of God's rule in all times and in places. Thus the footsteps of pilgrims approaching this particular place at any particular moment "reverberate to infinity."[205]

If this sounds strange to Christian readers of Psalms, they need only consider how the same paradox, the same scandal of particularity, lies at the heart of Christianity. For Christians, a particular event in time (the crucifixion of Jesus) at a particular place (Golgotha) becomes the central event of history. What appeared to be an ordinary execution of a common criminal is for Christians the focal point of all space and time. In a way just as particularist and strange and scandalous as the Zion theology of Psalm 48, Christians profess the incarnation of God in Jesus, a first-century Jew from an out-of-the-way place called Nazareth. Essentially, what Christians proclaim is "Christ crucified, a stumbling block to Jews and foolishness to Gentiles, but to those who are called, both Jews and Greeks, Christ the power of God and the wisdom of God"

203. Alter, *The Art of Biblical Poetry*, 133.
204. Elie Wiesel, *A Beggar in Jerusalem* (New York: Pocket Books, 1970) 19.
205. Wiesel, *A Beggar in Jerusalem*, 20.

(1 Cor 1:23-24 NRSV). What Psalm 48 and Elie Wiesel say about Jerusalem is what Christians profess about Jesus: No one can see him and go away unchanged. Indeed, the early followers of Jesus were known as ones "who have been turning the world upside down" (Acts 17:6 NRSV; see also Mark 13:1-2; 14:58; 15:29, where the Gospel writer suggests that Jesus has replaced the Temple, that Jesus is the new locus of God's revelation in space and time).

To be sure, neither the theology of Psalm 48 nor the Christian proclamation of Jesus is a facile utopianism. The psalmists knew, the apostles knew, and we still know that we live in time and space as part of a world that is fragile and troubled, terrified and terrifying. Yet, in the midst of it all, we join the psalmist in proclaiming a new reality: God rules the world! What's more, we claim to live by that reality above all others. For the psalmist, the vision of Jerusalem, the city of God, reshaped time and space. For Christians, the life, death, and resurrection of Jesus of Nazareth have reshaped the world, reshaped our time and space into a new reality. Thus, amid the same old realities of trouble and turmoil, we are changed and are able to discern by the eye of faith the dimensions of a new creation (see 2 Cor 5:17). In short, we live eschatologically. (See Commentary on Psalms 2; 46; Introduction.)

PSALM 49:1-20, GOD WILL REDEEM MY LIFE

COMMENTARY

Psalm 49 is a wisdom psalm (see v. 3) or a didactic poem that functions as a profession of faith in God. If v. 4 is a reliable indication, apparently the psalm was presented as a song accompanied by the harp (see Ps 33:2). The introduction consists of an invitation for everyone in the world to hear (vv. 1-2) and a characterization of the subsequent song (vv. 3-4). The song itself can be divided into two major sections (vv. 5-12, 13-20), each ending with a similar refrain.

Since Psalms 46–48 form a coherent sequence (see Commentary on Psalm 48), it is natural to ask whether Psalm 49 is a part of that sequence. At first sight, it does not appear to be; yet, given the fact that Psalms 46–48 proclaim God's universal sovereignty, it is at least significant that Psalm 49 addresses "all you peoples" (see Ps 47:1). Furthermore, the message of Psalm 49 complements from the human side the message of Psalms 46–48: that rich and powerful human beings, despite their illusions of grandeur and the status accorded them by others (vv. 6, 18), are *not* really in control of the world, or even of their own lives and destinies (vv. 7-9). In short, only God rules the world and ultimately determines human destiny (v. 15). The fundamental message of Psalm 49 may

have been particularly pertinent in the postexilic era, when God's people were perennially subject to richer and more powerful peoples; however, the message of Psalm 49 is also eminently relevant in the contemporary era, when our abundance tempts us to trust in our wealth and to overlook our finitude and fallibility (see Reflections below).

49:1-2. Although perhaps performed in the Temple or synagogue, the psalm intends to offer a message of universal significance (v. 1). Verse 2a reads literally, "also children of a human, also children of a man," but the idiom probably connotes high and low status (see Ps 62:9). The parallel in v. 2b reinforces this interpretation. The word "rich" (עשיר ʿāšîr) becomes a key word in the psalm (see vv. 6, 16), and the proper attitude to wealth lies at the heart of the psalm's message.

49:3-4. The psalmist's intent to "speak wisdom" (v. 3) indicates an educational purpose. Of course, the psalmist's interest is not primarily intellectual. Rather, wisdom and understanding have to do with God's instruction and thus with the orientation of one's life to God (see Pss 19:14; 37:30, where what one should speak and think has to do with God's "instruction" [תורה tôrâ, or "law"]; see also Deut 4:6; Ps 111:10; Prov 1:7; 3:13;

9:10; 15:33). The subsequent instruction will have to do with wealth, but it will also make very clear that one's stance on wealth is inseparable from one's stance on God. Verse 4 more specifically indicates the psalmist's educational approach or lesson plan. The message will be communicated by way of a "proverb." The Hebrew root of the noun translated "proverb" (משל *māšāl*) also occurs in the refrain as a verb, "are like" (vv. 12*b*, 20*b*). Thus the lesson will involve a comparison that takes the form of a riddle (see Ps 78:2 NIV "hidden things," NRSV, "dark sayings"; Ezek 17:2 NIV "allegory"; Prov 1:6). If the answer to the riddle is contained in the refrain, then we can state the riddle as follows: How are human beings and animals alike? The answer is basic to the psalmist's message about relating to wealth and to God.

49:5-12. The question raised in vv. 5-6 already implies an answer. The persecutors need not be feared, because, having cut themselves off from God, they have no future (see Ps 52:5-7). The only proper object of trust is God (see Pss 4:5; 9:10; 40:4; Introduction), but the persecutors trust their own resources. The only proper object of boasting is God (see Ps 34:2), but again the persecutors boast essentially in themselves. In short, they view themselves as sovereign and autonomous, denying God's claim on their lives and futures. Such self-centeredness, such dependence upon one's own resources, may give the appearance of success (see v. 18), but it is ultimately an illusion.

Verses 7-12 explain why. In a word, as vv. 7-8 suggest, life cannot be bought. Verses 7-8 seem to allude primarily to the provision made in Exod 13:11-16 for redemption of the firstborn; God will allow the sacrifice of an animal to take the place of the sacrifice of a firstborn male child. In this sense, a human life might be bought. Even so, as vv. 7-8 suggest, one should never conclude that the payment is adequate or that such a provision removes God's sovereign claim on human life. Verses 7-8 may also allude to the provisions made in some legal cases involving death; that is, the death of the victim might be redeemed by the payment of an appropriate ransom rather than by the death of the person responsible (see Exod 21:28-32). Here again, in a sense, life could be bought. But

while payment may suffice in the realm of human relations (see also Prov 13:8), no payment will suffice to compensate God.

There is one unambiguous sign of the human inability to buy life: death (v. 9). Everybody dies, wise and foolish, rich and poor (vv. 10-11; see Ps 39:4-6; Eccl 2:12-26). Death thus exposes the illusion of human sovereignty. The sense of v. 12 is captured more accurately by the NIV. No amount of money will enable a person to escape death (the NIV's "riches" is from the same Hebrew root as "costly" in v. 8). In this sense, humans and animals are alike. Although humans were given dominion over the animals (Gen 1:28), this did not make humans into gods. Death is a reminder that human dominion is derivative of and not a replacement for God's sovereignty (see Commentary on Psalm 8). Therefore, those persons who would trust or boast in their own resources are not finally to be feared. Verse 12 thus answers the question of vv. 5-6 and anticipates the advice given in v. 16.

49:13-20. As the book of Ecclesiastes demonstrates (esp. 2:12-26), the realization of the universality of death is not necessarily comforting and encouraging. It can be, insofar as it serves to cut the wealthy and the powerful down to size, which is the intent of vv. 5-12. But what about those who have not trusted their own wealth and have not sought to buy life? Whereas vv. 5-12 have portrayed death as the great equalizer, vv. 13-20 move in a different direction by distinguishing between how death will affect the "foolhardy" (v. 13; see "fool" in v. 10) and the "upright" (v. 14). As a comparison of the NIV and the NRSV of vv. 13-14 indicates, the text is very difficult and is subject to several construals. Given the reference to sheep in v. 14*a*, the NRSV is probably correct to suggest that death is personified as shepherding the foolish to Sheol (see Pss 6:5; 9:17; 31:17), but the NIV is probably correct as well in reading the Hebrew more literally in v. 14*b*, thus preserving the reference to the upright and their ultimate dominion over powerful, wealthy persons. At any rate, v. 15 maintains a distinction between the future of the foolhardy, who are destined to Sheol (v. 14), and the psalmist's own future. The concept of ransom is reintroduced in v. 15. Whereas human beings cannot purchase ultimate security (vv. 7-8), God "will ransom." The enigmatic assertion that God "will receive me" is reminiscent of Enoch and Elijah (Gen 5:24; 2 Kgs 2:1-12; see also Ps 73:24). The affirmation that the power of God is finally greater than the power of Sheol is a departure from the usual Israelite view of life and death. While v. 15 probably does not represent a developed doctrine of resurrection or afterlife, it certainly does, like Psalm 22:29, push beyond the normal limits (see also Ps 16:10-11). The psalmist trusts that nothing, not even death, will finally be able to separate the faithful from God (see Rom 8:38-39; 14:7-8).

On the basis of this conviction, the psalmist can instruct others not to fear the rich (v. 16; see also vv. 5-6). Although they and their admirers may delude themselves into thinking they have it made (v. 18), they will soon discover that they cannot take it with them (v. 17; see also vv. 10-11, where the same thought precedes the first occurrence of the refrain). The second occurrence of the refrain highlights the difference between vv. 5-12 and 13-20. Although the NRSV translates v. 20 exactly the same as v. 12, the Hebrew in each verse is different, as the NIV recognizes. The word "understanding" (בין *bîn*) recalls v. 3. The answer to the riddle has been given a twist. To be like the animals finally means to fail to understand, and thus to die without hope. The wise, who know what the psalmist has affirmed (v. 15) and who entrust themselves to God, will die with the assurance that the power of God is greater than the power of death.

REFLECTIONS

We have all heard and probably said what vv. 10-11, 17 suggest: "You can't take it with you." We know this, of course, intellectually speaking. But existentially speaking, it is very difficult for us to believe this obvious assertion, because we live in a society that systematically teaches us to define ourselves in terms of our incomes, our bank accounts, our stock portfolios, and our possessions. Despite all the blessings and remarkable achievements of capitalistic economic systems, our economy has moved far beyond the simple principle of supply and demand—that is, the principle of providing what people *need* to live. Rather, our economy thrives on the creation of demand, and we are very good at it. Advertisers convince millions of people every day that they can neither be happy nor really have lives worth living unless they drive the right car, drink the proper beverage, roll on the most effective deodorant, choose the best pain remedy, or use the most widely accepted credit card. In short, our economy aims not to meet people's needs but to stimulate people's greed. As Reinhold Niebuhr put it, "Greed has thus become the besetting sin of a bourgeois culture."[206] In other words, the very success of our economic system subtly tempts us to seek security in our wealth; in effect, we become our own gods. With good reason as responsible spouses and parents, we purchase securities and life insurance, almost as if we believe that we really can buy life (see vv. 7-8)! In short, it is exceedingly difficult in our culture, if not impossible, to avoid the conclusion that life *does* consist in the abundance of possessions (see Luke 12:15). For this reason, Brueggemann concludes, "In the consumer capitalism of our society, this poem is important."[207]

To be sure, as the reference to Luke 12 suggests, greed has always been a problem. In fact, the philosophy of the rich fool in Jesus' parable could serve admirably as a statement of the American dream as well as a restatement of the description of the wealthy in Ps 49:6. Not surprisingly, Jesus says that God reminds the rich fool, in keeping with Psalm 49, that he cannot take it with him (Luke 12:20; see also Matt 6:19-21, 24). Psalm 49 is reminiscent, too, of the story of the rich man who refuses to

---

206. Reinhold Niebuhr, *The Nature and Destiny of Man* (New York: Charles Scribner's Sons, 1964) 1:191; see also 139.
207. Brueggemann, *The Message of the Psalms,* 110.

follow Jesus because of his "great wealth" (Mark 10:17-22). Following this incident, Jesus tells his followers how difficult it is for the rich to enter the kingdom of God (Mark 10:25). Wealth inevitably tempts people to depend on themselves and to convince themselves that life can be bought. To the disciple's question, "Then who can be saved?" (Mark 10:26 NRSV), Jesus replies that "for God all things are possible" (Mark 10:27 NRSV). This is what the psalmist knew! What we humans cannot achieve or purchase, God can and does provide for those who are humbly willing to receive it: life (Ps 49:15).

Life is not a prize to be earned or another possession to be bought. Rather, it is a gift to be received (see Mark 8:36-37). The good news of Psalm 49 and the Gospel is that God wills that we live, so much so that Christians profess that God has paid the price by sending Jesus Christ "to give his life as a ransom for many" (Mark 10:45 NRSV; see 1 Tim 2:6). Those who enter the reign of God will live not by greed but by gratitude; they will live in the assurance that the exalted are humbled, and the humble are exalted (see Luke 18:14); they will see in the death and resurrection of Jesus Christ the ultimate embodiment of the affirmation of Ps 49:15 that the power of God is greater than the power of death. True wealth is the wisdom that understands that God is the only giver and ultimate guarantor of life.

PSALM 50:1-23, OFFER TO GOD A SACRIFICE OF THANKSGIVING

COMMENTARY

Neither a song of praise nor a prayer, Psalm 50 is often labeled a prophetic exhortation (see also Psalms 81; 95), and many scholars have suggested that its original use was some form of covenant renewal ceremony. The mention of "covenant" (vv. 5, 16), however, does not necessarily imply a special covenant renewal ceremony. The proper relation to God is an appropriate concern for any worship service. Thus Gerstenberger more simply calls Psalm 50 a liturgical sermon, and he links its origin and use to the post-exilic synagogue, where instruction was a paramount concern and, in his view, a regular feature of liturgy.[208]

To be sure, the accusatory tone of Psalm 50 does not accord well with contemporary homiletical theory, but as Gerstenberger rightly points out, "Accusatory and threatening rhetoric still today is part and parcel of many a Christian sermon."[209] In any case, the function of the accusatory rhetoric is certainly legitimate: to call the people away from self-centeredness to proper relationship with God. In addition, Psalm 50 has much

to commend it homiletically. For instance, it appears that the preacher has assessed the congregation well, identifying and addressing two problems in the two parts of the sermon: (1) a misunderstanding of sacrifice (vv. 7-15) and (2) the failure of congregational members to live lives consistent with the beliefs they profess (vv. 16-22). In short, the preacher criticizes the congregation's worship and its work. The two parts of the sermon are introduced by vv. 1-6, and v. 23 is a summary and conclusion. The superscription attributes the psalm to Asaph, the first such attribution in the psalter (see Psalms 73–83; Introduction). It is not clear why Psalm 50 is separated from the other Asaph psalms, unless perhaps the editors of the psalter wanted representatives of both Levitical collections (that is, Korah and Asaph) to introduce the Davidic collection (Psalms 51–72), since representatives of both Levitical collections follow the Davidic collection (see Psalms 73–83; 84–85; 87–88).[210]

50:1-6. The psalm begins by naming God three times, starting with the ancient

208. See Gerstenberger, *Psalms: Part 1*, 210.
209. Gerstenberger, *Psalms: Part 1*, 209.
210. See Wilson, "Shaping the Psalter," 76-77.

Canaanite name for the supreme deity and concluding with Israel's personal name for God: "El, Elohim, Yahweh" (אל *'ēl;* אלהים *'ĕlōhîm;* יהוה *yhwh).* The effect is to emphasize Yahweh's authority to speak, since God speaks throughout most of the psalm. Yahweh's speech in the first instance is a summons (vv. 1, 4), first to the earth and then to the heavens and the earth. That God can summon, in effect, the whole creation is indicative of God's sovereignty. The heavens and earth are to serve as court officials and perhaps witnesses in God's trial against the people (see Deut 32:1; Isa 1:2; Mic 6:1-2, where the heavens and earth also are called to witness to God's speaking or acting). They summon the people to court (v. 5). The mention of a covenant "by sacrifice" recalls the covenant ceremony following the giving of the Decalogue (Exod 24:1-8), where sacrifice accompanied the reading of "the book of the covenant" (Exod 24:7 NRSV). In that setting, the people promised, "We will obey" (Exod 24:7 NIV). Psalm 50 suggests that God's people have not obeyed; rather, they have violated the covenant. God may have kept silent (v. 21) in the past regarding the people's breach of the covenant, but God will keep silent no longer (v. 3). Therefore, God is coming to judge them (vv. 4, 6; the Hebrew words for "judge" [דין *dîn,* v. 4; שפט *šōpēṭ,* v. 6] differ but are essentially synonymous).

As Mays suggests, it is a "trial whose proceedings can be seen only by the eye of faith."[211] In other words, the trial scenario serves as a rhetorical device for bringing the word of God to bear upon the congregation. As in v. 1, the theophany imagery in vv. 2-3 communicates God's authority to speak and judge. As in Deut 33:2, God "comes" from a mountain—although here it is Zion (see Amos 1:2)—and God "shines forth" (cf. Ps 18:7-15). The storm imagery in v. 3 continues the memory of Sinai, where God appeared in order to establish the covenant and to give the commandments, which the people disobeyed (see Exodus 19, esp. vv. 5-6, 8, 16, 18). The heavens, which God has summoned, "declare [God's] righteousness" (v. 6). The heavens do the same thing in Ps 97:6, again following the description of a theophany (97:2-5). Psalm 97

begins with the affirmation that "The LORD is king!" Psalm 50:5-6 also proclaims God's sovereignty as the basis for God's authority to speak and to act to set things right, beginning with God's own people.

50:7-15. With the exception of v. 14, vv. 7-15 are framed in the divine first person—that is, the prophet or preacher delivers the Word of God. Verse 7 recalls a key text from the book of Deuteronomy—the Shema, "Hear, O Israel" (Deut 6:4 NRSV), which follows immediately the repetition of the Decalogue. Just as the whole book of Deuteronomy serves as a covenant renewal as the people prepare to enter the land, so also Psalm 50 is a call for renewal. In this context, the issue of the misuse of the sacrificial system (see vv. 8-15) need not be viewed as a call to abolish the system. In fact, "a sacrifice of thanksgiving" (v. 14) still involved the slaughter of animals. Rather, the call is to put sacrifice in proper perspective (see Pss 40:6-8; 51:16-19; Isa 1:12-17; Hos 6:6; Amos 5:21-24). Instead of bringing their sacrificial offerings out of gratitude to God, the people were doing so as a means of asserting their own merit and self-sufficiency, as if God needed them instead of their needing God (see vv. 12-13). In response to this misunderstanding, God, through the preacher, proclaims divine ownership of all animals (v. 10; see also Ps 104:14-18, 24-25, 27-30). Thus the proper sacrifice is really the thanksgiving itself (v. 14; see the NRSV's note), which is often associated with the payment of vows (see Pss 22:25; 61:8; 65:1; 116:14, 17-18). In short, the proper approach to God begins with gratitude. Verse 15 reinforces the message of v. 14: What God asks is that the people seek their security not in themselves but in God. This will prevent self-glorification, for the people will honor God (see v. 23; see also Pss 22:23; 86:12).

50:16-22. The translations of v. 16*a* may be misleading, for they suggest that vv. 16-22 are addressed to a different group than are vv. 7-15. But it is precisely God's people who have become "the wicked." They apparently say the right things (v. 16) but fail to act in accordance with their covenant identity (v. 17). In short, they are hypocrites. The "you" that begins v. 17 is emphatic. The people actually "hate discipline" or "instruction" (cf.

211. Mays, *Psalms,* 194.

Deut 11:2; Jer 17:23), and they discard God's word (see Neh 9:26). Verses 18-20 illustrate how the people have violated the covenant. The preacher alludes to the Decalogue, specifically the commandments against stealing, adultery, and bearing false witness (see Exod 20:14-16; Jer 7:9-10; Hos 4:1-3; see also Mic 7:5-6, where kinship ties are disrupted by disobedience). Verse 21 returns to the legal imagery of vv. 1-6. As v. 3 has already suggested, God breaks the divine silence and indicts the people for their faithlessness. The fundamental problem is that the people have forgotten God, thus inviting destruction (v. 22; see also Deut 8:19; Hos 8:14; 13:6). The imperative that begins v. 22 is more literally, "Understand." It represents the same root that occurred in the closing verse of Psalm 49

(see the NIV's "understanding"). Thus Psalm 50 joins Psalm 49 in inviting an understanding that consists of gratefully entrusting one's life and future to God rather than trusting wealth (49:6) or even one's own religious behavior (50:7-16).

50:23. This verse concludes the sermon with a brief summary of the two sections and a declaration of good news. Verse 23*a* summarizes the critique of sacrifices (vv. 7-15; see esp. vv. 14-15), whereas v. 23*b* summarizes the people's failure to obey the covenant (vv. 16-22; "way" suggests behavior or life-style). God's will is to save, and God will "show . . . salvation" to those who can forget themselves long enough to understand their neediness and insufficiency.

REFLECTIONS

Like all good sermons, Psalm 50 challenges its hearers to make a decision. The basis for decision is, like Jesus' preaching, grounded in the reality of God's claim on the world (Ps 50:1-6). Lest the sermon sound simply judgmental, we should remember that God's purpose in judgment is to set right people and things—that is, to establish justice (vv. 4-6; see 1 Pet 4:17). We should recall, too, that Jesus in his preaching did not hesitate to identify hypocrisy, the discrepancy between profession and behavior (see Matt 9:10-13; 12:1-7; 23:1-36; cf. Ps 50:16-17). Indeed, in his Sermon on the Mount, Jesus recognized the insufficiency of simply going through the right motions or saying the right words. The same call to decision contained in Psalm 50 (esp. vv. 14-15, 22-23) is implicit in Jesus' words, "Not everyone who says to me, 'Lord, Lord,' will enter the kingdom of heaven, but only the one who does the will of my Father in heaven" (Matt 7:21 NRSV).

The apostle Paul articulated the same call to decision. His dual appeal to the Christian congregation in Rome parallels themes in Psalm 50: (1) "present your bodies as a living sacrifice, holy and acceptable to God, which is your spiritual worship" (Rom 12:1 NRSV), and (2) "Do not be conformed to this world, but be transformed by the renewing of your minds, so that you may discern what is the will of God" (Rom 12:2 NRSV).

The call to decision presented by Psalm 50, by Jesus, and by Paul is still a crucial one. Hypocrisy is a persistent temptation. Good faith is always in danger of becoming bad religion—a mechanistic system to put God at our disposal and to give us the illusion of merit and self-control. If we think that we are deserving, and if we think that we have things essentially under control, then there will be no need for us to call upon God or to live in dependence upon God. All that is left is to glorify ourselves (see v. 15). The issue, then, is this: Will we live to gratify ourselves? Or will we live in gratitude to God?

PSALM 51:1-19, ACCORDING TO YOUR STEADFAST LOVE

COMMENTARY

Dominated by petition, Psalm 51 is ordinarily classified as a prayer for help or an individual lament/complaint. What sets it apart is that the psalmist's complaint involves his or her own sinfulness. Thus the church has with good reason included it among the seven penitential psalms (see also Psalms 6; 32; 38; 102; 130; 143). Indeed, with the possible exception of Psalm 130, Psalm 51 is the most dramatic and familiar of the Penitential Psalms. As Kraus suggests, it "stands out in the Psalter. Its peak statements are unique. And its fullness of insight is incomprehensible."[212]

The superscription is the first clue to what Psalm 51 is about: sin and forgiveness. Although it is possible to conclude that the superscription dates the psalm accurately,[213] it is much more likely that it was added later by the editors of the psalter to invite readers to hear Psalm 51 against the background of the story of David's taking of Bathsheba and murder of her husband Uriah (2 Samuel 11), as well as the subsequent confrontation between Nathan and David (2 Sam 12:1-14; cf. Ps 51:4 and 2 Sam 12:13). This story is as much or more about God's character than it is about human sinfulness, both of which are in view in Ps 51:1-6. The series of imperatives in vv. 7-12 petition God for forgiveness and re-creation. The series is broken by v. 13, and vv. 13-15 anticipate the psalmist's transformed existence. Verses 16-17 offer the psalmist's concluding observations about sin and sacrifice, while vv. 18-19 seem to be a second conclusion, perhaps an addition to an original vv. 1-17.

51:1-6. In the story of David and Bathsheba, what is finally determinative is not David's sinfulness but God's grace. To be sure, David's sin had grave consequences; the first child born to Bathsheba died (see 2 Sam 12:16-19), and David's family nearly fell apart

(see 2 Samuel 13–1 Kings 1). Nevertheless, David's sin was forgiven; he was allowed to live and to remain king (2 Sam 12:13), despite having broken at least half of the Ten Commandments, including the ones prohibiting adultery and murder! Because God's amazing grace is the most outstanding feature of the story of David and Bathsheba, it is appropriate in view of its superscription that Psalm 51 begin with a focus on God. Before any mention of the vocabulary of sin that dominates vv. 1-5, the psalmist appeals to God's character using three key Hebrew words that communicate God's grace. The NIV and the NRSV usually translate the first, "mercy," as "gracious" (חנן *ḥānan*; see the frequent plea "be gracious" in Pss 4:1; 6:2). The second word, "steadfast love" (חסד *ḥesed*), is virtually a one-word summary of God's gracious, self-giving character (cf. Pss 5:7; 6:4; 13:5; 25:6-7, 10; 33:5, 18, 22; Introduction). The third, "compassion" (רחמים *raḥămîm*), which might more accurately be translated "motherly compassion" (see Commentary on Ps 25:6; Introduction), often appears in conjunction with "steadfast love." Indeed, because all three key words appear in Exod 34:6-7, along with three of the four terms for sin found in Ps 51:1-5 ("iniquity," "transgression," and "sin"), it is appropriate to read Psalm 51 against the narrative background of the golden calf episode of Exodus 32–34 as well as against the background of the story of David and Bathsheba. Both stories are about God's forgiveness of grievous sin. Just as in 2 Samuel 11–12, so also in Exodus 32–34, God's character is determinative and keeps relationship intact. Both Israel and David are justified, made right with God, by God's grace. So it is with the psalmist, who quite rightly admits that God is "proved right" in God's judgment (v. 4) but later affirms also that "my tongue will sing of your righteousness" (v. 14). The psalmist has been or anticipates being set right, being justified by God's grace.

212. Kraus, *Psalms 1–59*, 507.
213. See Goulder, *The Prayers of David (Psalms 51–72)*, 24-30, 51-69.

After appealing to God's character, the psalmist turns to his or her own sinfulness. Israel's basic vocabulary of sin pervades vv. 1-5 (cf. Ps 32:1-5). In these verses, the most general Hebrew word for "sin" (חטא *ḥāṭā*, vv. 2-4) appears with one of three more specialized words: "iniquity"/"guilty" (עון *ʿāwôn*, vv. 2, 5; see also v. 9) involves the personal guilt or culpability of the sinner; "transgressions" (פשע *pešaʿ*, v. 3; see also v. 1) suggests willful rebellion; and "evil" (רע *raʿ*) conveys the injurious effects of sinful behavior. The repetition drives home the point. Sin and its consequences are pervasive. The emphatic "you, you only" in v. 4 is not meant to indicate that the psalmist's sinful behavior did not have destructive consequences for other people; rather, it suggests that sin has its origin in the failure to honor God. The climactic v. 5 has traditionally been cited in discussions of "original sin," and rightfully so. It is not intended to suggest that sin is transmitted biologically or that sexuality is sinful by definition. Rather, it conveys the inevitability of human fallibility. In each human life, in the human situation, sin is pervasive. We are born into it, and we cannot escape it. While sin is a matter of individual decision, it also has a corporate dimension that affects us, despite our best intentions and decisions.

Three of the four terms for sin in vv. 1-5 also occur in Exod 34:7, recalling again the narrative context of Exodus 32–34. Furthermore, David's behavior is characterized in 2 Sam 12:9 as "evil" (cf. Ps 51:4; "evil" is the one term that does not appear in Exod 34:7), and David admits in 2 Sam 12:13, "I have sinned against the LORD" (NRSV). Again, the recalling of these narrative contexts suggests that the reality of God's steadfast love (see Exod 34:6-7; 2 Sam 7:15) is more fundamental than the reality of human sinfulness. In short, God forgives sinners. Appropriately, each of the repeated words for sin in vv. 1-5 appears as the object of an imperative addressed to God in vv. 1-2—"blot out" (v. 1*d*; see also v. 11; Isa 43:25; 44:22), "wash" (v. 2*a*; see also v. 7; Jer 2:22; 4:14), "cleanse" (v. 2*b*; see also vv. 7*a*, 10*a*; Lev 16:30; Jer 33:8; Ezek 36:25, 33; 37:23). Verse 6 also suggests that sin is not the final word about humanity. God desires not sinfulness but faithfulness (אמת *ʾĕmet*; NIV and NRSV, "truth"; see Pss 26:3;

45:4). The wisdom that the psalmist requests consists of openness to God and dependence upon God (see Pss 37:30; 49:3; 90:12; Prov 1:7; 9:10). While sin is inevitable and pervasive in the human situation, it is not ultimately the determining reality.

51:7-12. Thus in these verses the psalmist prays for forgiveness and re-creation. The imperative "purge" (v. 7) is from the same Hebrew root as the word "sin" in vv. 2-5, 9. It occurs elsewhere in this particular verbal form in conjunction with purifying rituals involving hyssop (see Lev 14:49, 52; Num 19:18-19). While it is clear that the psalmist alludes to ritual practices in vv. 1*d*-2, 7-9, the language is figurative. The real point is that by God's action, the psalmist has been or will be forgiven and transformed. Sin and guilt will not be the final words; they will give way to joy (vv. 8, 12).

The psalmist's faith in God's transforming power is particularly evident in vv. 10-12. The verb "create" (ברא *bārāʾ*) is used in the OT only of God's activity. It is particularly prominent in the opening chapters of Genesis (1:1, 21, 27; 2:3, 4) and in Isaiah 40–55, where God's creative activity involves the doing of a "new thing" (Isa 43:15-19; 48:6-7; see also Isa 41:20; 45:7-8). It is significant, too, that "create" is used in the context of God's self-revelation in Exodus 34. Immediately following God's words to Moses in Exod 34:6-7, Moses appeals to God that "the LORD go with us" and "pardon our iniquity and our sin" (34:9 NRSV). God responds by making a covenant and by promising to "perform marvels, such as have not been performed [lit., "been created"] in all the earth or in any nation" (34:10 NRSV). In short, it is God's fundamental character to restore, rehabilitate, re-create sinners. In the context of Exodus 32–34, Israel's life depended on it; in the context of 2 Samuel 11–12, David's life depended on it; and in Psalm 51, the psalmist affirms that his or her life also depends on God's willingness to forgive and God's ability to re-create sinners.

The association of the terms "clean," "heart," "new," and "spirit" calls to mind Ezek 36:25-27, which also testifies to God's willingness to forgive and ability to re-create. The repetition of the word "spirit" (רוח *rûaḥ*) in vv. 10-12 reinforces this message. The mention of God's "holy spirit" is unusual (see elsewhere only Isa 63:10-11), but God's Spirit elsewhere is also suggestive of God's creative activity. In Gen 1:2, God's Spirit moves over the deep; God's Spirit is responsible for all life and its sustenance (Job 34:14-15). For the psalmist to receive a new spirit (v. 10) and to live in the presence of God's Spirit (v. 11) means nothing short of new life. In biblical terms, to be saved means to be restored to conditions that make life possible, and for the psalmist, forgiveness means salvation (v. 12; see also v. 14). What precisely is meant by "a willing spirit" is unclear, but it may connote generosity (see Exod 35:5, 22). In Isa 32:5, 8, the Hebrew word for "noble" (נדיב *nādîb*) is the opposite of "fool" (נבל *nābāl*; recall "wisdom" in Ps 51:6), and the noble are those who attend to the needs of others (see Isa 32:6).

51:13-17. The psalmist directs his or her thoughts to others in v. 13. Having been made new, the psalmist promises to share this experience with others. The vocabulary that dominates vv. 1-5 recurs in v. 13, but with a twist. The chief among transgressors and sinners will be the *teacher* of transgressors and sinners. The reconciled will bear the message of reconciliation (see Ps 32:8). Because sheer grace is always a scandal, those who faithfully witness to God's grace will always need to pray, "Deliver me from bloodshed" (v. 14). This may especially be the case for one who has been known previously as a notorious sinner. As a comparison of the NRSV with the NIV suggests, v. 14*a* can be interpreted differently. The Hebrew word in question (דמים *dāmîm*) can mean "bloodshed" or "violence," but it can also mean the guilt incurred from shedding blood. This meaning would also be suitable for one who has presented oneself as chief among sinners, especially if Psalm 51 is heard in the context of David's murder of Uriah. In this case, v. 14*a* continues the appeal for forgiveness in vv. 1-2, 6-12. Perhaps the ambiguity is intentional, but even if not, it is quite appropriate.

Despite opposition or anticipated opposition, the psalmist is committed to making a public witness. An inward transformation is not sufficient. The clean heart and new spirit will be accompanied by outwardly visible and audible proclamation. God's "new thing"

must be declared (see Isa 48:6). Every organ of speech will participate—"my tongue," "my lips," "my mouth" (vv. 14-15). This outpouring of praise is apparently intended to replace what may customarily have been offered as a public witness—namely, a ritual sacrifice (v. 16). At this point, Psalm 51 recalls Ps 50:14, 23, where the proper sacrifice is identified as "thanksgiving"—that is, humble gratitude accompanied by faithful words and deeds (see Ps 50:17-21). Verse 16 also recalls the prophetic critiques of sacrifice that communicate God's desire that ritual actions be accompanied by personal commitment and transformation (see 1 Sam 15:22; Isa 1:12-17; Hos 6:6; Amos 5:21-24; Mic 6:6-8); in short, God desires the whole self.

And this is exactly what the forgiven, transformed psalmist affirms in v. 17 and, at least implicitly, offers to God (see NIV and NRSV notes). What God desires is "a broken spirit; a broken and contrite heart." The two occurrences of "broken" (נשבר *nišbār*) translate the Hebrew root very literally; and that translation may be misleading. Contemporary persons tend to hear "broken," when used in regard to people, as something like "dysfunctional." Even elsewhere in the OT, brokenheartedness is not a desirable condition but something from which God delivers (see Ps 34:18, Isa 61:1). What brokenheartedness means in Ps 51:17, however, is captured by the word "contrite," which is a more interpretive translation of a word that literally means "crushed" (see v. 8). God does not want "broken" or "crushed" persons in the sense of "oppressed" or "dysfunctional." Rather, God desires humble, contrite persons who are willing to offer God their whole selves. If pride is the fundamental sin that leads to idolatry, then the transformed psalmist now evidences a humility that inevitably leads to praise. The psalmist's offering to God is the whole self. The psalmist has much to proclaim, but it is not about self. It is about God (vv. 14-15). The psalmist's public witness is directed in precisely the same direction as was the urgent appeal: at the character of God.

51:18-19. These verses may be a later addition to clarify the perspective on sacrifice in vv. 16-17. In any case, the effect of the final form is to give the intensely personal testimony of vv. 1-17 a corporate dimension, one that perhaps has been prepared for by the similarity in terminology between vv. 10-12 and prophetic texts like Ezek 36:16-36, which envisions the restoration of Israel after the exile. Because of the prayer for Zion and Jerusalem in v. 18, several scholars suggest that vv. 18-19 were added in the post-exilic period to make Psalm 51 more suited for corporate use in that era. (See the Introduction for a description of evidence that the psalter as a whole was shaped in response to the crisis of exile.) In any case, these verses are an apt reminder that sin is never simply a matter of individual decision; it is also a matter of corporate, institutionalized evil. They suggest also that the justification of the individual sinner does not obviate the need for participation in the worship of the community but enables proper participation. "Right sacrifices" will be offered by those who have first offered their whole selves to God. By the mercies of God, even the traditional rituals, the same old order of worship, will be transformed.

REFLECTIONS

1. Psalm 51 calls to our attention a perennial feature of the human situation: sin (see Commentary on Psalm 32). As A. Whitney Brown has said of human history, "Any good history book is mainly just a long list of mistakes, complete with names and dates. It's very embarrassing."[214] This characterization is preeminently true of the Bible. Israel's story is indeed a long list of mistakes. Claus Westermann pointed out that Exodus 32–34 proves to be paradigmatic of the whole history of Israel.[215] David's story and the history of the subsequent monarchy are indeed very embarrassing. So is the psalmist's story in Psalm 51. So is the behavior of the disciples in the Gospels (see Matt 26:56). So is the situation of the early church, revealed in the letters of Paul (see esp. 1 Corinthians). So is the history of the Christian church throughout the centuries. So are the denominational and congregational lives of the contemporary church. So are the details of our life stories, if we are honest enough to admit it. In short, Psalm 51 is not just about Israel or David or some unknown ancient psalmist; it is also about us! It is about who we are and how we are as individuals, families, churches—sin pervades our lives. It's very embarrassing.

That is the bad news. But the good news of Psalm 51 is even more prominent. Psalm 51 is not just about human nature; it is also about God's nature. And the good news is that God is willing to forgive sinners and is able to re-create people. Israel's corporate life is an example (see Ezek 36:16-36). David's life is an example. And the psalmist here offers his or her own life as an example as well. To be sure, sin is a powerful and persistent reality, but God's grace is a more powerful and enduring reality. By the grace of God, a persistently disobedient people become partners with God in "an everlasting covenant" (Isa 55:3 NRSV). By the grace of God, dull and disobedient disciples of Jesus become known as those "who have been turning the world upside down" (Acts 17:6 NRSV). By the grace of God, Saul, the former murderer, becomes Paul, ambassador for Christ. Grace is fundamental. That is the good news.

2. It should not surprise us that the apostle Paul knew Psalm 51. He quoted it in Rom 3:4 as part of his argument for the universality of human sinfulness. But this argument is the prelude to Paul's proclamation of justification of the sinful by God's grace (see Rom 3:21-31). Paul, of course, saw this reality revealed in Jesus Christ. What Paul proclaimed to the Corinthians (2 Cor 5:17-20) is reminiscent of Ps 51:10-13:

> So if anyone is in Christ, there is a new creation; everything old has passed away; see, everything has become new! All this is from God, who reconciled us to himself through Christ, and has given us the ministry of reconciliation; that is, in Christ God was

---

214. A. Whitney Brown, *The Big Picture: An American Commentary* (New York: Harper Perennial, 1991) 12.
215. See Claus Westermann, *Elements of Old Testament Theology,* trans. D. W. Stott (Atlanta: John Knox, 1982) 50, 54.

reconciling the world to himself, not counting their trespasses against them, and entrusting the message of reconciliation to us. So we are ambassadors for Christ, since God is making his appeal through us; we entreat you on behalf of Christ, be reconciled to God. (NRSV)

Psalm 51 is also an invitation to "be reconciled to God." As Paul knew, reconciliation happens as a result of God's willingness to forgive; the result is a new creation (see Ps 51:10-12), and the reconciled are entrusted with the message of reconciliation (see Ps 51:13). Like the psalmist, too, Paul must have found it necessary to pray often, "Deliver me from bloodshed" (Ps 51:14; see 2 Cor 6:4-5). Jesus also, of course, experienced the violence of persons who opposed what they perceived to be the scandalous proclamation of God's grace.

In the final analysis, Psalm 51 is a proclamation of the good news of the justification of sinners by God's grace. As suggested above, Paul's fullest exposition of this good news is his letter to the Romans. Following the exposition in Romans 1–11, Paul laid out the implications for response in 12:1-2. His appeal is reminiscent of the point at which the psalmist arrives in 51:17 and the direction taken to get there (see Reflections on Psalm 50):

I appeal to you therefore, brothers and sisters, by the mercies of God, to present your bodies as a living sacrifice, holy and acceptable to God, which is your spiritual worship. Do not be conformed to this world, but be transformed by the renewing of your minds, so that you may discern what is the will of God—what is good and acceptable and perfect. (NRSV)

The psalmist has anticipated Paul's advice. By the mercies of God (v. 1), the psalmist presents his or her whole self as a living sacrifice (51:17). The transformed psalmist (vv. 10-12) then is able to discern the will of God (v. 13*a*) and begins to participate with God in transforming the world (v. 13*b*). By the grace of God, amid the persistent reality of human sinfulness, there is a new creation.

3. As testimony to the pervasiveness of sin and as a call to be reconciled to God, Psalm 51 is clearly appropriate for its assigned use on Ash Wednesday and during the season of Lent. As a powerful proclamation of God's grace, this psalm is clearly also a psalm for all seasons, and it is appropriate that it is used often in worship. Paraphrases of Psalm 51, especially of vv. 1-5 and 10-12, are frequently used as confessions of sin. Many persons would recognize v. 15 as a call to worship, and perhaps they would appreciate it even more if they knew its source and context.

PSALM 52:1-9, I TRUST IN GOD'S UNFAILING LOVE

COMMENTARY

Like Psalm 50, Psalm 52 is neither prayer nor praise directed to God. Rather, vv. 1-5 are addressed to a "mighty one"—who appears to be a powerful person who intends to practice his or her wicked ways on the psalmist and perhaps others of "the righteous" (v. 6). The superscription identifies this "mighty one" as Doeg, one of Saul's servants, who informed Saul of David's locale and killed the priests of Nob at Saul's command (see 1 Samuel 21–22; 22:9 is quoted in the superscription). While Psalm 52 makes sense as the words of David in such a situation, it is much more likely that the superscription should be taken illustratively rather than historically. In short, Psalm 52 may have served and still can serve as the words of God's faithful but threatened people in a variety of times and places (see Reflections below).

Following the address to the "mighty one" in vv. 1-5 is an affirmation about the righteous (v. 6), a quotation of their words (v. 7), and the psalmist's profession of faith (v. 8). God is addressed directly only in v. 9. Because of its unique structure, Psalm 52 "resists form-critical analysis." It is sometimes categorized as a prophetic exhortation (see Psalms 50; 81; 95), although Gerstenberger suggests communal instruction, the use of which he locates in the post-exilic synagogue for the purpose of fortifying the community against threatening opponents.[216] Gerstenberger's proposal offers further evidence of the suitability of this psalm to a variety of historical contexts.

52:1-5. The content of the psalm's exhortation or instruction involves the nature of true security, wealth, and power. Verse 1 clearly contrasts the alternatives for seeking security, although the NIV and the NRSV unnecessarily obscure the matter by failing to follow the Hebrew text (see the NRSV note). The Hebrew of v. 1 could be translated more literally, "Why do you boast about evil, you mighty one? The steadfast love of God lasts all the day." In other words, security can be sought either in doing evil or in God's love. Verses 2-4 explore the first alternative that the mighty one has clearly chosen—to pursue security by self-assertion at the expense of other persons. The mighty one has no qualms about perpetrating "destruction" (הוה *hawwâ*, v. 2; the Hebrew word recurs in v. 7, as the NIV suggests; see also Pss 5:9; 38:12; 55:12). Both v. 2 and v. 4 mention "tongue" and "deceit"/"deceitful" (cf. Pss 10:7; 35:20; 36:3; 38:12; 55:23). Verse 3 repeats the word "evil" from v. 1, and it also portrays the mighty one as a liar (see Pss 7:14; 31:18; 109:2). The mighty one has no love for doing "good" (v. 3; see also v. 9; Pss 34:15; 37:3, 27; Amos 5:14-15; Mic 3:2) or for speaking "righteousness" (v. 3). The mighty one is willing to use any means to get ahead, regardless of how destructive. In short, the mighty one represents the essence of wickedness in the

216. Gerstenberger, *Psalms: Part 1*, 216.

Psalms: autonomy, self-rule (see Commentary on Psalm 1).

The psalmist affirms that the alternative to autonomy is dependence upon God and God's steadfast love. Verse 1 has indicated that this alternative is the only true and enduring one; v. 5 illustrates the reason why (see Ps 73:18-20). In contrast to the affirmation that God "will uproot" the wicked, the psalmist uses the self-portrait of a stable, fruitful tree in v. 8, which also contains the affirmation that the psalmist has chosen the proper alternative: God's steadfast love. The psalmist knows the nature of true security: Life ultimately depends on God rather than on ourselves or our possessions (see Luke 12:13-21, esp. v. 15).

52:6-7. The righteous will see the judgment announced in v. 5, and they will interpret it as confirmation of their choice to trust God (v. 6; see "see and fear" in Ps 40:3). Just as God laughs at those who oppose the divine will (see Pss 2:4; 37:13; 59:8; Prov 1:26), so also do the righteous. Their words indicate their understanding of the proper direction of trust (v. 7). As the NIV suggests, the Hebrew root that the NRSV translates "refuge" in v. 7 means basically "strength" (מעוז *mā'ôz*; see Ps 27:1). The so-called mighty ones seek their strength not in God but in destroying others. The psalmist recognizes that such a strategy is finally futile (see Pss 37:1-11, 37-40; 49:5-6; 62:10). Verses 5-7 do not describe a reward/punishment scheme that operates mechanistically. The punishment of the wicked is that by pursuing wealth they have cut themselves off from God, who is the source of life. Conversely, the reward of the righteous is that they are grounded in God and thus connected to life's source and destiny (see Commentary on Psalm 1).

52:8-9. Verse 8 articulates both the psalmist's connection to the source of life and the faith on which it is founded. Like a long-lived olive tree growing on the temple grounds, the psalmist's life is firmly rooted in God's love (see Pss 1:3; 92:12-15; Jer 17:5-8, 11). In explicit contrast to those who trust their own ill-gotten gain (v. 7), the psalmist trusts God's steadfast love "forever and ever" (v. 8; see also v. 1 and note "forever" in v. 5). Thus, while the life of the wicked is characterized by greed (vv. 2-4, 7), the life of the psalmist is characterized by gratitude to God (v. 9*ab*). The psalmist's relationship to others involves not exploitation (see v. 7) but witness (v. 9*cd*). The term "faithful"/"saints" (הסיד *ḥāsîd*) is from the same root as "steadfast love," and it may be translated "the steadfastly loving [or loved] ones." In short, trust in God's steadfast love creates a community shaped by God's character or "name" (see Ps 54:6, where "good" is associated with God's "name"; elsewhere God is described as "good" in association with God's steadfast love, as in

Pss 100:5; 106:1; 107:1; 118:1, 29; 136:1; 145:8-9). The verb in v. 9*cd* means "to wait for," "to hope" (קוה *qāwâ*; see Pss 25:3, 5, 21; 27:14; 37:34; 40:1; 130:5). The community of God's people is eschatological. It lives, surrounded by opposition from mighty ones, not by what it sees but by what it believes and hopes for. In doing so, it experiences already the abundant life that is greater than any earthly treasure or possession (see Matt 6:19-21; Luke 12:13-21).

REFLECTIONS

The words of Psalm 52 would be appropriate in various settings, ranging from the life of David to the post-exilic era to the contemporary scene. In other words, the central issue with which Psalm 52 deals is a perennial one: the nature of enduring security, wealth, and power. The temptation to live for ourselves at the expense of others is both as ancient as humanity itself (see Genesis 4) and as contemporary as today's date. Mays describes the depiction of the "mighty one" in vv. 1-4 as follows: "The portrait is that of a person who turns human capacities and possession into the basis of his existence."[217] This, of course, is precisely what much of contemporary society consistently presses us to do—to ground our lives in nothing but ourselves and our possessions (see Commentary on Psalms 1; 2; 49).

In other words, contemporary culture confronts us with the same alternatives that we find in Psalm 52. We can choose to live for ourselves, or we can choose to live for God. We can trust ourselves and our own resources, or we can entrust our lives and futures to God. The choice is not an easy one.

Psalm 52 is a reminder that there has always been hostility to the gospel. And, of course, the psalmist—whether we think in terms of David or of some unknown post-exilic poet—is not the only faithful servant to be threatened by rich and powerful opponents. We need only consider, for instance, Amos (see Amos 7:10-17), Jeremiah (see Jer 26:10-19; 38:1-13), and Jesus. Those who are called to follow Jesus can expect opposition as well (see Mark 8:34). The alternatives presented in Psalm 52 are still very real, and the psalmist's words and example are a timely witness for those of us who live in circumstances in which trusting God will be both increasingly difficult and increasingly important.

217. Mays, *Psalms*, 205.

PSALM 53:1-6, NO ONE DOES GOOD

COMMENTARY

Psalm 53 is nearly identical to Psalm 14, with the exception of 53:5 (cf. 14:5-6). The superscription of Psalm 53 is longer than that of Psalm 14; the noun translated "acts" (עול *ʿāwel*) in 53:1 differs from the noun in the

corresponding position in Ps 14:1 (עלילה *ʿălîlâ*); and the opening verbs of 53:3 and 14:3 differ. The divine name also differs in Psalms 14 and 53, since Psalm 53 is part of the Elohistic Psalter (Psalms 42–83; see

Introduction). The two versions of essentially the same psalm were apparently parts of separate collections that were both included in the book of Psalms.

The opening line of Ps 53:5 is the same as 14:5, but then the two psalms diverge briefly. Whereas 14:5-6 affirms God's presence with the righteous who find their refuge in God, Ps 53:5 develops the concept of "terror" (פחד *paḥad*). There are textual problems with v. 5 (see the NRSV notes); however, its apparent purpose is to portray God's judgment upon the "evildoers" mentioned in v. 4 (see Ps 141:7). This difference in Psalm 53 makes it a particularly suitable companion to Psalm 52, which also portrays God's judgment upon the wicked (see 52:5). Likewise, the content of Ps 14:5-6 has specific connections with its particular context, especially with Ps 12:5-7. (For further commentary, as well as Reflections, see Psalm 14.)

PSALM 54:1-7, SURELY, GOD IS MY HELPER

COMMENTARY

Psalm 54 is a prayer for help or individual lament/complaint. It opens with petition (vv. 1-2), followed by complaint (v. 3), affirmation of trust (vv. 4-5a), renewed petition (v. 5b), and vow to praise (v. 6) with accompanying reason (v. 7). Scholars disagree as to whether v. 7 indicates that the psalmist has already been delivered. It seems to do so, but it may allude to past deliverances that form the basis of the present confidence, or it may indicate that the psalmist is so sure of an anticipated deliverance that he or she can speak of it as already having occurred. The ambiguity has theological significance (see Reflections).

Attention is drawn to v. 3c by the *selah* following it, as well as by the fact that it is the third part of the only three-part line in the poem. Regardless of whether v. 3c is a later addition, as several scholars suggest, its present position serves to set up the sharply contrasting affirmation in v. 4a. Verse 4 is the middle line of the psalm, and, perhaps not coincidentally, it contains the central theological assertion: "God is my helper." It is significant, too, that v. 4 is surrounded by references in vv. 3 and 5 to those who oppose the psalmist. Structurally speaking, the affirmation comes in the midst of opposition. Experientially speaking, the same is true.

The superscription assigns the prayer to David (see 1 Sam 23:19) at a point when Saul "had come out to seek his life" (1 Sam 23:15 NRSV; cf. Ps 54:3). As with other such superscriptions (see Psalms 3; 51; Introduction), this one should be taken illustratively rather than historically. The editors of the psalter recognized the appropriateness of Psalm 54 for that particular moment in David's life; however, the prayer is also appropriate for and was certainly used in a variety of circumstances. Several commentators suggest that it may have been used by persecuted persons seeking refuge in the Temple (see Psalms 5; 7), while Gerstenberger maintains that it was "rooted in small-group ritual and employed in order to save and rehabilitate suffering group members."[218] On the other hand, several scholars approach Psalm 54 as a communal prayer of the embattled post-exilic community. In short, the characteristic inability to define a precise origin and setting testifies to the open-endedness and adaptability of the prayer.

54:1-2. The opening petition is a frequent one in Psalms (see Pss 3:7; 6:4; 7:1). The appeal to God's "name" is often interpreted as evidence of a late Deuteronomistic name theology (see Deut 12:5, 11, 21; 1 Kgs 8:16-20). While this is possible (see "name" also in v. 6), it perhaps more simply indicates an appeal to God's fundamental character, which includes both "might" (v. 1b; see also Pss 21:13; 65:6; 66:7; 71:18; 80:2; 89:13; and esp. 106:8) and "faithfulness" (v. 6; see also Exod 34:6; Pss 40:11-12; 57:3; 85:10-11; 86:15). The petition for God to "vindicate" is used less frequently (see Ps 7:9), but God is elsewhere described using this particular

218. Gerstenberger, *Psalms: Part 1*, 222.

word as one who judges or sets things right as a manifestation of divine sovereignty (see Pss 9:8; 50:4; 96:10). In essence, the psalmist's appeal in v. 1 demonstrates that she or he trusts that the power and purposes of God are greater than the power and purposes of the enemy, a conviction that is reinforced in vv. 4-5, 7. Thus the psalmist asks God to hear and to give ear (v. 2; see Pss 17:1; 39:12; 84:8; and esp. 143:1, where these requests are linked to God's faithfulness).

54:3-5. In v. 3a, the NIV follows the Hebrew, a reading that is often cited by those who emphasize the communal dimension of the prayer, since the word "strangers" (זרים *zārîm*) usually designates foreign enemies (see Isa 1:7; Hos 7:9; 8:7; cf. Ps 109:11). The NRSV follows several manuscripts that read a similar word that means "insolent" (זדים *zēdîm*; on enemies rising, see Ps 3:1). The same word occurs in Ps 86:14, as does the Hebrew word translated "ruthless" here (עריצים *'ārîṣîm*; "ruffians" in 86:14 NRSV). In both verses, the ruthless, failing to attend to God, seek the psalmist's life (see also Pss 35:4; 38:12; 40:14; 63:9; 70:2). The editors of the psalter apparently had v. 3b in mind in linking Psalm 54 with David (see 1 Sam 23:15), but others also had their lives threatened by enemies—Elijah (1 Kgs 19:10, 14), Jeremiah (see Jer 11:21), the people of Jerusalem (Jer 21:7), Jesus. Thus v. 3b is another reminder of the adaptability of Psalm 54.

Verses 3c and 4a provide a sharp contrast between the enemies and the psalmist. That contrast is made even more emphatic by the alliteration of "strangers" (*zārîm*) and

"helper" (עזר *'ōzēr*). The psalmist entrusts her or his life to God (see God as "help"/"helper" in Pss 10:14; 22:19). The syntax of v. 4b is difficult, but the translations seem to capture the proper sense (see Pss 3:5; 37:17, 24; 51:12; 119:116; 145:14). Again, the psalmist's life depends on God. God will deal with the psalmist's opponents, who in v. 5a are literally called "watchers" (שורר *šōrēr*; see the same Hebrew word in Pss 5:8; 27:11; 56:2; 59:10; 92:11). The appeal in v. 5b is based on God's character—"faithfulness"—just as the same petition in Ps 143:12 is based on God's steadfast love. The issue is not so much personal revenge as it is the psalmist's conviction that God wills to do justice, to give life, to set things right (see v. 1). If God does not deal with the enemies, then God's will is thwarted.

54:6-7. In apparent anticipation of the enactment of the divine will, the psalmist promises in v. 6 a "freewill offering" (see 2 Chr 31:14; Ezra 3:5; Ezek 46:12). The motive is gratitude for the manifestation of God's character (see "name" in v. 1; see also Pss 44:8; 52:9; 99:3; 138:2; 142:7). Although it is not clear whether deliverance has already occurred or is still anticipated, it is clear that the psalmist entrusts the future to God. The phrase "in triumph" is not in the Hebrew text (see also Pss 59:10; 118:7). While it may be an acceptable interpretive translation, it may also be too suggestive of the element of personal revenge. The real point is that God has or will set things right as the psalmist requested in v. 1.

REFLECTIONS

On the basis of vv. 5 and 7, the psalmist is sometimes understood as vengeful and vindictive. Weiser, for instance, says of the psalmist, "Human self-will and man's low instincts of vindictiveness and gloating retain their power over his thoughts."[219] Such a conclusion, however, overlooks the fact that the psalmist does not personally seek revenge but appeals to God's character and will to give life and to enact justice among human beings. In situations of injustice and oppression, in order for things to be set right, oppressors must be opposed. It is precisely this for which the psalmist prays. In short, the psalmist is not necessarily being vengeful but simply realistic. As Marvin Tate concludes: "The message of the psalm is clear enough: the Name of Yahweh will not

219. Weiser, *The Psalms*, 416.

---

fail the suppliant in a time of crisis. The enemies will not prevail. Yahweh will make a necessary connection between act and consequence, and the power of ruthless foes will be turned back against themselves."[220]

In essence, the psalmist demonstrates the same faith and prays the same way Jesus taught his disciples: "your will be done, on earth as it is in heaven . . . deliver us from the evil one" (Matt 6:10, 13 NIV). The perspective of the Lord's prayer is eschatological, as is that of Psalm 54—that is, the psalmist prayed and Christians pray in the midst of opposition and suffering. Yet, to affirm that "God is my helper," entrusting life and future to God, is already to be in touch with the source of enduring life and strength.

This tension between "already" and "not yet" makes the ambiguity of v. 7 theologically significant for us. In other words, persons who live in dependence upon God will experience the life that God intends, yet always in a world where brokenness and pain and disobedience are real. It is theologically appropriate that we not try to resolve the ambiguity of v. 7, for it reminds Christian readers of the truth that the cross and the resurrection are experienced not as separate but as simultaneous realities (see Commentary on Psalms 13; 22; Introduction).

220. Tate, *Psalms 51–100*, 49.

PSALM 55:1-23, CAST YOUR BURDENS ON THE LORD

COMMENTARY

Although this prayer for help contains typical features of the individual lament/complaint—petition (vv. 1-2a, 9a, 15), complaint (vv. 2b-8, 9b-11, 12-14, 20-21), expression of trust (vv. 16-19, 22-23)—it is also "astonishingly unique."[221] Not only are there many unusual words and difficult expressions, but also the movement of the poem seems abrupt and disorderly, to the extent that Kraus even suggests that vv. 1-18a and vv. 18b-23 are two separate poems that were joined because of the prominent theme of betrayal by a friend (vv. 12-14, 20-21).[222] It seems preferable, however, to view the structural irregularity as an apt representation of the chaotic conditions that prevail in the life of the psalmist.

Several attempts have been made to specify what these conditions may have been. It has been suggested that the psalm articulates the experience of exile, either of an individual or of the people, who find themselves in a strange and hostile city. Because of the military imagery and the betrayal theme, Psalm 55 is sometimes associated with the betrayal of David by Ahithophel as part of Absalom's revolt (see 2 Sam 15:31). While such proposals provide interesting background for the reading of Psalm 55, they remain very speculative. The theme of betrayal by friends also occurs in other prayers (see Pss 31:11; 35:12-15; 38:11; 41:9; 88:8, 18), and it is simply not possible to identify precisely the situations behind these prayers. Besides, Psalm 55 and other prayers were preserved and transmitted because of their ability to function liturgically and devotionally in a variety of times and places (see Reflections below). They articulate universal human experiences of opposition (vv. 2-3), danger (vv. 10-11), fear (vv. 4-5), and betrayal (vv. 12-14, 20-21), as well as assurance (vv. 16-19) and trust (vv. 22-23). As Gerstenberger suggests, Psalm 55 "summarizes liturgically the archetypal expressions of an ultimate anxiety in the face of death that is regularly experienced in situations of extreme danger."[223]

55:1-5. The psalm begins with four imperatives: "Give ear" (see Pss 5:1; 17:1), "do not hide" (see Ps 10:1), "attend" (see

221. Gerstenberger, *Psalms: Part 1*, 223.
222. Kraus, *Psalms 1–59*, 519-20.

223. Gerstenberger, *Psalms: Part 1*, 224.

Pss 5:2; 17:1), "answer" (see Pss 27:7; 86:1). Having requested God's attention, the psalmist immediately shares his or her troubling "thoughts"/"complaint" (see v. 18; Pss 64:1; 142:3). The "enemy" (v. 3; see v. 12) causes trouble "to totter" upon the psalmist (v. 3; see the NRSV note), but in the end the psalmist realizes that God will not allow "the righteous to totter" (v. 22, author's trans.). But for now the complaint continues in vv. 4-5, where the language suggests precisely the opposite of deliverance. "Terrors" (v. 4) and "trembling" (v. 5) are what the Egyptians experienced as a result of opposing God (see Exod 15:15-16), and overwhelming horror is what Ezekiel promises as a result of God's judgment (see Ezek 7:18).

55:6-11. It is understandable that the psalmist wants to escape (vv. 6-8). Speaking for God apparently, Jeremiah voices a similar sentiment in Jer 9:2-3; Jer 9:4-8 warns about betrayal by neighbors and kin, and Jer 9:9-10 announces a punishment from which the birds flee (see also Jer 4:25). Thus Jeremiah 9 recalls the content and movement of Psalm 55. The wilderness is seen as a place of refuge that contrasts with the violent city that is mentioned in vv. 9-11 (cf. Ezek 17:23; 31:13, where nesting birds are an image of safety). The wicked elsewhere are associated with violence (Pss 7:16; 11:5; 18:48; 27:12; 73:6; 74:20) and strife (Pss 18:43; 31:20), as well as with the other personified problems in vv. 10-11. For instance, the words the NRSV translates as "iniquity," "trouble," "oppression," and "fraud" all occur in Ps 10:7 to describe the speech of the wicked ("mischief" = "trouble" and "deceit" = "fraud"), who disrupt life in the villages (Ps 10:8). In Psalm 55, the city is characterized by "destructive forces" (v. 11), a condition elsewhere caused by the wicked (cf. Pss 5:9; 52:2, 7). The psalmist's plea in v. 9*a* recalls Gen 11:1-9 and the city of Babel (see esp. Gen 11:7, 9). The wicked threaten both the psalmist and God.

55:12-15. Verses 12-14 introduce a new dimension to the problem. The generally chaotic conditions of vv. 2*b*-5, 9-11 are accompanied by personal betrayal. Beginning with the personal pronoun "you," v. 13 designates the betrayer with three more terms that emphasize former intimacy. As suggested above, the theme of betrayal occurs in several

other psalms and prophetic texts (in addition to Jer 9:4-8, see Isa 3:5; Jer 20:10; Mic 7:5-6). The shift from "you" in v. 13 to "them" in v. 15 returns the focus to the larger problem. Apparently, the disruption of intimate relationships is a part of the larger societal breakdown. Verse 15, which essentially tells the enemies to "Go to hell," recalls Numbers 16, where Korah and his company "go down alive into Sheol" (Num 16:30 NRSV; see also Num 16:33), which represents the realm and power of death (see Pss 18:5; 88:3; 116:3).

55:16-19. In the face of circumstances that are deadly (v. 4) and destructive (vv. 9-11), terrible and terrifying (v. 5), the psalmist looks to God for life (see "save"/"deliver" in Pss 3:7; 6:4; 7:1; 31:16; 54:1; 57:3). The emphatic personal pronoun "I" begins v. 16, effectively contrasting the psalmist with the treacherous "you" of v. 13. The psalmist is constantly in communication with God (v. 17*a*) in the confidence that God "will hear" (vv. 17, 19) and "redeem" (v. 12; see also Pss 26:11; 31:5; 34:22; 44:26; 69:18). The word for "unharmed" (בשׁלום *bĕšālôm*) in v. 18 is more literally translated "in peace," and suits the military imagery (see "battle" in v. 18 and "war" in v. 21). It was the responsibility of a monarch to establish peace; thus God's sovereignty is affirmed in v. 19 (see "enthroned"/"sits" in Pss 2:4; 9:7; 29:10; 102:12). The phrase "humble them" or "afflict them" (יענם *ya'ănēm*) is similar in sound to "answer me" (ענני *'ănēnî*) in v. 2. God's answer will involve opposition to oppressors. Verse 19 makes explicit what was implied in vv. 9-11: The enemies of the psalmist are also opponents of God. Verses 16-19 profess the eschatological faith that pervades the book of Psalms: The power of God is ultimately greater than the power of the wicked. Although it may appear otherwise for now, God rules the world (see Psalm 2; Introduction).

55:20-23. On the basis of this conviction, despite human faithlessness and unreliability (vv. 20-21), the psalmist can invite others, including contemporary readers, to "Cast your burden on the LORD" (v. 22*a*). While it is possible to construe v. 22*a* as the sarcastic words of the enemy addressed to the psalmist (see v. 21), it is more likely that it should be understood as the psalmist's encouraging word to others, and this is certainly the way v. 22 has been appropriated in the history of its interpretation. The invitation is followed by an affirmation of God's care for the righteous. The pronoun "he" is emphatic; *God* will provide. Amid the chaos caused by the wicked, God offers stability. The righteous will not "totter" (see above on v. 3; see also "be moved"/"shake"/"fall"/"slipped" in Pss 13:5; 16:8; 17:4; 62:2, 6). The correlate occurs in v. 23, which recalls v. 15. Again,

the personal pronoun "you" is emphatic; *God* will deal with the wicked, who are here described as "bloodthirsty" (see Pss 5:6; 26:9; 59:2; 139:19). "Treachery" represents the same Hebrew word as "fraud" in v. 11. The psalmist's difficult experience has clearly shown that human beings cannot be trusted, but it apparently has served to solidify the psalmist's trust in God (see Pss 4:5; 13:5; Introduction). Life and future belong with God.

REFLECTIONS

1. In a notable sermon, preached shortly after the death of his son, William Sloan Coffin pointed to the impossibility of using the Bible to explain tragedies: "As the grief that once seemed unbearable begins to turn now to bearable sorrow the truths in the 'right' biblical passages are beginning, once again, to take hold: 'Cast thy burden upon the LORD and he shall strengthen thee.' "[224]

Coffin's citation of v. 22a as a "right" biblical passage is testimony to the ability of Psalm 55 to function as a powerful prayer and affirmation of faith, regardless of the exact situation in which it originated and was used. In other words, human life is lived now as it was then, amid persistent opposition. Whatever the cause—whatever or whoever the enemy happens to be—we know from experience the realities of anguish, death, fear, horror, violence, oppression, betrayal. It is not surprising that 1 Pet 5:7 quotes v. 22a as the author exhorts those who are suffering (see 1 Pet 4:13, 19; 5:10).

2. Indeed, the complaint sections at several points sound strikingly contemporary. For instance, our cities are still full of violence and strife (v. 9). As Psalm 55 suggests, too, the generally chaotic conditions of our society are reflected in our difficulty in maintaining personal relationships. The experience of personal betrayal is not new, but it is particularly prevalent among us (see Luke 22:48). Psalm 55 may help us to acknowledge that reality and begin to address it. Pastor Stephen P. McCutchan made this suggestion as he narrated the thoughts of a recently betrayed spouse who entered the Sunday service as the congregation was "invited to pray Psalm 55 slowly, pausing after each verse as the choir intoned the refrain, 'Cast your burden on the Lord, and God will sustain you.' " The woman's thoughts in part are as follows:

> How could the psalmist have known so long ago the deep anger that betrayal generates? How could the psalmist have understood that unless such anger is released to God, it will surely destroy either victim or victimizer? And now the congregation knew too. The unbearable pain was being borne by a larger body than hers. She felt the deeper anger that she had wrestled with alone and the relief that it was no longer hers alone.

McCutchan points out that psalms like this one encourage us to acknowledge our own pain and that of others and thus "to emerge from isolation." If they were used regularly in worship, "it might encourage people to consider worship as the appropriate place to cast their burden upon the Lord."[225] In short, Psalm 55 can still function as a faithful prayer and as a powerful profession of the faith that the sustaining power of God is ultimately greater than the power of human sin and its painful effects.

224. Quoted in Long, "Preaching About Suffering," 14.
225. Stephen P. McCutchan, "A Parable in Liturgy," *Reformed Liturgy and Music* 26 (Summer 1992) 139-40.

PSALM 56:1-13, IN GOD I TRUST

COMMENTARY

While v. 13 suggests that Psalm 56 could be viewed as a song of thanksgiving that looks back upon and narrates former distress, it is more likely that the psalm is a prayer for help or an individual lament/complaint. Such prayers regularly turn to expressions of trust and praise, thus making it difficult to determine whether deliverance has occurred or is anticipated. This ambiguity has theological significance (see Commentary on Psalm 54). In any case, it is clear that expressions of trust predominate in Psalm 56 (vv. 3-4, 8-11). These expressions follow sections of petition and complaint (vv. 1-2, 5-8), and the psalm concludes with the promise to make a thank offering in response to deliverance (vv. 12-13).

The superscription connects the psalm with David's presence in Gath (see 1 Sam 21:10-14). As with similar superscriptions, it is likely that this one should be taken illustratively rather than historically, and it is certain that the prayer was used in various settings. The titles in the LXX and the Targum, for instance, offer the setting as being "for the people far removed from the sanctuary." In other words, like many other prayers in the psalter, Psalm 56 would have served as an appropriate communal prayer in the exilic and postexilic eras. Some scholars suggest that it may have been used by any persecuted person who sought comfort and found encouragement by entrusting her or his life to God. As with other prayers, the inability to specify the origin and setting of Psalm 56 suggests its adaptability to a variety of situations. Illustrative of the flexibility of the prayer is Prothero's report that during the English civil war, an imprisoned Charles I used Ps 56:1-2 to answer the taunts of his captors, whose insults in turn were drawn from Ps 52:1.[226] While this may not be the most edifying illustration, it demonstrates the dynamic nature of the prayers in the psalter.

The opening petition is a frequent one in Psalms (see Pss 4:1; 6:2), as is the situation

of opposition by enemies. As usual, the precise nature of the circumstances is unclear. The Hebrew root that the NIV translates "attack"/"attacking" (לחם lāham, vv. 1-2) suggests a military setting. The repeated word "trample" (שאף šā'ap, vv. 1-2), on the other hand, could indicate socioeconomic abuse (see Ps 57:3; Amos 2:7; 8:4), and the word "oppress" (לחץ lāhas, v. 1) could indicate either (see Exod 3:9; 22:21; 23:9; Judg 2:18; 4:3; Ps 106:42; Amos 6:14). The military imagery is probably metaphorical, but in any case, the vocabulary is open-ended enough to be appropriate in a variety of settings. As a comparison of the NIV with the NRSV suggests, the textual problem at the end of v. 2 has been approached differently. The syntax is difficult. The last word in v. 2 is a noun that means "height" (מרום mārôm). While the NIV construes its grammatical function as an adverb and gives it a figurative sense, the NRSV interprets it as a reference to God and suggests that it belongs to the beginning of the next line, where it functions as a vocative.

The exact situation behind the complaint is no clearer in vv. 5-7. Whereas petition led to complaint in vv. 1-2, the complaint in vv. 5-6 culminates in petition in v. 7, which would be particularly appropriate as a communal prayer. Whatever the problem is, it is a constant one, as the repeated phrase "all day long" indicates (vv. 1-2, 5). As the NIV suggests, the noun in v. 5a is literally "words" (דברים dĕbārîm), but the verb usually means "to hurt," "to grieve" and is unusual in Psalms (see Ps 78:40). More typical is the complaint in v. 6 about the enemies' "thoughts" or "plotting" (see "devise," "plan," "conceive," or "plot" in Pss 10:2; 21:11; 35:4, 20; 36:3; 52:2; 140:2, 4 NRSV; in 140:2, the verb the NRSV translates as "stir up strife" in v. 6 also occurs). Verse 6 suggests the vigilance with which the enemies seek to destroy the psalmist's life ("lurk" occurs in Ps 10:8; see "watch" in the superscription of Psalm 59 and in 71:10). The word "hoped" (קוה qāwâ) in v. 6c is elsewhere a theologically significant word that usually indicates trust

226. Prothero, *The Psalms in Human Life and Experience*, 183.

in and reliance upon God (see "wait [for]" in Pss 25:3, 5, 21; 27:14; 37:34; 40:1 NRSV). Whereas the faithful place their hope in God, the psalmist's opponents find hope only in exploiting other people. Thus v. 7 is not so much a request for revenge as it is a plea that God set things right (see Ps 55:23; see also Commentary on Psalm 54).

What is clear about the opposition described in vv. 1-2, 5-7 is that it evokes fear in the psalmist (see "afraid" in vv. 3-4, 11). In contrast to the enemies, who seek security in taking advantage of others, the psalmist trusts God. Indeed, each occurrence of the word "afraid" (ירא *yārē*) is accompanied by the word "trust" (בטח *bāṭaḥ*), effectively and emphatically contrasting these two possible responses to threat (see Pss 4:5; 13:5; Introduction). The arrangement of the key terms in vv. 3-4 is chiastic (see Introduction): "afraid" /"trust"/"word"/"trust"/"not afraid." The movement is from fear to being unafraid, and it is a movement that takes place structurally and existentially through trust, with the focal point being God's word. The psalmist's praising of God's word here is unique in the OT, but it is clearly important, as the repetition in v. 10 indicates. The "word" may consist of the whole body of tradition concerning God's relationship with God's people—that is, what we would call Scripture. More specifically, however, it seems to refer to the "word" delivered elsewhere in situations of distress: "Do not fear, for I am with you" (Isa 41:10 NRSV; see also Exod 14:13; Josh 10:25; Ps 49:16; Isa 40:9; 41:13-14; 43:5; Jer 30:10).

In other words, the psalmist professes that true security is a divine gift rather than a human achievement. The fundamental mistake of the wicked is their belief that they can make it on their own, that they can find hope in exploiting others (v. 6; see Isa 47:10). The psalmist knows better. Because security is ultimately a gift from God, no human action can take it away. This affirmation is made by means of the similar questions (vv. 4, 11) that conclude the two expressions of trust (vv. 3-4, 8-11). In a sense, the psalmist knows all too well what others can "do to me"—trample, oppress, fight, plot, conspire, lurk (vv. 1-2, 5-6). But in a deeper sense, the psalmist knows that her or his life is known by God (v. 8, reading the verb in v. 8*a* with the NRSV as an indicative, the subject of which is an emphatic *you*; on "tears," see Ps 6:6; on God's keeping a "record," see Ps 40:7). And the psalmist knows "that God is for me" (v. 9). Essentially the same affirmation occurs in Ps 118:6 (NIV, "with me"; NRSV, "on my side"; see also 118:7), where it is accompanied by the same question as in vv. 4, 11 and followed by an affirmation of the proper object of human trust—God, not humans, even the most powerful humans (118:8-9).

The fact that the psalmist trusts God makes irrelevant the scholarly discussion of whether deliverance from the current distress has already occurred (see v. 13; see Commentary on Psalm 54). Even if it has, a new threat is inevitably on the horizon. The point is that, regardless of outward circumstances, the psalmist has been transformed by trust. While current or future opposition may cause fear, the psalmist will always be able to say, "I will not be afraid" (vv. 4, 11). This ability is not an act of human bravery or courage but a result of the conviction that the life God offers is beyond the reach of human threat (vv. 4, 11). Thus, in the face of every threat, the psalmist will be able to live with gratitude (v. 12; see also Pss 50:14, 23; 107:22; 116:17). To "walk before God" (v. 13), or more literally, "to the face of God," means an unfading source of light (see Job 33:30; see "light" in Pss 4:6; 27:1; 43:3; 89:15) and life (see Pss 116:8-9; 36:9).

REFLECTIONS

Psychologists and theologians alike tell us that we must believe in something. A perennial human question is not *whether* we shall trust but *what* or *whom* we shall trust. It is this question that Psalm 56 helps us to address. A persistent temptation, of course, is to trust ourselves, our abilities or achievements, our resources, as do the psalmist's opponents (see also Pss 49:5-6; 52:7-8; 62:10; Isa 47:10). In this regard, it is particularly significant that the word "hoped" (v. 6) is used to summarize the purposes of the enemy. They stake their lives and futures on what *they* can do at the expense of other people; they trust themselves. In contrast, the psalmist trusts God and God's promises.

Psalm 56 does not suggest that God suddenly or even eventually removes the conditions that cause the psalmist to be afraid. What it and the other prayers teach us is that human life is always lived under threat, in the midst of opposition, either from ourselves or from others or from some external circumstance. The good news, however, is that because God is for us (see v. 9), we can say with the psalmist, "I am not afraid" (vv. 4, 11). Long before Franklin D. Roosevelt said it, and in a far more profound sense, the psalmist knew that the only thing to fear is fear itself.

The psalmist's affirmation of a trust that moves the self from "afraid" to "not afraid" suggests that the opposite of faith is not so much doubt as it is fear. Jesus seemed to reinforce this conclusion when he said to Jairus in a moment of great distress, "Do not fear, only believe" (Mark 5:36 NRSV). Such a response is possible, according to Psalm 56, because we both are known by God (v. 8) and know that God is for us. Again, Jesus also encouraged his followers not to fear for the same reason: God knows, and God cares (see Luke 12:4-7; see also Reflections on Psalm 27).

The NT writers saw and heard in the life, death, and resurrection of Jesus the same good news proclaimed by Psalm 56. In considering that human life is always lived amid opposition—"the sufferings of this present time" (Rom 8:18 NRSV)—the apostle Paul affirmed, "If God is for us, who can be against us?" (Rom 8:31 NIV). To be sure, Paul was aware of and had experienced the things that human enemies can do (see Rom 8:35), but he was convinced that nothing could separate us from God (Rom 8:38-39). Such is the trust that enables us not to be afraid.

The final phrase of Psalm 56 cannot help reminding Christian readers of Jesus' words in John 8:12, "I am the light of the world. Whoever follows me will never walk in darkness but will have the light of life" (NRSV). Again, Jesus did not promise his followers a life free of threat (see John 15:18-25; 16:33; 17:14-15), but he did promise a peace greater than the world can give, a peace that means ultimately living unafraid (see John 14:27). This peace is the real subject of Psalm 56.

PSALM 57:1-11, BE EXALTED, O GOD, ABOVE THE HEAVENS

COMMENTARY

Like Psalm 56, Psalm 57 is a prayer for help or an individual complaint/lament, in which the element of trust is prominent. Immediately following the opening petition (v. 1*a*), the psalmist expresses trust in God (vv. 1*b*-3). The complaint is voiced in vv. 4 and 6, separated by the first occurrence of the refrain, which also concludes the psalm (vv. 5, 11). Verses 7-10 begin with a statement of loyalty (v. 7*ab*), continue with a promise to praise God (vv. 7*c*-9), and conclude with an expression of trust (v. 10) that features the

same attributes of God as in v. 3: steadfast love and faithfulness.

The superscription of Psalm 57 associates the prayer with a crisis in David's life (see 1 Sam 22:1; 24:3). As with other such superscriptions (see Psalms 3; 51; 56; Introduction), this one should be taken illustratively rather than historically. The actual circumstances of the origin and use of Psalm 57 are unknown. Relying primarily on v. 4, several scholars suggest that this psalm may originally have been the prayer of a falsely accused person who sought asylum in the Temple (see

v. 1; see also Psalms 5; 7; Introduction). Others detect evidence for the use of Psalm 57 in a night vigil (see v. 8; see also Psalm 17). Gerstenberger concludes more generally that Psalm 57 was probably "used in a communal situation such as synagogal worship for the suffering person."[227] As with other prayers, the very variety of proposals is indicative of the adaptability of Psalm 57 and its ability to function in a variety of settings.

57:1-3. Although the NRSV obscures it, this psalm begins with the same petition as does Psalm 56 (see also Pss 4:1; 6:2); even more quickly than Psalm 56, Psalm 57 moves to an expression of trust. Although the word "trust" (בטח *bāṭaḥ*) is not used, the repeated term "refuge" (חסה *ḥsh*) clearly communicates this concept (see Commentary on Psalm 2; see also 2:12; 7:1; Introduction). That is, the psalmist depends on God for life and future. The phrase "shadow of your wings" may be an allusion to the winged creatures who attended the ark, God's earthly throne, and who elsewhere announce a message similar to the refrain of Ps 57:5, 11 (see Isa 6:1-3). This may indicate an original temple setting, but it is also possible that the phrase is purely metaphorical (see Pss 17:8; 36:7; 63:7). At any rate, the psalmist trusts that his or her life is secure with God (v. 2; see also Ps 138:8, where the same affirmation occurs, as here, in the context of a celebration of God's steadfast love, faithfulness, glory, and saving power). God will "save" (v. 3; see Pss 3:7; 6:4; 7:1) the psalmist from the enemy (see Ps 56:1-2). The repetition of "send" in v. 3 suggests that God's saving action is a manifestation of God's essential character and purpose for humanity (see Exod 34:6-7; Introduction; "steadfast love" and "faithfulness" are also paired in v. 10; Pss 25:10; 40:10-11; 61:7; 85:10; 89:14; 115:1; 138:2). The psalmist affirms, in effect, that the love of God is the most powerful force in the universe. The enemies may attempt to enact their purposes, which include opposition to the psalmist, but God's purposes will prevail.

57:4-6. The actual complaint comes in vv. 4 and 6. It is not unusual that the enemies are described as ravenous beasts (v. 4; see Pss 7:2; 10:9; 17:12; 22:12-13, 16, 20-21; 34:10; 35:17; 58:6; 59:6-7, 14-15; 68:30;

227. Gerstenberger, *Psalms: Part 1*, 232.

91:13). The references to weapons reinforce their violent purposes (see Pss 11:2; 64:3; 91:5) in preparation for v. 6, where the enemies have "set a net" (see Pss 9:15; 10:9; 25:15; 140:5; cf. Lam 1:13) and have "dug a pit" (see Pss 7:15; 9:15; 119:85; Jer 18:22) in order that the psalmist be "bowed down" (see Pss 145:14; 146:8). Unexpectedly, the first occurrence of the refrain interrupts the complaint. The effect is to set the appeal to God, which at least implicitly is an affirmation of God's sovereignty (see the NIV's "exalt" in Exod 15:2; Pss 99:5, 9; 145:1 and "glory" in Pss 24:7-10; 29:1-3, 9; 96:3, 7; 97:6; 145:11, both of which occur in the context of the proclamation of God's reign), in the midst of a section that implies the sovereignty of the wicked. In short, as is always the case in the psalter and in Scripture as a whole, the sovereignty of God is asserted amid opposition. The proclamation is eschatological and calls for a decision (see Commentary on Psalm 2; Introduction).

57:7-11. The psalmist's decision is clear. In the midst of opposition, the psalmist takes a stand with God. As was the opening petition, so the psalmist's complaint is followed by an expression of trust (vv. 7-10), which lends the final occurrence of the refrain an added dimension (v. 11; vv. 7-11 occur in nearly identical form in Ps 108:1-5). The repetition in v. 7*ab* emphasizes the psalmist's loyalty to God; the decision is firm (cf. Ps 112:8, where the same idea is expressed with different words; cf. also Ps 78:37). Trust is accompanied by praise (v. 7*c*), to which the psalmist poetically summons his or her own self (v. 8*a*, lit., "my glory"; see "soul" in Pss 7:5; 16:9; 30:12 NRSV) as well as the instruments of praise (v. 8*b*; see also Ps 33:2). The phrase "awake the dawn" could suggest several things. It may express simply the psalmist's eagerness and intent to get an early start in praising God. Such eagerness may have been related to the belief that a new day promises God's help (see Pss 46:5; 59:16; 90:14; 143:8). It is also possible that v. 8*c* is an allusion to a beneficent Canaanite god "Dawn" (see Isa 14:12). In any case, one need not be able to state precisely what v. 8*c* means in order to appreciate its lyric quality. Like all good poetry, it evokes a variety of images and possibilities.

In any case, it is clear from v. 9 that the psalmist intends his or her praise to be heard not only by God but also by others, perhaps precisely by those who represented the threat described in vv. 3-4, 6. Recalling v. 3, v. 10 again asserts that God's loving purposes pervade the cosmos (see Ps 36:5), providing a fitting introduction to the refrain in v. 11. Coming immediately after the psalmist's expression of trust and intent to praise, the refrain serves this time to emphasize the psalmist's recognition of God's cosmic sovereignty (note that v. 11 represents the fourth occurrence of "heaven[s]"; see vv. 3, 5, 10). Opposition or no opposition, the psalmist already experiences the new world of God's rule. Such a conclusion renders moot the scholarly debate about whether Psalm 57 anticipates deliverance or celebrates a deliverance that has already occurred (see Commentary on Psalms 54; 56). In either case, the psalmist finds security by entrusting his or her life to God.

REFLECTIONS

Psalm 57 articulates the remarkable conviction that God's steadfast love and faithfulness are the pervasive, fundamental realities in the universe (vv. 3, 10; see Commentary on Psalms 19; 36). It would have been easy for the psalmist to conclude otherwise (vv. 1, 3*b*, 4, 6). Similarly, it would be easy for us to conclude otherwise as we look out upon a world full of hatred and hostility and that seems bent on destroying itself.

But this is precisely the reason why Psalm 57 is such a crucial contemporary witness. It is a reminder that the rule of God has always been experienced and proclaimed amid opposition. The clearest reminder of this reality for Christians, of course, is the cross of Jesus Christ. Not surprisingly, Jesus taught his disciples both to proclaim the reign of God—"thine is the kingdom"—and to continue to pray for its coming—"thy kingdom come." In short, just as the psalmist is *"one who simultaneously possesses and yet expects,"*[228] so also are the followers of Jesus.

Indeed, the simultaneity of possession and expectation creates the possibility for Christians to be realistic about the world without becoming totally pessimistic. Because we trust that God ultimately rules the world and that God's purposes for us will finally be fulfilled (vv. 2-3, 5, 10-11), we dare to perceive the mystery of love where others can see only the misery of life. Because we trust that love is the basic reality in the universe, we are able in the face of evil, sin, and death not just to sigh resignedly but to sing rousingly enough to wake the dawn.

228. Weiser, *The Psalms*, 428.

PSALM 58:1-11, THERE IS A GOD WHO ESTABLISHES JUSTICE

COMMENTARY

Like the two immediately preceding Psalms, Psalm 58 expresses the conviction that God ultimately rules the world and that God's purposes will prevail (see vv. 10-11). Although not entirely unique, Psalm 58 is unusual in that it begins by directly addressing the perpetrators of evil rather than God (vv. 1-2). Verse 3 shifts to a third-person description of the wicked that continues through v. 5. Verses 6-9 are a prayer for justice, and vv. 10-11 articulate the assurance that justice will be done. Because of its unusual structure, Psalm 58 has been categorized in diverse ways. In view of the complaint (vv. 3-5) and prayer (vv. 6-9), it is possible to view this psalm as a modified prayer for help or as an individual or communal lament/complaint. Some scholars suggest, however, that Psalm 58 should be seen as a prophetic judgment speech (see vv. 1-2), perhaps delivered by a cultic prophet and aimed at oppressing nations, or as communal instruction, which originated among disaffected elements in the post-exilic community and was directed at unjust community leaders. Certainty is impossible.

58:1-2. Certainty is also elusive in v. 1 in the attempt to identify precisely the apparent addressee. The meaning of the Hebrew word אֵלֶם (*'ēlem*) is uncertain. It may mean "silence" or "when you speak, justice is silent."[229] This translation leaves the identity of the addressee unsettled. Most translations emend the word slightly and construe it as a vocative. The identity of the addressee, though, is still unsettled, because the emendation involved can mean either "gods" or "mighty ones," including human beings. The NRSV and the NIV represent the two most frequently adopted solutions. The NIV's translation is probably to be preferred, since v. 3 clearly has human beings in view and since Psalm 52 also begins by addressing a wicked, powerful human being (the NRSV's "mighty one" in Ps 52:1 is a different Hebrew word [גִּבּוֹר *gibbôr*] that clearly designates a human being). If the NRSV's translation is correct, then Psalm 58 has a clearer affinity with Psalm 82, in which God accuses the gods of injustice.

In any case, the question in v. 1 has to do with whether righteousness and justice are being done. These concepts are frequently paired in the speeches of the prophets, who did not hesitate to call to account the leaders of their nation and of other nations as well (see Amos 5:7, 24; Mic 3:1, 8-9). The enthronement psalms indicate that righteousness and justice are the hallmarks of God's reign (see Pss 96:13; 98:9; the NRSV's "fairly" in v. 1 also occurs in Pss 96:10; 98:9, where it is rendered as "equity"), and Ps 58:1 suggests

that they should characterize human governance as well. But v. 2 indicates that they do not. Instead, there are "wrongs" (see Pss 7:3; 37:1; 43:1, "unjust"; 53:2, "abominable acts"; 82:2, "unjustly") and "violence" (see Pss 7:16; 11:5; 27:12; 55:9; 73:6; Jer 6:7; 20:8; Amos 3:10; 6:3; Mic 6:12). In short, the governance of the wicked (see vv. 3-5) is a reign of terror, the antithesis of the reign of God. Despite the reality of wickedness, the psalmist stakes his or her life and future on the reality of God's rule, the affirmation of which climactically concludes Psalm 58 (vv. 10-11; note the recurrence of the concepts of righteousness and justice in v. 11).

58:3-5. It is likely that the addressees in vv. 1-2 are human beings, and they are designated "wicked" in v. 3. Whereas persons who look to God for help are aware of God's presence "from birth" and "from the womb" (see Ps 22:10), the wicked have never known God, according to the psalmist. The hyperbole is intensified as the psalmist claims that the wicked are, in effect, born liars (see "lies" in Pss 4:2; 5:6). Verses 4-5 indicate that these persons' incorrigible behavior has destructive consequences (see Ps 140:3; Jer 8:17).

58:6-9. The hyperbolic intensity continues in these verses as the psalmist turns to God. Lest the prayer sound unnecessarily brutal, one must realize that the "teeth" (v. 6) of the wicked represent their weapons, the means by which they carry out their violence (v. 2) and destruction (see Pss 3:7; 57:4; 124:6). As in Ps 57:4 (although a different Hebrew word is used here), the enemies are portrayed as ravening lions. The prayer in v. 6 is not a request for personal revenge but a petition for protection. In effect, it is a prayer for the justice and righteousness that v. 1 has suggested are God's will, and this is confirmed by v. 11. There are problems with the vocabulary of vv. 7-9 (cf. v. 7*b* NIV and NRSV), but it is clear enough that the images in these verses communicate the heart of the matter; the psalmist prays for the disappearance of all that opposes God's will for human life. The request is indicative of the psalmist's loyalty to God and God's ways, and it is in keeping with Ps 1:4-6 and its affirmation that wickedness will not endure.

58:10-11. Indeed, the psalmist moves from the prayer of vv. 6-9 to precisely this

229. See Bratcher and Reyburn, *A Translator's Handbook on the Book of Psalms*, 516; the authors present seven major proposals for construing v. 1.

affirmation. The main characters are the same as in Ps 1:4-6: the righteous, the wicked, and God. Verses 10-11 must be heard in close relationship to vv. 1-2. Verse 10 affirms that the apparent sovereignty of the wicked (vv. 1-2) will be put to an end. Thus "violence on earth" (v. 2) will be replaced by the work of a God "who establishes justice on earth" (v. 11 author's trans.). As the repetition of "earth" suggests, the real issue is this: Who rules the world? For the wicked, they themselves are the only authority (see Pss 3:2; 10:4, 11; 73:11); but v. 11 asserts God's rule. The role of judging or establishing justice is elsewhere closely associated with God's reign (see Pss 9:7-8; 11:4-7; 96:13; 98:9). The imagery of v. 10b is harsh, but it is a typical ancient Near Eastern symbol for defeat of oppressors (see Deut 32:42-43; Ps 68:23), and it is an apt reminder that oppressors do not simply give up without a fight. The establishment of justice for the oppressed means the experience of judgment for the oppressors—the wicked. As suggested above concerning v. 6, the issue is not personal revenge. As Mays points out: "The notion of 'vengeance' (v. 10) is a feature of the vision of God as ruler. The term does not mean vindictive revenge; it refers to an action to do justice and restore order where the regular and responsible institutions of justice have failed."[230]

It is revealing, too, that the righteous do not carry out the vengeance but are witnesses to it. Vengeance belongs to God (see Deut 32:35; Ps 94:1), not to humans (see Lev 19:18). The word "reward" (פרי *pĕrî*, v. 11) is literally "fruit"; thus living in dependence upon God will ultimately bear fruit (see Ps 1:3). As Mays suggests, the reward of the righteous is "not some sort of earned payoff, but the knowledge of the vindication of God's reign in spite of the power and arrogance of injustice."[231]

230. Mays, *Psalms*, 212.
231. Mays, *Psalms*, 212.

REFLECTIONS

1. As is the case throughout the book of Psalms and throughout the Bible, the proclamation of God's reign is eschatological; it is proclaimed amid circumstances that seem to deny it—the power of the wicked (vv. 1-2; see Commentary on Psalm 2; Introduction). It was no different for Jesus. The "reward" for his proclamation of God's reign was a cross, and he promised his followers the same (see Mark 8:34). Yet, Jesus taught that to live in dependence upon God, which is the essence of being righteous (see Commentary on Psalm 1), is the fullest possible experience of life (see Mark 8:35). In short, the reward of the righteous is living, in dependence upon God, the life that God intends. To assert that "there is a God who establishes justice on earth" (v. 11 author's trans.) is to profess, in essence, that right makes might. To be sure, worldly wisdom is just the opposite—might makes right. But the righteous know with the apostle Paul that "God's weakness is stronger than human strength" (1 Cor 1:25 NRSV). So the righteous dare to assert in the face of the powers of evil (vv. 1-2) that God rules the world (vv. 10-11).

What the righteous assert, they also pray for, and Jesus taught his disciples to pray in the same way. Although it may sound offensive at first hearing, the prayer for justice in vv. 6-9 is, in essence, what Christians pray in the Lord's prayer: "thy will be done on earth as it is in heaven . . . deliver us from evil." Verses 6-9 are likely to sound less offensive when one realizes that the psalmist does not enact revenge but submits the complaint to God for action.

2. Other dimensions of vv. 6-9 are also quite positive. As Tate points out: "The imprecatory elements in the psalms are also evocative, challenging the reader to identify with oppressed and suffering people, even though the reader may be quite comfortable. . . . The language of these psalms evokes in us an awareness of the terrible wickedness that is in the world."[232] In other words, Psalm 58 can serve to remind us

232. Tate, *Psalms 51–100*, 89.

that our world is every bit as violent and unjust as that of ancient Israel. It may also serve to remind us that we bear some responsibility for the state of the world. Or, as Tate puts it: "The imprecatory psalms are likely to convict us of our own guilt. When we ask for divine judgment on our enemies, we are liable to an identity switch: We are often the enemies!"[233] Especially if wickedness in the psalms is understood essentially as self-centeredness and self-sufficiency (see Commentary on Psalm 1), we are all in danger of standing among the wicked.

Psalm 58 may be particularly relevant in view of Kraus's comment: "The psalm-singer suffers under a corrupt world order."[234] So do we; in some cases, perhaps, we must admit that we are the beneficiaries of a corrupt world order. In either case, the conviction that God will ultimately establish justice on earth is of greatest consequence. It calls us simultaneously to both joy and repentance, as did Jesus (see Mark 1:14-15).

233. Tate, *Psalms 51–100*, 90.
234. Kraus, *Psalms 1–59*, 537.

PSALM 59:1-17, THE GOD WHO SHOWS ME STEADFAST LOVE

COMMENTARY

Psalm 59 contains the typical elements of a prayer for help or lament/complaint. Scholars have long commented on the unusual structure of Psalm 59, but, in fact, the prayers for help show a variety of arrangements of the typical elements; and the arrangement of elements in Psalm 59 is actually quite symmetrical. In the two main sections (vv. 1-10, 11-17), initial petition and complaint (vv. 1-5, 11-13) are followed by an additional complaint, introduced by a refrain (vv. 6-7, 14-15). Both sections conclude with an expression of assurance (vv. 8-10, 16-17), in which vv. 9 and 17a are nearly identical and also feature the concept of steadfast love. In a sense, this repetitive structure, including refrains, reinforces the content of the first refrain—that is, the structural elements of the poem "return" (vv. 6, 14) just as the psalmist's enemies "return" every evening. Thus the persistence of the threat is emphasized, as is the psalmist's perseverance in living in dependence upon God's steadfast love in the midst of distress.

The precise circumstances of the poem's origin and ancient use are unrecoverable. The superscription associates the psalm with Saul's threats against David (see 1 Sam 19:11), but as with similar superscriptions (see Psalms 3;

51; 54; 56; 57; Introduction), this one should be taken illustratively rather than historically. Several scholars suggest that Psalm 59 could have been the prayer of a falsely accused person (see vv. 1-4a) who fled to the Temple for asylum (see vv. 9-10, 16-17), especially since it contains a brief protestation of innocence (vv. 3b-4a; see Psalms 5; 7; Introduction). There is evidence, too, that this psalm may have been edited for use—or at least could have been appropriately used in its final form—as a prayer of the oppressed post-exilic community (see vv. 5, 8, 13). Gerstenberger says of v. 13, "The passage reflects, in my opinion, the transition of personal complaint into the worship situation of the early Jewish community."[235] As with other prayers in the psalter, the variety of proposals for understanding the origin and setting of Psalm 59 is testimony to the open-endedness of its language and imagery, as well as to its adaptability to a variety of settings, including contemporary ones (see Reflections below).

59:1-3. The psalm begins with a fourfold petition (vv. 1-2), emphatic by virtue of the repetition of "deliver" in vv. 1a and 2a and by the chiastic structure (see Introduction) of each verse. In Hebrew the verbs are the first

235. Gerstenberger, *Psalms: Part 1*, 238.

and last words of each verse; that is, the poetic structure suggests that the psalmist's defense is to surround the enemies, who are given four different names (see "rise up"/"rising" in Ps 3:1; "bloodthirsty" in Ps 26:9; and "evil" again in v. 5), with pleas to God. This is particularly appropriate, since the enemies "surround" the city ("prowling" in vv. 6, 14 is more literally "surrounding"). The petition "protect" in v. 1*b* is from the same Hebrew root as "fortress" in vv. 9, 17. Thus the opening verse anticipates the climactic expressions of assurance. The plea for God to save is a frequent one (see Ps 3:7).

Verses 1-2 have implied the psalmist's complaint, which is explicit in vv. 3-4*a*. The enemies "lie in wait" (see Ps 10:9) and "stir up strife" (see Ps 56:6). This time the enemies are called "the mighty," which also anticipates the climactic expressions of assurance. The word "mighty" is from the same root as "might" (v. 16) and "strength" (vv. 9, 17). These latter occurrences give the designation in v. 3 a sarcastic ring. The enemies may appear mighty, but the psalmist takes a stand upon and celebrates God's might (see discussion of v. 9 below). Lest there be any question that the psalmist's misfortune is deserved, he or she emphatically affirms innocence by employing the three major Hebrew words for sin (see Commentary on Psalms 32; 51; the word rendered "fault" [עוֹן *'āwōn*] is usually translated "iniquity" or "guilt"). The word "sin" is repeated in v. 12; the blame for the psalmist's distress lies with the enemies.

59:4b-5b. Just as the psalmist surrounded the enemies with pleas in vv. 1-2, so also now he or she surrounds God (v. 5*a*) with petitions in v. 4*b* and v. 5*b*. The urgency is suggested by the initial petitions in v. 4*b* (see Pss 7:6; 35:23; 44:23) and v. 5*b* (see Pss 35:23; 44:23) that suggest God is asleep. If God will "see" (v. 4*b*), God will eventually also "cause me to *see* those watching me" (v. 10*b* author's trans.). In a sense, then, God's seeing will lead to a divine appearance for which the psalmist watches (v. 9*a*) and a revelation that exposes those who have had their evil eyes on the psalmist (v. 10*b*). In short, God's *seeing* will put all other seeing and watching in proper perspective. As suggested above, the focal point of vv. 4*b*-5 is v. 5*a*, where the pronoun "You" is emphatic and is followed

by three additional designations: God's personal name (Yahweh); God's military name ("God of hosts" or "God of the armies" [אלהים צבאות *'ĕlōhîm ṣĕbā'ôt*], which is apt for this conflict situation; see Commentary on Ps 24:7-10); and a relational phrase ("God of Israel" [אלהי ישראל *'ĕlōhê yiśrā'ēl*]). The latter prepares for the mention of "the nations" in the next line (see also v. 8) and gives the psalm a corporate dimension. The final petition, "show no mercy," stands out by virtue of its position and its negative form. It is the opposite of the frequent petition the psalmists make on their own behalf: "be gracious"/"be merciful"/"have mercy" (see Pss 4:1; 56:1; 57:1).

59:6-7. The refrain in v. 6 portrays the enemies as aggressive dogs (cf. 1 Kgs 14:11; 16:4; Ps 22:16, 20; Isa 56:11; Jer 5:3), who surround the city (see Ps 55:9-10 NRSV, where personified "violence" and "strife" "go around," literally surround, the city). They "spew" (v. 7; see Ps 94:4) threatening words that are metaphorically described as "swords" (see Ps 57:4). Their question in v. 7*c* demonstrates their arrogance. Accountable to no one but themselves, the enemies display the essence of wickedness—autonomy, or literally, "a law unto oneself" (see Commentary on Psalm 1; see also the questions or conclusions of the wicked in Pss 10:4, 6, 11; 14:1; 35:25; 42:3, 10; 73:11).

59:8-10. But God hears! And God responds. Both of the verbs in v. 8 occur also in Psalm 2:4, which is fundamentally an assertion of God's sovereignty over rebellious peoples and nations (see Commentary on Psalm 2). In the face of the self-assertion of the enemies, the psalmist emphatically proclaims God's rule (the "you" that begins v. 8 is emphatic). The psalmist's trust in God's reign is expressed too by the vocative "O my strength," since "strength" elsewhere is closely associated with God's sovereignty (see Exod 15:2, 13; Pss 29:1, 11; 93:1; 96:6-7). Because God—not the enemies—rules the world, the psalmist looks to God for protection (see above on v. 1). The noun translated "fortress" (משגב *miśgāb*) in v. 9 occurs twice in Ps 9:9 ("stronghold") in the context of the assertion of God's rule (see Ps 9:7). God's reign—indeed, God's very being—is characterized by steadfast love (see Exod 34:6-7;

Pss 5:7; 13:5; 98:3; Introduction). Verse 10*c* suggests that God's loving purposes will ultimately prevail over the hateful devices of the enemies (see Ps 54:7*b*). The phrase "in triumph" is not in the Hebrew, and perhaps suggests too much an element of personal revenge, as does the NIV's interpretive translation "gloat." The real point is that God will set things right for God's people (see Commentary on Ps 58:6-9).

59:11-17. To be sure, the petitions in vv. 11-13 also seem to contain an element of vindictiveness, especially v. 11, which seems to suggest something like, "Let them twist in the wind awhile before cutting them down." But even this request seems to be motivated by the psalmist's desire to have the destiny of the wicked be a reminder of God's sovereignty, and v. 13 states this desire even more explicitly. The disappearance of the wicked will be testimony to God's rule (see Pss 22:27-28; 67:7; 98:3). As in the preceding verses, the psalmist celebrates God's protecting power (v. 11; see Ps 3:3). The occurrence of "mouths" and "lips" in v. 12 recalls v. 7, which portrayed the destructive speech of the

wicked and their self-assertion. Both themes are elaborated upon in v. 12 with the mention of the pride of the wicked, which is especially manifested in their speech (see Ps 10:7).

Verse 14 is identical to v. 6. Whereas v. 6 was followed by a verse depicting the arrogance of the wicked, v. 14 introduces a verse that portrays the persistence of the wicked. The Hebrew root of "growl" (לין *lîn*) can also mean "lodge," "spend the night." In short, the wicked do not go away. Nevertheless, the psalmist lives under God's reign and, in the face of opposition, celebrates God's strength (v. 16; see also vv. 9, 17; cf. v. 3) and steadfast love (v. 16; see also vv. 10, 17) and protection (see also vv. 1, 9, 16-17; the Hebrew word translated "refuge" [מנוס *mānôs*] also occurs in Pss 18:2; 142:4). It is possible that morning was generally viewed as a time for receiving help or offering praise (v. 16; see Pss 46:5; 57:8; 90:14; 143:8). It is appropriate that the final word of the psalm is "steadfast love" (חסד *ḥesed*), for the psalmist stakes life and future on the divine sovereignty that is perfected in love.

REFLECTIONS

1. Several young people have told me that their attempts to live out their faith at school have resulted, in effect, in their being alienated from and verbally attacked by their classmates. The causes may seem small—befriending a person others have deemed unpopular or refusing to wear trendy clothes. We are likely to dismiss all of this as normal teenage "peer pressure." But the young people I have talked to were trying seriously to represent God's claim on their lives and their priorities—to live under God's rule. It is precisely this same kind of peer pressure that perpetuates the consumeristic, narcissistic culture that we live in, a culture that regularly encourages us to "look out for number one" and do whatever it takes, or at least whatever we can get away with, to succeed. What we end up with, to borrow the imagery of Psalm 59, is a dog-eat-dog world, a culture of cut-throat competition in which we're convinced that no one will look out for us if we don't look out for ourselves.

This is what we ordinarily call "the real world," and its philosophy is really not much different from that espoused by the psalmist's enemies in Psalm 59—do anything to get ahead. One commentator has described Ps 59:6-7 as "a picture of disgusting, self-seeking, and hateful activity."[236] Unfortunately, this description applies to much of what passes in our society for good business or the necessities of politics or perhaps peer pressure. In other words, the portrayal of the enemies in Psalm 59 puts us in touch with the way things still are among us. It reminds us of the evil in ourselves and in our society—the so-called real world (see Commentary on Psalm 58).

236. F. Nötscher, quoted in Kraus, *Psalms 1–59*, 541.

2. But Psalm 59 also reminds us of a deeper reality, an alternative world, which is driven not by the lust for power but by the power of love. This world is the world of God's reign, and Psalm 59 proclaims it as the authentic "real world." So did Jesus as he invited people to enter the reign of God (Mark 1:14-15). To be sure, the proclamation and embodiment of the reign of God do not make wickedness suddenly go away. Psalm 59—along with the cross of Jesus Christ—reminds us of the persistence of evil in self and society, but it also reminds us that we can confront that evil as transformed people.

In short, Psalm 59, like Psalms 2 and 56–58 and the whole psalter (see Introduction), is eschatological. It affirms the reign of God amid circumstances that seem to deny it; thus it calls us to decision, as Jesus did. Confronted by "the mighty" (v. 3) of the so-called real world, we profess to find true strength in God. Faced by the seemingly overwhelming forces of evil, we profess to be met by a God who comes to us in love. Tempted by a dog-eat-dog world to join those who live only for themselves and by their own resources, we profess to find a "fortress" in God, and we yield our lives to God in grateful praise (vv. 16-17).

PSALM 60:1-12, HUMAN HELP IS WORTHLESS

COMMENTARY

Marvin Tate states at the beginning of his comments on Psalm 60: "This psalm is plagued with difficulties, and all interpretation is tentative."[237] Most scholars agree, however, that Psalm 60 is a communal lament/complaint. While it does not display the typical structure of such prayers, its structure is relatively clear. Verses 1-5 contain complaint accompanied by petition, the final one of which is "answer us" (v. 5). Quite logically, vv. 6-8 offer an answer in the form of a divine address; however, the content of the answer—God owns all the peoples and nations—is problematic in view of the crisis described in vv. 1-5. Thus v. 9, which some scholars include with vv. 6-8 and others with vv. 10-12, raises a question that seems to suggest that Edom is particularly responsible for the crisis. In the light of vv. 6-8, the only possible answer to the questions in v. 9 is "God." But, as vv. 1-3 have made clear, God is the problem. Thus the final section of the poem renews the complaint (v. 10; see "rejected" in v. 1) and petition (v. 11; the NRSV's "help" [תשועה *těšûʿâ*] in v. 11*b* is the same Hebrew root as in the opening petition of v. 5*a*); the psalm concludes with an affirmation of faith that recalls vv. 6-8.

The inclusion of so many geographical terms, including the singling out of Edom, has proved particularly tantalizingly to scholars. That is to say, it seems that Psalm 60 could be dated fairly accurately, but such has not been the case. Taking the superscription seriously, and noting that vv. 6-8 describe roughly the core of David's empire, many scholars have dated the psalm to David's time. The editors responsible for the superscription apparently had 2 Samuel 8 in mind (see esp. 2 Sam 8:13-14), although all the details do not correspond (see 1 Chr 18:12-13). Other scholars have dated Psalm 60 as late as the Maccabean revolt, 800 years later than the previous proposal. Then, too, a strong case can be made for an early post-exilic date. G. S. Ogden, for instance, notes the verbal links between Psalm 60 and Isa 63:1-6 (cf. v. 9 with Isa 63:1; v. 11 with Isa 63:5; v. 12 with Isa 63:6); Ogden concludes that the two texts "belong in the same fundamental historical and liturgical context." More specifically, he comments that "Isa. 63:1-6 is a prophetic response to the lament ceremony in which Ps. 60 was sung to seek God's vengeance upon a treacherous neighbor."[238] But even if

237. Tate, *Psalms 51–100*, 103.

238. G. S. Ogden, "Psalm 60: Its Rhetoric, Form, and Function," *JSOT* 31 (1985) 93.

Ogden is correct, it is possible that Psalm 60 could have originated much earlier, in which case it would have been deemed particularly relevant to the early post-exilic generation. In short, certainty is impossible, and, as with other prayers, the very variety of proposals is testimony to the flexibility and adaptability of the prayer. Further evidence in this regard is the fact that vv. 5-12 are essentially the same as Ps 108:6-13.

60:1-3. These verses make it clear that the people perceive their misfortune to be a result of God's anger (see Ps 79:5). God has "rejected us," a frequent theme in the communal complaints (see v. 10 and Pss 44:9, 23; 74:1; 77:7; 89:38 NIV). It implies God's judgment, as does the second verb in v. 1a (see "Broke[n] out" in Ps 106:29; 2 Sam 6:8 NIV). Ogden suggests that the petition at the end of v. 1 be rendered "return to us," thus appropriately implying God's absence (see v. 10).[239] Verse 2 uses the imagery of an earthquake, perhaps to suggest the magnitude of the crisis as well as the extent of destruction. The verbs that the NRSV translates "quake" (רעש *rā'aš*) and "tottering" (מוט *môṭ*) also occur in Ps 46:2-3 to portray a cosmic crisis. In Psalm 46, God offers protection during the crisis, but here God causes the crisis. All the people can do is plead for help, and like v. 1, v. 2 ends with a petition (lit., "heal"; see Deut 32:39; Jer 30:17). The noun "hard things" (v. 3) recalls enslavement in Egypt (see Exod 1:14; 6:9; Deut 26:6); that is, God has reversed the exodus and is acting as taskmaster over the people. The cup God offers is not for refreshment (see Ps 75:8; Jer 23:9; 25:15-16; Zech 12:2).

60:4-5. Verse 4a is problematic, since it seems to say, in apparent contradiction to vv. 1-3 and 5, that God has already offered divine help. Thus several scholars construe v. 4a as a petition, and this may be the best solution. As the NRSV note suggests, there are difficulties with v. 4b as well. Verse 5 clearly returns to petition. The first petition is translated more accurately by the NIV. When the plea "save" is heard in conjunction with "right hand," it calls to mind the exodus (see "save" in Exod 14:30; "right hand" in Exod 15:6, 12). A new exodus is needed. Both the NIV and the NRSV reverse the order of the two parts of

v. 5. In Hebrew, the final word is the imperative "answer" (ענה *'ānâ*), which sets the stage for vv. 6-8.

60:6-8. The NIV more literally translates v. 6a with "God has spoken," but the NRSV's more interpretative translation captures the tone of the divine speech. Gerstenberger describes vv. 6-8 as "a homiletical device," or in effect, a brief sermon (see Ps 50:7-23).[240] The good news is that all peoples and lands belong to God. It is the prerogative of an owner or a victor to divide up the land (v. 6; see Exod 15:9; Josh 19:51). The names listed in vv. 6-7 are clearly Israelite places. Ephraim and Judah, designations for the northern and southern kingdoms, are paired and are assigned similar metaphors (see Gen 49:10, where the scepter is also associated with Judah). Traditional enemies are cited in v. 8. The metaphors in v. 8ab are not as transparent. They may be intended as insults, but perhaps the intention is simply to say that Moab is owned by God, like a personal possession, and that Edom has been acquired by transaction (see Ruth 4:7, where sandals were exchanged to confirm transactions). The word translated "shout in triumph" (רוע *rûa'*) can designate a signal to prepare for battle or the victor's joyful cry (see Jer 50:15). In short, God controls Philistia as well. In view of the above-mentioned recollections of the exodus, it is significant that the three places mentioned in v. 8 also are named in Exod 15:14-15. Their defeat by God (Exod 15:16) led to the people's possession of the land (Exod 15:17), all of which is a sign of God's reign (Exod 15:18). In the midst of a crisis that calls for a new exodus, vv. 6-8 effectively proclaim just that. As in the other prayers for help, individual and communal, the proclamation is eschatological. God's sovereignty is asserted amid circumstances that seem to deny it (note that vv. 6-8 are surrounded by complaint and petition in vv. 1-5, 10-12).

60:9-12. Verse 9 is another of the difficulties of Psalm 60. By singling out Edom from among the enemies listed in v. 8, however, the psalmist seems to indicate that Edom is heavily involved in the crisis described in vv. 1-3 and that God needs to lead someone to Edom to take corrective action. The problem with this, however, is that the real cause of

---

239. Ogden, "Psalm 60," 85.

240. Gerstenberger, *Psalms: Part 1*, 240.

the crisis described in vv. 1-3 is God! So v. 10a returns to the complaint of v. 1. The pronoun "you" is emphatic; God is the real problem. Like the concluding petition of v. 1, v. 10b suggests God's absence. It will do no good for anyone to go anywhere if God does not accompany the forces (see Num 14:42-45; Judg 4:14-15, which articulate this aspect of the theology of holy war). All that is left is for the people to ask for God's "help" (v. 11a; see this Hebrew root for "help" [עזר 'zr] in Pss 22:19; 38:22), while denying the utility of all

human "help" (see Ps 146:3), or as the word is often translated elsewhere, "salvation" (see Ps 40:10; Isa 45:17; 46:13). Despite current appearances, the people continue to trust God and to entrust their lives and future to God. With God's help, they will "do valiantly" (v. 12a; see Num 24:18; Ps 118:15-16). The God who rejected them will also be the God who finally deals with their oppressors (see Ps 44:5; Isa 63:6). The God who wounded will be the God who heals (see Deut 32:39 and discussion above on v. 2).

REFLECTIONS

At first sight, a psalm so closely tied to ancient military conflict and Israel's theology of holy war (v. 10) might seem to offer our contemporary era nothing edifying "for instruction" (see superscription). In fact, it might seem to reinforce in a dangerous way the all too pervasive temptation to equate national policy with God's will and to claim God as our ally in every cause. But a close reading of Psalm 60 subverts this possible approach. In fact, as Kraus points out, Psalm 60 is the prayer of a congregation that "trusts the sole efficacy of its God."[241] It is precisely this recognition of the inadequacy of human initiative and help that undercuts any temptation toward military triumphalism in the name of God (see Reflections on Psalm 20).

To put it somewhat differently, we must take seriously that Psalm 60 is the prayer of suffering and oppressed persons (see v. 3). Their prayer is not that of the powerful, who seek to claim God's sanction to enforce the status quo. Rather, their prayer is the desperate plea of those who turn to God as the only possible hope in an apparently hopeless situation (v. 11). As Tate puts it, "the psalm is a stark reminder that the limits of human power are easily reached and that salvation is God's work."[242] In other words, the assertion of God's sovereignty (vv. 6-8, 12) relativizes all human claims to sovereignty.

The proclamation of the good news in Psalm 60 is eschatological, as it is throughout the psalter and throughout the Bible (see Psalms 2; 56–59; Introduction). As we proclaim God's reign, God's defeat of oppression and oppressors (vv. 6-8, 12), we also pray for it and await it (vv. 1-5, 10-11). In an era in which political, social, ethnic, economic, and religious conflicts desperately threaten the security of people's lives and the well-being of the world, our hope is not that we can somehow manage to pull things together; instead, our only real hope is in the reality of a God who lovingly claims all peoples and nations (see vv. 5, 6-8) and who cares for the future of the whole world, beginning with the suffering and the oppressed.

241. H.-J. Kraus, *Psalms 60–150: A Commentary*, trans. H. C. Oswald (Minneapolis: Augsburg, 1989) 6.
242. Tate, *Psalms 51–100*, 108.

PSALM 61:1-8, THE ROCK HIGHER THAN I

COMMENTARY

Psalm 61 is usually classified as a prayer for help or an individual lament/complaint. Typical elements are present: petition (vv. 1, 2c, 4, 6-7), followed in each case by an affirmation of trust (vv. 3, 5) or promise to praise (v. 8), as well as a brief complaint (v. 2ab). Some scholars suggest on the basis of vv. 5 and 8 that the psalmist's prayer has already been answered, but this is not clear. Finally, however, this matter is not crucial. The pervasiveness of petition suggests that the psalmist will live constantly under some kind of threat, yet the affirmations in vv. 3 and 5 (see also "rock" in v. 2 and "refuge" in v. 4) indicate that the psalmist already experiences God as a present and enduring source of security (see Commentary on Psalms 54; 56; 57).

The circumstances of the origin and ancient use of Psalm 61 are unclear. Taking v. 2 literally, some suggest that the psalmist prayed in exile. On the basis of vv. 2c-5, others propose that the psalmist seeks asylum in the Temple from persecution of some sort (see Psalms 5; 7; Introduction). Noteworthy, too, is the prayer for the king in vv. 6-7 (see Pss 28:8; 63:11; 84:9). Do these verses indicate that the original speaker was the king? Or is the psalmist, having prayed for self (vv. 1, 2c, 4), now praying for the king? Verses 6-7 seem to indicate a pre-exilic origin for Psalm 61. If this is true, the psalm would almost certainly have been used in the post-exilic era as a communal prayer for help, in which case the prayer for the king would have been understood messianically or perhaps symbolically as a prayer for the future of the whole people. In any case, the reference to the king has presumably not prevented Psalm 61 from serving as a prayer for help or an expression of trust for generations of God's people over the centuries.

61:1-3. The opening petitions are commonly used in Psalms (see 5:2; 17:1; 86:6). Verse 2a need not be understood geographically. It is just as likely that it suggests metaphorically a situation of extremity, a conclusion reinforced by v. 2b (see "faint" in the superscription of Psalm 102 and Pss 77:3;

107:5; 142:3; 143:4 NRSV). The source of the problem is not clear, although faintness elsewhere is caused by hunger and thirst and persecution by enemies (see v. 3). In any case, the psalmist needs help and knows that her or his own resources are not sufficient (see Ps 60:11). As the petition and accompanying affirmation suggest (vv. 2c-3), God is the only source of help. The psalmist prays to be led (see Ps 23:3). God, or perhaps God's Temple, is the "rock" (צור *ṣûr*; see Pss 27:5; 31:2) that is "higher than I" (ירום ממני *yārûm mimmennî*; see Pss 113:4; 138:6; Isa 57:15). God is also a "refuge" (מחסה *maḥseh*; see Pss 2:12; 5:11; 14:6; 46:1; 62:7-8; Introduction) and a "strong tower" (מגדל-עז *migdal-'ōz*; see Prov 18:10). These three concepts— rock, refuge, strength—also occur together in Ps 62:7b ("my mighty rock" is literally "rock of my strength").

61:4-5. The request in v. 4a apparently involves entrance into the Temple (see Ps 15:1a), although the imagery can certainly be taken as a symbol of God's presence. Indeed, it is possible that the author intended it to be metaphorical. The same can be said of v. 4b, which repeats "refuge" from v. 3 and which may allude to the winged creatures associated with the ark (see Pss 17:8; 57:1; 63:7). Verse 5 is sometimes cited as evidence of God's removal of the distress articulated in v. 2. To be sure, the psalmist's vow or promise has been heard (see Pss 22:25; 50:14; 56:12; 65:1; 66:13; 116:14, 18), and the psalmist has been given "the heritage of those who fear your name." But exactly what this means is unclear. The root of the noun "heritage" (ירש *yāraš*) almost always designates possession of land, but this too may be heard symbolically. To possess the land meant to have the resources necessary to sustain life, and v. 5b would then affirm the psalmist's conviction that God has given him or her life (see Commentary on Psalm 37, esp. the discussion on vv. 9, 11, 22, 29, 34). Thus v. 5b may serve as the basis for the petitions in Psalm 61, not necessarily as an indication that the distress is past.

61:6-8. As suggested above, it is not clear whether vv. 6-7 indicate that Psalm 61 was originally the king's prayer. In any case, vv. 6-7a are similar to Ps 72:15, 17 (see also Pss 21:4; 89:29, 36-37), and v. 7b recalls other royal psalms. Psalm 89, for instance, features God's steadfast love and faithfulness, which are specifically said to accompany the king (see vv. 24, 33; see also Ps 21:7). In short, the king depends on God for life and future just as all people do, which is fitting, since the king was the symbolic representative of the whole people. In fact, vv. 6-7 may well have been understood in the post-exilic era as a prayer for the whole people of God, especially since it appears that the promises attached to the Davidic dynasty were transferred to the people as a whole (see Isa 55:1-3; cf. Ps 72:10-11, 15-17; see also Ps 105:15; Introduction). Verse 8 recalls v. 5 by way of repeating the words "vows" and "name." The phrase "day after day" also recalls v. 6 (lit., "Days upon days of the king may you increase"), and the repetition of "day(s)" may form an envelope structure for the final section. The repetition suggests at least that the continuing life of the king/people/psalmist will be lived joyfully and faithfully. In the final analysis, then, Psalm 61 invites readers of every generation to the faith and joy that derives from the conviction that life is sustained and secured by God's loving and faithful presence.

REFLECTIONS

1. Like the other prayers for help, Psalm 61 juxtaposes petition and trust in a manner that suggests they are simultaneous rather than sequential. The effect is to convey a perspective that is eschatological; the psalmist proclaims and entrusts the self to God's sovereign providence in the midst of circumstances that seem to deny God's sovereignty. Such a perspective always calls for decision, and the psalmist's decision is clear. He or she both possesses (vv. 5, 8) and simultaneously awaits (vv. 1-4) the aid of God (see Commentary on Psalms 54; 56; 57; 58; 59). This dynamic also characterized the preaching of Jesus, who taught that the kingdom of God was both to be entered immediately and to be yet awaited. In other words, Christians are simultaneously both people of the cross and people of the resurrection (see Commentary on Psalms 13; 22).

2. The distinctiveness of Psalm 61 may well lie, as Tate suggests, "in its metaphorical richness," the value of which is to "assist us to incorporate our own experience into the experience of prayer."[243] The "rock . . . higher than I" is a particularly striking and evocative image. The Hebrew root of the word "higher" is used in conjunction with God's sovereignty in Pss 99:2 and 145:1; thus the metaphor may be particularly pertinent in a culture that encourages one to make human potential and human achievement the highest measure of security. In short, it is especially important that this metaphor put us in touch with a presence and a power beyond ourselves and that it invite us and assist us to experience a source of security beyond our own achievement and potential. That source is God, to be sure, but it is also significant that the psalmist looks to God's sanctuary where the whole people gathered for worship. Bellinger concludes that Psalm 61 serves to "press us toward the *community at worship as the context for searching out genuine hope of protection.*"[244] In short, Psalm 61 encourages faith in God rather than in self, a reality that will be experienced communally and not in isolation.

This encouragement is not just a challenge to a thoroughly secular and individualistic society; it is also good news. One of the great ironies of our time is that its remarkable demonstration of human potential and achievement has left the human race anxious and on the brink of despair. But perhaps this is a perennial human condition, as

---

243. Tate, *Psalms 51–100,* 116.
244. W. H. Bellinger, Jr., *A Hermeneutic of Curiosity and Readings of Psalm 61,* Studies in OT Interpretation 1 (Macon, Ga.: Mercer University Press, 1995) 114.

Dahood suggests on the basis of v. 2: "The psalmist is here describing the human condition in existentialist terms: man constantly stands at the edge of the abyss, and only divine assistance can prevent his falling into it."[245] If this be the case, then the good news of Psalm 61 is for all seasons: We are not alone, for there is a presence and a power higher than we, which is ultimately made known to us as love and faithfulness. If we can manage to trust this good news, we shall undoubtedly join the psalmist and "always sing praises" to God's name (v. 8).

245. Mitchell Dahood, *Psalms II (51–100)*, AB 17 (Garden City, N.Y.: Doubleday, 1968) 84. Dahood translates the beginning of v. 3 as: "From the brink of the nether world."

PSALM 62:1-12, TRUST IN GOD AT ALL TIMES

COMMENTARY

Psalm 62 makes an excellent companion to Psalm 61 (see discussion above on the repetition of "rock," "refuge," and "strong" from Ps 61:2-3 in Ps 62:7 *b*, plus note "steadfast love" in 61:7 and 62:12), and it also anticipates the content and tone of Psalm 63 (see "power" in 62:11 and 63:2; "steadfast love" in 62:12 and 63:3; and "soul" in 62:1, 5 and 63:1, 5, 8). Indeed, Kraus notes "a certain interrelation of these three psalms."[246] Whether intended or coincidental, Psalms 61–63 form a sort of trilogy of trust with Psalm 62 at the center. In fact, Psalm 62 is most frequently categorized as a song of confidence or trust. The direct address of the enemies in v. 3 and the description of them in v. 4 suggest circumstances similar to those underlying the prayers for help (see also Pss 6:8-9; 52:1-5; 55:12-14). Some scholars suggest that the psalmist was sick (see Psalms 6; 38; Introduction); some suggest that the psalmist was persecuted and had fled to the Temple for asylum (see Psalms 5; 7; 61); and some even classify the psalm as a prayer for help. But God is not directly addressed until v. 12, and even here there is not a petition but an expression of trust. The whole psalm has the character of a profession of faith with an explicitly instructional intent (vv. 8-10).

The most striking structural feature of Psalm 62 is the similarity of vv. 1 and 5 and the nearly exact equivalence of vv. 2 and 6. Taking this repetition as a structural clue,

one may divide the psalm into three sections: (1) vv. 1-4, expression of trust followed by address to and description of the enemies, (2) vv. 5-10, expression of trust followed by address to the "people," and (3) vv. 11-12, the basis for trust and concluding prayer. Some scholars suggest two main sections: (1) vv. 1-7 and (2) vv. 8-12. Either proposal can be justified; in fact, the structure may move at more than one level. For instance, without necessarily contradicting the previous proposals, it is possible to view v. 7 as the center and turning point. It is at or very near the structural center of the poem, preceded and followed by eight lines. Two key words in v. 7 have already occurred in vv. 1-6 (see "salvation" in vv. 1, 2, 6 and "rock" in vv. 2, 6 NIV), and neither occurs again after v. 7. Verse 7 also anticipates vv. 8-12. Two key words in v. 7 recur in vv. 8-12 (see "refuge" [מחסה *maḥseh*] in v. 8 and "power" [עז *ʿōz*] in v. 11, which is the same Hebrew word as "mighty" in v. 7), and neither has occurred in vv. 1-6. In short, v. 7 functions as a structural and theological center, culminating the profession of faith in vv. 1-6 and serving as the foundation for the didactic call to decision in vv. 8-10 as well as the conclusion in vv. 11-12.

62:1-7. If it is permissible on some level to construe v. 7 as the central poetic line, then the similar professions of faith in vv. 1-2 and vv. 5-6 surround the address to and description of the enemies in vv. 3-4. The psalmist's trouble is real, but it exists only in the midst of—it is

246. Kraus, *Psalms 60–150*, 8.

circumscribed by—the psalmist's faith. Verses 1-6 thus move from faith to faith. Despite opposition, the psalmist will not "be shaken" (vv. 2, 6; see Ps 13:4 and NRSV "moved" in Pss 15:5; 16:8; 21:7; 30:6; 112:6; cf. 10:6). The opposite of being "shaken" is being "still unto God," as Weiser renders vv. 1a, 5a.[247] The NIV's translation is more helpful than that of the NRSV at this point, and the NIV also accurately maintains the imperative in v. 5a. As the NRSV suggests, however, patient waiting could be an aspect of the psalmist's inner repose (see Pss 4:4; 37:7; 131:2). The psalmist can be calm, because he or she trusts in God alone. In biblical terms, salvation (vv. 1b, 2a; see vv. 6-7) means life, and God is the source (v. 1b) as well as the protector and guarantor (v. 2; see "rock" in Pss 19:14; 28:1; 31:2; 61:2; see also "fortress" in Pss 46:7, 11 [NRSV, "refuge"]; 59:9, 16-17). The Hebrew particle with which the psalm actually begins occurs five times as the first word in poetic lines in vv. 1-6 ("alone" in vv. 1-2, 5-6 and "only" in v. 4). This repetition emphasizes the alternatives between which the psalmist has chosen and calls others, including the reader, to choose—that is, to live by trusting "God alone" or to live as if one's "only plan" were the destruction of other people.

The repetition of the particle that links vv. 1-2, 5-6 to vv. 3-4 also serves to emphasize that the threat to the psalmist is real and continuing. The ongoing reality of threat is also indicated by the subtle difference between vv. 1 and 5; "salvation" in v. 1 has been replaced by "hope" in v. 5 (see the noun in Pss 9:18; 71:5, as well as the verb translated "wait for" [קוה qāwâ] in Pss 27:14; 37:9; 39:7). The faith of the psalmist is not something attained after the crisis has passed. Rather, that faith endures throughout the ongoing threat. Verses 1-2, 5-6 are also linked to vv. 3-4 by the imagery of motion. The psalmist is "still" (v. 1) and not "shaken" (v. 2), even though the opponents are trying to "topple" the psalmist (v. 4) like a "tottering fence" (v. 3). As usual, the precise nature of the threat and identity of the opponents are unclear. Deceit is involved (see Pss 4:2; 5:6; 58:3; 109:28). Beyond this, however, one can only conclude that the threat is serious and ongoing. The phrase "How long . . . ?" suggests

247. Weiser, The Psalms, 445.

the duration of the crisis. The NRSV's "batter your victim" is more literally "kill," "murder" (רצח rāṣaḥ; see Exod 20:13). The language may be metaphorical, as the NRSV implies, but its intensity serves to indicate the urgency of the crisis. The psalmist's movement from faith to faith apparently leads through the valley of the shadow of death. The call to decision in vv. 8-10 must be heard in this context.

As already indicated, v. 7 both culminates the profession of faith in vv. 1-6 and anticipates the call to decision in vv. 8-10. Here the psalmist professes that everything he or she is and has depends on God—life itself (NIV, "salvation"; see vv. 1-2, 5-6), substance and reputation ("honor" or "glory" can denote both material wealth and reputation; see Pss 3:3; 4:2), sustaining strength ("mighty rock" or "rock of my strength"), security ("refuge"; see Ps 2:12; Introduction). The structure of v. 7 reinforces this all-encompassing profession. The two prepositional phrases—"on God" and "in God"—begin and conclude the verse. All references to the psalmist are in between. Structurally and theologically, the reality of God encompasses the psalmist.

62:8-10. In this call to decision, the psalmist commands what he or she has experienced (cf. "my refuge" in v. 7 and "our refuge" in v. 8). To take refuge in God means to trust God, and "trust" (בטח bāṭaḥ) is the first verb in both v. 8 and v. 10 (see Pss 4:5; 9:10; Introduction); it introduces the positive alternative in v. 8 and the negative alternative in v. 10. To "pour out your heart" means to pray, especially prayers of petition in distress (see 1 Sam 1:15; Lam 2:19). In short, the psalmist calls others to trust God and pray. This advice seems rather weak in view of the alternative introduced by the second occurrence of "trust" in v. 10. Verse 10 indicates that the psalmist's opponents trust their own resources, whether honestly or dishonestly gained. For the psalmist, to trust in the self is a lie (v. 9; see also v. 4). In other words, trust in oneself is finally ineffective; it amounts to "a breath" (v. 9; the same Hebrew root lies behind "set no vain hopes" in v. 10). Human achievement, honest or dishonest, cannot secure life (see Pss 49:16-17; 52:7; 60:11).

62:11-12. These verses articulate the foundation of the psalmist's faith. In affirming that "power belongs to God" (v. 11), the psalmist asserts that God rules the world (see "power" or "strength" in Exod 15:2, 13; Pss 29:1, 11; 93:1, passages that explicitly proclaim God's reign). It is revealing that the first direct address to God is a celebration of God's steadfast love (v. 12a); that is, the psalmist trusts that God's sovereign purposes will ultimately be experienced as love (see Exod 15:13, where "steadfast love" and "strength" are also linked; see also Ps 98:1-3). The verb in the final assertion (v. 12b) is a form of the Hebrew root from which is derived the familiar word *shalom,* "peace." Perhaps v. 12b should be rendered, "For you will give peace to all according to their work," which allows for a more nuanced understanding. This conclusion obviously does not mean that God rewards the faithful with an easy and materially prosperous life. The psalmist's own experience is testimony to that. What v. 12a does suggest is that the way one lives affects one's destiny. For instance, life is "a lie" (v. 9) for those who live by "lies" (v. 4). In other words, v. 12b teaches that there are different kinds of peace or repayment or reward. Psalm 62 commends the rewarding experience of finding refuge in God alone (see Commentary on Psalms 1; 2).

REFLECTIONS

1. Like the psalter as a whole, the perspective of Psalm 62 is eschatological. It affirms God's power or reign amid circumstances that seem to deny it (vv. 3-4; see Commentary on Psalms 2; 56; 57; 58; 59; 60; 61; Introduction), and thus it calls for decision. Unlike many other psalms, the call for decision in Psalm 62 is explicit (vv. 8-10), and it is as applicable and relevant to contemporary readers as it was to the psalmist's ancient contemporaries. The vocabulary of the psalm encourages us to hear its call to decision in a variety of ways. For instance, the repetition of "trust" and "heart" in vv. 8 and 10 enables us to hear the call to decision as: Where do we set our heart? Where is our ultimate loyalty? In whom or in what do we trust? In whom or in what do we seek security?

The psalmist's choice is clear: Trust in God at all times. But the alternative seems so much more concrete and compelling: Trust your own resources; trust your own buying power; trust whatever you can get your hands on. The psalmist rejects this alternative as "but a breath" (v. 9), suggesting other ways to word the call to decision: What is real and enduring? Are those who get ahead unjustly really deluding themselves? What kind of life is truly "abundant" life (see John 10:10-11)? The psalmist takes a stand on God's power and love, seeking peace in God, and thus suggesting again a way to put the call to decision: What is true power, and who are the truly powerful? What is peace, and where do we seek it and find it? I can envision the psalmist singing the final verse of the hymn "They Cast Their Nets in Galilee":

> The peace of God, it is no peace,
> but strife closed in the sod.
> Yet . . . [people] pray for just one thing—
> The marvelous peace of God.[248]

To decide to seek the peace of God clearly involves also a decision about the pursuit of power. As the psalmist knew, and as Jesus and Paul knew as well, to seek the peace of God will be to experience "power . . . made perfect in weakness" (2 Cor 12:9 NRSV).

2. The prominence of the call to decision in Psalm 62 reminds us that Jesus' preaching clearly involved a similar call (see Mark 1:14-15). The reality of God's reign means the creation of a new world with new priorities and values. Like the psalmist, Jesus

---

248. William Alexander Percy, "They Cast Their Nets in Galilee" in *The Hymnbook* (Richmond, Va.: Presbyterian Church in the U.S., UPCUSA, and the Reformed Church in America, 1955) 355 (#421).

calls people to trust and to follow (see Mark 1:17). Not surprisingly, Jesus and his followers found opposition at every turn, as did the psalmist. Jesus' enemies sought to topple him. Jesus' response was a perfect embodiment of the psalmist's call to decision; he trusted God at all times, and he prayed (see Mark 14:32-36). It seemed like a weak alternative to the disciples (see Mark 8:31-33), and it led to a cross. But the cross and the resurrection have created a whole new world (see Acts 17:6)—a world in which to be powerful is to become like a child (Mark 10:13-16), to be great is to be the servant of all (Mark 9:33-37), to know peace is to bear a cross (Mark 8:34), to experience abundant life is to give oneself away (Mark 8:35). In short, Psalm 62 presents alternative paths to peace or repayment or reward (see v. 12*b*). Jesus said of the hypocrites who gave alms only to be seen and praised by others: "They have received their reward" (Matt 6:2 NRSV). Presumably, their reward is not the life and peace that Jesus offers. For the psalmist, peace is found in trust and prayer. This peace is by no means incompatible with suffering, but "surpasses all understanding" (Phil 4:7 NRSV), for it is not "as the world gives" (John 14:27 NRSV).

3. Psalm 62 recognizes that one of the greatest hindrances to entering and finding peace in the new world of God's reign is wealth (v. 10). It still is today. The psalmist's honor and wealth are in God (v. 7), but that is not the case with the opponents. It is significant that much of the vocabulary of Psalm 62 relates explicitly or implicitly to making money. Balances in v. 9 can be used to weigh money as well as people (see Jer 32:10). Extortion and robbery are obviously ways to get money, and v. 10 goes on to mention riches. The word "repay" (שׁלם *šalēm*) in v. 12 can mean to repay money (see 2 Kgs 4:7; Ps 37:21), and "work" (מעשׂה *maʿăśeh*, v. 12) can mean the activity by which one earns money (Gen 46:33). The preponderance of this imagery reminds us that money is one of the greatest obstacles to living under God's rule (see Mark 10:17-27, esp. v. 23; Luke 12:15; 1 Tim 6:7-10). To be sure, the problem is not money itself; rather, wealth lures us into thinking we are autonomous, *self*-ruled. Psalm 62 thus gives us an opportunity to reflect upon the question of how our "work" actually does "repay" us. Does God have anything to do with our work? What would it mean if our work were carried out with a primary awareness of God's claim upon us and upon our world? These and similar questions are vitally important in a culture that regularly discourages us from locating our life and substance in God (v. 7). To be sure, it is difficult for most of us even to imagine being countercultural, but then again, "all things are possible with God" (Mark 10:27 NIV).[249]

249. Portions of the above treatment of Psalm 62 appear in substantially the same form in McCann, "Psalm 62:5-12: Psalm for The Third Sunday After Epiphany," *No Other Foundation* 11/1 (Summer 1990) 43-48.

PSALM 63:1-11, YOUR LOVE IS BETTER THAN LIFE

COMMENTARY

Scholars have offered a bewildering variety of proposals for classifying Psalm 63: song of praise (see v. 4), song of thanksgiving (see v. 5, a possible allusion to the meal that accompanied thanksgiving sacrifices), individual lament/complaint (see the complaint implied in vv. 1, 9-11), song of trust (see vv. 7-8), royal psalm (v. 11), and psalm for a night vigil (see v. 6). Each of these proposals entails, of course, a different understanding of the origin and ancient use of the psalm. What seems clear is that the psalmist has sought an experience of God's presence (v. 1; see Ps 27:4, 8 where the Hebrew verb translated "seek" is different from but conveys the same idea as the one used here), which the psalmist describes in terms of seeing God in the Temple (see "beholding" in v. 2 and "behold" in 27:4 NRSV). This description can be taken more or less literally. Several scholars, for instance, suggest that the psalmist spent the night at the Temple awaiting an answer to prayer at dawn. Mark Smith even suggests that v. 2 describes a solar theophany; that is, the psalmist "looked upon" God when the sun arose over the Mount of Olives and illuminated the Temple, which faces east (see Ezek 43:1-5, as well as Psalms 11; 17; 27; 42–43, which Smith also associates with solar theophanies).[250] On the other hand, the description in vv. 1-2 can be taken metaphorically. The editors of the psalter, for instance, associated Psalm 63 with David's experience in the wilderness, perhaps associating v. 9 with Saul's attempts to kill David (see 1 Sam 23:14; 24:2).

What we must conclude from this variety of proposals for the origin and use of Psalm 63 is that it is suitable for use in a variety of settings. Regardless of how, where, and when it originated, it continued to function powerfully for generations of Jews and Christians over the centuries (see Reflections below). In other words, more important than the categorization and possible original settings for Psalm 63 is the psalmist's claim that his or her life depends on God. As Smith concludes, "These words belong to a person who, thanks to God, is at rest and peace within."[251] In short, Psalm 63 articulates an experience that many persons from many places and times have had or can have as a result of their relationship to God. Psalm 63 is fundamentally about life and its true source. This fact is suggested by the fourfold occurrence of the Hebrew word נפש (*nepeš*), which is translated "soul" (vv. 1, 5, 8) and "life" (v. 9), but which means fundamentally "vitality," "being"; in some contexts, it may even connote "appetite," a nuance that would be especially appropriate in vv. 1, 5. In the face of a threat on his or her life (v. 9), the psalmist finds sustenance, satisfaction, and security in the experience of God's presence. As the key

word in Psalm 63, "soul"/"life" in vv. 1, 5, and 9 marks the beginning of the three sections of the psalm.

63:1-4. In v. 1, the psalmist expresses need in terms of thirst, a universal human necessity that can lead to faintness (see Isa 29:8). The only solution in this case is to see God (v. 2; see Ps 42:2, where the psalmist's soul "thirsts" and where the apparent solution is to "behold the face of God"). "Power" and "glory" are elsewhere associated with God's sovereignty; in Ps 29:1, the Hebrew words occur together but are there translated "strength" and "glory." The word for "power" also recalls Ps 62:11, where it was followed immediately by "steadfast love" (62:12). The same is true here (v. 3; see Commentary on Psalm 62 on the links among Psalms 61–63). The psalmist's entrusting of life to God's rule is expressed in a remarkable and memorable way in v. 3. "Steadfast love" is a primary feature of God's character as a forgiving and redeeming God (see Exod 15:13; 34:6-7; and Ps 5:7, where steadfast love is associated with entering God's house; see also Ps 61:7; Introduction). In other words, the psalmist recognizes that human life depends ultimately on God's faithfulness. The appropriate response is unending praise (vv. 3*b*-4*a*; see "bless" in Pss 16:7; 26:12; 34:1; 103:20-22), the joyful yielding of the whole self to God, and prayer, the humble entrusting of life and future to God (v. 4*b*; see Pss 28:2; 134:2; and 62:8, where different terms articulate a call to continual trust and prayer).

63:5-8. Whereas thirst symbolized the psalmist's need in v. 1, that need is hunger in v. 5. The psalmist's whole being is "satisfied" (see Pss 81:16; 107:9; 132:15; and especially 17:15, where satisfaction is derived from "beholding" God's face, and 65:4, where being satisfied involves entering the Temple). "Mouth" and "lips," ordinary organs for eating, here become instruments of praise as well. In the light of v. 2, v. 6 could suggest that the psalmist spent the night in the Temple, and "your wings" in v. 7 may allude to the creatures that attended the ark (see Pss 17:8; 36:7; 57:1). But such conclusions remain speculative, and it is not necessary to take the imagery so literally. Verse 6 may be a way of emphasizing that the psalmist constantly, even throughout the night,

250. Mark S. Smith, *Psalms: The Divine Journey* (New York: Paulist, 1987) 54.
251. Smith, *Psalms*, 62.

remembers and meditates on God (see Ps 1:2, where meditation on God's instruction is to be continual, day and night). The experience described is sacramental; that is, the memory of God's help (Pss 22:19; 27:9; 40:17; 46:1) is inseparable from the current experience of God's real presence. Verse 8 articulates the immediacy and intimacy of the psalmist's relatedness to God (see Gen 2:24; see also Deut 10:20; 11:22; 30:20). It also reaffirms the psalmist's dependence upon God (see Ps 41:12; Isa 42:1). The joy in the experience is emphasized by the repetition in vv. 5*b*, 7.

63:9-11. The joyfulness of vv. 5-8 is even more striking after the transition to the final section, which indicates that it is not superficial cheeriness but a profound joy that endures ongoing threat to the *nepeš* (see Heb 12:2). As one whose life is sought by enemies, the psalmist joins the good company of Moses (Exod 4:19), David (1 Sam 20:1; 22:13; 23:15; 2 Sam 4:9; 16:11), Elijah (1 Kgs 19:10, 14), and Jeremiah (Jer 11:21) in the OT (see also Pss 35:4; 38:12; 54:3), and Jesus in the NT (see Mark 11:18). In these cases, the one threatened with death is given

life, and so it is in Psalm 63. The psalmist finds sustenance and life in God's presence while the enemies "go down" to the realm devoid of God's presence (v. 9; see also Pss 86:13; 88:6). Whereas the psalmist's hunger is satisfied (v. 5), the opponents will become food for jackals (v. 10). The contrast between the destiny of the psalmist and that of the enemies is emphasized by the alliteration between the Hebrew words for "stopped" (סכר *sākar*, v. 11) and "seek" (שחר *šāhar*, v. 1). The psalmist seeks God and lives; the enemies seek the lives of others and will be stopped. To seek God is to know the truth (v. 11*b*; "swear" and "satisfied" are also linked by alliteration), but to live at the expense of others is to live a lie and ultimately to invite destruction. The mention of the king in v. 11 leads some scholars to conclude that he should be understood as the speaker throughout. While this is possible (see Ps 61:6-7), it is also possible to see the king as being representative or exemplary of the person who seeks God; it is clear that v. 11 did nothing to restrict the use of Psalm 63 by all kinds of persons in many places and times.

REFLECTIONS

1. The contrast between the uses of the word "mouth" in vv. 5 and 11 is significant. While the mouths of the enemies "will be stopped," the psalmist's mouth is open in joyful praise. The psalmist's open mouth seems to symbolize his or her orientation to God throughout the psalm: thirsting for God, hungering for God, praising God, praying to God. The open mouth indicates openness to God, which means life. In sharp contrast, the mouths of the enemies are closed so that they are unable to praise God, incapable of being satisfied, and unable to live, since to be closed to God is to be dead. The psalmist thus serves as a model of those who, in Jesus' words, "strive first for the kingdom of God" and find that "all these things [food, water, clothing] will be given . . . as well" (Matt 6:33 NRSV; see also Isa 55:1-9; Matt 5:6).

This remarkable openness to God is strikingly expressed in v. 3. It articulates the faith stance that persons in times past tried to elicit with a question reportedly asked to candidates for the ordained ministry in Calvinist churches: "Are you willing to be damned for the glory of God?" That this question now sounds so silly to us may be an indication of how difficult it is for persons in a self-centered culture to understand the intimacy of relatedness to God described in Psalm 63. Mays comments that:

> Trust becomes for a moment pure adoration that leaves the self behind as any participant in the reason for adoration. In the interpretation of patristic times this confession was associated with martyrs who valued God more than life and gave up their lives rather than deny their testimony. But in a salvation religion there is always the danger for all believers

to take the value of their own lives as the primary reason to trust God. This verse leads us in prayer to the point of devotion to God alone that must be the goal of all true faith.[252]

Psalm 63 thus illumines Jesus' call to a discipleship that involves self-denial and cross-bearing (Mark 8:34), but that finally constitutes life as God intends (Mark 8:35-37).

This life is possible in the presence of what Charles Wesley called "Love Divine, All Loves Excelling," and of which he wrote words that recall Psalm 63:

> Come, Almighty to deliver,
> Let us all thy life receive;
> Suddenly return and never,
> Nevermore thy temples leave.
> Thee we would be always blessing,
> Serve thee as thy hosts above,
> Pray and praise thee without ceasing,
> Glory in thy perfect love.

The final phrase of the hymn aptly describes the kind of self-denial voiced by v. 3: "lost in wonder, love, and praise."

2. Perhaps in continuity with its ancient Israelite use, or because the verb "seek" in v. 1 apparently meant originally "to look for dawn," Psalm 63 has been used from earliest Christian times as a morning psalm. Given its widespread use and its eloquent and powerful expression of faith in God, it is not surprising that it has been a favorite of persons as varied in time and place as John Chrysostom, Thomas à Kempis, and Theodore Beza, who, in keeping with v. 6, regularly recited the psalm at night.[253] This history of use is testimony to the adaptability of the psalms and their ability to transcend the circumstances of their origin and to be perennially available to express the praises, prayers, and piety of the people of God.

252. Mays, *Psalms*, 218.
253. See Prothero, *The Psalms in Human Life and Experience*, 77, 141.

PSALM 64:1-10, WHAT GOD HAS DONE

COMMENTARY

Psalm 64 shows the characteristic features of a prayer for help or individual lament/complaint. Petition (vv. 1-2) is followed by complaint, which takes the form of a description of the enemy (vv. 3-6). Verses 7-9 consist of an affirmation of faith in God's activity, and v. 10 calls for joyful trust and praise. As usual, it is impossible to determine the precise circumstances of origin and use. To be sure, destructive speech is employed to threaten the psalmist. But how and by whom? It is possible that the persecuted psalmist has sought refuge in the Temple from persecution or false accusation (see Psalms 5; 7; 61; Introduction), and it is possible that Psalm 64 was used in some

sort of restoration ritual within a family or small-group setting. We simply do not know. As Tate judiciously suggests, "In any case, the psalm is a literary entity, apparently without any strong ties to a specific ancient context. The text generates its own context in interaction with the reader."[254]

64:1-2. The psalmist characterizes this prayer as a complaint (v. 1*a*), and it apparently arises out of a frightening, threatening situation (v. 1*b*). The need to be hidden (v. 2*a*) reinforces the urgency of the threat (see 2 Kgs 11:2; Pss 17:8; 27:5; 31:20; Jer 36:26).

254. Tate, *Psalms 51–100*, 133.

The word that the NRSV translates "secret plots" (סוד *sôd*) usually designates consultation for good purposes, but clearly not in this case (see also Ps 83:3). The NIV's translation of v. 2*b* is probably more accurate, and by suggesting a sort of mob scene as opposed to a quiet conspiracy, it makes v. 2*b* a more all-encompassing request.

64:3-6. Verse 3 is similar to Pss 57:4 and 140:3, which suggest that the wicked use words as weapons. The bow-and-arrow imagery of v. 3*b* continues into v. 4. The word "ambush" in v. 4 is from the same Hebrew root (סתר *str*) as "hide" in v. 2; thus the wicked do their own sort of hiding, but the psalmist desires to be hidden by God. The wicked may shoot (see Ps 11:2), but the psalmist trusts that God shoots back (see v. 7). In short, the psalmist entrusts his or her life to God. Such trust is the real essence of being blameless or innocent (see Commentary on Psalms 15; 18). In contrast to the psalmist's dependence upon God, the wicked trust their own plans (v. 5*a*). They are convinced that they can do things secretly (v. 5*b*); the question in v. 5*c* further indicates their belief that they are autonomous (see Commentary on Psalm 1) and thus are accountable to no one (see Ps 10:13). Therefore, they continue to pursue "injustice" (v. 6*a*; see also Ps 58:2 NIV), convinced that they can do so with impunity (v. 6*b*) because of their own human capacities (v. 6*c*). Verse 6*ab* is made emphatic by the threefold repetition of a Hebrew root (חפש *ḥpś*) translated "plot," "devised," or "plan," and v. 6*c* prepares for the rest of the psalm. The word "heart" (לב *lēb*) anticipates the final line of the psalm, and the affirmation of human capacity sharply contrasts with the psalmist's focus on God, which begins in v. 7.

64:7-9. The shift at v. 7 is also marked by a reference to God in the third person, which gives the affirmation of faith in vv. 7-9 a sort of instructional tone. The repetition in vv. 7-10 of several words from vv. 3-6 serves to sharpen further the contrast between the psalmist's faith in God and wicked persons' faith in themselves. For instance, the words "shoot," "arrow," and "suddenly" in v. 7 recall vv. 3-4. God has arrows, too (see Ps 7:12-13). Thus the irony is that those who "shoot suddenly" will be "wounded suddenly." Verse 8*a* is difficult, but the word "tongue" (לשון *lāšôn*) recalls v. 3. Again, what the wicked perceive as their strength will be the cause of their undoing. The word "see" (ראה *rā'â*) in v. 8*b* recalls the question in v. 5*b*; that is, those who thought they could not be seen will become a public spectacle. Those who improperly had no fear (v. 4*b*) will engender a proper fear in others (v. 9*a*), and the crowning irony is that the lives of those who fancied themselves all-powerful will end up leading others to proclaim and wisely recognize God's powerful activity (v. 9*bc*).

64:10. The reversal between vv. 7-9 and vv. 3-6 is matched by the reversal between v. 10 and vv. 1-2. The psalmist's complaint has become an invitation for others to "rejoice" and "glory" (see Ps 34:2). The righteous (see Pss 1:5-6; 97:11) and the "upright in heart" (see Pss 7:10; 11:2; 32:11; 36:10; 94:15; 97:11) are those who live in dependence upon God rather than self. As the psalter has suggested from the beginning, to take refuge in God is the true source of happiness and joy (see Ps 2:12; Introduction). As with the other prayers for help, the movement from complaint to praise is not sequential or chronological; indeed, trust in God allows the psalmist to experience God's protection and to rejoice amid ongoing threat and the continuing reality of evil. In short, the perspective is eschatological, summoning readers in every time and place to trust and to have joy in the midst of human self-assertion that threatens both individuals and the security of our society and the world.

REFLECTIONS

The talk of swords and arrows and snares, as well as the portrayal of God's taking direct retributive action against the wicked, makes Psalm 64 seem rather far-removed from our contemporary world. Tate proposes, however, that it is more relevant than we might care to realize: "The psalm communicates a sense of anxiety and perplexity about the nature of human society that is at home in every generation. The supposed sophistication of modern society is not immune to deep awareness of destructive forces which threaten to reduce our semi-ordered world to chaos."[255]

In fact, the bold affirmation of human capacity and autonomy in vv. 5*b*-6 characterizes the way that most people, including Christians, routinely operate. Individual decision making and public policy making rarely include consideration of anything beyond our own interests. Although we may not be quite as crass as the wicked are in v. 5*b*, we seldom make accountability to God and others a major factor in our deliberations. This, of course, goes a long way toward explaining the existence of the "destructive forces" that Tate mentions—poverty and the unrest it breeds, oppression of women and minorities and the hostility it generates, warfare to protect ethnic claims or national interests and the chaos it produces, and so on. In a real sense, Psalm 64 calls us to recognize and to confess the evil within ourselves and our society.

It is also a call to faith—not to trust our own inclinations or capacities but to entrust our abilities and destiny to God. The structure of the psalm belies any facile understanding of divine retribution. For Christians, of course, the cross is a constant reminder that God does not exercise power by suddenly eliminating all evil and opposition. Rather, God's power is made perfect in weakness (see 1 Cor 1:25; 2 Cor 12:9-10). For Christians, the resurrection is the sign of God's victory, but we are called to live as people of the cross as well as of the resurrection (see Commentary on Psalms 13; 22; Introduction). Like the psalmist, we shall always find ourselves pleading and complaining as we confront the reality of evil (vv. 1-6), but because we ultimately trust God's power rather than human power (vv. 7-9), we shall also find that even now joy is possible (v. 10). We trust that evil is sowing the seeds of its own destruction, and we greet signs of evil's unraveling as what God has done (v. 9). Indeed, trusting God rather than self, we find the joy that liberates us for praise.

255. Tate, *Psalms 51–100*, 135.

PSALM 65:1-13, YOU CROWN THE YEAR WITH YOUR BOUNTY

COMMENTARY

Psalm 65 is usually categorized as a song of praise or a communal song of thanksgiving, and it is frequently associated with the autumn harvest festival. It is possible, however, to construe the verbs in vv. 3-5, 10 in an imperative sense, and on that basis several commentators interpret the psalm as a prayer for the rain that will produce an abundant harvest.

Although it is sometimes suggested that vv. 9-13 were originally an independent poem, there are clearly unifying features in the final form of Psalm 65. God is addressed directly throughout the psalm, and each section describes in a different way the reasons why God deserves to be praised (v. 1). Verses 1-4 center on God's answering of prayer (v. 2*a*), which means forgiveness (v. 3) and the ability to approach God's house (v. 4). Verses 5-8

recall more generally God's saving and creating activity, and vv. 9-13 offer a specific example of God's "awesome deeds" (v. 5) or "signs" (v. 8)—the provision of rain that makes the earth bountiful. Both the second and the third sections conclude with various elements of creation's offering the praise "due to you" (v. 1*a*).

65:1-4. The psalm begins in a striking way. The phrase "to you" begins the first two poetic lines (vv. 1*a*, 1*c*), and a similar phrase also begins the third poetic line (v. 2*b*). The effect is to make God the emphatic center of attention from the beginning, and this effect is reinforced by the emphatic pronoun in v. 3*b*, "*you* forgive." Verse 1*a* seems to read, literally, "To you silence is praise," perhaps a case of hyperbole, but it is probably better, as the NRSV and the NIV have done, to follow the reading of several ancient versions. God deserves praise, and people should keep their promises to God (that is, fulfill their vows; see Pss 22:25; 61:8; 66:13; 116:12-14, 17-18). This is the case, because God has heard their prayers and apparently has responded favorably (v. 2). This has been the case, despite the people's willful rebellion, which is suggested by the word "transgression" (פשע peša', v. 3). The NIV note suggests that the word translated "forgave" here (כפר kipper) is not the one usually used. It occurs elsewhere in the Psalms only in 78:38 and 79:9, but it is much more frequently used in Exodus and Leviticus in the context of people's engaging in ritual activity to effect atonement. The striking thing here is that God makes the atonement. As suggested above, the focus remains emphatically on God. Here God's gracious initiative is primary. Sinful people do not simply decide to approach God with their rituals. Rather, people are chosen (see Pss 33:12; 78:68) and brought near by God. The verb "bring near" (קרב qārab) is often used in the context of bringing offerings (see Lev 3:7, 12). In effect, God brings the people to God's own self as an offering. If the people offer anything, it is their gratitude, possibly in the form of a thanksgiving sacrifice. The payment of vows (v. 1b) often took the form of a thanksgiving offering (see Ps 116:17-18), and the ritual involved a communal meal, which may be alluded to in v. 4. In any case, literally or figuratively or both, the people "shall be satisfied" in God's house (note "Zion" in v. 1 and "courts," "house," and "temple" in v. 4). God is the gracious host who invites people in to live and to eat at God's table (see Pss 22:26; 23:5-6; 36:8; 63:5; Matt 26:26-29).

65:5-8. The mention of "all flesh" in v. 2 has anticipated the broadening of perspective in vv. 5-8. Although God has a specific place to which people are invited, God's influence and power extend to "the ends of the earth" (v. 5; see v. 8, where "bounds" translates the same Hebrew root [קצה qṣh] as "ends"). The mention of God's "awesome deeds" recalls the exodus (see Exod 15:11), when God proved to be the "God of our salvation" (v. 5; see Exod 15:2), and after which God's everlasting reign was proclaimed (Exod 15:18). God's sovereignty is implicit in v. 5, for "righteousness" elsewhere designates God's royal policy (see

Pss 96:13; 97:6; 98:9). The exodus was a public event that was not simply for Israel's benefit but was intended to fulfill God's creational purposes (see Commentary on Psalms 33; 66). Thus it is not surprising that the "power" God revealed to Pharaoh (Exod 9:16) is mentioned in v. 6 as that which "formed the mountains." The chaotic waters and the unruly peoples are also subject to God's sovereignty (v. 7; see Ps 46:10, where God is exalted over the nations and the earth, which 46:3, 6 have described using the same root that is translated "tumult" [המה hmh] in 65:7). Just as God provided for the invited guests in vv. 1-4, so also God is the "security of all the ends of the earth" (v. 5 author's trans.). Thus the creation joins in praising God in recognition of God's gracious rule (v. 8).

65:9-13. Here the psalmist offers a specific example of the way God provides satisfaction (v. 4) and security (v. 5): by sending the rain that makes the earth fruitful and productive. Mays comments that we have here a remarkable poetic portrayal of God as a "cosmic farmer" who carefully tends and waters the earth (vv. 9-10) so that it produces abundantly (vv. 11-13).[256] The word "bounty" (טובה ṭôbâ, v. 11) is from the same root as "goodness" (v. 4). Both in God's place and throughout the earth, God is the gracious provider. The verb in v. 11a suggests that God, the cosmic ruler, gives the earth royal treatment (see "crown" in Pss 8:5; 103:4). In recognition of God's rule and God's role in sharing the benefits of God's sovereignty, the created elements again offer their joyful praise (v. 13c; see v. 8). The verb "shout" (רוע rûa') specifically designates elsewhere the acclamation of God's reign (see Ps 47:1; see also Pss 95:1-2; 98:4, 6). As Kraus concludes, "The psalm fits best in the situation of the prostration before the creator and king of the world . . . who is enthroned on Zion and is worshiped in hymnic adoration (Pss. 95:6; 96:9; 99:5, 9)."[257] Psalm 65 is thus another affirmation of the theological heart of the psalter: God reigns! (See Psalms 2; 93; 95–99; Introduction.) It is also a reminder to us that we praise God, as also we live, in partnership with heaven and earth and all creation (see esp. vv. 8, 13; see also Psalms 8; 104; 143).

256. Mays, *Psalms*, 220.
257. Kraus, *Psalms 60–150*, 28.

REFLECTIONS

It is frequently suggested that vv. 9-13 have a polemical thrust, that the role of the Canaanite fertility God, Baal, is clearly occupied by Israel's God (see Hos 2:8, 16-20). Throughout Psalm 65, attention is directed clearly and often emphatically to God rather than to the gods or to human achievement. By worshiping Baal, the Canaanites—and frequently the Israelites—sought to secure by their own efforts a prosperous agricultural year. While we contemporary folk are not tempted to worship Baal, we are lured by Baalism's basic appeal (see Reflections on Psalm 29). In terms of security, we are convinced that we either do have or should have things under control. As for prosperity, we are generally convinced that we have earned it. From this perspective, of course, praise is due not to God but to ourselves. In short, we exalt ourselves, and the results are humbling. As Brueggemann puts it, "the loss of wonder, the inability to sing songs of praise about the reliability of life, is both a measure and a cause of our profanation of life."[258]

Psalm 65 is often read at observances of the national Thanksgiving holiday in the United States, a setting that clearly raises the issue of to whom our praise and gratitude are due. What Reinhold Niebuhr wrote about a community Thanksgiving service in 1927 is still true today: "Thanksgiving becomes increasingly the business of congratulating the Almighty upon his most excellent co-workers, ourselves. . . . The Lord who was worshiped was not the Lord of Hosts, but the spirit of Uncle Sam, given a cosmic eminence for the moment which the dear old gentleman does not deserve."[259]

Thus the polemical thrust of Psalm 65 is still relevant. It reminds us that neither we nor the government of the United States (nor any other country) rules the world. God rules the world. To direct our praise and gratitude toward anything or anyone less will finally mean either self-congratulation or a misguided patriotism—idolatry, in either case.

If we were less idolatrous about our national life, we might even be able to do what Israel did in v. 3: admit publicly that we are sometimes wrong! As Brueggemann says of v. 3:

> Let us not miss the dramatic claim. The whole people (together with the king, presumably) concedes its guilt and celebrates its forgiveness. Such a scene is nearly unthinkable in our public life. . . .
>
> . . . Psalm 65 reflects a public imagination capable of a troubled spirit, not so full of self, but able to reflect on its life in light of the majesty of God, a community forgiven and therefore ready to begin afresh.[260]

Obviously, this posture is a far cry from the frequently heard slogan "My country, right or wrong." Citizenship in the reign of God allows persons to look beyond mere national security to the one who is the security of all the ends of the earth (see v. 5).

258. Brueggemann, *The Message of the Psalms,* 136.
259. Niebuhr, *Leaves from the Notebook of a Tamed Cynic,* 147-48.
260. Brueggemann, *The Message of the Psalms,* 135.

PSALM 66:1-20, GOD HAS KEPT US AMONG THE LIVING

COMMENTARY

Psalm 66 follows nicely upon Psalm 65. In fact, the same verb ("shout" [רוע *rûa*]) appears in Pss 65:13*c* and 66:1*a*. Psalm 65 had proclaimed God to be the security of all the ends of the earth (v. 5), and Psalm 66 begins by bidding all the earth to praise God. Like Psalm 65, Psalm 66 is an eloquent affirmation that God rules the world (see esp. vv. 1-7), and, like Psalm 65, it is usually classified as a communal song of thanksgiving. It is easy to picture the use of Psalm 66 in a liturgical setting, but much more difficult to identify this setting with any certainty. Because of the allusions to the exodus and perhaps to the crossing of the Jordan (see vv. 1-7, esp. v. 6), Kraus suggests that the psalm may have been used at Gilgal in a festival commemorating these events (see Joshua 3–4; Psalm 114).[261] Other scholars, however, citing vv. 13-15, suggest the use of the psalm accompanying the offering of a sacrifice in the Temple.

These divergent directions, plus the shift from first-person plural to singular in v. 13, have led some scholars to question the unity of Psalm 66. But there are parallels and verbal links between vv. 1-12 and vv. 13-20, indicating that they should be heard as a whole. Furthermore, when the unity of the psalm is maintained, an important theological lesson is to be learned (see Reflections).

66:1-12. The psalm opens with an invitation to all the earth to praise God (v. 1), and reports that this praise does occur (v. 4). The mention of God's "name" (vv. 2, 4) is suggestive of God's character. Human beings worship God because of who God is, which is revealed by what God does (v. 3; see "cringe" in Pss 18:44; 81:15)—i.e., God rules the world. One should not be surprised, then, that the vocabulary of the invitations to praise frequently occurs in contexts explicitly affirming God's reign: "make a joyful noise"/"shout with joy" (v. 1; see Pss 95:1-2; 98:4, 6; 100:1); "glory" (v. 2; see Pss 24:7-10; 29:1-3, 9; 96:3, 7-8; 145:5, 11-12); "power"/"strength"

(v. 3; see Exod 15:2, 13; Pss 29:1, 11; 93:1; 96:6-7); "worships"/"bows down" (v. 4; see Pss 95:6; 99:5); "sing praises" (v. 4; see Pss 47:6-7; 98:4-5). Since God rules the world, all the earth is God's congregation (see also v. 7).

Like vv. 1-4, vv. 5-7 begin with a plural imperative, suggesting that the addressee is still "all the earth" (see the similar invitations in Ps 46:9). The focus is again on God's activity (v. 5), which is described again as "awesome" (vv. 3, 5), the same adjective used of God's activity in delivering Israel from Egypt (Exod 15:11; see also 47:2; 65:6; 96:4; 99:3; 145:6, where it occurs in contexts that explicitly proclaim God's reign). The exodus comes into even sharper focus in v. 6 (cf. Exod 14:16, 22, 29). Especially in view of vv. 1-4, it is important to realize that the exodus was ultimately not just for Israel's benefit but for the enactment of God's will for all the earth. As Terence Fretheim suggests:

> While the liberation of Israel is the focus of God's activity, it is not the ultimate purpose. The deliverance of Israel is ultimately for the sake of all creation (see 9:16). The issue for God is finally not that God's name be made known in Israel but that it be declared to the entire earth. God's purpose in these events is creation-wide. What is at stake is God's mission for the world, for as 9:29 and 19:5 put it, "All the earth is God's" (cf. 8:22; 9:14). Hence the *public character* of these events is an important theme throughout.[262]

As in the book of Exodus, here all the earth is summoned to "come and see" (v. 5). God's activity is not just for Israel but for all people! God intends that the nations (v. 7) will recognize God's reign (see "rules" in Pss 22:28; 59:13; 103:19). Those who "see" (v. 5) God's sovereign, creationwide purposes,

261. Kraus, *Psalms 60–150*, 36.

262. Fretheim, *Exodus*, 13.

will not exalt themselves but will join Moses and the Israelites in exalting God (Exod 15:2; see discussion of v. 17 below).

Another plural imperative begins v. 8, and the repetition of "praise" (see v. 2) also reminds us that all the earth is invited to "bless our God" (see v. 20, another link between vv. 1-12 and 13-20). As in vv. 1-7, the focus of God's activity is on Israel, but the deliverance related in vv. 9-12 is again paradigmatic and is thus cause for all people to praise God. The deliverance involves rescue from death (v. 9a). In this sense, it is like the exodus, but the vocabulary in vv. 9-12 is not specifically reminiscent of the exodus. God has not allowed the people to "slip" or to "be moved" (v. 9b; see also Pss 16:8; 17:5; 38:16; 55:22; 94:18; 121:3). The specific distress being faced is not described. Whatever it may have been, Israel is so sure of God's sovereignty that the trouble cannot be given a non-theological explanation. Thus the people affirm that God has "tested us" and "tried us" (v. 10). Tests and trials need not evoke the concept of punishment; indeed, they most frequently suggest that God is examining a person for the purpose of vindicating him or her (see Job 23:10; Pss 11:4-5; 17:3; 26:2; 139:23; Jer 12:3; Zech 13:9). In any case, the emphasis in vv. 10-11 is on God's deliverance of the people, made clear by the fact that vv. 9 and 12c envelope the description of distress.[263] Verse 12b is similar to Isa 43:2, which is a reminder that Isaiah 40–55 portrays the deliverance from exile as a new exodus. While v. 12b may be taken as a historical

clue to the date of the psalm, also it indicates that Israel understood that "the exodus recurs again and again, in new circumstances."[264]

66:13-20. While the shift that occurs at v. 13 can be taken as a sign of discontinuity, it can also be construed as the psalmist's presentation of her or his life as a witness to God's recurring activity in new circumstances of delivering persons from death to life. As in vv. 8-12, the exact nature of the trouble (v. 14) is not specified, but the deliverance from it is given a public character. The psalmist invites others to "come and hear" (v. 16) about God's activity, echoing what the whole people had done (v. 5). In keeping with the people's counsel to the nations (v. 7), the psalmist has not been rebellious (v. 18). It is not so much a matter that this prayer has merited attention but that the psalmist has opened the self to God's recurring activity. In any case, God has "listened" (v. 19) and has not removed "steadfast love from me" (v. 20). As did vv. 5-7, so vv. 19-20 recall the exodus (see "listen" in Exod 3:7 and "steadfast love" in Exod 15:13). For the psalmist, the old, old story of deliverance has become the new, new song. The psalmist joins Moses and all Israel in exalting God (cf. v. 17 with Exod 15:2). Thus the psalmist's life is an example of heeding the counsel of v. 7. As the nations have been invited to do (v. 8), the psalmist declares God "blessed" (v. 20) on account of who God is and what God does—steadfastly loving (see Exod 34:6-7; Introduction) in the fulfillment of God's creational purposes for all the earth (vv. 1, 4).

263. See John Bracke, "Psalm 66:8-20: Psalm for the Sixth Sunday of Easter," *No Other Foundation* 13/2 (Winter 1992–93) 42.

264. Brueggemann, *The Message of the Psalms,* 138.

REFLECTIONS

Rowland Prothero has written the following about John Bunyan's use of Psalm 66: "In his *Grace Abounding to the Chief of Sinners,* which bears the motto, 'Come and hear all ye that fear God, and I will declare what he hath done for my soul' [Ps 66:16], he has recorded, with a pen of iron and in letters of fire, his own passage from death to life."[265] Psalm 66 is about this "passage from death to life" (see esp. v. 9), so much so that the LXX and the Vulgate even provide this psalm with the title "Psalm of the resurrection," and it is still associated liturgically with the season of Easter. In the exodus (vv. 5-7), in recurring exoduses in new circumstances (vv. 8-12), and in individual

265. Prothero, *The Psalms in Human Life and Experience,* 185.

experiences of deliverance (vv. 13-20), God is at work bringing life out of death. For Christians, of course, the ultimate paradigm of God's life-giving activity is found in the death and resurrection of Jesus (see Commentary on Psalm 118).

Just as Christians affirm participation in the paradigmatic death and resurrection of Jesus (see Rom 6:1-11), so also the psalmist affirms participation in the paradigmatic event of exodus. Finally, what God has done for all God's people (v. 5) is inseparable from what God has done for the individual (v. 16), and vice versa. Such is the lesson of Psalm 66 when it is read as a whole. As Brueggemann puts it, "This psalm shows the move from communal affirmation to individual appreciation, which is what we always do in biblical faith."[266]

266. Brueggemann, *The Message of the Psalms,* 138.

PSALM 67:1-7, THAT GOD'S WAYS MAY BE KNOWN ON EARTH

COMMENTARY

Psalm 67 has ordinarily been classified either as a communal song of thanksgiving, possibly associated with a harvest festival (see v. 6), or as a prayer for God's blessing (vv. 1, 7). Perhaps it is both. In any case, its universal perspective fits well with that of Psalms 65–66. An earlier generation of scholars associated Psalm 67 with the annual celebration of God's enthronement. While it is clear that the central v. 4 asserts God's sovereignty, it is not clear that we can be very certain about the precise origin and ancient setting of the psalm. It would have been appropriate on a number of occasions, especially as a benediction. The traditional Jewish practice, for instance, was to recite it at the end of every sabbath.[267]

The psalm is usually divided into three parts (vv. 1-3, 4-5, 6-7), the first two of which end with an identical refrain. It is also possible, however, to discern a chiastic structure (see Introduction) that focuses attention on v. 4:

A	vv. 1-2	blessing and the knowledge of God among "all nations"
B	v. 3	refrain
C	v. 4	central profession of God's sovereignty
B´	v. 5	refrain

267. Tate, *Psalms 51–100,* 155.

| A´ | vv. 6-7 | blessing and the reverence of God by "all the ends of the earth" |

Verses 1-2, 6-7 feature the concept of blessing, which is somehow to involve "all" (vv. 2, 7; note too the repetition of "earth" in vv. 2, 6-7). The chiastic structure has the literary effect of surrounding the assertion of God's sovereignty (v. 4) with the acclamation of "all the peoples" (vv. 3, 5); that is, structure reinforces theological content, for the sovereign God deserves to be surrounded with praise. Verse 4 can be construed as a three-part poetic line, the only one of the poem; this, too, serves to set it apart.

67:1-2. In addition to the frequent petition that God "be gracious" (see Pss 4:1; 6:2), v. 1 introduces the thematic concept of blessing (see vv. 6-7; see also Pss 5:12; 28:9; 29:11). Verse 1 clearly recalls the so-called Aaronic or Priestly Benediction in Num 6:22-27. There as here, God's blessing is inseparable from God's presence or "face" (Num 6:26; see also Pss 4:6; 31:16; 80:3, 7, 19; 119:135) and ultimately from a knowledge of God's "way(s)" (v. 2; see also Ps 119:135, where the request that God's "face shine" is accompanied by the request that God "teach me") and from God's "salvation" (v. 2; see also Ps

80:3, 7, 19, where "let your face shine" is to result in being "saved").

While Israel is the primary object of God's blessing ("us" is the actual object in each case), it is clear that God intends the blessing somehow to be shared by "all" (vv. 2, 7; see also vv. 3, 5). Psalm 72 in particular portrays what blessing involves: "peace"/"prosperity" (שלום *šālôm*, vv. 3, 7) accompanied by "justice" and "righteousness" (72:1-2, 6-7; cf. "judge," which could be rendered "establish justice," in v. 4). As in Psalm 67, the blessings experienced by the king and his people (72:15) are to involve ultimately "all nations" (72:17; cf. 67:2).

67:3-5. As suggested above, the central profession of God's sovereignty is surrounded and set off by the refrain (vv. 3, 5). This central structural feature makes the fundamental profession that represents the theological heart of the book of Psalms: God rules the world (see Psalms 2; 93–99; Introduction). Judging or establishing justice is the primary responsibility of a monarch, human or divine (see Pss 9:8; 72:1-7; 96:13; 97:2; 98:9; 99:4; see "equity" in 9:8; 96:10; 98:9; 99:4). Only a sovereign God can "guide the nations upon earth" (see Exod 15:13, 18, where the celebration of God's guidance of Israel culminates in the proclamation of God's reign). This central profession of God's sovereignty underlies the request for a blessing that will have worldwide effects. This theme of universality is evident in the refrain. The verb translated "praise" (ידה *ydh*) is often translated "give thanks"; thus the psalmist's wish is that all the peoples acknowledge with gratitude God's rule. The word "all" (כל *kōl*, vv. 3, 5 as well as vv. 2, 7) emphasizes the universal perspective, as does the sevenfold occurrence of the words "peoples"/"nations," one occurrence for each of the poetic half-lines in vv. 3-5.

67:6-7. The psalm returns to the theme of blessing (cf. v. 6 with Lev 26:4), and the theme of universality is given its most comprehensive statement. The phrase "ends of the earth" occurs also in Pss 2:8 and 72:8 (see also Isa 52:7-10), both of which suggest that the sovereignty of God is exercised through God's chosen agent, the king (messiah). Even so, it is ultimately God who is to be revered or feared (v. 7; see Ps 2:11).

REFLECTIONS

The theme of blessing and the universal perspective of Psalm 67 recall Gen 12:1-3, the promise of blessing to Abraham and Sarah and their descendants, a blessing that will somehow involve "all the families of the earth" (Gen 12:3 NRSV). The promise is echoed throughout the OT (see Exod 9:16; Ps 22:27-28; Isa 2:2-4; 19:23-24; 49:5-7), including Psalm 67, and in the NT as well, where the apostle Paul cited it as support for his leadership in taking the gospel to the ends of the earth and for opening the church to all nations (see Gal 3:6-8, 28; Rev 22:1-5). As Kraus suggests concerning the message of Psalm 67, "The community of God here learns how to break away from all narrowness in the reception of salvation."[268]

In our contemporary world, plagued by injustice and divided by extremes of poverty and wealth, it is crucial that we hear the message of Psalm 67: God rules the world and intends blessing for all the world's people. This means that God wills justice for all (v. 4), including the equitable distribution of the earth's "harvest" (v. 6). It is crucial, too, that we hear the message of Psalm 67 in a contemporary world that is torn by racial, ethnic, and national exclusivism and strife. In short, Psalm 67 can assist us, in the words of Cain Hope Felder, as we "engage the new challenge to recapture the ancient biblical vision of racial and ethnic pluralism as shaped by the Bible's own universalism."[269] The psalm reminds us that God so loves the whole world (John 3:16), and that God's choice of a particular people is so that the world may know (John 17:23; see Ps 67:2).

268. Kraus, *Psalms 60–150*, 42.
269. Cain Hope Felder, *Stony the Road We Trod: African American Biblical Interpretation*, ed. Cain Hope Felder (Minneapolis: Fortress, 1991) ix.

PSALM 68:1-35, MY GOD, MY KING!

COMMENTARY

Psalm 68 is generally known as the most difficult of all the psalms to interpret. It contains fifteen words that occur nowhere else in the OT as well as numerous other rare words. As Tate puts it, "The difficulties of interpreting Ps 68 are almost legendary."[270] Not surprisingly, opinions diverge widely concerning the structure and movement of the psalm. At one extreme, some scholars conclude that Psalm 68 has no discernible unity or regularity of structure, while at the other extreme, some discern a regular pattern of strophes and stanzas. The truth probably lies somewhere in between. The unity of the psalm is suggested by the obvious correspondence between v. 4 and vv. 32-33, which provide a bracket around the psalm. Furthermore, while there are no verbal links, vv. 34-35 celebrate the power that God is invited to manifest in vv. 1-3. The "righteous" (v. 3) correspond to "his people" (v. 35), who have been given "power and strength" (v. 35) and thus finally have good reason to "be jubilant with joy" (v. 3).

This psalm is often divided into three major sections (vv. 1-10, 11-23, 24-35), which are sometimes associated with the place featured in each: Sinai (v. 8), Bashan (vv. 15, 22), and Jerusalem (v. 29). An alternative is to view vv. 1-3 as an introduction, followed by two major sections (vv. 4-18, 19-35), each of which consists of four smaller sections (vv. 4-6, 7-10, 11-14, 15-18 and vv. 19-23, 24-27, 28-31, 32-35). The movement of vv. 4-18 proceeds geographically. Alluding to the exodus, vv. 4-6 describe the kind of God revealed in that event. Verses 7-10 recall Sinai and the provision made by God for the people in the wilderness. Verses 11-14 recall the entry into and conquest of the land, which meant God completed the journey of accompanying the people from Sinai to Jerusalem, bypassing other mountains that might have provided a home for God (vv. 15-18; see Exod 15:1-18, which also moves from exodus to God's choice of Zion). The repetition

of "blessed" (ברוך *bārûk*, vv. 19, 35) provides an envelope for the second major section, in which God's victorious presence in Jerusalem is proclaimed (vv. 19-23), celebrated liturgically (vv. 24-27), invoked in prayer (vv. 28-31), and proclaimed again in the form of an invitation for all the earth to recognize God's sovereignty (vv. 32-35).

The origin and ancient use of Psalm 68 are also disputed. It has been identified as a victory hymn (cf. vv. 7-8 with Judg 5:4-5) as well as a communal song of thanksgiving. It finally celebrates God's reign from Jerusalem (see vv. 24, 32-35) and gives several indications of liturgical use (see the mention of God's abode or sanctuary in vv. 5, 16-18, 24, 29, 35). Verse 1 recalls Num 10:35, suggesting a possible association with the ark, which may have been involved in processional celebrations of God's reign (vv. 24-27; see Pss 24:7-10; 132:8). While there is no solid evidence for Mowinckel's theory of an annual enthronement festival, it is likely that Israel celebrated liturgically God's sovereignty on some occasion. What is clearer than reconstructed cultic settings, however, is the actual literary content with its proclamation of the victory and reign of God. Thus Psalm 68, along with Psalms 65–67, is another voice that proclaims the message that pervades the psalter: God reigns (see Psalms 2; 93–99; Introduction).

68:1-3. As mentioned above, v. 1 recalls Num 10:35, suggesting an association of Psalm 68 with the ark. Verse 1 thus prepares for the remainder of the psalm, which will portray God in battle as the divine warrior. The conflict is framed in vv. 2-3 in terms that recall Psalm 1, in which the righteous are promised life and "the way of the wicked will perish" (1:6). The transience of the wicked is also associated elsewhere with smoke (Ps 37:20) and the melting of wax (Ps 12:10). Later in the psalm, the righteous will rejoice (vv. 19-20, 24-27), but they will also pray for help (vv. 28-31). Thus Psalm 68 is another reminder that righteousness consists

270. Tate, *Psalms 51–100,* 170.

essentially in living in dependence upon God (see Commentary on Psalm 1).

68:4-6. In anticipation of the victory that will be described in vv. 5-18, v. 4 invites the righteous to sing and to praise (see Exod 15:1-2). It also introduces the ancient Near Eastern mythic background, which is prominent in Psalm 68 along with the outline of Israel's basic story—exodus, Sinai/wilderness, conquest/possession of Jerusalem. In Canaanite literature, it was Baal "who rides upon the clouds." But here, Yahweh is specifically named (see also Deut 33:26; Ps 18:9-13; Isa 19:1; see below on vv. 32-33). The specificity of the expression "his name is the LORD" is indicative of a polemical thrust (see Exod 15:3). "Name" is also suggestive of character, which is in view in vv. 5-6. The intent here is polemical as well; Yahweh fulfills the ancient Near Eastern ideal of the king as protector of and provider for the poor (see Pss 10:14, 18; 94:6; 113:7-9; 146:9). Verses 4-6 also seem to allude to the exodus (cf. v. 4 with Exod 15:1-3; the verb "leads out" [יצא *yāṣāʾ*] in v. 6 is often used of the exodus), which would be especially appropriate in view of the more specific allusions to the wilderness and to Sinai in vv. 7-10.

68:7-10. The verb "went out" in v. 7*a* is the same Hebrew root as "leads out" in v. 6, again recalling the exodus. Verse 7*b* specifically mentions "the wilderness" (see Deut 32:10; Pss 78:40; 106:14), and v. 8 mentions Sinai. Verses 7-8 also recall the possession of the land, since they are nearly identical to Judg 5:4-5, a portion of the Song of Deborah. Furthermore, the word "heritage" (נחלה *naḥălâ*, v. 9) occurs frequently in Joshua; it can designate either the land or the people (see Deut 32:9; the NRSV's "restore" in v. 9 and "provided" in v. 10 translate the same Hebrew verb [כון *kûn*], which also occurs in Deut 32:6 as "established"). Yahweh, not Baal, provides renewing rain for the land and its people. The "you" in the final clause of v. 10 is emphatic. In short, God did everything necessary for the welfare of the people.

68:11-14. These verses are difficult, but they seem to allude to the military actions described in Numbers–Judges as part of Israel's entry into Canaan (and perhaps more specifically the battle against Sisera in Judges 5; see Judg 5:19). The expression "bore the

tidings" (v. 11) came into Greek as "gospel," "good news"; elsewhere, the good news has to do with God's reign (see Ps 96:2; Isa 52:7). By scattering the kings (vv. 12, 14), God proves to be the true sovereign. Dividing the spoil (v. 12) indicates victory (see Judg 5:30). Verse 13 is obscure, as a comparison of the NIV and the NRSV makes clear. It may mean that despite Israel's inactivity (v. 13*a*), the victory has been won. The dove may refer to a jeweled object captured in battle (part of the spoils, perhaps even a statue of Astarte, who was represented by a dove); it may designate Israel (see Ps 74:19; Hos 7:11; 11:11), who has captured the wealth of the opposing kings; or it may indicate the release of birds to celebrate a victory.[271] Verse 14*b* is also obscure. The location of Zalmon is unknown; this verse is best understood metaphorically rather than geographically or historically.

68:15-18. The completion of God's journey from Sinai (v. 17) is related here. Victorious over all opposition, God ascends to the chosen place of residence to receive universal acclaim (v. 18; see Ps 47:5-9), even from "the rebellious" (see v. 6). Although some scholars suggest that vv. 17-18 may not have referred originally to Zion, they clearly do in the final form of the psalm (see v. 29; Ps 132:13-14). In choosing Zion, God apparently passed over other prime locations (vv. 15-16). Bashan was known for its luxuriance and desirability (Jer 22:20). Mount Hermon (elevation 9,000 feet) could be the particular mountain behind the references in vv. 15-16, but the real point is that Zion is the place "where the LORD will reside forever" (v. 16*c*).

68:19-23. Because God is enthroned in Zion, the celebration can begin (see "Bless[ed]" in vv. 26, 35; Pss 28:6; 31:21, and esp. 66:8, 20, where it is associated with preservation of life). Like v. 4, vv. 19-20 recall the victory song that begins in Exod 15:1-3 (see esp. "salvation" in Exod 15:2). The verb "escape" is the same root as "leads out" (v. 6) and "went out" (v. 7), and it is often used specifically of the exodus, which was an escape from death. The mythic background and polemical thrust are evident in v. 20 as well. The Hebrew word for "death" (מות *māwet*) is the equivalent of Mot (מות *môt*), the Canaanite god of death, whom Baal defeated yearly

---

271. Tate, *Psalms 51–100*, 178-79.

to ensure fertility of the land. Here it is Israel's God, not Baal, who defeats death. And as vv. 21-23 suggest, God defeats all other enemies as well (see vv. 1-3, 11-14, 30-31; Num 24:8; 1 Kgs 21:19, 23-24; Pss 58:10; 110:5). In short, Israel's God is sovereign.

68:24-27. Not surprisingly, God is addressed as King in v. 24 (see Pss 5:2; 44:4; 47:6; 74:12; 84:3), which describes a liturgical celebration of God's reign (see Pss 24:7-10; 42:4; 132:8-9, 13-14), complete with singing, music, and percussion (v. 25; see also Exod 15:20-21; Pss 33:3; and esp. 149:2-3, where God is also addressed as King). Verse 26 can be understood as a quotation of the singers, who address God as Israel's "fountain" or source of life (see vv. 6, 20; Ps 36:10; Jer 2:13; 17:13). The four tribes listed in v. 27 are apparently intended to represent all of Israel (see Judg 5:14, where Benjamin is also in the lead).

68:28-31. It is significant that this section shifts to petition. The sovereignty of God is not questioned, but present circumstances apparently call for a new manifestation of God's "power" (עֹז ʿōz, v. 28). The imperative "show your strength" in v. 28b represents the same Hebrew root (עזז ʿzz) as the noun "power" in v. 28a; that root will recur four more times ("mighty" in v. 33b, "power" twice in v. 34 and in v. 35). It frequently occurs in the context of proclamations of God's reign (see "strength" in Exod 15:13; Pss 29:1, 11; 93:1; 96:6-7). In short, it is clear from vv. 28-31 that God's reign does not go unopposed. The verb in v. 29 should probably be heard as a jussive, "let the kings bear gifts"; that is, it, too, is petitionary, and a tension exists between v. 18 and v. 29. As the NRSV note indicates, v. 30 is problematic. It is clear enough, however, that it requests God to deal with powerful opponents, who are symbolized as beasts (see Pss 22:12-13, 16,

20-21; 17:12; 57:4; 58:6; 59:6, 14; 74:12-14; 89:10). The mention of reeds may indicate Egypt, which is named in v. 31, but the real intent seems to be to ask God to subject all opponents, including those from the farthest reaches, which is what Cush probably represents (see Zeph 3:10).

68:32-35. Congruent with this conclusion concerning vv. 28-31, v. 32 addresses the broadest possible invitation to recognize God's sovereignty (cf. v. 4). Verse 33 also recalls v. 4. God's voice is probably meant to be understood as thunder. In the ancient Near East, thunder was associated with Baal, the god of the storm (see also v. 9 concerning rain). In Psalm 29, as here, it is a sign that Yahweh is to be greeted as sovereign. Like Psalm 29, v. 34 invites recognition of God's rule over the earthly and heavenly realms (see also "majesty" in Deut 33:26). Awesomeness is an attribute of God as sovereign (v. 35; see also Exod 15:11; Pss 47:2; 65:5; 66:3, 5; 96:4; 99:3). Like Psalm 29 as well (see vv. 9-11), v. 35 situates God in the divine sanctuary, which seems to refer to God's heavenly and earthly abodes, and it envisions God sharing God's power with the people (see 29:11).

It is revealing that the six occurrences of the Hebrew root meaning "strength," "power," "might" occur in the final eight verses after the people's need has been expressed in petition (see also vv. 1-3). In other words, as is always the case, the proclamation of God's rule occurs amid circumstances that seem to deny it (see Psalm 2; Introduction). The perspective is eschatological. As such, Psalm 68 finally calls readers in every generation to live in dependence upon a God whose sovereignty is revealed not in sheer force but in the power of compassion, which some might mistake for weakness (see vv. 4-6; see also 1 Cor 1:25; 2 Cor 12:9).

REFLECTIONS

1. As long ago and far away as Psalm 68 seems in many respects, it deals with a perennial theological issue: how to talk about a transcendent God in human terms. Commenting on the movement of God from Sinai to Jerusalem in this psalm, Mays states that it represents "the coming of the reign of God in time and space."[272] Such

272. Mays, *Psalms,* 228.

particularity is scandalous, but it is not unusual to Christians. The preaching of the historical Jesus apparently featured precisely this claim. Jesus proclaimed that the kingdom of God was present in human time and space, and he invited people to enter it (Mark 1:14-15). Jesus' followers were convinced that he had not only rightly proclaimed the reign of God, but had also fully embodied God's wisdom and power in such a way that to enter the realm of God meant to do so through Jesus. In short, God was in Christ, and so Jesus is Lord. The particularity was transferred from a place—Jerusalem—to a person—Jesus. But the particularity is no less concrete or scandalous.

2. Psalm 68 and the psalter as a whole illustrate what is clear from the NT as well— namely, the proclamation of the reign of God in space and time is always eschatological. The reign of God is never fully manifested; it is always opposed. The people of Israel and Jerusalem were regularly assaulted; Jesus was crucified. Or, to put it in slightly different terms, the proclamation of God's reign is always polemical. For the psalmist, to say that Yahweh is sovereign means that Baal is not. For first-century Christianity, to say that Jesus is Lord meant that Caesar is not. For contemporary Christians, to say that God rules the world and that Jesus is Lord is to deny ultimacy and ultimate allegiance to a host of other claims—national security, political parties, economic systems, ethnic heritage, job, family, self. Indeed, the underlying temptation represented by Baalism is perhaps more prevalent than ever—that is, to conclude that human beings can manipulate the deity and thus ensure security by our own efforts (see Commentary on Psalms 29; 65). By its polemical proclamation of the reign of God, Psalm 68 undercuts the gospel of human progress. Ultimately, salvation is to be found in submission to God rather than in the assertion of self (see vv. 19-20).

The eschatological, polemical dimension of Psalm 68 is crucial, for it puts the militaristic image of God as divine warrior in a particular perspective. The fact that Psalm 68 begins and finally returns to petition (vv. 1-3, 28-31) indicates that God does not simply step in and wipe out God's opponents, a lesson that is reinforced by the cross of Jesus Christ. To be sure, God fights back against God's enemies (vv. 1-2), against those "who delight in war" (v. 3c). But God fights in an unexpected way—with love and compassion. For worldly strategists, might makes right. But for God the divine warrior, right makes might. Mays concludes of this psalm:

> In spite of its militant character and victorious confidence, such is not its spirit. There is a self-understanding and self-description in the psalm's measures that belies such a reading. The uses assigned to the power of the LORD as divine warrior are crucial. The God who dwells in his holy habitation as victor is father of orphans and protector of widows, who gives the desolate a home and liberates prisoners (vv. 5-6). . . .
> . . . The song belongs to the lowly, who in the midst of the powers of this world remember and hope for the victory of God.[273]

In short, Psalm 68 calls us not to triumphalism but to the humble enactment of God's justice that is born of compassion for the needy (v. 10; see also vv. 5-6).

3. Thus the biblical description of life is very different from what our culture portrays as the so-called good life. For the psalmist, life is not the achievement of our own ends but dependence upon God and openness to God's ways (vv. 19-20). In this regard, the liturgical dimension of Psalm 68 is instructive. In worship, we say who rules the world and thus to whom we belong. Worship in the spirit of Psalm 68 will not simply be something that reinforces cultural values. Rather, as J. David Pleins suggests on the basis of Psalm 68, "The words we use in worship must open us to the God of justice and awaken us to the world's desperate need for hope and genuine social change."[274]

273. Mays, *Psalms*, 228-29.
274. J. David Pleins, *The Psalms: Songs of Tragedy, Hope, and Justice* (Maryknoll, N.Y.: Orbis, 1993) 95.

4. To be an advocate of justice and hope in a desperate, broken world requires a motivation and a source of energy beyond ourselves. The good news is that God gives power and strength to God's people (v. 35). Christians understand this finally to be nothing less than the power of the resurrection (see the use of Ps 68:18 in Eph 4:8), and thus Psalm 68 is appropriately associated with the season of Easter. To trust in and represent the claims of God's reign in a desperate, broken world will mean, as it always has, that we will encounter opposition. Appropriately, therefore, John Knox concluded the Scots Confession with a prayer that begins with Ps 68:1 and alludes to vv. 32 and 35 as well: "Arise, O Lord, and let thine enemies be confounded; let them flee from thy presence that hate thy godly name. Give thy servants strength to speak thy word with boldness, and let all nations cleave to the true knowledge of thee. Amen."[275]

275. Cited in Mays, *Psalms*, 229.

PSALM 69:1-36, FOR YOUR SAKE I HAVE BORNE REPROACH

COMMENTARY

Similar in many ways to Psalm 22, Psalm 69 is one of the longest and most impressive of the prayers for help or individual laments/complaints. Like Psalm 22, its first extended section (vv. 1-29) consists of alternating petition (vv. 1a, 6, 13-18, 22-25, 27-28, 29b) and complaint (vv. 1b-5, 7-12, 19-21, 26, 29a). And as the intensity of Psalm 22 is created in part by a sort of doubling (vv. 1-11, 12-21a), so it is with Psalm 69. Leslie C. Allen points out that the first major section consists of two smaller sections that are roughly parallel.[276] Allen's results can be summarized as follows:

	Verses 1-13b		Verses 13c-29
v. 1	Save me	v. 13d	your sure salvation
	waters	v. 14	do not let me sink
v. 2	I sink		deliver . . . from
	miry depths		deep waters
	deep waters	v. 15	do not let . . .
	floods		foodwaters
	engulf me		engulf me
v. 4	those who		depths
	hate me	v. 14	those who hate me
	my enemies	v. 18	my foes
v. 5	you know	v. 19	you know
v. 6	not be		
	disgraced		
	not be put		
	to shame		scorned

276. Leslie C. Allen, "The Value of Rhetorical Criticism in Psalm 69," *JBL* 105 (1986) 577-82. See the similar table in Tate, *Psalms 51–100*, 193. Tate also summarizes additional details of Allen's analysis.

v. 7	scorn		disgraced
	shame		shamed
v. 9	insults of those who insult you	v. 20	scorn
v. 10	scorn		
v. 11	when I put on	v. 21	they put
v. 13a	but I	v. 29	[but] I am

Obviously, the correspondence is not exact. Notably, vv. 22-28 are not represented at all. Even so, the parallels are too striking to be coincidental, and the doubling creates an impressive intensity. As in Psalm 22 as well, the promise to praise is especially outstanding after the prolonged complaint. It also consists of two parts (vv. 30-33, 34-36), the first of which is especially reminiscent of Ps 22:22-27. It is possible that vv. 34-36 were added to an original form of Psalm 69 to make it more explicitly relevant to the post-exilic situation.

As is usually the case, the circumstances that have given rise to the complaint are unclear, as is the identity of the enemies. Some scholars hypothesize terminal illness (see vv. 1-3, 26), which others interpret as a sign of sinfulness and as warrant to alienate (v. 8) and persecute the psalmist (v. 26). Other scholars suggest that the psalmist has been falsely accused (v. 4). But the language of the complaints is metaphorical, hyperbolic, and stereotypical. Tate recognizes, citing Psalm 69 that, "the probability of the usage of psalms in multiple contexts is high."[277] More accessible than reconstructed original settings for the psalm, and more important as well, is the psalmist's assertion that suffering is intimately related to God—even caused by God (v. 26)—so that the further suffering inflicted by others is for God's sake (vv. 7, 9-11). While this claim does not completely clarify the circumstances and characters involved, it does suggest larger literary settings in which Psalm 69 should be heard—the book of Job, Isaiah 53, the book of Jeremiah, the accounts of Jesus' passion (see Reflections below).

69:1-3. The opening petition links v. 1 to the beginning of the second section of complaint (v. 13*cd*), forms with v. 29 an envelope around the whole complaint, and also links the complaint to vv. 30-36 (see v. 35). To be saved (see Pss 3:2, 7, 8; 6:4) means to live, and the psalmist appears headed for death. She or he is about to go under (see Job 22:11; Pss 18:16; 32:6; 66:12; 144:7; Isa 43:2; Lam 3:54). The word translated "neck" in v. 1 (נפש *nepeš*), which is usually translated "soul" or "life," seems to have meant originally "neck" or "throat." At any rate, the psalmist asks God to save her or his neck. Nearly sunk (v. 2) in a "mire" (see Ps 40:2) of "depths" (v. 2*a*; see Exod 15:5; Ps 88:6; Jonah 2:3), there is no touching bottom. "Waters" (מים *mayim*) occurs in both vv. 1 and 2, and a second Hebrew word for "deep"/"depths" (מעמקים *ma'ămaqqîm*) occurs in v. 2*c* (see Ps 130:1; Isa 51:10). The psalmist is about to be swept away (see v. 15; Ps 124:4). All she or he can do is appeal to God and wait (see Pss 31:24; 38:15), which has been done, but time is rapidly running out (v. 3; see Ps 6:6).

69:4-5. In addition to the actual threat, the psalmist must contend with people who make the situation worse (see "without cause" in Ps 35:7, 19). Verse 4 does not necessarily suggest that the psalmist has literally been accused of stealing. Rather, the psalmist suggests that she or he cannot make up for something that she or he has not done. In other words, there is no pleading guilty when one is actually innocent. Verse 5 indicates that the psalmist is willing to admit that she

or he is not perfect. The point is that *God* knows the psalmist's shortcomings (the first "you" in v. 5 is emphatic), yet the psalmist is perfectly willing to rest the case with a loving and merciful God (see vv. 13, 16). In short, the problem is not that God condemns the psalmist. The problem is that other people condemn the psalmist. Job's friends come immediately to mind.

69:6-13b. Verse 6 indicates that the psalmist feels in some sense exemplary. The word "hope" (קוה *qāwâ*, v. 6) is essentially synonymous with "waiting" in v. 3. If the psalmist's suffering in waiting has produced only an adverse reaction (v. 4), then other God seekers could receive the same kind of discouraging treatment in their time of need. The psalmist thus prays that this will not happen. Verse 7 introduces a key word in the psalm, "reproach" (חרפה *herpâ*), which will be repeated five more times (NRSV, "insult[s]"/"insulted" in vv. 10, 11, 19, 20; see also Pss 31:11; 109:25; Jer 20:8). The psalmist suffers the insults of others not because she or he is unfaithful but precisely because she or he *is faithful* (see Ps 22:7-8). The NRSV's "dishonored" (v. 6) and "shame" (v. 7) represent the same Hebrew root (כלם *klm*; see Ps 4:2). Verse 8 describes what was perhaps the epitome of shame in ancient cultures: alienation from one's family (see Job 19:13, 15; Pss 38:11; 88:8, 18; Jer 12:6). It also illustrates the cruelty of a strict application of the doctrine of retribution. Suffering that is viewed as punishment from God justifies exclusion of the sufferer, thus compounding the plight. Verses 9-12 reinforce the unfairness of the situation. The faithful psalmist, the one who has entrusted life and future to God, is insulted (vv. 9-10), belittled (v. 11; see Ps 44:14), and taunted (see Job 30, esp. vv. 9-15). Nevertheless, the psalmist stands firm, looking to God in prayer (v. 13*ab*). The concluding line of this section (vv. 1-13*b*) should probably be translated "for a time of favor" (see Pss 5:12; 30:5, 7; 106:4; Isa 49:8).[278]

69:13c-18. The first section of complaint has documented that human character cannot be trusted, so the second begins with a focus on the character of God, beginning with the one attribute that is the

---

277. Tate, *Psalms 51–100*, 196.

278. See Tate, *Psalms 51–100*, 187, 189.

most fundamental: steadfast love (v. 13c; see also v. 16; Exod 34:6-7; Pss 5:7; 13:5; 86:15; Introduction). As is often the case, "steadfast love" is paired with "faithfulness" (v. 13d; see Exod 34:6; Pss 25:10; 40:10-11; Lam 3:22-23), and it is associated with "mercy" (v. 16; see Exod 34:6; Pss 86:15; 103:4). As suggested above the vocabulary of vv. 13c-15 parallels vv. 1-2, but goes beyond it as well. In effect, the psalmist asks not to be treated like an enemy of God—for instance, not to be swallowed up (see Exod 15:12; Num 16:30, 32, 34; Ps 124:3-4). Rather, like Job (31:5), the psalmist wants God to answer (vv. 13, 16-17). Indeed, the psalmist dares to ask to see God's face (the verb "turn" [פנה *pānâ*] in v. 16b and the noun "face" [פנים *pānîm*] in v. 17a are from the same Hebrew root; see Pss 22:24; 27:9; 102:1). The psalmist is postured as one whose life depends solely on God, and thus appropriately refers to self in prayer as "your servant" (see Exod 14:31; Job 1:8; 2:3; Pss 19:11, 13; note also Pss 27:9; 31:16, where servanthood is associated with God's face). Because the psalmist belongs to God, God is in a position to "redeem" (גאל *gā'al*, v. 18), an act customarily carried out by one's next of kin (see Lev 25:25; for God as redeemer, see Exod 15:13; Job 19:25; Isa 41:14; 43:14). This relational term recalls v. 8. Human kin have abandoned the psalmist, but she or he trusts God to act as next-of-kin (see discussion of 19:14 in Commentary on Psalm 19). The verb "set free" (פדה *pādâ*) is also frequently translated "redeem" (see Pss 26:11; 31:5; Jer 15:21).

69:19-21. Just as God knows the psalmist's shortcomings (v. 5), so also God knows all that the enemies have inflicted upon the psalmist (v. 19; see Jer 15:15). Insults (vv. 19-20; see vv. 7, 9) have broken the psalmist's heart (Ps 147:3) and have led to despair (see Jer 15:18). The psalmist has found no human relief. The Hebrew roots of "pity" (נוד *nûd*) and "comforters" (נחם *nḥm*, v. 20) occur in Job 2:11 to designate what Job's friends came to do. They were not successful, and the psalmist's experience recalls that of Job—nothing but bitterness from the human side (v. 21; see Mark 15:23; on the image, see Jer 8:14; 9:15; 23:15).

69:22-29. Thus the extended petition against the enemies (vv. 22-28) is understandable from a psychological point of view. In terms of the structure of the psalm, vv. 22-28 are roughly parallel to vv. 8-12, which describe how the psalmist has been mistreated. Thus, in essence, the psalmist simply asks for the opponents to experience what they have inflicted on others. Even so, the issue is not primarily personal revenge (see Psalms 35; 58; 109). Rather, from a theological point of view, the issue is justice or righteousness. The NRSV's "acquittal" (צדקה *ṣĕdāqâ*) in v. 27 is more literally translated "righteousness." In other words, the psalmist asks God to set things right. Again, the basic appeal is to God's character as loving, faithful, and compassionate. God wills justice for the poor, the lowly, and the oppressed (see Exod 3:7; Pss 9:18; 10:17-18; 68:4-6), and the psalmist is "lowly" and "in pain" (v. 29; see Exod 3:7; Job 2:13; Ps 39:3). Instead of exercising compassion, however, the opponents respond with persecution and attack (v. 26). Thus, for God's will to be enacted, they must be opposed. In effect, then, the psalmist prays, "thy will be done." By their actions, the opponents invite God's wrath (v. 24). In fact, they have already removed themselves from the company of the living and the roll of the righteous, for life and righteousness in biblical terms consist of dependence upon God (v. 28; see Exod 32:32-33; Ps 139:16; Dan 12:1; see also Commentary on Psalm 1).

69:30-33. The transition from petition/complaint to praise at v. 30 is characteristic of the prayers for help. It is possible to explain the shift psychologically or cultically, but the theological significance lies in the effect of the final form of the psalm—the juxtaposition of complaint and praise (see Commentary on Psalms 13; 22; 31; Introduction). In the book of Psalms, to live is to praise God, and to praise God is to live. Thus, even though the psalmist remains threatened and persecuted, he or she lives by entrusting life and future to God. The perspective is eschatological. The psalmist continues to wait and pray for the enactment of God's will, and yet she or he already lives amid adversity by the power of God. This witness serves to magnify God (see "magnify" in Ps 34:3 and "great" in Pss 35:27; 40:16; 70:4). God's greatness elsewhere is associated with God's sovereignty (see Pss 47:2; 95:3; 99:2-3); that is, the experience of God's power is finally not incompatible with suffering (see Reflections below). The thanksgiving in v. 30 could take the form of a sacrifice, but apparently does not in this case (v. 31). Rather, the psalmist offers her or his life as a witness to God's character (see "name" in v. 30) and as a witness to others. The NRSV's "oppressed" (עֲנָוִים *'ănāwîm*) in v. 32 is from the same Hebrew root as "lowly" in v. 29. Again, the psalmist's life is somehow exemplary (see v. 6). Other people in the same condition will see; they will share in the joy, and they, too, will live (v. 32; see Ps 22:26), knowing that, as is the case

for all those "in bonds" (see Pss 68:6; 79:11; 102:20; 107:10; Lam 3:34), God is on their side (v. 33; see Pss 9:18; 12:5; 22:24; 35:10; 140:12).

69:34-36. These verses may be a later addition, yet they are linked closely to the preceding verses. All creation joins the psalmist in praise (vv. 30, 34). God's saving work extends to other people as well (v. 35; see vv. 1, 13*d*, 29; in relation to Zion, see v. 9), and other "servants" (v. 36; see v. 17) will participate in God's gift of life, which is made possible by God's character, or "name" (vv. 30, 36).

REFLECTIONS

Theological reflection on Psalm 69 is assisted by the "liturgical-theological profile" that Mays compiles of the psalmist and that is summarized in seven points: (1) The psalmist identifies herself or himself as God's "servant" (v. 17; see v. 36) and one of the "lowly" (v. 29; see v. 32). (2) The psalmist views her or his suffering as deriving from God (v. 26), perhaps because of the behavior mentioned in v. 5. (3) The psalmist waits amid suffering for God's saving action (vv. 1, 3, 13*d*, 29). (4) The psalmist waits with humble but fervent devotion to God and to God's house (vv. 9-11). (5) The psalmist is insulted, derided, and alienated because of this fervent waiting (vv. 8, 10-11, 19-21). (6) The psalmist, therefore, bears reproach that is actually directed to God (vv. 7, 9). (7) The psalmist is a representative figure, both in the condition of affliction and in being saved by God (vv. 29, 32-33).[279]

Mays further suggests that while this profile discourages identification with any one particular historical figure, it clearly calls to mind several persons or groups: Jeremiah (see especially the so-called Confessions in Jer 11:18-20; 15:15-18; 17:14-18), the lamenting voice in Lamentations 3, the afflicted community of Psalm 44 (see vv. 22, 24), the Suffering Servant of Isaiah 53, and Job. Although precision and certainty are impossible, it is likely that all of these texts have been informed and shaped in one way or another by the experience of exile. Mays concludes: "Out of the anguish of the exile and its aftermath an understanding of affliction that goes beyond punishment and fits into the saving purpose of the LORD began to emerge. Psalm 69 is one piece of the pattern."[280]

For Christians, the ultimate piece in this emerging pattern is the cross of Jesus Christ. While Psalm 69 should not be interpreted as prophetic in a predictive sense, it is not surprising that this psalm was used several times by those who told and interpreted the story of Jesus' life, death, and resurrection. Like the psalmist, Jesus was persecuted not for being faithless but for being faithful (cf. v. 9 with John 2:17; v. 4 with John 15:25). Jesus was rejected by his own (see v. 8), mocked and insulted (see vv. 7, 9, 19-20), and received bitter treatment at human hands (cf. v. 21 with Matt 27:34; Mark 15:23; Luke 23:36; John 19:29-30). The familiarity of the psalm in the early church is indicated by the fact that even the petitions against the enemies (vv. 22-28) were cited in an attempt to explain the rejection of Jesus (cf. vv. 22-23 with Rom 11:9-10; v. 24 with Rev 16:1; v. 25 with Acts 1:20). The concluding verses of

279. Mays, *Psalms*, 230-32.
280. Mays, *Psalms*, 232.

Psalm 69 also anticipate the joy and promise of new life that came with the resurrection of Jesus (see esp. v. 32).

Like the other prayers for help (see Reflections on Psalms 13; 22; 31), Psalm 69 finally communicates God's intimate, incarnational involvement with the lowly and the oppressed. The juxtaposition of complaint/petition and praise creates an eschatological perspective; that is, the psalmist lives, and the people of God will always live, in perpetual and painful waiting (see vv. 3, 6) that is simultaneously joyful assurance and life (vv. 30-36; see Matt 5:10-11). In other words, suffering and glory, pain and joy, crucifixion and resurrection are ultimately inseparable realities for God's people and for God's own self. God's sovereignty is ultimately the power of love and compassion (see vv. 13, 16).

PSALM 70:1-5, O LORD, DO NOT DELAY!

COMMENTARY

Psalm 70 is almost identical to Ps 40:13-17. Some scholars think that Psalm 70 was an independent poem that was adapted for use as a conclusion to Psalm 40, while others view Psalm 40 as the older work and suggest that Psalm 70 was formed by borrowing the conclusion of Psalm 40. Certainty is not possible. It is interesting, though perhaps coincidental, that Ps 40:13-17 and Psalm 70 occur very near the ends of Books I and II. In fact, if Psalms 70 and 71 were originally meant to be one psalm (note that Psalm 71 lacks a superscription), then Ps 40:13-17 and Psalm 70 would be parts of the next-to-the-last psalm in both Books I and II.

The literary links between Psalms 70 and 71 reinforce the possibility that they were originally one psalm, or at least that someone intended them to be read as companions (cf. 70:1b, 5b with 71:12b; 70:2 with 71:10, 13; 70:1a with 71:2; 70:4c with 71:19c). In addition, the Hebrew word translated "memorial offering" (הזכיר *hazkîr*) in the superscription of Psalm 70 (see also the superscription of Psalm 38), is a causative form of the verb "remember" (זכר *zākar*), which occurs in a similar form in 71:16b. Psalm 70 also has affinities with Psalm 69. In both, for instance, the psalmist identifies herself or himself as "lowly"/"poor" (69:29; 70:5; the Hebrew word is the same), and the word "needy" (אביון *'ebyôn*) occurs in 69:33 and 70:5. Both psalms also feature the concept of "salvation" (69:1, 13cd, 29, 35; 70:4), the response to which is similar in each case ("magnify" in 69:30 and "great" in 70:4 represent the same Hebrew root [גדל *gādal*]).

The major difference between Ps 40:13-17 and Psalm 70 is found in a comparison of 40:17b and 70:5b. The word "thought" (חשב *ḥāšab*) in 40:17b recalls 40:5, while "hasten" (חוש *ḥûš*) in 70:5b recalls 70:1b. In short, the divergent content is appropriate in each case to its own context.

REFLECTIONS

Psalm 70 is traditionally used during Holy Week. In this setting, the quotation of the enemies in v. 3, "Aha, Aha!" (cf. Ps 35:21, 25), recalls the mocking words that onlookers directed to the crucified Jesus (see Mark 15:29). This liturgical setting is another reminder of the adaptability of the prayers for help to a variety of circumstances, and it is testimony, too, to the Christian conviction that Jesus ultimately embodied the role of the faithful sufferer who fully entrusts life and future to God (see Commentary on Psalms 22; 31; 41; 69). In other words, Jesus revealed the shape of God's sovereignty—greatness that is constituted by the power of suffering love (v. 4). (For further commentary and Reflections, see Psalm 40.)

PSALM 71:1-24, I WILL HOPE CONTINUALLY

COMMENTARY

Psalm 71 contains the typical elements of a prayer for help or individual lament/complaint: petition (vv. 1-4, 7*a*, 9, 12-13, 18), complaint (vv. 10-11), and expressions of trust (vv. 5-6, 7*b*, 17, 20-21) and praise (vv. 8, 14-16, 19, 22-24). It has numerous similarities to other prayers for help and is even sometimes viewed as a collage of quotations from other psalms, especially Psalm 22 (cf. v. 6 with 22:9-10; v. 12 with 22:11, 19; v. 18*b* with 22:30-31) and Psalm 31 (cf. vv. 1-3 with 31:1-3; v. 9*b* with 31:10; v. 13 with 31:17), but others as well (cf. v. 12*b* with 38:12 and 40:13; v. 13 with 35:4, 26; v. 19 with 36:6; v. 24 with 35:28). There are also several verbal links to Psalm 70, and it is possible that Psalms 70 and 71 were originally a single psalm (see Commentary on Psalm 70). Besides Psalm 43, Psalm 71 is the only psalm in Book II without a superscription.

Although Psalm 71 contains all the typical elements of a prayer for help, its arrangement of them is unique. For example, this psalm moves from petition/complaint to trust/praise, as is typical for this genre, but the psalm does so *three* times:

vv. 1-4	petition
vv. 5-8	trust/praise
vv. 9-13	petition/complaint
vv. 14-17	trust/praise
v. 18	petition
vv. 19-24	trust/praise

This movement is significant. Without minimizing the reality of distress and opposition, the psalmist displays pervasive faith and hope (v. 14*a*) and persistent praise (v. 6*c*; note the NRSV's "continually" in vv. 6*c*, 14*a*). The effect, in Kraus's words, is that "the psalm radiates tremendous assurance."[281]

71:1-4. This assurance is articulated in the opening words of the psalm. To "take refuge" in God may be related to the ancient practice of seeking asylum from accusers or persecutors in the Temple (see vv. 4, 10-11, 13;

1 Kgs 1:49-53; Psalms 5; 7; Introduction); however, the language may well be metaphorical. Some scholars suggest that the psalmist was ill (see v. 20) or was suffering the setbacks of old age (see vv. 9, 18), but this language may be metaphorical. What is clear is that, regardless of the circumstances, the psalmist's life depends on God. It is this dependence upon God that "refuge" communicates (see Pss 2:12; 5:11; 7:1; Introduction). It is reinforced by the series of imperatives in v. 2—"deliver" (see Ps 22:5, 9), "rescue" (see v. 4; Ps 7:2), and "save" (see Pss 3:2; 6:4; 7:1). The same word for "refuge" (מחסה *maḥseh*) recurs in v. 7, and the four nouns in v. 3 also communicate the psalmist's trust in God—"rock" (צור *ṣûr*; see Pss 18:2, 31, 46; 19:14, 28:1; 31:2); "refuge" (a different Hebrew word from that in vv. 1, 7; see also Ps 27:1; cf. Ps 31:2, although the Hebrew word in 71:2 actually differs slightly and means "dwelling place"); a second Hebrew word translated "rock" (סלע *selaʿ*; see Pss 18:2; 31:3; 42:9); and "fortress" (מצודה *měṣûdâ*; see Pss 18:2; 31:3). The NRSV suggests a fifth noun (v. 3*b*; see NRSV note); the NIV has tried to render this difficult phrase more literally.

The psalmist's assurance and appeal rest on the foundation of God's righteousness (v. 2), which becomes the major theme of the psalm (see vv. 15-16, 19, 24). The word "righteousness" (צדקה *ṣědāqâ*) designates what God wills and enacts as ruler of the world, and it involves justice and equitable treatment for the oppressed (see Pss 9:7-9; 96:13; 97:2, 6, 10-12; 98:9). As a victim of injustice and cruelty (v. 4), the psalmist trusts that God will set things right by shaming those who seek to shame the psalmist (see "shame" in vv. 1, 13, 24). In short, the psalmist trusts that God—not the wicked—rules the world (v. 4). Although v. 24 gives the impression that God has already shamed the wicked, it is not specified whether the wicked have actually experienced a reversal of fortunes or whether the psalmist speaks with a certainty of God's help that allows the psalmist to envision it as already having occurred. In any case, it is

281. Kraus, *Psalms 60–150*, 73.

clear that trust in God's righteous reign exists amid opposition for most of the psalm. In other words, the wicked (v. 4)—those who view themselves as self-sufficient rather than dependent on God—are a persistent reality (see Commentary on Psalm 1). Thus, as usual, the perspective is eschatological. God's rule is trusted and proclaimed amid powerful and persistent opposition (see Psalm 2; Introduction).

71:5-8. Verse 5 begins with the personal pronoun "you," which also occurs in vv. 3, 6-7 and focuses attention emphatically upon God. The psalmist's confidence is not self-confidence; it derives from "hope" (v. 5; see Ps 9:18) and "trust" (see Pss 4:8; 16:9; 40:4; 65:6). Verses 5-6 also introduce the theme of youth (vv. 5, 17) and old age (vv. 9, 18). While the language may be metaphorical, it expresses the psalmist's conviction that he or she has belonged to God from the day of birth and will always belong to God (see Ps 22:9-10; note especially that the word "trust" (בטח *bāṭaḥ*) occurs in 22:9, as the NIV makes clear). The proper response to God's sustaining care ("leaned" in v. 6*a* suggests sustenance; see "sustains" in Ps 3:5) is praise (vv. 6*c*, 8*a*,14*b*; see vv. 16, 22-23, where different Hebrew words for "praise" occur). For those who know their lives belong to God, praise is not just an occasional liturgical act. Rather, it is a life-style offered continually (v. 6*c*; see also v. 14 as well as the phrase "all day long" in vv. 8, 15, 24), even in the midst of adversity.

The meaning of "portent" (מופת *môpēt*) in v. 7*a* is unclear. The verse may articulate the psalmist's complaint that the suffering is so great that others see it as a warning (see Deut 28:46). The word for "portent" usually designates something more positive, however, often the exodus (see "wonders" in Exod 7:3; Deut 4:34; 6:22). Thus v. 7*a* could suggest that the psalmist's example of trust amid adversity is an encouraging sign to others. Perhaps the ambiguity is intentional, or at least appropriate. As Tate suggests, "Some members of the community would have seen the supplicant as a 'sign' of God's providential care; others would have understood his or her condition as a divine judgment."[282] In any case, the psalmist apparently intends to

282. Tate, *Psalms 51-100*, 214.

be a public witness to God's reign by praising God and testifying to God's "glory" (v. 8; see "beauty" in Ps 96:6 NRSV, a verse that also contains the word "strong"/"strength" [עז *'ōz*], found in 71:7). This intent is another major theme of the psalm (see vv. 15-19, 24).

71:9-13. The psalmist returns to petition and complaint. Verse 9 anticipates v. 18 (see also Ps 31:10), and the verb "forsake" (עזב *'āzab*) also prepares for vv. 10-11. Verse 11, which recalls Ps 3:2, indicates that some people interpret the psalmist's suffering as a sign of divine punishment. But even though the psalmist cannot understand the suffering apart from God's causation (see v. 20), he or she does not interpret it as punishment. Thus the appeal to God is persistent. Verse 12 recalls Pss 22:19 and 70:1, 6, and "shame" in v. 13 recalls v. 1 and anticipates v. 24 (see also Pss 31:17; 70:2). This look backward and forward at the center of the psalm is appropriate, and it seems to mark a turning point. Whereas vv. 1-13 consist of two sections of petition/complaint (vv. 1-4, 9-13) surrounding an expression of trust and praise, vv. 14-24 consist of two expressions of trust and praise (vv. 14-17, 19-24) surrounding a brief petition (v. 18). The movement is toward assurance.

71:14-18. In a real sense, v. 14 states the psalmist's perspective throughout the psalm: continual hope and praise (see vv. 6, 8, 15-17, 22-24). The Hebrew word for "hope" (יחל *yḥl*) in v. 14 differs from the one in v. 5, but they are essentially synonymous and occur elsewhere in the same context, often with one or the other of them being translated "wait" (see Ps 130:5, 7). Like v. 14, v. 15 recalls v. 8 (see "mouth"); and like v. 13, v. 15 recalls the beginning of the psalm (see "righteousness" and "save" in v. 2) and its conclusion (see "righteous" and "all day long" in v. 24). The effect is to focus attention on v. 14 as a kind of theological center. As vv. 15-17 suggest, continual hope inevitably issues in witness to God's righteous (vv. 15, 17), life-giving activity. The NRSV's "praise" (אזכיר *'azkîr*) in v. 16*b* is more literally, "cause to remember" (see Ps 77:11). The psalmist's role as witness is reinforced by the verb "proclaim" (נגד *ngd*) in v. 17. Even the petition in v. 18 is supported by the psalmist's desire to share the story. The verb *nāgad* is repeated, and the psalmist's stated concern is not for self-preservation but for the transmission of the faith.

71:19-24. At the heart of the psalmist's faith is the conviction that, despite appearances, God ultimately rules the world. The psalmist's proclamation focuses on God's righteousness (vv. 15-16, 19, 24) and "mighty acts"/"might" (vv. 16, 18), both of which are associated elsewhere with God's sovereignty (on "righteousness," see discussion above on v. 2; on "might," see Ps 145:4, 11-12 NIV). God's ability to do "great things" is also an attribute of God's sovereignty (v. 19; see Pss 47:2; 70:4; 95:3). In short, there is *no one* like God. Indeed, God's rule is so pervasive that the psalmist cannot help attributing his or her suffering to God (v. 20; see Deut 32:39), but does so in the confidence that God finally wills life (see "revive" in 69:32) and wholeness. The word "honor" (גדולה *gĕdûllâ*) in v.

21 is from the same root as "great things" in v. 19; thus the psalmist trusts that God's greatness is ultimately put at the service of human greatness. This in itself is a source of continual hope and "comfort" (see Ps 23:4). Thus the psalm ends with a crescendo of praise directed at God's faithfulness (see Exod 34:6; Ps 138:2; see esp. Pss 57:8-10 and 92:2-3, where harp and lyre are involved) and accompanied by another statement of resolve to be a constant witness to God's righteousness (v. 21; see Ps 35:28). The verb "tell" (הגה *hāgâ*) in v. 24 recalls the beginning of the psalter (in 1:2 *hgh* is translated as "meditate"), where it is made clear that what one meditates upon is crucial. In other words, the verb describes the orientation of one's whole existence, and the psalmist is consistently oriented to God and to God's righteousness. Precisely this orientation makes life possible and enables the psalmist to "hope continually" (v. 14).

REFLECTIONS

1. The psalmist's constant orientation to God and to God's righteousness recalls the words of Jesus as he spoke about the sustaining care of God: "But strive first for the kingdom of God and his righteousness, and all these things will be given to you as well" (Matt 6:33 NRSV; cf. Ps 71:5-6). Jesus knew that persons who strive for the kingdom of God will face adversity (see Matt 5:10-11), but he trusted and taught others to trust that God's providence is sufficient. The psalmist knew that same trust, and he or she, too, was committed to teaching it to others (vv. 17-18). Like Jesus, the psalmist lived with adversity (vv. 10-11), but the psalmist also lived in constant trust and hope that issued in praise (vv. 5-6, 14-17, 19-24). The structure of Psalm 71 represents the reality that faith lives amid adversity. Praise is not the celebration of the powerful and the prosperous; rather, it is the language and the life-style of those who know at all times and in every circumstance that their lives belong to God and that their futures depend on God.

2. Because of the psalmist's trust, hope, and faithful witness in the midst of threat and suffering, and perhaps because of the similarities between Psalm 71 and Psalms 22 and 31, Psalm 71 has customarily been associated with Jesus' passion and traditionally is used during Holy Week. It is also traditionally used during the season of Epiphany, for which the theme of the proclamation of God's righteousness (vv. 15-19, 24) makes it very appropriate. The psalmist also does the equivalent of what Christians customarily do during the season of Epiphany: We remember our baptisms. To remember our baptisms is to profess to the world that God claims us at birth and that we shall always belong to God (see vv. 5-6). In our *self*-centered, achievement-oriented culture, that simple profession is remarkable and radical. It means that we view life not as a reward to be achieved but as a gift to be received (see vv. 20-21). Thus praise becomes a life-long response and calling, from birth to old age. To praise God is to do as the psalmist did, even in the face of adversity—to look back and say "it was you who took me from my mother's womb" (v. 6) and to look forward and say, "You will . . . comfort me once again" (v. 21). As A. Hale Schroer has put it, "Praise is to declare even when the evidence seems stacked against it that this is God's world. . . . Praise is the posture of Epiphany for it keeps us open to the new ways God is manifesting Godself in our world."[283]

3. Although having grown old, the psalmist expects new things; indeed, the psalmist is intent on proclaiming God's deeds to "generations to come" (v. 18). Commentators have speculated that the psalmist was a member of one of the temple guilds, and thus was a specialist in writing songs for religious use. In our day and time, however, we cannot afford to leave the educational task to specialists. All who belong to God are called to praise God continually (v. 6) in joyful gratitude for God's faithfulness and righteousness (vv. 22-24), to witness to all the generations to come (v. 18) that ultimately nothing "will be able to separate us from the love of God" (Rom 8:39 NRSV).

283. A. Hale Schroer, "Having Confidence in God," *No Other Foundation* 9/2 (Winter 1988) 16.

PSALM 72:1-20, MAY RIGHTEOUSNESS FLOURISH AND PEACE ABOUND

COMMENTARY

As v. 1 suggests, Psalm 72 originated as a prayer for the king. The attribution to Solomon is understandable (cf. v. 15 with 1 Kgs 10:10, and vv. 1-4 with the emphasis on Solomon's justice in 1 Kings 3, esp. v. 28); it is possible that the psalm was actually written for Solomon. We simply cannot date the psalm with any certainty, but it is likely that it was written for use at the coronation of Davidic kings in Jerusalem, in which case it would have been used repeatedly, along with the other royal psalms (see esp. Psalms 2; 18; 20–21; 45; 89; 110; 132; Introduction). Obviously, Psalm 72 continued to be used after the disappearance of the monarchy. Such ongoing use was possible, because what Psalm 72 prays for ultimately is the enactment of *God's* reign and *God's* will for the world. Thus the way was open for Psalm 72 to be interpreted eschatologically within Judaism and Christianity (see Reflections below).

After the initial imperative, the psalm continues with a series of verbs that can be construed either as indicatives (NIV) or as petitions (NRSV). The ambiguity is appropriate, since Psalm 72 probably functioned both as a charge to and a prayer for the new king. The psalm is usually divided as follows: vv. 1-7,

vv. 8-14, vv. 15-17, vv. 18-20. Verses 18-19 serve both as an appropriate conclusion to the psalm and as a doxology for Book II, and v. 20 marks the conclusion of the collection that started with Psalm 51. It is significant that royal psalms (Psalms 2; 72; 89) appear at the seams of the psalter; they focus attention on God's reign at crucial points, and they lead up to the climactic proclamation of God's reign (Psalms 93; 95–99) that forms the theological heart of the psalter (see Introduction).

72:1-7. Verse 1 clearly marks the beginning of Psalm 72 as a prayer, and it introduces the two key words and concepts: justice and righteousness. Roland E. Murphy argues that the grammatical structure of v. 1 and subsequent verses serves as a clue to the programmatic significance of v. 1; that is, every section of the poem is to be heard in relation to v. 1.[284] But even apart from this grammatical clue, it is clear that v. 1 has overarching significance. Everything said about or wished for the king depends ultimately on *God's* justice (the Hebrew word משפטים [*mišpāṭîm*] is plural, but the singular sense is appropriate,

284. Roland E. Murphy, *A Study of Psalm 72* (Washington, D.C.: Catholic University Press, 1948) 6-14.

since the purpose of God's "judgments" is to enact justice) and *God's* righteousness. Justice and righteousness are first and foremost characteristic of God's reign (see Pss 96:13; 97:2, 6; 98:9; 99:4; 146:7); they describe God's royal policy, or in more theological terms, God's will. In short, the role of the king is to enact God's rule. The crucial significance of justice and righteousness for God, and thus for the king, is reinforced by repetition in vv. 1-7. The word "righteousness" (צדק *ṣedeq*) occurs in vv. 1-3 as well as in v. 7, where it marks the conclusion of the first section. The word "justice" occurs in v. 2; the verb "defend" (שפט *šāpaṭ*) in v. 4 represents the same Hebrew root, while "judge" (דין *dîn*) in v. 2 is a synonym (see Pss 7:8; 9:8; 96:10). Syntax enters the picture as well; the chiastic structure (see Introduction) of vv. 1-2 has the effect of literarily surrounding the king and his people with justice.

When God's will is done—when justice and righteousness are enacted—the result is *shalom* (v. 3 [NRSV, "prosperity"]; v. 7 [NRSV, "peace"]). The shape of *shalom* is suggested in vv. 2-7. It has primarily to do with the condition of the poor and of the needy (for "poor," see vv. 2, 4; see v. 12; see also Commentary on Psalm 9, esp. discussion of 9:18; and Psalm 10; for "needy," see v. 4; see also vv. 12-13). In fact, the *only* stated responsibility of the king in vv. 2-7 or vv. 12-14 is to establish justice for the oppressed, to "save" the needy (v. 4; see v. 13). Such salvation was what God did in the exodus (see Exod 15:2, 18), and this function is the measure of royalty, whether human or divine (see Psalm 82). The significance of justice and righteousness is further indicated by the mention of the cosmic elements in vv. 3, 5-7; only in the presence of justice and righteousness does the whole world operate as God intends (see Pss 36:5-6; 82:5; and the involvement of cosmic elements as well in Psalms 93, 96–99). Both the NIV and the NRSV follow the LXX in v. 5*a*, thus maintaining the focus on the earthly king. The Hebrew reading (see NIV and NRSV notes) has the advantage of grounding the king's work even more explicitly in God's reign.

72:8-14. Whereas vv. 5 and 7 envision the extension of the king's rule in time, vv. 8-11 envision its extension in space.[285] The river in v. 8 may be the Euphrates, or it may refer to the mythical river that flowed from God's throne in Jerusalem (see discussion of Ps 46:4 above). Tarshish is usually located in Spain (see Gen 10:4; 1 Kgs 10:22; Ps 48:7; Jer 10:9; Jonah 1:3); the isles probably refer to Mediterranean locales or perhaps to generally distant places; Sheba designates an area in the southern Arabian peninsula (see Isa 60:6; Jer 6:20; Ezek 27:22-25); and Seba may refer to generally the same area (see Gen 10:7; 1 Chr 1:9; Isa 43:3; 45:14; Joel 3:8).[286] In any case, vv. 8-11 envision the king's sovereignty as encompassing the whole world—all its rulers and all its people. The phrase "ends of the earth" recalls Psalm 2 (v. 8), which also describes the king's universal dominion over the other kings and nations. The words "bow down" (שחה *šāḥâ*) and "serve" (עבד *ʿābad*) in v. 11 designate responses ordinarily reserved for God (see Ps 2:11). Thus they are another reminder that the king's purpose is to enact God's reign.

The conjunction "for" (כי *kî*), which begins v. 12, connects universal political dominion not to clever strategy or to superior military might, as one might expect, but to the king's care for the oppressed. The vocabulary of vv. 12-14 recalls v. 4. And as v. 4 already began to suggest, the king does what is ordinarily attributed to God: He "delivers" when people cry out (see Exod 2:23); he "saves" (see Exod 15:2); he redeems (see Exod 15:13). He values the lives of those entrusted to his care (v. 14*b*; see Ps 116:15).

72:15-17. Given the correlation between the king's action and God's will, the acclamation "Long may he live!" (v. 15) is essentially a prayer that God enact God's will. As vv. 1-7 have already shown, the poet sees a connection between the work of the king and the operation of the cosmos—agricultural productivity and human productivity (v. 16). Verse 17 connects the rule of the king with the promise to Abraham in Gen 12:1-3. Scholars have traditionally dated the Yahwist (J) source in the Pentateuch, to which Gen 12:1-3 probably belongs, to the time of Solomon; Wolff even suggests that it was written to encourage the monarchy to be something

---

285. See Alter, *The Art of Biblical Poetry*, 129-33.
286. See Tate, *Psalms 51–100*, 221.

other than simply self-serving.[287] While this conclusion may be tenuous, and while the evidence is too slim to make a historical connection between Gen 12:1-3 and Psalm 72, it is at least clear that Psalm 72 views the ultimate purpose of the monarchy in terms of the fulfillment of God's purposes for the whole creation (see Ps 47:8-9; Isa 2:2-4; 19:23-25).

72:18-20. As suggested above, vv. 18-19 seem to serve as the concluding doxology for Book II, but they also form a very appropriate theological conclusion to Psalm 72. That

287. Hans Walter Wolff, "The Kerygma of the Yahwist," in *The Vitality of Old Testament Traditions* (Atlanta: John Knox, 1975) 41-66.

is to say, they make it explicit that praise for the king's activity belongs ultimately to God, for God alone is the real actor. The word "glorious"/"glory" (כבוד *kābôd*, v. 19) is often associated with God's reign (see Pss 29:1-3, 9; 24:7-10). In short, vv. 18-19 are a reminder that only God is ultimately sovereign and that the king's rule derives from and is intended to be a representation of God's reign.

Verse 20 originally may have marked the conclusion of the Davidic collection, Psalms 51–72. However, in the final form of the psalter, it also serves to mark the division between Books II and III (see Introduction).

REFLECTIONS

Perhaps the most obvious observation to make about Psalm 72 is the disparity between its portrayal of the king and the actual behavior of the kings of Israel and Judah. To be sure, such a disparity could tempt one to dismiss this psalm as part and parcel of ancient Near Eastern political propaganda (it does show marked similarities to other ancient documents, such as the Code of Hammurabi). But such a view would overlook the theological dimension of Psalm 72 in its role as Scripture. The disparity between Psalm 72 and the actual monarchy represents the disparity that always exists between the will of God and every attempt to implement the will of God concretely in space and time. The same disparity is evident, for instance, when we call the church "the body of Christ" and then observe the actual behavior of the church.

In other words, the disparity invites an eschatological understanding of Psalm 72. Even after the final failure and disappearance of the monarchy, Psalm 72 continued to be read and heard as a proclamation of God's reign and a portrayal of God's royal policy—God's will—for the world. By the time the psalm took its place in the psalter, it almost certainly was already understood messianically. For some Jews in the postexilic era, Psalm 72 probably expressed the longing for the historical restoration of the monarchy by a king who would finally get things right. For a later generation of Jews who would become Christians, Psalm 72 expressed the conviction that Jesus was that messiah, that king. They saw in Jesus one who proclaimed the reign of God (Mark 1:14-15) and embodied it in a ministry to the poor and the needy. They were convinced that Jesus' birth signaled peace on earth (Luke 2:14; see Commentary on Psalm 29) and that Jesus left peace with his disciples (John 14:27). And these disciples went out and invited all nations (that is, the Gentiles) to find their blessing in Jesus (see Galatians 3, esp. vv. 8-9, 27-29). While Psalm 72 is not specifically quoted in the NT, its association with the seasons of Advent and Epiphany is testimony to the Christian conviction that Jesus ultimately fulfilled the vision of the king portrayed in Psalm 72. When Christians pray this prayer through Jesus Christ, they are still asking essentially what Jews are asking when they pray this prayer messianically: "Thy kingdom come, thy will be done on earth as it is in heaven."

It is important, too, in the contemporary use of Psalm 72 that we not forget the similarities between it and other ancient Near Eastern expressions of the desire for justice, righteousness, and peace. As Patrick D. Miller points out, the vision of peace expressed in Psalm 72 is universal and still calls for actualization:

The potential of this shared vision for providing spiritual "weapons" in the struggle for peace was not realized in those days and has not been even until now. It still may be, however, that the wishes and hopes expressed in this psalm have their greatest possibility for actualization as they are joined with similar hopes, wishes, and prayers articulated by sisters and brothers of other religions and uttered in the hearing of all the human governments that rule our lives for good or ill, peace or war, righteousness or injustice, blessing or curse.[288]

In other words, Psalm 72 finally calls us as citizens of God's realm to remind every human ruler, politician, and government that "the way to peace and well-being is found only when power assumes responsibility for justice and is clothed in compassion, regarding as precious and valuable the life of every citizen in the land."[289] Or, to use the key word in Psalm 72, *right* makes might! The cruciform power of love, weak though it seems, is ultimately the greatest power in the world (see 1 Cor 1:25; 2 Cor 12:9).

288. Patrick D. Miller, "Power, Justice, and Peace: An Exegesis of Psalm 72," *Faith and Mission* 4/1 (1986) 66.
289. Miller, "Power, Justice, and Peace," 69.

PSALMS 73–89

BOOK III

PSALM 73:1-28, IT IS GOOD TO BE NEAR GOD

COMMENTARY

Given the apparent intentionality to the shaping of the psalter, it is not surprising that Psalm 73, which begins Book III, recalls the very beginning of the psalter. The wicked are prominent characters in Psalm 73 (see esp. vv. 3, 12) as they are in Psalm 1 (vv. 1, 5-6). The conclusion of Psalm 73 also echoes Psalm 1 (see "perish" in 1:6; 73:27), and it recalls Psalm 2 by way of the repetition of "refuge" in Pss 2:12 and 73:28. In fact, Psalm 73 is a sort of summary of what the reader of the psalter would have learned after beginning with Psalms 1 and 2 and moving through the songs and prayers of Psalms 3–72; that is, happiness or goodness has to do, not with material prosperity and success, but with the assurance of God's presence in the midst of threat and suffering. Quite properly, Brueggemann suggests that Psalm 73 plays a crucial role in the movement from Psalm 1 to Psalm 150: "Thus, I suggest that in the canonical structuring of the Psalter, Psalm 73 stands at its center in a crucial role. Even if the Psalm is not literally in the center, I propose that it is central theologically as well as canonically."[290] At a prominent point in the psalter, Psalm 73 reinforces the central message already offered in Psalms 1–72: that goodness means to live not in dependence upon oneself but in taking refuge in God (Pss 2:12; 73:28). The highest good is to be near God (v. 28).

This message would have been particularly relevant during the years following the exile. Thus it is significant that, even though the psalm narrates the experience of an individual "I," it has "Israel" in view from the beginning (see v. 1 NIV, which follows the Hebrew text). Not coincidentally, Psalm 73 introduces a book that is dominated by communal psalms of lament/complaint (Psalms 74; 79; 80; 83; and at least elements of 85 and 89). It seems likely that the experience of the "I" was offered, or at least was eventually understood, as a model for the whole people in confronting the prosperity of the wicked (see Commentary on Psalm 74).

The circumstances of the actual origin and ancient use of Psalm 73 are unclear. Because of the apparently instructional intent, many scholars classify it as a wisdom psalm. But others consider it a song of thanksgiving, a lament/complaint, a song of trust, or a royal psalm. There is also a wide range of opinion concerning the original setting of the psalm. The discussion usually focuses on v. 17, which apparently mentions the Temple and may indicate a cultic setting. If so, it is not clear what may have happened in the Temple to change the psalmist's mind—perhaps a priestly oracle of salvation, some sort of festal presentation, a Levitical sermon, or some kind of mystical experience. We simply cannot be sure. In any case, Psalm 73 finally has the character of a profession of faith, and it could easily have been used for religious instruction, for liturgy, or for both.

What is much clearer is that the structure of Psalm 73 reinforces the conclusion that the psalmist underwent a remarkable transformation of perspective. While scholars offer a variety of proposals, it seems best to divide the psalm into three major sections, each beginning with the same Hebrew particle (אַךְ 'ak):

---

290. Walter Brueggemann, "Bounded by Obedience and Praise: The Psalms as Canon," *JSOT* 50 (1991) 81.

(1) vv. 1-12   the problem (12 lines)
    vv. 1-3   the plight of the psalmist
                   (3 lines)
    vv. 4-12   the prosperity of the
                   wicked (9 lines)
(2) vv. 13-17   the turning point
(3) vv. 18-28   the solution (12 lines)
    vv. 18-20   the plight of the wicked
                   (3 lines)
    vv. 21-28   the prosperity of the
                   psalmist (9 lines)

As the outline suggests, the division on the basis of a stylistic criterion yields a symmetry that highlights the reversal of the psalmist's perspective. The central section (vv. 13-17) serves as the turning point. This section includes the much discussed v. 17, but, as suggested below, v. 15 may be just as crucial. It is the actual mid-point of the psalm; it represents the first instance of direct address to God, and it is linked conceptually to v. 1 and by repetition to v. 28, both of which are key verses, linked to each other by the repetition of "good."[291]

73:1-12. The psalm begins with the rehearsal of what sounds like a traditional affirmation of faith (v. 1*a*; see Ps 24:4). But the psalmist immediately professes doubt (v. 2) that is caused by the prosperity or peace (שלום *šālôm*) of the wicked (see Ps 1:6). The statement of v. 2 will be elaborated upon in vv. 13-14, but first comes an extended description of the wicked (vv. 4-12). It emphasizes that their pretentious (vv. 6*a*, 9) and oppressive (vv. 6*b*, 8) life-style is lived with impunity (vv. 4-5, 7, 9, 12). Verse 10 is difficult, but it seems to suggest that the wicked attract followers from among God's own people. The Hebrew of v. 10*a* can be read literally, "Therefore, his people turn away from here." These converts experience the apparent rewards described in vv. 4-5, 7, and they join the wicked in asserting their own self-sufficiency apart from God (v. 11; see Pss 3:2; 10:4, 11; 35:21, 25; 42:3, 10). The psalmist, too, seems almost to have yielded to this temptation, as the next section indicates.

73:13-17. The occurrence of "heart" (לבב *lēbāb*) in v. 13 recalls v. 1 (see also v. 7) and

291. See J. Clinton McCann, Jr., "Psalm 73: A Microcosm of Old Testament Theology," in *The Listening Heart: Essays in Wisdom and the Psalms in Honor of Roland E. Murphy, O. Carm.*, ed. K. G. Hogland, E. F. Huwiler, J. T. Glass, R. W. Lee, JSOTSup 58 (Sheffield: JSOT, 1987) 247-51.

anticipates v. 26. Like v. 1, v. 13 recalls Ps 24:4 ("innocence" [נקיון *niqqāyôn*] in v. 13 is the same as "clean" in 24:4). The psalmist is having trouble seeing the purpose of remaining faithful (see vv. 2-3). Whereas the wicked are "not plagued" (v. 5), the psalmist is constantly "plagued" (v. 14). To use the key word found in vv. 1, 28, we can paraphrase vv. 13-14 in the form of a question: "What good is it to be faithful to God?" While v. 15 does not answer this question, it does mark a turning point that is at least as significant as v. 17. It is important that v. 15 marks the psalmist's first direct address to God. Apparently, the encounter with God also renews the psalmist's awareness of God's family. The psalmist realizes that if he or she were to keep on talking the way expressed in vv. 13-14, then it would be a betrayal of God's family—that is, Israel (see v. 1). What brings the psalmist through the crisis of faith, then, is apparently his or her identity as a member of God's people. This sense of identity, of belonging to God and thus belonging to God's people, is subsequently solidified in worship (vv. 16-17). But the psalmist would never have gotten as far as the Temple (the word "sanctuary" [מקדשים *miqdāšîm*] in v. 17 is actually plural but nonetheless seems to indicate the Temple) if he or she had not already decided to remain faithful (v. 15). Thus what actually happened in the Temple—which is irrecoverable anyway—is less important than the sense of solidarity expressed in v. 15.

73:18-28. That vv. 13-17 have, indeed, been the turning point of the psalm is indicated by the structure and content of the final section. Whereas formerly the psalmist was on slippery ground (vv. 1-3) and the wicked were secure (vv. 4-12), now the wicked are on slippery ground (vv. 18-20) and the psalmist is secure (vv. 21-28). The reversal involves not a change in outward circumstances but a change of understanding. The psalmist now realizes that the apparent prosperity of the wicked is not true peace at all. Consequently, the psalmist has discovered a true and lasting peace that is not "as the world gives" (John 14:27 NRSV). This peace is founded on the simple but profound good news that God is present (see Pss 23:4; 46:7, 11). This good news is emphasized by the repetition in Hebrew of the prepositional phrase "with you" (עמד 'immāk in vv. 22-23; 'immĕkā in v. 25). Although the psalmist had been a "beast *toward you*" (v. 22; lit., "with you"), his or her behavior had not caused separation from God: "Nevertheless I am continually *with you*" (v. 23; see Ps 139:10). A third occurrence of the phrase is found in v. 25 *b*, which reads literally, "and *with you* I have no desire on earth." The two occurrences of "heart" in v. 26 recall vv. 1 and 13. More fundamental than the traditional notions of being pure in heart (v. 1) and keeping one's heart clean (v. 13)—which apparently were associated with entering the Temple, the sphere of God's presence (see Ps 24:3-4)—is the assurance that God is always present and thus the enduring "strength of my heart" (lit., "rock of my heart"; see Ps 19:14). The word "portion" (חלק *ḥēleq*) elsewhere designates the share that every Israelite was supposed to have in the land and that, therefore, meant access to life and future (see Josh 15:13; 19:9). The psalmist now knows an even greater portion: God's own self (see Num 18:20; Ps 119:57; Lam 3:24), which promises life and future.

Verse 24 also articulates the good news of God's presence (see Ps 23:3), and v. 24 *b* is often interpreted as a promise of life and future that transcends the boundary of death. Many scholars hear v. 24 *b* as an allusion to the assumptions of Enoch and Elijah (Gen 5:24; 2 Kgs 2:11; see also Ps 49:15), and Dahood even contends that "the psalmist finds the solution to the inconsistencies of this life in the final reward of the righteous after death."[292] The precise meaning of v. 24 *b* is unclear, and most interpreters find no evidence here for a developed doctrine of resurrection; however, v. 24 *b* clearly pushes the boundaries of the usual Israelite conception of life and death (see discussions on Pss 22:29; 49:15 above).

Verses 27-28 underscore the significance of God's presence. Death is essentially alienation from God (v. 27; see Ps 1:6). The phrase "But as for me" (v. 28) recalls the psalmist's precarious position in v. 2, while the repetition of "good" recalls v. 1. Now it is clear what "God is good to Israel" really means. It does not mean the material prosperity and ease enjoyed by the wicked (vv. 4-12). Rather, the essential goodness of life is to be near God (see Deut 4:7; 30:14; Pss 75:1; 145:18), to make God one's refuge (see Pss 2:12; 46:1; Introduction). The psalmist now knows the truth, and the truth has set him or her free "to tell of all your works" (v. 28 *c*). This final phrase of the psalm recalls the central verse. Both refer to God in the second person, and the verb "tell" in v. 8 is the same as "talk" in v. 15. The psalmist's talk has changed from self-pity (vv. 13-14) to praise (v. 28). No longer focused on the self, the psalmist affirms that he or she belongs to God (vv. 23-28) and thus belongs in the circle of God's children (v. 15). This nearness to God is the essence of goodness, happiness (see Pss 1:1; 2:12), assurance, and life.

292. Dahood, *Psalms II (51–100)*, 195.

REFLECTIONS

Given the psalmist's initial dilemma (vv. 2-3) and the elaboration of it in vv. 13-14, we must reflect on the concept of reward and punishment. The psalmist almost lost faith, because he or she thought that good behavior should be materially rewarded; but it was not (vv. 13-14). What the psalmist came to realize is that true goodness, happiness, and peace consist of a different kind of reward—the experience of God's presence (vv. 23-28). In a sense, faithful behavior (vv. 1, 13) is its own reward; it is rewarding, not because it earns God's favor, but because it derives from and expresses the power and presence of God in our lives, individually (vv. 25-26, 28) and corporately (v. 15). The psalmist knew already the happiness Jesus would proclaim, "Blessed are the pure in heart, for they will see God" (Matt 5:8 NIV; see Ps 73:1, 28).

This experience of God's power and presence—in effect, this seeing God—finally convinced the psalmist that faithfulness was not in vain. While Psalm 73 probably does not embody a doctrine of resurrection, Christian readers cannot help being reminded that for the apostle Paul the resurrection of Jesus was the assurance that his labor in this life was not in vain (1 Cor 15:58; cf. Ps 73:13-14). The powerful testimony to God's power and presence in Psalm 73 also anticipates Paul's affirmation that nothing "in all creation, will be able to separate us from the love of God in Christ Jesus our Lord" (Rom 8:39 NRSV). This assurance is for our living and for our dying. Paul's words in Rom 14:7-8 (NRSV) capture the spirit and good news of Psalm 73: "We do not live to ourselves, and we do not die to ourselves. If we live, we live to the Lord, and if we die, we die to the Lord; so then, whether we live or whether we die, we are the Lord's."

PSALM 74:1-23, DO NOT FORGET YOUR AFFLICTED PEOPLE

COMMENTARY

Psalm 74 is a communal lament/complaint that confronts in corporate terms the same problem faced by the individual in Psalm 73: the apparent triumph of the wicked. Not surprisingly, there are several literary links between Psalms 73 and 74, including the name "Asaph" in the superscription, "sanctuary" in 73:17 and 74:7, "violence" in 73:6 and 74:20, "right hand" in 73:23 and 74:11, and "ruin(s)" in 73:18 and 74:3 (the only two occurrences of the plural form in the OT). These links suggest that Psalms 73 and 74 should be heard together, and they reinforce the impression that Psalm 73 offers a model for the whole people in confronting the prosperity of the wicked (see Commentary on Psalm 73). It is probably not coincidental that Psalms 42–44 open Book II in the same way that Psalms 73–74 open Book III (see Commentary on Psalms 42–43; 44). The pattern of an "I" psalm (Psalms 42–43; 73) followed by a communal lament (Psalms 44; 74) provides a context for reading the rest of the psalms in Books II and III. It would have made both books not only particularly suited for addressing the situation following the exile, but also suited for ongoing use by the perpetually threatened people of God (see Introduction).

The rejection and destruction described in vv. 1-11 are usually associated with the fall of Jerusalem to the Babylonians in 587 BCE, although Psalm 74 has sometimes been dated as late as the Maccabean era. In particular, the lament over the absence of a prophet (v. 9) seems congruent with 1 Macc 4:46; 9:27;

and 14:41. However, this feature could apply to an earlier setting as well (see Lam 2:9), and an earlier origin is more likely, in which case the psalm would have taken on renewed significance during the Maccabean era as well as during other crises throughout the centuries. In fact, the post-exilic community lived under constant threat and domination, as do the people of God in every age, and Psalm 74 has the ability to speak in a variety of times and places (see Reflections below).

The psalm is usually divided into three major sections: (1) vv. 1-11, (2) vv. 12-17, (3) vv. 18-23. The questions in vv. 1, 10-11 provide an inclusio[293] for the first section (see esp. "why" in vv. 1, 11), which also consists of petition (vv. 2-3) and more direct complaint that describes the destruction of the Temple (vv. 4-9). Verses 12-17 shift to praise of God as king and of God's past activity on behalf of Israel and the whole creation. Verses 18-23 return to petition with accompanying complaints that serve as motivation for God to take renewed action against opponents of God's reign and thus on behalf of God's afflicted people.

74:1-3. The opening questions in v. 1 attribute the current crisis to God's anger. The language is typical of other complaints, both individual and communal (see "cast off"/"reject" in Pss 43:2; 44:9, 23; 60:1, 10; 88:14; 89:38; on smoking anger, see Deut 29:20; Pss 18:8; 80:4). Elsewhere,

---

293. *Inclusio* is a technical term for a biblical passage in which the opening expression, phrase, or idea is repeated, paraphrased, or in some other way returned to at the end.

too, the people are called God's sheep (see Pss 79:13; 95:7; 100:3; Ezek 34:31). The first petition, "Remember," will recur twice more (vv. 18, 22; see also Exod 2:24; 32:13; Pss 25:6-7; 98:3). The vocabulary of v. 2 recalls the Song of the Sea and the exodus, in which God originally "acquired" the people (see Exod 15:16), having redeemed them from slavery (see Exod 15:13) to bring them to Mount Zion (see Exod 15:17; note "inheritance" in Exod 15:17 and Ps 74:2 NIV). Verse 2 also anticipates vv. 12-17, where the exodus will be poetically described (see "of old" in vv. 2, 12). The Song of the Sea culminates in the proclamation of God's reign "forever" (Exod 15:18), but the only "forever" perceived by the people in Psalm 74 involves rejection and ruin (see "forever"/"everlasting"/"perpetual" in vv. 1, 3, 10, 19). In other words, it appears that God's opponents, rather than God, are sovereign. They have destroyed God's sanctuary.

74:4-11. Verses 4-9 describe the destruction in some detail. Roaring to signal their victory (see Ps 22:13; Jer 2:15), God's opponents also install in the Temple signs of their own rule (see "emblems" in vv. 4, 9 NRSV). Interpreting v. 5 is difficult, but along with v. 6, it seems to describe one of the means of destruction (see "carved" in 1 Kgs 6:29). Verses 7-8 mention another means: fire. The variety of synonyms for the Temple in vv. 4-8 emphasizes the point that the opponents have completely prevailed in Jerusalem and beyond. The NRSV's "meeting places" (מועדים *môʿadîm*) in v. 8 is the plural of "holy place" (מועד *môʿēd*) in v. 4, and the Hebrew word may designate other holy sites outside Jerusalem, perhaps forerunners of the synagogue (see 1 Macc 3:46). In short, there is no sign of God's rule anywhere (v. 9a). A comparison of the NIV and the NRSV translations of v. 9a reveals two possible senses of the Hebrew word usually translated "sign" (אות *ʾōt*). It can designate either a physical emblem, such as a flag (see "ensigns" in Num 2:2 NRSV) or a revelatory action of God. In either sense, there is no visible sign of God and no prophets to deliver a word from God (v. 9b; see Lam 2:9). In short, no one knows anything, including how long God will be absent (v. 9c). All that is left to do is ask, and the questions in vv. 10-11 thus reveal a remarkable

depth of faith. They reveal that the people still trust God and God's sovereignty, despite a total lack of evidence for God's rule. Thus the perspective is eschatological. God's rule is assumed and asserted in the midst of powerful opposition that certainly seems to prevail. In other words, the question is not *whether* God is powerful (see v. 11; see also "right hand" in Exod 15:6, 12) but *when* God will show God's power—"How long?" (see Pss 79:5; 89:46). In the meantime, God's foes will continue to "scoff" (v. 10; see vv. 18, 22; see also "taunt"/"scorn"/"reproach"/"insult" in Pss 22:6; 31:11; 42:10; 44:13, 16; 55:12; 69:9-10; 89:41) and "revile" (v. 10; see "renounce" in Ps 10:3, 13).

74:12-17. The sovereignty of God, which is asserted implicitly in the questions of vv. 10-11, is explicitly proclaimed in v. 12 (see Pss 5:2; 10:16; Introduction). As in the exodus, to which the following verses will allude, God's activity involves salvation (see Exod 15:2). Verse 13a describes the event more or less as a historical phenomenon that reveal's God's might, an attribute elsewhere associated with royal sovereignty (see "strength" in Exod 15:13; Pss 29:1; 93:1; 96:6). The description, however, immediately spills over into the realm of the mythic in vv. 13b-14. The sea itself, as well as the "dragons" (see Gen 1:21; Job 7:12; Ps 148:7; Isa 27:1; 51:9) and Leviathan (see Job 3:8; 41:1; Ps 104:26; Isa 27:1), represent the chaotic forces over which God is sovereign. In some ancient Near Eastern creation stories, the supreme deity defeats a monster and uses its body parts to fashion the universe. Such mythic imagery lies in the background of vv. 13-14 (see also Pss 77:16-19; 89:9-11; 93:3-4; 104:5-9; 114:1-6; Isa 51:9-11). The emphasis on creation is even clearer in v. 15 ("cut" [בקע *bāqaʿ*] is the same verb as "divide" in Exod 14:16; see also Ps 104:10), v. 16 (see Gen 1:14-16), and v. 17 (see Gen 8:22; Ps 104:9). In short, God is ruler of the cosmos (note "earth" in vv. 12 and 17, forming an inclusio for the section). The merging of exodus and creation imagery suggests that God's creative activity is in itself salvific and that God's activity in the exodus was not simply on behalf of Israel but involved the fulfillment of God's purposes for the whole creation (see esp. Exod 9:16; see also Commentary on

Psalms 33; 65; 66). Both God's saving and creating work, which should not finally be separated, are testimony to God's reign. The sevenfold occurrence of the Hebrew pronoun "you" (אתה 'attâ) in vv. 13-17 is emphatic, perhaps corresponding to the seven-headed chaos monster in some ancient Near Eastern myths, but in any case suggesting that God alone is sovereign.

74:18-23. The proclamation of God's universal sovereignty in vv. 12-17 serves as the basis for the petitions in the next passage. Twice God is asked to "remember" (vv. 18, 22) and "not forget" (vv. 19, 23). It was the special calling of a king to provide for the poor (vv. 19, 21) and the needy (v. 21; see Pss 72:1-7, 12-14; 82:1-4), and the final section serves to remind God of this responsibility in view of the apparent triumph of the wicked and their arrogant behavior (vv. 18, 22-23; see v. 10). In other words, the "cause" of the poor and needy is *God's* cause as well (v. 22*a*; see

Ps 43:1; Lam 3:58). Thus God can reasonably be asked to "rise up" (v. 22; see Pss 3:7; 9:19; 10:12) against those who have arisen against God (v. 23; the NRSV's "adversaries" [קמים *qāmîm*] is more literally, "those who arise"). Verses 19-20 are notoriously difficult and have given rise to a variety of translations and interpretations. Both the NIV and the NRSV translate the Hebrew literally, which is probably the best alternative in this case. The word "dove" (תור *tôr*) probably designates Israel in its current poverty or affliction. The mention of covenant also serves to recall God's past actions and the relationship God had established with the people (see Exod 24:1-8; Ps 44:17). Given the people's faith in God's cosmic sovereignty (vv. 12-17), the petitions in vv. 18-23 function finally as an affirmation of the people's trust that God will "not forget the life of your poor forever" (v. 19; see Ps 9:18).

REFLECTIONS

It is particularly significant that Psalm 74—the voice of suffering faith—contains not only the complaints and petitions that one might expect (vv. 1-11, 18-23) but also a rousing, hymnic affirmation of God's sovereignty (vv. 12-17). The paradox is instructive, for it reinforces the eschatological perspective that is present throughout the psalter and the entire Bible (see Introduction). That is to say, the reign of God is always proclaimed amid circumstances that seem to deny it: the destruction of the Temple and, in a later time, an executioner's cross. In the worst of times, when the forces of evil seem to prevail, the people of God profess their faith in a cosmic sovereign whose power seems to be no power at all, whose "power is made perfect in weakness" (2 Cor 12:9 NRSV; see 1 Cor 1:25). Of course, faith in a God who exercises sovereignty in this way profoundly affects one's understanding of suffering. Not surprisingly, the exile, out of which Psalm 74 seems to have arisen, produced several profoundly new expressions of the role of suffering in the life of the faithful—Isaiah 40–55, the book of Job, and certain psalms (see Commentary on Psalm 44).

As several commentators recognize, Psalm 74 has important ecclesiological implications, and these implications are related to the new understanding of the role of suffering. Mays comments:

> As for the self-understanding of the congregation in this prayer, is it of no importance that they have learned to think of themselves as the lowly [vv. 19-21]? This may be a form of the transformation worked in the character of the congregation by judgment for which Jeremiah and Ezekiel looked (Jer 31:33; Ezek 36:26). "Blessed are the poor in spirit . . . the meek . . . " (Matt. 5:3, 5).[294]

294. Mays, *Psalms,* 247-48.

In other words, Psalm 74 anticipates Jesus' eschatological proclamation of the reign of God (Mark 1:14-15) and his invitation to be disciples, not by the avoidance of suffering but by taking up a cross (Mark 8:34). As in Psalm 74, the life of faith will be lived amid constant scoffing and continual opposition (vv. 10, 18, 22-23), as was Jesus' life.

It is interesting that Psalm 74 contains no confession of the sins that led to the destruction of the Temple and the exile. But in a sense, once the Temple had been destroyed and the people's "penalty . . . paid" (Isa 40:2 NRSV), confession of sin became irrelevant. The real issue then became the one that is at the heart of Psalm 74: Who is sovereign? Can the foes who carried out the destruction of the Temple be put in their place? Can God ultimately enact God's purposes for the whole creation? The voice of suffering faith in Psalm 74 dares to answer yes. In the face of dominant evil, then and now, such an affirmative answer appears foolish. But Psalm 74 asserts that the real foolishness is to deny the character and power of Israel's God (see vv. 18, 22). Then and now, the people of God assert that "God's foolishness is wiser than human wisdom" (1 Cor 1:25 NRSV), and so we continue to pray and to trust that God will not forget the lives of the poor and the needy, among whom we must always include ourselves.

PSALM 75:1-10, GOD SAYS TO THE ARROGANT, "DO NOT BOAST"

COMMENTARY

Given the linguistic links between Psalms 73 and 74 (see Commentary on Psalm 74), it is interesting that Ps 75:1 clearly recalls Ps 73:28 (see "near" and "tell" in both verses). In addition, in the divine speech (vv. 2-5), God addresses "the arrogant" (v. 4), who were the source of the problem in Psalm 73 (see 73:3; the only other occurrence of this word in the psalter is 5:5; see also "the wicked" in 73:3, 12; 75:4, 8, 10). While there are no striking verbal links between Psalms 74 and 75 (but see "name" in 74:10, 18; 75:1), it is almost as if 75:2-5, 10 is a direct response to the petitions in 74:18-23; Psalm 75 develops the proclamation of God's sovereignty that is found in Psalm 74, portraying God as savior (vv. 2, 7, 10; see Ps 74:12-13) and cosmic creator and ruler (v. 3; see Ps 74:14-17). Thus, even if the sequence of Psalms 73–75 is coincidental, there are literary and conceptual links that suggest their coherence (see Introduction, concerning the shape of Book III).

Because of the existence and content of the divine speech in vv. 2-5, 10, Psalm 75 is frequently labeled a prophetic judgment speech (see Psalm 82). It begins, however, like a song of praise (v. 1), and the response to the divine speech (vv. 6-8) is a profession of faith that has a didactic character. Verse 9 recites the psalmist's promise that results from the faith expressed in vv. 6-8. Despite the variety of forms, Psalm 75 is clearly a unit. The promise in v. 9, for instance, clearly recalls v. 1, even though the vocabulary of praise and proclamation differs. Furthermore, both the divine speech and the response focus on God's establishment of justice (see the forms of "judge" in vv. 2, 7), especially as this involves dealing with the apparent power (see "horn" in vv. 4-5, 10) of the wicked (vv. 4, 8, 10). Unity is provided by the sixfold occurrence of a Hebrew root (רום *rûm*) translated "lifting up" (vv. 4-7), "high" (v. 5), and "exalted" (v. 10).

75:1. The word "name" (שם *šēm*) suggests God's character and presence, and as in Ps 73:28 the experience of nearness to God is accompanied by proclamation of God's activity (see also Deut 4:7; 30:14; Ps 145:18). The Hebrew word translated as "wondrous deeds" (נפלאות *niplāʾôt*) elsewhere designates the exodus (Exod 3:20; 34:10), the crossing of the Jordan (Josh 3:5), and other acts of deliverance. In Psalms, giving thanks and proclamation of God's wondrous deeds often go together (see Pss 9:1; 26:7).

75:2-5. As the NIV more clearly suggests with its insertion of "You say" and its use of quotation marks, v. 2 marks the beginning of the divine speech that runs through v. 5. In the light of v. 1, the word for "set time"/"appointed time" (מועד *mô'ēd*) could be an echo of the exodus event (see Exod 9:5). It also occurs in Hab 2:3, where, as in Psalm 75, it involves divine judgment upon arrogant opponents (see 2:1-5)—namely, the Babylonians. Scholars often note other similarities between Habakkuk and Psalm 75 (see the concern for justice for the wicked in Hab 1:4, 12-13; cf. Hab 2:15-16 with Ps 75:8). And if Psalms 74–75 are read together, there is even more reason to think of the Babylonians as "the wicked," since they destroyed the Temple in 587 BCE. Of course, the possible historical connection between Psalm 75 and Habakkuk remains elusive, but Habakkuk provides an illustrative context for hearing Psalm 75 without limiting its application or usefulness to that particular historical setting (see Reflections below).

In any case, what God will eventually do is establish justice, which will mean judgment upon God's opponents. God's will to "judge with equity" is elsewhere associated with the proclamation of God's reign (see Pss 9:8; 96:10; 98:9; 99:4). In short, God will exercise sovereignty on a cosmic scale (v. 3). When the world is threatened with chaos, God holds things together (see Psalm 46). The second "I" in v. 2 (אני *'ănî*) and the "I" in v. 3 (אנכי *'ānōkî*) are emphatic in Hebrew;

therefore, *God* and no other rules the world. This means that powerful human beings, who think that they rule the world (see Pss 10:3-4; 94:4-7), must be told not to boast (v. 4*a*) and must be warned not to exert their power (v. 4*b*; see "horn" in Jer 48:25). The NRSV's "on high" (v. 5) sometimes designates heaven. In other words, God warns the arrogant and the wicked not to oppose God's own sovereignty (see 1 Sam 2:3; Pss 2:10-11; 66:7).

75:6-8. Repeating key words from vv. 2-5, the response to the divine speech recognizes that God alone establishes justice (v. 7*a*; see also v. 2) and that God alone has the power to put down and to lift up (vv. 6, 7*b*; see also vv. 4-5; 1 Sam 2:7-8, 10; Pss 113:5-7; 147:6). Verse 8 portrays this divine activity with the metaphor of a cup from which the wicked drink (see Ps 11:6; Isa 51:17; Jer 25:15; 49:12; Ezek 23:32-34; Hab 2:15-16; Rev 14:10; 16:19; 18:6; cf. Pss 23:5; 116:13; Mark 14:23-25).

75:9-10. The response of vv. 6-8 is personalized in v. 9. In contrast to the wicked, who exalt themselves, the psalmist praises God. As a comparison of the NIV and the NRSV makes clear, the verb in v. 9*a* is attested differently. The Hebrew makes sense, although an object needs to be supplied, and it also has the effect of making v. 9 a closer parallel to v. 1. The "I" in v. 10*a* could be understood as the psalmist, but the activity described is better attributed to God, especially in view of vv. 6-8. Thus v. 10 returns to the divine speech of vv. 2-5. (On the contrast of the wicked and the righteous and their respective futures, see Commentary on Psalm 1.)

REFLECTIONS

Like Psalm 1 and many other psalms, Psalm 75 portrays the righteous as those who live in dependence upon God and the wicked as those who live by self-assertion, and it contrasts the outcomes of these two ways of living. Just as do Psalm 2 and many others, so also Psalm 75 asserts that the futures of the righteous and the wicked differ, because God rules the world. As is regularly the case in the book of Psalms, Psalm 75 does not precisely identify the wicked except by their boasting and self-centeredness. When Psalm 75 is read in the context of Psalm 74 and the book of Habakkuk, it is possible to identify the wicked as the Babylonians. Such an identification would have made Psalm 75 a particularly useful resource for facing the crisis of exile and its aftermath, and there is reason to think that Book III of the psalter was shaped with this in mind (see Introduction). But the psalm itself looks beyond this specific identification to "all the wicked of the earth" (v. 8).

If the wicked are understood as nations that take selfish pride in being world powers—perhaps even superpowers—then the problem of the wicked is just as real today as it was in the sixth century BCE. United States intervention in global conflicts may sometimes be morally healthy and helpful, but it also may serve as an excuse to protect national interests at any cost. Among all nations, there is a persistent temptation to identify as the will of God what simply seems to promote selfish concerns and goals, which are often given the high-sounding label of "national security."

If, on the other hand, the wicked are understood as powerful individuals who pride themselves on being self-sufficient, then the problem of the wicked is still just as real today as ever. Indeed, our culture generally teaches us to strive for autonomy and self-sufficiency, to look out for ourselves and our own above all else (see Commentary on Psalm 1).

In short, however wickedness is viewed, the truth is that it is well-represented in us and in our institutions at all levels, including nation and church. Thus, when Psalm 75 proclaims the rule of God, which will bring to justice "all the wicked of the earth," the message is eschatological. That is to say, as always, in Psalms and in the preaching of Jesus, the reign of God is proclaimed amid powerful opposition (see vv. 4-5; see also Commentary on Psalm 2; Introduction). And as always, the proclamation calls for a decision. Indeed, Psalm 75 invites the same commitment that Jesus invited when he said, "All who exalt themselves will be humbled, and all who humble themselves will be exalted" (Matt 23:12 NRSV; cf. Ps 75:7, 10). Psalm 75 reminds us that in God's reign, worldly values are turned upside down (see 1 Sam 2:1-10; Luke 1:46-55; 1 Cor 1:26-31). What this reversal means, as the apostle Paul recognized, is this: "Let the one who boasts, boast in the Lord" (1 Cor 1:31 NRSV; cf. Ps 34:2; 2 Cor 11:16-32; 12:1-10).

PSALM 76:1-12, GOD INDEED IS AWESOME

COMMENTARY

Because of the celebration of Zion as God's dwelling place and the site of God's victory (vv. 2-3), Psalm 76 has been traditionally classified as a song of Zion (see Psalms 46; 48; 84; 87; 122). Although scholars have sometimes tried to tie the victory to a specific historical incident—e.g., David's taking of Jerusalem (2 Sam 5:6-10) or the deliverance of Jerusalem from Sennacherib in 701 BCE (2 Kgs 19:35; Isa 36:1–37:38)—the present literary setting of Psalm 76 discourages such attempts. That is to say, when Psalm 76 is heard in the context of Psalm 74 (see also Pss 78:67–79:13), it clearly has an eschatological thrust. It asserts God's power and sovereignty, but it does so in a context where opposition and defeat are

evident. While it may allude to Zion's past, it is more about the future that God will create for the people and for the earth. As Mays suggests, "the psalm is more about the resident of Zion than about Zion itself."[295]

The psalm falls into four sections. Verses 1-3 introduce God's greatness and association with Zion. Verses 4-6 describe how God's power affects God's opponents. Verses 7-9 proclaim the purpose of God's power: justice for all (see "judgment" in vv. 8-9 NRSV; two different Hebrew words are represented). Alluding to the opposition (v. 10), the final section also describes God's power (v. 12) and invites recognition of and response to God's

295. Mays, *Psalms*, 250.

sovereignty (v. 11). The key word in vv. 7-12 is "feared" (ירא *yārēʾ*, vv. 7-8, 11-12).

76:1-3. The opening line already suggests a focus on God's sovereignty. It recalls another song of Zion in which "the great King . . . has shown himself a sure defense" (Ps 48:2-3; "shown" [ידע *yādaʿ*] represents the same verb used in 76:1). The verb "known" (*yādaʿ*) is a reminder that the purpose of the exodus, also a demonstration of God's reign (Exod 15:18), was that the Egyptians "know that I am the LORD" (Exod 14:4 NRSV). God's greatness is elsewhere an attribute of God's sovereignty (Ps 95:3); as in v. 2, it is explicitly associated with God's residence in Zion (see Pss 48:2-3; 99:2-3). The words used for Zion are used elsewhere to designate a lion's den or lair, and they may suggest that God is being portrayed as divine warrior in the form of a mighty lion. Such an image would be congruent with other passages where God "roars from Zion" (see Jer 25:30; Joel 3:16; Amos 1:2). In any case, God uses God's power to destroy the implements of war (v. 3; cf. Ps 46:9-10, another song of Zion; see also Isa 2:4; Mic 4:3). The word "there" (שמה *šāmmâ*) seems to refer to Zion, but the description of God's activity recalls God's work in a variety of settings, especially the exodus (see v. 6). Thus the reader is reminded that Zion in Psalm 76 not only refers to a specific place, but also functions as a symbol of God's sovereignty in all times and places (see Commentary on Psalm 48).

76:4-6. The opening word of v. 4 is derived from the Hebrew root that means "light" (אור *ʾôr*); it is frequently associated with God's presence (see "light"/"shine" in Num 6:25; Pss 4:6; 27:1; 31:16). The Hebrew pronoun "you" focuses attention on God, and it anticipates the beginning of the next section where "you" actually occurs twice in v. 7a. The adjective "majestic" (אדיר *ʾaddîr*) also describes God in Ps 8:1, 9, as well as in 93:4 in the context of the proclamation of God's reign. The metaphor of God as a lion in vv. 1-3 makes the Hebrew of v. 4b more understandable. Verses 5-6 recall v. 3 in that God's intervention ends the battle. Verse 6 recalls the exodus with its mention of "horse and rider" (see Exod 15:1). The power of God's "rebuke" is indicative of God's sovereignty and was also manifest in the exodus, especially in God's command of the sea (see Pss 18:15; 104:7; Isa 50:2).

76:7-9. Although not obvious in translation, the opening verbs of vv. 1, 4, and 7 are the same Hebrew form (*niphal* participle), drawing even further attention to God and the divine attributes. As suggested above, v. 7a represents the first of four occurrences of the root "fear" (*yārēʾ*), and not surprisingly, it, too, is explicitly associated elsewhere with God's reign (see "awesome"/"to be feared"/"to be revered" in Exod 15:11; Pss 47:2; 96:4; 99:3; 145:6). God's royal policy as cosmic sovereign is expressed here, as elsewhere, as justice (vv. 8-9; see Ps 96:10, 13 where the two Hebrew words occur in the context of the proclamation of God's reign). God's justice will be worldwide (see vv. 8-9; see also v. 12). Verse 8 suggests that the result of God's justice will be peace (see Zech 1:11; see also Ps 46:10). The conditions for peace in biblical terms include provision for the lives of the oppressed (see "afflicted"/"poor"/"meek" in Pss 9:9, 12, 18; 10:12, 17-18; 74:19, 21), the prototypical example of which is the exodus (see "save"/"salvation" in Exod 14:30; 15:2; Pss 6:4; 7:1; Isa 11:4).

76:10-12. The sense of v. 10 is elusive, as a comparison of the NIV with the NRSV suggests. The verb "praise" (תודה *tôdâ*) in v. 10 is often rendered "give thanks." A noun form of the root means "thanksgiving offering," and such offerings were apparently accompanied by the making and performance of vows (see Ps 116:17-18). By perhaps suggesting that even human wrath or recalcitrance eventually ends up honoring the sovereign God, v. 10 may provide the background for the explicit invitation in v. 11 to recognize and respond to God's claim on the whole world (v. 12; see Pss 2:10-11; 48:4-6).

Reflections

At first sight, it may seem that the particularity of a song of Zion like Psalm 76 would make contemporary application very difficult. However, Zion functions in Psalm

76 as a symbol of God's sovereignty in all times and places (see Commentary on Psalms 46; 48). As is always the case, the assertion of God's reign is eschatological; it is made in the presence of powerful opposition (see Commentary on Psalm 2; Introduction). In fact, no one in the ancient world would have known this any better than the residents of Jerusalem, which was just as much a source of contention then as it is now.

Nevertheless, there arose in Judah what is often called the doctrine of the inviolability of Zion, the conviction that Jerusalem could not be destroyed because it was God's dwelling place. Needless to say, this doctrine required major reformulation after the destruction of Jerusalem in 587 BCE (see Commentary on Psalm 74). In all likelihood, however, the doctrine of Zion's inviolability was never intended to be taken literally; rather, it was to function symbolically. As J. David Pleins suggests, "the Zion image is far more dynamic: God's presence in Zion launches a new era in which warfare comes to an end." Pleins also points out that this "dramatic interpretation" of Zion is articulated also in Isa 2:2-4 and Mic 4:1-3, and he concludes:

> For the psalmists and these prophets, Zion is the image of the power of God's transformative peace in the face of war. The weaker doctrine of inviolability might leave one thinking that peace stops at Zion's walls. The sentiment that rings so clearly in the hymns of Zion and in Isaiah and Micah is that Zion is the starting point of a new way of living and worshiping in a world filled with war. The image of Zion broadens the definition of security to encompass not only city walls and towers, but also divine presence, the breaking of the bow, and hope for an end to war.[296]

In other words, Psalm 76 is finally an invitation to live under God's sovereignty (v. 11), to adopt God's values and God's ways (vv. 8-9). But to stand for justice and peace in a world filled with war and injustice requires a particular understanding of sovereignty. God's sovereignty is exercised not as sheer force but as the power of love. The world does not understand this kind of power, but it is power nonetheless (see 1 Cor 1:25). The invitation in v. 11 is ultimately an invitation to respond to God's love. William C. Placher declares that God's strength is finally God's very vulnerability. He concludes, "We worship God, then, not intimidated by sheer divine power, but because, in the face of a love that reaches literally beyond our human imagination, we are 'lost in wonder, love, and praise.'"[297] As children of God, we are inevitably peacemakers (see Matt 5:9), for we dare to tell the world of and commit our lives to a power that is greater than weapons and generals and princes and prime ministers and presidents (see vv. 3, 6, 12)—the power of God's love symbolized by Zion and made known ultimately in the cross of Jesus Christ, whom Christians profess was and is the new earthly locus of God's presence and power (see Commentary on Psalm 48).

296. Pleins, *The Psalms*, 122-23.
297. William C. Placher, "Narratives of a Vulnerable God," *The Princeton Seminary Bulletin* 14/2 (1993) 149.

PSALM 77:1-20, GOD'S FOOTPRINTS WERE UNSEEN

COMMENTARY

The first ten verses of Psalm 77 have the character of a lament/complaint or prayer for help, but God is not addressed directly except in v. 4. It is as if the psalmist has become so discouraged that prayer has become impossible (see v. 4b) and has given way to anguished meditation (v. 6; note the past tenses in vv. 1-6 NIV). The meditation culminates in the wrenching questions of vv. 7-9 and the apparently hopeless conclusion in v. 10. Verses 11-20 are so unexpected after vv. 1-10 that some scholars conclude that vv. 1-10 and vv. 11-20 should be considered separate psalms; however, a common vocabulary unifies the two sections. Most notably, the psalmist continues to remember (v. 11; see also vv. 3, 5-6) and to meditate (v. 12; see also vv. 3, 6). John Kselman argues that the two occurrences of the Hebrew "my voice" in v. 1 are matched by the two references to God's "voice" (NIV, "thunder") in vv. 17-18 and that a further mark of unity is the repetition of "hand" in vv. 3, 20. He also detects a chiastic structure (see Introduction) in vv. 8-20 that cuts across the usual division of the psalm between vv. 10 and 11. In his view, vv. 8-9 raise questions that are answered in vv. 16-20, the conclusion of v. 10 is answered in vv. 14-15, and attention is thereby focused on vv. 11-13, which celebrate God's incomparable greatness.[298] While it is difficult finally to deny the distinct division between vv. 1-10 and 11-20, Kselman's insights certainly contribute to the understanding of the unity of Psalm 77, and it is possible that the structure and movement of the psalm should be understood on more than one level.

77:1-3. The nature of the "trouble" or "distress" in v. 2 is not specified. Given the magnitude of the crisis and the literary placement of Psalm 77 (see Commentary on Psalms 73; 74; Introduction), many scholars conclude that the psalmist voices questions and doubts raised by the exile. This is a sound conclusion, but it is also clear that the usefulness of Psalm 77 is not limited to this setting. It has continued to articulate the fears and the faith of the people of God throughout the centuries (see Reflections below).

The urgency of the situation is indicated in v. 1 by the repetition in Hebrew of the phrase "my voice unto God" (קולי אל־אלהים *qôlî ʾel-ʾĕlōhîm*). The verb in v. 1*a* is used elsewhere in situations of grave distress (see Exod 14:10, 25; Deut 26:7; Josh 24:7; Pss 88:1; 107:6, 28). The psalmists elsewhere affirm that

those who seek God will be answered and satisfied (see Pss 9:10; 22:26; 34:4, 10), but the constant seeking in Psalm 77 (see "day" and "night"), including unceasing prayer, has led only to the conclusion that no comfort is possible (see Gen 37:35; Jer 31:15)—another indication of the severity of the situation. Whereas remembrance of God elsewhere puts the psalmist in touch with God's loving care (see Ps 42:6-8), such is not the case here—at least not at first (cf. v. 3 with v. 11). Memory leads only to moaning (see Pss 42:5, 11; 43:5; see also Ps 55:17, where "moan" is accompanied by "complaint," which also occurs in 77:3 as "meditate"), and meditation leads only to further weakness (see Pss 107:5; 142:3; 143:4; Lam 2:12, 19).

77:4-10. Verse 4 describes characteristic signs of depression: inability to sleep and unspeakable distress. All the psalmist can do is think (see Ps 73:16), apparently about more auspicious times in the past (v. 5; see Ps 42:4). But the psalmist's sleepless nights and searching spirit (v. 6) produce no resolution, only agonizing questions that strike at the very heart of the biblical faith (vv. 7-9). The verb "spurn"/"reject" (זנח *zānaḥ*) occurs frequently in complaints (see Pss 43:2; 44:9, 23; 60:1, 10; 74:1), and v. 7*a* directly calls into question the affirmation of Lam 3:31 (see also "steadfast love" and "compassion" in Ps 77:8-9; Lam 3:32 NRSV). Indicative of the seriousness of the doubt are the references to time in vv. 7-8—"forever" (vv. 7-8; two different Hebrew words [לעולמים *lĕʿôlāmîm*, v. 7; לנצח *lānesaḥ*, v. 8]) and "for all time" (לדר ודר *lĕdōr wādōr*, v. 8). Perhaps even more indicative is the particular choice of vocabulary in vv. 8-9, which contain three of the key words from God's self-revelation in Exod 34:6: "steadfast love" (חסד *ḥesed*; see Introduction), "gracious" (חנות *ḥannôt*), and "compassion" (רחמים *raḥămîm*; "merciful" in Exod 34:6). In short, the psalmist questions God's fundamental character, or, as v. 10 summarizes the crisis of faith, the psalmist is "sick" (a more literal translation of the verb) that God has apparently "changed" (see Ps 89:34; Mal 3:6).

77:11-20. Although the psalmist is apparently again remembering and meditating in vv. 11-12 (see vv. 3, 5-6), the result is remarkably different. Verse 11*b* shifts to direct address,

298. John Kselman, "Psalm 77 and the Book of Exodus," *Journal of the Ancient Near Eastern Society of Columbia University* 15 (1983) 51-58; see the summary in Tate, *Psalms 51–100*, 272-73.

which perhaps is not coincidental (see Reflections below). In any case, the psalmist comes to a new awareness of God and of God's "way" (vv. 13, 19). The words "wonders" (פלא *pele'*) in v. 11 and "holy" (קדש *qōdeš*) in v. 13 call to mind the exodus (see Exod 15:11), and between the two references to God's "way" lies a hymnic celebration that is full of allusions to the exodus, especially to the song in Exod 15:1-18, which celebrates the crossing of the sea (see "great" in v. 13 and "might" in Exod 15:16; "wonders" in v. 14 and Exod 15:11; "might"/"strength" in v. 14 and Exod 15:2, 13; "arm" in v. 15 and Exod 15:16; "redeemed" in v. 15 and Exod 15:13; "waters" and "deep[s]" in v. 16 and Exod 15:8; "trembled" in vv. 16, 18 and Exod 15:14; see also "sea" and "mighty waters" in v. 19 and Exod 15:10). The words "might"/"strength" (עז *'ōz*) and "great" (גדול *gādôl*) also occur frequently elsewhere in the context of explicit proclamations of God's sovereignty (see Pss 29:1-3, 9; 48:2; 95:3; 96:6-7; 99:2-3; see also Exod 15:18). In other words, the psalmist finally affirms that God reigns and that God is powerfully present. Verses 16-18 recall not only the exodus but

also other accounts of God's appearing (see Pss 18:7-15; 114:3-8), and the vocabulary and shepherd imagery of v. 20 are associated elsewhere with both God's sovereignty and God's gracious presence (see Exod 15:13; Ps 23:3; Ezek 34:12).

Particularly significant are the affirmations about God's "way" that frame the retelling of the exodus story. God's way is "holy" (v. 13), and God's "footprints were unseen" (v. 19), suggesting the otherness and mystery of God. The latter phrase is particularly important because it has no parallel in Exod 15:1-18. What the psalmist apparently realizes in the process of recalling the exodus in the light of the experience recounted in vv. 1-10 is that God's way is not always clearly visible or comprehensible in terms of human ways (see Isa 55:8-9). As Tate suggests, the psalmist learns that God has God's "own schedule and often the faithful must endure the anguish of waiting."[299] Psalm 77, then, like the psalter as a whole (see Commentary on Psalm 2; Introduction), is eschatological; it affirms God's rule in circumstances that make it appear that God does not reign.

299. Tate, *Psalms 51–100*, 276.

REFLECTIONS

For the psalmist, the transition from despair to hope seems instantaneous, which raises the question of how to account for this sudden transition. Brueggemann has suggested that the transition marked by vv. 11-12 involves "a shift from 'I' to 'Thou.'" Thus the shift to direct address in v. 11*b* is of crucial significance, and it is reinforced when the affirmation of v. 14*a* begins with an emphatic pronoun, "you." Thus begins the remembrance of the exodus, which "takes the mind off the hopelessness of self." Brueggemann proposes that this transition is not an achievement of the individual psalmist. Rather, the psalmist takes part in a communal process of remembering. As Brueggemann concludes, "Everything depends on having the public, canonical memory available which becomes in this moment of pain a quite powerful, personal hope."[300]

As Mays points out, the recital of the exodus story in worship evokes God's presence: "The LORD is there in the recital as the God whose right hand has not changed. The hymn [vv. 13-19] does what praise and confession are meant to do—to represent the God of revelation as the reality and subject of truth in the face of all circumstances and contrary experience."[301] For Mays as for Brueggemann, the psalmist is still in the midst of "the day of trouble" (v. 2). What has changed is the psalmist, not the circumstance. No longer merely an isolated self (see v. 6), the psalmist is one of "your people" (vv. 15, 20) and is nurtured by the community's canonical memory.

300. Brueggemann, *Israel's Praise*, 138, 140.
301. Mays, *Psalms*, 253.

Most commentators, including Brueggemann and Mays, interpret Ps 77:13-19 as genuine praise. Tate, however, disagrees; he considers these verses to be the psalmist's continued "anguished meditation." Thus the questions of vv. 7-9 are left open for the reader to answer. For Tate, although vv. 11-20 provide the basis for answering no to the questions of vv. 7-9, "the decision is ours."[302] Thus, like the psalter as a whole, Psalm 77 issues a call to decision. In every age, the people of God are called to proclaim and to embody the reign of God in the midst of circumstances that make it appear that God does not reign. Tate's perspective also raises the question of whether the movement from vv. 1-10 to vv. 11-20 need be understood sequentially. At the least, the presence of vv. 1-10 invites the honest expression of our doubts and fears. Indeed, in a broken and sinful world, there is a sense in which a mature faith cannot exist apart from doubt.[303] In any case, Psalm 77 reminds us that we are people of memory and of hope. Faith is no guarantee against the possibility of despair, but even amid despair, the faithful will remember that God has been our help in ages past and will be our hope for years to come.

302. Tate, *Psalms 51–100*, 275-76.
303. See Paul Tillich, *Dynamics of Faith* (New York: Harper & Row, 1957) 1-29, esp. 16-22.

PSALM 78:1-72, TRUSTING IN GOD

COMMENTARY

Along with Psalms 105, 106, and 136, Psalm 78 is usually classified as a historical psalm. There is good reason for this designation, since Psalm 78 consists largely of a recital of crucial elements of Israel's story, but the label may be misleading. The recital in Psalm 78 is not history the way that we ordinarily understand it in the modern world—a recounting of names, events, and dates as accurately and objectively as possible. Rather, Psalm 78 is a creative retelling of Israel's story, and it has a particular purpose. In the broadest sense, the purpose is to teach (v. 1), but not simply in the sense of imparting information. Rather, the psalmist's teaching is intended to inspire hope and obedience in the hearers and, indeed, in all subsequent generations (vv. 6-8). In other words, this kind of history is as much or more concerned with the present and the future as it is with the past.

The same is true of the other historical psalms. Borrowing a phrase from Martin Buber's commentary on a Hebrew root (פלא *pl'*) that appears four times in Psalm 78 (see "wonders," "miracles," "marvels" in vv. 4, 11-12, 32), Brueggemann proposes that the purpose of the historical psalms be understood in terms of "abiding astonishment." By recalling God's formative activity in the past, "they seek to make available to subsequent generations the experience and power of the initial astonishment which abides with compelling authority." As is especially the case with Psalm 78, which continues the story up through God's choice of Zion and David (see vv. 67-72), the lesson suggests that every historical moment "is to be perceived in the same modes and categories of astonishment." By re-creating and perpetuating a sense of awe and wonder in the hearers, the teacher intends to evoke a response that will involve *"obedience, petition, gratitude, and new political possibility."*[304] The teacher intends anything but an objective recital. Rather, he or she intends the hearers and readers in every generation to respond with their whole lives to a subject matter that is supremely important: God and God's claim upon the world (see Reflections below).

Proposed dates for the origin of Psalm 78 range all the way from the time of David to the post-exilic era. Several scholars contend

304. Walter Brueggemann, *Abiding Astonishment: Psalms, Modernity, and the Making of History* (Louisville: Westminster John Knox, 1991) 34.

that v. 67 reflects the destruction of the northern kingdom in 722 BCE, and they also suggest that the origin of Psalm 78 would be particularly understandable in the time of Hezekiah, especially after the deliverance of Jerusalem from the Assyrians in 701. Certainty is impossible, however, and arguments can be made for the appropriateness of the use of Psalm 78 in a variety of circumstances. In any case, regardless of when the psalm originated, it would have been put to continuous use, and in the post-exilic era, for instance, Zion could have functioned symbolically and the references to David would have increasingly been understood messianically.

Scholars disagree on the literary structure and movement of Psalm 78 as well. Several outlines have been proposed, but one of the most helpful and widely accepted is that of R. J. Clifford, who divides the psalm into an introduction (vv. 1-11) and two recitals (vv. 12-39, vv. 40-72). Each recital follows a similar pattern—description of God's gracious activity (vv. 12-16, 40-55), rebellion of the people (vv. 17-20, 56-58), God's anger and punishment (vv. 21-32, 59-64), restoration of relationship by God (vv. 33-39, 65-72).[305] The paragraph divisions in the NIV and the NRSV indicate that it is perhaps better to extend the introduction only through v. 8. At any rate, Clifford's proposal has the advantage of highlighting God's graciousness as much as or more than Israel's sinfulness, thus inviting the reader's attention more to constructive possibilities for response than to the criticism of Israel's past.

78:1-8. The psalmist's didactic intent is evident from the beginning. He or she describes the poem in terms that are at home in Israel's wisdom literature—"teaching" (see Prov 1:8*b*), "parable(s)" (see Prov 1:6), "hidden things" (see Prov 1:6). The latter two terms also occur in Ps 49:4. The word here translated "parable(s)" (משל *māšāl*) connotes literally a comparison, and it communicates the psalmist's desire for the psalm's hearers to compare themselves to their ancestors in order not to make the same mistakes (see "be like" in v. 8). The repetition in vv. 3-8 emphasizes knowing (v. 3; see v. 5, where "teach"

is literally "cause to know" [הודיע *hôdîa*]; see also v. 6) and telling (vv. 3-4, 6; see also Deut 6:20-25; Pss 44:1; 73:28; 79:13), an ongoing process that involves "ancestors" (vv. 3, 5, 8) and "children" (vv. 4-6) from generation to generation (vv. 4, 6, 8). The content of the proclamation involves God's "praiseworthy deeds" (v. 4; see Ps 79:13), God's "power"/"might" (v. 4; see vv. 26, 61), and the "wonders" God has done (v. 4; see vv. 11-12, 32). The latter two words especially recall the exodus (see "wonders" in Exod 3:20; 15:11; and "strength" in Exod 15:2, 13), an event that led soon after to Sinai, which is recalled in Ps 78:5 and is also to be proclaimed. In short, every generation is to know God's sovereignty and God's sovereign claim, not simply as a matter of information but as a matter of life-saving hope (v. 4; see "confidence" in Prov 3:26). Interestingly, the ancestors who told their children the right things (v. 3) were apparently not able to do the right things (v. 8). Knowledge does not guarantee faithfulness; the ancestors were "stubborn" (see Jer 5:23; Hos 4:16), "rebellious" (see vv. 17, 40, 56; Jer 5:23), not steadfast (see v. 37), and "not faithful" (see vv. 22, 32, 37), as the rest of the psalm makes clear.

78:9-16. The first recital probably starts in v. 9, meaning that vv. 9-11 would correspond with vv. 40-42 and that both recitals begin by noting the people's unfaithfulness before describing God's gracious activity. If v. 9 refers to a specific episode, the allusion is now lost to us. It is perhaps best to construe it as an indication of Israel's characteristic behavior, as is the case with v. 10 (see v. 37). The people do precisely what the ongoing process described in vv. 1-8 was designed to prevent—they forget (see v. 7) God's wondrous activity (see v. 4). So vv. 12-16 recite what God has done. Zoan (v. 2) is not mentioned in the book of Exodus but is often identified with Rameses (Exod 1:22). The NIV's "wonders" (v. 11) and "miracles" (v. 12) represent the same Hebrew root (*pl*; see Exod 15:11), and the event in view is clearly the exodus (see Exod 14:21-29; 15:8; cf. Josh 3:13, 16). Verses 14-16 move on to God's provision for the people in the wilderness (see Exod 13:21-22; 17:1-6; Num 20:10-13), which remains the focus through the remainder of the first recital.

305. R. J. Clifford, "In Zion and David a New Beginning: An Interpretation of Psalm 78," in *Traditions in Transformation*, ed. F. M. Cross (Winona Lake: Eisenbrauns, 1981) 127-29.

78:17-20. Recalling v. 8, v. 17 introduces the section describing the people's sinfulness (see v. 32; see also Deut 9:16) and rebellion (see also vv. 40, 56; Num 20:24; 27:14; Deut 9:7, 23-24). Israel tested God at Massah (a name derived from the verb "test" [נסה *nissâ*] in Exod 17:2, 7; see also v. 41; Num 14:22; Deut 6:16; Ps 95:8-9) by demanding water (see also Exod 15:22-25). God responded by providing water from a rock (see vv. 15, 20; Exod 17:6; Num 20:10-11), having already provided bread and meat (Exod 16:4-36, esp. v. 12) in response to the people's complaints (vv. 18, 20; see also Exod 16:1-3; Num 11:4-6).

78:21-32. Verse 21 introduces God's angry response to the people's faithlessness (see vv. 8, 32, 37) and lack of trust in God's "deliverance" or "salvation" (v. 22; see Exod 15:2; Ps 3:8). But the bulk of vv. 21-32 is still devoted to God's gracious activity (vv. 23-29; see also Exod 16:13-36; Num 11:7-9, 31-32) before the section returns to God's wrath (vv. 30-31; see also Num 11:33-34) and notes again the people's sinfulness (v. 32).

78:33-39. The boundary between sections is fuzzy, but the final verses of the first recital mention again God's punishment of the people (v. 33) and their faithlessness (vv. 34-37) before concluding with a proclamation of God's grace (vv. 38-39). The vocabulary and content of v. 38 are reminiscent of the golden calf incident in Exodus 32–34, one of the major episodes in the wilderness (see "compassionate"/"merciful" in Exod 33:19; 34:6; "iniquity" in 34:7, 9; "restrained" in 32:12; "anger" in 32:10-12). At the conclusion of the golden calf episode, God reveals God's self to be a forgiving God, yet one who "by no means clears the guilty" (Exod 34:7). The same tension is evident in Psalm 78 (see Reflections below).

78:40-55. The second recital also begins by recalling the people's rebellion (v. 40; see also vv. 8, 17, 56) and their testing of God (v. 41; see also vv. 18, 56). Verse 42 contains the third occurrence of the verb "remember" (זכר *zākar*, vv. 35, 39, 42). Just as God's faithfulness—not the people's—is crucial for the continuation of the story, so also God's memory is determinative (v. 39). As if to stimulate the people's failed memory, the psalmist again returns to recital (vv. 42*b*-55). Edward

L. Greenstein comments that "through the rhetoric adopted by the psalmist for jogging the people's recollection, he exercises their memory by exercising his own."[306] The prominence of memory in Psalm 78 recalls Psalm 77, in which remembering is at first ineffectual (vv. 3, 6) but eventually becomes a stimulus to praise (v. 11). Although the juxtaposition of Psalms 77 and 78 may be coincidental, it is as if the psalmist wants to instruct future generations with Psalm 78 in how and what to remember, so that remembering will be an effective and powerful source of hope and obedience (see vv. 7-8).

Like the first, the second recital begins with the mention of Egypt and Zoan (v. 43; see also v. 12); however, the emphasis now is on the plagues, which elsewhere are called "signs" (see Exod 7:3; 8:23; 10:1-2) and "miracles" (see "wonders" in Exod 7:3; 11:9-10). The plagues are rehearsed in vv. 44-51— water turned to blood (v. 44; see Exod 7:17-21; Ps 105:29); flies (v. 45*a*; see Exod 8:20-24; Ps 105:31); frogs (v. 45*b*; see Exod 8:1-7; Ps 105:30); locusts (v. 46; see Exod 10:1-20; Ps 105:34-35); hail (vv. 47-48; see Exod 9:18-26; Ps 105:32-33; Ps 78:48 may also recall the death of the cattle in Exod 9:1-7); and the death of the firstborn (vv. 49-50; see also Exod 11:1–12:30; Ps 105:36). Obviously, the order of the plagues differs in Psalm 78 from the Exodus account, but this matters little since the psalmist's concern is less with the past than with the present and the future. The recital continues with brief references to the crossing of the sea and guidance in the wilderness (vv. 52-53; see also v. 13) as well as to the entry into Canaan and possession of the land (vv. 54-55).

78:56-72. The response of the people is again to test God (see vv. 18, 41), to rebel (see vv. 17, 40), and to disobey (see v. 5). The form of their disobedience this time is one that was manifest after entry into the land (see vv. 54-55)—idolatry (v. 58). Again, God responds with wrath (v. 59; see v. 21), abandoning Shiloh (v. 60; see also Josh 18:1; 1 Sam 1:3; Jer 7:12), which probably housed the symbolic seat of the divine power, the ark (v. 61; see also 1 Sam 4:1-22). With God's

306. Edward L. Greenstein, "Mixing Memory and Design: Reading Psalm 78," *Prooftexts: A Journal of Jewish Literary History* 10/2 (1990) 209.

having left them, the people are easy prey for their opponents (vv. 62-64, which may allude to the defeat of the Israelites by the Philistines in 1 Sam 4:10-11). But a compassionate and forgiving God (see v. 38) will not be content finally to abandon the people, so God awakes (v. 65; see also Pss 35:23; 44:23) and effects a reversal of fortunes, which may be intended to mean the victories of Saul and David against the Philistines (v. 66).

Given the historical references and probable allusions in vv. 60-66, and given the fact that Shiloh was in Ephraimite territory, v. 67 may be an allusion to God's abandonment of Shiloh and eventual move to Jerusalem (vv. 68-69) and the establishment of the Davidic dynasty (vv. 70-72). Verses 67-72 may have originated and functioned as a theological rationale for the priority of Zion and David. After 722 BCE, however, it is likely that v.

67 came to be heard as an allusion to the destruction of the northern kingdom. And after the destruction of Jerusalem in 587 BCE, an event that the shape of Book III seems to reflect (see Psalms 74; 79; Introduction), it is likely that the names "Zion" and "David" functioned primarily as religious symbols that communicated God's gracious commitment to the people in the past (2 Sam 7:15) and the promise of ongoing compassion and forgiveness in the future. Indeed, the primary purpose of the historical recitals seems to be the creation of a community that, despite its own failures and faithlessness, will live in hope (v. 7) as a result of the faithfulness and forgiveness of God (v. 38). In fact, this may be the solution to the psalmist's riddle (v. 2), which by inference can be stated as follows: "How can the recollection of a history of failure lead to a future of hope?"

REFLECTIONS

The shape of the recitals in Psalm 78 preserves a pattern that pervades the entire biblical story of the sovereign God who lives in the tension between justice and mercy—that is, gracious acts of God are followed by human disobedience, which in turn creates destructive consequences and necessitates God's gracious forgiveness and restoration if the story of God and God's people is to continue (see Genesis 6–9; Exodus 32–34, the shape of the prophetic books in their final form; see Commentary on Psalms 99; 103). For Christians, this pattern that portrays God's dilemma is stamped most clearly and decisively in the shape of a cross, which demonstrated just how far God is willing to go to forgive and to reclaim sinful humanity. For Christians, to recite Psalm 78 is to confess our own sinfulness and to profess our conviction that we are saved not by our merit or efforts but by the grace of God. Psalm 78 thus invites humility, gratitude, and the exercise of power in the form of love, not of force.

In highlighting the importance of teaching, knowing, and telling the story of the wonders God has done (vv. 1-8), Psalm 78 is a lesson in the crucial importance of religious education and evangelism. It is true in every era that the faith of the people of God is only one generation away from extinction. Psalm 78 invites us to share the good news, and it reminds us that our own children are an essential place to start (see Deut 6:4-9, 20-25; Josh 4:1-7). To be sure, Psalm 78 is also a reminder that knowledge does not guarantee faithfulness; however, it insists that knowing the story is the foundation for faith and hope and life. The church in recent years and throughout its history has often been so self-absorbed and preoccupied with institutional maintenance that it has forgotten what God has done (v. 11) and has failed to tell the old, old story that is so full of new possibilities for responding with gratitude and service to God's persistent and amazing grace.

PSALM 79:1-13, THE NATIONS SAY, "WHERE IS THEIR GOD?"

COMMENTARY

Psalm 79 is one of several communal laments or prayers for help (see Psalms 74; 80; 83–85; 89) that give Book III the appearance of having been decisively shaped by the experience of exile (see also Psalms 77; 81; Introduction). The juxtaposition of Pss 78:67-72 and 79:1-5 is especially jarring (see "inheritance" in Pss 78:62, 71; 79:1), and it suggests that the traditional Zion-David theology had to be reformulated in the light of the exile, just as the exile necessitated more generally a rethinking of the role of suffering in the life of the faithful (see Commentary on Psalms 44; 73; 74; 76). For other links between Psalms 78 and 79, see below.

As already suggested, most scholars relate the catastrophe described in this psalm to the destruction of Jerusalem by the Babylonians and the beginning of the exile (587 BCE). Some scholars, however, speculate that some other event accounts for the origin of Psalm 79, perhaps even the desecration of the Temple by Antiochus IV Epiphanes in the second century BCE. Portions of vv. 2-3 appear in the second-century 1 Maccabees as a comment on the murder of sixty faithful Jews (1 Macc 7:17). In that text, however, Psalm 79 is cited as "the word that was written" (1 Macc 7:16 NRSV), suggesting a much earlier origin for the psalm. It is most likely, then, that Psalm 79 was written as a response to the events of 587 BCE and that it was particularly relevant in later times as well, including the Maccabean era and beyond (see Reflections below).

While scholars propose several ways to outline the structure of Psalm 79, the most cogent and helpful is as follows: vv. 1-5, vv. 6-12, v. 13. As Mays points out, the complaint and petitions follow a " 'they, we, you' pattern" that highlights the major actors— the nations, the people, God—"and keeps the focus on the painful problem of this three-sided relationship."[307] Verses 1-5 voice the complaint; the focus moves from the nations (vv. 1-3) to the people (v. 4) to God (v. 5).

Verse 6 initiates a series of petitions with accompanying reasons; the focus, especially of the reasons, again moves from the nations (vv. 6-7) to the people (v. 8) to God (v. 9). Verse 10b initiates a second series of petitions with a similar movement; and the effect is to center attention on the question in v. 10a, which Mays calls "the climax and theological theme of the psalm."[308] Verse 13 concludes the psalm with the people's promise of perpetual gratitude and praise.

79:1-5. Verses 1-3 describe in graphic detail the desecration and destruction suffered by Jerusalem and its people at the hands of the nations (the repeated "they" of vv. 1-3; see Ps 74:4-7; Lam 1:10). The words "defiled" (טמא *ṭāmē*) and "holy" (קדש *qōdeš*) are used elsewhere for ritual purity or cleanness. God's place—the focus of Israel's purity—has become unclean; Jerusalem is in ruins (see Jer 26:18; Mic 3:12). The use of "your inheritance" in v. 1a in conjunction with the Temple in v. 1b recalls Exod 15:17-18, which affirms that the people will be "planted . . . on the mountain of your inheritance" (NIV) and that God "will reign forever and ever" (NRSV). When Ps 79:1 is heard in the light of Exod 15:17-18, the theological issue becomes clearer: The destruction of Jerusalem calls God's sovereignty into question. The nations are not alone in asking, "Where is God?" (v. 10; see also Pss 42:3, 10; 115:2). As Tate suggests, Psalm 79 echoes Israel's "deepest doubts and fears."[309]

The very entrance of the nations into the Temple was defilement enough, but the impurity is made worse by the presence of unburied bodies (see 2 Kgs 23:16), which bespeaks the ignominy of defeat and even divine punishment (see Deut 28:26; 2 Sam 21:10; Jer 7:33). In this regard, although v. 3 says the nations have poured out the blood of the faithful (see v. 10), the imagery could only have recalled Ezek 22:1-12, suggesting that the nations are simply completing a process that a corrupt people set in motion (see the admission of sin in vv. 8-9, an element that is unusual in the communal laments).

The language of v. 4 appears frequently in other complaints. Just as the individual sufferer is sometimes a "taunt" (see also Pss 22:6; 31:11; 69:7), so also are the whole people (Ps 44:13) or their representative, the king (see Ps 89:41; see also 89:50, where the verb appears and where the king is called "your servant," as are the people in Ps 79:2, 10). What is particularly interesting is that v. 4 anticipates v. 12, which suggests that the taunts against the people are really taunts against God. So what is at stake is not just the people's reputation but also God's "name" (v. 9)—that is, God's reputation or character. God's anger or "jealousy" (v. 5) is mentioned elsewhere in the context of covenant making, where it is clear that God wants Israel's exclusive allegiance (see Exod 20:5; 34:14; Deut 4:24; 5:9; 6:15; Josh 24:19). God the lover wants Israel to love no other gods (see Ps 78:58). God's jealousy, therefore, is ultimately a manifestation of God's love. Having experienced the tough side of God's love, the people will appeal in v. 8 to the side of God's love that is experienced as "compassion" or "mercy" (רחמים *raḥămîm*). For now, the question is, "How long?" (see Pss 6:3; 13:1-2; 89:46).

79:6-12. If God is angry at the people, God should also be angry at the nations for their treatment of Jerusalem and its people (vv. 6-7; see Jer 10:25). Upon those who have "poured out" blood (v. 3), God should "pour out . . . anger" (v. 6; see "outpoured" in v. 10; see also Ezek 36:18). The people do not claim to be innocent (vv. 8-9). Rather, having been "brought very low" (v. 8; see also Pss 116:6; 142:6), they appeal to God's compassion for the lowly, God's "mercy" or "motherly compassion" (see Commentary on Psalm 25, esp. the discussion of vv. 6-7). God willingly forgives sinners, as evidenced in Exod 34:6, where God's character is described as merciful after God has forgiven the people, even after they had constructed and worshiped another god (see Exod 32:1-14). The words "mercy"/"merciful" (רחום *raḥûm*) and "forgive" (כפר *kipper*) also occur together in Ps 78:38, which rehearses at length "the

iniquities of our ancestors" (79:8). That is to say, the good news of God's faithfulness and forgiveness proclaimed in Psalm 78 is also the basis of the appeal in Psalm 79. Given the appeal to God's fundamental character in v. 8, the two occurrences of "name" in v. 9 are readily comprehensible. In effect, the people suggest that God's delivering them from their distress would be an opportunity for God's character to be proved to the nations (v. 9; see also Exod 9:16). The nations, who do not know God (v. 6), will come to know God if God will act to avenge Israel (v. 10; see also Ps 94:1; Ezek 25:14). Thus the form of the requests in v. 9 does not simply mask the people's selfish concern (see "help" in Ps 22:19). Rather, as they "waive the right of all self-help,"[310] they subordinate their well-being to the request that God be glorified (see Ps 115:1). The request to be delivered "for your name's sake" (v. 9) may suggest the people's humble recognition of their sin as well as their concern for God's reputation, even above their own (see Ezek 36:21-23). Or, as v. 12 suggests, when the nations ask, "Where is their God?" (v. 10*a*; see also Ps 115:2), it is not just a taunt against the people but one against God as well.

The people's apparently genuine need (vv. 1-3, 8*b*), as well as their willingness to entrust themselves fully to God's help and to seek first God's glory, puts the petitions of vv. 10*b*, 12 in a particular light. That is, these verses are not simply selfish requests for personal revenge. Rather, they ask God to set right things that are obviously wrong (vv. 1-3), both for the people (v. 10; see vv. 2-3) and for God (v. 12; see also v. 1). Verses 10*b*, 12 realistically realize that when the lowly are liberated, then their oppressors must be judged. This is precisely the way God has always operated, as the allusion to the exodus in v. 11 recalls (see "strength of your arm," which also occurs in Exod 15:16). There, too, God saved people (see v. 9; Exod 15:2) who were prisoners and doomed to die (see Ps 102:20; Zech 9:11). And, as Psalm 79 suggests as well, God acted both for the sake of the people (Exod 3:7-8) and for the sake of God's name (Exod 9:16).

79:13. The word "then" (ו *wa-*) at the beginning of v. 13 is misleading; it appears too much as if Israel is simply trying to cut a

---

310. Kraus, *Psalms 60–150*, 135.

deal with God. If the Hebrew conjunction is translated simply as "and," v. 13 becomes the people's affirmation that they will always be grateful for God's compassion and that they will witness to God's praiseworthy deeds (see Ps 78:4). In the light of vv. 1-5, this is a remarkable promise. But biblical faith *is* remarkable! It is about a God who will not tolerate unfaithfulness (v. 5), but whose deep compassion will not let go of unfaithful people (v. 8). It is about a people who suffer miserably, although due to their own unfaithfulness (vv. 8-9), but who continue to pray to live (vv. 8-9) and live to praise (v. 13).

REFLECTIONS

Despite its origin in a specific ancient event, Psalm 79 continued and continues to be useful to the people of God. Psalm 79 is alluded to in Rev 16:6; it was cited by Jerome in response to the invasion of Rome by the Visigoths; it was frequently on the lips of Christians as they died in the religious conflicts of sixteenth- and seventeenth-century Europe, and it was and is used by Jews on the ninth of Ab, which commemorates the destruction of Jerusalem, and in weekly services as well. As Mays suggests, "In all these ways the psalm continues to voice the prayer of those who raise the question, 'Why should the nations say, Where is your God?' "[311] As suggested above, this question articulated not just the taunts of the nations but also the doubts and fears of God's people. And as we look around ourselves and see a broken world haunted by monstrous evil, we still ask the question, "Where is God?" As we do, we can be instructed by Psalm 79 and its insistence that suffering be seen in the perspective of faith. The psalmist never loses sight of the harsh realities facing the people of God (vv. 1-5). But the psalmist likewise never loses hope. As Brueggemann concludes: "Biblical faith is not romantic. It reckons with evil, and it knows that evil strikes at all that is crucial and most precious. Nevertheless it does affirm."[312]

The temptation was and is to view the suffering of the faithful as a sign of God's weakness—God no longer rules—or as a sign of God's punishment—God is forever angry. But in the face of catastrophic suffering, the psalmist continues to affirm. Such affirmation in the faith of contrary signs is eschatological (see Commentary on Psalms 2; 74; Introduction). It opens the way for a new understanding of God's sovereignty as power made perfect in weakness (see 2 Cor 12:9). It opens the way to the claim that God's love will ultimately be experienced as compassion, not jealousy. It opens the way to an embrace of suffering as something other than an indication of alienation from God (see Commentary on Psalms 44; 74). In short, the psalmist's affirmation in the face of adversity prepares the way for a time when a cross—the emblem of suffering and shame—will become a symbol of power and grace, the ultimate answer to the question, "Where is God?"

311. Mays, *Psalms*, 262; see also Prothero, *The Psalms in Human Life and Experience*, 31, 146-47.
312. Brueggemann, *The Message of the Psalms*, 74.

PSALM 80:1-19, RESTORE US, O GOD

COMMENTARY

A communal lament like Psalm 79, Psalm 80 also continues the flock/shepherd imagery from Pss 77:20; 78:70-72; and 79:13. Like Psalm 79, too, Psalm 80 bases its appeal on the good news of God's faithfulness and forgiveness that is proclaimed in Psalm 78 (see below on the refrain, esp. v. 14). The flock/shepherd imagery culminates in Psalm

80 with the opening address of God as "Shepherd of Israel"; despite a sordid past (Psalm 78) and a devastating present (Psalm 79), Israel still addresses God as its sovereign, its hope for light and life.

There is disagreement among scholars about the calamity that lies behind the origin of Psalm 80. The mention of Ephraim and Manasseh in v. 2 has led several scholars to conclude that it was produced in the northern kingdom, perhaps during the final years before the conquest of Samaria by the Assyrians in 721 BCE. The LXX's superscription, "Concerning the Assyrians," may support this view. Certainty is impossible, however, and proposed dates of origin range from the tenth to the second centuries BCE. It is likely that if Psalm 80 did not actually originate as a response to exile, it was placed in its present literary context to function as such (see Commentary on Psalms 73; 74; 79; Introduction). In any case, as Mays puts it, "Whatever the original historical setting, the psalm in its continued use belongs to the repertoire of the afflicted people of God on their way through the troubles of history."[313] The structure and movement of Psalm 80 are dominated by the occurrence of a refrain (vv. 3, 7, 19; see also v. 14). After the opening plea (vv. 1-2) and initial complaint (vv. 4-6), each of which is followed by the refrain, vv. 8-13 present a historical allegory or parable. A variation of the refrain (v. 14) marks a return to petition, which culminates in the final occurrence of the refrain.

80:1-2. A series of imperatives that indicate the dimensions of the problem opens the psalm. In the psalms, the directive to "give ear" often accompanies the object "my prayer" (Pss 17:1; 55:1; 86:6; cf. 84:8; 141:1-2). The need for this plea suggests that the people believe that God is inattentive (see v. 4). The verb "shine forth" (יפע *yp'*) is the language of theophany, and it is used to describe the appearance of God on mountains (Deut 33:2; Ps 50:2). The plea suggests that the people also believe that God is absent (see Ps 94:1). Two additional pleas in v. 2 convey the urgency of the situation. God seems to be asleep (see Ps 44:23). Since to be saved in OT terms means to remain alive (see Pss 3:8; 6:4), if God remains inattentive, inactive, and

313. Mays, *Psalms,* 264.

absent, the people will face death (see v. 18). The truly remarkable thing about these pleas in vv. 1-2 is that they are addressed to the same God who is perceived to be inattentive, inactive, and even absent, expressing a belief that even if God is the problem, nonetheless God is the solution. In spite of God's inattention and inaction, therefore, the people address God in the most exalted of terms. The appellation "shepherd," a royal title (see 2 Sam 7:7; Ezek 34:1-16; Ps 78:70-72), and the designation of God as the one "enthroned upon the cherubim" (see 1 Sam 4:4; 2 Sam 6:2; Ps 99:1) emphasize God's sovereignty. The imagery is associated elsewhere with the ark, God's earthly throne, a symbol of God's presence and power (see Commentary on Ps 24:7-10). Despite appearances to the contrary, the people still affirm that God reigns supreme.

80:3. This verse, which continues the series of imperatives, is related thematically to vv. 1-2. It is notable, however, because it contains the first occurrence of the refrain. The plea "Restore us" (השׁיבנו *hăšîbēnû*; more lit., "cause us to return") has several dimensions of meaning that are appropriate for Psalm 80. The word is used elsewhere to describe God's bringing the people back from exile (see 1 Kgs 8:34; Jer 27:22; cf. Dan 9:25). The word may also denote repentance, literally "causing people to return" to God (see Neh 9:26; Lam 5:21), as well as causing persons to return to life (2 Sam 12:23; Job 33:30). The plea "let your face shine" communicates much the same thing as "shine forth"; it is a request that God "be present for us." In Num 6:24-26, this phrase is paralleled by the terms "bless," "keep," "be gracious," and "give peace" (see also Pss 4:6; 31:16; 67:1).

80:4-6. The problems implied by vv. 1-3 come to the fore in vv. 4-6. The poignant question, "How long?" characteristic of both individual and communal complaints (see Pss 13:1-2; 74:10; 79:5; 94:3), sets the mood. God is angry with the people's prayers (lit., "smokes against"; see Deut 29:20; Ps 74:1) and refuses to listen to them (see v. 1). Like v. 4, v. 5 also recalls v. 1. Just as a shepherd feeds the flock, so also the king as shepherd should feed the people (see Ezek 34:1-16). The complaint of v. 5 becomes more poignant in the light of both the refrain, "let your face shine," and the existence in the Temple of the "bread of the face" (or "bread of the Presence"; see Exod 25:30; 1 Sam 21:16; 1 Kgs 7:48). In the present situation, the bread of God's face, symbolic of God's sustaining presence, has been replaced by the "bread of tears" (see Ps 42:3). The complaint is concluded in v. 6 with characteristic language. The NRSV's "laugh" represents the same Hebrew word (לָעַג *lā'ag*) that the NRSV translates as "mocked" in Ps 79:4 and "derision" in Ps 44:13; both are communal laments. The NRSV's "scorn" is more accurately "source of contention," which is a preferable translation in view of the similarity between the refrain and the priestly benediction in Num 6:24-26. The same Hebrew verb translated "give" (שִׂים *śîm*) in the phrase "give you peace" (Num 6:26) is rendered "made" in the phrase "made us a source of contention" (v. 6). Thus the people experience the opposite of the priestly benediction.

80:7. With the exception of the longer divine name, the refrain of v. 7 is identical to v. 3. The effect of the repetition is to express the urgency of the plea that pervades the psalm. The following allegory of the vine serves to remind God of past actions on Israel's behalf, and such recollections are typical in communal prayers for help (see Exod 32:11-12; Pss 44:1-8; 74:2, 12-17).

80:8-11. These verses are a brief review of Israel's history, starting with the exodus (v. 8*a*; "ordered . . . to set out" in Exod 15:22 NRSV translates the same verb as "brought . . . out" [נָסַע *nāsa'*]), moving to the conquest (v. 8*b*; see "drove out" in Josh 24:12, 18; Ps 78:55), and concluding with the growth and culmination of the Davidic empire, which stretched from the Mediterranean Sea to the Euphrates River (vv. 9-11). The metaphor of the vine indicates careful planning, preparation, and patient nurturing, which makes possible growth and fruitfulness. Thus the metaphor appropriately represents the commitment that God shows to God's people (see Isa 5:1-7; Jer 2:21; 6:9; Ezek 17:1-10; 19:10-14; Hos 10:1; 14:7; John 15:11; and see the use of "plant" even when the vine image is absent, as in Exod 15:17; Ps 44:2).

80:12-13. These verses continue the allegory, exploring the question of why, after all of the careful planting and nurture, God would break down the walls around the vineyard (see Isa 5:5; Ps 89:40) and allow the vine to be devoured (see Ps 89:41). The question recalls the previous question, "How long?" (v. 4). The word "feed" (רָעָה *rā'â*, v. 13) is particularly poignant as it recalls v. 1, where the word for "shepherd" (רֹעֵה *rō'ēh*) is literally translated "feeder." God, who traditionally has been the one to feed Israel, is allowing Israel to be devoured.

80:14-18. The poignant question in v. 12 receives no answer. Instead, the psalmist renews the petition, "Turn again" or "Repent, O God of hosts" (v. 14*a*). The sequence is not surprising, however, if one considers such passages as Exod 32:11-12 and Isa 5:1-7. Following Israel's apostasy, Moses twice asks "Why?" before requesting that God "turn" (Exod 32:12). Thus the renewed request in Ps 80:14 implies that the answer to the question in v. 12 is that God is punishing Israel for its sin. This view is reinforced by the people's promise in v. 18*a*, which also implies that the people have sinned previously, although there is no direct confession of sin. The people's sin, as well as the placement and construction of v. 14, makes clear that the initiative for restoration rests exclusively with God. The reader might expect the refrain again at v. 14; instead, "turn" is a different form of the same Hebrew verb translated "restore" in vv. 3, 7, 19. This seemingly intentional variation draws attention to v. 14 and, coupled with the absence of any confession of sin by the people, makes the message clear: There can be no life (v. 18) or future for God's people without *God's* repentance. The fourfold imperative in v. 14 serves to emphasize the need for God, not the people, to act. Just as in both major episodes of the exodus event, the deliverance from Egypt and the forgiveness following the golden calf episode, God's activity was determinative, so also now God must "turn," "see" (Exod 3:7), and "have regard for" Israel (Exod 3:16; 4:31).

The petition in v. 17 reinforces v. 14. To have God's hand upon one is to experience deliverance and protection (see Ezra 8:31). The phrases "one at your right hand" and "the one whom you made strong" are sometimes understood as references to a king or a future king. The Hebrew word translated "one whom" is literally "son of a human" (בֶּן־אָדָם *ben-'ādām*). This expression probably refers to Israel (Israel is elsewhere referred to as a son; see Hos 11:1; see also Gen 49:22, where Joseph, represented by a plant, is called a "son of a fruit-bearer," or "fruitful bough"; note also the repetition of "right hand" and "son" in vv. 15, 17).

80:19. The final petition, the refrain in v. 19, differs from vv. 3, 7 by the inclusion of the more personal divine name, Yahweh. Verse 19 indicates that the promises of v. 18 are not just Israel's attempt to bribe God; rather, Israel has already been calling on God's name throughout the psalm in deathly circumstances. Thus, even while Israel pleads for life, the very plea itself indicates that life is, at least in some sense, already a present possession.

REFLECTIONS

John Calvin introduced his comment on Psalm 80 with the following words: "This is a sorrowful prayer, in which the faithful beseech God that he would be graciously pleased to succour his afflicted Church."[314] Psalm 80 is, indeed, "a sorrowful prayer," but as Calvin implies, it is surely an act of faith and hope. In short, Psalm 80 is eschatological (see Commentary on Psalm 2; Introduction). Amid calamitous circumstances, which seem to belie their affirmation, the people of God dare to affirm that God reigns (vv. 1-2). That was an act of faith, and because the people trusted God to transform their circumstances and restore them, this act of faith was also an act of hope (see Rom 8:24-25; Heb 11:1).

In the exilic and post-exilic eras, the people of God may have envisioned their future restoration primarily in political terms—that is, the restoration of statehood and monarchy (see v. 17, which many commentators suggest refers to a present or future king, and which was apparently read messianically within Judaism). If so, that hope was disappointed, and the royal vision was pushed further into the future (see Mic 5:2-5a) and was later claimed by and for Jesus (see Matt 2:6, which quotes Mic 5:2). As a king was supposed to do, Jesus embodied both the experience of his people (see John 15:1-11 in relation to Ps 80:8-13) and the reign of God. His crowning glory appeared to be a God-forsaken exile—a cross. In an act of faith and hope not unlike that of Psalm 80, the followers of Jesus dare to affirm that in Jesus the light of God shines and that through Jesus we are restored and have life. Like those who prayed Psalm 80 long ago, Christians dare to see and expect the reign of God where others see only chaos and expect nothing.

The conviction that one confronts God in every circumstance, both good and bad, lies at the heart of the ancient Israelite prayers for help. This conviction is the ultimate paradox of the laments (see Commentary on Psalms 13; 22). The language and imagery of Psalm 80 suggest that the people think that God is inattentive and inactive, if not entirely absent. At the same time, they seem to belie this position by continuing to address God and by attributing their present circumstances to God's action (see vv. 5-6). The belief that God is in some way confronted in suffering and death as well as for prosperity and life is a remarkable affirmation—especially in a time when the pious are apt to view suffering as evidence of alienation from God, and secular folk are loath to attribute their prosperity and life to God. Psalm 80 is traditionally associated with the season of Advent, the celebration of God's coming and continuing presence. There is no better way to express belief in the reality of God's sovereignty than to address God out of our individual and corporate afflictions and to continue looking to God as the only source of light and life.

Advent is a season of preparation and repentance, and lest we be tempted to focus on our own efforts in these matters, Psalm 80 proclaims that our lives ultimately depend on God's gracious willingness to repent (see v. 14). So does the birth, life, death, and resurrection of Jesus. What human repentance amounts to, at best, is turning to accept the loving embrace of the God who gives us life. As Jesus indicated in his extension of the image of the vine, "apart from me you can do nothing" (John 15:5 NRSV; see also Phil 1:6).

314. Calvin, *Commentary on the Book of Psalms*, V:3:295.

PSALM 81:1-16, IF MY PEOPLE WOULD ONLY LISTEN TO ME!

COMMENTARY

Often categorized as a prophetic exhortation, Psalm 81 may more helpfully be labeled a liturgical sermon (see Psalms 50; 95), in which the preacher delivers the word of God (cf. vv. 6-16 with Ps 50:7-23). As in Psalm 50, the sermon in Psalm 81 divides into two parts (vv. 5c-10, 11-16) preceded by an introduction. Verses 1-5b clearly suggest a liturgical setting, seemingly the beginning of one of Israel's festal celebrations (see vv. 3-5b), and it is possible that the sermon was preached on one of Israel's holy days. Joyous praise marks the beginning of the festival (vv. 1-2). The reference to blowing "the trumpet at the new moon" (v. 3) accords with the prescriptions in Lev 23:23-24 and Num 29:1-6 regarding the first day of the seventh month (sometimes called the Festival of Trumpets). The conviction of the people for their faithlessness (vv. 8, 11-13) would also be an appropriate rite for the Day of Atonement. The references to the opening of the Decalogue (vv. 9-10b) and the harvest (vv. 10c, 16) would be appropriate for the Feast of Booths or Tabernacles. Since all of these observances were held in the seventh month (see Lev 23:26-36; Num 29:7-39), Psalm 81 originally may have been related to this festal season.

Following two communal complaints and placed in the midst of Book III, which recalls the crisis of exile (see Commentary on Psalms 73; 74; 79; 80; Introduction), Psalm 81 serves both as an explanation for the people's suffering (vv. 11-12) and as a hopeful, encouraging word if Israel will but listen and respond (vv. 8-10, 13-16). Beyond its possible original festal setting and its literary setting, Psalm 81 can function as a call to commitment at all times and in all places.

81:1-5b. Psalm 81 begins like a song of praise instead of a sermon. In the light of the joyous season, people are encouraged to "sing aloud" (רנן *rnn*; see Ps 145:7; see also 5:11; 67:4; 95:1; 96:12; 98:4; 149:5), to "shout for joy" (רוע *rûaʿ*; see also Pss 95:1-2; 98:4, 6; 100:1), and to "raise a song" (שאו־זמרה

śěʾû-zimrâ; see Exod 15:2; Pss 33:2; 47:6-7; 95:2; 98:4-5) with instrumental accompaniment (see Exod 15:20; 2 Sam 6:5; Pss 33:2-3; 149:3; 150:3-4). Although this type of joyful praise was appropriate for a festival, the same invitations occur often in contexts that make clear that what is really being celebrated is the reign of God over all creation. It should not be surprising, then, that many of the psalms cited above either contain the exclamation "The LORD is king!" (Ps 96:10) or in some other way address God as king (Pss 5:2; 47:2, 7-8; 95:3; 98:6; 145:1; 149:2). Furthermore, the song of praise in Exodus 15 culminates in the affirmation of God's reign (v. 18), and 2 Sam 6:2 states that God is "enthroned on the cherubim" (NRSV). When the psalmist invites the people to celebrate God's sovereignty (vv. 1-2), the psalmist anticipates one of the main themes of the sermon that follows: Only Yahweh is God (see esp. vv. 9-10). As noted above, blowing the trumpet may signal the beginning of a festal day (v. 3), but a trumpet blast was also the way to greet a king, either human (see 1 Kgs 1:34, 39) or divine (see Pss 47:5; 98:6). Worship always involves the recognition and celebration of God's claim upon the world.

81:5c-10. Verse 5c is problematic, but it should probably be understood as the immediate introduction to the sermon. The preacher is claiming to be delivering *God's* word rather than the preacher's own words, a statement that may be similar to the contemporary "Listen for the Word of God." In any case, God speaks in the first person for the remainder of the psalm, first reminding the people of their gracious deliverance from slavery in Egypt (vv. 6c-7a; the Hebrew word translated "burden" [סבל *sēbel*] is found in Exod 1:11; 2:11; 5:4-5; 6:6) and then of further gracious dealings during the wilderness wanderings. Verse 7b seems to allude to Sinai; the phrase "secret place of thunder" may be meant to recall the cloud engulfing the mountain (see Exod 19:16; note also the mention of a trumpet blast in this verse). Verse 7c recalls the incident at Meribah, although the preacher seems to be giving Israel the benefit of the doubt, for Meribah is remembered elsewhere as a place where Israel tested God (see Exod 17:7; Ps 95:8). The recalling of the journey to Sinai (v. 7c) and of Sinai itself (v. 7b) would be an appropriate anticipation of the clear recollection of the Decalogue in vv. 9-10. Following v. 9, which is a rephrasing of the first commandment (Exod 20:3; Deut 5:7; see also Jer 2:4-13), v. 10 is an almost direct quotation of the prologue of the Decalogue (Exod 20:2; Deut 5:6).

A central motif of the first section of the sermon is God's desire that the people hear—"listen to me!" (v. 8; the same Hebrew root [שמע *šāma*] lies behind both "hear" and "listen"). Since God had heard the people's cries for deliverance in Egypt (Exod 3:7), it is reasonable that now they obey the command to hear God (see Deut 6:4; Ps 95:7). Indeed, abundance awaits their hearing (v. 10c). The two key elements of vv. 6-10—God's desire to be heard and the promise of abundance—will recur in the second section of the sermon (vv. 13, 16). The choice belongs to the people.

81:11-16. The second part of the sermon starts by stating the people's response to God's call to hear; they "did not listen" (v. 11; see also vv. 8, 13). God's reaction is to give them exactly what they have chosen: their own "stubborn hearts" and "their own counsels" (see Jer 7:24, where these terms are used in the context of the prophet's condemnation of the people; see vv. 6, 26). In effect, God's desire to supply good things, to "fill" and to "satisfy" (v. 16) the people has been thwarted by their refusal to accept God's gracious actions. God's pain is like that of a rejected lover. The occurrence of "hear"/"listen" in v. 13 is an urgent repetition of God's desire. The setbacks the people experience are the result of their own choice not to listen, and not the result of God's will. God wills abundance, not just manna in the wilderness, but the "finest of wheat" (v. 16; see also Ps 147:14), and not just water from the rock (Exod 17:6-7), but honey (see Deut 32:13-14).

In view of the preceding psalms, it is especially noticeable that each time the key word "hear"/"listen" appears, the people are addressed as "my people" (vv. 8, 11, 13). Psalm 80, for instance, has suggested that the people's future depends ultimately on God's repentance. Similarly, Psalm 81 suggests that even in the absence of the people's choice to listen to and to follow God (vv. 8, 13), they are still "my people." The people will live finally by grace, by God's compassion and willingness to forgive (see Pss 78:38; 79:8).

REFLECTIONS

1. Citing Abraham Heschel, Tate reflects on the theological significance of Psalm 81: "The divine pathos of Yahweh is expressed in v. 14 [English v. 13]. . . . Yahweh is not a God of abstract absoluteness, who holds himself aloof from the world. He is moved and affected by what his people do or do not do. He has a dynamic relationship with his people, his family, and their welfare."[315] Thus, in the absence of the people's response, God begs and pleads that they listen. So important was hearing that this imperative was constantly put before the people, followed by Israel's fundamental profession of faith. The formulation is known as the Shema, "Hear, O Israel: The LORD is our God, the LORD alone" (Deut 6:4 NRSV). It captures the message of Psalm 81.

2. The repeated admonition to "hear"/"listen" to God calls to mind for Christian readers the story of Jesus' transfiguration (Mark 9:1-8). Both Psalm 81 and the NT transfiguration story recall the events at Sinai: the "mountain" (v. 2), the presence of Moses, the cloud (v. 7). The divine voice in the transfiguration story identifies Jesus as "my Son," the bearer of the divine will, and says, "Listen to him" (v. 7). Jesus proclaimed the reign of God and invited people to enter it (Mark 1:14-15; see also

315. Tate, *Psalms 51–100*, 327.

Ps 81:1-3). We are bombarded today by more competing voices than any other generation in the history of the world. In this din of voices vying for our attention and allegiance, Psalm 81 calls us to discern the pained but persistent voice of the one who says simply, "Follow me" (Mark 1:17 NRSV; cf. Ps 80:13*b*; John 10:4).

3. Listening to God is crucial. Psalm 81 thus becomes, in Mays's words, "a paradigm for what should happen in every religious festival."[316] Its emphatic call to hear/ listen is a reminder, too, that the revelation of God is not a static entity confined to the past. Rather, it is a dynamic process that continues in the present as God is moved and affected by what God's people do (see Reflections on Psalm 119). It is still the role of preaching, teaching, and pastoral care to challenge people to hear and to respond to God's exclusive claim upon their lives. Listening to God is still at the heart of what it means to be the people of God.

316. Mays, *Psalms,* 268.

PSALM 82:1-8, SHOW JUSTICE TO THE WEAK

COMMENTARY

As if to supply a rationale for Ps 81:9, Psalm 82 portrays the death of all other gods. In so doing, it offers a clear picture of the ancient Near Eastern polytheistic culture that formed Israel's religious background. In Canaanite religion, the high god El convened the council of the gods (see this concept also in 1 Kgs 22:19-23; Job 1:6-12; and perhaps Ps 58:1-2). In v. 1, Israel's God has displaced El and convenes what proves to be an extraordinary meeting. Israel's God proceeds to put the gods on trial (see the trial metaphor also in Isa 3:13-15; Hos 4:1-3; Mic 6:1-5). After the gods are indicted and charged (vv. 2-4), the case against them is summarized in v. 5, and the sentence is announced (vv. 6-7). The psalmist then pleads for God to claim the dominion once held by the gods and to rule justly (v. 8). In short, the council of the gods is permanently adjourned, and so Psalm 82 affirms again the message that forms the theological heart of the book of Psalms: God rules the world (see Psalms 2; 29; 47; 93; 95–99; Introduction).

82:1-4. The key issue in the trial of the gods is the way they "judge" (שׁפט *šāpaṭ,* v. 2) or administer "justice" (v. 3; note the two other occurrences of the same Hebrew root—"holds judgment" in v. 1 and "judge" in v. 8). Acting as both prosecutor and judge, God accuses the gods of judging unjustly and showing partiality (v. 2). The inadequacy of such behavior is apparent in Leviticus 19, part of the Holiness Code, as well. There God commands the people of Israel to "not render an unjust judgment" and to "not be partial" (Lev 19:15 NRSV). Indeed, Lev 19:2 exhorts, "You shall be holy, for I the LORD your God am holy" (NRSV). Thus injustice among humans, and certainly among the gods, violates the very nature of divinity and the divine will for the world.

The importance of justice in the human realm is emphasized in vv. 3-4. The series of imperatives functions not to exhort the gods but to indict them. As the series unfolds, it becomes clear that justice is a matter of ordering the human community. In v. 3, "give justice" and "maintain the right" are parallel, just as the nouns "justice" and "righteousness" are frequently parallel (see Amos 5:7, 24; 6:12). Justice and righteousness are not just abstract principles or ideals; rather, they have to do with the very concrete matter of how human beings relate. For the God of Israel, the criterion of justice involves what is done for the weak, the orphaned, the destitute, the needy (see Pss 9:7-9, 18; 10:17-18; 68:5-6; 113:7; 146:7-9). Not surprisingly, justice and righteousness also appear as parallels in the psalms that proclaim God's reign or describe the reign of God's earthly agent, the king (see Pss 72:1-2; 97:2; 99:4; see also 96:10, 13; 98:9). Here again, the establishment of justice and righteousness is the measure of divinity and of human life as God intends it.

Verse 4 allows even more specificity. Justice and righteousness involve the very concrete matter of how power is distributed in the human community, and thus the matter of who has access to life. In biblical terms, only persons whose lives are threatened need to be rescued or delivered. For instance, the psalmists often plead in life-threatening situations for God to rescue them from the wicked (see Pss 17:13; 71:2, 4). The verb "deliver" (נצל *nṣl*) is used to describe what God did to save the Israelites "from the hand of the Egyptians" (Exod 18:9-10 NIV). The word "hand" describes "grasp," or more to the point, "power." The gods should have delivered the weak and needy from the power of the wicked (v. 4), but it was precisely the wicked to whom the gods have been partial (v. 2). For the God of Israel, things are right in the human community when power is distributed in a way that all persons, especially the powerless, have access to the resources that enable them to live.

82:5. The speaker in v. 5 could be interpreted as the psalmist acting as narrator, but it is more likely that God continues to speak here. The "they" in v. 5 refers to the gods,

and the case against them is summarized. The result of their ignorance and failure is disastrous. The shaking of "all the foundations of the earth" represents a worst-case scenario. In the ancient view of the world, the mountains were the foundations that held up the sky and held back the waters from flooding dry land. The shaking of the foundations meant that the whole creation was threatened by the return of chaos (see Isa 24:18-19; Ps 46:1-3). In short, v. 5 suggests that injustice destroys the world! Where injustice exists, the world—at least the world as God intends it—falls apart. L. K. Handy argues that v. 5 is the structural center of Psalm 82, and its claim is certainly of central importance.[317]

82:6-7. Because the gods have failed to do justice, they are guilty of destroying human life and community as God intends them. Thus they deserve to die (vv. 6-7).

82:8. The death of the gods opens the way for God's reign of justice, for which the psalmist prays in v. 8 (see "rise up" in Pss 3:7; 9:19; 10:12). Having affirmed God's sovereignty, the psalmist also prays for and awaits God's rule; that is, the perspective is eschatological (see Commentary on Psalm 2; Introduction). But the psalmist is sure of the outcome. The final "you" is an emphatic pronoun; *God* rules the nations and the cosmos.

317. L. K. Handy, "Sounds, Words, and Meanings in Psalm 82," *JSOT* 47 (1990) 62-63.

REFLECTIONS

Psalm 82 raises the question of how we are to hear such an overtly mythological text in our very different world. The first step is to approach the psalm as a poetic expression of faith rather than a literal description of a trial in heaven. The truth of the psalm's message lies in its ability to illumine reality, which it does in a remarkable way—so much so that in our day, and with our distance from the ancient Near Eastern worldview, it is possible for us to appreciate the psalmist's conviction that injustice destroys the world. Indeed, we see it happening all around us—in our cities and neighborhoods, in our schools and churches and homes. That the foundations of the earth are still shaking reinforces that Psalm 82 does not literally describe the death of the gods, but instead denies ultimacy to any claim on our lives other than God's claim. The apostle Paul said it well in 1 Cor 8:5-6: "Indeed, even though there may be so-called gods in heaven or on earth—as in fact there are many gods and many lords—yet for us there is one God, the Father, from whom are all things and for whom we exist, and one Lord, Jesus Christ, through whom are all things and through whom we exist" (NRSV). Paul also refers to these so-called gods as "the rulers and authorities" (Eph 3:10; Col 2:15; see RSV "the principalities and powers"). These "rulers and authorities" are still with us in diverse forms—wherever and whenever anyone benefits from denying the God-given humanity of others. As Mays suggests, "As long as nations and their peoples do not see the reign of God as the reality that determines their way and destiny, there will be other gods who play that role."[318]

While such gods are still with us, Psalm 82 affirms, in Paul's words, that "for us there is one God." J. P. M. Walsh argues that the Canaanite polytheistic system elevated economic survival to ultimacy at the expense of compassion.[319] Thus the religion of the gods legitimated a hierarchical social system in which those at the top prospered and those at the bottom suffered. The religion of the one God, the God of Israel, countered by affirming that God's very nature is compassion. The faith of Israel was founded on the conviction that the one God hears the cries of victims and acts to deliver them from death to life (see Exod 3:7). The followers of the one God became an alternative community on the ancient Near Eastern scene. For them, the gods were dead.

For Christians, all rulers and authorities other than the one God have been dethroned; the gods are dead. We profess to live solely under the rule of God, which Jesus announced and embodied in a ministry of justice and righteousness, directed especially to the weak and to the needy. (See John 8:34-38, where Jesus cites Ps 82:6 in defense of his claim to be one with God on the basis of doing God's works; the sense of the argument depends on the Jewish custom of understanding "gods" in 82:6 as the people of Israel rather than divine beings.) We cannot help hearing the plea of v. 8 in terms of the prayer Jesus taught his disciples: "Your kingdom come. Your will be done, *on earth* as it is in heaven" (Matt 6:10 NRSV, italics added).

318. Mays, *Psalms,* 271.
319. J. P. M. Walsh, *The Mighty from Their Thrones: Power in the Biblical Tradition* (Philadelphia: Fortress, 1987) see esp. chap. 2.

PSALM 83:1-18, LET YOUR ENEMIES KNOW

COMMENTARY

Psalm 83 is one of several communal complaints/laments or prayers for help in Book III, which seems to have been shaped by the corporate afflictions of exile (see Psalms 74; 79; 80; Introduction). While Book III clearly reflects the experience of suffering, it also articulates the experience of God's nearness (see Ps 73:28) and a hope deriving from trust in God's sovereignty (see Pss 74:12-17; 76:7-9; 82:8). Psalm 83 does the same thing. Following the opening petition (v. 1), which already implies a crisis, the threat is described (vv. 2-5) and the enemies are named (vv. 6-8). Petition resumes in v. 9. Verses 9-12 appeal to past instances of help, while vv. 13-18 ask for vengeance upon the enemies that will demonstrate God's universal sovereignty (v. 18).

Whether Psalm 83 actually originated as a response to exile is not certain. If so, it is striking that the list of peoples and countries in vv. 6-8 does not include Babylon. Some commentators take the mention of Assyria as a primary clue to dating the psalm between the ninth and seventh centuries BCE; however, the name may have been intended to function symbolically, and thus many commentators suggest a post-exilic origin for the psalm. Certainty is impossible. Israel lived under persistent threat, and the psalm would have been a timely prayer at many critical points, but especially during the exile and beyond.

83:1. The threefold opening plea recalls similar petitions in other prayers for help (see Pss 28:1; 35:22; 109:1), and God's saving presence is elsewhere described as God's not keeping silence (see Ps 50:3; Isa 62:1-2, 6-7). The NRSV preserves the chiastic structure (see Introduction) of the verse, with "God" being the first and last word. While perhaps coincidental, this structure itself may imply the confidence that God surrounds the psalmist's pleas even as hostile nations apparently gather to surround Israel (vv. 6-8).

83:2-5. These verses describe the crisis. The enemies are first designated as God's enemies, and, as threatening foes are described elsewhere, here too they are "in tumult" (v. 2; see also Ps 46:6; Jer 6:22) as they assert their own sovereignty (see the idiom of raising the head in Judg 8:28). Verses 2-3 are reminiscent of Psalm 2, and the NRSV's "plans" (סוד *sôd*) in v. 3 represents a Hebrew root that is similar to the one that appears as "take counsel together" in Ps 2:2. As the NIV indicates, the verb "plot" (יעץ *yā'as*) occurs in vv. 3*b*, 5*a*. Elsewhere, it is God who plots or makes plans against nations (see Isa 19:17; Jer 49:20), but here the nations assert themselves against God and God's people. Between the repeated verb in vv. 3*b*, 5*a*, v. 4 indicates the enemies' intent to obliterate Israel (see Jer 11:19).

83:6-8. The list of enemies in these verses is unusual in the book of Psalms (but see Ps 60:6-8), and its exact origin and purpose remain elusive. The names in vv. 6-7 occur elsewhere in the OT—e.g., Edom (Pss 60:9; 137:7; Isa 34:5-6; 63:1; Ezek 35:1-15); the Ishmaelites (Gen 17:20; 25:18; 37:25-28); Moab (Judg 3:12-30; 1 Sam 14:47; 2 Sam 8:12; 2 Kgs 3:4-24); the Hagrites (1 Chr 5:10, 19-20); Ammon and Amalek (Exod 17:8-15; Judg 3:13; 1 Samuel 15; 2 Kgs 24:2; Jer 41:15); Gebal (Ezek 27:9; see "Giblites" in Josh 13:5; 1 Kgs 5:18, possibly ancient Byblos); Philistia (Exod 15:14; 1 Samuel 4–6; 14; 17; Ps 60:8); Tyre (Isaiah 23; Ezekiel 27–28; Amos 1:9-10). Assyria was a persistent enemy, especially powerful in the eighth and seventh centuries, to which several scholars date Psalm 83. Given the comprehensive and probably hyperbolic character of the list, however, it is likely that Assyria functions as a symbol or stereotypical example of a world power (see Ezra 6:22; Lam 5:6; Zech 10:10). The mention of Edom first may suggest an exilic origin, since Edom was often targeted as a major foe shortly after the exile (see Ps 137:7; Obadiah); however, Edom also was a frequent foe. Tate suggests "the possibility that the peoples listed form a rough circle around Israel, beginning in the south, up the Transjordan region, over to Tyre (and Gebal), and back down the coast to Philistia."[320] In any case, the effect of vv. 6-8 is to indicate that Israel needs major assistance.

320. Tate, *Psalms 51–100*, 347.

83:9-12. The remainder of the psalm indicates to whom Israel looks for help. Verses 9-12 recall outstanding instances of God's deliverance of the people, focusing on the book of Judges. The narrative in Judges 6–8 goes to great lengths to emphasize that the victory over Midian was a result not of Gideon's leadership but of God's leadership (cf. Judg 8:28 with Ps 83:2*b*). The defeat of Sisera and Jabin (vv. 9*b*-10) recalls Judges 4–5 (on v. 10*b*, see Jer 8:2; 9:22). Verse 11 returns the focus to Midian (see Judg 7:25; 8:15). The story in Judges 6–8 does not record the words (v. 12) attributed to the figures mentioned in v. 11; however, v. 12 recalls v. 4, and the intent seems to be to indicate that the current crisis is on the magnitude of the ancient ones.

83:13-18. The severity of the opposition explains perhaps the vehemence of the prayer as it continues in vv. 13-18. The imagery of v. 13 is similar to that of Ps 1:4; Isa 17:13; 40:24; 41:2; Jer 13:24. Verse 14 recalls Ps 97:3; Isa 10:17-18; 47:14, and the imagery of v. 16 is also used elsewhere to describe God's wrath (see Isa 29:6; Jer 29:13; Hos 8:7; Amos 1:14). The words "terrify" (v. 15) and "dismayed" (v. 17) translate the same Hebrew root (בהל *bāhal*) that is used elsewhere to assert God's sovereignty over enemies of God and the people (see Exod 15:15, which also mentions Edom and Moab; Pss 2:5; 48:5). The verb "perish" (אבד *'ābad*) also recalls Ps 2:12, where it occurs after the kings and rulers of the nations have been warned to subject themselves to God's rule.

While the petitions in vv. 9-18 are shockingly violent (although we hardly live in a less violent world!), vv. 16 and 18 suggest that the ultimate purpose of God is not to destroy but to reconcile (note the repeated "name" linking the two verses). The personal pronoun "you" provides emphasis on God's sovereign claims (v. 18*a*) and recalls the final verse of Psalm 82 as well (see "earth" also in Pss 82:8; 83:18). What God wills is that all the earth "know"—that is, recognize who truly rules the world (see Exod 5:2; 7:5; 14:4, 18; 1 Kgs 8:43; Ps 79:6, 10; see also Exod 9:16). The result will be a reign of justice and righteousness that characterizes God's rule as opposed to the rule of autonomous nations or the rule of the gods (see Psalm 82; Isa 2:1-4; Mic 4:1-3). Such constitutes the will of God.

Reflections

Psalm 83 is eschatological; its real purpose is to pray for and express trust in the fulfillment of God's reign over all the earth (v. 18) in the midst of opposition (see Commentary on Psalm 2; Introduction). To be sure, the prayer for deliverance from violent oppressors uses the language and imagery of violence. This in itself constitutes a valuable lesson, for it illustrates how persons are likely to respond when they have been victimized (see vv. 4, 12; see also Reflections on Psalms 109; 137). Verses 16 and 18 suggest, however, that the violent imagery is hyperbolic and that the real desire of God's people and God's own self is to enact God's reign of righteousness and justice. This is especially the case when Psalm 83 is heard in conjunction with Psalm 82. But as Psalm 82 also recognizes, God's will for justice and righteousness does not go unopposed. Thus both Psalms 82 and 83 very realistically recognize that oppressors do not give up without a fight. Pharoah, for instance, did not easily bend to the Israelites' request for liberation (see Exodus 1–15). Similarly, political equality for African Americans was achieved only by a long and costly struggle, and the white minority government of South Africa did not agree to dismantle apartheid without a prolonged and bitter fight.

Because of this recognition, the metaphor of God as divine warrior is appealed to by threatened people (see Exodus 1–15; Deuteronomy 32; Pss 66:3; 68:1, 21; 74:4, 18-23; 89:10). While the metaphor is understandable in the context of violent oppression, it can nonetheless be dangerous. Mays comments: "It is of course venturesome and dangerous for the people of God to see those who threaten them as enemies of God and to invoke God's vengeance against them. Such prayers can easily become the language of a self-serving, blind ideology."[321] This warning means that Psalm 83 finally calls the people of God themselves to humility—to humble enactment of God's ways of justice and righteousness.

Some may suggest that the violent imagery of Psalm 83 and its prayer for vengeance render it unusable for Christians. Properly warned, however, the church can hear this psalm as a cogent reminder that the reign of God and the divine purposes have never gone and never go unopposed. Israel knew this, of course, as did Jesus, Paul, and the early church. We should know it, too, for the contemporary world is hardly less inclined to violence than was the ancient world or more inclined to enact God's will for justice, righteousness, and peace. As Mays concludes: "Modern history is punctuated with attempts by secularized powers to dispossess the people of the Lord in both synagogue and church. Psalm 83 is in the psalter as the prayer of his people whose existence is the work of his reign and who leave the vengeance to God (see Psalm 94)."[322] In short, in our world of violence and oppression, we still pray as Psalms 82–83 suggest and as Jesus taught us: "Your kingdom come. Your will be done" (Matt 6:10 NRSV).

321. Mays, *Psalms*, 273.
322. Mays, *Psalms*, 273.

PSALM 84:1-12, HAPPY ARE THOSE WHOSE STRENGTH IS IN YOU

Commentary

Psalm 84 is perhaps the most expressive and beautiful of all the songs of Zion (see Psalms 46; 48; 76; 87; 122). Like the others, it may originally have been recited or sung by pilgrims as they made their way toward, arrived at, or walked about Jerusalem. Verse

1 seems to offer the psalmist's enthusiastic response upon first seeing the city or the Temple, an experience that the psalmist reflects on in v. 2. Verses 3-4 are linked by the repetition of the word "home"/"house" (בית *bayit*), which may derive from the psalmist's contemplation of the happiness of the priests and other cultic personnel who resided in the Temple. The word "happy" (אשרי *'ašrê*) becomes a key word in the psalm (see vv. 4, 5, 12), and vv. 5-7 extend the experience to the pilgrims who will see God in Zion. Verses 8-9 consist of petition. Verse 10 shifts from direct address of God to reference to God in the third person; and with v. 11, the psalm has the character of a profession of faith. The profession is made explicit in the concluding verse, which at least implicitly invites others to share in the psalmist's experience of God. The two initial and concluding sections (vv. 1-4, 8-12) each consist of seven poetic lines. While this may be coincidental, the effect is to focus attention on vv. 5-7 as the central unit, thus highlighting the experience of the pilgrim. It may not be coincidental that v. 5 begins with the word "happy," which is featured in the concluding verses of the surrounding sections. By the end of the poem, the beatitudes in vv. 4-5, 12 have constructed a compelling portrait of a faithful follower of God.

The canonical placement of Psalm 84 is worthy of note. It occurs immediately following a psalm that concludes both the Asaph psalms (Psalms 50; 73–83; see Introduction) and the Elohistic psalter (Psalms 42–83). Even though Psalms 84–85 and 87–88 are psalms of Korah (see also Psalms 42–49, the beginning of the Elohistic psalter), they do not significantly change the character of Book III. Psalms 84 and 87, both songs of Zion, recall Psalm 76, and each is sandwiched between complaints that effectively call for deeper understanding—that is, how should the enthusiastic hope and trust of the Zion songs be understood in view of the stark realities voiced in the complaints? This question, prompted by the ordering of psalms in Book III (see Commentary on Psalms 73; 74; 78; 79; 80; Introduction), encourages an eschatological understanding of Psalm 84. In short, its use was not restricted to ancient pilgrims to Jerusalem. Rather, it effectively articulates the experience of generations of pilgrims, who, trusting God (v. 12), have "seen" God (v. 7) in various times and places and have derived from their experience of God a strength that transforms them and their lives (vv. 5-7; see Reflections below).

84:1-4. The translation "lovely" (ידידות *yĕdîdôt*) in v. 1 is adequate, because the psalmist's experience involves visual admiration of Zion, but the experience creates a bond between person and place that might be better expressed with the word "beloved" (see the Hebrew word translated here as "dwelling place" [משכנות *miškānôt*] in Pss 43:3; 46:4; 132:5, 7). The title "LORD of hosts" is associated elsewhere with the ark, God's earthly throne (see Commentary on Psalm 24, esp. the discussion of vv. 7-10), and it occurs elsewhere in contexts where God is addressed as "King" (v. 3; see also Ps 48:8; Isa 6:5). Verse 2a further communicates the power of the place (see "courts" also in v. 10; Pss 65:4; 96:8; 100:4; 116:19; 135:2; Isa 1:12; 62:9), for which the psalmist "longs" (see Gen 31:30, where Jacob longs for his father's house, and note "home"/"house" in Ps 84:3-4) and "faints" (see "fail" in Ps 73:26; 119:81). As v. 2b indicates, the place derives its power from the presence of "the living God" (see Ps 42:2, where longing for God is also eloquently expressed but with different vocabulary and imagery). The verb in v. 2b usually indicates a joyful cry (see Pss 5:11; 67:4; 95:1; 96:12; 98:4), but it occasionally has a more plaintive sense (see Lam 2:19).

As Gen 31:30 suggests, longing is what one naturally feels for home. In other words, the psalmist is homesick for the true home: God's house. The sight of birds nesting within the temple complex (v. 3) and of the cultic officials at work leads the psalmist to reflect upon the appropriateness of literally finding a "home" in the Temple (see Pss 23:5-6; 27:4). The address of God as "my King," along with the repetition of the phrase "LORD of hosts" from v. 1 (see also vv. 8, 12), suggests that the psalmist's praise is not ultimately of the place but of God. The experience of the particular place puts the psalmist in touch with God's sovereignty over all places (see Commentary on Psalm 48).

84:5-7. The transformational power of Jerusalem is evident in the affirmations of vv.

5-7. The noun "strength" (עז 'ōz) indicates elsewhere an attribute of the sovereign God (see Exod 15:13; Pss 29:1; 93:1; 96:6-7), but it is also regularly imparted to God's people (see Exod 15:2; Pss 29:11; 68:35; 81:1; 86:16). Here the psalmist apparently claims that God bestows strength upon those traveling to Jerusalem, although the sense of v. 5*b* is uncertain (see NRSV note and cf. NRSV and NIV). Verse 6 also seems to connote transformation, although the precise sense is again unclear. "Baca" [בכא] is usually taken as a proper noun. Its location is unknown, but apparently it was a dry place, to which the pilgrims bring relief. The word is similar to the word בכי (*běkî*), which means "tears," in which case another sort of transformation is suggested. The mention of springs and rain may imply a connection with pilgrimage to the Feast of Tabernacles, which is associated elsewhere with rain (see Zech 14:16-19). Such a conclusion is uncertain, however, and it is possible to read the whole verse symbolically. The final form of the Hebrew text actually encourages this, since it has vocalized a set of consonants that could mean "pools" (ברכת *běrēkôt*) so that they mean "blessings" (*běrākôt*). In short, wherever the pilgrims go, they bring blessings. Enlivened and empowered by the vision of God's awaiting them (v. 8; see "saw"/"seen" in Ps 48:5, 8) or perhaps by the hope of being seen by God (see v. 9), the pilgrims gain strength (the Hebrew words differ in vv. 5 and 7; see also 1 Sam 2:4). They themselves are transformed.

84:8-12. Verses 8-9 move to petition, and apparently the pilgrim prays for the king. The word "shield" (מגן *māgēn*) which is used of God in v. 12 (see also Ps 3:3), can also be used of human rulers (see Ps 47:9), and the word "anointed" refers even more clearly to the king (see Ps 2:2). In the post-exilic era, the "anointed" (משיח *māšîaḥ*) could also have referred to the high priest (see Num 3:3). In either case, it would have been natural for those visiting Jerusalem to pray for the leaders of the people (see Ps 61:6-7).

Verses 10-11 again return to the psalmist's own experience (see vv. 1-4; note "courts" in v. 2 and "home"/"house" in vv. 3-4). The poetic hyperbole in v. 10*a* expresses the same longing as in v. 2. In v. 10*b*, "doorkeeper" probably does not refer to the office of that description (see 2 Kgs 12:9), but to anyone waiting to enter the Temple. Kraus translates as follows, "I would rather lie on the threshold at the house of my God than live in the tents of the wicked."[323] The "tents of the wicked" need not refer to a specific place, but to any place characterized by self-serving rather than to the service of God (see discussion of "the wicked" in Commentary on Psalm 1). To await entrance into God's house, by contrast, means to be one "whose walk is blameless" (v. 11). It is significant that precisely this kind of person is mentioned in Ps 15:2 in response to the question in 15:1, "Who may dwell on your holy hill?" To walk blamelessly means not absolute perfection but humble dependence upon God for life. Or, as v. 12 suggests, it means ultimately to trust God (see Ps 40:4 and the essentially synonymous beatitudes in Pss 2:12; 34:8*b*). Verse 11 articulates the content of this trust as the psalmist affirms God's providing "favor" and "honor" (see Prov 3:34-35, where these two words also occur together)—everything necessary for the sustenance of life. The same Hebrew word (טוב *ṭôb*) underlies "better" (v. 10) and "good thing" (v. 11), thus framing the two verses. The confidence expressed is not in a retributional scheme whereby good things are guaranteed as a reward. Neither is the happiness promised a facile or carefree cheeriness. Rather, happiness consists of taking refuge in God (see Pss 2:12; 73:28; note 84:5, 7), and the repetition of "good" recalls the affirmation of Ps 73:28 that ultimate goodness is to be near God (see also Ps 63:3). In a word, this is also the message that pervades Psalm 84.

323. Kraus, *Psalms 1–59,* 166.

REFLECTIONS

1. One of the most beautiful of contemporary musical arrangements of the psalms is "How Lovely, Lord," a metrical paraphrase of Psalm 84 by Arlo D. Duba that has been set to music by Hal H. Hopson (*Merle's Tune*). The auspicious wedding of text and tune captures movingly both the psalmist's longing for communion with God and the experience of well-being that results from encountering the living God. In other words, although our symbols for and understandings of God's presence in space and time may differ from those of the ancient psalmist, Psalm 84 can continue to function effectively and powerfully.

2. Citing Jon Levenson's conclusion that in Psalm 84 "physical ascent is also a spiritual ascent," Tate suggests that the pilgrimage experience described in Psalm 84 is sacramental—"visible actions become the means of grace and revelation of the presence of God."[324] For Christians, the visible actions may differ, but we still regularly engage in visible actions that we profess to be means of grace, modes of experiencing God's real presence and of finding our true home. For instance, we come regularly to what forms the centerpiece of any real home: a table. But for us, this is the Lord's table, where we eat and drink with Christ and with one another as a sign of our belonging. At the Lord's table we not only remember but are also re-membered; that is, we profess to receive a strength that derives not from ourselves but from God (see vv. 5, 7). In essence, as Psalm 23 suggests as well, church is home (see Commentary on Psalm 23, esp. discussion of vv. 5-6).

And so we go to church to profess that our lives are not our own but are lived under God's sovereign claim (see vv. 3-4; see also Reflections on Psalms 46; 100). We go to church to profess that insofar as we are powerful people, our strength derives not from ourselves but from God (see vv. 5, 7). We go to church to profess that our worthiness, insofar as we have any, derives not from what we manage to accomplish but from what God bestows (vv. 10-11). We go to church to profess that happiness is not the ceaseless pursuit of material well-being that our culture promotes but the entrusting of our lives and futures to God (see v. 12). As Mays suggests:

> Every visit to a temple or church or meeting of believers is in a profound sense a pilgrimage. We "go" [see v. 7 and the same Hebrew word translated "walk" in v. 11], not just for practical or personal reasons; we go theologically. Christians have read and sung Psalm 84 and through it praised the God to whom we "go" in different ways.[325]

Psalm 84 thus proclaims the good news that our destination, daily and eternally, lies in God. This good news contains the transforming power by which we profess to find strength, value, and life itself (see Commentary on Psalm 48).

324. Tate, *Psalms 51-100*, 362; see Jon D. Levenson, *Sinai and Zion: An Entry into the Jewish Bible* (San Francisco: Harper & Row, 1985) 178.
325. Mays, *Psalms*, 275.

PSALM 85:1-13, SURELY GOD'S SALVATION IS NEAR

COMMENTARY

Another of the communal prayers for help or laments/complaints that give Book III a particular character (see Psalms 74; 79; 80; 83; 89; Introduction), Psalm 85 is known primarily for its striking portrayal of God's promise of peace and salvation in vv. 8-13. The promise is delivered in the midst of current distress (vv. 4-7) that has followed a more favorable time (vv. 1-3). This sequence means that Psalm 85 makes especially good sense as a corporate prayer for help in the early post-exilic era. Indeed, the phrase "restored the fortunes" (שׁוב שׁבית *šûb šĕbît*, v. 1), is often used to describe Israel's return from exile (see Jer 30:3, 18; 31:23; 33:7, 11; Ezek 39:25). Furthermore, the prophet of the exile proclaimed that God had forgiven the people (Isa 40:1-2; see also Ps 85:2-3) and brought them home; but the glorious vision of Isaiah 40–55 did not materialize. The prophet Haggai lamented the people's failure to rebuild the Temple, and using the same verb as in Ps 85:1*a* ("showed favor" [רצה *rāṣâ*]), he suggests that this failure accounts for the lack of God's favor in the early restoration era (520 BCE; see Hag 1:8). Perhaps not coincidentally, the deficiencies Haggai detected are the very things promised in Ps 85:8-13. The "glory" of God did not dwell in the Temple (see Hag 2:7, 9; cf. Ps 85:9). The land yielded no crops (Hag 1:10; cf. Ps 85:12). There was no peace (Hag 2:9; cf. Ps 85:8, 10). In short, Psalm 85 may well have originated as a prayer of the people amid the disappointing circumstances of the early post-exilic era (see also Zech 1:12-17). The people had recently been restored (v. 1), but they soon found themselves again in need of restoration (v. 4; see also Ps 80:3, 7, 14, 19).

85:1-7. In terms of the above scenario, the relatively rapid change of fortune that necessitated the petitions of vv. 4-7 is not really surprising in the light of Israel's history. For instance, shortly after the deliverance from Egypt, the people's idolatry necessitated Moses' prayer that God "turn from your fierce anger" (Exod 32:12 NIV; see also Ps 85:3, 5). Moses' petition is accompanied by his reminder to God of the promise of land (Exod 32:13; see Ps 85:8-13, and note especially the mention of "land"/"ground" in vv. 1, 9, 11-12). God does indeed "turn" (שׁוב *šûb*; see Ps 85:3; the same Hebrew verb also underlies "restore[d]" in vv. 1, 4 and "again" in v. 6), allowing the people to live and finally revealing the divine character to consist of steadfast love and faithfulness (Exod 34:6; see also Ps 85:7, 10-11). The pronoun "you" in v. 6*a* is emphatic; it is God who must give life (see Ps 80:18).

The affinities between Psalm 85 and Exodus 32–34 do not necessarily indicate another historical setting for Psalm 85, but they do demonstrate that Psalm 85 is an appropriate prayer for a variety of circumstances. While the phrase "restored the fortunes" suggests the likelihood of a post-exilic prayer, it can indicate more generally any "reversal of Yahweh's judgment."[326] Like Psalm 126, which also contains the phrase in v. 1 and then petitions for further restoration (Ps 126:4; see also 85:4), Psalm 85 is perpetually appropriate for the people of God. That is to say, the people of God always stand in need of salvation (note how "salvation" in vv. 4, 7 frames the section of petition; see also v. 9; Exod 15:2; Pss 24:5; 25:5; 27:1, 9; 51:14; 95:1; 118:25).

85:8-13. The gifts prayed for in vv. 4, 7—steadfast love and salvation—are promised in vv. 8-13. An individual voice, perhaps that of a prophet or liturgical preacher (see Commentary on Psalms 50; 81), delivers the good news of peace (v. 8*ab*) and calls for a response (v. 8*c*). God's "salvation is at hand" (v. 9), and steadfast love is one of the four personified attributes in v. 10. In a sense, the gifts are conditional; God's salvation will be experienced by those who fear God (v. 9; see also v. 8*c*; Commentary on Psalm 103). But in a deeper sense, the remarkable description in vv. 10-13 exceeds any possibility of human merit or accomplishment. The focus is clearly on God's character and activity. Steadfast love (vv. 7, 10) and faithfulness (vv. 10-11) are at the heart of God's character (Exod 34:6-7; see also Pss 25:10; 40:10-11; 57:3; 61:7; 86:15; 89:14; 115:1; 138:2; Introduction). Righteousness (vv. 10, 13) is the fundamental policy that God wills and enacts as sovereign of the universe (see Pss 96:13; 97:2; 98:9), and the result is "peace" (שׁלום *šālôm*; vv. 8, 10; see also Pss 29:11; 35:27; Isa 60:17; Ezek 34:25). God's character and activity will fill the universe, from ground to sky (v. 11; see also Ps 36:5-6). The repetition of "righteousness" (צדק *ṣedeq*) emphasizes the point: God *will* set things right. The vivid poetic description affirms, in essence, that God will be with and for the people; God's "glory," symbolic of God's presence, will "dwell in our land" (v. 9; see also Exod 33:18, 33; Ps 97:6; Isa 40:5; 60:1-2; Ezek 43:2). And, as previous

326. John Bracke, "*šûb šebût*: A Reappraisal," *ZAW* 97 (1985) 242.

psalms have made clear, the experience of God's presence is the essence of "what is good" (v. 12; see also Pss 73:28; 84:10-11).

For similar descriptions of God's presence and its effects, see Pss 43:3, 89:14; Isa 32:16-18; 45:8; 58:8-9.

REFLECTIONS

It is a revealing observation about Psalm 85 that it was a major inspiration both to the contemplative Thomas à Kempis, who relied on it heavily in the third book of *The Imitation of Christ,* and to the militant activist Oliver Cromwell, who found it "instructive and significant" as he proclaimed his intent that seventeenth-century England embody the reign of God on earth.[327] In other words, Psalm 85, especially vv. 8-13, captures the reality that Christians *already* know and experience in Jesus Christ, but that exists amid the ongoing brokenness of the world and the sinfulness of persons and of our society. Thus, as Mays points out: "The vision has an eschatological reach. It needs the coming of God himself to realize it fully (vv. 9, 13). The psalm therefore is a judgment on any easy satisfaction with life under the conditions created by human character and a summons to look for and pray for the time and life created by the character of God."[328]

For Christians, of course, the birth of Jesus Christ was the very coming of God, and his ministry was an embodiment of love, righteousness, faithfulness, and peace (see John 1:16-17; 14:27; Rom 1:16-17; 1 Cor 1:30). In short, we already know and experience salvation in Christ. But Christ promised to come again, and Christ taught disciples to continue to pray, "Your kingdom come. Your will be done on earth as it is in heaven" (Matt 6:10 NRSV). Thus Christians also live perpetually awaiting salvation—between the already and the not yet. It is always appropriate that we pray with the psalmist, "Restore us again" (v. 4).

With good reason, Psalm 85 has been traditionally associated with the season of Advent. While Advent is a season of awaiting the celebration of the birth of Jesus, its focus is even more clearly on the second coming of Christ. Thus, by its nature, Advent encourages us both to celebrate salvation and to pray for salvation, as does Psalm 85 (see Commentary on Psalm 126).

327. See Prothero, *The Psalms in Human Life and Experience,* 76-77, 190, 196.
328. Mays, *Psalms,* 277-78.

PSALM 86:1-17, YOU ALONE ARE GOD

COMMENTARY

Psalm 86 stands out in Book III as one of only two individual complaints or prayers for help (see Psalm 88) and the only psalm attributed to David. This, plus the fact that it seems to interrupt a small Korah collection (Psalms 84–85; 87–88), seems to suggest intentional placement; however, the exact reasons are unclear. Given that Book III seems to reflect the experience of the exile and its aftermath (see Commentary on Psalms 73; 74; 85; Introduction), we can at least say that the individual prayer in Psalm 86 would have been a very appropriate one on behalf of the whole people, since Psalm 86 recalls a narrative context in which the people disobeyed and were forgiven (Exodus 32–34).

Because it alludes so often to other psalms and key biblical texts (cf. v. 1*b* with Pss 40:17; 69:29; 109:22; cf. v. 4*b* with Pss 25:1; 143:8; cf. v. 11*a* with Pss 27:11; 143:8; cf. v. 14 with Ps 54:3; cf. vv. 5, 15 with Exod 34:6), the originality of Psalm 86 and the creativity of its author have sometimes been questioned. Psalm 86 demonstrates, however, a unique structure, including the sixfold repetition of the Hebrew pronoun "you" that functions as a structuring device. While it is possible simply to divide the psalm into two (vv. 1-13, 14-17) or three sections (vv. 1-7, 8-13, 14-17), several scholars have detected a chiastic arrangement on some scale (see Introduction). At the simplest level, the complaints and petitions in vv. 1-7 and vv. 14-17 (see esp. vv. 7, 14) surround the hymnic affirmation of vv. 8-13. On a more elaborate scale, G. Giavini has suggested the following outline:

A vv. 1-4 (see "your servant" in vv. 2, 4)
  B vv. 5-6 (see "abounding in steadfast love," v. 5)
    C v. 7 (complaint)
      D vv. 8-10 (see "glorify your name" in v. 9)
        E v. 11 (central verse; note especially "your name")
      D´ vv. 12-13 (see "glorify your name," v. 12)
    C´ v. 14 (complaint)
  B´ v. 15 (see "abounding in steadfast love")
A´ vv. 16-17 (see "your servant," v. 16)[329]

The effect of this structure is to focus attention on the center of the psalm, thus highlighting the concept of God's name (vv. 9, 11-12) or character. The focus on God's character is reinforced by the vocabulary of Psalm 86, which is strongly reminiscent of God's self-revelation in Exod 34:6-7. It is further reinforced by the sixfold repetition of the Hebrew pronoun "you," referring to God (vv. 2, 5, 10, 15, 17). As Brueggemann points out, these occurrences also show a chiastic arrangement. The pronouns in vv. 2 and 17 claim God as belonging to or acting on behalf of the psalmist (note the nearly synonymous verbs for "save" [ישע yšʿ] in v. 2 and "helped" [עזר ʿāzar] in v. 17). The pronouns in vv. 5 and 15 are each accompanied by the title "Lord" as well as by a creedal statement recalling Exod 34:6. At the center is the double occurrence of "you" in v. 10, which proclaims God's exclusive sovereignty.[330] While the structural

proposals differ slightly in details, they are similar enough to warrant the conclusion that the poet was intent upon focusing the reader's attention on the center of the psalm—v. 10 or v. 11, or perhaps the two together.

86:1-7. Immediately following the opening plea (see Ps 17:5), the psalmist includes herself or himself among those for whom God has special concern (see Ps 9:9, 18; 10:12; 82:2-3). The word "devoted" (חסיד ḥāsîd) in v. 2 is from the same Hebrew root as the word "steadfast love" (חסד ḥesed, vv. 5, 13, 15), suggesting that the psalmist's identity is bound up with God's identity. In essence, the psalmist belongs to God, an identity also suggested by the repeated phrase "your servant" (vv. 2, 4, 16). Only God can "save" (see Pss 3:8; 6:4)—that is, give life—so the psalmist entrusts her or his life to God (v. 2b; see Pss 4:5; 9:10; Introduction). Or, as the final phrase in v. 4b could be translated, "I offer you my life" (see Commentary on Psalm 25, esp. discussion of v. 1; see also Ps 143:8).

The psalmist's life is secure with God because of the way God is. So the focus in vv. 1-7 is not only on the psalmist's identity but also on God's identity, as suggested by the first two occurrences of the emphatic "you" (vv. 2b, 5a). Petitions in vv. 3, 6 appeal to one crucial attribute of God that is mentioned in Exod 34:6: mercy (see "gracious" in Exod 33:19; 34:6). Other key aspects of God's identity are clustered in Ps 86:5—goodness (see Exod 33:19; Pss 54:6; 85:12), willingness to forgive (see Exod 34:9), abundant steadfast love (see Exod 34:6-7; Ps 5:7; Introduction). Because God is merciful, good, forgiving, and loving, the psalmist appeals to God for life, and by v. 7, the repeated verb "answer" (ענה ʿānâ; see v. 1) indicates the psalmist's growing assurance.

86:8-13. The focus is even more clearly on God's identity in vv. 8-13, beginning with a proclamation of the incomparability of God's being (v. 8a; see also Exod 15:11; Ps 35:10) and activity (v. 8b; see also Deut 3:24). Verse 9 indicates that the nations recognize God's sovereignty and respond appropriately, bowing down (see "bow down" or "worship" in Pss 29:2; 95:6; 96:9; 99:5, 9—all psalms that proclaim God's reign) and glorifying (see Ps 29:1-2, 9). Verse 10, with its two occurrences of the emphatic "you," represents the culmination of the psalmist's proclamation about God. The word "great" (גדול *gādôl*) is elsewhere associated with the recognition of God's reign (see Pss 47:2; 95:3; 99:2-3; 145:3), and "wondrous things" (נפלאות *niplā'ôt*) recalls the exodus (see Exod 3:20; 15:11; 34:10; Ps 77:13-15), the paradigmatic demonstration of God's rule (see Exod 15:18). Brueggemann translates the phrase in v. 10a with "doing impossibilities"; the sovereign God can make things new.[331] The final phrase of v. 10 summarizes the theme that began in v. 8: God alone (see Ps 83:18).

It was the prerogative and responsibility of monarchs to lead persons into participation in the realm of peace that was supposed to result from their reign (see Pss 72:1-7; 85:8-13), and so the psalmist requests such direction in v. 11a. Having offered the self to God (see v. 4), the psalmist is open to God's instruction (see Commentary on Psalm 1; the verb "teach" [ירה *yārâ*] here represents the same Hebrew root as the noun for "instruction" [תורה *tôrâ*] in 1:2). Not surprisingly, in both of the other instances where the psalmist lifts up the soul to God, the context focuses on God's steadfast love and contains both the psalmist's profession of trust in God and a request to be taught by God (see Pss 25:1-2, 4-6, 10; 143:8, 10, 12). The word "truth" (אמת *'ĕmet*) in v. 11 is the same as "faithfulness" in v. 15. Again (on "devoted," see above discussion of v. 2), the psalmist desires life and identity to be shaped by God's will and God's way. In other words, the psalmist gladly submits to God's sovereign rule. Undivided allegiance belongs not to self but to God (see "individual heart" and "whole heart" in vv. 11-12 NRSV; see "all your heart" in Deut 6:5 and "one heart" in Jer 32:39). The psalmist embodies personally the response of the nations (cf. vv. 9b, 12b). Life is gladly submitted to God, because the psalmist trusts that God's sovereign character—God's name (vv. 9,

11-12)—is ultimately manifested as love that leads to life (v. 13; see also Pss 30:3; 56:13).

86:14-17. Psalm 86 manifests the same tension that is evident in the other individual prayers for help. While v. 13 implies that the psalmist has been delivered, v. 14 returns to complaint and vv. 16-17 to petition (see vv. 1-7). As usual, the precise nature of the trouble is unclear, except to say that the psalmist is opposed by people who are also opponents of God (v. 14; see above on Ps 54:3). The first petition in v. 16 could be translated "Face me" (see Pss 25:16; 69:16). The petitions to "be gracious" and to "save" recall vv. 2-3, as does the phrase "your servant" (see also v. 4). "Strength" regularly characterizes God (see Exod 15:13; Pss 29:1; 93:1; 96:6-7), and the psalmist desires to live by God's provision (see Exod 15:2; Pss 81:1; 84:5). The psalmist's description of self in v. 16c may be intended to emphasize the psalmist's long-standing dependence upon God—that is, to the point of servanthood's being an inherited status (see Ps 116:16 GNB: "[Save me because] I serve you just as my mother did"). The "sign" in v. 17a seems to be the deliverance that the psalmist prays for and anticipates—that is, God's help (see Pss 10:14; 22:19; 30:10; 54:4) and comfort (see Pss 23:4; 71:21).

In any case, as the psalmist prays for and awaits God's help, she or he remains convinced of God's sovereignty, which will finally be revealed as love. In the midst of both series of petitions and complaints (vv. 1-7, 14-17) is an affirmation of faith that recalls the very heart of Israel's faith (vv. 5, 15). In fact, v. 15 reproduces Exod 34:6 almost exactly. As Brueggemann concludes about Psalm 86: "In the midst of the darkness, in the season of disorientation, Yahweh is affirmed, known to be the one who abides, who is not intimidated or alienated by the disorientation. The creedal claims of Yahweh are still credible in the darkness, perhaps especially credible here."[332]

331. Brueggemann, *The Message of the Psalms,* 63.

332. Brueggemann, *The Message of the Psalms,* 63.

REFLECTIONS

1. Although the word *righteous* is not used in Psalm 86, the psalmist's words illustrate the essence of what it means to be righteous: to entrust one's life and future to

God in openness to God's direction and instruction (see vv. 2, 4, 10; see also Commentary on Psalm 1). Such trust does not guarantee a life free of troubles and opposition (see vv. 7, 14); yet in the midst of such opposition, the psalmist somehow knows, experiences, and proclaims God's goodness, mercy, faithfulness, and love (vv. 5, 15). Truly, the psalmist knew what it meant to be justified by faith—to be rightly related to God by completely entrusting life and future to God. In terms of the psalmist's self-description, he or she was "your servant" (vv. 2, 4, 16), and on the basis of the psalmist's experience (vv. 7, 14) we must conclude that he or she was a suffering servant. In this sense, then, the psalmist's witness anticipates the life and ministry of Jesus, who, entrusting life unreservedly to God, proclaimed God's faithfulness and love amid persistent opposition. For Christians, the life, death, and resurrection of Jesus represent the ultimate sign of something that the psalmist had already discovered: For the faithful, suffering and glory are finally inseparable (see Commentary on Psalms 13; 22). In the apostle Paul's words, nothing in all creation "will be able to separate us from the love of God" (Rom 8:39 NRSV; see also Ps 86:5, 15).

2. As several commentators point out, the nature of the psalmist's witness also makes her or his words a model of prayer.

> Prayer is the utterance of an identity that is lived out. It is not mere language but brings to expression the role of servant adopted in existence. . . .
> Prayer is the voice of dependence [see v. 1]. . . .
> Prayer is the voice of trust [see v. 2]. . . .
> Prayer is not only a plea for life, it is a submission of life. The servant can serve only one master (see Matt. 6:19-34). Prayer is the voice of commitment [see vv. 11-12].[333]

In teaching his disciples to pray, Jesus also taught them to submit their lives—"thy will be done." As in the psalmist's case, such submission is possible, because we trust that God rules the world—"thine is the kingdom, the power, and the glory forever." Like the psalmist, we attempt to live out our faith in a broken world that opposes us and opposes God. This reality means we wait as we pray—"thy kingdom come."

333. Mays, *Psalms,* 280.

PSALM 87:1-7, THIS ONE WAS BORN IN ZION

COMMENTARY

Psalm 87 is known for its many interpretive difficulties, and scholars and translators have often resorted to rearranging the text in an attempt to achieve a smoother reading. Kraus, for instance, suggests the following sequence: vv. 2, 1*b*, 5*b*, 7, 3, 6*a*, 4*b*/6*b*, 4*a*, 5*a*.[334] The NEB's alteration is less radical: vv. 1-2, 4-5, 6, 7, 3. The REB has returned to the traditional ordering of the verses, as have most recent commentators, and this clearly is the best policy. Even so, the comment by Booij is not unusual: "I think the question of what Ps lxxxvii essentially means to say can be answered only tentatively."[335]

While caution is in order, it is safe to say that Psalm 87 is a song of Zion (see Psalms

334. Kraus, *Psalms 60–150,* 185.

335. T. Booij, "Some Observations on Psalm LXXXVII," *VT* 37 (1987) 22.

46; 48; 76; 84; 122). Like other songs of Zion, it asserts that Jerusalem is God's city (vv. 1-3; see Pss 46:4-5; 48:1; 76:2; 122:1-2). As such, Jerusalem has worldwide significance (vv. 3-7). The other songs of Zion suggest this as well when they relate God's residence in Zion to God's sovereignty over all the earth, including kings and nations (see Pss 46:6, 10; 48:2, 4-8; 76:8-9, 12; see also Isa 2:2-4; 45:22; Mic 4:1-3; Zech 2:10-11). To be sure, the striking imagery that Psalm 87 employs to assert Jerusalem's worldwide significance gives the psalm a poetic power that makes it unique.

As noted above, the structure of Psalm 87 has been much debated. The simplest proposal is to divide the psalm according to its two major themes: (1) vv. 1-2, Zion as God's city, (2) vv. 3-7, Zion's worldwide significance. A case can be made for taking v. 3 with vv. 1-2 (see the NRSV, and note the placement of the first *selah*); however, Mark Smith argues convincingly that the adverbs and prepositional phrases in vv. 3-7 are the clues to discerning a chiasm (see Introduction) that focuses on v. 5:

A "in you" (v. 3; NIV and NRSV, "of you")
  B "there" (v. 4; NIV, "in Zion")
    C "in her" (v. 5; NRSV, "in it")
  B´ "there" (v. 6; NIV, "in Zion")
A´ "in you" (v. 7)

As Smith concludes, "Theme and structure are one: God's establishment of Zion is a central fact of the divine order on earth."[336] It is possible, too, that the structure moves at more than one level, so it is not necessary to view varying proposals as mutually exclusive.

In its place in the psalter, Psalm 87 can be understood as an illustration of Ps 86:9. At the same time, however, the larger literary context of Book III suggests that the songs of Zion (Psalms 76; 84; 87; see also 78:67-72) be heard in the light of the communal prayers for help and their laments over the destruction of Jerusalem (see Psalms 74; 79; 80; 83; 85; 89). In other words, the context encourages the reader to construe Psalm 87 eschatologically and to hear its claims for Jerusalem symbolically.

---

336. Mark Smith, "The Structure of Psalm LXXXVII," *VT* 38 (1988) 357-58.

87:1-2. The syntax of v. 1 is problematic, but essentially v. 1 affirms that Jerusalem is God's city (see "foundations" in Ezra 3:11; Isa 44:28). Elsewhere, too, the site is called a holy mountain or hill (see Pss 2:6; 3:4; 15:1; 24:3; 48:1; 78:54). Verse 2 recalls Ps 78:68-69 (note "founded" in 78:69 in relation to 87:1; see also Ps 132:13). The exact phrase "gates of Zion" (שַׁעֲרֵי צִיּוֹן *ša'ărê ṣiyyôn*) is unique, but the gates of the city are mentioned elsewhere (see Pss 9:14; 24:7, 9; 122:2). The mention of the gates, along with the singers and dancers in v. 7, has led some scholars to propose that Psalm 87 was used originally as part of a processional liturgy (see 2 Samuel 6; Pss 24:3-10; 68:24-27). This is certainly possible, but the origin and ancient use are elusive.

87:3-7. Just as God's name is glorified (see Ps 86:9, 12), so also are "glorious things" said about God's place (see Isa 62:2; Lam 1:8; Hag 2:3). In other words, the city itself makes God known (see Psalms 48; 122). Thus the ambiguity concerning the speaker in vv. 4-5 is appropriate; it could be the personified city, or it could be God. To know the city is to know God, and vice versa. Elsewhere, the stated purpose of God's acts of deliverance is that people will "know that I am the LORD" (Exod 14:4 NRSV; see also Exod 9:16; 10:2; Pss 46:10; 59:13; 100:3). In these contexts, to know God means to recognize God's sovereignty and to live under God's rule. What is striking about the list of nations that know God—and thus count Jerusalem as their hometown (see "born" in vv. 4-6)—is that it consists of traditional enemies. Rahab elsewhere designates Egypt (see Isa 30:7), a major opponent, as was Babylon; but the other three nations were enemies as well (on Philistia and Tyre, see Ps 83:7; on Ethiopia, see Isa 20:3, 5; 37:9; Jer 46:9; Ezek 30:4; Nah 3:9).

The quotation in v. 4c is sometimes interpreted as something that individual Jews in the diaspora may have said as a matter of honor; however, it should not be taken so literally. Rather, v. 4 should be understood in the light of v. 6 (see the chiastic structure outlined above) as the beginning of God's roll call of the peoples (on God's keeping records, see Exod 32:32-33; Pss 69:28; 139:16; Dan 7:10; Rev 20:12). In other words, the nations call Jerusalem their home (v. 4), because the God of Zion claims them as God's own people (v. 6; note that vv. 4c and 6b are identical). Actually, this perspective should not be as surprising as many commentators find it, for it is a recurrent claim that God's choice of Abraham and Israel meant that "in you all the families of the earth shall be blessed" (Gen 12:3 NRSV). This claim follows from God's worldwide sovereignty, which is proclaimed throughout the psalter (see Psalm 2; Introduction) and is in view in Ps 87:5 in the title "Most High" (עליון 'elyôn). The prophetic books also regularly assert God's claim upon all the peoples and nations. Psalm 87 is particularly reminiscent of Isa 19:18-25 (see esp. Isa 19:23-25; see also Isa 2:2-4; Jer 1:10; Mic 4:1-3; Zeph 3:9-13; Zech 8:20-23).

The syntax of v. 7 is difficult. The Hebrew lacks the verb "say," but it is reasonable to conclude that the psalm ends with a quotation of the worshipers whom God gathers in Jerusalem as God's own people. In other words, the psalm concludes with a sample of the "glorious things" spoken about Zion (note the chiastic structure in which vv. 3 and 7 correspond). The word "springs" (מעינות ma'yānôt) elsewhere describes sources of water that God provides to sustain life (see Pss 104:10; 114:8), and Joel 3:18 even poetically depicts the spring as flowing from God's house (see Isa 12:3; Pss 36:9; 46:4, although the Hebrew vocabulary differs in these cases). In Prov 5:16, "springs" is part of a larger metaphor bespeaking intimacy and relatedness. In other words, persons who gather to worship God acknowledge their belonging to God and profess that the sovereign God is the sole source of their life and well-being.

REFLECTIONS

1. Kraus entitles his comment on Psalm 87 "Zion I Call Mother."[337] This is also how he translates v. 5a, based on the LXX of v. 5a, which actually contains the Greek word for "mother" (μήτηρ mētēr). Although the Hebrew text does not explicitly call Jerusalem "mother," the image is a helpful interpretation of the birth metaphor in vv. 4-6, for it captures the message that all nations and peoples are God's children (see above on Gen 12:1-3, Isa 19:23-25). Jerusalem—a specific place—became the symbol for God's sovereignty over all places, times, and peoples (see Commentary on Psalm 48; see also Gal 4:26; Heb 11:10; 12:22-24; Revelation 21–22).

The simple message that all people are God's children has sweeping and profound implications, including political and religious ones. In view of Psalm 87, it is not surprising and somehow appropriate that Jerusalem is a sacred place for Jews, Christians, and Muslims. Unfortunately, these groups have often treated each other as enemies, instead of allowing their very diversity to be a reminder that Jerusalem symbolizes a God who welcomes and claims all peoples and nations. If we must somehow view each other as opponents, then Psalm 87 at least calls for us to view the others as "fraternal opponents."[338] In other words, at the very least, Psalm 87 calls us, as Jesus called his followers, to love our enemies (see Matt 5:43). To take Psalm 87 seriously, then, would have a profound impact on the international policy of the nations of our world. The dehumanization of other people—a tactic that feeds hostility and warfare—cannot claim God's approval. The only permissible goal of "Christian soldiers" is love, for God claims all peoples as God's children. God so loves the world!

2. The structural embodiment of this good news was made in the early church by the welcoming of all the nations—the Gentiles (see Matt 28:19-20; Luke 24:47). The theological rationale was that God had "broken down the dividing wall, that is, the hostility between us" (Eph 2:14 NRSV), so that there are no longer "strangers to the

337. Kraus, *Psalms 60–150*, 184.
338. This expression is used by Pinchas Lapide to characterize the relationship of Jews and Christians. See Karl Rahner and Pinchas Lapide, *Encountering Jesus—Encountering Judaism: A Dialogue*, trans. Davis Perkins (New York: Crossroad, 1987) 109.

covenants of promise" (Eph 2:12 NRSV). To be sure, the author of Ephesians is not specifically citing Psalm 87, but the universal perspective of Psalm 87 is surely akin to what the author discerns in Jesus Christ. In fact, the church as an inclusive community is described as "a holy temple in the Lord; in whom you are built together spiritually into a dwelling place for God" (Eph 2:21-22 NRSV).

3. Johanna W. H. Bos points out that Psalm 87 has traditionally been used as a baptismal psalm in Dutch Calvinist congregations.[339] And how appropriate it is! Not only does Psalm 87 anticipate the gathering of the nations on the Day of Pentecost (see Acts 2, esp. vv. 8-11, 37-39), but it also reminds us of the essential good news that baptism proclaims. In short, our fundamental identity is not one that we eventually achieve; rather, it is one with which we are born and that we share with every other human being. We are children of God.

4. The ability of Zion to function symbolically, thus proclaiming God's sovereign claim upon all places and times and peoples, is evident in the frequent use by Christians of John Newton's hymn "Glorious Things of Thee Are Spoken." The hymn departs from Ps 87:3, capturing well the symbolic dimension of the psalm. In short, this ancient song of Zion continues to articulate the Christian conviction of God's gracious claim upon the whole world.

339. Johanna W. H. Bos, "Psalm 87," *Int.* 47 (1993) 281.

PSALM 88:1-18, THE DARKNESS IS MY CLOSEST FRIEND

COMMENTARY

Psalm 88 is classified as a prayer for help or an individual lament/complaint, but it has several features that make it distinctive, chief of which is the extent and severity of the complaint, which occupies virtually the whole psalm. Petition is limited to v. 2, and there is no explicit profession of trust or vow to praise.

Scholars have often insisted that the origin of the complaint in Psalm 88 can be traced to the psalmist's apparently terminal illness (see Commentary on Psalms 6; 38; 41). To be sure, the psalm is pervaded by vocabulary associated with death, but it is not necessary to conclude that sickness definitely accounts for the origin of the psalm, nor is it necessary to limit the psalm's relevance to situations of illness. The language is metaphorical and stereo-typical enough to express other life-threatening situations. For instance, the history of interpretation of Psalm 88 reflects the opinion of both Jewish and Christian

interpreters that this psalm was used as an exilic or post-exilic prayer to articulate the plight of the whole people. This use would be in keeping with the conclusion that the character of Book III has been shaped by the experience of the exile and its aftermath (see Commentary on Psalms 73; 74; 79; 80; Introduction), and it would make Psalm 88 an especially fitting anticipation of Psalm 89 (cf. v. 3 with Ps 89:48; vv. 7, 14a with Ps 89:38; v. 14b with Ps 89:46a; v. 11 with Ps 89:49; vv. 8, 18 with Ps 89:41, 50).

The structure of Psalm 88 is governed primarily by the three instances of the psalmist's crying out or calling to God (vv. 1, 9b, 13). Three different Hebrew words for "cry"/"call" (צעק *ṣāʿaq*, v. 1; קרא *qārāʾ*, v. 9b; שוע *šwʿ*, v. 13) are used, as if to indicate that the psalmist has exhausted every approach. To be noted, too, is that each of the psalmist's cries is accompanied by a chronological reference. In other words, every possible approach, at every possible moment, has been tried, and the result is "darkness," which is literally the final word of the psalm. Each section of the psalm contains a form of the Hebrew root for "darkness" (חשך *ḥōšek*, vv. 6, 12, 18). Darkness thus pervades both the psalm and the psalmist's experience.

88:1-2. Although Psalm 88 is pervaded by and ends in darkness, it begins with the psalmist addressing God as the one "who saves me" (see Exod 15:2; Pss 68:19-20; 89:26). The psalmist knows that God has traditionally responded when threatened persons "cry out" to God (see Exod 3:7, 9; Deut 26:7; Josh 24:7; Pss 9:12; 77:1; 107:6, 28). Thus the very fact that the psalmist bothers to make an appeal to God is indicative of an underlying trust in God's fundamental character, which the psalmist will also specifically refer to in vv. 10-12. In short, the psalmist's prayer (see also v. 13) is an act of faith and hope.

88:3-8. These verses are an indication that faithful, hopeful prayer need not sound "positive." The psalmist's complaint is bitterly and brutally honest. The bitterness is evident in v. 3*a*, where the Hebrew idiom employed (lit., "my soul is satisfied with" [שבעה נפשי ב *śābĕ'â napšî bĕ-*]) often communicates something good (see Pss 63:5; 65:4), but here the only thing that the psalmist has enough of is trouble. The words "Sheol" (שאול *šĕ'ôl*, v. 3*b*) and "Pit" (בור *bôr*, v. 4) indicate that the trouble is life-threatening (see Pss 6:5; 28:1; 30:3; 143:7). Indeed, the psalmist is apparently treated as one who is as good as dead (vv. 4-5). It is interesting that the verb "cut off" (גזר *gāzar*) is also used in the climactic Servant Song in Deutero-Isaiah to describe the plight of the servant (see Isa 53:8). The servant is often identified as the whole people, and this connection may have something to do with the use of Psalm 88 as a corporate prayer in the exilic and post-exilic eras. The verb is also used of the exiled and suffering people in Ezek 37:11 (see also "grave"/"graves" in Ps 88:5, 11; Ezek 37:12) and in Lam 3:54, where it is followed in Lam 3:55 by the same phrase used in Ps 88:6: "depths of the pit."

Verse 5 anticipates the shift in v. 6 to direct accusation of God. God has put the psalmist in the Pit (cf. v. 4). Since v. 1 has already alluded to the exodus (see "my salvation" in Exod 15:2 and "cry" in Exod 3:7, 9), it is not surprising to hear allusions to the exodus in vv. 6-9*a*; but this time they are in a negative direction. The word "deep" (מצלות *mĕṣôlôt*, v. 6*b*) designates the place where God put the Egyptians (Exod 15:5). Whereas God caused the Israelites to escape from Egypt (see "brought . . . out" in Exod 18:1; 20:2), the psalmist cannot escape (v. 8). Thus the psalmist remains in affliction (v. 9*a*; see Exod 3:7 NRSV, "sufferings"; 4:31 NRSV, "misery"; Deut 26:7), the state out of which the enslaved Israelites also cried to God. Apparently abandoned by God, the psalmist is also deserted by friends (v. 18; see Pss 31:11; 38:11; Job 19:13; 30:10; Jer 11:18-19; 12:6).

88:9-12. But the psalmist's prayer is constant. The phrase "every day" in v. 9*b* could also be rendered "all day long," and v. 9*c* describes the posture of prayer. The prayer in vv. 10-12 indicates that faithful, hopeful prayer need not be devoid of questioning. Like the opening address to God in v. 1, the questions in vv. 10-12 recall God's fundamental character. The repeated "wonders" (vv. 10, 12) again recalls the exodus (see Exod 3:20; 15:11; Pss 77:11; 78:12), and "steadfast love" and "faithfulness" (v. 11) recall God's self-revelation to Moses in Exod 34:6-7 (see Pss 5:7; 13:5; Introduction; see also Exod 34:10). The word the NIV translates as "righteous deeds" (אמונות *'ĕmûnôt*) denotes the work that God does as sovereign of the universe (see Ps 98:2). The question, however, is whether God can manifest God's characteristic being and activity with the dead (v. 10; see also Job 26:5; Isa 14:9; 26:14) or within the realm of the dead—"the grave" (v. 11*a*; see v. 5), Abaddon (v. 11*b*; see Job 26:6; 28:22; 31:12), "darkness" (v. 12*a*; see vv. 6, 18; Ps 143:3; Lam 3:6), "the land of oblivion" (cf. Job 10:21). The intended answer to the questions in vv. 10-12 is no, but the very questions themselves reveal the psalmist's implicit faith and hope. The questions are sometimes viewed as the psalmist's selfish appeal to God's own self-interest; however, it is better to view them as indicative of the psalmist's love of life and as an appeal to a God whom the psalmist knows as one who wills and works for life for God's people (see

Commentary on Psalm 30, esp. discussion on v. 9).

88:13-18. The questions in vv. 10-12 are framed in general terms, but v. 13 begins with the emphatic Hebrew pronoun "I" (אני *ʾănî*), thus focusing attention on the psalmist's own plight and cry (see Exod 2:23; Pss 18:6; 22:24). Not surprisingly, therefore, the questions in v. 14 are framed very personally. The verbs in both questions are characteristic of other prayers for help (on v. 14*a*, see "cast off"/"reject"/"spurn" [זנח *zānaḥ*] in Pss 43:2; 44:9, 23; 60:1, 10; 74:1; 77:7; 89:38; on v. 14*b*, see Job 13:24; Pss 13:1; 27:9; 30:7; 44:24; 69:17; 102:2; 143:7). In a word, they sum up the psalmist's situation; she or he has cried out in affliction, but God has not responded. Thus the psalmist remains "afflicted" (v. 15*a*; see v. 9), and the psalm concludes with an unremitting complaint. The psalmist experiences the "terrors" that God elsewhere inflicts on God's enemies (v. 15*b*; see Exod 15:16; Job 9:34; 13:21). The psalmist knows not God's salvation but the wrath God elsewhere shows to enemies (v. 16*a*; see Exod 15:7; Ps 2:5); the psalmist is under attack by God just as Job perceived himself to be (v. 16*b*; see Job 6:4). The psalmist is completely overwhelmed (v. 17; see also v. 7; Job 22:11; Ps 69:1). The psalm ends with another reminder of the psalmist's complete alienation (v. 18*a*; see also v. 8) and with the pitiful statement that "the darkness is my closest friend" (see the NIV, which makes better sense of the difficult Hebrew syntax than does the NRSV).

REFLECTIONS

1. The psalmist's situation is similar in many ways to that of the servant of Isaiah 53 and of Job; like Isaiah 53 and the book of Job, Psalm 88 prompts a re-evaluation of suffering, both human and divine (see Commentary on Psalms 8; 44). The theological problems and possibilities are posed most sharply, perhaps, by the two verses that conclude each of the psalmist's complaints (vv. 8, 18). God has caused the psalmist's suffering and isolation (as the NRSV's "caused . . . to shun" suggests, the Hebrew verb is a causative form). In short, God is the problem (see also vv. 6-7, 14, 16-17). But God is also the solution! The psalmist's prayer itself is evidence that she or he is convinced that even life's worst moments somehow have to do with God. So the psalmist's cries continue to arise out of the depths (see Ps 130:1).

2. Two statements by Brueggemann help to define the primary theological issue: "Psalm 88 is an embarrassment to conventional faith" and "Psalm 88 shows us what the cross is about: *faithfulness* in scenes of complete *abandonment*."[340] These statements may sound contradictory, until we realize that there was and is nothing conventional about the cross, "a stumbling block to Jews and foolishness to Gentiles" (1 Cor 1:23 NRSV). To be sure, Psalm 88 is not a prediction of Jesus' suffering, but it serves to articulate the same experience that Jesus would live out. Facing the cross, Jesus' soul was "full of troubles" (v. 3; see Mark 14:33-34). He was shunned even by those closest to him (vv. 8, 18; see Mark 14:50). As it turned out, his closest friend was darkness (v. 18; see Mark 15:33). Like the psalmist, who out of the darkness still appealed constantly to God, Jesus was faithful and hopeful. In the midst of abandonment, his cry was still, "My God, my God" (see Mark 15:34, which quotes Ps 22:1 but which is also reminiscent of Ps 88:1). In other words, from the Christian point of view, Psalm 88 not only provides us words to articulate the pain of life's worst moments, but it also offers testimony to the extremes to which God was willing to go to demonstrate faithful love for humanity. Just as the psalmist in Psalm 88 suffered, so also God's Son suffered life's worst for us. That is what the cross is finally about; it shows us how much God loves the world. And there is nothing conventional about that kind of love, for it is neither

---

340. Brueggemann, *The Message of the Psalms*, 78, 81.

fair nor just. Sheer grace is always a scandal. It is precisely this scandal that prompts the re-evaluation of the conventional view that suffering is a sign of God's punishment or a sign of alienation from God. Because God in Christ claimed the suffering of the psalmist in Psalm 88, we are invited to view suffering in a new way—invited, in fact, to take up a cross and follow Jesus (Mark 8:34), who in turn followed the way of the psalmist (see Commentary on Psalm 22).

3. The exceptional, extreme character of Psalm 88 makes it a valuable theological resource at all times, but especially perhaps when we have trouble perceiving any ecstasy at all accompanying our agony (see Commentary on Psalm 13). In his novel *Sophie's Choice,* William Styron depicts the main character, Stingo, returning to New York to confront a terrible tragedy. Stingo and an African American woman sitting beside him on the train begin to read the Bible, a "prescription for my torment," as Stingo puts it:

> "Psalm Eighty-eight," I would suggest. To which she would reply, "Dat is some fine psalm." . . . We read aloud through Wilmington, Chester, and past Trenton, turning from time to time to Ecclesiastes and Isaiah. After a while we tried the Sermon on the Mount, but somehow it didn't work for me; the grand old Hebrew woe seemed more cathartic, so we went back to Job.[341]

To read Psalm 88 may well be cathartic, but it is more. It is also faithful and instructive. To read Psalm 88 is to remind ourselves that even when we stand in utter darkness, we do not stand alone. We stand with the psalmist of old. We stand with Christ on the cross. To cry into the darkness, "O LORD, God of my salvation" (v. 1) is an act of solidarity with the communion of saints. It is indeed an act of faith and hope that God's will for life is greater than the reality of death.

341. William Styron, *Sophie's Choice* (Toronto: Bantam Books, 1979) 614-15; Brueggemann calls attention to Styron's use of Psalm 88 in *The Message of the Psalms,* 81.

PSALM 89:1-52, LORD, WHERE IS YOUR STEADFAST LOVE OF OLD?

COMMENTARY

A major interpretive issue for Psalm 89 is its unity, which many scholars have questioned on form-critical grounds. Because it deals with the Davidic king, Psalm 89 is ordinarily classified as a royal psalm, but it is clearly composed of varied kinds of material. Verses 1-2, 5-18 have a hymnic character; vv. 3-4, 19-37 are presented as an oracle from God (see esp. vv. 3, 19); and vv. 38-51 have the character of a lament, with vv. 38-45 narrating the circumstances behind the complaint and petition, which are voiced directly in vv. 46-51. Verse 52 is a doxology that closes Book III. Despite this diversity, there are compelling reasons to consider Psalm

89 as a unit, and most recent commentators have taken this approach. A primary indication in this regard is the repetition that links the three sections, especially the repetition of "steadfast love" (חסד *ḥesed,* vv. 1-2, 14, 24, 28, 33, 49) and the forms of a Hebrew root usually translated "faithfulness" (vv. 1-2, 5, 8, 14, 24, 28, 33, 37, 49). One of the effects achieved by this and other instances of repetition is to portray the reign of the Davidic king (vv. 19-37) in the same terms used to describe the reign of God (vv. 5-18). This effect is not accidental, and it demonstrates the unity of Psalm 89. It also sets the stage for the striking reversal that occurs at v. 38, and

thus it contributes to the reader's appreciation of the magnitude of the crisis described in vv. 38-51. In short, the failure of the monarchy seems to bespeak the very failure of God.

The seriousness of this crisis raises the question of the origin and ancient use of Psalm 89. For other royal psalms, it makes sense that the psalm would have been used at the coronation of a king or possibly at an annual celebration of the king's reign (see Commentary on Psalms 2; 72), but this does not seem as likely for Psalm 89 because of vv. 38-51. In an attempt to surmount this difficulty, an earlier generation of scholars suggested that vv. 38-51 do not describe an actual historical setback. Rather, they were part of an annual ritual humiliation of the king that was enacted as a reminder that the king's sovereignty was derived from God. This view, however, is very unlikely. There is no evidence for such a ritual, and the intensity of vv. 38-51 indicates a real, not contrived, crisis of faith. The most likely precipitating event was the destruction of Jerusalem in 587 BCE and the consequent disappearance of the Judean monarchy.

To be sure, it is possible that Psalm 89 originated earlier than 587 BCE following the defeat of a Judean king. The likelihood of this possibility is increased by vv. 47-51, in which a surviving king seems to speak. Of course, this may be an exilic or post-exilic literary device, and finally the origin and ancient use of Psalm 89 remain elusive. What is more accessible is the literary context of Psalm 89 in Book III. Given that Book III seems to have been decisively shaped by the experience of exile and its aftermath (see Commentary on Psalms 73; 74; 79; 80; Introduction), it is especially likely that Psalm 89 eventually would have been read and heard as an articulation of the theological crisis posed by the exile. As Gerald Wilson suggests, the appearance of royal psalms (Psalms 2; 72; 89) at the seams of the psalter suggests a shaping of Books I–III that both encourages an articulation of the theological questions raised by the exile and anticipates the "answer" offered by Books IV–V: God reigns (see Introduction; see also Reflections below).

Actually, Psalm 89 itself contains this answer in vv. 5-18, but the linkage of the sovereignty of God and the sovereignty of the earthly king required re-evaluation of both concepts in the light of the exile. Psalm 89 is a piece of this process of re-evaluation that led to an eschatological understanding of both God's reign (see Commentary on Psalm 2; see also Reflections below) and the concept of an earthly king. The latter eventually developed into the expectation of an anointed one (messiah)—a hope that was open-ended enough to allow the suffering of the anointed one (see vv. 50-51) to be understood in some circles as an essential aspect of his work (see Reflections below).

89:1-4. Verses 1-2 introduce the two key words in Psalm 89: "steadfast love" and "faithfulness." The pattern of repetition between vv. 1-2 and vv. 3-4 immediately links God's steadfast love and faithfulness to the origin and continuity of the Davidic dynasty. The repetition is captured more clearly by the NIV. God's love will be proclaimed "forever" (v. 1), and David's throne is "forever" (v. 4). God's faithfulness will be made known, and the Davidic throne will last "through all generations" (vv. 1, 4). God's love is "firm," as is David's throne (vv. 2, 4), and God "established" the divine faithfulness as God "will establish" David's line (vv. 2, 4). The content of vv. 1-2 will be developed in vv. 5-18, while the content of vv. 3-4 will be developed in vv. 19-37 (see "covenant" in vv. 28, 34; "chosen" in v. 19; "sworn" in v. 35; "my servant David" in v. 20; "establish"/"sustain"/"remain" in vv. 21, 37; "descendants"/"line" in vv. 30, 36; "throne" in vv. 29, 36).

89:5-18. Verses 5-14 celebrate God's sovereignty, and vv. 15-18 describe the appropriate recognition of and response to God's rule.

89:5-8. The background of ancient Near Eastern polytheism is evident in vv. 5-8, which are reminiscent of Psalm 82, in which God convenes the council of the gods and condemns the gods to die. That is not the case here, but Israel's God is clearly preeminent (for the concept of a divine council, see 1 Kgs 22:19; Jer 23:22; Psalms 29; 82; 97:7, 9). The title "LORD God of hosts" may also reflect God's sovereignty over other divinities as well as earthly beings; it is associated elsewhere with God's reign (see Ps 24:7-10; Isa 6:1-5). In any case, the heavens are to praise God for God's "wonders," which elsewhere demonstrate God's sovereignty (see Exod 15:11; Pss 9:1; 88:10, 12). The gods are to praise God for God's faithfulness (vv. 5, 8; see also vv. 1-2, and note the gods' unfaithfulness in Psalm 82). Verses 6-8*a* are in the form of questions, although their rhetorical effect is to affirm God's incomparable sovereignty (see Exod 15:11; Pss 18:31; 35:10; 71:19; Mic 7:18; see also Ps 86:8-10).

89:9-14. Lest any doubt be implied by the questions of vv. 6-8*a*, vv. 9-14 offer a rousing affirmation of God's cosmic rule. The most obvious rhetorical feature is the fivefold repetition of the emphatic Hebrew pronoun "you" (vv. 9*a*, 9*b*, 10*a*, 11*b*, 12*a*), which focuses attention on God's activity: *"You* rule . . . *you* stilled them . . . " and so on. In addition, the pronominal suffix "your(s)" occurs nine times in vv. 9-14, occupying the first position in the poetic line in vv. 11, 13. Content reinforces style. God asserts divine rule (see Pss 22:28; 66:7; 103:19; Isa 40:10) over the cosmic waters (v. 9; see Ps 65:7; Mark 4:41). The name "Rahab" (v. 10) recalls both God's victory over Egypt at the exodus (see Ps 87:4; Isa 30:7) and God's cosmic conquest of the forces of chaos. Myth and history are merged in the assertion of God's reign (see Exod 15:4-8, 10, 18; Ps 74:12-15). The mention of "mighty arm" (vv. 10, 13) and "right hand" (v. 13) also recalls the song in Exodus 15 that culminates in the proclamation of God's rule (see Exod 15:6, 12, 16, 18). God's rule in history is evidence of God's cosmic power. The whole world belongs to God (v. 11; see Pss 24:1-2; 93:1), and God's creation will join in recognizing God's sovereignty (v. 12; see Pss 96:11-13; 97:6; 98:7-9). Mount Tabor and Mount Hermon could simply represent well-known mountains, but it is likely that they were associated with worship of the gods (see Judg 3:3; Hos 5:1), so their praise of God would have added significance (see the NRSV's note on v. 12; see also commentary on Ps 48:2 for the possible significance of Zaphon in this regard as well). The climactic reference to God's throne in v. 14*a* also bespeaks God's reign, the basic policies of which are righteousness and justice (see Psalm 97:2*b*; see also Pss 82:1-4; 93:2; 96:13; 98:9). Verse 14*b* returns to the particular themes of Psalm 89, but these, too, are elsewhere characteristic of God's sovereignty (see Ps 98:3; see also Ps 33:3-4).

89:15-18. These verses describe the appropriate response to God's sovereignty. Verses 15-16 seem to depict a liturgical celebration. Happiness results from submission to God (see commentaries on Pss 1:1; 2:12), and it is enacted in the liturgy. In keeping with the focus of vv. 5-14, it is significant that a festal shout specifically accompanies God's enthronement in Ps 47:5 (see also Ps 33:3). The "shouts of joy" also have a liturgical context in Ps 27:6, where they occur in conjunction with a celebration of God as light (27:1) and with a desire to seek God's "countenance" or "presence"—more literally, God's "face" (פנים *pānîm*, 27:8-9). People join the created order in praising God's "name" (v. 16; see v. 12)—a particularly appropriate designation, since it calls to mind God's character, which is in view not only in v. 16*b* but throughout the psalm as well. Verse 17*a*, in which the "you" is again emphatic (see above on vv. 9*a*, 9*b*, 10*a*, 11*b*, 12*a*), may affirm that God is the glory (see Ps 71:8; Isa 46:13) and strength (see Ps 84:7) of the people (on "horn," see v. 25; Pss 75:10; 92:11). On the other hand, "strength" (עז *ʿōz*) and "horn" (קרן *qeren*, v. 17), along with "shield" (מגן *māgēn*, v. 18*a*; see also Ps 47:9), may refer to the earthly king. In either case, vv. 17-18, which start with the same Hebrew particle and seem to belong together, mark the shift of focus to the earthly sovereign, who will be featured in vv. 19-37.

89:19-37. The word "vision" (חזיון *ḥizzāyôn*) in v. 19 recalls the word that Nathan delivered to David in 2 Sam 7:4-17 concerning the future of the Davidic house. The addressee here is unclear, since Hebrew manuscripts disagree as to singular (see NRSV) or plural (see NIV). The difference is immaterial, for what is crucial is the content, which affects both king and people. Every aspect of the promise to David and his descendants is covered in vv. 19-37. Verses 19-20 recall 2 Sam 7:8, which in turn recalls the story of God's choice of David and the anointing of David by Samuel in 1 Samuel 16 (see "anoint[ed]" in 1 Sam 16:3, 12-13; see "chose[n]" in 2 Sam 16:18; 1 Kgs 11:34). Verses 21-27 recall primarily 2 Sam 7:9-11*a*, which promises God's help against enemies; however, v. 24 is similar to 2 Sam 7:15, and vv. 26-27 recall 2 Sam 7:14. To be noted is that the mention of the sea in v. 25 recalls v. 9; the claim is that the king participates in the exercise of God's sovereignty, even on the cosmic scale. Verses 28-37 correspond primarily to 2 Sam 7:11*b*-16, the provision for a Davidic line. "Steadfast love" is mentioned twice more (vv. 28, 33; see also v. 24; 2 Sam 7:15), and the emphasis is on the eternity of the promise (see "forever" in vv. 28-29, 36-37; 2 Sam 7:13, 16). Both texts make provision for punishment but never for removal of steadfast love (cf. Ps 89:30-33 with 2 Sam 7:14-15). Actually, Psalm 89 is even more emphatic about the promise than is 2 Samuel 7. The psalm explicitly names God's promise a "covenant" (vv. 28, 34; see also vv. 3, 39). Moreover, that covenant will not be violated (v. 34); God has sworn it (v. 35*a*; see v. 3), and God will not lie (v. 35*b*). To the contrary, one of God's prominent attributes is "faithfulness" (v. 33), a word that does not occur in 2 Samuel 7. Because God is faithful, the Davidic throne will be like the sun; and like the moon, it will be a "faithful witness in the sky" (v. 37; see "skies" in v. 6). Again, the metaphor suggests that the Davidic dynasty is an enduring structure of God's cosmic rule.

89:38-52. The emphasis on God's faithfulness throughout Psalm 89—as well as the insistent claims concerning the reliability of God's word (vv. 34-35) and the exalted status of the Davidic throne (vv. 25-27, 29, 36-37)—makes the transition at v. 38 all the more unexpected and remarkable. Verses 38-45 describe the occurrence of the unthinkable. This is not just punishment; this is rejection (see "reject"/"cast off"/"spurn" in Pss 43:2; 44:23; 77:7; 88:14; and esp. 74:1, which links conceptually the fate of Jerusalem with the fate of the Davidic king). The supposedly inviolable covenant has been broken (v. 39; see also vv. 3, 28, 34). The king's enemies are triumphant (vv. 40-43; cf. vv. 21-24). The

eternal throne has been cast down (v. 44; cf. vv. 29, 36). The emphasis on "forever" has been replaced by a note of transience (v. 45*a*), and glory (v. 17) has become shame (v. 45*b*).

In vv. 46-52, the king prays. The question in v. 46*a* is typical of other complaints (see Pss 13:1; 44:24; 69:17; 88:14; 102:2; 143:7). In terms of v. 46*b*, Ps 103:9 affirms that God's anger is not forever, but time is running out for the king, as vv. 47-48 suggest. The climactic question is the one in v. 49, which employs for the seventh time each of the two key words in the psalm. The number seven often symbolizes completion, and Psalm 89 had earlier described God as completely loving and faithful. But not now! As if to emphasize a final time the incongruity between the promise to David and the present reality, the word "taunt[ed]" (חָרַף *ḥārap*) is used three times in vv. 50-51 (see also "scorn" [חרפה *ḥerpâ*] in v. 41). In terms of the shape of the psalter, it is significant that the king's final appeal also recalls Psalm 74 and its final appeal on behalf of the people. There, too, God is asked to remember "how the enemy scoffs" (v. 18; "scoffs" is the same verb translated "taunt[ed]" in 89:50-51; see also Ps 74:10, 22). In other words, Psalms 74 and 89 provide a sort of frame for Book III. This frame suggests that Book III invites the reader to consider the question of God's sovereignty in view of the destruction of Jerusalem (Psalms 74; see Psalm 79) and the disappearance of the Davidic monarchy (Psalm 89), as well as the attendant humbling of God's people (Psalms 80; 83; 85). Given its place as the final word in Book III, it is significant that Psalm 89 does not, as Tate points out, answer the question: "The perplexity and hurt are not resolved in this psalm; the matter is left open."[342] It is precisely this openness that calls for further theological reflection.

342. Tate, *Psalms 51-100*, 429.

REFLECTIONS

Psalm 89 may have originated before 587 and the actual disappearance of the monarchy. If that is so, it certainly came to be read as a commentary on the events of 587, and it is extremely interesting and significant that the editors of the psalter chose to retain it and to give it a prominent place. It virtually forces the reader of the psalms to reflect upon the nature of God's reign, especially in the light of the destruction of God's city, the captivity of God's people, and the disappearance of the earthly agent of God's rule. The open-ended conclusion of Psalm 89 has crucial implications for understanding the shape of the psalter. It invites the reader to look for a solution to the dilemma in the following psalms, especially Book IV and its explicit affirmation of God's reign (Psalms 93; 95–99) in a context that is clearly Mosaic rather than Davidic. In fact, Psalm 90 is the only psalm attributed to Moses, the man who proclaimed God's rule *before* there even existed a monarchy, a temple, or a land (see Introduction; Commentary on Psalm 90).

In other words, the book of Psalms does not abandon the conviction that God rules the world. In fact, this message pervades the psalms, from Psalms 1–2 onward (see Commentary on Psalm 2; Introduction). But the persistent juxtaposition of this claim with psalms like 89 (and other communal and individual complaints) means that the assertion of God's rule is to be heard eschatologically. In short, God always rules amid opposition, which means that it does not appear that God reigns. God's sovereignty is a strength made perfect in weakness. The apparent incongruity between God's sovereignty and the prosperity of the wicked calls the reader to decide: Will I acknowledge God's rule and live under God's claim in fundamental dependence upon God? Or will I choose to be self-rooted and to live in fundamental dependence upon myself? In the psalter's own terms, the choice is between righteousness and wickedness (see Commentary on Psalms 1; 2). The lack of resolution in Psalm 89 contributes to the eschatological orientation of the psalter.

What then can be said of the Davidic monarchy, which is tied so closely in Psalm 89 to God's rule? The response to this question must be carefully nuanced. It is tempting to conclude that Psalm 89 points ultimately to the conclusion that the monarchy was a mistake. But if so, it is a mistake for which God bears major responsibility. While the narrative sources in 1 Samuel 8–12 reflect the ambiguity surrounding the monarchy, it was ultimately given divine sanction (see 1 Samuel 16; 2 Samuel 7; Psalm 2). Positively, it was an attempt to implement very concretely *God's* policies of justice and righteousness. In this sense, its purpose can be described as *incarnational*—an attempt to embody in the lives of real people, places, and times the will of God for the world. To be sure, in actual practice, the monarchy failed to accomplish this purpose. From this perspective, one may view it as a divine experiment that failed—a mistake. But because the language and conceptuality of the monarchy expressed so clearly God's purposes for the world, this language and conceptuality were retained.

The intentional retention of the language and conceptuality of the monarchy after the disappearance of the actual institution obviously called for reinterpretation. The reinterpretations differed then and still differ now. In some circles, the privileges and responsibilities of the monarch were apparently transferred to the whole people (see Pss 105:15; 144:9-15; 149:6-9; Isa 55:3-5; 61:1-3). Some Jews looked for a restoration of the monarchy as a political institution and looked for an anointed one (messiah) who would effect such a restoration; some Jews are still looking and waiting. Some Jews are less literal about the expectation of a messiah; they see the Jewish people as agents of God's rule, and they work toward the fulfillment of God's purposes and a messianic age. Christians claimed the language and conceptuality of monarchy for Jesus of Nazareth, who was hailed as Jesus Messiah or, to use the Greek equivalent, Jesus Christ. They viewed the triumph of the king's enemies (vv. 41-42), the king's suffering (v. 45), and the taunts of others (vv. 50-51) as essential aspects of the messiah's work (see the passion narratives in the Gospels). In short, Jesus incarnated the re-evaluation of sovereignty that is called for by the open-endedness of Psalm 89. In this sense, Psalm 89 is properly read as a text for Advent.

But even while seeing in Jesus a kind of completion to the open-endedness of Psalm 89, Christians would do well to continue to read the psalm as testimony to the difficulty of embodying concretely in space and time the justice and righteousness that

God wills for the world. In this sense, Psalm 89 may function finally as a call to humility, for the church—the body of Christ—often does no better than the monarchy did in furthering God's will in and for the world (see Reflections on Psalm 72). Thus the church, too, is only a provisional institution, at least in the sense that it lives not by its own sufficiency or merit but by the steadfast love and faithfulness of God. As in Psalm 89, these fundamental realities are ones that we simultaneously celebrate (vv. 1-2) and await (v. 49).

PSALMS 90–106

BOOK IV

PSALM 90:1-17, HAVE COMPASSION ON YOUR SERVANTS

COMMENTARY

salm 90 is the only psalm attributed to Moses. This alone might indicate its significance, but this is especially the case since Psalm 90 opens Book IV of the psalter. Book III is heavily weighted with prayers that lament the destruction of Jerusalem, and Psalm 89 concludes Book III with the announcement of God's rejection of the covenant with David and with the anguished questions of vv. 46 and 49. Thus it seems more than coincidental that Book IV immediately takes the reader back to the time of Moses, when there was no land or Temple or monarchy. Indeed, Book IV can be characterized as a Moses-book, and in response to the crisis of exile and its aftermath, it offers the "answer" that pervades the psalter and forms its theological heart: God reigns! (See Introduction.) In short, even without land, Temple, and monarchy, relatedness to God is still possible, as it was in the time of Moses.

Thus the superscription of Psalm 90 should be taken seriously—not as an indication of Mosaic authorship, but as a clue to read Psalm 90 in the context of the stories about Moses in the Pentateuch. For instance, D. N. Freedman notes the similarity between Ps 90:13 and Exod 32:12, where Moses tells God to "turn" or "repent" from God's anger; Freedman considers it likely "that the composer of the psalm based it on the episode in Exodus 32 and imagined in poetic form how Moses may have spoken in the circumstances of Exodus 32."[343] The superscription in the Targum supports Freedman's conclusion; it reads, "A prayer of Moses the prophet, when

the people of Israel sinned in the desert." Given the canonical placement of Psalm 90, however, it is more likely that the editors of the psalter intended for readers to hear this psalm as a poetic imagining of how Moses might have spoken to the monumental crisis posed by the loss of land, Temple, and monarchy. In any case, it is important to attempt to hear Psalm 90 as an imagined prayer of Moses. (Further connections between Psalm 90 and the Pentateuch will be noted below.)

This is not the way interpretation of Psalm 90 has been approached in recent years. It has sometimes been classified as a communal lament/prayer for help, a categorization that is at least congruent with its placement in the psalter. Several commentators note that vv. 13-15 in particular indicate a prolonged period of distress, which the exile certainly represented. Psalm 90, however, has more often been viewed as a wisdom psalm, a poetic meditation on the transience of human life (see esp. vv. 3-10). To be sure, this approach has merit, and it should not be ignored. Proponents of this approach have virtually ignored the attribution to Moses, however, and it is not necessary to do so. In a sense, Moses' problem was time—namely, his time was too short. One of the most incredibly surprising aspects of the whole biblical story is that the illustrious Moses dies before entering the promised land. The reason given is that God was "angry" with Moses (see Deut 3:26, where the word "angry" [עבר *ʿābar*] is from the same Hebrew root as "wrath" [עברה *ʿebrâ*] in Ps 90:9, 11). Moses thus became a paradigm for Israel's existence and human existence. We always come up short, in terms of time, intentions, and accomplishments.

343. David Noel Freedman, "Other Than Moses . . . Who Asks (or Tells) God to Repent?" *Bible Review* 1 (Winter 1985) 59.

What initially seems like a depressing message, however, is actually an encouraging one. If the great Moses came up short, then perhaps it is not such a disaster that we do too. Moses' death was a reminder that God, not Moses, would lead the people into the land (see Deut 31:3; 32:52). *Our* time, therefore, is not all there is to measure. *God's* time is primary, and as Psalm 90 suggests, our time must be measured finally in terms of God's time. The focus on time in this psalm will be elaborated upon below.

The structure of Psalm 90 can be outlined in several ways, but the simplest division is this: vv. 1-2, vv. 3-6, vv. 7-12, vv. 13-17. Verses 1-2 focus primarily on God, while vv. 3-6 focus on humanity. Verses 7-12 then explore the matter of human transience. The word "anger" in vv. 7, 11 provides an envelope structure for this section, suggesting that v. 12 is really a sort of transition. The tone of vv. 13-17 is markedly more hopeful than the preceding verses.

90:1-2. Although Psalm 90 focuses primarily on time, it begins with an affirmation involving place as well. As a response to exile, v. 1 is a particularly pertinent and powerful affirmation: God is really the only "dwelling place" that counts (see "refuge" in Ps 71:3; see also Ps 91:9). Indeed, such has always been the case—"in all generations." This phrase directs attention to the passage of time, as do the two verbs in v. 2, each of which is used elsewhere to speak of childbirth (see NIV). Here God is portrayed not as Mother Earth, but as mother of the earth.

Verses 1-2 already make the crucial juxtaposition of human time ("all generations") and God's time ("everlasting to everlasting"). The chiastic structure (see Introduction) of the two verses is striking, especially considering that the use of the Hebrew pronoun "you" in vv. 1-2 is often used for emphasis:

A   "Lord, *you* . . . " (God)
  B   "all generations" (time)
    C   "mountains" (space)
    C´   "earth and the world" (space)
  B´   "everlasting to everlasting" (time)
A´   "*you* are God" (God)

The literary structure makes a theological point. The divine "You" is all-encompassing

of time and space. Human life and the life of the world find their origin and destiny in God.

90:3-6. The vocabulary of vv. 3-6 continues to call to mind the passage of time—"back to dust" (v. 3), "children" (v. 3; NRSV, "mortals"; NIV, "sons"), "years" (v. 4), "yesterday" (v. 4), "watch in the night" (v. 4), "morning" (vv. 5-6), "evening" (v. 6). Verse 3 is usually taken to be an allusion to Gen 3:19, and it may be, even though the Hebrew words for "dust" differ in the two verses. The Hebrew word in Ps 90:3 (דכא *dakkā*ʾ) appears to mean something like "crushed," "pulverized (particle)," perhaps suggesting the crushing weight of time upon human existence. On the other hand, the meaning of v. 3 may not be quite so negative. The Hebrew root elsewhere means "contrite" (see Ps 51:17; Isa 57:15); the servant in Isaiah 53 is "crushed" (vv. 5, 10), but will still effect God's will for the benefit of other people. Similarly, God's command to humans to "turn back" may not be as cruel as it sounds; the imperative could also be translated, "Repent." To be sure, v. 3 is unremittingly realistic about human finitude and transience, but it anticipates the good news of v. 13, where the same Hebrew word (שוב *šûb*) is used to call upon God to "turn" or "repent."

The poetic structure of vv. 4-6 emphasizes the reality of human transience. In v. 4, which Alter contends "is one of the most exquisite uses of intraverset focusing in the Bible" (a verset is what Alter calls one component of a poetic line, and the focusing involves the increasingly smaller units of time in each component of v. 4), the movement from God's time to human time highlights the juxtaposition already begun in vv. 1-2.[344] For God, a thousand years are like three hours! The focusing in v. 4 leads directly into vv. 5-6, the chiastic structure (see Introduction) of which re-creates the progression of a day:

A   v. 5*a*   "like a dream" (night)
  B   v. 5*b*   morning
  B´   v. 6*a*   morning
A´   v. 6*b*   evening

344. Alter, *The Art of Biblical Poetry*, 127.

Poetic structure imitates the inexorable passage of time, which is what Psalm 90 is about (see Isa 40:6-8).

90:7-11. Like v. 3, vv. 7-11 are often interpreted in the light of Genesis 2–3. Indeed, both Psalm 90 and Genesis 2–3 do make a connection between sin and death, but the connection is difficult to define precisely. In Genesis 2–3, for instance, it is not at all clear that the humans would have lived forever even if they had not sinned. According to the text, the punishment for sin was not physical death but banishment from the garden (Gen 3:23). It is entirely possible to conclude that physical death was always a part of God's plan for humanity. From this perspective, then, the question for Psalm 90 is this: If death is not simply punishment for sin, what does Psalm 90 mean by associating human transience with the anger and wrath of God in vv. 7, 9, 11? Mays's perspective is helpful:

> The wrath of God is a linguistic symbol for the divine limits and pressure placed against human resistance to his sovereignty. . . . Eternity belongs to the sovereign deity of the LORD as God . . . Death is the final and ultimate "no" that cancels any pretension to autonomy from the human side.[345]

In biblical terms, death means fundamentally to be alienated from God. In this sense, sin always results directly in death. The first humans sinned; they alienated themselves from God, and so do we. Therefore, the limitation of physical death becomes a problem. If we accepted our lives and our allotted time as gifts from God, and if we entrusted the future of our lives and the life of the world to God, then physical death would be no problem. It could be accepted as part of God's plan. But in the presence of sin, human transience is a problem. Normal human limits are experienced as wrath (see vv. 7, 9). Failing to trust God, we fear physical death, and the fear of death itself becomes "death-serving."[346] That is, it motivates us to further self-assertion and thus further alienates us from God. Thus,

while sin and death are related, the relationship is not necessarily causal. Sin does not cause physical death. Rather, sin involves alienation from God, which makes physical death a problem. And when physical death is feared, then it becomes necessary to conclude that death causes sin!

The words "anger" (אַף *'ap*, vv. 7, 11) and "consume" (כלה *kālâ*) also call to mind a Mosaic context as background for hearing vv. 7-11 (see Exod 32:10-12). When the people's sin evoked God's anger and God's threat to consume the people, Moses prayed that God "turn"/"repent" (Exod 32:12; see Ps 90:13). In Exodus 32, the people's sinfulness and God's anger were not the final words. God repented, eventually revealing the divine self to be gracious, merciful, faithful, and steadfastly loving (see Exod 34:6-7; see also Ps 90:14). This is also the direction in which Psalm 90 moves. The despair of vv. 7-11 moves toward hope (vv. 13-17), and the transition occurs in v. 12.

90:12. If God's wrath and the reality of transience were all that could be said of human life, it would be insufferably sadistic of God to "teach us to count our days" (v. 12). But v. 12 is obviously meant to be hopeful and encouraging. God is not implored to teach us how oppressive life is, but to teach us how to accept our allotted time as a *gift*. If v. 12 is heard in the Mosaic context of the story of gathering manna in the wilderness (see below on v. 14), v. 12 may even be paraphrased, "teach us to live day by day," as the Israelites had to do in the wilderness when manna was received daily. When this is done—when life is accepted as a gift and entrusted daily to God—then a "heart of wisdom" is gained, and physical death is no longer a problem. Human transience—the reality of death as part of God's plan—becomes not an occasion for despair but an opportunity for prayer.

90:13. While the entire psalm has been addressed to God, the prayer takes an obviously different direction in v. 13. The first imperative recalls v. 3, where "turn" was used twice. There God's turning seemed to contribute to human transience, but v. 13 suggests that God's turning can take a different form. Verse 13 is not a request to undo human transience, for that is part of God's plan. Rather, v. 13 is a request for God to

---

345. Mays, *Psalms*, 292.
346. See Douglas John Hall, *God and Human Suffering: An Exercise in the Theology of the Cross* (Minneapolis: Augsburg, 1986) 62.

forgive human sinfulness, which alienates us from God and makes finitude a problem. The request is a bold one! God is being asked to do what human beings consistently fail to do: to turn or repent. The alienation caused by *human* sinfulness must be overcome by *God's* turning toward humanity, which is precisely what God's steadfast love (v. 14) is all about. Verses 13-14 especially recall Exodus 32–34, where Moses boldly requests God to repent (Exod 32:12), and God does (Exod 32:14), revealing that God's fundamental character involves steadfast love, which takes concrete form in the forgiveness of sins (Exod 34:6-7).

Verse 13 also has a connection with the Song of Moses in Deuteronomy 32, where Moses affirms that God will "have compassion on his servants" (v. 36). The verb translated "have compassion" (נחם *nḥm*) in v. 13 and Deut 32:36 also occurs in Exod 32:12, 14. In fact, Exod 32:12, 14 and Deut 32:36 represent two of the four times in the Pentateuch where God is the subject of this verb. Interestingly, one other occasion is Gen 6:6-7, where God is "sorry" that God created humankind. The shift in the sense of the verb (signaled by a different form of the Hebrew verb) from the beginning to the end of the Pentateuch is revealing. It is as if the use of this verb signals a shift in God's dealing with humanity; the same sort of behavior that grieved God in the beginning now moves God to compassion. The psalmist appeals to God's compassion in Ps 90:13 as Moses had also appealed in the Pentateuch. In terms of the suggestion that Psalm 90 imagines Moses' words for the exilic situation, it is also significant that the verb in question is a key word in other texts that address the exile. For instance, Isa 40:1 starts with this verb, "Comfort, comfort my people"; the prophet is commissioned to proclaim what Moses prays for in Exodus 32 and Deuteronomy 32 and Psalm 90: God's compassion upon the people in the form of the forgiveness of sins (see also Isa 49:13; 51:3, 12).

90:14-17. The request in v. 14 also calls to mind a Mosaic context, the wilderness episode in Exodus 16, where the people were indeed satisfied in the morning (see Exod 16:8, 12; the NRSV translates the verb as "your fill"). To be sure, the satisfaction is different in the two cases. In Ps 90:14, it involves steadfast love, which, as suggested already, has strong Mosaic connections (see Exod 34:6-7). The plea of v. 14 is also particularly appropriate for the exilic situation, especially in the light of Psalm 89, where "steadfast love" occurs seven times, culminating in the crucial question of v. 49 (see Commentary on Psalm 89). For a new wilderness experience—the exile—Psalm 90 offers Moses as intercessor.

Whether the situation is the Babylonian exile and its aftermath or contemporary experiences of alienation and despair, Psalm 90 finally affirms that God's faithfulness in the face of human unfaithfulness is redemptive. In particular, God redeems time. Verses 13-17, like vv. 1-12, are still a prayer about time, but the perspective on time has been remarkably transformed. Whereas previously the passage of time could be perceived only as "toil and trouble" (v. 10), now there are new possibilities. Because God is faithful, "morning" can "satisfy" (v. 14) rather than mark a fleeting moment on the way to our demise (cf. vv. 5-6; see also Lam 3:19-24). Because God is faithful, "days" and "years" can bring gladness rather than tedium (v. 5; cf. vv. 9-10). The occurrence of the word "children" (בנים *bānîm*) in v. 16 recalls v. 3, and again the perspective has been transformed. Whereas children in v. 3 are involved in the dissolution of life, in v. 16 they represent the continuity of human life. There will be a future! And as has always been the case, that future belongs first to God. It is God's work that humans need to perceive (v. 16) and upon which human life depends. The word "splendor" (הדר *hādār*) in v. 16 occurs frequently elsewhere in the context of the proclamation of God's reign (see Pss 29:4; 96:6; 145:5). In short, what humans need to perceive is that God reigns; God is "Lord" (v. 1), and humans are God's "servants" (v. 16; see v. 13).

To be sure, humans also have work to do (see Ps 8:5, where God bestows splendor upon humanity; NIV and NRSV, "honor"), but "the work of our hands" is finally the object of God's activity—God must "establish" it (v. 17). While Psalm 90 ends with this plea, the clear implication is that God will turn, satisfy, make glad, manifest God's own work, and establish humanity's work, as God did in answer to Moses' intercession in

Exodus 32–34. Indeed, Ps 91:16 affirms that God will act (see Commentary on Psalm 91). In the wilderness, God's possibilities were not thwarted by human sinfulness; in the exile, God's possibilities were not thwarted by human sinfulness. The conclusion of Psalm 90 suggests that God's purposes will never finally be thwarted by human sinfulness. That is our hope and the hope of the world, as Isaac Watts's paraphrase of Psalm 90 captures so well: "O God, our help in ages past, our hope for years to come."

REFLECTIONS

Because Psalm 90 is in itself a sort of theological reflection, the commentary has already begun the process of reflection; however, there is more to be said. The priority of God's activity and the priority of God's time reshape human activity and human time.[347] Our days and years are not simply moments to be endured on the way to oblivion; our efforts are not simply fleeting and futile. Because God is eternal and faithful and eternally faithful in turning toward humanity, our allotted time becomes something meaningful, purposeful, joyful, enduring.

1. In the final analysis, Psalm 90 functions like the songs of praise as a call to decision. We are called to entrust ourselves and our allotted time to God with the assurance that, grounded in God's work and God's time, our lives and labors participate in the eternal (see John 3:16-17, where trust in God's forgiving love results in "eternal life"). Psalm 90 is finally, therefore, not an act of futility but an act of faith. And it is also an act of hope. Without having to see it happen, the psalmist trusts that God can and will satisfy and make glad and manifest God's work and establish the work of our hands (vv. 14-17). And Psalm 90 is also an act of love. The psalmist's trust puts him or her in communion with past generations who found a dwelling place in God (v. 1) and with future generations, the children, to whom the work of God will be manifest (v. 16). For the psalmist, sin and death are inevitable realities. But so are forgiveness and life! Psalm 90 is a profession of faith that invites us and instructs us to live the only way it makes any sense whatsoever to live—in faith and in hope and in love. The words of Reinhold Niebuhr provide an excellent summary of the good news of Psalm 90:

> Nothing that is worth doing can be achieved in our lifetime; therefore we must be saved by hope. Nothing which is true or beautiful or good makes complete sense in any immediate context of history; therefore we must be saved by faith. Nothing we do, however virtuous, can be accomplished alone; therefore we are saved by love. No virtuous act is quite as virtuous from the standpoint of our friend or foe as it is from our standpoint. Therefore we must be saved by the final form of love which is forgiveness.[348]

2. Because Psalm 90 moves from despair to hope, it is quite appropriate for what is probably its most frequent contemporary setting in life: funeral services. To be sure, these services of worship confront us starkly with our finitude, as does Psalm 90 (see vv. 3-11). But the funeral service is not a witness to human mortality; it is a witness to the redemptive power of God, as is Psalm 90 (see vv. 13-17). This is not to say that the author of Psalm 90 possessed a doctrine of resurrection. Rather, trusting God's sovereignty (vv. 1-2, 16), the psalmist was empowered to entrust life and future to God, which is what the resurrection also invites people to do. The psalmist trusted that God's redeeming love was greater than human sinfulness and human finitude. Christians articulate this same trust by affirming faith in the resurrection. For us, the

347. See Alter, *The Art of Biblical Poetry*, 129.
348. Niebuhr, *The Irony of American History*, 63.

resurrection, above all else, makes God's work manifest (see v. 16). And the resurrection assures us that God establishes the work of our hands. In the words of the apostle Paul: "You know that in the Lord your labor is not in vain" (1 Cor 15:58 NRSV).

PSALM 91:1-16, THE SHELTER OF THE MOST HIGH

COMMENTARY

Psalm 91 consists of an eloquent profession of faith (vv. 1-13) followed by a divine speech that confirms the faith of the psalmist (vv. 14-16). Verse 1 states the theme of the psalm, and in v. 2 the psalmist directs personal profession to God. The profession continues in vv. 3-13 as testimony offered to an unidentified "you," with the exception of v. 9a, which in Hebrew reads, "Indeed, you, O Lord, [are] my refuge." This direct address to God matches v. 2; Tate suggests that v. 9a does double duty, both forming with v. 2 an envelope around vv. 3-8 and initiating a second section of the psalmist's testimony (vv. 9-13).[349]

With good reason, Psalm 91 is ordinarily classified as a psalm of confidence or trust. Scholars disagree, however, concerning its ancient origin and use. Some suggest that the testimony arises from a person who had sought refuge in the Temple from persecutors (see below on vv. 3-4; see also Psalms 5; 17; Introduction). Others propose that the psalmist offered thankful testimony after recovery from a serious illness (see vv. 5-7; see also Psalms 6; 38). More specifically in this regard, one scholar even suggests that Psalm 91 may have been the verbal accompaniment to the purification rituals prescribed in Leviticus 14 for restoration of persons into the community.[350] Still others contend that Psalm 91 originated and was used as a liturgy for entrance to the Temple (see Psalms 15; 24), or that it should be viewed as a liturgy used by the king before a battle, or that it can be traced to testimony offered by a recent convert to Yahwism. The very variety of these proposals indicates that the language and

imagery of Psalm 91 are open-ended enough to be relevant and powerful in many situations; indeed, Psalm 91 has served throughout the centuries and continues to serve as a source of encouragement and strength for the people of God (see Reflections below).

More accessible than the ancient origin and use of Psalm 91 is its literary setting. A. F. Kirkpatrick argued long ago that Psalms 90–92 belong together and that Psalm 91 responds with assurance to Israel's voice out of exile (Psalm 90).[351] This proposal is congruent with the interpretation of Psalm 90 offered above and with the conclusion that Book IV responds to the crisis of exile portrayed in Books I–III, especially Book III and Psalm 89 in particular (see Commentary on Psalms 73; 74; 79; 80; 89; Introduction). The relationship between Psalms 90 and 91 is established by the occurrence of the relatively rare word "dwelling place" (מעון mā'ôn) in Pss 90:1 and 91:9. Even more striking is that two of the concluding petitions of Ps 90:13-17 are explicitly answered in Ps 91:16, where God promises to "satisfy" (see Ps 90:14) and to "show" (see Ps 90:16). The promise of satisfaction with "length of days" (author's trans.) is particularly apt after Psalm 90 and its focus on human transience (see "days" in Ps 90:9-10, 12, 15).

91:1-2. Verse 1, the syntax of which is better captured by the NIV, summarizes the message of the psalm: God provides security. The word "shelter" (סתר sēter) occurs also in Pss 27:5; 31:20; and 61:4; and "shadow" (צל ṣēl) occurs in Pss 17:8; 36:7; 57:1; and 63:7. These words often occur in conjunction with and are virtually synonymous with those in v. 2: "fortress" (מצודה mĕṣûdâ; see

349. Tate, *Psalms 51–100*, 449, 453.

350. See Herbert J. Levine, *Sing Unto God a New Song: A Contemporary Reading of the Psalms* (Bloomington: Indiana University Press, 1995) 67-68.

351. A. F. Kirkpatrick, *The Book of Psalms* (Cambridge: Cambridge University Press, 1951) 553-54.

Pss 18:2; 31:2-3; 71:3; 144:2) and the more frequent "refuge" (מחסה *maḥseh*), which is repeated in vv. 4 and 9 ("refuge" is a key word throughout the psalter; see Pss 2:12; 5:11; 11:1; 14:6; 16:1; 17:7; 31:3; 36:7; 51:1; 61:3-4; 63:7; Introduction). The four nouns in vv. 1-2 express metaphorically what the psalmist affirms directly in v. 2 *b* : God is worthy of trust (see Pss 4:5; 9:10; Introduction). The noun "refuge," especially when it is associated with God's "wings" (v. 4; see Ruth 2:12; Pss 17:8; 36:7; 57:1; 63:7), originally may have referred to the practice of seeking sanctuary from persecutors in the Temple (see 1 Kgs 1:49-53) or to Israel's experience of finding security in worship. If either is the case, the image was broadened to mean the entrusting of one's whole self and life to God in every circumstance.

91:3-13. These verses affirm the effectiveness of trusting God in every circumstance, even the very worst. Brueggemann points out that God provides the psalmist both a "safe place" (vv. 1-2, 9-10) and a "safe journey" (vv. 3-6, 11-13); God's protection is effective everywhere.[352] Verses 5-6 assure the reader that God will protect him or her at all times as well—"night," "day," "darkness," "noonday." In addition, every manner of danger and difficulty is covered in vv. 3-13 (see Exod 23:27-29 for a possible source of some of the imagery)—surprise attack (v. 3 *a*; see also Pss 124:7; 140:5; 141:9; 142:3), disease (see "pestilence" in vv. 3, 6), demonic powers (see vv. 5-6, which may refer to such entities), violence and war (v. 7 and perhaps v. 5 *a*; see "arrow" in Pss 11:2; 57:4; 64:3), wicked enemies (v. 8), wild animals (v. 13; see Pss 35:17; 58:4, 6). It is not essential that we be able to identify precisely all the references and allusions in vv. 3-13. The poetic hyperbole and allusion are meant more to evoke than to specify; thus the psalmist affirms that no place, no time, no circumstance that befalls us is beyond God's ability to protect us. God's "angels" or messengers will "guard you in *all* your ways" (v. 11; see also Exod 23:20). God's faithfulness (v. 4) knows no bounds, an especially timely affirmation if Psalm 91 joins Psalm 90 in responding to Psalm 89 (see Commentary on Psalm 89, esp. discussion of v. 49; see also Ps 5:12 for the image of covering with a shield).

352. Brueggemann, *The Message of the Psalms,* 156.

91:14-16. The comprehensiveness of the psalmist's profession of trust (vv. 1-13) is matched by a more compact but equally comprehensive divine promise of protection in vv. 14-16. Seven first-person verbs surround a verbless clause in v. 15 *b* (the number seven often symbolizes comprehensiveness or completion). It contains an emphatic personal pronoun: "with him [am] *I* in trouble" (author's trans.). The only other use of the emphatic pronoun in this psalm is in the pivotal v. 9 *a*, in which the Hebrew pronoun refers to God. Using the two emphatic pronouns and the seven first-person verbs, the psalmist locates the source of life in God alone.

The Hebrew verb translated "love" (חשק *ḥāšaq*) in v. 14 *a* connotes as well "to be attached to," "to be connected with." The verb "know" (ידע *yāda'*, NRSV) in v. 14 *b* also conveys the intimacy of relation to God. Rather than suggesting that God's deliverance and protection are a reward for loving God, then, v. 14 suggests that relation to God *is* deliverance—it is life. In Ps 9:10, those who know God's name "put their trust" in God, and this is also the case here (see v. 2). It is they who experience God as protector (see Ps 9:9, where the two occurrences of "stronghold" [משגב *miśgāb*] represent the same Hebrew root as "protect" in Ps 91:14; see also Ps 20:2). The mention of God's "name" may recall vv. 1-2, where the psalmist moves from more general names for God to the more personal "Yahweh" (or "LORD"). In any case, vv. 14-16 describe the life of one who has entrusted the whole self to God. Such trust constitutes life, which is the meaning of deliverance and rescue and salvation (see Exod 15:2; Pss 3:2, 7-8; 13:5). It may seem unusual for God to "honor" human beings (see 1 Sam 2:30; Ps 8:5), but this action, too, bespeaks the closeness of the relationship God promises. The perspective is thoroughly God-centered; in this regard it is significant that the psalm ends with the divine speech. As John Bracke concludes: "While the psalm's first word was of human trust, the psalmist reserves the last word for God. . . . By ending the psalm in God's word of promise, the psalmist points to the ultimate ground of human confidence, security, and hope. We are finally grounded in God's sovereign power and promise."[353] Thus Psalm 91 finally invites the reader to

follow the psalmist's example of trust (v. 2), in the assurance that those who humble themselves will be exalted (v. 15; see Luke 18:14).

353. John Bracke, "Psalm 91:1-10: Psalm for the Third Sunday After Pentecost," *No Other Foundation* 10 (Winter 1989–90) 50.

REFLECTIONS

1. The sheer eloquence and comprehensiveness of the psalmist's affirmation of faith make Psalm 91 powerful. These same attributes, however, can also be a source of misunderstanding. For instance, many Jews and Christians have copied passages of the psalm and worn them in amulets to magically ward off danger; indeed, vv. 11-13 have been used to support the notion that guardian angels protect us from harm.[354] Illustrating such misuses of the psalm, in Luke 4:9-12 the devil quotes Ps 91:11-12 to tempt Jesus to jump from the pinnacle of the Temple, but Jesus refuses to claim God's promise of protection for his own benefit. For, Jesus says, to do so would be to test rather than to trust God (see also Matt 4:5-7). We should not use Psalm 91 as a magical guarantee against danger, threat, or difficulty. Rather, this psalm is a reminder to us that nothing "will be able to separate us from the love of God" (Rom 8:39 NRSV). Neither Jesus nor the apostle Paul sought to avoid danger or difficulty at the expense of being faithful, and Jesus warned his followers not to abuse the promised power of God (see Luke 10:19; cf. Ps 91:13). In fact, Jesus' and Paul's faithfulness to God and to God's purposes impelled them into dangerous situations (see 1 Cor 6:4-10); when Jesus did claim the assurance of the psalms, it was *from the cross* (see Luke 23:46, where Jesus quotes Ps 31:5). Jesus' life, death, and resurrection demonstrate the self-denial and humble trust (see Ps 91:2) that lead to being exalted by God (see Ps 91:15).

2. Psalm 91 is traditionally used at the beginning of Lent, and its thoroughly God-centered perspective makes it appropriate for this season. It warns us not to reduce Lenten disciplines to trivial, self-help schemes. Genuine self-denial begins with the kind of radical affirmation of trust that is found in Psalm 91.

354. See Mays, *Psalms,* 297.

PSALM 92:1-15, BUT YOU, O LORD, ARE EXALTED FOREVER!

COMMENTARY

Psalm 92 is the only psalm assigned to a specific day—the sabbath. Given the overwhelming significance of the sabbath in the Pentateuch (see, e.g., Exod 20:8-11; Deut 5:12-15) and in the history of Israel and Judaism, it is not surprising that the sabbath should be singled out in this way. Rabbinic sources confirm the use of Psalm 92 in the Temple on the sabbath following the daily offering, but they also cite Psalms 24; 48; 81; 82; 93; and 94 for use on the other six days of the week. Since the superscriptions of none of these other psalms reflect such use, Nahum M. Sarna concludes that the unique superscription of Psalm 92 "must be indicative of deliberate selection for the Sabbath day, prior to, and independent of, the other six."[355]

355. Nahum M. Sarna, "The Psalm for the Sabbath Day (Ps 92)," *JBL* 81 (1962) 156.

This is not to say that Psalm 92 was written for use on the sabbath. At some point, though one cannot with certainty say why, the psalm was deemed appropriate for such use. God's "works" (vv. 4-5) may refer to the creation, with which the sabbath was also associated (see Gen 2:1-3; Exod 20:8-11; see also v. 9, which may reflect the mythic notion of creation by God's combat with the forces of chaos). But there are other reasons for linking the psalm to the sabbath: Psalm 92 reflects God's will for the righteous ordering of human society (see vv. 7, 11, 12-15), and the sabbath was associated with the proper treatment of human beings (see Exod 23:12; Deut 5:12-15); and the sabbath day was devoted to praising God (vv. 1-3) and gathering for worship (v. 13). One might even see a link in that the name "Yahweh" ("LORD") occurs seven times in the psalm, and the sabbath was the seventh day.[356]

Psalm 92 is usually categorized as an individual song of thanksgiving, and in vv. 1-3 the psalmist at least implicitly invites others to share in thanksgiving; vv. 4, 10-11 may be construed as a description of the psalmist's deliverance, also typical of thanksgiving songs. It is unclear, however, whether one should translate the verbs in vv. 10-11 in the past tense or the future tense. Has the psalmist already been exalted and the enemies defeated, or do these events still lie in the future? This uncertainty brings to light another major aspect of Psalm 92: its concern is not just with the individual psalmist (vv. 10-11) but more generally with the life and future of the righteous (vv. 12-15) and the wicked (vv. 7, 9). Because the psalmist recognizes that the wicked flourish, at least for a time (v. 7), and because a strong case can be made for translating the verbs in vv. 10-11 in the future tense (as in v. 9), it is best to approach Psalm 92 not so much as a celebration of a particular deliverance, but as affirmation of the sovereignty of God and the deliverance of God's people.

Indeed, the structure of Psalm 92 focuses attention on God's sovereignty. The very middle verse (v. 8; note how the NIV sets it apart) further stands out by virtue of the emphatic pronoun "you." To affirm that God is "on high forever" is to affirm that God rules

the world (see Ps 93:4, which contains the phrase "on high" and which initiates a series of psalms that proclaim God's reign; see the same Hebrew root in Pss 99:5, 9; 145:1). Tate even suggests that v. 8 is the pivotal verse in a chiastic structure (see Introduction) in which vv. 1-3 correspond with vv. 12-15 (joyful celebration of God's character; see "proclaim"/"proclaiming" in vv. 2, 15 NIV), vv. 4-6 with vv. 10-11 (the work of God), and v. 7 with v. 9 (both are three-part lines dealing with the wicked).[357] This proposal may be too elaborate; however, it does have the advantage of suggesting that Psalm 92 is not simply a typical song of thanksgiving, and it thus allows for the didactic tone that scholars often detect (see vv. 5-7, 12-15, which are especially reminiscent of Psalms 1; 37; and 73, which also have a didactic character).

As suggested above, Ps 92:8 anticipates Ps 93:4 and the subsequent series of psalms proclaiming God's reign (Psalms 95–99); it also is linked literarily to the two preceding psalms (see Commentary on Psalms 90; 91). Psalm 92:1-4 especially recalls Psalm 90 with the mention of proclaiming God's "steadfast love in the morning" (v. 2; see also 90:14). The word "faithfulness" (אמונה *ĕmûnâ*) in v. 2 recalls Ps 91:4, and all three psalms are concerned with day and night (90:4-6; 91:5-6; 92:2). Furthermore, 92:4 answers the requests of 90:14-15; in both cases, joy and gladness are associated with God's work (90:1b; 92:4). In part, this work has to do with God's opposition to the wicked (see Pss 91:8; 92:11). Thus Psalm 92 joins Psalms 90–91, as well as the subsequent psalms in Book IV, as a response to the theological crisis posed by the exile and especially articulated in Book III (see Commentary on Psalms 73; 74; 79; 80; 89; Introduction).

92:1-6. Both verbs in v. 1 occur also in Ps 7:17, which immediately follows an affirmation of the downfall of the wicked (7:12-16; see also 92:7, 9, 11). Verses 1-2, as well as the reference to musical instruments in v. 3 (see Ps 33:2), support an original liturgical setting for Psalm 92 (see above on the superscription).

As in the hymns, the offering of praise is supported by reasons for praise (vv. 4-6). The

---

356. See Sarna, "The Psalm for the Sabbath Day (Ps 92)," 157-68.

357. Tate, *Psalms 51–100,* 464; Tate relies on the insights of R. M. Davidson.

Hebrew word translated "work" (פעל *pō'al*, v. 4*a*; NIV, "deeds") usually designates God's saving work on behalf of the people (see Deut 32:4; Pss 44:1; 90:16; 95:9; Isa 5:12). The word "works" in vv. 4*b*, 5*a* also refers often to God's saving activity (see Josh 24:31; Judg 2:7, 10; Ps 33:4), but it refers as well to God's activity in creation (see Pss 8:3; 19:1; 103:22; 104:24). Either nuance is appropriate, for both God's creating and saving activities testify ultimately to God's universal sovereignty. The word "great" (גדל *gādal*) is also associated frequently with the proclamation of God's reign (see Pss 47:2; 95:3; 96:4; 99:2). Thus vv. 4-5 anticipate the pivotal v. 8. Although the NIV and the NRSV link v. 6 syntactically to v. 7, it can also be understood in relation to vv. 4-5; that is, the recognition of God's sovereignty constitutes true understanding (see Job 28:28; Ps 111:10; Prov 1:7; 9:10).

92:7-9. It is both structurally and theologically significant that v. 8 is surrounded by two verses that focus on "evildoers" (vv. 7, 9; the "doers" component of this compound word is the same as "work" in v. 4*a* NRSV, thus contrasting God and the wicked). In terms of the structure of the psalm and of the reality of the psalmist's world, the affirmation of God's rule is made in the midst of evil. Thus the perspective is eschatological (see Psalm 2; Introduction). Appearances seem to deny God's reign, for the evildoers flourish (v. 7; see also vv. 12-13). But, the psalmist affirms, they shall perish (v. 9; see also Pss 1:6; 37:20; 73:27).

92:10-15. The Hebrew verb forms do not change between vv. 9 and 10, so it is likely that the verbs in vv. 10-11 should be translated in the future tense (and probably those in vv. 12-14 as well). The correlate of the wicked person's perishing is described by the psalmist first in personal terms (v. 10) and then more generally. The psalmist will be "exalted" (see Ps 75:7). The wicked will flourish, but only briefly, "like grass"; the righteous will flourish like trees that are planted in God's garden (cf. v. 7 with vv. 12-13; see also Ps 1:3; Jer 17:7-8). The righteous are able to take root, grow, and be fruitful, because God is both their foundation and their constant source of nourishment. Whereas the righteous trust God, the wicked trust themselves (see Jer 17:5, 7). Psalm 92 affirms that trust in self alone is illusory and ultimately leads to destruction (vv. 7, 9, 11). But trust in God brings true understanding (v. 6) and connects one to the unfailing source of life (see Commentary on Psalm 1, esp. discussion of v. 3). The integrity, vitality, and joy of the righteous (vv. 4, 12-14)—who exist *even now* amid the flourishing of evil—offer testimony to God's character (v. 15; see also v. 2). God is "upright" (see Deut 32:4; Pss 25:8; 33:4), and unlike other so-called authorities, God does "no unrighteousness" (see Ps 58:2; 82:2). The life of the righteous also testifies to God's strength (see "rock" in Deut 32:4; Pss 19:14; 28:1; 31:2; 73:26; 95:1), for the righteous have discovered that trusting God is precisely what constitutes life.

REFLECTIONS

1. The eschatological perspective of Psalm 92 is in keeping with the orientation of the whole psalter (see Commentary on Psalm 2; Introduction), but Psalm 92 is especially reminiscent of Psalms 1; 37; and 73. Its message that trusting oneself alone is illusory and destructive offers a sobering warning to a generation that generally "cannot understand this" (v. 6). As much as or more than any generation before in the history of the world, we are inclined to trust our own intelligence, strength, and technology more than we trust God or each other. From the perspective of Psalm 92, the irony is that the more sophisticated and self-sufficient we think we are, the more stupid and more insecure we actually are. A renewed sense of the greatness of God's works, of the stunning depth of God's design for the cosmos, and of the breadth of God's sovereign claim upon humankind, is urgently needed (see vv. 5-9).

2. As with Psalms 1–2; 37; 73; and many others, the eschatological affirmation of God's rule challenges us to find our security in God rather than in ourselves, which suggests another dimension to Psalm 92 as a sabbath song. According to the Heidelberg Catechism, the Fourth Commandment requires that one "cease from my evil works all the days of my life, allow the Lord to work in me through his spirit, and thus begin in this life the eternal sabbath" (Question 103). In recognizing and yielding to God's rule (Ps 92:8), we experience at once "the eternal sabbath," the peace God intends and will bring about (vv. 4, 12-15; see also Isa 55:10-13).

3. The theme of proclaiming makes Psalm 92 especially appropriate for Epiphany (see vv. 2, 15). What is to be proclaimed gets at the very heart of God's character—steadfast love and faithfulness (v. 2; see also Exod 34:6-7; Pss 89:50; 98:3; 138:2; Introduction), as well as God's righteousness (v. 15). The proclamation is to be made throughout every day (see "morning" and "night" in v. 2) and throughout a lifetime (see "old age" in v. 14). It involves both liturgical activity (see vv. 3, 13) and style of life (see v. 14). By their worship and by their work, the people of God proclaim that their lives and futures belong not to themselves but to God. Indeed, the content of this proclamation is the essence of being "righteous" (v. 12; see also Commentary on Psalm 1). This message was liberating good news to ancient exiles, and it is still liberating good news to contemporary persons captivated by themselves, alienated from God, and isolated from one another.

PSALM 93:1-5, GOD HAS ESTABLISHED THE WORLD

COMMENTARY

Psalm 93 is the first in a collection of enthronement psalms (Psalms 93; 95–99; on the apparent intrusion of Psalm 94, see Introduction and Commentary on Psalm 94), which forms the theological heart of the psalter (see Introduction). To be sure, its fundamental claim—"the LORD is king" (v. 1)—pervades the psalter; there have already been other enthronement psalms (see Psalms 29; 47). The strength of this collection, however, is impressive, and it comes at a crucial point in the psalter in response to the theological crisis articulated by Book III (see Commentary on Psalms 73; 74; 79; 80; 89; 90; Introduction).

The origin and ancient setting of the enthronement psalms are much debated. While there is no solid evidence for Mowinckel's view that they were used at a New Year festival where God was annually enthroned, it is entirely likely they were used in some liturgical setting (see Commentary on Psalm 47). There are affinities between the enthronement psalms and the poetry of

Isaiah 40–55 (see Isa 52:7-10; see also Commentary on Psalm 96), but the direction of the influence is unclear. In their present setting, the enthronement psalms do seem to respond to the same crisis to which Isaiah 40–55 is directed: the exile. Their literary context in the psalter also gives the enthronement psalms an eschatological orientation; they assert the reign of God in the face of circumstances that seem to deny it (see Commentary on Psalm 2; Introduction). It is finally not possible or necessary to view as mutually exclusive the cultic, historical, and eschatological approaches to Psalm 93 and the other enthronement psalms (see Commentary on Psalm 96).

While the enthronement psalms share much in common, each one is unique. Psalm 93, for instance, features God's role as creator and the attendant ancient Near Eastern mythic background. Verses 1-2 describe poetically the reality of God's kingship, while vv. 3-4 use the image of water to portray the response. Verse 5, which at first sight may appear unrelated to vv. 1-4, then addresses the privilege and responsibility that fall to a monarch to order justly and rightly the lives of those subject to his or her rule.

The translation of the Hebrew verb form in the opening affirmation has been the subject of prolonged debate. Several scholars have defended the translation "has become king," and this rendering fits nicely their view of an annual enthronement or re-enthronement of God. This translation is grammatically possible, but so is the present tense, which is preferable in view of the affirmation in vv. 1c-2 that God has *always* been king. Verse 1 continues with a figurative description of God's royal garments (see Isa 51:9, where the NIV's "clothe" and the NRSV's "put on" represent the same verb as "is robed" [לבש *lābaš*] here, and where "strength" is also involved; see also Ps 104:1; Isa 59:17). First is "majesty" (גאות *gēʾût*), which interestingly in view of vv. 3-4 is used of waters in Ps 46:3 and of the sea in Ps 89:9. But God has subdued the chaotic waters (vv. 3-4) and thus demonstrated God's sovereignty. It is significant, too, that God's majesty is also celebrated in the Song of the Sea in Exodus 15 (see Exod 15:7), where God defeats not only the Egyptians (a historical foe), but also the waters (v. 8). The whole episode is a demonstration of God's strength (vv. 2, 13), and the song culminates in the proclamation of God's reign (v. 18). The song in Exodus 15 is also framed by a verbal form of the root that appears in 93:1 as "majesty" (see Exod 15:1, 21).

93:1-2. To be "girded" usually denotes preparedness for battle, as the NIV more clearly suggests (see Pss 18:32, 39; 65:6). As in Exodus 15, "strength" is elsewhere associated with the proclamation of God's reign (see Pss 29:1; 96:6-7). In short, the depiction of God's royal attire as "majesty" and "strength" amounts to the portrayal of the king as divine warrior. Verse 1c follows logically from this portrayal, since creation in the ancient Near East was often viewed as a battle between God and the forces of chaos—the sea or the waters or the deep (see Ps 74:12-17). In this battle, God has proven victorious; so chaos is ordered, and the world is "established" as solid and immovable (see Pss 24:1-2; 96:10; see also 46:5, where Zion is the solid point

in the chaotic swirl described in 46:1-3; see also 15:5; 16:8, where individuals will not be moved on account of God's presence). The verb "established" (כון *kûn*) links vv. 1 and 2, and thus provides another conceptual tie between God's sovereignty and the ordered existence of the world (see other references to God's throne in Pss 47:8; 89:14; 97:2; 103:19). Verse 2 shifts to direct address of God; in a case of unusual syntax, the last word in the line is the Hebrew pronoun "you," which emphatically focuses attention directly on God.

93:3-4. That the cosmic battle with chaos lies in the background of vv. 1-2 is confirmed in vv. 3-4 with the mention of "floods" (see Ps 98:8), "waters," and "the sea." The threefold occurrence of "floods" and "lift up" may be intended to suggest the repetitive motion of large bodies of water. In any case, the sound of the waters ("voice" in v. 3 and "thunder[s]" in v. 4 are the same Hebrew word [קול *qôl*]) seems to be viewed poetically as their way of paying homage to God (see Isa 24:14). The NIV's "pounding," however, may point in a different direction. The form is difficult, but the word seems to derive from a root that means "to crush." Its appearance in Ps 94:5 may suggest that the noise of the sea indicates its hostile intent. If so, however, God's power is greater, as v. 4 makes clear. The repeated "majestic" (v. 4) occurs in Exod 15:10, where it also describes "waters" ("the sea" also is present in this verse). The affirmation is that God's majesty/might is greater than that of the chaotic waters, which were actually personified as gods in Canaanite literature. Thus God rules the world (see "majestic" also in Pss 8:1, 9; 76:5; and see "on high" in Pss 7:7; 68:18 NIV).

93:5. As suggested above, the movement from vv. 1-4 to v. 5 is not unnatural. The affirmation of v. 5a is virtually identical to that of Ps 19:7b; like Psalm 93, Psalm 19 also moves from creation to God's instruction (cf. vv. 1-6 with vv. 7-14). In fact, the exodus narrative, to which Psalm 93 alludes, makes a similar movement from the proclamation of God's sovereignty (Exod 15:1-21, esp. v. 18) to Sinai and the proclamation of God's will (Exodus 19–24). God's decrees are "sure" (אמן *ʾāman*), which translates the Hebrew root that lies behind the noun "faithfulness."

That is, God's will embodies faithfulness. It was precisely God's faithfulness that the exile called into question (see Ps 89:49), and Psalm 93 is part of the response that Book IV provides: God reigns, and God's will is faithful (see Pss 92:2; 98:3).

God's "house" in v. 5 is apparently the Temple. Elsewhere, too, the Temple (or Zion or God's throne) is called "holy" (see Pss 2:6; 3:4; 5:7; 11:4; 15:1; 24:3; 47:8). Holiness in its root sense connotes unapproachability, so it is significant that holiness here has to do with the communication and enactment of God's will—that is, God's will to *relate*. The same complex of ideas recurs in Psalm 99, where the repeated assertion is that God is holy (vv. 3, 5, 9), but where God has again communicated God's decrees (v. 7) for the relational purpose of enacting justice and righteousness (v. 4). Such was and is the true calling of the powerful, divine and human (see Commentary on Psalms 72; 82).

REFLECTIONS

1. The probability that Psalm 93 was placed literarily to respond to events that called into question God's faithfulness and love (see Ps 89:49) is significant, for rampant evil in our world still raises similar questions in people's minds. In other words, the affirmation that God reigns is eschatological; it is always made amid circumstances that seem to deny it—exile, evil, alienation, sin, suffering, death. Yet, Psalm 93 joins the psalter as a whole in asserting unequivocally and enthusiastically that God alone rules the world and that God's purposes can be trusted. In short, the real and fundamental truth about the world is simply this: God reigns. The disparity between this proclamation and the so-called real world calls for a decision. Weiser, noting that Psalm 93 offers through the eyes of faith a very particular view of God and the world, says that "He is the God who was, who is and who is to come, and before whose reality the barriers of time disappear so that what happened long ago and what will come to pass in the future both simultaneously call for a decision at the present moment."[358] In fact, this decision is the same one Jesus called for when he announced the presence of God's reign and invited people to enter it (Mark 1:14-15). Of course, to most of his contemporaries, Jesus seemed out of touch with the "real world," and his cross was an offense. But again, the reign of God is always proclaimed amid circumstances that seem to deny it.

2. The certainty that Psalm 93 was used liturgically in some setting is also significant, for it suggests that worship affords us the opportunity to affirm that we trust that God rules the world. It is an exceedingly difficult affirmation to make. On the one hand, the very existence of monstrous evil in the world leads many Christians to attribute equal, if not superior, power to the devil (which, of course, offers a convenient excuse for our own failings). This, in turn, raises a second source of difficulty. Our culture teaches us essentially that there is no need to talk about God anyway; God is a projection either of our own guilt or of our own will to power, and it is really we who are in control of the world and of our destinies for good or ill. Because of these two different but persistent temptations, it is crucial that our worship incorporate the fundamental message of Psalm 93: God reigns.

This astounding good news has profound consequences. It means that we belong fundamentally not to ourselves, but to God. And so does the world. The ecological implications alone are staggering, not to mention the social, economic, and political ones! (See Commentary on Psalms 2; 8; 29; 47.) But Christians profess that the place to start is by following the one who invites people to enter God's reign by denying self and taking up a cross (Mark 8:34). Jesus' disciples thought it was a strange way to acknowledge God's sovereignty, and the world still thinks it strange! All of this suggests

---

358. Weiser, *The Psalms*, 618.

that the most important thing we can do, repeatedly in our worship and work, is to affirm God's fundamental claim upon our lives and our world—God reigns. In the words of Hauerwas and Willimon: "We would like a church that again asserts that God, not nations, rules the world, that the boundaries of God's kingdom transcend those of Caesar, and that the main political task of the church is the formation of people who see clearly the cost of discipleship and are willing to pay the price."[359]

359. Hauerwas and Willimon, *Resident Aliens*, 48.

PSALM 94:1-23, JUSTICE WILL RETURN

COMMENTARY

Mays suggests that the message of Psalm 94 is captured in the familiar hymn "This Is My Father's World": "Though the wrong seems oft so strong, God is the ruler yet."[360] Thus, even though Psalm 94 does not directly say that God reigns, it reinforces the proclamation explicit in Psalms 93; 95–99. Psalm 94 also recalls Psalm 92; both psalms are concerned with the lives and futures of the righteous (92:12; 94:21) and the wicked (92:7; 94:3, 13), the latter described twice in each psalm as evildoers (92:7, 9; 94:4, 16). Both psalms have an instructional intent (cf. 92:6 with 94:8); they share several items of vocabulary (see the NRSV's "steadfast love," 92:2; 94:18; "upright," 92:15; 94:15; "rock" 92:15; 94:22); and they both reinforce the explicit proclamation of God's reign. The similarity suggests that the apparent intrusion of Psalm 94 into the series of enthronement psalms (93; 95–99) may serve the purpose of binding this collection more explicitly to Psalms 90–92, which open Book IV (see Introduction).[361]

Psalm 94 is often categorized as a communal lament or prayer for help; however, this designation applies well only to vv. 1-7. Verses 8-15 are addressed not to God but to foolish people (vv. 8-11) and to the righteous (vv. 12-15). Verses 16-23 consist of direct address to God (vv. 18-21), framed by references to God in the third person that have the character of professions of faith (vv. 16-17, 22-23). The structure is usually outlined according to the above divisions: vv. 1-7, vv. 8-15,

vv. 16-23. Several scholars, however, suggest a chiastic arrangement (see Introduction), in which vv. 1-2 are an introduction, vv. 3-7 correspond to vv. 20-23, vv. 8-11 to 16-19, and vv. 12-15 form the focal point.[362] While the first proposal is simpler, the second has the advantage of highlighting a unit that seems to summarize the message of the psalm. The two proposals need not be viewed as mutually exclusive.

94:1-7. As the juxtaposition of the major concepts in vv. 1-2 suggests, vengeance has to do with God's establishment of justice. Elsewhere, too, God is characterized as a "God of vengeance" (see Deut 32:35, 41, 43; Pss 58:10; 79:10; Jer 51:6; Ezek 25:12, 14, 17), and it is especially significant that Ps 99:8 describes God as avenging the people's wrongs as part of the exercise of God's reign (see 99:1). God's role as judge—God's establishment of justice—also belongs to the exercise of God's rule (see Pss 9:7-8; 96:13; 97:2; 98:9; 99:4). The plea that God "shine forth" uses the language of theophany (see Deut 33:2; Pss 50:2; 80:1), and it reveals the psalmist's trust that when God appears, God will set things right. That is to say, God will deal with the wicked (v. 3), who are elsewhere characterized by pride or arrogance (v. 2; see also Pss 10:2; 31:18, 23; 36:11; 73:6). The same Hebrew root behind "proud" (גאה *g'h*) underlies the translation "majesty" in Ps 93:1, thus linking the two psalms in a way that suggests the wicked assert their own sovereignty while the psalmist requests God to make known God's sovereignty.

360. Mays, *Psalms*, 302.
361. See Wilson, "Shaping the Psalter," 75-76.

362. See Tate, *Psalms 51–100*, 486.

The wicked are characterized by arrogant speech (v. 4; see also Pss 31:18; 59:7; 73:8; 75:5) as well as oppressive behavior (v. 5; see also Exod 1:11, 12; 2 Sam 7:10; the psalmists often used this Hebrew root [ענה 'ānâ] to complain of being afflicted, poor, or oppressed, as in Ps 10:2, 9). The verb "crush" (דכא dākā) also appears to be related to the word that designates the activity of the floods in Ps 93:3, thus providing another link between the two psalms and tying the activity of the wicked to the chaotic forces that God orders in the role of sovereign. Verse 6 illustrates the oppressive behavior of the wicked; they afflict precisely those for whom God has particular concern (see Exod 22:20-23; Pss 68:5-6; 146:9). Verse 7 illustrates the arrogant speech of the wicked; they view themselves as completely autonomous, accountable to no one, not even God (see Pss 10:4, 11; 14:1; 53:1; 73:11).

94:8-11. Using the same verb that the wicked have just used in v. 7*b*, the psalmist in v. 8*a* calls them to attention (the verb is more literally "understand," as in 8*a* NRSV; see also Ps 92:6). The imperative is followed by a question in v. 8*b*, which recalls Ps 2:10 (see also Ps 14:1), where being wise also involved recognizing God's sovereignty (see 2:11). In Psalm 73, the psalmist describes himself or herself as dull or senseless (v. 22) when he or she failed to "know" (v. 22; see Ps 94:10) or to "understand" (v. 17) God and God's dealings with the wicked. The psalmist eventually reached the proper understanding (vv. 17-20; 27; as the NIV suggests, the verb in Ps 73:27*b* is the same as in 94:23), and it is the same knowledge that the psalmist also seeks to impart in Psalm 94. The question in v. 8*b* is followed by a series of questions, which really function as affirmations. God is not oblivious, as the wicked had claimed (v. 7). God does hear and see (v. 9), and God does respond (v. 10). The verb "disciplines" (יסר yissēr, v. 10*a*) also recalls Ps 2:10, thus offering another reminder that the real issue is who is sovereign. The wicked claim that they are, but the psalmist claims that God is. God "teaches knowledge" (v. 10), because God "knows" (v. 11). Verse 11 should be heard in relation to v. 7. It is not an abstract affirmation of God's omniscience, but an affirmation that the arrogantly stated intentions of the wicked will come to nothing (see Ps 39:11). God will deal with humanity's evil "thoughts" (see Gen 6:5). In short, God is sovereign.

94:12-15. Whereas vv. 8-11 have recalled Psalm 2, vv. 12-15 recall Psalm 1. The beatitude in v. 12 contains two key words from Ps 1:1-2: "happy" and "law," or better, "instruction." The vocabulary of v. 12 also recalls that of vv. 8-11 (see "discipline" and "teaches" in v. 10). The crucial claim is that happiness derives not from pursuing one's own intentions, as the wicked do, but from being instructed by God (see Commentary on Psalm 1). Such openness to God's instruction does not offer immunity from trouble (v. 13*a*), but it does provide "respite" or "relief" while the wicked pursue their evil intentions (v. 13*b*; on a pit for the wicked, see Pss 7:15; 9:15; 35:8). In Isa 32:17, the Hebrew root of "respite" is used to designate one of the results of God's reign (see Isa 32:1) of justice and righteousness—"quietness" for God's people. The "respite" in Psalm 94 is also tied conceptually to "justice" and to "righteousness" (v. 15; see the NIV, which follows the Hebrew text, while the NRSV follows a variant reading). Justice and righteousness are the hallmarks of God's reign (see Pss 96:13; 97:2; 98:9; 99:4). God's "heritage," God's people, may suffer affliction (see v. 5; see also Ps 34:19), but because God is sovereign and not the wicked, God's people will not be forsaken (v. 14). The "upright in heart" are the ones who experience life as God intends it (see Pss 7:10; 32:11; 36:10; 64:10; 97:11).

94:16-19. The questions of v. 16 (see Pss 9:19; 10:12) are answered in v. 17. It is God who helps (see Pss 22:19; 27:9; 38:22; 40:13, 17; 46:2). The "land of silence" (v. 17*b*; see also Ps 115:17) designates Sheol, the realm of the dead. Verse 18 returns to direct address; it and the following verses express gratitude and trust. The verb translated "slipping" (נטה nāṭâ) is used often in expressions of both threat and confidence (see also "moved"/"shaken" in Pss 13:4; 15:5; 16:8; 30:6; 38:1). God is a solid support for the psalmist (see Pss 18:35), as God is also the solid support for the world (see Ps 93:1). It is a matter of God's character, which is expressed in a word by "steadfast love" (see Pss 5:7; 13:5; Introduction; in the more immediate context, see 90:14; 92:2; 98:3; 100:5; 103:4, 8, 11, 17; 106:1, 45).

94:20-23. Verse 20 is difficult. The NIV offers a more literal reading of v. 20*a*, which the NRSV has rendered more interpretively. Verses 20-21 recall vv. 5-7 and seem to suggest that the oppressive, deadly activity of the wicked is institutionalized. But in the face of such ingrained evil, the psalmist asserts trust in God (vv. 22-23). God is the psalmist's source of protection (see "stronghold"/"fortress" in Pss 9:9; 18:2; 62:2, 6) and strength (see "rock" in Pss 31:2; 62:7; 92:15; 95:1)—in short, the psalmist's "refuge" (מחסה *maḥseh*) a word that also recalls Psalm 2 (see Pss 2:12; 5:11; 7:1; Introduction). As for the wicked, God "will return upon them their iniquity" (v. 23*a*, author's trans.). Thus the wicked suffer from delusions of grandeur (see v. 7); they are actually sowing the seeds of their own destruction (see Pss 7:15-16; 73:27).

REFLECTIONS

It does not appear that God reigns, for the wicked prosper, and crime does pay. The psalmist does not deny appearances (vv. 3-7, 13, 20-21), but neither does he or she waver from the conviction that God rules (vv. 1-2, 8-15) and that God is the help and hope of God's people (vv. 16-19, 22-23). In short, the perspective is eschatological. God's reign is proclaimed amid circumstances that seem to deny it, and the reader is thus called to decision—either to choose the self-assertion of the wicked or to find happiness (v. 12) and consolation (v. 19) and refuge (v. 22) in God (see Reflections on Psalms 1; 2; 93; Introduction).

As Mays suggests, the psalmist has the conviction of a prophet and the voice of a pastor. Like the prophets, the psalmist calls God to deal with injustice (vv. 1-2) and announces punishment for the wicked (v. 23). But it is even more evident in Psalm 94 that "the psalmist had a pastoral calling to encourage and support the discouraged and hurt in their life as the people of God."[363] That calling is still a timely one. We are still familiar with the arrogance and oppression that derive from self-assertion (vv. 3-7), and it is still discouraging and hurtful. So Psalm 94 can perhaps serve as a model for contemporary pastors, who are called upon not to deny appearances (vv. 3-7) or to acquiesce with institutionalized oppression (vv. 20-21), but to find ways of honestly encouraging and supporting God's people. In a world that teaches and rewards self-assertion (see Commentary on Psalm 1) and is usually content to acquiesce with oppression, the pastoral task seems like an insurmountable one. As Psalm 94 suggests, it must be rooted in the proclamation that God reigns, and it must involve the invitation to live under God's rule as the first step toward the pursuit of the elusive goal of being "happy" (v. 12). This proclamation and invitation were, after all, the essence of Jesus' ministry as well (see Mark 1:14-15).

Part of the difficulty of such a task involves the issue of how to preach judgment without being judgmental, and how to preach vengeance without being vengeful (see vv. 1-2). The psalmist apparently avoided the pitfalls of this dilemma by holding firmly to the conviction that *God* is judge and that consequently, "Vengeance is mine" (Deut 32:35 NRSV; see also Rom 12:19; Heb 10:30). For those who are convinced that preaching must refrain from any mention of judgment and vengeance, Psalm 94 is a reminder that it is not possible. In a world of oppression and institutionalized evil, to preach the judgment and vengeance of God is to profess our hope and our conviction that God rules the world and that "justice will return" (v. 15).

363. Mays, *Psalms,* 304.

PSALM 95:1-11, LISTEN TO GOD'S VOICE

COMMENTARY

Psalm 95 is often categorized as an enthronement psalm, because it begins (vv. 1-7b) with a song of praise to God, the "great King" (v. 3), and because it adjoins a collection of similar psalms (Psalms 93; 96–99). The unique conclusion to Psalm 95 (vv. 7c-11), however, has led some scholars to label it a prophetic exhortation or a liturgy of divine judgment. Actually, vv. 1-7b are somewhat unusual as well. The typical elements of a song of praise are present—invitation to praise (vv. 1-2, 6) and reasons for praise (vv. 3-5, 7ab)—but they appear twice. In fact, some scholars detect three separate invitations (vv. 1, 2, 6), each of which they associate with a different liturgical movement. Taken together, in these scholars' view, the three movements constitute a processional that would have culminated with entrance through the temple gates or into the Temple (vv. 6-7ab), at which time the prophetic exhortation would have been heard. If this scenario is correct, then Psalm 95 has strong affinities with Psalm 24, which also celebrates God's role as creator (cf. 24:1-2 with 95:4-5) in the context of hailing God as king (cf. 24:7-10 with 95:3) and could easily have originated or been used as a liturgy for entrance into the Temple (see Commentary on Psalm 24).

The literary or liturgical movement from praise to the hearing of God's word also makes Psalm 95 similar to Psalms 50 and 81, especially the latter (cf. 81:8, 13 with 95:7c). Indeed, Psalms 50; 81; and 95 have often been viewed as festival psalms, but there is no consensus on their precise liturgical setting. While there is no solid evidence for an annual enthronement festival in conjunction with the New Year (see Introduction), it is likely that Psalm 95 would have been used in some liturgical setting, perhaps the Feast of Booths. At some point, its use would have been adapted for worship in the synagogues; rabbinic sources associate its use with the beginning of the sabbath. In keeping with this Jewish usage, Psalm 95 was and is used in Christian liturgy as a call to worship. Scholarly views of vv. 7c-11 vary in accordance

with the way one views the setting and ancient use of the psalm. These verses can be construed as an oracle delivered by a cultic prophet, but it is probably more accurate to view them as representative of a Levitical sermon (see Commentary on Psalms 50; 81).

As part of the enthronement collection that occupies a prominent place in Book IV, Psalm 95 participates in the response to the theological crisis raised by the shape and content of Books I–III (see Commentary on Psalms 73; 74; 79; 80; 89; 90; 93; Introduction). Psalm 95:8 also contributes to the character of Book IV as a Moses-book (see Psalm 90; Introduction), and it is possible that Psalms 95 and 100 are intended to serve as a frame around Psalms 96–99, the core of the enthronement collection (cf. 95:1-2, 6 with 100:1-2, 4; 95:7ab with 100:3).[364]

95:1-2. The invitations in vv. 1-2 anticipate the explicit proclamation of God's kingship in v. 3. The repeated "make a joyful noise" indicates an appropriate way to respond to God's sovereignty (see Pss 47:1; 66:1; 81:1; 98:4, 6). The other Hebrew roots used in vv. 1-2 also occur in explicit proclamations of God's rule (for the NRSV's "let us sing," see Pss 96:12; 98:4, 8; for "songs of praise," see Pss 47:6; 98:4-5). The "thanksgiving" in v. 2 could mean a sacrifice that accompanies other expressions of gratitude, or it could indicate the non-sacrificial expressions themselves (see Pss 50:14, 23; 100:3; see also the title to Psalm 100). In any case, the thanksgiving is to be presented to God's "face" (see Ps 27:8-9). The metaphor of God as a rock is a frequent one in the psalms (see Pss 31:2; 62:2, 6; 89:26; 92:15; 94:22).

95:3-5. Reasons for praise follow in vv. 3-5. Verse 3 assumes the polytheistic background of the ancient Near East (see Pss 82:1; 96:4; 97:9), but Yahweh is preeminent among the gods—the "great King" (see Ps 47:2; greatness is frequently associated with God's sovereignty, as in Pss 96:4; 99:2). God's

364. See Tate, *Psalms 51–100,* 475; D. M. Howard, Jr., *The Structure of Psalms 93–100* (Ann Arbor, Mich.: University Microfilms, 1986) 78, 134, 174-76, 207-8.

sovereignty extends throughout the cosmos. The repetition of "his hand(s)" in vv. 4a, 5b has the literary effect of surrounding all the elements of the cosmos with references to God's hands. Structure reinforces content; that is, the whole world is in God's hands (see Pss 24:1-2; 138:7-8).

95:6-7b. Verse 6 again invites actions that were appropriate for greeting a king. The first verb (שׁחה šāḥâ) means more literally "bow down" (see 1 Sam 24:8; 2 Sam 14:4, 22; 1 Kgs 1:31 for earthly kings; Pss 29:2; 96:9; 99:5 for God), which is also the meaning of the second verb (see 2 Chr 7:3; 29:29; Pss 22:29; 72:9). It is followed in several instances by the noun "knees" (see 1 Kgs 8:54; Isa 45:23), thus anticipating the third verb, which in other conjugations of the root means "to bless" (ברך bārak; see Pss 96:2; 100:4; 145:1). The address of God as "our Maker" recalls the verb "made" (עשׂה 'āśâ) in v. 5a, and the repetition highlights the two possible senses of "made." It can mean God's salvific activity (v. 6: God made Israel by way of the exodus, which is already alluded to in v. 5 and will be again in v. 9; see Pss 100:3; 118:24), as well as God's activity in creation (v. 5). Indeed, ultimately the two senses are inseparable, for the making of Israel was for the purpose of enacting God's creational purposes (see Commentary on Psalms 33; 66). In this regard, it should be noted that "sea" in v. 5 not only recalls creation but also is reminiscent of Exod 15:1, 8, and "dry land" calls to mind both creation (see Gen 1:9, 10) and exodus as well (see Exod 14:16, 22, 29; 15:19). Appropriately, just as God holds the world in God's hands (vv. 4a, 5b), so also Israel represents "the sheep of his hand" (v. 7b). In the ancient Near East, kings were known as the shepherds of their people (see Jer 23:1-4; Ezek 34:1-10), so it is especially fitting that this metaphor appears in a psalm that celebrates God's kingship (see also Pss 23:1; 74:1; 79:13; 80:1; 100:3; Ezek 34:11-16). The "great God" (v. 3) is "our God" (v. 7a).

95:7c. Verse 7c is really a transitional verse. Sheep are supposed to listen to the voice of their shepherd (see John 10:3-5, 14, 16), so v. 7c could be considered the culmination of vv. 1-7. But v. 7c also introduces the issue illustrated negatively in vv. 8-11. The three-part poetic line of v. 7 also has the effect of isolating, and thus emphasizing, v.

7c as a call to attention and obedience (see Ps 81:8, 13). The word translated "listen" in v. 7c often has the sense of "obey," especially in Deuteronomy. The emphasis on "today"—on reactualizing the past—is also characteristic of Deuteronomy (see 4:40; 5:3; 6:6; 7:11).

95:8-11. These verses recall places and events in the wilderness shortly after Israel had been "made" ('āśâ, Exodus 1–14; see the Hebrew root of "made" in Exod 14:31 [NRSV, "did"; NIV, "displayed"]) and God's reign proclaimed (Exod 15:1-21, esp. v. 18). Meribah and Massah are mentioned together in Exod 17:1-7 (see also Massah in Deut 6:16; 9:22; Meribah in Num 20:13, 24; Pss 81:7; 106:32; and both in Deut 33:8), which could be considered the text for the sermon in vv. 8-11. Exodus 17:1-7 does not say that the people hardened their hearts, although the Hebrew root translated "hardened" (קשׁה qāšâ) is used elsewhere to characterize the behavior of the people in the wilderness. In a different form, it appears as the first element in the term "stiff-necked" (see Exod 32:9; 33:3, 5; 34:9). Against the background of these references to the book of Exodus, "my work" in v. 9 certainly refers to the exodus itself (see Pss 44:1; 77:12). Thus, the whole exodus event and the people's response lie in the background of vv. 8-11. In the book of Exodus, the sequence of deliverance (Exodus 1–14) and proclamation of God's reign (Exod 15:1-21) should have led to immediate obedience, but instead it led to immediate complaining and testing of God (Exod 17:1-7; see also Exod 15:22-27). The people even ask, "Is the LORD among us or not?" (Exod 17:7 NRSV). Against this background, Psalm 95 says, in effect, "Do not repeat that mistake." In other words, in your place and time— your today (v. 7c)—listen to God's voice. In response to the proclamation of God's reign (v. 3), submit instead of rebelling (v. 6), and obey instead of complaining (v. 7c). Verses 10-11 conclude the sermon with a reminder of past consequences for disobedience— namely, God's displeasure (see Num 14:33-35) and failure to enter the land (see "rest" in Deut 12:9; see also Num 10:33)—which is intended to serve as a warning for the present. The call for a decision in response to God's reign is an urgent matter—indeed, a matter of life and death.

Reflections

1. The message that pervades the psalter is explicit in Psalm 95: God reigns. As the shape and content of the book of Psalms demonstrate, the proclamation of God's reign is eschatological; it is always made in circumstances that seem to deny it (see Commentary on Psalms 2; 29; 47; 93; Introduction). It is revealing that in Psalm 95 it is not the forces of chaos that resist God's claim (as in Psalm 93), nor is it the wicked or the nations (as in Psalm 94). Rather, God's own people resist God's claim. This situation is significant, for it reveals something crucial about how God exercises sovereignty. God does not coerce obedience; God invites obedience. God warns that the consequences of disobedience are severe, but God refuses to be an enforcer. It leaves God in the vulnerable position of having to implore the people to obey (v. 7c), but such is the price of integrity and of love.

2. God's invitation to obedience is particularly clear in Psalm 95. The proclamation of God's reign always calls for a decision, but that call for decision is highlighted by the structure and movement of Psalm 95 (see esp. v. 7c). As with Psalm 93, it is significant that the call to decision appears in an explicitly liturgical context. Thus this psalm teaches us about worship. In worship, we profess who is sovereign, and we actualize today the reality of God's claim upon us. To be sure, worship has something to do with the past, but it also clearly has to do with the present. Worship really is a "service" in the sense that we act out our servanthood, our submission to the God whom we profess rules the world and our lives. Worship is a matter of word and deed (see Matt 7:21-23).

3. There is a rabbinic tale that culminates in a reference to Psalm 95:7c and emphasizes the significance of its call to decision. Rabbi Yoshua Ben Levi finds the prophet Elijah and asks him when the Messiah will come. Elijah tells the rabbi where to find the Messiah so that he can address the question to him.

> Peace be unto you, my master and teacher."
> The Messiah answered, "Peace unto you, son of Levi."
> He asked, "When is the master coming?"
> "Today," he answered.
> Rabbi Yoshua returned to Elijah, who asked, "What did he tell you?"
> "He indeed has deceived me, for he said, 'Today I am coming' and he has not come."
> Elijah said, "This is what he told you: 'Today if you would listen to my voice.'"[365]

The reign of God represented in the tale by the coming of the Messiah is experienced as a decision made *today*. While the eschatological character of God's reign means that we await its full manifestation, it also means that we can enter and live in God's realm right now, as Jesus proclaimed (Mark 1:14-15).

4. The author of Hebrews, who claimed Jesus as Messiah, used Ps 95:7c-11 as the text for a Christian sermon (Heb 3:7–4:13). That author heard in Psalm 95 encouragement to persevere in trust and obedience (see 3:12-14), based on the assurance that God's rest is still available for the people of God (see 4:1-3, 6-7, 9-11). Thus, in keeping with the intent of Psalm 95, the author uses it to call to decision and accountability the people of his or her "today."

---

365. Cited in Henri J. M. Nouwen, *The Wounded Healer* (Garden City, N.Y.: Image Books, 1972) 94-95; see also 71-72. The story is from the tractate *Sanhedrin*.

PSALM 96:1-13, GOD IS COMING TO ESTABLISH JUSTICE

COMMENTARY

Psalm 96 is part of an impressive collection of enthronement psalms (Psalms 93; 95–99) that are strategically placed in Book IV to respond to the theological questions raised by Book III, especially Psalm 89 (see Psalms 73–74; 79–80; 89; 93; Introduction). In proclaiming God's reign, Psalm 96 shows the typical structure of a song of praise; that is, invitations to praise (vv. 1-3, 7-10a, 11-12a) are followed by reasons for praise (vv. 4-6, 10b, 12b-13), which together describe the nature and consequences of God's rule.

The ancient origin and use of enthronement psalms have been the subject of extensive scholarly debate, which can be summarized briefly by considering the primary options for identifying the "new song" in Ps 96:1a : (1) The new song perhaps should be understood as Psalm 96 itself as it was sung in the Temple upon the occasion of the re-enthronement of God at an annual New Year festival (see 1 Chr 16:23-33, where most of Psalm 96 appears as part of the praises accompanying David's movement of the ark to Jerusalem). Actually, there is almost no solid evidence for such a festival; however, it is certain that God's rule was regularly proclaimed anew in some setting; a liturgical song like Psalm 96 would have re-actualized for the present moment for the present worshipers the reality of God's reign. Thus Psalm 96 itself could be viewed as the new song, insofar as "it is the evocation of an alternative reality that comes into play in the very moment of the liturgy."[366] (2) The "new song" may also be understood as the response to a historical event, such as the return of the exiles from Babylonian captivity. In this regard, it is significant that Isaiah 40–55, which originated as a response to exile, also invites the people to "sing to the LORD a new song" (Isa 42:10 NRSV) in response to the "new thing" (Isa 43:19; see 42:9) that God is doing in returning the exiles to their land. Just as the exodus

of old was celebrated in a song proclaiming God's reign (see Exod 15:1-21, esp. v. 18), so also a new exodus should be accompanied by a new song. The relationship between Psalm 96 and Isaiah 40–55 is reinforced by several other parallels. Both texts are concerned with the proclamation of "good tidings" or "good news" (Isa 40:9; 41:27; 42:7; the same Hebrew root [בשר *biśśar*] underlies "proclaim" in Ps 96:2b) involving the reign of God (Ps 96:10; Isa 52:7), the proper response to which is singing for joy (Ps 96:12; Isa 52:8). And in both texts, God's purpose is justice (Ps 96:10, 13; Isa 42:1, 3-4) for the earth and its peoples (Ps 96:7, 10, 13; Isa 42:1; 45:22-23; 49:1-6; 52:10; 55:4-5). While a relationship between Psalm 96 and Isaiah 40–55 is clear, it is not clear which text originated first or even whether one text directly influenced the other. (3) The new song may be sung not so much in celebration of what God has done or is doing but in anticipation of what God will do. Especially in v. 13, it seems that God's coming is still in the future, as is God's establishment of justice and righteousness. In this view, the new song would have an eschatological orientation.

In actuality, the above three options are not mutually exclusive. The liturgical celebration of God's reign in the present is related to experience of God in the past, and both the past and the present dimensions lead to the anticipation of a transformed future. In other words, a liturgical or historical reading of Psalm 96 will also inevitably have an eschatological dimension (see below on v. 13 and Reflections).

96:1-3. Of the six imperatives in vv. 1-3, three invite the people to "sing" (שיר *šîr*, vv. 1-2a; see also Exod 15:1, 21; Pss 13:6; 27:6; 33:3; 104:33), a joyful response to God that involves but goes beyond simple speech. As suggested above, the new song (see Pss 40:4; 98:1; 144:9; Isa 42:10), as well as the very act of singing, recall the song that Moses, Miriam, and the people sang after deliverance

366. Brueggemann, *The Message of the Psalms,* 144.

from Egypt (Exod 15:1-21). Allusion to the past is accompanied by actualization in the present and anticipation of the future. God was, is, and will be king. The directing of the invitation to "all the earth" (v. 1; see also v. 9) bespeaks the cosmic scope of God's rule, and it anticipates the further invitations to and reasons for praise in vv. 10-13 (see also Pss 97:1; 98:4; 99:1). The fundamental sense of "bless" (ברך *bārak*, v. 2) seems to be to kneel in homage (see Ps 95:6; see Pss 100:4; 145:1, 21, where blessing God's name is involved; see also 16:7; 26:12). The invitation to recognize God's sovereignty is accompanied by the invitation to communicate it to others. The Hebrew root of the verb "proclaim" (*biśśar*, v. 2) came into Greek as the word usually translated "good news," "gospel";[367] Mays rightly observes that Psalm 96 "has a definite evangelical cast." *Biśśar* is most frequent in Isaiah 40–55 (see 40:9; 41:27; 52:7; see also Ps 40:9; Isa 60:6; 61:1). The good news has to do with God's life-giving work; the word "salvation" (ישועה *yĕšûʿâ*) again recalls the exodus (see Exod 15:2; Pss 3:2, 7-8; 98:1-3). Also to be declared (see Pss 44:1; 73:28; 78:3-4) are God's "glory," which bespeaks God's sovereignty (see Pss 24:7-10; 29:1-3, 9; 97:6) and God's "marvelous works." The latter once more recalls the exodus as well as the subsequent series of God's acts of deliverance (see Exod 3:20; 15:11; Josh 3:5; Judg 6:13; Pss 9:1; 26:7; 77:11, 14; 78:4, 11-12; 43; 98:1).

96:4-6. The reasons for praise begin with God's greatness (see Pss 47:2; 48:1; 70:4; 77:13; 86:10; 95:3; 99:2-3; 138:5), an attribute that means God's sovereignty is exclusive (see Exod 20:3; Pss 86:10; 95:3). Other so-called gods are but idols (see Ps 97:7). Whereas vv. 1-3 had recalled the exodus, v. 5 points to creation as evidence of God's rule (see Commentary on Psalm 95; see also 97:6). While vv. 4-5 seem to partake of the ancient Near Eastern concept of a council of the gods (see Ps 82:1), v. 6 perhaps moves toward the de-divination of these gods by surrounding God with only the divine attributes themselves. These attributes are elsewhere explicitly associated with sovereignty—"honor"/"splendor" (see Pss 21:5; 45:3; 145:5), "majesty" (see Pss 21:5; 29:4;

45:3; 145:5), "strength" (see Exod 15:2, 13; Pss 29:1; 93:1), and "beauty"/"glory" (see 1 Chr 29:11).

96:7-10a. Perhaps also in the direction of de-divination of the gods, vv. 7-9 take up the invitation of Ps 29:1-2, but it is addressed this time not to "heavenly beings" (29:1) but to "families of the peoples." The invitation of Ps 29:1-2 is expanded in 96:7-9 (see vv. 8*b*, 9*b*; on "tremble," see Pss 97:4; 29:9), and apparently what is envisioned is a procession of the nations to Jerusalem (see Isa 2:2-3; Mic 4:1-2; Zech 8:20-23). What is at stake is the universal recognition of and proclamation of God's reign (v. 10*a*; see Pss 93:1; 97:1; 99:1).

96:10b-13. What God's cosmic rule means is stated in v. 10*bc*: stability for the world (see Ps 93:1) and justice for all the world's peoples. The whole cosmos participates in and celebrates God's just ordering of the world (vv. 11-12; see also Pss 97:6; 98:7-8). The Hebrew word translated "judge" (דין *dîn*) in v. 10*c* is different from the one translated the same way in v. 13 (שפט *šāpaṭ*), but they are essentially synonymous, and both designate the prerogative and responsibility of a sovereign. In short, a king is to establish justice and righteousness (see Ps 72:1-2, where the root in Ps 96:10 appears as "judge" in v. 2, and the root in 96:13 appears as "justice" in vv. 1-2). It is precisely the failure to establish justice and righteousness that indicts the gods (see Ps 82:1-4) and threatens the earth with chaotic instability (see Ps 82:5, where "shaken" [מוט *môṭ*] is the same word as "moved" in Ps 96:10), and the establishment of justice and righteousness is the hallmark of God's reign (see Pss 97:2; 98:9; 99:4). God's justice and righteousness mean "equity" (see Pss 9:8; 98:9; 99:4) rather than partiality (see Ps 82:2), faithfulness (v. 13; see also Pss 89:49; 92:2 for a different form of the same Hebrew root) rather than neglect (see Ps 82:3-4).

As the NIV suggests, the references to God's coming in v. 13 can be understood in a present as well as a future sense. The ambiguity is appropriate. Israel affirmed God's just and righteous rule as a present reality, and yet the experience of God's justice and righteousness was for Israel and is for us always in the midst of ongoing injustice and brokenness. In short, the affirmation of God's reign, here as always, is eschatological.

367. Mays, *Psalms*, 308.

REFLECTIONS

1. Psalm 96 articulates the good news that forms the theological heart of the book of Psalms: God reigns (see Psalms 2; 29; 47; 65–68; 93; 95; 97–99; Introduction). Because God rules the world, it is not sufficient to gather a congregation less than "all the earth" (vv. 1, 9). This includes humans, to be sure (see v. 7), but it also includes "the heavens," "the earth" itself, "the sea," "the field," and "all the trees" (vv. 11-12). The ecumenical and inter-faith implications are profound; we are somehow partners with all the "families of the peoples" (v. 7). The ecological implications are staggering; we humans are somehow partners with oceans and trees and soil and air in glorifying God. The destiny of humankind and the destiny of the earth are inseparable. We—people, plants, and even inanimate entities—are all in this together (see Ps 150:6; Hos 4:1-3; see also Psalms 8; 104).

2. The invitation to praise in Ps 96:7-9 is essentially the same as that in Ps 29:1-2, except that the invitation in 96:7 is extended to the "families of the peoples" rather than to the "heavenly beings." This difference suggests at least that God's sovereignty is to be effective on earth as well as in heaven. To hear Psalms 96 and 29 together is to be taught to pray, in effect, "thy kingdom come, thy will be done on earth as it is in heaven." Like that of Psalm 96, the perspective of the Lord's Prayer is eschatological. Reciting it, we both affirm the present reality of God's reign—"thine is the kingdom"—and pray for the coming of God's reign—"thy kingdom come."

3. The emphasis in vv. 2-3 on proclaiming the good news makes Psalm 96 especially appropriate for Epiphany. Psalm 96 is also traditionally used on Christmas Day. This use articulates the Christian conviction that Jesus' birth manifests God's rule (see Psalms 29; 97; 98). Not surprisingly, the basic message of Psalm 96 is the same as that proclaimed by Jesus: God reigns. And like the preaching of Jesus, Psalm 96 calls for a decision; it invites us to submit ourselves to God's sovereignty, to enter the reign of God (see Mark 1:14-15). The shape of the psalter makes it clear that the sovereignty of God is asserted in the face of opposition (see Introduction), and so it was with the preaching of Jesus and the proclamation of the early church. In the face of severe persecution came this proclamation:

> "The kingdom of the world has become
> the kingdom of our Lord and of his Christ,
> and he will reign for ever and ever." (Rev 11:15 NIV)

Such an assertion is, as Brueggemann says of Psalm 96, "an act of profound hope." But, he adds, it is also "more than hope."[368] The conviction that God rules the world empowers us even now, in the face of old injustice and brokenness, to defy such realities as we live under God's claim and sing "a new song" (v. 1; see Rev 5:9; 14:3).

368. Brueggemann, *The Message of the Psalms,* 145.

PSALM 97:1-12, REJOICE THAT THE LORD REIGNS

COMMENTARY

Like the other enthronement psalms (see Psalms 29; 47; 93; 95–96; 98–99), Psalm 97 features the affirmation that forms the theological heart of the psalter: God reigns (see Introduction). It shares much of the vocabulary and themes of the other enthronement psalms; Tate even considers Psalms 96 and 97 to be "twin-psalms."[369] Even so, Psalm 97 is unique. The first section (vv. 1-5) is written in the style of a theophany (a description of God's appearing), as if to portray the coming of God mentioned in Ps 96:13. Verses 6-9 present the response to and consequences of God's appearing. Verses 6-7 show a chiastic structure (see Introduction), moving from the heavenly realm (v. 6a) to the earthly sphere (vv. 6b-7ab) and back to the heavenly (v. 7c). Verse 8 focuses on the response of God's own people as it shifts to more intimate direct address of God, and v. 9 asserts again God's sovereignty over the earthly (v. 9a) and heavenly realms (v. 9b). The occurrence of "earth" (ארץ 'eres) in v. 9a is the fourth one in the psalm (see vv. 1, 4-5). The occurrences in vv. 1, 4-5 form an envelope structure for the first section; however, it is possible to construe the occurrences in vv. 1, 9 as an envelope for a larger section consisting of vv. 1-9. In either case, vv. 10-12 form the final section, the effect of which is to extend the invitation to respond to the readers of the psalm in every generation.

Another unique aspect of Psalm 97 is the way that the themes of joy/gladness and righteousness are unifying features. To be sure, these themes occur in other enthronement psalms (see joy/gladness in Ps 96:11, and righteousness in Pss 96:13; 98:9; 99:4), but here they are pervasive. Rejoicing is for the earth (v. 1), for God's own people (v. 8), for all the upright/righteous (vv. 11-12; see also "glad" in vv. 1, 8). The theme of rejoicing occurs in every section of the psalm, as does the theme of righteousness (vv. 2, 6, 11-12). The first two occurrences refer to God's

righteousness, and the final two suggest that those who submit themselves to God's rule will derive their character from God's character. Because God rules, there is the possibility that people can be righteous too.

The origin and ancient use of the enthronement psalms have been and are the subject of extensive scholarly debate (see Commentary on Psalms 29; 47; 93; 95–96; Introduction). Regardless of the conclusions one reaches on these matters, however, the final form of the psalter suggests that Psalm 97 and the others should be heard eschatologically (see Reflections below). The final form of the psalter also suggests that Psalm 97, as part of the collection including Psalms 93–99, participates in the response to the theological crisis of exile that is articulated by Books I–III (see Commentary on Psalms 89; 90; Introduction).

97:1-5. In v. 1, the earth (see Pss 96:1, 9, 11; 98:4; 99:1) and "the distant shores" (see Ps 72:10; Isa 41:5; 42:4, 10; 49:1; 51:5) are the first invited to respond to the proclamation of God's rule, making it immediately evident that God's reign has cosmic significance. God's appearance is surrounded by manifestations of the natural order—dark clouds (v. 2), lightning (vv. 3-4a), and thunder that shakes the earth (vv. 4b-5; see also Pss 29:3-9; 96:9). The same poetic imagery is used elsewhere in the OT to depict God's appearing (see Exod 13:21-22; 19:6-20; 20:18-21; 24:16-17; Pss 18:7-15; 50:3; Mic 1:4; Hab 3:3-12). Yet the psalm also affirms God's relatedness to humankind in suggesting that righteousness and justice are the foundational principles of God's rule (see Ps 89:14; see also 96:13; 98:9; 99:4). God's will for the right ordering of human society is embodied in the very structure of the cosmos; this suggests that in the presence of the injustice perpetrated by the gods (see vv. 7, 9), the very existence of the world is threatened (see also Pss 82:5; 93:1; 96:10).

97:6. A comparison of the NIV and the NRSV suggests that v. 6 can be understood

369. See Tate, *Psalms 51–100*, 508.

as related more closely to vv. 1-5 (NIV) or to vv. 7-9 (NRSV). In contrast to v. 1, where the earth was called upon to respond, v. 6 is the response of the heavens to God's appearing. "The heavens" and "the earth" designate the whole cosmos (see Gen 1:1); therefore, the whole universe responds to God's reign. It is significant that the heavens proclaim God's "righteousness" (צדק ṣedeq), a term used frequently to describe God's will for human relatedness (see Ps 50:6; cf. Ps 19:1). As in v. 2, the psalmist links God's rule of the cosmos with the right ordering of humankind (see v. 6b). In beholding God's "glory," we also confront God's presence (see Exod 16:7, 10; 24:16-17; 33:18, 22) and are invited to acknowledge God's sovereignty (see Pss 24:7-10; 29:1-3, 9; 96:3, 7-8).

97:7-9. In v. 7, the psalmist recognizes that not all persons do acknowledge God's sovereignty; rather, such persons are "put to shame" as their gods "bow down before" the true God (see Pss 95:3; 96:4). Like the heavens and the earth, God's people—Zion and Judah—celebrate God's "acts of justice" (v. 8). Thus God's people are in tune with the cosmos. As the focus narrows to God's own people, the form of address becomes more intimate. The direct address of God continues in v. 9, and it is accentuated by the appearance of the Hebrew pronoun "you" (אתה 'attâ). The phrase "most high" (עליון 'elyôn) and the word "exalted" (נעלית na 'ălêtā) translate the same Hebrew root, emphasizing the affirmation that God rules both the earthly and the heavenly realms. This same Hebrew root also occurs at two crucial points in Psalm 47 (see vv. 5, 9), another enthronement psalm.

97:10-12. The reader should follow the NIV translation of v. 10 (see NRSV note).

Here the worshipers are directly addressed, as are the readers of Psalm 97 in every generation. Those who recognize God's rule are called upon to hate evil. The prophets, persistent advocates of justice and righteousness, made the same appeal (see Amos 5:15; Mic 3:2). In any generation, those who hate evil out of allegiance to God's rule will face opposition from "the wicked." The appearance of "the wicked" in this psalm is a reminder that, like the other enthronement psalms and the psalter as a whole, Psalm 97 is eschatological; it proclaims God's rule in circumstances in which one may think that God does *not* rule (see Commentary on Psalms 1; 2). Those who are "faithful" (v. 10), "righteous" (vv. 11-12), and "upright in heart" (v. 11; see also Pss 7:10; 94:15) will not go unopposed, but God will guard and ultimately deliver them from the power of the wicked (see Ps 82:4). God rules, not the wicked. Light, another cosmic element that is used as a symbol for God's presence and protection (see Pss 4:6; 27:1; 43:3; Mic 7:8), "is sown for the righteous" (v. 11; see the NRSV note). Thus people who live by God's rule instead of by self-will are at one with the universe as God intends it. The righteous can rejoice that, despite the wickedness around them, it is possible to be joyous (vv. 11-12; see also vv. 1, 8). The righteous are invited to acknowledge with gratitude "the remembrance of his holiness" (author's trans.; see above on Ps 30:4; note also that Psalms 93 and 99 conclude with mention of God's holiness). The good news is that God's holiness connotes not unapproachability but the willingness of the "most high" God (v. 9) to enact justice and righteousness on earth as it is in heaven.

REFLECTIONS

1. Psalm 97 is honest. It acknowledges the reality of evil and the power of the wicked, who oppose God's rule (v. 10). But behind this view of the so-called real world, the psalmist discerns and celebrates an even deeper and more profound reality: God reigns (v. 1). Like the other enthronement psalms, then, Psalm 97 is eschatological; it is an act of hope. Mays puts it as follows: "The psalm's proclamation of God's reign offers the righteous hope in their opposition to evil. When the kingdom of God is proclaimed, the righteous take courage."[370] In this sense, then, Psalm 97 is also more

370. Mays, *Psalms*, 312.

than an act of hope. It is the proclamation of and participation in a new reality in which joy and gladness are possible even *now* in the midst of evil.

Not surprisingly—since Jesus' fundamental message was identical to that of Psalm 97 (see Mark 1:14-15)—Jesus also invited his followers amid opposition and persecution to "rejoice and be glad" (Matt 5:12; cf. Ps 97:1, 12). This invitation makes sense only for those who acknowledge God's reign and accept the invitation to live under God's rule (see "kingdom of heaven" in Matt 4:17; 5:3, 10, 19-20).

2. Like Psalm 96, Psalm 97 is traditionally used on Christmas Day, and appropriately so, as Brueggemann suggests: "In Christmas the Church does not simply celebrate the birth of a wondrous baby. Through that birth we celebrate the cosmic reality that God has entered the process of the world in a decisive way that changes everything toward life. That entry of God into the process of the world is the premise of the poem in Psalm 97."[371] Christmas is also known as the festival of the *incarnation*; so involved is God in the process of the world that "the Word became flesh and lived among us" (John 1:14 NRSV). Jesus incarnated what it means to love God, to hate evil, to enact justice and righteousness. It landed him on a cross, but Jesus affirmed that this difficult way is the way that leads to life (see Matt 7:13-14; see also Mark 8:34-35).

In what we Christians profess is the ultimate demonstration of God's sovereignty, Jesus arose. God delivered him from the power of the wicked (see Ps 97:10), and light shone into what appeared to be utter darkness (Ps 97:11; see also Mark 16:2; John 1:4-5). Appropriately, Psalm 97 is also used during the season of Easter. From cradle to cross to empty tomb, God's incarnational entry into the process of the world still invites our joyful pursuit of justice and righteousness—our submission to the God we love and our opposition to the evil God calls us to hate (see Rom 12:9). To hear Psalm 97 is to make Christmas and Easter and any season "a time to reflect on the transformation wrought by God and the ethical possibility offered us in that transformation."[372] Such reflection promises a radiant joy that will not fade (v. 11).

371. Walter Brueggemann, "Psalm 97: Psalm for Christmas Day," *No Other Foundation* 7 (Winter 1986) 3.
372. Brueggemann, "Psalm 97," 6.

PSALM 98:1-9, JOY TO THE WORLD

COMMENTARY

Similar in many ways to the other enthronement psalms, especially Psalm 96 (cf. 96:1*a* with 98:1*a*; 96:11*b* with 98:7*a*; 96:13 with 98:9), Psalm 98 is nonetheless unique. The first section (vv. 1-3), for instance, features an occurrence of the word "salvation" (ישע *yš'*) in each verse, and this section primarily elaborates reasons for praise that allude to God's saving activity on behalf of Israel (vv. 1-3). The middle section (vv. 4-6) consists entirely of invitation to praise, framed by the imperative "Make a joyful noise" in vv. 4*a*, 6*b*. The invitation continues in vv. 7-8, but it is directed to elements of the created order.

The word "righteousness" (צדק *ṣedeq*) in the subsequent section (v. 9) recalls v. 2, thus linking the whole creation and "the house of Israel" (v. 3) as spheres for God's work of setting things right—that is, "salvation."

On the possible origin and ancient use of the enthronement psalms, see the Commentary on Psalms 29; 47; 93; 95; 96; and the Introduction. As for its present literary setting as part of a collection of enthronement psalms (Psalms 93; 95–99), Psalm 98 participates in the response of Book IV to the theological crisis articulated in Book III, especially in Ps 89:38-51 (see Commentary on Psalms 73;

74; 79; 80; 89; Introduction). In particular, v. 3 sounds as if it could be a direct response to the question of Ps 89:49 (see also "remember" in Pss 89:47, 50; 98:3). In addition, the recollection of the exodus in Ps 98:1-3 fits the characterization of Book IV as a Moses-book (see Psalm 90; Introduction), and the similarity between Ps 98:1-3 and Isa 52:7-10 also reinforces other indications that Book IV has been shaped in part to respond to the crisis of exile and its aftermath (see Psalms 89; 90; Introduction). Even so, as Tate suggests, "The psalm encompasses the whole range of Yahweh's victories."[373] That is to say, while it may recall the exodus and celebrate the new exodus from Babylon, Psalm 98 and its affirmation of God's reign had, and still has, ongoing significance for the people of God (see Reflections below).

98:1-3. Verse 1 is itself a brief song of praise, with an invitation (v. 1*a*; on "new song," see Ps 96:1) and reasons for praise. Every major item of vocabulary recalls Exodus 15: "song" (see Exod 15:1, 21), "marvelous things" (see Exod 15:11), "right hand" (see Exod 15:6, 12), "holy arm" (see Exod 15:11, 16), "salvation" (see Exod 15:2). The stated purpose of the exodus was that the Egyptians might know God's sovereignty (see Exod 7:5; 8:10; 9:14; 14:4, 18). Thus Ps 98:2 is also reminiscent of the exodus, and v. 3 recalls Exod 9:16, which suggests that the ultimate purpose of the exodus was to make God manifest "through all the earth." As suggested above, vv. 1-3 are also similar to Isa 52:7-10 (cf. Ps 98:3*b* with Isa 52:10*b*), and more generally, the universalistic perspective of Psalm 98 is like that of Isaiah 40–55 (see Commentary on Psalm 96). Psalm 98 thus reinforces the analogy drawn in Isaiah 40–55 between the exodus and the return of the exiles from Babylon. In effect, both events are revelatory of God's basic character, which is best summarized by the word pair "steadfast love and faithfulness" (see Exod 34:6-7; Pss 25:10; 86:15; 89:2, 14, 24, 49; 92:2; 100:5; Introduction; see also "remember" in Exod 2:24). Because the perspective of Psalm 98

373. Tate, *Psalms 51–100,* 524.

is finally eschatological (see v. 9), it invites its readers to extend the analogy as they discern manifestations of God's reign that result in justice and righteousness for the world (see Reflections below).

98:4-6. The universal perspective opened up in vv. 1-3 is reflected also in the invitation in v. 4 addressed to "all the earth" (see Pss 96:1, 9; 97:1; 100:1). Each invited action is an appropriate way to acknowledge God's sovereignty and to pay joyful, enthusiastic homage—"make a joyful noise" (see Pss 47:1; 95:1-2), sing a "joyous song" (see Pss 95:1; 96:12; Isa 52:8), "sing praises" (see Pss 47:6-7; 149:3*a*). The human voice is to be accompanied by full instrumentation (see Pss 33:2-3; 47:5; 149:3; 150:3).

98:7-8. But a human choir and its instrumental accompaniment are not sufficient response to God's reign. The whole creation will respond (vv. 7-8; see also Ps 96:11-12). In ancient Near Eastern creation accounts, the sea and the "floods" represent chaotic forces that oppose in battle the sovereignty of the supreme creator-God (see Ps 93:3-4). Thus vv. 7-8 call to mind the image of God as divine warrior, who subjected hostile forces to create the world (vv. 7-8) as well as to create and re-create God's people (vv. 1-3; the NRSV assumes this background with its decision to use "victory" instead of "salvation"). Psalm 98 is a witness, therefore, to a God whose choice of a particular people, and whose activity on their behalf, are for the ultimate purpose of fulfilling God's purposes for the whole creation (see Gen 12:1-3; Isa 2:2-4; 19:19-25; 42:5-9; 49:6; see also Commentary on Psalms 33; 65; 66; 93).

98:9. This verse points to the same conclusion (see Ps 96:13). God's coming is to establish justice for "the earth" and to set things right (see v. 2) for "the world." It is no mere local action that is envisioned. God's equitable treatment (see "equity" in Pss 9:8; 96:10; 99:4) includes not just *a* people but *the* peoples. God so loves the world.

REFLECTIONS

Psalm 98 proclaims exuberantly the message that pervades and forms the theological heart of the psalter: God reigns (see Introduction). Like other enthronement psalms, Psalm 98 presents justice and righteousness as the essence of the worldwide policy that God wills and enacts (vv. 2, 9). Psalm 98 also makes it clear that this policy is motivated by God's faithfulness and love (v. 3). In short, the good news is that God rules the universe with faithfulness and love, and the ecumenical, ecological, economic, social, and political implications of this message are profound (see Reflections on Psalms 29; 47; 93; 95; 96; 97; 99; see also Psalms 2; 19; 65–68).

Although the enemies of God are not explicitly mentioned in Psalm 98, they are implied, and the larger literary context of the psalter makes it clear that the assertion of God's sovereignty never goes unopposed. In short, Psalm 98 is eschatological. Its eschatological orientation (see Commentary on Psalm 2; Introduction), as well as the way it draws an analogy between the exodus and the return from exile, encouraged the people of God to continue to apply it analogically and to use it to profess their conviction that God reigns. For instance, the early Christians, who knew that Jesus proclaimed the reign of God (see Mark 1:14-15), also saw in Jesus the ultimate embodiment of God's reign. They experienced in Jesus a king/messiah who lovingly and faithfully enacted justice and righteousness for all people; they experienced his ministry as salvation; and they sang Psalm 98 as a song about Jesus. In response to the announcement of Jesus' birth, Mary interpreted the upcoming event as God's "remembrance of his mercy" (Luke 1:54 NRSV; see also Ps 98:3).[374]

Appropriately, then, Psalm 98 is traditionally used on Christmas Day (see also Psalms 96–97). Such use affirms the Christian conviction that the birth of Jesus Christ belongs with exodus and return from exile in the sequence of God's marvelous doings (v. 1). In fact, although they may not recognize it as such, most Christians are probably familiar with Psalm 98 primarily in the metrical version through Isaac Watts's hymn "Joy to the World." To sing Psalm 98 to greet the birth of Jesus affirms that this event had and has cosmic significance (see Commentary on Psalm 29); it changed and changes the world. To be sure, it seems strange that the birth of a humble baby should signal God's cosmic rule, but the strangeness is a hint of things to come. This baby would finally enact from a cross God's sovereign claim upon the world. The cross of Christ reveals a strength made perfect in weakness (see 2 Cor 12:9), and so it is appropriate that Psalm 98 is traditionally used at the Easter Vigil and during the season of Easter. This rhythm of liturgical use is a reminder that the incarnation, the crucifixion, and the resurrection together proclaim the good news that God so loves the world and that together they portray a divine sovereignty manifest, not as sheer force, but as sheer love.

374. See Mays, *Psalms*, 314.

PSALM 99:1-9, THE LORD OUR GOD IS HOLY

COMMENTARY

Psalm 99 is the conclusion of a collection of enthronement psalms (Psalm 93, 95–99) that form the theological heart of the psalter and appear to be strategically placed to respond to the crisis articulated in Book III, especially Ps 89:38-51 and its lament over the failure of the Davidic covenant (see Commentary on Psalms 73; 74; 79; 80; 89;

Introduction). Book IV responds to Book III by proclaiming God's reign and by offering a pre-Davidic, Mosaic perspective—a reminder that Moses proclaimed the reign of God (Exod 15:18) before there was land, Temple, or monarchy. In this regard, it is crucial that Book IV begins with the only psalm attributed to Moses (Psalm 90), and it is significant that Psalm 99, the climactic enthronement psalm, explicitly mentions Moses and Aaron (v. 6; see also Pss 103:7; 105:26; 106:16, 23, 32), as well as Samuel, who opposed the formation of the monarchy on the grounds that only God could properly be considered Israel's king (see 1 Sam 8:1-18).

It is revealing, too, that there are numerous verbal links between Psalm 99 and Exod 15:1-18, the song of praise that Moses and the Israelites sang after being delivered from Egypt. Both songs celebrate God's reign (v. 1; Exod 15:18). In both, God is to be "exalted" (vv. 2, 5, 9; Exod 15:2), because God is "great" (vv. 2-3; see "might" in Exod 15:16 NRSV), "awesome" (v. 3; Exod 15:11), "mighty" (v. 4; see "strength" in Exod 15:2, 13), and "holy" (vv. 3, 5, 9; Exod 15:11, 13). In both songs, people "tremble" (v. 1; Exod 15:14), and in both, God is established in God's own place (vv. 1-2, 5, 9; Exod 15:13, 17). It seems as if Psalm 99 intentionally recalls Exod 15:1-18 as a way of affirming for a later generation—discouraged by events like those described in Book III—that God *still* reigns. In the context of the book of Psalms, and in the context of the world as we know it, this affirmation is made in the face of opposition to God's reign. That is to say, it is eschatological, and it calls every generation to make the decision to live under God's rule (see Psalm 2; Introduction). On the possible origin and ancient use of Psalm 99 and the other enthronement psalms, see the Commentary on Psalms 29; 47; 93; 95; 96; and the Introduction.

While Psalm 99 has much in common with the other enthronement psalms, including the theme of holiness (see Pss 29:2; 47:8; 93:5; 96:9; 97:12; 98:1), it is unique in its use of the theme of holiness as a pervasive structuring concept. The phrase "Holy is he!" in vv. 3, 5 divides the psalm into three sections: vv. 1-3, vv. 4-5, vv. 6-9. Verses 5 and 9 are nearly identical, and v. 9 has two more

occurrences of the key word "holy" (קדוש *qādôš*). Holiness, in its fundamental sense, designates the awesome presence of God that evoked fear and required human beings to keep their distance or to approach God only after making special preparations or taking special precautions (see Exod 19:7-25, esp. v. 23; 20:18-21). This fundamental sense is reflected in Ps 99:1-3; the presence of God causes people to "tremble" and the earth to "quake" (v. 1; see also Exod 19:16; 20:18, although the Hebrew words translated "trembled" are both different from the one in Ps 99:1; the same observation also applies to Pss 96:9; 97:4). As the psalm proceeds, however, holiness is defined in very different terms. Rather than keeping humans at a distance, God relates to them, doing justice and righteousness (v. 4), answering cries (vv. 6, 8), and both forgiving and holding accountable (v. 8).

99:1-3. In addition to reflecting the fundamental sense of holiness, vv. 1-3 introduce the striking claim that while God's sovereignty is universal, it is focused "in Zion" (v. 2). God's enthronement "upon the cherubim" (v. 1) also indicates the centrality of Jerusalem. The reference is apparently to the ark, which was understood symbolically as God's throne (see Ps 80:1). The particularity of v. 1 continues throughout the psalm. God's "footstool" is another reference to the ark (v. 5; see also 1 Chr 28:2; Ps 132:7), and God's "holy mountain" is Zion (v. 9; see also Pss 2:6; 15:1; 43:3; 48:1). In short, Jerusalem is the earthly locus of the presence and power of God (see Psalms 46; 48; 76; 84; 87; 122), who is nonetheless a cosmic sovereign (see "awesome" in Ps 47:2 and "great" in Pss 47:2; 95:3; 96:4).

99:4-5. By insisting on the particularity of Zion, vv. 1-3 have already begun to suggest that the holy God is not entirely separable from human places and matters. Verses 4-5 now indicate just how intimate God's involvement actually is. As the NRSV note suggests, v. 4a is somewhat problematic, but it can be construed as follows: "The strength of a king (is to be) one who loves justice" (see Ps 72:1-2). The implication is that God loves justice, for God does "justice and righteousness" (see Pss 9:7-8; 96:13; 97:2; 98:9; see "equity" in Pss 9:8; 96:10; 98:9). In other words, God is not enthroned above the struggle for rightly ordered human relatedness; rather, God is intimately involved in it. The shift to direct address of God in v. 4 reinforces this message, and the personal pronoun provides emphasis: *"you* have done. . . . " As the prophetic books make clear, justice and righteousness have to do with the concrete, daily realities of human existence and relatedness, especially provision for the poor and needy (see Amos 5:7-13, 21-24; Mic 3:1-12; 6:6-8). Indeed, as Psalm 82 suggests, doing justice and righteousness is the fundamental criterion of divinity. For God, holiness ultimately means not transcendence but immanence, not inseparability but involvement.

99:6-9. These verses portray even more clearly the tension between transcendence and immanence. In other words, for the holy God to be involved with humankind means that God has a problem. What Moses, Aaron, and Samuel called on God about was the people's sinfulness (see Exod 32:7-14; Num 16:20-22; 1 Sam 7:5-11). The "pillar of cloud" (v. 7; see also Exod 13:21-22; 14:19, 24; 33:9-10; Num 12:5; 14:14) represented God's presence with the people throughout the exodus and wilderness experience. Although v. 7 indicates that the people "kept his decrees . . . and statutes," the wilderness was actually characterized by distrust, complaining, and disobedience (see v. 8) that necessitated intercession by Moses and Aaron. God "answered" (vv. 6, 8), and that answer inevitably involved forgiveness (note the shift to direct address of God in v. 8 and another emphatic "you" in v. 8*a*). Only by God's grace did the people continue to exist (v. 8*b*), but God continued to demand the people's obedience (v. 8*c*). Herein lies God's problem: how to be both a forgiving God and "an avenger of their wrongdoings." Verse 8 portrays the same tension that is evident in God's self-revelation to Moses in Exod 34:6-7. God's holiness ultimately involves not God's avoidance of sin and sinners but God's willingness to bear the burden of sin (v. 8; the Hebrew word translated "forgiving" [נשׂא *nāśā*] means lit. "to bear," "to carry") and to love sinners.

REFLECTIONS

What has been said about the other enthronement psalms applies to Psalm 99 (see Reflections on Psalms 29; 47; 93; 95; 96; 97; 98); however, it is fitting that the final enthronement psalm brings into sharpest focus the issue of the nature of God's sovereignty. A popular notion of sovereignty equates it with the fundamental sense of holiness—that is, absolute freedom, transcendence, and unapproachability. Thus it is significant that Psalm 99 pushes toward a redefinition of holiness in the direction of involvement and committed, forgiving love.

1. In a word, the theology of Psalm 99 is *incarnational* (see Commentary on Psalm 97). God is involved with a particular place (vv. 1-2, 5, 9) and with particular people (vv. 6-8) in the struggle for justice and righteousness (v. 4). Christians affirm a scandalous particularity that is analogous. Replacing Zion and the Temple (see Mark 13:1-2; 14:58; 15:29), Jesus became the earthly locus of God's presence and power, the focus and revelation of God's glory (see John 1:14-18). The incarnation of Jesus is the ultimate redefinition of holiness: God resides in human flesh! Psalm 99, however, evidences already the redefinition of God's holiness, which culminates in the incarnation. And in the tension represented in v. 8 between God's forgiving and God's holding accountable, it is not difficult to discern the shape of a cross. God's sovereignty is manifested ultimately in suffering love, a manner that appears to the world to be weakness (see 1 Cor 1:22-25; 2 Cor 12:9).

2. Psalm 99 is used traditionally on Transfiguration Sunday. The association of Psalm 99 with the transfiguration may be due to the Gospel accounts' mention of Moses and the cloud (see Matt 17:1-8; Mark 9:2-9; Luke 9:28-36), but there is a deeper connection. The transfiguration is a scene that partakes of the fundamental sense of holiness; Jesus is set apart and unapproachable, and the disciples are terrified. In each Gospel, however, the transfiguration follows immediately Jesus' first announcement that he must go to Jerusalem to suffer, die, and be raised. Like Psalm 99, this juxtaposition pushes toward a redefinition of holiness and sovereignty in the direction of committed involvement and suffering love. Defying the conventional notion of holiness and the worldly definition of royal power, God is the Holy One who is persistently present in our midst (see Hos 11:9). Because the Holy One is committed to being with us and enacting justice and righteousness among us, it is fitting that Jesus taught us to pray, "hallowed be thy name; thy kingdom come, thy will be done, *on earth* as it is in heaven."

PSALM 100:1-5, KNOW THAT THE LORD IS GOD

COMMENTARY

Although Psalm 100 is not ordinarily considered a part of the collection of enthronement psalms (Psalms 93; 95–99), it has many affinities with this collection. Given the similarity between Psalms 95 and 100 (cf. Pss 95:7 with 100:3), one can reasonably conclude that they are intended to form a frame around Psalms 96–99, which seem to form the core of the collection.[375] In any case, Psalm 100 shares much of the vocabulary of the preceding psalms (see references below), and it certainly serves admirably as a conclusion to the preceding collection, regardless of whether it was intended to do so. (On the literary placement of the collection and the role of Psalms 93–100 and Book IV as a whole, see Commentary on Psalms 90; 93; 99; Introduction). It is not clear exactly how to construe the superscription. The Hebrew word rendered "thanksgiving" (תודה *tôdâ*) can designate an actual sacrifice, but it can also denote liturgical expressions of gratitude that apparently served as substitutes for sacrifice (see Ps 50:14, 23). The word recurs in v. 4 (see also Ps 95:2), and the same root in verbal form also occurs in v. 4 (see Ps 97:12). Thus the origin and ancient use of Psalm 100 are unclear, but it is certain that Psalm 100 would have been used in some liturgical setting (see "gates" and "courts" in v. 4), perhaps in conjunction with Psalms 93; 95–99. (See Commentary on Psalm 96 for the possible origin and use of the enthronement psalms.)

In a sense, Psalm 100 demonstrates the typical structure of a song of praise: invitation to praise (vv. 1-4), followed by reasons for praise (v. 5). In this case, the invitation is predominant. Within this apparently regular structure, however, v. 3 stands out. Like vv. 1, 2, 4, it begins with an imperative, but the invited action is different. It invites the hearer to "know" something that underlies all action, and it is followed immediately by instruction about God and God's people. Furthermore, v. 3 is the central verse in the psalm; the imperative in v. 3 is the central one in a series of seven (there are three imperatives in vv. 1-2 and three in v. 4). In short, while all the songs of praise are implicitly instructional (note the reasons for praise), the structure and content of Psalm 100 focus attention on v. 3, which gives the psalm an explicitly instructional quality.

100:1-2. In keeping with the perspective of the enthronement psalms and other songs of praise, the invitation in v. 1 is addressed to "all the earth" (see Pss 66:1; 96:1, 9; 97:1; 98:3; 99:1). The underlying rationale is that a cosmic sovereign deserves nothing less than a cosmic response. To "make a joyful noise" is an appropriate way to acknowledge and to greet a monarch (see Pss 95:1-2; 98:4, 6). To summon any congregation less than "all the earth" is to misunderstand the identity of Israel's God.

The imperative "worship" (עבד *'ābad*) in v. 2 also bespeaks God's sovereignty. While

---

375. See Tate, *Psalms 51–100*, 535.

the Hebrew root can mean "worship," this translation probably does not convey satisfactorily the comprehensiveness of the term. The word means to orient one's whole life and existence to a sovereign master, to be the servant or slave of a monarch. The word always occurs in the psalter in relation to a royal figure, either human or divine (see Pss 2:11; 18:43; 22:30; 72:11; 97:7; 102:22).[376] The imagery of royalty also includes the imperative to "come into his presence" (see 1 Kgs 1:28, 32), as well as to "bless" in v. 4 (see "kneel" in Ps 95:6; see also Ps 96:2). The inseparability of service and sovereignty is also clear in other contexts. For instance, the culminating affirmation of the people following the exodus is "the LORD will reign forever and ever" (Exod 15:18 NRSV). This proclamation of God's sovereignty is congruent with the stated goal of the exodus that the people may "serve" God (see Exod 4:23; 7:16; 8:20; 9:1, 13; 10:3; 12:31). Thus it is probably not coincidental that one of the only two occurrences of the imperative "Serve the LORD" is in Ps 100:2, immediately following the explicit proclamation of God's reign in Psalms 93; 95–99. In terms of the shape of the psalter, it is revealing that the other occurrence is in Ps 2:11. In short, Psalm 100 and the other songs of praise are fundamentally about precisely what Psalm 2 suggests the whole psalter will be about: the reign of God (see Introduction).

100:3-5. As suggested above, the lone imperative in v. 3 stands out; Psalm 100 explicitly intends to teach. A literal translation of v. 3 makes the nature of the teaching even clearer:

Know that YHWH, he (is) God,
He made us, and not we,
  his people (are we) and the sheep of his
  pasture.

The clustering of personal pronouns and pronominal suffixes in v. 3 is striking, as is their sequence: "he . . . he . . . us . . . we . . .

his . . . his." This arrangement dramatically suggests that the question of human identity must begin and end with God. This is what the psalm intends for us to "know." As Mays points out, v. 3 is a variation on what Zimmerli identified as the "recognition formula" ("and you will know that I am Yahweh"), which always follows a description of God's activity (see Ezek 5:13; 6:7; see also Exod 7:5; 8:10; 9:14; 14:4, 18; see above on Ps 98:2).[377] Here the imperative introduces a description of God's activity. There is a rich ambiguity in the word "made" (עשׂה 'āśâ); it could refer to God's creation of the world and all living things (see Pss 95:5; 104:24), or it could refer to God's "making" or electing Israel as God's own people (see Deut 32:6, 15; see above on Ps 95:6, where the same ambiguity is present). The ambiguity is appropriate, for Israel could never tell the story of its election apart from an understanding of God's intention for "all the earth" (v. 1; see Commentary on Psalms 33; 65; 66; 93; 98). The reasons for praise in v. 5 also point in both directions. The word "good" (טוב ṭôb) recalls the recurrent evaluation of God's creative activity in Genesis 1, while "steadfast love" (חסד ḥesed) and "faithfulness" (אמונה 'ĕmûnâ) recall God's self-revelation to Moses (see Exod 34:6-7; Introduction) immediately prior to the reestablishment of a covenant with the people (see Exod 34:10).

Verse 5 also recalls Ps 98:3, where steadfast love and faithfulness to Israel are mentioned in the context of the proclamation of God's reign (see also Pss 86:15; 89:2, 14, 49; 92:2; 117:2). The same proclamation is implicit in Psalm 100, and it is reinforced by the sheep/shepherd imagery in v. 3. In the ancient Near East, kings were known as the shepherds of their people (see Ezek 34:1-10). Psalm 100 wants us to know that God is shepherd both of God's people and of the whole cosmos (see Pss 23:1; 74:1; 80:1; 95:7; Ezek 34:11-16). The only proper response is joyful gratitude and praise (vv. 1-2, 4; see also Pss 95:1-2; 96:11; 97:1, 8, 12; 98:4-6) that bespeaks the offering of one's whole self in service (v. 2) to the ruler of the world.

---

376. See James L. Mays, "Worship, World, and Power," *Int.* 23 (1969) 321.

377. Mays, "Worship, World, and Power," 319.

REFLECTIONS

1. Psalm 100 is perhaps the most familiar of the songs of praise. Mays observes: "Were the statistics known, Psalm 100 would probably prove to be the song most often chanted from within the history that runs from the Israelite temple on Mount Zion to the synagogues and churches spread across the earth."[378]

Psalm 100 is certainly the banner hymn of the Reformed tradition. A metrical version of the psalm, "All People That on Earth Do Dwell," was composed by William Kethe, a friend of John Knox, in 1561. The tune by Louis Bourgeois, musical composer for John Calvin, became known as *Old Hundreth,* even though it was originally composed for a paraphrase of Psalm 134.[379] *Old Hundredth* is now the tune that accompanies words that many Christian congregations know simply as "The Doxology" (lit., "the word of glory/praise").

2. The appeal of Psalm 100 may lie in part in its brevity and simplicity, as well as in its explicitly instructional tone. The lesson itself is remarkably simple yet deeply profound: God rules the world, and consequently we belong to God. This message lies not only at the heart of the book of Psalms but also at the heart of Jesus' preaching and of the whole of Scripture (see Commentary on Psalms 29; 47; 93; 95–99). In a quite different context, the apostle Paul taught essentially the same lesson: "Or do you not *know* that your body is a temple of the Holy Spirit within you, which you have from God, and that *you are not your own?* For you were bought with a price; therefore *glorify God* in your body" (2 Cor 6:19-20 NRSV, italics added).

We are not our own! This is a difficult lesson to hear and to get across in a culture that encourages us to be "self-made" men and women. Most of us seem to believe the popular saying, "It's *my* life to live." The Bible insists, however, that our lives are not simply our own to live. Genuine life is found in submission to God. In biblical terms, to live is to praise God, and to praise God is to live. As Claus Westermann puts it, to praise anything or anyone other than God "must disturb and finally destroy life itself."[380]

From this perspective, Psalm 100 is an "act of sanity," as Brueggemann calls it:

> Obviously our world is at the edge of insanity and we with it. Inhumaneness is developed as a scientific enterprise. Greed is celebrated as economic advance. Power runs unbridled to destructiveness.
>
> In a world like this one, our psalm is an act of sanity, whereby we may be "reclothed in our rightful minds" (cf. Mark 5:15). . . . Life is no longer self-grounded without thanks but rooted in thanks.[381]

Brueggemann cites Geoffrey Wainwright, who has pointed out what is undoubtedly true: "The world is not an easy place in which to live doxologically."[382] But as difficult as it may be, to live doxologically is of paramount importance, for to praise anything or anyone other than God "must disturb and finally destroy life itself." At this point, Psalm 100 offers essentially the same instruction as Psalms 1–2. To be happy means submission to God—openness to God's instruction (1:2) and primary dependence on God rather than self (2:12). To be wicked is to be an autonomous self, and "a wicked life leads only to ruin" (Ps 1:6).[383]

---

378. Mays, "Worship, World, and Power," 316.
379. See Prothero, *The Psalms in Human Life and Experience,* 114.
380. Westermann, *Praise and Lament in the Psalms,* 161.
381. Walter Brueggemann, "Psalm 100," *Int.* 39 (1985) 67.
382. Geoffrey Wainwright, *Doxology* (New York: Oxford University Press, 1980) 425; see Brueggemann, "Psalm 100," 69.
383. The translation is that of Gary Chamberlain, *The Psalms: A New Translation for Prayer and Worship* (Nashville: The Upper Room, 1984) 26.

Because the Reformed tradition has so treasured Psalm 100, it is fitting that its essential instruction is contained in the first question and answer of the Westminster Shorter Catechism:

Question: What is the chief end of humankind?
Answer: The chief end of humankind is to glorify God and enjoy God forever.

PSALM 101:1-8, I WILL SING OF YOUR LOVE AND JUSTICE

COMMENTARY

Psalm 101 has always been something of an enigma to commentators. It is best viewed as a royal psalm in which the king was the original speaker. The king's question in v. 2, which the NIV translates more accurately, is primary for considering the origin, ancient use, and literary setting of Psalm 101. Without the question, Psalm 101 would make good sense as a pledge or oath of office that the king might have recited at his coronation, following the assumption of office (see Psalm 2) and perhaps appropriate ceremonial prayers (see Psalm 72). Indeed, it is possible that the psalm was written and used for this purpose, but the question in v. 2 seems inappropriate. If it is not considered a later addition or emended somehow, it has the force of a plea for help and gives the rest of the psalm the character of a complaint (see the questions in Pss 42:2; 119:82, 84 and the similar "How long?" in Pss 6:3; 74:10; 94:3). That is to say, the king professes his loyalty and good behavior as a basis for asking when he will experience God's presence and favor—a reasonable question in view of Ps 18:20-30, another royal psalm (see Ps 18:25, where "loyal" and "blameless" occur as in Ps 101:1-2). In fact, in view of the similarities between Psalms 18 and 101, Leslie Allen categorizes Psalm 101 as a royal complaint and concludes:

Psalm 18 looks back to God's intervention in response to the king's appeal and testimonial, and gives thanks that he was delivered from a situation of distress. Psalm 101 is set at an earlier stage in royal experience.[384]

384. Leslie C. Allen, *Psalms 101–150*, WBC 21 (Waco, Tex.: Word, 1983) 6.

While this conclusion makes sense chronologically, it raises questions about the literary placement of Psalms 18 and 101: If Psalm 101 reflects an earlier stage of royal experience, why is it placed after Psalms 18? Then, too, since Psalm 89 suggests the failure of the covenant with David and the disappearance of the monarchy (see Commentary on Psalm 89; Introduction), why are there any royal psalms at all in Books IV and V (see Psalms 110; 144)? Assuming the placement is not simply haphazard, one can respond that in its current literary setting, the royal complaint in Psalm 101 is a response to the destruction of the monarchy, as are Psalms 90–100 (see Commentary on Psalms 90; 93; Introduction). The voice of an imagined future king says, in effect, "I shall do everything right," implying that the monarchy should be restored; the question in v. 2 thus asks when the restoration will occur. The cogency of this approach is strengthened by the juxtaposition of Psalm 101 with 102, which, while it starts out as an individual prayer (perhaps still to be heard as the voice of a king?), suddenly in v. 12 becomes an expression of hope for the restoration of Zion, the seat of the monarchy (cf. 101:2 with 102:13), as well as an expression of hope for the return of the exiles (vv. 18-22). Thus Psalms 101–102 together address the three key elements of the crisis of exile—loss of monarchy, Zion/Temple, and land. This loss is documented in Book III, to which Book IV responds (see Psalm 90; Introduction), and Thus Psalms 101–102 can be construed as a part of that response. Even if this proposal is incorrect, it is clear that as years passed without the restoration of the monarchy, Psalm 101 would have been read either messianically or perhaps as a recital of what God intends for the whole people, as well as for faithful individuals (see Reflections below).

Scholars offer a wide variety of proposals for understanding the structure and movement of Psalm 101, probably because the frequent repetitions point in several directions. The complexity may suggest that the structure moves on more than one level. Verses 1-2a introduce what the whole psalm is about, which can be summarized with the key word "blameless"/"integrity" (תמים *tāmîm*, vv. 2ab, 6). Many commentators take vv. 2b-4 as the next section (the king's own behavior), and vv. 5-8 as the final section (the king's enforcement of integrity). This makes sense, but the sevenfold listing of negative behaviors in vv. 3-5 also suggests that vv. 2b-5 form a coherent unit that begins and ends with the word "heart" (לבב *lēbāb*, vv. 2b, 5b; see also v. 4). In this view, vv. 6-8 form the final section, which begins and ends with the word "land" (ארץ *'ereṣ*, vv. 6a, 8a). The two sections are characterized by four repeated terms or phrases that occur in the same order in each: "blameless"/"integrity" (vv. 2b, 6b), "in my house" (vv. 2b, 7a), "before my eyes"/"in my presence" (vv. 3a, 7b; see "eyes" in vv. 5b, 6a NIV), and "destroy" (vv. 5a, 8a).

A further structural feature is a chiastic pattern of repetition (see Introduction) that also links the two sections (my literal translations):[385]

A v. 3a "before my eyes"
  B v. 3a "*speech* of worthlessness"
    C v. 3b "those *doing* crooked (things)"
      D v. 5b "haughtiness of *eyes*"
      D' v. 6a "my *eyes* (are upon)"
    C' v. 7a "those *doing* deceit"
  B' v. 7b "those *speaking* lies"
A' v. 7b "before my eyes"

The word "eyes" (עינים *'ênayim*) lies on the boundaries and at the center of the chiastic pattern, thus suggesting that the king sees all (vv. 3a, 7b) but watches out for "the faithful" (v. 6a) in contrast to the arrogant.

385. See John S. Kselman, "Psalm 101: Royal Confession and Divine Oracle," *JSOT* 33 (1985) 47.

Each poetic line at the center of the pattern is linked by repetition to the verse that either opens or concludes each major section of the poem but does not figure in the pattern (see "heart" in vv. 5b, 2b, and see "land" in vv. 6a, 8a). Again, the effect is to contrast integrity with arrogance (vv. 2b, 5b) and faithfulness with wickedness (vv. 6a, 8a). The king chooses and supports God's values—the way of integrity, which embodies loyalty and justice (vv. 1-2a).

101:1-2a. Singing indicates celebration (see Pss 47:6; 96:1; 98:1, 4-5), and what the king celebrates are the characteristics of God's reign. The word translated "loyalty" (חסד *ḥesed*) is usually rendered "steadfast love" in the NRSV; it characterizes God's very being (see Exod 34:6-7; Pss 5:7; 13:5; Introduction) as well as the way God exercises sovereignty (see Pss 89:1-2, 14; 98:3), including the way God relates to the king, the earthly agent of God's rule (see Pss 18:25; 18:50; 21:7; 89:24, 28, 33, 49; 2 Sam 7:15). The word "justice" (משפט *mišpāṭ*) also describes the policy that God wills and enacts as sovereign (see Pss 9:7-8; 89:14; 96:13; 97:2; 98:9; 99:4), as well as what God intends for the earthly king to will and enact (see Ps 72:1-2, 4). Similarly, blamelessness or integrity is rooted in God's character, as Psalm 18 makes clear. God's way is one of integrity (18:30), and God deals with integrity with those who have dealt likewise with God (18:25), and this includes the king (18:23). God's integrity or blamelessness involves God's faithfulness and dependability; human integrity or blamelessness means not moral perfection but the commitment to live according to the priorities of and in dependence upon God (see Commentary on Psalms 15; 18). The king implies this commitment in v. 1 and indicates it more explicitly in v. 2a. The verb translated "study"/"be careful" (שכל *śākal*) recalls Ps 2:10, where it is used as a warning to all kings of the earth to "be wise"—that is, to serve God (see Ps 100:2).

Having made this commitment, the king asks when he can expect the treatment promised in Ps 18:25. This question in its current literary setting may once have functioned as a plea for restoration of the monarchy; in any case, it gives the psalm a future orientation. Other interpreters view the question in v. 2 as evidence of the king's ritual humiliation in an annual cultic drama or as a general plea for assurance or as the king's request for the kind of revelation that Solomon received in a dream in 1 Kings 3.[386]

101:2b-5. After the reaffirmation to pursue integrity (v. 2*b*), vv. 3-5 offer a list of seven things that the king will avoid or abolish. Seven is often symbolic of completeness, and this symbolism would be very appropriate in a psalm in which a key word is "integrity" (תמים *tāmîm*), the Hebrew root of which means "to be complete, whole." In other words, the king completely avoids evil. There is a similar list of seven in Prov 6:16-19, and several scholars detect the influence of the wisdom literature here. This is not unlikely, but several of the negative behaviors are also mentioned elsewhere in the psalms. For instance, "vile thing" in v. 3*a* occurs as "vile disease" in 41:8, and "perverse(ness)" in v. 4*a* occurs in Ps 18:26. This word occurs also in Prov 10:9; 11:20, where it is explicitly the opposite of "integrity"/"blameless." Perversity or crookedness, along with arrogance (v. 5*b*; see also Ps 138:6), forms the primary contrast to the integrity that the king advocates and embodies. Silencing or destroying the wicked (v. 5*a*; see also v. 8*a*) is something ordinarily reserved for God (see Pss 54:6; 94:23), but the king is to be the agent of God's rule (see Ps 18:40). The list of behaviors in

vv. 3-5 is reminiscent of Psalm 15 (see 15:3-5), where the issue of entrance to the Temple begins with integrity or blamelessness (see 15:1-2*a*). Kraus even suggests that Psalm 101 casts the king in the role of "the guardian of the Torah of the [temple] gate."[387]

101:6-8. Using much of the same vocabulary as vv. 2*b*-5, vv. 6-8 drive home the point. The king will support and surround himself with people of integrity. The gatekeeping function of the king is called to mind again by the mention of "deceit" (רמיה *rěmiyyâ*) in v. 7*a*, since deceitfulness also disqualifies one from entering the Temple in Ps 24:4. Given what could be considered the redundancy of vv. 2*b*-5 and vv. 6-8, Kselman suggests that vv. 6-8 be considered a divine oracle delivered to the king by a cultic prophet—the answer, as it were, to the king's question in v. 2 about God's coming to him.[388] To be sure, this is a possible construal of vv. 6-8, since what may be intended as divine speech can occur with no introduction (Kselman cites Ps 32:8-9). Kselman's proposal has the advantage of emphasizing clearly the ideal that the earthly king be the embodiment of divine sovereignty, but this is clear enough from Psalm 101 without Kselman's proposal, which remains highly speculative. The king pursues God's way of integrity, which is embodied in love and justice.

386. See Th. Booij, "Psalm CI 2—'When Wilt Thou Come to Me?'" *VT* 38 (1988) 460.

387. Kraus, *Psalms 60–150*, 279.
388. Kselman, "Psalm 101," 52-57.

REFLECTIONS

1. Psalm 101 may have originated as a king's oath of office, and it was probably placed in Book IV to serve as a hopeful plea in the aftermath of exile. Even so, Psalm 101 has the potential to speak to and be useful for the people of God in a variety of circumstances. With the disappearance of the monarchy and the eventual realization that it would never be reinstituted, Psalm 101 could at least be understood as an articulation of the values that God wills to be concretely embodied among humans—love, justice, integrity. Furthermore, the psalm is implicitly a profession of faith in God's sovereignty. The psalmist begins by affirming God's steadfast love and justice, aspects of God's reign, and the psalmist makes a commitment to pursue love and justice, even in the apparent absence of God (see the question in v. 2*a*). In short, the psalmist depends ultimately not on his or her good behavior but on God's coming.

2. Because the early Christians saw in Jesus a representation of God's values and a commitment to pursue love and justice even in the apparent absence of God—the cross (see Mark 15:34, quoting Ps 22:1)—they heard Psalm 101 as Jesus' instruction to the faithful in all times and places. In a sense, the psalm has been democratized, as Mays suggests, although he also recognizes that it remains especially pertinent for those who govern:

> The psalm teaches that it is not enough for those who lead to live by the legalities and govern by codes. It is the character of the governor and the character of those in his government that really determine what the effect of their governing is on the governed. In this the psalm is radical, but history is replete with examples that prove it is right. The psalm also teaches that conduct depends on character and character is shaped by ultimate commitments. It would insist that "you cannot be good without God," a lesson for more than rulers.[389]

In a society where the word *politician* has become almost synonymous with *crooked* and where much speech—for instance, advertising—is designed to mislead, the invitation of Psalm 101 is particularly timely: that we speak and embody the truth in love as a witness to God's claim upon our lives and our world (see Eph 4:15).

389. Mays, *Psalms*, 322.

PSALM 102:1-28, GOD HEARS THE PRAYER OF THE DESTITUTE

COMMENTARY

Psalm 102 begins like an individual prayer for help or lament/complaint (vv. 1-11), but then it makes a sudden shift. A brief ascription of praise is followed by an expression of hope for and confidence in the restoration of Zion (vv. 12-17) and of hope for the return of the exiles (vv. 18-22). Verses 23-24 return the focus to individual complaint and plea, but then vv. 25-28 again shift to praise, followed by an expression of confidence in the people's future. The presence of both individual and corporate material has been particularly problematic for form critics. As Allen states, "A bewildering multiplicity of interpretations have been offered for this complex psalm."[390]

It is possible, for instance, to conclude that the king was the original individual speaker (see Psalm 101) and that he spoke on behalf of the whole people. Or perhaps the prayer of an individual, seemingly one who was sick, served as the basis for post-exilic additions to create a corporate prayer. Or perhaps an individual in the post-exilic era simply included a prayer for the nation in the midst of his or her prayers for self. Certainty concerning the origin and ancient use of Psalm 102 remains

390. Allen, *Psalms 101–150*, 11.

elusive. What should be noted is that the character of Psalm 102 is quite appropriate for its present literary setting in Book IV, which serves as a response to the crisis of exile and its aftermath, and is presented in Book III (see Commentary on Psalms 73; 74; 79; 80; 89; Introduction). Like Psalm 90, which it recalls at several points (see vv. 4, 10-11, 23-28), Psalm 102 grounds hope for the future in God's eternity. And like the enthronement psalms, which serve as the core of Book IV (see Psalms 93; 95–99), Psalm 102 is a proclamation of God's reign (see esp. vv. 12, 15-16). Psalms 101–102 together deal with the three crucial aspects of the exilic crisis—loss of monarchy, Temple/Zion, and land (see Commentary on Psalm 101)—by grounding hope in God's coming (101:2) and God's enduring presence (102:26-28).

The superscription is one of the very few that accurately describes the actual content of the following psalm. The state of affliction applies to both sections—Zion's need (vv. 12-17) as well as that of the individual (vv. 1-11, 23-24)—and the word "afflicted"/ "poor"/"oppressed"/"weak" (עני *ʿānî*) is used frequently in the psalms to designate a category of people whom God is particularly committed to helping (see Pss 9:12, 18; 10:2, 9, 12; 25:16; 35:10; 37:14; 74:19, 21; 86:1; see also Exod 3:7, 17; 4:3). The sufferers in the psalms also describe themselves elsewhere as "faint" (see Pss 61:2; 77:3; 142:3; 143:4; 107:5; see also Lam 2:11-12, 19, which describe the effects of the destruction that led to exile), and they describe their prayers as "lament" or "complaint" (see Pss 55:2; 64:1; and esp. 142:2, which uses the idiom of pouring out the complaint).

102:1-2. As is often the case, the prayer begins with petition that God hear (v. 1*a*), and the prayer is more specifically designated a "cry for help" (v. 1*b*; see also Exod 2:23; Pss 18:6; 34:15; 39:12; 145:19; Lam 3:56). The petitions in v. 2 are typical as well: "Do not hide your face" (see Pss 13:1; 27:9; 69:17; 88:14; 143:7); "Incline your ear" (Ps 17:6); "answer . . . quickly" (see Pss 69:17; 143:7). The repetition of "day" in v. 2 introduces the theme of time (see "days" in vv. 3, 11, 23-24 NIV); the psalmist will eventually discover hope for fleeting human life in God's eternity (see "years" in vv. 24, 27; see also Psalm 90).

102:3-11. These verses are the complaint proper, marked by an envelope structure formed by the repetition of "days" (vv. 3, 11) as well as "wither(ed)" and "grass" (vv. 4, 11). The psalmist portrays the brevity of life with the metaphors of smoke (see Ps 37:20; Hos 13:3) and withering grass (see Ps 90:5-6; Isa 40:6-8). These metaphors—as well as the mention of burning bones (v. 3*b*; see also Pss 6:2; 31:10; and esp. Lam 1:13, where the pain expressed involves Jerusalem's destruction), a stricken heart (v. 4*a*; see also 1 Sam 5:12; Isa 53:4), an apparent loss of appetite (v. 4*b*; see the NIV's more literal translation), and perhaps a loss of weight (v. 5; see Job 19:20)—often lead scholars to conclude that the psalmist was gravely ill (see Psalms 6; 38; 88). To be sure, this is possible. Sickness elsewhere leads to isolation and alienation (vv. 6-7; see also Pss 38:11; 88:8, 18) and persecution (v. 8; see also Pss 6:8; 38:12, 16, 19-20), which in turn causes feelings of humiliation and grief (v. 9; see "ashes" in Isa 6:3; Lam 3:16; see "tears"/"weeping" in Pss 6:8; 42:3; 80:5). Disease is also attributed to God's anger (v. 10; see Pss 6:1; 38:1-2; 88:7; see also Pss 90:7-11, where human transience is associated with God's anger).

But it is possible, too, that the language and imagery were intended to be metaphorical, or at least came to be understood metaphorically. Similar imagery in Lamentations (see references above) supports this conclusion, as does the juxtaposition of vv. 3-11 with vv. 12-17. That is, vv. 3-11 were certainly capable of being heard as an articulation of the pain, alienation, grief, and despair of exile (cf. v. 10*b* with Deut 29:28, where the same vocabulary is used to describe what happened with the destruction of Jerusalem). The exile apparently made Israel particularly aware of the general frailty and transience of human existence (see Ps 90:5-11; Isa 40:6-8; on the simile of the shadow, see Job 8:9; 14:2; Pss 109:23; 144:4). Thus the transition marked by v. 12 may not be quite so abrupt and problematic as it first seems.

102:12-17. In fact, v. 12 seems intended to play off of vv. 3-11. The focus on the psalmist is shifted dramatically to God as both v. 12 and v. 13 begin with the emphatic Hebrew pronoun "you," and the name Yahweh (LORD) occurs for the first time since v. 1. Whereas human transience was the subject of vv. 3-11, v. 12 affirms God's eternity (see "forever" and "all generations"). In keeping with the dominant emphasis of Book IV (see Psalms 93; 95–99), v. 12 also proclaims God's sovereignty (see "sits"/"enthroned" in Pss 2:4; 9:7; 29:10). Because God is eternally sovereign, God's "name"—literally, "remembrance" (זכר *zēker*)—will always endure. The same word occurs in Ps 111:4 (see also Exod 3:15; Ps 97:12), where the accompanying affirmation is that God is "gracious and compassionate." The same two Hebrew roots occur in Ps 102:13 ("compassion" [רחם *rḥm*] and "favor" [חנן *ḥnn*]) to describe God's anticipated action toward Zion, and they get at the essence of God's character revealed to Moses after the episode of the golden calf (see Exod 34:6). This allusion implies that the psalmist's hope is grounded in the earlier exodus event, which also aimed at manifesting God's universal sovereignty (Exod 9:16; 15:18; see also Ps 102:15; Isa 40:5; 66:18) and was celebrated as the first step in God's and the people's movement to Zion (Exod 15:17; see also Ps 102:16; Isa 45:13; 60:10). The two occurrences of "prayer" in v. 17 recall the superscription and v. 1, suggesting again that the hope expressed in vv. 12-16 is somehow related to vv. 1-11.

102:18-22. While the hope expressed in vv. 12-17 alludes to the exodus, the vocabulary of vv. 12-17 also is reminiscent of the way Isaiah 40–55 anticipates the return from exile, and the return of the exiles is even more clearly in view in vv. 18-22. The theme of time is again evident in v. 18 as the psalmist anticipates a future for God's people (see Pss 22:30-31; 90:13-17). It will be because God "looked down," as God had "looked down" to defeat the Egyptians (Exod 14:24) and as God was regularly requested to do to ensure the life of the people (see Deut 26:15; Ps 113:5-6). This looking down will be to liberate prisoners, who elsewhere also are the beneficiaries of God's saving work (see Pss 68:6; 69:33; 107:10). In Ps 79:11, which is very similar to v. 20, the prisoners seem to be precisely the victims of the destruction of Jerusalem and the subsequent exile (see also Isa 49:9; 61:1; Lam 3:34; Zech 9:11). In short, the return of the exiles to a restored Zion (vv. 12-17) will be the prelude to the universal recognition of God's sovereignty (vv. 21-22; the word "worship" [עבד '*ābad*] suggests more literally to "serve" a superior; see Isa 66:18-23).

102:23-24. These verses return the focus to the psalmist, as in vv. 1-11. The fact that the individual prayer encloses vv. 12-22 suggests again that the two sections should not be sharply separated. Someone—the original author or an editor—intended them to be read together. In view of the explicit address of exilic concerns in vv. 12-22, it is significant that v. 23 *b* recalls Ps 89:45 *a*, which is in a section of lament over the failure of the Davidic dynasty. In Ps 89:46 the voice of an apparently deposed Davidic king inquires how long God will hide God's face (see Ps 102:2) and be angry (see Ps 102:10). The king then asks God to remember his own (and human) transience (89:47-48; see also 102:3-4, 11) and to remember the taunts of his enemies (89:50-51; see also 102:8). These similarities may be coincidental, but they increase the likelihood that the individual voice in Psalm 102 should be heard as a Davidic king, albeit a deposed one (see Psalm 101), or at least that the individual complaint in Psalm 102 be heard in relation to the exile.

102:25-28. Verse 24 *b* already shifts the focus back to God, where it remains in vv. 25-28. Two occurrences of the emphatic "you" (vv. 26 *a*, 27 *a*) match those in vv. 12-13. Whereas vv. 12-13 alluded to the exodus, vv. 26-28 look to God's creative activity as a sign of God's enduring sovereignty (on v. 25, see Pss 24:1-2; 104:5; on v. 26, see Ps 104:6). God's enduring "years" (vv. 24 *b*, 27) contrast with the psalmist's "days" (vv. 2, 3, 8, 11) and are the hope of God's people. The language of v. 28—"children," "your servants," "established"—recalls Ps 90:13-17, where essentially the same hope is expressed. As eternal sovereign, God is in a position to "establish" things, and God does—the work of human hands (Ps 90:17), the world (Ps 93:1), and the future of God's people (102:28).

REFLECTIONS

1. In the face of exile and subsequent crises throughout the generations, the people of God have found hope and strength in the conviction that because God reigns, the future can be entrusted to God. Psalm 102 is the fifth of the church's seven Penitential Psalms (see also Psalms 6; 32; 38; 51; 130; 143). It contains no explicit confession of sin, although one may be implied in v. 10. But the Penitential Psalms are about more than confession of sin; they are ultimately testimony to God's grace. This is certainly the case with Psalm 102. The future of Zion, which symbolizes the future of the people, depends on God's compassion and favor (v. 13)—or as these Hebrew roots are translated elsewhere, God's mercy and grace.

2. This message is reinforced if the psalm is heard as a plea out of exile or out of the despair of the early post-exilic era. While Israel viewed the exile as deserved punishment, Israel also concluded at some point that enough was enough (see Isa 40:1-2).

At that point, the reality of exile became viewed as an opportunity for God to perform a new exodus (see Isa 49:8-26)—to have "compassion on Zion" (Ps 102:13; see also Isa 49:13, 15). That v. 13 recalls Exod 34:6 is significant, because God revealed God's nature as merciful and gracious after the people had sinned by worshiping the golden calf. This episode proved to be paradigmatic of Israel's whole history; Israel proved constantly disobedient, making it necessary for God to bear the burden of their sin. In short, the ongoing existence of Israel was testimony to God's mercy and grace. The church professes to be heir to Israel's story, and its history certainly demonstrates that it continues to live not by its own merit or worthiness but by the grace of God.

In Psalm 102, Zion is the symbol of God's willingness to be concretely present in space and time with a particular people (see Commentary on Psalms 46; 48; 76; 84; 87; 122). For the church, the symbolism of Zion has been transferred to Jesus (see Heb 1:10-12, which views Ps 102:25-27 as testimony to Jesus' lordship). For Christians, Jesus' life, death, and resurrection are the ultimate demonstration of God's reign, which takes the form of mercy and grace. Jesus is the seal of God's constancy (see Heb 13:18; cf. Ps 102:27), and the church professes to find its hope in these words of Jesus, which make essentially the same promise for the future as Ps 102:28: "I am with you always, to the end of the age" (Matt 28:20 NRSV). The good news for individuals (vv. 1-11, 23-24) and for the whole church (vv. 12-22) is that by the grace of God we are indeed "established in your presence" (v. 28).

PSALM 103:1-22, BLESS THE LORD, O MY SOUL

COMMENTARY

Psalm 103 is one of the most familiar and beloved of all the psalms. One of its most frequent words is "all" (כל kōl, vv. 1-3, 6, 19, 21-22), for Psalm 103 intends to be comprehensive. It affirms that God, who rules over all and does all good things for all persons in need, is to be praised in all places by all creatures and things with all of their being. Although not an acrostic, its twenty-two lines—the number of letters in the Hebrew alphabet—also suggest the psalmist's intent to say it all.

Scholars disagree on the categorization of Psalm 103 and its original setting. Some label it an individual song of thanksgiving that celebrates the psalmist's recovery from a serious illness (see vv. 3-5). The liturgical setting of the thanksgiving ceremony would have included the invitation to others to praise God (vv. 1-22), as well as testimony to God's character (vv. 6-19), which has been revealed in the psalmist's experience. Other scholars suggest that Psalm 103 is a song of praise, celebrating not a specific deliverance but God's general activity (vv. 3-5 or 3-6) and character (vv. 5 or 6-18 or 19) as reasons for praise. As a hymn, Psalm 103 could well have been used at large festal gatherings. Some scholars, however, view it as a late imitation of hymnic forms, and thus they suggest that it may have been used in small gatherings of the pious. Certainty on these matters is not possible.

The structure of Psalm 103 is often outlined as follows: vv. 1-5, vv. 6-18, vv. 19-22. The first and last lines are identical, thus forming an envelope structure, which can be expanded to vv. 1-2, 20-22, all of which contain the verb "bless" (ברך bārak) in the imperative. Many scholars further divide vv. 6-18 into three sections on the basis of style and content: vv. 6-10, vv. 11-14 (note the symmetrical pattern of the opening words of each verse, "For . . . as . . . As . . . for"), vv. 15-18. The criteria, however, are ambiguous. For instance, "works" in v. 6 is a participle, as are all the verbal forms in vv. 3-5a. One could argue, therefore, that v. 6 should not be separated from vv. 1-5. On the other hand, the participle in v. 6 is the only one that has a subject ("LORD") with it, so perhaps this variation signals the beginning of a new section, or perhaps v. 6 is meant to be transitional. The same could be said of v. 19. On the one hand, it seems to belong with vv. 20-22 (see "all" in vv. 19, 21-22; plus "rules" in v. 19 and "dominion" in v. 22 translate the same Hebrew root [משל *mšl*]); however, the syntax of vv. 15a and 19a is similar, perhaps suggesting that the psalmist's intent is to contrast human instability with divine stability. Again, v. 19 may be transitional.[391]

Only recently have scholars confronted the question of the literary placement of Psalm 103. If Book IV is a response to the crisis of exile elaborated in Book III (see Commentary on Psalms 73; 74; 79; 80; 89; 90; Introduction), then Psalm 103 is extremely well-placed. In fact, Psalm 101 and especially Psalm 102 (see vv. 12-22) have just rehearsed the problem again—loss of monarchy, Zion/ Temple, and land. In this literary context, it is possible to hear Psalm 103 as the praise anticipated in Ps 102:15, 18, 21-22 (see "name" in 102:15, 21; 103:1). Part of the strategy of Book IV is to return the reader to the perspective of the Mosaic era, in which the reign of God was celebrated without land, Temple, or monarchy (see Psalm 90; Introduction), and Psalm 103 is congruent with this perspective (see v. 7). In particular, Ps 103:8-10 recalls God's self-revelation to Moses in Exod 33:12–34:7 (cf. esp. Exod 34:6 with Ps 103:8), and two key words from this episode become key words in Psalm 103: "steadfast love" (חסד *ḥesed*, vv. 4, 8, 11, 17) and "mercy"/"compassion" (vv. 4, 8, 13). Of course, the good news of God's love and compassion, manifest in God's willingness to forgive, is precisely what the exiles needed to hear (see vv. 9-13; see Commentary on Psalm 89, esp. discussion of v. 49). Not coincidentally, it seems, Psalm 103 is reminiscent of the prophetic preaching found in Isaiah 40–66 (cf. v. 5 with Isa 40:31; v. 9 with Isa 57:16; v. 11 with Isa 55:9; vv. 15-16 with Isa 40:6-8;

see also "steadfast love" in Isa 54:10; 55:3; 63:7; and "mercy"/"compassion"/"pity" in Isa 49:10, 13; 54:7-8, 10; 55:7; 60:10; 63:7). Furthermore, like the prophet of the exile (see Isa 52:7-10) and like the core of Book IV of the psalter (see Psalms 93; 95–99), Psalm 103 proclaims God's universal sovereignty (see vv. 19-22). This theme will also be continued in Psalm 104, which is verbally linked to Psalm 103 by its opening and concluding invitation.

103:1-5. These verses have the form of a hymn—invitation to praise (vv. 1-2), followed by reasons for praise (vv. 3-5). The word "bless" (*bārak*) seems to have meant originally to bend the knee before—that is, to bow in homage to one's sovereign (see Pss 16:7; 26:12; 34:1; 63:4; 95:6; 96:2; 100:4; 145:1, 21). The psalmist, in effect, invites his or her whole self to bless God and God's "name," which is suggestive of God's essence or character (see vv. 8-13, where the subject is specifically God's character). In other words, the psalmist owes his or her whole life to God, and this is exactly what vv. 3-5 will say. The word "benefits" (גמול *gĕmûl*) in v. 2 almost always elsewhere indicates a negative consequence—God's recompense or retribution (the same root underlies "repay" in v. 10). Its use here makes the content of vv. 3-5 all the more pleasantly surprising. God's recompense is first of all forgiveness! It is significant that this particular word for "forgiveness" (סלח *sālaḥ*) ties Psalm 103 to the literary contexts mentioned above; it occurs in both Exod 34:9 and Isa 55:7. Similarly, several of the other "benefits," which could be understood simply as individual terms, are reminiscent of what God has done (and will do again) for the whole people, especially in reference to the periods of exodus and return from exile—healing (see Exod 15:26; Deut 32:39; Isa 57:18-19; Jer 30:17; 33:6), redeeming (Exod 6:6; 15:13; Pss 74:2; 77:15; Isa 43:1; 44:22-23; see esp. Isa 51:10, where the people are called "the redeemed," and 51:14, where "the Pit" is a metaphor for the threat represented by the oppression of exile), and satisfying (see Exod 16:8, 12; Isa 58:11; Jer 31:14; see also "goodness" in Exod 33:19). In Lam 5:16, the exile is characterized as the crown "fallen from our head" as a result of sin and iniquity (see Lam 5:7).

391. For a more detailed discussion, see T. M. Willis, " 'So Great Is His Steadfast Love': A Rhetorical Analysis of Psalm 103," *Biblica* 72 (1991) 525-37.

To this situation, Ps 103:4*b* (along with vv. 3, 8-13) would offer a fitting response.

103:6. This transitional verse presents a climactic description of what God has done and will do again. "Righteousness" and "justice" are what the sovereign God wills and works to enact for all humanity (see Pss 9:7-8; 89:14; 96:13; 97:2; 98:9; 99:4). These words are not used specifically to describe the exodus, but they are found frequently in Isaiah 40–55 to designate God's work in returning the exiles (see esp. Isa 51:1-8 NIV, where "justice" occurs in vv. 4-5 and "righteousness" in vv. 1, 5-6, 8). The Hebrew root of "oppressed" (עשׁק *'āšaq*) in v. 6 also occurs in Isa 52:4, where it is applied to the Egyptian captivity as well as to the more recent exile, and in Isa 54:14, where the removal of oppression is designated as "righteousness."

103:7-18. While v. 6 belongs with vv. 3-5, it also anticipates vv. 7-10 and vv. 11-18. What God works to enact implies the nature of God's character, which is described more fully in vv. 8-18. Elsewhere, too, "righteousness" is associated with the attributes of God listed in v. 8 (see Pss 85:10-13; 89:14; 98:3, 9; 111:3-4; 116:5). Verse 8 quotes Exod 34:6 (see also Pss 86:15*b*; Introduction), but the whole golden calf episode (Exod 32:1–34:9) is in the background, especially its conclusion, beginning at Exod 33:12 (see "know"/"known" in Exod 33:13; Ps 103:7 NIV). The people's idolatry provoked God's anger (see Exod 32:7-14), but the episode culminates in Exod 34:6-7, thus illustrating the affirmations of v. 9 (see also Jer 3:5, 12) and vv. 10-18. God forgives "sins," "iniquities," and "transgressions" (vv. 10, 12; see also Exod 34:7). Two of the attributes in Exod 34:6 get further attention: "steadfast love" (vv. 11, 17) and God's "mercy" or fatherly "compassion" (רחם *rāḥam*, v. 13; see also Exod 33:19; and see above on Ps 25:6 for an explanation of why the Hebrew root fundamentally suggests motherly compassion).

The revelation of God's steadfast love and compassion in Exodus 32–34 required *God's* repentance or change of mind (see Exod 32:12-14), and Moses concludes the episode by reminding God of the nature of the people with whom God must deal (Exod 34:9). The whole episode is reminiscent of Genesis 6–9, where God's realization about human nature prompts the promise never again to destroy all creatures (cf. Gen 6:5 with 8:21). Psalm 103:14 also recalls the opening chapters of Genesis, and in Psalm 103, as in Genesis 6–9 and Exodus 32–34, God's willingness to forgive is tied to God's realization about human nature. To the sinful, transient creature (vv. 14-16; also see Pss 89:47; 90:3-11; 102:3-4, 11; Isa 40:6-8), God continually shows God's steadfast love and righteousness (v. 17; see also v. 6). The mention of steadfast love in v. 17 means that there is one occurrence for each major division of the poem, except vv. 19-22.

While the structure of Psalm 103 communicates the pervasiveness of God's steadfast love, there seems to be a qualification. Three times the psalmist reserves steadfast love or compassion for those who fear God (vv. 11, 13, 17; see also Pss 25:14; 33:18; 34:7, 9; 85:9; 111:5; 115:11; 145:19; 147:11), and righteousness is reserved for those who are obedient (v. 18; see also Exod 20:6). There seems to be a contradiction: How is it "mercy" if finally it is deserved? And what need is there for forgiveness? This contradiction, or better perhaps, tension, represents the inevitable dilemma for God, who both wills and demands justice and righteousness and yet who loves and is committed to relationship with sinful people. This tension is present already in Genesis 6–9, and it is clearly expressed in Exod 34:6-7, where the affirmation of God's willingness to forgive is followed immediately by the announcement that God "does not leave the guilty unpunished." It cannot be otherwise for God, who is both just and merciful (see above on Ps 99:6-9; see also Reflections below).

103:19-22. As in Psalms 90; 102; and Isa 40:6-8, where the experience of God's wrath awakens an acute sense of human transience, the solution is to be found in the affirmation of both God's transcendence and God's immanence—God's eternity and unbounded sovereignty (Ps 103:19-22; see also Pss 90:1-2; 102:12, 25-27; Isa 40:8; 55:8-11) as well as God's compassionate love, which is manifested in forgiveness (Ps 103:6-18; see also Pss 90:13-17; 102:13; Isa 40:1-2; 55:1-7). The concluding verses of Psalm 103 recall both the opening verses of the psalm and other psalms that proclaim God's reign. For instance, v. 19 echoes Ps 93:2, and along with v. 22, it anticipates Ps 145:10-13. Because God's sovereignty is "over all" (v. 19), all beings (the ancient Near Eastern notion of a divine council of attendants is in view here as in Pss 29:1-2; 82:1; 97:7, 9; 148:2) and all things are invited to praise God (see Pss 96:11-12; 98:7-8; 148:1-12). The sequence of invitations concludes by focusing attention again on the individual psalmist. In other words, one puts oneself in tune with the whole cosmic order by acknowledging God's reign and by joining all beings in conforming to God's word and will (see vv. 18, 21, where the NRSV's "do" links human behavior with that of the heavenly beings). The cosmic dimension of God's reign and the significance of conformity to it are evident in Psalm 104, to which Psalm 103 is linked (see 104:1, 35).

REFLECTIONS

Psalm 103 is a good place to start when talking with persons who perceive God in the OT to be simply a God of wrath and judgment. In fact, in his *Elements of Old Testament Theology,* Claus Westermann begins his discussion of God's compassion with an interpretation of Psalm 103. Westermann recognizes the tension between God's justice and God's mercy, and he addresses it as follows:

> The poet has no intention of contesting God's activity in wrath. But he makes a distinction. God's activity in wrath is limited; God's goodness knows no boundaries (v. 17). . . . The same is true of sin and its forgiveness. If God compensated man commensurate with the way he sins, then one might despair. But here too, God is inconsistent; his forgiving goodness is immeasurable. One might even say that the entire Psalm deals with the incomprehensible excess of God's goodness.[392]

As Weiser puts it, the poet "has been granted an insight into the heart of the majesty of God, and what he has found there is grace."[393]

The immeasurability of God's grace does not dissolve the tension between God's radical demand for obedience and God's willingness to forgive. This is the dilemma with which God, as a loving parent (v. 13), must always live, and it is one that human parents know as well. It cannot be otherwise for God, else grace would be cheap (see Rom 6:1). For Christians, God's dilemma is in sharpest focus on the cross of Jesus Christ. Christian theology has traditionally interpreted the cross as an event to satisfy God's demand for justice, but the satisfaction is made by the offering of God's own self, *not* by human obedience—"while we still were sinners Christ died for us" (Rom 5:8 NRSV). The cross thus seems to compromise God's justice at the same time that it seems to compromise God's sovereignty. Such is the mystery of sovereignty and the miracle of grace, which for all the world looks like weakness (see 1 Cor 1:25; 2 Cor 12:9). But Psalm 103 knows better (see Reflections on Psalm 99).

The mystery and the miracle do not mean that grace is cheap, as Psalm 103 also recognizes. On the contrary, the cross indicates the great cost to God, and the cross demands our whole lives as well (see Mark 8:34-35; see also Ps 103:1, 11, 13, 17, 22). Yet for us self-centered, sinful people who know that even our very best is not enough, our hope is finally not in our ability to measure up but in the immeasurable, incomprehensible excess of God's goodness. We dare to profess that the ruling power in the universe (v. 19) is One who treats us like a loving father, a compassionate mother (see Isa 49:15). Such love demands our soul, our life, our all.

392. Westermann, *Elements of Old Testament Theology,* 139.
393. Weiser, *The Psalms,* 663.

PSALM 104:1-35, GOD AS CREATOR AND PROVIDER

COMMENTARY

Linked to Psalm 103 by the only occurrences in the psalter of the invitation "Bless the LORD, O my soul" (103:1, 22; 104:1, 35), Psalm 104 is an eloquent poetic elaboration on the cosmic reign of God that is proclaimed in Ps 103:19-22. Psalm 103 asserts that God "rules over all" (v. 19), and Psalm 104 agrees (see "all" in vv. 24, 27), exquisitely depicting how all God's "works" (Pss 103:22; 104:24a) effectively bless God simply by taking their rightful place in an intricate ecosystem that originated with and constantly depends on its sovereign Maker. In fact, the Hebrew root of "works" (עשׂה 'āśâ) is the key word in Psalm 104, occurring five more times— "make(s)"/"made" in vv. 4, 19, 24b and "work(s)" in vv. 13, 31. Thus Psalm 104 focuses on creation, whereas Psalm 103 had given more attention to God's saving mercy and love (vv. 4, 8, 11, 13, 17). But together the two psalms are another reminder that God's creating work and God's saving work (see "works" in Ps 103:6) are finally inseparable; God's activity on behalf of Israel was toward the enactment of God's purposes for the whole creation (see Commentary on Psalms 33; 65; 66; 93; 95; 98). Together, then, Psalms 103–104 affirm God's cosmic sovereignty in response to the theological crisis articulated in Psalms 101–102 (see Commentary on Psalms 101; 102; 103). And in concert with Psalms 93; 95–99, Psalms 103–104 contribute to the response of Book IV to the theological issues raised in Book III (see Commentary on Psalms 73; 74; 79; 80; 89; 90; Introduction).

Scholars have traditionally debated at length the origin of and influences on Psalm 104. It is obviously reminiscent of Genesis 1, but there is no warrant for attempting to discern a seven-day structure in Psalm 104 or even for positing direct literary influence in either direction. Such is possible, of course; but if anything, Psalm 104 appears to be an exuberant poetic reflection on the evaluation of creation that is found in Gen 1:31: "it was

very good" (NRSV). Psalm 104 is also similar in some ways to Psalm 8, but the affirmation of the exalted status of the human creature (see Ps 8:4-8) is absent in Psalm 104, in which the human is one among many creatures that depend on God for life. In addition, there are striking similarities between Psalm 104 and the Egyptian hymn of Amenhotep IV to Aten, the sun disc. While direct literary influence cannot be ruled out entirely, it is more likely that the similarities can be traced to the common stock of cosmological ideas that were extant in the ancient Near East. Psalm 104 actually reflects the influence of a variety of ancient Near Eastern materials, including Egyptian lists of cosmological phenomena and Canaanite accounts in which creation is the result of a battle among the gods and the subsequent ordering of the forces of a watery chaos (see below on vv. 1-9). In each case, these ideas have been adopted and stamped with Israel's faith in the exclusive sovereignty of Yahweh. The elements of the cosmos are objects of God's action, not gods in themselves (see vv. 2-9, 19, 26); it is clear throughout that God "made them all" (v. 24).

The structure of Psalm 104 can be perceived in several ways. Attention to stylistic detail suggests division as follows:

vv. 1-4	God and the heavens
vv. 5-13	God and the earth (see "earth" in vv. 5, 13)
vv. 14-23	God and people (see "people" in vv. 14, 23 NRSV; the same Hebrew root also appears in vv. 14, 23 NIV as "cultivate" and "labor")
vv. 24-30	"all" God's works (see "all" in vv. 24, 27)
vv. 31-35	conclusion: God's joy (v. 31) and human joy (v. 34)

Allen even suggests that this outline constitutes a concentric structure that focuses attention on vv. 14-23, and he notes that the key word "work(s)"/"made" appears in either the first or the last verse of each section (vv. 4, 13, 24*ab*, 31), except for the central section, where it occurs in the middle (v. 19).[394] This may be coincidental, however, and the actual content of the sections tends to overlap considerably. The focus shifts from heaven (vv. 2-4) to earth (vv. 5-6) to waters (vv. 7-10) to wild animals (v. 11) to birds (v. 12) to earth again (v. 13) to plants that feed animals and people (vv. 14-15) to trees (v. 16) to birds (v. 17) to wild animals (v. 18) to heavenly bodies (vv. 19-20*a*) to wild animals (vv. 20*b*-22) to people again (v. 23). It is as if the psalmist cannot quite control an effusive, joyful flow of observations and words that culminate in the exclamation of v. 24*a*, only to overflow again in vv. 25-26 before the psalmist is able to manage a conclusion that expresses what has been evident throughout: All creatures depend on God for sustenance and for life itself (vv. 27-30). An even more reasoned response is represented by the psalmist's wishes and promises in vv. 31-35. It is possible also, as Mays suggests, to consider vv. 1-9 under the rubric of creation and vv. 10-23 under the rubric of providence, both of which are in view in the summary observations of vv. 24-30 before the actual conclusion.[395]

104:1-4. These verses affirm God's sovereignty. To say that God is great is to say, in effect, that God reigns supreme, for greatness is frequently associated with sovereignty (see Pss 47:2; 48:2; 95:3; 96:4). This more abstract profession is reinforced with the metaphor of God's clothing (vv. 1*b*-2*a*) and the description of God's activity (vv. 2*b*-4). God wears "honor"/"splendor" and "majesty," the attributes of royalty (see Pss 21:5; 45:3; 96:6; 145:5), as well as "light." Light is regularly associated with God's presence (see Pss 4:6; 27:1; 43:3; 44:3), sometimes in the context of language and imagery that affirm God's sovereignty (see Ps 76:4 in connection with 76:1; 89:15 in connection with 89:14). "Light" also indicates the cosmic dimension of God's rule (see Gen 1:3). The description of God's activity begins in vv. 2*b*-3*a* with God's establishing a dwelling place. The word translated "tent" (יריעה *yĕrî‘â*) seems to

mean more specifically the curtain of a tent, and by far the majority of its uses designate the curtain of the tabernacle (see Exod 26:2). With this dimension of the word in the background, v. 2*b* then suggests that God's real house is not the Temple but the universe (see 2 Sam 7:6; 1 Kgs 8:27), which is only appropriate for a cosmic sovereign. The verb in "set the beams" (קרה *qārâ*) and the noun in "upper chambers" (עליה *‘ăliyyâ*, see v. 13) in v. 3*a* are architectural terms. That God builds God's house upon the "waters" suggests also the mythic background of a created order resulting from the divine warrior's defeat of the chaotic waters (see Pss 74:12-15; 93:3-4). The mythic background is even clearer in vv. 3*b*-4. In the Canaanite worldview, Baal, god of the storm, rode the clouds and commanded the winds (vv. 3*b*-4*a*) and the lightning. But here Baal has been dethroned and his forces de-divinized. Yahweh reigns, and God asserts sovereignty over elements that have resulted from God's own creative work (see Pss 18:15; 29:3-9; 68:4; 97:1-5; Isa 19:1; cf. Job 22:14).

104:5-13. As suggested above, v. 5 seems to start a new section, either a major unit (vv. 5-13) or at least a subdivision of vv. 1-9. In any case, God's creative work is still in view. It results in a stable world. As were vv. 3*b*-4, v. 5 is at least implicitly polemical. According to Ps 82:5, the rule of the gods resulted in the shaking of the earth's foundations, but the work of the truly sovereign God holds the world together (see Pss 24:1-2; 93:1; 96:10). The mythic background is again evident in vv. 6-9. God controls "the deep" (see Gen 1:2; Exod 15:8; Pss 33:7; 77:16). The waters obey God's voice (v. 7; see "rebuke" in Job 26:11; Pss 18:15; 76:6) and perform God's will for them (v. 8). The NRSV's "appointed" (יסד *yāsad*) in v. 8 is the same Hebrew root as "set" in v. 5; thus earth and the waters are under God's rule. The chaotic forces have been tamed (v. 9*a*; see also Job 38:8-11, although the vocabulary differs), and the earth is safe (v. 9*b*; see also Gen 9:11, although again the vocabulary differs).

The occurrence of "earth" in v. 9 may mark a subdivision of the larger vv. 5-13 (see "earth" also in vv. 5, 13). In any case, God's control of water is still the subject (v. 10), and under God's rule, water becomes not a threat to but a sustainer of life (vv. 11-13*a*).

394. Allen, *Psalms 101–150*, 31-32.
395. Mays, *Psalms*, 332-35.

The NIV's "give water" (v. 11a) and "waters" (v. 13a) represent the same Hebrew verb (שקה *šqh*). God provides for animate and inanimate things alike; the earth has what it needs. This theme of God's providence will be echoed by the repetitions of "satisfied" in v. 16 ("watered abundantly") and v. 28.

104:14-23. Human beings enter the picture for the first time in v. 14, and the words "people" (אדם *'ādām*) and "cultivate"/"labor" (עבדה *'ăbōdâ* / פעל *pā'al*) in vv. 14, 23 may form an envelope structure for this section. The subject is still God's provision. By way of plants, God provides "food" (לחם *leḥem*, v. 14; "bread" in v. 15 translates the same Hebrew word), but more as well. Plants also yield wine—a source of pleasure as well as sustenance (see Sir 31:27-28)—and oil, the purpose of which is not clear here. The use of oil occurs elsewhere in contexts that suggest hospitality, honor, and joy (see Pss 23:5; 45:7; 92:10; Luke 7:46). God "satisfies" not just people but trees—God's trees! (v. 16)— which in turn provide hospitality for animals (vv. 17-18; see also v. 12; Prov 30:26).

Each creature has not only its place but also its appropriate time, according to God's design and implementation (vv. 19-23). Perhaps it is not coincidental that the key word "made" occurs in v. 19 with its object "the moon." The moon and the sun were widely regarded as deities. It is possible that the sun played a legitimate part in Israelite worship at some point (see Commentary on Psalm 63), and whether legitimate or not, worship of the sun apparently occurred rather frequently (see Jer 8:1-2; 19:13; Ezek 8:16). But here the sun simply serves God's purpose of ordering the lives of the creatures.

104:24-30. Containing two occurrences of the key word "works"/"made," v. 24 is an exclamatory summary of vv. 1-23. *Everything* derives from God. The heavens, the earth, plants, animals, people—God made them all, and the whole creation is a witness to God's wisdom (see Prov 3:19; 8:22-31; Jer 10:21). The word "wisdom" (חכמה *ḥokmâ*) can mean not only knowledge, but also technical skill in construction (see Exod 31:3, 6). Both senses are appropriate here (see above on vv. 2b-3a); God is both architect and artisan. The exclamation overflows into a further observation about the sea, which perhaps

not coincidentally is called great as God was called great in v. 1. In the Canaanite view, the sea was a god who represented chaotic power. Psalm 104 has already suggested that God orders the chaotic waters into life-giving rivers and springs (vv. 6-13). Verses 25-26 affirm that even the mighty and mysterious oceans are subject to God (see Ps 29:10; Isa 51:9-10). The "great" living thing (v. 25) that resides in the sea is Leviathan (v. 26), a version of the divine chaos-monster known in other ancient Near Eastern sources. Here Leviathan is a creature who simply plays in the water. Or is Leviathan, in effect, God's water toy? The grammar is ambiguous, but in either case, Leviathan has been rendered harmless (see Job 41:1-11; Ps 74:12-15; Isa 27:1; 51:9-10).

The "all" in v. 27 refers to the "all" in v. 24. Every creature, human and otherwise, depends on God. Food is a gift from God (see "give" in vv. 27b, 28a). The description of the creatures gathering their food recalls Israel's gathering of manna in the wilderness (see Exodus 16). In both instances, God satisfies (v. 28; see also vv. 13, 16; Exod 16:8, 12). Verses 27-28 occur in a similar form in Ps 145:15-16. Psalm 145 brings together the perspectives of Psalms 103–104, and it may be significant that the concluding psalms of the psalter explicitly recall Book IV (see Introduction and Commentary on Psalms 145; 146 for further similarities between them and Psalms 103–104).

God provides not only food but also the very breath of life itself (vv. 29-30). The words "breath" and "spirit" (the capitalization in the NIV should be avoided) are the same Hebrew word (רוח *rûaḥ*). The vocabulary—"breath"/"spirit," "dust," "created," "ground"—recalls Genesis 1–2. The breath of the creatures is not identical to God's breath, but God is responsible for giving life to the creatures (see Gen 1:2; 2:7; Job 34:14-15; Ps 146:4). Verses 29-30 also suggest that God's creating is an ongoing process. God's breath brings new creatures into being (v. 30a); God's "face" (v. 29) serves to "renew the face of the ground" (v. 30b).

104:31-35. Just as vv. 1-30 have asserted God's sovereignty, so also the psalmist's first wish is for the eternity of God's rule. Elsewhere, "glory" is associated with both God's rule (see Pss 24:7-10; 29:1-3, 9-11; 145:1, 5, 12; Isa 6:1-5) and God's presence (see Exod 24:16-17; 33:18, 22; Pss 26:8; 102:16; Ezek 10:4, 18; 43:4-5), each of which is manifested in God's ongoing creation of the world—in God's works (v. 31). Verse 32 is the language of theophany—God's appearing (see Exod 19:18)—and the psalmist hopes that God's appearing will afford God joy (v. 31 *b*). This also seems to be the thrust of v. 35; the psalmist wants no one to interfere with the operation of the world as God intends it (see Pss 145:20; 146:9; see also Reflections below). The psalmist is certainly committed to that end, responding to God with unceasing praise (v. 33), which involves the yielding of the whole self to God in liturgy and life. The psalmist hopes that his or her meditation—seemingly a reference to the preceding poem—will be an acceptable offering to God (see Ps 19:14) and an indication that the psalmist intends to enjoy God forever (v. 34*b*). Thus the psalmist's joy reflects the joy of his or her creator (v. 31), just as the psalmist intends his or her life to reflect what God intends for the life of the whole creation.

REFLECTIONS

1. Thousands of years before smog, acid rain, global warming, and the so-called butterfly effect—the awareness that a butterfly flapping its wings has at least some tiny physical impact on the environment on the other side of the planet—the poet who wrote Psalm 104 was an environmentalist. The psalmist knew about the intricate interconnectedness and subtle interdependence of air, soil, water, plants, and animals, including humans. The psalmist knew the truth revealed in the etymological connection between the Hebrew word for "humanity" (אדם *'ādām*) and the word for "ground" (אדמה *'ădāmâ*): Human beings really are creatures of the earth. The origin and destiny of humankind is inextricably tied to the origin and destiny of the earth. The same truth is revealed in the etymological connection between the English word *human* and the Latin word *humus,* "soil." But, as it were, we have forgotten our roots, both etymological and physical.

Of course, the psalmist's awareness was grounded not in etymology, not in a knowledge of physical sciences like botany, zoology, geology, hydrology, and meteorology. Rather, the psalmist's awareness was grounded in *theology.* The psalmist was convinced of the profound interdependence of air, soil, water, and all living things, because he or she believed that *everything* derived from and was ultimately dependent upon God: "the Lord God made them all," as a familiar hymn also puts it ("All Things Bright and Beautiful"). "Nature," as we often call it today, is not divine, but it is sacred. It does not and cannot exist apart from God and God's renewing breath. Because for the psalmist life derives from God, it follows that our lives belong to God (see Psalm 100). Because for the psalmist we live in God's world, it follows that everything we do has an effect on God's world and thus on God. Ecology and theology are inseparable.

2. The psalmist's environmental consciousness is of a different sort from that of most contemporary folk. To be sure, regardless of what motivates it, any concern for the environment is better than none at all. Still, it is important to realize that much of our concern for the future of the earth is motivated by our desire to maintain our current standard of living without trashing things so terribly or depleting natural resources so severely that we cannot pass the same style of life on to our children. In other words, our primary concern is ourselves, and our major motivation is fear. While this kind of environmental consciousness may be better than none at all, our efforts to "save" the earth are surely misguided and doomed to failure as long as the focus is on ourselves and our motivation is fear.

The psalmist demonstrates another way. For the psalmist, relating to the world—in our terms, perhaps, an environmental consciousness—begins with praising God. The motivation is not fear but rejoicing in the Lord (vv. 33-34). Praise involves the acknowledgment of God's sovereignty and the commitment to live under God's rule (see vv. 1-4, 33-34). Taking the psalmist as an example, we would have to conclude that concern for the environment begins with praising God. To be sure, this sounds hopelessly simplistic, scientifically and technologically naive. But such a starting point—and its underlying conviction that the world belongs to God—is the only thing that will dislodge our arrogant assumption that *we* can *save* the world, as if it were ours to save! In biblical terms, salvation means life, and in biblical terms, the world does not need to be saved. God has already done that! Psalm 104 affirms that God has made every arrangement and provision for the life of the world. The only problem will be if someone disrupts God's design and destroys the delicate balance God has put in place. For the contemporary world, v. 35 may be the key verse in the psalm. To paraphrase a famous line: We have seen the wicked, and it is us!

The environmental crisis will be addressed by nothing short of praising God, exalting God, and humbling ourselves (see Commentary on Psalm 8). It may be telling that Psalm 104 uses the phrase "trees of the LORD" (v. 16) but not "people of the LORD." In a profound sense, Psalm 104 puts us humans in our place—with springs and hills and trees and creeping things. If our motivation for facing our own future and the future of the earth were to glorify God, we might even have the humility to ask ourselves what it would really mean to live in partnership with a tree or with a wild goat or with the thousands of species whose disappearance causes hardly a ripple of attention, primarily because we are convinced that nature exists to serve humanity. Quite simply, Psalm 104 asserts that this is not the case. Rather, to serve God will mean ultimately to serve God's creation (see Gen 2:15, where the vocation of the human in the garden of Eden should be translated "to *serve* it and keep it"). Psalm 104 counsels praise of and rejoicing in the Lord, but it cannot help adding its own word of warning that may evoke in us legitimate fear, especially since the warnings of our scientists give a whole new dimension of meaning to the scenario of "sinners [being] consumed from the earth" (v. 35). As for us, we can do no better than the psalmist's own response to this scenario: "Bless the LORD, O my soul./ Praise the LORD [הללו־יה *halĕllû-yāh,* "Hallelujah"]!" As Mays asks concerning this first instance of *Hallelujah* in the psalter: "Could a more appropriate place be found?"[396]

3. Psalm 104 is traditionally used on the Day of Pentecost to celebrate the gift of God's Spirit, which gave new life to a discouraged and dispirited band of disciples (Acts 2), who then went about "turning the world upside down" (Acts 17:6 NRSV). At first glance, it may seem as if the spirit of God in Psalm 104 (v. 30) has little to do with Pentecost, the celebration of the coming of God's Holy Spirit. But the spirit of God in Psalm 104 is associated with ongoing creation and renewal (v. 30), which is also what Pentecost is about. To use Psalm 104 on Pentecost is to affirm that God is the source of all life—the physical life of the world, the eternal life offered in Christ, the life of the church—and, indeed, that these spheres of life are finally inseparable. Psalm 104 is a reminder also that, like all of God's creations, the church lives by the power of God's renewing Spirit, not by its own ability, merit, or ingenuity. The church exists, like all of God's works, to praise the Lord (v. 35).

396. Mays, *Psalms,* 336.

PSALM 105:1-45, ALL GOD'S WONDERFUL WORKS

COMMENTARY

Like Psalms 78; 106; and 136, Psalm 105 is usually classified as a historical psalm. As in the others, the recital of history in Psalm 105 is a selective and creative retelling of Israel's story. Psalm 105 is sometimes labeled a didactic hymn, and its purpose may be to educate. But if so, the subject matter is not just names, places, and events out of Israel's past. Rather, the real subject matter is praise (vv. 1-6) and obedience (v. 45). In other words, the psalmist's intent in retelling the old story is to evoke the people's grateful and faithful response to God's choice (see "chosen" in vv. 6, 26, 43) to be related to them (see "covenant" in vv. 8-10), a choice supported by the "wonderful works" (vv. 2, 5) that God has done on their behalf (vv. 12-43). Thus the psalm is not primarily about the past. Rather, it is about the present and the future (see Commentary on Psalm 78, especially Brueggemann's observations about the historical psalms).

In form, Psalm 105 may be considered a song of praise, with vv. 1-6 constituting the invitation to praise and vv. 7-45 giving the reasons. In content, Psalm 105 is similar to Psalm 136 in that both psalms focus exclusively on what God has done. This is in sharp contrast to Psalms 78 and 106, which recount at length the people's unfaithful response. Of course, the juxtaposition of Psalms 105 and 106 makes the contrast particularly obvious, an effect apparently intended by the editors of the psalter. The two should be read together. On the one hand, Psalm 105 makes the people's faithlessness look all the more grievous. But on the other hand, Psalm 106 makes God's grace look all the more amazing (see esp. 106:45). This too may well have been the intent of the editors of the psalter, especially since the conclusion of Psalm 106 apparently situates the people in exile. The hope for the exiles lay in the possibility that God would again hear their cry and turn away from wrath, as God had repeatedly done in the story, which is told in two different ways in Psalms 105–106.

The intent of Psalms 105–106 to address the crisis of exile is in keeping with the apparent purpose of Book IV (see Commentary on Psalms 90; 93; 94; 95; 96; 97; 98; 99; 101; 102; Introduction) to respond to the theological crisis of exile elaborated in Book III (see Psalms 73–74; 79–80; 89; Introduction). This does not necessarily mean that Psalm 105 was written in the exilic or post-exilic era, but in addition to its connection with Psalm 106, several features of Psalm 105 would support such a conclusion. For instance, due to the loss of the land, possession of the land was a preeminent exilic concern (see vv. 11, 44). It was natural, therefore, to look back behind the failed Davidic covenant (see Commentary on Psalm 89; Introduction) to the covenant with Abraham (vv. 9-10). The prophet of the exile does the same thing (see Isa 41:8; 51:1-2), apparently transferring the notion of a Davidic covenant to the people as a whole (see Isa 55:3). A similar move may be suggested by Ps 105:15, where the people are referred to with a term often applied to the Davidic kings: "my anointed" (מְשִׁיחָי *měšîḥāy*; see Pss 2:6; 18:50; 20:6). In addition, the chronicler assigns the use of Ps 105:1-11 to Asaph upon the occasion of David's transfer of the ark to Jerusalem (1 Chr 16:8-18). It is generally thought that the chronicler reflects the concerns and practices of his own era more so than those of earlier periods, and this may indicate the currency of Psalm 105 in the post-exilic setting. In any case, the usefulness of Psalm 105 was not limited to whatever circumstances may have occasioned its origin and ancient use. It continued and can still continue to call the people of God to grateful praise and faithful obedience.

105:1-6. The same imperative opens Psalms 105–107, suggesting that the relationship between Psalms 105 and Psalm 106 should be extended (see Commentary on Psalm 107; see also Pss 44:8; 97:12; 100:4). The psalmists affirm elsewhere that

God makes known God's own deeds (see Pss 77:14*b*; 98:2; 103:7; 106:8), and the people are called upon to join God in this public witness (v. 1*b*; see also Pss 78:5; 145:12). God's "deeds" are testimony to God's sovereignty (see Ps 9:11), which is appropriately greeted with singing and praise (see Pss 96:1; 98:1, 5). "Wonderful works" (vv. 3*a*, 5*a*) recalls the exodus as well as other saving manifestations of God's sovereignty (see Exod 3:20; 15:11; Josh 3:5; Pss 77:11, 14; 78:4, 11-12, 32; 106:7, 22), thus anticipating what the psalmist will remember (see v. 5) and tell (v. 26; the root is the same as "meditation" [שִׂיחַ *śîaḥ*] in Ps 104:34) in vv. 12-45. The word "miracles" (מוֹפֵת *môpēṭ*) in v. 5 refers often to the plagues (see Exod 7:3; 11:9-10; Ps 78:43), an aspect of the demonstration of God's sovereignty over Pharaoh that will also be featured in Psalm 105 (see v. 27). The word "judgments" (מִשְׁפָּטִים *mišpāṭîm*, vv. 5-7), or better "acts of justice," designates the policy God wills and enacts as cosmic ruler (see Pss 96:13; 97:2; 98:9; 99:4).

Another appropriate response to the demonstration of God's sovereignty is invited in v. 3*a*. The word "glory" (הִתְהַלְלוּ *hithāllû*) represents the Hebrew root that, in a more frequent conjugation of the verb, means "to praise" (הִלֵּל *hillēl*, see 104:35). In this form, it has the nuance of "boast," which is proper only if directed to God (see Pss 34:2; 106:5; Isa 41:16; 45:25; cf. Ps 75:5). The phrase "his holy name" (שֵׁם קָדְשׁוֹ *šēm qādšô*, v. 3*a*; see Pss 106:47 and 97:12, where a different Hebrew word underlies "name") recalls v. 1*a*; "name" directs attention to the character of God revealed in God's "wonderful works." Two different Hebrew verbs underlie the three occurrences of "seek" [בקשׁ *biqqēš*; דרשׁ *dāraš*] in vv. 3*b*-4 (cf. v. 4*a* NIV). To seek God's "face" may suggest to approach God in worship (see Pss 24:6; 27:8), perhaps indicating a cultic setting for the psalm. More broadly, however, to seek God means to entrust one's whole existence to God in recognition of God's sovereign claim (see Pss 9:10; 34:5, 10; 40:16; 69:6). God's "strength" bespeaks God's sovereignty (Pss 29:1; 96:6), but it is also a gift shared with God's people (see Pss 29:11; 68:35; 84:5; 86:16). Thus the act of remembering (v. 5*c*; see also Pss 77:11; 106:7), which Psalm 105 itself represents, is

a fundamental first step toward participation in the paradox of being strong by yielding the self in order to be God's servant (v. 6*a*; see also v. 42), which is what the sovereign God intends the "chosen ones" to be (v. 6*b*; see also vv. 26, 43).

105:7-11. Before the actual rehearsing of God's "wonderful works" in vv. 12-45, vv. 7-11 lay the foundation for God's action on behalf of Israel: the covenant with Abraham, Isaac, and Jacob, involving the promise of the land (see Gen 12:1-3; 15:1-19, esp. vv. 18-19; 17:1-14, esp. vv. 2, 7-8; 24:7; 26:3; 28:13; 35:12; 50:24; see also Deut 1:8; 4:31; 8:1). The "he" that begins v. 7 is emphatic, and God is the subject of every verb in vv. 7-11. Verse 8 is especially reminiscent of Exod 2:24, where God remembers the covenant just prior to initiating the series of events that lead to the exodus (see also Exod 6:2-5; Ps 106:45). The covenant is termed an "everlasting covenant" (v. 10) elsewhere only in sources that are generally considered exilic or post-exilic (see Gen 9:16; 17:7; Isa 55:3; 61:8; Jer 32:40; Ezek 16:60; 37:26), except perhaps 2 Sam 23:5.

105:12-25. These verses recall the wanderings of the patriarchs and matriarchs, who are called "strangers" (or "alien") in Gen 19:9; 26:3; 35:27. Verse 14 may have in view the stories in which Sarah is threatened by Abraham's deception (Gen 12:10-20; 20:1-7; cf. Gen 26:6-11). Abraham is called a prophet in Gen 20:7 (see above on v. 15). Both prophets and kings ("anointed ones") were known as God's servants, the primary identification of the whole people in Psalm 105 (vv. 6, 25, 42; see also "slave" in v. 17). Verses 16-22 summarize the story of Joseph (Genesis 37–50), whose unlikely release from captivity and rise to power might have been a particularly encouraging example to the exilic and post-exilic generations. Jacob/Israel arrived in Egypt toward the conclusion of the Joseph story (v. 23; see Genesis 46). The people remained there and prospered (v. 24; see Exod 1:1-7), provoking the hatred of the Egyptians (v. 25; Exod 1:7-22).

105:26-38. Here the psalmist rehearses the rest of the exodus story (Exod 2:1–15:21), focusing primarily on the plagues (v. 27; see also Ps 78:43)—darkness (v. 28; v. 28 should probably be translated in accordance with the NRSV note, understanding the subject as personified darkness;[397] see Exod 10:21-29), waters to blood (v. 29; see Exod 7:14-25; Ps 78:44), frogs (v. 30; see Exod 8:1-15; Ps 78:45b), flies and gnats (v. 32; see Exod 8:16-32; Ps 78:45a), hail and lightning (vv. 32-33; see Exod 9:13-35; Ps 78:47-48), locusts (vv. 34-35; see Exod 10:1-20; Ps 78:46), and death of the firstborn (v. 36; see Exod 11:1-10; 12:29-32; Pss 78:51; 135:8; 136:10). The number and order of the plagues differ in Psalm 105 from both Exod 7:14–12:32 and Ps 78:44-51, perhaps reflecting a different tradition and illustrating that the poet's purpose was not historical accuracy. Verses 37-38 recall Exod 12:33-36.

105:39-44. The cloud and fire led the people even before the crossing of the sea (see Exod 13:21-22; 14:24) and continued with them into the wilderness (see Num 9:15-16; 14:4), which is also the setting for v. 40 (see Exod 16:13; Num 11:31-32) and

v. 41 (see Exod 17:1-7; Num 20:2-13). Verse 42 recalls v. 8 ("promise" [דבר dābār] in v. 42 is more literally "word"), and v. 43 perhaps looks back over the whole exodus/wilderness story ("brought out" is often used of the exodus; see Exod 18:1–20:2) in anticipation of the recollection of the entry into the land in v. 44. Verse 43, however, is similar to the description of the return from exile in Deutero-Isaiah (see Isa 55:12), who saw the return as a new exodus. Verse 43 is probably another indication that Psalms 105–106 were intended to address the crisis of exile.

105:45. Along with vv. 1-6, v. 45 indicates the real purpose of the psalm: to evoke praise and obedience. Verses 1-6 point to God's sovereignty, and it was the responsibility of a sovereign to establish justice, righteousness, and peace among his or her servant people (see Pss 72:1-7; 82:1-4; 106:3). It is to this end that v. 45 is directed (see Deut 26:16-19; Ps 78:7). Verse 45 also prepares the reader to hear Psalm 106, which will document at length the people's failure to respond to God's "wonderful works" (Pss 105:2, 5; 106:7, 22).

397. Th. Booij, "The Role of Darkness in Psalm CV 28," *VT* 39 (1989) 211-12.

REFLECTIONS

A familiar hymn asks the question, "Why should the wonders He hath wrought be lost in silence and forgot?" (Isaac Watts, "Bless O My Soul! the Living God"). In answer to this question, Psalm 105 resoundingly proclaims, "They shouldn't!" Rather, the people of God are called upon to "make known . . . tell . . . remember" (vv. 1-2, 6). By asserting God's sovereignty and inviting people to praise and obey God (vv. 1-6, 45), Psalm 105 subverts every human claim to power and privilege (see Commentary on Psalm 78). In other words, the primary identity of God's people is that of servant (see vv. 6, 26, 42), and the good news is that persons who submit their lives to God's claim will be strong (v. 4; see also Mark 8:35; Luke 18:14).

By focusing exclusively on God's activity, including God's choice of a people (vv. 6, 26, 43) and the establishment of a covenant with them (vv. 8-10), Psalm 105 articulates the priority of God's grace. God does call for obedience, but only *after* God's choice of the people and the performance of "wonderful works." In this regard, Psalm 105 is like the Pentateuch, which is featured in the psalm. That is, exodus precedes Sinai; deliverance precedes demand; grace comes first. God's choice precedes all human choices.

Not only is grace the first word, but as the juxtaposition of Psalms 105 and 106 affirms, grace is the final word as well (see Commentary on Psalm 106). Even after a long and sordid history of faithlessness and disobedience, God will still remember the covenant God made with the people (Ps 106:45; see also 105:8, 42), and God will act "for their sake" (106:45). Thus, by telling the story of God's "wonderful works," Psalms 105–106 not only rehearse the past but also anticipate the future. For Christians, God's "wonderful works"—the story of God's acting "for their sake"—continue in Jesus Christ. He is taken to be the ultimate sign of the good news already evident in Psalms 105–106: the priority and perseverance of God's amazing grace (see Rom 3:24; 5:1-2; 6:14-15).

PSALM 106:1-48, OUT OF GREAT LOVE, GOD RELENTED

COMMENTARY

Like Psalm 105, with which it should be heard, Psalm 106 rehearses Israel's story, but it includes a very different series of episodes. To be sure, the psalmist is aware of the "wonderful works" that are featured in Psalm 105 (see 106:7, 22; see also 105:2, 5), but what the psalmist tells about are Israel's reprehensible works, the result of not remembering God's work (vv. 7, 13, 21) and consequently not trusting God's word (see v. 24b; cf. v. 12). Whereas God remembers God's word and the covenant it bespeaks (Pss 105:8, 42; 106:45), the people constantly forget, and their forgetfulness leads to a history of faithlessness that is costly to the people (vv. 40-43) and painful for their spurned lover—God. Indeed, only the abundance of God's steadfast love has kept the story going (vv. 1, 7, 45; see Introduction) and serves as the basis for the hopeful appeal in v. 47.

Verse 47 situates the people and the psalm in the exilic or post-exilic era. This is in keeping with the whole of Book IV (see Commentary on Psalms 90; 93; 101; 102; Introduction), which confronts and responds to the theological crisis of exile that is presented in Book III (see Commentary on Psalms 73; 74; 79; 80; 89; Introduction). The pattern presented in Psalms 105–106—God's "wonderful works," followed by the people's disobedience, followed by God's compassion (see vv. 43-46)—was the only hope the exiles had. While concluding Book IV, Psalm 106 also anticipates the opening of Book V. Psalms 106 and 107 begin the same way, and Psalm 107 recounts precisely the experience for which Ps 106:47 prays (see "gather[ed]" in 106:47; 107:3; see also Commentary on Psalm 107, which also features several other words from Psalm 106, including "steadfast love" and "wonderful works").

Scholars cannot agree on the proper form-critical categorization of Psalm 106. Thus it is variously viewed as a song of praise (see vv. 1-2), a communal lament or prayer for help (see vv. 4-5, 47), a liturgy of penitence (see vv. 6-7), and a sermon, as well as its more frequent designation as a historical psalm. Like the other historical psalms (see Psalms 78; 105; 136), the purpose of Psalm 106 is not to impart information about the past. Rather, it is to invite gratitude, faithfulness, and obedience in the present as the prelude to a transformed future (see Commentary on Psalm 78). Psalm 106 grounds the hope for a transformed future, however, not in the people's willingness or ability to be faithful and obedient but in God's abundant love. Thus it finally has the character of a profession of faith in God and God's compassionate, faithful, forgiving love.

106:1-3. Actually, v. 1 is itself a basic profession of faith (see 2 Chr 5:13; 7:3; Pss 107:1; 118:1, 29; 136:1; Introduction), as well as an invitation to praise (see the return to the vocabulary of praise in v. 47). While in the form of a question, v. 2 is actually an affirmation that no one is capable of adequately praising God. Verse 3 suggests that in the absence of this capability, what we are called upon to do, for our own sake as well as God's, is to conform to God's will—justice and righteousness (see Deut 16:19-20; Pss 96:10, 13; 97:2; 98:9; 99:4; Mic 6:8). Happiness is to be found not in acting selfishly but in doing what God intends (see Ps 1:1-2). Of course, most of the rest of the psalm documents Israel's failure in precisely this regard.

106:4-5. But before turning to the confession of sin and accompanying recital, the poet or worship leader voices in vv. 4-5 an individual petition that points to the end of the psalm and its hopeful conclusion (see "remember" in vv. 4, 45; "people" in vv. 4, 40; "deliver"/"save" in vv. 4, 47; "glory"/"praise" in vv. 5, 47; "heritage" in vv. 5, 40). The brief prayer also recalls v. 1 ("good" in v. 1 and "prosperity" in v. 5 are the same Hebrew root [טוב *ṭôb*]), and the mention of "saving"/"delivering" (ישע *yāšaʿ*) becomes thematic (see also vv. 8, 10, 21). The designation "chosen ones" is a link to Psalm 105 (see 105:6, 26, 43), as is the word "glory" (see 105:3).

106:6. This verse introduces both the first historical episode and the penitent character of the whole psalm. It contains three of the major Hebrew roots that convey "sin" (see Commentary on Psalms 32; 51). Verse 6a reads, literally, "We have sinned with our ancestors," perhaps recalling Exod 20:6; 34:7, which suggest that the parents' sins have ongoing effects (cf. Jer 31:27-30; Ezek 18:1-4). While the subsequent recital will focus on the past, the psalmist demonstrates from the beginning the same concern evident in the book of Deuteronomy: to actualize the experience of past generations for the present generation. The extended confession of sin also recalls the Deuteronomistic speech placed on the lips of Solomon in 1 Kgs 8:33-40, 46-53; from the perspective of its imagined tenth-century BCE setting, it anticipates the people's sin and the loss of land, both of which are presupposed in Psalm 106 (see also Neh 9:9-37; Isa 63:7–64:12; Dan 9:3-19).

106:7-12. Although the Song of the Sea celebrates God's "wonderful works" (see Exod 15:11), Psalm 106 is correct to trace the people's failure of memory and faith all the way back to Egypt (v. 7; see Exod 14:10-12). "Consider" (שכל *śākal*) in v. 7 means more literally "to be wise," and the beginning of the psalter defines wisdom as recognition of God's sovereignty (see Ps 2:10). Israel's foolish self-reliance—their rebellion (see vv. 33, 43; see also Pss 78:8, 17, 40, 56; 107:11)—does not prevent God's acting for God's own sake (v. 8; see "know" in Exod 14:18). Verses 9-11 briefly rehearse the sea crossing (see Exod 14:21-29; cf. v. 28 with Exod 14:28), and v. 12 correctly recalls Israel's initial belief (see Exod 14:31) and praise in song (Exod 15:1-21).

106:13-15. The "soon" in v. 13 is an understatement. Only three verses after the conclusion of the Song of the Sea, the people are already complaining (Exod 15:24). The psalmist may have this episode in view, as well as several other similar scenes in the wilderness, especially Num 11:4-34 (cf. Ps 106:14a with Num 11:4; see also Exodus 16). Verse 14b also recalls Exod 17:1-7 (see "tested" in v. 7). Verse 15a recognizes that God did provide water, manna, and quail; the difficult v. 15b, if the NIV and the NRSV are followed, recalls Num 11:33. Verse 15b can be construed more positively as conveying God's provision for the people: "he cast out (the) leanness in their throat." That vv. 13-15 recall several episodes should not be surprising. The psalmist does not follow the canonical order of events and is not intent upon accurate historical presentation.

106:16-23. Verses 16-18 offer a summary of the rebellion in Num 16:1-35 (see esp. Num 16:1-3, 30-35). The omission of Korah is surprising and perhaps indicates that the psalmist was working with a different or earlier form of the tradition. Verses 19-23 recall the beginning of the golden calf episode in Exod 32:1-14. In addition, v. 20 is similar to Hos 4:17 and Jer 2:11. Later in the psalm, there will be an allusion to the conclusion of the golden calf episode, in which God "showed compassion" (v. 45; see also Exod 32:14) or "relented," ultimately revealing God's self as a God of abundant "steadfast love" and pity/mercy (Exod 34:6; see also Ps 106:45-46).

106:24-27. These verses are a summary of Num 14:1-25, where the people refuse to accept the report of those sent to spy on the promised land (cf. v. 24 with Num 14:11; v. 25 with Num 14:22; Deut 1:27). As v. 26 suggests, the people's grumbling was the catalyst for God's decision that the wilderness generation would not enter the land (see Num 14:22-23; Deut 1:34). Like the golden calf episode, the spies episode also ends with Moses' appeal for God's forgiveness, based on God's steadfast love (cf. Exod 34:6b-7 with Num 14:18-19; see Ps 106:45). Verse 27 draws an analogy between the consequences experienced by the wilderness generation and the present experience of the people (see v. 47; Lev 26:33; Ezek 20:23).

106:28-33. These verses cite the episode described in Num 25:1-13 (see Hos 9:10). Numbers 25:2 does not associate the sacrifices with ones "offered to the dead" (Ps 106:28); however, there is some evidence that the worship of the Canaanite gods was associated with funeral observances—the *marzeaḥ* feast seemingly alluded to in Jer 16:6-9 and Amos 6:4-7.[398] Verses 32-33 summarize Exod 17:1-7 (see also Num 20:2-13). The NIV is closer to the Hebrew text in v. 33*a*, but the Hebrew words for "rebel" (מרה *mārâ*; see vv. 7, 43) and "bitter" (מרר *mārar*) are similar, and many translators go with the NRSV translation.

106:34-39. These verses turn to the people's disobedience after they had entered the land—syncretism and idolatry (vv. 34-35; see Num 33:50-56; Deut 7:1-6; 13:6-18; 17:2-7; 20:16-18; 32:15-18), including child sacrifice (vv. 37-38; see Lev 18:21; Deut 12:31; 2 Kgs 16:3; 21:6; 23:10; Jer 7:31; 19:5). The verb in "be unclean" (טמא *ṭāmē'*, v. 39) is used often in Leviticus of temporary ritual impurity, but the prophets also use it to describe the results of Israel's idolatry (see "defile"/"pollute" Jer 2:7, 23; Ezek 20:30-31, 43; Hos 5:3; 6:10). The verb "to prostitute" (זנה *zānâ*) is used the same way (see "prostitute"/"play the whore" in Exod 34:15-16; Deut 31:16; Jer 2:20; 3:1; Ezek 23:3, 19; Hos 4:10; 5:3).

106:40-46. These verses are particularly reminiscent of the Deuteronomistic pattern repeated several times in the book of Judges (see Judg 2:11-13; "moved to pity" in

Judg 2:18 NRSV is the same verb as "showed compassion" in Ps 106:45), but they could well describe the vicissitudes of Israelite and Judean history recounted in the books of Judges through 2 Kings. As v. 44 reminds the reader, the pattern is related to the exodus (see Exod 3:7). But after the exodus, the problem became not just external oppression but the internal faithlessness that is described at length in vv. 13-39. In the book of Exodus, the question became, "Will God put up with this rebellious people?" (see Exod 32:7-10). The answer is yes, not because the people ever do any better, but because God is steadfastly loving and merciful (see Exod 34:6-7), the attributes celebrated in vv. 45-46. God's character—not their own—was the people's only hope, especially in exile and beyond (v. 47). The word "name" (שם *šēm*) in v. 47 often stands for character, and its occurrence at the end of the sorry story in vv. 6-46 is another reminder that God's holiness consists finally not in God's separation from sin and sinners but in God's bearing the burden of sin and forgiving sinners (see Commentary on Psalms 99; 103).

106:47-48. While Ps 105:1-11 opened with the prayer offered on David's behalf in 1 Chr 16:7-36, Ps 106:47-48 provides its conclusion (1 Chr 16:35-36). This envelope structure is an appropriate reflection in the chronicler's work of the reality of the exile and its aftermath. It is interesting that v. 48, the doxology concluding Book IV, occurs also in 1 Chr 16:36. This seems to suggest that the divisions of the psalter were already in place, unless one concludes that the doxologies in the psalms occur coincidentally and have no editorial significance (see Introduction).

398. See Neil H. Richardson, "Psalm 106: Yahweh's Succouring Love Saves from the Death of a Broken Covenant," in *Love and Death in the Ancient Near East*, ed. J. H. Marks and R. M. Good (Guilford, Conn.: Four Quarters, 1987) 198.

REFLECTIONS

1. Whereas Psalm 105 affirmed the priority of God's grace (see Commentary on Psalm 105), Psalm 106 proclaims the perseverance of God's grace. This good news is clearly what Israel needed to hear in the midst of the exile and its aftermath; but, as Psalm 106 demonstrates, this good news had been evident from the beginning and throughout Israel's history (see esp. vv. 8, 43). Indeed, there would have been no story to rehearse, apart from the way God is—steadfastly loving, ceaselessly compassionate, abundantly merciful (vv. 45-46). Israel was saved by grace!

2. This good news did not stop with Israel's story. The apostle Paul saw in v. 20 not only a comment on Israel's character but also a comment on the character of all humanity (see Rom 1:23). To be sure, Paul could cite episodes from Israel's wilderness experience as "examples for us" (1 Cor 10:6; cf. 1 Cor 10:5, 7-11 with Ps 106:19-23, 28-31), in order to encourage Christians to be obedient. Paul knew, however, that humankind is fundamentally sinful (see Rom 1:18-28; 3:9-20; 7:14-25). And Paul proclaimed ultimately that we are justified by God's grace (Rom 3:24-26; 5:1-2)—"while we still were sinners Christ died for us" (Rom 5:8 NRSV). Humankind is saved by grace!

3. Lest Israel's story sound too bad to be true, Christians should be reminded that the same basic story was played out by Jesus' disciples. In the Gospels, especially in Mark, the disciples are incredibly foolish (see Mark 8:31-33; 9:30-37; 10:32-44) and incurably faithless (see Mark 14:50, 66-72). Yet these same disciples are later empowered to be the church (see John 20:19-23; Acts 2). The church was created by grace. And lest we look askance at Jesus' disciples and the early church, we need only remind ourselves of the many sorry chapters from the annals of church history, or of the many embarrassing realities that characterize the contemporary church—racism, sexism, greed, cultural accommodation, disunity, reluctance to proclaim the good news and to embody it in selfless love for all people and all creation. Indeed, some have proclaimed the beginning of the post-Christian era, noting that the church is awash in an overwhelming sea of cultural influences—a contemporary exile perhaps. If so, then Psalm 106 may be even more timely than ever: "Save us, O LORD our God,/ and gather us from among the nations,/ that we may give thanks to your holy name/ and glory in your praise" (v. 47).

Self-centered as we are, and priding ourselves on being powerful people, we are likely to want to respond to the current crisis by trying to program our way out of it—in short, trusting ourselves instead of entrusting ourselves to God. But praise is about trusting God. Mays points out:

> The voice of trusting praise is the sound and sign of a people restored by the LORD's salvation (vv. 12, 47). The litmus test for the spiritual health of the people of the LORD is the integrity and actuality of their praise, whether they "remember the abundance of the LORD's steadfast love" (v. 7) or forget his deed and let themselves be determined by dangers or desires or the ways of the nations.[399]

The current crisis facing the church is not really new; it is simply another chapter in the ongoing story told in Psalm 106. Now, as then, the best possible news is that God loves us steadfastly (see Commentary on Psalms 32; 51). We are saved by grace! "Praise the LORD!" (vv. 1, 48).

399. Mays, *Psalms,* 342.

PSALMS 107–150

BOOK V

PSALM 107:1-43, CONSIDER THE STEADFAST LOVE OF GOD

COMMENTARY

P salm 107 opens Book V with what appears to be a direct response to the concluding plea of Book IV (see "gather[ed]" in Pss 106:47; 107:3). Psalm 107 also features in an impressive way one of the key words in Psalm 106 and the psalter as a whole: "steadfast love" (חסד *ḥesed*; see Ps 106:1, 7, 45; Introduction). The word occurs in the first and last verses of Psalm 107 (note that 106:1 and 107:1 are identical), and it occurs in the second of the psalm's two refrains (vv. 8, 15, 21, 31). There are still more literary and conceptual links between Psalms 106 and 107—"wonderful works" (106:7, 22; 107:8, 15, 21, 24, 31), "rebel" (106:7, 33, 43; 107:11), "redeemed" (106:10; 107:2), "counsel" (106:13; 107:11), "subjected" (106:42; 107:12), "distress"/"trouble" (106:44; 107:2, 6, 13, 19, 28), "iniquity" (106:43; 107:17). Indeed, Psalm 107 can be regarded as further illustration of the pattern evident throughout Psalm 106 and summarized in 106:43-46. In other words, Book V begins in a manner that suggests that the editors of the psalter intended it, like Book IV (see Commentary on Psalms 90; 93; Introduction), to serve as a response to Book III and its elaboration of the theological crisis of exile and its aftermath (see Commentary on Psalms 73; 74; 79; 80; 89; Introduction). Psalm 107, for instance, serves as a pointed response to the question raised in Ps 89:49: "Lord, where is your steadfast love of old?"

Psalm 107 is usually categorized as an individual song of thanksgiving, based on v. 1, the second refrain (vv. 8, 15, 21, 31), and the expansion of this refrain in vv. 22, 32. It may have been used as a congregational liturgy (v. 32) accompanying a thanksgiving sacrifice offered in the Temple (v. 22). Most scholars who propose this idea, however, also suggest that an original core of Psalm 107 (vv. 1, 4-32) has been expanded by the addition of vv. 2-3, 33-43 in order to explicitly address the exilic or post-exilic era. This conclusion is congruent with that suggested above concerning the canonical placement of Psalm 107.

In considering the structure of Psalm 107, it is helpful to think of it as a sermon on God's steadfast love, beginning with an invitation for congregational response (vv. 1-3), followed by four narrative illustrations (vv. 4-9, 10-16, 17-22, 23-32), and concluding with a hymnlike summary based on the four illustrations (vv. 33-42) and an admonition to continue to attend to the message about God's steadfast love (v. 43). The whole psalm effectively conveys what God's steadfast love is all about: compassion for people in need, including forgiveness, since the distress in two instances is the result of human sinfulness (see vv. 11, 17). Jorge Mejía suggests that the four illustrations are arranged chiastically (see Introduction). Arguing that the desert and the sea are symbolic of chaos, Mejía concludes that "two acts of salvation from sin [vv. 10-16, 17-22] are framed by two acts of salvation from chaos [vv. 4-9, 23-32]." The result, especially in the light of the addition of vv. 33-43, is "a fairly complete theology of salvation."[400]

107:1-3. Verse 1 not only ties Psalm 107 conceptually to Psalm 106, but also introduces its major theme: steadfast love. Verse

400. Jorge Mejía, "Some Observations on Psalm 107," *Biblical Theology Bulletin* 5 (1975) 58, 66.

2 introduces the countertheme: trouble. Each of these key words is featured in one of the refrains. Given the definition of "the redeemed" as those "gathered" from exile, it is not surprising that the post-exilic generations were known elsewhere as "The Redeemed of the Lord" (Isa 62:12; see also Isa 43:1; 44:22-23; 48:20; 52:9).

107:4-9. While these verses may be read as the experience of any person or group, the reader may also find allusions to Israel's experience of exodus/wilderness and return from exile. Each involves wandering (see "go astray" in Ps 95:10; Isa 35:8 NRSV) in a "desert" (see Exod 15:22; 16:1; Isa 40:3) or "wastelands" (see Deut 32:10; Ps 78:40; Isa 43:19-20). Each involves hunger (see Exod 26:3; Isa 49:10) and thirst (Exod 17:3; Isa 41:17), which are filled or satisfied by God (see Exod 16:12; Isa 55:2). Each involves God's leading the way (see Exod 3:18; 5:3; Isa 11:15; 48:17), and each may be described or anticipated as "wonderful works" (see Exod 3:20; 15:11; Mic 7:15). In short, even if vv. 4-9 originated in the experience of some people (v. 4), these verses were easily adaptable to corporate experiences of deliverance, such as exodus and return from exile. The verb "cried" (צעק $\check{s}\bar{a}'aq$, v. 6) is particularly reminiscent of the exodus (see Exod 3:7, 9; 14:10; Deut 26:7), but it is not limited to that experience (see also Judg 3:9, 15; 6:6-7; Neh 9:4; Ps 142:5). In fact, the people's crying out is always a feature of the experience of salvation, as its repetition in Psalm 107 suggests. As Mays puts it:

> What sets the *ḥesed* ["steadfast love"] of the LORD in motion in every case is the cry to the LORD in trouble. The psalm sees the *ḥesed* of the LORD manifest in salvation completely in this way. It elevates the prayer for help, the voice of dependence on God, to the central place in the relation to God.[401]

107:10-16. These verses could describe anyone's experience of oppression. See "darkness," for instance, in Pss 18:28; 143:3; Isa 9:2; Mic 7:8, and see "gloom" in Ps 23:4 (NIV, "shadow of death"; NRSV, "darkest");

Isa 9:2. But both of these words are used also of exile (see "darkness" in Isa 42:7; 49:9; Jer 13:16; Lam 3:2; and see "gloom" in Ps 44:19; Jer 13:16). Similarly, the word "prisoners" (אסירים $\check{a}s\hat{i}r\hat{i}m$) need not designate the condition of the exiles (see Ps 68:6), but it can (see Isa 49:9; Lam 3:34; Zech 9:11; and perhaps Pss 79:11; 102:20), as can the word "misery" (עני $\check{o}n\hat{i}$; see v. 17 NIV and NRSV, "affliction"; v. 41 NRSV, "distress"; see also Ps 44:24; Lam 1:3, 7; 3:19). The attribution of the oppression to rebellion (v. 11) is also appropriate for the exile, and v. 11 also recalls Psalm 106 (see vv. 7, 13, 33, 43), reinforcing the conclusion that Psalm 107 also intends to address the exilic crisis and its aftermath by presenting the same pattern that pervades Psalm 106. In keeping with God's character, God helps those who have "no one to help" (v. 12; see also Ps 22:11 and Commentary on Psalm 3). God is steadfastly loving.

107:17-22. A comparison of the NIV with the NRSV of v. 17*a* reveals that the NIV retains the Hebrew text. Because of the description in v. 18 and the mention of healing in v. 20, however, many translators emend the text in the direction of the NRSV. This is not necessary, nor is it advisable in the light of the mention of "wise" in v. 43. Even if sickness is the subject of vv. 17-22, sickness elsewhere is associated with disobedience (see Psalms 6; 38), which in turn is elsewhere a manifestation of foolishness (see Prov 1:7; Isa 19:11; Jer 4:22). It is possible that the imagery of sickness is a metaphorical description of an urgent, life-threatening situation (see "gates of death" in Ps 9:13; cf. Isa 38:10, however, where sickness is the problem). In any case, it is God who heals, literally (see 2 Kgs 20:5) or figuratively (see Jer 3:22; Hos 6:1; 11:3; 14:5). In fact, the figurative use of the verb can portray the forgiveness that enables return from exile (see Isa 57:18-19; Jer 33:6). Again, even if vv. 17-22 originated as a general description of deliverance, these verses were easily adaptable to the return from exile. The means of God's deliverance is God's "word" (see Isa 40:8; 55:11). In contrast to the first two illustrations, the concluding verse of this one is an invitation for response (see v. 32). The delivered are to proclaim publicly what God has done (see Ps 73:28*c*).

401. Mays, *Psalms*, 347; see also Richard N. Boyce, *The Cry to God in the Old Testament*, SBLDS 103 (Atlanta: Scholars Press, 1985) 68-69.

107:23-32. "Works" in v. 22 recurs in v. 24*a.* God's "works" are seen by sailors at sea. While the previous three illustrations have affinities with other material in the psalms, nowhere else in the psalter is there a description of deliverance from distress at sea (see Jonah 1–2; the words "deep" and "depths" in Ps 107:24, 26 also occur in Jonah 2:3, 5). This scenario, however, gives the psalmist the opportunity to assert God's ability to deliver even from hostile cosmic forces, which are symbolized by "the sea," "the deep" and "the depths," "the storm," and "the waves" (see v. 29 and above commentaries on Pss 74:12-15; 93:3-4; see also Gen 1:2; Exod 15:5, 8; Matt 8:23-27; Mark 4:35-41). The phrase "were at their wits' end" (v. 27*b*) is more literally, "all their wisdom was swallowed up," perhaps another allusion to Jonah (see Jonah 1:17). In any case, "wisdom" anticipates v. 43. True wisdom is to cry out to God, to acknowledge one's utter dependence upon God and to know that God's steadfast love is sufficient for even the worst possible scenario (see Commentary on Psalm 46). The appropriate response to this good news is praise, which is a public liturgical response that bespeaks the yielding of one's life to God (v. 32; see also Ps 106:47). To "extol" or "exalt" God involves the fundamental recognition of God's sovereignty, which is manifest in God's acts of deliverance like those illustrated in Psalm 107 (see Exod 15:2; Pss 99:5, 9; 145:1).

107:33-43. Many scholars consider this section to be an exilic or post-exilic updating of an original core of the psalm (vv. 4-32). This proposal is strengthened by the fact that portions of vv. 33-43 are based on previous verses (cf. v. 36*a* with vv. 5, 9; v. 36*b* with vv. 4, 7; v. 40 with v. 4; v. 41 with vv. 10, 17). On the other hand, all good poets and storytellers regularly employ repetition. In any case, vv. 33-43 are reminiscent of other exilic material (cf. v. 33*a* with Isa 50:2; v. 35 with Isa 41:18), and they serve as an apt poetic description of the return from exile (see vv. 2-3). Earthly sovereigns are made subject to the sovereignty of God (v. 40; see also Pss 47:9; 118:9; 146:3) as part of God's great reversal of fortunes (v. 41; see also 1 Sam 2:8; Ps 113:7; 146:8). Those who acknowledge God's sovereignty—"the upright" (v. 42*a;* see also Pss 11:7; 33:1)—can rejoice as injustice is thwarted (see Pss 52:6-7; 58:10-11; 63:11).

It may be coincidental, but just as the first psalm in Book IV portrayed wisdom as humble, daily dependence upon God (see Ps 90:12), so also Ps 107:43*a* asserts that wisdom consists of heeding the lesson of the preceding illustrations: Those who renounce self-sufficency and cry to God will be the beneficiaries of God's "wonderful works," which reveal God's enduring steadfast love (v. 43*b;* see vv. 1, 8, 15, 21, 31). Such was the only hope for exiles, as it had been Israel's only hope throughout its history (see Psalm 106). It is our hope as well (see Reflections).

REFLECTIONS

The probability that vv. 4-32 originated in the experience of some and were claimed by the whole people (or simply the fact that vv. 4-32 apply to a variety of experiences) is theologically significant, for it suggests that Scripture is a "living word that . . . is not exhausted in an ancient situation nor does it require repetition of history to become valid again, but runs freely, challenging a new generation of believers to see a fresh correspondence between word and experience."[402] To put it differently, the four illustrations in vv. 4-32 not only apply to a variety of ancient settings, including the crisis of exile and its aftermath, but also became "open paradigms."[403] Psalm 107 suggests, therefore, that there are certain typical things we can count on as we look for fresh correspondences between our experience and God's word and work. For instance, the four narrative illustrations assert the essential weakness, neediness, and sinfulness of humanity. Persons who are "wise" and "heed these things" (v. 43) will realize that

402. Allen, *Psalms 101–150,* 65.
403. Mays, *Psalms,* 346.

there is never a time when they are not in "trouble" (vv. 2, 6, 13, 19, 28). Thus, crying out to God, living in dependence upon God, is not simply an emergency measure but a way of life (see Commentary on Psalms 1; 2; 3).

This message is diametrically opposed to what much of contemporary North American culture teaches people. In modern culture, maturity is often measured by how *self-sufficient* we are. We are taught that we earn what we have (see vv. 4-9); we are taught that we must pull ourselves up by our bootstraps when we are down (see vv. 10-16); we are taught that wisdom is getting ahead in whatever way we can manage without getting caught (see vv. 17-22); we are taught that our security results from careful planning, investment, and management (see vv. 23-32). In short, we are taught to be self-made persons—no need to cry to God for help, and consequently no need to thank God for anything. Seldom, if ever, does it occur to us that human life depends on God.

Thus the message of Psalm 107 is simple but radical: There is ultimately no such thing as self-sufficiency, for human life depends on God. The good news is that we can depend on God. God is good (v. 1), and God shares God's goodness (v. 9). God loves us with a steadfast love, and Christians profess that this love is manifested in the life, death, and resurrection of Jesus Christ. Thus it is not surprising that Jesus does the same kinds of things that God does in the four narrative illustrations: feeding the hungry in the wilderness (Mark 6:30-44; 8:1-10; see Luke 1:53), liberating those bound by demonic powers (Mark 1:21-28; 3:20-27; Luke 4:16-21), healing and forgiving the sick (Mark 2:1-12), stilling storms at sea (Matt 8:23-27; Mark 4:35-41). Jesus called people to acknowledge and to live under God's sovereignty (see Mark 1:14-15), to renounce self-sufficiency and to walk the way of the cross in dependence upon God (see Mark 8:34-35). Indeed, as Paul recognized, the cross is precisely the sign that God chooses the foolish, the weak, the low, and the despised—that is, the very kind of people featured in the four narrative illustrations in Psalm 107. Using one of the key words in Psalm 107, Paul proclaims that the cross is "the power of God and the wisdom of God" (1 Cor 1:24 NRSV; see Ps 107:43). This kind of wisdom means that no one should "boast in the presence of God" (1 Cor 1:29 NRSV). Rather, the fundamental attitude and activity of the faithful will be gratitude for God's goodness and steadfast love. It is precisely this that Psalm 107 encourages and invites: "O give thanks to the Lord" (v. 1; see vv. 8, 15, 21, 31; see also Commentary on Psalm 50). The invitation to humble gratitude makes Psalm 107 appropriate for the season of Lent and for all seasons.

PSALM 108:1-13, WITH GOD WE SHALL DO VALIANTLY

COMMENTARY

Psalm 108 has apparently been composed by the joining of Ps 57:7-11 (Ps 108:1-5) and Ps 60:5-12 (Ps 108:6-13). While scholars agree that Psalms 57 and 60 represent the earlier versions of this material, they have reached no consensus concerning the reason for the use of portions of Psalms 57 and 60 to create Psalm 108. Kraus even suggests that it is "difficult, indeed almost impossible," to discern the reasons for and intent of the new composition.[404]

While there is clearly no room for absolute certainty, it is possible to find good reasons for the composition and current placement of Psalm 108 in the light of the intent of Books IV and V to respond to the crisis of exile and

404. Kraus, *Psalms 60–150*, 333.

its aftermath (see Commentary on Psalms 90; 107; Introduction). Psalm 107 celebrates God's redemption of the people and the return from exile (vv. 2-3), calling for grateful praise in response to God's steadfast love (vv. 1, 8, 15, 21-22, 31-32). Ps 57:7-11—now Ps 108:1-5—supplies precisely that. The verb "give thanks" (ידה *yādâ*) from Ps 107:1, 8, 15, 21, 31 recurs in Ps 108:3. Then, too, the word "steadfast love" (חסד *ḥesed*), which accompanies each occurrence of "give thanks" in Psalm 107, is the stated reason for praise in Ps 108:4. This verse can also be viewed as a direct response to Ps 89:49, the question with which Book III leaves the reader. Furthermore, "be exalted" (Ps 108:5) recalls Ps 107:32. Again, Ps 108:1-5 articulates the praise that Psalm 107 invites, and given the celebration of the return from exile, it is especially fitting that the praise is offered "among the peoples, and . . . nations" (v. 3). In Psalm 57, vv. 7-11 immediately follow an announcement that the psalmist has been delivered from enemies (57:6). Given the introduction (vv. 2-3) and conclusion (vv. 39-42) of Psalm 107, these verses have found a similar setting in Psalm 108—they offer exuberant praise and thanksgiving in response to God's steadfast love.

The skillful joining of portions of Psalms 57 and 60 is indicated by the fact that vv. 5-6 of Psalm 108 form a section of petition consisting of the last verse of the quotation from Psalm 57 (57:11) and the first verse from the quotation from Psalm 60 (60:5). The repetition of "glory" (v. 1, NIV and NRSV "soul"; v. 5) marks the beginning of the first two sections of the psalm (vv. 1-4, 5-6) and also signals the shift of attention from the psalmist's activity to God's activity. Following vv. 1-6, there is an oracle (vv. 7-9), a complaint (vv. 10-11), a further petition (v. 12), and an expression of trust (v. 13). In other words, following praise in celebration of deliverance (vv. 1-4), there is renewed complaint and petition for deliverance (vv. 10-12). This sequence is unusual but not entirely unique (see Psalms 40; 118; 126), but what is of particular interest here is that the sequence fits exactly the situation involved in the return from exile and subsequent events. Whereas the return itself was cause for celebration (vv. 1-4; see Psalm 107; Isaiah 40–55), the actual conditions following the return were far from ideal (see Isaiah 56–66; Haggai; Zechariah 1–8). In short, further help was needed and further petition became necessary as well, and Ps 60:5-12—now Ps 108:6-13—supplies precisely that. It seems to have been chosen because of its focus on Edom, which apparently rejoiced over and perhaps participated in the defeat of Jerusalem that led to the exile (see Ps 137:7; Obadiah 10–14) and therefore was a target of hostility in the exilic and post-exilic eras (see Obadiah 15–21). (For more detailed comment on Psalm 108, see the Commentary on Psalms 57; 60.)

REFLECTIONS

1. As was the case with Psalm 107, Psalm 108 illustrates the dynamic life and use of the psalms. In Allen's words, "The combination of earlier psalms illustrates the vitality of older scriptures as they were appropriated and applied to new situations in the experience of God's people."[405] In this case, Psalms 57 and 60 were brought together to form Psalm 108 as a response to the post-exilic situation. But Psalm 108 remains vital and applicable to the life of the people of God. By following initial praise with ongoing petition, Psalm 108 teaches us that the people of God never live beyond trouble and the need for God's help (see Commentary on Psalm 107). In a word, the perspective of Psalm 108, like that of the psalter as a whole, is eschatological, for it simultaneously celebrates and asks for God's help (see Commentary on Psalms 2; 57; 60; 93; 95; 96; 97; 98; 99; Introduction). Renouncing human help, it affirms that human life and the life of God's people depend finally on God (vv. 12-13).

405. Allen, *Psalms 101–150*, 70.

2. One is tempted to conclude that in addition to the reasons suggested above, Ps 57:7-11 was chosen to begin Psalm 108 on account of its splendid poetry; indeed, this could have been a consideration. In any case, the continuing artistic appeal of these verses is demonstrated by Leonard Bernstein's choice of Ps 108:2 to open the first movement of his *Chichester Psalms.* Bernstein juxtaposes Ps 108:2 with Psalm 100, another psalm that articulates both dependence upon God (100:3) and gratitude for God's steadfast love and faithfulness (100:4-5; see 108:3-4). Bernstein's work is testimony, too, to the vitality of the psalms as scripture and to their ability to be applied creatively to new situations in the life of God's people.

PSALM 109:1-31, GOD SAVES THOSE WHO ARE NEEDY

COMMENTARY

Hermann Gunkel considered Psalm 109 to be the only pure psalm of imprecation in the psalter, and many commentators note its peculiar character.[406] While it begins and ends with elements that are typical of a prayer for help or individual lament/complaint—petition (vv. 1*a*, 20-21, 26-29), complaint (vv. 1*b*-5, 22-25), vow to praise and profession of trust (vv. 30-31)—the verses in between (vv. 6-19) constitute what Brueggemann aptly calls a "song of hate."[407] Lest Psalm 109 be too quickly dismissed as nothing but an expression of desire for unlimited revenge, it is important to consider the context of vv. 6-19. Verses 1-5 suggest that the psalmist, although innocent, has been put on trial. Several scholars assert that the trial would have taken place in the Temple before priestly judges (see Commentary on Psalms 5; 7; see also Exod 22:8; Deut 17:8-13; 1 Kgs 8:31-32). Whether the psalm actually records the psalmist's prayer in such a setting or whether such a setting should be interpreted metaphorically is unclear. In either case, it is crucial to hear the psalmist's words as those of an unjustly accused person; in short, the psalmist comes to God as one who is "poor and needy" (v. 22; see vv. 16, 31).

A major interpretative issue, reflected in a comparison of v. 6 in the NIV and the NRSV, is whether vv. 6-19 should be understood as the words of the psalmist against the accusers (NIV), or whether they should be construed

as the psalmist's quotation of what the accusers have said about him or her (NRSV; NIV note). Since the psalmist has been referring to a plurality of accusers (vv. 2-5), the switch to the singular in v. 6 seems to support the NRSV. Furthermore, if v. 6 begins the words of the accusers, then v. 31 would be an eminently fitting reply by the psalmist. Whereas the enemies wish for an accuser to stand on the psalmist's right (v. 6), the psalmist professes that it is God who "stands at the right hand of the needy" (v. 31). On the other hand, there is nothing in the text to indicate specifically that vv. 6-19 are the words of the accusers; it is entirely possible that the psalmist switches to the singular simply to address more specifically the last accuser who pointed the finger at him or her. Certainty is not possible, and commentators are divided almost equally on the issue. In either case, it should be noted that the option chosen by the NRSV does not remove the necessity of confronting the psalmist's desire for vengeance, because in v. 20 the psalmist claims the "song of hate" as an expression of his or her own desire for the accusers (even if it was the accusers who originally uttered the words). In the comments below, I shall follow the NIV's decision on this matter.

The placement of Psalm 109 may be entirely coincidental, but its major concept—steadfast love (vv. 21, 26; "kindness," vv. 12, 16 NIV and NRSV)—is also one that is featured prominently in Psalm 107 (vv. 1, 8, 15, 21, 31, 43) and appears in Psalm 108 as well (v. 3). Anticipating deliverance, the psalmist

406. Gunkel, *The Psalms,* 35.
407. Brueggemann, *The Message of the Psalms,* 83.

vows in v. 30 to do exactly what Psalm 107 enjoins: to give thanks to God (107:1, 8, 15, 21, 31) and to praise God publicly (107:32). In effect, the psalmist's anticipated deliverance in Psalm 109 can be added to the four narrative illustrations of God's saving love in Psalm 107 (vv. 4-32). Then, too, the psalmist, while vehemently expressing the desire for vengeance, apparently leaves the actual activity to God, as in Psalm 108 (vv. 21, 26-27, 31; see Ps 108:12-13). Furthermore, it may not be coincidental that the grounding of vengeance in God's love for the poor and needy (vv. 21-22) follows immediately the mention of Edom in Ps 108:10. If Psalm 109, like Psalms 107 and 108, is intended to address the post-exilic situation (see Introduction), then desire for vengeance against Edom would have been a major issue (see Ps 108:10; Obadiah 15–21; see also Ps 137:8-9, where the desire for vengeance is directed against Babylon, but apparently intended for Edom as well, as 137:7 suggests). It would have been important to articulate and ground this desire carefully, especially since Israel also remembered Edom as a brother (see Gen 25:30; see Ps 109:4-5). Whether intended or not, Psalm 109 could have this effect.

109:1-5. After a brief initial petition (v. 1; see Pss 28:1; 35:22; 83:1), the psalmist voices the complaint that he or she has been falsely accused. Although the phrase "deceitful mouths" is unique in the psalter, the psalmists frequently complain about deceitful persons and their speech (see Pss 5:6; 10:7; 35:20; 36:4), which is sometimes specifically described as "lying" (see Pss 27:12; 31:18; 101:7). This latter term often refers to testimony offered in court, so it may be particularly apt here (see Deut 19:18). In any case, the enemies' hateful words are not justified (v. 3; see Pss 35:7, 19; 69:4). The occurrence of "without cause" in Lam 3:52 is particularly interesting, because there a prayer upon the destruction of Jerusalem is voiced by an "I," who makes some of the same complaints and appeals as in Psalm 109. This indicates that Psalm 109 may have been understood corporately, especially following Psalms 107–108. The Hebrew root underlying "accuse(r)" in vv. 4, 6 (שטן śāṭan, see also vv. 20, 29) later became used of a superhuman adversary or accuser—Satan (see NIV note; 1 Chr 21:1;

Zech 3:1)—but the word in v. 4 simply designates an accusing witness (see Pss 38:20; 71:13). The enemies' accusations are even harder to take, because the psalmist has shown them not hatred but love (vv. 4-5).

109:6-19. Verses 4-5 describe a situation that cannot get any worse. Thus in v. 6 the psalmist asks for redress, suggesting in effect that the accusers get a dose of their own medicine. As they have proven themselves "wicked" (v. 2), so let the wicked get after them (v. 6a). As they have accused (v. 4), so let an accuser stand on their right—the position of closeness and help (v. 6b; see v. 31). Verse 6 could be understood as a request for due process, but v. 7 leaves due process behind. In other words, there is really no need for a trial, because the enemies are clearly "guilty" (רשע rāšāʿ, v. 7a, which translates the same Hebrew word as "wicked" in vv. 2, 6). Verse 7b also attempts to turn the tables on the accusers; just as the psalmist's prayer has been to no avail (v. 4b), so also let the enemies' prayer "miss the mark" (the fundamental sense of the NRSV's "sin").

In other words, the psalmist has put the enemies on trial (vv. 6-7), and vv. 8-19 can thus be understood as the sentence that a representative enemy deserves. The psalmist's desire for vengeance covers all the bases, to say the least. Not only is the enemy the direct target (vv. 8, 11-12, 17-19), but so also are his wife (v. 9), his children (vv. 9-10, 12), his posterity and any future remembrance of his name (v. 13), and even his ancestors (v. 14). The hyperbole would be comic were it not for the utter seriousness of the psalmist's request—let the enemy be annihilated. Even so, it is important to notice that the psalmist's request is in accordance with what most persons, then and now, would say is only fair—the punishment should fit the crime (see Exod 21:23-24; Lev 24:19-20; and esp. Deut 19:18b-19, 21). In particular, the enemy deserves no kindness (v. 12, or "steadfast love"), because he showed no kindness (v. 16). The enemy deserves to be impoverished (vv. 8-11), because he mistreated the poor and the needy (v. 16; see Ps 10:2). The enemy deserves to be cursed, because he cursed others (vv. 17-19, 28-29; see Ps 62:4). In short, the enemy deserves to die (v. 8), because he pursued others to their death (vv.

16, 31; see "pursue"/"persecute" in Pss 7:1; 31:15; 35:3; 119:84, 86, 157, 161; 142:6; 143:3).

109:20-31. The case against the accusers is summarized in v. 20, and in v. 21, the psalmist turns his or her case over to God. The "you" that begins v. 21 is emphatic, introducing the contrast between the character of the accusers and the character of God, who can be trusted to act in accordance with the divine character—"for your name's sake" (see Ps 23:3). If any one word describes God's character, it is "steadfast love" (חסד *hesed*; see Exod 34:6-7; Pss 5:7; 13:5; 103:4, 8, 11, 17; 107:1; Introduction). So the psalmist entrusts the self to God. Whereas the accusers showed no steadfast love (or kindness), God's steadfast love is "good" (v. 21; see also v. 26.) Whereas the accusers pursued the poor and the needy, God can be trusted to "deliver" them (v. 21), to "help" them (v. 26), to "save" them (v. 26). Whereas the accusers cursed, God can be trusted to bless (v. 28; see Gen 12:3; 5:12; 29:11). In other words, the psalmist professes the faith that pervades the psalter: God will hear the cries of the oppressed, and God will act (see Pss 9:18; 10:17-18; 11:7; 12:5; 14:5-6; 17:13-15;

107:39-43; 108:12-13). So the psalmist stresses his or her oppression and neediness (v. 22*a*; see Pss 35:10; 40:17; 70:5; 74:21; 86:1) in language reminiscent of other prayers for help—"pierced"/"wounded" (v. 22*b*; see Ps 69:26; Isa 53:5), "like a shadow" (v. 23*a*; see Job 17:7; Ps 102:11), "weak" knees (v. 24*a*; see Pss 31:10; 107:12; see also Isa 35:3-4, where this condition evokes God's vengeance against the perpetrators), "an object of scorn" that turns people's heads (v. 25; see Pss 22:6-7).

Recalling v. 21, the "you" in v. 27 is again emphatic; it is *God* who effects the great reversal of fortunes. (The NRSV's "act" [עשׂה *ʿāśâ*] in v. 21 and "done" in v. 27 are the same Hebrew verb, and both verses also mention God's steadfast love; note also the reversal in Ps 107:39-43.) There is another emphatic "you" in v. 28—*God* will bless, despite the enemies' curses. God's purposes will not be thwarted. Those who sought to shame the psalmist will themselves be ashamed (vv. 28-29; see Ps 35:26), and the psalmist will respond with joy (v. 28*b*), gratitude (v. 30*a*), praise (v. 30*b*), and trust in the God who loves and saves the oppressed (v. 31).

REFLECTIONS

1. In recent years at least, Psalm 109 has been largely ignored in Christian liturgy; in fact, it is often criticized as being morally inferior. This is a very interesting response, because most Christians seem to support what underlies the psalmist's expression of desire for vengeance in vv. 6-19—that is, that the punishment should fit the crime. Indeed, most Christians seem to support the death penalty for capital offenses. It would seem, therefore, that Psalm 109 should not present much of a problem. Yet, most Christians seem to think the psalmist's sentiments are somehow "unchristian," especially in the light of Jesus' admonition to love enemies, turn the other cheek, go the second mile. The psalmist does not measure up. The disparity between the standard we affirm (and legislatively embody in our legal system) and the standard to which we hold the psalmist is the initial clue to what Christians can learn from Psalm 109. If we are honest, we must conclude that the psalm teaches us about ourselves. *We* are vengeful people. As Brueggemann puts it:

> The real theological problem, I submit, is not that vengeance is *there* in the Psalms, but that it is *here* in our midst. And that it is there and here only reflects how attuned the Psalter is to what goes on among us. Thus, we may begin with a recognition of the acute correspondence between what is *written there* and what is *practiced here*. The Psalms do "tell it like it is" with us.[408]

408. Brueggemann, *Praying the Psalms*, 68.

2. Psalm 109 not only tells it like it is with us, but it also tells us how it is with the world. The psalmist had been victimized, and when persons become victims, they are bound to react with rage. C. S. Lewis says that Psalm 109 shows "the natural result of injuring a human being."[409] When persons are treated unjustly, we can expect them to lash out. We can expect them to express vehemently the desire for an end to the violence that has made them a victim. In other words, we can expect them to demand justice (the word "tried" in v. 7 could be translated "brought to justice"). When we hear Psalm 109 as a victim's appeal for justice, then "what we thought was a poisonous yearning for vengeance sounds more like a just claim submitted to the real judge."[410]

3. The psalmist's submission to God of rage, hurt, and demand for justice is not only to be expected, but it is also to be accepted as a sign of health. At this point, Psalm 109 teaches a basic principle of pastoral care: Anger is the legitimate response to abuse and victimization, and appropriate anger must be expressed. Such catharsis is healing. What Psalm 109 represents, however, is not merely a therapeutic movement. Rather, this is *theological* catharsis as well. The anger is expressed, but it is expressed in prayer and thereby submitted to God. While it is not explicit, we may assume that the psalmist's submission of anger to God in prayer was sufficient (see vv. 21, 27). This angry, honest prayer thus removes the necessity for the psalmist to take actual revenge upon the enemy. It seems that the psalmist honors God's affirmation in Deut 32:35, "Vengeance is mine" (NRSV; see also Psalm 94). Thus this vehement, violent-sounding prayer is, in fact, an act of nonviolence.

4. In the final analysis, then, Psalm 109 teaches us not only about ourselves and the world but also about God. It suggests that evil, injustice, and oppression must be confronted, opposed, hated because God hates them (see Psalm 82). From this perspective, the psalmist's desire for vengeance amounts to a desire for justice and righteousness in self and society—"Your will be done." God wills not victimization of persons but compassion for persons, as the fourfold occurrence of "steadfast love" indicates (vv. 12, 16, 21, 26). The psalmist's enemies had failed to embody God's fundamental character and will—"steadfast love." Thus their actions led to death for others instead of life. The psalmist grounds this appeal for help precisely in God's steadfast love (vv. 21, 26) and his or her own oppression and neediness (v. 22; see v. 31; cf. v. 16). The psalmist affirms that God's steadfast love means judgment upon victimizers for the sake of the victims—the poor and the needy. Psalm 109 thus teaches us who God is, what God wills and does, and what God would have us do. To be instructed by Psalm 109 is to take our stand with God, which means we shall stand with the poor and the needy as well (see v. 31).

5. To be sure, there is nothing morally inferior or unchristian about Psalm 109 as instruction. But what about Psalm 109 as a prayer? Can it be a Christian prayer? Most North American Christians have never been so completely victimized as the psalmist had been, so perhaps they will not need to pray this prayer for themselves. But can Psalm 109 then be a prayer for others? In speaking about the psalms as prayers, Mays suggests this possibility:

> Could the use of these prayers remind us and bind us to all those in the worldwide church who are suffering in faith and for the faith? All may be well in our place. There may be no trouble for the present that corresponds to the tribulations described in the psalms. But do we need to do more than call the roll of such places as El Salvador, South Africa, and Palestine to remember that there are sisters and brothers whose trials could be given voice in our recitation of the psalms? The old church believed that it was all the martyrs who prayed as they prayed the psalmic prayers.

409. Lewis, *Reflections on the Psalms*, 24.
410. Walter Brueggemann, "Psalm 109: Three Times 'Steadfast Love,'" *Word and World* 5 (1985) 154.

Would it be possible to say them for the sake of and in the name of the fellow Christians known to us? We do make intercessions for them, but perhaps these psalms can help us do more than to simply, prayerfully wish grace and help for them, can help us to find words to represent their hurt, alienation, failure, and discouragement. . . .

The apostle said "If one member suffers, all suffer together" (1 Cor. 12:26) and he also said "Bear one another's burdens." Can these prayers become a way of doing that?[411]

Yes, they can. To pray Psalm 109 is a commitment to bear one another's burdens, to stand in solidarity and in suffering with the abused, the victimized, and the oppressed, because that is where God stands (v. 31).

6. Psalm 109 has not always been ignored by the Christian church. Not surprisingly, given the similarities between Psalm 109 and other texts that figure more prominently in the story of Jesus' passion (cf. v. 2 with Ps 31:18; v. 3 with Ps 69:4; v. 22*b* with Ps 69:26; Isa 53:5; v. 24*a* with Ps 31:10; v. 25 with Ps 22:6-7), Psalm 109 was also seen as a reflection of the suffering of Jesus, who was also victimized by accusers and their hateful, deceitful words. Evidence in this regard is Acts 1:20, which cites Ps 109:8 to describe Judas's fate. As Allen says of Psalm 109: "Behind its use in Acts 1:20 lies an understanding of the psalm, as in the case of so many psalms of innocent suffering, whereby it found its loudest echo in the experience of Jesus. From this perspective Judas became the fitting heir of its curse, as history's archetype of wanton infidelity."[412] Like Psalm 109, Jesus' life and death are testimony to the good news that God stands with the poor and the needy.

411. Mays, *The Lord Reigns*, 52-53.
412. Allen, *Psalms 101–150*, 78.

PSALM 110:1-7, SIT AT MY RIGHT HAND

COMMENTARY

Commentators generally agree that Psalm 110 is a royal psalm (see Psalms 2; 18; 20–21; 45; 72; 89; 101; 132; 144), but that is where the agreement ends. Most scholars suggest that Psalm 110 was probably used originally at the coronation of Judean kings (see vv. 1, 4; see Psalms 2; 72), but some conclude that Psalm 110 was written to be used either in preparation for a battle or to celebrate the king's victory in battle (see vv. 2-3, 5-7; see Psalms 18; 20–21; 144). Proposed dates for Psalm 110 range over a period of 800 years, from the time of David to the Maccabean era.

Obviously, those who date the psalm in the post-exilic era do not associate its original use with the actual monarchy. Rather, they suggest that the psalm was composed to express messianic hopes. Certainty on matters of date and original use is impossible. It is likely that Psalm 110 existed before

the exile, but it is clear that the disappearance of the monarchy in 587 BCE would have necessitated a reinterpretation of the psalm. Indeed, its close proximity to Psalms 107–108 (see Commentary on Psalms 107; 108; Introduction) also encourages the reader to hear Psalm 110 in the light of the exile. That Psalm 110 did survive suggests that it was understood as articulating hope for the future—perhaps hope for a literal restoration of the monarchy or for continued existence of the whole people as God's chosen or anointed ones (see Ps 105:15). In any case, Psalm 110 would have been understood as an affirmation of the trust that God continues to manifest God's reign in some concrete way among God's people. Concluding that the placement of Psalm 110 probably reflects how the editors of the psalter construed it, Mays suggests that "it is a sequel to Psalm 89 and its lament over the rejected Messiah. It is a prophetic voice repeating and affirming the promises of Psalm 2 that the LORD will claim the nations through the Messiah. Until God has defeated his enemies, the Messiah is 'seated on the right hand.' "[413]

This trusting hope obviously was rather open-ended, as witnessed by the fact that the early Christians heard Psalm 110 as testimony to Jesus as Messiah (see Reflections below).

Discernment of the structure of Psalm 110 is hindered by the difficulty of understanding vv. 3, 7. As Mays says about these two verses, "For the purposes of preaching and teaching, it is best to admit that the perspicuity of Scripture is missing here."[414] Nevertheless, it is simplest to divide Psalm 110 into two sections: vv. 1-3, vv. 4-7. Each section then begins with an oracle, perhaps uttered originally by a cultic prophet ("says" occurs mostly in the prophetic books), followed by elaboration in subsequent verses. Unfortunately, the climactic verses of each section are the very ones that are so difficult to understand.

110:1-3. The repetition of "right hand" (ימין *yāmîn*) in Pss 109:31 and 110:1 may be coincidental; however, the juxtaposition is interesting. Psalm 109 concludes by affirming that God stands at the right hand of the oppressed (see also 110:5), presumably including the whole people in their time of need (see Ps 107:2-3, 39-43). Psalm 110 begins by affirming that the king—the representative of the whole people (or perhaps the whole people is now understood as a corporate anointed one in view of Ps 105:15)—is to sit at the right hand of God. In other words, the two psalms together portray a mutuality, an intimate relationship, between God and God's needy people. God offers protection from enemies (Ps 110:1-3, 5-6; see also 107:39-41; 108:12-13; 109:26-27, 31), and the people offer themselves as partners in the embodiment of God's reign in the world.

As suggested above, the oracular announcement of v. 1 may originally have played a part in the coronation of the king. The predominant theme in vv. 1-3 is God's subjugation of the king's enemies, a theme that also plays a major role in Psalm 2 (see

vv. 1-5, 8-11). The word "footstool" (הדם רגלים *hăḏōm roglayim*) is ordinarily used of God's footstool, probably the ark, which served symbolically as God's earthly throne (see Pss 99:5; 132:7). It is even possible that the king's coronation involved a visit to the ark, to stand symbolically at God's right hand. In any case, the allusion to God's reign is appropriate, since the earthly king (and/or people) ultimately represented God's reign in the world (see Commentary on Psalm 2). While "mighty scepter" (v. 2*a*; see Jer 48:17) bespeaks the king's royal authority, and while the king is enjoined to have dominion or to exercise royal rule (v. 2*b*; the NRSV accurately translates the Hebrew; see "dominion" in Ps 72:8 and "ruled" in Ezek 34:4 NRSV), it is actually God who initiates the action in v. 2. Although quite problematic, v. 3 also seems to promise God's provision of willing warriors.

110:4. Like v. 3, v. 4 has its share of uncertainties as well. Like v. 1, it is an oracle, but it is not clear who is speaking. While some scholars suggest that the newly crowned king now addresses the high priest, it is more likely that the addressee is still the king. That he is called a priest is surprising perhaps, but not too unusual. The king officiated at liturgical functions (see 1 Kings 8); Melchizedek (king of pre-Israelite Jerusalem) is identified in Gen 14:18 as both priest and king (if, indeed, Melchizedek here is intended to be a proper name; see the NRSV note). The priestly designation also would have presented no problem for a post-exilic understanding of the whole people as God's anointed one (see Exod 19:6). If the NRSV note is followed, the stress would again be on God's initiative. The word "rightful" (צדק *ṣedeq*) is usually translated "righteousness," and it is a fundamental aspect both of God's reign (see Pss 96:13; 97:2; 98:9; 99:4) and of what God wills for the earthly king (see Pss 45:4, 7; 72:1-2, 7).

110:5-6. Repeating "right hand" (see v. 1; Ps 109:31), v. 5 reiterates the intimate relationship between God and the king/people. The "he" in vv. 5*b*, 6*ab* is apparently God. Even more clearly than in vv. 1-2, vv. 5*b*-6 recall the holy war traditions in which God does all the fighting on behalf of the people. God deals with opponents of the divine reign, establishing justice (v. 6*a*), which in this case

413. Mays, *Psalms,* 353.
414. Mays, *Psalms,* 352.

means judgment upon oppressors (see Pss 9:8b; 96:10b, where the same word for judgment is used). The NRSV's "shatter" occurs in both vv. 5 and 6. In another royal psalm, the king does the shattering of the enemies after being instructed by God (see "struck down" in Ps 18:38a NRSV), but in Ps 110:5-6 the initiative even more exclusively belongs to God. The brutal imagery reflects the standard ancient Near Eastern practice of warfare, or at least of describing literarily one's preeminence in battle (see 2 Kgs 8:12; Ps 137:9; Hos 10:14; Nah 3:3).

110:7. The "he" that begins v. 7 apparently should be understood as the king. The significance of the action involved is not clear. It may indicate that the battle is over and that the king can pause and drink now that the victory is won (see the image of lifting up the head in Pss 3:3; 27:6). Or there may be some ritual significance behind v. 7, perhaps related to coronation. (See 1 Kgs 1:38-40, where Solomon's anointing takes place beside a stream, although it is not clear that the stream itself played any part in the ritual.)

REFLECTIONS

1. It is likely that Psalm 110 was already understood messianically when it found its place in the psalter—that is, it was viewed as an expression of the trust that God would manifest God's sovereign claim upon the world. Because the actual monarchy had disappeared, the messiah's role as an agent of God's sovereignty was not clear. To state the matter more positively, the hope was open-ended, and different groups within Judaism drew different conclusions. By the first century CE, for instance, Josephus could claim the Roman Emperor Vespasian as the fulfillment of Jewish messianic hopes. Many other Jews drew almost precisely the opposite conclusion; the messiah would arise to throw off Roman oppression. Still others were convinced that God's sovereign claim upon the world had been truly proclaimed and embodied by Jesus of Nazareth, whom they hailed as Jesus Messiah or, in its Greek equivalent, Jesus Christ.

Not surprisingly, Psalm 110 entered the first-century CE debate concerning the identity of the Messiah (see Matt 22:42-45; Mark 12:35-37; Luke 20:41-44). For Christians, the matter was settled, and they thus claimed Psalm 110 as testimony to Jesus' messiahship. In fact, Psalm 110 is the most frequently used psalm in the New Testament. It was used by the first-century Christians to affirm their faith that the life, death, and resurrection of Jesus were and are the ultimate demonstration of the concrete manifestation of God's sovereignty in the world. Thus it is Jesus to whom God must finally have addressed the words "sit at my right hand" (see Matt 26:64; Mark 14:62; Luke 22:69; Acts 2:34-35; 7:55-56; Rom 8:34; Eph 1:20; Col 3:1; Heb 1:3, 13; 8:1; 10:12; 1 Pet 3:22). Christians continue to make this affirmation every time they recite the Apostles' Creed: "I believe . . . in Jesus Christ, who . . . sitteth on the right hand of God."

2. What slips so easily off our tongues without a thought is actually a profoundly radical affirmation. The Christian appropriation of Psalm 110 "holds the enthronement of Jesus in relation to the question of political power in the world."[415] Jesus threatened then and threatens now politics as usual. After all, he was not crucified for spouting innocuous religious niceties. Rather, Jesus subverted both the power of Roman legions and the authority of Jewish tradition when he announced the simple good news that God rules the world (see Mark 1:14-15). This radical good news allowed tax collectors, sinners, lepers, prostitutes, children, women, and men to sit down and eat at the same table in the realm of God. Thus Psalm 110 is no mere artifact of ancient political propaganda. Rather, in relation to Jesus Messiah, it is a world-transforming challenge to every form of politics and power that does not begin with submission of the self to

415. Mays, *Psalms*, 354.

God's claim. Jesus, messiah and priest (see Heb 5:6; 7:17, 21), guarantees all people access to God. Those who would deny such grace and its claims set themselves up as enemies of the reign of God; the exalted will be humbled. Persons who accept such grace and submit to its claims open themselves to abundant life; the humble will be exalted (see Psalms 113; 115).

PSALM 111:1-10, GREAT ARE THE WORKS OF THE LORD

COMMENTARY

Psalms 111 and 112 belong together. Each is an acrostic; that is, each poetic line (each half-verse in English) begins with a successive letter of the Hebrew alphabet. In form, Psalm 111 can be categorized as a song of praise. An invitation to praise (v. 1a) and a statement of intention (v. 1bc) are followed by reasons for praise, the theme of which is stated in vv. 2-3—God's work (see "works" [מעשים * maʿăśîm*] in vv. 2, 6-7; the same root occurs as "gained" in v. 4 NRSV, and a synonym occurs as "work" in v. 3 NRSV), which bespeaks God's sovereignty (see below on v. 3). God's saving work from exodus to entry into the land is reviewed in vv. 4-6, and God's work of instructing the people and establishing the covenant is covered in vv. 7-10. The key word used four times of God's work (vv. 2, 4, 6, 7) is used twice more in vv. 8, 10 to describe the people's response ("performed" and "practice"). Performing God's precepts is summed up in the phrase "fear of the LORD" (v. 10), which then becomes the point of departure for Psalm 112. Whereas Psalm 111 focuses primarily on God's work, Psalm 112 focuses on human response and consists of a description of the happiness of those who fear the Lord. What is remarkable is that the same thing is said of both God and those who fear God: Their "righteousness endures forever" (Pss 111:3; 112:3, 9). In other ways, too, the character and life of those who fear God conform to God's own character and life (cf. 112:2b with 111:1c; 112:4b with 111:4b; 112:5b with 111:7a; 112:6b with 111:4a; 112:7b with 111:1a; 112:9a with 111:5a). Indeed, in the most profound sense, this is the reward of fearing God (see Commentary on Psalm 1).

The individual voice in Psalm 111 joins the ones in Pss 108:3 and 109:30 in giving thanks to God (v. 1b), as Psalm 107 had enjoined (see 107:1, 8, 15, 21, 31). If the opening psalms in Book V are read sequentially, the effect of Psalms 111–112 is to put the return from exile (Psalms 107–108) in line with all God's saving work on behalf of the oppressed (Psalm 109) and in particular with the classical historical sequence of exodus through entry into the land (Psalms 111–112). Psalm 113 initiates a series of psalms that again celebrate God's saving work in general (Psalms 113; 115; 116; 117) and the exodus in particular (Psalms 114; 118). Perhaps not coincidentally, the culminating Psalm 118 recalls Psalm 107 (cf. Pss 118:1, 29 with 107:1), and it has the effect of putting even anticipated future deliverances in sequence with the exodus (see Commentary on Psalm 118). Also not coincidental, perhaps, is the fact that the vocabulary of Psalms 111–112 anticipates Psalm 119 as well.

111:1. The psalmist offers thanks with the "whole heart" (v. 1b; see Ps 86:11-12, where the phrase also occurs in the context of fearing God; see also Pss 9:1; 119:2, 10; 138:1). Praise involves the whole person, and it is the essence of true security (see Ps 112:7-8). Praise is intensely personal but not private; it is offered in the gathered congregation of God's people (v. 1c). The word "congregation" (עדה *ʿēdâ*) recalls Ps 1:5 and is the first of several verbal and conceptual links between Psalms 111–112 and Psalms 1–2. The "upright" (ישרים *yĕšārîm*; see v. 8; Pss 112:2, 4) are the same as the "righteous" (צדיקים *ṣaddîqîm*) in Ps 1:5-6 (see Ps 112:6).

111:2-3. The next link, in fact, occurs in v. 2: "delight" (see Pss 1:2; 112:1; 119:35). Those who delight in God's works, which include God's instruction (see 111:7), study them (see "seek"/"sought" in Ps 119:2, 10, 45). Verses 2-3 bespeak God's sovereignty. Greatness is an attribute of a monarch (see Pss 47:2; 48:1; 95:3), as are "honor and majesty" (see Ps 96:6), and "righteousness" describes the royal policy God wills and enacts (see Pss 96:13; 97:2; 98:9; 99:4). It was the prerogative and responsibility of a sovereign to follow up acts of deliverance with measures to enact justice and righteousness among his or her subjects. God's "works" include both of these spheres—deliverance (vv. 4-6) and establishment of the conditions for justice (vv. 7-10).

111:4-6. While the word "wonderful deeds" (נפלאות *niplā'ōt*) in v. 4*a* does not refer exclusively to the exodus, it often describes the exodus (see Exod 3:20; 15:11; Ps 77:11, 14). The word that the NIV translates "to be remembered" (זכר *zēker*) also recalls the climactic plague (see Exod 12:14; see also Ps 112:6*b*), and the words "gracious and merciful" (חנון ורחום *ḥannûn wĕraḥûm*, v. 4*b*) are reminiscent of Exod 34:6, God's self-revelation to Moses following the golden calf episode (see also Ps 112:4*b*). Verse 5*a* maintains the focus on the wilderness (see Exodus 16; Numbers 11), and v. 5*b* recalls Exod 2:24 as well as Exod 34:10, 27. The word "power" (כח *kōaḥ*) in v. 6*a* recalls Exod 9:16; 15:6; as v. 6*b* suggests, the ultimate result of the exodus was the possession of the land. Verse 6*b* also recalls Ps 2:8. It is revealing, perhaps, that the promise made to the king in Ps 2:8 is now articulated in terms of the whole people (see Commentary on Psalms 105, esp. v. 15; 110).

111:7-10. Verse 7*a* could actually serve as a climactic summary of vv. 4-6 or as an introduction to vv. 7*b*-10. Perhaps it is intentionally transitional, linking conceptually God's saving works (see v. 6) and God's works that take the form of instruction (see

v. 2, where both meanings seem to be present). The word "justice" (משפט *mišpāṭ*; NIV and NRSV, "just") also points backward and forward. Along with righteousness (v. 3), it is a fundamental aspect of God's sovereignty (see Pss 96:13; 97:2; 98:9; 99:4). God's saving work establishes justice for the oppressed (see vv. 4-6), and God's "precepts" (פקודים *piqqûdîm*) are intended to enable God's people to maintain justice. The word "precepts" is not used frequently in the psalter (see elsewhere only Pss 19:8; 103:18 NIV; 119); it is synonymous with God's instruction.

The words "faithful" (אמת *'ĕmet*) and "trustworthy" (נאמנים *ne'ĕmānîm*) in v. 7 are from the same Hebrew root. God relates faithfully to God's people (see Exod 34:6), and God expects faithfulness in return (v. 8*b*)—both God's work of redemption (v. 9; see Deut 7:8; 13:5; Pss 25:22; 78:42) and the people's work of obedience (see "performed" in v. 8 and "practice" in v. 10) are integral to the covenant that God intends. In addition to the repetition of "works"/"performed"/"practice" (vv. 2, 6-8, 10) and "faithful(ness)" (vv. 7-8), the repetition represented by "awesome" (נורא *nôrā'*, v. 9) and "fear" (יראה *yir'â*, v. 10) stresses the mutuality of the covenant. God's awesomeness derives from God's sovereignty (see Exod 15:11; Pss 47:2; 76:7; 96:4; 99:3; note also the pairing with holiness in Ps 99:3 as in 111:9). Here, as elsewhere, God's awesomeness and holiness are not intended to keep people at a distance (see Commentary on Psalm 99). Rather, God's awesomeness calls forth the people's "fear of the LORD" (see Pss 2:11; 25:12, 14; 34:9)—their recognition of God's reign issues in praise (v. 10*c*; see v. 1*a*) and obedience (see the NRSV note for v. 10, where "them," i.e., "precepts," is the object of "practice"). Precisely such yielding of the self to God's claim constitutes wisdom and understanding (see Deut 4:5-6; Job 28:28; Prov 1:7; 9:10). It also constitutes true happiness, according to Psalm 112, which takes 111:10 as its point of departure.

REFLECTIONS

1. Psalm 111 begins and ends with praise. The only action involving the psalmist is the expression of intent to give public thanks to God with the whole being (v. 1). This complete dedication of the self to God, of course, is the essence of praise. As such, it inevitably involves obedience. This posture toward God—praise, gratitude, obedience—is captured by the phrase "fear of the LORD." It is the fundamental human "work"—a "work" not in the sense of a meritorious accomplishment but in the sense of human vocation or calling in response to God's grace. While "fear of the LORD" clearly involves performance and practice (vv. 8, 10), the structure and movement of Psalm 111 make it clear that human works (vv. 8, 10) are evoked by God's works (vv. 4-6). In terms of the history of Israel, exodus precedes Sinai. In short, grace is prior. Salvation is a gift to which God's people make grateful response with their whole hearts. Praise, therefore, is both liturgy (v. 1) and life-style (vv. 8, 10).

2. Indeed, praise is the foundation of the psalmist's epistemology—true knowledge begins with grateful praise and obedience! The psalmist's closing affirmation is a radical challenge to our ways of knowing and our definitions of knowledge. From the scientific point of view, for instance, the acquisition of knowledge requires the shedding of all values and commitments in order to try to become completely objective. Reaction to scientism leads in precisely the opposite direction—to the claim that knowledge does not exist apart from subjective human experience. The psalmist's affirmation contradicts both of these perspectives. True knowledge—wisdom—is not grounded in ourselves but in God, and it involves the embrace of God's commitments and values. Thus wisdom will take concrete shape in righteousness, grace, and mercy (see vv. 3-4), and those who fear the Lord (Ps 112:1), therefore, will be "gracious, merciful, and righteous" (Ps 112:4; see Commentary on Psalm 112). For Christians, the One who perfectly embodied God's character and values also is professed as "the wisdom of God" (1 Cor 1:24 NRSV).

PSALM 112:1-10, HAPPY ARE THOSE WHO FEAR THE LORD

COMMENTARY

Psalm 112 clearly belongs with Psalm 111. Both psalms begin with the same phrase, and both are acrostic poems. Furthermore, Psalm 112 offers a more developed description of those who fear the Lord (see Pss 111:10; 112:1). The remarkable thing is that the same is said of both God and those who fear God: Their "righteousness endures forever" (Pss 111:3; 112:3, 9; see Commentary on Psalm 111 for other verbal links between Psalms 111 and 112).

As suggested above, Psalms 111–112 recall Psalms 1–2. For instance, if its opening invitation is viewed as a sort of superscription (see Pss 111:1; 113:1), Psalm 112 begins and ends with exactly the same words that open and close Psalm 1: "happy" and "perish" ("come[s] to nothing," 112:10). In addition, Psalms 1 and 112 feature the same characters—"the righteous" (1:5; 112:6) and "the

wicked" (1:1, 5-6; 112:10). Indeed, Psalms 111–112 are a sort of mirror image of Psalms 1–2. Whereas Psalm 1 portrays the life of the righteous and Psalm 2 grounds it in the sovereignty of God (see esp. Ps 2:12), Psalms 111–112 reverse the pattern. Psalm 111 asserts the sovereignty of God as the foundation for the life of the righteous. It is as if Psalms 111–112 serve as reinforcement for Psalms 1–2 after the prosperity of the wicked—including the crucial reality of exile and its aftermath—has been clearly confronted and articulated in the preceding psalms (note the preponderance of complaints in Books I–III, and see esp. Psalms 42–43; 73; 74; 89–90; 105–108; see also Introduction).

Discussion of the structure of Psalm 112 usually focuses on its acrostic pattern; most translations, including the NIV and the NRSV, give no indication of structural divisions. This may be the best policy, but several scholars suggest that the identical vv. 3*b*, 9*b*, as well as the similar v. 6, divide Psalm 112 into three equal sections, each of which focuses on the life of the righteous and its outcome. Verse 10 shifts the focus to the life of the wicked and its outcome as the psalm concludes.

112:1-3. As in Ps 1:1-2, happiness in Ps 112:1 is associated with "delight." In Ps 1:1-2, it was delight in God's "instruction" (or "law"); here it is delight in God's commandments. In both cases, therefore, happiness has to do not with self-fulfillment but with the orientation of life to God's purposes. Fear is essentially the recognition of God's sovereignty that leads to the entrusting of life and future to God (see "fear" in Ps 2:11 and "happy" in Ps 2:12). Despite what vv. 2-3 seem to suggest, such happiness does not consist essentially of material reward or of a life free of trouble and opposition (see Ps 49:6; Prov 3:16; 8:18; 13:7). Rather, such happiness consists of being right with God, a condition that neither "bad news" (v. 7*a*) nor opposition (v. 8*b*) can ever dislodge (vv. 3*b*, 6*a*, 9*b*). In short, trusting God (see v. 7*b*) is true might (v. 2; see Ps 37:11; Matt 5:5) and true wealth (v. 3; see Ps 49:5-7). Happiness is not a reward that is earned but is the experience of being connected to God (see Commentary on Psalms 1; 2).

112:4-6. Those who fear God, who trust God and whose lives are oriented to God's purposes, become like God. Like God, they are sources of light for others (v. 4*a*; see Pss 27:1; 36:9). Their character embodies God's character (v. 4*b*; see Ps 111:4*b*), including gracious provision for others (v. 5*a*; the NRSV's "deal generously" is the same Hebrew root as "gracious" [חנון *ḥannûn*] in v. 4*b*; see Pss 37:26; 111:5*a*) and the establishment of justice (v. 5*b*; see Ps 111:7*a*). Fearing God

means entrusting life to God and embodying God's values and purposes, and it provides a stability that is both effective in the present (v. 6*a*; see Pss 15:5; 16:8; see Commentary on Psalm 1) and enduring forever (v. 6*b*; see Ps 111:4*a*).

112:7-10. Verses 7-8 make it clear that the happiness of the righteous is no facile, carefree existence. The righteous are not immune from bad news and opposition. Rather, because they fear God, they need not fear evil (see Ps 23:4; "evil" in Ps 23:4 and "bad news" [שמועה רעה *šĕmûʿâ rāʿâ*] in Ps 112:7*a* NIV have the same Hebrew root). The imagery of stability that is present in v. 6 continues in vv. 7-8 (see Commentary on Psalm 1). The repeated "heart(s)" (לב *lēb*) in vv. 7-8 recalls Ps 111:1. The grateful, faithful heart is the secure heart. Faith triumphs over fear and foe (v. 8; see Pss 54:7*b*; 59:10; 118:7). Those who humble themselves (v. 9*a*) will be exalted (v. 9*c*; see Pss 75:10; 92:10).

Verse 8*b* suggests that the perspective of Psalms 111–112, like that of Psalms 1–2, is eschatological. That is to say, the reign of God and the consequent security of the righteous are asserted in the midst of ongoing opposition. Thus the disagreement between translation of the verb tenses in vv. 9*c*-10 is appropriate. As the NRSV suggests, the exaltation of the righteous and the demise of the wicked are *already* a reality, but as the NIV suggests, this reality is a process that is not yet complete. The reign of God is always both now and yet to come. The purposes of the wicked will not endure (see Pss 1:5; 37:12-13); their desires will ultimately perish (see Pss 1:6; 10:3). Thus those who know this and who align themselves with God's purposes—in short, those who fear God—are truly wise (Ps 111:10) and genuinely happy (Ps 112:1).

REFLECTIONS

In a secular culture, where wisdom is divorced from faithfulness and where happiness is often viewed superficially as material prosperity and ease, it is crucial to hear Psalms 111–112. They are a vivid reminder that faithfulness to God and to God's purposes is not a guarantee of success and security as the world defines these concepts. Happiness and security are derived not by conformity to the standards of the world but by transforming ourselves to be like God. In a similar world-negating stance, Jesus pronounced happy those whom the world would consider unfortunate and most likely to be unhappy (see Matt 5:3-11). This teaching, of course, appears in the context of Jesus' proclamation of the reign of God (see Matt 4:17; 5:3, 10, 20; 6:33). Jesus, too, was an eschatological preacher, announcing the reign of God amid persistent opposition and demonstrating God's sovereignty most clearly on a cross (see Commentary on Psalms 1; 2).

Such a stance is indeed countercultural, a witness to the transforming power of God. This perspective accounts for the psalmist's remarkable attribution to the righteous of God's own characteristics (see esp. Ps 112:3*b*, 4, 5*b*, 6*b*, 9*b*). As Mays says of Psalm 112, "Its composer believes so profoundly that the works of God take shape in the life of the righteous that for the psalmist the commendation of the latter becomes also the praise of God."[416] This perspective recalls not only Jesus' beatitudes but also the apostle Paul's admonition to his readers to "join in imitating me" (Phil 3:17 NRSV). This admonition is not the arrogant self-assertion of an egomaniac but the bold challenge of one who was convinced that "it is no longer I who live, but it is Christ who lives in me" (Gal 2:20 NRSV). In short, like the psalmist, Paul was convinced that by the transforming mercy of God (see Rom 12:1-2), the works of God take shape in the life of the righteous. For Paul, this is no cause for boasting, except insofar as one boasts in God (see 1 Cor 1:31). The transformed lives of the righteous become the praise of God.

416. Mays, *Psalms*, 361.

PSALM 113:1-9, WHO IS LIKE THE LORD OUR GOD?

COMMENTARY

Psalm 113 is a song of praise that Jews and Christians have given "a special place in their repertoire of praise."[417] For Jews, it begins the Egyptian *Hallel* (Psalms 113–118; *Hallel* means "praise," as in the phrase, *Hallelu-yah,* "Praise the LORD!"), a collection used at all major festivals but especially at the beginning and conclusion of the Passover. For Christians, Psalm 113 is used for the celebration of Easter. While the association of Psalm 113 with Psalms 114–118 is traditional (see *Hallelu-yah* in Pss 113:1, 9; 115:18; 116:19; 117:2), it is often overlooked that the phrase *Hallelu-yah* also links Psalm 113 to Psalms 111–112 (see 111:1; 112:1). To be sure, Psalm 113 is an appropriate introduction to Psalms 114–118 and their theme of deliverance, especially exodus (see Psalms 114; 118). But it is also an appropriate culmination to Psalms 111–112. Like Psalm 111, it articulates God's sovereignty (see below on vv. 1-4;

417. Peter Craigie, "Psalm 113," *Int.* 39 (1985) 70.

see also 111:2-6, esp. v. 4, which recalls the exodus), and it offers an especially appropriate response to the exclamation of 111:9*c* (see "name" in 111:9*c;* 113:1-3). Furthermore, like Psalms 111–112, Psalm 113 asserts that God's power is manifested in gracious, compassionate provision for the poor (see Pss 111:4-5*a;* 112:9*a;* 113:7-9; the words "poor" in 112:9*a* and "needy" in 113:7*b* represent the same Hebrew word [אביון *'ebyôn*]). This theme also ties Psalm 113 to Psalm 107, which begins Book V (see esp. 107:39-42). Thus Psalm 113, as well as the *Hallel* collection it initiates, also would have served as an appropriate response to the crisis of exile and its aftermath (see Commentary on Psalm 107, esp. vv. 2-3; Introduction). As such, it is also testimony to God's enduring character and typical activity (see Psalms 107; 118; and Reflections below).

While it is clear that Psalm 113 was (and is) used liturgically, its origin and original setting are uncertain. Psalm 113 shows striking similarities with the Song of Hannah in 1 Sam 2:1-11 (cf. esp. Ps 113:5 with 1 Sam 2:2; Ps 113:9 with 1 Sam 2:5*b*; Ps 113:7-8 with 1 Sam 2:7-8); however, the similarities do not allow a certain dating of the psalm. Scholars disagree also on how to describe the structure and movement of Psalm 113. As the NIV suggests, it is possible to divide the psalm into three sections (apart from the opening and closing *Hallelu-yah*): (1) vv. 1-3, which function as a call to praise and are bound together by the repetition of "praise" (vv. 1, 3) and "name"; (2) vv. 4-6, which focus on God's identity as reason for praise; and (3) vv. 7-9, which focus on God's activity as reason for praise. On the other hand, as the NRSV suggests, it is possible to conclude that the question in v. 5 begins a new section, in which case the psalm consists of vv. 1-4 and vv. 5-9. It is possible that the structure moves at more than one level. For instance, it is possible that v. 5, the center line of the poem, serves as a sort of pivot. Each of vv. 1-5*a* contains the divine name "Yahweh" ("LORD"), culminating in the question of God's identity in v. 5*a*. Beginning with v. 5*b*, the rest of the psalm is intended to answer the central question. After v. 5*a*, there are no further occurrences of the divine name (except the final *Hallelu-yah*). Instead, God's identity is described in terms of God's activity. Verses 5*b*-9 are bound grammatically by the fact that each of the six verbal forms is *hiphil*, a causative form of the verb. A more literal translation captures the effect: God "makes God's self high in order to sit" (v. 5*b*), "makes God's self low in order to see" (v. 6*a*), "causes the poor to arise" (v. 7*a*), "makes exalted the needy . . . to cause them to sit with princes" (vv. 7*b*-8*a*), "makes a home" (v. 9*a*). In short, God is active. God's character is known, and God is to be praised (vv. 1-5*a*), because God makes particular things happen (vv. 5*b*-9).

113:1-4. Beginning with the designation "servants" (v. 1), vv. 1-3 bespeak God's sovereignty. "Servants" are persons who are subject to a sovereign master (see "serve" in Pss 2:11; "worship" in 100:2), and the appropriate response of servants is to submit their whole selves—that is, to praise (see vv. 1, 3*b*)

or to bless (v. 2*a*; see Pss 96:2; 100:4; 145:1, 21). The occurrence of "name" in each of vv. 1-3 suggests not only the mode of God's presence but also the issue of God's character. Verse 4 reinforces the conclusion that God is to be praised because of God's sovereign character. God is "exalted" or "high above all nations"—that is, sovereign on earth (v. 4*a*; see "exalt" in the context of the proclamation of God's reign in Pss 99:5, 9; 145:1 NIV). And God's "glory," a word elsewhere explicitly associated with God's reign (see Pss 29:1-3, 9; 96:3, 7-8; 97:6), is also "above the heavens" (v. 4*b*).

113:5-9. After the central question of v. 5*a*, which also explicitly raises the issue of God's character (see Exod 15:11; Pss 35:10; 86:8; Mic 7:18), vv. 5*b*-9 make it clear that God's sovereignty—God's "aboveness" or "highness" (v. 4)—is manifest in a very particular way. To be sure, God's enthronement is real (v. 5*b*; see also Ps 2:4), but God "makes God's self low to look upon the heavens and the earth" (v. 6 author's trans.). Note that the same two spheres of God's sovereignty are present in v. 6 as in v. 4—earth and the heavens—but God exercises God's sovereignty from below! The immediate consequence is that God "raises the poor" and "lifts the needy" (v. 7). The occurrence of the same Hebrew root in vv. 4 and 7 is particularly revealing (see "exalted" in v. 4*a* and "lifts" in v. 7*b* NIV); the exalted one has chosen to be humbled, and the humbled are thus exalted.

Another crucial dimension of God's activity is indicated by the repetition of the Hebrew root (יָשַׁב *yāšab*) that the NIV translates "sits enthroned" in v. 5*b*, "seats" in v. 8*a*, and "settles" in v. 9*a*. God gives a home to the homeless. Again, the exalted God is involved in the activity of exalting the humbled. Because Israel's God exercises sovereignty from below in order to exalt the poor and the needy (vv. 6-9), Israel's God is like no other (see v. 5*a*; see Commentary on Psalm 82). Therefore, this God deserves enduring and unlimited praise (vv. 1-3).

REFLECTIONS

1. Psalm 113 is testimony to who God is, revealed by what God does. Not surprisingly, therefore, Psalm 113 is similar to other biblical psalms, especially the Song of Hannah in 1 Sam 2:1-11 and Mary's song, the Magnificat, in Luke 1:46-55. Like Psalm 113, both of these songs celebrate God's exaltation of those who are humbled (see 1 Sam 2:4-5, 7-8; Luke 1:48, 51-53). The apostle Paul also detected God at work in the same way in Jesus Christ (see Phil 2:5-11) and in the formation of the church (see 1 Cor 1:26-29). The Gospels suggest that Jesus and the disciples would have sung Psalm 113 at their last supper (see Mark 14:26), and Jesus' teaching affirms the pattern evident in Psalm 113: The humble will be exalted (see Luke 18:14).

2. Especially when heard in sequence with Psalm 112, which suggests that human character and activity are to conform to God's character and activity, Psalm 113 is an invitation to the people of God to join God at God's work in the world on behalf of the poor and the needy. At the same time, however, Psalm 113 is a warning against the persistent temptation to leave God out of the picture. As Hauerwas and Willimon put it: "Most of our social activism is formed on the presumption that God is superfluous to the formation of a world of peace with justice. Fortunately, we are powerful people who, because we live in a democracy, are free to use our power. It is all up to us."[418]

The nature and subtlety of this temptation is portrayed movingly by Flannery O'Connor in her story "The Lame Shall Enter First." In the story, Sheppard, a well-intentioned City Recreation Director, goes to great lengths to assist a lame juvenile delinquent, Johnson. Sheppard takes the boy into his home, gets corrective shoes for him, attempts to give him every possible advantage. In a conversation with Johnson, Sheppard's son Norton says of his father:

"He's good," he mumbled. "He helps people."
"Good!" Johnson said savagely. He thrust his head forward. "Listen here," he hissed.
"I don't care if he's good or not. He ain't *right*!"

What Johnson means becomes clear as the story unfolds. When Johnson refuses to cooperate easily with Sheppard's helpfulness, Sheppard initiates the following exchange:

"I'm stronger than you are. I'm stronger than you are and I'm going to save you. The good will triumph."
"Not when it ain't true," the boy said, "Not when it ain't right."
"My resolve isn't shaken," Sheppard replied. "I'm going to save you. . . ."
Johnson thrust his head forward. "Save yourself," he hissed. "Nobody can save me but Jesus."

Johnson finally sums up Sheppard's motivation with the conclusion: "He thinks he's God."[419] Thus he illuminates the temptation to which Sheppard has yielded. For Sheppard, God is superfluous. In his view, it was all up to him. His actions, well-intentioned as they are, are fundamentally selfish. He may be good, but he is not right.

As a powerful testimony to the sovereignty and transcendence of God (vv. 4-5), Psalm 113 is also a powerful warning against the temptation to conclude, "It is all up to us." Psalm 113 affirms that God's character is known in God's activity; God makes things happen. To be sure, God's people may, indeed must, join God at God's work in

418. Hauerwas and Willimon, *Resident Aliens*, 36.
419. O'Connor, *The Complete Stories*, 454, 474, 480.

the world. But as Hauerwas and Willimon point out, "The moment that life is formed on the presumption that we are not participants in *God's* continuing history of creation and redemption, we are acting on unbelief rather than faith."[420] In the final analysis, Psalm 113 encourages faith—submission to God's reign that is manifest in praise and participation in God's continuing story of creation and redemption.

420. Hauerwas and Willimon, *Resident Aliens,* 36-37, italics added.

PSALM 114:1-8, TREMBLE, O EARTH, AT THE PRESENCE OF THE LORD

COMMENTARY

While Psalm 114 is usually categorized as a song of praise, it is a distinctive one. There is no invitation to praise, except perhaps v. 7, which is addressed not to persons but to the earth. Most of the psalm could be considered an elaboration of reasons for praise, but they are not simply listed in the usual manner following an invitation to praise. Rather, Psalm 114 consists of a series of poetic allusions to the basic elements of Israel's story: exodus (vv. 1, 3*a*, 5*a*), God's provision in the wilderness (v. 8), the crossing of the Jordan to enter the promised land (vv. 3*b*, 5*b*), and the choice of the people and their establishment in the land (v. 2).

The exuberant tone of Psalm 114 suggests liturgical use; we know that Psalms 113–118 were eventually used at the major festivals, including Passover, for which the allusions to the exodus make Psalm 114 particularly fitting (see Commentary on Psalm 113). When Psalm 114 originated, and how and where it may have been used originally, we do not know. In its present literary setting, it serves to put the exodus and entry into the land (see also Ps 111:4-6) in sequence with the return from exile (see Psalms 107–108) and other divine acts of deliverance (see Psalms 109; 115–116). The sequence of Psalms 107–108 would have served as a hopeful response to the exile and its aftermath (see Commentary on Psalm 107; Introduction). Beyond that, however, the sequence serves to encourage the oppressed people of God in any age, as well as to give them words to articulate their faith in and praise for God's ongoing story with God's people (see Commentary on Psalm 118).

As both the NIV and the NRSV indicate, the structure of Psalm 114 is best described as four pairs of poetic lines. Verses 1-2 lay out the movement from exodus to settlement in the land, and vv. 3-4 are a poetic commentary on these events. Using the same vocabulary as vv. 3-4, vv. 5-6 ask the questions to which vv. 7-8 offer a response. In so doing, vv. 7-8 highlight the crucial concept that accounts for Israel's election, deliverance, and establishment in the land: the presence of God (see below on v. 7).

114:1-2. The verb in "went out" (יצא *yāṣāʾ*, v. 1*a*) is used frequently of the exodus (see "bring out" in Exod 3:10-12; 14:11; 18:1; 20:2). The phrase "strange language" (לעז *lōʿēz*, v. 1*b*) is unique, but similar phrases are used elsewhere to designate Israel's opponents (see Deut 28:49; Isa 33:19; Jer 5:15). The precise sense of v. 2 is unclear, but it appears to mean that God has chosen Judah both as God's own people and as the place of God's dwelling. The movement from exodus to God's dwelling place is also present in the song the people sang immediately following the crossing of the sea (see Exod 15:1-18, esp. vv. 13, 17, where "holy" and "sanctuary" represent the same word as "sanctuary" [קדש *qōdeš*] in Ps 114:2). The sanctuary was the place where God's presence could be experienced most immediately, so v. 2 perhaps anticipates v. 7. In Exodus 15, the mention of the sanctuary (v. 17) is juxtaposed with the affirmation of God's reign (v. 18). Both concepts are present in Ps 114:2 as well. The word "dominion" (ממשלה *memšālâ*) represents a different Hebrew root than does "reign" (ממלכה *mamlākâ*), but they are essentially synonymous and occur together in Ps 145:13.

114:3-4. Verse 3*a* is clearly recognizable as a poetic description of the parting of the waters that allowed the people's crossing of the sea (see Exodus 14, esp. vv. 21-29). In Exod 14:25, 27, it is not the sea but the Egyptians who flee. That fleeing is here attributed to the sea is indicative of a mythic dimension already present in Exodus 14; thus God's deliverance of the Israelites by commanding the sea indicates God's sovereignty not only over Pharaoh but also over all chaotic forces, including cosmic ones (see above on Pss 74:12-17; 77:16-19). The ultimate implication is that God's creative work (see Ps 104:7) and God's saving work are united. The exodus is an enactment of God's creational purposes (see Commentary on Psalms 33; 65; 66). Verse 3*b* alludes to the people's crossing of the Jordan and subsequent entry into the land (see Josh 3:1-17), an event perceived as analogous to the exodus (see Josh 4:23-24). Although not as clear, v. 4 may be a poetic allusion to Sinai (see Exodus 19). In any case, it is a poetic description of the effects of God's appearing. Elsewhere, too, God's appearing affects the mountains and hills (see Hab 3:6), even causing them to "skip" (see Ps 29:6, which is part of a description that culminates in the affirmation of God's cosmic sovereignty).

114:5-8. Verses 1-4 do not explicitly mention God (see the NRSV note in v. 2). Thus the questions in vv. 5-6 build toward the climactic v. 7. The events described and alluded to in vv. 1-4 happened because of "the presence of the LORD." The Hebrew syntax gives this phrase the emphatic position in the line, and the repetition of "presence of" has the poetic effect of surrounding the imperative with the two references to God's presence. Poetic structure reinforces content, for the poet intends to affirm that the whole earth is pervaded by God's presence and thus is subject to God's sovereignty. The appropriate response to God's sovereign presence is indicated by the imperative "tremble" (חולי *ḥûlî*). This is precisely what the earth does in Ps 97:4*b* in response to God's appearing as king (see 97:1-4*a*). The same verb also describes the effects of God's appearing in Pss 29:8-9; 77:16. Apparently, the verb implies a mixture of fear and joy in response to the awesome presence and power of God. The mention of water in v. 8 alludes to God's provision for the people in the wilderness (see Exod 17:1-7; Num 20:2-13; Deut 8:15). As in v. 3, water is involved, although in a different form and context. Even so, the event alluded to in v. 8 is another indication of God's cosmic sovereignty, manifested in gracious provision for human need (see Commentary on Psalm 113).

REFLECTIONS

Psalm 114 is a poetic affirmation of the faith that lies at the heart of the whole Bible: the God who rules the cosmos is made known in space and time for the purpose of properly ordering the world and the human community. Indeed, this affirmation is made in Psalm 113, as well as in Psalm 115, with which Psalm 114 belongs in some manuscript traditions; whereas Psalm 114 invites the earth to tremble (v. 7), Psalm 115 invites the specifically human response of trust (see 115:9-11).

The specific events in view in Psalm 114 constitute the basics of Israel's story: exodus, provision in the wilderness, entry into the land as God's people. But the fundamental trust articulated in Psalm 114—that the sovereign God reveals God's self concretely in space and time—contributed to the discernment of an ongoing story of God with the world. The return from exile was understood as a new exodus; later, the early Christians perceived the cosmic God at work in quite ordinary events, like the birth of a child (see Commentary on Psalm 29, to which Luke 2:13-14, like Psalm 114, has affinities), as well as scandalously concrete events, like the cross. Consequently, as Mays concludes concerning Psalm 114: "The church has read and sung the psalm in the light of what happened in Judah and Israel through Jesus Christ. It sees in his death and resurrection yet another and a climactic theophany of the divine rule in which the Presence assumes a new relation to people and place."[421]

421. Mays, *Psalms*, 365.

PSALM 115:1-18, TRUST IN THE LORD

COMMENTARY

Not surprisingly, since Psalms 114 and 115 are a single psalm in some textual traditions, Psalm 115 portrays the human equivalent of the earth's trembling at the sovereign presence of God (see Ps 114:7)—namely, humble submission (v. 1), trust (vv. 9-11), assurance (vv. 12-13), and praise (vv. 3, 16-18). These elements, plus the presence of complaint (v. 2) and petition (vv. 14-15), make Psalm 115 difficult to classify. Verses 9-13 suggest the probability of liturgical use (see Commentary on Psalms 113; 114), and the polemic against idolatry (vv. 4-8; see also v. 2) may indicate a post-exilic origin (see Isa 40:18-20; 44:9-20). While certainty concerning origin and original use is impossible, it is clear that Psalm 115 is congruent with the apparent purpose of Book V to address the crisis of exile and its aftermath (see Commentary on Psalms 107; 108; 111; Introduction).

Because of its variety of elements, Psalm 115 is subject to a diversity of structural proposals, usually based on division by content. Attempting to take stylistic criteria seriously and noting a cluster of repeated words toward the beginning and end of the psalm (see "not" in vv. 1, 17; "does"/"made"/"make" in vv. 3-4, 15 NIV; "human" in vv. 4, 16 NRSV; "heaven(s)" in vv. 3, 15-16), Allen proposes the following divisions, which have a particular symmetry:

A   vv. 1-4
  B   vv. 5-8
    C´ vv. 9-11
  B´   vv. 12-13
A´   vv. 14-18

In this view, vv. 9-11 and vv. 12-13 also correspond by virtue of the repetition between and within the two sections.[422] Although perhaps coincidental, vv. 9-11 stand at almost the exact structural center of the poem, thus emphasizing the repeated term "trust" (בטח *bāṭaḥ*).

---

422. Allen, *Psalms 101–150*, 109-10.

115:1-2. The unusual syntax of v. 1*a* emphasizes the opening negation, which suggests the people's recognition that "glory" belongs properly to the sovereign God (see Pss 29:1-3, 9; 79:9). Even so, God's glory will include the manifestation of God's basic character (v. 1*b*; see Exod 34:6; Pss 89:49; 92:2; 108:4; Introduction), and thus will be of help to God's people (see vv. 9-13) amid the hostility of the nations (v. 2; see Pss 42:3, 10; 79:9-10).

115:3-8. This assurance is reinforced in v. 3. Neither v. 3*a* nor v. 16, which it anticipates, should be understood geographically. God is not restricted to "the heavens"; rather, the heavens symbolize God's cosmic sovereignty (see Ps 113:4-5). Verse 3*b* articulates this sovereignty as well; it should be heard in the light of v. 1*b*. That is, it does not intend to say that God is whimsical but that God has the power to enact God's faithful, loving purposes. In contrast, the idols of the nations have no power (vv. 4-8; see Ps 135:15-18). The contrast is emphasized by the repetition of the Hebrew root "do," "make" (עשה *ʿāśâ*) in vv. 3-4, 8 (see also v. 15). That is, while God *makes* things happen, the idols are *made* by people. Those who make and trust in idols, the psalmist asserts, become like the idols (v. 8; see Ps 97:7; Isa 45:16-17). In other words, those who presume to make their gods will find themselves powerless as well, or at least limited to the power that they themselves can muster. In short, those who exalt themselves will be humbled (see Psalm 113).

115:9-11. The illusion of trusting in idols leads the psalmist to encourage trust in God (see Pss 4:5; 9:10; 25:2; 62:8; Introduction). Such trust puts people in touch with a source of help beyond themselves (see "help and shield" in Ps 33:20, where these concepts are also associated with trusting God). It is possible that different groups are represented in vv. 9-11 (see Ps 135:19-20), perhaps the worshiping congregation (v. 9) and the priests (v. 10). Scholars sometimes suggest on the basis of late sources that those "who fear the LORD" are proselytes, but it is more likely that this phrase is a designation for the whole people (see v. 13; Ps 112:1).

115:12-15. God's remembrance of the people is a crucial element in experiences of deliverance (see Gen 9:15; Exod 2:24; 32:13; Pss 9:12; 74:2, 18, 22), and the people express the confidence that God remembers and therefore "will bless" (vv. 12-13; see Pss 5:12; 29:11; 67:1, 6-7; 107:38). The mention of "small and great alike" (v. 13; see Jer 31:34) makes it clear that the people have not earned the blessing, for unlike the worshipers of idols, they live in dependence upon God rather than self. The request for blessing in vv. 14-15 also reinforces this perspective. While the nations "make" idols (v. 8), God's people look to the "Maker of heaven and earth" (v. 15).

115:16-18. The transcendence of God is also in view in v. 16. To be sure, human beings also have a God-given sphere of influence (v. 16; see Commentary on Psalm 8). But as vv. 17-18 suggest, the earth is not a realm for unbridled human self-assertion but for praising (v. 17; see Pss 6:5; 30:9; 88:10) and blessing God (v. 18; see Pss 103:1-2, 20-22; 104:1, 35). The "we" in v. 18 is emphatic, as if the community of God's people wants to distinguish itself as sharply as possible from those who make and trust in other gods. Appropriately, the psalm concludes with the people's promise to offer unlimited praise to the God whose sovereignty is unlimited (see Ps 113:2).

REFLECTIONS

Psalm 115 begins and ends with an emphatic focus on the community—"us" (v. 1) and "we" (v. 18)—but in each case, the community looks beyond itself. In its intent to glorify and bless God (vv. 1, 18), the community denies itself (see Mark 8:34); it renounces reliance upon itself and its own resources and places its trust in God (vv. 9-11). Such humbling of self, it trusts, will be its exaltation (vv. 12-15; see Luke 18:14).

Trust in God sets the community apart from those who make and worship idols. As Mays points out, the polemic in vv. 4-8 "is hardly an accurate and fair description of the religions of the nations around Israel who made images to be representations and symbols of the person and presence of their deities."[423] Even so, the exaggeration is not without a point. The polemic is grounded in the first and second commandments, which state Israel's conviction that no material image can properly represent God. The inevitable tendency of the use of human-made images is to limit God. In effect, people create gods in their own image, and the human self becomes preeminent (see v. 8). It is important to note, too, that because the polemic is part of the liturgy of the congregation, it also serves to remind the community of the persistent temptation toward the idolatrous self-centeredness that it professes to renounce.

The presence of the polemic in vv. 4-8 may well indicate the exilic or post-exilic origin of the psalm—that is, a period of domination by the nations (see v. 2). In any case, Allen reaches the following conclusion, "Psalm 115 is a stirring lesson to the people of God in every age concerning survival in an alien, hostile environment."[424] As such, it can be a particularly valuable resource for the contemporary church, which confronts a culture that is increasingly alien and hostile. To be sure, the hostility may not always be overt, but much in modern North American culture systematically teaches self-groundedness and self-centeredness; it assigns primary importance to enjoying ourselves rather than to glorifying God (see Commentary on Psalms 1; 100).

In such a culture, it is an increasingly radical act to profess faith in God—to say the Apostles' Creed, to which Ps 115:15*b* has contributed a crucial phrase (see also Gen 14:19, 22; Pss 121:2; 124:8; 134:3). To profess faith in God, "Maker of heaven and

423. Mays, *Psalms*, 366.
424. Allen, *Psalms 101–150*, 111.

earth," is to affirm that we intend to live first and finally to God's glory rather than to our own (see v. 1). It is to affirm that we live by trusting God rather than ourselves (see vv. 9-11). In such a culture, it is also an increasingly radical act to pray as the community prays, to say the concluding line of the Lord's Prayer, which is reminiscent of Ps 115:1: "For thine is the kingdom and the power and the glory forever. Amen."

PSALM 116:1-19, I WILL LIFT UP THE CUP OF SALVATION

COMMENTARY

Psalm 116 is a song of thanksgiving (see Psalms 30; 32; 34). It is clear from vv. 1-2 that the psalmist's prayer for help has been answered (see also vv. 6b, 7b, 8-9, 12, 16c). The psalmist can now look back on the former threat (vv. 3-4, 8, 10-11, 15), celebrate God's goodness and the deliverance God has effected (vv. 5-6a, 7), profess devotion to God (vv. 1a, 2b, 16ab), and make a public response of gratitude in the Temple (vv. 12-14, 17-19). While the traditional elements of a song of thanksgiving are present, they seem to be presented in no particular order; scholars disagree on the structure of the psalm. In fact, the LXX and the Vulgate transmit vv. 1-9 and vv. 10-19 as two separate psalms. Even so, there are clear indications of the unity of Psalm 116—for instance, the repetition of "call" in vv. 2, 4, 13, 17; the repetition of "death" in vv. 3, 8, 15; and the repetition of "bountifully"/"bounty" in vv. 7, 12.

Taking the repetition in vv. 13b-14 and 17b-18 as a major clue, Allen divides Psalm 116 into three sections: vv. 1-7, vv. 8-14, vv. 15-19.[425] Each section looks back to the former distress (see vv. 3-4, 8, 10-11, 15; note esp. "death" in each section), and if v. 7a is properly construed as a statement of the psalmist's intent to go to the Temple, as Mays suggests, then each section also concludes with what Mays calls "a performance statement"—the psalmist's promise to respond gratefully to God (vv. 7, 13-14, 17-19).[426] The psalm was probably originally used by an individual as an expression of gratitude and faith following deliverance from some life-threatening distress, perhaps sickness (see

Psalms 6; 38), but the language is open-ended enough to apply to a variety of crises. It was apparently performed at the Temple (v. 19) and accompanied by sacrifice (vv. 13, 17). At some point, Psalm 116 became a part of the *Hallel* collection (Psalms 113–118), which was used at Passover, and it also became associated by Christians with the Lord's supper (see Reflections below). Its theme of deliverance is in keeping with the thrust of Book V (see Psalms 107; 109; 111; 113–115; 118; on the purpose of Book V, see Commentary on Psalms 107; 111; Introduction).

116:1-4. The beginning of Psalm 116 is unique (see Ps 18:1, where a different Hebrew verb is translated "love"), and the psalmists only rarely speak elsewhere of loving God (see Pss 5:11; 31:23; 40:16). As subsequent verses indicate, the psalmist's love for God grows out of the realization that God has saved his or her life (v. 4). As elsewhere in the psalms, death is described in conjunction with a place, Sheol, the realm of the dead (v. 3). Sheol is sometimes portrayed as a place beyond even God's reach (see Pss 6:5; 30:9; 88:3-7, 10-13), but at other times, Sheol is viewed as a sort of power that invades life and from which God can rescue (see Pss 30:3; 49:15; 56:13; 86:13; see also Ps 139:8). As Mays points out, there is a tension between these points of view.[427] The tension may be testimony to the diversity of Israelite views of life and death, or perhaps to the development of differing perspectives over time (see Commentary on Psalms 22; 49). In any case, the psalmist is convinced that he or she is alive because of what God has done. Thus what the psalmist did in the time of distress—call

425. Allen, *Psalms 101–150*, 114-15.
426. Mays, *Psalms*, 369.
427. Mays, *Psalms*, 370.

on God's name (v. 4)—has become a life-long commitment (v. 2). To love someone is to be in constant conversation with him or her.

116:5-7. Love also motivates one to communicate enthusiastically to others the character of the beloved (v. 5). The word "name" (שׁם *šēm*) in v. 4 has already suggested the importance of God's character, and the words "gracious" (חנון *ḥannûn*) and "merciful" (מרחם *měraḥēm*) are used elsewhere to describe God's fundamental character (see Exod 34:6; Pss 86:15; 111:4). The word "righteous" (צדיק *ṣaddîq*), too, describes what God fundamentally is and wills (see Pss 9:8; 96:13; 97:2; 98:9; 99:4); it does not usually occur in conjunction with "gracious" and "merciful," but it is certainly an appropriate grouping (see Ps 111:3-4). Motivated by compassion, impelled by grace, God sets things right for "the simple" (v. 6*a*)—that is, the powerless—and those "brought low" (v. 6*b*; see Ps 79:8, where Israel appeals to God's "mercy"/"compassion" when "brought very low"; see also Ps 142:7). God helps those who cannot help themselves (see Psalms 3; 107; 109; 113; 118). This is the bounty (vv. 7*b*, 12) the psalmist has experienced (v. 6*b*) and to which he or she intends to respond (v. 7*a*; cf. Ps 95:11).

116:8-11. Verse 8 rehearses the deliverance. The threat of death is elsewhere symbolized by "tears" (see Pss 6:6; 39:12; 56:8) and "stumbling" (see Ps 56:13). The psalmist does not stumble but walks (v. 9*a*); the psalmist does not die but remains "in the land of the living" (v. 9*b*; see Pss 27:13; 52:5; 142:5; Isa 38:11; 53:8; Jer 11:19). In looking back over this experience, the psalmist recalls articulating the severity of the affliction (v. 10; see Ps 31:22). But the psalmist's words are not indicative of resignation or despair. In the light of v. 10, v. 11 should be viewed not so much as evidence that the psalmist has been the victim of deceit but that he or she did not place hope in human help (see Ps 62:9).

116:12-14. Recalling v. 7, v. 12 raises the question of an appropriate expression of gratitude. It was apparently customary to accompany public expressions of gratitude with sacrifices, and the "cup of salvation" (v. 13) seems originally to have been some form of sacrificial offering (see Exod 29:40; Num 28:7). In good times (vv. 13*b*, 17*b*; see v. 2) as well as in bad (v. 4), the psalmist calls upon the name of God. The material and verbal expressions of gratitude fulfill the vow the psalmist would have made as part of a prayer for help during the time of distress (vv. 14, 18; see Pss 22:25; 61:5, 8; 65:1).

116:15-19. The NIV and the NRSV make v. 15 sound as if God welcomes the death of the faithful, but the whole point of the psalm is that God wills life and works to make life a reality. Thus the Hebrew word translated "precious" (יקר *yāqār*) should be understood in the sense of "costly." Because God does *not* welcome the death of the faithful, the psalmist professes emphatically his or her relatedness to God as servant (v. 16*ab*; see above on Ps 86:16), and recalls again God's intervention to deliver (v. 16*c*; see Ps 107:14). Like the previous two sections, the final one concludes with a performance statement. Verses 17*b*-18 are identical to vv. 13*b*-14, but v. 17*a* cites a different sacrificial act than does v. 13*a*: "a thanksgiving sacrifice" (see Lev 7:12; 22:29; Pss 27:6; 107:22). Verse 19 specifies the public setting as the Temple (see "courts" in Pss 65:4; 84:2, 10; 96:8; 100:4; 135:2), and the final *Hallelu-yah* links Psalm 116 to the rest of the *Hallel* collection (see Commentary on Psalm 113).

REFLECTIONS

1. Like other songs of thanksgiving, as well as songs of praise and prayers for help, Psalm 116 is testimony to the gracious character and righteous purposes of God. Contrary to conventional worldly wisdom, the psalmist asserts that God helps those who cannot help themselves (see Commentary on Psalm 3). Psalm 116 thus invites, not self-reliance, but dependence upon God—in short, trust (vv. 2, 10; see Ps 115:9-11; see also Commentary on Psalms 1; 2). Genuine faith in God inevitably involves loving God (v. 1); as the psalmist's life demonstrates, love of God is manifested in witness to God's character (vv. 5-6), gratitude (vv. 12-14, 17-19), and humble service (v. 16). Such faith is also manifested in the ability to endure every affliction (v. 10; see Ps 34:19; see also 2 Cor 4:8 and note that Ps 116:10 is alluded to in 2 Cor 4:13).

2. Although originating apparently for use by an individual in response to deliverance by God, Psalm 116 eventually came to be used in wider liturgical settings. The exact reason why Psalm 116 became part of the *Hallel* collection is not known. Perhaps it was because of its theme of deliverance from death (see Pss 115:17; 118:17-18), or if the *Hallel* collection had an original connection with Passover, perhaps Psalm 116 was chosen because of its mention of a cup (v. 13). In any case, the Passover meal involves the lifting up and blessing of four cups of wine; rabbinic sources connect the reading of Psalms 115–118 with the fourth cup. Thus the lifting of "the cup of salvation" (v. 13) would have come to be understood in this setting as a celebration of the exodus (see Psalms 114; 118). The Passover liturgy encourages the reactualization of the exodus by every subsequent generation.

3. Jesus, of course, reactualized the Passover meal in a way that transformed its significance for Christians. Not surprisingly, Psalm 116 became associated by Christians with the Lord's supper, which is also known as the eucharist—that is, thanksgiving. In particular, Psalm 116 is traditionally the psalm for Holy Thursday. In this liturgical setting, Christians are encouraged to hear the psalmist's experience as an anticipation of Jesus' faithful suffering (v. 10) and ultimate deliverance from death in the resurrection (vv. 3-4, 8-9, 16). Jesus' lifting of the cup and his new interpretation of it (see Matt 26:27-28; Mark 14:23-24; Luke 22:20; 1 Cor 10:10; 11:25) point to his own death as the sacrifice (v. 17) and to a new dimension of the affirmation of what it means for him and for his followers to be delivered from death into "the land of the living" (v. 9).

PSALM 117:1-2, PRAISE THE LORD, ALL YOU NATIONS

COMMENTARY

Although the shortest of all the psalms, Psalm 117 manages to demonstrate in two verses the typical structure of a song of praise: invitation to praise (v. 1) and reasons for praise (v. 2). For all its brevity and typicality, Psalm 117 makes a claim that is long on significance and anything but routine. The claim is simple but breathtaking: Praising God is the proper vocation and goal of human life!

The invitation in v. 1 points to this claim. It is extended not to Israel or to Judah or to some group of the faithful, but to "all you nations" and "all you peoples." Underlying this invitation is the conviction that the God of Israel is the God who rules the world. Not surprisingly, the psalms that explicitly proclaim God's reign also address their invitations to praise to a universal audience (see Pss 47:1; 96:1, 7, 9, 11-12; 97:1; 98:4, 7-8; 99:1-3; 100:1). Praise is what God intends for everybody. Because God rules the world, God's congregation must include all peoples and nations along with all creatures and all creation (see Pss 148:1-4, 7-12; 150:6).

Given the universality of the invitation, one might expect the accompanying reasons to depart from the opening chapters of the book of Genesis (see Pss 86:9; 150:6), but the reasons for praise recall instead the book of Exodus. The words "steadfast love" (חסד *ḥesed*) and "faithfulness" (אמת *ʾĕmet*) are two of the key words in God's self-revelation to Moses, which forms the culmination of the golden calf episode (see Exod 34:6; see also Pss 25:10; 36:5; 40:10; 57:10; 85:10; 86:15; 89:14; 92:2; 98:3; 100:5; 108:4; 138:2; Introduction). The recollection of this narrative context is important, because by this point in the story, God is clearly aware that the creation of humankind and the choice of a particular people leave God no other option than to be related to a sinful humanity. By recalling Exodus 34:6, therefore, Psalm 117 grounds the reasons for praising God in God's fundamental identity. Because God is steadfastly loving and forever faithful,

God can do no other than love the world and its sinful inhabitants. In relation to the sovereignty of God, implied in v. 1, the word translated "great" (גבר *gābar*) in v. 2 is particularly interesting (see Ps 103:11). The Hebrew root is often used to indicate the power of a military conqueror. Here it also affirms that God conquers the world, but that God does so by the power of faithful love.

REFLECTIONS

1. Psalm 117 communicates the good news that God loves the world, all nations and peoples (see Psalms 19; 87; John 3:16-17), and that God rules the world with the power of faithful love (see John 16:33). Thus it also teaches that human life is incomprehensible apart from God and from God's love for the world. To praise God is to understand and affirm that genuine life consists ultimately in submission to God rather than assertion of self. In our world, which seems either unable or unwilling to praise God, the message of Psalm 117 is crucial (see Commentary on Psalms 8; 100).

2. Like every affirmation of God's rule, explicit or implicit, Psalm 117 must be heard eschatologically (see Commentary on Psalms 2; 93–99; Introduction). As Mays puts it: "The call to the nations reaches toward an eschatological horizon when nationality and race shall be comprehended and healed in a larger unity that can be constituted only by the faith spoken in praise of God."[428] To live under God's rule, to live eschatologically, means that God's future affects the human present. On the basis of the eschatological horizon glimpsed in Psalm 117, for instance, the apostle Paul insisted that the Christian church be open to the Gentiles, to the nations (see Paul's citation of Ps 117:1 in Rom 15:11).

3. In our age, in which the church transcends the barriers of race and nation, Psalm 117 invites us perhaps to conversation with persons of other faiths or of no faith at all. William C. Placher suggests that Christians enter such dialogue to represent the truth we perceive but also to learn from other traditions and practices. The success of such conversations should not be measured by the goal of conversion, but simply by the effort to speak honestly and listen carefully to a variety of persons, who, as Psalm 117 suggests, are also children of God.[429]

428. Mays, *Psalms,* 372-73.
429. William C. Placher, *Unapologetic Theology: A Christian Voice in a Pluralistic Conversation* (Louisville: Westminster John Knox, 1989) 115-18, 143-49. Placher does not cite Psalm 117, but it would support his appeal to texts like Gen 1:26 and Acts 17:23 (p. 116).

PSALM 118:1-29, THIS IS THE DAY ON WHICH THE LORD HAS ACTED

COMMENTARY

As the opening and closing verses might suggest, Psalm 118 is ordinarily categorized as a song of thanksgiving. Like others of this type (see Psalms 30; 34; 116), it recounts (see

vv. 5-18) and publicly celebrates an experience of deliverance (vv. 19-28). But Psalm 118 is unique. While the speaker for most of the psalm is an individual "I" (vv. 5-21), the distress recounted seems to suggest a crisis of national proportions (see esp. vv. 10-14). This has led many scholars to conclude that the "I" is the king speaking on behalf of the people, but certainty is elusive. The speaker actually shifts to the plural in vv. 23-27, leading scholars to disagree as to whether the song should be viewed as individual, communal, or both. Further complicating the interpretive task is the fact that Psalm 118 is especially reminiscent of the celebration of the exodus and return from exile, plus the psalm shifts to petition at v. 25 before concluding with thanksgiving again.

All of these features of Psalm 118 must be considered in addressing the question of its original use and setting. It seems that some sort of liturgical procession, perhaps culminating in a thank offering, originally lay behind vv. 19-28. And it seems that some sort of national victory or deliverance was the focus of the original celebration, perhaps led by the king (see Commentary on Psalms 18; 20–21). But it is difficult to be any more specific than this.

What is more certain is that Psalm 118 is the concluding psalm of the *Hallel* collection (Psalms 113–118), which came to be used at Passover (see Commentary on Psalm 113). In this setting, its recollection of the exodus is especially significant (see Psalm 114). But its allusion to the return from exile and the shift to petition in v. 25 suggest that both exodus and deliverance from exile served as bases for hope that future deliverance would also occur. This gives Psalm 118 an open-endedness that would have made it particularly relevant to the post-exilic era, during which the aftermath of exile persisted and the people continued to be dominated by the nations. Indeed, this feature of Psalm 118 makes its placement in Book V readily understandable. Book V begins by establishing a post-exilic perspective (see Ps 107:2-3) and by commending consideration of God's steadfast love (see 107:43). Not coincidentally perhaps, Psalm 118 begins and ends with the same verse that opens Book V (107:1), suggesting the possibility that Psalms 107–118 together offer a perspective from which to face the reality of continuing oppression: recollection of God's past activity as a basis for petition and grateful trust in God's future activity on behalf of the people (see Commentary on Psalms 107; 108; 111; Introduction). The open-endedness of Psalm 118 is also evident in the way that the early Christian church heard it and understood its speaker and subject to be Jesus (see Reflections below).

118:1-4. The opening and concluding invitations (vv. 1-4, 29) provide a framework for the recital (vv. 5-18) and celebration of deliverance (vv. 19-28). Each verse of the framework features the word "steadfast love" (see Pss 106:1; 107:1; 136:1), a word that describes the very essence of God's character that is revealed in acts of deliverance like those described and alluded to in Psalm 118 (see Exod 15:13; 34:6; Introduction). Verses 2-4 anticipate the communal dimension, which is explicitly present in vv. 23-27 (on the three different addressees, see Pss 115:9-11; 135:19-20). The communal dimension is also evident in vv. 1, 29. The other three psalms that begin with this same verse conclude by associating their theme of deliverance with the situation of the whole people following the return from exile (see Pss 106:44-47; 107:33-41; 136:23-24).

118:5-18. The recital in vv. 5-18 can be divided into three sections: vv. 5-9, vv. 10-14, vv. 15-18. Verse 5 offers a succinct account of the deliverance. The Hebrew root of the noun "distress" (מצר *mēṣar*, v. 5a) has the sense of "restricted," "narrow," "tight." When the psalmist was in a tight spot, God gave space (v. 5b; see "broad place" in Pss 18:19; 31:8 NRSV). Verses 6-9 relate what the psalmist has learned from the whole experience. "On my side" (לי *lî*, vv. 6a, 7a) is more literally "for me." The psalmist's knowledge that God is "for me" (see Pss 56:9; 124:1-2; Rom 8:31) meant that the psalmist need not fear other people (see Ps 56:4, 11), even enemies (v. 7b; see Pss 54:7b; 59:10b; 112:8b). The psalmist has experienced God's help (v. 7a; see v. 13; Pss 10:14; 22:19; 37:40; 115:9-11; 121:2; 124:8; 146:5), and so the psalmist can affirm what the psalmists elsewhere assert makes for genuine happiness: taking refuge in God (see Pss 2:12; 34:8; Introduction), trusting God (see Ps 84:12) rather than even the most powerful humans.

Verses 10-12 again recount the deliverance. The word "surrounded" (סבב *sābab*) links these verses (see Pss 17:11; 22:12), but the description of the distress is intensified with each recounting. Even so, each verse ends with the identical phrase; that is, God's help remains constant amid the growing threat. The verb "cut off" (מול *mûl*) is used most frequently of circumcision, an especially interesting nuance given that the threat comes from the nations. At the crucial moment, God helps (v. 13), just as God did at the exodus, which is recalled very specifically in v. 14. In fact, v. 14 quotes Exod 15:2*ab*, a portion of the song that Moses and the Israelites sang immediately after crossing the sea (see also Isa 12:2*cd*, where the same affirmation occurs in a context that presents it as celebration of return from exile and dispersion).

The words "salvation" (v. 14) and "victory" (v. 15) represent the same Hebrew word (ישועה *yĕšû'â*; see also vv. 21, 25), and the allusions to the exodus continue in vv. 15-18. The three occurrences of "right hand" (ימין *yāmîn*) in vv. 15*b*-16 recall the three occurrences in Exod 15:6, 12 (see also Isa 41:10 in the context of God's returning the exiles). The word "exalted" (רוממה *rômēmâ*, v. 16*a*) again recalls Exod 15:2 (see below on v. 28). The Hebrew root (עשה *'āśâ*) represented by "does" (vv. 15-16) and "deeds" (v. 17) also occurs in v. 6 and v. 24. The effect of the repetition is to contrast human deeds, which threaten the psalmist and the people with death, with God's deeds, which offer life (vv. 17-18; see Pss 115:17; 116:8-9). The mention of punishment/chastening/disciplining in v. 18*a* indicates that the psalmist or the people interpret the distress as God's doing as well (see v. 13*a*; see NRSV note), but there is no specific indication of wrongdoing (see Pss 6:1; 38:1; 94:12; Jer 30:11; 31:18; see also Ps 2:10).

118:19-29. Verses 19-28 have several features of a public worship service, including indications of alternating voices and a liturgical procession (vv. 19-20, 26-27). This section is framed by the individual speaker's expression of intent to "give thanks" (vv. 19, 28; see vv. 1, 29). Verse 28 clearly recalls Exod 15:2*cd* (see above on v. 14; and see v. 16, where "exalt" is the same as "extol" in v. 28). Thus the speaker again suggests that the present deliverance is analogous to the exodus. He or she apparently intends to enter the temple gates to make the appropriate expression of gratitude (see "gates" in Pss 24:7, 9; 100:4; Jer 7:2). Verse 20 appears to be a response to v. 19 by a priest or some temple official (see 1 Chr 16:42). As is the case throughout the psalms, "the righteous" are not persons who have proven themselves worthy (see v. 18) but those who acknowledge that they owe their lives and futures to God (see vv. 8-9; see also Commentary on Psalm 1). Indeed, this is precisely what the psalmist gratefully acknowledges in v. 21 (see "answered" in v. 5 and "salvation"/"save" in vv. 14-15, 25).

Verse 22 seems to be a congregational response that interprets the psalmist's experience of deliverance from death to life; it would have served in the post-exilic era to interpret the experience of the people as well (see Isa 28:16; Jer 51:26). The shift to a plural speaker is clear in vv. 23-27. The reversal of fortunes is unambiguously attributed to God, and the vocabulary of vv. 23-24 continues to recall the exodus as a prototype. The root of "marvelous" (פלא *pālā'*) in v. 23*b* occurs as "wonders" in Exod 15:11, and the focus on "the day on which the LORD has acted" (v. 24*a* NEB) recalls the crossing of the sea (see Exod 14:13).

The shift to petition in v. 25 is unexpected. The plea "Save us, we beseech you" is a real and urgent petition (cf. Mark 11:9-10, where the similar "Hosanna" appears to have been a celebrative cry; see also Reflections below). The psalm's earlier testimony (vv. 5-18, 21), though written in the first-person singular, is the basis for prayer in the midst of communal distress. As psalmist and people had been saved in the past (vv. 5, 13-14, 15-18, 21), so now the people need to be saved again. The plea for "success" is not a request for abundant material prosperity but an appeal to God to provide resources for life amid the current threat (on "prosper," see commentary on Ps 1:3). The petition in v. 25 orients the psalm to the future as well as to the past and thus gives the psalm an open-endedness that is evident in the history of its use.

The blessing and affirmation of vv. 26-27 recall vv. 19-20 ("comes" [בוא *bô'*] in v. 26 is the same verb as "enter" in vv. 19-20), but they should also be heard in the context of the petition of v. 25. The "one who comes in the name of the LORD" represents the possibility of blessing in the midst of the current threat (v. 26), and the present crisis does not diminish the people's trust that "the LORD is God" or their memory of God's past faithfulness in giving light (v. 27; see "light"/ "shine" in Pss 4:6; 27:1; 31:16; 67:1). Thus v. 27 seems to express the people's confidence in God's illuminating presence in the midst of their current need. In any case, the people are apparently intent upon celebrating even during the moment of threat, although the precise nature and significance of the activity described in v. 27 b are unclear (see NIV and NRSV notes). The mention of "branches" may suggest an origin in or allusion to the Feast of Tabernacles (see Lev 23:40).

In v. 28, the psalmist echoes in an emphatic and very personal way the communal affirmation of v. 27 a : "My God (are) you" (v. 28 a, author's trans.). The psalmist also reaffirms the intent to give thanks (see vv. 1, 19, 21), again alludes to the exodus (see Exod 15:2 cd), and invites the community to participate in giving thanks (v. 29; see v. 1; Pss 106:1; 107:1; 136:1).

REFLECTIONS

The failure of Psalm 118 to identify the speaker in vv. 5-18, 28 contributed to the open-endedness of the psalm. So did its juxtaposition of clear allusions to past saving events—exodus and return from exile—with the petition for help in v. 25. Regardless of the circumstances of its origin and original use, Psalm 118 became a part of the *Hallel* collection, which was used at Passover, a recollection of the exodus and an anticipation of God's continuing presence and ongoing help (see Commentary on Psalms 113; 114; 115; 116; 117).

1. The same factors that contribute to the open-endedness of Psalm 118—in particular, the movement from thanksgiving to petition back to thanksgiving in vv. 19-29—also make it, in Brueggemann's words, "a model for evangelical prayer."[430] Praise and petition join in affirming God's sovereignty and the persistent reality of human need. As Mays indicates, Psalm 118, which serves as a model for prayer, suggests too that human need and God's saving activity "are not tied to a particular historical occasion or social setting or festival, but are read as functions of the canon." To view this psalm in the context of the biblical canon "opens the psalm to use and interpretation in later and other times by the community for whom the canon of scripture is the guide to faith and life."[431]

2. Thus the early Christian community identified the speaker in vv. 5-18, 28 as Jesus. According to the Gospels, when Jesus entered Jerusalem shortly before his crucifixion, he was greeted by a crowd in a manner reminiscent of Psalm 118. In Mark 11:9, the first part of the greeting consists of Ps 118:25 a, 26 a. The use of Psalm 118 at this point is not really surprising, since Jesus enters Jerusalem during the week of Passover. But this observation does not exhaust the significance of Mark's use of Psalm 118. Verses 22-23 were understood within first-century Judaism to refer to the Messiah.[432] In fact, Matt 21:42 cites these verses to suggest that Jesus is the rejected Messiah (see also Luke 20:17; Acts 4:11-12). In the story of Jesus' entry into Jerusalem, the Gospel writers have extended the messianic interpretation to vv. 25-26. Mark 11:10 and Matt 21:9 make this clear by mentioning "the kingdom of our father David" (NRSV) and "Son of David" respectively, while the parallel accounts in Luke and John record that the crowd addresses Jesus as "King" (Luke 23:38; John 12:13). For all the Gospel writers, Psalm 118 is a means of understanding and articulating the significance of Jesus.

430. Walter Brueggemann, "Psalm 118:19-29: Psalm for Palm Sunday," *No Other Foundation* 10 (Winter 1989–90) 16.
431. James L. Mays, "Psalm 118 in the Light of Canonical Analysis," in *Canon, Theology, and Old Testament Interpretation*, ed. G. M. Tucker, D. L. Petersen, R. R. Wilson (Philadelphia: Fortress, 1988) 310.
432. See H.-J. Kraus, *Theology of the Psalms*, trans. Keith Crim (Minneapolis: Augsburg, 1986) 196.

In other words, by articulating the significance of Jesus through Psalm 118, the Gospel writers profess that the life, death, and resurrection of Jesus are an extension of God's saving activity in the exodus and return from exile. Psalm 118 has become in Christian liturgical tradition not just a psalm for Palm/Passion Sunday, which celebrates Jesus' entry into Jerusalem, but also for Easter Sunday. For Christians, Easter is above all "the day on which the Lord has acted" (v. 24 NEB). God was active in the exodus; God was active in returning exiles; God was active in the life, death, and resurrection of Jesus. So the Gospel writers affirm in their use of Psalm 118. As a traditional call to worship, v. 24 is a reminder to Christians that every Sunday is a celebration of the resurrection, the Lord's Day, the day on which the Lord has acted and is still active. Thus Psalm 118 can be seen as a focal point for discerning the continuity between the Old and the New Testament witnesses that God is "for us" (see vv. 6-7; Rom 8:31) and that God's "steadfast love endures forever" (vv. 1-4, 29; see Rom 8:38-39).

3. Not surprisingly, the special appeal that Psalm 118 had for the Gospel writers has continued throughout centuries of Christian interpretation. Martin Luther, for instance, viewed Psalm 118 as "My own beloved psalm."[433] Not surprisingly either, v. 17 has been heard by Christian interpreters as an affirmation of the resurrection both of Jesus and of believers. That is to say, in view of the extension of God's saving activity to include Jesus Christ, Christians hear v. 17 with a fuller sense. Luther, for instance, called v. 17 "a masterpiece," and concluded that "all the saints have sung this verse and will continue to sing it to the end."[434] Given the rich historical allusions and open-endedness of the psalm, as well as the history and currency of its use in Judaism and Christianity, one might make the same conclusion of Psalm 118 as a whole—all the saints have sung it and will sing it to the end.

433. Quoted in Ronald M. Hals, "Psalm 118," *Int.* 37 (1983) 277.
434. See Hals, "Psalm 118," 280. These quotes and the previous one are from Luther's *Works,* Vol. 14: *Selected Psalms III*, ed. J. Pelikan (St. Louis: Concordia, 1958) 45, 87.

PSALM 119:1-176, HOW I LOVE YOUR INSTRUCTION

COMMENTARY

Simply by virtue of its length, Psalm 119 is impressive and imposing, perhaps even intimidating. Leslie Allen aptly calls it "a literary monument raised in honor of Yahweh's revelation . . . to Israel."[435] As is the case with any imposing structure, some people like Psalm 119, and some people do not. Leopold Sabourin, for instance, reflects the opinion of many commentators when he describes Psalm 119: "Tedious repetitions, poor thought-sequence, apparent lack of inspiration reflect the artificiality of the composition."[436] In contrast, Dahood detects "a freshness of thought and a felicity of expression" throughout the psalm.[437]

To be sure, Psalm 119 is repetitive, but repetition is not necessarily tedious. By "artificiality," Sabourin means the acrostic structure of Psalm 119, comprising twenty-two sections, one for each letter of the Hebrew alphabet (see NIV). Each poetic line in the first section begins with the letter *Aleph* (א), each line in the second section begins with *Beth* (ב), and so on. This kind of repetition is accompanied by another: the repeated use of eight Hebrew terms that designate God's revelation. The frequent use of eight terms

435. Allen, *Psalms 101–150,* 141.
436. Leopold Sabourin, *The Psalms: Their Origin and Meaning* (New York: Alba House, 1994) 381.
437. Mitchell Dahood, *Psalms III (101–150),* AB 17a (Garden City, N.Y.: Doubleday, 1970) 172.

may explain why each section contains eight verses; however, not every verse contains one of these terms. The first and most frequently used (twenty-five occurrences, at least once in every section except vv. 9-16) is *torah* (v. 1*b*; NIV and NRSV, "law"), which should be translated "teaching" or "instruction" or "law" (see Commentary on Psalm 1). The other seven can be considered synonyms of *torah* (תורה *tôrâ*; for the nuances of each term, see below). In order of their first appearance in the psalm, they are as follows: "decrees" (or "statutes," עדת *'ēdōt*, v. 20, twenty-three occurrences), "precepts" (פקודים *piqqûdîm*, v. 4, twenty-one occurrences), "statutes" (or "decrees," חקים *ḥuqqîm*, v. 5, twenty-two occurrences), "command(ments)" (מצות *miṣwōt*, v. 6, twenty-two occurrences), "ordinances" (משפטים *mišpāṭîm*, v. 7 NRSV; NIV, "laws"; twenty-two occurrences, usually plural, but singular in vv. 84, 121, 132 where it is translated differently), "word" (דבר *dābār*, v. 9, twenty-two occurrences), "promise" (אמרה *'imrâ*, v. 11, nineteen occurrences). With the exception of vv. 3, 37, 90, and 122, every line in Psalm 119 contains one of these eight words.

When commentators consider this repetition tedious, they are missing the point. Psalm 119 is more artistic than artificial. As a literary artist, the psalmist intended the structure of the poem to reinforce its theological content. In short, *torah*—God's revelatory instruction—is pervasive and all-encompassing. It applies to everything from A to Z, or in Hebrew, *Aleph* to *Taw*. As Westermann recognizes, "If a person succeeds in reading this psalm's 176 verses one after the other at one sitting, the effect is overwhelming."[438] This is precisely the effect the psalmist intended! For the psalmist, the importance of God's instruction is overwhelming. It applies to everything at every moment, and apart from it, there is nothing worthy to be called life (see Commentary on Psalm 19). This being the case, the proper stance toward God is constant openness to God's instruction (see Commentary on Psalm 1); Jon Levenson suggests that the repetition in Psalm 119 is intended to create a psychological condition—the proper state of mind and heart—which is conducive

to concentration upon God and thus openness to God's revelation:

> It seems likely that the psalm was written to serve as an inducement for the kind of revelation and illumination for which it petitions. Its high degree of regularity and repetition can have a mesmerizing effect upon those who recite it, with the octad of synonyms functioning like a mantra and providing a relaxing predictability while banishing thoughts that distract from the object of contemplation. If the goal of the author was to create the psychic conditions conducive to the spiritual experience he seeks, then those commentators who wish the psalm were shorter have missed the point of it . . . there are liturgies that are best short, and others, like Psalm 119, that work only if they are long.[439]

The psalmist's concept of *torah* is an expansive one. While Psalm 119 has several verbal and conceptual affinities with the book of Deuteronomy and the Deuteronomistic history, including the importance of obedience to God's commandments, it is striking that the psalmist never considers *torah* to be simply a body of legislation, Mosaic or otherwise, and certainly not a book—that is, not the Pentateuch or an emerging core of the Pentateuch. In this regard, the psalmist seems to have more in common with how *torah* was understood by the prophets or wisdom teachers. Levenson summarizes: "We have seen that the author of Psalm 119 recognizes three sources of *tôrâ*: (1) received tradition, passed on most explicitly by teachers (vv. 99-100) but including perhaps some sacred books now in the Hebrew Bible, (2) cosmic or natural law (vv. 89-91), and (3) unmediated divine teaching (e. g., vv. 26-29)."[440] In short, while oral and written tradition were very significant for the psalmist, he or she remained open to God's ongoing instruction, to God's further revelation, to new experiences of the divine Word. This openness has profound implications for current discussions of the inspiration of and authority of Scripture as a written word (see Reflections below).

438. Claus Westermann, *The Psalms: Structure, Content, and Message,* trans. R. D. Gehrke (Minneapolis: Augsburg, 1980) 117.

439. Jon Levenson, "The Sources of Torah: Psalm 119 and the Modes of Revelation in Second Temple Judaism," in *Ancient Israelite Religion,* ed. P. D. Miller, Jr., P. D. Hanson, S. D. McBride (Philadelphia: Fortress, 1987) 566.

440. Levenson, "The Sources of Torah," 570.

While Psalm 119 demonstrates affinities with Deuteronomy, with wisdom materials, and with the prophets (especially Jeremiah), it is not possible to identify the psalmist easily with any particular figure, body of material, or perspective. Will Soll argues that Psalm 119 makes sense as a prayer of the exiled King Jehoiachin for the restoration of the Davidic monarchy.[441] But Levenson points out that the psalmist's concept of *torah* is quite similar to that of Ben Sira, who taught and wrote some four hundred years after Jehoiachin.[442] This disparity points to the difficulty, if not the impossibility, of recovering the circumstances of the origin and original use of Psalm 119. It probably originated during the post-exilic era, but what is more recoverable is the setting implied by the content of the psalm itself. Mays suggests on the basis of Psalm 119 (as well as Psalms 1 and 19, which also highlight the concept of *torah*) that the setting for *all* the Psalms is "a type of piety . . . that used the entire book as prayer and praise." This torah piety was characterized by "faithfulness through study and obedience and hope through prayer and waiting."[443]

The identification of the setting of Psalm 119 as a type of piety explains why the psalm would have been an appropriate prayer for Jehoiachin or Jeremiah or Ben Sira or Israel in exile/dispersion. While the psalmist does not claim to be perfect (see v. 176), it is clear that he or she is committed to obedience. Even so, the psalmist is scorned and persecuted (vv. 22-23, 42, 51, 61, 69, 84-87, 95, 110, 121, 134, 141, 150, 157, 161) and experiences sorrow and affliction (vv. 28, 50, 71, 75, 92, 107, 153). Thus the psalmist lives in waiting as a suffering servant (see vv. 17, 23, 38, 49, 65, 76, 84, 91, 122, 124, 125, 135). In other words, the perspective of Psalm 119 is eschatological. Life is entrusted to the sovereign God in circumstances that seem to belie God's sovereignty (see Commentary on Psalms 1; 2; Introduction).

The eschatological dimension of Psalm 119 makes it a fitting anchor for Book V, which, along with Book IV, responds to the crisis of exile and its aftermath by proclaiming God's sovereignty, by recalling past

deliverance, and by praying for future deliverance (see Commentary on Psalms 107; 111; 118; Introduction). Psalm 119 also clearly recalls Psalms 1-2 (cf. 119:1 with 1:1; 2:12), which from the beginning of the psalter commend openness to God's instruction and the entrusting of life and future to God. The eschatological dimension of Psalm 119 also gives the psalm the character of a prayer for help or individual lament/complaint, and some commentators classify it as such. Most commentators, however, consider Psalm 119 a torah psalm, along with Psalms 1 and 19. In a sense, Psalm 119 belongs in a class by itself. Because of its length, it contains elements of all types of psalms. This in itself is appropriate, since Psalm 119 articulates so eloquently and powerfully the torah-piety that pervades the whole psalter.

The acrostic pattern of Psalm 119 is its most prominent structural feature and some would say its only organizing principle. Indeed, some scholars suggest that Psalm 119 would make as much sense read backward as it does forward. Soll, however, detects a larger coherence. He suggests the following divisions designated by the letters of the Hebrew alphabet, featured in each eight-verse section:

I.   *Aleph-Bêt* (vv. 1-16): Prologue
II.   *Gîmel-Wāw* (vv. 17-48)
III. *Zayin-Yôd* (vv. 49-80)
IV.   *Kaph-Sāmek* (vv. 81-120):
      Central section
V.   *'Ayin-Ṣādê* (vv. 121-144)
VI.   *Qôph-Tāw* (vv. 145-176):
      Concluding section

In Soll's view, Psalm 119 is an individual lament, and it shows the characteristic movement of such prayers—from complaint and petition (vv. 17-24) to praise and assurance (vv. 169-176), with the turning point coming at vv. 89-96. This turning point, which Soll considers the zenith of the poem, occurs in the central division immediately following the section that Soll identifies as the "nadir" of the poem (vv. 81-88). Soll recognizes that complaint and petition continue to occur after the central division, but he attributes this to the length of the poem, suggesting that the basic movement from complaint/petition to praise is recapitulated in each division, as

441. Will Soll, *Psalm 119: Matrix, Form, and Setting*, CBQMS 23 (Washington, D.C.: Catholic Biblical Association, 1991) 152-54.
442. Levenson, "The Sources of Torah," 567-68.
443. Mays, "The Place of the Torah-Psalms in the Psalter," 12.

in Psalm 31.[444] While Soll finds significantly more coherence in Psalm 119 than do most other commentators, his proposal is a welcome corrective to those who assert that Psalm 119 shows no coherence or logical movement. After all, it only makes sense that the psalmist's careful artistry would extend beyond the measure of the individual poetic line or section.

119:1-8. It is not surprising that Psalm 119 uses several items of vocabulary from Psalms 1 and 19. In fact, every word of v. 1 occurs in either Psalm 1 or Psalm 19. It is clear that the blamelessness (see Ps 19:13) involved is not moral perfection, for the psalmist later confesses, "I have strayed like a lost sheep" (v. 176, lit., "perishing sheep"; "perish" [אבד *'ābad*] is the same word used to describe the way of the wicked in Ps 1:6!). Likewise, the psalmist's being "happy" (see Pss 1:1; 2:12) must involve something very different from simply reaping material benefits for obedience. Somehow, the psalmist's happiness cannot be incompatible with the persecution, scorn, sorrow, and affliction he or she experiences. In short, happiness has to do with entrusting life to God, which means constant openness to God's life-giving *torah* (see Pss 1:2; 19:7).

Subsequent verses introduce other terms for God's revelation. Verse 2 is reminiscent of Deuteronomy, where God's "decrees" (see Ps 19:7) are to be heard and kept (see Deut 4:45; 6:17, 20) and where God is to be sought wholeheartedly (see Deut 4:29; Ps 119:10). Verse 3 is unusual in that it does not contain one of the eight major synonyms. Rather, God's "ways" indicate God's revelation in this case (see also vv. 15, 37), and the image of walking in God's ways is again reminiscent of Deuteronomy, occurring often in parallel with keeping God's commandments (see Deut 8:6; 10:12-13; 11:22; see Ps 119:6). While "precepts" (*piqqûdîm*, v. 4) occurs elsewhere only in the psalms (see 19:8; 103:18; 111:7), "statutes" (*ḥuqqîm*, vv. 5, 8) and "ordinances" (*mišpāṭîm*, v. 7) again recall Deuteronomy and other portions of the Pentateuch (see Exod 18:16; Deut 6:1; 7:11). The word "ordinances" is the plural of a noun usually translated "justice" (see vv. 121, 156), a reminder that the purpose

of God's instruction is to order rightly (see "righteous" or "right" in vv. 7, 62, 75, 106, 121, 137, 164) the human community (see Pss 97:2; 99:4). While the repeated terms in Psalm 119 can and certainly do elsewhere suggest written formulations of God's will, and while the psalmist may have such written codes in mind, the obedience he or she seeks should not be understood as a simple matter of following a set of rules. Verses 1-8 communicate the sense that the psalmist continually seeks God, which means seeking new and deeper understandings of how God intends justice and righteousness to be enacted in the world. This seems clear as well in vv. 9-16.

119:9-16. The question of cleanness or purity in v. 9*a* (see Ps 73:13; Prov 20:9) is answered by reference to another of the eight synonyms: "word" (*dābār*). While *torah* seems to be the most important of the eight (vv. 9-16 is the only section in which it does not occur), "word" seems to be next in line. Not only does it provide an envelope structure for the second introductory section (vv. 9, 16), but it also appears in the first line of fully half of the psalm's twenty-two sections. While "word" can suggest written revelation (see Exod 34:27-28; Deut 4:13), it also designates God's communication beyond any current written formulation (see 1 Kgs 6:11; 13:20; Jer 1:4; Ezek 1:3) and thus suggests a dynamic revelatory power that will not finally be thwarted (see Ps 33:6; Isa 40:8; 55:11). The psalmist apparently is open to both God's past and future revelation.

Verse 11 introduces the final of the eight synonyms and the one that occurs least often. The noun is derived from a verb that means "to say," "to utter" (אמר *'āmar*), and it never clearly designates a written formulation of God's revelation, except perhaps in Deut 33:9 (see "word"/"speak"/"promise" in Deut 32:2; Pss 12:6; 105:19; 138:2; 147:15; Prov 30:5; Isa 5:24; 28:23; 32:9). For this reason, perhaps, the word is usually translated "promise" in Psalm 119 (of the nineteen occurrences, the NIV uses "promise" thirteen times and the NRSV fourteen times; otherwise, they use "word," except for "command" in v. 158 NRSV). In the psalmist's mind, "word" (vv. 9, 16) and "promise" appear to be associated, perhaps because they are the most dynamic of the eight synonyms.

Of the nineteen occurrences of "promise," eight occur in verses immediately preceding or following occurrences of "word" (see vv. 41-42, 49-50, 57-58, 81-82, 89-140, 147-148, 161-162, 169-170). Another six occur within two verses of "word" (see vv. 9, 11; 65, 67; 74, 76; 101, 103; 114, 116; 158, 160), and only five times does "promise" occur any further apart from "word" (vv. 38, 123, 133, 154, 172).

Verse 11 is reminiscent of Jer 31:33, a verse in which God promises to write "instruction" on the people's hearts. In short, God will teach the people directly (see Jer 31:34), a conviction also evident in Ps 119:12 and throughout the psalm. The implication is that the psalmist has more to learn and that God has more to reveal.

119:17-24. While vv. 1-8 have hinted that the psalmist lives under threat (see vv. 6a, 8b), vv. 17-24 clearly have the character of a complaint. The section begins with petition (vv. 17-18) and moves to complaint (v. 19); it also introduces a regular feature of the prayers for help—the enemies (vv. 21-23; see Pss 22:6; 31:11; 44:13). The desire to see "wondrous things" (v. 18; see vv. 27, 129; Exod 3:20; 15:11) suggests the need for deliverance, as does the psalmist's description of his or her "alien" status (see v. 54), an allusion perhaps to the plights of Abraham (see Gen 13:4) and Moses (see Exod 2:22; 18:3). Verse 23a also calls to mind the plight of Jeremiah (see Jeremiah 36–38). Princes and kings regularly employed advisers and counselors, but the psalmist professes to be advised by God's revelation. Verses 23-24 perhaps anticipate v. 46, where the psalmist dares to speak before kings, because he or she looks to a higher authority. The plight described in vv. 17-24 is one with which the exilic and post-exilic generations could have readily identified, but it is also one that regularly confronts the people of God (see Reflections below).

119:25-32. The complaint continues. Verse 25 communicates urgency, for "dust" is associated elsewhere with death (see Ps 22:15, 29). Life resides in God's "word" (see v. 17, where "live" [חיה ḥāyâ] represents the same Hebrew word as "revive" in v. 25 NRSV). "Grief"/"sorrow" in v. 28 is also frequently associated with death (see Gen 42:38; 44:31; Pss 31:10; 116:3), and

again it is God's word that offers strength ("strengthen" [קימני qayyĕmēnî] in v. 28b is lit., "cause me to stand," which is reminiscent of the literal meaning of "resurrection," which is "to stand up again"). As in vv. 9-16, God is the teacher (see vv. 26-27, 29), and God's teaching means life. Thus, while the psalmist's "soul clings to the dust" (v. 25), he or she is expressing the intent to cling to God's revelation (v. 31). God's word is life (see Commentary on Psalms 1; 19).

119:33-40. The marked difference between vv. 33-40 and vv. 17-32 supports Soll's contention of a logical movement in Psalm 119. Verses 33-40 are dominated by petition. In fact, each of the first seven lines begins with a *hipil* imperative. As suggested above (see vv. 12, 26), God is the teacher (v. 33; the Hebrew verb "to teach" [ירה yārâ] underlies the noun *torah,* which occurs in v. 34). God is the primary actor, and the psalmist's actions are in response to God's previous activity. The psalmist prays that God's instruction permeate his or her whole being (v. 34) and that he or she not be distracted by "selfish gain" (v. 36; see Exod 18:21; 1 Sam 8:3; Prov 1:19; 15:27; Isa 56:11; Jer 6:13; 22:17) or "worthless things" (v. 37), a word that sometimes implies idolatry (see Ps 31:6). In other words, only God is sovereign—not the self or other gods. Both "servant" and "fear" in v. 38 suggest further the psalmist's recognition of God's claim and rule. Those who deny God's sovereignty may "scorn" the psalmist (see v. 22; "disgrace" in v. 39 is from the same Hebrew root), but the psalmist remains oriented to God (v. 40) and convinced that only God can "give me life" (vv. 37, 40; see also vv. 17, 24). As the imploring stance in vv. 33-40 makes clear, life is a gift to be received rather than a reward to be earned.

119:41-48. The movement in Psalm 119 continues, since vv. 41-48 have a different tone from vv. 33-40. Petition recurs (vv. 41, 43a), but the dominant note is assurance (vv. 42a, 45), based on trust (v. 42b; see Pss 4:5; 9:10) and hope (v. 43b; see vv. 49, 74, 80, 114, 147; "wait" in Ps 31:24) and manifested in freedom (v. 45a; lit., "in a broad place"; see Ps 118:5), courage (v. 46), and joy (v. 47). Verses 46 and 48b recall v. 23, thus highlighting the movement from complaint to trust—or at least the juxtaposition of the two—that is characteristic of Psalm 119 and establishes its eschatological perspective. The occurrence of "steadfast love" in v. 41 is the first of seven (see vv. 64, 76, 88, 124, 149, 159). Its appearance here and throughout the psalm is eminently appropriate. To trust God's word (v. 42) is to trust God's very self, the essence of which God revealed to be steadfast love (see Exod 34:6; Pss 5:7; 13:5; Introduction). The psalmist may still be taunted (v. 42; "taunt" is the same Hebrew word as NRSV "scorn" in v. 22 and "disagree" in v. 39), but lives joyfully by trusting the truth that sets people free.

119:49-56. According to Soll's outline, vv. 49-56 initiate the next major division (vv. 49-80), which is characterized by retrospection. This direction is set by the three occurrences of the verb "remember" (זכר *zākar*) at the beginning of vv. 49, 52, 55. Remembrance does not suddenly eliminate suffering (see vv. 50-51) or the existence of the wicked (v. 53). As is always the case, memory is inseparable from hope (v. 49*b*; see above on v. 43); together, they are a source of comfort (vv. 50*a*, 52*b*).

Levenson says that v. 54*b*, which reads literally "in the house of my sojourning" (the same Hebrew root as "alien" in v. 19 NRSV) "implies an identification of the *persona* of the psalmist with a homeless Israel, trusting in an unfulfilled promise."[445] This kind of identification reinforces the conclusion that Psalm 119 would have been particularly meaningful to the exilic and post-exilic generations, but it also makes Psalm 119 forever timely. It is always the case that the faithful live inevitably by hope. The image of home/homeless also provides a link between vv. 49-56 and v. 57, which begins the next section.

119:57-64. Perhaps the most meaningful profession that a homeless Israel could make is that "the LORD is my portion" (v. 57*a*). The word "portion" (חלק *ḥēleq*) designates elsewhere the allotment of land that each Israelite, except the priests and Levites, was supposed to have (see Num 18:20; Josh 15:13; 18:7; 19:9). To entrust one's life and future to God—in effect, to have God as one's "portion"—is to be never without a home (see Pss 16:5; 73:26; 142:5; Lam 3:24) and, furthermore, never without a community (see

445. Levenson, "The Sources of Torah," 568.

v. 63). This means praise is possible at all times (v. 62), even in distress (v. 61). To have God as one's "portion" means that nothing—not time, not place, not circumstance—can separate one from God's steadfast love (v. 64; see above on v. 41; see also Rom 8:38-39).

119:65-72. This good news is articulated in vv. 65-72, in which the key word is "good" (טוב *ṭôb*, vv. 65 [NRSV, "well"], 66, 68, 71, 72 [NRSV, "better"; NIV, "precious"]; in fact, each of these verses begins with the word "good"). God's goodness is celebrated amid current affliction (vv. 67, 71). In view of v. 67, it seems that the affliction could well have been interpreted formerly as divine punishment (see v. 75). If so, however, it can be no longer. The psalmist is now faithful and obedient, even though the affliction persists. The motivation, therefore, cannot be fear of retribution, but the conviction that genuine life is found in openness to God's instruction and reliance upon God's help. No amount of material reward can truly constitute life (v. 72; see Ps 19:10; Luke 12:15).

119:73-80. This section begins with the psalmist's profession that, in effect, he or she belongs to God; life is in God's hands. This, plus the affirmation of God's righteousness (see v. 7), becomes the basis for the petitions in vv. 76-80. Verse 75 recalls vv. 67, 71 and seems to reinforce the conclusion that the psalmist viewed the current affliction as justifiable punishment (see Ps 51:4). This, of course, would provide another analogy between the *persona* of the psalmist and Israel, which was persistently deserving of punishment (see Commentary on Psalm 51). Or, to state it from the other side, Israel consistently stood in need of God's steadfast love (v. 76) and mercy/compassion (v. 77). Only God could comfort (v. 76; see vv. 50, 52; Isa 40:1-2). Fortunately, steadfast love and mercy/compassion lie at the very heart of God's character (see Exod 34:6-7; Introduction). As the psalmist recognizes, his or her life depended on it (v. 77; see vv. 17, 25, 37, 40, 50, 88, 93, 116, 154, 156, 159, 175), and so did Israel's life. In the context of this understanding, to be "blameless" (v. 80) can ultimately mean nothing other than to be forgiven (see v. 1; Pss 15:2; 18:25; 19:13; 37:18). As in other psalms in which the psalmist has been forgiven or anticipates forgiveness, the psalmist also anticipates being an example, a teacher, or a witness to encourage others (vv. 74, 79; see Pss 32:8-9; 51:13).

119:81-88. According to Soll's outline, vv. 81-88 begin the central division of the psalm (vv. 81-120). The petition of vv. 76-80 gives way to the most extended and bitter complaint in the psalm—its nadir. Indicative of the urgency of this section is the threefold occurrence of the verb meaning "to fail," "to be finished," "to be spent" (see "languishes" in v. 81; "fail" in v. 82; "made an end" in v. 87; see also v. 123; Pss 31:10; 69:3; 73:26). The questions in vv. 82, 84 also contribute to the sense of urgency, as does the departure from the psalmist's regular pattern in v. 84; the NRSV's "judge" represents the singular of the word that is usually plural ("ordinances"). While the singular occurs also in vv. 121, 132, 149, it does stand out. The questions in v. 84 are essentially a plea for help. The petition is direct in vv. 86*b*, 88*a* (see "persecute" in vv. 84*b*, 86*b*, linking the questions and the direct petition), but its abbreviated statement gives the impression of an urgent shout (see the punctuation at the end of v. 86 NRSV).

As is the case throughout the psalm, the psalmist looks to God for life (v. 88; see above on v. 77) and comfort (v. 88*b*; see above on v. 76). He or she continues to live in hope (v. 81), but vv. 81-88 portray very clearly the psalmist's existence as a suffering servant. Not surprisingly, v. 85 recalls Jer 18:20, 22, the prayer of another servant who suffered precisely because he was an instrument of God's word.

119:89-96. From its nadir, Psalm 119 moves to its zenith. Complaint has given way to a profession of faith in God's sovereignty for all time (vv. 89*a*, 90*a*), in all places (vv. 89*b*, 90*a*), and over "all things" (v. 91). The profession is highlighted by the uniqueness of v. 90, which does not contain one of the eight synonyms. Rather, the word "faithfulness" (אמונה *ʾĕmûnâ*) occurs instead (see v. 75). Often paired with the word "steadfast love" (חסד *ḥesed*, see v. 88; Pss 25:10; 57:3; 85:10; 98:3), it communicates the way in which God exercises sovereignty—with faithful love that issues in forgiveness (see Exod 34:6-7; Introduction). Thus the psalmist, who would have perished (v. 92; "misery" is the same root as "humbled" in vv. 67,

71, 75), remains alive (v. 93; see above on v. 77). Verse 94*a* articulates again the psalmist's conviction that his or her life belongs to God. The petition and renewal of complaint (v. 95), following the marvelous affirmation of vv. 89-93, indicate that there will never be a time when the psalmist will be self-sufficient. He or she will always depend on God. Verse 96 returns to the expansive perspective of vv. 89-91. The meaning of the word translated "perfection" (תכלה *tiklâ*) is not entirely clear, but v. 96 could be paraphrased as follows: "I am weak, but you are strong." In short, it seems to be another profession of dependence upon God.

119:97-104. Following the zenith of the psalm, it is appropriate that vv. 97-104 are effusive in their expression of love for and joy in *torah* (see esp. vv. 97, 103), as well as in their description of the effects of God's instruction (see esp. vv. 98-100, 104). Verses 97-104 stand in the middle of what Soll identifies as the central division of the psalm (vv. 81-120), so perhaps they should be considered the real focal point of the psalm. The exclamations in vv. 97, 103 are downright sensual. The psalmist is in love with God's revelation (v. 97*a*; see vv. 47-48, 113, 119, 127, 132, 159, 163, 165, 167). As is always the case with a beloved person or thing, the psalmist has God's revelation always in mind (v. 97*b*). The word "meditate" (שׂיח *śîaḥ*) occurs several times in Psalm 119 (see also vv. 15, 23, 27, 48, 78, 99, 148), but this is the only place where the meditation is "all day long" (see also the chronological references in vv. 55, 62, 147-148, 164). Thus v. 97 is reminiscent of Ps 1:1-2 (although the Hebrew words translated "meditate" are different), where those who meditate on God's instruction are pronounced "happy." The psalmist in Psalm 119 exemplifies such happiness; it is not a superficial cheeriness (see vv. 81-88) but the happiness of a person who is in love with the one who truly offers life. Not surprisingly, v. 103 employs the sensual language of the Song of Solomon (see 2:3; 4:11; 5:1, 16; 7:9; see also Ps 19:10; Prov 24:13-14). The psalmist has an emotional attachment to God's word that is indicative of his or her love for and commitment to God.

The wisdom tradition is drawn upon in vv. 98-100 to describe the benefits of God's instruction ("wiser," v. 98; "insight," v. 99; and "understanding," v. 100; see v. 104; Pss 2:10; 14:2; 19:7; 94:8; Hos 14:9). Instructed by God (see v. 102), the psalmist need not fear the foe (v. 98) or be intimidated by the friend (vv. 99-100). The authority figures in the psalmist's life—"teachers" and "the elders"—are subordinated to God's ultimate authority. This theme is paralleled in Deut 4:6, where Moses tells the people that obedience to the "statutes and ordinances" (Deut 4:5) they are receiving "will show your wisdom and understanding to the nations" (NIV). Thus "this entire law" (Deut 4:8 NRSV) is to govern the people's existence. The psalmist's wisdom is a personal witness and example of what it means to hear and to heed God's instruction.

The correlate of loving God's *torah* (v. 97) is hating "every false way" (v. 104; see vv. 29, 128). The psalmist had complained about being the victim of falsehood (see v. 86). In other words, the psalmist hates what works toward death, and he or she loves what works toward life: God's revelation.

119:105-112. As if to indicate again that human life never stands beyond threat, or beyond need for God's help, vv. 105-112 return to complaint and petition (see esp. vv. 107, 110; see above on v. 94). But this section starts with the memorable profession of v. 105. God's revelation is the truly reliable guide to life (see v. 130; Prov 6:23). It is not surprising, since God's word reveals God's very self, that the word "light" (אור *'ôr*) is used as a metaphor for both (see Pss 4:6; 27:1). As is the case throughout the psalm, eloquent expressions of trust like v. 105 are juxtaposed with forthright complaint. "Afflicted" (v. 107*a*) recalls vv. 67, 71, 75, and 92, and the petition "give me life" (v. 107*b*) pervades the psalm (see above on v. 77). After the complaint of v. 110 (see Pss 91:3; 124:7; 140:5; 142:3), v. 111 offers another expression of trust that recalls v. 57. Like "portion" in v. 57, the word "heritage" (נחלה *naḥălâ*) designates the allotment of land that each Israelite, except the priests and Levites, was supposed to have (see "inheritance" in Josh 11:23; 14:3). This inheritance was precious, because land represented access to life and a future (see 1 Kgs 21:3). In v. 111, the psalmist

affirms that God's revelation itself guarantees a future.

119:113-120. The final section of the central division of the psalm, these verses articulate primarily loyalty and trust. This section uses words and themes from earlier in the psalm—"love" (vv. 113, 119; see vv. 47-48, 97) and "hope" (יחל *yāḥal*, v. 114; see v. 43; the word translated "hope" [שבר *śābar*] in v. 116 differs and recurs in v. 166). But it also introduces new vocabulary—"hiding place" (v. 114*a*; see "cover" in Ps 27:5 and "shelter" in Pss 31:20; 91:1) and "shield" (see Ps 3:3). Amid the expressions of trust, the presence of opposition is evident (vv. 113, 115, 118-119), and as always, it is necessary to pray for life (v. 116; see above on v. 77). The NRSV's "judgments" in v. 120*b* translates the word usually rendered as "ordinances"; the NIV of v. 120*b* is more helpful.

119:121-128. This section is the first of three in the fifth major division of the psalm. Like the other divisions, it moves generally from complaint (vv. 121-128) to petition (vv. 129-136) to affirmation (vv. 137-144), but each section contains all three of these elements. The petitions in vv. 121-122 imply the complaint (see "oppress" in each verse; see also v. 134), which is voiced directly in v. 123*a* (see v. 82). The word "just" (משפט *mišpāṭ*) in v. 121 is the singular of the word the NRSV translates as "ordinances" (see vv. 84, 132). Verse 122 is the most irregular in the psalm. It contains none of the eight major synonyms, nor a variant form of one of them (as in v. 121), nor even a substitute as in vv. 3, 37, 90. This irregularity perhaps replicates the disorientation caused by the reality of oppression. In any case, the psalmist appeals to God's loving character (v. 124; see above on v. 41) and for a benefit celebrated earlier (v. 125; see v. 100). While v. 126 recaptures some of the urgency of vv. 81-88, v. 128 indicates that the psalmist has not become totally disoriented as he or she waits. Furthermore, the psalmist already experiences a reward (v. 127; see v. 72; Ps 19:10) that is greater than the material wealth oppressors might gain by their dishonest ways (v. 128; see v. 104): the love of God's revelation, which constitutes life.

119:129-136. The tone of vv. 127-128 continues in vv. 129-130. Verse 129 recalls

v. 18; v. 130*a* recalls v. 105; and v. 130*b* recalls v. 100 at the same time that it seems to respond to v. 125. The imagery of vv. 131, 136 portrays again the necessity of waiting— that is, the eschatological dimension—and thus vv. 131, 136 serve as an appropriate frame for the petitions in vv. 132-135. The NRSV's "custom" (v. 132) represents the singular of the more frequent plural translated "ordinances" (see vv. 84, 121). More literally, the psalmist asserts that it is God's "justice" to be gracious. This assertion reinforces the psalmist's conviction that his or her life depends ultimately on God's mercy and love (see above on vv. 76-77). The subsequent petitions indicate that the psalmist entrusts life to God, depending on God for guidance (v. 133), liberation from oppression (v. 134; see vv. 121-122), and illumination (v. 135; "Make . . . shine" [האר *hāʾer*] is the same Hebrew root as "light" in v. 130; see also v. 105; Num 6:25; Pss 4:6; 31:16; 67:1).

119:137-144. Occurring five times (vv. 137, 138, 142, 144), the key word is this section is "righteous(ness)" (צדק *ṣdq*); the word "right" (ישר *yāšār*) in v. 137 is from a different Hebrew root. God is "righteous" (vv. 137, 142; see Pss 7:9, 11; 11:7; 116:5), and God's "decrees are righteous" (v. 144; see v. 138 as well as vv. 7, 62, 75, 106, 160). The word "righteousness" is used elsewhere to describe the policy that God wills and enacts as ruler of the universe (see Pss 89:14; 96:13; 97:2, 6; 98:9; 99:4). In keeping with the conviction of God's universal reign (see above on vv. 89-91), the psalmist proclaims that God's righteousness is "everlasting"/"forever" (vv. 142, 144). As in v. 75, righteousness is inextricably associated with God's faithfulness (vv. 138, 142; "truth" [אמת *ʾĕmet*] represents a word usually translated "faithful").

As a servant (v. 140), one who recognizes God's sovereignty, the psalmist is bothered by the same thing that bothers God: disloyalty. The word "zeal" (קנאה *qînâ*), used to describe the psalmist's response to the people's forgetting "your words" (v. 139), is also used to describe God as a "jealous" God who will tolerate no rival (see Exod 20:5; 34:14; Deut 4:24; 6:15; Ps 79:5). Others may forget, but the psalmist does not (v. 141; see vv. 16, 61, 83, 93, 109, 153; Deut 4:23; 26:13).

At the same time proclaiming loyalty to God, the psalmist is also complaining about troubles (see vv. 141, 143). The juxtaposition of the proclamation of God's righteousness and the psalmist's complaint reminds us once again of the psalmist's eschatological perspective. While "delight" is a present reality (v. 143*b*; see vv. 24, 47, 70, 77, 92, 174), so are "trouble and anguish" (v. 143*a*). God and God's will are righteous, but not everything in the world is yet right. God and God's servants are opposed (vv. 139, 141). Thus the psalmist is inevitably a suffering servant, delighting already in God and in God's will, but constantly awaiting the consummation of God's reign. Appropriately, this section ends with a petition that indicates again the psalmist's dependence upon God for life and future (v. 144; see above on v. 77).

119:145-152. Like the other major divisions of the psalm, vv. 145-176 recapitulate the movement from complaint (vv. 145-152) and petition (vv. 153-160) to affirmation (vv. 161-168) and praise (vv. 169-176). Again, however, all these elements are interspersed in each section. Verses 145-152 begin with vocabulary that is typical of complaint (see "call" in vv. 145, 146; "save me" in v. 146; "cry for help" in v. 147). The chronological references in vv. 147-148 emphasize that the psalmist is in constant conversation with God (see vv. 55, 62, 97, 164). As always, the psalmist looks to God's steadfast love (v. 149*a*; see vv. 41, 76) and justice (v. 149*b*; see vv. 132, 156) for life (see v. 77). And as always, this is necessary because of the presence of opposition (v. 150; see "persecute" in vv. 84, 86 as well as in the next two sections in vv. 157, 161). Verses 150-151 play on the opposites "near" (vv. 150*a*, 151*a*) and "far" (v. 150*b*). The complaint of v. 150 issues in the emphatic affirmation of v. 151: "you are near." In the final analysis, God's nearness is all that the psalmist needs and all that really matters (see Ps 73:28). Verse 152 seems to be a response to the plea of v. 125, since the psalmist here affirms that he or she long "has known" (a more literal translation) God's decrees.

119:153-160. This section begins with and is dominated by petition (see vv. 153*a*, 154*a*), especially the one that pervades the psalm: "give me life" (vv. 154, 156, 159; see above on v. 77). This plea is associated in vv. 156, 159 with God's mercy/compassion and steadfast love (see vv. 76-77), as well as with God's justice (v. 156b; see vv. 132, 149). As affirmed throughout, God's justice ultimately takes the form of merciful love. Verse 160 again associates God's faithfulness (see NIV, "true"; NRSV, "truth"), another attribute regularly associated with God's mercy and love (see Exod 34:6-7), with God's righteousness (see vv. 75, 142). The righteousness God intends will be effected ultimately by God's faithful love.

119:161-168. Although this section starts with complaint (see vv. 23, 150, 157), it moves quickly to expressions of joy (v. 162) and commitment (v. 163; see vv. 104, 128). The word "praise" (הלל *hillēl*) is relatively rare in Psalm 119, but its occurrence in v. 164 anticipates the two occurrences in the final section (vv. 171, 175). It is not clear whether the "seven times" is meant literally or whether it is figurative for something like "all day long" (see v. 97). The eschatological perspective of the psalm is again evident; the one persecuted without cause (v. 161) knows simultaneously "great peace" (v. 165a) and security (v. 165b). The faithful life inevitably involves both hope (v. 166; see v. 116; Ps

146:5) and the present experience of God (v. 168b; see v. 151a).

119:169-176. The final section contains several pleas that by this point are familiar: pleas for understanding (v. 169b; see v. 100, 125), for grace (v. 170; "supplication" [תחנה *těḥinnâ*] represents the same root as "be gracious" in vv. 58, 132), for help (vv. 173, 175; see v. 86), as well as the all-embracing plea for life (v. 175; see vv. 17, 25, 37, 40, 77, 88, 107, 116, 144, 149, 154, 156, 159). The psalmist anticipates and promises praise (vv. 171, 175), but it is striking, especially in view of all the expressions of loyalty and obedience throughout the psalm (see v. 176b), that the psalmist includes in the final verse another plea for help that follows what sounds like a confession of sin. The word "lost" (אבד *'ōbēd*) is more literally "perishing." Thus, just as Ps 119:1 was reminiscent of the first verse of Psalm 1, so also Ps 119:176 recalls the final verse of Psalm 1. But—and this is the remarkable thing—in Ps 1:6, it is the wicked who are to perish! The final verse of Psalm 119 is, therefore, a final reminder of what the psalmist has affirmed all along: The faithful are saved by grace. Their lives and their futures belong to God (see Luke 15:1-7).

REFLECTIONS

1. Like Psalm 1, Psalm 119 has often received bad scholarly press. Not infrequently, it has been criticized not only as artificial and tedious, but also as the product of a self-righteous psalmist who exhibits the legalism that supposedly characterized post-exilic Judaism. The charges against Psalm 119 should be dropped. They are not fair to either the psalm or the psalmist—or to Judaism. To be sure, the psalmist exhibits an unmistakable torah piety. The psalmist is thoroughly devoted to God's word and is intent upon a faithfulness to God that includes obedience. But the psalmist shows no trace of legalism or self-righteousness. Rather, the psalmist is thoroughly aware of his or her own failings, of the need for grace and mercy, of dependence upon God for life and future. It is likely that the psalmist's view of God's torah, "instruction," included recognition of written sources of revelation that constituted the core of a developing canon of Scripture. But, as Levenson points out, "Psalm 119 lacks any trace of book consciousness," and the psalmist is open to a variety of sources of the revelation of God's word and will, including "unmediated divine teaching."[446] In short, the psalmist is open in the broadest sense to God's instruction.

2. If there is no trace of book consciousness in Psalm 119, neither is there any trace of the psalmist's commitment to a rigid retributional scheme. In this regard, the final verse of the psalm is particularly striking. While it reaffirms the psalmist's loyalty

446. Levenson, "The Sources of Torah," 565, 570.

to God and commitment to obedience, it also employs language used elsewhere to describe the wicked. It leaves the psalmist utterly dependent on God's grace. Furthermore, the psalmist has repeatedly appealed to God's steadfast love and mercy—to divine attributes that manifest themselves in forgiveness (see Exod 34:6-7). Also, the psalmist's regular juxtaposition of complaint and profession of trust indicates that he or she could not support a simple retributional scheme. While the psalmist admits wrongdoing, the psalmist must also have considered himself or herself more deserving than those who are described as the wicked, the insolent, the arrogant, evildoers, "my oppressors," and "my persecutors." Yet, it is precisely the psalmist who *is* persecuted and oppressed. In a word, he or she is a suffering servant, "who waits and looks for Yahweh's effective word of power."[447] The perspective is eschatological. The sovereignty of God and God's word is upheld amid circumstances that seem to deny it.

3. The psalmist clearly reminds us of figures like Jeremiah and Elijah, who suffered as a result of their faithfulness to God's word and will. Christian readers of Psalm 119 will also inevitably be reminded of Jesus. The psalmist's commitment to discerning the word of God and doing the will of God anticipates the life and ministry of Jesus, who even as a boy is depicted "among the teachers" (Luke 2:46; see Luke 2:42-51; note esp. "understanding" in v. 47 and "wisdom" in v. 52; cf. Ps 119:98-100). Jesus upheld the *torah* (see Matt 5:17-20), but he was not bound to specific formulations (see Matt 12:1-8; 15:1-20). Rather, he sought to extend the *torah* to represent God's sovereign claim upon all of human life (see Matt 5:21-48). The psalmist was no legalist, and neither was Jesus. Rather, both the psalmist and Jesus were open to God's instruction in a variety of forms—Scripture, tradition, and ongoing events and experiences that reveal God's way and represent God's claim upon humanity and the world. By constantly affirming that he or she lives by the word of God, the psalmist anticipates Jesus' articulation of the motive for his faithful, hopeful obedience to God (Matt 4:4; see also Deut 8:3):

"One does not live by bread alone,
but by every word that comes
from the mouth of God."

4. This kind of torah piety has profound implications for the life of the church in the world. For instance, in a scientifically oriented and education-obsessed culture, Psalm 119 has radical epistemological implications. That is to say, it points to generally unacceptable conclusions about what we know and how we know it, for it asserts that true knowledge is not achieved through detachment and objectivity. Rather, wisdom grows from passionate involvement with God and commitment of one's whole self to God (see 1 Cor 1:18–2:16). In short, Psalm 119 claims that as people of God, we believe in order to understand (see Commentary on Psalm 111).

This claim, of course, should not be understood to be anti-intellectual or anti-scientific. Rather, it is an invitation for us to recognize the inevitable limits of human knowledge, human power, and human technology. It is an invitation to accept the biblical claim that human life is finally a gift of God and that it depends ultimately on God. The proper human prayer is the one that pervades Psalm 119: "Give me life."

5. The claim of Psalm 119 is certainly not a warrant to retreat into a narrow view of the inerrancy of Scripture, a position that amounts to making the Bible an idol. While the psalmist included written formulations as one source of God's Word, he or she by no means limited God's revelation to written sources. The psalmist's openness to God's Word has profound implications for understanding Scripture as the Word of

447. Kraus, *Psalms 60–150*, 420.

God. While Scripture is to be honored as a source of God's revelation, it is always to be heard in conversation with the theological tradition of the church and within the context of the contemporary place and time. Apart from such a hearing, God's ability to speak to God's people is anchored entirely in the past, and there is no possibility of God's continuing to reveal God's self. In short, Scripture is not a dead letter but a dynamic, living word. It is to be read and heard and proclaimed in openness to the Holy Spirit—what Levenson might call "unmediated divine teaching"—who leads the church to discern the Word of God for our place and time.

PSALMS 120–134, SONGS OF ASCENTS

OVERVIEW

Psalm 120 is the first of fifteen consecutive psalms that bear the title "A Song of Ascents." While certainty is not possible, it is likely that this collection was originally used by pilgrims on their way to Jerusalem or as part of a festal celebration in Jerusalem. Each psalm is relatively short (except Psalm 132) and thus capable of being memorized, and a variety of types and themes is represented. The noun translated "ascents" (מעלות *ma'ălôt*) is from a Hebrew root meaning "to go up" (עלה *'ālâ*); as Ps 122:4 points out, it was decreed that "the tribes go up" regularly to Jerusalem (see Deut 16:16; see also 1 Kgs 12:28; Ps 24:3; Isa 2:3). The noun can also mean "steps" or "stairs," and it is elsewhere used for the steps of the Temple (Ezek 40:6) and the steps to the city of David (Neh 3:15; 12:37).

The likelihood that Psalms 120–134 were used by pilgrims on the journey to Jerusalem or during a celebration in Jerusalem is increased by the frequent references to Jerusalem and Zion (see Psalms 122; 125–126; 128–129; 132–134). Also, the alternation between singular and plural references to the people suggests group participation, as do the frequent liturgical elements, such as invitations for response (124:1; 129:1; 130:7; 131:3), professions of faith (121:2; 124:8; 134:3), and benedictions (125:5; 128:5-6; 134:3). These elements also represent verbal links among the psalms that suggest the unity of the collection. Even if some of these elements are redactional, as several scholars suggest, this in itself suggests that an editor provided further indications of unity to a collection that he or she already recognized as a unit.

Scholars frequently observe that Psalms 120–134 deal often with matters of daily life—place of residence (120:5-6), routine activities (121:8; 127:2; 128:2), the importance of spouse and children (128:3-4), as well as larger family and friends (122:8; 133:1). This, too, increases the likelihood that the collection was originally used by ordinary persons on the way to or upon arrival at Jerusalem. The juxtaposition of psalms reflecting daily concerns with those reflecting national concerns (Psalms 123–126; 130–132; 134) also makes sense in the context of festal celebrations, where individuals and families from all over would have been brought together by loyalties that transcended the personal and familial.

Several scholars also detect evidence of a pilgrimage orientation in the shape of the collection, especially the beginning and end. Psalm 120:5, for instance, has the effect of locating the speaker outside Jerusalem and even outside the land, even though the geographical references may have been intended metaphorically. The imagery of Psalm 121 makes especially good sense in the context of a journey—seeing mountains in the distance (v. 1), the concern with stumbling and with safety in general (vv. 3-4), the need for protection from the heat of the sun and the dangers of darkness (vv. 5-6), the mention of departure and entrance (v. 8). The joyful tone of Psalm 122 gives the impression of just having arrived at Jerusalem, and Psalm

134 would have served well as a benediction upon departure. To be sure, this arrangement may be coincidental, but in conjunction with the above considerations, the shape of the collection increases the likelihood of its use by pilgrims.

Psalm 120:1-7, I Am for Peace

COMMENTARY

The psalm's location of the speaker outside the land (metaphorically, at least) and in a situation of hostility (vv. 6-8) may also explain the placement of the Songs of Ascents in Book V; at least it makes their perspective congruent with that established in Psalms 107–118 as well as in Psalm 119. Along with Book IV, Book V seems to respond to the theological crisis of exile that continued into the post-exilic era of dispersion; and Psalm 107 begins Book V by establishing this setting (see also 106:47). Especially when Psalms 107 and 108 are read together, the impression left is that the return from exile has not solved the problem; the people still need help. This is also the message suggested by Psalm 118, which is linked verbally to Psalm 107 (see 107:1; 118:1, 29). While alluding to exodus and return from exile, Psalm 118 concludes with a petition for salvation; that is, the people still need help. Psalm 119 leads to the same conclusion. While the psalmist clearly celebrates God's presence and power as mediated through God's instruction, the psalmist still needs help. Indeed, the imagery at several points portrays the psalmist as an exile or alien who finds a place only in God's revelation (see vv. 19, 54, 57, 111). Not surprisingly, then, Psalm 120 also portrays the psalmist as an alien; furthermore, vv. 1-2 preserve in brief the same pattern evident in Psalm 118: recollection of past deliverance (v. 1; the verbs should be rendered in the past tense) that serves as the basis for petition in the midst of a new crisis (v. 2; see Commentary on Psalm 118 on the transition from v. 24 to v. 25; and on Psalm 126 on the transition from v. 3 to v. 4).

The question of how to translate the tenses of the verbs in vv. 1, 5-6 is the most debated one in the psalm. It is possible to render them all in the past tense and thus to conclude that the crisis lies completely in the past. In this case, v. 2 can be considered a quote from a past prayer, and Psalm 120 can be construed as a song of thanksgiving.[448] Although both the NIV and the NRSV use present tenses in v. 1, both also suggest that the crisis is current and that Psalm 120 is a lament/complaint or prayer for help. While there is clearly room for disagreement, this seems to be the most reasonable conclusion; it also makes Psalm 120 congruent with the perspective of the preceding psalms.

120:1-4. Elsewhere, too, the psalmists relate the experience of God's answering a prayer out of distress (v. 1; see Ps 118:5). The description of the new distress is also a familiar one in the psalms (v. 2; see Pss 31:18; 52:2-3; 64:8; 109:2; the word translated "lying" [שֶׁקֶר šeqer] in v. 2 also occurs as "false[hood]" or "lies" in Ps 119:29, 69, 104, 128, 163). In v. 3, the "deceitful tongue" is personified and addressed with a question, which is answered in v. 4. Verses 3-4 express poetically the psalmist's conviction that the enemies will eventually be brought to justice. The psalmist petitions God for the same judgment upon enemies in Ps 140:10 (see also Prov 25:22). These enemies have shown themselves with their tongues and lips (140:3; cf. 120:2) to be proponents of war (140:2; cf. 120:7), and the petition for judgment upon them is followed by a profession of faith in God's execution of justice for the victimized (140:12). Verses 3-4 profess this same faith.

120:5-7. These verses elaborate upon the distress that has already been articulated in v. 2. Because most scholars locate Meshech significantly to the north of Israel and Kedar to the south, it is likely that the two names were intended as metaphors for "those who hate peace" (v. 6; see Meshech in Ezek 32:26; 38:2-4; 39:1-3; and Kedar in Isa 21:16-17). The Hebrew verb forms in vv. 5-6 would ordinarily be translated with English

---

448. See Kraus, *Psalms 60–150*, 422-25.

past tenses. If this is done, however, the verbs should be understood to indicate a current situation of long standing rather than a situation that no longer exists. The psalmist's attempts to be conciliatory have been met only with hostility (v. 7; see Ps 109:2-5). Verses 6-7 anticipate the theme of peace in 122:6-8, a link that perhaps supports the detection of a pilgrim sequence involving Psalms 120–122.

Another noteworthy feature of vv. 5-7 is what scholars often call stairlike repetition.

That is, the verb "live" (שכן *šākan*) in v. 5*b* recurs in v. 6*a*, and the noun "peace" (שלום *šālôm*) in v. 6*b* recurs in v. 7*a*. Thus the repetition leads the reader along step by step as up a flight of stairs. This pattern of repetition is particularly appropriate for a poem labeled "A Song of Ascents," or "A Song of the Steps." Not coincidentally, it seems, this pattern of repetition occurs frequently in Psalms 120–134 (see, e.g., 121:1*b*-2*a*, 3*b*-4, 7*b*-8*a*; 122:4*ab*, 5).

REFLECTIONS

The juxtaposition of deliverance recalled (v. 1) with ongoing petition (v. 2) and complaint (vv. 5-7) is characteristic of Book V, and it would have been particularly meaningful to the post-exilic generations. More generally, this juxtaposition is in line with the eschatological perspective of the whole psalter—indeed, the whole Bible. God's establishment of justice for the victimized is both affirmed on the basis of past experience (vv. 1, 3-4) and prayed for and awaited (vv. 2, 5-7). As Allen correctly recognizes, Psalm 120 not only would have been particularly meaningful for Jews in dispersion, but it also expresses a perspective that is characteristic of Scripture generally: "The psalm hovers between divine promise and fulfillment, like so much of the Bible."[449]

In short, Psalm 120 leaves the people of God between "already" and "not yet." So does Jesus' proclamation of the eschatological reign of God, which is now a reality (Mark 1:14-15) but which is experienced amid persistent opposition from the world, as Jesus' own cross so clearly demonstrates. This "betweenness" is evident also in the teaching of Jesus, in which "Blessed are the peacemakers" is followed immediately by "Blessed are those who are persecuted for righteousness' sake" (Matt 5:10 NRSV). In short, the experience of the psalmist (vv. 6-7) proves to be the persistent experience of the people of God. The peace God gives is real, but it is not a peace that the world recognizes or accepts (see John 14:27). Thus the church will always, in a real sense, lead an alien existence; it will always be in the world but not of the world (see John 17:14-18; 1 Pet 1:1-2; 2:11-12). Its efforts for peace and reconciliation will be met with hostility, because they threaten the ways of the world.

It is still true, and examples abound. In the United States during the 1950s and 1960s and in South Africa in the 1980s and 1990s, legislation ending racial segregation and apartheid came only after an extended and often violent struggle. Christians of various nations who promote and work for world peace are frequently labeled unpatriotic, and those who side with the victimized are often dismissed as bleeding hearts. To be for peace is to invite a battle (v. 7); to follow Jesus is to bear a cross (see Mark 8:34).

449. Allen, *Psalms 101–150*, 150.

Psalm 121:1-8, God's Protective Care

COMMENTARY

The second of the Songs of Ascents (Psalms 120–134), Psalm 121 is an eloquent profession of faith in God's providence and protection. The circumstances of the psalm's origin are unknown. Noting the military significance of mountains or hills (v. 1; see 1 Kgs 20:23), Anthony R. Ceresko proposes that Psalm 121 may have originated as a prayer or profession of a warrior, and that it was reread as a pilgrimage psalm when it became a part of the ascents collection (see Overview on Psalms 120–134).[450] James Limburg, on the other hand, suggests that the psalm originated as a "farewell liturgy," in which vv. 1-2 should be heard as the words of one who is about to depart and vv. 3-8 are the response of one who is staying behind.[451] In any case, Psalm 121 is in an auspicious position, if, as is likely, Psalms 120–134 form a collection that was used by pilgrims on their way to or upon arrival at Jerusalem. Its language and imagery are readily understood in terms of a journey—seeing mountains in the distance (v. 1), the concern with stumbling and safety in general (vv. 3-4), the need for protection from the heat of the sun and the dangers of darkness (vv. 5-6), and the mention of departure and entrance (v. 8). It is even possible that the sequence of Psalms 120–122 is intended to re-create the movement from dispersion (120:5-7) by way of a journey (Psalm 121) to the gates of Jerusalem (122:1-2). The dialogical character of Psalm 121 would have made it suitable for an exchange between priest and pilgrim upon arrival at Jerusalem or perhaps in preparation for departure home. In any case, vv. 7-8 expand the journey concept to the whole of life. Thus the usefulness of Psalm 121 has transcended the circumstances of its origin as well as its ancient role as a pilgrim song (see Reflections below).

The structure of Psalm 121 is disputed. A few scholars suggest dividing it into three sections: vv. 1-2, vv. 3-5, vv. 6-8. Most prefer

four two-verse sections. A prominent stylistic feature is the stairlike or steplike repetition that occurs in vv. 1-2, vv. 3-4, and vv. 7-8 (see Commentary on Psalm 120, esp. discussion of vv. 5-7). This pattern is especially appropriate for a psalm about a journey, which in ancient times would literally have proceeded step by step. Even more prominent perhaps is the sixfold occurrence of the word "keep" (שמר *šāmar*, vv. 3, 4, 5, 7*ab*, 8). The pervasiveness of this key word matches the pervasiveness of God's protecting presence.

121:1-2. Verse 1 is sometimes translated as a statement, but it is better rendered as a question that is answered in v. 2. The exact referent of "hills" is not clear. "Hills" could indicate simply an unspecified destination, as in the contemporary idiom, "head for the hills." If the speaker were on a journey, "hills" could refer to elevated terrain in the distance that perhaps promises a difficult climb and possible danger. In the context of the Songs of Ascents, the hills in the distance might be intended to include Mount Zion, a symbol not of danger but of divine help (see Deut 33:7, 26, 29; Pss 22:19; 33:20; 54:4; 63:7; 70:1, 5; 115:9-11; 124:8), since it is the place where the cosmic God (see v. 2*b*) sits upon an earthly throne (see Pss 48:1-2; 125:1-2; 132:8, 13-14). Psalm 123 also begins with the psalmist lifting up his or her eyes, and there it is specifically to the cosmic God. The similarity between 121:1 and 123:1 may support the conclusion that we should construe 121:1 as an indication of the psalmist's looking toward Zion. In any case, it is significant that the Lord is identified both very personally—"my help"—and cosmicly. The phrase "Maker of heaven and earth" both anticipates the expansive conclusion to the psalm in vv. 7-8 and provides one of the threads of unity for the collection (see Pss 124:8; 134:3; see above on Ps 115:15).

121:3-4. The image in v. 3*a* is obviously appropriate for a person traveling on foot. The traveler could literally "slip," but the image also functions metaphorically. For instance, the same image is used in Ps

450. Anthony R. Ceresko, "Psalm 121: Prayer of a Warrior?" *Biblica* 70 (1989) 501-5.
451. James Limburg, "Psalm 121: A Psalm for Sojourners," *Word & World* 5 (1985) 183.

66:9*b* in parallel with God's activity to preserve people "among the living" (see also "moved"/"shaken" in Pss 16:8; 55:22; 62:2, 6; 112:6). The verb "moved" (מוט *môṭ*) recurs in Ps 125:1*b*, where it communicates the stability of Mount Zion, which is to be a symbol of the people's security (see 125:1*a*, 2). The verbal links between Psalms 121 and 125 increase the probability that "hills" in 121:1 should be understood to include Mount Zion (cf. 121:8 with 125:2*c*). Verse 3*b* contains the first occurrence of "keep" (*šāmar*). This word recalls God's protection of the whole people following the exodus during the journey to the promised land (see Num 6:24; Josh 24:17). Both it and the verb "slumber" (נום *nûm*) create the steplike repetition in vv. 3-4, which affirm God's eternal vigilance. The addition of "sleep" (ישׁן *yāšēn*) in v. 4 intensifies the assurance. God will definitely not do what the people sometimes fear God might be doing (see Ps 44:23).

121:5-6. Ceresko points out that v. 5*a* is preceded and followed by exactly the same number of syllables and that it is the center of the psalm.[452] Thus structure serves to reinforce the repetition of "keep" to emphasize the psalm's central theological affirmation. Not surprisingly, the subject—"the LORD"—is in the emphatic position. Verse 5*b* introduces another metaphor, which occurs in Ps 91:1 (see "shadow"), another psalm that celebrates God's protecting presence (note, too, that "guard" in Ps 91:11 is the same verb rendered "keep" in Psalm 121; see also "day" and "night" in Pss 91:5; 121:6; as well as "foot" in 91:12; 121:3). The metaphor of God as shadow occurs most often in the

452. Ceresko, "Psalm 121," 499.

phrase "shadow of your wings" (see Pss 17:8; 36:8; 57:1; 63:7), an image that may derive from the winged creatures that decorated the ark in the Temple. Thus v. 5*b* may hint at the destination of the pilgrim's journey—Jerusalem—while at the same time affirming that the God who resides in Zion is also present on the journey. Especially for the traveler on foot, the sun could be deadly (see Isa 49:10), and people in antiquity apparently believed moonlight to be harmful, a notion evident in Matt 4:24; 17:15, where "epileptic(s)" literally means "moonstruck" (the English word *lunatic* derives from the Latin word for "moon"). In any case, vv. 5-6 again affirm God's constant vigilance. God is always in a position to help (see "right hand" in Ps 109:31).

121:7-8. These verses each begin with the subject—"the LORD"—in the emphatic position, thus recalling v. 5. The emphatic and expansive character of vv. 7-8 is also communicated by three more occurrences of "keep," each of which broadens the scope of God's protection. Verse 7*a* indicates that vv. 3-7 have merely been illustrative. God will protect from "all evil," because the psalmist's very life is the real object of God's care. Verse 8 culminates this movement by making it clear that the real journey on which the psalmist has embarked is the journey of life. Every departure and arrival will be under God's care (see Deut 28:6)—now and forever (see Pss 125:2; 131:3). No place, no time, no circumstance will be able to separate the psalmist from God's loving care (see Rom 8:38-39). The direction of vv. 7-8 points to the adaptability of Psalm 121 to a variety of settings and provides a textual grounding for the psalm's ongoing use throughout the human journey of many centuries.

REFLECTIONS

1. Although short in length, Psalm 121 has been long on influence. It has contributed a phrase to the Apostles' Creed (v. 2*b*; see also Pss 115:5; 124:8; 134:3), and, except for Psalm 23, with which it shares the same fundamental message, Psalm 121 is probably recited from memory as often as any other in the psalter when people of faith reach for words of assurance amid the trials and turmoil of their life journey. Like the folk song, which moves from God's "got the whole world in his hands" to God's "got you and me, sister/brother, in his hands," Psalm 121 affirms that the sovereign ruler of the cosmos has a personal concern for the lives of all God's people (v. 2).

2. In keeping with what was perhaps its original use, Psalm 121 has remained a psalm for travelers. Upon the morning of his departure from England to do missionary work in Africa, David Livingstone is said to have read Psalm 121.[453] But Psalm 121 finally has in view all of life as a journey. Thus it is appropriate that it has been traditionally used in the Evangelical Lutheran Church as part of the baptismal liturgy and that it is used by many traditions in funeral services. From birth to death and beyond, Psalm 121 is a psalm for the journey of life.

3. James Limburg calls Psalm 121 "A Psalm for Sojourners."[454] Not only does this title explain why Psalm 121 would have been particularly meaningful to dispersed post-exilic generations (see above on Pss 119:19, 54, 57, 111; 120:5-7), but it also serves to remind every generation of God's people that while the earth is our home, because God made it, it is housing each of us only temporarily (see Ps 39:12). This reality is not an excuse to grab all the gusto we can get on our one time around (see Luke 12:13-21), but an invitation to live fully in the present on the basis of a promise. Like Abraham and Sarah, we are called to live as sojourners, as people always on the way (see Gen 47:9; Heb 11:9-10). With good reason, the early church was known as "the Way" (see Acts 9:2; 19:23; 22:4; 24:22). In the Gospel of Mark, to be a disciple is to follow Jesus "on the way" (see Mark 8:27; 9:33; 10:52). Jesus characterizes his own existence as that of a sojourn rather than a settled existence (see Luke 9:57-62), and Jesus' instructions to those he sent out do not allow for the implements or provisions of a settled existence (see Mark 6:7-13). While this orientation may have an other-worldly thrust, it does not lend itself to a pie-in-the-sky-by-and-by escapism. For Jesus, the unsettledness he advocated led to a radical undermining of the social arrangements that supported power and privilege and that his contempories sought to maintain by claiming divine sanction.[455] Thus Jesus' journey led finally to a cross, but the good news is that God was there too, keeping his life. And as we follow Jesus on that way (Mark 8:34), God is our keeper as well.

453. See Prothero, *The Psalms in Human Life and Experience*, 264.
454. Limburg, "Psalm 121," 180, 186-87.
455. See John Dominic Crossan, *Jesus: A Revolutionary Biography* (San Francisco: Harper, 1994) 102-22.

Psalm 122:1-9, The Peace of Jerusalem

COMMENTARY

Psalm 122, the third of the Songs of Ascents (see Overview on Psalms 120–134), is the only psalm in the collection that is explicitly a pilgrimage song. However, the sequence of Psalms 120–122 may be intentional. The sequence moves the psalmist from dispersion (120:5-7) by way of a journey (Psalm 121) to Jerusalem (122:1-2). Because it locates the speaker(s) in Jerusalem, or at least focuses the reader's attention squarely on Jerusalem, Psalm 122 is usually categorized as a song of Zion (see Psalms 46; 48; 76; 84; 87). Its attention to the architectural features of the city is particularly reminiscent of Psalm 48 (see "the house of the LORD" in

vv. 1, 9; "gates" in v. 2; "thrones" in v. 5; "walls" and "towers" in v. 7).

Scholars propose various structural outlines for Psalm 122, but most favor the three-fold division followed by the NIV and the NRSV. Verses 1-2 describe the setting. They are followed by two sections, each of which begins with a reference to Jerusalem and contains four poetic lines. Attention to other features of the psalm, however, yields a different division, and it is legitimate to analyze the structure and movement of the psalm at more than one level. For instance, references to "the house of the LORD" encompass the psalm (vv. 1, 9), as if to say that the beginning and end, the motivation and destination, of the ascent to Jerusalem is the Temple, God's house. At the same time, there is a focusing of attention on the center of the psalm by means of a chiastic structure (see Introduction) and the repetition of the word "house":

A vv. 1-2 the psalmist, his or her companions ("I"/"us"), and "the house of the LORD"
  B vv. 3-4 Jerusalem
    C v. 5 "house of David"
  B´ vv. 6-7 Jerusalem
A´ vv. 8-9 the psalmist, companions, and "the house of the LORD"

There were two houses in Jerusalem— "the house of the LORD" and "the house of David"—just as Jerusalem was known as both "the city of God" and "the city of David." The structure of Psalm 122 calls attention to both houses. While "the house of David" is central, its position in the psalm and thus its authority are encompassed by "the house of the LORD." In other words, the power of the Davidic house is derivative. The three occurrences of the key word "house" (vv. 1, 5, 9) recall the narrative of 2 Samuel 7 in which "house" is also a key word. Second Samuel 7 makes it clear that David did not build God a house (that is, a temple); rather, God built David a house (that is, a dynasty). Thus the reign of the Davidic house is but an agency of God's reign, and the fundamental purpose of the Davidic administration is to enact the fundamental purpose of God's rule: justice (v. 5; see Ps 48:11). The psalms that explicitly proclaim God's reign also portray God's royal policy as "justice" (see Pss 96:10, 13; 97:2, 8; 98:9; 99:4; see also 82:1-3, 8). The structure of Psalm 122 suggests what other psalms also indicate: The Davidic reign is to manifest God's reign (see Psalms 2; 72). To experience Jerusalem is ultimately to experience the reality of God's reign and God's purposes for the world (see Ps 123:1).

122:1-2. These verses make it clear that the pilgrimage to Jerusalem was indeed a special experience. Verse 1 apparently reflects the typical invitation for a pilgrimage (see 1 Sam 14:11; Isa 2:3; Jer 31:6), and v. 2 seems to convey the sense of joy and excitement that would have accompanied a pilgrim's arrival. Since the verb in v. 2 would ordinarily be translated by an English past tense

("were" instead of "are"), however, some scholars conclude that Psalm 122 looks back over the whole experience after the pilgrim has returned home. While this is possible, vv. 6-9 also convey an immediacy that suggests the speaker's presence in Jerusalem. But the chronological issue is not crucial; the centrality of Jerusalem is evident in either case.

122:3-4. The word "Jerusalem" ends v. 2 and begins v. 3, representing another case of the steplike repetition that characterizes the Songs of Ascents (see Pss 120:5-7; 121:1-4, 7-8). The translation and sense of v. 3 are problematic. Both the NIV and the NRSV suggest an observation concerning Jerusalem's architectural quality, and this makes good sense in the context of a pilgrimage that involves the celebration of that particular place (see Commentary on Psalm 48, esp. discussion of vv. 12-14). The word translated "bound"/"compacted" (חבר ḥābar), however, is never used elsewhere of buildings. Rather, it is used of human compacts or alliances (see "allied" in Ps 94:20). Thus it is possible that it is not so much Jerusalem's architecture that is being praised but Jerusalem's ability to bring people together. Thus, the NEB translates v. 3b: "where people come together in unity." This too makes good sense, especially in view of v. 4, which describes the gathering of the tribes (cf. Exod 23:14-7; Deut 16:16; 1 Kgs 12:28). It is conceivable that the ambiguity is intended as a play on the possible senses of the verb. At any rate, v. 4 maintains the focus on Jerusalem. The NRSV's "it" is literally "there" (שם šām), a word that occurs regularly in the songs of Zion (see Pss 48:6; 76:3; 87:4; 132:17; 133:3). The repetition of "tribes" continues the steplike pattern.

122:5. While certain features of the psalm point to the centrality of v. 5, it is also true that v. 5 is not to be sharply separated from vv. 3-4. The word "there" recurs in v. 5, and the mention of "the name of the LORD" in v. 4 perhaps anticipates v. 5 and its focus on justice, a central attribute of God's "name" or character. The repeated plural "thrones" (כסאות kis'ōt), another instance of the steplike pattern, has been puzzling to commentators. It is probably a figurative way of saying that the Davidic house and its bureaucracy were responsible for justice in the city and throughout the land (see 2 Sam 8:15; 15:2-6; Isa 1:21-23; Mic 3:9-12).

122:6-9. Justice, which the Davidic house was to enact in accordance with God's reign, was supposed to result in *shalom,* "peace" (see Pss 29:10-11; 72:3, 7), which is the key word in vv. 6-8. Continuing the step-like pattern, it occurs once in each verse; the Hebrew root is also a component of the name "Jerusalem," which may mean "possession of peace" or "foundation of peace." The Hebrew word for "pray" (שאל *šā'al,* v. 6) and the word translated "secure"/"security" (שלוה *šalwâ,* v. 7) both contain the first two consonants of the root of "peace." This makes for what is probably the most striking example of alliteration in the whole psalter; the effect is to emphasize even further the concept of "peace."

The psalmist's invitation in v. 6*a* and his or her prayer for Jerusalem and those who live in it (vv. 6*b*-7) clearly imply that Jerusalem is not peaceful. In fact, Jerusalem has always been one of the most contested and conflicted cities in the world. Especially in the post-exilic era, during which it is likely that the Songs of Ascents were collected, Jerusalem existed in anything but "security" (v. 7*b*; see "prosper" in Lam 1:5; see also Neh 1:3; Jer 15:5). Yet, for the pilgrim who experiences conflict outside of Jerusalem (see Ps 120:5-7), Jerusalem is the consummate sign and symbol of peace. How can this be? Is the psalmist nostalgically recalling the former glory of Davidic and Solomonic times, or is the psalmist simply engaging in patriotic wishful thinking? So some might conclude, but on a deeper level, the psalmist's prayers for the peace of Jerusalem, as well as the commitment to seek its good (v. 9), are indicative of the recognition of God's reign and the intent to live under God's rule. Such recognition and commitment do not represent facile optimism or merely patriotic wishful thinking. Rather, the psalmist's motivation and conviction are eschatological. For the psalmist, to enter Jerusalem *really does* mean to enter a new world. The joy is real (v. 1). To live for God's sake (v. 9) and for the sake of others (v. 8) is to experience, to embody, and to extend the justice that God intends as ruler of the world. This life-style, this commitment, *is* reality. To be sure, the same old so-called realities will still be present—hatred and war (see Ps 120:5-7), trouble and turmoil (see Neh 1:3)—but they will no longer be determinative. To enter Jerusalem, to acknowledge God's reign and to commit oneself to live under it, is to be transformed and enabled to live in an extraordinary manner in the ordinary world of daily reality that is frequently reflected in the Songs of Ascents (see Overview on Psalms 120–134 and the Reflections below). The transformation of the pilgrim may be represented by the movement from v. 1 to vv. 8-9. While the psalmist articulates in v. 1 the benefit Jerusalem can have on the self, the focus in vv. 8-9 is on what the psalmist can do for the benefit of others and of God.

REFLECTIONS

1. Given the ongoing unrest in the Middle East and the uneasiness of peace accords that have been reached, the psalmist's invitation in v. 6*a* is remarkably contemporary in its literal sense. Yet even as we pray for the peace of Jerusalem, it is crucial to realize that Jerusalem represents in the psalms not just a place but a symbol of God's presence in space and time. Ironically, much of the ongoing controversy surrounding Jerusalem stems from the failure to discern its symbolic function; the city has often been viewed only as a *place* to be possessed rather than a symbol of the concrete presence in the world of a God who *cannot* ultimately be possessed and whose presence certainly cannot be limited to a particular place (as Psalm 121 proclaims!). To enter Jerusalem is ultimately to experience the reality of God's reign and to be transformed to represent God's just purposes in God's world. In short, to enter Jerusalem is to live eschatologically, because God's claim and God's purposes are always opposed (see Commentary on Psalms 48; 84).

What it means to enter Jerusalem, to live eschatologically, to live under God's reign, is illustrated powerfully by one of Walker Percy's characters, Will Barrett, in the novel *The Second Coming.* Will's father had committed suicide when Will was a young man, and Will's own life has been a persistent battle with a voice inside him (his father's voice perhaps) that tells him to do the same. The voice knows what the so-called real world is like:

> Come, what else is there [except suicide]? What other end if you don't make the end? Make your own bright end in the darkness of this dying world, this foul and feckless place, where you know as well as I that nothing ever really works, that you were never once yourself and never will be or he himself or she herself and certainly never once we ourselves together. Come, close it out before it closes you out because believe me life does no better job with dying than with living. Close it out. At least you can do that, not only not lose but win, with one last splendid gesture defeat the whole foul feckless world.[456]

Will's answer to the voice is a simple no, based on an experience of genuine love between him and another human being, which he takes as a sign that "the Lord is here."[457]

What the psalmist saw in Jerusalem was, in effect, a sign that "the Lord is here," amid the dark, daily realities of a dying world, a frustrating world where nothing ever really works out completely right and we are never all that we can be. Walker Percy does not take the story of Will Barrett beyond his discovery of the sign, but the reader assumes that Will discontinues his frantic search for the second coming of Christ and begins to live in the new world created by the good news that "the Lord is here." As for the psalmist, this good news is also transformational, enabling people to live in an extraordinary manner among the often dark and difficult daily realities of the world.

2. Psalm 122 is appropriately used by the church during the season of Advent. Advent maintains a dual focus on Christ's second coming and Christ's first coming—his birth—and so it effectively celebrates the good news that "the Lord is here" and will be here forever. Indeed, for the Gospel writers, Jesus represents what the Temple had symbolized; Jesus is the new locus of God's revelation in space and time (see Mark 13:1-2; 14:58; 15:29). Because this is the case, the Christian reader cannot help hearing Psalm 122 in the light of Jesus' reaction as he made a final pilgrimage to Jerusalem. When Jesus "saw the city, he wept over it," because it was evident to him from his own reception that the people did not recognize "the things that make for peace!" (Luke 19:41-42 NRSV). Tellingly, Jesus moves directly to the Temple, where he pronounces it a means of fleeing from justice rather than furthering the just purposes of God's reign (Luke 19:45-46). As Mays concludes concerning a Christian hearing of Psalm 122:

> When we return to the psalm from this scene in Luke we have to read it and sing it tutored by his [Jesus'] questions. As we pray for the peace of church and city, have we recognized the things that make for peace? Do we know that unless we go with him the pilgrimage toward peace will find no Jerusalem?[458]

Thus, as the good news always does, Psalm 122 leaves us with a challenge that is appropriate for Advent and for all seasons.[459]

---

456. Walker Percy, *The Second Coming* (New York: Ivy Books, 1980) 307.
457. Percy, *The Second Coming*, 328.
458. Mays, *Psalms*, 394.
459. Portions of the above treatment of Psalm 122 appear in substantially the same form in J. Clinton McCann, Jr., "Preaching on Psalms for Advent," *Journal for Preachers* 16/1 (Advent 1992) 11-16.

Psalm 123:1-4, Our Eyes Look to the Lord

COMMENTARY

Fourth among the Songs of Ascents (see Overview on Psalms 120–134), Psalm 123 is the first complete prayer in the collection (see Ps 120:2, a brief petition characteristic of the prayers for help; portions of 122:6-8 also could be construed as prayer). The opening profession of trust begins in the first-person singular (v. 1a) but concludes in the plural (v. 2b), and the accompanying petition (v. 3a) and complaint (vv. 3b-4) are also in the plural. Thus Psalm 123 is traditionally categorized as a communal lament/complaint or prayer for help.

The shift from singular to plural makes sense in the context of a pilgrimage (see Commentary on Psalms 120; 121; 122), during which individuals or small groups of travelers became part of a much larger group upon their arrival at Jerusalem. Psalms 120–122 seem to form an intended sequence, moving the pilgrim from dispersion (120:5-7) by way of a journey (Psalm 121) to Jerusalem (Psalm 122). Psalm 123 makes sense as the culmination of this sequence; that is, if Ps 120:5-7 describes the conflicted circumstances of those dwelling in dispersion, then it makes sense that the first thing they would do upon arrival at Jerusalem (Psalm 122) is to look to God (123:1-2) and ask for help (123:3-4). Indeed, the complaint in vv. 3-4 portrays a situation similar to that described in 120:5-7, although there are no verbal links. As several scholars observe, the situation certainly sounds like that of the post-exilic era (see, e.g., Neh 2:19; 4:4, where "ridiculed" and "despised" represent the same Hebrew root as "contempt" in Ps 123:3-4; "scorn" in 123:4 also occurs in Neh 2:19; 4:1 as "mocked"). This means that Psalm 123 is consistent with the character of Book V, which from the beginning (see Ps 107:2-3) appears to be a response to the theological crisis and the need for help that persisted even after the return from exile (see Commentary on Psalms 107; 108; 111; 118; 120; Introduction).

123:1. The NRSV preserves the Hebrew word order of v. 1a. The phrase "to you" is in the emphatic position, suggesting the

psalmist's complete orientation to God. To lift up the eyes can indicate arrogance (see 2 Kgs 19:22; cf. Ps 131:1), but that is clearly not the case here (see Ps 141:8). Rather, God is viewed and addressed as cosmic sovereign (v. 1b; see "sits"/"enthroned" in Pss 2:4; 9:7; 29:10; see also 11:4; 115:3). Thus Ps 123:1 reinforces the direction that is implied in Psalm 122; to enter Jerusalem is to acknowledge God's sovereignty and commit oneself to live under God's rule.

123:2. The two metaphors in v. 2 clearly portray the humble dependence that characterizes the psalmist's approach to God. Because God is sovereign (v. 1), God's people are in the position of "servants" (see Pss 34:22; 69:35-36; 79:2, 10; 86:2, 4, 16; 90:13, 16; 113:1; 116:16) of their "master" or "mistress." The word translated "master" (אדון *'ādôn*) is used frequently of God elsewhere (usually translated "Lord"; see Ps 97:5b), but the feminine imaging of God here is striking, although not unprecedented (see Isa 66:13; Hos 11:4; see also Commentary on Psalm 131). The repetition of "eyes" (עינים *'ênayim*), which occurs in each of the four poetic lines in vv. 1-2, is another instance of the steplike pattern that characterizes the Songs of Ascents (see Pss 120:5-7; 121:1-4, 7-8; 122:2-5). This pattern of repetition also cuts across the two sections of Psalm 123; "mercy" at the end of v. 2 occurs twice more in v. 3a.

123:3. The double petition "have mercy" (חנן *ḥānan*, v. 3a) has the emphatic literary effect of surrounding the Lord with pleas for help. The petition is a frequent one in the psalms, often translated "be gracious" (see Pss 4:1; 6:2; 9:13; 25:16; 26:11; 27:7). While it may imply the specific need and desire for forgiveness, it more generally is an indication that the psalmist or the people depend on God for life itself. The Hebrew verb recalls Exod 34:6 (see also Exod 33:19), where God reveals the divine self to be fundamentally gracious. In this case, God's grace does specifically involve forgiveness (see Exod 34:7), but it includes more broadly God's willingness to be present with the people to make life possible (see Exod 34:9).

123:4. The need in Psalm 123 is stated in terms of the people's experience of "contempt" (vv. 3*b*, 4*b*) and "ridicule" (v. 4*a*). The particular situation is not known precisely, but it makes sense to hear the complaint in the narrative context of the post-exilic book of Nehemiah (see Neh 2:19; 4:1, 4). Similar complaints also appear in other psalms, where the psalmists or people are victims of contempt (Pss 31:18; 119:22; "pride" in Ps 31:18 is also from the same root as "proud" [גאון *gā'ôn*] in 123:4*b*) and ridicule (see Pss 22:7; 44:13; 79:4). The similarity of the complaint in Ps 123:3-4 to those in 44:13; 79:4 is particularly suggestive, since Psalm 79 laments the destruction of Jerusalem and since Psalm 44 is also a communal complaint that follows

a prayer that apparently belongs to a person who is absent from Jerusalem (Psalm 42) and who states his or her intention to make a pilgrimage to Jerusalem (Psalm 43). Thus the similarity of Psalm 123 to Psalms 44; 79 would support the hearing of Psalm 123 in a post-exilic context. The "proud"/"arrogant" also appear as opponents of God and/or the psalmist in Pss 94:2; 140:5. Not surprisingly, the complaint continues the steplike pattern of repetition (see "endured much" in vv. 3*b*, 4*a* as well as "contempt" in vv. 3*b*, 4*b*).

As is more common with the communal complaints than the individual complaints, Psalm 123 ends with the complaint itself. While praise has been implied and trust expressed in vv. 1-2, there is no concluding movement in this direction. What Psalm 123 may lack, however, Psalm 124 will supply.

REFLECTIONS

1. While Psalm 123 makes sense in the historical context of the post-exilic era, it also has affinities with prayers for help that originated and were used in circumstances that simply cannot be determined. This in itself suggests the appropriateness of Psalm 123 for a variety of settings. John Calvin, for instance, unable to determine the authorship of and historical circumstances behind Psalm 123, concluded that its real importance is that it "calls upon us to have recourse to God, whenever wicked men unrighteously and proudly persecute, not one or two of the faithful, but the whole body of the Church."[460] In other words, Psalm 123 can be the prayer of the people of God in every generation.

2. North American Christians in particular may never have experienced persecution or "contempt" on account of their faith. If this is the case, it is because we have not faithfully proclaimed and embodied the radical good news that God so loves the whole world and intends it to be rightly ordered so that all may know life and peace (see Commentary on Psalms 31; 120). It was precisely because he proclaimed and embodied this good news that Jesus ended up on a cross, and he calls people to follow him (Mark 8:34). Insofar as it is faithful, the church will win no popularity contests judged by the standards of the world. While the church is called to be in the world, it can never be of the world (see John 17:14-18). Thus Psalm 123 calls the church to the kind of humble servanthood that lives in utter dependence upon the sovereign God (see vv. 1-2) and that will inevitably be like Jesus' suffering servanthood (see Commentary on Psalm 44). Paradoxically, only at the point that we know the contempt of the world can we know the grace and peace that overcomes the world (see John 16:33). It is for this grace and peace that Psalm 123 prays. And in so doing, it may begin to teach us self-centered folk to turn away from ourselves long enough to be able to say that "our eyes look to the LORD our God" (v. 2).

460. Quoted in Kraus, *Psalms 60–150*, 437.

Psalm 124:1-8, If the Lord Were Not for Us . . .

COMMENTARY

Psalm 124 is the fifth of the Songs of Ascents (see Overview on Psalms 120–134). While its position following Psalm 123 may be coincidental, the sequence is an auspicious one. Psalm 123 is a prayer for help in the face of hostility and opposition, while Psalm 124 reports deliverance from enemies and publicly proclaims that help comes from the Lord (v. 8). In fact, v. 8 represents the entire people's affirmation of what an individual traveler had professed in Ps 121:2, suggesting the possibility that the sequence of Psalms 120–124 is intentional. In any case, the sequence in its current form seems to say that the individual faith professed in Ps 121:2 is confirmed by the pilgrim's arrival at Jerusalem, where his or her voice is joined with that of all Israel (see 124:2). In other words, just as Psalm 123 recalls Psalm 120, so also Psalm 124 recalls Psalm 121. In the midst of opposition, individual or corporate, God is the one who helps. Along with Psalms 120–123, Psalm 124 would have been an effective response to the realities of the post-exilic era. Thus it is in keeping with the apparent intent of Book V (see Commentary on Psalms 107; 108; 111; 120; Introduction).

Psalm 124 consists of three sections. Verses 1-5 consist of what can be rendered as one long conditional sentence with two *if* clauses (vv. 1-2) and three *then* clauses (the NRSV more accurately conveys the fact that each of vv. 3-5 begins with the same Hebrew word). Verses 6-7 offer praise for the deliverance described in vv. 1-5, while at the same time offering another metaphor for the deliverance. Verse 8 concludes with a profession of trust.

124:1-5. Verses 1*a*, 2*a* can be translated more literally as, "If God had not been *for us.*" Both the syntax and the content recall Ps 94:17, and the particular phrase "for us" recalls Ps 118:6. Verse 2*b* can be translated more literally as, "when humans rose *against us*" (see "rise" in Ps 3:1 NIV). In short, vv. 1-2 set up a contrast between the power of God and the power of humans, a contrast that is also present in Ps 118:6 (see the NRSV's

"mortals"; see also Pss 9:19-20; 56:4, 11). The real issue is "help" (עזר *'ēzer*). Whose help is ultimately effective? The answer present in vv. 1-5 and vv. 6-7 is given memorable expression in v. 8 (note "help" also in Pss 94:17; 118:7; see also Psalm 3, although the Hebrew word behind "help" in 3:2 differs from the one in Pss 94:17; 118:7; 124:8). As suggested above, the apparently liturgical invitation in v. 1*b* makes sense in the context of a festal gathering attended by pilgrims (see also Ps 129:1*b*).

Without God's help, the hostile actions of other humans would have resulted in the people's demise. Verses 3-5 do not specifically identify the disaster that would have occurred. The verb "swallow" (בלע *bālaʿ*) is used in Jer 51:34 to describe Babylon's defeat of Zion (see Jer 51:35). Verses 3-5 certainly make good sense as a description of what the Babylonian exile could well have been: the end of God's people. Whether such specificity is intended here, however, is not clear. The verb "swallow" is used in a variety of other contexts as well (see Exod 15:12; Num 16:30, 32, 34; Jonah 1:17). Similarly, the water imagery in vv. 4-5 is used to describe the threat to Jerusalem (see Isa 28:17, where "overwhelms" is the same as "swept . . . away" in Ps 124:4*a*), and the prophet of the exile promises that waters will not "overwhelm" (Isa 43:2 NRSV) the people on their return from Babylon to Jerusalem. But again, the particular verb in v. 4*a* and the general image are used elsewhere of either unspecified or clearly different threats of chaos (see Pss 42:7; 69:1-2; Jonah 2:3, 5); God's sovereignty over the chaotic waters is affirmed elsewhere as well (see Pss 74:12-15; 89:9-10; 93:3-4). "Us" (נפש *nepeš*) in vv. 4*b*, 5 translates a Hebrew word that is usually translated "soul" but seems to have originally meant "neck," a translation that would be appropriate here (see Ps 69:1). The NRSV preserves the chiastic poetic structure (see Introduction) of vv. 4-5; it visually represents the threat, as the two occurrences of "waters" (vv. 4*a*,

5b) surround the two occurrences of "us" (vv. 4b, 5a).

124:6-7. Verse 6a offers praise to God for being "for us" (see "bless" in Pss 28:6; 31:21; 103:1-2, 20-22; 104:1, 35; 115:18), and v. 6b introduces another image for the deliverance (see Job 29:17; Pss 3:8; 57:4; 58:6). Just as the chiastic structure of vv. 4-5 represented the threat, so also the chiastic structure of v. 7 visually represents the escape. The two occurrences of "we have escaped" (see Isa 49:25) surround the two occurrences of "snare" (see Pss 64:5; 91:3; 140:5; 141:9). The people are no longer trapped. Rather, as Kraus translated

the final phrase of v. 7, "we are free!"[461] The "we" that begins v. 7 translates the "us"/"our neck" that was surrounded in vv. 4-5, and the "we" in the final phrase of v. 7 is the emphatic personal pronoun. Thus poetic structure, the pattern of repetition, and the effective choice of personal pronoun combine to reinforce the good news: "We are free!"

124:8. This verse climactically affirms the answer to the question implied in vv. 1-2: Where or who is our help? It is no mere earthbound mortal, but the cosmic sovereign "who made heaven and earth" (see Pss 121:2; 134:3; see also 115:15; 146:6).

461. Kraus, *Psalms 60–150*, 439.

REFLECTIONS

The affirmation in v. 8 has perhaps been made so familiar by traditional use that we fail to grasp its profound and radical implications. To profess that God is our fundamental help means to profess that we are not sufficient to create and secure our own lives and futures. In short, we need help. Of course, this is something that most people are hesitant to say or even to admit, for it undercuts one of the primary principles that seems to drive our individual lives as well as our social and economic institutions— namely, "God helps those who help themselves." Psalm 125 teaches just the opposite; God helps those who *cannot* help themselves (see Commentary on Psalm 3). Apart from this teaching, it is not possible to speak with any integrity about what lies at the heart of the biblical message: the grace of God (see Psalm 123). Indeed, discipleship and servanthood (see Ps 123:2) really begin with the profession that we owe our very lives to God (see Mark 8:34-35).

The fundamental trust that God secures our lives and futures—that God is "for us" (vv. 1-2) and is "our help" (v. 8)—is what empowered Israel to claim the role of suffering servant in the post-exilic era (see Commentary on Psalm 44); it is what empowered Jesus to bear a cross as a suffering servant; and it is what has empowered, does empower, and will empower the church to continue to serve even when it means suffering at the hand of those who oppose God's reign and God's will (v. 2). As the apostle Paul put it with his words and embodied with his sufferings, "If God is for us, who can be against us?" (Rom 8:31 NIV).

Psalm 125:1-5, Those Who Trust in the Lord

COMMENTARY

Psalm 125 is the sixth of the Songs of Ascents (see Overview on Psalms 120–134). While it is not possible to demonstrate conclusively that the sequence is intentional, it is possible to detect a pattern in the opening psalms of the collection. The first three psalms

have the effect of moving an individual pilgrim from dispersion (Psalm 120) by way of a safe journey (Psalm 121) to Jerusalem (Psalm 122). The next three psalms approximate this same movement, but they do so in the plural rather than the singular. Psalm 123 articulates the contempt that was evident in Ps 120:5-7; Psalm 124 expresses trust in God's help, as did Psalm 121 (cf. 121:2 and 124:8, as well as 121:8 and 124:2); and like Psalm 122, Psalm 125 focuses on Jerusalem and concludes with petition aimed at the establishment of peace. To be sure, this pattern may be coincidental, but at least it suggests that Psalm 125 fits comfortably in the context of the Songs of Ascents. That is to say, it makes sense to conclude that it was originally used by pilgrims on the way to or upon arrival at Jerusalem.

Like Psalm 123, Psalm 125 is usually classified as a communal lament/complaint or prayer for help, and it begins with an expression of trust (vv. 1-2). Verse 3 continues the expression of trust but concludes with a clause that implies complaint and petition. The petition is explicit in v. 4. Verse 5 returns to trust in the form of a warning, and the psalm concludes with a declaration of peace. Scholars frequently suggest, especially on the basis of v. 3, that Psalm 125 reflects the people's domination by the nations in the post-exilic era. This makes good sense and also makes Psalm 125 congruent with its immediate context in the Songs of Ascents and with the larger context of Book V (see Psalms 107–108; 111; 118; 120; Introduction); however, the usefulness of Psalm 125 and its ability to speak for and to the people of God are not limited to an ancient setting. It continues to reflect both the faith and the struggle of the people of God in every generation (see Reflections below).

125:1-2. While the word "trust" (בטח *bāṭaḥ*) has not occurred in the Songs of Ascents until Ps 125:1*a,* the concept has been clearly portrayed in the preceding psalms (see Pss 121:1-8; 123:1-2; 124:1-5, 8). In fact, v. 1*b* explicitly recalls Ps 121:3 (see Pss 16:8; 55:22), and the stability of those who entrust their lives to God is a central theme throughout the psalter (see "trust" in Pss 4:5; 9:10; see the related theme of "refuge" in Ps 2:12; Introduction). The use of geological imagery also is characteristic of the psalter. The metaphor of God as rock may derive from the prominence of Zion (see above on Pss 18:2, 46; 31:2), but here Zion is a simile for the people's stability, which, of course, derives from God (v. 2). Verse 2 makes it easy to picture pilgrims in Jerusalem looking out toward the surrounding mountains (see Ps 121:1) and then interpreting the panoramic view as a metaphor for God's eternal protection (see Pss 121:8; 131:3). The repetition of "surround(s)" continues the steplike pattern that characterizes the Songs of Ascents (see Pss 120:5-7; 121:1-4, 7-8; 122:4-8; 123:1-2).

125:3. The Hebrew particle (כי *kî*) that begins this verse should probably be translated "surely" rather than "for" (note that the NIV simply omits it). While v. 3 continues the expression of trust, it does seem to stand apart from vv. 1-2. Carol Bechtel Reynolds even suggests that "the entire psalm seems to pivot on this verse," the conclusion of which should be translated with the KJV, "lest the righteous put forth their hands unto iniquity."[462] In other words, v. 3 implies that the wicked do wield authority in the land and that their persistent influence tempts the righteous to adopt their ways (see Ps 73:10). Because the Hebrew word translated "land allotted" occurs frequently in the book of Joshua as the land is being settled (see Josh 15:1; 17:1), scholars frequently conclude that v. 3 reflects the situation of the post-exilic era, when the people and the land were dominated by other nations. This is a reasonable conclusion, especially since other Songs of Ascents seem to reflect the same situation (see Pss 120:5-7; 123:3-4). The interpretive significance of v. 3, however, should not be limited to the ancient setting. The effect of v. 3, especially in the light of the petition in v. 4, is to give the psalm an eschatological orientation; it suggests that the people of God always live amid circumstances that make it appear that the wicked are in control (see Commentary on Psalms 2; 93; 96; 97; 98; 99; Introduction).

125:4-5. The reality of wickedness makes necessary the petition in v. 4. God's "doing good" is elsewhere associated with the people's possession of and prosperity in the land, so the verb may reinforce the conclusion that Psalm 125 originated amid the oppression of the post-exilic era (see Deut 8:16; 28:63; 30:5; see also Mic 2:7). But in keeping with the broader relevance of Psalm 125, it should be noted that the contrast between "the righteous"/the "good"/"the upright" and "the wicked"/"those who turn

---

462. Carol Bechtel Reynolds, "Psalm 125," *Int.* 48 (1994) 273.

aside"/"the evildoers" is introduced in Psalm 1 and pervades the psalter. The real issue is this: Who rules the world? While it appears that the wicked rule (note that "scepter" or "rod" in v. 3 occurs often in contexts where the subject is sovereignty, as in Judg 5:14; Pss 2:9; 45:6; Isa 14:5), the expressions of trust in vv. 1-2, 3a, 5 indicate the psalmist's conviction that God reigns.

Thus it is fitting that the final line of the psalm declares "Peace," which describes the conditions that prevail when God's sovereign rule is recognized and enacted (see Pss 29:10-11; 72:3, 7). In longing for peace (Ps 120:7), in praying for peace (Ps 122:6-7), in declaring peace (Pss 122:8; 125:5; 128:6), the psalmists identify themselves as faithful citizens of the reign of God.

REFLECTIONS

The peace derived from service (see Ps 123:2) under God's sovereignty is no ordinary peace. It surpasses all understanding (see Phil 4:7), and it is greater than the world can ever give (see John 14:27). Like the peace Jesus left with his disciples, so the peace the psalmist declares is experienced amid opposition from the world, the apparent sovereignty of the wicked (v. 3). Thus, as the NT also makes clear, the faith of the people of God (v. 1) is inseparable from hope (see Rom 8:24-25; Heb 11:1). In short, the people of God always live eschatologically, proclaiming God's rule in the face of wickedness, attempting to embody the peace that God offers in the midst of a hostile world (see Commentary on Psalms 2; 31; 120; Introduction).

The opposition to God's rule is as evident in the contemporary era as it was in the post-exilic era. Thus Psalm 125 continues to speak to and for the people of God. In his essay "Are We Afraid of Peace?" Elie Wiesel addresses the ongoing opposition to the peace that God wills for the world:

> Though temporary in nature, war seems to last forever. In the service of death, it mocks the living. It allows men to do things that in normal times they have no right to do: to indulge in cruelty. A collective as well as individual gratification of unconscious impulses, war may be too much a part of human behavior to be eliminated—ever.[463]

In a similar direction, Reinhold Niebuhr reminds us that moral people are far more inclined to do immoral things—like indulging in cruelty—in the name of their society or nation.[464] And the characters in novelist Walker Percy's novels constantly confront the reader with the observation that human beings do not seem to tolerate very well the ordinariness of daily life: "War is better than Monday morning."[465]

Given these trenchant and realistic assessments of human nature, we can begin to appreciate the profound importance of Ps 125:3. Because the dynamic of evil seems to have a subtle way of luring the righteous, it is all the more important that human hostility and cruelty be identified, named for what they are, and opposed. It is crucial that the people of God, who know a more excellent way, be just as faithfully determined as the psalmist that evil not prevail (v. 3a), that they pray for God's goodness (v. 4), and that they display the psalmist's confident courage in declaring a peace that opposes the declaration of war and every other impulse toward cruelty (v. 5; see Ps 120:5-7).

463. Elie Wiesel, *From the Kingdom of Memory: Reminiscences* (New York: Summit Books, 1990) 225.
464. See Reinhold Niebuhr, *Moral Man and Immoral Society: A Study in Ethics and Politics* (New York: Charles Scribner's Sons, 1960).
465. Walker Percy, *The Last Gentleman* (New York: Ivy Books, 1966) 74.

Psalm 126:1-6, Restore Our Fortunes, O Lord

COMMENTARY

Psalm 126 is the seventh of the Song of Ascents (see Overview on Psalms 120–134). Given the unifying features of the collection and even the possibility of the intentional arrangement of Psalms 120–125 (see Commentary on Psalm 125), it is not surprising that Psalm 126 reflects the perspective of the preceding psalms—that is, the people have experienced God's deliverance in the past (Ps 126:1-3; see Pss 120:1; 124:1-7), but now confronted with another crisis in the present, they petition God for help (Ps 126:4-5; see 120:2; 122:6-7; 123:3-4; 125:4) and profess their trust in God's help (Ps 126:6; see Pss 121:1-8; 123:1-2; 124:8; 125:1-2, 5). Of course, this construal of the psalm depends on a translation similar to that provided by the NIV and the NRSV, and the translation of the verb tenses in Psalm 126 is often disputed. For instance, some translate all the verbs in vv. 1-3 (as well as those in vv. 5-6) in the future tense, thus making the psalm consistently a prayer for help. Others translate all the verbs in vv. 4-6 (as well as those in vv. 1-3) in the past tense, thus making the psalm consistently a song of thanksgiving. Such strategies appear to be forced attempts to remove the tension between vv. 1-3 and vv. 4-6, but it is precisely this tension that is reflected in Psalms 120–125 and that gives Psalm 126 its continuing theological relevance to the people of God in every generation.

Historically speaking, the tension between vv. 1-3 and vv. 4-6 makes very good sense in the post-exilic era. The likelihood of a post-exilic origin for Psalm 126 is increased by the appearance of the phrase the NRSV translates as "restored the fortunes" in v. 1a. While this more general sense is preferable, it is likely that the phrase refers to the return of the exiles from Babylon to Jerusalem (see Deut 30:3; Jer 30:3, 18; 32:44; Ezek 39:25). This glorious pilgrimage ran up against hard historical realities. The vision of Isaiah 40–55 did not materialize, and soon the disillusioned people found themselves again in need of restoration (see the books of Ezra; Nehemiah; Haggai; and Zechariah). The same phrase

that occurs in Ps 126:1, 4 also occurs in Ps 85:1 (see also the verb in 85:4); Psalms 85 and 126 share the same movement, and they can be reasonably understood in the same historical context (see Commentary on Psalm 85). Even so, it is not necessary to tie Psalm 126 inextricably to a specific historical occasion. The phrase "restored the fortunes" can refer more generally to any reversal of God's judgment, and it is clear that Psalm 126 has continued to speak to and for the people of God throughout the centuries (see Reflections below).

126:1-3. It is easy to imagine how the return of the captives from Babylon would have been like a dream come true (v. 1b), especially in the light of the exalted interpretation of this event by Isaiah 40–55 as a second exodus, God's "new thing" (Isa 43:19). While there is support in the ancient versions for an alternate reading of v. 1b (see the NIV note), the Hebrew makes perfectly good sense (see Isa 29:7-8; Joel 2:28; Acts 12:9). The return to Jerusalem was also a source of great joy (v. 2ab), and joy becomes the dominant note of the psalm (see "songs of joy" [רנה rinnâ] in vv. 2, 5-6). Not surprisingly, the Hebrew root of "songs of joy" occurs frequently in Isaiah 40–55 to describe the appropriate response to the return from exile (see Isa 44:23; 48:20; 49:13), but it is also used more generally to portray the appropriate emotion for approaching the house of God (see Ps 42:4) and for worship in response to divine deliverance (see Pss 47:1; 118:15). The joyful tone is reinforced by the mention of "laughter" (v. 2a; see Job 8:21) and by the verb "rejoice" in v. 3b (the root is different from the one behind "songs of joy").

According to Isaiah 40–55, the return from exile was to be universally proclaimed (see Isa 41:1; 48:20); indeed, it was effected by God's use of other nations (see Isa 45:1-7) so that God's people might become "a light to the nations" (Isa 42:6 NRSV). Again, this background helps to make sense of what the nations say in v. 2cd, especially since the nations usually are portrayed as saying something quite different (see Pss 79:10; 115:2; see above on Pss 120:5-7; 123:3-4). Continuing the steplike pattern of repetition that characterizes the Songs of Ascents, the people echo what the nations have observed (see Joel 2:20-21).

126:4-6. The retrospective look of vv. 1-3 is left behind in vv. 4-6, which have the present need in view. The recollection of v. 1*a* in v. 4*a* sharpens the contrast between past and present, as do the occurrences of "tears" (v. 5) and "weeping" as antonyms to "songs of joy" (vv. 5-6; cf. v. 2). But the present is not without hope. The image of the "streams in the Negev" (v. 4*b*) communicates both the people's neediness and their confidence in God. While often dry, even today these stream beds can suddenly become rushing torrents when the seasonal rains arrive. So the simile used here functions to convey not only the people's current dryness but also their expectation of the life-giving deliverance of God. In Ps 42:1, as well, the need for God is represented in terms of the desire for "streams of water"; Joel 3:18 depicts future deliverance by using the same imagery.

The imagery shifts to sowing and reaping in vv. 5-6 (see Amos 9:13-15, where similar agricultural imagery depicts future deliverance). That the people "sow in tears" and go out "weeping" is often interpreted as a reflection of ancient Near Eastern rituals of mourning for a dead fertility god, whose burial is represented by the sowing of seeds into the ground. While such a background is possible, it is just as important to observe that sowing is always an act of anticipation and hope. The mention of tears and weeping in this case may simply emphasize the urgency of the need already articulated in v. 4, and thus the fervency of the people's hope. Appeals for help from God are made elsewhere in the OT with "tears" and "weeping" (see 2 Kgs 20:5; Pss 39:12; 42:3; 56:8; Jer 9:1, 18; 13:17; 31:16; Lam 1:16; 2:18; Joel 2:17). Just as the people's need is real, so also is their hope real. Like v. 6, v. 5 can also be translated with an indicative force. The repetition of "songs of joy" in vv. 5-6 is emphatic; there will be a joyful harvest.

REFLECTIONS

1. While Psalm 126 makes good sense against the background of the post-exilic era, its relevance and use are much broader. Concerning the key phrase, "restored the fortunes," Kraus maintains that it can be properly understood as "an expression for a historical change to a new state of affairs for all things."[466] In other words, v. 1 articulates the remembrance of a past deliverance that evokes laughter and joy among God's people. Similarly, the prayer in v. 4 is perpetually appropriate for the faithful—both individuals and the whole people. No matter how often we proclaim that God "has done great things for us" (v. 3; see also v. 2), we will still find ourselves in need of God's help and renewed deliverance (see Commentary on Psalms 123; 125). Thus Psalm 126 reminds us that we live in the hope of God's help, always remembering what God has done in the past (vv. 1-3; see also Psalm 124) and always anticipating what God will do in the future (vv. 4-6; see Isa 43:19; 65:17; Rev 21:5; see Commentary on Psalms 2; 93; 96; 97; 98; 99; Introduction).

2. Given the several similarities between Psalm 126 and the book of Joel (in addition to the references cited above, cf. Ps 126:1, 4 with Joel 3:1), Walter Beyerlin argues that the author(s) of Psalm 126 actually used the book of Joel as a source in the attempt to address the disappointing circumstances that prevailed in Judah following the return from exile.[467] Even without this possible historical connection, however, it is instructive to read the book of Joel alongside Psalm 126. Like the psalm, Joel moves from an articulation of need (1:2–2:17) to the promise of God's response (2:18–3:21).

466. Kraus, *Psalms 60–150*, 450.
467. Walter Beyerlin, *We Are Like Dreamers*, trans. D. Livingston (Edinburgh: T. and T. Clark, 1982) 41-58.

Thus Psalm 126 and Joel join in proclaiming the good news that God will ultimately provide for God's people. This theme, along with the harvest imagery, makes Psalm 126 an appropriate reading for Thanksgiving Day.

3. Psalm 126 is also appropriately associated with the seasons of Advent and Lent, because it communicates the reality that the people of God always live by both memory and hope. During Advent and Lent, we remember the humble and humbling circumstances of Jesus' birth and death; yet we do so in the joyful hope represented by his resurrection and the promise of the renewal of all things. The hopeful, joyful tone of Psalm 126 points to the possibility that dreaming in v. 1 involves not simply the incredulous response to a divine act of deliverance but the suggestion that every divine act of deliverance evokes a joyous vision of the future out of which the people of God live (see Joel 2:28 and its use in Acts 2:17). The joyful tone of the hymn "Bringing in the Sheaves," based on Psalm 126, suggests the effect of living as a visionary, through which anticipated joy becomes a present reality even amid the distressing circumstances that lead us to pray, "Restore our fortunes, O LORD." In other words, "Blessed are those who mourn, for they will be comforted" (Matt 5:4 NRSV).

Psalm 127:1-5, Unless the Lord Builds the House

COMMENTARY

Psalm 127 is the eighth of the Songs of Ascents (see Overview on Psalms 120–134). The eighth position represents the middle of the collection, but it is not clear how much significance should be attached to the shape of the collection. It does seem to be the case, though, that while expressing trust in God's help (Psalms 121; 124), Psalms 120–126 articulate primarily the ongoing need of the people in a hostile environment (see Pss 120:5-7; 122:6-9; 123:3-4; 125:3-5; 126:4-6). While Psalm 127 continues to articulate the importance of trusting God and living in dependence upon God (see esp. vv. 1-2), it introduces the possibility of happiness (v. 5). This vocabulary is picked up in Ps 128:1-2, which also seems to offer assurance in response to the petition of 125:4 ("Do good" in Ps 125:4 and "go well" in 128:2 translate the same Hebrew root). Psalm 128 also introduces the concept of blessing as applied to humanity (v. 5), a concept that does not occur in this sense in Psalms 120–126 (cf. Ps 126:6) but recurs several times in subsequent psalms (Pss 129:8; 132:15; 133:3; 134:3). Psalms 130–131 encourage hope (130:7; 131:3), and Psalm 132 is an encouraging word about Jerusalem. All in all, then, the tone of Psalms 128–134 is more upbeat than that of Psalms 120–126, and the people's

opponents are seldom in view (see only Psalm 129). If anything, what threatens the people are their own misplaced priorities (127:1-2), sinfulness (130:3), and pride (131:1). Hence, Psalm 127 does seem to represent something of a turning point. Its function in this regard may be marked by the unique attribution of the psalm to Solomon.

Earlier generations of scholars had difficulty perceiving the unity of Psalm 127, and they often concluded that it was composed of two independent wisdom sayings (vv. 1-2 and vv. 3-5). Recent scholarship has detected a unity between the two parts on a structural and a conceptual level. For instance, on the structural level, the verb "build(s)" (בנה *bānâ*) in v. 1 begins with the same two Hebrew letters that form the word "sons" (בנים *bānîm*) in vv. 3-4, thus signaling a unity. On the conceptual level, to build a house can refer not only literally to the physical construction of an edifice, but also figuratively to the establishment of a family. This latter sense is in view in vv. 3-5; in both vv. 1-2 and vv. 3-5, the ultimate accomplishment belongs to God.

Verses 1-2 display the steplike pattern of repetition that is characteristic of the Songs of Ascents (see Pss 120:5-7; 121:1-4, 7-8; 122:4-8; 123:1-2), as the words or phrases "Unless the LORD," "build(s)," "guard(s)," and "vain" are repeated. Three activities are described as "vain"—that is, ultimately purposeless and worthless—without God's involvement. As suggested above, building a house could include several things, from physical construction of a house (Gen 33:17; Deut 8:12) or the Temple (2 Sam 7:13) to having children (Deut 25:9; Ruth 4:11). When God builds a house, the reference is to the establishment of a priestly or royal dynasty (see 1 Sam 2:35; 2 Sam 7:27), a direction that points toward vv. 3-5. Guarding or keeping is a characteristic activity of God (see Num 6:24; Pss 25:20; 34:20; 86:2; 97:10; 116:6; 121:3-5, 7-8). Patrick D. Miller points out that the reference to "the city" is "richly ambiguous": "It may be Jerusalem, or it may be any city, that is, the city of those who sing this song."[468] The third activity involves excessive work, which is accompanied by needless anxiety. Although the sense of v. 2d is not entirely clear (see NIV and NRSV notes), the message is that God ultimately provides what humans need without their excessive striving. While the word "sleep" (שנא šēnā) is well-attested (see Pss 3:5; 4:8), J. A. Emerton suggests an emendation that yields a word meaning "glory" or "honor" or "wealth."[469] In either case, the sense is that provision for human life is a result, not of extraordinary human effort, but of the grace of God. As Miller suggests, we should hear in v. 2 an echo of Gen 3:17-19, although v. 2 is really "a counterword to Gen 3:17-19," in that it promises provision beyond what human beings can manage to produce.[470]

Even if building a house (v. 1) is not heard in the sense of establishing a family, there is a connection between vv. 1-2 and vv. 3-5. All the activities cited are ordinary necessities of life—securing a home (v. 2ab), establishing a safe neighborhood (v. 1cd), working for a living (v. 2), having children (vv. 3-5). Each activity can, of course, be approached simply in terms of human effort and accomplishment, but the psalmist insists that each be viewed in relation to God. In the case of children, they are God's gift. The word "heritage" (נחלה naḥălâ) often refers to God's gift of land (see "inheritance" in Josh 14:3),

which represented access to life and a future. Here, children represent much the same thing, and it is God who gives them (see Gen 15:1, where "reward" involves the promise of children in Abram's future; see also Gen 30:2, where "the fruit of the womb" is God's prerogative to give). They represent strength (v. 4) and apparently a security that comes from sheer numbers, although the precise sense of v. 5 is unclear (the NIV's "they" translates the Hebrew accurately). The city gate functioned like a courthouse (see Deut 21:19; 25:7; Amos 5:12), and perhaps a person with a large family had guaranteed allies in settling disputes.

Given the central position of Psalm 127 in the Songs of Ascents, it is probable that its context affected the way the community heard and construed "house," "city," and "sons." As pilgrimage songs (see Overview on Psalms 120–134), Psalms 120–134 show particular interest in the Temple (see Pss 122:1, 9; 134:1), Jerusalem (see Pss 122:2-3, 6-9; 125:1-2; 126:1; 129:5; 132:13), and the Davidic dynasty (Pss 122:5; 132:1-5, 10-12). Thus it is likely that "the house" (v. 1) was construed as the Temple or perhaps the Davidic dynasty, that "the city" (v. 1) was understood to be Jerusalem, and that the "sons" (vv. 3-4) were taken to be royal descendants. Perhaps Ps 127:2 was even heard in the light of the words attributed to David in Ps 132:3-5; that is, David's determined attempt to build God a house actually resulted in God's building David a house (see 2 Samuel 7). In any case, this reading of Psalm 127 probably accounts for the attribution of Psalm 127 to Solomon, who carried out numerous building projects, including the Temple (see 1 Kgs 3:1-2; 7:1-11; 8:13; 9:1). Given that Solomon's motives may not have been the purest—he spent thirteen years building his own palace and only seven years on the Temple (see 1 Kgs 6:38; 7:1)—and that his policies led to the split of the kingdom (see 1 Kgs 5:13; 12:1-16), it is perhaps proper to view Solomon in some sense as a negative example. Thus without God's involvement, human efforts and achievements, even those as great as Solomon's, are finally fleeting and empty.

468. Miller, *Interpreting the Psalms*, 133.
469. J. A. Emerton, "The Meaning of šēnā' [שנא] in Psalm cxxvii 2," *VT* 24 (1974) 15-31.
470. Miller, *Interpreting the Psalms*, 133-34.

REFLECTIONS

1. Given that Psalms 120–134 are probably a pilgrimage collection, it is not surprising that several psalms reflect the realities of daily living, such as work and family (see Psalms 122; 127; 133). The effect of grounding such realities in the will of God and of construing them ultimately as the work of God is to give the ordinary realities of life an extraordinary significance. That is to say, God cares about the so-called routine matters, such as home, community, work, and family.

While making this affirmation, Psalm 127 is also an insistent challenge to a purely secular reading of human experience. While some people need to be reminded that home, community, work, and family are not simply necessities to be tolerated, other people need to be reminded that neither are these realms of experience the be-all and end-all of human existence. Having a nice house may be part of the American dream, but it does not necessarily fulfill the will of God (see Luke 9:57-62). Having a crime-free neighborhood does little good if we have nothing to live for except our possessions, and making a living means nothing if we do not know what life is really all about (see Luke 12:15). Family can become an idolatrous means of escaping God's will if it is defined too narrowly (see Mark 3:31-35; see also Commentary on Psalm 133). As Miller concludes, "The word of the psalm is that unless such enterprises become God's enterprises as those who build, watch, and labor seek the will and way of God and invoke God's presence and purpose in these activities, then there is an emptiness to them."[471] Or worse, there is a demonic, destructive side to them when these activities become means of expressing self-sufficiency rather than dependence upon God (see Commentary on Psalms 1; 121) and means of pursuing greed rather than generosity. In the final analysis, Psalm 127 functions as an invitation to entrust our lives to God and so not to be anxious about our lives, but to pursue God's claim upon us and strive to embody God's will (see Matt 6:25-34).

2. The corporate construal of Psalm 127, signaled by the attribution to Solomon, reminds us that what applies to our individual lives also applies to our lives as a community of God's people. As Mays concludes, "Unless the LORD builds the church, they labor in vain who build it."[472] Quite properly, Psalm 127 is widely used in liturgies of dedication of new church buildings. The subtle temptation is to make even church buildings into monuments to human achievement. Psalm 127 opposes the pervasive temptation to take personal credit for God's activity among us.

471. Miller, *Interpreting the Psalms*, 137.
472. Mays, *Psalms*, 402.

Psalm 128:1-6, You Shall Be Happy

COMMENTARY

Psalm 128 is the ninth of the Songs of Ascents (see Overview on Psalms 120–134). Although scholars continue to debate whether there is an intentionality to the shape of the collection, it seems that Psalm 127 represents a sort of turning point. In any case, it is clear that Psalm 128 should be heard as a companion to Psalm 127. The two psalms are linked by the occurrences of "happy" in 127:5 and 128:1-2; verbal links also highlight the fact that both psalms deal with the subjects of work (see "eating"/"eat" in 127:2; 128:2) and family (see "sons"/"children" in 127:3-4; 128:3, 6). Both psalms affirm that fruitfulness of family (see 127:3; 128:3; "fruit" in 128:2 is a different Hebrew word) and of work derives from God.

The NIV follows the usual structural division of Psalm 128: vv. 1-4 and vv. 5-6. In this view, the word "fear(s)" serves to mark the beginning and end of the first section. Allen divides the psalm into vv. 1-3 and vv. 4-6, suggesting that the beginning of each section is marked by the word "fear(s)" and that both sections display the same movement from third person (vv. 1, 4) to direct address (vv. 2-3, 5-6) while repeating the major concept of each section (see "happy" in vv. 1-2, "blessing" in vv. 4-5).[473] The NRSV offers yet another proposal: vv. 1-2, vv. 3-4, vv. 5-6. In this view, vv. 1-2 focus on the happiness derived from work; vv. 3-4 focus on the blessings of family; and vv. 5-6 put both within the context of God's blessing from Zion (see "prosperity" in vv. 2, 5 NIV and "children" in vv. 3, 6 NRSV). In short, several structural proposals can be justified, depending on which clues one considers most important.

128:1. The psalm begins with a beatitude that is very similar to Ps 112:1 and recalls Ps 1:1-2. Although, like Psalm 112, Psalm 128 seems to suggest that happiness consists largely of material reward—the benefits of one's work (v. 2) and a large family (v. 3)—the matter is clearly not so simple or superficial. To fear the Lord means fundamentally to recognize God's sovereignty and so to entrust life and future to God (see Pss 2:11; 25:14; 31:19; 33:18; 34:9, 11; 60:4; 112:1; 115:11, 13; 118:4). It is to orient one's whole life to God's ways rather than one's own ways (v. 1*b*; see Deut 8:6; 10:12, where walking in God's ways is also parallel to fearing God; see also Ps 119:3). While the psalmist properly maintains that such orientation of one's life affects what one experiences in life, he or she does not intend to advocate a mechanistic system of rewards or punishment, as the

literary context of Psalm 128 makes clear (see Pss 120:5-7; 123:3-4; 126:4-6). Rather, as in Psalms 1–2, happiness is ultimately the connecting of one's life to the true source of life: God.

128:2-4. The inability to enjoy the fruit of one's own labor was a traditional sign of God's disfavor (see Deut 28:33; Pss 78:46; 109:11), as was barrenness (see Gen 30:1-2; 1 Sam 1:5). Similarly, fruitfulness of work (v. 1) and of family (v. 3) was understood as God's blessing (v. 4; see Ps 115:13). The psalms regularly make it clear that faithfulness to God does not guarantee such blessings in any mechanistic way (see Pss 3:1; 34:19). For instance, the petition in Ps 125:4 ("Do good" represents the same Hebrew root as "well" [טוב *ṭôb*] in 128:2) implicitly indicates that the faithful frequently stand in need. Even so, Ps 128:1-4 encourages the faithful to view the so-called ordinary daily benefits of life in relation to God. Those who fear God will know a blessedness that endures in all circumstances.

128:5-6. These verses are sometimes construed as a priestly benediction (see Num 6:24-26; Ps 134:3). While it is easy to imagine the blessing of the people by a priest within the context of a pilgrimage to Jerusalem (see Overview on Psalms 120–134), the ancient setting of Psalm 128 remains uncertain. What is clearer is that the mention of Zion in v. 5 connects Psalm 128 to its literary context (see Pss 122:1-2, 6-9; 125:1-2; 126:1; 129:5; 132:13; 134:3), as does the theme of blessing (see Pss 129:8; 132:15; 133:3; 134:3) and the proclamation of peace that concludes the psalm (see Pss 120:7; 122:6-9; 125:5). The proclamation of peace is appropriate by those who fear God, who live under God's rule, since it describes the conditions that prevail when God's sovereignty is recognized and enacted (see above on Ps 125:5).

473. Allen, *Psalms 101–150*, 184.

REFLECTIONS

Claus Westermann distinguishes between God's activity in saving—extraordinary moments that involve deliverance from death to life—and God's activity in blessing—God's ongoing provision for the ordinary necessities of daily life.[474] While this distinction

474. Westermann, *Elements of Old Testament Theology*, 35-117.

can be pressed too far, it can also be helpful. And in these terms, Psalm 128 articulates a theology of blessing as it celebrates the daily realms of work and family as gifts of God. In this regard, it is similar to Psalm 127. Together, the two psalms resist our persistent tendency to view the world purely in secular terms (see Commentary on Psalm 127).

The possible danger of a theology of blessing is that people are tempted to turn it into a mechanistic system of reward and punishment. The immediate literary context of Psalm 128 and its larger canonical context resist this tendency. For instance, when Psalm 128 is heard in conjunction with Psalm 125 (cf. Pss 125:5 with 128:6), the proclamation of peace must be understood eschatologically; peace always exists amid the hostility of those who do not fear the Lord (see Commentary on Psalm 125). This does not make it any less real, but the peace God gives surpasses all human understanding (see Phil 4:7), for it is not "as the world gives" (John 14:27 NRSV). In this context, the experience of the blessing and peace of God is cause not for self-congratulation but for gratitude (see Commentary on Psalms 50; 67).

Psalm 129:1-8, God Has Cut the Cords of the Wicked

COMMENTARY

Psalm 129 is the tenth of the Songs of Ascents (see Overview on Psalms 120–134). It has been categorized in several ways by scholars—communal lament/complaint, communal thanksgiving, and communal song of assurance. In any case, the invitation for the people's participation in v. 1 recalls Ps 124:1 (see also Ps 118:2-4), and the openings of the two psalms relate a similar story of threat and deliverance ("attacked" in 124:1-2 and 129:1-2 translates two different Hebrew words). The pattern of an individual voice joined by the voice of the community makes good sense if the Songs of Ascents were originally used by pilgrims on the way to or upon arrival at Jerusalem (see Commentary on Psalms 120; 124). So does the focus on Zion (v. 5), which is frequent in the collection (see Pss 122:6-9; 125:1-2; 126:1; 132:13; 134:3).

The NIV follows the usual division of the psalm into two roughly equal sections. Several scholars suggest, however, a division into vv. 1-3 and vv. 4-8, since the first-person perspective extends only through v. 3 (note that the NRSV includes vv. 1-3 in quotation marks, although it indicates no structural divisions at all). Of course, it would be possible to extend the quotation at least through v. 4. Allen, for instance, suggests that vv. 2-4 can be understood as the speech of a personified Zion. He finds support for this proposal in Micah's prophecy that Zion will be "plowed" (see Mic 3:12), and he notes that a personified Zion also speaks elsewhere (see Isa 49:14; Jer 4:31; Lam 1:9).[475] In short, as is often the case, the structure and movement of Psalm 129 can be described on more than one level, depending on which clues are taken to be the most important (see Commentary on Psalm 128).

129:1-4. A comparison of the NIV with the NRSV shows that the adverb at the beginning of vv. 1-2 can be construed to indicate either the frequency of the opposition or its severity. In either case, vv. 1-2 recall the occurrences of the same adverb used earlier in the collection, where it also suggests both length and severity of opposition (see Pss 120:6; 123:4). Thus vv. 1-2 articulate the reality of the persistent opposition, which has been and is being experienced by the people of God and which is described figuratively in v. 3 (see Isa 51:23). Even so, the people have continued to exist (v. 2b); as v. 4a indicates, their ongoing existence is testimony not to their own achievement but to God's righteousness (see Pss 7:9, 11; 11:7). The attribution of righteousness to God occurs often in the context of the proclamation of God's sovereignty (see Pss 9:7-8; 96:13; 97:2; 98:9; 99:4); the mention of "cords" in v. 4b

475. Allen, *Psalms 101–150*, 189.

also raises the issue of sovereignty (see Ps 2:3; see also 46:9, where God "cuts" the spear). The affirmation of God's sovereignty (v. 4) in the context of persistent opposition (vv. 1-3) means that Psalm 129 shares the eschatological perspective that characterizes the Songs of Ascents (see Commentary on Psalms 120; 123; 124; 126) and that pervades the psalter (see Commentary on Psalms 2; 46; 93; 96; 97; 98; 99; Introduction).

129:5-8. The mention of Zion in v. 5 probably recalls the original pilgrimage setting of Psalm 129. It also is a reminder that opposition to God's people was also opposition to God, since Zion was God's place (see Commentary on Psalms 46; 48; 76; 84; 87; 122). Verses 5-8 may be construed as a wish or a prayer, in which case they recall the petitions in Pss 123:3; 125:4; 126:4-6. On the other hand, the verbs can be translated with an indicative sense, in which case vv. 5-8 would have the character either of a prophecy concerning Zion's future or of a further expression of trust in God's sovereignty (see v. 4; Pss 121:3-4; 124:8; 125:5). In either case, the perspective is still eschatological, for it assumes the existence of those who hate Zion and who constantly assail the people of God (vv. 1-2). It is not clear how to construe v. 8. The NIV and the NRSV include both v. 8*b* and v. 8*c* in the quote of the saying, which the wicked will not hear; however, it is possible that v. 8*c* should be heard as a concluding benediction offered by or for the people of God (see Pss 128:5-6; 134:3).

REFLECTIONS

From its earliest to its latest chapters—from the struggles of the patriarchs and matriarchs to the embattled generations of the post-exilic era—the story of God's people is one of persistent opposition. This reality, of course, is another way of articulating an eschatological perspective; God's sovereignty is always opposed. Thus the people of God experience the opposition directed at God. Inevitably, Israel lived by both memory and hope (see Psalms 77; 126). Jesus, too, invited his followers to live eschatologically, to enter God's reign (Mark 1:14-15) by taking "up their cross" (see Mark 8:34). It will always be so. Insofar as they faithfully embody God's claim, the people of God will experience the hostility of the world (see John 17:11-19; see also Commentary on Psalms 31; 120; 125).

The juxtaposition of Psalms 129 and 130 is fortunate. Lest the people of God be tempted to self-righteousness by their suffering for God's sake, Psalm 130 is an eloquent reminder that the opposition to God is internal as well as external. The history of Israel may be one single passion narrative, but it is also one singularly marked by Israel's persistent faithlessness and disobedience (see Commentary on Psalms 51; 78; 106). The people of God live ultimately by the grace of a steadfastly loving God, who is willing to bear opposition from all sides, including Israel and the church (see Ps 130:7-8).

Psalm 130:1-8, Out of the Depths

COMMENTARY

Psalm 130 is the eleventh of the Songs of Ascents (see Overview on Psalms 120–134). While it is not certain that the arrangement of the collection is intentional (see Commentary on Psalm 127), the juxtaposition of Psalms 129 and 130 serves an important purpose: to address any temptation toward self-righteousness by reminding the people that, although they suffer for God's sake at the hands of oppressors (see Ps 129:1-2), they must also confront their own "iniquities" (Ps 130:3, 8; see Reflections on Psalm 129).

Quite appropriately, Psalm 131 begins with a profession of humility; not coincidentally, Ps 131:3 recalls Ps 130:7.

Psalm 130 is usually categorized as an individual lament/complaint or prayer for help. It starts in typical fashion (vv. 1-2), but the question in v. 3 makes it clear that "the depths" have something to do with the psalmist's own sinfulness (see Psalms 32; 51). The psalmist's affirmation in v. 4 responds to his or her own question. It also prepares for the profession of faith in vv. 5-6, which are no longer addressed directly to God. This shift prepares for the psalmist's direct address to Israel (v. 7a), which is followed by another profession of faith (vv. 7b-8) that focuses clearly on the character of God and amounts to nothing short of a proclamation of the good news that lies at the heart of the whole Bible. While vv. 7-8 are often viewed as a later addition to an earlier portion of the psalm, they are linked to vv. 1-6 by the repetition of "iniquities" (vv. 3, 8) and "hope" (vv. 5, 7), as well as by similar syntactical uses of the preposition "with" (vv. 4, 7), each occurrence of which communicates a crucial aspect of God's character. Furthermore, the movement from individual to communal perspectives is characteristic of the Songs of Ascents (see Psalms 121–124; 129; 131).

130:1-4. In a real sense, the memorable opening phrase of Psalm 130 expresses the location or condition from which all the laments arise; the psalm is often known simply by the Latin rendering of this phrase, *de profundis*. The word "depths" (מעמקים *ma'ămaqqîm*) names the chaotic forces that confront human life with destruction, devastation, and death, and that are regularly symbolized by water (see NRSV, "deep waters" in Ps 69:2, 14). The exodus is described as being evoked by the people's crying out to God (see Exod 3:7, 9), and the prophet of the exile recalls the exodus as God's making "the depths of the sea a way for the redeemed to cross over" (Isa 51:10 NRSV). Given this pattern, it is crucial that the psalmist cries out to God, asking for a sort of personal exodus and perhaps encouraging Israel to anticipate a new exodus as well (see vv. 7-8). The repetition of "voice" (vv. 1-2) demonstrates the steplike pattern that is characteristic of the Songs of Ascents (see Pss 120:5-7; 121:1-4,

7-8; 122:4-5, 6-8; 123:1-4). The final word in v. 2 (תחנון *taḥănûn*) can mean more generally "supplications," but as the NIV suggests, the root contains the nuance of "mercy." This nuance is particularly appropriate here, since v. 3 makes it clear that the destructive forces confronting the psalmist are to be traced in part to his or her own sinfulness (see also v. 8).

In concert with the vocabulary of vv. 3-4 and vv. 7-8, "cry for mercy" in v. 2 recalls God's self-revelation to Moses in Exodus 34, an episode that brings to a culmination the story of the people's disobedience in making the golden calf (see Exod 32:1-14). There God reveals the divine self to be "gracious" (Exod 34:6; the same root lies behind the NIV's "cry for mercy" in Ps 130:2) and "abounding in steadfast love" (Exod 34:6 NRSV; see Exod 34:7; Ps 130:7), and these attributes are manifested concretely in God's forgiveness (see Exod 34:9; Ps 130:4) of the people's "iniquity" (Exod 34:7, 9; see the plural in Ps 130:3, 8). God's willingness to forgive makes possible the renewal of the covenant and thus the continuation of the "awesome thing" that God will do with God's people (Exod 34:10; the *niphal* of the same Hebrew root [ירא *yārē*] appears in Ps 130:4 as "may be revered"). Thus the psalmist's question (see Ps 143:2) and response in vv. 3-4 constitute an eloquent affirmation of God's essential character, and the echoes of Exodus 34 prepare for the direct address of Israel in v. 7. Apparently because of the unusual form of the verb in v. 4b, but perhaps because the translators had a different text, the LXX of v. 4b reads, "according to your law." This reading contains the profound theological insight that God's law is ultimately grace; it might also serve to call further attention to the allusions to Exodus 34, which is part of "the law," or the Torah. The Hebrew, however, is to be preferred.

130:5-6. The syntax of these verses is unusual. For instance, v. 6a has no verb, and the word "waits" has to be supplied from v. 5. Furthermore, the apparent redundancy of v. 6bc leads some translators to omit v. 6c. The repetition in v. 6bc, however, draws out the poetic line; thus it reproduces literally the effect of waiting (see Ps 5:3, although the verb the NRSV translates "watch" differs).

Furthermore, this steplike pattern of repetition is characteristic of the Songs of Ascents (see above on vv. 1-2), and it is evident as well in the repetition of "wait(s)" (קוה *qwh*, v. 5) and "my soul" (vv. 5a, 6a). The psalmist can "watch" (v. 6bc) with anticipation, because God does not "watch iniquities" (v. 3, author's trans.). This instance of repetition thus calls attention again to the character of God. The psalmist's waiting is based on the conviction that God is fundamentally gracious and forgiving. Waiting is the persistent posture of God's servants (note the servant-master relationship implied by the address of God as "Lord" in vv. 1b, 3b, 6a), whose own sinfulness appears to belie God's sovereignty and who also experience the destructive effects of the sinfulness of others (see Ps 129:1-2). In short, the psalmist's waiting articulates the eschatological perspective that pervades the psalter, which regularly proclaims God's sovereignty among persons and in circumstances that seem to deny it (see Psalms 2; 13; 93; 96–99; 126; Introduction). In the midst of their troubles, self-imposed or inflicted by others, the psalmists wait and encourage others to wait as well (see Pss 25:3, 5, 21; 27:14; 37:34; 52:9; see also the NRSV note). The verb "hope" (יחל *yḥl*) is synonymous with "wait" (see Isa 51:5, where they occur together; see also Pss 31:24; 33:18, 22; 71:14; Lam 3:21, 24). Because God's Word relates and represents God's grace, to hope in God's Word is to hope in God, as v. 7 will suggest (see Pss 119:74, 81, 114, 147).

130:7-8. As elsewhere, the psalmist's faith and hope impel him or her to encourage others to be faithful and hopeful (v. 7a; see Pss 22:22-23; 27:14; 31:23-24; 32:8-11; 34:3, 5, 8-14; 51:13-14; 131:3). The repetition of "hope" connects the conclusion of the psalm to vv. 5-6, and the recurrence of the preposition "with" (עם *'im*) links the final profession of faith to the earlier one in v. 4, while at the same time suggesting that the experience of God's forgiveness and love and redemption is nothing less than the experience of God's own presence (v. 4, for instance, can be construed to mean that people experience forgiveness when they are "with you"). As suggested above, the focus is on God's character. Israel's future does not depend on its own worthiness or ability to save itself but on God's faithful love and ability to redeem. The words "steadfast love" (v. 7) and "iniquities" (v. 8) recall Exodus 34, which narrates this same good news. The psalmists regularly celebrate God's steadfast love in songs of praise (see Pss 33:5, 18, 22; 98:3; 100:5; 103:4, 8, 11, 17; 117:2) and appeal to God's steadfast love in prayers for help (see Pss 25:6-7; 31:7, 16, 21; 32:10; 51:1; Introduction).

It may be coincidental, but the word "great" (הרבה *harbēh*) in v. 7 represents the same Hebrew root as "greatly" in Ps 129:1-2. Even if coincidental, this verbal link encourages a sequential reading of the two psalms, and it suggests that the greatness of the opposition to Israel is more than matched by the greatness of God's will and ability to redeem. The repetition of "redeem," as well as the adjective "all" (v. 8), make the final profession impressively comprehensive (see Ps 25:22, and note "wait" in 25:3, 5, 21). No sin or setback will be of sufficient depth to separate God's people from God's amazing grace and faithful love (see Rom 8:38-39).

REFLECTIONS

1. The power of Psalm 130 has been evident throughout the centuries of its use. Given its honest confrontation of sinfulness (vv. 3, 8) and the psalmist's humble professions of dependence on God's mercy (vv. 4-8), it is understandable that Psalm 130 became by the fifth century one of the church's seven penitential psalms (see Psalms 6; 32; 38; 51; 102; 143), an ecclesiastical grouping that perhaps originated with Augustine. Not surprisingly, Psalm 130 was one of Martin Luther's favorites; one of Luther's most well-known hymns is his metrical version of this psalm. Another of the early Reformers, Theodore Beza, is said to have died with the words of Ps 130:3 on his lips.[476]

476. See Prothero, *The Psalms in Human Life and Experience*, 141.

It is also said that John Wesley heard Psalm 130 performed as an anthem on May 24, 1738, at St. Paul's Cathedral. According to R. E. Prothero, "the psalm was one of the influences that attuned his [Wesley's] heart to receive that assurance of his salvation by faith, which the evening of the same day brought to him in the room at Aldersgate Street."[477] By Wesley's own account, his heart was "strangely warmed," not unlike, perhaps, those two disciples on the Emmaus road, who felt their "hearts burning within" them as Jesus interpreted to them what was written about him "in the law of Moses, the prophets, and the psalms" (Luke 24:32, 44 NRSV).

2. This is not to say that the psalms are predictions of Jesus, but psalms like 130 certainly do testify to the kind of God whose presence in "the depths" would ultimately be expressed by the death of Jesus on a cross. After all, the really striking thing about Psalm 130 is the psalmist's conviction that God is somehow present in the depths, or is at least within earshot. This is the paradox of the prayer, since the depths represent the forces of all that oppose God and since the psalmist's own turning away from God is at least partially responsible for his or her present despair. The good news is that God will not so easily be rejected; God's presence and power can be, must be reckoned with in every human experience—even in the depths, even on a cross! At this point, it may be helpful to distinguish, as Terence Fretheim does, among varying intensifications of God's presence. As he puts it, "The Old Testament language of absence (e.g., 'hide,' 'withdraw,' 'forsake,' etc.) always entails presence at some level of intensification, albeit diminished."[478] In any case, the psalmist's cry from the depths *to God* articulates the conviction that led Israel to cry out from bondage in Egypt and from exile in Babylon, and that led Jesus to cry out to God from the cross—no place or circumstance is beyond the reach of God's forgiving, loving, redeeming presence and power (see Commentary on Psalms 13; 22; 69; 139).

3. This conviction has profound implications for understanding God and ourselves. It means, as Miller suggests, that God "is subject to being moved, responsive, affected by the human cries out of the depths."[479] This kind of God opens the divine self to the vulnerability of being in relationship with a sinful humanity. God's sovereignty, therefore, cannot be the exercise of sheer force but the power of committed love. For the people of God, it means that we shall live not only with the destructive effects of our own sinfulness (vv. 3, 8) but also with the suffering we experience from others when we do manage to be faithful and obedient (see Ps 129:1-2). In other words, the faithful life inevitably involves waiting upon the Lord and hoping in God's word. Because God's "power is made perfect in weakness" (2 Cor 12:9 NRSV), we, empowered by faith and hope, are able to say with the apostle Paul, "Whenever I am weak, then I am strong" (2 Cor 12:10 NRSV; see Isa 40:30-31).

477. Prothero, *The Psalms in Human Life and Experience*, 230.
478. Fretheim, *The Suffering of God*, 65.
479. Miller, *Interpreting the Psalms*, 140.

Psalm 131:1-3, Like the Weaned Child That Is with Me

COMMENTARY

Psalm 131 is the twelfth of the Songs of Ascents (see Overview on Psalms 120–134). The repetition of the exhortation to hope (Pss 130:7; 131:3) indicates that Psalms 130 and 131 should be read together. Furthermore, Psalm 130 calls for a posture of humility that

Ps 131:1-2 eloquently expresses. The metaphor of a child with its mother is not unexpected in a collection that may have derived from or been used by groups of pilgrims on their way to Jerusalem (see Overview on Psalms 120–134) and that displays elsewhere a concern with families and children (see Pss 122:8; 127:3-5; 128:3, 6; 133:1). Even so, v. 2 is striking, because a straightforward translation of v. 2c (see NRSV) suggests that the psalmist is almost certainly a woman. Several scholars even suggest that Psalm 131 may have originally been uttered by a woman as she carried her young child along the way to Jerusalem, perhaps even up the steps toward the Temple. While it is difficult to be too confident about such specific proposals, it is clear that the imagery in v. 2 involves the experience of a mother and child; most likely, the psalm was authored by a mother on the basis of her own experience of comforting children. Other songs and prayers were, of course, written and spoken by women in various contexts (see Exod 15:20-21; 1 Sam 2:1-10; Jdt 16:1-7; Luke 1:47-55).

131:1. The psalm begins with a series of three negatives that eschew pride and arrogance. The word "heart" (לב *lēb*, which could also be translated "mind") in the first clause suggests internal matters; the psalmist is free of destructive pride and haughty thoughts (see 1 Sam 2:3; 2 Chr 26:16; 32:25; Pss 101:5; 138:6; Prov 16:5; 18:12; Ezek 28:2, 5, 17; Hos 13:6). The word "eyes" (עינים *ĕnayim*) in v. 1b suggests external things; raised or haughty eyes are associated in Prov 6:16-19 with destructive behaviors (see Prov 21:4; Isa 2:11; 5:15). In other words, the psalmist affirms that in both thought and deed, she has been humble. The words the NIV translates as "great matters" and "things too wonderful" are ordinarily understood to designate arrogant, self-centered pursuits that the psalmist properly avoided. This may be the correct interpretation, but Miller points out that these words elsewhere refer almost exclusively to God's great and wonderful works. Therefore, he suggests that the third clause of v. 1 may well indicate the "inappropriateness on the part of the woman and

mother to care about and bother with theology," and he considers it likely that v. 1 is "an indication of the role restrictions placed upon women in the patriarchal structure of Israelite society."[480] Indeed, this restriction may account, at least in part, for the struggle implied in v. 2—that is, the woman's need to find a calmness of soul, a peace of mind and heart, that is denied her by her social setting.

131:2. The woman finds peace in her acceptance by and dependence upon God. The grammatical construction that begins v. 2 is emphatic. Despite restrictive circumstances—ones that perhaps made humility as much coercion as choice—the psalmist affirms that she *really has* found a certain equilibrium (the first verb in v. 2 seems to mean literally "to be even," "to be smooth") and security with God, like her child (a member, of course, of another devalued class in the ancient world as well as the modern world) has found with her. The child is not an infant but a "weaned child." Having once found acceptance and satisfaction (the Hebrew root of "weaned child" [גמל *gml*] means fundamentally to "deal fully with") and nurture at the mother's breast, the weaned child returns for comfort and security to the mother's loving embrace.

131:3. As Mays points out, "Verse 2 prepares for and interprets verse 3."[481] In short, the image of the loving, comforting mother embracing her needy child portrays Israel's hope (see Deut 1:31; Isa 66:13; Jer 31:20; Hos 11:1-9). The vulnerable God (see Commentary on Psalm 130), whose choices are restricted by the rebellious stance of the wicked (see Ps 129:1-2) and by the iniquities of God's own people (see Ps 130:3, 8), will finally do nothing other than lovingly embrace God's children, including both the victims of pain and those who by their iniquities have inflicted pain upon other people and upon God. Such incomprehensible love and amazing grace are the hope of Israel and of the world (see Ps 130:7)—then, now, and forever (see Pss 121:8; 125:2).

480. Patrick D. Miller, *They Cried to the Lord: The Form and Theology of Biblical Prayer* (Minneapolis: Fortress, 1994) 240.
481. Mays, *Psalms,* 408.

REFLECTIONS

1. Remarkable in its beauty and its brevity, Psalm 131 performs the valuable service of eloquently enlarging the stock of metaphors that most people ordinarily use for understanding God—God is the loving, compassionate, comforting mother, who, although regularly pained and aggrieved and fatigued by her own children, welcomes them back into her arms and bears them up along a difficult way (see above on Ps 25:6). As for the human side, Psalm 131 commends the style of life that the psalms regularly describe as "righteous" and "happy"—utter trust in and childlike dependence upon God for life and future (see Commentary on Psalms 1; 2). Thus, for the Christian reader, Psalm 131 cannot help being a reminder that Jesus performed the mother's role of Psalm 131 as he took children into his arms and commended them as models for entrance into the reign of God (Matt 18:1-4; Mark 9:33-37; 10:13-16).

2. Consider further the probability that as a woman in a patriarchal society, the psalmist's humility was in some sense forced upon her (see above on v. 1). That the psalmist's experience of oppression impelled her to seek and find comfort with God should in no sense be taken as justification for oppression. Rather, Psalm 131 gives us a glimpse of the beginnings of women's experience of equality in God's sight. It is no coincidence that as he proclaimed and embodied the reign of God, Jesus readily accepted and befriended women and children (see Mark 9:33-37; 10:13-16; 15:40-41; John 20:11-18). Therefore, it is not surprising that in a remarkable reversal of social practices in the ancient Near Eastern world, women were among the leaders of the early church (see Acts 18:26; Rom 16:1, 3; 1 Cor 16:19). In short, as she experienced the liberating acceptance of God, the humble and humbled psalmist experienced the revolutionary, hopeful good news that to be set free by God means never to be a slave again to human masters. The only proper master of humans is God, the recognition of whose sovereignty creates, not patterns of human domination, but a community of sisters and brothers who are *mutually* servants, each of the other (see Mark 10:41-45; Gal 3:28).

Psalm 132:1-18, For the Lord Has Chosen Zion

COMMENTARY

The thirteenth of the Songs of Ascents (Psalms 120–134), Psalm 132 stands out in the collection, because it is noticeably longer than the others. Its length seems to signal its special importance. The Songs of Ascents probably originally served as a collection used by pilgrims on the way to or upon arrival at Jerusalem (see Overview on Psalms 120–134), and Psalm 132 impressively articulates the theological rationale for making the pilgrimage—namely, Zion is God's chosen place (vv. 13-14; see Pss 122:1-2, 9; 125:1-2; 126:1; 128:5; 129:5; 133:3; 134:3), as well as the site of the Davidic throne (see Commentary on Psalm 122, esp. vv. 4-5).

The connection between Zion and the Davidic dynasty is implied in Psalm 122 and perhaps in Psalm 127 (see the superscription), but Psalm 132 clearly articulates the connection (see also Ps 78:67-72). For this reason, Psalm 132 especially recalls 2 Sam 6:1-19, the account of David's bringing of the ark to Jerusalem (see Ps 132:1-10), and 2 Samuel 7, Nathan's announcement that David would not build a house for God but that God would build a house for David (see Ps 132:11-12, 17-18). The precise relationship between 2 Samuel 6–7 and Psalm 132 is not clear, and opinions vary widely. Some scholars conclude that Psalm 132 is very early, to be dated to the time of Solomon. In short, they suggest that the chronicler's account of Solomon's use of Ps 132:8-9 (see 2 Chr 6:41) at the dedication of the Temple is essentially accurate historically, in which case Psalm 132 pre-dates the final form of 2 Samuel 6–7. The chronicler's account is a post-exilic retelling of Israel's story, however, and the chronicler's use of Psalm 132 may suggest its late origin. Thus some scholars conclude that the psalm originated as a poetic rendering of the material in 2 Samuel 6–7 for the purpose of expressing hope for the post-exilic generations.

The latter view is more likely, especially considering the place of Psalm 132 in the psalter. Psalm 89, the final psalm in Book III, rehearses at length the rejection of the Davidic dynasty; Books IV–V seem to have been shaped to respond to the crisis of exile and its aftermath, which included the ongoing loss of the monarchy (see Commentary on Psalms 89; 90; 107; Introduction). In this regard, "all the hardships" (v. 1) of David may refer not only to the trouble he took to rescue the ark but also to the apparent rejection of the Davidic dynasty, recounted in Psalm 89. Furthermore, vv. 17-18 seem to suggest that no king currently is in place; perhaps not coincidentally, the word "disgrace" (בשת *bōšet*) in 132:18*a* recalls Ps 89:45, where the disgrace belongs to David and the pronouncement concerning David's "crown" in 132:18*b* reverses the reality stated in Ps 89:39. In any case, Psalm 132 would eventually have been understood in the context of the realities of the post-exilic era, and these realities are articulated very well in the immediate context of the Songs of Ascents—namely, the subjugation of God's people by their enemies (see Pss 123:3-4; 126:4-6; 129:1-2) and the people's acute awareness of their own iniquities (see Ps 130:3, 8). As Allen suggests, the placement of Psalm 132 encourages the reader to hear it as an articulation of the hope called for in Pss 130:7; 131:3. Thus the references to David are to be heard messianically; they are a way of symbolizing concretely the hope for the future of God's people.[482]

The structure of Psalm 132 is that of a prayer (vv. 1-10) and a response to the prayer (vv. 11-18). The content and movement of the first section are paralleled in the second. Verses 1-5 are David's vow to God, while

482. See Allen, *Psalms 101–150*, 209.

vv. 11-12 are God's vow to David (see "swore" in vv. 2, 11). After vv. 6-7 report the discovery of the ark, v. 8 appears to invite the Lord to accompany the ark to "your resting place." Verses 13-15 correspond to vv. 6-8 as they report the Lord's acceptance of the invitation and God's blessing of Zion (see "resting place" in vv. 8, 14). The prayer for priest and people in v. 9 is answered in v. 16, and the prayer for David in v. 10 is answered in vv. 17-18. The repetition represented by the NRSV's "turn away" (v. 10) and "turn back" (v. 11) serves as a hinge between the two main sections.

132:1-10. The imperative "remember" (זכור *zĕkôr*) in v. 1 recalls Ps 89:47, 50 where the rejected anointed one makes the same plea. The Hebrew word translated "hardships" also recalls Psalm 89. The same word appears in the promise that no one "will oppress" (v. 22) the anointed one, but Ps 132:1 seems to assume, in accordance with Ps 89:38-51, that the anointed one has indeed been oppressed. As the NIV suggests, v. 1 should not be linked so closely with v. 2; that is, the word "hardships" (ענות *'ūnôt*) suggests something more severe than the efforts of David described in vv. 3-5.

The vow recorded in vv. 3-5 does not appear elsewhere. These verses seem to be an imaginative poetic rendering of the kind of sentiments David expresses in 2 Sam 7:1-2; however, the remainder of the psalm shows no interest in David's specific concern, which is so evident in 2 Samuel 7—that is, the building of a house for the Lord. In fact, vv. 6-7 allude more clearly to 2 Samuel 6, the account of the bringing of the ark to Jerusalem. The precise sense of vv. 6-7, however, is elusive. For instance, it is not clear what the antecedent of "it" is supposed to be. Is it the ark (see v. 8)? Or is it David's oath (vv. 3-5)? Furthermore, it is not entirely clear that "Ephrathah" and "Jaar" are intended to designate specific geographical places; even if they are, the precise locations are unknown. The most frequent conclusion is that the first term refers to the environs of Bethlehem, David's home, and that the second is a poetic designation of Kiriath-jearim, where the ark is located in 1 Sam 6:19–7:2. Thus vv. 6-7 seem to have in view David's movement of the ark from Kiriath-jearim to Jerusalem (cf. 1 Sam

7:1 and 2 Sam 6:3). But who are the "we" of v. 6 and the "us" of v. 7? This, too, is unclear, but the most compelling suggestion is offered by Elizabeth F. Huwiler, who concludes that vv. 6-7 both recall David's story and articulate the current experience of worshipers in Jerusalem—for instance, pilgrims who are on the way to or have arrived at Jerusalem (see Overview on Psalms 120–134). As she puts it: "The 'we,' the voice of the worshiping community, functions both to bring the David story from the historical past into the liturgical present and to transport the congregants from current worship setting into that same historical past."[483]

In other words, vv. 6-7 may indicate that pilgrims to Jerusalem understood their journey as being analogous to David's earlier journey to Jerusalem with the ark; they, too, are accompanied by the presence of God (see Psalm 121). At the same time, of course, they would have realized that God had already taken up the divine residence in Jerusalem (see Pss 99:5; 122:1).

Verse 8 can also be understood as both an allusion to the past and a present petition. With an eye to the past, v. 8 would be heard as a poetic invitation to God to join David on the journey to Jerusalem. The grammatical construction of v. 8 actually makes this sense unlikely, however (there is no "and go" or "and come" in the Hebrew of v. 8*a*); since, from the perspective of present worshipers, God is already present in Zion, v. 8 can also be heard as a request for God to protect or deliver Zion. This is the more usual sense of "rise up" (קום *qûm*, v. 8*a*; see Ps 3:7). Verse 8*a* could thus be translated, "Rise up, O LORD, for the sake of your resting place." This construal would also be congruent with the frequent role of the ark in protecting or delivering God's people (see Num 10:35).[484] It also puts the request in v. 8 more in line with those of vv. 9-10, especially v. 10, which sounds like a plea for protection or deliverance. The references in vv. 1, 10 to David and to David's apparent need provide an envelope structure for the first section.

132:11-18. As suggested above, David's oath to God (vv. 2-5) is matched by God's oath to David (vv. 11-12). In general terms, vv. 11-12 again recall 2 Samuel 7, but with glaring exceptions. For instance, the key word in 2 Samuel 7—"house" (see Commentary on Psalm 122)—is missing in Psalm 132. Furthermore, 2 Samuel 7 does not use the word "covenant" (ברית *běrît*) to describe the promise to David. This word more clearly recalls Psalm 89 (see vv. 3, 28, 34, 39). Psalm 132:11-18 would have made especially good sense in view of the exile and its aftermath, during which the monarchy remained extinct but Zion was recovered. The conditional sentence in v. 12 would have served to explain the disappearance of the monarchy—the Davidic descendants disobeyed God. Verses 13-16 focus on the aspects of the pre-exilic era that were recovered—Jerusalem (including a rebuilt Temple), the priesthood, and an identity as God's people. Of particular interest is the clear emphasis on God's initiative. *God,* not David, "has chosen Zion" (v. 13); the repetition of "desired" (vv. 13*b*, 14*b*) reinforces the point. In v. 15, God promises to do what David himself did in 2 Sam 6:19.

Just as references to David envelope vv. 1-10, so also promises to David provide an envelope for vv. 11-18 (see vv. 11-12, 17-18). The language of v. 17 strongly implies that the monarchy no longer exists (see Ezek 29:21, where the image of a horn sprouting suggests the restoration of something that has been destroyed; see also 2 Sam 2:17, where "lamp" represents the possibility of a future). Thus the psalm concludes on a note of hope, but it is open-ended enough to have been understood in several ways as the post-exilic era unfolded. Some, no doubt, looked toward a literal restoration of the Davidic monarchy. Others seem to have applied the Davidic ideology to the people as a whole (see Pss 105:15; 149:5-9; Isa 55:3). Still later, the early Christians would claim to see in Jesus of Nazareth the fulfillment not only of the Davidic hope but also of the Zion theology as well. Thus Jesus would be proclaimed both a son of David (see Matt 1:2) and the one whom God had chosen for the divine habitation (see John 1:14).

---

483. Elizabeth F. Huwiler, "Patterns and Problems in Psalm 132," in *The Listening Heart: Essays in Wisdom and the Psalms in Honor of Roland E. Murphy, O. Carm.,* ed. K. G. Hogland, E. F. Huwiler, J. T. Glass, R. W. Lee, JSOTSup 58 (Sheffield: JSOT, 1987) 207.

484. See Huwiler, "Patterns and Problems in Psalm 132," 204.

REFLECTIONS

1. Because of its focus on both David and Zion, Psalm 132 has traditionally been classified as either a royal psalm or a song of Zion (or both). Like other royal psalms (see Psalms 2; 18; 20–21; 45; 72; 89; 110; 144; Introduction) and songs of Zion (see Psalms 46; 48; 76; 84; 87; 122; Introduction), Psalm 132 articulates Israel's conviction that the rule of God was manifested concretely in the world of people, space, and time (see Reflections on the above-listed psalms). The traditional use of Psalm 132 on the Sunday that celebrates the Reign of Christ is a reminder that Christianity has not abandoned the scandalous particularity of the royal psalms and the Zion songs, or the inevitable connection between David and Zion. Rather, Jesus has been proclaimed pre-eminently as *the* royal son (see Ps 2:7), who both proclaimed and concretely embodied God's justice and righteousness (see Ps 72:1). Furthermore, the incarnation of Jesus presents him as the successor of what Zion symbolized—the earthly locus of God's presence and power (see Mark 13:1-2; 14:58; 15:29; see also Commentary on Psalms 48; 122).

2. As Mays suggests, Ps 132:1 is particularly worthy of note in view of the larger canonical context. He notes that where the NIV and the NRSV translate "all the hardships," the Jewish Publication Society translates "his great self-denial." He then further observes:

> His [David's] self-denial served the dwelling of the LORD in the midst of his people. A resonance sets in with another poem that speaks of one who took the form of a servant, and, being found in human form, humbled himself, and in his obedience unto death (Phil. 2:6-8) has become God with us and God for us, the presence and power of the kingdom of God. The need for a Messiah who keeps the covenant and promise of horn and lamp for David to appear in Zion are fulfilled in him.[485]

485. Mays, *Psalms*, 412.

Psalm 133:1-3, In Praise of Unity Among God's People

COMMENTARY

Psalm 133 is the fourteenth of the Songs of Ascents (Psalms 120–134). Given the probable origin and use of the collection by pilgrims on the way to or upon arrival at Jerusalem (see Overview on Psalms 120–134), it is not surprising that Psalm 133 is akin to several other Songs of Ascents in its use of the imagery of family (v. 1; see Pss 122:8; 127:3-5; 128:3, 6; 131:2). But as in the others, family concerns are set within the larger context of God's whole people (v. 3; see Pss 122:6-8; 128:3-6; 131:2-3). Adele Berlin even argues that the main theme of Psalm 133 is "the reunification of the country"—that is, "the dew of Hermon," representing the people of the northern kingdom, is to flow down upon Zion, the center of the southern kingdom.[486] While absolute certainty is elusive, it is clear that the focal point of Psalm 133 is finally not on local families but on Zion (v. 3), which is the rallying point and gathering place for God's larger family (see Pss 122:4; 125:1-2; 126:1). The pilgrims gathered there to receive God's blessing (v. 3). Not coincidentally, it is precisely the climactic themes of Zion and blessing that link Psalm 133 closely with Psalms 132 (see vv. 13-15) and 134 (see v. 3).

Verse 1 may have circulated at one time as a proverbial saying. In any case, it introduces

486. Adele Berlin, "On the Interpretation of Psalm 133," in *Directions in Hebrew Poetry*, ed. Elaine R. Follis, JSOTSup 40 (Sheffield: JSOT, 1987) 145.

the concept of unity or harmony; v. 1 itself does view family on a local level. The only other occurrence of the expression "when kindred live together" is in Deut 25:5, where the concern is with the responsibilities attendant upon members of an extended family in order to provide for and perpetuate the family. As Deut 25:5-10 makes clear, and as everyone knows from experience, harmony does not always prevail within extended families. When it does, v. 1 asserts, it is "good and pleasant" (see Ps 135:3, where the same two adjectives describe God; Ps 147:1, where they describe what it is like to praise God; see also Ps 128:2, 5).

The effect of the similes of oil and dew in vv. 2-3 is to broaden significantly the focus of v. 1. The Hebrew repetition represented by "good" (טוב ṭôb, v. 1)/"precious" (ṭôb, v. 2) links vv. 1 and 2. The steplike pattern is characteristic of the Songs of Ascents (see Pss 120:5-7; 121:1-4, 7-8; 122:6-8). An even more noticeable instance is evident in vv. 2-3, where the verb "to go down" (ירד yārad) occurs three times in an identical form (NIV, "running down," twice in v. 2, and "falling" in v. 3). This repetition re-creates literarily and visually the effect of oil or dew slowly flowing downward, as does the repetition of "beard" (זקן zāqān). The question remains, of course, as to what the two similes intend to communicate. The pouring of oil over the head seems to have been an act of hospitality, signaling joy and relatedness (see Pss 23:5; 92:10; 141:5), as well as an official act of consecrating kings and priests. Both senses would be appropriate here, but the mention of Aaron especially calls to mind the latter

(see Exod 28:41). Insofar as v. 2 looks back to v. 1 (note the repetition in vv. 1-2), the message would be that family unity is a joyful, even a holy, thing.

It is likely, however, that the poet intended v. 2 to look forward to v. 3 as much as or more than backward to v. 1 (note the repetition of "running down"/"falling"). The allusion to Aaron's consecration has already served to begin to broaden the focus beyond the local extended family, and the mention of Zion in v. 3 goes even further in this direction. Mount Hermon, located in the north some 200 kilometers from Jerusalem, was known for its abundant dew. In other words, the abundance of outlying areas properly belongs with Zion. While this may be, as Berlin suggests, an appeal for national unity, it serves clearly also to shift the focus from the local family to the whole people. The shift is completed by "there"—Zion—in v. 3. The word "blessing" (see Pss 128:4-5; 132:15; 134:3) gathers up the meaning of the phrase "good and pleasant" from v. 1, but by the end of the poem it is clear that the ultimate goodness that God intends is the gathering of God's larger family, the whole people of God. When God's people gather in Jerusalem, God's place, they experience their true family and home, for they are in touch with the true source of their life—God's presence. As Mays concludes: "It is this abundant life, which Israel can receive only in its unity, and only from the Presence at this place that is the *summum bonum* [that is, "the greatest good"; see v. 1]. The life that the Lord gives his people in their unity is the supreme family value."[487]

487. Mays, *Psalms,* 414.

REFLECTIONS

1. Psalm 133 reflects an obvious concern in ancient Israel that is a perennial concern in every culture: family values. The family is a crucial institution. It affects everyone, for good or ill. By its very nature, it can be the place where one experiences and learns intimacy, love, and growth, or it can be the place where one experiences and learns resentment, abuse, and destructive behavior. Clearly, v. 1 commends the former, but the expansive perspective of vv. 2-3 puts the consideration of family values in the larger context of the relationship between God and God's people. The effect is to relativize the importance of the individual family; it cannot be in any unqualified sense the most important institution in a society.

The teachings and actions of Jesus move in the same direction as does Psalm 133, and they serve to bring into focus the radical implications of this direction. In the Gospel of Mark, for instance, when Jesus' mother and brothers come to see him, he looks at those around him and says, "Here are my mother and my brothers! Whoever does the will of God is my brother and sister and mother" (Mark 3:35-36 NRSV). In short, the most important sphere of relatedness is defined as the larger family of God's people (see also Luke 11:27-28; 12:51-53). John Dominic Crossan captures eloquently the radical implications of Jesus' words and deeds, ones that are in keeping with the direction of Psalm 133:

> The family is society in miniature, the place where we first and most deeply learn how to love and be loved, hate and be hated, help and be helped, abuse and be abused. It is not just a center of domestic serenity; since it involves power, it invites the abuse of power, and it is at that precise point that Jesus attacks it. His ideal group is, contrary to Mediterranean and indeed most human familial reality, an open one equally accessible to all under God. It is the Kingdom of God, and it negates that terrible abuse of power that is power's dark specter and lethal shadow.[488]

As Crossan rightly recognizes, "most human familial reality" has not considered the critique of Jesus and Psalm 133. In other words, a focus on the family may well serve to do nothing other than reinforce cultural patterns that regularly exploit women and marginalize children (see Commentary on Psalm 131). Indeed, if the discussion of family values begins and ends with the individual family, apart from the vision and experience of God's larger family, open and accessible to all, then such values will inevitably promote exploitation and abuse.

2. The church's use of Psalm 133 has upheld the psalm's portrayal of God's family as the true definition of familial reality and the true source of blessing and life. While Augustine surely oversimplified the matter, he attributes the origin of monasteries and their brotherhoods to Psalm 133. To be sure, these family orders engendered problems of their own, but they were grounded in the affirmation of a family structure that transcends that of the biological family. The traditional association of Psalm 133 with the Lord's supper makes the same affirmation, for the Lord's supper brings the whole people of God to a family table where all profess their unworthiness and yet all are welcome. Some traditions also suggest the use of Psalm 133 in services of Christian unity, in which "the psalm is a witness that God is at work building a family that transcends all the given and instituted barriers that separate and diminish life."[489] Thus Psalm 133 affirms that life derives ultimately from God's ordaining and blessing and in communion with the whole body of God's people. This profession radically undercuts our pervasive tendency to conclude that life derives from human effort and achievement and that we can successfully manage it on our own (see Commentary on Psalms 1; 2). Psalm 133 is, therefore, an appropriate psalm for the season of Easter, during which we especially celebrate the reality of a life-giving power that both transcends and transforms human efforts and human structures: the resurrection of Jesus. To profess the resurrection is to take our place in God's family, and it is thus to receive an identity that prevents our making an idol of human familial reality in any of its various cultural forms.

488. Crossan, *Jesus*, 60.
489. Mays, *Psalms*, 414.

Psalm 134:1-3, May the Lord Bless You from Zion

COMMENTARY

Psalm 134 is the final Song of Ascents (Psalms 120–134). Given the probable origin and use of the collection among pilgrims on their way to or after arrival at Jerusalem (see Overview on Psalms 120–134), it is evident that Psalm 134 forms a fitting conclusion. After Psalm 133 has celebrated the unity of the gathered people of God in Zion, Psalm 134 addresses the gathered congregation, inviting them to do what they had come to Jerusalem to do: praise the Lord (vv. 1-2). Verse 3, then, has the character of a benediction, which would have effectively sent the people forth with what they had come to Jerusalem to receive: the blessing of God.

While the original cultic setting must remain speculative, it is clear that Psalm 134 has close connections with its literary context, including both the preceding Songs of Ascents and the following psalms, especially Psalm 135. For instance, the congregation is portrayed elsewhere as blessing the Lord (see Ps 124:6); it is described earlier as standing in the house of the Lord (see Ps 122:1-2). The blessing of the people by God is also a theme of the Songs of Ascents (see Ps 128:5, where the blessing is also "from Zion"; 132:15 and 133:3, where the blessing is "there"—in Zion), and God is twice described earlier as "Maker of heaven and earth" (v. 3; see also Pss 121:2; 124:8). The possibility that Psalms 135–137 form an appendix to the Songs of Ascents is suggested by the fact that Ps 135:1-2 also address the people as "servants of the LORD" as they "stand in the house of the LORD." The conclusion of Psalm 135 (vv. 19-21) also recalls Psalm 134 as it invites all the people to "bless the LORD!" and as it repeats the phrase "from Zion" (although this time it is the Lord who is blessed "from Zion"; cf. Ps 134:3).

The verb "bless" (ברך *bārak*) occurs in three of the four poetic lines of Psalm 134. The two imperatives to "bless" (vv. 1a, 2b), addressed to the whole congregation, form an envelope for vv. 1-2, which are structured chiastically (see Introduction)—that is, the two imperatives surround two references to the Temple (vv. 1b, 2a). The people thus surround God with blessing. The final poetic line repeats the word "bless," but the direction is reversed—from God to people. The repetition clearly communicates the mutuality of blessing, and this mutuality points to the remarkable theological claim of the psalm (see Reflections below).

The Hebrew root that the NRSV regularly translates as "bless" (*bārak*) originally meant more literally "to kneel," as in paying homage to a superior (see above on Ps 95:6; see also Pss 16:7; 26:12; 34:1; 63:4; 103:1-2, 22; 115:18; 135:19-20; 145:1, 10). Thus the characterization of the gathered worshipers as servants is especially appropriate in this context (see Pss 31:16; 34:22; 35:27; 113:1; 135:1, 14); it is not necessary to view the imperative as addressed exclusively to priests. The lifting up of the hands could indicate a gesture of praise (see Ps 63:4, where the same gesture is also parallel to "bless"); but it could also indicate the posture of intercessory prayer (see Ps 28:2; Lam 2:19). In either case, the posture indicates loyalty to and dependence upon God.

In terms of the possible original setting and use of Psalm 134, v. 3 makes good sense as a priestly benediction (see Num 6:23-25; Deut 21:5; 2 Sam 2:20; Ps 118:26), pronounced as the pilgrims prepare to leave Jerusalem on the night before they set out (see Isa 30:29). As such, it recalls the affirmation of God's cosmic sovereignty that the pilgrims perhaps made on the journey to (see Ps 121:2) and upon arrival at Jerusalem (see Ps 124:8, where the affirmation also follows the people's blessing of God). More significant, however, are the theological implications of the mutuality of blessing between God and the people, a mutuality that bespeaks the genuine relatedness between God and the people, based ultimately in God's redeeming love (see Ps 130:7-8).

REFLECTIONS

The double call to "bless the Lord," the characterization of the people as servants, and the description of God as "maker of heaven and earth" communicate clearly the people's conviction of God's sovereignty and thus of their dependence upon God (see Commentary on Psalms 1; 2). It is to be expected that the people kneel before God— that is, bless God. What is striking, however, is the mutuality of blessing that is antici- pated in v. 3. Thus there is a sense in which God will kneel before the people! In other words, God will voluntarily take on the servant role that properly belongs to the peo- ple. This mutuality, which ultimately means God's willingness to be vulnerable, results from God's risky choice of Zion (see Ps 132:13-14) and from God's choice to take on the responsibility of providing for Zion's people (see Ps 132:15-18). What promises blessing for God's people promises suffering for God, for the very people committed to blessing God regularly end up burdening God with their iniquities (see Ps 130:3, 8). In short, the mutuality between God and God's people means ultimately that God reveals the divine character to be essentially forgiving and steadfastly loving (see Ps 130:4, 7). Such love explains how a persistently sinful people can dare to anticipate that the cosmic God will bless them from Zion. Such love, in other words, is their only hope (see Pss 130:7; 131:3), a hope that Christians profess to be sealed in Jesus' incarnation of God in the form of a servant (see Phil 2:5-11).

PSALM 135:1-21, YOUR NAME, O LORD, ENDURES FOREVER

COMMENTARY

Although the Songs of Ascents conclude with Psalm 134, it is as if the editors of the psalter intended for Psalms 135–136 to artic- ulate the praise invited by Ps 134:1-2. For instance, like Ps 134:1, Ps 135:1 addresses the worshipers as "servants," and "stand" in Ps 135:2 also recalls Ps 134:1. Furthermore, Ps 135:19-21 uses the key word "bless" (ברך *bārak*) from Psalm 134. Similar themes and concerns connect Psalms 135 and 136 (cf. 135:5 with 136:2-3; 135:8-12 with 136:10- 22), prompting several scholars to suggest that Psalms 135–136 (and perhaps Psalm 137, since, like the Songs of Ascents, it fea- tures Zion) form an appendix to the Songs of Ascents.

It is perhaps not coincidental that Psalms 135–136 also recall Psalms 111–118, which precede Psalm 119 and the Ascents collec- tion. For instance, the opening and conclud- ing *hallelu-yah* of Psalm 135 occurs also in Pss 111:1; 112:1; 113:1, 9; 115:18; 116:19; 117:2. And at several points, Psalm 135 clearly recalls Psalm 115 (cf. 135:6 with 115:3; 135:15-18 with 115:4-8; 135:19-20 with 115:9-11). As for Psalm 136, v. 1 is identical to Ps 118:1, 29. The central theme of Psalm 135—God's universal sovereignty, especially over the gods—is congruent with the apparent purpose of Books IV–V to respond to the crisis of exile and its aftermath (see Commentary on Psalms 90; 93; 95; 96; 97; 98; 99; 107; Introduction). In this regard, too, it may be especially significant that Psalm 135 alludes to several crucial Pentateuchal texts (cf. Ps 135:5 with Exod 18:11; v. 13 with Exod 3:15; v. 14 with Deut 32:36) and summarizes in vv. 7-12 the movement from creation to exodus to entry into the land. In short, despite appearances to the contrary, God rules the world.

Psalm 135 is a hymn or song of praise, but its structure can be outlined in several ways. The fivefold division of the NIV and the NRSV is compelling. As Allen points out, the elements are concentric; that is, vv. 1-4 correspond to vv. 19-21 (invitations to and reasons for praise), and vv. 5-7 correspond to vv. 15-18 (polemic against idols and God's sovereignty).[490] The effect is to focus on vv. 8-14 as the central section; it illustrates the divine sovereignty (vv. 5-7, 15-18) that makes praising and blessing God the appropriate response (vv. 1-4, 19-21).

135:1-4. The imperative "praise" occurs three times in v. 1 and once in v. 3 (see Pss 22:23; 107:1; 148:1-5; 150:1-6). The word "name" (שֵׁם šēm) also occurs in vv. 1 and 3. Connoting "reputation" or "character," it becomes a key word in Psalm 135, occurring again in v. 13. In essence, the whole psalm is a defense of God's character or reputation, especially over against the gods (see vv. 5, 15-18). God is fundamentally "good" (see Pss 100:5; 106:1; 107:1; 118:1, 29). The syntax of v. 3b is ambiguous, but it is syntactically possible to construe the adjective as descriptive of God (see the same ambiguity in Ps 147:1). As v. 4 suggests, God's identity and thus reputation are bound up with God's choice of Israel (see Exod 19:5; Deut 7:7-11). Thus the movement from vv. 1-3 to v. 4 anticipates the movement from v. 13 to v. 14. True to the divine character (v. 13), God will set things right for God's chosen people (v. 14), as opposed to those who make and trust in idols (v. 18).

135:5-7. Verse 5 recalls Jethro's profession of faith in the Lord in the light of the exodus (see Exod 18:11). The issue raised by the bondage in Egypt was "Who is sovereign?" The exodus revealed the Lord's sovereignty (see Exod 15:18). Not surprisingly, God is frequently described as "great" in contexts that explicitly proclaim God's reign (see Pss 47:2; 95:3; 96:4; 99:2). The title "Lord" also communicates sovereignty; its correlate, "servants," occurs in vv. 1, 14. The sphere of God's sovereignty is unlimited, encompassing every dimension of the three-storied universe as it was portrayed in ancient Near Eastern cosmology—heaven, earth, depths (v. 6; see Ps 115:3). The elements of the most impressive and powerful natural phenomenon—the thunderstorm—are under God's control (v. 7; see Exod 19:16; Jer 10:13; 51:16; see also Commentary on Psalm 29). Control of these phenomena was regularly attributed to the Canaanite god Baal, so v. 7 is clearly polemical. That is, it is another way of affirming that

490. Allen, *Psalms 101–150*, 226.

"our LORD is above all gods" (v. 5). The NRSV's "does" in v. 6 and the second "makes" in v. 7 translate the same Hebrew root (עשׂה 'āśâ), which recurs as "work" in v. 15 and "make" in v. 18. The effect of this repetition is to contrast even more sharply the true God who *makes* things happen as opposed to the idols, which are *made* by humans.

135:8-14. The vocabulary of v. 5 has already alluded to the exodus, the culmination of which involved God's "wind" (v. 7; see Exod 14:21; 15:10) driving back the "seas" and the "deeps" (v. 6; see Exod 14:21-22; 15:4, 8, 10), so that God could lead the people to Sinai, where "clouds" and "lightning" awaited them (v. 7; see Exod 19:16; see also Commentary on Psalms 19; 33; 65; 66 for more on the importance of discerning a unity between creation and exodus). In short, vv. 5-7 have amply prepared for the specific focus on the climactic plague in v. 8 (see Exod 13:29-32; Pss 78:51; 105:36; 136:10) and then for the summary of God's actions against Pharaoh in v. 9 (see Exod 4:8-9, 21; Deut 4:34; 26:8; Pss 78:43; 105:27). Pharaoh's people are called "servants" (v. 9), recalling v. 1 and anticipating v. 14, thus sharpening the focus on the issue of sovereignty. The verb "struck down" (נכה nkh) is repeated in v. 10 (see Ps 136:17) as vv. 10-11 continue the recital that culminates with Israel's possession of the land (v. 12; see also Ps 136:21-22). God's defeat of two persons identified by the title "king" (v. 11ab; see Sihon and Og in Num 21:21-35; see also Ps 136:17-20), and indeed God's defeat of "all the kingdoms of Canaan" (v. 11c), further emphasize God's reign. The central section of the psalm culminates in vv. 13-14. The exodus and subsequent victories demonstrate God's enduring "name" and "renown" (see Exod 3:15, where the same two nouns occur). In short, God's actions reveal the content of God's character as one who will set things right for the oppressed and have compassion for people (see Deut 32:36).

135:15-18. In striking contrast to the wondrous activity of God, the idols do absolutely nothing (note the series of negations in vv. 16-17; see also Ps 115:4-7). Verses 15-18 are framed by the occurrences of "work" (v. 15) and "make" (v. 18), which recall "does" and "makes" in vv. 6-7. The idols do not create, because they have been created. The final negation (v. 17b) involves "breath" or "wind," thus recalling v. 7. The "wind" serves God's command, but the idols have no "wind"—no vital power. As v. 18 suggests, the real issue is trust (see Ps 115:8-11). Those who trust their lives to nothing will experience nothingness, whereas those who entrust their lives to the sovereign God will participate in God's enduring future (vv. 12-14).

135:19-21. Thus it is appropriate that God's people "bless the LORD!" (vv. 19-21). The word "bless" (*bārak*) appears originally to have meant "to kneel," as in acknowledging the sovereignty of another (see above on Ps 134:1-2). The repetition effectively makes the point: God eminently deserves the people's allegiance and praise. The different designations in vv. 19-20 may indicate different groups of worshipers (such as priests in v. 19b, temple personnel in v. 20a), or they may all be designations for the whole assembly (see above on Pss 115:9-11; 118:2-4). The phrase "from Zion" in v. 21 recalls Ps 134:3, but the blessing here moves in the opposite direction. Thus Psalm 134–135 together portray the mutuality of blessing that is already evident in Psalm 134. By the end of Psalm 135, the movement has been from praise (vv. 1-4) to praise (vv. 19-21; note especially the opening and closing *hallelu-yah*), the fitting response to the God who is "above all gods" (v. 5) and whose name "endures forever" (v. 13).

REFLECTIONS

Psalm 135 articulates again the conviction that pervades the book of Psalms: God reigns! This conviction, of course, is intimately connected to the first two of the Ten Commandments—no other gods and, in particular, no human-made idols (see Exod 20:3-4). This conviction is always polemical and always pertinent. Israel's immediate inclination was precisely to make an idol and to worship other gods (see Exod 32:1-6), and this inclination seems to be an inevitable human tendency. To be sure, contemporary forms of idolatry may be more subtle but hardly less crass. Idolatry is finally an elevation of the human self to the status of God, and we are masters of that art. The word *masters* characterizes the way we tend to see ourselves. By virtue of our sophisticated scientific knowledge and incredible technological achievements, we are inclined to view ourselves as masters of the universe rather than servants of a universal God.

This confusion is a dangerous one, indeed a deadly one, for to place ultimate trust in ourselves is to consign our destiny to nothingness (v. 18). What, after all, have we accomplished with our amazing scientific discoveries and dazzling technological achievements? *We have created* a situation in which it appears that the future of human civilization hangs in a delicate nuclear and ecological balance. If we can manage not to blow ourselves away suddenly, we appear to be in danger of slowly poisoning the earth and ourselves to death. The irony is that the more powerful we become, the less secure the human future seems to be.

The current situation is obviously complex, and there will be no simple solutions. Indeed, there will be no solutions at all apart from our relinquishment of the seemingly inevitable drive to be masters of the universe. Given the history of humankind, ancient and modern, there is little room for optimism in this regard. But the Bible, including Psalm 135, dares to affirm that there is room for hope—not in ourselves, but in God. Hope for the world will begin not with scientific knowledge but with what the psalmist knows: "The LORD is great . . . above all gods" (v. 5), including ourselves. That kind of knowledge begins and ends where Psalm 135 begins and ends: with praise, the yielding of the human self to God in liturgy and in life. To praise God (vv. 1-3), to bless God (vv. 19-20), means that we shall not be masters of the universe but servants of a universal master. It will mean considering first not what we desire but what "the LORD pleases" (v. 6)—"thy will be done."

The current endangered state of the earth and its peoples is a reminder that the proclamation of God's reign is eschatological; it always is made amid circumstances and people (including ourselves) who deny it. Thus God's sovereignty is what the world considers a strange form of power, not sheer force but the force of suffering love. To praise the Lord is to choose, as Jesus showed, to be a suffering servant. It means that we shall live by faith, not trusting ourselves (v. 18) but entrusting life and future to the God whose name "endures forever" (v. 13; see Commentary on Psalms 8; 100; 104; 115).

PSALM 136:1-26, GOD'S STEADFAST LOVE ENDURES FOREVER

COMMENTARY

Psalm 136 is clearly related to Psalm 135, with which it seems to form an appendix to the Songs of Ascents (see Commentary on Psalm 135). Both are songs of praise, and both begin by citing the Lord's goodness as a basic reason for praise (135:3; 136:1). Furthermore, Ps 136:2-3 recalls Ps 135:5, and Ps 136:5-9 can be viewed as an expansion of Ps 135:6-7, while 136:10-22 are an extended version of 135:8-12. Because of its expanded recital of God's "great wonders" (v. 4), Psalm 136 is often categorized along with Psalms 78; 105–106 as a historical psalm. This label is helpful so long as it is clear that these psalms are not merely objective rehearsals of Israel's story. Each of these four psalms features the Hebrew word translated "wonders" (נפלאות *niplā'ôt*) in 136:4 (although the translations of it differ; see Pss 78:4, 11-12, 32; 105:2, 5; 106:7, 22). Borrowing from Martin Buber's reflection on this Hebrew word, Brueggemann suggests that the historical psalms be viewed under the rubric of "abiding astonishment." Their focus is not so much on the past as on the present as they seek to evoke a response of "*obedience, petition, gratitude, and new political possibility.*"[491] In short, Psalm 136 articulates God's claim upon the world, and it calls for the reader's response (see Commentary on Psalms 78; 105; 106).

The most obvious feature of Psalm 136 is the identical refrain that concludes every verse. Psalm 136:1 itself forms a brief hymn that occurs several times elsewhere (see

1 Chr 16:34; Pss 106:1; 107:1; 118:1, 29). Nearly identical but briefer formulations occur in 2 Chr 5:13; 7:3; 20:21; and Ezra 3:11, where the context indicates that they were used by the congregation as liturgical responses during worship services. Thus the concluding portion of an apparently standard liturgical formula forms the refrain of Psalm 136, which consequently bears the mark of a responsorial liturgy. That is, the congregation probably sang the refrain in response to a leader's singing of the first part of every verse. While absolute certainty is not possible, Psalm 136 more than any other psalm demonstrates the probability of responsorial liturgical use. The precise setting of its ancient use remains elusive.

When Psalm 136 is considered as a literary product in its current placement within the psalter, the effect of the refrain is to give an explicitly theological dimension to this recital of Israel's story. As suggested above, the rehearsal is not meant to be objective. Rather, by way of the refrain, the psalmist affirms that every aspect and moment of Israel's story—from creation (vv. 5-9) to exodus (vv. 10-15) to wilderness journey (vv. 16-20) to possession of the land (vv. 21-22) to the present moment (vv. 23-24), including the daily meal (v. 25)—is pervaded by and dependent upon God's steadfast love. As several scholars suggest, vv. 23-24 seem to take the story beyond the exile to the return from Babylon. This would make Psalm 136 congruent with the perspective of the Songs of Ascents and with the apparent purpose of Books IV–V to

491. Brueggemann, *Abiding Astonishment,* 34.

respond to the crisis of exile and its aftermath (see Commentary on Psalms 90; 107; 120; Introduction). In any case, Israel's fundamental response is to be gratitude (vv. 1-3, 26; see Reflections below).

While it is obvious that the refrain is the most important structural feature of Psalm 136, scholars disagree in their discernment of an outline of the psalm. As suggested above, structural divisions could be made by content (creation, exodus, etc.). Attention to grammatical forms, however, yields a different outline. For instance, following the introductory imperatives (vv. 1-3), the subsequent reasons for praise are introduced in several lines by a preposition followed by a participle. If this pattern marks structural divisions, they would be as follows: vv. 4, 5, 6, 7-9, 10-12, 13-15, 16, 17-22. A different pattern exists in vv. 23-25 before v. 26 returns to an imperative. Such irregularity might aptly represent the irregularity of Israel's history; however, many scholars are intent on finding a more symmetrical structure. Several propose, for instance, four major sections. Each of the first two, vv. 1-9 and vv. 10-18, consist of three triads of verses, and the final two sections, vv. 19-22 and vv. 23-26, consist of four verses each. Jacob Bazak even suggests that regular geometric patterns are formed by the small divisions as well as the whole.[492] Obviously, the scholarly proposals differ markedly. Because they attend to different criteria in each case, they need not be considered mutually exclusive. More significant, in any case, are the refrain and its claim that the origin and history of the world and of Israel are inextricably tied to the love of God.

136:1-9. The titles for God in vv. 2-3 (see also v. 26) recall Ps 135:5. Again, the issue is sovereignty, and exclusive sovereignty is reserved for Israel's God (see Psalm 82). Israel's God alone does the "great wonders" (v. 4) that are recounted in vv. 5-22. Unlike the other historical psalms, God's "wonders" in this case include creation (vv. 5-9). In other words, as in the Pentateuch, Israel here professes that its story begins with creation. The affirmation is a crucial one, for it suggests that Israel's specific story is part of God's wondrous and comprehensive purpose for the whole

cosmos. God's steadfast love lies behind and accounts for the origin of the world. Actually, the recital does not really conclude until v. 25, which returns to the creational perspective of vv. 5-9. This conceptual envelope means that the recital of Israel's story is surrounded by affirmations of God's love for the world and all its creatures. That is, God's steadfast love is also responsible for God's providence for all creation (see Pss 33:5; 36:5-9). God has the whole world in God's hands! (See Commentary on Psalm 19; see also Psalms 33; 65–66; 135; 145–146, which also insist that the creation of the world and the origin of Israel are parts of the same story.)

Verse 4 is linked to vv. 5-9 by repetition of the verb "does"/"made" (עשׂה ʿāśâ, vv. 4-5, 7; see also Ps 135:6-7, 15, 18). The verb makes clear that God's character, the essence of which is steadfast love, is made known by God's creating, redeeming, sustaining activity. Verse 5 calls to mind Prov 3:19, and, of course, it and vv. 6-9 are reminiscent of Genesis 1. The verb "spread out" (רקע rāqaʿ, v. 6) appears as the noun "expanse" in Gen 1:14-15, 17 (see Isa 42:5). Also, "the great lights" (v. 7) are mentioned in Gen 1:16, where their function is also described in a manner similar to Ps 136:8-9 (Gen 1:16 does not name them "sun" and "moon," however; see also Ps 148:3-4). The effect of vv. 5-9 is to affirm that God's wisdom and God's power are ultimately motivated by and are manifestations of God's love.

136:10-22. In one sense, the focus narrows in vv. 10-22 (see Exod 12:29–15:21; Num 21:21-35; Josh 12:1-6; Pss 78:12-16, 23-30, 51-55; 105:26-45; 106:8-12; 135:8-12), but the refrain effectively communicates that in another crucial sense the focus remains as broad as it was in vv. 5-9. In other words, the story of Israel's deliverance from Egypt (that is, from death) and entry into the land (that is, into life) is still the story of the fulfillment of God's creational purposes. To be sure, the particularity is scandalous, and many persons find it particularly problematic that God "struck down great kings" (v. 17) and "killed famous kings" (v. 18) like Sihon and Og (vv. 19-20; see Ps 135:10-11). To many people, this does not seem to be very loving, but the stark realism indicates that God's love is not simply sentimental. God's

---

492. Jacob Bazak, "The Geometric-Figurative Structure of Psalm CXXXVI," *VT* 35 (1985) 129-38.

creational purposes, God's will to grant life to the threatened and the disposessed (see vv. 23-24), cannot finally be opposed with impunity. Egypt and Pharaoh found this out (vv. 10, 15); other famous kings found this out (vv. 17-20); and, to put this dynamic in proper perspective, God's own people and their kings found this out, too—the exile saw the destruction of the monarchy, the death of many persons, and the dispersal of God's people (see Psalm 137).

136:23-26. While it is possible that vv. 23-24 refer simply to the exodus and subsequent events recounted in vv. 10-22, it is likely that they carry the story further by reflecting the return from exile. To be sure, they would certainly have been understood this way in the post-exilic era. In other words,

opposition from neither great and famous kings nor from God's own chosen people could thwart God's steadfastly loving purposes. God remains at work, doing what God had done previously—turning things around for the oppressed (see Exod 2:24). Lest God's activity be perceived too narrowly, v. 25 is a reminder that God's work is for the benefit of "all flesh" (see above on vv. 5-9; see also Pss 104:14-15, 27-28; 145:15-16; 146:7; 147:9). God so loves the world.

In view of the fact that vv. 10-22 in particular have described God's work on earth, it is significant that v. 26 addresses God as "the God of heaven" (see vv. 5, 7-9). Thus v. 26, which recalls vv. 1-3, is a final reminder that Israel professes its God to be the cosmic ruler of the universe.

REFLECTIONS

1. As Bratcher and Reyburn point out, the word "steadfast love" is "the one word which more than any other expresses Yahweh's attitude toward his people."[493] But more than that, according to Psalm 136, steadfast love characterizes the attitude of God toward the whole cosmos, including the earth and all its features and all its creatures. There can be no more profoundly good news than this—that God's attitude toward the world and God's motivation for action are summarized by steadfast love. This concept, of course, is crucial throughout the book of Psalms and elsewhere in the OT (see, e.g., Exod 34:6-7; Pss 5:7; 13:5; 23:6; 25:6-7, 10; 33:5, 18, 22; 103:4, 8, 11, 17; Introduction). As Exod 34:6-7 makes eminently clear, steadfast love inevitably involves God's grace. Thus Psalm 136 ultimately affirms that the origin, continuity, and destiny of the cosmos are dependent upon the grace of God.

2. This expansive profession of faith is crucial for construing the scandalous particularity of vv. 10-22, lest these verses be dismissed simply as ancient nationalistic propaganda or be misused to support the notion that God is partial to one particular group of people. Particularity is necessary and desirable, but any construal of God's will is misguided if it fails to take into account God's love for the whole creation (vv. 5-9) and God's intention to provide for "all flesh" (v. 25). In other words, Psalm 136 proclaims that God rules the world. Thus it joins the other historical psalms as "determined challenges to the autonomy of reason and the autonomy of power."[494] The gratitude to which Ps 136:1-3, 26 invite us will take the form of humble submission of our wills to the will of God. Our lives and the life of the world will be received as loving, gracious gifts of God. Psalm 136 calls us to live in dependence not upon ourselves but upon God (see Commentary on Psalms 1; 2).

3. The use of Psalm 136 at the Easter Vigil is an illustration of the reality that this historical psalm continues to speak to people in and concerning the present. Its use in this liturgical context also affirms the Christian conviction that God's steadfast love continued and continues to be manifested in the life, death, and resurrection of Jesus.

493. Bratcher and Reyburn, *A Translator's Handbook on the Book of Psalms*, 1108.
494. Brueggemann, *Abiding Astonishment*, 44.

Like Psalm 136, Jesus announced God's claim upon the whole world, and he invited people to enter God's reign (see Mark 1:14-15). Jesus proclaimed, represented, and embodied God's amazing grace and the incomparable good news that God steadfastly and eternally loves and provides for the world (see John 3:16-17). Noting the movement of Psalm 136 from God's creation of the cosmos (vv. 5-9) to God's provision of daily bread (v. 25), Mays concludes:

> That brings the story down to every meal and makes the recitation of the LORD's mighty works a preface to every blessing said over the food we eat. It becomes apparent here why our LORD taught us to pray for the coming of the reign of God and the gift of daily bread in one short prayer. They are both part of the continuum of God's mighty works. All of history and each day of living are contained in the story of the LORD's steadfast love.[495]

495. Mays, *Psalms*, 421.

PSALM 137:1-9, BY THE RIVERS OF BABYLON

COMMENTARY

H.-J. Kraus calls Psalm 137 "the only psalm in the psalter that can be dated reliably."[496] If it was not composed in Babylon during the exile (587–539 BCE), it must have originated shortly after the return to Judah, when the pain of exile was still fresh in the minds and hearts of the people. It is quite possible that it was written by a member of the Levitical guilds, which were responsible for music and singing in the Temple (see 2 Chr 25:1-8; Ezra 2:40-42).

The combination of first-person plural and singular voices, the focus on Jerusalem, and even the length of the psalm make it similar to the Songs of Ascents (Psalms 120–134). Given the similarities between Psalms 134 and 135, as well as Psalms 135 and 136, it is likely that Psalms 135–137 form a sort of appendix to the Songs of Ascents (see Commentary on Psalms 135; 136). In view of Pss 135:12 and 136:21-22, the sense of loss and grief articulated by Psalm 137 is all the more acute. The clearly exilic or early post-exilic perspective of Psalm 137 is congruent with the apparent purpose of the Songs of Ascents and of Books IV–V to respond to the crisis of exile and its aftermath (see Commentary on Psalms 90; 107; 120; Introduction).

496. Kraus, *Psalms 60–150*, 501.

The structure of Psalm 137 is debated, but most scholars suggest three divisions. Those suggested by the NIV and the NRSV are acceptable, but it is probably better to combine v. 4 with vv. 1-3. According to this view of the psalm, vv. 1-4 express the exiles' grief, and vv. 7-9 express the exiles' rage and desire for revenge. In between, at the literary and conceptual heart of the poem, vv. 5-6 focus on the crucial activity of remembering. This central concept links vv. 5-6 to vv. 1-4, in which the exiles remember Jerusalem (v. 1), and to vv. 7-9, in which the Lord is called upon to remember Jerusalem as well (v. 7). Thus the importance of memory is pervasive, both literarily and conceptually. For the exiles, remembering Zion means faithfulness to God's place and to God's ongoing purposes. It is an act of resistance; "in a foreign land" (v. 4), they could not sing, but they could and must and did remember.

137:1-4. Babylon was nothing like home for the exiles, and the psalmist expresses the painful reality of remembering Zion in vv. 1-4. The geographical strangeness of the land, with its system of canals between the Tigris and the Euphrates—the "rivers of Babylon"—may have exacerbated the grief when Jerusalem was remembered. Of course, things were only made worse by their captors' sarcastic invitation (v. 3), the effect of which was to ask, "Where is your God?" (see Pss 42:3, 10; 79:10). There was nothing to do but weep, for singing was out of the question in their present location (vv. 2, 4; see Lam 1:2, 16, where the personified Jerusalem weeps at the devastation of exile, and note Lam 1:7, where Jerusalem also "remembers"; see also Ps 42:3). The "LORD's song" (v. 4) would perhaps have been one of the joyful "songs of Zion" (v. 3; see Commentary on Psalms 46; 48; 76; 84; 87; 122). They could be sung only in Jerusalem, the Lord's place, and not in Babylon.

137:5-6. Although the people could not sing in Babylon, they could remember their homeland. The chiastic structure of vv. 5-6a emphasizes this crucial activity:

A   *If I forget you,* O Jerusalem,
 B   *let my right hand* wither!
 B´   Let *my tongue* cling to the roof of my mouth,
A´   *if I do not remember you,*

Addressing the personified Jerusalem as "you" in vv. 5-6, the individual voice asserts that if Jerusalem is not remembered, then music and song will become impossible *forever.* The withered right hand will not be able to pluck the strings of the harp (see v. 2), and the paralyzed tongue will not be able to sing. As painful as it is for the people to remember Jerusalem (v. 1), it would be more painful for them not to remember, for these memories offer hope, indeed life, amid the pain (vv. 1-4) and devastation of exile (vv. 7-9).

137:7-9. The people's request for God to remember them (v. 7) is a plea for God to

share in their suffering. Whereas the psalmist expresses that pain as grief in vv. 1-4, the psalmist voices that grief as anger and outrage in vv. 7-9. The anger is directed first at Edom (v. 7), which apparently took particular advantage of Jerusalem's misfortune at the hands of the Babylonians (see the book of Obadiah, esp. vv. 10-14; Ezek 35:5-15; see also Lam 1:20-22; 3:64). Not surprisingly, since it was the Babylonians who destroyed Jerusalem and took the people into exile, the psalm concludes by addressing a personified Babylon (cf. the personification of Jerusalem in vv. 5-6). While vv. 8-9 shock our sensibilities, and rightfully so, it is necessary to point out that they merely express a sentiment that most Americans would claim; this is clear in v. 8. The Babylonian conquest of Judah certainly involved the deaths of many Judeans, including children, who represent the future of a people. Verse 9 suggests that the Babylonians deserve the same. As Kraus suggests concerning v. 9, it should be understood not only as the expression of a particular individual but also as "a reference to the cruelty of ancient warfare generally,"[497] the typical practices of which are reflected in 2 Kgs 8:12; Isa 13:16; Hos 10:14; Nah 3:10 (see also Revelation 18, esp. vv. 6, 20-24, for another expression of the desire for revenge against "Babylon"). Thus, in view of the cultural context, the wish expressed in vv. 8-9 represents a principle that most Americans routinely espouse: The punishment should fit the crime. Those who have deprived others of a future deserve no future themselves (see Commentary on Psalm 109).

497. Kraus, *Psalms 60–150*, 504.

REFLECTIONS

1. Perhaps because it is a psalm about singing ("songs"/"song" is used five times in vv. 3-4), Psalm 137, with the omission of vv. 7-9, has often been set to music and used in worship services. The psalm in its entirety, however, including its shocking conclusion, has much to teach us about prayer, about ourselves, and about God. One thing it teaches us, for instance, is the lesson that in extreme situations, grief and anger are both inevitable and inseparable. The worst possible response to monstrous evil is to feel nothing. What *must* be felt—by the victims and on behalf of the victims—are grief, rage, outrage. In the absence of these feelings, evil becomes an acceptable commonplace. In other words, to forget is to submit to evil, to wither and die; to remember is to resist, to be faithful, and to live again.

From this perspective, the psalmist's outburst in vv. 8-9 is both a psychological and a theological necessity. The psalmist is motivated toward revenge out of loyalty to Jerusalem—indeed, loyalty to God! John Bright claims of the psalmist, "It would not be too much to say that he hated so because he loved so."[498] Yet, there is no evidence that the psalmist did act out the expressed desire for revenge. Rather, the psalmist expresses these feelings to God in prayer (v. 7) and apparently leaves them with God. Thus the cycle of violence is broken by the psalmist's honesty with God (see Commentary on Psalm 109).

Psalm 137 as a whole, then, is an "invitation to a kind of prayer that is passionate in its utter honesty."[499] To pray is to offer ourselves and our desires—anger as well as grief—to God and to know that God loves us as we are. This aspect of Psalm 137 represents "a drive toward incarnation"; God chooses to be revealed through people "of like passions with ourselves."[500] We must acknowledge that we are no less vengeful than the psalmist was. But the good news is that God loves us and chooses to use us anyway. Thus Psalm 137 points ultimately to forgiveness. It is even possible that the psalmist's cathartic expression of vengeance represents a first step toward forgiving the victimizers. Similarly, after proclaiming God's forgiveness of the sins that led to the exile (Isa 40:1-2), Isaiah proclaims God's word that the mission of exilic and post-exilic Israel is to be "a light to the nations, that my salvation may reach to the end of the earth" (Isa 49:6 NRSV). The desire for revenge gives way to a mission to save. Hate has been replaced by hope.

2. In our time, Psalm 137 cannot help reminding us of the Holocaust, the monstrous victimization of the Jewish people during World War II. Holocaust survivor Elie Wiesel has dedicated his life to making sure the world remembers what happened. Wiesel says frequently that he can tolerate the memory of silence but not the silence of memory. In other words, the Holocaust can be remembered in unutterable horror—silence. But it *must* be remembered. To remember is painful; grief is always painful. To remember is unsettling; anger always unsettles. But to remember is also to resist the same thing's happening again. To remember is to choose to live and to be faithful to God's purpose of life for all people.

Given the mention of "little ones" in v. 9, it is especially revealing to consider Elie Wiesel's special concern for children. It is, perhaps, a clue to the ultimate direction and significance of remembering in Psalm 137—namely, grief and rage energize a memory that eventually takes the form of compassion. Although it is not explicit, we may assume that the psalmist's submission of anger to God obviates the need for actual revenge upon the enemy. It is encouraging, at least, to think that Wiesel's life provides support for this assumption. His remembrance of victimization, a remembrance sustained certainly by grief and rage, is now expressed as compassion for the vulnerable and as faithfulness to God's purpose of life for all God's children. Consider Wiesel's own words:

> When I see a child, any child, I have tears in my eyes [see Ps 137:1]. Especially my own, especially Jewish children, but any children. . . . We [Holocaust survivors] want to caress our children 24 hours a day. We want to shelter them, to show them nothing but joy and beauty. And yet we want them to know. . . .
>
> When I speak of life, I mean, children. To me, nothing is more sacred, nothing more divine, than a child's life. There are two absolutes, life and death. I choose life.[501]

For survivors of victimization, ancient or modern, to express grief and outrage is to live. If Wiesel's life can be taken as evidence, such expression is a necessary first step

498. John Bright, *The Authority of the Old Testament* (Grand Rapids: Baker, 1975) 237.
499. James S. Lowery, "By the Waters of Babylon," *Journal for Preachers* 15/3 (1992) 29.
500. Bright, *The Authority of the Old Testament,* 236.
501. "Elie Wiesel and the Two Who Saved His Life," *The St. Louis Post-Dispatch,* October 5, 1988, E6.

in a lifelong process of remembrance, which ultimately issues in a compassion for others that is grounded in God's compassion for all.

3. A psalm about remembrance that both expresses the pain of death and harbors hope for life cannot help reminding Christians of the Lord's supper and Jesus' words, "Do this in remembrance of me" (Luke 22:19). Remembering Jesus' self-sacrifice is painful, for it must recall his death. But in remembering there is hope, for "you proclaim the Lord's death until he comes" (1 Cor 11:26). The final stanza of Ewald Bash's metrical paraphrase of Psalm 137 captures this sense of hope:

> Let Thy cross be benediction
> For men bound in tyranny;
> By the power of resurrection
> Loose them from captivity.[502]

Remembrance, which is at the heart of Psalm 137, is also at the heart of the Christian faith. In a profound sense, Psalm 137 can be a Christian prayer. It can be prayed as an act of honesty about our own vengefulness; it can be prayed for victims, for those in captivity, and for ourselves, since we know that we are inevitably both victims and victimizers. As we pray and reflect upon Psalm 137, we remember and are retaught the pain of exile, the horror of war, the truth about ourselves, the terror of despair and death, the loneliness of a cross. But as we pray and reflect upon Psalm 137, we are also taught to submit our frailty and finitude to God; we begin a journey that transforms grief and anger into compassion; we affirm that life is lived and promised in the midst of death; and we anticipate and celebrate a resurrection power that frees us from captivity.

---

502. Ewald Bash, "By the Babylonian Rivers," in *The Worshipbook* (Philadelphia: Westminster, 1978) no. 328.

PSALM 138:1-8, THANKSGIVING AND PRAISE FOR GOD'S DELIVERANCE

COMMENTARY

Psalm 138 has traditionally been classified as an individual song of thanksgiving, and v. 2 has often been taken as a clue to its original setting and use. Having been delivered from distress (v. 3), the psalmist has come to the Temple to offer praise (vv. 1-2), perhaps along with a sacrifice of thanksgiving. While this proposal is plausible, it does not fully address the uniqueness of Psalm 138, nor does it explain a fundamental ambiguity; it seems that the psalmist has already been delivered (v. 3a), but the psalmist continues to pray for deliverance. This ambiguity opens the way to a theological approach to Psalm 138 (see Reflections below).

The attempt to discern the original setting and use of Psalm 138 also fails to take into

account the possible significance of its present literary placement. One of the unique features of Psalm 138—the psalmist's offering of praise not simply before the congregation of Israel but also "before the gods" (v. 1)—recalls Pss 135:5 and 136:2-3. There are additional connections to Psalms 135–136 as well. For instance, the psalmist's praise is directed to God's "name" (v. 2; see Ps 135:1, 3), and both psalms proclaim God's greatness (see 135:5; 138:5). Furthermore, in giving thanks to God (vv. 2-3), the psalmist does precisely what Ps 136:1-3, 26 invite, and the psalmist is grateful for God's "steadfast love" (vv. 2, 8; v. 8 especially recalls the refrain of Psalm 136). Given the connections between Psalm 138 and Psalms 135–136, and considering as well the intervening Psalm 137, it is reasonable to conclude with Mays that Psalm 138 "can be understood as a general song of praise by the restored community in the postexilic period, written under the influence of the prophets whose words are gathered in Isaiah 40–66"[503] (see below for similarities to Isaiah 40–66).

Especially in its present literary context, then, the message of Psalm 138 is in keeping with the apparent purposes of Books IV–V to address the crisis of exile and its aftermath (see Commentary on Psalms 90; 107; 120; Introduction). While conclusive proof is not possible, it seems that Psalm 138 serves as a sort of transition between the Songs of Ascents (Psalms 120–134), including their appendix (Psalms 135–137), and the subsequent Davidic collection (Psalms 138–145). This collection draws to a close with a psalm that also sounds like the praise (see 144:1-10) and prayer (see 144:11-15) of the postexilic community. Psalm 145 then recalls Psalm 138 as it explicity asserts God's sovereignty and celebrates God's steadfast love. In between Psalms 138 and 144–145 are five psalms characterized by complaint and petition for deliverance from the wicked. This placement of Psalms 139–143 in Book V, including their framing by Psalms 138 and 144–145, encourages a corporate reading of these psalms by the post-exilic community. While these psalms may have originated as individual prayers, they certainly were capable of speaking to the crisis of the exile and its aftermath in keeping with the response of Book V (see Commentary on Psalms 107; 108; Introduction).

The structural divisions indicated by the NRSV are to be preferred. In vv. 1-3, the psalmist describes his or her own approach to and relationship with God. The focus shifts to "the kings of the earth" in vv. 4-6, although, as the NIV suggests, it is possible to relate v. 6 more closely to vv. 7-8. Perhaps it is intended to be transitional. In any case, vv. 7-8 clearly focus again on the psalmist and God.

138:1-3. The first section of the psalm begins with the psalmist presenting his or her whole self to God in thanks—"with my whole heart" (v. 1*a*; see 1 Kgs 8:23; Pss 9:1; 119:2, 10, 34, 58, 69, 145; Jer 3:10; 24:7).

503. Mays, *Psalms,* 424.

The unique v. 1*b* has a polemical tone, which is perhaps best captured by a literal translation that yields the contemporary idiom "in your face." The psalmist offers praise "in the face of the gods," almost contemptuously denying them sovereignty (see Pss 58:1-2; 82:1). For the psalmist to "bow down toward your holy temple [or palace]" is to profess that God alone is sovereign, the sole provider for his or her life (v. 2*a*; see also v. 7).

The psalmist is able to present his or her whole life to God, because the psalmist trusts that it is God's character to manifest "steadfast love" (חסד *ḥesed*) and "faithfulness" (אמת *'ĕmet,* v. 2*b*; the word "name" can connote character or reputation). These two words are used in God's self-revelation to Moses (Exod 34:6-7), and they became part of a basic profession of Israel's faith (see Introduction). They are paired frequently in the psalms as the basis for an appeal to God for help (see 40:11-12; 115:1-2), or as a profession of trust (see 57:2; 85:10-13). God's dependability is also emphasized in v. 2*c*. The Hebrew is difficult (see NRSV note), but could perhaps be translated interpretively as "your promises surpass even your fame" (NJB). However God's "word" is construed—as God's revelation generally or as God's promises in written form (see Ps 119:11, 38, 41)—it is apparently perceived by the psalmist as a very personal address (v. 3*a*). Again, v. 3*b* is difficult, but it appears to be the psalmist's affirmation that he or she is strengthened. God's word gives life (see Deut 8:3; Matt 4:4).

138:4-6. The second section of the psalm (vv. 4-6) suggests that the psalmist's experience is universal (see the NRSV as opposed to the NIV, which construes vv. 4-5 as petition). Somehow, "all the kings of the earth" have been reached by God's "words" (אמרה *'imrâ,* v. 4; see "word" in v. 2), and they join the psalmist in giving thanks to God ("praise" in v. 4 translates the same Hebrew verb as "give thanks" in vv. 1-2). Verse 5*a* asserts that the kings yield their sovereignty in recognition of God's sovereignty (see Isa 49:7; 52:15). They celebrate "the ways of the LORD" rather than exercising their own wills. This is precisely what Psalm 2 at the beginning of the psalter admonished the kings of the earth to do in order not to perish (2:10-12). For the kings of the earth as for the psalmist, the word of God gives life.

Not surprisingly, "glory" (כבוד *kābôd*, v. 5*b*) elsewhere is associated with the recognition and celebration of God's reign (see Isa 6:1-8; Pss 24:7-10; 29:1-3, 9-11; 97:1, 6; 145:10-13; see also Isa 40:5), as is the word "great" (גדול *gādôl*; see Pss 47:2; 48:1; 95:3; 135:5; the same Hebrew root also appears in 138:2 as "exalted"). Lest the kings of the earth or anyone else misunderstand, however, the nature of God's strange sovereignty is clarified in v. 6, which is reminiscent of 1 Sam 2:1-10 and Ps 113:4-9 (see also Isa 57:15). Verse 6 thus articulates the topsy-turvy values that prevail in the reign of God (see Reflections below).

138:7-8. As the NIV division of the psalm suggests, v. 6 at least prepares for the return to the psalmist's personal situation in vv. 7-8. Those who relinquish self-sufficiency and commit themselves to the reign of God will undoubtedly experience trouble and have enemies (v. 7). The psalmist affirms that God "gives me life" in the midst of the struggle, not beyond it. Deliverance/salvation/life (see Ps 3:2, 7-8) is both a present reality and yet something that awaits fulfillment (v. 8*a*; see Ps 57:2-3, where the same affirmation is made in the context of trust in God's steadfast love and faithfulness). As in v. 2, the psalmist's ability to entrust life and future to God is grounded in God's steadfast love (v. 8*b*). The "not yet" dimension of deliverance is evident in the final petition (v. 8*c*). The Hebrew word translated "forsake" (רפה *rāpâ*) more literally means "to let fall," "to drop," a meaning that is appropriate in a context that refers to hands three times (vv. 7-8). The petition thus implicitly affirms the psalmist's trust that he or she is in God's hands. The "works of your hands" (v. 8*c*) certainly includes the psalmist (see Job 14:15, where an individual person is so designated). But the phrase should also be understood more inclusively, especially in the light of the affirmation of God's sovereignty in vv. 4-5. In terms of the post-exilic hearing of the psalm, the phrase can designate the whole people (see Isa 64:8), and God's "works" elsewhere includes all the creatures and, indeed, the whole creation (see Ps 104:24). God—not the gods (v. 1)—rules the world.

REFLECTIONS

1. The final petition of Psalm 138 implicitly affirms what Christians affirm with the singing of a well-known folk song: God's "got the whole world in his hands." Like the psalmist, we make this affirmation in the midst of all kinds of trouble, opposition, and apparent evidence to the contrary. In other words, the proclamation that God rules the world is eschatological (see Commentary on Psalms 2; 65; 66; 67; 93; 95; 96; 97; 98; 99; Introduction). Amid the "not yetness" of our lives and our world, it is our way of professing our trust that God will fulfill God's purposes for us and for our world.

The eschatological perspective of Psalm 138 means that we shall always live in the midst of the fundamental ambiguity that characterizes the psalm. That is to say, we shall always find ourselves simultaneously professing God's deliverance (v. 3) and praying for God's deliverance (v. 8*c*)—"thine is the kingdom" and "thy kingdom come." The apparent ambiguity is actually a representation of the reality of the life of faith. As faithful people, we know that experiences of grace do not alter our essential and perpetual neediness. Psalm 138 thus ultimately teaches us about and calls us to fundamental dependence upon God. Such dependence upon God rather than upon ourselves or the gods of our own making (see v. 1*b*) enables us to live in the present with assurance (v. 7; see Ps 23:4), offering our whole selves and lives to God (v. 1*a*).

2. Verse 6 is a particular reminder that to acknowledge God's reign and to live in dependence upon God means a transformation of what and whom the world generally values. Hannah's song (1 Sam 2:1-10), which v. 6 recalls, is taken up by Mary in anticipation of the birth of Jesus (see Luke 1:46-55, esp. vv. 51-53). Jesus embodied God's strange sovereignty and world-transforming values, distancing himself from the proud and powerful in favor of the lowly. Jesus showed us what it means to live in fundamental dependence upon God, to offer one's "whole heart" gratefully to God.

3. The profession that God rules the world is clearly appropriate for the season of Epiphany, with which Psalm 138 is associated. Like all proclamations of God's rule, Psalm 138 calls us to decision. It invites us to join the psalmist and the kings of the earth in praising God and offering ourselves to God with our "whole heart."

PSALM 139:1-24, SEARCH ME, O GOD, AND KNOW MY HEART

COMMENTARY

The key word in Psalm 139 is "know(n)"/ "knowledge" (vv. 1-2, 4, 6, 14, and twice in v. 23). It may be entirely coincidental that it occurs seven times—the number indicating fullness or completion—but such a pattern appropriately reinforces the message that the psalmist is fully and completely known by God. This message pervades the first eighteen verses of the psalm, and it serves as the foundation for the petitions and affirmations in vv. 19-24. Scholars frequently suggest that these concluding verses offer a clue to the origin of Psalm 139. It is possible that the psalmist had been accused of idolatry and that the appeal in vv. 23-24 serves as the psalmist's affirmation of innocence (see Psalms 7; 17; 26). In any case, the psalmist's assurance of being known by God and of belonging inseparably to God transcends the particular circumstances of the psalm's origin. It has communicated good news to persons in all places and times. Indeed, the literary placement of Psalm 139 suggests the possibility that it served to express both the assurance and the wishes of the post-exilic community (see Commentary on Psalm 138; Introduction).

While Psalm 139 has been analyzed structurally in a variety of ways, the simplest conclusion is that represented by the NRSV. Verses 1-6 focus on God's knowledge of the psalmist's actions, thoughts, and words. The question in v. 7 introduces a new section, and the response in vv. 8-12 affirms God's knowledge of the psalmist in the form of an inescapable presence. Verses 13-18 trace God's intimate knowledge of the psalmist to God's creative activity. The shift that takes place at v. 19 is signaled by the introduction

of "the wicked" and "bloodthirsty," who are enemies of the psalmist and of God; vv. 19-24 effectively contrast the rebellious behavior of those enemies with the psalmist's loyalty to God.

139:1-6. The very first word of the psalm is the divine name "Yahweh," and the first word of v. 2 is the emphatic Hebrew pronoun "you." While vv. 1-6 are often described as a statement of God's omniscience, what really matters about God to the psalmist is that the divine "you" knows "me." Four of the seven occurrences of the word "know" (ידע *yāda'*) are in vv. 1-6, and both verbs in v. 1 recur in v. 23, indicating that the psalmist desires to be and is fully known by God. As Patrick D. Miller puts it, "From beginning to end it is 'I' and 'you.' "[504] Verses 2-4 make it clear that God knows the psalmist fully—deeds (vv. 2; see "way[s]" in vv. 3, 24), thoughts (v. 2*b*), and words before they are even spoken (v. 4). "Such knowledge," which the psalmist describes as "too wonderful" (v. 5; see Ps 131:1), could easily be perceived as threatening. Indeed, there seems to be some ambivalence in the psalmist's mind. For instance, the verb in the phrase "hem me in" (צור *ṣûr*, v. 5) can have the sense of "besiege," "confine" as well as "protect." Ambivalence would be understandable, for it is risky "to dismiss the deceptive coverings under which most men take refuge," as John Calvin describes the psalmist's posture.[505] To be fully known is to be completely vulnerable, but on the whole, the psalmist certainly celebrates as good news

504. Miller, *Interpreting the Psalms*, 144.
505. Calvin, *Commentary on the Book of Psalms*, VI:5:206.

the marvelous and mysterious reality that his or her life is accessible to God in every way and at every moment.

139:7-12. From the beginning of the Bible, the word "spirit" (רוח *rûaḥ*, or "wind"/"breath") is a way of indicating God's presence (see Gen 1:2; see also the proximity of "spirit" and "presence," or more literally "face," in Isa 63:9-10). Indeed, the mention of "heaven," "morning," and "sea" recalls God's creative activity (see below on vv. 13-14). While vv. 7-12 are often construed as a statement of God's omnipresence, the crucial thing for the psalmist is that God's presence is inescapable. Again, the "I" and "you" are preeminent; again, there is a possible ambivalence. For instance, the word "flee" (ברח *bāraḥ*, v. 7) usually indicates an attempt to get away from (see Amos 9:2-4, which is similar to vv. 7-12 and where God's inescapable presence is clearly bad news). But again, the conviction of God's presence is fundamentally good news for the psalmist (cf. Job 23:8-10), who is convinced that God will "lead me, and . . . hold me" (v. 10; see Ps 73:23-24). In a case of enthusiastic poetic outreach (see above on Pss 22:29-31; 49:15), the psalmist affirms that God is "there" even "in Sheol" (v. 8), an affirmation that contradicts the more usual view of Sheol as a realm beyond God's reach (see Job 17:12-16; Pss 6:5; 30:3, 9; 88:3-7). There seems to be a mythic background to v. 9, but in any case, the imagery communicates a situation of extremity. The word "dark(ness)" (חשך *ḥōšek*), which occurs four times in vv. 11-12, is associated elsewhere with the forces of chaos and death (see Job 12:22; 17:12-13; Pss 23:4; 88:6, 12, 18). But the forces of darkness are dispelled by God's light (see John 1:5). Light is elsewhere associated with God's "presence" or "face"/"countenance," so vv. 11-12 recall v. 7 (see also Num 6:25-26; Pss 4:6; 27:1, 8-9; 44:3; 89:15). But aside from alluding to other texts, vv. 11-12 communicate by their poetic beauty the pervasive brilliance of God's presence.

139:13-18. Like v. 2, v. 13 begins with the emphatic Hebrew pronoun "you." In short, God's activity is emphasized, and vv. 13-18 are an eloquent presentation of the biblical view that human life is not simply a natural, biological occurrence but is the result of the will and work of a benevolent creator. The verb translated "formed" (קנה *qānâ*) in v. 13 is used elsewhere of God's gracious activity of constituting the whole people (Exod 15:16; Ps 74:2; Deut 32:6). God's creation of Israel is also proclaimed elsewhere as one of God's wonderful works (v. 14; see Exod 3:20; 15:11; Pss 77:11, 14). That the same language is used here to describe God's creation of an individual human being affirms God's loving care for every person (see Ps 138:8; Matt 6:26). As for the mode of creation, the psalmist does not use the more familiar image of God as potter (see Gen 2:7; Jer 18:11) but the more unusual metaphor of God as weaver. The psalmist has been "knit together" (v. 13; see Job 10:11).

Verses 15-16a seem to move in a different direction as it appears that God is portrayed as more an observer of a process, the details of which are unclear. It is possible that "depths of the earth" (v. 15b) is a metaphor for the womb, or perhaps v. 15 alludes to ancient Near Eastern mythic material in which human beings originated from below the earth. If so, according to v. 16, God is ultimately in control of even this process. Yet another alternative is that the poet intends to say that God is not just an observer. Rather, in keeping with the weaver image of v. 13, God is the one who has "intricately woven" (v. 15) the psalmist together. Certainty is elusive. The Hebrew word that the NRSV translates "my unformed substance" (גלמי *gōlmî*) occurs only here in the OT. The NIV proposes a more specific rendering, and some translators even use "embryo." Such specificity is probably misleading, since we do not know the precise background of the imagery in vv. 15-16a or the real meaning of the word. In any case, it is clear that the poetic, evocative language of vv. 15-16a does not answer the kind of question that is often posed in contemporary debates over abortion—that is, when does human life begin?

At the same time, the fundamental affirmation of vv. 13-18 is certainly relevant to any consideration of ethical questions. In other words, both v. 13 and vv. 15-16a are congruent with the affirmation in v. 14a, where the psalmist says that she or he is "fearfully and wonderfully made." The psalmist knows (v. 14b; cf. the RSV, which reads the conclusion of v. 14 as another statement that God knows the psalmist) that each human life belongs to God in every aspect—past (vv. 13-16*a*; see Jer 1:5) and future (v. 16*b*; on God's "book," see Exod 32:32-33; Ps 69:28; Mal 3:16), as well as present (see below on vv. 23-24*a*). Whereas God knows human thoughts (v. 2), humans cannot begin to comprehend God's thoughts (v. 17). Because the Hebrew verb in v. 18*b* means "awake" (קִיץ *qîṣ*), some scholars propose that the psalmist spent the night in the Temple as protection from accusers or to await an answer to prayer (see Commentary on Psalm 73). While this is possible, it is finally not really important. What matters is the psalmist's realization that she or he is always "with you" (see Ps 73:23*a*). Thus v. 18 serves to summarize the affirmation of vv. 7-12, while v. 17 recalls vv. 1-6 (see esp. v. 6). The psalmist's origin and destiny lie with God.

139:19-24. Whereas in v. 14 the psalmist properly responds with gratitude to God's creative activity (the verb translated "praise" is the same one translated "give thanks" in Ps 138:1, 3), his or her response in vv. 19-22 seems quite different. Commentators have often concluded that these verses do not really belong with vv. 1-18; liturgical use of the psalm has often omitted these verses, apparently because of their direct request for revenge. In their present place, however, vv. 19-22 join vv. 23-24 as the culmination of the psalm. They articulate the way things always are; people who belong to God (vv. 1-18) and who try to live as God intends (vv. 23-24) will always be opposed by those who oppose God (see Pss 26:9; 55:23; 59:2). While vv. 19-20 inevitably sound like a request for personal revenge, their import is much broader and deeper; they request that God set things right in the world; in other words, "thy will be done." As in other psalms that contain requests for vengeance, the matter is apparently entrusted to and left with God rather than taken into human hands (see Commentary on Psalms 58; 109; 137). Similarly, the hatred expressed in vv. 21-22 is not simply a matter of personal feeling but the psalmist's way of saying that he or she opposes those who oppose God, in effect, "I am on the LORD's side" (see Pss 26:5; 31:6; 119:158).

The psalmist's oath of loyalty is sealed by vv. 23-24, where in language recalling vv. 1-3, the psalmist lays himself or herself open to God's examination. Having been searched (v. 1), the psalmist wants to be continually searched. Having been known (vv. 1-2, 4), the psalmist wants to be continually known. Having been seen (v. 16), the psalmist wants to be continually seen. Having experienced God's leading (see v. 10), the psalmist wants to be continually led. In short, by the end of the psalm, there is no hint of ambivalence. The psalmist fully entrusts her or his life to God, for now (vv. 23-24*a*) and forever (v. 24*b*), secure in the conviction that he or she has been, is being, and will be "fully known" (1 Cor 13:12).

REFLECTIONS

1. Explicitly theological concepts like omniscience and omnipresence are often applied by interpreters to Psalm 139. Almost inevitably these terms will fail to do justice to the psalm, since the psalmist did not intend to articulate systematically a doctrine of God. Rather, the psalmist affirms that God *knows me* and that God is *with me.* Similarly, the discussion of Psalm 139 in terms of the doctrine of predestination will inevitably be misleading if this doctrine is heard in its classical sense; however, the word *predestination* may be appropriately applied to Psalm 139 if it is understood fundamentally as an affirmation that our lives derive from God, belong to God, and find their true destination in God's purposes. In Romans, the apostle Paul suggests that to be "predestined" (8:29) means essentially that nothing "in all creation, will be able to separate us from the love of God in Christ Jesus our Lord" (8:39 NRSV). While obviously not appropriating the message through Jesus Christ as Paul was, the psalmist knew essentially the same good news about God. Although unable to comprehend God's thoughts (vv. 17-18), the psalmist is sure of one thing: "I am still with you" (v.

18*b*). This assurance that God is Emmanuel ("God-with-us"; see Matt 1:23; 28:20) enables the psalmist to entrust her or his life and future to God, inviting God's searching gaze (v. 23) in openness to God's "way everlasting" (v. 24). Such trust means, in effect, that the psalmist displays what Psalm 1 calls "happy"—an openness to God's instruction that derives from the assurance that God *"knows* the way of the righteous" (1:6*a* RSV; see Commentary on Psalms 1; 2).

2. Not surprisingly, Psalm 1 affirms exactly what the psalmist prays for in 139:19: "The way of the wicked will perish" (1:6*b*). The affirmation and the prayer are evidence that the perspective of the psalter is pervasively eschatological; it affirms God's claim on the world (see Psalms 2; 93; 95–99; 145–146; 148) and on every individual life at the same time that it acknowledges the existence of the wicked and their opposition to God and to God's people (vv. 19-20). This perspective means that the faithful in all times and in all places will find themselves doing precisely what the psalmist does in Psalm 139—professing that they belong to God, entrusting their lives and futures to God on the basis of the experience of God's pervasive presence, and praying for God to set things right. For this reason, to be sure, Psalm 139 is a profoundly important theological resource, although, as Miller suggests, "it may translate into the poetic expression of Francis Thompson's 'The Hound of Heaven' as easily as or better than into a systematic theological expression."[506] In short, God actively pursues us and will not let us get away (see above on Ps 23:6). The presence of such love invites both fierce loyalty (vv. 19-22) and sweet surrender (vv. 23-24).

506. Miller, *Interpreting the Psalms,* 144.

PSALM 140:1-13, A CRY FOR PROTECTION FROM VIOLENCE

COMMENTARY

Psalm 140 is ordinarily categorized as a prayer for help or individual lament/complaint. The occurrences of *selah* after vv. 3, 5, and 8 suggest a fourfold division of the psalm, but scholars often conclude that vv. 12-13 should be separated from vv. 9-11. Still others prefer a threefold division (vv. 1-5, 6-11, 12-13) or a different fourfold structure (vv. 1-5, vv. 6-8, vv. 9-11, vv. 12-13). As Allen points out, it is certainly possible that there is "more than one artistic scheme in the psalm."[507] He detects, for instance, a chiastic arrangement (see Introduction) of terms in vv. 1-11, as follows:

v. 1	"evil(doers)," "violent"
v. 3	"lips"
v. 4	"wicked"
v. 8	"wicked"
v. 9	"lips"
v. 11	"evil," "violent"

The effect is to focus attention toward the center, which Allen identifies as vv. 6-7. He also points out that the phrase "in the day of battle" (v. 7) recalls "wars every day" from v. 2. At the same time, "head" in v. 7 anticipates "heads" in v. 9. Again, the effect is to focus attention toward the center of the psalm. Thus the psalmist's petitions for protection against and deliverance from the violent (vv. 1-5, 8-11) surround the psalmist's profession of trust in God (vv. 6-7). This profession also anticipates and is tied conceptually to the conclusion of the psalm (vv. 12-13).

In an attempt to arrive at the origin and ancient use of Psalm 140, scholars often suggest that the psalmist was falsely accused and

507. Allen, *Psalms 101–150,* 267.

that he or she came to the Temple to seek vindication and help from God (see Commentary on Psalms 5; 7; 139). While this is possible, certainty is elusive. In the present literary setting, the petitions in Psalm 140 can be understood as an elaboration of Ps 139:19-22 (see Pss 139:19; 140:4, 8), and the assurance expressed in Psalm 140 corresponds with Ps 139:1-18 (see Pss 139:7; 140:13; note also the emphatic pronoun "you" in Pss 139:2, 13; 140:6). Psalm 140 also anticipates the similar prayers in Psalms 141–143 (see Commentary on Psalm 141), and Psalms 139–143 are framed by psalms that make good sense as testimony and petition offered by the post-exilic community (Psalms 138; 144–145). This framing may have provided literary encouragement to the post-exilic community to hear the individual expressions of petition and profession in Psalms 138–145 as pertinent to the whole community. If so, then Psalms 138–145 would be congruent with the purpose of Book V to address the ongoing crisis of the exile and its aftermath (see Commentary on Psalms 107–108; 111; 118; Introduction).

140:1-5. The opening petitions are typical of the prayers for help (see Pss 6:4; 25:21; 40:11), as are the descriptions of the perpetrators (see the first, lit., "a man of evil," in Ps 10:15; see "violent"/"violence" in Gen 6:11, 13; Pss 7:16; 11:5; 55:9; 72:14; 73:6). The further description of the violent in v. 2a recalls Ps 35:4, 20, where the NRSV's "devise" and "conceive" translate the Hebrew verb rendered "plan[ned]" (חשב ḥāšab) in Ps 140:2, 4. Verse 2b is reminiscent of Pss 56:6; 59:3; 120:7. Three of the four words in v. 3a contain an "sh" sound, thus creating the onomatopoeic effect of a snake hissing (see Ps 58:4). The mention of "tongue" (see v. 11) and "lips" (see v. 9) in v. 3 suggests verbal violence (see Pss 57:4; 64:3; 73:8).

Verbal abuse is inevitably part of a larger pattern of destructive activity, and this is indicated in vv. 4-5. The word "hands" (ידים yādayim) in v. 4a connotes "grasp" or "power" (see Ps 82:4). Verse 4b repeats v. 1b; the violent do not stop at verbal abuse. They have "planned" (v. 4c; see also v. 2) to bring the psalmist down. The NIV's translation of v. 4c is more literal and conveys how the imagery of v. 4 carries into v. 5, which

also indicates that violent speech (v. 3) is accompanied by violent action (see Pss 9:15; 10:9; 31:4; 37:6; 64:5; 141:9; 142:3). Verse 5 also introduces another designation of the enemies—the "proud" or "arrogant" (see Pss 94:2; 123:4).

140:6-7. While it would appear from vv. 1-5 that the violent are in control, the psalmist affirms in the central section of the psalm (vv. 6-7) that God is sovereign. The title "Lord" in v. 7 indicates a sovereign master, and the Hebrew root translated "strong" (עז ʿōz) is regularly associated with God's reign (see Pss 29:1; 93:1; 96:6-7; 99:4). In Exod 15:2, as here, it appears in conjunction with God's saving activity (see "salvation" in Exod 15:2; the phrase in Ps 140:8 is more literally "strength of my salvation"); the song in Exodus 15 also culminates in the proclamation of God's reign (v. 18). Furthermore, the sovereign God is "my Lord" (v. 7) and "my God" (v. 6). The appearance of the Hebrew pronoun "you" in v. 6 emphasizes the point. Like the psalm as a whole, which juxtaposes petition and profession, so do vv. 6-7. The petition in v. 6b is followed by profession in v. 7b (see Pss 5:11 and 91:4, where God also covers the psalmist). In short, the psalmist simultaneously celebrates and prays for deliverance; the perspective is eschatological (see Reflections below).

140:8-11. Petition is resumed in v. 8. The "desires of the wicked" involve violence, oppression, and destruction (see vv. 1-5, 9, 11; see also Pss 10:3; 112:10)—that is, the antithesis of "justice" (v. 12). Their behavior is further described in vv. 8-11 as an "evil plot" (v. 8b; see Gen 11:6; Pss 31:13; 37:12), "mischief" (v. 9b; see Pss 7:14, 16; 10:7; 55:10), and "slander" (v. 11a, lit., "a man of tongue," recalling v. 3). The psalmist's prayer in vv. 8-11 is not a request for personal revenge. Rather, the psalmist asks that God set things right. Of course, "justice for the poor" (v. 12) will necessarily mean judgment upon the victimizers. Repeating the words "evil" (see vv. 1-2) and "violent" (see vv. 1, 4), v. 11b requests simply that the violent experience the results they intend to inflict upon others. Again, the matter is not revenge but justice (see Commentary on Psalms 109; 137; 139).

140:12-13. These verses state positively what the psalmist has prayed for in vv. 8-11. Verses 6-7 have asserted God's sovereignty, and vv. 12-13 present the royal policy that God wills and enacts—justice. The word the NRSV translates "cause" (דין *dîn*) in v. 12*a* appears elsewhere in contexts that explicitly proclaim God's rule (see Pss 9:4 in the context of 9:7; 96:10). So does the word "justice"/"judge" (משפט *mišpāṭ*; see Pss 96:13; 97:2; 98:9; 99:4; see also "presence of the LORD" in 98:9). The beneficiaries of God's justice are those who are the victims of the violent: the "poor" and the "needy" (see Commentary on Psalms 9; 10; 82; 109). These same persons can also be called "the righteous" (see Commentary on Psalm 1) or "the upright" (see Pss 33:1; 111:1; 112:2, 4). They depend for life not on themselves but on God. Thus their fundamental posture is gratitude to God (v. 13*a*; see Ps 138:1-2), and their "salvation" (v. 7) is to "live in your presence" (v. 13*b*; see Pss 23:6; 27:4; 73:28).

REFLECTIONS

As is the case throughout the book of Psalms, the juxtaposition of petition and profession of faith in Psalm 140 creates an eschatological perspective. That is, the reign of God is proclaimed amid circumstances that appear to deny it (see Commentary on Psalms 2; 13; 22; 138; Introduction). It was, of course, no different for Jesus, whose proclamation of and embodiment of the reign of God (see Mark 1:14-15) led him to a cross.

1. While Psalm 140 represents a theological perspective that pervades the psalter, indeed, the whole Bible, many people might question the appropriateness of Psalm 140 as a Christian prayer on account of the petitions in vv. 8-11. As suggested above, however, the issue in vv. 8-11 is not personal revenge but justice for the victimized. If we are not victimized to the point that we feel the need to pray as the psalmist does in Psalm 140, then we should pray Psalm 140 on behalf of others who are victims (see Reflections on Psalm 109). If we prayed Psalm 140 on behalf of others, we would perhaps be reminded of some of the stark realities of our culture—the frequency of spousal and child abuse, for instance. In our midst, there are millions who daily need to pray literally, "Protect me from those who are violent" (vv. 1*b*, 4*b*).

2. But there is a further dimension to the use of Psalm 140 as a contemporary prayer. In Rom 3:13, Paul quotes Ps 140:3*b* to support his claim that all people "are under the power of sin" (Rom 3:9 NRSV). From this perspective, Psalm 140 becomes a prayer requesting that we be delivered *from ourselves!* That is to say, Psalm 140 forces us to consider that all of us are victimizers. For instance, most contemporary persons give at least implicit approval to a culture that all but glorifies violence. Even children watch violence daily on television, and violence is a staple of adult entertainment. When we seek solutions to domestic and international problems, those solutions frequently amount to fighting violence with violence. In short, violence is not just a problem for and with *other* people; it is a problem for and with *all of us* (see Commentary on Psalm 109). Many philosophers convincingly argue that violence, hostility, and war are inevitable human realities, for peace is simply too boring and too costly in the so-called real world (see Commentary on Psalms 120; 125). In the face of such conclusions, Psalm 140 is ultimately a reminder that, as people of God, we profess that the true real world is the world of God's reign (vv. 6-7), and it is a confirmation of the faithfulness of the contemporary slogan "If you want peace, work for justice." Violence will never effectively be fought with violence. It will only effectively be answered with the justice that God wills and works to enact (see vv. 12-13).

PSALM 141:1-10, DELIVER ME FROM WICKEDNESS

COMMENTARY

Like Psalms 140 and 142, with which it has several similarities, Psalm 141 is ordinarily classified as an individual lament/complaint or prayer for help. As is typical, the psalmist prays for deliverance from specific threats (v. 9), but less typically, the psalmist also prays for deliverance from the temptation represented by the very existence of the wicked and their apparent prosperity (vv. 3-5).

While the origin and ancient use of Psalm 141 are uncertain, it is evident that it continues the focus on the wicked that is present in Psalms 139–140. In this regard, the verbal links between Psalms 140 and 141 are significant—see "wicked" in Pss 140:4, 8 and 141:4, 10 (see also 139:19); "righteous" in 140:13 and 141:5; "guard" in 140:4 and "guard"/"keep" in 141:3, 9; "lips" in 140:3, 9 and 141:3; "evil" in 140:1-2, 11 and 141:4, 5; "my Lord" in 140:7 and 141:8; and "trap(s)," "net(s)," and "snares" in 140:5 and 141:9-10. Psalm 141 also anticipates Psalm 142, especially by way of the repetition of the important word "refuge" (חסה *ḥāsâ*) in 141:8 and 142:5 (see also "voice" in 141:1 and 142:1; "righteous" in 141:5 and 142:7; "trap" in 141:9 and 142:3). In short, it appears that Psalms 140–142, or perhaps 139–143, form the core of the Davidic collection, which includes Psalms 138–145. Framed by Psalms 138 and 144–145, this Davidic collection makes especially good sense against the background of the postexilic era (see Psalms 138–140; 144). Thus Psalm 141 participates in the response of Book V to the ongoing crisis of exile and its aftermath (see Commentary on Psalms 107; 108; 111; 118; 140; Introduction). This crisis involved not only the need for protection against powerful enemies (see Psalm 140) but also the persistent temptation to conclude, in effect, "If you can't beat them, join them." It is to this temptation that Psalm 141 is particularly addressed (see Commentary on Psalm 125, esp. discussion of v. 3). Of course, the

seductive power of evil is a perennial temptation, so Psalm 141 remains a timely prayer for the people of God (see Reflections below).

Psalm 141 is outlined by scholars in a variety of ways. This variety stems in part perhaps from the textual difficulties in vv. 5-7 (see NRSV notes). Pointing out that vv. 5-7 have been "understood and translated in the most diverse ways possible," Bratcher and Reyburn conclude that these verses are "extremely obscure, not to say unintelligible."[508] Artur Weiser even chooses to leave vv. 5*c*-7 untranslated on the grounds that they are finally incomprehensible (see below for a literal translation).[509] In any case, the NIV and the NRSV offer two different fourfold divisions of the psalm. Some scholars prefer a division in two sections (vv. 1-5, vv. 6-10), while others suggest three (vv. 1-2, vv. 3-6, vv. 7-10). On the basis of content, it is also possible to divide the psalm into vv. 1-2, vv. 3-7, vv. 8-10. In vv. 1-2, the psalmist requests to be heard. Verses 3-7 focus on the psalmist and the wicked. Verses 3-5*b* request help to oppose temptation, while vv. 5*c*-7 may be a profession of trust in God's justice or perhaps a complaint. Verses 8-10 begin with a profession of trust, which is followed by petition for deliverance.

141:1-2. The language of v. 1 is typical. The "call" to God indicates prayer (see Ps 4:1, 3), which is mentioned specifically in v. 2. The two occurrences of "I call" surround two more pleas—"come quickly" (see Pss 22:19; 38:22; 40:13) and "give ear" (see Pss 55:1; 86:6; 143:1). Verse 2*b* depicts a posture of prayer (see Pss 28:2; 63:4; 134:2). This verse may indicate an original cultic setting, but it is often taken as indication of the spiritualization of sacrifice (on "evening sacrifice," see 2 Kgs 16:15; Ezra 9:4-5; Dan 9:21). In Ezra 9:5, though, Ezra prays immediately following the evening sacrifice, a sequence that

---

508. Bratcher and Reyburn, *A Translator's Handbook on the Book of Psalms,* 1142, 1144.
509. Weiser, *The Psalms,* 811.

would make good sense in terms of v. 2. In any case, there is simply not enough evidence here to suggest a movement to replace sacrifice by prayer (see Commentary on Psalm 50). As Mays succinctly concludes, "Word and sacrament are not at odds here."[510]

141:3-5b. The vocabulary of these verses recalls Psalm 140. Whereas Psalm 140 contains the psalmist's prayer for deliverance from the destructive "lips" of the wicked (vv. 3, 9), here the psalmist prays that her or his own "lips" be kept from destructive behavior (v. 3b). Whereas the psalmist prayed in Psalm 140 for deliverance from "evil" (see vv. 1-2), here the prayer is that she or he be prevented from joining the wicked in their "evil" (v. 4). The psalmist desires to be counted among "the righteous" (v. 5a), even if this means being disciplined by their rebuke (v. 5b). The NIV translation of v. 5a is more literal, and the word rendered "kindness" is the same word the NRSV ordinarily translates as "steadfast love." In short, the psalmist will welcome the loving correction of his or her brothers and sisters. The NIV also attempts a more literal translation of the difficult v. 5b, connecting it more closely to v. 5a than does the NRSV (see the NRSV note). While faithfulness is clearly a matter of proper speech in v. 3, the issue is broader in v. 4 and includes even what is eaten. While the vocabulary differs, v. 4 recalls Daniel 1, where Daniel's faithfulness is also a matter of refusing to eat the king's royal food (see Dan 1:8-18). While Psalm 141 should not be connected historically to the book of Daniel, Daniel 1 does provide a narrative illustration of the logic of Ps 140:4; it may also illustrate how Psalm 141 would have been an important resource in facing the ongoing crises of the post-exilic era. In any case, the petition of v. 4 amounts fundamentally to what Jesus taught his disciples to pray: "Lead us not into temptation, but deliver us from evil."

141:5c-7. Although v. 5c is again difficult (see the NRSV note), it seems to be the psalmist's affirmation that her or his intent is congruent with what the psalmist has just prayed for in vv. 3-5b. The textual difficulties are multiplied in vv. 6-7, which read literally:

510. Mays, *Psalms,* 431.

v. 6   Their judges were thrown
         down into the hands of
          the rock,
     and they heard
         my words, for they were
          pleasing.
v. 7   Like one clearing and
         plowing the earth,
      our bones have been
         scattered at the mouth
          of Sheol.

While these verses appear to make no sense, the scholarly proposals amount to little more than speculation. It may do just as well to try to make sense of the Hebrew as it appears. Although certainty is impossible, vv. 6-7 may be a highly poetic complaint. That is, those who could have served to punish the wicked (v. 6a) and reward the psalmist for his or her pleasing words (v. 6b; "pleasing" [נעם $n\bar{a}'\bar{e}m$] is from the same root as "delicacies" in v. 4) have been brutally dealt with (v. 6a). Thus the psalmist and his or her associates have been effectively driven into the ground (v. 7a) and are as good as dead (v. 7b; see "Sheol" in Pss 30:3; 55:15; 116:3). In contrast to this attempt at a literal reading, the NIV and the NRSV turn vv. 6-7 into the psalmist's affirmation that God will ultimately deal with the wicked, in which case vv. 6-7 anticipate v. 10. Construing vv. 6-7 as a complaint, however, seems to make more sense of the Hebrew particle at the beginning of v. 8, which both the NIV and the NRSV render in an adversative sense.

141:8-10. In other words, despite the brutal treatment of those who seek justice (v. 6) and despite the resulting setback expressed by the psalmist (v. 7), the psalmist affirms, "But my eyes are turned toward you" (v. 8a; see Ps 123:1). Whereas it appears that the wicked are sovereign, the psalmist addresses God as "my Lord" (v. 8a; see Ps 140:7). Whereas the wicked appear to prosper and promote evil with impunity (v. 6), the psalmist refuses to join the wicked and chooses instead to "seek refuge" in God (v. 8b). That is, the psalmist resists the seductive temptation of wickedness and professes to live in dependence upon God (see Pss 2:12; 5:11; Introduction). The petition in v. 8b could be rendered more literally "do not leave my life naked." Nakedness elsewhere is indicative of punishment and even recalls the plight of the destroyed Jerusalem (see Lam 1:8; Ezek 16:37; 23:10, 29). Petition continues in v. 9 (see Ps 140:5; 142:3), and the corollary of God's defense of the vulnerable is God's destruction of the wicked (v. 10; see Ps 1:6).

Like other requests for the destruction of the wicked (see Pss 7:9-11, 15-16; 12:3-4; 17:13-14; 58:6-9; 109:6-19; 137:8-9; 139:19-22), v. 10 is the psalmist's way of pleading for God to set things right, in effect, a way of praying, "Thy will be done."

REFLECTIONS

Because of the reference to an "evening sacrifice" in v. 2, Psalm 141 was used from earliest Christian times as an evening prayer, and it still is. Its contemporary use is appropriate, indeed very timely, in a culture that surrounds us with both subtle and blatant temptations to do evil. People are taught to use speech as a weapon to intimidate, as a tool to get ahead and to get their own way (see v. 3). Millions of dollars are spent daily by advertisers who want to convince us to "eat . . . their delicacies" (v. 4) or to drink the coolest beverage or to drive the hottest car. In short, we are bombarded daily with messages that both subliminally and overtly assert that life does consist in the abundance of possessions (see Luke 12:15) and that happiness consists of getting what we want and accomplishing what we desire. The "American dream" amounts essentially to having the power and the resources so as to be answerable to no one but ourselves.

In biblical terms, however, this is the essence of wickedness, from which the psalmist prays to be delivered (vv. 3-5b; see Commentary on Psalms 1; 2). For the psalmist, the pursuit of happiness involves not material abundance or unbridled self-assertion (vv. 3-4) but the fundamental orientation of life to God (v. 8a). Rejecting the temptations of the wicked and their outward prosperity, the psalmist prays for and apparently finds the strength to live in humble dependence upon God (v. 8b). Thus the psalmist can articulate the intention to live as part of a community of loving discipline (v. 5a) rather than as an isolated self. Even so, it is revealing that the psalmist continues to pray for help (vv. 8b-10), including the request that she or he not be left exposed to the pervasive enticements of the wicked (v. 8b). The psalmist's example is instructive, and it reinforces Jesus' instruction that his disciples constantly need to pray, "Thy will be done; . . . lead us not into temptation, but deliver us from evil."

PSALM 142:1-7, NO ONE CARES FOR ME

COMMENTARY

An individual lament/complaint or prayer for help, Psalm 142 is linked verbally to Psalm 141. Its vocabulary also anticipates Psalm 143 (see "supplication[s]" in Pss 142:1; 143:1; "spirit grows faint" in 142:3; 143:4; "save me" in 142:6; 143:9; "pursue[s]" in 142:6; 143:3; and perhaps "refuge" in 142:5; 143:9, but see the NRSV note). It makes sense to view Psalm 142 as part of the core of the Davidic collection (Psalms 139–143) framed by Psalms 138 and 144–145, which

would have been especially appropriate for the post-exilic community. Thus Psalm 142 participates in the response of Book V to the ongoing crisis of exile and its aftermath (see Commentary on Psalms 107; 108; 111; 118; 138; 140; 141; Introduction).

Whether Psalm 142 originated as a response to the exile or to the post-exilic situation is unclear, since the origin and ancient use of Psalm 142 are unknown. What is clearer is that Psalm 142 would have been an appropriate exilic or post-exilic prayer, although its usefulness cannot be limited to that setting (see Reflections below). Indeed, the superscription suggests a narrative context within David's life as the background for hearing Psalm 142 (see 1 Sam 22:1; 24:3-4). It recalls the superscription of Psalm 57, which also features the concept of "refuge" (see v. 1). The superscription should not be understood historically but as illustrative of a narrative context for hearing the psalm (see Commentary on Psalms 3; 7; 18; 34; 51; 52; 56; 57). The appearance in Book V of a Davidic collection, especially one that includes a royal psalm (Psalm 144), reinforces the necessity to reinterpret the traditional Davidic theology (see Commentary on Psalms 89; 110; 132; 144; Introduction).

The structure of Psalm 142 can be outlined in several ways, as the difference between the NIV and the NRSV indicates. Allen suggests a division into vv. 1-4 and vv. 5-7, based on the pattern of repetition between these two sections (see "I cry" in vv. 1, 5; the emphatic pronoun "you" [אתה *'attâ*] in vv. 3, 5; and "me" [נפש *nepeš*] in vv. 4, 7).[511] Still another possibility is to divide the psalm into vv. 1-3a, vv. 3b-5, vv. 6-7. In this case, each section begins with complaint or petition and moves toward assurance (vv. 3a, 5, 7b). In short, as is often the case, various proposals can be justified, depending on the criteria one chooses to emphasize. It is possible that the structure and movement operate at more than one level, so the various proposals need not be considered mutually exclusive.

142:1-3a. Although the Hebrew root translated "cry" (זעק *zāʿaq*) in vv. 1, 5 does not occur often in the psalms (see Pss 22:5; 107:13, 19), it is an important theological word. For instance, it recalls the exodus (see Exod 2:23); it is a crucial part of the pattern in the book of Judges (see Judg 3:9, 15; 6:6-7); indeed, it became understood as a typical element in God's dealing with God's people (see Neh 9:28). The very act of crying out to God bespoke the trust that God hears and that God cares; this trust is evident in the movement toward assurance in each of three sections of Psalm 142. This trust was particularly necessary during the aftermath of the exile, and it is significant that the word "cry"

occurs twice in Psalm 107 (see Ps 107:13, 19; a nearly identical variant also occurs in Ps 107:6, 28), the first psalm in Book V. As the NIV suggests, the verb in v. 1b derives from a root that means "to be merciful," "to be gracious" (see Pss 4:1; 6:2; 9:13). It is God's mercy upon which the psalmist depends, and his or her assurance is communicated effectively by the chiastic structure of v. 2. The two occurrences of the prepositional phrase "before him" (lit., "to his face") surround the two words that describe the psalmist's situation—"complaint" (see Pss 55:2; 64:1; and the superscription of Psalm 102, where the words "pour out" and "faint" also occur) and "trouble." In other words, the psalmist's problem is encompassed by God's presence, and this assurance is stated explicitly in v. 3a. Needy and weak (see Pss 61:2; 77:3; 107:5; 143:4; Lam 2:12), the psalmist is assured of God's presence. The "you" in v. 3b is emphatic; the psalmist is sure that God knows. Such knowledge is not simply informational but relational (see Ps 139:1-2, 4, 23).

142:3b-5. The complaint becomes specific in the second section of the psalm. The psalmist is targeted by enemies (v. 3b; see Pss 140:5; 141:9), and there is no one in the traditional position for helping—at the "right hand" (v. 4a; see Ps 109:6, 31). In the struggle against the enemies, the psalmist has no one to turn to (v. 4b, 4d) and no place to hide (v. 4c). Verse 4c reads literally, "a refuge perishes from me"; this same expression occurs also in Job 11:20; Jer 25:35; and Amos 2:14. In short, the situation appears to be hopeless.

But for the psalmist, faith is "the conviction of things not seen" (Heb 11:1 NRSV; see 142:4a). So the psalmist emphatically says to God, *"You* are my refuge" (v. 5b). The appearance of the Hebrew pronoun recalls v. 3a. The Hebrew words translated "refuge" differ in vv. 4 and 5 (מנוס *mānôs*, v. 4; מחסה *maḥseh*, v. 5). The latter is the more frequently used one and is present from the beginning of the psalter. In the worst possible circumstance, the psalmist can affirm what Ps 2:12 presents as true happiness: entrusting life and future completely to God (see also Pss 5:11; 7:1; 141:8; Introduction). Although not seen, God's help is as dependable and tangible as the "portion" of land that was intended

511. Allen, *Psalms 101–150,* 276-77.

to represent every Israelite's stake in life and in the future (v. 5c; see Num 18:20; Pss 16:5; 73:26; 119:57; Lam 3:24). The psalmist is faced with death, but God offers life (see Ps 27:13).

142:6-7. The beginning of the final section of the psalm again returns to petition and complaint. The request to be heard (v. 6a; see Ps 5:1) is accompanied by complaint (v. 6b; see Pss 79:8; 116:6), as is the first request for deliverance (v. 6cd; see Ps 18:17). A second request for deliverance is made in v. 7a. The act of bringing out is what God did in delivering the people from Egypt (see Exod 18:1; 20:2) and from exile (see Ezek 20:34, 41; 34:13). The psalmist asks for a personal exodus from "prison." To be sure, some commentators take this word literally and find in it a clue to the original setting of the psalm (see Lev 24:12; Num 15:34), but it is likely that the word should be heard metaphorically and certainly came to be understood that

way. In Isa 42:7, it seems to designate the exile (see also Ps 88:8; Lam 3:7); this dimension of meaning would be especially appropriate for the placement of Psalm 142 in Book V. Whereas the first request for deliverance was accompanied by complaint, the second is supported by the psalmist's promise to praise God (v. 7b). Perhaps not coincidentally, the wording recalls Ps 138:1-2, the beginning of the present Davidic collection. In view of the complaint in v. 4 of total isolation from help, it is fitting that the psalmist states the final assurance in vv. 7cd in terms of being surrounded by the "righteous" (see Pss 140:13; 141:5). This company of friends, helpers, and fellow worshipers will be a sign of God's bountiful treatment of the psalmist (see Pss 13:6; 116:7; 119:17). Similar gatherings are depicted in the conclusions of other prayers for help or songs of thanksgiving (see Pss 22:22-26; 116:14, 17-19).

REFLECTIONS

Like the other complaints or prayers for help, Psalm 142 portrays the simultaneity of trouble and assurance. It is thus another reminder of the inseparability of complaint and praise; to put it in explicitly Christian terms, Psalm 142 represents the inseparability of cross and resurrection (see Commentary on Psalms 13; 22; 69). Jesus invited his followers both to take up their crosses and to go forth empowered by the resurrection (see Matt 16:24; 28:19-20). These are not separate invitations. Rather, the resurrection offers both assurance for the difficult present and promise for the future. Inevitably, therefore, like the psalmist, Christians live by a power we cannot see (see v. 4)—we live by faith and by hope (see Rom 8:24-25; Heb 11:1). We live in fundamental dependence upon God, and so, despite appearances, we shall never be alone (John 14:18-19).

Living by a power that cannot be seen (v. 4) means that Christians have a unique epistemology, a unique way of knowing (see Commentary on Psalms 111; 119). For the world and perhaps especially in our scientifically oriented culture, "seeing is believing." But for us, as for the psalmist, the opposite is true—believing is seeing! Trusting God, we know and experience the very power of God (see John 20:29). Thus things are not as they appear. Apparent weakness is strength (see 1 Cor 1:25; 2 Cor 12:9), for instance, and those with no visible means of support actually have an ever-present refuge in God (v. 5) and in the community of God's people (v. 7).

This assurance, however, is not meant to be an excuse simply to dismiss the needy with pious reminders that their help is in God (see James 1:14-17). Most Christians are fortunate enough to have sufficient power and resources at their disposal so that they may never need to pray v. 4 literally. But this verse should be a reminder to us of the pain of the world, especially in places where plenty of persons are reduced to the status of non-persons. Psalm 142 affirms that God hears persons whom nobody else bothers to hear, and that God cares for those whom nobody else appears to care for (v. 4d)—the homeless, the destitute, the low, and the despised. In a nearly incomprehensible statement for most of us, Jesus even said, "Happy are you destitute, for yours is the kingdom of God" (Luke 6:20, author's trans.). This is no romanticizing of poverty. Rather, it is a powerful affirmation of what Psalm 142 also affirms: God helps those who cannot help themselves (see Commentary on Psalm 3)! From this perspective, Psalm 142 is ultimately a warning to the wealthy, the privileged, the self-sufficient. Although it may appear that they have no advocates at their "right hand" (see v. 4a), the needy find that God stands at their right hand (see Ps 109:31). This is precisely what the psalmist knew (v. 5), and her or his knowledge calls us to renounce self-sufficiency for dependence upon God, and thereby to renounce isolation from the needy for solidarity with the needy (which now includes us!). In short, Psalm 142 calls us "righteous" folk to "surround" and be surrounded by our needy brothers and sisters as a sign of our mutual dependence on God's bounty (v. 7cd).

PSALM 143:1-12, NO ONE LIVING IS RIGHTEOUS BEFORE YOU

COMMENTARY

Linked literarily to Psalm 142, Psalm 143 joins Psalms 139–142 as the core of the Davidic collection, framed by Psalms 138 and 144–145. Its current placement means that Psalm 143 participates in the response of Book V to the exile and its aftermath (see Commentary on Psalms 107; 108; 138; 140; Introduction), but this is not to say that it originated with that purpose in mind. While Psalm 143 can be classified as an individual lament/complaint or prayer for help, the circumstances of its origin and original use are unknown. Because of the reference to "morning" in v. 8, some scholars have suggested that the psalm was prayed as part of a ritual that involved the psalmist's spending the night in the Temple to await God's answer. This remains speculative, however, and it is likely that the open-endedness of the imagery contributed to the use of Psalm 143 in a variety of ways and circumstances throughout the generations (see Reflections below).

As Allen points out, the pattern of some of the repetition in Psalm 143 suggests a division into two major sections: vv. 1-6 and vv. 7-12. For instance, "answer" occurs in v. 1 and again in v. 7; "not" occurs in vv. 2, 7; "before you"/"your face" (the same word in Hebrew) also occurs in vv. 2, 7; "in your righteousness" is found in vv. 1, 11; and "your servant" occurs in vv. 2, 12.[512] As the NIV

and the NRSV suggest, these major sections can be subdivided. Verses 1-6 move from petition (vv. 1-2) to complaint (vv. 3-4) to a sort of profession of loyalty and desire for God (vv. 5-6). Verses 7-12 form an extended series of petitions. They may be treated as a single unit or divided into three parts (NRSV) or into two parts (see the NIV's break after v. 10). Still another alternative is to construe the emphatic "you" in v. 10 and the emphatic "I" in v. 12 as an envelope structure, in which case the subdivisions are vv. 7-9 and vv. 10-12.

143:1-2. The requests to be heard in v. 1ab are typical (see "hear my prayer" in Ps 4:1; see "give ear" in Pss 5:1; 86:6; 140:6; 141:1). "Cry for mercy" (חנן ḥānan) in v. 1b (see Pss 28:2, 6; 31:22) already suggests that the psalmist's plea will be based on God's character. The underlying Hebrew root occurs as "gracious" in Exod 34:6—God's self-revelation to Moses—as does the root of "faithfulness" (אמן 'mn). The phrase "in your righteousness" in v. 1c anticipates not only v. 12 but also v. 2. The words "righteous(ness)" and "justice" (v. 2 reads lit., "Do not enter into justice") often occur in the same context to indicate God's character in action—God's sovereign will (see Pss 89:14; 96:13; 97:2). What is striking about v. 2a is that the psalmist does not want justice! What she or he needs is mercy, because "no one living is righteous" (v. 2b). The theological implication is

512. Allen, *Psalms 101–150,* 283-84.

clear: In attempting to set things right among human beings, God's will must ultimately be manifested as grace. In prayers of complaint about pursuers, it is more frequently the case that the psalmist proclaims innocence or righteousness (see Psalms 17; 26). But this is not the case in v. 2, which Kraus characterizes as "most remarkable."[513] Interestingly, v. 2b is not the personal confession of sin one might expect following v. 2a but an appeal to the sinfulness of all humanity (see Ps 39:11; cf. 39:7; see also 130:3). It later serves well Paul's argument in Rom 3:20 (see also Gal 2:16; Reflections below).

143:3-4. Verse 3 introduces two more terms that are repeated throughout the psalm: "enemy"/"enemies" (איב 'ōyēb; see vv. 9, 12) and "me"/"my" (נפש nepeš, vv. 3, 11-12; "soul" in vv. 6, 8), which means fundamentally "vitality," "life." In the light of v. 2, it seems that the general unrighteousness of humanity is manifested when some persons ("the enemy") threaten the lives of others (in this case, the psalmist). The psalmist has already identified herself or himself as a "servant" (v. 2; see also v. 12), and v. 3 makes it clear that the psalmist is a suffering servant, ("pursued"; see Ps 142:6) and, like the suffering servant in the book of Isaiah, crushed (see Isa 53:5, 10; see also Ps 94:5; Lam 3:34). The phrase "in darkness" also describes the condition of the people in exile in Isaiah 40–55 and Lamentations (see Isa 42:16; Lam 3:6), as does the verb "faints" (see Lam 2:11-12, 19; see above on Ps 142:3). As suggested above, this does not mean that Psalm 143 originated as a response to the exile or to conditions in the post-exilic era, but it does suggest that the post-exilic community could easily have found in Psalm 143 the language to articulate its complaint.

143:5-6. The language of vv. 5-6 clearly recalls Psalm 77, in which the psalmist also complains that "my spirit faints" (Pss 77:3; 143:4) and stretches his or her hands to God in the posture of prayer (Pss 77:2; 143:6; see also Exod 9:29, 33; Ps 141:2; Lam 1:17). There, too, the psalmist remembers (77:3, 11 NIV) and meditates (77:12 NIV) and considers (77:3, 12; the translation is "mused" in v. 3 NIV); as in Psalm 143, these activities are directed to "the days of old" (77:5; see

513. Kraus, *Psalms 60–150*, 536.

Isa 63:9, 11) and to God's "works" (77:12) and to what God has "done"/"performs" (Ps 77:14; 143:5). The allusions are most likely to the exodus. Thus the psalmist's longing in v. 6b (see Ps 63:1) is for an analogous deliverance from deadly threats, and her or his prayer would have been and has been found to be appropriate amid a variety of crises, personal and corporate.

143:7-9. The first plea in v. 7 recalls v. 1 as it opens the second major section, and "spirit" recalls v. 4 (see "fails" in Pss 31:10; 73:26). Although the psalmist realizes that no living person is righteous before God's face (v. 2, "before you"), she or he also pleads that God not hide God's face (see Pss 13:1; 22:24; 27:9; 69:17; 88:14; 102:2), lest she or he die (see Pss 28:1; 30:3). In other words, the psalmist obviously trusts that God is steadfastly loving, an attribute that means God shows compassion for the afflicted and willingness to forgive the sinful (see Exod 34:6-7; Pss 5:7; 13:5; 25:6-7, 10; 86:5, 13, 15; 138:2, 8; Introduction). Thus, although both sinful (v. 2) and afflicted (vv. 3-4), the psalmist can confidently entrust the whole self to this kind of God. The plea that God "teach me" (v. 8) is indicative of the psalmist's total dedication of the self to God, as is the statement that concludes v. 8. The verb translated "lift up" (נשא nāśā) is used elsewhere of offering sacrifices, and the statement could also be translated "to you I offer my life." The same formulation also occurs in Pss 25:1; 86:4; just as in Psalm 143, so also in Psalms 25 and 86 the psalmist appeals to God's steadfast love (25:6-7, 10; 86:5, 13, 15) and prays to be taught by God (25:4-5; 86:11). The same depth of trust is expressed in v. 9, in which the petition is again followed by a statement of confidence. The NIV of v. 9b attempts to read the Hebrew more literally (see NRSV note), although the NRSV's "refuge" has some manuscript support and would certainly be appropriate in this context (see Pss 2:12; 5:11; 141:8; 142:5; Introduction).

143:10-12. As suggested above, these verses are set off by the complementary affirmations in vv. 10b and 12c (see Ps 86:2, 14, 16). Verse 10 begins with another request for God's teaching (the Hebrew verbs differ in vv. 8 and 10, as the NIV suggests). Because the psalmist belongs to God, she or he desires to know God's "will" (see Pss 40:8; 103:21) and to experience the leading (see Pss 23:3; 31:3; 73:24; 139:10) of God's "good spirit" (see Neh 9:20, where the "good spirit" also plays an educational role) toward "level ground" (see Pss 26:12; 27:11). As the beginning of v. 11 indicates again, the issue is fundamentally one of God's character (see Pss 23:3; 25:11). God is righteous (v. 11b) and steadfastly loving (v. 12), attributes that have already been mentioned in such a way as to demonstrate that they involve God's grace (see vv. 2, 8). As vv. 11-12 indicate, for God to set things right will involve both life for the psalmist (v. 11a; see Pss 80:18; 119:37, 77) and destruction of the enemies (v. 12; see Pss 1:6; 54:7; 73:27; 94:23; 101:5, 8). The psalmist's plea is not a matter of personal revenge but of God's will for righteousness and justice. The oppressors do not yield themselves as servants to God's will as the psalmist does (see vv. 2, 10, 12). Thus the psalmist's personal exodus (see

"bring me out" in v. 11; Exod 18:1; 20:2) will necessarily involve the same treatment of oppressors as in Israel's exodus from Egypt— that is, their decision to cut themselves off from God and God's will means ultimately that they choose their own destruction (see Commentary on Psalms 58; 94; 139; 141).

In the final analysis, Psalm 143 demonstrates the tension that pervades the psalter and the whole Bible: God demands submission to God's will but is ultimately gracious (see Commentary on Psalms 99; 103). While the psalmist is well aware that she or he does not completely embody God's will (v. 2), the psalmist at least affirms that she or he belongs to God (v. 8) and is open to God's will and to God's guidance (vv. 8, 10). In a word, the psalmist sees herself or himself not as the master of her or his own destiny but as God's "servant" (v. 12c). To be God's "servant" is to profess to live finally by the grace of the Master.

REFLECTIONS

1. While the circumstances of its origin and original use are unknown, Psalm 143 provides an apt commentary on and prayer for use by post-exilic Israel. The exile, after all, was understood to be a result of the people's own sinfulness (see v. 2a). But the prophets proclaimed that Israel's sins had been forgiven (see Isa 40:1-4). Thus the protracted suffering of the people in the post-exilic era was viewed in terms of the disobedience of the nations, as evidence of the general unrighteousness of humankind (v. 2b). It is clear that the exile and its aftermath forced Israel to rethink many things, including the nature of suffering and sin and their complex interrelatedness (see Commentary on Psalms 44; 89).

2. While Psalm 143 seems to have assisted Israel to rethink and express its theology in the post-exilic era, it clearly served such a purpose for the apostle Paul. In Rom 3:20, Paul cites Ps 143:2 in support of his conclusion that all "are under the power of sin" (Rom 3:9 NRSV). For Paul, therefore, as for the psalmist, God's activity of setting things right—including the justification of humanity—is finally a manifestation of God's grace. Paul's insight, of course, led to a radical re-formation of the shape of the people of God. Not surprisingly, Psalm 143 later became one of the church's Penitential Psalms, a grouping that can perhaps be traced to Augustine (see Psalms 6; 32; 38; 51; 102; 130). While Psalm 143 does not contain a direct, personal confession of sin, it clearly does assert the sinfulness of humankind. It also eloquently articulates the basis for penitence: the conviction that God is steadfastly loving and that we can therefore offer our whole selves to God (v. 8). Such trust leads to transformed lives that are lived in openness to God's instruction (vv. 8, 10) and that manifest concretely the fruits of repentance. Not surprisingly again, Martin Luther's fresh hearing of the psalms, of Paul, and of Augustine contributed mightily to another radical re-formation of the shape of the people of God in the sixteenth century and beyond.

3. Psalm 143 is assigned for liturgical use as part of the Easter vigil. In this setting, the psalmist's example of suffering servanthood can be an apt and powerful reminder of the life, ministry, death, and resurrection of Jesus, as well as a reminder of Jesus' call for disciples to follow him by taking up their crosses. This kind of discipleship will be possible, however, only as we trust in the ultimate power of God that is manifested as faithful, forgiving love. As an embodiment of God's power and, indeed, God's very character and being, Jesus revealed the depth of God's love and the lengths that God is willing to go to on behalf of sinful humanity. The good news is that God is ultimately the exemplar of suffering servanthood!

In the face of such love, perhaps we may find the motivation and the courage to confront our own individual sinfulness and the corporate sinfulness of humankind. Both dimensions are important, but in our time and place, the latter is crucial. As Douglas John Hall points out: "Most people in the churches seem still, despite half a century of serious and critical reflection on the subject, to think of sin in rather crudely moralistic terms—in terms, to be explicit, of *private* morality, with special emphasis on private *sexual* morality."[514] Hall calls for the church to reexamine its tradition of thinking about sin, including rediscovery of the awareness of the corporate and tragic dimensions of human sinfulness. Our psalmist certainly knew of her or his shortcomings (v. 2*a*), but the psalmist also knew about the corporate sin of humankind (v. 2*b*). Perhaps the psalmist's prayer can begin to put us in touch with the terrible truth about ourselves in order that we may, like the psalmist, rest our case on the wonderful truth about God and God's amazing grace (see Commentary on Psalms 32; 51).

514. Hall, *God and Human Suffering,* 77-78.

PSALM 144:1-15, HAPPY ARE THE PEOPLE WHOSE GOD IS THE LORD

COMMENTARY

Psalm 144 has proved to be quite an enigma to form critics. Because of the numerous similarities to Psalm 18 (cf. vv. 1-2 to Ps 18:1-2, 34, 46-47; v. 5 to Ps 18:9; v. 6 to Ps 18:14; v. 7 to Ps 18:16, 44-45; and v. 10 to the superscription of Psalm 18), Psalm 144 has traditionally been categorized as a royal psalm. At the same time, however, form critics have recognized that this label really does not fit. In particular, the shift from singular to plural speaker in vv. 12-14 is anomalous if Psalm 144 were intended for actual use as a liturgy for kings.

What is puzzling and problematic from a form-critical perspective, however, makes more sense when one considers the placement of Psalm 144 within the psalter. As the final Davidic collection in the psalter (Psalms 138–145) draws to a close, Psalm 144 offers, in effect, a rereading of Psalm 18. It is significant that this rereading reflects the realities of the exile and its aftermath. This

is especially the case in vv. 12-14, but this perspective is reinforced by the fact that Ps 144:5-7 has transformed the affirmations of Ps 18:9, 14, 16, 44-45 into petitions. It is particularly noticeable that the "aliens" (בני־נכר *běnê-nēkār,* vv. 7, 11) whom God had dealt with on the king's behalf in Ps 18:44-45 are precisely the problem in Psalm 144. Again, this situation accurately portrays the perennial reality of the post-exilic era (see the same Hebrew term in Neh 9:2; Isa 56:3, 6; 60:10; 61:5; 62:8; Ezek 44:7, 9). As Mays concludes concerning the use in Psalm 144 of Ps 18:44-45: "The composer of Psalm 144 must have found in these verses a promise for his own time . . . . By re-praying Psalm 18 in a new version, he appealed to the LORD to do for his people what the LORD had done for his servant David."[515] As Mays implies, and as Allen

515. Mays, *Psalms,* 436.

also asserts, Psalm 144 reflects a situation in which the Davidic monarchy had disappeared and in which the promises formerly attached to the monarchy had been transferred to the people as a whole (see Isa 55:3-5 and Commentary on Psalms 105; 110; 132; 149; Introduction).[516]

The perspective of Psalm 144 is thus congruent with that of Books IV-V, which respond to the failure of the Davidic covenant that is articulated in the concluding psalm of Book III, Psalm 89 (see above on Psalms 89; 90; 107; Introduction). In the face of the failure of human monarchs, the people realized that their true and ultimate hope lay in God's sovereignty. Thus, it is not surprising that the phrase "new song" in v. 9 recalls Psalms 96 and 98, both of which explicitly proclaim God's reign. But v. 9 even more clearly recalls Ps 33:2*b*-3*a*. Furthermore, v. 15*b* recalls Ps 33:12*a*. Psalm 33 also asserts God's sovereign claim over all the world and its peoples; and in view of the re-reading of Psalm 18 in Psalm 144, it is not surprising to find these recollections of another psalm from Book I. Indeed, there is still at least one more clear indication that the psalmist was re-reading Book I—namely, v. 3 recalls Ps 8:4. The answer in v. 4 to the question in v. 3 obviously departs from the direction of Psalm 8, but it is very much in keeping with exilic and post-exilic expressions of the awareness of the transience of human life (see Isa 40:6-8). Not coincidentally perhaps, Ps 89:47-48 also articulates an awareness of human transience as the prelude to an appeal for God's help. The same movement is present in Psalm 144, where vv. 3-4 are followed by the petitions of vv. 5-8.

The implicit affirmation of God's sovereignty in Psalm 144 is followed by the explicit affirmation in Ps 145:1, which addresses God as "King." Thus, it seems that Psalms 144-145 form a pair which participates with Psalm 138 in framing the prayers in Psalms 139-143 that form the core of the final Davidic collection in the Psalter (see above on Psalm 138). The effect is to highlight the appropriateness of the individual prayers in Psalms 139-143 for expressing the communal plight of the exilic and post-exilic eras.

144:1-11. As suggested above, the shift of persons in v. 12 serves to divide Psalm 144

516. Allen, *Psalms 101-150,* 290.

into two major sections (see NRSV). As the NRSV indicates, it makes sense to further divide vv. 1-11 into sections of praise (vv. 1-2), reflection (vv. 3-4), petition (vv. 5-8), and further praise and petition (vv. 9-10). The NIV and NRSV disagree on the construal of the role of v. 11. As I have suggested, the NRSV takes it as the conclusion to the first major section; but the NIV interprets v. 11 as a petition which initiates the second major section of the psalm. The NIV's construal apparently envisions the speaker in vv. 11-14 as an imaginary Davidic descendent (see above on Ps 89:46-51). In any case, the situation presupposed is still the one which prevailed in the post-exilic era.

As suggested above, vv. 1-2 recall Ps 18:1-2, 34, 46-47. The major departure from the vocabulary of Psalm 18 is the first word in v. 2—"my steadfast love" (חסד *ḥesed*; see NRSV note). The NIV has stayed with the Hebrew at this point, but the NRSV has chosen to harmonize Ps 144:2 with Ps 18:2. This choice is understandable, but the NIV is to be preferred. After all, the psalmist's use of Psalm 18 is not slavish. The word "steadfast love" represents a creative departure from Psalm 18; and it both recalls the occurrences of "steadfast love" in Psalm 138 (vv. 2, 8) and anticipates the occurrence in Psalm 145 (v. 8). Thus, the three psalms that frame the core of the Davidic collection (Psalms 139–143) all contain the word "steadfast love" (see also Ps 143:8, 12), effectively linking the collection to the beginning of Book V (see Pss 107:1, 8, 15, 21, 31, 43; 108:4; 109:12, 16, 21, 26; Introduction). The word "refuge" in v. 2 links Psalm 144 to the core of the Davidic collection (see Pss 141:8; 142:5), and it also represents what is a key word from the beginning and throughout the Psalter (see Ps 2:12; Introduction). Psalm 2 is also a royal psalm which proclaims God's sovereignty over "the peoples" (Ps 2:1).

But Psalm 2 also recognizes that "the peoples" and their rulers are rebellious, and the transition from vv. 1-2 to vv. 3-4 of Psalm 144 suggests that the rebellious peoples have clearly gained the upper hand. Verses 3-4 recall not Psalm 2 but Psalm 89, another royal psalm but one which recounts the rejection of the Davidic line (see Ps 89:38-51, especially vv. 46-48). Thus, the affirmations found in yet another royal psalm, Psalm 18, have become petitions in Ps 144:5-7 (cf. Ps 18:9, 14, 16, 44-45). The allusions to Psalm 18 in Ps 144:5-7 are drawn from the theophany section (Ps 18:7-15) and from descriptions of the king's deliverance from threat, including "foreigners" or "aliens" (Pss 18:44-45; cf. 144:7, 11). In effect, Psalm 144 requests a new divine appearance and a new deliverance, to which the proper response will be a "new song" (v. 9). Verses 9-10 indicate that the post-exilic community has not given up on the sovereignty of God, despite the dominance of those who are their enemies and God's enemies. As is the case from the beginning and throughout the psalter, the perspective is eschatological; that is, the sovereignty of God is asserted and trusted amid circumstances that seem to deny it (see above on Psalms 2; 65–67; 93; 95–99; 138; Introduction).

144:12-15. The people are left in waiting, anticipating the fulfillment described in vv. 12-14 (see Deut 8:12-13; 28:4). Verse 15 reinforces the conclusion suggested above that Psalm 144 represents a re-reading of Psalm 18 that applies to the whole people the promises formerly attached to the Davidic dynasty. Verse 15 also indicates that happiness is a present possibility even as the people await deliverance, for happiness ultimately involves belonging to God. Not coincidentally, Psalm 33, to which Ps 144:15 alludes (cf. 144:15*b* with 33:12*a*), also leaves the people hoping and waiting (see 33:18-22), as well as praying for God's steadfast love (33:22; see Ps 144:2). The double beatitude in v. 15 also recalls Pss 1:1; 2:12. Amid the existence and apparent prosperity of the wicked, true happiness involves an openness to God that seeks and finds refuge in the sovereign God.

REFLECTIONS

1. Although Psalm 144 would have had special relevance to the post-exilic community, it portrays the position which the people of God perpetually occupy. Like the psalmist, Jesus accompanied his proclamation of God's reign with the announcement that even now happiness belongs to the poor and the persecuted (see Matt 5:3-12). Such happiness consists fundamentally of recognizing God's sovereignty and accepting the invitation to live in the new world of God's reign—that is, of belonging to God. We continue to announce God's claim upon the world amid circumstances that seem to deny it. In short we continue to live eschatologically—in waiting.

2. The process of the composition of Psalm 144 has theological significance. As Mays concludes concerning Psalm 144:

> This psalm, then, is an illustration of the practice of using psalms to compose hymns and prayers, combining earlier material into new compositions for new needs. . . . Revising the material of Psalms for new hymns and prayers is a practice that continues to this day. By it the power and beauty of psalmic material continuously make a canonical contribution to worship.[517]

Psalm 144 is thus an invitation to treat the Psalms not as historical artifacts but as living words which can continue both to address us with God's claim upon our lives and our world and to express our hopes and fears, our praises and prayers.

517. Mays, *Psalms*, 437.

PSALM 145:1-21, GOD IS GREAT AND GOOD

COMMENTARY

Psalm 145 is the only psalm identified by its superscription as "Praise" (NRSV). This uniqueness is appropriate, since Psalm 145 concludes the final Davidic collection in the Psalter (see above on Psalm 138). It is even possible that the Psalter originally ended with Psalm 145. But even as the Psalter now stands, Psalm 145 is, in the words of Gerald Wilson, "the 'climax' of the fifth book of the Psalter, with the final *hallel* (Pss 146–150) drawing its impetus from 145:21."[518] Given the apparent intention of Book V to address the crisis of exile and its aftermath (see above on Psalms 107–108; Introduction), and given the post-exilic perspective reflected in Psalm 144, it is especially significant that this climactic psalm features from its beginning the kingship of the Lord (see NIV, which translates v. 1*a* more accurately). In so doing, it not only recalls the theological heart of the psalter in Book IV (see above on Psalms 93–99; Introduction); but it also, as Wilson suggests, anticipates the explicit proclamation of God's reign in Pss 146:10; 149:2. In view of the disappearance of the monarchy and the accompanying theological crisis, it is highly significant that this climactic Davidic psalm asserts God's comprehensive sovereignty in such an emphatic way.

The proclamation of God's sovereignty is made emphatic by the fourfold repetition of the Hebrew root of "king" (מלך *mlk*, v. 1) in vv. 11-13. In fact, in the Hebrew word order, the word "kingdom" (מלכות *malkût*) occurs three times in succession—once at the end of v. 12 and twice at the beginning of v. 13. This repetition is particularly noticeable since it occurs near the center of the poem. In fact, Barnabas Lindars suggests that vv. 10-13 form the central panel of Psalm 145 (see below). This means that vv. 11, 12, and 13*a* are the central poetic lines. Reading from the bottom upward, the first Hebrew letters of each of these poetic lines combine to spell מלך (*mlk*), the Hebrew root from which the words "king" (*melek*) and "kingdom" (*malkût*) are

derived.[519] While this circumstance may be coincidental, it was probably intended by the clever poet who carefully structured Psalm 145. Its effect is to further emphasize the message that God is king.

That the poet intended to structure Psalm 145 carefully is suggested by its acrostic pattern (see above on Psalms 25; 34; 37; 111; 112; 119). The major Hebrew textual tradition does not contain a poetic line beginning with the letter *nûn* (נ, "*n*", a circumstance that would have called attention to the *mlk* sequence mentioned above), but both NIV and NRSV have supplied the missing line as v. 13*b* on the basis of strong manuscript evidence, including the appearance of the *nûn* line in a Hebrew text from Qumran (see NIV and NRSV notes). The acrostic pattern also serves to reinforce the message of Psalm 145. It suggests completeness or comprehensiveness, and thus it is appropriate for a psalm which proclaims and praises God's comprehensive sovereignty. In this regard too, it is significant that the word "all"/"every" occurs seventeen times!

While the acrostic pattern is the most obvious structural feature of Psalm 145, it is likely that other features also exist that serve to divide the psalm into sections. The traditional observation has been that Psalm 145 is composed of four sections: vv. 1-3, vv. 4-9, vv. 10-13*a*, vv. 13*b*-21. In this view, the first three sections consist of announcements of praise (vv. 1-2, 4-7, 10-12) followed by descriptions of God's character (vv. 3, 8-9, 13*a*). The final section reverses this pattern. An extended description of God's character (vv. 13*b*-20) is followed by a brief but climactic announcement of praise (v. 21). This proposal has the advantage of identifying clearly the alternation between praise and reasons for praise, and it also calls attention to the expansive progression in the first three sections from the individual psalmist's praise (vv. 1-2) to the praise of "All your works" (v. 10 NRSV). This movement is highlighted also in

518. Wilson, *The Editing of the Hebrew Psalter,* 225.

519. Barnabas Lindars, "The Structure of Psalm CXLV," *VT* 29 (1989) 26-28.

v. 21, which combines the perspective of the individual with that of "all flesh" (NRSV).

Attention to other features of Psalm 145, however, yields a different structural proposal. Lindars, for instance, notes the repetition which links vv. 1-2, 21 (see "bless" in vv. 1-2, 21 NRSV; "praise" in vv. 2, 21 NRSV; "forever and ever" in vv. 1, 21); and he concludes that these verses stand apart as a framework for the psalm. Verse 3 then belongs with vv. 4-6, and the words "Great" (v. 3) and "greatness" (vv. 3, 6 NRSV) form an envelope for this section. The words "goodness" (v. 7) and "good" (v. 9) do the same thing for vv. 7-9. The central section consists of vv. 10-13; it is bounded by a double envelope (see NRSV "works" and "deeds," which translate the same Hebrew word; see also "faithful" in v. 10 and "gracious" in v. 13 NRSV, which translate the same Hebrew root). The beginning of the central section is tied to the framework of the poem by means of the repetition of "bless" (NRSV), and this section features the concept of kingship which is introduced in v. 1 (see above). According to Lindars, vv. 14-16 form a three-line section corresponding to vv. 7-9, and v. 17-20 form a four-line section corresponding to vv. 3-6, thus providing symmetry for the poem and focusing attention toward the center.[520] Lindars's proposal and the traditional proposal need not be considered as mutually exclusive. Rather, it is possible to view the structure and movement of Psalm 145 on more than one level. Each proposal highlights different, but equally important, aspects of the poem.

145:1-6. The word "praise" (תהלה *tĕhillâ*) in the title sets the tone for the whole psalm (see vv. 2-3, 21). As the psalmist addresses "my God the King" (v. 1 NIV), he or she announces three actions, each of which communicates the recognition of God's sovereignty: "extol"/"exalt" (see Exod 15:2 in relation to 15:18; Ps 99:5, 9), "bless" (NRSV; see Ps 96:2 in relation to 96:10), and "praise" (see Ps 22:26 in relation to 22:28, where the NRSV's "dominion" is from the same root as "King"/"kingdom" in 145:1, 11-13). The mention of God's "name" in vv. 1-2 anticipates the attention which will subsequently be directed to God's character (vv. 3, 8-9), including God's activity (see

"works"/"made"/"deeds"/"doings" in vv. 4, 9, 10, 13, 17 NRSV; "fulfills" in v. 19 also translates the same Hebrew root).

The attribute of greatness is regularly associated with God's reign (vv. 3, 6; see Pss 47:2; 95:3; 99:2 and especially 48:1; 96:4). So are the words in the phrase "glorious splendor of your majesty" in v. 5 (see vv. 11-12; the same three words occur in Ps 96:6-7 as the NRSV's "honor," "majesty," and "glory"). While God's greatness is finally "unsearchable" (NRSV; see Job 5:9; 9:10; 36:26; Isa 40:28), there is much that can be seen and understood—God's "works" (vv. 4, 9, 10, 13, 17, 19; see above), "mighty acts" (see "mighty" and "mighty acts" in vv. 11-12 NIV; and see Pss 106:2; 150:2), "wondrous works" (v. 5 NRSV; see Exod 3:20; 15:11; Pss 9:1; 26:7; 77:11, 14; 78:4; 106:22), and "awesome deeds" (v. 6 NRSV; see Exod 15:11; Pss 47:2; 66:3, 5; 68:35; 76:7; 106:22). As is always the case, the reality of God's reign is good news that must be and is communicated (see NRSV "declare" in v. 4; "meditate," which can also connote telling, in v. 5; "tell" in vv. 6, 11 NIV; "proclaim" in v. 6 NIV; "speak" in vv. 11, 21 NIV; "make known" in v. 12 NRSV).

145:7-9. God's activity reveals God's character, to which vv. 7-9 direct attention. NRSV "fame" (v. 7) is more literally "remembrance"; it is associated elsewhere with God's activity and character (see NRSV "name" in Pss 30:4; 97:12; "renown" in 111:4). As in God's revelation to Moses, so here God's goodness (vv. 7, 9; see Exod 33:19; Pss 25:7; 27:13; 100:5; 106:1; 107:1; 118:1) takes the form of grace, mercy/compassion, and steadfast love (vv. 8-9; see Exod 34:6-7; Pss 25:6-7; 86:15; 103:8; Introduction). In short, it is God's gracious love which finally yields "righteousness" (v. 7), one of the hallmarks of God's reign (see Pss 89:14; 96:13; 97:2; 98:9; 99:4). The repeated "compassionate" in vv. 8-9 (NIV) underscores the astounding message—God's power is manifest as motherly love (see above on Psalm 25; 131). The two occurrences of "all" in v. 9 anticipate the expansive perspective of vv. 10-21, which contain fourteen more occurrences of "all"/"every" (see above).

145:10-13. The psalmist and the generations are joined by "All your works" in

520. Lindars, "The Structure of Psalm CXLV," 25-29.

expressing thankful praise (v. 10; see Psalm 148). This is only appropriate, since "all" God "has made" has been the recipient of God's motherly compassion (v. 9; "made" in v. 9 and "works" in v. 10 are the same Hebrew word). The experience of God's gracious love produces witnesses to God's sovereignty, to God's particular way of exercising power. The word "kingdom" occurs four times in vv. 11-13. God's sovereignty is central both structurally and theologically (see above). Its spatial and temporal reach is unlimited (vv. 12-13a; see Dan 4:3). Its character is unwavering; in word and deed, God's power is manifest as faithful love (v. 13b; NRSV's "faithful" and "gracious" represent the Hebrew roots behind the word-pair "steadfast love and faithfulness" in Exod 34:6; see Introduction).

145:14-20. These verses provide concrete illustrations of the divine activity which reveals God's grace, compassion, and love. In this sense, Lindars is correct to correlate vv. 14-16 with vv. 7-9 and vv. 17-20 with vv. 3-6; however, vv. 14-20 lack the verbal clues that would clearly distinguish vv. 14-16 from vv. 17-20. But Lindars admits that throughout Psalm 145, the sections overlap. In this case, for instance, vv. 14-16 and vv. 18-20 seem to surround the central v. 17, in which "righteous" (NIV) recalls v. 7 and "loving" (NIV) recalls vv. 8, 10, and 13b. In any case, vv. 14-17 assert that God shows steadfast love by upholding or sustaining the threatened (v. 14a; see Pss 3:5; 37:17, 24; 54:4), by lifting up the oppressed (v. 14b; see Ps 146:8), and by providing for all creatures (vv. 15-16; see Ps 104:27-28). Without contradicting this universalistic perspective, vv. 18-20 focus more narrowly on those who explicitly recognize God's sovereignty—those who "call on" (v. 18), "fear" (v. 19a; see 22:23; 25:12,

14; 103:11, 13, 17; 112:1), "cry" to (v. 19b; see Exod 2:23; Pss 18:6; 34:15; 39:12; 40:1), and "love" God (v. 20a; see Pss 31:23; 116:1). They will experience God's presence (v. 18; see Pss 34:18; 75:1), provision (v. 19), and protection (v. 20a; see NRSV "keep" in Ps 121:3-5, 7-8).

In short, those who acknowledge God's sovereignty experience salvation or life (v. 19b; see above on Ps 3:2, 7-8), while the wicked are destroyed (v. 20b). Verse 20b in particular seems to contradict v. 9 and the universalistic perspective of vv. 10-17. The sharp distinction between the wicked and those who love God recalls Psalm 1, and what applies to Psalm 1 applies to Psalm 145 as well. That is, the happiness or prosperity of the righteous (see Ps 1:1, 3) is not so much a reward as it is their experience of being connected to the true source of life—God. Similarly, the destruction of the wicked is not so much a punishment as it is the result of their own choice to cut themselves off from the source of life. The compassionate God does not will to destroy the wicked (see Ps 145:9), but their own autonomy leads to their ruin (see above on Psalms 1–2).

145:21. The psalmist's choice is clear. She or he "will speak the praise of the LORD" (v. 21a NRSV; see the superscription and vv. 2-3). It is the vocation that the psalmist envisions for "all flesh" (v. 21b NRSV). Thus v. 21 prepares for the crescendo of praise which follows in Psalms 146–150, culminating in the similar verse which concludes the psalter (150:6). To praise God—that is, to acknowledge one's own insufficiency and the sovereignty of God's loving purposes—is ultimately the only mode of being that truly constitutes life (see Commentary on Psalms 8; 100; 103–104).

REFLECTIONS

As Mays points out concerning Psalm 145, "the Talmud showed its estimate of the psalm's worth by saying, 'Every one who repeats the *Tehillah* of David thrice a day may be sure that he is a child of the world to come' (*Berakot*, 4b)."[521] To repeat Psalm 145 is to confess the insufficiency of self and the sovereignty of God. It is, in a real sense, to live in a different world—not in an escapist sense, but in the sense that God's claims, values, and priorities inevitably put us at odds with a prevailing culture

521. Mays, *Psalms*, 437.

that promotes autonomy (see Commentary on Psalms 1; 2). In other words, Psalm 145 invites us to live in the world of God's reign, the world where the fundamental reality and pervasive power is the gracious, compassionate, faithful love of God. It is to life in this world that Jesus also invites his followers, reminding them that the decision to enter involves repentance (Mark 1:14-15) and the denial of self in order to experience true self-fulfillment (Mark 8:34-35). As Jesus reminds his followers, and as Psalm 145 also asserts, the world of God's reign is a topsy-turvy world where the poor and the persecuted are happy, where the humble are exalted, and where the last are first (see Ps 145:14-20; Matt 5:3-11; Mark 8:33-37; 10:41-45; Luke 18:9-14). To live in this world is to live eschatologically (see Commentary on Psalms 2; 93; 95; 96; 97; 98; 99); amid the wicked and their opposition to God (see v. 20b), those who love God dare to live by God's claim, under God's watchful care, and into God's promising future.

Not only do classical Jewish sources recognize the value of Psalm 145, but so do Christian ones. Augustine, for instance, opens his *Confessions* by quoting Ps 145:3 (see also Pss 48:1; 96:4). In his opening paragraph, Augustine claims that because human beings are God's creation, they cannot experience contentment apart from praising God, "because you made us for yourself and our hearts find no peace until they rest in you."[522] As Augustine recognized, the psalmist knew this great truth; and Psalm 145 invites us and "all flesh" to know it as well. What's more, Psalm 145 invites us to live by this truth, and to join all creation in making known to all people the good news that God's power is manifest in gracious, compassionate love (vv. 7-13; see Matt 28:18-20; John 17:20-23; and above on Psalms 8, 100, 103–104, 117).

522. Augustine, *Confessions*, 21.

PSALM 146:1-10, JUSTICE FOR THE OPPRESSED

COMMENTARY

Psalm 146 is the first in a series of hymns or songs of praise (Psalms 146–150), all opening and closing with "Praise the LORD!" (*Hallelu-yah*), that brings the book of Psalms to a conclusion with a crescendo of praise. Psalm 145, especially v. 21, has prepared for Psalms 146–150, including anticipation of several themes that are present in Psalm 146 as well as in Psalms 147–150. For instance, like Psalm 145, Psalm 146 recalls both the beginning of the psalter (Psalms 1–2) and the theological heart of the psalter (Psalms 93; 95–99). In particular, Psalm 146 is explicitly instructional (vv. 3-5), recalling Psalm 1, which orients the reader to hear the entire collection as *torah*, "instruction" (Ps 1:2; NIV and NRSV, "law"). The content of the instruction in Psalm 146 is essentially the same as that of Psalm 2: Trust God, not human rulers. Because human rulers and their plans perish (v. 4; see also Pss 1:6; 2:12), "happy" are

those who entrust their lives to God (v. 5; see also Pss 1:1; 2:12). The message of Psalm 2 anticipates the theological heart of the psalter: The Lord reigns (see Psalms 93; 95–99; Introduction); thus it is not surprising that this message is echoed clearly at the conclusion of the psalter, including Ps 146:10 (see also Pss 145:1, 11-13; 149:2). The contrast between "the righteous" (v. 8) and "the way of the wicked" (v. 9) also explicitly recalls Ps 1:5-6. This contrast pervades the psalter (see Commentary on Psalms 1–2; Introduction), and again, it is not surprising that it is clearly echoed as the psalter concludes (see also Pss 145:20; 147:6; and the same contrast presented in different terms in 149:5-9).

The NIV's divisions reflect the traditional structural analysis of Psalm 146. Following the initial *hallelu-yah,* vv. 1-2 introduce the psalm by both inviting and announcing praise. Verses 3-4 offer instruction concerning what praise means: exclusive loyalty to and trust in God rather than human rulers. The beatitude in v. 5 initiates a section that continues with an extended series of participial phrases (vv. 6-9*a*) and is rounded off by a return to finite verb forms in v. 9*bc*. The NRSV's division between v. 7*ab* and v. 7*c* marks the point where the participles begin to be accompanied by a subject, "the LORD" (vv. 7*c*-9*a*). Returning to the political vocabulary of vv. 3-4 (see "princes"), v. 10 offers a climactic concluding affirmation of God's eternal reign, followed by the final *hallelu-yah*.

John Kselman proposes an alternative structural analysis. Paying particular attention to the didactic dimension of the psalm, he proposes a chiastic structure in which vv. 1-2 correspond to v. 10; vv. 3-4 correspond to vv. 8*c*-9, both of which Kselman labels "Wisdom"; and vv. 5-8*b* form the central section, which Kselman calls "God Creator and Redeemer."[523] Kselman's proposal has the advantage of highlighting the instructional intent of Psalm 146 (vv. 3-4, 8*c*-9). Given the participial series in vv. 6-9*a*, it seems unlikely that a division should be made between v. 8*b* and v. 8*c*; however, the words "righteous" (צדיקים *ṣaddîqîm*) in v. 8*c* and "wicked" (רשעים *rĕšā'îm*) in v. 9*c* form a conceptual envelope that lends support to Kselman's analysis. In the final analysis, it is not necessary to view the traditional proposal and Kselman's proposal as mutually exclusive. As is often the case, attention to varying stylistic criteria yields alternative proposals that may be equally legitimate and helpful in calling attention to the various features of a poem.

146:1-4. As is typical for a song of praise, v. 1 begins with an invitation in the imperative, although it is unusual that it is addressed to "my soul." This happens elsewhere only in Pss 103:1, 22 and 104:1, 35. Not coincidentally perhaps, v. 2 is also reminiscent of Psalm 104 (see v. 33), a psalm that eloquently portrays God's cosmic sovereignty over "the heavens" (v. 2), "the earth" (v. 4), and "the sea" (v. 25). These same three realms will be mentioned in Ps 146:6. Praise—the offering of the whole self to God in worship and work—is the lifelong vocation of the human creature in response to God's cosmic

sovereignty and thus God's comprehensive claim on human life and the life of the world (see Reflections; see also Psalms 8; 100; 103; 104; 145; 150).

The antithesis of praising God is trusting oneself or trusting human agencies and institutions in place of God. It is precisely this that the psalmist warns against in v. 3 (see Ps 118:8-9; Jer 17:5-7; see also Pss 9:10; 25:2; Introduction). Thus, while all the songs of praise are implicitly instructional, Psalm 146 is very explicitly so (see above on Ps 100:3). The Hebrew play on words in vv. 3-4 emphasizes the transience of human life and human "help" (v. 3*b*); that is, "mortals" (אדם *'ādām*, v. 3) soon revert to "the earth" (אדמה *'ădāmâ*, v. 4). As the NIV suggests, the NRSV's "help" is often translated "salvation" or "deliverance." This word is key in Psalm 3 (see vv. 2, 7-8), and thus Psalm 146 recalls Psalm 3 as well as Psalms 1–2. As suggested above, "perish" (v. 4) recalls Pss 1:6; 2:12, where "the way of the wicked" (1:6; see 146:9) and the way of those who refuse to "serve the LORD" (2:11) will "perish." In the book of Psalms and the Bible as a whole, wickedness is essentially a matter of trust. It involves the decision to trust someone or something other than God, and the results are empty and destructive, as vv. 4, 9 suggest (see above on Kselman's structural proposal, which posits a correspondence between vv. 3-4 and vv. 8*c*-9). Given the recollection of Psalm 104 in vv. 1-2, it is not surprising that v. 4 is reminiscent of Ps 104:29. This common feature of vv. 1-2, 4 is another link between Psalm 146 and Psalm 145, in which vv. 15-16 recall Ps 104:27-28 (see below on Ps 147:8-9).

146:5-10. In Ps 40:4, as in Psalm 146, happiness is also a matter of whom one trusts (see Jer 17:7). In Ps 33:20-21, confidence in God's help is articulated as "trust" (see also the beatitude in Ps 33:12). Thus, the beatitude in v. 5 is not unexpected. In fact, as the final beatitude in the psalter, it effectively summarizes all the others (see 1:2; 2:12; Introduction). As the whole sweep of the psalter makes clear, happiness is not the absence of pain and trouble but the presence of a God who cares about human hurt and who acts on behalf of the afflicted and the oppressed. The series of participial phrases in vv. 6-9*a* portrays precisely such a God. Verse 6 cites

523. John S. Kselman, "Psalm 146 in Its Context," *CBQ* 50 (1988) 591.

Israel's two basic traditions, which are finally inseparable (see Commentary on Psalms 33; 65; 66)—God is creator (v. 6a; see Genesis 1–2; Psalms 8; 104), and God is deliverer (v. 6b; see Exod 34:6, the self-revelation of God that forms the real culmination of the exodus story). Verse 7a represents what Brueggemann calls "the main claim for Yahweh" (see Ps 103:6, where the nearly identical claim is the climactic element in a series of participles).[524] Not surprisingly, v. 7a features the concept of "justice," which elsewhere characterizes the royal policy or will of the sovereign God (see Pss 89:14; 96:13; 97:2; 98:9; 99:4). The remainder of the participial series tells how God exercises sovereignty—namely, by loving service on behalf of persons in need. Verses 7b-9a offer concrete illustrations involving those whom God helps—"the hungry" (see Ps 107:9; Isa 58:7), "prisoners" (see Isa 61:1), "the blind" (see Isa 42:7), the "bowed down" (see Ps 145:14), "the alien" (see Exod 23:9; Ps 94:6; Jer 7:6). While it

524. Walter Brueggemann, "Psalm 146: Psalm for the Nineteenth Sunday after Pentecost," *No Other Foundation* 8/1 (Summer 1987) 28.

may seem that "the righteous" (v. 8c) do not belong in this series, we must remember that it is precisely "the righteous" in the psalter who are constantly besieged, assaulted, and oppressed (see Ps 34:19). Verse 9bc returns to the use of finite verbs, but the affirmation is the same: God helps the needy (see Pss 68:5; 94:6; Jer 7:6; 22:3) and opposes "the way of the wicked" (see Pss 1:6; 145:20; 147:6).

In view of v. 10, which explicitly affirms the eternal reign of God (see Exod 15:18; Pss 29:10; 96:10; 97:1; 99:1; 145:1, 13), vv. 6-9 come into focus all the more clearly as a policy statement for the kingdom of God. The sovereign God stands for and works for justice, not simply as an abstract principle but as an embodied reality—provision for basic human needs, liberation from oppression, empowerment for the disenfranchised and dispossessed. Whereas in v. 1 the psalmist invites her or his own self to praise God, the psalmist addresses Zion in v. 10. The proper response—individually and corporately—to God's sovereign claim on the world is simply this, "Praise the LORD!"

REFLECTIONS

1. Since it introduces the final collection of the psalter, it is fitting that Psalm 146 recalls Psalm 1–3 in such a way that it summarizes the fundamental message of the book. Like Psalm 1, Psalm 146 pronounces "happy" those whose lives are completely oriented to God. Like Psalm 2, Psalm 146 asserts God's sovereign claim on the world. Like Psalm 3, Psalm 146 makes it clear that God's help does not mean a carefree existence for the righteous. In other words, by characterizing "the righteous" as being oppressed and hungry and imprisoned and so on (vv. 7-9), Psalm 146 conveys the eschatological perspective of the psalter: God's reign is proclaimed amid circumstances that seem to deny it (see Psalms 2; 93; 95–99; Introduction).

2. The eschatological proclamation of God's reign calls for a decision. To use a key term employed by Psalm 146, the issue is this: Whom shall we *trust?* The question is as timely and crucial now as it ever has been. To trust in "princes" and "mortals" is a perennial and pervasive temptation, especially in a thoroughly secularized society like ours. Human help seems so compelling and immediate and effective. Self-help schemes abound, and the credo of our culture has virtually become, "God helps those who help themselves" (see Commentary on Psalm 3). Such a credo, however, results inevitably not in praise of God but in self-congratulation. The results are ruinous (v. 9c). As Claus Westermann puts it: "The praise of God occupied for Israel actually the place where 'faith [that is, *trust*] in God' stands for us . . . the directing of this praise to a man, an idea, or an institution must disturb and finally destroy life itself."[525]

525. Westermann, *Praise and Lament in the Psalms,* 155, 160-61.

3. Psalm 146 is, therefore, an urgent call to praise—indeed, a call to life (see Commentary on Psalm 100). In biblical terms, to praise God is to live, and to live is to praise God. Praise is thus both liturgy and life-style; the two are inseparable. Brueggemann makes this clear as he reflects upon Psalm 146, taking "sing praise" in v. 2 as a point of departure:

> Israel holds doxology against the powerful staying force of the rulers of this age. Israel sings, and we never know what holy power is unleashed by such singing. Israel sings, and we never know what human imagination is authorized by such singing. One reason we may not sing is that such hope is intellectually outrageous. Another reason we may not sing is that such an alternative is too subversive. But the Church and Israel do sing! This singing is our vocation, our duty, and our delight. We name this staggering name—and the world becomes open again, especially for those on whom it had closed in such deathly ways—the prisoners, the blind, the sojourner, the widow, the orphan. The world is sung open. Against this Holy One and this song, death cannot close the world into injustice again.[526]

4. By way of its call to praise (v. 1) and its instruction (vv. 3-4) and proclamation of God's reign (v. 10), Psalm 146 anticipates Jesus' preaching of the reign of God (see Mark 1:14-15), as well as Jesus' teaching about happiness (see Matt 5:3-11) and his enactment of God's will in a ministry of justice, feeding, liberation, healing, and compassion (see Matt 11:2-6; Luke 4:16-21). As the church faces the same kind of opposition to God's values and policies that Jesus faced, Psalm 146 is an encouragement to God's people to sing and to pray as Jesus taught, affirming "thine is the kingdom" even as we pray, "thy kingdom come, thy will be done on earth as it is in heaven."

526. Brueggemann, "Psalm 146," 29.

PSALM 147:1-20, GOD SENDS OUT GOD'S WORD

COMMENTARY

Psalm 147 is a hymn or song of praise that is part of the final collection in the psalter (Psalms 146–150), each psalm of which begins and ends with *hallelu-yah.* In several ways, Psalm 147 follows well upon Psalm 146. In fact, v. 1 seems to serve as much as an evaluation of the preceding psalm as it does an introduction to the rest of Psalm 147 (see 142:6; 147:1). Furthermore, Ps 147:6 recalls Ps 146:9, and more generally, Psalm 147 focuses alternately upon the two conceptually distinct but ultimately inseparable spheres that are introduced in Ps 146:6: creation and deliverance (see Commentary on Psalm 146 and below on the structure of Psalm 147). Besides recalling Psalm 146, Psalm 147 also anticipates Psalms 148 and

149, each of which will concentrate on one of the two alternating spheres in Psalm 147. Psalm 148 invites all creation to praise God, while Psalm 149 extends the invitation to Israel (see esp. 149:2, 5).

Given the establishment of a post-exilic perspective from the beginning of Book V (see Ps 107:2-3), it is not surprising that the concluding collection also clearly articulates this perspective. In particular, Ps 147:2-3, 12-14 conveys the same good news that was announced in the exilic and post-exilic eras. The Greek and Latin textual traditions associate Psalm 147 with Haggai and Zechariah, although scholars are more inclined to associate it with the time of Nehemiah. The psalm also has affinities with the material in Isaiah

40–66. All of this suggests the post-exilic origin of this psalm, although precision is not possible. In any case, its placement reinforces the conclusion that Book V was shaped in response to the ongoing crisis of the post-exilic era (see Psalms 107; 108; 111; 120; 137; 138; 149; Introduction).

Psalm 147 is usually divided into three sections: vv. 1-6, vv. 7-11, vv. 12-20. The beginning of each section is marked by an imperative. In the Greek and Latin traditions, vv. 12-20 actually constitute a separate psalm; some commentators have even suggested that three separate psalms have been joined to form Psalm 147. But the unity of Psalm 147 is evident. Not only is it bounded by *hallelu-yah,* but also each section gives attention to both creation (vv. 4-5, 8-10, 15-18) and deliverance (vv. 2-3, 6, 11, 13-14, 19-20). In fact, the first and last sections show a similar pattern—deliverance (vv. 2-3, 6 and vv. 13-14, 19-20) encompasses creation (vv. 4-5 and vv. 15-18). Thus the very noticeable juxtaposition of vv. 18-19, marked by the repetition of "word," is simply the climactic instance of a pattern that characterizes the whole poem (see Ps 146:6-7).

147:1-6. After the initial *hallelu-yah,* v. 1 offers an observation about praise that is unusual but not entirely unique (see Ps 92:1). As a comparison of the NIV with the NRSV suggests, the conclusion of v. 1 is ambiguous. The adjective "fitting" (נאוה *nā'wâ*) certainly seems to describe the act of praising God (see Ps 33:1), but does the adjective "gracious"/"pleasant" (נעים *nā'îm*) describe God or the act of praising God? The same ambiguity is present in Ps 135:3; in all likelihood, it is intentional. James Kugel even suggests that v. 1 is an instance of "strangeifying"—that is, using language in an unusual way for special effect and to pose an interpretive challenge.[527] Thus it is appropriate that different possibilities are offered for construing v. 1.

Reasons for praise follow in vv. 2-6. Verse 2 in particular suggests an exilic or post-exilic perspective. In these eras, Jerusalem was rebuilt (v. 2*a*; see Neh 12:27), and the exiles or "outcasts" were gathered (v. 2*b*; see Deut 30:4; Neh 1:9; Isa 11:12; 56:8; Jer 30:17; Ezek 34:16; Mic 4:6). The language

527. Kugel, *The Idea of Biblical Poetry,* 92.

and imagery of v. 3 are also used elsewhere of God's redemptive handling of the exiles, who are characterized elsewhere as "broken-hearted" (see Isa 61:1), whom God "heals" (see Ps 107:20; Isa 57:18-19; Jer 30:17) and "binds up" (Isa 61:1; Ezek 34:16). The same can be said of v. 6*a* (see also Isa 61:1). Verses 2-3, 6 encompass vv. 4-5, which cite God's creative activity as reason for praise. Similar juxtaposition of God's creative and redemptive activity is found frequently in Isaiah 40–66 (see Isa 40:28; 41:14; 45:18-21), which can be dated to the exilic and early post-exilic eras. In fact, vv. 4-5 are very similar to Isa 40:26. The word "great" (גדול *gādôl*) in v. 5*a* is expressive of sovereignty (see Pss 48:1; 95:3; 96:4; 99:2; Jer 10:6-7), as is the word "power" (כח *kōaḥ*; see Exod 9:16; Ps 29:4; Jer 10:10-12). In the face of the stark realities of the exilic and post-exilic eras—including the loss of the Davidic monarchy—the prophet of the exile proclaimed the sovereignty of God (see Isa 52:7). The book of Psalms appears to have been shaped to offer the same response (see Commentary on Psalms 2; 89; 90; 93; 94; 95; 96; 97; 98; 99; 107; Introduction), and it is appropriate that the concluding collection returns explicitly to this proclamation (see Pss 146:10; 149:2). The NRSV's "number" (v. 4*a*) and "measure" (v. 5*b*) translate the same Hebrew root (ספר *sāpar*), thus providing an envelope structure for these two verses and emphasizing the message that God's "understanding" exceeds human comprehension (see Isa 40:28; see a similar idea in Ps 139:17-18, where "count" in v. 18*a* represents the same Hebrew root as "number" and "measure" in 147:4-5).

147:7-11. The return to imperatives in v. 7 marks the beginning of the second section. The verb translated "sing" (ענה *'anâ*) is unusual in the psalms (see only Ps 119:172). Its very infrequency may call attention to Israel's deliverance from Egypt, since it is used to introduce Miriam's song in response to the sea crossing (Exod 15:21), a song that follows immediately the proclamation of God's reign in Exod 15:18. To sing "with thanksgiving" is an appropriate response to God's sovereignty (see the title to and v. 4 of Psalm 100). The second imperative, "make melody," also indicates an appropriate response to God's sovereignty (see Ps 149:3; see also v. 1; Pss

47:6-7; 98:5). The lyre is specifically involved in such responses in Pss 98:5; 149:3 (see also Ps 33:2). As is often the case, the assertion of God's sovereignty in vv. 8-9 is at least implicitly polemical (see Pss 96:5; 97:7). Here God does what the Canaanites routinely attributed to Baal—sending the rain that provided growth for plants and food for animals (see Commentary on Psalms 29; 104). Verses 8-9 especially recall Ps 104:14, 27. Psalms 145 and 146 also recall Psalm 104 (see Pss 145:5, 15-16; 146:1-2, 4), thus providing a further link between Psalms 145–147 and increasing the likelihood that these concluding psalms are relatively late and were written in part as artistic anthologies of earlier psalms. In this regard, v. 10 recalls Ps 33:16-17 and v. 11 even more clearly recalls Ps 33:18. God does not need impressive displays of human power; rather, God is pleased when persons yield themselves to the divine rule (see Pss 25:12, 14; 33:18; 103:11, 13, 17). Because God's sovereignty consists of the power of faithful love (see Pss 5:7; 25:6-7, 10; 33:5, 18, 22; 103:4, 8, 11, 17; Introduction) rather than sheer force, God's people will live inevitably by hope and in waiting (see Pss 25:3, 5, 21; 33:18, 22). The repetition of "pleasure" in vv. 10b, 11a anticipates Ps 149:4 and also recalls another exilic text, Isa 42:1.

147:12-20. Two more imperatives in v. 12 mark the beginning of the final section. The mention of Jerusalem recalls v. 2, as does the content of v. 13a (see Neh 3:3, 6, 13). Jerusalem was the place where God's blessing was sought (v. 13b; see Pss 129:8; 132:15; 133:3; 134:3) and peace was anticipated (v. 14a; see Pss 125:5; 128:6; Isa 60:17). Verse 14b recalls Ps 81:16. Verse 15 introduces the word that provides conceptual unity for the rest of the poem: God's "word" (see vv.

18-19; see also Pss 33:4, 6; 107:20). As in the conclusion to the preceding section (vv. 10-11), vv. 15-20 appear to have been influenced by Psalm 33 (see esp. 33:4-9), in which God's "word" also indicates and enacts God's sovereignty (see also Genesis 1; Isa 40:8; 55:10-11). God is sovereign over the "earth" (v. 15a; see Pss 146:6; 148:7-10) and all the forces that are still impressive to modern people but would have been especially impressive and important to ancient folk—snow and frost (v. 16; see Job 38:29; Isa 55:10), hail (v. 17a; see Job 37:10; 38:29), cold (v. 17b; Job 37:9). The mention of God's "word" in v. 18a makes it clear that these phenomena cannot be subsumed simply under the category of meteorology. For the psalmist, because God rules the world, even the weather is a theological matter! Thus, while "wind" in v. 18b is a proper translation, we should hear in it another nuance. The word is רוח (*rûaḥ*), often translated "spirit." As in Gen 1:2 and Exod 14:21, the wind is not simply a meteorological phenomenon. It somehow contains and conveys the power, presence, and purpose of Israel's personal God. Verse 19 reveals the personal dimension of the divine word. God's word—formerly addressed to snow and hail and wind—is now addressed to Israel. To know God's word is to know God's will and, indeed, God's very self. The NRSV's "ordinances" (משפטים *mišpāṭîm*, vv. 19b, 20b) could more literally be translated "justices," and God's establishment of justice is a hallmark of God's reign (see Pss 89:14; 96:13; 97:2; 98:9; 99:4; 146:7; 149:9). The word God sends out marks God's sovereign claim on the earth and everything in it (vv. 15-18; see Ps 148:7-8), including Israel (vv. 19-20) and ultimately all the earth's rulers and peoples (see Ps 148:11-12).

REFLECTIONS

Verses 15-20, especially the juxtaposition of vv. 18-19, convey in a particularly clear way a crucial theological insight: the ultimate inseparability of creation and redemption. To put the matter in slightly different terms, God's dealing with a particular people—Israel and the church—is for the fulfillment of God's purposes for all creation. To be sure, this conviction is not unique to Psalm 147. It is evident in Israel's choice to begin its story with creation rather than with exodus, and it is evident in the sweep of the biblical witness from the OT to the NT in the direction of "a new heaven and a new earth" (Rev 21:1 NRSV) and "the healing of the nations" (Rev 22:2 NRSV). Furthermore, this insight is conveyed in several other psalms as well (see Commentary on Psalms 19; 33; 65; 66; 96; 97; 98; 99).

Even so, Psalm 147 articulates this conviction in a striking way that brings home its remarkable significance. The force that drives the universe, producing rain and snow and heat and cold (vv. 15-18), is not just something we observe and experience but *someone* we know (vv. 19-20). At the heart of the biblical faith is the astounding claim that the power that has strewn the stars into their courses (v. 4) is the same power that—or better, *who*—"heals the brokenhearted" (v. 3), "lifts up the downtrodden" (v. 6), and declares an intelligible, personal, life-giving word to Israel (vv. 19-20). In short, our trust—indeed, our only hope—is that the power behind the universe has a personal face that is turned toward us in "steadfast love" (v. 11 *b*). Although this word will not be used until the NT, Psalm 147 articulates the *incarnation* of God's word (see John 1:1, 14). The cosmic God is personally, intimately, inextricably involved in the lives and futures of human beings. With good reason, Psalm 147 is regularly used during the season of Christmas, the Festival of the Incarnation. The only proper and fitting response to the good news of God's incarnational involvement with the world is to stand in awe (v. 11 *a*) and to sing the words that convey the grateful offering of our lives, "Praise the LORD!"

PSALM 148:1-14, LET THEM PRAISE THE NAME OF THE LORD

COMMENTARY

Psalm 148 is the third in a collection of hymns or songs of praise, each bounded by *hallelu-yah,* that concludes the psalter (see Commentary on Psalm 146). Of the two alternating spheres of God's activity in Psalm 147—creation and deliverance—Psalm 148 focuses on the former as it calls all creation to praise God. Only in v. 14 does Psalm 148 turn to the sphere of deliverance, thus anticipating the focus of Psalm 149 (see 148:14; 149:1, 5, 9). Although neither Psalm 147 nor Psalm 148 contains the word "reign" or "king," they are bounded by two psalms that do (see Pss 146:10; 149:2), and the effect of both Psalms 147 and 148 is to articulate God's universal sovereignty (see below on v. 13). Thus Psalm 148 participates in the final collection's recalling of the theological heart of the psalter: God reigns (see Commentary on Psalms 93; 95; 96; 97; 98; 99; Introduction). And thereby it contributes to the response of Books IV–V to the theological crisis of the exilic and post-exilic eras (see Commentary on Psalms 90; 107; Introduction).

In a sense, Psalm 148 displays the typical structure of a song of praise—invitation to praise followed by reasons for praise. But in this case, the invitation is greatly elaborated, thus anticipating Psalm 150. Every half-line of the psalm up through v. 4*a*, for instance, begins with an imperative summons to praise. The invitation is resumed in v. 5*a* with a jussive verbal form ("Let them praise"), and then reasons for praise follow in vv. 5*b*-6. The return to the imperative in v. 7*a* marks the beginning of the second section of the poem. Whereas vv. 1-6 focus on praise "from the heavens" (v. 1), vv. 7-14 focus on praise "from the earth" (v. 7). As in the first section, a jussive invitation to praise (v. 13*a*, which is identical to v. 5*a*) immediately precedes the reasons for praise in vv. 13*b*-14. By the end of the psalm, the word "praise" (הלל *hillēl*) has occurred eleven times as a verb and once as a noun (v. 14). This impressive repetition in itself suggests the inclusivity of praise, which Psalm 148 invites. The intent to be inclusive—indeed, *universal*—is reinforced by the prepositional phrases in vv. 1,

7 (see also NRSV, "above earth and heaven" in v. 13) and by the repetition of "all" in vv. 2-3, 7, 9-11, 14. Then, of course, there is the actual listing of beings (heavenly and earthly) and things (animate and inanimate) that are invited to praise God. The effect of the structure and stylistic features of Psalm 148 is even more inclusive than the climactic final verse of the psalter, for in Psalm 148 it is not just a matter of "everything that breathes" praising God (150:6). Rather, it is also a matter of *everything that is* praising God.

148:1-6. In the first section, God is to be praised "from the heavens" (v. 1) by the beings and objects that inhabit the heavens (vv. 2-3), as well as by the heavens themselves (v. 4*a*, lit., "heaven of heavens"; see Ps 19:1). As will be the case in the second section, praise is invited from both the animate and inanimate spheres—"angels" (v. 2*a*; see Ps 103:20) and God's "host" (v. 2*b*; see Pss 24:10; 103:21) as well as sun and moon and stars (v. 3; see Pss 8:3; 19:4-6; 136:8-9; 147:4). The list is reminiscent of Genesis 1–2—"heavens" (see Gen 1:1; 2:1), "host" (see Gen 2:1), "stars" (see Gen 1:16). All the heavenly beings and bodies are to praise God's "name" (vv. 5*a*, 13)—that is, God's essential character and purposes, which represent God's very self (see Pss 8:1, 10; 23:3; 29:2; 135:1, 3, 13). The character and purposes of God are revealed in what God has done as creator, and such is the focus of the reasons for praise in vv. 5*b*-6. The verb "created" (ברא *bārā*) recalls Gen 1:1–2:4, as does the mode of creation by speech, although the verb "command" (צוה *şiwwâ*) does not occur in Gen 1:1–2:4 (see also Job 38:10; Pss 33:6-9; 104:5-9; Prov 8:29).

148:7-13. The second section invites praise "from the earth" by beings, objects, and elements in this realm, both animate and inanimate. Not unexpectedly, v. 8 recalls Ps 147:15-18, both in terms of the elements of creation involved and of the creative power of God's "word." The list again is reminiscent of Genesis 1–2—"earth" (see Gen 1:1; 2:1, 4; the phrase "earth and heaven" occurs only in Gen 2:4*b* and Ps 147:13); "sea monsters" (see Gen 1:21); "deeps" (see Gen 1:2); "fruit trees" (see Gen 1:11); "wild animals and all cattle, creeping things and flying birds" (see Gen 1:21, 24-25). As in Genesis 1, the

culminating focus in Psalm 148 is on humanity (see vv. 11-12). Those whom human beings recognize as sovereign are to acknowledge the ultimate sovereignty of God (v. 11), as are all general categories of people (v. 12). Verse 11 recalls Ps 2:1-2, 10-12, which at the beginning of the psalter calls for recognition of God's sovereignty (see also Ps 149:5-9). Quite appropriately, the reasons for praise in v. 13*b* proclaim God's sovereignty. The word "exalted" (שגב *śāgab*) occurs elsewhere in the context of the proclamation of God's kingship (see Isa 33:5 in the context of 33:17-22), and the word "glory" (הוד *hôd*) regularly describes royalty, both human (see Pss 21:5; 45:3) and divine (see Pss 96:6; 145:5). In keeping with the two divisions of the psalm, v. 13*b* affirms that God's sovereignty is over "earth and heaven." In short, God rules the cosmos.

148:14. This verse continues the reasons for praise, but it moves in a different direction. The cosmic God has chosen to fulfill the divine purposes through a particular people. To "raise up a horn" seems to mean to protect or to strengthen (see Pss 75:10; 89:17, 24; 92:10; 112:9). The two occurrences of this image in Psalm 89 are particularly interesting, because Psalm 89 concludes Book III with a rehearsal of the failure of the Davidic covenant, to which Books IV–V offer a response (see Commentary on Psalms 89; 90; 107; Introduction). That the concluding collection of Book V returns to this image may be more than coincidental. It is as if Ps 148:14 asserts a reinstatement—*not* of the Davidic king, however (see Ps 89:24), but of the whole people, "all his faithful" (see Ps 89:17). Interestingly in this regard, "the faithful" play the key role in Psalm 149, which reserves for them the role assigned to the king in Psalm 2 (see below on Ps 149:5-9). Thus Psalms 148–149 offer further warrant to conclude that the Davidic theology was transferred in the post-exilic era to the whole people (see Commentary on Psalms 105; 110; 132; 144; Introduction).

It is unclear what is meant precisely by the phrase "praise for all his faithful" in v. 14. In view of the placement of Psalm 148 in Book V, it seems to suggest, along with the preceding horn imagery, the reinstatement of God's people represented by the return from exile and reoccupation of Jerusalem (see Ps 147:2-3, 12-14). But the noun "praise" cannot help recalling the eleven verbal occurrences that have preceded in vv. 1-13. In short, Israel is one among many participants in the cosmic praising of God; its unique role, perhaps, is to articulate intelligibly the unspoken praise of the rest of creation (see Ps 19:1-4). Terence Fretheim suggests, although the exact meaning is elusive, that v. 14 recalls Ps 22:3 and that it perhaps should be construed as follows:

God has made God's people strong, indeed has made them a praise in the earth, for the purposes of the universal praise of God. . . . Just as the various other creatures show forth the praise of God by being what they are as God's creatures, so Israel having been made what it now is by God, shows forth God's praise by being who they are, the redeemed people of God. . . . God's people in every age are called upon to continue showing forth the praise of God because of what they have been made by God. In this way they will join with that vast chorus of God's nonhuman creatures in honor of God and in witness to God.[528]

Because God rules the cosmos, God's praise is incomplete without the participation of every voice, human and nonhuman, in heaven and in earth and in all creation.

528. Terence E. Fretheim, "Nature's Praise of God in the Psalms," *Ex Auditu* 3 (1987) 29-30.

REFLECTIONS

1. While the songs of praise generally push toward universality (see Pss 67:1-7; 100:1; 103:20-22; 117:1; Introduction), Psalm 148 takes inclusivity to the limit, surpassing even the final climactic verse of the psalter (150:6). The inclusivity of the invitation to praise God has profound implications that demonstrate the inseparability of theology and ecology (see Commentary on Psalms 8; 96; 98; 104). We human beings, we people of God, are partners in praising God with a multitude of other living beings and inanimate things as well. For this reason, Psalm 148 recalls not only Gen 1:1–2:4, but also Genesis 9. In Genesis 9 the covenant after the flood is established not just with Noah and his descendents (Gen 9:9) but also with "every living creature" (Gen 9:10, 12, 15-16), indeed, with "the earth" (Gen 9:13). This covenant, along with the all-inclusive invitation to praise in Psalm 148, suggests that the human vocation of "dominion" (Gen 1:26, 28) involves not just a stewardship *of* creation but a partnership *with* creation. Francis of Assisi had it right when, on the basis of Psalm 148, he composed his *Canticle of the Sun,* in which he addresses the sun and wind and fire as brother, and the moon and waters and earth as sister. Psalm 148 is not a call to pantheism, but on the basis of Psalm 148, we must speak of a "symbiosis in praise" involving humans and nature; we can hear in Psalm 148 "an implicit call to human beings to relate to the natural orders in such a way that nature's praise might show forth with greater clarity."[529] In short, human beings are called to exercise their God-given "dominion" or sovereignty in the same way that God exercises power: as a servant. To so fulfill our vocation is to praise God by, in effect, imitating God.

2. Several other hymns that proclaim God's reign also invite heaven and earth and the beings and objects therein to praise God (see Pss 29:1; 96:11-12; 97:1; 98:4, 7-8). Indeed, the movement of Psalm 148 is similar to that of Psalm 29; the praise of heavenly beings (Pss 29:1-2, 9; 148:2-4) is accompanied by a prayer for or the affirmation of God's strengthening or blessing of God's people (Pss 29:11; 148:14). The same movement is also found in Luke 2:13-14, where heavenly beings proclaim both God's glory and peace on earth. The angels' song communicates Luke's conviction that the birth

529. Fretheim, "Nature's Praise of God in the Psalms," 28-29. Fretheim also calls attention to two contemporary hymns that capture the message of Psalm 148: "Let All Things Now Living" and "Earth and All Stars."

of Jesus represents God's enthronement, God's cosmic sovereignty. Its parallel movement with Psalm 148 suggests the appropriateness of Psalm 148 for the season of Christmas. The church affirms that Jesus the Christ not only announced but also embodied the cosmic reign of God in a ministry of suffering servanthood. But for this very reason, Jesus is to be exalted, so that "at the name of Jesus every knee should bend, in heaven and on earth and under the earth" (Phil 2:10 NRSV; cf. Ps 148:13). One of the church's cherished Christmas hymns, "Joy to the World," is a paraphrase of Psalm 98, another hymn that proclaims God's reign and invites universal recognition in praise. To greet Jesus as Lord is to recognize God's sovereign claim on our lives and on the whole created order, and it is to commit ourselves to exercise God-given sovereignty over the earth as God demonstrated divine sovereignty in Jesus—the power of suffering servanthood. Thus Psalm 148 is a psalm for Christmas and for Easter and for all seasons.

PSALM 149:1-9, THE JUSTICE THAT IS WRITTEN

COMMENTARY

Psalm 149 is the fourth in a collection of hymns or songs of praise, each bounded by *hallelu-yah,* that concludes the psalter (see Commentary on Psalm 146). The psalm begins like a typical song of praise—invitation to praise (vv. 1-3), followed by reasons for praise (v. 4). The renewed invitation to praise in v. 5 is also not unusual, but then vv. 6-9 offer "an unparalleled departure" from the typical form.[530] These verses have been an enigma to scholars and somewhat difficult for readers who are offended by the psalmist's call for vengeance. The uniqueness of Psalm 149 has given rise to a variety of proposals for understanding its origin and ancient use, including the suggestion that vv. 6-9 indicate its use accompanying a sword dance at a victory celebration or perhaps a cultic celebration of God's kingship (see vv. 2-3). Read figuratively, however, vv. 6-9 represent a radical call for the faithful to enact and to embody the reign of God, which is celebrated in vv. 1-4, thus making Psalm 149 particularly appropriate for use on All Saints Day (see Reflections below).

That "an unparalleled departure" should characterize the penultimate psalm in the psalter is probably not coincidental. In short, the uniqueness of Psalm 149 invites careful consideration of its placement within

the book. For instance, vv. 6-9 recall Psalm 2, where the concern is also with rebellious "nations" and "peoples" (Ps 2:1; cf. 149:7) and "kings" (Ps 2:2, 10; cf. 149:8). Psalm 2 is ultimately an affirmation of God's sovereignty (see Commentary on Psalm 2, esp. discussion of vv. 10-12; Introduction), and so is Psalm 149. Both assert that those who attempt to exercise their own sovereignty (see Ps 2:3) will be called to account (Pss 2:8-12; 149:7-9; note "iron" in 2:8; 149:8). Thus, whereas Psalm 2 anticipates the theological heart of the psalter, Psalm 149 clearly recalls it—namely, Psalms 93; 95–99 and their affirmation of God's reign (see Introduction). The invitation in Ps 149:1 to sing "a new song" echoes Pss 96:1; 98:1, and 149:2 addresses God as "King" (see Pss 95:3; 97:1; 99:4).

Book IV, of which Psalms 93–99 form the core, responds to the crisis of exile that is articulated in Psalm 89. As Psalm 89 makes clear, a major aspect of this crisis was the disappearance of the Davidic monarchy. Besides proclaiming *God's* kingship (see Commentary on Psalms 90; 93; 95; 96; 97; 98; 99), the response of Book IV moves in the direction of transferring the Davidic theology from the monarchy to the whole people (see Commentary on Psalm 105). Thus the royal psalms became appropriated messianically—that is, as affirmation of God's sovereignty that is and

530. Allen, *Psalms 101–150,* 319.

will be made manifest through the whole people rather than through the Davidic monarchy (see Introduction). This kind of appropriation is especially clear in the final royal psalm in the psalter, Psalm 144 (see also Psalms 110; 132 in Book V), to which Psalm 149 is linked by the repetition of "new song" (144:9; 149:1). In a real sense, then, Psalm 149 completes the movement of transferring the Davidic theology to the whole people, since after asserting God's sovereignty (vv. 1-3), it assigns to the "faithful" the task of concretely implementing God's sovereignty in the world, a task Psalm 2 assigns to the monarchy. Not surprisingly, the faithful will be addressed several times in Psalm 149 in royal terms (see below on vv. 4-5, 9).[531]

Since Psalm 149 participates fully in the psalter's response to the crisis of the exilic and post-exilic eras, it is also not surprising that it has many affinities with Isaiah 40–66 (see Commentary on Psalms 96; 98). In particular, Allen cites six verbal links between Psalm 149 and Isaiah 61: "humble"/"oppressed" (Ps 149:4; Isa 61:1); "pleasure"/"favor" (Ps 149:4; Isa 61:2); "vengeance" (Ps 149:7; Isa 61:2); "crowns" (Ps 149:4), which occurs twice in Isa 61:3 as "crown of beauty" and "splendor" (NIV); "Zion" (Ps 149:2; Isa 61:3); and "judgment"/"justice" (Ps 149:9; Isa 61:8). In addition, he sees parallels between Psalm 149 and Isa 45:14; 46:13; 60:1-3, 9, 11-12, 14; 66:14-16, 18-21. Contending that Psalms 96; 98 partake of the same tradition as Isaiah 40–66, Allen concludes: "It is difficult to avoid the conclusion that like Pss 96–98 this psalm is building upon the motifs of the future victory of Yahweh over the nations and of the exaltation of Israel. The psalm appears to have emanated from a similar tradition to that of Pss 96–98 and to develop its themes."[532] While, as Allen suggests, there is a future dimension involved, Psalm 149 is eschatological in a more fundamental sense; it proclaims God's present sovereignty amid ongoing opposition by nations and their kings (see Commentary on Psalms 2; 93; 96; 97; 98; 99; Introduction).

Scholars have reached no consensus concerning the structure of Psalm 149. Some suggest a threefold division: vv. 1-3, vv. 4-6, vv. 7-9. But most favor a division into two sections, with the break occurring either between vv. 4 and 5 or between vv. 5 and 6 (see NIV). Interestingly, Psalm 149 is one of the few psalms for which the NRSV suggests no divisions. Observing that v. 5 seems to go equally well with vv. 1-4 or vv. 6-9, Anthony R. Ceresko argues that v. 5 should be understood as a "pivot" or hinge.[533] Furthermore, v. 5 is precisely the central poetic line, and along with vv. 1 and 9, it contains one of the three occurrences of "faithful," thus providing a further mark of symmetry.

Ceresko argues convincingly that the conceptual unity of Psalm 149 lies in its allusions to two crucial historical events: the exodus (vv. 1-4) and the possession of the land (vv. 6-9). For instance, "Maker" [עֹשֶׂה 'ōśeh] in v. 2 probably refers not to creation but to God's formation of Israel as a people (see Pss 95:6; 100:3), and the constitutive event was the exodus (the Hebrew root of "Maker" occurs in Exod 14:31). The people's immediate response was to sing (Exod 15:1), and the "new song" of Ps 149:1 probably alludes to the Song of the Sea in Exod 15:1-21. Other verbal links make this interpretation plausible: "praise" (Ps 149:1; Exod 15:11), "dancing" and "tambourine" (Ps 149:3; Exod 15:20), and "victory" (Ps 149:4; Exod 15:2). In addition, the word "reign" (מָלַךְ mālak) in the climactic Exod 15:18 represents the same Hebrew root as "King" (melek) in Ps 149:2. In short, both the Song of the Sea in Exodus 15 and the "new song" called for in Ps 149:1 are celebrations of God's sovereignty.

149:1-4. While these verses are reminiscent of the exodus, the psalmist's assertion of God's sovereignty in a new context also recalls Isaiah, the prophet of the exile (see Isa 43:15; 52:7; see above on other parallels with Isaiah 40–66). The prophet interpreted God's ongoing commitment to the people as a new exodus (see Isa 43:1-7), a "new thing" (Isa 43:19; see also Isa 42:9; 48:6). The appropriate response would thus be "a new song" (Ps 149:1; Isa 42:10). The affirmation that God "takes pleasure in" the people

531. I am indebted to the insights of Gary Martindale, "Vengeance, the Tie That Binds: An Intratextual Reading of Psalm 149," unpublished paper presented to the Society of Biblical Literature, Nov. 21, 1994, Chicago, IL.; and Rich Brzowsky, "Exegesis and Reflection: Psalm 149," unpublished paper, Eden Seminary, May 18, 1993.

532. Allen, *Psalms 101–150*, 319-20.

533. Anthony R. Ceresko, "Psalm 149: Poetry, Themes (Exodus and Conquest), and Social Function," *Biblica* 67 (1986) 185.

(v. 4*a*; see Ps 147:10-11) further recalls Isa 42:1, where the servant—who should almost certainly be understood as the whole people—has a mission to establish justice among the nations (see also Isa 42:3-4, 6; see below on Ps 149:9). Like vv. 6-9, the mission of the servant in Isa 42:1-9 casts the whole people in the role formerly assigned to the monarchy. In this regard, it is significant that v. 4*b* asserts that God "crowns the humble." The Hebrew root behind "crowns" (פאר *pā'ar*) is associated elsewhere with royalty (see Exod 8:9; Esth 1:4), including the Davidic monarchy (see Zech 12:7). Even more significantly, it occurs as a verb in Isa 55:5 to describe what God has done for the whole people; that this occurrence comes immediately after Isa 55:3 suggests the transfer of the Davidic promise to the whole people (see also Isa 60:9). In short, v. 4*b* is further evidence for the transfer of the Davidic theology to the whole people.

149:5. The same can be said of v. 5*a*, where "glory" is also a word that is regularly associated with sovereignty, both human (see Pss 8:5; 21:5*a*) and divine (see Pss 24:7-10; 29:1-2, 9; 96:3, 7-8). To be sure, v. 5*a* invites a recognition of God's sovereignty (see Ps 96:4), so "glory" could refer primarily to God's glory. In view of v. 9, however, it seems that the glory is at least shared by the people, an interpretation the NIV makes more explicit. Singing for joy (v. 5*b*) also describes elsewhere the proper response to God's reign (see Pss 96:12; 98:8). What it means for the people to celebrate God's rule "on their beds" is not clear. Several emendations are often suggested, but they have no manuscript support. The phrase is sometimes taken as evidence that the ancient worshipers spent the night in the Temple (see Pss 27:4; 139:18) or that they were being called to prostrate themselves as an act of obeisance. Another possibility is that v. 5*b* exhorts the people to recognize God's sovereignty in every sphere of their existence, public as well as private (see "on their beds" in Mic 2:1).

149:6-9. These verses continue to invite the recognition of God's reign (v. 6*a*) as well as to suggest the people's participation in God's reign (vv. 6*b*-9). The NRSV's "high praises" (v. 6*a*) is from a root that elsewhere describes the response to God's sovereignty (see Pss 99:5, 9; 145:1). Verse 6*b* begins, however, to suggest the people's participation. "Vengeance" ordinarily belongs to God (see Deut 32:35; Ps 94:1), but v. 7 indicates the people's role. They are now assigned the part formerly played by the Davidic kings (vv. 7-8; cf. Ps 2:9). This sharing in the enactment of God's reign in order to establish justice (v. 9*a*; see also Pss 96:13; 97:2; 98:9; 99:4; 146:7) is the people's "glory" (v. 9*b*). Thus v. 9*b* recalls v. 5*a*, although the two words the NRSV translates "glory" differ. The word in v. 9*b* is also regularly associated with sovereignty, including God's sovereignty (see Pss 29:4; 96:6). More interesting here, however, is that the faithful possess the glory formerly reserved for the Davidic kings (see Pss 21:5; 45:3). It is they who share in the responsibility for justice—not the Davidic kings (cf. Ps 72:1-2).

In the NIV and the NRSV, it is almost inevitable that vv. 6*b*-9 sound triumphalistic, perhaps dangerously so (see Reflections below). It is important to remember that in the book of Psalms, vengeance always serves the purpose of justice (see, e.g., Psalms 94; 109). A different translation of v. 9*a* will also help to avert triumphalist tendencies. For instance, v. 9*a* could be rendered, "to enact among them the justice which is written." This translation means that the actions of God's people can never be self-serving or simply punitive but must constructively serve the establishment of justice (see Isa 42:1-4). The proposed translation raises the question, of course, of what precisely is the "justice written." In terms of the shape of the book of Psalms, it may well refer to the affirmations found earlier in the book that the sovereign God wills justice and righteousness (see Pss 96:13; 97:2; 98:9; 99:4). God's justice and righteousness always encompass all peoples and, indeed, all things, as Psalms 96–99 suggest and as the immediately preceding psalms have made clear (see esp. Pss 145:10-13; 146:7; 148:11-12). When Psalm 149 is heard in this literary context, vv. 6-9 may even take on an ironic ring, especially insofar as Psalm 149 recalls Psalm 2. That is to say, the whole people have displaced the kings as partner in God's sovereignty, because *their own kings* have been brought to justice! That is to say, the monarchy disappeared with the exile (see Psalm 89).

In the larger canonical context, the "justice written" may refer to earlier traditions, perhaps the book of Judges, in accordance with Ceresko's suggestion that vv. 6-9 allude to the narratives of Israel's possession of the land. In this perspective, vv. 6-9 recall Judg 3:16-23, where Ehud uses "a double-edged sword" (Judg 3:16 NIV) to kill King Eglon of Moab as part of Israel's consolidation of its settlement in the land (see also Num 31:2-3, another episode in the possession of the land). If Psalm 149 does allude to the book of Judges, one must note that Judges credits Israel's victories to God, and not to Israel or to its leaders. Like the book of Judges, then, Psalm 149 is ultimately an affirmation of God's sovereignty—only God is king (see Judg 9:7-20).

REFLECTIONS

1. As suggested in the Commentary, vv. 6-9 may sound dangerously triumphalistic—a call to violence against the enemies of God. Indeed, Psalm 149 has been used to promote violence. Prothero points out that Psalm 149 was cited by Caspar Schopp as he called Roman Catholic princes to a holy war against the Protestants; the result was the Thirty Years War. And Thomas Müntzer appealed to Psalm 149 to incite the German peasants to revolt.[534] There is no question that the military imagery of vv. 6-9 is problematic and even positively dangerous if taken literally as a call to arms.

But vv. 6-9 should not be taken literally. Rather, their theological thrust is to assert God's universal sovereignty and to invite God's people to join God at God's work in the world. That work, as the whole book of Psalms makes clear, consists fundamentally of justice (see v. 9) and righteousness (see Psalms 96–99), the result of which is peace (see Ps 72:3, 7). Thus, again when understood figuratively, vv. 6-9 are a profoundly theological call to discipleship. To be sure, the military imagery will always require careful interpretation, but its value is to convey the reality that the faithful will always face opposition insofar as they really do represent and work to enact God's justice and righteousness in the world (see Eph 6:10-17). In short, the proclamation of God's sovereignty is eschatological; it is always made in the midst of opposition and circumstances that seem to deny it (see Psalms 2; 93; 96–99; Introduction).

Because the proclamation of God's reign is always eschatological, the call to discipleship is a call to bear a cross (Mark 8:34). Entrance into the reign of God invites opposition, as Jesus' life and death demonstrate. The faithful life will always involve a struggle, a battle. In this sense, the people of God will always be "Christian soldiers," but they will always be waging peace instead of war (see Eph 6:15). As John Calvin concludes concerning Psalm 149, citing Eph 6:17, "As to the Church collective, the sword now put into our hand is of another kind, that of the word and spirit."[535] To proclaim that God rules the world is to invite opposition from those who want to claim power for themselves, as Israel knew, and as the early Christians knew, and as is still true today. As Hauerwas and Willimon put it, we live in a "world [which] has declared war upon the gospel in the most subtle of ways."[536] The battle will mean for us what it meant for exilic and post-exilic Israel, which discovered its identity as a servant (see above on Isa 42:1-9), and what it meant for Jesus: suffering. The good news is that such suffering is our "glory" (Ps 149:9; see Rom 8:17).

2. Not surprisingly, since it arose in a situation in which the church was being persecuted by the Roman Empire, the Revelation to John draws upon many of the concepts present in Psalm 149 and in related passages, such as Psalms 96; 98; and Isaiah 40–66. Although it appeared that Rome ruled the world and that Caesar was Lord, the church

534. Prothero, *The Psalms in Human Life and Experience*, 115.
535. Calvin, *Commentary on the Book of Psalms*, VI:5:316.
536. Hauerwas and Willimon, *Resident Aliens*, 152.

dared to proclaim that God was still sovereign (see Rev 11:15). Because God rules the world, the faithful can "sing a new song" (see Rev 5:9; 14:3). The Revelation is less a vision of the future than it is a profession of faith about the present—God reigns. And as in Psalm 149, the author is convinced that the faithful reign with God (see Rev 4:10; 22:5) toward the end of fulfilling God's purpose of drawing in all nations and peoples and kings (see Rev 21:24-26; 22:2), and indeed all creation (see Rev 21:1). What greater glory could there be for us than God's permitting us to participate in enacting among all peoples and nations the justice, righteousness, and peace God wills for all creatures and all creation? The only possible response from all the saints is "Praise the LORD!"

PSALM 150:1-6, PRAISE THE LORD!

COMMENTARY

With a rousing and uninterrupted invitation to praise, Psalm 150 concludes the final collection of the psalter (Psalms 146–150) and the psalter itself. Every half-line begins with an imperative form of the verb "praise" (הלל hillēl), except the final one, which puts the subject first—"everything that breathes"—and switches to a jussive form of the verb ("Let everything . . . praise"). The uniqueness of Psalm 150 is fitting for its placement. Not only does v. 6 recall Ps 145:21 and thus provide a cosmicly oriented envelope around the final collection, but also the psalm serves as an appropriate doxology to conclude Book V (see Pss 41:13; 72:19; 89:52; 106:48) and the whole psalter. Just as Psalm 149 is an apt counterpart to Psalm 2 (see Commentary on Psalm 149), so also is Psalm 150 for Psalms 1 and Psalm 2. From the beginning, the psalter has commended openness to God's instruction (Psalm 1) and recognition of God's sovereignty (Psalm 2). Praise is the offering of one's whole life and self to God, and Psalm 150 is an enthusiastic invitation to all creatures to yield themselves to God (see also Psalm 148). Thus the whole psalter moves toward its climactic crescendo of *hallelu-yah* psalms (Psalms 146–150), and Psalm 150 provides the final, breathtaking and breath-claiming note. Although the prayers for help actually outnumber the songs of praise along the way, the book of Psalms is aptly known in Hebrew as תהלים (*tĕhillîm*, "Praises").

Scholars often divide Psalm 150 into vv. 1-2, vv. 3-5, and v. 6. What sets vv. 1-2 apart is that the summons here at least implies what is usually an explicit feature of the songs of praise—that is, reasons for praise. Verses 3-5 are unified by their references to musical instruments, and v. 6 provides the conclusion. In other words, Psalm 150 tells who is to be praised (v. 1), why God is to be praised (v. 2), how God is to be praised (vv. 3-5), and who is to offer the praise (v. 6).[537]

150:1-2. These verses suggest reasons for praising God by way of their vocabulary, which elsewhere in the psalter is associated with God's reign. God's sovereignty is the fundamental affirmation that pervades the psalter (see Psalms 2; 5; 93; 96–99; Introduction), and it is especially prominent in Psalms 145–149 (see 145:1, 11-13; 146:10; 149:2). Although the Hebrew root for "to reign" or "to be king" (מלך *mālak*) does not occur in Psalm 150, the vocabulary of vv. 1-2 affirms God's rule. For instance, "sanctuary" (v. 1) elsewhere designates where God dwells as king. God's throne is there (see Ps 11:4, where "holy" represents the same word as "sanctuary" here), and God is explicitly greeted as "my king" as God enters "into the sanctuary" (Ps 68:24). It is not clear whether the sanctuary here should be understood as God's heavenly abode or the earthly Temple. Perhaps both senses are intended (cf. Pss 11:4; 68:24). As Kraus suggests, "At the holy place heaven and earth touch each other."[538] The word "firmament" (רקיע *rāqîaʿ*) suggests heaven, but it is not clear whether v. 1*a* and v. 1*b* should be construed as completely parallel.

537. Mays, *Psalms*, 450.
538. Kraus, *Psalms 1–59*, 570.

The Hebrew roots behind the words "mighty" (עז *'ōz*, v. 1*b*) and "mighty deeds" (גבורה *gĕbûrâ*, v. 2*a*) occur together as the phrase "strong and mighty" in Ps 24:8 to describe God as "King of glory." The word "mighty" occurs often in the context of the proclamation of God's reign (see Ps 99:4; see "strength" in 29:1; 93:1; 96:6 NRSV), as does the root behind "greatness" (גדל *gādal*, v. 2*b*; see Pss 47:2; 48:1; 95:3; 99:2; see also 147:5). In short, all creatures are summoned to praise God, because God rules the world.

150:3-5. Praise involves all aspects and spheres of life, including liturgy. In this section, worship of God in the Temple is in view, and music is featured. Every section of the orchestra—horns, strings, pipes, percussion—is invited to join in a symphony of praise. Given the direction to which the vocabulary of vv. 1-2 points—that is, toward the proclamation of God's sovereignty—it is significant that elsewhere the sound of the trumpet announces God's reign (see Pss 47:5-7; 98:6). Furthermore, several of the instruments in vv. 3-5 are involved in the liturgy of 2 Samuel 6, where the ark on which God is "enthroned" (v. 2) is brought to Jerusalem (see, e.g., 2 Sam 6:5; 1 Chr 13:8; 15:28; 2 Chr 5:13; Neh 12:27; Pss 33:2-3; 68:24-25; 149:3). As is still often the case in more contemporary symphonic arrangements, the loud clash of the cymbals marks a climactic moment. The repetition of "cymbals" in v.

5*a* provides emphasis, preparing the way for the mention in v. 6 of the only thing that can surpass the praise of the full temple orchestra: the uplifted voice of every creature!

150:6. In addition to its final position, the switch in syntax and verbal form makes this verse emphatic. As it makes clear, the symphony of praise must ultimately include all creatures. The songs of praise regularly push toward universality, inviting "all you nations" (Ps 117:1) and "all the earth" (Ps 100:1) and indeed everything in heaven and on earth (Psalm 148) to praise God. Along with Ps 145:21 and Psalm 148, v. 6 is the ultimate extension of that invitation. The word "breath" (נשמה *nĕšāmâ*) recalls the creation of the world and of human life (Gen 2:7) as well as the flood story, in which the destiny of human and animal life went awry (Gen 7:22). Against this background, Psalm 150 proclaims that the proper goal of every creature is praise—life shaped by God's claim and lived under God's rule. As Mays puts it: "No other use of breath could be more right and true to life than praise of the LORD. No other sound could better speak the gratitude of life than praise of the LORD."[539] The final verse of the psalter is an eloquent reminder of the book's pervasive message: To praise God is to live, and to live is to praise God (see Commentary on Psalms 8; 100; 103; 104; 145).

539. Mays, *Psalms*, 451.

REFLECTIONS

Psalm 150 clearly indicates that the praises of God's people are meant to be sung to the accompaniment of musical instruments. Indeed, Israel and the church have always sung and still sing the psalms as well as other songs of praise and prayer. As Mays says of Psalm 150: "It is a witness to the power of music, its amazing potential for evoking beauty and feeling and for carrying vision beyond the range of words into the realm of imagination. That we sing the praise of God is no accidental custom."[540]

A concrete illustration of the power of music is the version of Psalm 150 performed by Duke Ellington. Jazz historian Stanley Dance describes the response to Ellington's rendition:

In Barcelona, in the ancient Church of Santa Maria del Mar, the enthusiasm was such that the congregation burst into the aisles to participate in the finale, "Praise God and Dance" [Psalm 150]. The music and the message of the concert seemed to transcend language barriers without difficulty.[541]

540. Mays, *Psalms*, 450.
541. From the album cover of Duke Ellington's *Sacred Sounds*, The Prestige Series, P-24045. See James Limburg, *Psalms for Sojourners* (Minneapolis: Augsburg, 1986) 91-92.

Dance's comment touches upon two complementary concepts that are important for reflecting on Psalm 150: music and message. Precisely because music is powerful and can transcend barriers without difficulty, it is an appropriate medium for conveying the message about the sovereignty of God, whose claim transcends all the barriers that separate peoples from one another and humans from other creatures and the whole creation (see Psalm 148). By virtue of its vocabulary, which richly alludes to God's reign (vv. 1-2), by its call for full and enthusiastic musical accompaniment (vv. 3-5), and by its final invitation to every creature (v. 6), Psalm 150 "expresses a lyrical self-abandonment, an utter yielding of self, without vested interest, calculation, desire, or hidden agenda."[542]

Such "lyrical self-abandonment" is precisely what Jesus called for in response to the reign of God (see Mark 1:14-15; 8:34-36). The resurrection is the validation of Jesus' claim that to lose one's life for the sake of the gospel is to save it (Mark 8:35). Thus the use of Psalm 150 during the season of Easter puts us in touch with Jesus' claim. In concert with Jesus' life, death, and resurrection, Psalm 150 and the psalter as a whole invite and commend "lyrical self-abandonment" in liturgy and in every moment of life (see Ps 1:1-2). Indeed, God wills that our worship and work become inseparable, symphonic expressions of our response to the simple but marvelously profound invitation, "Praise the LORD!"

542. Brueggemann, "Bounded by Obedience and Praise," 67.

INTRODUCTION TO WISDOM LITERATURE

RICHARD J. CLIFFORD, S.J.

DEFINITION OF WISDOM LITERATURE

In biblical studies, "wisdom literature" designates the books of Proverbs, Job, Qohelet (Ecclesiastes), and, in the Apocrypha or deuterocanonical books, Sirach and the Wisdom of Solomon. Other biblical literature is sometimes put under the wisdom umbrella. Tobit in the Apocrypha has been called a sapiential short story because of its concern with the morality of everyday life. The Song of Songs is often included on the grounds that it, like the wisdom books, is "of Solomon" (Cant 1:1). Psalms such as 37, 49, 73, 112, and 127 are aphoristic, or meditate on the problem of the innocent righteous person; but to call them wisdom psalms broadens the category unduly in the opinion of many scholars; moreover, there is no consensus on which psalms belong to the group.

Scholars have occasionally regarded whole sections of the Bible as being influenced by wisdom themes, such as wisdom and life, worldly success resulting from shrewdness, or the inherent consequences of human actions. Genesis 1–11 is indeed concerned with cosmic order and with wisdom and life (esp. chaps. 2–3), but these themes come more from "international" epics like *The Epic of Gilgamesh* and the story of Atrahasis than from wisdom books. Genesis 37–50, detailing Joseph's rise at court through sagacity and skill at interpreting dreams, resembles court tales like Ahiqar and Daniel more than wisdom books. The sophisticated court history (2 Samuel 9–20; 1 Kings 1–2) portrays Yahweh as being hidden in the course of human events, as one finds in the wisdom portrayal, but such a shared perspective is no argument for literary dependence. Finally, some think that Deuteronomy and wisdom literature are related because both were written by the Jerusalem scribal class. Such a view is possible, for these literatures share common vocabulary, and Deuteronomy reckons obedience to Yahweh as wisdom (Deut 4:5-8; 32:6, 21, 28-31). Rather than wisdom books influencing other biblical books, however, it is more likely that wisdom thinking was in the main stream of biblical literary production from whence its style and ideas radiated throughout biblical writings.

Jerome (died 420), in his *Prologue to the Books of Solomon,* attributed the unity of the traditional wisdom books to their connection with Solomon, although he was aware that the connection is loose in some instances. The Christian Bible groups the wisdom books together (with the psalms) after the historical books and before the prophetic books. The Jewish Bible places the wisdom literature in the third section of the Tanakh—the Writings (a miscellaneous collection)—after the Torah and the Prophets.

There are good reasons for grouping the wisdom books together. First, few of the books except the latest wisdom books, Sirach 44–50 and the book of Wisdom 10–19, say anything about the history of Israel, its major institutions of covenant and kingship, and its great personalities, such as Abraham and Sarah, Moses, and David. The name of Israel's God, Yahweh, does not even occur in Qohelet and the Job dialogues (Job 3–37; Yahweh in Job 12:9 is anomalous). Righteousness in the books is not linked to observance of the law and covenant or to performance of rituals as it is elsewhere in the Bible. Genres and themes of neighboring literatures are far more obvious in the wisdom books than in other sections of the Bible. Second, the books all share a strong didactic tone. The word *wisdom* pervades all the books: forty-two times in Proverbs, eighteen times in Job, twenty-eight times in Qohelet, sixty times in Sirach (σοφία *sophia*), and thirty times in the book of Wisdom; the numbers are much higher if synonyms of *wisdom* are counted. There is persistent attention to wisdom in itself, which makes these biblical books different from their canonical counterparts. The books are, of course, concerned with practical wisdom—knowing how to live well, how to perform one's tasks, and how to understand the secrets of the universe. But the Bible goes beyond specific instances of wisdom to explore the nature of wisdom, its importance and limits, and its relationship to Yahweh.

Within this grouping of canonical wisdom literature, there are considerable differences deriving from the presence of distinct literary genres and from the different meanings of wisdom in antiquity. Proverbs includes the distinct genres of wisdom poem, instruction, and proverb; Job is a dialogue on divine justice set within a narrative; Qohelet is (among other things) a royal pseudo-autobiography; Sirach is a vast compendium of instructions and proverbs; and the book of Wisdom is a philosophical exhortation to a way of life (λόγος προτρεπτικός, *logos protreptikos*).

Each major genre develops different themes in a distinctive way. The concept of wisdom is not univocal; it may signify aphorisms, instructions for the younger generation, magical knowledge derived from the gods (as in oaths), royal and judicial discernment (as of Solomon), and critical, skeptical inquiry. All of these different concepts are included under the umbrella of ancient wisdom.

Modern interest in wisdom literature has gone through several phases since the foundations of contemporary biblical scholarship were laid in the sixteenth century. Renaissance creativity was based on freeing human activity from connection with ultimate and hierarchical patterns of order. Reformation theology was interested in the God of history rather than in the Author of a static system; human destiny was perceived as the realization of spiritual capacities in time. Given the presuppositions regnant at the dawn of modern historical-critical study of the Bible, it is no wonder that wisdom literature took second place to the study of the Pentateuch, historical and prophetic books, and Psalms. Sapiential writings were regarded by many as derivative, a quasi-philosophical distillation of the law and the prophets. Dependence on the prophets was, in fact, thought to account for two traits of wisdom: the doctrine of retribution and the (alleged) suspicion of cult that surfaces in Prov 15:8: "The sacrifice of the wicked is an/ abomination to the LORD,/ but the prayer of the upright is his delight" (NRSV; cf. Prov 21:27; Eccl 5:1; Heb 4:17). It is important to remind ourselves that this neglect of the wisdom literature is relatively modern and that it reflects neither the outlook of the Bible nor that of many centuries of Jewish and Christian interpretation, which have considered every aspect of the world to have been created for the divine purpose. To regard wisdom literature as a foreign body in the Bible, as some scholars still do, is a hermeneutical decision based on the assumption that the historical and prophetic books are normative for what is genuinely biblical.

Three twentieth-century developments have pushed wisdom books to the forefront of scholarly interest:

First, Hermann Gunkel (1862–1932), applying his new form criticism, proposed that much wisdom literature came from ancient oral models and originated in a particular group in Israel: the sages. Thus was introduced the impulse to search for the social location of the wisdom books, an impulse that has become stronger in recent times. Second, the recovery (beginning in the mid-nineteenth century) of texts comparable to biblical wisdom literature in Egypt and Mesopotamia, civilizations far older than Israel, challenged the old assumption that the biblical wisdom books were late systematizings of traditional teaching in accord with a view of religion as obedience to the law. Third, the theological bias against wisdom books was challenged by prominent scholars, such as Walther Zimmerli and Gerhard von Rad, who found a basis for the theological study of wisdom books in the concepts of creation and cosmic order, which attest that every aspect of God's world is good and worthy of study. Their discernment of wisdom literature's theological value prepared the way for the lively interest it holds today.

WISDOM LITERATURE IN THE ANCIENT NEAR EAST

The title "wisdom literature" has been applied to certain literary genres from Egypt and Mesopotamia. Were it not for the example of the biblical wisdom books, however, the extra-biblical texts probably would not be regarded as constituting a special group. Comparison between these other texts and their biblical counterparts is fruitful, nonetheless, chiefly because the foreign examples illuminate two vitally important topics: literary genres (the set of conventions ruling the work) and the social location of the writers. On these points the Bible provides scant information.

Wisdom texts comprise some of the most ancient literature. Some wisdom genres, such as the instruction and the proverb collection, are attested from the first appearance of *belles lettres* (c. 2600 BCE for Mesopotamia, some two centuries later for Egypt) and continued in use long past the biblical period. The following section surveys Mesopotamian, Egyptian, and Canaanite parallels as they are relevant to the Bible, with particular attention to genres and the social location of the scribes.

Mesopotamia. Many wisdom texts entered the "stream of tradition" of cuneiform literature—i.e., texts controlled and maintained by generations of professional scribes, who copied them as part of their elaborate training. Preserved in temple archives and private collections, the works were widely known and accepted, in other words "canonical." They were widely distributed throughout the East including the Levant, and some of them influenced the Bible.

The oldest genre relevant to the Bible is *instruction.* The *Instructions of Šuruppak* was widely known and is extant in two archaic Sumerian versions dating to 2600–2400 BCE: a "classical" Sumerian version of c. 1800 BCE and two Akkadian translations of c. 1500–1100 BCE.[1] Šuruppak was king of the last antediluvian city (reminiscent of the biblical Noah) and was endowed with the divine wisdom of that privileged time. The text was used in schools, where students practiced cuneiform writing by copying it. In this collection, the father instructs his son, the customary recipient of ancient instructions. Some scholars believe that the father is a personification of the city of Šuruppak. The advice is not as specific and literal as Egyptian instructions, which are generally imparted through metaphor and indirection. Most of the counsels appear in a twofold structure: a command and a reason—e.g., "Do not go surety for another. They shall seize you." Incidentally, the fact that agricultural concerns are prominent in this and other instructions does not mean that instructions originated with peasants rather than with the scribal class. The productivity of the land was such an abiding concern for all classes of an agrarian society that herds and crops occur often in the sayings of urban scribes. Šuruppak advises even the nobles to do their share at harvest time: "At the time of the harvest, days are precious. Collect like a slave girl, eat like a queen!"

Another well-attested genre was the *proverb collection.* No less than twenty-four collections are attested in Sumerian, though only a few survive in bilingual (Sumerian and Akkadian) translations.[2] A few independent

---

1. See Bendt Alster, *The Instructions of Šuruppak: A Sumerian Proverb Collection* (Copenhagen: Akademisk Forlag, 1974).
2. B. B. Foster, *Before the Muses: An Anthology of Akkadian Literature*, 2 vols. (Bethesda: CDL, 1993) 1:337-48.

Akkadian examples are extant.[3] Kassite scribes of the late second millennium BCE for some reason did not consider these texts worthy of copying. Biblical proverbs were not directly influenced by Sumerian collections, though there are general similarities in form and content.

Some literary works represent a skeptical and critical spirit for which the *edubba* ("tablet house," Sumerian for "the academy") was renowned. The sufferer in the "Sumerian Job" complains bitterly of his treatment by others and of his fate; the composition ends happily with the god's return.[4] The Babylonian Theodicy of c. 1000 BCE, an acrostic poem of twenty-seven stanzas, each of eleven lines, is a Job-like dialogue between a sufferer and a friend.[5] In one stanza, the protagonist complains of his sufferings, and in the next, his friend counters with the conventional pieties: Suffering is the fate of all, justice will ultimately be done, and the gods are remote and inscrutable. Eventually the friend concedes that the righteous poor are vulnerable and unhappy, and the sufferer utters a prayer for divine protection. Another poem, often compared with Job since its partial publication in 1885, is the "Babylonian Job," sometimes cited by its first line: "I will praise the lord of wisdom" (*Ludlul bel nemeqi*).[6] The full publication of its first tablet in 1980 shows that it can no longer be used as a parallel to Job, for it is not a treatise on the problem of suffering but a bold proclamation of Marduk as the supplicant god. In the midst of terrible personal anguish, the sufferer rejects his personal god in favor of Marduk. (Marduk had become important in the late second millennium BCE.)

Another Mesopotamian genre only recently recognized as relevant to the Bible is the pseudo-autobiography of a king, in which the king makes a lesson of his life and records it for posterity. Especially relevant to the Bible is the standard version of the *Epic of Gilgamesh* in eleven tablets, apparently completed around the thirteenth century BCE.[7] A didactic purpose was imposed on the Old Babylonian version by a new introduction and conclusion as well as the inclusion of wisdom themes. Gilgamesh's opening and closing speeches in the standard version emphasize not his strength but his experience and knowledge gained through sufferings. The work addresses the reader as "thou" as it instructs. The flood story, which has been added in tablet XI, omits giving a reason for the flood (although the tradition attested in the Atra-hases epic did include a reason) to underline the wisdom theme of the inscrutability of the gods. The plant of life that slips away from the hero instances another wisdom theme: the fragility of life. Qohelet quotes the alewife's advice to Gilgamesh as he seeks immortality: "You will not find the eternal life you seek. . . . Go eat your bread with enjoyment. . . . Enjoy life with the wife whom you love" (Old Babylonian version). The book of Proverbs may also draw from Gilgamesh; the goddess Ishtar's false offer of life to the hero seems to have influenced the depiction of Woman Folly's false offer of life to the young man in Prov 5:3-6; 7; and 9:13-18.

Mesopotamian literature reflects the world of the scribes. Despite their various specializations, scribes are described with one term: *ţupšarru*, "scribe." They wrote the literature and saw to its transmission. Literature was by definition what they copied and kept in libraries. This practice accounts for multiple copies of the limited number of works in the stream of tradition. Scribes had three functions—bureaucrat, poet, and scholar. As bureaucrats, they recorded the intake and outflow of palace goods; as poets, they composed literary works, such as hymns, epics, annals, and inscriptions; as scholars, they recorded and arranged omens and practiced divination. For the writing of literature, the royal court was far more important than was the temple; the latter lost its economic and political importance to the palace at an early period. The king sponsored the cultural establishment as an ongoing part of his responsibility to uphold political and economic order and stability.

In contrast to other societies, Mesopotamian scribes were not *ex officio* connected with sanctuaries or other religious

3. See *Ancient Near Eastern Texts Relating to the Old Testament*, ed. James B. Pritchard, 3rd ed. (Princeton, N.J.: Princeton University Press, 1969) 595-96.

4. Pritchard, *Ancient Near Eastern Texts Relating to the Old Testament*, 595-96.

5. Pritchard, *Ancient Near Eastern Texts Relating to the Old Testament*, 601-4; Foster, *Before the Muses*, 2:806-14.

6. Foster, *Before the Muses*, 1:308-25.

7. *ANET*, 72-99.

institutions, nor did they operate with a body of normative or "classical" texts. They functioned within the palace organization or, with the economic prosperity of the first millennium BCE, independently, selling their "scholarly" services (omens and divination) to wealthy individuals.

Egypt. Literature comparable to the biblical wisdom books was composed as early as the mid-third millennium in Egypt. Egyptologists include three major genres under the heading of wisdom: *instructions, laments* or *complaints,* and *political propaganda.* The first two, instructions and complaints, are relevant to the Bible. Since instruction is such an abundant source of information on the scribal profession, information on the social context will be provided within the discussion of instructions.

Instruction was a pervasive genre; seventeen examples are extant.[8] The oldest is the *Instruction of Prince Hardjedef* (composed c. 2450–2300 BCE),[9] and the youngest is the *Instruction of Papyrus Insinger* of the first century CE, written in Demotic, the vernacular language.[10] One instruction, that of Amenemope, dating to c. 1100 BCE,[11] has directly influenced Prov 22:17–24:22.

Instructions gave advice to enable the young person to lead a life free of undue difficulties and costly mistakes. Instructions make concrete and pragmatic suggestions rather than hold out abstract ideals to live up to—e.g., Don't lie to a judge, since telling the truth will render the judge benevolent the next time around, and in the long run lies don't work anyway. Such pragmatic counsels provide no indication that Egyptian instructions were secular. On the contrary, they were thoroughly religious. Like other ancient peoples, Egyptians believed that God implanted order (*ma'at*) in the world. *Ma'at* can be variously translated—"truth," "order," "justice"—and is found in nature (the seasons, fruitfulness) no less than in the human world (civic and social order, laws, right relationships within families and professions, among neighbors, and in relation to the

king). In mythology, *Ma'at* is the daughter of Re, the god of the sun and of justice. She is portrayed as crouching with a feather on her knees or head. *Ma'at* was not revealed directly to humans, but "read off" the course of the world and communicated through the maxims and exhortations of instructions. To help readers fulfill the demands of *ma'at* in every walk of life was the aim of the instructions. Some scholars see *ma'at* as the model for personified Wisdom in Proverbs, though it must be noted that Wisdom in Proverbs, by her vigorous speeches and pursuit of her lovers, goes far beyond the abstract Egyptian goddess. Finally, the scope of the instruction is the guidance of the individual rather than the reform of society; one accepted the world and lived according to its rhythms.

Some themes of the instructions are explained by their context in Egyptian society. The career of the young person was played out, at least initially, within the *famulus* ("private secretary") system; one entered the household of high officials (mostly of royal blood) who trained their successors in their household. The young person served the great personage, establishing a solid relationship, like Joseph with Potiphar (Gen 39:2) and with Pharaoh (Gen 41:40). Eventually formal classes came to be conducted at the royal court. In that world, fidelity to one's master was important. The apprenticeship context explains exhortations to deliver messages accurately, to avoid (domestic) quarrels, and to guard against entanglements with women of the household.

In portraying human beings, the instructions use the "heart" as the seat of feeling and, especially, of intelligence. A "hard-hearted" person lacks good sense rather than compassion. Human beings are characterized by a fundamental polarity—the wise person and the fool, the hot and the silent person. Fools do not follow the advice of their "father," or elder, and thus do not act according to *ma'at.* The cleverness of the wise is the result of education, nature, and their own shrewd assessment of people and situations. "Hearing" (in the sense of heeding) is an important verb in the exhortations. Egyptian society was open, allowing poor and ambitious young people to rise to positions of power. Such people needed guide books to success.

---

8. Helmut Brunner, *Die Weisheitsbücher der Ägypter: Lehren für das Leben* (Munich: Artemis, 1991).

9. Miriam Lichtheim, *Ancient Egyptian Literature,* 3 vols. (Berkeley: University of California Press, 1973–1980) 1:58-59.

10. Lichtheim, *Ancient Egyptian Literature,* 3:184-217.

11. *ANET,* 421-25; Lichtheim, *Ancient Egyptian Literature,* 2:146-63.

Instructions were composed in every period during the three millennia of Egyptian history, and they reflect changes in society. The genre arose with the Egyptian state in the third millennium BCE, when the need to administer vast territories required the king's servants to leave behind their village routine to travel and to respond to situations requiring more than just their personal experience. Instructions of the Old Kingdom (2650–2135 BCE) arose within the court and revolved around the king, but with the decline of the monarchy and the social disorder of the First Intermediate Period (2135–2040 BCE), the instructions turned from royal service to private concerns. With the restoration of monarchy in the Middle Kingdom (2040–1650 BCE), instructions once again stressed loyalty to the king. New Kingdom authors came from all levels of society, for daily business was now conducted by a broad range of people. With the *Instructions of Any* in the Eighteenth Dynasty (c. 1550–1305 BCE), concern for the individual and for the acquiring of inner peace reappears and dominates the genre down to Hellenistic and Roman times. Another reflection of societal change is the way success was interpreted. In the Old Kingdom, when courtiers were the intended readers, success meant getting ahead at court. When the readership became less tied to a particular social class, exhortations became more general and more personal—how to avoid suffering, conflicts, and disappointments in life.

In contrast to the Egyptian principle that artists be anonymous, instructions name their authors, presenting them as real people—kings or prominent scribes. The authority of instructions, after all, rested on the repute of their writers no less than on their antiquity. Reverence for authority and for antiquity did not, however, prevent critical editing and recasting of the ancient wisdom.

Composing, studying, teaching, and copying texts took place in a kind of academy known as the House of Life, which was usually located near a temple and had a cultic function. Instructions were copied out by school children as they learned the Egyptian script; their frequently faulty copies are often the chief manuscript source for instructions. Instructions were never meant solely to be school texts, however. The addressee in

instructions was a "son," a broader term than its English equivalent, one that expressed any close relationship with a younger person—one's child, student, or successor. The texts reveal a high level of personal involvement, for the prestige of the "father" depended on the success of the "son." The instructions were class-specific up to the first millennium, at which time general formulations became more common.

At the end of the third millennium another type of writing appeared: pessimistic and cynical attacks on traditional ways of thinking. The *Admonitions of Ipu-wer*, after a grim recital of the troubles of the land (a common topos), blames the creator-god using the form of dialogue.[12] *The Protests of the Eloquent Peasant* is a confrontation in nine speeches between a peasant and a high official.[13] *A Song of the Harper* urges one to enjoy today, for who knows about tomorrow.[14] The *Satire on the Trades* criticizes non-scribal activities to glorify the profession of the scribe.[15] The *Dispute of a Person with His Ba* (i.e., vital force) vividly describes the miseries of life.[16] These works show that scribes in Egypt, as in Mesopotamia, were free to criticize the tradition. One should not regard skeptical works *ipso facto* as the products of alienated or marginalized groups, therefore; they could arise within the scribal guild.

Canaan. The larger context for Israel was in the "Canaanite" culture common to the entire Levant (with local variations). Unfortunately, few wisdom writings survive from this culture. The Ugaritic texts, which provide a northern sampling of Canaanite culture, contain a few didactic texts. Most such texts are Babylonian: the *Counsels of Shube'awilum,*[17] collections of sayings, and a hymn of trust to Marduk (similar to the Babylonian "I will praise the Lord of wisdom"). These and other Babylonian texts appear in the Akkadian language, showing that the Ugaritic scribes read and appreciated Mesopotamian literature. One wisdom text, the book of Ahiqar, originally written in

12. *ANET,* 441-44; Lichtheim, *Ancient Egyptian Literature,* 1:159-63.
13. *ANET,* 407-10; Lichtheim, *Ancient Egyptian Literature,* 2:146-63.
14. *ANET,* 467; Lichtheim, *Ancient Egyptian Literature,* 1:194-97.
15. *ANET,* 432-34; Lichtheim, *Ancient Egyptian Literature,* 1:184-92.
16. *ANET,* 405-7; Lichtheim, *Ancient Egyptian Literature,* 1:163-69.
17. Foster, *Before the Muses,* 332-35.

Aramaic around the eighth or seventh century BCE, is possibly of Canaanite origin. The book contains the tale of Ahiqar, an official of the Assyrian king, and a collection of his sayings. The tale is similar to stories of courtiers such as those of Joseph and Daniel, in which the courtier loses his high position at court through the envy of others and then regains it through his patience and sagacity. Ahiqar has some links to the book of Tobit. It is noteworthy that the courtier Ahiqar, who has experienced many things and suffered much, is celebrated as the author of sayings, exhortations, and wisdom poems. Practical wisdom is connected with age and experience.

SOCIAL CONTEXT

Form criticism, from its beginnings in the early twentieth century, has inquired about the origin of literary forms in specific arenas of human life. Recent scholarship, with its consciousness of class interest lurking in literary works, asks even more intensely about the social location of authors and their works.

Who were the authors of the wisdom books, and what social class interest(s) did they promote? Were they scribes on the staff of palace and temple, or teachers in schools? Were they elders of tribes or families inculcating tribal traditions and values onto the younger generation? Unfortunately, the Bible does not provide sufficient information about everyday life to answer these questions with certainty.

The complicated writing systems of Mesopotamia and Egypt virtually ensured that authors of literary works were professional scribes and poets. The scribe in Mesopotamia and Egypt belonged to a well-defined profession. Egypt had its House of Life, and Mesopotamia its tablet house.

Scholars have theorized about two different settings for Israel's wisdom literature: the school (under royal sponsorship) and the tribe. Some scholars, on the basis of foreign examples, suggest that the monarchy, beginning in the tenth century BCE, built up a skilled or "wise" bureaucracy for the keeping of records and accounts, for diplomatic correspondence with foreign powers (requiring a knowledge of Akkadian and Egyptian),

and for composing didactic material. From this circle would have come the authors of the instructions and other wisdom literature. King Solomon was recognized by the historian both for establishing administrative structures and for possessing pre-eminent wisdom (cf. 1 Kings 3; 4:29; 11:41). His name is associated with wisdom books (Prov 1:1; 25:1; Eccl 1:12; Cant 1:1; Sir 47:13; Wisdom 7–9).

Proponents of the tribal theory point out that the wisdom books do not mention any class of sages. Noting the strong family and tribal traditions of Israel, they propose that the admonitions and warnings of the wisdom books have their roots in prohibitions laid down by tribal elders that regulated social relations within the tribe. A variant of the tribal theory finds the folk element not so much in the admonitions and warnings as in the sayings and comparisons. The latter arose from real-life experiences of ordinary people; the sayings were made concise and memorable by removing details of their originating situations.

In assessing the origin and context of wisdom writings, indeed of other biblical writings, one must concede some influence from tribal tradition on wisdom material, for the family was a dominant institution in ancient Israel. Nonetheless, it is likely that professional scribes or poets, under the general sponsorship of the king, composed the biblical wisdom books, since all of these books represent genres well known in the ancient literary world. Only people able to read and appreciate such writings could have adopted their conventions with the skill and sophistication so evident in the biblical books. References to rural life and farming cannot be used as evidence for tribal origins, for they reflect almost universal anxiety about crops and herds in the precarious economy of the ancient world. Many Israelites, it is true, were able to read the relatively simple alphabetic Hebrew, and they would have constituted a broad readership; but the authors of the biblical books came from the ranks of professional scribes and sages. Skeptical and critical books like Job and Qohelet could have come from these ranks also, for a critical and skeptical spirit was at home among ancient scribes, as is clear in the writings from Mesopotamia and Egypt. The author of Qohelet is called a sage, a collector, and a sifter of maxims (Eccl 12:9-11). Ben Sira, in the first quarter of the second century BCE, was a professional sage, though not necessarily in the employ of temple or court. He lauds the profession of scribe (Sir 38:24–39:11) and invites young people to his school (Sir 51:13-30). The role the Israelite sage played is difficult to detail, however. Like the Mesopotamian scribe, some Israelite scribes may have been in the employ of the royal court, whereas others may have been privately employed. African societies, where proverb experts provided the king with appropriate maxims, may offer a valuable analogy. Given the small population of Judah and Jerusalem and the limits on the monarchy (and later to the high priesthood) from tribal loyalty and ancient religious traditions, however, one cannot in simple fashion apply to Israel observations about the scribe in neighboring cultures.

FORMAL CHARACTERISTICS OF WISDOM LITERATURE

Biblical and other ancient literatures were ruled by conventions, far more so than is the case with modern literature. Attention to the major genre and smaller genres or forms of each work as well as to other formal features sheds considerable light on biblical wisdom literature. Genre refers to the kind of literature, the literary species of a complete work, such as comedy, tragedy, biography, law code, or instruction. Unfortunately, ancient Near Eastern authors did not commit their theories of literature to writing, forcing modern readers to infer each text's category.

Discussion of the precise literary forms in each work will be found in each commentary. Only the large-scale genres, those that incorporate smaller genres, will be noted here: instructions, proverb collections, dialogues on divine justice and human suffering, pseudo-autobiographies, and philosophical exhortations to a certain way of life.

Instruction. This widely attested wisdom genre is found in both Egypt and Mesopotamia from the mid-third millennium to the beginning of the common era. Most such writings are Egyptian. Formally, Mesopotamian and Egyptian instructions are of two types: those with a title and main text, and those with a title, prologue, and main text (with subtitles and other divisions). The author is always referred to in the third person, often with titles and epithets. There is always a direct address of the son in the prologue, sometimes also in the body of the work. The main text is made up of units consisting of one to seven lines, the two-line couplet by far the most common. The couplet (also called distich or bicolon) occurs in synonymous, antithetic, or synthetic parallelism, or in balanced phrases. Because early instructions are lengthy and sophisticated, attempts to show historical development from short sayings to long essays, or from simple to complex argumentation or forms, are not persuasive. Instructions always contain proverbs and exhortations.

Proverb Collections. Although proverbs or pithy sayings were part and parcel of all ancient literature, *collections* of proverbs were not always present. Besides sayings, the many Sumerian proverb collections contain anecdotes, extracts from works of literature, short fables, and other unidentifiable material. Some sayings occur in parallel lines, whereas others consist of just one line.

Dialogues on Divine Justice and Human Suffering. From a formal point of view, the Egyptian *Dispute Between a Man and His Ba* (second-millennium BCE) mingles prose, symmetrically structured speech, and lyric poetry. From the same period, *The Protests of the Eloquent Peasant* consists of nine carefully framed petitions in poetic form (with prose explanation) framed by a prose narrative describing the injustice done to the peasant. The whole is shaped and unified by irony and contrast. The Mesopotamian "Sumerian Job" has a brief introduction and ending, between which a sufferer addresses god in a long complaint, using pithy sayings. The Babylonian Theodicy has a remarkably regular structure—twenty-seven stanzas of eleven lines, one stanza for the sufferer's complaints, and one stanza for the friend's notions of divine justice. The argument proceeds with concrete examples of justice and injustice and short sayings rather than with abstract reasoning.

Pseudo-Autobiography. The Akkadian genre of autobiography narrates the great deeds of a hero, drawing morals from them. Related to this form of writing is the genre of royal pseudo-autobiography, narrated partly in the first person, in which legendary and historical elements blend. Both adventures and interactions between characters appear in it.

Philosophical Exhortation. Exhortations to follow a particular philosophy or life of wisdom, known as protreptic in classical Greek and Latin literature, employ a variety of arguments and styles to persuade their audience. Some forms of writing that fall within this genre are the diatribe, in which imaginary opponents are chided, and the (elaborate) comparison. The biblical book of Wisdom is such an exhortation.

Brief Forms. The most pervasive small forms in wisdom literature are the *saying* and the *command* or *prohibition.* The saying is a sentence, usually written in the indicative mode. It can be divided into three types: the proverb, the experiential saying, and the didactic saying. The definition of a proverb is controverted, but the following is widely accepted: a concise statement of an apparent truth that has currency. The word *apparent* is used because a proverb is not always and everywhere true but proven so by context— e.g., "Many hands make light work" and "Too many cooks spoil the broth" are true according to the situation. *Currency* means that people "use" proverbs; they are not just clever sayings. The experiential saying presents some aspect of reality, "telling it like it is," and lets the hearer or reader draw the practical conclusions from it. The saying, "Some pretend to be rich, yet have nothing;/ others pretend to be poor, yet have great wealth" (Prov 13:7 NRSV), is open to further verification or qualification. The didactic saying is more than a statement about reality; it characterizes an action or attitude so as to influence human conduct—e.g., "Those who oppress the poor insult their Maker" (Prov 14:31 NRSV).

The sages can impose their will directly through commands (imperative or jussive mood) and prohibitions. Occasionally a command is placed parallel to a saying, moving the saying from observation to command.

MAIN TEACHINGS OF WISDOM LITERATURE

The theology found within the wisdom books does not add up to a system, for the writers did not have a speculative aim; rather, they sought to instruct the next generation, to solve specific problems, to collect, critique, and hand on ancestral traditions. The central assumption of all the books is that God made the world, an order within which the human race must learn to live. That order was given privileged expression on the day of creation. Through wisdom, human beings can cope with the world and live happy and successful lives. Of great concern to the sages was the consequences of human choices ("retribution") upon individuals and society. Wisdom authors saw human beings as active agents, often dramatizing the moral life as involving two ways: the way of the righteous and the way of the wicked. Experience of life forced the sages to confront that surd in the cosmic system, the problem of evil. The sages recognized wisdom to be more than human ability to master life; it was hidden with God and had to be given to human beings. Attempts to consider wisdom in itself led to the personification of wisdom as a woman. Such are the themes constituting a theology of wisdom.

God. The word for "God"—אלהים (ʾĕlōhîm), יהוה (Yahweh), or one of the several names for God in the Joban dialogues (e.g., "the Almighty" [שדי šadday, Job 6:4])— occurs throughout the wisdom books, naming One who creates, sustains the universe, and brings all human acts to completion. Although the wisdom mode of understanding the divine presence differs from that of the historical and prophetic books, it is no less real. Scholarly hypotheses that early wisdom was profane and only later made religious by incorporation into Yahwism have rightly been rejected, for all ancient Near Eastern wisdom presupposed the gods even when gods and worship of gods are not mentioned. Skeptical Qohelet, who avoids the name "Yahweh," mentions "Elohim" four times in twelve chapters. In the monotheism of orthodox Yahwism, according to which the Bible has been edited, there is no order beyond Yahweh's will, unlike neighboring cultures.

Cosmic Order. Wisdom literature assumes that there is a divinely implanted order in the universe, embracing the "natural" and the human worlds. The modern, dichotomous distinction between human beings and nature (deriving largely from Greek thought) was unknown in the ancient Near East. The purposeful activity of a colony of ants is as much an example of order as is the purposeful activity of human beings (see Prov 6:6-11). Job's claim that he, as a righteous man, had not experienced any order in the universe (Job 38:2) is refuted by Yahweh's listing of the activity of the inanimate and animate spheres. Analogies are constantly being drawn between human and non-human beings and activities (Prov 5:15; 11:28-29; 26:21; 27:17, 21). These dispositions are all "righteous" examples of the way the world works.

Cosmic order was perceived in two basic ways in the ancient Near East: order as the result of divine planning and order as being above and beyond divine plans and powers. In the first perspective, the gods in their wisdom justly reward or punish an individual with success or failure in this life. Coexisting with this view, in an existential contradiction, is the second perspective—a deterministic view according to which the course of one's life is fixed from birth. An Akkadian word illustrates well this notion. *Šimtu* (Sumerian *namtar*), inexactly rendered "fate" or "destiny," was "a disposition originating from an agency empowered to act and to dispose, such as the deity, king, or any individual"; it refers to the share of fortune and misfortune that determines the direction and temper of life. Other Mesopotamian vocabulary is even more deterministic; e.g., Akkadian *uṣurtu* (Sumerian *gišḫur*), means "drawing" or "design." These two views of cosmic order reflect diverse, even contradictory, experiences of the world.

Israel's monotheism affected, at least implicitly, this ancient Near Eastern interpretive blend of fate and freedom. Instead of an interplay between unchangeable order and divine decree, the sole God, Yahweh, is consistently portrayed as all-powerful and all-wise, utterly responsive to human actions. Yahweh is not capricious, for there are always reasons for divine action. Cosmic order in

the Bible, therefore, must be understood as less absolute than elsewhere in the East; it is associated closely with Yahweh's will (on occasion even personified as Yahweh's word or a female friend).

Creation. Unlike modern scientific concepts of creation, which envision only the physical world (typically in its astral and planetary aspects), ancient cosmogonies narrated the creation and organization of human society within the universe. In all cosmogonies, the gods created the world to benefit themselves; humans were slaves of the gods, their task being to ensure that everything operated for the divine service. Elements of the universe were given their purpose on the day of creation; the origin of a reality was its essence. Thus it is not surprising that cosmogonies were common in the ancient world, narrated to ground or to legitimate realities important to human life, such as the stars, the sun, and the moon, which determined time (especially sacred time), temple, king, and other institutions. Cosmogonies or cosmogonic language appear frequently in the Bible (see Genesis 1–11; Psalms 33; 77; 89; 93; 96–98; 104; Isaiah 40–66; and the wisdom literature).

Each wisdom book devotes considerable attention to creation. Proverbs has two cosmogonies: Prov 3:19-20 and 8:22-31. Job contains many allusions to creation, especially in chaps. 38–41. The opening of Qohelet (Eccl 1:3-11) presents a cosmology grounding the sage's ethical teaching about God and human actions. Sirach treats creation in 16:24–18:14; 39:12-35; and 42:15–43:38. In Sir 16:24–18:14, Yahweh creates the world, determining boundaries and arranging forever all their works that never disobey the divine word (Sir 16:26-28). The created world includes human beings whose obedience is not automatic but is given freely to their creator. Formed with a fixed number of days and with "fear of the Lord" and understanding, they are called to live obediently and worshipfully within the covenant (Sir 17:1-17). A lengthy address to the human race follows the cosmogony: Turn back to your righteous and merciful God (Sir 17:17–18:14). For Ben Sira, the nature and purpose of human beings (including Israel) were fixed at creation. The book of Wisdom develops the parallel between creation and redemption that the books of Genesis and Exodus had already drawn through cross-referencing. According to Wisdom, the world was created as salvific by wisdom (Wis 1:14); the cosmos itself is intrinsically involved in the divine judgment that restores the original righteous order (Wis 19:18-21).

Proverbs 8 and Job 38–41 are worth singling out to show the relation between wisdom and creation. The cosmogony in Prov 8:22-31 legitimates the speech of Woman Wisdom in which she promises her friends life and prosperity. Proverbs 3:19-20 likewise grounds the promise of wisdom in Prov 3:13-18. The full cosmogony in Prov 8:22-31 is structured chiastically:

> A Yahweh creates Wisdom in honored first place vv. 22-23;
> > B Creation "negatively" described vv. 24-28;
> > B´ Creation "positively" described vv. 28-30*a*;
> A´ Wisdom's intimacy with Yahweh vv. 30*b*-31.

The final two verses (vv. 30*b*-31), which come after the actual creating, are crucial for understanding Wisdom's appeal:

> and I was daily [his] delight,
> > [playing] before him at all times,
> [playing] in his inhabited world
> > and delighting in the human race. (NRSV)

The chiastic placement of "delight" and "play" makes Wisdom's delighting in Yahweh parallel to Wisdom's delighting in the human race. Just as Wisdom is Yahweh's delight "daily" in v. 30*b*, so also her friends are to wait at her doors "daily" in v. 34. The intimate relationship between Woman Wisdom and human beings on earth is a reflection of the intimate relationship between Woman Wisdom and Yahweh in heaven. Woman Wisdom might be expected to ground her authority on the fact that she has seen Yahweh create and can communicate to her friends the secrets of how the world works. Yet she bases her authority solely on her intimacy with Yahweh; from the beginning she has been with God. She enables those who love her to know the all-wise God as well.

Proverbs 8 goes a step beyond Prov 3:19-20 by personifying wisdom, which the sages traditionally associated with the divine act of creation and the cosmic order. Now the vivid personification in Proverbs 8 grounds Wisdom's claim that only those who court her will enjoy blessing. The search for wisdom in Proverbs 8 becomes more than performing or avoiding certain actions. Rather, one is to seek Wisdom herself. To court her is to touch a quality of Yahweh the creator, and to enter into a relationship with her is to receive every divine blessing. This cosmogony explains how life may have a more profound meaning; it may be not only life in the sense of enjoyment of health, good name, and family happiness, but also "life with" association with Yahweh.

In Job, creation themes and language are vital to the argument. God's first speech (Job 38:1–40:2) refutes Job's denial of order, and the second (Job 40:6–41:34) refutes his charge of injustice (in the sense of God's being unable to restrain evil). The first speech is a list of created things, showing them to be a mix of the useful, the bizarre, and even the playful. God, it appears, creates not for human beings (Job) but for the divine pleasure, which is inscrutable. The second speech simply describes the two primordial beasts, Behemoth and Leviathan. Any cosmogony based on the combat myth, as it was then current in Canaan, would have told how God defeated the primordial monsters as the first act of creation (cf. Isa 51:9); but in Job they are not defeated, and their cosmic menace and hostility to the human race are actually celebrated by the deity! Rather than destroying them to create an orderly world, Yahweh chooses to let them be (although on a leash). God tells Job that these monsters, the very symbols of evil, are alive and well, and that Job must live in the universe where they roam. Creation language here and elsewhere in Job shows paradoxically that the universe is not orderly as some traditional sages had thought. Yahweh remains, however, the powerful if inscrutable friend of such stalwarts as Job.

Wisdom. The rules or laws structured into the world at creation can be discovered through wisdom. Moreover, these norms can be expressed in artful words and communicated to others. Although wisdom cannot be defined solely as a response to cosmic order, the literature accepts this order. The sages hoped to instruct others about how to live in accord with wisdom (see Proverbs), to investigate scandal in that order—namely, the failure of a righteous person to enjoy appropriate blessings (see Job)—to point out why tradition cannot explain the world or ensure happiness (see Ecclesiastes), to anthologize and arrange ancient wisdom and relate it to Israel's literary heritage (see Sirach), and to locate wisdom in a seemingly unjust world for an audience familiar with the philosophical tradition of middle Platonism (see book of Wisdom).

Wisdom cannot be satisfactorily captured in a single brief definition because it has at least four aspects. First, it is practical, involving knowledge about how the world works so that one can master and enjoy life fully. This aspect of wisdom is expressed well in the French term *savoir-faire,* "to know how to act or do," rather than "to know" in an absolute sense, divorced from action. Practical knowledge can involve judicial activity, as when kings exercise their role as judge. David discerns the true intent of the woman from Tekoa (2 Sam 14:1-24, esp. v. 20), and Solomon shrewdly decides which of the two prostitutes is telling the truth (1 Kgs 3:16-28). It can mean skillful composition of proverbs and songs (1 Kgs 4:32) or cataloging related objects (1 Kgs 4:33). Jewelers and artisans can be "wise," like the artisans who constructed the tabernacle (Exod 35:30–36:1). More generally, wisdom designates knowing how to live life; human life, as such, is a constant theme in wisdom literature. Most of the sayings in the wisdom books do not give advice but state a thesis about the world. "Hope deferred makes the heart sick,/ but a desire fulfilled is a tree of life" (Prov 13:12 NRSV) is not advice to finish projects for the sake of psychological health; rather, it states the way people ordinarily respond to disappointment and fulfillment of desires. Life is sufficiently regular that the sage can discover its rhythms and formulate them into theses or statements.

Second, human wisdom has limits. Proverbs, which is sometimes regarded as naively optimistic, has as its heroine Woman Wisdom, who from her place with God gives wisdom to those who wait upon her. Proverbs 26:4-5 wittily expresses the limits of wisdom sayings to fit every occasion: "Do not answer fools according to their folly,/ or you will be a fool yourself./ Answer fools according to their folly, or they will be wise in their own eyes" (NRSV). Wisdom in Proverbs involves the careful application of the tradition to individual situations. Job, that legendary wise man, refutes the traditional wisdom of his friends by using his own case; yet, he in turn is refuted by God's description of a vast, complex, and totally theocentric universe. Qohelet poses as the weary king who has seen all in order to put down any claim of wisdom to master life. The moments of life are hidden with God and parceled out to the foolish and the wise alike (Eccl 3:1-15). Ben Sira, though confident in the wisdom project, nonetheless writes long hymns to the divine wisdom (Sir 16:29–18:14; 39:12-35; 42:15–43:33) and pays court to her (Sir 51:13-30). The book of Wisdom focuses on divine wisdom; the model sage (Solomon) desires and prays intensely that it will be given to him (Wisdom 7–9).

The third point develops naturally from the foregoing one: Wisdom generally is both a human task and a divine gift, acquired through experience and obedience *and* given by God. Reconciling divine sovereignty with human freedom may be a major problem in the Western philosophical tradition, but the Bible does not perceive this dual affirmation to be a problem requiring a solution.

Fourth, wisdom in the Bible is itself an object of constant reflection. A major difference between the wisdom books of neighboring cultures and those of Israel is the constant occurrence of the word *wisdom* (חכמה *ḥokmâ*) in the biblical books. Job 28 declares that wisdom is hidden with God and that the only way to wisdom is fear of the Lord (Job 28:28). Proverbs 1–9 goes further and personifies wisdom as an attractive woman who offers to share with her friends the life she shares with God (Proverbs 8–9). She shares in the divine governance of the world, doing what Yahweh elsewhere is depicted as doing. Sirach 24 identifies wisdom with "the book of the covenant of the Most High God" (Sir 24:23 NRSV), part of Ben Sira's project of incorporating wisdom into the other literature of Israel. In the Wisdom of Solomon, wisdom is closely associated with God and is like an ether permeating the cosmos (Wis 7:22–8:1); wisdom is revealed to human beings after prayer and pursuit (Sir 7:1-22; 8:2–9:18).

Consequences of Human Choice. Because biblical wisdom is so linked to action, the sages were much concerned with the effects of human action on each individual and on the community. The term "retribution" is often used to describe the relation between deed and consequence, but its negative connotation in English (punishment from an external source) makes it an unsatisfactory term to use. The effects of actions, according to the sages, could come from the very actions themselves as well as externally— i.e., directly from God, who sees all. Klaus Koch has emphasized the deed/consequence side of human acts: The deed creates its own effect, that consequences are latent in all significant good and evil actions.[18] The theory is an instance of cosmic order applied to human activity. God acts as "midwife" (Koch's term) to the law. A good example is the parent's warning to their offspring not to join a band of robbers on the grounds that a life of brigandage is inherently self-destructive. The robbers

> lie in wait—to kill themselves!
> and set an ambush—for their own lives!
> Such is the end of all who are greedy
> for gain;
> it takes away the life of its possessors.
> (Prov 1:18-19 NRSV)

Another example of inherent outcomes is Prov 26:27 (NRSV): "Whoever digs a pit [to trap enemies] will fall into it,/ and a stone will come back on the one who starts it rolling." Inherent outcomes, however, are only one side of human action, for God is depicted as intervening directly: Yahweh "does not let the righteous go hungry,/ but he thwarts the craving of the wicked" (Prov 10:3 NRSV; cf. Prov 15:29; 16:4; 17:15). Job disproves his friends' belief that the deeds of the wicked always come back on them even as God is the ultimate source of Job's undeserved

afflictions. The internal and the external perspectives that seem exclusive to modern readers remain valid for the biblical authors.

Doctrine of the Two Ways. The Bible, especially the book of Proverbs, imagines the moral life as presenting two ways, each with an intrinsic dynamism. Sometimes the two ways are explicitly contrasted, as in Woman Wisdom and Woman Folly in Proverbs 1–9 (esp. Prov 4:10-19) and in the persistent contrast in the sayings between the wise or the righteous and the fool or the wicked; Psalm 1 is also a good example of the inherent dynamism of two ways of life. The parental warning that opens Proverbs (1:8-19) envisions the future of the child as a way of life (Prov 1:15) shared with others ("we will all have one purse" [Prov 1:14 NRSV]). The doctrine of the two ways has sometimes been interpreted statically, as if it described a class of people who meticulously observe the law and a class who do not; but this reading is incorrect. The concept is dynamic: There are two ways of living, one blessed and the other cursed, and people are invited to follow the way of the righteous and to avoid the way of the wicked. There is no room for pride or smugness, for one can leave the righteous way at any time. The way of the righteous is protected and guaranteed by God, but people must walk in it—that is, act accordingly. The doctrine is implicit in Job, where the point at issue is the result of righteous living, and also in Ecclesiastes, where, since one cannot fully understand human behavior, Qohelet denies the epistemological basis for the two ways. The book of Wisdom contrasts the wicked (Wis 2:1-24; 4:20–5:23) with the righteous child of God, interpreted individually (Wis 2:12-20; 5:15-16) or corporately as Israel (Wisdom 19). In the Qumran texts and in the New Testament, the notion of two ways is expressed in the concepts of the children of light and the children of darkness.

The Problem of Evil. A skeptical and critical thread runs throughout ancient wisdom literature. The problem of evil was often formulated as a case—the sufferer who is not aware of having sinned or, conversely, the prosperous scoundrel. Proverbs does not subject the problem of evil to explicit reflection, though it does not necessarily regard its sayings as the ultimate answer to life's mysteries.

---

18. Klaus Koch, "Is There a Doctrine of Retribution in the Old Testament?" in *Theodicy in the Old Testament,* ed. James L. Crenshaw (Philadelphia: Fortress, 1983) 57-87.

Job narrates a case of the innocent just person. Qohelet's skepticism and criticism of traditional wisdom attempts to explain inconsistencies in the world. Ben Sira is aware of inexplicable evil in life but simply affirms the divine origin of evil as well as good (Sir 39:12-35), and he insists that God has created all things in pairs, corresponding to the human ability to choose between right and wrong (Sir 15:11-20; 33:7-15). The suffering of the innocent just person is so important in the book of Wisdom that it led to the teaching on immortality as its solution.

Biblical exploration of inexplicable suffering differs from that of Israel's neighbors. In Mesopotamia there was, strictly speaking, no such thing as a righteous sufferer. If one is afflicted without apparent reason, it can only be that one has infringed upon the sovereign order of the gods. This perception continues throughout the history of ancient Mesopotamia:

> In the Old Babylonian period this theology may find expression in a simple confession of bewilderment and ignorance of what one has done, or in the acceptance of one's sinfulness, along with its necessary consequences, as another manifestation of *fragilitas humana* common to all men. Later, one may infer from a clear conscience and a life re-examined and found, according to the known rules, faultless, that the gods hold men to the observance of other rules that he cannot know. To these thoughts one may join a contempt for man as the minion of many moods, a creature that may live gloriously only to die miserably. Or one may make the problem of the mind a problem of the heart, and solve it with reasons of the heart. Instead of wisdom, belief; instead of reflection and argument, a hymn to paradox and contraction. *Credo quia absurdum.* Attitudes and expression change; the theology does not.[19]

Against that background, Job is unique: "An explicit, unyielding declaration of innocence is not found before the book of Job."[20] The

Bible's confession of one God, all-wise and all-powerful, makes its exploration of the problem of evil and of the righteous sufferer more pressing and more poignant than that of neighboring cultures. Who but God is ultimately responsible for whatever happens in the world?

Personification of Wisdom. Israelite wisdom literature attended to wisdom itself alongside pragmatic wisdom. This "theoretical" interest is first clearly visible in Proverbs 1–9 (also in Job 28), where traditional teacher-disciple instructions exhort one not only to proper conduct but also to the acquisition of wisdom, which is portrayed as the source of long life, wealth, honor, and closeness to Yahweh. Although Israel had long singled out divine attributes such as power, love, and fidelity, occasionally even personifying them ("love and faithfulness go before you" [Ps 89:14 NRSV]; "Awake, awake, put on strength,/ O arm of the LORD!" [Isa 51:9 NRSV]), the consistent and vivid personification of wisdom as an attractive woman in Proverbs 1–9; Sirach 24; Bar 3:9–4:4; and Wisdom 7–9 stands on a different level. Wisdom acts and speaks, threatening or promising her audience, exulting in her intimacy and privileged place with Yahweh. For explanation, scholars have adduced venerable parallels such as an alleged Canaanite goddess; Ma'at, the Egyptian goddess of order; or the type scene found in the Mesopotamian Gilgamesh epic, the Canaanite Aqhat epic, and the Greek *Odyssey* (Calypso in Book V and Circe in Book X), in which a goddess offers life to a young hero only to destroy or transform him later on. Although personified Wisdom probably has non-Israelite roots, one must also reckon with influences from the social roles of real women in Israelite history and literary traditions about them—e.g., wife, harlot, wise woman—and with folk literature motifs such as the "sought-for person" (princess/bride).

In Prov 1:10-33 and chap. 8 (the frame for Proverbs 1–9), Wisdom invites the young disciple into a relationship with her, using language of love and courtship that is found also in Song of Songs (seeking and finding amid danger, waiting for the beloved). Her intimacy with Yahweh is the model of her relationship to the disciple; it enables her to give other

19. W. L. Moran, "Rib Adda: Job at Byblos?" *Biblical and Related Studies Presented to Samuel Iwry* (Winona Lake: Eisenbrauns, 1985) 176-77.

20. Moran, "Rib Adda," 177n16.

gifts as well (Prov 8:30-36). Scholars grope for the right term for this presentation of Wisdom in Proverbs. Is it a hypostatization of a divine attribute or of the divinely implanted order in the world, or is it straightforward literary personification? Whatever explanation is adopted, Proverbs provides the primary interpretive context: Wisdom is a symbol of divine presence as well as of revelation; she is closely related to the instruction of the human teacher and to wisdom; a countervoice parodies Wisdom's message (Prov 2:16-19; 5; 6:20-35; 7; 9:13-18); and the quest for her is modeled on human love.

Personified wisdom appears in later books of the Bible as well. Sirach 24 (written c. 180 BCE) develops the link of wisdom and Yahweh and the old question of where wisdom dwells (Job 28) in a narrative in which Wisdom tells how she "came forth from the mouth of the Most High" (Sir 24:3 NRSV) and, at God's command, settled with Israel in Jerusalem (Sir 24:10-12). The author then identifies Wisdom with "the book of the covenant of the Most High God" (Sir 24:23 NRSV). Baruch 3:9–4:4 similarly identifies wisdom with the Torah. Wisdom of Solomon (c. first century BCE) combines the tradition of personified Wisdom living at God's side with Greek philosophical notions to assign a cosmic role to wisdom. The famous twenty-one qualities of Wisdom enumerated in Wis 7:22-23 highlight her pervasive agency in all things. For the influence of Wisdom on early Christian reflection about the cosmic role of Christ, see the section "New Testament" below.

THE CONTINUATION OF WISDOM LITERATURE

Judaism. The wisdom genres of instruction, saying, dialogue, and its themes of the blessed life and of cosmic order continued in the writings of early Judaism. Many literary works of the period used the technique of "relecture"—that is, rereading and recasting the classic texts. In the second century BCE, Sirach 24 rereads Proverbs 8, and Sirach 44–50 rereads the historical books, viewing the great personalities of Israel's history as individuals inspired by wisdom. Baruch 3:9–4:4 rereads Job 28 and Sirach 24, showing how the rulers of nations never found Wisdom, unlike Israel, who finds her in the book of the commandments of the law (Bar 4:1). Wisdom 10–19 interprets the books of Exodus and Numbers in seven great comparisons. *Pirqe 'Abot* (*The Sayings of the Fathers*) is a collection of sayings from the "men of the Great Assembly" (between the late fifth and the third centuries BCE) down to the descendants of Rabbi Judah the Prince in the third century CE. One of the treatises in the Talmud became the object of commentary in *'Abot de Rabbi Nathan*. Its opening sentence places the men of the Great Assembly in a line from Moses, Joshua, the elders, and the prophets. The wisdom text of the Cairo Geniza, which some date in the first century CE but more likely dates to the early medieval period, continues the old wisdom tradition. Hebrew ethical wills, in which parents hand on to their children their wisdom, draw on traditional wisdom instruction.

The New Testament. Early Christians saw Jesus as a wisdom teacher and employed the tradition of personified wisdom to express his incarnation. Among the various influences on the New Testament was the wisdom teaching of "the Scriptures" (i.e., the Old Testament)—the themes of wisdom hidden with God and revealed to human beings, its identification with divine Spirit, Word, and Law, as well as the forms of instruction and admonition.

Unique among New Testament writings is the Letter of James, for it is an instruction. Although classed among the seven catholic epistles, it is a letter only in its opening address, "James, a slave of God and of the Lord Jesus Christ, to the twelve tribes in the dispersion, greetings" (Jas 1:1 NAB). The rest of the work comprises a series of instructions using the familiar exhortatory verbs (imperatives, jussives), followed by reasons, which are often sayings or proverbs. Old wisdom themes appear: the dangers of an unbridled tongue (James 3; cf. Prov 10:18-21), of presumptuous planning (Jas 4:13-17; cf. Prov 16:1), or of ill-gotten wealth (Jas 5:1-6; cf. Prov 10:2-3). Although commonsensical in the style of the instruction, James nonetheless exalts "wisdom from above" (Jas 3:13-18 NRSV; cf. Jas 1:17), invoking the tradition of wisdom beyond human capacity but graciously given to human beings (see Job 28; Proverbs 8; Sirach 24). In Jas 3:17, wisdom from above is designated by seven qualities, recalling the famous twenty-one qualities of wisdom in Wis 7:22-23. The wisdom instruction does not remain unchanged, however, for it is altered by the addition of prophetic denunciations of the callous rich (Jas 1:27; 2:1-13; 4:1-10; 5:1-6).

Paul's argument against those who are scandalized by the cross (1 Cor 1:17–2:13) employs the traditional wisdom literature contrast between the wise and the foolish as well as that between human wisdom and divine wisdom (see Job 28; Proverbs 8): "For since in the wisdom of God the world did not come to know God through wisdom, it was the will of God through the foolishness of the proclamation to save those who have faith" (1 Cor 1:21 NAB). So harsh is Paul's judgment on the ability of the sage to know Christ that one may question whether this passage singlehandedly eliminated wisdom genres as vehicles for the early Christian message.

Wisdom traditions influenced the putative written source of the synoptic Gospels Matthew and Luke: Q, for *Quelle,* the German word for "source." Most scholars believe that Q emphasized Jesus' teachings rather than his death and resurrection. A few scholars even hypothesize a trajectory of the genre "words of the wise" from early collections of wisdom sayings, such as Proverbs, to gnostic collections of sayings, such as the *Gospel of Thomas* (late first century BCE), with Q falling somewhere in the middle of the trajectory. In its pure form the hypothesis runs into serious problems, for Q at some stage had eschatological statements incompatible with gnostic timelessness and lacking distinctively gnostic sayings. Wisdom themes nonetheless are strong in Q, as is illustrated by Matt 11:27// Luke 10:22: "All things have been handed over to me by my Father. No one knows the Son except the Father, and no one knows the Father except the Son and anyone to whom the Son wishes to reveal him" (NAB). The saying is part of the Jewish (and early Christian) debate about what and where wisdom is. Is it to be identified with the law (Sirach 24), with heavenly mysteries (*1 Enoch* 42:1-3), or with Christ (John 1:1-18; Col 1:15-20)?

Is wisdom to be found in the Jerusalem Temple (Sir 24:8-12), everywhere in the cosmos (Wis 7:24-26), in heaven (*1 Enoch* 42:1-3), or in the church (Col 1:18)? Jesus in the text is divine wisdom incarnate, for to know him is to know God, who is wisdom itself. The immediately following verses, "Come to me, all you that are weary and are carrying heavy burdens, and I will give you rest. Take my yoke upon you, and learn from me" (Matt 11:28-29 NRSV), echo Sir 51:23-30, which is an invitation to attend Ben Sira's school and become his disciple. Matthew, therefore, answers the question of the early debate: Wisdom is found in Jesus and in his teaching.

Of all the Gospels, John is the most persistent in regarding Jesus as incarnate wisdom descended from on high to offer human beings light and truth. The Gospel expresses Jesus' heavenly origin by identifying him with personified Wisdom. Just as Woman Wisdom was with God from the beginning, even before the earth (Prov 8:22-23; Sir 24:9; Wis 6:22), so also Jesus is the Word in the beginning (John 1:1), with God before the world existed (John 17:5). Just as Wisdom teaches human beings heavenly secrets (Job 11:6-7; Wis 9:16-18) and shows them how to walk in the way that leads to life (Prov 2:20-22; 3:13-26; 8:32-35; Sir 4:12) and immortality (Wis 6:18-19), so also Jesus functions as the revealer in John. Jesus speaks in long discourses, as did Woman Wisdom (Prov 1:20-33; 8). Wisdom invites people to partake of her rich banquet, where food and drink symbolize life and closeness to God (Prov 9:2-5; Sir 24:19-21). Jesus does the same: "I am the bread of life. Whoever comes to me will never be hungry, and whoever believes in me will never be thirsty" (John 6:35 NRSV; cf. Prov 9:1-6, 11). Just as Wisdom seeks friends (Prov 1:20-21; 8:1-4; Wis 6:16), so also Jesus recruits followers (John 1:36-38, 43), though an individual might reject Wisdom (Prov 1:24-25; Bar 3:12; *1 Enoch* 42:2) or Jesus (John 8:46; 10:25).

Two early Christian hymns identify Jesus with God's creative Word and with heavenly wisdom: John 1:1-18 and Col 1:15-20. The Greek word λόγος (*logos,* "word") in John 1 has more in common with Old Testament wisdom than with merely a word. Sirach 24:3 ("From the mouth of the Most High I came forth," NAB) and Wis 9:1-2 had already made "wisdom" and "word" parallel. Proverbs 8:22-23 ("The LORD created me at the beginning. . . . Ages ago I was set up . . ." [NRSV]) and Sir 1:1 affirmed that Wisdom comes from God and remains with God forever. The Johannine prologue states that the Word was always with God. Wisdom as an aura of the might of God and pure effusion of the glory of the Almighty (Wis 7:25-26) seems to be echoed in John 1:14, where Jesus is the refulgence of eternal light (cf. Heb 1:1-2). Wisdom 7:22 says that Wisdom is unique (μονογενής, *monogenēs*), and the prologue declares that the Word is God's unique (*monogenes*) son. Wisdom sets up her tent in Sir 24:8, as does Jesus in John 1:14 (ἐσκήνωσεν *eskēnōsen*, "to tent"). In Sir 24:16, Wisdom has "glory" (δόξα *doxa*) and "grace" (χάρις, *charis*), as does Jesus in John 1:14.

The hymn about creation in Col 1:15-20 (NAB) applies to Christ the creative role of wisdom:

> He is the image of the invisible God,
>   the first born of all creation.
> For in him were created all things in
>   heaven and on earth,
>
> . . . .
>
> He is the head of the body, the church.
>   He is the beginning, the firstborn from
>   the dead.

He is the beginning, the firstborn from the dead. As in John 1, the hymn combines vocabulary of Genesis 1 with ideas from Proverbs 8 and Wisdom 7 to show that Christ, who created and governs the world, is now redeeming it. Creation and redemption stand in structural parallelism. Colossians 1:15-17 affirms that Christ was the model for the human race (created in the image of God, Gen 1:27-28) and is now the model for all members of the body, the church, and the means by which they are reconciled and exist together.

SUMMARY

The people of the ancient Near East, like people today, were interested in learning how to live optimally in a world they found only partially understandable. They took note of successful and unsuccessful ways of coping with life, stated them memorably, and handed them on to others. They also observed that life is often inexplicable and the lot of human beings is to be miserable, and they explored such problems in complaints and dialogues. It was the human task to observe carefully the world the gods had made and to record their observations. Because of this common commitment to attend to the world and its rhythms and laws, there is remarkable continuity among the wisdom literatures of antiquity.

The people of Israel lived in that world and responded to it in literature similar to that of its neighbors. Belief in the sole God, Yahweh, made things different, however. The relation of wisdom to Yahweh had to be explained. The problem of evil was an especially vexing problem, because there were no demons to blame or a fate beyond God; there was only Yahweh, whom they celebrated as all-wise and all-just.

The wisdom books now appear in the Bible, a book of books. In the perennial dialectic of the Bible, the wisdom books "charge" other books and themselves receive a charge from them. They are incorporated into a story, which Christians and Jews regard as still ongoing. The wisdom books remind readers that one must take hold of life as both gift and task, that there are many possibilities but also profound limits, and that honest observation and fidelity to one's experience of life can put one in touch with a wondrous order whose source is God. The wisdom books' starting point of everyday experience and honest observations creates common ground for Bible readers to engage with other people just as it once did for ancient Israel and its neighbors.

BIBLIOGRAPHY

Ancient Near Eastern Wisdom Literature:

Brunner, H. *Die Weisheitsbücher der Ägypter: Lehren für das Leben.* Munich: Artemis, 1991. Annotated translations of all the extant instructions, with a fine general introduction.

Foster, B. B. *Before the Muses: An Anthology of Akkadian Literature.* 2 vols. Bethesda: CDL, 1993.

Lambert, W. G. *Babylonian Wisdom Literature.* Oxford: Clarendon, 1960. Authoritative introduction and translations.

Lichtheim, Miriam. *Ancient Egyptian Literature.* 3 vols. Berkeley: University of California Press, 1973–1980. Excellent commentary and translation of many wisdom texts.

Pritchard, J. B., ed. *Ancient Near Eastern Texts Relating to the Old Testament.* Princeton: Princeton University Press, 1955. Standard translations of many wisdom texts from Egypt and Mesopotamia. Lichtheim (below) is generally preferable for Egyptian texts.

Biblical Wisdom Literature:

Barré, M. L. " 'Fear of God' and the World View of Wisdom," *BTB* 11 (1981) 41-43. Effective argument that ancient wisdom was always religious, against some recent scholarship.

Crenshaw, J. L., ed. *Studies in Ancient Israelite Wisdom.* New York: KTAV, 1976. Influential scholarly essays.

———, ed. *Theodicy in the Old Testament.* Philadelphia: Fortress, 1983. Essays, some not previously in English, on the problem of God's wisdom and justice in the world.

Gammie, J. G., and L. G. Perdue, eds. *The Sage in Israel and the Ancient Near East.* Winona Lake, Wis.: Eisenbrauns, 1990. Essays on biblical and other wisdom books with special attention to their social context.

Murphy, R. *The Forms of Old Testament Literature.* FOTL 13. Grand Rapids: Eerdmans, 1981. Good form-critical analysis of all the wisdom books, with bibliography.

———. *The Tree of Life: An Exploration of Biblical Wisdom Literature.* 2nd ed. Grand Rapids: Eerdmans, 1996. Comprehensive and judicious introduction with annotated bibliography.

Smalley, B. *Medieval Exegesis of Wisdom Literature.* Edited by R. Murphy. Atlanta: Scholars Press, 1986. Solid historical studies.

Vanel, A. "Sagesse," *Supplément au Dictionnaire de la Bible* (1986) 7:4-58. Thorough and recent survey of the major question.

von Rad, G. *Wisdom in Israel.* Nashville: Abingdon, 1972. A seminal work, full of fresh insights, and extremely influential on theological discussion of wisdom literature.

Whybray, R. N. *The Intellectual Tradition in the Old Testament.* BZAW 135. Berlin: de Gruyter, 1974. An argument that the authors of wisdom books were from a class of intellectuals rather than professional sages.

THE BOOK OF PROVERBS

INTRODUCTION, COMMENTARY, AND REFLECTIONS
BY
RAYMOND C. VAN LEEUWEN

THE BOOK OF
PROVERBS

INTRODUCTION

E very human needs wisdom for living, and every healthy society hands its wisdom on to the next generation. Proverbs is a literary anthology of Israel's traditional wisdom, gathered from diverse spheres of life. The book's purpose is to help people become wise and godly (1:2-7). Yet its writers were aware of a hermeneutical circle of living and reading, in which one needs godly wisdom to get wisdom (2:1-6; 8:9). The book's entry into this circle of life and learning is generational. In traditional oral cultures, mothers and fathers, teachers and leaders pass on their own life experience and ancestral wisdom to their "children," both real and figurative (1:8; 4:3-4; 6:20; 31:1). Proverbs is a literary gathering of such diverse wisdom. Its readers are invited to walk the path of wisdom and "the fear of the LORD."

Although many readers find Proverbs full of "common sense" with which they can connect, there are still many difficulties in a book whose world, culture, and language are ancient and foreign. We often find ourselves listening in on a fragmentary conversation intended for someone else and filled with hidden assumptions and references. In addition to the challenges faced by all readers, feminism has made us aware that women face additional barriers in appropriating the wisdom of Proverbs, because it is addressed to men and presents women in terms of their relations with men. In the Hebrew of Proverbs, the word translated "my child" or "children" (NRSV) is invariably literally "my son" (בני *běnî*) or "sons" (בנים *bānîm*). Presumably, Israelite parents taught daughters as well as sons, but this book gives no sign thereof. Many readers today find this androcentric focus objectionable. Moreover, some women declare Proverbs to be oppressive because of its ancient patriarchal worldview, because it lacks a (nonpatriarchal) woman's voice, and because of its portrayal of women.[1] It is, perhaps, important to remember that the male focus of Proverbs is a reflection not only of patriarchal culture but also of the book's genre (see below).

---

1. Sharon H. Ringe lists a variety of women's approaches to interpretation of the Bible in her essay "When Women Interpret the Bible," in Carol A. Newsom and Sharon H. Ringe, eds., *The Women's Bible Commentary* (Louisville: Westminster, 1992) 4-5.

Proverbs is a challenge to all modern and postmodern readers whose world and worldviews can make it difficult to connect with aspects of this ancient book. Biblical scholars have shown the naivete of selectively domesticating the Bible to fit present cultural patterns (so that the Bible's own voice is silenced, as we assume it means what we mean), or of attempting to transform the present society into an ancient Israel (so that the particularity of the present culture and society is not taken seriously). Wisdom, however, requires that we see new situations fittingly (see Commentary on 26:1-12). This means seeing not just the different or the particular in a new situation, but also recognizing in it those old fundamental patterns of life described by the sages of Proverbs. Wisdom requires a humble, earnest effort to hear what the other says and a willingness to see our world in the other's terms (18:13).

TITLE AND DATE

The English title "Proverbs" stems from *Proverbia,* the Latin title that Jerome gave the book in the Vulgate. In Hebrew, the book is known by its first word, [שלמה] משלי (*mišlê* [*šĕlōmōh*]), "The Proverbs [of Solomon]." *Mišlê* (sg., *māšāl*), however, has a wider range of reference than English "proverb." The word's meaning suggests "comparison," though some think it connotes "mastery" (over life or language). It is used to refer to a variety of oral and literary genres, including not only sayings and admonitions, but also parables, poems, and songs (see Num 21:27; 23:7; Ps 49:5; Isa 14:4; Ezek 17:2; 21:5).

The title "Proverbs of Solomon" is traditional and honorific, for it is clear that Solomon is not the author of the book in its present form (see 25:1; 30:1; 31:1), though some have argued for the origin of sections of the book in the Solomonic court. Solomon is Israel's paradigmatic wise king (1 Kings 3–4; 10). To him the ancients ascribed not only Proverbs, but also the Song of Songs, Ecclesiastes, the book of Wisdom (written in Greek!), and other works. In much the same way, all psalms are conventionally ascribed to David and all of Israel's laws to Moses. The issue for the ancients was not authorship in the modern sense, but the authority of works written in the "spirit" of the archetypal lawgiver, psalmist, or sage.

Proverbs is a collection of collections, organized and edited with an Israelite character of its own. It was compiled over several centuries and bears the stamp of its diverse origins in the headings of its subcollections and sections (1:1; 10:1; 22:17; 24:23; 25:1; 30:1; 31:1) and in the variety of its materials.

Generally scholars consider the "Solomonic Collections" (10:1–22:16; 25:1–29:27) to be the earliest monarchical sections of the book. Though some have pointed out early ancient Near Eastern parallels to the personification of Wisdom in Proverbs 8,[2] the first nine chapters and the thirty-first chapter are usually dated in the early Persian period, after the return from the Babylonian exile (538 BCE).[3] However, the possibility of a Greek-Hebrew wordplay in 31:27 (see Commentary) may mean that the final sections of the book were composed after Alexander the Great's conquest of Palestine (332 BCE). The Septuagint (LXX), with its different ordering of the last sections and its pluses and minuses, constitutes in effect another edition of the book. Thus different versions of the book existed during the Hellenistic period.[4]

The nature of this literature makes it extremely difficult to date. Proverbs (sayings and admonitions) refer to the common structures and patterns of human life. Sayings and admonitions are traditional and can preserve wisdom from earlier times in fossilized form (as in English, "Pride *goeth* before a fall"). The problem is made more difficult by the extremely brief scope of the various sayings and admonitions. In addition, there are virtually no historical "hooks" on which to hang a secure date or dates for the whole and its parts. Aside from the references to Solomon (1:1; 10:1) and to Hezekiah (25:1), there are no specific historical references in the book (Lemuel and Agur are otherwise unknown). Proverbs is entirely silent concerning Israel's

---

2. Christa Kayatz, *Studien zu Proverbien 1-9,* WMANT 22 (Neukirchen-Vluyn: Neukirchener Verlag, 1966); G. von Rad, *Wisdom in Israel* (Nashville: Abingdon, 1972) 143-76.

3. Claudia V. Camp, *Wisdom and the Feminine in the Book of Proverbs* (Sheffield: JSOT, 1985) 179-208, 233-54.

4. E. Tov, *Textual Criticism of the Hebrew Bible* (Minneapolis: Fortress, 1992) 337.

history of redemption (patriarchal promises, covenants, exodus, law, gift of the land, exile and return—but see 2:21-22; 10:30; 22:28).

This silence does not imply that the various authors of the book had no interest in matters of redemptive history or in other biblical books (see Commentary on 16:5-6; 25:18; 30:4-5). Like most books, Proverbs does not reveal the full range of its authors' concerns. Similarly, the New Testament wisdom book called James bypasses the events of the life of Jesus, a matter that displeased Martin Luther. Such silences in wisdom writings are a function of their genre and purpose, and too much should not be concluded concerning the isolation of the sages from Israel's historical traditions. To borrow a remark on Psalm 119, the sage "so focuses upon *ethos* that he barely notices *mythos*, in this case, the history of redemption."[5] The same holds true for the book's infrequent mention of worship.[6] The clues for dating that remain are the uncertain ones of language, culture, and social location.

SOCIAL LOCATIONS: ORAL AND LITERARY

Like the quest for firm dates, the attempt to establish the social location of the book, its sections, and sayings has proved difficult.[7] Arguments in these matters are especially prone to circular reasoning: One posits a date and social location for a section of the book and then proceeds to explain that section in terms of the proposed location. Neither have scholars always clearly distinguished among (1) the original *sources* of sections and proverbs (whether oral or written); (2) the *persons, processes,* and *places* of literary collection; (3) editorial *composition*; and (4) the Hebrew book in its final form, embodying all the earlier collections, but reflecting the shape, scope, and purpose of the final editors and ultimately of the Holy Spirit (see Commentary on 30:5-7).[8] These writer-editors have put all their materials together for a new purpose, in which the whole is more than the sum of its parts.

The embodiment of oral traditions in literary works raises problems with which biblical scholars still struggle.[9] A number of scholars have compared sayings and admonitions in Proverbs to oral traditions from Africa to argue that the source of the biblical sayings and admonitions is the Israelite "folk," in family, clan, and village.[10] For R. N. Whybray, many of the sayings reflect the perspective of the Israelite peasant. For them life was hard and difficult, a matter of survival. Yet he notes that chaps. 1–9 and 22:16–24:22 have a more aristocratic social level, as does chap. 31.[11] Others believe that the book reflects the aristocratic world of the royal court. Although the sayings and admonitions of the Solomonic collections appear to arise from a variety of social locations and periods, the royal court remains the most plausible location for their literary compilation (10:1; 25:1; cf. 31:1). Even a scholar such as F. Golka (an advocate of the "folk" origin of proverbs), who claims to show that sayings about the king do not require a courtly origin, assumes that the sayings were collected and redacted in the royal court.[12]

The theory that the book (or its parts) arose from a school setting remains disputed, suffering from a lack of conclusive evidence that Israelite schools existed independently in the pre-exilic

---

5. Jon D. Levenson, "The Sources of Torah," in *Ancient Israelite Religion*, Patrick D. Miller, Jr., Paul D. Hanson, and S. Dean McBride, eds. (Philadelphia: Fortress, 1987) 568, 559-74. See J. J. Collins, "Proverbial Wisdom and the Yahwist Vision," *Semeia* 17 (1980) 1-17.

6. See Leo G. Perdue, *Wisdom and Cult* (Missoula: Scholars Press, 1977).

7. R. E. Murphy, "Form Criticism and Wisdom Literature," *CBQ* 31 (1969) 481; J. L. Crenshaw, "Wisdom," in John L. Hayes, ed., *Old Testament Form Criticism* (San Antonio: Trinity University Press, 1974) 236.

8. For an astute defense of God's speaking in the diverse texts of Scripture, see N. Wolterstorff, *Divine Discourse: Philosophical Reflections on the Claim That God Speaks* (Cambridge: Cambridge University Press, 1996).

9. Walter J. Ong, *Orality and Literacy: The Technologizing of the Word* (London: Methuen, 1982); Jack Goody, *The Logic of Writing and the Organization of Society* (Cambridge: Cambridge University Press, 1986). For the ancient Near East, see J. Bottero, *Mesopotamia: Writing, Reasoning, and the Gods* (Chicago: University of Chicago Press, 1992) 4, 67-137.

10. Most recently, C. Westermann, *The Roots of Wisdom: The Oldest Proverbs of Israel and Other Peoples* (Louisville: Westminster John Knox, 1995).

11. R. N. Whybray, *Wealth and Poverty in the Book of Proverbs* (Sheffield: JSOT, 1990); and *The Composition of the Book of Proverbs* (Sheffield: JSOT, 1994).

12. Friedemann W. Golka, "Die Königs und Hofsprüche und der Ursprung der Israelitischen Weisheit," *VT* 36 (1986) 13-36, here 13. See Michael V. Fox, "The Social Location of the Book of Proverbs," in Fox et al., eds., *Texts, Temples and Traditions: A Tribute to Menahem Haran* (Winona Lake: Eisenbrauns, 1996) 227-39.

period.[13] The probable final editing of the book took place in the early Hellenistic period (after 322 BCE; see Commentary on 31:27). The final editors of Proverbs were among the scribal sages who gave the Hebrew Bible its canonical shape. Parallels to these redactors may be found in literary sages like Ben Sira and the poet-writers of Qumran.[14]

The foregoing uncertainties about dating and social location are partly due to the variety and even contradictory character of sayings gathered in the book. It is likely that differing social groups produced and made use of originally independent sections and that the final author-editors collected, augmented, and edited the parts to provide a complex and diverse compendium of wisdom.[15] One group learns from another, borrowing and adapting its wisdom for its own ends. This is entirely in keeping with the amazing mobility of proverbial wisdom. Each group in a society produces its own sayings, some of which become universal. For example, everyone today knows the computer proverb, "Garbage in, garbage out." Proverbs not only cross social boundaries within a society, but they can even cross linguistic and cultural barriers as well.[16] Erasmus domesticated ancient and medieval Latin proverbs in his *Adages.* Western anthropologists and missionaries have collected sayings throughout the world.

When proverbs are contradictory, it is not necessarily a sign of different origins or conflicting worldviews. Proverbs even from a single group or person can be contradictory, because life is complex. In a proverb collection, or in the collective oral memory of a culture, we find a "universe" of wisdom, a world of discourse. The collection is undergirded by a common view of reality, but may be diverse and even contradictory in its particulars. Thus users of proverbs must choose from the diverse sayings and admonitions the one that best "hits the nail on the head." With proverbs, one may say, "If the shoe fits, wear it" (see Commentary on 25:7, 9). Proverb use is always situational.

Another factor is at work in a written compendium of wisdom such as Proverbs. Whether individual units were originally oral or written, their juxtaposition cheek by jowl in a book creates a *literary* context for the reader. Their original oral settings have disappeared; we have only a literary context to clarify their meaning. Often proverbs are juxtaposed in such a way that one "comments" on its neighbor (see Commentary on 17:17-18; 26:4-5). Among these "proverb pairs," the Yahweh sayings are particularly sharp in qualifying their fellows (see Commentary on 18:10-11).

In addition, within each section of Proverbs, certain themes, genres, or patterns are more prominent than in other sections. While the differences among the collections are not absolute, they are significant, for they create typical patterns of emphasis and concern. For example, the contrast between righteous and wicked in chapters 10–15 is typical of the first Solomonic subcollection (chaps. 10–15). It creates an orderly view of reality and justice in which good and bad actions are met with corresponding consequences. In contrast, the second Solomonic subcollection (16:1–22:16) presents a more complex view of acts and consequences. Here the focus on God's freedom and on the king (16:1-15) introduces the notion of limits to human wisdom and of mystery in the divine disposition of events. Here we see that sometimes the righteous suffer while the wicked prosper (see Commentary on 16:8).

A further, crucial aid to interpreting Proverbs is the existence of long-distance literary context, created by repetitions of themes, of phrases, and even of lines and couplets.[17] This literary context is first of all within and among sections of Proverbs itself, but the alert reader will find many connections among Proverbs, the rest of the Bible, and other Jewish and Christian writings (see below, "On Using This Commentary"). Finally, comparative study of ancient Near Eastern and Egyptian cultures greatly enriches our understanding of Proverbs.

13. See James L. Crenshaw, "Education in Ancient Israel," *JBL* 104 (1985) 601-5; S. Weeks, *Early Israelite Wisdom* (Oxford: Clarendon, 1994) 132-56. Cf. Andre Lemaire, "The Sage in School and Temple," in *The Sage in Israel and the Ancient Near East,* ed. John G. Gammie and Leo G. Perdue (Winona Lake: Eisenbrauns, 1990) 165-81.

14. See R. C. Van Leeuwen, "Scribal Wisdom and Theodicy in the Book of the Twelve," in Leo G. Perdue et al., eds., *In Search of Wisdom: Essays in Memory of John G. Gammie* (Louisville: Westminster/John Knox, 1993) 31-49.

15. James L. Crenshaw, "The Sage in Proverbs," in Gammie and Perdue, *The Sage in Israel,* 205-16. See also the essays by Camp, Fontaine, Whybray, and Lemaire in the same volume.

16. The classic, essential work remains Archer Taylor, *The Proverb* (Cambridge, Mass.: Harvard University Press, 1931; reprint edited by W. Mieder [Bern: Peter Lang, 1985]). See also W. Mieder, *Proverbs Are Never Out of Season: Popular Wisdom in the Modern Age* (New York: Oxford University Press, 1993).

17. Daniel C. Snell, *Twice-Told Proverbs and the Composition of the Book of Proverbs* (Winona Lake: Eisenbrauns, 1993).

GENRE AND CONTENT

Proverbs has affinities in genre and content to a long list of Egyptian "instructions" and other ancient Near Eastern works.[18] Indeed, many scholars believe that the section titled "Sayings of the Wise" (22:17–24:22) adapts parts of the Egyptian *Instruction of Amenemope* for its own purposes.[19] The book begins with a brief title, an extended statement of purpose, and a motto: The fear of the Lord is the beginning of knowledge (1:1-7). The remainder of Proverbs 1–9 comprises a series of speeches by parents to a young son. These speeches especially are akin to the Egyptian "instructions" in which a royal father left a testament of wisdom to his heir. A similar medieval Jewish genre is the "Ethical Will." This sort of literature is based on oral "rites of passage." The parent—often portrayed as being on the point of death—gives advice to a son (occasionally a daughter) about to enter the responsibilities of adulthood (see 1 Kgs 2:1-9; Tob 4:1-21; Sir 3:1-16).[20]

Within the book, however, chapters 1–9 have a literary function. Together with chapters 30–31, they form an interpretive "frame" through which to view the small wisdom utterances they enclose. The worldview of these chapters—to change the image—gives the reader lenses through which to read the diverse sayings and admonitions in chapters 10–29. Even when contemplating the minutia of table manners, of farming, or of the law court, all of life expresses "the fear of the Lord"—or lack thereof (1:7; 9:10; 31:30). No aspect of reality is irrelevant to wisdom, because the Lord made all things through wisdom (3:19-20; 8:22-31).

The wisdom of Proverbs requires a knowledge of the common structures and patterns of the world and of human life as ordained by God. Globally, this is presented in the imagery of chaps. 1–9, in which "ways," "women," and "houses" in relation to the young male addressee form a metaphorical system for Wisdom and Folly that communicates the basic character of life in God's world (see Overview on 1–9). On a smaller scale, this is often true of the sayings and admonitions as well (chaps. 10–29). Sayings are often narratives in a nutshell; they distill the manifold patterns of life down to their basic elements. Thus Mario Puzo can expand the insight of Prov 10:21b into an entire novel.[21] The reader familiar with biblical stories will find in them many proverbs "writ large," as the commentary attempts to show.

Wisdom requires reverence for God and a general knowledge of how the world and humans work. Wise folk know the way things "ought to be," and they have a sense of right and wrong.[22] Wisdom also demands an understanding of concrete situations, of particular institutions and persons with their individuality and quirks (this job, this company, this boss, this employee, this woman or man, this teacher, this country, etc.). Wise people know what the present moment and its constituents require. Wise action and speech are *fitting* (see Commentary on 26:1-12). Consequently, proverbs can be contradictory on verbal and social levels because different sayings apply to different persons, circumstances, and times. The wise person recognizes which is which and acts appropriately. The conceptual adequacy of Proverbs to illumine reality comes only when the rich diversity of proverbs is wisely exploited (see 26:7, 9).

The use of proverbs can be even more complex or subtle than suggested so far. The same proverb can be legitimately used for quite different purposes and to communicate quite different things, depending on who speaks, to whom, and in what way and circumstances. For a disadvantaged poor person to say, "Money talks," has a different meaning than when someone rich and powerful says it.[23] Social location and relations matter.

Even on something so basic as the "act-consequence connection" (the basic wisdom doctrine that people reap what they sow), the book of Proverbs can be contradictory. Its basic teaching

---

18. Weeks, *Early Israelite Wisdom*, 162-89; Miriam Lichtheim, *Ancient Egyptian Literature*, 3 vols. (Berkeley: University of California Press, 1973–80) and *Late Egyptian Wisdom Literature in the International Context* (Freiburg and Göttingen: Vandenhoeck & Ruprecht, 1983).

19. Harold C. Washington, *Wealth and Poverty in the Instruction of Amenemope and the Hebrew Proverbs*, SBLDS 142 (Atlanta: Scholars Press, 1994).

20. See Fox, "The Social Location of the Book of Proverbs," 232. For examples, see *Ancient Near Eastern Texts Relating to the Old Testament*, ed. James B. Pritchard, 3rd ed. (Princeton, N.J.: Princeton University Press, 1969).

21. Mario Puzo, *Fools Die* (New York: Putnam, 1978).

22. Cornelius Plantinga, Jr., *Not the Way It's Supposed to Be: A Breviary of Sin* (Grand Rapids: Eerdmans, 1995) 113-28.

23. Barbara Kirshenblatt-Gimblett, "Toward a Theory of Proverb Meaning," in *The Wisdom of Many: Essays on the Proverb*, W. Mieder and A. Dundes, eds. (New York: Garland, 1981) 111-21; Peter Seitel, "Proverbs: A Social Use of Metaphor," 122-39 in the same volume; Carole R. Fontaine, *The Use of the Traditional Saying in the Old Testament* (Sheffield: JSOT, 1982).

(chaps. 1–15) is that right living produces wealth and well-being. Folly and wickedness produce poverty, disgrace, and even death. This is true because God made the world in wisdom, and God is faithful to its principles. But as the book proceeds (chaps. 16–29), we learn that there are exceptions to the general rules of life. Not even the wise can comprehend all the contradictions and mysteries of life, of God and cosmos. The wicked can prosper, especially in a time of chaos, and the righteous can suffer unjustly. (These themes are developed more extensively in Job and Ecclesiastes.) Still, Proverbs insists that it is better to be poor and godly than rich and wicked (see Commentary on 15:16; 16:8). Ultimately Proverbs is a book of faith (1:7), insisting on the reality of God's justice and righteousness, even when experience seems to contradict it (see Hebrews 11).[24] God's justice often remains hidden, since much of life—and God's own self—is beyond human grasping (see Commentary on 16:1-9; 21:30-31).[25]

The bulk of the book is devoted to short, mostly two-line indicative "sayings" or "sentences" of the sort commonly called "proverbs" (esp. 10:1–22:16; 25:1–29:27). A middle section of the book (22:17–24:22) is largely devoted to "admonitions," brief second-person precepts that usually provide reasons or motive clauses for doing or not doing something. These motives can be practical (looking at positive or negative consequences) or explanatory (appealing to the nature of things). Ultimately, and sometimes explicitly, they are theological, rooted in the God who made and rules all things wisely. Both genres, sayings and admonitions, appear throughout the book, sometimes embedded in larger structures.

This diversity of sayings and admonitions constitutes one of the main problems in understanding the book (see below, "On Using This Commentary"). A master scholar of world proverbs has declared that "the proverb in a collection is dead," because readers have no direct access to the life situation in which they are used.[26] Proverbs (both sayings and admonitions) are generally short, pithy utterances that require a social and cultural context for us to understand them fully. Proverbs are addressed to particular people in particular situations, and yet, they embody common human truths, recurring patterns in ordinary life. Wisdom applies old truths to new situations, because in a certain sense, "there is nothing new under the sun" (see Matt 13:52). A mother tells a sluggish college student that "the early bird catches the worm." A Nigerian father tells a teenager who hangs out with the wrong crowd that those "who sleep with puppies catch fleas." One child needs to be told, "Look before you leap," another, "She who hesitates is lost."

Proverbs also embody a culture's commitments, contradictions, and myths. Many Americans believe that "money talks" and that "sex sells." Yet we emblazon "In God we trust" on our currency, perhaps to remind ourselves that "money isn't everything." And advertisers fervently exploit our belief that "the sky's the limit"—meaning that for us there are no limits, whether ecological, moral, or divine—to self-gratification.[27]

THEOLOGY

Some scholars believe that the God of Proverbs was a mere variant of the deities in other ancient Near Eastern wisdom writings. An extreme form of this view argues that the God of Proverbs is *not* the God of the rest of the OT.[28] This position, however, presupposes the widespread (and mistaken) belief that the uniqueness of Israel's God had to do with Yahweh's involvement in history; it also entailed a corresponding marginalization of creation.[29] A related position, using the method of tradition history, separates creation of the cosmos from creation of humans, so that the theology of Proverbs 1–9 (cosmos) has little to do with Proverbs 10–29 (humans).[30] This position, however, ignores the actual coexistence of both traditions in Proverbs and the

24. R. C. Van Leeuwen, "On Wealth and Poverty: System and Contradiction in Proverbs," *Hebrew Studies* 33 (1992) 25-36.

25. G. von Rad's work remains basic, *Wisdom in Israel*, 97-110.

26. Wolfgang Mieder, cited by Fontaine, *The Use of the Traditional Saying in the Old Testament*, 54.

27. Alan Dundes, "Folk Ideas as Units of Worldview," *American Journal of Folklore* 84 (1971) 93-103.

28. H. D. Preuss, "Das Gottesbild der älteren Weisheit Israels," *VTS* 23 (1972) 117-45.

29. See H. G. Reventlow, *Problems of Old Testament Theology in the Twentieth Century* (Philadelphia: Fortress, 1985) 59-124; Rolf P. Knierim, "Cosmos and History in Israel's Theology," in *The Task of Old Testament Theology: Substance, Method, and Cases* (Grand Rapids: Eerdmans, 1995) 171-224.

30. P. Doll, *Menschenschöpfung und Weltschöpfung in der alttestamentlichen Weisheit*, SBS 117 (Stuttgart: Verlag Katholisches Bibelwerk, 1985); Westermann, *The Roots of Wisdom*.

editors' evident intent in chaps. 1–9 to create a cosmic context for understanding the sayings of chaps. 10–29. It is also anachronistic because, unlike the modern West with its separation of nature and culture, ancient Near Eastern anthropologies presuppose cosmologies, which may be largely implicit (as in chaps. 10–29) or explicit (as in chaps. 1–9). On another front, some scholars seek in Lady Wisdom evidence for an Israelite goddess whose existence was suppressed by the monotheistic editors of the book.[31] One's hermeneutical approach to these theological-exegetical questions greatly influences one's reading of the evidence and the conclusions drawn from it. On this point leading scholars are divided. James L. Crenshaw, writing in honor of Roland E. Murphy, put it succinctly: "For me, the crucial issue concerns whether or not ancient sages accepted the world view of Yahwism. Murphy thinks they did; I am not able to accept that position."[32]

Yet, the writer-editors of Proverbs clearly considered the God of wisdom to be Israel's God, Yahweh. This is evident in their almost exclusive reference to God by that name (see Commentary on 1:7; 16:5-6). That there are features common to both Israel's God and the gods of the nations is a theological problem not unique to Proverbs and the wisdom literature.[33] The evidence of Proverbs itself and its inter-textual relations within the larger canon leads one to see these commonalities in the light of the particular grace given to Israel.[34] At the same time, these commonalities, and the cosmic context of Israel's wisdom, lead one to recognize the God of Israel as the wise creator of all things and persons. Thus this commentary will begin with the book as a whole and assume it and the OT are the primary, though not only, literary context for theological interpretation.[35]

ON USING THIS COMMENTARY

Because proverbs presuppose both specific life situations and a larger cultural context to make sense of them, their interpretation can be difficult. Consequently, there is an abundance of cross-references in this commentary; and perhaps more than any other book, Proverbs requires that one pay attention to them. The great German poet Goethe once said of languages that "whoever knows only one, knows none." This saying is all the more true of proverbs. Because the sayings and admonitions are so short, they require some larger context for understanding. For ancient Israelites that larger context came naturally. Their sayings reflected their own culture and experience. Moreover, they used sayings (as do we) to comment on real-life situations. The truth of many sayings is only realized when they are "fittingly" applied.[36] Unfortunately, we do not have access to these life situations, though certain biblical stories and cross-cultural comparisons can give us some idea of how the Israelites actually used their proverbs.[37]

Consequently, finding the meaning of ancient biblical proverbs can be difficult. Sometimes knowledge of archaeology and ancient Near Eastern cultures and languages can help us. But our main resource is the language of the sayings themselves. Proverbs, in any language, never exist in isolation. One proverb comments on or contrasts with another. Thus proverbs can happily "contradict" each other: "Haste makes waste," but "whoever hesitates is lost." Again, when it comes to marriage and friendships, a recent authoritative study tells us that "birds of a feather

---

31. B. Lang, *Wisdom and the Book of Proverbs: An Israelite Goddess Redefined* (New York: Pilgrim, 1986); C. Camp, "Woman Wisdom as Root Metaphor: A Theological Consideration," in *The Listening Heart,* ed. K. G. Hoglund et al. (Sheffield: JSOT, 1987) 45-76.

32. James L. Crenshaw, "Murphy's Axiom: Every Gnomic Saying Needs a Balancing Corrective," in *Urgent Advice and Probing Questions: Collected Writings on Old Testament Wisdom* (Macon, Ga.: Mercer University Press, 1995) 352, 344-54. See Roland E. Murphy, "Wisdom and Yahwism," in *No Famine in the Land,* ed. J. Flanagan and A. Robinson (Missoula: Scholars Press, 1975) 117-26; "Wisdom and Creation," *JBL* 104 (1985) 3-11.

33. Bertil Albrektson, *History and the Gods* (Lund: Gleerup, 1967); J. J. M. Roberts, "The Ancient Near Eastern Environment," in *The Hebrew Bible and Its Modern Interpreters,* Douglas A. Knight and Gene M. Tucker, eds. (Chico, Calif.: Scholars Press, 1985) 75-121.

34. Von Rad, *Wisdom in Israel,* remains basic. See also L. Bostrom, *The God of the Sages: The Portrayal of God in the Book of Proverbs* (Stockholm: Almquist & Wiksell, 1990); R. E. Clements, *Wisdom in Theology* (Grand Rapids: Eerdmans, 1992).

35. See Raymond C. Van Leeuwen, "Heuristic Assumptions," in *Context and Meaning in Proverbs 25–27* (Atlanta: Scholars Press, 1988) 29-38; Jon Levenson, *Hebrew Bible, Old Testament, and Historical Criticism: Jews and Christians in Biblical Studies* (Louisville: Westminster/John Knox, 1993) 106-26, 177-79.

36. C. E. Carlston, "Proverbs, Maxims, and the Historical Jesus," *JBL* 99 (1980) 87-105.

37. See Fontaine, *The Use of the Traditional Saying in the Old Testament;* Susan Niditch, *Folklore and the Hebrew Bible* (Minneapolis: Fortress, 1993) 67-91; Mieder and Dundes, *The Wisdom of Many.*

---

flock together."[38] Yet, there are some marriages in which "opposites attract." Indeed, without the latter truth, the sexes would never get together.

Again, for proverbs, "whoever knows only one knows none." One proverb may not fit a situation, but another will. One saying calls for another to qualify it, or for a biblical story to flesh it out. Hence the many cross-references in this commentary. Often a proverb theme will appear more than once. Frequently, the reader will find that the information needed to understand one saying is given in the commentary on another. Hence the frequent appearance of the words in parentheses, "see . . ." or more important, "see Commentary on . . ." The former reference means that one can find a worthwhile parallel in another proverb or biblical passage. The latter reference means that the comment on another particular passage will provide crucial information for the passage at hand. Brief as proverbs are, no one saying contains the whole truth. Reality is too rich and complex for that.

38. Robert T. Michael, John H. Gagnon, Edward O. Laumann, and Gina Collati, *Sex in America: A Definitive Study* (Boston: Little, Brown, 1994).

BIBLIOGRAPHY

Commentaries:

Alonso-Schökel, L., and J. Vilchez. *Proverbios.* Madrid: Ediciones Cristiandad, 1984. For Americans with facility in Spanish, a valuable commentary with insightful literary observations.

McKane, William. *Proverbs: A New Approach.* OTL. Philadelphia: Westminster, 1970. A long commentary on a short genre, useful in linguistic matters and for international wisdom.

Toy, Crawford H. *The Book of Proverbs.* ICC. New York: Scribner's Sons, 1902. A classic, comprehensive commentary, still valuable for text, language, and insight.

Whybray, R. N. *Proverbs.* NCBC. Grand Rapids: Eerdmans, 1994. Valuable for close attention to problems of translation and for exploring the issue of literary context among the sentences.

Other Works:

Camp, Claudia V. *Wisdom and the Feminine in the Book of Proverbs.* Sheffield: Almond, 1985. A pioneering feminist reading of Proverbs.

Fontaine, Carole R. *Traditional Sayings in the Old Testament.* Sheffield: Almond, 1982. Very useful for the literary portrayal of Israelite proverbs in action, and for introduction to broader (non-biblical) proverbs research.

Mieder, Wolfgang, and Alan Dundes, eds. *The Wisdom of Many: Essays on the Proverb.* New York: Garland, 1981. A collection of essential essays on non-biblical proverbs.

Van Leeuwen, Raymond C. *Context and Meaning in Proverbs 25–27.* Atlanta: Scholars Press, 1988. A study of the problem of literary context in Proverbs.

Von Rad, Gerhard. *Wisdom in Israel.* Nashville: Abingdon, 1972. This book remains the most profound theological treatment of Proverbs available.

Washington, Harold C. *Wealth and Poverty in the Instruction of Amenemope and the Hebrew Proverbs.* Atlanta: Scholars Press, 1994.

Weeks, Stuart. *Early Israelite Wisdom.* Oxford: Clarendon, 1994. A recent study of key issues in wisdom and Proverbs, with bibliography.

Whybray, R. N. *The Book of Proverbs: A Survey of Modern Study.* Leiden: Brill, 1995. A valuable overview and bibliography.

——. *The Composition of the Book of Proverbs.* Sheffield: JSOT, 1994.

———. *Wealth and Poverty in the Book of Proverbs.* Sheffield: JSOT, 1990.

Williams, James G. *Those Who Ponder Proverbs.* Sheffield: JSOT, 1981.

OUTLINE OF PROVERBS

I. Proverbs 1:1–9:18, The Parental Legacy: Wisdom's Worldview

    A. 1:1-7, Title and Prologue
    B. 1:8-19, Warning Against Outlaws
    C. 1:20-33, Wisdom's Prophetic Warning
    D. 2:1-22, The Search for Wisdom
    E. 3:1-12, Instruction in the Fear of the Lord
    F. 3:13-35, On Wisdom: Blessing, Creation, Admonitions
    G. 4:1-27, Tradition, Wisdom, and Ways
    H. 5:1-23, Adultery as Folly; Marriage as Wisdom
    I. 6:1-19, Money, Sloth, Good, and Evil
    J. 6:20-35, Teaching Against Adultery
    K. 7:1-27, A Tale of Seduction and Death
    L. 8:1-36, Wisdom's Cosmic Speech
    M. 9:1-18, Two Houses at the End of the Road

II. Proverbs 10:1–22:16, The First Solomonic Collection of Sayings

    A. 10:1–15:33, The Antithetical Collection
        10:1-8, Introduction to the Antithetical Collection
        10:9-32, Sayings on the Antithesis of Good and Evil
        11:1-31, Further Sayings on the Antithesis of Good and Evil
        12:1-28, Whoever Loves Discipline Loves Knowledge
        13:1-25, On Listening to Wise Counsel
        14:1-35, The Wise Woman Builds Her House
        15:1-33, The End of the Antithetical Collection
    B. 16:1–22:16, The Royal Collection
        16:1-33, Introduction to the Royal Collection
        17:1-28, Bettter a Dry Crust with Peace and Quiet
        18:1-24, A Fool Takes No Pleasure in Understanding
        19:1-29, Better a Poor Man Whose Walk Is Blameless
        20:1-30, Wine Is a Mocker, Strong Drink a Brawler
        21:1-31, All Deeds Are Right in the Sight of the Doer, but the Lord Weighs the Heart
        22:1-16, The Royal Collection Concluded

III. Proverbs 22:17–24:34, The Sayings of the Wise

    A. 22:17–23:35, Listen to the Sayings of the Wise
    B. 24:1-22, Sayings of the Wise Concluded
    C. 24:23-34, An Appendix: More Sayings of the Wise

IV. Proverbs 25:1–29:27, The Second Solomonic Collection of Sayings

A. 25:1–27:27, On the Court, Fools, and Friends
    25:1-28, On God, King, Court, and Conflict
    26:1-28, On Fools and Fittingness
    27:1-22, On Friendship and Paradox
    27:23-27, On Tending One's Flocks
B. 28:1–29:27, On Justice and Torah
    28:1-28, Torah, the Righteous, and the Wicked
    29:1-27, More on Torah, the Righteous, and the Wicked

V. Proverbs 30:1-33, The Words of Agur, Curses, and Numerical Sayings

VI. Proverbs 31:1-31, The Words of Lemuel and a Hymn to the Valiant Woman

A. 31:1-9, The Words of Lemuel
B. 31:10-31, Hymn to the Valiant Woman

PROVERBS 1:1–9:18

THE PARENTAL LEGACY: WISDOM'S WORLDVIEW

OVERVIEW[39]

After a brief prologue (1:1-7), Proverbs 1–9 presents a series of instructions addressed to "my son" by a mother or father (1:8-9). This advice is designed to guide young men as they step into the adult world, with its problems and possibilities (see Reflections on 1:1-7). The instructions form a literary "testament," modeled after oral instructions given at key life transitions. But more than this, they introduce readers to the book's worldview, to its fundamental framework of meaning. The seemingly random and scattered events of life, so richly described in the tiny sayings of chaps. 10–29, are here given an interpretive context. Chapters 1–9 provide a moral map of the world, a portrait of the "universe" as made by God with wisdom (3:19-20; chap. 8).

This divinely ordered cosmos comprises the conditions that make life possible. It provides the arena within which humans find freedom. The writers employ a set of repeated metaphors to create a symbolic representation of reality.[40] The dynamic, purposeful character of life is signaled by good or bad paths and by legitimate or misdirected male desire for women and material goods (1:10-19; 3:9-10). Life is thus a journey whose motive force is a quasi-erotic desire for real or bogus goods, whose end is determined by the "woman" one chooses to love. At the end of the journey, the young man finds a "house." In Wisdom's house there is life (9:1-6), but to cross the "threshold" of the "strange woman" or "Folly" is death (2:16-19; 9:13-18).

These pervasive metaphors illustrate and embody basic reality principles. The proper desire of a young man for his wife (5:16-19) is contrasted to desire for another woman (2:16-19). Love of wife embodies wisdom, but to fulfill one's desire for another is folly. This interplay of literal and metaphorical relationships among men and women, roads and houses, spells out the authors' view of cosmic and human reality (see Commentary on chap. 8). Life is a matter not only of created structures and limits (signaled by God's setting limits to the sea [8:29]), but also of ultimate "loves" for one "woman" or another. When love is misplaced, when one loses direction, when boundaries are violated, when creation's goods are misappropriated, then the good becomes harmful and damage is done. Consequently, wisdom implies love within limits, freedom within form, and life within law.[41]

---

39. See also the section "Genre and Content" in the Introduction.
40. R. C. Van Leeuwen, "Liminality and Worldview in Proverbs 1–9," *Semeia* 50 (1990) 111-44.

41. R. L. Cohn, *The Shape of Sacred Space: Four Biblical Studies,* AAR Studies in Religion 23 (Chico, Calif.: Scholars Press, 1981).

PROVERBS 1:1-7, TITLE AND PROLOGUE

COMMENTARY

These verses state the pedigree, essence, and purpose of the book called Proverbs. Similar beginnings are found in non-Israelite wisdom books.[42] The prologue also makes

42. See R. Clifford, "Introduction to Wisdom Literature," 1-15, in this volume.

clear the primary audience of the book: young, inexperienced males on the threshold of adult life (1:4). Secondarily, the book serves to confirm and increase the wisdom of the wise (1:5).

1:1. The opening verse is the book's title; several subtitles head sections in the book (e.g., 10:1; 22:17; 24:23; 25:1; 30:1; 31:1). The title identifies Solomon as the spiritual fountainhead of the wisdom compiled in Proverbs (cf. 1 Kgs 2:6; 3:3-28; 4:29-34; 10:1-25; Eccl 1:1; Cant 1:1; Wisdom 7–9; Sir 47:12-17). As with the Davidic psalm headings, Prov 1:1 cannot be taken as a simple assertion of authorship in the modern sense. This is clear from the composite character of the book and its subtitles. For example, Hezekiah's men (Prov 25:1) are active some two hundred years after Solomon's death. Whatever the origins of the book's sayings and sections, the whole now claims the heritage of Solomon, David's son, to whom God gave wisdom and the covenant promises (2 Samuel 7; 1 Kings 3; 10; Psalm 132). The title communicates that this book is endued with the same "spirit of wisdom" that animated Solomon (see Moses and Joshua, Deut 34:9).

"Proverb" (מָשָׁל *māšāl*; 1:1, 6; 10:1; 25:1) can refer to a variety of genres, such as parables, taunt songs, and the like. In Proverbs, it includes several genres. Foremost among these are instructions (mainly chaps. 1–9), admonitions (see esp. 22:17–23:28; 24:1-29), and sayings (esp. 10:1–22:17; 25:1–29:27).

1:2-6. These verses state the book's purpose and primary audience. In a series of purpose clauses (interrupted by 1:5, an editorial link with 9:9), the writer heaps up key wisdom terms that are repeated throughout the book (e.g., 1:3*b* and 2:9; 1:2 and 23:23). The basic concepts conveyed by these terms, however, are often present in proverbial images and actions even when the terms are not used. Proverbs 28:15, for example, does not mention righteousness, justice, or equity (1:3), but these are nonetheless the standards by which rulers are judged. Moreover, by such key terms the final editors of Proverbs sought to link this wisdom book with key concepts in the Torah (Gen 18:19; Deut 4:5-8; 34:9), the Prophets (Isa 11:1-5; Hos 14:9), and the other Writings, such as Psalms. For example, Ps 99:4 declares that Yahweh "has

established *equity*" and done "*justice and righteousness* in Jacob" (see also Psalms 1; 25; 34; 37; 111–112; 119; and the "Solomonic" Psalm 72).

Verse 6 includes in the book's purpose the mastery of the forms, language, and thought patterns of "the wise." Through study of the book, one gains understanding of its sayings. The book itself provides the needed context, since as a book its sayings can be compared and contrasted. The book, however, affords no example of a genuine "riddle," though perhaps the words of Agur provide one (30:1-9). Perhaps the term here refers to any puzzling, thought-provoking utterance (see Hab 2:6) and to the mental effort required to use proverbs rightly (see 26:7).

1:7. This verse is the book's motto and states its theological theme (variants are 9:10; Job 28:28; Ps 111:10; cf. Prov 13:19; 15:33; 16:6, 17; 31:30). Here God and humans, wisdom and folly, knowledge and discipline borne of parental urging are all related in eight packed Hebrew words. To fear Yahweh means to hate evil and turn from it (3:7; 8:13; Job 28:28; cf. Psalm 1). But "fools" disdain wisdom and discipline.

The great phrase "the fear of the LORD" grounds human knowledge and wisdom (cf. 9:10) in humble service of Yahweh. This phrase frames the first section of the book (1:7; 9:10), as well as the whole book (1:7; 31:31). The book of Proverbs is meant to teach humans wisdom. But the fear of the Lord relativizes human wisdom, because the mysterious freedom of God can subvert human plans and purposes (16:1, 9; 19:21; 21:30-31; 27:1). Without the God of Israel, the best human wisdom becomes folly, because God alone holds the world and all outcomes in God's hands (2 Sam 16:15–17:23; 1 Cor 1:18-31, with its OT quotations). Although this phrase has its origin in the experience of God's numinous majesty (as at Sinai, Deut 4:9-10), it eventually has come to express the total claim of God upon humans and the total life-response of humans to God. In the covenant context of Deuteronomy (a book with wisdom concerns, Deut 4:6) we find:

So now, O Israel, what does the LORD your God require of you? Only to fear the LORD your God, to walk in all his ways, to love him, to serve the LORD your God with all your heart and with all your soul, and to keep the commandments of the LORD . . . for your own well-being. (Deut 10:12-13 NRSV; see also Deut 10:14-20; 8:6; Mic 6:8)

This command succintly elaborates the meaning of fearing God. Similarly, Ps 34:7-14 describes this divine-human relationship (see 1 Pet 3:10-12). On the divine side, the Lord protects and provides for those who fear God (vv. 7-9). On the human side, those who fear God pursue moral good and shun evil (vv. 13-14). This in turn produces enjoyment of life (v. 12). In sum, the fear of Yahweh is not just *worship* (a topic hardly mentioned in Proverbs), but *religion* in the comprehensive sense of life in its entirety devoted to God's service. Here, *all* human activities are undertaken in the light of God's presence and purposes in the world (see Psalms 90; 139; Matt 28:16-20).

With very few exceptions, Proverbs refers to God as "the LORD" (Yahweh), the God who made covenant with Israel and led the people throughout history (cf. Gen 20:11; Eccl 12:13). Proverbs never uses אל (*'ēl*, "god") and uses אלהים (*'ĕlōhîm*, the most common word for "god" or "gods") only three times: 2:5, par. to "fear of the LORD"; 3:4; 25:2. The editors of Proverbs are very consistent in avoiding the suggestion that the God of the sages is any other than Israel's covenant God, Yahweh (see Exod 3:15; 33:18-20; 34:6-7; John 1:14-18). Proverbs has profound similarities to ancient Near Eastern wisdom. Perhaps the consistent use of "Yahweh" was meant to forestall the idea that the God of Proverbs was not Israel's covenant God.

REFLECTIONS

1. The word *beginning* in the book's thematic motto (1:7) contains the hint, to be elaborated throughout the first nine chapters, that life is not static, but a journey whose end is found in its God-centered beginning. One may recall the profound lines from T. S. Eliot's *Four Quartets*:

What we call the beginning is often the end
And to make an end is to make a beginning.
The end is where we start from. . . .
    We shall not cease from exploration
And the end of all our exploring
Will be to arrive where we started
And know the place for the first time.[43]

The fear of Yahweh is the absolute beginning and foundation of wisdom. On this foundation, the opening verses lay down the great concepts that give order and coherence to the bewildering diversity of insights and admonitions in Proverbs as a whole. Without basic biblical concepts such as righteousness and justice, wisdom and discipline, all of them grounded in the fear of God, we cannot think wisely about life or live it well. These concepts are not random, unrelated ideas but building blocks for a Christian worldview and praxis. Oliver O'Donovan has seen this clearly:

We will read the Bible seriously only when we use it to guide our thought towards a *comprehensive* moral viewpoint, and not merely to articulate disconnected moral claims. We must look within it not only for moral bricks, but for indications of the order in which the bricks belong together.[44]

---

43. T. S. Eliot, *The Complete Poems and Plays: 1909–1950* (New York: Harcourt, Brace & World, 1952) 144-45.
44. Oliver O'Donovan, *Resurrection and Moral Order* (Grand Rapids: Eerdmans, 1986) 200.

It is the function of 1:1-7 (and chaps. 1–9) to point to the order of the many bricks in wisdom's house. Mastery of these fundamental concepts in an often confusing world is the goal of the book's teaching.

2. In Proverbs, faith is not opposed to reason, but constitutes its possibility, its connection to reality.[45] Proverbs 1:7 contradicts an assumption basic to most current worldviews—namely, that knowledge of the real world is independent of the "fear" or "knowledge" of God. This modern assumption is expressed, even in works of biblical scholarship, by a variety of separations of "sacred" and "secular" realms: public vs. private, facts vs. values, science vs. religion, reason vs. faith, "objective" vs. (merely) "subjective."[46] But the critique of modernity in 1:7 is not just a matter of ideas or perspectives. The very patterns, structures, and institutions of our public and private lives have been largely shaped by reason, science, and technique in the service of modern idols such as wealth, power, pleasure, nation, and unbridled individual "freedom." Technology, with its focus on specific outcomes, without consideration of the whole fabric of existence, often does life and creation much harm.[47]

For Proverbs, all of reality is God's reality (cf. 8:22-31) and is subject to God's cosmic order for good (cf. Genesis 1). Although we may legitimately distinguish between worship and secular affairs, for Proverbs, "life is religion." That is, the ordinary affairs of daily life as well as cult and worship are to be lived in service of God and according to God's norms or "ways." Anything else is arrogant folly (1:7*b*). Thus the various "worldly" activities of the "valiant woman" are not opposed to or separate from her "fear of the LORD," but are its living embodiment (31:10-31; cf. Ruth 3:11).[48]

The great scholar Gerhard von Rad put it well: "Humans are always entirely in the world, yet are always entirely involved with Yahweh."[49] Again, "The experiences of the world were for [Israel] always divine experiences as well, and the experiences of God were for her experiences of the world."[50] (This does not entail erasure of the Creator-creature distinction.) Thus, "folly is practical atheism." Israel was "of the opinion that effective knowledge about God is the only thing that puts a man in a right relationship with the objects of his perception, that it enables him to ask questions more pertinently, to take stock of relationships more effectively and generally to have a better awareness of circumstances."[51]

3. Women are conspicuously absent from the address of Proverbs; they appear mainly in relation to the young males whom it addresses. It thus requires an extra act of interpretive imagination for women to appropriate the wisdom of Proverbs. Yet, Israelite mothers taught wisdom (1:8; 6:20; 31:1), Lady Wisdom is personified as a woman (1:20-33; 8:1-35; 9:1-6), and the human incarnation of wisdom is a "capable woman" (31:10-31). Ultimately, it is our common humanity that enables all who are different to gain wisdom from Proverbs, concerning both ourselves and others who are ethnically, culturally, or personally different from us. Our humanness is more basic than our gender and other differences (Gen 1:27). The same Creator has made us all and placed us in a creation governed by wisdom (Prov 3:19-20; 8:22-31). We modern folk are not ancient Israelites, nor are most modern males courtiers (25:1-7). Wisdom seeks to overcome such differences. In new and different situations, the wise speak and act appropriately because they have learned the common structures and patterns of life (see Commentary on 26:1-12). Wisdom sees the universal through the particular and judges the particular for what it is.

---

45. Von Rad, *Wisdom in Israel,* 53-73.
46. W. McKane, *Prophets and Wise Men,* SBT 44 (London: SCM, 1965). For critique, see S. Weeks, "Was Early Wisdom Secular?" in *Early Israelite Wisdom* (Oxford: Clarendon, 1994) 57-73.
47. J. Ellul, *The Technological Society* (New York: Random House, 1967).
48. Al Wolters, "Nature and Grace in the Interpretation of Proverbs 31:10-31," *Calvin Theological Journal* 19 (1984) 153-66.
49. Von Rad, *Wisdom in Israel,* 95; Van Leeuwen's translation.
50. Von Rad, *Wisdom in Israel,* 62.
51. Von Rad, *Wisdom in Israel,* 65, 67-68.

Still, some scholars believe that benefit can be gained from Proverbs 1–9 only by subverting its patriarchal discourse. Carol A. Newsom has written a brilliant essay in this vein.[52] For Newsom, the fundamental opposition in Proverbs 1–9 is male versus female. However, the fundamental opposition in the biblical text is wisdom versus folly, which is not gender specific (see on 2:12-19), though gender relations illustrate it.

In my judgment, several issues are at stake here. Most basic is whether Proverbs 1–9 is merely a patriarchal construct or a revelatory, symbolic representation of reality; whether—despite being subject to the limitations of all human discourse—its metaphors illumine a real order of creation that impinges on humans, to which they are accountable, and within which they may find freedom and life;[53] and, finally, whether God can speak truth about God's own self and reality through the medium of a patriarchal culture.

According to Hebrews, God "spoke in many and various ways" and has finally spoken in Christ, through whom all things were created, and by whose powerful word all things are sustained (Heb 1:1-3). If so, the second, difficult hermeneutical issue lies in distinguishing mere cultural variation from abiding standards for behavior and truth. Clearly, one cannot simply appeal to human behavior (in or out of Scripture) to determine right from wrong, for two reasons. Humans are endowed with an enormous freedom to name and shape created reality (Genesis 2). In addition, humans have an enormous capacity for sin and self-deception. Not only do we have difficulty living in harmony with creation, but also we are not at peace with ourselves and our neighbors.

On the one hand, Christians have often erred on the side of self-righteous legalism and moralism by making the boundaries of creation more restrictive than they need be. This stifles God-given creativity and freedom. On the other hand, people today often act as if there are no created norms for culture and society. Our contemporary prejudice against an external, normative order of meaning is profound and pervasive.[54] This is perhaps the most fundamental way in which current worldviews differ from that of Proverbs.

4. The prophets called on sinful men and women to reflect on their relation to God by using the shocking metaphor of Israel as God's unfaithful wife (Hosea 1–3; Jeremiah 3). In a different cultural setting, Ephesians used the metaphor of marriage to illustrate the positive relation of Christ and his church (Eph 5:22-33). In a somewhat similar way, male and female readers of Proverbs 1–9 are challenged to imagine the common human quest for Wisdom in terms of a young man's disciplined search for a good wife, "forsaking," as the wedding liturgy has it, "all others." Admittedly, metaphors are only partial reflections of the realities they point to. Yet these biblical metaphors portray the moral ambiguity of life and the need for fidelity. Humans can be unfaithful, they can choose folly or wisdom, Yahweh or Baal. Proverbs 1–9 invites all humans to love wisdom and eschew folly. The fact that wisdom relates to humankind as woman to man, and that Yahweh relates to Israel as husband to wife, is a metaphoric representation of reality whose depths remain unplumbed.

---

52. C. A. Newsom, "Woman and the Discourse of Patriarchal Wisdom," in *Gender and Difference in Ancient Israel*, ed. Peggy L. Day (Minneapolis: Fortress, 1989) 142-60.

53. For the view of metaphor assumed here, see Janet M. Soskice, *Metaphor and Religious Language* (Oxford: Clarendon, 1985). For a different view, see Sallie McFague, *Metaphorical Theology: Models of God in Religious Language* (Philadelphia: Fortress, 1982).

54. Charles Taylor, *Sources of the Self: The Making of the Modern Identity* (Cambridge, Mass.: Harvard University Press, 1989).

PROVERBS 1:8-19, WARNING AGAINST OUTLAWS

COMMENTARY

The first parental instruction (vv. 8-19) begins with a typical call to listen, followed by a motivating metaphor (vv. 8-9; cf. 6:20-21; Deut 6:4-8). A mother or father addresses a young man on the threshold of adult life (see Overview). "My son" is a literal translation of the Hebrew and better fits the male-oriented focus and symbolism of sexual attraction running through chaps. 1–9 than does the NRSV's "my child." Together with Wisdom's first speech (1:20-33), this instruction establishes several key images and issues in the conflicts of good vs. evil, wisdom vs. folly, which preoccupy Proverbs 1–9.

The instruction proper begins at v. 10 with a warning against joining a murderous gang of "sinners" (חטאים *ḥaṭṭāʾîm*; see Ps 1:1) who entice the naive with get-rich-quick schemes based on murder and a community of "honor among thieves" (v. 14). The parent recognizes the need for independent judgment on the part of the youth. Her persuasive speech lays out the options and appeals to the son to make up his own mind. The parent subverts the sinner's invitation (vv. 11-14) by encapsulating it within her own better invitation to wisdom and reality. She sees through wicked arguments, because she has a more comprehensive vision of right and wrong, of acts and consequences, of the way the world works. She appeals to her son to see for himself the way things are. The adolescent is no longer solely under parental influence. There are other voices out there, and he must now choose for himself which voice to listen to, which community to belong to. But in the end, the voice and the reality of cosmic justice and wisdom (1:20-33; 8) will shatter unreal promises of worldly success.

The sinners' speech is a masterful invitation (cf. 9:4-6, 16-17) to cross the threshold into a community of crime. The concrete invitation is to a roadside ambush (1:11, 16; cf. 4:14-17). This "path" (דרך *derek*, v. 15—a key metaphor throughout chaps. 1–9) leads away from law-abiding society, and its violence marks the threshold the young man

must cross to join the gang. Thus would he be incorporated into a society from which, like death, there is no return. In contrast to the segmented society of Proverbs, with its degrees of honor, the company of sinners presents itself as a successful community with egalitarian and utopian claims: share and share alike (vv. 13-14). Unfortunately their offer of equality and wealth is a lie.

Some scholars put this poem in the troubled time of Ezra and Nehemiah (see Introduction).[55] The redactional quotation of Isa 59:7 in Prov 1:16 shows at least that its editing is post-exilic (see also 4:10-19, which the present poem anticipates). This quotation also ties the independent poem in 6:16-19 to its context in Proverbs 1–9 through the near duplicates in 6:17*b*, 18*b* (see also 1:13; 6:31).

In literary terms, this invitation into a community of death finds its parallel in the deadly invitations of the "strange woman" and Woman Folly to cross their thresholds (7:10-27; 9:13-18; see Commentary on 2:12, 16). But the promises of sinners are unreal. They promise a wealth that belongs properly to wisdom (1:13; 8:18; 24:4; 31:11*b*), and they seek to gain it by trespassing upon the goods and lives of their neighbors. True life and wealth are found only within the righteous limits set by wisdom. The parent warns the son of the inherent instability of such anti-societies (cf. 24:23-24). While sinners seek abundant life, their ironic end is death because they step outside the conditions of life, like a fish out of water. The sinners, greedy for gain, think to ambush and kill others (Mic 7:2), to swallow them alive, like *Sheol* ("the grave"; cf. 5:5; 7:27; 9:18; 27:20; Num 16:30-33; Isa 5:14; Hab 2:5). Instead, they trap themselves (v. 18). The wickedness of these sinners is revealed as folly. Birds, at least, can see a net spread before them (v. 17), but sinners are blind to the consequences of their own actions.

55. See Camp, *Wisdom and the Feminine in the Book of Proverbs*, 233-54.

REFLECTIONS

For some readers, the sinner's invitation to violence may seem far removed from their secure, middle-class world. Indeed, some scholars think the parent's vignette of violence is an exaggerated didactic lesson, "an extreme case" that "cannot be generalized."[56] But to hear the relevance of this text for the human condition, it is necessary to attend to its literal sense. The parent who speaks in 1:10-19 is from the upper stratum of Israelite society. But the problem of evil the parent addresses is universal. Our own century has known two world wars, a flood of smaller ones, and countless terrorist acts both political and private. Violence is a human reality. As M. Scott Peck's analysis of the Mylai massacre in Vietnam has shown, American violence may be a *systemic* problem.[57] It invades all social groups. It implicates even "good people" who are not overtly immoral, because there are no innocent bystanders to societal evil.[58]

The parent of 1:10-19 knows that evil is a real option for the son, that anyone can cross the line from good to evil (cf. Gen 8:21). The parent does not assume that "good families" are innoculated against evil or that godly virtue automatically continues from generation to generation. The speech is brutally realistic about the possibilities that lie before the son.

This dissuasive speech speaks to many situations. Shakespeare used it and Wisdom's prophetic warning (1:20-33) to shape his account of the moral education of young Prince Hal.[59] It would be suitable as well on the lips of a mother on Chicago's South Side today, or of a father to a potential Nazi SS recruit in the 1930s. It could have served a mother of an Israelite lad about to join one of the bloody rival gangs in the days of Abimelech (Judg 9:4, 25, 29). It might serve Christian parents of a bright young son or daughter tempted to join a firm whose profits rest on exploitation of laborers, on destruction of the environment, or on success at the expense of justice and truth.

---

56. O. Plöger, *Sprüche Salomos*, BK 17 (Neukirchen-Vluyn: Neukirchener Verlag, 1984) 15, 17, 20; cf. Lang, *Wisdom and the Book of Proverbs*, 15.

57. M. Scott Peck, *People of the Lie: The Hope for Healing Human Evil* (New York: Simon and Schuster, 1983) 212-53.

58. See D. Bonhoeffer, *Ethics* (New York: MacMillan, 1965).

59. See Shakespeare *King Henry IV* I.ii.98-100; cf. Prov 1:20-21, 24.

PROVERBS 1:20-33, WISDOM'S PROPHETIC WARNING

COMMENTARY

1:20-21. Wisdom's first speech as personified woman begins with a two-verse introduction. In vocabulary and setting, these verses are parallel to 8:1-5 and 9:1-6. This parallelism makes clear that personified wisdom in chaps. 1; 8–9 is the same figure. But it also establishes a contrast over against Dame Folly (9:13-18) and her symbolic counterpart, the "strange woman" (5:3-6, 20; 7:5; cf. 5:15-19). For example, among the verbal echoes are "busiest" or "loud" (המיה *hōmiyyâ*; cf. 7:11; 9:13). These parallel passages (1:20-21; 8:1-5; 9:1-6) thus contribute to the metaphorical equivalence among "house" (15x), "city,"

and "[woman's] body," all of which one enters through "openings" (פתח *petaḥ*; 1:21; 5:8; 8:3, where "mouth" should not be emended, 34; 9:14), either for good or for ill.

As is common in the symbol systems of many cultures, in Proverbs 1–9, "house," "city," and "body" have cosmic cultural implications (see Commentary on Proverbs 8; 9:1).[60] Via their connection with wisdom

---

60. Mary Douglas, *Purity and Danger* (London: Routledge and Kegan Paul, 1966) 115; and *Implicit Meanings: Essays in Anthropology* (London: Routledge and Kegan Paul, 1975) 47-59. For house and city building as a repetition of creation, see M. Eliade, *The Myth of the Eternal Return or Cosmos and History* (Princeton: Princeton University Press, 1971).

and folly, these images represent the world of divine norms for creatures, in contrast to a world of norms violated by human folly and delusion. This symbolic world includes what moderns call nature as well as human history and society. To enter the house/body of folly is a cosmic trip into Sheol, the underworld (see Commentary on 1:12; cf. 5:5; 7:27; 9:18). At stake in Proverbs 1–9 is nothing less than the nature of reality as created by Yahweh. What is such a world like? What are the conditions for living well in it?

1:22-31. Wisdom addresses young men (qualified here as "mockers" and "fools") in the public square, perhaps in contrast to the secret invitation of sinners (v. 14). She also first raises the recurring theme of love and delight, which pervades chaps. 1–9. Humans are responsible for the loves they choose. The body of Wisdom's speech (vv. 22-31) adopts the genre of a prophetic judgment for purposes of instruction. She speaks to those who have heard her before, but have rejected her (vv. 22, 24; cf. Ps 82:2-7; Jer 23:26-32). One may compare God's mouthpiece, Moses, speaking to Pharaoh after several plagues have already been sent (Exod 10:3-6). Other prophetic motifs here are the reciprocal calling and not being heard (v. 24; cf. v. 28; 21:13; Isa 65:12; 66:4; Mic 3:4), seeking and not finding (v. 28; Amos 8:12; Hos 5:6, 15; cf. Prov 8:17; Matt 7:7-8).[61] But Wisdom speaks for herself. She takes her stand at the center of communal life, in the gates of the city, in the highway. She addresses all humans. No one can claim that he or she has not heard Wisdom's voice, that they did not know (the reasons for this are made clear in Proverbs 8; cf. Ps 19:1-4; Rom 1:18-20; 2:14-15).

1:22-25. These verses function as a prophetic accusation. The "simple" have been hearing Wisdom, but they have not been listening. Indeed, they have rejected her message (cf. Jer 6:19). The translation of vv. 22b-23 is problematic. In line with the argument of the passage as prophetic accusation and the grammatical possibilities, it is best to translate, "You refused my reproof; I poured out my thoughts to you; I made known my words to you"[62] (cf. Ps 107:11; Zech 7:8-14).

1:26-28. The consequences of rejecting Wisdom are spelled out: calamity like a storm (v. 27; 10:24-25), accompanied by the laughter of Wisdom, who responds in kind to the mocking young (v. 22; see Deut 28:63; Pss 2:4; 37:13; 59:8). Verse 28 shows that timing in life is essential (Eccl 3:1-8). There are points of no return; when the storm is upon us, it is too late to seek shelter. Moments of decision pass and are gone forever. Timing is all.

1:32-33. The final passage briefly describes the consequences of rejecting and of listening to Wisdom's advice: death or security in life (cf. Jer 17:23, 27).

61. Roland E. Murphy, *Wisdom Literature: Job, Proverbs, Ruth, Canticles, Ecclesiastes, Esther,* FOTL 13 (Grand Rapids: Eerdmans, 1981) 52.

62. R. E. Murphy, "Wisdom and Eros in Proverbs 1–9," *CBQ* 50 (1988) 600-603.

REFLECTIONS

1. Wisdom addresses the paradoxical mixture of naivete and scorn that sometimes afflicts the young and arrogant (cf. 1:29; 5:12; 12:1). When people persist in ignorance, in defiance of Wisdom's teaching, they become culpable. It is not wrong to be young and naive; it is blameworthy, though, to want to stay that way (1:22). There is no hope for "scoffers" and "fools," who "know it all," yet "know what they like" and only "love what they know" (15:12; 26:11-12; 28:26; Isa 5:21)! Sometimes, "I like myself just the way I am" is not a healthy affirmation of self-respect, but a denial that life requires growth and correction from external forces: "When I was a child, I spoke like a child . . . [but now] I put an end to childish ways" (1 Cor 13:11).

2. The laughter of Wisdom is shocking. It is perhaps to be understood as a response to the absurdity of those who flaunt reality, who "spit into the wind" and are puzzled when they get wet. It is also, perhaps, a fierce joy that the goodness of the world order and justice have been vindicated when the wicked reap what they have sown.[63] When a tyrant falls, the people rejoice (11:10; cf. Job 22:19; Isa 14:4-20; Rev 18:20). It is important to note that the persons whom calamity overcomes are themselves responsible for it (1:18). When they refuse to eat Wisdom's fruit (3:18; 8:19), they are stuffed with the "fruit of their [own] way" (1:30-31 NRSV; 14:14; 18:20-21; Isa 3:9-11). Such self-induced calamities befall not just individual persons, but entire nations (Jer 6:16-19; cf. Prov 26:3 LXX). Wisdom is a matter of life and death not just for individuals but for families, corporations, universities, nations, and cultures. They, too, reap what they sow.

63. See Abraham Heschel's classic work on the pathos of God, *The Prophets,* vol. 2 (New York: Harper & Row, 1962).

PROVERBS 2:1-22, THE SEARCH FOR WISDOM

COMMENTARY

This brilliant poem comprises one elaborate sentence of twenty-two lines, corresponding to the length of the Hebrew alphabet (see 31:10-31).[64] Its sections are marked off by the first and twelfth letters of the Hebrew alphabet, א (*'alep;* 2:1, 5, 9) and ל (*lamed;* 2:12, 16, 19). This instruction plays off the speeches by the parent (1:8-19) and by Wisdom (1:20-33), just preceding. It also states the themes that will occupy the parental instructions (excluding the "Insertions," 3:13-20; 6:1-19) until Wisdom herself returns to speak in chap. 8.[65]

The parent speaks in his own voice (v. 1), but urges the son to listen to "Wisdom" and "Understanding" (v. 2; cf. 8:1). The parent thus points beyond himself to wisdom, which (or "who") is the goal of parental teaching. Through repetition of terms from 1:20-33, the instruction shows that the relationship between humans and Wisdom is reciprocal. In the previous speech, Wisdom "cried out" and "raised her voice" (1:20*b*-21*a;* cf. 8:1). Now, in the same words, the son is urged to do the same (v. 3). Wisdom's call to humans is echoed by the call of humans for Wisdom, like lovers seeking each other in the street (Cant 3:1-2 LXX; 5:6; cf. Prov 7:4).

The opening verses also play upon the search for treasure. The son is to "treasure up" the words of the father (2:1*a;* cf. 1:11, 19; 2:7 Hebrew), and to "seek" and "search" for wisdom "like silver" and "hidden treasures" (v. 4), which the Lord "stores up" for the good (v. 7). The search for wisdom begins with mastery of parental "words" and "commandments" (v. 1).[66] In the poem's second half (vv. 12-22), Wisdom will rescue the young from the parallel evils of wicked men (vv. 12-15) and the "strange" woman (vv. 16-19) who will play such an important role in the symbolism of these chapters. The chapter concludes with a call to goodness and a final promise and warning (vv. 20-22).

2:1-4. The long condition ("My son, if . . .") has two global outcomes, both governed by wisdom. The first concerns the son's relation to God ("then," vv. 5-8) and the second his positive relation to humans ("then," vv. 9-11). This second, principled relation to others is contrasted with two negative relations that Wisdom enables the young to avoid. These dangerous, parallel relations are with "wicked men" (vv. 12-15) and the "strange woman" (vv. 16-19).

2:5-9. The first outcome of the son's search is, somewhat surprisingly, practical insight into "the fear of the LORD" (see Commentary on 1:7). The son will "know"

64. See Dennis Pardee, *Ugaritic and Hebrew Poetic Parallelism: A Trial Cut ('nt and Proverbs 2),* SVT 39 (Leiden: Brill, 1988). For a different assessment, see R. N. Whybray, *Proverbs,* NCB (Grand Rapids: Eerdmans, 1994) 49-51.

65. So A. Meinhold, *Die Sprüche,* Zücher Bibelkommentare (Zürich: Theologischer Verlag, 1991) 1:46.

66. Michael V. Fox, "The Pedagogy of Proverbs 2," *JBL* 113 (1994) 233-43.

(ידע *yāda'*) God (v. 5). "Knowledge of God" here is not due simply to individual activity or to immediate divine revelation. Humans get to know God somewhat as they get to know a language, through interaction with parents and others who speak and act in the ordinary activities of life. As parents relate to God, world, and others, they communicate a certain understanding of God and reality. The child's business is gradually to take responsibility for his or her life in response to parents, persons, the world, and God.

The quest for wisdom is necessarily a quest for God, for wisdom comes from God (vv. 6-7). Like the prophets, Proverbs 2 resolutely refuses to separate right living from knowledge of God (see Jer 22:13-16; Hos 4:1-3). The poet communicates this by the parallel outcomes in vv. 5 and 9 ("then you will understand . . ."). God's giving of wisdom, however, is complex. It comes through tradition, teaching, experience, and the disciplined practical learning of how things work in God's world (Isa 28:23-29). God gives wisdom through the ordinary.

God "stores up" (or "hides") "sound wisdom" for the "upright," and protects those who walk with integrity (= "blameless," v. 7). "Sound wisdom" translates an obscure Hebrew word (תושיה *tûšîyâ*), which appears in Proverbs only at 2:7; 3:21; 8:14; 18:1. It "denotes clear, proficient thinking in the exercise of power and practical operations." It has connotations of "stability, efficacy, confidence, and resilience." It is a "power . . . used in determining a course of action and dealing with difficulties."[67] Such resourceful competence is not automatic, for God ultimately dispenses it. A blameless walk (v. 7) is defined by the "paths of justice," which God's "faithful ones" negotiate, step by step (v. 8). The standard for integrity is justice as determined by God (see 1 Kgs 9:4). Wisdom and justice are inseparable, each being rooted in God's ordering of reality (see Commentary on 8:20). God preserves those who walk in tune with God's requirements.

Verse 9 repeats the opening of v. 5 ("then"), thus marking the move from God (vv. 5-8) to humanity, whose existence is subject to the cosmic-social norms of "righteousness and justice and equity" (v. 9; see 1:3; 8:20).

2:10-11. Wisdom enters the core of one's being or "heart" (see Excursus, "The 'Heart' in the Old Testament") and thereby enables right conduct toward God and neighbor. Wisdom here is already personified, and a cluster of parallel terms is used to designate her (cf. 8:1). Among them is the word translated as "prudence" or "discretion" (מזמה *mĕzimmâ*), which actually is the capacity for private, hidden thought.

It is to be used in keeping your own counsel and thinking for yourself. This power will protect you from the temptations of the wicked man and woman (2:11f.; 5:2f.), because when they try to seduce you to their ways, you will be able to look inward, maintain independence of thought, and stand up to their inveiglements.[68]

When Wisdom enters the son (v. 10), she protects him from two parallel evils: the communal "way of evil" (v. 12; cf. 8:13), represented by "those who speak perversely" or "topsy turvy" (תהפכות *tahpukôt*; see also 1:11-19; 4:14-17; cf. Isa 5:20-21); and "the strange woman" (NRSV margin, vv. 16-19).

2:12-15. The masculine evil is portrayed by the bad path, found first in the parental speech on sinners (1:15-16, 19; cf. 3:31) and developed throughout chaps. 1–9 (the vocabulary for "path" and "way" is the most frequent of any in these chapters, the terms for "wisdom" coming second). The young "choose" their life's path (v. 13) and do not merely fall into it. "Path" here is not simply the course of events in a life, but the religio-ethical manner in which people negotiate the events that come their way. Yet, by just or unjust conduct, we humans also manufacture the events that come to us (1:18, 31-33). Some tread "ways of darkness" (v. 13)—a metaphor developed in 4:19 (cf. 7:9)—in contrast to the sunlit "path of the righteous" (4:18 NRSV; cf. 6:23; Ps 119:105). The wise and the wicked desire contrary pleasures; they delight in opposite paths (vv. 10, 14; cf. 5:18).

2:16-17. This logic of desire (and of forsaking good paths for worse, v. 13)

67. Michael V. Fox, "Words for Wisdom," *Zeitschrift für Althebräistik* 6 (1993) 149-69, see also 162, 164-65.

68. Fox, "Words for Wisdom," 160. Cf. *Amenemope*, chap. 1 in Lichtheim, *Ancient Egyptian Literature*, 2:149.

leads naturally to the figure of the "loose woman"/"adulteress" (v. 16). The NRSV and the NIV paraphrase the two parallel terms used to describe the strange woman. Literally she is "strange" and "alien" (זרה *zārâ*; נכרי *nokrî*; see Commentary and Reflections on 5:3, 9-10). The allurements of the strange woman are powerful, but they can be avoided through the deeper and nobler love of wisdom (v. 16). Greater passions displace lesser ones. The "stranger" herself embodies the failure of fidelity, for she "forsakes the partner of her youth"—that is, her husband (v. 17; cf. 4:17). The forsaking of proper sexual love is a problem not only for men but also for women. This abandonment of proper love entails ignoring her "sacred covenant" (lit., "the covenant of her God"). This reference to "covenant" is unique in the Proverbs. The phrase "of her God" also begs explanation. The closest verbal and conceptual parallel to 2:17 is Mal 2:14-16.[69] The issue there is faithfulness in marriage, with God appearing as witness to the "covenant" between the marriage partners (see Gen 2:24). In other passages, Israel (metaphorically a bride) is bound by a marriage covenant to Yahweh (cf. Jer 3:4; Ezek 16:8; Hos 2:18-20; Mark 10:2-9; Eph 5:21-33). Proverbs 2:17 perhaps alludes to such prophetic use, as well as to the aged folly of Solomon, led into spiritual adultery by his foreign wives to violate his covenant with Yahweh (1 Kgs 11:1, 4, 11).

But the issue in Proverbs is not directly that of breaking a marriage covenant with the Lord, for OT covenant-as-marriage imagery always portrays Yahweh as husband and Israel as wife. In contrast, the portrayal of faithful and unfaithful marriage in Proverbs 1–9 has as its analogue, not Israel's relation to Yahweh or to a foreign god, but humanity's relation to female Wisdom or Folly. In this symbolic context, all humans, male and female alike, are portrayed in the image of young males attracted to females.

Neither is the problem of literal exogamy with "foreign women" (as in the days of Ezra and Nehemiah) the direct concern of these chapters. Here the woman in v. 17 is chastised, not for the foreignness of her religion (as with Solomon's wives), but for ignoring the covenant of "her God" (i.e., Yahweh) through being unfaithful in literal human marriage (with metaphorical repercussions throughout Proverbs 1–9). The poet of Proverbs 1–9 would probably share Ezra's aversion to marriage to foreign women, and his choice of "stranger"/"alien" may allude to that aversion (cf. Ruth 1:16 and Ps 45:10, which honor women who forsake pagan gods for Israelite religion and marriage).[70]

2:18. The Hebrew has a grammatical conflict of gender in verb ("sinks," fem. [שחה *šāḥâ*]) and subject ("her house," masc. [ביתה *bêtāh*]). This may be due to the metaphorical equivalence of the strange woman's "body," "pathway," and "house"; to enter one is to enter all (see v. 19). Although she herself is not Sheol (the grave), her body/house/path is the "entrance" (5:8; 9:14; cf. 8:34) to Sheol (7:27; 9:18). There may also be a punning relation between the verb שוח (*šûaḥ*, "sink down") and the conventional image of the strange woman as a "pit" (שוחה *šûḥâ*; 22:14; cf. 23:27).[71] For the "shades," see 9:18; 21:16; 1 Sam 28:8-19; Isa 14:9; 26:14. Apparently Israel, like its ancient Near Eastern neighbors, pictured the dead as having a shadowy, impotent existence of some sort. There is no real life (Isa 26:14), and thus no praise of God in the gloomy netherworld (Ps 6:5).

2:19. To "go [in] to her" is a phrase with sexual connotations (see 6:29; Judg 15:1), but the activity here symbolizes all irrevocable deeds, from which there is no turning back. This verse echoes the language of sinners in 1:12, but it also reveals the fate of sinners seduced: They are themselves swallowed.

2:20-22. The parental speech ends with a purpose statement and warning. The outcome of pursuing wisdom (vv. 1-4) is a life in the company of "the good" (plural) and "the righteous" (plural, v. 20), in contrast to the deadly path of sinners (1:19). Although each person must walk his or her own path, we humans travel in companies gathered and directed by ultimate loves for either wisdom or folly. Life is not neutral and static, but a movement toward good or ill, however

---

69. Gordon Paul Hugenberger, *Marriage as a Covenant: A Study of Biblical Law and Ethics Governing Marriage Developed from the Perspective of Malachi*, SVT 52 (Leiden: Brill, 1994) 296-302.

70. Cf. J. Blenkinsopp, "The Social Context of the 'Outsider Woman' in Proverbs 1–9," *Bib* 72 (1991) 473-75.
71. See the Mesopotamian "Dialogue of Pessimism," in Pritchard, *Ancient Near Eastern Texts Relating to the Old Testament,* 438.

hidden and subtle that may be.[72] This view of the collective nature of the human journey (v. 20) leads to vv. 21-22, which focus on "the land"/"earth" (ארץ *ereṣ*), the place where humans live together.

Connections with Israel's historical traditions are unusual in the wisdom books (cf. 10:30; 22:8; Job 15:18-19). But Prov 2:20-22 seems dependent on traditions concerning the "land": promise to the patriarchs, conquest under Joshua, loss in exile, second exodus in the return from Babylon (Isaiah 40–55). However, these verses do not merely repeat

old traditions concerning the land (Deut 8:1, 19-20; 30:11-20; Ps 69:35-36). Rather, they move toward considering the final justice of God over the entire earth (cf. Pss 96:10, 13; 98:7-9). Proverbs 2:21-22 is linked especially with Zech 13:8 and Psalm 37 by vocabulary and by the conviction that evil will be cut off from God's land/earth and that only good will remain (Ps 37:3, 9, 11, 20, 22, 29, 34, 38; Matt 5:5). As with Deuteronomy, where Israel can choose for or against the Lord's covenant, so the choice for wisdom or folly (here for the first time defining the "righteous" and the "wicked") is an ultimate one, a matter of life and death.

72. See M. Scott Peck, *The Road Less Traveled* (New York: Simon & Schuster, 1978).

REFLECTIONS

1. In Prov 2:9, the poet repeats the opening of 2:5, thus moving from God (2:5-8) to humans, who are subject to the cosmic-social norms of righteousness, justice, and equity (2:9-11; see 1:3; 8:20). This move, from the divine to the human and cosmic, is fundamental for biblical faith. The same move will determine the sequence of Proverbs 3. It reflects the fundamental principle that "the fear of the Lord is the beginning of knowledge" (1:7 NRSV). Only when humans "begin" with God in all their thinking and doing does humanity, the world, and all within it fall into harmony (Ps 24:1; Matt 6:33).

Central passages of Scripture follow the same pattern. For example, it determines the order of the Ten Commandments (cf. Matt 22:37-40). Exodus 20:1-7 concerns God; Exod 20:8-11 concerns the sabbath, during which human action is to emulate the divine "rest"; and Exod 20:12-17 concerns right dealing with others. Similarly, the Lord's Prayer begins first with God's name, kingdom, and will (Matt 6:9-10), followed by the more obvious human needs for provision, forgiveness of sins, and protection from evil (Matt 6:11-13). Again, Hosea laments the lack of knowing God and documents it by Israel's failure to keep the commandments that concern the neighbor (Hos 4:1-2; see also Hos 6:6). Although there is an order in reality (God before creatures, and creatures "according to their kind,"[73] Genesis 1; Psalm 104; Prov 16:4), God and creation are inseparable, for the world reflects God's glory and righteousness (Pss 19:1; 97:6). Consequently, our relationship to God is manifested in our conduct toward others and toward the creation itself. And our worldly conduct, no matter how moral, eventually goes awry without God: "Fear God and keep the commandments" (see Eccl 12:13).

2. In 2:7-8 God dispenses wisdom to those who are faithful and live wisely. This sort of interactive circle of divine and human synergy is not uncommon in Scripture (cf. 8:9). For example, in Leviticus, the process of sanctifying persons or things (making them "holy") is both a human moral-ritual responsibility and an act of God (Lev 21:8).[74] God gives what humans actively seek, whether for ill or for good (see Commentary on 11:27; Matt 7:7-11). In this respect, gaining God's gift of wisdom is not unlike putting on "the whole armor of God" (Eph 6:10-17 NRSV).

73. This phrase should not be identified with medieval concepts of hierarchy. See O'Donovan, *Resurrection and Moral Order*.
74. See Gordon J. Wenham, *The Book of Leviticus* (Grand Rapids: Eerdmans, 1979) 22-23.

In the same way, wisdom is both a gift of God (2:6) and a human achievement (2:1-4; 4:7; cf. Phil 2:12-13). Its result is personal transformation and the ability to live with integrity, unswayed by various temptations. For example, justice and righteousness (2:9), which can be experienced as external and alien to oneself (cf. Hos 4:1-2), now become "pleasant" (2:10) instead of onerous. This picture of personal transformation may be compared to Jeremiah and Ezekiel. These prophets placed the divine transformation of the human "heart" in a redemptive-historical perspective. After Israel's failure to keep the Sinaitic covenant (Jeremiah 11), God promised to give Israel a new heart that would transform the people and enable them to keep the "new covenant" (Jer 24:7; 31:31-34; 32:37-41; cf. Ezek 36:26-27).[75] These prophetic traditions become the basis for New Testament views of human transformation in the image of Christ (Rom 5:5; 12:2; 2 Cor 4:6, 16). Yet also for Ezekiel, a new heart is not merely a result of divine fiat, but requires human initiative (Ezek 11:18-21; 18:31; cf. Rom 12:1-2).

3. Wisdom "saves" the young from both the evil way of the "bad man" (2:12) and the "strange woman" (2:16). The parallelism of wickedness here is crucial for understanding the metaphorical role of woman in Proverbs 1–9. In Hebrew, Prov 2:12, 16 begin with exactly the same expression, and both male and female use speech to persuade to wrong. For the writer-editors of Proverbs 1–9, good and evil are not primarily a matter of gender. Rather, the writer uses gender relations, in the cultural context of that day, as a primary metaphor for understanding the bipolar attraction humans have for good (i.e., one's spouse, wisdom, and justice in general) or for what seems to be good (i.e., "thy neighbor's wife" or husband, folly, and sin in general). Warnings against adultery in these chapters do function as literal advice to sexually volatile young men. But literal woman and metaphorical woman (Wisdom or Folly) interanimate each other's meaning.

75. See G. von Rad, *Old Testament Theology* II (New York: Harper & Row, 1965) 211-17.

PROVERBS 3:1-12, INSTRUCTION IN THE FEAR OF THE LORD

COMMENTARY

Proverbs 3, like chaps. 8–9, is composed of three parts: (1) an instruction on the "fear of the LORD" (vv. 1-12); (2) a blessing that praises Wisdom's benefits and role in Creation (vv. 13-20; cf. chap. 8); and (3) an instruction on relations with other people (vv. 21-35). Proverbs 3 is a summary of right human behavior toward God (vv. 1-12) and toward other people (vv. 21-35). Thus these instructions develop the first two themes stated in chapter 2's programmatic instruction. Verses 13-20 add the essential cosmic dimension to these relations, because creation is the arena in which divine and human concerns are played out.

3:1-2. The chapter opens with a negative and positive admonition to keep the parent's

"instruction" and "commandments" (see 6:20; 7:2). "Keep . . . in your heart" means both "learn by heart" and "take to heart," in the sense of living out of what is learned, as Jacob and Mary do (Gen 37:11; Luke 2:19). The admonition promises a long and good life ("abundant welfare" [שלום *šālôm*]; see 4:10; 6:20-23; cf. Moses' speeches to Israel, Deut 8:1, 18-20; 30:16, 20). The logic that connects admonition and blessing here is similar to the command to honor parents in Deuteronomy with its promise of long life (Deut 5:16; cf. Exod 20:12; Eph 6:2). This extravagant promise of life assumes that the parental teaching faithfully mediates the teaching of Lady Wisdom and thus her rewards (3:16-18; 8:35; 9:10-11; cf. 10:27). The authority of the parental speech defers to Lady Wisdom and is accountable to her cosmic standards. This is not spelled out, but simply assumed in the logic of a promise that only God and Wisdom can fulfill. Behind the parent stands Wisdom, not as authoritarian cudgel, but as reality and reason (see 2:1-4). In a similar but grander vein, even the Mosaic law only reflects cosmic norms imperfectly (Matt 19:3-19; in Sir 24:23, cosmic Wisdom and Mosaic law are identified, but there, too, Wisdom has priority).

3:3. The first clause of this verse appears to be an editor's elaboration. Grammatically, two readings of "loyalty and faithfulness" are possible. The phrase may continue the promises of v. 2, and the clause may be translated, "loyalty and faithfulness will not forsake you." On this reading, reference is to the essential attributes of Yahweh once revealed on Mount Sinai (Exod 34:6; Pss 25:10; 57:3; 67:7); "bind them" refers to the instruction and commandments of v. 1 (cf. 6:20-21; 7:1-3; Exod 13:9, 16; Deut 6:6, 8). In ancient Israel, as in orthodox Judaism today, amulets with sacred writing were bound about the neck (1:9; 6:21), thus close to the heart, as spiritual reminders. But writing "on the tablet of your heart" is also metaphorical for memory at the deepest level of one's being (3:1; 7:3; Jer 17:1). What penetrates to the depths of the heart determines one's very character and actions. Thus to transform the heart is to transform the person (Jer 31:33; Rom 12:2; 2 Cor 3:3; see Commentary on Prov 4:23). But, more probably, "loyalty and faithfulness" stand as parallels to "instruction" and "commandments" and refer to human attributes that sum up the whole of our religio-ethical life (so NIV and NRSV). Thus in Hos 4:1-3, these two terms summarize the radical and comprehensive nature of Israel's moral-spiritual failure.

3:4. The author spells out the consequences of heeding the previous admonition: divine and human approval. This cliché indicates that one's life meets the standards of God and society. The phrase presupposes that human identity is formed through two fundamental relationships, with God and with other humans (1 Sam 2:26; Luke 2:52; Acts 2:47; Rom 14:18). Ancient Israel was a shame-and-honor culture, in contrast to modern Western societies, which often exercise social control through blame and guilt.[76] In the former, one's status and honor are public matters (see Commentary on 26:1), openly given or taken away by a (hopefully healthy) community. This is in contrast to the self-evaluation of those who trust in themselves (28:6; cf. 18:10-11), who are "wise/good/right in their own eyes," but ignore the perceptions of God and others (3:7; 26:12; cf. 27:2; Judg 17:6; 21:25). Good repute is literally "good sense" (שכל־טוב *śēkel-ṭôb*), which leads to a good reputation (see Commentary on 12:8; 13:15). So the Hebrew says that heeding the admonitions of 3:3 not only leads to social approval, but also enables one to acquire good sense. Matthew Poole, a seventeenth-century divine, commented: "The serious practice of religion is an excellent mean to get a solid understanding of it; as, on the contrary, a vicious life doth exceedingly debase and darken the mind, and keep men from the knowledge of truth."[77]

3:5-8. These verses teach the inner spirit of the "fear of the LORD" (see Commentary on 1:7). Essential is first a total (cf. Deut 4:29; 6:5) trust in the Lord (3:5; 16:20; Ps 37:3), which is contrasted to a self-reliance that trusts in its own insight (28:26), power, and wealth (11:28; Ps 52:7; Jer 9:23-24), quite unaware of human limits. Mighty Sennacherib's attack on Jerusalem (2 Kgs 18:17–19:37) is a tale of King Hezekiah's trust in Yahweh (2 Kgs 18:5, 19-24; 19:10) when no human power could save (Pss 33:16-17; 118:8-9; 146:3). It illustrates most of the issues at stake in Prov 3:5-6 (cf. 29:25).

Literally, "In all your ways know him" (v. 6; cf. 1 Chr 28:9, of Solomon). "Ways" refers to human conduct in the world in its diversity: our behavior in various activities and circumstances, none excluded (16:2-3). This ordinary world is the arena in which human knowledge of God, or lack thereof, is revealed by human responses to the divine standards of justice and righteousness (1:3; 16:12; Jer 22:13-16; Amos 5:21-24). Knowing and doing justice are not the same as being in relationship with God, but the two are inseparable (28:5, 9).

76. See Victor H. Matthews and Don C. Benjamin, *Social World of Ancient Israel: 1250–587 BCE* (Peabody, Mass.: Hendrickson, 1993) 142-54.
77. Matthew Poole, *A Commentary on the Holy Bible II* (McLean, Va.: MacDonald, n.d.) 218, on Prov 3:4.

Verses 7-8 form another admonition with a promissory motive, at the center of the series in vv. 5-10, that lays down the essentials for a God-fearing life. The first precept of v. 7 warns against being "wise in your own eyes." This phrase is used to express one person's subjective evaluation of things in implicit contrast to some other person's evaluation. The "other" must always be kept in mind. The first is usually a positive or negative adjective (good, just, right, wise, evil, wicked). The "other" is sometimes other people (12:15; 28:11), but most important it is some higher judge of what is right or wise (cf. 16:2, 25). Ultimately this judge is the Lord. In Judges, when each person does what is right in his or her own eyes (Judg 17:6; 21:25), it is because there is no king to ensure that what is right in his eyes is done. The human king is in turn accountable to Yahweh, the divine king (cf. 1 Kgs 11:33, 38). Since Yahweh is the creator, Yahweh's view of things is true, the way things are, and to go counter to this view is to flout reality (Isa 5:20-21). The folly of being wise in one's own eyes (3:7; 26:12, 16; 28:11) is parallel to the notion of relying on one's own heart (cf. 3:5), as the proverb pair in 28:25b-26 makes clear.

Verse 7b complements v. 7a. The opposite of overblown self-assurance and pride (see 1 Cor 8:1) is to "fear the LORD, and turn away from evil" (see Commentary on 16:5-6). This positive and negative precept is the sum of a godly and good life (Job 1:1, 8; 28:28; see Commentary on Prov 1:7), for to shun evil is to turn toward God and the good (16:6; Amos 5:4b, 14-15). The issue is a lifelong journey of "conversion" (16:17). Such a mindset (a Hebrew might say "heart-set"; cf. Pss 57:7; 78:37) promises life and well-being to one's very self, both inner and outer, "body" ("flesh" or perhaps "navel" as the body's center) and "bones" (3:8; 16:24; cf. Isa 66:14; Rom 12:1). Such promises have often been misused by the purveyors of a "health-and-wealth" gospel (see Reflections on 3:11-12). The promise here is more modest and qualified. It means that a godly and good life is a healthy one, one that ought to be a matter of common sense, not wholly unlike Benjamin Franklin's *Poor Richard's Almanac* entry, "Early to bed, early to rise, makes a man healthy, wealthy and wise" (cf. 1 Tim 4:7b-8

and the qualifications in 1 Tim 6:5-10, which set sharp limits on the goal of well-being for its own sake). Well-being and wealth, like the more elusive happiness, when God grants them, are natural by-products of a quest for more ultimate goods.

3:9-10. The text moves naturally from the inner dispositions of the heart (3:1, 3, 5, 7) to the practical "payoff." Money talks, and it shows the heart's true home (Matt 6:21). Our use of world and wealth reveals our true commitments. Specifically, by it we show either honor or scorn to God (14:31; 19:17; 1 Sam 2:29; Dan 11:38). For Israel, this meant that the "first fruits," the first produce of a new harvest and symbolically the best, were dedicated to God alone, sometimes for the use of the priests (Lev 23:10; Num 18:8-15) or for lay folk (Deut 26:1-11).

Such first fruits are part of a symbol system that includes the firstborn of human and beast (Exod 13:1-3, 11-16) because Israel, God's people, has been graciously elevated to the status of God's firstborn (Exod 4:22; Hos 11:1) and first fruits (Jer 2:3). All things and persons belong to God, Israel's creator and redeemer, and the gift of the first fruits and the redemption of the firstborn acknowledges this (Deut 26:1-11). But first fruits/firstborn also are a sign and a promise of the full harvest to come, a matter taken up in New Testament representations of Christ and his people (Matt 2:15; Rom 8:29; Rev 1:5).

Verse 10 presents an abundance of crops and wine as a natural outcome of giving honor to God. There is a sort of natural symmetry between the gifts to God (cf. Num 18:27, 30) and the blessings of barn and vat, which ensue (3:10; cf. Sir 35:9-13). Similar language and thought also appear in Deuteronomy (cf. Deut 15:13-14; 28:8). Proverbs 3:9-10 is one of the few places in the book of Proverbs where cultic language and matters are presented (see 15:8; 28:13; cf. Mal 3:8-12). Worship and liturgy in the narrow sense are not the focus of Proverbs. The book takes Israel's covenant faith as a given (see the section "Theology" in the Introduction). Its particular concern is daily life lived in the presence of God.

3:11-12. The solemn precept and explanatory motive here present a sharp, deliberate contradiction to vv. 9-10. Sometimes those who honor the Lord find their barns empty and their vats dry, so that joy and gladness flee away (cf. Isa 17:10). This alternative, godly, Job-like experience of life sometimes finds an explanation in the loving discipline and reproof of God the parent (cf. 1:7-8; 13:24; 15:5).

REFLECTIONS

1. Proverbs 3:11-12 presents a direct contradiction to glib "health-and-wealth" (sub)versions of the gospel, which appeal to vv. 9-10. Proverbs 3:11-12 shouts "No!" to promises of wealth made by preachers who exploit the naive, the desperate, and those who practice religion as a means of gain. Genuine faith is sometimes called upon to "fear God for nothing" (see Job 1:9-11). On Prov 3:11-12, the best commentaries are Deuteronomy 8 and Hebrews 12. Moses' profound sermon on the wilderness sufferings of Israel provides one explanation of the meaning of human suffering (esp. Deut 8:5), and also warns of the dangers of material prosperity (Deut 8:11-20). Hebrews 12 follows upon the grand story of godly heroes in Hebrews 11, with its litany of human promises kept through faith and suffering, and its litany of divine promises left unfulfilled by God. Then the writer of Hebrews quotes Prov 3:11-12 and encourages readers who also suffer: "Now, discipline always seems painful rather than pleasant at the time, but later it yields the peaceful fruit of righteousness to those who have been trained by it. Therefore lift your drooping hands" (Heb 12:11-12 NRSV).

2. This section also deals with the matter of trust and reliance. Ralph W. Emerson's classic essay "Self-Reliance" established that concept as a basic American virtue. But the Bible presents a paradox. The more one relies on God, the more independent one becomes. Paradoxically, then, it is the most God-dependent persons who are the most independent of external controls and coercion. For the writer of Proverbs to say, "Get understanding, get wisdom" (see 4:7), is not incompatible with "Lean not on your own understanding."

Humans have a marvelous capacity to understand and live meaningfully in the world. But life is riddled with evils, mysteries, and troubles beyond human grasping or fixing. Some of these troubles are due to sin, but some are not. There are gaps between what humans expect and what actually happens. More sharply, there are gaps and contradictions between what God promises and what humans receive in life (Hebrews 11). This fact of life is presented but not resolved in the great works of Ecclesiastes and Job (see also Psalm 73). The problem is already present in Proverbs (3:9-12; 16:1, 9; 19:21; 21:30-31; 27:1).[78]

Thus there is no true wisdom without humble recognition of our limits and of God's transcendence (Psalm 131; Jer 9:23-24). God is the ultimate reality with which humans have to deal in the thick of life. The Bible does not present God as a quick and easy answer to human terror, as many would wish. Rather, God's involvement in the mystery of evil renders God mysterious to us, for evil seems to call divine goodness and truth into question. This paradox is powerfully expressed in the contradictory formulations of Genesis, where the evil actions of Joseph's brothers are attributed to God's saving purposes and action: "It was not you who sent me here, but God" (Gen 45:8 NRSV; cf. Gen 50:20).

The consistent biblical answer to this dilemma of life is faith or trust in the One we do not and cannot fully comprehend (Job 28:28; Eccl 12:13-14). The gospel says that the solution to evil lies mysteriously beyond us; according to the "foolish" wisdom of the cross, it lies with God in Christ (1 Cor 1:18-31; 2 Cor 4:18). Meanwhile,

---

78. See von Rad, *Wisdom in Israel,* 97-110; Van Leeuwen, "Wealth and Poverty," 25-26.

Christians, like ancient Israel, live in hope (Rom 5:1-5), being enjoined to trust and obey where they cannot clearly see. We walk by faith, not by sight (2 Cor 5:7).

3. Walking in the knowledge of God is motivated by the promise that God will "make straight your paths" (3:6*b* NRSV). The use of this phrase in 9:15 suggests that "straight paths" does not necessarily mean a life free from difficulties. It does mean that one's life has a clear direction and goal that a Godward person will attain (11:3, 5; 15:21; cf. 4:25). A divine and human synergy occurs when humans are in tune with God and with God's purposes. Thus Isaiah can tell the Babylonian exiles to "make straight in the desert a highway for our God" (Isa 40:3 NRSV; cf. Prov 15:21). The desert is not a place of abundant life, but the purposes of God and humans may be fulfilled there. The German theologian and martyr Dietrich Bonhoeffer wrote from a prison cell:

> Not everything [evil] that happens is the will of God, yet in the last resort nothing happens without his will (Matthew 10:29), i.e., through every event, however untoward, *there is always a way through to God.*[79]

Abraham set off on a journey, not knowing where he would go, only that God would go with him on the way (Gen 12:1-3; cf. Heb 11:8).

79. Dietrich Bonhoeffer, "Letter of December 18th, 1943," in *Letters and Papers from Prison,* E. Bethge, ed. (London: SCM, 1953) 84; italics added.

PROVERBS 3:13-35, ON WISDOM: BLESSING, CREATION, ADMONITIONS

COMMENTARY

After the preceding instruction in the fear of the Lord (vv. 1-12), there follow a blessing (vv. 13-18) and a saying on creation (vv. 19-20). Formally, vv. 13-18 comprise a blessing. (The root אשר [*'šr,* "happy," "blessed"] marks the beginning and end of the section, an inclusio; cf. 8:34.) But the blessing functions here to praise the benefactions of wisdom in hymnic fashion. In vv. 19-20, as in 8:22-31, the role of Wisdom in creation grounds the preceding account of her benefits (3:13-18; 8:1-21). Another instruction follows (vv. 21-35), comprising two parts. The first part (vv. 21-26) is a summary instruction based on the foregoing teaching (vv. 1-20; cf. 7:24-27; 8:32-35). The second part (vv. 27-35) concludes the chapter with six practical admonitions and a divine curse (v. 33), which contrasts with the blessing of vv. 13-18.

3:13-18. The blessedness ("happy," vv. 13, 18; 8:34; Ps 1:1) of those who find wisdom and get understanding is here detailed. This language links this section and its message to chap. 2 and especially to chap. 8. It repeats the search-and-find motif that in Prov 2:2-6 (cf. 8:17*b;* 1:28*b*) entailed the fear of the Lord, a topic treated at length in 3:1-12. The quest for wisdom is inescapably a journey in the presence of God. The vocabulary of v. 13 is also repeated in the beginning and ending of Wisdom's great speech (8:1, 34-35). Again, creation through Wisdom (vv. 19-20) is more fully elaborated in 8:22-31.

The language of v. 13 is also used of the acquisition of a wife, who symbolizes wisdom (18:22; cf. 8:35). Hence, it is not surprising that the language of vv. 13-18 reappears to describe the "capable wife" of Proverbs 31. Her children call her "blessed" (31:28; cf. 3:13, 18; 8:32, 34). The rewards of Wisdom are priceless (vv. 14-15; see 8:11*a,* 19; 16:16; 31:10, 18, with parallel vocabulary), and nothing one might desire is comparable to her

(v. 15b = 8:11b; 31:10). These verbal and thematic parallels create a three-way link among 3:13-20; 8:1-35; and 31:10-31. Through repetition, they forge a long-distance, interactive parallelism among cosmic wisdom and human cultural activities, especially as exemplified in the earthy, life-enriching activity of the "capable woman" (31:10-31).[80]

In Wisdom's hands are long life (vv. 16-17; cf. 3:2; 4:10; Ps 91:16) and riches and honor (v. 16; 8:18). Verse 16 perhaps alludes to Solomon's request for wisdom and God's surprising gift of what Solomon did not ask for (1 Kgs 3:5-14). The image of Wisdom holding "life" in her hands has an Egyptian counterpart in *Ma'at*, the goddess of world order and justice, who holds the *ankh* ("life") sign in one hand and the *was* scepter, symbol of wealth and honor, in the other (see Commentary on 8:27).[81] Wisdom's "ways" (v. 17) are pleasant (cf. 2:10; 9:17), "paths of peace."

Within Proverbs 1–9, שלום (*šālôm*, "peace and prosperity") appears only here and in 3:2. This repetition suggests that Wisdom's gifts (vv. 16-17) may be gotten through parents (v. 2). Again, "way" and "path" reinforce the theme of life as a journey governed by either Wisdom or Folly.

The "tree of life" (v. 18) is a cosmic image known throughout the ancient Near East. In the Bible, outside of Proverbs, this tree is present only at the beginning and the end of all things, in the Garden of Eden (Gen 2:9; 3:22, 24) and in the city-garden of the new creation, where it bears its fruit in season (cf. Ps 1:3) and its leaves are for the "healing of the nations" (Rev 2:7; 22:2, 14). In Proverbs, the phrase has become a metaphor for the good life offered by Wisdom (3:18; 11:30; 15:4) or even by hope fulfilled (13:12). In the context of vv. 19-20, the cosmic overtones of this image are still active, though the everlasting life of the Garden of Eden is not (Gen 3:22-23). Nonetheless, the human imperative here must not be overlooked; one must "lay hold" of wisdom and "hold her fast." If Wisdom in a fallen world does not afford eternal life, she does offer the best and fullest life humans can possess. One should not wait for the plums to fall from the tree (cf. Eccl 9:10)!

3:19-20. The double naming of Wisdom as "Wisdom" and "Understanding" is repeated from v. 13 (cf. 8:1) and marks a shift from the human (vv. 13-18) to the divine relationship with wisdom. It provides the cosmic warrant for all the blessings just described (vv. 13-18; cf. 8:22-31). The passage has affinities with Ps 104:24 and Jer 10:12. "Earth," "the heavens," and "the deeps" are a tri-part way of summing up the entire creation (cf. Exod 20:4; the opposites, "heavens" and "earth," can also have such a summary function, Gen 1:1). The verbs of v. 19, which are used of God's creating acts (see also Job 38:4; Ps 24:2; Isa 14:32; 45:18), are also used of "founding" and "establishing" a city or a house, whether a domestic domicile or a temple (1 Kgs 6:37; 1 Chr 17:24; Ezra 3:12; Isa 14:32). Building a house is a human echo of God's wise work of creation (see Commentary on 9:1; 24:3-4).[82]

Verse 20 presents another bi-polar figure of the universe, life-giving waters from below and above ("dew"). The "deeps" were divided at creation so that the dry land and the waters were separated into their proper domains (8:29; cf. Gen 1:9; Job 38:8-11; Ps 104:9). This separation of the waters from the dry land represents the cosmic stability of the world, in which potentially destructive and chaotic forces, symbolized by the deeps, are kept harmless, in their proper sphere. But the ongoing order of creation, represented by the waters, also enables life to flourish. In arid Palestine, a water source is a natural symbol of life (10:11; 13:14; 14:27; 16:22; cf. Jer 2:13). Thus for Israel, God's disposal of water was one of the surest signs of divine wisdom. The land is dry; lack of rain in season can bring famine. In the rainless summer months (see Commentary on 26:1), the heavy dew, brought from the Mediterranean by the west wind, can keep crops alive. Thus the cosmic imagery here is not fortuitous, but comports with the imagery of vegetative life from v. 18.

3:21-35. These verses belong together as an instruction that develops the second theme from the programmatic instruction in Prov 2:9-11—namely, correct relations with other persons. The return to instruction is signaled by "My son" (v. 21), a general

80. For the cohesive effect of repetition in distant parallelism, see Pardee, *Ugaritic and Hebrew Poetic Parallelism*.
81. Kayatz, *Studien zu Proverbien 1–9*, 104-5.
82. M. Eliade, *Cosmos and History or the Myth of the Eternal Return* (Princeton: Princeton University Press, 1971).

admonition with promissory motivations (vv. 22-26), a series of negative admonitions concerning relations with other people (vv. 27-31), and is concluded by an extended theological grounding of the series (vv. 33-35). The overall pattern of this instruction is thus similar to that of vv. 1-12.

3:21-26. In v. 21, the instruction is something the son must "keep," but in 2:11 prudence and understanding "keep" the son. (For "prudence" [= one's inner thought], see the Commentary on 2:11.) There is a mutuality between wise humans and the cosmic Wisdom they seek and keep (see Commentary on 2:1-4). But what is the relation between the security that comes from keeping "sound wisdom and prudence" (v. 21*b*, 23-25, alluding backward to Wisdom's speech in 1:26-27 and forward to 4:19) and the security that Yahweh affords (v. 26; cf. v. 5)? Through human wisdom "your foot will not stumble" (v. 23; cf. Ps 91:12, Hebrew), but Yahweh "will keep your foot from being caught" (v. 26). This parallel suggests that Yahweh stands behind Wisdom, as her ultimate guarantor. Conversely, the unwise and sinners are caught by their own folly (5:21-23; 6:2; 11:6). Yahweh's protection, mediated through wisdom, does not save from that! The focus here is not on the Lord's extraordinary deeds of salvation, but on the ordinary connections between human responsibility and life in the world as ordained and ordered by God.

Verse 22 echoes the imagery of v. 3 (cf. 1:9; 4:9). In Hebrew there is also a double pun that exploits the imagery of the necklace: "they will be life for your soul [throat]" and "adornment [favor] for your neck" (נפש *nepeš* can mean "soul"/"life" and the "throat" that a necklace adorns; see Isa 5:14; Jonah 2:5; חן *ḥēn* means "favor," but can also be a [beautiful] ornament, such as a necklace; cf. Prov 3:4). The security wisdom provides (v. 23) recalls 1:33 and, more broadly, the covenant promises of dwelling in the land (2:21; 10:30; cf. Lev 25:18; Psalm 37; Matt 5:5).

3:27-35. Verses 27-31 are a row of negative admonitions, all beginning with the command, "Do not," an example of anaphora. Verses 28-29 also end with the same Hebrew terms ("with you"/"near you"), an epiphora. The issue in each is not mere advice that may or may not be followed, depending on the situation (cf. 26:4-5). Rather, these admonitions, like the Ten Commandments, lay down basic, non-negotiable rules for dealing with others.

Verses 29-30 are linked to the foregoing by anaphora and the key word *neighbor* (רע *rēa*ʿ), and also form a thematic pair in themselves (*harm* [רעה *rāʿâ*] is a key word that also forms a wordplay with "neighbor" in Hebrew). Verse 29 moves from the withholding of "good" (v. 27) to the active plotting of evil against one's neighbor, where the thought is parent to the crime (Ps 7:14-16). The neighbor, meanwhile, lives in naive security, like the innocent inhabitants of Laish, destroyed by the tribe of Dan (Judg 18:7-10, 27-28). Thus this cluster of admonitions moves from sins of omission to those of commission against the neighbor for personal advantage (cf. 1:11-12).

Verse 30 broadens the venue from neighbor to the more inclusive "anyone" (אדם *ʾādām*, "human," "man") in a way reminiscent of the contrast between Lev 19:18 ("neighbor") and Lev 19:34 ("stranger"). The focus is on the unjustified "quarrel" or "lawsuit" (ריב *rîb* means both; see Commentary on 25:7*b*-10).

The summarizing precept (v. 31) and the motive clauses that follow (vv. 32-35) provide depth to the foregoing admonitions. Actions of greed (vv. 28-29) or assault (vv. 29-30) are "ways" of the violent. The violent are immoral persons whose might is their right, who use whatever force they command, whether moral or not, to expand their own kingdom at the expense of their neighbors. The parent's parable on sinners (1:10-19) is only a flagrant example of this human tendency to envy (cf. 4:16-17).

Verses 32-35 give grounds for not envying the violent of v. 31 in a series of contrasts between the good and the bad vis-à-vis their relations to God. A stock series of terms describes the opposed parties. "Perverse" or "devious" (cf. 2:15) people are an "abomination" to God, and thus they are far from God (see Commentary on 11:1). But God is near to the upright, the "straightforward" who partake, almost in prophet-like fashion, in God's inner "counsel"/"council" (סוד *sôd* means both; cf. Job 15:8; 29:4; Ps 24:14; Jer 23:18; Amos 3:7). The stories of Noah before the flood (Gen 6:9-22) and Abraham before Sodom and Gomorrah (Gen 18:17-19) illustrate Prov 3:32*b* (cf. John 15:15).

Verse 33 continues the series of motivational oppositions, contrasting "the LORD's curse" with God's "blessing" (10:6-7, 22; cf. Job 42:10-16; Zech 5:3-4). The contrast of blessing and curse in consequence of obedience and disobedience was basic to Israel's covenant relation with Yahweh as spelled out in Deuteronomy (Deut 11:26-28; 27:14–28:68). It is by the Lord's blessing that houses, domestic and dynastic, get built (2 Samuel 7; Psalm 127; Luke 2:4).

God deals with humans in kind (v. 34*a*; Job 34:11); as we give, so we get. Compare the American proverbs, "What goes around, comes around" and "Violence begets violence." Like is related to like in actions, in consequences, and in relations with God and with other humans (cf. 24:23). Yet God's grace or favor can surprisingly reverse human expectations dimmed by evil in the direction of justice and *shalom* (v. 34*b*; cf. 1 Sam 2:4-8; Luke 1:51-55). The logic compressed in v. 34*b* is laid out more fully in Ps 18:24-27, though there is little overlap of vocabulary (cf. Prov 30:5 with Ps 18:30). God "scorns scorners"—that is, God shows them no respect (for the verb, see 19:28*a*). The LXX of 3:34 is quoted in Jas 4:6 and 1 Pet 5:5. The quotation in James follows upon a passage on coveting whose logic is similar to Prov 3:31-34.

Verse 35 appropriately closes the passage with a contrast of "wise" and "fools" who receive "honor"/"wealth" (see Commentary on 11:16) and "disgrace" respectively, rewards appropriate to each life-style. Thus, by giving fitting rewards, God helps the "humble" (v. 34*b*), while subverting the wrongful attempts of the wicked to get gain at the expense of their neighbor.

REFLECTIONS

1. As so often in Proverbs, 3:13-35 considers life in terms of two antithetical directions: toward God, wisdom, righteousness, and life (3:13-26) or toward sin, folly, and death, with the loss of all the former (3:27-28). The implications are not just individual (though the passage speaks personally), or merely ecclesiastical. They are cosmic in scope (3:19-20; also the tree of life) and social in the broadest sense.

With concrete, albeit negative, examples, 3:27-28 expresses principles of justice essential to any society's health. First, as the Western legal proverb has it, one must give "to each his own." Humans have a general claim on certain things that their humanity entitles them to. Life, food, shelter, and dignity are among the most obvious of these things essential to our humanness.

Each person is unique. But part of that uniqueness stems from membership in families, countries, and various groups. Part of it stems from our roles as workers, clients, students, employers, spouses, and so forth. In short, justice requires not only that individuals receive what is their due simply as human beings, but also that they receive what is theirs as unique individuals who stand in a rich array of relationships. The short admonition of 3:27-28 thus casts a very wide umbrella over human existence. Perhaps no aspect of social and personal life is not touched by it. Wisdom consists in knowing what properly belongs to my neighbor, at the proper time, and in the proper way, by virtue of who he or she is and my relationship to that neighbor.[83] Teachers, for example, owe their students a journey into the truth. This journey should happen in a way pedagogically appropriate to the students' age, development, training, and abilities. Justice (and love) consists of granting what is properly yours to you, *when it is in my power to do it.*

The second principle appears in 3:27*b*. Our actions, also with respect to God, to rulers, and to our neighbor (cf. 3:9; 24:21; Matt 22:21; Rom 13:7-8), are determined both by our ability (3:27*b*-28) and by our responsibility according to the standard of

83. See Aristotle *Nicomachean Ethics* III.i.16, 1111*a*; O'Donovan, *Resurrection and Moral Order.*

justice (3:27a). Justice determines that when I have something that I owe to my neighbor, I am responsible to him or her for it. (In some cases, we may owe good to God or to our neighbor but be unable to meet our obligation.) The present admonition considers a case in which I am able to give good, in which my sphere of influence matches my sphere of responsibility. It is at this point that we may be tempted to deceive ourselves and our neighbor—but not God (3:28; cf. 24:10-12). By committing sins of omission, we neglect to do what is right and deny our responsibility for it. Finally, the disposition of obligations must be timely (3:27b-28). While v. 27 refers to one with a claim on you, v. 28 may also refer simply to a neighbor in need who asks for help that you can render, whether that neighbor has any legal claim to it or not (cf. 14:21, 31; Exod 22:25-27; Jas 4:17; 1 John 3:17-18). There are sins of omission against the command to love one's fellow human beings (Lev 19:18, 34), as the parable of the good Samaritan illustrates (Luke 10:29-37).

2. Proverbs 3:29-30 considers active wrongs instead of sins of omission. Verse 29 discusses the inward malice that comes to the surface in actions that harm a neighbor, whether in violent or legal ways. Quarrels and litigation can be used wrongly to seek personal gain from another who has done you no harm. For instance, a man picks a fight with a newly arrived, confused tourist, while his associate picks the tourist's pocket. But the more common and significant application of this admonition is in the legal arena, where false accusation and irresponsible litigation can do great harm to others, even as they erode the fabric of civility and justice that binds a society together in harmony. In the litigious United States (with 4 percent of the world's population and one-half of the world's lawyers), one would wish this saying were inscribed on the portals of every courthouse and on the hearts of all who enter there.

3. The writer of Proverbs reveals the spiritual source (3:31) of the sins warned against previously (3:27-30); they are rooted in "envy"[84] (see 24:1-2, 19-20; Psalm 37). Beginning with Adam and Eve and their progeny, Cain and Abel (Genesis 3–4), the Bible repeatedly describes humans as being smitten with envy of God and of neighbor. "The grass seems greener on the other side of the fence." We covet what others have (Exod 20:17; cf. Col 3:5; Jas 4:2). And we envy those who have what we have not, even when their goods have been gained by wrong. This is the disease described by Shakespeare:

And look upon myself and curse my fate,
Wishing me like to one more rich in hope,
Featured like him, like him with friends possess'd,
Desiring this man's art, and that man's scope,
With what I most enjoy contented least. (Sonnet 29)

84. Cornelius Plantinga, Jr., "A Select History of Envy," in *Not the Way It's Supposed to Be*, 157-72.

PROVERBS 4:1-27, TRADITION, WISDOM, AND WAYS

COMMENTARY

4:1-9. These verses present an extended parental invitation to get wisdom, an expansion of the usual introduction to an instruction. Its language is stereotypical, with slight variations (e.g., a plural address). The central theme is tradition itself, the notion that wisdom is something passed on from generation to generation. Israelite culture, strongly traditional and oral in character, revered the aged as treasure houses of wisdom (cf. 8:22-31; 16:31; 20:29; Job 15:7-10).

4:1-4. Wisdom from the past, refined in the crucible of experience, is passed on from parents to children, from teachers to pupils, and from craftspeople to apprentices. This notion has left its traces in the word *learning* (לקח *leqaḥ*, v. 2), which connotes something received from another, something handed on, accepted, and finally made one's own by the recipient (cf. 1:5; 9:9; 16:21, 23; as verb, 2:1; 4:10; 24:32). The great rabbinic wisdom work *Pirqe 'Abot* ("Sayings of the Fathers") captures this traditional notion of learning by its repeated, "So and so received [the tradition] from so and so." More than any inheritance of wealth and property, parental teaching is to be "treasured" (2:1; 7:1; 10:14; see Commentary on 19:14) and used by the next generation as they make their own way through life. The chain of tradition is made explicit by the father-son-father-son links in vv. 3-4. What the father was taught, with verbal variation, he now adapts and teaches to his own son (v. 4; cf. 2:1; 3:1; 7:2).

Several biblical and ancient Near Eastern scenes portray or allude to the drama of a father (figurative or literal) who, as he approaches death, passes on his wisdom and commands to the next generation. Such transmission may be to the next leader or to a son (Deut 34:9; Josh 1:7-9; 1 Kgs 2:1-9; cf. Luke 1:17; 2 Tim 2:2).[85] The parental wisdom and commands are sometimes explicitly linked with the Mosaic Torah (תורה *tôrâ* means "teaching" or "instruction," and, secondarily, "law"). The language in v. 2*b*, "do not forsake my teaching," resonates with passages on the forsaking of Yahweh's law as received by the ancestors. In Ps 89:30 the concern is with the royal sons in the line of David; in Jer 9:13, it is with Israel generally.

4:5-9. Here is an extended admonition to "get wisdom" first and foremost. The juxtaposition with the foregoing verses (vv. 1-4; cf. v. 5*b*), which urged children to listen to

their parent's teaching, is not accidental. The assumption is that the parent, as portrayed in Proverbs, is a faithful mediator of wisdom to the young. But even so, the young are to get wisdom. They are responsible for laying hold of the wisdom offered them. The issue is not the parent's authority and tradition for its own sake, but rather Wisdom herself. All good parental teaching seeks to put children in touch with reality and its norms (cosmic Wisdom) and to engender those habits of the heart and mouth and hands that constitute the good life (human wisdom). Human wisdom is fostered by pointing to Wisdom as something "out there" to be gotten hold of, to be loved, embraced, and prized (vv. 6, 8), like the wife in 5:15-20. Human wisdom is love of reality, of the world, and of its excellent "norms." And those who embrace Wisdom are in turn kept, guarded, and honored by her reality (vv. 6, 8; for the imagery of v. 9, cf. 1:9). The love affair of humans and Wisdom is reciprocal and mutual (see Commentary on 8:17, 31, 35).

4:10-19. These verses provide additional instruction on the theme of the two ways. It begins with the traditional call to listen (v. 10) and contrasts the "way of wisdom" (vv. 11-13) with the "path of the wicked" (vv. 14-17), a negative anti-reality illustrated most vividly in 1:10-19. It concludes with a two-verse summary, again contrasting the two ways, this time in terms of cosmic light and darkness.

4:10-13. The parent refers beyond herself to Wisdom (v. 11), whose way sets the child free to run the path of life unfettered. Verse 10, with its promise of increased life, suggests that the parent's teaching is a conduit of Wisdom, who, as God's cosmic agent, is the true source of life (cf. 3:16, 18, 22; 4:4, 13, 22; 8:35). Instruction (v. 13) is not a hindrance to freedom but its precondition. ("Instruction" is literally "discipline" [מוסר *mûsār*], which does not here imply punishment, as the term often does in American English.) To "keep hold" of "discipline" is like committing oneself to an athlete's regimen of a wise diet, exercise, and training. By limiting themselves in this way, athletes are set free to run in top form and speed, without "stumbling" (4:12; cf. 4:16, 19). The encouragement given here, when compared with the language of 3:6 and

85. Leo G. Perdue, "Liminality as a Social Setting for Wisdom Instructions," *ZAW* 93 (1981) 114-26; "The Testament of David and Egyptian Royal Instructions," in *Scripture in Context II: More Essays on the Comparative Method*, W. W. Hallow, J. C. Moyer, and L. G. Perdue, eds. (Winona Lake: Eisenbrauns, 1983) 79-96.

Isa 40:30-31, is a reminder that a life of forward momentum is a matter of both wisdom (attained by human effort) and divine grace. Thus the argument emphasizes both the responsibility of the hearer for discipline (v. 13) and the gift-character of Wisdom's way as straight and free of obstacles (vv. 11-12; cf. 2:13; 3:6, 23; 10:9). The feminine pronouns ("her," "she") in v. 13*b* do not refer to "instruction" (which is masculine in Hebrew), but to the feminine "wisdom" of v. 11*a* (cf. 3:16; 4:6; 8:35).

4:14-19. This unit begins with a verbal and thematic echo of 1:10, 15. The "path of the wicked," like the house of the adulterous woman, should not be entered, but avoided. One must "turn away from it and pass on" (v. 15). Similar admonitions and language are applied to the adulterous woman as a symbol of folly (7:25; cf. 2:19; 5:8; 7:8; 9:15-16). For v. 16, see Commentary on 6:4-5. Verse 18, with its image of the rising sun, may be compared to the description of the righteous ruler in 2 Sam 23:4.

Verse 19 suggests that sin is blind, "in the dark" about the path it walks: "They do not know what they stumble over." This not knowing is an essential part of sin. Folly lives unaware of consequences, of what lies ahead in the path chosen (28:22). The young man seduced does not know "it will cost him his life" (7:23 NRSV; cf. 9:18). The adulterous woman wanders from the path of life and joy (cf. Ps 16:11), "and she does not know it" (5:6 NRSV). And those who sin by omission, who deny responsibility for their neighbor, claim, "We did not know. . . ." Meanwhile, God knows it and will "repay all according to their deeds" (24:12 NRSV).

4:20-27. The chapter closes with a short instruction with a call to listen motivated by a promise of life. The positive and negative admonitions that follow are linked by body parts used for good or for ill. Such lists of parts of the body function to convey the unity and diversity of human actions (see 6:12-15, 16-19).

4:20-21. The parent's "words" are to be kept in the "heart," that inner receptacle and fountain of the self (see Excursus, "The 'Heart' in the Old Testament," below). The translation "keep them within your heart" is somewhat misleading, for it might seem as if the teaching were only an inward, private matter, not affecting life. The sense (to anticipate v. 23) is, rather, "memorize" these words (cf. 3:3; 7:3) and set them at the center of your consciousness, so that your life flows from them. In an oral culture, only what is "known" is remembered.[86] Hence, the tremendous emphasis on remembering the parent's utterances and the memorable, poetic form in which the instructions and, especially, the short sayings are couched. The astounding brevity of these sayings often does not survive translation (see Introduction). "To those who find them" is another phrase that sets the parent's teaching parallel to Wisdom as something that must be sought and "found" (cf. 1:28; 3:13; 8:17, 35; 19:8).

4:22. This verse provides the fundamental, rock-bottom motivation for listening and keeping the parent's words: They bring "life" and "health"/"healing," a common pair stemming from Wisdom (14:30; 15:4; cf. 3:8, 18; 4:10).

4:23. The writer here presupposes the utter importance of the "heart" or the "mind" (see Excursus, "The 'Heart' in the Old Testament," below). Because the heart is the center and wellspring of the self, to guard it is to care for one's very life.

86. Ong, *Orality and Literacy.*

EXCURSUS: THE "HEART" IN THE OLD TESTAMENT

The Hebrew term for "heart" (לב *lēb* or לבב *lēbāb*), often translated as "mind," is easily misunderstood in English translation. In both languages, the heart can simply be the organ in one's chest. But of greater interest biblically is its metaphorical use for the internal wellspring of the acting self. In the modern West, heart and head are often opposed as the loci of feeling and thinking respectively. But the ancient Hebrews used "heart" comprehensively to indicate the inner person, the "I" that is the locus of a person's will, thought (Prov 16:1, 9; 19:21), and feeling (Prov 14:10, 13; 17:22). Thus all of a person's actions (Prov 15:13; 2 Sam 7:3), especially speech (Prov 16:23), flow from the heart, expressing its content, whether good or bad (Gen 6:5; 8:21; Sir 37:17-18; Matt 12:33-35; 18:18-19). Scripture can use related terms, such as "belly" and "kidneys" (כליות *kĕlāyôt*; Jer 11:20; 17:10), in much the same way as "heart" (cf. John 7:38 NRSV).

Most important, one's basic disposition toward God is a matter of the "heart" (Prov 3:5; 19:3; Deut 6:5; 1 Sam 12:20). Like a deep well, the heart has a hidden depth (Prov 20:5). Its deepest depths, what modern psychologists might call the subconscious or the unconscious, only God can plumb (Prov 25:2-3), though hidden even from the heart's owner and friends: "The heart is devious above all else, and beyond cure—who can understand it? I the Lord test the mind and search the heart" (Jer 17:9-10 NRSV and NIV collated; cf. Prov 21:2; 15:11). When seeking to replace Saul, the Lord finds in David "a man after his own heart" (1 Sam 13:14 NRSV). But even the seer Samuel is not able to recognize the Lord's chosen, because mortals "look on the outward appearance, but the Lord looks on the heart" (1 Sam 16:7 NRSV). In Proverbs, since the heart is the locus of wisdom, it often stands in metonymy for wisdom: Those who are not wise "lack heart" (Prov 7:7; 10:13). Israel shared the general structure of its anthropology concerning heart and other bodily members with its neighbors. The famous "Memphis Theology" from Egypt illustrates the biblical conception well:

> The sight of the eyes, the hearing of the ears, and the smelling the air by the nose, they report to the heart. It is this which causes every completed (concept) to come forth, and it is the tongue which announces what the heart thinks.[87]

Against this background, we can understand the absolute urgency of the admonition in Prov 4:23: "Above all else, guard your heart" (NIV). This is a fundamental precept, like Socrates' "know thyself"; but it goes beyond Socrates in depth and scope. For Israel, all human hearts are inescapably related to the one Lord, whether in loving service, in uncertain vacillation (1 Kgs 18:21; Ps 86:11), or in grievous rebellion (Prov 19:3). Thus in a prayer that plumbs anthropological depths, the psalmist, wary of personal sin and self-deception, concludes, "Search me, O God, and know my heart" (Ps 139:23 NRSV). Augustine understood the biblical heart well: "Our hearts are restless until they find their rest in thee."[88] And when the prophets anticipate God's final renewal of a wounded and disobedient human race, they do it in terms of the heart, as it is the hidden seed of the new humanity: "A new heart I will give you, and a new spirit I will put within you. . . . I will put my spirit within you, and make you follow my statutes . . . and you shall be my people, and I will be your God" (Ezek 36:26-28 NRSV; cf. Ps 51:7-11; Jer 24:7; 31:33).

Even though the heart can stand in metonymy for the whole person in its "mental," inner aspect (what my heart thinks is what I think), there is in the admonition to guard one's heart an awareness of the mysterious reflexivity that humans possess: I can look at myself and make even my inmost self the object of care, reflection, improvement, and betterment. Some commentators have looked upon guarding the heart (Prov 4:23) as equivalent to keeping it from sin. The admonition is more comprehensive than that, but certainly does not exclude it, as is evident from Prov 4:24.

87. Pritchard, *Ancient Near Eastern Texts Relating to the Old Testament*, 5; cf. Prov 6:12-19.
88. Augustine *Confessions* 1.1.

4:24. The close connection of the heart and the external organs and actions that give expression to it are revealed here. "Crooked speech" is literally a "crooked mouth" (עקשות פה 'iqqĕšût peh), perhaps the most important part of the wicked person's crooked life-style (2:15; 6:12). "Put away" (הסר hāsēr; lit., "turn aside") is part of the larger conversion from evil that fools find so difficult (3:7; 4:27; 13:19; 16:6; cf. Col 3:7-10).

4:25. This verse pictures the single focus required of those who pursue wisdom. The saying does not advocate tunnel vision, which is blind to broad reality. Rather, one's vision must be focused, like a navigator who does not lose sight of the star that guides the ship, lest the course be lost and the ship come to a bad end.

4:26-27. These verses continue the thought of v. 25. One may translate the admonition in v. 26a, "Examine the path of your foot" (author's trans.), since "examine" (פלס pālas) is the same verb used in 5:6a, 21b. Compare the psalmist, for whom God's word was a "lamp to my feet and a light to my path" (Ps 119:105 NRSV). The NRSV and the NIV differ in the second line over how to take the verb—as a simple future or as continuing the admonition respectively. Both are grammatically possible. Most commentators go with the NRSV, but the NIV version has the advantage of not interrupting the sequences of precepts. In v. 27, the singleminded pursuit of the right path is reiterated in an image best known from the deuteronomic tradition of not turning aside from the law of God, either to the right or to the left (cf. Josh 1:7).

REFLECTIONS

1. "Tradition," Chesterton wrote, "means giving votes to the most obscure of all classes, our ancestors. It is the democracy of the dead. Tradition refuses to submit to the small and arrogant oligarchy of those who merely happen to be walking about. . . . We will have the dead at our councils."[89]

Human wisdom is a matter of tradition, the knowers passing on what they know to those who need to know, whether in medicine, law, or family. Most of what we do in life is based on what we have observed or have been taught, on what is commonly accepted by our culture and, more narrowly, by the overlapping subcultures and groups to which we belong. Without such cultural common sense, our lives would be reduced to constantly reinventing the wheel. A true "permanent revolution" is unlivable. In spite of massive changes in the modern era, much in life remains traditional, handed down from the past. Culture is inherently, necessarily conservative—as in, "If it ain't broke, don't fix it." The question for a wise society, however, is this: *What* from the past should be retained and conserved? What from our fathers and mothers should we embrace, and what should we reject? Wisdom also asks, By what criteria do we distinguish the ancestral dross from the gold? Labels like "progressive," "conservative," and "liberal" are not helpful here, because they do not tell us what is to be conserved or changed, or why.

Biblical wisdom appeals to creation order and the distilled experience of past generations to provide the insight for meeting new situations. The abiding patterns of reality, including human nature, provide a context, or frame, within which we can recognize the new.

> Wisdom is the perception that every novelty, in its own way, manifests the permanence and stability of the created order, so that, however astonishing and undreamt of it may be, it is not utterly incommensurable with what has gone before. This does not imply a pretense that the unlikeness of the new to the old is unreal. Even unlike things can be seen as part of the same universe if there is an order which embraces them in a relation to one another.[90]

89. Quoted by Barbara Grizzuti Harrison, "Arguing with the Pope," *Harper's* (April 1994) 56.
90. O'Donovan, *Resurrection and Moral Order*, 189-90.

Wisdom is the ability to perceive the new appositely, in terms of something humans have met before. A new scam on the stock market can be recognized by someone who understands the market's principles and processes and remembers the shenanigans of the 1920s and 1980s. The wise, in any area of life, know "there is nothing new under the sun."

Thus the great importance of history and tradition and the pervasive biblical insistence that we remember and not forget the past (Deuteronomy 8; 1 Cor 11:23-26). Through the godly experience and wisdom of the past, we are equipped to recognize the things that matter, the cast of characters, the events and situations that make up the dangers and opportunities of life for good or for ill. None of us lives long enough to experience enough of God, world, and humanity to be adequately equipped without the wisdom of the past.

2. The idea of "two ways" is fundamental to the piety and worldview of both Proverbs and Psalms (see Psalm 1). The sharp polarity of the two ways is a teaching tool parallel to the sharp contrast between "righteous" and "wicked" in Proverbs 10–15. The point is not so much that people can be neatly separated into "good guys" (us) and "bad guys" (them), as in some simple "cops and robbers" film, wholly unaware of the moral ambiguity that runs through every human heart. Rather, we all are constantly placed before choices or "steps" (4:12) that eventually shape paths, patterns, habits, a way of life, a form of culture that settles into character. Like the footpaths that cut across campus greens, such paths are formed over time by the steps of many generations, each person, on a smaller scale, pursuing the goal of wisdom or unwitting folly. The steps we make and the paths we take depend not only on what we have inherited, but also on where we want to go. Paths are also tradition.

3. Traditions can do damage. Traditions are especially powerful among those who assume them as self-evident and ultimate and have no higher norm by which tradition can be corrected and renewed as circumstances change. Thus Mark 7:1-13 may be taken as a sharp critique of the Christian church whenever it elevates tradition above the dynamic word and purposes of God. Traditions also damage those who reject them. Ironically, in this case, tradition limits people's choices to what is *not* the tradition, thereby cutting people off from their roots; the baby gets thrown out with the bath water. This happens not only with individuals, but also with generations (Judg 2:10). Among those who flee from tradition, sometimes the content changes, but the interpersonal processes remain (as when a dogmatic fundamentalist parent raises a dogmatic liberal child, or vice versa). The French say, "The more things change, the more they remain the same." On a larger scale, one may consider the historical continuities and discontinuities of the French Revolution, with its reign of terror and devotion to the goddess of reason. In their wholesale rejection of a flawed Christianity, the revolutionaries were unable to separate the wheat from the chaff. T. S. Eliot once wrote that the surest thing to drive out old evil is new evil.

4. "The beginning of wisdom is this: Get wisdom,/ and whatever else you get, get insight" (4:7 NRSV; cf. 1:7; 9:10). Scripture has a number of statements about "the one thing needful": Love the Lord your God with all your heart, soul, and might (Deut 6:5). Seek first the kingdom of God and his righteousness (Matt 6:33). What does the Lord require of you but to do justice, and to love kindness, and to walk humbly with your God (Mic 6:8)? Fear God, and keep his commandments; for that is the whole duty of everyone (Eccl 12:13). Proverbs puts the getting of wisdom first, because wisdom is the key to God's reality (Proverbs 8).

Finally, Christ is the wisdom of God, revealed in the person of Jesus (1 Cor 1:24, 30). Thus the getting of wisdom and the knowing of God in Christ are inseparable, fulfilling the sense of Prov 9:10, "The fear of the LORD is the beginning of wisdom" (NRSV).

5. Proverbs 4:17 represents moral-spiritual activity under the universal figure of food: "bread of wickedness," "wine of violence" (see 30:8-9, 14-15, 20, 22, 25). Leon Kass has shown that "literal" eating itself is a bodily activity that lays bare human nature and its cultural propensities for virtue and vice.[91] For humans, eating is never merely nourishment, no more so than sex is ever merely sex (see 30:20). When we eat, we ingest creation, and this activity speaks more convincingly than can words of our most deeply held commitments concerning creation, God, and human relations. A serious consideration of who in our world eats and who goes hungry is fundamental to a biblical view of justice.[92] A German proverb declares, "What you eat is what you are." Like all proverbs, this one does not tell the whole truth. Yet, what and how we eat reveals who we are and shows that material things are vehicles of spirit. In the profound film *Babette's Feast,* for example, we see culturally shaped creation (food) as a means of grace, reconciling estranged sinners.

Food is everything that nourishes us as persons. Jesus said, "My food [bread] is to do the will of him who sent me" (John 4:34 NRSV). The "capable wife" of Proverbs 31 "does not eat the bread of idleness" (31:27 NRSV). These images represent the nourishment with which humans feed their souls. Our spiritual food and drink (both good and bad) is thus any cultural product that shapes and fills our inward self, whether music, speech, film, literature, advertisements, urban architecture, or the daily experience of commuting in bumper-to-bumper traffic, breathing smog.

The paradoxical tendencies of humans to eat what is not good for them, to eat too much (25:16) or too little, or to covet a neighbor's piece of pie are all signals of human distress and folly, signals of our painful alienation from our bodies, from that personal piece of cosmos that is I and you. What we do with real food, we also do with metaphorical food. Contemporary Americans need only to turn on the TV or radio to be flooded with the "wine of violence" and stuffed with the "bread of wickedness."[93] Christian folk need to turn away from junk food for the soul and cultivate space and time for rumination on "whatever is true . . . honorable . . . just . . . pure . . . pleasing, whatever is commendable, if there is any excellence and if there is anything worthy of praise" (Phil 4:8 NRSV).

6. Proverbs 4:20-21 employs the conventional "call to hear" and begins a sequence of bodily organs that stitch the instruction together. In a certain sense, the ear is obviously for hearing and the eyes for seeing (20:12; cf. Ps 94:9). But hearing and seeing are by no means automatic. Scripture is full of admonitions to hear, because people can choose not to and sometimes are simply unable to (Exod 6:9, 12; Deut 29:4). Alternately, the blind lead the blind (Matt 15:14), and a "foolish and senseless [lit., "heartless"] people . . . have eyes but do not see . . . have ears but do not hear" (Jer 5:21 NRSV; cf. Ps 115:6; Isa 6:9-10; 43:8; Mark 4:9-12). Hearing and seeing, or their lack, are reflexes of an open or recalcitrant "heart" (see Excursus, "The 'Heart' in the Old Testament," and the parallelism of 2:2; 18:15). The hymnic confession, "Once I was blind, but now I see," concerns the inner self. Proverbs speaks of a "listening ear" (15:31; 20:12; 25:12), but Solomon, wisest of kings, is given a "listening heart" to judge the people and to distinguish right from wrong (1 Kgs 3:9). Jesus, knowing of resistance to his teaching (Mark 4:9-12), ends his parables in wisdom fashion: "He who has ears to hear, let him hear" (Luke 14:35 NRSV).[94]

7. The world and life are filled with distractions, and "the eye is not satisfied with seeing" (Eccl 1:8 NRSV; cf. Prov 27:20). Jesus made the point more radically: "If your right eye causes you to sin, pluck it out" (Matt 5:29 RSV). The admonition of Proverbs

91. Leon Kass, *The Hungry Soul: Eating and the Perfecting of Our Nature* (New York: Macmillan, 1994).

92. See Rolf P. Knierim, "Food, Land, and Justice," in *The Task of Old Testament Theology: Substance, Method, and Cases* (Grand Rapids: Eerdmans, 1995) 225-43.

93. See Neil Postman, *Amusing Ourselves to Death: Public Discourse in the Age of Show Business* (New York: Penguin, 1985).

94. See David L. Jeffrey, "Ears to Hear," *A Dictionary of Biblical Tradition in English Literature* (Grand Rapids: Eerdmans, 1992) 219-20.

4:25 is concerned first with avoiding sin, but its message is broader. One must avoid not only sin, but also anything that impedes the path to excellence (Phil 4:8): "The good is the enemy of the excellent." Only those who resolutely "put first things first"[95] gain their goal. But "a fool's eyes wander to the ends of the earth" (17:24 NIV).

95. Stephen R. Covey, *The Seven Habits of Highly Successful People* (New York: Simon and Schuster, 1989) habit number 3.

PROVERBS 5:1-23, ADULTERY AS FOLLY; MARRIAGE AS WISDOM

COMMENTARY

This parental speech contrasts adultery and marriage as the right and wrong modes of sexual love. The passage functions not only literally, but also as metaphor and illustration within Proverbs 1–9. Literally, we have a warning against adultery and a frank invitation to the erotic delights of married love, expressed in liquid images. Metaphorically, desire for someone who is not one's spouse is similar to the love of Folly, while love of Wisdom is represented by desire and delight in one's spouse. Finally, as illustration, the opposition of adultery to married love concretely shows that sin and folly cross created boundaries, while the play of eros within marriage illustrates freedom within form. Underlying these metaphors is the cosmic principle that God has set good limits to human play and freedom, just as God has set limits to the watery powers of the sea (see Commentary on 8:27-29).

Chapter 5, an instruction, begins with the usual call to hear (vv. 1-2), followed by a warning against the "loose woman" (lit., "strange woman" [זרה *zārâ*], NRSV margin) in vv. 3-14. A contrasting, metaphor-rich invitation to enjoy one's own spouse (vv. 15-19) leads to an appeal to the son to draw his own conclusions from the foregoing (v. 19). Finally, the argument is grounded theologically (vv. 20-23). God's eyes see the course of a person's life. God sees to it that habits have consequences.

5:1-2. The opening verses are a variation on the typical invitation to hear. The pairing of "my wisdom" and "my understanding" is especially important, for it suggests that the parent's wisdom communicates cosmic wisdom and understanding (8:1, the two terms

refer to aspects of one reality). Heeding the parent's wisdom will help the son in "prudence," the capacity for private thought (see Commentary on 2:10-11), and will enable his "lips" to "guard knowledge" (cf. Mal 2:7). This unusual image suggests that the organs of speech are the public guardians of the heart's deep truths. The lips, so to speak, are the border guards that allow thoughts to be released or to remain unspoken (cf. 17:27-28; 18:2; Ps 141:3). The issue here is not duplicity of our inner and outer, private and public selves (on which see 26:22-26). Rather, there are times to keep silent and times to speak (Eccl 3:7). Through their lips, fools and the wise distinguish themselves (15:1-2, 7; 18:6-7).

5:3. This verse uses "lips" as a pivot to shift from the son to the seductress. The verse as a whole is highly sensual, a fact somewhat disguised by the translation "speech" in v. 3*b* (lit., "mouth"/"palate" [חך *ḥēk*], with a pun on "lap"/"bosom" [חיק *ḥêq*]; see 5:20; Deut 28:56; Mic 7:5). One may translate, "her mouth is slicker than olive oil." The imagery is suggestive on several levels. The liquid image of lips dripping honey appears more elaborately in Cant 4:11 (cf. Cant 2:3; 5:13, 16). On one level, it refers to the "smooth talk" or "sweet talk" that flows from the woman's lips (26:28). What she says is easy to swallow; she competes with Wisdom in sweetness (24:13-14). On another level, "lips" and "mouth" evoke the liquid delights and organs of love (see Commentary on 5:15-19; 20:14; 30:20), which turn into a deadly trap when offered by the "strange woman," who is out of bounds (2:16).

The image of honey is especially telling in its ambiguity. It is not quite solid, not quite liquid. It does not hold its shape or stay in place. Its boundaries are not firm. It represents what is sweet and good (16:24; 24:13-14), and also what is addictive and potentially dangerous. To eat too much honey is not good (25:27a). Greedy flies get stuck in it, and it sticks to greedy children. Honey certainly sweetens life. But by itself, it neither makes a square meal nor quenches one's thirst. A satisfied person disdains honey (27:7). It is crucial to take only the honey that is properly yours and only the right amount for you, lest it make you sick (see Commentary on 25:16).

Consider the story of Samson (Judges 13–16), though it employs a symbol system for holiness that is not found in Proverbs. Samson was a Nazirite, separated for divine service. As a holy person, he had forsworn all that is "unclean" (Num 6:1-8). But when he got honey out of the lion's carcass, he crossed the boundary between holy and unclean, for what is dead is especially unclean. The carcass is contagious and will render the honey (good in itself) unclean. In the Samson narrative cycle, this episode mirrors Samson's unfaithfulness in getting his sexual "sweets" from ritually unclean Philistine women. But it also symbolizes Israel's sin in leaving its calling as a holy nation, while seeking its cultural "sweets" from the foreign societies around them. Samson, in language that echoes Gen 3:6, gives some of the unclean honey to his parents, who eat it (Judg 14:9).

Thus v. 3 vividly portrays the reality and the ambiguity of temptation, both to illicit love and to the love of folly, in line with the larger metaphorical system of Proverbs 1–9.

5:4. This verse follows the tale begun in v. 3 to its end. The sweet has become bitter, and slippery softness has become sharp. Literally, "her end" is bitter as wormwood, sharp as a "sword with mouths" (i.e., two-edged sword; Judg 3:16; Ps 149:6). A sword has two edges, or "mouths," that "devour" those it kills (Isa 1:20). The imagery here ironically reverses the devouring roles of deadly male sword and female mouths (literal and metaphorical). In addition, the language intersects with the "way" imagery pervasive in chaps. 1–9. To enter the "door" of the forbidden woman's body (or "house," 5:8; cf. 8:3, 34; 9:14; Job 31:9-10) is the end of the road called Folly (cf. 14:12; 16:25; 24:13-14). Her body/house

is a place of no return on a dead-end street where Sheol swallows fools alive (see Commentary on 1:12; 2:18-19; 7:27; 9:13-18).

5:5-6. The writer makes the connection of wrong woman, ways, and death explicit in these verses. "Her feet" may also be rendered "her legs" (sometimes a euphemism in Hebrew; see 2 Kgs 18:27; Isa 7:20), which themselves "go down to death" even as they lead young men on the same path. Those who walk the path of folly are blind. The woman herself wanders toward death and "does not know it" (see Commentary on 4:19). For "Sheol," see Commentary on 1:12.

5:7-14. The focus turns to the son and spells out the consequences of yielding to seduction by the "stranger" of vv. 3-6. A brief call to hear (v. 7) leads to an admonition (v. 8), followed by an extended account of the negative consequences of not heeding the warning (vv. 9-14). These consequences are both social (vv. 9-10) and psycho-spiritual (vv. 12-14), as the youth becomes remorseful about past actions whose present consequences must be lived with. Hindsight is clearer than foresight. Verse 14 perhaps affords a glimpse of grace.

5:7-8. The parent speaks with profound awareness that the sons are themselves responsible for what they do with his words (see Commentary on 8:9). They can listen, but they can also "depart from the words of [his] mouth" (a contrast to the "mouth" of the temptress). So he appeals to their growing maturity and ability to discern consequences and to take appropriate action.

Verse 8 spells out the required evasive action in the light of the highly visual nature of male sexuality (6:25; Matt 5:27-29): "Keep your way far from her." The father assumes that his son, like any immature male, may be tempted to have sex without love. He advises the son to take responsibility for this weakness (a conflict of biology and humanity) and set his course in another direction. "The door of her house" represents the threshold, the point of entry and no return. This is where one crosses the borderline and enters a new and deadly world (see Commentary on 5:4).

5:9-11. The writer warns of the social and personal consequences of trespassing limits. The "cruel" one may be the outraged husband (cf. 6:34-35) or perhaps Sheol, which devours the dead (1:12). The heaping up of masculine parallels in vv. 9-10 makes the reference indeterminate: "others"//"cruel one" [sing.]//"strangers"//"alien." It is not clear who the others are. Nor is it specified how the personal loss will take place. This open-endedness permits the reader to apply the admonition to his or her own life-world, whatever the circumstances may be. The same open-endedness appears also when the same vague adjectives ("strange"/"alien") are used to describe any woman who is not one's proper sexual partner (2:16; 5:3).

The son who transgresses sexual limits is himself responsible for loss of fortune, health, reputation, and vitality. It is not just that others take and enjoy it (v. 10; cf. Job 31:9-10), but that he foolishly gives to others what is essential to his own existence (cf. 31:3). The terms "honor," "best strength," "wealth," "years," and "labors" are also suggestive of a variety of possibilities, including venereal disease. This latter prospect is explicitly included in v. 11, "when your flesh and body are consumed." This clause, with its traditional components, may also refer literally and metaphorically to a variety of psychosomatic illnesses (cf. Job 33:21; Pss 71:9; 73:26).

5:12-14. These verses conclude this section of the instruction with a future autobiographical speech, in which the (potentially) erring son owns up to his folly. In daring fashion, the parent enters empathetically into the life-world of the son. The rhetorical strategy is hypothetical and dangerous: How does the parent know what might be in the mind of a child, especially in relation to events that are only potential? Wisdom knows that acts have consequences. You reap what you sow. The parent can "know" what the son will experience because the invented speech here reflects the pattern first described by Wisdom herself (1:24-25, 29-31).

In vv. 12-14 the son's folly is first the rejection of community "discipline" and "reproof" (see Commentary on 12:1) as mediated by parents and teachers (vv. 12-13; cf. 3:11-12 of the divine "parent"). The son's words reflect first on his behavior and conclude with its consequences: near ruin in the community (v. 14).

5:15-19. The instruction here takes a joyful turn, enjoining delight in one's wife, while continuing the warning against the strange woman. As in v. 3, sexuality is portrayed in liquid images. But a sharp contrast exists between the deadly portrait of honey and oil in v. 3 and the life-giving well and waters of married sexuality in vv. 15-19. These verses also repeat the pattern of spending personal honor and goods for "strangers" (vv. 9-10), in the image of "scattering springs . . . abroad" (vv. 16-17).

In this passage, all the water sources mentioned are parallel metaphors for "the wife," as is finally made clear in v. 18. The poem plays on the life-giving and joy-enhancing qualities of water. In arid, hot Palestine (cf. 30:16), water is exceedingly precious. Thus water flowing freely down the street is a disaster (v. 16). Water spilled is life lost.

Palestine is generally arid, especially in the south. In summer rain does not fall; all is hot and dry (26:1). Water is experienced as the very stuff of life and joy. Cisterns are usually carved out of solid rock; they are used to collect and store rain water, either for the community or (as here) for private use. The young husband may drink only from his own "cistern." A well is dug in the ground to tap the aquifer. Once dug, a well might be hotly contested (Gen 26:18-22). Wells, like cisterns and suitable wives, are hard to acquire. Cities and individuals jealously guarded their water sources in order to preserve the life of the community or family in times of war, siege, or drought. The strange woman's "honey" (v. 3) and the sweet "waters" of Lady Folly (9:17) are deadly and produce conflict precisely because they are stolen.

There is a gradual progression in the quality of water sources pictured in vv. 15-16. A cistern stores water and is liable to contamination (though cistern water is better than no water at all).[96] But a well continually receives fresh water from the aquifer and produces running or "living water" (נזלים *nōzĕlîm*). No sensible person would prefer a cistern to a "fountain of living water" (Jer 2:13 NRSV; cf. Cant 4:15). The images continue to grow in clarity and desirability. The "fountains" flow with "streams of water" (v. 16; cf. Ps 46:4; Ezek 47:1-12) and prefigure the fountains made by God (8:24). These

---

96. See "Water Works," in *Anchor Bible Dictionary*, 6 vols. (New York: Doubleday, 1992).

sequential, parallel images do not stand in contrast with each other, as if several wives were portrayed. Rather, they cumulatively picture the one wife as a personal source of life, sexual delight, blessing, and fecundity. They also reinforce the parallel of wife and wisdom (cf. "fountain" in 13:14; 14:27). The "springs" of marriage are parallel to the life-giving "springs" of creation (8:24, 29).

Verse 17 makes clear that the water sources in vv. 15-16, 18 do not refer to male fluids (cf. Sir 26:19-21) or to progeny. Some have argued that the shift from singular water sources to plural in this verse indicates a shift in subject. Instead, the plural serves to intensify the notion of abundance found in the wife (the word *water* [מים *mayim*] itself is plural in Hebrew; cf. "all my springs are in you," said of the Lord in Ps 87:7). As v. 18*b* makes explicit, the water images all refer to the wife (cf. Cant 4:12, 15). A wife is "for her [husband] alone." Sexual exclusivity is basic to human well-being in marriage, family, and society (cf. Exod 20:14). But fidelity is also essential to healthy and joyous sexual love. In the Song of Songs, this point is beautifully made by the joyous refrain, "My beloved is mine and I am his" (Cant 2:16 NRSV; 6:3; cf. Cant 6:9; 7:10; 8:12), by the imagery of "a garden locked, a fountain sealed" (Cant 4:12, 15 NRSV), and by the private vineyard (Cant 8:12).

Verses 16-17 present an implicit picture of retributive correspondence, a sort of poetic justice. The husband's (potential) unfaithfulness is answered by the wife's sexual exploitation, willingly or unwillingly, by "strangers"—that is, those who are alien to the marriage bond and its privileges (cf. v. 10). This sort of correspondence, in which the "punishment fits the crime," appears not only in wisdom literature, but also in other biblical genres (see Job 31:9-10; Amos 7:17).

The "riddle" of the water sources in vv. 15-17 is answered in v. 18 by spelling out the reference as "the wife of your youth." This fountain, when faithfully loved, is blessed—that is, a source of blessing (cf. 3:13, 18, of the man who finds Wisdom; Ps 128:3). The young man is commanded to "rejoice" (שׂמח *śāmaḥ*) in his wife. The same verb is used of mutual divine and human delight in each other and the good (Ps 104:15, 31; Cant

3:11; see also Commentary on Prov 8:30-31; cf. Isa 62:5).

The image of the beloved wife shifts to that of "a lovely deer, a graceful doe" (v. 19). The use of animal metaphors to portray lovers is universal. Song of Songs 2:8-9 uses similar figures for a male beloved, and Cant 4:5 portrays the young woman's breasts as twin fawns.[97] There is a wordplay in "may her breasts satisfy you." The Hebrew for "breasts" (דד *dad*) plays on "love" (דוד *dôd*, 7:18), while "satisfy" (רוה *rāwâ*) also connotes "drinking one's fill," an echo of the liquid images in vv. 15-18 (see Isa 60:16, where restored Israel "shall suck the breasts of kings" [NRSV]). "Be intoxicated" (שׁגה *šāgâ*) generally means "wander," "go astray" as when drunk (20:1; Isa 28:7). This verb links vv. 19, 20, and 23. Here it conveys the unfettered passion of love. Through repetition, however, it creates a contrast between marital and extra-marital love (vv. 19-20) and reinforces the parallel between love out of bounds and folly (v. 23).

5:20-23. These verses draw the moral from the preceding instructions. The language recapitulates earlier moments in the chapter (cf. v. 3 with v. 20; vv. 6, 8 with v. 21; v. 5 with v. 22; vv. 5, 12 with v. 23). In the light of married realities (vv. 15-19), the unreal pleasures of the "stranger" make no sense. So "Why be . . . intoxicated" (lit., "led astray") by "another woman" (lit., "strange" [זרה *zārâ*])? The rhetorical question invites the son to draw his own conclusions, to "own" the logic of the parental instruction. In view of the divinely approved delights of marital love, wandering is simply folly.

Verse 21 grounds the preceding wisdom in the Lord. God has created all things good, including male and female sexuality (Genesis 1; 2:18-25). But humans are accountable and transparent to their Maker, before whom even the cosmic depths lie open (15:3, 11; 16:2; 24:12; cf. Jer 16:17-18). The Lord judges human actions and ways (cf. 5:6), the myriad acts and steps that comprise a life and its fundamental direction. Finally, the parallel language of 4:26 and 5:21 reveals that divine oversight and human responsibility are correlates.

97. See Othmar Keel, *The Song of Songs* (Minneapolis: Fortress, 1994) 22-29.

The principle underlying the example of seduction is summarized in v. 22 (cf. Sir 23:16-21). People get caught in the netlike toils of their own sin, like a spider strangely stuck in the web it has spun (see 1:17-18, 31-32; cf. Job 18:7-10). The juxtaposition of vv. 21 and 22 conveys something of the mystery of God's justice. While God's are the eyes that see, and God is the one with whom we have to do, the working out of human good and evil is generally a mundane, even banal thing (see Commentary on 13:6).

The instruction concludes by returning to basic themes of discipline (self-control and self-denial for a higher good) and the threat of death for one led astray by folly (v. 19).

REFLECTIONS

1. In the Lord's Prayer, Christians pray, "Lead us not into temptation." With respect to the "strange woman," the parent specifies the human task of avoiding temptation, whatever that may be (5:8). Both the prayer and the task of watching our step are necessary. The ancient Latin proverb says, "Pray and work" (*Ora et labora*). That is, work at what you pray for, knowing that the gift of grace is often the gift of work (Phil 2:13). The particular sins we pray about and work at avoiding vary according to our position and personality. Wise recovering alcoholics avoid bars and go to AA meetings; godly traveling salespersons avoid singles bars; smart gluttons stay away from ice cream parlors; members of Congress who have integrity shun lobbyists with money (see Commentary on 17:23). If the shoe fits, wear it.

2. Chapter 5 again reflects on a person's way. Although life patterns have been traced by the feet of our forebears, each new generation and individual is responsible for making their own way in the world. Cultural or familial traditions and patterns of behavior, like paths, may help or hinder, may lead to weal or to woe. But the responsibility for choosing and the determination to walk the chosen path rest with each new generation. It may be difficult to break out of unhealthy or dysfunctional family paths. But blaming the past does not obviate present responsibility to make our own way as humans.

3. The Lord limits the potentially destructive powers of the sea by keeping its mighty waters within boundaries (8:29; see 2 Esdr 4:13-19). The shore limits the "play" of the waves. But just as when the sea surges onto land as a hurricane or typhoon, great harm is done, so also human sexuality is a great and good power that turns destructive when out of bounds. But within the safety zone of marriage the liquid play of sex is a life-generating, life-enhancing delight (5:15-19). Marriage is not an arbitrary (and thus dispensable) human invention, one of several possibilities for taking care of sexual drives, procreation, and the rearing of the next generation. In the cosmic-social terms of Proverbs 1–9 (cf. Gen 1:27-28; 2:21-24; Matt 19:3-9), marriage is a divine creation that sets the parameters within which human cultural and personal variations may take place. Similarly, the Ten Commandments, which set limits, are basic boundaries within which humans are free to function. Outside those divine, cosmic boundaries, humans cause damage to themselves and to others.

4. Some readers object to the limited portrayal of women in these chapters—either as desirable wife or as desirable temptress in relation to the son whom the parents address.[98] There is also concern that the book seems not to protest against the exploitation of women who may be forced to prostitution by social marginalization or poverty (23:26-28; see Genesis 38).[99] However, it is characteristic of the proverb genre to focus

---

98. See C. Osiek, "Reading the Bible as Women," in *The New Interpreter's Bible*, vol. 1 (Nashville: Abingdon, 1994) 181-87.

99. See Carole Fontaine, "Proverbs," in Carol A. Newsom and Sharon H. Ringe, eds., *The Women's Bible Commentary* (Louisville: Westminster, 1992) 146-47.

on one aspect of an issue and not treat all. The proverb genre often portrays evils without comment, because the reader is assumed to know they are evil (e.g., 26:20-23). Moreover, the book's appeal to God's defense of the widow, the orphan, and the poor shows that vulnerable women must be provided for and protected from exploitation (15:25; 22:16, 22-23; 23:10-11).

The book's focus on woman as wife/mother or temptress arises largely from its male-oriented symbolism of wisdom and folly (see Overview to chaps. 1–9). This focus also stems from Israel's commitment to marriage and family as created realities (Gen 2:24), a commitment that some women echo today.[100] Because these chapters are directed at males, the genesis of female prostitution and adultery is largely ignored, except in as much as male behavior makes them possible. If males heeded the parental advice to be faithful in marriage and to avoid illicit liaisons, female prostitution and adultery would obviously cease. The writer is concerned with the damage that male promiscuity can do to family, society, and self. The problem for the writer is to persuade young males not to yield to their promiscuous sexual impulses. In the same manner that dreams of illicit wealth were shattered (1:10-19), the parent exploits adolescent male fantasies of illicit sexual bliss to debunk them (7:10-27). Male sexual desire is a force that needs to be disciplined and set within the context of lifelong commitment and love (5:15-19).

100. See Osiek, "Reading the Bible as Women," 186.

EXCURSUS: DEATH AND THE STRANGE WOMAN IN PROVERBS 1–9

Who is the figure in Proverbs 1–9 designated by the parallel terms "strange woman" (אשה זרה, *'iššâ zārâ*; NRSV, "loose woman") and "alien" (נכריה, *nokriyyâ*; NRSV, "adulteress")?[101] And how are we to understand the constant connection between this woman and death (2:16-19; 5:5-6, 20; 7:5, 22-27; cf. 9:18)?

Compare the meaning of death in Proverbs 1–9 to the paradise story of the first temptation: "Of the tree of the knowledge of good and evil you shall not eat, for in the day that you eat of it you shall die" (Gen 2:17 NRSV). The tree itself, as Eve saw, is simply "good" (Gen 3:6), an echo of "God saw that it was good" in the creation story of Genesis 1. But because God has put the tree "out of bounds" with respect to eating, the good tree becomes a source of disorder and death.[102]

The "strange woman" in Proverbs 1–9 is, in the first instance, "your neighbor's wife" (see Commentary on 6:24, 29). A woman (or man) other than one's spouse, like the fruit in the garden, may be "good . . . a delight to the eyes." But she is not good as a mate for anyone other than her own husband. Her strangeness is a function of the exclusivity of the marriage relation (cf. Jer 3:25, of spiritual "adultery" with "strangers," where the foreignness of the Baals is secondary). In this (sexual) regard, the creator has placed the strange woman off-limits, out of bounds. To eat this fruit

101. See Whybray, *Proverbs,* 72-73 and bibliography.
102. See Richard D. Nelson, *Raising Up a Faithful Priest: Community and Priesthood in Biblical Theology* (Lousiville: Westminster/John Knox, 1994).

causes disorder and death (see Reflections on Proverbs 4, number 5). In the second instance, the strange woman is a metaphorical illustration of folly.

The exact (male) semantic counterpart of the "strange woman" is the "strange man" of Deut 25:5. According to the law of levirate marriage, a widow may not marry a "stranger" (איש זר *'îš zār*)—that is, someone outside the family—but is restricted to the brothers of her dead husband. The strange woman of Proverbs, like the "strange fire" offered by Aaron's sons (Lev 10:1), is something God has not "commanded" or allowed (cf. "illicit fire," Num 3:4 NRSV). Again, only the priests are allowed to touch holy things or to make offerings. With respect to these functions, even fellow Israelites are called "strangers" or "outsiders" (Num 1:51; 16:40[17:5]; 18:4 [זר *zār*, the word used in Proverbs]). This common usage of *zār* in the sense of "another," or of one who stands outside a specific relation, appears also in Prov 27:2 (cf. 6:24; 14:10; 1 Kgs 3:18; Job 19:27). The stereotypical parallel of "strange" and "alien" does not affect this usage of *zār*. God's work, when it is contrary to human expectations, is "strange" and "alien" (Isa 28:24; cf. Prov 27:2).

To step beyond the boundaries of freedom set by God is to attempt the impossible: to live outside the very conditions that make life possible. In the end, humans can no more live outside God's moral order than can the proverbial "fish out of water" live outside God's biotic order. Outside the ordinances of God we find not life but, ultimately, death. Humans have little difficulty seeing this truth in the so-called natural world. We cannot leap off a building, flap our arms, and fly. If we eat poison, we get sick or die. But humans are more easily confused in the moral sphere because of the great freedom God has entrusted to us—freedom to shape culture, language, art, and even created institutions as fundamental as marriage and family in a variety of ways. Nevertheless, a culture that thinks there are no limits to freedom finds itself in the "out of bounds" territory of death and chaos. Death is the ultimate limit to freedom. It drives us to accept reality and to find the good within its limits. It is this truth that Pharaoh was unwilling to learn, when plague after plague confronted him (Exodus 5–11).

The freedom to shape the world and our way in it has thus led to opposite errors. On the one hand, there is legalism, which attempts to prevent evil and ensure life by making laws on top of God's laws, to avoid coming close to sin. Since sex is dangerous, we will forbid dancing. Alcohol is dangerous, so we will forbid drinking. Such an approach to religion has only the appearance of wisdom; it errs when it identifies human conventions with God's will. The apostle Paul condemns it (Col 2:20-23). Much of the New Testament attacks legalism, which reduces religion to morality. Ironically, churches have often made asceticism mandatory rather than voluntary.

The modern age, however, makes an opposite error. As never before, modernity has become aware of freedom, of the human role in social formation, and of the consequent diversity of cultures. But this important insight has been accompanied by the erroneous belief that culture is purely the creation of human ingenuity. The eminent anthropologist Clifford Geertz put it this way: "Believing that . . . man is an animal suspended in webs of significance he himself has spun, I take culture to be those webs."[103] But even spiders need twigs to hang their webs on and flies to come their way and bodies made for spinning. Taken to its conclusion, this view suggests that there are no created limits, that culture is arbitrary, and that everything is permitted as a matter of personal or collective preference—a view advertisers constantly exploit.

---

103. Clifford Geertz, *The Interpretation of Cultures* (New York: Basic Books, 1973) 5. See also Peter L. Berger and Thomas Luckmann, *The Social Construction of Reality: A Treatise in the Sociology of Knowledge* (Garden City, N.Y.: Doubleday, 1966).

This collective tendency rebels against realities that limit human freedom.[104] Often arguments against such a knowable reality, which holds humans accountable, exploit the protean ambiguity dwelling on the margins of language. Yet, though language shapes humans' grasp of reality (Gen 2:19-20), only God orders a reality for Adam to name and to shape (Gen 2:21-23). Consequently, it is possible to shape reality truly or falsely.

104. See Taylor, *Sources of the Self*; G. von Rad, "The Age of Jeremiah," in *Old Testament Theology* (New York: Harper & Row, 1965) 2:212-17.

PROVERBS 6:1-19, MONEY, SLOTH, GOOD, AND EVIL

COMMENTARY

6:1-5. The focus turns from sexuality to another prime mover in human affairs: money (cf. 1:13-14). This brief instruction advises not to "put up security" for a "neighbor" ("another" [זָר *zār*] here is literally "stranger," the same term used in 5:10, 17). This warning is common in Proverbs (11:15; 17:18; 20:16 = 27:13; 22:26-27). These sayings are not against commerce and for agriculture. Rather, the issue is the wise conduct of fiscal and related affairs. (See Commentary on 11:15 for the image of "striking hands.")

While the exact mechanisms and persons involved in the financial transactions described in Prov 6:1-5 are disputed, the wisdom issues are clear and subtly treated. More is at stake than financial advice. The "son" has put himself at financial and personal risk by making a rash commitment to another. Wisdom requires that the mistakes be corrected, if possible. But at this point it is difficult even to recognize that a mistake has occurred, for negative consequences have not yet occurred. The damage is only potential, though the parent portrays the son as already caught in another's power. Wisdom requires insight into the whole situation: the nature of the investment, the character and reliability of the "neighbor" (see Commentary on 17:17-18), possible future outcomes, and the son's ability to sustain loss (22:27). Without specifying details, the parent has judged the financial transaction a mistake. The son needs to overcome his reluctance to admit error caused by shame ("humble yourself," v. 3), and to overcome the inertia of laziness, perhaps intensified by shame (cf. vv. 4 and 9-10). The mistake concerns poor judgment and a failure to maintain proper personal boundaries; the son has let himself be engulfed by the agenda and power of another, a "stranger" (see Excursus, "Death and the Strange Woman in Proverbs 1–9"). While the wicked are "caught" by their own iniquity (5:22), here the son is "caught" by foolish commitments (18:7; cf. 12:13; 24:16; 29:6; Ps 124:7).

Verse 3 urges the hapless son to regain control of his existence from the stranger to whom he has foolishly given it. In relation to others, personal responsibility is essential, as well as a clear sense of the limits of one's own "turf." This entails rejecting what lies outside the limits of our competence (including fiscal competence) and affirming what is properly ours to dispose of.

Verses 4-5 urge fiscal self-redemption. To gain financial control of one's life can be to "save" oneself (v. 5), because control of material goods is life's foundation. Moreover, our heart is where our treasure is (Matt 6:21; see Excursus, "The 'Heart' in the Old Testament"). Money matters. By denying oneself sleep (v. 4), one may gain soul, self, and life. This image anticipates the discussion of sleep and sloth that follows in vv. 9-10. But it also sets up an ironic contrast with the wicked (4:16), who often seem more shrewd and more zealous in wrongdoing than the righteous in well doing (Luke 16:8; cf. Ps 132:3-6, of David's wish to build the Temple).

6:6-11. This passage is a reproving poem addressed to the "sluggard." The lowly ant serves as a moral example. The admonition is gently humorous but ends with a stern warning. (The LXX version adds a section on the bee as well.) In Hebrew, the word for "ant" (נמלה *nĕmālâ*) is grammatically feminine and singular, a fact obscured by the NRSV and the NIV, which translate "she" as "it." This small detail reveals yet another female symbol of wisdom in Proverbs. The use of the singular is also important, for the example concerns individual responsibility (the collective nature of ant behavior is ignored). Each ant does its own job within the socio-cosmic system. In the biblical world, non-human animals are seen as creatures of God (Genesis 1–2) who inhabit and respond to the same world order that impinges upon humans. Thus their behavior serves as models and analogues for humans (30:24-28; Job 12:7-9; Isa 1:3; Jer 8:6-9). In the prophets, animals are often in better harmony with reality than are humans.

Proverbs devotes three poems to the "sluggard" (6:6-11; 24:30-34; 26:13-16) as well as scattered sayings (10:26; 13:4; 15:19; 19:24 = 26:15; 20:4; 21:25; 22:13; cf. 19:15; 31:27). The topic is clearly important. Sloth is folly by default, for the sluggard avoids the hard work done "in season," which wisdom requires (Eccl 3:1-8; Isa 28:23-29). To imitate the ant's ways makes one wise (6:6), because the ant acts in harmony with the cosmic rhythm of the seasons (6:8). The ant's diligent work is a model for the son of 10:4-5, a saying that repeats the language of 6:8 (cf. 20:4; 30:24-25).

The ant (v. 7) is proactive, a "self-starter." She needs no boss to tell her what has to be done. By being responsible for her task, she blesses her community.

The ant acts in harmony with reality, seen in the rhythm of the seasons (v. 8). Palestine has basically two seasons: the cool, rainy season (roughly October through May) and the warm, dry season, which includes three or four months of no rain at all (see Commentary on 20:4; 26:1). Harvest occurs during the dry season as crops ripen. Thus the ant's actions are not determined by present appearances, whether of bounty or of blight. Rather, she uses the present (harvest with its bounty) to provide for the future and its different circumstances (the rainy season). The ant is not beguiled by present abundance, but uses it for the future. Such a creature lives in faith that the good order of the world will continue (see Gen 8:22) and that present faithfulness will establish a future. The story of Joseph's wise administration of the abundant and lean years (Genesis 40–45) is a version of Prov 6:6-8 writ large.

Verses 9-11 begin with a warning question, "How long . . . ?" designed to prod the sluggard to wake up. The question throws the responsibility where it belongs, but gives the sluggard freedom to make up his own mind. The question, "When will you rise?" also holds out the option of personal change through action, as if to say, "You need not continue in your present impotence." The question appeals to the sluggard to "come to himself" like the prodigal son (Luke 15:17), but before the damage is done. A word to the wise is sufficient, though fools only learn from hard knocks. Sleep, like sexual desire and ambition for gain, must be kept within its proper limits, lest opportunity fly away and one come to poverty (10:5*b*; 19:15; 20:13). In other words, "Make hay while the sun shines."

Verses 10-11 are a stock couplet (see 24:33-34; cf. Eccl 4:5). It mocks the false security of a "lazy bones" in his bed (see 26:13-14), suddenly overtaken by calamity (see v. 15; 1:27). In contrast, the sleep of the wise is secure (3:24; cf. Pss 3:5-6; 4:8). Verse 11 portrays poverty and want as an armed robber. The Hebrew (איש מגן *'îš māgēn*) suggests a "highwayman" who appears when least expected (cf. 1:11; Judg 9:25; Matt 24:43) and takes by force what belongs to his victim. Ironically, the sluggard is his own victim.

6:12-19. Verses 12-15 and 16-19 are poems that sketch the inside and outside of human evil. The first poem presents bodily members as "instruments of wickedness" (Rom 6:13), while the second presents sin as what God hates. The diversity in the first list is united by its representation of a single person with a full panoply of evil acts. Verse

15 describes the disastrous consequences of the person's evil. The second poem employs a similarly diverse list of evil deeds, now united by the Lord's opposition to them. The interaction of the two poems is facilitated by repetition and parallelism, especially of the two lists of body parts (cf. 4:20-27). To the bodily members may be added two actions, for a total of seven parallels.[105] The list follows the order of vv. 17-19, which explicitly identify "seven things" abominable to the Lord:

Verses 17-19	Verses 12-14
17*a*, eyes	13*a*, eyes
17*a*, tongue	12*b*, mouth
(speech organs)	
17*b*, hands	13*b*, fingers
18*a*, heart	14*a*, heart
devising evil	devising evil
18*b*, feet	13*a*, feet
19*a*, lying	14*a*, upside-down
	deceit
19*b*, sowing discord	14*b*, sowing discord

In Hebrew, the "scoundrel" is literally a "man of *belial* [בליעל *běliyya'al*]"; so 1 Sam 25:25 KJV). The precise sense of *belial* is elusive; its significance is best gained contextually.[106] The term appears to have a mythic background in the powers of chaos, death, and Sheol (Ps 18:4-5 ["perdition," NRSV] = 2 Sam 22:5-6; Ps 41:8 ["deadly thing," NRSV]). It is applied to persons who disrupt the social and moral order (1 Sam 25:17, 25). One who neglects the poor is guilty of *belial* (Deut 15:9). Hannah fears she is mistaken for a "daughter of *belial*," when Eli thinks she is drunk in the holy tabernacle (1 Sam 1:16; cf. Lev 10:8). Psalm 101 is a "mirror for princes" in which the righteous king rejects all that is *belial* ("base," Ps 101:3). In several instances, *belial* refers to wrongdoing by legal manipulation. Honest Naboth is "legally" murdered through Jezebel's employment of false witnesses, "sons of *belial*" (1 Kgs 21:10, 13; cf. Prov 19:28). Verses 12-19 deal with legal matters, but are not restricted to them.

"Crooked speech"/"mouth" (also 4:24) heads a list of bodily agents of wrongdoing.

Such a mouth is basic equipment for the life journey ("goes about") of a *belial* person. In human affairs, there is nothing more powerful than an open mouth, whether for good or for ill (see Commentary on 18:21; cf. Sir 37:17-18; Jas 3:1-12). Greater violence can be done with the tongue than with the fist (10:11*b*; 12:18; cf. 25:15*b*). The "crooked mouth" twists reality upside down and inside out (6:14); it calls "evil good and good evil," it puts "darkness for light and light for darkness" (Isa 5:20 NRSV). "Crooked" is regularly opposed to "integrity" (11:20; 19:1; 28:6). Wicked magistrates abhor justice and make crooked what is right (Mic 3:9). The speech of Wisdom herself has nothing crooked in it (8:8). But the crooked mouth distorts reality and breaks the implicit covenant that governs our relations with our neighbor.

Three further agents of wrongdoing, "eye," "feet," and "fingers," are listed in v. 13. The actions described seem to be body language, non-verbal communication whose precise character and significance are uncertain. One scholar suggests the reference is to magical acts that damage the neighbor (cf. 10:10; Ps 35:19).[107] These signals probably refer more generally to any gesture that communicates for malevolent purposes. The Hebrew verbs for "shuffling" (מלל *mālal*) and "pointing" (מרה *mōreh*) are wordplays on "speaking" and "instructing" respectively (4:4, 11). In these verses, the agent of evil moves from the mouth (6:12) to the more elusive body language (6:13). With a shrug of the shoulders, one can deny responsibility for what one has said, as if to say, "I said nothing wrong."

Verse 14 is the climax of the first poem, for it gets at the inner source, or "heart," of human evil (see Excursus, "The 'Heart' in the Old Testament"). *Belial* persons have deceit in their hearts. (In contrast to 12:20, "deceit" [תהפכות *tahpukôt*] here is lit. "things upside down"; see Commentary on 6:12; 30:21-23.) Their inner disposition distorts reality, like a drunkard who perceives and speaks things upside down (23:33). Since evil resides in the spiritual core (heart) of such persons, wrong is not incidental, but basic to their character. They do not grow weary in wrongdoing. Their sins are not passive neglect of duty, but

105. See L. Alonso-Schökel and J. Vilchez, *Proverbios* (Madrid: Ediciones Cristiandad, 1984) 213-15.
106. See Nicholas J. Tromp, *Primitive Conceptions of Death and the Nether World in the Old Testament* (Rome: Pontifical Biblical Institute, 1969) 125-28.

107. William McKane, *Proverbs: A New Approach*, OTL (Philadelphia: Westminster, 1970) 325.

the active "devising [of] evil" (see v. 18; Mic 2:1-3).

Verse 15 portrays the sudden demise of the *belial* person in stock terms (cf. 1:26; 3:25; 29:1*b* = 6:15*b*). The calamity without remedy "descends" (יבוא *yābôʾ*, "comes") like the warrior in 6:11. The persons and mechanisms that underlie this retribution for wickedness are not spelled out. In the monotheistic world picture of Proverbs, the Lord is the ultimate guarantor of justice. If there were any doubt about this, the following poem presents the Lord in fundamental opposition to wickedness. The implicit logic here is that of Mic 2:1-3, which portrays the Lord as devising evil in response to those who have first devised wickedness against their neighbors.

Verses 16-19 are an extended numerical saying of the form N/N + 1. This simple pattern of two numbers in sequence is common in the ancient world. It was popular with the ancient Canaanite poets of Ugarit, who wrote nearly a millennium before the editing of Proverbs (cf. 30:15-31; Amos 1:3–2:8).[108] The effect is something like saying, "Not only this, but also that."

Outside of Proverbs, the term "abomination" (תועבה *tôʿēbâ*) is used mostly in connection with Yahweh (see Commentary on 3:32; 11:1). The wisdom writers use it to refer also to human relations. What the Lord hates here is bodily members turned from their good use to the service of wrongdoing.

"Haughty eyes" (v. 17) fail to balance the glory of humankind (God's viceroy over the earth, Psalm 8) with a realistic humility. Similarly, pride was considered the chief of the seven cardinal sins in medieval Christian theology. But lowered eyes before a superior are a universal gesture of shame, modesty, or proper humility. One does not look God in the eye (Exod 33:20, 23; cf. Gen 32:30; John 1:18). Yet humans can "lift up their eyes" to God and expect that God will take them seriously and deal with them kindly (Psalm 123; cf. Ps 61:2-3). In the face of sin and death, and of humanity's limited wisdom and radical dependence on God, supercilious pride is out of place. Humans have difficulty even in understanding their own ways and heart

108. See "The Legend of King Keret," in Pritchard, *Ancient Near Eastern Texts*, 142-49.

(Jer 17:9-10). But the Lord, who does know human hearts, "brings down haughty eyes" (Ps 18:27; cf. Ps 131:1; Isa 2:11; Jer 23-24; Sir 23:4).

The juxtaposition of "haughty eyes" with a "lying tongue" (also 12:19; 21:6; 26:28) is suggestive. Liars disdain reality, which they misrepresent, and other people as being unworthy of being told the truth. The lying tongue, like a weapon (25:18), damages both the external world and other people, because humans act upon representations of reality embedded in speech. Psalms 64:2-6 and 109:2-19 provide excellent examples of this evil dynamic at work. False legal accusations (cf. Prov 6:19; Ps 25:18; 1 Kgs 21:8-14) and seemingly pious curses (cf. 26:2; Ps 109:17) against the neighbor are mainstays of verbal evil (cf. also 10:18; 12:22; 17:7).

"Hands that shed innocent blood" (v. 17*b*) parallels "feet that hurry to run to evil" (v. 18*b*; cf. 4:27). Together, these lines are an expansive echo of 1:16. Evil possesses an impulsive energy arising from a crooked will to power, "a heart that devises wicked plans" (see Commentary on 4:23; 6:14). Evil also does wrong to the innocent, who do not deserve it (cf. Ps 109:2-5).

Verse 19*a* is repeated in 14:5*b* (cf. 14:25; 25:18; Exod 20:16; Ps 27:12). While a false witness may appear in any arena of life, its defining setting is the law court. Israelite justice at different times and places was variously administered by local elders, royal officials, and priestly functionaries. But the role of witnesses in establishing guilt and innocence was basic. To prevent false testimony, multiple witnesses were stipulated (Deut 19:15-21). But the sad tale of Naboth's vineyard shows that this legal safeguard did not always succeed, particularly when the powerful and the wicked were in collusion (1 Kgs 21:8-14). A number of tales recount how judicial wisdom is able to expose the false witness (1 Kgs 3:16-28; Susanna).

The various vices listed in vv. 16-19 culminate in "sows discord in a family" (lit., "incites quarrels among brothers"; see 6:14; 16:28). Evil disrupts the natural bonds of society—family, clan, tribe—and the secondary bonds that evolve as society becomes more differentiated. "Quarrels" (מדון *mādôn*) can refer to various sorts of conflict (cf. 21:9, 19, of marital conflict), but the primary reference here is to litigation, that last resort in settling the conflicts generated by human wrongdoing (cf. 26:21). "Brother" (אח *'āḥ*) is a term with a wide range in ancient Hebrew. It refers not only to male siblings but also to extended kinship relations. Thus the naming of Israel's tribes after twelve siblings communicates that all Israelites are brothers (cf. Exod 2:11; Deut 15:12). By extension, "brother" can also refer to persons bound to one another in voluntary associations, ranging from friendship (2 Sam 1:26) to political and economic pacts (1 Kgs 9:13; 20:32-34; Amos 1:9). Yet, (il)legal conflict can also arise among siblings, especially in matters of inheritance, as in the stories of Esau and Jacob (Gen 25:19-34; 27:1–28:9; 32:1-17); of Absalom and Amnon, with its bloody repercussions (2 Samuel 13–18); and of the Solomonic accession to the throne (1 Kings 1–2). A fine example of legal conflict over inheritance is found in Hesiod's archaic Greek wisdom book *Works and Days,* which tells the tale of Hesiod's dispute with his brother Perses.

REFLECTIONS

1. Proverbs constantly reminds us that the arena in which wisdom and folly contend is this world, with its goods and powers. According to Proverbs 1–9, the way we use our material resources, particularly our sexuality and our money, reveals either godly wisdom or its lack: "Money talks." The matters in which our spirituality is most commonly manifested are the goods and activities of ordinary life outside of worship (see Commentary on 31:30).

2. Laziness is a subset of folly and the opposite of wisdom. The sluggard is out of tune with the cosmic rhythms of reality. The sluggard does not realize that human existence is historical, that circumstances change, that opportunities pass, and that one must act in the present to ensure one's well-being in the future.

3. The juxtaposition of Prov 6:12-15 and 6:16-19 is significant. It suggests that sin involves a combination of reality-rejection, active malice, and a rejection of the Lord as the creator and master of reality. Scripture portrays several such evil characters. Perhaps the archetypal figure is the pharaoh of Exodus, in his tyrannical persecution of the Israelites, his tenacious refusal to face the reality of the plagues, the "hardening" of his own heart, and his denial of the Lord (Exod 5:2)—all this in spite of plague upon plague designed to make him know who the Lord is (Exodus 5–11). Another is the king of Babylon (Isa 14:4-20). Because such figures are both malicious (Prov 10:12) and at odds with reality, they incite conflict wherever they go (Prov 6:14*b*, 19*b*; 16:28). When they possess great power and position, they wreak devastation on the earth among humans, as Stalin and Hitler in the twentieth century show.

PROVERBS 6:20-35, TEACHING AGAINST ADULTERY

COMMENTARY

This section opens with an appeal to keep the parent's "commandment" and "teaching," followed by praise of the same to motivate the appeal. The passage then turns to its specific topic, adultery. The previous section (6:1-19) had provided a kaleidoscopic view of human wickedness; the present section focuses on that sin that, for the author of Proverbs 1–9, symbolizes the essence of human folly: unfaithfulness and the destructive desire for good things "out of bounds." For Proverbs, this sin represents turning away from wisdom to folly.

Undergirding this representation is the insight that wisdom and the Lord are intimately related (1:7; 9:10). Thus being unfaithful to one's spouse (and so to wisdom) is tantamount to ignoring God and God's ways for humans. The lesson against adultery in vv. 23-35 can stand by itself. But its full import is sensed only within the larger, bipolar metaphoric system concerning opposed ways, women, and houses. The literal teaching on adultery and the larger metaphorical message reinforce each other. This message may be summed up as: freedom within form, life within law, and love within limits.

6:20-23. The instruction begins with an admonition to keep the father's "commandment" and the mother's "teaching." Both parents have the authority and responsibility to instruct young males (31:1). "Commandment" and "teaching" (תורה *tôrâ* can also mean "law") are terms usually associated with Israel's legal traditions. Here they are wisdom terms denoting parental authority to command and to instruct. Yet the passage develops these ambiguous terms in a way that evokes the Decalogue's prohibition against adultery, theft, and coveting (Exod 20:14-15, 17) as well as its admonition to honor one's parents (Exod 20:12; cf. Deut 5:16-21). This implicit appeal to the divine law is strengthened by verbal and conceptual parallels between Prov 6:20-23 and Deut 6:1-9. Proverbs 6:23 also borrows the language of light from Ps 119:105 in praise of the divine law/word (cf. Ps 19:7-8). Thus underlying parental authority in Prov 6:20-35 is an implicit appeal to the divine law given through Moses. This contrasts with the usual grounding of parental teaching in cosmic wisdom (see Commentary on 2:1-22; 3:1-3). In sum, the highly allusive language of 6:20-35 connects its parental wisdom to the Mosaic law (*tôrâ*), which is also Israel's "wisdom" (Deut 4:5-8). Parental authority always has a norm above and beyond itself, to which it must appeal and to which it is accountable. For Proverbs that norm may be cosmic wisdom or, in this case, the "law" of Moses.

Verse 21 uses images of bodily ornamentation similar to those in Deut 6:8 and Prov 3:3. The parent's teaching finds its home in the hidden "heart" (see Excursus, "The 'Heart' in the Old Testament"), as well as on the "neck," where it is publicly visible in the form of actions. Moreover, this teaching is to be an abiding reality in the son's life, ever present like a wedding band.

Verse 22 exactly parallels Deut 6:7 in its sequence of walking, lying down, waking. The last two terms form a merism—that is, two opposites used to indicate totality. All of life's activities are under the umbrella of the parental/divine teaching. Parental teaching here is personified (cf. 2:11; 4:5-9); "she" guides, watches over, and talks to the son.

Verse 23*a* is richly ambiguous and allusive. In its context, it picks up "commandment" and "teaching" from v. 20 (caught by the NIV's "these"/"this"). But "teaching" is *tôrâ*, or "law," as well. As it stands, this half verse describes the commandment and teaching in metaphors identical to Psalm 119's description of the divine word: "Your word is a *lamp* to my feet and a *light* to my path" (Ps 119:105 NRSV, italics added; cf. Ps 19:8). Thus v. 23*a* helps to evoke the divine *tôrâ* underlying the parental *tôrâ*. Although the parental "law" is a light, it also sets limits on youthful conduct, the "reproofs of discipline" that keep one on the "way of life" (cf. 4:11; 10:17; 15:24; for "way" and "light," see 4:18).

6:24. The NRSV translation "wife of another" (lit., "neighbor" [רע *rēaʿ*, whose consonants also can mean "bad," "immoral"]) is preferable to the NIV's "immoral woman" for several reasons. First, the parallel term is "foreign" (NRSV, "adulteress"). Second, the bound grammatical relation of "woman"/"wife" to "neighbor"/"bad" (*rēaʿ*/ רע *raʿ*) in every other biblical instance (12 times) refers to the neighbor's wife. Third, vv. 26 and 29 provide the variant "wife of another." Finally, vv. 24-25 allude to the Mosaic command against coveting the neighbor's wife. The adulterous wife of another captures hearts by "smooth talk," by her beauty, and by the silent speech of her eyes (v. 25; cf. Sir 26:9, 11). The use of eye makeup in the ancient Near East is well known through art and archaeological finds of cosmetic palettes and tools. Jezebel prepared for the arrival of Jehu by making up her eyes (2 Kgs 9:30).

6:25. The admonition "Do not desire" ("covet") combines with "neighbor's wife" from v. 24 to form an echo of "Do not covet your neighbor's wife" in the Ten Commandments (Exod 20:17; Deut 5:21). Jesus takes up the phrase "in your heart" when he radicalizes the command against adultery (Matt 5:28).

6:26. The Hebrew of v. 26a is uncertain. The NIV and the NRSV give two possibilities: A prostitute brings one down to poverty (NIV), or she can be had at a small price (NRSV). The verse's point is found in the second line, which employs the logic of "how much more so." If prostitution is costly and damaging, adultery is even more so. Adultery can cost one's life. It is akin to theft, as the next verses (vv. 30-31) indicate.

6:27-29. These verses are a series of rhetorical questions (cf. Amos 3:3-6; 6:12) to suggest the absurdity of adultery and the impossibility of "not getting burned."

6:30-35. Here the writer compares adultery to thievery and spells out the inevitable disaster that awaits the adulterer. But sexual "theft" is a more destructive breach of faith than is the stealing of material goods. Material goods can be restored, but the adulterer "destroys himself" (v. 32; cf. 1 Cor 6:18). An offended husband's jealousy and fury (v. 34; cf. 27:4) will not be placated.

REFLECTIONS

1. Israel's culture is largely oral; without reference books, only what has been kept in memory is truly known. The teaching is so deeply internalized that it becomes part of the inner dialogue that forms the self. Willy-nilly, for better or worse, even today parental discourses make up the inner, authoritative voice with which children must deal, positively or negatively, over the course of a lifetime. But the parental voice presented here is grounded in the divine Word and law.

2. The end of chapter 6 resumes the theme of sexual fidelity in marriage. The writer uses theft of material goods as the foil for speaking of that transgression of limits, that invasion of a neighbor's "turf," which is adultery. As in some forms of "family-systems therapy," the concept of appropriate boundaries is crucial to the worldview and "personview" of Proverbs (see Commentary on Proverbs 8).[109]

This lesson is crucial because self-limitation (discipline) and deliberate acceptance of interpersonal and cosmic limits are basic to biblical wisdom. When humans practice self-discipline in relation to created goods and other persons (sex, food, sleep, exercise, work, play, speech), it promotes self-knowledge, self-mastery, and, paradoxically, freedom. Bonhoeffer saw this clearly in his poem "Stations on the Way to Freedom":

Self-discipline
If you set out to seek freedom,
    you must learn before all things
Mastery over sense and soul,
    lest your wayward desirings,
Lest your undisciplined members
    lead you now this way, now that way.
Chaste be your mind and your body,
    and subject to you and obedient,
Serving solely to seek their appointed goal and objective.
None learns the secret of freedom
    save only by way of control.[110]

---

109. See Harriet G. Lerner, *The Dance of Anger: A Woman's Guide to Changing the Patterns of Intimate Relationships* (New York: Harper & Row, 1985).

110. Reprinted by permission of Simon & Schuster from *Ethics* by Dietrich Bonhoeffer, translated from the German by N. H. Smith. English trans. copyright © 1955 by SCM Press, Ltd. Copyright © 1955 by Macmillan Publishing Company.

Self-denial (to use a NT formulation, Mark 8:34) is an implicit recognition that life must be lived within limits not created by us for purposes not invented by us and that life ends in death. It is fundamental to following Christ, the paradoxical wisdom of God.

3. In this section, the language continues to be directed at males. In addition, for didactic reasons (see Overview on Proverbs 1–9), the roles in which women appear continue to be limited to sexual partner in or out of marriage (see Commentary on 5:15-19; chap. 7). Clearly, this does not exhaust the multiplicity of roles in which women function not only in ancient Israel, but also in the modern world. Some biblical glimpses of role diversity for competent women with authority appear in Prov 31:10-31 and in biblical stories such as those about Deborah, the judge and prophetess (Judges 4–5), and Huldah, the prophetess (2 Kgs 22:14-20). According to Carol Meyers, apart from the minority urban population, Israelite life was largely agricultural and did not exhibit significant gender polarization.[111]

In order to balance the male priority in this portion of Scripture, in addition to exploring passages that show women in diverse roles, it is necessary to remember those biblical passages that express mutuality in marriage and sexuality (see Commentary on 31:10-31). The young woman's refrain in the Song of Songs comes to mind: "My beloved is mine and I am his" (Cant 2:16 NRSV; 6:3; 7:10). Again, Paul wrote, "The wife does not have authority over her own body, but the husband does; likewise *the husband does not have authority over his own body, but the wife does*" (1 Cor 7:4 NRSV, italics added; cf. Eph 5:21). Most fundamentally, the creation of male and female in God's image grounds the dignity of both (Gen 1:26-28).

111. Carol L. Meyers, "Everyday Life: Women in the Period of the Hebrew Bible," in Carol A. Newsom and Sharon H. Ringe, eds., *The Women's Bible Commentary* (Louisville: Westminster, 1992) 249-50; see also Myers, *Discovering Eve: Ancient Israelite Women in Context* (New York: Oxford University Press, 1988).

PROVERBS 7:1-27, A TALE OF SEDUCTION AND DEATH

COMMENTARY

This exquisitely crafted instruction contains a vivid cautionary tale (vv. 6-23) set within a frame of a parental call to hear (vv. 1-5) and a concluding warning with a call to hear (vv. 24-27; see 8:32-36; 7:24*a* = 8:32*a*). The passage resumes the warning against adultery in the last chapter (6:24-35). The seductress is juxtaposed to Lady Wisdom (chap. 8) to intensify the double opposition of wisdom/folly and wife/seductress, which pervades chapters 1–9.

The parent quotes the smooth words of a temptress (vv. 14-20) and uses verbal echoes of the first parental speech (1:10-19), which had quoted male tempters (1:11-14). Thus the first and last parental instructions are parallel and form an envelope around the parental speeches. This parallelism suggests again that sin and folly are the issue, not gender per se (see Commentary on 2:12, 16; 4:10-19). The main character in chap. 7 is the adulterous woman, who represents Folly, in contrast to Lady Wisdom in chap. 8. With Proverbs 7, the parental instructions come to an end. The prologue of Proverbs climaxes in Wisdom's own voice (chap. 8) and concludes with the opposed voices of Wisdom and Folly in chap. 9.

7:1-5. Verse 1 parallels the language of Ps 119:11: "I treasure [store up] your word in my heart" (NRSV). The similar expressions concerning the parental and the divine "word" and "commandments" continue the perspective of 6:20-23. The parent's words are not the divine Word, but they are faithful reflections of it and are thus a means of life (v. 2 echoes 4:4). The "binding" imagery of v. 3 appeared earlier (3:3; 6:21) and reflects the practice of binding the law upon one's person. "Fingers" and "heart" (v. 3) denote the external, acting person and the inner, secret self respectively. And while the parent's words echo the law, they are more immediately connected to wisdom and to understanding, which are personified here as the object of love (v. 4). "Sister" and "kinsman" (NIV; see Ruth 2:1; 3:2; Cant 4:9; 5:1; Tob 7:15) are tender terms addressed to a bride or wife.

The urging to "Wisdom" as a "sister"/ "bride" and "kinsman" (v. 4), provides the clue that the seductive adulteress in vv. 6-23 functions as more than just a moral object lesson against adultery. The contrast of Wisdom/bride as a love object maintains the bipolar symbol system of the prologue (see Overview on Proverbs 1–9).

Verse 5 states the teaching's purpose, repeating 2:16 and 6:24 with slight variation (cf. 5:3, 20). Again, the repetition reinforces the symbol system. A "slick mouth" is an identifying characteristic of the "strange woman" (2:16; 5:3; 6:24; 7:21). It is probably a mistake to try to establish one, totally consistent identity for the "strange woman" in the prologue.[112] She is something of a composite picture, showing traits of the harlot, of the adulterous wife, and perhaps on occasion even of a literal foreigner, whose husband is a traveling merchant ("Canaanite" can refer either to an original inhabitant of the land or to a "merchant"; cf. 31:24). That she is a cultic prostitute devoted to a goddess of love is too much to conclude from the vows and sacrifices in 7:14. The problem of the worship of foreign cults does not appear as a significant issue in these chapters.

Rather, the common feature in all the appearances of the strange woman is that she is sexually and spiritually out of bounds. This constitutes her "strangeness," her violation of the created order of marriage. A wise "son" will recognize her in any of her guises. Later (v. 21), her seductive words will ironically be described as "teaching" ("persuasive words"), to contrast with parental "teaching" ("learning," 1:5; 4:2; 9:9) on behalf of Wisdom.

7:6-9. The parent's speech is introduced in stylized autobiographical fashion.[113] The parent, perhaps the mother, watches a disaster in the making from the window of her house. (The LXX, with its third-person feminine verbs, seems to have the seductress looking out of the window. There may be a type-scene of a royal woman looking out the window; cf. Judg 5:28; 2 Sam 6:16; 2 Kgs 9:30. If a royal type-scene underlies this passage, it may suggest a queen mother; cf. 31:1-9.)[114] With symbolic key words, the naive young man is said to take "the road to her house" (v. 8), thus disobeying 4:15. He does so as day becomes night and twilight descends into darkness (v. 9; cf. 4:18-19). In the dark, boundaries are blurred, and people do "not know" what they do (v. 23; see Commentary on 5:6). The implication of these allusive references to earlier teaching is that the young man is naive and lacks sense (lit., "heart"), because he has not taken parental instruction to heart (see Commentary on 4:4).

7:10-13. These verses describe the woman in action, with language that reinforces her symbolic role as foil to Wisdom/ wife. She is "loud" (המיה *hōmiyyâ*), a term in Proverbs that appears only of the "foolish woman" (9:13) and of the bustling streets where Wisdom speaks (1:21). She goes out to meet the young man as an aggressor, "wily of heart." She wears a "prostitute's" garb. This does not indicate her profession but her crafty purpose (cf. Gen 38:14-15 and below). "Her feet/legs do not stay at home/in her house" (v. 11). The alternate translations are literal. The term for "legs" (רגלים *raglayim*) anticipates the purpose of her roaming, for "legs" is a common euphemism for private parts (Judg 3:24; 2 Kgs 18:27; Isa 7:20). Moreover, that she does not stay in her house suggests symbolically that she has left the sexual place proper to her as a married woman (see Commentary on 2:18; 5:4; 7:19; Reflections on Proverbs 9 for the symbolism of the "house"; cf. 7:19; 27:8, which are applied to "men"). She bustles about precisely where Wisdom gives her call, precisely where the young husband was warned not to let his waters run: in the street and squares (v. 12; see 1:20; 5:16). She lies in wait, like the robbers of 1:11.

---

112. See Gale Yee, "'I Have Perfumed My Bed with Myrrh': The Foreign Woman (*'iššāh zārāh*) in Proverbs 1–9," *JSOT* 43 (1989) 53-68.
113. See Tremper Longman III, *Fictional Akkadian Autobiography: A Generic and Comparative Study* (Winona Lake: Eisenbraun's, 1991).

114. McKane improbably suggests Wisdom herself. See McKane, *Proverbs*, 335-36.

Sexually, both men and women are meant to dine at home (see 30:20).

7:14. Her actual words may or may not be false (cf. v. 13 with 21:28-29). She claims to have settled her religious obligations of vows and fellowship offerings, which must take place in a state of ritual purity. This is perhaps an indirect way of communicating her sexual availability (cf. 2 Sam 11:2, 4, where Bathsheba "sanctifies herself from her impurity"). In any case, the irony is great: She has presumably made herself right with God and now is ready to violate her sacred marital covenant through committing adultery (see Commentary on 2:16-19).[115] A "fellowship offering" leads to a feast, for the meat of this sacrifice was eaten and shared. But the issue here is not a sacred meal (the meal takes place after the sacred activities); rather, sex is on her mind. Having paid her "vows" and "sacrifices" means she is free, it seems, to have a feast and a liaison.[116]

7:15-17. Words of flattery to the young fool suggest he is the "only one" she wants. However, "seeking" and "finding" are characteristic of Wisdom, of Folly, and of their respective lovers; humans are in a courtship dialectic with either one or the other (v. 15; cf. 1:28; 2:4; 3:13; 8:17, 35). Not only does she offer food and sex (cf. 30:20), but also the sort of wealth that belongs properly to Wisdom in the form of exotic foreign furnishings (for the bed, of course) and the perfumes of love (vv. 16-17; cf. 31:21-22, 24; Ps 45:8; Cant 3:6; 4:12-14; 5:1).

7:18-20. The strange woman's language is a twisted echo of the legitimate love delights in 5:19-20, which anticipates chap. 7 by warning of the stranger. With the ancient equivalent of "out of sight, out of mind," she tells the youth that her husband is not in his house but has gone on a long "road," and will not "come into his house" (both dwelling and woman's body, since the verb connotes

intercourse) until the new moon (see v. 8; 27:8).

7:21-23. With a series of animal images—ox, stag, bird—the youth on the prowl for a girl heads instead to the slaughter. He had fancied himself a hunter ready to pierce his prey. Instead, he is himself hunted, "pierced," and caught, totally unawares. The animal images convey the youth's loss of his humanity; he has abandoned the wisdom that enables him to be human, to know what he is getting into (v. 23). Sin here is blameworthy folly, a deliberate ignorance of consequences. Although the young man is portrayed as a senseless beast, usually even animals know better (1:17-18: cf. Isa 1:3; Jer 8:6-7).

7:24-27. These verses are a summarizing warning and call to listen. It draws the moral from the cautionary tale: Keep your "heart" (the center of your selfhood) from her "ways." Learn from the victims who have gone before! Her "house" is the way to Sheol, going down to the chambers of death (v. 27).[117] Sheol, then, is a subterranean house whose chambers are filled with death.[118] This conclusion of the parental speeches powerfully draws together the symbols of woman, house, way, and cosmos (Sheol, the underworld) and so prepares the way for Wisdom's cosmic discourse in chap. 8 (cf. 1:12-13; 2:18-19; 5:5, 8; 9:18). At stake in the symbolism of women, ways, and houses is the very structure of the universe itself, a world where life is a journey (way) motivated by love for either Wisdom or Folly, whose end is life or death. The conditions for life in this world are thus: freedom within form, love within limits, and life within law. To try to live outside the (moral) order of existence is to enter the realm of death. The expression "chambers of death" reinforces the imagery of body and house (see Commentary on 18:8; 20:27).

---

115. See Hugenberger, *Marriage as Covenant,* 296-302.
116. For another view, see K. van der Toorn, "Prostitution (Cultic)," *Anchor Bible Dictionary,* 5:511.

117. The combination of "ways" and "her house" in 7:27*a* needs no emendation. Cf. Job 38:19-20.
118. For the cosmos as a metaphorical house with chambers, see Commentary on 9:1; 24:3-4; see also Job 9:9; 37:9. The "chamber" is also the place of lovemaking; cf. Judg 15:1; 1 Kgs 1:15; Ps 45:13; cf. also Ps 19:4-5, with its cosmic images (though a different term for "chamber").

REFLECTIONS

1. In this autobiographical instruction, the parent says, in effect, "This is what I have seen; learn from my observation and experience." The speech is an artistic "fiction," for the parent does not have access to the woman's intimate words or to the outcome of the tryst. Sometimes the literary genre of fiction, as in Ecclesiastes, best tells the truth about reality. The autobiographical form also models the passing on of experience from generation to generation. Those who are older offer the fruits of their living, hearing, remembering, and communal reflection to a younger generation of persons who have not lived long enough to learn for themselves what only life can teach (see Reflections on Proverbs 4).

2. This chapter presents an ancient, archetypal portrait of a *femme fatale* (see Commentary on 11:16). However, Proverbs 7 does not try to make a general statement about women's sexuality. Any attempt to stereotype women based on this specific portrait is mistaken, for Proverbs also portrays the woman as Wisdom and as a capable wife.

The literal point of chap. 7 is that sexually volatile men must learn to master their desires and fantasies, and not be overcome by them. For Proverbs, marriage is the relationship of commitment within which sexual freedom and delight are to be found (5:15-19). The metaphorical point of chap. 7 is that humans should avoid Folly and seek Wisdom instead. Because sexuality is such a powerful force in male experience, it serves in Proverbs as a paradigm for that self-limitation that human beings need in relation to all earthly goods. In New Testament terms, "There is great gain in godliness combined with contentment" (1 Tim 6:6 NRSV).

PROVERBS 8:1-36, WISDOM'S COSMIC SPEECH

COMMENTARY

The great poem of cosmic Wisdom falls into seven subsections of five verses each. These five-verse units then combine to form the larger structures of the poem:

vv. 1-5, Introduction: Location and Addressees
vv. 6-26, Wisdom's Priceless Virtues
    vv. 6-11, Her Righteous Words
    vv. 12-16, Her Role in Civil Order
    vv. 17-21, Her Gifts for All Who Love Her
vv. 22-31, Wisdom and the Creation of the Cosmos
    vv. 22-26, Her Genesis Before Creation
    vv. 27-36, Her Role in Cosmic Order
vv. 32-36, Final Invitation and Warning

Proverbs 8:11, in the third person, and 8:13*a* are editorial additions. Proverbs 8:29*a* is thematic and not an editorial expansion (although the LXX lacks it). Rather, the tricola in 8:29-30 are climactic. Verses 1-5 combine a description of Wisdom's location and her first words, but these establish all humans as her audience. Proverbs 8:6 then begins with the usual call to hear.

8:1-5. This section presents Wisdom as virtually omnipresent in the human city: on the heights, in the streets, at the crossroads, and especially at the gates. It was at the gate, in ancient cities, that people would come and go, congregate, and conduct the business of life. There, folks could buy and sell, settle disputes, and arrange marriages (vv. 1-3; cf 1:20-21; Ruth 4:1-12). The city gate is the place for justice (Deut 21:19; 2 Sam 15:1-6; cf. Job 29:7-25). Here, the wise "open their mouths" (24:7) and prophets advise kings (1 Kgs 22:10). These "openings" of the city are places of encounter, where life's basic transactions and transitions occur. Here decisions are made and people "enter into" new situations and embark on new journeys. Where thresholds are crossed and the issues of life are decided, there Wisdom takes her stand and speaks. But so does Folly (7:11-12; 9:13-15).

Personified wisdom (חכמה *ḥokmâ*) is more precisely specified by its parallel term, understanding (תבונה *těbûnâ*). "Understanding" designates the practical competence, or know-how, by which actions are accomplished (see Commentary on 3:19-20; 24:3-4).[119] This term anticipates the active role of Lady Wisdom in "building" creation (8:27-31; 3:19; cf. Ps 136:5; Jer 10:12; 51:15; see Commentary on 9:1).

Through its vocabulary and phrases, the poem in Proverbs 8 establishes links with other parts of Proverbs 1–9 and with the book as a whole. Most of the key terms in the densely compacted prologue (1:1-7) reappear, sprinkled throughout Wisdom's speech (8:1-36; cf. 1:4 and 8:12; 1:7 and 8:13*a*). Such verbal links communicate that the book's teaching is grounded in cosmic wisdom.

The "body" language of vv. 1-3 suggests that "city" also belongs to the metaphorical interaction of "way," woman's "body," woman's "house" (see Commentary on 8:24; 9:1; cf. Ps 127:1), and "cosmos." Both the wise and the foolish women are located in the "openings" of the city or house. So women are not identical with the city or house (or cosmos) but inhabit it and speak from within it. Folly and Wisdom inhabit the same world, and they affect the son's experience of the world for good or for ill, because his relation to the women reflects his relation to reality and its goods. To enter the "doors" of the wrong woman's body or house is to leave the path of life and enter Sheol, the underworld realm of death and damage (see Commentary on 2:18-19; 5:5-6; 7:25-27). On the other hand, to embrace Wisdom is to embrace reality and life (8:17-21, 34-35); her house contains a life-giving feast (9:1-6). In this, too, the houses reveal the structure of the cosmos, with its places, persons, and activities

permitted or forbidden, life-enhancing or stultifying. The women (good or bad) represent the ordered or disordered goods of the cosmos, those that are legitimate and those that are off-limits and deadly.

In its own way, then, this poem continues to play the "intricate game with 'house' and 'way'" so prominent in Proverbs 7.[120] Lady Wisdom is the foil to the seductress of chap. 7, an opposition repeated again in chap. 9. The symbolic equivalences among "city," "woman," and "Wisdom" as cosmic order are now fully operative. The "crossroads" where Wisdom takes her stand is literally "the house of ways" (בית נתיבות *bêt nětîbôt*; cf. 7:27). The heaping up of terms for entrances to the city ("gates," "entrance," "portals") uses words elsewhere used of the openings of the strange woman's body/house. In 8:3 (the NRSV unnecessarily emends the text to read "in front of the town"), the Hebrew actually calls the city gate the "mouth of the town" (פי־קרת *pî-qāret*; see Commentary on 22:6). "Portals" (פתחים *pětāḥîm*) is literally "openings," a term used for both the entrance into the strange woman's deadly "house" (5:8; see Commentary on 5:4; 9:14; 30:20; cf. 31:26) and the entrance into Wisdom's house of life (8:34-35; cf. Sir 14:22-27).

In sum, the city is the culture-shaped world of humans, a reflection in miniature of the world itself where Lady Wisdom has been active from the beginning (8:22-31), and where she presently speaks to all humans (8:4, 31) in their condition of moral and spiritual ambiguity (8:5; see Commentary on 9:1).[121] Here, as throughout chaps. 1–9, human beings are represented under the figure of young men ready for wife and Wisdom, yet prone to illicit loves. The point is that Wisdom speaks everywhere, to everyone with ears to hear. In this she is much like the mysterious voice of divine origin that "goes out through all the earth" (Ps 19:1-4 NRSV), reveals God's righteousness, and finds expression in Israel's *tôrâ* (v. 4; cf. Pss 50:6; 97:6;

119. Michael V. Fox, "Terms for Wisdom," *Zeitschrift für Altthebräistik* 6 (1993) 149-69, see esp. 153, 158.

120. Robert Alter, *The Art of Biblical Poetry* (New York: Basic Books, 1985) 60.

121. In house and city building, a person "must create his own world and assume the responsibility of maintaining and renewing it. . . . The house . . . is the universe that man constructs for himself by imitating the paradigmatic creation of the gods, the cosmogony." So M. Eliade, *The Sacred and the Profane: The Nature of Religion* (New York: Harcourt Brace Jovanovich, 1959) 56-57, see also 172-79.

Rom 1:18-20; 2:14-15).[122] Whatever Wisdom is, no one can claim not to have heard her voice. Like the Stoic personification of virtue, "she is open to all, admits all, and invites all."[123] Wisdom, as God's agent, speaks in and through the creation and its creatures, which all give indirect testimony to her norms (cf. Job 12:7-10; Isa 28:23-29; Jer 8:7-9).[124] In contrast to the other speeches in chaps. 1–9, Wisdom specifies her addressees as all humans, but especially naive ("simple") and foolish people, who may yet change (8:3-5; cf. 1:22).

8:6-21. These verses (along with vv. 22-31) are Wisdom's self-presentation. Self-praise seems strange to Westerners today, for whom it seems immodest and naive. But the function of such speech is like a modern résumé, in which people present their qualifications for a position. Not to know Wisdom leaves one open to choosing Folly. Through her self-presentation, Wisdom enables humans to seek and to find the truth about reality, since she herself is its key. Her self-praise is not self-indulgent (as if Wisdom were insecure and needed to boast), but for the benefit of people who need to know her for their own well-being. In similar fashion, the Lord is presented to the defeated exiles in Second Isaiah, to folk who have become uncertain about the identity of the master of the universe (Isa 42:8; 43:14-21, 25; 44:6-8, 24-28; 45:5-7; 51:12-16; cf. Exod 20:1).

There are parallels to Wisdom's self-presentation from other ancient Near Eastern lands. Various Egyptian gods and goddesses engage in self-presentation and self-praise: Re, Isis, Hike (= magic power).[125] Maat, the goddess of world order and justice, presents herself as being present at the beginning of creation, much like Wisdom in Proverbs 8.[126]

Characteristic in these self-presentations is the declaration, "I am so and so," or "I am such and such." Examples are also extant from Mesopotamia. One of these is a speech of Gula, wise goddess of healing:

I am noble, I am lordly, I am splendid and
    sublime.
My station is on high, I am a woman of dignity.
I excel among goddesses. . . .
I am the physician, I can save life,
I carry every herb, I banish illness . . .
I give health to mankind. . . .
At a word from me, the feeble one arises.
I am merciful, [I am] kindly. . . .
I am a warrior and am skilled through
    experience . . .
I make decisions, I give commands . . .
I have mercy on the weak, I enrich the
    destitute,
I bestow life on the one who reveres me.
I make straight the path of the one who seeks
    after my ways,
I am the great one, daughter of Anu
[= the high god].[127]

Yet the speech of Wisdom employs a broader range of utterances than the "I am . . ." formula. These range from first-person action verbs and participles to prepositional phrases such as "by me."

8:6-11. These verses focus on the quality of Wisdom's words. They open the body of Wisdom's speech with the conventional "hear," but the imperative is plural. Cosmic Wisdom's address is universal; her audience is not restricted (v. 4). This section employs key terms from the prologue (1:1-7) to characterize Wisdom's teaching (cf. 8:12 and 1:4; the roots for "justice" and "righteousness" in 1:3 appear in 8:15-16). But vv. 6-10 are not rich in specific allusions to other passages (cf. the praise of divine law in Ps 19:8-11). Yet, the editorial addition of v. 11 links this section to 3:15 and to the virtuous woman in 31:10.

This section insists on the verbal character and quality of Wisdom's teaching. Human wisdom is revealed by what people say (13:14; 15:7; 16:23-24). Similarly, Wisdom's words reveal her insights. Wisdom's words

122. The juxtaposition of cosmic voice in Ps 19:1-6 with the "law" (Torah) in vv. 7-13 is an early development in traditions that give a cosmic (Wisdom or Word) setting to Israel's Torah (cf. Ps 147:15-20; Sir 24:23; Bar 4:1; John 1:1-3, 14-18; Col 1:5-6, 15-20). See von Rad, *Wisdom in Israel*, 53-73, 78, 92, 144-76.

123. Cited by M. Hengel, *Judaism and Hellenism*, vol. 2 (Philadelphia: Fortress, 1974) 98n296.

124. Lang calls this the "language of things" and gives a fine Ugaritic example: "I have a tale that I would tell you, a word that I would repeat to you, a tale of trees and a whisper of stones, the sighing of the heavens to the earth, of the oceans to the stars." See Lang, *Wisdom and the Book of Proverbs*. See also Pritchard, *Ancient Near Eastern Texts Relating to the Old Testament*, 136; cf. Ps 42:8; Hos 2:23.

125. Kayatz, *Studien zu Proverbien 1–9*, 86-93.

126. Coffin Text 80, cited in J. Assmann, *Ägypten—Theologie und Frömmigkeit einer frühen Hochkultur* (Stuttgart: Urban, 1984) 211. See also H. Ringgren, *Word and Wisdom: Studies in the Hypostatization of Divine Qualities and Functions in the Ancient Near East* (Lund: Hakan Ohlssons Boktryckeri, 1947) 27.

127. "Gula Hymn of Bullutsa-Rabi," in Benjamin R. Foster, *Before the Muses: An Anthology of Akkadian Literature* (Bethesda, Md.: CDL, 1993) 2:491-99.

mediate God's wisdom for life in the cosmos and are reflected in human language and tradition (see Commentary on 6:20-23; 7:1-3; 30:4-5). Crucial to this poem is the idea that Wisdom speaks in and through the cosmos and its creatures.

The poem accentuates the bodily instruments of speech by repetition and variation: "lips," "palate" ("mouth"), "lips," "mouth" (vv. 6-8). These terms previously appeared as instruments of the strange woman's seduction (see Commentary on 5:3). Although Wisdom's words are "right" (as in Ps 19:8), they are only so "to one who understands . . . to those who find" (v. 9; cf. the Gula hymn above). In the self-presentation of Hammurabi, king of Babylon (c. 1750 BCE), a similar perspective appears:

I, Hammurabi, am the king of justice,
to whom Shamash [god of justice] committed law.
My words are choice; my deeds have no equal;
it is only to the fool that they are empty;
to the wise they stand forth as an object of
wonder.[128]

Humans betray a contrariness to Wisdom (and to God, Wisdom's source). Humans can not only recognize and embrace, but also distort, reject, ignore, or rebel against what is right (Ezek 18:25; Amos 5:7, 10). It is as if we need wisdom before wisdom makes sense to us (14:6; 17:16). Wisdom's first speech held human beings responsible for stubbornly rejecting her counsel (1:20-33; cf. Isa 6:9-10; 1 Cor 2:14-16). Here the problem seems to be people who are not so much rebellious but, as it were, tone deaf. Such folk are unable to recognize the good, the true, and the noble when they hear it (cf. Phil 4:8). They are out of tune with reality and the right. Wisdom and goodness make no sense to them. Only those with "ears to hear" actually hear (Matt 10:13-17).

This section concludes with advice to "take my instruction" rather than silver or gold. The editorial v. 11 comments on v. 10 by quoting 3:15. In this way, Proverbs 8 is explicitly linked with the earlier parental instruction on the virtues of cosmic Wisdom. At the same time, v. 11 foreshadows the human embodiment of Wisdom in the valiant woman of Prov 31:10, at the book's very end.

8:12-16. Here Wisdom presents her indispensable role for civil or social order. In the ancient Near East, kingship was the organizing social principle for every sphere of life.[129] Each verse of this unit begins or ends with a similar-sounding, self-referential pronoun, "I"/"me" (cf. v. 17). The repeated "I"/"me" creates a powerful rhetorical effect of insistent self-assertion. There is no escaping Wisdom in the courts of the high and the mighty. She is the standard and norm for government.

8:13a. The pattern of first-person speech by Wisdom is broken. The verse thus appears to be an editorial addition, designed to link Wisdom to the "fear of the LORD" (see Commentary on 1:7; 9:10). In combining the fear of the Lord with turning from evil, v. 13a has a close parallel in 3:7 and Job 28:28 (cf. Job 1:1, 8; 2:3; Prov 14:16). The remainder of v. 13 expresses Wisdom's hatred of "pride and arrogance" and "evil," to which high and mighty rulers are prone. (In Hebrew, "pride" [גאה *gēʾâ*] and "arrogance" [גאון *gāʾôn*] punningly allude to the height [*gāʾôn*] of the powerful.) Like the Lord, Wisdom hates evil and arrogance (6:16-19; cf. 2:12, 14).

8:14. The way is prepared in this verse for vv. 15-16 as Wisdom claims for herself those qualities that are indispensable for successful government: counsel, sound wisdom (see Commentary on 2:7), and strength. In 21:30-31, these things are subordinate to the Lord or are possessions of the Lord (the word for "sound wisdom" [תושיה *tûšiyyâ*] in v. 14 is translated "victory" in 21:31). Here and increasingly in the following verses, Wisdom's closeness to Yahweh is revealed.

8:15-16. When Wisdom says, "By me kings reign," she claims that all royal functions are done in accordance with her authority and gifts. (For these functions of justice and righteousness and the cosmic blessings that attend justice, see Psalm 72 and Isa 11:1-9.) Her words and speech convey these gifts to humans (vv. 1-11). Wisdom is an active agent in creation, including human affairs. The expression "by me" (or "with me") has an exact, albeit negative, counterpart in a hymn to Marduk, the Babylonian creator god who is the counselor among the gods (like his father, Ea).

128. *ANET*, 178, italics added.

129. See H. H. Schmid, *Gerechtigkeit als Weltordnung* (Tübingen: Mohr-Siebeck, 1968).

Without you, Shamash judges no case,
Without you, no verdict is rendered for the
    land . . .
Without you, the destitute and widow are not
    cared for.[130]

In the ancient Near East, kings ruled, judged, waged war, protected the weak, and gave laws by means of the authority and gifts of the gods. They mediated divine blessings to the people and ensured peace and prosperity. Thus the great king of Babylon, Hammurabi, could say that he carried out the various functions of kingship:

With the mighty weapon which . . . Inanna
    entrusted to me,
with the insight [wisdom] that Enki allotted
    to me,
with the ability that Marduk gave me.[131]

Similarly, in a setting where Yahweh alone was to be worshiped, Wisdom declares that all the kings and rulers of the earth (v. 16b NIV) carry out their functions "by/with me"—that is, by using Wisdom's gifts of insight, justice, and state craft according to her cosmic standards, as determined by Yahweh at creation. This cosmic connection with human government is a common presupposition of ancient Near Eastern and biblical thought. In this text it is spelled out by means of a series of wordplays on the thematic Hebrew root חקק (ḥqq). Just as the Lord "marked out" (חקק ḥāqaq) "the horizon on the face of the deep" and "gave to the sea its boundary" (ḥāqaq), and as God "marked out" (ḥāqaq) "the foundations of the earth" (vv. 27, 29), so also do human rulers "decree" (ḥāqaq) "what is just" (v. 15).[132]

8:17-21. These verses turn to the motif of seeking and finding, in the context of mutual love between Lady Wisdom and her human suitors, portrayed throughout these chapters in the figure of a young man ready for marriage (see Commentary on 2:1-4, 11-19; 8:35; cf. 4:6, 8; 29:3). This language also recalls the contrary love of the stranger (7:15, 18). Language of love marks the beginning and the end of this section. Wisdom promises her devotees wealth within the path of justice and righteousness (vv. 18-21). That is, the material goods of creation are not acquired by doing violence to others or by cleverly, perhaps even legally, expanding one's own little "kingdom" at the expense of a neighbor or by violating the good order of the creation itself.

8:22-31. This section provides the warrant for the extraordinary claims made by Wisdom in vv. 6-21. The warrant falls into two parts: vv. 22-26 establish her temporal priority before all created things, and vv. 27-31 establish her active presence at God's work of creation.

8:22-26. Verse 22 has inspired much argument over the centuries, because the verb קנה (qānâ) bears several meanings. Besides "create" (Gen 14:19, 22; Ps 139:13; Ugaritic cognate), it can also mean "to acquire" and so "to possess." (The NIV's "brought forth" appears to be a meaning derived from the birth imagery of its context, vv. 24a, 25b; cf. Gen 4:1; but in Ps 139:13 it makes no sense to say, "You brought forth my inward parts.") In v. 22, Wisdom appears to have been created by the Lord, but she exists prior to and on a different plane from all other creatures (see Reflections). Since Wisdom determines cosmic order and addresses human beings concerning that order, she is the prior condition for the existence and functioning of all things.

The temporal priority of Wisdom is crucial because being wise requires knowledge of reality and the events that take place in it, and this can only be gained over time. Events happen in time, and, other than God, only one who has been there from the absolute beginning knows the whole story. Only Wisdom can be completely wise, since she has seen it all from the beginning. In the human realm, only long experience gives insight into human nature and knowledge of individuals. Consequently, much of the Bible comprises narratives that expand our experience of reality beyond what is possible in one brief lifetime. Thus the OT, the only Bible the early

---

130. Foster, *Before the Muses*, 2:607-8. Shamash is the sun god, the god of justice. Twelve lines begin, "Without you . . ." The hymn presents a variety of cultural functions that cannot take place without Marduk. Cf. John 1:3, "Without him not one thing came into being" (NRSV).

131. Epilogue to the *Code of Hammurabi*, in *ANET*, 178. Inanna is the goddess of love and war; Enki/Ea is the god of wisdom, counselor to the gods; Marduk is the god of Babylon, son of Enki and endowed with Enki's wisdom.

132. Words based on the root חקק (ḥqq) appear four times (vv. 15, 27, 29 twice). The effect of this repetition is strengthened by the repetition of the root's sounds in other words in the immediate context: שחקים (šĕḥāqîm, v. 28); משחקת (mĕśaḥeqet, vv. 30-31).

church had, can serve to make humans wise (so the Greek) for living (2 Tim 3:15-17). Similarly, many of the short sayings in Proverbs 10–29 may be seen as narratives in a nutshell that compress typical human events into their essence.

Wisdom's priority in time fits with the ancient view that only the old can be wise, for only they have experienced the world and life. They have gone through the "school of hard knocks." Thus wisdom is the province of the old: "The glory of youths is their strength, but the beauty of the aged is their gray hair" (20:29 NRSV, where gray hair symbolizes wisdom; cf. 16:31). Rehoboam's great mistake was to ignore the advice of the wise old counselors, and instead follow his foolish young friends (1 Kgs 12:1-19). In language similar to Prov 8:25, the "friends" of Job attack his claims to wisdom: "Are you the firstborn of the human race? Were you brought forth before the hills?" (Job 15:7 NRSV; cf. Ps 90:2). In the NT, the language of Wisdom's priority and involvement in creation is applied to Christ (Col 1:15-20; cf. John 1:1-3).

8:27-31. The presence of Wisdom at God's primordial creation and ordering of all things is equally important. This means that she not only knows all the particulars and individual quirks revealed in the history of humankind from the beginning, but that she also knows equally the basic structures, components, patterns, and functions of reality (cf. Wis 9:9, 11). These are the constant, unshakable conditions of human and cosmic existence, within which change and development take place. These regularities of reality (like the separation of sea and dry land and the daily rising of the sun) make life possible. Without knowing the fundamental, normative patterns of reality, no one can evaluate historical change or judge whether rulers indeed "make laws that are just" (8:15). Wisdom's knowledge of the cosmos (including human nature and justice) provides a stable point of reference by which to judge the new things that occur in human history and behavior.

The writer does not arbitrarily or casually describe some of God's cosmic acts. Rather, through the use of terms like "heavens," "deep," "sea," and "earth," the entire

universe is depicted as Wisdom's province (vv. 27-29, 31). These words represent the three realms (sky, waters, land) that for the ancients encompassed all of reality (cf. Exod 20:4; Ps 24:1-2). Various key words and images show that the grand ordering of God's cosmos was done in wisdom (3:13-20), and that human society is regulated by similar cosmic principles.

Some examples may show this correlation between the macrocosmos (world) and the microcosmos of human existence. According to v. 27, the Lord established the heavens. An Egyptian parallel shows how loaded such a phrase is with implications for human life, because the cosmic order establishes the human. Othmar Keel describes an Eighteenth Dynasty (1570–1345 BCE) wall painting from west Thebes:

A qualified village elder, or perhaps the owner of the field himself, takes the following oath while holding the *was* scepter: "As surely as the great god endures in the heavens, this boundary stone is properly erected." From ancient times, the *was*-scepter symbolized the immovability of the pillars of the heavens . . . the *was*-scepter held by the person taking the oath may illustrate the stereotyped saying: "I have set such and such a boundary stone as firmly as the heavens are established." . . . The earthly order emulates the heavenly, and like the heavenly, it is guaranteed by the deity.[133]

Israel too believed that God had made firm the structures of heaven and earth. In similar fashion, human structures and boundaries ought to be fair and stable (cf. 15:25; 22:28; 23:10-11; Deut 19:14; 27:17). Just as the cosmic realms are firmly in place, so also should just human boundaries be observed and protected.

Perhaps the most frequent image of God's setting cosmic limits has to do with God's putting a boundary to the chaotic, playful waters of the sea (v. 29). This verse has parallels in the majestic hymn on creation (Ps 104:9), in God's speech from the whirlwind (Job 38:8-11), and in Jeremiah's prophetic word to a "foolish and senseless people" who, unlike

133. O. Keel, *The Symbolism of the Biblical World: Ancient Near Eastern Iconography and the Book of Psalms* (New York: Seabury, 1978) 96. See further, Van Leeuwen, "Liminality and World View in Proverbs 1–9," 119. Cf. Jer 31:35-37.

the sea, do not know how to stay within God's limits (Jer 5:21-29). In God's economy, all things, including human beings and their various activities, have their proper place and limits. This wisdom principle, grounded in creation thinking, is nicely spelled out in the parable of the war between the sea and the forest in 2 Esdr 4:13-21. In the context of the imagery of Proverbs 1–9, with its focus on sexual relations, God's limits on the cosmic waters in chap. 8 provide a model for the limits on human sexual "waters" (5:15-20) and on human behavior generally.[134]

The grounding of human order in cosmic order is emphasized in Proverbs 8 also by the repetition of the thematic root *ḥāqaq,* which is used both of God's ordering of the cosmos and of the ordering of human affairs (see Commentary on 8:15-16). Jeremiah 31:35-37 is comparable, where the stable decrees of nature are a standard for God's covenant promises—that is, for the social order and obligations that obtain between Yahweh and Israel.

Verse 30 is famous among exegetes for the uncertainty surrounding the rare word אמון (*'āmôn*).[135] The main interpretations are that the word here means (a) "little child" (NRSV margin); (b) "master worker" (cognate with Akkadian *ummānu* and Aramaic *'umān*;[136] cf. Cant 7:2; Jer 52:15, with a disputed text); (c) "architect's plan," something like a builder's blueprint for the cosmos (so *Genesis Rabbah* 1.1, identifying Wisdom and Mosaic *tôrâ*); and (d) that the grammar may be read differently, *'āmôn*, so that the word refers to God: "Then I was with [God], the master worker."

The first view (a) appeals to Egyptian Maat, the goddess of cosmic and social order, who is portrayed as playing before her father, the creator god Re. This parallel appears to accommodate the apparently strange association among world order, a personal being, and play with delight. Position (c) is simply derived from (b) by way of narrative elaboration: an architect needs plans—i.e., the Torah in its written and oral forms—to build the cosmos. Position (d) has not found wide support.

It seems best to take the *'āmôn* of v. 30 in terms of position (b), based on the Akkadian cognate *ummānu,* but understood in a broader sense than "master worker." The Akkadian word generally means "wise," "expert," "skilled"; it can refer to a wide range of wisdom, practical skill, and expertise. The *ummānu* can be a counselor, adviser, or scribe.[137] The Hebrew term for "wisdom" (חכמה *ḥokmâ*) bears a similar broad semantic range, including the practical skill to make a temple (Exod 31:1-6; 1 Kgs 7:13-14). A first-person speech by Enki (Akkadian Ea), the Sumerian god of wisdom, may illustrate the role of an *ummānu* (or *apkallu,* a related designation that applies to the primordial wise men before the flood).[138] Although the text is in the Sumerian language and does not use the term *ummānu,* its conceptual world fits it precisely and illustrates certain aspects of Proverbs 8.

My father, the king of the universe,
Brought me into existence in the universe,
My ancestor, the king of all the lands,
Gathered together all the "me's," placed the
      "me's" in my hand. . . .
I brought craftsmanship to my Abzu of Eridu . . .
I am the first born son of An . . .
I am he who brings full prosperity, . . .
I am he who directs justice with the king An
      on An's dais [i.e., as royal counselor, or
      apkallu].[139]

---

134. Besides the general emphasis of liquids in 5:15-20 and 8:22-29, note the vocabulary common to these two passages: "springs," "waters," "abroad" = "fields" (חוץ *ḥûṣ*, 5:16; 8:26; cf. 1:20; 7:12), "at all times" (5:19; of sexual delight) = "always" (8:30). "Streets" and "squares/abroad" link 5:16 not with chap. 8, but with Wisdom in 1:20 (in contrast to 7:12; cf. 8:1-3).

135. R. B. Y. Scott, "Wisdom in Creation: The *'āmôn* of Proverbs VIII 30," *VT* 10 (1960) 213-33.

136. The Aramaic term, like its Akkadian forebear, has a wide semantic range and can refer to a person practicing almost any skill, craft, or profession. In some Palestinian synagogue inscriptions, the word is used of synagogue builders (whether architect, builder, or both is not clear). See Joseph A. Fitzmyer and Daniel J. Harrington, *A Manual of Palestinian Aramaic Texts* (Rome: Pontifical Biblical Institute, 1978) 254-57. In *Targum Neophyti* to Exod 31:5, a cognate term is used for skilled work in metals and precious stones for the tabernacle.

137. See M. Fishbane, *Biblical Interpretation in Ancient Israel* (Oxford: Clarendon, 1985) 26n11.

138. The *apkallu* served to "insure the correct functioning of the plans of heaven and earth." After the flood, the role of *apkallu* is subsumed by the *ummānu.* "This is not an easy term to translate since it covers a broad spectrum including 'scribe, scholar, master craftsman, officer.'" J. C. Greenfield, "The Seven Pillars of Wisdom (Prov. 9:1)—A Mistranslation," *JQR* 76 (1985) 15-17.

139. "Enki and the World Order," in S. N. Kramer, *The Sumerians: Their History, Character, and Culture* (Chicago: University of Chicago Press, 1963), 174-83. The Sumerian word *me* designates basic units of world order that apply to and regulate divine and human social institutions and practices. The one who controls the "me's" "fixes the borders, marks off the boundaries" (issues of justice, see the discussion of *ḥāqaq* in the Commentary on 8:15, 29), and takes "charge of the crook, staff, and wand of shepherdship" (= kingship).

Just as Enki is the wise counselor of the divine king Anu, who orders the universe and the arts of civilization, so also Proverbs 8 personifies Wisdom as the architect associate of Yahweh at the creation of the world. The 'āmôn in v. 30 is Wisdom personified as the king's architect-adviser, through whom the king puts all things in their proper order and whose decrees of cosmic justice are the standard for human kings and rulers (v. 15).[140] This interpretation accords with pictures elsewhere in the OT where God as king consults the heavenly court in carrying out decisions (esp. Gen 1:26; cf. Deut 32:6b-9; 1 Kgs 22:19-22; Job 1–2; Isa 6:1-9).

This reading of Wisdom in Proverbs 8 has an antecedent in the book of Wisdom, where the human king needs Wisdom's presence both to rule wisely and to build a temple, because "she knows your works and was present when you made the world" (Wis 9:1-12; cf. 8:4). Wisdom 7:21 and 8:6 allude directly to Prov 8:30 and call Wisdom the "fashioner" of the world (which does not exclude God as "fashioner," Wis 13:1; cf. Prov 3:19).

Scholars have often been puzzled by the delight in v. 31, uncertain as to how it might fit with the "architect-adviser" ("master workman") reading of 'āmôn in v. 30. Hence many have taken 'āmôn as a "nursling" who plays before the Lord. This inference is unnecessary, however. A counselor who gives good advice is a source of delight to the one counseled: "Your decrees are my delight, they are my counselors" (Ps 119:24 NRSV). And Israel, pictured as a vineyard created by God's hard work, is called the "garden of his delight" (Isa 5:7 NIV).

In the ancient Near East, building projects, especially cities, palaces, and temples, were a source of delight both in execution and at their completion. Ashurnasirpal II rebuilt the city of Calah "in that wisdom of mine, the knowledge which Ea . . . has bestowed upon me." Its palace was "a palace of joy and (erected with) great ingenuity." In addition to this joy in the process of "creation," there was celebration and feasting upon completion. So Ashurnasirpal, his palace finished, prepared a giant banquet, slaughtered many beasts (listed in detail), and claimed a total of "69,574 invited guests."[141] Again, an inscription of Assyrian king Tukulti-Ninurta I reads: "I built a temple and completed it and set up a dais. Annunita my Lady in joy and happiness I seated on her dais."[142] Similarly, in Jer 30:18-19 and 31:4 the same pattern (and verb) of playful rejoicing after the (re)building of the city appears (cf. Zech 8:5). When Solomon completed the "house" of the Lord (a microcosmic mirror of the universe), a seven- (or fourteen-) day feast was held, and the king sent the people on their way, "joyful and glad in heart" (1 Kgs 8:62-66 NIV).

This move from cosmic construction to joy, delight, and feasting is basic to Proverbs 8 and 9:1-6, which follow a widespread ancient pattern that combines joy in building with celebration at its completion and inauguration. Indeed, this pattern is universal. In 8:21-30, we have the "building" of the cosmos, employing verbs commonly used of human building projects. The joy in 8:30-31 is joy at the construction and completion of the ordered world, including the human world (cf. Job 38:7). In keeping with the cosmic symbolism of "house," the banquet scene in 9:1-6 must also be understood against this background (see Commentary on 9:1).

The above data suggest that the Lord's delight is in Wisdom, but not because of her playful performance as a "little child."[143] Rather, the Lord delights in Wisdom's active role in creation (8:27-29, 31). Ultimately, the arena of Wisdom's delight and rejoicing is the inhabited world of human beings— that is, the completed creation. Wisdom delights in the world of human culture, and to humans she speaks, so that they may live according to the wisdom she imparts (8:3-21, 31-36). The conclusion of creation is delight. This delight arises from creation's goodness, which is celebrated every sabbath (Genesis 1; Exod 20:8-11; 31:7). When God put the creation in order, "all the heavenly beings shouted for joy" (Job 38:7 NRSV; cf. Ps 104:15, 31, 34; Bar 3:34).

140. For the *ummānu* as "royal counselor," see Bottéro, *Mesopotamia,* 246-49.

141. *ANET,* 558, 560. In the Ugaritic Baal cycle, Kothar wa-Khasis, the wise artisan god, builds Baal's "house" in seven days with fire. Thereupon beasts are slaughtered, guests invited, and the banquet is held (*ANET,* 134).

142. Cited in V. Hurowitz, *I Have Built You an Exalted House: Temple Building in the Bible in Light of Mesopotamian and Northwest Semitic Writings* (Sheffield: JSOT, 1992) 100.

143. See Othmar Keel, *Die Weisheit Spielt vor Gott: Ein ikonographischer Beitrag zur Deutung des mahaqät in Sprüche 8, 30f.* (Fribourg: Universitätsverlag, 1974).

8:32-36. The closing section gives a final invitation and warning and prepares the transition to chap. 9, with its banquet scene upon completion of the "house." The reference to Wisdom's "doors" in v. 34 anticipates the metaphor of the two houses, which dominates 9:1-6, 13-18, especially 9:13-14, where the "foolish woman . . . sits at the door of her house" (NRSV). Between the chapters there is implicit movement from waiting (8:34) to entry upon invitation (9:1-6, 13-18; cf. Matt 25:10).

Conventional wisdom language is used in this sermon. The "blessed" of vv. 34-35 repeats the blessing and love imagery ("seek," "find," "embrace") from 3:11-18. Wisdom is to be sought and found like a wife. The symbolic equivalence of Wisdom and woman/wife is once again reinforced, not only for chaps. 1–9, but for the entire book in its final form as well. Both Wisdom and wife are gifts from God, and to love them faithfully puts one in touch with God (18:22 par. 8:35; 19:14; 31:10-31). This notion of Wisdom as bride is richly developed in Wis 8:2-16.[144] The final line of Proverbs 8 is staggering in its bluntness: "All who hate me love death."

144. See David Winston, *The Wisdom of Solomon,* AB 43 (New York: Doubleday, 1979) 192-96.

REFLECTIONS

1. The identity of personified Wisdom is much debated. Indeed, her metaphorical portrayal should caution against finding a simple referent for the poem. She exists both as a person who speaks and as cosmic reality. Like some other parts of Scripture, this poem is multireferential. One may compare the famous Immanuel prophecy. Christians maintain that, in some profound sense, Jesus is the fulfillment of the Immanuel ("God with us") prophecy in Isa 7:14 (see Matt 1:23). Yet Isaiah's prophecy clearly refers to events and persons in Isaiah's day and was fulfilled some seven hundred years before Christ. Similarly, while Proverbs 8 is background for Christian understandings of Christ as the Wisdom and Word of God, our first task is to understand this female personification of Wisdom in Proverbs; she was present at creation and, abiding in creation, addresses all humans.

Some have thought that Wisdom is a poetic personification of God's attribute of wisdom, by which God created the world (cf. 3:19-20; Ps 104:24; Jer 10:12). Others think the divine attribute of wisdom has here become a hypostasis, or independent personal being, somewhat like an angelic power. Such moves toward personification are common in the ancient Near East, in Second Temple Judaism, and in early Christianity.

Recently, Wisdom (often with the Greek name *Sophia*) has come to play a significant role in feminist theology. An important example is the work of Elizabeth A. Johnson. Appealing to the portrayal of Wisdom in Proverbs, Sirach, Wisdom, and Baruch, Johnson argues that "Sophia is a female personification of God's own being in creative and saving involvement with the world. The chief reason for arriving at this interpretation is the functional equivalence between the deeds of Sophia and those of the biblical God. . . . Sophia is Israel's God in female imagery."[145]

The poem itself, however, clearly distinguishes Wisdom from the Lord, for Wisdom was "created" by God (8:22) and was with God during the process of creation (8:30). Wisdom is intimately associated with Yahweh and is instrumental in creation (3:19-20). However, she is not identified with Yahweh. Wisdom is an independent entity. This association-with distinction has parallels in such expressions as "the angel of the Lord," "the word of the Lord," "the Name (of the Lord)," and "the Presence." These entities express the working or presence of Yahweh in the world and cannot be separated from God's being; and yet they are not identical with it. A remarkable example is the personified divine Word in Wis 18:15-16 (cf. Isa 30:27, of the Name). This passage

145. Elizabeth A. Johnson, *She Who Is: The Mystery of God in Feminist Theological Discourse* (New York: Crossroad, 1992) 91.

is a significant parallel to Proverbs 8, because the book of Wisdom understands the Word of God and the Wisdom of God as variant expressions of the same reality.[146] The scene is Israel's exodus from Egypt:

> Your all-powerful word leaped from heaven, from the royal throne,
> into the midst of the land that was doomed,
> a stern warrior
> carrying the sharp sword of your authentic command,
> and stood and filled all things with death,
> and touched heaven while standing on the earth. (Wis 18:15-16 NRSV)

Here the divine Word is portrayed as a personal, independent being that not only carries out the divine will in history, but also has a cosmic scope, touching "heaven while standing on earth" (cf. Sir 24:5, of Wisdom). God's Word is an immanent intermediary between God and creation. Similarly, Wis 8:1-2 strikingly juxtaposes the cosmic and personal aspects of Wisdom. The Word or wisdom of God put the world in order; it pervades the cosmos (cf. Sir 24:3-6; Wis 8:1-2); it regulates human affairs. Thus Wisdom is "in" the creation; she addresses human beings, but is not of the same kind as other created things. G. von Rad put it as follows:

> This wisdom, immanent in creation, was differentiated . . . from the "real" work of creation (wind, springs, sea, mountains, etc.). This ontological separation of the phenomena within creation is the most interesting element. Obviously what the teachers perceived as a "summons from creation," as the "self-evident nature of its order," was not simply identical with the "real" works of creation.[147]

In the NT, Christ, in his cosmic, creative functions, will be described as the Word and the wisdom of God. Many of the attributes of the "Word made flesh" are framed in the cosmic and personal terms of OT Wisdom (cf. John 1:1-3, 10; Col 1:15-20; Heb 1:2-3; 11:3).[148]

2. For Israel, the order of divine creation set limits and determined the norms for human activity. Human culture and society are embedded in the matrix of the world God made, and this matrix was designed to keep humans from folly and to foster goodness. Just as the sea has freedom within the limits marked out by God, so also do humans. This principle is easy to recognize in the physical realm (human beings cannot breathe in outer space); it is much more difficult to recognize the more subtle and complex limits set by God on human moral and cultural behavior.

Whatever cosmic norms there are, their concrete articulation is culturally specific and variable. We experience cosmic norms mediated through human culture. This makes it deceptively easy to imagine that the norms are purely human creations. For example, the norms for good Baroque music and for good jazz are quite different. Human languages also display great variety. And yet, this rich variability should not obscure the created conditions that make music and speech possible. This is, perhaps, easiest to illustrate with languages. They universally conform to certain limits (e.g., phonemic) and fulfill certain functions and patterns (e.g., of topic and comment) required by communication. Although actual speech performance varies greatly in adequacy (as when a baby lisps), our knowledge of language norms enables us to understand what is meant and even to supply what is lacking.[149] Such imperfect speech is

---

146. Winston, *The Wisdom of Solomon*, 317.
147. Von Rad, *Wisdom in Israel*, 171-72; see also 80, 83, 92, 107, 144-76.
148. See Raymond Brown, *The Gospel According to John I–XII*, AB 29 (Garden City, N.Y.: Doubleday, 1966) cxxv.
149. Linguists speak of "performance" (*parole*) and "competence" (*langue*). See John Lyons, *Introduction to Theoretical Linguistics* (Cambridge: Cambridge University Press, 1968) 51-52.

different from sinful speech (e.g., lies). Again, marriage and family show wide variation among cultures (even within the Bible), but according to Matt 19:3-9, the norms and ideals for their basic structures and functions are given with creation—norms such as fidelity, lifelong partnership, love and respect, sexual exclusivity (even in polygamous settings), and the rearing of healthy, appropriately socialized children. Needless to say, human beings continually struggle with and fall short of creational ideals for marriage and family, even as articulated within their specific societies. Many of the marriage and family stories in the Bible are profound tales of sin and dysfunction commingled with redemptive grace and growth (e.g., Genesis 12–50; 2 Samuel 11–1 Kings 2; 2 Tim 1:5).

Thus, for human affairs to be conducted wisely, freedom and form, love and limits, vital life and cosmic law have to be balanced. Very often in history, the rich and powerful have identified the cultural status quo, which serves them well, with the will of God and the order of creation. So the culturally specific, the culturally relative, and even things unjust have been preached as the very word of God or the structure of the world. Cosmic thinking has often served to defend a tyrannical status quo.[150] Sinful, relative human order is too often identified with divine order. And yet, for better or worse, human order and behavior are always responses to the divine order, from which we can learn. We sometimes gain a sense of how things *ought* to be from critical assessment of what *is.*

To conclude from the imperfection and relativity of human responses that there is no (culturally mediated) cosmic order for behavior can be disastrous:

> For the recognition of universal principles forces man to judge the established order, or what is actual here and now, in the light of the natural . . . order; and what is actual here and now is more likely than not to fall short of the universal and unchangeable norm. The recognition of universal principles thus tends to prevent men from wholeheartedly identifying themselves with, or accepting, the social order that fate has allotted to them.[151]

Any reformation of a status quo needs a higher, stable standard by which to judge it and the changes advocated by the proponents of reformation or revolution, lest new evil replace old evil.[152] The difficult human task is collectively to recognize those genuine boundaries and reality principles that are non-negotiable givens, so that true human freedom and the goods of creation may be preserved.

3. Proverbs 8 is also significant for the role it played in doctrinal controversy over the centuries. In particular, it was central in the controversy between orthodox and Arian Christians in the fourth century CE. Many Christians sought too simply and directly to apply statements in Proverbs 8 to Christ. And in the divergence of Judaism and Christianity, Proverbs 8 also played its role. For Judaism, Wisdom became elaborated as Torah, for Christians as Christ.

This Christian development occurred first in the NT writings that describe Christ in cosmic terms as God's Word or Wisdom (John 1; 1 Cor 1:24, 30; Col 1:15-20; 2:3; cf. Heb 1:1-3). In the fourth-century Arian controversy, a battle raged over the verb in Prov 8:22a. It is perhaps best to accept the ambiguity of the verb קנה (*qānâ*) as part of the richness of the text. (In English, the verbs "get" and "beget" display an ambiguity similar to *qānâ*.) On the one hand, God has "possessed" Wisdom from the beginning (cf. Prov 8:30). So also humans, in their own fashion, are to acquire and possess or

150. But see J. Richard Middleton and W. Brueggemann, "Is Creation Theology Inherently Conservative? A Dialogue with Walter Brueggemann," *HTR* 87 (1994) 257-89.

151. Leo Strauss, *Natural Right and History* (Chicago: University of Chicago Press, 1953) 13-14. On historicism, see also O'Donovan, *Resurrection and Moral Order*; and Jon D. Levinson, *The Hebrew Bible, the Old Testament, and Historical Criticism* (Louisville: Westminster/John Knox, 1993).

152. Knierim's essay "Cosmos and History in Israel's Theology" is indispensable here. See Rolf P. Knierim, *The Task of Old Testament Theology: Substance, Method, and Cases* (Grand Rapids: Eerdmans, 1995) 171-224.

"get" wisdom (the same verb appears in Prov 1:5; 4:5, 7; 16:16; 23:23). But more profoundly, the verb suggests that God has "created" or "formed" Wisdom as the beginning of God's ways, before the other works of creation. (In Gen 1:1 the same word for "beginning" opens the Bible. In Job 40:19, the awesome creature Behemoth is called the "beginning of God's ways" as a prime example of God's wisdom in creation.) Thus the creation of the universe and all creatures in it was undertaken in, by, and through Wisdom (3:19-20; Ps 104:24; Jer 10:12).

Using Prov 8:22-31, the Arian party argued that Christ (as Wisdom) was the first creation of God, the unique creature before all other creatures. But as created, the Arians reasoned, Christ was not God in the same sense as the Father was God. The orthodox party, which defined subsequent Christian dogma through the centuries, preferred to take the verb in Prov 8:22*a* as "possessed," so following the ancient Greek LXX version. Alternately, the orthodox took the verb as meaning "to beget," so that Christ was not created but, as in the Nicene Creed of 351 CE, eternally "begotten, not made." Again, conceding the possibility that the verb meant "to create," Athanasius took pains to say that what was created was not Christ per se, but his position as the "first of God's works/ways."[153]

Christian tradition has thus in various ways identified Wisdom in Proverbs 8 and Christ as one. A better move, perhaps, would be to understand Christ as the hidden reality underlying and fulfilling the cosmic and personal imagery of Wisdom in Proverbs 8, without positing a direct one-to-one correspondence in all particulars. This seems to be the New Testament procedure.

In Jewish tradition, the move has been to identify Torah (the written and oral law or teaching given to Moses by God at Mount Sinai) with Wisdom. The correlation of Torah and cosmic wisdom (or Word) is suggested already in several biblical passages (Deut 4:6-8; Pss 19:1-10; 33:4-9; 119:89-104; 147:15-20). But the explicit equation of Torah and cosmic wisdom is developed later, in Sir 1:4; 24:3, 9; Bar 4:1. By the time of the great rabbinic midrash on Gen 1:1,[154] the opening word(s) of Genesis are made to intersect with Prov 8:22, 30.

4. God's delight in the goodness and order of the created world is variously expressed in the Bible. It provides the background for human enjoyment of the goodness of creation (cf. 1 Tim 4:4). It also contrasts with most worldviews that find evil somehow intrinsic to (some part of) reality. In the creation account of Genesis 1, God repeatedly sees that what God has made is "good," even "very good." The psalmist prays that the Lord may "rejoice in his works," for "in wisdom you have made them all," including Leviathan, which God "formed to frolic" in the sea (Ps 104:31, 24-26). The verb for "frolic" is translated "rejoicing" or "playing" in Prov 8:30.

O'Donovan speaks, in Christian terms, of the love and delight that permeate Proverbs 8:

> Classical Christian descriptions of love are often found invoking two other terms which expound its sense: the first is "wisdom," which is the intellectual apprehension of the order of things which discloses how each being stands in relation to each other; the second is "delight," which is affective attention to something simply for what it is and for the fact that it is. Such love is the fruit of God's presence within us, uniting us to the humanity of God in Christ, who cherishes and defends all that God the Father has made and thought.[155]

---

153. See Jaroslav Pelikan, *The Emergence of the Catholic Tradition (100–600)*, vol. 1 of *The Christian Tradition* (Chicago: University of Chicago Press, 1971) 191-200.

154. *Genesis Rabbah* 1.1. For the text of *Genesis Rabbah*, see Commentary on Proverbs 9:1-18.

155. O'Donovan, *Resurrection and Moral Order*, 26.

PROVERBS 9:1-18, TWO HOUSES AT THE END OF THE ROAD

COMMENTARY

Chapter 9 forms a carefully constructed conclusion to the first nine chapters. It falls into three six-verse sections (A, vv. 1-6; B, vv. 7-12; A´, vv. 13-18). Of these, section B, which interrupts the parallel sections A and A´, signals that chap. 9 forms an envelope around the nine chapters through its repetition of key phrases from 1:1-7 (1:7 and 9:10 on "the fear of the LORD"; 1:5 and 9:11) and from Wisdom's first speech in 1:20-33 (1:22, 29 and 9:7-8; 1:29 and 9:10). The city scene in sections A and A´ also echoes the one in 1:20-21, which strengthens the envelope effect. Through their contrast of Lady Wisdom and Dame Folly, sections A and A´ summarize key images and themes in chaps. 1–9: opposed ways, women, and houses. This summary function appears in verbal echoes from earlier passages that reinforce the connection between literal and figurative invitations to wisdom and folly (cf. 5:8 with 9:14; 1:21 with 7:11 and 9:13; 5:6 with 9:13, 17 and 7:23; 4:17 with 9:17). Literal adultery or fidelity (5:18-20; 7:6-27) are now definitively revealed in their metaphorical function as symbols of folly and wisdom. Folly's house of death has been anticipated in the house of the "strange woman" (see Commentary on 2:18; 5:5; 7:27; 9:18). Wisdom's banquet house is the cosmos created in 8:22-29 (see below). Wisdom spoke previously in 1:20-33 and 8:3-36. Folly spoke in the figure of the "strange woman" and the adulteress of 7:14-20.

Although the invitation to banquets is a new element, the fit of chap. 9 within the symbol system of Proverbs 1–9 makes unlikely the older view that sacred prostitution or a fertility cult is being portrayed in 9:13-18 (or in 7:14-20). Indeed, some doubt the reality of sacred prostitution in the ancient Near East.[156] The "house" built by Wisdom is not a temple, nor is her meal sacrificial. Though it has been argued that Wisdom in Proverbs 1–9 was originally an ancient Israelite goddess of learning (disguised by the monotheistic editors of Proverbs), the evidence for this theory is inadequate.[157]

Evidence from Proverbs suggests that its final editors provided clues to the meaning of Wisdom's mysterious house building. They have created a set of parallel passages that present cosmos building in the same terms as house building. A literal translation makes these parallels clear:

A Yahweh *by wisdom* founded the earth,
  B Establishing the heavens *by understanding,*
    C *By his knowledge* the depths were split. (3:19-20)
A *By wisdom* a house *is built,*
  B *By understanding* it is established,
    C And *by knowledge* its chambers are filled (24:3-4)
A *Wisdom has built her house* (9:1)
A *Wisdom* of women *has built her house*
    D But Folly with her hands tears it down (14:1)

In the first two passages, house building (24:3-4) is parallel to cosmos building (3:19-20). Both God and humans operate by the architectural and practical skill indicated by the trio wisdom-understanding-knowledge (see Commentary on 8:1). This exact sequence of attributes is given by God to the builders of the Mosaic tabernacle and of the divine "house" built by Solomon (Exod 31:3; 35:31; 1 Kgs 7:14). These cultic houses are also microcosmic reflections of the macrocosmic world of God's creation (cf. Ps 78:69). Moreover, both the cosmos and human houses are "established by understanding" (Prov 3:19*b*; 24:3*b*). To the "filling" of the house (24:4*a*), one may compare Ps 104:24, where all the works of the Lord are made "by wisdom," and "the earth is full of [God's] creatures" (employing the same verb). On

---

156. See "Prostitution (OT)" and "Prostitution (Cultic)," in *Anchor Bible Dictionary,* 6 vols. (New York: Doubleday, 1992) 5:505-13.

157. See Lang, *Wisdom and the Book of Proverbs,* 90-93.

this reading, "house" (9:1) and "city" (9:3b) are concentric microcosmic analogues of the cosmos.

This understanding of Wisdom's house in Prov 9:1-3 as a symbol of the world was anticipated long ago in the Babylonian Talmud. The Talmud explains the purpose of Adam's creation on the eve of sabbath in terms of Proverbs 9. Its purpose was

that he might straightway go in to the banquet. The matter may be compared to a king of flesh and blood who built palaces and furnished them, prepared a banquet, and thereafter brought in the guests. For it is written . . . Wisdom "hath builded her house—this [Wisdom] is the attribute of the Holy One, blessed be He, who created the world by wisdom.[158]

In many cultures, the building of cities and houses is an analogue of cosmos building, and in the OT similar vocabulary is used for all three. The order of the house, whether secular or sacred, should partake of and mirror the wise order employed by the Creator of the cosmos.[159] The parallelism among the texts quoted above shows that this pattern is operative in Proverbs. These texts also underline the fundamental intersection of woman, house, and wisdom or folly, which governs the symbolic world of this book in its final form (see Commentary on 31:10-31). The analogy of house and cosmos was also anticipated in Proverbs 8. After the cosmos is built (8:22-29) we hear of Wisdom's "doors" (8:34)—that is, of her house.

In Proverbs 8, however, Yahweh is the creator of the cosmos, while in Prov 9:1, Wisdom is the builder of the cosmic "house." This sort of dual agency is not uncommon in Scripture (cf. Gen 45:4-8; 50:20; Exod 9:34–10:1; Phil 2:12-13). Furthermore, in various ways God is said to build the Temple, the city, and ordinary houses (Pss 78:69; 127:1; Isa 14:32; cf. Heb 3:3-6). This dual agency in Proverbs 8–9, whereby Wisdom's house building is also the Lord's cosmos building, is nicely captured by the ancient Midrash on Gen 1:1, which identifies Torah with Wisdom:

'āmôn [from Proverbs 8:30] is a workman (uman). The Torah declares, I was the working tool of the Holy One, blessed be He. In human practice, when a mortal king builds a palace, he builds it not with his own skill but with the skill of an architect. The architect moreover does not build it out of his head, but employs plans and diagrams to know how to arrange the chambers and the wicket doors. Thus God consulted [lit., looked into] the Torah and created the world.[160]

9:1-6. Scholars have been much puzzled over the "seven pillars" of Wisdom's house (v. 1). Over the centuries, the pillars have provoked much fanciful speculation: the seven gifts of the Holy Spirit, the seven liberal arts, the seven churches of Revelation, and so on. Other scholars have simply taken the seven to be a cipher for "many." Archaeologists have found parallels to the seven pillars in the homes of wealthy patricians.[161] In the present cosmic context, however, the pillars are most likely a reference to the "pillars of the earth" (Ps 75:3; cf. 1 Sam 2:8; Job 9:6; 26:11). Perhaps the general symbolic function of the number seven is also operative here. Seven is widely present in the OT as a symbol for completeness, perfection, and fullness. In this passage, seven would refer to the perfection and stability of the creation.

But the seven pillars may also be a case of inner-biblical allusion to Gen 1:1–2:3. Jewish tradition, including the Talmud passage cited above, saw in the seven pillars an allusion to the six-plus-one pattern of creation and celebration (sabbath) in the days of Genesis 1. This may not be as farfetched as it first seems. The text of Proverbs 8–9 appears to be playing with the pattern six plus one equals seven.[162] In vv. 1-6, the preparation of the house and its feast takes six actions (past tense verbs), and the invitation to celebrate in the completed house takes one action, "she calls" (present-continuous verb). In the preceding chapter, the account of creation falls into two connected sections. The first (8:22-26) has six verbs of creation; the second (8:27-29) has six infinitives of creation. These sections

158. I. Epstein, *The Babylonian Talmud: Seder Nezikin* (London: Soncino, 1935) *Sanh.* 38a, 240-41.

159. See M. Eliade, *The Sacred and the Profane: The Nature of Religion* (New York: Harcourt Brace Jovanovich, 1959) 20-65.

160. H. Freedman, *Midrash Rabbah: Genesis* (London, Soncino: 1951) 1.1, 1; italics added to show words translating the root אמן ('mn).

161. See Lang, *Wisdom and the Book of Proverbs*, 90-93.

162. See U. Cassuto, *A Commentary on the Book of Genesis, Part One: From Adam to Noah* (Jerusalem: Magnes, 1961) 13-15, for the number seven in the verbal patterns of Gen 1:1–2:3.

are followed by two identical verbs ("I was," 8:30) referring to Wisdom's joyful presence in creation. This creates a verb pattern of twice six plus twice one, equalling twice seven. In 9:7-12, the root for "wisdom" (חכמה *ḥokmâ*) appears six times, in addition to the reference to Wisdom in the phrase "by me" (9:11; patterned after 8:15-16). Significantly, in the disordered world of Folly (9:13-18), there are no patterns of six plus one to be found.

This sequence of building, preparing for a feast, and inviting people to the feast is a common pattern (see Commentary on 8:30-31 for parallels). In contrast to the adulterous feast implied in 7:14-20, this feast is not the by-product of a sacrifice. It is simply an ongoing celebration at the completion of the building of the house (cf. modern "housewarming" parties). Its language is that of a wealthy woman providing a lavish meal.[163] In the Bible, the closest verbal parallels to Wisdom's festal preparations of meat and wine occur in the story of the rich fool Nabal, who refuses to share his feast with deserving David (1 Sam 25:11). Perhaps not so ironically, it is Nabal's wise wife, Abigail, who sends her servants before her and provides David and his troops with a feast (1 Sam 25:18-19).

In contrast to the bustling activity of Lady Wisdom is the inaction of Dame Folly, who sits on her seat, catching those who come by. Wisdom offers meat and wine, but Folly offers bread and water. The metaphorical use of food and drink for moral, sexual, and religious choices is common (Job 20:12-14; Prov 1:31; 4:17; 5:15; 7:18; 20:17; 30:20; Sir 23:17; John 6:35). Wisdom offers her goods without guile. Folly's offer is deceptive; she promises secret delights, but hides death. Wisdom urges from death to life (9:6a) and invites the simple to walk in blessing (the Hebrew puns on "blessed"/"happy" [אשרי *'ašrê*] and "walk" [אשרו *'išrû*]; cf. 3:13, 18; 8:32, 34).

The double invitation of Wisdom and Folly highlights the ambiguous character of the goods of this world. The poet conveys this ambiguity by using the long-established pattern of similarity between the two women. Especially striking are the identical descriptions of their invitations: "'You who are simple, turn in here!' And to those without

sense she says . . ." (9:4, 16). All sin, all folly, it would seem, are temptations to acquire legitimate created goods (sex, wealth, honor, power) by illegitimate means. The goods of this world are ambiguous; in the wrong context they become problematic. The power of speech is a great good, but its power can bring life or death (8:21; cf. Jas 3:1-12).

9:7-12. This section is an interlude whose presence delays the final contrast between Wisdom and Folly (A and A´). To this point, Proverbs 1–9 has been mainly concerned with presenting the message of Wisdom. The speeches of parents and of Wisdom herself have invited the listener to a banquet of life and have warned about Folly and her counterinvitation to sugarcoated death. Now the author advises wise humans, in the second person (vv. 8-9), concerning the reaction their teaching will provoke in others. Those who are wise and righteous respond to instruction and correction by growing wiser (vv. 8b-9). But scoffers and the wicked hate those who correct and admonish them (vv. 7-8b). Verses 10-11 interrupt this advice with a variation of the book's theme verse on wisdom and the fear of the Lord (see Commentary on 1:7). This is followed by an utterance from Wisdom ("by me"), reminding readers that she offers long life. The section concludes with advice that returns to the contrast between the wise and scoffers (v. 12).

At first glance, this section appears to add little that is new; the passage seems merely repetitive. But this conclusion would mistake its function in the book. Through repetition of key phrases and themes, these verses create links both forward and backward in the final form of Proverbs. In form these verses anticipate the short sayings and admonitions that will predominate in chaps. 10–29. Through parallelism of terms these verses also equate the wise with the righteous, in contrast to the wicked. This equation links the focus on wisdom and folly of chaps. 1–9 with the focus on righteous and wicked, so characteristic of chapters 10–15. Verses 7-12 thus help to connect chaps. 1–9 to the subsequent sentence collections formally and by establishing thematic equivalence. Within chaps. 1–9, Prov 9:11 forms links with Wisdom's speech ("by me" in 8:15-16) and with the parental gift of "years of life" (3:2; 4:10). The envelope function of 9:7-12 with chap. 1 has been discussed above.

---

163. See Camp, *Wisdom and the Feminine in the Book of Proverbs*, 271.

9:13-18. The chapter and the book's first major section now conclude. Dame Folly is an explicit contrast to Wisdom in v. 16, even to the point of making an identical invitation (v. 4 = v. 16). But this passage also sums up virtually every theme expressed in Proverbs 1–9 by means of its repetition of key words. In particular, Dame Folly masterfully integrates the portrait of Folly as a seduction to bogus good, in contrast to the genuine good of Wisdom.

REFLECTIONS

1. The food and drink prepared by Lady Wisdom are metaphors for the life-giving gifts of creation (9:6). Her "house" is full, and she offers, in effect, to fill the "house" of her guests (cf. 8:21; 24:4; 27:27; 31:15; cf. 1:13; 17:1; Job 22:18). To enter Wisdom's house is to enter the life-giving center of the cosmos, a Garden of Eden where creation's goods are most intensely present and accessible. Here, the cosmos is in order and humans are in harmony with its life-giving principles. Lady Wisdom is an edenic "tree of life" (3:18; cf. 8:35) whose fruits (or meat and wine) are eagerly to be enjoyed. In Wisdom's house all the goods of creation are to be found, for God made them all "by wisdom" (cf. Ps 104:24). Negatively, to enter Wisdom's house requires that one leave "simpleness" behind. To choose is to lose. But those who give up their foolish self-direction (see 1:22-33) for love of Wisdom, gain genuine life. They continue to walk "in the way of insight" (9:6).

2. Proverbs 9:1-6 shows that the goal of the wise person's path is life in Wisdom's house, in contrast to the deadly house of the strange woman or Folly (9:18; see also 2:18-19). And yet the goal of Wisdom is not something achieved by humans, once for all. Those who enter and feast in Wisdom's house continue to walk "in the way of insight" (9:6). Similarly, one can enter into a marriage and over time travel more deeply into the reality of that relationship. Our ongoing love affair with either Wisdom or Folly gives direction and sets the goal of our life-journey. Over time, we grow in wisdom or folly, according to the ultimate loves and commitments that move us. What we love determines where we are headed, where we end up, and who we become. It determines how we journey (see Commentary on 1:7). Lovers of Wisdom are on the way to Wisdom's banquet house, and they are already in it—a paradox that should not be strange to Christians, who know the gospel paradox of a kingdom that is already and not yet. Augustine captured this insight well in talking of Christ as both the way and the goal of the Christian life: "Thus, though Wisdom was himself our home, he made himself also the way by which we should reach our home."[164]

3. The contrast between Lady Wisdom's house and Dame Folly's house is complex. On the one hand, Wisdom's house designates a world in order, full of life. Folly's house is a world in disorder, descending into Sheol, the realm of death. The fool is free of the very conditions that make life possible. Folly's house represents those things in creation that are out of place, out of bounds, and off-limits. Conduct outside Wisdom's limits and order destroys the self and damages others; ultimately it is deadly. Thus food and drink are good, but too much or the wrong type can be harmful (25:16, 27). One cannot really live in Folly's house, for the stolen water and bogus bread she offers are deadly.

On the other hand, Wisdom and Folly inhabit the same cosmos and even the same places in the world. They both make their pitches in the same places (cf. 1:20-21; 7:11-12; 8:2-3; 9:3*b*, 14*b*). Paradoxically, the world that Wisdom has built is also the house where Folly dwells. It is not Folly's house by right but by usurpation. Folly and sin are always parasitic of the good that God by Wisdom has made. Folly takes the goods and

---

164. Augustine *De Doctrina Christiana* 1.11.11, cited in Jeffrey, *A Dictionary of Biblical Tradition in English Literature*, 833.

destroys their goodness by ripping them from their proper place in the coherence of things. She tears down the ordered human world that Wisdom makes (see Commentary on 14:1). Folly has not built her house; she has stolen it, like the cowbird steals and befouls the songbird's nest.

The identical language in the mouths of Wisdom and Folly (9:6, 16) underscores the parasitic ambiguity of evil. It masquerades as good (Isa 5:20). When humans are tempted, it is by something God created good. But it is a disordered good, because we humans, as Augustine saw it, are driven by disordered loves to disorder reality. Christ, the Wisdom of God, came to set our love right.

PROVERBS 10:1–22:16

THE FIRST SOLOMONIC COLLECTION OF SAYINGS

PROVERBS 10:1–15:33, THE ANTITHETICAL COLLECTION

OVERVIEW

On titles and the divisions of Proverbs, see the Introduction. The first "Solomonic" collection of sayings (10:1–22:16) can be divided into two parts: 10:1–15:33 and 16:1–22:16.

The first part moves from the extended instructions of chaps. 1–9 to the two-line sayings that predominate in the Solomonic collections. Its sayings are with few exceptions antithetical—that is, the parallel lines present topics and comments using a rich interplay of synonymous and contrasting terms. For example, wisdom is contrasted with folly, sloth with diligence, joy with sorrow, so that issues are illuminated from more than one side. In particular, this section pervasively contrasts "righteous" (צדק *ṣdq*) and "wicked" (רשע *rš*ʿ). These concepts are active even when the terms are not used, because they are commonly portrayed in concrete words, actions, and images. To move the widow's boundary stone is "wicked," even if that term is not used (15:25; 22:28).

In the book of Proverbs, there is some overlap in meaning between the opposed pairs righteous/wicked and wisdom/folly (which dominated chaps. 1–9), as 10:1-8 shows. In general, righteousness, like wisdom (see Commentary on chaps. 8–9), is a cosmic concept (cf. Pss 50:6; 72:3, 16; 97:6).[165] In the human realm, it carries connotations of social-moral-spiritual-legal right and wrong and is a narrower concept than "wisdom"

165. H. H. Schmid, *Gerechtigkeit als Weltordnung;* "Creation, Righteousness, and Salvation: 'Creation Theology' as the Broad Horizon of Biblical Theology," in Bernhard W. Anderson, ed., *Creation in the Old Testament* (Philadelphia: Fortress, 1984) 102-17.

(חכמה *ḥokmâ*). One can do what is righteous (care for the poor, for example), but do it in an unwise manner. But one cannot be wise without being righteous. There is no way to steal, lie, or murder wisely, because these deeds are wicked and contrary to cosmic-moral order. Wicked deeds are not wise; they produce damage and death; they do not foster goodness and life. In this regard, Proverbs is different from other OT books, because it has shaped its understanding of wisdom and righteousness in terms of the "fear of the LORD" (see Commentary on 1:7). Proverbs would not call wicked Jonadab "very wise," though 2 Sam 13:3 does (perhaps ironically?).

For Proverbs, righteousness is an indispensable but minimal reality requirement. Wisdom includes it, but goes beyond it. The wise do righteous things well, in the best way, in harmony with the requirements of the situation, the time, the persons, and other circumstances. In wisdom, righteous humans exercise their freedom in the best possible way.

Another important feature of Prov 10:1–15:33 is its simplicity with regard to the act/consequence connection. It relentlessly insists that "you reap what you sow." In Proverbs 10–15, good acts predominantly produce good consequences, and bad acts produce bad consequences. This is the ABC of wisdom, the basic rules the young need to live well. Starting with chap. 16, the exceptions to the basic rules of life will appear much more frequently (see Introduction).

Proverbs 10:1-8, Introduction to the Antithetical Collection

COMMENTARY

Verses 1-8 form a patterned introduction to the fundamental issues of 10:1–15:33 (see Commentary on 16:1-9, 10-15). Through repeated key words, the introduction sketches the horizon of meaning for the sayings that follow. Many of these terms appear throughout 10:1–15:33, or are elaborated by appropriate images and actions. The concentric pattern of key words is here diagrammed using simplified English forms (in 10:1, 8, the Hebrew terms for "fool" [כסיל *kĕsîl*] are different).

A   v. 1,
  B   vv. 2-3,

    C   vv. 4-5,
  B´   vv. 6-7,

A´   v. 8,

Wise ⟍⟋ Fool
Wicked ⟍⟋ Righteous
Righteous   Wicked
Illustrations of key terms
Bless Righteous/   Wicked

Righteous Bless/   Wicked
Wise   Fool

Verses 1 and 8 frame this introduction with the basic opposition of wisdom and folly; vv. 2-3 and 6-7 introduce the righteous and the wicked; and v. 3 makes explicit the all-encompassing involvement of God in human affairs.[166] Wisdom and ethical order are inseparable from the divine source of order (see Commentary on 1:7). Verses 4-5, at the center of the introduction, focus on human responsibility and on the consequences of human habits and actions, setting them in their cosmic context.

10:1. The opening verse (variant in 15:20; see Commentary on 13:1) assumes that wisdom is a matter of generations. By taking up this insight from chaps. 1–9 (see Commentary on 29:3), the proverb creates a strong link between chaps. 1–9 and the first Solomonic collection. Wisdom is handed down by parents and received (v. 8, "accepted" NIV; cf. 2:1; 4:3) or rejected (13:1) by children. Each generation (and individual) must choose for itself wisdom or folly, and these choices come in terms set by previous generations. Moreover, children's choices can bring joy or sorrow to their parents (cf. 17:21, 25; 19:26; 23:15-16, 22-25; 27:11; 28:7; 29:3, 15; Eccl 2:18-21; Sir 3:1-16). In keeping with the character/consequence schema (humans reap what they regularly sow), v. 1 uses general categories (wise/foolish, parents/son) to focus on specific consequences within the parent-child relationship (cf. v. 5*b*). This saying is illustrated by the poignant stories of the old priest Eli and his wicked sons (1 Sam 2:12–4:18), of Samuel and his sons (1 Sam 8:1-9), and of King David and his sons Amnon and Absalom (2 Sam 13:21; 18:33).

10:2-3. Verse 2*a* suggests that wicked wealth is unstable, of no profit in the long run. "Ill-gotten treasures" is a prophetic phrase (Mic 6:10-11; cf. Prov 11:1). But righteous human behavior "delivers" from death (see 11:4), a rescue operation elsewhere ascribed to the Lord (Pss 33:19; 56:13). In later Hebrew, "righteousness" (צדקה *ṣĕdāqâ*) can refer to "alms" (Sir 16:14; cf. Matt 6:1-4, where "alms" is a specification of "righteousness" in 6:1).

Verse 3 sets up one of the theological problems of wisdom: Does God never let the righteous go hungry (cf. Pss 34:10; 37:25; Matt 6:11)? One proverb is never adequate to describe all of reality; here we find a statement of God's fundamental and usual mode of dealing with humans. Other sayings (and various psalms [44; 73], Job, and Ecclesiastes) show that the situation is more complex (see Commentary on Prov 16:8). There is a

166. See Alonso-Schökel and Vilchez, *Proverbios*, 256.

pun in v. 3*b* on הוה (*hawwâ*), a word that means both "desire" and "disaster": The Lord "thrusts forward the disaster of the wicked!"

10:4-5. These verses link laziness to poverty and hard work to success, as causes to effects. Again, no one proverb provides a complete picture (see Commentary on 13:23). In this introductory section (as in chaps. 10–15 generally) the ABC's of wisdom are being taught; the exceptions to the rules will come later. Without hard work, there can be no success, and laziness destroys the best of circumstances. The imagery is simple: The "slack hand" and the "diligent hand" each has its consequences. But the image is suggestion rich. "Hand" (יד *yād*) is a standard Hebrew metaphor for power. The proverb says to the young, in effect, that success or failure is in your hands. One must be proactive and take responsibility for one's own existence.[167]

Verse 5 sets the issue of personal responsibility and labor in the context of the created order (see Commentary on Proverbs 8). To be wise and good requires that humans be in touch with reality, that their actions be in tune with the rhythms of the cosmos as well as the nature of individual things (Isa 28:23-29; Rom 1:18-25; 2:14-15). The imagery is drawn from the world of the Palestinian farmer. "Summer" and "harvest" are parallel terms, since the crops ripen, each in its order, during the dry hot months of summer (cf. 26:1). To harvest at the appropriate time is an instance of basic wisdom. This truth—obvious except to the one who ignores it—is built into the fabric of creation itself. The parallel passage in 6:6-11 (cf. 20:4) seeks to teach the sluggard by using the lowly ant as an example of wisdom (on laziness, a subspecies of folly, see 24:30-34; 26:13-16).

10:6-7. The consequences of righteousness and wickedness are generalized in terms of blessing—that is, the divine act of granting success and *shalom* (peace and prosperity) to humans in tune with God and reality. The implicit divine action in blessing further strengthens the concentric parallel with vv. 2-3. The relation of v. 6*b* to v. 6*a* is difficult to establish; the fit of the repetition in v. 11*b* is more obvious. Perhaps 11:26 provides a solution: The good person receives public blessing while the wicked person conceals his or her ill intentions.[168] (For the NIV translation, cf. Ps 140:9; Hab 2:17.)

10:8. This verse is elliptical; the consequences of heeding commandments are not spelled out, but the ruin that follows unbridled speech is. In the OT, the word for "ruin" (לבט *lābaṭ*) appears only in 10:8, 10 and Hos 4:14, where it is applied to Israel as a people lacking understanding.[169] The nexus of character, acts, and consequences applies not merely to individuals but to nations, societies, and cultures (cf. the LXX reading of 26:3, "a rod for a lawless nation").

---

167. See Covey, *The Seven Habits of Highly Successful People*, 65-94.

168. Alonso-Schökel and Vilchez, *Proverbios*, 261.
169. Cf. the Qumran hymn 1QH 2:19.

REFLECTIONS

1. Proverbs assumes that the wise formation of children is the work of mothers and fathers. It portrays women as authoritative sources of instruction and models of wisdom also for males (cf. Proverbs 1–9; 23:22-25; 31:1). In contemporary North America, however, the work of parenting suffers generally from deficient or absent fathering, with too much of the burden placed on the shoulders of women, whether single mothers or married. Some research suggests that the sons of absent or aloof fathers may more frequently grow up with a "macho," or authoritarian identity, especially in relation to women.[170] More than that, individualistic Americans need to remember that "it takes a village to raise a child."

It should perhaps also be noted that analyses of Israel's patriarchal society need to account for the role of both women and men in maintaining and handing on a

---

170. See Mary S. Van Leeuwen, *Gender and Grace* (Downers Grove: Inter-Varsity, 1990) 125-63; Samuel Osherson, *Finding Our Fathers: How a Man's Life Is Shaped by His Relationship with His Father* (New York: Fawcett Columbine, 1986).

worldview and its norms. In addition, the role of Israel's mostly agrarian material culture in limiting gender roles must be given serious consideration, lest the complexities of life be reduced to a play of ideas, as if only male ideas shaped society.[171] This is not to deny wicked male misogyny, violence, and oppression of women past and present. It is, rather, a plea for analysis of a cultural system in which both women and men are responsible, (inter)active agents. One explanation is that women have internalized dominant male attitudes, including "male fear of women."[172] But such an explanation begs explanation. How does this happen? Does it imply bad faith on the part of women in patriarchal cultures? Or is it a function of their status as victims? Does the "elite mother" (perhaps writer) of 31:1-9 experience herself as a victim? Family and cultural dysfunction or health, the frenzy or felicity between the sexes, the war or peace between the generations—these are systemic matters that need to be analyzed and addressed on many levels by divine grace and human labor.[173]

2. Wisdom and folly are not merely intellectual or spiritual qualities; they are inseparable from actions of virtue or vice, as the repetition of key terms in these verses shows. If the good are not wise, their goodness is ineffectual. If the wise are not good and godly, their wisdom is eventually unmasked as folly by the flow of history. For example, the wise but unscrupulous Jonadab sets in motion events that culminate in Absalom's revolt (2 Sam 13:1-22; 14:32-34). It is such overweening "wisdom" that the prophets and the apostle Paul attacked (Isa 5:18-25; Jer 8:4-12; 1 Cor 1:18-31). The classic narrative of wisdom undone by God's superior judgments is the tale of Ahithophel (2 Sam 16:15–17:23). Indeed, virtually the entire narrative of David's reign, from his sin with Bathsheba until his final decline, may be read as a tale of royal folly, pregnant with disasters narrowly averted, thanks to God's stern covenant mercy (2 Samuel 11–20; 2 Kings 1–2).[174]

171. See Myers, "Everyday Life," 244-51.
172. Cf. the views of Newsom, "Woman and the Discourse," 151.
173. See Lerner, *The Dance of Anger.*
174. R. N. Whybray, *The Succession Narrative: A Study of II Sam. 9–20 and 1 Kings 1 and 2,* STB 2nd series 9 (London: SCM 1968).

Proverbs 10:9-32, Sayings on the Antithesis of Good and Evil

COMMENTARY

10:9. Psalm 26 elaborates the character of one who "walks in integrity" (see 2:7; 20:7; 28:6, 18; Job 1:1). The psalmist prays that God will deal with him according to his inner and outer, godly integrity (Ps 26:1-3). Such oneness of direction in life ("walk") and unity of character is associated in Psalm 26 with "trusting" the Lord (i.e., finding one's security in God; 26:1-3, 11; Ps 23:4; Isa 33:15-16). The inner and outer person are of one piece (Ps 26:2; cf. Prov 26:23-26, where outward action conceals inner evil). Such integrity is often contrasted with "twistedness" (Prov 11:20; 17:20; 19:1; 28:6). The "twisted" or "crooked" person will eventually be exposed

(Prov 26:26). Crookedness, like murder, will out. Since the righteous psalmist must request God's vindication, the security promised in Prov 10:9a is not necessarily the same as a trouble-free, prosperous life.

10:10. "Winks the eye" refers to some secretive, non-verbal communication meant for ill (Prov 6:13; Ps 35:19; Sir 27:22-24). The body and its parts express and are agents of good and ill (Prov 6:17-18; Mark 9:43-48). The Hebrew text of v. 10b seems misplaced from v. 8 (NRSV margin), since it breaks the pattern of antithesis in these chapters and the connection between v. 10a and v. 10b is unclear. Most scholars follow the LXX (e.g., NRSV).

10:11-12. These verses form a proverb pair ("conceals" and "covers" are the same word in Hebrew [כסה *kāsâ*]; for NIV, see Hab 2:17) and are part of a cluster of verses on good and bad speech (vv. 11-14; see vv. 18-21). Verse 11 contrasts the effects of a righteous or wicked "mouth." "A fountain of life" (see Ps 36:9[10]; Prov 13:14; 14:27; cf. Jer 2:13; 17:13) is a powerful image in hot and dry Palestine, where life is impossible without water (cf. 3:18; 15:4, "tree of life"). The parallels suggest that God and human agents are not to be artificially separated as sources of life (see Ezek 47:1-12; John 4:13-14; 7:37-39). The righteous mouth brings life because wisdom flows from it (see 3:13-18; 10:13, 31; Ps 37:30).

Deceptive speech "conceals violence" (v. 11*b*) against others (v. 18), but ultimately also against oneself. "Here is a double opposition between the righteous and the wicked; first in the contrary effects, the former causeth life, the latter mischief and death; and secondly in the manner of producing them, the righteous doth it by uttering his words, and the wicked doth it by concealing his mind."[175]

Whether concealed (v. 18) or open, hate stirs up conflict (6:14), while love can remove it by covering offenses (in the sense of forgiving them; see Ps 85:3; cf. Prov 11:13; 17:9; Jas 5:20; 1 Pet 4:8). In this sense, one cannot cover one's own sin (28:13; Job 31:33; Ps 32:5). Alternately, "covering" has the sense of "ignoring" as in 12:16.

10:13. "Lacks sense" (חסר–לב *ḥăsar-lēb*) is literally "lacks heart," the central organ of insight and understanding (see Commentary on 26:3). This idiom occurs 11 times in Proverbs, while the Hebrew for "heart" (לב *lēb*) occurs 99 times (see Excursus, "The 'Heart' in the Old Testament").

10:14-15. The mouth has tremendous power for good or for ill, whether to oneself or to others (see 2:1-2; 7:1-3). Verse 15 is linked to v. 14 by the term "ruin" (חתת *ḥātat*; see 13:3; 18:7). Here wealth and poverty are portrayed as strength and disaster respectively, with no moral or spiritual judgments attached (cf. v. 4). But the picture is

more complex, as the proverb pair in 18:10-11 shows (cf. 10:29).

10:16-17. Wage(s) and gain foreground the character/consequence nexus (cf. Paul's "the wages of sin is death," a good wisdom saying [Rom 6:23]). The same Hebrew word can refer to sin proper or to sin's consequences, punishment and ultimately death. The ambiguity ought not to be eliminated, since the wealth of the wicked can embroil them in further wickedness.

Verse 17 is linked to v. 16 by the phrase "to life" (see 6:23; 15:10; and the Overview to Proverbs 1–9 on path imagery). In the expression "Goes astray/leads others astray," the Hebrew verb form is ambiguous, and its causality can be either internal (damage to self, 12:26; cf. Isa 47:10) or external (damage to others; cf. Isa 3:12; Jer 50:6).

10:18. Now begins a second cluster of verses on good and bad speech (vv. 11-14; 11:12-13, 18–21; 26:26). The NRSV and the NIV differ on the grammatical subject of v. 18*a*: "Lying lips" or "He who conceals"; the latter supplies a better antithesis to the second line. Usually, a person's inner character and convictions are expressed in word and deed (1 Sam 24:13; Luke 6:43-45). There is an integrity of the inner and outer person. But the heart is able to conceal its hatred (see 26:23-28, where "enemy" and "hatred" share the same Hebrew root; cf. 2 Sam 13:22). The wise will be aware of this phenomenon and beware. Conversely, honest conflict is better than hidden love (Prov 27:5-6; Lev 19:17-18). In the light of this verse, the young Joseph may have been a fool (Gen 37:2, 5, 9).

10:19. These thoughts continue in the tradition: "All my days I have grown up among the Wise, and I have not found anything better than silence; and not study is the chief thing but action; and whoso makes many words occasions sin."[176] Appropriate, timely expression or restraint of what is in the heart is essential to wisdom (12:23; 15:2; 17:27-28; 18:2; Eccl 5:2-7). Compare the World War II proverb, "Loose lips sink ships."

10:20. Monetary metaphors are here juxtaposed with body parts ("tongue"/"choice silver" vs. "heart"/"little worth") in an attempt to communicate the surpassing worth

---

175. Poole, *A Commentary on the Holy Bible II*, 2:231.

176. Mishnah tractate *Abot* 1:17; cf. Jas 3:1-12; *APOT* II, 694.

of righteous speech (cf. 8:19). Even in ancient Israel, "money talks." The connection of heart and organs of speech is once again assumed (see Commentary on v. 18). This verse contains a lovely wordplay on "tongue" (לשון *lāšôn*), because the word also can refer to a tongue-like ingot of gold or silver (cf. Josh 7:21, 24: "bar," "wedge").

10:21. The contrast of life and death is implicit in "feed many" versus "die." But the relationship between the two lines of the saying needs to be determined. "To feed many" employs a verb (lit., "to shepherd" [רעה *rā'â*]; see Psalm 23), which is a metaphor of kingly rule throughout the ancient Near East, including Israel. Psalm 8, however, portrays the democratization of kingship. Thus the righteous here are those persons in various positions of responsible authority (parents, teachers, pastors, rulers, employers, etc.) who care for and nurture their "flock" with wisdom and justice (Jer 3:15; 23:1-6). In the "peaceable kingdom," the wise shepherd is implicitly present (Isa 11:1-9). But fools who "lack heart" (v. 13) will die like errant sheep in spite of "pastoral" nurture (29:19). "A word to the wise is sufficient," but not for fools.

10:22. Verse 22*b* is ambiguous (see NRSV margin), and this ambiguity has profound theological and practical implications. The way one interprets and contextualizes this proverb may say much about the reader's own world and life view. The NRSV and NIV translations suggest that God grants blessings unadulterated with sorrow or trouble. Yet in the real world even the blessed suffer. One might attempt to escape the problem by suggesting that sorrow comes not from God but from elsewhere. But in the monotheistic OT, this theological move is countered by the prologue of Job 1–2 and many psalms of lament (e.g., Psalms 22; 35; 44), which hold God ultimately responsible for the welfare of the people.

The variation suggested in the margin of the NRSV is preferable, even though it brings its own complications. On the surface, "toil adds nothing" contradicts the wisdom principle that toil produces wealth (10:4; 14:13).

10:23. This verse states a mystery of folly: Its pleasure is to do evil (1:16; 2:14; 15:21; 26:19). It is also a mystery to fools

that wisdom may give delight. "Sport," "pleasure," and "delight" are the same word in Hebrew (שחק *śāḥaq*), which appears only in the first line and functions elliptically in the second. Just as a primary love determines the character and direction of individuals, groups, and societies (a basic theme of Proverbs 1–9 as well as of Augustine's *City of God*), so also the "sport" of persons and cultures shapes their character and reveals their ethos.[177] Our tendency toward good or evil depends on what we delight in (2:14; 15:21; 26:19; cf. Matt 6:21).

10:24-25. These verses form a proverb pair (see v. 28). The wicked stand in a love/hate relation with evil. By the evil done to others, they hope to gain personal good. Yet such persons dread that what they do will be done to them, that the punishment will fit the crime (cf. 11:27*b*; 21:13; Isa 66:3-4; cf. Job 3:15). But since the desire of the righteous conforms to the order of reality and to God's own purposes, it will surely come to be (11:23; Pss 20:4; 21:2; Matt 6:33). It will "be granted" (יתן *yittēn*, used in ellipsis; cf. 12:12, 14; Job 36:6; Ps 121:3), that is, by God.

Verse 25 contrasts righteous and wicked in the context of cosmic imagery (see Commentary on 10:30; Pss 93:1-2; 96:10; Wis 5:14-15). The expansion of this proverb in Jesus' parable suggests that the wicked and the fool are close kin (Matt 7:24-27). "Storm"/"tempest" (associated with God's theophany in judgment, Isa 29:6; 66:15; Nah 1:3) in the first line contrasts with "established"/"stand firm forever" in the second. The latter phrase (lit., "a lasting foundation"), corresponds to declarations concerning the stable foundation of creation itself (Pss 78:69; 104:5; cf. Job 38:4; Ps 24:2; Prov 3:19). But the wicked do not survive the storms of life (cf. 1:27; Job 27:20-21; Ps 73:18-19; but note Prov 25:26 and Job's complaint in Job 21:18).

10:26. This is one of several sayings on the incongruous or unfitting (25:20; 26:1, 6-7; 27:14). Ancient Israel did not possess modern dentistry. Thus vinegar would cause pain to teeth that were broken or decayed.

---

177. For a modern Augustinian analysis of history, see E. Rosenstock-Huessey, *Out of Revolution: Autobiography of Western Man* (Norwich, Vt.: Argo, 1969). See also J. Huizinga, *Homo Ludens: A Study of the Play-Element in Culture* (Boston: Beacon, 1950).

"Employers" (NRSV) is literally "those who send him" (NIV; see 13:17; 25:13). For "fittingness," see Commentary on 26:1-12.

10:27-28. The "fear of the LORD" (1:7), wisdom, and parental teaching are of one piece in their effects (3:1-2, 16; 9:11), the latter two as the objective reality and the first as its subjective appropriation (2:5). As is usual with proverbs, this saying needs to be qualified, for the life of the righteous is sometimes cut short (Ps 102:24-25). Compare Isa 57:1, which offers one explanation for this phenomenon, and Ps 44:22 and Wis 4:7-20, which offer others. The problem's ultimate resolution requires a developed view of life after death.[178]

Verses 27-28 form a proverb pair on the alternate futures of the righteous and the wicked. Verse 27 concerns the future's objective realization, v. 28 inner expectations for the future, which are realized or not (cf. 10:24; 11:7, 24; Job 8:13; 11:20; Ps 112:10*c* [= Prov 11:28*b*]; John 5:45). The sure object of godly hope is joy, though at present the reality may be absent (see Ruth 1:12; Pss 9:18; 33:18; Rom 8:24-25; Heb 11:1). For "comes to nothing" (lit., "perishes"), see Commentary on 11:7.

10:29. "The way of the LORD" occurs only here in Proverbs. Does it refer to God's action or "way" (8:22; Exod 33:3) or to the "way" revealed by God for human conduct? Delitzsch suggests that it is "the way which the God of revelation directs men to walk in [Pss 27:11; 143:8], the way of His precepts [Ps 119:27], His way of salvation [Ps 67:2]."[179] In the NT it appears as "the way of God" (Matt 22:16; Acts 18:25-26) or simply, "the Way" (Acts 9:2; 24:14). In Proverbs, one must also think of the way of Wisdom (cf. 3:17; 4:11; 8:20). Thus revealed religion (including general revelation, as in Proverbs 8) is comfort and protection to those of integrity, but a source of destruction to evildoers (cf. 2 Cor 2:14-16).

Alternately, the verbal parallels between 10:29 and 21:15 suggest that "the way of the LORD" may refer to God's judgments on human conduct. Compare the wisdom saying that concludes Hosea (Hos 14:9) and

Isa 55:8-9. Finally, the Hebrew of v. 29*a* permits the translation, "Yahweh is a fortress to the man whose conduct is blameless" (see 11:20; 13:6).

10:30. This verse has strong thematic and verbal connections to Psalm 37 (esp. Ps 37:9, 11, 22, 27-29; see also Ps 125:1; Prov 10:25; 12:3). Wisdom rarely intersects explicitly with Israel's historical theological concerns: promises to the patriarchs, covenants, exodus, Sinai, and the gift of or exile from the land (but cf. 22:28; Job 15:18-19; 24:2, 18). The possession of the land (of Canaan), or "earth" (the Hebrew term ארץ [*'ereṣ*] means both), is here not related to Israel per se (Gen 15:18; 17:8) but to the contrast of "righteous" and "wicked" (see Commentary on 2:21-22; note the condition of obedience in Deut 4:1; 8:1; 25:15; 28:36-37, 49, 64; cf. Jer 7:7; Amos 7:17). Thus this proverb belongs to that matrix of traditions that grows into Israel's and the church's eschatology (Matt 5:5; Rom 4:13). "Will never be removed/uprooted" is literally "totter," "slip" (25:26; Pss 93:1; 96:10; see Commentary on 12:3). Experience sometimes contradicts this statement (25:26), and past commentators have resolved the tension in various ways. The steadfastness of the righteous may refer to individuals whose fall is only temporary (24:15-16; Ps 34:21-22), to their posterity (Pss 89:29; 102:28), or to the future life.[180] The first two options appear already in the medieval Jewish commentators Rashi and Moses Kimchi.

10:31-32. The final verses are a proverb pair, related by parallelism of speech organs and the opposition of righteous and wicked.

v. 31	Mouth-righteous	Perverse-tongue
v. 32	Lips-righteous	Mouth-wicked
		(perverse)

"Brings forth" (v. 31; cf. 10:11, 21; 15:28) is literally "to bear fruit" (נוב *nûb*; cf. 11:30; 15:4; Ps 92:14). "Perverse" (תהפכה *tahpukâ*; used nine times in Proverbs, and elsewhere only in Deut 32:20) refers to what is "upside down," here to speech that inverts and distorts reality (cf. 2:12; 6:14; 8:13; 23:33; Isa 5:20).

178. F. Delitzsch, "Proverbs," in C. F. Keil and F. Delitzsch, *Commentary on the Old Testament,* vol. 6 (Grand Rapids: Eerdmans, 1975) 226.

179. Delitzsch, "Proverbs," 227.

180. Examples may be found in Matthew Poole, *Synopsis criticorum* (1671) 2:1549. On the conflict of experience and faith, see Van Leeuwen, "On Wealth and Poverty."

"Cut off" seems a gruesome image when applied to the tongue (used only here and Ps 12:4). The ancient Assyrians actually tore out the tongues of rebels.[181] But "tongue" is used here in a literary device called synecdoche, in which the part stands for the whole (see Gen 9:11; Num 15:31). "Acceptable"/"fitting" (v. 32) is what delights both God and humans (see 8:35; 11:1, 27; 12:22; 14:35; 16:13; Rom 12:1-2; Phil 4:9).

181. See Pritchard, *Ancient Near Eastern Texts Relating to the Old Testament*, 288.

REFLECTIONS

1. The topics of Proverbs 10 are diverse. What unites this and the following chapters is the relentless opposition of "righteous" and "wicked," good and evil. Every verse (including v. 10 if we follow the LXX) presents an opposition, in one form or another, of good and evil. This polarized world corresponds to the two ways in chapters 1–9. In this world humans have to find their way, and they do so by making and keeping ultimate commitments. Human beings are an ambiguous mixture of good and evil (see 20:9). But this does not erase the fundamental opposition between two directions in life.

2. The chapter also forces us to face up to reality—first, in the sense that there is an objective, created order that sets the terms in which humans are responsible to God, to others, to self, and to creation itself: Sow in season; harvest in season. Human habits and actions, including words, have consequences for which we are accountable. Both folly and sin begin with denial and distortion, with the embracing of irreality.[182] Second, to face up to reality requires that we acknowledge the conflict of good and evil in the world and in ourselves and not try to paper it over. Americans, still enamored of myths of progress, tolerance, and the innate virtue of the United States ("America: love it or leave it"; "My country, right or wrong"), are tempted to ignore internal evil and the tremendous labor and sacrifice that are required to achieve personal or corporate good.

The gospel here is that God has made this world good and, in spite of quirks, quandaries, and sin, it runs with a certain reliability that rewards the wise, the diligent, and the righteous (Gen 8:22). If this were not true, ordinary work, success, love, and life would not be possible.

3. Proverbs 10:22 suggests that a theology that holds that God "does it all" can lead to passivity or to ritual magic (like anointing one's wallet, advocated by some televangelists). This is an abdication of the power and responsibility given to human beings. Yet a secular "untheology" of human achievement also misses reality (Deut 8:17-18), for it neglects the mysterious role of divine blessing (Gen 1:22, 28) in the fecundity of creation and the felicity of life. Human action and divine providence are not in tension (cf. the paradoxical formulation in Gen 45:8). Rather, toil, which has no independent power to add to God's blessing, is nonetheless the means of its realization (Pss 127:1-2; 128:1-6; Phil 2:12-13, a passage pertaining not so much to eternal destiny as to life in this world). For humans, this paradox is resolved in the old Latin proverb, *Ora et labora,* or "Pray and work." Blessing is a grace that does not annul or contradict nature (including human work) but is its ground and sole possibility.[183] The godly worker, having prayed and labored (Ps 90:17), experiences the fruit of labor as a gift (Eccl 3:12-13, 22; 5:18-19).

182. See Peck, *People of the Lie.*
183. The grammar of Prov 10:22*a* is emphatic, specifying "the blessing of the LORD" as the ultimate source of wealth.

4. If we consider the cross of Christ in relation to sinful acts and consequences (see Commentary on 10:16), we may say that the cross does not annul this connection, but reroutes the consequence of death to Christ, while releasing his life for humans. A similar logic of grace obtains in OT sacrifice.[184]

184. See Wenham, *The Book of Leviticus*, 25-29.

Proverbs 11:1-31, Further Sayings on the Antithesis of Good and Evil

COMMENTARY

11:1. This saying brings righteousness into the marketplace and grounds economic fair play in the good pleasure of Yahweh (see 20:10, 23). Its language echoes Israel's legal codes (Lev 19:35-37; Deut 25:13-16) and the prophetic condemnation of commercial greed and deception (Ezek 45:10; Hos 12:7-8; Amos 8:5; Mic 6:11). Because God "created" commerce, money matters to God (16:11). Abomination/delight is a standard antithesis, referring occasionally to human standards (16:12; 29:27; cf. 13:19), but more usually to Yahweh as the ultimate judge of good and evil (6:16; 11:20, 27). However, besides eleven occurrences in Proverbs, the phrase "abomination to the LORD" appears only in Deuteronomy (8 times, usually of cultic matters; cf. Prov 15:8). Crooked commerce is an "abomination" to the gods also in Egyptian wisdom.[185]

11:2. This verse is a variation on "Pride goes before a fall" (see 15:33*b*; 18:3, 12 for the form). Our English saying is a condensation of 16:18. Verse 2*b* associates wisdom with the humble (cf. 13:10), while 22:4 associates humility with the fear of the Lord. Although one should avoid self-praise (27:2; Deut 8:17-18), the requirement here is not for false modesty, but for "sober judgment" of self, including a realistic assessment of both one's gifts and limitations (26:1, 8), with a view to service of God and neighbor (Rom 12:3-8; 1 Cor 12:12-26). God ultimately humbles the proud (1 Sam 2:3; Isa 10:12-19).

11:3. Here the writer describes lives ruled by contrary inner principles: integrity versus

185. See "Amenemope," in Lichtheim, *Ancient Egyptian Literature*, 2:156-57.

unreliable crookedness. Integrity ("blameless," Job 1:1; 9:20-22) is what Job struggles to maintain in the face of calamity and God's apparently unjust silence. Since "practice makes perfect," these principles build character over time. Consistency of character either guides one's journey through thick and thin or destroys one (10:9; 19:3; Rom 5:3-5). As Aristotle said, "We are what we repeatedly do. Excellence, then, is not an act, but a habit." Here "treacherous" is the same as "faithless" (see Commentary on 13:15).

11:4. Language and thought from the prophetic tradition of the "day of the LORD," when Yahweh judges nations on a cosmic scale (Isa 13:9, 13; Ezek 7:19; Zeph 1:15, 18), are used here (see 16:4; Sir 5:8; 11:18-19). Although the saying does not exclude such a cosmic reference, a focus on people is more typical of Proverbs. This proverb may be applied to the "end" of individuals: Money will not help when death threatens (Ps 49:7-9, 16-20; Luke 12:15-21). At that moment, only one's righteous standing before God will matter (see Ps 49:15, though the sense is uncertain). Thus "death" may refer simply to calamities and mortal threats in the course of life (Ps 33:18-19).

11:5-6. These verses form a proverb pair closely tied to vv. 3-4 ("blameless" and "integrity" translate the same Hebrew root [תמם *tmm*]). In v. 3, integrity guides; in v. 5, righteousness clears one's way (see 3:6; cf. Commentary on 11:31).

Verse 6 forms a pair with v. 5 through verbal, formal, and thematic parallels; and v. 6*a* is a more general form of v. 4*b*. Verse 6*b* contains a wordplay on "desires" (הות *hawwat*; see Commentary on 10:3; Ps 5:10):

"the treacherous are trapped in [or by] their [own] chasm/ruin/desires" (see 26:27; Pss 7:15-16; 9:15-16; 38:12; see also Commentary on 13:6). For "treacherous," see Commentary on 11:3; 13:15.

11:7. Death is God's final "no" to evil (cf. v. 23; 10:28). The destructive projects of the wicked perish with them, while Yahweh's purposes continue (Ps 73:18-20; Isa 40:6-8, 22-24). In "Godless" and "from his power," the NIV and NRSV translations chose alternative possibilities for an obscure Hebrew phrase.

11:8. The righteous do not lack for troubles, but God rescues them (Exod 2:23-25; Pss 34:4, 19; 107:2). The saying as a whole, however, implies a more complex narrative of poetic justice. Unlike most sayings, which use generalizing verb forms, v. 8 uses the narrative verb sequence for specific events in the past. Literally, "A righteous person was rescued from trouble, and a wicked one got into it instead." Thus this saying, more clearly than most, is a narrative in a nutshell that summarizes the way God's justice sometimes works (see Sir 10:14). The hanging of wicked Haman on the gallows intended for Mordecai perfectly realizes this proverb (Esth 5:14; 7:10; 9:1-10), as does the story of Daniel in the lions' den (Dan 6:23-24). The parable of Lazarus and the rich man moves the pattern into the realm of the afterlife (Luke 16:25).

11:9. This passage begins a cluster of sayings exploring the interplay of social and political relations; it also has a backward verbal tie to v. 8 in "delivered." The ancient Greek translation (LXX) intensified the political focus of these verses by translating "neighbor" (vv. 9, 12) as "citizen." The "godless" or "profane" person is one who goes through life ignoring God (Job 8:13; Isa 32:6). But profane persons show their godlessness in dealing with their neighbors. The life-style of the godless reflects the dictum of Dostoyevsky: "If God does not exist, everything is permitted." Strangely, such practical atheism may be masked by "pious" worship (Isa 1:12-17; Jer 22:16; Amos 5:21-24) or even prophetic preaching (Jer 23:15). In this saying, the destructive power of speech (see also 18:21) is contrasted with the ability of righteous knowledge to rescue. The knowledge that saves may include knowledge of God, of

oneself, of others, or of a particular situation and the wisdom that applies to it (see Eccl 9:14-15, with its ironic qualification).

11:10-11. These verses form a pair that move us from interpersonal relations (v. 9) to the city as a symbol of political reality in general (see 14:34; Gen 11:1-9). This move suggests that the political realm is founded on the personal and that its health presupposes the vitality and integrity of the latter. Verse 10, like most sayings, is open to various applications. The prosperity of the righteous may refer to their own wealth, by which they promote civic good. It may also refer to the good they do directly for the people. Again, the righteous and the wicked may be ordinary citizens, or those who rule and govern (28:12, 15-16, 28). The good of good people makes the city rejoice, but so does the departure of the wicked, because their destructive power dies with them. The story of Haman and Mordecai illustrates v. 10 well (Esth 3:15; 8:15-17).

The Hebrew for "is exalted" (רום *rûm*, v. 11) may also mean "is built up" in contrast to the "overthrow" or "tearing down" of the city, both physically and as the symbol of the body politic. "Blessing" (ברכה *běrākâ*) in this verse displays the same ambiguity as the prosperity of the righteous in v. 10; but "mouth" in v. 11*b* suggests that it refers to the verbal act of blessing. Such blessing functions as a prayer that calls God to act on behalf of the people: "Pray for the peace of Jerusalem" (Ps 122:6 NRSV; see 1 Kgs 8:14, 55; Pss 51:18; 128:5-6; 133:1-3).

11:12-13. These verses form another pair (see Commentary on 10:12, 18; 11:9). For "lacks sense," see Commentary on 10:13. To "belittle" or "deride" one's neighbor is a human impulse that violates the essence of biblical religion (14:31). It is also, in merely practical terms, deeply foolish and counterproductive. The Hebrew word (בוז *bûz*) connotes an attitude that despises (14:21) another human being, for real or imagined flaws and failings.

Verse 13 applies the matter raised in v. 12 to gossip, echoing the law of Lev 19:16 (see Prov 20:19; Jer 6:28; Sir 27:16). This legal parallel opposes gossip to the great command to love the neighbor as oneself, from the heart (Lev 19:16-18; Matt 22:39; Rom 13:9).

Several other sayings contrast verbal destruction of the neighbor to wise love, which knows when silence is right (Prov 10:12, 19; 12:16; 17:9; 20:19).

11:14. What follows is one of several sayings on the need for wise counsel, especially in affairs of governance, state craft, and the waging of war (15:22; 20:18; 24:6). "Guidance" refers to the art of steering, of giving direction to things, as God does to clouds pregnant with moisture (Job 37:11-12).

11:15. This saying and related ones concern the obvious danger of being a direct or indirect guarantor of a loan (see Commentary on 6:1-5), especially to a stranger (20:16; 22:26; 27:13). To strike hands is a symbolic action that seals a deal.

11:16. It is difficult to understand the connection between the two lines of the Hebrew text of this verse. The NIV adds "only" to suggest that a "kind-hearted woman" is worth more than the ruthless who only gain wealth (see 22:1, where "favor" is the same word as "kind-hearted"). The NRSV solves the problem by adding to the Hebrew text lines from the Greek (LXX) and Syriac versions. But the Hebrew term for "kind-hearted"/"gracious" (חן *ḥēn*), when referring to a woman, generally means "beauty" (5:19; 31:30; cf. 1:9; 4:9; 17:8; Nah 3:4). Sirach 9:8 uses the identical Hebrew phrase to mean "beautiful woman." "Honor"/"respect" (כבוד *kābôd*) is usually translated "glory," but the term includes "wealth" as well. The saying is probably to be understood as a shrewd observation on beauty (see 11:22) and violence: "A beautiful woman gets 'glory'; ruthless men get wealth." The point of the comparison is that beauty can be the instrument by which a woman gains glory—that is, status, power, wealth, and the splendid symbols thereof (cf. 26:1). In the same way, ruthless/aggressive men find ways to get riches. ("Glory" and "riches" are parallel in 3:16; 8:18; 22:4; see also 1 Kgs 3:13; 1 Chr 29:28.)

11:17. The text implies that our disposition and behavior toward others, for good or for ill, affect our very selves in boomerang-like fashion (see 21:21). The Hebrew uses two different terms for the repeated English "themselves"; the first (נפש *nepeš*), sometimes translated "soul" (Ps 103:1), denotes the whole human person from an inner

perspective, as does the second (שאר *šĕʾēr*) from an outer, or "bodily," perspective. Literally, the verse may read, "The cruel trouble their own flesh" (see v. 29). Here the ethical problem of self-love finds its proportion and resolution. Contrary to the myth of rugged individualism, human solidarity is such that to love or harm others is to do the same to oneself. Moreover, the closer the human bond, the more intense the blessing or bane to the self (see 1 Cor 7:4; Eph 5:28-29).

11:18. Here the writer contrasts deceptive versus true wages earned by the efforts of the wicked and the righteous respectively (see 10:2, 16). "All that glitters is not gold." The contrast here of appearance and reality lends complexity to the basic act-consequence pattern, by providing one explanation of the anomaly of wicked wealth. The fruits of wicked labors may seem impressive, but they cannot be relied upon (Psalms 49; 73), even as one cannot rely on deceptive words. The imagery of sowing and reaping is a basic biblical metaphor for the character-consequence pattern (Job 4:8; Ps 126:5; Prov 22:8; Hos 10:12; 2 Cor 9:6; Gal 6:7). Because sowing and reaping are general patterns (not every seed bears the expected fruit, Jer 12:13; Mic 6:15; Matt 13:3-8, 24-30), the metaphor allows for anomalies and exceptions to the general rule. Sowing righteousness appears also in Hos 10:12-13 (see Prov 22:8; Jas 3:18).

11:19-20. Verse 19 has a small uncertainty in its first line. Perhaps "steadfast"/"truly" is a particle ("Thus righteousness . . .") linking v. 19 to the preceding verse. This saying repeats the basic life issues central to chaps. 10–15. The end (good or evil) one pursues over the course of a lifetime determines the outcome (see Commentary on 11:4-5, 27; see 13:21; 15:9; 21:21). For "abomination"/"delight" (v. 20), see v. 1; for the contrasts "crooked"/"blameless" and "heart"/"way," see Commentary on 10:9.

11:21. The phrase "will not go unpunished" (used 7 times in Prov 6:29; 11:21; 16:5; 17:5; 19:5, 9; 28:20) is one of several that connect wisdom with the great revelation of the name of Yahweh in Exod 34:6-7 (see also Exod 20:7). The phrase affirms the ultimate justice of God, not on the basis of empirical observation, but on the basis of

God's nature. Verses 20a and 21a together find a near duplicate in 16:5.

11:22-23. Ancient Israelite women wore nose rings for beauty and ornament (Gen 24:47; Ezek 16:12), but the shock of a pig's snout bedecked with gold provokes insight. Without good sense, beauty in a wife or woman (the Hebrew means both) is out of place. Beauty and wisdom may combine, as with Abigail (1 Samuel 25) and the heroines in Esther, Susanna, and Judith. But just as wisdom prohibits one from worshiping wealth (23:4-5), so also it cuts short the human tendency to idolize female beauty (31:30). Verse 23 is a variant of 10:28 (on "wrath," see v. 4).

11:24-26. These verses form a trio on economic relations between rich and poor. "Gives freely" (v. 24) is literally "scatters" (מפזר *měpazzēr*, see Ps 112:9)—that is, to the needy. The verse plays on a surface paradox that confirms the deeper principle of reaping as one sows. Generosity would seem to diminish one's resources but, in God's economy, brings gain (3:9-10; 19:17). To withhold more than is just, conversely, does not preserve wealth but brings lack. Verse 25 may be seen as an explication of the paradox in v. 24, according to the correspondence of acts and consequences (see 22:9).

Verse 26 completes the trio with a move from alms to commerce (see 11:1). The saying refers to a time of need, when hoarding staples can lead to personal profit at the cost of public starvation. The people's curse and blessing are in effect prayers to God (2 Sam 16:5-12; Prov 26:2), that God right injustice (24:24) or prosper the generous, who sell to the needy though the latter have only their labor to offer. The story of Joseph may serve as a general illustration of the positive second half of this saying (Gen 41:56; 42:6; 47:25; 49:26b). For profiteering (and the collapse thereof) in time of famine, see 2 Kgs 6:25; 7:1, 16.

11:27. "Favor" (רצון *rāṣôn*) is happily ambiguous, referring to what pleases God and humans (3:4; 1 Sam 2:26; Luke 2:52) and to the goodwill evoked thereby, though divine favor is infinitely uppermost (8:35; 12:2; 18:22; see 11:1, 20, where "delight" = "favor"). "Evil" (רעה *rā'â*) is unhappily ambiguous, referring to the wrong done by folks in their errant search for good (Gen

3:6), and to the trouble that comes to them instead (10:24a; Pss 7:16; 9:16; Sir 27:26-27). Beneath this saying lies the question, "What do I seek?" and the realization that no human has fully arrived (Phil 3:12-16). (The NRSV, with its double "seeks" in v. 27a, hews closer to the Hebrew than does the NIV.) So the search for "good" and for God are parallel, inseparable, with life and death at stake (v. 19; Amos 5:6, 14-15). For Jesus, such a search is the one thing needful: "Seek first the kingdom of God and his righteousness" (Matt 6:33 NRSV; 7:7).

11:28. Other things being equal, wealth is good (10:15), but without righteousness it is worthless (v. 4; 16:8). To make riches—any sort of human power really—into a source of security is to fall into unreality (18:11; Psalm 49; 1 Tim 6:17) and to separate the fruits from their root (15:20; 28:25; 29:25; Deut 8:17-18; Hos 2:8). Ultimate security and blessing are with God (3:5-8). The thought, antithesis, and botanical imagery of this saying parallel Psalm 1 and Jer 17:5-8 (see also Pss 52:7-8; 92:6-7, 12-14). The variation in translation of "whither" and "fall" perhaps reflects a deliberate pun in the Hebrew.

11:29. Literally, the Hebrew reads, "He who troubles his house," a rather open-ended phrase (= 15:27a; for the verb, see Gen 34:30; 1 Sam 14:29; 1 Kgs 18:17). The Hebrew for "house" (בית *bayit*) can mean "house(hold)" as well as "family." One's "house" is an inheritance from one's parents (19:14), to be built up by wisdom, labor, and care (24:3-4, 27). One's "house" is that microcosmos of God's greater world for which we are most immediately responsible (see Commentary on 9:1-6). As an ill bird fouls its own nest, so humans can trash their own "house" and thus "inherit the wind"—that is, nothing. The second line suggests a further descent: Fools who fail to exercise responsibility over their own turf will serve the realm of those who do (see 12:24; 14:1, 19; 17:2; and the peculiar development of wisdom themes in Matt 25:14-30; Luke 19:11-27).

11:30. For "tree of life," see Gen 2:9; 3:22; Prov 3:18; 13:12; 15:4. The difficulty of the second line is reflected in the two translations. The rendering by the NIV, with its view to gaining souls for eternal life, has its forerunners in medieval Jewish commentators.

The NRSV, however, is aware that to "take lives" (lit., "get/take souls" לקח נפשות *lāqaḥ nĕpāšôt*) in Hebrew often means "to kill" (1:19b; Ps 31:13, though the rabbis appeal to Gen 12:5 for a positive sense). Thus the NRSV changes the Hebrew subject to violence. This, however, destroys the text to be explained. A fully satisfactory solution remains to be found.

11:31. It might seem that the righteous here are repaid for their righteousness, while the wicked are repaid for their sins. But on such a reading, the move from minor to major (how much more) remains unexplained. The point is, rather, that since during their life (on earth; see Ps 58:11) even the righteous receive judgment for their sins (Num 20:12; 2 Sam 12:10-12), surely the wicked will as well. (The Greek translation taken over in 1 Pet 4:18 may be a paraphrase in this vein.) Verse 31 thus qualifies a too simplistic reading of the many sayings that, for pedagogical purposes, employ "righteous" and "wicked" as unnuanced, primary character types. (Such agonistic, "heavy" portrayal of types is characteristic of oral cultures.)[186]

186. See Ong, *Orality and Literacy,* 43-45, 69-71.

REFLECTIONS

1. While continuing the antithesis of righteous and wicked, Proverbs 11 introduces a few sayings that are not antithetical (11:7, 16, 22, 25, 29) and presents a richer variety of antitheses. Prominent in this chapter is a turn to the interwoven public arenas of commerce (11:1, 15, 24-26) and the sociopolitical commonweal (11:9-14, 24-26).

It is common for scholars to note in these chapters a straightforward connection between goodness and success and between wickedness and failure. Here, goodness leads to prosperity and badness leads to calamity (see Overview to 10:1–15:33). They further assume that such a simplistic view of acts and consequences must reflect a secure, almost complacent, social setting, perhaps among the scribes of the royal court. But the severity of the calamities (death and destruction, the "day of wrath," the fall of cities and nations) suggests that these sayings have currency even beyond a complacent middle-class world of decency and order.[187]

Whatever their social origin in ancient Israel, the application of these sayings certainly stretches to times of crisis and chaos. Perhaps especially in crisis and chaos it is necessary for the righteous to insist on the reality of justice, of consequences that follow upon good and evil. Such a view of meaning and order in life is grounded in the goodness and justice of the Creator, who calls human beings to account. Such a faith maintains belief in the God of justice, even when it does not experience justice. Such a faith was typical of Israel, as the psalms of lament eloquently attest.

For this American son of Dutch immigrants, the proverb clusters of chapter 11 evoke parental stories of life in the Nazi-occupied Netherlands during World War II. Others will have other tales to tell: of America's inner cities, of Vietnam, of Bosnia, of Ireland, of Rwanda, or of the former Soviet Union. In times of socioeconomic distress or oppression, the distinction of "righteous" and "wicked" becomes more visible, and the fence-sitting majority find it more difficult to maintain their posture of uncommitted respectability. These proverbial observations are also illustrated by Langdon Gilkey's wise first-person account of life in the microcosm of a war-time prison camp. When human goodness costs personal sacrifice, it becomes a rare commodity.[188] Trouble tests the heart's true mettle. In times of crisis and injustice, whispered words become more potent to destroy (Prov 11:9a, 11b, 13a); silence saves lives (Prov 11:12b, 13b); and shrewd ploys rescue the perishing (Prov 11:89b, 14b). And when the righteous triumph and the wicked finally fall, there is dancing in the streets (Prov 11:10).

187. See Whybray, *Wealth and Poverty in the Book of Proverbs.*
188. Langdon Gilkey, *Shantung Compound: The Story of Men and Women Under Pressure* (New York: Harper and Row, 1975).

2. To have contempt for other human beings is to insult their Maker (11:12-13; 17:5; see 14:31; 22:2). Although Proverbs does not make the connection, something like the priestly theology of humans' being created in the image of God's glory is operative here (Gen 1:26-28; Psalm 8; Jas 3:9). No doubt "other" people are flawed, weak, poor, and doers of what is despicable. Self-knowledge, however, ought to remind us that we belong to "them" (Prov 20:9). There is a twofold human solidarity that transcends race, sex, class, culture, and any other difference. First, God has made us all of one flesh, in God's image, to reflect the glory of God (see Acts 17:26). Second, there is the fragmented solidarity of sin, which prohibits pride and reveals our common need of grace (1 Cor 4:7). It is precisely defective and deficient humans, the failed and the unlovely, who receive God's compassion: "a broken and contrite heart, O God, you will not despise" (Ps 51:17 NRSV; see also Pss 22:24; 102:17; Isa 57:15; Matt 9:13; Rom 5:6-8).

On the practical level, to belittle another person is to damage the bond of common humanity, to sever ourselves from our own flesh. In marriage and family, in corporate and civic life, to belittle the other destroys the ability to continue our common work, whatever that may be. It is a form of win/lose thinking that ultimately redounds to our own loss. The person I insult, directly or in secret, is unlikely to help me in my time of need. Understanding knows when to hold its tongue (11:12*b*; 10:18-19; 17:27-28).

3. Lurking behind sayings on guidance and counsel (11:14) is the apparatus of the royal court and a variety of counselors on whose wisdom the success or failure of the nation in no small part depends. Before projects can be born in reality they must be conceived in the mind. But such deliberation must be communal, for "two heads are better than one." No one, not even the king, has all the answers, thus the need for counselors. But even the sharpest and shrewdest human wisdom has its limits. The best wisdom of the earthly court may be utterly undone by the contrary plans of the heavenly court (16:1, 9; 19:21; 21:30-31; Isa 29:14-16). Such sayings in Proverbs anticipate the intense discussion of the limitations of human wisdom found in Ecclesiastes and Job. The stories of David and Ahithophel (2 Sam 16:15–17:14) and of Ahab and the prophet Micaiah (1 Kgs 22:19-28) illustrate the failure of human wisdom in the face of the divine counsel.

4. The advice implicit in 11:15 has universal validity (like "let the buyer beware"), even though forms of financial risk taking change. It speaks also to a culture of stocks, (junk) bonds, failed savings and loans, and of leveraged buyouts. "The more things change, the more they stay the same." Nonetheless, there are times when it is proper to risk oneself as guarantee (the Hebrew term is not limited to loans) for another, as the Judah and Benjamin episode in the Joseph cycle indicates (Gen 43:9; 44:32-33; John 15:13; see Commentary on Prov 17:17-18).

5. Two sayings concern women and beauty (11:16, 22). In his autobiographical book, *Telling Secrets,* F. Buechner notes how his mother failed to develop character because she was able to trade upon her extraordinary beauty.[189] Proverbs is aware of the goodness and power of beauty and wealth. Yet, it steers us away from evaluating persons (even ourselves) on the basis of wealth or beauty; for human beings, male or female, other attributes are more important (see Commentary on 16:8). Wealth is no ultimate source of security (11:28). In spite of the widespread male idolatry (and fear) of beauty, wisdom does not value women according to mere appearance (11:22; 31:30; 1 Pet 3:3-5*a*). Men too frequently render themselves fools and sinners on account of a woman's beauty (2 Sam 11:2-27; 13:1-21; Prov 7:4-27; Matt 5:27-30). In general, according to social scientists, humans are inclined to attribute intelligence and other virtues to those who are of striking appearance (1 Sam 16:7). If beauty is skin deep, wisdom requires that we look deeper.

---

189. F. Buechner, *Telling Secrets: A Memoir* (New York: HarperCollins, 1991) 11-20.

---

6. It is a pervasive biblical principle that people reap what they sow and that the punishment, in the negative instance, will fit the crime (Exod 21:23-25; Pss 7:15-16; 9:15-16; Prov 11:29). What the evil folks do will come back to haunt them (1:18-19). The tales of Joseph's wicked brothers (Genesis 37–50) and of David's adultery with Bathsheba and murder of Uriah, her husband (2 Sam 11:2-17) may be considered extended instances of Prov 11:5*b*, 31*b*. Joseph's brothers are caught in the net they wove by selling Joseph to Egypt. And the saddest result of David's sins is his impotence in dealing with the similar sins of his sons Amnon and Absalom, an impotence that enables the latter's revolt and the near loss of David's kingdom. In the end, lusty King David is merely impotent (1 Kings 1). In both these stories, it is only God's grace and purpose that break the fateful chain of consequences for Joseph's brothers and for David (Gen 45:4-8; 50:15-21; 2 Sam 17:14). In the pedagogy of grace, people inclined to be wicked become righteous.

Proverbs 12:1-28, Whoever Loves Discipline Loves Knowledge

COMMENTARY

12:1. Aristotle begins his *Metaphysics* by observing that all people naturally desire knowledge. He illustrates his point by referring to our "love" of the senses, especially sight, which "best helps us to know things, and reveals many distinctions." Verse 1, however, has a focus characteristic of oral cultures: Wise knowledge comes through verbal interaction with others in the midst of life. Chapters 1–9 explored the theme of rebuke and correction in the figure of Lady Wisdom (1:25, 29-30). In this verse, the focus is on love of discipline (the broader term) and correction as essentials on the road to life (10:17). Paradoxically, discipline is a "station on the way to freedom."[190] In and of itself, our natural inclination is not to love discipline, but to reject and resist it (5:12; 9:7; 13:1, 18). Discipline is difficult, for it requires self-limitation at the behest of another (Heb 12:3-13; cf. Deut 8:5; Prov 3:11-12). But discipline may be loved for its fruit: knowledge. Knowledge makes us human; without it we are mere beasts ("stupid" in 30:2; in Ps 92:6 the term means "beast-like").

12:2. This verse employs language that resonates with key moments in the book. The "good" person receives the Lord's favor or goodwill (11:1, 27)—that is, life in the bosom of Lady Wisdom (8:35). This finding

and receiving has its mundane parallel in the divine gift of a wife (18:22; 19:14). In such a woman, but not in man, the human incarnation of wisdom is manifested (31:10-31).

But God "condemns the crafty." To be crafty is not in itself bad (1:4; 3:21; 8:12). But in this context, the Hebrew word for "crafty" (זמה *zimmâ*) signals those who rely on the devices of their own mind while ignoring God—the ultimate form of unreality (16:9; 19:21). Alternatively, the crafty are those who actively plan evil (24:8; Gen 6:5; 8:21; Eccl 7:29). The psalmist prays that such people be "caught in the schemes they have devised" (Ps 10:2 NRSV). God's justice "condemns" them, providing the model for human judges (17:15; Exod 23:7).

12:3. This verse democratizes a cosmic principle of divine and human kingship (Pss 89:14; 93:1-2; 97:1-2). On pillars such as these the house of Wisdom is built. Whereas the divine and Davidic thrones are "established through righteousness" (16:12 NIV; 25:4-5), this verse asserts the same of humankind in general, but in negative form.

12:4. As noted before, the original audience of Proverbs was male. Thus the possibility of a spouse's being good or bad is portrayed in terms of a good or bad wife. The phrase "a good wife of noble character" appears only three times in the OT (and also Sir 26:2). It receives a full description in the heroic hymn

190. Bonhoeffer, *Ethics*, 15. See also Reflections on Proverbs 6.

of Prov 31:10-31. Boaz uses it to describe the enterprising young widow, Ruth (Ruth 3:11), whose book immediately follows Proverbs in the Hebrew canon. The phrase seems to lie behind Paul's statement in the NT that a wife is her husband's glory (1 Cor 11:7), for "crown" and "glory" are closely associated (Prov 4:9; 16:31; Isa 28:1, 5; Jer 13:18).

12:5. The righteous and the wicked are here characterized by the thoughts and advice that preoccupy each. The Hebrew word translated as "advice" (תחבלות *taḥbulôt*) more precisely denotes stratagems that steer or govern life and its activities, such as battles (20:11; 24:6; see Commentary on 11:14, "guidance"). "Just" (משפט *mišpāṭ*) is literally "justice"; the mind of the righteous is focused on justice, which is God's basic intention for the descendants of Abraham (Gen 18:19; see Commentary on 21:3).

12:6. The positive and negative powers of speech are contrasted (see Commentary on 12:13; 18:21). The first line continues the thought of v. 5b by giving a concrete instance that echoes the invitation to murder in 1:11 (see NIV). The second line varies the language of 11:6.

12:7. The word root of "overthrown" (הפך *hāpak*) is used elsewhere of the destruction of Sodom and Gomorrah (Deut 29:23; Isa 13:19; Jer 49:18; Amos 4:11). On "are no more," see Job's lament that he is treated like the wicked (Job 7:7-10, 21). "House" can refer to a dwelling, to one's turf, or to one's posterity (15:25; 23:10-11). For further discussion, see the Commentary on 10:25; 12:3; 14:11.

12:8. For Israel, praise and life are inseparable partners. Where there is life, there is praise: praise of all things bright and beautiful (see Ps 104:24), praise of persons (31:10-31; 2 Sam 23:8-39; Sir 44:1–50:21), and ultimately praise of the Lord God who made them all (see Psalm 148; Sir 50:22-24). Only with death, in the grave, does praise cease and silence reign (Pss 6:5; 115:17). To use an imperfect anthropological typology,[191] Israel's culture is a shame-and-honor culture, in which persons are publicly affirmed and celebrated for the virtues and well-being they bring to the community, and conversely they are condemned for the havoc they wreak (see

Commentary on 3:4; 10:5, 7; 22:1; see also Eccl 7:1). Such praise and blame express the speaker's delight or dismay in the other person and powerfully enforce the community's standards of good and evil upon the recipient of praise or blame. It is foolish to praise oneself (27:2, 21), a thought that provides a link to the next verse.

12:9-11. These verses form a triplet linked by their rootage in the agricultural life on the land. Verse 9 is the first of many better-than sayings that offer paradoxical comparisons that invert conventional judgments of value, especially regarding wealth and poverty (cf. 15:17; 16:8). The laconic Hebrew of v. 9 may be understood in several ways. The NIV and the NRSV translations contrast two types of persons. The first are poor peasants, lightly esteemed by society, who have the means and initiative to support themselves. The second also lack social status, for they pretend to have social weight or wealth. Perhaps because they consider themselves to be above working, they go hungry (12:11//28:19; see Commentary on 6:6-11; 20:4). The medieval Jewish commentator Rashi takes this saying as follows: "Better is a person of little account (in his own eyes) who works for himself, than one who honors himself but comes to lack food" (author's paraphrase; see Commentary on 25:6-7). However the saying is taken, it provokes the reader to wrestle with the question of societal versus personal perceptions and with the related problems of self-knowledge and realism about oneself, one's circumstances, and one's legitimate responsibilities (see Commentary on 13:7; 26:1, 12, 16).[192]

Verse 10 uses the Hebrew "know" (ידע *yāda'*) to convey understanding and insight into as well as care for one's animal (see 27:23). Domestic animals are utterly dependent upon their master's benevolence. They cannot clearly articulate their needs or desires (the Hebrew word often translated "soul" [נפש *nepeš*] also connotes needs and appetites; see 16:26). Yet, the righteous, who are in tune with reality, can read what is "on the mind of" their animals and provide for them. So the righteous hear and answer the voice of those who have no voice (Job 12:7-10). "Cruel mercy" is a deep oxymoron (see Jer 6:23).

191. Geertz, *The Interpretation of Cultures*, 400-403.

192. See "Discipline" in Peck, *The Road Less Traveled*.

Verse 11 (par. 28:19; see also 13:25; 20:13) reflects the world of the small farm, on which life is maintained only by wise, hard work.[193] Wise humans are responsible realists who "work" (lit., "serve" [עבד (*ābad*); see Gen 2:15; 1 Kgs 12:7) the turf God gives them (Lev 25:2, 23), whatever that may be, to earn their daily bread (20:13; 30:8-9), the fruit of God's good creation. Those who serve the creation and its creatures are in turn served by it. "Fantasies" (ריקים *rêqîm*) is literally "emptinesses" or "nothings." Not to work with what is ours is to flee the real to chase the unreal. To lack judgment is literally to lack heart, without which one cannot acquire wisdom (17:16; see Pss 51:6; 90:12). The heart, in OT psychology, is the burning center of our humanity from which flow our thoughts, words, and deeds (see Excursus, "The 'Heart' in the Old Testament"; see also 10:13). It is thus the deepest home of wisdom, where knowledge of God and the world meet (see Commentary on 1:7).

12:12. The Hebrew of this verse has found no satisfactory explanation. The NRSV and the NIV translations are two of many educated guesses. The saying may mean that the wicked desire a source of security ("stronghold," see 18:10-11) built of evil, but that God grants (10:24; 12:14) security (see v. 3) only to the righteous.

12:13. Verse 13*a*, with its reference to lips, is a more specific variant of 29:6 (see also 1:17-18; 6:2; 12:6; 18:7). It may also be translated literally, "In the transgression of the lips is an evil trap" (see Eccl 9:12). The story of Susanna illustrates both halves of this saying. The two lustful elders are caught by their false testimony, while innocent or righteous (the Hebrew word means both) Susanna escapes death (see Ps 34:17-19). The connection between the verse halves may be this: When people are in trouble, they are tempted to escape their plight through false speech. But such speech is itself a deadly trap, because it distorts reality. Sinful speech may move one from the frying pan into the fire.

12:14. In 15:4, the tongue is a "tree of life," presumably for others who can pluck its healing fruit or leaves (Rev 22:2). In this verse (see also 13:2; 18:20; Isa 3:9-11), our deeds affect not only others but also ourselves

(see Commentary on 11:17); we are sated with the "fruit" of our own speech. This saying focuses on good eating and thus implies good fruit. But the more general form of the saying in 18:20 suggests that the produce of mouth and hands may be either good or evil (18:21), because good and evil each bears its own fruit. The NRSV and NIV translations convey a natural sequence of act and consequence. But one of the two traditions preserved in the Hebrew text, the *Qere*, implies that God is the one who rewards human works (see Commentary on 10:24; 12:12). Theologically, this ought not to be an either/or, for God's mysterious hand is present in the processes of the world God has made (Pss 7:11-16; 9:15-16).

12:15-16. These verses concern the fool. Verse 15 is a more specific variant of 16:2 and 21:2 (see also 14:12; 16:25). Literally, "The way of a fool is right in his own eyes." The Hebrew expression "X in the eyes of P" denotes a subjective perception that is implicitly in contrast to the judgment of some other, "X in the eyes of Q." This "other" may be human, as here and in 28:11, but most important it can be God, the ultimate judge of right and wrong, of wisdom and folly. When in Judges each person does what is right in his or her own eyes (Judg 17:6; 21:25), the narrative shows that these people are actually doing "evil in the eyes of the Lord" (see, e.g., Judg 2:11; 3:7; 4:1). In the monarchy, the human king is to do what is right in the eyes of the divine king (1 Kgs 11:33, 38; see Prov 25:2-3). In v. 15, fools are individualists, satisfied with their lives, because they are satisfied with their own standards. Wise persons know the limits of their own understanding and listen to the wise (15:12, 22). Fools, however, do what is right in their own eyes even when they consult others, because they listen only to people like themselves (1 Kgs 12:1-16; see Commentary on 3:7; 26:12).

Fools lack self-control when provoked. Yet wounded rage is impotent; it shows the opponent's power, and it lends credence to an insult. Inner strength and wisdom are needed to refrain from expressing self-defeating emotions. The ability to keep silent often distinguishes the prudent from the foolish (12:23; 13:16; 18:2), but not always (17:27-28)!

193. See Whybray, *Wealth and Poverty in the Book of Proverbs.*

There may be more than one reason for covering over personal injury (10:12).

12:17. This verse moves speech into the legal arena (see 6:19; 14:5, 25; 19:5, 9, 28; 21:28; 25:18). In predominantly oral cultures, legal disputes and criminal cases are decided primarily through the testimony of witnesses (Deut 17:6; 19:15-18; 1 Kgs 21:8-14; Matt 26:57-66). Matthew 18:16 applies this principle to life in the church, where "honest testimony" is literally "righteousness"—that is, testimony in harmony with reality. The frequency of this topic in Proverbs reflects its tremendous importance; in the law court, truth and falsity can rescue or kill (see Commentary on 25:18, which links this insight to the Ten Commandments).

12:18. "Reckless words" may occur in any setting: in the making of vows (Lev 5:4), or in a fit of rage (Num 20:10; Ps 106:33). The tragic story of Jephthah and his daughter illustrates the rash vow (Judges 11), as does the nearly tragic tale of Saul and Jonathan (1 Sam 14:24-45). Once a word has been uttered, it cannot be called back. At v. 18, the juxtaposition of v. 17 and the parallel in 25:18 underscore the deadly power of words in the law court. The tongue can cut like a sword (Pss 57:4; 64:3-4; the Hebrew term חרב [*ḥereb*] covers both the long sword used in war and the dagger, the most dangerous and intimate weapon known to the ancients [see Judg 3:16-23]). But the wise tongue heals wounded persons (15:4; 16:24) and broken communities (15:1), a fact that underscores again the ambiguity of the Hebrew (see Commentary on 12:14; cf. Jas 3:1-12).

12:19. This verse contains observations similar to vv. 3, 7, but continues the present focus on speech. "Lips" and "tongue" stand for those who speak. They endure, or not, because their words do, or do not, reflect reality. What goes counter to reality is shattered by it in a moment, like a ship on the rocks. In Hebrew, "only a moment" (עד–ארגיעה *'ad-'argî'â*) contains a nice pun on the word for "witness" (עד *'ēd*, v. 17), suggesting that a liar will be a short-lived witness.

12:20. Those who plan evil (see 6:14; 14:22) do so in their heart, the hidden center of the human person (see Excursus, "The 'Heart' in the Old Testament"). The heart's deceit includes self-deception (Jer 17:9-10) as well as distortion of reality. It bears unreliable fruit in the real world (Job 4:8; "plan" and "plow" are the same Hebrew verb). Similarly, the joy of those who "counsel peace" (see 12:22; Ps 120:6-7) may be internal or external, when their advice is enacted (21:15).

12:21. This verse is typical of Proverbs 10–15 (see Overview to Prov 10:1–15:33; see also Pss 32:10; 91:10; Sir 33:1 *a*): good leads to good, and bad leads to bad. The rhetorical force of the verse is to encourage and remind readers of the basic pattern of good and evil consequences in the world (see Commentary on 10:3).

12:22. The psalmist prays for deliverance from lying lips, whose power to hurt is like a weapon of war (v. 20; 25:18; Ps 120:2, 4). Those who act faithfully are literally those "who do truth." Although speech can be deadly, this saying moves from negative words to positive deeds backed respectively by the power of God's abomination or delight (see Commentary on 11:1; Zech 8:16-17). This contrast of word and deed parallels James's opposition between hearing and doing the word of truth (Jas 1:22-23, 25; see *m. 'Abot* 1:15, 17).

12:23. This verse is a companion to 10:18; 11:13; 12:16; and 13:16. Concealing and revealing are highly complex and ambiguous actions, whose good or evil, wisdom or folly is highly dependent upon the motives, persons, matters, and circumstances in question. Here, as in 13:16, the wise act with knowledge (keeping silence is such an action), while fools involuntarily reveal their folly. When Saul begins to lose his royal wisdom, he reveals every matter to his son Jonathan (1 Sam 20:2; see Commentary on Prov 25:2-3).

12:24. Although the inertia of institutions and social systems is massive, social status is not simply static (see Commentary on 10:4; 17:2; 30:21-23). Character and drive, or lack of same, can elevate or lower one socially. Sayings such as this one criticize passive proponents of the status quo (see 17:2; 22:29). The indolent rich should not expect to enjoy power forever, nor are the diligent poor doomed to perpetual poverty. This general point is given a political edge in v. 24. "Rule" and "forced labor" refer to the opposite extremes of political power. The NIV's "slave labor" is misleading. The reference is to an ancient form of taxation in the form of obligatory labor, or corvee, required of citizens or subject peoples (see Judg 1:28-30; 1 Sam 8:10-18; 1 Kgs 5:13-17; 15:22; Isa 31:8). Yet, the human diligence that gains lordship does so only in the context of God's direction of history. This larger lesson is sung by Hannah and Mary (1 Sam 2:2-10; Luke 1:46-55; see also Pss 90:17; 127:1-2).

12:25. The NIV and NRSV translations of this verse concern a common human experience (see 15:30*b*; 25:13, 25; Gen 45:25-28; Ps 94:19). But the Hebrew grammar of this psychologically profound verse is not completely clear. Following rabbinic traditions, it may be translated, "A man tries to suppress the care in his heart, but a good word turns the care to joy."

12:26-28. Verse 26*a* begins a series of obscure verses. The NRSV and NIV margins follow the ancient Syriac translation of v. 26. The hiphil verb form may be more closely

rendered, "The righteous help their neighbors find [their own way], but . . ." This reading makes a clear antithesis with the second line. (For the contrasting way of the righteous and the way of the wicked, see Commentary on 1:15.)

Verse 27 concerns the contrast of "lazy" and "diligent" (6:6-11; 12:24). The sense seems to be that, even when food is brought home, the sluggard is too lazy to take advantage of what he or she has gotten (see 26:15). The NRSV and the NIV share a common understanding of v. 28*b*, but the NIV's "immortality" is an unlikely interpretation of the Hebrew (אל–מוח *'al-māwet*), rendered more literally by the NRSV as "no death." Immortality is improbable in Proverbs, since the teaching of resurrection (Dan 12:1-3) is very rare in the OT and does not become widespread until the last two centuries BCE. This saying renders in positive terms the thought of 10:2*b*; 11:4*b*.

REFLECTIONS

1. A frequent, sometimes implicit, metaphor for humans (both male and female) in the OT is that of a democratized kingship in service of Yahweh the great king. All human beings (collectively and individually) have a limited sovereignty and accountable freedom over the little "kingdom" that God has given to each (e.g., body, mind, land, wealth, relationships; see 12:11; Gen 1:26-28; Psalm 8). This view comes to the surface, from time to time, in the language of Proverbs. For example, humans are not "established through wickedness" (12:3). This proverb uses the vocabulary of kingship in a negative, antithetical way. Positively, a king's throne "is established through righteousness" (16:12 NIV; see Commentary on 16:12). Humanity's royal freedom is limited by the constraints of righteousness, service of God, and the good of creation. Outside these constraints is the unstable realm of wickedness. Like the tree of Psalm 1, the righteous person is rooted in the creation and will never be moved, a phrase that also has a cosmic backdrop (see Commentary on 10:25, 30).

2. A considerable cultural gap separates us from 12:4, whether we are inclined to affirm the saying as supporting family values or to reject it as hopelessly patriarchal. On the one hand, the "good wife" (lit., "woman of valor") is not a mere domestic housewife who finds her identity through her husband and who leads a mainly private existence at home, excluded from the public business of life. This is clear from the stories of a variety of public women in the Bible (see Judges 4–5; Ruth; Prov 31:1, 10-31), and from powerful queen mothers, such as Bathsheba (1 Kings 1). On the other hand, there is in this saying a profound sense of the mutuality of husband and wife, of their being one flesh (see Commentary on 11:17). This saying runs counter to modern perspectives that conceive of human existence in individualistic fashion.

3. The "mercy of the wicked is cruel" (12:10), because they do not "know" or "listen" to their animals. What applies to the relation between humans and animals applies so much more to the relation between wealthy, powerful people and their neighbors (14:31) who are needy, dependent, or marginalized (19:17; 1 Cor 9:9-10). The kind deeds of the wicked may be cruel because they arise from self-interest imposed on the other, who has not been truly heard or known. There are also those who are cruel simply because they are cruel. Bonhoeffer, his insight honed by the Holocaust, says that the bad deeds of a good person are better than the good deeds of the wicked.[194]

4. The "good word" that cheers a human heart is spoken by another (12:24). Although there is something inscrutably single about the human heart (14:10), words can join person to person, so that the solitary heart is made whole (12:18; 15:4 NIV; 16:24). There is more. We are also bearers of the divine Word, which heals (Ps 107:19-20; Wis 16:12; Luke 7:7; 9:2, 6; Acts 9:34). "A Christian needs another Christian who speaks God's Word to him. . . . The Christ in his own heart is weaker than the Christ in the word of his brother; his own heart is uncertain, his brother's is sure."[195]

194. Bonhoeffer, *Ethics*, 64-65.
195. D. Bonhoeffer, *Life Together* (London: SCM, 1954) 12.

Proverbs 13:1-25, On Listening to Wise Counsel

COMMENTARY

13:1-4. These verses are bound together in several ways. Actions and organs of speaking and hearing link vv. 1-3. The Hebrew catchword נפש (*nepeš*, "craving," "life," "craves," "desires") connects vv. 2-4, appearing twice in v. 4. Verse 3 follows logically upon v. 2, a connection reinforced by the repetition of "mouth" (פה *peh*; "lips," NIV). Verses 2 and 4 are linked by "craving" and "desire," negated or fulfilled.

The NIV best construes the Hebrew of v. 1, taking the "listen" in v. 1*b* as double duty ("heeds"). The saying reinforces the pattern of parental training or discipline presupposed or expressed throughout chaps. 1–9 and in the sayings (see Commentary on 10:1; 12:1).

Proverbs 12:14 is a near duplicate of 13:2*a* (also 18:20). Here the bodily imagery of eating and desire forms an elaborate conceit over both lines. One's mouth (NIV, "lips"), like a "tree of life," produces the very fruit one eats with the mouth and is nourished (see 3:18; 11:30*a*; 15:4). That is, speech that nourishes others (10:21) produces good social consequences for the speaker. But the treacherous cannot be relied upon to keep their word (Jer 3:20); their speech destroys their neighbor (11:9). They have an inner appetite for destruction (see Commentary on 10:11). "Craving" can also refer to the inner self, which chooses to move from desire to action (6:30). In 16:26, *nepeš* is parallel to "mouth."

Verse 3 follows logically upon v. 2. Since speech bears good or bad fruit, the organs of speech must be carefully controlled (10:19; 17:27-28). But v. 3 raises the stakes: Speech is a matter of life and death (18:21). Each person possesses and must take responsibility for these powerful organs, by which we harm or help ourselves, first of all. But words knit us to others. So the thought may be broadened to the societal sphere, as suggested by the World War II saying, "Loose lips sink ships." Proverbs 21:23 expands on 13:3*a*.

The sluggard's desire is frustrated because he or she does not do what reality requires (v. 4; see 21:25-26). A lazy person becomes heartsick because of unrealized dreams (v. 12). Such lives are botched by sins of omission. As often, the issue here is taking responsibility for one's own turf—whatever that may be— and working it in season (see Commentary on 6:6-11; see Reflections on Proverbs 12). But those who work hard are satisfied when they reap what they sow. The saying, "God helps them that help themselves," is not far from the mark. Nor is "Make hay while the sun shines."

13:5. The NRSV and the NIV differ on the rendering of the hiphil verbs in v. 5*a*; the NIV, with a causative sense, seems closer to the mark (see 10:5; 19:26). The wicked may bring shame or odium onto others by the false word or deed (דבר [*dābār*] can refer to both) that the righteous hate (see 8:13; Pss 101:7; 119:163).

13:6. Righteousness and wickedness are personified as agents that hold sway over someone's existence, guarding or overthrowing the one under their power (see 5:22; 11:3-6; 19:3). In 22:12 these functions are ascribed to God, using the same verbs (see also 21:12).

13:7-8. These verses are linked by Hebrew roots for "rich" (עשר *ʿāšar*) and "poor" (רוש *rûš*). Their meaning may also be connected. Verse 7 is wonderfully ambiguous. Literally, it reads, "One makes himself rich, yet nothing at all; another makes himself poor, yet great wealth." Thus the saying may deal with deception of self and of others (see 12:9) or the contrast between what is and what appears. There are some who think themselves rich and do not know their poverty (Rev 3:17-18). Others are too blind to work with what they have, letting it lie useless and barren (Luke 19:11-27). Again, the saying may refer to one who began with nothing but became wealthy. Or it may refer to a greedy person who becomes rich, yet in the end has nothing (Luke 12:13-21). This paradoxical saying would then be parallel to 11:24 (see Ps 112:9). Finally, there is the Christian paradox of rich poverty, which we find in both Christ and Paul (2 Cor 6:10; 8:9).

How to link the two lines of the saying in v. 8 is difficult. Verse 8*b* is identical to v. 1*b*, except for the substitution of "poor" for "scoffer" (lit., "The poor does not hear rebuke"). The rich are subject to criminal threats where the issue is "Your money or your life!" (1:11-13). But the poor do not hear such threats, for they have nothing to give. If this interpretation is correct, then v. 1*b* and v. 2*b* bear different meanings because of their changed context. Elsewhere, גערה (*gĕʿārâ*) refers consistently to a rebuke by which one sets constraints on another. Here the sense would be extended to include a threat of death. The Torah allows for ransom for life (Exod 30:12), but forbids it in the case

of deliberate murder (Num 35:31). In the ultimate sense of the death all humans die, wealth affords no ransom, so as to buy God off (Ps 49:7-9). But one may ask if Ps 49:15 holds open the possibility that God will provide a ransom to redeem human life (Matt 20:28).

13:9. Verse 9*b* is repeated in 24:20 (see also 20:20; Job 18:5-6; Ps 38:10), while the thought of v. 9*a* is close to 15:30. Light is a metaphor for life, vitality, and goodness; its natural companion is joy (4:18; Ps 19:5; Eccl 11:7-8). The Lord is the ultimate source of light as life (29:13; Ezra 9:8; Pss 18:28; 27:1; 36:9). To lose the light of the eyes is to lose vitality, joy, even life itself (Ps 38:10).

13:10-11. The Hebrew of v. 10*a* is not entirely clear (see Commentary on 11:2; 12:15). Several scholars read, "An empty [of no account] person creates conflict by pride." The translations of v. 11 are unclear on the sense of the Hebrew behind "from vanity" (NRSV suggests the word can connote "nothing") and the versions reflect a variety of textual options or emendations (see 20:21; 21:6; 28:22). But in the economic realm, the ideas of haste, easy money, something for nothing, and what is dishonest are not unrelated. When we speak of get-rich-quick schemes, fraud and deceit come to mind. It appears these associations also existed for the ancients. The proverb states a paradox of the sort "Slow and steady wins the race," and the tortoise outruns the hare. Limits are set to clever greed here, and the homely truth that connects steady work and success is affirmed.

13:12-19. Verse 12 and v. 19 form an envelope construction around vv. 13-14, 18 (on instruction), which in turn envelope vv. 15-17 (examples of successful or failed instruction?). Thus vv. 12-19 form a relatively patterned cluster of sayings.

13:12. This verse may provide an implicit, paradoxical contrast to v. 11 concerning the quick or slow realization of human aspirations. Verse 11 suggests that the slow and steady pursuit of a good goal wins the race. But hope delayed can crush the spirit. Verse 12, however, does not specify the type or moral quality of hope in question, a matter taken up in v. 19.

13:13-14. These verses are a proverb pair. Scholars quibble over whether v. 13 refers to a divine or a human word and command (see 2:6; 6:20; 16:20; Deut 30:11-15). A contextual reading of the proverb pair suggests the topic is human instruction ("teaching of the wise") of the sort found in Proverbs (3:1-2; 7:15). Yet the ambiguity of "word" and "command" should be maintained. Divine imperatives are mediated through humans, whether by Moses on Sinai or by wise generations of parents and teachers (Deut 4:6, 9; 6:6-9; 30:11-20; 32:46-47). Such "teaching" (תורה *tôrâ*; 6:23; 28:4, 7, 9; 29:18) has life-and-death consequences, depending on its reception by the next generation (for "despise," see 1:7-8, 29-33; 23:9). The biblical tradition that understands Mosaic Torah ("law") as an expression of wisdom (Deut 4:6) is explicitly developed in Sir 24:23; 45:5. Proverbs 14:27 is identical to 13:14 but has "the fear of the LORD" (see also 19:23) for "the teaching of the wise" (see Commentary on 2:1-5; "fountain of life," 10:11*a*; 16:22*a*; Ps 36:9).

13:15. "Good sense" has connotations of general human competence and excellence, which produces success and earns one honor (see Commentary on 12:8). The decisive Abigail is a "woman of good sense" (1 Sam 25:3). But the way of the faithless or treacherous (cf. 11:3, 6) is to speak and act in ways that betray basic human commitments in marriage (Exod 21:8; Jer 3:20; 9:2), in business, or in politics (Judg 9:23). Like a brook that runs dry (Job 6:15), they cannot be relied upon (25:19). The final word, "ruin"/"hard" (איתן *'êtān*) is uncertain, as reflected in the NIV and NRSV translations.

13:16. The NIV attaches "all"/"every" to the subject of the sentence (which is grammatically more plausible), while the NRSV makes it the verb object (see Commentary on 12:23; 15:2; 18:2; 29:11). "Out of knowledge" (lit., "by/with knowledge") is parallel to "by/with wisdom" (see 3:19-20; 9:1; 14:1; 24:3-4; Ps 104:24). These parallels suggest that wise humans imitate not only God but also Wisdom by acting according to knowledge. But fools broadcast folly (17:12; 26:4-5), because that is what is in them (Luke 6:43-45).

13:17. In the ancient Near East, messengers possessed an important role scarcely comprehensible to modern people. Messengers could belong to the highest social strata, such as members of the royal family or court. They might function as ambassadors and conveyors (with armed guards) of large sums of tribute. Prophets functioned as royal messengers from the heavenly court to the earthly one (1 Kgs 22:13-23; Isa 6:1-8; 7:3). But messengers could also be go-betweens for common folk. Messengers generally possessed considerable responsibility and freedom in representing the mission of their (absent) senders. They might bring news good and bad, reports accurate or false, or even misstate their master's intentions. Thus messengers variously made their senders and hearers glad or sad (10:26; 22:21; 25:13, 25; 26:6). One of the models of the Christian life is that of the messenger as well (Matt 28:18-20; John 20:21; 2 Cor 5:18-21). The NRSV repoints the vowels of v. 17*a* to make the antithetical parallel with v. 17*b* more symmetrical. The NIV translates the traditional medieval (MT) pointing.

13:18. In Hebrew, this proverb begins with "poverty and disgrace" and ends with "honored," a root (כבד *kbd*) that connotes "wealth" (see Commentary on 5:10-12; 11:16; 13:13-14; 15:32). This opposition concerns not only social status in the community, but also the substance of a person, which may or may not find social recognition (16:8; 19:1; 28:6; Eccl 8:14; 9:13-16). The public and private sides of disgrace and honor find subtle expression in a common Hebrew wordplay on "light" and "heavy," implicit in "disgrace" versus "honored" (roots קלל [*qll*] and כבד [*kbd*]; e.g., 3:35; Job 40:2; Isa 3:5; Hos 4:7; Hab 2:16; Sir 3:6-12). The paradox is that the path to becoming a human of "weight" begins by submitting to the formative discipline of another self. Character formation requires parents, teachers, and mentors who know what makes a solid person and how to help others become solid people (see Commentary on 12:1).

13:19. As noted earlier, this verse is a subtle companion to v. 12. A longing satisfied is certainly sweet, at least initially (9:17; 20:17). "Soul" (נפש *nepeš*) here has the sense of "appetite" (see Commentary on 16:24). Longings generally seek some limited good (cf. 4:5, 7; Matt 6:33), but this good may not be good for me (see Gen 1:31; 3:6).

13:20. This verse follows naturally upon the teaching of vv. 13-14, 18. Human beings are social creatures. Our self-identity and fate are profoundly shaped by our fellow travelers (see Commentary on 14:7). Even more, our formation is influenced by the communities and families that laid down the paths, traditions, and modes of being we grow into and then travel in, happily or brokenly, consciously or blindly, willingly or rebelliously. To turn from a bad path is very difficult (v. 19). Indeed, grace may be defined as the gift that makes such turnabouts possible (Eph 2:1-10; Phil 2:12-13).

13:21-22. These verses form a proverb pair, linked by the repetition of "righteous" and by a chiasm (in Hebrew) of the first and last words of each line: sinners/good/good/sinners. People are sometimes portrayed as pursuing good or ill (15:9; 21:21; Pss 34:15; 38:20; 119:150). What people chase generally comes to them (see Commentary on 10:24; 11:19, 27; 28:19). This ought to give sinners pause, but often it does not (vv. 19-20). Verse 21, however, personifies misfortune (רעה rā'â, a general term for "evil," "trouble") as hunting down sinners (see Sir 27:10). Psalm 23:6 is similar, but positive: "goodness and mercy will pursue me." The underlying conception is that good and evil are active powers in God's world. These cosmic, moral realities pursue humans whose actions correspond to them, as lovers rush to meet each other. We find what we love, and it finds us. Again, Wisdom or Folly and humans, good or bad, mutually call out and seek each other (see 1:24; 2:2-3; 7:15; 8:17, 35; 9:3, 14). In a different context, Paul personifies sin as an active cosmic, spiritual power (Rom 7:7-11, 14). Verse 21*b* has no explicit subject. It is perhaps best to take Yahweh as the implicit subject: "The Lord recompenses the righteous with (the consequences of their own) good" (so the medieval Rabbi Moses Kimchi; see Commentary on 10:24; 12:12, 14). If this is correct, Yahweh appears as the hidden agent behind the character-consequence schema (see Reflections number 2 below).

Verse 22 (see 28:8) extends the act-character-consequence schema of v. 21 to reflect on God's faithfulness over generations.

Eventually good is passed on to children's children; and in unexpected ways the good inherit what sinners wrongly took or used (11:8; 28:8; Job 27:13-17; Eccl 2:26; cf. Eccl 6:2; Sir 11:18-19). There is a fine wordplay in "stored up" (צפן ṣāpan), for the Hebrew connotes what is "hidden," as in buried treasure that comes to light for those who least expect it (Matt 13:14). Verse 22 thus provides one solution to apparent failures in the pattern of retribution: Things will be made right in the generations to come (14:26; 20:7). Israel did not think in merely individualistic terms. Proverbs 2:20-22 develops this theme in the direction of a cosmic, eschatological hope.

13:23. The Hebrew of this verse is difficult and susceptible to various readings. The NRSV and the NIV understanding of the verse seems most likely (see v. 25). Through hard work and God's blessing, the "freshly broken field" (ניר nîr; Jer 4:3; Hos 10:12; *m. 'Abot* 3:9) of the poor produces abundant food. But injustice (see 16:8; Jer 17:11; 22:13; Ezek 22:29) robs the poor of the fruits of their land and labor. This scenario violates the principles of justice expressed in the Law (Leviticus 25) and the Prophets (Isa 5:7-8; Amos 8:4-6; Mic 2:1-2; 3:1-3).

13:24. This verse (see Commentary on 22:15; 23:13-14) comes from an ancient Near Eastern culture that recognized the human inclination toward sin and folly, and used physical discipline as a means to keep older children, fools, and wrongdoers from destructive paths (Deut 25:1-3). In Egyptian, the word for "education" was accompanied by the hieroglyph of a striking man or arm (see Prov 17:10; 19:18; 29:15, 17; Sir 30:1-2, 11-13).

13:25. Verse 23 is linked to this verse by root and sound repetition (אכל 'kl), and by implicit contradiction, if the interpretation of v. 23 is correct (see Commentary on 10:3). Instead of promising wealth to the righteous, v. 25 modestly suggests that they will have enough to eat (see Commentary on 30:8). The wicked come to lack because their lifestyle runs counter to the good order of creation (see Commentary on 10:4-5).

REFLECTIONS

1. The implied author of the book speaks in the voice of an inspired parent (13:1). This construction functions as an ideal that defines the office of parent: to pass on wisdom and life to the next generation (Gen 18:19; Deut 6:4-7), who then become responsible for their use of the tradition (Ezek 18:1-32). Only a know-it-all scoffer rejects wise parental reprimands. Yet this ideal, which governs the shape of Proverbs, is susceptible to authoritarian misuse (see Commentary on 13:24; 23:13-14), for Proverbs never explicitly portrays a parent as being in the wrong (see Commentary on 29:15). In the light of widespread familial dysfunction and abuse, Paul's corrective to an authoritarian reading of these sayings must be heard: "Fathers, do not provoke your children to anger, but bring them up in the discipline and instruction of the Lord" (Eph 6:4; Col 3:21). Discipline aims at hope (19:18) and freedom (see Reflections on Proverbs 6).

2. Israel saw the act-character-consequence schema both as a natural pattern in life and as the work of God's justice (see Commentary on 13:6). We moderns tend to exclude the divine mystery from history, leaving only natural connections between acts and consequences. But ancient Israel saw God as the hidden actor even in the mundane (see Commentary on 5:22). The parallelism of Ps 9:15-16 (see also Ps 7:15-16) perhaps expresses the mysterious presence of God in ordinary consequences most clearly:

> The nations have sunk in the pit that they made
>
> .   .   .   .
>
> The LORD . . . has executed judgment;
>   the wicked are snared in the work of their own hands. (NRSV)

3. Arrogance produces conflict (13:10), because the inflation of one ego occurs at the expense of the dignity and worth of others, who naturally fight back to protect themselves. *All* people possess worth as God's creatures (14:31; 29:13), and we instinctively react against whatever diminishes that worth. When both parties are arrogant, the conflict is all the worse. But the wise know the limits of their own insight and that "two heads are better than one" (see Commentary on 11:14; 12:15; 21:30-31; 26:12). Genuine wisdom is not egotistically independent but realistically inter-dependent.

4. Human beings become sick at the core of their being (heart) when hope suffers delay (13:12*a*). But with desire fulfilled, life flourishes as in paradise (see Commentary on 3:18). When the Lord fails to deliver Israel out of Egypt quickly, the people stop believing Moses, "because of their broken spirit and their cruel slavery" (Exod 6:9 NRSV). The Scriptures are filled with the cries of people, sick at heart, who ask, "How long, O Lord?" (e.g., Pss 13:1; 35:17; 74:10; 89:46; Hab 1:2; Rev 6:10). Biblical faith constantly struggles with the tension between what is promised and hoped for, but not yet come. We walk by faith and not always by sight (see Hebrews 11).

5. Humans naturally delight in legitimate goods (13:19). But goods wrongly attained or used turn bad, like cream that sours. Yet fools hate to give up such evils. The mysterious addiction of fools to evil is perhaps explained by evil's parasitic dependence on the good. Gradually the acids of folly transform good into something corrupt, even as they erode the fool's awareness of the difference. So it is that fools delight in vomit (26:11). To turn from evil is basic to wisdom because it sets one's path and life in a new direction (3:7; Job 28:28; cf. Amos 5:14-15). It is an act of conversion of the sort required by incarnate Wisdom (Luke 5:27-28; 9:57-62).

6. Agricultural injustice (13:23) is still common today, for example, in tropical lands in which coffee or bananas are grown for export to the United States. But the saying may be applied wherever greed, wealth, and power deprive others of opportunity, labor, or the fruits thereof. Americans need not look abroad.

7. The imagery of 13:24 makes it offensive to many. Today, violent parents and child abuse are commonly reported in news media, so that any form of corporal punishment seems repugnant and wrong in principle (see Commentary on 17:10). The deeper issue in this proverb is the paradox of "tough love," both in the family and in society. Parents may be compelled by love to be severe with a child "for the child's own good" (see 3:11-12; Deut 8:5; Heb 12:5-11). If human nature has been distorted by sin, to let a child do as it pleases is no kindness. To let a child grow up with no sense of boundaries or consequences is cruel. It seems better to spank the hand of a headstrong toddler than to allow him or her to burn a hand by touching a boiling pot. Discernment and wise love are crucial here; the same slap may be abusive in one case (with a particular child) and not in another.

In society, one of the functions of punishment is to redress wrongs justly. An ancient Israelite might consider our contemporary practice of incarceration more dehumanizing and unjust than the momentary, painful humiliation of a caning. Prison deprives people of the responsible freedom that is essential to their humanity. Bonhoeffer, during his long confinement in Hitler's Tegel prison, noted that Israel did not use imprisonment as punishment. He observed that imprisonment over the long term was utterly demoralizing, especially for the young. Instead, Bonhoeffer sought to make the punishment fit the crime.[196] A judicial caning (of one who assaulted another, for example) might permit the offender to resume life in society as God's image, rather than wasting life in confinement. C. S. Lewis argued that by appropriate punishment government honors the image of God in a person—that is, their capacity as responsible agents. When legitimate authority fails to punish, we treat wrongdoers as less than human. This problem today is made more complex by theories concerning rehabilitation, as opposed to punishment of wrongdoers,[197] and by the inhumane conditions in American prisons. This matter bears communal reflection in America, with its burgeoning prison population.

196. Bonhoeffer, *Letters and Papers from Prison*, 134, 164, letters of 20 November and 15 December 1943.
197. See C. S. Lewis, "The Humanitarian Theory of Punishment," in *God in the Dock* (Grand Rapids: Eerdmans, 1970) 287-300.

Proverbs 14:1-35, The Wise Woman Builds Her House

COMMENTARY

14:1. Verse 1a has a difficult text. Its consonants are identical to 9:1a except for the addition "of women." Underlying this verse we may assume an original saying: "Wisdom has built her house, but Folly tears it down with her own hands." This earlier version of v. 1 would be a concise statement of Folly's negative relation to Wisdom's good work of cosmic house building. Folly reduces the house to chaos by the works of her hands (11:11). Folly tears down the house built by

Wisdom, not her own house (with NRSV, against NIV; see 11:11, of a city).

The difficulty in this verse is the addition "of women." "Wisdom of women builds her house" (NRSV margin). The sense is that womanly wisdom builds her house.[198] Since "of women" is an editorial expansion of 9:1a, it seems best to seek an explanation in terms of the editing of the book as a whole. The

198. A genitive of genus. See Bruce K. Waltke and M. O'Connor, *An Introduction to Biblical Hebrew Syntax* (Winona Lake: Eisenbrauns, 1990) 153, ¶9.5.3i. See also Prov 14:8; 15:20.

addition "of women" creates a distinction between human wisdom and cosmic wisdom as personified in 8:1 and 9:1. Proverbs 14:1 now well suits its context among the small sayings that characterize chaps. 10–29. Here the focus is not cosmology but anthropology. The point of this shift is that human wisdom imitates the divine creative Wisdom.

In a similar vein, v. 1a anticipates 24:3-4. As allusions to 9:1, these passages represent humans as being engaged in the imitation of Wisdom. Elsewhere Scripture presents humans as being made in God's image and assumes human life in manifold ways to be the imitation of God. A well-known example of this pattern is the motivation for sabbath rest, based on God's rest from the work of creation (Exod 20:11; Eph 5:11; 1 Thess 1:6).

There is dispute as to the meaning of "house" in this verse, based on the idea that Israelite women were not literal house builders. (In truth we know little about who built houses in ancient Israel.) The Hebrew term for "house" (בית *bayit*) is very broad in its referential range. It can refer to buildings as varied as a temple, a palace, or a peasant dwelling. It can also refer to a family, a dynasty, or a household. Thus women can be said to "build a house" by bearing children (Ruth 4:11; see Exod 1:20-21, where "family" = "house"). The "capable woman" oversees the well-being and provision of her house (31:15, 21, 27). When David wishes to build the Lord a house (temple) the Lord counters with the promise of a lasting Davidic dynasty, or house (2 Samuel 7; Luke 2:4). Yet the folly endemic in the Davidic house, beginning with David's adultery and the murder of Uriah, nearly tears his royal house to the ground. In general, the building of houses and cities apart from God is labor in vain (Psalm 127).

14:2. This verse is composed of two nominal clauses, where the subjects and predicates are noun phrases simply juxtaposed as follows (in a literal rendering):

A One walking uprightly
  B One fearing the Lord
A´ But one twisted in his ways
  B´ One despising him (i.e., the Lord]

In each clause it must be determined whether A or B is predicate or subject. The NRSV and

the NIV both take the A lines as subjects in their clauses. But there is reason to think that the predicate phrase precedes in A, so that we may translate: "One who fears the Lord walks uprightly" (see 10:9; 20:7). There may be grammatical reasons for this rendering,[199] but there are also logical grounds. Not everyone who "walks uprightly" fears the Lord; even those who do not know Israel's God can do good deeds. The implication is that those who fear the Lord will live uprightly (see Commentary on 1:7) and that an unjust life gives the lie to claims of fearing the Lord.

With the second half-verse the order of predication is not so clear, again for grammatical and logical reasons. One cannot be a person of consistently twisted behavior and genuinely fear the Lord. In the long run, the two are mutually exclusive, though all humans suffer from varying degrees of inconsistency in the implementation of their basic beliefs and commitments (consider David and Bathsheba, and Peter at Jesus' trial). Conversely, one cannot despise the Lord and not end up a person of twisted and devious behavior.

14:3. Both the NIV and the NRSV follow a conjecture in v. 3a (see 10:13; 26:3b); the Hebrew is literally, "In a fool's mouth is a shoot of pride." The word for "shoot" (חטר *ḥōṭer*) appears only here and in Isa 11:1, "A shoot shall spring up." The sense of the original is perhaps that a fool's speech "sprouts" arrogance and that this "fruit of the mouth" (12:14; 18:20-21) typifies some sorts of folly. Speech is frequently the instrument and revealer of human pride. God and Wisdom are opposed to human arrogance (8:13; 15:25; 16:5), so that pride goes before a fall (16:18). On the other hand, v. 3b declares that their speech protects the wise.

14:4. The first line of this verse is uncertain. The NIV and the NRSV express one option in which v. 4a and v. 4b are two sides of the same coin. Another likely reading of the Hebrew is, "Without oxen there is [only] a crib of grain." That is, you either have oxen who constantly eat up the grain in the crib, or you have a crib full of grain, but no oxen whose work in the field both fills the crib and feeds the household. If this reading is right, v. 4a is an either/or saying, like,

199. See Waltke and O'Connor, *An Introduction to Biblical Hebrew Syntax*, ¶8.4.2.

"You can't have your cake and eat it too." In any case, the saying underscores the mutuality of humans and their domesticated beasts. In God's creation, the earth, animals, and humans are part of one vast fabric (Psalms 8; 104). Wise humans care for the creatures that God has placed in their care, for the good of both (12:10; 27:23-27).

14:5. This verse seems tautological. Does it say more than "Honest folk don't lie, but liars do"? Tautological sayings convey more than their literal meaning, as in "Business is business" (see Commentary on 14:24). Perhaps the point of this verse is that it is the way things are, and wise persons (including judges) will accordingly distinguish truth tellers from liars (1 Kgs 3:16-28). Verse 5 *b* duplicates the first line of 6:19 from the catalog of things the Lord hates (see 19:5, 9). "False witness" is an expression based in Israel's legal traditions and principles (Exod 20:16; Deut 19:18; see also Commentary on 12:17; 14:25).

14:6. The writer distinguishes two types of persons in this verse. Mockers figured prominently in 9:7-12. Because they do not accept correction (15:12), their seeking for wisdom is not genuine. In wisdom and religion, people generally find what they truly seek (11:27; Matt 7:8). Mockers like the idea of having wisdom but are not willing to pay the price of discipline and submission to the educational authority of another. The mocker is like the fool who lacks the capacity for wisdom (17:16). Like the lazybones, who seek for food without result (13:4; 20:4), so the actions of mockers undermine their search for knowledge. For "one who understands," however, learning comes naturally (8:9).

14:7. An exception, this verse is an admonition in the midst of the sayings that dominate chaps. 10–15. The advice is common sense: Do not keep company with fools because the knowledge you need cannot be found with them. Proverbs 13:20*a* provides the positive corollary: One becomes wise by joining others already en route to wisdom.

14:8. The clever have a certain practical wisdom that knows what it is up to, considers well the path to take, and understands the consequences of taking it (vv. 14-15; 22:3). "Clever(ness)" (ערום *‘ārûm*; the NIV's "prudent" is moralizing) is the talent for devising

and using adroit and wily tactics in the attaining of one's goals, whatever these may be.[200] It is something approved by Wisdom herself (1:4; 8:12), but like many good things it is susceptible to corruption (Gen 3:1). Implicit here is the notion that humans are responsible for their lives, their choices, and their actions. The wise use their brains and their resources. They set goals, work hard, and, "weather permitting," they achieve them like a fine harvest. They succeed because their way accords with reality (see Commentary on 10:4-5 and Overview on Proverbs 1:1–9:18). On the other hand, the folly (the same term personified in v. 1) of fools has skewed perceptions of reality, whether of the world, of others, or of self. The deceit may be deliberate and perverse. It may be unconscious, the product of a general moral-spiritual blindness. What looks good to a fool is not actually good (12:15; 14:12 articulates a different point). Yet the best human wisdom can fall short (see Commentary on 20:24; 21:29-31).

14:9. A satisfactory explanation of the Hebrew of this verse has not yet been found. The NIV and the NRSV present conjectural translations. Literally it reads, "Fools [plural] mocks [singular] guilt; and between upright persons is favor." If God is the implicit subject (see NRSV), one might translate, "God mocks fools [with] guilt, but between upright persons is [divine] favor."

14:10. No description of human solitude is more exact or penetrating (see Commentary on 13:12; 14:13). In our inmost self, we are single (see Excursus, "The 'Heart' in the Old Testament"; 1 Cor 2:11; Rev 2:17). In this solitude we suffer, but it is also a sacred preserve, a garden of the self, where others cannot intrude. The topic of this proverb is not the contrary emotions of joy and bitterness (see 1 Sam 1:10; 2 Kgs 4:27), nor is it a pre-modern statement of existential isolation. The topic is the self-reflective singleness of the heart in all circumstances. The opposition of joy and sorrow is a cipher (merismus—two opposites used to express totality) for the entire spectrum of human emotions. While bitterness is often a lonely state (Ruth 1:11-13, 20-21), joy makes obvious claims on community. Gladness invites others to join in (Ps 122:1; Luke 15:6, 9, 23). But this

200. Fox, "Words for Wisdom," 158.

verse says that even in gladness—perhaps surrounded by revelers—the heart is alone. No matter how close humans come to knowing one another, even in the one flesh that is marriage, we remain individual persons, unique centers of consciousness and responsibility, each with his or her own hiddenness. In its depths, this hiddenness lies open only to God (15:11; 17:3; 1 Sam 16:7; Ps 44:21; Jer 17:9-10). This saying is not a denial of human community (see Commentary on 13:20; 14:7), but a statement of its limits. The admonition of the apostle Paul to those who are one body remains valid: "Rejoice with those who rejoice, weep with those who weep" (Rom 12:15 NRSV, from Sir 7:34-36). Verse 10a does not tell us what to do with the heart's bitterness. The psalmist shows a way in the prayer, "Search me, O God, and know my heart" (Ps 139:23 NRSV). Similarly, the old spiritual that laments, "Nobody knows the troubles I've seen" continues with "nobody knows, but Jesus." This move from solitude toward God is beautifully captured in the story of Hannah. In "bitterness of soul" she prays, and God hears her (1 Sam 1:10-15).

14:11. With a lovely irony, this saying moves from the destruction of the well-built house (14:1; 24:3-4) to the abiding fruitfulness of the more fragile tent. As usual in chaps. 10–15, there is a sure declaration of the consequences of good and evil. Here the character-consequence connection is extended beyond the individual to include family and clan ("house"). The imagery of humans as fruitful plants (or gardens) is common but profound (11:28; Pss 1:3; 92:12-15; Isa 5:1-7; Jer 17:8; John 15:1-17; see also 3:33; 12:3, 7, 12).

14:12. Parallel to 16:25, this verse is similar to 12:15 but says something different from that passage. In 12:15, it is understandable that a fool considers a path to be right, though it is not. Fools and sinners deceive themselves, misread reality (21:2), and ignore consequences (14:15-16; Ps 73:17-20). However, in itself, abstracted from its literary context, v. 12 refers to any person, not necessarily godless or foolish, who considers a way to go. "The best laid schemes o' mice an' men/ Gang aft a-gley." The outcome of any human venture is uncertain. The reasons why are various: the limits of human knowledge and power,

the destructive power of self-deception, the sometimes absurd combination of events, and ultimately the inscrutable workings of providence (see Commentary on 16:1-9; 21:30-31). The sharpest examination of human limits and the inscrutability of things occurs in Ecclesiastes and Job. In view of the different literary context of 14:12 and 16:25, it is probable that this saying's radical possibilities are not intended in chap. 14 (vv. 8, 11, 14-15). That awaits its second appearance, where Prov 16–22:16 explores the problem of limits and the absurd (see Introduction).

14:13. Like v. 12, this verse has an unexpected, paradoxical end in view. Both the NIV and the NRSV translations are grammatically possible. But the NRSV better reflects the nature of proverbs: to state something sharply in universal terms and to leave the application to the user. The more absolute form (NRSV) provokes deeper and broader reflection; it makes the proverb maximally versatile. Since humans die, joy inevitably ends in grief (see 27:1). The party always ends; acts of love cease. Because we are creatures with a limited future and are conscious of it, "even in laughter the heart is sad." Operative here is the gap that can exist, whether purposely or unconsciously, between our inner selves and our outer persona (see Commentary on 26:23-26). Ecclesiastes 7:1-5 appears to further develop implications of this saying. Less ultimate observations also lie at hand: Even in an exuberant allegro, Mozart's music is borne along on an undercurrent of sadness.

14:14. The NRSV correctly translates this verse according to a root and sense found in Isa 3:10-11 and Hos 12:2. "Perverse" is literally "a backslider in heart" (סוג לב sûg lēb) and continues the focus of these verses on the human heart. It is another expression of the theme of character (here at the deepest level) and consequences in human life (see v. 12 and the common term "way"). Related sayings include 1:31; 12:11, 14; 22:8; and Job 4:8. Psalm 44:17-19 provides a paradoxical exception to this consequential rule. Although exceptions occur, one should not base one's life on them.

14:15. This saying is paired with the next through a contrast of careless confidence and appropriate caution or fear. The young, in contrast to the prudent (v. 18), are gullible because they have no experience to judge words, persons, and situations. One purpose of Proverbs is to give the young vicarious experience, and thus to make the simple prudent (1:4; 9:4-6). Several scenes from the prologue illustrate this saying (4:14-15; 7:7-8; see also 14:8, 12; 16:9; 22:3; 26:25).

14:16. The first line of this verse is probably elliptical (lit., "the wise one fears"), so that the NIV translation, which adds "the LORD," captures the sense on the analogy of 3:7 and Job 28:28, which also links "fear of the LORD" with "turning from evil" (see 8:13; 13:19; 16:6, 17). The NRSV reading remains on the horizontal plane, by contrasting caution with heedless folly. Verse 16*b* is also ambiguous. The fool gets either angry or out of line ("throws off restraint"), or perhaps gets involved with trouble ("evil," v. 16*a*; see LXX and Syriac, with an inversion of consonants; see also Commentary on 26:17). Fools are careless, because they are groundlessly confident (lit., "trust," as in 28:26). In 3:5 "trust" refers to confident trust in God. Here it forms a parallel with "believes" (v. 15*a*).

14:17. "Quick-tempered" is literally "quick to anger" (קְצַר־אַפַּיִם *qĕṣar- ʾappayim*), the opposite of "slow to anger" or "patient" (v. 29; 25:15). Verse 17*a* states a common human failing. Of themselves, emotions are morally neutral. Their value is in reflecting the personal significance of things for us, whether good or ill. Their limitation is that they possess neither wisdom nor restraint, since that is not their function. Emotions present information that may need responsible consideration and restraint (11:12; 17:27). Overly hasty, intemperate reactions to others do damage, because, without reflection, angry people do foolish things they later regret. On the other hand, the schemer who masters feelings while inwardly plotting personal advantage is eventually hated (see 12:2).

14:18. Here the writer returns to the opposition of the simple and the clever (v. 15). Verses 15-18 illustrate aspects of this contrast with alternative vocabulary. The NRSV emends the text of v. 18*a*, but its reading appears in no ancient version and is unnecessary; the NIV better reflects the Hebrew. The two lines are connected in that both folly and kingship ("a crown") are passed on in families; the first to shame, the latter

to honor (see 3:35; 19:14; 28:10). Abstract qualities can be metaphorically worn as clothing (1:9; Ps 73:6)—i.e., "He wears his heart on his sleeve." Ancient kings were expected to be wise and knowledgeable; the proverb slyly suggests a royal dignity for all who are "crowned with knowledge" (see Commentary on 14:24; cf. Psalm 8).

14:19-24. This section of Proverbs 14 is a cluster of sayings about relations among people who differ morally or socioeconomically.

14:19. This verse is a didactic saying about the superiority of goodness over evil. The lesson is made concrete and visible in the oriental images of a person bowing down before a superior or begging at the gate of the prosperous (see Lazarus in Luke 16:19-31, a story of reversal).

14:20-21. These verses form a proverb pair within vv. 19-24; v. 21 comes as a sharp qualification after the bluntly realistic observation in v. 20. That the poor are disdained ("hated") is a sorry commentary on humankind. People seem to shun those who reflect the fragility of the human condition to them. If the evil of poverty is located in the other, we can distance ourselves from it (Luke 10:29-37; 16:19-21, 25). That people curry favor with the rich, the beautiful, and the powerful—those who seem to possess life to the full—is a converse comment on the drive to seek security and life on the horizontal human plane rather than in God (see 18:10-11; 22:16; Psalms 49; 62:9-10; 146:3-4). Ultimately, human differences are merely relative. They are leveled by that judgment of God that is death (Job 3:13-19; Isa 14:10-11). Verse 21*a* bluntly condemns the behavior of v. 20*a* as sin. It is also stupidity (11:12), because the Lord, who made all, is compassionate to all and will not tolerate cruelty (14:31; 17:5; 22:2; 29:13-14). Verse 21*b* may be compared with Ps 41:1-2. The verb "is kind" (חָנַן *ḥānan*) here refers to humans, but is one of the basic attributes of the Lord ("merciful" in Exod 34:6). In this regard, good people practice the imitation of God (19:17; 21:10*b*; 28:8; see "merciful" in the twin psalms 111:4 and 112:4; Matt 5:7). The wisdom of these sayings was also found outside of Israel:

God prefers him who honors the poor
To him who worships the wealthy.[201]

14:22. Like v. 21, this verse borrows key terms ("kind," "love," and "faithfulness") from the list of divine attributes found in Exod 34:6 (and repeatedly in the OT; e.g., Num 14:18; Neh 9:17; Pss 86:15; 103:8; Joel 2:13; Jonah 4:2; John 1:14, 17; see Commentary on 16:5-6). Those who plan evil (3:34; 6:14; 12:20; the verb is used of a smith's work of shaping metals) are opposed to those who plan good (only here); this opposition echoes the contrast of good and evil in v. 19. The relation of love and faithfulness to those who plan good is not spelled out. Grammatically, the phrases are simply juxtaposed in a non-verbal sentence. One might supply, "Those who plan good do love and faithfulness." But the NIV and the NRSV translations may also be followed; they suggest that God's love and kindness come to those who plan good (see Commentary on 3:3-4).

14:23. This verse repeats the common theme that hard work and success or sloth and failure are connected as acts are to consequences (see Commentary on 10:4-5). For theological issues connected with this verse, see Commentary on 10:22. Sloth is here nicely pictured as mere talk (lit., "a word of the lips"). In other words, "all talk and no action."

14:24. The NRSV of v. 24a follows the LXX, though πανοῦργος (*panourgos*) reflects the Hebrew word for "cleverness" (ערמה *'ormâ*) rather than the usual term for "wisdom" (חכמה *ḥokmâ*). The NIV translates the Hebrew with the sense that wealth is a consequence, or "crown," of wisdom (see 3:16; 8:18; 12:4; 16:31; 17:6; 1 Kgs 3:13). In v. 24b the Hebrew reads, "the stupidity of fools is stupidity" (see 16:22b). This seems too tautological and produced a variety of translations already in ancient times (see Commentary on 14:5). The NIV adds "yields," while the NRSV, with many commentators, slightly emends "folly" (אולת *'iwwelet*, the same word used for "stupidity" above) to get "garland" (ולוית *wĕliwyat*) as a parallel to "crown," as in 4:9. Perhaps the tautology is to be retained; while wisdom produces a

crown, stupidity is and remains merely stupidity. Such utterances appear elsewhere and require some context, either social or literary (like the first contrasting line), to make them work. Note the ancient proverb, "An ape's an ape, a varlet's a varlet, though they be clad in silk or scarlet."

14:25. This verse is one of a number of sayings on true and false witnesses (see Commentary on 12:17b; 14:5). These sayings have nearly interchangeable parts (e.g., 12:17 and 14:25b) and do not produce startling insights. Their frequency, however, is a reminder of the great importance of justice and of the significance of witnesses in legal and criminal procedures.

14:26-27. These verses are a pair of sayings on the fear of the Lord (see Commentary on 1:7; 14:2). Verse 26 has strong links with the theology of the psalter, which also combines "the fear of the LORD," trust/confidence, and "refuge." Psalm 25 combines all these themes from v. 26 and includes the believer's children (Pss 25:2, 12-14, 20; 34:8-9, 11, 22). The God-fearing pass on the faith to their children by example and by precept (see 20:7; Exod 20:6; Deut 6:2). The theme of refuge is important in the editing of the psalter (see Pss 2:12; 37:40).[202] In the psalms, as in Proverbs, the root בטח (*bṭḥ*) regularly expresses ultimate trust or confidence, either in God or in human beings (Pss 26:1; 37:2, 40 ["refuge"]; 40:3-4; 56:3-4, 11; see Prov 3:5; 11:28 18:10-11; 28:25-26).

Verse 27 moves to a different metaphor for the fear of the Lord. It is a "fountain of life," because through it one is connected with the Lord, who, indeed, is that fountain (10:27; 19:23; Ps 36:9; Jer 2:13). Elsewhere in Proverbs, the wise themselves are such a fountain of life. This logic of derivation, whereby humans mediate divine goodness, is a common one in Proverbs and elsewhere (see Commentary on 10:11). Proverbs 13:14 is nearly identical to 14:27, except that teaching of the wise takes the place of fear of the Lord. It is impossible to say that one of these two sayings has temporal priority over the other. In Ps 34:11, the fear of the Lord is

201. *Amenemope*, in Lichtheim, *Ancient Egyptian Literature*, 2:161. Cf. Prov 22:16.

202. Gerald T. Sheppard, "'Blessed Are Those Who Take Refuge in Him' (Psa. 2:11) Biblical Criticism and Deconstruction," *Religion and Intellectual Life* 5 (1988) 57-66.

something that can be taught (see Prov 2:5; 15:33).

14:28. The first of many references to a king in the saying collections (roughly chaps. 10–29), this verse follows upon a Yahweh saying, thus presenting a frequent and important linkage in Proverbs (20:26-28; 21:1-4; 22:11-12; 25:2-7; 29:12-14; see Commentary on 15:33; 16:1-15).[203] Proverbs 25:2-3 in particular links "the glory of a king" with Yahweh's glory.

In Judah, kingship or government had its ultimate basis in the rule of Yahweh (see Commentary on 16:12). Large kingdoms (and their rulers) have more glory and power than do small ones. This fact plays a role in David's proud desire to number his populace and in his general Joab's response, " 'May the LORD your God increase the number of the people a hundredfold. . . . But why does my lord the king want to do this?' " (2 Sam 24:3 NRSV). The saying may also imply, conversely, that the glory of a king does not consist in the splendor of his court, in his army, or in his wealth, but only in the well-being of the ordinary citizens whose care, justice, and prosperity are his responsibility (Psalm 72).[204] Except for brief moments in its history, as under David and Solomon, Judah (Israel) was a very small kingdom. The amazing impetus toward universal claims to sovereignty in Judean royal theology has its basis in the universal scope of Yahweh's kingdom (see, e.g., Pss 2:8; 18:43; 22:27-28; 72:11, 17; 103:19; 145:11-13; Luke 1:33; 4:5).

14:29-30. These verses reflect on the damage unrestrained emotions can do. Verse 29 provides an antithesis to v. 17*a* and complements its reflections on being quick to anger (see Commentary on 15:18 for "slow to anger"). The principle of self-restraint is not unique to Israel. It is a commonplace, for example, in the ancient Egyptian contrast of the "heated man" and the "silent" one, which runs throughout the *Instruction of Amenemope*.[205] Wisdom about the human condition is not restricted to Israel or the church.

While v. 29 considers the social consequences of emotional restraint and excess,

v. 30 looks at the impact of inner emotional life on a person's bodily well-being (15:4, 13; 17:22). In this area, too, "the springs of life" flow from the heart ("mind," 4:23). For "envy"/"passion," see Commentary on 27:4. Because of the intimate connection of husband and wife, a difficult spouse can also be a "rottenness in the bones" (12:4). "Flesh" and "bones" together are a conventional way to express the whole, bodily existence of a person (4:22; 16:24). Today the insight of v. 30 is expressed in terms of psychosomatic illness, though the implicit anthropologies underlying modern theories and the biblical observation may be different.

14:31. The fundamental principle of kindness to the weak and vulnerable is emphasized in Israel's wisdom writings, in its laws, and by its prophets (see 17:5). It was also affirmed by Israel's neighbors. The Babylonian king Hammurabi, famous for his law code, claimed "to cause justice to prevail in the land, to destroy the wicked and the evil, that the strong might not oppress the weak . . . that justice might be dealt the orphan [and] the widow."[206] For Israel, this principle rested in the compassionate ("kind") nature of God, who made humans (see Commentary on 14:21; Exod 22:27; Sir 18:13; Matt 9:36; Luke 7:13; 10:33). Such proverbs are deepened by awareness that human beings are made in God's image (Gen 1:26). Thus to accord the needy their dignity as human beings is indirectly to honor God, whose representatives on earth are the poor—along with all humans (see Reflections on 15:25). In this verse, the intimate bond between the needy and God is emphasized; the Lord is his Maker (Hebrew singular), and each poor person can claim God's special protection (22:22-23; 23:10-11).

14:32. The NRSV clearly renders v. 32*a*, but it is inexactly translated by the NIV. The thought is a common one, that people reap what they sow and that the wrongdoing of sinners does damage to them (see Commentary on 13:6; 26:27). The second line is textually difficult. The NRSV transation, "in their [his] integrity," is based on the ancient LXX and Syriac versions, which read an inversion

---

203. See Whybray, *Proverbs*, 221.

204. See Alonso-Schökel and Vilchez, *Proverbios*, 323.

205. Lichtheim, *Ancient Egyptian Literature*, 2:143-46. See esp. chap. 4 (150-51), with its contrast of two trees, as in Psalm 1.

206. Pritchard, *Ancient Near Eastern Texts Relating to the Old Testament*, 164, 178. See also "Amenemope," chap. 25 in Lichtheim, *Ancient Egyptian Literature*, 2:160.

of two consonants (metathesis) where the MT has "in his death." But never does the verb "find refuge" (חסה *ḥāsâ*) have an abstraction like "integrity" as its object. Indeed, the verb actually means "to seek refuge" in or under something, and not "to find."[207] It makes no sense to say that the righteous seek a refuge in the death of the wicked (which is what a literal translation of the MT requires; the NIV without reason omits the pronoun referring to the wicked in both lines. The attempt to find a reference to life beyond death ["refuge"] is unwarranted here). In the OT, by far the most common object of "to seek a refuge (in)" is the Lord (30:5; Ps 2:12). The verb never appears without a preposition ("in" or "under") except here and in Ps 17:7, which is textually suspect (see the LXX). In Ps 64:10, "the righteous rejoice in the LORD and take refuge in him" (NRSV). Something of this sort is to be expected in v. 32*b*. By a slight emendation the following translation is possible, "and the righteous person seeks refuge in him [the Lord], when he [the wicked] dies."[208] The elements of this non-antithetical proverb would then have an illustration in David's song of thanksgiving (2 Sam 22:1-3, 21-22, 38-43).

14:33. The MT of the second line appears to lack a word. The NRSV supplies "not" (following the LXX and the Syriac). The Targum adds "stupidity" as the subject of "is known." One scholar suggests translating the second line as a question, "But can it [wisdom] be known in the inner being of fools?"[209] The NIV translation presupposes the idea that Wisdom speaks to all people alike (see Commentary on 8:1-5), although "among fools" is more probably "in the inner being of fools," parallel to "in the heart of one" (cf. 15:31). Egyptian wisdom also recognized that insight could be found in unexpected places:

Don't be proud of your knowledge,
Consult the ignorant and the wise . . .

Good speech is more hidden than
    greenstone
Yet may be found among maids at the
    grindstones.[210]

But the paradox is that the untutored maids are actually wise, not fools, as in the NIV. The ancient solution followed by the NRSV seems best to capture the sense of the saying. Wisdom finds a home in some hearts, but is a stranger in others.

14:34. The focus turns to concern for the moral-spiritual character of the largest of human social-cultural units: the nation. Although Proverbs speaks mostly to (young male) individuals, its principles can be applied to other persons and to groups (see also 11:10-11, 14).

14:35. This verse is another royal saying (see 19:10; 30:22); its position after v. 34 is significant, for the king is the moral-spiritual heart of the nation. In Israel, the word for "servant" and "slave" (both עבד *'ebed*) is a fluid term, having multiple references, depending on social location (see Commentary on 25:2-3.) Thus a servant of the king may be a nobleman or a relative in the king's court, while a small landowner's servant may share in his poverty. The servant is responsible to the king for loyalty, obedience, and for specific functions within an office (soldier, administrator, etc.). In North American culture, an egalitarian ethos often obscures or fails to illuminate necessary inequalities in specific, limited social relations: employers and employees, teachers and students, the commander in chief and the armed forces, magistrates and citizens. Verse 35 looks candidly upon one such relationship and suggests that the king's well-being depends on the quality of his servants, in whom he either delights or is angry, as the case may be (see 10:1, 5; 16:13; 17:2). The king's ability to carry out the weighty tasks of his office depends largely on the quality of his servants. Reciprocally, a king's disposition can bring good or ill upon his servants (16:15; 19:12).

207. McKane, *Proverbs*, 475.
208. Reading וחסה בו במותו צדיק (*wĕḥōseh bô bĕmôtô ṣaddîq*) with haplography of ב (*b*) and consequent loss of ו (*w*). The antecendent for "in him" may be found in the previous saying, "his Maker."
209. Meinhold, *Die Sprüche*, 1:242.
210. *Ptahhotep*, chap. 1, in Lichtheim, *Ancient Egyptian Literature*, 1:63.

REFLECTIONS

1. The saying "The proof of the pudding is in the eating" also applies to faith (14:2; Jas 2:14-26). True godliness is incompatible with an unjust life-style. The same religious logic animates the opening of Psalm 128: "Blessed are all who fear the LORD, who walk in his ways." Fearing the Lord entails a just walk.

One's relationship to God and one's behavior are two sides of the same coin. The practice of life is not indifferent to religion, for God is not indifferent to the practice of life. On this, the writers of the wisdom literature and the prophets agree. Indeed, daily life is the practice of religion in things ordinary, in contrast to the practice of religion in divine worship. God is the creator and Lord of all things, and our disposal of all things is inextricably related to our disposition toward God.

2. Proverbs assumes that human beings are shaped by the company they keep and by the common goals and way of life they share with others (14:7). Thus, when God renews the people, they will have "one heart and one way" (Jer 32:39 NRSV). Shared commitments animate a people in a common way of life and create communities, some good, some bad. This insight also leaps forth from the beginning of Psalm 1: Blessed are those who do not become increasingly enmeshed (walk, stand, sit) in the company of the wicked (see 1 Cor 15:33). The question of individual identity is always also a question of community, from family and church, school and business, all the way up to nation and state. Communities create the paths we walk.

3. In the ultimate order of things, goodness and right prevail over wickedness and wrong (14:19). For Proverbs, the most important difference among persons concerns not their wealth or social status, but their moral-religious character (see Commentary on 14:21). The young need to learn these patterns of reality lest they try to build a life based on those inverted instances where wickedness overturns good (see Commentary on 25:26). Similar in function are the American proverbs "Crime doesn't pay" and "Honesty is the best policy." Such principles are ultimately moral and spiritual convictions about God and reality. Good folk commit themselves to such principles even when temporal evidence seems to contradict them. They do good because it is good.

4. All human groups, whatever their size, can be characterized in terms of their spiritual-moral behavior (14:33). In the bare-bones language of Proverbs, such behavior is simply righteousness or sin. The Hebrew word for "righteousness" is closely associated with Yahweh (Ps 72:1-4). Yet, since the Lord is creator of the universe (3:19-20), this saying applies not just to Israel, but to all nations, which are subject to God's standards for human conduct (Amos 1:3–2:16). A nation is a unit, a body politic. But in a nation as large and diverse as the United States, good and moral people are easily tempted to distance themselves from segments of the nation they consider violent or sinful. About this problem, M. Scott Peck wrote:

> Any group will remain inevitably potentially conscienceless and evil until such time as each and every individual holds himself or herself directly responsible for the behavior of the whole group—the organism—of which he or she is a part. We have not yet begun to arrive at that point.[211]

211. Peck, *People of the Lie*, 218.

Proverbs 15:1-33, The End of the Antithetical Collection

COMMENTARY

Proverbs 15 concludes the first Solomonic sub-collection (10:1–15:33), and its distribution of sayings creates a number of significant relations with other chapters. Several sayings here echo elements of Proverbs 10, creating a verbal and thematic envelope to mark off the first Solomonic sub-collection (cf. 10:1 and 15:5, 20; 10:2-3 and 15:6, 16-17; 10:17 and 15:5, 10, 12, 31-32; 10:27 and 15:33). The sayings on heeding rebuke (15:5, 10, 12, 31-32) also connect with the redactional section 9:7-12 and embody principles running throughout chaps. 1–9. Proverbs 15 also frequently mentions the Lord (vv. 3, 8-9, 11, 16, 25-26, 29, 33), thus anticipating the series of Yahweh sayings that opens the second Solomonic sub-collection (16:1–22:16).

15:1-2. Verse 1 simply observes human interaction, with the intent that people use its twofold insight (on speech, see 15:23, 28; 25:11-12, 15). A harsh word is one that causes another person pain (see "sorrow," 10:22; Gen 3:16), but may also embody the speaker's pain, just as a gentle answer embodies the speaker's calm and healing presence (12:18; 14:29; 15:4, 18).

Verse 2 follows naturally upon v. 1. Wisdom not only speaks in the proper manner (v. 28), but also delivers the insight and know-how that a particular situation, task, or problem needs (10:31; 13:16; 15:7; see Commentary on 24:3-4).

15:3. This verse states a fundamental precept of biblical thought, that the Lord knows all things, including the human heart (see Excursus, "The 'Heart' in the Old Testament"), and that God is especially concerned with human good and evil, which God judges as King of the universe (v. 11; 16:2; 17:3; Ps 7:9; Jer 17:9-10; Rev 2:23). Whereas systematic theology speaks abstractly of divine omniscience, the Bible uses concrete images or metaphors like "the eyes of the LORD" (2 Chr 16:9 NRSV; Job 31:4; Ps 139; Jer 16:17; see Heb 4:13).

15:4. Here the text picks up from vv. 1-2. The NRSV rendering "gentle" translates the same adjective (מרפא *marpēʾ*) as "tranquil" in 14:30; its root connotes "health." The NIV translation "that brings healing" understands "healthy" in a causative sense; right speech restores hurt, damaged relationships (as in 12:18; see 10:11; 13:17; 16:24). Each translation captures a nuance of the original. For "tree of life," see Commentary on 3:18; such trees bring healing (Ezek 47:12; Rev 22:2). The opposite situation is a tongue whose talk is "twisted." Such perverseness in speech distorts reality and causes damage (11:3; 19:13 uses the same root), in this case despair in another's inmost being (see v. 13; Ps 51:17; Isa 65:14). The psalmists pray against enemies who do damage with their tongues (Pss 5:9; 12:1-4; 73:8-9).

15:5. People are known by what they love and by what they disdain (1:7). A fool rejects parental discipline and thus is cut off from the chain of tradition and from Wisdom herself (1:30; see Commentary on 10:1; 15:12, 20, 31). The ability to accept criticism, however, marks one who will grow and succeed (9:7-9). "Is prudent" (ערם *ʿārûm*) is more accurately "become clever," in the sense of someone able to work out solutions to life's problems.

15:6. The main theme of chaps. 10–15 continues: Righteousness leads to well-being, and wickedness to trouble (10:2, 16; 15:25). "Treasure" (חסן *ḥōsen*) indicates what is stored over time (Isa 23:18 uses this root), while "income" (תבואה *tĕbûʾâ*) suggests the precarious character of existence based on earnings or produce. Job raises objections to the facile application of this saying (Job 21:7-26), but it is already qualified within Proverbs, especially in the next Solomonic sub-collection (see Commentary on 16:8).

15:7. This verse is a variant of v. 2, using the frequent connection of "heart" and organs of speech (see Commentary on 16:1, 9). The second line may also be rendered, "the hearts of fools are not steadfast [or "right"]" (see 11:19 NRSV; 28:2, "order").

15:8-10. Verses 8-9 form a proverb pair, linked by the contrast of divine "abomination" and "delight"/"love" (see Commentary on 11:1). The first saying is one of very few that mention the essential acts of worship: prayer and sacrifice (v. 29; 21:3, 27; 28:9, 13). Proverbs assumes the ordinary practice of worship in Israel, but does not elaborate upon it. The book also ignores Israel's history with God. These omissions are a matter of the genre and function of wisdom sayings and admonitions (see Introduction). A sacrifice (something costly and ordinarily pleasing, 3:9-10; Lev 12:8) is rendered repugnant to God because wickedness pollutes the holy gift (see Commentary on 21:3, 27).[212] By contrast, a mere prayer of the upright, which involves no material cost, pleases God. The Hebrew word for "prayer" (תפלה *tĕpillâ*) is used of the Davidic psalms, which are predominantly laments requesting divine help (Ps 72:20). The juxtaposition of v. 9 to v. 8 shows that sacrifice and prayer do not please the Lord, unless one also "pursues righteousness" (see Matt 6:33). As in chaps. 1–9, what one loves and pursues determines the character of one's life journey (11:19). Thus, without righteousness, one has neither God nor wisdom (8:20). Indeed, God desires righteousness in ordinary life more than worship or personal piety (see Commentary on 21:3; 28:9). On this point, the sages and the prophets agreed (1 Sam 15:22-23; Ps 50:7-23; Isa 1:10-17; Amos 5:21-24).

Verse 10 is linked to v. 9 by the words *way* and *path* and by the standard opposition of "love" and "hate." These connections suggest that an abomination leads to severe discipline and ultimately death. The appearance of Sheol and God as judge in v. 11 confirms this movement of thought. Verse 10 is ambiguous and can be taken several ways. Some suggest that discipline seems bad to one who leaves the path (of "right" or "life"; 2:13; 10:17; see Commentary on 8:9). This reading lessens the connection of the two lines. Alternatively, "severe discipline" is parallel to "will die" (so NIV, without the adversative "but"), thus portraying death as the Lord's ultimate device of corrective instruction. Such a pattern of

212. See Nelson, *Raising Up a Faithful Priest,* 17-38, 55-82.

education through death and disaster appears in the plagues of Exodus, with their repeated purpose, "that you may know . . . the LORD" (Exod 10:2 NRSV; cf. Exod 7:3-5; 18:11). Resistance to "rebuke" (or "reproof") typifies those who spurn Wisdom (1:25, 30; 15:5), as does the consequence of death (1:32).

15:11. This verse resonates with v. 3. The God who knows the depths of the cosmos, for whom the mysteries of the underworld lie exposed, has no difficulty in knowing human hearts. Sheol and Abaddon ("Destruction") are a hendiadys (two nouns describing one referent) for the realm of death (27:20; Job 26:6; 28:22). The cosmic scope of divine knowledge appears in Amos 9:2-4, but Psalm 139 most magnificently displays God's knowledge of the cosmos and of the human heart.

15:12. This verse has close affinities with vv. 5 and 10*b* and with 9:7-8. Literally, the first line reads, "Mockers do not love the one who rebukes them." Scoffers do not love those whose criticisms require them to mend their ways. This hatred of correction is most pernicious when it enters the law courts, where the lives of ordinary people can be destroyed (Amos 5:10). The conflict of good and evil entails conflict between persons and determines the company we keep (see Commentary on 14:7; 13:20; see Reflections on Proverbs 28–29).

15:13-17. These verses are stitched together by word repetitions. Verses 13-14 are a proverb pair, each beginning with "heart" ("mind" [לב *lēb*]); this proverb pair is similar to 18:14-15. Verse 15 seems to have a pivot function, for it contains the word *heart* (looking back) and also "good"/"better," a Hebrew term that begins the next two sayings (the root appears in v. 13). Finally, vv. 16-17 conclude with the phrase "with it."

Verse 13 finds a near duplicate in 17:22 and is the basis for Sir 13:25-26 (see 14:30; 15:4). What is in one's heart will come to the surface, where it can be seen (v. 13*a*). The relation of the heart and the spirit in v. 13*b* is puzzling because both refer to closely related inner capacities. The word for "spirit" (רוח *rûaḥ*) also means "wind" and connotes the wind's force and energy. Here it seems best to take "spirit" in the sense of one's vital powers, the inner energy and drive by which a person succeeds in life (see 18:14). A troubled heart quenches the spirit, so that one's vital energy cannot flow. The logic of v. 13*b* implies that the heart is the more profound and abiding dimension of a person; it affects the spirit, which, like wind, comes and goes (John 3:8). Conversely, the advent of spirit brings life and power to the heart.[213] The transitory character of wind/spirit is typical of OT usage (Judg 3:10; Job 34:14-15; Ps 104:29; see Acts 1:8).[214] Without the movement of spirit, life ceases.

The discerning heart (v. 14) has a drive to know (see Commentary on 10:14; 12:1; 18:15), but God does not give such a heart to all (Deut 29:3-4; 1 Kgs 3:9, 12). The mouth of a fool "feeds on" folly like a sheep feeds on grass (the verb is a shepherding term). The wise and the foolish appear to seek and pasture on different mental and spiritual food. Less plausible is the view that the verbs are doubly transitive: The wise shepherd seeks out good pasture for the sheep, but fools feed the sheep folly.[215] In the metaphor, "heart" and especially "mouth" correspond better to sheep than to shepherd (see 18:15*b*).

Verse 15 (see v. 13) begins a series of three paradoxical sayings connected by themes of wealth and poverty, contentment, and the truly "good" (a key word, "good" and "better" (טוב *ṭôb*) are the same in Hebrew). The inner person can overcome external circumstances, a paradox powerfully expressed by Paul in a vision of divine grace (see 2 Cor 4:6-10, 16-18).

A paradoxical proverb pair on wealth and poverty follows (vv. 16-17; 16:8; 27:8).[216] Ordinarily, the fatted oxen are good; they are included in wise Solomon's provisions (14:4; 1 Kgs 4:23). But without godliness, the goods of this world become disordered; they exist in turmoil—a reference to troubled and unjust personal and social relations (Ezek 22:5; Amos 3:9). Verses 16-17 are parallel and interpret each other. Verse 16 is not a pious overlay, commenting on the secular proverb in v. 17. Rather, v. 17 portrays the fear of the Lord, or its lack, with vivid images: a plate of greens or a fatted ox, seasoned with love or hate. This picture of contrasting meals shows that the ordinary affairs of life are not apart from good or bad religion, but are their living manifestation (see Commentary on 31:30).

15:18. The idea of troubled relations, implicit in the contrast of "love" and "hate" in v. 17 (see 10:12), is the focus of this verse. It contrasts the hot-tempered person (lit., "angry man") with one slow to anger (see Sir 28:8-12). Each of these types has a characteristic effect on social relations; the first brings conflict (6:14, 19; 22:10; 29:22); the second brings peace and cooperation because slowness gives one freedom to think before speaking or acting (v. 28). Thus one's words and deeds can heal rather than hurt (vv. 1, 4; 17:27; 25:15). Such persons control their spirit or passion (16:32; Eccl 7:8-9). Mastery of emotions is essential to wisdom (19:11; 25:28). While the phrase "slow to anger" is at home in wisdom (14:29; 16:32; 25:15), its most striking use is in the series of attributes that describe the essential character of Yahweh (Exod 34:6-7; see Commentary on 14:21-22).

15:19. This verse presents a variation on the theme of the two ways (see Overview to Prov 1:1–9:18). The parallelism opposes the sluggard to the upright. This unusual pairing suggests that there is moral deficiency in laziness but wise virtue in diligence (see Commentary on 6:6-11). How the sluggard's way is "blocked with thorns" (lit., "like a thorn hedge") is not clear. Perhaps they imagine obstacles to possible undertakings (see 22:13). Alternatively, the sluggard's way is in fact overgrown with obstacles because the work needed to make a clear path ("highway") has not been done (see 24:31; Isa 40:3-4).

15:20. This is a variant of 10:1. Its appearance near the end of the first Solomonic collection contributes to the envelope structure of this sub-section (see Commentary on 9:10). To "despise" a parent was a heinous crime in Israel (20:20; 30:11, 17; Deut 21:18-21; 27:16; Ezek 22:7). The deficient character of a foolish man (see 21:20) seems rooted in his failure to honor his parents by heeding their advice and instruction about life (1:8; 12:1; 13:1; Deut 5:16).

15:21. This verse repeats the root שמח (*śmh*, "joy," "glad," "delights") from v. 20, but in a different context (see v. 23). Here

213. See Knierim, "The Spirituality of the Old Testament," in *The Task of Old Testament Theology*, 269-97.
214. See H. W. Wolf, *Anthropology of the Old Testament* (Philadelphia: Fortress, 1974) 32-39.
215. Whybray, *Proverbs*, 230.
216. See *Amenemope* IX, 5–8, in Lichtheim, *Ancient Egyptian Literature*, 2:152.

something is desperately wrong: Folly is pleasure to one who lacks heart (see Commentary on 10:13). But one with discernment walks by (v. 21 *b*). This thought reflects the imagery of Proverbs 1–9, where the wise walk by the seductions of Folly and the strange woman (see 4:25-27).

15:22. For a discussion of the themes of this verse, see the Commentary on 11:14; 14:7 (see also Tob 4:18).

15:23. This is one of many sayings on speech. An answer suggests the dialogical character of speech in community (see vv. 1, 28; 18:21; 24:26; 25:11). A comparative reading of the lines seems unlikely (people may be self-satisfied with their talk, but much better is speech that fits the occasion). The NIV and the NRSV supply "apt," which is not in the Hebrew, apparently reading v. 23*a* in the light of v. 23*b*. There is "joy" in speech that fits the moment (see Commentary on 26:1-12; Eccl 3:1-8). Proverbs themselves, in their verbal artistry and apt use, exemplify this point.

15:24. The "upward . . . path of life" is not an ascent to heaven (cf. Isa 14:13-15; see also Prov 12:28; 15:25), but simply employs the common Israelite imagery of high and low to contrast the goodness of an abundant life with the grave tendency of foolish humans toward Sheol or death (see Reflections on Proverbs 5). A similar use of the expressions "upward" and "below" appears in Deut 28:13, 43, where the Israelites have success or failure depending on their obedience to the law. In other words, "Onward and upward!" (See 2:18-19; 5:6; 7:27; 10:17.)

15:25. God gives judgment against the proud and justice for the widow (see Commentary on 22:28; 23:10-11). Wisdom's opposition to pride is rooted in its understanding of humility and the fear of the Lord— notions that conclude this chapter (v. 33; see 16:18-19). Oppression is a form of pride that is especially incompatible with godliness (14:31). The widow represents all those who are vulnerable to the arrogant wicked. Similar thoughts are found in the law (Exod 22:22-24), in the prophets (Isa 5:8-10; Hos 5:10), in historical literature (1 Sam 2:1-10; Luke 1:46-55), and in Psalms (Pss 75:6-7; 113:5-8). Several of such passages use the high/low imagery of v. 24 (Isa 2:12-17).

15:26. "Evil plans" or "thoughts" (12:5; see 24:8) run counter to God's nature and purposes for reality. The source of such plans is the heart (6:18; 15:21; see Excursus, "The 'Heart' in the Old Testament"). Verse 26*b* forms a puzzling contrast to v. 26*a*. The NIV avoids the problem by translating the Greek from the LXX rather than the Hebrew. Inner plans and outer speech ("words"), however, are often contrasted (vv. 14, 28; 26:23-25), as are various expressions for good and evil. "Pleasant" or "gracious" words stand in opposition to "evil plans," and "abomination" is opposed to what is pure and pleasing in the Lord's eyes (for "abomination," see Commentary on 11:1; see also Commentary on 22:11; cf. Hab 1:13). The root for "gracious" or "pleasant" (נעם *n'm*) is related to what is good (Gen 49:15; Job 36:11) and lovely (Cant 1:16; 7:6). Thus Wisdom's ways are pleasant (3:17), and the attributes of "gracious"/"pleasant" words are associated with wisdom (16:24; 24:13-14). The "words" ("promises") of the Lord are pure (Ps 12:6).

15:27. This verse refers to Israel's judicial system, in which the gift (here translated "bribe") was considered compensation for services rendered (18:16) or for damages (6:35). But the practice was easily corrupted, as greedy judges or witnesses accepted bribes in exchange for rendering unjust verdicts or testimony favoring the rich (28:16; Exod 23:6-8). Sometimes Proverbs condemns the gift or bribe, sometimes it simply observes its power (18:16; 19:6; 21:14; see Eccl 7:7; cf. the related term for "bribe" [שחד *šōḥad*], 6:35; 17:8, 23; 21:14). Ezekiel 22:12-13 connects greed "for unjust/dishonest gain" with ignoring God, a matter that God will judge (see 1:19). Such persons damage themselves and their households (see Commentary on 11:29). This contrasts with the promise, also found in the law, that the judge who rejects bribes will live (28:16; Deut 16:19-20). The phrase "to hate bribes" also appears in the law (Exod 18:21; see Reflection number 1 on Proverbs 18).

15:28-32. These verses comprise a cluster of sayings closely linked by word repetitions and themes of speaking and hearing: ear and eye, heart and mouth. Verses 28-29 contrast the speech of righteous and wicked people toward others and toward God (see 10:31-32). Verses 29-32 are linked by the root for "hear" (שׁמע *šmʿ*, also "news," as in "something heard," in v. 30).

15:28. The righteous consider how to answer fittingly (but see Commentary on 16:1; 26:4-5). This inner capacity to reflect, rather than to react emotionally, defines the wise person and produces the sort of speech described in vv. 1*a*, 2*a*, and 23*a*. Compare the folk advice to "count to ten" before responding to an affront (see 15:18; 19:11). A malicious mouth, however, "pours out" harmful words like unrestrained waters (17:14; 19:28; see also 1:23). "Evil" here is plural—"evil things"—perhaps because the behavior and speech of the wicked are not one sort of evil, but diverse. "Heart" and "mouth" are emblems of the inner and outer person (see Commentary on 15:14, 26); what is on the inside will come out (1 Sam 24:13).

15:29. Implicit in prayer and other forms of worship is the spatial image of nearness to God. It is ironic that even when the wicked "come near" in prayer, God is "far" from them (see v. 8; 28:9; Isa 1:15; 29:13). Distance implies the absence of God's loving help and blessing (Pss 22:1, 11; 35:22; 71:12).

15:30. Once again the contrast of the inner and outer person appears. Here, two of the sense organs, eyes and ears, are gateways for light and good news (25:25; see also 12:25) as vivifying influences from the outer world upon the inner person ("heart" and "bones" are in synecdoche for the "body" in its inner aspects). "Light" is a metaphor for life and joy (4:18; Pss 38:10; 97:11) and, naturally, is associated with righteousness (13:9; Matt 6:22-23). For Israel, the laws of God make the heart rejoice and enlighten the eyes (Ps 19:8-9). Yet the Lord gives light to the eyes of both the rich and the poor, the oppressor and the victim (29:13). However,

until the early modern period, the eyes were generally pictured as having and emitting their own light, like a lamp (see 13:9; Matt 6:22-23).[217] Wine, another external influence, also gladdens or "rejoices the heart" (Ps 104:15). One's inner self influences one's outer, bodily being (v. 13), but the world and external body also influence the soul.

15:31-32. These verses reflect on the heart and the ears as organs that receive or reject discipline and correction (see Commentary on 12:1; 4:20, 23; 25:12). The latter action is literally to reject or to despise oneself, or "life" (נפשׁ *nepeš*). In antithetical contrast is v. 31*b*: To gain understanding is literally to gain "heart" (לב *lēb*)—the vital, wise center of life and selfhood (cf. "keeping oneself/life" in 16:17). In Israel's highly oral culture, the organs of understanding and wisdom were the heart, mouth, lips, eyes, and ears (see Rom 10:5-17 for a NT discourse that assumes much the same view, even while it speaks of Moses' writing).

15:33. This verse appears to be a redactional conclusion to the first Solomonic sub-collection (10:1–15:33). Its first line derives its vocabulary entirely from the book's motto in 1:7 (see NRSV; the NIV is very free), so as to link "the fear of the LORD" inseparably to the instruction and wisdom the book teaches. These key words were anticipated in vv. 31-32. Verse 33*b* is derived from 18:12*b*. Reverence for God gives a person a proper sense of self, of realistic humility (16:18-19; see Commentary on 11:2, which uses a different term to the same effect). This verse sets the anthropological stage for the contrast of human limits and divine freedom, which opens the next Solomonic sub-collection (16:1-9).

217. W. D. Davies and Dale C. Allison, *The Gospel According to Saint Matthew I,* ICC (Edinburgh: T. & T. Clark, 1988) 635-37.

REFLECTIONS

1. To put Prov 15:1 into practice is difficult because human emotions naturally react to anger and pain in kind. Emotions themselves know no morality; they just are. The way we deal with our emotions, however, is a moral-social issue, because human beings are more than their feelings. Harsh words reveal a lack of self-discipline, a failure of boundaries (25:28).

Another difficulty in practicing Prov 15:1 stems from distorted views concerning genuine strength versus perceived weakness (16:32). In this category are some macho views of manhood. Such styles of masculinity, in whatever cultural context, may plaster over insecurity and inner weakness. They disrupt human relations, often to the detriment of both parties. The story of Rehoboam's harsh answer to the northern tribes, with its disastrous consequences, illustrates this problem (1 Kgs 12:1-16; see also Prov 20:29). But Gideon's proverbial response to angry Ephraim brings peace (Judg 8:1-3). Again, Nabal's harsh words stir up David's wrath (1 Sam 25:10-13), while Abigail's gentle answer deflects it (2 Sam 25:23-31). Abigail's story illustrates the divine origin of wise speech (2 Sam 25:32-35, 39), as does Prov 16:1.

2. The two halves of Prov 15:15 qualify each other in paradoxical fashion. A central task of the king (and of government today) is to do justice by defending the rights of the poor (see Commentary on 29:14; 31:8-9). Poverty or affliction can render every day a bad day and can crush those made in God's image. Thus Scripture consistently looks upon poverty as an evil thing, with negative spiritual consequences. For example, when Israel is overwhelmed by oppression, the people cannot believe God's good news of grace and liberation (Exod 6:9). Those in prosperity should not glibly underestimate the constraints that hobble the poor (see Commentary on 15:13). And yet, there are rare people whose inner disposition, a cheerful heart, renders them always content. The rich person is defined in *m. 'Abot* 4:1 as one "happy with his lot."[218] Because of his existence in Christ and the effect this has on his inner being, the apostle Paul could say he had learned to be content in all circumstances (Phil 4:11-13; see also 2 Cor 4:6-10, 16-18). Most people, including self-professed Christians, fall short of this transcendent goal.

3. Better-than sayings (15:16-17; see 16:8) set conventional understandings of wealth and poverty on their head. They do not deny the goodness of wealth, but they relativize goods by placing them beneath the fear of the Lord. The mutual realities of wisdom, righteousness, and the fear of the Lord are the indispensable foundations of a good life, even if—contrary to usual expectations—they entail suffering or self-limitation. The first better-than sayings in the book stated that wisdom was better than wealth (8:11, 19). Proverbs 15:16-17 is the first of a number of comparative sayings (mostly found in 16:1–22:16) that assert that the fear of the Lord and its moral-spiritual concomitants are better than good things obtained or held without righteousness. These proverbs undermine simplistic readings of Proverbs that say that the book is unrealistic in its portrayal of the causal connections linking virtue to wealth and vice to poverty. In normal circumstances, these connections of acts and consequences hold true—and life would be impossible without them. But in a broken world where injustice and the absurd can prevail, faith persists in belief and obedience even when its rewards remain unseen (Heb 11:1). Christians walk by faith, not by sight, and our conduct must show this. Faith (represented here by "love" and the "fear of the LORD") can transform a "meal of vegetables" into a "continual feast" (15:15).

4. Human delight in the wrong is a grievous mystery (15:21; see 10:23), but the imagery of the strange woman as Folly in Proverbs 1–9 may render it somewhat less mysterious. Sin and folly always tempt us with some created good. If sin did not offer the semblance of good, people would not be tempted. But Folly's goods are distorted and dangerous, because they are gotten at the expense of other goods and of the comprehensive good of cosmic order, or righteousness (see Commentary on 15:17-18). The consequences of sin are disastrous, "in folly ripe, in reason rotten." Those with understanding recognize such pleasures for what they are and proceed straight on their way (see 11:5a). Proverbs 3:6 sees the ability to walk such a straight path as

---

218. R. H. Charles, *The Apocrypha and Pseudepigrapha of the Old Testament* (Oxford: Clarendon, 1913) 2:703.

a gift rooted in one's relation to God. The ability to say no to pleasant follies is rooted in commitment to that one great good that gives direction to one's life and places all lesser goods in their proper place (see Matt 6:33).

5. To consult others is not necessarily "a mark of conservative society which mistrusts individual initiative" (see 15:22).[219] Rather, it is an acknowledgment that no one has enough wisdom even for his or her own life. This saying is all the more striking because of the strong social relations in which ancient Israelites existed. If the Israelites needed such advice, how much more do we modern individualists! The problem is not merely our individualist mind-set (see Commentary on 14:10). The structures and patterns of our lives conspire to isolate us. In contemporary society, the automobile dismantles neighborhoods and mass media isolate even family members from one another; when the TV is on, who really talks? Paradoxically, the media create a bogus sense of community and shared values,[220] even as they alienate us from those closest to us.

In such a life-world, Christians (and people in general) need to create places and naturally recurring situations in which families and neighborhoods can seek and share counsel (15:22) within genuine communities based on common commitments. This goal may also require that citizens work creatively to change the shape of neighborhoods, the architecture of cities, and the patterns of our commuter lives. (Is not "freeway" an oxymoron?) Since God created us as bodies in a physical world, these issues, too, are concerns of biblical wisdom and obedience. The shape of our life-world should not be dictated by commercial interests and technological forces; it should be based on wise, responsible public counsel and action.

6. The idea of boundaries (15:25) is fundamental to Israel's understanding of justice. Justice is rooted in cosmic order and reflects it (see Commentary on 8:27). The law stipulates that boundary markers (usually heavy stones) may not be moved (Deut 19:14; 27:17; Prov 22:28). In agrarian Israel, a family's land was necessary for survival, but also for its collective, familial, and personal identity as God's royal vassal(s). Thus the land was central to Israel's covenant role as God's servant (Lev 25:38, 55). To steal land—by means legal or illegal—was to steal the foundation of a family's humanity, because human beings—Israel and the church included—serve God in and with the fruitful earth God created. By exercising responsible stewardship over that earth, we represent God as servant-kings (Gen 1:26-28; Psalm 8).

To each of these servant-kings (men and women), the Lord has given a little kingdom, a bit of turf, with which to serve God. The psalmist responds to this reality with gladness, linking the oath of loyalty to Yahweh to delight in his portion of land:

I say to the LORD, "You are my Lord;
I have no good apart from you."

. . . .

The LORD is my chosen portion and my cup;
  you hold my lot.
The boundary lines have fallen for me
  in pleasant places;
I have a goodly heritage. (Ps 16:2, 5-6 NRSV)[221]

To trespass on our neighbor's God-given kingdom, to violate boundaries, is to violate the righteousness that God's kingdom on earth demands (Matt 6:10, 33). On a

219. Whybray, *Proverbs*, 233.
220. See Postman, *Amusing Ourselves to Death*; and Robert N. Bellah et al., *Habits of the Heart: Individualism and Commitment in American Life* (Berkeley: University of California Press, 1985) 279-81.
221. See J. Clinton McCann, Commentary on Psalms, in *The New Interpreter's Bible Commentary*, vol. 3 (Nashville: Abingdon, 2015) 343-44.

personal level, it attacks our neighbor's status as God's image (see Commentary on 14:31).

In the United States, most people do not farm the land. In our world, the boundaries that get violated are not made of stone and dirt. For us, Prov 15:25 must be applied, for example, to the boundaries that concern bodies, emotions, jobs, reputation, and the natural limits of earth's environment. Proverbs 15:25 and related sayings (22:28; 23:10-11) may also speak to the way in which modern commerce and technology invade and trample upon other spheres of life for their own narrow purposes. Wealth and power can invade and subvert politics, democratic processes, and criminal and civic justice. Overweening commercial interests can do violence to the integrity, variety, and quality of sports, arts, and entertainment and to the communication of truth by the mass media.[222] Education also can be subverted when learning and research serve what President Dwight Eisenhower termed the military-industrial complex. The drive to maximize profits needs to stay within the cosmic limits of justice, where every creature and human function has its proper space to flourish. When boundaries are trampled, damage is done (see Commentary on Proverbs 8).

Job, in his extreme situation, complains that God is not judging those who violate boundaries in their drive for wealth and power (Job 24:2). But Isa 1:23-28 declares that God will act against those who do not vindicate the widow and the orphan (see 23:10-11). Eventually, God will straighten out all violated boundaries, because the integrity of the divine name and kingdom requires it.

7. Proverbs, like the law and the prophets, insists on God's fundamental passion for justice and equity among humans at law (Prov 15:27; see Isa 1:23-24; 5:23; 10:1-4; Amos 5:12; Mic 3:11; 7:3). The doing of impartial justice is a way in which Israel imitates its maker (Deut 10:17-18). The sometimes subtle, sometimes blatant influence of money on the practice of justice and on the conduct of legislators, lawyers, and judges is also a prominent reality in our time. It is often taken for granted as just the way things are done. Jews and Christians who claim biblical roots for their ethics should not tolerate it, because these are not sectarian issues. They are universally human.

222. See Neil Postman, *Technopoly: The Surrender of Culture to Technology* (New York: Knopf, 1992).

PROVERBS 16:1–22:16, THE ROYAL COLLECTION

Proverbs 16:1-33, Introduction to the Royal Collection

COMMENTARY

16:1-15. These verses, which introduce the second Solomonic sub-collection, occur just before the physical center of the book (16:17, according to the MT verse count). It is the lengthiest cluster of sayings on God (and king) in the book. This section exhibits more redactional care in its composition than do many other sections of Proverbs, where themes and poetic patterns are not so tightly organized, especially at such length (but see 26:1-12). This section of the book may have been one of the last to be edited in the Masoretic tradition, for the ancient LXX translation presents 16:6-9 MT interspersed among verses in 15:27-30, omits 16:1, 3 MT, and has significant differences in the verses that do correspond. A different Hebrew text underlies the LXX translation of 16:1-9.

In the MT, vv. 1-9 are filled with repeated sounds, words, and phrases that reinforce the coherence of the whole. The initial words of vv. 2-4, for example, are כל/גל/כל

(*kol/gōl/kōl*), with another *kol* appearing in the first line of v. 5.

Verses 10-15 focus on the king as the earthly administrator and agent of God's righteous rule. In Israelite thought, as throughout the ancient Near East, God and king are closely linked (24:21; 1 Kgs 21:10, 13), although Israel's Lord set a particular covenantal stamp upon the God-(Davidic)king relationship (2 Samuel 7; Psalm 132). Both God and king are agents of justice (16:10, 33). Both God and king abominate wickedness (15:9; 16:12). There is as well a social hierarchy of God, king, and subjects (see Commentary on 25:1-3).

16:1. Verses 1 and 9 provide the theological frame and theme for the tightly knit cluster in vv. 1-9 (see v. 33; 19:14, 21; 20:24; 21:30-31). The human heart makes "arrangements" or "plans" that are ordinarily expressed in action or speech (see Commentary on 15:13). Earlier proverbs had given counsel about the different sorts of answers that wise or foolish folk make (see Commentary on 15:1, 23, 28; see also Sir 33:4). But here the presence of God is revealed precisely where humans believe themselves most in control: "Man proposes, and God disposes."

16:2. Deity and humanity are contrasted, setting an individual's self-deception (not just ignorance) against God's unerring evaluation of the evanescent "spirits" of us all (see Commentary on 15:13; see also 17:3; 21:2; 24:12). On the contrast between divine and human perception, see Commentary on 14:12 (see also 15:3, 11; 21:2; 24:12).

16:3. This verse seems to reverse normal causal sequence. We—the reader is directly addressed—may commit our plans to the One who knows our ways and expect that God will establish our works (see 3:6; Ps 90:17). But this verse reverses the order of "plans" and "works" (see 4:26*b*). Why? Perhaps the logic is like that of Psalm 127. Even our works (which naturally embody our plans) will fail unless the Lord is at work to make them efficacious (v. 1). "Commit" (lit., "roll") translates an idiomatic metaphor found also in Pss 22:8; 37:5; Sir 7:17 (MS A). One might translate, "Turn your works over to the Lord" (see Ps 55:22; 1 Pet 5:7). The ancient versions repointed the verb "commit" (גל *gōl*, from the root גלל *gll*) as "reveal" (גל

gal, from the root גלה *glh*); what this might mean is uncertain.

16:4. The direct objects and object phrases in v. 4*a* are ambiguous and may be translated several ways:

> The Lord makes everything/all for its purpose
> The Lord makes everyone for his purpose
> The Lord makes everything/one for his purpose
> The Lord makes everything/one to answer him

The NIV's "works out everything" is patterned after Rom 8:28 and seems designed to ward off the misreading that God, who creates wicked persons, must be culpable for their wickedness (see Eccl 7:29). The first three translations all make good sense. Less likely is the fourth translation, which would mean that all creatures (Psalms 19; 148), but especially humans, are created to answer or respond to God. Rashi, however, took this to mean that all things are created to praise God (referring to Ps 147:7 with the same Hebrew root) or to "bear witness" to God. Even the wicked will give their account to God in a way that vindicates God's goodness and justice. Jeremiah confesses that God is his refuge in the "day of disaster" and prays that it come upon his persecutors as their just deserts (Jer 17:17-18).

16:5-6. To be "proud [lit., "high"] of heart" is an "abomination" (see Commentary on 11:1) because it renders one incapable of that fear of the Lord that causes one to "turn from evil" (see Commentary on 3:7; 16:17). It connotes a lack of realism about oneself and one's place in the world, vis-à-vis God (17:12; 18:12; 2 Chr 26:5; 32:25; Ps 131:1; Ezek 28:2, 17). Deuteronomy 8 provides a good example of such self-deception. When one's "heart is lifted up" (Deut 8:14 KJV), one forgets God and says, "My power and the might of my own hand have gotten me this wealth" (Deut 8:17 NRSV; see Commentary on 11:2).

Some scholars wonder whether "loyalty" and "faithfulness" (v. 6) refer to divine or human actions (see Commentary on 3:3; 14:21-22; 15:18). It appears that they refer to God in this passage, for vv. 5*b*-6*a* contain clustered terminology drawn from Exod 34:6-7, the central biblical description of the name Yahweh. This list of divine attributes conveys the mysterious union of God's justice and compassion (see Exod 20:5-7), which chap. 16 places in the context of God's inscrutable freedom. Allusions to this list of divine attributes play a significant role in various biblical books and in an ancient Israelite inscription. The relevant expressions here are "will not go unpunished" (see 6:29; 11:21; 17:5; 19:5, 9; 28:20), "love" and "faithfulness" (see 3:3; 14:22; 20:28), and "iniquity [is atoned for]." Several texts combine the verb for "atone" (כפר *kipper*, which does not appear in Exod 34:6-7) with "iniquity." Psalm 78:38 describes Yahweh as compassionate—the first epithet from Exod 34:6—and as one who "atones iniquity." Moreover, two parallel verses in the golden-calf story show that the verb for "atone" in Prov 16:6 (see also 16:14*b*) is a substitute for "forgive" in Exod 34:6 (see also Exod 32:30, 32). The allusions to Exod 34:6-7 at the heart of Prov 16:1-9 remind the reader that Yahweh, the God of Proverbs, is both merciful and just. God's actions and judgments are grounded in the attributes revealed in God's name, "Yahweh" (see Sir 2:11; 5:4-7). The God of the wise is the same Yahweh known in the Prophets, the Psalms, and revealed in the narratives of Israel's salvation history.[223] That "one avoids evil" (lit., "turns from evil") through the "fear of the LORD" is obvious, else one's religion is not genuine (see Commentary on 1:7; 3:7*b*, 14:16).

16:7. What is pleasing to the Lord (root רצה *rāṣâ* appears as a noun, "delight"/"favor," in vv. 13, 15) is the opposite of an abomination (vv. 5, 12; see Commentary on 11:1). This vocabulary links God and king in vv. 1-15 (see v. 8). God's power to bring peace between enemies is frequently recounted, and it is presupposed in some places where it is not explicitly mentioned (Gen 26:26-32; 2 Sam 10:12, 19; 1 Kgs 8:50). Enemies may also be pacified through conquest (Ps 110:1; Luke 20:43). Ultimately, God makes peace with and for human enemies (Rom 5:1, 10).

16:8. Verses 8*a* and 16*a* are near duplicates, alternating "righteousness" for "the fear of the LORD" respectively. These two expressions describe two inseparable, though

223. Fishbane, *Biblical Interpretation in Ancient Israel*, 347n80; J. Clinton McCann, Jr., *A Theological Introduction to the Book of Psalms* (Nashville: Abingdon, 1993) 54-55n9; Van Leeuwen, "Scribal Wisdom and Theodicy in the Book of the Twelve," 31-49. See, however, J. L. Crenshaw, "The Concept of God in Israelite Wisdom," in Van Leeuwen, "Scribal Wisdom and Theodicy in the Book of the Twelve," 1-18.

distinct, aspects of one religious mode of human existence. This close relation of righteousness and reverence for Yahweh and the paradoxical character of v. 8 mean that this verse properly belongs in its present context, though Yahweh is not mentioned. It also anticipates the frequent mention of justice or righteousness in vv. 10-13, further tying the passages on Yahweh and the king closely together (see v. 7). To be righteous is to live in harmony with the righteous order that God has established in the cosmos. It also means that one's relationships with the earth, with other creatures, and with other people are as they ought to be. But such righteousness is inseparable from a right relation ("fear of the LORD") to the God who made, cares for, and judges all things wisely and rightly (3:19-20; 8:22-31; 16:14; Psalms 93–99; 104:24). Engagement with God is what sets humans in a right relation to this world and all that is in it (see Psalms 24; 119; 147). Verse 8 and related better-than proverbs state in a newly radical way the old truth that wisdom is better than wealth (see Commentary on 15:16). When wealth is a product of injustice (13:23), it becomes precarious and unstable (10:2; 11:4). The disordering of God's world, represented by wealth with wickedness or righteousness with little, will not forever endure (1 Sam 2:3-10; Ps 37:16-17; Luke 1:51-53). In the meantime, faith maintains its lived commitment to righteousness, even when the fruits of righteousness are not visible (Heb 11:39).

16:9. This verse is conceptually and verbally linked to v. 1 (see also v. 3); the two verses form an envelope around the theological themes of divine sovereignty and freedom in this passage. "Way" (דרך *derek*) here picks up a key idea from Proverbs 1–9: Life is a journey undertaken step by step, day by day, until we reach our goal. To plan our way is to take the long view of things; we plan a journey to accomplish something significant (Jas 4:13-16). But v. 9 presents a fine irony: God is master of things big and small, immediate and eternal. God makes secure each tiny, cumulative step, out of which a long journey is made (Pss 66:9; 91:11-12; 121:3). Conversely, one false step, one slip, and all a person's grand plans can come to naught (27:1). In combination with 20:24, this proverb appears in the dark anthropological reflections of Jer 10:23 and the Qumran texts.

> I belong to evil humankind
> to the assembly of wicked flesh . . .
> For to man (does not belong) his path,
> nor to a human being the steadying of
>   his step.[224]

16:10. The meaning of this verse is disputed. The root of "oracle" (קסם *qsm*) is elsewhere in the Old Testament translated "divination," a Gentile and Israelite practice generally disapproved of (Deut 18:10; 1 Sam 6:2; 28:8)—perhaps because prophecy became the means of divine revelation during the monarchy. But here *qesem* has a positive sense, seeming to suggest that the king's judgments are indisputable, endowed with God's wisdom (so NRSV's "inspired decisions" and the indicative "does not sin" in v. 10*b*; see 1 Kgs 3:9, 12, 28; Ps 72:1). Josephus asserts that the Hasmonean John Hyrcanus possessed not only the offices of ruler and high priest, but also a reliable prophetic gift.[225] However, in 2 Sam 14:17, 20, where the wise woman of Tekoa suggests the king is infallible, "like the angel of God, discerning good and evil" (NRSV), her irony is great (see Prov 29:26), because she has just shown how fallible the king's judgment has become. Often Israel's kings were less than Solomonic in their judgments. The NIV seeks to solve the problem by translating the verb in v. 10*b* modally, "should not betray." In this reading, the saying does not express what necessarily is, but what ought to be, since the king is God's representative for justice (8:15-16; 16:12; 25:5; 29:4; Psalm 72). Perhaps the best solution is to take seriously the idea of divination in *qesem.* Apparently, this word of itself is religiously neutral (even though most biblical occurrences put it in a negative context). It is here used to refer to a legitimate means of consulting God, such as with the Urim and Thummim. Then the sense is as follows: In a judicial case, when the king's lips report a divine judgment (conveyed by the casting of lots or some other device), his judgments do not err (see v. 33). An example is Saul's use of the lot in determining his son Jonathan as

the one who violated the royal curse (1 Sam 14:37-42; see Josh 7:13-20).

16:11. The only proverb in vv. 10-15 that does not mention the king, v. 11 continues the mixture of divine and human work (v. 3) that runs throughout the two parts of vv. 1-15. The insertion of this Yahweh proverb among the royal sayings sets limits to the mighty powers of the king. In human terms, weights and measures are the king's responsibility; he must ensure that they are honest and consistent throughout the land (2 Sam 14:26). But the norms and practice of economic justice are a creation of God, even though they are carried out by humans (see Commentary on 11:1; Sir 42:4, 7). Economics is a particular, important instance of the broader principle that the world of human culture is a divine creation, placing human freedom within divine limits of justice and righteousness (see Commentary on 8:15-16; cf. Ps 33:4-5). The Hebrew word for "honest" (משפט *mišpāṭ,* or "justice") links vv. 8, 10-11; the closely related root for "righteous(ness)" (צדיק *ṣaddîq*) further links vv. 8, 12-13.

16:12-13. These verses comprise a proverb pair, linked in Hebrew by the initial opposition of "abomination of kings" versus "delight of kings" (see Commentary on v. 7; see also 14:35) and the stereotypical opposition of "wickedness" ("evil") and "righteousness" at the end of the first lines of these verses. Yahweh's justice (v. 11) is followed by the king's. The NRSV's "to do evil" better captures the ambiguity of the Hebrew in v. 12*a.* While it is obvious that for others to do evil is an abomination for kings (the primary point of the saying), it is also an abomination for kings themselves to do evil—a pattern abundant in Judah's and Israel's history. The ground for this pronouncement follows: righteousness establishes the "throne" (place of justice). In Egypt this principle was visually represented by the placement of the hieroglyph for *Maat* (cosmic order, justice = "righteousness") under the pharaoh's throne. This is one of the most basic principles of Judean kingship, for as agent of justice, the Davidic king imitates Yahweh, the heavenly king. The same terms describe Yahweh's throne and the earthly king's throne (Pss 9:4, 7-8; 89:14; 97:2; see Commentary on Prov 12:3; 20:8; 25:5).

224. 1QS XI:10-13, in F. G. Martínez, *The Dead Sea Scrolls Translated,* 2nd ed. (Grand Rapids: Eerdmans, 1996) 18-19, 323. See also 1QH VII [= XV], 12-17.

225. Josephus *Antiquities of the Jews* XIII.299-300.

Verse 13 flows from v. 12 because the speech the king "loves" is naturally understood as "honest" ("righteous") testimony in cases of law or justice. In this way also the king imitates Yahweh, the divine king (see 12:22).

16:14-15. The section on the king concludes with another proverb pair, which follows naturally upon the preceding one. Verse 14 presents death as a judicial consequence of what the king detests in v. 12 (see 25:4-5; 1 Kgs 2:24-46). Verse 15 portrays the life-giving favor of the king in terms of light from his face and the gracious clouds that bring spring rain, thus ensuring a fruitful summer harvest (see 19:12; 20:2; Jer 5:24; Hos 6:3). Once again the king's power to do good or ill reflects prerogatives of the heavenly king, Yahweh (negatively, see 2 Kgs 6:32-33; Ps 78:49-50; positively, see Num 6:25; Pss 4:6; 44:3; 89:15). The wise person in v. 14*b* appeases the king's wrath; the verb here is the same translated "atone" in v. 6. Once again the parallelism of God and king is reinforced.

16:16-17. The medieval Jewish scribes marked v. 17 as the middle verse in the book of Proverbs. Verse 16 appears to be an editorial link to themes from chaps. 1–9. Proverbs 3:13-14; 4:5, 7; and 8:10-11, 19 supply most of its vocabulary and ideas (see Commentary on 3:13-18; 8:11). The effect is to link the center of the book (which is also near the center of the Solomonic subsections, 10:1–15:33 and 16:1–22:16) to chaps. 1–9 as the book's hermeneutical prologue with its pervasive instruction to "get wisdom."

Verse 17 picks up the symbolism of life as a journey, which pervades Proverbs 1–9 (see Overview to Prov 1:1–9:18). Proverbs 15:19*b* provides the clue to the unique expression "highway of the upright." In Hebrew, the predicate "avoids evil" is an infinitive phrase, "to turn from evil." This predicate is ambiguous, as is its relation to the upright's highway. The word translated "evil" (רע *rā*ʿ) can indicate greater or lesser trouble (13:14; 14:27), which would fit this verse's connection with 15:19*b*. To paraphrase v. 17*a* in this sense, "the leveled road of the upright is a highway that avoids trouble." This goes nicely with v. 17*b*: The upright take good care of the path that is their life's journey, and thus they preserve themselves (for "guard" used in the sense of "take good care of," see 27:18; Job 27:18; Isa 27:3). But more often to avoid evil in Proverbs refers to turning from what is ethically wrong, an action that befits the fear of the Lord (3:7; 16:6; the related idea, "to hate evil," is uniquely connected with the fear of Yahweh in 8:13). To paraphrase, "to turn from wrongdoing is a crucial means by which the leveled road of the upright is created and guarded." By turning from wrongdoing in this sense, the upright preserve the integrity of their life-journey and of themselves (נפש *nepeš* connotes both "life" and "self"; see 19:16; 22:5). For the "upright," there is a dual, divine-human agency to guarding one's way (see 2:6-8; 16:9).

16:18-19. These verses form a proverb pair, for which 25:6-7 provides a concrete illustration. Proverbs 18:12*a* is a condensed variant of v. 18. The contrast of pride and humility is conveyed in the imagery of high and low: a "haughty spirit" versus "a lowly spirit" (see Commentary on v. 5). "Poor in spirit" conveys a similar idea (Matt 5:3). The Lord has little tolerance for the proud (3:34; 15:25). Thus proper humility is a matter not only of human relations, but also of godly wisdom. It is the only realistic posture in a world that we do not ultimately control, though we remain responsible agents (see Commentary on 6:17; 11:2; 15:33; 16:1-9; 26:12). "To share the plunder" usually has a military context (Exod 15:9; but see 1:13; 31:11). The Hebrew terms for "pride" and "proud" (גאון *gāʾôn*) provide another link between this section of chap. 16 and chap. 8 (8:13, "pride" and "arrogance").

16:20-24. These verses are intensely intertwined thematically and verbally, and they possess a certain logic concerning wisdom communicated by speech. One must first hear a "word" and trust God (v. 20) before one is recognized as wise in heart and speech (vv. 21, 23). The root שׂכל (*śkl*, "to have insight or understanding") is a key word uniting vv. 20 and 22-23. It suggests that understanding is a "fountain of life" (v. 22; see 10:11) not just to those who have it, but also to those who hear it through the medium of wise speech (vv. 20, 21-24; see 10:11; 13:14). The seemingly unrelated v. 22*b* (lit., "but the instruction of fools is folly"), then, finds its place as a negative contrast to wise speech (see Commentary on 14:24).

16:20. In v. 20*a*, the NIV and NRSV translations are interpretations of a deceptively simple Hebrew text. The somewhat literal KJV reads, "He that handleth a matter wisely shall find good." This interpretation joins wise conduct of human affairs with trusting God. But "matter" translates דבר (*dābār,* also "word," "thing"). Thus v. 20*a* may also refer to paying proper attention to a spoken word that refers to some significant matter, perhaps a legal case (see 18:13*a,* 17; 25:2). In v. 20, however, *dābār* more naturally refers to God's Word, since this makes better sense of the whole proverb and its literary context. This reading joins obedience to God (v. 20*a*) with trust in God (v. 20*b*). Giving heed to a word is never merely cognitive; it entails obedience, as in 1 Sam 3:9-10. While the word may be from a wisdom teacher (so NIV's "instruction"), *dābār* in Proverbs by itself never clearly conveys this (see Commentary on 13:13, the only parallel). In keeping with the elliptical style of Proverbs, Yahweh, who is implicit in v. 20*a*, becomes explicit in v. 20*b*. The Lord blesses the persons who trust in the Lord (a variant of 3:5; see 28:25, 29; 29:25). The phrase "shall find good" (not "will prosper") is also used of those who find a good wife (18:22), which in turn is parallel to the "blessed" activity of finding Wisdom as wife (see Commentary on 3:13; 8:35; 19:8; 31:10). Such verbal links further strengthen the ties connecting chaps. 3; 8; and 16.

16:21-23. In Hebrew, vv. 21 and 23 exhibit verbal/thematic repetitions in their beginnings ("heart"/"wise," in chiastic sequence; see 10:8) and endings ("lips"/"promotes instruction"). Pleasant speech is literally "sweetness of the lips." "Sweetness" as a metaphor for wise, persuasive speech is common and links vv. 21 and 24 (see 24:13; 27:9?). Compare the American proverb, "You catch more flies with honey than with vinegar." The expressions "wise," "promotes instruction" (= "add . . . learning"), and "discerning" all appear in 1:5, of which 16:21 may be an editorial echo (see 9:9).

16:24. In Proverbs, honey and sweetness are significant symbols of true or bogus wisdom and of the verbal or nonverbal packaging

in which they come (see Commentary on 5:3; 9:17; 16:21; 24:13; 25:16, 27). "Soul" (נפש *nepeš*) is also "appetite" (as in 13:19; 16:26), "life," or "person" (for "health to the body" see 3:8; 4:22; 14:30; 15:4, 30; "pleasant words" appears in 15:26, but not in 16:21, contrary to the translations).

16:25. For details on this verse, see the Commentary on Prov 14:12; 16:2.

16:26. The NIV and the NRSV provide a straightforward translation of this verse, although the Hebrew is not entirely certain. The need to eat drives one to work (Eccl 6:7; 2 Thess 3:10).

16:27-30. These verses form a group of sayings on negative speech as being destructive of community (v. 28*a*; see 6:14, 19; 17:9). In its terminology and ideas, it has many connections with the two catalogs of vice in 6:12-15, 16-19. Verses 27-29 all begin with איש (*ʾîš*), "a man of . . ." The form of v. 30 is different, but reveals some signals by which the wicked are known (see 6:13). In v. 27, for the term "scoundrel," see Commentary on 6:12. For "the violent" who verbally entice their neighbor into a wicked way (v. 29), see Commentary on 1:10, 15.

16:31. Gray hair was a symbol of wisdom throughout the ancient Near East. Traditional cultures believe that only those persons with abundant life experience can be wise (see Commentary on 8:22-31; 20:29). But the sages were also aware that "there's no fool like an old fool." Thus they add that such wisdom is gained only through a righteous life (lit., "way of righteousness"). The image of the way once again suggests that only through the consistent, persistent long haul is a life crowned with glory and wisdom. Yet, from another perspective, such a crown is a gift (4:9).

16:32. This verse is a better-than saying that subtly praises the quiet, inner mastery of oneself over the more macho public conquest of the warrior-hero. Without the disciplined, wise conquest of oneself, mastery of the external world and its problems—in any area and of every sort—is not possible. The self can be an unruly city inhabited by rebellious feelings that disturb its effective integrity and destroy its self-preserving boundaries (see Commentary on 25:28). Proverbs 24:5-6 and Eccl 9:13-18 take the contrast of might and wisdom in different directions. For "slow to anger," see Commentary on 15:18; 25:15.

16:33. The chapter ends with a return to the theme of its beginning: the mystery of divine sovereignty in the midst of human plans and actions (see esp. Commentary on 16:1, 9). For the "lot" as a means of reaching decisions, see Commentary on 16:10; 18:18. The practice was apparently common in various contexts in which human powers of discrimination and decision were inadequate (see Exod 28:30-31; Lev 16:8-10; Jonah 1:7).

REFLECTIONS

1. Proverbs 16:1-9 focuses on the Lord in a way that sets radical limits to human wisdom. The juxtaposition of these sayings generates a theological dialectic whose sense is greater than that of the individual sayings. To this point the book has largely focused on the ABC's of wisdom: the nature of the world, the need to fear the Lord, the nexus of acts and consequences, and the conflict of wise and foolish, wicked and righteous. But the focus on Yahweh in 16:1-9 marks a shift in pedagogy and profundity that makes the wisdom of Proverbs as a whole more rich—and difficult. Here the book begins to develop a theological depth and complexity it has not possessed to this point. In God's freedom and sovereignty, human wisdom—for all its goodness and indispensability—finds its radical limits.[226] In the mystery of world and humankind, the sages encountered the mystery of God, who answers finally to no one else. God is not answerable to us humans, nor subject to our manipulations and theological demands (cf. Rom 3:3-8; 11:33-36).

Consequently, in this second Solomonic sub-collection the reader begins to encounter the exceptions to the rules of acts and consequences laid out so simply in chaps. 10–15. Far from providing a warrant for a health-and-wealth gospel, these chapters show that sometimes the wicked prosper and the righteous suffer, contrary to all normal expectations.[227] Here it becomes clear that even believers do not have God or reality figured out. Thus the fear of the Lord (see 1:7; 3:5-8) is here coupled with humility and discipline (see Commentary on 15:33). This section calls for obedient faith without presumptuous arrogance.

2. We are responsible for the plans of our hearts, for the steps we take, and for the answers on our tongue (16:1, 9). And so, at first glance, the route from inner heart to outer speech and action seems direct and unproblematic to us. Yet God is sovereignly present even here (see 21:1). This mysterious reality comes to the fore in two opposite ways. On the one hand, being overly confident in human outcomes can be unexpectedly subverted by an unintended slip. Here, to our dismay, the limits of our control over even our inner and outer selves may be painfully evident (cf. Jas 3:1-12; Excursus, "The 'Heart' in the Old Testament").

On the other hand, sometimes persons in situations of great moment or difficulty are graced to speak more wisely and bravely than they or others could imagine (see Matt 10:19-20). Of this phenomenon and proverb, von Rad writes that

the road from . . . plans to the . . . appropriate word . . . "at the right time," is a long one and much can happen in the meantime which is outside [human] control. But God is there precisely in this incalculable element, and at a single stroke which you have scarcely noticed, he has taken the whole affair out of your hands.[228]

226. Von Rad's chapter on "The Limits of Wisdom" remains indispensable. See von Rad, *Wisdom in Israel*, 97-110.
227. On this theme, see Van Leeuwen, "On Wealth and Poverty."
228. Von Rad, *Wisdom in Israel*, 100.

3. Human self-delusion about what is pure (16:2; 20:11; 21:8) ranges over every area of our lives, but what looks good to us is not necessarily so in God's eyes (see Commentary on 3:7-8). Proverbs 16:2 does not portray the arrogant evil of those who plot wrong and imagine God does not see it (Ps 64:68). Rather, this is the deception of hypocrites, who sense the requirement of purity, but deceive themselves about their conformity to it (20:9)—hypocrisy being the homage vice pays to virtue. The story of David's anointing sharply reveals the absolute superiority of divine over human perceptions (1 Sam 16:6-7; 17:28). The apostle Paul applies the principle of 16:2 to himself (1 Cor 4:3-5).

4. When God works good through wicked persons, the wickedness is theirs and the goodness God's (16:4). All creatures, wicked persons included, have their ground of being and goal in God alone. Having made them, God takes them up into the unfathomable divine plan and makes them subservient to good ends (Gen 45:4-8; 50:20; Exod 9:16; Eph 1:5-11). In a similar vein, God has made the poor, a fact that points to their dignity, while leaving the causality of their poverty unspecified (22:2; 29:13). When Isa 45:7 says that God makes peace and creates evil ("evil" = "trouble" in Prov 16:4; see Amos 3:6), it is to make God's justice known (Isa 45:6; Ezek 38:22-23). The mysterious thought of Prov 16:4 plays an important role in early Judaism and Christianity alike. It provides a base for reflection on the justice of God, especially when painful history renders God's justice difficult to believe. Sometimes the approach is to develop a rational theodicy. The Jewish sage Sirach develops such a theodicy based partly on this verse (Sir 39:16-35; see Sir 33:7-15). Ecclesiastes 7:13-14 insists on human limits, but the hymns of the Qumran community develop Prov 16:4 in the direction of an earnest double predestination: The righteous are predestined to life, but

the wicked you have created for the time of wrath,
from the womb you have predestined them for the day of annihilation.
For they walk on paths that are not good,
they reject your covenant

. . . .
Instead they choose what you hate.[229]

Paul also wrestles with the mystery of 16:4 in Rom 9:19-24, and this leads him, eventually, to the great doxology of Rom 11:33-36.

229. 1QH 7[15]:21-23, in Martínez, *The Dead Sea Scrolls Translated*, 323.

Proverbs 17:1-28, Better a Dry Crust with Peace and Quiet

COMMENTARY

17:1. This chapter opens with a better-than saying (see Commentary on 15:16-17). In a family or "house," amiable relations are more important than bounty (15:17). The troubled history of David's house amply displays the insufficiency of bounty (2 Sam 13–19; 1 Kgs 1–2). In the subsistence economy of Israelite peasants, this proverb has a sharpness and depth that may escape affluent readers. The morsel of bread is dry because there is no sauce or olive oil to dip it into (19:24). "Feasting with strife" is literally "sacrifices of conflict" (ריב *rîb*). The principal occasions for eating meat were religious festivals or ceremonies at which sacrifices were offered and then consumed. Only the wealthy could afford abundant ("a house full," see 1:13) sacrifices of meat (see Deut 12:7; 1 Sam 9:12-13, 22-24; 20:6, 29). The picture is of a "religious," wealthy household in which public piety is married to internecine conflict—a topic taken up in the next verse. Perhaps the religious activity and conspicuous consumption are a cover for family dysfunction.

17:2. Like v. 1, this verse subverts ordinary Israelite expectations about family values. It asserts that wisdom is a higher good that reverses the usual evaluation of son over slave. At the same time, it reaffirms the family virtues by implying that sons must measure up to certain standards. (In Israel, women generally did not inherit property, but see Num 27:1-11; 36:1-12.) It does this by calling the servant "wise" (see Commentary on 16:20-24) and the son "disgraceful," perhaps because of laziness, as in 10:5 (see also 12:24). Ordinarily, it would be considered outrageous for a social inferior from outside the family to take a son's place. Thus 19:10*b* and 30:21-23 object to the idea that a servant (see Commentary on 14:35; 22:7) will rule.

17:3. Verse 3*a* is identical to 27:21*a*. Precious metals are tested and purified through smelting and pouring off dross. The process is used here as an image of God's knowing, and perhaps refining, the quality or purity of the human heart (see Excursus, "The 'Heart' in the Old Testament"). For God's knowledge of the inner person, see Commentary on 15:11; 16:2; 20:27; 21:2; 24:12. This (divine) testing may work through human agency (27:21).

17:4. This verse may be compared to the portrait of the wicked in Ps 52:1-4. Even the wicked, whether king or commoner, are known and shaped by the company they keep (see Commentary on 14:7; 29:12; see also Ps 101:5, 7). Our character determines to whom we listen and is in turn determined by those to whom we listen. This circle can be either vicious or virtuous (13:20). Speech is the instrument that shapes good or bad community (see v. 7).

17:5. The writer condemns malicious laughter at a poor person as a mockery of God (see Commentary on 14:31). The laughter of Wisdom at calamity is different (see Commentary on 1:26-27). Verse 5*b* expands the

thought to condemn any joy at another person's misery.

17:6. This verse expresses the generational and familial perspective of biblical thinking (see Commentary on 13:22; 27:10-11; see also Psalms 127–128). Three generations are joined in a chain of fathers and sons (so the patriarchal Hebrew) in which one link finds its "glory" and "crown" in another (these terms are joined in 16:31). This picture of an unbroken family, lasting over the generations, contrasts with the sad collapse of family seen in vv. 1-2.

17:7. This verse is one of three sayings on things unbecoming or not fitting (see 19:10; 26:1; for things not good, see 17:26; 18:5; 19:2; 20:23; 25:27; 28:21). The principle of fittingness is basic to wisdom (see Commentary on 26:1-12). "Fool" here translates a term used infrequently in Proverbs, נבל (*nābāl*; elsewhere in Proverbs only 17:21; 30:22; see 1 Sam 25:25; Job 30:8). Whybray states that the term denotes someone who "takes a negative stance in every area of life, contributes nothing . . . gives no help, respects nothing, is a nothing, and who ought therefore to be excluded from normal society."[230]

"Fine speech" (not "arrogant lips"), which does good to others, is simply out of character for such a person. Even more unfitting is that a ruler (or "person of noble character"; see v. 26) should lie, because the lies of the powerful, especially when they are trusted, do all the more damage (see Ps 120:2). Conversely, those in power should not listen to lies, no matter how persuasive (see v. 4; 12:22; 15:4; 29:12). The famous opening of Socrates' defense is a masterful illustration of this saying.[231]

17:8. Bribes are regularly condemned in the OT as a means of perverting justice (see Commentary on 15:27; 17:23). The parallelism in 21:14 shows that the line between what is a bribe and a legitimate gift could be difficult to draw. This verse, however, seems ironic, because the bribe's success is assessed in terms of the briber's opinion—which could be quite wrong (for "in the eyes of," see Commentary on 12:15). So, while this saying may simply observe bribery in action, its more

---

230. Whybray, *Proverbs*, 255-56.
231. See Plato *Apology*.

likely target is human blindness that does not see God, who "takes no bribe" (Deut 10:17 NRSV).

17:9. This verse is one of a group of sayings about love or hate covering or revealing things, rightly or wrongly, foolishly or wisely (see also 10:12, 18; 11:13; 12:16, 23). Whether revealing or covering something (also in the sense of forgiving or passing over; see 19:11), what is right or wrong depends on motive (love or hate), on what fits the concrete situation (26:1-12), and on the results: social strife or harmony. To "repeat a matter" is gossip that disrupts friendship (16:28).

17:10. "A word to the wise is sufficient" implies that many words are not enough for a fool. Some people learn only from painful experience, the "school of hard knocks" (see Commentary on 19:29; 26:3-5). The second line is hyperbole, since the law forbids more than forty lashes, lest a person be demeaned (Deut 25:3; 2 Cor 11:24). The fool here is one who is self-satisfied, verging on "wise in one's own eyes" (26:12). Because they "know it all," such persons resist correction and admonition (13:1; 15:10, 12, 31-32). For the problem of corporal punishment, see Commentary on 13:24 and 23:13-14.

17:11-15. A section concerning situations of conflict begins (implicitly) and ends (explicitly) with the mysterious judgment of God operating in and through human conflict. Verse 15 is a particular (legal) instance of the inversion of right and wrong, stated more broadly in v. 13 (see Isa 5:20, 23).

17:11. The word translated "rebellion" (מרי *měrî*) consistently refers to defiance of God, as in 1 Sam 15:23 (cf. Isa 30:9; Ezek 2:8; 44:6). Since the Creator defines good and evil, wrongdoers necessarily set themselves in opposition to God. Sin is not simply moral disorder; it is rebellion against the Creator. The second line refers vaguely to God's judgment against rebels, much on the political model of 16:4 (see Ps 78:49, where "angel" = "messenger").

17:12. "A bear robbed of her cubs" is a proverbial expression for a bitterly angry and dangerous enemy (2 Sam 17:8; Hos 13:8). The proverb is ironic and playful; to meet a fool is even worse. But the hyperbole suggests that the quiet, often unnoticed, damage done to people by fools can be more hurtful

than the spectacular calamities that make the headlines. There may be a connection between vv. 11 and 12. In 2 Kgs 2:23-24, bears are sent in judgment, one might say as cruel messengers from God. For the damage done by fools, see 1:32; 10:1; 13:20; 17:21; 18:6-7; 26:6.

17:13. Returning evil for good is an outrageous inversion of the way things should be (Ps 109:5; Jer 18:20). David rages that Nabal (see Commentary on 17:7) has returned him evil for good, and David wrongly plans to get revenge (1 Sam 25:21; cf. 1 Sam 24:17). Eventually God vindicates David and judges Nabal and Saul, Nabal's royal counterpart (see Prov 20:22; 25:21-22; Lev 19:17-18). Joseph makes the same accusation against his brothers (Gen 44:4), but in his story grace breaks through the reproductive cycle of evil begetting evil. Even with grace, repentance, and forgiveness, a certain amount of trouble gets passed on through the generations of a family or house (2 Sam 12:7-12).

17:14. A quarrel is best stopped before it has begun. Once water has broken the dam, you cannot put it back in.

17:15. This verse provides a significant example of the difficulty of translating OT terms into English. The roots usually translated "righteous" (צדק *ṣdq*) and "wicked" (רשע *rš'*), when used in a legal context as here, refer to the innocent and the guilty. Similarly, the verbs "justifies" (מצדיק *maṣdîq*) and "condemns" (מרשיע *maršîa'*)—which tend to have theological connotations for Protestant NT readers—translate the same roots as "innocent"/"righteous" and "wicked"/"guilty" respectively; the NRSV obscures the forensic context, as the NIV does not. Judges who invert justice (18:5; Exod 23:6-8; Deut 25:1; Isa 5:23) are an abomination to God (see Commentary on 11:1).

17:16. It is implied here that wisdom was taught by paid teachers, though the practice is not attested in Israel before Ben Sira in Hellenistic times. The matter is uncertain, for the proverb itself may be as late as the Hellenistic period, or it may use the image of purchasing as a metaphor (see Isa 55:1-3). It seems unlikely, however, that monarchical Israel, with its highly sophisticated literature, should lack paid teachers (see Mic 3:11, where the priests teach for pay but should not). The main point is that money cannot buy wisdom, if a person lacks the intellectual-spiritual equipment to get it (lit., "heart"; see 16:16; 19:8; 23:23; 24:7).

17:17-18. These verses are a proverb pair whose connection in English is obscured because the same Hebrew word (רע *rēaʿ*) is translated "friend" in v. 17, but "neighbor" in v. 18. The determination of *rēaʿ* in v. 17 by the definite article "the friend" strengthens the connection between the verses, since *rēaʿ* in v. 18 is also definite. The definiteness shows the closeness of the relationship in each case.[232] Together the sayings communicate more than they would individually.

The true character of love is revealed by its constancy over time, but especially by its conduct in adversity (v. 9). The *rēaʿ* in v. 17 is compared to a brother who is obligated to his siblings by birth. Alternately, "brother" is a metaphor for a friend who has become like family. The friendship of David and Jonathan is an example (1 Sam 18:1-4; 2 Sam 1:26). While people are given their siblings, they choose their friends. Yet some friends reveal more of faithful love than siblings do (18:24*b*; 27:10). Such persons are not "fair-weather friends."

Verse 18, however, shows that the *rēaʿ* (true "friend" or greedy "neighbor"?) is an ambiguous relation (see 14:20; 19:4, 6-7). To one you can entrust your life; to the other you should not trust your cash (19:4). Wise persons know what sort of *rēaʿ* they are dealing with and act accordingly. On putting up security for one's neighbor/friend, see Commentary on 6:1-5.

17:19. The translation of this verse is obscure because the expression "to make one's opening/door high" is not understood. The NRSV is somewhat loose; the door/opening is not a threshold, and "bones" is not in the Hebrew. This translation interprets the metaphor: If you raise your threshold too high, people will trip over it and get hurt. On this reading, the wicked intentionally set up obstacles that create conflict in relationships. The NIV is straightforward, but also obscure. Some think the "high gate" is a metaphor for pride (see Commentary on 16:5, 18). Finally

the "opening" may refer to a (proud) mouth (see 1 Sam 2:3; Mic 7:5). The matter remains uncertain. Verse 19*a* simply juxtaposes "one loving transgression" and "one loving strife." Thus the ambiguity reflected in the NIV's and the NRSV's inversion of subjects and predicates. Some people love to stir up trouble (10:12).

17:20. The "crooked of heart" (cf. v. 10) are an abomination to God (11:20). The phrase "will not prosper" is literally, "will not find good" (see Commentary on 16:20). The person here portrayed is also twisted in tongue, the heart's outer expression. The two lines express a simple character-consequence connection. But v. 20*b* is ambiguous; it may be translated, "one perverted by his tongue [i.e., of the crooked of heart; see 21:6] will fall into trouble." This makes the saying more complex: the speech of one crooked person twists another to make him or her fall.

17:21-22. Like v. 25, v. 21 is a variant, perhaps editorial, on 10:1. "Fool" in v. 21*b* translates נבל (*nābāl*; see Commentary on 17:7).

Verse 22 is closely parallel to 15:13 (see also 14:30). The first lines are identical, except here the uncertain word גהה (*gēhâ*) replaces "face" in 15:27*a*. The word possibly refers to a body part, like the face. The NRSV translation, "is good medicine," relates the word to a rare verb, "to heal," used in Hos 5:13. "Bone" (singular) refers to the inner person, deprived of the vital juices of the spirit.

17:23. This verse portrays the blatant corruption of justice (see 1 Kgs 21:8-14, where bribery of witnesses is to be assumed). The problem is not that there is a bribe (or "gift," 15:27), but that it is concealed—that is, it does not conform to public standards concerning just and appropriate payment for services rendered. Such sayings show that proverbial wisdom is in harmony with Israel's legal and prophetic traditions concerning justice (18:5; 21:14; Exod 23:6-8; Deut 16:18-20). For the "bribe," see Commentary on 15:27; 17:8.

17:24. Wisdom is near to one who is discerning, but distant and inaccessible for the fool who seeks it at "the ends of the earth" (see Commentary on 8:9; 14:6; Deut 30:11-13). The first line of the verse may be

---

232. The definite article in 17:17 virtually functions as a possessive, "one's friend" rather than "a friend." See Waltke and O'Connor, *An Introduction to Biblical Hebrew Syntax*, 243, ¶13.5.1e.

translated, "Wisdom is in front of the discerning person."

17:25. For discussion of this verse, see the Commentary on Prov 10:1; 17:21.

17:26. Again the inversion of good and evil is given attention here, specifically in the crucial arena of justice (v. 15). It is one of several sayings using the predicate "not good" (see Commentary on 17:7). The proverb does not explain why these things are not good, but assumes it is obvious. It is wrong to "punish" or "fine" (see 21:11; 22:3) an innocent person (see Commentary on 17:13, 15). Similarly, to flog officials (see 8:16) or persons of "noble" character is wicked, especially when they are flogged for their integrity (properly, "uprightness"). The Hebrew term for "noble" (נדיבים *nědîbîm*) has somewhat the range of the English (see v. 7; 19:6; Isa 32:5-8).

17:27-28. These verses are a proverb pair on the complex relationship between wisdom and folly, speech and silence. The ability to refrain from speech, to speak only with deliberation, is an indispensable aspect of wisdom (see Commentary on 15:28; 10:18-19). Job wishes his false comforters would show their wisdom by keeping silent (Job 13:5). But silence is only a sign of wisdom; even fools can fake it. Yet there may be some gentle, pedagogical irony here: If you are a fool, at least act wise by keeping silent—though it may be difficult (18:2). Others will consider you wise, and, curiously, in recognizing your own personal limitations, you will have made a crucial step on the road to wisdom (see Commentary on 15:33; 16:18-19).

REFLECTIONS

1. In contrast to American individualism, in which individuals choose to join groups, or leave them,[233] the Israelites believed that families are an inescapable given, prior to and more lasting than the individual.[234] In this regard, Americans are profoundly at odds with the biblical worldview, often without being aware of it. Our individualism is like a blinder that obscures the critical light the Bible sheds on our society. If we can discard our cultural blinders and learn from ancient Israel, we might see our own society more critically and seek to change ourselves and it for the better.

Proverbs, and the Bible generally, understands family differently and more profoundly than is possible with individualistic assumptions. From Scripture we learn that even when we flee from our families, or are divorced by them, we take them with us—as the Jacob and Joseph stories so profoundly show (Genesis 26–50). In the beginning, we get our identity, even our language, in and through family. In the course of life, we inevitably find and mold that identity in terms of those relations.

Yet, from within Israel's collectivist culture, Prov 17:2 asserts that there are realities more basic than family. Wisdom, godliness, and divine grace can override such natural relations. The stories that exemplify 17:2 often concern women. Rahab and Ruth are wise outsiders who enter the Israelite family at its messianic, Davidic center (Joshua 2; 6:17-25; Ruth 4:13-22; Matt 1:5; Jas 2:25). Grace regularly promotes younger brothers over their elders: Abel, Isaac, Jacob, David, and the nation Israel over its international older "sibling," Egypt (Exod 4:22-23). And grace can break the power of canceled sin that binds one generation to another (see Exod 34:6-7).

In a wisdom speech equally as sharp as Prov 17:2, Jesus insists that discipleship is greater than family (Mark 3:31-34). For Paul, Christians are slaves who have become heirs and children of God by adoptive grace (Gal 3:26–4:7). Christians should thus neither underestimate nor overvalue the importance of the family. Individualistic Americans need to repent of their neglect of family. But for those whose families have been

---

233. Bellah et al., *Habits of the Heart*, 142-95, esp. 167; and *Individualism and Commitment in American Life: Readings on the Themes of Habits of the Heart* (New York: Harper & Row, 1987).

234. The standard, highly illuminating work on this general topic is Harry C. Triandis, *Individualism and Collectivism* (Boulder, Col.: Westview, 1995).

---

instruments of violence and abuse, the good news is that grace makes us members of God's family, even as it makes us new persons (Rom 12:2).

2. Do those who mock the less fortunate (17:5*a*) imagine that they themselves are immune to woe (Psalms 49; 73:4-9)? Rich and poor, good and bad, black and white, we all share one Maker and die one death (22:2; 29:13). Joy at another's calamity (17:5*b*), what Germans call *Schadenfreude,* is a twisted child of envy. It is not even covetousness, which desires another's goods, hoping that "if you lose, I win." Envy simply takes pleasure in another person's ill fortune.[235.] Against such sins, Prov 17:5 levels the same warning as given elsewhere against godless pride and blasphemy: It will not go unpunished (see Commentary on 16:5-6; Deut 5:11).

235. See Plantinga, *Not the Way It's Supposed to Be,* 157-72.

Proverbs 18:1-24, A Fool Takes No Pleasure in Understanding

COMMENTARY

18:1-2. These opening verses are a proverb pair that appear to build on an implicit contrast between an isolated (and therefore foolish) individual and the wisdom that can be gained only in community. The meaning of v. 1 is not wholly certain because some of its terms are obscure. Its subject is literally, "one separated" (see the verb in 16:28*b*; 17:9*b*; 19:4*b*), probably from one's proper companions. Rabbi Hillel, a contemporary of Jesus, counseled against separating oneself from the community.[236] Rashi compared it to Lot's separating himself from Abraham to live in Sodom. One may translate, "One who is alienated seeks his own desire; he breaks out [17:14; 20:3] against competent [communal] planning" (for "sound judgment" [תושיה *tûšîyâ*], see Commentary on 2:7; for "counselors," see Commentary on 11:14).

Verse 2 continues the topic of one who resists communal wisdom and is further linked to v. 1 by a wordplay between יתגלע (*yitgallā',* "defies," "breaks out against") and התגלות (*hitgallôt,* "expressing"). The fool "knows it all" and takes no pleasure in the "understanding" of others, but merely lays bare his own heart or personal opinion. In Hebrew, the irony of this is laughable, because a fool is one who lacks heart—that is, the capacity for understanding (see 11:12).

236. See *m. 'Abot* 2:5.

18:3. This verse is near in form and theme to 11:2. When one thing comes, another follows; the pairs are inseparable. The connection of "wickedness" and "contempt" in v. 3*a* is suggestive. Wickedness entails a devaluation of some created good or creature, even of other persons (11:12; 14:21, 31). Wickedness fails to love and value what God made good and still loves (Gen 1:31; John 3:16). But v. 3*b* seems to point the proverb in a different direction, though its sense is uncertain. The terms "dishonor" and "disgrace" are so similar as to obscure the point of their connection. Is it because one dishonors another that one receives disgrace from society (see 6:33; 9:7)? Then also the first line may be understood differently. When one is wicked, then one earns and receives contempt from others (see Commentary on 12:8; 13:18; 26:1, concerning honor and shame in Israel's culture).

18:4. This verse may be read in two ways. The first line conveys the inscrutability of human words, as expressing the hidden depths of the human heart (see 20:5; 21:1; 25:3). This is somewhat paradoxical, because words would seem to be on the surface and open to all. The depth dimensions of words and persons is at least partially susceptible to human understanding (20:5*b*), but ultimately only God knows the heart behind the words (16:2; 17:3). Verse 4*b* may be read as a nominal, somewhat independent sentence:

"A fountain of wisdom is a flowing stream." But more likely is that "fountain of wisdom" qualifies the "mouth" of one whose words are "deep waters" (see 10:11; Sir 21:13). Through the opening of the mouth, the waters flow to enrich others. Such a wise person emulates Lady Wisdom, who "pours out" her spirit and words (1:23) for listeners. Similar imagery is taken up in John, where believers, through the Spirit, also become a source of "waters" (John 7:38-39).

18:5. This verse is a "not good" saying (see Commentary on 17:7). The perversion of justice in the law courts violates the fundamental principles of 17:13a, 15 (see Commentary on 17:23, 26; 24:23; 28:21). The idiom "to be partial" (שׂאת פני śĕ'ēt pĕnê) is literally, "to raise the face," as when a supplicant, head bowed to the ground, is given permission to rise (see 6:35; Mal 1:8; 2:9). People are prone to dispense preferential treatment to persons who impress them by wealth, class, or beauty (see Commentary on 11:26). But personal advantage, like a bribe, can also be a powerful persuader. Partiality is forbidden in the law (Lev 19:15; Deut 1:17; 16:19; see also 1 Sam 8:3; Sir 42:1-2; Jas 2:1-7). Partial judges set themselves on the side of the wicked and against the innocent. But impartial judges mirror the Creator (Deut 10:17; Sir 35:12-13; Acts 10:34; Rom 2:11).

18:6-7. A proverb pair concerning the trouble that fools get into by talking is the focus of these verses (see also 26:1-12). There is a chiasmus of speech organs setting off the two verses: lips/mouth/mouth/lips. Unconsidered speech creates social conflict and calls for punishment. A fool's mouth is his or her downfall, the lips a dangerous trap (see Commentary on 12:13; 20:25; for נפשׁ [nepeš], see Commentary on 16:17; cf. 1:18). The mouths of fools are their own worst enemy.

18:8. Gossip is like junk food (see 16:28), delicious to taste before it settles inside to do its destructive work (16:28; 26:20, 22). It ought to give both the gossiper and the listener pause that God searches everyone's inmost being (lit., "all the rooms of the belly," 20:27). The image of the body as a house with rooms is used in chaps. 1–9 in connection with the "strange woman" (see 7:27). The prophets "eat" and digest God's words before

speaking them to the people (Jer 15:16; Ezek 2:8-3:3; Rev 10:9-10; see Prov 18:20).

18:9. The NIV offers a more literal translation than does the NRSV. This is strong condemnation of laziness, because in a subsistence agrarian society, laziness can mean hunger (see Commentary on 10:4-5; 12:11; 28:19). But just as "Strike while the iron is hot" speaks far beyond the blacksmith's shop, so also this saying speaks to many situations (see 22:29). It presupposes that humans are to work and do good with the gifts given them. Not to do so makes a person one who destroys (see 28:24).

18:10-11. The text shifts to a proverb pair that relativizes wealth as a source of security, in contrast to trust in God's name (see also v. 12). The imagery in both verses is taken from the military world of civil defense. In 10:15, which has the same first line as 18:11, wealth appears simply as a "strong city." Wealth does provide a certain level of security. But the security of wealth and power (21:22) is not ultimate—as anyone with a life-threatening illness knows. Verse 10 speaks of Yahweh's name (see Commentary on 16:5-6) as a "strong tower" to which the righteous run and are safe. But "safe" is literally "high" (נשׂגב niśgāb), the same word used of the rich person's "high wall." In case of enemy attack, folk retreat to the city, whose elevated location and secure walls place them "high" above danger (see Pss 61:2-3, 5, 7-8; 91:14b). Thus the proverb pair contrasts trust in God (see 14:26a; 28:25-26; 29:25-26) with a false security based on wealth (Luke 12:15-34). A high wall can be breached (Isa 30:12-14). Thus the security of wealth is only apparent, in contrast to the absolute security of trust in Yahweh's gracious name. The illusory character of the rich person's wealth becomes apparent only in the last line of the proverb pair: Wealth is like a high wall of defense only "in their imagination" (the Hebrew phrase is best taken in this sense; see Ps 73:7). Job as well declares that he has not made wealth his trust (Job 31:24-25).

18:12. Verse 12a is a condensed parallel to 16:18, while v. 12b duplicates 15:33b (see Commentary on those verses). Perhaps the saying in its present context is a backward comment on the fate of one trusting in riches (v. 11) and a forward comment on the arrogance of answering without first listening (v. 13).

18:13. The original reference of this saying may have been to legal proceedings (see Commentary on 18:17). In ancient Israel, as in the contemporary United States, a court case is a "hearing" (see Sir 11:7-9). But the issue applies to all human relationships. One of Covey's seven habits of highly effective people is, "Seek first to understand, then to be understood."[237]

18:14-15. These verses seem to be a proverb pair that, like 15:13-14, moves from psychosomatic concerns to a focus on the heart as an organ of knowing. Verse 14 is one of several psychological sayings showing profound awareness of the interrelation of the human spirit (or heart) and bodily well-being. Verse 14b intensifies v. 14a. Bodily sickness is a hard, but not impossible, burden for a healthy spirit. A broken spirit, however, can seem impossible to bear (see Commentary on 15:13; 17:22 for this expression; Ps 51:17 uses a different Hebrew adjective for "broken"). "Who can bear" is a rhetorical question that expects the answer, "No one" (see 27:3-4). Physical maladies can stem from a sick spirit, and the spirit shows in a body weighed down as if by an invisible burden. Although Hans Selye coined the term "stress" in relation to such "psychosomatic" phenomena, the concept is ancient (see Commentary on 13:12, 19).[238]

The two lines of v. 15 are variants of 15:14a. The chief means by which the wise gain knowledge in an oral culture is the listening ear (see 4:20; 20:12; 25:12). In the cognate language of Assyria and Babylon (Akkadian), one of the terms for "wisdom," *uznu,* simply means "ear." Jesus' admonition that those who have ears to hear should hear stands in this broad wisdom tradition. Also in legal matters, hearing is essential (vv. 13, 17). The didactic language here echoes the introduction (1:5) and may be a sign of pedagogical editing.

18:16-17. A proverb pair whose verses implicitly comment on each other comprise this saying (see 19:6). Verse 17 follows a proverb on the power of gifts. The juxtaposition of

vv. 16-17 implies that a wealthy person's gift ought not to distort the free, due process of law (see 28:11).

In pre-industrial societies such as ancient Israel, gifts played a major role in the general exchange of goods and services.[239] The land of Canaan itself was a royal gift of Yahweh to Abraham and his descendants (e.g., Gen 12:7). Gifts were used in social interactions of almost every sort, from legal transactions (Prov 15:27), to prophetic consultation (1 Sam 9:7), to marriage arrangements (Gen 34:12; Exod 22:16-17; 1 Sam 18:20-27), and the acquisition of a burial plot (Genesis 23, where the verbs translated as "sell" or "pay" are נתן [*nātan*], "give"). A person who did not give the appropriate promised gift would be condemned (25:14). A gift could also mean access to persons of power (v. 16). This use of the "gift" was especially prone to corruption. Hence, Israel's prophets and sages had to warn against the danger of corrupt gift-giving (see Commentary on 15:27; 17:8, 23).

In legal proceedings, what seemed true on one person's testimony may be exposed as false by the other's cross-examination (v. 17). A case should not be judged after hearing only one side (see Commentary on 18:13). When David fled Jerusalem and Absalom's army, David unjustly condemned Mephibosheth on the word of Ziba alone (see Deut 19:15-21). This is one of several instances where David failed to act wisely and justly as royal judge (2 Sam 16:1-4; 19:24-30; see Commentary on 16:12; 25:2-5).

18:18. This saying continues the legal topic. For Israel, the ultimate decider of obscure cases was the "lot" (see Commentary on 16:10, 33). Perhaps the lot was used when the arguments of each side seemed equally matched. Like a referee in a boxing match, the lot separates the combatants. When powerful persons contend at law or other matters, much damage can be done to property and to the innocent bystanders who are associated with the powerful.

18:19. The Hebrew grammar of this verse has received no satisfactory explanation, even though many of its words appear in the surrounding verses, and all of them are well known. The saying is either extremely

237. Covey, *The Seven Habits of Highly Effective People,* 236-60.
238. See Hans Selye, *The Stress of Life* (New York: McGraw-Hill, 1976).
239. See Marcel Mauss, *The Gift: Forms and Functions of Exchange in Archaic Societies* (New York: Norton, 1967).

elliptical or corrupt. The general sense seems to be that it is more difficult to win over a brother offended or "sinned against" (the sense supplied by the KJV) than it is to conquer a strong city. One cannot gain entrance because quarrels create barriers like a barred door.

18:20-22. In its present context, v. 20 introduces a trio of related sayings that all begin with the same letter. Verses 20-21 concern the metaphorical fruit of speech organs, and vv. 21-22 are linked by images of women and Wisdom that recall chaps. 1–9. Verse 21 discusses the ambiguous "tongue" in terms that echo the love of Wisdom and Folly (see Overview on Proverbs 1:1–9:18). Verse 22 explicitly echoes 8:35, reaffirming the wife as a symbol and, as it were, the incarnation of Lady Wisdom.

Verse 20 is a near duplicate and expansion of 12:14a and 13:2a. "To be filled" or "satisfied" (שׂבע *śāba‘*) both translate the same Hebrew word, and the object of filling can be negative or positive (see 1:31; 14:14; 18:21). The imagery is playful and punning, as if one can eat words that then go down into the belly (see Commentary on 18:8).

Verse 21 takes up the image of fruit produced by the organs of speech from v. 20 (see Sir 37:17-24). Here, however, the imagery suddenly becomes complex and allusive. The tongue is portrayed as a woman (it is feminine in Hebrew) who has male lovers—a thought that anticipates finding a wife in v. 22. But love of the tongue can entail either life or death—just as love of a woman does in Proverbs 1–9 (see 2:18-19; 4:6; 5:19; 8:17, 35-36). Literally, the verse reads, "Death and life are in the hand of the tongue, her lovers will eat her fruit" (see 8:19; 31:16b concerning the fruit of Lady Wisdom and of the capable woman).[240]

Verse 22 is crucial to the interacting theme of woman and wisdom in the book (see Commentary on 8:35; see also 3:13; 19:8b, 14;

31:10-31). The affirmation of ordinary life, including marriage, is essential to a biblical view of God as Creator and of the creation as good. Proverbs throughout addresses young men and here considers a wife from a male perspective. But the affirmation of a spouse as divine gift may apply equally to wives. In its present masculine form, however, the saying may combat perennial male tendencies to deny the importance that wives have their husbands' weal or woe (12:4; 19:13; 21:9; Sir 26:1-4, 13-18).[241]

18:23. This saying presents a sharp portrayal of the power difference between rich and poor and of the temptation to arrogance that comes with wealth (see Commentary on 11:24; 14:31; 18:10; 22:7). The poor person who pleads for mercy is likely to be rejected by the rich, but God hears such pleas (Pss 28:2, 6; 116:1). Humans may separate themselves from the misfortunate, thus ignoring their common existence as God's creatures (22:2; 29:13). There is a sharp judgment for such people, a *lex talionis,* in which the punishment fits the crime (21:13).

18:24. The Hebrew of v. 24b is clear (see Commentary on 17:17; 18:19), but v. 24a is open to a stunning number of readings, reflected in the variety of translations it has occasioned. These possibilities reflect linguistic ambiguity in the original: "There are friends who mutually harm one another." "A man of *many* friends comes to harm" (see NIV; see also 19:4). "There are friends who *merely* chatter." "There are friends who are *merely* friends" (see 22:24). The final reading is perhaps correct (see NRSV). There seems to be a contrast between the appearance and the reality of friendship, but it is difficult to say more than this (for "friend," see Commentary on 17:17-18). In 12:9 and 13:7 hithpael verb forms generate similar ambiguities, though without the added problem of an obscure root.

240. For a different view, see Camp, "Woman Wisdom as Root Metaphor," 45-76, esp. 52-53.

241. See Frank S. Pittman's wise book, *Man Enough: Fathers, Sons, and the Search for Masculinity* (New York: G. P. Putnam's Sons, 1993).

REFLECTIONS

1. On occasion, a biblical concept or practice that seems obvious and familiar to us may conceal something foreign. The "gift" is such a concept (18:16). Gifts in ancient societies had more than a merely personal function—unlike capitalist societies where most exchange of goods and services is purely economic. As in the United States, in ancient Israel gifts were used to establish and cement relationships. But unlike the United States, for Israel most exchanges of goods and services bore a "gift" character (see Commentary on 18:16). As a gift, any economic transaction would entail a multi-faceted personal relationship of mutual moral and spiritual obligations in a context of community standards.

In our society, however, the ordinary exchange of goods and services has largely lost the biblical sense of mutual personal obligation attached to gift giving. Economic exchange has been rationalized and made impersonal by money, mail, telemarketing, and credit cards. Both buyers and sellers suffer from lack of trust, because transactions are not based on personal relationships. "Let the buyer beware" is an ancient Latin proverb, but it seems ever more relevant today. On the other hand, a real estate agent's proverb in the Philadelphia area complains, "Buyers are liars." Without mutual trust grounded in personal relationships, there is little sense of obligation to fair play and fair dealing. Employers and employees also view their relation in purely economic terms. "To downsize" is a new verb that connotes a company's abandoning employees to their fates. The fiscal "bottom line" and "maximization of profits" devour other human values.

A biblical answer to such problems is not quick and easy. At the very least, it requires that Christians begin to think hard about the implications of biblical faith for shaping community that is more than just a Sunday thing. The obstacles to such community in a highly mobile, TV-saturated, technologized society are immense. But a beginning might be made by striving to deal with all people in the light of their divine creation, dignity, and calling (see Commentary on 14:31; 15:25).

If most economic transactions in our society have become rationalized and impersonal, the converse problem of distorted gift giving has grown to extraordinary proportions. The use of the gift as a means of unjust access to the great and the powerful is a constant feature of our national life. Political access and influence are purchased by wealthy individuals and by powerful corporations whose lobbyists exert undue influence on the legislative process.

The gift as problem is evident in the persistent unwillingness of our legislators to enact genuine campaign finance reform. It is evident in the way that wealthy lobbies manage to subvert legislative action for the common good, while socially harmful or unjust favors are granted to special interest groups of dubious merit. The giving of gifts, without the moral restraints, can do much to undermine a just and democratic society.

Enactment of appropriate legislation is obviously needed. But the solution to such problems cannot be achieved by legal means alone. It requires a turn from mammon to God, from evil to good (Amos 5:6, 14-15). It requires a spiritually and morally healthy humanity such as only God can make (Jer 31:31-34; Ezek 36:25-32; see 2 Corinthians 3–5). This reality may not happen for our nation, but it does define the new humanity in Christ, which is light and salt to the world (Matt 5:13-16; John 8:12).

2. Like the prophets, Proverbs has a persistent concern for righteousness and justice, not only in personal life, but also in the public arena of the law court (18:5, 17). The modern relegation of religion to the private and personal would have been incomprehensible and abhorrent to ancient Israel's prophets and sages. Public justice and righteousness are integral expressions of the "fear of the LORD" (1:3b; Jer 22:13-17).

For America, with its millions of Christians, this means that claims of biblical piety and godliness are empty unless they bear fruit in collective Christian action for equity between rich and poor, and among races and ethnic groups in our criminal justice system (see Commentary on 13:24).[242]

242. See Dan Van Ness, *Crime and Its Victims* (Downers Grove: Inter-Varsity, 1986); Donald Smarto, ed., *Setting the Captive Free: Relevant Ideas in Criminal Justice and Prison Ministry* (Grand Rapids: Baker, 1993).

Proverbs 19:1-29, Better a Poor Man Whose Walk Is Blameless

COMMENTARY

19:1-3. Each of these proverbs uses imagery of "way" or locomotion. Verse 3 may be a radical instance of the general problem put in v. 2.

Verse 1 is a better-than saying that inverts ordinary valuations of wealth and poverty (see Commentary on 15:16; 16:8). It is almost identical to 28:6, with two differences. Verse 1*b* presents a person who is perverse in regard to the lips (see 8:8; 17:20; 19:5, 9), while 28:6*b* has one perverse in regard to "double ways." For "perverse" and "integrity," see Commentary on 10:9. "Lips" and "ways" each represents action in the world. The more general term "way" designates one's life conduct; it includes "lips" as a specific form of conduct. Proverbs 28:6*b* seems to provide a more natural (and obvious) contrast to the poor person in 19:1*a* (see 18:23; 19:7). Thus the ancient Syriac version and some commentators emend "fool" in v. 1*b* to the "rich" of 28:6*b*, but this is probably hypercritical. That the fool here must be rich is an obvious expectation, which the proverb subverts. The substitution of "fool" for the obvious term "rich" creates in the hearer's mind an implicit comment: Yes, there are rich fools, though one does not always say so out loud (see 28:11).

"Zeal" and "desire" (v. 2) translate נפש (*nepeš*; see Commentary on 13:4, 19; 16:24; 19:15). Desire drives one to activity (16:26), but without considered reflection, even well-intentioned, "spiritually" driven activism can be harmful rather than helpful. Those whose "feet are hasty" (see 1:16) miss the way or sin (חוטא *ḥôṭē'* means both; see 8:36; the words "the way" are not in the Hebrew). For "not good," see Commentary on 17:7, 26.

Verse 3 may be a radical instance of v. 2. Literally, it reads, "A man's folly subverts his way, and his heart rages against Yahweh." Folly and sin are cognitive as well as practical dysfunctions. It is an error in thought to shift blame, but the practice is as old as the primeval pair (Gen 3:12-13). Human beings ruin (11:3 has the same root) their own lives but get angry at God.

19:4. The topic of human relations resumes, especially friendships, as they are affected by wealth and poverty (see 18:23-24; 19:1). Modern folk may be culturally disposed to read this saying cynically: "Money talks," and all that counts is "the bottom line," even in human relationships. But the matter was more complicated in ancient Israel. The exchange of gifts cemented relationships and communicated mutual respect and fulfilled moral obligation (see Reflections on 18:1-24). The gifts of the wealthy can be a means by which goods and services are redistributed, so that society benefits. Thus, on special occasions, the king gave gifts to the people (see 2 Sam 6:19; Eph 4:7-13).

19:5. This verse is one of several sayings, whose lines are near duplicates, against bearing false witness (6:19; 12:17; 14:5, 25; 19:9; 21:28). The topic was an important one in Israel's oral culture, in which false testimony could do great damage (25:18). For "will not go unpunished," see Commentary on 16:5.

19:6-7. These verses are an antithetical proverb pair, presenting opposite sides of one social reality (see v. 4). The effects of wealth and poverty on human relationships is presented in terms of nearness and distance. The phrase "to seek favor" is literally, "to seek the face of someone" (יחלו פני *yĕḥallû* *pĕnê*)—that is, to come close to someone. It is often used with reference to God as the ultimate benefactor of humans (Pss 24:6; 27:8). The face represents the main organ through which humans (and God) communicate the character of their relationship to others (see Num 6:25-26). Thus "curry favor" may be too negative in its connotations. For "generous" (NRSV)/"ruler" (NIV), see Commentary on 17:7, 26. In contrast, people distance themselves from a poor person (v. 7*b*; see v. 4*b* and related verses): "Nobody knows you when you're down and out." Even relatives (lit., "brothers") shun (lit., "hate" [שׂנֵא *śānē*], but the Hebrew has a broader range than the English term) their poor sibling. This may be a form of shaming that seeks to reform the lazy (see Commentary on 10:1, 5; 12:8; 17:2) or is simply a neglect of family responsibility to take care of their own (17:17). Translation of v. 7*c* (two lines in NIV) is uncertain.

19:8. A literal translation brings to light important verbal links with key ideas in Proverbs: "He who gets heart loves himself; he who keeps understanding tends to find good." "Getting heart" is the same as getting wisdom (see 4:5; 16:16), for the heart is the organ of wisdom (see Excursus, "The 'Heart' in the Old Testament"). The ideas of love and "finding good" connect v. 8 with the themes of love for Wisdom/wife and "finding good" (see Commentary on 8:17, 35; 18:22). "Understanding" (תבונה *tĕbûnâ*) is a parallel term for Lady Wisdom (5:1; 8:1). When the young male addressee of the book "keeps" or "cares" for her, then good ensues, because she in turn watches over or guards him (see 4:5-6). To love oneself is to love one's נפש (*nepeš*; see Commentary on 16:17; cf. 13:3; 15:32; 16:17; 19:16). Self-love here appears in its appropriate sense: wise regard, respect, and responsibility for oneself as God's creature.

19:9. This verse is nearly identical to v. 5, but v. 9*b* shares the predicate of 21:28*a*. Repetition indicates the importance of the topic of false witness.

19:10. Essential to wisdom is a sense of propriety, of "fittingness" (see Commentary on 17:7; 26:1-12). This verse presents a world upside down, where social order is inverted and people possess things not fitting to them (see Commentary on 17:2; 20:22;

29:2; see also Eccl 10:6-7). This saying has an anti-revolutionary thrust, as does 30:21-23 (but see Commentary on 17:2).

19:11. This verse belongs to those sayings that insist on the human capacity to reflect before responding to a stimulus (see Commentary on 15:28). "To overlook" (lit., "to pass over" [עבר *ʿābar*]) an offense is akin to the covering of offenses that love does (see Commentary on 10:12; 17:9). More than this, being slow to anger and "passing over offenses" are characteristics of Yahweh (see Mic 7:18, which is based on Exod 34:6-7; cf. Joseph as a quasi-king in Gen 50:17). The person who so acts imitates the goodness of God (see Commentary on 15:18). This is a form of "glory" or "splendor," such as God and kings possess. Thus this saying implicitly comments on the next. Both sayings concern anger as a response to offense, but the perspective of the first saying may be seen as a guide to the king in dealing with wrong.

19:12. The first line of the verse is a near parallel of 20:2, which also compares the king to a roaring lion (the NRSV translates the same Hebrew differently in each case). Verse 12*b* is a variant of 16:15*b*, and 16:14-15 develops the contrast of the king's wrath and favor in a different direction. Morning dew in dry Palestine was an important source of moisture for plants. While a king's wrath could wrongly harm the innocent, the reference here (like the life-giving dew) may be a positive one. As a judge, the king's anger removes the wicked (see Commentary on 25:4-5). David's anger at the rich man in Nathan's parable is an ironic example of judgment gone awry (2 Sam 12:5-6).

19:13-15. These independent proverbs are cunningly juxtaposed around the topic of family relations. The three sayings are rife with vocabulary that echoes the introduction to the antithetical collection (10:1-5, "foolish son, craving/ruin"; see Commentary on 10:3*b*, "father," "hunger," "prudent," "sleep," "slack," "person," "appetite" [*nepeš*, untranslated in 10:3; see 19:15]). There is also a playful contrast between positive wet weather (dew, v. 12) and the negative dripping of constant rain (v. 13).

Verse 13 combines the calamity of a foolish son (see Commentary on 10:1; Eccl 2:18-21) with that of a quarrelsome wife (see Commentary on 27:15, an expansion of 19:13*b*). In the male-oriented address of Proverbs, the father-son relation and the husband-wife relation are the family connections most important for well-being.[243] These relations could be sources of great good or distress. Wives can embody not only wisdom (see Commentary on 8:35; 12:4; 18:22; 31:10-31), but also chaos (21:9, 19; 25:24; 27:15). The "dripping" may refer to a perpetually leaking roof (see 27:15; Eccl 10:18).

Israel conceived of life in terms of family and land—that is, generations of family, in cosmic space, extended through time. Thus v. 14 is a significant deepening of and contrast to v. 13. The transition of possessions and land—whether much or little—from father to son occurs in predictable fashion (v. 14*a*). But the greatest source of male happiness is God's gift of a "prudent wife" (v. 14*b*; see 18:22; her opposite appears in 12:4*b*; 10:5 applies the same contrast to sons). For the mysterious, yet non-coercive presence of God in all human activity, see Commentary on 16:1, 9, 33; 19:21.

Verse 15 may possess an implicit connection with the foregoing proverb pair through the association of "deep sleep" with the implicit laziness of the foolish son (opposite of "prudent") who sleeps in harvest (10:5; see also 10:1). The threat of hunger also appears in 10:3. Sleep as a deterrent to energetic, successful work gives rise to such sayings as, "The early bird gets the worm" and "Rise and shine!"

19:16. This verse is similar in form and thought to v. 8. There the focus was on keeping wisdom and understanding, here, literally, "He who keeps the commandment keeps his life" (*nepeš*). The commandment may be parental (4:4; 7:2), but in the background looms the commandment of God as the ultimate standard of good and evil (see Commentary on 6:20-23; 13:13). Some scholars see v. 16*b* as damaged and emend "his ways" to correspond to "word" in 13:13 ("those who despise the word will die"). The change is unnecessary and is not supported by the ancient versions. God's Word and "ways" (for humans to live) correspond (see the use of "ways" in Ps 25:4-10; Mic 4:2). This reading supposes that the possessive pronoun "his"

refers to Yahweh (implicit in "commandment"? Cf. "despises him" in 14:2, though there "his ways" refers to a person's conduct). Alternately, we must attend to our own ways, though the threat of death seems an extreme punishment for failure to do so. Moreover, to "despise one's own ways" seems too strong an expression to indicate merely being heedless of one's conduct (see 1:7*b*; 14:2).

19:17. This verse is one of many sayings that directly relate one's treatment of the poor to one's relationship with God (see Commentary on 14:21, 31; 21:10; 28:8). The present saying provides a theological explanation for the mystery of profitable generosity (11:24; see also 3:9-10). Its logic (a gift to the poor is a loan to God) underlies Jesus' saying that "whatever you did for the least of these . . . you did for me" (Matt 25:40). This saying may be an example of keeping the commandment (v. 16; see Deut 15:4-6).

19:18-20. These verses form a cluster of three admonitions, an unusual occurrence in these Solomonic sayings. Verse 18 is advice to a father; v. 19 confirms the need for discipline and for not protecting people from the consequences of their actions; v. 20 then gives advice to young persons to receive (parental) advice (see Commentary on 11:14; 15:22) and instruction (the root [יסר *ysr*] is translated "discipline" in v. 18). Thus both parent and child are addressed as partners in the instructional process.

Verse 18*a* concerns the timeliness of instruction and discipline (see Commentary on 13:24; 17:10; 23:13). In this, as in all activities, there is a fitting or right time (Eccl 3:1-8). Developmental biology and psychology have become aware of critical periods in which certain developmental tasks must occur. Once the phase has passed for developing a language-specific accent, for example, it is gone and the opportunity does not return. It is too late. The adage "as the twig is bent, so grows the tree" conveys a similar idea of timely formation of a child's mind and character. Verse 18*b* is not so clear. It may mean, "Do not pay attention to his [a son is meant] moaning" (see TNK, המיתו *hemyatô*; see also Isa 14:11) or "Do not set your heart on his death" (המיתו *hămîtô*), perhaps by letting him continue on a deadly way (see 23:13-14). The saying may also refer to the legal

243. See Pittman, *Man Enough*.

process described in Deut 21:18-21, which does eventuate in death, though the implementation of this law is dubious (see 30:17). A few scholars believe that v. 18*b* literally warns against beating a child to death. Most who accept the second translation, however, see it as typical proverbial hyperbole, meaning "Do not chastise him excessively."[244] Deuteronomy sets limits on paternal authority to harm a child (see Deut 21:18-21, which requires communal judgment). In contrast, the Roman *pater familias* did have life-and-death power over his children.

Verse 19 begins as a saying but ends as an admonition. Though v. 19*b* is obscure in Hebrew, the NIV and the NRSV reflect the most natural reading of it. It appears to be a warning against enmeshment in another person's dysfunctional life. When one person prevents another from bearing the consequences of his or her own actions, one actually interferes with the act-consequence sequence, and so keeps the person "great of anger" (*Qere*) from becoming responsible for his or her own actions. That one must engage in the process again shows that it does not work; it only prolongs the problem. Ironically, the person who "rescues" another is now caught in the unhealthy dynamics of another person's life; you will have to do it again.

The admonition in v. 20 has affinities with counsel to become wise in chaps. 1–9, but some of its elements and its formulation are new. "Listen to advice" has a near parallel only in 12:15*b*; the term "accept" (instruction) occurs only here in Proverbs, and the formulation of the purpose clause after imperatives is also unique. "In the end" is literally, "in your end," an expression found otherwise only in 5:11, but with near parallels in 23:18; 24:14. "The end" may refer to a person's death (5:4-5), but also, as here, to a less ultimate outcome of a specific course of action ("future").

19:21. This verse comments on v. 20 through a play on the double meaning of the word *advice/purpose* (עצה *ʿēṣâ*). God's purpose overrides all human advice and planning, even that of wise parents (see Commentary on 16:1, 9, 33; 21:30-31).

19:22. The difficulty of v. 22*a* is reflected in the differing translations. Literally, it is, "A

man's desire is his kindness/shame." The last two terms reflect two homonyms in Hebrew. חסד (*ḥesed*) frequently means "kindness" (see 16:6). But *ḥesed* is used twice to mean "shame" or "disgrace" (14:34; Lev 20:17; cf. Prov 25:10). This is the probable sense here. One should probably translate according to the NIV margin. Excessive desire (18:1) is shameful, so it is better to be poor than corrupt (see Commentary on 19:1; 28:6; 30:8). The NIV text is also possible, but less likely.

19:23. Verse 23*a* is a conventional declaration concerning "the fear of the LORD" (see Commentary on 1:7; 14:27). Verse 23*b* is less clear, and translators grasp its sense through its relation to the first line of the verse, by filling in the gaps. The general thought seems to be that with a genuine relation to God, one is content, gains security, and avoids trouble (see 16:6*b*).

19:24. This saying has a close variant in 26:15 (see Commentary on 6:6-11; 26:13-16). The comical picture is based on the Eastern custom of dipping bread into a dish of oil or "soup." There is food to be had, but the sluggard is too lazy—or sleepy—to profit from it. Even when sluggards desire what is before them, they remain unsatisfied (v. 15).

19:25. This saying is reminiscent of 9:7-9 (see 21:11). To discipline mockers through corporal punishment (19:29; 26:3) may not help them, because they are too stubborn to learn. But the simple can learn from such an object lesson and gain some "street smarts" (see 1:4; 14:15). Verse 25*b* is literally, "He who rebukes a discerning man (he) understands knowledge." That is, the subject of "understands knowledge" may be either the one who rebukes or the discerning person who is rebuked. In the first reading, rebukers understand knowledge because they do not waste time verbally rebuking a mocker (see 9:7-8; see Commentary on 19:19). In the second reading, the wise get wiser; to those who have, more is given (1:5; Matt 13:12). The punishment of mockers is taken up in vv. 28-29.

19:26. Israel's shame-and-honor culture (see Commentary on 12:8; 13:18) had as one of its most significant expressions the principle—fundamental to all ancient cultures—of honoring one's parents (10:1, 5; Exod 20:12). This principle is implied through portrayal of

244. See Whybray, *Proverbs*, 283.

its violation, through violence (not robbery) done to parents (see 20:20; 28:24; 30:11). For "cause shame and bring reproach," compare the intransitive translation in 13:5.

19:27. Unusual in its construction, this verse has given rise to many conjectural emendations. The form is an admonition with a result clause addressed to "my son," which occurs nowhere else in 10:1–22:16, but is typical of chaps. 1–9 (see Commentary on 19:18-20). The NRSV, following Rashi's old suggestion, inverts part of the two lines to get its translation. The NIV takes the two lines as given, but reads the admonition in v. 27a as though it were a protasis, "If you stop listening . . ." followed by v. 27b as the apodosis, or result clause. Some take the admonition ("Stop listening to instruction") as ironic (see 1 Kgs 2:22; Amos 4:4). The verse remains uncertain.

19:28-29. A "worthless witness" is a belial witness (עֵד בְּלִיַּעַל ʿēd bĕliyyaʿal; see Commentary on 6:12; 16:27; 1 Kgs 21:10), on which "devour" (lit., "swallow" [בלע bālaʿ]) makes a pun. The mouth can pour out things good and bad, but figuratively it also eats them (see Commentary on 18:8). Compare our sayings, "She swallowed it, hook, line, and sinker," or "He really ate it up," used of untruth or gossip. "Mock/mocker" appears in vv. 25, 28-29 as a key word (see 9:7-12) and also creates a link with the next chapter (20:1).

In v. 29, the threat of punishment for mockers is juxtaposed as a warning to the false witness in v. 28 who "mocks" at justice. Literally, "Judgments [שפטים šĕpāṭîm] are prepared," unless the word is a dialectical variant of "rods" (so that the פ [p] of "judgments" equals the ב [b] of שבטים [šĕbāṭîm, "rods"]), which would make a good parallel to v. 29b (see 10:3; 26:3). In v. 25 also the mocker is punished by striking.

REFLECTIONS

1. Spirit, zeal, and desire for good things are no substitute for careful analysis and understanding of reality (19:2; see Commentary on 1:7; 12:1). This is also a central thrust of Mark Noll's *The Scandal of the Evangelical Mind*.[245] Too often, says Noll, evangelical Christianity in North America has been characterized by a simplistic activism that shows zeal without a regard for reality and manifests action without insight into the complexities of life. But activism without reflection or knowledge is not unique to evangelicals; it defines a broad stream in North American culture and human nature in general.[246] We fail to look before we leap. We make haste and waste. We want answers and action before we have understood the questions. We often fail to see issues in terms of a comprehensive biblical worldview, and thus we fail to consider the cosmic-social inter-relatedness and implications of things.[247] Too often we are indifferent to the truth, because we are unwilling to suffer for the sake of truth, both in the gaining of it and in the living out of its consequences.

Exacerbating these problems is the (understandable) rift between ordinary Christians and mainstream North American intellectual culture.[248] The problem is also manifested in the quality and scope of books read by educated Christians and in the often weak financial support of Christian colleges and seminaries.

The wisdom literature insists that God's human servants develop their intellects and use them in every aspect of life, so that—to speak in New Testament terms—we may "destroy arguments and every proud obstacle raised up against the knowledge of God, and . . . take every thought captive to obey Christ" (2 Cor 10:4-5 NRSV). Paul's great discourse on Christ as the Wisdom of God is not intended to support

245. Mark Noll, *The Scandal of the Evangelical Mind* (Grand Rapids: Eerdmans, 1993).
246. Richard Hofstader, *Anti-Intellectualism in American Life* (New York: Knopf, 1963).
247. See O'Donovan, *Resurrection and Moral Order*; Brian J. Walsh and J. Richard Middleton, *The Transforming Vision: Shaping a Christian World View* (Downers Grove: Inter-Varsity, 1984); Albert M. Wolters, *Creation Regained: Biblical Basics for a Reformational Worldview* (Grand Rapids: Eerdmans, 1988). Walsh and Middleton provide an extensive bibliography.
248. See George M. Marsden, *The Soul of the American University* (New York: Oxford University Press, 1994).

anti-intellectualism, otherworldly pietism, or fundamentalism (inasmuch as it continues nineteenth-century scientism).[249] Rather, it intends that every human thought, action, and institution be converted from foolish rebellion (disguised as "wisdom") and so be made subject to the mind of Christ (1 Cor 1:18–2:16).

2. To drive out one's mother is particularly heinous (19:26), since she is a defenseless widow (object of God's special concern, 15:25). In Israel, a mother would reside with a son only upon the death of her husband. Shakespeare's *King Lear* provides a pre-modern instance of driving out a parent. This issue has become exceedingly difficult in modern, technological societies in which the medical and personal care of the aged is often beyond the capacity of a nuclear family. The basic principles of 19:26 still hold, but wisdom for their implementation has become more difficult to obtain, given the rapid changes in society and medical technology.

249. George M. Marsden, *Fundamentalism and American Culture* (New York: Oxford University Press, 1980).

Proverbs 20:1-30, Wine Is a Mocker, Strong Drink a Brawler

COMMENTARY

20:1. The opening saying takes up the word *mocker* from 19:28-29 to personify wine and beer as bad company and destroyers of wisdom (see Commentary on 23:19-2, 29-35; 31:4-5). Strong drink is also a "brawler" (המה *hmh*), the root used to describe the seductive or foolish woman (7:11; 9:13). In 1:21 the root describes the tumultuous city where Wisdom's cry goes unheeded. This connection of crazy-making drink and Woman Folly is strengthened by their common effect on young males: They both tempt young men to be led astray (see Deut 27:18; Isa 28:7) or intoxicated (שגה *šāgâ*; see 5:19, positively of one's wife; 5:20-23, negatively of the strange woman). Alcoholic and sexual intoxication—except within the passionate bonds of marriage—robs one of wisdom. That is, those drunk with wine or lust cannot discriminate the limits of creation and conduct (cf. Lev 10:8-11). Lemuel's mother makes a similar association of drinking and lust for women (see Commentary on 31:3-5). These verbal links suggest that this verse is part of the thematic, final editing of the book.

20:2. Verse 2*a* is a variant of 19:12, but v. 2*b* offers indirect advice about not rousing the king's anger (see Commentary on 14:35; 16:14-15). This advice speaks to all situations where a powerful person has the ability to damage a weaker one (though it does not

always succeed, 18:23). For instance, young offenders had best not sass the judge presiding over their drug trial. For the expression "angers him," see Commentary on 14:16*b*, where the verb is translated differently. "Forfeit life" is literally "miss life" (חוטא נפשו *ḥôṭēʾ napšô*), as in "miss me" (8:36 NRSV).

20:3. See 17:14 on stopping a quarrel before it starts, and 15:18 on the qualities of a person who stills a quarrel. For honor and shame in Israel's culture, see Commentary on 12:8; 13:18; 26:1. For the verb here translated as "quick to quarrel," see 18:1 ("defies" or "break" out in 17:14).

20:4. Agricultural life, lived in harmony with the cosmic order of seasons, is a model of wisdom. "In season" is literally, "in late fall" (חרף *ḥōrep*)—that is, the cooler, rainy season when one plows and sows in order to reap in the summer harvest time. This saying varies the act-consequence idea of reaping what one sows. Its focus, however, is on the crucial timing of actions. The famous Gezer calendar shows that each season had its appropriate tasks.[250] On the sluggard, see Commentary on 6:6-11; 10:4-5; 13:4.

250. Pritchard, *Ancient Near Eastern Texts Relating to the Old Testament,* 320; R. de Vaux, *Ancient Israel* (New York: McGraw-Hill, 1961) 1:184.

20:5. Traditionally, what is in the king's heart is too deep for humans to search out (25:3), but no heart is hidden from God (15:11; 21:1; see Excursus, "The 'Heart' in the Old Testament," and 18:4 for "deep waters"). Wise persons can bring to the surface what others have in mind, even when there are attempts at concealment (28:11). The image is of a well into which one descends in order to get life-giving water (see Commentary on 10:11; 13:14). Often in ancient cities (Megiddo is a good example) there is a long stairway carved through rock in order to get down to the protected well at the base of the city mound. No little effort was required to go down, get the water, and carry it back up to the surface for use.

20:6. This verse shows how little humans heed the wisdom of 27:2. It also should make honest folk cautious (see Commentary on 17:17-18) about those who proclaim their reliable love, or חסד (ḥesed), a word often associated with faithfulness (see Commentary on 16:5-6). The Lord approves faithful, or "reliable," persons (12:24), and this quality is especially important in witnesses (12:17; 14:5) and messengers (13:17). "Who can find?" is a rhetorical question to express rarity. The idiom expects a negative answer, "no one" or "hardly anyone" (see 31:10).

20:7. For "walk in integrity," see Commentary on 10:9 (see also 19:1). Verse 7b again embodies the connection of the generations so basic to biblical thought. This is often conveyed by the word *son* (בן *bēn*), which occurs sixty times in Proverbs (see Commentary on 10:1; 13:22; 14:26; 17:6). Good begets good and is blessed (see Commentary on 3:13) from one generation to the next.

20:8. The throne (1 Kgs 7:7; Ps 122:5; Isa 16:5) symbolizes the most basic function of kingship: the doing of justice (2 Sam 15:2-4). Justice had an external aspect, the military and diplomatic defense of the nation, as well as a domestic one. In Israel, the latter function entailed the defense of the poor and the needy (28:15; 29:14; 31:8-9; see Psalm 72) and the removal or punishment of the wicked according to the norm of righteousness (16:12; 19:26; 25:4-5). In 2 Samuel 8–9 (cf. Prov 8:15), David is portrayed as a good and wise king who secures the national boundaries against enemies and shows kindness to the crippled Mephibosheth, a survivor from the house of Saul. This saying has "leap-frog" connections (where two or more related verses are separated by intermediate verses) with vv. 10, 12; there also Yahweh appears as judge and creator.

20:9. Set between a proverb on royal judgment and another on divine standards, this verse is a reminder of the universality of sin (see Gen 6:5; 8:21; Psalms 14; 32; 51:5; Jer 17:9-10; Rom 3:9-19). "Who can say . . . ?" expects the answer, "No one."

20:10. Verses 10 and 23 are variants of the same saying and are closely related to 11:1. The repetition of such sayings reinforces God's deep concern for integrity and fair play in matters of money and commerce (Deut 25:13-16; Amos 8:5). Often the use of money and material goods is the best indicator of the operative beliefs of a culture or a person. "Faith without works is dead"; that is, only those beliefs that shape everyday life are genuine (Jas 2:17, 20; 5:1-6; see Commentary on 20:12).

20:11. Along with the NIV and the NRSV, another possible translation of this text (based on another meaning of the root נכר *nkr*) is "A child may be dissembling in his behavior/ Even though his actions are blameless and proper" (TNK; see 26:24a). For the vocabulary of v. 11b, see 21:8b.

20:12. In the sayings of chaps. 10–29, Yahweh often appears as the Creator of humans (14:31; 17:5; 22:2; 29:13), in contrast to chaps. 1–9, where God appears mainly as Creator of the cosmos—including human beings (3:19-20; 8:22-31). The "hearing ear" is the basic organ through which wisdom enters the heart (see Commentary on 15:31; 25:12; see also 2:2; 18:15). But the "seeing eye" is not portrayed as an organ for getting wisdom. It is much more ambiguous, often representing mere perception or self-deception (see Commentary on 3:7; 26:12). The fool's eyes and ears do not function rightly (17:24; 23:9). That God creates these organs means that God holds humans accountable for their use (Exod 4:10-16; Ps 94:8-9). The Exodus passage reflects mutual divine-human involvement in speech (see Commentary on 16:1). The ending, "them both," links this verse to v. 10.

20:13. This saying has a catchword link to the "eyes" of v. 12 (and v. 8?). The contrast of sloth and industry is a particular case of the opposition between folly and wisdom (see Commentary on 6:6-11; 19:15). Proverbs 12:11 and 30:22*b* use similar Hebrew expressions for "plenty of bread." Psalm 127:2 provides an important qualification to this saying: Without God's blessing even sleepless labor profits not.

20:14. Here the NRSV better catches the pithy sharpness, though not the poetic genius, of the Hebrew—an ironic observation on devious behavior in the business of buying and selling. In ancient Israel, as in many non-Western countries today, most transactions were achieved through bargaining over the price of goods. The bargaining ritual was well-known to both buyer and seller. The buyer offers a low initial price, and the seller asks for a higher one. Usually a satisfactory compromise is then reached. Here the buyer condemns a deal as bad, only to boast afterward. Although the issues are judicial rather than commercial, Abraham's negotiating with God for Sodom and Gommorah is a strangely inverted example of negotiating a "price." A gracious God keeps accepting lower offers from Abraham (Gen 18:22-33)!

20:15. Like v. 14, this verse concerns the value of things. Taken together, the two sayings present an ironic contrast between the goods for which one haggles and priceless wisdom (see 3:15; 8:10-11). This verse praises the value of lips as an instrument of wisdom (see 25:11-12). They are not so much a precious jewel but "instruments" or "vessels."

20:16. The NIV follows the MT vowel pointing of this verse and introduces the "strange woman" from Proverbs 1–9 (see 27:13, which is nearly identical). The NRSV translates the *Ketib,* or consonantal text, moving the parallelism from masculine singular "stranger" to masculine plural "foreigners." These words may simply refer to a second party, "another" (see 27:2), with a hint that they are not known well to the guarantor (see Commentary on 17:18). The *Ketib* is probably original here, and its warning echoes common advice (see Commentary on 6:1-5; 11:15). A person's cloak could be taken as surety for a debt, but the law placed restrictions on the practice (Deut 24:10-13, 17; Amos 2:8; see Prov 22:26-27). The admonition to take is probably pedagogical irony, the real target of the saying being one who foolishly gives security for a loan.

20:17. This verse is linked to v. 16 by wordplay on "security"/"sweet." The verbal connection suggests that someone can be enticed by a "sweet deal" but has in fact swallowed a bad deal. "Bread gained by deceit" is literally "deceptive bread" (cf. 23:3). Only afterward is the true nature of the "meal" evident (see 9:17). Job 20:12-23 is a baroque elaboration of the metaphor of swallowing something bad that seems initially sweet. Similarly, the "deceptive bread" of this verse should not be limited to bad business deals or to ill-gotten gain, but may refer to any wickedness or deception that someone "swallows" (see 4:17; 18:8; for "gravel," see Lam 3:16).

20:18. The interest unexpectedly turns to advice appropriate for a king, who is militarily responsible for the integrity of the nation's borders (see Commentary on 11:14; 15:22). Proverbs 24:6 provides a near parallel.

20:19. Another admonition, this verse picks up themes encountered earlier (see Commentary on 11:13*a,* a variant of 20:19*a*; see also 25:9). The principle that humans are shaped by the company they keep (14:7) is given a specific focus here. One should not keep company with gossips and slanderers. It is ironic to associate with those whose speech destroys community (18:8).

20:20. The honoring of parents is a fundamental obligation in ancient cultures (see Commentary on 19:26; Exod 21:17; Lev 20:9). The opposite of honoring parents (כבד *kābēd*) is cursing them (קלל *qālal*; see Commentary on 26:2), a term that also connotes treating them with contempt (see Sir 3:1-16). The punishment of having one's lamp snuffed out befits the wicked (13:9). But there may be a wordplay here, since "lamp" is used as a stereotyped metaphor for the continuance of a family (1 Kgs 11:36; 15:4; 2 Kgs 8:19). If this reading is correct, then the punishment fits the crime. Those who dishonor the parents who gave them the light of life may have their own line extinguished (see 2 Sam 18:14-18). When Eli "honors" his sons rather than God, this inversion of honor receives a similar judgment (1 Sam 2:29-31, 34).

20:21. Ordinarily an inheritance is not gained through activity but as a parental legacy (19:14). This verse may refer to anyone who wrongfully acquires (*Ketib*) the familial land of another. Ahab's acquisition of Naboth's vineyard is the classic case (see Leviticus 25; 1 Kings 21; Isa 5:8-9). Alternatively, the saying refers to sons who hasten the demise of their parents to get the inheritance. If so, vv. 20-21 form an editorial proverb pair that mutually reinforce each other. The manner in which the inheritance is "quickly gained" (*Qere*) is not spelled out (see 13:11; 28:22).

20:22. This admonition to wait patiently for Yahweh provides the theological foundation for vv. 20-21, because God is the ultimate source of justice (see Commentary on 24:29; see also Deut 32:35-36; Psalms 27; 37). The intent of this verse is not pacifist or anti-judicial, since divine authority for international and domestic justice devolves on human officials appointed to those tasks (Psalm 72; Rom 13:1-7). Rather, it warns victims against arbitrarily taking justice into their own hands (see Lev 19:17-18). David is a model of this principle when he refuses to kill Saul, though he narrowly escapes violating it in the case of Nabal (1 Samuel 24–26). This verse also encourages victims of crime, when human justice fails them (see 29:26; for NT allusions, see Matt 5:38-39; Rom 12:17; 1 Thess 5:15).

20:23-24. These verses are variants of other sayings within Proverbs. The present location of v. 23, a variant of v. 10, reinforces the theme of Yahweh's justice in vv. 20-22. Verse 24 is a variation on themes from 16:1-9 (see also Ps 37:23*a*, a duplicate of v. 24*a*). There are limits to human understanding, even of one's own life journey (see Commentary on 27:1; cf. 14:8). Proverbs presents a paradox by insisting on the importance of human wisdom and responsibility (see Commentary on 21:29) even as it insists that God's guidance of life is beyond human understanding or control. This paradox is essential to the book of Proverbs and to biblical faith. Jeremiah bitterly alludes to a form of this proverb (Jer 10:23; see also Jer 9:12, 23; 17:9-10).

20:25. Here the writer portrays the evil of inattention to God and the created world. To declare something holy is to dedicate it voluntarily, on oath, as a gift to God (the verb is rare, but its general sense seems clear).

Such gifts could be animals, money, land, or other property (Lev 27:9-25). Oaths were often made in thanks to God for rescue from trouble (Gen 28:20-22; Jonah 1:16; 2:9). But to do so casually or hastily is a form of taking the Lord's name in vain, of not taking God seriously enough, as if God would not call one to account (Exod 20:7; Lev 19:12; Num 30:2; Deut 23:21-23; Eccl 5:1-6). Such vows are also a form of inattention to (or of self-deception about) the created world, for the use of whose goods we are responsible. To offer God what we cannot pay thus dishonors God and devalues the world entrusted to our care. In the Gospels, Jesus repeatedly discusses the games that people play with vows and other obligations to God (Matt 5:33-37; 15:3-9; 23:16-24). Money talks, also, in its religious deposition.

20:26. This verse is tied to v. 8 and the judicial image of winnowing (lit., "scattering"), by which the righteous and the wicked, like wheat and chaff, are separated (see 25:4-5 for a different image). The image of v. 26*b,* however, is disputed. The NIV supplies "threshing" (not in Hebrew) to explain the metaphor of the wheel. This is probably correct. Various mechanical means were used to separate the husk from the kernel, depending on the nature of the grain (Isa 28:27-28). Verse 26*a* is a summary statement of the process, focused on its conclusion. Verse 26*b* sharpens the severity of judgment with the image of the threshing wheel, though temporally that action precedes winnowing.

20:27. Literally, the Hebrew reads, "The breath of man is Yahweh's lamp,/ searching all the rooms of the belly." Verse 27*a* is a nominal sentence (without a verb), so that either phrase could be subject or predicate. The NIV understands the verb from v. 27*b* to govern v. 27*a* (a double-duty construction). This reading is possible but improbable, and it obscures the suggestive richness of the proverb's imagery. The NIV reflects the common thought that God searches and knows the inmost being of persons (see 15:11; 16:2; 17:3; 18:8 for this phrase). Human breath is given by God at creation and taken away at death (Gen 2:7; 1 Kgs 17:17; Isa 42:5). "Breath" (נשמה *nĕšāmâ*), however, "is not only the principle of life . . . but also the principle of wisdom" (Job 26:4; 32:8, 18; see

20:3).[251] In this regard, "breath" is similar to "spirit" (רוח *rûaḥ*; see 1:23). Breath typically goes in and comes out of a person, giving life; but it also comes out as wisdom and words. Lamps give light for seeing and searching. But light is also a symbol of life (6:23; 13:9; 16:15; 20:20; 29:13). The imagery of lamp and breath thus communicates a person's possession of and responsibility for the life and self-reflective insight that God gives. As often in the second Solomonic sub-collection, God is present in the inmost being and actions of persons (see Commentary on 16:1, 9; 21:1). The proverb thus suggests both God's knowledge of humans and human self-knowledge as a gift of God, not either one or the other.

20:28. Verse 28*a* parallels the prayer in Ps 61:8. Love and faithfulness are gifts from God to the king (see Ps 89:33), which the king displays in his own rule (see Commentary on

3:3). Verse 28*b* is a variant of 16:12*b*, with "kindness" in place of "righteousness" (the NRSV translates the LXX).

20:29. This text presents a profound contrast between the characteristic virtues of youth and age. Gray hair is a symbol of wisdom, since only the old have experienced enough reality to be wise (see Commentary on 16:31; Sir 25:3-6). Rehoboam sins against this wisdom principle when he listens to the advice of the young men and ignores the wise old advisers associated with his father, Solomon. This folly costs him the ten northern tribes (1 Kgs 12:6-20).

20:30. Details of this verse are uncertain, but the NIV and the NRSV seem to capture its general sense. Corporal discipline was seen as a means to correct wrongdoers and errant youths. "Evil" in v. 30*a* may be a word for (inner) "thoughts" (see 17:10; 23:13; Ps 139:2, 17). The external discipline of the body affects the inmost being (see Commentary on 20:27).

251. E. Dhorme, *A Commentary on the Book of Job* (Nashville: Thomas Nelson, 1984) 378.

REFLECTIONS

1. Israelite society was often sinfully violent and brutal, as the inter-tribal wars, the conflict between David and Saul, and the separation of northern and southern kingdoms demonstrate. And yet it promoted an ethos of civility, community harmony, cordiality in personal relations, and the avoidance of conflict. These qualities are related to Israel's deep sense of honor and shame (see Commentary on 20:3). Perhaps ancient Israel is closer to Japanese culture and history in these matters than it is to that of the United States. Americans seem to tolerate an ethos of violence fed by the mass media, and too often lack healthy restraint in personal relations. Lack of shame and proper personal boundaries in our society is regularly exposed on television talk shows.

In this context, one of the tasks of the church is to become a counterculture that fosters a biblical sense of the nobility and dignity of persons—without being naive about sin (see Reflections on 15:25). The issue is that we are called to be in the world but not *of* it (John 15:19; 17:6-19), and that we are not to be conformed to this world but renewed by the Word and Spirit of God (Rom 12:1-2).

This task requires that ordinary Christians commit themselves to being shaped by Scripture and Christian wisdom in their daily life (see Phil 4:8-9). Conversely, it requires that Christians be willing to discipline their use of entertainment media. It especially requires that children be provided healthy (not boring!) alternatives to the spiritual trash that panders to them in some television programs (see Commentary on 22:6). It requires that the "body of Christ" be an extended family that helps overstressed parents to rear their children (see Reflections on 15:22).

2. Proverbs 20:9 is a corrective to those who believe that they can maintain their own purity in evil times (see Commentary on 16:2; 26:5-6), while implicitly relegating others to the ranks of the impure and sinful.[252] We are morally ambiguous creatures,

252. See Bonhoeffer, *Ethics*, 67.

and inevitably we are implicated in society's immorality. None of us will be whole until Christ makes humanity whole. Nor can we be pure or fully redeemed until the creation itself is pure and redeemed (Rom 8:18-25). In the meantime, righteous and wicked, pure and impure are standards of judgment to which people more or less conform. A person is only relatively one or relatively the other. The line between wisdom and folly, good and bad, cuts through the heart of us all. What matters is that one is on the road of progressive righteousness and wisdom (see chaps. 1–9). In addition, terms such as "righteous" and "wicked" (see Commentary on 17:15) are often applied to very limited matters.[253] In a criminal case, for example, the thief is called "wicked" or "guilty," and the falsely accused is called "righteous" or "innocent," only with regard to the particular matter at hand. Unfortunately, a person who is righteous or pure in one area may be wicked in another (see Jas 2:8-13).

3. Parents sometimes note that a child's character is present at a very early age (20:11). Ancient Greece and Rome sometimes saw character (and class) as a lifelong, immutable given. Ancient Israel had a more complex view. The Israelites recognized that character in many respects was something given. Yet they also recognized that persons can change morally and spiritually, either for better or for worse.[254] Many of the biblical stories recount the growth, or decline, of such people as Abraham, Saul, David, and Esther. One of the factors in character development is early training (22:6). Another is collective and personal discipline (13:24). But undergirding all our attempts to improve ourselves and our world is the power of divine grace (Gen 39:2-3, 5, 21, 23; 1 Cor 1:26-31; Phil 2:12-13), which can mold ordinary people and families into great ones.

In this fact lies the immediate hope and joy of biblical salvation for all who struggle with woundedness and imperfection. We are all the victims of others, and we are all victims of our own sin. At a certain point the allocation of guilt and blame becomes a futile exercise. The gospel—in both the Old and the New Testaments—urges us to become responsible for our own life journey (1:10-19; see also Reflections on Proverbs 9), to lay hold of divine grace and forgiveness (28:13-14), to join with like-minded Christians, and to press forward knowing that we do not have to remain helplessly stuck in our misery (Phil 3:10-17, 20-21).

4. Kings and rulers need wise counsel in the event of war (20:18). But this admonition applies to any struggle or conflict in human life. Humans need counsel especially when things are difficult. Those affected by a situation may be least able to see the whole picture or to think clearly about it. Jesus applies the metaphor of Prov 20:18 to counting the cost of discipleship (Luke 14:31-33; for the limits of this saying, see Commentary on 21:30-31).

---

253. See Lyons, *Introduction to Theoretical Linguistics*, 465-66.
254. See Erich Auerbach, *Mimesis: The Representation of Reality in Western Literature* (Garden City, N.Y.: Doubleday, 1957).

Proverbs 21:1-31, All Deeds Are Right in the Sight of the Doer, but the Lord Weighs the Heart

COMMENTARY

21:1. In arid Palestine, irrigation channels can make the desert bloom (see Isa 32:2, of righteous rulers). Here the image portrays God's inscrutable mastery of the king, who otherwise appears uniquely superior to other people. This saying asserts God's mysterious sovereignty precisely where humans are most free and potent, in the thoughts of their "heart" (see Excursus, "The 'Heart' in the Old Testament"). The king is cited as that person who is most able to claim such power and freedom (see Commentary on 20:5; 25:2-3).

21:2. This verse is a variant of 16:2, and its repetition suggests—as does the dialectic of Yahweh and royal sayings throughout 20:22–21:4—a close affinity between 16:1-15 (on Yahweh and the king) and this verse. It links with the "heart" of the preceding verse.

21:3. Although it does not mention the king, the similarity of v. 3*a* and 16:12*a* (as opposites) also reinforces the connection of this passage and 16:1-15. This saying does not reject sacrifice as such, but worship by the wicked (15:8-9).

21:4. "Haughty eyes" (see Commentary on 6:17; 30:13) go naturally with a "proud heart" (lit., "broad heart"; see 28:25*a*; Ps 101:5) as "the lamp of the wicked" (see Commentary on 15:30; cf. Matt 6:22-23). These stand in implicit contrast to "the lamp of the Lord," which searches humans (see Commentary on 20:27 for the double sense of "lamp" as "life" and "wisdom"). In the case of the wicked, their "lamp"—including their "wisdom"—is sin (see 26:12; Isa 5:20-23). Such lamps are doomed to being extinguished (13:9; 20:20). The above understanding may resolve the disputed question as to the relation of the two verse halves.

21:5-6. Together these verses consider opposite ways of getting—or losing—material goods. Verse 5 contrasts the diligent (see Commentary on 10:4-5; 12:24), who make plans, with the hasty, who presumably do not. The former get gain ("profit" should be taken in a broad sense, for agrarian Israel was not a society with capital investments in the modern sense), while haste leads to want or lack (cf. 13:11; 14:23). A farmer's success does not come quickly. The verb for "haste" (אץ *'āṣ*) does not have moral connotations per se (see Josh 10:13), but haste in human affairs generally is negative. In monetary matters, haste connotes greed (28:20; cf. 11:24), and haste in speech connotes a lack of reflection (29:20; see Commentary on 15:28; 19:2). One might say that "haste makes waste," or

"Make haste slowly," or "Look before you leap."

Verse 6 describes an evil means of getting rich, "a lying tongue." Treasures gained through deception stand under God's judgment (10:2). Verse 6*b* is textually problematic, as reflected in the NIV and NRSV notes. The solutions suggested rest on emendation and the ancient versions, but remain uncertain.

21:7. The wicked do the opposite of the righteous (see vv. 3, 15) as a matter of deliberate choice ("because they refuse" is an explanatory clause, as in v. 25; see also 2:14). Violence (24:2) begets violence, and the wicked are carried away by it, like fish in a net (see Hab 1:15). As we do to others, so it will happen to us (1:17-19; 11:6*b*). Similar is the saying that those who "take the sword will perish by the sword" (Matt 26:52 NRSV).

21:8. The NRSV and the NIV take the uncertain and unique word וזר (*wāzār*) to be cognate with an Arabic word meaning "to be laden with guilt." But this is uncertain. Two ancient versions (Syriac and Vulgate; see also Targum) take the word as the copula *w* ("and") plus *zār,* "strange." Then the saying may be rendered, "Confused is the way of a man and strange,/ but the pure—his work is right." Somewhat along these lines, the TNK translates, "The way of a man may be tortuous and strange,/ Though his actions are blameless and proper." But rendering "blameless and proper" as a coordinate predicate requires the insertion of the copula. There is no wholly satisfactory solution here.

21:9. A duplicate of 25:24 and one of several on the "quarrelsome wife" (v. 19; 27:15; cf. 19:13), this saying has a humorous edge and assumes that relations with a spouse profoundly affect one for good or for ill (see Commentary on 11:17; 12:4). The image is of a hut on a flat roof where one is exposed to the elements—whether rain or withering sirocco winds. A house "shared" may be correct (so LXX and Vg). Or the word may mean a "noisy house."[255] The point is that one is better exposed to nature than to a wife's "storms" (see 27:15). These sayings provide exceptions to the basic perspective in this male-oriented book that a wife is a divine gift to a man (5:15-20; 12:4; 18:22; 31:10-31; see Gen 2:18).

---

255. Taking חבר (*ḥbr*) as cognate with Akkadian *habrum,* "noisy."

21:10. People may be known by their appetites and desires, by their choices and ultimate loves (see 1:16, 28-29; 4:16-17; 8:17, 35). The soul, an organ of appetite (16:24, 26), wants what it wants, even if other people are injured, because addictive desire tolerates no obstacles to its gratification (for the opposite virtue—kindness or mercy, see 14:21, 31; 19:17; 28:8). The story of Amnon's rape of Tamar illustrates the proverb in the sexual arena (2 Samuel 13). The Hebrew of this verse makes a sad wordplay; orthographically both "evil" (רע *rāʿ*) and "neighbor" (רע *rēaʿ*) are רע (*rʿ*). Verses 12-13 provide theological perspective on this verse (see Commentary on 12:10).

21:11-12. Either the "simple" and the "wise" are contrasted in their mode of learning (v. 11), or the simple learn both by observing the fate of mockers and by heeding the instruction of the wise (see 1:4-5; 19:25). In Hebrew, "observes" (משכיל *maśkîl*, v. 12) picks up the word for "instructs" in v. 11. The words *wicked* and *evil* (רשע *rāšāʿ* and רע *raʿ*) also link v. 12 to v. 10, on which it offers theological comment. Both the NIV and the NRSV take "righteous" as referring to Yahweh, on the ground that God is the judge of the wicked (see 22:12, where "overthrow" and "cast down" translate the same verb). While God is often described as righteous, the use of the term as a title is disputed.

21:13. This saying is a sharp warning against active indifference toward the unfortunate (see v. 10; 3:27-28; 18:23; 24:11-12). The not-hearing is willful, since the culprit shuts his ears (see 28:27). The not-being-heard is a classic example of the *lex talionis*: as people do, so it happens to them (see Commentary on 21:7; see also Jas 2:13). The hidden agent of justice is God (see 1:28; Isa 58:9; 65:12, 24; Mic 3:4; and Job's complaint in Job 19:7). When humans ignore the cry of the desperate, God hears them (Exod 22:22-24). People who are not gracious to the needy have no part in God's love (see Commentary on 19:17; 1 John 3:17).

21:14. The practice of making a concealed bribe is somewhat like a modern out-of-court settlement. The gift takes care of a problem without public exposure and embarrassment (see 6:35, where the practice fails; cf. 15:27; 17:8, 23; 18:16; 19:6).

21:15. The NIV and the the NRSV take the doing of justice passively ("When justice is done"), so that the righteous have joy as mere observers. But a better reading is that they take pleasure in doing justice themselves (see Commentary on 20:23; cf., negatively, 2:14). With respect to justice, people do what corresponds to their character (see vv. 3, 7, 10).

21:16. This verse says in few words what is developed at length in chaps. 1–9 (see Commentary on 2:18; 7:25-27; 9:18; see also 4:14-19, where the way of righteousness leads to life).

21:17. This saying is an ancient parallel to "You can't have your cake and eat it too." Wine and oil go with festivity and joy (Judg 9:9, 13; Ps 104:15; Eccl 9:7-8). Oil is used cosmetically for adornment and to soothe dry skin. Later, vv. 20-21 will assert that wisdom and righteousness, which include hard work, are the way to abundance (see 10:4-5).

21:18. Isaiah 43:3 affords a parallel to this puzzling verse. The sense seems to be that justice is achieved by a reversal of positions (see Commentary on 11:8; cf. 1 Sam 2:2-10; Luke 1:51-53), but the meaning of "ransom" (כפר *kōper*) remains puzzling. Its usual sense is a substitute payment for punishment when one is guilty (see 6:35; 13:8; Exod 21:30; in 1 Sam 12:3, it refers to a judicial bribe). Scholars question why the righteous should need a ransom. On the other hand, Psalm 49 states both that no person can by a ransom evade death and that "God will redeem my life from the power of Sheol" (Ps 49:7-9, 15, paraphrase of NIV and NRSV).

21:19. Verse 9 is a variant of this verse. Here the desert is the place of disorder and drought where life is not possible (Deut 32:10). The contrast of the dry desert and the promised cultivated land, with its life and water, is fundamental to Israelite thought and experience (Deut 8:2, 7-10, 15-16).

21:20-21. Oil is a symbol of wealth and luxury, and the link with v. 17 creates an evident contrast of life-styles. The message of these verses is similar to "seek first [God's] kingdom and his righteousness, and all these things will be given to you as well" (Matt 6:33 NIV). Because the world is ordered according to wisdom and righteousness, to pursue them sets one in a right relation with material things (see 8:18; 11:19). The wise and the fool differ in their disposal of goods; one gathers, and the other squanders (cf. 14:1). The NRSV's "remains" only partly follows the Greek (it omits "mouth"). The NIV supplies "food," which is lacking in Hebrew (see 8:21; 10:2; 21:6).

21:22. Unlike most proverbs, which generalize, this saying is a miniature narrative in the past tense (so NRSV; cf. NIV). Ecclesiastes 9:13-16 provides a similar narrative. Wisdom is more powerful than strength of arms (8:14; 16:32; 20:18; 24:5) and than fortified walls in which people trust (18:10-11). Perhaps David's conquest of the well-defended city of Jerusalem by the stratagem of climbing up the water shaft reflects such wisdom (2 Sam 5:8). A modern equivalent of this verse may be "The pen is mightier than the sword." "Warriors" better reflects the Hebrew (גברים gibbōrîm) than does "the mighty," however.

21:23-24. Verse 23 is an expansion of 13:3a and 18:21. Although the syntax of v. 24 is difficult to determine, its general sense is clear. The Hebrew heaps up expressions for pride and arrogance to define the essential character or name of the mocker (see 9:7-12). Such heaping up of terms is not tautology (a logical problem), but a rhetorical means of intensification, as in "boys will be boys." See Sir 10:6-18 for an expansion of the theme of this verse.

21:25-26. Since v. 26a lacks a subject of its own, it seems best to take it as continuation of v. 25 (NIV). The NRSV partially follows the expansive LXX text of v. 26: "An impious person craves bad cravings all the day." The sluggard desires but does not work (v. 17; see also 6:6-11). The contrast with the righteous person is indirect. While the sluggard is consumed with unfulfilled desire, the righteous person (who is implicitly wise and diligent) has enough to share generously (see Commentary on 11:24 within the cluster 11:23-25; 28:27).

21:27. Verse 27a is a near duplicate of 15:8a (Yahweh is implicit, not explicit). Worship without a corresponding righteous life is execrable to God (see Commentary on 21:3). But v. 27b takes the saying in a different direction. With an obvious how-much-more logic, it exposes the internal mental hypocrisy of such sacrifice, which thinks it can buy

God off. "Evil intent" is here the internal scheming (see 24:9a) of those whose secret thoughts belie the apparent meaning of their deeds. The same word for that expression (זמה zimmâ) is misleadingly translated "evil conduct" and "wrong" in 10:23.

21:28. Verse 28a expresses a common thought (19:5, 9). Some argue a double sense for "perish"—that the testimony of a liar will not succeed, while honest testimony will endure. Verse 28b may refer to the judge (lit., "the man who hears") in a judicial hearing, rather than to someone who listens well (see Commentary on 25:10). Several suggestions for an alternative translation of the predicate in v. 28b have been made (e.g., "will have descendants," and the NIV's "will be destroyed") to provide a contrast with "perish," but this appears unnecessary. The sense may be that the "one who listens" will speak (as witness or judge) with enduring consequences and will thus "have the last word." The NIV margin takes "listen" in the sense of "obey," thus following the Vg. Verse 28b is not certain.

21:29. Like the seductress of 7:13, "a wicked man [masc. sing.] puts on a bold face." In v. 29b, both translations follow the Qere (MT) correction of the traditional verb, "gives thought to [or understands] his way(s)" (see Commentary on 14:8). This same verb (בין bîn) also occurs in 20:24, which asks, "How can anyone understand his way?" The Ketib (or received) text has "establishes his ways," which creates a link with the important verse 16:9 (see 4:25-27). "Way(s)" is another Qere/Ketib variation, of which the singular seems preferable. If the Qere reading is followed, then vv. 30-31 appear to set limits on even the planning of the upright (v. 29b), much in line with 16:1-9. The relationship and contrast between vv. 29a and 29b are not certain. They may refer to "putting on a mask" of duplicity in contrast to having a straightforward life plan.

21:30-31. This profound couplet insists that ultimately only God's wisdom and purposes prevail, even though the book of Proverbs seeks to train young and old to get wisdom and live by it (see Commentary on 19:21; 20:18; 24:6). Yet there is no contradiction, for an essential part of wisdom is knowing one's limits and facing up to reality.

Because people are limited in wisdom and power, the beginning of human wisdom is necessarily the fear of the Lord, who alone has ultimate wisdom (see 1:7; 3:5-8, 19-20; 8). Verse 30 does not merely have in view wisdom that opposes God, as suggested by the translation "against the Lord." Rather, the Hebrew expression is more general, meaning "before" or "over against." Its purpose is simply to contrast human wisdom, whether good or bad, with God's. Verse 31 uses the proud imagery of war horses, a technological innovation that gave surpassing advantage to those armies that had cavalry units.

REFLECTIONS

1. Proverbs makes no attempt to explain the paradox of divine mastery and responsible human freedom (see 21:1; Phil 2:12-13). Several stories illustrate the issues of this saying. In Genesis, Joseph's brothers plan and execute evil against Joseph for their own purposes, but their actions ultimately serve God's good purposes of salvation (see the paradoxical formulations concerning "who did it" in Gen 45:5-8; 50:19-21). In other cases, Yahweh "hardens" Pharaoh's self-hardened heart (Exodus 5–11) and ordains that Absalom choose the wrong counsel against David (2 Sam 15:31; 16:23; 17:14). Proverbs 21:1 again raises the issues of 16:1, 9 and 20:27. Its main thrust, however, is positive, because irrigation waters, like royal wisdom, cause the land and the people to flourish (see 18:4).

Practically, 21:1 gives hope to those who pray for rulers and all in positions of authority (1 Tim 2:1-8)—hope that God will guide and move them to act in wisdom for the common good. In evil times, this proverb may comfort those whose lives are afflicted by capricious tyrants or cruel magistrates. The Lord can indeed turn the hearts of the wicked to do what is right, thereby working God's own good purposes even when human beings intend evil.

Yet in our reflection on the genocidal "ethnic cleansing" perpetrated by the Nazis, by the warring factions in Bosnia, by the Khmer Rouge in Cambodia, by Amin in Uganda, and by opposing sides in Rwanda and Zaire, we ask the anguished question, Why has God not made good the hearts of the mighty and the common folk alike? "Why, O Lord, do you make us / stray from your ways / and harden our heart, so that / we do not fear you?" (Isa 63:17 NRSV). Perhaps the most terrible judgments of God are those in which God confirms the hardness of human hearts and leaves us to our own devices:

> Surely the arm of the Lord is not too short to save,
>   nor his ear too dull to hear.
> But your iniquities have separated
>   you from your God;
> your sins have hidden his face from you,
>   so that he will not hear. (Isa 59:1-2 NIV)

2. "To do righteousness and justice" (21:3) is God's basic requirement for Israel and its king and for humans in general (see 15:9; Gen 18:19; Ps 119:121; Amos 5:24; Matt 5:6, 10; 6:33; 1 Pet 3:13).[256] This the wicked refuse to do (21:7, 15). The prophets also insist that worship or sacrifice without justice is not pleasing to God (1 Sam 15:22-23; Isa 1:11-17; Hos 6:6; Mic 6:6-8). The basis for this is that Yahweh is Creator and Lord of every inch of reality, which God made in wisdom and righteousness.

---

256. See Moshe Weinfeld, *Social Justice in Ancient Israel and in the Ancient Near East* (Minneapolis: Fortress, 1995).

3. Not only does Proverbs warn Israel of the limits to human wisdom, but it also warns against overconfidence in power and technology (21:30-31). Israel was repeatedly warned not to rely on horses, just as modern nations might be warned not to trust in military technology (see Pss 20:6-9; 33:16-17; Isa 30:15-16; 31:1-3). Deuteronomy forbade the king to acquire horses (17:16). The theological basis for these warnings about human limits and against arrogance is that the outcome of events, sometimes counter to the odds, rests with Yahweh (see 16:33; 29:26). This is also the theological point of the narrative of David and Goliath (1 Sam 17:37, 45-47), of Deut 20:14, of Gideon's radically reduced band of warriors (Judg 7:1-23), and of the fall of Jericho without human military action (Joshua 6). This proverb couplet and such stories can encourage God's people in adverse circumstances of any kind, even as they humble arrogant self-confidence.

Proverbs 22:1-16, The Royal Collection Concluded

COMMENTARY

22:1. The NIV and the NRSV follow most ancient versions in adding "good" to "name." But "name" includes reputation, as in "let us make a name for ourselves" (Gen 11:4; see also Gen 6:4, lit., "men of name"; 2 Sam 23:22). Israel was an honor-and-shame culture, and one's name meant personal identity as it was recognized and respected (or not) in the community (see Commentary on 12:8; 13:18; 26:1). Usually—but not always—wealth is linked with wisdom, goodness, and honor (see 8:16; 22:4; see Commentary on 11:16 for a contrary case). This better-than saying (see Commentary on 15:16; 16:8) limits the status of wealth by placing wisdom and righteousness above it. To find favor or grace with someone is to be a *persona grata,* accepted and esteemed (3:4; 28:23; cf. 13:15; 1 Sam 2:26; Luke 2:52). Ecclesiastes puts the worth of a name in the context of death, believing—in contrast to others—that even one's name does not remain (Eccl 2:16; 7:1, "good" is again added to the text; 9:5; Sir 41:11-13).

22:2. Several sayings focus on Yahweh as Creator of persons, not at the beginning of time, but in their present concreteness, especially as "rich" or "poor" (see Commentary on 14:31; 17:5; 29:13; see also Job 34:19; Sir 11:14). The intent is to qualify and mitigate the social and economic divisions that humans are prone to make so much of, thereby denying the humanity that binds them to one another and to their Maker. The

saying has a prophetic edge to it, implicitly calling for socioeconomic justice.

22:3. Proverbs 27:12 is a variant of this verse. A crucial part of wisdom is the ability to see what is coming before it arrives. Like 14:15, 18, this saying contrasts the naive or simple, who have little life experience, with the clever, who do (see Commentary on 14:8). It takes the form of a past tense narrative, which is obscured by the English translations (see Commentary on 21:22). Literally, the Hebrew reads, "A clever man [masc. sing.] saw trouble and hid, but the simple [pl.] continued on and suffered."

22:4. The Hebrew word underlying "reward" (עקב *ʿēqeb*) has the sense of "consequence" (cf. the paraphrase in NIV). Verse 4*a* lacks the word for "and," which the translations add. Thus several ancient versions include "the fear of the LORD" among the consequences of humility. But humility and reverence for Yahweh naturally go together in the realism that is essential for true wisdom (see Commentary on 11:2; 15:33; 18:12). Contrary to views that expect godliness to produce only suffering, this saying asserts that godly humility leads to well-being (see 3:13-20; 8:18). The underlying logic is that wisdom puts one in harmony with reality. This proverb should neither be absolutized (as in a prosperity gospel, which says, "God wants you to be rich"), nor should the creational benefits of a realistic godliness be minimized (see Commentary on 10:3; 16:8).

22:5. The Hebrew word translated "thorns" (צנים *ṣinnîm*) is obscure and odd in combination with "snares." The Syriac version and the Targum take the Hebrew term to mean "net" or "trap," which forms a better parallel to "snares." The general sense is clear, however, with a return to the common image of life as a positive or negative journey. For "perverse" as "twisted," see Commentary on 10:9. "Cautious" (שומר נפשו *šômēr napšô*) is literally, "one who guards his life" (see Commentary on 16:17, 24; 19:16).

22:6. This verse is linked to v. 5 by the key word *way* (דרך *derek*). As translated, this admonition's concern for training the young is like that in 19:18; 29:17; and throughout the book. The verse may have a slightly different focus, however. The root for "train up" (חנך *ḥnk*) is always used in biblical Hebrew and Aramaic for the dedication or initial use of a house or temple (Deut 20:5; 1 Kgs 8:63 = 2 Chr 7:5; see also the related nouns). This suggests that the verb in v. 6*a* refers to a rite of passage (such as the later Bar-Mitzvah celebration) through which an adolescent gains adult status. Hildebrand argues that the child (נער *na'ar*) is primarily a social classification ("a squire"), designating a person attendant on someone of high social status. This is less certain, for the term can connote both "servant" and "youth." "The way he should go" is literally "according to his way"—a phrase that may mean "in the way that is appropriate to his status." In any case, this proverb should not be used to induce guilt in good parents who have errant children. Proverbs are not absolute promises (see Commentary on 10:3).

22:7. This verse is a straightforward observation on the fundamental effect that credit and debt have on relationships, using the metaphors of political rule and servitude (see Commentary on 14:20; 12:24; 17:2; 18:23; but see the reversal in 28:11). The saying may be used to warn against going into debt (see Commentary on 6:1-5). The poor could sell themselves into servitude in order to provide for themselves and their families (Exod 21:2-7; Neh 5:5).

22:8. This proverb applies the rule of sowing and reaping to the moral and spiritual realms (see Job 4:8; Hos 8:7; 10:13; Gal 6:7-10; see also Commentary on 22:9). Its present placement creates a warning against the potential for abusive rulership inherent in the power of wealth, as described in v. 7. Verse 8*b* is much like Isa 14:5-6, where Yahweh puts an end to the tyrannical "rod" of the king of Babylon (see Habakkuk 2). The saying also offers comfort to the oppressed, assuring them of God's justice. "Rod" (שבט *šēbeṭ*) is a metaphor for rulership (see v. 7), not of punishment, as it is usually used in Proverbs (see 10:13; 26:3). "Fury" (עברה *'ebrâ*) may also connote "excess." The NRSV omits the pronoun "his," thus obscuring the connection between the two lines (see NIV).

22:9. This verse forms a clear contrast to the two previous verses. "Generous" (טוב-עין *ṭôb-'ayin*) is literally "good of eye," an idiom whose opposite, "stingy," is "bad of eye" (23:6; 28:22; Deut 15:9; Matt 20:15 margin). The saying appears related to Deut 15:9-11, which forbids stinginess and commands generosity, promising the latter will be blessed by God (see 11:26; 14:21; 19:17; Sir 7:32). The NT (2 Cor 9:6-10) combines the teaching of this verse with the imagery of sowing and reaping, found in v. 8.

22:10. The mocker is arrogant, cynical, and "knows it all" (see 9:7-12; 21:24). Similar to this admonition is the idea that without kindling a fire goes out (see 26:20-21). "Quarrel" refers to litigation, but is not restricted to it. At times the Israelite community, including small local groups such as villages, excluded wrongdoers (see Commentary on 25:4-5) in order to preserve the well-being and integrity of the sociospiritual group—as did the early church (1 Cor 5:1-13; see Deut 7:17). In a morally clouded situation, Sarah uses the same imperative, "drive out," when she tells Abraham to send Hagar and Ishmael away (Gen 21:10). The matter of boundary definition, of inclusion and exclusion, is always difficult. Yet it is crucial, for without it no group, even the family of God, can have identity with integrity.

22:11. The Hebrew grammar of this verse is difficult. Underlying the NIV and NRSV translations is a literal understanding: "He who loves purity of heart [or "one pure of heart"]/ whose lips are grace, his friend is the king." A parallel thought can be found in 16:13. Psalm 101 documents the sort of persons who are and who are not acceptable in the court of a righteous king. Some translators (following the LXX and the Syriac) supply "God" as the subject of "loves," but this makes the difficulties even greater. Others follow Rashi and make "king" from v. 11*b* the subject of v. 11*a*.

22:12. The "knowledge" in question is that which a judge needs in order to effect justice in the land (see 1 Sam 2:3; see also Commentary on 15:3; 21:12).

22:13. This verse has a near duplicate in 26:13, but unlike that version of the saying, the present verse possesses a wonderful word music that imitates the sound of tearing, as the sluggard imagines being torn limb from limb. Note especially the *r, ḥ,* and *ṣ* sounds in the words for "lion," "outside," and "murdered!" For the "sluggard," see Commentary on 6:6-11.

22:14. This verse brings the reader back to the world of the strange woman of chaps. 1–9 (see Commentary on 2:16-19). The image of woman as a well of water is positive in 5:15-20. Here it is used negatively, as a hole one may fall into. The same idea appears in the Babylonian *Dialogue*

of Pessimism.[257] New in this saying is the thought that such a woman might be an instrument of God's wrath.

22:15. The word *boy* is the same as in v. 6*a* and 23:13 ("child"); the reference is probably to an adolescent or servant. The saying is not a statement of universal youthful depravity, with beating as the remedy of choice for adolescents. The proverb is probably best taken as a conditional sentence: "If folly is bound up in the heart of a boy, then the rod of discipline will drive it far from him." (Cf. 23:13-14 and see Reflections on 13:24 concerning corporal punishment.)

22:16. The end of the first Solomonic sub-collection attacks that evil wherein "the rich get richer and the poor get poorer." The needy are made by God and receive God's jealous care and protection (see Commentary on 14:31; 17:5; 22:2). Verse 16*b* attacks the giving of wealth to those who already have it. This act is not fitting, like "carrying coals to Newcastle" (see 26:1-3).

257. W. Lambert, *Babylonian Wisdom Literature* (Oxford: Clarendon, 1960) 147.

REFLECTIONS

1. Proverbs 22:7 speaks of the profound effect debtor and creditor status has on personal relations. Even in the United States—which is deeply committed to the myth of individual freedom and equality—economic status greatly determines one's freedom and class and the degree to which equality under law is actually available. The proverb makes no moral pronouncements; it simply observes a fact of life. Yet, Israel's law consistently forbade lenders from taking interest from the poor (see Commentary on 28:8). By implication, 22:7 in its biblical context sharply condemns one of today's common banking practices. When banks charge usurious interest rates on their freely offered credit cards—while knowing that generally the financially vulnerable are driven to amass credit-card debt—they offend the God who cares for the poor (14:31; 22:9, 16).

Perhaps this proverb applies also to international relations, a possibility that time will answer for America. In the 1980s, the United States went from being the world's largest creditor nation to being the largest debtor nation. Wealthy America may become a "servant" to its international creditors, its freedom to act in international affairs compromised by its financial obligations (see Commentary on 6:1-5). This issue is of even greater moment for poor, developing nations with large foreign debts. Often cash crops for export (coffee, cocoa, opium poppies, and the coca leaf used to make cocaine) are grown instead of foodstuffs desperately needed by the native population. The Lord of the nations also judges nations that exploit those weaker than themselves.

2. Wealth gained by wronging, oppressing, or taking advantage of the poor stands under God's condemnation. In ancient Israel, this happened when the wealthy bought up—and kept—the land of the destitute, so depriving them of their heritage in the land of promise (Leviticus 25; Isa 5:8-10; see Reflections on 15:25). But Proverbs also condemns giving to the rich (22:16). On planet Earth, where resources are limited, the excessive increase of goods for some means loss for many others, both domestically and internationally. This happens when damage to human beings and to the environment results from the manufacture and use of earth-destructive technological products.[258] It happens when executives are paid exorbitant sums as their companies downsize, merge through debt-increasing buyouts, and overwork their remaining employees. It happens when jobs are shipped to sweatshops hidden in inner cities or overseas. It happens when a country's tax code and other laws promote a massive shift of wealth from ordinary people to the nation's richest inhabitants. We expand our little kingdoms at the expense of our neighbors and at the expense of the natural kingdoms—plant, animal, and mineral. Thus we disrupt the righteous order of God's kingdom's coming on earth (Matt 6:10). This we do to our own peril. In the long run, such activities lead to the opposite of what they are intended to do, to loss instead of to gain.

258. See Lester Brown et al., *The State of the World* (Washington: The Worldwatch Institute, published annually); Loren Wilkinson et al., *Earthkeeping in the 90's* (Grand Rapids: Eerdmans, 1991); H. Paul Santmire, *The Travail of Nature: The Ambiguous Ecological Promise of Christian Theology* (Philadelphia: Fortress, 1985).

PROVERBS 22:17–24:34

THE SAYINGS OF THE WISE

OVERVIEW

When the Egyptian *Instruction of Amenemope* was discovered in the 1920s, the study of Israelite wisdom was revitalized. The present section of Proverbs (esp. 22:17–23:11) appeared to be dependent upon that Egyptian work. Though contrary theories exist (that the Egyptian and Israelite works each borrowed from an earlier work, or that the Egyptian work borrowed from the biblical Proverbs), most scholars believe that this section of Proverbs shows a creative use of *Amenemope,* a work written late in the second millennium BCE.[259]

The "Sayings of the Wise" are generally admonitions, brief positive or negative precepts followed by positive or negative motive clauses that provide reasons for obeying the precepts. The admonitions are much briefer than the long instructions in chaps. 1–9, and also much more diverse in the topics of their advice. The reader is addressed directly in the second person, implying that one cannot be an uninvolved observer of wisdom (as if its teaching pertained to someone else), but must make a personal response to wisdom's demands.

259. See Glendon Bryce, *A Legacy of Wisdom* (Lewisburg: Bucknell University Press, 1979); Washington, *Wealth and Poverty in the Instruction of Amenemope and the Hebrew Proverbs*; cf. Whybray, *Wealth and Poverty in the Book of Proverbs.*

PROVERBS 22:17–23:35, LISTEN TO THE SAYINGS OF THE WISE

COMMENTARY

22:17-21. These verses are an extended invitation to hear, opening a series of admonitions, much like an ancient Egyptian *seboyet,* or "instruction," and like the instructions of Proverbs 1–9. It is strongly personal in its address ("yes—to you," 22:19) and makes rare mention of the written, and not merely oral, character of the instruction (v. 20). The text offers many difficulties. "Words of the Wise" has been identified as a title (cf. 24:23*a*). It is actually embedded in the call to hear (as in NIV). The NRSV has rearranged the text to identify the phrase as a title. "In your heart" is literally "in your belly," an image also found in Egyptian wisdom literature (see Commentary on 18:8). "Ready on your lips" means that what is internal will

come to expression in action and speech (see Excursus, "The 'Heart' in the Old Testament"). Verse 19*a* reminds readers that wisdom is based on trust of Yahweh (see 1:7) and that the book's purpose is to foster such trust, even in mundane aspects of life.

Verse 20 contains one of the most discussed words in the book (see NIV margin). The *Ketib* (reading implied by the consonantal text) has שלשום (*šilšôm*), "formerly," an idiom developed from "three" days ago, and the *Qere* (the MT's preferred reading) has שלישים (*šālîšîm*), "officers," which does not make sense. The ancient versions understood the word to mean "in three ways" (LXX, Vg) or "three times" (Syriac, Targum). The latter reading is close to the *Ketib*'s "formerly." Since the discovery of Amenemope's "Thirty Chapters," many commentators have emended the word to "thirty" (שלושים šělôšîm) and have taken it to refer to "thirty sayings" (see Overview). This too is problematic, because the thirty sayings cannot be clearly identified.

"True answer" (v. 21) may have the sense of a "reliable answer." "To him who sent [you]" is a stereotypical expression for someone who employs a messenger (see 10:26; 25:13; 26:6). This mode of speech was still current in Jesus' day (John 1:22).

22:22-23. The first in a series of admonitions, these verses have a negative precept (v. 22) followed by a theological motive (v. 23; cf. Exod 22:22-27). Warnings against robbing or otherwise harming the poor are common to Israel's laws, prophets, and wisdom writings (see Commentary on 14:31; 22:16; Deut 24:14-15, 17-22; Amos 5:11-12; 8:4-6). The wicked "crush the afflicted" (or "needy") at the gate. The city gate is the place where public business, including justice, is done (see Commentary on 8:1-3; Amos 5:12). The widow and the orphan are the archetypal representatives of all poor and disadvantaged people, whose ultimate defender is God (see Commentary on 15:25; 22:28; 23:10-11). Yahweh contends for the poor, especially when legitimate authorities fail in their duty to do so (see Isa 1:23; "pleads their cause" = "fights their fight," often used in the legal sense of vindicating a person in court; see also 23:11; 1 Sam 24:15; Mic 7:9). Verse 23b uses a rare verb (קבע qāba', "despoil," "plunder"), otherwise only in Mal 3:8. Its repetition indicates that the Lord will do to the wrongdoers as they have done to others, and more (*lex talionis*). The NRSV captures the severity of God's judgment better than does the NIV, for God "despoils" the oppressors of their "life" (נפש nepeš; see Commentary on 16:17).

22:24-25. This unit is another two-verse admonition with negative precepts and motive clauses. The admonition parallels the logic of the first parental address (1:10-19) by warning against bad company (see Commentary on 14:7), specifically angry persons (see 15:18; 27:4; 29:22), lest one accommodate oneself to "their ways" and suffer the consequences (see 1:19). Those consequences are deadly, for *nepeš* is the final word of the

admonition, although neither the NIV nor the NRSV translate it thus.

22:26-27. These verses form another negative admonition with a precept and, unusually, a rhetorical question (see NRSV), preceded by a condition, as a motive clause. See the Commentary on 6:1-5 for the general warning against giving surety for a debt (see also 11:15; 17:18; 20:16). The present admonition clarifies that one should not venture capital or goods beyond one's ability to pay—advice still valuable in our credit-driven society. The snatching of one's bed is probably humorous exaggeration, as if the foolish creditor was caught sleeping, literally and figuratively. Entering a debtor's house to get a pledge is forbidden in Deut 24:10.

22:28. In a culture without modern surveying techniques and records, the displacement of ancient boundary markers was a way of robbing others of the land given by God to each of Israel's families (see Deut 19:14, on which this saying may depend). Also Israel's neighbors took very seriously the sanctity of boundary markers, whether of persons and families or of nations and city-states. To violate boundaries was an offense against divinely established order (see Commentary on 8:27-29).[260] This proverb is aware that placing boundary stones was human work ("set up by your forefathers"). Yet the historically established social order—though human and flawed—was seen as a work of God, inasmuch as it protected the weak and powerless and fostered justice and righteousness. For the sake of the vulnerable, boundary markers come under God's protection (see Commentary on 15:25; 23:10-11). The archetypal story of the violation of ancestral land is Ahab's bloody appropriation of Naboth's vineyard (1 Kings 21).

22:29. This verse breaks the series of negative admonitions. It is a second-person rhetorical question that begins, "Have you seen . . . ?" (see 24:32; 26:12; 29:20). The question's purpose is to involve readers in the observation so that they may appropriate the lesson personally. A pun on "his work" (מלאכתו měla'ktô) and "kings" (מלכים mělākîm) uses the closeness of sounds to

---

260. See O. Keel, *The Symbolism of the Biblical World: Ancient Near Eastern Iconography and the Book of Psalms* (New York: Seabury, 1978) 96-100.

reinforce the closeness of the skilled person to the king. "Work" is used of God's creation in Gen 2:2 and can refer to a variety of arts, crafts, and activities. Ezra is described as a "scribe skilled in the law of Moses" (Ezra 7:6; see Ps 45:1, apparently a standard phrase for a skilled scribe).[261] In Isa 16:5, the Davidic king is skilled, or "zealous," for justice. "Serve" is literally "stand before," an idiom describing the privilege of being present in court (see 25:5). Verse 29c is unusual, but its sense as translated seems satisfactory. This saying uses the general opposition between good and bad traits in human undertakings: diligent/skilled/competent versus lazy/inept/incompetent. Wisdom is concerned not with piety alone, but with responsible excellence in all of God's creation. The opposite of this saying appears in 18:9, and similar thoughts appear in chap. 30 of *The Instruction of Amenemope* (see Overview).

23:1-3. This section continues the theme of interaction with rulers or kings. This admonition is addressed to one who is of high enough status to eat at the ruler's table. It urges alert observation and conduct appropriate to one's situation, especially restraint of appetite. The ruler presumably observes bodily greed and intemperance in subordinates as indicators of similar failings in other, more important matters. "What is before you" may also be "who is before you." A knife to the throat is apparently a proverbial expression for curbing one's appetite.

23:4-5. These verses are a humorous but pointed warning against wearing oneself out in the pursuit of uncertain wealth, which might sprout wings and fly away! Though the topic is different from 22:1-3, both admonitions concern setting limits to the greedy pursuit of good things (like food or wealth). At a certain point they become harmful and damage other goods, such as one's place in court or the well-being of one's family. This point is made more somberly in Eccl 4:7-8 and 5:13-17; Eccl 5:18-20 as well provides some counsel of joy, nonetheless. The image of wealth as birds in flight appears in "Amenemope" (chap. 7).[262] It is found already in the early second millennium BCE: "Possessions

are sparrows in flight which can find no place to alight" (see Commentary on 26:2).[263]

23:6-8. These verses are similar to vv. 1-3, and the two admonitions share a line (v. 3a = 6b); but the circumstances are different. The host is not a ruler scrutinizing a would-be courtier, but one who is stingy (lit., "bad of eye"; see Commentary on 22:9; 28:22). Although "bad of eye" is an idiom for "selfish," the literal connotation of "bad" is also at work here, for the host (masc.) is not well intentioned toward his guest. What he says in friendly fashion and what he thinks in his heart are not the same; he is duplicitous (see Commentary on 26:23-25).[264] Perhaps Simon, who invited Jesus to dinner with bad motives, is an example of such a host (Luke 7:39-48). Saul's malevolent wish to have David at table in order to kill him is another example (1 Sam 20:24-34). God complains about people who "honor me with their lips, while their hearts are far from me" (Isa 29:14).

Verse 7a is highly uncertain. The NRSV takes it in relation to the vomiting reaction in 22:8a, "a hair in the throat" ("hair," שֵׂעָר *sēʿār*). This also reinforces the connection with "Amenemope," chap. 11: "A poor man's goods are a block in the throat,/ It makes the gullet vomit."[265] What seemed tasty has a bad consequence. The NIV paraphrases a rare verb (שֵׂעָר *šāʿar*, "to calculate") to refer to the host, who thinks more of expenses than of people. The NIV's first marginal note offers an alternate, traditional reading of the same verb. The meaning of the line is uncertain, but the sense of the whole admonition is fairly clear (cf. Sir 13:8-13).

23:9. This verse belongs with 26:1-12, which gives advice on dealing with fools. The refusal to listen to wisdom from others is a defining characteristic of folly (see Commentary on 26:4-5).

23:10-11. This saying duplicates 22:28a before it fills out the thought with a reference to orphans and a theological motive clause. God "fights the fight" of the poor, and here their redeemer does the same for orphans ("plead their cause"; see Commentary on 22:23). The entire motive clause has a parallel in Jer 50:34, but see Job's complaint in

261. But see McKane, *Prophets and Wise Men*, 28-36.
262. Lichtheim, *Ancient Egyptian Literature*, 2:152.
263. Whybray, *Proverbs*, 333.
264. Cf. *The Instruction of Ani* 8:11-14 in Lichtheim, *Ancient Egyptian Literature*, 2:142.
265. Lichtheim, *Ancient Egyptian Literature*, 2:154-55.

Job 24:2-12. The topic is similar to "Amen-emope" 6, which refers to a widow's boundary marker. Accordingly, some scholars have emended "ancient" to "of a widow." This makes a good parallel to "orphan," but the MT makes good sense as it is, and there are no ancient textual variants.

23:12-35. The remainder of Proverbs 23 introduces a minor subsection (23:12-28), followed by an extended riddle about drinking (vv. 29-35). The section of close parallels to "Amenemope" has ended with the preceding verse. The present subsection repeatedly focuses on the parent-son relation in a way that echoes chaps. 1–9. The stereotyped vocabulary of v. 12 is entirely borrowed from those chapters. These factors suggest the hand of a redactor working to integrate the book as a whole. The poem on drinking is anticipated in vv. 15-16.

23:12-14. These admonitions belong together as an introduction to the minor subsection of vv. 12-28. Verse 12 advises a son to yield himself to discipline (see chaps. 1–9; see also 23:15, 26). Verses 13-14 give corresponding advice to a father (second-person masc.) not to withhold discipline from his son (see Commentary on 13:24; 19:18). Verses 15-28 then provide a composite representation of speech fragments, portraying key themes in parental discipline.

Verses 13-14 reflect Israel's view of corporal punishment, which is different from that of modern Americans. For some, however, "Spare the rod and spoil the child" remains a self-evident proverb (see Commentary on 13:24). The admonition seems to have an ironic motive clause that says that a properly restrained parental lashing does no harm. Instead, it does the youth good in the end, keeping him (masc.) from Sheol (see 7:25-27). Perhaps similar is our advice to a child reluctant to take bitter medicine, "Come now, it's not going to kill you!" This motive clause expresses a typical ancient Near-ern idea (see the Aramaic *Words of Ahikar* and the later Egyptian Papyrus Insinger).[266] On the other hand, Exod 21:20-21 contains a law concerning a beating that turned deadly (see Commentary on Prov 19:18).[267]

---

266. Pritchard, *Ancient Near Eastern Texts Relating to the Old Testament*, 428; Cf. *The Instruction of Ani* 8:11-14 in Lichtheim, *Ancient Egyptian Literature*, 3:192.

267. See W. Brueggeman's commentary on this law in *The New Interpreter's Bible Commentary*, vol. 1 (Nashville: Abingdon, 2015) 423-24.

23:15-16. The four lines of these two verses form a chiastic (ABB´A´) pattern of condition, two consequences, and a parallel condition, concerning parental joy in the wise son (in Proverbs, the term is gender specific; see the Overview on Prov 1:1–9:18; for this theme, see Commentary on 10:1). The son will speak what is right (מישרים *mêšārîm*; "equity" in 1:3; 2:9)—a standard of goodness that is established by God (Ps 99:4). Moreover, when the son's lips speak what is right, he imitates Lady Wisdom (8:6; cf. 16:13; Isa 33:15; see also 23:19).

23:17-18. These verses comprise an admonition with a negative and positive precept followed by motive clauses promising a future. They also echo chaps. 1–9, urging the fear of the Lord (1:7; see 24:21) and warning against envy of sinners (1:10-19; 3:31). The language and topics anticipate 24:1, 14, 19-20 and parallel Ps 37:1, 37-38. A more complex dismay at the prosperity of sinners comes to expression in Psalm 73 and Job 21. The motive clauses promise a future and hope for those who fear the Lord (the afterlife is not in view here; see 19:20). Because ancient Israel thought collectively and in terms of generations yet to come, such hope may well apply to future generations and not just to individual persons.

23:19-21. The call to hear (v. 19) returns to the parent-son relationship of vv. 15-16. It insists on honoring both mother and father (see Commentary on 19:26; 23:22). This is fleshed out by a warning against failing to observe wise limits in eating and drinking (see vv. 1-3). Drowsiness is the natural consequence of overindulgence, and it is a typical problem for the lazy (see 6:9-11). The admonition uses language, perhaps conventional (28:7), that is found also in Deut 21:20, where a rebellious son is liable to stoning by the covenant community (see Commentary on 19:18). Here, however, the threat is poverty. Concerning drinking, see the Commentary on 20:1; 23:29-35; 31:4-5.

23:22-25. These verses continue the theme of parent-son relations with an extended admonition to listen, get wisdom (see 4:5, 7; 17:16), and so give joy to one's father and mother (see Commentary on 10:1; 17:21; 23:15-16). The parallelism of "righteous" and "wise son" in v. 24 echoes the larger parallelism of the two categories in the first two major sections of the book.

23:26-28. This section contains an implicit contrast between dedication to the father's wisdom and to a prostitute (perhaps "strange woman"; see the LXX) or alien woman (so NRSV margin). The latter term appears regularly in chaps. 1–9 in parallel to the "strange woman" (see Excursus, "Death and the Strange Woman in Proverbs 1–9"). Thus, like Wisdom in 2:16, the father's wisdom here saves the son from an out-of-bounds woman who symbolizes folly incarnate. "Deep pit" is a conventional ancient Near Eastern slur for a (bad) woman (see Commentary on 22:14). But "pit" also suggests the underworld (Sheol), to which the strange woman's house leads (2:18; 5:5; 7:27). Some commentators wonder how she can add to the number of the faithless. Perhaps she does so in the same manner that the invitation of sinners can add to their number (1:10-19). The request that the son give his heart in v. 26 is perhaps the most intimate address of a parent to a son in the book (see "Excursus, The 'Heart' in the Old Testament"). As often, the inner life ("heart") has its counterpart in one's conduct, which is to be patterned after the father's ways.

23:29-35. These verses form an extended humorous riddle-poem on drinking. It begins with a series of six questions (v. 29), followed by an answer (v. 30) and a negative admonition (v. 31), with explanatory motive clauses describing the effects of drinking (vv. 32-34), and it concludes with a speech by the addict, who wakes from a stupor only to seek another drink (see Commentary on 23:20-21; 26:9; 31:4-5). While some of the details of the poem are obscure or multivalent, the thrust of the whole is clear.[268] In v. 33 the ancient versions take the feminine plural ("strange things") to refer to strange women (Vg; LXX and Syriac have singular; see Commentary on 23:27-28). The meaning of v. 34 is highly uncertain.

268. See Wilfred G. E. Watson, *Classical Hebrew Poetry: A Guide to Its Techniques* (Sheffield: JSOT, 1984) 20-30.

REFLECTIONS

1. The status and importance of the messenger in Israel and the rest of the ancient Near East cannot be exaggerated (22:21; cf. 25:13; 26:6). There was no postal service or instant communication. Thus messengers had to be trustworthy, since they often conveyed money and goods. They also had to be able to speak and negotiate on behalf of the sender, since the sender could not be consulted, being at some distance away. Consequently, the messenger had to have sufficient rank, integrity, and wisdom to represent the sender, much like an ambassador today. If the sender were a king, the messenger would be a high courtier, perhaps a member of the royal family. In Israel, prophets functioned as ambassadors from the heavenly court of Yahweh to the earthly court of a human king. In the New Testament, Christ is the one "sent" from the Father; he in turn "sends" his followers into the world (e.g., John 3:17, 34; 17:18-25; 20:21); and apostles are literally "sent" as ambassadors of Christ.

Christians are sent into this world as God's messengers, commissioned to act on God's behalf and to carry out God's purposes in this world (2 Cor 5:16-21). Christian existence is thus a responsible existence, requiring that we be ready to give "a sound answer to him who sent [us]" (22:21).

2. To modern minds, instruction on etiquette may seem out of place in a book on godly wisdom (23:1-3). But even table manners and food are part of the overall order of things, connecting us to the physical world that sustains us, connecting various people to one another, and giving expression to their varied relationships. Who sits where, for instance, is of great importance, for it usually suggests hierarchy, even in an egalitarian society (see Commentary on 25:6-7).

The life of the Christian community, therefore, will not be fully "Christian" until our entire life-style is shaped in harmony with God's order for creation and consciously dedicated to honor and serve the Lord. In the end, nothing, even table manners, is indifferent to the service of God, even though God gives us servants immense freedom to shape cuisine and culture in various ways (see Reflection number 2 at Proverbs 8:1-36).

PROVERBS 24:1–22, SAYINGS OF THE WISE CONCLUDED

COMMENTARY

24:1-2. This admonition echoes 23:17 and anticipates 24:19-20, all warning against envy of the wicked, presumably because of their success (see also 3:31-32). The function of these admonitions is to strengthen and encourage godly persons to remain faithful to God and to what is good in times of adversity. On "nor desire to be with them," see Commentary on 1:10-19; 14:7. What is in the heart comes to expression on the lips (see Commentary on 4:23).

24:3-4. These verses begin a series of third-person sentences that, for the most part, abandon the second-person address of the admonitions (but see v. 6a). On the surface this is a straightforward, four-line saying about building with wisdom. But it uses the language of creation, in which God and Wisdom build the cosmos like a house. The point is that human enterprises should take place in harmony with the order of the cosmos laid down by God through Wisdom. For this larger conception and the parallels in language, see the Commentary on 9:1-3 and 14:1. This saying also is connected verbally with the parent's opening speech, though this is obscured in the English translations. Sinners promise a house filled with all kinds of costly things (1:13). Identical Hebrew terms for "all precious" and "riches" are used in these verses. Thus a contrast is once again suggested between two ways to achieve prosperity (see Sir 1:17).

24:5-6. Verse 5 is uncertain, though its general point about wisdom's being superior to or essential to strength seems clear. While the superiority of wisdom and righteousness to wealth is often asserted (15:16; 16:18), occasionally their superiority to strength and power is declared (16:32; 20:29; 21:22; Sir 40:25-26). Wisdom gives guidance to

strength, and in war that means the taking of counsel (see Commentary on 11:14; 20:18; Eccl 9:18; Sir 37:16). Yet there are radical limits to human wisdom, counsel, and strength (see Commentary on 21:30-31). Verse 6a slips back into second-person address.

24:7-9. The final verses in the series that began with vv. 3-4 are a loose cluster of sayings on folly and sin. Wisdom is beyond the capacity of a fool (see Commentary on 17:16), just as the mysteries of God are beyond human capacity (see Commentary on 25:2; Psalm 131). For "in the gate," see Commentary on 8:1-3 (see also 31:23). "Open one's mouth"—that is, with something worth saying—is used of the king and of the capable woman in 31:8-9, 26. Verse 8 has language similar to Ps 21:11, where "those who devise evil" come under God's judgment (see Commentary on Prov 12:2, where "mischief-maker"/"crafty" translates a parallel expression). The NIV translates זמה (*zimmâ*) as "schemer" and "schemes" to capture the root repetition linking vv. 8-9, while "folly" is repeated from v. 7. The line between mere folly and sin is a theoretical one. The two can be distinguished but are practically inseparable because folly generally entails a refusal to recognize one's limits, or reality in general. This pride is tantamount to sin.[269] The character of such persons is recognized by the community, which names the evil. Usually bad things are an abomination to God (see Commentary on 11:1), but here the mocker (3:34; 13:1; 14:6; 15:12; 22:10) offends the sensibility common to humans.

24:10-12. Verse 10 introduces this passage with a conditional sentence applying the admonition to difficult times. There is a

269. See Plantinga, *Not the Way It's Supposed to Be*, 113-28.

pun linking "trouble" (צרה ṣārâ) and "small" (צר ṣar). In such situations great strength and courage are needed to do what is right (see Reflections on Prov 11:1-31). Verse 11 begins with an imperative (so NIV). The syntax of the admonition is difficult. It may be taken as an anacolouthon, or interrupted syntax. It may be translated, "Rescue those being taken away to death . . . if you hold back (from helping), if you say, 'Look we did not know this.'" The person "taken away to death" is not specified.

24:13-14. This admonition to eat honey is a figure for getting wisdom. For the ambiguity of "honey," see Commentary on 5:3. Here it symbolizes wisdom (see 16:24), as the good that consists (among other things) in knowing the right proportion, the proper limits of things (see Commentary on the related admonition in 25:16-17). Honey is good, but eating too much honey is not good (25:27)! "Find" (מצא māṣā´) is a key word in the book's final form, but especially in chaps. 1–9. It is regularly used of finding a wife or wisdom (1:21; 3:13; 8:17, 35; 18:22; 31:10) or good (16:20; 17:20; 18:22). Finding honey or wisdom means finding a future and hope (see Commentary on the parallel in 23:18; see also 24:19-20). This thought appears to be an editorial variant of the idea that finding Wisdom is tantamount to finding life, the theme of chaps. 1–9 (e.g., 3:18; 8:35; 9:11). There is probably also here an awareness that the good (honey or wisdom or "wife") that humans find is specific to them. It is something I have found and not another; it is proper to me. Part of wisdom is joy and contentment with the specific "honey" that we find in life (cf. 5:3; 9:17). This idea is fundamental to Ecclesiastes' insistence on joy in one's lot, even amid life's difficulties (Eccl 5:18-20; 9:7-10).

24:15-16. These verses form an admonition against attacking the righteous (see 1:11; 23:10-11). Its point is in the motive clause: Although the righteous are not free from troubles, even though they fall again and again, they get up and go on (Ps 20:7-8). The wicked, however, are brought down (lit., they stumble and fall), like the wicked in

4:12, 16, 19 (see also 24:17). The underlying premise is that God rewards people according to their deeds (see vv. 12, 29).

24:17-18. These verses are linked to vv. 15-16 by the catchwords *fall* and *stumble*, and they qualify that admonition. When one's enemy suffers God's just anger, one must not gloat (see 17:5; Job 31:29). This is what the wicked do (Ps 35:15-16). The righteous, who depend on God, must not become smug. A further step on this dangerous path is to take God's justice into one's own hands (see Commentary on 20:22; 24:29). Such sayings move in the direction of loving one's enemy (see 25:21-22; Exod 23:4-5; Matt 5:43-48). The motive clause (v. 18) has caused some consternation. It seems to say that one may hope for God's wrath on one's enemies, in apparent contradiction to the warning in v. 17. But the issue is leaving something to God's justice, the righting of wrongs (for which one may legitimately hope; see 2 Tim 4:14), as opposed to presuming self-righteous superiority. If one sins against an enemy in this matter, then both are subject to God's judgment—or mercy. The psalmists and the sages were aware that they themselves could move from righteousness and wisdom to folly and sin (Pss 19:12-13 NIV; 139:23-24; Prov 26:5-6).

24:19-20. The focus returns to the topic of fretting and envying evildoers (see Commentary on 23:17-19; 24:1-2). Once again the motivating concern is a "future" (אחרית ’aḥărît) or lack thereof (23:18, 32; 24:14, 20), a term that appears several times in this subsection of Proverbs. On a lamp's being put out, see Commentary on 13:9 and 20:20.

24:21-22. This admonition concludes this subsection of the book. The reading of v. 21b is uncertain. The NRSV margin gives a literal translation, whose sense the NIV also follows, interpreting "those who change" as "rebellious" persons who foment insurrection. The NRSV text follows the LXX. In v. 22 the two translations solve the grammar in different ways, but the sense is not significantly changed. (See Reflections at 24:23-24.)

PROVERBS 24:23-34, AN APPENDIX: MORE SAYINGS OF THE WISE

COMMENTARY

24:23-25. Verse 23a is an editorial heading, introducing this brief section as an appendix to the larger "Sayings of the Wise" (22:17–24:22). In the LXX this section comes after 30:14, a bit of evidence for the book's obscure process of growth. It consists mostly of admonitions, concluded by a didactic poem on the sluggard (see 27:23-27, another poem concluding a subunit).

Verses 23-25 are an expanded "not-good" saying against partiality in the law court (see Commentary on 18:5; 28:21a is a near duplicate of 24:23b). The language is legal (Deut 1:17; 16:19). In 17:15 the inversion of justice (pronouncing the guilty innocent and vice versa) is an abomination to the Lord. Here peoples and nations curse the unjust magistrate, because perverted justice hurts ordinary people. The unusual reference to "nations" reflects the universal recognition of basic standards for justice, something all ancient Near Eastern kings claimed to provide. With the advent of the monarchy in Israel, the responsibility for justice shifted to rest ultimately with the king (see 2 Sam 15:1-6). In Israel's long history, town elders or priests were variously the agents of justice as well.[270] A curse is essentially a prayer to God to do justice when human institutions—and those responsible for them—fail to provide it (see Commentary on 26:2). The just magistrate receives blessing (the opposite of a curse). Although God is not mentioned, the deity is the implicit source of "rich blessing," a phrase that appears in a prayer for the king (Ps 21:4).

24:26. This verse may be related to the judicial speech of vv. 23-25, but the saying's general character suggests its independent origin. It plays on the role of lips in good speech. An explicit reference to kissing the lips appears nowhere else in the OT, but is implied in Cant 4:11; 5:13. Its use here may be an idiom that is no longer understood (cf. the obscure Hebrew of Gen 41:40, which

refers to kissing the mouth; see Job 31:27 for a different idiom). Nonetheless, it suggests the dialogical, give-and-take character of speech. It has been argued that the verb here refers instead to sealing or silencing lips.[271] In that case, the point is that honest speech has the last word. "Give an . . . answer" is a standard expression (see 18:13; 22:21; 27:11; Ps 119:42); Wisdom's words are also honest (8:9).

24:27. Related to vv. 3-4, this admonition has no motive clause, but it argues for right (temporal) order in major life undertakings. Agriculture was the basis of ancient life, in which most of society was actively involved. The procuring of food comes prior to getting a shelter of one's own. A similar logic appears in the Egyptian *Instruction of Any*.[272] The advice is agrarian (see 12:11; 24:30-34), but the principle of setting and accomplishing right priorities applies anywhere.

24:28. This verse is one of many warnings against false testimony in court (14:5; 19:5; 25:18). "Without cause" means that the object of the testimony is innocent (see Commentary on 26:2; cf. 3:30).

24:29. Some commentators wish to take this verse with the preceding one, so that "neighbor" provides an antecedent to "him." More probably, it is an independent admonition (see Commentary on 20:22; 24:17-18). The statement (lit.) "I will pay him back according to his deed" shows a human arrogating a prerogative that is God's (v. 12; Rom 2:6; 12:19).

24:30-34. This saying is a first-person didactic narrative that appeals to personal observation to make its point (see 4:3-9; 7:6-23; Ps 37:25-26, 35-36; Eccl 1:12). The topic of the sluggard is a regular one in Proverbs (see Commentary on 6:6-11; 10:4-5). The narrator's conclusion, drawn from observing the sluggard's farm, is a conventional one

270. For basic data, see de Vaux, *Ancient Israel*, 1:150-57.

271. J. M. Cohen, "An Unrecognized Connotation of *nsq peh* with Special Reference to Three Biblical Occurrences," *VT* 32 (1982) 418-24.
272. Lichtheim, *Ancient Egyptian Literature*, 2:139.

borrowed from 6:10-11. Extended poems on the sluggard thus link chaps. 1–9, the present "Sayings of the Wise," and the second Solomonic sub-collection (26:13-16). In addition are the numerous sayings scattered about the first Solomonic sub-collection. The extended poem gives closure to the present sub-collection. This lesson on the gone-to-ruin property of the sluggard forms a sharp contrast to houses built wisely (24:3-4, 27).

REFLECTIONS

1. The true test of a person's strength or mettle is adversity; almost everyone can survive the good times (24:10-12). This principle also applies to families, to social groups and institutions, and to nations. Even when taken literally, this admonition invites wide application. It may refer to victims of theft (see 1:11-12, 16) or to any situation where one is called upon to help a neighbor in trouble (see Commentary on 21:13). Those in a position to help in difficult, dangerous circumstances are tempted to deny reality in several respects. They may deny that innocent people are in danger of harm or death. They may deny that they are responsible for rescuing others who cannot help themselves. Some people think that any potential danger to self or family frees them from moral obligation to do good. This view, in thought and deed, entails the moral and spiritual collapse of a society. It stands under the judgment of the One who sees through human self-deception and denial of reality (see Commentary on 16:2; 21:2). God knows even when we deny that we know. God appears here as a just judge who repays people "according to their deeds" (see the prayer in Ps 28:4; see also Matt 16:27; Rom 2:6). In the United States the infamous case of Kitty Genovese, who was assaulted and left to die on a sidewalk in New York City while her neighbors listened and did nothing, comes to mind. In our time, the complicity of ordinary people in the mass murders during World War II is the ultimate example of the banal brutality of sins of omission.[273]

2. In several key passages, Proverbs associates God and the king (16:1-15; 24:21-22; 25:2-5). The underlying premise is that human governments are ordained by God to be earthly agents in doing justice and righteousness (Ps 72; Rom 13:1-8; 1 Tim 3:1-3; Titus 3:1; 1 Pet 2:13-17; see also Commentary on Prov 21:3). Thus honor is their due. To give honor or respect is the opposite of cursing God or a ruler (Exod 22:28). Yet, a government is not God; its authority is sharply limited to its task and is subject to God's standards for right government (see Reflections 1 on Prov 28:1–29:27).

273. For a retelling of Kitty Genovese's story, see Plantinga, *Not the Way It's Supposed to Be*, 182-84, a chapter on "flight" from responsibility.

PROVERBS 25:1–29:27

THE SECOND SOLOMONIC COLLECTION OF SAYINGS

OVERVIEW

The second Solomonic collection[274] begins with an editorial heading that echoes 1:1 and 10:1 and shares stylistic features with 24:23. Scholars generally recognize two main subunits in this collection (chaps. 25–27 and 28–29), as they do in the first Solomonic collection (chaps. 10–15; 16:1–22:16). The last two chapters of the second collection display a special interest in the king and justice. This section has been called "a mirror for princes," because it reflects the standards and behaviors proper to royalty. The collection begins with attention to God, king, and court/subjects (25:1-7), followed by sayings on speech and social

conflict of various sorts (25:8-15). The address of 25:2-7, if not the whole chapter, is to the young men of the royal court. The last half of the chapter (25:16-27; 25:28 seems isolated) is concerned with conflict and strife brought about by wickedness or the failure of wisdom. These are the problems the king, his court, and all people must handle with wisdom and justice. The collection on the "fool" (26:1-12) explores the wisdom theme of fittingness. A subunit on the sluggard follows (26:13-16), and chap. 26 ends with a return to the theme of conflict (26:17-28). Chapter 27 consists of miscellaneous sayings and concludes with a monitory poem on farming (27:23-27). Like the poem in 24:30-34, this one serves to close off a subunit of the book.

274. For a fuller account, see Raymond C. Van Leeuwen, *Context and Meaning in Proverbs 25–27* (Atlanta: Scholars Press, 1988).

PROVERBS 25:1–27:27, ON THE COURT, FOOLS, AND FRIENDS

Proverbs 25:1-28, On God, King, Court, and Conflict

COMMENTARY

25:1. The chapter opens with an editorial heading. It locates the work of proverb collection (as opposed to proverb creation) in the royal court of Hezekiah (c. 728–700 BCE), who was sometimes seen as a second Solomon (2 Kgs 18:1–20:21; 2 Chr 29:1–32:33; Sir 48:17-23). Although questions have been raised about the historicity of the heading,[275] there seems no reason to doubt it (see

275. See, Michael Carasik, "Who Were the 'Men of Hezekiah' (Proverbs xxv 1)?" *VT* 44 (1994) 289-300.

Introduction). The exact meaning of the term translated as "copied" (עתק *'tq*) is not known ("transcribed" or "transmitted"?).[276] Most probably it refers to the work of editing and arranging sayings and admonitions.

25:2-3. These verses are linked by repetition of "(un)search(able)"; together they show not only the close relation of God and king, but also the ultimate difference between them. There is a hierarchy of social

276. See Fishbane, *Biblical Interpretation in Ancient Israel*, 33.

position: God inscrutably above all, the king, and then the rest of society (see the subsequent sayings). God can both reveal and conceal (Deut 29:29), and humanity, led by the king, searches out what God has hidden in reality. The verb "search" (חקר ḥāqar) may refer to the king's judicial function of bringing to light the truth in criminal cases (18:17; 1 Kgs 3:28). The hiddenness of the king's heart is compared to the far reaches of the cosmos. Elsewhere the expression "unsearchable" is used only of God and the vast creation (Job 5:9; 9:10; Ps 145:3; Isa 40:28; cf. Job 11:7-10).

25:4-5. These verses form another pair, depicting the king as a judge who removes the wicked to ensure the nation's stability and integrity (see Commentary on 29:4).[277] If the "things" the king searches out in 25:2 refer to judicial matters, then there is a natural flow from vv. 2-3 to vv. 4-5. Verse 4 provides a metaphor for the process of cleansing society and making government stable, like a well-built throne. When a metal is smelted, its impurities rise to the surface, are poured off, and the remaining purified metal is poured into a mold to make a vessel or "implement" (כלי kělî) for the smith. The wicked are like the impure dross (see Isa 1:21-26; Jer 6:27-30). When the wicked are removed from the king's court (from his presence, the center of national power), "his throne will be established in righteousness." The three key Hebrew words in this clause are central to the royal creation theology of the Davidic house (see Commentary on 16:12). This proverb pair is not addressed to members of the court, but speaks to the duty of the king. Perhaps the best example of this proverb pair is the "wisdom" (1 Kgs 2:6, 9) of young King Solomon in removing those who would undermine the stability of his kingdom. This is not seen by the biblical writers as negative, but as the proper way to "establish" the kingdom (1 Kgs 2:12, 46).[278]

25:6-7b. This unit is an admonition addressed to young members of the court, jockeying for position and status (see 18:16; 19:6; 22:29; Sir 7:4-7; 11:1). It is tied to the

previous pair of sayings by the phrase "the king's presence." The expressions "place of the great" and "the presence of a noble" do not refer to different locations, but are parallel designations of the court.

25:7c-10. While the preceding admonition used horizontal and vertical spatial images to convey movement up and down socially, now follow two admonitions linked by a concern for legal disputes among equals. Perhaps the connection is that success in legal disputes can lead to social or political advancement (see 2 Sam 15:2-7). There is also a movement from "seeing" in the first admonition to "hearing" in the second. Both admonitions concern wrongly bringing something hidden (whether seen or heard) out into the open. The avoidance of frivolous lawsuits was already in the ancient Near East a conventional wisdom topic. In vv. 7c-8, the warning is against becoming unnecessarily involved in a dispute that is really not one's business (see Commentary on 26:17; 27:8). This is a form of ignoring proper boundaries, of being enmeshed with another person's affairs. The negative conclusion of the case (see 18:17) suggests that one may not understand what one has merely seen; appearances can be deceiving, especially if one is not closely acquainted with a situation. Proverbs 20:3 makes a more general warning against hasty litigation (cf. 24:28).

Verses 9-10, by contrast, suggest that if one must be in a dispute, it should be one's own legitimate concern (the NRSV's "directly" is puzzling and is not in the Hebrew; for the legal idiom, see 22:23; 23:11; Ps 43:1). Nor should it entail the unnecessary exposure of what is best kept private, an act typical of gossips (see Commentary on 11:13; 20:19; cf. Matt 18:15). "Your ill repute will have no end" is literally, "The accusation against you does not return (to your accuser)"; cf. Isa 55:11 for the "word" that does not "return" to God "empty" but has its intended effect. "One who hears" may refer to a judge, similar to the modern practice in which a court case is a hearing.

25:11-12. These verses are two artfully constructed sayings that compare fine speech to well-crafted jewelry. In v. 11, the translations have reversed the order of the two lines; in Hebrew the imagery comes

277. Cf. the Babylonian "Advice to a Prince," in Lambert, *Babylonian Wisdom Literature*, 113-15.
278. P. Kyle McCarter, Jr., "'Plots, True or False' the Succession Narrative as Court Apologetic," *Int* 35 (1981) 355-67; Perdue, "Liminality as a Social Setting for Wisdom Instructions," 114-26.

first, then comes the reference to speech. "Apples" (תפוח *tappûaḥ*) refers to some kind of fruit, but not the apple we are familiar with. A likely candidate is the apricot, which has a golden color (Cant 2:3, 5; Joel 1:12). "A word . . . spoken" may refer to a judicial decision. "Fitly" (על-אפניו *al-'opnāyw*) is uncertain, perhaps literally, "upon its *turning*" (if the word is related to "wheel"). Some think it means "according to circumstances" and thus "fitly." Others relate it to an Arabic word for "time," thus a word spoken "at the right time" (see 15:23). The intent remains uncertain.

Verse 12 is delightfully clever, for the gold ring (11:22) hangs, as it were, "on a listening ear" (see 20:12). There is art in wise reproof (27:5), and also in serious listening (12:15; 15:31-32)! In keeping with the apparent judicial background of the preceding admonitions, however, the participle translated "a wise man's rebuke" is literally, "a wise *reprover.*" This may be a technical legal term referring to an arbiter or judge, as in Amos 5:10: "They hate *the arbiter* in the gate, and detest him whose plea is just" (TNK).

25:13-14. These verses are linked by weather images. In v. 13, a person of lower social status wins favor from a superior; in v. 14, the failure to deliver what is promised leads to loss of face, or worse, with respect to equals or superiors.

Faithful messengers give relief to their masters (v. 13), who in some way are stressed as if by summer heat (see Commentary on 25:25; 26:1). In Israel and in the ancient Near East in general, messengers were of a status commensurate with those who sent them (see Commentary on 13:17; 22:21). The imagery of cold snow in the hot harvest time may be based on the practice of runners bringing down compacted snow or ice from the mountains to cool the wealthy.[279] For "refreshes the spirit" (נפש *nepeš,* "soul" or "throat"), see Commentary on 16:24 (cf. Exod 31:17; Pss 19:8; 23:3*a* for the idiom).

In v. 14, the clouds do not deliver what they promise: rain for the thirsty ground (cf. 25:23; Jude 12). A literal illustration appears in the Elijah cycle. After a long drought,

Elijah sends his servant to look for a cloud as a harbinger of rain (1 Kgs 18:41-45). Worse is a person who does not give what is promised (see Commentary on 18:16, where a gift is the means for access into the circle of "the great"; cf. 25:6).

25:15. The thought returns to one's relation to a ruler, the ultimate social superior (see "king" and "the great" in vv. 2-7), and to the sort of behavior that will move them favorably (see 16:13-16). Patience is a variant of "slow to anger" (see Commentary on 15:18). In the delightful oxymoron of v. 15*b,* the softest organ, the tongue, breaks the hardest organ, the bone.[280] The NIV's "gentle" translates the word for "soft" as in 15:1. Sirach 28:17-18 moves this saying in the direction of the English expression, "The pen is mightier than the sword" (see Ps 55:21). That brains are better than brawn is a recurrent theme in Proverbs (see Commentary on 16:32; 20:29; 21:22).

25:16-17. These verses warn against good social relations going bad. Finding and stuffing oneself with too much honey is compared with presenting oneself too often at a neighbor's door. Both are failures to recognize proper limits to behaviors that are perfectly good in themselves. Too much of a good thing makes one sick. It is possible to wear out one's welcome. The repeated phrase "too much of" in the NIV nicely captures the Hebrew parallelism of the two admonitions. For the symbolism of honey, see Commentary on 5:3 (see also 24:13; 25:27).

25:18. This verse contains an allusion to the "ten words" as found in Exod 20:16. A false witness in a court procedure can initiate the judicial process as an accuser or join it once begun (see Commentary on 6:19; cf. 1 Kgs 21:13). For honesty in testimony, see the Commentary on 12:17; 14:5. The weapon images convey the deadly force of lying words (see 26:18; Pss 57:4; 120:3-4).

25:19. The tooth is one that breaks, and the foot is one that shakes or "slips" (מעד *m'd*). Humans depend on "reliable" body parts. A healthy society is also interdependent, in that each member must play his or her role reliably, especially in times of crisis. The story of Hezekiah under Assyrian attack

---

279. B. Lang, "Vorläufer von Speiseeis in Bibel und Orient. Eine Untersuchung von Spr 25,13," in *Mélanges bibliques et orientaux en l'honneur de M. Henri Cazelles,* ed. A. Caquot and M. Delcor (Neukirchen-Vluyn: Neukirchener Verlag, 1981) 218-32.

280. A similar image appears in *Ahiqar* 105-106, in Pritchard, *Ancient Near Eastern Texts Relating to the Old Testament,* 429.

uses the same root for "trust" and "reliable" (בטח *bṭḥ*) as a thematic key word (see 2 Kgs 18:20-24; 19:10).

25:20. This verse is difficult. It appears to portray things or actions that do not "fit" their object in character or in time (see Commentary on 26:1-3; cf. 10:26; 27:14). The saying is not a simile ("like" does not appear in Hebrew); the metaphorical images are simply juxtaposed to the point of the saying in the last line (so also in vv. 18-19). The NRSV largely follows the versions, but the shorter Hebrew text can stand. On a cold day one's body should not be exposed, nor should acidic vinegar be poured on a wound (reading נתר [*nāter*] after Arabic *natratu*).[281] Wounds were soothed with oil or balm (Isa 1:6). The NIV translation, "vinegar poured on soda," provides a simple example of incompatibility. These images of pain (or of unfittingness) show the damage done by inappropriate levity to a sad or heavy heart (see Isa 40:2). Sirach 22:6*a* provides a parallel, "Like music in time of mourning is ill-timed conversation" (NRSV). Similarly, an Assyrian hymn to the god Shamash ends with the following curse: "May his string-playing be painful to people,/ May his joyful songs be the prick of a thorn."[282]

25:21-22. In effect, the concrete terms of v. 21 tell the reader to love not only neighbor and stranger, but also one's enemy (cf. Lev 19:18, 34; Matt 5:43-48). The law in Exod 23:4-5 embodies a similar principle (cf. Deut 22:1-4; see Sir 28:1-7). There are further parallels to this principle in ancient Near Eastern writings.[283] Unfortunately, the expression "heap burning coals on his head" remains obscure. Its use in 2 Esdr 16:53 suggests God's punishment of the sinner. A modern suggestion compares an Egyptian rite of contrition, but this has no known resonance in Israelite culture. Another (unlikely) suggestion is to translate, "then you will be snatching coals (from) upon his head." That is, the water you give relieves your enemy of heat, and God will reward you. Another is that the fiery coals represent the red-faced shame of

your enemy in response to your kindness.[284] David's encounter with wicked Saul illustrates both the attitude required of the righteous and the theological point of this admonition (1 Sam 24:8-22). The apostle Paul quotes this text in the context of arguing love ("overcome evil with good") and leaving vengeance to God (Rom 12:20; see Commentary on Prov 20:22; 24:17-18). God takes note of those who do good and right wrongs.

25:23-24. Both of these sayings concern bad relations and may have a subtle link in imagery. There is bad weather in v. 23; in v. 24 the husband on the roof is exposed to bad weather (see Commentary on 27:15-16). There is a problem in v. 23, in that rain generally does not come from the north. The solution may lie in a pun. "North wind" can also be read as "hidden wind," and "sly tongue" is literally a "secret tongue." Thus rain storms and emotional storms can both arise from unexpected (hidden or secret) sources (see Job 38:22-23).

Verse 24 appears several times with minor variations (see Commentary on 21:9, 19). One may compare the humorous story in which Socrates' wife, Xanthippe, gave him a scolding and then doused him with water. Socrates remarked that after the thunder comes the rain. Apparently exposure to the elements was considered better than exposure to the storms of a tempestuous wife. The remarks in Proverbs about a quarrelsome wife are tempered by its pervasive affirmation of the wife as wisdom (see Commentary on 31:10-31); moreover, these remarks are mild in comparison to the misogyny of Sirach (see Sir 25:13-26).

25:25-26. These verses are linked by water images, one positive, one negative. Both sayings presuppose the hot and dry climate of Palestine, where drinkable water is a precious, even life-saving, commodity (see Commentary on 5:15-19). Good news (see 12:25; 15:30) from afar is like water that restores a person worn out by thirst (see Commentary on 25:13). נפשׁ (*nepeš*, "soul") may suggest "throat" here and in v. 13. When David is in distress he longs for water from his ancestral spring, and his mighty men get him some (2 Sam 23:13-17).

281. McKane, *Proverbs*, 588-89.

282. Foster, *Before the Muses*, 2:726.

283. See *Amenemope* 5, 1-6 and "Papyrus Insinger" 23, 6, in Lichtheim, *Ancient Egyptian Literature*, 2:150 and 3:203, respectively. See also "Counsels of Wisdom," 41-48, in Lambert, *Babylonian Wisdom*, 101.

284. See Van Leeuwen, "On Wealth and Poverty," 60; Meinhold, *Die Sprüche*, 2:430.

Verse 26 expresses an inversion of the way things ought to be. The "wicked" or "guilty" succeed at the expense of the righteous or innocent. This saying contradicts the truth claim of 10:30, which says that the righteous shall never be moved (see Commentary on 10:30; 12:3; cf. 10:3; Ps 55:22). Things in this world do not always work out justly. The image is of cattle who so trample and befoul a watering place that one cannot drink from it. Something good and essential has been ruined so that the spiritual and social "waters" necessary for communal well-being are polluted and undrinkable. Without divine and human justice, the fountains of life are corrupted.

25:27. Verse 27 *a* is related by theme and verbal repetition to v. 16, as is v. 27 *b* to v. 2. These links, and the reversed repetition of "righteous" and "wicked" in vv. 5 and 26, appear to create a double envelope around vv. 2-27. The sense of v. 27 *a* is straightforward (see Commentary on 25:16). But v. 27 *b* is extremely difficult. Literally it reads, "and to seek/search for their glory is glory," or "is *not* glory," if the negative in v. 27 *a* does double duty. A shifting of consonants and a repointing of vowels permits the translation, "and to seek difficult things is [no] glory." If this is correct, then the meaning has to do with accepting one's limits (see Psalm 131; Sir 3:21-22; 2 Esdras 4).

25:28. The concluding verse is similar in theme and imagery to 16:32 (cf. 14:29; 17:27). Wisdom is superior to strength; lack of self-control leaves one exposed and without defense (cf. 10:15; 18:10-11).

REFLECTIONS

1. The OT often uses spatial images to convey aspects of the human condition. The imagery of high and low is used frequently in the psalms to indicate security and well-being or, alternatively, misery and calamity (Pss 18:16; 27:5; 30:1, 3, 9; 36:12; 38:6; 40:2; 130:1; see Commentary on Prov 18:10-11). God, who dwells on high, lifts up the lowly and brings down the high and mighty (1 Sam 2:6-8; Isa 2:12-17; 5:15-16; 6:1; Luke 1:52). In Proverbs 25, the inscrutable glory of God and king are conveyed by cosmic height and depth (25:2-3).

Spatial imagery also conveys social position and boundaries. Wisdom at court, or anywhere, requires a recognition of social limits and propriety. This includes self-knowledge (What is my proper place and function in the scheme of things?) and awareness that powerful others also form judgments about who we are. When the one judging us is God, a human ruler, or an employer, realistic humility is called for (see Commentary on 11:2; 16:18-19; 29:23). Jesus expands the admonition of 25:6-7 into a parable on choosing places of honor at table (Luke 14:7-11). Israel's shame-and-honor culture (see Commentary on 12:8; 13:18) made explicit social dynamics that are often present but are obscured in our more egalitarian culture.

2. Proverbs 25:2-10 concerns the social scale in ancient Israel, especially in the royal court, Israel's center of power (like America's Washington, D.C., and New York City). It looks at where people, both good and bad, fit into the "pecking order" and the things they do to climb higher or descend lower on the social ladder. Where there is social mobility, there are also social conflict and competition. People can use litigation and conflict to further their own ends. The restraints that Proverbs here puts on social climbing through devious means and on unwarranted litigation speak a word of caution to our litigious and contentious culture.

3. When body parts crumble, we get hurt (25:19). If those we depend on prove unreliable in times of trouble (see Commentary on 24:10), we are especially vulnerable to injury. Proverbs 25:19 has wide application, from marriage and family in times of personal or cultural crisis to business and military in times of economic distress or war. Given the interdependence of human communities, much depends on mutual reliability and warranted trust. Whether in the body politic or in the church as a body (Rom 12:3-8; 1 Cor 12:12-30), we need one another. Individualistic persons need to reflect on this fact. Christians especially must strive to build a society that raises reliable persons, deeply aware of their role and importance in the community. While this saying focuses on the need for reliable people in times of crisis, we must nevertheless rely wholly on God in times ordinary and extraordinary (see Commentary on 3:5; 16:20; 28:25*b*).

Proverbs 26:1-28, On Fools and Fittingness

COMMENTARY

The coherence of this passage is evident from the appearance of "fool" (כסיל *kĕsîl*) in every verse but the second. On a deeper level, the passage uses the problem of interaction with fools to teach about the need to properly "read" other people, situations, and even oneself (v. 12). In doing so, it also teaches about the nature of proverbs and their use (vv. 7, 9). Wise interpretation of proverbs, of persons, and of circumstances should lead to fitting relations and actions in every area of life. The passage also shows a structural unity in the regular construction of its sayings (vv. 4-5 are admonitions). The sayings present similes or metaphors in the first line that are figurative comments on the topics (usually concerning a fool) in the second line. (The translations in vv. 6-7, 9-10 turn metaphors into similes with "like.") In vv. 6-11, the B lines alternately present unfitting actions in relation to fools (26:6, 8, 10) or unfitting actions committed by fools (26:7, 9, 11). More precisely, the first group (vv. 6, 8, 10) provides instances of honor or position being given to a fool, as v. 8 spells out. Verse 12 concludes the whole with a saying that has an important relation to other passages in the book.

26:1-3. These verses introduce the theme of fittingness. The first two verses are similes, but the third follows the same pattern of two images followed by the saying's true (human) topic. In each image and topic, the point of comparison is whether two related things "fit."

26:1. Palestine has a warm, dry climate with fall and spring rains. The summer (also the time of harvest) is hot and dry. Rain at that time is such an anomaly that it is a frightful

inversion of the cosmic order, a world upside down (see Commentary on 30:21-23; 1 Sam 12:16-18). It is not fitting (see 17:7; 19:10; Sir 10:18; 14:3; 15:9). Rain in harvest time is not only an anomaly, but it can also do damage by destroying crops or rotting them. Similarly, the proper order of things is inverted when a fool receives honor (כבוד *kābôd*, "glory" in 25:2, 27).

26:2. At first glance, the saying does not seem to fit its context, because it lacks the key word *fool*. Yet it has the same structure as vv. 1, 3, and fittingness is its implicit theme. In v. 1, something good (honor) was given to someone bad (a fool). In v. 2, an inversion takes place. Something bad (a curse) is given to someone good (an innocent person). In v. 3, finally, something bad (a rod) is fittingly given to someone bad (a fool). The person who is cursed here is innocent because the curse was undeserved (lit., "causeless"). In the same way that a bird does not "come to rest" as long as it flies, a curse will not "stick" to an innocent person (see Commentary on 23:4-5). A curse is implicitly a prayer that God will right wrongs, when human justice fails (11:26; 24:24). God does not honor unjustified prayers—that is, when they do not "fit" their object (Ps 109:17, 28).

26:3. In the third instance, things "fit" their objects. For corporal punishment, see Commentary on 13:24; 17:10. This verse is more compact than vv. 1-2 and imitates a beating rhythm when recited in Hebrew. Fools do not learn from reason and advice, hence the comparison with stubborn animals (cf. Ps 32:8-10; Jas 3:3). This saying leads directly into the next verse, an admonition that draws a logical conclusion from the stubbornness of the fool.

26:4-5. These verses are a contradictory pair of admonitions that present the problem of fittingness in the most radical way. The contradiction of these verses nearly kept Proverbs out of the Jewish canon of biblical books, but the Talmud argued that the admonitions refer to different matters.[285] The solution to the contradiction does lie in this direction: Wisdom does not always mean doing the same thing, even in superficially similar circumstances. Yet the juxtaposition of these admonitions drives one to reflect on the limits of human wisdom, for no clue is given to help the reader identify which fool should be ignored and which spoken to. Of two viable courses of action, we do not always know which is "fitting." The first verse of the pair gives the standard "majority" advice for handling fools (see 23:9; Matt 7:6). Since they do not listen (v. 3), and since they are attached to their folly (v. 11; see 13:19), to join them in discussion is to be dragged down to their level and to allow them to dictate the terms of the debate. Thus one becomes like them.

Verse 5 gives "minority" advice: "Answer a fool," because sometimes to leave self-deluded fools unanswered does greater damage than would exposing their folly. The practical difficulty of vv. 4-5 is knowing whether to speak or to be silent when confronted by a fool. There is, indeed, "a time to be silent and a time to speak" (Eccl 3:7 NIV). Wisdom is a matter of fittingness and timing. But here, no clues are given for making the right decision. This general problem is explored more extensively in the Babylonian *Dialogue of Pessimism,* in which a wise but cynical slave offers equally plausible reasons to his master for doing or not doing a variety of actions.[286] While the "Dialogue" concludes in pessimism, Proverbs arrives at a different outcome (see Commentary on v. 12, "wise in his own eyes").

26:6. A person in authority sends someone on a mission for which that person is not suited (see Commentary on 26:1, 8; 25:13, 25). The lack of diligence (10:26) or competence for the job renders the person—and

his or her employer—a fool. The images of v. 6*a* are ironic; instead of the messenger's being an extra pair of feet for the master, the failed job in effect cuts the master's feet off. The drinking of violence is an unusual image (see 4:17), but it suggests that senders of fools harm themselves.

26:7. Here the writer shows that knowledge of proverbs does not automatically make one wise (see Commentary on 26:9; cf. Sir 20:18-20). Good proverbs can be put to a lame, ineffectual use. The wise make proverbs, and fools repeat them.

26:8. The imagery of v. 8*a* has not received a satisfactory explanation, but v. 8*b*, which is the verse's true topic, is a variant of v. 1. Thus by repetition it emphasizes the theme that holds this passage together. Giving honor to a fool is illustrated concretely in vv. 6, 10.

26:9. This verse repeats v. 7*b*, but changes the figurative comment in v. 9*a*, which is not entirely clear. Literally it reads, "A thorn(bush) goes up [עלה *'ālâ*] in(to) the hand of a drunkard." The NRSV suggests that the drunkard brandishes a thornbush (or "hook" [חוח *ḥôaḥ*]; see Job 41:2[40:26]), but "brandished" seems a far-fetched rendering of "goes up." The Hebrew may mean that the thorns do damage to the drunkard's hand (see the more ambiguous NIV). In any case, dangerous implements are not fitting in the hands of one robbed of reason by drink. In contemporary terms, "If you drink, don't drive."

26:10. This verse is textually corrupt, but the NRSV offers a plausible solution, based on slight emendation. To hire a drunkard (a link with v. 9) or someone otherwise unfit for a task does damage, sometimes deadly damage, in society. Similarly, in North American society, granting the privilege or "honor" (see Commentary on v. 1) of driving to those who drink kills tens of thousands of people every year.

26:11. There is a certain sharp humor here, based on acute observation of both humans and animals. The wise learn from their mistakes, but fools do not.

26:12. An ironic close to this section on fools and fittingness, the direct question of v. 12*a* (see 22:29) forces the reader to become personally involved in the issues of

285. See *m. Sabb.* 30*b.*
286. Lambert, *Babylonian Wisdom Literature,* 139-49; *ANET,* 600-601.

the passage. The saying is linked conceptually and verbally to vv. 4-5. There, the reader was in danger of becoming a fool (v. 4), and the fool was in danger of "being wise in his own eyes" (v. 5). This verse sharpens the point by explicitly raising the problem of self-perception as opposed to perception of the other. Those who consider themselves wise are worse than fools, because they think they are superior. They do not recognize their own limits, the fragility of human goodness, or the limits that relativize all human wisdom. The insoluble contradiction of vv. 4-5 is designed to promote awareness of these limits and to inculcate proper humility. In the larger context of Proverbs, the repetition of the phrase "wise in his own eyes" (see 26:5, 16) should drive readers to ultimate trust in the Lord rather than in themselves (see Commentary on 3:5-8; 28:25-26). The idiom "X in the eyes of P" denotes a person's subjective valuation of something, in contrast to someone *else's* valuation. The X slot in the idiom can be variously filled with terms like "good," "right," "wise," "bad," "great," or "pure" (see 12:15; 16:2; 28:11; 30:12). What ultimately matters is how things appear in God's eyes (e.g., Deut 4:25), rather than how things seem in merely human eyes (Judg 17:6; 21:25).

26:13-16. These verses comprise a short collection of sayings on the sluggard, a subclass of fool. It is related to vv. 1-12, for both sections use repetition of a key word and end with a comparative observation about being wise in one's own eyes. The sentences on the sluggard can exist independently (19:24 and 26:15 are near duplicates, as are 22:13 and 26:13), but their conjunction makes a larger, more humorous statement (see Commentary on 6:6-11; 24:30-34). In v. 13, the sluggard cannot get out of the house; in the next verse he (the Hebrew is masc.) cannot even make it out of bed; in the third, all the tossing and turning in bed has made him too weary to eat. He turns like a door tied to its hinges, but he will not open the door, for fear a lion might be walking the street. Yet, he thinks himself wiser than seven who can render a commonsense account of things. Thus he places himself under the judgment of v. 12. The seven may be an allusion to the proverbial seven wise men of antiquity. Laziness can thwart talent, position, wealth, and power.

Sluggards stand in need of wisdom (6:6); in contrast to the wise son (10:4-5), they do not obey the order of the seasons (6:6; 20:4) but reject reality (22:13; 26:13). In vv. 6, 12, and 16 (see also 10:26), "fool" and "sluggard" occupy similar semantic positions.

26:17-28. The remainder of the chapter may be divided into four groups of three verses. The section as a whole concerns conflict between neighbors and the behaviors and characters that underlie conflict. Deceit and the duplicity that can exist between the outer and the inner person receive special attention.

26:17-19. The section begins with a vivid, commonsense reminder of what happens when one gets involved in fights that are not one's own (see Commentary on 25:9). One might, so to speak, get bitten. The implicit advice is obvious, yet people are notorious for simultaneously diffusing their energies in the business of others while neglecting their own responsibilities. The next two verses compare lying speech to deadly weapons, much in the manner of 25:18. The claim that a damaging lie was only a jest adds insult to injury.

26:20-22. These verses continue reflection on the power of words to create conflict, but begins this passage's movement toward exposing the inner malice that is the source of deception. The word *whisperer* translates a root (רגן *rgn*) that includes malicious gossip, but goes beyond it. The word suggests a wrongful verbal attempt to damage the rights, reputation, or authority of another in order to achieve one's own ends (see 16:28; 18:8; Deut 1:27; Ps 106:25; Isa 29:24). Falsehood, slander, gossip, distortion of reality—these are the fuel of interpersonal conflagration. Verse 21 accents the parallel of "fire" and "quarrelsome person" with a pun (אשׁ־אישׁ *'eš- 'îš*). Verse 22 continues the topic of the whisperer, but moves it toward the next trio of verses, with their focus on the hidden, inner dimensions of conflict (see Commentary on the duplicate in 18:8).

26:23-25. The contrast between the (hidden) inner and the (visible) outer person is basic to biblical wisdom. Here it appears in the contrast respectively of lips/lips/speech with heart/within/heart (so the Hebrew; see Excursus, "The 'Heart' in the Old Testament").

914

The "glaze" (v. 23; this translation is based on a putative Ugaritic cognate to an otherwise unknown Hebrew word) is literally "silver dross," which suggests that the shiny surface of the pot is itself corrupt: "All that glitters is not gold." In any case, the gloss on the pot shows the superficiality and malice of "fervent" (lit., "burning" [דלקים *dōlĕqîm*]; see 16:27) lips disguising a corrupt heart. (The NRSV's smooth is an unnecessary emendation similar to "flattering" in v. 26.) Enemies use the power of speech to hide their true intentions and character (see 6:14; 12:20; 26:26; Ps 62:4; Jer 9:8). Wise folk see through the facade of hypocricy, withhold trust, and do not take liars at face value. For "seven abominations," see Commentary on 11:1 (cf. Matt 12:45).

26:26-28. These verses expose inner hatred as the source of duplicitous, hurtful behavior (see Commentary on 10:12, 18), but affirm the act-consequence scheme of just recompense. Verse 27 uses traditional images to show that "what goes around, comes around" (see Eccl 10:8; Sir 27:25-26, 29). The psalms make clear that when people (individuals or nations) dig a hole to harm others and fall into it themselves, God's justice is at work (Pss 7:15-16; 9:15-16; 35:7-8). The image of the rolling stone suggests that things we set in motion assume a life of their own, beyond our control. The logic of the three conjoined verses is much like Ps 28:3-5. Our translations correctly see that v. 26 is connected with v. 25, but provide verbal connectors that are stronger than the Hebrew warrants. Verse 28 is linguistically difficult; the NIV comes close to a viable literal rendering of the Hebrew. "Those it hurts" is literally "those it crushes."[287] In line with the logic of v. 27, v. 28*b* may mean that "a slick mouth works its own ruin." "Flattering" (חלק *hālāq*) is literally "slick" or "smooth," with connotations of falsity.

287. See Van Leeuwen, *Context and Meaning in Proverbs 25–27*, 112n5.

REFLECTIONS

1. "Honor" (or "glory") designates one's place in society (26:1, 8). It encompasses such things as power, authority, position, office, prerogatives, and even wealth (see Commentary on 11:16; 12:8; and on 13:18 for honor and shame). God (Mal 1:6), kings (Ps 21:6), rulers (Gen 45:13), as well as ordinary men and women—all have a glory that is proper to them (3:35; 11:16; 15:33; 18:12; 20:3; 27:18; 29:23; Sir 10:23-24, 27-31). Paul even argues, on the basis of the diversity of "kinds" in God's original creation, that in the age to come each person and creature will have a glory proper to it (1 Cor 15:35-49).[288]

Proverbs 26:1 is an ancient version of the "Peter Principle," in which persons are promoted to their level of incompetence. When persons who are not gifted, trained, or "fit" for a particular position of power, responsibility, and authority are nonetheless given that position, damage results (see 26:6, 8, 10).[289] This is true of musicians without a sense of pitch, of basketball players without depth perception, and of preachers without faith or morals. The principle of giving honor only to those to whom honor is due (Rom 13:7) is especially crucial in the sphere of government (Prov 29:1, 12; Eccl 4:13; 10:5-7). The allocation of honor (including wealth) is a key indicator of a society's true values. When a society showers wealth and adulation on sports figures and entertainment celebrities without morals and underpays those who educate their children, something is desperately wrong with that society's value system. Proverbs 26:1 implies that Christians must respect the diversity of gifts in the body of Christ and in society at large. But it also condemns us for giving glory to fools.

288. See Raymond C. Van Leeuwen, "Christ's Resurrection and the Creation's Vindication," in Calvin B. DeWitt, ed., *The Environment and the Christian* (Grand Rapids: Baker, 1991) 57-71.

289. See "Ankhsheshonq" 5.1, in Lichtheim, *Ancient Egyptian Literature*, 3:163-64.

2. Proverbs 26:7, 9 raises the problem of practical hermeneutics or interpretation. It is not enough to read and understand proverbs rightly. One must also rightly "read" life situations, persons, and events in order to use the sayings fittingly. A proverb's wisdom is useless unless it is used at the right time, in the right way, with regard to persons and circumstances that correspond to the saying. When this happens, a situation or problem is suddenly illuminated. The wise have a sense of appropriate context, of what times and circumstances require (Eccl 3:1-8).

This wisdom principle may be applied more broadly to the problem of biblical interpretation. An old adage says that "the devil can quote Scripture for his own ends." Because Scripture presents the most varied circumstances and situations over a great span of cultures and history, one cannot simply pick and choose from the Bible as one pleases. The reader of the Bible needs a sense of the whole—and of the parts. Only a knowledge of the "whole counsel of God" can enable the church to recognize and understand its present circumstances in the light of the appropriate biblical analogies and principles. God's word to discouraged slaves in Egypt, for example, may not fit white male, tenured, well-paid academics.

Proverbs 26:1-12 requires that readers interpret the text, themselves, others, and their present world rightly. But it is not true, as some postmodern folk suggest, that everything is interpretation. There can be quite different, equally valid performances of a Beethoven sonata with regard to tempo, dynamics, phrasing, room acoustics, etc. Yet, if Beethoven wrote G sharp, it is not interpretation to play F sharp! It is simply wrong. On the other hand, some interpretations can be note perfect—but all wrong, because the reading does not "fit" the composer's style or "spirit," however difficult that may be to explain. Of jazz, they say, "It don't mean a thing if it ain't got that swing."

The all too human conflict of interpretations often arises regarding situations that are ambiguous (26:4-5), that lie on the fringes and margins of things. The conflict also arises when human action or insight requires that we have a right sense of both the whole (a worldview, if you will) and the particulars that lie before us. Wisdom requires that we see reality rightly regarding both the overall patterns of existence and the individual circumstances before us, for which we are responsible.

Wisdom and valid interpretation can be distinguished from their opposites. Yet Proverbs insists that human wisdom is not omniscient (26:4-5, 12). None of us transcends reality, to "know it all" from above. We see the world only from below, from that small place where we stand, and our vision is blurred by sin and finitude. Thus, as Calvin argued, we need Scripture as the lens through which we can clearly see the difference between non-negotiable boundaries and truths of reality (G sharp, not F sharp; Yahweh, not Baal) and those legitimate areas of interpretation where wisdom and insight are called into play.

Proverbs 27:1-22, On Friendship and Paradox

COMMENTARY

The twenty-two proverbs here gathered are the last in the first half of the Hezekian collection (see Commentary on 25:1), and they have much the character of a proverb miscellany. Two topics do receive emphasis, however: friendship and paradoxical twists in human relations. The proverbs of this section are generally joined as pairs, but in some instances they are connected in "leap-frog" or "plaited" fashion, with one saying linked to the second saying following (see also Proverbs 29). The poem in 27:23-27 rounds off the subcollection; compare the poems in 23:29-35; 24:30-34; and 31:10-31, which ends the entire book.

27:1-2. These verses are linked by a common term; in Hebrew, "praise" and "boast" are the same word (הלל *hālal*). Verse 1 sounds much like Ecclesiastes, with its pervasive focus on the limits of human life and knowledge. The advice (an admonition with motive) is obvious and has parallels in many societies. For instance, "Don't count your chickens before they hatch." Yet we frequently ignore such obvious common sense. The proverb in 1 Kgs 20:11, with its surrounding narrative, gives similar advice in the context of preparing for battle: "One who puts on armor should not brag like one who takes it off" (NRSV). Confidence regarding the future must be realistic, modest, and grounded in the fear of the Lord (31:25, 30; see Commentary on 20:24). Only God is master of the future (16:1, 9; Jas 4:13-17). Thus Jeremiah urges the wise, the mighty, and the rich to boast only in knowing Yahweh (Jer 9:23-24; for "knowing" God, see Jer 22:13-16).

Verse 2 is another "obvious" admonition. It, too, is routinely ignored by people who may be insecure, feel undervalued, or are vain and proud—perhaps all at the same time. This admonition gives no grounds for the advice, but a little observation shows how much people resent others who are "full of themselves" or who "toot their own horn." Self-praise is generally counterproductive. On the other hand, some Christian bodies fail to affirm their various, diverse members, perhaps for fear of "making" others proud (see Commentary on 12:8). In such communities mutual praise grows silent and unity of spirit flags. The words here for "another" and "stranger" also describe the "strange" or "foreign" woman (see 2:16 and Reflections at 5:1-23).

27:3-4. Another pair, these verses are linked in form and in presenting a crescendo of emotions culminating in jealousy as the most unbearable (see Gen 49:7). The images of v. 3 generate a paradox: Heavier for humans than stone or sand is the "immaterial" burden of a fool's provocation (see Job 6:2-3; Sir 22:14-15). "Provocation" can also refer to "anger" (see v. 4) and to "grief,"

such as what a foolish youth can give parents (17:25; see 21:19). In v. 4, "jealousy" arises out of an offended, properly exclusive love's being violated (6:34; see 14:30). The rhetorical question, "Who can stand?" expects the answer, "No one."

27:5-6. These verses are a pair of paradoxes on the "tough love" that is sometimes required in faithful relationships. The pair are linked by repetition of the root for "love" (אהב *ʾāhēb*, "friend" in v. 6), so that v. 6 comments on the paradox of v. 5. The word translated "profuse" or "multiplies" (עתר *ʿātar*) is uncertain, but may mean "excessive" in the transferred sense of "false."[290] Kisses from an enemy are the ultimate betrayal (Matt 26:48-50).

27:7-8. Although v. 7 at first glance appears isolated, it shares an alliterative use of נ (*nun*) with v. 8 and continues the sequence of paradoxes. In juxtaposition with v. 8, there may be an allusion here to honey as an erotic metaphor for the "strange" or "foreign woman," whose end is "bitter" (see Commentary on 5:3-4; 9:17; 24:13-14). If this is correct, then vv. 7-8 have been paired editorially (note also the mention of jealousy, love, and kisses in vv. 4-6 and of the foreign woman in v. 13*b* [NRSV margin]; cf. 6:32-34; 7:13, 18). The satisfied husband is content and does not wander like an errant bird from the nest (see 7:19). People controlled by lust or hunger cannot or do not discriminate.

Verse 7 can also stand independently as an astute observation into human behavior and as a suggestive metaphor with many applications: "Appetite is the best pickle," and "Hunger is the best cook." In contrast, the wealthy may have a spoiled appetite. At a deeper level, the inversion of "bitter" and "sweet" serves as a metaphor for moral and spiritual confusion. The wise should be able to tell the two apart, because they know the proper order of things (Isa 5:20-23). In extreme cases, as survivors of war and famine know, all-consuming hunger can utterly confuse human judgments of what is right and what is wrong (see 2 Kgs 6:24-31).

When read as an independent saying, v. 8 evinces a profound regard for human roots in place and history. It has a parallel in

290. Nahum M. Waldman, "A Note on Excessive Speech and Falsehood," *JQR* (1976–77) 142-45.

Isa 16:2-3, which refers to the homelessness of exile ("home" here is lit., "place").

27:9-10. These verses form a pair linked by the key word *friend* (רע *rēaʿ*). The LXX adds "wine" to those things that make the heart glad (see 27:11; Ps 104:15). Wisdom also knows, however, that too much love of good things is folly (see 21:17). The Hebrew of v. 9*b* (ומתק רעהו מעצת-נפש *ûmeteq rēʿēhû mēʿăṣat-nāpeš*) is notoriously difficult. The NRSV thus opts to translate the LXX, which provides a good antithesis to v. 9*a*. There are good reasons for attempting to make sense of the Hebrew, however. The image of sweetness has already appeared in v. 7, in collocation with "appetite"/"soul"/"person" (נפש *nepeš*), a combination also appearing in v. 9*b*. Verse 9*b*, as noted, is also tied to v. 10 through repetition of "friend" (for this term, see Commentary on 17:17-18). The Hebrew may be translated either as in the NIV or as "a friend's sweetness (gladdens) more than one's own counsel," with the verb from v. 9*a* doing double duty.[291] On this reading, "sweetness" refers to a quality of speech or counsel (see 16:21, 24; 24:13-14; Ps 55:14). Some suggest that "sweetness" (מתק *meteq*) actually means "counsel." Thus, "a friend's counsel [with a pun on "sweetness"] is better than one's own advice"—"two heads are better than one." The line remains uncertain.

Verse 10 is an admonition that insists on solidarity both in the extended family and among friends and neighbors (see Commentary on 17:17-18). Although siblings are one's most natural allies, one needs to avoid over-reliance on them or (in the extended sense of "brother") on clan and covenant partners (see 25:16-17). The somewhat unusual addition of a third line (see 25:13) sharpens the point that family alone is not enough for well-being. It observes realistically that a distant brother can do less good than a close neighbor, a thought that partially corroborates the earlier observation on wandering from one's "place" (v. 8).

27:11. This verse concludes the first half of the twenty-two verses (see Commentary on 23:15). Like v. 10, it is an admonition, addressed to "my son" and urging him to be wise (see Commentary on 10:1).

For the expression "makes the heart glad," see Commentary on 27:9. The admonition reflects an intense sense of family solidarity and the mutual pride of the generations in one another (see 17:6). In Israel's patriarchal honor-and-shame culture, one needed to be able to answer those who sought to bring shame on the family (for the idiom, see Ps 119:42). Thus the honor of a "father's house" is preserved.

27:12-13. With minuscule variations, v. 12 duplicates 22:3, and v. 13, another admonition, repeats 20:16. Together these verses may partially spell out what the parent in v. 11 understands a wise son to be. A son who does not look ahead (v. 12) is likely to end up in the predicament described in v. 13. The variant in v. 13*b* refers to the foreign woman, which may be an editorial attempt to connect this passage with chaps. 1–9.

27:14. The focus turns from the "stranger" (v. 13) back to the "neighbor" of v. 10. It portrays a humorous failure of fittingness (see Commentary on 25:20; 26:1-12), where a blessing is received as if it were a curse, because it is delivered at the wrong time ("early in the morning," perhaps a gloss, but see Sir 22:6) or in the wrong manner ("with a loud voice").

27:15-16. Verse 15 is related to a number of sayings on the quarrelsome wife (see Commentary on 21:9, 19; 25:24), and the entire verse is an expansion of 19:13*b* (see vv. 12-13, which are also variants of other sayings). Verse 16, however, has not been satisfactorily explained, though its connection with v. 15 is patent.

27:17. This verse is another saying on friendship, with a leap-frog link to v. 19. The saying is simple and profound with its metallurgical metaphor of sharpening (the translations assume minor repointing of the verbs). "The wits of another" is literally "the face of his friend" (רע *rēaʿ*; see Commentary on 27:9-10). "Face" is puzzling, but it may be explained as a continuation of the metaphor of sharpening, since the working edge of a sword or knife is called its "face" (Eccl 10:10; Ezek 21:21).[292] Another solution is to presume a different root for the second verb and translate, "one man makes the face of his

291. See Van Leeuwen, *Context and Meaning in Proverbs 25–27*, 124.

292. Whybray, *Proverbs*, 384.

friend glad" (cf. 15:13a for a similar idiom).[293] But this damages the parallel and point of the sharpening metaphor.

27:18. The writer assumes that every person has an honor or glory appropriate to his or her calling, no matter how humble, and that faithful service receives its reward. Often this is an increase in status and responsibility, as in the well-known stories of Joseph and Daniel in foreign courts. See the Commentary on 26:1 for the meaning of "honor" and its social misapplication.

27:19. This saying is a somewhat cryptic, non-verbal sentence; lit., "as water, the face to the face, so the man's heart to the man." The translators have supplied "reflects," assuming that it or something similar is implicit. The translations of v. 19b reveal the major interpretative problem in the verse. Does a man's heart (see Excursus, "The 'Heart' in the Old Testament") reflect the man (האדם hā'ādām) to himself (NIV)? On this reading, one comes to self-knowledge by internal

293. Meinhold, *Die Sprüche*, 2:455.

self-examination. Or does one heart reflect another person's heart (NRSV)? The latter reading is preferable, because it reinforces the link in form and meaning with v. 17 and the theme of friendship, which dominates this section.

27:20. This verse is simple but deep. For "Sheol" and "Abaddon," see Commentary on 15:11. The grave is never satisfied or filled with the generations of the dead; it never says, "Enough" (30:15b-16).

27:21-22. Both sayings concern the possibility of personal refinement. Verse 21 forms an envelope on "praise"/"boasting" with vv. 1-2 (see also 12:8; 31:30). It uses a metallurgical image to portray the process by which persons are tested. Verse 21a is a duplicate of 17:3, but v. 21b heads in another direction. The thought seems to be that praise is a test of a person's mettle. Will it "go to one's head," or will the person remain even-keeled with realistic self-assessment (11:2)? Verse 22 uses the image of a mortar and a pestle to show the impossibility of separating fools from their folly.

REFLECTIONS

1. "Open rebuke" may be the means by which a true friend wounds a loved one, as a surgeon wounds a patient to do good in the end (27:5-6; see 28:23; Deut 8:16). Rebuke can be given and received in a spirit of wisdom (13:18; 15:31-32; 25:12). Though painful, it is better than hidden love, which remains useless, like some treasure buried in a field (Matt 13:44; 25:25). It is not just the thought that counts. Rather, if actions speak louder than words, then they speak immeasurably louder than mere thoughts. Love must manifest itself in wise, appropriate action, because we humans are embodied creatures, made of earth and air. To assert that only one's heart or soul matters is a form of gnosticism that devalues God's good creation. It is true that Paul championed faith without works, but he did so only to assert the indispensability and sufficiency of grace. Nonetheless, Paul also insisted on faith with works, endurance based in hope, and love that labors and suffers in concrete, visible ways (1 Thess 1:3; cf. Rom 5:1-5). The paradox of Prov 27:5-6 is explored in Shakespeare's great tragedy *King Lear*. Though even his fool knows better, Lear prefers false flattery to Cordelia's silent, but honest, love.

2. To stray or wander away can have a variety of causes (27:8; Sir 29:18-28; 39:4). In the biblical story, Cain is the first to wander the earth (Gen 4:12-16). Cut off from the roots that nourish us (geography, family, nation, culture, and community), we are diminished. In these realities, we find our home, our work, our vocation, our blessing. The rootlessness of modern life is an affliction all the more acute because we often suffer it unawares and confuse it with freedom. And yet, Abraham left his home to find a new home, a new city whose maker and builder was God (Gen 12:1-3; Heb 11:8-10).

A basic tension of human life is that we are earthlings, made from the earth (Gen 2:7); and yet we have no abiding home here, until all things will be made new in a new creation in which "righteousness is at home" (2 Pet 3:13).

3. Friendship is a major concern of Proverbs 27. Verse 17 focuses on the sharpening effect friends have on one another, presumably because they are not afraid to exercise tough love (27:5-6). Verse 19 treats a related aspect of friendship, the mutuality of self-knowledge and knowledge of the other. We know ourselves as we know, and are known by, others. The self refracted through another self becomes richer and is more clearly seen. Through such a dialectic of personal knowledge, two souls can be knit together in love (1 Sam 18:1-4). In another cultural setting, Aristotle observed that the good person relates to a friend as to oneself, for a friend is "another self."[294] This mutuality of hearts and souls should not be restricted to voluntary friendship. It is utterly essential to the state of being one flesh in marriage. On a much larger scale, when God renews the chosen people, they will be given "one heart and one way" (Jer 32:39 NRSV).

4. The comparison of Sheol to the insatiable human eye (27:20) should give pause on two counts. The Preacher says that the eye is never satisfied with riches (Eccl 4:8; see 1:8), even though death is inescapable. More than that, it is as if the eye feeds on death, and this may be the main point. The "lust of the eyes" (1 John 2:16 NKJV) turns the good things of creation into something deadly to the self. Advertising in our industrial-capitalistic society ceaselessly stimulates visual desire and promotes unwearying covetousness of things and persons (as objects for sex or control). Delitzsch quotes an old Arab proverb, "Nothing fills the eyes of man but at last the dust of the grave."[295]

294. Aristotle *Nicomachean Ethics*, 1166a30.
295. Delitzsch, *Proverbs*, 216.

Proverbs 27:23-27, On Tending One's Flocks

COMMENTARY

This brief poem may be read in a straightforward fashion as an exhortation to care for one's flocks and to work hard in the fields, with the reward of good provision for family and household (cf. 24:30-34). Yet, sayings and admonitions are designed for application beyond their ostensive reference, as the agricultural proverb in v. 18b shows. (Cf. also the wisdom poem in Isa 28:23-29, which uses agricultural imagery to illustrate Yahweh's fitting action in history.) Several factors suggest that this poem has a royal reference in its present context. In particular, the reference in v. 24b to a crown (often emended to "treasure") implies an oblique address to the king or ruler as metaphorical "shepherd" of the people.[296] The metaphor of the king as shepherd was widespread in the ancient

296. Van Leeuwen, *Context and Meaning in Proverbs 25–27*, 131-43. Cf. Bruce V. Malchow, "A Manual for Future Monarchs," *CBQ* 47 (1985) 238-45, esp. 243-45.

world, including Israel (cf. Psalm 23). Also, the poem's setting in the Hezekian collection naturally connects it with the royal concerns of 25:1-15 and of chaps. 28–29. Moreover, the references to riches, servants, and the purchase of a field all convey a social setting at the upper reaches of society (as does the related poem in 31:10-31).

A good shepherd knows the condition (lit., "face" in the sense of "appearance") or "soul" of his animals and cares for them appropriately (see Commentary on 12:10; the LXX supplies "soul" in v. 23). Such diligence leads to the well-being of all that belongs to the shepherd. Finally, the poem's general interest in domestic economy and the close relation of v. 27b to 31:15b suggest that there may be a redactional relation between these two poems. In this regard, it is striking that "servant girls" appears only in v. 27 and in 9:3 and 31:15.

REFLECTIONS

Whether applied to a landholder or to a ruler, this little poem (27:23-27) reminds all people that God has given them a quasi-royal responsibility for a bit of this earth (see Reflections at 15:1-33). Our stewardship requires that we know intimately those things, creatures, and persons entrusted to our care (27:23). Governments need to understand the people, the land, and justice. Teachers need to know and love their students and their subjects. Workers and artists need to know their materials and their craft. Pastors ("shepherds" in the religious sense!) also need to know and tend their "flocks." Those in authority should not exercise power for their own glory or ego, but for the good of those persons and things entrusted to them. The quiet warning of this poem is that those who abuse their little kingdoms lose them (27:24), but those who work the earth with wisdom (note the rhythm of the seasons, 27:25; see also Commentary on 10:4-5) enjoy its fruits (27:26-27).

PROVERBS 28:1–29:27, ON JUSTICE AND TORAH

OVERVIEW

Scholars have long seen that the second Solomonic collection (Proverbs 25–29) falls into two parts, with the poem in 27:23-27 marking the divide. While the poem has often been seen as the conclusion to chaps. 25–27, which began with a focus on kingship, some have argued that it introduces chaps. 28–29 as "A Manual for Future Monarchs." What is clear is that these chapters represent a return to the antithetical proverb style of chaps. 10–15, with a similar emphasis on the opposition of "righteous" and "wicked." As Malchow has shown, the thematic character of this opposition in the sub-collection is apparent from the close linkage in thought and vocabulary in four significant verses where it occurs (28:12, 28; 29:2, 16).[297] In addition, the rhetorically important beginning and end of the sub-collection (28:1; 29:27) also employ this opposition. Although 29:7 stands outside the central group of four, it shares their opposition of "righteous" and "wicked" (here singular) and the pervasive concern in these chapters for just rule. Although the two key words are not often repeated, the various characters that appear in these chapters embody the two opposed life-styles.

Another repeated thematic term is תורה (tôrâ). While the word in wisdom contexts often refers to the "instruction" or "teaching" of the wise (1:8; 3:1; 4:2; 7:2), it is also used of God's "instruction." In chaps. 28–29, tôrâ always appears in the absolute form (28:4 twice, 7, 9; 29:18), without specifying whose teaching it is (see Commentary on 6:23, the only other absolute occurrence of tôrâ in Proverbs). While teaching is no doubt mediated by humans, it is likely that the primary reference here is to God's instruction or law, as the NIV and the NRSV translations consistently render it (see Commentary on 28:9). God's law includes the Mosaic law (Genesis–Deuteronomy), but is not limited to it. It should be remembered that the Mosaic books contain not only guidance for moral living and Israelite worship, but also stories that instruct us concerning the gracious character of God and the purpose of human life—as Paul recognized (1 Cor 10:1-13). Though the explicit use of the Mosaic books in Proverbs is not frequent, occurrences should not be ignored (e.g., see Commentary on 16:4-5; 17:15; 18:5; 25:18; 28:8; perhaps 28:1). In a wider sense, tôrâ refers to all of God's instruction, grounded in creation and discovered in history, however such instruction is mediated

297. See Malchow, "A Manual for Future Monarchs"; and Meinhold, *Die Sprüche,* 2:464-65.

(see Isa 28:23-28; and the Torah piety of the psalms, esp. 1; 19; 119; cf. Sir 24:23).[298]

298. See Levenson, "The Sources of Torah"; and J. Clinton McCann, Jr., Commentary on the Book of Psalms, in *The New Interpreter's Bible Commentary*, vol. 3 (Nashville: Abingdon, 2015) 286-95, and 304-5 on Ps 1:2.

Thus Proverbs 28–29 distinguish righteous and wicked, teach pious obedience to God's instruction, and urge justice among citizens and rulers. In short, they contain the key elements necessary for a healthy society.

Proverbs 28:1-28, Torah, the Righteous, and the Wicked

COMMENTARY

28:1. The wicked person is out of touch with reality, just as fools and sluggards are (17:16, 24; 26:11, 13). Verse 1*a* may allude to Lev 26:17, 36, where God's face is set against wicked Israel: "You will flee even when no one is pursuing you. . . . I will make their hearts so fearful . . . that the sound of a windblown leaf will put them to flight." This suggests that beneath the bold facade of wickedness stirs an uneasy conscience. Even the wicked have a suppressed awareness of divinely ordained right and wrong and the consequences of each (cf. Rom 1:18-20; 2:12-15). "Are bold" is better translated as "are confident." This confidence is based on trust (the usual translation of the verb בטח *bāṭaḥ*) in the Lord and God's Word (see Commentary on 3:5; 16:20; 28:25-26). The lion is the "king of beasts" who has no need to fear (19:12; 30:29-30). On the opposition of "wicked" and "righteous," see Commentary on 17:15.

28:2. "Rulers" translates a term (שר *śar*) that can refer to a variety of government officials, from judge to general to prince. Cohen cites a proverbial Arabic curse, "May God make your sheiks many!"[299] The saying is one of several that explore the well-being of the body politic and the correlation between authorities and those subject to them (vv. 12, 28; 29:2, 4). Land (ארץ *'ereṣ*) is the created environment for society; here it includes the people who live on it (29:4; 30:21; Amos 7:10). The moral-religious health of the people has an impact on the natural order (Jer 3:1; Joel 3:18-20; Amos 1:2).[300] In Hosea's

299. A. Cohen, *Proverbs: Hebrew Text and English Translation with Introduction and Commentary*, The Soncino Bible (London: Soncino, 1945) 185-86.
300. See H. H. Schmid, "Creation, Righteousness, and Salvation: 'Creation Theology' as the Broad Horizon of Biblical Theology," in Anderson, *Creation in the Old Testament*, 102-17; Ronald A. Simkins, *Creator and Creation: Nature in the Worldview of Ancient Israel* (Peabody, Mass.: Hendrickson, 1994); Knierim, "Cosmos and History in Israel's Theology."

day in the rebellious north, rulers were multiplied in serial fashion, through murder (Hos 4:2-3; 7:3-7; 8:4). Verse 2*b* is unclear; the NIV gives a fairly literal translation, taking כן (*kēn*) in the infrequent sense of "order" or "right" (see Commentary on 15:7).

28:3. This verse is clear and direct; it gives the converse of Psalm 72. The word *ruler* here (רש *rāš*) is different from that in v. 2, and it requires a repointing of the consonants that otherwise mean "poor." Scholars generally make this minor emendation to fit with v. 2, because the Bible does not emphasize that the poor can oppress one another. Yet city life all over shows that the poor can prey on the poor. A driving rain can destroy the grain (cf. 26:1).

28:4-5. Here the absolute use of *tôrâ* ("law" or "teaching") appears twice to announce another thematic key word in this subsection (see Overview and Commentary on 6:20-23). The search for Yahweh in v. 5 reminds the reader that the norms for human existence cannot be separated from God (cf. v. 9). These verses divide humanity into two camps: those who seek God and those who do not. This human division is most clearly manifested in the responses people make to the divine law. Some obediently keep it; some forsake and reject it; some seek God and understand justice (see 1 Cor 2:14-16); but others oppress the poor (v. 3). In lawless times, love becomes difficult to maintain (Matt 24:12), and the conflict between the godly and the lawless becomes more evident (v. 4*b*; see Reflections on Prov 11:1-31). In his catalog of sins, Paul takes up the idea that the lawless praise the wicked (Rom 1:32).

Although rulers are not mentioned, the saying in v. 5 has obvious relevance to them (see vv. 2-3). Without justice in human relations and society, there is no true knowledge of God (see 29:7; Jer 22:13-16). Conversely, to seek God without seeking social justice is an exercise in bad faith (Amos 5:46, 14-15).

28:6. This verse is a variant of 19:1. The repetition of the consonants רשׁ (*rš*) in vv. 3-6 (inverted in v. 5) links this verse to its context. This repetition also emphasizes the words *poor* and *wicked*, since both words begin with these same consonants. The rich may be tempted to misunderstand justice and so to be crooked in their ways (see Mark 10:25). For the paradoxical situations in which poverty is "better than" wealth, see Commentary on 16:8. "Whose ways are perverse" (see 10:9) is literally, "perverse (in regard to) double ways." The dual form is unusual, but see Commentary on 28:18 (see also Sir 2:12, "the sinner who walks along two ways"). In contrast to integrity or unity of heart (Ps 86:11), the Israelites recognized the duplicity of the "double heart" (Ps 12:2) and of limping along a conflicted path of double opinions (1 Kgs 18:21).[301]

28:7. This verse reinforces v. 4 on keeping God's law (see Eccl 12:13) and returns to the theme of the wise or "discerning" son, the opposite of the one who "brings shame" (see Commentary on 10:1, 5, 8). Loose living of various sorts is a perennial theme in wisdom literature of many cultures (see 29:3; Luke 15:13). For the powerful effect of "the company we keep," see Commentary on 13:20.

28:8-9. These verses form a proverb pair. Verse 8 is a clear reference to a consistent biblical legal principle that forbids lending at interest to a fellow Israelite (Exod 22:24; Lev 25:36-37; Deut 23:20; Ps 15:5; Ezek 18:8; 22:12).[302] By translating the Hebrew hendiadys ("interest and increase") as exorbitant interest, the NIV and the NRSV obscure the sociocultural gap between Israel's pre-industrial economy and our modern system of capital investment. The hendiadys apparently refers to interest on money or material goods, such as grain or oil. The OT unanimously forbids lending at interest, in order to protect the poor from exploitation and hunger. This fact led to an intense hermeneutical discussion in the Reformation period, as capital loaned

at interest became necessary for economic development. Recognizing that he lived in a social situation different from that of ancient Israel, John Calvin grudgingly allowed the necessity of lending at interest, but strongly warned against using it to take advantage of the needy.[303] Ezekiel 22:12 includes taking interest in a list of major sins that show that the people have forgotten God, because they do what is displeasing to God. The one who is kind to the poor pleases God, imitates God, and receives a reward (see 13:22; 14:31; 19:17; cf. Pss 111:4-5; 112:4-5).

Verse 9 follows upon v. 8 (with its legal language) to remind the reader that piety without kindness to the poor is hated by God and repudiated in the law. For the logic of the verse, see Commentary on 15:8.

28:10. This verse employs the infrequent triplet form (see 25:13), the third line supplying an antithesis. Its warning against leading others astray is varied in the wisdom teaching of Jesus (Matt 5:19; Luke 17:1-2). The image of falling into the pit one has made is a proverbial expression of poetic justice (see Commentary on 26:27).

28:11. "Rich" and "poor" are contrasted, to the latter's advantage (see Commentary on 16:8), because the poor person has discernment, while the rich person may mistakenly think that wealth automatically confers wisdom (see Commentary on 18:10-11; 26:12). A slang saying also expresses the common assumption that associates wealth and wisdom: "If you're so smart, why aren't you rich?" "Sees through [one]" translates the same verb (חקר *ḥāqar*) used in 18:17*b* and 25:2*b* for "to search" (something or someone) out.

28:12. This is the first of several thematic sayings on the weal or woe of the body politic in relation to the rising or falling of the righteous or the wicked (see Overview; 28:28; 29:2, 16). That righteous folk go into hiding when the wicked rise to power has been a common occurrence throughout history, from the time of Abimelech (Judg 9:5) to the present day. Verse 12*a* is literally, "When the righteous rejoice," presumably in response to the defeat of wicked enemies or some other good (see Commentary on 11:10; cf. Ps 68:1-4).

301. See Alonso-Schökel and Vilchez, *Proverbios*, 485.

302. See John I. Durham, *Exodus*, WBC 3 (Waco, Tex.: Word, 1987) 329; P. C. Craigie, *The Book of Deuteronomy*, NICOT (Grand Rapids: Eerdmans, 1976) 302-3; Moshe Greenberg, *Ezekiel 1–20*, AB 22 (Garden City, N.Y.: Doubleday, 1983) 330.

303. See John Calvin, *Commentary on Exodus*. Calvin's treatment is a masterful demonstration of the inadequacy of literalistic interpretation.

28:13-14. These verses are probably best understood as a couplet, for together they echo vocabulary and themes from Psalm 32, a psalm that ends in a wisdom instruction. As the second of the church's seven "penitential psalms," Psalm 32 (see also Psalms 6; 38; 51; 102; 130; 143) may also be the best OT commentary on these two verses (see also 1 John 1:5-10). Verse 13 contrasts covering up sin—something Job claims not to have done (Job 31:33)—with confessing and forsaking it, and so receiving mercy. One is to understand that such mercy comes from the One whose name is "merciful and gracious . . . forgiving iniquity and transgression and sin" (Exod 34:6-7). Verse 14 pronounces a blessing on the one who always fears; the NIV rightly supplies "the LORD" as the implicit object of fear (see Commentary on 1:7, though 28:14 uses a different root for "fear"). One of the patriarchal names of Israel's God is "the Fear of Isaac" (Gen 31:42). Pharaoh is the classic example of one who stubbornly "hardens his heart" (and has it hardened—a variety of verbs are used), thus buying for himself and his people the trouble of the plagues (Exod 7:3; 9:34; cf. Ps 95:8). In contrast to "hardhearted," the Hebrew idioms of the "hard heart" and the "stiff neck" do not mean cruelty or lack of kindness, but instead "stubbornness," especially against God (29:1; cf. Ps 95:8). A corollary of the hard heart is trust in one's own heart (v. 26).

28:15-16. These verses illustrate v. 12*b* and juxtapose the wicked ruler and the ruler without sense; both treat their subjects cruelly, the first by malice, the second by incompetence (see Commentary on 26:1). The lion and the bear are powerful and dangerous animals (17:12; 22:13), fitting images for rulers, whether good or evil (see 19:12; Dan 7:1-8). In v. 15*b*, the adjective "poor"/"helpless" (דל *dal*) also connotes the powerlessness that attends poverty. Israelite rulers were responsible for justice, the righting of wrongs (2 Sam 14:4-11; 15:1-6). They especially were required to do justice for the poor, who have no earthly defender (see 22:22-23; 23:10-11; 29:4, 14; Psalm 72). For this purpose, God has given these rulers authority and power, and they are accountable to God in their exercise of that power (see Wis 6:1-9;

Rom 13:1-7). For "who hates unjust gain," see Commentary on 15:27.

28:17. Translation of this verse is obscure. Literally, it reads, "If a man is oppressed by life blood, let him [or "he will"] flee to the pit. Do not hold him back [or "support him"]." It is linked to the verses on either side by repetition of the root עשק (*'šq*, "oppress," "do wrong to"). Since the use here of "oppressed" is unique, the NIV and the NRSV give it an extended meaning, "burdened," though this is uncertain. The idea is that one guilty of murder ("blood," see 1:10-19; 12:6; Gen 9:6; Sir 34:21-22) will be "oppressed" by anxiety (see Commentary on 28:1; cf. Job 20:25; Isa 38:14). The verb in v. 17*b* (תמך *tāmak*) can mean either "support" or "hold back."

28:18. Verse 18*b* reads literally, "One twisted (with regard to) double ways will fall by one (of them)." "Pit" is a variant reading of "one," based on the Syriac (see Commentary on 10:9; 19:1; 28:6).

28:19. But for its ending, this verse is a duplication of 12:11. Note the implicit contrast with v. 20.

28:20. In an agrarian context, the contrast of a faithful person and one "in a hurry to get rich" (see 29:22) implies that haste in acquiring wealth involves skullduggery, unlike the honest work of the diligent farmer (v. 19). "Blessing" is often associated with fertility of land, animals, and humans (see 10:3-7; Gen 1:22, 28).[304] While Proverbs warns against the too zealous pursuit of wealth (13:11; 20:21; 23:4-5), it also notes that wealth can be a blessing from God (10:22).

28:21. Verse 21*b* is perhaps hyperbole designed to show how little it takes to get a person to sin. The saying refers to bribery (see Commentary on 17:23), and it fits well between vv. 20 and 22 as an example of getting money too hastily (see Commentary on 18:5; 24:23).

28:22. The "miserly" person is literally "bad of eye," apparently an idiom for a greedy person (see Commentary on 23:6). For the idea that the wicked do not know the consequences of their actions, see 7:23; 9:13, 18. In a more comprehensive way, Ecclesiastes develops the limits of all human knowledge

---

304. C. Westermann, *Blessing in the Bible and the Life of the Church* (Philadephia: Fortress, 1978).

as a major theme (see Prov 27:1; see also Commentary on 13:4; 20:21).

28:23. This verse should be compared to 9:8; 19:25; and 27:5-6. The emphasis is on the difference time makes. At first the pain of reproof may provoke a negative reaction. Its good results may appear only later. For "flattery," see Commentary on 7:5; 29:5.

28:24. In Israel, an adult male who took what belonged to his parents—when they were no longer able to defend themselves—might claim that there was no sin involved. After all, what is theirs is (eventually) his by right of inheritance (19:14). In this case, a sinful rationalization ignores the role of time and circumstance in determining what is right. A similar violation of this principle appears in the prodigal son's wish to have his inheritance before his father has died (Luke 15:11-32).[305] Such actions stand under the judgment of 19:26 and 20:21. The teaching of Jesus in Mark 7:10-13 also deals with a hypocritical avoidance of obligation to parents. "One who destroys" is more accurate than "a thug" (see 18:9b).

28:25-26. This proverb pair is linked by the middle lines, which contrast one who "trusts in the LORD" with one who trusts in oneself (lit., "in his own heart"). The latter trust is a form of being "wise in one's own eyes" (26:12; 28:11). For the concepts here, see Commentary on 1:7; 3:5-8; and Excursus, "The 'Heart' in the Old Testament." The antithetical structure of the sayings implies that those who trust in God will not

be greedy (see 28:20, 22, 24). Trust in God frees people from the compulsive drive to find security in material goods and power. Acquisitive greed causes conflict, because it robs the neighbor's little "kingdom" (23:10-11) in its anxious drive to expand its own. Literally, the greedy are "wide of throat/appetite"; like Sheol, they are ready to swallow up their neighbors whole (see 1:12). Paradoxically, those who trust in God are enriched (lit., "made fat," v. 25b, a symbol of well-being in the subsistence world of the ancient Near East; cf. 11:25; 16:20). Trust and "walking in wisdom" (or "integrity") go together and have similar results (see v. 18a; 29:25b).

28:27. The paradox of giving to the poor and having no lack is characteristic of one whose trust is in God (v. 25; see Commentary on 11:24; 22:16). Turning a blind eye is akin to shutting one's ear to the cry of the poor (see Commentary on 21:13).

28:28. This verse (with v. 12; 29:2, 16) is thematic for chaps. 28–29 (see Overview). Verse 28b is a variant of v. 12b. In the present verse, a pun between "people" (אדם *ʾādām*) and "they perish" (אבדם *ʾobdām*) links the two lines and accents human mortality. This verse, with its thematic companions, links the weal or woe of common people and society to the ascendancy of the righteous or the wicked respectively. The righteous increase in the sense that they thrive, "as do plants, when the worms, caterpillars, and the like are destroyed."[306] (See Reflections at Proverbs 29:1-27.)

---

305. See Kenneth E. Bailey, *Poet and Peasant & Through Peasant Eyes* (Grand Rapids: Eerdmans, 1976/1987) 158-206.

306. Delitzsch, "Proverbs," 240.

Proverbs 29:1-27, More on Torah, the Righteous, and the Wicked

COMMENTARY

29:1. The opening saying is reminiscent of Lady Wisdom's warnings in 1:25, 30 about the calamity that comes to those who stubbornly refuse to listen to (her) wise counsel and rebuke (also 13:18; 15:10; cf. 28:23). Verse 1b replicates 6:15b, where the villain of 6:12 receives his fate. To be "stiff-necked" is a common idiom for stubborn rebellion

toward one who deserves obedience. Thus when Israel rebels against Yahweh, their new covenant Lord, they are stiff-necked (Exod 32:9-10; cf. Jer 7:25-26; 17:23). This saying illustrates the patience of the reprover and the persistence of the rebel, for the rebukes are multiple. As Delitzsch notes, "The door of penitence, to which earnest, well-meant admonition calls a man, does not always remain open."[307] Individuals can finally be broken beyond healing, but so can nations (Jer 19:10-11).

29:2. Here is another thematic verse on the weal or woe of the body politic in relation to righteous and wicked rulers (see Commentary on 28:12-28; 29:16). Here the emphasis is respectively on the joy people feel when right has the upper hand and the acute suffering of ordinary people when wrong reigns. Our century has illustrated both sides of this proverb, though one wonders if the second line does not predominate (see Commentary on 11:10-11 and Reflections on Proverbs 11:1-31).

29:3. The saying applies to all people (10:1; 28:7), but in the context of vv. 2 and 4, it may apply especially to the royal son (see 31:3). The contrast between "loves wisdom" and the illicit love of prostitutes (6:26) evokes the pervasive symbolism of chaps. 1–9, which associates the love of wisdom or folly with love of wife or the "strange woman" (see Overview on 1:1–9:18).

29:4. This verse is a specific illustration of v. 2. "Justice" (משפט *mišpāṭ*) is a word whose range of meaning includes "customary [and thus normative] practice," "law," and the giving of justice within and outside of the law court (see 29:14).[308] Lit., the king's justice "makes the land stand (firm)." "Country" (ארץ *'ereṣ*) or, rather, "land," also means "earth," and the cosmic overtones of the word should not be ruled out here. Social injustice leads to cosmic catastrophe (see Commentary on 30:21-23), but justice leads to blessing and a fruitful earth (see Psalms 65; 72).[309] The alternative translations, "who makes heavy exactions" (NRSV) or "who is greedy for bribes" (NIV), each interprets a unique Hebrew phrase, lit., "a man of gifts." The difficulty is that gift (תרומה *tĕrûmâ*) is a term that elsewhere consistently refers to sacral contributions. NIV understands a ruler or judge who takes bribes; NRSV suggests a ruler whose taxes are extreme. In either case, the issue is the government's misuse of income (perhaps intended for the sanctuary?) in a way that compromises its responsibility

to do justice. For "tears it down," see the same verb in 11:11; 14:1.

29:5. The NIV better captures the ambiguity of the masculine gender Hebrew: Is the flatterer spreading a net for his own feet or for his neighbor's? The next verse suggests that, while the net is intended for the neighbor, it actually snares the flatterer (see 1:17-19; Pss 9:15-16; 57:6). For "flatterer," see Commentary on 26:28.

29:6. Verse 6a ("snare") picks up on the previous verse; the thought is similar to 12:13. Verse 6b conveys the joy of those who escape from trouble (cf. Ps 67:5; Jer 31:7; Zech 2:10). Because the connection of the two lines is not entirely obvious, some scholars emend "sing" (ירון *yārûn*) to "run" (ירוץ *yārûṣ*; i.e., free of trouble) and are glad (cf. 4:12; 18:10).

29:7. "Know" here refers to active, caring concern, as is clear from 12:10 and 27:23. The just have compassion even for their cattle; how much more for their fellow humans, who are sometimes treated worse than beasts.[310] "Rights" (a term laden with modern, Enlightenment connotations) does not quite capture the sense of the Hebrew, which is closer to "cause" in a legal dispute (see Commentary on 23:10-11). The "knowing" of the righteous entails that they defend and rescue the poor from the powerful who have wronged them (see Commentary on 24:10-12). This happens especially in juridical but also in other ways.[311] Verse 7b is not entirely clear; lit., "a wicked person does not understand knowledge." Our translations convey the general sense.

29:8. The writer provides here another political observation. The Hebrew phrase underlying scoffers appears also in Isa 28:14, where it refers to rulers who have filled Jerusalem with lies—until that time when God will make justice and righteousness the standard (Isa 28:17; cf. Prov 29:12). Wrongdoers set the city on fire with conflict (see 26:18-21; Sir 28:8-12). It takes the wise to restore order and peace (see Commentary on 15:1-2).

29:9. This verse presents one of a number of reasons for the advice in 26:4: "Do not answer a fool according to his folly" (NIV).

307. Delitzsch, "Proverbs," 240.
308. See Weinfeld, *Social Justice in Ancient Israel and in the Ancient Near East*, for these terms.
309. Schmid, *Gerechtigkeit als Weltordnung*.
310. See Delitzsch, "Proverbs," 245.
311. Weinfeld, *Social Justice in Ancient Israel and in the Ancient Near East*, 44-49.

The general point is to avoid conflict, especially with fools, if possible (see also 13:20; 14:7; 26:17-19). NIV supplies "fool" as subject in the second line (probably rightly, see 29:11); NRSV renders the verbs impersonally. Because v. 9*b* lacks an explicit subject, some translations identify the subject as the "wise" person: "he [the wise man] may rage or laugh but can have no peace" (NAB).

29:10. Verse 10*b* is difficult and uncertain. At first glance, it means "and the upright [pl.] seek his life" (i.e., to kill him), which makes no sense. This has led to a number of emendations. NRSV and NIV have the advantage of not modifying the text.[312] The issue is the murderous rancor that the wicked have toward the good. For descriptions of the "bloodthirsty" (lit., "men of blood"), see Pss 26:9-10; 139:19-20.

29:11. The reading of NRSV is closer to the Hebrew than is the NIV, for the object of "holds it back" is "anger" (lit., "spirit," cf. Eccl 10:4), not the person. The restraining of rampant emotion is a frequent theme in Proverbs; it separates the wise from the foolish (12:16; 14:17; 15:1-2, 18; 16:32 18:2; cf. Sir 20:7; 21:26).

29:12. Citizens, like children, will generally do what they are permitted to do. Here the abdication of the ruler's responsibility leads to the corruption of his officials, with the consequent ruination of the land (29:4; see Commentary on 17:4). Psalm 101, as a "mirror for princes," demonstrates the care with which a righteous king chooses his servants. A king must search out the truth of things and judge accordingly (14:35; 25:2). Sirach 10:1-4 provides a generalized form of this saying with commentary.

29:13. This verse is a variant of 22:2, but the juxtaposition of "poor" and "oppressor" adds sharpness to the theology of this saying. The point is that God judges those who wrong the poor (see Commentary on 14:31). "Gives light to the eyes" is the same as giving life and the joy of life, because "to see light" means to live (see Job 3:16; Pss 13:4; 38:10; 49:19; cf. Prov 15:30).

29:14. This verse outlines one of the basic duties of government: the protection and defense of the poor from those stronger than they (Ps 72:4; Isa 11:4; Jer 22:16). This protection lies at the heart of royal "justice and righteousness"[313] and gives stability to the king's throne or government and to the land (see Commentary on 16:12; 25:5; cf. 28:2, 15-16; 29:2, 4).

29:15-21. Delitzsch notes that vv. 15-18 alternate the topics of household and people.[314] In the ancient world, relations in marriage and family, between masters and servants, and in the body politic were generally conceived as parallel hierarchical structures, a fact still evident in the so-called domestic codes of the NT (Rom 13:1-7; Titus 2:1-3, 8; 1 Pet 3:13-22; see Commentary on 30:21-23).[315] The pattern seen by Delitzsch may be extended as far as v. 21, for v. 15 is linked, leap-frog fashion, with 29:17, 19, 21, all of which concern the discipline of sons or servants. Verses 19 and 20 reflect on two of the many functions of words.

29:15. For the context of this verse, both cultural and literary, see Commentary on 13:1; 23:13. The ancient oriental mode of corporal punishment is presupposed (see Commentary on 13:24). The proverb warns of "permissive" child rearing, for it assumes that children need to be trained because what is right and wise does not always come to them "naturally" (22:15). Sirach expands this saying and renders it more severe (Sir 22:3-6; 30:1-13).

29:16-17. Verse 16 is similar to 10:19, though the cause of transgression is different in each case. This verse is part of the thematic repetition noted in the Overview (see Commentary on 28:12; 29:2). It promises that tyrants will fall. The belief that God's justice will ultimately prevail is implicit. Psalms 11 and 12 may be seen as meditations on this point. For v. 17, see the Commentary on 10:1; 19:18; 29:15.

29:18. This verse is the only place in Proverbs where prophetic "vision" (חזון *ḥāzôn*) is mentioned. "Vision" can refer to various types of prophetic revelation (Ps 89:19; Dan 1:17; 8:1), and usually occurs as a dream

---

312. For the grammar implicit in the (somewhat paraphrastic) NIV and NRSV translations, see Waltke and O'Connor, *An Introduction to Biblical Hebrew Syntax,* ¶4.7, 76-77, ¶16.4.b, 303.

313. Weinfeld, *Social Justice in Ancient Israel and in the Ancient Near East,* 45-74.

314. Delitzsch, "Proverbs," 250.

315. See David L. Balch, *Let Women Be Submissive: The Domestic Code in 1 Peter,* SBLMS 26 (Chico, Calif.: Scholars Press, 1981) 28, 33-34, quoting Aristotle *Politics* 1.1253*b*.1-14.

(Isa 29:7; Mic 3:6). A sage can claim such a revelatory vision (Job 4:13 uses a cognate term). A vision can be written down (Hab 2:2), thus the term appears in the titles of prophetic books (Isa 1:1; Obad 1:1; Nah 1:1; cf. 2 Chr 32:32; Amos 1:1; Mic 1:1; only Hab 1:1 uses the verb).

There is diversity of opinion on 29:18. Many feel that its vocabulary should be understood in terms of typical wisdom concerns, so that "vision" and "law" refer to political guidance and wise instruction respectively (cf. 11:14). Others note that "vision" appears here in parallel with *tôrâ* (law or instruction)—a key word in this subsection of Proverbs (see Overview to chaps. 28–29). Thus, taken together, these terms represent the "law and prophets" as twin, written sources of guidance for the people of God. [316]

If this is correct, 29:18 may represent editorial, "innerbiblical" reflection on the first two sections of the Hebrew canon: the law (of Moses) and the Prophets. The third section, Writings, includes Proverbs itself (see Commentary on 30:1-9 for intra-biblical references in Proverbs). The overall concern in this subsection of Proverbs for rulers, politics, and justice brings to mind the deuteronomic dependence of the king on the Mosaic law (Deut 17:18-19; cf. 1 Kgs 2:2-4), and of king and people on prophecy (Deut 18:15-22; cf. 2 Sam 24:11). A comprehensive study of language common to Proverbs and the Pentateuch, Proverbs and the Prophets, and Proverbs and the other Writings remains to be written. It should be noted, however, that toward the end of canon formation, wisdom becomes an increasingly literary and learned scribal phenomenon, as is evident also from Ben Sira, Qumran, and the NT.[317] Judaism and Christianity in their formative periods were already "religions of the book."

Another view is that with the Babylonian exile active prophecy ceases, as does priestly teaching of the Mosaic law. At that time, Jerusalem's "king and princes are among the nations; the law is no more, and her prophets

obtain no vision from the Lord" (Lam 2:9; cf. Ps 74:9; Jer 18:18; Ezek 7:26; 12:22). In such a situation, the individual (the Hebrew is singular) "who keeps the law" will still be blessed (see Commentary on 28:4, which uses the plural; see also Ps 1:1). McKane emends v. 18*b* to read, "but a guardian of the Law keeps it [the people] on a straight course."[318] The emendation is unnecessary (cf. 28:4, 7).

29:19. In the matter of discipline, the ancients believed that "actions speak louder than words." The servant (sg., masc.), like many people, follows the line of least resistance: he gets away with what he can (29:12; cf. 17:2). Without sanctions authority has no power to command obedience. Sirach 33:24-33 treats the handling of servants ambiguously, advising not only harsh discipline, but also kindness (see Commentary on 29:15, 17, 21).

29:20. This verse is a near duplicate of 26:12 (cf. 22:29); it substitutes "who speaks in haste" for "wise in his own eyes." Haste in speech is an eminent form of folly (10:19; Eccl 5:1; Jas 1:19; see 19:2 for haste in general). It is better to be silent than to speak an ill word that cannot be called back (17:27-28).

29:21. This saying is the end of the leap-frog series on discipline and training of sons and servants. The final word in Hebrew is otherwise unknown and, despite many conjectures, uncertain. Thus, "bring grief" and "come to a bad end" are guesses. A possible solution is that מנון (*mānôn*) was an error for מדון (*mādôn*), "strife" (see 29:22). The general sense of the saying, against permissive indulgence, is clear.

29:22. Verse 22*a* is nearly identical to 15:18*a*. Verse 22*b* expands the thought, using vocabulary similar to 29:16, a key verse in this subsection.

29:23. The reversal of high and low, proud and humble is a topic encountered before (see Commentary on 15:33; 16:18-19; 18:12).

29:24. (See Commentary on 13:20; 14:7.) The saying is not entirely clear. The partner of a thief, lit., "who shares [the spoils]," hates his own life, that is, puts his life at risk as in 1:18 (cf. 8:36). An Israelite's obligation is to help restore goods to their

---

316. W. O. E. Oesterley, *The Book of Proverbs* (London: Methuen, 1929) 263.

317. See, comprehensively, M. J. Mulder, ed., *Mikra: Text, Translation, Reading and Interpretation of the Hebrew Bible in Ancient Judaism and Early Christianity,* CRINT 2.1 (Philadelphia: Fortress, 1988); cf. Van Leeuwen, "Scribal Wisdom and Theodicy in the Book of the Twelve," 31-49.

318. See McKane, *Proverbs,* 640-41.

rightful owner(s), to break with wrongdoers, and to give testimony against them in court. Not to fulfill these obligations is a sin of omission that renders one subject to a curse (Lev 5:1; Judg 17:1-3). The accomplice of a thief prefers ill-gotten gain to the well-being of the community and disdains the curse that falls on wrongdoers. It is not clear that such a person has actually been put under oath.

29:25. The "fear of man" in v. 25*a* may be taken in one of two senses. In the first, the genitive "of" is objective, contrasting fear of other humans to trust in God (see Commentary on 28:25-26). This topic is familiar from the psalms: "In God I trust; I will not be afraid./ What can man do to me?" (Ps 56:11 NIV; cf. Psalm 27). In the second, the genitive is subjective, as in the NRSV margin. Here the reference is to human terrors of any sort, with the implication that those who trust in God do not need to fear, for they are secure in him. The imagery is of a fortress or tower,

literally "high" and thus safe (see Commentary on 18:10-11). The meaning in both cases is similar, though the second applies to any frightful human situation. This verse and the next contrast humans with Yahweh.

29:26. This saying contrasts the ruler—as that powerful human who is entrusted with the responsibility of giving "justice" to the many—and God as the ultimate source of justice. This is so, even when human rulers are the agents of God's justice on earth (20:22; 21:1-3; Ps 72:1-2; Rom 13:1-7). The contrast between God and humans (see 29:25) is a foundation of OT thought and is expressed in a myriad of ways (Job 38; Psalms 8; 62; Eccl 5:2; Isa 55:8-9).

29:27. The final verse contrasts the mutual abhorrence of righteous and wicked humans, rather than God's abhorrence of the latter. For "abhorrent" ("abomination"), see Commentary on 11:1; cf. 11:20.

REFLECTIONS

1. Proverbs 28–29 casts a penetrating gaze at the interaction of government, money, justice, and poverty. These chapters call Christians to social and governmental reflection and reform. To reflection because uninformed reform does damage. To reform because much in the land is wrong and crooked. The sages were not prophets, but their standards for government and civic life have a prophetic ring. Their concern extends far beyond the red flag moral issues that exercise many religious folk in America today: (other people's sexual) immorality, abortion, and drugs. These issues are important, and in a pluralist society their resolution is complex. Unfortunately, passion about them is no substitute for a biblically informed, wise view of the government's task. Here Christians are desperately divided.[319]

Curiously, evangelical Christians, who rightly proclaim the authority of Scripture, often restrict its message to the realm of private, personal conversion and the family-related moral issues noted above. But mainline Christians, who rightly proclaim the social, public relevance of the gospel, often struggle with biblical authority. And both camps struggle with ignorance of Scripture in a television culture. In both camps Scripture does not function as a reality guide for public and private life. In this regard, Abraham Lincoln's monumental second inaugural address shows that this need not be so. It provides a prophetic example of biblical wisdom illuminating the life of the nation in time of crisis.

The OT insists that the basic task of rulers is to do justice internationally by preserving the nation's boundaries and integrity, and domestically by protecting the boundaries of widows and orphans (see Commentary on 15:25) and righting wrongs. Royal justice, like Yahweh himself, is especially dedicated to the cause of the weak and defenseless (28:27; 29:7, 14; Psalm 72).[320]

---

319. See James W. Skillen, *The Scattered Voice: Christians at Odds in the Public Square* (Grand Rapids: Zondervan, 1990).
320. See Keith W. Whitelam, "King and Kingship," *Anchor Bible Dictionary*, 6 vols. (New York: Doubleday, 1990) 4:40-48.

To move to one example in our American context, the perennial debate about the size of government requires a clear understanding of its task. Christians cannot say that government is too big or too small without serious, biblically informed analysis of that part of creation that is government and politics (see Commentary on 8:15-16).[321] Government should be big enough to do its job and small enough to do it without inappropriate trespass into other spheres of life (28:2, 15-16; 29:2; 1 Sam 8:10-18). Indeed its delicate, necessary task includes the adjudicating of relationships among various persons and spheres of life and the prevention of one sphere from dominating others (e.g., does industry exploit workers; are products safe for consumers; are drivers competent to drive a car; may minors buy tobacco and alcohol?).[322] To do its task, government must often intrude into other spheres "for the sake of justice and righteousness" (e.g., when parents neglect or abuse their children; when a large company unfairly restricts trade; when Christian schools fail to meet public educational standards; when another country invades its borders). These issues and the tasks of justice are complex and crucial. Too often today Christian minds and hands neglect them.

Not only do Christians need clarity as to government's nature and task, they also need a sense of its right practice. For example, the Scriptures, including Proverbs, consistently warn that money diverts the government from heeding the truth and doing justice (see Commentary on 15:27b; 17:23; 28:16, 21; 29:4, 12). Thus Christians ought not to be silent when Congress perpetually fails to enact campaign finance reform, so allowing special interest lobbies to distort legislation. Again, Christians ought not to be silent when civil and criminal justice is affordable only to wealthy individuals and corporations who can afford expensive lawyers and professional "expert" witnesses.

Biblical wisdom and biblically informed common sense concerning government will grow, not by proof-texting this or that specific issue, but when God's people learn to read the Bible as a book of justice and to see their world in its light. For Proverbs 28–29 the "law" is both the "Torah" of Moses and the "teaching" of the wise (see Overview of 28:1–29:27). These chapters imply that knowledge of the Scriptures and wisdom concerning practical politics and good government cannot be separated (cf. Josh 1:6-9; 1 Kgs 2:1-4). We need to saturate our minds and imaginations in the Scriptures and then open our eyes to the reality around us. We need to act, not rashly, but wisely and decisively, not out of partisan interest, but with a humble passion for "justice and liberty for all."

2. Proverbs 28:5 and 29:27 portray the mutual intolerance of the righteous and the wicked. The assumption is that righteous folk understand and align themselves with the divine perspective on good and evil (28:5; 29:7). Wicked folk and wickedness are abhorrent to God (6:16-19; 8:7; 21:27), and in this the righteous imitate God. God's enemies are their enemies, because God's enemies do evil. This thought comes to strong expression in Ps 139:19-22 (from the divine side, cf. Gen 12:3; Num 24:9). Such sayings portray a world apparently without a middle ground, a world with a fundamental conflict between good and evil. In our tolerant, pluralistic society, such thinking seems troublesome, especially when we see the violence done by groups seeking to impose their understanding of good and evil on others. Should we not rather "live and let live"?

Yet Jesus also spoke in terms of conflict. "Whoever is not with me is against me, and whoever does not gather with me scatters" (Matt 12:30). How are we to understand such biblical language today?

321. See Paul Marshall, *Thine Is the Kingdom: A Biblical Perspective on the Nature of Government and Politics Today* (Grand Rapids: Eerdmans, 1984); Oliver O'Donovan, *The Desire of the Nations: Rediscovering the Roots of Political Theology* (Cambridge: Cambridge University Press, 1996).

322. See Michael Walzer, *Spheres of Justice* (New York: Basic, 1983) 3-30; Peter L. Berger, "In Praise of Particularity: The Concept of Mediating Structures," in *Facing Up to Modernity* (New York: Basic, 1977) 130-41.

Two extreme currents compete in contemporary culture, and yet they seem to feed on one another in a strange symbiosis. On the one hand there is a strong insistence—itself often dogmatic—on tolerance and avoiding dogmatic truth claims.[323] No one person or group may presume to have the truth because such claims are actually covert bids for power and self-aggrandizement.[324] A moral corollary, especially in the media, seems to be that "anything goes." On the other hand there is a fanaticism in which one's position or the position of one's group is absolutely right; nothing is ambiguous, and divergent views should be destroyed. To the extent that such thinking is theologically aware, human thought is identified with God's thought, ignoring that even divine revelation must be interpreted by fallible humans. In such thinking "the end justifies the means," including violence. All balance is lost; public discourse is destroyed.

Proverbs 29:27 offers a reproof to the first current rather than the second. And yet, unless this proverb is taken seriously, the second, fanatic current will be given free play. Proverbs reminds us that we may not elevate moral ambiguity and religious mystery to the point of relativism, where the lines between right and wrong, good and evil, true and false, are erased (see Isa 5:18-23). At that point tolerance is no longer a virtue, but moral indifference in the face of evil. It is an abandonment of the social responsibility to which the God of the Bible continually calls us. Christians cannot, for example, remain silent and inactive in the face of oppression or racial hate—whether in Nazi Europe or in America with its burning of black churches. Tolerance is not an adequate response to evil.[325]

The Scriptures insist that in and through creation God has shown *all* humans enough of God's own self and of good and evil that we are "without excuse" (Rom 1:18-20; 2:14-15). No one may say, "We did not know" (24:12; see Reflections on Prov 8:1-36). God has shown humans what is good, and what God requires is especially open to those who have the Scriptures (Mic 6:8; see Commentary on 29:18).

323. See Lesslie Newbigin, *The Gospel in a Pluralist Society* (Grand Rapids: Eerdmans, 1989), for an invaluable discussion of these issues.
324. On these themes, see Anthony C. Thiselton, *Interpreting God and the Postmodern Self: On Meaning, Manipulation, and Promise* (Grand Rapids: Eerdmans, 1995).
325. Bonhoeffer's *Ethics* is a crucial resource. In a public television interview, Philip Hallie, author of *Lest Innocent Blood Be Shed* (New York: Harper & Row, 1979), revealed that he no longer believed that the heroic pacifism described in his book was an adequate response to the Holocaust. It did not stop Hitler. See Bill Moyers, "Facing Evil: Light at the Core of Darkness," Videotape (KERA Dallas: Public Affairs Television, Inc., 1988).

PROVERBS 30:1-33

THE WORDS OF AGUR, CURSES, AND NUMERICAL SAYINGS

COMMENTARY

30:1-9. The "Words of Agur" is one of the most difficult and controverted sections in Proverbs. Not only does it present serious textual and exegetical problems (especially in v. 1), but also its very meaning and purpose have received radically contrary interpretations.[326]

Some find here the words of a skeptic (vv. 1-4) who is either agnostic (denying human knowledge of God) or atheistic (denying God's existence). The next verses would be the words of a pious Jew who answers the skeptic in an orthodox way (vv. 5-6), praying to be spared similar impiety or sin (vv. 7-9).[327] A contrary reading—the view taken here—believes that the entire section needs to be taken as a whole and reflects a humble piety (cf. Job 42:1-6), recognizing the immense gap between God and humans (vv. 2-4). The arena in which this gap is revealed is creation itself, much as in Job 38–39 and Isaiah 40–55. And like Isa 55:8-11, vv. 5-6 assert that the answer to the cosmic gulf between God and humans is a form of God's Word, prophetic and canonical Scripture respectively.

The main sections of the passage are linked by hymnic rhetorical questions based on the name of God (see Commentary on 30:4, 9). Moreover, in the light of God's provision for life, the sage prays that God give neither luxury nor poverty, lest faith be tempted to violence against the Giver's holy name.[328] Finally, there is an implicit contrast between the faithful Word of God (v. 5) and what

faithless humans may say (v. 9—the Hebrew uses the same root [אמר *'āmar*]; cf. Rom 3:4).

Even the boundaries of the passage are disputed. The LXX version of Proverbs places vv. 1-14 before 24:23 and places vv. 15-33 (plus 31:1-9) after 24:34 (using the Hebrew chapter and verse numbers). It is clear that vv. 1-14 comprise several subunits. Are they merely juxtaposed, or is there an implicit editorial logic that links them into a larger whole? Crucial here is the question of genre or genres in the passage.

Verses 1-3, 4, 5-6, 7-9 should be read together as an editorial, "anthological" poem. Reference to other passages of Scripture is an essential feature of this passage, and these allusions and quotations have a deliberate theological and canonical function. In this composite literary whole, the central issues arise from the questions concerning God's name and the believer's need to be free of sin regarding that name, lest one say contemptuously, "Who is the Lord?" (i.e., "Yahweh," which is the proper name of Israel's God; see Exod 3:14-15; 34:6-7). Conspicuously, the passage does not use the name until its last verse. As numerous commentators have noted, in contrast to the rest of Proverbs, which almost always uses "Yahweh"/"LORD," this passage avoids that name by using alternative terms for "God."

The passage begins with the limits of human knowledge, which nearly drive the writer to despair (vv. 1-4); yet it ends with a fervent prayer of faith (vv. 7-9), made possible by confidence in the written revelation of God (vv. 5-6; see also 29:18).

Verses 1-9 comprise several parts, but they are linked by rhetorical questions and their implicit answer, by thematic catchwords, and by an overarching, implicit logic. Skehan

326. James L. Crenshaw, "Clanging Cymbols," in Douglas A. Knight and Peter J. Paris, eds., *Justice and the Holy: Essays in Honor of Walter Harrelson* (Atlanta: Scholars Press, 1989) 51-64.
327. R. B. Y. Scott, *Proverbs–Ecclesiastes,* AB 18 (Garden City, N.Y.: Doubleday, 1965) 175-76.
328. See P. Franklyn, "The Sayings of Agur in Proverbs 30: Piety or Scepticism?" *ZAW* 95 (1983) 237-52; A. Gunneweg, "Weisheit, Prophetie und Kanonformel: Erwägungen zu Proverbia 30, 1-9," in *Alttestamentlicher Glaube und biblische Theologie: Festschrift für Horst Dietrich Preuss zum 65 Geburtstag,* Jutta Hausmann et al., eds. (Stuttgart: W. Kohlhammer, 1992) 253-60.

argued that v. 4 was a riddle pointing to the Creator and that "his son" must be taken seriously. For Skehan, the riddle is resolved by seeing in "the Holy One" a reference to Yahweh, and in "Agur son of *YQH*" a reference to Jacob/Israel as Yahweh's "son" (What is his name and his son's name, if you know?), since Israel is God's "son" (Exod 4:22; Deut 32:19; Hos 11:1; cf. Matt 2:15). *YQH* is then an abbreviation for יהוה (*YHWH*, *Qadôsh Hû*, "Yahweh, Holy is He"), a precursor of the familiar later phrase, "The Holy One, blessed be He."[329]

Against Skehan's position, it may be noted that these questions are not true riddles concerning Yahweh's name, which every Israelite knew. Rather, they concern the greatness of the Creator and the smallness of the creature. As questions about Yahweh's name, their counterpart is the triumphant hymnic declaration often found in creation contexts: "Yahweh (God of hosts) is his name!" (e.g., Isa 47:4; 48:2; 51:15; 54:5; Jer 31:35; Amos 4:13; 8:7-9; 9:6). As questions about divine activity in creation, they correspond to the rhetorical hymnic questions in Isaiah 40–55 (e.g., Isa 40:12, 26; 45:21). Agur's questions, like their counterparts in Job 38, are designed to exalt God and to humble human pretensions to knowledge (Job 38:4-11).

30:1. This opening verse abounds with difficulties. "Agur son of Jakeh" is unknown. "Agur" itself is not a usual Hebrew name. Again, "Jakeh" (properly, יקה *yāqeh*) is unknown. Agur's sayings are called not "an" but "the" oracle (המשא *hammaśśâ*); this term reappears, without the article, in 31:1. Many commentators prefer to make a minor emendation so that the word (in one or both cases) refers not to a prophetic utterance but to a north Arabic tribe to which Agur and Lemuel, both apparently non-Israelites, belonged (see Gen 25:14; 1 Chr 1:30). The most vexing part of the verse, however, is "to Ithiel, to Ithiel and to Ucal" (NIV) or "I am weary, O God, I am weary, O God. How can I prevail?" (NRSV). The only other occurrence of the Hebrew name "Ithiel" ("God is with me"; cf. "Immanuel") is in Neh 11:7. The NRSV makes one of many attempts to

divide the consonants differently and repoint its vowels to give some coherent meaning that fits the context. Another, less plausible, attempt reads the text as Aramaic (see Dan 3:29): "There is no God, there is no God, and I can [not know anything]" (see Ps 14:1; Dan 2:10).[330] The phrase "thus says the man" (lit., "an oracle of the man") is a prophetic formula found only in Num 24:4, 15 and 2 Sam 23:1. The allusion to Numbers is nicely ironic. There Balaam, a prophet for hire, uses wisdom modes of speech. He "takes up his saying"—the same word found in the title of Proverbs (משל *māšāl*; not "oracle")—and gives a conventional invitation to hear, used frequently in Proverbs 1–9 (Num 23:18). Balaam claims to be one who sees clearly, who "hears the words of God" (Num 24:4, 16; cf. Prov 30:5). He claims to have visionary "knowledge of the Most High" (Num 24:16; cf. Prov 30:3). Yet, Balaam is "son of Beor," a name that punningly may be read as "son of Stupid," the same root as in v. 2.

30:2-3. The writer does not mean to say that Agur considers himself subhuman. Rather, it is a hyperbolic and ironic confession of the limits of human existence and understanding, like the psalmist's "I am a worm and not a man" (Ps 22:6 NIV; cf. Ps 49:10, 12, 20). The same metaphorical denial of human understanding of God appears in the psalms.

How great are your works, O LORD,
how profound your thoughts!
The senseless man does not know
[בער לא ידע *ba'ar lō' yēdā'*],
fools do not understand.
(Ps 92:5-6 NIV)

Again, when the faith of the pious poet of Psalm 73 was tried, he failed to understand God's justice:

I was senseless and ignorant [בער ולא אדע
ba'ar welō' 'ēdā'; cf. Jer 10:14];
I was a brute beast before you [see Prov 26:3].
Yet I am always with you. (Ps 73:22-23a NIV)

There are people like Eliphaz and Balaam who think they know divine mysteries by personal revelation (Job 4:12-17). However, in

329. P. W. Skehan, "Wisdom's House," in *Studies in Israelite Poetry and Wisdom*, CBQM 1 (Washington, D.C.: Catholic Biblical Association of America, 1971) 42-43; Murphy, *Wisdom Literature*, 80.

330. Scott, *Proverbs–Ecclesiastes*, 175-76.

the light of vv. 5-6, the specific focus of Agur's ignorance appears to be his failure to learn the wisdom that Moses taught to Israel (Deut 4:1, 6) and for which one does not need to ascend to heaven (Deut 30:11-14).

30:4. The four questions in this verse all presuppose the obvious answer: No one, except God or heavenly agents. These cosmic questions are traditional and rhetorical; they reveal the gap between God (or gods in the ancient Near East) and human beings. To ascend to and come down from heaven is impossible for humans (Gen 11:4-5, 7; 28:12-13; Deut 30:12; Judg 13:20; Bar 3:29-32; 2 Esdr 4:8; John 3:12-13), and this question was a standard proverb in the ancient Near East.[331] It is mere presumption for humans to contemplate ascending to heaven (Gen 11:1-9; Job 11:7-9; Isa 14:13-15). In the Hellenistic period, however, apocalyptic claims to have seen hidden things, which had been revealed uniquely to them, arose in the name of heroes like Enoch (Gen 5:21-24):

I know everything; for either from the lips of the Lord, or else my eyes have seen from the beginning even to the end . . . I know everything, and everything I have written down in books, the heavens and their boundaries and their contents. . . . What human being can see their cycles and their phases [i.e., of the heavenly bodies]? . . . I measured all the earth . . . and everything that exists. I wrote down the height from the earth to the seventh heaven, and the depth to the lowermost hell. . . . And I ascended to the east, into the paradise of Edem [i.e., into heaven].[332]

Perhaps an important function of vv. 1-9 is to reject such claims to know hidden things by directing readers to trust in God's scriptural word (v. 5) and to humble acceptance of the limits of the human condition (vv. 8-9).

The whole span of creation is covered in the four questions. The sequence of elements from "heaven" to "earth" spans reality from

top to bottom and sets the four ancient elements in order (fire = heaven, air = wind, earth, water; cf. Eccl 1:4-11). Like the divine speeches in Job 38–41, these questions contrast the almighty Creator with puny humans (cf. Job 26:8; 28:26; Isa 40:12).

30:5. This saying is a quotation from 2 Sam 22:31 (= Ps 18:30; cf. Pss 2:12; 18:2), but uses an infrequent term for "God" in place of the original "Yahweh" (cf. Ps 18:31). This psalm in effect supplies the answer for Agur's questions, for immediately after the verse quoted here, David asks, "Who is God but Yahweh?" (2 Sam 22:32 = Ps 18:31). Significantly, the psalm portrays Yahweh as descending from the heavens (2 Sam 22:10, 17; for an ascent, see Judg 13:20; see Commentary on Prov 30:4).

30:6. The writer here alludes to the canonical formulas in Deut 4:2; 5:22; 12:32. The purpose, in line with the questions asked in v. 4 and the confession about God's Word in v. 5, appears to be to exclude apocalyptic speculation and additions to the Scriptures held as authoritative by the editors of Proverbs (see Commentary on Prov 30:4).

30:7-9. This is the only prayer in Proverbs. It asks God for two seemingly unrelated things: first, to be kept from falsehood; second, to be given neither wealth nor poverty. Expressed in positive form, it is a request for one's daily bread. The petition from the Lord's Prayer has its background here (Matt 6:11), as the NIV translation suggests. But the Hebrew term חק (*ḥōq*) here means a portion that is fitting (see Commentary on 26:1-12) or appropriate to one's needs and situation as a servant (31:15)—in this case, a servant of God.

Verse 9 provides the motive clauses that explain the reasons for the prayer's unusual requests. The one who prays knows that being poor is better than being a rich liar (19:22), who, like Pharaoh, thinks that Yahweh is an impotent nobody: "Who is the LORD?" (Exod 5:2 NRSV; cf. 3:13-15, "What is his name?" leading to the revelation of the name "Yahweh"). But the one who prays also knows that grinding poverty can break a person and lead to theft, which does violence to God's name. The verb here (and "deny" you) is linked elsewhere to "stealing" as something disloyal or unfaithful to God (Josh 7:11;

331. F. Greenspahn, "A Mesopotamian Proverb and Its Biblical Reverberations," *JAOS* (1994) 33-38; Lambert, *Babylonian Wisdom Literature*, 41, 149, and esp. 327. See also *ANET* 79 (Gilgamesh), 101-2 (Adapa), 103, 508 (Nergal and Ereshkigal), 601 (Dialogue of Pessimism), 597 (I Will Praise the Lord of Wisdom).
332. 2 Enoch 40, 41 [J], in J. H. Charlesworth, ed., *The Old Testament Pseudepigrapha*, 2 vols. (Garden City, N.Y.: Doubleday, 1983) 1:164, 168. See M. Stone's important study, "Lists of Revealed Things in the Apocalyptic Literature," in F. M. Cross, W. Lemke, P. D. Miller, eds., *Magnalia Dei* (New York: Doubleday, 1976) 414-54.

Hos 4:1-2). But it can refer also to greedy, idolatrous reliance on wealth (Job 31:24-28; cf. Col 3:5). Joshua 24:27 uses the same verb to signal denying God by failing to keep all the "words of the LORD" (cf. v. 5; Job 6:10). In Hos 4:1-2, "stealing" and "lying" ("denying") are among the actions that demonstrate that Israel does not know God. Significantly, v. 9 provides the first explicit instance of God's revealed name, "Yahweh," in this passage. Its question, "Who is the Lord?" echoes the rhetorical questions of v. 4.

30:10. This verse is loosely linked to vv. 11-14 by the theme of blessing and cursing (see Exod 21:17), while vv. 11-14 form a subunit, each beginning with "There are those . . ." The remainder of the chapter, separated in the LXX, contains a variety of numerical sayings.

There are curses that are deserved (see Commentary on 26:2). Servants are in a vulnerable position with respect to their masters; the servants' only recourse may be the curse as an appeal to God for justice. Ecclesiastes 7:21 and Deut 23:15-16 appear to take note of the power imbalance between master and servant, so as to protect the servant. The saying in this verse assures the weak that God will give them justice when they are wrongly accused (cf. 22:22-23). The story of Joseph and Potiphar's wife provides a good illustration (Gen 39:6-23).

30:11-14. These verses form a catalog of vice, reminiscent of the numerical saying in 6:16-19. "There are those who" is literally, "A generation of those who" or perhaps, "A circle of . . ." Although this unit is in the third-person indicative, there is here a note of prophetic urgency and indignation. The focus is on the collective character of sin; wrongdoing is done in "packs" inspired by a common spirit of wickedness (cf. Jer 2:31; 7:29; Matt 3:7; 12:34). The cursing of parents is forbidden in the Torah (Exod 20:12; 21:17; see Commentary on 10:1; 20:20; 30:17). The deception of self-appraisal is a frequent theme in wisdom literature, signaled by the phrase "[pure] in their own eyes" (see Commentary on 16:2; 20:9; 26:12). "Lofty" eyes are a symbol of pride (see Commentary on 6:17; see also Ps 131:1). For the image of teeth as swords, see Ps 57:4. The rapacity of

the powerful against the weak is a frequent OT theme (see 14:31; Ps 14:4; Mic 3:1-3).

30:15-16. Here begins the first of a series of explicitly numerical sayings, though one should note the number in v. 7 and the implicit numerical catalog in vv. 11-14. Numerical sayings, especially those that use the pattern x, x + 1, are common in the ancient world, including the Homeric poems of Greece (see 6:16-19; Amos 1–2). Verse 15a appears to have been added to the three-plus-four saying in vv. 15b-16. Common to both is the insatiability of things, whether human or cosmic. Instead of the four elements—fire, earth, water, and air (see Commentary on v. 4)—here we have the addition of Sheol, the grave, which is never filled with the dead (see 27:20; Isa 5:14). For a related metaphorical use of "fire," see 26:20-21. The juxtaposition of Sheol and the "barren womb" is poignant, since it cannot replace what the grave devours. Rachel, Hannah, and Elizabeth each express the depth of an Israelite woman's longing for children (Gen 30:1-2; 1 Samuel 1–2; cf. Luke 1:5-25).

30:17. This verse corresponds to v. 11. The reference to eyes graphically portrays the law of retribution, in which the punishment fits the crime. When a corpse is abandoned, it is eaten by beasts or by the birds of the air (cf. 1 Sam 17:44, 46; 1 Kgs 14:11; 21:23-24), and the brutal harshness of this act means to convey the utter wrongness of cursing parents.

30:18-20. These verses portray simple wonder at marvelous phenomena in God's creation, culminating with the mystery of sexual love. If vv. 2-3 expressed the limits of human knowledge with regard to God above, then these verses declare that even the marvels of creation are beyond human comprehension. Verse 20 is linked to the preceding verses by the catchword *way* (דרך *derek*) and by a poignant awareness that the same activity can excite wonder and dismay. For a discussion of "way," see the Reflections on Prov 4:1-27.

The typical pattern of three and four is used here with reference to created phenomena. They are beyond understanding, not so much in a scientific sense, but in the sense of joyful, aesthetic awe at what God has made indescribably beautiful. Some scholars have thought that the four ways are linked by the disappearance of what has passed, as suggested by Wis 5:7-13. Here, however, each way somehow excites the poet's amazement and joy. And each image subtly suggests the most wonderful thing of all: "the way of a man with a girl." "Eagle" is from the same word translated "vultures" (lit., "sons of the vulture"—i.e., birds of the vulture class) in v. 17b. Birds, which fly and soar through the air, have a way that, in its freedom and artlessness, seems to be no way at all. The snake moves mysteriously without feet; it is, not coincidentally, a universal phallic symbol. The ship makes its way, literally, "in the heart of the sea" (23:34; Exod 15:8), an image that suggests rhythmic movement as the ship plunges through wave after wave of waters with unfathomable, hidden depths.

The ways move from three realms of creation (again earth, air, water; see Commentary on 30:4, 16) to culminate in the human realm. Of all the creatures made by God, God's image, male and female, is the crown. The translations obscure some of the parallelism of the images. Both the three natural images and the image of human love share the same pattern, and (except for the snake on a rock) use the same Hebrew preposition, ‏ב‎ (b). This preposition can mean both "in" and "with," and the translators choose the latter in the last line only: a vulture "in the sky, a ship on . . . the sea," but a man "with" a girl. The term "girl" is that used in the well-known passage Isa 7:14, where it refers to a young woman without specifying virginity or lack thereof. Using delicate imagery for love, this small poem sings implicit praise to God for the glories of creation, especially for sexual love (see Commentary on 5:15-20; Song of Songs).

Like 5:15-20, the present passage moves from delight and wonder at sexuality as a created good to a disturbing picture of good gone wrong. Adultery is not the way the Creator intended. Sex is compared to eating (a common trope, see Reflections on Proverbs 4:1-27; 5:1-23; Sir 26:12), and the casually wiped mouth may be literal or figurative. Perhaps more horrifying than the deed itself is the lack of guilt or remorse, as if the deed might be wiped away and leave neither physical nor moral tracks, like a ship on the seas.

30:21-23. These verses form another three-plus-four saying. Though some have seen this passage as merely humorous, it is an instance of the world upside down, a pattern of inversion or chaos that is found throughout the world from ancient times to the present.[333] Such pictures of inversion have a variety of functions ranging from the comic to the serious and sometimes combine both. Many a true word is spoken in jest. The ancients linked the natural world to the human world of culture and society (see Reflections on Prov 8:1-36). Chaos or harmony in one was correlate to chaos or harmony in the other. When God's messiah (anointed one) comes, people of low status are elevated and the high and mighty are brought low (see 1 Sam 2:4-8, 10b; Luke 1:51-53). But whether social inversion is good or bad depends upon the situation (see Isa 3:4-5). "The Bible delights in fruitful reversals of fortune . . . but has no use for upstarts."[334] If the wicked are in power, inversion is good, but if the good are brought low, the world upside down is bad. Moreover, the various spheres of life were seen as linked. Thus the political world of king and royal servant is parallel to the domestic world of husband, wife, and domestic servants (cf. Esth 1:16-22; see Commentary on 29:15-27).

The earth is meant not to tremble, but to be stable and carry its load (Amos 1:1; 7:10; 8:8; 9:5-6). The elevation of a royal servant to the position of king represents social anarchy (14:35; 19:10; Eccl 10:5-7), something that especially plagued the northern kingdom of Israel (but see Commentary on 17:2 for a contrary saying). A fool is here someone who behaves contrary to right custom and social norms (17:7), as does Nabal in 1 Samuel 25. In a subsistence farming society, fools do not work appropriately and so lose the right to scarce resources (10:4-5; 19:10; 28:19; cf. 2 Thess 3:10).

The case of the unloved woman (lit., "disliked") may refer not to one gaining a husband, nor to one being divorced, but rather to a second wife in a polygamous household (see Deut 21:15-17) who comes to "lord it over" the household, as Peninnah did to Hannah (1 Samuel 1). The last instance of a topsy-turvy

333. R. C. Van Leeuwen, "Proverbs 30:21-23 and the Biblical World Upside Down," *JBL* 105 (1986) 599-610.
334. Derek Kidner, *Proverbs,* TOTC (Downers Grove, Ill.: InterVarsity, 1964) 181.

world is the case of a female servant displacing her mistress as mother of an heir. This pattern appears in the conflict of Hagar and Sarah (Genesis 16; 21) and often in the competition of royal wives or concubines to set their son on the throne (see 1 Kings 1). Here the domestic and the political combine.

30:24-28. Only the number four is mentioned in this passage, and the subject turns to the world of nature as a source of wisdom (see vv. 15-19; Job 12:7-10; Psalm 19). The sayings exploit the paradox that the small, weak, and insignificant can be wise and accomplish great things. The description of ants and (rock) badgers (Ps 104:18) as a people suggests that part of their wisdom and success lies in their grassroots social organization and cohesion, a point that is explicit in the case of the locusts, who have no king (contrast Judg 17:6 and Jotham's parable, Judg 9:7-15). The devastating, quasi-military order of a myriad of locusts in the Near East is well known (Joel 1:4-7; 2:2, 4-9, 11). Their strength lies in their unity. The ant has already had a parable devoted to it (6:6-11). At key, perhaps editorial, points in the book, the advance preparation of food (lit., "bread"; 6:8; 12:11; 20:13; 27:27; 31:14, 27) and especially the building or care of a house have a powerful resonance as instances of fundamental wisdom (9:1; 14:1; 24:3, 27; 27:27; 31:15, 21, 27). Again, a lizard is small, insignificant, yet has free run of the king's palace. Though one can take it in one's hand, one does not harm it, for it serves the king by controlling noisome insects.

30:29-31. This unit is another three-and-four animal saying, which, if correctly translated, affords comparisons for the king in his majestic dignity. There are a number of linguistic uncertainties, however, and the last line is obscure. Verse 30 is quite clear. Even in English the lion is "king of beasts," known for its fearlessness (see Gen 49:9-10). "Strutting rooster" follows the ancient versions but is uncertain (lit., "loins girded"?). The LXX amplifies, "the rooster marching boldly among his hens." If this reading is correct, it signals (perhaps with humor) the king's proud bearing: the rooster knows it rules the roost. In Dan 8:5-8, another word for "he-goat" is used as a metaphor for a leader, and this appears to be the point here, although the word used here appears only four times in the Bible.

30:32-33. These verses present a humorous sketch with a serious point. There is danger in elevating oneself (see Commentary on 25:6-7). If you've made that mistake, silence yourself by putting "hand to mouth," a symbol of dismay and humiliation (Job 21:5; 29:9). The pressing of the hand to one's mouth leads to a humorous chain of parallels in v. 33, nicely captured by NRSV's repeated "pressing . . . produces." There are here some delightful puns. The word for "curds" plays on a word for "wrath." And in the last line, "pressing anger," which makes no real sense in English, puns in Hebrew because the word for "anger" is the dual form of the word for "nose"!

REFLECTIONS

1. To some readers, the Words of Agur (vv. 1-9) seem to offer biblical warrant for skepticism. Such a position appeals partly to uncertain readings of the very difficult first verse. But the thought of skepticism in the Bible is somehow appealing in our culturally uncertain times. We are often uncomfortable with those who possess more certainty than seems humanly appropriate. In my understanding, vv. 1-9 give no warrant for skepticism, but it does humble many of our proud certainties. As Ecclesiastes notes, God is in heaven and we are on earth (Eccl 5:2). The writer (or editor, if fragments have been combined) refuses even to claim the knowledge of divine things that other religious specialists of his day claim to know (vv. 2-3). But with the rhetorical questions of v. 4, he exposes their claims to superhuman, perhaps apocalyptic, knowledge as bogus: No human has made the journey to heaven and back.

The writer/editor's response to the limits of human knowledge is threefold. First, he points to the reliable, now written or canonical word of God (vv. 5 *a,* 6). This is not something up in heaven and out of reach, but near at hand. Humans can know it and do it (Deut 30:11-14). However vast human ignorance of God and cosmic mysteries may be, this they can and must know. The writer quotes a canonical formula that warns against adding to (or subtracting from) the written word of God (v. 6). The scriptures provide the norm, the limit, the circle of truth within which human thought may operate, "lest you be found a liar." The writer is profoundly aware of the human tendency to (self) deception and denial of reality. Denial and deception were not discovered by Freud.[335]

Second, our source of security is not found in the perfection of our knowledge, but by taking refuge in the God who is made known in Scripture (v. 5, quoting Ps 18:30 = 2 Sam 22:31). This does not diminish the importance of human wisdom and knowledge (the focus of Proverbs), but puts it in an ultimate perspective.

Third, the writer prays for daily, ordinary bread—not too much and not too little (vv. 8-9)—for he knows how deeply we humans are embedded in this created world and how easily our earthly circumstances sway our devotion to God and distort our perception of the truth (cf. Luke 8:14). Thus the rich are tempted to rely on their wealth and to ignore God and deny God's radical requirements (vv. 8-9; cf. Deut 8:17-18; Luke 18:18-29). Conversely, the poor are tempted to mistrust God's goodness and promises. So they may offend the integrity of God's name (cf. Exod 6:9; 34:6-7) because hunger drives them to break the requirements of God's law (v. 9; cf. 6:30-31).

2. To ask a person's name and that of his or her son is not a Hebrew way of asking for someone's full identity (v. 4). That would require a person's name and his or her father's name (and a mother's name, if royalty). One's child does not establish identity; even King David is "the son of Jesse" (1 Sam 20:30; 2 Sam 23:1). Some scholars conclude that the point is ironic; there is no such (human) person. But if the answer to the rhetorical questions is Yahweh, then a plausible candidate for "his son" must be found. In Israel there were two possibilities: Israel itself (Exod 4:22-23; Hos 11:1) or David and his royal heirs, sons of God by covenant (2 Sam 7:14; Pss 2:7; 89:26-27). In the New Testament, the identity of Israel is encompassed in Jesus Christ (Matt 2:15). There Jesus is known both as "son of David" (Matt 22:41-45) and as the "Son of God" who ascended into heaven (John 3:12-13; Heb 4:14). In his Pentecost sermon, Peter is at pains to point out that "David did not ascend to heaven," but Christ did (Acts 2:33-34; cf. Eph 4:7-10; Heb 4:14; see Commentary on v. 5 and note the messianic ending in 2 Sam 22:51).

---

335. See the exposition of the classic Reformation creed, The Belgic Confession (1561), Article 7 ("The Sufficiency of Scripture") on this point. Concerning human opinions it declares, "All human beings are liars by nature and more vain than vanity itself."

PROVERBS 31:1-31

The Words of Lemuel and a Hymn to the Valiant Woman

Overview

The final chapter of the book begins with the words of a king, taught him by the queen mother (vv. 1-9). These verses are separated from vv. 10-31 in the LXX by chaps. 25–29, perhaps indicating they were once independent. Yet these passages are related in various ways. Through echoes and allusions, both passages, but especially the second, create an envelope around the book with Proverbs 1–9.[336] More immediately, the royal focus in vv. 1-9 has been anticipated by the numerical sayings of the previous chapter, with their frequent reference to kings (30:21-31; cf. chaps. 28–29). The genre in vv. 1-9 is the royal instruction, a sub-category of the instruction form pervasive in chaps. 1–9.[337] The royal instruction also appears in Egypt and Mesopotamia, but the attribution to the queen mother (a position of no little importance) is exceptional.[338]

The last section of the book is formally an acrostic (alphabetic) hymn in praise of a "capable wife." It begins with an introduction of the woman (vv. 10-12), is followed by a catalog of her heroic deeds (vv. 13-27), and concludes with an invitation to join the poet in praise of his subject (vv. 28-31).[339] One may compare the extended "praise" (הלל *hālal*, vv. 30-31; Sir 44:1) of distinguished men in Sirach 44–50. (When Sirach speaks of the good wife, however, his focus is relentlessly on her benefits to her husband, and the praise is commingled with fear of the bad wife; Sir 26:1-27.) The twenty-two letters of the Hebrew alphabet sum up wisdom, as it were, from A to Z, just as the extended acrostic in Psalm 119 sums up Torah piety. Wisdom is here embodied in a noble woman. And so the symbolism of wife as wisdom, which runs through Proverbs, is brought full circle (see Introduction).

336. See Camp, *Wisdom and the Feminine in the Book of Proverbs*, 186-208.

337. See James L. Crenshaw, "A Mother's Instruction to Her Son (Proverbs 31:1-9)," in *Urgent Advice and Probing Questions: Collected Writings on Old Testament Wisdom* (Macon, Ga.: Mercer University Press, 1995) 383-95.

338. N. A. Andreasen, "The Queen Mother in Israelite Society," *CBQ*

45 (1983) 179-94. Cf. Carole R. Fontaine, "Queenly Proverb Perfomance: The Prayer of Puduhepa," in *The Listening Heart*, ed. K. G. Hoglund et al. (Sheffield: JSOT, 1987) 95-126.

339. Al Wolters, "Proverbs XXXI 10-31 as Heroic Hymn: A Form-Critical Analysis," *VT* 38 (1988) 448-57.

PROVERBS 31:1-9, THE WORDS OF LEMUEL

Commentary

This instruction, like those in Proverbs 1–9, addresses "my son." Besides formal affinities, the passage has thematic connections with chaps. 1–9. The queen mother instructs her royal son not only concerning his duty to do justice (see Commentary on 8:14-16; Reflections on 28:1-18; 29:1-27),

but reverts to the preoccupation with women found in chaps. 1–9.

31:1-2. Lemuel is otherwise unknown; for the alternatives, "an oracle" or "king of Massa" (NIV margin), see Commentary on 30:1. The foreign character of Lemuel is perhaps suggested by the Aramaic forms in this passage (which alternate with the corresponding Hebrew forms) and by the Aramaic word for "son" (בר *bar*). Similar literary mixing or alternating of Hebrew and Aramaic appears in Job and Daniel, for example. "No" or "O" is literally, "what?" and this form has not been adequately explained. An appeal to an Arabic expression, "Take heed," is far-fetched. Like Hannah (1 Samuel 1–2), this mother has dedicated her son to God.

31:3. "Your ways" seems an odd parallel to "your strength," and alternative explanations have been offered. But "ways" may simply allude to chaps. 1–9, where ways is a basic metaphor for the conduct of life, especially in relation to women.

31:4-5. This passage warns the king against the subversive effect of alcohol on memory and judgment (cf. Lev 11:10). To "pervert the rights" is literally to "change the judgment," a judicial idiom known also in Mesopotamia.[340] On things decreed, see Commentary on 8:15, which employs the

royal terms used here. The concern is that the government protect those who cannot protect themselves and "speak for those who cannot speak" (see vv. 8-9, 20; 16:12; 28:3, 15; 29:4, 7, 14; Ps 72:1-4, 12-14; Jer 22:16).

31:6-7. In classic wisdom fashion (see Commentary on 26:4-5), these verses follow the warning against misuse of alcohol with an opposite, positive use. Wisdom is too perceptive to offer simplistic solutions to problems like alcohol abuse. To make an absolute prohibition of alcohol or other drugs would be to remove their proper use. The picture here is of a less chemically sophisticated society, where alcohol has an anesthetic function: Those in bitter anguish may drink to forget their sorrow, in contrast to kings who should not (v. 5; cf. Lev 10:11:10; Jer 16:7-8).

31:8-9. The mother's instruction to the young king concludes with a positive admonition not to be passive, but to be active and zealous in seeking the well-being of the poor and helpless. It has strong verbal and thematic connections with v. 20, precisely at the center of the next passage.

---

340. See "The Code of Hammurabi," Law 5, in Pritchard, *Ancient Near Eastern Texts Relating to the Old Testament,* 166.

PROVERBS 31:10-31, HYMN TO THE VALIANT WOMAN

COMMENTARY

This section comprises a great wisdom hymn in praise of the "capable woman/wife." This phrase, which is variously translated, is the female counterpart to "capable men," persons who evidence a wise competence and vigor in a variety of tasks (Gen 47:6; Exod 18:21, 25 [with fear of God, see 31:30]; 1 Chr 26:8, 12-14), including warfare (2 Sam 11:16; Jer 48:14; cf. Isa 5:22, which is ironic: "heroes" at drinking). The acrostic Psalm 112 (see also its acrostic twin, Psalm 111) is somewhat parallel to vv. 10-31 and describes a man who fears the Lord.

Throughout vv. 10-31 the focus is on the woman's wise and energetic activity. The poem is rich in words of action. The common Hebrew root for doing and making, working and acting (עשׂה *'sh*), appears five times (vv. 13, 22, 24, 29, 31), culminating

in the declaration that her very works praise her (v. 31). The adjective "capable" is from the same Hebrew word (חיל *ḥayil*) translated "strength" in v. 3 and "noble things" in v. 29. This repetition creates a thematic envelope linking the two sections of chap. 31, as well as an envelope marking the beginning and ending of the acrostic poem. The two poems in chap. 31 are also linked by the care for the poor and needy that king and capable woman exhibit, each in ways appropriate to them (vv. 9, 20). The expression "capable woman" appears only three times in the Bible (v. 10; 12:4; Ruth 3:11). Significantly, Ruth follows Proverbs in Hebrew Bibles.[341]

31:10. This verse picks up the love language of finding wife and wisdom that has

---

341. Thomas P. McCreesh, "Wisdom as Wife: Proverbs 31:10-31," *RB* 92 (1985) 25-46.

been pervasive in chaps. 1–9 (cf. 8:35; 18:22). The point of the rhetorical question, which expects the hyperbolic answer "no one," is not that such women do not exist, but that they are, as it were, a rare find and priceless, like Lady Wisdom herself. Pious Jewish husbands still recite this poem every Sabbath eve in praise of their own wives. "The sense is: Whoever has married such a woman knows from his experience how priceless is her worth."[342] The same rhetorical question appears with a male object in 20:6*b* (cf. Gen 41:38). A similar rhetorical idiom seems to inform Eccl 7:28, a passage often read as misogynist (cf. the numerical hyperbole in 1 Sam 18:7). The comparison to jewels/rubies links the woman to Wisdom (3:13-15; 8:11; cf. 20:15; Job 28:18).

31:11-12. These verses lay out the good the wife does for her husband (see vv. 23, 28; 12:4), because the book as a whole is addressed primarily to young men on the verge of marriage and adulthood (see Overview on chaps. 1–9). As the wise trust in God, so also a wise husband, on a human level, trusts in his wife, because she "brings him good, not harm" (for the phrase see 1 Sam 24:18; cf. 16:20; 28:25-26). "Gain" ("booty") contrasts with the ill-gotten gain of brigands in 1:13 (cf. 16:19). This term— unusual in this context—suggests the woman is like a warrior bringing home booty from her victories.

31:13-20. This section (to the end of the first half of the alphabet) details the woman's great industry and wise competence in a dialectic of acquisition and provision. The wife seeks/selects the raw materials that her hands will work into cloth; the verb used here connotes careful inquiry and investigation (see Ps 111:2; Eccl 1:13). The woman understands the nature of things; she knows the quality and use of the materials she acquires (see v. 16). The ending of this section (vv. 13-20) forms an envelope with its beginning, for her hands make yarn from the materials she sought (see Commentary on vv. 19-20). Throughout the poem, cloth, clothing, and cloth goods are symbols of industry, intelligence, and, when worn, of the glory (see Reflections on 26:1) appropriate to the woman and her house—also a key word

342. Cohen, *Proverbs,* 211.

(vv. 5, 21 [twice], 27). As Wisdom builds and supplies her house, so also the capable wife builds and fills her house with good (see Commentary on 9:1; 14:1; 24:3-4).

31:14. The woman's scope of action encompasses the entire creation: Both land and sea provide resources for her house as she brings goods from near and far (v. 14). She is like a trader's ship faring over the awesome sea (see Pss 104:24-26; 107:23-32). Israel was not a seafaring nation, but it made use of the Phoenician traders of Tyre, Sidon, and Byblos (see Commentary on v. 24; 1 Kgs 5:9). The Phoenician ships plied the coast, bringing grain from Egypt to the Levant. The woman, who appears to live in the rocky Judean hills (see Commentary on v. 21), probably brought grain for her household from the Jezreel Valley in the north, Israel's bread-basket. Her activity also spans night (vv. 15, 18) and day (vv. 12, 25). Verse 14*b,* however, turns from acquisition to provision.

31:15. This verse continues the turn to provision for the house and anticipates the nocturnal activity of v. 18. More important, this verse (of which the last phrase may be an editorial expansion) contains important links with other passages in Proverbs. "Portions" rather than tasks (for her servant-girls) better translates חק *ḥōq,* for the point is provision of house(hold) members, each according to their appropriate measure (see Commentary on 30:7-9; cf. Job 24:5*b*). The phrase is parallel to 27:27, and the reference to servant girls (only three times in Proverbs) links it also to Lady Wisdom's house (9:3). Abigail, a wise, energetic, and godly woman, had such servant girls ("maids," 1 Sam 25:42).

31:16. The woman astutely surveys and evaluates a field to see what it is good for and how it may be developed. The text probably does not describe the acquisition of the field, for Israelite women did not own land (cf. 27:26). Rather, she is like a general who conquers territory and subdues it (she takes it; this verb refers only rarely to buying; for conquest, see Gen 48:22; Deut 3:14). To transform a Judean highland plot (as large as 10 acres) into a vineyard is a difficult, massive undertaking (Eccl 2:4; Isa 5:1-5, 10). It is done on rocky, hilly ground, not good for much else (Mic 1:6). The woman takes part in humanity's task to "master the earth" (Gen

1:28-29).[343] From the "fruit of her (working) hands," probably her textiles, the woman gains yet more (see 18:20-22) by financing and planting a vineyard to produce literal fruit. Commerce and creation join to produce prosperity.

31:17. "She girds her loins with strength" is an act that prepares one for heroic or difficult action, often for warfare (1 Kgs 18:46; 2 Kgs 4:29; Jer 1:17). It is a masculine image (see Reflections and 8:14; 24:5; 31:25; Job 38:3; 40:7).

31:18. This verse describes the wife with language attributed to Lady Wisdom; "that her merchandise is good" is identical in Hebrew to "for she is more profitable" in 3:14. The verb in v. 18*a* is literally, "She tastes" (see Gen 1:4; Ps 34:8). The beautiful woman in 11:22, however, lacks taste, that is, good sense. That the capable woman's light does not go out refers partly to rising early, while it is still dark (v. 15), but mainly to the adequate provision of oil, which keeps a lamp burning through the night, as in the temple. One may compare the foolish and wise virgins in Jesus' parable (Matt 25:1-13).

31:19-20. These two verses are a carefully constructed chiastic couplet that forms the heart of the poem. In Hebrew, the woman uses her hands/palms/palm(s)/hands both to produce and to provide for the needy. There is no evidence for the use of the distaff, however, in the ancient Near East. Also, a distaff is not grasped with both hands. The Hebrew term probably refers to a "doubling spindle."[344] "She puts her hands to" is an idiom that has military connotations of mastery, thus reinforcing the heroic character of the woman's activities. Moreover, her provision for the poor and needy links her activity to King Lemuel's (v. 9). The hands that grasp to produce open wide to provide.

31:21-31. The second half of the acrostic forms an envelope, beginning with "no fear" and ending with "a woman who fears the Lord" (v. 30).

31:21-25. Here the focus is on the woman's provision for her house (v. 21 twice, see v. 27), especially of the splendid clothing she

makes, sells, and—with her household—wears (contrast 23:21). Snow was for Israelites an infrequent (except in the mountains of Lebanon) and awesome phenomenon (Ps 147:16-17). Its presence places the woman in the Judean hill country (2 Sam 23:20; 1 Macc 13:22). Because of her clothing, the woman has no fear; so she "laughs at the days to come" (v. 25; see Job 5:21-22; 39:22).

"Coverings" (מרבדים *marbaddîm*, v. 22) is an exotic word appearing only twice in the OT. It forms another link between the capable woman and the women of Proverbs 1–9, and a contrast with the wealthy adulteress (7:16). Purple, a foreign word, is another luxurious cloth, made with the famous Phoenician dye derived from shellfish.

At first glance, the appearance of the husband (v. 23; lit., "lord" [בעל *ba'al*], vv. 11, 28) seems unmotivated. Its explanation is probably to be found in v. 21*b* (see 2 Chr 18:9). The household, including the husband, are bedecked in clothing worthy of their status and glory (see Commentary on v. 13; Exod 28:2, 40; Ps 45:13-14; Dan 5:7, 16). From Exodus it is clear that to make garments that bespeak glory requires a "wise heart" (= "skill") and a "spirit of wisdom" (Exod 28:3; Jer 10:9), just as does building a tabernacle (see Commentary on Prov 9:1-18). For the significance of the city gate, see Commentary on 8:1-3 and 24:7 (see also Lam 5:14). For "elders of the land," see 1 Kgs 20:7 and Jer 26:17.

"Linen garments" (v. 24) is another foreign term of uncertain meaning; it occurs in contexts that convey splendor (Judg 14:12-13; Isa 3:23). She sells her goods to merchants (lit., "Canaanites," a term that came to mean "trader," from the renown of the Phoenician merchants; see v. 14; Job 41:6; Zech 14:21). "Sash" is a noun of the same root as "girds" in v. 17.

Verse 25 returns to the woman's own clothing (vv. 17, 21-22), but in a metaphorical sense. "Strength and dignity" (though not in combination) are clothing worn by the king (Pss 8:5; 21:5) and even by Yahweh (Pss 29:1; 93:1; 104:1). "She laughs" is an envelope parallel to "she has no fear" (see Commentary on vv. 21-25).

31:26. This forms the center of the second half of the poem. The woman's wisdom

---

343. See Jeremy Cohen, *"Be Fertile and Increase, Fill the Earth and Master It": The Ancient and Medieval Career of a Biblical Text* (Ithaca, N.Y.: Cornell University Press, 1989).

344. Al Wolters, "The Meaning of Kîšôr (Proverbs 31:19)," *HUCA* 65 (1994) 91-104.

is not simply evident in her actions (though that is the hymn's main focus). The phrase "opens her mouth" with wisdom (see v. 23a; 24:7) again links the capable woman to King Lemuel (vv. 8-9; see Commentary on vv. 19-20). It also suggests that she partakes of Wisdom's splendid words (see Commentary on 8:1, 6-10). The "teaching of kindness" or "faithful instruction" (cf. Mal 2:6) is a phrase that in the Bible only occurs here. If the former meaning is correct, one may think of Lemuel's mother, who teaches her son compassion for the destitute and afflicted (vv. 5-9; see also 1:8; 6:20). The woman herself practices what she preaches (v. 20).

31:27. A clever bilingual pun appears here. In v. 27a, the first Hebrew word forms a transliteration of the Greek word *sophia*, or wisdom; the Hebrew word for wisdom appears in the previous verse. The line may then be translated, "The ways of her house are wisdom."[345] Similarly, v. 27b may be read, "and idleness [in the concrete sense of "idlers"] will not eat bread" (cf. 30:22). Along with clothing, food and eating are a recurrent theme in the poem (vv. 14, 15; vv. 16, 18, 31 use metaphors of food and eating). The provision of food is a sign of wise diligence and not idleness (see 6:6-11; "sluggard" translates the same Hebrew root).

31:28-31. The final verses turn to those who praise the woman and conclude with a hymnic invitation to praise. Her children (lit., "sons," the audience of vv. 1-9 and chaps. 1–9) "call her blessed" (see Ps 112:1) because she, like Wisdom, is a source of blessing (see 3:13-18). Perhaps "children" is another double entendre, meaning also that her works praise her (see v. 31b; Matt 11:19; parallel Luke 7:35). Her husband praises her (the Hebrew verb [הלל *hālal*] is familiar in English as "Hallelujah" or "Alleluia," "Praise the Lord") in the words of v. 28.

Verse 29 quotes the husband's words of praise, which express the wife's incomparability; similar idioms are often used in hymns praising Yahweh. "Women" is literally "daughters" (בנות *bānôt*), which echoes the "sons" of the previous verse. "Do noble things" captures the envelope structure of the poem (noble = capable, חיל *ḥayil*; see

345. Al Wolters, "Sôpiyyâ (Prov 31:27) as Hymnic Participle and Play on *Sophia*," *JBL* 1054 (1985) 577-87.

Commentary on v. 10), especially in combination with woman/wife in v. 30. This expression can refer to gaining wealth (Deut 8:17-18; Ezek 28:4), and to heroic military exploits, (Num 24:18; 1 Sam 14:48). Significantly, the "elders at the gate" encourage Ruth to "do noble things/valiantly" in the context of building a house (Ruth 4:11; the verbal parallel is obscured in the translations). "You surpass them all" uses an idiom (עלה על *'ālâ 'al*) that often refers to military activity.

The standards according to which the capable woman is to be praised are summarized in v. 30. Verse 30a may be seen as an implicit attack on the ancient (and modern) valuations of women only according to their external beauty and sex appeal (see Commentary on 11:16, 22). The ancient literature in praise of women is consistently erotic in focus, and the hymn in praise of the capable woman is a profound corrective to this. That she does her husband good "all the days of her life" is a reminder that a wife is also a treasure in old age. Finally, this woman fears the Lord. This is the ultimate source of her energetic and joyous wisdom. This gives coherence, wholeness, and meaning to the activities of her life. Moreover, this phrase creates in Proverbs a grand envelope structure, not only with regard to women (chaps. 1–9 and 31), but with regard to its theological key: the fear of the Lord (see Commentary on 1:7; 9:10).

Verse 31 contains yet another rich wordplay. Since this is a heroic hymn, the primary sense of v. 31a is "extol her for the fruit of her hands" ("extol" = root תנה *tnh*, see Judg 5:10[11]; 11:40). This reading provides the appropriate parallel to "praise" in v. 31b. The NIV and the NRSV, as well as the ancient versions, record the secondary sense of the line, probably because the verb for "extol" is rare (see Isa 3:10 for the thought). Finally, the woman's works—no doubt suffused with piety (see 16:3)—praise her in the center of life, at the city gates (see Commentary on 8:1-3; 31:28). This is a human parallel to the cosmic praise that Yahweh's works accord to him (Ps 145:10).

REFLECTIONS

1. If in the earlier chapters the strange woman could subvert ordinary males, here it is the king, cornerstone of ancient society, whose person and duty may be damaged by wine and women (vv. 1-9). This admonition speaks only indirectly to or about women. Rather, it is a warning to powerful men who are tempted to indulge themselves sexually. It is easy for the powerful to think that divine standards for conduct do not apply to them and that what is possible is permitted. The royal stories of David and Bathsheba, Amnon and Tamar, Solomon and his harem show that the problem was not imaginary (2 Samuel 11; 13; 1 Kings 11). It is no less a problem in our society, as well as in the church, where the vitality of Christ's body and the credibility of the gospel are damaged by sexual misconduct (see 1 Cor 5:1-12; 6:9-20).

One respected commentator has said that "the elite mother, if this passage is indeed by a woman, has internalized the male fear of women so prevalent throughout the book (31:3a)."[346] To this male author it seems that interpretation misreads the book's warnings about sex and does a disservice to the queen mother and her wisdom. If men are afraid of women, their fear is misplaced and dysfunctional. What people should fear is, rather, their "disordered passions" (Augustine), by which they inordinately desire created goods (wealth, wine, property, attractive sexual partners, etc.) that are not proper to them. To say that men fear attractive women is a little like saying the male robbers of 1:10-19 fear jewels and money. A reformed robber, I suppose, would say he fears and fights his greed for what is not his. To blame the beautiful jewels is a projection of his problem onto the object. No doubt men often engage in such rationalization and projection, especially with regard to wine and women. It makes no sense, however, for an alcoholic to say, "The glass of wine led me astray" (cf. 20:1). In the perspective of Proverbs, the male line, "She was asking for it," is no excuse for sexual misconduct, even in those cases where a woman offers a sexual invitation (see 7:10-21).

Testosterone-flooded men do have a problem, but it is not women. It is themselves. Proverbs challenges them to take responsibility for their sexual selves and to love and enjoy their wives with thanks to God.

2. Some commentators have been puzzled by the appearance of the phrase "fears the LORD" in the poem on the capable woman (v. 30), since it has been totally occupied with praising the woman's mundane activities. The woman's wisdom and fear of the Lord, however, come to expression precisely in her worldly activities.[347] For Proverbs there is no sacred-secular split. All of human life and action is to manifest reverence and obedience to God and show harmony with his cosmic order. This biblical perspective that ordinary life is to reflect and serve the Creator's glory and wisdom was especially prized in the early modern period by English and Dutch Calvinists. John Milton put this ideal succinctly:

> To know
> That which before us lies in daily life
> Is the prime wisdom.[348]

This view, with its biblical roots and elaboration in various Christian traditions, had a powerful shaping role in forming the modern mind.[349] And yet, when such an affirmation of ordinary life is severed from a wise love and service of the Creator and

---

346. Fontaine, "Proverbs," 151.
347. Wolters, "Nature and Grace in the Interpretation of Proverbs 31:10-31," 153-66.
348. John Milton *Paradise Lost* VIII.192-94.
349. See Taylor, "The Affirmation of Ordinary Life," in *Sources of the Self,* 211-302; Lee Hardy, *The Fabric of This World: Inquiries into Calling, Career Choice, and the Design of Human Work* (Grand Rapids: Eerdmans, 1990).

creation, it eventually descends into that confused worship and degradation of the creation that Paul described in Romans 1.

3. Like Wisdom in 9:1-6 and Abigail in 1 Samuel 25, this woman is a great lady, a wealthy member of the aristocracy. Her counterpart may be found in other cultures, among the noble ladies of archaic Greece, for example.[350] She has a great deal of authority and power. In all her dazzling activity, she manifests a vital joy in doing good. And yet, the ideal that she embodies should not be restricted to the upper classes. Such ideals of energy and wisdom can and should pervade all strata of society.[351] An ordinary person can model himself or herself after a great man or woman, and grow thereby (cf. Phil 3:17; Heb 11:1–12:13).

4. The use of masculine images in praise of a woman (vv. 17, 25) must be considered in the light of the poem's masculine audience. If ancient Israel admired the man of war (even Yahweh in Exod 15:1-3) who defended God's people from their enemies, and if Israelite males, like men throughout history, were sinfully prone to demean women as "the weaker sex," the praise of woman here is designed to alter errant male perceptions of women. The heroic terms of strength usually applied to men are here given to a woman so her splendor and wisdom may be seen by all.

350. See Werner Jaeger, *Paideia: The Ideals of Greek Culture* (Oxford: Basil Blackwell, 1965) 1:22-24.
351. On this point, see the cogent argument of Simon Schama, *The Embarrassment of Riches: An Interpretation of Dutch Culture in the Golden Age* (Berkeley: University of California Press, 1988) 4-6.

THE BOOK OF ECCLESIASTES

INTRODUCTION, COMMENTARY, AND REFLECTIONS
BY
W. SIBLEY TOWNER

THE BOOK OF
ECCLESIASTES

INTRODUCTION

E cclesiastes has always had its fans among the original thinkers of the Jewish and Christian communities: skeptics, people with a dark vision of reality, recovering alcoholics. The rest of us know and love some of its individual epigrams and its more lyrical passages. On the whole, however, believers have found it at least baffling and at most wrongheaded. From the beginning serious efforts were made to exclude it from the list of sacred books, and even now in liturgical practice it enjoys only a very small place. The Revised Common Lectionary would have us read Eccl 3:1-13 every New Year's Day—not a day for much pious observance, except when it falls on Sunday—and offers Eccl 1:2, 12-14; 2:18-23 as the Old Testament alternative to Hos 11:1-11 on Proper 13 in cycle C. That's it! Theoretically, its place in Jewish liturgical practice is greater because it is one of the five "scrolls" (*megillot*) that are read during festivals. The book of Ecclesiastes is to be read in its entirety during the Feast of Sukkot (Tabernacles), but the number of worshipers who will sit still to hear all twelve chapters through or even, in modern synagogues, will have the opportunity to do so is surely small. Frequently this book excites talk about its partial grasp of the truth, its need for fulfillment, and its function as the dark background against which the light of the gospel shines forth.

All dismissive talk about the book of Ecclesiastes is banned from the following pages. This commentary has been written in the conviction that we need to hear the author of Ecclesiastes out. Time and time again one is driven to admit the truth of what Ecclesiastes has to say, even though one might not want to hear it. Here is the most real of the realists of the sacred writers. Here is the Hebrew writer least comfortable with conventional wisdom, and the most willing to challenge unexamined assumptions. No faith can survive long that is founded on the slippery slope of conceptually muddled piety, and in Qohelet, God has given us a tonic for our biblical faith.

Following this minimal, stage-setting introduction, each unit of the scriptural text will be discussed in a Commentary section designed to remove as many barriers to understanding as possible so that the communication of that unit can be set forth clearly. Technical discussions of philology, redactional history, ancient Near Eastern background, and the like are kept at a minimum, not because they are unimportant for understanding, but because they are available elsewhere. This interpretation has another task: to allow the clarifications of each commentary to flow directly into a Reflections section. The most original contributions of this commentary to the literature on Ecclesiastes are to be found in these Reflections. That must inevitably be the case, for these paragraphs move across more than two millennia from what the Teacher taught to what the Teacher's teachings can teach us.

THE NAMES OF THE BOOK: QOHELET AND ECCLESIASTES

We know the writer of the book of Ecclesiastes not by name but by the title קדלת (*qōhelet*). In two of its seven occurrences in the book, that title even appears in Hebrew with the definite article (7:27 [as amended]; 12:8). Traditionally this title has come over into English as "the Preacher." The real identity of the author is masked by this title, however. True, the word *qōhelet* offers slight warrant for claiming that the author was a woman, because it has the form of a feminine singular participle of the Hebrew verbal root קהל (*qhl*, "assemble"). Arrayed against this suggestion, however, are two weightier considerations: (1) Other titles, presumably of male persons, can be found in the Hebrew Bible in exactly the same grammatical form (e.g., Hassophereth ["the leatherworker"]; Pochereth-hazzebaim ["the gazelle-tender"] in Ezra 2:55, 57). This leads to the conclusion that the "feminine" form of the participle is merely an alternative form of the masculine. (2) A clearly male appellation, "the son of David," is appended to the title in Eccl 1:1, and the verbs accompanying the title here and in two of its other appearances (Eccl 12:8-9) are masculine. For better or for worse, then, in this commentary the speaker in the book of Ecclesiastes will be referred to as "him."

Now, one of the functions of the Hebrew participle is to serve as the noun that names the one who does the action of the verb. So a *qōhelet* is the agent of "assembly," the "assembler." If what he assembles is a קהל (*qāhāl*, "congregation"), one can translate *qōhelet* as "leader of the assembly" (see NIV note) or even, to use the title most frequently given by us to such a functionary, "preacher" (see NRSV note). Already in antiquity, the Greek translators of the Hebrew Bible accepted this sense of the term *qōhelet*. Their Septuagint translates it as Ἐκκλησιαστής (*Ekklēsiastēs*), "one who leads a congregation [ἐκκλησία *ekklēsia*]," and it is from them that the name reached the English language.

Working from the basic root meaning of "assemble" for the verb קהל (*qāhal*), some argue that a *qōhelet* is one who assembles sentences or proverbs or wisdom."[1] The translation "Teacher," favored by both the NIV and the NRSV, attempts to capture some of both of these senses of the term. A teacher not only assembles information to convey to students but also carries out this function in an assembly, perhaps even in a place of congregational worship. There are other perfectly good and far more common Hebrew words for "teacher," of course, and whether *qōhelet* would have been understood as a synonym for them is difficult to judge because this title occurs only in the book of Ecclesiastes. If this writer is essentially a teacher, then by the standards of the wisdom literature of the Hebrew Bible he is a highly original thinker, capable of uncommonly sustained argument.

A title always implies a social setting. No one is called "judge" except in a place in which decisions are handed down. People receive the title "pilot" by virtue of their vocation in the maritime or aeronautical industries. If we could be sure which way to construe it, we could provide Qohelet with at least a sketchy sociological setting from his title alone. If it is taken to mean "Preacher," the name Qohelet conjures up a social setting of a congregation of believers—e.g., an early synagogue. Taken to mean "Teacher," it suggests a place of instruction for one or more pupils—e.g., a tutor's chamber in a royal or high priestly household or another early school. Unfortunately, we know next to nothing about either places of worship (other than the Second Temple) or schools in third-century BCE Judea. So whichever way we go with the title, we gain only a hint about the work of the man.

---

1. James L. Crenshaw, *Ecclesiastes*, OTL (Philadelphia: Westminster, 1987) 33-34.

It makes sense that the author of the book of Ecclesiastes should be referred to by his title, "the Teacher," only four times in the book: in the superscription (1:1) and in its reprise (12:8), once in the main body (7:27), and once in the epilogue (12:9). After all, he is presented as having written the book, and having done so mostly in the first person! In these four instances, some narrator or editor of the teacher's work butts in to say something about the man. Although the definite article appears in the Hebrew only in 7:27 (as amended) and 12:8, the NRSV and the NIV make all four occurrences definite: He is always "the Teacher."

LANGUAGE AND GENRE

The Hebrew language in which Qohelet wrote is distinctive. Either it is a late dialect peculiar to his place and time or, because his task was to offer a philosophical discussion of issues, he had to shape a new language for the purpose. Ancient Hebrew was not a literature given to abstract philosophy; however, if there was a philosopher in ancient Hebrew, Qohelet was the one, and to him fell the task of making the language of his people work for the purpose of sustained reflection.

Like other post-exilic writings in the Hebrew Bible, Qohelet's Hebrew betrays significant influence of the Aramaic language. Because Aramaic, like Hebrew, is a member of the family of northwest Semitic languages, the two always drew on a common vocabulary base. Periodically, however, new words or grammatical constructions would flood into Hebrew from Aramaic, leaving behind enriched linguistic soil. This happened during the period of the divided monarchy, especially in the northern kingdom of Israel, which had much intercourse with the Aramean kingdoms of Damascus and Hamath. It happened again after the exile. From the seventh century BCE down into Hellenistic times as late as 200 BCE, Official or Imperial Aramaic was the lingua franca of the Near East. The royal epistles and decrees preserved in the book of Ezra are written in this language. The Hebrew spoken and written in Judea during these years in this Aramaic milieu is distinctive enough to have been given its own name, Late Biblical Hebrew. Probable Aramaisms that occur only in Ecclesiastes in the Hebrew text of the Bible (though they often become common in Mishnaic and even modern Hebrew) include עִנְיָן (ʿinyan, "business"; 1:13 and seven other times as a noun); כְּבָר (kĕbār, "already"; 1:10 and eight other times); חֶשְׁבּוֹן (ḥešbôn, "sum"; 7:25, 27; 9:10); פֵּשֶׁר (pēšer, "interpretation"; 8:1); and גוּמָּץ (gûmmāṣ, "pit"; 10:8). Many other Aramaic loanwords and grammatical forms occur as well, including the synonymous terms רַעְיוֹן (raʿyôn) and רְעוּת (rĕʿût), "chasing [after wind]," alternatively translated "feeding [on wind]" in the NRSV note (1:14 and seven other times). In all, 3.1 percent of Qohelet's vocabulary consists of Aramaisms.[2]

Quite apart from linguistic evidences of origin in late post-exilic culture, Qohelet simply forged his own distinctive literary style out of a repertoire both of standard clichés and of unique words or inflections of words. Five of his favorite terms are discussed below (see the section "The Vocabulary of Qohelet's Thought"), and others are pointed out along the way.

The very genre of the book of Ecclesiastes is a matter of debate. The editors of the NIV consider 60 percent of the text to be poetry, while the NRSV thinks it is 75 percent prose. The translators of the Good News Bible and the Revised English Bible think the only poetic passage in the entire book is 3:2-8. The criteria for identifying poetry in biblical Hebrew are subtle, and with Ecclesiastes they function hardly at all. As to the literary form of the book as a whole, von Rad's proposal that it follows the Egyptian genre of "royal testament" is now generally rejected because the pretense of kingly authorship is dropped after chap. 2. The Hellenistic genre "diatribe," too, has failed to convince critics, largely because of the absence of any explicit dialogue. Numerous sub-genres can be recognized (e.g., autobiographical narrative, rhetorical questions, parable, curses and blessings, proverbs), but for the book as a whole the very general rubrics "instruction" and "reflection" seem to be most satisfactory.[3]

---

2. Crenshaw, *Ecclesiastes*, 31.
3. Roland E. Murphy, *Ecclesiastes*, WBC 23A (Waco, Tex.: Word, 1992) xxxi-xxxii.

AUTHORSHIP, DATE, AND HISTORICAL SETTING

The language of Ecclesiastes demands that it be placed among the later books of the Hebrew canon. Its language is not as late as that of Daniel, however. Almost half of Daniel is written in the so-called Middle Aramaic dialect that slowly displaced Official Aramaic in written texts after Greek became the more widely used official language in the Hellenistic period (after 200 BCE). Embedded in that Aramaic and in the Hebrew half of Daniel as well are loanwords from Greek; furthermore, that book is rich with veiled historical allusions to the Ptolemaic and Seleucid successors of Alexander in Egypt and Antioch respectively. Indeed, because of those allusions, we can date Daniel in its canonical form quite confidently to 164 BCE. The language of Ecclesiastes shows no discernible influence from Hellenistic Greek, nor is it particularly reminiscent of the Hebrew of Daniel. It should, therefore, be dated earlier than 164 BCE. This *terminus ante quem* (the date before which it must have been written) is supported by the presence of fragmentary Ecclesiastes texts among the Dead Sea Scrolls of Cave 4, dated mid-second century BCE.

The book exhibits the "philosophical" spirit of the Hellenistic period to a degree more pronounced than any other book of the Hebrew canon, even though none of the Teacher's ideas can be directly linked to Greek originals. All things considered, it seems sensible to date the book to the period between 332 BCE, when Alexander the Great put an end to Persian political dominance in the Middle East and cemented the hold of Greek cultural influence in the area, and 200 BCE. Had Qohelet known of the wrenching political crises associated with the change from Ptolemaic to Seleucid suzerainty in Palestine around that time, he might have alluded to them. Without attempting a definitive statement on the matter, this exposition will assume that Ecclesiastes was written in the middle of the third century BCE, perhaps around 250.

Other books, such as Daniel, offer historical evidences that corroborate linguistic judgments about their dates. The narrator of the final form of the book of Ecclesiastes also offers a historical setting to the reader, though without reference to the Egyptian Ptolemies of his own day or to their rivals, the Seleucid monarchs of Antioch in Syria. Instead he reaches over centuries to the era of monarchy in Jerusalem. It is no surprise that the superscription (Eccl 1:1) attributes the book to a king. That a king would concern himself with wisdom might surprise people today, but it certainly would not have done so in antiquity. The importance of circles of scribes, seers, and teachers at the courts of Babylon, Persia, and Egypt can hardly be overestimated. In ancient Israel the court—whether royal, gubernatorial, or high priestly—was paired with the Temple as the center of learning, the patron of scribes and teachers, the arbiter of etiquette. Joseph and Daniel in their respective times act the parts of wise and learned courtiers. The wisdom writer, Jesus ben Sira, who may even have been a late contemporary of the author of Ecclesiastes, instructed the patrician youth of his age in the things that make for successful living, boldly claiming, "Hear but a little of my instruction,/ and through me you will acquire silver and gold" (Sir 51:28 NRSV).

It comes as no surprise either that "the Teacher" is not only a king but is, in the literary presentation given to his work, no other than "the son of David," King Solomon. After all, it was Solomon who, having asked God for the gift of wisdom, received it so abundantly that it "surpassed the wisdom of all the people of the east, and all the wisdom of Egypt." It was he who "composed three thousand proverbs, and his songs numbered a thousand and five." It was to hear his wisdom that "people came from all the nations . . . [and] from all the kings of the earth who had heard of his wisdom" (1 Kgs 4:29-34 NRSV). Pre-eminent among these visitors was the queen of Sheba, who exclaimed to him, "Your wisdom and prosperity far surpass the report that I had heard" (1 Kgs 10:7). His father, David, might have been both warrior and lyricist, but to Solomon were attributed, among the canonical books, whole sections of the book of Proverbs, Ecclesiastes, and the great lyric of erotic love, the Song of Solomon (NRSV), or Song of Songs (NIV). Apocryphal works attributed to the wise king include a long sapiental book, the book of Wisdom, the *Psalms of Solomon, Odes of Solomon,* and a pseudepigraphical *Testament of Solomon,* which touts his greatness as a magician.

However, when all is said and done, one person who almost certainly was not the author of the book of Ecclesiastes was Solomon. First of all, the author drops any pretense of being a king after the fictional narrative of the royal experiment (Eccl 2:1-11). In the middle of the book, he offers advice to courtiers who come into the presence of the king as if he were standing beside them and whispering words of etiquette into their ears (Eccl 8:2-6; 10:4). He expresses views of monarchy very unlikely to have emanated from any actual royal throne (Eccl 4:13-16; 5:8-9). Finally, he is identified in the epilogue as a wise man or sage, who worked among the people (Eccl 12:9). Apart from these bits of internal evidence that the writer of Ecclesiastes, or the Teacher himself (if they are not one and the same person), was not a king of any kind is the linguistic evidence already alluded to, which places the book well after the time of any monarchy in Israel.

Who, then, was the author of Qohelet? For the purposes of this commentary, let us assume that the author of the bulk of the book is also the one who speaks in the first person. Only the epilogists and the author of the first verse of the book stand apart from the man who teaches through the rest of the text, and their identities are too pallid to obscure the thought and personality of the Teacher in any significant way.

He is a "sage" (Eccl 12:9). It is generally agreed that sages played important roles in the royal courts of the ancient Near East. This does not necessarily mean, however, that Qohelet was either a member or a servant of the elite, or that he shared their "upper-crust" attitudes. Some commentators find the bent of a patrician in passages like 7:21 and 11:1-2, but others dismiss as routine the references to a personal servant and investment of capital. The assertion that he worked among the common people (Eccl 12:9) might suggest a link with the traditional wisdom circles of the rural folk of Palestine. Nevertheless, a man who could read and write and who could draw even indirectly upon resources of the ancient Near Eastern sapiental tradition seems unlikely to have been a common peasant. At the same time, too little is known about the sages as a class (if, indeed, they constituted anything as definable as a class in ancient Israel) to make generalizations about their place in the social order.[4]

As for the provenance of the book of Ecclesiastes, efforts to show settings as diverse as Egypt and Phoenicia have not gained much support. While nothing in the book requires that its author had worked in Judea or Jerusalem, neither is there any compelling reason not to make that assumption.

THE CANONICITY OF QOHELET

Although not much is known about the process by which Qohelet came to be regarded as sacred scripture, controversy evidently surrounded its candidacy for the first few centuries. Fragments of Ecclesiastes from about 150 BCE appear at Qumran, but a book did not have to be regarded as Scripture in order to be included in the library of the Dead Sea community. The Mishnah reports challenges in rabbinic circles to the sacredness of Qohelet down to the time of Rabbi Akiba (died c. 135 CE). After setting forth the general principle that "all the holy writings render the hands [ritually] unclean," *M. Yad* 3:5 states, "The Song of Songs and Ecclesiastes render the hands unclean." The rabbis argued about the matter, however. Rabbi Akiba gave a ringing endorsement of the canonicity of the Song of Songs with these words: "God forbid!—no man in Israel ever disputed about the Song of Songs [that he should say] that it does not render the hands unclean . . . for all the Writings are holy, but the Song of Songs is the Holy of Holies." Then, as if to suggest that the argument about Qohelet continued on, the passage concludes, "And if aught was in dispute the dispute was about Ecclesiastes alone."[5] Ecclesiastes is mentioned in the very earliest Christian lists of canonical writings as well, such as that of Melito of Sardis (died c. 190 CE).

QOHELET'S RELATIONSHIP WITH ANCIENT WISDOM

The book of Ecclesiastes belongs to that third part of the canon of the Hebrew Scriptures known as the Ketubim ("Writings"). Into this section of the Bible the scribes of ancient Israel

4. Murphy, *Ecclesiastes*, xxi.
5. Herbert Danby, trans. and ed., "The Mishnah" (Oxford: Oxford University Press, 1933) 782.

gathered all sacred texts that were neither Torah nor prophets: Ezra, Nehemiah, and the books of Chronicles (late historical writings); the book of Psalms (hymns of the Second Temple, though certain ones, such as Psalms 1; 37; 49; 73; 112; and 128, are recognized as "wisdom" psalms); Lamentations (a collection of laments or dirges over the loss of Judah that are traditionally treated as an appendix to Jeremiah); Daniel (placed among the prophets in the order of the Christian canon); Ruth and Esther (short stories); and the Song of Songs (nuptial poetry). Only the remaining three "Writings"—Proverbs, Job, and Ecclesiastes—remain in the true "wisdom" canon of the Hebrew Bible.

That Ecclesiastes belongs in the company of Job and Proverbs cannot be doubted. The genres of writing, the strongly secular perspective, the sophisticated quarrel with conventional piety and theology—all belong to the effort of wisdom writers to make sense of life based on observation and practical experience. Like all of wisdom literature, both courtly and popular, the focus is on human nature, and the goal is to guide human beings into the path of successful living. Rules of proper behavior (i.e., etiquette), observations of natural phenomena, and even some sustained theological reflections (such as those on Dame Wisdom in Proverbs 1–9 and on theodicy in the book of Job) are the stuff of the classical sapiental writings of Israel.

The world of wisdom, however, stretched far beyond the narrow borders of Israel. Any reflection on the wisdom bed in which Ecclesiastes nestles, therefore, has to take account of this larger environment. The relationship was richer and more complex than a few sentences can indicate; the examples given here are merely illustrative. Mesopotamian wisdom traditions must have been known to writers and thinkers in Israel for nearly the first millennium of its existence as a people, since Assyria, Babylon, and finally Persia dominated the Levant during most of that time. The Babylonian exile may have given the displaced intellectuals of Jerusalem fresh purchase on the actual sapiental texts of their conquerors—the image of Daniel and his friends successfully gobbling up learning while picking delicately at their victuals in the Babylonian Academy of Wisdom (Dan 1:3-7, 18-21) might not be far off the mark. Among several witnesses to Babylonian theological pessimism about fair treatment for the righteous at the hands of the gods is *A Dialogue About Human Misery,* or "The Babylonian Ecclesiastes."[6] Ecclesiastes 3:11 resonates in a particularly striking way with v. 24 of this text, which says: "The mind of the god, like the center of the heavens, is remote; His knowledge is difficult, men cannot understand it."

Even a document as different in genre from Qohelet as the Mesopotamian epic of the primeval hero Gilgamesh provides evidence of the ubiquity of sage advice. The alewife, Siduri, tries to deflect the hero's quest for immortality with words of realism that have often been compared to the wisdom of the Teacher in Eccl 9:7-10:

> Gilgamesh, whither rovest thou?
> The life thou pursuest thou shalt not find.
> When the gods created mankind,
> Death for mankind they set aside,
> Life in their own hand retaining.
> Thou, Gilgamesh, let full be thy belly,
> Make thou merry by day and by night.
> Of each day make thou a feast of rejoicing,
> Day and night dance thou and play!
> Let thy garments be sparkling fresh,
> Thy head be washed; bathe thou in water.
> Pay heed to the little one that holds on to thy hand,
> Let thy spouse delight in thy bosom!
> For this is the task of [humankind]![7]

6. James B. Pritchard, ed., *Ancient Near Eastern Texts Relating to the Old Testament,* 3rd ed. (Princeton, N.J.: Princeton University Press, 1969), 438-40.
7. Pritchard, *Ancient Near Eastern Texts Relating to the Old Testament,* 90.

How the sapiental tradition of Egypt was mediated to the late post-exilic intellectual community in Judah is not entirely clear, although we know that a great deal of intellectual and cultural exchange between the two cultures took place right alongside commercial enterprise and the usual military incursions. That the sages of Egypt served in the ancient and universal role as counselors to nobility is demonstrated conclusively in wall paintings, tomb furnishings, and in such written works as *The Instruction of Amenemope*.[8] It is a role with which Qohelet was evidently familiar as well (e.g., Eccl 8:2-6). Other commonalities, if not direct influences, can be demonstrated in such works as *The Song of the Harper*,[9] which sounds the theme of *carpe diem* ("seize the day!") with words like these: "Fulfill thy needs upon earth, after the command of thy heart, until there come for thee that day of mourning" (cf. Eccl 7:14). *The Instruction of Ani*[10] offers admonitions about the proper approach to God, similar to those found in Eccl 5:1-7.

As far as relationship with Greek tradition, the consensus of scholars is that the parallels of ideas are frequent and broad enough to justify the contention that Qohelet was very much influenced by the Hellenistic culture that had spread throughout the domain of the Ptolemies, including Judea, in the third century BCE. Attempts to identify specific Greek influences in the terminology of the book or to discern overt borrowing by Qohelet from Greek philosophers or literature have all failed. It is clear, however, that he shared the quest of Greek philosophy in general, which was to help a human being live happily in a world that is not very friendly to human happiness.[11]

It remains to say something of the relation of Ecclesiastes to the two great deuterocanonical Jewish sapiental works of the last centuries before the turn of the era, Ecclesiasticus (the Wisdom of Ben Sira) and the book of Wisdom (also known as the Wisdom of Solomon). Many efforts have been made to link Qohelet's work with that of Ben Sira, whose book is dated about 180 BCE. Certainly, the two authors held one pedagogical objective in common: Both wished to imbue their students with ideas and etiquette sufficient to move successfully in the highest levels of society. Ben Sira differs markedly from Qohelet on the major wisdom theme of retribution by generally following the conventional expectation of his age that the system will requite fools and knaves for their deeds. Qohelet, of course, will have none of that. The two do agree that justice, if there is any, has to be achieved here and now because there is no life after death and in Sheol there is neither hope nor praise.

As far as the relationships with the first-century CE book of Wisdom, much effort has been made to show that it is in part an intentional refutation of Ecclesiastes. This polemic is centered particularly in Wisdom 2, which seems to target such passages in Ecclesiastes as 3:16-22 and 9:5-6 that speak of non-existence after death. One major innovation by the Wisdom of Solomon over against Ecclesiastes (and the rest of the canonical Hebrew wisdom writings, as well as Sirach) is the doctrine of blessed immortality. That doctrine, of course, takes care of a number of the laments raised by Ecclesiastes, including the obscure but poignant agnostic statement about the wise and the righteous in the hands of God: "whether it is love or hate, one does not know" (Eccl 9:1). The writer of Wisdom knows. He believes that in the life beyond death a loving God makes good with those who trust that God.

Nevertheless, rather than argue that the writer of the book of Wisdom is specifically attacking Ecclesiastes on this point, it seems preferable to take the later work as simply a fresh meditation for another generation on the great themes of justice and death, which were perennially raised by the Israelite wisdom tradition and were addressed powerfully in his own time by Qohelet.

THE PLOT OF THE BOOK

Every piece of literature, down to and including one's laundry list, has a plot. That is to say, it moves according to some logic. It aims at some end and follows some structure in order to

8. Pritchard, *Ancient Near Eastern Texts Relating to the Old Testament*, 421-25.
9. Pritchard, *Ancient Near Eastern Texts Relating to the Old Testament*, 467.
10. Pritchard, *Ancient Near Eastern Texts Relating to the Old Testament*, 420-21.
11. M. V. Fox, *Qoheleth and His Contradictions*, BLS 18 (Sheffield: Almond, 1989) 16.

reach that end. Certain essays and books display their plots prominently, while others conceal them in elaborate ways. People tend to enjoy reading the former more than the latter. The same is true of biblical texts. They all have internal emphases, main points, punch lines, and the like. Some, such as Jonah or the Joseph narrative, are novellas with rising action, climactic moment, and falling action—just like *Tom Jones* or *A Farewell to Arms.* Others, such as the epistles of Paul, follow a more tortuous route toward their main emphases.

Either the book of Ecclesiastes has one of the most tortuous plots of any book of the Hebrew Bible, or else it has an extremely minimal one. The latter seems to be more likely. There is no story line. Unlike any one of the prophetic books, the seams between individual units in Ecclesiastes are often invisible. In fact, it is more difficult to identify most of the individual pericopes of Ecclesiastes than in any other book of the Hebrew Bible, except perhaps the book of Proverbs. This much, however, is agreed upon by all: There is a narrator of all the material between Eccl 1:2 and Eccl 12:8. All of this material presents itself as being the thought of Qohelet, whose book it is. Ecclesiastes 1:1 is always conceded to be a superscription or title for the book, probably by some other hand, and nearly all commentators agree that the last two units of the book (12:9-11, 12-14) are by one or two other persons who have added some words at the end of the work of Qohelet to integrate that work somehow into the stream of canonical literature. Beyond this, there is no universally agreed-upon analysis of the structure of the book.

Efforts to provide such an analysis range from claims that the book is a systematic philosophical treatise with a discernible architecture,[12] through proposals that it is a series of intentionally created antitheses or "polar structures" by which the Teacher set his thought off against conventional wisdom,[13] to proposals that the book is given unity by one concept or another (e.g., ephemerality, goodness, divine freedom), to denials that any overarching structure is demonstrable.[14] Crenshaw simply lists twenty-five units, comparing their sequence to the apparently random but sometimes illuminating configurations of a kaleidoscope.[15] Murphy, on the other hand, adopts and adapts the structural analysis of Addison G. Wright.[16] This approach, based initially on repetition of key phrases, was elaborated by Wright's discovery of a numerological pattern that places the conceptual midpoint of the book exactly where the Masoretes, who were only counting verses, placed it—namely, after 6:9 (the 111th of the 222 verses in the book).

More recent commentators seem less eager than those of a generation ago to invoke a slew of editors and glossators (as Barton, e.g., did)[17] or extensive cryptic quotations from other sources (as Gordis did)[18] to account for the numerous and often-remarked-upon contradictions within the book. Now its tensions strike people more as the natural inevitabilities of experience than as a dialectic between various voices. From one angle or another, everything that is said is true. Indeed, one might ask whether the failure of experience and observation to convince the writer of the truth either of traditional reward-and-punishment ideology or of an untraditional outlook of total moral randomness may have led him to despair of ever arriving at a working philosophy of life. Perhaps it led the writer to what is now called, in psychological jargon, "the doubting syndrome," in which he found reason to question everything simply because its opposite could also be found.

The outline of the book used in this commentary is merely descriptive of the contents and discerns no major organizing structure in the work. Certain structural features do stand out, however. (1) Specialized vocabulary, clichés, and refrains often signal the presence of major teachings. (2) Several important units can easily be demarcated: the thematic statement (Eccl 1:2; 12:8), the poem on times and seasons (Eccl 3:1-8), the sad but beautiful evocation of the ravages of old age (Eccl 12:1-7), and many individual epigrams and proverbs. (3) Elsewhere, it seems to be the case that the practice of gathering thematically related materials together in little collections is operative. (4) Beyond that, it is noteworthy that some sentences are stated in the

12. Norbert Lohfink, *Kohelet, Die neue Echter Bibel* (Würzburg: Echter Verlag, 1980).
13. J. A. Loader, *Ecclesiastes,* Text and Interpretation (Grand Rapids: Eerdmans, 1986).
14. R. N. Whybray, *Ecclesiastes,* NCB (Grand Rapids: Eerdmans, 1989).
15. Crenshaw, *Ecclesiastes,* 47-49.
16. Murphy, *Ecclesiastes,* xxxviii-xli.
17. George A. Barton, *A Critical and Exegetical Commentary on the Book of Ecclesiastes,* ICC (New York: Scribner's, 1908).
18. Robert Gordis, *Koheleth: The Man and His World,* 1st ed. (New York: Schocken, 1951; 3rd ed., 1968).

first-person singular as if they were "reflections" by the author, and others, which can be called "instruction," are directed to the student in the second-person singular or even with the use of the imperative mood of the verb. These "reflections" and "instructions" interface throughout the book in a way that is almost as seamless as the tongue-and-groove joining of a good oak floor.

Perhaps Ecclesiastes is best viewed as a notebook of ideas by a philosopher/theologian about the downside and upside of life. In this notebook he reports much of his own inner life and then turns to his students or his public with instructions that flow from that inner life. All of this reflection and instruction is framed by the famous slogan of the book, "Vanity of vanities! All is vanity" (1:2; 12:8 NRSV). Perhaps that slogan itself, together with a few other key terms, provides the most solid principle of organization that we can grasp. As G. von Rad puts it, "There is . . . an inner unity which can find expression otherwise than through a linear development of thought or through a logical progression in the thought process, namely through the unity of style and topic and theme. . . . A specific, unifying function is fulfilled by a small number of leading concepts to which Koheleth returns again and again, concepts such as 'vanity,' 'striving after wind,' 'toil,' 'lot,' etc."[19]

THE VOCABULARY OF QOHELET'S THOUGHT

"All" (כל *kōl*). In the opening thematic statement of the book (Eccl 1:2), Qohelet uses the word *all*, and he never lets up after that. The word occurs in 41 percent of the 222 verses of the book. The text of Ecclesiastes constitutes about 1.2 percent of the volume of the Hebrew Bible, and yet 2.1 percent of the verses in which "all" is used are in this book, almost double the expected rate. This frequency of the use of "all" in Ecclesiastes far outdistances any competitor in the Hebrew Bible. Other wisdom texts do not stress it. In Proverbs it occurs in 8.3 percent of the verses, and in Job 6.2 percent. This statistical study suggests that the universal perspective conveyed by the word *all* belongs in a very special way to Qohelet, the philosopher and theologian. It is useful to him because of his determination to reflect on the meaning of all of life—not just Israelite life, not even just human life, but all of life. Alone within the canon of the Hebrew Bible, Qohelet makes this kind of meditation a central concern; more than any other book of the Old Testament, this one attempts to arrive at understandings that will work everywhere and in every time.

"Vanity" (הבל *hebel*). The noun *hebel* occurs some sixty-nine times in the entire Hebrew Bible, five of which can be subtracted because they are the name of Abel, Cain's unfortunate younger sibling. Of the sixty-four remaining occurrences, thirty-eight, or almost 60 percent, occur in the book of Ecclesiastes alone, beginning in the opening thematic statement (Eccl 1:2). As if the great partiality of the Preacher for this term were not enough to drive home the centrality of the concept to his thought, the locations of most of its occurrences further underscore its importance. Usually it appears at the end of a discussion in the position of a punch line or a coda; furthermore, it is often used in longer formulas with one or both of two other stock expressions, "a chasing after the wind" and "under the sun."

In the light of this high visibility, one would suppose that the meaning of the Hebrew term *hebel* would be clear to all translators and interpreters. But such is not the case. This can quickly be illustrated by looking at the words used by various English versions simply to translate the first clause of Eccl 1:2: "Vanity of vanities" (KJV, RSV, NRSV, JB); "utterly vain, utterly vain" (Moffatt); "emptiness, emptiness" (NEB); "futility, utter futility" (REB); "it is useless, useless" (GNB); "utter futility!" (TNK); "nothing is worthwhile" (TLB); "utterly absurd" (Fox); "a vapor of vapors!" (Scott); "meaningless! meaningless!" (NIV).

These English renditions of the Hebrew word *hebel* do not all mean the same thing. They are not even all the same part of speech. Although most translators take the word to be a noun, the NIV treats it as an adjective. To say that something is a "vapor" captures a sense of ephemerality, but ephemerality and "utter futility" are not really the same thing. Something can be extremely

---

19. Von Rad, *Wisdom in Israel*, 227.

substantial and not at all vaporous but still be utterly futile. Similarly, something can be meaningless without necessarily being worthless or vain. Perhaps the least satisfactory translation of the term *hebel,* because of the broadness of its meaning in English, is the traditional "vanity of vanities." What does that mean? That things are proud and stuck up? That things are a waste of time? That they are ineffectual?

Here, then, is the most important term in the book of Ecclesiastes, and its English equivalent is not agreed upon. No wonder. Even in Hebrew its sense is ambiguous. One way, of course, to make precise the meaning of the term in Ecclesiastes would be to go to the other 40 percent of its occurrences elsewhere in the Hebrew Bible to see what kind of sense can be made of it there. The standard biblical Hebrew dictionary gives the root meaning of the word as "vapor" or "breath"; that sense of the term in fact fits best with its use in Isa 57:13, where, in a polemic against idols, it is used in parallel with wind: "The wind will carry them off,/ a breath [*hebel*] will take them away" (NRSV). This sense of the term can also be found in post-biblical Hebrew texts. Other occurrences translated by the NRSV as "breath" (Job 7:16; Pss 39:5-6, 11; 62:9; 78:33; 94:11; 144:4; Prov 21:6) do not demand this rendition alone. The parallel with "shadow" in Pss 39:5-6 and 144:4 and the comparison with weightlessness in Ps 62:9 suggest "ephemerality." Qohelet, too, uses the term in this sense at least once (Eccl 11:10). Other texts imply a meaning of emptiness or worthlessness, as in Jer 10:15: "They are worthless, a work of delusion" (NRSV; see also Job 35:16; Jer 51:18). Elsewhere *hebel* means "falsehood" (e.g., 2 Kgs 17:15; Job 21:34; Zech 10:2).

From these comparisons it is evident that the term *hebel* describes something that is without merit, an unreliable, probably useless thing. Perhaps, in the manner of creative thinkers everywhere, the Teacher has welded new meaning onto this already extant term so that it can better serve his special purposes. Michael Fox thinks so, arguing that the most appropriate English rendition of *hebel* as Qohelet uses it is "absurd," "absurdity." In order to define "absurd," he appeals to the contention of Albert Camus that absurdity arises when two ideas that ought to be joined by links of causality and harmony are in fact divorced from each other. Something that is absurd just makes no sense. "To call something 'absurd' is to claim a certain understanding of its nature: It is contrary to reason."[20] That, says Fox, is what *hebel* is in Ecclesiastes. (Murphy agrees with the sense of "absurd, absurdity" for Qohelet's *hebel,* but thinks that "irrational" goes one nuance too far for the meaning of "absurd." "Incomprehensible" is plenty for him.)[21]

Fox follows the many uses of the term *hebel* in Qohelet as it is applied to human behavior, living beings, and divine behavior and finds that this sense of "absurdity" for the notion of *hebel* best comprehends them all. Human labor produces goods and achievement, and yet all avails for nothing in the face of chance and death. It is possible to find pleasure, wisdom, and the like, and yet they do not guarantee happiness or long life. Even the behavior that, according to the normal piety of ancient Israel and of many people today, ought to be rewarded by God appears instead to be punished: The system of reward and punishment is out of order. In all of these things a disparity exists between what people expect and what actually happens to them. By his widespread application of *hebel,* "there is not, Qohelet avows, a single unspoiled value in this life."[22]

"Toil" (עמל *'āmāl*). This Hebrew noun occurs some fifty-five times in the Bible. It has nothing to do with the honest, goal-oriented labor of what we know as the "work ethic," but almost always conveys such negative ideas as trouble (Job 3:10; 5:6), weariness (Ps 73:16), sorrow (Jer 20:18), mischief (Job 4:8; Ps 140:9), and even oppression (Deut 26:7). In Ecclesiastes alone the term appears twenty-two times as a noun (40 percent of its usage), which means that, as in the case of *hebel,* it supplies a major motif to the message of this book. The accents of suffering and pain remain even though the Teacher uses the term in a more focused way to refer to hard labor of the sort best conveyed in English by the word *toil* (see also Ps 107:12). For Qohelet, toil and life are practically identical.[23] Like the writer of the story of the fall in Genesis 3, he places human beings in a world from which both the presence and the friendship of God are withdrawn and people are left to fend for themselves on an accursed ground in lives of toil that end only in death.

20. Michael V. Fox, "The Meaning of *Hebel*," *JBL* 105 (1986) 413.
21. Murphy, *Ecclesiastes*, lix.
22. Murphy, *Ecclesiastes*, lix.
23. Fox, *Qoheleth and His Contradictions*, 54.

"Wisdom" (חכמה *ḥokmâ*). This noun occurs some twenty-six times in Ecclesiastes, beginning with 1:13. The related noun/adjective חכם (*ḥākām*, "sage," wise") also occurs nearly as frequently (22 times), and the verb occurs four times, twice in its usual stative sense, "to be wise" (2:15; 7:23), once in the unique preterit sense of "to act wisely" (2:19), and once in a reflexive form (7:16). These terms are part of the distinctive semantic repertoire of the Teacher, though their occurrence is not uniform throughout the book but clusters in those pericopes in which he reflects on the value of "wisdom" as such (1:12-18; 2; 7:10-13, 15-25; 9:10-18). Qohelet does not employ the entire semantic range that the word *ḥokmâ* enjoys elsewhere in the Hebrew Bible. For example, he does not use it to mean the inspired skill of a craftsman (cf. Exod 35:35; 36:2, 8; 1 Kgs 7:13-14); nor does he personify it as Dame Wisdom, God's first creation and co-worker in the making of the world (cf. Prov 8:22-31; Sir 24:1-12; Wis 7:22–8:18).

Unlike the other "wisdom" books of the Hebrew Bible, Ecclesiastes never explicitly identifies wisdom as "the fear of the LORD" (cf. Job 28:28; Ps 111:10; Prov 15:33; Sir 1:14), though he often recommends fearing God (e.g., Eccl 5:7; 7:18; 8:12); nor does he use it as a synonym for Torah, God's revealed will (cf. Sir 24:23; Bar 4:10). By *ḥokmâ* Qohelet never means the rich tradition of mantic wisdom—the interpretation of dreams, the solution of riddles, and other occult arts at which, for example, the Jewish sage Daniel excelled (Dan 5:11) and with which Solomon was credited by later generations (Wis 7:15-22).

For all that, however, the Teacher does mean a variety of things by the term "wisdom." It is an intellectual skill to be used in the discovery of truth (e.g., 2:3; 7:23), or at least the discovery that truth is undiscoverable (1:12-14). It is the mental endowment of "wise" people (e.g., 2:9), from whose instruction one gains great profit (7:5; 9:17). It can be construed as a moral value, the opposite of folly (e.g., 10:1). Perhaps most frequently, it is a rich body of lore (1:16) that, because it provides the only possible avenue to the understanding of all of life (8:16), is a most precious asset (2:9; 7:11), even though the training necessary to acquire it can only be called vexing (1:18). The first epilogist sums up the work of the "wise" Teacher under the headings of teaching knowledge, studying, and "arranging" (i.e., writing down) proverbs (12:9).

Not only the intense preoccupation with "wisdom" as demonstrated by the frequency of the term but also the literary style and subject matter of the book won Ecclesiastes its place alongside Job and Proverbs in ancient Israel's canon of sapiental literature. As Israel practiced it in these books, and in the deuterocanonical books of Sirach and Wisdom, wisdom aimed at "practical knowledge of the laws of life and of the world, based upon experience."[24] Many of the values that are prominent in the earlier sections of the Hebrew Bible—Torah and Former and Latter Prophets—are largely absent in this wisdom canon: covenant, election of Israel, sacrificial cultus, God's action in history. The outlook of these books is anthropocentric rather than theocentric and universal rather than particular. God is not mentioned very often, but stands in the background as the providential upholder of a world of such orders as the connection of deed to consequence and the certainty of death. These orders work themselves out dependably and inexorably, without any need for direct divine intervention.

As is quite evident, Qohelet shares these same understandings. However, he radicalizes them in that he rejects the commonly held conviction of his age that the linkage of cause and effect can be resolved in the moral sphere into a scheme of distributive justice by which good is rewarded and evil punished. For him, bad things happen to good people, too. The only transcendent truths are God's sovereignty over all things and the universality of death. All other supposed moral orders are absurd. No wonder orthodox theologians have found this book objectionable!

In short, the "wisdom" this book seeks and offers bears the distinctive accents of the Teacher. Although challenging to standard thinking, this wisdom was, nevertheless, recognized by Israel as a gift from God. It won and maintained its place in the sacred canon in spite of attempts to purge it.

"Fate" (מקרה *miqreh*). At the end of 2:14, the Teacher mentions for the first time the word *miqreh*, "fate," "chance," "destiny." Seven of the ten biblical occurrences of the word are in Ecclesiastes. The other three occurrences of the word are in more or less mundane contexts:

---

24. Gerhard von Rad, *Old Testament Theology* (New York: Harper & Row, 1962) 1:418.

---

(1) When David, suspecting a plot against his life, fails for two days to turn up at Saul's table, Saul says to himself, "Something has befallen him; he is not clean, surely he is not clean" (1 Sam 20:26 NRSV). (2) Ruth happened to glean in the part of the field that belonged to Boaz (Ruth 2:3). Of course, neither of these was really a random and mysterious event, for which our word *fate* would be the appropriate translation. The protagonist and the reader can easily see that these occurrences have been engineered very consciously. (3) Readers know that the great harm the Philistines suffered after they captured the ark of God was not mere "chance"; however, the Philistines themselves could be sure of that fact only by putting the ark on an ox cart and letting it go (1 Sam 6:9).

In Ecclesiastes, the outcome of life's struggles is described with the same word (2:14-15; three times in 3:19; 9:2-3). Here, too, the "fate" that awaits human beings is far from mere chance or a random event, though from our point of view it may seem purely contingent since it overtakes us without apparent connection either to our behavior or to our wishes. For the Teacher, "fate" is fact. It is decreed by God, even though one can learn nothing about this decree; it is death.

THE IDEOLOGY OF THE BOOK OF ECCLESIASTES

The thought of any book flows out of its vocabulary. The five components of the vocabulary of Qohelet discussed in the preceding section are pillars upon which its view of the world rests. "All" of human experience is "absurd"—i.e., incomprehensible, even senseless. Life is "toil." With the help of "wisdom" a person may find happiness amid the toil, but only if that person is utterly realistic about the inevitable "fate" of death.

Murphy sagely remarks that "the message of Ecclesiastes has suffered from excessive summarizing."[25] The epilogist, perhaps even the Teacher himself, started doing it right within the book itself ("All is absurd" [1:2]; "The end of the matter . . . Fear God, and keep his commandments" [12:13]), and the practice has continued to this present day. Yet, what are we interpreters to do? We need handles on this book of Scripture. We need pedagogical and homiletical strategies that flow straight out of the book's own current of thought and ultimately make confluence with our own.

Ecclesiastes is not a book about God; it is a book about ideas. That is why one speaks of its ideology in preference to its theology. Its ideas are about human survival in a world in which work is pain, overwork is foolish, pleasure soon pales in the face of death, and wisdom is unable to comprehend even the simplest sequences that would make possible real understanding of the world. Such a world is absurd. Yet life in the face of the absurd did not create a Qohelet who, with desperate shouts of *carpe diem* ("seize the day!"), merely snatches at a few shreds of superficial happiness or lives a few fitful moments of bright joy against a relentlessly dark background. No, he comes forward as the Teacher, with sober and yet caring countenance, ready to help his pupils deal with such a world. He holds God in profound respect but will never claim to know too much about God. Above all he will not commit God to the program of distributive justice that Job's friends advocated. Is his God just, then? Is his God even good? Qohelet does not tell us, perhaps cannot tell us. His is not a book about God.

In his magisterial commentary on Qohelet, Robert Gordis identifies four themes that are basic to the thought of Qohelet: (1) Human achievement is weak and impermanent; (2) the fate of human beings is uncertain; (3) human beings find it impossible to attain to true knowledge and insight into the world; (4) the goal of human endeavors needs to be joy, which is the divine imperative.[26] Clearly, the fourth theme is the only one that boldly affirms life. The other three only point to the limitations and impossibilities within which human beings live. For Gordis, too, the book has no proper "theology" or doctrine of God other than that God exists in limitless sovereignty; its ideology is "anthropology." Deep within human nature is "an ineradicable desire for happiness," planted there by God.[27] To live a moral life by doing the will of God, then, is to pursue happiness.

25. Murphy, *Ecclesiastes*, 1viii.
26. Gordis, *Koheleth*, 252.
27. Gordis, *Koheleth*, 113.

Other commentators introduce at least a theological dimension into their summations of the meaning of the book of Ecclesiastes. Gerhard von Rad, for example, finds that the book continually circles around three basic ideas: "1. A thorough, rational examination of life is unable to find any satisfactory meaning; everything is 'vanity.' 2. God determines every event. 3. Man is unable to discern these decrees, the 'works of God' in the world."[28]

The notion that "God determines every event," based in large part on the famous passage in Eccl 3:1-8 (see Commentary), leads Murphy to write an entire section on who is the God of Qohelet.[29] He agrees that Qohelet teaches that whatever God is doing in the world is unintelligible to human beings and that little personal relationship with God can, therefore, exist apart from human attitudes of fear and awe. God is not revealed in any way in history. However, Murphy is convinced that Qohelet's God is not simply a god of origins who sets into motion inexorable natural laws and then walks away. Such a god is not the God of Israel, and Qohelet—though he never calls God "Yahweh," the name revealed to Moses at Sinai, and uses only the generic name אלדים (ʾĕlōhîm)—is an Israelite writer who stands squarely within the give and take of Israel's tradition of theological reflection. Qohelet believes that "everything happens because of the Lord's action. . . . God is portrayed as intimately involved in all that occurs."[30] Murphy quotes with favor L. Gorssen's remark that "God is utterly present and at the same time utterly absent. God is 'present' in each event and yet no event is a 'place of encounter' with God. . . . Events do not speak any longer the language of a saving God. They are there, simply."[31]

Here is the ideological crux of the book. Von Rad and Murphy are by and large correct in saying that for Qohelet events are both impenetrable and preordained by God. There can be no question of mastery of events, because they are out of human hands. The position is deterministic, but not fatalistic, as Murphy understands it, because human beings are still perfectly free and responsible to act. At the same time, it seems unnecessary to insist that this assertion about the predetermination of times by God is the central idea of the book. True, God "has made everything suitable for its time . . . yet they cannot find out what God has done from the beginning to the end" (Eccl 3:11 NRSV). Nevertheless, charges that God is arbitrary and capricious or even just plain absent pale beside the positive assertion that, by taking charge of what they can in their lives, human beings can find joy and happiness (Eccl 2:24-26; 3:12-13; 5:18-20; 8:15; 9:7-10; 11:7-10). This advice culminates in the remarkable sentence, "Follow the inclination of your heart and the desire of your eyes, but know that for all these things God will bring you into judgment" (Eccl 11:9 NRSV), in which the latter clause should be taken to mean that God holds every person responsible for following the heart and the eyes to find happiness (see Commentary on 11:7-10). Even in the middle of a maddeningly absurd world in which the fatal shadow of death hangs equally over the wise and the foolish (Eccl 2:10), human being and beast (Eccl 3:19), this passionate possibility exists for those who, with prudence and respect for the unknown and all-determining God, can seize it!

By the simple device of shifting the emphasis from the admitted determinism of an order in which God has already ordained everything to the human responsibility or freedom that Qohelet also admittedly affirms, the weight comes down not on a tragic fatalism—human beings in the hands of a distant, all-powerful, and arbitrary God who causes good and evil alike—but on the opportunity for human happiness in a world in which God is utterly sovereign and people are truly free.

Can we have it both ways—divine sovereignty over all things *and* human freedom? Let us hope so! Every book of the Bible mixes these ingredients of theological truth in different proportions. In the Hebrew Bible, the books of Samuel and Kings, Esther, and Ruth concern themselves largely with the free actions of human beings in the world, while the book of Daniel hints at a plan for the ages set down before ever a king or a saint began to act. Ecclesiastes pours heavy doses of sovereignty and predestination into the theological mixture, but it too reckons with the responsive human heart and the obedient human will. Even though God remains cloaked in

---

28. Von Rad, *Wisdom in Israel,* 227-28.
29. Murphy, *Ecclesiastes,* 1xviii-1xix.
30. Murphy, *Ecclesiastes,* 1xvi.
31. L. Gorssen, "La cohérence de la conception de Dieu dans l'Ecclésiaste," *ETL* 46 (1970) 314-15; quoted in Murphy, *Ecclesiastes,* lxviii-lxix.

obscurity, God's predetermination sometimes seems more like prevenient grace; sometimes the ordained times and seasons seem more like the blessed and secure orders of nature. It is good that divine sovereignty and human freedom find a blend in this book, too, because faith assents to both ideas and finds each vital. If Qohelet spoke only for predetermined necessity, synagogue and church alike might have to put it aside, for most of us find such a doctrine both theologically obnoxious and intellectually impossible. But he does not; in the end, he seeks to lead his pupils to their own decision to walk humbly, sensitively, harmoniously with their God.

THE TEACHER FOR THE PREACHER

No attempt at an introduction to the Reflection sections of the book will be made here. To do so would be abstract; the move from Scripture to contemporary thought and preaching is best made in the presence of specific texts that raise burning questions one by one.

This section will serve, therefore, simply as a brief index of theological topics discussed in the Reflections that follow. Readers are invited to turn directly to them.

Topic	See Reflections on:
Absurdity of life	1:1
Advantage of the wise and rich	6:1-12
Death	3:16–4:8; 7:1-14; 9:1-12; 11:7–12:8
Envy	3:16–4:8
Fame	1:3-11
Feelings	7:1-14
Folly	9:13–10:7
Freedom to act	10:8–11:6
Happiness	1:1; 2:1-11, 24-26; 9:1-12; 11:7–12:8
Hatred of life	2:12-23; 3:16–4:8
Hopelessness	9:1-12
Moral perfectionism	7:15–8:1
Newness	1:3-11
Orders	3:1-15
Predetermination by God	3:1-15; 5:8-20; 6:1-12; 7:1-14
Resurrection, immortality, sheol	3:16–4:8; 9:1-12
Solidarity with the animals	3:16–4:8
Talk	4:9–5:7
Universal fate	2:12-23
Vocation	3:16–4:8; 8:10-17
Wisdom	1:12-18; 7:15–8:1; 12:9-14
Work	1:3-11

BIBLIOGRAPHY

Barton, George A. *A Critical and Exegetical Commentary on the Book of Ecclesiastes.* ICC. New York: Scribner's, 1908. Long a standard, still useful especially in philological matters.

Crenshaw, James L. *Ecclesiastes.* OTL. Philadelphia: Westminster, 1987. Careful exegesis, thorough documentation; stresses discussion of literary features.

Farmer, Kathleen A. *Who Knows What Is Good? A Commentary on the Books of Proverbs and Ecclesiastes.* ITC. Grand Rapids: Eerdmans, 1991. A more conservative viewpoint, aimed at preachers and teachers in the church.

Fox, M. V. *Qoheleth and His Contradictions.* BLS 18. Sheffield: Almond, 1989.

Gordis, Robert. *Koheleth: The Man and His World.* 1st ed. New York: Schocken, 1951; 3rd ed., 1968. Rich in command of the literature, Gordis offers fresh insights that have achieved wide acceptance. (Page references in this commentary are to the first edition.)

Murphy, Roland E. *Ecclesiastes.* WBC 23A. Waco, Tex.: Word, 1992. The most recent commentary, richly documented. Considerable theological reflection as well.

Rankin, O. S., and G. G. Atkins. "The Book of Ecclesiastes." In *The Interpreter's Bible.* Vol. 5. Edited by George A. Buttrick et al. Nashville: Abingdon, 1956.

Scott, R. B. Y. *Proverbs, Ecclesiastes.* AB 18. Garden City, N.Y.: Doubleday, 1965. Concise general introductions to the wisdom canon and to Ecclesiastes; commentary skimpy.

Whitley, C. F. *Koheleth: His Language and Thought.* BZAW 148. Berlin: de Gruyter, 1979. Intense work with philology.

Whybray, R. N. *Ecclesiastes.* NCB. Grand Rapids: Eerdmans, 1989. Nontechnical, compact, and readable. Intended for use in lay teaching.

OUTLINE OF ECCLESIASTES

I. Ecclesiastes 1:1, The Superscription

II. Ecclesiastes 1:2–12:8, The Wisdom of the Teacher

    A. 1:2, Theme
    B. 1:3–2:26, Illustrations of the Theme of Absurdity
        1:3-11, The Tedious Cycle of Nonachievement
        1:12-18, A King Gains Nothing from Wisdom
        2:1-11, Pleasure Is an Absurdity
        2:12-23, Wisdom Is an Absurdity
        2:24-26, Living Happily Pleases God
    C. 3:1-15, Reflections on the Meaning of Time
    D. 3:16–4:8, Reflections on Justice and Death
    E. 4:9–6:12, Aphorisms
        4:9–5:7, On Competition, Cooperation, and Vows
        5:8-20, On the Love of Money
        6:1-12, On Lowering Expectations
    F. 7:1–8:17, A First Miscellany
        7:1-14, Things That Are Good for Human Beings
        7:15–8:1, Common Sense
        8:2-9, Instructions on Appearing Before the King
        8:10-17, Retribution Is an Absurdity
    G. 9:1-12, Time and Chance Befall All
    H. 9:13–11:6, A Second Miscellany
        9:13–10:7, Wisdom, Folly, Kings, and Fools
        10:8–11:6, The Certainty of Cause and Effect
    I. 11:7–12:8, Instructions for a Young Person and Conclusion

III. Ecclesiastes 12:9-14, The Epilogues

ECCLESIASTES 1:1

THE SUPERSCRIPTION

COMMENTARY

The superscription, or headline, of Ecclesiastes (1:1) appears to give us its social and historical settings. The appearance is deceptive, however. The lateness of the Hebrew language of the book puts its composition well after the time of Solomon or, for that matter, any later royal "son of David" (see Introduction). Nor does the title "Qohelet" reveal much about the author or the social setting of the book. (For more on this title, see Introduction.) In fact, the book was written by an unknown author, not the one to whom it is attributed in the superscription. This author created a main character, Qohelet, who impersonates the wise and pleasure-loving king Solomon from 1:1 through 2:11. Because of the sustained exploration of ideas he offers to the readers of his book, he is best known as "Teacher," the translation of his title used by both the NRSV and the NIV.

ECCLESIASTES 1:2–12:8

THE WISDOM OF THE TEACHER

ECCLESIASTES 1:2, THEME

COMMENTARY

The major theme of the entire book is set forth in 1:2. We can be certain of the importance of this verse because it introduces the term הבל (*hebel*; NRSV, "vanity"; NIV, "meaningless"), which becomes a veritable refrain throughout the book. Furthermore, if we set aside 1:1 as a headline and 12:9-14 as an epilogue by other hands, then the notion of *hebel* forms a literary bracket (1:2 + 12:8) around the body of the Teacher's work.

Of the many proposals advanced by scholars about the precise meaning in Ecclesiastes of the key word *hebel* (see Introduction), the translation "absurdity"[32] best conveys the Teacher's meaning across the millennia into contemporary English. Under the impact of existentialist philosophy, an "absurdity" has become for our age more than simply a silly, foolish thing; it is a thing that cannot be made intelligible through any of the rubrics that people usually invoke to explain the meaning of their experience. An absurdity is not necessarily ephemeral ("a vapor"). It may in fact go on and on. But it makes no more sense at the end than it did at the beginning.

That is the very conviction with which Qohelet approaches his reflections on meaning in life. Everything is *hebel*. Nothing can be counted on to work out the way it ought to; nothing makes any ultimate sense. Certain things can be done; certain achievements can be made. Happiness is possible. However, over all experience stands the Teacher's general rule: "All is absurd." This judgment is "not cosmic, but designates the worldly realities with which humans must deal."[33] (For the significance of the lowly word *all* for the universalism of Qohelet, see Introduction.) The traditional system by which life could be understood does not work, and randomness, pain, loss, failure, and death may break out unexpectedly and inexplicably.

The doubling of the word *hebel* into the form "vanity of vanities" creates a superlative; it heightens the absurdity to its ultimate possible degree. Similar constructions can be seen in Exod 26:33, "holy of holies"; Cant 1:1, "song of songs"; and Ezek 26:7, "king of kings."

32. Fox, *Qoheleth and His Contradictions*.
33. Murphy, *Ecclesiastes*, 4.

REFLECTIONS

It is ironic that the best-known single verse in the book of Ecclesiastes is also the most maligned and despised. Sometimes the artistic and literary images that are the most mocked and parodied are those that are the most painfully true. Take, for example, Grant Wood's painting of the elderly Iowa farm couple, *American Gothic*. We hate it, we laugh at it, and some of us know in our hearts that we are in that picture, too. The case is similar with the slogan in the book of Ecclesiastes: "Vanity of vanities, says the Teacher,/ vanity of vanities! All is vanity." Since time immemorial the possibility that life really is absurd, that no sense can be made of it, has haunted human consciousness. In the heart of Herman Melville's novel *Moby Dick,* which is the story of a chase after evil that, because it is so futile and destructive, becomes evil and absurd in itself, Melville reveals his partiality for the book of Ecclesiastes. He rightly recognizes that the slogan of the book stands as a perpetual warning against superficiality and foolish, giggling hilarity.

> That mortal man who hath more joy than sorrow in him, that mortal man cannot be true—not true, or undeveloped. With books, the same. The truest of all men was the Man of Sorrows, and the truest of all books is Solomon's and Ecclesiastes is the fine hammered steel of woe. "ALL is vanity." ALL. This wilful world hath not got hold of un-christian Solomon's wisdom yet. But he who dodges hospitals and jails, and walks fast crossing grave-yards, and would rather talk of operas than hell . . . not that man is fitted to sit down on tomb-stones, and break the green damp mould with unfathomably wondrous Solomon.[34]

Twentieth-century literature, too, reflects the malaise of a Western culture in which boredom and meaninglessness squeeze the joy out of life. The despair and hollowness of Willy Loman in Arthur Miller's *Death of a Salesman,* the blurring of falsehood and truth in George Orwell's *1984,* the plight of T. S. Eliot's "Hollow Men"—all testify to the very real consciousness in our time that life might just be absurd. Interpreters do well not to play down the slogan in the book of Ecclesiastes.

At the same time, we do well to acknowledge that this truth is only a partial one. Life is absurd until, and unless, meaning is thrust upon it in acts of courage and faith. Even the author of this slogan, the Teacher, will cautiously propose responses to the challenge of absurdity in his own teachings. One of the salient themes of his book is that God wills that we enjoy our lives (see Introduction), and in that teaching lies at least an existential, if only temporary, respite from absurdity. Other biblical writers are not so cautious. The teller of the story of Esther (who worked at a time not far distant from that of the Teacher himself) relates how a Jewish woman and her uncle parlayed her potentially absurd position as a member of the king's harem into a powerful victory for justice against tyranny. The stories of Daniel 1–6 show how obedience and trust in the power of God can transmute scenes of pitiful persecution into scenes in which the very oppressor praises God. The man born blind (John 9) finds that his blindness is an occasion wherein the glory of God might be manifested. By his steadfastness in suffering for others, the man on the cross turned an instrument of torture and tragedy into a symbol of hope.

Our modern writers, too, sometimes believe that meaning and purpose can be forged out of the raw material of absurd pain and tyranny, not by the giggling words of Pollyanna, but by the faithful love of those who are determined here and now in their own lives of obedience to give foretastes of what life is like in the kingdom of heaven. One example of this juxtaposition of absurdity and meaning is P. D. James's novel *The Children of Men,* in which, against the background of the end of human reproduction and the slow demise of the human race, a flawed but brave couple bring forth a savior in a manger.[35]

---

34. Herman Melville, *Moby Dick,* chap. 96.
35. P. D. James, *The Children of Men* (New York: Alfred A. Knopf, 1993).

ECCLESIASTES 1:3–2:26, ILLUSTRATIONS OF THE THEME OF ABSURDITY

Ecclesiastes 1:3-11, The Tedious Cycle of Nonachievement

COMMENTARY

Having established a general but unconventional rule by which all life can be interpreted, the Teacher moves on to reflect on the first of a number of specific instances in which experience proves conventional wisdom to be absurd. In a haunting and melancholy poem (1:3-11), he poses a rhetorical question: "What do people gain from all the toil/ at which they toil under the sun?" The expected answer is, of course, "Nothing." In nature's endless round there is neither innovation, variation, nor remainder. For all their claims of unique creativity, human beings cannot escape this universal futility.

Clearly he had hoped that the עמל (ʿāmāl, "toil"; see Introduction) of a humble, righteous struggler would enjoy a payoff somewhere. After all, the psalmist had construed Israel's own history as such a reversal of fortune: "He gave them the lands of the nations,/ and they took possession of the wealth [עמל ʿāmāl] of the peoples" (Ps 105:44 NRSV). Qohelet's observation that toil gains nothing confounds all notions of distributive justice.

The rhetorical question of v. 3 concludes with another formula, "under the sun." Used twenty-nine times in Ecclesiastes and nowhere else in the Hebrew Bible, this cliché, too (together with the variant "under heaven" found in 1:13; 2:3; and 3:1; see also Gen 6:17; Exod 17:14; Deut 7:24; 9:14), is part of the distinct repertoire of the Teacher. Like the "all" of 1:2 and 12:8, the expression points to all that human beings ever have to face and deal with. It is a gloomy assessment of the light of day.

Having established that nowhere on the face of the earth does hard labor produce the expected effect, the Teacher proceeds through a number of details illustrative of the point. In

vv. 4-11, one of the most lyrical passages of the book, the Teacher draws upon the four elements of ancient cosmology—earth (v. 4), fire or sun (v. 5), wind or air (v. 6), and water (v. 7)—to describe repeating cycles of inevitability that touch upon all things except the earth itself. Just like the ever-repeating cycles of nature, human generations go and come. The sun also rises eastward and sets westward, then "hurries" to start over again.[36] The wind blows south, then north (unusual wind directions for Palestine), and the streams flow tiresomely and uselessly to the sea (v. 7). Just as endless and just as ineffectual as the endless cycles of nature are the futile efforts by human beings to observe and express these things (v. 8). In despair, the Teacher can only deny the possibility of any novelty or any randomness. All is predictable, for "there is nothing new under the sun" (v. 9). When some unseen adversary objects and says, "See, this is new" (v. 10), Qohelet once again affirms that whatever today seems innovative and fresh is only the latest manifestation of something that has always been around. By this point in the poem, readers are exhausted with the monotony of it all.

The passage 1:3-11 concludes with the devastating assertion that the "remembrance" of people past, present, and future will fail as well (v. 11). Considering that for Qohelet and all Israel before him this was the only form of immortality for which a person could hope, and was in fact a kind of reinstatement or recapitulation of the thing remembered, this is truly a hard saying. It calls into question the one means available for transcending death.

---

36. Gordis contrasts the sun's weariness here with the joy with which it runs the course ordained for it by God in Ps 19:4-6. See Gordis, *Koheleth*, 196.

REFLECTIONS

At least three major challenges to conventional piety lurk in the poem of Eccl 1:3-11. Contemporary faith will be enriched to the degree that these challenges can be faced squarely in theology and preaching.

1. *The Folly of the Work Ethic.* The implied answer "nothing" to the rhetorical question of v. 3 confounds more than simply the Protestant work ethic and other such propensities of modern readers. It confounded the ethic of the sages of ancient Israel as well. Their usual line was, "In all toil there is profit" (Prov 14:23). Teachers and parents have echoed that idea ever since. In contrast, Qohelet teaches that hard work is only an absurd waste of effort. He would have blessed the appealing heroine of Larry McMurtry's novel *Leaving Cheyenne,* Molly Taylor White, who always believed in living fully while she was alive (see Eccl 2:24); and he would have chastised the hard-working, driven hero, Gideon Fry, who never learned how to quit and enjoy.[37]

2. *Nothing New Under the Sun.* The notion of the wearisome cycle of all things and the claim that "what has been is what will be" (vv. 8-9) capture an experience of *ennui* with which we are familiar. In another sense, however, they are dead wrong. To say that what has been is what will be is not the same as saying *Que será será,* "Whatever will be, will be." The latter is not only empirically justified, but it is also affirmed in biblical thought, even by Yahweh, who says, "I am what I will be" or "I am what I am becoming" (Exod 3:14). But to say that what has been is what will be is to speak of an eternal round of natural and moral orders that admits of no variation or innovation. Such a world truly would be absurd, for there would be no room for individualism, creativity, or contingencies of any kind. But the world is not really like that; although Qohelet may have captured a well-known feeling, he did not capture a physical reality. As far as the death of all living organisms goes, yes, that is an order that has been and will be true. Jerome caught the irony of v. 4 when he wrote, "What is more vain than this vanity: that the earth, which was made for humans, stays—but humans themselves, the lords of the earth, suddenly dissolve into dust?"[38] We now know, however, that the orders of creation do not move in cycles, but more nearly in spirals, never returning to the beginning point. The new science of chaos studies begins with evidence that even in physics there is a place for new things under the sun, for random, chance events and genuine innovations. What casts a pall of absurdity over our experience is neither the endless round that Qohelet imagines nor the relentless, invariable operation of natural laws that Newtonian physics has bequeathed us; rather, it is the knowledge that we are hurtling toward the end of the cosmos—the very thing the Teacher said does not happen (Eccl 1:4b)! Our faith ought to challenge us to face up to this ultimate absurdity. If the great monuments we construct and the great literature and art we pass on are all destined ultimately for the cosmic scrap heap, it becomes more urgent than ever for us to impose meaning upon existence through acts of courage, loving-kindness, and compassion. Although the memory of such acts will not survive, the acts themselves transcend the perishing nature of the world because they participate in the eternal reality of the love of God, which is revealed in the courage and compassion of Jesus Christ.

3. *No Abiding Fame.* The quest for fame, too, is brought under scrutiny by this passage. That people struggled since time immemorial to achieve for themselves a lasting name as a hedge against oblivion is acknowledged in the story of the Tower of Babel: "Come, let us build ourselves a city, and a tower . . . and let us make a name for ourselves" (Gen 11:4 NRSV). The ensuing story of the call of Abram counters Babel

---

37. Larry McMurtry, *Leaving Cheyenne* (New York: Simon & Schuster, 1979).
38. Cited by Crenshaw, *Ecclesiastes,* 63.

by teaching that a lasting name is a gift of God: "I will . . . make your name great" (Gen 12:2 NRSV). The Teacher, however, trusts neither the efforts of human beings to attain immortality through their works nor the promise of God to grant that "remembrance" that is a lasting heritage.

Ecclesiastes 1:12-18, A King Gains Nothing from Wisdom

COMMENTARY

The Teacher who was also the "king" now addresses himself to the worth of wisdom. The structure of the passage (vv. 12-18) falls into two parts: A report by the Teacher culminating in the formula "all is vanity and a chasing after wind" is followed by a proverb quoted with approval, perhaps from a traditional source.[39] The same pattern is then repeated in vv. 16-18. The phrase "a chasing after wind,"[40] which occurs nine times in Ecclesiastes with slight variations in the Hebrew, conveys a sense of extreme intellectual futility and frustration.

1:12-15. Following a formula of royal declaration, "I, Qohelet" (v. 12; cf. Dan 4:4, 37), the Teacher-king "applies his mind" (v. 13 NRSV) or "devotes himself " (NIV) to see what wisdom will gain for him. His search is far-reaching. He will "study" and "explore" (TNK, "probe") experience, verbs that in Hebrew suggest that the effort has both breadth and depth.[41] In fact, he sets for himself a goal both universal and impossible in scope: Using wisdom as his instrument, he will examine "all that is done under heaven."

Now for the first time in the book, the Teacher-king mentions God (v. 13). He discovers that God has "laid upon" human beings "an unhappy business" (NRSV) or "a heavy burden" (NIV). What are we to make of this judgment? In one sense, the proverb of v. 15 helps to answer this question. We live in a world in which providence reigns supreme. The rules by which existence is structured are firm and reliable; however, they also dictate that some of the things against which we rail and struggle, such as crookedness and deficiency, remain.

1:16-18. In these verses, a similar point is made. Although the Teacher-king says, no doubt in all candor, that his wisdom exceeds that of anyone before him, he has learned that all wisdom leads to sorrow and knowledge to grief. The puzzling v. 17 may suggest the universality of the Teacher's quest for knowledge, which carries him into both the light and the shadow side of human experience. A better construal of the four Hebrew nouns in the verse—"wisdom" (חכמה *ḥokmâ*), "knowledge" (דעת *da'at*), "madness" (הוללות *hôlēlôt*), and "folly" (סכלות *siklût*)—would be to take them as doubly compound objects of the infinitive "to know" (לדעת *lāda'at*)— that is, "to know that wisdom and knowledge [are] madness and folly."[42]

In any case, the entire effort comes to naught. Perhaps the closing proverb of the passage, "the more knowledge, the more grief" (NIV), was originally meant to be taken quite literally. If the cane was used liberally in school, the educational process might truly have been painful.[43] Qohelet radicalizes the teaching, however: The wiser one becomes, the more troubled and unhappy one is. Nevertheless, he pushes on.

39. Gordis has argued that Qohelet quotes extensively from otherwise unknown Israelite wisdom sentences, using them sometimes as evidence and sometimes as foils for his own argumentation. See Gordis, *Koheleth*, 95-108. Whybray, too, thinks Qohelet cites other sages, but he can positively identify only eight examples. He believes Qohelet used each of these sayings because he agreed with it. See Whybray, *Ecclesiastes*, 35-40.

40. Scott translates "clutching at the wind." See R. B. Y. Scott, *Proverbs, Ecclesiastes,* AB 18 (Garden City, N.Y.: Doubleday, 1965) 216.

41. Crenshaw, *Ecclesiastes,* 72.

42. Gordis, *Koheleth,* 203.

43. Crenshaw, *Ecclesiastes,* 76.

REFLECTIONS

It is true that what is by nature crooked cannot be made straight (v. 15a). Who would want to live in a world that was any different than that? To say that something that is absent can nevertheless be counted present (v. 15b) would be to say that the world is unreliable and crazy. However, things that should not be crooked or absent are, and people want to know why. The intellectual restlessness God placed in human beings that causes them to search for answers to such "Why?" questions is not a happy dimension of life.

Why not quit school, then, and just remain innocent? After all, "the more knowledge, the more grief" (v. 18). The notion has had echoes in traditional thinking ever since:

> . . . where ignorance is bliss,
> 'Tis folly to be wise.[44]

and:

> From ignorance our comfort flows,
> The only wretched are the wise.[45]

Yet the heart resists such a conclusion. A modern writer answered these counsels of despair with the aphorism, "Ignorance is not bliss—it is oblivion."[46] Even though the quest of the Teacher-king led him close to embracing ignorance, in the end he too cannot reject wisdom (Eccl 9:13-18).

44. Thomas Gray, "On a Distant Prospect of Eton College" (1742).
45. Matthew Prior, "To the Hon. Charles Montague" (1692).
46. Philip Wylie, *Generation of Vipers* (New York: Farrar & Rinehart, 1942).

Ecclesiastes 2:1-11, Pleasure Is an Absurdity

COMMENTARY

Having reasoned from experience that the acquisition of wisdom is an absurdity (which is to say it does not result in the happy outcome that its proponents had touted for it), Qohelet determines to "make a test of pleasure" (2:1). As before (1:13), he gives the result (vv. 1b-2) before he describes the experiment: Pleasure is vanity and of no use. The reward of uninhibited hedonism is unbounded disillusionment; it is all absurd and futile (v. 11).

According to 1 Kgs 10:1, the queen of Sheba came to Jerusalem to "test" Solomon with riddles. True to form, the "Solomon" of Ecclesiastes readily subjects himself to tests in order to find the answer to the great riddle, Is anything in life not absurd? In vv. 3-8 the Teacher-king becomes a whirlwind of energy in carrying out his experiments. After fortifying himself with wine (v. 3) and putting folly under the control of wisdom for the time, he acts in grand style, filling his days by acquiring houses, vineyards, gardens,[47] parks, pools, slaves and cattle, silver and gold, servants of all kinds, and concubines[48] (vv. 4-8). He does not do all this in order to wallow in

47. The Hebrew word used here, פרדס (*pardēs*), is probably a corruption of a Persian word meaning "[forest] enclosure." A similar word meaning "park" also occurs in Akkadian. The Greeks borrowed the word as well (παράδεισος *paradeisos*), from whence we got our word *paradise*. If its presence here betrays Persian influence, as seems likely, we have additional evidence that Qohelet's Hebrew is post-exilic, from the period when Persia was dominant in the Middle East.

48. The Hebrew word שדה (*šiddâ*) has been variously rendered "cup bearers" (LXX), "goblets" (Vg), and even "music" (Luther; see KJV). Its relation to "sad," "breast," and other considerations have led recent translators toward the women of the royal household. The NIV's "harem" captures the sense of abundance that the double use of the Hebrew term conveys.

sensuality, but because "he is taking the measure of a life of pleasure."[49]

The royal perquisites are writ large here. The model is the fictional Solomon of the Song of Songs, whose "gardens" were veritable paradises (see Cant 4:12-15; 5:1; 6:2) and whose appetites were renowned. But the profile is also consistent with the report of Solomon's largeness and largesse in 1 Kgs 4:20-34 (see also 2 Chr 9:13-28). We are not told there that he planted forests and made reservoirs to provide irrigation for them (cf. 2:6), but such works were the king's to command. The mention in 2 Kgs 20:20 that King Hezekiah built a pool and a conduit in the Jerusalem water system (confirmed archaeologically by the eighth-century BCE Siloam inscription found on the wall of the conduit) and the mention of the king's pool in Neh 2:14 are evidence of royal interest in that

49. Murphy, *Ecclesiastes*, 18.

precious commodity, water, in ancient Israel. It is no surprise, then, to read that "I became great and surpassed all who were before me in Jerusalem" (v. 9). We readers take hope when we hear that "my heart found pleasure in all my toil, and this was my reward for all my toil" (v. 10). Experience does not deny the possibility of pleasure and the possibility of reward. Yet the very word חלק (*ḥēleq*, "reward," "portion," "lot") provides a transition from the good news that pleasure is real to the bad news that follows. Qohelet uses the term eight times, usually in a positive sense. But what did his "reward" really amount to? The result of the Teacher-king's effort to escape from absurdity through pleasure replicates the outcome of his quest for meaning through wisdom; it is "vanity and a chasing after wind, and . . . nothing to be gained under the sun" (v. 11).

REFLECTIONS

Teachers of creative writing say that one should not give away the point of a story before the conclusion lest readers be deprived of an opportunity to imagine. Qohelet pays no attention to that rule, and tells us right away that the "test of pleasure" the king undertakes will prove that pleasure ultimately is meaningless (2:1-2). Had he not done so, we might have held our breath until the dénouement in v. 11. Many of us see a familiar sight as the Teacher-king sets out determinedly to do all the things that pleasure-loving people, hedonists, even affluent upper-middle-class Americans have always done. He tries to find meaning and happiness in property, produce, wealth, and sex. Furthermore, he craftily brings the whole effort under the rubric of a work ethic. Because he can say, "I made . . . I bought . . . I gathered . . . I got," he rightly gets to enjoy the fruits of his labor (v. 10). What is wrong with that?

Even though we readers knew the enterprise was doomed from v. 2 onward, we may have hoped for the best and found ourselves unprepared for the total rejection of the entire search for pleasure as absurdity or vanity, chasing after wind, and more of the same old thing (v. 11). That message will not play well in Peoria; in fact, it may not even be entirely true. Human beings all over the world, from the poorest peasants of Sudan to the teeming masses on the Ganges to the affluent residents of penthouses in New York, all agree that food, drink, comfort, and intimacy are goals to be pursued and are likely to produce a measure of human happiness. The notion is not foreign to our religious tradition either. The Song of Songs is a canticle to bounty and sensual pleasure. Jesus did not scruple to enjoy himself thoroughly at the wedding in Cana, and he added further pleasure to the occasion by improving the water (John 2:1-11).

Underlying the pessimistic assessment by the Teacher in this passage is the view later to be articulated (2:24-26) that the capacity to enjoy life is a gift of God alone. Unless God has made that gift, he believes, the most relentless struggle for wealth and the satisfaction of sensual appetites will fail. That view raises the difficult question of the predetermination of all things (see Introduction; Reflections at 2:24-26); but it also enables us to put something of a positive spin on the passage before us. It requires not that we deny the love of human beings for pleasure, but that we place human pleasure in its proper context. Qohelet is not too far from the faith of Torah or Gospel when he teaches that happiness is not a product of our own concupiscence, but of the prevenient grace of God.

Ecclesiastes 2:12-23, Wisdom Is an Absurdity

COMMENTARY

Running through this section, and marked by numerous uses of the slogans with which Qohelet structures his meditations on meaning and absurdity, is the underlying theme of the common fatal destiny of all things. That common destiny, hateful death, keeps the rich entrepreneur awake at night, seething in anger at the prospect that some unknown knave may live to enjoy the windfall of his inheritance. Although wisdom must be valued (vv. 13-14), it does not bring peace and happiness to one who contemplates this fate. In fact, it is not even attainable (7:23-24).

2:12-13. The exact meaning of v. 12*b* is difficult to ascertain. The NIV specifically identifies the speaker as the successor to the Teacher-king, who finds that he cannot improve on what his predecessor has done. Gordis, who translates the passage, "Of what value is a man coming after the king, who can only repeat what he has already done?" is surely correct in saying, "Koheleth, in his assumed role of Solomon, wishes to assure the reader that he has experienced the ultimate in both wisdom and pleasure and that there is no need for anyone else to repeat the experiment."[50]

2:14-17. In v. 14, the Teacher swings to the other side again, affirming the enterprise of wisdom, saying it is superior to folly, and even offering a proverb that, by use of antithetical parallelism, gives the edge to the wise who "have eyes in their head." Fools are as good as blind, because they walk in darkness. This is, of course, conventional wisdom, and it is consistent with the general drift of the metaphors for "light" (wisdom, goodness, Torah) and "darkness" (folly, evil) in the sapiential literature. But with his dialectical

"Yet . . ." (v. 14*b*), the Teacher swings back to negate the values of wisdom that he has just briefly affirmed.

At v. 14*b* the Teacher uses for the first time another of his favorite words, "fate" (see the section "The Vocabulary of Qohelet's Thought" in the Introduction). Powerful, predetermined "fate" is perhaps the major component of his sense of absurdity. Once again the Teacher's meditations drive him to the encompassing "all." Death, the great leveler of all distinctions between wise people and fools, workers and drones, "befalls all of them."

2:18. Who is the one that will come after the Teacher? The Hebrew text of this verse reads literally, "I must leave it to the individual who will be after me." (Here is a case in which the NRSV, in its effort to eliminate generic pronouns, obscures the meaning. The verse is improperly understood when one reads it as "I must leave it to those who come after me," because the Masoretic text speaks only of האדם [*hā'ādām*], "the [individual] human being," but not of a whole class. The NIV gets it right.) If this verse intends to continue the literary fiction that Ecclesiastes is the work of "the son of David who is a king in Jerusalem," this could be an oblique reference to Rehoboam, the unfortunate successor of Solomon, who inherited only half of his father's kingdom. However, one of the manuscripts from the Cairo Geniza[51] eliminates the article, thereby making the rule a general one: "I must leave it to whoever comes after me." This scribe was probably correct in understanding that Qohelet intended to teach

---

50. Gordis, *Koheleth*, 211.

51. During the second half of the nineteenth century, a trove of Hebrew manuscripts, some as early as the eighth century CE, was extracted from a forgotten storeroom (*geniza*) in the ancient Karaite synagogue of Old Cairo. Variant readings in the biblical texts from Cairo are now incorporated into the critical apparatus of the standard *Biblia Hebraica Stuttgartensia*.

a universal truth—even a truism—here. What finally happens to one's worldly goods after one dies lies beyond the reach of the "dead hand" of the grave.

2:19. The question, "Who knows?" is rhetorical in Ecclesiastes (which uses the expression four of the ten times it occurs in the Bible). The expected answer is "No one!" No one can say whether the beneficiary of a bequest will prove to be wise or foolish. But it really does not matter. Qualified or not, the successor will "be master" (NRSV) or "have control" (NIV; the cognate verb in Arabic gives rise to the noun "sultan") over all of one's hard-earned wealth. That is why toil is absurd.

2:20-23. The absurdity of inheriting the property and wealth of another person without working for it is underscored in v. 21. Crenshaw remarks, "The sages' egocentric perspective stands out here, for there is no indication that the donor derives genuine pleasure from bestowing happiness on someone else."[52] Perhaps Qohelet is selfish, but realism is on his side. The illusion that the goods and properties for which one has labored so mightily are inalienable is stripped away by the realization of death. When that occurs, it is possible to despair, even if one fantasizes that one's legacy gives happiness to the heir and contributes to the common good. Literally translated, the Hebrew of v. 23 reads, "Even at night his heart will not lie down." Because the biblical writers have no interest in the brain and make no reference to it, the seat of all the emotions is always the heart. Such a heart is the mind of a person, and, as we all know, the mind can be restless and worried. Like the proverbial rich person who tosses and turns at night in anxiety over all there is to lose (see 5:12), Qohelet makes sleeplessness the rule for anyone contemplating the disposition of a life's accumulation.

52. Crenshaw, *Ecclesiastes,* 88.

REFLECTIONS

This section is so rich with theological and homiletical possibilities that any discussion of it must necessarily be selective. Only two issues are explored here: (1) Qohelet's universalism and the fool's paradise; and (2) the painful cry of the truth seeker.

1. *An Unhappy Universalism.* In that he recognizes no exceptions to the fate of human beings, Qohelet is a genuine universalist. In 2:14b-17, he looks with clear vision and great pain on the fact that the attainment of wisdom offers no guarantee of an enduring name. Two centuries before Qohelet flourished, the Greek philosophers undertook a threefold quest for knowledge, virtue, and happiness. Often knowledge held pride of place. Socrates, for example, held the highest good to be knowledge of the self; from that knowledge flowed all the rest. For Qohelet, in contrast, knowledge brings the tragically clear vision of universal obliteration. These verses elaborate the theme that in later times Paul will use as a foil to christology: "For as all die in Adam, so all will be made alive in Christ" (1 Cor 15:22 NRSV). Even though the Teacher has access to only the gloomy first half of that antithesis, he is not willing to deny the truth that his wisdom has brought him to see. Neither virtue nor happiness flows from this truth, but he intends to face it squarely and unhesitatingly. Herman Melville, whose poem "A Spirit Appeared to Me" takes its cue from these verses, was more prepared to pretend:

A spirit appeared to me, and said
"Where now would you choose to dwell?
In the Paradise of the Fool,
Or in wise Solomon's hell?"
    Never he asked me twice:
    "Give me the Fool's Paradise."

2. *A Painful Cry: "I Hate Life."* For Qohelet, who had no notion of a meaningful afterlife, death leveled the distinction between the wise and the foolish. Are you wise? So what! Why bother? It will not make any difference at all in the end; death relativizes, even trivializes wisdom. Until resurrection makes its first appearances late in the Old Testament period (see Isa 26:19; Dan 12:1-3), the hope of ancient Israelites for any transcendence of death lay only in "enduring remembrance" (v. 16). The individual life would be extinguished at death, but the memory of good deeds and wise words would linger on. Now, however, the utter realist—no detached observer here, but an anguished victim—arises to say what everyone knew anyway: that memory is short and the monuments raised by wise people and fools alike do not long endure. Fate is not kind to some and hard on others; it is hard on everyone. Was he wrong? Here the realism of the Teacher emerges to clear away any self-delusion about our common destiny of death. Modern Jews and Christians usually deny his premise of no afterlife, but as far as what we leave behind here, the man was absolutely correct. All of us have to say, "I must leave it to those who will come after me—and who knows whether they will be wise or foolish?" (See vv. 18-19.)

So bitter is this pill of absurdity that the Teacher claims that he hates life altogether (v. 17). The cry is the most extreme in the entire book, yet it is not a choice of death over life (Deut 39:19). In fact, the claim is hard to accept at all, for this central character of the book has a mind so lively and zeal so apt to challenge every orthodoxy that mere contact with him quickens the spirit of his readers. Even in his extremity, Qohelet continues to prefer light over darkness (v. 13), which means "life lived without self-deception, without despair, life lived in full questioning awareness."[53]

53. Kenneth R. R. Gros Louis, "Ecclesiastes," in *Literary Interpretations of Biblical Narratives*, ed. K. R. R. Gros Louis et al. (Nashville: Abingdon, 1974) 280.

Ecclesiastes 2:24-26, Living Happily Pleases God

COMMENTARY

In the desert of absurdity baking everywhere around him under the sun, Qohelet now discovers a small but important oasis. Verse 24 introduces one of the principal themes of Qohelet (see Introduction): the commendation of eating, drinking, and pleasure in life (reiterated in 3:13; 5:18; 8:15; 9:7). The conventional wisdom scheme of distributive justice that Qohelet may have taught his students and in which he seems also to have wished to place his trust animates v. 26: God rewards those who please God with "wisdom and knowledge and joy," and even with the fruits of the labors of sinners who end up turning their gains over to the righteous. The familiar refrain "This too is meaningless, a chasing after the wind" (NIV), with which the paragraph closes (v. 26*b*), may sum up the self-serving effort of the "sinner." The word is probably without moral connotation; the Hebrew word that the NIV

and the NRSV translate as "sinner" (חוטא *ḥôṭeʾ*) can also mean "fool," "bungler"—i.e., someone antithetical to wisdom (see 9:18). It might even mean simply an "unlucky" person. A fool misses the mark by denying God's will that human beings should enjoy life. An unlucky person discovers that in God's utter freedom, the fruits of that person's toil just may end up in the hands of a "lucky" person.[54] For the Teacher, one's moral purity never guarantees that one gets the goods.

Nevertheless, the possibility of enjoying life remains open. True, that enjoyment is subject to the limitations of discretion (cf. 7:26); furthermore, it is evanescent. In the end all roads lead to the grave. However, in this passage we encounter the counterpoint to the Teacher's great theme of absurdity.

54. H. L. Ginsberg, "The Structure and Contents of the Book of Koheleth," in *Wisdom in Israel and the Ancient Near East*, ed. Martin Noth and D. W. Thomas, VTSup 3 (Leiden: Brill, 1955) 139.

There is a small space in life that, though not large enough to accommodate an abiding monument of any kind, is nevertheless tolerable. One can enjoy simple things such as food, drink, and life itself. If, in fact, these pleasures are "from the hand of God" (v. 24) and cannot be enjoyed apart from God (v. 25, as amended on the basis of the ancient Greek and Syriac versions), then surely it is the duty of human beings to receive them gratefully and to enjoy them. Putting the best spin on vv. 24b-26 leads the interpreter to say that, according to Ecclesiastes, it is the will of God that we should enjoy our life, pitching our tents in an oasis of peace and happiness in the middle of a desert of absurdity. While pleasure may fall short of an absolute goal for human life, "it remains the only practical program for human existence."[55]

55. Gordis, *Koheleth*, 216.

REFLECTIONS

This unit opens with advice that sounds like an echo of the words of Qohelet's contemporary Greek philosopher Epicurus (341–270 BCE). However, it was not he who first taught "Eat, drink and be merry for tomorrow we die," but the Hebrew Bible itself. Perhaps Isaiah was quoting the ironic words of an already well-known drinking song when he pictured the endangered inhabitants of Jerusalem partying on the eve of the Day of the Lord, saying, "Let us eat and drink, for tomorrow we die" (Isa 22:13 NRSV). Wherever he may have gotten the slogan, he put the stamp of prophetic disapproval upon it. Paul did not think much of this attitude, either, when he quoted Isa 22:13 in order to dismiss the hopelessness of those who denied the resurrection of the dead (1 Cor 15:32). Jesus, too, criticized this attitude in his parable of the rich fool, who was a fool precisely because he did not take the last clause of the saying seriously and died that very night (Luke 12:19).

Qohelet provides a needed canonical counterpoint to this criticism of existential despair. As contemporary theologians, we can be gratified that he identifies food, drink, and enjoyment as gifts of God and anodynes for upcoming death. The problem for us may be the muted, but implicit, notion (made explicit in 5:19; 6:2) that one can enjoy one's present moment only if God elects one into the happy company of those who can do so. If not only the values of "wisdom and knowledge and joy" (v. 26) are gifts of God, but also the very ability to enjoy these gifts, then an atmosphere of utter determinism and predestination lingers around even this one hopeful motif of the book. If one cannot even choose to enjoy what is given, but is given that capacity, too, as a gift, then Gordis is perhaps overly optimistic in thinking that Qohelet wants a person to reach out and take the glass of wine and the loaf of bread from the festive table as a religious duty, a *mitzvah*, that one eagerly and happily embraces. How could one answer for a willingness to enjoy life if that very capacity of enjoyment is bestowed on only a few by God? In the larger canonical context, particularly in the wisdom literature, the capacity to enjoy the good things of life is mated with more individual moral responsibility in decision making. To take pleasure in life is a choice that lies within the reach of every individual (e.g., Ps 1:1-3; Prov 12:20; 21:15; Matt 5:3-12; see also Sir 1:12, a variant of which reopens the "gift of God" theme).

As is true of so many beloved slogans, this one has enjoyed a life of repetition and paraphrase. The third of the three terms in Qohelet's version of the saying is "enjoyment." That third term is the one that has been most volatile in the replays through literature. In Isa 22:13 and 1 Cor 15:32, the third term is "death": "Let us eat and drink, for tomorrow we die" (NRSV). In *Don Juan*, Byron turned it into "love": " 'Eat, drink, and love, what can the rest avail us?' / So said the royal sage, Sardanapalus" (2.207).

Arthur Hugh Clough, in his poem "Easter Day," turns the third term into "play":

Eat, drink, and play, and think that this is bliss.
There is no heaven but this;
There is no hell
Save earth, which serves the purpose doubly well.

The list goes on and on. The theme of imposing meaning on fading life through eating, drinking, and merriment is reiterated in our modern literature in many ways. Irving Berlin's popular song "Let's Face the Music and Dance" captures the sentiment as well as any:

Before the fiddlers have fled,
Before they ask us to pay the bill,
And while we still have a chance,
Let's face the music and dance!

If inexorable, divine predetermination is the notion guiding the mind of the Teacher, the strange conclusion of the passage makes more sense. A sinner is simply one whom God has chosen to regard as a sinner, and the appropriate spirit of the onlooker is bafflement! (For another angle on the issue raised by 2:24-26, see the Reflections at 9:7-10.)

ECCLESIASTES 3:1-15, REFLECTIONS ON THE MEANING OF TIME

COMMENTARY

3:1-8. This is perhaps the best-known passage in Ecclesiastes, the beloved list of things for which there is a proper time. The topic of time was a favorite one with wisdom writers. In Sir 39:16-34, as also elsewhere in Qohelet (e.g., Eccl 3:14-15; 6:10), time marches strictly to God's command. But not here. In these verses, God plays no explicit role in setting the "seasons" and "times." In this passage, Qohelet does not say why things occur at their appropriate times. They just do. Only as he reflects further in the enigmatic ensuing prose passage (vv. 9-15) does the Teacher invoke God's role in the matter of time.

The distinctive style of the passage may indicate that Qohelet drew it from another source. The seven verses 2-8 contain fourteen antitheses,[56] encompassing twenty-eight experiences known to all human beings, all organized under the twofold synonymous heading, "For everything [phenomenon] there is a season, and a time for every matter

under heaven" (v. 1). Like 1:3-11, this pericope is simply a list of empirical observations. Except for the bracketing words "be born . . . peace," the list offers no order of importance or any other evaluation at all other than the principle stated in the heading. None of these times and seasons is a pregnant, potential-filled καιρός kairos. The "times" are moments of human-scale appropriateness intricately interwoven with implicit cosmic orders. The first item on the list, "a time to be born, and a time to die" (v. 2), is clearly out of human hands, but the rest involve human choices. The wise person's task evidently is to know when the right time has come and to move visibly with whatever invisible program there may be.

In v. 3, the reference to "a time to kill and a time to heal" seems to give society two ways to respond to individual transgression. The first is capital punishment; the second is the work of physicians and other kinds of helpers to improve the life of an ailing person. Since sickness was regarded as a punishment from God, some may have thought nothing should

---

56. Cf. Sir 33:15, "Look at all the works of the Most High;/they come in pairs, one the opposite of the other" (NRSV).

be done for the sinner/invalid. Qohelet, however, seems to affirm the right of physicians to intervene in the sequence of cause-and-effect and to heal when it is time to do so.

The medieval midrash *Qohelet Rabbah* interprets the reference to scattering and gathering stones (v. 5*a*) as a strict parallel to embracing (v. 5*b*)—i.e., both are metaphors for sexual relations. Given the fact that stichs *a* and *b* of each verse in the series are closely related to stichs *c* and *d* of each verse, this seems preferable to taking v. 5*a* as a reference to the preparation of a field of rocky Palestine for farming (see Isa 5:2).

Surely the teaching that there is "a time to keep, and a time to throw away" (v. 6*b*) intends to do more than simply warn "pack rats" to get serious about cleaning out the attic. In a broader sense, this antithesis suggests that both prudence and providence— that boundless outpouring of help to other people—are genuine human virtues. If v. 7*a* refers to the ancient Israelite mourning custom of rending garments (see Gen 37:29; 2 Sam 13:31, then v. 7*b* would authorize the family to sew the rips back up again when the mourning was over. Mourning customs could also explain the coupling of v. 7*ab* with v. 7*cd,* "a time to keep silence and a time to speak," for as Job 2:13 suggests, silence was appropriate in the presence of bereavement. If, on the other hand, the picture is of a sewing bee, even in that context silence might, from time to time, be golden. When Ben Sira thought about this subject, he too tied talk to time: "The wise remain silent until the right moment" (Sir 20:7 NRSV).

The culminating v. 8, which raises the human experiences of love and hate, war and peace, reverses the order in the final clause, putting peace in the position of a "punch line." Thus do peace and birth (v. 2*a*) bracket the entire list. By this simple device, their antitheses, death and war, are demoted to realities that, though both profound and universal, have neither the first nor the last word.

3:9-15. In the prose section, which follows the poem of vv. 1-8, the notions of the rhythm and rightness of time are pursued further. "What gain have the workers from their toil?" the Teacher asks in v. 9. His answer takes the form of religious truth claims about human endeavor. In 1:13, the "business" that God gave human beings to do is "unhappy" or even "evil." Not so in v. 10, because now Qohelet has supplied an important context for human striving: It all takes place within "suitable" (יפה *yāpeh*) time. God "has made everything suitable for [NIV, beautiful in] its time" (v. 11 NRSV) and has given human beings a sense of having a place in the stately unrolling of the universal ("everything"), predetermined providential plan of God. The good news is that the (presumably) good God has provided direction, even finality, to the course of history (vv. 14-15). The bad news is that people "cannot find out what God has done from the beginning to the end" (v. 11). Withholding this knowledge is within the sovereign authority of God. By refusing to show the trump cards of the future, God keeps humanity—who want to know good and evil (Gen 3:22), who want to have an unassailable name (Gen 11:4), who want to compete with God—in awe and submission. It goes without saying that what cannot be known by human beings also cannot be changed by them. Verse 11 is the very epitome of one of Qohelet's principal themes: the impossibility of knowing what is truly going on in the world (see the section "The Ideology of the Book of Ecclesiastes" in the Introduction; see also Eccl 6:10-12; 7:14, 27-28).

Both the NRSV and the NIV take the much debated word העלם (*hā'ōlām*) in v. 11 to refer to time (NRSV, "sense of past and future"; NIV, "eternity"; cf. Eccl 3:14). Taken this way, the picture is of human creatures endowed by God with a keen consciousness of the passage of time, yet not endowed with the capacity to make any sense of it. In Murphy's words, v. 11*b* "is a fantastic statement of divine sabotage."[57]

The other meaning of the word *hā'ōlām,* "world," has been advocated in modern times by such scholars as Ewald, Voltz, H. L. Ginsberg, and Gordis. Although the latter meaning of the word is largely a development in post-biblical Hebrew (see Sir 3:18; *M. 'Abot 4:17*), Ecclesiastes uses a number of other words of which the same could be said. For Gordis, this meaning yields a teaching that reinforces his proposal that enjoyment of life is at the heart of the message of the book: "He

---

57. Murphy, *Ecclesiastes,* 39.

has also placed the love of the world in men's hearts, except that they may not discover the work God has done from beginning to end."[58] Scott relates the term back to the root sense of "that which is obscure, hidden," and translates, "Yet he has put in their minds an enigma."[59] Whitley suggests "ignorance."[60]

In favor of viewing *hā'ōlām* as "eternity" (NIV) are the facts that this is the usual meaning of the noun in the Hebrew Bible and that the context establishes "time" (v. 11*a*) as the subject under discussion. The problem is to arrive at the exact nuance of time in this sentence. "Eternity" can be misleading, too, if a reader thinks of immortality or the spiritual contemplation of divine timelessness rather than history in its most inclusive sense. The paraphrase of the NRSV suggests frustration with the One who fixed the times of all things and gave humankind a sense of that reality, yet who withheld the timetable from those who might otherwise have understood it. Faced with this problem, Rankin argues for a

revocalization of *hā'ōlām* to העלם (*hā'elem*), "forgetfulness." The sense, then, would be that although God made everything excellent in its time, God also burdened people with "the inability to remember and record all the generations of human history," thereby depriving them of the means of making history comprehensible.[61]

Within the awful incomprehensibility of the big picture (v. 14), however, God has made a "gift" of the possibility of human happiness. It is a gift made to "all" (כל *kōl*, v. 13)—a teaching that omits the deterministic reservation voiced in 5:19 and 6:12 that God "enables" only some to enjoy life. As Gordis has pointed out, Qohelet teaches that "joy is God's great commandment for man."[62] Verses 2-13, therefore, are ethical teachings. When the Teacher says, "Be happy and enjoy . . . eat and drink and take pleasure in . . . toil" (vv. 12-13; see 2:24), he means that to accept God's gift of life is to be obedient to the will of God.

58. Gordis, *Koheleth*, 146.
59. Scott, *Proverbs, Ecclesiastes*, 220.
60. C. F. Whitley, *Koheleth: His Language and Thought*, BZAW 148 (Berlin: de Gruyter, 1979) 31-33.

61. O. S. Rankin and G. G. Atkins, "The Book of Ecclesiastes," in *The Interpreter's Bible*, 12 vols., ed. George A. Buttrick et al. (Nashville: Abingdon, 1956) 5:48-49.
62. Gordis, *Koheleth*, 118.

REFLECTIONS

In 3:1-8, the Teacher does not describe the inexorable cycling of times as another absurdity, nor does he frame it with despair. On the contrary, he endorses it. Time is not out of joint: "For everything there is a season." Here at last he finds solidity and dependability. It is good that there is order in life. It is good that there is a time to die that stands over and against the time of birth, for to have it any other way would be to admit that there is no order at all but only arbitrary and erratic events. In 3:1-8, the Teacher is able to affirm that the polarities within which life must be lived are both discernible and secure.

One can wax enthusiastic about the moral possibilities of some of the items on Qohelet's list of things for which there is a proper time. For example, that there is "a time to keep, and a time to throw away" (v. 16) invokes the two virtues of prudence and providence. It is good to know that the cosmic orders provide a place for saving against a future rainy day (even ants do it! see Prov 30:25). Qohelet seems to open the door to prudential moral behavior.

There is also a time to throw away. Now, the virtue we call generosity is about throwing away, about the unstinting pouring out of good things on those around about. We call God's generosity "providence"; the Bible also knows that human behavior can be providential. The idea reaches a keen point in Jesus' difficult teaching "Be perfect, therefore, as your heavenly Father is perfect" (Matt 5:48 NRSV). Taken by itself, that verse has served some people as a disastrous invitation to excessive scrupling and perfectionism. But taken in context, it is clear that the God-like perfection (i.e., "reaching the mark") that Jesus advocates is in human giving, "throwing away." The context of the saying in the Sermon on the Mount reads, "[God] makes his sun rise on the evil and on the good, and sends rain on the righteous and on the unrighteous. For if you love those who love you, what reward do you have? Do not even the tax collectors do the same?" (Matt 5:45-46 NRSV). For the Gospel writer, perfection consists in being like God in pouring out providential generosity onto others. In teaching that there is a time for divestiture, Qohelet, too, opens the door to providential moral behavior.

Similar discussions can be advanced about the other antitheses of the poem, as if they invited the individual to be sensitive to appropriate times for action and then to act, morally, perhaps decisively, to kill, to heal, to keep silence, to speak, to love, to hate, to make war, and to make peace. However, if we read this list through the lens of predetermination, as vv. 9-15 suggest we do, a number of things change radically. First of all, there can be no quarrel with any members of the list, such as hate and war. If everything occurs on the God-given schedule, then this list cannot be weeded. Second, there is little real possibility of moral action. If a time to make love is not a matter of a conscious human choice to act appropriately, but merely a matter of a timetable set forth in advance by God for organisms or even for human individuals, then there can be no question of moral agency in the lovemaking, but simply answering responses to the call of the hormones. All of the earlier remarks about perfection in giving (v. 6*b*) become simply nonsense. There simply comes a time to throw stuff away, no doubt because of the approach of death.

Commentators and preachers alike have generally not wanted to consign the beautiful poem of 3:1-8 into the grim jaws of necessity, and they have warrant. The uniqueness of its style and its logical coherence invite attention to this pericope in its own terms. Even if only for heuristic reasons, much can be gained by reading it independently of context—at least of vv. 9-15—and thereby seeing it in a different light from that given it through the (tinted) lens of predetermination. If one reads the poem with the understanding that the fixed orders provide structure rather than calendar, then individual human moral decision making is possible. One can then hear in this poem a challenge to be wise, to be ethical, to discern when one's actions are in keeping with God's time and then to act decisively.

Reading vv. 1-8 through a positive lens focuses on the grace inherent in the periodic structure of life. What would the gift of life be, for example, without the concomitant gift of death (v. 2)? Without the knowledge of death, life would lose its urgency and savor. Without death no poetry would be written, no music composed, no monuments raised, no children begotten. This is not to say that people actually welcome death, except those in the most dire states of emotional and physical distress. Nevertheless, a healthy acknowledgment that "there is a time to die" leads people "to improve each shining hour." In that sense, even if taken as a list of grim necessities, Qohelet's hymn serves as a gift of truth. And truth is grace!

A predestinarian rereading of the poem of 3:1-8 does seem to occur in the prose context in which the poem is now placed within the book of Ecclesiastes. For example, v. 15 situates life squarely in the middle of an endlessly repetitive and rigid scheme that cancels any intention by vv. 1-8 to make place for human free will: "That which is, already has been; that which is to be, already is." No innovation or creativity seems to be possible under those rules! Yet, the Teacher maintains a slight ambivalence even in this passage. The key to this chink in the armor of predisposition is the declaration "It is God's gift that *all* should eat and drink and take pleasure in all their toil" (v. 13, italics added). Not only is this option available to *all*, as opposed to only those who have been specially enabled for the task of enjoyment (contra 5:19; 6:2), but also it seems to be phrased in terms of a choice. If there is a choice, there is also the possibility of moral behavior. If there is a choice, then the Teacher's student can be as happy and as wise as the Teacher, if the student chooses gratefully to accept the small daily pleasures of life as gifts of God.

The tension between a radical predisposition of all things into an inexorable sequence of times and seasons, on the one hand, and, on the other hand, a small but secure place for human choice has troubled adherents of Islam—that most predestinarian of the Western religions. The tension is exemplified in the seventy-third stanza of the *Rubáiyát of Omar Khayyám*:

> With Earth's first Clay
> They did the Last Man knead,
> And there of the Last Harvest sow'd the Seed:
> And the first Morning of Creation wrote
> What the Last Dawn of Reckoning shall read.

In this view, nothing happens that was not already determined on the day of creation. That cannot easily be squared with any human initiative in happiness. What a way to make a world! Omar's sad yearning to reorganize the world along very different lines, expressed in his ninety-ninth stanza, might have struck a chord of response in Qohelet, too:

> Ah Love! could you and I with Him conspire
> To grasp this sorry Scheme of Things entire,
> Would not we shatter it to bits—and then
> Re-mould it nearer to the Heart's Desire!

ECCLESIASTES 3:16–4:8, REFLECTIONS ON JUSTICE AND DEATH

COMMENTARY

The Teacher has new shocks in store in 3:16–4:8. He has come to see that the conventional law of retribution, *jus talionis,* in which his contemporaries believed and perhaps he taught his students, is not operative. How could it be, if everything is predetermined? On the other hand, he seems unwilling to charge God with being tolerant of evil.

3:16-22. Qohelet ferrets out the answer to the absurdity stated in v. 16 through the device of a dialogue with himself, punctuated by the formula "I said in my heart" (NRSV) or simply "I thought" (NIV). Prior even to these clichés is the formula "I saw," which unifies the entire pericope (see also 3:22; 4:1, 4, 7). At first he relates the issue back to the theme of appropriate times (v. 17*a*; cf. 3:1), with this nuance: At the time God appointed for it, God will judge the righteous and the wicked. This will not occur, of course, in an afterlife of bliss or torment, but here in this world.

Nevertheless, it may not happen right away. In fact, on a day-to-day basis, neither justice nor righteousness, but wickedness prevails. So much for the standard theodicy!

The insight of vv. 18-19 may not be very original, but it is profound, perhaps in more ways than Qohelet himself understood. The mysterious origins of life's experiences lie in God, who uses them to "test" humankind. The sense moves from testing as "proving" (as in "proving ground") to testing as "proving to"—driving people to the conclusion that they belong to the realm of beasts. Death, the common fate that animals and human beings share, is the final proof of this: "as one dies, so dies the other." In Qohelet's view, this lack of advantage of human beings is "absurd" (הבל *hebel*). We who stand near the place of angels (Ps 8:5) and who have been invited into the council of heaven (1 Kgs 22:19-23) must all "turn to dust again" (see Gen 3:19;

Job 10:9; Ps 104:29; Sir 40:11). In vv. 20-21, echoes of the Yahwistic creation story in Genesis are present. Qohelet assumes that the רוח (*rûaḥ*, "wind," "breath," "spirit") that God breathed into the original terracotta humanoid (Gen 2:7) is the animating principle of all living creatures and can be withdrawn by God from one species just as well as another (see Ps 104:27-30).

Upon the lowly but omnipresent word *all* (כל *kōl*, vv. 19-20; see Introduction) rides Qohelet's universal vision. There are no exceptions to this rule of death. In v. 21 the Teacher pleads ignorance on the question of the ultimate destiny of the human spirit. The discussion is introduced by a second use of the formula "Who knows?" (see 2:19; 6:12; 8:1). The question is not exactly rhetorical; that is, it does not seem to anticipate a particular answer. In fact, the formula is often invoked in the Hebrew Bible precisely when the question is to be left totally open-ended (see 2 Sam 12:22; Joel 2:14; Jonah 3:9). When the pupil asks, "Is there life beyond death?" the Teacher answers, "Who knows?"

The ancients believed that at death everything returns to its source. Consistent with that model, in 12:7 Qohelet distinguishes between the dust that descends to the ground from whence it came and the "breath" that arises to God, from whom it came (see Gen 2:7). However, the question of the continued existence of the creature that can live only because it is a *combination* of dust and life-breath is left totally unanswered. The logic of the Teacher's argument is to forge a solidarity in death between animals and human beings. There is no discernible reason why the "breath" of the former should behave differently at death than would that of the latter. The Hebrew underworld, Sheol, is not the source of the animal spirit, and there is no reason why it should descend thither after death in antithesis to the upward, "heavenly" movement alleged for the human spirit (v. 21).[63] Chances are good that the same fate awaits us all.

63. Rankin points out that this is the first reference in the Hebrew Bible or any other Jewish source to "immortality"—i.e., the direct ascent of the human "breath" to God without resurrection or at least an interim state in Sheol. See Rankin and Atkins, "The Book of Ecclesiastes," 5:52. The notion was present in Mesopotamian astral religion as well as in Greek thought, and it may have reached Israel from the east. In any case, Qohelet reports the view only to reject it. The reference in 12:7, too, does not suggest a life after death for the individual, but only the reclamation by God of the "life-breath" that had belonged to God in the first place.

Contemplation of ultimate destiny or fate is of no comfort to Ecclesiastes, so he reverts to the comfort already set forth in 3:9-15: Happiness in their doings is the lot of human beings. That is not bad; it is a gift of God (v. 13). However, it is possible only when human beings accept the premise that they cannot know what lies ahead (v. 22*b*). The question, "Who can bring them to see what will be after them?" is, of course, a rhetorical one. The answer is, No one! For Qohelet the high probability exists that there is nothing after death. However, he refuses to speculate beyond that and instead carves out for human effort a little island of happiness in the midst of a sea of unknowability and, finally, nonexistence.

4:1-8. Qohelet continues his dialogue with himself by further meditations (vv. 1-3) on the intertwined themes of death and justice, introduced by the unifying formula "I saw." Oppressed people find no comfort from any quarter. Job, too, longed for an advocate, and even dared hope for a divine one (Job 9:33; cf. Job 16:18-22; 19:25-27). Qohelet holds out no such hope. In vv. 2-3, the Teacher returns to the theme of death. He divides all people into three categories according to an ascending order of happiness: those who are now living, those who have died, and those who were never born. The latter are happiest of all because they never have to see the horrors that occur in human history (see 7:1; Job 3:11-19; Jer 20:14-18). Therefore, nonexistence is preferable to existence, though the Teacher does not advocate suicide.

The Teacher's high estimation of the power of "envy" (קנאה *qin'â*, v. 4) to drive the engines of competition ought to gladden the hearts of capitalists everywhere. It does not gladden his heart, however, for in his judgment this is an absurd way to make a living. The NRSV's literal translation of the traditional saying of v. 5 leads one to contemplate self-cannibalism (the language is a figure of oppression in Isa 49:26; Mic 3:2-3), though no doubt it describes the fool who will not work, therefore cannot eat, and so destroys himself (see Prov 6:10-11; 19:15). This teaching seems to contradict the doubts about economic drive in v. 4, insofar as the person who takes it easy is judged to be a fool. It connects better with the proverb in v.

6, which advocates modesty in consumption (see Prov 15:16-17; 16:8; 17:1). With whom is the Teacher more sympathetic, then, the workaholic or the skinny fool? Or is v. 6 his mediating position? Gordis discerns here another unattributed quotation that serves as an opponent to be refuted. He thinks that v. 5 should be introduced with "Some say" and v. 6 with "But I say."[64] Murphy, in contrast, thinks both sayings may be traditional and, in Qohelet's opinion, valueless.[65]

The case of the lonely person whose lust for riches is never satisfied and who never simply enjoys life (v. 8) leads to the plaintive question, "For whom am I toiling?" (On "toil," see Introduction.) Reflecting on a similar situation, Ben Sira remarks, "If one is mean to himself, to whom will he be generous?" (Sir 14:5 NRSV). Crenshaw, who accused the sage of selfishness in his account of the royal experiment (2:1-11), remarks that here "sapiental . . . egocentrism weakens appreciably."[66]

64. Gordis, *Koheleth*, 231.
65. Murphy, *Ecclesiastes*, 39.

66. Crenshaw, *Ecclesiastes*, 51.

REFLECTIONS

This interesting passage provokes reflection on four of the Teacher's themes that continue to resonate in our lives: (1) the hatefulness of life; (2) our solidarity with the animals in death; (3) the ethics of envy; (4) the human need for a cause.

1. *The Hatefulness of Life.* How the mournful tenor of this pericope is supposed to square with Qohelet's recommendation to "eat and drink and take pleasure in all their toil" (e.g., 3:13) can only be guessed at. Perhaps he would simply have had his angst-ridden readers laugh in the face of onrushing doom. True, the attitude squares with the hatred of life the Teacher voiced in 2:17—a hatred that arose from the absurd fact that the righteous suffer oppression and justice seems blind. The orthodox faith he has abandoned would not have had it so. But it is so, and it is hateful. At the same time, this writer takes care, even delight, in exploring from all sides the meaning of life, and he does so with sustained energy. He does not behave as one who feels, like Macduff in Macbeth, that he should have been "from his mother's womb/ Untimely ripp'd"; he is more like his own model figures who "take pleasure in all their toil" (3:13). Besides, as he will later observe, "a living dog is better than a dead lion" (9:4 NRSV). For anyone today who seeks theological guidance from the Teacher, it is fortunate that the latter observation may be as close to his last word on the subject as this one is. After all, the view that it would have been better to never have been born is antithetical to most other biblical teaching. Modern theology, too, which often makes existence or being itself its central value, would cry out against a preference never to have been born. From Tillich's point of view, for example, because being is rooted in God the very Ground of Being, it stands in ontological opposition to the most profound antivalue, which is nonbeing.

2. *Our Solidarity with the Animals in Death.* Qohelet's expansion on his hatred of life is doubly interesting because it is articulated by a declaration of solidarity in death with all living things (3:19). He was right in making this identification, of course. He simply did not go far enough in talking about the commonalities that we share with the animal kingdom. We know now that we are made of the same stardust—carbon, oxygen, nitrogen—that makes up the cells of all living things and that our genetic makeup differs very little from that of the great apes. But even in the third century BCE, Qohelet knew that the gulf that continues to separate humankind from God is a great one in spite of human efforts to bridge it (Genesis 3). He knew that that gulf is far greater than the one that separates humankind from baboons and shrews. Qohelet's remark that all are driven by the brutal fact of death means that the world does not take moral sides, and we can no more manipulate our fate with virtue or with wickedness than can the animals.

In short, modern Jews and Christians have much to agree with in Qohelet's exclamation in 3:19 that the fate of all animals is the same. Our dispute with him comes more in relation to the following v. 20, in which he says, "All go to one place; all are from the dust, and all turn to dust again." Physically, of course, he is correct, but he means also to deny the possibility of any existence beyond physical death. In his own time, the dawn of the alternative doctrine of resurrection was at hand (Isa 26:19 probably predates him slightly, and Dan 12:2 follows not long after). The alien doctrine of blessed immortality had also begun to find acceptance in Judaism. At about 100 BCE, the writer of the book of Wisdom quoted a remarkably Qohelet-like opponent as saying:

> For our allotted time is the passing of a shadow,
> and there is no return from our death,
> because it is sealed up and no one turns back.
> Come, therefore, let us enjoy the good things that exist. (Wis 2:5-6 NRSV)

His answer to this opponent is clear: "God created us for incorruption, and made us in the image of his own eternity" (v. 23 NRSV). For Christians, the resurrection of Jesus of Nazareth tips the scale definitively away from blessed immortality and toward resurrection faith in the renewal of all things at the day of God's victory over death and evil (1 Cor 15:20-28).

Do we have an argument with 3:21-22? Does the human spirit go upward and the spirits of animals go downward at death or at a general resurrection? That is a fascinating question that remains surprisingly open in twentieth-century theology. A Tillichian approach, for example, assumes that anything that has being is finally reunited with the source of all being and that God wastes nothing. That would include animals, too, though the details remain sketchy.

3. *The Ethics of Envy.* Perhaps the Teacher intended to be cynical in attributing all effort and accomplishment to envy (4:4). Then again, perhaps he had grabbed human nature by the same lapel that Adam Smith and other capitalists seized it by in later times—competition (= envy) drives the engines of commerce. One wonders, however, how this insight fits with the conviction expressed in 3:11 that everything is predetermined. If time and chance are absolutely neutral, if the world is driven on by destiny, and if meaningful moral choice, therefore, is impossible, then a decision to push ahead of others in moneymaking because the time is right would be based on illusion. To compete out of envy is an ethical choice. It may be a perverse ethic, but it is a choice. It is a choice that is consistent with the kinds of energy that, released by the knowledge that death is inevitable, give rise to such human activities as empire building and childbearing, which seem to offer a way of transcending the inevitability of death (see Reflections at 3:1-8).

In short, Qohelet is inconsistent in his remarks about work that imply choices—even bad ones. Readers sometimes fault Qohelet for being inconsistent; some even postulate an editor who inserted occasional glosses to correct some of the Teacher's more egregious unorthodoxies. Perhaps the most we can say about the dissonant teachings of the book is to suggest that, as an assembler of proverbs (12:9), Qohelet was aware that the folk had spoken about the same subject in quite different ways on separate occasions. Perhaps he was ambivalent himself and could see both sides of such an issue as competition versus cooperation.

Actually, it is remarkable that so many contradictory thoughts about the same subject can have the ring of truth. On the one hand, it strikes the reader as true that we live in a web of fixed orders (3:1-8) and that, at the same time, we can make choices that are good and bad. It strikes one as true that people are urged on to toil and skill because they fear death and because they envy their neighbors. By nature, truth is multifaceted.

Modern literature explores this fact frequently, perhaps nowhere more successfully than in Akira Kurosawa's 1951 film *Rashomon.* In that film a murder in a forest is viewed from the perspectives of the victim, the murderer, and others. In the end, the viewer, who witnessed the original crime, is no longer sure what really happened because the same set of facts takes on different contours depending on who tells the story. Most of the things that Qohelet is saying about life are true, and a preacher ought not to ignore the fact, even though the same realities viewed from a post-resurrection perspective can be described in other ways.

4. *The Human Need for a Cause.* The delightful story in 4:7-8 tells about the lonely childless person who, like Ebenezer Scrooge after Marley's ghost had finished with him, asks, "Why am I joylessly struggling to acquire goods and property that I have nowhere to put in the end?" (His case is almost worse than that of the person who has to leave it all to some fool [2:19]!) None of us can prove that the deferred gratification that we practice now will have some payoff in the years ahead or in the world to come.

To be set alongside Qohelet's insight, however, is the equally important biblical realization that human beings require a cause, something bigger than themselves, in order to live happily and effectively. Both creation accounts in Genesis establish this as an ontological reality. In the J account (Gen 2:4b-25), there can be no plant of the field, no agriculture, no husbandry, until there is a human being. God plants the garden of Eden only after God creates Adam to be its farmer and keeper. Human beings are created with a vocation, and that vocation is essential to the larger cause of earth-keeping. The Priestly writer, too, recognized that human beings have a vocation from the very moment of their creation. Probably the best translation of Gen 1:26 is "Then God said, 'Let us make humankind in our image, according to our likeness, so that they may have dominion over the fish of the sea'" (NRSV). In other words, God's image in humankind is to be expressed in God-like, loving rule in the earth on God's behalf. This is our human vocation.

This biblically acknowledged need for a cause that is bigger than the self is confirmed by modern social science. Psychiatrist Robert Jay Lifton, for example, identifies a capacity toward resiliency and self-transformation present in all of us that enables us to survive personal and cultural traumas and to connect ourselves with the rest of humankind.[67] By effecting change in our self-preoccupation, we can join in community in working to end warfare, to enhance ecological safety, in short, to ensure human survival. This is our human vocation.

Put the insight of Genesis alongside that of the Teacher, and you have valid and useful doctrine. To put everything off to some future time while spending the present enslaved to moneymaking is foolish. Just say no to that! On the other hand, it is also true that we want to feel that our lives contribute to a larger good. Perhaps within the Teacher's doctrine of times and seasons there is a place for this truth, too, especially if moral choice survives within his scheme (3:6):

There is a time to seek [one's self-interest] and a time to lose [one's life in the vigorous pursuit of a cause].

67. Robert Jay Lifton, *The Protean Self: Human Resilience in an Age of Fragmentation* (New York: Basic Books, 1993).

ECCLESIASTES 4:9–6:12, APHORISMS

Ecclesiastes 4:9–5:7, On Competition, Cooperation, and Vows

COMMENTARY

4:9-16. This passage opens with pairs of people. Here are explored the virtues of companionship—perhaps even marriage—and teamwork. The imagery of vv. 10-12 suggests travel, though the "falling" of v. 10 may be metaphorical for "failing." The shift from ordinary narrative description to the metaphor of the three-stranded cord suggests that at least v. 12b is another popular proverb. If by cooperating two persons can ensure their mutual safety, three would offer even greater security. (If the bed in v. 11 in which the two snuggle to keep warm is a marriage bed, perhaps the third strand in v. 12 is a child.) Altogether, these three verses offer a positive alternative to the envy-driven rivalry declared absurd in 4:4.

Verses 13-16 also focus on two persons: a wise youth juxtaposed to a foolish king. (As the NRSV notes indicate, the Hebrew text seems to include both a first and a second successor to the original king.) The Joseph-like jail-to-throne motif of these verses is enhanced in the NRSV by considerable emendation of the obscure Hebrew text. The result fits the context, however. The fame and power based on popular acclaim is evanescent. The "doubting syndrome" of the Teacher reasserts itself when he points out that even the success of the youth who replaced the king is of limited duration and that hopes for generations yet to come to continue to grant him enduring praise are merely "chasing after wind." So much for the enduring legacy of Joseph, wise vizier to the pharaoh!

5:1-7. The last verse of chap. 4 in the Hebrew text is 5:1 in the English translations. The latter division makes sense, however, because the subject of 5:1-7 is coherent— all the aphorisms have to do with the vanity of speech. A literal translation of the beginning of 5:1 could be, "Watch your step when you go to the house of God" (lit., "the god"). In the presence of God (presumably in the Temple), sincere listening is more pleasing to God than the sacrificial gestures of "fools." (Note that the condemnation of fools in v. 1b results from an emendation of the Hebrew text, which literally reads, "They do not know how to do evil." Murphy offers a helpful alternative: "They have no knowledge of doing evil.")[68] We do not know to what kind of preaching or instruction the contemporaries of the author of Ecclesiastes had the opportunity to listen in their temple environment, but evidently discourse was available for those who had ears to hear. Perhaps chanting of psalms and recitation of weekly portions of the Torah were what Qohelet had in mind. Even though his book makes little reference to worship in the Temple or elsewhere, the central cultic institution would very likely have been part of his experience. Gordis, who consistently finds evidence of social elitism in the Teacher's work, finds it here as well: "Koheleth here reflects the proto-Sadducean upperclass viewpoint, which regards the Temple as essential to the established order, and therefore required."[69] However he may have experienced it personally, Qohelet knew that in the presence of God a person's heart, ears, and mouth are all under scrutiny. Each person needs to be chastened by the humility of being an earthling (v. 2), subject to a heavenly sovereign who cannot be manipulated by words: "He does whatever he pleases" (Ps 115:3 NRSV).

Prophets and sages alike had always warned that cultic worship without serious intention and obedience is foolish and dangerous (see 1 Sam 15:22-23; Prov 15:8; 21:27; Jer 7:22-23; Hos 6:6; Mic 6:6-8). The cautionary note "let your words be few" (v. 2) may refer to prayer; if so, it anticipates Jesus' warning to his disciples not to "heap

68. Murphy, *Ecclesiastes*, 46.
69. Gordis, *Koheleth*, 236.

up empty phrases as the Gentiles do" (Matt 6:7 NRSV). The linkage of dreams with cares (v. 3a) is less germane to the context than is the voice of the fool (v. 3b). The point is that excess—whether of business or of words—means trouble. Meaningless verbiage is the mark of a fool (10:12-14) and is inappropriate public behavior (Sir 7:14).

Verse 6 suggests that to tell the messenger who arrives to collect on a vow that you did not mean it is not at all wise. (The word translated "mistake" [שגה šāgâ] is used elsewhere to designate unintended sin; e.g., Num 15:22.) To do so would only alert God to the need for punitive action. The law was

clear: "If you make a vow to the Lord your God, do not postpone fulfilling it; for the Lord your God will surely require it of you" (Deut 23:21 NRSV). Even though Qohelet pleads ignorance about what God is doing all the time (3:11), evidently he still believed that God would judge and punish human actions. Ben Sira, too, saw the danger of reneging on a vow (Sir 18:22), and the sages advised careful thought before even making one (Prov 20:25). The seven verses that caution against empty vows and excessive verbiage conclude with a simple admonition that, when taken seriously, negates both pomposity and carelessness in speaking: "Fear God!" (v. 7).

REFLECTIONS

In 5:1-7, the organ at issue is the mouth. Qohelet warns his students against the hollow, outward observance of religion, and he cautions them to be particularly careful in taking vows. In issues of faith and philosophy alike, having a big mouth can get one into a lot of trouble: "Do not let your mouth lead you into sin" (v. 6a). Perhaps it was this warning that vacuous words are also culpable words that led G. K. Chesterton to compose his poem "Ecclesiastes":

There is one sin: to call a green leaf gray,
    Whereat the sun in heaven shuddereth.
There is one blasphemy: for death to pray,
    For God alone knoweth the praise of death.

There is one creed: 'neath no world-terror's wing
    Apples forget to grow on apple-trees.
There is one thing is needful—everything—
    The rest is vanity of vanities.

Ecclesiastes 5:8-20, On the Love of Money

COMMENTARY

The second section of aphorisms offers a number of reflections on profit and wealth, all of which throw an unfavorable light on the person who makes the gain of wealth a high priority.

5:8-9. In the light of the teachings that follow it, we may take v. 8 to be a commentary not on political oppression as much as on economics. Every official "watches" those lower on the chain of authority in order to secure a percentage of the tax or bribe

revenue. The enigmatic v. 9 leaves translators and exegetes with serious problems, as the comparison of the NIV with the NRSV will demonstrate. The NIV solution fits best with the sense of the section: The heavy hand of taxation extends to the king at the very top, who claims revenue for the crown from fields worked by even the lowliest peasants. The king is devoted to agriculture all right (which may be the notion at work in the NRSV), but that devotion is self-interested. There is no reason to see in this sentence any positive affirmation by the Teacher of the institution of kingship. If the king, who, according to the prophets, had to guarantee that the system worked justly for all, had his own hand in the till, then no one should anticipate any recourse from unfair treatment by officials.

5:10-17. The plight of the acquisitive person is explored further in these verses. In 3:8, Qohelet linked greedy eyes to riches; here he speaks of unfulfilled passion, "love," for wealth of all kinds. Furthermore, with increased productivity and profitability come increased demands by interested parties. Sometimes the owner merely gets to look at personal gains before they are consumed by others (v. 11). The Teacher is then moved to restate an idea that he first raised in 2:23: Those who have nothing to lose sleep sweetly even on half-empty stomachs, while those who have more than they need lose sleep worrying about protecting their assets—or perhaps because they have overeaten.

The theme of vv. 13-17 is an echo of 2:18-23. It describes the evil effects of riches, on both the hoarder and the disappointed heirs of an estate. In words reminiscent of Job 1:21, the Teacher laments that we exit from the world just as naked and vulnerable as we entered it and that we have nothing to show for all of our toil. We work only for wind (v. 15). The passage culminates in v. 17 with the textually difficult reference to the one who eats in darkness "with great frustration, affliction and anger." One pictures an ancient Scrooge who, in his unpleasantness and obsessiveness having driven off all friends and family, sits down to his supper alone.

5:18-20. These next verses, in contrast, bring the passage to a close with a reprise (see 2:24-26) of the only consistently positive theme of the book: that the proper goal of all human endeavor is joy (see Introduction). A good life of enjoyment of the fruits of human labor is possible if people will simply look on food, drink, and money as gifts from God and accept their "lot" (חלק ḥēleq, v. 18; cf. 2:10, "reward"; 3:22). This term, not to be equated with "fate" (מקרה miqreh, 2:14), refers to the individual's share of personal history and of earthly goods. God "enables" some to enjoy these gifts (v. 19), even though the gifts are limited both in quantity and in duration. Because God makes this available, acceptance of one's lot as a gift of God to be enjoyed becomes a moral responsibility.

The meaning of v. 20 is elusive, partly because the Hebrew verb "remember" (זכר zākar) is susceptible of various interpretations. By translating it as "brood," the NRSV suggests that the "remembering" in view here is not quite healthy and that it is better for human beings not to examine seriously the situations in which they find themselves. God keeps them so "occupied" (ענה ʿānâ; taking the verb in the sense unique to Ecclesiastes; cf. 1:13; 3:10) that they do not have time to brood and despair, and so their "days flit pleasantly past."[70]

---

70. Rankin and Atkins, "The Book of Ecclesiastes," 5:60.

REFLECTIONS

This collection of aphorisms on the theme of the acquisition of wealth (5:8-20) seems contemporary in many ways. Verse 8, which cynically says that there is no need for surprise at the oppression of the poor by the rich and the powerful, could well be a text for one of today's liberation theologians. Systemic violation of the have-nots by the haves is as crucial an issue in our time as it ever was. Similarly, v. 10, "The lover of money will not be satisfied with money," expresses the very sentiment on which consumerism is built. In giving one of the simplest reasons why the rich tend to get richer, Qohelet incidentally discloses one of the bedrocks that underlie Wall Street.

A matter of more philosophical interest grows out of Qohelet's remarks in vv. 18-20. The fact that good things come from God suggests that Qohelet thought of God as more than simply a distant power, an omnipotent but amoral fabricator of the universe. God also appears here as the author and source of all that is available to human beings to make life joyous. To accept God's gracious gift is, in fact, the only moral responsibility laid by Ecclesiastes upon the reader of the book. The disturbing aspect of this otherwise positive situation is, of course, that the decision by God as to who gets wealth and who is "enabled" to enjoy it seems totally arbitrary. Although such a radical claim squares with Qohelet's general preference for a closed predestinarian system, the choice of the verb *enables* rather undercuts the moral possibilities inherent in doing God's will by humbly and gratefully accepting God's gifts. If even the very ability to make that choice is a gift of God, those who do not receive it will never find happiness.

A more positive spin on the word *enables* might take it this way: People cannot earn their happiness through good works, as the authors of the Hebrew Bible had sometimes imagined they could do (e.g., "The reward for humility and fear of the LORD is riches and honor and life" [Prov 22:4 NRSV]; see also Pss 19:11; 62:12; Isa 3:10). Like Job, who found that all his good deeds did not save him from the dunghill (Job 29:11-20), Qohelet realizes that there is no sure and certain hope and that one must simply have faith that God will make happiness possible. Whether this election by God of some people requires the rejection by God of others, whether that rejection follows as a consequence of human behavior or is simply God's arbitrary choice—these are questions of which Qohelet makes nothing. The conundrum he raises remains alive and well. Who among us has not puzzled at why some people who "have it all" struggle with self-doubt, low self-esteem, and general misery while others do not? We may attribute the difference to family systems, jumbled genes on some chromosome, or simple brain chemistry, though the definitive answer remains beyond our reach. Here Qohelet attributes the difference simply to God's "enabling."

Ecclesiastes 6:1-12, On Lowering Expectations

COMMENTARY

Chapter 6 picks up the note upon which chap. 5 concluded: that possessions are gifts of God and that the ability to enjoy them is also a gift of God. This chapter follows through four stages the plight of those who do not have that gift of enjoyment: (1) Verses 1-2 present us such persons as the counter-image of the happy rich person of 5:18-20; (2) vv. 3-6 tell the story of two characters, a thwarted rich man who does not have the gift and a lucky stillborn child; (3) vv. 7-9 use the anatomical images of mouth and eyes to bring forward the painful truth that advantage is no advantage; (4) vv. 10-12 picture the human community in the grip of inexorable predetermination, true knowledge about which is not available to humankind.

6:1-2. The formula with which the chapter opens, "There is an evil that I have seen under the sun," echoes the language of 5:13. The evil is the situation of the individual whom God has not "enabled" to enjoy "wealth, possessions and honor." God's refusal to "empower" the rich man means that a "stranger" ends up enjoying the estate.

Gordis points out that this stranger need not be a foreigner or even an unknown person: "For Koheleth, the individualist, each man is a stranger to his fellows, even to members of his own family. There is a distinctly modern implication here of the essential loneliness of the individual personality."[71]

6:3-6. At v. 3 the contrast is drawn between the man who ostensibly has the things that constitute blessing—many children (e.g., Gen 24:60; Deut 11:21; 28:4) and a long life (e.g., Exod 23:26; Deut 30:20; Ps 91:16; Isa 65:20)—with the stillborn infant. The latter is better off, says the Teacher, because it finds rest more quickly than does the rich man. Although the stillborn child's progress through the world is from vanity to darkness (v. 4), that journey is mercifully brief. The passage culminates in a rhetorical question: "Do not all go to one place?" The intended answer is yes. If the distance between now and then is only a course of suffering, then why not recognize that the

71. Gordis, *Koheleth*, 247.

shorter life is the better? Like its precursor in 4:3, this text brings to mind Job's wistful longing to have ended his life "like a stillborn child,/ like an infant that never sees the light" (Job 3:16 NRSV). It raises questions about whether long life is in fact always a blessing. Indeed, with a consistency rare to him, Qohelet repeatedly expresses doubt about it (see also Eccl 8:12; 11:8).

The NRSV and the NIV do not reveal the difficulty in the semi-final clause of v. 3, translated by NRSV "or has no burial." It is true that a decent burial is one of the marks of blessing and that to be deprived of it is a curse (see Isa 14:19; Jer 22:19). The importance attached to the moving of Joseph's bones from Egypt (Gen 50:25; Exod 13:19) and to the proper burial of Saul and Jonathan (1 Sam 31:11-13; 2 Sam 2:5-7) illustrates the point. The problem with v. 3 is both logical and philological. Is it logical to suppose that a rich man who had a miserable life but an elaborate funeral could therefore be said to have been a happy man? Surely not. Crenshaw construes the pronoun implied in "and [he/she/it] does not receive proper burial" as anticipatory of the stillborn child. His result, then, is "but he is not satisfied with good things, then even if it does not have a burial, I say that the still-born is better off than he."[72]

However the verse may be fine-tuned, the point of the story remains the same. The rich man who does not enjoy his riches, whether he was properly buried or not, is less well off than the stillborn fetus who may not be buried at all.

6:7-9. These verses seem to be an amalgam of a traditional saying (v. 7) that is approved and enlarged upon by Qohelet (cf. Prov 16:26, "The appetite of workers works for them; their hunger urges them on," NRSV). Human beings struggle to stuff their mouths full, and yet they cannot satisfy their cravings. Some interpreters suggest that because "mouth" (פה *peh*) is modified by a possessive pronoun ("his" or "its") in Hebrew, the "mouth" must be that of Sheol, the place to which all go (6:6*b*). The notion that Sheol has a hungry, gaping maw that swallows up the dead is graphically acknowledged in the list in Prov 30:15-16 of three and four things that never say "Enough" (see also Isa 5:14;

Hab 2:5). Certainly the gaping mouth of hell (pictured as Leviathan, as Jonah's whale, or just as a cavelike opening into which the damned are flung) became a staple feature of medieval Christian art. However, the fact that "appetite" (נפש *nepeš*) lacks the possessive pronoun rather tips the interpretive scale back to seeing the proverb as a generalization about the human condition: Satiety can never be achieved.

The response to the problem of nonsatiety seems to be 6:9, which commentators take essentially to mean "a bird in hand is worth two in the bush." The seat of desire in the Hebrew Bible is the נפש (*nepeš*), the "soul" or "life force" (see Cant 5:6). So the reference to "pursuing *nepeš*" (v. 9*a*) is no doubt correctly translated "wandering of desire" (NRSV) or "roving of the appetite" (NIV).

Bracketed by verses 7 and 9 is the rather puzzling v. 8. Does v. 8*b* describe a poor man who knows how to conduct himself in the face of opposition, or is Scott right in amending the text to read, "How then is a wise man better off than a fool? [Only] in knowing how to conduct himself during his life"?[73] In either case, v. 8 seems intended to give yet another painful example of the truth that the advantaged person finally has no advantage. Even if wisdom and wealth are joined, as Qohelet urges they be (see 7:11; 9:15), nothing necessarily is gained; nor is the humble virtue of the poor person of lasting merit.

6:10-12. These verses appear to comprise a separate, transitional unit devoted entirely to one of the Teacher's major themes: the impossibility of knowing what is truly going on in the world (see Introduction). It opens with the enigmatic statement that "it is known what human beings are." Assuming that the one who is stronger than the human individual is God (v. 10*b*; the NRSV obscures this possibility), this verse joins Job in decrying the uselessness of words spoken against God even while longing to enter into "dispute" with God. (In such passages as Job 9:32-35 and 16:18-22, Job tries to get God into court for a full hearing and adjudication of their dispute.) The Teacher—a lover of words in spite of his declarations against rhetoric—puts it with beautiful alliteration: "the more words, the more vanity

72. Crenshaw, *Ecclesiastes*, 120.

73. Scott, *Proverbs, Ecclesiastes*, 231.

דברים הרבה מרבים הבל] *děbarîm harbēh marbîm hābel*]" (v. 11).

"Who knows" indeed what is good for mortals in the present moment (v. 12*a*)? Long ago Zimmerli credited Qohelet with having stated the "central question" faced by the wisdom writers of the Hebrew Bible: "What do people gain from all the toil at which they toil under the sun?" (1:3). How can a wise person gain "practical mastery" over life?[74] By

74. Walther Zimmerli, "Concerning the Structure of Old Testament Wisdom," in *Studies in Ancient Israelite Wisdom*, ed. James L. Crenshaw (New York: KTAV, 1976) 175-207, esp. 176, 198.

this point in his book it is clear that Qohelet will be unable to answer his own question and will be forced to leave it as an unanswerable conundrum. Nor can anyone say what lies in the future for human beings (v. 12*b*). Yet they can no more leave alone the question of the future than they can the question of the proper task of the present moment. Because of his curiosity about the fate of his descendants, Job could not live in peace: "Their children come to honor, and they do not know it;/ they are brought low, and it goes unnoticed" (Job 14:21 NRSV).

REFLECTIONS

Like the ancient dialectical theologian that he was, the Teacher circles once again around the themes of the means of joy in life, the illusory advantage of power and wealth, and inescapable predetermination.

1. In 6:1-2, the fatalistic dilemma into which Qohelet's radical logic carries him is restated in negative terms. In 5:19 the problem was stated softly and positively: To have the gift of enjoying good things is a grace of God. Now it is put harshly: To have it and never enjoy it is "an evil" that "lies heavy upon humankind." Unlike the rich fool in Jesus' story whose free choice it was to build ever bigger barns before he ate, drank, and was merry (Luke 12:13-21), the rich and famous people of Qohelet's tale could not have escaped their discontent and despair in any way. One sympathizes with Scott's effort to weaken the dilemma by describing this as the "case of a man who has everything that heart can desire, but is prevented by circumstances, or by his own attitude, from enjoying life."[75] Elsewhere the Teacher allows freer play to human choice and responsibility (see, e.g., Commentary and Reflections at 3:1-15). In this passage, however, Qohelet's mood is deterministic. God and God alone decides who will be able to enjoy and be happy—and faithful obedience, moral rectitude, prayer, and fasting will not affect this outcome in any way.

2. As Qohelet sees it (6:3-6), the stillborn or aborted fetus enjoys the advantage in the game of life by never having played it. Yet he does not advocate resigning the game by committing suicide. "Tough it out!" is his recommendation.

Someone among his contemporaries must have been advocating an afterlife as a way of offering advantage upon those who were willing to play the game fair and square now. Why else would the Teacher keep raising that possibility, only to reject it with a rhetorical question (v. 6*b*)? Now, even though we Christians are on the side of Qohelet's adversary because we accept Easter as the first step toward the renewal of all things, we need not scoff at Qohelet's gloomy assessment of non-advantage to anyone who stands before death. Our hope of participation beyond this life in the life of the kingdom of heaven is not based on any reward we may feel we have earned or have been given. It is based solely on God's love of us and commitment to our lives. So Qohelet's gloom can serve us in good stead when the snake oil seller or our own longings promise us the advantage. The fact is that we all do die, and, but for God alone, we probably would all lie forever in the same narrow bed of extinction. The game

75. Scott, *Proverbs, Ecclesiastes*, 232.

of life is always a deuce game; ultimate advantage lodged in the assertion of ourselves really is an illusion.

3. At the end of chap. 6, Qohelet conveys the sense that human beings move almost as automatons within the inexorable orders of the One who is stronger than we are (v. 10). We cannot know the future, but we know that whatever it will hold has already been named. As so often elsewhere, echoes of Qohelet's ineluctable doctrine reverberate in the rhymes of the Islamic predestinarian Omar Khayyám.

> We are no other than a moving row
> Of Magic Shadow-shapes that come and go
> Round with the Sun-illumin'd Lantern held
> In Midnight by the Master of the Show;
> But helpless Pieces of the Game He plays
> Upon this Chequer-board of Night and Days;
> Hither and thither moves, and checks, and slays,
> And one by one back in the Closet lays.

The view is an obnoxious one to modern Jewish and Christian sensibilities. Only if we construe Qohelet's line on predetermination as not so much a hard one involving election and rejection, but something more commonsensical, perhaps involving a softening of the heart into an attitude of grateful acceptance of life's allotment, does it begin to have possibilities for us.

ECCLESIASTES 7:1–8:17, A FIRST MISCELLANY

Ecclesiastes 7:1-14, Things That Are Good for Human Beings

COMMENTARY

At the end of the preceding chapter (6:12), the Teacher abandoned the search for "what is good for mortals." Apparently the mention of the word *good* jingled his memory or that of his compiler, for, having just abandoned his search, he promptly offers in 7:1-14 a collection of seven sayings precisely dealing with what is "good" (or even "better") for human beings (concluding with v. 14*a*, "When times are good, be happy"). No absolute good is proposed, and no perfection is attainable, but now (in contrast to 6:10; 7:14) Qohelet imagines that within their limits human beings do have competency to make moral decisions and to act accordingly. The "goods" that are discerned are behavioral virtues, things that a wise person should cultivate. They do not

differ from the standard teachings of the sages except that they offer no guarantees, no certain outcomes; even the good of wisdom itself is limited in its capacity to comprehend the outcome of life (vv. 11-14). Verse 14 offers the perspective from which the Teacher guides his students through this examination of what is good for mortals. That verse says, as it were, *"Carpe diem,"* "Seize the day." If a day is good, be good with it—be happy. You can know neither the etiology of this good thing nor its outcome; all life is tangled in a web of divine orders that can neither be known nor altered. God made both the good and the bad days, and one can expect to experience both, whether one's morals and etiquette bear the marks of wisdom or not.

The appropriate way to approach life, then, is with realism, sobriety, and a low profile.

7:1. The series of epigrams begins with this beautifully crafted verse, the alliterative first stich of which reads in Hebrew, טוב שם משמן טוב (*ṭôb šēm miššemen ṭôb*): "A good name is better than good ointment." The relationship of v. 1*a* to v. 1*b* becomes clear only when one recognizes that the "good name" and the "day of death" are given preference respectively over "precious ointment" and "day of birth" (the logic being A > B : A′ > B′). This means that A and A′ also explicate each other, as do B and B′. Perhaps one can never really attain a "good name" prior to the completion of one's life: "Call no one happy before his death; by how he ends, a person becomes known" (Sir 11:28 NRSV). The Hebrew Bible is full of stories of people's efforts to make for themselves a good name or its near equivalent, a great name. The builders of the Tower of Babel were led into sin by their zeal to "make a name for ourselves" (Gen 11:4 NRSV). In Gen 12:2, the Lord offers as a precious gift to Abram and his descendants the very thing the tower builders could not achieve: "I will . . . make your name great, so that you will be a blessing" (NRSV). The sages did not leave the good name strictly up to God, however. Human beings have responsibility and can attain the goal: "A good name is to be chosen rather than great riches" (Prov 22:1 NRSV). If "good name" and the "day of death" are thus related, then so are "precious ointment" and "day of birth." This pairing of terms may refer to the actual practice in ancient Greece and Egypt of anointing infants at birth with fragrant unguents. Although the Bible does not describe this act narratively (Ezek 16:4 speaks only of bathing an infant and rubbing it with salt), we know that adults anointed themselves with oil after bathing (Ruth 3:3; Ezek 16:9; Jdt 10:3; see Luke 7:38), and there is reason to suppose that infants were similarly anointed. Perhaps v. 1*a* was a traditional proverb and v. 1*b* is Qohelet's expansion of that proverb in an unconventional direction. The resulting combination is similar to Hillel's teaching, "Trust not in thyself until the day of thy death."[76] Although elsewhere Qohelet is

76. M. 'Abot 2:5.

prepared to say that it is better never to have been born at all than to suffer the frustrations of life (6:3), here the "good name" and the "day of death" are linked into a rounded-out life history that includes an element of satisfactory achievement. There is a place for human responsibility and action after all!

7:2. The second "good" saying extends this direction of thinking in recommending visitation at wakes during the seven-day period of mourning (Sir 22:12) in preference to attendance at "the house of feasting" ("drinking house" [בית משתה *bêt mišteh*]). The modal auxiliary verb "should" (NIV) accurately captures the idea: A wise person should approach all of experience with a keen sense of mortality, aware that death "is the end of everyone." The same idea, that all behavior should be colored by the reality of death, is expressed by the well-known line in Ps 90:12: "So teach us to count our days/ that we may gain a wise heart" (NRSV).

7:3-4. The third of the "good" sayings introduces the notion that "a sad face is good for the heart." If we allow Scripture to be its own interpreter, this apparently absurd teaching takes on life because of its relationship to the other six sayings in the series. The overriding theme of the series is that one should be busy at all times preparing for days of adversity, rather than trying to deny their inevitability or drown the awareness of them in foolish mirth. In 1:18, Qohelet already observed that the suffering that accompanies wisdom is so intense that wisdom hardly seems worth seeking. This is not the same message as that brought to Job by his friends—namely, that suffering has pedagogical value and should be welcomed as a moral benefit (Job 5:17). Qohelet speaks here in a simple declaratory manner: Given all that one comes to know in life, sadness is more appropriate than laughter.

7:5-6. These verses make up the fourth of the "good" sayings in this pericope. Now the metaphor involves sound and hearing. It is possible that the "song" (Vg, *adulatio*) of fools is simply the insincere praise that the Teacher's student will receive from others. (Other instances in which "song" is synonymous with "praise" include Ps 149:1; Isa 42:10.) This kind of "song" would be the perfect antithesis to the rebuke of the wise. In an expansion of this theme, Qohelet once again employs the literary device of alliteration. In v. 5 he spoke of the "song" (שיר *šîr*) of fools; in v. 6 he speaks of the "thorns" (סירים *sîrîm*) that crackle under the "pot" (סיר *sîr*).[77]

7:8-10. The fifth of the "good" sayings reverts to the claim of v. 1 that the best perspective one can hope to attain on a matter is the perspective of its outcome (v. 8*a*; see King Ahab's message to the king of Aram: "One who puts on armor should not brag like one who takes it off" [1 Kgs 20:11 NRSV]). To do so requires patience (v. 8*b*); in turn, this requires resistance to quick, hot flashes of anger (v. 9; see Prov 16:32). Finally, a perspective from the end of life precludes the need to hark back to the good old days (v. 10). The maturity and realism of age do not long for the past, because, from the perspective of the end (v. 8), they are able to assess the meaning of all of life and not simply its fresh beginnings. From such a perspective, it is clear that there is no general progress in justice and righteousness, no ethical evolution, but only individual examples of wise persons who acted prudently.

7:11-12. The Hebrew of v. 11, the beginning of the sixth "good" saying, reads, "Wisdom is good with an inheritance, and profitable to those who see the sun." This literal translation seems to make the point that wisdom is good, but wisdom with cash is even better. The idea is paralleled in *M. 'Abot* 2:2: "Excellent is study of the Law together with worldly occupation, for toil in them both puts sin out of mind." In other words, even such positive values as wisdom and Torah

can benefit from the parallel practical responsibility of making a living. The NIV takes the Hebrew preposition "with" (עם *'im*) to mean "like" in this instance and sees a simile here: "Wisdom, like an inheritance, is a good thing." This places wisdom and money on a par; therefore, the value of wisdom can be illuminated by comparing it to an inheritance. By creating a comparison using the formula "as good as," the NRSV plays down the value of money in comparison with wisdom and says, in effect, that even without any money at all, one could still have in wisdom a possession of great value. Verse 12 tips the scale toward the more literal understanding, especially if one follows Gordis (and Ibn Ezra) in translating v. 12*a*, "For there is the double protection of wisdom and money."[78]

7:13-14. For Gordis these verses present the epitome of Qohelet's thought.[79] Because God is all-powerful and cannot be challenged, human beings have to take whatever comes in stride, knowing that both the good and the bad are from God. In reference to what God "has made crooked" (see also 1:15), Crenshaw remarks, "The universe has wrinkles."[80] Some things out there seem to us not to be the way we would want them to be, but we cannot alter what God has made.

This then leads to the last of the seven "good" sayings (v. 14), the somewhat tentative affirmation that it is possible to find things that are good for human life (a rejoinder to 6:12); however, one has to reckon that God, who structures life by opposites (see 3:1-8), sends evil times along with the good ones. No reason exists, therefore, to hope that life will go on to perfection.

---

77. Barton's translation of v. 6*a*, "As the crackling of nettles under kettles," wonderfully preserves alliteration but diverts the eye of the mind away from the spiny desert plants and cacti that surely were in Qohelet's mind to the nasty stinging weeds of Bryn Mawr, where Barton taught. In Hos 2:6, *sîr* seems to mean a cactus hedgerow, like those still in use on farms in the Middle East. See Barton, *A Critical and Exegetical Commentary on the Book of Ecclesiastes*, 140.

78. Gordis, *Koheleth*, 264.
79. Gordis, *Koheleth*, 265.
80. Crenshaw, *Ecclesiastes*, 139.

REFLECTIONS

The collection of aphorisms that makes up 7:1-14 is not as miscellaneous as it might seem at first. Whether original with Qohelet or borrowed by him, all of these sayings have to do with what is good for the human being. Reflections on three facets of that discussion now follow.

1. It is well and good to contemplate the end of life. The first three "good" sayings (7:1-4) stress the superiority of sober contemplation of death to any giggling, foolish hilarity about life. Underlying these verses that juxtapose wisdom and foolishness, sobriety and mirth, is yet a deeper juxtaposition: birth and death. Verse 1 makes that juxtaposition explicit: The happiest outcome of life is to arrive at one's destiny with a good name and a record of probity rather than by virtue of being born to plunge the whole household into rejoicing and feasting (v. 2). Underlying this juxtaposition are the sacramental acts of mourning the dead and anointing the newborn child. The contrast between these two major life events and their liturgical accompaniments remains alive in both the Jewish and the Christian communities and in their respective houses of worship.

One of the most dramatic moments in the life of any Christian congregation is the baptism and chrismation of a child. This is particularly the case in Eastern Orthodox congregations in the modern Middle East, when the priest sweeps the infant three times through a great copper basin filled with warm water—once in the name of each of the members of the blessed Trinity. Then, with the child wrapped in a cozy towel, the priest makes the sign of the cross on the forehead, lips, ears, eyes, and feet of the child with the chrism, the sacred oil of unction. After communing the infant from the altar, priest and family parade around the sanctuary with the infant raised on high for all to see, accompanied by that peculiar gobbling shriek of women, called ululation. All of this signals reception of a new human being into the bosom of church and community.

Evidently Qohelet saw whatever version of that process was practiced in Jewish antiquity and was not impressed. He soberly concluded that it is more important to participate in the solemn ritual acts that even to this day accompany the end of life in the Middle East, when the professional mourners go wailing through the streets to mourn the departure of a loved one—if one is to live life with the gravity and care that it deserves.

2. It is worth noting that Qohelet teaches his student here that there is a discrepancy between the outer and the inner reality: A glad heart hides behind a sad face. This contradicts the usual exact proportionality between physiognomy and passion in the Hebrew Bible. Physical manifestations of inner states begin at least as early as Cain's nose burning (he was very angry) and his countenance falling (depression?) in Gen 4:5. Positive or negative feelings welling up from that innermost of organs, the heart, are also reflected in the voice and face (e.g., Ps 45:1; Prov 15:13; Sir 13:26). Even God's emotions are written straightforwardly on the divine countenance (e.g., Num 6:25-26).[81] Here, however, the sage turns the link inside out and teaches his students that they can identify persons whose hearts are whole and secure by their long faces. Other sages had seen the same reality, of course. Something similar to Qohelet's reversal of the usual congruence of the heart and the face is evident in Prov 14:13: "Even in laughter the heart is sad,/ and the end of joy is grief" (NRSV).

In his poem "Do Not Go Gentle into That Good Night," that quintessential voice of modernity, Dylan Thomas, challenged a war-torn and weary world to value life and make the most of it.

> Do not go gentle into that good night,
> Old age should burn and rave at close of day;
> Rage, rage against the dying of the light.
> Grave men, near death, who see with blinding sight
> Blind eyes could blaze like meteors and be gay,
> Rage, rage against the dying of the light.[82]

81. See Meyer I. Gruber, *Aspects of Nonverbal Communication in the Ancient Near East,* 2 vols. (Rome: Biblical Institute, 1980).
82. Dylan Thomas, from *The Poems of Dylan Thomas.* Copyright © 1952 by Dylan Thomas. Reprinted by permission of New Directions Publishing Corp.

Thomas's sensibility is utterly opposed to the counsel of the Teacher. When the latter gentleman heard anyone ask him not to pull a long face all the time but to plunge vigorously back into the struggle, his response was, "Sorrow is better than laughter,/ for by sadness of countenance the heart is made glad" (v. 3). In short, Qohelet's advice is: Go gentle!

3. Verses 13-14 contain an essentially obnoxious doctrine—everything is from God—which, as has been pointed out, has to be put into some kind of canonical context in order to be used (see Introduction; also Reflections at 3:1-15). Although the verses may epitomize Qohelet's theodicy, it remains hard to accept that God made the bad times as well as the good ones. Is it possible to agree with Qohelet that "nothing can challenge God's sovereign power or secure human existence,"[83] and still deny the premise underlying vv. 13-14 that God conjured up everything—the good and the bad alike?

Now, in the larger canonical context this problem has been examined many times, and a variety of solutions has been offered. One solution is that human beings create their own destiny by their deeds, which are theirs alone and not God's. The notion that the wicked die prematurely or suffer injury and that the righteous prosper underlies the great retributional scheme of the deuteronomistic history and is hymned as an article of faith in the "psalms of the two ways" (Pss 1; 37). Qohelet is in business to deny that scheme its simplistic appeal with the message that "we have no sure and certain hope." He has to be heard on this point. The Christian, too, standing on the far side of the incarnation and the cross, only sees through a "glass darkly" when it comes to making iron-clad assertions about who has earned salvation. We do not have God in a box, and we are not able to predict what God will do. No formula exists by which we can assure our lives after death or even victory and success here. It is necessary that Qohelet be heard, for his teaching is profoundly true: "Who can tell [mortals] what will be after them under the sun?" (Eccl 6:12 NRSV).

However, the corollary Qohelet offers in 7:13-14 is not a mandatory one. The corollary to the premise that we do not have God in a box and cannot force our own salvation is not that all the bad stuff is sent on us by God. Even the writer of Job shied away from saying that, because it makes God the author of evil. (Job came very close to saying it, of course, when he cried, "The arrows of the Almighty are in me;/ my spirit drinks their poison;/ the terrors of God are arrayed against me" [Job 6:4 NRSV].) Even if we grant God a shadow side, we cannot go against the profound conviction of our tradition that God and God alone is good (Matt 19:17; Mark 10:18; Luke 18:19) and that God is good (Pss 100:5; 135:3; 136:1) without admixture of evil (1 John 1:5).

Biblical faith is theologically monistic and ethically dualistic. That means that God is good and good alone; we human beings are capable of both moral good and moral evil. This reality about human nature means that we need help from God when we confront the choice of good or evil. The appropriate corollary to the premise that we cannot know what lies ahead for us is the faith that when we confront crises in our life and have to make profound ethical decisions, God will be alongside, ready to muddle on through with us. Even though we cannot know what will happen, in the full context of the canon of Scripture we are assured that we can walk the road into the future with a friend. That is the message of the story of the man born blind in John 9. Jesus rejects the premise that the blindness is punishment for anyone's sin. Instead, it is an occasion wherein "God's works might be revealed in him" (John 9:3 NRSV). That is a far different way of looking at the adversities that inevitably confront us than to say, "God has made the one as well as the other."

83. Crenshaw, *Ecclesiastes*, 139.

Ecclesiastes 7:15–8:1, Common Sense

COMMENTARY

7:15-18. The expectation promoted by conventional wisdom (e.g., Pss 1; 37; Prov 10:28; 11:21) that righteousness and wickedness respectively reap their just rewards is refuted once again in v. 15 (cf. Eccl 3:16). The Teacher then advocates a kind of wise moderation (vv. 16-17). It is impossible to know whether he had firsthand knowledge of Solon or Aristotle, but concepts such as "the golden mean" were in the air of third-century BCE Palestine. He urges realism about both righteousness and wickedness, wisdom and foolishness. Why should one be fanatically righteous or try to go on to moral perfection? Such proto-Wesleyan piety might only cause one to be set upon by others!

This first section concludes with the enigmatic indefinite pronouns of v. 18a, "the one . . . the other . . ." This sounds for all the world as though Qohelet were advocating a modest ownership of the shadow side of life, anticipating Jung by several millennia! In any case, v. 18 appears to be the point of the entire discussion—namely, that by reverencing God one can keep a grip on righteousness and wisdom even though one will certainly—even prudently—fall short of perfection. If fanatical scrupling and perfectionism give way to modesty in well-doing, moral excellence is possible.

7:19–8:1. A series of reflections that culminates at 8:1 begins at 7:19, and the first and last verses of this series bracket the pericope with lofty evaluations of wisdom. Embedded in this frame are two proverbs that offer acknowledgment of human shortcomings as a component of wise behavior (vv. 20-21) and sad truths about human nature, which wisdom discerns (vv. 22-29).

7:19-20. Verse 19 itself sets a tenfold premium on the power of wisdom to strengthen the sages (cf. Prov 21:22; 24:5-6). Verse 20 echoes a line from the intercessory portion of Solomon's great prayer of dedication of the Temple (1 Kgs 8:46: "There is no one who does not sin" [NRSV]). Commentators suggest that it is placed here as an answer to v. 19,

lest some sage claim too much for the advantage conferred by wisdom; however, the theme of v. 20 is righteousness, not wisdom, and the two are not synonymous. Perhaps this teaching of realism is simply one facet of the empowering wisdom a sage possesses.

7:21-22. Another may be the discretion in the handling of slander that the Teacher advises: A genuinely wise person knows that even to listen to gossip is to borrow trouble (v. 21). Furthermore, because the wise person knows that his or her own record on cursing others is not spotless (v. 22), the recommended style is acceptance rather than criticism. Crenshaw points out that the reference here to the sage's servant (v. 21) allows us to extrapolate to an element of the social setting of Qohelet and his pupils: They must have belonged to an elite, propertied, slaveholding class. Furthermore, he notes that the reference to "what your heart knows" (v. 22) comes close to being a discussion of conscience, though that term itself occurs for the first time in Jewish literature only in the first-century BCE extracanonical book of Wisdom (Wis 17:11).[84]

7:23-25. Although vv. 23-24 issue a caveat suggesting that theoretical wisdom is beyond the grasp of human beings, the remainder of the subsection, vv. 23-29, sets forth some specific advances in understanding made by the principal character of the book, Qohelet the sage. The latter are the kind of learnings that assist in getting on with the business of life; only God possesses the former. The same contrast of wisdoms animates the book of Job and comes to the fore in the meditation on wisdom in Job 28. Only God knows the way to the secrets of the cosmos, but God imparts knowledge sufficient for human needs with these words: "Truly, the fear of the LORD, that is wisdom; and to depart from evil is understanding" (Job 28:28 NRSV). The theme that ultimate wisdom is elusive to humankind is sounded frequently in the sapiental writings of the ancient Near East as well as elsewhere

84. Crenshaw, *Ecclesiastes*, 143n107.

in Jewish wisdom (Prov 30:1-4; Sir 24:28-29; Bar 3:9–4:4).

7:26-28. Qohelet turns to relations between the sexes and immediately warns against that standard character of ancient Near Eastern wisdom literature, the ensnaring woman (see Prov 5:4; 6:26). There is no use pretending that Qohelet's attitude toward women measures up to the standards of equality and respect we now expect. It is true that in 9:9 he recommends love and marriage for life; here, however, his attitude is grouchy, to say the least. The two characters who confront the woman here are not necessarily a good man and a sinner; the Hebrew terms would also support the translation "a lucky one" and "an unlucky one" (also true in 2:26).

The problem of vv. 27-28 is to make sense of the phrase "adding one thing to another to find the sum." Is this a description of the work of a "collector" (קהלת *qōhelet*) of proverbs? Or does it refer to Solomon and his collection of 700 wives and 300 concubines? Commentators often suggest that the verse points forward to v. 28*b*, where the result of the Teacher's research is given—i.e., that among a thousand persons, only one man (0.1 percent) is found worthy. Although the Hebrew term used here is the generic "human being" (אדם *'ādām*), it has to be translated "man" in this case, because it is antithetical to אשה (*'iššâ*), "woman," not a single worthy one of whom (= 0 persons) was to be found. Does this mean that, in Qohelet's view, males are only infinitesimally better than females? Or does it mean that they are infinitely better? The same statistics could be read either way. Males have nothing to crow about in any case, for the ratio of good ones to bad ones is extremely low!

7:29. The conclusion of the subsection puts the responsibility for human behavior squarely on human beings themselves. God made people "straightforward" (NRSV) or "upright" (NIV), but they have "schemed" or devised many questionable things. This news that human beings are responsible for their own perversity is not new in the Hebrew Bible (see Job 5:6-7; Lam 3:31-42), nor does it come as a shock to Jews and Christians of later eras. In spite of his avowal of the radical predetermination of all things by God (6:10; 7:14), even Qohelet makes theological allowance for human freedom and, therefore, for human error and malfeasance, for which human beings must be deemed responsible.

8:1. As understood here, this verse closes out the passage. The verse begins with two rhetorical questions and concludes with a twofold statement about the effect of wisdom on outward human appearance. The verse closes the bracket opened by 7:19 and thus helps to embrace the more restrained and gloomy evaluations of human performance in 7:20-29.

In v. 1*a* the term פשר (*pēšer*, "interpretation") is used only in this place in biblical Hebrew. It is relatively common in the Aramaic text of Daniel and becomes a major concept at the Qumran community, whose Teacher of Righteousness had the key to *pēšer* and whose *Pēšer Habakkuk* is the most perfectly preserved of the sectarian documents from the Dead Sea Scrolls.

The shining face of the wise person in v. 1*b* reflects God's shining face in the context of a right relationship of blessing (see "the priestly benediction," Num 6:25). The "impudent look" is something simply to be masked (see Sir 13:24).

REFLECTIONS

1. *Modesty in the Attainment of Virtue.* The delightful realism of 7:15-18 has struck a chord with people through the centuries. It has the ring of realism, even humanism, in its willingness to acknowledge human limitations. Qohelet already expressed great dissatisfaction with the idea that the reward of virtue and the vindication of wisdom were sure and certain outcomes (e.g., 2:15-21). For him, no one-to-one relationship between piety and payoff exists either here or in some world to come. All through their lives, human beings need to be pushed to see that they have no advantage even over the animals (3:18-19). The world itself is morally neutral, and human history produces no mechanism that will respond positively to superscrupulous sanctity and perfectionism. Qohelet counsels, therefore, that we take it easy, do the best we can, and not make ourselves miserable trying for moral superiority when there is no point in it. To make that effort might be to miss the most fundamental moral direction God gives us, that "all should eat and drink and take pleasure in all their toil" (3:13 NRSV).

2. *The Difficulty of Attaining to Wisdom.* When the writer of Deuteronomy contemplated the accessibility of the truth that saves human life from death and disaster, he said:

> Surely, this commandment that I am commanding you today is not too hard for you, nor is it too far away. It is not in heaven, that you should say, "Who will go up to heaven for us, and get it for us so that we may hear it and observe it?" . . . No, the word is very near to you; it is in your mouth and in your heart for you to observe. (Deut 30:11-14 NRSV)

Other writers of Scripture have not been as sanguine when they have contemplated ultimate and saving truth. Job 28:12-28, for example, teaches that the true meaning of things, "the reality below all changing phenomena,"[85] cannot be known (see also Sir 24:28-29; Bar 3:15-23; Rom 11:33). No one stated this pessimistic point of view more dramatically than did the Teacher, who, when undertaking to know the reality behind the realities, cried out, "That which is, is far off, and deep, very deep; who can find it out?" (7:24).

In our time we have discovered that reality lies even deeper than Qohelet imagined. Against the apocalyptists of his day, for example, he was quite willing to assert that he knew that the earth would endure forever (1:4) and that the great cycles of nature would perdure (1:5-11). Beginning with the seventeenth century, we have lived with Newtonian physics, which in a secular way made the same assertion—that immutable laws provide for stable cycles in the natural order and allow us to predict the long-term behavior of objects as large as our planet and even the universe as a whole. Now the truth about matter has become "deep, very deep; who can find it out?" From meteorology to paleontology to astrophysics, science gives us evidence of flux, of chance occurrences, of randomness and chaos. Science and Scripture converge now, not at Eccl 1:4 ("the earth remains forever" [NRSV]), but at Eccl 7:24 ("That which is, is far off, and deep, very deep" [NRSV]). Order there is in the natural world, but it is a malleable order, the complexity of which grows exponentially as we learn more about it.

85. Barton, *A Critical and Exegetical Commentary on the Book of Ecclesiastes*, 146.

Ecclesiastes 8:2-9, Instructions on Appearing Before the King

COMMENTARY

In this short passage the Teacher instructs his pupil on court etiquette. The writer makes no effort to validate the king's authority; he merely notes that it is real, it is supreme, and a wise person will approach the king accordingly. This leads, of course, to the dangers of obsequiousness and opportunism, alongside the achievements of survival and success.

Surely the king in view here is neither Solomon nor a member of the Davidic dynasty. In fact, he is probably not a Jewish king at all. Assuming a third-century BCE date for the book of Ecclesiastes, it is quite likely that his contemporaries among the wealthy merchant or priestly Jewish families would be involved in intercourse with the suzerain of the Ptolemaic family of Egypt. The Zeno Papyri and Josephus[86] describe exactly such affairs between the rich tax farmers, the Tobiad family of Qasr al Abd (a few miles west of modern Amman, Jordan), and the Ptolemies. Other clues in the book suggest that Qohelet either belonged to that class himself or worked for them. His counsel about court etiquette thus fits with the times and with the needs of his clients; the king in question, then, might have been an Egyptian.

8:2-5. If we understand that the last phrase of v. 2, literally translated "on account of an oath of God," refers not to an oath God made to legitimate the king but rather to an oath the client made or would make to the king in the name of God, then v. 2 is clear enough. Verse 3, however, is not. Gordis suggests that the sense of the whole verse is something like: Do not leave your post when events are unfavorable.[87] The NIV takes the two parts of the verse as separate instructions in prudential etiquette. In v. 3a, the Teacher may mean that to dash suddenly out of the king's presence is to arouse suspicion. In v. 3b, he counsels the pupil to avoid espousing causes in which the king has no interest or about which he holds a different opinion. If such counsel sounds like an invitation to become a sycophant, to seize every opportunity to please the foreign despot, so be it. Proverbs 16:14, too, advises appeasement of the king's anger. After all, the position before the throne of the conquered subject has always been precarious, to say the least. This picture of the prudent Jew in the presence of the king belongs to a diverse collection of biblical stories about courtiers who range from the ideal servant of the king, Joseph, to the impressive but resistive young sages Daniel and his friends in the Babylonian court, to Esther and Mordecai, who were not above using stratagems to get their way with the king, to Judith, who simply tricked the leader of the enemy to death. Up to a point, but not beyond, all of these would have accepted Qohelet's advice of v. 3: Go along to get along. After all, the king's word goes (v. 4)! Bearing in mind the spirit of 7:16-17, Qohelet's advice in 8:4-5 may amount to saying, "It is better to violate your own scruples than to disobey the king's command." Where would he draw the line?

8:6. The Teacher believes that timing is everything (v. 6a). As he demonstrated in the beautiful poem of 3:1-8, the notion of the proper time was as fundamental to the thinking of Qohelet as it was to that of earlier wisdom teachers. Ben Sira epitomizes the usual sapiental attitude toward time when he says, "Watch for the opportune time, and beware of evil" (Sir 4:20 NRSV). For Qohelet, however, there is no comfort in the concept of the proper time, for unlike other wisdom teachers, he believes that one can do little on one's own to discern the proper time. Things are not a random jumble because God has predetermined them. On the other hand, one cannot discern the hand of God anywhere because God does not reveal that hand (v. 7). The strange dilemma in which he is left is summed up by Gerhard von Rad: "To Koheleth, the world and events appear to be completely opaque and . . . on the other hand . . . they are completely within the scope of God's activity."[88]

It is no wonder that Qohelet couples with the announcement that everything has its proper time (v. 6a) a further reference to the misery human beings experience (v. 6b). But what exactly does this half verse mean? Are the "troubles of mortals" referred to there from this implacable conundrum of divine predetermination and divine secrecy, or are they simply the things people generate for themselves? Perhaps the "troubles" referred to here are not moral failures as much as they are human defects and ailments, like Job's boils (Job 2:7). The sense of v. 6 might be, therefore: Bide your time and wait until someone messes up and gives you your opening. Even if the meaning is ethically evil, as it is in v. 11, the sense may still be the same: When someone else slips up, the wise courtier can move in at that "proper time" to win the king's favor.

8:7-9. These verses restate one of Qohelet's major themes (see Introduction; cf. 9:3, 11-12; 11:6). Whatever decisions people may make, be they pragmatic, prudential, or highly principled, they cannot know the outcome because they cannot know the future. This is a painful truth. The NIV understands the sequence of v. 8 as a set of two analogies.

---

86. Josephus *Antiquities of the Jews* 11.4.
87. Gordis, *Koheleth*, 278.

88. Von Rad, *Wisdom in Israel*, 229.

Just as people have no power over the "wind" (or "the spirit [of life]"), so they also have no say about when they die. Just as there is no exit when a battle is underway, even though the law (Deut 20:1-9) exempts certain people from war duty, so also wickedness does not exempt its perpetrators from its consequences (see 10:8-11).

REFLECTIONS

The closing observation of this unit weaves the reflections on court etiquette back into the fabric of the book as a whole using the key phrase "under the sun." The reader is left not with the usual message of absurdity but with something worse. Whatever else may happen, the abuse of the marginals by the powerful will continue. Qohelet offers this as a universal and timeless rule that applies not only to the relationships of kings and subjects, but also even more generally to those between the powerful and the vulnerable. The NIV debates whether the Hebrew pronoun at issue in the last clause refers to the abuser or to the one being abused, while the NRSV is clear that the teaching is not a moral homily (the bad person will get it in the end) but simply a gloomy reality check (the bad person will continue hurting other people).

Ecclesiastes 8:10-17, Retribution Is an Absurdity

COMMENTARY

Even though Qohelet closed the preceding unit on the note that wickedness cannot be guaranteed to pay, he is not prepared to say that righteousness will do so either. The section that follows, vv. 10-17, includes a complex interplay between the accepted wisdom set forth in vv. 12b-13 and his own profound doubts that the mechanism for rewarding wickedness according to its just deserts is in place. Although all of the themes in this passage have been stated before, it brings them together in a combination that sets forth with considerable pathos the failure of retributional theology to operate dependably, the impossibility of discerning the reason why this should be, and the retreat into the by now familiar advice to eat, drink, and be merry (v. 15) that is Qohelet's only positive recommendation. Rankin sums up the thought of this section succinctly: "There is no moral purpose working itself out in human destiny."[89]

8:10. With help from the LXX, scholars conclude that this obscure opening verse intends to say something like this: "I have seen the wicked brought to their grave with pomp; and when people walk from the holy place, they are praised in the city where they acted thus." The sense, then, is that even though the community knew these people were wicked, it gave the villains a decent burial (a mark of a successful life, according to Eccl 6:3). Before they are even cold in their graves, in the very city in which they committed their evil deeds, their names are being honored (another mark of distinction, according to Eccl 7:1). In short, the wicked do not get what is coming to them; they get much more! This Qohelet finds to be absurd.

8:11-15. Although it is clear that Qohelet advocates sentencing sinners in order to deter sin, vv. 11-12a offer no assurances that they will certainly be caught and treated appropriately. In spite of the optimism of the traditional teaching of vv. 12b-13, the Teacher recurs to his own line in v. 14. In this topsy-turvy world, the very opposite of what ought to happen may in fact happen. In the light of these grim injustices, Qohelet once again advocates his type of hedonism (v. 15), sounding the hitherto unheard note that the pleasures of food and drink will accompany individuals into the difficult struggles of their lives. Whether this accompaniment into toil is simply a matter of memory or whether it is a full stomach or even genuine happiness and

89. Rankin and Atkins, "The Book of Ecclesiastes," 5:71.

peace of mind cannot be determined from the text; however, the Teacher does seem to allow the possibility that times of leisure and pleasure positively affect the rest of life.

8:16-17. The passage closes with Qohelet's familiar diatribe against the claims of sages to have penetrated to the heart of life and to the work God is doing in the world (see Job 12:2, where Job sardonically mocks his friends for claiming to know such things). It is a canon of the preacher's faith that God's actions in history cannot be discerned.

REFLECTIONS

Advocates of the summary execution of judgment can no doubt take heart from the sentiments expressed in vv. 11-12a. In these verses, the Teacher might be heard to say, in effect, that crime and wickedness are rampant because there is too much parole, that too many offenders are let off with light sentences or released early from jail, and that deterrents of crime cannot be operative in such a climate. Perhaps he did toy with such ideas. At the same time, in the context of God's predetermination of the times and refusal to share the plan, there seems to be relatively little space for vigorous legal and moral action. The wages of sin are not necessarily death, nor are the wages of righteousness life; things happen when they must happen. Even though the spectacle of the wicked person's going unpunished and even prospering is sickening, one tires of looking at it. Then one turns to the swimming pool and to the lunch spread on the grass and to the enjoyment of such small things as are available to people who live with total lack of knowledge of the future and total lack of ability to shape or structure it. There is no use trying to get out ahead of events, to anticipate the future, be it economic, political, or personal. *Que será, será*: Whatever will be will be.

Such a climate seems to inhibit the building up of much enthusiasm for ridding a community of evil and building a better world. It drives one to quietism in the search for a little piece of happiness with food, drink, and loved ones. Even though there is a time to kill (3:3), and that might include the speedy execution of justice against evildoers (8:11), on the whole there is not much point in taking too many people before the firing squad. Innumerable others will spring up. By getting involved one only loses time to "eat, and drink, and enjoy" (8:15), which is the one sphere of real human freedom and autonomy that the Teacher is able to discern.

ECCLESIASTES 9:1-12, TIME AND CHANCE BEFALL ALL

COMMENTARY

This section is a happy amalgam of two of the major themes of the book: The same fate happens to everyone, and *carpe diem* ("seize the day") and enjoy life (see Introduction). The passage also weaves together traditional proverbs with fresh reflections by Qohelet; it combines prose and poetry; it punctuates the entire mix with two of the slogans of the book, "all is vanity" and "under the sun." The overarching theme upon which the writer expands in this section is that the ultimate destiny of the good person is no better than that of the evil person and that all the achievements of life do not guarantee escape from death or obliteration. In no way does good behavior guarantee good results. In short, it is a sadly realistic, almost despairing passage; yet, it is animated by the lovely sentiments of 9:7-10. The combination of familiar elements makes those verses sound almost like a programmatic statement for the entire book.

9:1-3. The love and hate that await an individual (v. 1) are the attitudes of God, though one cannot know the divine verdict in advance. The last clause of the verse, which literally reads, "Everything is before them," is combined by the NRSV with an amended version of the beginning of v. 2. The NIV rightly decides to avoid the emendation and keep the two verses separate, making clear that the task of v. 2 is to expand on the gloomy theme of the common destiny of all humanity.

The list of "righteous" people in v. 2 has a somewhat antiquarian flavor. Perhaps Qohelet reached out for examples from the ranks of the superreligious. By his time, for example, sacrifice had begun to yield to prayer as the most basic act of personal piety. As for the swearing of oaths, including the curious custom of placing the hand on the genitals of the other oathtaker (see Gen 24:2-9; 47:29), the practice was coming into increasing disfavor in the later period of the Hebrew Bible and in the intertestamental period. Qohelet did not personally recommend it (5:5). Josephus[90] says that the turn-of-the-era Essenes banned oath taking, except for the binding vow taken upon entry into the covenant community. Nor did Jesus look upon the practice with favor: "Let your word be 'Yes, Yes' or 'No, No'; anything more than this comes from the evil one" (Matt 5:37 NRSV). In the background of this development stands the ninth commandment, against false testimony (Exod 20:16; Deut 5:20), which was Israel's safeguard of the integrity of sworn witnesses in court. Qohelet's point may be that even people who have become so scrupulous about the truth that they fear to take an oath have destinies neither more nor less positive than the moral leper who has sworn an oath and then violated it. Against the standard but flawed reward-and-punishment mentality of his day—and every day—he asserts that what one does has no bearing on what finally happens to one. "The same fate comes to everyone" (v. 3): Everyone dies.

9:4. After the extremely dark picture of human beings painted in v. 3b, a ray of hope shines out of this verse—if, that is, "hope" is the correct translation of בטחון (*biṭṭāḥôn*), which in its other occurrences in biblical Hebrew (2 Kgs 18:19 = Isa 36:4)

eans "trust" and in modern Hebrew means "security." Perhaps v. 4a simply means that whoever is alive can have confidence in life, at least for the present moment. This is followed in v. 4b by another popular proverb that stresses the superiority of any kind of life at all over death. The dog is not admired in the Hebrew Bible (1 Sam 24:14; 2 Sam 3:8; 16:9), whereas the lion is the very emblem of royalty (Gen 49:9) and a metaphor for God's power (e.g., Isa 38:13; Lam 3:10; Hos 5:14; 13:7-8). Yet the nod is given to life, for "consciousness on any terms is preferable to non-existence."[91]

9:5-7. Nevertheless, the advantage of the living human being quickly deteriorates into the pain of knowing what lies ahead. The dead vanish in memory as if they never were. This is the theme of Qohelet that sticks in the craw of his putative antagonist, the author of the Wisdom of Solomon. The latter includes this motif in his condemnation of those who reason cynically that we can eat, drink, be merry, rob, and extort because:

Our name will be forgotten in time,
and no one will remember our works;
our life will pass away like the traces of a cloud,
and be scattered like mist
that is chased by the rays of the sun
and overcome by its heat.
For our allotted time is the passing of a shadow.
(Wis 2:4-5 NRSV)

Against this view, so profoundly asserted by Qohelet, the writer of Wisdom advocates a doctrine of blessed immortality and a dependable connection between righteousness and salvation: "But the souls of the righteous are in the hand of God, and no torment will ever touch them" (Wis 3:1 NRSV).

In response to the gloomy future sketched in vv. 1-6, vv. 7-10 sound the affirmation of Ecclesiastes that the goal of humankind is to seek joy in all endeavors. Because all passions are extinguished by death (v. 6), it is imperative to seize the hour for happiness now. Appended to the injunction to eat, drink, and be merry is the extraordinary remark that "God has long ago approved what you do."

---

90. Josephus *The Jewish War* 2.8.6; confirmed by 1QS 5:8.

91. Grodis, *Koheleth*, 295.

At issue between the NRSV and the NIV is the meaning in this verse of the word כבר (kĕbār, "already"). Using the perfect or completed tense, the Teacher claims that God has accepted or approved the hearer's deeds. (The same Hebrew verb is used when God accepts an offering; e.g., Deut 33:10-11; Amos 5:22.) The use of the perfect (completed) tense is not definitive inasmuch as Qohelet sometimes uses it to refer to present and uncompleted acts as well (e.g., "gives," 2:26; "exercises authority," 8:9), but the word *already* seems intended to underscore the completedness of the divine decision. Thus the verse appears to be giving the hearer a blank check to spend on a life of gaiety and pleasure. The NIV tries to avoid this implication, it seems, by discerning the nuance "now" in the word kĕbār and by using an imperfect or uncompleted sense of the verb "accepted," "approved": "for it is now that God favors what you do." The NRSV comes closer to the literal understanding: Long ago God declared it to be morally correct that human beings should enjoy bread, wine, and life itself. It is not that God foreordains or approves of everything that one might do, but that God created human life good from the beginning and wills that human beings take legitimate pleasure in being alive. This approach differs from that of Crenshaw, who dismisses the problem by saying, "Since one's capacity to enjoy life depends on a divine gift, anyone who can eat and drink must enjoy divine favor. . . . Divine approval preceded human enjoyment."[92] Crenshaw's interpretation is indebted to 5:16 and 6:2, where the word השליט (hišlîṭ, "empowered") is used to describe God's role in human pleasure. But here God's role is described by the verb רצה (rāṣâ, "approved"). If approval equals empowerment, the Teacher would not need to offer this instruction.

9:8. The passage continues to describe the joyful person as being clothed in white, the festal color throughout the ancient Near East. Mordechai wears "robes of blue and white" on the day of the liberation of the Jews (Esth 8:15). The togas of the worshipers on the walls of the third-century CE synagogue at Dura Europas are white. White is the color of the garments of the saints (2 Esdr 2:40)

and of the clothing of the transfigured Jesus (Matt 17:2 and parallels). The garments of the angels at the tomb of Christ (Matt 28:3 and parallels) and in Rev 3:4-5 and 7:9 are all white. When this invitation to wear the clothing of the holy ones is combined with the injunction to use oil freely (see Ps 133:2), the effect is a call to exuberance.

9:9-10. Qohelet reaches the zenith of his very restrained praise of women in v. 9. Evidently addressing an all-male audience, he links happiness with "a woman you love" (TNK) to the other means of happiness that are given to humankind. In this fourth and final use of the term "love" (אהב 'āhab), the Teacher for once is unambiguous. Elsewhere love may be opposed by hate (3:8; 9:1) or may be described as fleeting (9:6). Here, however, the love of a man for a woman is a simple component of joy. Both the NRSV and the NIV make the indefinite Hebrew word "a woman," "wife," definite, "the wife," and "your wife," respectively—no ambiguity for them! One need not go so far in the opposite direction as does Gordis, who says, "Koheleth was almost surely a bachelor, and was certainly no apologist for the marriage institution."[93] Yet the Teacher's analysis of how joy and morality intersect might not have been the same as those of today's Jews and Christians. The point here is not the exact arrangement within which a man and a woman find happiness in each other, but rather the importance of the ability to love amid the fleeting absurdity of life. This is because the destiny that confronts all people is Sheol (v. 10).

Sheol, the abode of the dead, is not the Hellenistic hades or the hell of later Judaism and Christianity. It is not the antithesis of heaven (although the reluctance of the NIV to use the term suggests that it wishes to reserve the concept of an underworld for later juxtaposition with heaven). Contra the NIV, it is not simply "the grave." Instead, it is a place in which all dead persons have a shadowy existence, a place to which the Lord can send people and from which God can also bring them back (1 Sam 2:2), a place from which the Lord could hear the cries of Jonah (Jonah 2:2). Sheol is mentioned some sixty-five times in the Hebrew Bible, and some of the writers allow the "shades" to continue to

---

92. Crenshaw, *Ecclesiastes*, 162.

93. Gordis, *Koheleth*, 296.

possess some kind of memory and existence in Sheol (e.g., Num 16:30-33; 1 Sam 28:8-14; Ps 143:3; Isa 14:14-17). One psalmist even imagined that God could be present in it: "If I ascend to heaven, you are there;/ If I make my bed in Sheol, you are there" (Ps 139:8).

But in this his only use of the term, Qohelet maintains the traditional view of ancient Israel: Sheol is a place from which no one exits, from which no prayers arise, beyond which there is no further hope (see Job 14:11-14; Ps 6:5). It is a place of nonbeing, where all consciousness and all passions have ceased (see 9:5-6). As we have seen (3:21), the Teacher maintains this view in the face of some of his contemporaries who were apparently already beginning to suggest that the dead might be resurrected to either of two places, one up and one down (see Isa 26:19; Dan 12:2). Perhaps Qohelet's view is a manifestation of a conservative, upper-class outlook, analogous to that of the patrician Sadducees of later times who denied the resurrection of the dead (Mark 12:18; Luke 20:27). Perhaps Qohelet's critic of a later generation, the writer of the Wisdom of Solomon, more accurately represented the hope of the rank and file of Jews even of Qohelet's day

when he wrote, "Righteousness is immortal" (Wis 1:15 NRSV).

9:11-12. The lyrical v. 11 systematically demolishes all of the assurances of success to which people cling. The object of a runner is to win the race; the object of a valiant soldier is to win the battle; the object of intelligence is to gain riches. According to the Teacher, however, there is no sure and certain hope that any of these objectives can be met, because over all loom time and "chance" (see Introduction). Through all of life one can only repeat, "Curses, foiled again!" In this stern judgment Qohelet runs against conventional wisdom, which saw a one-to-one correlation between good sense and success—e.g., "Good sense wins favor,/ but the way of the faithless is their ruin" (Prov 13:15 NRSV). Although righteousness is not listed as one of the virtues that is demolished by time and chance, presumably Qohelet would include it as well (see 7:16), thereby confounding even hopes as fond as those expressed by the psalms of the two ways: "In all that [the righteous] do, they prosper" (Ps 1:3 NRSV). Sudden entrapment, sudden calamity, sudden death are the fates of human beings just as they are those of innocent fish and birds (v. 12), and one cannot anticipate, prevent, or gainsay this reality.

REFLECTIONS

Qohelet's characteristic ambivalence about life permeates 9:1-12. "The same fate comes to everyone" (v. 3), he says, and yet "whoever is joined with all the living has hope, for a living dog is better than a dead lion" (v. 4). The latter sentence is not exactly a thumping affirmation of life, but it is a reluctant admission that a bird in the hand is better than two in the bush (to maintain the idiomatic flavor of the discussion). The notion that life even at an attenuated level is better than no life at all has been affirmed by theologians and poets alike (see Reflections at 3:16–4:8). Thoreau, for example, in the conclusion to *Walden,* criticizes those who say that "we Americans, and moderns generally, are intellectual dwarfs compared with the ancients, or even the Elizabethan men. But what is that to the purpose?" He continues: "A living dog is better than a dead lion. . . . Let every one mind his own business, and endeavor to be what he was made." Somerset Maugham evidently thought Americans had a propensity to go for the main chance and that Eccl 9:4 describes that propensity. In his *Cakes and Ale,* when two young American literati prefer to tour the home of the deceased writer Edward Driffield with his widow rather than in the company of a distinguished younger writer, Maugham has the latter remark to a friend, "You don't know America as well as I do. . . . They always prefer a live mouse to a dead lion. That's one of the reasons I like America."

The poet Louis Untermeyer gave a rather different spin to the passage in question. In his poem entitled "Koheleth," he relates the message of the entire book to 9:4. He takes the living dog to be a moral midget that survives the moral giant, who perishes. Although he does not say it explicitly, to him this is vanity.

I waited and worked
To win myself leisure,
Till loneliness irked
And I turned to raw pleasure.
I drank and gamed,
I feasted and wasted,
Till, sick and ashamed,
The food stood untasted.
I searched in the Book
For rooted convictions
Till the badgered brain shook
With its own contradictions.
Then, done with the speech,
Of the foolishly lettered,
I started to teach
Life cannot be bettered:
That the warrior fails
Whatever his weapon,
And nothing avails
While time and chance happen.
That fools who assure men
With lies are respected,
While the vision of pure men
Is scorned and rejected.
That a wise man goes grieving
Even in Zion,
While any dog living
Outroars a dead lion.[94]

As noted in the exegetical discussion, the clause "for God has long ago approved what you do," the most original and unexpected comment in this passage, is woven into the familiar advice of Qohelet to eat, drink, and be merry (9:7-10). Because the meaning is elusive, the interpretive possibilities are many! If Qohelet's point is that God foreordains everything, then even what one does by way of play has already been written in the book of life before history ever began. If Qohelet's point is that God gave advance approval in general terms to the things that make for human happiness, then interpreters can enlarge on the possibility of having a good life, if it is lived within those preapproved parameters.

The most likely construal of v. 7*b* is this: In the midst of the uncertainties and even the absurdity in which people live and in the face of the personal extinction that most certainly lies ahead, the best thing they can do now is to "eat . . . bread with enjoyment and drink . . . wine with a merry heart." Then they will be obeying the will of God for their lives and can enjoy divine approval. The nuances of how one eats bread and drinks wine and enjoys life are many, of course, and we heirs to the puritanical tradition will no doubt busy ourselves developing criteria by which to grade the degree of approval that God gives to our various modes of doing these things. Even so, the

---

94. Louis Untermeyer, "Koheleth," *Burning Bush.* Copyright © 1928 by Harcourt Brace & Company and renewed 1956 by Louis Untermeyer. Reprinted by permission of the publisher.

previous approval of vigorous, happy, human living seems to be the singular plus in the message of Qohelet. God knows there are many long faces and much unhappiness out there, some of which derives from the malpractice of religion. Qohelet's plus, therefore, is a gift from which contemporary Jews and Christians can take heart.

When Qohelet reverts to his theme of the certainty of death for everyone in 9:11-12, he sees no escape from the sudden onset of calamity. Virtue, wisdom, skill, riches, and strength cannot alter that immutable decree, expressed to our minds as "time and chance." When D. H. Lawrence read these verses, his reaction was to advocate a modest acceptance of fate even while clinging to the fragile beauty of life. In other words, he read 9:11-12 in terms of the life affirmation of vv. 7-10:

> The race is not to the swift
> but to those that can sit still
> and let the waves go over them.
> The battle is not to the strong
> but to the frail, who know best
> how to efface themselves
> to save the streaked pansy of the heart
>   from being trampled to mud.[95]

Christians have a basis for optimism about the future, because we are convinced that it belongs to God. By our eschatological vision of the New Jerusalem, we are drawn as with a magnet into that future. Having had a foretaste of the new age of peace and justice in the life, ministry, death, and resurrection of Jesus Christ, we are eager to get on with our work of building a world that looks as much as we can make it look like the kingdom of heaven on earth. Even so, there is a place in our faith for the kind of realism that Qohelet offers us and that D. H. Lawrence captures: In the misery of warfare and persecution or in the doldrums of secularization and consumerism, sometimes the best we can do is to acknowledge the limits of our human capacity to achieve great ends and "save the streaked pansy of the heart."

95. "Race and Battle" by D. H. Lawrence from *The Complete Poems of D. H. Lawrence* by D. H. Lawrence, ed. V. de Sola Pinto and F. W. Roberts. Copyright © 1964, 1971 by Angelo Ravagli and C. M. Weekley, Executors of the Estate of Frieda Lawrence Ravagli. Used by permission of Viking Penguin, a division of Penguin Books USA Inc.

ECCLESIASTES 9:13–11:6, A SECOND MISCELLANY

Ecclesiastes 9:13–10:7, Wisdom, Folly, Kings, and Fools

COMMENTARY

There is no need to regard this section as an intentional unity. It seems highly likely that a number of verses are quotations from popular wisdom (e.g., 9:18; 10:1), while others have been grouped together because of thematic commonalities. However, running through this section are the contrasts of wisdom and foolishness and of kings and commoners. As the NRSV understands it, the passage is bracketed on either end by little prose passages that can almost be called parables (9:13-16; 10:5-7).

9:13-16. These verses tell the story of a poor wise man who saved an entire city during a powerful siege by an enemy king, and yet in the end the poor man was overlooked. This passage almost has the quality of an apophthegm, a story developed to provide a narrative context for an already extant teaching or proverb. In this case, it enlarges on the difficulty a poor person has in being listened to with respect (cf. Sir 13:23). The punch line is the Teacher's gloomy dialectical reflection in v. 16. As elsewhere (e.g., 4:5-6; 9:18), he is able to make two contradictory points simultaneously. Perhaps he achieves this by quoting a traditional saying and then answering it; in any case, he seems to agree with both positions: "Wisdom is better than might," and, at the same time, "Wisdom is despised." If Qohelet is speaking as a teacher of the children of the rich and powerful, he is warning them not to be too sanguine, not to expect that the rewards of wisdom will be acknowledgment and esteem. He will go on to urge realism. Even with such good attainments as wisdom, wealth, and power there is no sure and certain hope in this life, and absolutely no hope in any other life.

9:17–10:1. The sage Qohelet comments further on the values of wisdom and its limitations. After affirming the efficacy of wisdom, he offers another contradiction: "One bungler [חוטא *ḥôṭe'*] destroys much good" (v. 18*b*). The NIV translates the term *ḥôṭe'* as "sinner." The rendition is possible, but it substantially changes the meaning of the proverb. The contrast in this section is not sinner/saint but fool/wise person. That a *ḥôṭe'* can be one who "misses the mark" and is therefore a fool and a bungler is demonstrated by Prov 19:2.

This little series of teachings about the superiority of wisdom over folly combined with the infernal capacity of folly to win the day concludes with the much-quoted proverb of 10:1. The problems of the Hebrew text of this passage have led interpreters both ancient and modern to propose many emendations. However, all agree on the main point of the proverb: Just as worthless insects can ruin valuable ointment, so also little specks of folly can pollute an entire mass of "wisdom and honor."

10:2-3. These verses continue the wise/foolish antithesis, followed by vv. 4-7, which are dominated by the image of the ruler. Verse 2 puts an unfortunate onus on the leftward

direction. Hebrew literature was not alone in this tendency. In many languages "left" is ominous and awkward (*sinister,* Latin; *gauche,* French), whereas "right" also means "balanced," "correct," "just" (*droit,* French; *recht,* German). Even God seems to be right-handed, for salvation is wrought by God's powerful right hand (Exod 15:6), which is "filled with victory" (Ps 48:10). When the Christ is raised to glory it is to sit at the right hand of God (Acts 2:33-34; Heb 1:3). From his throne of judgment, the Son of Man separates the saved sheep from the damned goats onto his right and left hands respectively (Matt 25:31-36). The judgment here, however, is not a moral but a practical one, for everyone can see the stupidity of the fool who drifts off in the wrong direction (v. 3). Although Qohelet was often unconventional, he was still a teacher of wisdom and often accepted standard ideas such as this one.

10:4. Gordis believes that in passages such as vv. 4-7 the conservative upper-class mentality of Qohelet the professional sage appears. Here, for example, he warns his prominent pupils that "an unstable society may give importance to upstarts and fools, while the rich and well-born (the contrast is instructive) may lose their positions."[96] The advice of this verse, aimed directly at the pupil in the second person, is in the mode of 8:1-9. It says, in effect, If you offend the ruler, do not run off, but face the music with composure. After all, "a soft answer turneth away wrath" (Prov 15:1, 4), and so on—conventional stuff.

10:5-7. These verses deal in reversals. Qohelet cautions his pupils that the world can easily be turned upside down and that the unpredictability of life may result in debasement of those whose wealth and social standing would normally have given them preferential seating at banquets and on steeds. The ruler himself may even sanction such reversals. Verse 6 juxtaposes an abstract noun, "folly" (הסכל *hassekel*), with a concrete noun, "the rich" (עשרים *'ăšîrîm*). In a similar juxtaposition in 9:18, abstract wisdom could be undone by the confusion of one specific bungler; here abstract folly dethrones the power of many leading citizens.

---

96. Gordis, *Koheleth*, 306.

Crenshaw points out that, because of their use in warfare, horses had prestige that mules and donkeys lacked, even though royalty, too, rode mules in earlier times (2 Sam 18:9) and perhaps even later in ritual processions (Zech 9:9).[97]

For members of the Jerusalem establishment, Jesus' Palm Sunday entry into the city—mounted on a donkey, not a horse—must have represented a reversal like that anticipated in this verse. See Matt 21:1-11 and parallels.

97. Crenshaw, *Ecclesiastes*, 172.

REFLECTIONS

History provides numerous examples of the validity of 9:17. In our own lifetimes many of us have seen the contrast between the German contemporaries Dietrich Bonhoeffer and Adolf Hitler. The quiet words of the jailed theologian have proved to be of enduring worth. But who can quote a single phrase of the endless rantings of the dictator? The antithetical parallelism of v. 18 makes for useful reflection. A wooden translation of the Hebrew, "More good is wisdom than implements of warfare; but one bungler destroys much good," reveals that the contrasting assertions are tied together by the word *good*. The effect is to say that the great quantity of good that wisdom can amass can be wiped out by one lowly fool. To express the theme in our vernacular wisdom, "One rotten apple can spoil the whole bushel."

The saying of 10:1 expands on this theme and in the process gives us our English adage "a fly in the ointment." Rottenness is manifested in folly as much as it is in outright sin. The historian Barbara Tuchman defines wisdom as "the exercise of judgment acting on experience, common sense and available information"; folly, in contrast, "is the pursuit of policy contrary to the self-interest of the constituency . . . involved."[98] Folly manifests itself in wooden-headedness, which is the source of self-deception, that fatal wish not to be deflected by the facts from a chosen course of action. Tuchman applies these criteria to the activities of kings and nations and in her book *The March of Folly*, subtitled *From Troy to Vietnam,* cites parade examples of public folly on a horrific scale. Qohelet's rule of 10:1 can be applied equally well to both the private and the public spheres, but it disagrees in no way with the insights of the modern historian. Wooden-headedness and self-deception can indeed overcome wisdom and honor! Nor need the folly be continuous and current; it can be a single act of long ago—a sexual contact with an HIV-infected person, a small unrepaid loan from a fund entrusted to one's keeping, a decision to invest in a fraudulent scheme. It all goes on the record, for every action has consequences sooner or later. The eighteenth-century English poet Matthew Prior addressed this in his poem "Pleasure: The Second Book of Solomon on the Vanity of the World," from which this stanza is excerpted:

> Oft have I said, the praise of doing well
> Is to the ear, as ointment to the smell.
> Now if some flies perchance, however small,
> Into the alabaster urn should fall;
> The odors of the sweets enclosed would die;
> And stench corrupt (sad change!) their place supply.
> So the least faults, if mixed with fairest deed,
> Of future ill become the fatal seed:
> Into the balm of purest virtue cast,
> Annoy all life with one contagious blast.

98. Barbara W. Tuchman, *The March of Folly: From Troy to Vietnam* (New York: Knopf, 1984) 4-5.

Ecclesiastes 10:8–11:6, The Certainty of Cause and Effect

COMMENTARY

The collection of miscellaneous proverbs found in 10:8–11:6 pivots around the theme of the inexorable tie of cause to effect. However, that theme is not explored in a theoretical, abstract way. By offering a number of examples of wise and foolish behavior and their results, the text shows that actions guided by prudence will enjoy success. Not once in this passage does the Teacher brand the outcome of good judgment and wise behavior an absurdity! Put another way, these proverbs assure the Teacher's student or reader that disaster assuredly will follow folly and that caution and good judgment help one to avoid such disaster.

10:8-11. The possibility that one might fall into a trap that one had dug for another person (v. 8) recurs rather frequently in the Israelite wisdom tradition (Pss 7:15; 9:15; 35:7; Prov 26:27; 28:10; Sir 27:26). In this and the following verses, the Teacher expands on the idea, saying, in effect, Do not blame anyone else if you are "hoist with [your] own petar." If the pit traps or the snake bites or the stones crush or the logs injure or the axe is dull, the fault lies in your own lack of preparation or even intellectual laziness, for "wisdom helps one to succeed" (v. 10b). This series of teachings on prudence culminates in the charming v. 11, which conjures up the humorous picture of "the master of the tongue" (the Hebrew idiom for "snake charmer"), a man with a wooden flute (or recorder) and a basket. Even today snake charmers entertain that way in Middle Eastern village markets. Biblical writers thought of the charmer as more than an entertainer, however, as someone necessary to control those pests that were susceptible to charming (apparently adders were not; see Jer 8:17). A certain skepticism about the efficacy of charming seems evident here, however. Either Qohelet's charmer came too late with too little or, as seems more likely, his charms just did not work. Ben Sira is skeptical not about the method but about the intelligence of the charmer, who has chosen such a high-risk vocation: "Who pities a snake charmer when he is bitten,/ or all those who go near wild animals?" (Sir 12:13 NRSV). We

are doubly doubtful now, especially when music is involved, because we have learned that snakes have no hearing apparatus. It may be that charmers wave their recorders from side to side so that the snake will strike the end of the flute and not the flutist!

10:12-15. The next little collection of sayings pivots around the theme of the talk of fools, which is self-destructive (v. 12), malicious (v. 13), and deceptive (v. 14; Qohelet repeatedly asserts that the future is unknowable; see 6:12; 7:14; 8:7; 11:6). The section culminates in the obscure teaching that fools "do not even know the way to town" (v. 15b). Commentators find parallels elsewhere in ancient literature, suggesting that in the category of fool is the barbarian or rube who does not "know the territory."

10:16-17. These verses contrast a happy land with an unhappy one, the respective states of mind of which are dependent on the status of their leaders. As the notes in both the NRSV and the NIV show, the Hebrew of v. 16a literally reads, "Your king is a lad" (or "child" [נער *nāʿar*]). Rather than attempt to find a boy-king in Qohelet's time to whom this might be a cryptic reference (the Egyptian ruler Ptolemy V Epiphanes, 203–181 BCE, is probably too late), it is better simply to say that Qohelet was interested in maintaining the social order. If he was a retainer of the upper class who looked down his nose at impropriety, he would, of course, have preferred a land in which the king was mature and dignified and the princes did not get drunk in the morning. As Gordis points out, ancient sources in and out of the Bible took morning drinking to be a sign of dissoluteness (e.g., Isa 5:11-13).[99]

10:18-20. The section culminates in these verses, which contain both bad news about laziness and good news about the gladness of feasts and the worth of money. We may suppose that the warning of v. 20 not to say curses out loud against the rich and not even to think curses against the king suggests the relative menace posed by each. The

---

99. Gordis, *Koheleth*, 315.

king's informants are so ubiquitous that even an unguarded comment stemming from an "attitude" toward the king might cause trouble. As for the rich, gossip may reach their ears. It seems unlikely that the Teacher really intended to warn against talking birds (v. 20*b*), as if a parrot or a crow might spread one's curses all over town.[100] The key to Qohelet's meaning is probably to be found in Ahiqar's metaphor: "A word is a bird; once released no man can re[capture it]."[101] As our idiom puts it, "a little bird told me." The little bird might really have the shape of a servant or a spouse.

11:1-4. The collection of prudential epigrams continues. Since ancient times the famous v. 1 has been taken to advocate liberality motivated by the promise of a good return on generosity—not sevenfold, perhaps, but at least at a break-even rate.[102] However, when vv. 1-2 are taken together, the teachings emerge as practical advice about how to invest money: Export of goods abroad can be profitable (v. 1), and (speaking almost in the mode of a modern-day mutual fund broker) investments should be diversified (v. 2). Verse 2 contains the literary device of the "graded numerical dictum." Qohelet does not offer

an actual list of seven or eight investment opportunities, though such lists often follow a headline like this. This literary device can be found in the prophetic canon (e.g., Amos 1:3–2:8; the figures seven and eight occur together in Mic 5:5), but it is used most commonly in sapiental texts. (In Prov 30:15-31, five full lists of three and four are given; see also Job 33:14, 29; Prov 6:16-19; Sir 26:5; 50:25-26.)

Verses 3-4 should be taken together, for they form a chiasm:

A rain;
  B wind (manifested in fallen tree);
  B´ wind;
A´ rain (clouds).

Although one can do nothing about the natural phenomena of the seasons, it is not prudent to stand gaping at the rain clouds and wind, perhaps waiting for the ideal moment in which to act. One has to sow and reap in harmony with these natural forces. Again, the Teacher affirms that "wisdom" is necessary for success.

11:5-6. The section culminates in two different teachings that reiterate Qohelet's major theme of the unknowability of the future (see Introduction). If one cannot figure out the miracle of conception, even though it is something that has happened to every human being, one cannot expect to know the workings of the Almighty (v. 5). This does not lead one to refrain from sexual activity, however. The same is true of agriculture: Sow your seed (not the sexual sense here; see v. 4) early and late. Even though you cannot be assured of any specific outcome (v. 6), your chances of harvesting a crop are immeasurably improved if at least you plant one!

---

100. It is, of course, conceivable that Qohelet meant it literally. The conceit was not unknown in his era, of course. Aristophanes used talking birds in his drama *The Birds* (601:4950). A note on the apocalyptic 2 Esdr 5:6 ("And one shall reign whom those who inhabit the earth do not expect, and the birds shall fly away together" [NRSV]) remarks, "Birds, possibly as creatures which soar aloft, were regarded in antiquity as possessing supernatural knowledge. They could foresee impending events." See R. H. Charles, *Apocrypha and Pseudepigrapha of the Old Testament*, vol. 2 (Oxford: Clarendon, 1913) 569.

101. Pritchard, *Ancient Near Eastern Texts Relating to the Old Testament*, 428*b*.

102. Rankin's suggestion that the exhortation to "send out your bread upon the waters" is an allusion to the popular practice in the cult of Adonis of flinging baskets of grain seedlings into streams or the sea in order to assure the fertility of the land has found little support. See Rankin and Atkins, "The Book of Ecclesiastes," 5:81.

REFLECTIONS

Every preacher ought to deliver a sermon on Ecclesiastes 10:8-11! Although this passage is not in any lectionary reading, it ought to be because it sets forth in a wonderful way the principle of the "destiny-producing deed."[103] In his realism, the Teacher finds no need to invoke God either as the proximate or the remote cause of things like snake bite, quarry and logging accidents, and the stupid and embarrassing position of a person who has fallen into the trap prepared for an enemy. In this text, a deed

---

103. For his seminal discussion of the "destiny-producing deed," see K. Koch, "Does the Old Testament Have a Doctrine of Retribution?" in J. L. Crenshaw, ed., *Theodicy in the Old Testament* (Philadelphia: Fortress, 1983) 57-87. See also W. S. Towner, "The Renewed Authority of Old Testament Wisdom for Contemporary Faith," in *Canon and Authority*, G. W. Coates and Burke O. Long, eds. (Philadelphia: Fortress, 1977) 132-47.

brings on its own unhappy destiny just as dependably as night follows day. No doubt, as Qohelet himself says (3:9-15), God is in ultimate control of the world and of history. That remains the faith of Judaism and Christianity. Within that large scheme, however, there is a circle of human hegemony in which we make our own decisions, shape our own immediate destinies, and have to act either foolishly or responsibly. In short, Ecclesiastes gives us canonical authority to give a certain secular, nonsacral interpretation to experience. God may have the whole world in the divine hands, but there is a sphere within that sphere in which human beings are fully responsible. In that sphere, people reap what they sow. In spite of the Teacher's highly predeterministic outlook, he secures a place for human autonomy.[104]

Writers from Jerome through Tolkien have been fascinated with the image of the pit (Eccl 10:8), which they usually take to be a metaphor for the commission of evil and its consequences. One who falls into a trap of one's own making experiences the appropriate self-inflicted penalty of sin. Even Sherlock Holmes offers us a sample of this long-lasting tradition. In "The Adventure of the Speckled Band," Holmes discovers that the villain, Grimesby Roylott, has been killed by the serpent that he intended to use to kill his stepdaughter. A. Conan Doyle has his sleuth remark, "Violence does, in truth, recoil upon the violent, and the schemer falls into the pit which he digs for another."

When, in his poem "All Is Vanity, Saith the Preacher," Byron contemplated Eccl 10:11, he thought of a snake more intellectual and spiritual than a real one that had failed to be charmed:

The serpent of the field, by art
And spells, is won from harming;
But that which coils around the heart,
Oh! who hath power of charming?
It will not list to wisdom's lore
Nor music's voice can lure it;
But there it stings forevermore
The soul that must endure it.

The proverb "Send out your bread upon the waters,/ for after many days you will get it back" (Eccl 11:1 NRSV) has made its way into the proverbial repertoire of the English language. No doubt there are people out there who think Benjamin Franklin first said it, but they are wrong; the credit goes to the Teacher. Although writers and preachers generally recognize that it is a call to providential behavior or disinterested benevolence, often it is used in an ironic sense. In his story "The Man Higher Up," for example, O. Henry renders for us a delightful cardsharp who, prior to a big gambling evening, bought every deck of cards in a small town and marked every card in every deck before he returned them to the shops for half credit (and for subsequent purchase by other gamblers). That caper cost him $75, but then, as he says, "trade and commerce had their innings, and the bread I had cast upon the waters began to come back in the form of cottage pudding with wine sauce."[105] An even more dramatic use of the maxim "bread upon the waters" to describe corruption is employed by Somerset Maugham in his story "The Fall of Edward Barnard," wherein he speaks of "the philanthropist who, with altruistic motives builds model dwellings for the poor and finds he has made a lucrative investment. He cannot prevent the satisfaction he feels in the ten per cent which rewards the bread he has cast upon the waters, but he has an awkward feeling that he detracts somewhat from the savor of his virtue."[106] In our own time, when television evangelists appeal for funds saying that they can guarantee that every dollar contributed will come back to the donor double or even sevenfold, we see a modern-day exploitation of the notion that charity is profitable.

104. Cited in David Lyle Jeffrey, ed., *A Dictionary of Biblical Tradition in English Literature* (Grand Rapids: Eerdmans, 1992) 336.
105. O. Henry, "The Man Higher Up," in *The Complete Works of O. Henry* (Garden City, N.Y.: Doubleday, 1953) 323.
106. Cited in Jeffrey, *A Dictionary of Biblical Tradition in English Literature*, 105.

The fallen tree of 11:3b, which is taken here to illustrate the need to act even when conditions are not completely favorable, was applied by Samuel Johnson and Boswell to the spiritual estate of a person on the deathbed. In the entry for Thursday, May 29, 1783, this colloquy is recorded. Boswell asked:

> Suppose a man who has led a good life for seven years, commits an act of wickedness, and instantly dies; will his former good life have any effect in his favour? JOHNSON. "Sir, if a man has led a good life for seven years, and then is hurried by passion to do what is wrong, and is suddenly carried off, depend upon it he will have the reward of his seven years' good life; GOD will not take a catch of him. Upon this principle Richard Baxter believes that a Suicide may be saved. 'If, (says he) it should be objected that what I maintain may encourage suicide, I answer, I am not to tell a lie to prevent it.'" BOSWELL. "But does not the text say, 'As the tree falls, so it must lie?'" [Eccl. 11:3]. JOHNSON. "Yes, sir; as the tree falls: but,—(after a little pause)—that is meant as to the general state of the tree, not what is the effect of a sudden blast." In short, he interpreted the expression as referring to condition, not to position. The common notion, therefore, seems to be erroneous; and Shenstone's witty remark on Divines trying to give the tree a jerk upon a death-bed, to make it lie favourably, is not well founded.[107]

107. G. B. Hill, ed., *Boswell's Life of Johnson*, rev. ed., vol. 4 (Oxford: Clarendon, 1934) 225-26.

ECCLESIASTES 11:7–12:8, INSTRUCTIONS FOR A YOUNG PERSON AND CONCLUSION

COMMENTARY

With the final panel from the hand of the Teacher, the book of Ecclesiastes reaches a lyrical climax. Although the NRSV prints 11:7–12:8 as prose, a strong case can be made to join the NIV in viewing it as poetry. With the exception of the concluding verse, the entire section is a lengthy exploration of Qohelet's most positive theme: To be happy in the present moment is the goal of human endeavor, and to be so is the will of God for human beings (see Introduction). Evidently these words are addressed to Qohelet's student ("young man," 11:9). Such a young person was also the student of the epilogist ("my child," 12:12, the traditional addressee of wisdom teachings; e.g., Prov 1:10; 2:1; Sir 2:1). Even though his listener is young, Qohelet offers him a realistic assessment of the losses and terrors of old age contrasted with the opportunities that are presented to youth.

11:7-10. Beginning with the images of "light" and "sun" (v. 7), frequently used in ancient literature when the subject is the praise of life, the Teacher proceeds to urge people really to live while they are alive (cf. 2:3, 24; 3:12, 22; 5:18; 8:15). "Rejoice" during a time of light, but "remember" that the darkness is coming. The announcement in v. 8 that "the days of darkness will be many" is not so much a threat as it is a justification for enjoying the "many years" that one might live. Beyond vital living comes the endless darkness, the oblivion of Sheol, which in its pitiful contrast to light and life is the ultimate absurdity (v. 8). Gordis makes perhaps his greatest contribution to the understanding of the ideology of Qohelet in the way he reads passages like vv. 9-10: "For Koheleth, the enjoyment of life becomes the highest dictate of life."[108] Unlike many more austere writers of the Bible (e.g., Num 15:39), Qohelet has no problem with desire and encourages his readers to "follow the inclination of your heart and the desire of your eyes." In fact, for Qohelet the enjoyment of life is an imperative, which requires the use of the imperative mood (e.g., four times in 11:9, twice in 11:10). For this

108. Gordis, *Koheleth*, 325.

urgency for the enjoyment of life he advances two reasons: Life is fleeting (vv. 8*b*, 10*b*; 12:1*b*), and it is God's will that we enjoy life (v. 9*c*). This approach to vv. 7-10 hinges considerably on the conjunction "but," which connects v. 9*c* to the rest of the verse in the NRSV and the NIV. "But," of course, is an adversative conjunction; however, the same Hebrew particle ו (*wĕ*) also means "and." Taken that way, v. 9*c* becomes a simple narrative sequence: "and know that for all this God will call you to account." In other words, instead of a pious warning against getting carried away, the text may well be an announcement that God holds you responsible to "follow the inclination of your heart and the desire of your eyes." Such advice might be unconventional, but not really radical. The spirit is rather like that of Sir 14:11, 14, 16: "My child, treat yourself well, according to your means,/ and present worthy offerings to the Lord. . . . Do not deprive yourself of a day's enjoyment;/ do not let your share of desired good pass by you. . . . Give, and take, and indulge yourself,/ because in Hades one cannot look for luxury" (NRSV).

If this reading is correct, the "judgment" of God (v. 9) is an evaluation of a life lived fully and not an *a priori* condemnation of desire and the love of life. Such a treatment of v. 9 is consistent with v. 10, in which the NIV and the NRSV substitute the psychological term "anxiety" for the more traditional renderings of "vexation" (RSV) or "sorrow" (KJV). Thus is manifested the changing influence of modernity on our reading of the unchanging ancient text! Anxiety and physical pain detract from happiness and challenge survival itself. Survival, God knows, is brief enough (v. 10*b*). The theme word הבל (*hebel*, "vanity") should be translated here as "ephemeral" or even "fleeting breath," on analogy with Job 7:16; Ps 144:4 (see Introduction). That makes it clear that v. 10*b* is really a motivation for v. 10*a*. The writer is not saying that "youth and vigor are meaningless" (NIV) or even that they are "vanity" (NRSV), but that they are painfully brief.

12:1-8. Such a reading accords well with this magnificent "allegory of old age," which is addressed to youth. Over the years, commentators have attempted to discern a consistent extended metaphor underlying the imagery of this passage. Some have imagined that the body

and its organs are being allegorically described here; others have supposed that the verses picture a storm; yet others see the prevailing metaphor as a house and estate in decline. There is, in fact, no pressing reason to insist that the allegory be entirely consistent. The most satisfactory understanding of the imagery may simply be to let each image remind the reader of what it will. Poets write that way, after all, not intending to exercise strict control over the range of impressions their images evoke.

12:1-3. In his opening address to the young person (v. 1), Qohelet unexpectedly adjures his student to "remember your Creator in the days of your youth." Murphy summarizes suggested alternatives to the Hebrew word for "your Creator[s]" (בוראיך *bôrĕ'eykā*; expressed in the plural form), including "your well" ("your wife"), "your pit" ("your grave"), "your vigor," or even "your health."[109] While it is true that "your Creator[s]" does not fit the context of vv. 1-7, the ancient manuscripts and versions do not support an emendation of the text. The Teacher has no illusions about old age.[110] Those are the "days of trouble," the days of joylessness. Since "the sun and the light and the moon and the stars" are not really darkened but only appear to the human observer to be so, v. 2 most likely refers to the progressive loss of vision and slow descent into depression that afflict the aged (although

109. Murphy, *Ecclesiastes*, 113.
110. Who would the Teacher have considered to be an "old" person? Put aside the idealized life spans of the prediluvian matriarchs and patriarchs and even the immediate pre-flood reduction to 120 years (Gen 6:3). The psalmist comes closer to human reality: "The days of our life are seventy years,/ or perhaps eighty, if we are strong" (Ps 90:10 NRSV). King David acted "old" with Abishag (1 Kgs 1:1-4) when David was seventy years of age (a figure arrived at by adding his thirty years at coronation in Hebron [2 Sam 2:15] to the forty years of his reign [1 Kgs 2:11]). The few physically superior persons who survived into their eighties would certainly fit the description of the losses of aging enumerated in Eccl 12:1-7. However, without the benefit of modern medicine, the decline of eyesight, hearing, potency, and general vitality no doubt occurred earlier for most people. An average life expectancy for ancient Israel, were a reliable one available, would not help us to calculate when "old age" would have been recognized in individuals because the average would be seriously skewed downward by the high infant mortality rate. Recent studies of tombs in Jerusalem and Jericho from the first century BCE to the first century CE have shown that about 65 percent of the people interred therein had died before the age of thirty, and nearly half of those had died in infancy and early childhood. (The sources are cited by Rachel Z. Dulin, *A Crown of Glory: A Biblical View of Aging* [Mahwah, N.J.: Paulist, 1988] 23.) Persons who survived into their twenties had a much better chance of attaining something like "old age," although even most of them would not have outlasted their forties. Even though kings suffered from the occupational hazards of warfare and assassination, presumably they also enjoyed the nutritional and medical benefits of the elite. The fact that the average age at death of the seventeen kings of Judah whose ages are given in the books of Kings is forty-four (Dulin, *A Crown of Glory*, 21-23) suggests a life expectancy of around forty for adult commoners who did not enjoy the same advantages. For the purposes of the discussion of Eccl 12:1-7, let us assume that people became "old" when their capacities began to fail in their late fifties and sixties, but that people in the category of "old" were a very small percentage of the population.

proponents of the storm metaphor find in this verse a picture of an approaching cloud-burst). Verse 3 offers quite a good picture of a decaying estate in which the servants have grown old and unable to work; however, the imagery works with the storm metaphor, too, when the house shakes, work ceases, and darkness settles in. Proponents of the human body allegory equate the "house" with the body, "the guards" with the legs, "the strong men" with the arms, "the women who grind" with the teeth, "those who look through the windows" with the eyes. Perhaps the writer deliberately left all of these possibilities in the rich imagery of the poem. In any case, what-ever prevailing metaphor one imagines to be at work here, the text conveys a powerful impression of creeping collapse.

The use of the word *windows* in v. 3 might mislead readers into imagining panes of glass in a frame. Glass is mentioned only once in the Hebrew Bible, and then it is listed next to gold in value (Job 28:17). It is doubtful whether any ancient Israelite houses had glass windows. The word translated "windows" (ארבות *'ărubbôt*) really means "lattices," no doubt similar to the decorative wooden *mushrabiya* still to be seen covering windows on old houses in Arab cities. These lattices enable women to look out on the scene in the street without being seen themselves.

12:4-5. The beautiful imagery continues in v. 4, allowing the body allegorists to find references to deafness ("the doors on the street"), to the digestive tract ("the sound of the grinding"), to inability to sleep in the morning ("rises up at the sound of a bird"), and to deafness again ("all the daughters of song [birds, not dancing girls] are brought low"). The same images can be applied to either the storm metaphor, taking them to refer to the cessation of activity and the shut-ting of doors, or the metaphor of the decay of a working household. The deterioration of the body seems to be the favored metaphor lying behind v. 5, for it culminates in death. The first clause is straightforward; the reference to the blossoming almond tree in the second perhaps refers to the white hair of old age, for almond blossoms turn quickly from pink to white. Much of the discussion of v. 5 has centered on the meaning of the clause "the grasshopper drags itself along." Some of the

versions take the verb סבל (*sābal*) to mean "to grow fat"; the Talmud thinks "grasshop-per" is a euphemism for "the rump."[111] If the clause is an allusion to the decline of sexual vitality, with the grasshopper's being a euphe-mism for male genitals, then the next clause of the verse, "and desire fails," follows logi-cally. The problem with the latter clause is that the key word translated by the NRSV as "desire" (אביונה *'ăbiyyônâ*) occurs in this sense nowhere else. An alternative meaning, supported by the ancient versions and the late second-century CE compilation of Phari-saic lore, the Mishnah,[112] is "caperberry," a plant believed to stimulate sexual appetite. With this culminating and tragic picture of an old person whose body has failed in many respects, the picture turns at the end of v. 5 to the funeral itself. The "eternal home" must be the grave (see Tob 3:6). The "mourners" (see 3:4) are those professional wailers who could be hired to provide a suitable lamenta-tion for the dead. Perhaps irony is intended: The man or woman who had enjoyed esteem and wealth in youth is honored at the end by hired hands!

12:6-7. Here the Teacher employs a differ-ent metaphor. The silver cord, golden bowl, pitcher, fountain, wheel, and cistern all appear to refer to the failure of a single well (although "silver cord" and "golden bowl" are exces-sive for a well rope and bucket and would better describe an elegant ceiling oil lamp). As elsewhere in 12:1-8, these verses contain rare or unique words and difficult textual prob-lems. However, the sense remains clear: Live now, young person, before the precious water of life becomes unobtainable and (in a clear allusion to Gen 3:19) "the dust returns to the earth . . . and the breath returns to God who gave it" (v. 7). This does not contradict 3:21, for there the Teacher merely expressed skep-ticism that the respective life forces of human beings and animals had different destinies at death. As Gordis points out, "This verse affirms what Koheleth does not deny[,] that life comes from God."[113] This is not, however, a teaching of immortality. The "breath" is not one's soul or one's identity, but simply the life

111. *B.T. Shabb* 152a.
112. *M. Ma'aś* 4:6.
113. Gordis, *Koheleth*, 339.

force that came from God in the first place (Gen 2:7; see also Job 34:14-15; Ps 104:29).

12:8. This lyrical section concludes with nearly an exact repetition of the opening thematic statement of the book (1:2), which now serves as a conclusion to the message of Ecclesiastes. If v. 7*b* led anyone to think that the Teacher hoped for blessed immortality, this section dispels the idea. The two verses are not identical, however. The phrase "vanity of vanities" is not repeated here as it is in 1:2, and in the Hebrew of v. 8, the word *Qohelet* bears the article as if it were a title, "the Qohelet" (see Introduction).

REFLECTIONS

Except for the marvelously uninhibited affirmation of life and light in 11:7, the remaining verses of chapter 11 (vv. 8-10) moderate their affirmative cries of joy about life and youth with cautionary remarks. Nevertheless, these four verses have an almost defiantly existential quality. Rejoice, rejoice, follow the inclination of the heart and the desire of the eyes, banish anxiety and pain—these are the positive recommendations of the Teacher. They are motivated not only by the grim realizations that the darkness of death lasts a long time (v. 8) and that youth and vigor are ephemeral (v. 10), but also by the joyous conviction that God wills that we live life up to the limit. Qohelet's ideal religionists would never be the pale and hollow people that Nietzsche described; far from moping around in despair, he would have us really live while we are alive.

The true counterpoint to the joyous affirmations of vv. 11:7-10 is the lyric of 12:1-7. If the NRSV punctuation accurately reflects the Masoretic system of conjunctive and disjunctive accents (which, by reflecting the way in which the text of the Hebrew Bible was recited, provided it with most of the very minimal punctuation that it had), then this entire passage of seven verses is all one sentence. Because Hebrew literature is, on the whole, given to short and pithy utterances, such a stylistic variation has to be taken as a serious clue to the intended understanding of the passage. Lectors, cantors, preachers, and those who read Scripture out loud need to practice this passage over and over to capture the richness of oral interpretation that it provides.

Oral interpretation is that kind of rendition of a text that recapitulates its content in the way it is read. It "performs" the sentiment of the text. Verses 1-7 should be "performed" in the mode of a clock running down. The pitch should lower, and the speed should drop as the reader moves from the memory of the Creator and the days of youth through the dawning clouds of trouble; the covering of the sun with darkness; the shaking of the household; the loss of desire; the arrival of the mourners; then the loss of the bowl, the cord, the pitcher, and the wheel at the cistern; dryness; and finally death. The poem is a great inclined plane dropping to the lowest range of the voice and the lowest decibel of sound and culminating in extinction! The voice of the Teacher has died, the voice of the reader has died, and only dark silence remains.

If the text of 12:1-7 is "performed" in this way, the new sentence of v. 8 rings like a tocsin bell. With rich sonority, the opening slogan of the book is repeated in the firm, clear voice of the narrator of the book of Ecclesiastes: "Vanity of vanities, says the Teacher; all is vanity." That this is meant to be the final assessment of the Teacher's thought is evident from the fact that it mates with the initial thematic statement in 1:2 to form a perfect bracket around the body of the work.

More can be said about these verses than simply the literary role they play in the dénouement of the book of Ecclesiastes as a whole. First of all, the power of the imagery of 12:1-7 is revealed in the response it has awakened in readers throughout the years. In the survey of literary uses of the image of the broken golden bowl in Jeffrey's work, no less than eight modern writers, mostly North Americans, are shown to have alluded to this passage.[114] Not only Herman Melville, who, as we have seen, drew heavily on Ecclesiastes, but also Washington Irving, Oliver Wendell Holmes, Henry James, and Lytton Strachey used the image quite straightforwardly as a metaphor for the end of life. One of the more notable allusions is found in the first lines of Edgar Allan Poe's "Lenore":

> Ah, broken is the golden bowl! the spirit flown for ever!
> Let the bell toll!—a saintly soul floats on the Stygian river.

The picture of desolation and ruin that the passage invokes for body, household, and world itself, culminating in the loss of access to water, which is tantamount to the loss of life itself, is reminiscent of some of the more desolate landscapes by Salvador Dali. The apocalypses of modern literature, too, spring to mind. In Russell Hoban's novel *Riddley Walker,* the descendants of the survivors of a holocaust wander around in a world in which dogs and people fight for food, in which language is degraded and memory unreliable. Memory is imparted by a wandering bard who recalls the time when the "one big one" caused the beauty and the glory of civilization to wind down toward extinction.[115] In Walker Percy's book *Love in the Ruins,* the little world of the protagonist is choked with kudzu-like vines that are a metaphor for the approaching end.[116]

These literary images of our own time tend to be political and cultural. They reflect the fears of a generation that has seen the demons that its own hands have unleashed. As far as the decline of individual life into those days of which one says, "I have no pleasure in them" (12:1), the images and expectations are radically altered. We have difficulty even imagining a world in which the average life expectancy was only forty-some years, as it was in Qohelet's day. Many more people survive now into really old age, and not all lose the abilities to walk erectly, to see clearly, to chew painlessly, to enjoy sexuality—the losses alluded to in this poem. At the same time, many experience to the full the sequence of decay described in 12:1-7. For us, too, then, Qohelet's appeal in 11:7-10 remains vital: Do it while you can! Live while you are alive!

It is perfectly sound Christian doctrine to say that God wills that we love life. It was to the end that we might live abundantly and that we might renew with vigor and enjoyment our vocation of earth keeping, peace making, and loving that Jesus came into our midst. When Qohelet says, "Banish anxiety from your mind, and put away pain from your body" (11:10 NRSV), his motivation is the brevity and transience of life. When Jesus says the same thing, he offers an entirely different motivation. Jesus says, "And can any of you by worrying add a single hour to your span of life? And why do you worry about clothing? Consider the lilies of the field, how they grow; they neither toil nor spin, yet I tell you, even Solomon in all his glory was not clothed like one of these" (Matt 6:27-29 NRSV). This is an invitation to a life of trust, gratitude, and courage, driven not by a melancholy sense of the fleetingness of it all, but by the nearness and greatness of the kingdom of God and God's righteousness (Matt 6:33).

Of course, with Qohelet-like realism, Jesus also acknowledges that "today's trouble is enough for today" (Matt 6:34 NRSV). That cautionary note aside, however, he urges his followers to get on with the business of being merciful, making peace, comforting those who mourn, and living life abundantly. The fact that we can expect to do these things more than thirty years longer on average than the original readers of the Old Testament could have done is truly a cause for rejoicing. Yes, it is a foretaste of the kingdom of God in which we participate already.

114. See Jeffrey, *A Dictionary of Biblical Tradition in English Literature,* 313.
115. Russell Hoban, *Riddley Walker: A Novel* (New York: Summit Books, 1980).
116. Walker Percy, *Love in the Ruins* (New York: Avon, 1971).

The time in life described by 12:1-7 is now called dotage. Its hallmarks are the decline in quality of life and, sometimes in the end, post-personal existence. The knowledge that frail old age is a possibility for us may serve as a useful goad, just as Qohelet meant it to do. Teaching us that one day the light will fade, the "daughters of song" will no longer be audible, the life force will fail, and death will come is surely his way of enabling us to enjoy the light of the moon and the stars now, to appreciate the sound of the birds and the taste of food now, and to savor intimacy and love now. Not only to quiet enjoyment does the Teacher goad us, but to action as well. While we have time, we have work to do—the work of conceiving and raising children, the work of building monuments, of writing poems and sermons, of performing music and creating needlepoint, and cooking delicious dishes—now—before "the golden bowl is broken, and the pitcher is broken at the fountain, and the wheel broken at the cistern" (12:6 NRSV).

ECCLESIASTES 12:9-14

THE EPILOGUES

COMMENTARY

The book of Ecclesiastes closes with two epilogues that are widely agreed to be the work of hands other than those of the Teacher. The most obvious reason for this idea is that in this section Qohelet is referred to in the third person, whereas elsewhere (except in 1:1 and in the clause "says Qohelet" at 1:2; 7:27; 12:8) the writer speaks in the first person. The phrase "my child" or "my son" appears only in this section (12:12), even though it is used very commonly elsewhere in the wisdom literature to address the client of a sage. Perhaps the epilogists added these concluding verses sometime between the time of the composition of the book in the third century BCE and the time of Ben Sira (c. 190 BCE), who, many commentators believe, regarded Ecclesiastes as sacred Scripture. By the time a book came to be regarded as Scripture, the opportunity to amend it was over; therefore, the supplements may have been attached during the years 250–200 BCE.

The writers of these last two short panels (vv. 9-11 and 12-14) use a form of Hebrew similar to that of Qohelet, thus they must have been reasonably close to the Teacher in time and place. It has often been asserted that the mission of the first epilogist was to bring the book closer to the mainstream of Hebrew thought, thereby to ensure its place in the library of sacred writings. He is not opposed to the ideas and temperament of the Teacher and gives valuable information about him in vv. 9-10. The second epilogist undertakes to correct certain key ideas of the book.

12:9-11. The first epilogist highlights the claim that Qohelet was a member of the royal family and calls him a "wise" man—i.e., a professional sage. More surprising, he claims that Qohelet "also taught the people" (v. 9). Evidently the Teacher reached out to an audience larger than the narrow circle of the court and the aristocracy. Perhaps he weighed and studied and arranged sapiental texts for this mass audience, improving them stylistically and gathering them into collections (v. 9); the book of Ecclesiastes itself, however, seems too sophisticated to have been part of Qohelet's popularizing work. Verse 10a may contain a slight criticism of Qohelet, since "pleasing words" can also be vacuous or manipulative ones. Nevertheless, there is no reason to join Ehrlich in translating v. 10b as if it were intended to contradict v. 10a—i.e., "but what should be written are words of truth."[117] Verse 11 has caused no end of trouble (see NRSV note), largely because several of its words are unique in the Hebrew Bible. Particularly difficult is the phrase "the collected sayings"; the KJV's "masters of learned assemblies" only demonstrates how obscure the Hebrew really is. Assuming that the "one shepherd" refers to God, the epilogist appears not only to have valued highly the "sayings of the wise," even those that were unconventional and controversial, but he appears also to believe sapiental works like Ecclesiastes should and did have the status of inspired Scripture.

12:12-14. The assumption that the phrase "anything beyond these" (v. 12) introduces a second epilogue lends more sense to the strange warning against too much study (v. 12). Efforts to understand which writings he was speaking of when he said, "Of making many books there is no end," have not achieved consensus. It may be that this writer intended to offer a more cautious and orthodox perspective on Qohelet. Some have suggested that vv. 11-12 are intended to contrast canonical writings (the "sayings of the wise") with apocryphal or even non-Jewish ones, to the disparagement of the latter. Murphy takes the warning against writing more books to be a way of praising Qohelet's work: "There is no need of more wisdom writings! In this view one should not postulate a second redactor responsible for vv. 12-14."[118]

---

117. Cited by Gordis, *Koheleth*, 342.
118. Murphy, *Ecclesiastes*, 126.

The book concludes with a standard formula for escaping the kinds of theological and moral dilemmas in which Qohelet has wallowed: "Fear God and keep his commandments" (cf. Ben Sira's summary of his thinking, Sir 43:27). This is followed by a ringing affirmation of the reliability of divine retribution, an affirmation that Qohelet himself was never able to make at all convincingly, though he allowed for the inevitable cause-and-effect sequence of the "destiny producing deed" (10:8-11). At this late date it is not possible either to affirm or to deny that the otherwise heterodox book made it into the canon because of the caveats contained in these verses. Certainly these last words would have been more familiar than other parts of the book to many of the readers of sacred Hebrew literature two centuries before the turn of the era. However, not only do they lack the nuance and probing energy of the rest of the book, but also they contradict two of its most important claims—namely, that human beings can know neither the future nor the activity of God (see 3:11; 7:14).

REFLECTIONS

The epilogists who added the last six verses to the book of Ecclesiastes achieved their apparent end of making the book more conventional and palatable. The traditionally pious confidence of vv. 13-14 that God will bring all deeds into judgment and will reward those who fear God feels more comfortable to many people even today than does anything else in the book of Ecclesiastes. It is ironic that much of the preaching and thinking about this fascinating book is based on the words of someone other than its real author.

The epilogists also coined what for many people, particularly students, is one of the best-known slogans in the book: "Of making many books there is no end, and much study is a weariness of the flesh" (12:12b). In the days before the printing press, people took the first remark to mean that the awesomely wearisome business of copying and binding books had to go on endlessly in order to support human culture. The sight of medieval books chained to their reading desks, which can still be found in old libraries in Europe, gives some legitimacy to this reading of the verse. The Puritans, however, took the second of the two clauses of v. 12b to be the guide to the proper understanding of the first. They tended to see this verse as cautioning readers against relying on teachings other than those of sacred Scripture. As Matthew Henry put it, "Let men write ever so many books for the conduct of human life, write till they have tired themselves with much study, they cannot give better instructions than those we have from the Word of God."[119] John Milton, on the other hand, though a Puritan, was also a liberally educated Cambridge rationalist who, in his *Areopagitica,* observed that the choice among books is one that God has placed within the sphere of our responsibility: "Solomon informs us, that much reading is a weariness of the flesh; but neither he, nor other inspired author, tells us that such or such reading is unlawful; yet, certainly had God thought good to limit us herein, it had been much more expedient to have told us what was unlawful, than what was wearisome."[120]

In our age of the explosion of knowledge and the difficulty of information retrieval, the words of Hugh of St. Victor ring as true as any: "The number of books is infinite; do not pursue infinity! When no end is in sight, there can be no rest. Where there is no rest, there is no peace. Where there is no peace, God cannot dwell."[121] Perhaps he had in mind the writing of commentaries on books like Ecclesiastes, which, if they are to prove their worth, have to shed at least as much light as does the original itself. Experience teaches that this is an accomplishment not easily attained!

119. Matthew Henry, *Commentary on the Whole Bible,* 4.1051.
120. Cited in Jeffrey, *A Dictionary of Biblical Tradition in English Literature,* 562.
121. Hugh of St. Victor *Didascalicon* 5.7.

THE SONG OF SONGS

INTRODUCTION, COMMENTARY, AND REFLECTIONS
BY
RENITA J. WEEMS

THE
SONG OF SONGS

INTRODUCTION

The content of Song of Songs, sometimes referred to as the Song of Solomon, represents a remarkable departure from that of other books in the Bible. To open the pages of this brief volume of poetry is to leave the world of exceptional heroism, tribal conflict, political disputes, royal intrigue, religious reforms, and divine judgment and to enter the world of domestic relations, private sentiments, and interpersonal discourse. Filled with language of sensuality, longing, intimacy, playfulness, and human affection, Song of Songs introduces the reader to the non-public world of ancient Israel. The relationships are private (i.e., a man and a woman), the conversation is between intimates (e.g., "darling," "beloved," "friend"), and the language hints of kinship bonds (e.g., mother, sister, brother, daughter). At last, readers of Scripture have the opportunity to focus not so much on the external politics that organized and dominated the lives of Hebrew people (e.g., palace intrigue, temple politics, prophetic conflict, international doom, natural disasters), but on the internal systems and attitudes that also shaped the lives of the people of Israel.

Song of Songs stands out in sharp contrast to the rest of the biblical books in two other ways. First, nowhere in its eight chapters is God mentioned. The book of Esther is the only work that shares this distinction. Although the religious significance of the latter is frequently debated as well, its religious significance is a little more self-evident, referring as it does to the rituals of fasting and prayer (Esth 4:16) and to the celebration of the Feast of Purim (Esth 9:20-32). A decidedly secular tone permeates Song of Songs; not only is God's name not mentioned in the book, but also no allusions are made to any of Israel's sacred religious traditions, be they covenant traditions (the Davidic or Sinai covenants) or God's saving acts in Israel's history (e.g., deliverance at the sea). One possible allusion to a religious theme may indicate that the book had "religious" origins: The lovers exchange their love poems against the backdrop of a pastoral, utopian garden setting where images of animals, hillsides, and exotic flowers predominate. Such allusions suggest intimations of the Garden of Eden story (Genesis 2), with its focus on the first human couple and their portentous dealings with each other. (More will be said about this topic below.)

Second, Song of Songs is the only biblical book in which a female voice predominates. In fact, the protagonist's voice in Song of Songs is the only unmediated female voice in all of Scripture. Elsewhere, women's perspectives are rehearsed through the voice of narrators, presumably male (e.g., Esther and Ruth), and their contributions are overshadowed by male heroism and assorted male-identified dramas. But in Song of Songs, where more than fifty-six verses are ascribed to a female speaker (compared to the man's thirty-six), the experiences, thoughts, imagination, emotions, and words of this anonymous black-skinned woman are central to the book's unfolding. Moreover, the protagonist is not merely verbal; unlike many of the women in the Bible, she is assertive, uninhibited, and unabashed about her sexual desires.

The book's pronounced and unrelenting female point of view is reinforced further by its strong female imagery. The several interjections of the Jerusalem daughters into the lovers' discourse (5:9; 6:1, 13*a*) and the repeated mention of the "mother's house" (בית אמ *bêt 'ēm,* 3:4; 8:2) as opposed to the customary "father's house" (בית אב *bêt 'āb*), the patriarchal household, contribute to the book's impression of giving readers insights into the decidedly private, unexplored world of Hebrew women's special viewpoints and private sentiments. The presence of such important female imagery allows Song of Songs to be seen as a collection of meditations from a woman's heart. Casting the book as the private, journal-like reflections of a female may provide us just the insight needed to unlock the mystery behind the decision to include such patently erotic and secular musings within the canon. As meditations of a woman's heart, Song of Songs might have been viewed as the feminine counterpart to a book like, say, Ecclesiastes. In the latter, an unnamed speaker, who is most likely male, reflects on the chasm between traditional wisdom teachings and actual human experience. He does not hesitate to express profound disdain for traditional wisdom, arguing that even the best of life is plagued with transience, unpredictability, absurdity, vanity, and ultimately ends in death. And he is openly cynical about the contradictions he has observed in life, one being that good deeds do not always lead to good consequences. In the light of the patent limitation of human wisdom, and in the face of death and vanity, the Preacher repeatedly urges his audience to indulge themselves in life's few genuine pleasures—food, drink, love, work, and play—as gifts of God.

One might argue that the protagonist in Song of Songs accepts the author of Ecclesiastes' invitation and revels in the joys of nature, work, and play when one is in love. In its own way, Song of Songs meditates, among other things, on traditional thinking about (female) sexuality and a certain protagonist's life experiences as a woman in love. Speaking in the first person, as does the protagonist in Ecclesiastes, the woman allows herself a few outbursts of impatience and effrontery (1:6; 6:13*b*; 8:1, 10), making it very clear that she is well aware that her own words and actions violate traditional teachings pertaining to womanhood and modesty. In the end, she is as impatient with traditional wisdom as her male counterpart in Ecclesiastes is scornful. But instead of expressing openly her contempt for and cynicism toward traditional wisdom, the speaker in Song of Songs takes the subtle approach and extols the erotic happiness she has found—despite all of its complications and limitations. One can see from both the striking amount of female speech and the decidedly female angle of vision of the book how easy it is to imagine that a female sage is responsible for the stirring meditations contained in Song of Songs.

AUTHOR AND TITLE

On the surface, the allusion to King Solomon in the superscription to the book (1:1) rules out a female as the author of Song of Songs. But the attribution to the last king of the united monarchy should not be taken as decisive. Because he was rumored to have married hundreds of wives (1 Kgs 11:3), many traditions inspired by Solomon's presumed vast knowledge about romance and matters of the heart no doubt emerged over the centuries. Song of Songs was likely one such composition. Attributing the love poems to Solomon probably represents an attempt by the scribes to associate the work with the wisest and most notorious king in Israel's history. Appending his name to the book would place it foremost within an intellectual stream of respected and authoritative theological reflection, the wisdom tradition. The king's reputation as a sage with more than several thousand wise sayings to his credit and a composer of more than one thousand lyrics (1 Kgs 4:32) lent to Song of Songs, especially in the light of the wisdom homily attached near the end of the book (Cant 8:6-7), the kind of sublimity and inspiration befitting royal compositions. This might explain one rendering of the book's title: "The Most Sublime of Songs."

There is no way to determine the gender of the person actually responsible for having written this collection of love poetry (although the preponderance of female speakers and experiences in the book has led me to refer to the lyricist throughout as female). But the book's class origins are conspicuous. Its author was acquainted with the accoutrements of the privileged class (e.g., the reference to the woman's vineyard in 1:6; the lavish royal wedding procession in 3:6-11; the scattered references to fine spices, fruits, and perfumes; the mention of Tirzah, once the capital city of the northern kingdom [6:4]). It is not far-fetched to imagine that the lyrics were inspired by someone (a woman) from an elite class who, at least modestly educated, was familiar with the Hebrew lyrical heritage and aware of prevailing assumptions about the role of women and the prohibitions against marriages crossing class and ethnic lines.

The title of the book (שיר השירים *šîr haššîrîm*) cleverly hints at the work's contents. Although its flat translation is better known among English-speaking audiences as the Song of Songs (NIV) and the Song of Solomon (NRSV), the title actually bears rich connotations ranging from the Song Comprised of Songs to the Most Excellent of Songs. (See Commentary on Cant 1:1.) The book is a collection of love lyrics filled with candid longing and tender expressions of desire and desperation by both the lover and her beloved.

Although it is difficult to discern any straightforward rationale or logic to the book's structure, the poems' lyrical quality is unmistakable. These brief, evocative, unpredictable units of material, which were brought together on the basis of alliteration, intonation, and possibly rhythm, surely made for memorable musical performances. In the second century CE, the lyrics to Song of Songs became a favorite in bawdy quarters, prompting Rabbi Aqiba (c. 135 CE) reportedly to protest that "he who trills his voice in chanting the Song of Songs in the banquet house and treats it as a sort of song has no part in the world to come."[1] We are not sure how successful the rabbi was in quelling secular enthusiasm for the lyrics. Nevertheless, for those who appreciate its subliminal nature, the content and character of Song of Songs continue to stir the religious imagination. Even today in some Jewish traditions, the text of Song of Songs is chanted at the end of the eight-day celebration of Passover. In other Jewish traditions, it is sung weekly in services prior to the sabbath. Even in many Protestant Christian traditions, some of the book's important themes continue to find their way into the church's most stirring compositions about human longing, divine compassion, and the beauty of creation.

LOVE LYRICS AND THEIR CONTENT

Lyrical poems cast as passionate dialogues, erotic soliloquies, and private dreams function in Song of Songs as the discourse of interior life and the rhetoric of heartfelt emotions. Hardly anything written in classical secular romance literature can match the exquisitely provocative exchanges between the anonymous female protagonist and her shepherd suitor in Song of Songs. To see Song of Songs merely as a collection of love poems that reclaim human sexuality and celebrates female sexuality, however, poems embodying gender balance and mutuality, is to fail to appreciate the deep and complicated emotions expressed in the book. Love lyrics are powerful forms of persuasion; they provide a modest way for communicating immodest sentiments, and they allow one to talk disingenuously about experiences and identities that defy official moral codes and fall outside the official cultural ideology. That being the case, the poetry of Song of Songs is the poetry of personal sentiment.[2] Its vocabulary and expressions are obscure because they are the private language of intimates. Identifying the speakers is complicated so

---

1. Tosefta, *Sanhedrin* XII 10.
2. For an illuminating discussion of the way poetry and songs are used to express personal, often unconventional sentiments in Arab bedouin communities, see Lila Abu-Lughod, *Veiled Sentiments: Honor and Poetry in a Bedouin Society* (Berkeley: University of California Press, 1986).

as to protect the privacy of the partners. The descriptions of human longing, vulnerability, dependence, and yearning are intended to capture the imagination and sympathy of the audience, forcing them to identify with the universal plight of lovers who want to be loved by the man or woman of their own choosing. Love poetry permits the speakers to comment on subjects from perspectives the audience might otherwise never consider. The woman argues for her right to pursue love, and her lover argues that in his eyes his maiden is beautiful.

When we compare the lyrics in Song of Songs with some of the psalms, we see that all lyrics are not the same. They differ according to their content, emotional tone, and social context. In our culture, gospel music, Scottish hymns, anthems, rap music, country music, hard rock, rock and roll, reggae, and jazz, to name a few, are all examples of oral literature that, while formulaic, ultimately originated out of very particular social contexts and represent unique forms of social commentary. The closest American musical parallel to the kind of material we find in Song of Songs may be the American blues tradition because of its comparable poignant interest in personal, individual struggles, the joys and sorrows of love, and the confounding chasm that exists between domestic reality and domestic fantasy. In both musical traditions, the speaker speaks in the first-person singular voice and the subject matter is deeply personal and gripping in intensity.

Many of the specific themes covered in Song of Songs also appear in classical women's romantic literature (e.g., personal relationships, thwarted love, sexual passion, the female body). In the classics, male self-identity develops and grows through a series of adventures that inevitably takes him away from his country and home, especially away from his intimate connections with women (e.g., mother, wife, sister). However, the female self in classic literature develops invariably through the woman's experiences with the impediments and frustrations of romantic love. In other words, women's education traditionally is "in or on the periphery of marriage."[3] Similarly, the lyrics of Song of Songs record the personal predicament of a certain black-skinned maiden—her struggles to love and be loved by a man for whom she has been deemed, for reasons not exactly clear to modern readers, an unsuitable mate. Readers are asked to understand the innocence of their love, to recognize the purity of their longing, and to empathize with the absurdity of the obstacles and frustrations, both internal and external, they are forced to endure. We watch the protagonist's selfhood unfold before our eyes as we observe her (1) as the innocent romantic who is propelled by her passion and her dreams of being loved and caressed by the man of her dreams (e.g., 1:2-4); (2) as defiant and impatient (1:5-6; 6:13b); (3) as a mature, intelligent, knowledgeable woman who passes on what she has learned in her experience of frustrated love to her impressionable female audience (2:7; 3:5; 8:4); and (4) as self-assured but pragmatic about the way the world operates and resolved to find happiness, despite the limitations imposed on her (8:10, 13-14).

The book's charm is its ability to elaborate on the erotic while at the same time critiquing prevailing cultural norms. In fact, the poet cunningly uses the former subtly to denounce the latter. So forward, so uncompromising, so urgent is the maiden's desire for and attachment to her lover that her comments border on the contentious in some places. Her insistence on three occasions that her beloved suitor belongs to her (2:16; 6:3; 7:10) is not mere assertion. Rather, seen in the context of her defense of her complexion (1:4), her bodily integrity (1:5; 6:13b), her small breasts (8:10), her continual adjuration (2:7; 3:5; 8:4), and in view of the Jerusalem daughters' continual skepticism (5:9; 6:13a), the protagonist's words have a polemical tone. For one thing, her black skin color, she suspects, immediately places her at odds with those around her (1:5-6).

The woman's daring love talk and explicit sexual longing invariably raise questions about the place of this book within the Bible. This is especially the case when one considers that the lovestruck female is as straightforward and aggressive about satisfying her libidinous urges as is her male suitor, or any other male character in Scripture. How, then, do we explain the radically different portraits of female sexuality in the Bible when we compare the sexually vivacious protagonist in Song of Songs with the sexually constrained women in so many other portions of Scripture? The former speaks openly and immodestly about her erotic desires, while the latter

---

3. Elaine Hoffman Baruch, "The Feminine *Bildungsroman:* Education Through Marriage," in *Women, Love, and Power: Literary and Psychoanalytic Perspectives* (New York: New York University Press, 1991) 122-44.

are portrayed as the archetypal other whose sexuality must be regulated and guarded against. These are not questions easily answered by cursory readings of the book. In fact, it has been difficult for scholars to arrive at answers to such important questions. Perhaps we are not supposed to come up with satisfying answers. Perhaps the fact that the book has been included in the canon is evidence enough of the rich, complex, and often ambivalent thinking about women, sex, and matters of the heart that existed in Israel throughout the centuries.

INTERTEXTUAL ALLUSIONS

Lyrical compositions, like all discursive forms, rely on a great store of intertextual comparisons for their affect and effect on their audiences. We have already seen how associating the book with King Solomon gave it an air of authority and legitimacy. When Song of Songs is viewed within its ancient Near Eastern setting, the influence of broader, extra-canonical texts lends the book a cosmopolitan note and situates it within the larger stream of internationally acclaimed compositions. For example, Song of Songs shares striking parallels with Egyptian love poetry. Both favor openness, tenderness, and frankness in their romantic speeches; the female lover in both traditions is referred to as "sister" (Cant 4:9, 10, 12) and is frequently addressed in superlative terms ("the most beautiful of women," Cant 5:9; 6:1).

Song of Songs also resonates with intertextual allusions to the story of the first human couple (Genesis 2–3).[4] Repeated mention of "garden" and garden-like settings in Song of Songs, whether used as a metaphor for the woman's sexuality (e.g., 4:12, 16; 5:1) or as a special location for the couple's lovemaking (6:11-12), may suggest that the book is a response to the "love story that goes awry"[5] back in the garden in Genesis 2–3. As a result of what happened in Eden, there is rupture in creation, disharmony between the first human couple, resulting in the subjugation of the woman and, by implication, the demise of mutual sexual fulfillment. In the garden of Song of Songs, by contrast, mutuality is reestablished and intimacy is renewed. Audiences encountering the content of Song of Songs for the first time would have had a repertoire of cultural information upon which to draw as they listened to the poems and placed them within the framework of what they understood love, relationships, and sex were or should entail.

A less commented upon, but equally suggestive parallel may be drawn between Song of Songs and Hosea 2.[6] Both use the trope of aggressive female sexuality to comment ambivalently on the relationship between love and power, on the one hand, and the erotic and the divine, on the other. In both texts, male figures threaten to imprison the women if they prove unchaste (cf. Cant 8:9 and Hos 2:6-7), and the women are beaten for pursuing the men they love (cf. Cant 5:2-8 and Hos 2:6-13). The woman in Song of Songs tells the woman's side of the drama; she is not depraved and incorrigible, as in Hosea. Instead, she is a woman in love and in trouble.

Whether Song of Songs was indeed written in response to these canonical examples of female/human sexuality is debatable. What is certain, however, is that like all poets, the author of Song of Songs appealed to what at that time was a store of cultural "texts" familiar to an ideal audience—some written and fixed, some oral and evolving, some ancient and tried, some contemporary and trendy, some expressly religious, and others, though secular, nevertheless inspired. Some of those texts are recoverable, such as the Garden of Eden story in Genesis and Egyptian love poems; but many of those intertextual allusions remain unrecoverable for the outsider. Regardless, they represent the kinds of material all readers bring to the reading process, consciously or unconsciously, that act as a sieve through which new information is assessed and organized, appropriated or resisted.

---

4. Phyllis Trible argues that Song of Songs was written as a counterpoint or response to the Genesis story and points to a number of remarkable resonances between the two in her work *God and the Rhetoric of Sexuality* (Philadelphia: Fortress, 1978) chap. 5.

5. This is the title of Trible's chapter on Genesis 2–3 in *God and the Rhetoric of Sexuality*, 72-143.

6. A frequently overlooked study of the parallels between Song of Songs and Hosea 2 that deserves more attention is Fokkelien van Dijk-Hemmes, "The Imagination of Power and the Power of Imagination," *JSOT* 44 (1989) 75-88.

THE "BODY" IN SONG OF SONGS

With abandon, the lovers in Song of Songs delight in the physical pleasures of love. They revel in each other's bodies: taste (2:3; 4:11; 5:1), touch (7:6-9), smell (1:12-14; 4:16), and the sound (2:8, 14; 5:16) of each other's voices. The female body poses no ethical problems in Song of Songs, although in other parts of Scripture it is problematic. It bleeds (cf. Leviticus 12; 15:19-30); it breeds (Leviticus 12); it confounds male wisdom (Numbers 5); and it has enormous power over the male imagination (Lev 21:7; cf. 2 Samuel 11), or so it seems. So mysteriously powerful is a woman's body that it can compete with a man's religious obligations (Exod 19:15). Only in Song of Songs is the female body extolled and praised for its difference and its beauty. With daring abandon the shepherd describes the maiden's eyes, neck, hair, feet, thighs, and navel using extravagant metaphors and sexually suggestive imagery. In fact, both lovers, using the genre of the *wasf*, or poetic passages describing with a series of images the various parts of the body, celebrate the integrity and uniqueness of the other's body. Four *wasfs* (Arabic for "description") can be found in Song of Songs (4:1-7; 5:10-16; 6:4-10; 7:1-9).[7] Three of the four *wasfs* praise the woman's form and flawless appearance, suggesting that the poet assumed that her audience might otherwise find some aspect of her physical makeup (perhaps her complexion?) objectionable (4:1-7; 5:10-16; 7:1-9). While only one *wasf* praises the man's body (6:4-10), nevertheless it stands out in both Song of Songs and in Scripture because it is the only description of masculinity and male beauty from the female point of view. No doubt drawn from the conventional stock of imagery and language poets and lyricists used during that period to describe the human body, *wasfs* do not attempt to be precise and concrete in their descriptions. They are deliberately imprecise and playful, where the intention is upon evoking the imagination and stirring the senses.[8] The focus on the human body allows both the poet and the audience to reflect simultaneously on at least three complex and highly symbolic themes that body imagery invokes in a culture: race, sex, and power.

The protagonist is unapologetic about the way she looks and relaxes in her beloved's desire for her. On one occasion she insists that her beloved's desire is for her only, presumably despite what others think (7:10). This is the talk of a woman under pressure both to conform and to relinquish her rights to be loved by the man of her choice. A possible context for the poem's origin was the post-exilic period, when the inhabitants of the tiny province of Judah were struggling to reestablish their identity. There are indications that canons of legal prescriptions were codified during this period to legitimate women's subjugation and that aggressive measures were taken to restrict social intermingling and to monitor marriage affiliations (Ezra 9:1–10:44; Neh 13:23-29; cf. Leviticus 12; 15; Numbers 5).

INTERPRETATION

Various proposals have been made for interpreting the book's secular and erotic contents. The major interpretations have viewed Song of Songs as (1) a dramatization of an ancient fertility rite in which the deity and humans were ceremonially united in sacred marriage;[9] (2) a single love poem structured around repetitive words, phrases, and motifs;[10] (3) a cycle of marriage songs;[11] and (4) an allegory idealizing, from the Jewish point of view, God's love for Israel, and from the Christian perspective, Christ's love for the church or for the individual's soul.[12] As for the latter, it is surprising to note that while Protestants have for the most part rejected the allegorical and tropological modes of interpretation that were characteristic of medieval biblical interpretation, when it comes to Song of Songs they are willing to rely on medieval and mystical allegorical interpretations to guide their thinking about the book's contents.

7. Richard N. Soulen, "The *Wasfs* of the Song of Songs and Hermeneutic," *JBL* 86 (1967) 183-90.
8. See Marcia Falk's keen insights on *wasfs* in *The Song of Songs: A New Translation and Interpretation* (San Francisco: HarperCollins, 1990) 125-36.
9. T. J. Meek, "Canticles and the Tammuz Cult," *AJSL* 39 (1922–23) 1-14.
10. J. Cheryl Exum, "A Literary and Structural Analysis of the Song of Songs," *ZAW* 85 (1973) 47-79.
11. Michael D. Goulder, *The Song of Fourteen Songs*, JSOTSup 36 (Sheffield: JSOT, 1986).
12. This line of interpretation began, of course, with the Targum, but one European Catholic scholar in modern times was very influential in arguing the claim. See Paul Joüon, *Le Cantique des Cantiques: commentaire philologique et exégétique* (Paris: Gabriel Beauchesne, 1909).

Readers tend to see the book as an allegory in part because the vocabulary of love poetry is obscure, the images are condensed, and the referents are ambiguous. The view that the lovers' pulsating passion and titillating sexual fantasies do not represent or point to any higher theological reality, that the book's significance is revealed in its literal meaning, and that the poet and editors who shaped the final poetry were not interested in elaborating on the nature of God and mediating sound religious doctrine has proved too incredible for those who remain bent on reading Song of Songs allegorically.

Today more and more interpreters are willing to read the book as a collection or anthology of love lyrics that capture the joys and sufferings of intimate relationships and of sensual love. The book chronicles one woman's journey to find fulfilling love with a man who, for reasons unknown to us, comes across as both enamored of her and forever elusive to her. Although the matter is never put so boldly in the poems, everyone who listens to the couple's plaintive outbursts empathizes with their dilemma, "to love or not to love." And although the drama appears to center around the heterosexual, erotic exchange between a woman and a man, Song of Songs is not in the end *about* heterosexual sex. Instead, it teaches us about the power and politics of human love. The lovers' humanity, not their genders, intends to captivate the audience. Audiences are supposed to recognize their own flawed demonstration and practice of love in these two characters, not because they recognize themselves in the characters' genders, but because they recognize themselves in their humanity. Audiences are first lured into contemplating the universal need by all to be loved, and then forced to confront their ambivalences about sexuality.

The black-skinned protagonist remains in many ways a product of her culture in her ambitions and her fantasies. Her continuous struggle to fulfill her desire to be loved and to retain her dignity as a woman invites audiences to ignore for the moment their inbred ethnic prejudices (against a Shulammite?), their class assumptions (about women who labor in the sun?), and their religious judgments about female sexuality, modesty, and impurity. The hope is that readers, whether male or female, will recognize themselves in this woman's very human need and desire simply to be loved.

STRUCTURE AND COMPOSITION

While the archaic grammatical and linguistic forms found in the book suggest that some version of the book dates back to the early period in Israel's history, lyrical compositions are notoriously difficult to date with any accuracy. In fact, much of their appeal is the result of their seemingly timeless, universal application to the human situation. The themes of Song of Songs are those that belong to the commonplaces of human courtship and human sexual attraction: yearning for the lover's presence, the joys of physical intimacy, coded speech, and elusive behavior, intoxication with the charms and beauty of one's lover, overcoming social obstacles and impediments to be together. Such themes are typical of love lyrics both ancient and modern. In fact, scholars have long noted the similarities between the mood and lyrics in Song of Songs and those of ancient Egyptian love poetry dating from the period of the New Kingdom (c. 1567–1085 BCE).[13] Observing particular stylized features of Egyptian love songs associated with the Ramesside texts, Michael Fox posits that these ancient songs may have been composed for entertainment and were performed by professional singers at private banquets and public festivals.[14] This music, performed over centuries and for generations, was created to charm audiences through its use of erotic allusions, veiled speeches, and extravagant imagery. Indeed, in the Song of Songs, audiences are at least implicitly invited to assume the identities of the lovers, to identify with their plight, to sympathize with their dilemma, to share their resolve, to relish their tenacity, to enjoy their clever disguises, to mourn their losses and flaws, to celebrate their joys and strength, and to endure with them unto the end.[15] The mood and tone of the

13. See Adolf Erman, *The Literature of the Ancient Egyptians*, trans. Aylward M. Blackman (London: Methuen, 1927); John Bradley White, *A Study of the Language of Love in the Song of Songs and Ancient Egyptian Poetry*, SBLDS 38 (Missoula, Mont.: Scholars Press, 1978).
14. Michael Fox, *The Song of Songs and the Ancient Egyptian Love Songs* (Madison: University of Wisconsin Press, 1985) 244-47.
15. Roland Murphy, *The Song of Songs*, Hermeneia (Minneapolis: Fortress, 1990) 47.

book change, sometimes within a few verses, as speakers move in and out of the drama, wooing, pleading, teasing, doubting, and interrupting each other. Audiences (and readers) are expected to be able to perceive within the poem's "progression" all the ambiguities, uncertainties, tensions, shortcomings, and suspense of love itself. In other words, drama and contents come together in the Song of Songs to create a poem intent upon gripping its audience.

Readers trained within the Western literary tradition invariably find a book like Song of Songs difficult to follow. Western readers expect literature to proceed in an orderly fashion and are frequently dismayed when a book like Song of Songs defies expectations of linearity, uniformity, transparency, and plot development. Whereas the presence of speakers, dialogue, and audiences gives the book an unmistakably dramatic quality, modern readers are struck by the way speakers, imagery, moods, and perspectives shift back and forth, seemingly without logic, sometimes within a span of one, two, or three verses. These otherwise oral speeches, which originally had their own performance quality, have been committed to a written form that has caused some tensions in its narrative development. Finding a uniform structure and consistent pattern to the book's content is not always possible. Those who perceive any literary unity to the poetry usually argue on the basis of their own aesthetic insights and not on the basis of any straightforward criteria. Commentators who divide the work into poems see it as a composition of fourteen, eighteen, twenty-eight, or thirty-one (to name just a few examples) units of poetry.

The position taken in this commentary to divide the poem into eleven lyrical units is not based on unassailable perceptions into its unfolding direction. Although the poem seems to be framed by an inclusio (the book opens [1:2-6] and closes [8:8-14] on similar themes; e.g., vineyard, the protagonist's brothers, her bodily integrity), the major indications of the book's "organization" are shifts in speakers and moods. The thirteen blocks of material commented upon in this commentary reflect what seem to be thirteen shifts in speakers, in some instances, and moods of speeches (in other instances). Of course, in the numerous instances where it is difficult to determine exactly who speaks and who is the referent (e.g., 2:1; 6:11-12; 8:11-12), guesses are hazarded.

Although we see changing sides of the protagonist (romantic, defender, sage, and pragmatist), she switches back and forth between these different shades of herself, depending on the obscure attitudes challenging her right to love and to be loved by whomever she chooses. By the poem's end, the protagonist is leaning in her lover's arms in a satisfying embrace (8:5). But her fulfillment is short-lived. The curtain closes on the lovers' thwarted passion; the maiden hurries her lover's pleasure for fear of retaliation. As a woman in the Hebrew culture, she is aggressive and audacious, but as a sage and observer of human nature she is also profoundly realistic. The homily on wisdom in 8:6-7 may be correct that love is a powerful force, one that in the end conquers everything that opposes it. But love's victory does not come without a price.

Finally, Western readers expect compositions to exhibit some interest in progression or development of character(s) and plot. This cultural expectation is only casually satisfied in the Song of Songs. In the first five chapters the lovers yearn for each other, delight in each other's charms, and sing each other's praises. In the last three chapters of the book, having defended their relationship against forces from without and from within, they eventually embrace, consummate their love, and pledge that their love, though costly, is more powerful than the forces opposing it. Under no circumstances can one argue that the book closes on a note of resolution or conclusion. At the end the maiden is forced to shoo her lover away, leaving the audience to wonder whether the two are ever allowed to relax and revel in their relationship. What could be the meaning of such an unresolved ending? Is love worth it? Perhaps that is precisely the question the song wants the audience to ponder.

BIBLIOGRAPHY

Commentaries:

Falk, Marcia. *The Song of Songs: A New Translation and Interpretation.* San Francisco: HarperCollins, 1990. Although not a commentary per se, this translation of the Hebrew text by a Jewish scholar represents one of the most sensitive, contemporary, and daring attempts to capture the nuances of Hebrew love poetry in English.

Murphy, Roland. *The Song of Songs.* Hermeneia. Minneapolis: Fortress, 1990. This commentary by a Catholic Carmelite adds helpful insight into neglected literary and theological themes in Song of Songs.

Pope, Marvin. *Song of Songs.* AB 7C. New York: Doubleday, 1977. This most celebrated commentary on Song of Songs represents a meticulously detailed exposition on virtually every conceivable Near Eastern mythological intimation in the little Hebrew book.

Other Suggested Studies:

Abu-Lughod, Lila. *Veiled Sentiments: Honor and Poetry in a Bedouin Society.* Berkeley: University of California Press, 1986. An exceptionally illuminating discussion of the structure, form, content, and social context of bedouin poems and songs reflecting the private sentiments of bedouin women in particular.

Baruch, Elaine Hoffman. *Women, Love, and Power: Literary and Psychoanalytic Perspectives.* New York: New York University Press, 1991. A social critique of prominent themes that recur in literature about women and romantic love from the Middle Ages to the present.

Biale, David. *Eros and the Jews: From Biblical Israel to Contemporary America.* New York: Basic, 1992.

Brenner, Athalya, ed. *A Feminist Companion to the Song of Songs.* Sheffield: JSOT, 1993. A collection of classic articles written on Song of Songs.

Merkin, Daphne. "The Woman on the Balcony: On Reading the Song of Songs," *Tikkun* 9, 3 (May–June 1994) 59-64.

Meyers, Carol. *Discovering Eve: Ancient Israelite Women in Context.* New York: Oxford University Press, 1988. An interdisciplinary look at the everyday lives of women in ancient Israel living in the Palestinian highlands during the Iron Age (1200–300 BCE).

Miles, Margaret R. *Carnal Knowing: Female Nakedness and Religious Meaning in the Christian West.* Boston: Beacon, 1989.

Nelson, James, and Sandra P. Longfellow, eds. *Sexuality and the Sacred: Sources for Theological Reflection.* Louisville: Westminster John Knox, 1994. A rich collection of writings reflecting a range of contemporary Christian thinking on sexuality.

Trible, Phyllis. *God and the Rhetoric of Sexuality.* Philadelphia: Fortress, 1978.

OUTLINE OF SONG OF SONGS

I. Song of Songs 1:1, Superscription

II. Song of Songs 1:2-4, Let Him Kiss Me

III. Song of Songs 1:5-6, I Am Black and Beautiful

IV. Song of Songs 1:7–2:7, I Compare You, My Love

    A. 1:7-8, A Simple Question
    B. 1:9-11, Precious Metaphors
    C. 1:12-17, Fragrant Metaphors
    D. 2:1-7, I Adjure You

V. Song of Songs 2:8-17, My Beloved Is Mine, and I Am His

VI. Song of Songs 3:1-5, I Looked for Him but Did Not Find Him

VII. Song of Songs 3:6-11, Who Is This Coming Up from the Desert?

VIII. Song of Songs 4:1–5:1, How Beautiful You Are, My Love

    A. 4:1-8, A Woman's Beauty
    B. 4:9-15, A Locked Garden
    C. 4:16–5:1, The Scent of a Woman

IX. Song of Songs 5:2–6:13, If You Find My Beloved

    A. 5:2-8, I Slept, but My Heart Was Awake
    B. 5:9, We Don't Get It
    C. 5:10-16, Do You See What I See?
    D. 6:1-3, But Where Is He?
    E. 6:4-10, One-of-a-Kind Beauty
    F. 6:11-12, The Garden of Love
    G. 6:13, The Daughters' Request

X. Song of Songs 7:1–8:7, Who Is This Leaning on Her Beloved?

    A. 7:1-9, The Shepherd's Seduction
    B. 7:10-13, The Shulammite's Surrender
    C. 8:1-5, In My Mother's House
    D. 8:6-7, The Power of Love

XI. Song of Songs 8:8-14, Epilogue

SONG OF SONGS 1:1

SUPERSCRIPTION

COMMENTARY

The Hebrew title שיר השירים (*šîr haššîrîm*), usually translated flatly, though literally, as "the Song of Songs" (NIV), identifies the work before us as an exemplary literary creation. The Hebrew is a typical way of expressing the superlative and might be more accurately translated as "the Most Excellent of Songs" or perhaps "the Most Sublime of Songs" (cf. "the God of gods and the Lord of Lords," Deut 10:17 NIV; "vanity of vanities," Eccl 1:2; 12:8 NRSV).

The book's further association with King Solomon (שיר השירים אשר לשלמה *šîr haššîrîm ʾăšer lišlōmōh*) situates it in the tradition of the wisest and most prolific king in Israel's history; hence the title in some translations, "the Song of Solomon" (NRSV). Less poetic, but equally defensible translations might be "the Song Composed of Songs" or "the Song of Many Songs." Each translation in its own way calls attention to the contents of the book as a special collection of songs or poems.

According to tradition, King Solomon uttered some three thousand "proverbs" (משל *māšāl*) and a thousand and five songs in his lifetime (1 Kgs 4:32[5:12]). It is unlikely that Solomon actually composed the Song of Songs, however, given many of the late linguistic forms scattered throughout the book. It is possible that the reputation of the infamous king as sage, composer, and husband to hundreds of wives inspired more than one composer through the centuries to draft provocative love lyrics in his memory. Rather than being viewed as an attempt to give a precise date and specific author, then, the superscription in 1:1 is best understood as a scribal effort to associate the book with a prominent figure in Israel's history and to place its contents within an established tradition of reflection—namely, the wisdom tradition.

Solomon's reputation as husband to seven hundred wives and three hundred concubines, both foreign and local women (1 Kgs 11:1-8; cf. Deut 17:17), must have made him a popular subject of folk tales and folk music. The six references to the king in the book may reflect some of the varied folk traditions that inevitably sprang up over the centuries about the king and came to be incorporated into a book under his name (1:1, 5; 3:7, 9, 11; 8:11). The many speculations about the king's love life, the banter about his powers of seduction and numerous marriages, and admiration of his godly insight into affairs of the heart made his name an ideal *nom de plume* to attach to the highly controversial, but profoundly human, contents of Song of Songs. Associating poetry luxuriating in human passion with such a renowned king accomplished three things: (1) It lent the work a semblance of authority, thus assuring its preservation and transmission; (2) it connected the book with a privileged school of thinking that was associated with Solomon—the wisdom tradition; and (3) it brought together for sacred reflection three topics (sex, power, and wisdom) that, combined, could evoke deeply felt emotions and tap into widely held social beliefs.

Biblical superscriptions, though rarely as precise about dating as modern interpreters would like, insist by their very placement at the opening of a work that the following material did not originate in abstraction. Its contents have been shaped by specific contexts, its conversations framed by shared histories and worldviews. "Let the reader beware," then, is the subtle warning behind every superscription; although the subject matter may appear oblique and quixotic in some places, downright obscure and baffling in others, and although its origin and apparent significance may seem puzzling, the following text has been judged sublime and urgent by past generations who were perfectly willing to wrestle with its message and whose patience is worthy of emulation.

REFLECTIONS

Throughout the ages in Jewish and Christian liturgy, the Song of Songs has played an important part of worship, being sung at Passover celebrations in the Jewish tradition and serving as sermon text to illustrate Jesus' love for the church in the Christian tradition. The melodramatic and highly passionate tone of the lyrics lends the book's contents to singing and reenactment in festive, celebrative gatherings where love and devotion are thematic.

Judging by the bits of songs and poetry scattered throughout the Old Testament, especially the 150 lyrical compositions assembled in the book known as Psalms, music and poetry were ideal media in biblical antiquity for chronicling profoundly sacred and profoundly human experiences. We find repeated examples of the people's attempt to articulate in song their greatest joys (e.g., "Sing to the LORD, for he has triumphed gloriously" [Exod 15:21a NRSV]), their deepest sorrows (e.g., "How shall we sing the LORD's song in a strange land?" [Ps 137:4 KJV]), and their most profound hopes ("Sing, O barren one who did not bear; burst into song and shout, you who have not been in labor! For the children of the desolate woman will be more than the children of her that is married, says the LORD" [Isa 54:1 NRSV]). According to tradition, King David, himself a musician, was so convinced of the powers of music to evoke the sublime that he made sure that music was a professional, institutionalized part of Israel's worship.

It is difficult to imagine worship without music. Certainly for those raised in traditions characterized by lively music, expressive chants, and dramatized sermons, music and worship are virtually synonymous. Music, as musicians are wont to insist, is the language of the soul. And a book like Song of Songs is ideal reading in ceremonies where men and women gather to celebrate the perfecting of human love here on earth as it is in heaven.

Because lyrics use the sparsest amount of language to appeal to the deepest of emotions, capturing our joys and fears, recording our creeds and contradictions, rehearsing our ambitions and failures with meter and measure that lull and grip the imagination, music and poetry reflect upon a society's images of itself that it can hear, appreciate, digest, react to, and correct. Perhaps that is why artists are the first to be silenced in totalitarian governments. Theirs is a potential to unmask falsities bit by bit, in portions manageable to the masses and in unforgettable language.

Some of the most memorable hymns, anthems, and praise songs make imaginable and comprehensible to our congregations ideas and notions that continue to elude our best exegetical sermons: God's amazing grace, Jesus' redemptive love at the cross of Calvary, the faith of our beloved ancestors, a people's prayers for their children's children. Epiphanies like these tend to break the back of mundane speech. Often, music and poetry are needed to bridge the gap between heaven and earth, the world of strangers and enemies, the world of women and men. Love lyrics, like those in Song of Songs, invite their audience into the private world of intimates.

SONG OF SONGS 1:2-4

LET HIM KISS ME

COMMENTARY

Turning to the initial full unit (1:2-6), readers are gripped by the first-person narration that opens the book: "Let him kiss me with the kisses of his mouth!" One experiences the uneasy, but exhilarating, feeling that attends a public performance where actresses and actors invite audiences into the deeply personal world of private secrets and pent-up emotions. The audience is invited to share in each actor's pathos. To do that, however, one must be able to distinguish the players from one another and to follow the direction of the performance.

The opening verses of Song of Songs plunge the reader directly and without delay into one of the features of the book that make it difficult to organize and frustrating to follow. Pronouns shift back and forth, as do verb forms, making it hard to identify speakers and subject matter from verse to verse. For example, the pronouns shift from the third person ("him") in v. 2 to the second person ("you") in v. 3, signaling a change from the narrative voice to direct address; and in v. 4 the verb forms change the speech from second-person narration to first-person singular ("Draw me after you") and first-person plural address ("We will exult and rejoice in you"). Readers are left to wonder how many speakers are involved in this drama and exactly who is being spoken to and about. This kind of suspense was evidently used by composers of ancient lyrics to entice the audience to strain forward and listen intently.

1:2. The first speech opens on a note of yearning. The speaker is female. She introduces herself to the reader, not by giving her name, but by announcing her wish to be kissed by her lover: "Let him kiss me with the kisses of his mouth!" In a culture where casual touch between the opposite sexes was rare, a kiss was fantasized as the climax of sexual pleasure. After addressing no one in particular, but everyone in earshot, the woman turns

to address her lover directly, beckoning him by speaking adoringly of his love, his scent, and his name (vv. 2b-3). She cherishes his "love" over wine (v. 2b)—no trivial matter when one considers that the black-skinned woman lives in a part of the world where vineyards were greatly prized and specially handled (cf. Exod 22:5; 23:11; Deut 20:6; 23:24). Comparing love to wine was common to male and female exchanges of love (cf. 4:10), much like the modern expression, "Your love is sweeter than honey."

Because the Hebrew words for "breast" and "love" share a similar consonantal spelling (דוד *dwd*), some ancient manuscripts, changing the vocalization of the noun, read "your breasts" (דדיך *daddayik*) over "your love" (דדיך *dōdeykā*), thereby rendering the verse as "your breasts are better than wine." But "breasts" is an unlikely translation. It assumes the speaker is male, and nothing in the remainder of the verse points indisputably to a male speaker. There *is* reason to believe that the woman remains the speaker. For one thing, the Hebrew word for "love" is a derivative of the same term she uses repeatedly in the poetry to refer to her suitor, דודי (*dôdî*), "beloved" (see 1:13, 14, 16).

1:3. The maiden insists that no one can escape her lover's powers: "No wonder the maidens love you!" (NIV). But she carefully refrains from divulging his name, simply comparing it to the perfumed oils of Mediterranean cultures. Such oils, regarded by the populace as powerful aphrodisiacs, were produced by combining perfumes with olive oil. Like spilled perfume, whose aroma fills the air, her lover's name is pleasant to the senses. Demonstrating in this verse her powers as a poet, the protagonist relies more on inference and imagination than on candor and the mundane to describe her love. She invites her audience to experience her suitor as she does, with the nose (e.g., perfume) and the taste buds (e.g., kisses and wine).

1:4. In this verse, the protagonist's voice becomes insistent, and her request is cast in the imperative: "Draw me after you." She speaks assertively, insisting that her suitor take her quickly to his chambers (lit., "Draw me after you—let us hurry [until] the king has brought me into his chambers"). Her reference to the king is probably an expression of endearment and esteem, although some commentators have thought that Solomon is being spoken of here. Whether "king" refers to an actual monarch or is a term of endearment for a special love, the sense of the verse is probably best captured by the NIV: "Let the king bring me into his chambers."

The narrative change from first-person singular to first-person plural in the next line ("We will rejoice and exult . . . extol your love") has prompted several translations and interpretations: Is this the speech of the maidens, presumably the daughters of Jerusalem (v. 5), who from time to time interrupt the speeches of the protagonist and suitor to challenge their views (5:9; 6:13)? Or is the protagonist speaking here, looking forward to the time when she and her suitor can frolic and luxuriate in royal or lavish settings, celebrating their love for each other and savoring each other's tastes ("we will extol your love more than wine")? Listening in on the private world of human passion, we can only guess that the latter is the case.

Modern readers might marvel at such a bold portrait of a woman in biblical antiquity. Such immodest desires on a woman's lips run counter to the passive, reserved, submissive image of Hebrew women one finds in many other portions of the Old Testament. Hebrew women do not initiate sex, one might suppose, except in the cases of women like Tamar (Genesis 38) and Ruth (Ruth 3), who wanted to become pregnant. Yet there is no hint in these verses, or elsewhere in the poem, that the female protagonist has procreation on her mind as she yearns for her suitor. Indeed, the protagonist presents a portrait of Hebrew women different from the one cast throughout much of the Old Testament—indeed, the entire Bible. She boldly longs for intimacy with a special lover and does not hesitate to pursue him.

REFLECTIONS

Perhaps our ancestors were not so squeamish about using the erotic to contemplate transcendence as we have supposed. In Song of Songs all of the created order is invited to join in this paean to human eroticism, where two souls pine for each other in a lyrical drama of suspense, intrigue, and desperation. Audiences are invited to identify with a female protagonist who longs to be kissed and swept away by her lover. Does the woman's voice in Song of Songs, which is unparalleled in the rest of Scripture, make us recoil or surrender? How, if at all, might we react differently had her suitor opened the book with the same words and his was the dominant perspective? If the male voice were predominant, would the work's religious import be more apparent or plausible?

We should not dismiss the importance of our initial shock at the woman's voice and longing in the first few verses of a canonical book. The composer of the poem undoubtedly was hoping to pique her audience's attention. After all, nothing seizes an audience like the topic of sex. A sensual sermon illustration is sure to make the person dozing in the third pew take notice of the remainder of a sermon. Hearing a woman talk explicitly about her sexual fantasies can arrest an audience's wandering thoughts.

The composer probably did not expect her poetry to fall into the hands of audiences for whom combining the topics of sex and religion was unthinkable. But she was likely quite aware that poetry detailing a woman's intimate fantasies was not the stuff of normal public discourse. And like any good composer of a literary work, she incorporated the song's probable effects upon her audience—discomfort, embarrassment, curiosity—into the meaning and significance of her poetry. Notice that the composer does not postpone the ribald topic of sexual longing until after she has won her audience's sympathies for the lovers; nor does she prepare her audience for the steamy erotic exchanges of the lovers by explicating in detail the nature of the difficulties obstructing their love (cf. Psalm 137, where the poet delays introducing a cruel outcry to slaughter the babies of his enemy [Ps 137:8-9] until after he has first lured the audience into empathizing with the social distress of the speaker [Ps 137:1-6]). The poet counts on the tensions experienced by audiences wanting to believe in both love and social propriety to create an arresting drama. Sex forces audiences to confront head-on their deepest convictions, their unspoken preconceptions, and their own complicated desires. When sex is combined with religion, boundaries are transgressed and lines are blurred, because sex is rarely about just sex. It is about needs, longings, fears, fantasies—in a word, human passion. And passion never quite conforms to the neat and tidy categories and labels of religion.

The opening verses of Song of Songs force the reader to face his or her deepest convictions about marriage, love, and female sexuality. The Bible is full of stories in which male sexual aggression is taken for granted and assimilated into some of the most notable moments in redemptive history. In Genesis 6:1-4, intercourse between women and the "sons of God" (referring either to mythic angels or to ancient warriors of renown) represents one final act of corruption leading to God's decision to blot out humankind with a flood (Gen 6:9–9:17). In the prophecies of Hosea, Jeremiah, and Ezekiel in particular, male fantasies of whoring wives, female lasciviousness, and rape are the backdrop for divine judgment and prophetic predictions of destruction.[16] And in Exod 19:15 the men of Israel, before receiving divine law, are ordered to observe rituals of purification, which included refraining from sexual intercourse with women (the inference being that sexual contact with women obstructs divine revelation). Female sexuality poses problems for men and, according to our male narrators, for God. Unrestricted contact with women threatens boundaries and portends turmoil. Repeatedly fathers warn sons against falling into the sexual snares of loose women (cf. Prov 2:16-19; 5:3-14, 20-21; 6:24-35; 7:1-27; 9:13-18); and in both canonical and non-canonical literature one finds male narrators openly declaring their contempt for women (Eccl 7:26; Sir 25:24; 42:14).

Song of Songs represents a remarkable departure from much religious literature because the book's opening verses hurl the unsuspecting reader straight into the clutches of a *woman's* sexual fantasies. It forces the reader to see herself or himself, the world, and God (for those who read the book as an allegory of God and Israel's relationship) in an unfamiliar way—namely, through a woman's libidinous cravings. Whatever ambivalences one may have about hearing from God or discovering the sacred through the messy mysteries of the female body are forced to the surface. By beckoning the reader into the private world of female imagination and longing, the poet gambles on her audience's curiosity about sex and romance and fascination with tales of obstructed love winning out over whatever squeamishness the readers may have about associating women's bodies with divine revelations. Hence, the meaning of the opening verses of Song of Songs lies not only in what they tell us about God, but also in what they tell us about ourselves.

16. Renita J. Weems, *Battered Love: Marriage, Sex, and Violence in the Hebrew Prophets* (Minneapolis: Fortress, 1995).

SONG OF SONGS 1:5-6

I AM BLACK AND BEAUTIFUL

COMMENTARY

A good example of how the poetry of this book provokes the cultural imagination appears in 1:5-6. It is one of those Bible passages whose interpretation has engendered a lively amount of speculation and discussion, even though the Hebrew text is relatively uncomplicated.

After romancing her lover with flattery in 1:2-4, the protagonist speaks with pride, self-confidence, and, contrary to what some have argued, without apology as she describes herself (v. 5). She is, in her own words, "black and beautiful" (NRSV). The Hebrew word she uses to describe her complexion (שחורה *šĕḥôrâ*) is unambiguous, despite the numerous efforts by translators to render it more euphemistically and palatably as "dark," "very dark," "swarthy," "blackish," and so on. Derivative adjectival forms of the word appear elsewhere in the Old Testament where the color "black" is the indisputable meaning. In Lev 13:31, 37, "black" hair as a sign of health and cleanness is clearly being contrasted to yellowish diseased hair. In Zech 6:2, 6 the adjective distinguishes the "black" horses of the second chariot from the red, white, and dappled horses driving the other chariots. And elsewhere in Song of Songs the adjective describes the color of her beloved's wavy hair, "black as a raven" (Cant 5:11). In its only occurrence as a verb, שחר (*šāḥar*) describes Job's blackened, parched skin, the result of a protracted fever (Job 30:30). If "black" is the uncontested meaning of *šāḥar* elsewhere in the Old Testament, then there is no basis for debate about its meaning in Cant 1:5. If there is any dispute, and there has been considerable, it centers on whether the protagonist describes herself as "black and beautiful" or "black, but beautiful."

In the Septuagint (LXX), the Greek translators of the Old Testament had no misgivings about the matter. The Greek translation reads, "Black am I and beautiful." Some commentators, construing the protagonist's comment in v. 5 as apologetic, point to v. 10 and Lam 4:7 to defend the view that the white and ruddy complexion was the prevailing standard of beauty at the time. That being the case, they argue, the accurate translation is, "I am black, but beautiful." Other evidence must be considered, however: (1) The word *black* appears five times in the emphatic position, suggesting that the woman's tone is confident and her posture assertive—not apologetic. (2) Throughout the poem the woman's physical beauty is both praised and celebrated, not only by her lover but also by the maidens of the city, which means that others regard her as indisputably attractive. (3) Although the Song of Songs and Lamentations (and other portions of Scripture) suggest that a ruddy complexion was prized in men, the same does not automatically apply to women, since women were commonly judged by a different standard of beauty.

No other woman in the Bible describes herself in the way the black-skinned woman in Song of Songs does. Unlike Leah and Rachel, she is not seen through her male narrator's eyes (Gen 29:17). Unlike Tamar, she does not disguise who she really is to avoid rejection (Gen 38:15). And unlike Ruth, she does not apologize for being noticed, conspicuous, or different (Ruth 2:10). She is the only woman in Scripture who describes herself in her own words.

She is careful to explain how she became the color she is. Her brothers, she insists, forced her to work outdoors in their vineyards. She is not a freak, she insists, but a casualty of the sun (v. 6). Although there is no mistaking the defensive tone in her words, there is no reason to believe that the protagonist is apologetic about her color. That she is not embarrassed by her complexion can be seen in the fact that she compares her color to the stark sable fabric characteristic of the imposing tents of the Syro-Arabian nomadic tribe known as Kedar (whose root connotes darkness; cf. Jer 8:21; 14:2; Mic 3:6), and to the striking curtains in Solomon's palace. The inference is that hers is a color of distinction and nobility (at least in her own mind), hence her insistence that she is beautiful (נאוה *nā'wâ*).

Despite the brief references to her color, the protagonist remains nameless and virtually clanless throughout the whole poem (notwithstanding the one oblique reference to "Shulammite" in 6:13). Likewise, no mention is made of her patronymic or matronymic, which could shed light on her ancestral lineage. We are left to take heart in her bold act of self-assertion and description: She speaks up for herself; she is the object of her own gaze: she is, by her own estimation, black *and* beautiful.

There remains the matter of her enigmatic statement in v. 6, "My brothers were angry with me and made me take care of the vineyards." Is this a reference to actual kindred? Familial terms are used casually throughout the book as literary devices and as part of cultural memory; the male lover refers to the protagonist repeatedly as his "sister" (4:9, 12; 5:1); she refers to "mother(s)" on several occasions (3:4, 11; 8:1, 5); and in 1:6 and 8:1 she alludes to the privileges a "brother" can take with his sister. But exactly why were her brothers angry with her, and, more important, what politely veiled cultural comment might she be making by claiming that her brothers forced her to tend "the vineyards"?

The protagonist's complaint that she was forced to labor in vineyards, a term with erotic overtones throughout Song of Songs (2:15; 7:12; 8:12), has led some commentators to draw sexual inferences from the verse. Marvin Pope, who has written an important commentary on the book, says, "The well-attested sexual symbolism of vineyard and field strongly suggests that the import of her statement is that she has not preserved her own virginity."[17] Specifically, Pope (and others) sees the protagonist as referring here to her body and sexual parts.[18] Taken this way, then, the woman admits here that she has not been able to safeguard her own virginity—as she ought or would have liked. Such an interpretation is consonant with the overall image throughout the book of a woman who persists in the face of incredible odds in pursuing an elusive relationship.

17. Marvin Pope, *Song of Songs*, AB 7C (New York: Doubleday, 1977) 329.
18. Pope, *Song of Songs*, 330.

REFLECTIONS

Curiously, God's name is never mentioned in Song of Songs. Neither is there any explicit comment on traditional religious themes. Readers are left to draw on their experiences of love, longing, mutuality, sensuality, and human connectedness to contemplate the book's meaning for conventional religious doctrines of faith, covenant, law, justice, hope, revelation, and reconciliation. We are invited to find God in ourselves, to perceive the parallels between human passion and religious pathos, to weigh our noblest ideas against our most senseless prejudices, and to let our deepest yearnings direct us to what is eternal. What better way of prompting audiences to probe the depths of their thinking about God, to examine their unexamined prejudices, and to dive below the surface of their narrow notions than to invite them to contemplate simultaneously love and bigotry? Indeed, to read the poetry of Song of Songs is to be caught up in unrelenting and enormous swings in emotions. The reader must be willing to switch from one emotion to another, sometimes in a span of one, two, or three verses, surrendering to passion and then playfulness, longing and then reserve, vanity and then defensiveness, awe and then anguish. It is also to be torn between one's deep cultural prejudices and one's noblest cultural ideals. We have already seen in vv. 5-6 that the reader follows the lovesick woman through at least two extremes of the human heart: confidence and defensiveness.

What is it about the color of a person's skin that can evoke the most banal impulses of the human heart? Why has color prejudice been such a pervasive and virtually universal mode of discrimination throughout the ages and around the world? Why in patriarchal cultures do foreign women whose physical characteristics deviate from the norm invariably become the subject of intense debate and condemnation? Addressing these questions would, perhaps, take us too far afield of our present study. But they are questions worth pondering as we reflect on the significance of Song of Songs for our cultural context. Time and again religious people have been at the forefront of campaigns to outlaw and subjugate people who think and look differently, and they have turned their heads when others were tortured, gassed, or hanged. The black-skinned woman in Song of Songs remains forever a meaningful trope for talking about the quest for authentic relationship and community.

Of course, this is not the first time in the Bible when a foreign woman becomes a reminder of how diverse is God's vision of covenant people (e.g., Ruth and Rahab). Nor is the protagonist in Song of Songs the first woman who functions as a mirror for self-scrutiny (e.g., Moses' Ethiopian wife, the Samaritan woman at the well). The stories of these deviant women, foreigners, harlots, and widows, who part from cultural norms, not so much by their actions (although they frequently engage in heroic or gallant feats on behalf of their community), but by nature of their physical and cultural differences, become important rhetorical lessons on the ecumenicity of God's vision of the kingdom.

Forced to get into the skin of this black woman, the reader is made to see her as neither Amazon nor demon, the two extreme fears of the bigot. Her quest for love, her desire to be loved genuinely, and her willingness to give herself unselfishly to love are so familiar that even the bigot can identify with the protagonist. All of us are reminded that love has its own logic. It refuses to succumb to the human will. It is rarely predictable, and it delights in the unexpected. It forces us to do things we never anticipated, to say things we never heard ourselves say before, to submit to feelings we never felt before, and to pair ourselves with people we never imagined for ourselves. Love helps us risk stretching beyond our comfort zones. Indeed, nothing exposes us for who we really are—and who we are not—or divulges our secrets and unmasks our preconceptions like love. Song of Songs, with its hint at color prejudice, taps into our deepest cultural prejudices by making us confront the way they keep us from seeing certain people as individuals with needs, desires, ambitions for love, and intimacy just like ourselves.

Finally, the lovelorn female in the Song of Songs calls out our noblest yearnings. She does this first by forcing us to face our prejudices about the other, making us confront a base impulse: the propensity to differentiate ourselves from those who deviate from our expectations and fall outside the norm. She challenges the dominant aesthetics. She pooh-poohs the hegemonic standards of beauty. She leaves us conflicted. Do we endorse her quest to find satisfying love, irrespective of where such a search might take her? Or do we, along with her gawking audience, allow our prejudices against black, aggressive, forward women to censure her, impose limits on her, and force her into vineyards not of her choosing?

SONG OF SONGS 1:7–2:7
I COMPARE YOU, MY LOVE

OVERVIEW

Turning to 1:7–2:7, we cannot help feeling that we are eavesdropping on an intimate tête-à-tête between lovers. It seems as though we are intruding upon a conversation intended for only the special ears involved. This is profoundly private talk between two people who share special intimacies and who have special intentions toward each other. Theirs is love talk, lusty and mischievous. Such talk is ablaze with mutual admiration and longing, while at the same time shrouded in cryptic references and secret allusions. What keeps it from careening toward the vulgar, besides the fact that it is consensual, is that love talk is not blunt speech. Lovers bristling with passion and yearning rarely talk about their desires forthrightly. Instead, they talk around them. They talk in codes, relying on analogies, hiding behind innuendos and figurative speech to convey what they are too shy, too embarrassed, too nervous, too straitlaced, or perhaps too modest to say outright. As for the subject of their whispers, why, it is sex, of course.

SONG OF SONGS 1:7-8, A SIMPLE QUESTION

COMMENTARY

1:7. One detects a petulant tone in the protagonist's voice as she inquires as to her lover's whereabouts, a query repeated in one way or another throughout the book. To soften her impatience and boldness in asking, however, the black-skinned woman addresses her lover with a term of endearment that melts away any possible taking of offense. The NRSV captures poetically her seduction: "you whom my soul loves." She inquires as to where he pastures his flock (which suggests that he is a shepherd), particularly where he leads his flock, as shepherds do, at the noon hour to rest. The implication is that midday might be the ideal time when she and her mate could steal away for some adventure.

Almost pouting, but maintaining a tone of seductiveness, the protagonist lets her lover know that she resents being in the dark as to his whereabouts, having to stumble about blindly, as if she wore a veil over her face,

groping for him: "Why should I be like one who is veiled beside the flocks of your friends?" (v. 7*b*). She is not comparing herself to a prostitute whose face is cloaked in order to hide her identity, as one might think. Some scholars point to the ruse Tamar was forced to resort to in her efforts to woo her father-in-law, Judah (Gen 38:15; cf. Hos 2:2). The protagonist's meaning, then, would be something like, "Why should I have to resort to duplicity (like the ancestress Tamar) in order to get your attention?"

But the poetry makes clear throughout that it is not the woman who is evasive, but her lover. She is continually looking for him, groping for him, inquiring about him (2:8; 3:1-2; 5:6; 6:1-2). He is elusive, but she is persistent. The veil that she speaks of is the figurative one she feels she wears, which keeps her always uncertain about him.

1:8. To her question about his where-abouts, he answers with a tease: "If you do not know, most beautiful of women, follow the tracks of the sheep and graze your young goats by the tents of the shepherds." Like other maidens in antiquity who resided in rural, bedouin-like, semi-pastoral cultures, the protagonist was responsible for her share of the chores in the household, which among other things included tending the fields, dressing vines, and leading the family goats to grazing ground during the day. Seen in the light of her duties, her lover's comment in this verse should be taken to mean: "I am right under your nose." One might be tempted to ascribe this verse to the chorus of Jerusalem maidens who from time to time interject their opinion

into the poetry (5:1 *b*; 6:1, 10, 13; 8:5). But her question is not directed at the maidens. It addresses her lover.

Such a forthright answer on the shepherd's part contradicts his reputation throughout the book as inaccessible and elusive. More likely, his comment represents the kind of cryptic retort that skittish, evasive lovers are wont to make when pressed for more accountability: "You know where to find me." But that remains to be seen. So far we have a typical scene in love poetry: One party is frantic with desire, and the other party feigns disinterest by remaining elusive, not to be mean, but to heighten the romance and to prolong the foreplay. (See Reflections at 2:1-7.)

SONG OF SONGS 1:9-11, PRECIOUS METAPHORS

COMMENTARY

Like the protagonist, the shepherd in Song of Songs relies on metaphors in these verses to describe his admiration: "I compare you, my darling, to a mare harnessed to one of the chariots of Pharaoh" (1:9). The numerical incongruity between the Hebrew word for "mare" (סוסה *sûsâ*, sing.) and the Hebrew word for "chariotry" (רכבי *rikbê*, plural construct) is not a problem to be solved by grammarians when one considers the Egyptian custom of sending a mare out among the stallion-driven chariots of the enemy to distract and waylay the enemy. The implication is that the beloved female in Song of Songs is as tempting and alluring as a mare. Her earring-adorned cheeks and bejeweled neck heighten her allure (v. 10).

While comparing a woman to a mare may elicit a blank stare from a modern, urban audience—we are, after all, totally ignorant of mares' unique contribution to chariotry tactics—we can assume that at the time of

its composition such a comment would have been easily understood by someone familiar with horses and their role in Egyptian tactical formations. A savvy audience knows a compliment when they hear one and knows when to swoon with appreciation. Now, whether the average maiden in antiquity was familiar with the roles mares played in military affairs is another thing altogether. More likely, this is one of those instances, so common in courtship rituals, in which a man compliments a woman with imagery borne of androcentric activities (e.g., sports, warfare) and based on androcentric values (e.g., power, domination), which are foreign to the woman's domain of activities and to her values. We can only guess the maiden's knowledge of mares' role in warfare maneuvers. The shepherd redeems himself, however, by going on to compare his maiden to precious stones (v. 10). (See Reflections at 2:1-7.)

SONG OF SONGS 1:12-17, FRAGRANT METAPHORS

COMMENTARY

It is the maiden's turn to return the compliment. Again, she affectionately refers to the shepherd as "king." But what exactly are we to make of "While the king was on his couch, my nard gave forth its fragrance" (v. 12)? Is she fantasizing about a future moment, recalling a past event, or describing a present happening? She leaves those eavesdropping to wonder. On the one hand, v. 12 is simply too tantalizing not to be taken literally. On the other hand, it is one of those cryptic allusions to private intimacies only the lovers are able to decode. As for its meaning, is it "an allusion to the sexual smell" the woman emits when aroused in anticipation? To her lover's exclamation of her beauty (vv. 9-10), does she comment explicitly on his power to excite her (v. 12)? The scene is irresistible: As he reposes under a tree on a makeshift "couch" of leaves, nestled between her breasts, presumably whispering his flirtations in his sweetheart's ear, she admits that he stirs her in ways that make her emit aromas (vv. 12-14).

In v. 13, the protagonist refers to her lover as "beloved" (דודי *dôdî*), a term she will use more than twelve times. She compares him to choice fragrances, myrrh and henna (vv. 13-14), which by and large were not native to Canaan and had to be imported. Myrrh was used, among other things, as a cosmetic treatment on young girls preparing for sexual relations with their husbands-to-be (Esth 2:12). Because the springs of En-gedi made it a fertile oasis, such a site would have been an ideal lush garden for myrrh to grow.

The Hebrew in vv. 15-17 leaves open the possibility that two voices are heard here. Their words are precisely the kind of sweet talk lovers whisper to each other as they relax together. He admires her beauty (v. 15); she compliments him on being handsome (v. 16). With large broad trees towering above them, and with their leafy, green couch (or nuptial bed) spread beneath them, they are presumably ready for love. (See Reflections at 2:1-7.)

SONG OF SONGS 2:1-7, I ADJURE YOU

COMMENTARY

2:1-4. The popularity of v. 1 in Christian traditions as a metaphorical epithet for Jesus makes it disappointing to have to admit that we do not actually know much about the plants mentioned in v. 1. The KJV translates them "rose of Sharon" and "lily of the valley," and modern translators tend to follow suit. Ancient versions have not been helpful in determining the precise plant life cited. The problem is that the rose is actually a late transplant to the region, and there is no evidence that lilies ever really flourished in the area in any abundance.

Nevertheless, it seems certain that the protagonist is feigning modesty when she compares herself to *a* flower among many— namely, to one of a number of flowers that grow in Sharon and in valleys. Her lover counters that, in fact, she is more unique than she gives herself credit; indeed, she stands out among her peers (v. 2). She returns the compliment in v. 3*a* by reminiscing or fantasizing about rendezvous that turned into love feasts (the Hebrew is literally "wine house"). On those occasions, she exclaims, his "intentions," as seen in his eyes or "glance," are unmistakable (v. 4).

Marvin Pope argues that strong funerary echoes are evident throughout Song of Songs, prompting him to interpret the book as a text associated with funerary feasts common to the ancient Near East. Such love feasts, held to invoke fertility of the land, were celebrated with wine, women, and song.[19] Song of Songs celebrates the power of love over death (8:6), and, as seen in vv. 3-13, echoes language found in Ugaritic mythological and ritual texts in which sacrificial banquets, full of revelry and excesses, take on a funereal character as the gods become drunk almost to death. While Pope's interpretation of the book remains daring and debatable, there is no doubt that revelry, fantasy, and lightheartedness permeate much of the poetry.

Again, the protagonist delights in tantalizing the eavesdropper. This time she uses what appears to be a *double entendre,* which allows her to praise her lover while leaving those listening in to figure out her meaning (v. 3*b*): "With great delight I sat in his shadow, and his fruit was sweet to my taste." Exactly what was sweet to the protagonist's taste? An apple from the apple tree, or was it some part of her beloved's body? It is obviously something for the two of them to know—and the rest of us to find out.

2:5-7. The mere recall of their escapades and the very thought of his touch leaves her faint, flushed, and wistful (vv. 5-6). But greater still, we learn in v. 7, is the knowledge that love brings: "Daughters of Jerusalem, I charge you by the gazelles and by the does of the field: Do not arouse or awaken love until it so desires." In classic romance literature, of which Song of Songs can be viewed as something of a precursor, love is explored as the agent of a woman's self-development. Whereas men obtained their education, developed their identity, and matured in their consciousness through danger and a series of adventures, women turned to romance to achieve knowledge and the development of a higher level of consciousness. Similarly, in Song of Songs, the love-struck woman who earlier in the poem was lightheaded with passion becomes by 2:7 the worldly woman and savvy teacher. She passes her knowledge on to her impressionable female admirers. Love has taught her a few things about herself, about the opposite sex, about stolen intimacy, about love itself. She has learned that love

must be allowed to run its course, neither interfered with nor prematurely provoked.

Scholars have offered various proposals for interpreting v. 7: "I adjure you, O daughters of Jerusalem, by the gazelles or the wild does: do not stir up or awaken love until it is ready!" The phrase appears in two other places in the poem (3:5; 8:4). It has been translated variously as an admonition (a) not to arouse love prematurely (NRSV, NIV), (b) not to awaken the male love until "he" determines (KJV), (c) not to awaken or rouse the female protagonist until she pleases (NEB), (d) not to disturb their lovemaking until it is satiated.[20] Each translation represents an effort to see in this recurring phrase the *crux interpretum* to unlocking the otherwise elusive message of the entire book. Whatever its message, it is clear that there is a searching, unfulfilled, desperately longing mood to the entire book. The maiden's adjuration was probably formulaic and common to those who dwelled in desert settings: e.g., "I charge you by the gazelles and by the does of the field." In other words, we might say, "I beg you with everything within me." Of course, some of the imagery in the admonition appears in other contexts throughout the poetry: The male lover is associated with the swiftness and agility of gazelles in vv. 9, 17; the woman's breasts are compared to young fawns who browse (meaning probably "bounce" or "leap") among lilies.

In the end, the woman's experiences are supposed to serve as a lesson to her Jerusalem female friends. The admonition in v. 7 by the black-skinned woman not to interfere with love should be understood as a typical feature of women's romance literature, which offers a portrait of the love-worn but savvy female whose moral example becomes a prophylaxis, a warning and guide to the path of love for her sister neophytes (the Jerusalem daughters). The admonition represents the wisdom of a woman who has learned a lot about life and about herself through her experiences with "impeded" love. What exactly about love has she learned? For one thing, there is a time for love—a time to love and a time to wait for love. Perhaps it is her attempt, as a sage, to round out the litany of Qohelet (Eccl 3:1-8).

19. Pope, *Song of Songs,* 210-29.

20. Marcia Falk, *The Song of Songs: A New Translation and Interpretation* (San Francisco: HarperCollins, 1990) 164-76.

REFLECTIONS

Song of Songs can be a frustrating text to read for those who take seriously the responsibility to study and scrutinize God's Word. Zealous to be scrupulous exegetes and faithful interpreters, conscientious students of the Bible turn to commentaries for sober guidance into these sacred texts; but their zeal is met with equivocation and conjecture. A battery of questions is applied to each passage, and every word is weighed and studied; nonetheless, the book and its content refuse to submit easily to the arsenal of learned procedures we put them through. Song of Songs insists that we approach it on its own terms. Proving above all that language is rarely precise and emotions are hardly translatable, the love lyrics in the Song of Songs force serious, humorless religious types to get back in touch with the playfulness of the human spirit and the intensity of religious longing. As we listen in on lovers flirting with and teasing each other, whispering their deliciously oblique fantasies in each other's ears, and as we witness them playing hide-and-seek in each other's dreams, we are reminded of how resilient and trusting, and hence inscrutable, is the human heart.

We are warned against obstructing love. This is not the same as disturbing love. The consequences of the former can be more dire. Those who disturb love can be forgiven because what they do is frequently unintentional. But those who obstruct love, impede love, interfere with love—because of their own prejudices and fears—should beware. They do so at the risk of crushing lovers' enthusiasm, destroying lovers' faith in life, and bruising their sense of esteem. In this case the cliché that deserves repeating is: Human beings are born to love and to receive love. We are our happiest, our strongest, our most creative and most forgiving when we are in love. We are also our most confident and secure about ourselves as individuals when we know that we are loved unconditionally. In fact, our ability to love makes us capable of transcending our finitude, our humanity, our creatureliness. Our ability to love is also what makes us most like God. Part of what it means to be created "in the image of God" is to be capable of transcending oneself and loving another person unconditionally. Small wonder that at the center of both the OT and the NT is the repeated reminder that being a covenant people means loving God with all that is possible.

We have no transcripts of what were surely the many lively discussions about the propriety of including the ribald poetry of Song of Songs in the biblical canon. We are left only to wonder how it made its way into Scripture. Based on what criteria did those responsible decide it qualified as sacred, holy writ suffused with divine truth? It is unlikely that Solomonic authorship alone warranted its inclusion in the canon. The astute reader perceives something more. Its tale of love, courtship, compassion, intimacy, longing, and mutual delight resounds with many of the elements that characterize, according to the larger biblical drama, God's dealings with God's people. Bawdy, titillating, cryptic, and bordering sometimes on the lewd as the book may appear, the lovers' unpredictable love affair, which the poet tries desperately to capture—characterized by halts, jerks, lurches, twitches, and inconstancy—shows remarkable parallels with the history of the relationship between human and divine love. Powerful lessons await its readers. Seeing our relationship with God through the eyes of frustrated, but desperate, lovers, however baffling their behavior, forces us to ponder the powerful emotions underlying the divine-human bond: what it means to be demanding, yet fickle, desperate, but timid; what it means to wound those we love and to be wounded by love; what it means to disappoint those we love and to be disappointed by love; and what it means to be hopelessly attached to each other and trying to hear what the other is saying.

The Song of Songs provides its audience glimpses into two human beings' efforts at perfecting human love and building intimacy and the lessons they learn about themselves and each other along the way.

MY BELOVED IS MINE, AND I AM HIS

COMMENTARY

L overs are notoriously possessive. They demand to know each other's whereabouts, they insist upon commitment, they expect accountability, and they take advantage of every opportunity to remind each other, and those in earshot, of their special claims upon each other. Nowhere is their possessiveness more apparent than in the choice of pet names they use to describe each other. The protagonist consistently refers to her anonymous male lover throughout the book, beginning in 2:1-3, as "my lover" (NIV) or "my beloved" (NRSV). Elsewhere she refers affectionately to him as "my friend" (5:16) and "he whom my soul loves" (1:7; 3:1-4).

The suitor's store of pet names for his love is more inventive and diverse. He relies on a plethora of epithets to address the woman: "fairest among women" (1:8; 5:9; 6:1); "my darling" or "my love" (1:9, 15; 2:10, 13; 4:1, 7; 5:2; 6:4); "my fair one" or "my beautiful one" (2:10, 13); "my dove" (2:14; 5:2; 6:9); "my perfect one" or "my flawless one" (5:2; 6:9), and so on. His epithets for her, and those she applies to him, all have one very important thing in common: They are preceded by the first-person singular possessive pronoun "my." Nine occurrences of the pronoun "my" within a span of nine verses (vv. 8-17) is not a trivial matter, even in Song of Songs. This is not simply an example of the romantic drivel typical of new lovers. Something more is at stake here and throughout the poem. In fact, the more than fifty occurrences of "my" throughout this brief poem strongly suggests that they are not just asserting their mutual devotion: The lovers are *insisting* on it. To her, he is "my lover" (vv. 8, 9, 10, 16, 17 NIV). But to him, she is "my darling" (vv. 10, 13), "my beautiful one" (v. 10), "my dove" (v. 14). Perhaps they expect their audience

to disapprove of their union. Perhaps they are aware that some might question the propriety of their relationship. Was theirs a forbidden union? Were they, because of class, ethnic, or economic differences, an unlikely pair? What did they have to prove? The poetry to this point is elusive, but tantalizing, about the matter. We will have to wait for answers. In the meantime, again and again the two lovers declare their exclusive affection for each other, a declaration that climaxes in the beautiful "formula of mutual belonging" that we find in v. 16 and in altered form elsewhere in the poem: "My lover is mine and I am his" (דודי לי ואני לו *dôdî lî waʾănî lô*; cf. 6:3; 7:10). Here the Hebrew is both elliptic and unequivocal: "My lover to me and I to him."

Taken as a whole, the unit rhapsodizes the feeling of love that spring brings. The gifts of spring rain are everywhere. The sight of sprinting animals (vv. 8-9), the smell of figs and vines (v. 13), the sound of birds singing (v. 12), the feel of fresh flowers and new buds (v. 12) are enough to arouse love in the most cynical of persons. With springtime comes belief in new adventures, new possibilities, and, most of all, a new outlook on life. Even forbidden love looks different when viewed against the backdrop of spring rain, sprinting animals, budding flowers and vines, and the sound of chirping birds.

Drawing on the intoxicating feelings that nature and spring arouse, the shepherd refers to this time as "the season of singing" (v. 12), when the sound of the turtledoves can be heard throughout the land. No one wants to be unloved at this time of year, when all of nature is aroused to newness. He beckons her to come away with him (v. 13). But as usual, he is vague and does not specify exactly where he wants to take her. He changes the subject by asking to hear her voice (v. 14).

In fact, this unit is filled with the sound of the lovers' voices. Each luxuriates in the sound of the other's voice. She hears his "voice" (lit., "sound" [קוֹל *qôl*]) before she actually sees him approaching from just over the mountains (v. 8). His words are what the ears of every lovestruck maiden yearns to hear: "Arise and come" (v. 10). We cannot be sure whether this is an actual quotation or simply what she imagines him saying on the day he arrives. From v. 10 to v. 15 the maiden replays the words of her beloved. Twice he encourages her to depart with him ("Arise, my love, my fair one, and come away," vv. 10, 13). With her safely in his arms, he imagines in v. 14 that he can luxuriate in the sound of her voice and in the loveliness of what both the NRSV and the NIV have translated as "face," but is more accurately "appearance" (מראה *mar'eh*; cf. 5:15). One might expect the shepherd to comment directly on the maiden's face or complexion in the light of her own defensive remarks in 1:5. But he does not. (For more discussion of his silence, see Commentary on 4:1–5:1.)

To keep the audience at bay, the lovers speak to each other in riddles: "Catch for us the foxes, the little foxes, that ruin the vineyards, our vineyards that are in bloom" (v. 15). One commentator has referred to this statement as "a saucy reply to the lover."[21] It may be saucy, but just how saucy, we may never know. The riddle's meaning is obscure. Some interpreters have understood it as a quotation of a well-known ditty that cryptically observes the manner in which foxes (young men) notoriously despoil the blooming vineyards (ripening female sexuality).[22] Others see in this verse a more ominous meaning, one in which the foxes are not prowling young men, but threatening city guards who take advantage of defenseless women on the streets (3:3).[23] The overall mood of this unit

seems not to support Falk's ominous reading of the riddle, however. From beginning (v. 8) to end (vv. 16-17), the protagonist is not emphasizing danger, but seduction. Throughout she tries to woo the shepherd with promises of her anticipation. Both delight in sustaining the suspense between them by talking in riddles and romantic cryptograms. The reference to "foxes" and "vineyards" is probably an allusion to their cunning stratagems to find opportunities to consummate their blossoming love while attempting simultaneously to avoid detection by others. They belong together; they belong to each other (v. 16). Her suitor rightfully "pastures," says the maiden, among the most delicate flower of all, the lily, the black-skinned maiden herself (cf. "lily of the valley" in 2:1).

Finally, the black-skinned maiden is not shy about trying to pin her elusive lover down on a time for them to meet. By the passage's end, she proposes the allure and romance of an evening rendezvous (v. 17) instead of a daytime tryst (1:7): "Until the day breaks and the shadows flee" (NIV). Her words from the beginning of the passage to its end echo one another. In both the opening (v. 8) and closing (v. 17) lines, she compares her lover to a gazelle and a stag who bound over hillsides. (The same imagery reappears in the final verse of the book, 8:14.) His swift, agile movements are of the sort that make young maidens imagine prowess and attribute strength to their lovers. The unit is dominated by her yearning, her imaginings of his presence, her fantasies of his seduction, her response to his diffidence, her imploring him to tread carefully. She commences her remarks by announcing his arrival (v. 8); she closes her remarks by shooing him away (v. 17). She urges him to hold off their consummation until a more opportune time, late evening. Her hesitation is unclear to us. But her passion is constant. As often as she beckons him to her, for reasons unknown she shoos him away until a later time.

21. Murphy, *The Song of Songs*, 141.
22. Murphy, *The Song of Songs*, 141; Pope, *Song of Songs*, 402-5.
23. See Falk, *The Song of Songs*, 178.

REFLECTIONS

The love lyrics in Song of Songs are ideal for examining the pull and tug of romantic and spiritual commitment. The story of the beguiling young maiden and her skittish shepherd lover can be used as a thoughtful text for probing the dread of living in committed, covenant union. The book reminds us that intimacy can be as frightening as it is fulfilling. It is fraught with dangers, unknowns, demands, and unforeseeable consequences. Not simply a commentary on the fragility of human intimacy, the work captures the dilemma of the divine-human drama.

The Bible is full of stories of people who play hide-and-seek with God's calling. Their faith falters, their obedience is short-lived, their worship wanes, and their commitment must be tested and reestablished again and again. The stories of Elijah withdrawing to a lonely cave, Jeremiah refusing to preach, Jonah sailing away to Tarshish, and Paul prowling the Damascus road are stories of men who went to extraordinary lengths to resist God's claim upon them. But before we see Song of Songs solely as an indictment of the inconstancy of commitment to and love for God, we would do well to pause and consider its honesty. These brief nine verses remind us that human-human relationships, like human-divine relations, must be cultivated, nurtured, safeguarded, and cherished. Special moments do not just happen; they are cultivated. Intimacy with God and with each other costs; it costs us our time and our energies. A willingness to be present, to remain, to be accountable, to see things through, to come out from hiding are necessary to nurture relationships.

Lovers cannot take their love for granted, no more than humans can take their relationship with God for granted. We must take care to spend time with those we love and to find time to talk with each other. Like lovers in search of the perfect time and place to mate, care should be given to creating an atmosphere in which conversation and intimacy can thrive. "Mindfulness," "attentiveness," and "dailiness" are popular terms within our culture to remind us that beauty, love, joy, abundance, the sacred, and the possibility for happiness surround us in the ordinary routines of human living if we would only take the time to notice and nurture them. The sound of children's laughter, the thoughtful gesture of a lover, the sound of church bells in the distance, the gentle breeze across the face after a day at the office, an unexpected call from a childhood friend, a helping hand from a stranger, a "thank you" from an admirer, the smell of fresh-baked bread, and the sight of fresh flowers on the nightstand are just a few of the gifts "angels" strew daily along our path. Straining as we do, like the lovers in Cant 2:14, to behold beauty and to hear the sacred in our routines, we must take care to lean closer and see God's face and to hear God's voice in our lives.

In preaching and teaching on this and other portions of the Song of Songs, modern interpreters should not be put off or intimidated by the titillating direction of the poetry. Readers should relax and enjoy the poet's playful use of language and exploration of human emotions. Allow the lovers' playful jostle back and forth and curious speech to inspire thinking about the way figurative and coded speech creates special memories for intimates. It might be a worthwhile exercise for preachers and teachers to listen to the way they try to tell their audiences about God's love for humankind. What imagery is repeatedly used? What language stirs an audience's emotions? From whence does language receive its power to make an impact on an audience? When do you know that the language has connected with your audience? Perhaps we should try rewriting the love story between God and human creation in our own modern jargon and imagery, comparing our images of God and ourselves, our symbols for love and passion with those of our biblical ancestors. What do human connectedness and intimacy look like to us? What do they feel like? To what do we compare them? What does this tell us about ourselves?

Song of Songs is an ideal text for comparing the changing history and context of romantic talk. The poet uses the language and imagery of a rustic, semi-pastoral culture to evoke passion and desire. Comparisons to goats, gazelles, and apple trees sound strange to those of us who reside in parts of the country where neighborhoods are treeless, apartment complexes have no lawns, and we ride underground in the earth's belly to get to our windowless downtown offices. We do not recognize seduction of the Song of Songs sort when we hear it. Our lives are too hurried and harried to bother with cryptograms from another time and another culture. And while it may be true that much of the speech in this little book is hopelessly lost on our modern ears because it does not speak to our experience, we must admit that our own language for intimacy is equally lost on those unfamiliar with our culture. How does a generation flatter and woo one another when they are raised on microwave ovens, computers, fax machines, voice mail, the Internet, camcorders, electronic games, space fantasies, and overnight express mail? How do they talk about love? "You've pushed the right button," perhaps. Or "My hormones are in warp speed for you"? The maiden and her suitor of Song of Songs would stagger down the slopes of En-gedi in amazement and laughter at the sound of twenty-first-century erotic speech.

I LOOKED FOR HIM BUT DID NOT FIND HIM

COMMENTARY

When evening comes and the shepherd has not arrived, the maiden takes to the streets to search for her lover. Desperation, supplication, and longing fill this unit, and the audience is invited to ponder the experience of the distraught woman.

Scores of questions race through the maiden's mind as she scours the streets and squares of Jerusalem searching for her lover. Has she shooed her lover away this time, only to lose him forever? Where is he? Is he lost? Is he hiding? Why can he not be found? Will he return? She wonders now about the wisdom of putting him off until evening, a time she thought more auspicious for lovemaking (2:17). "Have you seen him whom my soul loves?" she anxiously inquires of the sentinels who guard the city at night (v. 3; the Hebrew actually reads more poetically and archaically: "Him whom my soul loves, have you seen?"). Her desperation touches her audience. Our emotions go out to her. We are as frustrated as she. "Where in God's creation is he?" we wonder aloud. How long will they continue to put each other off?

At last, it seems, the black-skinned woman finds her lover (v. 4*a*). We sigh with her. She holds him close, promising never again to let him go, determined to bring him into the house of her mother, into the very chambers where she herself was conceived (v. 4*b*). This expression "to my mother's house" (אל־בית אמי *'el-bêt'immî,* v. 4; 8:2) is odd, given the enormous emphasis throughout the Old Testament on the "father's house" (בית אב *bêt 'āb*), the patriarchal family compound.[24] With the emphasis in Song of Songs on family

and with imagery drawn from the private omain, one would expect some reference to *bêt 'āb,* the place where a daughter's chastity was protected and controlled by the father or male head of household. But the Song of Songs is the poetry of domesticity and not the poetry of domination (cf. Gen 24:28; Ruth 1:8). It focuses on the private world of women's interior emotions and experiences. The references to the "mother's house" symbolize the private, enclosed world of women's secrets and sexuality. Where the maiden intends to lure her lover is no place for fathers, brothers, uncles, or other male guardians. The "chambers of her who conceived me" are where women's secret rituals, fantasies, speech, and private dramas (e.g., bathing, having babies) take place.

Once the maiden finds her lover, we hold our breath. We wonder if in her "mother's house" the two lovers will finally be able to consummate their love. She holds him, but can she keep him? She has him now, but will he stay? Is this a dream, or is it real? What is the point of the cat-and-mouse game the two lovers seem bent upon playing? How are contemporary audiences, accustomed to tales of speedy romance and uninhibited passion, supposed to read this story of frustrated love?

In a culture where casual sexual relations were virtually unheard of, where it was difficult for lovers to find opportunities to satisfy their lust, where social contact between the sexes was strictly limited, where lovers exchanged glances more than they did kisses, love songs about thwarted love affairs took on mythological proportions. (The kind of myths mentioned above tend also to reinforce the culture's attitudes about courtship and romance.) Delayed gratification was the rule in antiquity, not the exception. Unmarried

---

24. For a helpful discussion of the presence of "mother's house" over the customary "father's house" in Song of Songs, see Carol Meyers, *Discovering Eve: Ancient Israelite Women in Context* (New York: Oxford University Press, 1988) 177-81.

couples were not free to indulge their appetites for each other when and however they wanted, nor could married couples, for that matter (see Lev 18:19). Ancient audiences, thus, were enthralled by poetry like Song of Songs because it captured the longing, heightened the tension, gave drama to the pursuit, and reinforced the promise of awaiting ecstasy. In antiquity, love lyrics were not expected to describe the consummation of love, but the anticipation of its consummation. Some things were better left to the audience's imagination. Whereas modern audiences cannot figure out why the two lovers do things that forestall their getting together—he comes, and she puts him off; she inquires about his whereabouts, and he does not say; he invites her to come with him, but he does not say where—ancient audiences would have been patient with their failed attempts at love and amused by their blunders. Impediments and obstacles were typical devices of ancient love lyricists, designed to sustain the audience's interest in the subject and heighten the tension of the drama.

Parallel accounts of searching and finding, or not finding, for example, appear in romantic lore of neighboring cultures in antiquity. In Mesopotamian hymns and myths, Ishtar, the goddess of love and sexuality, supposedly travels to the netherworld in search of her lover, Dumuzi. On the way she contends with inimical forces and eventually meets up with him. Their meeting ends in a sacred marriage that was ritualized in the mating of the king with a sacred prostitute as a way of regenerating the fertile forces of nature. A similar motif appears in the Ugaritic myth of Anat's search for the body of her consort, Baal, who has been killed by Mot ("Death"). Upon finding Baal, Anat buries him and mourns him by inflicting wounds upon her own body. When the irate Anat avenges her lover's death and destroys Mot, Baal is revived and restored to power. In each of these texts, the female protagonist is the fierce, aggressive, and zealous one who sets out on a dangerous journey to find her missing comrade, rescuing him from opposing forces, restoring him to his rightful place of power, or, as in the case of Song of Songs, receiving him into her arms as her consummate lover.

Finally, when the maiden exhorts her audience again to be patient with love, not to interfere prematurely with love, not to launch into love unadvisedly (v. 5), she is cautioning an audience already accustomed to postponing sexual pleasure. She is reminding them of what they know only too well: Love is a powerful force that should not be rushed into or provoked.

REFLECTIONS

Modern readers may tire of this roller-coaster love affair—now you see him, now you don't; now she has him, now she doesn't. We are not accustomed to delaying our passion. We are impatient with indecisive lovers and bored by repeatedly frustrated love scenes. In our sexually liberated culture, we do not understand unconsummated love affairs. "What is the problem with these two people?" we ask ourselves. Now that the protagonist has finally seized her lover and suggestively beckoned him and her audience toward the room where her own mother conceived her, do we dare allow ourselves to anticipate their passion?

The challenge for preachers and teachers alike is to use the Song of Songs as a way of reclaiming some of the virtue of patience, the wisdom of delayed gratification, and the joy of exploring each other's hearts long before we explore each other's bodies. This text is ideal for exploring new ways of discovering and building human intimacy, because it begins by celebrating and delighting in the human body. We are not asked, as in so much banal religious literature, to deny our need for physical contact and communion. Song of Songs takes the body seriously. But it also takes seriously that we are more than a body. Relationships cannot survive when they are based solely on physical attraction. Song of Songs, with its constant use of dialogue and conversation, riddles and allusions, reminds us of the importance of learning how to talk and how to listen to each other. Those who turn to this poetry for profound theological insight into the nature of God, the character of the divine, the lessons of the Christian faith (e.g., grace, mercy, free will, sovereign love) should not dismiss its teachings about what it means to live and to love as human beings. We can learn from the ancient audiences. One thing we can learn is to listen for the unspoken gestures of human communication.

One cannot help admiring the aggressive measures the protagonist takes to find her missing lover. She risks her life and reputation to find him (3:1-3). She is not daunted by the fact that she is female and that certain aggressions in women are unacceptable in her culture. She knows what she wants, and she goes after him. Better yet, she knows what belongs to her, and she searches for him. Love forces us to stretch beyond our boundaries, beyond our narrow self-interests, beyond our comfort zones. Love encourages us to take risks, to embrace other ways of thinking, other ways of being, and other ways of doing.

Again, our ability to love is the very quality that makes us most like God. We learn what it means to go to extraordinary lengths to reclaim our lovers. The search for a lover reminds those of us who read this poem with theological eyes how very precious love is. When you find it, do everything in your power to keep it. God, who is love, has created us to be able to give and to receive love.

Song of Songs reminds us that nothing in our upbringing prepares us for love's rocky journey. It is a journey filled with valleys and peaks, requiring of the lovers enormous patience with and commitment to each other. Love is something that must be worked at, sought after, and fought for. When it eludes the lovers, disappearing from their bedroom, escaping their embrace, it must be pursued, hunted down, recaptured, and brought back into their domain. Not only with lovers, but also in humans' relationship with God, closeness and intimacy must be nurtured. It cannot be taken for granted, nor is it a given. Human beings must be as vigilant about their relationship with God as they presumably are about their relationships with each other.

SONG OF SONGS 3:6-11

WHO IS THIS COMING UP FROM THE DESERT?

COMMENTARY

Scholars have frequently observed that this section interrupts the poetry with its description of an ornate wedding ceremony. In the preceding unit, the woman describes her desperate search for her lover (3:1-5). In the unit that follows (4:1–5:1), the man describes the physical charms of the woman. At first glance, the lofty procession recounted in vv. 6-11 seems premature, if not out of place. Seeing the unit, however, as the protagonist's fantasy about her wedding day, when she will finally be given license to do precisely what she can only wish to do in v. 4—that is, to steer her lover into her secret chambers—we can forgive the unit its abruptness. Fantasies are by nature unpredictable.

The scenery described in these verses is her daydream, a wedding scene reminiscent of the days of Solomon, when, in the light of the king's marriages to hundreds of women, lavish wedding processions with imposing military formations were a common sight on the streets of Jerusalem. Although we have no information from the OT about how ancient wedding ceremonies were actually conducted, we can see here in Song of Songs, especially in the description of the ornate carriage with its silver, gold, and purple upholstery and its cedar (v. 10), just how lavish and imposing a sight royal weddings were. (The pomp and circumstance associated with royal weddings are hinted at in Psalm 45.) Undoubtedly, special lyrics were composed for the occasion, parts of which have been incorporated into the book of Song of Songs.

Exactly who or what is being hailed by the speaker in v. 6? Solomon? The female protagonist? The "litter" (bed) of Solomon? The NIV translates the interrogative literally as "who." But one does not find in v. 7 a specific person stepping forward and identifying himself or herself, as one does in Isa 63:1, where a similar phrase appears. Instead, a procession is described ("Look!"), one associated with Solomon, which has led some translators to render the interrogative, following an Akkadian precedent, more accurately as, "What is this coming up from the wilderness?"

The question in v. 6 is the kind posed by sentries to persons, parties, or caravans as they drew near the city gates, or by inhabitants as strangers drew near their quarters. In this context, the question may have been ceremonially posed to an approaching wedding caravan, hailing the arrival of an awe-inspiring wedding procession as it drew near the awaiting guests. The military procession described in vv. 7-8 suggests that the bridegroom's party is arriving. Exactly why the procession is described as originating in the "desert" (NIV) or the "wilderness" (NRSV) remains uncertain. (If v. 6 represents the manner in which the bridegroom would have been hailed upon arrival at the ceremony, the parallel greeting for the approaching bride and her bridal procession may be found in 6:10: "Who is this that looks forth like the dawn?"; see note there.)

Although one is tempted to see the bridegroom and his party as the subject of vv. 6-11, the mention of an approaching "litter," or bed, naturally suggests a woman's being hoisted upon a canopy and carried ceremonially and suggestively into the wedding service. It seems, however, that the bridegroom is being hoisted onto the bed and carried to his awaiting bride. Such imagery would certainly be in keeping with the protagonist's earlier wish (3:4) that her lover be brought into her intimate chambers.

Furthermore, the mention of Solomon's name in v. 7 should not be taken literally, but as part of the lyrics of the song. It is yet another oblique term of endearment that a bride might use to compliment her lover for his dashing, romantic, regal side. A modern parallel might be to call a man "Romeo."

By now, the royal bridegroom is decked in attire befitting a king and warrior who is confident in his power. Surrounded by a swarm of virginal attendants, the bride, herself of royal heritage according to her daydream, is brought before the king adorned in embroidered garments and gold ornaments. So resplendent is the whole occasion that the Jerusalem daughters are urged to come out (vv. 10-11) and behold the bridegroom ("Solomon") and the entire wedding party, which by now presumably includes the bride.

"The crown with which his mother crowned him" (v. 11) does not apply exclusively to royal wedding ceremonies, but, as Robert Gordis has pointed out, to the standard headpiece worn during marriage ceremonies by both bride and groom in antiquity.[25] As for the reference to Solomon's mother (v. 11), mothers figure prominently in the protagonist's development of her female and sexual

identities in Song of Songs. On the one hand, her own mother serves as the role model for her sexual identity, providing her with the charms and chambers for seduction (v. 4). On the other hand, the mother who gave birth to the bridegroom "crowned" him with life and conjugal possibilities. In a patriarchal culture, a mother's approval of her son's marriage was not necessary, since arranging marriages was largely in the hands of the male head of the house. However, it was signally important to have the mother-in-law's blessing, since brides upon marriage moved to their husband's locality, frequently in the compound where his father and mother lived.

Wedding ceremonies in ancient Israel were meant to be lavish occasions where each class attempted to approximate as much as it could afford the most ideal of all ceremonies, the royal wedding. In every culture and in every generation, women (and men) imagine their wedding day, when in the pageantry and splendor befitting their love, they are united with their sweethearts in everlasting bonds. We see here in the sketchy details of 3:1-5 how very much the black-skinned woman, in her fantasy of her wedding day, was a product of her culture.

25. Robert Gordis, *The Song of Songs: A Study, Modern Translation, and Commentary*, TextsS 20 (New York: Jewish Theological Seminary of America, 1954) 56.

REFLECTIONS

For those who are married, Song of Songs is a reminder of how naive and idealistic we were on our wedding day. We look back on our wedding photos at the slim, dashing young man with a full head of hair and the svelte, glowing young woman, and we say to ourselves, "Gosh, were we naive!" By luring those of us who are married into reliving our wedding day, and by enticing those not married to imagine that day, Song of Songs reminds us of what it means to pledge to live one's life with only one other individual. A man and a woman pledge to submit to each other and to expose his or her wounded self to each other for scrutiny and healing. We promise to allow our two lives to be melded into one brand-new life together. The man and woman in Song of Songs remind us of how much passion, enthusiasm, and utter idealism it takes to believe such things are even possible.

Throughout the Bible, marriage is viewed as the most sublime metaphor for the relationship between God and human beings. Old Testament prophets—Hosea, Jeremiah, Ezekiel—and others used marriage to symbolize the intimacy, love, and devotion characteristic of the covenant union between Yahweh and Israel. The author of the book of Ephesians relied on marriage imagery to describe the union between Christ and the church (Eph 5:25-33), noting that the union between man and woman, like the one between Christ and the church, is a mystery. Jesus himself told a parable in which a wedding feast became the symbolic setting for the coming of the kingdom (Matthew 22). Marriage is an apt metaphor for capturing the divine-human relationship because it captures best all the vicissitudes of trying to live faithfully and spontaneously with the Other. It is the closest bond possible for two human beings, one that teaches both partners lessons about grace, forgiveness, constancy, submission, and love. The love poetry in Song of Songs reminds us of how crazy, how innocent, how ardent is the passion that brings human beings together. But this one glimpse into the protagonist's fantasy also reminds us of how preposterous, how unthinkable, how supernatural is the actual union that takes place, often years after the ceremony is over, when passion fades and true love has a chance to emerge.

In marriage, each partner is given the opportunity to see one person as he or she has never seen another person before. Living as a child in a parent's home does not quite prepare a person for marriage. Neither does living with someone outside the bonds of marriage ensure that once married, one has a jump on marriage. Marriage, as a union of articulated vows and commitments, allows an individual the context in which to glimpse into the heart and soul of another, to behold another's nakedness and vulnerabilities, to handle and to nurse another's wounds and bruises. A covenant vow is needed to embark on this kind of undertaking, for it acknowledges that it takes an act of will *and* a power greater than two frail parties to prevent either or both from abandoning the tedious work that lies ahead. Physical attraction may draw the two together, but it will take a supernatural attraction to keep them together—in love. And while it is true that living in covenant union with another human being may prove the most unglamorous, exacting, and excruciating work a person will ever undertake, it is also the most extraordinary effort one can engage in. Behold, it is a mystery!

SONG OF SONGS 4:1–5:1

HOW BEAUTIFUL YOU ARE, MY LOVE

OVERVIEW

I f there is any connection between the wedding scene that the protagonist fantasizes about and the lover's celebration of the beloved's body in 4:1–5:1, it is this: The flattery and praise he lavishes upon her in this unit are the stuff of wedding-night seductions. The shepherd extols the woman's beauty (4:1*a*), he admires her eyes (4:1*b*), he praises her hair (4:1*c*), he compliments her teeth (4:2), he relishes her lips and mouth (4:3*a*), he delights in her cheeks (4:3*b*), he loves her neck (4:4), and he fawns over her breasts (4:5). Hers is the kind of beauty, he says in 4:6-8, that draws him to her. As a

shepherd, he uses the native gifts of the desert to describe his lover's beauty (e.g., fauna, pomegranate, the landscapes of Gilead). His lavish bodily compliments, known as *waṣfs*, based on parallels with Syrian nuptial songs that poetically describe and celebrate a beloved's body, are unheard of elsewhere in Scripture. Of the four *waṣfs* in Song of Songs (4:1-7; 5:10-16; 6:4-10; 7:1-9), three focus on the beauty of the woman's body (4:1-7; 6:4-10; 7:1-9). This one, belonging as it does to a larger paean to her beauty, is striking in both what it says and what it does not say.

SONG OF SONGS 4:1-8, A WOMAN'S BEAUTY

COMMENTARY

After luxuriating in her beauty, the beloved hastens to the woman's scented bosom (v. 6, "mountain of myrrh and hill of frankincense"). The Hebrew word for "frankincense" (לבונה *lĕbônâ*), which appears also in 3:6, plays on the mountain name "Lebanon" and reappears in vv. 8 and 15. Overcome, the beloved beckons his "bride" to depart with him from known mountain sites to unspecified parts.

In his eyes, the maiden is perfect. But judging by the kind of imagery he uses to describe her, one thing is certain: Beauty is in the eyes of the beholder. Even more, seduction and erotica are culturally specific. For example, comparing beauty to the slopes of Gilead, halves of pomegranate, flocks of goats and ewes coming up from the washing, and

a thousand bucklers on the tower of David is alien to the modern (Western) reader. Not only are seduction and erotica contextually determined, but also love talk can be especially frustrating to decode. While it is obvious that Lebanon, Amana, the peak of Senir, and Hermon are mountainous regions, exactly why these are peculiarly ominous places for his beloved to be wandering is all but lost on us. Presumably, predatory animals roam the peaks of these mountains, making them dangerous for both lover and beloved.

Even so, might these place-names be his way of talking metaphorically about what he sees as her own inaccessibility? Typical twelfth-century courtly love poems, for example, focused on the theme of *amor de lonh,* love from far away, where love between a knight and his lady was unattainable and endlessly frustrated. Lovers in these lays are perpetually confronted externally and internally by obstacles, dangers, and impediments.[26] This theme continues to influence even modern androcentric literature, in which "men idealize women as the beautiful but unattainable *object*."[27] Nevertheless, his lover's inaccessibility and unattainability only add to the feverish desire of her beloved: "You have ravished my heart, my sister, my bride, you have ravished my heart" (v. 9).

Idiosyncratic as his descriptions of her body are, we have every reason to believe that comparisons to goats and slopes, to crimson thread and buckler shields, and to dangerous mountainsides were enough of an aphrodisiac to woo the heart of a young maiden and melt any resistance on her part. They were probably also stirring enough to convince any detractors of the shepherd's sincerity.

Oddly enough, the lover's compliments of his maiden stand in sharp contrast to her own defensive comments. In 1:6 she demanded that her onlookers not stare at her. While she did not apologize for her complexion, she did defend her black skin tone. So lavish is the shepherd's praise of the maiden's body, however, that one cannot help wondering who he is trying to convince. His beloved? Himself? Outsiders? Probably the latter. After all, lyrical poetry is frequently written to sway audiences as much as to entertain them.

26. Baruch, *Women, Love, and Power*, 49.
27. See Elaine Hoffman Baruch and Lucienne J. Serrano, *Women Analyze Women: In France, England, and the United States* (New York: New York University Press, 1988) 327; see also Baruch's chapter, "He Speaks/She Speaks: Language in Some Medieval Love Literature," in *Women, Love, and Power*, 31-51.

One clue that something more is at stake in his poetry is the lover's claim that his darling is not only "altogether beautiful" in his eyes, but also "flawless" (v. 7). That is strong language, spoken perhaps to counter strong reservations on the part of his audience. He is quick to elaborate on his opinion of his lover's physical virtues (vv. 9-15).

Notice, however, that while the black-skinned woman defends her complexion in 1:5, the shepherd extols every part of her body except her complexion. While the woman's race or complexion is not the chief focus of the book, it would be inaccurate to assume that color played no role in standards of beauty, health, and social acceptability (cf. Miriam and Moses' Ethiopian wife in Numbers 12). Ancient lyricists were indeed aware of color differences and preferences. But the emphasis of Song of Songs is not on color so much as it is on the pain and power of love. Although the book opens with the maiden's somewhat defensive comments about her skin color (1:5-6), it seems odd that her suitor never addresses directly the matter of her color. With so much care given in this praise song to elaborating on the details of her body, one would expect to find in 4:1-15 some flattering comment about her complexion. One cannot deny the significance of his silence. Perhaps he did not think the matter worth commenting on; or perhaps dwelling on other aspects of her beauty and charm (i.e., eyes, hair, teeth, lips, cheeks, neck, scent) was the shepherd's way of rebuffing his critics and making it clear what attributes had for him the greater allure. In his eyes, she is "flawless" (v. 7). (See Reflections at 4:16–5:1.)

SONG OF SONGS 4:9-15, A LOCKED GARDEN

COMMENTARY

The Hebrew verb (לבב *lbb*) used in v. 9 to describe the maiden's effect upon the shepherd can be interpreted in two ways: "to hearten" or "to dishearten." In this case, "hearten" makes the most sense, and both the NRSV ("you have ravished my heart") and the NIV ("you have stolen my heart") make gallant

efforts to capture the meaning here. Put differently, his "sister" and "bride" has turned him on. "Sister" is a popular term of endearment in Egyptian love poetry. It no more suggests that the two lovers are siblings than does the word *baby*, shared by modern lovers, suggest an incestuous relationship between the two.

"Bride" picks up on the wedding imagery introduced in chapter 3. Interestingly, of the ten times in the OT in which the word *bride* appears, six are in Song of Songs. All six occurrences appear in 4:8–5:1. Both "sister" and "bride" are terms not only of endearment, but also of intimacy.

In vv. 9-15, the lover abandons fauna metaphors and takes up flora metaphors. Not only is he a skillful lover, but also he is a versatile poet. Because the fruits and spices to which he compares his beloved are more familiar to us, we modern readers are better able to appreciate the scents and taste of romance evoked here: wine and spice (v. 10), nectar (v. 11a), honey and milk (v. 11b), cedar wood (v. 11c, "scent of Lebanon"), pomegranates and henna (v. 13), myrrh and aloes (v. 14). These are the fragrances and spices one expects to find in a "garden."

The repeated mention of "garden" in Song of Songs has prompted more than one feminist scholar to interpret the latter as an echo of and a redeeming counterpoint to the "love story that goes awry" in the garden in Genesis 2–3.[28] Indeed, this entire poetic unit in Song of Songs has been categorized by more than one scholar as something of a "garden poem" in which the garden metaphor extends throughout as the ideal symbol of love. Lush with erotic imagery (e.g., flowers, spices, and delectable fruits), the garden is both the ideal place for sexual consummation and a metaphor for the woman's fertility. As for the physical garden described in Song of Songs, the unlikelihood that such a lush, variegated growth of plants and trees could have grown or been sustained in this region should pose no problem for the imagination. But that is the whole point of poetry: It specializes in the exaggerated, the extreme, the evocative—not in statistics, formalism, and the concrete. Rightly called a "utopian, fantasy-garden,"[29] the emphasis here is not on the known entity, but on an unknown, mysterious, unique place for love. The garden, therefore, is both the place to which they escape together and the place mentioned as a "well of living water" (v. 15), perhaps hinting at the flood of human body fluids that accompany arousal.

More interesting information could be cited on the garden image in the Song of Songs. Repeatedly, the woman, or some part of her anatomy, is referred to as a "garden" (4:12, 15-16; 5:1; 6:2, 11). In one instance, she is a "garden locked, a fountain sealed" (NRSV), a subtle allusion to the black-skinned woman's mystery and chastity. (The Targum, Midrash Rabbah, and Christian interpreters have interpreted "locked" and "sealed" as emphasizing the woman's virginity.) The NIV follows other ancient manuscripts (e.g., the Septuagint, the Vulgate, and Syriac) in changing the parallel word from "garden" (גַּן *gan*) to "spring" or "fountain" (גַּל *gal*). Of course, seeing it as the latter picks up the connotation in Proverbs, where, in a series of warnings against adultery, "fountain" can be understood as referring to sexual intimacy:

> Should your springs be scattered abroad,
>   streams of water in the streets?
> Let them be for yourself alone,
>   and not for sharing with strangers.
> Let your fountain be blessed,
>   and rejoice in the wife of your youth,
>   a lovely deer, a graceful doe.
>   (Prov 5:16-19 NRSV)

(See Reflections at 4:16–5:1.)

---

28. See, e.g., Trible, *God and the Rhetoric of Sexuality*, 144-65.

29. Murphy, *The Song of Songs*, 161.

SONG OF SONGS 4:16–5:1, THE SCENT OF A WOMAN

COMMENTARY

Whether the black-skinned woman is mysterious or virginal (or both), the shepherd-lover will not be deterred. With the fragrance of her body stirring in the breeze (4:16), he gladly comes and immerses himself in the maiden's taste and smells (5:1). For the reader who appreciates subtlety and modesty, the man's language invites the mind to volley between the literal and the figurative. What in his "garden" might he be eating and drinking that tastes of myrrh and spice, honeycomb and honey, wine and milk? We can only guess and blush.

Finally, an anonymous but welcome voice encourages "friends" to eat and drink until they are satiated. Taste your fill of love, the anonymous voice admonishes. Is it the voice of the daughters of Jerusalem (5:1*b*)? We do not know.

REFLECTIONS

It is curious to note that a book that on the surface seems to celebrate human sexuality and luxuriate in the female body would come to be interpreted over the centuries by some parts of Christendom as a tract for renouncing fleshly passions. For example, for many years ascetics have seen in 4:1–5:1 a call to renounce the prevailing sociopolitical hegemonic structures of their day and to withdraw into the austere, disciplined life of monasticism. For these "dissidents," Song of Songs has epitomized the pleasures one experiences when bodily passions are subjugated for the blessed reward of achieving mystical union with God. Song of Songs 4:6-8 is particularly important because of its alleged call to a life of chastity and austerity. It progresses "from the many to the one, for the more we draw near to God in fleeing the world, that much more are we gathered into the one."[30]

Even Protestant preachers and teachers, who are otherwise ardent champions of setting biblical passages within their concrete historical settings in establishing the parameters of their interpretations, have rarely resisted the temptation to rehearse the allegorical and tropological interpretations of their ascetic counterparts. The blatantly sexual tone of the book has embarrassed the Protestant and the Catholic churches alike. Thus the shining peak of Lebanon, in the tradition of both, has become the hope and heart of the spiritual life, the embodied peak of the union between the Bridegroom (God) and the Bride (the human soul). The journey, therefore, is away from the carnality of the lion's den and the leopard's cave—that is, away from the temptations of the female body and female impurities—and toward the spiritual peaks of Mount Seir and Mount Hermon.

In fact, in a great deal of Catholic and Protestant theological thinking, nothing in the world is as tempting as the female body. She is, as one feminist representation theorist has argued, "both desirable body and fascinating subjectivity. She is difference and *diffe'rance,* mysterious, and unknown. She localizes, focuses, reduces all temptation to the time and space occupied by her body. She is the litmus test of his ascetic practice, the 'trial of seduction' that proves his accomplishment."[31] All of the sexual pleasure and charm associated with the female body in Song of Songs are transferred onto a spirit relationship with God in androcentric interpretation, where union with God is a garden delightful and inviolable (4:12), and the process of union is one of perpetual wooing (4:1, 9), surrender (4:16), and luxuriating (5:1). This shows, perhaps, the extent to which both Protestant and Catholic male interpreters have tended to agree with one particular maxim that was popular during the medieval period: "A woman's body is fire."[32]

We see, then, that the lone book in the Bible that celebrates human sexuality and praises the female body has become in some hands the guiding tract for denying human desires and for mortifying human flesh. Why are we still inclined to read it so?

---

30. A quotation from medieval Christian literature, found in Ann Matter's study of the medieval perspectives on Song of Songs, *The Voice of My Beloved: The Song of Songs in Western Medieval Christianity* (Philadelphia: University of Pennsylvania Press, 1990) 136.
31. Margaret R. Miles, *Carnal Knowing: Female Nakedness and Religious Meaning in the Christian West* (Boston: Beacon, 1989) 136.
32. Matter, *The Voice of My Beloved,* 33.

The reasons are many and complex, but the first and easiest answer would be to say that the human body continues to embarrass us by its insistence upon bleeding and decaying. It disobeys us with disease and lust. It disappoints us by refusing to shape up to certain ideals. Even God, according to the purity laws in Leviticus 12–26, cannot countenance the discharges and messiness of the human body. The female body, being the messiest of all, poses the greatest problem when it comes to control (cf. Lev 12:1-8; 15:19-30; 18:1-20).

Song of Songs can be, if we allow it, an ideal book for guiding the Christian interpreter into reflecting on bodily integrity and religious meaning. It gives us permission to accept our bodies as gardens for exploring the human and divine parts of our nature. In Song of Songs, the female body poses no threat to the created order. It is a blank form on which many of the gifts of nature (flora and fauna) are inscribed. Reading Song of Songs in this way forces us to an entirely new bodily theology, one that acknowledges and celebrates the bodily self as an integral part of what it means to be human.

A second reason why modern readers continue to read Song of Songs in ways that shift the focus from sexual intimacy toward spiritual intimacy between God and human beings is the book's lack of moral precepts and divine law. It remains the one book in the Bible (hence, in our lectionaries) that continues to be elaborated on at a level beyond its apparent meaning, even though reading the Bible allegorically is no longer as popular as it was from the fourth century to the early Middle Ages. There is no mention of God by name or allusions to any of Israel's sacred historical traditions. Readers desperate to understand the book's religious significance are left to wonder whether beneath the sexual surface there might be hidden meanings and deeper revelations in the Song of Songs. Perhaps there are. Yet if the book was written to valorize the integrity of the human body and the mutual blessedness of human sexuality as gifts from God, why should that not be sufficient?

Because sex and power are virtually synonymous in our culture, we are in continuous need of material that helps us to model and celebrate intimacy that does not abuse power. In a society in which virtually every public debate about sexuality becomes a debate about power (e.g., rape, sexual abuse, pornography, incest, abortion marches, teenage pregnancy), it is refreshing to read an account of love in which lovers love without domination. The love songs of the beloved speak, among other things, of mutual love as the context for empowering the human spirit and for sharing bodily humanity. The shepherd in 4:1–5:1 praises the body of the black-skinned maiden without any attempt to dominate or subdue her. He just appreciates his beloved's beauty. That alone should be enough to give modern readers pause.

Finally, Song of Songs does not anticipate all of our questions and equivocations about human sexuality. The book celebrates the love of a man and a woman—in this case a man and a woman of, presumably, different skin colors. It does not argue against same-sex love, nor for that matter does it argue against sex between lovers of the same hue. The human body is relished and praised throughout the book, despite the fact that in much of Scripture, particularly the New Testament, the body poses a problem for those who desire to approach God. In the Song of Songs, a woman's sexuality is the delight of God's creation, despite overwhelming efforts elsewhere in the Bible to manage, regulate, and subjugate the chaos that female sexuality poses for the cult (Numbers 11; cf. Leviticus 12). A black-skinned woman is elevated as beautiful and desirable, although "black" and "dark" are associated elsewhere with things negative, sinister, and evil. Song of Songs does what it does well: It inspires modern audiences to find ways to bridge the chasm that divides lovers and to perfect human intimacy. Plain and simple.

SONG OF SONGS 5:2–6:13

IF YOU FIND MY BELOVED

OVERVIEW

As the longest poetic unit in the book, 5:2–6:13 (MT 7:1) has the trappings of a real drama. One gets the feeling of some progression of thought, action, movement, and speech. The lovers have an encounter; there is misunderstanding. The shepherd departs, and the maiden searches after him; in her pursuit she is attacked by city guards. She enlists help from the daughters of Jerusalem. They hesitate at first, but, upon hearing her song of adoration for the shepherd, the daughters of the city relent. The young man reappears, if only through his words (his whereabouts remain uncertain), and once more he speaks in strong seductive tones about his lover's beauty. The two lovers exchange endless adulations and confessions of their undiminished desire for each other. Although the language remains highly evocative and refuses to yield easy answers, the poem's sense of suspense, frustration, uncertainty, and tragedy was intended to keep the audience invested in the lovers' fate. With the words, "I slept, but my heart was awake," the writer conveys to the audience the feeling that at last the two lovers will meet. They will defy the odds and consummate their love.

The entire meaning of the unit seems to hinge upon how one interprets the opening scene in 5:2-8. Is this a "dream scene" as many have supposed,[33] or an account of an actual set of events[34] that helps to give the entire passage a note of dramatic unity? Is the black-skinned maiden asleep or awake, fantasizing or describing real events? The poet is ambiguous; she leaves open the possibility that the maiden is both asleep and half-awake, fantasizing about what almost took

place and also trying to discover what went wrong. Her opening line, "I slept, but my heart was awake," is not meant to draw an audience into a discussion of whether these are actual events (although there is no reason to reject out of hand the possibility that what she describes did take place). Rather, her comment is meant to admit that not all the impediments facing the lovers stem from their environment and their culture. Just as the shepherd, though effusive in his seductive remarks, remains strangely elusive, even slippery, is always running and hiding and must always be searched out, the maiden must carry her share of responsibility for the state of their romance. Whether a real or imaginary event, the description of her failure to rouse herself fully from her sleep in order to respond to her lover's knock at the door may be her own encrypted way of admitting her inability to separate fantasy from reality; when given the opportunity to face the love for which she has wished, she tends to prolong the coquetry and is reluctant to answer the call.

The poem is a complex structure of voices, changing scenery, shifting moods, drama, and dénouement. The shepherd comes for his beloved. Yet each, for his or her own reasons, recoils. The nighttime, when this all presumably takes place ("I slept"), is a fitting backdrop for their hapless disappointments. If what we have in some earlier passages are accounts of the protagonist's dreams and fantasies about her beloved (e.g., their wedding, his wedding-night seduction, the consummation of their love), then what we have here in 5:2–6:13 (MT 7:1) is what invariably follows upon fantasy—namely, the rude awakening of reality. It is the most bitter lesson of all young love: Reality hardly matches fantasy. Whether the events the long unit describes actually took place is beside the point. What matters

---

33. Falk refers to it as the only self-proclaimed dream poem in the entire collection. See Falk, *The Song of Songs,* 121.

34. Some have proposed seeing it as the actual events on the night after the wedding (4:1-7), or shortly afterward, when the bride is only half-awake and too sluggish to open the door when the bridegroom taps. See Goulder, *The Song of Fourteen Songs,* 40-43.

is the torrent of emotions the lyrics invite the audience to relive. Here, the two extremes of the human heart are the focus: the joy of hope and the bitterness of disappointment.

SONG OF SONGS 5:2-8, I SLEPT, BUT MY HEART WAS AWAKE

COMMENTARY

5:2-5. The sound of his knock at her door rouses the maiden from her sleep (v. 2). The Hebrew word קוֹל (*qôl*) is translated in both the NIV and the NRSV as the exclamation "Listen!" although the actual meaning is something like "noise" or "sound." The same word appears in 2:8 and in Isa 40:3, where the meaning has more to do with a human noise, specifically an "outcry" or "yell" that portends someone's approach. From the look of things, the Palestinian dew, which is characteristically heavy and frigid (see Judg 6:38; Hos 13:3), has left her suitor's head drenched. The protagonist hesitates and protests, even though the suitor prefaces his request with a string of pet names: "my sister," "my darling," "my dove," "my flawless one" (v. 2). "Will she open, or will she not?" the audience wonders as the song unfolds.

But before satisfying her audience's curiosity about the outcome of the lovers' encounter, the poet cleverly raises in her audience's minds other equally engaging questions. Is the maiden dreaming about her lover's visit, or is this an actual encounter between the two? Is she fantasizing about finding his hand thrust through the opening to her door, or speaking seductively about an intimate sexual touch?[35] Is the shepherd trying to get into the portal to the woman's home or into the portal to her womb? How do we explain her reluctance to open the door? After all, her response, "I have taken off my robe—must I put it on again? I have washed my feet—must I soil them again?" (v. 3), does not sound like the response of the lovesick woman elsewhere in the book (see 5:8). Whether their encounter is real or imagined, and whether their remarks are literal or figurative, neither shepherd's nor maiden's wishes are granted. She delays, and he goes away dejected—leaving the audience

disappointed and perplexed. But, then, love and lovemaking rarely are as convenient, tidy, or graceful as they are in our dreams.

Proposals for translating the second half of v. 4 prove fascinating: "my heart began to pound for him" (NIV); "my inwards seethed for him";[36] "my heart leaps for him";[37] "my innermost being yearned for him" (NRSV); "I trembled to the core of my being" (JB). The noun is literally "inward parts" (מֵעֶה *mēʿeh*), as in the belly, but the more poetic translations (NIV and JB, e.g.) have tried to capture the emotional timbre of the poetry. Proving again that the literal translation is not necessarily the most accurate, the KJV translation borders on the comical: "My bowels were moved for him." In this case, the meaning of the verse is completely lost. The verse can be taken to mean (a) upon hearing her lover fumbling with the door lock, the maiden confesses that his efforts stir her to her senses; or (b) the feel of his hands fumbling to unlock her sealed sexual parts is part of the steamy adventure of foreplay, which leaves her body trembling at and surrendering to his touch. In either case, it is not the maiden's bowels, but her genitals that respond.

5:6. Further, the maiden's disappointment in v. 6c is as heartrending as her description of ecstasy in v. 4 was titillating: "my heart sank at his departure" (NIV); "my soul failed me when he spoke" (NRSV); "I swooned when he left";[38] "my soul failed at his flight" (JB). The Hebrew reads literally, "my life went out," as in Gen 35:18, where Rachel dies while giving birth to Benjamin. The protagonist in Song of Songs does not die, but feels as though she had when she discovers that her beloved shepherd has left without her.[39] A better way of capturing her meaning

35. "Hand" (יד *yād*) appears in one other place in the OT as a euphemism for the male sexual organ. See Isa 57:8-10.

36. Pope, *Song of Songs*, 517-21.
37. Falk, *The Song of Songs*, 184.
38. Murphy, *The Song of Songs*, 164.
39. Falk omits the line altogether. See Falk, *The Song of Songs*, 184.

might be "something inside me died when he left" (perhaps it was the same something that had earlier yearned for him). Once again, she sets out to search for her beloved (cf. 3:1-4). She searches, but cannot find him; she calls, but there is no answer. This time, love is not just elusive; it is all but gone forever. At least, that is what the audience is led to think.

True to its form, love poetry delights in the provocatively ambiguous. The composer of Song of Songs relishes words that leave her audience wondering. Ancient audiences would have known that wooden keys were needed to unlatch doors from the outside (Judg 3:25; Isa 22:22). But the composer of this work, like composers of love lyrics everywhere, exploited her audience's fascination with love and lighthearted attitude toward love lyrics. By using polyvalent language and oblique descriptions, she invites her audience to probe every statement, weigh every option, and imagine every possibility. The lyricist uses a variety of devices to invite the audience to ponder possibly different layers of the poem.

In the end, the maiden's excuses cost her her fantasies. Her suitor leaves dejected. She learns something about herself, perhaps: She is not the woman of her dreams.

She learns something also about the man of her dreams. He is not the dogged lover she has imagined him to be. At the slightest rejection he withdraws and walks away. While it is true that he attempts to open the lock and fails, still the man in the rest of her dreams is much too gallant, too persistent, and too smitten with her to give up so easily.

5:7-8. This time the sentinels of the city are less forgiving at the sight of a woman roaming the city streets at night alone. Before they apparently did not interfere (3:3), but this time, as with the woman in Prov 7:11-12, whom the sentinels mistake for a prostitute, they attack the protagonist, beating and wounding her (v. 7). Not only does her heart suffer, but her body suffers as well. The mention of her torn cloak may be a veiled reference to the sentinels' having raped her. If gang rape is her payment for reluctance to open the door to her lover, then her adjuration to her Jerusalem girlfriends in v. 8 is understandably different from those elsewhere in Song of Songs (2:7; 3:5). She is not merely faint with love; love has made her sick (v. 8).

REFLECTIONS

Stories of women in love and in trouble abound in the Bible. Indeed, themes and imagery introduced in stories about women echo back and forth across chapters and books in the Bible as a way of binding books and women together. In Song of Songs we hear echoes of the first lovers in the garden in Eden, of the battered prostitute in Proverbs 7, and of the ever faint whisper of the bludgeoned concubine in Judges 19. Like the protagonist in Song of Songs, the latter is high-spirited and independent-thinking. The fates of both eventually hinge on the other side of closed doors, however. In a disgusting scene of extravagant violence against a woman, the concubine returns to the door from which her Levite husband had thrown her out, raped and brutalized by the perverse men of the town. She is left to die on the doorstep with her hands clasped to the threshold. Obviously, the mere recounting of this story can leave an audience reeling with outrage and sorrow. The informed listeners recognized the terrorizing echoes of Judges 19: both high-spirited women, both left to fend for themselves, both raped and abused, both left "dying" at the door, and both searching in vain for their lovers.

There is one difference between the concubine in Judges 19 and the black-skinned maiden in Song of Songs. The concubine in Judges is never given the chance to speak for herself. The maiden in Song of Songs speaks throughout the work. Interpreters should resist the urge to regard the story of the protagonist in Song of Songs as redeeming that of the concubine in Judges 19. The black-skinned maiden in Song of Songs has no more power over her relationship with her lover than did her counterpart in Judges. Although her speech extends beyond the mention of her rape, she is nevertheless raped by the sentinels in the city. Besides, she, too, never quite finds what she's looking for on the other side of the door.

What are we to do, then, with these stories of extravagant terror against women?[40] The fact that some are probably pure artistic creations with female characters who embody literary types—stories that do not recount the lives of real women in antiquity—does not get us off the hook. That the violence against women like Hagar, Jephthah's daughter, the Levite's concubine, Gomer, and the black-skinned protagonist was *thinkable* is strangling enough to the senses. The question these stories ought to raise concerns the pervasive portrait of violated women in the Bible.

In a story like the Song of Songs, where the mood is largely playful and seductive and the social conflict behind the book is well disguised, what and how does the protagonist's beating contribute to the book's general meaning? Its mention is so oblique that it can go unnoticed. Why do repeated accounts of women's castigation and victimization appear in the biblical narratives? What is it about the lives and bodies of women that lends them to the mutilating purposes of writers? What is the cultural fascination with a woman's ravaged body? For one thing, it lends enormous emotional power to the plot of a book. Because of the attitudes attached to the female body, violence against it evokes great passion in audiences. One can manipulate a number of intense and contradictory emotions when trying to retain an audience's attention. Moved by feelings as contradictory as compassion, desire, rage, and disgust, audiences are gripped by these tales. Feelings reinforce themes, and themes reinforce feelings. Here, the maiden's regret at hesitating to open the door, her longing to be embraced by her beloved, her insistence upon searching for love become even more palpable in the light of the extent to which she goes for love. She is willing to lose her virtue to be with her beloved.

Texts that describe plundering and rape are not for the fainthearted reader. They are to be read, shared, and explored in settings in which the reader is unafraid to tap into the volcano of emotions lying just beneath faith. We should not overlook these tales for the more palatable stories that reinforce the religiously inspired fiction that bad things happen only to bad people. Bad, ugly, crushing things happen to good people also, sometimes for no apparent reason.

A cryptic, barely noticed line in Song of Songs like 5:7 does not have to be made to carry the weight of violence against women everywhere. In its own context, this passage is clear: With love come suffering and disappointment. To love someone is to open oneself to the risk of being hurt and disappointed by that person. Indeed, it entails giving someone access to hurt you and discloses knowledge about you that only comes with intimacy—that is, the knowledge of what hurts you most. Song of Songs reminds us that the journey to satisfying love may bring us face-to-face with our greatest torment and disappointment.

40. See Phyllis Trible, *Texts of Terror: Literary-Feminist Readings of Biblical Narratives* (Philadelphia: Fortress, 1984).

SONG OF SONGS 5:9, WE DON'T GET IT

COMMENTARY

The Jerusalem daughters act as interlocutors; they goad the speakers and action along with questions and instigations. "What is so special about your beloved?" they ask. "Why should we get involved?" they want to know. Even more, "If we are to help you find him (v. 8), how are we to recognize him?" After five chapters of listening in on the lovers' longing, the Jerusalem daughters remain unconvinced. "How is your beloved better than others?" they ask in this verse. They are made to ask the unspoken sentiments and reservations of the audience. The Jerusalem daughters verbalize the audience's doubts about the propriety and implication of the lovers' affair.

The Jerusalem daughters' query functions as a welcome interjection into this protracted drama about the bewitching nature of love. "Explain to us, what is so special about your love?" Or better yet, "What makes your love so different from others?" The audience obviously does not get it.

SONG OF SONGS 5:10-16, DO YOU SEE WHAT I SEE?

COMMENTARY

The protagonist patiently takes the time to describe her lover's charms in these verses. Of the four *wasfs*, or poetic descriptions of the body in Song of Songs, this one alone focuses on the man's body (cf. 4:1-7; 6:4-10; 7:1-9). The maiden begins her description with the upper part of his body (his hair and face) and proceeds from there to the lower part of his body (his legs and feet). It is not an actual description of her lover, of course, but a portrait of ideal masculinity and male desirability according to ancient standards of physical beauty. The aim of her poetry is to persuade her audience to see what she sees in the shepherd.

This paean to male beauty is the only one of its kind in the Bible. It represents our only look at the male body through the eyes of a woman. It is a woman's subjective construction of male beauty: healthy complexion (v. 10); luxuriant black hair (v. 11); translucent eyes (v. 12); sweet-smelling cheeks (v. 13); brawny physique, with strong legs (vv. 14-15); tall, like the cedars in Lebanon (v. 15); and charming (v. 16). Strong white teeth should probably be added in view of v. 12*b* ("bathed in milk, fitly set"); we know from the shepherd's description of the maiden in 4:2 that healthy teeth were important to good looks. She describes him as she experiences him, using imagery her audience is sure to understand because it is inspired by the sights, sounds, and smells of their rural, pastoral, bedouin culture.

No one part of her description stands out, except perhaps her descriptions of his "body" in v. 14 (מעה *mēʿeh*). The word usually refers to the internal organs, but in this context it obviously refers to the external region of the man's body. Some translators have translated it more precisely as "belly"[41] or more erotically as "loins."[42] The parallel clause "decorated/encrusted with sapphires" intensifies the description of the external region between the man's thighs and chest. In all likelihood the maiden is discreetly referring to the man's genitalia, hinting that his loins are a work of consummate firmness, rare and precious as gems.

When applied to the shepherd in v. 15, both the NRSV and the NIV translate *marʾeh* as "appearance." The maiden compares his appearance to choice timber. But the same word, in feminine form, when applied in 2:14 to the maiden, is translated "face." The translators probably chose "your face is lovely" because it is paired with "your voice is sweet." But the shepherd is requesting to see more than her lovely face; he desires to behold her full "form" or "body." Male commentators have tended to see the poetic imagination at work in this *wasf* as "less sensuous and imaginative" than the other three *wasfs*, which all describe the female body (4:1-7; 6:4-10; 7:1-9).[43] Whether the description of the man's physique and loins is "less sensuous and imaginative" than the descriptions of the woman's breasts and long hair may just be a matter of opinion.

To the maiden, the shepherd's most enduring and distinguishing quality is not his genital area, however, but his speech (v. 16).

41. Murphy, *The Song of Songs*, 164.
42. Pope, *Song of Songs*, 411.
43. Soulen, "The *Wasfs* of the Song of Songs and Hermeneutic," 183-90.

Twice in this unit, once indirectly (v. 13) and once explicitly (v. 16), the protagonist basks in the taste of and sounds from her beloved's mouth. Earlier in the book the shepherd pined for his soul mate's sweet-sounding voice (2:14) and admired her lips, which drip honey (4:11). Here in chap. 5, the maiden imagines the smell of spices on the shepherd's cheeks (v. 13*a*) and the taste of lips that drip honey (v. 13*b*). (A fragranced beard was perhaps common among Hebrew men, as noted in Ps 133:2, which describes the precious ointment the Aaronide priests wore on their beards.) In v. 16 she moves from her lover's smells and tastes to the sound of his speech (cf. "His conversation is sweetness itself" in the JB).

According to some biblical narrators, men in love speak in a certain tender way to the women they love and wish to woo (see Gen 34:3; Hos 2:14). Throughout Song of Songs the voice and sounds of the shepherd inspire the protagonist to act and react. His sound captures her attention in 2:8, and his beckoning in 2:10 arouses her. His silence sends the maiden searching the Jerusalem streets for him (3:1-2). Again in this chapter his words rouse her from her sleepy stupor and once more prompt her to take to the streets in search of him. This attention to speech and voice coheres within the very structure of the book. In a poem sculpted along the lines of soliloquies and dialogue, it is not surprising that compliments abound between the two lovers about their sweet-talking ways.

Although it would be futile to read the *waṣfs* in Song of Songs literally, as precise descriptions of the lovers, we should not overlook what may be a very important allusion in v. 10. The maiden begins her one and only poetic sketch of her lover's body with a remark about his complexion. His complexion is the same as that of the shepherd boy turned king, David. Both are described as "ruddy," which refers to the color red (1 Sam 16:12; 17:42). A ruddy complexion was probably associated with the healthy tan of shepherds, whose work kept them under the sun's rays. But what are we to make of the different descriptions of the lovers' complexions? Hers, the result of laboring in the vineyard under the sun (1:5-6), is "black" and evidently odd; but his handsome, ruddy complexion, common to shepherds who labor in pastoral settings under the sun, is charming and handsome. Is this a hint of different standards for male and female beauty, different interpretations of the same physical characteristic?

Finally, after summing up the shepherd's charms, the protagonist closes contentedly and smugly, "This is my beloved and this is my friend, O daughters of Jerusalem" (v. 16*b*). In other words, "Now do you see what I mean?"

REFLECTIONS

In recent years feminist writing on the spiritual meaning of female body experiences has been rich and voluminous. Feminists have sought to create new frameworks for understanding women's embodiedness, showing how women's experiences of their body selves, from their anatomical parts (e.g., breasts, uterus, clitoris) to their biological potentials (e.g., menstruation, orgasm, pregnancy, labor and childbirth, infertility, and menopause), can be a resource for understanding and relating to God and to the larger world. What remains virtually uncommented upon in this new movement to reclaim embodied knowledge is the spiritual meaning of the male body, especially the moral significance of male genitalia.

It is, indeed, a great loss to those of us who want to affirm body experiences as good that, whereas the female character in Song of Songs claims her body as positive, good, and important—contrary to those who attempt to make her feel inferior because of her dark complexion (1:5-6) and small breasts (8:8-10)—the male character never comments upon his own body. Our only description of his body is from the woman's perspective. His thoughts about his appearance, his sexuality, his embodiedness remain unknown to us. What does it feel like, women may wish to know, to live inside a male body? What does it feel like to have a penis? More important, how do men experience and commune with God in the day-to-day bodily experiences of their maleness?

For example, if the experience of pregnancy puts many women in touch with the creative powers of God, and menstruation reinforces for others the atoning and purifying power of Christ's blood, then what analogous bodily experiences of spiritual revelation can men point to? In Song of Songs we perceive the male body from the female point of view. Her description is telling. We discover that standards of beauty and handsomeness and definitions of masculinity and femininity vary according to context. Not only is it true that "beauty is in the eyes of the beholder," but also what you see depends upon where you are standing. Human beings, depending upon what they have been taught, tend to ascribe different values to different shades of skin complexion. Likewise, we are taught to ascribe different values to different body shapes and builds, and we are taught to associate certain physical and emotional characteristics with women and others with men. The lovers in Song of Songs do not necessarily teach us new ways of thinking about beauty. Indeed, we discover from the poetry just how long prejudice against "black" complexions has existed in the world. But this book of poetry does allow us to come face-to-face with one couple's efforts to challenge color prejudice and cultural biases and stereotypes about what makes someone a suitable partner. In our own culture, men are expected to marry women who are shorter, younger, physically weaker, less educated, and who earn less money. Says who?

The lovers' odes to each other reinforce the notion that the singular most important thing about love is their experience and perceptions of each other. Although those experiences and perceptions may sometimes be influenced by the culture, they are not hopelessly determined by it. Love by its very nature arouses lovers to see and hear each other in ways no other ever has. We should recognize in the maiden's description of the shepherd her effort to describe what she sees as special about her lover. Yes, her imagery is conventional. Of course, her description is generic. But her experience of otherwise conventional beauty is unique: "This is my lover, this is my friend" (v. 16b). We should not dismiss their descriptions of one another because they focus on physical characteristics, with hardly any mention of the things we value in potential mates: character, social ambitions, family background. After all, theirs was a culture where physical contact, though not impossible, was rare and kissing was the stuff of sexual fantasy. Sex was a fantasy, and kissing was a pleasure that demanded one's most ingenious talents for hiding, sneaking, and talking abstrusely. If we tire of their endless elaborations, it is perhaps because we cannot understand their delay. Song of Songs reacquaints the modern reader with the art and pleasure of old-fashioned courtship.

SONG OF SONGS 6:1-3, BUT WHERE IS HE?

COMMENTARY

The Jerusalem daughters' interest is piqued: "Where has your beloved gone, O fairest among women? Which way has your beloved turned, that we may seek him with you?" (6:1). They want a glance at him for themselves. But the protagonist is oblique about his whereabouts, alluding once more to the image of the garden, their private and sensuous utopia, insisting that the two of them belong to each other and to no one else (6:3).

SONG OF SONGS 6:4-10, ONE-OF-A-KIND BEAUTY

COMMENTARY

In these verses the shepherd extols his black-skinned lover's beauty. Here he repeats and expands upon much of the imagery he used to describe her in 4:1-3. He admires the maiden's flowing hair (like "a flock of goats moving down the slopes of Gilead"), her perfect teeth (like "a flock of ewes . . . all of them bear twins and not one of them is bereaved"), and her blushing cheeks ("like halves of a pomegranate"). In his eyes, the maiden is beautiful. Indeed, if there is one thing the Jerusalem daughters and the shepherd agree on, it is that she is physically striking. Both use various Hebrew word forms to describe the maiden as "beautiful" (יפה *yāpâ*; Jerusalem daughters: 1:8; 5:9; 6:1; the lover: 1:15; 2:13; 4:1; 6:4). In this *waṣf* praising the woman's beauty, the shepherd reinforces the idea that the maiden is unique, one of a kind.

As lovers tend to do, the shepherd gushes with hyperbole and rattles on indecipherably when he talks about his love. For example, it is unclear exactly what similarities he has in mind when he compares the black-skinned maiden to "an army with banners" (v. 4c) or "bannered troops." In Hab 1:7 a different form of the same Hebrew word for "banner" (אים *'āyōm*) appears, referring to the formidable invading Chaldean troops (translated variously as "terrible," NRSV; "majestic," NIV; "formidable," JB). Whatever its exact translation, the sense in Song of Songs is that the woman's beauty is captivating and arresting. The idiosyncratic manner in which he compliments her should probably be viewed as the typical blather of the lovestruck.

Contrasted with the protagonist's defensive comments in 1:6 ("Do not gaze at me because I am black"), the descriptions of her beauty by her observers are noteworthy. Is there a conflict in perspectives here? Does the black-skinned woman see herself in a way (e.g., stigmatized, object of scorn and ridicule) that is different from the way her lover and friends see her (e.g., beautiful, striking, unrivaled)? Why do the others repeatedly make reference to the protagonist's beauty? Must the black-skinned woman be convinced of something she sometimes doubts herself? Why does one of the only two comments she makes about her own body (the other in 8:4 comments obliquely on her breasts) pertain to her complexion? Why does her lover remark again and again about her beauty, insisting in 6:9 that hers is a bodily self that is unique, perfect, and flawless? Should we see this simply as the conventional formulaic romantic gush of a lovestruck paramour? Or might this be a clue that theirs was a romance that violated the boundaries and norms of acceptable coupling, transgressing class, ethnic, or tribal barriers, which forever necessitated defense and special pleading before a disapproving audience?

The comparison of the protagonist's beauty to two capital cities, Tirzah and Jerusalem, though less remarkable, has left a number of commentators baffled. It should not, however, since one finds capital cities symbolized as female throughout the OT (see Ezekiel 16; 23). Influenced by ancient Near Eastern mythology, which understood the capital city as the patron city of the deity, the prophets, for example, characterized Jerusalem, and frequently Samaria as well, variously as a bride, a widow, a pubescent girl, a promiscuous wife, a woman raped, a whore, and a mother writhing with labor pains. Whether in the first three chapters of the book of Hosea or in chapters 16 and 23 of Ezekiel, or in scattered texts throughout Jeremiah, the capital cities Jerusalem and Samaria are repeatedly depicted as women, loose, wanton, brazen, and shocking in their indifference to the social norms regulating female sexuality. Song of Songs 6:4 stands out because it is the only occurrence where, in the language of linguists, the tenor (the subject) and the vehicle (the figurative language) are reversed. Usually in the OT the capital city (tenor) is compared to a woman (vehicle). Here in v. 4, however, a woman (tenor) is compared to a capital city (vehicle).

The mention of Tirzah (v. 4) instead of Samaria, which one would expect in parallel with Jerusalem, has prompted different interpretations. First, one can point to v. 4 as strong evidence for dating the book to the period of Solomon's reign. Tirzah was the capital city of the northern kingdom from the time of Jeroboam, just after the division of the united kingdom to the time of Omri, when the latter built Samaria as the new capital (see, e.g., 1 Kgs 14:17; 15:21, 33; 16:6). A second approach to this verse follows the lead of the LXX and other ancient manuscripts in translating the Hebrew as a nominal form of רצה (rāṣâ), meaning "pleasing." A third approach regards Tirzah as a gloss inserted in place of Samaria, either because of the circumstances surrounding its destruction or because the long-standing aversion to the Samaritans made Samaria unmentionable in polite settings. Although each is a likely explanation for the verse, none can be proven correct.

Lovers everywhere boast that their beloved is somehow different from others.

If the beloved is male, his courage and stature are unlike other men's. If the beloved is female, her beauty, poise, and modesty are unparalleled. The reference to "sixty queens and eighty concubines" (v. 8) is a way of talking about the countless number of women among whom the black-skinned woman stands out as unique. Not only is the maiden praised by countless royal and peasant women alike, but also she is the apple of her mother's eye ("the darling of her mother," NRSV), says the shepherd lover.

In v. 10, the shepherd quotes what likely was a conventional way of hailing a beautiful or exceptional person when the latter entered a room: "Who is this that looks forth like the dawn, fair as the moon, bright as the sun, majestic as the stars in procession?" In fact, this greeting is probably the parallel to 3:6, which hailed the bridegroom's arrival. In 3:6, the "sixty mighty men" and other skilled swordsmen in Solomon's litter are mentioned as surrounding the bridegroom. Here sixty maidens and eighty concubines (vv. 8-9) surround and praise the black-skinned maiden. (See Reflections at 6:13.)

SONG OF SONGS 6:11-12, THE GARDEN OF LOVE

COMMENTARY

Verses 11-12 are easily the most difficult in the entire book. They stand apart from the preceding unit and do not fit with what follows. The greatest difficulty with these verses has to do with identifying the speaker. A case can be made that the shepherd continues to speak, albeit obliquely, about his love affair with the maiden. A case can be made also that the black-skinned woman is the speaker. Of course, the allusion to the garden in v. 11 is reminiscent of repeated references throughout the book to the woman as a garden (cf. 4:12, 16; 5:1), and of her own fantasies of endless hours of lovemaking amid the fertile fields and villages. She fantasizes in 7:12 of just such lovemaking, using language and imagery similar to what we find in 6:11. The LXX editors obviously understood the woman

as speaker in 6:11; on the basis of 7:13, they added to 6:11 the additional line, "There I will give my love to you."

Even if one can reasonably ascribe v. 11 to a female speaker and determine that the inference of the verse is about lovemaking in the springtime, there remains the matter of v. 12. The latter invariably brings even the most intuitive interpreter to her or his exegetical knees.

Various emendations have been offered to restore the meaning of v. 12, but none has achieved a consensus among interpreters. With the NRSV and the NIV, these are among the speculations:

"Before I knew my desire had hurled me onto the chariots of Amminadib." (JB)

"Before I knew it, my heart made me (the blessed one) of the prince's people."[44]

"Unawares I was set in the chariot with the prince."[45]

"Or ever I was aware, my soul made me like the chariots of Ammi-nadib." (KJV)

44. Roland Murphy, following a NAB rendering. See Murphy, *The Song of Songs*, 176.

45. Pope, *Song of Songs*, 584-91.

Falk admits defeat and simply refuses to hazard a guess about the translation or the meaning of the verse. In a bold move, she omits the line from her translation.[46] But we should allow the verse to stand as an eloquent reminder (1) of the cultural distance between our world and the ancient world of biblical love poetry; (2) of how formidable love poetry can be to the rigid, unimaginative exegete; and (3) of how imprecise language often is.

46. Falk, *The Song of Songs*, 187.

SONG OF SONGS 6:13, THE DAUGHTERS' REQUEST

COMMENTARY

Translators differ as to whether this verse (MT 7:1) belongs with the preceding unit or with the *wasf* that follows in chapter 7. Where do the words of the Jerusalem daughters belong? Indeed, theirs are the words of the interlocutors who play each partner off the other. In 5:9 they questioned the protagonist about what she saw in the shepherd lover. This time they wish to know what the shepherd sees in the maiden. Their request to examine the maiden for themselves comes between the shepherd's two praise songs (*wasfs*) and acts to heighten the tension in the drama. Because they are not quite convinced of his reasons, the shepherd must once again defend what he sees in the Shulammite.

But first the woman is forced to (re)turn (from the nut orchard? v. 11) and face her doubters: "Come back, come back, O Shulammite; come back, come back, that we may gaze on you!" (NIV). This is the first time an epithet is applied to the protagonist that does not necessarily signify her as a sexual object (e.g., "my darling," "my bride") or refer to her by her physical looks (e.g., "fairest one," "perfect one"). Unfortunately, the word does not show up anywhere else in the Old Testament, so its meaning is difficult to determine. One way to view the epithet is to see it as a feminine form of the name of the monarch with whom the book is associated, King Solomon.[47] Another possibility is to view it as a title of nobility, reinforced by the parallel appellation בת-נדיב (*bat-nādîb*), which is translated as "queenly maiden."[48] Regardless of how one understands her new epithet, the inference of the daughters' request is unmistakable: "Let us find out for ourselves what is so special and unique about this Shulammite!"

Before the shepherd can resume his defense, the protagonist speaks up in v. 13b. She is prepared to challenge anyone who tries to undermine her sense of self (see 1:5; 8:10). Her rebuff in modern idiom might be something like, "Why are you looking at me as though I were a freak or something?" The dance she mentions, "the dance of two armies," while unknown to us, was probably outstanding for its unusual, spectacular, exotic choreography. Regardless, the black-skinned Shulammite refuses here, as in 1:6, to be an object of people's stares and speculations.

In summary, a look at the unit as a whole, from its opening (v. 4) to its closing (v. 13) lines, shows that the emphasis is on asserting in sundry ways the protagonist's inherently unique beauty and worth. The

47. H. H. Rowley, "The Meaning of 'the Shulammite,'" *AJSL* 56 (1939) 84-91.
48. For a helpful history of interpretations given to this term, see Pope, *Song of Songs*, 596-600.

shepherd finds different ways to defend his lover's attractiveness: He first asserts that she is beautiful (v. 4) and then enumerates the many physical attributes that prove it (vv. 5-7); even when compared to other women, say, those of royal or privileged circumstances, she stands out as unique (v. 8). Not only is she uniquely favored in her own mother's eyes (v. 9), but also she captures the attention of onlookers whenever she enters the room (v. 10). In the end, we discover that she

does not need the shepherd to plead her case and defend her self-worth. The black-skinned maiden is quite able to defend herself. He can speak about her, but he cannot speak for her. To those who remain skeptical about what he sees in her, the black-skinned woman steps forward and speaks for herself (v. 13). She is not something to be gawked at and pointed to as though she were a freak show. The implication is that she is a person with value and an identity apart from her appearance.

REFLECTIONS

1. Song of Songs 6:4-10 portrays a man who defends the depth of his love and sentiments for a certain unknown young maiden who, for reasons unclear to us, has been deemed an unsuitable mate. We hear his defense of this maiden as unique and his defense of their love as special. This is a rare glimpse at male love. Accounts of men driven by anger, jealousy, hatred, and cynicism, all in the name of God, abound in the Bible. But by comparison only a few stories exist in the Bible about men falling in love: Adam rejoices at Eve's creation (Gen 2:23); Jacob falls for Rachel (Gen 29:9-11); Shechem is smitten by Dinah (Gen 34:3); David lusts after Bathsheba (2 Sam 11:2). But outside the poetry of Song of Songs there are no descriptions of what it feels like to be a man in love. This is the case despite the fact that the biblical story of salvation is often inspired by, and sometimes thwarted because of, the romantic entanglements of many of the male protagonists. Indeed, the sage of Proverbs all but warns of the mysterious effects that love has on the male psyche:

> Three things are too wonderful for me;
>   four I do not understand:
> the way of an eagle in the sky,
>   the way of a snake on a rock,
> the way of a ship on the high seas,
>   and the way of a man with a girl. (Prov 30:18-19 NRSV)

That the shepherd uses much of the same imagery he employs elsewhere to describe his true love should not be surprising. How many ways are there to describe one's love? This explains why love poetry repeats time-worn expressions. It draws from a repertoire of stock themes, phrases, and imagery to talk about topics otherwise risqué and immodest. Borrowing this traditional language makes erotic talk both legitimate and honorable. His descriptions of his beloved's spellbinding gaze, her flowing hair, perfect teeth, and blushing cheeks were the stuff of the Mediterranean man's dreams. And we should take heart in knowing that the shepherd is as eager to defend his love for the maiden as she is to defend her love for him.

2. As for the maiden herself, it is interesting to note that her harshest words in the entire poem (6:13) are directed at her female peers, the Jerusalem daughters. Their views represent the cultural prejudices against which the lovers must defend themselves. And while the maiden is not a radical feminist, we do witness some remarkable things about her character. Here, for example, she defends her integrity as a person; she is not an object to be stared at and inspected. Interpreters should resist the temptation to portray the black-skinned protagonist in Song of Songs as something of a feminist and independent thinker in her day. She is sassy and aggressive, to be sure. But she is not asserting the universal right of women to be judged according to their character, rather than their physical looks and bodily functions. For what it is worth, she is insisting on her right to love the man of her dreams.

Still her portrait provides us a glimpse of a rare female self. The maiden belongs both to herself and to her lover (2:16; 6:3). The woman, or man for that matter, who is able to experience sensuous autonomy and selfhood and at the same time be present to another person is not plagued by the kind of dualistic tension so characteristic of Christian patriarchal thinking. This kind of thinking leaves us feeling as though we must continually choose between autonomy and dependence, between the self and the other to be whole. Patriarchy so frequently leaves us "split at the roots," forcing us to choose between domination and submission, power and powerlessness, sex and intimacy, friendship and eroticism, spirituality and materiality. The black-skinned Shulammite woman in Song of Songs insists upon the integrity of her physical, bodily self as the source and resource for her understanding of herself and her relationship with others.

3. Finally, the guiding premise throughout this commentary is that Song of Songs is about more than just sex. To the extent that it is *about* anything, it is especially about male and female expressions of love and intimacy, the communion of self with the other, and the riddled journey toward mutuality. If this little book of love poetry can teach the church anything about sex, it is that sex is more than what we do with our genitals. Thus the church's sometimes hysterical outbursts against sexuality (e.g., adult unmarried sex, homosexuality, teenage sex) frequently completely miss the point. Sex is a physical reenactment of our emotional, physical, cognitive, and spiritual need to experience intimate communion with other(s). Making love involves partners exploring and searching for *their* own expressions of love for each other without the detractions of naysayers, without the diminishment of oneself in order to enhance the other, and without being forced to live up to or according to certain predetermined roles. Those who are rightly distressed by many of the abusive and extreme expressions of human sexuality we regularly witness in our culture (e.g., rape, pornography, pregnant teenagers) must face the fact that we have lost touch with the true meaning of love. Inasmuch as the perfecting of human love has always been a recognized goal of religion, Song of Songs—with its spotlight on the trials of impeded love and the pleasures of "making love" beyond the impediments—is an appropriate text for modern readers to consider again and again.

WHO IS THIS LEANING ON HER BELOVED?

OVERVIEW

This block of material, which contains speeches by the protagonist (7:10-13; 8:1-4, 5*b*, 6-7), the shepherd (7:1-9), and the maidens (8:5*a*), propels the entire book toward yet another climactic possibility: The lovers at last experience the passion they have longed for throughout the book. This section consists, then, of four subunits (7:1-9, 10-13; 8:1-5, 6-7), which are organized around the shifts in speeches. After an unusually explicit seduction speech by the shepherd (7:1-9), there follows an intimation of the maiden's surrender (7:10-13) and her subsequent fantasy of the ideal circumstances for their affair and the reply of the Jerusalem daughters (8:1-5). The section ends with a wisdom homily (8:6-7) extolling the power of love.

SONG OF SONGS 7:1-9, THE SHEPHERD'S SEDUCTION

COMMENTARY

In the final seduction scene, the shepherd yearns for his lover, praises her bodily charms once more, and teeters close to violating the codes of decency and public performance by talking explicitly about his fantasies of his lover's breasts. He begins this *wasf* by praising her feet (v. 1). This is the first time in the book that the man compliments a body part below the woman's waistline. And what he has to say about her thighs, navel, and belly is much too personal to take lightly. In fact, his luxurious comments do not sound like the talk of a man who is keeping the required distance between himself and a veiled, or even diaphanous veiled, virgin. The body parts he describes in this *wasf* are of a more intimate nature than those described elsewhere. By poeticizing her feet, thighs, and navel, the shepherd's sweet talk has moved from blather to daring. If his daring details of her intimate places were without feeling, commitment, and genuine adoration for the maiden, his description would be pornographic. But he is not a voyeur, peeping vulgarly at a naked woman; he is a man smitten by a woman others overlook.

The setting of these verses has been seen as a reference to the dance before the two armies (מחנים *maḥănayim*) alluded to in 6:13. Drawing on parallels with modern Near Eastern sword dance ceremonies, the bride, who supposedly wields a sword on her wedding day, presumably wears an outfit that exposes significant portions of her body, especially her mid-section. This might explain the shepherd's racy remarks about her feet, thighs, navel, and belly. Another context might be the palace dance, which was common during festival seasons, when the king showed off the beauty of the women in his harem by asking them to dance. (King Ahasuerus's summons of Queen Vashti to display herself before his guests may reflect just such a ceremony [Esth 1:10-13].) Although commentators are inclined to see hints of just such dance rituals, the parallels are in the end unconvincing. Indeed, in 6:13b the protagonist seems to reject any efforts to associate her with exotic exhibitionism. Her sentiment on the matter throughout is unmistakable (see 1:6): While she is perfectly willing to revel in her lover's exploratory glances, she refuses to be an object of other people's fantasies. What we have here then is not the raucous shouts of male revelry at the sight of a woman's gyrations. It is a man who is gingerly, carefully, discreetly fantasizing about the contours of his lover's frame. He explores her body with poetic relish.

Beginning his remarks in v. 1 with yet another pet name for his lover ("O prince's daughter," NIV; "O queenly maiden," NRSV), the shepherd describes a body that has form and definition, flesh and sinew, shape and cultural meaning. In the other three *wasfs*, the direction of description was from top to bottom (e.g., 4:1-7; 5:10-16; 6:4-10). Here the shepherd begins his compliments from the bottom up, beginning with the woman's feet. (In a rustic, pastoral, bedouin environment people's feet surely take an incredible beating, since women and men stand on their feet for long periods of the day on rocky, uneven surfaces and in brutal weather.) His description of her thighs ("legs," NIV), her navel, and her belly suggests that hers is the body of a round, full-figured, fertile woman. Her breasts, like "two fawns," are firm and supple (v. 3). Ivory ornaments adorn her long graceful neck (v. 4). This woman stands in sharp contrast to the image of the ideal Western woman in contemporary times, who is gaunt, curveless, and boyish in form. As disquieting as it may be to read such erotic descriptions of a woman's body parts in the Bible, it is important that we savor the descriptions. Such careful delineation of her body reinforces the notion that the woman in Song of Songs is a real flesh-and-blood woman with emotions, desires, ambitions, and bodily integrity. She is not a convenient blank form, like the concubine in Judg 19:27-30. She is more than the sum total of her body parts, to be sure, but at the same time she will not be dismissed because of her body.

To describe the maiden's face, the imagery moves from the mundane to the ethereal. Before the shepherd was content to compare the maiden's beauty generally to the glory and splendor of capital cities (6:4). In vv. 4-5, however, he elaborates upon each part of her face by drawing comparisons with ancient place-names, each no doubt renowned for its own wondrous features. Unfortunately, those unique features are all but lost on most modern Western readers: Heshbon (v. 4b), Bathrabbim (v. 4c), Lebanon (v. 4d), Damascus (v. 4e), Carmel (v. 5a).

In the end, the maiden's elegant pose is like that of a palm tree (v. 6).[49] The maiden had compared the shepherd to the trees in Lebanon, erect and tall (5:15b). Here he uses the same tree to describe her as graceful and smooth. Each lover has a gender-biased way of understanding trees: For him their forms sway gracefully with the wind; for her their upright, unbowed nature is striking.

Accentuating the woman's body are her breasts (vv. 7-8). The shepherd dreams out loud of mounting the black-skinned woman's body and clutching her breasts (v. 8)—which surely must have been a shockingly explicit statement for a Mediterranean man, governed by modesty and honor, to have uttered. He longs in v. 8 to taste her mouth and smell her breath, imagining both to bring to his mind the fragrance of apples and the taste of a smooth wine (v. 9). (See Reflections at 8:6-7.)

49. Three women in the Old Testament share the name "Tamar," which in Hebrew means "palm tree" and symbolizes poised beauty. See Gen 38:6; 2 Sam 13:1; 14:27.

SONG OF SONGS 7:10-13, THE SHULAMMITE'S SURRENDER

COMMENTARY

The woman interrupts the man's speech in v. 10. She stakes her possessive claim upon him ("I am my beloved's, and his desire is for me") as she did using similar language in

2:16 and 6:3. If part of God's curse upon the woman in Gen 3:16 was that she be ruled by her "desire" (תשוקה *těšûqâ*) for her husband, then certainly the woman in Song of Songs comes to restore mutuality to life outside Eden, where the man's desire for a woman is equally determinative. She repeats his invitation to join in a pastoral tryst (2:10), but this time she has a tryst of her own in mind and beckons him into the fields and villages (lit., "henna flowers") to survey the plants that bloom there (e.g., vines, grapes,

pomegranates, mandrakes), each of which was associated with sensuality and fertility. In v. 11 she openly beckons him to the fields and leaves no doubt in the audience's mind as to her intentions: "There I will give you my love" (v. 12*d*). In a book filled with coded, figurative speech between lovers, this is perhaps the protagonist's boldest, most open declaration. She recalls the image of the mandrake as a recognized aphrodisiac in Israel's national fiction (see Gen 30:14-16). (See Reflections at 8:6-7.)

SONG OF SONGS 8:1-5, IN MY MOTHER'S HOUSE

COMMENTARY

8:1-2. The shepherd does not seem to be aware of or fazed by any restraints on his fantasy of kissing his lover (7:8-9). The protagonist, however, hints that the circumstances are not quite right for engaging in their fantasies. In Mediterranean cultures, where consanguinity usually provides the only culturally approved basis for forming close social relationships and where the cultural ideal for many tribal societies is the marriage of patrilateral parallel cousins (preferably the children of brothers), it is likely that we have in v. 1 the first hint that the tension in the shepherd and black-skinned woman's romance has to do with the possibility that it violates the norms governing marriage affiliations. The maiden wishes that her lover were her "brother," by which in all likelihood she means a close relative. That would be the ideal circumstance for their union in that culture.

The protagonist's complaint in v. 1 that had the shepherd nursed at her mother's breasts their intimacy would have been permissible brings several possibilities to mind. Perhaps we have here an indication that matrilineal unions were allowable during the time of the composition of the Song of Songs. Of course, such a supposition flies in the face of overwhelming evidence in the OT that Israelite tribal societies were based on patrilineal lineage. Indeed, in most Middle Eastern societies, kinship is usually reckoned patrilineally (through the male line) and

kinship-based family units are structured patrilocally around what in Hebrew is called the בית אב (*bêt 'āb*), the "father's house." The wife leaves her *bêt 'āb* to reside within the *bêt 'āb* of her husband.[50]

But there is evidence that matrilineal unions were not unknown in biblical Israel. In Genesis 28–29, the story of the marriage of Jacob and Rachel (and Leah), we see an instance in which a matrilineal kinship-based relationship was arranged and encouraged, in this case between a son and his mother's brother's daughter. Some commentators have taken the protagonist's references to her mother in vv. 1-2, particularly the expression "mother's house" (בית אם *bêt 'ēm*), as an indication of the possibility of just such a union.

The other kinship possibility that the protagonist may be alluding to brings under the control of one *bêt 'āb* a variety of women (e.g., co-wives, sisters-in-law, nieces, aunts, wives of dependent hired workers) who share collectively in the domestic affairs of the household and in the care and upbringing of children. In this household arrangement, common in Mediterranean cultures, marriage among some children of the same "household" is permissible. The emphasis here is on the close bond that exists between families

---

50. For a helpful discussion of this topic, see Meyers, *Discovering Eve*, chaps. 5 and 7; Naomi Steinberg, *Kinship and Marriage in Genesis: A Household Economics Perspective* (Minneapolis: Fortress, 1993).

raised in the same compound/household. Because they are bound by shared blood and common interests, and typically have been raised in the same household (since close genealogical kin ideally live near each other), cousins in Eastern cultures are considered ideal marriage partners. They frequently know each other and have had sufficient contact with each other to be virtual sisters and brothers. (The marriage of Abraham and Sarah was probably a marriage of cousins, since more than once Abraham refers to Sarah as his "sister" [Gen 12:10-20; 20:2-18; cf. Gen 26:7-11].)

On a more poetic level, of course, the protagonist's reference to her "mother's house" (*bêt 'ēm*) may be a veiled reference to a private, secret chamber in her imagination, if not actually in her house, where female passion could be explored and luxuriated in (see Commentary on 3:4).

The protagonist is brazen in her courtship, but when the time comes for actual consummation of the relationship, she remains a product of her culture. She would like to be able to embrace her beloved freely and without public hassle. If they were kin, she imagines, she could invite him into her mother's house and there be instructed by him in the ways of lovemaking (v. 2). It is not clear in the MT whether she means, "I would lead you and bring you to my mother's house—she who has taught me" (NIV), or "I would lead you and bring you into the house of my mother, and into the chamber of the one who bore me" (NRSV), or "I would lead you, I would take you into my mother's house, and you would teach me!" (JB). Following the example of similar statements in 3:4 and 8:5, one would have to emend the Hebrew to read "she who bore me." The more conservative position, however, would be to leave the Hebrew as is and to follow the unusual statement, "she who [has] taught me."

8:3. Despite her apprehension, the black-skinned Shulammite still yearns for her beloved's embrace, his left hand under her head, his right hand clasping her. In a book of poetry filled with passionate verses, this is one of the few explicit references to the lovers actually touching each other. There are plenty of steamy descriptions of their bodies and several veiled references to tastes and smells, but hardly any direct talk about embracing, kissing, or stroking. Allusions abound, of course (cf. 2:4; 5:1, 4; 7:8), but they are just that—allusions. The only other explicit reference to body contact is in 1:2, where the maiden opens the poetry by expressing her desire that her lover kiss her. Only intimates dared touch each other openly (Isaac and Rebecca, Gen 26:8; Jacob and Rachel, Gen 29:11).

8:4. The protagonist repeats her earlier adjuration (2:7; 3:5). Her accumulated wisdom about love, her lover, and lovemaking results from her experience of obstructed, but now consummated love. She is a wiser, more experienced woman by chap. 8 than she was in chap. 1. Her message to her peers, however, is constant: For everything there is a time and a place. There is a time and a place for love(making). And it is best not to hurry or interfere with the natural course of love.

8:5. We can only imagine that by now the Shulammite has consummated her dreams. She emerges from her chambers of blossom and budding refreshed, energized, inspired, and a little fatigued, possessed of new knowledge about herself and fascinating knowledge about him. The maiden arrives embraced by her shepherd lover, and the look on their faces captures the attention of the Jerusalem daughters. The city women hail the lovers' arrival with a conventional question: "Who is this coming up from the wilderness, leaning upon her beloved?" (see 3:6; 6:10). It is a moment of joy, to be sure; but it is also, after journeying in the wilderness, the look of post-coital relaxation. (See Reflections at 8:6-7.)

SONG OF SONGS 8:6-7, THE POWER OF LOVE

COMMENTARY

The contemplative mood of this passage is a curious change from the flirtatious tone that dominates most of the other portions of the book. Cast as a homily on the power of love, this piece of worldly lyrics is reminiscent of the aphoristic material one finds in the wisdom texts of Proverbs and Ecclesiastes. This unit alone lends to the entire poem a kind of wisdom-like quality, where the object of the lyrics' message, like that of Proverbs and Ecclesiastes, is to transmit a very important lesson about life. In this case, vv. 6-7 impart one of the most important lessons of love: Love is possibly the most powerful force on earth. Even chaotic forces (i.e., fire and flood) cannot subdue it. Whereas the sages who stand behind books like Proverbs and Ecclesiastes use aphorisms and irony to impart such hard-earned wisdom, the sage behind the Song of Songs uses love lyrics to ponder the lessons of human experience.

The "seal" the maiden wishes to be placed upon her lover's heart (v. 6) signals her desire to be inseparably united with the shepherd by a sacred oath. The "seal ring" was a symbol of the kind of oath new lovers tend to make with each other when, after lovemaking, they awaken to the reality of the immense risk they have taken in exposing such intimate knowledge of themselves. (Tamar asked for just such an object from Judah before having sex with him [Gen 38:18].) Lovers pledge themselves in love, the only force on earth believed capable of circumventing the inexorable power of death and the grave. In other words, say the lovers, may our love outlive death and destruction.

Death and the grave (v. 6) are paired elsewhere in the Bible, notably in the other book renowned for its ambivalent message about love and passion: the book of Hosea. In Hos 13:14, death is personified in language reminiscent of Canaanite mythology, in which Mot, god of death, engages in battle with Baal and loses. Also in that verse, however, Israel's

God boldly proclaims victory over the forces of death and the grave:

> Shall I ransom them from the power of Sheol?
> Shall I redeem them from Death?
> O Death, where are your plagues?
> O Sheol, where is your destruction?
> (Hos 13:14 NRSV)

Sheol, the Hebrew word for "grave" (שאול *šĕʾôl*) in both Song of Songs and Hosea, is the underworld where the departed go according to Hebrew cosmology, and it should not be confused with the modern notion of hell. The idea of hell—namely, a place of endless punishment, especially by fire—derives from Greek mythology, whose influence we see in both intertestamental literature (*1 Enoch* 18:11-16; 108:3-7, 15; 2 Esdr 7:36-38) and Christian writings (Rev 19:20; 20:14-15; 21:8). In Song of Songs, and elsewhere in the Old Testament, it is a force that is powerful and devouring. Like divine love, human love, according to v. 6, is capable of overcoming the negative natural forces (i.e., death/grave, fire, water) that threaten human existence.

But the seal upon the shepherd's heart is not merely a pledge; it also carries a warning. Beware, for "human passion" (קנאה *qinʾâ*) sometimes manifests itself in a number of intense and indistinguishable shades. "Jealousy" (NIV), which is frequently the translation of the Hebrew word (*qinʾâ*), is the dark, dangerous side of love, as unrelenting as the grave itself and as vehement and intense as a blazing fire. The last part of v. 6 is perhaps deliberately multivalent. Human passion is compared to "a mighty/raging flame" or "a flame of fire from Yahweh/God." Human love can be as intense as divine love, but divine jealousy can be as intense as human jealousy. This kind of intense love cannot be put out by another force of nature, the "floods" (מים רבים *mayim rabbîm,* v. 7). Nor can this love be bought with a price.

Verses 6-7 address the wise, contemplative souls who are prepared to reckon with the impediments and frustrations to love, the social norms and cultural opinions that legislate love, and the changing mutations and irrational sides of love. This is not knowledge that one acquires through hearsay. This kind of knowledge, acquired through experience and careful observation of life's rhythms, is savored by the wise.

REFLECTIONS

For all of its titillating descriptions of the male and female anatomy, for all of its lush intimations about erotica and lovemaking, Song of Songs does not mislead its readers about the dark, dangerous, and complicated sides of human passion. Couples who clamor to include sections of the poetry in their wedding vows and to reproduce portions in their wedding announcements, without reflecting on its ominous undertones, have missed a valuable look into the future that awaits them. Unwed, casual lovers who glibly take the book as divine permission for their unbridled sexual appetites patently profane its purposes. Song of Songs is about neither romance nor sex, not entirely, anyway. It is about love struggling against the odds. In this unit, where the shepherd speaks for what perhaps is the last time (7:1-9) and the maiden speaks in the boldest of fashion (7:10-13), theirs is a love that has been beset by powers and forces that have threatened to overwhelm them (8:6-7).

SONG OF SONGS 8:8-14

EPILOGUE

COMMENTARY

This unit consists of disparate pieces of material that seem to lack any obvious coherence to one another and that fail to show any obvious dramatic connection to the unit that precedes it. Three distinct subunits make up this final section: vv. 8-10, vv. 11-12, and vv. 13-14. Intriguing as each element is, the unit itself comes off as anticlimactic after the wisdom homily in 8:6-7, which summarizes what seems to be the conspicuous contents of the book. The material in this unit repeats or elaborates upon themes presented elsewhere in the book (vineyard, breasts, Solomon), yet it does not seem to bring any further closure to the poetry, as one would expect. A possible exception may be vv. 8-9. If the protagonist's brothers are the speakers of this first segment ("We have a little sister, and she has no breasts"), then their words act as an inclusio, or repetition of closure, echoing the reference to the brothers in 1:6. Their words bring the poem full circle.

Aside from the obscure remarks about the maiden's breasts, there is the matter of the meaning of v. 9. As her male guardians who safeguard or avenge their "sister's" chastity (see Dinah's brothers in Gen 34:25-31; and Absalom, Tamar's brother, in 2 Sam 13:20-22), the speakers, presumably the maiden's brothers, promise to reward their sister with silver adornments on her wedding day ("the day when she is spoken for") if she has remained chaste ("if she is a wall"). If, however, she fails to be chaste ("if she is a door"), they threaten to hem her in with cedar to prevent her from chasing after her lovers. A similar warning appears in Hos 2:6, where the prophet threatens to build a wall of thorns so that his wife cannot get to her lovers.

The brothers' taunt and threat are in all likelihood quoted here by the maiden, who replies impudently in v. 10 that she has been chaste ("I am a wall"); and as for her breasts, they are ample enough, thank you. The only person whose opinion matters is her lover, and in his eyes she is "whole" (שלום šālôm). Here again the black-skinned maiden is sassy and headstrong. She resists the efforts of those around her, including her male guardians, her brothers, to define her, to censure her, or to meddle in the affairs of her heart. Her protest here is in keeping with repeated admonitions in the book not to interfere with the course of love.

It is impossible to say with certainty who is speaking in vv. 11-12. This boastful song, if it is comparing the speaker's vineyard, or sexual property, to King Solomon's vineyard, is the kind one might expect from a male lover. Despite Solomon's larger holdings, the speaker presumably has the choicest woman. The unknown site "Baal-hamon" (בעל המון baʿal hāmôn) means literally "possessor of abundance" and may be a *double entendre* referring to what was then a well-known private vineyard owned by King Solomon. Again, cryptic references to vineyards and royal sexual encounters echo material already introduced in the book.

In the final moment of this dramatic poem (vv. 13-14) the protagonist warns her beloved of impending danger. She shoos him away from "the gardens"—that is, his intimate exploration of her body (see Commentary on 4:1–5:1). Conventionally these verses are interpreted as the protagonist's effort to shoo her beloved away for fear they will be caught together. Unidentified persons around her watch for his arrival ("my companions are listening for your voice"). She is concerned for the shepherd's safety. This conservative, straightforward way of interpreting these final verses has a lot to commend it, for it follows the literal wording of the verse. Yet such an interpretation leaves the audience dangling and mystified about what all this means, even though it coincides with the larger theme of coming and going, hasty departure, and fleeting encounters, which marks much of the poetry.

Another admittedly daring way to interpret these final verses considers the cryptic edge of the overall poem and sheds light on the entire epilogue: the maiden's and the shepherd's words as exchanged in the context of their lovemaking. In these final verses, the maiden is hurrying her lover's sexual climax. Her defiant exclamation in vv. 8-10 and his boastful outburst in vv. 11-12 are the stuff of lovers' intimate exchanges in a moment of special privacy. Referring to herself as a "garden" (v. 13), she awaits the sound of his culminating pleasure in v. 14. She encourages him to hurry like a swift and graceful young antelope (gazelle) and stag (male deer) "upon

a mountain of spices" who must come and go quickly and gracefully to avoid becoming prey for dangerous animals. Her brothers, or other male relatives, lurk in the background determined to catch not only the shepherd's dishonorable advances toward their sister, but also their socially unacceptable attempt to unite. Seen in this way, the epilogue concludes the book with a description of the consummation of their love as the protagonist's continual defiance of the social norms. Or, on a more realistic note, the ancient audience is left to contemplate the final episode in their thwarted passion. That is, rebellion against cultural norms—no matter how moving, inspiring, and legitimate—is in the end *very* costly.

REFLECTIONS

The composer who brought together this little book of love poems known as the Song of Songs was not an idealist. She was quite aware of the cost lovers must pay for defying social customs. Despite the homily on the power of love in 8:6-7, she is not saying simply that love conquers all. Love may conquer all, but not without a price. It will have to survive the forces of cultural ideology, family beliefs, outside opinions, and the lovers' own individual quirks and limitations. The poet is apparently sympathetic to the lovers' desire to plead for their right to love whom they choose, irrespective of norms and prejudices, and to their desire to explore their love. But the composer also respects the power that the combined weight of custom, tradition, and attitudes has to distort even the most laudable attempts at reform. No matter how noble their cause, because of the power and influence of culture, nonconformists must always look over their shoulders.

Song of Songs is for the contemplative and the realist. It does not lend itself easily to some of the "God said it, and I believe it, and that settles it" preaching that bellows from so many pulpits every Sunday morning. Its lessons are not that banal. It demands introspection and honesty on the part of its audience. It invites them to explore the complicated world of emotions and feelings that clash with inherited values and cherished traditions. Nothing is as simple as it seems, not even falling in love.

Finally, Song of Songs can teach modern audiences a lot about the power and politics of love. It invites its audience to weigh the risks of love and asks us indirectly whether love is worth it. Those of us who think that it is worth it must decide so wisely. The recurring narrative plot of the Bible is that of the power of divine love to subvert the external systems that oppress human existence. The poetry of Song of Songs gives us a glimpse into the battle of human love to subvert the internal systems that thwart human relations.

ABBREVIATIONS

BCE	before the Common Era
ca.	circa
CE	Common Era
cent.	century
cf.	compare
chap(s).	chapter(s)
d.	died
Dtr	Deuteronomistic historian
esp.	especially
fem.	feminine
HB	Hebrew Bible
l(l).	line(s)
lit.	literally
LXX	Septuagint
masc.	masculine
MS(s)	manuscript(s)
MT	Masoretic Text
n(n).	note(s)
neut.	neuter
NT	New Testament
OG	Old Greek
OL	Old Latin
OT	Old Testament
par(r).	parallel(s)
pl(s).	plate(s)
SP	Samaritan Pentateuch
v(v).	verse(s)
Vg	Vulgate
\\	between Scripture references indicates parallelism

Names of Pseudepigraphical and Early Patristic Books

Apoc. Abr.	*Apocalypse of Abraham*
2–3 Apoc. Bar.	Syriac, Greek *Apocalypse of Baruch*
Apoc. Mos.	*Apocalypse of Moses*

Ascen. Isa.	*Ascension of Isaiah*
As. Mos.	*Assumption of Moses*
Barn.	*Barnabas*
Bib. Ant.	Pseudo-Philo, *Biblical Antiquities*
1–2 Clem.	*1–2 Clement*
Did.	*Didache*
1–2–3 Enoch	Ethiopic, Slavonic, Hebrew *Enoch*
Ep. Arist.	*Epistle of Aristeas*
Gos. Pet.	*Gospel of Peter*
Herm. Sim.	Hermas, *Similitude(s)*
Ign. Eph.	Ignatius, *Letter to the Ephesians*
Ign. Magn.	Ignatius, *Letter to the Magnesians*
Ign. Phld.	Ignatius, *Letter to the Philadelphians*
Ign. Pol.	Ignatius, *Letter to Polycarp*
Ign. Rom.	Ignatius, *Letter to the Romans*
Ign. Smyrn.	Ignatius, *Letter to the Smyrnaeans*
Ign. Trall.	Ignatius, *Letter to the Trallians*
Jub.	*Jubilees*
POxy	B. P. Grenfell and A. S. Hunt (eds.), *Oxyrhynchus Papyri*
Pss. Sol.	*Psalms of Solomon*
Sib. Or.	*Sibylline Oracles*
T. Benj.	*Testament of Benjamin*
T. Dan	*Testament of Dan*
T. Iss.	*Testament of Issachar*
T. Job	*Testament of Job*
T. Jud.	*Testament of Judah*
T. Levi	*Testament of Levi*
T. Naph.	*Testament of Naphtali*
T. Reub.	*Testament of Reuben*
T. Sim.	*Testament of Simeon*

Names of Dead Sea Scrolls and Related Texts

CD	Cairo (Genizah text of the) Damascus Document
DSS	Dead Sea Scrolls
8HevXII gr	Greek scroll of the Minor Prophets from Naḥal Ḥever
Q	Qumran
1Q, 2Q, etc.	numbered caves of Qumran, yielding written material; followed by abbreviation of biblical or apocryphal book
1Q28b	Rule of the Blessings (Appendix b to 1QS)
1QH	Thanksgiving Hymns (Qumran Cave 1)
1QM	War Scroll (Qumran Cave 1)
1QpHab	Pesher on Habakkuk (Qumran Cave 1)
1QpPs	Pesher on Psalms (Qumran Cave 1)
1QS	Rule of the Community (Qumran Cave 1)
1QSa	Rule of the Congregation (Appendix a to 1QS)
1QSb	Rule of the Blessings (Appendix b to 1QS)
4Q175	Testimonia text (Qumran Cave 4)
4Q246	Apocryphon of Daniel (Qumran Cave 4)
4Q298	Words of the Sage to the Sons of Dawn (Qumran Cave 4)
4Q385b	fragmentary remains of Pseudo-Jeremiah that implies that Jeremiah went into Babylonian exile. Also known as ApocJer[C] or 4Q385 16. (Qumran Cave 4)

4Q389a	several scroll fragments now thought to contain portions of three pseudepigraphical works including Pseudo-Jeremiah. Also known as 4QApocJer[e]. (Qumran Cave 4)
4Q390	contains a schematized history of Israel's sin and divine punishment. Also known as psMos[e]. (Qumran Cave 4)
4Q394–399	Halakhic Letter (Qumran Cave 4)
4Q416	Instruction[b] (Qumran Cave 4)
4Q521	Messianic Apocalypse (Qumran Cave 4)
4Q550	Proto-Esther [a-f] (Qumran Cave 4)
4QFlor	Florilegium (or Eschatological Midrashim) (Qumran Cave 4)
4QMMT	Halakhic Letter (Qumran Cave 4)
4QpaleoDeutr	copy of Deuteronomy in paleo-Hebrew script (Qumran Cave 4)
4QpaleoExod	copy of Exodus in paleo-Hebrew script (Qumran Cave 4)
4QpNah	Pesher on Nahum (Qumran Cave 4)
4QpPs	Psalm Pesher A (Qumran Cave 4)
4QPrNab	Prayer of Nabonidus (Qumran Cave 4)
4QPs37	Psalm Scroll (Qumran Cave 4)
4QpsDan	Pseudo-Daniel (Qumran Cave 4)
4QSam	First copy of Samuel (Qumran Cave 4)
4QTestim	Testimonia text (Qumran Cave 4)
4QTob	Copy of Tobit (Qumran Cave 4)
11QMelch	Melchizedek text (Qumran Cave 11)
11QPs[a]	Psalms Scroll (Qumran Cave 11)
11QT	Temple Scroll (Qumran Cave 11)
11QtgJob	Targum of Job (Qumran Cave 11)

Targumic Material

Tg. Esth. I, II	First or Second Targum of Esther
Tg. Neb.	Targum of the Prophets
Tg. Neof.	Targum Neofiti

Orders and Tractates in Mishnaic and Related Literature

To distinguish the same-named tractates in the Mishnah, Tosefta, Babylonian Talmud, and Jerusalem Talmud, *m., t., b.,* or *y.* precedes the title of the tractate.

'Abot	'Abot
'Arak.	'Arakin
B. Bat.	Baba Batra
B. Meṣ.	Baba Meṣi'a
B. Qam.	Baba Qamma
Ber.	Berakot
Dem.	Demai
Giṭ.	Giṭṭin
Ḥag.	Ḥagigah
Hor.	Horayot
Ḥul.	Ḥullin
Ket.	Ketubbot
Ma'aś.	Ma'aśerot
Meg.	Megilla
Menaḥ.	Menaḥot

Mid.	Middot
Mo'ed Qat.	Mo'ed Qaṭan
Nazir	Nazir
Ned.	Nedarim
p. Šeqal.	pesachim Šeqalim
Pesaḥ.	Pesaḥim
Qidd.	Quddušin
Šabb.	Šabbat
Sanh.	Sanhedrin
Soṭah	Soṭah
Sukk.	Sukkah
Ta'an.	Ta'anit
Tamid	Tamid
Yad.	Yadayim
Yoma	Yoma (=Kippurim)

Other Rabbinic Works

'Abot R. Nat.	'Abot de Rabbi Nathan
Pesiq. R.	Pesiqta Rabbati
Rab.	Rabbah (following abbreviation of biblical book—e.g., Gen. Rab. = Genesis Rabbah)
Sipra	Sipra

Greek Manuscripts and Ancient Versions

Papyrus Manuscripts

$\mathfrak{P}^1$	third-century Greek papyrus manuscript of the Gospels
$\mathfrak{P}^{29}$	third- or fourth-century Greek papyrus manuscript
$\mathfrak{P}^{33}$	sixth-century Greek papyrus manuscript of Acts
$\mathfrak{P}^{37}$	third- or fourth-century Greek papyrus manuscript of the Gospels
$\mathfrak{P}^{38}$	fourth-century Greek papyrus manuscript of Acts
$\mathfrak{P}^{45}$	third-century Greek papyrus manuscript of the Gospels
$\mathfrak{P}^{46}$	third-century Greek papyrus manuscript of the letters
$\mathfrak{P}^{47}$	third-century Greek papyrus manuscript of Revelation
$\mathfrak{P}^{48}$	third-century Greek papyrus manuscript of Acts
$\mathfrak{P}^{52}$	second-century Greek papyrus manuscript of John 18:31-33, 37-38
$\mathfrak{P}^{58}$	sixth-century Greek papyrus manuscript of Acts
$\mathfrak{P}^{64}$	third-century Greek papyrus fragment of Matthew
$\mathfrak{P}^{66}$	second- or third-century Greek papyrus manuscript of John (incomplete)
$\mathfrak{P}^{67}$	third-century Greek papyrus fragment of Matthew
$\mathfrak{P}^{69}$	third-century Greek papyrus manuscript of the Gospel of Luke
$\mathfrak{P}^{75}$	third-century Greek papyrus manuscript of the Gospels

Lettered Uncials

ℵ	Codex Sinaiticus, fourth-century manuscript of LXX, NT, Epistle of Barnabas, and Shepherd of Hermas
A	Codex Alexandrinus, fifth-century manuscript of LXX, NT, 1 and 2 Clement, and Psalms of Solomon
B	Codex Vaticanus, fourth-century manuscript of LXX and parts of the NT

C	Codex Ephraemi, fifth-century manuscript of parts of LXX and NT
D	Codex Bezae, fifth-century bilingual (Greek and Latin) manuscript of the Gospels and Acts
G	ninth-century manuscript of the Gospels
K	ninth-century manuscript of the Gospels
L	eighth-century manuscript of the Gospels
W	Washington Codex, fifth-century manuscript of the Gospels
X	Codex Monacensis, ninth- or tenth-century manuscript of the Gospels
Z	sixth-century manuscript of Matthew
Θ	Koridethi Codex, ninth-century manuscript of the Gospels
Ψ	Athous Laurae Codex, eighth- or ninth-century manuscript of the Gospels (incomplete), Acts, the Catholic and Pauline Epistles, and Hebrews

Numbered Uncials

058	fourth-century fragment of Matthew 18
074	sixth-century fragment of Matthew
078	sixth-century fragment of Matthew, Luke, and John
0170	fifth- or sixth-century manuscript of Matthew
0181	fourth- or fifth-century partial manuscript of Luke 9:59–10:14

Numbered Minuscules

33	tenth-century manuscript of the Gospels
75	eleventh-century manuscript of the Gospels
565	ninth-century manuscript of the Gospels
700	eleventh-century manuscript of the Gospels
892	ninth-century manuscript of the Gospels

Names of Nag Hammadi Tractates

Ap. John	Apocryphon of John (also called the Secret Book of John)
Apoc. Adam	Apocalypse of Adam (also called the Revelation of Adam)
Ep. Pet.	Letter of Peter to Philip
Exeg. Soul	Exegesis on the Soul
Gos. Phil.	Gospel of Philip
Gos. Truth	Gospel of Truth

Ancient Versions

bo	the Bohairic (Memphitic) Coptic version
bo^{mss}	some manuscripts in the Bohairic tradition
d	the Latin text of Codex Bezae
e	Codex Palatinus, fifth-century Latin manuscript of the Gospels
ff^2	Old Latin manuscript, fifth-century translation of the Gospels
Ir^{lat}	the Latin translation of Irenaeus
latt	the whole Latin tradition (including the Vulgate)
mae	Middle Egyptian
sa	the Sahidic (Thebaic) Coptic version
sy	the Syriac version
sy^s	the Sinaitic Syriac version

Other Abbreviations

700*	the original reading of manuscript 700
$\aleph$*	the original reading of Codex Sinaiticus
$\aleph^1$	the first corrector of Codex Sinaiticus
$\aleph^2$	the second corrector of Codex Sinaiticus
$\mathfrak{M}$	the Majority text (the mass of later manuscripts)
C²	the corrected text of Codex Ephraemi
D*	the original reading of Codex Bezae
D²	the second corrector (c. fifth century) of Codex Bezae
f 1	Family 1: minuscule manuscripts belonging to the Lake Group (1, 118, 131, 209, 1582)
f 13	Family 13: minuscule manuscripts belonging to the Ferrar Group (13, 69, 124, 174, 230, 346, 543, 788, 826, 828, 983, 1689, 1709)
pc	a few other manuscripts

Commonly Used Periodicals, Reference Works, and Serials

AAR	American Academy of Religion
AASOR	Annual of the American Schools of Oriental Research
AB	Anchor Bible
ABD	*Anchor Bible Dictionary*
ABR	*Australian Biblical Review*
ABRL	Anchor Bible Reference Library
ACNT	Augsburg Commentaries on the New Testament
AcOr	*Acta Orientalia*
AfO	*Archiv für Orientforschung*
AfOB	Archiv für Orientforschung: Beiheft
AGJU	Arbeiten zur Geschichte des antiken Judentums und des Urchristentums
AJP	*American Journal of Philology*
AJSL	*American Journal of Semitic Languages and Literature*
AJT	*American Journal of Theology*
AnBib	Analecta Biblica
ANEP	J. B. Pritchard (ed.), *The Ancient Near East in Pictures Relating to the Old Testament*
ANET	J. B. Pritchard (ed.), *Ancient Near Eastern Texts Relating to the Old Testament*
ANF	*Ante-Nicene Fathers*
ANRW	*Aufstieg und Niedergang der römischen Welt*
ANTC	Abingdon New Testament Commentaries
ANTJ	Arbeiten zum Neuen Testament und Judentum
APOT	R. H. Charles (ed.), *The Apocrypha and Pseudepigrapha of the Old Testament*
ASNU	Acta Seminarii Neotestamentici Upsaliensis
ATANT	Abhandlungen zur Theologie des Alten und Neuen Testaments
ATD	Das Alte Testament Deutsch
ATDan	Acta Theologica Danica
Aug	*Augustinianum*
AusBR	*Australian Biblical Review*
BA	*Biblical Archaeologist*

BAGD	W. Bauer, W. F. Arndt, F. W. Gingrich, and F. W. Danker, *Greek-English Lexicon of the New Testament and Other Early Christian Literature*, 2nd ed. (Bauer-Arndt-Gingrich-Danker)
BAR	*Biblical Archaeology Review*
BASOR	*Bulletin of the American Schools of Oriental Research*
BBB	Bonner biblische Beiträge
BBET	Beiträge zur biblischen Exegese und Theologie
BBR	*Bulletin for Biblical Research*
BDAG	W. Bauer, W. F. Arndt, F. W. Gingrich, and F. W. Danker, *Greek-English Lexicon of the New Testament and Other Early Christian Literature*, 3rd ed. (Bauer-Danker-Arndt-Gingrich)
BDB	F. Brown, S. R. Driver, and C. A. Briggs, *A Hebrew and English Lexicon of the Old Testament*
BDF	F. Blass, A. Debrunner, and R. W. Funk, *A Greek Grammar of the New Testament and Other Early Christian Literature*
BEATAJ	Beiträge zur Erforschung des Alten Testaments und des antiken Judentum
BETL	Bibliotheca Ephemeridum Theologicarum Lovaniensium
BEvT	Beiträge zur evangelischen Theologie
BHS	*Biblia Hebraica Stuttgartensia*
BHT	Beiträge zur historischen Theologie
Bib	*Biblica*
BibInt	*Biblical Interpretation*
BibOr	Biblica et Orientalia
BJRL	*Bulletin of the John Rylands University Library of Manchester*
BJS	Brown Judaic Studies
BK	*Bibel und Kirche*
BKAT	Biblischer Kommentar, Altes Testament
BLS	Bible and Literature Series
BN	*Biblische Notizen*
BNTC	Black's New Testament Commentaries
BR	*Biblical Research*
BSac	*Bibliotheca Sacra*
BSOAS	*Bulletin of the School of Oriental and African Studies*
BT	*The Bible Translator*
BTB	*Biblical Theology Bulletin*
BVC	*Bible et vie chrétienne*
BWA(N)T	Beiträge zur Wissenschaft vom Alten (und Neuen) Testament
BZ	*Biblische Zeitschrift*
BZAW	Beihefte zur Zeitschrift für die alttestamentliche Wissenschaft
BZNW	Beihefte zur Zeitschrift für die neutestamentliche Wissenschaft
CAD	*The Assyrian Dictionary of the Oriental Institute of the University of Chicago*
CB	*Cultura Bíblica*
CBC	Cambridge Bible Commentary
CBOTS	Coniectanea Biblica: Old Testament Series
CBQ	*Catholic Biblical Quarterly*
CBQMS	Catholic Biblical Quarterly Monograph Series
ConBNT	Coniectanea Neotestamentica or Coniectanea Biblica: New Testament Series
ConBOT	Coniectanea Biblica: Old Testament Series
CP	*Classical Philology*
CRAI	Comptes rendus de l'Académie des inscriptions et belles-lettres

CRINT	Compendia Rerum Iudaicarum ad Novum Testamentum
CTM	*Concordia Theological Monthly*
DJD	Discoveries in the Judaean Desert
EB	Echter Bibel
EI	*Encyclopaedia of Islam*
EKKNT	Evangelisch-katholischer Kommentar zum Neuen Testament
Enc	*Encounter*
EncJud	C. Roth and G. Wigoder (eds.), *Encyclopedia Judaica*
EPRO	Etudes préliminaires aux religions orientales dans l'empire romain
ErIsr	*Eretz-Israel*
EstBib	*Estudios bíblicos*
ETL	*Ephemerides Theologicae Lovanienses*
ETS	Erfurter theologische Studien
EvQ	*Evangelical Quarterly*
EvT	*Evangelische Theologie*
ExAud	*Ex Auditu*
ExpTim	*Expository Times*
FAT	Forschungen zum Alten Testament
FB	Forschung zur Bibel
FBBS	Facet Books, Biblical Series
FFNT	Foundations and Facets: New Testament
FOTL	Forms of the Old Testament Literature
FRLANT	Forschungen zur Religion und Literatur des Alten und Neuen Testaments
FTS	Frankfurter Theologische Studien
GBS.OTS	Guides to Biblical Scholarship. Old Testament Series
GCS	Die griechischen christlichen Schriftsteller der ersten [drei] Jahrhunderte
GKC	Emil Kautzsch (ed.), *Gesenius' Hebrew Grammar*, trans. A. E. Cowley, 2nd ed.
GNS	*Good News Studies*
GTA	Göttinger theologischer Arbeiten
HALAT	*Hebräisches und aramäisches Lexikon zum Alten Testament*
HAR	*Hebrew Annual Review*
HAT	Handbuch zum Alten Testament
HBC	*Harper's Bible Commentary*
HBT	*Horizons in Biblical Theology*
HDB	*Hastings' Dictionary of the Bible*
HDR	Harvard Dissertations in Religion
HeyJ	Heythrop Journal
HNT	Handbuch zum Neuen Testament
HNTC	Harper's New Testament Commentaries
HR	*History of Religions*
HSM	Harvard Semitic Monographs
HSS	Harvard Semitic Studies
HTKNT	Herders Theologischer Kommentar zum Neuen Testament
HTR	*Harvard Theological Review*
HTS	Harvard Theological Studies
HUCA	*Hebrew Union College Annual*
IB	*Interpreter's Bible*
IBC	Interpretation: A Bible Commentary for Teaching and Preaching
IBS	*Irish Biblical Studies*
ICC	International Critical Commentary

IDB	*The Interpreter's Dictionary of the Bible*
IDBSup	supplementary volume to *The Interpreter's Dictionary of the Bible*
IEJ	*Israel Exploration Journal*
Int	*Interpretation*
IRT	Issues in Religion and Theology
ITC	International Theological Commentary
JAAR	*Journal of the American Academy of Religion*
JAL	Jewish Apocryphal Literature Series
JANESCU	*Journal of the Ancient Near Eastern Society of Columbia University*
JAOS	*Journal of the American Oriental Society*
JBL	*Journal of Biblical Literature*
JETS	*Journal of the Evangelical Theological Society*
JJS	*Journal of Jewish Studies*
JNES	*Journal of Near Eastern Studies*
JNSL	*Journal of Northwest Semitic Languages*
JPS	Jewish Publication Society
JQR	*Jewish Quarterly Review*
JR	*Journal of Religion*
JRH	*Journal of Religious History*
JSJ	*Journal for the Study of Judaism in the Persian, Hellenistic, and Roman Periods*
JSNT	*Journal for the Study of the New Testament*
JSNTSup	Journal for the Study of the New Testament Supplement Series
JSOT	*Journal for the Study of the Old Testament*
JSOTSup	Journal for the Study of the Old Testament Supplement Series
JSP	*Journal for the Study of the Pseudepigrapha*
JSS	*Journal of Semitic Studies*
JTC	*Journal for Theology and the Church*
JTS	*Journal of Theological Studies*
KAT	Kommentar zum Alten Testament
KB	L. Koehler and W. Baumgartner, *Lexicon in Veteris Testamenti libros*
KEK	Kritisch-exegetischer Kommentar über das Neue Testament (Meyer-Kommentar)
KPG	Knox Preaching Guides
LCL	Loeb Classical Library
LTQ	Lexington Theological Quarterly
MNTC	*Moffatt New Testament Commentary*
NCBC	New Century Bible Commentary
NHS	*Nag Hammadi Studies*
NIB	*The New Interpreter's Bible*
NIBC	*The New Interpreter's Bible Commentary*
NICNT	New International Commentary on the New Testament
NICOT	New International Commentary on the Old Testament
NIGTC	The New International Greek Testament Commentary
NJBC	*The New Jerome Biblical Commentary*
NovT	*Novum Testamentum*
NovTSup	Supplements to Novum Testamentum
NPNF	*Nicene and Post-Nicene Fathers*
NTC	New Testament in Context
NTG	New Testament Guides
NTS	*New Testament Studies*
NTT	*Norsk Teologisk Tidsskrift*

OBC	*The Oxford Bible Commentary*
OBO	Orbis Biblicus et Orientalis
OBT	Overtures to Biblical Theology
OIP	Oriental Institute Publications
Or	*Orientalia* (NS)
OTG	Old Testament Guides
OTL	Old Testament Library
OTM	Old Testament Message
OTP	*Old Testament Pseudepigrapha*
OTS	*Oudtestamentische Studiën*
PAAJR	*Proceedings of the American Academy of Jewish Research*
PEFQS	Palestine Exploration Fund Quarterly Statement
PEQ	*Palestine Exploration Quarterly*
PGM	K. Preisendanz (ed.), *Papyri Graecae Magicae*
PTMS	Pittsburgh Theological Monograph Series
QD	Quaestiones Disputatae
RANE	Records of the Ancient Near East
RB	*Revue biblique*
ResQ	*Restoration Quarterly*
RevExp	*Review and Expositor*
RevQ	*Revue de Qumran*
RSRel	*Recherches de science religieuse*
RTL	*Revue théologique de Louvain*
SAA	State Archives of Assyria
SB	H. L. Strack and P. Billerbeck, *Kommentar zum Neuen Testament aus Talmud und Midrasch,* 6 vols. 1922–61
SBAB	Stuttgarter biblische Aufsatzbände
SBB	Stuttgarter biblische Beiträge
SBL	Society of Biblical Literature
SBLDS	SBL Dissertation Series
SBLMS	SBL Monograph Series
SBLRBS	SBL Resources for Biblical Study
SBLSCS	SBL Septuagint and Cognate Studies
SBLSP	SBL Seminar Papers
SBLSS	SBL *Semeia* Studies
SBLSymS	SBL Symposium Series
SBLWAW	SBL Writings from the Ancient World
SBM	Stuttgarter biblische Monographien
SBS	Stuttgarter Bibelstudien
SBT	Studies in Biblical Theology
SEÅ	*Svensk exegetisk årsbok*
SJLA	Studies in Judaism in Late Antiquity
SJOT	*Scandinavian Journal of the Old Testament*
SJT	*Scottish Journal of Theology*
SKK	Stuttgarter kleiner Kommentar
SNTSMS	Society for New Testament Studies Monograph Series
SOTSMS	Society for Old Testament Studies Monograph Series
SP	Sacra Pagina
SR	*Studies in Religion/Sciences religieuses*
SSN	Studia Semitica Neerlandica
ST	*Studia Theologica*
SUNT	Studien zur Umwelt des Neuen Testaments
SVT	Supplements to Vetus Testamentum

SVTP	Studia in Veteris Testamenti Pseudepigraphica
SWBA	Social World of Biblical Antiquity
TB	Theologische Bücherei: Neudrucke und Berichte aus dem 20. Jahrhundert
TD	*Theology Digest*
TDNT	*Theological Dictionary of the New Testament*
TDOT	*Theological Dictionary of the Old Testament*
TextS	Texts and Studies
THKNT	Theologischer Handkommentar zum Neuen Testament
TLZ	*Theologische Literaturzeitung*
TOTC	Tyndale Old Testament Commentaries
TQ	*Theologische Quartalschrift*
TSK	*Theologische Studien und Kritiken*
TSSI	*Textbook of Syrian Semitic Inscriptions*
TToday	*Theology Today*
TynBul	*Tyndale Bulletin*
TZ	*Theologische Zeitschrift*
UBS	United Bible Societies
UBSGNT	*United Bible Societies Greek New Testament*
UF	*Ugarit-Forschungen*
USQR	*Union Seminary Quarterly Review*
UUÅ	Uppsala Universitetsårsskrift
VC	*Vigiliae Christianae*
VT	*Vetus Testamentum*
VTSup	Supplements to Vetus Testamentum
WA	M. Luther, *Kritische Gesamtausgabe* (= "Weimar" edition)
WBC	Word Biblical Commentary
WBT	Word Biblical Themes
WMANT	Wissenschaftliche Monographien zum Alten und Neuen Testament
WTJ	*Westminster Theological Journal*
WUNT	Wissenschaftliche Untersuchungen zum Neuen Testament
ZAH	*Zeitschrift für Althebräistik*
ZAW	*Zeitschrift für die alttestamentliche Wissenschaft*
ZNW	*Zeitschrift für die neutestamentliche Wissenschaft und die Kunde der älteren Kirche*
ZTK	*Zeitschrift für Theologie und Kirche*